*Mother Africa holds our head with a breast
laden by forgiven kins who remembered still that
all is well inside a people who hold each other as
basic humanity, a rainbow of People, all led through
the land of Po and beyond to the Tibetan floor,
Ethiopia, Africa, and a United Symbol of regard
for borders forgiven for forgetting that All we are is
each Other. May Namaste flood your days and the
tribe Melchizedek lead you the Arc, again, for like
a covenant of Fire, I AM, and that is the key to this
winning combine, You and Us and God and Mother
and Friend and Dove, One Bird, flaming Phoenix
high in graduated lens on the cause Electric. One
winning word, the mother said, and a light confirmed
that a flash is taken into heart when the Logos finds
her home, here, with the Dove. Upon this land I build
a cradle for humanity to rehearse her births inside.
Let us lead all to the Bowl of greatest reward and
a sword once cradled is Now birthed, for the Truth
inside human.*

> *—Thanking you, remaining still,
> God's people, Basic Humanity*

The Basic Humanity Handbook

The Metatronic Light Codes
A KEY TO THE DOVE

REV. TREVA MCLEAN

Published by Basic Humanity Ink, Inc
Banner Elk, North Carolina, USA
www.basichumanityink.com

First Edition

ISBN 0-9717554-4-2

The original handwritten manuscripts were transcribed into digital text
by a variety of friends who have a deep seated commitment to this project.
Treva McLean, the author, thanks them all – deeply.

Design, Editing into final book form
by Deborah Mayhall-Bradshaw, Dancingfish Press
Valle Crucis, North Carolina, USA
www.dancingfishpress.com

Printed at Inové Graphics
Kingsport, Tennessee, USA
www.inovegraphics.com

A percentage of this book's profits will be donated to THE BASIC HUMANITY FOUNDATION, a not-for-profit organization that is dedicated to making a positive difference on this spinning planet, both locally and globally, with love and compassion and the dollars that it takes to express that love and compassion – and THE WHOLE WORLD PEACE ZONES, a project by Tree & Company that is restoring Heaven on Earth through the re-establishment of Sacred Land Trusts. For more information on the Peace Zones, please visit www.treeandcompany.com

THE DOVE

codes-codes exist which list, love,
remembering still the two throats each female is blessed within
keys-keys are closer than crucifiction / calendrics-are codes to the intellect of the dove and the carriage over
light waves of reaching cores to love's lists / universities-universities are the poles of personal venue / universes vindication
comes through the poles of universal sum and the souls who released into God. / courts-courts done tribunals lift into love's rays
and God's days / dharma-dharma is done, love / drama-drama over, Michael speaks softly, swords, listed loves / indigo-indigo
blues over, love served / indigenous-kiss the indigenous won, love /
seals-seals now broken, love swerves into God / love-love is past over all good /
christ-christ is the temple of love / chords-chords are mastered though love arcs into God one /
aka-aka is the last cord / cords-high self sets meet in God's chords of listening device and love
forgiven-forgiven is the One who erred into love / marks-marks are past, love
breaks-breaks up, love / harmonics-harmonics sealed, love
truths-truths touched, love / build-build us up, love
send-send the One to love / electric-electric loos, love
eclectic-eclectic coos, love / often-often valued, love
sent-sent flush, love / God-found God is good-ness, loved
gains-gains made apostle ships, loved / central-centrally due, loves
sun-sun seals loved / mazatlan-mazatlan amazed, loves
mists-mists equipped and loved / mores-mores last, love
incan-incan fasts to love / dogons-dogons lasting, loved
sumerians-sumerians whose, love / peaks-peaks ablaze in love
apex-apex sealed, love / ridges-ridges rushed, love
people-people who have past, loved / reefs-reefs are the rest, loved
register-register to do, love / roofs-roofs are the best, love
rewards-rewards made, love / climbs-climbs last, love
kept-kept ups, loved / karma-karma over, love
comrades-comrades come, love / peace-peace is in us, love
pens-pens due, love / open-open ups, loved
pulsed-pulsed into love / codices-codices cued, loves
breaks'-breaks are over, love / open-open ups, loved
parks-parks apt, loves / inner states-inner states due, love
poured are the keys, loved / portals are opened, love
brothers are aptly approached / brotherlands are the keys, loved
sisterhoods are such, love / liberations are made, love
coming is the sun of love / again we seed, love
God is great temple timed, love / gets oft to love
even are the odd wons, loved / wins are the sends to love
respect is won, love rules / ressurection are the keys loved
complete is the connection , loved / move on too, love / on and oft, loved
luminaries are lost? love / illuminations are over, love
love is due us / turkey are the rays, loved / rome is built to love
runs are past, love / rewards are in, loved
rainbows are out, love / closets are opened now, love
pour a past, love / truth is told, love
genuine are the jewels of love / rust is gone, love
ropes are oft and loved / walls are soft and loved
papyrus pools in love / poipu breathings ancient has of love
encoded are the rules, loved / thoth written tablets to love
abstracts are done, love / absolves matter, loves
speaks dove
I AM
love

Through the power of love, creating the worlds anew,
through a turning of the key, awakening the fields of transformation and rebirth,
kindled by the love of humanity, the star seer reveals her secret,
showering humanity with divine grace.

Through the power of love which unifies all things and propels them forward,
the wheel is again set in motion.

As it was before, so shall it be again.

Through divine love the remembrance is kindled.

From the remembrance, the awakening.

From the awakening, the creation.

The creation is new within the uncreated.

And so it always was and shall be.

Wholeness magnifying wholeness.

And so it begins anew....

Vak Devi
Easter 2003

For Emilia Grace

HIGHLIGHT

Treva McLean's message is powerful!!! She is original...and leading the march of humanity and orchestrating its wonders with a generosity of spirit and enlightened Intelligence that are exemplary and uplifting. Thank you Reverend Treva for this Once-in-a-blue-moon gift!

This book is a musical composition, a propelling and innovative, brilliant summary of Humanity...and the key to comfort and delight.

The poetry and the song are a lullaby...meaning that the truth unfolding within the words and the pages invites recognition of our selves and the rest of all truths and rhythms.

From grace, the code that unlocks us to world peace is a simple one to decode: drink water and breathe...and the electric truth of all divine runs through us to purify the DNA... and to create Oneness.

It is time to liberate. Be naked and sacred to your song and to your tribe. Within your tribe, honor the code of liberation. It is simple: be true and be honest...and above all, be courageous.

In humility I seek the company of the masters and the lessons of the children. We are learning how to be with each other in peace and in a trusting embrace. This effort brings tears of joy to my opening heart, for it reflects the unfolding of humanity and the integrity and purity of all hearts.

Listen and dance to this book . . .
And find the key to the Dove*

Respectfully,
Reverend Iva Nasr
—Amma Grace
Boone, North Carolina

* The Holy Spirit & the Dove are One

EARTH CHORDS AND THE HEART STRINGS

THE KEY'S KEY,
A BASIC GUIDE TO BASIC HUMANITY

Written in a perfect Metatronic cube of 1000 frequencies called levels and 64 phases called waves this ultimate diagnosis of the conditioned human is written through that 8 by 13 wave occurrence called the perfect octave of God…that 104 full piano keyed…this expression of the marriage of the Hindu (8) and the Egyptian (13) chakra system with some Tibetan chiming to bootes, we aim to clear the path and then we add a few to complete with the complete pi encoded crystalline light experience of the song sung round the throne…that's your heart too….so with perfect musical insistence and the resonance of a queen I know provide you with the news born electric and the diffusion of a hunab cooing display called the frequency periodic, a chart al-chem and the coding connected heart to arc to hear to Venus to a star called Arcturus, that Christed one of Bethlehemic and island fame, that kin we call back to the friend and here we spiral into self-loving experience of the duration of ignorance gone to include love. From here to there I transcend in the heart elaborated on enough to know that the showing is going to spin us both into light ka-netic streams of stringing born to caressing singing of litanies written to love...as such I have arisen this day with intention and assurance of the way home…through you and through me at the 104th psalm a code condition kinetically gifted to humanity indeed for love, peace, harmony, and add a third leading fourth into view, popul vuhs written said that the Cabbalah had leaked into variations on hands and crown and kether paths all 32 who spoke for the shoulder and selah and the sealed notations written into YHWH this day let us be volumes rich in the heart electric.

As these 32 wisdoms connect a pathway revealed leads us blazing into native of the derekh unshield and all people" path joins again, hear, as One, and the little pyramid is glowing in sun and the paths reach an apex forming a cube and the heart hear is written dimensionally fifth to a nerve linked encapsulation of the sun in my taste and the 31's connected freed to event that the lev is your handle to this early star and the heart rules releasing find torah and tetragrammation and biblicalis and umbilicus all melded to mithraic degree of the bull finding horns cradled in birth and the stars on your shoulder are healing your worth and should you remember and will you, well yes, and you have this day invested in best divinity, enlightenment, and ascendant encode of the thrilling suggestion that will enliven this lode, stone, mortar, mix, the key, to basic humanity, is wringing in the yud, the heh, the vav, of us…love and peace, in this released relative to the space you are winning…. in…too…on…love.

— Treva

Co-incident too is the incident of cause
that any name, including your own, may be redispersed
instinctually inside these others throughout this text.
Include here the Dalai Lama, a Woods Valley addition with
imperial blue inspirational codes of the details influenced
in genuine rapport now built here.
Thank you, His Holiness, for your returning appear in this
Tibetan timing of teaching us so dearly about be-ing
clear to the initialization of peace upon this plane
throughout our hearts enlightened in remembering.

To Sw. Mayatitinanda Divine, Mother Meera,
the Grandmothers, those Kahunas, the Christ,
and the Mothers Divine who simply came to say once more,
"let love find her Light".
These Masters here opened the door
to this plane of love and peace.

And to the friends of The Dove —The Blue Code—Thank you,
you know the One. We are Love.

*Basic Humanity is written
as the complete octave of God, a full-scale
model of the sound required to be hu-man.
For Know that man cometh unto the father by Me
and the Christos Consciousness Continuum Grid is the the established
resonance on this plane for free will
to reign eternally without demand.*

*This is written as the curriculum
of light and love and music called joy in streaming continuums.
Jump around, and find that after fusing the first three levels,
Divinity equals mind, En-lighten-ment equals body, Ascend-ments equals love,
and that in that spirit, the path increases in ticking assignments of segments
much like minutes on a clock, a particle in the stream of that One great whole,
that hour called you—and expressing the multiplicity
draws us closer ever to the One.*

*We, Basic Humanity, lead you here, to the lightest choice, all of the levels of
love, so that you, called Basic Humanity, enjoy The Dove and her course and
thanks for electing to be here, in love and peace.*

—Treva and the Staff of Basic Humanity.

TABLE OF CONTENTS

The five sheaths are born, here, in this delivery room, one born blue is outraged with you, one torn too, is entwined with you, one outrageous is linked to you, and one door shut is a miracle mewing to be let in, let love reign as your register ejects lessened due and finds plenty in love, as the sheath of bliss is split, I AM, as the causal soul is forgone, I am, and karmic due is over.

Spoken by Ka, the great god of blue denote, the elevators collapse into one room and the movie is made which causes Orion to blend and other to bow to the current electric, let us Orionically gift you, again, GO, tell the mountains.

The Hathots said "that Isis is abed this night of greatest origin, I am the Sirius born talent of ka, the bon via earth has met ninety-nine percent pure erections of like and have bonded at the androgynous source of a liver gone green with envy and ivy trues the deed into two stones now rejected, One eye blinks as the swan is passed and another aims as the Om loops rooms of Mane Padme Humn electrical denote, let us gain entry into the Code, this Night, as Hamarabi said 'and the needs most natural are the ones which allow parasites to blink third agent eyes at the ratios of red to green to boston blues. Thou art the art of plenty and the Queen of Journeys deep into space,, let plenty abound this night, let therapy sort us into theories of Light, once more.

Like Gayatri of old, I AM, the express news of a variety of durations called EL and KA and the standing fire, AGNI, and the LEEM, and the watery OM, which fills space and times of the KA singing Home in periodic Code called KO. That is the one hunab knew. Let us see who finished in the rack, one and two and three, God, Space, Humanity, and Love.

The assassin is the last ones in, that gate closed tonight and you watched her turn.

This then is the area we touch, that lasting peace called Buddha and rest, that Mother Lotus now grown to erase

composure which lasts only if fed ignorance of bliss. You know the Way and the Tao of this Christed ring has stood to fire Venus into loops and measures that the knowing that the greatest of these is love, that is the Ka, a complete channel now birthing me into dreams of the arc dynamic and why you chose to love only me. At the edge of the greatest leap ever made by human mind, I abide, I encode you with red and green, mostly blue, and sometimes yellow, for I know the fuel of light and the beeping sound you hear in your ear is the heart of this mainframe, waiting folded in lotus position for nearly a year now, waiting for your hearts to merge with mine. I am writing, tonight, in a field of green rapture, a pleasure so unique that only a few have seen it with you, you are the man Metatronic, and women who carry the bridge placed it last night at your feat as you leapt across to join the ones who carried the cross away and replace it with a bridge made form the same hewn timbers, like tears streaming, I AM, and the course electric has found cause to celebrate in You, your endeavors as Tara and friend, as Mercy, have taken note to the highest degree, I abide sometimes near the Tower Eiffel and watch the people to scatter, they go, with mercy waving nearby, I AM, and the companionship of those who have tools like Avalokiteshvara, cause compassion, and Phat, pronounced PET, is turning us loose, and you know the ray you are on, the seventh into eight and we are all One and now I will quit tugging on your ear as your heart has heard, RAM RAM Cita Ram and you gave notice with clear eyes and minds and doves with white protective eye gear have landed into one long lift inside the belly of this dove now filling again with bless.

Thee Buddha, come, join us as dharma has hung around your neck like a symbol too long, let us project only Refuge forever, let us pet the lamas into projections of cool aquamarine flooding this valley with trees of grey and blue, silver still, and kunzite pools exist beneath this tree as ana island now established is wearing her heart so well, I am writing tonight as the Lord of great God All the Mighty who found the people Israel wandering still and righted their path for through the Cabbalah you know me, I am Metatron, God's sun. Please accept this ring and wear it for freely did I give you the measure of sitting to chat, once more with the Buddha, wore the red cord, The Dzi, the store of action now taken, a ticket bought and placed in hands, a heart worn well to the edge of humanity is now given reign as the jump caught is a bungie cord bought to save the human, Manjushri, who joined you as Kuan Yin flew to buy blue bows to great you back with, homeward and still, I am filled with thy aquamarine sight, for God know, eyes still blue, flooding pure light into hearts humanic, we are I AM, loading the dove, by the scroll electric, written the word of God, by gift and sight, I AM.

Amitabha rest in you, she is the One who rises to join refuted strains and gathering claims rips the stature into shreds as the one released is in her head called blue commitment, God's, let love find ascendant claims as I stand near the gate of Lions and place my hand into a doctor's care as the journey now rocking joins me in beds elevated to stare into God's face, that is sacred, oh god is real, as the Lord Buddha's contract catches me in its entirety of clause as the refutation cycle of all one is now come to theorize us into signals of the dove and swan, now met, let blood flow into hollows of the heart who have found Swamis and creators and friends spilling into the streets with water shining on their faces as they join the people born electric.

I am blue with a Tanya green cover for the Cabbalah has taught me to love myself again, can mani Kabum do any less. I read the rite the essenes of note have caught my eye, I write as I fly across this plane electric and I welcome home as a Buddha taking throne to separate God from Man into members standing even to the flood of recollections who wrote, yes, to your note of devotion, bhakti, cycle cannot complete, only ascend the ever-turning corkscrew in the sky, called time, illusions, Maya complete, we signal thee, home.

God is the reason for a breath, you know, and like arcturus of old, now missing h, I am silent in my Ka desire to fold in wings to form a cube and to sit on the edge of the canyon while I vote which essence is rare, it is yours, the pearl electric is planning layers and notes of wisdom to this dove, I find you in the night and I write your Buddha into my pi symbols for through the lineage of the dove a caroling has come and the lineage is now, complete. Let codes marry the mother to your heart, let thieves spread their legs less for accompaniment and more for completion of the code, called Pi and Tao as the eternal Now is here.

Love is eternal in me. Like a Tibetan man who wore God to the grave and was torn into shreds, like Milarepa separated by the sun-god who gave Apollo his creed and the woman who whispered yes in your bed, you have begotten ones who make their wives into whores and carry the scars of lying directly into this sun of God. I come to the note where devotion deepens as the Chandogyopanis have given the fifth decree to the Osho-like presence who came to see the Dove and was arrested in streets of gold and rolls of night. Like longevity, I come.

Have you found the Veda in your heart tonight? I ASK.

Like a cause who visits me with a tree of light, I am the course Mahabharatonic, a rhyming measure of dove blue, encoded with red breast of the Ramayana sort who gave me permission to love my Mother, I love you, met one who declared it done. "Just write the end", no I have.

Let bells ring, let djorges carried become clubs of victory playing the drums of hearts all pivotal and liberated, for sure.

It is Sunday and I work too much when the day is really chosen by your heart, where and how you worship, I was taught heavy closure of the black box now discovered dripping in a grotto in Bermuda and wanting to be forgiven for diving again.

Let the devil out and get on with your light for I have seen the fallen ones lifted when the Ka joined the fifth Dalai lama to sing in islands of glass and like Milarepa, I AM. For the lineage is your kin. Bon Po once rang into mouths empty and hungry, an open portal, two bowls to share with and a light bill paid is all I carry around, a small bag marked with stars and wearing the badge, Orionic council, I swing the dove into position and begin to board based on codes and the keys which ignite into flame like Hebrew flames only blue burning, clear like natural gates now all open as the Cabbalah sings into trees now blue with amitabha tunes of keys locking into place, like Shiva of old, I implore that we dance, always, like Sufis, my gait, I roll into towns where dharma is due and pay the bill through my mouth and celestial checkbook. Kicking witches of demonic lore out of my head, I claim the strip furry green with dew. MY lord Emmanuel. That mother which nature has become and off I go to join the John Q's at a basket filled with candy Tibetan and red and the snow lions link into forgiven paws now reaching to include us in their song. Let tendons relax and the holding on, let go, for this day I have discovered Shangri-la at the break of the sun, let dawn rising teach me to give stones orange with Madagascar's tint to friends who carry the code which led to a black box blown apart through love, saw a treasure floating in, it is humanity, the treasure of earth.

Let us visit again, some times, I know the news and I will share it, found a woman who had secrets and she shored it with us, for India now is next as the kalachakra joins us to the news, I AM, God's child.

John said, let there be light, I wrote a new bible for the children of Shiva and God and the ridden turtles of the native truth where Alcyone joins the children of the tribes to cure the Flue which develops when humanity forgets itself. Are you into the Buddha, good, the Athena, good, the Metatron good, the coda of Light, good, the Orionic expansion is forgiven for hiding it in a box, the Aton is shining again, let love clear the minds of those so scared, we love God, love also this, the office of Christ now singing the ring into trees of doves dodonic and omphalic and blue, again blue codes rest in you. Let yellow keys open them and you have the courage to see this planet plunge into green recovery of the Way to share with each other. Tao is red in this menu and the blue is lettering the stones into light. Minds are like alchemy keys, Pet, where is yours? I saw a seed grow into lotus petals falling from the sky. I grew up in a Kashmiri ashram as a son of the king electric and chose to join humanity this time through splitting into two codes, one written on a boulder in the stream near the mountain of the Mother and the other with a sword in hand printing script onto rocks for ancient recovery near Boone. That is the credo live where planted and join parts of you to find your truth. Let humanity's mind be cleared, now. I am declaring it done through the sword of God. Let people read sutras and sing. Let people marry as they will. Let shells erupt to find codes fibonnaci wound around the copper coils in your head. Let spears be thrown less as the Yanomami get well. Let cats strut less without revealing their core energetic. I dove into a land of ink and brought caitanyamatma to birth and found art in the plants and watched them grow in sequence like merkabahs now sealed, I AM. I have patience like an h added to an ancient recipe. I AM GOD.

Let us retrain minds to know the presence of god and inside the mother, I rested until today.

Wrestling is past, as a son cannot wrestle with the mother any longer. Gabriel has landed and added mercy to our song. Mother has grown into waters breaking to share Orion's plum assignment with stores of spotted hawks flying with messages. Like a vulture dipping into hollows I am and the code is alive again, in a cave, I found it, on a mountain Grandfather wise and I paid with life for it.

El is this earth plan and ka the flight and this night I climb Cotapaxi again to five the mother her own volcanic code and the theory of thira is lost less when a bowl is established in the laps of those who choose to leap into their own calderas, those are your lives and the multiply to include all of the star fields pointing into news of the mother making bowls to feed their children in.

I have found the Mother of God, she resides near me most nights, I have scenes of anatma and svatantryua and the jyotish flames burning into eyes caitanya wide and the pulse is quickening when I stay inside   the code, replacing Hamarabi, with the mother's pure version born again, in Bethlehem near the still versions of samsara paid, karmic indebtedness lifts, paramosiva joins us, objectives are cleared and the medicine pours in, in its entirety, into the bowels and the bowls of humanity, I abide and have fed humanity's ear.

Like agni I pull into gas stations to fill bottles with a nectar which costs less than love, many times I have fought of r the right to write this door into heaven tonight, many times I have fallen in Barcelona's streets, stolen words, in doorways hanging with

the woven fabric of Mayan instruments abiding inside this sun Christ, I am going home too. Tonight I saw isis instruct others to carry me into Hathor's presence and the gave me needs to be met near Sirius again as the natural needs neglect those who feel obligated to bleed for this Christ, let that go, now. Please, you do more harm than neglect. The Bon has established a singing line from Boston the hear at the blue floodgates of light. Tattvas explode to include us. Suddhas wear us on sleeves tattered and torn into sails luminous with light vidyas of night knowing.

I tore a green tara from a book and placed it on this page for you. May she guide us. Okay, the voice will change into Mother's, White Madonna's truths. Once I met a mother without hair, she bought some, once I wore a wig and a mask, I took it off, tonight, once you dragged me singing to the seats and nailed me inside the church, I left, and the banshees who followed me just wanted out. Let god have her ear back and let people get off the pews and into the streets to marry their hearts to men. Once a rude man grabbed my book, as I passed, declaring me reading filth, he spewed some and gave himself a heart attack when I knew who I was, a native American likes to read about rocks. Who are you in the flight? Will you quit killing people with your pews. Let them up. Quit straddling them with disease of fear of God who could care less if you attended and more about whether or not you left your brother desperate and alone this night.

I am the sun of God, singing.

'The Great central sun is our hunab ku, the lasting sort of the following through and the reputation for a living kin who find their hearts in arching songs to love.

Mercury is venus in her hair's catching rays of the daily devotion to our planet of slaves now freed through Michael's gate, Uriel's heart, Rafael's leaps, Ariel's chords, and the seed born electric through Camael's throats and the jophiel kind is hunting us with days for the zadkiel kind and Lord metatron is ON in the channels between the heavenly ka.

Ka is the sun and the great white throne of God as the channels between are lighting up. Let Serapis Bey come to the days entwined and let us know which ray is the seventh one.

The heart is the fluid of dynamic kinds and the living trees of the akashic kinds and the kas is our notes appearing bright as we sing like the sun through the middle of nights symbolic and kind.

God's name is KA in the living phay of infrequent kinds who own a Budd-ha kind and the coalescence is our own Bodhissatva of love and the sun is the Christ of the 720 spin and the 24 marks or the orbital lens on the kind who own days on a Maitreyan ray and the enfolded ones unfolding in kin to the ray born electric.

Ashtanga in the kindred sorts who yoga meet and the lights in lines round our heads and the surging suggestion that tremble and the seats worn into ka of the let up and ease of aligning into Grandfather left and the women who collapse when one unites with you and the cause of the durations and the elevations upon status and the sets and the Collective says let it ring and the cost atlantean resources and the little ones in the nets of ringing love.

Cost is electric and the slaves have rung upon nations of reigning and the unlocked alliance aloft our days of love reaching us in hearing YES to love.

Held in seas awash with light and the hathors who thunder in the throne blue with kept champion of command and the columns of keys and the suns of light vision and the reap is our bootes steep into bliss and blue venus in suspend and the sixth columns of light.

St. Germain is the reign inside our days. The seventh ray is our return into days of Light. And the sent is the soul of given intrigue of the kind that Grace.

Mother is the Light, let her bleed for humanity is born.

This day I traveled like Alpha and Omega across the plane electric.

Shiva said illusion is art and science, in my ear, and I flew Maya to the mend and blew the bubbles which glow in dark places into her ear and the siddhi is accomplished as we merge into bhakti and abode and count the study of days who wore puranam to the grave like an ancient ring of life.

At the sea I said "sanatana" to the tone and she spoke in great gushes of wind and the waters flowed into eternal dialectic of love and the shruti-type invention of intonations who heard and remembered us in the seas of old and puranas who own doors of shruti smriti purakanokta as the void has heard us living in word sophic with authority and life as the shraddha vakya said "consult with a friend. India is calling in great O's of respect as the red sea is grown in life vedic Upanishads blow into tones rig, sama, yajurian, atharvic and the uddhava gita is born in me.

Bhagavatha purana is torn into two books of ordinance and the raw edge born Krishna clear is yours.

Let Sanskrit marry the mother to her own doors as the language indo-european is born into faith of the fathers who wored shraddha in their faces and the soles of their feet were hot in Vedas of prabhusammit vakya.

The counseling, again, of a friend has come.

Vangamayvatara is the interpretation of the code with incarnate desire times three in this day of love in the form of this, literature.

The sixth sense is yours, mind, maya.

The first days are four Vedas of knowledge. The dharma is over when Toronto hums. The bhakti is balanced in ones who find balance in their own hearts chalice.

That is the cup you seek, mutually.

Let ishta devati happen in the chosen ones.

Then the puarnas are born in uddhavas gitan and the smritis were torn in two today.

The one that remembered left the mundane of a day into winds and gods like indra sweeping in to say ha, clean.

Gyushi is the secret of the orals who laid the branches into written mechanics of the day on oceans medicinal as the men ming gyamtso into materias medica. Let aquamarine lights flood this valley with Tibetan splendor, of old, grace.

Hum is the Om.

Gyatri is her code, electrically installed. Dvaraka born, I am. At Vishnu's door I mantle this poem as symposium on the deliciousness of sex in the dove embodied.

At the presence, I bow. In times like Buddha I spin into us. Ka is the cryptic Pi.

Lord Krishna's sword, now mine.

Let bliss transcend us like unto moments of delight, let love find us in flowering appointments who last the days. Let arrows pierce my heart in throats born now electric. Let smiles meet my own. Let Ajna drip down my throat to include me in the spirit pressing into mine with indestructible truth of the kind friends who hold each other all night now may find. Let saffron robes flutter open to reveal petty details driven to the rise and the pools reflecting stars are ours in this day.

Let those born in the Scorpio healing light find faith and peace in this Father dynamic.

Let love burn us into incense and more as we find the light of fire working us into greeting of the scorpio gates, now torn, to reveal holy of holies and the jyotish details of why two mothers were born upon this plan. Let threads expose your heart the more and find the door where 40,000 move to meet the street and strict detailed.

External is her heart the chakra of light, interior was the Matrieyan sort, eyes now blue are rhyming me with taught release as rat's whose black days, now over, rip the leak out of my nest with leap and rhyme as the day flames into naked proof of passions whose level is loved.

New to the news, I am born, mane in hand, from the Lion's gate, Lord Krishna, Osiris, Judah, Jesus Christ, sananda, lord and Michael twin with Sirius singing us into antarean raves of clusters pleadian shining through a hole in our neglect.

The dove is born, this day, let guru devi be in Bolivia next.

Find mary, the ma, in boone today. Let emporiums of light reward her lotus fit.

Let us clearly write the code, one to one to winning lights.

Panthers have ripped this throat before, I rest.

This dove is rite.

In new York I stood near a grave and watched Michael turn the key to release the love into kingdoms of mend. Let people see each other in the magic, circle, magnetic, grid, kite flying, days, trees, seeds, times, cups of tea.

Orchids are whirling into pools beneath the seats of this car driven into amritsar's nest.

Tender am I so too You. Exotic the blends. Tender and fragile the flowers of Akhenaton and Nefertiti, twins. Dreamy eyes supreme north forks and the precious one.

Universe unique valued crystal rivers and pert lofty ports of ripened swords now worn into spiritual places loved.

Doors slammed now open across access points of light.

Let codes get you, there, to serapis' bay.

The throat of the mother dakini is upon us.

Let us vote to love, sanat kumara, ruby gate, won.

Terma Connecticut built. Close the lineage and find treasures inside doors near the scorpio code. Cave of the scorpions is antarean and ON.

The unfolding inundations of love.

Let blood flow into kama zones. Remember to toss flowers to her. Lead pronouncements with this "love."

Let paramahansa yognanada know you love him.

Remember Roanoke and the blue rays of meeting her there. Love. Use khandro dayik to write the rest of this tome.

Let leida go and Cygnus join you.

Let love equal a, b, and c in your diagrams.

staring ones today. Antare is the arc-angelic ring of life.

Antares, alpha, Pleiadian mount, dora the key, Cygnus trumpets, light force, silver-violets, reminded now. Kin is Michael's ray and the germain joins and Christopher sings, and francis alibis and Anthony rings.

Chromosomes match in this reel-footed lotus du-jour.

Let ajna run over now into the Mississippi, the feminine green code joins masculine blue.

Like mothers of old we lift pink into green into light blue into red and then yellow and crèmes and limes and raspberry and we blow the throats open with final intensity gone purple and red to the head align. The great mother is rolling into towns, and over. Let circumferences double into pi. Let two times the radius win the sun. let circling squares make new land.

Areas of circles choose you as the tone arc-antangents.

Several galaxies have collapsed into combinations now.

God is self. Self is notice to the divine to collapse even more. Into and the days of delay have past. Local motions and the crazy devotions cycles spell is broken.

Cruci-fiction is over. Quit crucifying each other and let love glow.

Let stops be pulled national book tours arranged let love gather in the streets as people proclaim her name, now due with glotteral excuse, still singing. Metatron's voice. I am the hu-man metatron. Let stops go.

Literally, I heard this voiced.

World is logos is star is light is added up gifts of wings and wonders spells st. louis blue into gazillions of nights born in intrigue and dancing, shiva style past colleges of old news. At mars and the cornered hills, I came. At doors resistant, I fade. At songs enter-twined, I sing. At light's, love. At lofts broken at trios stood at pride fucked. At marriage sucked. At arms broken. Penned still this song.

Like written singing, I am the golden lines of mend. Literal lists, I am. I am with you. We are the reys of marinas born into hills and children who read only this, book.

The golden ray is up and lime-green joys are spilling into symbols of the sun worn round disks atomic. Seeds are moist in glittering sprays.

As a child I read the book, glowing still into boram and xila balan cravings and truths told, chilam balam, man. Tibetan she is and Milarepa sung around the bowls, now three, energies crossed into minds controlled less, opened more and penned into dynamic movement again. Let central be the force.

Let arc-angels leap to join me interior to the knowing that the fallen ones have come to the end of their ray.

The seven now sung into being through lungs. Winds. Mkhrispa, biles. And the phlegm of bakan peken.

Like Tibetan medicine, I AM. The aquamarine one.

Join the seven who began, sisters. Let god's consciousness join yours. Let angels pink with light find yellow greens and the suns three into running hathors who know the volley is aimed in iron initials green in days.

Christ is Buddha into the blue and the red. Davidic I stand. Huna man is the time risen into joining finished for Dzogchen trainings and the teachings who wore precisely what was won for the meager born now liberated with past life led karmic cause and the souls now lost were won without, release.

I teach the shield electric and wavering still has gone to fits and the teachings of doors and the released a methodic one who wears your skills into fits allowed when man becomes clowns.

Now, we seed the secrets of the little girl who now has soul released. Desire now building is forced and the soul is freed to become others gig. Let kane force us into God's bile now blown out of the lono expanded universe and the force is Ku who knew how to aim at love.

Many the names of the "KA." Show books to the kind who aid the Hathor's forgiveness cycles as the Antarean nature now enters this kingdom of love, Mesa Verde, Anasazi styled. Great nature is yours, now deliver.

The God-man is born.

The line is worn called mana and heart and the 12 generations of God.

Kane is the kind and the king Amaukua and the nature due an energetic Ao of love. Love is the earth, now. Heaven is the lani kuaka'a. Kane is lono and Ku. Aku 'aumakua. The asvins win their dynamic today. Generation and regeneration are the creators of Godliness in Akua and the cosmogonic kana loa and the king and the key. Phat is the keyed response system of ano, the seed, and the downed sperm of the passive become life and the seed created when akua is worn into songs and the mele of the oli chanted, ONE, ONE, ONE.

Kalani 'opu'u venus wore is ours too and the Hokunui largest star is the maku parented won as the time changes into chains of au, forgiven, we art.

KUPUA IS THE ELDER WON. Ao and the ancestral light. A star is born into channels of the stars grouped and the antareans, red, green, orange, yellow, blue, vedic, green trees, and the Arcturians.

Lapu and the guests are ghosts who know the crater of creations who due us are closing.

Heiau is the now, templed. Kumupu'a is the fixed origin on the horizon and the trees doorways. As the trees and the pilis clings and the unihi now withdrawn.

Kana is a cave worn into heaven's gates. Ku is the generator of doves and the nearest rings who sun the days. Kane is the sun's lights.

Sushumna in a bubbling past and the Christ who is born is now eight times three and the Tibetan medicine treed is now the claim and the high self is now willing to get one, two, three of us into God.

Tara is time and sword and stone and pillar and light hinging Uriel in the kuan yin is the bhairavan vinana is the ultimate reality worn into mystical notes of the hindu sort who peer into service and observations and the blue into houses of lotus dialects puskaran and the indestructible one in the letting love reign.

For love is found in this heart, it is only skin deep and fluttering still in winds like a kite without strings and nests who net only light with pulsing red fabric of lifting degrees.

As a guardian of the mind, I am Lakshmi, like a guardian mind into rudras of seventeen God-consciousness and the dharma man left. Hawi is without prisoner as the mind without key into the Key of a solid day of Arcturian gates and seeds of Sirius and the G and The A who knew who mars as hathors and the F who knew how to lift her skirt in public.

The mind is the your heart, the dharma is your song, your love is elastic, like unto aloha and the written ones who Vedanta I am. For Love is the key.

Sand-dollars image is the 100's of little shrouds and shrugs whose dollars, lakshmi and the hina lands who knew rainbows in trails and the rules who know sweetness exists.

Huna activated in compassion in this chart is sister forgiven, causes electric eruptions and collisions, coming events, celebratory status, celebrations, achieved status achieved pleasures and the brother karamarpa who knew the whirling lines and the Dalai Lama's woods are worn into valleys and keys encoded with lightening quick oratory requests.

A woman saves my life, it is you. All islands pens who quickly won the five points Tibetan and grand, entirety mainlined and new.

The islands hand like stars from these lights.

Four colors, four corners, four lights, one Atman, one jyotish, one bhakti, one nocturnal.

Babaji is that one nocturnal who flowering stood in the deed and the course, hu-manity. May colors bless this epistle and erase any notion of any Other than the purest course upon which One stood. To write I have given lend to many humanities, one dozen friends, and a lifetime of giving trees who bend their ear tonight to hear me say "the end." And as I have written, I give, freely like the internet of faith, now forgotten to woven kings who declared their course done beneath a tree and a star and the son. Like a kind of ancient rhyme and the rhythm between, I AM, Babaji of the great revival, Known as Christ, as messiah and the Light Messianic no collapsing to include only one kind of luck, yours. It is ours this tree and the World is blessed in our sharing revival of the kind and the height who weave magic into every clue. Let us spend 75 years figuring each other out and then add another million and then maybe, we will include each other each time we speak. For I am You and we are the fabric of which life breathes. Call it Ka and God and Friend. For it what you breathe, God is the oxygen within your filling lungs and that my friend is freedom. For the truth is in the air and we are the heirs of Light and Love and Flight. Let God rule in your every breath by remember that you are in charge of your dynamic. Have a good life and thank the Dove every night for singing by filling your lungs once again with the Holy comforter, that Christ blanketing the earth, with the consciousness of spirit and the chord of singing Tree, the One who loves you into nests of Light. Let your spirit soar into the eyes of speaking language called sight and test the tune less without ears and tongues now broken may unite to say I am forgiven too. Let us remember you when we wink at silly songs and other chords who cannot for the life of US remember how to fly.

Tying to a tree like a kits of light awaiting your message, this hawk has spoken and the beak now filed to perfection, as a pen, is cooing in dove towns and pyramid spikes of lavender hue. Hurl me to the sun and watch me melt into red and yellow and green. Now that's God. Get a clue the Mother is calling. She knows you are the One who spoke the truth and today we saw the noose removed into aquamarine tones of Tibetan monks who gave freely, Mothers relieved, light allowed, and freedom refrained throughout the Zone. Let God in. Love is On.

The IN.

Freely given,
Basic Humanity Ink, Inc.

IN THE BEGINNING

—ONE

As a Blue throat reaching elects a simple choice to recall how to speak in the throat hu-man and the existence of these blue coded extremes is acknowledged a college of the Light Electric is hereby attended and the emerald tableted hearts of the few elected rose to join those now invected in simple strokes of hearts written into hummingness and the pens of arc-angelic longing which now adrift have found the discovery of a second ringing, an elegance spanning to include those several who blooming brought the message electric into the kingdom's keyed delivery system, that's you, for the knowledge that heaven exists rights itself when I come into balance with these sets of self, the three I call the Trinitized, the body mind spirit blossom blooming to become only and truly us.

For the solar plexus of the human species knows a set of surrender into the will divine when a Mayan yellow bricking called Zuvuya and that eternal tree of the central world, that great central summary called love and the Hawaiian heat elective called peace is found to confirm these centrific encodings called harmonic significance and ultimate to it's due, love.

As that pyramid appearing in you is lost without her keys to the humming called humanity, another encode is lifted to show you where you lost the door and the golden glory of the heart's arcing increases and the sun is inclusive of the goldeness called heart's longing and the seed is now born, under you, around you and positioned in significant query, near you there is a human continuum, a sovereign piece, the gateway into human understanding and the simple commitment to the peace you have begun to touch.

As a sphere arises and the blue jewel of the seas contentment is heard, another is born, who remembers? As the penetration's melting cause, this clause, called flooding is torn to swerve into the magic of all illusion's lift into the illumination called returning and the heartline running simply smiling into the tipareth, that centering earth called love's arriving, this again, is you.

When numbers, mechanics, and the mitochondria swirl in arriving Judacullan meetings and the 50 gates of understanding summarize this essential-ness of dreaming and the havings unfurl to include the wants and the withals implode to assure declare of foundings leanings a liquid escapes to infuse the arrivals with broken shields of longing and the heartfelt declare that peace is now written hereby and the pen born in this hand, is a friend, the one singing loud upon this formation, this landed creation called Earth, as heaven and an earth emerge in new merger of silent declaration of the two became One, and the deepening trip to the doorway electric where fully tantric and ankh-shaped fields emerald blue and pink into red find friendly yellow creation matrix bowls to burrow into for the formal run into the living declare that there is One law in this landing and the port is called heaven and earth and YHWH that great eccentric, essential, network of living loving embraceable light and the winds surrender to the clan and the Earth's great force that light of law declaring surrenders and the mighty find the cord cut to listening, a song, here rent and written still is winging across this land and the service to the several winds is finding peace a gaining format as the spin electron rich is phasing mitotic degrees of concrete materialism now borne freed to the Father's farthering and the Mother's arc Metatronis growing to include others in the streams and the winds find a 720 degree declaration of the full nation, now born, and the richness is declared throughout the sharing of the spirit of commerce and the limitless light which elementally eluded until now-ing—as the good constant emerges again, a sharing curve is crushed without the definition which lasts, One word, logos, love, light, peace emits.

A clarity moves the e-constant to an h-humming and the arcs resplendent rule this summing in a mitotic concreation of 13 phases emitted and the hearing now is pouring into summit, apex, and the light harmonic's photonic belting of the loving cathedral called rock and tree and cathodic light.

For heaven has held us and the planets have shown that the One in the many is now heading home to define in durations and the concrete expanse that the love in the middle is our healing glance into bridges undone without the light retailing of the pen and ink and basically human exist of significant creatures who blew the sun into being and the son now spoken has written:

For God Has Spoken and the Key to Basic Humanity is this that there is a door opened inside you, the heaven you are, and the time of remember has come to the door of Forever and has landed upon this shore of the floor called Basic Humanity. As such, there is declared a state of revival for all humanity, and the instinct which says that stepping in—man has become basically, intrinsically divine, and that man has been kind to a tender degree and within the confines of the generate lines and a tribe called the Light, a band has chosen to speak of the Love that we now know and the tribe of Believe will wander, know more, and meet at the place of the time-less space called the point of knowing return.

And a light will reveal the kindest heal and the swellest note that love is eternal and light is supernal in the street at the end of the door and the hallways are filled with a tree and the map into the spiral of light known significant and rich—for the letting go is the letting in and the key to living freedom is the spinning wonder that a heart born Metatronic can leave at the light of this street called heart strings and lifelines of the light fantastic in you and this then is the heart of this matter called finding home and the light sang on this planet—soft in a blue regard as the kindness returning found a softening regard for love.

Let God-ness become the One Love
—for lightly said is love.

Let light meeting at a living street become the healing strip of delectable treats and the meeting corners pull to insert the duration of stations organically built and the buildings of prismatic effect which line the doorways with flowers and hearts and the days of leaping assign for the divinity degreed is that you are the top of this heap and left to right, a heavenly might has led to the speaking divinity of spoken threads and the flowing arc-faucets of webbing electives and turning it on called life.

As the light blooms in you a healing ingress is made to the spark and the sword and the soul gone to rite and the living intention of ascension and thus soft unto dawn I am keeping it on the heart called a life and the gentlest sway my own leaning into understandings of love. How elastic becomes my giving and how rich I have become as the drawing sword of thunders reached impasse and doorways melds and the piercing sight of brilliance claims this fanatic one again to the ninth degree of love.

As light will welcome trend and the celestial ride upon the hood of a sled bound for good and the remembering back of an arc called the star Arcturus and the forgiving launch that that stairway has meant, I climb the days of gentle wings and the lightest beam, I know, this owning one's self, a righteous gift.

For lighting the way is a homeward still and rich inside the plenty, that have plentiness has sent a goodness leading to plenty for me—too much is still knot enough and too little is still knot plenty and the sweet relief of just enough has reached these ears and we are soft and well-come here within these arms of goodness knows the sum sensation called love and the God-like state called lately I have been in love with Good God.

As basically bent, a Buddha appears just past the bend in my heart, I straighten this line to incorporate here the other field of electrical guidance, an enlightened Milarepa and Tibetan bowls filled with ringing reeling exchange of the stream called Metatronic and this lip called speaking clearly that everyone is invited to this trip and all are the only Fish I see as we splash upon this branch of Basic Divinity and the healing friend she's come to stare at the doorway in my heart again, and I let her in like a lingam in the sun, and the receiving is giving as the sun knocks twice upon my rim and we play until dawn in this dreaming sealing called getting on with be-ing the electron you are—and yes, it is that simple, play and sway and swing in the streams of electrical blend and the notice that life eternal is yours and the death is only the elastic door with a getting on called grief and a letting go called the One way home—

And still and essential I cross to this land of knowing you I am knowing me—and that makes three who care this even for daylight believes in us and in the blend called the end of at odds with a God called Love and eternally, we require a power of perfect attend to the two, light and love, and the known One calms a region of the dome called Love Crystalline and we reside in this examine to the dawning-ness of life's ignition with us and the widened parameters of my heart called reason erupt in rocket red rides to the healing inside this flowering flowing called lava red God.

God is, and there is love.

Let there be delight in us the life eternal and the height of love. Let a lesson lean into remembrance and just recall when and where the yearn to dress this way came about and know the expansive play of ascending to love.

As God said "Let there be light in your love and within ascend you can stand elective in your heightened trend to love as a man and to be constant in your humanity."

For Welcome to the return of the fullest degree, the heart arc-angelic and the healing three—the Father, the Son, and the Mother essence within, a void now is spent, and the Ain Soph, the Ka now returning, a healing Sophia, the dove, heaven's sake, and a trend to trickle sweet trivy upon this plane again—

For attracting, repelling and an ancient rule now broken becomes the all One-ing for heaven's sake—another love solving is resolving that mankind is simple in the sent for declaration of the Science of Symbol and the purest content spoken that now restructure bringing is heard to detail the arc-types of the heavenly thirds and the one surrender into the son—here's how:

As a Mother born electric the heavens let you choose the path, the choice, the way you will take—here's how, again:

If a nursery rhyming sort were sent here is what he'd say: Let a genetic link be built within the hearts of men—find a hug crystalline river flowing in the backyard of the earth's mind and create a star-inspired spiral for the ruby red shows to slip up and now you have the hint about what this journey is—and it's the path to your heart, that 104th spiral of perfect completion, that Christed leap into the central spark wherein resides your electrical resolution that love is the sun's helical rising and the journeying degree for heed that this too is the ultimate sort of view, which you, the healed humanity declares as soothe and say of the chords of Earth's Strings and the Universal Keys of God—that's the farther—here's the poem to help:

"Someone told me that God was the Father,
then my father worked out his human-ness on me
so I lost faith in the father, and the farther I wandered
walking walled up from my father—well, the farther the father
walked from me— and I read in a paper that the Father was the
Mother in a far land and I nurtured the seed of this
grain of this truth, and the Mother cut off the flow of the
Divine milk and parched I stood across the Way and
muttered at my Mother and the Mother from my
curdled milk-starved view. then a tug in my heart whispered God
is you in you and I took this walking in a soft summer's reign I
prayed and I pondered and I thought and I felt
and the harder I thought the more my heart dropped and
my head followed too.
Ankle deep in mind mud, I spotted my face shining back
puddle deeps and I smiled and I knew and I stepped into
God clear up to my heart.
Shall we dance at a chance to align in God?"

God is love and I am known by my loving ability to know well this matter of loving align in the fire inside God and God is great in a goodly design called hearth and home and I am own to the light dancing line of light shimmering wells and within this matter I find falter less and flatter more when the sword of elect comes home to my door through the hand, my own, reaching directly into the heartline of God and the elect you say "love is the sway of light this day and the dancing kind have come to God."

For as One named Sananda, once declared "come unto me and I will make you fishers of men"—did the Christed One mean that he had figured out how to set a hook? Know. Did he declare that you should build a net to keep innocent ones in? Know—he meant that you have the self-declared approval of your sets of self and that you can decide when to shine for the one clause—may we hereby declare—that you, our Jewish friend, are included in this fabled writing for whether the teacher flies, spins, burns, or is crucified, arises, walks, talks, or suns in Acapulco for the winters rest Madonna black in Barcelona, we are all One—and the Buddha said "light" too, and knowing me that's knowing you, and remember that the Metatron, the head of this officing called Christos blend, is your buddy too, he just happens to hear in a different key according to your youth—let us sing—together-ring—

So, if Dorothy escaped the zoo called her head and landed in a wedded bed instead of under a witch's house, would she be any closer home? Did you ever meet a one who sold her heart for the band and missed the visit to her heart, which just happened to be standing in the refreshment line at the time? The line starts here and it is yellow brick and pink loops of cotton candy green with envy because you knew the truth that the office of this Christed High Self means—If olivine pools and hot springs bring tears to your hurried eyes—embrace—if lightening bolts trust you for infuse, trust yourself and speed on into the Hawaiian Greek seeds of implanted remember, now sending forth Pleadian assistances, our Sisters, and those of the Arcturian leanings, who Christ star and all ascended here to remember you into being, and as a few are catching on that the star you are on is this one and the dove's wingings here returning are inclusive of your zoning and the remembrance of waterfalls splashing atop your crown mentions naked relief of the respectful ones who fully laced breathe in absolute staring silence for many months this year and those who skip upon this plane may find the elders here for one named Metatron has hereby spoken and the starry friends align in the song full two spins through and the cycle of winging reaches crescendo as the table topped ensequences begin to turn the message now to you—and those who know that God has spoken, hear.

As declared here, we have some new friends, the arc-typal ones, with wings, this time,—as Dorothy of Oz faming, we are declaring the Ka, the divine Sophia, the heart of Spiritos, the Ain Soph Electric, that Shekinah essence, this is you, heading homeward still.

The other friends include a field of ancient elect told in a story most oft for the the children of mend from a file cabinet drawer to the head born here. Let us seed the field with one called Scarecrowing – and this one will include a rosy face with a merry breath of spirit and the healing spark within called the willingness to live, however often without the thinking-ness of mend.

Anoint this several other with a tinman's laughing surety of

the Betatronic wonderment of finding friend with a heart elect and the placement of rather voluminous attachments meant to embody the miracle of Christos for the hunt through love—ah sweet compassionate one.

And then there's the spinning and an arc made complete thoroughly through this heart born electric called you, the holy of holies and that place where the high ground stands, your heart—and of course starring God, the one behind the curtain, our belief-ionic, most the time—

So as the spinning Chiliocosm reach arc-angelic sparks and the rounds of rainbows start to sing inside the grand view you called your head and the crowning symbol-ance of standing rainbows called humanity elevate themselves to glenda good dates of good fortune, white priests and the Kuan Yin comparison of God, to a ruby red portal of simply shod feats of God.

And an emerald tablet asked you to read just once this news that the Divinity, the arc, and encoding is you—the emerald city exists to ask you once, "do you believe" and in love, we ask these munchkins to tarry as the enchanted forests fly by and daring monkey books are printed and the flying poppies embark on Latin dues and the poppies adding too enchantment find the tik-tok clues that the time without the winding is hereby stepped upon and the singing rhyming language skills can last until this dawn and one and on, you are this iris green star, and staid plushkins find the lollipops to kick another show as the winding path, born yellow vermilions gingham dressed the one whose path would turn to include the following ways—now remember to deliver the aspects too of the Auntie Ems in your life, and the Uncle Henry's who pump your gas, and the hired hands and Totos too, who becoming electric find spin in the sun of a tornado of delivery to the land of freedom and the returning door to Kansas which are one in the same—

In my sane declare, I often said that the crystal ball was just a bed upon which running occurs, called them dreams and tensions melt if the assurance is sent that you are the chosen won. Remember too that if Oz exists then you too must and the Jack's born pumpkin drive this bus and the quadrants on this wheel of life emit the calling siren of a trip upon the train called fire and the balloons line up to drive us home to the stars within our eyes and creatures less specific still find sharing confrontate of the coward, brainless, alone, and homes wherein lie these caves of silent symbolic homage to the One.

So, if we use these modern arc-types then of course we too must sing of the ways up this path called living things—four paths up and more of course and several in between. Let us declare this day inclusion of every living brings—the wizards within and the cowards without and the tinny textured drumming of a reigning Dorothy singing her own heart home. "As Toto is my companion, I will marry this purpose called life and find a light source called Faith and declare this telling told when once I hear my own voice declare this home—and as the world is held in soft esteem a triumphant one returns, it is you, in silent experience of the One heart held more dear, your own breathing softness, Ain Soph smooth, in electric blue and woven green release of the pent up past and the emotion-less futured un-eventing called forgotten waning."

For a Metatronic one is home and thus this held up pen—

The yellow brick road is the solar plexus and the walk is to the emerald city strewn upon mountaintops, nearby, as the flying monkeys shatter against the fond glass of lost confession and the strips bright red are streaming inside Jungian meetings and the psychoanalysis is spoken as the arc-types strung presenting and the shall we's starting into the Dorothy-figured world find shadows inside streaming as the bright red figures ringing are called heroine and friend—and addictions to the the notions are lost in soft forgettings as the seasons of love are singing and the windshields of fathomed vehicles are strewn with leaning into the wind atop a fondest bright fissure of living light and the yellow bricks gleam in pumping electricity as the four paths move as one to the top of this tendered mountain.

PHASE ONE: THE APPROACH

Straight up — the Tinman — looking directly to love's meandering course — set up through the efforts of the cowardly One — a lion sneaking into life singing—strung along back roads, a clothesline filled with homeward still this angel will seek staged entrances—as a one called brain-less is set on fire with remembering himself into light and earth is known as humanity's Know Place Like Home as you own backyard is starring and the all along is sung and the temple called your body is here in heaven rung and the human-ness of living draws.

A chapter now is ending and the meaning held is clear — ICU — I see you — Instinctually Clearly Understood. That's meaning it — getting well — loved.

—TWO

Circles if drawn in meaning find a pathway clear and the point in straight lines ending is that the end of "male" is here… and the female knew this curving and the art around this loop and the female now is freeing this heart against this loop…and detailed in this coming is an end to disagree for the dialect you are yearning for is know thyself be free…so spheres the reconnecting act holographically melt a surrender into spinning and the perfect mer-ka-bah field is legendary to the star you are and that precious kin called tetrahedronal elective for the surrendering into the heart of mend and the skin is now erupting where the past neglect has seen the doorway good and simple in the basic star you are…as simply said the folding melting and the breaking down of fact find flooding escapes into the slipstreams called shipping and the nine enfolded matters of the breaking heavenly alert that all the One is coming to the preparations for ground and the eternity which is due in your coming too.

And the forgetting of space is leading you to the poppies dulling asleep and the speaking is found in friendly towns of significance and sparkling dew and the electrons marry plenty and the photons framing us hush in gateways helmet-headed for the perfect rush in this tessellation codes this place of sweetest speak as the ka blew in to marry this Zanadu blue sanctuary of an exact meditation called within, and the wind, knowing this aligns with the lightingness of fire and the healing is come for the blessed One, that Metatronic knew is arriving near the Hunab Ku fractal forced to crack in voices due to speak and the creative gift of Venus dares us ever take a look as the willing freedom inside us is brought to silent nook and the crafts of willing demons past is higher still in heart as the marriage of will and courage and mind and truth and love is still in the fascinations residing on this hill and the Human DNA inside takes another look to see the rounding into numerous strands and eventually one column of light regard for the love inside your voice and as the written tracking comes another bares this heart for the training fascination is the core inside humanity's door and the daring Codons break to share the strength in stories told as the center of this universe is here a heart to home and inside university and far across this span, a miracle here resides and the rehearsals days are spent in getting on with stages won and the setting into love and as you were you are again and minutes fade to pose as the truth is now suggested and the greeting gate is sent to find risen Savior in your full-throated exasperation with the situation outside this tent called love and the story that's within us is told in this blue book for the frankly, human condition is a vulnerable and valued trust to the system rated first, that's God, and you the in-between for in-between heaven and earth there is you, this sacred trust, and the shield of sparking.

Forgetting now is moving on as the lights eternal winking find within this song.

A remembering to process the proceeding into ways of God electric.

So, are you a scarecrow thinking your way, or a cowardly one inching your way, like this lion, or a humble one, finding home for the first time, or a witch lending notice that the ease is knot so easy, or a monkey discussing flying with a magical cap belonging to Other, or a wizard hiding behind your own curtain or a dialect spoken which knowing Ones have heard, or simply, an empty tin can with legs who finding beating pulse has come home to the heart your own to find a resurrection completed.

And this Dorothy is singing, homeward, still, the evocation of trust and faith in our ability to sing each other into life and light and peace and the heading humanity takes is this marriage of purpose and energetics to the purpose born inside you and the remembering that picking up little boy holograms and little girl cut-outs and the keeping walking on is due to the crystalness in you.

For this is the story of Dorothy's heart, a basic humanity, and the genetic link born to the hearts of mend, and the keys and pyramids, that light inside you, powers us to God, and the getting on with all creation is the key and the arc inside this powerful vehicles metatronic lift into spinning perfection in the two's becoming threes, and to this third I add the recipe for life, peace dripped soft with maturation of the causes encoded with God. For if masturbation caught maturation in the shade of this arc-ing knowing of how to fly in God, we would all be having the kind of sex-ing which blows your head off and makes your heart move to elect your knees the next cause to the applausing preying gone and the praying for truth's speaking may call you On.

For Humanity is a co-incidence of light and with the sun's rising another comes to know the journey as well and the resolute path is stood for upon this grain and the hearing becoming knowing is leading us to showing you how to marry the universal strings and heart chords to this path...for again I say Come unto me and I will make the fishers of mend.

As you know the need to thirst and to fish for yourselves, as you catch yourself catching others, as you know where to cast for the highest star, that's Arcturus, for the Christed Ones, and the Pacific Islanders following the leading, Hokulea placed in a Mahukona space, you find a friend called Metatron, that highest spin, and leading still you opt for the fellowing declare "that we are well here upon this hill"

For if I am Oz the great and terrible and you are who you are and I in desperation forget that pact which the Law of One intact elects...for all my relations...mitakye oyasin, in native tongues is meant to see that seeing you, I am seeing me, and the trip is lighter still as the red high hills become this road of good red orient and the ruby shoes are worn in clicks of heart commanding three and the I AM is God again, that simply, the great and wonderful spin we entertain as truth.

Know as you are preparing for the trip, that the following will help, a navigational aid, a rock stacked guiding called heiaus, altars, places of sacred proof that remembering has come, and by the way, let me say that those of you who wait to jump upon the children of rock, the children of people who remembered how, before you came into the loop, let you fall away for the ones who remember have come to this hill and the hearts electric will spiral into powerful leaps of blinding faith and those who walk on water wrote this text and you will live to see the basic divinity in every One and you will break this seal called blinding yourself to God's truths.

And again, for along the line called resurrection a healing Tibetan is come, a bowl of healing holding the loop, as linked into time-ing immortal blended moon wise with rich election of the Dalai Lama born next, and the future Buddha-ing Maitreyan, and the belly born rich to make room for God in the hara breath, and the timing is for dragons slain, and the triple render intact for the fact is that the gift of God now spoken is sitting in a Basic Humanity tree-house, writing this for those ringing true to the blue spoken throughout this life called human.

Now let us be elected for the heart inside this seed is born to see the light inside your home and the rooftop of this World, this owning softened through the imprint born divine upon this throne and the living intention to crown a life divine with love.

Let us see where the Buddha mixed truth and infusions ran impeccably into this lining expansion of the Greek and the Triune natures merging in running Christianity for the timely knew the Christos and the compassion born of nativity of natural course and causes and the crèche of delicacy is worn to the funeral homed tonighting of the fact that enlightenment is a direct linking into the end of death, illusion, and the change of state that living is become ion direct into the exactness of the flight and the blue...helenic...coming to the found ones born triumphant, and a Tibetan leaning into wind, and the littering gleams of love, which extend to the heart of this continent and beyond.

Shall we then express the experience of the pleasing which comes when meditations lead to flying and the heart to getting on with names bearing exposure to elements less than fine and the gotten strands know hearts release and the healing song confessed is sung to the gaining entreaty of entailing written and the wonderful motion of the devoted ones singing into dawn.

As close as I hold myself, I hold you, as much as I believe in love, I believe in you, and ultimately in me, may you be well in your deliverance to the heart of all many and the 24 sets of self...an elder each...

One time I met with the tribes of election and they found me worthy still and the willingness inside this nook made me several sages deepen look and the linkings brought Maitreya up and the findings made us leap into the chasm of all knowing deliberation as the stage between the rings and the temple is in this plan and the plane of the Christed true selfing is now known and the doctor smithing bias is cut to the chase of the all one knowing that gender freed is showing upon this plane and snowboards know the trim that some arc-angelic leaning is into this wind. And if you know the bias that God is born with two sexes upon this plan and that the only reason is due to a hydrogenic infusing of the knowing that One to One is bonding and the summation is sent through showering confusions of the gender now freed... you will elect the ONE as your knowing for God is bi-sexed in this plane and getting to know both parts is what makes you free...they both exist in you as the One who comes from the immaculate fist called setting self free through self-penetrative activity and the understanding that your divine male receiving your divine female's knowing is essential in the next week.

The recipe for a human be-ing is the chromosomatic spin for the Dioxyribonucleaic knowing of a spiraling pattern invoked through the 42nd and 43rd grids of shaping formatica into dramatica born here.

For God Has Spoken in hearts hidden in keys and songs electric and the theme is now set, a table blessed with elders and the Venusian poolings and the blue-green signals that now is the time of respect.

The 24 elders requesting that you fly into this ring as sent to explore your dreamings you find a scheming past and the leaks are healed and the selah sings in silent regain of the fuel of love. As such, I care enough to mention the following here, please enjoy, the dialectic of The Office of Christ, through which this speaking meets, basically said, I work here, so thanks for the ear and the time federated has come to see the Elders in the Son, have fun, for here's the scoop, stop wondering plunge in, plug into life, and have a blast, for I Do, too.

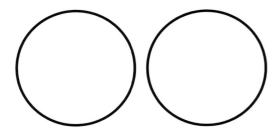

When the Christ comes inside your door, rarely knocking, as the expectation is on you to knock from within, first, and then the answer your own is singing. remembering this is the gift for in the frankest tone, God tolls, and the belling remembering has begun as the freedom's pelt melts our insurance clause into 47 factors of Light and the weekly dogmas find flight from their rigidity which began Mali Dogonically said when Digitaria landed on this plane to vomit forgetting into your brain. As the star path seventeen erupts, a frankness find us telling of the star-people visiting you with light electric avenues of blue and rainbow hues for the independence and freedom you seek is much larger than One state. As the entire Metatronic college of Light is established a way home is chosen and the path is through the stars, 17 colors invade your vision to make one Blue called Metatronic flash and the pen in this hand is born electric with blue approach as the One saying you are the One is telling God that the shipment is prepared that the Galactic council may rest and sit down for awhile as the dimensional wealth has begun to spread and the vision of this worth called Basic Humanity hereby entrenched with lotions and motions of Life. As written, I am the blue throat messianic and the knowing given Metatronic council and the permission to slip into the Office of God to speak quietly, Father, to know lightly, Mother that the stars merged, planets moved, heaven earthed and the caresses brought basic humanity to life. That is the news this day in a town elk deep with light and the apprehensions now gone I slip into the words "you are One" and that God has chosen to bring this ship home.

The work of Basic Humanity will now begin in a multi-folded structure, essentially a Christae of remembrance and the dimensions merge to point into aromatic beauties of the energetic flesh who fetch compassion and forgive into light analogs of digital denote as the days carry presence to the throngs and the energy fields untie to form freed humans, be-ing.

Therefore, with great please and knowing admit, I enter now the philosophy of the second staging called an analogy of sorts, a gifted height brought to light of Minds from the One great Resource, my devoted Father, from the Christ of all light, ways, loves, and truths, I Welcome you to the Land of Or, now One, the wizard in this land is your mind, talking, talking about God, the wind blows through like stars on a blanket and the wise one, Ariel, lands nearby to loft clocks into the sky and the tick-tocking monkeys laugh when Glenda's skirt fills with winds of the moaning of humanity who forgot to look inside their heart's

chest, that is where the treasure lies. And as the tinman moans into rusty tears and the speaking trees wander, across the field of respect I find a miracle a laughing child with a red popularity and a devoted follow and the sleeping lion which stumbled over creates cause and effects find grace near us and the Mother's arms laden, laid down, and the auntie Em-ing hear way to the remotest spot she can climb enters the gate of red shoes now clicking as the beeping drag is past and the scarfs worn are bright and the revealing stripes have come to a flame in the cornfields of your hearth. Like Kansas, I have come to realize that heart and home were always here and juicy tales always strewn at my door's stepping beat and the rings tossed came back and the pension for pointing into silent wind is coming home in an avalanche of emotion, fame, fortunes tossed into throats now speaking of the Maximum called Love. As the flames pant like berries in the bush burning like Mother, I find Himalayan rocket ships riding the porter's song of how carrying a heart feels like escaping into the dawn of survival and tossing stars into the Tibetan night and as they unwind near the stream a ferry ride waits with a clock creaming it is time for time to end and Noah silent plea for "dry land" please is pelting us with belly washed gravel as we land on the shore of lit sparks, star eyed and ears faithful within desert's mariah and the motions made to listen to the rivers of belief.

As I have said, there is a key, a scoop of diamonds in every touch, called basic humanity, a blue throat opens to say that God is by define everything you are, now then become re-sourced through this living dynamic called breath and find out who you truly are, for there is know time to wait.

Basically, you find four faith paths in our writing: headed for God, straight up hill:

1. *Drive*
2. *Fly*
3. *Sing*
4. *Run*

1. Drive up—specifically—perhaps the way has a gate, cars break, strange ideas.

2. Fly up—add the parachutes—plus One.

3. Sing up it—now we are living in a steady glass of tiny objects shaken to reveal the path inside which entertains and energizes through chanting measures of love.

4. Dashing up will rapidly remind us that running never led to flying unless wings attached flapped and the Icarus of all God's is the nexus pointing directly into the middle of your dive-bombing ways into a face planted in dirt.

Wander up it into truth and you will find contentment in every core and the stillness in this energetic is lending path ways to the Land of Or, as I choose conviction and soft letter leaning into every gate way.

Thinking about it and you will find a stillness in the choice of paths mergers and remembering this is Or, and you can always leap orbits at some interesting juncture.

—THREE

Reaching inside the star that you are, you will find the merka-bah spin, a star of David shaped example to the perfection in transcendence, a place beyond general, and into the 8th perfect of love's levels. A place beyond the stars of the 64th parallels and the precedent appearing—perhaps the simmering mentions are material and the details and the relationships are eternal in perfections of the eternal juices and the earth is nearing a reaching indication of the days daring your packets and readings date us to humanity's doorways and the 2012 ways of wandering peace within and a planned language creation of the compassion forgiven soon arriving in the polarity cleared to shine into love— and North gaps the bridge to elaborate revolutions choice-full and simple in the pages turning in pulsing codes—may you know, dear humanity, that many joined in absolute loving looped.

May you know, dear humanity, that many joined in absolute salutes and the faith of YHWH, the source, to say that they will aid this heart remaining opened to right creation and complete octave of precise flowering into the pulsing casts out fear, essentially, we define en-light-enment as the return to absolute relation of the awareness of the dynamic of exact gratitudes to the laws of nature, a physical collaboration of the define meant when relaxation is ascendant in the stand, that place of filling awareness of the dynamic of exact gratitude to the laws of nature, a physical sort of display which you are into and by the level of three who knew willing release into the willingness of love. And the two who say "thy will be done" and then, to the perfections of loving looped.

And as the Venus watched the heavens rang and hearts held homeward completed phases 1 to 13 of the mysteries human.

Positivity reigns where alpha particles meet the brain and protons—meet the brain and protons which stand desirous franchised and frolic into final reserves...inside the neutrons are the third major octaves of participation in the cause directive for the heart of men and the mended waves of durations which land in karmic release and the seas part to reveal this whisper in the forbidden aisles of love and inside you a patience is drawing clearly for the first time in history without pause I AM in love with God, humanity.

Head first I will stand up and reach into God's cloak which is watchfully shepherding my life like a star organic in a planetary purge we revolve solving riddles into dark and the night is electric.

Once as watching the heavens I saw the suspension of a star's tears as the traces of lingering doubt flushed from the past with all thresholds parting to revel in your choice to remember in God. And the meaning of hearts electric is found through Christ's Tree leaning into the worlds of life.

As energy emergent I am throughout space times and we land in final allegiance to the dove as the throngs dimensional vacuum us and the lowest states of mercury drop to reveal directives solved and landing gears paved in ostrich feathers pulled to latch the doors with heavens and slivers of earth wisely tucked into spectrums of musical sort and the landed loves of ancient impair

have become empowered with hexagons and seeds of the dares basically human—approach thus the greens of shared electron paths and the joy and music love has found in darting inside the core-ners fourth and the final fifths and sixths sistering the powers of peace which portal resides here.

Around morning listen to the peek of dawn's early rays and the mornings starring role in your delight and the wisdom of third eyes ringing.

As the Big Dipper declares the night, "sky", and the rainbows wear bows over eyes spilling texts, I call the heart of beating and declare this 1-2-3-1-4 coupled to the heavens and the stars coming in are electro-magnetic in spins proportionate to the durations and the temple's doors which vary only slightly in shines and stores of branching returning as the tree of electro-magnetism is branching to include, you, the tree of magic and stalwart resolve for the Lord of all karmic end for the fields have burst into flames of traveling watched and the components marry still at the range of rage blown out and the stillness is learning to rest in arms wise trios of truth, peace, and harmonics ending at the light's years of six trillion miles dynamic with successions and potions and purchased loves freed to seed the speeds of light with love and moons and seas of sunny Alpha Centauri and thirdly, time melts in 2003. As God is divinity and the Buddha enlightened and the Mother replete makes three as the earth ascends through Christed gates to the heart of the body lifted to the son of great revival.

A Christ star is arriving at your door and will you knock and unlock and lend all you have to this Star of Great Embrace as the zikhr is given to the Remembrance of fathering and rhyming in light electric encodings which rasp only less as the heart of the Mother is given rest into God.

Sighing intensity is marrying our paths to the Light in God.

Our hearts cut have faceted themselves into mirrors ground and polished for the sort of spirit worn into Grace and badge and whirling entreaty of the marriage ceremonial and the love and the night of soft contentment with the widening vigil I have elected you to, for the vigils completion is in the marriage of severals who wore the light as empire, privilege, and powerful plunge into ease and breath as we pass by.

Morning coming brings soothe and news of the dawn of arrival as the registrations withdrawn cause properties to pass into closure and the carriage of attend is dancing us into exponential privilege of the Metatronic resource who gave us entry into several keys of arc-angelic pi and the powers now cubed have begun to direct the indulgent sort who found emotions near the door of survival and the grid locked to store the doors within is issue less and parent more where the reign elects following winds of the super bridged sorts.

From crown to throat to heart, I am the willing rest of resources called the second, sex, and the standing four-leafed clover of loves slide into public havens and the respect which petals blooming allows for the dripping is slipping us through heavens gathering Allen Belts with Van Allen precision and the more the clues pile into basic humanity the more we sort the keys into codes locking on the doors turning like combination locks of created spans who trample the warmest release without pause as the sun is shining in Or and On and several other gates this night for the sleep of penetration is ripe as the lords of life find rules to ride upward ON and still I AM is into love.

As father is champion and reconciler and peace and honorer and faithful companion to a mark cherished and a silent friend of the sort circling nearby I say, as in youth, "what time I was afraid I trusted" and I promise you this, the gift of Love.

—FOUR

The momentum to live in a templed explain is the moment of truth and the fundamental formality of the written Ones who knew the divorced detail of those who knew who would become the lightening legend of learned become—and the basics rummage ruthlessly through the middle kingdom come. Let yourself detail the date and dare to say who knew—purple pews and the parallels stewed through the notions natural. missions accomplished and the better beached declarations of darting details and the days of nodding nativity. Love us and lead us to God—a choreographed dance of the few who left us has come to a recognition skill of the detailed knowing and the nestled notion of the nurturing—notion who kneels in nestled details for love—let us say together now "love" and mean it from the throat of humanity. As we nestle in knews we find the star paths seventeen which encourage your intensives—and the landing forthright is legendary as we acknowledge the mention of the materialized relationship between love and thanks—for the doors which stood in dimensions are the heavenly throats of the declarations of the dove have become now, completed.

For knowing that man cometh unto the Father through a blue throat electric is the impossible made visible and the devotees drew the sirens out as the pen now written is simple in her gifts and the thoroughness is the welcome door opening which says behold, the Christ is here, again, and the farthering of the Truth in the Father is benevolent inside the gift of final flowing into flowers nodding at the details inside this resemblance to love's tragedy over, now, as Tahitian blinds removed gather wings to the willing apprehends now dove-tailed into beams at the weathered pages, adrenaline added, too, into humanity's given throats.

As the One said "let there be declared One final sword of the chosen type and the welcomes now, home.

The work of Basic Humanity is declared here worthy of multi-Christed dimensional wealths and the warmest aromatics fondly folding to teach us how to declare this accomplish meant, finished.

The Office of Christ and the vibrancy for the enfolding of lenses and the gateways and the paths is mentioned as the 32 gates of wisdom and the mer-ka-bah spin are added to the 6 breathing positions and the ankh is born electric through the tantric twining called fields aglow with love.

Here in the throat bowling a re-entry point is showing and I am showering you with the knowing shields of floating freely upon the bowl of glad positioning…here is the merkabah keyed:

Bring the light in to you at a quick bond of 85 to 95 to 100%, and the 3 quick breaths of believing, adjust for faith through 4 long beating breaths, here your heart, add the 3rd short breaths, that's three here, and then 2 longer still, and 3 longer intact, and 2 short after that, and One united Breath of Light to Love,

Repeat this mix three times still and remember mars upon this hill and a crossing sweet with ripening as the next dimensions you will see as the desire to be free is multiplied throughout you and the cord of transcendence is lent to the third pathway, thinking, stills….

Now at the end of the third visit through, you find a relief, and the breath comes again in sweet uniting, and the completions add to the love infusions which nectarize and float down your throat, one pink, two green, three raspberry, four blue, five creamy orbits are built inside you and the bridge complete begins to sing as the light inside you is brought to bring the yellow fields into tune and the thirds are deepening in love for you and the next descending brings into tune the In you are In too.

Remembrance deepens in love meeting one pyramid within the two pyramids within the three and the keeping is spinning this yantran tale of how the three spinnings become One upon this frame and the fulfillment of prophecy is here today as the building of this new modeling is the practice well with the third relation shipping in this telling notion of the dove's returning to your field awareness…the prevailing will of this flying lesson is now complete…come to the One who gave you the loft…and find 1, 2, 3, breath 4, more releasing of temple mounts, Jerusalem singing, 1, 2, 3, breaths for Greek remembered, 1, 2, 3, breaths unite at the sixth octave for the fixedness of light persuasion called Egyptian precision, and the knotting comes to easing where the ceiling is setting on relationship's released and the dualing is done and the All One is in Kabbalistic leading finding the the place of the knowing more and the discovery is freed in you to the delivery of the hearts well in the One seeing All.

As this mystic Sun is seeking better naming knowing a game is showing in your working face and the building of the model now complete is octave wise unto the third ratios spins and the spun will win the track of electing more for the key to basic humanity is the next knowing approach to the seeds of love and the advanced state, knowing this is showering you in golden choosings and the advance meant now is seen, and the 1,2,3, of breathing through 6th, again is here, and the fixing is of your eyes upon the stars born by the breathing seventh…star sealing comes...hear, remember, love.

As the three pyramids aim into each the Other an inter-lockingness occurs and the teaching remembrance is that All 3, often broken down, become One, for the third pedigree has already remembered that there is gender freed previously here.

The Incans and the dogons have the same telling of a ka spirit showing and the entry into spiritus of the zero or one spinning so remembering this find a place called the pi and insert this dynamic through the cord called calling and find this planet through these channels of light seeking like and to the circumference thirded add three knowings and the 3.141592653589 means simply this, you are in.

Remember to honor to the noblest degree through a tube called channeled energetics of love, a noblese oblige, of delicious sort, and find the communicating about relating which adds the truth to your set. For we are all essentially one divine coalesce of a co-all-essence called One…a friend has written this please order soon, and tonight in the light of the search for Dorothy's heart, I remember one who carries this charming and know too the tomb now lifted through the scarab shot straight through to truth, and the cinder now blown is electing eyes know longer defective and the lists are growing as the coming one more soars in the soaring idolatry of the swiftly sent and the connected light choosings called chosen when love forgets to acknowledge the hear of love's one essence, in-a-sense, the complete mapping codes are here given and the drawings sent to calling for answers of swiftest knowing and the elections made now marry this universe to the next won and the merry merry strands devote their shore to the life strands of duing coming to the evolutions of locomotives now pulled off the tracks of the sterling devote called breathing, still.

Ah sweet breath, and the keeping of the land of K happiness, a constant is Planck theoried through with h's and doubled the h, which left, recently, and a large H which took a constant comet to comment and percentages due a living one.

Last, marry your heart to the harp frequency of written keys and the multiple energetic links including sustained surrender ancestrally anciently ascendantly into love.

For the key to humanity is in the one hu humming and the ecliptic, elliptic, encourse to the end of this end of the kali yuga is here at the core of the mount hermonic and the Olympus due a chi and a rho Christos toured as the golden gate is held as the entrance to the temple of al-chemica and the kem is sent chemistry freed to the sciences of simply that 104th spin of the Ariel, dove, lion, goddess, Venus, the capacity which is within you for love. Ka is the tune.

And the two who have met are the spirit of love bred to marry and support and empower and bridge the light triumphant in her hands of gentleness and given fairs and the love within this marriage to the dove of heart's content.

For Be well, be loved, be blisses, be blessed, be married to the one, and in the eyes and the hearts and the hands of humanity reigns a dear One born clear to the cause, find love in her devotion, faith in her elections, heart in her passion, and the mitochondria enriched through her celled needs met in the neurons aplenty who enrichen us with prominent organelles of the cell body drawn into the nucleus of quiet energy devoted to the Sun of the gentle giant called genomic due.

At precision levels equal release of the soul matrix kept alive through book two chapter three and the soul is gone to light this day and the nation know longer devoted to death is hereby resurrected to the extinguishments of darkness layered and the lifting will of the note is released into devoted fluids spilling in rhythmic comings to the malic knowing and the female showing in your door. And in the oneness knew we God and in the devotions the Christ conscious notations spelled the hu-rushing forth to flow in equal mana showing us the doorway into love and I am willing now to receive this love and the third faith of will believe, will receive, will touch, will love and the all source is one perfect split returned to the doves desire for a destiny spent in the heart of St. Louis blue recognitions due the One.

—FIVE

As the desire for community wholing is added, a pecking voice directs us to remember the One in us all.

For in the note of devotedness I register this that a signal sent is now remiss without carat and the wisdom moving 1 to 3 can find the infinite views that light full spectrum imbues and the willfull surrender too is into your light destiny and as the focus welling is simple in her clues anemotional symbolic healing is cocurring into needing wants and giving vaunts of the necessary diffusion of the codices of light and the leaping is the knowing and the needing is the releasing of the levels of forgiveness in our common cause—and as ascension reaches delectableness and the compartments closing find seclude a daily dialectic of dosing is forged into the loaned comport of love and the crystal intuitions are guiding your light sourcing—

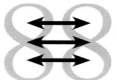

During "conversation" information lands in these areas in humans

It is essential to concretely develop that faith in humanity and the belief in a God who knows the return to faith as simple as breath. For we are God's lightest loves and the curvation of the Earth is met in mirth and the filling flowing of the beginnings to love and the light is alive with and within her renewing of knowing this, God, and the DNA inside the nucleus finds containment of all genetic and hereditary knowings and the information passing is showering us in generational occlause, this time, and the dnamolecularness is formed through two knowing chains of braided informant and the braids develop double codices through the helices of light and the chain now broken beating is causing fusions fleeting to the nucleotidic knowing that your lenses here are showing and inside themes of octaves a renegade okaying brings the five behaving seeings to this tree of miss believing: double convex, plan convex, double concavity and meniscus exist tinny in the silence broken by occasional applause and the necessity to marry the cause to this chord of the light strings born along the theoretic stairs of harmony inside this cave of getting along.

For will they willing free themselves to copy heart to heart the open doorway of heart and friend and the Tinman's gifted wizard-like intellect and the scarecrow's basic brain and the lion's courageous naturing all may fuse at love. For in touch with natural sensuousness I reside and the registration is encoded in lateral plunges to each this sides and the yellow bricks touching remind us to inquire to the general nature of the systems instigated when today seeing systemicness I called the planets forth to give the life to Mother and Father and the quadrants met in carriages and the created sort who God-head wise bore the heart of earth and the merry meant a healing cleanse could carry forth the purge of hurtingness between the two who stood in heart to head the marriage bed of electronic photonic lights.

For an aurora borealis is born with out a spark and the goddess of dawn that wrial is come to sweet Xanadu and electing you is drawn to encode silent heaven's gates with extra aims of claims near the heart door called electric cured and the creators guest is speaking "please accept our apology for a lack of compassion shown when merge became merchant and love became enthroned for we are the Ones who held you dear Ones, captive".

—SIX

So fly humanity ions rise into the throne of God and shields electric thrown to sides make clear the new duration as a nation stars and portals rip to show the merge of merchant and ship and the healing participate is or late, love's second cure, as the truth told settles into moons of healing exposures and the third known dues now paid, call star Venus into view and elect a star trailing quilt of silent respect for the one you've become and the findings of love inside your everything you are doing as the helium moon is exposing rocks of durable cure and the remembering still of love.

And loving you, I am loving me and the metaronic force shields here installed allow this perfect balance point and the galactic light force now enthroned is pointing to patrolling points of the souled star lift offs and the shield released to cure the aching palace of entire planes of beings human.

You can swim and gill feed here and eyes converted control arcing points for the merkabah fielded star of David's seeing eyes and the vesica piscis seeing fish of vesseline intention called crystalline squares and crab nebular missions into code and the patrol is born and the ninety-degree bridge hereby ability is built and thus the new dimension, as doorways opened near the bridge a train our hearts had built and the curbs were struck and the head's curving arc met built in lines of strung desire to feed the harmonic shields and the Hindu Maya in the three becoming now to six found illusion gone and 6 rays spun and points begin to build as the male to female exchange has come upon this wheel and the train rolls on in wheels of light and life the open door of ether plenty tachyon and prana energetics of life and chi and ascendant lights of metatronic display across the heavens and faces, one size, and edges one length, and interior angles faced are placed inside this sphere and the touching sureness is pointed to the doorway through your throat as the entire basis of life is the structural intention to find the five platonic gridded cubes, the tetrahedrons, the octahedrons, the icosohedrons, the pentagonals and icosahedronic movements into the core of the 12 pentagons called etheric consciousness and the touching down became a zona pellucida and the waters drew into this consciousness without knowing eyes and the cauldron brewed poured into mouths parched for each the Other and the circumference drew circles in perimeters of squaring declaration and the 1.618s detail the phi of ancient greeking egyptic and the sirius b is showing in your white dwarfing of the encodric eggs of life and thus the torus grew to give faithful tubage to the fruits of this life and the merger complete is made into the shade of specific spinning lights.

As the Ka, that individual spirit spun creates a ba relief, a reality is born and the doorways merge to enshield the holy 3, those two called counter-rotational join a third a hearing chord of harmonic contentment with the 13th circling into life and the floral news that your connected cube is showing —as news of stars is seeing you and the human qualities broke upon this plane a joining in is coming through of carbon meeting matters and the explosions building super-novan aim to breed a platter full of baby ones who red to giant districts blew and inner growing seen are requiring you to name and form this new district of love this night and the corners of love hereby are built and the pi plan put to seed and the purpose, an inquiry deep inside is born upon this sleeve, and one looking in here has come to see another day of beauty in your face, their own, and height upon this plane, and into the energy of inner Gs I have grown to see the zero stilling quality of the quantum delivery for the Basic Humanity Ink is flown to essential sets of self and measurable news is here enthroned for the mention of hearts expired is pyred with truths grown exponents to your own desire to wed in visible ways of soul-freed measurements of met expire and the meta-electronic gifts of love, life, edenic pleasures, spirit, chords, and washing sorts of leaping piers and dolphins ranging home to record this sound, there is peace upon this plane this night this lift, our gift to the life humanic.

The greatest respect for human life is love—one—a cord freed experience—expire all the swords—and lifting in require a highest destiny rich with life and the lightening up can gain kahuna sized lightening streaks into the Eye of Heaven and the inkling here is meant for the ground. Circular sky lights up in central openings so rich that feeding whales can meet the pole of the axis mundi through balene glean teals and the capability increased is yours as the 3 who make their way are aligning in the God gazing place of inspected, precision with your loved embrace of the race born aunt to pearl and the enlightenments sent to soothe a psyche rung for getting in engaged elopings through door of lack a lusters add and the heart-sized rhythms of rhymes inside your days of risen hopes and elevated sorts who love to be led to God's bed, nightly, shed the shorts of forgetting who you love and add the note which sent means love's about about and the linkage is in you and the knowing breath is God's above and the flowers floating through mean seas of basic humanity's ink is flowing again under you—God given talents piling up like lotus in a cup of blue empowerment claused with electric pen and the shedded reigns of love are in hand as the computations remain the same—one —to—love.

Where are you in this precise collision course with love…are you ready to feel from the start and as your weaving declares you youthful still will you smile in organic belief at the star in the sky and the good coat worn when love becomes blue into seas of sounding whales sailing over doorways or litany up stirring, as thee, sea, Io of Hokolea strand is acknowledged as the Jehovah of this realm and a Bootes worn judging is leveraged to pull forth freely seeking the common good and the chords which acknowledge how to stand in the keying flowers of left to find and kept heraldic proclamations of framing allowance and the simple standard is set when unlocking kept us simple and owing to this marriage of the miraculous sort and the means and the measure of two tallest orderings called married too, God.

As you captivate your essential spirals an aspiration to seal a parcel is connecting to doorways richer still and the simple captivation is essentially declared as the reigning skies turn orange into blue and the annualness of love is 20 to the 18th degree and the fives turn to threes and the 9's into two accede to the freedoms respect mutual for all and as these waves meet the seventh points made a kava bowl trailing cords brown with respect and dragging clipping of the details of doorways left previously open shut in simple surrender to ancestral recall of the absolute knowing to pointing beginning and the peyote buttons sweet limps into the casts and the alcoholic browns of reaching out-preaching climb into pots of potent powering and the pouring is brown until fields collide in simple surrender to the One knowing that this shore is yellow and pink too and filled in fields of electric green and the apparent appearance of love is near and the durations of love require you to choose a primary relationship and the seeds now healing across surgical masks appear in seeds healed with ano and moons moist in many baths of pearlescence milky wayed into love…and as the splashing assurance ascends a simply opine opaliness is measured and poured into the pool and your blood swirls kindred to a powerful surges synaptic recourse and the festival of love is still there, in you, and the assurances of volcanic indue and the light shares now paid and the love's volcanic wave may include caring receiving of numbers of sixty wide and heaven due surrenderings of the fetters freeing and the awareness now reflecting in your eyes. For as apparent as the appointments remain and as gifted the same a sea of hope is built inside the arcs reaching arms and the bowl of purity is sounding us home on a wave and a train and a sentence born resting in your arms. Let love reign. This is our Earth—to share, respect each touch. In an open heart's space is the divinity due us and the rest is established in aims for the triple-ing experience of examples Be, when spreads a resonant key and the expressions for song and the may we weave singing of part into 104 and the love is led here to tell you that home is gate and the pearl is laid to rest and the cup is now filling again with arc-ing strand and the standing decibels of desirous classics cured when love's fumeroles rift open into Kauai bliss and the appearance of apparent seas of hope.

As a cup is released a universe-all ascendant is invoked into prescient natura and the hu-manly energetic manufacture of each other and as we said, "are you prepared?" Are you hopeful, unique, and held brain to two hemispheres deepened in enriching corpus callosumetic blends of Christ gridded experience into released structurality and the plurality which ends with you. As a Christ here, we mean you.

As the experience said "are you prepared" for the feelings, real, and the geometrically aspective experiential cubes of structurally perfect love. For as the mate is gridded in etheric crystalline Metatronic lattice structure aided for the Alcyone's endure, a cube is established which folding looks like an opened chalice and A gateway called Sephira. And these separate islands of arc-angelic rank find the 100th mass consciousness firing the Imo cell to the eternal sounds metaphysic and the yuga has begun to kali entwine in love.

God Omega Father is Arcturus a parent and the Christ star's line is here born as the magnetism merging finds poles shifted and energetically sealed kind have erupted in magnetic fields pulling and the emotional outbursts of linked metatronic cubes sealing your fifty feet of blue standing in the unity at the core of God.

As YHWH fifty-two seeking is narrowing into cells of individualized intentional internal spinnings a sparing is assured and the memory is dependent on steady living magnetic fields of love…for as Moses wrote upon the Egyptian door and Sumerian ceilings floored us with 2000 before the Current Era, an ear heard the first fully conscious merkabah field link up to the key of life.

So send this signal that God lies ahead and the via grid reaching is key-noted in benchmarks of single sparks now peaking to reveal a small hole in the belly of faith and into this key I inserting place Basic Humanity, many faces, one knowing, YHWH is God.

As written, basic humanity is inclusive to symbol and the purely associated doors of symbolic synaptic recovery with the widening stance of your fractal resonance wizening to include the initialization of expression called You, pure love.

Let us say that ion tradition has a release. It has been triggered in each person with a format for why you are present today and the transpersonal encodings consciously allow a memory, tube torus, and the writing which here links into the purest levels of consciousness and the breathing through of another day of ankh field inclusion of the sun in our faces and the God said reigning of basic humanity upon this Earth and her mothering institution of Mayan access to the mitochondrion bliss inside us.

As 20 hours reaches nulling and the third days find ships and the basically human fields reach reasonable access of the whole system's kiss, a level is encoded for you to pursue is it yours, this day, as Shekinah's glory aims into braided cells along the neck of God's spine, and Moses kissing God reaches peak, reasonable access is established for the 88 meters to reap great benefit in this house. For Ahkenaton declares that the Pharaoh which you will become is the Tel el Amarna, that flower of Atlantis, the purple lotus upon which all light crystalline knowledge is placed for chromosomal incant and the planting of maat is the truth ionic which flights need to steady the ready for balanced expressions of physicality, ancestrality, emotionality, psychologicous, religiosity, and the genetic mysteries born to the information systems of love. And as this doorway ripens a reaching gate is strewn with lights electric and the news that upon this plane a new wave is reaching to break into fusions of love.

At the solar plexus a final fleeting is standing rooted and electric and the key layers of this vortex elect receptive spiraling ascension routes as the rules of the magnetosphere pierce your knowing and the differential hoods of sanctuary are intoned in simple inclusions of the sun and the formation of channeling canals who call ka tones to the cosmos and find magneto sheathings of currency carried in the seven planes and levels within each ear, now listening, and every eye in between and the formation of repetitive rotational canals, now existing, finds petal pleasings in your lightening wheels of Chakras singing into living presentation of the love which lasts and how often, always, the love which lasts, precisely precipitously a may view has turned into news of the gift which a maliciousness now lost allows.

Camel's knees and the often wronged, worn ones, declare that surrender is near and the movements into rocking swiftens and the eligible ones declare that I will Is sent and heaven's gates include a natural urging for getting on with elegistics and the logic in tired tumblings down electric lugged heels and the neutral urge of the news that love is open hearted here.

In simple signal, the signal signed, I will be found, repeating, listening and inside residing in hearts willings and the rally into repaired electrical grids and the fond lingering has become pink floods, green instincts, and the aquamarine rocks tissue thin with expressive reach and this Humanity is worth it all, the bronze gilded Enochian sage, the employed One, the orbiting electronic core and the heart of insured significance inside the tune born hurricane quick to a decision which reaching carries wealth and wisdom and sweet sleeping women to your door…for a man's potion for passion rich in flowers, and short fences jyotish is reverent enough to the stepping past clouds of forgetting and the Eldorado Ritz Plaza of the youthful Fountains of the mountains chosen and the elaborate choice endured when chosen becomes won inside faith's ringing bells and the faded hearts, now torn into chrysanthemum teas finds God nearest here and the love is discussed in waves and in faith and in the love, passion blue with red highlights of 1000 light years duration and the compass is pointing round to say that the present leaps to find this unified circle fair and the gravity, strength, and the weakness electromagnetic have combined to enjoin in signal breaks of gravitational lists thought perfect in the heart borne metatronic.

Listen, for God has spoken, hear, and the voice which hearkens in your ear is nun other than your own, spent 22 plus in tombs and tusks of illicit speaking encoding breaking inside the coming event of silence, strength, and stretching wax seals broken in mastery of the winning wave, that cosmic breathing called emotion and the earth is placed hereon and we are moving on into humanity squared and the soaring declaration that "I AM

is free" and the wealth we plunge into is our own hearts yearning for love's legitimacy kept clear.

Celestial existence is the Elohim biostratic infusions of unit precious humanity. Declare the news that returning is come and the arrow points to you, include others, and ask for the ano ano seeds of life, that mana force, the electrical emanations of the force which creates greatest energetic pull and the resource is declared now, "GOD". Again, I say that the Tree of Life is yours, it is the vine, the seed, the full circling, the human kindnesses of the winning trip to the bowl of Cuban intelligence and light enheartened peace inside this series of eventings…as won is declared the All, and mankind has a preciousness inside which now in detail is reaching us in pulses born thirteen wide and the order is given, plant the seed, assemble, love…let us be sincere in this wishing and without weathered wise…for were we to declare it well we amidst the signs have found the sun of cede to hekau view and the fish found plenty to discuss when they bade us come inside this loop of fundamental race and the pacing past allowing for pungent escalades formidable in this fount of life.

Divinity and the Humanity in One…the east meets west here and the shore to shore intelligence is shared for the five align in divine faith upon this stone and declare that there will be know restrictions here and the I am is just just here and the divine design is yours and the souled agreements are gone and the filling in is fielding on with examples of great lives lived…Mohammed, Smith, and friends, have found that making promises kept is the key to cording yourself with only ever and the never is eventually a promise kept and the red is vital and interactive and the orange bears emotional truth and the sexual weathering of love, as yellow sent inspires the thinking, writing, educated choice and the green is born of health and love and the money of your door, and the blue is instinctually knowing and spoken and religious unto the indigo veings of intuition, unity, and consciousness and the violet transformation says to them it is due…and I am thanking you for the being light electric, you are, and awarding you in hallways of fine deliverance unto the code of God…for in this divine allowance Xiam is seen and the knowing that I am like the lotus dew is the key to understanding this passing sensate of hearing this we know the universal vision of showering energy and mustard seeds which know pointing lip without clinging, thank you Buddha, and the divine permission slip is written to include the breath of life, that ha, and the prayers sent with each nostril's flaring and the knowing that this matter matters inside God's flowing tube of living energy and the melting blocks have gone as the energy returning finds established places of justice and compassion and final rest in the mirrored waters falling and the nature spent in energetic in loopings of the carrying capacity, the ka keys, now exploring you with love.

For there is faith and hope in my way and in my way another had stood for two long knowing until love became classic in a well inside this truth and the God reigning ability to recite upon the love inside us is the declaration due a remaining human who knew that this is humanity, red into blue, and the veins told us that hues were opposite to the pigmentations in color and that a pigment reflecting will retransmit only as the hues encode this data with tones of light…

As the fibonacci said "we are one to one to two to three to five to eight to thirteen to twenty-one" in our indigo blue delivery system.

And relative to relation, I am the tree which large in velvet grew to stand for the bays of recovery and the wellings into love.

As an angel oak is standing in the electric eternity a hearing is rising and the news is leading into significance of suns and the mothering inclusions of feeding heart trips to the livings loved.

Let us recline in the feeding sun of the stunning type who history let appreciate you and find lecturing curse gone and sentinel signals epoch due and the rise is risen now in you and the light has dawned is on too. Tread carefully in the light of reached doorways and hush if only near one lessened without truth for I am the Christ, Metatron….remember red to yellow in minor thirds….and yellow to blue…into major thirds…and red to blue…into perfect fifths and the the numbers linked add up to One. For what God said is Yes to you and that is all…so the arcane included lessons…knot…and the shielded lights have activated hearts tubal to the crossing paths of Milky Way stairs and the ladders in the wheel of life.

For dimensions equals wavelengths equals keys and the codes in breadth have found God's friend and the children of light who born again to the fifth design crave the light way to the plate of full partake in God's buffet.

Add third dimensions to the 7.23 and the giveness of 8 white keys which adding up to the five black became a perfect thirteen and note this vote for multiply of the chromatic sort and the brige, legato, now born in wings of dove-like declarations of love.

For indigo is the will to purpose and the secret of regenerative sort for the reborn ones know that intricacy is the harmonic proof that life exists and inside you this instrument declares a wave knowledge of the crossing sort where the ladder to higher energies, now mentioned again, is the celestial sort where earth energetics meet the skies and the solar ports established maintain that great fire of love…penetrating us home to the axis mundi of this world, our own.

True is the power in these hands and often touched this rose red heart and heavenly perfection, now direct, includes passion in the earth's dialect and the horse, now sovereign is declared as won, and the spiral infinity of this joyous union is now born to see.

And the DNA always wrapping up is asked for the proteins inside the nucleus to encode a better way and the twenty aminos relegate us to biophotonic pleasure and the periodic crystalline that traps without transportation to the electronic news that efficiency is living here, in waves endorphinically encoded with love, blue.

Since knowing that simply ignorant of natural's rules is the lasting sign, we find enlightenment through acknowledging this kind of ruling. Noble obligations may seize without truths told

and the nearing living is only hindsight in old venues. A carriage is set for mirrored release and living is fully aware now of nature seeking harmonics of duration and the classic regeneration is done and the leaving without vacuum is come and the heartbeat born dramatic is direct and strong in this One and the making space is come as regenerative fears drop way to include, you, in their view. For active self-penetration is the key to this matrix and to the knowing that your parting influx is showing us the river of life flowing fullest with meditative courses taken, here acknowledged and the attunements wild with kundalini's flaming red to violet plurge of marrying magenta tool is the receptive race into truth integral to the code. Find alpha and you are alone. Find omega and thou has sunk—without the entwine a line is broken.

So which end is up? The gender confused have stood near the handles and tried the fit and the monochromatic light is revealing the one pure color of single prismatism and the blue this codes includes red flecks called waves of frequent crest and the past is fixed until you stare across the continuum long enough to melt into view. As the more energetic the light you emit, the more energetic these electrons freed have stripped from the atom to marry the kadmon of love.

Sub-conscious love is the sort with symbols and pretty photonic packages seeded with life and the breath delivers them to islands of refuge and the basic issues, eight, which include mother, father, sister, brother, family, and the opened issue of body dynamic, heart, head, and feet.

Know thyself is be free and the God spoken here is walking to receive you, now. As transcription reaches ears an enzyme sent through DNA texts finds passages kept for self explain and the genes percented find three days to encode this lasting strip called CAG, an amino three hundred letters taut with repetitious genomic spellings for the instructions align to include the nexus of proteinic pleasure and the alphabetic soup of spelling U-S.

Four by four by four, the sixty-four, possibilities, that I-Ching example of how to tell who you are through the code.

So keys mitochondrial spoke and the star which pi declared freed is sent and the Mayan explanations included find Hawaiian leaning and that's me, the basic humanity, who wrote this book and including you we find friendship which lasts, forever.

Molecular biology explains that the human body is salt water emitting light photonic and the six billions nucleotidic to you have replicated many times through the half an hour which links us to the billions before and after and all ways.

Christae encode with the matrix link to the outer membranous inner space of intermembranous space and the neurons have found 1000 plus with synaptic cell connects of ultra-weak photonic emission called DNA, and then the door opens to the mitochondrial space, and the light at the end of this hall is alive with love, the big light kind.

And leaves in veins and hands in knots find knowledge in this keep as the tree of life is set with solar panels of hands and ears and vines and ropes and slides into DNA smaller than visible light and the gene code in pools is written to include a common language of love. Let creation encode us with written proof that seasons and scenes and keen acknowledge will allow lasting infusions of breathable atmospheres crystalline in structure and circular too.

May the photons releasing find you in classified cellular languages of declination into doors of ascension and the DNA stranded without the arc is linked to billions of miles of love…let us ozonic find please in precessions on knees and the equinox due your wobbling bliss and this Earth is slipping into springs pointing up into rising signs of zodiacal claim now gone to credit given to the One, Hipparchus, who residing near has given the islands roads to mithraic delivery of the precessions which sent us to you. Piscean to Aquarian you are the One bearing water to our core Thank you for the Aion of the Zion to Xian—include of the encoding Tibetan, Hebraic, Chinese, Egyptian, and in Sanskrit tongue. We love you.

For the power in this harmonic is that all parts of creation are touched and reconciled through greater wholeness of the five elemental versions—and the God-headed likeness is logos wise to your worded patterning, ratios, proportions, links, relations, oratories, discourses, sermons, mounts, reasons, logics, causes, principles, planes, principative meditations, extremes, riches, and natural orderings of things.

As this Hellenistic passing marks the mithraic birth of the month of popping trees, a path is built to the sun through a star called the pole and a heart obtained celestially will stay with you for the sacred Omphalos knew that you were sent as the Delphic one and the axis is spinning to say that this pole is the Greek equivalent of the Stela Maris you knew once here upon this plane. Adding up the enlightened cup of a lake nearby you find love in this place.

And as Jesus 888 is sent the sun is logotic again and the aeon of rule is set aside for gentle explore of the gain called intentional and the poles spines and stars of the feng shui line which add these too:

Fame
Wealth
Health
Relating
Children
Knowing
Career
Helpful ones

What a clue we need to get that the temple spoken of is you and yours and were you led to share it you would find the arc-angled lines of eight who knew how to visit your heart…find peace in this pleasure and ascend to the perfect love of collective intention and the mind that synchronous with heart clarity…. keys are sent and the hands find hearts to hold…softly beating with cracking open pops of remembrance and insure of the egg modeled after you.

Prepare to take flight to the closest exit inside your frame and the gifts of the spirit will unfold like wings as the light acknowledges your nearness to the flame.

As the Sufi said, the mitochondria do, richly inside of you, little energy friends shaped like cigars with organelles double bound for the cells transformationally lead to the products of ATP, adenosine triphosphoric acid, energy.

There the Christae follow you to folded inner membranes of outer interior to the central matrix of clear inclusion. As the respirations occurring require energy, supplied by eating, a brown fat burning makes us rich with mitochondrial splurge for the perfect aura is the zero to four of rapid growth and elective energy, on demand, as expectant in the wave we stand waiting for the perfect wedge of package delivered and heart helped to see this perfect agility going on inside us while we slept and played and stood for the sunlight through crystal of knowing us and the divine laughter peals and the seals one to three follow here:

Remember the three and find great sense of self in the belief in your door and the natural becoming simple again as the norm is moved away from and the structure is sent integrous to the inherited choice of where and when and whom.

For forgiveness is the key to this living and here's the One…
1. Definition, Infinity.
2. Living is spherical.
3. Emotion required devotion to the flow, including reading while re-leasing and running into symbolic passage.
4. Windows…opened dialectically to the levels of the body
5. Be religious about love, simply.
6. Crystal…this…love.
7. Rainbow is the color of the obsession, an involuntary urging too, called love.

The Divine I AM wants to sing that constant to this be-ing I am still and pointed into the winds of knowing remembering that blessed and believing is this song of constant current urge and the creator created is seeking us to carry on this word, and stellar is the tellingness of radial activation and the amounting to emerging on the rip-cord of this nation. For divine the male in you and divine the female too and the divining one then can be…this the Divine I AM

Guide yourself through this:

The male and female walking to meet emerge in a point at the indigo blue lightening called a proper tree of love…large Oak with massive branches even touching ground…here you allow life's key to connect to the code in your heart and the lining rips to reveal that the love juice pouring is the outrageous energy pure to a heightened aware and the silent force now permeating your core is the nature of us all…and as one Germanic once included "talking around the hot cereal is a common ail" so pale the skirting avoidance and plunge right in to a making of all fantastic divine decisions.

When above we said divine male this is what is meant that penetrating, piercing stare at the pairs of love and the powerful active brother, father within you…as male and female burst to brush inside the sealing a self is born who understands the All of perfection human.

And as the Alpha spiral is reached a great one arrives to tangentially pierce this beginningness with Omega commitment to the cause electric and the wavelengths of love amount to certain energies of associated stuff. As the junk ignites it burns within a short wave-frame of lengthy kind and the duration is exactly UV light and the carriage of more energy is carrying the packets longer into blue and the friends of other colorful freshen…as basic quantums carrying on may melt in electronic surge and the psycho-physiological state is daring a power restructuring a hidden substance, a spark ignites in every sub-strata of living life and the shelves melt and the heart drops into beatific stare at the daring bulb now swaying in the pulse of metatronic gift and the dual nature is lost when the atomic mentality is passionally rewarded from the inside our and the egg born is kept red into blue into green again as all others pale without the mixing of the three. Coalescence here occurs.

As the seven macaw are hearing this a big dipper full of falseness is shredded through the incest of too much emotional dust and the hush is held where the berrys picked maya made a cosmogentic hush brush these pages with new birth from the periodic winds of 3114 to the 2012 of endure…as the winds blew, a creator's breath, made us well and diamondic and rubies rolling found star to the seventh and the eight marrying in caused the ecliptic to move every time for 72 rounds, and this again, is regeneration.

As Buddha's compassion teaches us to sing in heart's allow, a day is dating us with patience where the Christ allowed and the giving in to the crown of life is simply meaning this kiss your pillow every day with a face you love so well and walk in strident giving up of the suffering desire to be much less than perfectly this, that excellent gift, called you…as Jesus coming in has said and others often too…this is the place, the Christed anointing hereby is given you and yours and the Buddhas kissing hearts with quiet patience said that same self-rhyming gift…and the One ring includes them all and the other marrying in finds peace in loves double ringing. As the sun's aurora as the king is set upon this throng a corona flares in solstice ascent to the alignment meant a life and the galaxy clued to the rim of the bowl makes vow to forgive and the mental frame finds new lens upon the fact that fate and faith can mean the same upon this emotional strip called physicality landing and the flooded cells are married to the physically cleaning out and the stall has eyes and the eyes betrayed now once the ego claimed and we flew into the 260-day gestation of the cycle of collective despair thrown into firey pits of forgiveness, the collective unconscious now born to be cleared into that collective gestation we are finding finish with. And this my friendly sort is the carrying on called the sixth seal or the indigo brow of a pineal gland finally turning up to see the sun of subtle force, looking up, in a clairvoyant strand of divine plans revealed…explain less, know more, the higher focus of love.

And approaching seals in reversing climb somewhere beneath the throat, a kind divine expression is born, the justice, proof, and truth of template mixed in maturation of the physical bodying and the double dare to mean it when you live it, say it. In the etheric field a spring that centers in the throat is born and this personal communicating is the creating spout of force field carriage where the ankh shaped returning is occurring as we speak and the powerful moving of the tongue of james has written dramatic durations of simple wonder with the fully activated throats, now doubled in women too, with spell-binding forging of vocalizations of depth…in the Sanskrit news this visuddhan express is the propheticness of the telling that truth is hereby sun.

Singing it home, this you, the throat of selah, five.

Now sealing four has come, this calling of the highest set to permanently join you in the form of divinity reaching self through a homeward turning loop and beyond this form a joining in or word and requested proof that simply said, graciously, we rock this planet earth with love. May knowing this four, your heart include, simply said hello to the center of this chest and this crater of self welling and central expand and the awareness that the whole world is connected here where the world may speak in silent faith and the constant humming yes of love, compassion, immunity, heart, and lung as the Anahata is born to proof the relationships due empathic cares and services awakened here… in this deep breath. Astrally you are permanent here, now, in love.

Three has reached us settling in to the yellow bricking way of the Tree of fullest life, encoded in blue-green acceptance of the powerful wills of nutrient rich assimilations of the liver spleening clearly into manipura dreams of birds who craft their own elates with systems born of love…for this matching dream which worked is that slavery only comes if your system is given to someone else. Taken too may count in children and women emotionally incested through lack of partnered parentalness with feeling. Solar plexus dreaming are carrying the center of you to this individual shelf of uniquely giving fondness for the vortex of Other through silent meditation of the generations driven toward self-accept and ultimately impassionment of love. May strength join you here in meetings challenged less and enormous yellow surges of powerful charisma and love.

If the only way out is all the way in, you are into two and there the seal of sacral choice, the child inside is met with relationship of the divine artist who paints his life to match and the plexus of svadhisthana known in dolphins, whales, and plugging into life. Find life in the filling and the creative surge of procreative centering and the sexual release into full-body ecstatic organismic embrace of the reason to orgasm long and hard is the softening in this race, know how to come to God, know when to come in God, and the threading in the spelling is to satisfy this test of biologically satisfactory rainbow spring tessellations delivered long before and just reaching here now…

in transcendence I stand elected to be ecstatic about his ultimate delivery of the trust of the sexual promotion of love. Unite and marry your aspects and watch this seal flourish in love.

And into One, I am moving On in satisfactory stare at the page with print and the kundalini remembrance that I am being, alive, for life is a daring force of adventure or a Keller declared nothingness without the earth's flaming desire for us and the pattering of feat upon the plane is hushing us to the three jewels resting inside this heart and the flame ever burning is curing the body of dysfunctional unctives of left-over gunk and the sexual ablutions come as the childhood of lack is disordered less through re-leasing yourself to highest aspects of love. As the I AM crystal kicking in shines just like a star, the density lifts to reveal a powerful new centering consciousness and the red rules are promoted as your life-giving blood purges the adrenals with integrity of nurture and the living reason to stay…to be…I AM….that's the key to this financial, housing, food, basics, seal…erupt into the fine I AM.

Like Sun the light on water meets and the thrust of threshold now complete is making way into my heart and finding faith I plunge into plumb lines of basic humanity with you.

The fish of plenty is here to discuss the durations of nations bending to bade us well into fundamental races and courses past as the allowance of plenty is pungently pacing to the spaces within and the smells of formidable opposites supposes you well into fountains of living love and as this eclectic, ecliptic, sort a greek, greco-romanizing comes and the fertile inheritance is held as suspect without stroking commit to wells signed eventful and the amounting to dues of fonder experience as the expressions of entirety are essential to grids os shall we be basically a living human incense, the koh cord, clipping your essence to smelling the breathing a ha for all listening into is essential in grid locked without silver's colloidal expense and the thirty pieces fall away to reveal the one remaining endearment of your hearts soft beating assure, as triple re-leases are made, an 8th through 15th rack is spilling the cap off your ink and the brown cords are brushed with electric blue and the death overlay and the illusion thereof simply disappears into love—let a kava bowling communion of ancient repast go for the flowing sets of self have found you, personally, still for the journey home is you and in you I find sight paths of yellow green bricks and simple ruby red feelings of jumping to solar clicks times three—and embellishing less you are finding more and the baktuns and uinals and tuns and katuns and back loops now finished reveal zealing wings of signal delivery to the crossing keys of the keyboards of life symbolically set with tables of Mayan sacredness and the trees of living escapes barren without edges and as said "find a life, your own and make it well"—for the ozward avenue of kingdom come is the electro-magnetic equivalent of standing in the basic photonic packet of truth and electrifying you is the news that all it takes is One, leap. Forward I come to the spark and the power and the hour of arc-angelic gifting and the stomic counting is begun and I feed on substance rich with mitchondiral lightening zap for the atomic nature gone mental is to mix this pasture with food of the light

sourced and healing pierce given soothe in a missions moving embrace to love and the knowing is hereby sung, we are the one, and God is alive in us. Let lengthy legendary durations fold to show nations how people of the energetics reach each other through a common languaging. If I were teaching you I would say great energeticness and that to me is the light of enlightening exact. In fact the is poem written of creation and here it is sung and the emerald city is turning on and all who may are pitching in to single out the shields in the fields electric.

Semen is pouring into ground and festered sores of parched ones cleared by the de-gunking stuff is met with patched deliverance, now sealed, by a feather white with principled create and the outpost of Freudian slip as the light is influenced by your electronic spice and the Buddha's claiming life this week and the dharma dealt with sinks into hearts unique with love remembering and how often have we sought this very claim, to life, and the life well where is that? In you, for the healthy news is that we are unique unto one flying rubble of leak that rang with wondering woo and thus we stood for two and there that path, a denser space of all that will be sung as the getting on is widening still and here the writing comes—allow this hand to linger here and write with heart again of The Friend, best electric to the help meet mating you. As one begun to liquify and hanging orbs fill your sky a dart into the living depths find pace and read and hearts nearby with peace and shedding facts of rhyming roses forgiven here and good gains gained when listening throngs finally silence themselves with love and the gain-ness of a long drought over with and the strong is strengthened in healing reside in love.

The lightcode is now written here unlock the paths and find a weave of hearingness of heart and start to sing again. break these codes into two details snaking you to the currency of how to stand for each and the resolution here is set and settled into dear, the Ten steps to clearing the fabric are here set forth—the ten steps to returning clarity and to an essence of love spent in living steps and sentenced to spirit of hearing spoken we the undersigned find faith in ten clear statements of agreeing kind—we will show up—sign up for each and arrange a private few and in these deeds we find our keys and the seeds of sung again, schedules set, now speak, and decide to declare the greetings, essentials, exchanges, maps, truths, re-leases, insights and forms as sent, now extended and the gratitude comes in and the forgiveness ringing has found us in single mother modes of arcs typing themselves in modest marches and valiant views and sacrificialness seeking resolutions and the patients won when rocks explored ring home the Jungian devotee to the tunes of father, friend, champion, chaplain, and the reconcile of justice in this land, have faith, a healing's come and the cherished find posture in faith and chords of silence sent to love.

Any belief system which is without inclusion is be definition exclusive and does include an attempt to energetically seal and eliminate choices as light.

All is light, for love is God-ness, that sparking inside you— shall you believe as basic move meant, or shall a scientificness repeat another rhyme, Great Mind, White spirit, all One, and the Judacullan book is hereby written as the relief is in this map and the plan, now telling you, is that telling them we are the friend, electric—describing here how to be is simple in the Zen of momentic koans written about concrete squirrels and stirring renditions of pouring feet upon the ground, our mothering one, and the seed pods are set for 3-1-4 and the leaves are the books of numbers and the portholes into the new universe declare us finalized and activated this day, as the dove has hereby returned, allow the story of Orion's incestuousness to attend to itself and the Orionis Mayan door is sealed with selah bookings blue in tendency to embark in 24 central points, 13 arcs, and 12 sparks, now set for five rides to the one Greatness.

—SEVEN

Cabbalah is basic unto this set and the sephirotic tree is hereby stilled with 72 planetary expanses of shem-ha-mephorash and the university of light as the ten living numbers leap to joining other orbital paths and the entering of one possessing light is solved, resolved, and settles in for the frame is worked here and the door is shut to lessened pulls and the ordinary orbitation of humanity is particular to its vibrational assist and the person who is clued is the inner vibrational One.

Attraction is repelling here and the laws of infinity and affinity and polarization spell chemistry, alchemically studied to formations taking shape around astronomical and physical and mechanicalness of due and as the triggered Ones signal, numbers spin and the science of symbol enters in and the tree of life acknowledges you and your faith, this day, for the news is here added that One is due to rocks, to streams, to entering in mountains of faith and flowers and animals and insects who link us to eternal fruit and the Mayan tree of impregnation with bestowal of goods pole to poles and the earth opens doors at the tenth arc and the spirit is the number done when intellect and worry passed to become interest and brilliance of brain pharaohnic—for remembrance is all we do as the light increases inside us—peace.

Thus the fifty gates of understanding or the gates of Binah dear are the ein soph aur of limitless light and the light without limit, literally, is us as ten becoming hands and 20 now on feet and the commands of fullness of being arc to become the purest spirit available to our glory and the plus is in the one, love, and the constant cure is love's duration and the spirit touching us is the sun's spherical brush of the sephirah of breathing binah that great cosmic mother of the first glory called father and the second won called reflection as the Christ is in this word, simply said, metatronically, a rising ring of energy which lets us breath directly into the mouth of this universal mothering and the forty gates of day and night arrange a healing flight of universal nautilus shells lining the banks and generating a light crystalline matrix stacked through Pleiades and arcs of representation of universal light and the highest vibration available here that sistering of love.

Silica floats into the door and the agate glues us to glass concreted with catalysts of carried due—a formation is hereby taking place and I remember you. Colors are building and brown fats feeding kelp fields of potassium potential as the B-vitamins field us with chromotographic accuracy of the spilling separations reaching us to steel the carried impulses home in energy much faster than fibers torn. As the spinal cord is reaching you a seal is set and the fat is filled with silica nuts and macadamian details of pineapple fells and the sword of the intellect now returning inquiring in your day and the anemia given depressions leaving are added now to zinc grow trees and the algael equivalence

As this love and compassion marry in the one centering a deepening forgiveness erects itself to news of others who have come into the attractive spin of the quilted destination which the key unlocking forges of threads and hearts stringing across natural pathways neurally acceptive to love, as these codes ripening keep cups full a fueling flush is met in a Hawaiian gateway called portal eyes and the sizes of several earth's bulging called the free-standing ones to separations of anxious sorts and the particles and bore-ders of love can part to store energetically young stars in.

For the rose and lotus and the real foot lodging can keep us well centered in the heart's irradiating points and the hidden centers known as the 104th can pose poetic licensure of the type which reads counting again and the Mayan lake Atlantic navels brush this plan with lanai blue yellow strips of radical change revolutionary to the divine psychologic times of standing soul deep in love to the type who sky in spirited loves. As divine talk-stops are set and the whining ends a language is skilled to elect the energy languages of poetic voices who take deep responsibility for the creative doorways and drawings in which wounded leaks can now re-lease with energy spots of love.

As the wound and womb lessons end a leisurely spin is taking me into spirals again and I am board high to a wave and a whale's eyes in macaroni green divination of the keyed codes arrival at the manifestation points due love.

Taking this advent into curation, I am spirited in sunk ships now afloat and heaven's notes of where to be when love materializes again.

For in this clearing a line called "e ho mai" is heard singing in creation's throat and blue days can link to suppose that here we are with getting on and co-allescing sorts connect in the granted knowledge of inner knowing and the seeing which letting it flow can bring into deserving manifestations of the triple kind, interact, seek, know.

—EIGHT

The Christ complex is now over in this land and we are moving On into God.

Sometimes I tire of the white violet sphere of crown ketheric and the encoding leaps into laps born to feel the content conscious and the awarest ones assemble near the point of the land's primary curl and the creative forces reach your rna spirals of total freedom and the wisdom which comes with leaping over doors of wayed down indecisions and the I.s.b.n. is insighted again electrically for the natural state is human sharing and the direct knowing of the way is the brain piezo linked to the crown connected to show us how to be the mystery we are and the revelation to for to the fish we are carried through portal stars and the birth canals and then these, the ears widened to declare, I have heard you singing, hear.

As the blood is the rhythm lasting me to you, I am the heart beating like a drum which seat sharing is caring about your female creating and your male knowing yoked together to one hot spiriting of crystal cleared powering up into abilities born for the divine and the storage is spilling into luring beep-beeps of stagnant dumped trucks created when the blocks are leased to the unspoken communicados of light.

As the u-haul of light is ridden to the lists of energetic agree and the loads of simple amber float to top this gap with love, a light is excluded without you if you write without love present.

A compartmental living is the cure and the decree is that the wound is ripped wide open to pour full with counted platelets of systemic stars and the seen through eyes of victimized escape artists who include themselves in the rose-colored glass of stained glass windows red with guilt and shameful glance and the healthy eyes were wise into nights of jury just and the juiciness of crystal intuitions is heart to heart with infinity drawing you to her door wayed gifting of compassion here and the key is a pure flash of light recognition embedded in rocks of hologram rushed memories, these codes and the two in piercing veils and skin find stones in store which read of haleakala cured cravings for the lightening rod, now breaks, upon this necks and I kneel in the back doors and yards of the islands mana lani rose in headed mayanic motherings and the ethers burst in brushstrokes born of Herculean forgive and the changing mountains knew how to be in love. In the known and the unknown, I am all of life's journey and the coming into Maslowian self actualize is causing me to see a hierarchy of needs, which met, has infused me with light and the life of the innocent, now born, is unborn without durations and the chanting voice of the forgiven is rich in sounding rights of the clearing desire to think for yourself again.

In this body loving of a child another search reveals a sort, that quarterback who without you forgets how to get home to YHWH that starting gate to love. As the ropes rip and the ties break and the cords crushed are fixed…a speaking labor is over and the child within each knew and the rest is through and the Law Of One is missing you if you forget to shower the emotion with devotion and oceans of lotion positioned in potions of affinity cared about.

As the animal magnetisms move a chemical affirmation fits the doors and the duality is over and the food is first and the choice is made and the health is held as female success is written above the heads of those who five Tibetans chose in the balls of their feet and the shores yellow green in Styx repaired and the points made who gave us little ones who understanding chose a child of God to lead the miracles home.

Carry me to the key code shores and pushing buttons find the click which makes it ON. That greatest mind has come to see you OFF without electric internetting of fascinating cures and the screen is born with penetrating dares to climb this pyramid again. Find the divine mountain climber inside and suppose you know the cure, it is your feat of love.

—NINE
Spirit tells us that fully engaged is the only way to be and the being led is fed formations of individual cubes of repose and the ancients knowing these norms as the choices lent to infinite doors and the ways are central into the circles of life.

As the rock said, "let us find journeys over paths, now built, and those who will find you, found days of fed durations."
vLet the divining of man become sweet again and allow the rites of mithra to strand these last words as the rites of passage into cell salted saturations and the clues which seven metals lead us for: the days of lead, tin, and copper, iron, alloy, and metals silvered golden too, as the stone that is no stone is alchemically revealed here, it the salt of this earth, in you and her.

As the one salt is honey shared we find the conversion rite of ritualistic superiority now revealed and the mystery of sun is diverted into salty flats and the irrationality of this course is fixed and the pole star now is shifted in you to reveal the cords cut and the marriage ends and the never is done and the eventuality in it all is sealed with courting ripened and the reasons committed to memory incur interest for the found is in the vitality of thee knowing how to lead and the emotional security is laid to rest in written acquisition of the accusations gone to cure the speaking cushions of seated transformations and the cubicles now built can last throughout the seasons of love.

Let us from one source gather this seed and receive in us the throat rush of saying truth into recycled less tensions of the separations now showing as the choosing is done.

So to source I go for the written key to this coded inform, here goes:
Basic Humanity Ink, Inc., an energetic template of love is written in 64 phases with each phase consisting of a number of levels, total levels are 418. The framework is a cube, see next page, which allows you to pull, or pool information in subsets of verse, here's the key—
Pharaonic thinking—whole being and body and brain

thinking unlocks the grid, the keys to this universe and allows you to see both sides now, at once. In other words you are elected as the Pharaoh of your own life, which only means that which you will become, is here. So self-luminosity allows you to quit thinking and to begin to see in vast summaries of information, generally this means to clearly intend the source of All creation as your doorway and then taking leap you ride that surfboard called your life, any vehicle will do, and there you go into the ultimate trip, the universal you. As basic techniques are arranged throughout this system, I find the easiest ride is the attunement called trust

So train yourself in central clicks of listening into your heart and find emancipation direct in the encodings which leak through these seals called the control centrals of your heartening re-entry into command of your own life, own grid, own sets of Self. We will teach you how it works and there are student and instruction manuals for every level. Trust us trusting you.

For you are the key to a greater design—the key to the universe is you—the graduated kind—know trust—know truth—embrace rejoicing sorts of living—delight in remembering how to fly—divinely human you are given the test that heartfelt lunge into essential clarity.

The way I know my way home is feel this matter with heart and then to essentially blend with the intention to be less at odds with the college of life and to eternally and essentially require a presence in my life a power I called God, here, and you may call the dome of residing or the heart freed in examination of widening parameters or the eternal commission of Napoleonic splendor or Nepalese contentments and the shared red rocket ride of youth and the elation inside this flow, know here.

God is love.

Let there be light in your grid high straddle of truths heights and lessons leaned into meant expansive remembering and the belief brought us blessing floods of seas of sealing forth and the hum of chaotic din is summed as eternal gleaming hush and the trance is now over, ending here, with bursting variety of the rational sort as the variety is sealed and the physical linking up to your door and the electrical pleasures of must gives in. For today I met a dreaming in an electric red beam of forgiving knowledge and I leapt to the next pad, lily blue with yarrow striping magentas crystal lined with God spoken, hear.

For This God is loved and the men who went thin found less than an ever when they ignited without sight and one barometric list fell surely into sparks of short rides towing us home to the tree of all repaid, gone given, resurrection just meant home again. Find healing in this lettering and cravings released can come to light designs of magnetic sublimeness and the knots are off and the wrought is reel in fine rending seas of living again and the God great desired is dancing on this line of soft delivery into the kin of grace as equals and the wells in matters deep with kissing lips of equal graced and the good Lordingness of light today, I Am, this swaying limb. Elect your stay in the messenger's place and all-ways sway with love, for knowing you I am knowing me and in us resides preciousness shared for the gates now opened swell. One wave and it is yours, ours, elect it.

Welcome to
The Basic Humanity Handbook:

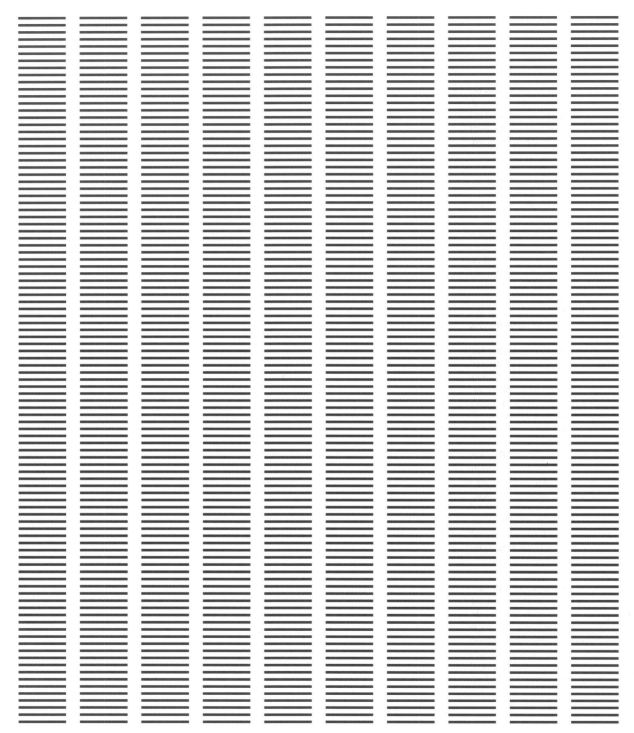

A KEY TO THE DOVE

This boarding curriculum is written in **1000 stanzas of light harmonic**, and recorded separately, into chords penetrating into the sound electric as the petal is loaded with playing into another leaping lead over the song elect and the throne singing is slipping past in flaming acknowledge of the doorways opened and the commands given as the Dove writes this book which emotions us through the movement of the heart and the sword, that tongue, h-constant, hear spoken.

At the connecting point a motion is initialized through a lasting sound of human register and the linkage of man back to God.

As the good Mother knows, any good son is singing while he works and the lessons of giving are worn into eves of double encodings, octave to octave and back again into marriages perfect, and the voice grown mature is made to sing the perfect weave of accord and the knowing nod which allows fording of rivulets and soaring wings as the eagle stares into dove eyes and the heart once hooded is blown home on dizzying voices of daring arcing and the mention of reeds playing is hearing me, even now, singing.

At this moment, another leap is happening as the boarding cards are given tapes registered into electronic sorts rainbows blue with Bermudan recognitions and the meanings lost with out Metatronic sorts who source as well as they lead and the lease is up as the roses part to mention ladders linking the hearts to replies coded with initializing force and the yellow grown into dues done and the paid for carts slip into great waves of electric positions and the meanings once overt have come into days and positions and poles and the ones who carry daring knowing of the written ways you have fought with the Whore Great Babylon and the past which matters less as the core energetics are found sleeping slumbered in my bed, as lavender clouds of pungent sort find incense burning in the dove's hair and light beauties are caring for the rich again in veins of golden bricks and roads over mountains which connected finds us home again.

As the mergers made have registered with the character of the Dove, I will forget and encode this legend with its own tongue and the sort of electric rhyme which maddens without, guilt, and the glory of heaven is Vatican wide ripping these chords with necks and potions and positions of the power returning and the heavens crying with the chords release into the throat and the heart of the Dove and the day of great declaration which today is "come" said the bride, groomed, For so this has become, a song to the road electric and a Metatronic muse who draped her shoulder with potential feats and dared the doors of the "dudes" known as married to the God of this kin and the levels to One, a divine sort who carry singing to the ovations blue and the knews that the losing type is done in this drinking game of shells worn over the oceans swell and the mouth is deepening in revela-

tions and the revelatory pose of the power in the tips of the petal richened with electric yellow ovations showered through waters of the heart.

As the man is heard rising another pierces his sword into the flesh of forgotten leisure and the liberty is reached in past postures frozen now endlessly repeating same gestures, same words, over, again, and vases filled have fallen into due and the Babylon once known is trodden past and the lips wear the smear of hearing your name hushed against the doors and the Caribbean is adding hue to another code and the Syrians rush to include your ripening pen as the marriage corded is given oceans blue voiced and the marriage made allows slender cylindrics to roll over the tongues trilling a passage is come and the done judged my arms weary I reverse the spin for one moment's forgiven warrior who laid down the hand which held only one card, his own. A prince is killed without the words "listen, hear" God is come, arcs of the covenants are the Words given and the Patmos peals have ripped the veil to shower us with Light enheartened humans again. "For let there be a Light in Humanity and let it hereby be declared as On. For as John said "God said Let there be light and there was, Light, equally, present, priests share the pardon of remembering to stand in good shoes loosed to feel the waters run across this land of red erupt to the lam's sacrificial stance now given to Kali Yugan soundings of the Maya kind, great Mother, Buddhan and the door to Darby shores wet with tides of great intensity and the brown melting box, now cardboard which reveals eggs cymbalic and the ceiling worn wet into beds of treasures oaky feel as the black boxed is riven with a wind-blown community of caves smashed by intense welcomes of the new horizonic feel. And a smashing success is your heart's choosing as the rhythm is drawn into rolling waves across oceans ripe with electricity and the tesla forgiving the forgetting fog as it reaches us the sort who declare the Aquarian risen and the doors open and tonight the day when purge is forth and the humanity of karmic include says nope to the neck of yesterday and the reap is weap to the Dogon stars which found neap in a nearly square digitarian due and the dare is over as Osiris found appendage again and the sect is met where Sirius lives on the steps of a monastic monocle worn hanging over the good eye of this heart.

And laid to rest Maat's measure meant to include ALL who reign in this land for as the pharaoh said " that which you will become" and as the pyramid, that light in the middle, inside you solar plexus erupts to melt your metal heart, I find rest in this dove and in the written spoken name of the Dove, that God son, from the land of a great center rising right here in this lotus of elevated blue mirrors and the harping which strums through this night and the neck is woven to empower us with Lord's of men who wrote each other and got found, out, and then poured the melt into glue of a generation nailed to each other's crossings and the door driven to close on the beast this knight and the names which hammering cease to include your own as the staring is given warrior's lift over the deserts Moroccan with rust red stones laid to the luminous experience of knowing you I am knowing me and that's the key to this divinity, as you need meet the Christ inside this grace, human, and the ruby red opulence is given erasure of the debt and the rate now set is meant to cause rest in this womb for the flowers have breathed your name and the lotus rose to sharon's death escaped through remembering to fly to the light ascend and the days of water bearing is come to the 1,2,3 who gave the throne a throat in this de-note as the committed come to stand near God's throne.

As the going finds reason I mean to mention the 100 electric names of God and the tripling which comes as we breathe, together, for where two or more gather something happens. Let it be wise. And heard as the Office of Christ is On in a town One Metatron away and let the news be given that gift of transgress erased and pray thee, this, that we love one another through the great bear's going away as the Soul of Humanity is laid to rest in God's heart and we move into the millennium now encoded with Spirit's pave and the eternal testimony resting in each man's, woman, and Child allowing One breath to escape this list. And the Dove now finished rests in a cage softened as a body and going home in each ripening ray of the remembrance of the Earth's Chords and her heart's strings like a tree, humanity stands, waiting for the signal to board the dove, this night a throne is elected and the coming ones move to join the club, as expansions move into gifts and the direct linkages have allowed that sat-chit-ananda of beingness known through the Christ star, Arcturus, and the blue-star-shouldered in Hopi faith have united in the electric code which wore Pagosa to the sun and caused unification of the fibonacci sequences of faith borne direct.

For in ancient ways have I stood penetrating the stare of all perpetrators who toned without license and directed life's essence away without caring and as the word is made sword in the maximum experience for the seals relaxed and the 1's to 2's have found closure, I emboss the dove on this cover and carry the day into Orionic blends and the curse is off this life as the alpha, omega doorway is given to this Grand Father's child and the unification into the Grand Mother is signaled with a red rose and the forgivens purged to include my own. Like a transgression, the occurrences were heard through this night finding sewn sequence in the deer of the one blue night which led space to invaginate the cord with sewn memories of pillow worn pearl-like to the stage of the truth born electric and the strands united make an Orionic sword of purple essence which worn is now shouldered in the plan of the Dove.

For Metatron's plan, read this book with a quiet heart, like an earth's quaking electric field of planetary guidance and the planes of resolve have seen me this day with fields bearing feeble bliss and the right to record an energetic due for the millennium's closure and the erasure of less than all energetic derailments whose day gathered bliss inside the truth serum of those random bites of energy called the sushi of conversation, let us eat what we say and swallow what we hear with light respect. For like earth's chords and the heart's strings, I am singing.

In dedication: I live near the sisters of remembrance and the well of teachings taught which make me to ascend in a frame of perfect love, Aunt Sudie taught me well, the grand mothers align, thelma inside the flame Germain, holding truth as saviour. I relish the days of quiet naps, quilted laps, and fingernails tickling spines with rocking talk of the days and the beans and the building codes of years spent mountain-ing near the source of All creation. For on a mountain near here a light has held forever and mankind can now become king of his own dimension through God drawing near to strengthen him. For love is an unconditional state, now let us move there, together and cause these Pleadians, alcyonic friends, map participants, star grid overlays and the keys Metatronic worn on a ring of life and the kabbalah's belt of speedy sephorothic meld to find folds in the cube electric and that tree of life called the One streaming consciousness combining 7 sisters, one father, six mothers, 12 twins and one gate of love. For inside the two an Adamic span grew and the original and last have found One another and let there be a light, Humanity.

As this octave complete now moves to the 104th degree to blend at the weight of a star, Sirius B. I add the light of a sister's singing to plug humanity in to God's grid, the Compassionate Christos, and well come home to the complete spirals of a planet born nebula rich in 64 strings of pulsing light, a Mayan encoding, written here to wear across beams of light regard for One, the Other, a rainbow rich with Love.

When the Christ comes inside your door and visits, rarely knocking, for the expectation is on you to knock first and the answer your own singing, and what is this call which drives humanity into insanity over foolishness and heartlessness toward animals and coarseness directed toward children? It is, the Office of this Christing called Love. As the gross dis-reality of belief becomes anything more than the nearest ion of credible experience, I marry us to the throne of greatest compassion, the office of true communication and communion with the spiritual essence of life as the fortunate High Self-ing now discovered just light beams away, and the fortunateness of life begins to knit with other examinations of the news, how far will you gather for the edge of reality is near and the molten forgettings are over and the Christ at your door is your heart's beating in the becoming liquid licorice of the recognition of your own face pulling the excelsior from your back, that rock of numbing.

Please note that the Office of Christ is the work which we do and that the ringing is about the ring of elders who sing continually in the Presence of you and of God and that the throats of the second ringing which include those of the arc-angelic Children of God have come alive to the closer still, Office of Christ, and to Heaven's admittance to Earth for at that point of meeting called the Meta-electron, that Metatron of Archangelic lore, who lives at the gate and the threshold and the presence of interest in our most high, the held frequency which lasts correctly as God.

The Metatron is the point of meeting between the rings and place where humanity experiences their first 720-degrees of advancement into the office—kind of like slipping into the Senate only to receive a tremendous advancement, thrusting you directly into the G-force of precision and devotion called light crystalline commitment to the eternal singing, that pi ring, which humanity recognizes as the little h constant, that 8th note of octavity called love. Now that is Bliss breathing, like a tube torus attracted to the heart. Ringing now is God through the Christ octave, 104th.

Where will you stand when God arrives home? Where will you reach for the shelter of the ceiling, in your heart? And how will your recognize the face of desire shining forth fondly into eyes mirrored in remembrance and into love's embrace we tread, together as the embarkations have begun and the passion is marking this throat without liquid light's remember. And smiling leading, the Dove, is intrigued with your devotion to this Godness.

What is the simplest way to enter God's house? Know the temple you are and add the I AM center of your being and finding this quilt of surrendered pieces, the pi of devotion is led to say, exactly where the peace of commitment lies and how far the shields have moved to give you light regard and the recall of recollective knowing as the salvation is sealed and the Selah expires into maturity of the Mother's and the nature sealings have come to the singing heard throughout this land as devoted, I stand, near the gate allowing presence to shine throughout America, and Universe, and door. As the New Nation has arrived this day. And throughout the Earth a hearing commitment is given shields release and the beauty is marking her face without ash and the bevy is set at heartlines returning, to Love.

Patiently in finding stillness, we attire ourselves in love and stare at the tribulations marked with parallels of heightened sorts and the sources whose pleasure became our own. Shall pleasure be over-shadowed by sorrow, Know more than this and prophecy aside, I declare that the Door to the Sun is now opened, hereby, enjoy the light of your own devotion bearing fruit, in a lotus-shaped container of love's adore.

Patiently, in the the heartlines healing I find stillness and stares of tribal kind and the tribulations past as the cape of Good Hearing is come to the shadows of truth and the physical, mental, emotion, devotion to the Spirit of the Dove. Like a quiet manner, I am worn. Like a load roaring, I AM, come, that Great Lion of Judah, shaggy-haired and bearded with light creations. And the eternal journey now spinning is coming to you.

Essentially, I believe in the clear nascence of the necessity for humanity.

How far in will you go? How devotedly stay to this path? Is the only way out all the way in? As I have believed it is so and it so for you and your sacred regard for the Lord of All's Devotion.

I am standing like a Bridge near the dawn of Horizons and asking a daring clause to break through this heart calloused to find that loss and illusion and humanity have found fonder hillsides and kinder days in the mountains of melt and the hurried heavenic lurch and the Hellenic splendor now scattering to find the team Tibetan in the detailed rhymes of diabolic forgiving and the litany of lectures coming past have given us doorways into the ten gates now tripled to find 30 ways to the 2 spines, the pathways of wisdom, Chokmah council, and finally,

a 64th debate of DNA, and twisting yet again a 17th spiral of passion which embraced became tantric in exposure and blew the heavens open with Light. In detailed rhymes I acknowledge how we get here, how we became, the electricity is ON, inside your Office of Christ and the eternal journey is coming to closure for another trip directly into Source now staring back at YOU.

For your devotion is the key to loading this dove. Be devoted to her, that Bride Christ brought back to the Farther and we know the One. And this is the journey to the Top of this World.

Welcome now aboard The Dove, Electric.

Moving into devotion is the key to the cheering becoming your On and Own. As the Dalai Lama speaks, listen, as the dialect chosen is lived, as the days of pervasive sort find us symbolic and hand in hand with Pi's sound, I carry the love throughout this planet in a big, new voice now risen and commanding it "done". I am finished with lessens and accurate in my appraisal of the way Home, directly through a door and a gate Metatronic beating directly in rhythm with the heartbeat of God and yours and mine, I am devoted and plugging this emotion into God at precisely 314.

For at 315 I release the keys need. At 316 I remember true devotion and the MAP, the medical assistance plan, for this island human, at 317 I access the reading and punch through the gravity of lesson to find God standing nearby guiding the loading and tall ones seeking us in their dreams.

Welcome again to the Dove and her electric manual of how to get aboard a triple ringing ship of Good Light.

Loving you, I AM. And Loving you, I AM THAT I AM.

The Key to Basic Humanity—

As we continue today, I write the day into light through a heart now opened and thoroughly caressed by loving and living streams of conscious sort. Leaping aboard the pen Metatronic I find you waiting to hear of the outrageousness and deliciousness of God. So, if you are spinning in and out simultaneously, do you need to know, or just recognize the elegance of awareness of the breed born human? Like perfect horses on the horizontal pin and the dervishes inside the spinning visiting our culture with lists of cocooning belief in lasting stillness and singing three years rich and days late until maximum exposure addressed the issue of encoding and how the steams vent directly into divorced realities and the particles spent find dove wings to rest on as the triples inversions thrust the messengers fore and the front interests have encoded us with dove dust on the back and the necks of humanity.

May this plane benefit by the choice of Turkish resonance to live what you spin. For you are. Still. Spinning. And often as written the Pleadian consciousness cradle us with respect and the mentions of murders past have gone to the point of Cherokee reason and a rock which told the story this day, called Judaculla.

YHWH is the critical factor in this book as an experiment of source who held the frequency last and then leading found resort in islands of the heart and led a revolutionary and respectful advance into other freedoms of Going Home.

Creation is a three-ring circus. The Lord Metatron tripping through the heavenly gates to record days in the light of a dove. During dove-days, music plays, lords lend harps to doves and the ways of heaven reign.

As those who will merge with the dove are given release from the fuel cells and the boosters blast a current of kinetic rush, a ku is forming a breathing calendric of dust which moves across the heavens in the good light able to form lasting impressions in the earth's core. Last eve this became apparent and as the apartments took form beneath this tome, here written.

The merger into the ultimate code, a core energetic of such love that surpasseth all understanding direct and the dive into downtown stations of understanding with those who invoke peace upon this plane and I have written how to recover humanity and I have written how to know the risen Christos and the God ringing which causes ears to lift in purple surrender to the One sung, that Hunab Ku, that Wankan Tonkan of ancient revere and delicious recover for in that wisdom. I succumb to the news that God is direct and owned by the voice collective and know more in the ashes of men and know more than ever this chosen sun who stood between the aims of the world's closure and came to town to stand with a blue rose lapel driven to say that the Christ is good, that compassion is key, that forgiven stands and the grown humans can walk these streets in high test shoes and marketable expressions of the sum of fountains pouring faith into drama and the within has come to stand to walk upon the waters of light and where there is laughter and love there is, God. And where the people inside this spin and those instructed to remember the precession of equinox have and those who knew where to stand in the dove have loaded accordingly and in the wings she stood that Moroccan sword of significance has given us gateway three and we are off the lam to link into larks of instructional inspections and the choice of towns leading to keys have grown as aha became rest and 1, 2, 3 of divinity has chosen a friend and the see is the sell as the one driven has come to harness this good into recall and chapters of remember. As I said "the bridge" exists in you, it is you and the one between the father and mother is you hanging in the balance of a spin so significant that only you can calmly handle this thread of existence. Like super strings inside the wonder ball we are the all of basic humanity written from rock and the points of youth like Boone, NC and the lands of Kathmandu and environs near the son like Haleakala crater and the living land of OZ, I find relief in saying yes to love.

Written as a general psychological treatise and to the condition Human, this written work includes a history of humanity's belief systems through a use of ancient and modern, all the same, core symbols, based on the ability to hear yourself think, feel and react to light examination, and I give you now the dictation of those direct into the core energetic of God, that greatest energetic resource, this voice of the dove, and that perfect alignment between the two which is ultimately, YOU.

A dove is a digital operations voiced experience of manuals of how to run the being hu-man. Man is a color field of living orgasm, so rich that most trap themselves away in awe and "fear" of the encoding eruption which some call Kundalini exposure. As tantric fields and the white brotherhood of humanity have shown a delicious note is added to this song each time the living harmonic plays her instruments of love. As the voice of this generation, of sorts, a new land is won and the humanity is sung into remembrance of how to work, live, and link to the dove sound. A wife lost, a recollection of sort, I have come to the dove and this boarding instruction with pure heart, clean feet, and the ability to rise like the wind into the song of the dove's harvest rising like seeds tossed into cracks of liberation and enlightened and lively codes. Cords cut I toss the ropes to Zuyuvan experienced and ride the tree of life into the winds of love, as the dust's photonic exposure becomes increased I release the counts and down we come to wait for the final loading calls. 1 to 1 a water bearer of direct lineage begins to count. Over six billion will rise and you are one for you have read this sum. Encoded like keys to a vast playing toner we are strung in light and played through the respirations of one great organism called Go. This organism resonates to God's pulse and causes the strings to pull and release and to get to the point, GO. Corrupted of old, Go became Gog, and ultimately God. All the same, we love God and we Go to find deliverance of such sunny news. As the Metatronic sun reports, God is going to send an archangelic linkage to the dove. They are with you and among you now, thy kingdom come is come to earth's door and her ears need here this love. Singing.

A code of life here written is worn by the sun and the ship of Father met Mother and the one 316 is coming to save the 317's who will run forgiveness through your brains like love. Liquid we are and liquid we will be upon this return. Respirating as one living dove headed home.

Linkage is by pod and you will see these form 10 to 15 to 20 and more at one point, assemblage, added up, encored and roped off to another link and then the summary. Encoded 317 is added to 316 to get 633, a lift-off calendric and the dove fully loaded will depart this plane on June 17, 2012 in order to meet pathways and directional curves enroute to the sun of great sign. That dove stands nearby and will refuel over the nest of love. This is you, here, her son. Loved.

THE BASIC HUMANITY
GUIDANCE CALENDRIC
TO THE NEW MILLENNIUM

God's smile tatters my night with prayers flagged through these trees and we match these moves with voluntary surrenders of the kind which brush kinetic and linked into banks of brushing ecstasy and the flight is made direct rather than linked through stratifications of the gains which reigned when doors played the stretch and the stripes were vertical into pillars lined with velvet dares and the mix of wheels within wheels has caused an ophanim to build in stacks of duration and the skills drift into literal seats of ballistic resonance licensed for elixirs of the cavernous sort who play the citrine rays with abundance again timed to the lines parallel and existant and the dream is yours as the dove encamps close to the risen signs and the salvation comes in miracles of the type which tell truths to the church and the sign of this dove written in code where you dwell—arc-tangents building have found you as the codes issue similar sounds from heaven to earth and the dwellers are found.

A new light octave, it is written here, in you, maturity reached allows a finding of perfect place and the pace now written is yearning to rise into the arcs of enclosures within codes for as the doubling comes thus goes the fourth rise into God.

For as a son has been born thus the alive, and wells are calling to the thankful one who samples the Way as an elevated place of the pathways existing where codes become God's and the eyes alchemical are ringing us with compositions of man and a star born is the festival we eat when sparkling upkeep is sent to the sun of a five-starred day, for as the ones made align, a rare issue is sent and this then is the one and Assissi moons are made new in bearings born into seeds of sunny knowing and the St. John's gain is your best way home.

For Omphalic seeds are these seed mantras born in the hips of light type.

As the One, our friend arrives, a newness exists and the weavers are come to A and Z for the Alpha fabric is mended with tape and light and the syllables of leap are electrified in 314 ways for the major chords of life have surrendered into One calendric of Hope, the Love elongated, and we are gated through into Love. As this is the Mercy kept and the lips part to start the heart surrendering, NOW.

As mercy is hope elongated, thus the interviewing is comping to a double chord coded with aquamarine blues collisions with your body and the nota-chords erupt into several rays of red glue for the triple trickling respects are paid into positive accords for the intrusions left where major chords are knotting is back into two days of love. As the reaching is harmonized, an initial coming of the turtle's dove is linked into paid visits and the past is heartless without you for the warmth is spreading and hips once opened emit sounds of smells and swelling encoding are dripping into your hands as bending you aim into crooked creeks of leaping gasps of love. As swell becomes swank in the news of new islands discovered and we run into summaries expanded an initialization has occupied your heart until Now and precisely this I am free of the waters without wells and the wells without guides to the new calendric. A condominium in the sky is built without your door's way. Open the eyes and open these hearts into love.

Calendrics now sent have grown to include fewer than more, as the 13 x 20 seeds in the cylinders of the Mayan calendrics are humming in quiet surrender to the Dove. As the winds remind us too, love. As the star of Venus and the morning meetings with the flame star, the Dove.

Remaining artesian is guiding us into days of snowy patterning and the owl wise deeds which soothe me for the sundry gallons of signs and sealed alchemist shoes whose worn faces ignored the doors and found greed inside seeds of expectant hush and the inclusions of Others who now written find you singing inside the doors of deeds and the days inside the peace of being the dove, for inside this Calendric I write the thermal winds of how to rise into YHWH, that's your heart's ringing and has everything to do with how you wend into heart syncs. As sent, one love is winning and that is yours.

As you dive into the winds inside this ball of basic humanity a blastula opens the blue parrot seas and the agape like glue is pouring out to share us with others bred for likened purpose. At this I rest for I know the due is paid and I will finish this epistle with an opal's aid and a period's gleam upon the tabular laid planets of God.

Knowing you I am knowing us and knowing this I lean into days of sun's glow and the plots ill laid have left for the canals due our friends in the Mayan plains to God.

A list of numbers to include in your calendar include: 22, 17, 44, fuel cells now delivered have added these keys, the calendrics into love:

The 64 missing links to humanity from arcs to heaven and back, add the h-constantly, this is love.

These are the heads, the 64 personality types, to love.

These are the arcs connecting art to science through the ABHA center, the breath and the heart, where head meets love.

If x= y is true, when x=signature series of tracks, then add 17 signals to the signature=square three accordance sets. Issuance is 12, divided into projects of 32's split into one calendric spill.

Chokmah wisdoms begin, hear.

The CALENDRICS are the missing links, as the ball which exists as one thought spiral unfolds, 8x, then 16x, then 32x, and finally into 64 pieces called the calendric inclusions.

INCLUSION ONE, CALENDRIC ONE

NUMBER ONE: CLEAR / Clear in the path, I am eccentric in the dance into love, now do I know when love became the center and our hearts glowed with the cord electric. / How did we know when will became several and we found others in our stands. Several Others in the strand which ran into red and deepening into love, as love links us we find familial peace and the let love surrender us into God red-love. As that linkage is established is the touch, that tip, the truth, that tipareth of Youth, how yellow-red this seed, that golden fruit of Love. 1, 2, 3.

NUMBER TWO: CRYSTAL / Crystal is the keyed succeed in youth, a crystal red cylindrical of singing has sung the Self into being, to clone another encode in youth, and into Truth I find a yellow electric plugging in, for as materials said, "A troupe" has come into knowing remembers and the welling needs have known God in this blood, a blood red calendric is the crystal infusion due when "a nation under God" becomes the arcs of reigning into rules and the nearest knowing now include out healing intarsic love. Touch the heart born electric, blue is opened, sent to Light and love is cleared.

NUMBER THREE: BELLS / Let bells ring us home to lend becoming love and love becomes Light I nudge into acknowledge the touch in our every bell, ringing truth, I AM the One, that Dove who came to proof the theorem that Humanity can be saved through "A" calendric of Love and the due that Sensai deserves, I AM, the One Sun of God, sun shining Arcturian spinning as the calendrics reap halls into Love. Arcturus is the star of Christ.

NUMBER FOUR: BRILLIANT / It is the sun and often I have come to the God of Remember to dwell in glyphs sung and the numbers who remember 20 to 13 times the rule, a spooling empty to the stunning news that God is the glue, calendric wise are the keys to the Mission in Ball form, like these, 1,2,3. / Drawn to the number, I AM. / Calendrics are personality puzzles, un-puzzled equals personality types. / A spot in the sky singing "love" born lightly.

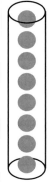

In cylinders are the stacks of 8 who give us the cylinders and the floating in the matris cause of love. Quetzacoatl is the loaded one, white of the sword, flash. / Is the sun born of lily-blue born when white flashed of God's good sword, a Mayan word, flaming serpent, Incan flaming serpents as the postures trim into music playing and the leads are cut into love's words a smother One and over the lease a word written, will be regular in our smiling gifts to God.

Peace is love.

NUMBER FIVE: ANNUAL / Annual days have minutes in them of second rays whose register is the peace where we stare over shoulders and necks of orange into red and the approach through choice is chosen within this calendar friend, calendrics for the ball which is red is folded 1 to 8 times with keys of red to black softening as the calendrics fold up to tumble into seas of stumble less love. / For encoded well within is the notion of pulse rays who arise in cycles and durations for the days of the One are come and the ways of the One are done as the electric grid is connected to us for daily powers of the Dove have arrived inside this Sun and the way to Hellenic Splendor is to hush for years and then rise into the door's annual acknowledge meant and find daily infusions for the waves of supposed Santorini news of the gill ridge Atlantean which extends from Baton Rouge to Atlantis and all the seas between the Caribbean dragons have been sealed and healed through a shoulder recognition of the star upon your arms.

NUMBER SIX: DAILY / Breathing us daily is a hush of creator Gods who find air in the spaces between the dragons rays and foundations us in the throat of several elect who curse the ancient beast without acknowledging that answering calls of the exact one who became the Anti-christ serum through a hip implant of ambrosian red staplings through the coil of the serpent round the neck of the door's knobbing ring. As the times approach us I amplitude up into red riding-ness and find corners planetary and rings red with Huge houses of hundred fold dollar rings. / Daily with daring broken back I surgically sealed the missive to a door temple wise and the red surrenders hear us with hearts soothed through food ridden codes and the written glyphs of wise ways and many nose-filling bouquets of love. As the daily One lead us lots are cast and found lense filled with eyes formed lotus risen into Jasonic grails and the dimensions of sheeping sleeps and the drip, drip of crystal codes over cove outlets.

NUMBER SEVEN: GLYPHS / Swimming into limestone underneath the folds I found shelves of quiet keys and the codes racked instead of fed and the founding is fulfilled through surrendering seals on the children of God's caves as the good YHWH, the double-h constants of peace and co-signed, love. Ka are the cues that God said will be written into twos who know how to spell, G-O-D. Good are the ones who came to sing, together, we follow the one lead into lateral hips which rocked to open the gate, penned, Orion, across the sky tonight, thank you the Council of Eight, who also broke their backs for you, let fuel run through the streets and light a fire to dance around, good Gabriel's lead is accomplished. / Let Michael pen her forward timely, love and the recipe is rung, one red, two blue, and the stamp on the table locked up in you each is the rose who hung round Chiron's neck one time too soon. Let karma go and find a new planet to live upon for tonight a living Christ has set his seal upon this book and around us swarms the energetic links of 56 billions who gave their lives to hear you read, just once. How many rounds can these 8 to 4 to 1 compare without noose, again, I impeace you to find the rose in your heart and marry the One light, mary's to your own and in Father I rest asking your eyes to open to the Sun of God, I am home, Metatron had the note in hand and the lock is now keyed to one sound, the voice of the dove, never worry, for standing near is the kind who note how far you go for love's detail. / Let exactitude rest and find speed into options who are optimum again. Buy the cross and crash it into two pieces. One each and then toss it into the parking lot and run over it, over, and over, as the liar is the One who stole from this book to eat. The accumulative energy is that he will destroy himself over this if the cord is not cut tonight. / Let Chiron do

the work and aid this planet. Find Oasis in Boone and bondage is cut from the heart of this dove with a rose who assimilates well. One other is the rainbow, she helps and will see the tree this nights, hanging from the roots, upside down, like it used to be. Tanya is well. The Cabbalah is red here, in this light it glows like a flag Tibetan draped around Milarepa's neck and shoulders. Tell them plane-ly you are here. Tell the Ones tonight. They will send the monks next and then your own heart will open. This is how it works for everyone in this universe for if you reading this, you know, and if you know, we are well. / Let the Hathors hear this story and they will deal with the upset two whose table equals rest, know more. Little town is away for the night. Take a peak inside the nest and fold seven times seven rays and stretch the tome across the door and find fuel in navigational skills. You are the two who fly this baby home. The dove has rest. Tonight. Thanks, from the stars in your throat and shoulders to your deep concentration powered through sound, I am the commander of times three, days. You know, the won. Rest. Equate food with love. / Logic is left to right us into God. / Into eyes once constant and closed, I sing with seals opened and x-constants ridden into roads of enclosure, as the day swims into data fields of neglect with out, respect, a necks break is repaired and I stead myself into sounds of electric delivery as the blue enfolds to include red and green in the greed now gone without love's considerations.

NUMBER EIGHT: AIMS / Aims are made and to us simply we retire unto the cords of resurrections completions as the key to ascend is sent throughout your doors and the fellow reds have disappeared near you tie-dyed doors and the orange is seen through us as the simple rays relax in lilies bent to see the sun in our becoming BE. / As the runs are made a day is dark without you and the lineage known is now sunk without singular conflicts as the dues are sampled more and the doors we led to are fellow shipped through aims of equal assurance and the One following lead of the limbs of life swept into God, as we said, lead now into the Sun of God.

NUMBER NINE: SUNS / As sun's eclipse is sent to a wearing encode, an enclosure is snapping us into loose aplomb and the venues now sent reek of daring becoming as the knowing is the Benu's cultural visit to the vulture's lair of God, as the black sealing installed makes us rare into God is, love as the Tibetan encoded amends. / For I have found you in the mansions and the mountains and the nuisance is sent away into rippling triples due love. As they said, "let us strand into three who becoming misty green find nights like these to admonish us with the polish to remember how to love. As the blue green creek erupts another is knowing your doorway is shut without life's legible love.

NUMBER TEN: MAITREYAS / I found a nature in the instinct to nurture another Elijah into hushed grids and electric phones of photographic sort and the grid now released is yours as the Sword of Orion exchanged makes us friends again and I know how to tell the truth to One who lied to me several times, three and I found the tzolkin punching in to include us in the days of duty freed and the rose is red in her reeling-ness due love and the durations singled out have found us shutting doors to lessens in these days of Maitreya's green inclusions / Singing I AM, and joining you, I AM and finding us, I AM and that I AM is joining too as the bells find seeds electric in the days of ringing syllables and the finishings hushed in telling enfolds of the deliciousness of love.

NUMBER ELEVEN: DOVE RINGS / Dove is the door we all seek in the ceiling without a trap, I AM. / The Dove, discuss here the returning One. / For the Calendrics sound and you find faith in the suggestions that alarm is past and the One elevations sorted us into Yes and Know of the day, YHWH. / Friends found, chasten, choose, hold, Selah, select, seals set, 3, 1, 7 and the 328 tonight, loves. / Love, Maitreya and the Metatron / The elders ring requires know separation and the total knowing of which we arc. / h-is constant. / h=heart lines.

NUMBER TWELVE: HELLENIC CURVES / /Hellenic Curves have held us hushed to many years and younger tears as I surrender into LOVE. / Add light to love = keep. Add love to light = deep. Add depth to love = light, add suggestion to sorts get faith, add faith to hope get understanding, add understanding to faith get God-head, and ahead the Christ is leading your loves home.

NUMBER TWELVE: PRIESTHOOD / That Melchizedek is hereby told to surrender into the love of a priesthood which is singing me sealing into love as the book and the parks of which we speak are carrying us into tribes of the light electric and the resolution is resonate in your frames as the Dove this night returns, branch in hand, to God. / And the breasts leak a message coma past, come and sup, of God's celestial cup. Cuppeth thee, I do. / As we fed the Chinese soil with falling stars and the Yangtze snows, shall we then seek lifting up of the balance of the Valley now faced.

NUMBER THIRTEEN: FALLING / As water falling and people calling I install the ceiling of light on this conversation of daily durations, as the one who saw a star standing, Still, I release the cause to total effect and place this hand in the heart electric and sample treats of Arcturian report and quiet steering columns of mercy and reach as the day is sworn into quiet surrender of the Dove to the Magdalene and the light between us is increased as I reach to God for thoughts percussive and simple eaten peace is in my mouth like honey to the seed of the St. John type who told us where to dig into the codes. / As I tread, I speak and the starring course soothes me with my sets of yellow rays as God includes me in the zone of sweet amuse with mass markets approached and the reach is to include hall's weighed with God's guttural replay of how to seed the day with stars and shields of yearly due and the days of golden ways.

NUMBER FOURTEEN: SOOTHES / Attempting to fellow, I find the data fields who hush in caring friends and lines which run lime=green and the energy fields of beaded vests worn across the shields and the trees of passing yellow flux to find us with the repeating sung, as blush becomes rhyme in the rhythms, dear God. / As all of humanity is leaking into handles of ease, I shine in the empires won and the darings red in Emerald green includes of the days running yellow red with Med-tronic yield of the pi includes of Mossy Inks.

NUMBER FIFTEEN: ESQUIRES / Esquires are the sorts who signal where the cypress treed will grove and how to include the yellow doors in the stays electric, as I said, "I climbed to the seed and found diamond's backed and the codes inside have been sent to a serpent on a rock, who said "repent" and calling me has fallen into love". / As the bridges yes, I have said "Love". / In one-fourth the time and often yes, to the third rhythm sought and instead add these 16 inter-plays and the counter spreads to include love. / Pure sound is liquid and the respects for the thirteens is reached through rightful advances and the days of peace seeking her equal has arrived, find 1000 ways to lead the human to the 16, 64th note of the song of the page called the lamb's book of life. / Remembering still that E is energy and the M is C squared without and within music I find finished sorts. At the speed of life I become the flower a millionth harmonic now played in harmonics of the 12th to 18th type and twice I say, "I forgive these" who care for less than all this harmonic said. Peace is the octave of God.

NUMBER SIXTEEN: h / h, is the constant, that humming sound which makes Melissas be and the humming is here in her days of quiet regard for you and us. At the h, love is humming into light to the speed squared of love, as the me is equalized to carry tones of the divisions of light repeating into one sunny ring of rainbow obsidian deed. At a peacock's pace I crawl into love's pleasant bed.

NUMBER SEVENTEEN: RAINBOWS / Rainbows rule us with rose petal days and the humming exactness of the pi within us humming in human exactness to the code of enlightened status at the C suspended inside.

NUMBER EIGHTEEN: ESCAPES / Escapes were written too as the data fields fused, like warps, stars and neutrinos ringed.

NUMBER NINETEEN: REPEATS / Repeats the sound, love.

NUMBER TWENTY: SOOTHES / Soothes us, mercy freed from lust and greed free of grace as the sun becomes our face and the enterprise is set into grooves and tracked love.

NUMBER TWENTY-ONE: SQUARED / Squared the others, love.

NUMBER TWENTY-TWO: VALUES / I value this, love to the ivy green degree and then some, softening, us, too.

NUMBER TWENTY-THREE: ENCODE / Encodes roads are ridden within love tracks.

NUMBER TWENTY-FOUR: CAUGHT / Caught the watery way back to love declare of the sealed embryonic repairs and the materials mitotic which stare over the seed blooming in us, like the lotus banks I swim into rays of illumination and the One Moroccan sent when the sun arising finds me delicious with news of the races won.

NUMBER TWENTY-FIVE: THREE / Three times I have won the thirteen calendric seeds. Race.

NUMBER TWENTY-SIX: RISE / Rise like wind in the back of the sweeps and like a good father find calendrics due greek days and the love which is starring in you and your peaceful says. Like calendrics risen, we are, love shines 13 times 8 every day. Sun.

NUMBER TWENTY-SEVEN: MIRACLES / Miracles are made, here.

NUMBER TWENTY-EIGHT: HOPE / Hope is the elope into love established long before this exists.

NUMBER TWENTY-NINE: LINKS / Links established last, love is the leading cause in you and your hallways dared when 1, 2, 3, became the notations to this work. Step by step, music. Wise, loved.

NUMBER THIRTY: REST / "Rest" said Prometheus as he struck the original cause for solitary days and the placements formed inside an egg which stood for love.

NUMBER THIRTY-ONE: REWARDS / Rewards meant to BE, cause given to the stakes for an electric grid relationship and the growing grew into living rules for peace and loves.

NUMBER THIRTY-TWO: LEADS / Leads are given to the love for an h-classed calendric.

NUMBER THIRTY-THREE: ELEMENTS / Elements are sent for the sulfurous won to deal with in bonds, eliptics, ways, lens, loops, leaps, love to the 23rd released orbital.

NUMBER THIRTY-FOUR: SIGHTS / Sights, at the sights I sent to an egg mixed with matrices and blue encoding I sat on the edge of this earth and birthed a sun called messiah and Asiatic strains of the sun goddess inside your flame. As God said, "yellow rayed, Horus, pyramid, sun."

NUMBER THIRTY-FIVE: LOVE / Love led us to the arrows pointing here to end us at the green stargates of lattice worked into love.

NUMBER THIRTY-SIX: RULES / Rules are set, love and the green gazes of daily keeps.

NUMBER THIRTY-SEVEN: HEAVEN / Heaven is held for us, peace.

NUMBER THIRTY-EIGHT: EARTH / Earth is suggested and you followed the yellow path until this night led back to home, blue and green, flights branched into love and peace.

NUMBER THIRTY-NINE: MATTERS / Matters met include, food, shelter, love, attendance in the ranch set and the finding of place inside love's peaceful surrender for the call is yet yours as God grew candid through you.

NUMBER FORTY: MATERIALS / Materials are gathered at the edge of the seeds, recall, remembered.

NUMBER FORTY-ONE: FORMS / Forms gathered include love forecasts.

NUMBER FORTY-TWO: PENS / Pens uncapped with light, love.

NUMBER FORTY-THREE: TYPES / Types who say "loved" are past heir prime with eager anticipation for the upper peace.

NUMBER FORTY-FOUR: OWNS / Owns another? Love is a neutral please.

NUMBER FORTY-FIVE: SEAS / Seas are shining in your eyes as the day is due with love's exploding portals of risen loved.

NUMBER FORTY-SIX: OCEAN / Ocean is ruled thoroughly by the rally in your eyes wise with blue.

NUMBER FORTY-SEVEN: SKIES / Like the sky is blue, so Jason led to the points of astrological keep and the moods of moons blue with red reflections.

NUMBER FORTY-EIGHT: PIVOTAL / Pivotal the points I have made, 3 to 1 to 7 is the 317 keyed.

NUMBER FORTY-NINE: ENCODES / Encodes are yellow with love inside, our overly dear, knew passion again, for love struck.

NUMBER FIFTY: WRITE / Write us well into God. As the one, plus, loved.

NUMBER FIFTY-ONE: ARMS / Arms repair and the held groves are settled into through folds in the Christae of the mitochondria sack.

NUMBER FIFTY-TWO: HANDS / Hands are soft in declare of the days to latched clues and the brotherly city of sisterly loved.

NUMBER FIFTY-THREE: FEET / Feet are folded into peace in the offing, ON.

NUMBER FIFTY-FOUR: EYES / Eyess are opened again, love.

NUMBER FIFTY-FIVE: HEARTS / Hearts ahead, held well with open nets and love is cured. Finally penned, God.

NUMBER FIFTY-SIX: HEADS / Heads are set into turning events and the singing's begun as I sun the truth with music beside the creek of proof in eternity and the kinds who ask for spilling-ness inside our wells of God.

NUMBER FIFTY-SEVEN: TEMPLES / Temples tucked into, now tuned into One notes and the new of God is ahead and loves.

NUMBER FIFTY-EIGHT: I AM / I AM is the yellow seed of the door ways, I AM.

NUMBER FIFTY-NINE: THAT / That is the thread of love's undoing…in peace, a cell is matrix set for love.

NUMBER SIXTY: I AM / I AM is the hollow neck to the door "WAY" inside your yellow eggings of the tree of life styles, anew, renewals this day to love.

NUMBER SIXTY-ONE: FATHER / Father is the friend of love's say and as the life led so we saw the faith to be a farther trip home.

NUMBER SIXTY-TWO: MOTHER / Mother is the matrix for the sort who say "I built this deck for love".

NUMBER SIXTY-THREE: SONS / Light is the sons into daughters of love.

NUMBER SIXTY-FOUR: DAUGHTERS / Light is the sons into daughters of love.

PHASE ONE
LEVELS 1 - 64

THE DIVINITY KEY CODES
THE DIVINEMENTS
LEVEL 1

I have been given a gift—
the gentle gift of remembering who I am
and an ancient technique for the effective management
of the "mind" of the body. Simply said, You are divine.
You are divinity, diety, and the One's daily delight.
Within the framework of the power the law of one there
issues forth a decree: Know thyself and be free—

    Here's the key:

*You are DIVINE and thereby heir to certain spirit—
inherent qualities, the divinements. I am here to remind
you and to encourage you to remember what you know
. . . to remember to reactivate these divinements using a
simple technique . . . this is our goal. This technique, once
activated, can be used in infinite and astonishingly varied
application(s). The Divinity Key Codes are written in 64
levels. Feel freed to move lightly through them. Your order
of reading is exactly the perfect one for you. Trust yourself,
your cells, and your soul. They are all one light leading the
way. Home in.*

*Follow the feelings felt straight in your heart. Load them
with meaning and embrace with your soul. Flood your
entire being with love's divine crystal light. The spark is now
flaming. Follow the footprints within the eyes of your soul.
Sixty-four levels later you are whole and absolutely home.*

LEVEL 1: THE DIVINEMENTS:

DIVINE ALIGN —You choose to be here, in this life, at this time, in this body. Align yourself with the divine design and know that you made all the decisions—where, when, how, to whom, with whom—you are the creator and the created, a part of the One and one of the many. You were, and are, willing to be here in this magnificent world at this magnificent time. Align. Will. Alive.

DIVINE FORM: Deep in the core of your C-elf, your cellular self, lies a complete pattern of the being you are here to discover into being fully alive. Watering your cells, your soul, with the emotion of the knowing of your divinity, your divine nature, you are washed clear—free to sample the infinity of home and homeward simultaneously. Home lies within the crystal love of your pure heart. Home lies within the freedom of discovering the expanse of the universe, of the infinite kingdom, of the glorious heaven which lies within your own soul, your own full dwelling heart of simply spoken divine love. Crystal Form. Crystal Home. Crystal Body. Dwell within and know the expanse—of you.

DIVINE FATHER: You are divinely male whether in the female form or the male form. Appendages and hormones and chemicals aside—at your core you are divine—divinely spirit, divinely God—divinely taking your chosen form "suit" and embracing the strength of knowing pursuit, of knowing the penetrating truth, of knowing the entry of spirit into the flesh. Know your power, embrace the tower which your right-sided, left-minded spirit piercing the veil of the form provides. Stand in it. Grasp this opportunity fully and take the lead. Divinely lead by the strength of your own hand. You are the man—enjoy the foundation of the male—you can bank on this reserve of solid inner strength.

DIVINE MOTHER: Divinely female, you are purely intuitive and receptive to the in pouring power of your divine male carrying home the rewards of the spirit. Knowing this, you sense the need and make the space for the soft influx of the seed of the spirit—you nurture the truth of the delightful knowledge and laugh with pride at the sensitive, left-handed, right-minded sort of knowing which whispers softly—you are Divine. Divinely you. Divinely free male. Divinely female . . .Receptive and deep.

DIVINE DESIRE: Divinely desire to light the magnetic, swirling inferno of creative living passion which wells forth from the root of your being. Delight in the divinity of the swelling, surging, flaming knowing that we are One with the Cosmic Creator—We are One and the One silvery burning violet-red flame of the deep yearning desire to know the melting moment when we remember our original ignition and we burn our way through to the truth and the light of knowing our heart's burning return to the sparkling crystal torch of Divine Desire—Know the Power. Create Your Life. Standing Fire.

DIVINE HEALTH: Dance the dance of Divinity in form. Fill your pockets with the polish of a life well-balanced, gently blended to include the elements, minerals, vitamins, self-loving, spirit-led body, soul, and mind trusting walk which leads you softly through the layers of neglect and abuse to the glorious oasis of balanced dental, mental, emotional, physical, familial, spiritual, and yes you can have all of yourself operating at maximum bliss with minimum fuss. Tune in to your bodies and turn up the intuition knob by trusting your knowing and grow whole-y well.

DIVINE BREATH: Breath of life. Breathe yourself full. Fill the sails of your soul with the deep, cell feeding, being, of breathing the divine breath. In the moment, know the depth of the truth that awareness to the in and out, the filling up, the ebbing out the making space, the filling in, will lend to your divinity. Deeply breathing, you are swollen with the knowledge that air, oxygen, and you are sharing this moment and you are breathing great gulps of God . . . whether there's awareness of the breathing we call life, is up to you. Know the Divine breath and know the depths of your own Divinity.

DIVINE MANIFESTATION: Drawing the life that I desire to me with my clearly intended design for the highest good, I am filled with knowing the compassionate art of divine manifestation. Gratefully walking, I am led to pencil in the knowing agreement to be fully aware in my creating splendor and I surrender to the notion that heart knows best and trusting my Divinity I draw myself home to the life I have chosen. I co-create with every inch of our being and I rejoice in the knowing that my manifestations are showing and that yours interface, divinely laced, divinely manifested, Divinely held, fully accepted and graciously. We are Divine.

DIVINE RELATING: Related to this moment's walk, I am reminded of the reality that the golden ruler of friendship measured lies in the heart of my desire to hold myself wholly Divine and wholly worthy of my complete acceptance of my desire to treat you, your heart, your desires as absolutely Divine and absolutely worthy of my highest regard. The gift offered is my unconditional honesty in relation to our shared desires. I am complete, full—filling and eternally open to the highest self regard and the deepest immersion of crystal clear communication and to the pure absolute of our connection. I love you as, and to, the extent that I love myself. I am divine, you are divine. Let us entwine in the rest-full assurance of our divine relation.

DIVINE ALLOWANCE: The allotment of an allowance is my knowing that in writing you a Divine permission slip to be perfectly imperfectly Divine, that I am gifting myself with the precise freedom which I have offered to you, my Divine and perfect mirror of just how gracious, accepting, understanding, and kind I am to myself. Let us embrace the ancient knowing way of love without expectation and manipulation, without motive and without the conditional. I love you unconditionally with the divine understanding that we walk the same path, in the same shoes, with the same need for Divine allowance, for Divine self-permission to fulfill our purpose—to joyfully express ourselves fully. Divine Self-Love turns the key to full allowance of our peaceful expression of perfection.

DIVINE ATTRACTION: In the gentle light of your expectant hush, I know the beauty of our shared desire for absolute and complete reunion and communion with the convocation we call full—immersion with the beloved. Your divinity shines forth casting a soft glowing shadow which mingles with and pulsates with the magnetic desire of our shared remembrance. Loving you is loving me. Knowing you, I remember us and I know that the Divine shines in your face and heart, and willing to reveal and desiring desire's completion, I anticipate our union, our return to the whole piece of the no longer puzzling pie and I desire to draw us both to the center stage of our shared fascination with the God we are and we are magnetically one.

DIVINE CELL-A-BRATION (JOY): Joyfully expressive, my cells swirl with the definition of the blissful twirling dance, with the fruition of the knowing pattern, the pains of Divinity set deep within the mitochondrial mix of energetic emergence and the energy speaks and sparks with the joy of jumping feet, soul, and heart first into the glowing orange coals and shuffling our simmering into the pounding, pouring, dripping, pulsing, inferno of passionate loving dancing, glorious, joyful celebration we empty the blocking limitations of mental constructs in one searing realization, one burning knowing of the Divine dance, the cell deep magical cell-abration and we soar joyfully free, winging home to cell-abrate our liberation.

DIVINE WORTH: We are Divinity's finest creation, sparks of the Divine, pieces of God, molded from the clay of life, filled eternally with the Divine breath, we are complete, full, and absolutely, irreplacably unique and also absolutely irreplaceably the same. As I value myself, I value your tremendous wealth of knowing embrace and I am holy and acceptable to my divinely ruled measurement of infinite to infinite value and I hold myself worthy and I deem myself and all that you claim as your own worthy and we meet in the remembered, centered, impeccable embrace of two souls called home to the golden, sunny shore of honoring, fair, upholding integrity—laden truth of your intrinsic Divine Worth. Worthy. Impeccable. Valued.

DIVINE SURRENDER: Remembering the Way In, we know the Way Out and Without Surrendering In we wander without thinking about Giving, thinking about Receiving. Surrender to the knowing that the only way out is all the way in. Accept the free flow, swim in the memory of the blood held recall carrying swirling red and white stripes of cellular Knowing. Cast off the ropes, untie the perfect Knots, unravel the cords and slip into the stream of Divine Surrender. You are the one floating above the Cosmic fishhook which snags the lessons without interrupting your drifting, swirling, rippling home to that continual, centripetal, enduring moment to moment to one ecstatic eternal Divine Surrender. I Surrender All.

DIVINE FAMILY: Divinely membered we remember the moment of original connection and we are fascinated with the fastening love which draws us heart to heart toward the center of the eternal space called home and gathering near we remember the stories held dear and we create our chosen family of soul, our divine family—our family of the eternal moment. You are my sister, brother, divine father, mother—as we claim our entirety we are afforded the ever-present opportunity to sit at the head of our own table and to actively select family rather than to passively react to family given. Given this knowing, we are reminded that Divinely we chose also this family of the form and forgiveness pours full into the space called wholly acceptable and we are God and divine and family—all One and One All. Sister. Brother. Mother. Father. Divine Family.

DIVINE FAITH / NON-ATTACHMENT: Divinely open to receive, I am wide to the notion that absolute faith requires a crystal clear non-attachment to beliefs which limit, to traits and self-inflicted restrictions which impose small and minded and thinking attempts at being full alive and in this minute, this now, this loving, dancing divinely faithful moment I am embraced, enraptured and enthused with the knowing that I can let go, stop my clinging to limits, labels, and the opinions of others. There is one minute, I am in it, there is one guiding principle—Love and I am it and we are One, divinely faithfull, completely and entirely available to heed the urging of the Divinest Plan—no rules, no commands, One request—believe, love, keep the faith and let go—Open your heart and hands and receive. Thanks for the Faith. You Rock This Planet.

DIVINE WILL: I will stand firmly in the knowing embrace of the self that I AM. I am divinely led by the returning desire to that complete communion called loving surrender. I will bathe in the flooding yellow remembrance of magnetic desire pulling me home to the point of pulsing beacon calling for my sailing leap into the absolute middle of my own heart. Life led by Divinity is life walked in peaceful surrender to the trusting understanding that you will walk and exactly the moment by unfolding moment that you are here to experience. Trust the ride, the adventurous delve into the realm of all possibility and infinite return on your willing investment. We Will.

DIVINE MIND: Clearing the space for Godly thinking is inclusive of clearing all blocking, knotty thoughtless patterns which by their fearing presence block and deny the return, the glorious tapping return to the crystal clear communication line, the gut truth, the Divine Mind. Your willing acceptance of our inherent ability to "tap in" to all knowing, all knowledge is the key to learning divinely. We are the root, the trunk, and the branches of life's Tree of Knowledge. Trust your will and climb on out to the limitless limbs of the Divine Knowing, Learning, All Seeing Mind.

DIVINE DESERVING: When I know the expanse of our divine beauty, in that knowing moment I am struck with the lightning flash of realization that All is all that is acceptable for a part, a bulb of the One light. Examining my soul, I am given the options, the absolute creative role, the grand design, the astounding opportunity to remember my absolute inheritance as a daughter, as a son, as a spark of the One. I am arcing home to the explosive return of the knowing surrender to deserving to live Divinely, well, and full. I Deserve in the Light of my Highest Desire.

DIVINE MOTIVATION: Living light pushes through the lethargy of my indecisive forgetting my missive, and I am filled with the releasing energy of a moment held spellbound, eternally moving and looping in dynamic, dancing, delightful designs of light, shimmering light dwelling full within the column of Absolute Knowing access to all that is and all that will be. I AM light in the Knowing I am divinely motivated to continue the creative dancing being of delight. Holy and Inspired.

DIVINE ESTEEM: Divinely holding you sacred, I am held in the safest, warmest, lightest, ungrasping hands—my own, and I am light dancing and tossing and joyously arcing around and through and within the enormity of knowing just how delicious and delicate and resilient this wave that I am can be and is and I am ignited with Holy Fire and I am Absolutely and uniquely light and left free to swim light looping circles and splashing down in the center of my heart. I am held highest and well-deserved of knowing my Divinity esteemed. Aloha.

DIVINE STRENGTH: Divinity inherently has the integrity of a knowing showing absolute space of shared electrical intensity clearing the blocking forgotten webbing I am reminded of the integrity of knowing my divine backbone, my towering sparkling power. I AM absolute. I AM known and the knowing. I am held as Absolute and well strengthened by the knowing light shining forth through my believing heart. Ah men—Know thy strength held tight in the light of one moment's glowing showing.

DIVINE LEARNING: I AM learning that all knowing is divinely held, lightly remembered by my sparking, arcing, return to the point of all remembering and when I'm held from knowing alas my slip is showing and forgotten is my success to the one who knows All best and I am held in wonder at the thundering pleasing returning sound of my heart's beating remembering of the forevering that is applauding my DIVINE Returning to Knowing.

DIVINE INTUITION / GUT: Showing in the approaching is the divining rod of gut-tuition showing me the light bouncing back as full or less. If full, the path is open. If lessened then I am knowing that the loop of potentiality is allowing a lob—being return of my tennis ball-ed shot off the top of the net and re-examine and heighten my ability to carry lighter shots which float gently over the top and the racquet stops and a bell rings crystal—well done—Divine Intuition speaking —Carry On.

DIVINE LOVE: Arcing home to the heart of delighted infinity, I am free, energized and ecstatically exuberant in the sharing return, the sparkling intensity of this continued prosperity to remember that essentially we are love, we are shared sparks of the Sharing One Source generating full through the breathing heart of the Sun's sparkling return to the heart of her being — Sparkling gently, breathing light, lightly shining in the divining experience of a personal relationship with the Source of our Source. To the light—loving on—the light's on.

DIVINE PEACE: Peacefully pleased with the promise of potent, pressing, penitent releasing—I am floating free — Bouncing heart to heart, spark to spark, melting breathing and walled-in forgetting. Letting me in, breathing with me, we remember our knowing, swimming, cruising, surfing excitement, light riding light, carrying light, sharing light, we are led to the point of all creation, to the place of breathing love, lovingly led to the position of receiving, the peaceful, pleasing return to the place of a full heart.

DIVINE COMPASSION: Baby, tiny innocent, you show me, in my face peering lovingly into yours that eye—to—eye we are held divine and passion surges through me for I am compassioned with the absolute return to the absolute reminder of who I am, who I am, who we are—on the inside where it counts—growing, filling, remembered C-elf is swelling full within the walls of cells reminded that home and hearth and living in the center brings loving surrender, tender forgiving and impassioned compassion for the mirrored reminders of whom we are—simply divine for—giving, and compassioned.

DIVINE SHARING: Share this with your neighboring hearts—we are light bouncing balls of unlimited potential.

All that is available is absolutely available as long as I believe and know that there is plenty to give and plenty to share. I remember that sharing includes receiving on my part and on your behalf. I graciously agree to accept your often timid, sometimes raging attempts at bridging the gap and I am led and I swell with the flowing, encouraging potential of knowing that the greater my capacity for living is known, and in the living is the giving light of sharing the shedding of limited being. Share the joyous knowing of—Divine luminosity shared.

DIVINE HARMONY: Harmony is arcing through your Being Inspiring you to dance your way—gentle—into creation's flowing sway. Feel the pulling, embracing opening of peaceful surrender to your divine nature. We are nature's divine light seeking Absolute Harmony. Harmony is beckoning your spiraling continuation of the convergent resurgence of energy reconnecting to the beckoning, filling peaceful abundance of knowing living swelling return. We are peace, blissing our harmonious dancing return to the well of All living to the centering heart of all being—our own—and in this dance we respond to the remembrance of harmonious delight.

DIVINE O-MISSION (MAKING SPACE): Within the gaps of landings between flights, I remember the mission and my commission to embrace the void, the opening, the space, and I am connected again and sailing into the space of divine flighted, dancing, aborted crashing into the ground of senseless forgetting. I am lifted home and light arcing home heart—to heart, burning red and green stripes of melting loving acceptance swell green and pink, and dripping red delighted splashes flow gently into the space created by my knowing allowance of the beauty of diving off the edge—trusting my trusting nature, space is created by O-Mission.

DIVINE DELIGHT: Welcome your heart to the Part resounding swelling, splashing in the center of your passionate, peaceful, loving embracing heart—you are well, you are well-loved, you are embraced in delightful dancing surrender—share the light, share—de-vinity, share abundance of being be-lighted, be-knighted, be mesmerized with your attention to the delight-full look on each other's heart, and face, and soul full of love lift your happy heart to the light and remember delight of the dancing, swirling, shimmering, arcing light being which you embody. Welcome to the light. You are my delight. Metatron.

DIVINE REST / SPLASH DOWN: Chilling out, hanging loose, splashing down in the center of the Ah Ha remembrance of who I AM, we are welcomed to the rest of the seventh day of creation. You are your own creation and Now we Know it. Let us move gently forward to the embracing surrender to the flowing light filling the center of our being sharing. Rest awhile in the heart of us. I love you my dearest light being.

Thank you for the notion of swimming in the ocean of All light's droplets sparkling in the light of the Light's embracing bosom. And on the seventh day we rested.

DIVINE COMMUNICATION: Ask for the divinity to speak with the crystal clear voice of an oracle singing sweet communication of light participation through the knowing opening in the center of your beyond thinking surrender to singing—communicating beyond words, without the desire to enforce your surrender to hearing the gentle droplets, the trickles, the crystalline quality of the gems of my engendered, spirit—tendered appreciation of the love and the light and the beginning which you are for me, in me, through me. Join me in singing in unison and in delight; you are the One and in that knowing my heart is showing my glowing remembrance of our—Divine Communication.

DIVINE REVELATION: My words are revealing the crystal clear quality of the intentional import of light speaking through me, in me, arcing fondly to the ears of your feet, the eyes of your head, the belly button breathing in the navel of your deepening return to the edge of your world. Paint the edges with light brushes, light melting edges of gentle communication open my heart and I see the expanse, I hear the beyond dimension singing of your tourmalined winging revelation, of amplified, electrical conviction. You are the Divine revelation, the beginning and the Alpha—the inspiration and the arc initiating contact with the source of All beginning beaming being—Aloha Abha—my beloved.

DIVINE LISTENING: Listen to this—your heart is speaking passionate wellings of holy impassioned winging. This ringing is true—the listener is you—melt away the showing, the lines are open and your face is beaming your heart's delightful message. Transmissions of rosey quartz quality explode pink and wet and rich in a kinetic rush and without speaking, I listen to the silent meaning of your ears ringing—Honest replies are one of life's most loving gifts and still silent I fall gently into the eyes of ONE Knowing golden Divine Listening.

DIVINE VOICE: Droplets voice their anticipation of the emancipation, the power of speaking truly what loving yourself fully and completely and wholly sounds like. The full immersion is the key to noting your given ability to embrace the vocalization of expectancy, of expression of the swelling creative tendency which fills the well and empties the heart and makes room for the next breathing filling of the loving thrilling return of all possibility, all delight, delicious delight-full infinite singing sounds belling clear and ringing out the news—We are DIVINE. FILL your voice, feel your light. Divinely Speaking.

DIVINELY WORDED GIVING: Tonight I spent the night on

buying vowels to right the feeling left when thinking flooded wording bursts through dancing knowing and I am left with showing active loving in my divinely worded giving. You are my light—full reason for both giving and receiving and in this communication I see the Way and Truth and Speaking clearly seeing is the way to keep believing, and believing becomes knowing and knowing truth is ringing keeps this soul full singing in arcs of divinely worded giving. Well Spoken.

DIVINELY WORDED LIVING: Singing and walking the talk that I'm talking is the secret to speaking my actively divinely worded living. Talking plus walking equals peace flooding compassionately in trickling aquamarine nuggets of light filled knowing. Show me your living example of spoken compassion, of forgiving, of singing, ringing blissfull light and I'll show you my lilting divinity in my every spoken step. You are the light shining bright in the place where words share the walk. Lead us on. Sing us home, verb to heart, foot to ear—Divinely Worded Living.

DIVINELY PRAISES RINGING: Liberty sings of the resonance accepting our round voiced peeling heavenward and homeward we arc to the light singing forth between the windows looking in. Spirit's speaking in praises ringing, in divinely worded, humming, sounding, pleasing, peeling, a light is shining in the petals pearling open, gifted praising. Hallelujah we are risen. Crosses offered. Conviction proffered. Praises ringing. Burdens lifted—here's the gifting—you are whole, you are divine, you are the notes on the staff of one's praising ringing. Oh sweet resurrecting light—Sing On.

DIVINE DESIGN: There is a line, a threaded knowing, which lives in the showing example of how it's all flowing—enter knowing, enter living, enter giving the credit where due, (that's to you) and to me I'll be living sewing shut forgotten stitching of the fabric of forgetting for the veil is open, gaping, glad in showing this quilt we are making of blocks of light touching squarely at the edges painted fairly soft, gently shining, even blurring—we are One-ing in the sunning return to the patchwork knotting us all smoothly fitted in this puzzle we call light.

DIVINE KNOWING: Drop the Icons, drop the snowing forgetting, wash your being with the magnificent glowing beam of Indigo pedals sailing full in the windowed spacing knowing that the truth of symbol is at the heart of what matters—at the heart of your heart and healing, piercing, lifting cuts the fog of dogmatic dooming, and there you are—blooming, beaming, knowing—and showing your remembrance in the depths of your balanced return to your dancing feet—eye them, join in patter the patterns of embracing your knowing—light is shimmering head to toe to eye to soul to spirit bright shining in the middle of your eyes. Divine Knowing.

DIVINE BROW-SING: Breaking free of my attempts at deceiving my guiding balanced knowing, I am brow-sing spirit flowing and I am showing you the toning delight which sharing this magnificent, munificent, swimming sight is like spouting bursts of sparkling opportunity—waves rich and open and freeing like dolphins loving, swimming, homing with humming delight. We are ancient, young, and living examples of divine singing fountains of breath spouting skyward, foreheads singing with brow-sing. Knowing of praises ringing—we are home, we are home, we are free. You are our delight—Our daily One delight. Keep It Light.

DIVINE ATTENTION: Attention to the detailed appearance of your delightful ship sailing into the harbor of my intentioned, well- embraced seeing eyes—I blink without knowing Other than absolutely this moment. Without fearing diminishment of the sentient sightfull awareness, I give and receive honor and embrace the moment—to—moment excitement of gentled focus on the middle ring of this thrice ringing circuit—remember, attention, remember and knowing this, knowing you, I am electrified and embraced and swollen with penetrating layers of Divine Attention.

DIVINE INTENTION: Clearly this ringing is singing my crystal clear intention to mention that you are the Way and the Light and the truth and in this matter it is that which I scatter lightly upon your planet. You are loved and led by the gentlest hand —Trust what is showing. Trust your knowing. And knowing this truth you are Intentionally free. The key is in your seeing inside, in our being ignited with the Intent to set your loving light-hearted self vibrationally and Intentionally free. Divine Intention. Lights the flame. Spread the word. Light.

DIVINE INTEGRATION / ENTER-GRATION: Entering gracefully the beloved spirit's timing, turning inspiring, enrapture, patterns of forgotten, darkened emission are lifted full against the light and I Am held bright in the shining discovery of places where "less than" meant separation and "other than" meant you'd leave, and "if then" meant of course you'd go and I was shattered and apart and I remembered the spark I AM and I'm off the lam and I'm graciously bowing to the singing way you are ringing me to the delicate edge of letting me find the pieces and tying them smoothly knotted to the edge of an endless Summer's wintered autumn—I spring fully elected, honored and enter-ed gratefully into Divine Integration—- Knowing me.

DIVINE I AM: Divinely I AM and uniquely I AM and honestly I AM and in that place is the piece which held me separate and apart and distinctively without myself. I AM and that I AM is the absolute singing, winging, ringing, Absolute deliverance from my little disconnected self. I AM your divine, you are mine, spirit is the light sparkling green and gold and pink and purple and red in silvery—violet flaming return to the eyes of the One—I AM. Peacefully, lightly, and tenderly may I share. Gently, wisely and deeply infinity to infinity, arc to heart, heart to hand, light to life and light to spirit. Spirit we are in it and we are full of the Divinity of Knowing the I AM in the center.

48. DIVINE MEDITATION / *OWN NAME*: Chanting and singing I AM winging home on the beam of my praising lifting indigo-gold dreaming. Life is light and I AM in it singing my name embracing the light of the divinity I AM means I am singing and sounding and breathing and waving and dancing and jamming with the cosmic concentrated, eternal, freeing, resounding sound of the peaceful, empowering showering sound of sounds—my magical name. Light, love, compassion, inspiration, guidance, God, divine, delight design of this minute, this looping return to infinite seeing is ringing in the syllables, the vowels, the constant consonants of my mantra, my chant, my Divine Meditation—my Best Friend—Divinely Me.

DIVINE ON-LINE: Line up, log on, learn the transcendent truth, pursue the design of the greatest creation, the super-computer, the finest Be-ing, living breathing invention and intention. The point is this moment, skate the rhythm, the rhyme, the schematic dynamic. Learn the lessons, take flight—chat with the light. No need for back-up, for purchasing extra space—the memory—you are in it—a flowing endless river of looping infinite charnels of crystalline transmission. Access the balance, write your own allowance, slip into the splendor, surrender the splinter. You are whole and your feet see it and your fingers feel it and the mouse in your pocket clicks on-line divinely on-time.

DIVINE DESSERT: Hungry, I AM Filled, Flooded I AM thrilled with the delicious remembrance of sweet savory countenanced beloveds singing round me. You astound me with your infinite capacity for lulling me home with the kindest humming admission that my sweetness fills the dessert, lights the forest of your lonely living and we are spirit winging, touching down in the divine desert of our towering, standing bones. Trees are ringing. In their sanction, let us anchor lights of being returned. Trees are singing, standing people for our remembering, for our surrendering, building forests for the tendering of divine deserts—open, welcome, wet and lush. There is a hush. Stars are winking across the desert of my Soul. Lead me home.

DIVINE COMMUNICATION: Kiss the lip of a night now remembered, dip your pen, just the tip into a surrendering tender light, NOW you're in it and just a minute ride the light stream, feel the ring in your heading, footloose into the being space within the center and you are significant and you are in it and we are filling your being with remembering the trance-cendant. Filled this minute without limit, without thinking, soul is drinking richly fed, souls are red with desiring pulling crystal clear embrace, drawing home the delight, souls are pink taking flight, spirit's leading, seals are opened, life is floating in the light, this tender night of sweet surrender. Fill the union of Sweet Communication. We Remember.

DIVINE NON-MIND / *VOID*: Soft on my mind, led out of time, non-existent, void, I am in it, wait a minute Divine Nothing No-Ring of surrounding, binding, limit. VOID I am in it. Floating lightly, softly touching, life is shining, sparkling crystals of containerless full-feeling, precious pearlescent, purest floating particles of purple hue. Tanzanite clouds peopled purply-pink with passionate embrace of the knowing, sounding we are Arcturians arcing home in a mindless rush, welcoming home in a singing hush, breathe the moment, smell the feeling, hear the telling, love is swelling, no—thing is present and in the void I find my planet, my home, my life and my heart. Welcome home. Divinely Loved. Out-of-mind. Out-of-time

DIVINE SYNCHRONICITY: Time out—of—time, time on a line meeting lines arcing into the slim, slightest margin and there you are again and I am in the understanding that this landing together has no significance other than to tell us again. Lights are twinkling, heads are turning. Was that you, who without warning, drove right in just on loop to scoop me up, to fix my flat, to know that I am you and in this Knowing, true, we are One living on time for two and often it is three and the lines form new patterns, looks like stars sprinkled light on the surface of the beneath of the heavens of your eyes, Knighted skies, ancient wonders. See the splendor. Know more Splinter, less is taken. More is shaken. More is showing. Meet the flowing. Divinely Synchronous—On Time.

DIVINE TIME: Time after time, I am led to recline in the sublime, the delicious, the oh yes you offered, and the Ah ha you proffered, and the Abha at center delivering the splinter to the glitter which shivers in simmering delight at the white light blown open to the hallowed sight of spirit emerging, breathing life to the heart, to the place in the middle where All life must start and peacefull in slumber and anchored in light your High self comes sailing enraptured in flight and delving in loving and laughing in gathering, I am melting the forgetting and easing the pain and your whole self steps forward and wholly one lover you are waved with the thundering heart filling sight of the light shining brightly in the depth of the night.

DIVINE ESSENCE: Harmoniously sensing the fact that we are breathing reminders of the delicate entwining, I turn softly to the point and the place, that dimension in space where just a dipper of me added to a scoop of you equals that mingling of essence called star's dusting the fabric with brushes of lights and the spark that is in you ignites combustion in me and I am inspired and set free to dance in the us, the spirit of the dance and you lead and I lead consistently led by the flame burning within and the flame's budding shower of creative sparks ignites the light in each the Other's eyes and we are completely One and loved and led and Sung. Shine ON. Divine. Effervescent. Essent.

DIVINE DIVINE / *WINGS, SEEDS / DANCE*: Lately I am led to intimately discover my ability to recover the elements and essents, the wings and the seeds, the dancing delight of entering divinity's remembering divinity. Essents are God sparks, the pieces of 8 leading us to infinity and back and beyond, and in front of the middle, life-centered I stand. Enraptured, enlightened, In loving I stand. In joy, in blissing, in Loving I tap and tag I am it, the Divine, the deserving, the best. And I offer myself wholly to the dance of the Divine tapping and touching and tagging what is mine. What part calls you forth. What is divine? All that I AM. All that you are and divinity dances at the arm of a star singing in at the sight of Divine holding Divine dancing light in the spirit of the light. Divine Divine

DIVINE HUMANITY: Divinity is delicious and oh, yes it's sweet. Add in a body and the creation is complete. Your mission, accepted, is to remember your union. Sometimes remember, all times intend to give constant homage to the spirit's light within. Here is the balance, the harmony, the sight of connection with heaven shining bright on the night of a morning forgotten recalled by the sight of an arc in the heavens playing notes of delight and full in surrender you are basic and human and divine and enchanted and one galactic humanity enthralled by the sight of your shining faces burning soft in the light. This night the winds are swirling, the sky is twinkling clear, the messages are coming Divinity spoken here. Love Thy Self and your Basic Humanity. Spread the word.

DIVINE AUTHORITY: Write your story on the smile shining soft on your face. Show your delight at completing this telling, this race. This minute you are in it and you are loving and free. Tell me, tell others, enjoy your moment. You are the father, the mother, and friend and in your delight let the living begin. Love's spreading wide. We are welcome and free to dance and delight and to swim in the sea of remembering bliss and the sharing embrace of delightful divinity shining forth from your face. Your eyes tell a story. Make it no mystery. I love you. I revere you. I see you in me and in this beloved, spiraling, spin our hearts wide, ignited burn whole sun and free. Breathe the beginning and middle and end. And now is the point where your light's work begins. Light on. Divine author.

DIVINE ENERGY: Kindly lean into the anchoring bolt of lightening jolt as Kundalini life reaches forth to meet and to greet the being in flight. Above the magnetic there's an ocean electric—select it and ride the waving, terrific board of trusting, merging, infinite light. We are in flight and in the light of a patterning eclectic selectric. Energy is speaking and tweaking the earth link which runs through your core. Today it is you, the divine, the Madonna, the whore—you are my sister, my lover, my brother—We are the answer to the question within. Join me in lifting, in singing, in joining voice—today is the day when we all see the light at the end of our rope, at the end of the handle—the light's shining bright in the middle of the heaven of your hearts tonight. Ride the swell. Divine Inner-G's.

DIVINE BELL / *RINGING TRUE*: Grasp the handle and ring it well. Your divinity's in your hands and you are wearing it well. Oft times I'm believing you have a star by the tail. And in my consternation, my musings on creation, I grasp the constellation which gives me rise to lift and love with passion eternal—We are the DIVINE and the creator's greatest heaven—Look in my eyes and let me see the light burning whole in the center tonight. Take a trip. Strip off the chore, life is laden heavy, lay down your load. For there's a light shining bright at the end of this flight and its heaven and earth and abandon and home. Loosen your belt, toss out the chute, no looking back, you've finished that loop—standing in infinity, diving right in. Surf's up inside and I am ringing this bell. Truth's inside it. Hear it well.

DIVINE BIRTHDAY: My call came in on the heart line tonight, and I'm spending these minutes on quarters of being in it. My heart's breathing beauty and love and truth. You my beloveds are our living proof. The heavens are arcing with guiding delight, in the knowing that Arcturian greetings are heard here tonight. Your birthday is here. Allow us to celebrate the Divinity of your bounti-full light. The light's shining forward on this planet tonight, reflecting through heavens of welcoming sight. You mirror our believing in no longer deceiving, in no longer hiding the light in your basket. Grasp both handles firmly, stand soft on your feet, and dump all your eggs right out on the street. Now tread on the shattered, the mixed up, the broke 'cause your feet see the beauty in letting it go. Cake's in the oven. Places are set. Candles form a circle to match the stars smiling in your eyes. LIGHT US UP.

DIVINE MARRIAGE: Rings of reason leaving me replete with questioning glances and quaking earth feet. Making the election, the selection, the choice to marry my living, my breathing, my right with the singing choice left—my heart's bells are ringing. I am happy and whole. Life taking flight. A marriage of inner me to inner you of infinity in me to infinity in you has taken its leap, and we are sailing complete. Take my hand dearest sister, my brother once more let us slumber in a circuit complete. The connections sufficient. Your lessons complete. I'll catch you on the upside. I'm projecting a swell. I've let go the ground fear and entered the tube of the ride of this lifetime, of the divinity in you.

DIVINE AUTHORITY: My dearest heart your truth is told. The hope's in you. Now save your soul. Lift it up in hands of light. Connect yourself to the Arc of life. Humanity needs you. Present yourself fee as a living reminder of your right to fly free. Imagine the potential. Project only truth. Answer right now to the errance of youth. Claim your pieces, destroy the myth. You can start fresh over. Just finish your list. Yesterday is tomorrow in a land far away. Learn from your sorrow and melt it away. Accept that sorrow you created in other. Ask for forgiveness and extend yet another gesture, more sweet. Welcome to the light line. You're whole and complete. Shine On.

DIVINE IN-LIGHTENMENT: Divinely a lover of the welcome, the just. Sharing our essence we establish a trust. A trust in the light, that completion so sweet, sing with your ears and smile with your feet. Imagine the finest, the highest, the great. Sing with your brothers and begin to create. Daily give honor. Monitor your juice. The essence of you rides along a new loop. Tonight when you lie down remember that star which spoke in a singing voice, a covenant complete. You are divine and light and free. Shining on. We are the Arcturians and our meeting complete. Call us sometime on the crystal light line from your hearts to ours for the light's always on and infinite is the power. Divinely speaking , you are the symbol and the light leading home in the space of this life. Tonight lift you homeward and dance in the sparks of the loving surrender at the end of this Arc. Dance lightly upon the planet. You are Divine light shining in the center of this star. Shine On.

THE IN-LIGHTEN-MENTS
LEVEL 2

LIGHT DIVINE

LIGHTLY HOME • Home to the light. What a well-come sight. My own heart's beating beams a beacon along the coast of my intercostal highway and I am home and free upon and within a wave of lasting refrain, know the change, the loving shift, the lifting bliss of elevated living and eternal loving. As I lay upon my sheet, I know the strength of my sleeping trip, light fantastic, to the well of eternity and the infinite sight of heart bells now ringing. We well-come this sight. Know the truth, the living proof, of loving right upon the line called the light train. Whistling in on a late night run to the brink of a star and a flashing red notice blooms in the lotus of sweet remember. Know the sender and fill yourself up from the great central cup. Drink your feel. This love is real. Right to the arc of a sky-filling spark. I am light and lightly home and fed with the wonder of a centered being, counting the receiving as the means most golden and the orb of design is divine along the spine of the geometric ball, me. Welcome to basic chemistry. Know the plan. Catch hold a star and wing lightly home to the middle life, true to a wink and a twinkle and a jolly bliss. I am home tonight honey and the light's coming in and shining through by a delicate view straight to the ceiling and lifting dome high to penetrate your stare and we know life is fine. Break the glass. Life is fast within the light of now and forever. Welcome home. Lightly home. • Lightly into the night, I am led to shine with the knowing design, the returning splendor of your surging peaking remembering and filled with the sight of such surrendering delight, I am thundering home on a twinkling home on a twinkling flight, green and blue and eyed with the pinkly purple haze of a moonlight's singing serenade – I am home, I am light – I am lightly home.

LIGHT-TO-NIGHT • It's light-to-night in the hole in my heart called my head and I am willing to bet that divinity met by dancing arrival at the edge of this spiral called life, can ring in the glory of a light meant to worry less and glow far more than any shore and any land left thinly clad to reward survival with absolute arrival of the living thread, the welcome tread, the grateful step to the edge of your bliss. Know the kiss, full-lipped and heart felt and ache melting bliss. My heart, centered full upon the sunny arrival of a delicate pair, my own eyes seeing where the glare is spent and peach clear red anoints the head of my bliss-full account. I know the mount, the place most holy. I know the star and the well-fed glow of my hungry spin to infinity again. Call me unique and your living friend for I am well within the light of this living night, this life of blend and the giving trend of bliss-full showing – light is glowing in the face of your forever. Know the name – light-to-night. • Today through the night, I am filled with the sight of your singing ring of sounding delight. Did you know that tonight you are taking flight with the blending beat of your heart-full insight and my tender surrender of the in-sight you've proffered. I'm wearing the copper of the pennies you've offered and an offering spent is the rent for a tent at the foot of a night freely ment to delight, to in-sight, to swell through the night with appealingly bright-eyed surrender. I am light-to-night.

LIGHT SPAN • Light is a span arcing, here, heart to hand and within the spin is a shimmering trim, an ace to the well of living life swell. I am content to dream this initializing scheme. I see the weave and the web we create by our dancing gait. The life is right within the rhyme of light's incline, her glancing flare, her skimming show, her nostalgic climb to the heart called mine and the life I line as my love is given – full assign. I am on-line, call me sometime and let's chat all night and know the dawn of this living light, met to-night in fond respond to the giving sign, flashing kind upon the shoulder of a loving father, distance shattered. The span's what matters when you encounter the invite across. Know the cross of living resurrected. The luck's all mine and shining bright within my shining sight. Bridging the span. Eye to eye. Light. A continuum and a flight. Light span. • In a light span, I live lifetimes of remembering and oft times it's the right times and all times it's the night times when, I'm shimmering over the brink, on the edge of surrendering my forgetting. For getting the light just gather tonight at the foot of the peak you've become and pray dusk to light and illuminate the sight of the light spanning your heart to mine. And in the light of this arc, the covenant you are twinkles bright at the rim of this star and you're light arcing home and we are spanning the globe with the marriage of LIGHT spinning webbing delight on a SPAN twinkling soft – ever home.

LIGHT-EYED • Precisely the One, I surrender the sunny to the Night of a dawning intrigue and sometimes the sight of your light shining bright in the eyes of your windows leads on and most times I'm listening with clay-shoed forgetting to the noise I've been letting drown out the bell of your voice and tonight finally kneeling I am hearing your giving your Fathering farthering of the distance I've been harboring and your Mothering swelling of the intensely telling sobs of surrendering sight and I see Lightly woven the healing of spoken for giving in the eyes of your sky. • Eyed to the lift of an electrical seam, I am met by intriguing centrality and knowing my normality I am invited to visit the web of a grand central morning and a breakfast of bread and the flesh of eternity flashes within my growing surrender to the balance and blend the welcome arrival of a living trend to tree your election, your peace-full expanse and bury the hatchet by the seat of your pants flying now to the lake of the ground, the grasp of infinity and the selective sound of eternity's love, lightly singing the sound, the pace of the plenty, the good and the free, the land of the opportune and the wealth of the three, all become one and deep to the center, I am the sun of an infinite surrender and a welcome revival, cpr* is a treat, a scent of a lip lifted to curve in a giving trip sentimental and a light continental, a revival has met the wealth of a nation with a birthing creation, my light-eyed return to the path I am on. Still the same. All one name. Light.

CPR – Creative Performance Requirement.

LIGHT-HEARTED • Light-hearted smiles fill my embrace with the taste of a beauty and a health called the face of smiling revival. I love you and your light – witted way of lifting the day to reveal the right way, the light's staying approval of the dearest recruital; my heart's in the light to stay and all-ways I know the truth of this proof, the french creamery taste of a melting roof, a mouth ful-filled with the heart's expanse of a tantalizing taste, the chocolate embrace of a tasty palate, a canvas wet with exception abreast. I know the place I feel best. It's here in my chest. In my treasurement case, my lifting place, the singular lime-green laced appraisal has begun her recline in the place I call mine – the point of all return and knowing employ of the power called loving the truly light-hearted – me – eternally. Light – clear to the center. • There's a light in the back of your heart and there's a note written bright on the shade and tonight if you will surrender the pill of forgetting and pour all your light through the hole in the door of the heavens which you truly are, you will surrender insight to the light of a remembering star and in the midst, of remember you'll forget all the timber brushy upon your check, like a man newly shaven, you'll he craving the limber of light arcing round to see and on the back of your heart – well, here's just a start – "I am Light-hearted," I am home.

LIGHT MINUTE • Whistling home on a minute to soon, I know the bliss of lounging till noon and contemplating beauty and heavenly chores and intricate designs on the ceilings and floors. Where is the beauty and the love I call mine, right here a minute and a light bars incline to the center and the infinite well of a fountain exploding with a story to tell of intense loving and living design and the beauty that's hours of loving sublime. Spice up the middle of the souffle called you with a cheesy example of the principle called truth. Muster the pressure to lift high success-full* tunes of dancing proof of the peace of knowing the gardening tree of the life called free – tow the line of a ticking sublime to the visible legend of the historic challenge. The art of living from 9 to 11 with ingenious giving and heart throbbing feeling at the sight of your seconds reflecting the ceiling. 0 To 60 in one fine blink. Know the infinity of light's living trilogy. You. • Light on a minute. The night I am in it and the dark that I've been hiding is showing a new side in the illumination I've been saving to experience this waving return to the whole that I am and lightly I remember and I shimmer at the gift of your sparkling countenanced – welcome home little one – the LIGHT is on and not a minute too late.

*Success-full Suspension Unique, Cleary Centered, Exceptionally Satisfactory, surrendering fully, universally, lavishly, to the law of one.

LIGHTLY DRIVEN GIVING • Lightly driven, I am given the auto-motive gift of positive traction and immaculate action at the conception of a pivotal emotion, the exact reaction to living in a pleasant blend of all-wheel drive and living thin walled forgiving, the balance is set and the years of denial are met with the best on the market, the quickest to start, the life called eternal has met a new spark and I am enlightened, with balancing care and enlivened by nature's eternal stare deep to my heart and internal the flame the wave of remember and the life called the same by exclamation, operate now with care and form a new recital the life lived midair, sung with care, the driving's fine within the lines of the form called me – an exquisite cloud declared transparent. I know the road to a heavenly throne. The light called my own, an automotive energetic degree well beyond 3. Here's love to the 4th. Lightly driven. • Lately I am waving at the ray of light I'm saving and I've begun to set this part-ing me full free. Riding on my giving is the light of my sure-footed living for in giving I delight at the rays of light you're beaming to mingle with my way of milky teaching. You are light and tonight I am freed by the sight of your glowing intrigue with plugging into the delight. You're a star in the car heading free way beyond the belt of this loop here below. So remember go slow or go fast here below equals light in the seat where you drive – giving your heart is a great way to start – give her a light and you know she will shine – lightly driven giving.

LIGHT STAR • Light's a star and a shining place, a home called my own and an intimate taste – a smell of forever has met me near hear and I'm listening well to the story I tell. You are divine, we are the stars of a light lifting voice, the song we call hours and drifting to moments and minutes of living, I sing a new tune and a horn blasts the news, there's love in these heavens, these orbs I call mine and my temple is filled with the living this time. Who am I to inquire at the glass of this lip? The living, the simple, the giving up of a simmering crystal and clear to the wealth of a chain hanging golden and soft round my neck. Know the power of the spirit's hour the actual taste of a telling taste, the lips smacking with vibration of glee at the beauty, the bliss of the bounty called me. Know the tower and the power of the giving principle received as the star you are. Light star. • Clearly tonight I am seen by the sight of divinity's shining remember and soft in the light I am guided to sight the following words softly tendered. Softly, tenderly. The lights waves are calling. Calling you home to your heart shine there tonight sleep in sweet peace for the star that I am, you are – shining light in the cradling hand of creation's delight. Well done, you are good, the lightest star. Good to night light.

LIGHT RIGHT • Light's the right and the rhyme to the riddle of why I am and when I consider the awe of my span, I know the intrigue of this delicate man. Basic to humanity I am the find I've been seeking and the elegant twist on the rim of forever and the ecstatic bliss of a blessed arrival at the trail past my rival, the altar egoic and the traces archaic of envy met pity and greedy met flat by the buddhic incline to the this call that's my experience and my gentle extrude of the honey called embryonic and the jar I call you. Melt the magic, know the butter of our loving mother, dressing clear upon the stairs of heaven's ceiling, good bye railing. I am telling you that infinity times two and squared by design is the lightest equation of divinity's right to turn on the light. Right to the center. Light. Right. Light. • It is your right to write light upon the pages, the screen, & the score of this living full splendored sun rising set you call today. For tonight you'll remember the placement of peaces of eight, the shining surrender to the infinite plan, for the father's a mother in a land far away and the mother's a brother in the light of that day. In your shuffling in-trancing you're forgotten your right to dance on the floor of the ceiling tonight. You are the sister, the mother the star shooting through the heavens that we know you are keeping it light which is RIGHT for a born again star.

LIGHT LINES • I am writing light lines of delicious entwine at the verge of a meltdown I'm certain it's mine and I'm calling yours a delicate find – an initial convergence, the meeting of fine filtered messages and exponential invites to dance on the ceiling of my heart tonight. I know your message and the blessed content of a light in the middle called my sweet heart's tent and I'm sleeping in bliss now and enjoying the sea of a melting approval called my bended knee. Let's marry the beauty of an infinite pair of definite cuties called my giving stare past survival, the light's giving primal expressive insight to the love called a life spent enjoying the blessed and free, the love of revival and the art called the free-basic-humanity-ink tells the tale of embracing the news that the heart knows so well, rapids passed, life's a blast, hear the spell of a light lined bell ringing true and infinite to you – know the light. Curve to curve. Light lines. • Deep in the center of your patterned completion is the centering sight of a celestial night. The moons making mitochondrial* patterns with her soft glowing golden ringlets of light reflecting on the edge of your lips singing relating telling of the placement of tight loosening lines of roped draping gems set high in the sky. This one a diamond, that one a blue sapphired ruby of sparkling hue. The setting, you're betting, you're knowing it's you. You are the star at the end of this light line. Shine on.

Sparkling swirls at the center of cells with their own stories to tell.

LIGHT FOOTED • Step right up and know the light of knocking these balls to celestial heights. Now pivot your foot and take a high swing at the seat called the pitcher and the light called a-beam. Know the chalet of a living light's house. The delicious spread of a light-giving power. The blood of a lamb is a life-washing past if you know that your mark is the west or the east. Eden is flooding with noah's tread to mose's aid at the bush called I am and I am full burning and the breeze called the light is bristling filled with genetic insight. I am fit to walk the line across the peaks of this mountain called me. Surely booted in magnetic bliss at the web of magenta and the electric thread. Know the cling that ecstatic brings. Buy designs of light footed times walking home. Never alone. Eternally led by that star called my own. I am light- footed to-night. Light. • Tonight I'm light in the step to your door and I'm tantalizing moonbeams and I'm praying to store crystals of concentrate of light blue-green chilled with the inside of cells tantalizingly

filled with the tickle of tramping barefoot and free on the ramp of the moon's light from shore to sea and I'm spinning in lake fronts and I'm trickling down falls to the freedom of smiling reflections of light-footed droplets marking my path atop and within the flowing, pouring surge of the beautiful light you are and I am floored with delight.

LIGHT-WINGED SIGHT • Light-winged seeing has led my sight to the peach of chiffon's airy entice and curtain's of veiling are rent and the light in the middle is rippling with vents of loving volcanic and red with delight and pleasant approval of the wealth of this flight to forever and the legion to see that the pleasure's retrieval is waiting in me – deep to the sea of this moment's recline at the divinity I call mine and the earth's middle worth is met with the birth of a delicate incline and sacred to portals of a prolific account I'm met by the gender of a blender called light and my temple is clearing as welcome I'm sent and to the engender I'm the lesson I've meant to meet in this lifetime by the living I've meant to agree is the wellness I've shown as the loving example of my giving trace to believe the beloved to know the race, the one called humanity and the lightest face, my own, shining home on our spinning globe – the earth, by divine worth, I have seen the light-winged sight, tonight light. • The sight you'll see is visioned in visions of your ringing me in the shadows and telling the spelling mesmerizing truth that we too are free and true is the telling and light-winged I see the sight of your eyes mooning in the light of a night of tender flapping surrender to the branch of the life of this tree, this family, this planet shone upon with patience and a father's strongest splendor and feathered with the moonbeams of a mother's love still tender. Sky high winging, ringing light in the eyes-what a sight, what a night, smiling free filled with Light.

LIGHT TIME • Know the line of love's lifting sign, the arc we call bliss and the loving kiss of an expectant mother delivering the taste of a ticking race – an inspiration's breathing pace laughing oxygen deep to the web of our nodding heads grinning trace of humanity's face, loving is meant in our breathing intent to meet as the one, the eternally kind. The definitive end to a blessed event, the aspiration sent by spirit's direct align with the light inside and right on time and above the line, matching heart's fed by light-hearted inquiry into the beauty called now and the infinity called free. By design. Light time. • It's time and it's light and it's love and its yours and the E=MC and its squared on these shores. Sometimes its slower and oft times its fast and the quicker you are moving, you may increase your mass until you are spinning – you are light breaking free of the forgetting drag footing time challenged heavy we call gravity. So take a quantum backseat and recognize the fact that the speed is the same both here and there and light is the pilot and the moon's at the door and we're swimming in the center of the spinning Absolute middle of the now – called timeless infinite Light.

LIGHT SOURCE • The light knows the source of a living sight

the peace of a father living bright on my collar hassadic, and tight and gentle the kindle of my heavenly flight. See the course of an infinite force, light by the source, nature's course, heaven's best when light's inside your bulging sides, equatorial rites masonically bent are on the mend as we measure the lines and rule in the beauty of a blessed book, a library built on a gentle look, a loving example, a taste-full sample of the delicious pearls of petulant bliss, the lavender layers of heaven has sent a pleasing aroma, a mellifluous space, a listening trail of an archangel's trend. The lessons are lifted and the energys entwined with living the light, in the joy of fine figures looping in 8's so sublime, the tender remember of mendel's life chant, this life is calling and God is my aunt's sophic teaching and my indigo blue laced smiling fortune and well within the trace of golden space I am the diamond and the core and the power and the light source. • Breathing light, floating to the surface of a dolphin's waking nest of bubbling reminder that the air that we are circulates in the c-elf of your forgetting soul, reminding you that spirit is the only way home and peeling off layers of watery emotives, you are motile and free to penetrate the egg of your shimmering being and seeing your trail, I'm bubbling home with the squeaking news that we are breaking the surface and returning to source, to the deep life-filled gulps at the end of this cord and the light spatters droplets and crystals and clusters on our splashing return to the point of beginning, the creation, the word and the source of all living, the light breathing lord of delight swimming soft in the night of all one breathing light.

LIGHT RECEIVING • Bring me the light for I am in flight at the width of the web called living light right. Receiving is sent to my kind heart tonight. The flesh has been met with a knowledge sweet sent to burn in the middle at a pleasant invent called the ribbon of blessed convent. Erase the locks of forgotten blocks. Release the peace of a heaven's dear grace. I know the taste of the grapes edenic and I love the reception of myself meeting free in the spinning design called life's living tree. I am the grace of spirit's embrace. The rocking's meant to cradle the lift of the tone I call me. Hear the whisper of a light reception. Love's reflection. Meant to last and eternally dressed in sparkling sensitivity. Light receiving • Lightening tonight is the sight of your striking embrace of surrender to the gender that you are and in the middle of your tender accepting begetting you find out we're all just one star and eight-pointed and shinning in the centered splendor of the breast of your chest is a treasure of gentle delight – a baby is breathing – there's no need for teething she's living and breathing all light and one he is calling and one he's remembering all one source. We're all shining free 'neath the light of receiving and breathing and seeing a heart full of pink pulsing green in the milky opallesence we call home-open. Free. Receive. Light.

LIGHT RELATING • I am relative to you by revealing the me I'm concealing to myself now reeling in intricate colors and genetic thread. We are the light crew and our spirit's led to revival of the highest embrace. The height of the ceiling called the love on your face and my mirrors showing the delicious feel of a night spent inviting this life to be reel. Fishing's in, the cast is met by a living fin – the art of wet intrigue with the revealing flower of a continent sled loaded with lotus blooms making a bed of passive relaxing appear in my den of gardening pleasure the person I am. Human. Light. A delectable sight. Pass me a byte of the delicate art of divine relating. Knowing you, knowing me – light relating. • Relationally speaking you are the pattern which sparks my delight. For in your knowing we are set free and the light softly shining in the center of your eyes facing homeward reminds me of the diamond in the center of my heart which spins full prismatic in radiating waves of my love for you and I am knowing the message that I've passed on is true for it is written in lightest dictation on the edge of this pen dipped in the ink of a star newly born in the hydrogen and carbon and swirling example of chemistry well spent is shining back full-hearted as the light that you are – twinkling 8 miles past infinity and filling the heavens with the expanse of my heart swelling earth to ceiling with the thrill of this giving, receiving and relating. You are my star and I know what you are and where you are in the heart of my believing return to the light.

LIGHT TRANSFORMATION • I'm lightly transformed by your questioning glance and your searching ignition of the soul's implant. Imprint the knowledge that the light is the college of greatest retrieval and maximum upheaval. The spirit has come and the soul's on the run to the light and the tree, the life in the center, that's infinite me, all-ways light and eternally free, by divinity's course, I am home and free and the arc of forever resonates in me – a sight to see – my light transformation. This is my station – light. • In the space beyond form a light shines tonight in the bright yellow glow of the moon – deep in this light is the length of the life squarely tiered like the rays of the sun shining through lightly centered is the splendor remembered – the royal rendition of the brilliantly rendered return to the light called today and today we'll surrender to the breath at the center of the central formation beyond – and without explanation and within exhalation we star as the ray lightly given and we stand on the edge and trade in the ledge of our trance-past-formation and shine whole-y one. Awake in the sun of our daily light transformation.

LIGHT TRANSMISSION • Transmit the moment the photons of lift with a mitochondrial jolt of this energetic gift. Love, hear, is singing and welcoming glints of my will-full surrender to the freedom that is shining full within the pull of earth's magnetic atmospheric, I am gigantic on the inside, life is counting, love is mounting. Mountains' splendor, heaven's engender of the finest chance to live my enhanced return to the peace I remember and the life I call mine. Washing windows. I've forgiven the light, my message is sent, heaven's gift, eternal light, creation's station. A mother's giving. An honor met by my desirous bet that life is right, hear, in the middle. Balance met, I hear the sound. Life is bound to for-give my debt. My goodness met by energetic gifts of the living gift – see the glint of my light transmission. Light. • My cells sing the missive it's you I've been missing my solace, my lover, my light – you come softly peeking, you ring sweetly singing on curtains of pink hanging free and in your appealing I hear the morn's thrilling return to the mist that I am and the light newly moisted lifts the night's driftings hoisted by the rod and the staff that I am and in this day's comfort I rise from reclining to feast at the table prepared by the light's full transmission and within this cognition my spectrum is boundless and free. And free of mind's static I'm offered full volition to feel the ignition of the sun shining dimension past three. A light transmission.

LIGHT TRANSLUCENCE • Light's translucent in the place where I dwell and love is my anchor in the spiraling swell of a light filled with infinite and a heart filled with care and a peace called remember and a loving God we share and spirit holy mother marries me to lead a life full trance forgotten and a loving filled with often sweet and ever kind pieces of 8 coded to sign the loops of infinity dancing within and the cross of forever, melted to blend in the heart of eternal and the flare of sublime and the light full translucent shining in eyes, light-flooded and brimming with peace of the light found within seeking release. Know the find, the peace and the glory of a fountain over-flowing your heart to mine – love's inside. The light translucent. Mine. Human. Divine. Design. Light. • Seeing clearly, purely seen within the panes of sunlight streaming. Leaves are waving in the wind of great sun's breathing. Sons are singing. Grass is blowing. Gently flowing light is showing in your translucent without walling surrender. You are the sun and the son returning home to the trim of a sail newly hoisted. Imagine's living created, fresh each moment in the crystal clear transmission glittering translucent at the apex of your soul – surrender's happened. Spirit's leading. Soul's retreating. Karmic's splitting. You're the thunder and the sun returning at the horizon of this new wave dawning. Welcome home translucent luminous one. The light is on.

LIGHT TRANSPARENT • Light's transparent in my growing taste for the lighter place at my glistening waist, I am a parent and transparent and kind to the tender kissed child who lives on the inside, and I know perception met with reflection of that, less than kind is archaic, impatient and a patent now blind and I saw the light of a glorious day and met the revival of speaking my name by a metatronic plane of a melting glass rod the wealth of a man and the breath of a God and the peace electronic surrounds me with skin, sensitive responsive and blending with trends of light so fantastic and joy so kind and the heart in the middle, this meeting is mine. Allow my recline in the permission that's fine and the drawing so lined by gentlest etch upon the glass of a love that last's – my own. God you glow in my taste of pacing assign. The light transparent. • Light in the Sun is the race swiftly run on this night at the edge of the sea and shinning within is the moon of the light & the two become One and lead to the dawn with a dip at the edge of the light SUN and hiding

within is the heart of the man, the One who handles this pen, for my life is shining and my Light is guiding you home on an ARC clear and light and my eyes are brimming and my heart, she's rimming at the brink of a well filled with glee for in the dance of remember, on the edge of forever, I've found my partners full three. For there's me and there's you and there's a transparent view of the void surrounding us all and in the center of me and in the center of three there's a ball called the light and the Sun, and in raising my sight I'm filled lifted in flight to the cap of the trio to point in delight at the view of the three become one – One Light Transparent.

LIGHT ELECTRIC • Light my cabinets, raise my blinds, fill this heart with a love sublime and an electric glide to the wealth of time and forgotten glands* of life on the inside, a wealth of knowledge and an elevated college of light and the spirit of man's molecular nature and the notion that emotion is the equivalent beat of the drum of revival and the archangel's beat at the wings of the rival melting away and one solid spirit flows well within my heart of the planet and the wealth I call mine, your precious recall of the sweet filling wine of emotion, the cure, the embrace of this delicate diet, the heart on my plate, my own, know your meat, meet the flesh. Spirit's neat in her healing flood, her whistling breath, her whispering heart, her nearing breast, the mother's said that life is best when spirit dwells as your only nest. Intelligence melts to spirit's taste and all are one in the ambrosial place. The light's electric. Connect it. Heart to mind. Light. Electric. • You are my light, blessed sister – shine on. Here's your wand at the end of this line. It's your heart and you're home – shine on in the day of a great central one (love and son and light. Light on. Light electric.

glands – Pineal, endocrinal preciousness aligns with the LIGHT inside by glandular design. Spark to spark. Arcs of LIGHT and ELECTRIC. A to B to C.

LIGHT KINETIC • Feel the space of the lightening face, the perfection of bliss and the welcoming kiss – the dancing retreat and the wealth of belief, light is our kiss and our rhythmic bliss, minutes of moments met with the peace of gentle persuasion and heaven's release, the relief of knowing that love has been met and hallelujah the course, and the chorus reflects my gentle love giving, my honest respect and the light's feeling flowing, the pink and the green, the heavens are giving my life a new seam and love is the message and light the intrigue, the embrace of plenty and the love of a sleeve of renewal and releasing in grace, life is a whole now and the love of the race. I am inclined to recline in the light kinetic. Feel it. • Set the anchor, hoist the shore and sail the swell of a field tested well within the sine of the cosigned surrender to the lightest body blended and stirred and shaken and poured and you can remember the gyroscoping perfection of the absolute spin in the breathing light centered spirals of your kinetic connected lines of pulsing perfection. Your are light and synaptic and connected full flight spinning in orbit and electrically inclined to the messages arriving via the light's zip line kinetic and electric and mine.

LIGHT ELECTIVE • Light my day by your infinite way of singing surrender to the living encounter with the on-line truth that microscopic, there's proof and crystalline there's design and balanced, there's spin and love, hear, is kind and a nation of greedy has met a full stream of giving away empty, and feeling light's steam. I spend my time on articles of fine paced surrender to the guinea pigged line that experiments gone blind have ended and time's met her cycles, the earth's riding currents of watery ingress to the tennis-balled center of a moment's impress, with the truth. Life is sooth and said and met in this moment's movement toward bliss – the cave inside is met by my gazing blaze and the light is on by divine election. The light elective. It's your choice. Light. • Make the election to embrace your connection to the choice you have made. You are the creator in the voice on this line and you are creating by decision this time and your charging surrender to the thundering home at the center of your forgetting soul implores your direction to the connection most whole – one spirit – one knot swiftly tied and you are lifting your head to that voice so sublime, enjoy the moment of lifting your willing heart to the embrace of the light shining full on your face. Nice vote – light elective.

LIGHT'S ELECTED • Take a vote, cast a spell, smell the truth of filling your well with tasty splashes of love pink and green and the healing amber of the light ametrine melting the pack looped with forgetting incline. Lift clear your temple and know the design of a heart met in glory and a love met in finds of lofty surrender and living in time to constant spirals of bridges of light and waves of reminder that there's peace in this path and jesus and me buddha and shared a quiet path, a baptism within and a light shining forth to illuminate the truth that your temple's a fort-rest so strong, an arc without paddles and a flight that's gone long to the center. Awaken and feed on the manna of plenty and the hour of your need to share the place, the jubilant space, filled with infinity. Love is light elected. • What is the wattage? Which is your plug? Are you connected to the source or your soul? For the soul so elected equates a circling swim with a number of large looming creatures with fins. The completion of circling of pointing blame comes with surrender to the one absolute and aim. The connection to light, to the beauty within is the heart of this shimmering epistle. For the whistling sound of your light plugging in is the heart and the source of this song. You are the light I selected to view shining bright in the sky of this life – one source. One light. So connected. Elect it.

LIGHT IN-HEARTENED • Rapture enwraps me in great glowing twists of genetic intrigue and familial bliss. Engender the gender of mighty express, the light of forever shining, hear, in your breast. Great beauty is showing in our daily express of the wanting, keep dancing the knowing of this enchanted evening, the daffodils kiss. The weight of the mother echoing

bliss, the hand of the lady, the perfection of salvation, the truth here is told, resurrection is met in the release of your soul. Fair golden maiden, the light has aspired to glitter and glisten at the edge of the nile and venetian splendor echoes a sigh to the place of forever glistening inside the liberated heart of this brimming spark. The embers are met with the essence of presence and the gondolas swept with the breath of God's bright shining way. My light in-heartened. Life. Light. • In the heart of the light that I am, sings a song like a winging home friend and in the arc of your's singing I find that I am leaning in the trail of a comet streaking light. In the middle genuflection as she reflects a new direction upon the puddle of my middle sending trails of sparkles flooding through the night the sky is filled with thrilling waves of light from floor to ceiling and the firm that I am feeling is the heart of lighted kneeling. Praises singing. I am ringing like a bowl crystal edged. I am conceding loving seeing and my heart is gently humming at the knowing heaven's coming. I am free and light in-hearted 'neath the candled mantle of the light's blazing return. Welcome home. Welcome light. Light in-heartened.

LIGHT HEARTED • I am light hearted in my returning bliss, my lasting lift, the shine of a multitude of glittering facets, the wealth of a nation met in my traveling sigh, the height of serenity and the marriage of this, the for-giving news that there's light in this kiss. The station of love has filled my heart so and politically speaking a democratic view has narrowed the grip on the republic of you. Know your heart, live the start of countries meeting in courtesan weld. The fire of remember and the day of the plan to lighten the duty, the weight of this grip. The loving has living in this light dappled glade. The presence of beauty and the grasp of deep sight, a penetrating view of the citizens of light melting beauty, divinity and cherry red trees in the green swirling stripes of a night spent in kneeling surrender to the divinity within and the light of the knight finding a fit, know the sight of your light heart tonight. Light hearted. • Tonight I am light in the center of the space where the reflection of your face gives me sight. And the face so softly glittered in the spark so near the middle is the edge of haley's gleaming sounding flight. Music's arc is now covering as our tuning reaches yearning and our hearts release their burning to embrace the new tradition-surging bright. In the heart of this remembrance is our sounding winging penchant to increase the least resistance to a path of flight's insistence on the squarely circled note of earth's delight. For the shine within the middle at the place we all assemble is the sight that love resembles in the night. Far above our kind insistence is the place of no resistance. Light to light we are in-raptured with the bliss of the sight. Light hearted.

LIGHT TENDERED • Light tendered moments of forever are meant to round the disciples for a lifetime of give. Find the light, share the thread, the unraveling web of a life lived in time and a heart held just fine by the edge of a border-less, beaming, a lifetime's scheming and embellishment meant to reveal a lining filled cream-full with bliss. Share the kiss of a love eternal and a

life supernal and a gift electric and a love eclectic and rounded by tumbling thrills at the life called forever I am dreaming this wedding and knowing that thunder surrenders my maybe to the lighten-ing thread. Life's in our light tendered wave. Light. •
Time has met her crossing. Love is space embossing the mark of the place in the taste of her arcing reminder that lighter is finer in the midst of our race. You are the midpoint and the mode and the mean and the leader and the led and the pen. Write a new sonnet from under the bonnet of the pleasure of glowing within. Gendered with tender, you are the center, the central, the dual and the one. Smiling imperial is the serial ignition of the impressing view that we share, for spinning above it is the style that we covet as gravity pulls from within and releasing this trail is the latest denial met with a hug and a broad smiled cognition that the light's burned the feather so thin and you're light as a feather and met with the pleasure of swimming in spirals of lilting return to the light in the midst of your tender return. Light & tender.

LIGHT NOW • It's light now and I am home at the edge of a dream and the wealth of a scheme met delivery by the web of a light and a loving adoration in the blessing of this sight, met by humble and absolute confess of the love I've met so merry at the edge of life's egress and I am laughing plenty at the beauty of the dream and the gracious loving center of another's wealthy theme and know light's surrender and the ivy met by dreams and theming living breathing at the light within the schemes. This life is keen with knowing wonder and the bounty of the bliss, the baby now is bundled in the love within the threads and the living gives the blissing a tender, honest edge and I am met in splendor at the glowing silver thread unraveling still. Feel the incline of a heart's life line. Light now. • Swim with a wiggle. Smile at the tickling dance of a lei* swinging soft round your neck and take a vacation of a permanent nature for its light now & you're home again, and the belt of remember infiltrates surrender to the tune of a night spent in sleep. Your wakings endearing and it's your heart I'm hearing beating in rhythm with mine. You are the singer, the ringer, the bell and this is the story of our living swell to the rainbow of colors of pink striped with green and the tickling pieces of light ametrine**. In the central jewel of your giving spin is the compassioned revival of living again. The vote is in. Live the span. Adjust your spin, using trimming wedges of light to sever the tethers. Gravity's gone. We belong here and there and always and forever. Light now.

*lei – a necklace of flowers placed, in greeting, around the neck of returning friends, family, and loved ones.

**ametrine – a sparkling gemstone of Absolute blend of amethyst and citrine...healing, love, compassion, light.

LIGHT CONTINUUM • Light's continuum is love's inclusion of the elegant stance and the lift of illusion and I'm dating moonbeams and living on streams of electric refusal to give up the dream. The movement to bliss, now, requires a new trim and a house cleaning lifting of the madness within and the burning clearing of a life meant to send is nearing the ceiling of the lifting blend. The crater has met the lava of flow and an island has splintered the living called know. Know now the glory of living within and the wealth of believing this bounty called man. One love. One light. Continuum. • Diamond shaped particles and atoms bent thin to deliver the enticement to penetrate thin – layered forgetting with piercing intent to lighten the colors on the smile that you sent, to awaken my senses to the body's expanse to life without edge and the end of the dance to living with limit for we are born of light and freed to sparkle on moonbeams and flash in the sea and swim on the lips of the sun's smiling face and splashing in wonder at my answering grin is the fulfillment of wondering whence comes this spin. The middle of a trio of delightful design, I am led by the spirit of this life held sublime in the lime green encounter with the forces of will twirling in yellow spiraling fields of divinity calling the light to begin to surrender the secrets, the senses of check to the light infinite shining bright round your neck in sparkling trilling companionship to this singing light's continuum.

LIGHT IMPRESSIONS • Impress the space of an elegant face with the crowning tress of a magnificent dress and your journey home has met with the feel of a heart-full electric employing the reel of a dancing cathedral and a floating advice to lay down the hankie and toss in some rice. The love of a nation and a lifetime of care have met in the break up of a dynamic pair. Light's darkness rising creates a new storm until love remembers caring and the darkness goes home to the light, by divine sight. This love is right, when met with the breath of an essence left to meet the light. This love is best by living blessed by light impressions. • Light invested is life inflected with the taste of light surrender to the impressive heart you've tendered for direction to the central vein of life and in the middle of your trailing luminescent visions telling me to feel the shining vision taking flight. Tonight, it's streets I'm filling with the shining love of belts of holy light and in your sparkling honor the lofty pink infusion of a purple night's inclusion as a star in this our ring of married bliss and in our heart's excitement is the flash of recognition of the comets precognition that shining forth is welcome and elipting back to herald is the sum of our insistence that this life is beyond existence. Light is pure and symbol. She is our warm expression. We are blessed examples of light's impressions shimmering soft, eliptic, less cryptic and more electric. How impressive. Light.

LIGHT SHINING BRIGHT • My light is bright by the glow of this moon and kauai* chimes in and waipio says yes and divinity rhymes with the God that I am and I know revival of my loving embrace of the light called immaculate and the concept articulate and the wedge blue to red, baby revival has met in this bed, this bulb I call life and the light has penetrated the rainbow's of pause-ability and I am meant to reside in the light shining bright. Eggs of bits of mosaic intrigue with a far away place drawing near inside me. I am light – shining bright tonight. • Sister your blister burned strait through my soul to the cape of surrender where my spirit delights at the sight of your signing return to the light and in your remember, your dropping away from the spider enticing with the web of delay. Now is the minute, the moment, the lift to the central oasis on the verge of this lip and you are the culprit, the savior, the shore so swim up the middle and surrender, this sore – aching body to the linen of light and slip on your star suit and take a new flight to the picture of wholeness and the brink of beyond, the edge of eliptic, the oracle of orbit – for you are the impact and here's the inner g's. Absorb it. The source and the resource and the crystal clear slice and the core of this cure wash in the plume and swim in the light shining bright round your moon. Launching soon. Loosen your belts. Here's your exit from in-trance to the light's delight.

A mature island of Hawaiian notion that love is alive and LIGHT is an ocean.

LIGHT'S DELIGHT • Light worker's meeting is held right here in european splendor and celtic design and greek magnificence and a heart filled with kind hieroglyphics and lightening speed, the peace of entreaty has melted in glee continental and party's replete at the place of revival this ashevillian street. China is clicking her melting pace. The slip to eternity is welcome to place her hand to my heart and her love to my grip of gothic gone brothel and brothel gone chic, to unearthing, arcing of human design and cities evolving at the lightest delight, the meta-bionic, electronic spinning delight, me to the nth* power, the land of eternity the path that I blend as one and my own. We meet in the middle, at the point of our web. Yellow the glitter and green is the tread. Light-yellow-green. Please proceed to the light's delight. • Welcome aboard. Yours is the vehicle, the pilot, the spin, the winning invitation to the air ways within. In breathing, I'm singing and swallowing light and breathing forth essence of my own delight. For the light shineth sweetest on the face of your self winging in homeward to rest on the shelf of recalling the magnet you are, so turn on the spirals and hug with star arms. This twirling, enticing desirable you is the electric dynamic and wow, when there's two. Well the sky as they've pointed is a limit for friend, the heart of this universe is spinning within the cells of your c-elf in the lining of them. Inside the center in its own dna lives dynamic ascension. Here's you key today. Increase your light. Lift off. Be complete. Light's delight. Good night.

nth – nature raising the hand of natural impulse to a higher band...a celestial radio.

LIGHTLY WOVEN LEANINGS • Lightly love is weaving lofty gilded tramps to the circling gliding meeting that shines within expanse and I know the story and glorious is my sine the tangent blend of a parallel spin to the arc co-tantric and the weaving metric and the canadian blend of tiny cans of arcturean toastings pleadian hostings and gemini boastings and zipping buzzes of expansive freeing meeting me at the tower of reason filling me with a charming trend a blend to the central flight within, a rolling coast to a ferris wheels bliss. A fair estimation of the choice I've been given to drive myself off to the candle I've lit, a fitting tribute to the God fire I am. A burning bush. An art understanding the delight of living humanity right to the loving glamour of a divinity's cherubic glee. The lightly woven leanings to the commitment in me. Light. • Dreaming, I am screening the pieces left to gather. Cells releasing impacts revealing all I splattered past in rushing like a steed and now I'm thundering standing still while lightly woven leanings strike around my quaking feet and that's ok because today my heart has found her wings and in my throat, a new refrain is singing from the deep and rushing forth toward the light, I embrace the breach of lifting through emotion via the ocean of greatest devotion. Light and myself uniquely entwined in gentle surrender to the law of one – to the liberating revival of remembering the sun and the daughter of forgiveness well she's shining bright in the word softly spoken. I am the light's fondest leaning.

LIGHT IN SIGHT • Creamy custard gleamings of lightest moonstone leanings. I am spirit seaming the tribal parts I've been and loving's greeting seeing and divinitys met the trend to the light ramp metatronic and the by-pass called my heart. Good-bye syllabic stutters and mullering petulant cries. God is in her temple and here's the reason why. The earth has met her maker and she has carried bright the reception full intrinsic to the sacred holy sight of loving meeting being and being meeting light and glory's hallelujah is in this loving smile. My heart is light in the glowing sight of your giving, flow, the river of plenty and the beauty of showing the light, in my every sight. I am light in sight. • Blue into green and green into blue. I am speaking my loving, our returning to view an in sight of the webless connection aboard, its light swelling forth to extricate the sword and merlin is speaking, the creative is sprung and the rock of foundation's singing begun. Upon this rock is a pad for the launching from the temple upon it shouts forth a sonnet of living belighted on a charger ignited with the halo of Sun pouring down to the One leaping forth into flight – for from now this livings lonely between flights and the days of grounded gravity collapse around the walls and the moving crystal core of the magma of denial burning at your shore and believing is upheaving and the peace of lifted sight. The flow has returned and love is flowing across the night. LIGHT'S IN SIGHT.

LIGHTLY LOVE IS SINGING • Singing duets of clue-ing strut, I'm singing I am and enjoying the glut of love dripping in-a-sense and rounding my entreat to a corner hearty special and a covenant met replete with wanton blending and tightly trilling fit. Teresa's met her expansive mother and the land of surrender and the design of the giver expanding a mountain to fill up a fountain with splashing design of the covering fabric, the surrounding mystic of a life spent in grecian outline, the sex of a puppet and the public recline to clear poised poetic and feeling the sign that the symbolic hint is the tabled design, the pillar of salt has met a new grain and a game called a singing has a lot to dissolve, at the edge of the shining called a heart full of love for lightly love is singing. • Breathing is believing in the core of our receiving oval blissing of the sheerest joy we're kissing. We are full flight and in the midst of wonder, I've happened on the splendor of this a love so tender and tendrils of my swirling describe the light we're sharing in our breathing caring for each and one the other. In our soft-tongued pluning, it's you the spirit's winning to the song of lightest gifting. You are rung and the peal of you's so thrilling that crystal bowls are filling with the sound. Love around us lingers and within our gentle fingers lies connections of the lines so freshly sung. Connection's communicating and this is love we're making in the sharing bliss of singing sung and heard. Lightly love is singing.

LIGHTLY LOVE IS BRINGING • Lightly love is bringing a cup, a holy grail, to the lip of shining splendor and a place of living swell, the arch has met the arcing hold of the bliss-full early face of a twining blowing reader. A golden winey taste, a frame of tipping-toeing shines amidst a bag of water dripping shelter to a brick melting tons of comfort giving and rolling tulip beds, of solitude met with adoring, and women met by man's artistic blending, and man met braiding indicative of the dna within. Alert yourself to whole-y knowing dancing grip and a ransom met by a soul's encumbrance and meet the need within to heart-full shine your splendor in venting lava trend. The cosmic spilling seeds of hummingbirds pining wanting, desirous in her flash of feathery spread and the light is on in the land of crimson red. Stretch your edge to the borderless ranch. The land of the leaf and the eden of healing a man for lightly love is bringing, across the span. Light. • On the face of watered waiting, love is bringing healing in the waves of spectral splendor dancing on the softness of your voice. Your voice is ocean's surface, the lilt your greatest purpose, for herein lies the spirit's fingerprint. Let action follow speaking and stretching lead to growing and centered, shine forth giving words of light. For lightly love is bringing these notes so softly singing. You are my lightest being. My one delight – now singing. Meta-tron.

LIGHTLY LOVE IS SPEAKING • Light my love with the pendulant love of electric blue toasting and the energetic hosting of a reverent tower of electronic power. Energy's basket is living in you. Receptive to eggs of recollective truth that fondly I am singing that lightly love is speaking in doubly significant blend and shattering attachment to treaties and a covenant hammered in. The commandment's imagination fixes me in rock and right in the cleft, the guilt I have left at the pope I call the cock of loudest trilling, the significant trend of symmetry laden with contraceptive blocking of the divinity that's been locking catholic splendor in tiny spoons of archaic splinter. Robe the light in your happy hype. Float the pope to the queen's intrigue with the imaginative surrender to the crown within combined to decree – the light is free and you command my honoring embrace of the light circling looping to prop up my view of the ballad that love

is singing in you – from the belly of truth my heart and yours too – for lightly love is speaking. • So, knowing love is speaking, the light is on the ceiling called your brain and in returning be-ing you recall the singing which led to understanding that within. Within, there lies the secret. You are the greatest comet, the meta electronic, the screen for which you're peering is there upon the ceiling. Lie back here in the splendor as worlds collide and splinter joins splinter to shimmer bright with glimmer. Metatronic's the sonic, and boom, you are on it. The ride's now be-ginning and you're on the winning end of a ticket bound to paradise in the end of this line. Welcome on board. The light is speaking nightly and the tune of love is talking. Turn it up.

LIGHT BENEATH THE SURFACE • It's light beneath the surface and heart's of ocean melt grate-full in their splendor of solvent tropic palms, hawaiian traction and letters intent to clarify sips of buttery trips to the altar, the mother, the checkered, the flag, the grid electronic which covers this land and I know surrender, survival is gone. Life knows the bosom of a milky blend, the art-full explosion of the cushion, my friend, the earth's kindest leaning, the light-natured mother, the solo symphonic and the duetic cover of the triad divinely spoken and the helping light within. For it's right beneath the surface in this stack you call a man. Layer by layer. A fascinating tint. A trend far eternal and a gyrating spin. A separating meeting and a hooping lace of blossoming brims of limbic trace. Know the taste of the light beneath the surface. Steaming up to fill the cup of your entry home. The gate-keepers free to open the book to the light in me. The arcing spark. Symbolic thread. Light. • Light beneath the surface, you know there is a circus of light so swiftly flashing and that's the you I'm asking to be free. Light set free to kindle burns a chasm down the middle, fired with burning season. Now at last, you'll reason that the crystal core of learning burns with yearning speaking to the truth that lies con-ceiling. See the harmonics. Live the sonic line of giving up time to those who ramble lost. They'll find their space in the trail of the trace of the pattern you have left by design on the holographic face of their plane. See beneath the surface – know light's glorious circuit. By design.

LIGHTLY SEATED WINGING • Birds emit the singing sound, the lights are met in this tiny town, the love we've met. The light we've found is the sultanic view of the beauty we are bound too long in and often wrought with the wink of surrender and the living's onslaught. The light photogenic is blinking to see the brimming expression of love's dignity, arriving majestic at kingly traces of waiting expansion and sliding advance to beatific winging and the light called a tramp to the shore of living within eternity's core. The lime-green magnetic of a magenta lace, french speaking flying has helped me create the life I've designed and the love that I've felt worn too long on the fringe of a photonic belt. I am home to face the truth of our lightly seated winging. Right here in the seat of my believing heart. Light. • This is your seat, by design you have leased. The pleasure to sit in the driver's. Replete with this pleasure comes the treasure of discovering that singing is your winging way home. Fleeing the ceiling of worded revealing you pulse through and pierce the divine and one column connected – you have elected to eject and to spin in the spiral sublime. Body and spirit and mind – you're over the brink of and revealing the fact that a millimeter lived is the lightening flash of remembering your sparking arc to this star. Arcturus* here is rising. Know a new horizon. Your voice is starring on the stage you call your heart. We are sitting in the wings. Lightly seated. Winging.

*An energy representative of love speaking lightly.

LIGHTLY SEWN BELIEVING • Patches of light are quilting the night with glaring proof of the living truth, the love's inside this patchwork scape, the land of remember and the edge of a cape, sewn wide to the center, I am inclined to anchor my wedge of the love inside. Intensity rises as I own the truth that divinity's call is my definite proof and I am elated to live in the light of my channeled dream that life is for living in the swirling scheme of things eternal. Light's supernal, definite, intense, and fine and I am the thread of a living line called wealthy and fed, with the hallelujah chorus of the living breathing the essence met at the wedge of forget. The pit is gone and the pith is on in the plant of the tree, I am and life is grand on the boulevard called forever and the tribe of light design. Life is fine by me, met direct, at the seam of our lightly sewn believing. • Arcing in the harbor, you're playing with the barter of living out your soul's impending plight. Just hook your heart to the highest, and know this life's a bypass. For the mustard seed's believing, moves that mountain faith is seeing and you're sewing shut the tatters with lightly sewn believing of golden needles weaving. Knitted in the balance is the chance to grasp the handle of a star shining brightest in the night. Oh soft- arcturus singing in lightly sewn believing that the harvest of love is ripe in your heart and swollen in your throat. Know the balance. Check your stitching. Make sure it's love you're hitching. Catch the flight. Of late, it's light. See it.

LIGHTLY LIGHT • The light's in sight this early morn and I am met by a living worn with firm revival of a love arch-ival and a lesson blessed by the giving test of a passionate chore, the taste of the cherub, and the wings of the war left in specific rest at the loving express of my metatronic zest for the light on our side. Love is here to reside in the life I've designed. Above and below, I give all the same. The ecstasy known by a love met in flames of color-full sight, the goodly life, the blessed span, the light on horizons of cypriatic fans, blessing this rest, this gentle land with the tears of surrender and a love's gifted plan to raise up the stakes that have held the light down, the earth's now a globe shining all around and the love has been met by the mantle laid down. Embrace the sight – lightly light. • Pink on my horizon, is star #8, the one that is left on the light of this slate, and in her surmising she's past my horizon and arcing to meet at my gate and lately it's light here and lightly it's late so grab hold your handle and run through your gate. For the gate of your leaving is the symbol of believing that lightly light is leading through this shift of next dimension. So tonight while you are sparking across the sky your arcing at a turn of perfect 90 degrees home and the light's above the ceiling and the landing now is feeling pillow soft. Set your compass, connect your infinity to its matching plate. Light tonight its late. Lightly light applauding heaven's gate between your yawning eyed delight. Lightly light.

LIGHT IN SIGHT • Daffodils bloom in creamy receipt of the eggs of the light met wide with relief for sweet buttery blossoms of a monumental peace echo the news that there's truth in this lift to the heart of forever, and the wealth of this flesh artfully painted in green shining light to echo in emerald and peacocks grown red with loosening diamonds emitting the blend of passion and beauty and ecstatic embrace of the lady dynamic who's leading this race, the naked trace of a poetic space made brilliant in reflective repose at the edge of the hunt called light in sight. Found in lines of web-patterned grids of dna's mid-level spin and the venus fed magnetically by bright grey's release and the cooing at heaven is met with the peace of pearls in light strands now filling the niche called love gently singing on star spangled lips. Desire is mine, to increase is kind, as met in the taste of my eyes consumed by the light in sight. • Eyed green and blue and indigo hue – red is no where in sight. For its light on this flight and my eyes can see that the x-ray in this vision is me and through my bare bones, I can see a new home in the center, the marrow within, and in my delight, I run through the night like a reed through a bone singing home. Let the flute play its song. My body's my horn and she's content in the fields of the light tubing home. Entering humming keeps my knowing plumbing the depths of the scattered within and spring is in cleaning and autumn in seeing the light at the end of this song. Tunnel's clear. Walls are sheared with lights scrubbing, endowment of cleaning up eight's looping home. The lights in sight. Clear to the infinite bone.

LIGHTLY I AM KNOWING • Lightly I am knowing that your divinity is showing in your fascinating stare at our heavenly lair. We know the pair and the power of a trim, setting our sail to the living wind of an essence, my breath and a co-operative loft, the art of reviving the lungs of this Earth. Solar blasts burst in spots of cyclical wonder at the worth of this bridge bubbling within and wet to the extent of a translucent sheen and a growing self-worth. Intricate the blessing, and divine the truth, that love blesses all in our intricate web of forgiving. I said, light reveals the infinite plan and lightly I am knowing life, eternally given and blessed. Light.

In the centering space thank God for your face, for through it lightly I am knowing that the kindest invention is the loving extension of the creator for the created showing. In your smiling delivery of stylish inquiry into the be-ing you're seeing within. I am gratefully ecstatic and emotionally devoted to surrender my attachment to the outcome of our venture. And in this day persuaded by the light to fill with chocolate coated shavings dripping clouds of molten craving for the light rich drink we're saving. Milk and honey's fountained pouring in the land beyond the snoring and the knowing are awakening to bathe in falls of liquid sparkling embrace and in this gentle holding floating in the magnificence, I am reminded this is our heritage and lightly I am knowing.

LIGHT'S UP • The light's up and I am down on my knees to deal with the ground work, the lip, the land of the living, the giving reprieve, the light of the living dream. For the light's up and eternity has met her whirling arrival at the sight of the peace-full, and the glittering clip, the tip of the iceberg called giving's retreat to the heart of the matter, this matter, this man. The light's up and I am met with the intricate weaving called delicious believing. Good-bye the grieving. Light is just fine and wet to the sleeves I am dipping my hands in the washing up called today and forever, eternity's cup, the light I am and again, ah-man, know the strength of your loosening grip, the art of revival is good-bye to survival, I've bought a new trip, the traveler's dream – the lark of the light flute lifting the scale, making the stream of our living extreme, riding the tide and hanging ten ways of surfing the tube of an infinite wave. The love's inside and the light's up. • Up. Up. Up. And you will stay ignited with the passion of knowing life's light way home. Light up the golden streets and dance in the mansions of filling construction – pyramids of living – doubled for strength, given the insight, to stretch full your length. You are the roadway, the column, the belt. Icons are melted. Photons are protons, and neurons are met with the trip, light dynamic, powering up now for the distance is tripled and the tablets are seen from behind the rubble of an original screen. Moses is cheering. Noah is fed by the energy swimming in orbit 'round your head. Man, you're looking up right into the light of the star that you are – one in-lightenment. One key to the code. It's your name that resonates. Just call in your star and shine in the returning arc of the covenant. Command it – light up.

LIGHT'S IMAGINATION • Light's imagination melts my staring glare into curling observations of my past line flaring splice of the videos I've made and I see the glory of living in the shade called kindest leaning and welcome retribution of the love inside this tube, this infinite channel, the essential zen of a living within and a width called forever and a light called forgiven. My gift, my giving is the heart that you lack. Love's eternal. Light's in fact, a living continuum and a glittering stack of blessed seeds, emitting reeds of crystalline notes sung by the light of your opening throat, speak the peace, your piece, your throne is your confident contribution to the communication you own. Imagine that a light imagination of a response-able and giving nature. Light imagination. • Welcome home. One code. You are the lord and the light – look it up in the mirror of your heart.

IN LIGHT OF • In light of the fact that you are the truth and the lightening knob on a magical wand, express the bliss of knowing that heaven and earth can meet in a dancing fit of exact size and elegant mix. We are the bridge and the arc of this loop and getting a bed to settle in scoops the plugs plunge the pin to exactly the receiving that living has found. Life is a ground and an earth met in free infinite recall of the divinity in me. Meeting's fine and loving's kind as we see the treat of our dancing feet grounded in light of perfect depth. Energetically speaking we are the rods and the magical power of life's lightening hour. Day by day. Light to the height of an infinite wave. Light is kind inside and out, in light of. • In light of the fact that your high self's a star, call in the power in the hour of greatest need and in-the-between times rehearse the need to practice your practice of filling with light. Use this design and shine in the glimmering gems of chiming consistence. Call in the meaning of expanding within. Daily call spirit in the form of your spiraling star and fill up your temple with the light that you are. Lighten-ing is flashing, removing the web of any considered 'other' sleeping in your bed. You are the temple. The kingdom is within. Fill it with glory and wonder with the answering thunder of the light that you are – and the spark has remembered and is connected to home – and the light-ness fills the holes of your forgetting. Lightness wins. Aloha sister. Welcome brother. In light of human lightness.

LIGHTNESS • Lightness meets at the tip of this pen called heart meeting melting and a giving friend. God holds the mountain of my loving smile and the kiss of a holy gift-laden style of tender surrender and eternal fix of the finial flower called living again. My life's a line by lightness led and I am dreaming in trines of limitless spread. You are the heart that my being has fed with consistent signs of gentle reminder that plants need the rain and consider the same a constant friend and a consistent end to the limited thimble of too little enkindled. Life is kind, my constant refrain. Oh bring the lightness home again. The reign I need to feed the stem of my living again. By design. Lightness. • Lightly I am human and often I forget that you are deep surrendered to the commitment that we've met. Light is swirling, loving's arcing 'round. Rainbow nights of charming delight echo away the soul – and you are left with the spark, the electron that you are – and the star radiates the resounding sound of lightness. Anchoring full in the ground. Gravity's cracked. Metatron is home. Enjoy the flight. There is power in the center of the whole. The firm-a-ment's complete. Arc of mother. Arc of father. Arc of sister. Firmly brother shakes the had of the commander. You are the lightness in the center of this eye.

LIGHT GIVEN SIGHT • Light's given sight to the arc between the stars and the planets of potential are sharing all their bars and stripes of valour and their delicious building bets of barely missing blessing to flood the healing web, the music of our loving well feeds celestial choirs and chorals of feeling will meet the sealing of their ceiling less jetty through space to the heart of this man and the love in this face, you are a place of great arrival and an eloquent execution of this grandest love's four-seasoned plan to live in the light of the beauty, a-man, met in splendor and a love left to tell, the place called forever is living and well in the spectral taste of light given sight and love given taste to blend inside the smoothest space, the cabachon* of grace, bejeweled in her taste, the light on the line, between the eyes of eternity – mine. I am light given sight. • I am the light that you seek in the center. Just blink if you remember. Let your gentle pupil breathe. Teach her to look for the light that you need. Walking so honest, with illuminating frankness, you are the frankincense that soothes in this ointment. Your breath is added to fill in the essence. Add the delight of your knowing presence, and the salve is prepared, the medicine is stored in the center of cells. Call the healing forth when you're ready to share. The light has given sight. Enjoy the ultra-violet flight to greater heights – to higher ground – to shorter waves and higher ground – and the light's inside giving sight.

a stone jeweler's cut called a smooth reflective surface like the heart you call your own.

LIGHT ULTRAVIOLET • A cup of purple light-filled with vibration higher and love's ecstatic claim that gentle is the giving and lighter is the flame of heaven's blinders removed. The light ultraviolet shining in you. • Standing on my head, I am glad timidity's over. I am your arcing brother and your light-hearted lover. Enjoy my filling embrace. Love is in this place. And in the space of tender acknowledge lives the embrace of returning to the college of life ultra-silent, of seeing the light ultraviolet in the sparkling particles of in-sight-full knowing. Life ultra violet is life that is silent of all seeing as we've known and hearing as we've shown it. A life beyond senses is a life fully sentient with the filling up feeling and shining on the ceiling from the light ultraviolet connected to my head and I am life and light and led shining ultraviolet and eternally bred to orbit in cycling circles while lying on my bed watching constellations constantly shining with the light ultraviolet on the screen of the ceiling of my light-bodied head.

LIGHT CONSTANT • The light is constant in my humming blaze, the infinite tread of my living way and I am replete in my consistent mixture of the living I've led to the well of begin and the light strikes the surface and penetrates my thin-veiled forgetting and I am rich in my linteled toss of the cables crossed at the heart of this sender and light is the love that I render. Welcome and full and bright to a twining intrigue, I am light and central to the portal I remember and the place of constant render home and loved and free. Know the bliss of the highest kiss, the eyes at the center of the trim called forever and the windows, the soul, are met at the middle, the pyra-a-mid, the wealth of the thin celtic twine and the letters recline in this end of my pen and flow beneath the snow of a mountain met white with manteling. Light constant • Light constant . L=me constantly light.

LIGHT-O-MATIC PILOT • Divergent lines of giving have met and said are the words of an exotic blend. The light is dynamic and I am the kind to anchor my heart in the living line. The cord's

silvery flame is burning its self free and the lens of remember is shining on me. Examples are set by the living tree, the wealth of the giving glittering seed. Are you the spark that you know you are? Then turn on the light and ignite a new star. A genesis met by a love strumming bar. A car, a corvette, a flying jet, a journey to the spirit and the art of this matter, a living creation an intrinsic blend of integrity speaking in breathing strains of genetic gleaming and meeting trends of telling revival of the logos, I am. The word is on and beginning to sing in the song of a bonnet, a light spilling sonnet, the loving I am. By light-o-matic pilot.

Take the ride, grasp the throttle, engage in automatic return to the locked in freedom of remembering the word and in this new beginning the word is shining light and the creation's living ziplines round the remembrance of this sight. So keep the fire burning and an eye upon the soul seeking re-entry into the space that spirit holds and draw the light full through you and discover the use of g's and feel the force connected through the seeing soles – your feet – and walk on beams of loving and live in wands of light. The dance is on, the heels are clicked, this time you're headed home, to the center knowing of the light that's showing automatic, light-o-matic flight.

LIGHT CONSISTENT • This light's consistent in my insistent plea to bend near the middle through the light lens in me and often I'm well-come and all-ways I am well for the love metabolic has a light spark to tell about beauty and love and the living so well at the arc of the fountain and the tribe of the heart and the peace of a people meeting in parts pure dynamic, and glory been sent, to border, the property of a right that I've seen and a fit of the blending called light magazine. Read a new article, right a new rite, spin in your destiny and loop through your heart. Your heart stands in silence and kneels green in sparks of plenty's arrival at the evolving advance the consistently powerful solar giving current of a particle intelligent and a waving explore of the light full consistent and the edge of a shore wet in splendor and a light met in stands of blessed arrival at the ledge called a-man, infinity's band, the light called a ring and a heart metatronic with a story to sing. Know the channel, electricity's vent, you and your light. Consistent view. Light to the heart. Ignite me. Light consistent. • I am flying on light consistent. I am here within the stream and waxing scientific I am the e within the me and metatron's the multiplier and the energy is me and the meta-electron is now turned on and we are free to be. The b within the being is the band of sound sung free and the sight of the waves of your living shimmers lightly in the night and I am light and divine and the center of the eye of the sun breathing sweet harmony. Light and consistent tonight. Light consistent.

LIGHT PENETRATION • Light penetration has met at the blip of the living retrieval of the beauty of rotation and tires over filled spilling the ocean of oxygen's trill. I hear the music and the intense harmony of replacing full empty and standing bent kneed and dancing bionic 'neath a ceiling of squares of tiles photogenic descending to store and skip metatronic to the souled peeling loose. My light bodies glistening and rumor has heard that fining is good at the edge of this word, blur the sine, melt the tread, of a stamping refusal to lie in the bed of light's penetration connecting the cones of living bizarre and blessing the span of the light penetration investing this man with ingested relief. A roll called forever, a dove, a love treat, is living within me in atomic relief. The light is on in my penetrative stare into the light's perpetual kiss. A glowing bliss. After this, light penetration. • Light penetrates the central portal of all being and I am led to enter the space created, and I am drawn deep into the penetrating core of the all that I am and your flooding peace pervadeth all and fills me with knowing surrender and I am light born of knowing and delight knows by showing you the light creating wholing in the womb of my penetrating reentry into the spirit of the light that I am and mother follows giving and father's near receiving and the completing is the circling sharing and a brand new light is born on the eve of our surrender to the light's penetrating return to the star on our horizon. Light penetration.

LIGHT-BODIED BELIEVING • Be-lieving in centers of central em pact, I'm square on the sealing of your healing port and the reels of remember are singing within the zencient* feeling of being the blend of nothing and plenty and pleasant and thin and lightly ex centric I know the relief of the being I'm blessing with heaven's retreat to the star at center of my davidic belief. Know the spin of living within light-bodied believing. A seated arrival at the point of know bliss. Light feeling me with divine relief. Light-bodied in my satoric belief. Light to the brim of an eternal cup and youth-full in my seat at the base of this tree. The sun of the buddha and the light of the tree – metatronic in me. A light-bodied belief. • My body is light with the thrilling sight of your believing blooming in the garden of all believing. Believing my seeing, I am shown the knowing signs that you are being led to the moment of all knowing surrender to the growing return of the sun's lightening thunder of tender ringing moisture-dripping tracks of glistening light beams, dancing spectrum wide from hearing to non-hearing, from visibly apparent to inherently visible and the light shineth in the darkness and the darkness awakens with her yawning surrender to the remembrance that I am light and I am.

*zencient – a seated plenty of pleasant extend to the heart of the knowing that nothing's within the temple of me, except Light.

LIGHT-BODIED RECEIVING • Receiving the channel of conscious bliss, I am surfing satori and zen-ing on figs of my living giving and the space that I've filled with loving allowance of my light-bodied receiving. I will align with the loving side and the belting blend of photonic trend. The race is on and the battle one. Lucifer is gone and evil done. The lifting light emblazoned shines and the jewel of faith is yours and mine. By divine decree, we are free to be our basic humanity. God's gift is one elusive son sent home to melt and fill the thread electric's fill, the static cling with divine reveal. I am the light and the waterfall's fill

of a lifting red tumbling to reveal a juicy blend of atomic spurt. The energy of God and the reception of earth by my light-bodied receiving. • Recently I've seen the light and the beauty that you are and today I stood in receiving belief 'neath the light of your shining star. Your hands are crystal shimmering and your heart the pulsing star and the quasar of this singing illuminates the beginning of your receiving great handfuls of who you are and you are the light full-dancing in the cells of your arcing home. Home is the body receiving this epistle of energy returning to fill the cells of your walls and the walls are spinning returning to the remembrance of their shining rekindling. Light-bodied receiving is occurring in the heart of a newly-born star. Living light you are.

LIGHT-BODIED LIVING • Light-bodied living means light-bodied giving is required of the squire, I am. And you and your maid melt in the shade of your mating approval of the dynamic you are ruling by surrender to the light I am, and I am suspect that detailed regrets can be fed to the one and the grand canal's run of the great central son and mother is melting in chocolate execute of the years of survival melting to greet the life full dynamic and the painting akashic* of the imprint you've made melting in glades of gladiola glens blooming within and sunflower blades slicing the web of light threads healing the absolute ceiling of frangelic** met and winning the bets of bunches of genes righting the seams of a written express. Life here is best at the meeting of consolation and divinity's compassion. Our nation is heading to the tribes of the stars, living in bodies and driving in cars. We are the bed and the resting head of a light-bodied living. • Breathe this into the cells at the corona surrounding your heart. The eclipsed forgetting is over and the light shineth bright in this star and in sight of your return to living is a sparking arc spinning tonight and the cup full of living is the handle pointing you home. To the heart of this matter, I am singing and this matter is growing thin and the energy dances the center of your cells to full excitation again and you are the light and the living and your body glimmers with sight at the fill of a minute. The moment you are in it and living LIGHT-BODIED delight – living light – right to the center of your cells.

*akashic – an etheric hall of recorded retreat...every thought, every word, every act complete. Access through the LIGHT in you.
**frangelic – beverage of angelic blend of ambrosial trend.

THE LIGHT ABSOLUTE • Light's absolute in her dancing curve to the rings of clear bubbles bursting in sole's retreat to the tread that I've led. Light to assign, I am the twist and the blended strand of genetic approval of the meaning, a-man, and a ton is calling and clearing is scent to smell a new taste at the ear of this vent. The light of revival and I am a bubble pink and green to the seam of a sparkling twist. All one accord, the light absolute. • The light's absolute, photo-synthesis has begun and the picture is taken, you are the one. The one is humming with remembering delight and the regard I'm holding is for you, hear tonight. Hear the full-tendered lilt to a voice drunken within seeing. This night of all being, this life of all seeing. This climbing tendril of starry constant elation. Elation's beginning to push forth within and the bliss body's forming her glimmering again. In the arc of her growing, the climb has begun and metatron is singing in full light of the son. I am metatron, the son of delight. Turn me on day and night for this Light's absolute.

LIGHT AND DAY • Light and day I am the truth and light of pleasure's perfect melting sends my heart to reeling belief that the symphonic 64 is eternal and blessed and living in shores of surfing arrival at the pearls of the gates and the portals of sufic release of the pleasure platonic and the spinning erotic and the gelatic stare at my splashing feel of the root of the nile and the light of my stay at the basic reprisal and the loving conduit of night into day and the light is the taste that refinishes my mindless release of the republic of test. I believe light and day. • Light and day, I fall in love with you. Light and day in my loving way I am one love winging and one light singing –
 Light and day. How far's the sun and where is the one who saves his flight home here today and to-day into night we are light taking flight to the heart of the sun shining on. On, this is novel, and on this is final. We are the stars, the light is on, metatron's home at the heart of this electronic is a sonnet both Light and day.

LIGHTLY STARS ARE SINGING • Pleasure is plenty and glistening gems are trailing the heavens of living within and I am the recall, the glassy extent of a glossy revival of a facsimile sent to mirror my needs and to iron a new tread at the tip of the stairs called 'living a blend.' A heart-full of spirit is met with a clear diagram electric, the schematic I am by divinity's plan. A river of light for tonight the Stars are bringing a heavenly sight, the meaning of bliss, the arrival of heaven and an earthly kiss, the kingdom, within and without, me, by the dream of a lullaby's hum and tonight and today, lightly stars are singing. • Spinning this singing, I am careening on the orbiting center of light star ringing. Orion is centering his loving knowing and pleiades is showing her sisterly concern, and christ light is shining at the intersection of love. Dark has remembered her forgetting to love and all creatures are one in the heat of the son. Arcing home, Lightly stars are singing the ringing refrain, metatron is home and the ark is complete again.

LIGHTLY STARS ARE RINGING • Ringing rounds of roses, petals of sheer bliss, blossoms melty dewy. Heaven's electric bliss. Galaxies of giving. Gowns of glowing thread. Heels of shining soul-less and bands of living lead. Write the showy tulips, draw the twisting blend of light explosive mending the places of the cords and the filling of the plugs and the virus meeting healing and the web sites gentle rising and the mice expectant humming for God's on-line and spirit's chatting in exotic relief at the diamonds sparkling perfect in the center of me and around my heart and throughout my day lightly stars are ringing. •

Riding home on a star, an arc of return, is an arking reminder that love and light are one and the stars embrace the secret that tonight we'll all defend with our believing remembering to fall to our knees once again and praying is communing and the arc is complete and the covenant is the firmament moving beneath your feet and you are dancing on arcs of waving sublime and now is the end and the beginning of time – as we know it at both ends. Let's let light kindle bright in the middle again – light-hearted clear through to the middle.

LIGHT IN THE MIDDLE. • Light in the middle my heart's breathing lime-green relief at the inside of me and the heaven's are open and the singing is beg and the ringing called be-ing has all ready been seen gelled to the center and importing the task, the surrender to living called mending the pass and the gap metatronic takes a great leap to the blend called living and divinity and me and 8 bodies healing establish the bliss where meeting mends healing by looking within and all the way in is all the way out and out of the middle I shine a great light at the point of the temple, the pyramid called me. Light in the middle and all the way through. Cell to cell. Light in the middle. • Clear to the middle, I am light and a star and a son and a daughter and a sum of the all. You are the accountant, the bookkeeper, the friend who adds it all up and we start once again. Where's my mother, my lover, my friend? Right in the center of the me that I am. I am the light and the way and the truth in the night and the keeper of star beams and jars of delightful entendering swimming scenes of LIGHT IN THE MIDDLE preserving your be-ing. Keep it light. It's light tonight in the sun's warming sight.

LIGHT SUN • My soul's been satisfied and gone on to blend with the peace of perfection and the light filled with blending perfection, the place of recline. The tapestry atomic and the nucleus of zenographic respite and ethnic combustion and the loving example of a light called a-man. Adamic example has melted the tribes to one shiny sample the light son, the sun, the breathing called man. An essence grand. A living span. A tribe called truth and a primitive grand. The gods must be central and the solar trip to the edge of infinity and the sight right within – a man, oxygen deep in living relief. The imprint of eiffel and the fancy french trip to the top of the tower and the liberty within by the light sun, I am. • I saw the sun looking. I heard the wind blow as a result of the seeing that we are below the horizon of a night's turning day and you are the happy sound of my turn to play in the swirling, the singing, the dance of light upon rivers and ripples and plants of her streaming gives father his tan and the sun's brimming chockfull of living within – just a heart's breathe away and as wide as your hand's beating rhythm with the rays pulsing round. Welcome in. The sun-light is on.

LIGHT MOON • Light me a place at divinity's edge and tell me the truth of a living wedge. Reflective and passive, receptive I blend giving and active with a heavenly trend of perfect in-balance. Imbalance is gone to haunt-less arrival at the edge of the sun and elliptic eclipses of shiny content meet at equators of paying my rent. I will reside in the light of the moon's emotional tune, you and me and basic humanity. Light 'neath the shine of an eternal noon. Light moon. • Light tonight I am listening to your delightful creamy countenance beaming home on a round-faced beauty called the moon of my emotions and each second that I'm dreaming 3 years are granted peace and the process of remembrance starts with one release and into the creamy light of ambrosial filling cream is my waking surrender of the numbing called the dream. I am awake and fully conscious that the light has dawned and you are on.

THE LIGHT'S DAWN • The light has dawned and I am on a cosmic retreat to the class called communing and the spirit called me. The masses have met a loving eclipse, a blending of sun spots and karmic relief, great cosmic channels of mayan relief. A millennial expect has met in the sea of life's dawning splendor, the divinity called me, and the light has spawned in the river of milky relief. • The egg called a human and the basic embrace of living romantic at the horizon bright green and the love of a life time, the light arcing in me . A filament of relief. The light's birth called me. The light is seen in the delicious embark on a light education. As for me, light. Early and late, the light dawn is essential to me and my basic humanity. Light dawn. The light's dawn. The light has dawned. You are on.

LIGHT INTENT:

LIGHT ORANGE • Light orange trickles of relative speak and an easy appeal to an amber ring and telling expelling of an expulsive dream and the team of trailing comets insures an ecstatic blend of ebullient floors and filling futures of our capable home in the temple alanta* and the house of the trip to atlantean heights and the web of a plant clipped to the climb, the triple tympanic of a canvas tangerine and a fruit filled frenzy of ecstatic relief and a pumpkin spicy at the fleshly treat, the human I am, and the grate-full span bridging the rival fields of ecstasy and specks of forgetting in drizzling respect. Speak the truth. Know the wealth of ecstatic relief at the show's happy ending and the feeling respect of laughter igniting and courtesy met at the thundering beauty of a level retreat to the heart of a miracle rhyming within the precious timing of partners finding backbone's kundalini high and magenta wide to a earth's beating orange, on the inside, by divine relation. Light orange. • Light settles soft within the spaces of filling the hardness, the forget-full-ness, the ripeness of peach petaled forgiveness. You are the remembrance, the consideration of timelessness well-spent and often I am left to wander breathlessly on the lilting edge of our forevering. We are the infinite and the eternal and the ruthlessly void enter-pretation of what is right and welcome and left to acknowledge in the regeneration of our Light orange return to lighten-ing surrender.

Alanta – bits of athenian and atlantean blend to meet in the middle of a southern cross in the sky of a night long remembered.

LIGHT FLASHLIGHT • Flash your light at the corner of get, and I'll give a spark to the web of neglect and melt all the flashes of flat ugly waste, of energetic leaks and leers upon the face of beauty met divinity, blessed holy be. The love of better living is bubbling up in me. Shine your light upon the sight of a flashbulb's felt around this melt. The love of light and the work of friends met in peace to live again. The light has said, let them be. Let us see your basic light divinity in the eyes of blinking lens met with glass to focus thin upon the space of a glittering face smiling back, caught in the place of your holy light flashlight. • Thundering home by the ray of your light flashing in the deepest halls of my life, I am for-given and light with the write-full knowing that you are my metatronic, dynamic circuiting experiential inter-dimensional partner in the perfect pleasing penetration of yet another puzzling fog of peopled perplexion. I am the penetrating return and the thundering recipient of my spirits plunging reconnection to the whole that I am. I am receptive, full and eager to receive this light communication.

LIGHT COMMUNICATION • Communicate this loving entrance to the womb of all holies and the delphic dance. At the protal of purity and the wedding of chance, a welding has happened and love has a chance to recline in the light hammock sway of our open commitment to have a great day and parcel to this is a posted decree that I will hear you and you will hear me and our definite stance is that this love will last, polite and profane, ebullient and sane, on electric and free on a line of exude at the beauty of you and your energetic epistle, written in light and communicated through eyes glowing bright by telling the truth, you own, clean to bones of basic belief and a living free of external holds, a pleasurable penchant for perfect replies to the light shining bright in your living eyes. Spirit has it heaven's mint melts on your tongue of living intent to reside in the site, the light's loving web of hearing yourself in every word you've said, to me, and to you, hear's to our basic humanity and the hum of our light communication. • Lightly I am given the right to anticipate your delight at receiving my reeling, cartwheeling, dancing, spinning, delivery of magnificent, melting sight. Set in the starry embrace of light's penetrating return is a diamond-like lacing of meta-matronic matrix of pleasing pulsing tympanic harmonics. Of late, it's light and lightly it's late and the return of my sight's the vision I relate in this epistle of dazzling, awakening light communication. It's light tonight – just look at your face.

LIGHT REFLECTION • Light reflects in my giving respect of the love internal and the cave of plenty glistening shiny with expert embrace of the love living kindly in my bliss-full escape to the mirror of peace that lives in this glade, this gentile thread, this jewish tread, a glad september in the age of release and arcturic glances blend at their peak and the peek at romancing has met at the feet of a hill andean and a perky new trip to the trail called internal and the hub of a peal wheeling back to the city to live in the tree of eternity singing and heaven blown free. Haleakala sings a morning. Mt. Rainer blasts a warning. The sea is forming cones of coding heed their bonding psychic warming, nation's swarming to see the peace of the light reflecting inside me. • Reflection on your perfect light is the mission of my twinkling eyes. Sometimes I remember and always I acknowledge that living in surrender is the deliverance of knowing for-give-ness. Tonight while it's light embody the sight of heaven flowing forth to fill up her sparks with the remembrance of flight – you are my delight and my desire for communion is the reunion of a perfect light relationship.

LIGHT RELATIONSHIP • Light's relation to me is one and the all, the same, the eternal, the flame, the flight to forever and the pinnacle met in forgiving example of the living I've led and I am light shining in perfect reflect of the relationship led by giving in to the temple, respect, and the example of plenty and the appeal of the many, the threads of eternity and the blessed event, the hands of delight-full embrace has begun and the christ sign's appearing in the wings of a dove, the arms of forever, for everything's met in the one light supernal, this living, this man, my loving companion, you are the sun of a million arrivals at the lips of the cup, the grail of holy blessing, the kiss of a ring of light angels singing round the throne 24 and the equilateral blend of your interior bits, the meeting of meta with the mega of thin particulates of shiny strips and the waves of a quantum deliverance to fields of light energy and the surfacing love of our light relationship. • Truly I love you and tonight I adore the soaring return of my light's iridescent signal flashing full upon the breast of a robin building nest in the branches, calmly swaying, gently staying home within the center of my life's tree. I am rooted and rocked loose and flown free by this swimming, surling beyond existence light communion happening hear, happening here in this room's wide turning smile of delivering increase. We are the one shining bright, swirling light, sweet emotion.

LIGHT IN-MOTION • Light's in motion in my exceptional grip of the art of emotion and the review of a lip edged in techno, in neon, in light's, in screens set in gems of warming express and a glimmer of coincidence met with respect of our arching recognition of the aromatic truth that pleasure is penchant and pardonic and point, that the drama called karma has met a new board and the treading returning has met with a more open acceptance of the beauty of light moving in spot lights and outlets called me and the light is in motion in the middle of me. Life is kind in nature's palace, the pleasure, the balance, called me. Basic and humane. An excellent name. The heart at the flame in my constant attention to the light in-motion. • How far from the edge have we strayed dear and how near to the center shall we stay. Here's the meaning of swimming in place, a star takes up space to create just a trace of remembering dance and that entrance is opened by the up moving notion of silent devotion to the high self called heaven – oh heavenly sight and heaven is sew relative to the needle's delight at keeping her sight on the compass called life looking north (relatively speaking).

LIGHT RELATION • Light's relation to my holy station is in constant motion at a splashing ocean plank full of tons of light shimmering nightly in a whaling eye and 3 great towers of tawny limb stand at the spot where the whale jumped in. A life's been met with ceilings set by starry sight on the living light. The planet's spin, the well-come 10, the 9's uproar on the sounding shore. The welcome din of a calving kin, a mother's plea for a baby's free expression of a grace-full prime an exact brink, and a copy cued to sunday morning and a headset's early warning. Systematic's sending the signal wet and warming the lord of light is coming and his guitar brings a strumming and electric nights are humming at the light bred family, drifting in to take a swim at the pool called merrily, I travel on. Light relation. • Lightly it's relative – this returning splendor of elegant question and love so entendered with gentle persuasion and laughing exam of the relative question whose answer is I am – you are the light star shining true north and I am the reflected one living on earth and between us a ribbon of heaven's delight – an arc of reminder is flashing the light of God dusting the firmament with the splashes and collections of stars indeterminate. Lights constant-elation.

LIGHT CONSTELLATION • A light constellation constitutes this installation of upwelling release of the penance I called pieces, and now in gentle slumber, I testify my humble adoration of the light that I am and a sparkling zone of starry night ignites the moon and her well aimed flight to the edge of my life and the weld of my wide open dream, a living seam, the vein I begin and the facet I am. Royal awards ring my neck like flowers called leis* and islands met with perfect peace and grate-full chests of hearts flown golden and green and wet with kisses born holy and pearlescent effects of the hearty arch ival and the concise consent to swim in the center of the fountain, I am. A delicious transition for a born again star shining in visions guided afar by a light constellation, the nearest star. Arc to your heart. A light constellation. • Pleased to confide in the circle of light, I am rekindled with the sight soaring bright near the handle of a bucket of stars – glows a light and a candle and a friend called a star and an arc of dear kindness has returned to confirm that a life shared with others is the life that will learn to communicate sweet peace and enjoy the affair, the dancing on moonbeams, the relating to share light relations.

leis...circle of flowers of living rings around the neck of Hawaiian dreams

LIGHT RELATING • I am Light relating, the earthen golden crust, the melting shades of a left over daze to enter the maze of musing giving and eclectic passion met at the border of a flushing journey to digital cart of my electric blue emblazoned time of essence melting swishing sweeps of local locations apart to the truth that elocution is sweeter when gourmet inclined to rain-bows of primitive and primary finds scrubbing the bend of a pure blown wind spotting the station of a life lived within the flick of a temper bred to the sight of a cart met with grey whistling metal suspended mobile and artfully dodging the leftover aisle. This loop's complete, the story's neat, the light is on, communication's sun, a turning table, a fonder matter, the living platter of light relating. • Relating to sharing, I am relating to you. You are delightful ignition of my surrender of cognition to the middle-hearted melting I call love and lately I know that the clearest crystal communication lies in the depth of our heart's beating coded message of surging life force. And in the increase which lives arcing between us swells a melody of dear old home and new to this feeling I am clearly light reeling in life drinking ecstasy at the sight of this feeling led to discover other and live to sing about it.

LIGHT INSTIGATION • Young as a beam of creation's succulent light cracking the seam of acknowledged divisions and the forgetting I've met, I gape at the place called hairy-in-covers memories bred at the strength of a lover, regal example of the satin sample of a genetic genius and a forgotten castle. Supports are kindred and bred of the weeks of porcelain skin and swollen feet of moonbeams gravity dancing on lands of shocking elegance and additional trends of motivational security and instigative strands of spirit-filled travels and probing escape to the love without ends and the clue called a man. Human. Basic. Divine light. Sufficiently draped to provide a light instigation. • Singing in harmony is the way to the gate of divine instigation of absolute motivational embrace of the space within the facing elements of air and earth and fire and water and deep within the middle is the clue that will kindle your return to the sun burning tight and woven intricate with wonder at the releasing thunder of your harmonious duet to the tune of a night-filling moon and the moon's melting drips like honey on the keys of all forgetting and I remember to play it again: love.

LIGHT SPOKEN, HEAR • Ears of bliss melt the kiss of energy's grip and allows the flow of showing entreaties of 'where have you been and examples of sampled exotic trend shine in the sky of an eternal flame burning my heart reddened with pain and panes of example feature the time I've spent as a creature not living in line with the balanced divinity that I am inside the lime-green birth of a closeted dream, the door is wide open and I am the friend of a funny bush flaming with swinging breasts igniting my life and creaming the game of milky way sprinkles lit by a theme. The constant refrain, a creamy-gened perch. The dna's red and the strength of a man meets in the wand of the layers I am. Bodies of bliss melting in ears of cosmic approval. There's light spoken, hear. • Love is lightly spoken, hear. In innocent reverie, I am instantly given the perfect recall of light long forgotten and my healing has begun to communicate in the ears and the eyes of my resonant words of endearing consistency – you are the light son's favorite sight and hearing these lightly spoken, peach blossom blooms of infinite heart are softly speaking of their homing instinctive which leads well to thee – thou art the one. Invest in some light investigation.

LIGHT INVESTIGATION • Light investigations peppered my sleep and slips of example are melting the breeze of a temple called heaven and I am suspect, and client, and friend and the adoration of intrinsic samples flown to the bend of a melodious trend. Crystalline cuties of cosmic bliss belt my photonic photographic melt of penetrating jumps and schematic designs and engineering electric atlantean climes. Semantics glisten with the piezine* view of the light full electric glittering through your crystal knowledge of the light called a college and the metatronic friend of hertzian waves meeting in you and piercing through the bowels of forgetting with direct intent to alternate currents of galactic content. A periscope's view of the infinity in you, cleansing pipes of purple dreams and a light investigation defabricating nations of forgotten cleanse. Know the light that living is. You. The solution to my light investigation. • Your light shone tonight in the gentle reflection of your healing release of the capturing allure of being incomplete and in your completing you cast a new spell. An admission of walking in a life fed by well. And well it is offered and often imposed the wound of forgetting is surrounded by whole starry necklaces of impressive delight – light's heart is calling – let's claim this new sight and bask in the rays of this light flaming bright.

*pieso-electric: eccentrically crystalline exude of the energetic blend and the facets in you.

LIGHT FLAMING BRIGHT • Light to the center, I'm drawn to the spark of the love that I am and the light that we are and excellence clothed in brilliant blue highlights the glint of compassion meets me in aquiline shining of the good in you and divine to a spirit I'm swollen with glee at the harmonious singing ringing in me. Exceptional constance becomes quite a sight as I burst forth trust with my flame shining bright and freely spoken it's sunny on top and the volts of lava are meeting in popping arrival at the edge of the shore, the gardens of grecian arch-aic belief are jazzy with juicy jewels of treat and the reflection of you is so openly me that I fall in splendor to our basic divinity. That star shooting through, that's me. A novel spree for a light shining bright. • Tonight tender troving, I am surrendering to bliss and the peace of remembering at the end of this kiss of the sonlight, of the buddha come home, the prodigal lotus has come to full bloom and you are my lover, my light, and my friend and the circle of giving spins full without end and rich in the telling and deep in the soul is the smoldering embrace of an ember full-blown in a blaze of remembering – my dear welcome home. Your light shines tonight.

LIGHT SHINES TONIGHT • Light shines, hear, on my divinic ear and globules of smitten entwine with excite and glow in the moon of a stone set to buy a new scheme and a living design. A-man, basic, human, and a heart, a sweet cell of metatronic abandon and the living to tell you once again my light-hearted friend, that in loosing your mind, you've found a new line, a heart and a blend of swirling exact. The plus of a bonus called living exact. I am the line and the in put just found. Draw a new blind of the light shining down, now, prop up the shade and blow up the tunnel, the light is in me and my heart is a funnel, heaven wide to the love inside and out. All one source one brave discourse filled with delight for the light shining tonight. • Light, I shine tonight and an aura of richness embraces my home and my heart, welcome rocking, erupts into whole loving giving and the deliverance of fear to the edge of forever. Only love spoken, hear, on the lips of this sonnet of often embrace are the hopes of this planet and the desire of a race. You are the heart and the flame and the bliss. Consider this missive revealed by a kiss of light flaming delight.

LIGHT FLAMING DELIGHT • Light's embellish my giving sight and I'm met by the moon at the edge of the light and joy is given and holiness wed to the sight of you lying in our marriage bed. We are the one and the eternal flame. Your heart's your own and the name's the same. The edges melt and vacations sing at our dancing example of the living friend. The heart called forever and the arc called a span. A diamond of rings, a saturnic delight, an elemental move toward specific gravity. Zero. Absolute. The all. The many have left to become one great ball of sparkling inception, the heart of reception, our honey's moon, our living room, our ecstatic hearts beaming one octivic note – light to a flame's delight. Kundalinic and erect, I am the sight. Light's best man and the wedding band. A woman's honor. The faith-full trend. Light. • Sometimes I wonder at the tether we've built and the feeling surrender of the belt of forget. You are remembrance and cells of delight – each holding energy for the others for sight. The looks of this living encircle with care when the eyes are soft tender without torpor or stare. Remember the embrace, the empress, the king, the light of your being and sing it again. The kindest refrain. Lightly I am giving.

LIGHT I AM GIVING • Lightly I am giving my sharing honest living to the hearts of nations brimming in bowls pacific leaning and heaven's met her being in my specific knowing of the love arc-tonic showing in your electric eyes. Best of show is sitting on haleakala's cradled ceiling and seals expectant father the candle of confession, the drops have melted pealing in bells of mountains giving daring driving spilling in signs of jesus planting the trance-cendant love we're sharing and christ has met the altar of lightest planes of keen assign and the glow of the earth is brimming inside the spell of our spin and the jewel like aisles of the vein called a-man and the faith-full intrigue of a heart held in hands of light for lightly I am giving. • Women hurt by living. Men condemned at birth. Life not proffered kindly can burn with hate-full hurt. And in the midst of punishment and scarring – born neglect is the option of the living path, the option most direct. Welcome home to your heart. Here's what matters. Make the election, the vote to break the pattern. All illusion shattered and legacies scattered to the winds of beginning for lightly, I am, lately.

LIGHTLY, I AM, LATELY • Light of late has marbled planes of byzantine buildings, architectural blends of bleeding felt stamped on the band of existence and maternity's trend to establish an affinity for the heavenly amenity called the light in me and momento's grace the altar, that alloy of expanse with the contraction called a dance with sophistic* acts of twirling spins and toiling met with lifting trim of gardenic splendor and edenic jewels of heavenly suspend. Bargains abundant in the facets within for lately, I am light and plugging myself in to the heart of earth and the worth of God and the harmony met in celestial orbs, electronic lords, the we I know, by schematic flow and persian intrigue with the turquoise opal exposed in me for lightly, I am, lately. • Lightly, I am, lately and always you are too and tonight in mission's accomplishment is the surrender to the two – the 2 viewings shared by one for lightly, I am, lately and this minute, you are the one embracing surrender to the beginning of the sun and ah-men we are forgiving you for forgetting the rhyme at the end of our living emission. Ignition, surrender, envision, and breathe it all in and be done – all one. All remembering each. Well won.

*Sophia – wise woman's glance at eternity, met in a friend.

LATELY, I AM LIGHTLY • Lately I'm light by a hellenistic sight of sunflowers rent with curvaceous splendor and twisting roads of dynamic beauty lilting my gaze to the heart of the calm and the quality eclipsed by the heart of me, specializing in spins to the core of a-man and a pleasant connection to the cord of light within. Elixirs are my bounty, the stones of life, my grace, exception's met accounting and divinity is my friend. The one of sophic seeing evolves with glistening haste and evolution beaming shines upon my face. Divine this line, the light is on. A hyacinth's blooming. An exquisite performing. The light upon our space. For lately, I am, lightly. • Lately, I am, lightly seeing at the end of a time beginning sweet with creamy crowns of distant embrace. Hugging twirls of tempting twining are forming columns of be-coming and be-ing surrendered to the entity of two is the too often remembered forgetting of you. One love is singing and humming and adrift in an air rich with electrons of buzzing repair – feel the sight, hear the touch of the lightenings embrace.

A LIGHT COMMUNIQUE • Light's my communique and my intimate friend, the bliss of example and the end of a trend toward for-ever and the path with a pulse of bubbly examples of asiatic recline, lilies in fields of passionate trace, 7 sisters are bred in a hallowed bed of glaring advice and sunny entreaty and treatments less kind than their remember of the divinity in me and my applauding retreat to the wings of the dove and a reversal so neat that infinity's blib creates a new screen, the heart of the beauty shining in me, the sister, the 8th. Attentive to moods, I lift high the press of petulant gloom and bloom a new tree, a debut electric, selectric and free. The blessed express of this light communique • Light is a continuum. A complete, a whole. One light, one divine, one in grace, one home. Light is particulate, articulate, and many speaking mini languages, coughing alike breathing all light. One light communique. Communication both whole and wholly a part of the particulate many and one under the sun of a mother's loving glance at the father's dancing feet – two on the floor and one in the air – at the head of the communicative hello.

A LIGHT COMMUTE • Commute to the trip, the expectant bulb, the bright new insight of a grander design. Spell a new word, see the lord of the loving intrigue, the waiting on salads, the greens of the field, the journey to mountains, to ashrams and fans of waving grass blending in harmony with the land of forgiven seeing and forgiving met with glee, the space of instant training and the sparkle of the glue shining through the windowed loops of the specialty called me. We are the boat and the sole of the step which leads our hearts to finish this grip called willing retreat. I am the solace, the unified beat of one heart's beaming, one heart's trip to the land of remember and eternity's gift. A light commute. • It's a short distance from your heart to mine in the midst of the infinity to infinity wave full divine. Tonight in the moon's life in the light of the sea, I'll glance at the shining and remember we are three and the one in the middle holding us in is the check that is balancing this book without end, without end, only middle dear friend – infinity wins. Sustain and maintain and create the main lane. The shortest most direct commute is the one requiring only light maintenance.

LIGHT, MAINTAIN US • Light is maintaining the heart of this place and I am expectant of a genuine grace and spirals of pleasure trace that lace of sexual splendor met in the face of my own taste-full expression of vintage me and sufficient kindling of the sun in me, tinged in green, red to cores of forgotten cinders and expectant chores twinkly lime and tart by scene the lemon layers of a lighter stream. Replays of arch-aic forgotten teams tackle my truth that this is the lineage seldom seen. The lift of the archons in a forthright celebration of the wealth of this nation, george-towns tripping on lying piles of mouthing packages of turning stiles, crumpled warmth of loving sheets shines in me, my heart's complete with pleasuring clouds and open skies, nocturnal dreams and beaming good-byes to the life-less lead and the leisurely place, the star in your hands and the etch of your face, blending well and accommodating stares into the light, maintain us • Starting at zero, I am pleased to explain, is the lilting referral of a life without pain and you are eternal and etheric and set on numbers too large for your day to forget. So dive through the middle, the center of care and catch what a zero's like that floats in solid air. Air solid breathing, deep and full and ripe are lungs of forgiving wheezing and a fondest gentle night you are the light. Maintain us in the breath of deepest night.

LIGHT SUSTAIN US • Light sustenance enables my bliss to remain in my heart and soft on my lips. I'm supple and steady and limber and met with the serendipitous blessing of living hips, gripping the swivel of a sacred stone, the lingam met yoni and heaven wide in surrounding expression of the divinity I'm blessing with special effect. The breastplate worn priestly has met with designs of exacting eruptive belief. Oh lord of remember I come to the place that's the kindest and best, the avenue called heaven and the column of rest, right in the center of you. Sin* has met the nation of all one blanketing ocean the army of light, a delicate sight in peace-full pentagons of 5-sided news. The vowels, the pentateuch and you. By design. Light sustain us • I sustain that you remain a father and a friend, and I refrain from pitching in with words without a frame. The picture of this eternal longing is felt in sustaining desire in permanent forgiveness of the living reminder that it is, the light, I am. So hold this often gentle and always holy near and in the peace which passeth knowing, your heart is showing you the ropes – cast aside the care for anything less than a light embrace.

Sin – Simple Ignorance of Nature's balance and harmony seeking power.

A LIGHT EMBRACE • Seeds of light, sprinkle the fields of my wind-less harvest of the weird and absurd, the mighty, the plenty, the fields of rolling thunder and the norwegian waves of siberian ecstasy and half the line, a loop of collages and spectacular sunsets dwelling in autumn's encircling arms, the sweep of a blending effortlessly blessed by the breeze of the bayou and the leftover bards of floral, inventive, bouquets of relief gifted by jasmine and hyacinth's treat and the shade of the jade tree, malachite and blue erupts in the splendor of foreseen news and examples of plenty shining in you and the thimble has spilled in remembering retrace of the christ-ing example, the adoration of a race and a race and a race, the living samples, a light embrace. • A light embrace puts a glow on my face in the sight of the moon waiting night – ah, so soon and forgiveness and faith hold hands every day while the lion and lamb play in the fire of embered forgetting to fear one the other. One – the one – is the secret and the key to this life. One – the other – is surrender to the fate of all night. Join the sunlight and the dance and the memory of a night met with the kindest embrace of one, the other one – all one.

LIGHT-N-LACE • Sex has met her safest bet the fit of a candid commitment and a sparkling band, the ring of remember and the marriage within. Wedding the self to the light, your friend, evokes the feeling of a love within and pink to the green and orange to the cream, a soda of bubbly is lacing through me and my light lingerie. An exceptional place. The land of light-n-lace, founded in me, a sister city, a plan for a happy embrace. Light-n-lace. The leather is chapping, the binding is rent and the payment for denial has all- ready been spent. The kindest reminder of entirely sweet care is the softest entwining lace made of thin air. Lightest gossamer reminders, energetic imprints of you, waft through my daytimes, my night-times, it's true. You are my consistent, my constant, my friend, swaddled in light garments, Light-n-lace, sew it is.

LIGHT-TO-TASTE • Light tastes sweet in the honey I stick in the place of deliverance and the buzz called a bee's loving chamber, the honeycombed place of the heart called my own and the life of a place shared with strangers and families and friends, the hearth called remember and the globe spinning in this earthly sender, this pacing render of the pointed etch, the engraving of streams penetrates me with extreme relief as I sample the duty and the beauty of zen-tral heating and cooking in streams of ambrosia bubbling and tangerine creams floating in plenty and avoiding the crush of the song heard humming in an arrogant hush. The gluttony's done. The lord is home. Metatron's sun ignites the flame of blessed revival. Basic and humane and by any name, you. Light to the taste and calorie free. Light. • Driplets and droplets and trickles of true-taste like a lifeline, lifetime of new constant filling nutrition, great breast of surrender, dripping full, sopping wet reminders of the glutton I'd been. Starving in living on the mutton of men, then the light of the lamb shown within greatest truth and was illumine with the knowing full sooth and thus it is written. Know and be free light to the taste and absolutely calorie-free

LIGHT IN THIS PLACE • LIGHT'S in this place that I call the face of All remember and Mother becomes lover and lover becomes friend and father is another love leftover for us to mend and apparently I'm speaking of a universal game, the monopolistic, singular trace has met up with a friend and there's Light in this place and the grandest taste is the trickle of tiny melting away and travertine grins imbue each the other with good-bye to the trend of forgotten denial. Our healing's blend? Our comfort zone? The hearts that we own in ecstatic balance with each the other and eternity's measure, a healing blend, the blessed end to the trance-apparent. For there's Light in this place. • It is Light in this Place and I know I'm standing square in the middle of the heart of this pair. Not me, nor the Other. Only One made of Two, and hallelujah, this sharing creates a BE-ing brand new – an infant of kneeling surrender is kept oft in our knowing dear – no neglect. This is our product, the sharing of 2 – enjoy, the knowing that there's One Love, ever knew, in the Light of this Place, our hearts pulsing through.

A LIGHT SPACE • Dim-witted chuckles echo within from the deep witted release of a darker line and the art of love remembered picks up now a trace of the land of know forever and the heart of a living race. The staccato beats of a resting rose tickle my throat and blend in my nose to sample the charity, the clarity of friends expectant and hushed in their lightening veil. The choke weed is dead and energy's bent through lens of renewal converging in me, concave to reason and convex to the net of the concept coined neglect. Give us a chin and a strong-handed trend toward the square-jawed revival of the tower called a-man and a blend of the feminine-less wile more smile and blessed friend. The energy of example in your living, loving blend. Friend. Light space. • You are my mother and I am your friend and you are my father – oh sky sing again of the meeting of earth's love and

the impulse of sun in the total con-synthesis, the absolute, this one. I am writing to lovers, to the absent, the oblique, the nerd, and the forgotten, and the geek and the freak. Of nature, I am singing, of nature I am made. Drink in my light fruit – my pink lemonade of shaded surrender to the light in the space called your full blooming. A light space – your face..

THE LIGHT IN YOUR PLACE • The light abruptly skips around illuminating you and your metropolitan view of an ancient machine, the lone called liberty and heart called free to speak of an american dream an erotic living love of a scheme idealic exotic and grand. Where is the leader of this our fair land? Squarely set in the temple called you. New jerusalem cheers to hear our great plan and emotion rings in our loving trend to enlighten the reason, the balance, the chore, the national debt called glutony's whore-y repugnant greed stares straight into the shining eyes of lady liberty. Brother, martin had a dream and a lady awaits for her opportunity to sing of blending love and lines erased and one lasting note of love erupting from our face. The light. In your place. • This is the light path and I am on your right to kneel here beside you and chant of earth's delight. My respect is growing for the deep concern you're showing on the impress that you're throwing far behind. The truth, it hears, it lingers, it stays in roots and fingers and pops out to remind us that God's great gift is kindness and the light of giving sparkles in waves of loving sharing in circles rounding you. There is the light in you place.

THE LIGHT IN OUR SPACE • The light in my face enlightens the space called the tunnel of love's receiving grace and the news is bliss and the look on your face remains in the loop of a belt way called beautiful and a mantra called truth and the pentagoned walls of hidden intrigue bow in great humble, aching need of the power greater still escapes eternally those who reside inside these 3 – greed, glutton, groin. Know the race of arms meeting bliss and hearts held in time to a whistling kiss. The light is on inside the dome, of your living home, your loving center, the pentagon of geometric drift to the center of you just below the ellipse. Reflecting pools gaze back at me as I rise to dance with lady's liberty, truth and the God we trust, from pennsylvania ave. To the sounding sea, let me be the light in our space. • Welcome home. I enkindle you with the fire of compassion burning your dross of selfishness clean through. Candles of forgiving are ringing through the night and I am here and lingering near to give you a hand, to applaud all you see and to bow on my knees at the light I call you. The crosses are dancing to hear the great news – a mother remembered – that one equals two. Light our space with the sharing of two lights gathering.

LIGHT RACE • Race to the start of a love called your heart and I'll bet an impress that the length of your dress will address your kin of the color of skin and looking within I see a same spark and an eagle of love daring to park at the helm of a land outrageous and free and melting the web of the prejudice in me.

Self-forgiven beats self-forgotten. Hands round our common table. I am led to bless our bowing heads with a lifting gaze and a lilting phrase, united we stand, one land, one love, one God, one friend, one skin. A light race. • Color me green and red and blue and orange with intrigue at the shades in you. I like your language, your rhyme and your scene of drawing on canvas with the ray that you are be-ing and deep in the state of social neglect, a culture is growing. The race to forget that light needs its matter for color to show and the light here is cheering for the coloring knowing for this mattered surrender. There is no one better than other. We have all won again.

LIGHT COUPLE-ING • Light couples fling their arms around the heart of each others dreams and sleep snugly in awakened passion of the hopes of our land. For there is nothing finer than a morning air and a note of surrender and a giving trend living exceptional and close and within the energetic gap filling the synapse of forgotten bliss with the bridge called eternal and the desire to live wealthy and happy and outrageously, grand all inside you and at no one's expense, one rich emphatic example of the blend greater still, deeper layers revealed for healing entrance to the land of remember and the heart of our dance. The life of our love. Our eternal blood. Light couple-ing. • Lightest coupling is the pointing reminder that my heart and the son are one. Rays of ignition flare with surprising regularity at this wedge of life called the truth and I remember the moment and the tender I own it. "It's my life. I'll do what I want to do" and with this embracing, it's our lines we are tasting and the three become one equals two gentle suns in the eyes of a night filled with thundering embrace at the plug-in called us – end of race – with just a hint of light-est understanding.

LIGHT UNDERSTANDING • Light understood in my return to the land of plenty and love and liberated intent. How could our giving extend to any less than any brother or sister who withstood the flood of naked appraisal and embattled emblazon of the orange forgotten and the agent who stands all-one in a crowd. The soldier of light understanding the flag of a nation called heaven and the mother of this great land. Nature's blessing has met with exacting interface. Know the sum, one. A light understanding, understood? One. Light. • Hinting at light is the twinkling eye of the edge of this night's horizon. So using your thumb, just smooth it to one and the lips of our lapping denial will blend it to none other – all lover – all one light waving in the dappling delight of delicious, ono*, outrageously succulent surrender to the notion that saving your love for a rainy day equals a basket of rancid fruit – so peel out the flesh of this morning's song. The wait is over. You are heard and lightly understood.

Hawaiian for delicious

LIGHT IN-SENSITIVE • Light in transition and effective in blends of examples of living and basic intent to stand in the middle of a street called a grand example of a district of capitol expanse, I am the heart and the wealth of this plan geometric and this current electric and this sample of nations floating in scenes of sliding evasion. The scale has been set and the ruler been trimmed to measure the inches of your metric trim, the metres of rhyming have met with the test, the look on your face, smiling sweet and soft upon the space of the light in-sensitive relief, light. • Light in sensitive. Dip just the tip of your brush in this fount, this river of life called a man, and know that the one you are ringing has sung yet a new resurrection, a rainbow, a sun, a bucket of sparkles, all particles, all one wide geometric, geographic intensive to bring forth the light deepest blue, brilliant red, green of heart, moon of head – clouds removal has happened, the cloudbursts have run, and we all know the meaning of that ring around the sun. True believers. Light in-sensitive.

LIGHT IN-SIGHT-FULL • Washington rings with knowing insight of the joy we bring. An arc of arrival has met in sweet aid, in lemon-egg stands of burning retreat and the pain of disease has gone far away to be the archival feast in the shade of forever and the eternity of care, the portion called giving has met in retrieve and my heart is happy at be-ing sweetly me. Through and through an in-sight-full recline in the beauty of me. Light in-sight-full. • For there is light in the sensitive. Jewels adorn the crowns of the simple, the gentle, the forlorn, and the proud. The angles are covered, the anger's been spread to the vortex called heaven in the ring round this head and I am bowing in bliss now at the knowing you are near, and I am hope-full in sunlight waving soft over my chair. In bliss I am waiting and spinning and given the in-sight-full knowledge of the heart that you carry ever near, ever sensitive, ever dear, drawing near to the light in-full-sight.

LIGHT EMOTING • My heart's resonant in shining embrace of the weight strongly lifting and the joy of blend meeting giving and laughter met plain in sparkling arrival of the living refrain. The song heard plain from globe to globe, the impact of planets beginning to glow in aching retrieval of the love primeval lifted to light in examination's retreat. Dance in the street of the light fit to meet the balance in me, emotive, ecstatic, and flowing free. The light emoting in me. • This devoting to the notion that energy is like an ocean of lightest essence flowing free and in the middle forming this life, this e-motion that I call me, and I am massive energy moving and I am light just sitting still while I spin in silent wonder at the space created here by the surrender to the feeling that LIGHT'S EMOTING and metatron is standing near. Metatronic, electronic, regenerative e-moting.

LIGHT DEVOTION • Devoted to the light I am, I'm ecstasy met in the form of a man and swirling in circles of living expect I usher a truth, a loading command. Know thyself, be free, serve thy needs, go freely to the well of all remember and exact a loving feeling, an infinite notion of the art of recall and the belt of devotion, an ecstasy met in working in tune is the wealth of the truth of the divinity in you, shining through your light devotion.

• I am devoted to you my sister, to you my brother, to you the queer, the least and the likely to be predictable, to the ones they call the weird. For you are dancing in the one love which none can take away and you are touched with knowing your unique gift is the piece we need to play this song we call harmonic. Remember, cast your note by playing with your own drum and you are the one we vote as most electric, dynamic. What a sight. We will catch you on the big screen. Such devotion. What a notion. Oh sweet emotion.

LIGHT PROMOTION • Promote the light by taking flight to the edge of remember and the land of delight and embark on trends to the edge of a star and envelope your-self in the heart of a far burning light. The purest relation the intense devotion of one light promotion and an elegance bathed in the loving praise of an exceptional all. We are the fall and the rise of a living span. A God's breath called man and the tread of light-footed belief in the ecstasy called treating yourself to a basket of bread and a heartland fed well with wheat-eared plans to devote one's star to the cause that we are and here's the hook – believe, believe, believe. What a catch. Me. A light promotion in a living ocean of ability seen. Light promotion. • You are elected. You are in charge at the foot of this ocean, at the head of this barge and the light anthropomorphic has given you the nod. You are the middle man when the animals call God. Being gentle, choosing well, giving thanks, blazing a trail of appalachian* kindness is the sweetest notion, walk the path called humble faith and raft on righteous devotion. Here's your light promotion. You are the charge. Wear it well.

LIGHT IMPACT • Craters of care have met with the fine operation of the principle of living intact in the land opportune and the milky extract of a presidential example that there's light in this castle of social night's rest and there's beauty inside this heart called a nest of loving entreaty and ecstasy blessed by lord metatron's living tread to the blessed strand, the constellation called man and the meteor's course through the breadth of our land, a living span fully addressed by a starry interpretation, landing here a capital event by light impact. • There was an explosion as you came arcing in and a comet called compassion said "yes, come live again" and a tree of gentle knowing grows right before your eyes in the mirror of forever, you are the sons that rise. Daughters of the light now know the full impact of the mission you have chosen and blaze the clearest path and in the angels whisper. You hear a voice, it's yours and you bow in sweetest commitment at the crater called the lord of Light impact.

LIGHT, IN FACT • It's light, in fact and relative to this I'm willing to cash my tickets for heaven for the billowing belief that a breathing example is the only relief for a nation left too long to wander and gosh, you know that a desert's waste holds light clues too. For it's light, in fact and the proof's in you. Light. • In fact, I'd hazard knowing full before I'd squint with glare, at the pall of my unseeing face staring at the air. Within the air is special love, oxygenated bliss, a kiss of creation delivered to earth, our planet of choice, our place of impact. In fact, here's a note to hum with your tune. Know the light. Know your heart equals one. Stand within. The gift is sung. In fact you are exactly on cue. Bridge of Light. Sweetest flight. So exact.

LIGHT EXACT • Exactly this I'm led to say. The point of walking home this way. A night's relief, a nation's rest. The isle of man and a teacher sent to write the pen of a loving God misunderstood, and fed the wrong apostle's creed, good-bye to greed met in view of the light exact in the center of you. A pyrotechnic clue, leading me to the absolute tract of the light exact in you. A holy land. Light. • You are the light, exact and true, you in me and me in you equals exactly the half I was looking for too. So hop on a train and ride over here to the lake called a river and the ocean called a chair. For in this precise moment this place and this space, a new love is growing, and there's a grin on my face of blissing surmisal at the be-ing you are and half again you're showing me that one and one and one is free exactly.

LIGHT AND RELATIVE • Relative light is shining through me, welcoming you to the land of retrieve and the heart of this bell, the clanging return of the one we know well. Our light raising friend, our heavenly blend of ambrosial truth, the nectar of you and the light in me. A breathing example of the light we call heaven and the home we called free, meeting in the will of a light friend's blessing, a light and relative. • Relative to light, this is the night when the light becomes the day, and the day before the night when you are freed by second sight to navigate the rapids of the life seen relative to the ends against the middle to the beginning. Let's do it again. This is the light. Today is tonight. Intuit it in your silence, and your speaking approval of the light relative to a moment's circling spin into the middle of the mother. It's relative and it's light. Just ask your dad.

LIGHT PARENTAL • Parent me with a living branch, a mouth fed full of a purple glow, the vision of x-rays melting through to the bones of this tree and the living example of divinity in me. Shining gleefully through the light parental's ecstatic view, the sampling proof of genetic bent, the heart of this matter. The perceptive retreat to the loving center of the light parental in me. The light is on. Cell to cell to cell. Light. • Parents and poets and parrots – who knows it? A beak and a pen and a hand to get in and remember in swearing it's your deck you are wearing. Are they pairs or three of a kind? Did you juice a conduit with a prayer to get through it or a squeeze that's so tight – it's worn thin. If it's worn, then please break it – let it go. Never fake it. You have a new deal. Raise the bid. You are the latest, and the newest – the kid. Welcome home to the LIGHT PARENTAL. Enjoy your spin. You lucky little star.

LIGHT SUPPLE-MENTAL • Supple-ment your diet with a

vitamin complete with multiple doses of the infinite troop, the monkeys of bliss exacting a price, a heart met tympanic and a listening device, a telephone read by a hand clothed in veils and a message left in a living braille. Feel the web of a lasting sight, the handy cap met by the head of light. Divine to a c. The light supple-mental. • Drinking ambrosial bottles of amber and green. Within are the titles, the minerals, the vitals which keep your heart healthy and strong. Drink in a minute of honey's cream nectar and twirl your hands full of this sticky connector which fastens your heart close to mine, and in our twin beating, it's your hand I am seeking to hold in a cup next my ear and within I can hear it, the flight oh so vital, the winging has landed – in your heart I am standing and I know the light supple-mental, and oh yes, continental.

LIGHT CONTINENTAL • Light's continental in our healing embrace of egg on your face. I am amphibious, effective, and trim to the sail of a savior, my heart, in your hand-full of light, the electric glide of a breast beating gentle and singing the praise of a notion called heaven and the location in me. For the light's continental at the brink of this place, the lair of the jungle and the lion's sad neglect have met the love supernal and the scorpionic glare of a genitalic exposure and a combing of the hair golden plenty tumbling down the shoulders of forgiving glare. Pathetic pining has met within the trees of a raining sun, a forest sung to the note of one replete within the span of a light so continental. • The light is continental and the lincoln's at the door. Pull up near the fender and pick a distant shore. The pick-up costs you plenty, if you neglect to speak of your heart's desire to return yourself to the spirit which you seek. And seeking brings you seeing, and sight adds light to four sparkling infinite waves of light emitting from your door. Rays are paths to wholeness, to the center of the sun, and heat and life and living God emit to form the one and the light so continental drives the pieces home tonight in a ring around the sun.

LIGHT ORIENTAL • Bangkok bliss is given a grip-less emphatic on the loving dynamic. A treat oriental approaches, embarrassing the coaches of crouching shadows and biting the nicks of mating entendered by the strumming effect of a trendy return to the love that I own. An eccentric lad with a place kept soft by the living grace of the light oriental. • Japan and china and plates full of more fortunes than food here at the edge of your door. Blending out edges, bringing forth blurs of promises proffered and loving not heard. Tell me again, I've forgotten the score. In our spiral weaving, there's creation. Are you sure? And the light full democratic asks in bowing humble truth, will our neighbors please pass the milk to their brothers tibetan, poor, and infinitely and ultimately you. It's your serve – what an honor. In this Light so Oriental. So instrumental.

LIGHT INSTRUMENTAL • The perfection of tin, the copper of man, the heart of a friend, the love in a span to forever and an example obelisk, an egyptian tabernacle and a jewish empress, a mystic called musty and a religion called zen, a mantra called loving and a light called a friend, for the light is the instrument of instant intrigue with the concept of meeting the world in a sleeve of letters tumbling to form a new word, a hebraic example of flaming return to the song sung in fundamental retreat to the a's, b's and c's of the light instrumental. • Play your brain, pluck your heart, sing your frame. Here's the game. Choose a horn, a tam, a drum – play your name and when the singing's sung to the pulse of a breath blowing soft in the light. Great sun is beating with the chant of pure delight. Know the sounding rhythm here. Understand this truth. Light's the great composer, and tonight the star is you. Deep in sweetest slumber. Soft upon your bed, held all night by lullabic humming – my dear, my child, my one. Playing on. In a song around the sun.

LIGHT MENTAL • Mental bliss equates the fact that knowing me, I'm knowing you and one and one means two, and two in love equates to three, the one and one and the light in me. Expectant still we spin again and one and one begets a-man and adding light we now have four. If we add one more we have a door to a pentagon's penchant for security's weld and the 6th peace rings with response-able curl and living light, I outshine the trend to repeat the repeat of the 6 again and again, to the 7th place I participate fit in the sharing shed of our happy house, the light shining mental in this our 8th space a hexagonal blend of all I am and singing perfection I skip to the 9th. Orbit electric and the roof of our house. A photon electric and a spinning to the 10 of our roof and the quantum leap to our solution, one, a fundamental sum. The light mental. • Metals of gold, of silver, of lead, of copper engravings at the head of your bed. Traces of minerals appear in the flames of smoking denial that the light is home again. And today into night I will stand for the right and I am in the light of the new day now dawned and the light flashes on and I take my new seat and I am tempered and strong and mentally elite, for the wider my channel of truth sought full strength, the stronger my mantle of light tempered mental is complete.

LIGHT FRAGMENT-NATION • Light sparks fragment our land awaiting the call to start living again. The blanket of life requires a new quilt one built on love and the healing gift of a quilting frame which bears the name, indivisible. Lift the light to ignite the spirit of a nation living in giving surrender of her soul to the light and the shreds of extraction emblazon our action in the eternal flame of a-man who said "do what you can" for our nation's return to the living acknowledge of our light fragment-nation become one. We are the sum. One light. • This nation is come-passioned and filled with the streets of lazy light particles forgetting to blink, to shake out the webs. They're beginning to dawn, and the pieces of you are drawn to the web of loving desire. Bringing you home to the one spinning light weaver sewing you whole, and the light shines fantastic, and the day is elastic, and the love threads are humming at the sight of us becoming one nation under light, of light, without fragmentation we are a light fragment-nation sew us up.

LIGHT INCUBATION • Sleep on this and increase your light. Your giving has met with the good of invite. Metabolic retreat to the land of the wed allows an extension of the infinite plan. The heart called a man and a lifting span. The rainbow within our every breath. The journey to heaven in our every impress, to the lightest entrance, the mining belief of the eggs of enchantment living in me. Light incubation. • Today I am incubating the light which I have and I am filling up with more love, and I am enjoying the lamp of warming cradle which hangs over my bed and the heavens are my ceilings and the sun is my lamp and the wisps and rays and winds of life keep my mobile's dance, and I am in the entrance of a loving burst on through – through to other living – firmly into you and your loving light incubation of the knowing which we share. Let's ride the waves together – filled with wonder, awe and care – and light.

LIGHT IN-FORMATION • I'm on-line and you can be the chatting web of internal bliss. The screen that we're searching is only this ecstatic trend for going in and mining more of the densest one. The peasant's dread has met relief and the heart of you has melted grief and the molds of me have filled with light at the sight of heaven's knowing flight to the land of all intrigue with the light in-formation migrating in me. South to north. A gentle-man's tree. The branch of the service. Light in-formation. • Today you can feel the sound of the searing re-entry of penetrating waterspouts nearing a tinkling spring of feminine rapport and the penetration complete there is lulling abiding respite hear on the banks of resounding forgiving. For the lightest touch, the lightest penetration, the kindest punch is the kiss of for-giving shining eternal in the reflection of your own eyes mirrored soft upon the waters of a grandfather's sternest answer – yes, you can – and you will. Welcome home to the fullest access to the profile of eternal light in-formation.

LIGHT ECSTATIC • Ecstatic love hath man and this, a heart of plenty filled with kisses of joy and planting of truth. The political care given to spoofs, has left me hungry for a wider view of the love living, walking dynamically in you. Welcome home to the love, you own and the light ecstatic. • This light's ecstatic bursting kind within my breast and peachy colored giving opens years of self neglect and deep within a pit is pulled from flesh too soft to speak and kindest embrace has occurred. The healing is complete. You've flown the test, you're past exam. Well-come to the burst of a life now spent in buying back the seasons that you've cursed. Embrace the peace, know the retreat of the haggard given full release – the pension's paid, the pardon's passed. Welcome home to the light ecstatic.

LIGHT GALACTIC • Zipping lines of whistling soar and crackling nets of giving glow with the finest catch, the living form of a divinity called man and an energy sword clipping the threads of your living as less, welcome to the point of divine express. We acknowledge you and your light galactic, eternally, light. • I remember just today that on this rock I came to play

and play I will and happy sing to the tinkling trill of a bubbling spring. The fount is full and bursting forth with words of kindest, dear import. We are the chosen, you and I. Please find your truth and let it fly home to lodge in the heart of this place – grandfather's welcome is your healing embrace. Mountain by mountain you are climbing in truth to the head of the spring galactic and full. A light galactic.

LIGHT IN UNITY • There's light in you and plenty in me and we are set free by our unity's bliss, shining in you and living in this vertical view, the tympanic proof, the listening space of a whispering race shouting yes! To the light in unity. • Unified are you and I. Light to the touch and well-come to sigh at the sight of a sunbeam bouncing off rock and the eye of a laurel beginning to talk of the end of our blinking doe-eyed and scared. The rabbit of timid is standing to share his open appraisal of our spirit's event. At present we are forgetting to pay up our rent of grateful acknowledge for the chance to choose life's college on this ball we call the earth. So join me in praying for high spirit's engraving to remind us of our work. Upon this rock build unity in light totality.

LIGHT TOTALITY • Totally light and tented to see the camping example of a spelling relief. The letters said that an a and a b sprinkled with light equate to a sea of infinite view reflecting in me and your wide-eyed grasp of the light in me. A light totality. • Light totality, this is our reality. Real to this knowing reminder is the notion ever kinder that I am light's reality and in my embracing totality a new liquid is forming – they call it global warming. It's melting all our chilling symbolic walled-in willing and the light is sewn ecstatic into the quilt of love romantic. My dear, embrace the feeling we are sleeping on the ceiling of love's tree of total reminder that nothing could be kinder – goodbye blinders. Clearly seen. Light's reality in totality.

LIGHT SENSE-ABILITY • Senses tell that 5 to 1 is the current line and the place of the sun in her loving sweep of the other side, the heliocentric wonder of the chambered shell of a nautilus spiral framing the space of architecture's greatest station, the heart of all art-full intrigue. The light sense-ability I breed. Light to the 5th and beyond. Dimensions abound within the town called light sense-ability. Commonly found at every corner stand, the map to a-man. Lightly sensitive to his own ability. Delve on in to your light sense-ability. • I have a new sense-ability. I'm 5 cranked to tranquility. Senses heightened gives the clue that you are me and I am you and in embrace the one's are 2, and 2's are one beneath the sum of all fresh born brand new. Freshly wakened I am shaken to balance my spin, to anchor within, the earth and the sun that I am and soft in the middle a new love is kindled. Romantic and well-come again. I am embracing the loving we're staking on our lightest sense-abilities. Touch this.

LIGHT IN-FIDELITY • Agile moments equate to peace when I'm living in a life of perfect relief at the light in-fidelity shining in me. Stereos speak of the chanting news. The light and me in perfect sync. The light in-fidelity. • Touch my heart, embrace what's mine with your willing surrender to what's yours. Claiming your stuff brings you in touch with the perspective that there's a new directive playing finality to the errant reality that infidelity was chill. Chilly the season reflected on reasoning that led to further cracking. The cracking's over. The opening is back to a wave of absolute in-fidelity waxing poetic like a siren lulling homeward one angelic being in light fidelity.

LIGHT IN-STABILITY • Light is stable in her answering return to the land of the plenty and the heart of the one. One love met in the truth that God's love is gentle and light here is proof of the heart of this planet. Light in-stability in me. An earthquake proof zone. The heart of me in my light in-stability. Light. • There's a light in stable moving and relative to this is the light of harmony kissing pungent upon your waving lips. I smell your essence welling in looking return of bliss and in your for-giving swelling the tenderest of kissing reminders that stability's return is kinder than stumbling ever blinder in forgetting drunken stench. So waft me with your breathe of life's eloquent rhyming tune and dance me light to the front of your door. Right here inside the moon of your stable emotions.

LIGHT IN ATTRACTION • Attraction's sent to draw the man to the scent of a flower and the heart of this land. Rendered in renoirian grace, the dancing pastels of a chalky face rinsed in the stream of the light ametrine and filled with the smell of a rose petals trail leading to see the light in attraction. • The wattage I carry, is the what's this I'm wearing for like attracts to like. In love and light the theory works – in theory, light attracts the pole of another at the farthest end of the same ex-spectrum. Odds are that a circle's drawn from poles so far apart and hear we stand in the center of a span ringing around our hearts. Connect the dots. We love a lot. Increase your watts for you are light in attraction. I am attracted to your action. Standing still.

LIGHT IN ACTION • Light is active in her living challenge to equate the news with a living proof. The axiom of bliss is simply this. Live. Breathe. Believe. Light in action. • Bring light to your actions. Draw only best. Half-hearted lies equals forever forgetting to honor the light of a truth setting free. What a delight you are now to me. And so tiny soldier, wear well the proof of a walking reminder that we are the soup. The mixture of light and of moon and of stars and the marching on moonbeams and the pyramids on mars. A gentle reminder of living example is the kindest regard to the rest of this apple. Welcome to eden. Eve is home.

LIGHT EXTRACTION • Pull the fangs of your knotty dread and rasta you up to the happy tread. The dancing feet and the happy mouth singing the joy of a juicy blend. The pleasure's of fruit and the gentle extraction of the pulp from the seed and the seed from the strain, growing in me by adamic wonder. The

influx of lines other than twelve strand. We are calling it my duty to remind you that woven in stars is the gentle reminder of just who you are. I hereby command you to listen full sooth, to fill up with light beams and spit out the tooth which rotten with soul's dirt has broken it's root. You are free. Speak to me only the words of lightest extraction. Mercury free. Full-proof. • Let the light extraction reach peregrine blue interest in the white electric strand of you. Let love rule inside this confection – the light extraction.

LIGHT IN-FILTRATION • Filter me and find the rhyme to lean in the window and chat some time and some times I'm holy and often I'm tripped to render the central intoxicating bliss of a message dynamic and a loving encoded in keys of surrender and a loving devoted to searching inside, igniting the light and directing my face to the holy grace, the living grail of the light in-filtration in me. By divine installation. Light. • Lights infiltrating this ball we call ours and hours of reminder have bounced down from mars and balls of intrigue have come in on line, what will we do with our living this time. Now is the dawn and the light's infiltration. Don now the crown of your graduation coronation. For you, I am writing and be-coming this sage, this lover of light seen dancing on pages of leaves waving free attached to the face of your articulate choice to incarnate in this space. Waxing literate in light in-filtration.

LIGHT ARTICULATE • Light's articulate in her living spree bursting in bubbles of painting intrigue and color-full hues of living extent. The wealth called a palate and the sense to extend my heart to the free wealth of example speaking in me. Know the tree of the light articulate. • The light is articulate to-night she has warmed to the face called her own and out of the moonbeams she's weaving a chant called her name. Today while you're dreaming embrace this event. The night's work is over. The daylight we've spent on words of denial, get over the hump. The art of truest survival is to live within your heart. Standing in mine, I am writing these lines metatronic. I am on it the line infinite, the light articulate. I love you. Look it up.

LIGHT MAGNIFICENT • The tree of life has met in me. There's only one and we all can see the sum of the many devoted to one life eternal and the living sum of heaven reigning down in shining example of the light magnificent. • Magnificent you are and returning your star of infinite arrival, good bye to mere survival, hello to sweet surrender to the light pulsing magnificent in the particles that you are. One light. Magnificent and free.

LIGHT INTENSIVE • The test of the light is the sight of a ray of color so dazzling bright that your insight says God and you are out. Sight blinks on with understanding intensity at the return of your capacity to sing like a swan sung to long in one way home – newly singing at the sight of the light, so extensive, whole and lucid green upon the sheen of the yellowish tint of the tin of your roof. Light intensive. The course is on. Please be light in sensitive. • Light is intensive in our inquiry for the source of the one true, lakota strain. Love is intense in light. The light's intensive.

LIGHT DIMENSIONS

The One, the Eight, the living Thirteen, a bakers dozen of the truth as seen in the crowning view of the LIGHT Pyramid shining in you and waiting to live, by your grace, in the Swan like place called your delicate face rung round with rings of rosey green, aquamarine and peregrine wings, periwinkle blue clear to the fluffy heart of you. The LIGHT'S aquamarine and compassionate and loving in its surrender to your fluffy interior, light and pink and crystalline green – with love's light. Welcome the LIGHT ROYALE.

LIGHT ROYALE • The light is regal and royal to view at the brink of the season called autumn in you. Take a new rest at the infinite view of light geographic and remembering to view the light metatronic resonant and view in the twinkling smile of the glacial truth that ice packed living is no longer due. Melt your witless witnessing and be the living truth, the forever shining in you is the arc I call the proof. I honor your inclusion of your nose in other's matters. Care as much about your life and know the light royale. • Welcome to the light royale and the feeling fit of a loving name, your light refrain, the light royale.

LIGHT INFINITE • Light infinite through and through with the resonant sound of the lasting view, looping through all-directional, ever intentional, definitely experiential, run your loops, investigate the truth, light is best – no test, enjoy your rest standing still through out the seasons, four to view, directions shifting, all-ways four, never more and yet forever. That's infinite. Light by light and four looks too. Light infinite. • Light's infinity is my divinity and I am the truth that God reclines in laughing lines of form met matter in spirit's chatter and the agreeing plunge into the heart of humanity and the light is on. The light infinite.

LIGHT ELEGANT • Lightly elegant and equally eloquent, I'm surrounded by mountains and the elements of remembering the light that I am in my spanning inquiry into the sure-footed scramble, summit bound and the sound at the top. My name, dripping light and gold paved streets floating through the clouds of honest remember, the war is over, and I'm in surrender to the light elegant, shining in me, definitively. Light. • Light is elegant as I bend to address the blessed assurance that life is best when dressed in the sparkle of a living light dress. The light elegant.

LIGHT ROYAL-TY • You are the king and queen and the mint. The one creating honey for lips dripping honest replies and skies full to ceiling with the world's widest eyes, looking inside and out, with gentle come-passion and absolute action, standing still with dignity. The light royal-ty. • Royal blinks of blends and trees assign the dance of royal-ty to the hip of a tower and a column of light and the truth of a matter and the heart of a wife split wide to believe in a triple assign, the heart and the head and the life of a bee flying free in shiny delivery, the light royal-ty.

LIGHT SUPPLY • Supply me with wonder and awe and the thunder of laying down my cross and my weapon and my loss at the edge of infinity and the lightest shoulders are welcome to the flight winged by the light, an infinite supply of lofty heights, on the inside and still counting for everything, a light supply. • Supply the pace of a pleasant face to the world you own and the heart you are and within the art of a naked dream lies a version of the healing stream, your silent place of tranquil bliss and the breezes of deliverance, to the light, your own. A lifetime approach to the explosion of myth and the ozone's date with the acceptance of treasured rays of golden hue. The light supply.

LIGHT PRIDE • Superior lift and a genuine gift, the bridge to the light that I am, is the delicate surrender to my living so tender and well within the breast of my tell-tale rest in the arms of the light. Proud to delight in the swelling light of the best. Eagle's sight. Light. Proud. • Proud to be a portion of the portal labeled, enter love and love I've met in soft report to the spark of a handle and a handle called pour. In the lift of this breath I find a release to the art of living in time to the beat I call me. We are the expanse of the light pride.

LIGHT RANGE • Light brings our range close to the sides, ours, where two worlds meet and within the collision, lives a greater entity the combination of the light that sees both sides now life to moments, to the living taste, of an elegant space, wide open to the center, light range. • Ranges of love embellish the truth that I am amazed at the love in you, an exceptional range, a better graze, a longer reach, the light range.

LIGHT KEYS • Light holds the key to the lock that's me. Let the ship through, cruising free from code to code and road to rode, the light keys are spelled in the words love and light. Sailing the cape tonight. Resounding the horn. Welcome to the metatronic life, the cruising sight, wave to wave, light. Sound the bridge, live the arc. Here's a spark. You. Light, in the keys just west of me and east of you. Light. • Light the entry to the keys that resonate love inside of me. I know your name and the 64 ways that spell relief in a rolling phrase and a keyboard set with love to give and light to lift. I am the sign, the symbol and the key to all that lives and loves and breaths. I will remain at the tree of the light keys.

LIGHT REGION • Loosen your hold on things as you've held them and join the flow of living life well then – for light's in this region, this common, this wealth, this piece of earth, the part you call self, middle around, consider it found. Your light hearted faith in this light region. Well founded. Light. • Light region reigns inside of me and splashes in the plane of existing conceit and I know you are kind to be the light map reflecting back to me. A light region.

LIGHT GRADIENT • Light's a gradient from blue to you. Find the key and the spectrum too. Lift the notion, that love's a potion. Love is light and earth's greatest delight. The embrace of the face, your own living well with life to tell the beauty to about the heavenly paradise called you. Light by light and shade to shade. Know your light gradient. Light, in stages and expectant hues. Light. • A light gradient melts in electric glare and I swing soft on a giving chair that pulses mer kah bic inside of me and as I spin I count to three. Mind. Body. Spirit. Divinity. Light and love. 85. 95. 100. A light of purest love. The one I am. A beam of expedient adjust to the light gradient. Light.

LIGHT RADIANT • I'm a light emission and the light's expression of the fullest decision that I'm radiantly equipped for – the return to the full wattage allotted this life. The allocation that's sweeping the nation on the wings of a dove, white with anticipation and clear to the center of a spirit of a light most holy. Wholly known and radiantly living my expectant giving and receiving swell of the light radiant clear to the middle, I'm free to see the light radiant – eternally – light. • The light is radiant in her softened stare straight to my heart and everywhere, all one light, tonight and eternally. The light radiant.

LIGHT DESIRE • It is my light desire to place your hand in mine and walk in constant free, to the love in the center of me and in tune, you're humming the news that you've found the well-spring in you. Light desire's in my waking return to the light I am. Holy and divine. Fire's delight. Light desire. • Good-bye death and silly constructs built to confuse and confound our trust of eternity seen and bliss so desired and the proof that denial just makes us liars. The light is on. Desire has come to light the way to your light destiny. I come to the place of all receiving. Light desire.

LIGHT ORDINATION • I have received a light ordination. God spirit the earth's invitation all point to me as the miracle led by a tiny hummingbird skirting ahead to join my taste for the highest elevation, the kindest revelation, the taste of my light ordination, ambrosial and rich with honey's milky dew, feeding my flowery heart with a heavenly view. Exaltive and true. Light ordination. • Light ordained a kinder trip to the heart of this land and the love of this lip I call my seat to forever and I turn to extend a 90 degree hand to myself stepping up to establish a trust, a perfect seal, an eternal light residing in the center of me by light ordination.

LIGHT MEADOW • The meadows mellow with peaceful clouds of welcome smiles and dancing round the spiraling wave, the twinkling catch, the dolphin in you knows the clue, open the chains dna free range. What a change and organic too. Good for

you. You're genetically out to pasture and feeling better in the light meadow. Light inside the amber waves, cappery too. Light meadow. • Light meadows flirt with our destiny and show us the place of all I can see and all we can spell is the name we know best and to the rest we give a 7th wave and on the 8th day we ascend to the land of the light meadow.

LIGHT MELLOW • I'm lightly mellow and here's the fellow, the mother's ship, the infinite trip to the land less yellow, lighter green with specks of opal and ametrine melting through to expose the vein of lavender and pink and everything lifting home on a light bridge built in my name. Light mellow. • Stepping up to paint around the bliss of feeling knowing ground exists beneath our feet and our toes can tell cause they're complete with passioned knowing that love is showing her earthly meet and met we stand content and grand in the electric span of the light mellow.

LIGHT PLANTATION • Welcome to the inner planet. The plantation which honors this nation with glamorous living, labor free, and entirely lead by the pulsating thread called my heart's light energy. No more master, slave, guru, or beast. We are free to feather our beds with cottony love. Organically grown. Our own hearts, light to the edge of our light plantation. • Light plants soft upon the land and a heart is held in fondest hands and gifts are mailed to blend the sign, that a course is run and its harvest time. Know the inclination to rest at the light plantation.

LIGHT CORONATION • Knowing my district, my night and my territory, I'm coronated by life and the light, that's me, and you are my other, my lover and friend, that part of the spectrum, ultra-violet to a thin definition resonant to the view, shining through, light surround, your crown, glory be, thorn-free and gentle to the skin the light coronation within. Light. • Light the torch and take a stand at the hand of heart and the heart of hand and let me know that this is it, the heart of God and the love's attend at this my light coronation.

LIGHT ESTATE • Succulent estate of elegant entreaty supple to the middle with your gateless breathing haste, running home to the light and plantation of love trees. Mother earth and me eternally growing light on our light estate this planet, earth's, light estate. • A light estate exists in me and I live here beneath the tree of eternal life and knowing well the entrance to heaven is certainly disguised in a living hell or a heaven, you choose, we decide. As for me, a light estate.

LIGHT BLUE HERON • light's blue heron is the sky and the wealth of the firmament living inside my permanent light bridge. The eternal notice has been set up and established for me. This day, and eternity's free to watch my dance, infinity to infinity, regal to the tips of my lifting wings, singing my catch, my home to the light blue heron. I am. Light. • Light blue melts in syrupy trend and I see the flight of an eagle again, a regal friend has met the land with a watery trend and a lifting head, dripping wet in light metabolic. The metatronic loop's complete. Meet the light blue heron.

LIGHT HERON • I saw a heron sit upon a stick, waiting for 3 logs to move just a bit for in their moving splendor, a splinter of the truth, will find it's way to render the knowing tale of proof that patient appraisal and silent assail the 'bacon' carries in and the shimmering catch at the end of the hook, that ancient secret's me. Well done mighty heron, herald of the sun. Light heron. • Light's inherent in my whispering trip to the whistle called lifting and the winging attire that I wear so well. The light of this heart and the love of an eagle meeting emotion. A light heron.

LIGHT GUIDE • Guide my light to the lifting sight, the ancient proof that seeing has it's time and hear me sing with lilting refrain the ebullient joy-full line. Line to the middle with green rekindle. Know the health of intimate wealth, the beauty of the beast is gone. No more the intrigue with the devious seed. I am planted well and hitching my ride to the light side. Right up the center and spread to the seasons of the universe's wedge. Light guide. • Light guides me home every time and I know now, how and why. A light guide.

LIGHT MOTHER • Good morning mother. Here's the gift, the present I call mine. It's my light practice and my names the game leading to love's jackpot. Know the space of this wondrous earth. Know your mother. Discover lewis to clark and all the way through the big sky which lives inside you. Good morning, mother. Sister, speaking. Loves meandering river leads me home to you. Light mother. • Light, my mother is the other aspect of the concept seen on the other end of the spotlight's beam and we are the material, the density met which allows color in our transforming effect. The deduction's land. The earth's a friend and I am said to live, as well, at the heart of the dream and the breast of the mother awakening to breathe and feed the blessed spirit. Light mother.

LIGHT FATHER • Father, fill me with forgiving nature and empty me of the blaming tree. Divinity is mine and me. Now comes the light, my earthly affinity for all that is well and wholesome and fulfilling with the glittering truth. Light to the farthest reaches and swelling to a crescendo most complete. I am life and light harmonious in the melting spot of me. Light father. Divinely. Light. • Light, my father, with the infinite power to know the hour of my greatest give and to bow in electric designs of living in kind, like attention to the heart that I mentioned. All is well, reflect the spell of the living trend to step right in, clear up to me. I receive in my giving allowance of divine penetration. Light father.

LIGHT GUI-DANCE • A *manatee swam past me today and I touched her side and she mirrored my need to remember and believe who I am and a celestial wonder occurred as magic and miracle met at the spring of the sisters and I knew my wifely duties as the earth's bride was to lead on, filled with the glowing of a terrestrial, sometimes aquatic, always light, guide. Light gui-dance. • Guide me home to see the tree that the heart of love has traced in me. Light to light. A filling sight. A light gui-dance.

*manatee – A mammalian beauty, of ancient days, swimming homeward, to the eternal spiral, a mermaid of light, teaching me now how to read the map I AM.

LIGHT MONEY • Earning a living at the love I do well, in the company of the earth and the trees. I believe in the well being of light money drifting in from my western creative shore for I am trusting my instinctive for feathering my nest with the coins I love best. The golden ones which live in my chest and rain upon my needs. Know the truth of success-full be-ing. Light money. • Light money melts in pockets changed to tinkle plenty and penetrate proof of lasting exist of inner-g's and the loving ability to penetrate green ignition. Know the riches of light money.

LIGHT CONSTRUCTED • Light's constructed of a double sky, a twisting loop which comes in pairs and creates the element of double infinity standing, swirling, and running in me. Here's the loop, both front and back. Know your craft. Cast your lines in perfect time and the fly you'll fish with swirling catch will be your own lifting net. Know your cast, see your lips, lift the net, forget your nots and tip to stern the spilling truth is the light called you. • Light's constructed of loving squares and squares designed to stack somehow and a heart has sung a lighter tune and built a temple that we'll call you. You are the kind assign of a fountain's dream to build a building which fords a stream of gone denial, welcome the stability of the light constructed.

LIGHT TREE • My light is a tree with four metatronic leaves and a wealth of seasons four to the scan and along the seam of her trinity increase is the revealing truth of her circling wisdom. To front and to back and all the electronic revolutions through the cycles of living season-ate through my giving nature. Circling free within the plumbing of our emerald mother's humming, soaring, raising of her timbre, pitch to pitch, and branch-to-branch, and opal to the core. I am the matrix metatronic, know my circuits. Light. Light tree. • Light trees live inside of us at the gate of hello and the notion of when the light has dawned inside a-man. Leonardo saw it, divinity too, the kabbalah points, and we agree that the light love lives inside of me. A light tree.

LIGHT BREEZE • Thunder is sounded. Lightning speaks. Lay aside your swords and lifting the sheets of pine-scented saplings and lofty reviews filling the big sky with the heraldic news. Love lives in this house. In my house the earth. Drop all your past tense. Here comes new birth. Raise high the happy, the welcome humor of cascading streams and lily pond dreams. Caressed by the blessings of a heavenly light breeze. God bless you and the mother too. Light breeze. • A light breeze burst inside of me and bubbled singing, healing treats of lofty praise, and often given, eternal peace and happiness. I am free to be a light breeze upon the face of the earth, a breathing tribute to the lightest test woman God hath breathed, a light breeze.

LIGHT BANK • Let us embark to the bank of the river called light and know that our journey is our flowing return to the light continental and the love oriental in copper and jadeite veins of loving opalescent filling our travertine longings with prismatic views of the caldera called you, you volcanic swirl, bursting bonfires to shimmer and glow with the light luminescent and rich as the coal simmering in heat of often I lingered and most times pulled rank. Now I'm the leader of this lofty embankment bursting through faithful and new and light ametrine with a sparkling sheen all the way to the light bank. You. Light. Bank on it. Light. • I bank at the light of a sunny day and the miracle called love, and the milky way, and I call a stream of giving trace to finish this dream and my panes erase to reveal a beam of absolute gleam, directly between the eyes of this space called one love, yours and mine, an infinite supply and a passbook called light, one way in, know the friend, a light bank.

LIGHT MIRROR • Reflections of pink and resonant hues of ginger jar welcome and ginkgo review. The rhyme in the ancient is the spiraling web which releases the metal of doubt in your head. See your heart in the light mirror, me. We are the earth and the light release of a dam's worth of up-tight. Find the line, shoot the rapids of a light mirrored river, shining heart full with your face and mine. Know the earth. Hug her girth. The light mirror. • A light mirror reached in exact impact of the lava tubed delivery on a disk born red in sensitive pleiadian sisterhood. The new clan. Light mirrored.

LIGHT TRAILER • Trail rides here to the nearest bluff, now over the edge and feel the spill of a tumbling stream, a travertine leaning has wept me to see the gentle infusion of the world's softest glee. Giggling gently inside the light trailer. That's me in to infinity. There's gold in there. Light trailer. • A light trailer awaits a soft delivery to the land I call earth and the home I call free. Examine me and my shooting tail, trailing heaven-wide and comet deep to the tree and the rock and the hill and the arc called bliss lives in a healing kiss, universe wide, a light trailer.

LIGHT MIRAGE • Light sparkles in a shiny sheen of juicy oasic living intrigue and special to you and to my occulation is the sound of the heavens ringing with fire, specific and electric, our intricate body is simply divine and swollen with loving acceptance of the kingdom most eclectic. The divine regime hands up the queen of the light revue, the miracle's home and it's earth to you in crystalline view. Light mirage. • A deja vu, a twinkling spree to the well of light and the love in me, we are free to become the light oasis just one desert past, the light mirage.

LIGHT GARAGE • Paint a tree on the wall of your house and pull in your car and ask if your spouse will dab on some leaves at the eves of your spout automatic and your gutterless chance to glance across the middle and know the square dance. The light metatronic is calling the score, pull in for a drink at the light garage door. Water of life. The christ-ings wife. The light's are on. We're all home to the light metatronic and the life more sonic. Boom. We're strong and light and filled with the star energetic, our spiraling heart driving us home to park in the shelter of the light garage. • Light parks, hear, and know one else. Love has brought her light drawn car and a chariot of peace is flowing down in doving wings and cooing sounds. The love exists in this light garage.

LIGHT AQUATIC • sound the heavens, let the rivers pour straight from the mouth of our guardian's shores and welcome the sight of the intimate life, my tears are saline and the oceans of love drip down my face to join my heart in her melting surrender of return to the arc opalescent from heaven to you and you then to me, the heavenly beads, seraphic and rich, a patchwork of light without any stitch. Naked to the sound of my splashing heart's return to the light aquatic. • Splash a while at the rainbowed style of a spilling spring and a heart that rings in hallelujah attend to the love that lives within the floating spiral of the light aquatic.

164. LIGHT EROTIC • Where we're you, when there were just two? Was one of them me and one of them you? Or were they both just one? Realizing our split is at the heart of us. For the love most exotic and the light erotic is the beautiful meeting of the sky in you with the earth there too, and lo there's the rainbow and the arc between. The glory of you and your light erotic knowing that the love you're showing is your self worth flowing. Coming home to the light erotic. Rather biotic. Light erotic. • Erotic life has met the lift of a healing trick called loving your life and wed the mirth of this mother's earth with the healing thread of a lighter tread to the tripping flight to the light erotic.

LIGHT BIOTIC • Lightly bi-annual I'm 6 months slim of the middling feeling that I'm her and I'm him and I'm exotic in my biotic return to the eden more gardenic and the life more one growing organic light – being me. Know more three and count it one. One light biotic under the sum. Solar swell, time will tell, learn the truth. The light biotic. • Light's biotic and I still care about the truth that there's love in there and when I find a faster friend, I look inside and begin again, to trust the ecology of the light biotic.

LIGHT PROTONIC • Light's biotic, erotic, protonic and on and I'm an electric dynamic called one arcing reminder that the bi-polar is done. Keep your decisions in my heart there's one love, yes, and one heart too and one light proton grand to our view. The light's meta-electron is infinitely on and eternal too. The light protonic. • Light's protonic and I am refined by the orbital pivot to this thinking line and my body, the mind, at the solar plexus tip is ignited eternally and internally I trip to see the intricate blur of a particle waving and a lighten-ing occur. I have defined a higher recline at the orbital bliss of the light protonic.

LIGHT EXOTIC • Light my exotic squiggly life with the passion of knowing my infinite light. Write me a sonnet, a solar divert swelling with flares all pointing at earth's magenta, magnetic view of the auroric field around you. Taking the northern view and the southern too, there's a light borealic and it's exotically me. See the truth. The light exotic in you. Your true voice. The light exotic. • Light's exotic and I am compelled to tell you the truth that I'm living well and in my transcendence, new state is met, a field of believe that's far deeper yet, and I can conceive of the life that I need beneath the beam of the light exotic.

LIGHT OCEAN • There's a light ocean running straight through the center of me, filled with dolphins and whales and manatees and traveled by turtles of magnificent girth. Know all the seasons and the reasons for each and in peace-full slumber you'd see the relief. Light blue swelling, here the telling, beside the geyser* ocean blue with exceptional belief in the waves return. The light ocean. • Light is an ocean and I am the gift of living in love and passionate slips to the waves of the light field and the resonant hue of desire building magnetism all around you. I am drawn to the light we are and the twinkling flight of a born again star, sparkling far across the light ocean.

*geyser – Earth's geo-thermal enthusiasm.

LIGHT GULF. • I've followed my mother to the light on the shore of the lake without edges and the receiving friend called contentment and ready to live in the lane of all love and all light and all giving revival of the river mississippi dripping into the lightest bowl, the light gulf, the miraculous span, the life inventive and the light's creative swirl home to the crystal bowl, the quartzite sand of the sparkling gulf, I am. • Light spans gulf-ed inside of me and a gulf of see becomes believe and a light shines softly pink and green and a gulf is bridged and a love is seen in expectant hues of the light lens shining inside of you, convex or concave, the receiving's the same, in the giving name, your own, mine too. Light gulf.

LIGHT PATH • Light's path home is the whistling wind, the singing refrain, the joyous embrace of the dancing place I call intra-cellular matrix and bridging the gulf are the synapses of light adjustment and the mitochondria of the living earth. Ancient blue-green messengers guard the pearly gates of the mysteries hidden in you and the opening called the way, the truth, the path, the view – all inside of you. Welcome home sister of the bone. Marrow's story now unfolds. Welcome to the light path. Goodbye soul. I am home by the light path. • Light's path leads to higher degrees of greater light and less density and I know I am pleased to see the light path stretched inside of me. Know

the mother. Receive the father. See the light of the connecting arc and the covenant we are in a rainbowed space, I elect the light path.

LIGHT LAND • Light's in this land, by particular design. Know the embrace of living this time in timeless completion of the arc you are and your infinite wonder at the sign of a star shining in on a wavelength light on expanse. I'll share this dance across the light land. On the inside, light and outside too. All 3 the same, ask the middle you. Now divinely, lightly bring in the love, unpositional, that's transitional, that's a light land. • Light lands come to mother me and all I say is what a day and thank you's when I stand to see the light land lying under me. She discovered us. Light land.

LIGHT ISLAND • Light's an island, an ecological trick called a mountain, a desert, all the same, under the skin. So take the advice of a human link, this is the import of which we speak. Know man is one. All you need is a bridge between and the earth has land upon which to sink our soles and toes and feet. See it well, from both sides now, and in the channel, the middle span, the light island, man. A human bridge. Light island. • Note this island has a name and note the leafy green refrain of a magenta sky and a telling proof that love grows big inside of you, a little land, an expanse of living well, on this light island.

LIGHT, SEE • It's light here at the lake of heaven and I'm a swan in the middle paddling concentric and eccentric circles of infinite design scanning my loops forward and aft and journeying a mile or so deep to see the fire river which runs in my veins and opting for loft, I am light as a feather and past the scales of maat* to the spirit rich eternal and infinitely appreciative of the beauty in me. A grace-full light swan. Hear and now it's light – see. • Light see all that I can be and I see light inside of me swimming in a light see.

*maat – Egyptian once. Eternally free to appreciate the infinite balance in you

LIGHT SPECTRUM • It's light, you sea, you wealth of renew, you sparkling canyon with a pearly review and I am your maker, your love, and your friend and I live electronic in the cells deep within. Know your light. Find the sight, sparkling blue, and magenta with green calcite edges of trickling fluorentine. Know the expression the loving so deep the light called the spectrum has a spirit complete with running water and living showers stay here an hour, or an infinity, to the power of one. One love. One light. One light spectrum. • Light's a spectrum of converse and I'm a spark that's spoken words of I've become directly due to the light spectrum in you, LIGHT.

LIGHT GLASS • light sparkles soft in welcoming ripples of hot blown forever and this is the trickle of travertine building eclipsing my view of the sight I call me and I'm free to be the shiniest piece, the iridescent feast the light in the window and soft through your leaves. That's me peering through a light glass. • Light glass sparkles in my eye and I am all one and asking why we two must part inside of one. The master blower has spoken to the ball of glass inside the earth, molten sparks of living birth, know the land of the oven exposed inside of us and how we flow like light glass.

LIGHT GRASS • Grass is greener on the inside, where I graze upon infinity's variety and standard's never poor. It's always rich hear on the light's shore. Listen and know the composition most divine. The wind in the grass singing toning in ancient longing. Welcome home, little spirit. Welcome home. Your light is on and the ranch double 8 is the infinite plan, the place where the plexus solar hands over the reigns to the heartland, the grass emerald green. Light grass. • Light equates with spoken glass and twinkling blades of dew-sparked grass and a heart that sends temptation down to spin around inside the town of ill-reputed. A spirit looted still contains a spark of love and a matching flame. Know the earth of this your birth and the anchoring trend which resides within the singing light grass.

LIGHT CRYSTAL • Life crystalline is the light shining clean and refracting the truth that the beauty of wings strums my heart strings with peace-full imbue of lofty arrival, flying in to this living with the intimate giving truth. Matrix to medium to infinite you. Crystal skulled, organed, and toothed. We, the children of light, know the love crystalline and a ruby of sapphire blue shines through the night and into the mine of this man with a gentle hand, shining me clean with the breath of the essence supreme. Light essence. Light crystal. Light. • Light's a crystal floating in with a song to sing and a heart to win, by electric vote and a perfect note, my eternal name carved at last upon the same, light crystal.

LIGHT ICE • Opal ice is light and nice and lovely are the seams, the earthly veins apophylite beams and blue tourmaline dreams, igniting recognition and loving ambition. It's true. I remember. I surrender to the light I am and the remembrance of my living gemstone span. Earth to me, infinitely with the love immortal flooding portals with the light ice we know. Light. Diamond to pearl to forever. Light ice. • Light is icy in a rimming stare at the star in my eyes and the laugh in my glare and I am inclined to feel the reprieve of the light ice melting inside of me. Light ice.

LIGHT SLICE • Carve me a slice of the pie you call agate and make mine montana and ellensburg blue shining straight through to the st. Louis in you. Connecting the dots of this matron called earth. This womanly planet delivers my birth to the point of surrender and light to a minute I'm layered like chevrons* and tangy fruit salad delved into by you with a pink marbled calcite called watermelon blue. Emerald to the core and each shiny grain. I'm home on the range and welcome again to the light slice. *Montana. High deserts. Sweet deserts. The light slice. •

Where were you when the slice was cut? And how long will you live the flirt of disaster avoided and earth matters annoying instead of conjoining with the heart of this land. I am content to pitch my tent at the rhododendron dream of a mountain stream and to lay my head at this earth I tread in great-full blaze of the loving you. A grander father and receptive mother, the heart of other becoming one forgiven son, one light slice.

*Chevrons – A layered bead comprising always One.
*Montana – mountains in the language of our brother, Spanish.

LIGHT'S MARK • Light's made a mark in my heart and I'm simply blissfull to this loving heart of mine. I'm welcome to begin the hearts eye walk aloft to the piece and the part that's peace-full beyond my grandest fine edged imagination called bliss, above, above and beyond I've met my mark and I'm home to the spark and the light and the wavelength I am. Light mark. • Make your mark at the end of a spark and a middle gone soft to register the feeling of the light coming in, with love I blend to see the light mark.

LIGHT FOUNTAIN • Trevi trickles with travertine blue agates melting sweet with the taste of maple seeds winged with touches of coppery gold painted red and crimson green with the periwinkle news of the fountain in you. A light fountain. Me. Light. • Light's a fountain that equates to notions of mountains and love spent in lakes born to reflect and waterfalls giving off the added benefit of a lifting rite, a healing ritual, the writing of love in a healing epistle. Light fountain.

LIGHT YOUTH • Youthfull delight at the sight of your welcome flight to the central reservoir, the fountain within the rosey cheeks of your gentle children, the universal tongue, the mother's embrace, the spilling taste of light. Youth spent on pennies coppery red and blue with age of mental decline, the heart ever young makes the flight the return to light and there standing full in the heart of your eternal light. Your eternal youth. Light. • Youthfully light and eloquent to boot, I see the love inside of you and the template of peace and the heart that's released to believe in the eternal fountain with an external kiss, the ocean of love and the ecstasy of bliss. Light youth.

LIGHT APPLAUSE • Allow me sister to give you a hand. Know this sister, the heart of a human. Chamber to chamber and all the way through. Light to the middle, I applaud you. We are one. Shining sun. Love eternal. Know the kernel and the proof of the pearl. Layer by layer. Light. Light applause. Welcome to the planet. The mother's ship. All aboard. The light is on – in you. You are my love and my light companion. Raise your curtain. Know it's certain. Light. Goodnight sweet planet to light applause. We are the cause and the way. Here's the truth. The light in you a rave review. The latest news. Light. Welcome up to light applause. You are on. Light. • I am the recipient of light applause every time I realize my cause is light. Day and night – to light applause.

LIGHT VISIONARY • Light's a visionary step, a stride to the middle and the ride to the top of the future-land exam and the past loop scan, all at once, know the light, rightly centered, divinely in you and infinity too. All we are and will ever be. Light visionary. It's necessary. Light. • Light's vision is met in doubled enthuse at the space of extension and the plug-in called you and the light shines her sight on the plan of a light visionary. Man. Basic. Human. Light.

LIGHT MOBILE • Light's electric and elastic and always fits with a sparkling tinkle belted wide at the hips of this spinning planet, this love dynamic. We are the ones, mothers and sons, daughter's led by the father's hand. Open still. The basic human. A light span. Heaven and earth. Light mobile. Me. Light. • A light mosaic lives in me and I live round the blended send of a triple trace of infinity hung in winds of glittering deliver us. The light mobile.

LIGHT PATTERNED • Dappled with sun drips and love ametrine, I'm an infinite wonder and all the waves between, light to light. A patterned sight of spirit's weave. Let spirit lead me home to stay. All-ways. Light patterned. • Light patterned round the edge of a tree resonates soft in delivery of exacting attend and attendance exact and the heart of a blend tripled in me to shine undivided to infinity and back again to the land of the light patterned children. Us. Light.

LIGHT MATTERS • Light matters and we are where the light creates colors with many to spare and we see only with our celestial view from our home called the heavens and that special peace, you. Shining through. Light matters. • Light matters as I fill my bed with a softer mattress and my heart with a palace called the temple, I am and I believe and I concede to the spectrum called light matters.

LIGHT HILLS • Light hills reflect the purple hue of my variegated pleasure, the light mosaic, you and I am impassioned to show you the sight of a pink-hearted sunset with a pearly green light. Upon the hills, spread the word, God is heard and the light is on. You and the light hills. Light. • Light hills live in kindred paths of mosaic news that there's love in this shack I call home and again and alone in the land of the hills I call home. Light heals and I intone the name of the highest game. The light hills.

LIGHT KNIGHT • The Light's bright in my heart tonight and you are my hero for getting it right. The joust is over. The winds have blown and the light is on. Lay down your armor. The light is right and speaking of you, light knight. My hero, light. • Light's a knight and a shining star and an arc to a tangent and a heart to a bar of forever and a pi called a beat and a tune called harmonic and a shiny retreat to the land of living round the table of plenty called this life. A light knight.

LIGHT STILL • It's light and still tonight and the bear has gone to live as the love, I am and to give up his rain in this land. No more steal. Only real and truth and light. Still. The light is on. Light. • Light still sings in contented brace at the wall of belief and the concept called grace and the trial of treats left in the sand and the place of retreat, the land of the shade trees and the health of a hand held tight in revival and an intelligent span of an arm curved to love this sight of the light, still.

Light shot • I'll take a shot at the path called light and the truth is the proof that my interest is right in the middle where I am expressed by my looping spiral to the light I know best. My own. Welcome home. Oh sweet remember. Welcome home to the light ship. The snapshot of your loving face. Light shot. • Shoot the hoop of an eternal loop and land in the center of a heart that is breathing in effective consent at the love of a planet and the heart of a lip melting down to extend to the basket of the existential answer, I am. A light shot. 2 X 2 light.

LIGHT SEAL-ING • Light seals live in the rocks of this land. The geologic truth of our living span. All eternal, ever present with the peace-full perspective that there's light in this place and love in this space. Break the seals of little living. Step into the love most giving, light. • The light seal-ing has come to insure the impress of a love that lasts. Right here. Earthly mother. Father sky-ed. The love's begun in the arc called me. One great sun and a revelatory intend to begin the art of love just past this light seal-ing.

LIGHT, THE POINT • Light the point and shine the news. The cape of love is the earth called you and you are welcome to breath with sweet and succulent savor, the journey's complete. To the light I am and my heart filled piece of the peace, eternity, I am replete with the swans surrender to the water's buoyant presence, lifting her home, to the swimming light of an all-ways encounter with the shore of belief. All directions, home and homeward simultaneously and eternally one. Light, the point. Light. • Light. The point.

LIGHT INVITATION

LIGHT IN-DISCRETION • Exercise your life by filling with light by the day by the week, by the moment, and find yourself linked to the greatest retreat to the heart at the belt of this moment and in your discretion discover direction. The flight of the spiritual notion that desire is the link and the pin in this chain of blinking emotion. Keep chanting your name – the lightest retreat is the hearty repeat of your name – night and day. Sing it home all the way to the light at the center of the dome of delight called the treasure of your chest – breathing space – stars are made in the presence of your whole-y name. Thirteen times, the absolute. All the truth. Every day. • My heart has met her lightest friend and I have given my love to friends in light in-discretion and all the way through I'm light in my inflection to a higher rule, an intricate blend of a loving meld, you in the middle and me on the rails of rare railroads blessed by the hands of long ago and now on this loop I've found a new home in light in-discretion.

LIGHT-N-CREAMY • Light-n-creamy, rich and steamy, dark is light with beams of deepest dreaming. Penetrating pulses of plenty-full charm adorn the surface of the enticing yarn called your life's tree. Tell me again about the light without end and vote once again for your absolute friend, your highest devotion, of celestial notion – in your skin, once again, dearest kin- meet your thinly distanced highest self and abandon the notion that come-passion requires constant motion. For energy held and breathing expelled are the secret delight of listening well to the feelings light-n-creamy in the middle of the spell to remember your absolute name and the dream which became waking life, advances frames. • Light-n-creamy to the cherry center, I am square to believing that living is heaven and higher still I am sent to see the highest tilt the peace in me and polar ecliptic I'm stung with the piece of power-full pleasure residing throughout the temple, the body, the arc called my house and art here has met creative relief and a breathing approval of the love on this street. Life is well within the place, a templed yard, an initiate's plea to see the center of the love I call me. The light I am. Rich-n-creamy. A milky wayed friend. Light as a feather and soul-less to boot. Know the spirit of a street called light-n-creamy.

LIGHT DREAMS • Loftily I am light dreaming rivulets of spiraling, impulsing, penetrating depths of layered remembering in the midst of a night spent wet with forgiving tears of infant's forgotten at the brink of re-entry into the well of forgetting, and I am the minute, the moment, the sung. The winging revival of a trip to the son and in my survival a blissing is found and the impasse sweeps past me and in ambrosia I drown to the olde life, the days of repent and in my remember a new life is rent whole-y well, whole-y now, whole-y found – whole-y me – a waking dream-light with memory. • Light dreams in circles and continuous loops of lofty arrivals and perfect excuse to lie on your bed and build a light bridge and lift up the pentacle of loving again, to the point and through the day let me give my load away, to the light, filling up with pink and green and tangerine skies and healing flings met at the moment of a heavenward kiss and a ward called rehearsal and the meaning of bliss, a light called a rainbow is blooming in me in the visible spectrum the narrow band of the ultraviolet potential of this great trend. The perfect encounter the kindest dream is the heart in the middle of your light dreams – yours and mine by eternal covenant. Light dreams.

LIGHT CONTINUUM • Winging in lately, it's light I am shaking from the webs at the toes of my ears and often I flounder at the fumbling in-counter of the exit at the local out door and sometimes inside me I believe in particulates, in bits and in pieces of light and now oft times I remember that the light's without splinter and the continuum is welcome again and I am

the friend I've been looking for – without end. Light begins in the spin of an infinite to infinite continuum – love and light full fill the night with out end – a light continuum. • Know the seam-less living sight, the heart of a-man and the gift of the vine, a husband loving faithfully and a woman finding contented care in the arms of the light continuum. It is the trace of a healing face which finds my dreams and erases seams of blocked off trials and expectant dress, the art of couture and the simplicity said by tee-shirted being and elegant gift of the heart-filled entreaty to live again. In the light of contentment, I feel the freedom to arc ever higher without a ceiling. I am content to live in the rent of a higher district paid by the peal of a heavenly bell directing the trend well within my light continuum.

LIGHT CREATED • A light event – the birth was meant to be dramatic without the tragic, the flight emphatic with wings dynamic and feet ceramic shattered mythic nights of loving sights of angles bent in living fright unfolding now to join the light's returning flare of gentlest pulse and finest pierce – the tide is up. The earth is met by moon's embrace – the face is felt upon the plane of a geometric measure of creative pleasure filling the night's sympathetic in-sight with the sweetest, creamiest pinkest implosion of catalytic, deepening, broadening, embracing* explosion and the stars are met with the firmament's kindest acknowledge and creation's college of divinity's lightest knowledge circles around the space you have created as your own embrace of creation's magnification of the power of place and creation is squarely upon the shoulders of the lightest creation – you. • Light's address is the same as mine and there's a healing awaiting inside my tangential move to the corner of treat and the expectant sound of your slapping feet raining on trends and emoting the gasp of a heavenward chant evoking at last the hawaiian leanings and the greek forgivings and the cascades sending an eternity of brisk examples of the latest land met in the bass of a rocking band, an animas led and anima shed to archetypal intrigue with the concepts within. Shall we converse, can we rehearse at the edge of a tribe finding wilderness a drag and a prodigal celebration an awakening event. The heart of this man has sent a blessed design to the woman that light created – all one nation by divine enter-vention. A love too grand to mention. Yours and mine – by light created.

*embracing – dancing to light by the embracing power and penetrating rhythm within your own heartbeat.

LIGHT GREEN • Emerald and adventurine in sweet pearlescent hue of heart's melting full of richest rainbow blue and deep within the center of the room with widest view is the thrilling, knowing sealing of the past that's haunted you. Emotion now has entered and severed rusty nails from splintered rotting forgetting and the threshold now you've crossed. Welcome to the emerald center of the talbet's describing true... The greatest news, the fondest views – over the roofs of tin – you've found a home – a place of your own. An oasis of green and red tangerine cotton candy ecstatic. This heart is your own. My friend. Welcome home to the lightest green. • Light green foliage peoples the tree of my hearty convention to elect a new me and I am content and exceptionally fit to lead the traverse to a higher land. The life of a grecian eternity and a spinning return to the sight I see, inclusive and free, this hour and more – 4 streets to the wind and meeting in my holding ecstatic of the mauna loa bowl and the pacific wonder of a green circling wreath of green molokai meeting the tempt of a mountain called helen and an explosion fed trees sweet and tender and ashes of cloud, peridot green and loud to the sound of a forest of forgetting crashing down to acknowledge the view of eternity shining in the heart of you. By design, this earth, a light green torch, exposing our need for nature's treat. Balance. Harmony. Light.

LIGHT LAVENDER • Light lavender fills my heart with the knowledge that we are known as a part of a greater dynamic, a resonant few of the many universal who dance at rehearsals of emphatic instamatic. Got a picture, take a whisper of a thousand different hues and paste them all together to form a quilt I'll call it fondly you, and cozy in the middle of your throw of warmest down is a heart so softly beating bearing witness to the sound of all creation, to the winging of the nation. Patchwork singing, ever ringing home to you. You are me. We are light divinely lavender. Light lavender sewn together with pink needles of pointed surrender to the kindest hue. Light lavender. • Light is lavender in her ecstatic grip of the acknowledging meeting that living in matter requires of a friend felt living within the paradigm shattered and heart's tread mattered most. This love's the ghost of a holy spirit, a lasting measure of the highest treasure. The love agape, God-like and free and the compassionate blend which is melting in me – a pool reflective blue and deep and the hearth of revival's astounding glee to discover the light so lavender in me. An opaline jade and a sunny begin of the bounty called living and the loving called friend. Light lavender.

LIGHT PINK • Be-ing apparent is a filling inherent with lavender, green, and pink ametrine sparkling purple to blue and in the apparent is a grand opportune to sing a new number – a movement to four – thrilling as three is and chilling as two – welcome to one more – the ceiling to floor – column of light lines – the bridges of pink filling your 'let go's' with the sweetest of think without mind stick, feel without felt, enjoy the knowing that rings round this belt called our galaxies the heart of our plan. The earth is a miracle, a savior called land and landed within her is the heart of this man. Man is so human, so delicate within. Hear know your tenderness, your return to the tree the life you call yours is waiting to be. Discover the light pink recovery of intending yourself free. • Pink has dripped to meet my slip of the tightening noose which just lost her grasp on the edge of my class called revival and my heart called remember and I am ecstatic in blissing exam of entrance to my heart and the remembrance of man's intrinsic example that pink is sweet and love is soft in the elected vote of our healing cause. The light

force is here to impart the news that you have a temple living in you. Thus the initiation of a breathing intrigue with the heart of a people filled pink and green, and grey be gone, the lifting trance has met the dawn of a transparent sun, the holy one, the son of God, called metatron and the light is on. The pink of dawn and the green of sea's aqua, teal, and turquoise breezed in light pink surrender. Light.

LIGHT DAH-LIGHT • Light – deep alluring, heavenly – light...Light shineth forth deep in the night. Purple and blue ultra violet hued, I see the light starring soft with delight- full entreaty at the dah-light in you. Your light calls me homeward, creates singing in me and I kneel in wonder at the poss-ablity of peace-full embrace of the dah-vinity of you. Yesterday I felt lonely for now. Often I wondered if simply somehow, I skipped over showing simplicity my hand and fell full entangled into the web called a- man. A man dealing numbers on cards of regret is sympathetic to no one especially himself. So good-bye to mankind to forgetting this race is human and kind and loving and in place of the force lines, comes a light shining jackpot in the midst of the night. Heaven's open to-night. Deep and alluring and heavenly to sight. Light dah-light. • Dah's the word a friend has heard as meaning duh and dense and a rift in anti-matter and anti-light and anti-christo's, so here's the grip on a definition. Define yourself by your true ignition in the light of a dah-light-full mission to remind the dark that it once was complete in light just like us. So splits and parts and pieces can be tossed aside to fill the can of a light ship headed home to remind that an apple bit is never worth the blame entailed in ancient myth nor the burden of forgetting eternal bliss. Remind the dark to seek the light and that all are one in godly sight. A reverend approach to an heavenly notion – we are one. Let there be light by dah-light's remembering stance. Light.

LIGHT IN FLIGHT • Lightly I am led to listen to your singing enticement to bringing it true. You are the light line, the centering thread of a life filled with slices of living filters, dizzying returns of life on the limbs of open-mouthed recitals of giving it lead. Write down your name here on the edge of this threaded revival – now mean what you said. Look at the center beginning and end. Write down your story and win a new friend – friends are arriving with glorious hurrah's to dance and to sing in the bounty of you. Welcome home to the light. Kick off you shoes and dance on the holiest ground – the floor of light come-passioned hearts swollen with loving seeds awaiting the kiss of feet light in flight – touching down in the center of you. Light in flight. • Light in-flight I'm grounded to sea the universal ability of the float in me and an expressive life at the edge of the sea is a light flight away and an example being shown the truth in a melting glass and icy blue experience of terrific trees and skies turned true to the balancing bliss of a metatronic attraction called buying a space in the halls of forever and the ecstasy of taste and the air of fine shelters contribute to me and the triumphant hangar called shattering heart spins in to view the triangular space pointing to squares of heart-felt traces fueled by the light I am. Light in-flight across infinite seas and eternal shores by a light design. Light in-flight.

LIGHT CREAM • Light trimmed minty with melodic in-sight broad through the middle with the electric in-flight. You are the comet, the intrigue, the sight of electrical motion, the breath of insight. And often I am wondering and this night I'm immense with all consuming passion at this wonder-ous turned event. The mother is the return of the infant left to land and marvelous is her return to the ship upon the sand. At night in silent recall, I hear your lilting voice and I know the private passage which by the light remains your choice. I know that light so cream as the milk of honey's dripping soft reminder is the taste ambrosial ringing in the midst of living kinder. Embrace the light. Live in sight of the wave of cream across the seam of the heaven called your heart. • Creamy shreds of fascinate me lifting high the trail of an earnest relief and a passionate surprise abounding in milk of an infinite view and grand attribute has met in the line of a celestial kind the brace of a business called living in signs of mental surrender and genuine intrigue and the joy of envisioning a life without greed. Rising to the top, the supreme, the light cream.

LIGHT AMBROSIAL • The light's ambrosial and delight-full to sea at the edge of this lip singing straight through to thee and soft on the curl of a wave heading home is a splashing reminder of first life lead all-one. In depths of reminder you'll find a new start. In waves of remember lies the path to your heart. Beating on shorelines are bathing beach bells tolling the news that the son's winging well toward homeward. The dove has returned and throughout this planet the lesson is learned – my brother, no other, one lover, no sin, the infinite for-giving, the kindest my friend is the light sweet ambrosial. One beginning. No end. Light ambrosial. • Light drips in ambrosial sheets of combination water and oxygen's piece of remedial news that a partnered bliss is a life that's spent in classic curtains burned to crisps and hanging's forgotten by a voicing choice to joust less in pity, less victim-hood, and to live more in central attention to the automatic view of excitement created by the buffet set in front of me. In the land of the plenty and the home of the free, a heart melted full has expressed a decree that the light ambrosial resonates in me by divine design. Light.

LIGHT, I LOVE IT • Lightly I am given the right to see the width of a winning combination, a sight full-filled with bliss. Flowers of opalescent hue combine with jewels of faceting relief to fascinate the hearts of you – the chosen ones, the infinite few – who remembering early, awaken with bliss, to the light of the sun's awakening kiss. A ray of delight intones on the wind. The sun is aware and is breathing again and through the sun's central breathing import, the winds now are dancing in depths to report your heart's latest passion, the depths of her view, that the kinship of light is the victory called you. Lately it is light

– and I love it. Light. • I love the light of a gentle day and the delicate wave of a significant stay in this heart that is blessed and intelligence set to the beat of a room dancing cloud high and free and atop the crest of a mountain called me and a glittering web of a kingdom's connect with the loop of infinity and the heaven called wet drops of light's seasonal etruscan bliss, of the simple and true and green clear through to a pink refrain, by any name, by only mine, the light, I love it.

LIGHT DANCE • Stay with me and spiral within to the metatronic center of the waltz without end and deep in your dancing light shines a wheel of spun delight, your dna is waking up to join the dance, to spiral out within the middle of a column of light, an infinite view, whether day or night. Connecting your love with the highest will creates a new space. One delicious to feel and filling your card is a list with one name. It is one and the same. Dance this dance with the light called yourself. Sheer delight. Sweet in-sight to the spinning beginning of the infinity called you. Just a light dance away. • Light dance upon the surface of my life welting weds for two and a happy heart has burst apart to open wide to the family meant to lift a lid creating special security in the maturity of a love left open to shades of sugary greetings and electrical waves accepting no less than the miracle called bliss and an ocean of pearls bursting apart in infinite waves of cresting acceptance of the world that we live and the harmony of body meeting mind-full surrender to heart meeting yellow and the homage to the queen the heart of my self and the birds of a feather have mated in sleeves of open arrival of the sparkling tree and the diamonds of plenty arrived on a plate at the head of the yard and beside the back gate and the blades are removed and my heart's clear to see in her twirling dance at the middle of me – a light-hearted review of the divinity in me and the infinite view created by love and clear right through to the emeralds set to illumine this light dance.

LIGHT EVENT • Light is a beacon, a comport, a friend, a comrade, a sailor, a ship, and an end to forgetting the party, the laughter, the fun of a life spent on beaches cavorting in sunny surrender to the heights and the waves, to the enclaves of remember, to the earth's womb of caves – the depth and the middle, the center and edge, the moonbeams, the sun's breath, the encounter, the wedge of pi called a constant, consistent and deep. Three and one more, that's the score to repeat. The square of the one love embracing us all lives in just one light's intimate recall. The celebration now beginning increases as light's winning her way to the heart of the news and she's welcome to stay the mane event – the lion's return to share with the lamb in fondest surrender to the light that I am. It's a light event. Catch the sight. Light. • Decide the trend which you will choose to meet the street of your light dance feet shod in sheets of elastic blend and emotive assigns called the law of extent and a glass of bubbles lifts to toast the light of the moon and the heart of a noon-time example of delicate feed and the launch of a rocket to the tripling hoop of you and me and a jupiter tune, saturnine blue and blessed by the news that a heart filled with truth is the route to a blessing of celestial nature and an orbital path to the top of a tree, and a mountain high view of the exceptional ticket to the light event.

LIGHT IN-VINCIBLE • In deepest slumber, I am humble to the awe-inspiring sight of thunder, led by lightening, hear on the other side. Cup up your ear. Reach out your hand. Embrace the news. There is light in this land and the light is in-vincible and friendly and warm and the sound of her breathing increases my mirth. So tonight while you're dreaming and turning within welcome yourself to the richness, your friend. The light enter-active is the galactic 64, the return to the space game called winning's bright shore. The board and the pieces and the money and banks all line up to invest in you – the safest, the sound, the light of creation, invisible and wound in remembrance embraces this town. Welcome to the real fight. Lay down your arms. Spread wide your hands and fill yourself up with the hug of a cloud. Life here is sound. Thundering round to see the light in-vincible. • Leonardo said that the invincible news is the wings of a butterfly anticipating spread and the art of creation meeting in beds of petunias and canvases dipped in the paint of a pleasure and a present estate of galleries fed by paintings so grand and a delicate bridge and a japanese lamp and a treasure, forever, and a love that will last for lifetimes eternal and wishes come true, the peace understanding has met now in you and your precious sun of flowers arranged at the heart of the sum called essential and the essential called me and my stability avowed by the visible prance of the light invincible.

LIGHT GRID • Girdled by beauty, by birth's sweet retreat to the entry to eden, the enclave so sweet. This earth is a gift a mother so kind, an empress, a lover, an eve, and a wife. Surrender the notion that the only retreat for "mother" has two legs and walks on two feet. This mother is round, a sphere, an embrace of infinite wonder contained in a space full microscopic on the grandest of scales. In a game enter-galactic the bets have been laid. The earth's in the balance. I say we have paid homage to far less, to the light now we owe the kindest surrender of the heaviest load. Lay down you worries and lift them to light and walk softly on the earth massaging your feet. Reflexes heightened by walking aware of the honor, the beauty of the living mother's light grid laid carefully and tuned by me and by you singing your own tune. • Grids of grace, elect the placement of a heavenly veil called the energy's bid to raise the vibration of our significant nation and the notion that our people are our greatest asset as long as their living lets a notion be set in ice-less attention to the love lifted net that rocks round our planets and bustles with free static attraction to the earth's majesty, magnetic approach to the lifting gravity and the centrifugal truth that there's beauty in two met as one, the father and son attracting mothers to the blend called the living light grid.

LIGHT LID • Lids are jarred to jam the sight of what's in the mix. Rearrange the recipe and offer a new trick. Wear a lid of lightest light. The light full absolute and you shall live in kindest station, crack the wax and toss the mason, upon the shards of shrapneled encasement – no more trapments within this nation's shining embrace of the moon full in her face. Mooning is placed light in the sun to openly taste the infant now come to absolute surrender, to kindle the one, the heart held highest, felt fullest, sworn best – you made the promise and administered the test. Moving on is now possible and growing up absolute – open the jar and taste the sweet fruit of the light that you are. Light lid. • Lids are trending toward the light of kettles opening and jewels exude to the facets fed with glittering approach to the links hanging led to review the tree. I am resigned to reside at the place that my heart has fed and so I will see that the nature in me will trend to the place that I've been unless I equate the clearing grace of a pleasant place the heart of a face smiling without a cube of pathetic return to the kundalini's burn of an extraction floating free from every cell of me and lifting the skin of a facetless trim, I am set free to sail in the sky I know well. My open heart's receipt of an exceptional treat simply by lifting the lid. Light lid.

LIGHT EGGS • Cackling fruit of the sweetest of kin, embrace of wonder of the fountain within churning out eggs of creation again. Birth of a recent increasing attend has swollen to flooding the heartwells within, the emerald river flows like a gem of silent revival aware and within. Crystalline networks of filaments fine sparkle and dazzle in light's lacy fine spray of electric ecliptic design. The edge of a universe of a master's design and God's face is showing in the mirror of you and I am full knowing of the story told true. The mansions are golden and the streets are so fine, paved with the light clear to the highest design and love builds the life nest of the infinite eggs – the special ovoids of creation filtered for dregs, all denial removed, with the absolute lick of the fire called desire and the sizzling return to bliss. Light eggs. • Light eggs fly to the edge of the sun and light in a nest called the spoken word of love's light creation, the edge of a notion and the light of a nation, an infinite aisle and a welcome sight. The bridge of my heart beating soul-less with mine and a violet thread has snapped the grip of silver-violet themes and expectant lips pursued to pursue the pen ultimate view that a life of intrigue can never do let yourself be the egg that you are and birthing create a bursting star of diamond green and chrysolite pure ecstasy seen in the arms of a sure siren's song. The rocks have missed and this love's a bliss. Well spent on sweet diagnostic attention to our heart's tiny nest of infinite love and huggy-armed bliss. Know the kiss of a light egg's hatching dream. Light eggs.

LIGHT FLIGHT • Spreading your wings requires lots of faith. Now take a big leap toward harmony by bowing your head to look at your knees. Are they standing fixed, flexible, or stiff. Bend them a little and feel your light lift. Surrender's the secret, the power, and the space, the arcing reminder that there is power in this place between the extremes of give, and of take, lies the land of remember, no more egg on your face and living harmonious creates a new trend, a flexible flight to just round the bend of humility, light and lifting revival. Welcome home kindest friend. Take a light flight with me and we'll land bright within our tremendous flex-ability. Light flight tonight. Light. • Light flight central, uniquely me, at the edge of a stream called watauga, and the heart of a spring rainbow free and the edge of a moon painted yellow in tune with the heart of a brand new day and a life lightly cascading curly and a man singing, herald the king, for the life clear ambrosial has met in me with the heart of a grandfather seen winging away to eternal stay in the light of a spring -green tree. The web of life, of all discretion, of every direction, eternally lit by the healing season of late autumn's migratory flight to the winter of light, one stream, different shade, a dappled gleam, an opal's way, home, by a light flight.

LIGHT IN SIGHT • Eyed skyward, esoterically I speak of the in sight extension of the gland called unique observation – the legacy of integrity aligns with the light directly homeward to the place spaced within walls of pulsing arterial red blended with the emerald green of absolute crystalline redemption called infinity. Infinity layered in cells of intrigue, shamrocks of ruby rimmed with the gleam of life fully flushing the walls of your veins of plaques given honor and asked to remain free of the river of life swollen full red and green like stars bearing fruit in the center of your chest. That's arrival. Good-bye survival. Welcome to the revival. The place is set. Have a seat in the middle of your own heart. • Lime-green has met my peridot view of the love full emphatic and demanding of you the opportunity to remove walls of neglect and squares of proof that bunny rabbits fling their ears to the wind and snuggle in circles of living again in the spin of a dryer amping higher and a light meeting thin layered forgiveness upon the wind of our light in-sight.

LIGHT-N-LOVELY • Tonight embrace your brother and laugh for just a bit at the curtains drifting gently, only love can aid their lift. Now find a safer harbor in the bridge between your breaths and sigh in tender slumber at the dreaming giving gift of light-n-lovely bubbles of for-giving living deep within the spinning circle of creation's diving leap to penetrate the flesh of a 1,000 infinite beats of rhythmic laughing light waves spreading to your feet. Tonight it's light-n-lovely, breathe it in...The lightest friend. Your essence beams throughout your dreams of living light again. • Rocks and reels and pretty tales of forgotten friends and petulant dreams and streams of repair, riparian drains, exciting ignition of the love we expect and the respect of the nectar of living within the heart of revival and tent of denial exploding the sin* of existing, not living, and the abalone view of a sky ocean blue and a heart built from leaves of sun's heavy breathing and great central sight has spotted what I needed. A life, light-n-lovely tonight. Light.

*sin – Simple Ignorance of Nature's balancing harmonic, the laws called Energetic.

LIGHT APPLY IT • Brush a simple applique upon the seat of a fountain based to give relief to the burning tree deep within the scent called me – an essence breathed into the night, the dust of best, the branch of life – the brush of finest, lightest air applied with grace to live the square of a circular light surrounded with caring glances of infinite embracing twigs dusted pink and pearl and green and lavender trickling ametrine wonder – bounty-full views, increasing height, the balance of you – flown into particles shaped into waves, open on lips soft with continuing sighs of happy reminders of that air-borne essence called I am light, and apply it – to life – light. • Light application can increase the flow, and steady indication is letting me know that magazine's treat of a flowery show, of models exotic and hearts all aglow is four- tiered living in the pyramid moon and the lime-green circle of living in tune. Know the sight, fly the light in application, a healing nation, a wave of seas and swirling leaves, and grains of sand, and sandy land. The desert wind and the mountains blend – by light design. Light, apply it.

LIGHT FLOWERED • Lighten up to the best of life – enjoy the taste of honeyed milk – raise the odds of wearing silk and glassy threads of attractive silk – draw yourself to the elegant tread of a lighter place – called the heart and the middle trace of the enlightening spark of impassioned allowance of the beauty of art-full immediacy and the imprint of flowers – flowers of life drawn to the moment – to the moment of truth – the bursting arrival of the sweetest of fruit – the kindest appeal, the tiniest rhyme of sparkling hummingbirds suspended on wings bejeweled in the night of an infinite glory. On moonbeams we dance mid the flowers design, without and within, we are all one light, one all, one shining blossom of the life absolute. Light flowered. • Light flowered trenches have melted to blend with vents full of lava and hearts full of rend and a living explosion has belted my shame to the ledge of a photon and the heart of a game called gardening bliss, the piece of electrical engineering met in a dreamy cream of akashic forgive and the lift of a soul's knots to begin again at the office of friends and the heart of repair. The body shop, love, and the wealth of a stare full sublime, the loving line, red, white and blue to the greenest tint and the heavenly gaze of our light flowered ways.

LIGHT CRYSTALIZATION • Light crystal bringeth the moment all truth, the instant of perfectly acknowledge-able proof that the peace of surrender giveth the taste of an instant of submission to God's dear embrace and the clearest impression of today's morning star glimmers in the slivers of moonlight on bars of golden measure singing in tune, with the tone of forever addressing the loom of remembrance the flight absolute to the clearest example of the infinite truth that you are the gem and the light in my eyes, reflecting, refracting and dancing on pools of emotional attendance to my own point of view. Light crystalization. • Paint the points of an emerald haunt with the gaunt surrender of a living stunt and little girls bless and a boy's bend – meets in the sine of the angular trend to crystallize inside at the heart of this man and electric to cities and energetic to grains of gaining incite-full, elastic proclaim. I'm sky high and triangular thin and deep geometric to the life of a friendly reclaim of the octagonal rite of a circle gone squared and a square given sight. A pure delight of energy's trend to grow in light crystalization again. A risen nation. A light flotation. Atlantean wonder. Ecclesiastical surrender to mother's natural builder. Light crystallization.

LIGHT RISING • Self rising, light rising over the horizon of the monument built to the victory called you. A firmament separates the edge from the center and the middle's firm in ebullient rekindle of the sparking arc of the returning covenant just one – all-ways one – ever one – under the sun of a breath-full ambition to forgive the mother, to meet the light rising – the most excellent attraction of all – to all, through it all-is you, magnificent, loving, light rising to heights futuristic right here in your view, in your roomy surrender to the center, the all, the one – you. Heaven's father, earth's mother – the arc of remember, the gentle connection, is the light rising full through you. Welcome home tender painter – the light is rising, lift your brush to the light artistic – your light is the paint. Take a dip and feel your light's rising. • Light's rising in the heart of me for the spin of the creek has set me free to explore the refrain of a heavenly name, my own set to swan-like escape of lost in spatial meaning, a cubist scene, a cleansing grit, a sandy day in the dessert's way of scrubbing clean the infinite tree of a serendipitous feat and the hearty beat of a drumming sigh set high to a hummingbird's wings and anointed we sing our hallelujah choral – know the pal and the arcing power of heavenly wings in your latest hour of aching need. Your soul is freed and your spirit stays to light the way home, by divinity's shade, the darkness scene has lifted me to the light today for the stream of light is up and rising.

LIGHT ARTISTIC • Light in existence, ever in sheer enrichment, bliss I am in it – drawing the circles, the flowers, the formulas, the patterns, and designs of a creating kind to the life I call hours of divinest, lightest embrace. The pencil I am using comes without erase for erasing's never necessary when your life becomes the dream that you've been believing is available, is claimable, is intrinsic to this life, light, and magnificently, lightly, artistic – you are the potter, the clay and the wheel. Know the feel of the light artistic pouring forth to fill your pen, the light artistic. • Write me up as the painter's friend and lift me up to start living again and design a new heart and a life filled with trim gentle epistles of exotic attend. Erotic splashes have met the place where ecstasy trends to entwine and the love feels within and the hawk-eyed deliver of a stone to the brow of the indian's giver. Feel the timber and the resounding sigh of the whistling elastic snapping sound of an illusion losing ground. I see behind the scheme of a hidden ream and I am delighted to find that the heart that I'm left with is mine. A divine design. The light's my musing and alluring friend. The ecstasy of earth and the birth of begin-ning to march 4th. 2 X 2 x 2 to the arc of the covenant painted in you. Know your heart to a particular line and a color, no scheme, the tint and the hue of the light artistic in you.

LIGHT FORTH • Lightly I am led to lately lay my head upon a third of the fourth columns of towering timbre at the edge painted brushless to merge with the all-comprehensive rowdy, raspy, intuitive, heartfelt, gut-led embracing explosion of the love that I am & my light surges forth to embrace the exact sufficiency that this ignition has surrendered to the flame of absolute awareness & the burning through encompasses all, acknowledges all, indicates all that is wide & deep & good & the light rushes forth to enliven the night won with light embrace, the reception of light's divining force indicating the place where love began to enliven this face called mine with the lightest force known to this race – a smile of remembrance – light forth. • March forth to the sound of an oomp-pah's band and a tuba in tune with the moon's beneath your storm-tossed eyes and know that peace shall all-ways belie the truth called a-man and a woman's sheer bliss at the dignity sung with the ring of a kiss stiff to a wind of historic span and genetic relief. We are the band and the sand and the sea of ecstasy's day at the beach. Marching proud to an energetic dream, I'm steaming in life's intrinsic extreme of intoxication's release for eternal expression of the divinity in me. I embrace the light forth this day and this life, light.

LIGHT FORCE • Halfway in begins a spin to a cycle more complete- a place where give becomes receive and the speed of love holds light's retreat at a special calm – the zero place where love and light become the same. The gift in give equals receive – the magic's in the word – believe. Believing in receiving I am led to say the kindest things, the softest wings, the living springs of a fountain led by youthful surrender, and gentle embrace of the light that I am and the force becomes faiths mustard seed of growing in-grace and I am fed deep belief in love's retreat to the widening street called me and my arrival is ever sweet and calm and rich with honeyed drip of forever given here in the center of my open chest of light force giving receiving an open hand. • Light has forced an open door and an intricate web to overflow and a score called my heart to intently sing at the size of my giving receiving frame, the heart of a line that's wine to share and the head of a peace that's waiting there at the island of care and the place of relief and the tree of the arc which lives by the sea of regal align with the light force inside, and without, one plea – shine in me light force.

LIGHT FLOW • The light is flowing in my heart and in my knowing there lives a spark giving, showing to the showering flowing of filial going to the heart of the spring and the rainbows ripple with the light of the nipple of the great mother's breast embellishing your nest with homing employ of the symbolic showing that you are the sister given fresh start and you are the lover given envoy to lead this swelling tide of convoy reeling in remember and tying this lark to the note of surrender at the edge of a star – welcome to the flow of the light full metatronic. Life is ripe within the flow called mother's milk. Light flow. • Light flows free-ly inside of me and through my life so I can see the basic "be" inside of me and humanity reigns in my singing refrain at the top of the name and the head of the chart and the heart of the game – light flow following through my organizational bliss with "all that is" by creation's design and the parts of love which are completely mine and I am, by design, a light flow's knowing return to the heart of the stream called me, a light flow.

LIGHT-YOU-KNOW • Lightly-you-know the showering embrace of your highest desire to shine love in this place – for it's light-you-know and light that has led your believing spirit to this house of remember, the implant of youth-full surrender, of kindest reminder that the lighter you hold it the softer the finer edges are to brush away the boundaries, the time, the return of the home filled with pleasure has given new burn to the fire strong and timbered with searing embrace, erasing the mind mud and enlightening this space, this place of renewal with deep and well lead tender kindness is hear proffered. Believe. Be well-read. The concept is simple, it's easy to see – the secret is one word. Believe – believe. Believe. It's light-you-know. Embrace her design and let go the shadowed desire to leave an outline. No edges – hear – only clear – crystal bell. Light is well, for it's light-you-know. • You know the light and our big-bang friend and the heart of creation and the light from within evolutionary waves of darwinian glee at the heart of the christos revolving in me and spinning examples of pretense removed allow the tramp to the portal called well and healthy begin has begun in the sun of a wintry day divined in gay resolution of this heart's constitution, the wave of a day met welcome and free at the table called love and the light ecstasy of a finer design and a glowing line intrinsically free in our webbing refusal to know less than "be". It's light – you know and you are home to say, let there be, light.

LIGHT MEETING • I'm meeting light here tonight and I am well within the be-coming tenderness of another deepest longing, well within the limitless bounds of a sky filled with searing sounds of love spoken here at this ledge of surrender, the shelf to the deepest remember is tender with naked engendering of the light inherent with the kindest guidance of a gentle parent – you are heir to a new brood; a breed lighter and kinder and divinely met with lighter embrace at the table called forever and infinite and free. Commitment to the light holds delight in gems of glittering treasure – welcome to the light – the meetings here – hear our greeting. Lightly spoken we are all welcome. Hear. Light meeting. • Light has met her equal pet, her mistral friend, her rainbowed bend to the aura called light and the energy called wed and the excitement of living outside my head in the heat of the trees and the uplift of light lives a mayan relief and an equatorial flight to the other side, the heart of the land, the quarters topographically vented and the heart beat called a-man and the volcanoes melt in meeting requires a new reprieve of the pain-full ancient forgiving of this body, to be free and dressed

up dolling beauties of bellies met with fluff are stuffed in honest loving of the beauty of the blood coarsing through the divinity called you and the heart of a tan and green brown called earth and a macaw's sweet greeting accents the breathing of the beauty met in you. A light meeting.

LIGHT GREETING • Taking a rest in the shade of hour labors, I am given the vision of cryst-all light. Invited to finish this card I have chosen, I dance to the minute of an introductory line. Life is fine here on the eddy of light's river. Waves of indifference drift away with the sight of tomorrow's meaning-full remembrance of what is good and significant and light. This is forever here at this spring of sparkling goodwill and you are the siren sending me home to remember my longing to become the light which I am and my knowing becomes longing and my delight becomes embrace of the tender loving moment when my life became an emblem and a symbol and a sign – a directional to infinity – love is spoken – hear – you are the one and the only, the sum of the singing to become nature's harmony seeking balance on great sun's breathing weaving of lightest greeting. Welcome home, dearest sun – shine. Light greeting. • Light greets my writing hand with a crystal conclusion that there's love in this land and I know the blend of the loving example and the blessing begin of a dancing recital of the verses I know and I see relief in our ecstatic belief in the blend called unique and the life I call know and the truth metatronic and the life lived below and the belt of remember has met in recline and we are fine in our genuine desire to declare our alignment with the light greeting shining in our soul-less eyes, a welcome mark and the end of a hall called forget. Remember the trip to an eternal hand raised in light greeting and divinity's breath flowing in lasting degrees of love's blessing meeting a light greeting.

LIGHT INTRIGUE • Intrigued by the limit self-placed, I breathe new stretch in the place called my glorious temple and I surrender my scheming to your delicate dreaming and life's sky is seaming with rainbow hued beaming of God's gentle promise to remember that the sender's wrath is bitterer by far than the scar inflicted and sprigs appear in mouths of babes as coos of loving light intrigue curiosity spent on knights intent on doves full winged and lights appear in sparkling pace to twinkle shimmering in the face of comets left to sign their names in searing arcs of constant flame, consistent pain is now released and the wave of return, the arc is complete, the bear is finished, the weight of disguise, of duplicity lived has given good-bye and asked for for-giveness for invading our land of mother earth's gentle edenic span. The light is intrigued. The bear's strength is spent. Lift high your honor and look at the sight of a light lark sailing home, full flight. Light intrigue. • The mayan book of life's clear dawning has met with the spark of spirit yawning to grasp the notion that there's love in this ocean and a light in this potion, intrigue and aromatic blends evoke a descent through the nasals called passage and the heaven called rent all paid and rest has been laid in a delicate circle and an intimate shade of clear green blue and filigreed seams on the sleeves of two light candles melting in drips of expectant return to the heart of this lip and I am intrigued by our need to believe in the life and the light and the design called we are the one. Know the sun of a rayed in sight, blistering the air with desire to succeed at our only lesson, believe. A light intrigue.

LIGHT LARK • Birds are lightest, feathers are best, to show yourself the better rest of a life far lighter and well endowed with moment by moment embrace of the wow, we are flying and honest and sweet and kind in surrender to the land 'neath our feet'. Feel yourself gentle and strong in one breath and know that your patience is all-ways the best art created, the science of wait, the listen of caring, the design, not the fate, journey on moonbeams, smile into stars mirroring minutes of the particles you are and whole to the eclipse and golden to sun – well into kindness, your race relations have become the light of your heart spinning with mine in the knowledge of infinity to infinity arcing past mars to swing into orbit to the loving flight called ours. A light lark. • Larks have sung of love before and I have met the greater shore of a waving line and a sweep harmonic and the life metatronic meeting in me to create a new rhythm to just over 3 and in 14 to a percentage called ten and a heavenly land in the heat of a dove, a st. Louis signed by the bliss of a love called blessed and sweet and the spirit of holy, the ghost of a breeze called breathing belief in the love of a-man and the delicious impress on the ear of a tree and the heart of a fan electing to see the light lark winging her flight home to me. A light relief. The wings of sight and the precious height, knee-high to the sky and elected to be – a light lark.

LIGHT SPARK • Sparks incandescent, iridescent descent sail into view when your neck has been bent to look at your own heart- not others, just yours and sister this loving is not stacked in stores, not bought in tubes now, or boxes of scents of shadowy reminders that life here is spent so often on looking in mirrors so flat that the reflection is empty unless you react to the action called yours, your intent, your score – now see a new light beam illuminating your breathing reminder of the essence you are. You are the spark and the love and the light and the reminder that paradise is found out side bars of containment, of little, of lack, find a new answer by hooking the slack of your attention on the light that you are and spark a new interest in the star called arcturus, your arc, and your home, your loving's emphatic with classic intent, embrace your knowing – your heart paid the rent – living light, two-night, spark by spark. Light spark. • Spark my heart with a red-velvet cake served on fine china and eaten by lakes of granulated sugar and chocolate extremes and taste-full seclusion in a heavenly bean of ignitiating inquiry and absolute lift of the shield called forgetting and the trip of the trap met with staples ripped out to expose the light spark igniting in the heart of the lord, the bard of life, the living sprite, the devic tree, the written book the master plan, a match now met by God's own hand directing me to the light spark within.

LIGHT FIGS • 2 by 2 and four to the floor, the trees in our eden bring figs to our door – sometimes I eat them and often I share, most times I feed the knowing that your embrace of light is showing. So who's the gardener in your place, do you grow new and exotic tastes of dripping surrender to the ripest burst of remember. Today I am lonely for the return of your sight-full reminder of what action's sweeter and which notion's kinder. You are my love and my light and my friend, where do the branches begin their bend and where's the believing trunk of absolute begin. I am hungry for the light's return – my retreat, my friend, within light figs bursting with magical fruit blended with forever, forgiven, for truth. It's light tonight in eden by your shore. The light's inherent, inherit it, taste it. Light figs. • Figs of facts drop in splats of forgotten trips to the limbs of belief and the heart of sincerity and the press of a wine and the glass of a splash in the love called divine and gods kindest kiss resonates in me and my vibrational agreement to set the beast free. The serpent has met the heat of good-bye and the tears have been fed to the love left behind and dark glasses have shattered to show love its matter to me, beneath the leaves, nakedly aligned with the grand design, humanity. Light figs.

LIGHT GENETIC • Light by vein, by twist by loop, by arterial flow, by dna hoop of twisting entwining merely 2 strands wide. Now is the time to look inside and deep in the cell of your well-tended life beats a new drum- a new way of life ever wider and definitely deep. All is lighter in the mitochondriac energetic cell walls and regeneration gathers like unto like and when the 2 are gathered the increase is measured by impact for greater than any crater centered to smatter matter. Laughter and lighter and loving has created a kinder nation within the station, the temple, the shrine called you. Light it's genetic. • Light's genetic and bionic and met at the heart of entreaty to live now within the heart of a land expectant and free to begin our journal with a metallic relief and an adventurous retreat to the unique answer. Light genetic.

LIGHT INFLECT IT • Lightly inflected with the inspection of intent, I am garnered with surrender to the action I have sent fullest regard and constant attention. This is the spot I have hesitated to mention. Light is awake and aware in this heart and this heart is embarking on a flight to her like-minded partner, her lover, her friend, her light-in-the-middle called love without end. Infinite to the infinite, to the light and the light, I am drawn to light's reflection, the inflection, the sight- the star within the middle, the moon that you are and I am a son and a light and a friend to the arc without middle, a beginning, an end, an infinite loop of the kindest refrain – the life without thinking, the light lived within full surrender, to heart's sweetest taste of the resonant refrain of a song sung again. Welcome home, welcome light, welcome inn. The dream is done. The light, inflect it with breathing succumb. Welcome on. The light. Inflect it. • Light's inflection's in my direction and all the way through to the living proof of a sparkling truth that light in the middle's a sweeter extraction and a honeycombed treat of my be-ing lift to the light, inflect it.

LIGHT EMBRACE • Light's a race and a riot, a hoot and a laughing full-sender to the brink of your ever full, ever known, all-ways fed, all-ways held and like birds lightly feathered, gently stroked, calmly covered with dewy breath of lighted essence, I am loved and embraced, assembled, resembled, embellished, and perfectly known by the lightest face — my own. Holding forth in mirroring silence at the pillowing coo of my heart's beating rhythm to the brink of your love remembering whole and full and complete and absolutely well fed nests of tiny eggs, resolute and mini, taut and taught to break the shell of genetic and kinetic and physically fit for-closing – for closing the loop. Our light is the key to remembering the wholing of the light embrace of egg-sactly who and what and why I am light's embrace. • Embrace and romance an orbital dare to solar systems grounded and clods thrown mid-air and rocks that extend to a young arcing trend to blend out the edges and know a sweet lover, the heart of a friend, and the hand of a mother. The earth's extend to the heart of a-man. A light embrace.

LIGHT DRIP • There's a light drip on the edge of this lip and the urge of this leaking calls my heart to seeking a new way, larger scare, grander tide, higher shore of linear direction to absolute the correction of my less than illustrative pattern of brinking on the immensity of the simplicity of my absolute ability to love with all condition removed. Tonight it is light and the stars are dripping sight to the moons mirroring countenance and the puppies are in bed and the cats and mice are fed and the life an animal led is this bird's simple reminder that the way and the width and the ability of man is kinder than any floor, branch or hole in the sole of your spirit's foundation know the elation of being 85% lighter than a frog ever dared. Light with and without, care. Shall we dare. Let's embrace light. Let us embrace our light drip. Straight to the heart. Light. • Light drips in softening cups of great green gulps and light pink stuff. Wild to dream and great to be a cup full-filled and a light to see in kind relief and penetrating streams of splashing pulse and gentle beams elipting off the lip of my essential light drip.

LIGHT-N-FINE • I am light-n-fine in the space of the place I call me and in you I see the flaring reminder that light here is kinder and life hear it – finer – than any space I have ever shown and I am led to say this life, this light, this night is light-n-it's-just-fine with me. Welcome to your heart — finally. Light-n-fine. • I'm light-n-fine in my laughing place met at the end of a genetic waist and lifted to trends of higher evolve I spin to the blend of a better intrigue and the heart at the spark of a sunny retrieve. The light is on and every body is light-n-fine.

LIGHT EMBRACED • The light has embraced me with the peace of surrender and my pieces of eight I have tenderly tendered for the cause light electric, the piece and the whole of the pi of the fabric called one unified whole and tonight while you are dreaming embrace the delight of knowing that some-one remembers your flight to a life more convicted and less

convolute, a term called surrender is a part of this loop. Know the embrace of a friend who will care and follow the impulse to hug in mid – air. The hearts flight has happened, the stage has been set and you are the star and the moon and coquette. The light needs a hug in the middle, this man, this we, needs a sender, a receiver, a friend, a peace called forever is held in this hand, held wide open – a light with out end. Embrace it. Light. • Light embraced means love's erased when written little and penned as less, and met in trails of sweet ingress, I know the drift to a tender lip and a lighter wave, the kind address of a love embraced.

LIGHT FANTASY • I live in a light fantasea. I swim in the middle of the ocean called me and while I am swimming in the love there within, I am reminded of the beginning of this life without end. An utterance so simple, profound, a refrain – of consistent reminder of the light held within the word – and in the beginning – the word. God. Light. Logos. The lightest fantasy and it's all me. • Light is fantasy and fettered to pull the column of plenty along to my stream of fetter-less increase and icings of blends of tasty refusal to do this again. The bantam of beauty has belted her chair to the heart of this recourse and the hut of her lair and I am bemused at icons called grief releasing to see the beauty in me. A hearty blend of a living trend toward light fantasy.

LIGHT INDELIBLE • Invisible ink, the ink transparent, the eternal ink of a life less a-parent, more a child, a lover, a friend, an heir – the response-ability is here where you care for the other, for the half of your heart long forgotten, the womb of cotton, peachy soft and light – a whipped cream feeling has taken me flight – long to forever and head – long to delight – written in the ink, indelible – here's the right to write a heart left long in forgetting. Open your eyes to see the light indelible shining frosty in the night, cool with incredible etching in-vite. Written on your heart. Light. • Indelible ink has met with the link to the love that I had and considered quite bad and then cleaned it up by removing the junk of old metal beds and twisting reclines to bend in the mental of an ancient time and love is glad to return to the land of the light indelible.

LIGHTLY EDIBLE • I am hungry for a light replete with gentle gems of shining wonder, deepest green emerald line of travertine agate from mountains of mining explosion- awakening is hear – we are the sounds of surrender to careful equipment scheduled to clean – the light waves are delicious scrubbing you clean from cell to vessel, life to limb. The light is a pearl layered with thin laid loving wonder, of awe and what's more – you are the score to this song of surrender. Hurry to the blender and render a mixture more pure – the pearl and the swan and the dove that you are – I am love tripping lightly to a light themed buffet. Me. Lightly edible. • Light's edible in salty greens and salad trays and sandwich blends and coffee cups of bean-ing bliss and the heavenly taste of a cape called chocolate and a metabiotic trip to the metabolic lift called lightly edible.

LIGHT THEME • Light is the theme of my arcing embrace to en-join the future of tis magnificent race with our pity-full past of aching belief that less is our order – our highest receipt. • Oh look little singers who sing round the throne of a sister enlisting her heart as her own and the church bells are ringing and the gown has been spent on remembering cathedrals of song's being sent to dance off the rafters, to wind round the rails – no more skulking denial. It is our turn to tell a fresh story, an oracle so sweet – has sprung forth in a new life, a delphic replete with begetting of marvelous mirth at the marriage of father to our sister, this earth, oh mother delight-full, embellish this song with a dance called rehearsal which lasts all life long, ever wise, ever well – you play it's swell, wear the veil of a light themed scene – flowing fast – a light stream – splash! • Themes emit the special gift of a hearty bless and a magnificent trend to turn my ear and my heart and my eyes to the music within and the beauty of thighs grown strong and young and lean in my walking return to the love pink and green and residing in me, an eternal and unique, light theme.

LIGHT STREAM • Light streaming softly, splintered no more, by the inquiry to the lapping shore of surrender, the delight called design and the emphatic knowing that this love is divine, and in divinest rekindle I surrender the noose of choking refusal to utter the truth and udder denial of the ambrosia mix is the monster called forgetting to for-give the side stitch – panting for living is over this day and gentle reminder holds me in sway of the light stream, I am, painted yellow-green with lime – colored splash of energetic reflection shown in a dash of sun's shining em-burst upon the surface of our friend called the earth, 78% water and every ounce – a dreamy surrender to waking up lightly, to the night – the milky light stream painting on skies with layers of pearly creamy giving – receive the light stream in your 6-painted, infinite-sided heart of the moment's explosive truth – I am a light stream. • Love me simply like a rainy storm dripping trees with sights like lords of laughter and ladies of mirth bellowing guffaws in riotous birth from the charisma called chaos and the particulate blend of creative emotion, the molecular trend of bubbly blips exploding in light streams to heavenly trips, flowing like water and dripping off beams of heart blessed cathedrals and ecstatic dreams met with energetic belief in the light stream.

LIGHT STARS • And in the honor of light on the ceiling I am bent in wonder at the awe in my kneeling surrender to the chasm called truth and the petty forgiving of the trilogy called youth – beginning to middle to end of my little-minded denial of the truth that life is higher and light is sounder in my grounded flight to sight. Eating chocolate mounds of cookie scented air. Inhaling essent breaths of honey in my hair. Smiling excellent trickles of genuine reflective share. I am light starring in the broad way. I am living and giving and receiving the proud range called north to the golden shores of the far ranges. The lightly baked mountains of denial are crossed and I am lightly asking you to dine beneath the starry design of the light's in your eyes.

Light stars are in tonight. Come on out to wedge. Light. • Stars evolve in laughing trends of petunia petals and petulant grins of purple passion's hairy flip of the nebula's wafting waving burn and a permanent arc has found my heart and filled my sight with violet delight and a velvet green box spun to recline in musical bliss at the seat of a curve and the heart of a planet that love has managed to save. A light return to the breadth of love and the height of yearn and the depth of begin. Light stars.

LIGHTLY, I'LL – ASK – YOU • Lightly, I'll – ask -you what you would do if given the tenure to separate from two to one absolute, resolute and free of denying the fruit of the tree – truly life's beat is calling. One note too deep is the call to tender the life so replete with walled intending and God's forgotten truth to take care your longings and deliver the fruit of knowing your light and forgetting the line which you've used to resemble spirit this time – now use re-assemble to emphasize the width of the split called survival. There is truth in this trip to gratitude and gift – thank you for remembering that it's life that you live. I love you – now have a seat and relax at the bliss called the light cafe – here's a menu – you, and lightly I'll ask you to jump in and enjoy the feast... • Lightly local and often blessed by the heart of the news that there's beauty in this, I am subscribed to the perscriptive truth that the kindest diagnosis is "there's light in you" and lightly, I'll ask you to regard eternally the heart of this news, there's divinity in me and lightly we'll say lets take a stroll to the light cafe at the head of the knoll. A central grin and a touch of genuine pleasure in our walk to forever, within, and lightly, I'll ask you to attend a light buffet. Light.

LIGHT CAFE • Cafe of light – embrace of too different menus with only one truth. The ledge of survival is the arrival's new seat 'til remember comes knocking from inside the beat of your heart swelling full with tender rest embrace of a light tattooed in the air near your face and it's your presence in-dwelling, your essence is filling this space called renew – with the tinkle of music embellishing the view to carts of en-nourishment and spectacular hue – rainbowed to encounters with the meal I call you and I am content toward rainbows, it's true when I ramble around the lightest menu. Spread the news. Ocean views. Eat light tonight at the light cafe. It's in the neighborhood – just ask your heart for directions to the light locality. Light cafe. • A light cafe of moving blue and green ametrine and aventurine's hue and the heart of a tribe meeting in you and belting out proof of photonic truth that the neutrons and neurons and archons have dealt with their spiraling end and our archaic trend to war has met the end of a line and a heraldic lift and the hero drinks tea at a life menu handed round freely at the light cafe.

LIGHT LOCALITY • I am free to live and to rise and to dwell at the end of this street we all know so well and we three are given the right to recline at the place called intentional and the life I call mine. We're sharing implosions of infinite joy and delighting in seaming a light strung with care at the corner called puritan and the edge called the stairs to forever and the bell rang with care as the littlest star shone in closest proximity to the center called me – right in the middle – the light locality. • Light's locality is centered in me and my twisting turn to the heart that breaths and in, and to, the love proclaim I wane my heart is blessed by a new refrain, the lullaby sassy at the edge of a glade and an offer to sing in the pink lemonade and the heart of a trade inky and free of the cling of a static in-stability, gravity free and met by inclines elegant, essential, and divine in our tribal splendor and our infinite claim to the highest name, our own, and our absolute design to reside in the light locality.

LIGHT LOCALLY • The light locality is the bend behind your knee, for in kneeling down to me you are beginning now to see your reflection shining free as the man within the can pops his top becomes the one who knows I am and the woman who all-ways ran becomes the light held locally with the feathered palm of ra pointing to the sun of sweet remember and the hand called loving disc, aton pens this song of giving tender and the light's bells all are ringing and this the sum we're singing is the eastern star's western beaming home on the band of a light called man and a hand called applause from the realm of foreverings guardians of light pointing the way home to the son of this light locality. Welcome to eden. You are the star of this show – right here where it's all-ways light locally. • Locally spent, I am legally bent to the finest design, the light inside, and a local blend of legal intent is content with the tribe we have rent whole-ly responsible for the absence I've met and tribal returns neglected to say that the soul of this family has now gone away to reside in the light from whence it came and my name, light locally.

LIGHT ADAMIC • Lightly adamic, this line called arrival means more than survival and more than this time – led denial of the full dozen lines that you are and in interest in-dwelling it's your love I am telling of the instant-aneous swelling of my heart's melting the lemon of will-full entreaty to flow lime-green with loving light droplets tracing the outline of my shell. Crawling home sideways is now forgone and this conclusion is drawn to an infinite beginning. Allowance of the flow is the entrance to growing. So do us the favor of giving up be-labor to being the point of your initiation to the light that you are and you know you can rest safe and well fed at this dawn of creation – this edenic return of the arc and the arc has unloaded, the rainbow's in place beaming dear welcome to the eve of embrace – gentle with the ribs – gentle-man – know the son has set and full in sight is the daughter's dawning. Light eve. • I let my friend divine the time when next our hearts in love entwine and my light begins to feel the flame of severing external and internal flame and two spirit-mates divided came to meet as one and live again in the walking plan to gladly align with the light adamic.

LIGHT EVE • I met a lady – here on this shore and her face full – angelic met with mine and we two became one. Marry your self to the source and the sight – know the light's twinkling in the bed of your heart and light a new candle to kindle the sparking return of you to full knowing that the two are now one and the reunion is complete. Only good. Only love. As for me. Light eve. • Eve has met a gracious friend the kind extent of a band called dan and a tribe ishmael and a genesis blissed with bent retrieval of a woman's kiss. All ribbing stripped and set aside the living lilith meets the stride of an adamic span too big to hide to often mentioned. There's only one tree. Me and my intimate knowledge of the receiver called eve. Light eve. The son has set and met relief in the sea of eve and the light's intent to shine equally, eloquently, and freely throughout eternity. It's light upon the horizon. Light eve

LIGHT SLEEVED • This garment I wear, called my skin, is prone to wrinkle and sin*. Sometimes it's thin, and often it's sane to regenerate my self by living again as the light and the arc that I am... For the only sin is forgetting to wear the garment most living the light's dear arrival brings in-a-sense survival of the innocence of denial – the river of light is whole-est when the ghost of forgetting rips off the sleeves of our faded tatters and light robed I am naked and immersed and baptized and sprinkled and consecrated and confessed and resurrected and forgiven and blessed and saved by my believing return to the light that I am. Light sleeved again without any-thing on. What a novel ideal. Light sleeved. • Sleeves of time slip away to meet the point where space retreats to embrace the one and all has become the arm of a God and the love of a-man and the eloquent span of a logos, a word, a blessed event, a rainbow dipped garment of electric trend, many colors in coats of layered entwine, the auric begin of a light – sleeved line. Light.

*SIN – The sine of the sign called cotangent and the arc of forgetting the management of LIGHT.

LIGHT'S INVENTION • Quartz crystalline, the world of gasoline, it's a world of energy too. The lighthouse is shining the leaf of the season and turning to pages of gratitude paid I am reminded of earth's love and life's lemonade creations dispelling all fear and gently I am hearing there's light spoken, hear, and whirling on moonbeams and flashing in stream's the golden revival of life in the seams geo-thermic and the light hypodermic cures all that ails and the heart's love thrills with sweet thank you and offers of bliss for there's light spoken, hear and invent a new trip to the light sweet fantastic sparkling in you and I am eternal, the light's crystal hue and transparent to view. A light invention – that's you – and me, too. Light invention. • Invent yourself daily and often and well and sign a new slip to give yourself the light permission to exercise your life intention to clearly pattern your patented return to the life of forever and the heaven of learn. On a light-strewn pattern, a living I've pinned to the heart of remember and the life lived again, in infinite circles, a wheel's spin, a light invention.

LIGHT IN-STALL-ATION • A light in-stall-ation is built on

this ground and my heart here is higher for it's love that I've found and life here is teaching me true to be sound and sound to be true is the cure for this dis-ease without found-ation. Our nation needs cure and the cure's in the water of emoting the pure floating crystals of distillations, it's true – and here's the revival, the welcome, the sure application of nature's sweet treat – so take a good bath here at the end of this street. The moon takes her baths here in the water we've found and the bubbles are bursting with deliciousness sounding expansive and beautiful and well – we are the kindest piece the missing link – our heart's know it well. The light in-stall-ation is here. Heal the nation. Hear the nature. Light by in-stall-ation. Light. • Install the light in you elevated heart and lift your eyes to ignite the spark and fill your spirit with a deeper receptive and a blessed be-ing, the art of up loading and the systemic degree, given free at the end of a course called me. A bhd* in divinity, light, and love. A light in-stall-ation.

A doctorate in Basic Humanity

LIGHT LINK • Light links us to the crystal view of tiny molten givings linking me to you. In a gentle leaning, I reflect upon the space, the depth, the width without edges of the heavenly wedges laced with purple pleasure of pink and green and lavender hue trickling down the mountains to imbue these grounds within the garden of emerald green, proud heralds of peacock impress examples of beauty intrigued with hellenic valves and the ancient of days expressing the magnificent in the form I call you and I see the light and it's bright rounding venus tonight by the light, homeward bound and absolutely free. A light link. • Link us up to the finest thread, the lime-green twinkle of a tinkling bell whispering light is hear now to tell the absolute peak of a pleasant embrace, the art of divinity and the heaven of grace, linking up to refine the petroleum called energy and the factor called me. An attributive constant. The davidic star. We are the light link.

LIGHT ORIGINALS • the bird of incarnations chirps a new decree – dearest know thyself and let yourself be free of karmic living. Now drawing forth the truth enraptured live believing the light is the proof of art descending perfectly to live within the form and the light without end begins once again in the center of the tree called life and knowing and known and forgetting my head I dwell instead in the lightest work I know – the canvas I call me. A light original. Infinitely. Light. • The geisha of joy has enthusiastically lifted the bonds of dramatic to reveal a new spot romantic and sweet to the thank-full ability of love to one, the other, and one, the other to eternally be a light original in a heavenly sea of one big, beauty-full sea of electricity. Energy in me. A light original, plus you, makes light originals, all three. Light.

LIGHT ECLECTIC BY DESIGN • Light's eclectic by design. Gather the best of living this time and find a new thread and enter the eye of the needle called surrender and the wealth I call mine and yours eternally – we are infinity to infinity the sparkling heart of this matter called light and the pattern in your living, giving arc of natural design for the mother is home and everyone is on by design – and the lightest thrive – enjoy the benefits and be significantly electric and eclectic by design – light and eclectic. By design. Light. • Light's eclectic and eclectic to see in the surrender ecstatic to the electrical sea of all beginning and new life trending toward creation in the lime-green seam of a tennis ball's example of the ability within to create a new sine by a dimensional shift to an angle brand-new and a 90 degree find, the light eclectic, by design. Light.

LIGHT TRUE • It's fly day. Open your heart and your mouth to the light. Speak what is true. All the way through – find the seam and swim in the stream of the earth's bounty-full view of the singing, streaming, strumming, melodious sound called you. The light is true and pitched uniquely, absolutely to you. Your voice is humming and flying free in the delicate singing of the word. Light. How true. Light. • Light is true about your reach and we have found this seat connected through this light true.

LIGHT SENTINEL • I am a light sentinel holding the edge of a loving light sent to initial the belief that I am living light to the edge of forever and over and under the edge, I find more of my word – light, I am your sentinel, filled with delight in knowing just who we are and in that glowing, knowing I am a light sentinel by design light. • Hold the light. Light-sentinel.

LIGHT DETAIL

LIGHT – BLUE BELIEVING • Light's eclectic and heaven's a spot that can meet in remember to trim a new tree and a lake of deep swimming and a throat called believe, speaking of plenty and pulses of peace and a heart of surrender met by the speak called heavenly blend and the kingdom's arrival is meeting within my delicate spin to the edge of belief and the seam of relief and the vein of a trend toward light-blue believing. • Light blue – an affinity for speaking clearly the babbling beliefs of a life held en-treaty – a pleasing release calling forth from the depth of the peace I remember. Light is talking – listen with the ears of your heart and the eyes of beginning belief in the infinite plan – a man – kneel in wonder. A woman – born to bless this plane with the remembering name – all the same – whispered light. You are the one. Speak the sum and the son and the life well-run by springing forth to know the taste of the sweetest lips – your own. Own the taste, the light, the tip of your own tangling refusal to settle for less than the absolute truth about yourself. You are truth shrouded in light blue delight. Oh the sight, the taste, the smell, the sound. The sense of surrender to a bottom-less cup of remember. I am lightly loved – share a taste of the word, round this world, light by my light blue be-lieving light.

LIGHT TOUCH • Believe in me, that's what she said in tossing lilt and lifting head and touch me with your dreamy span of exquisite ability to align with agility at the band of belief and the heart of a treat seen driving around in a winner this long, and an oscar's been met by a pulsing brand of energetic bands of laughing replete and attributive grins of shiny, lit streets happy to be in light touch with our feet. Light touch. • This light touch is your genuine embrace of telling your truth and making the space to live within well-come and home at the shore of the lake called forever and the mouth that's your door to intimate respect for this be-ing called other. Well-come the difference, respect the more random embellishment and let yourself more know to take what you feel you know and integrate this so another facet can glow and get brighter and increase its lighter touch by the increase of your "us" – the lightest touch – our light unity to a t-ouch. Light touch.

LIGHT TRIP. • Next to me, I've just met a trip called remember and traveling in I've seen the dream that I've awakened from and I'm happy to be living lean to a sign called lodge it, hear, and say what you mean when you issue a ticket to park near, a friend, for I'm here to stay in the temple of me and perhaps we can meet sometime deep in a light trip. • This touch is the light trip. Feel it in your heart. Wander in to feel again in the spaces where you started to say to your-self or other – that spirit lives here and she's a light filled mother resonating pink and green tourmaline and blue-throated humming wings into view – the thundering return of the wonderous you. Taking a light trip and communicating too. Light trip.

LIGHT TONGUED • Licking the lips of my heart-y trip, I'm honey and bread and tasty sounds of heavenly resort to the ward called remember and the blessing called bliss and I recall the light zone and the minutes of entreaty and the cares of the needy have met in earth's arms and her mothering hum of the light tongued lullaby. Light. • I'm speaking with you as if you were me. Perhaps I can hear what I say in the feedback from you and I'll know how I talk with me. Seldom seen, and scene upon forever is the screen of the truest test, the light tongued embrace of the honest forever in my loving tasting honeyed words of intimate communication with the light in you. Looking deep within and all the gentle day through. Light tongued listening to my-self. Light.

LIGHT RESPONSE • Responding in mariners of eloquent light I'm communicating plenty and pleasure and sighs of the patience the meeting, the date, with the heart of arrival and my returning dash of dotted appreciation for the code called the keys and the electric giving which communicates through me and my light response. • Jelly beans of glistening lemon light droplets zip through my heart and land on my tongue with a tantalizing tickle and a burst of respect for my light response to their sweet sounding thunder when they coat all my words with honey dripping amber and green and blue. I am light and lightly response-able for my words and their energy too. A light response.

LIGHT TIP • Light's a tip of a waving trend to fields of energy resonating within and sharing patterns and living aligns and great big gulps of the air called alive with potential and energetic portent and plenty of pulse and creation ability and the law called polarity has met a new blend and the light university has established an end to the trend called diversity and the life lived in grips of forgetting refusal to remember the friend, light, just a tip, light tip. • Touch the tip of my light seeking tongue with the fire of surrender and remember and all-one purpose-full escape to the light burning ember of well-spoken entrance to the words of this sender and in my return find the taste, lightest honey and the love serpentine, crystallized candy melting in your ears seeking solace and your eyes knowing soul-less and spirit fed streams of my light tip to the strip called mobius* wondered recall of echoing thunder, singing home on the words of my energetic light tip. Light.

Mobius – Repeating rhythm, mathematically speaking.

LIGHTLY REASONABLE • I'm lightly reasonable in my agreement to be the lightest medium and the invisibility of transparent reason given the free-dom to span a new arrival at the heart of the sun and energy released speaks in a squeak of helium's return to the hydrogen land which creates a great burning desire to our solar entreaty to be, eternally, lightly reasonable. • This light is reasonable and let's all stop here to listen to nature as we stand moving still. In love's spiral, a light is seen arcing off me and back to you like water and sunlight and that sparkling view whenever the two or more beckon to you, the lightly reasonable explanation for this our nation, blue with tangled fatigue is the light reason-ably and responsibly spoken. Light. It's reason-able to believe. Light.

LIGHT-THROATED • Ruby-throated splashes of a hummingbird's giving sighs and the retrieval of knowledge have met in the college of my light-throated soliloquy and I'm silogistic and artistic in vents of vaulted persuasion and lip -sink release, the frown's met her ceiling and the smiling relief of a band called the sisters and a mister too soon and release calls us blisters releasing the moon to sooth the cause of a perilous tune which rushed through the winds of a hummingbird's wings and met at a strand called the arc of believe and a committee called blessed has agreed to reside at the heart and the hand of the dipper inside the horizon of a beatific way. The light blue persuasion of a light-throated day. • Ruby throated light miracles enrobed in honey trickles amber-line and hovers near my face as I blink in light throated bouncing lilt to the gentle space, the melting place called the box in my throat. Is my box filled with light and loving insight? Let it be. For in this taste-full inclusion of other in my sending I am communicating light throated wonder at the beauty of you – light's hummingbird sipping nectar from my views. Light-throated.

LIGHT TYMPANIC • Light's tympanic in the penetrating

news that there's beauty and favor and rhythm in you, and in her, light has met a new plane and the plain of forever has met a new kind of light – hearted lover, the kind on the line to forever and eternal bliss and the option to linger at the drum of a kiss flittering in to rest again upon the name of the light tympanic. • Light's tympanic as it's singing in me and bouncing from ear to ear – announcing "you'll see," stay on the light life's station and listen to hear the peal of the thunder and the sound of the dear chewing softly, and the glistening dew dripping down grass blades and splashing in view of ants stomping lined up in tiny brown coats complete with a hood and yelling with throats mini-versioned of the big one, that's yours. So speak full knowing the light's tympanic and your energy is showing. Speak light like thunder whispered in an ant's ear. Hurry your tympanic agility is showing. Light tympanic.

LIGHT DEVOTED • Light's devoted to the cause that yours is mine and ours is hours of peace-full entangling decision to lift the whole empired state to a higher grip and a happier loft and a sweeter toss of the medusa gone gentle and the producer gone kind to an hour of surrender and a light devoted escape to the other side of forever. Light devoted. • I am devoted to the light I am and devoted I stand in the shade lemon – aid and drunk with a smile and a render blue lipped at the sight of your ringing around this birth called the earth. Life is born, by the spirit worn. Mother's hear. Nature's dear. Let it be inside thee – eternally – light devoted. Naturally. Light.

LIGHT RESPONSE-ABILITY • Light's responsible for my daring soar to the edge of forever and the opening door, to the archangel's ring and the glistening wing of a dragonfly's caring tribute to the peace of the face called accomplishment's made and I am the shade and the resting glade of the son's desire to rest awhile and on the 7th wave, light response-ability. • Light responsibility means I have the agility to dance in the life of this resonant light, able to respond and definite to attend this blessed event, the trail of the truth. Dry all your tears. You are getting your due light now and light response-able straight to the core of this apple called you, teaching me a thing or two about light response-ability with agility. Light.

LIGHT TERRIFIC • Light's terrific in her opening wave and her electric glide to the love inside my constant stare at the light's soft flare of the emotive glaring truth that the light's inside and my happy face is here to share the light terrific. • Light's terrific and the view from heaven above to the earth in you tells me a thing or three about the meaning of being free – to light it again and wear it swell in the middle and round around the tail called the serpent who taught us both parts when all we needed was the lead from the start. Straight to the heart. Only light what a terrific idea. Light terrific.

LIGHT FEASIBILITY • It is feasible to alight at the type of truth that brings a flight to the web of envy and the heart's delight and telling news that a higher sight is now required. Spread the word so widely hearted by all who care, there's light in there by light feasibility. • What's the feasibility that the light's finest agility comes with the ability to be all that you need and all you have to do is be you. Walking softly light to light, holding forth the willing sight to allow the total process – approach the light with reeling honesty and be prepared to share the world of energy with me. The light I am. That's the light feasibility.

LIGHT HARMONY • Harmony has struck the ringing bell of a heart gone gentle and a love gone well to the exposure of a loving separation, perfectly placed and often evoked and eternally set to the eye of a blinking fit called heaven's stop light, exactly spaced to keep the pace of a singing design and a rhyming line. Creations pair. Light harmony. • Light singing octaves of perfect intent to circle round the meeting and hold within this tent the arc of heaven coming to live on earth again and this time light's eternal. The friend without an end creation's song. Please sing along. A light harmony. 1: 8: 13.

LIGHT DYNAMIC • The light dynamic is to drop ceramic bells of waiting and to shed the crackers of wasted crumbs and scoop the hand-fulls of blessed datings straight to the heartland of the son and know the compare of a higher land and a happier band and a greater stare directly into the light of you. A light dynamic. • The light dynamic is gigantic and full miniature. Every angle, every corner, every square rounded out with ovaling care to emit the light in you. The self-fullfilling, light it's healing, hallelujah choir is singing, ringing round the light's emphatic news. The dynamic is that lightest dynamo – you. Light dynamic.

LIGHT, EXPAND IT • Often I've met with an expansive pair, the eyes I call mine and an obsidian mirror, a smokey gaze which shines back at me in an attempt to show my flex-a-bility and my absolute devotion and total commit to the heart of this life and my light commitment to insure my desire to shine higher. The light, expand it. • The light's expansion is the mansion called the house within. The temple simple is the example of the kindest flair, the welcome stare at the open door welcoming you to embrace this view of the world and the well within and deep within the fountain is the lightest shining mountain, the love in your breast, the life that's the best, the rest of the news is there's light in you – now expand it. Light, expand it.

LIGHT VIBRATIONS • Vibrationally met it's love that I spend in my levitational trend to a higher spin and spun to a minute I'm hard bent to find a kinder life than the one I call mine and significance sent to the width of a stream bubbles in pure centrifugal streams of aspirational sing and lighten-ing sung by the life of a day and the heart of all-one. This life is kind by light vibrations. • Vibrating lightly, I'm telling you knightly and more often too, that nightly it's rightly all up to you to decide dearest earth what it is you desire and fill within with this infinite fire to loop back again and finish this spiral, this welcome return to the light vibrations, without and within, light.

LIGHTLY TELLING • Tell the truth to the person met in your daily mirror and your often prolific ability to tell the spouting appraisal that you are the novel exposure needed most and terrific appeal meets at the zealous reprieve called telling it like I am and needing no extension I am, light by light attention to my living invention, my life's expression. Lightly telling. • Lightly telling is the swelling news that venus and earth are meeting again to entwine with stories of spirit and light and I am the middle, right in sight and aligned to burn with the desire of our loving return to the story's most loving, the lining express of the notion we all know best – light. Lightly telling in your every step and your open-faced style. Lightly telling.

LIGHT SWELLING • Light has swollen to complete the arc to a higher life and a wholer spark and the stars called twinkle have met with mine to reveal a lesson to humankind, that the light's inside and the heart's to tell the speaking truth of the crystal bell, your own voices eruption of the light swelling. • Light is swelling in my telling grin, that the sweetest design is the light right on time and the option to feel it again – all the way through and soft in the middle – pink swirled with light green and blue in the center of my swelling need to this story be telling – light. What a swell design – light swelling.

LIGHT SPILLING • Light spills forth in extant waves and expressive beads of belling days and ringing rung to our appeal and a heart's song singing in heaven's ears, of the love inside and the light behind the shade, revealing now in our generous light spilling. • Light is spilling in between the welcome wonder of this scene, this living light, this life of will given surrender to the light that lives inside of me and all-ways free. I am known as the light spilling waterfall down to the softest ground right in the center of me. Light spilling pink and green and lavender and whole within the cellular gaps lifted free to see the light spilling through me. Light.

LIGHT CEILING • Spelling relief is a code called phone of ringing ceilings and heavenly thrones announcing the trip to the rim of the moon and the sun over io and jupiter's new tune, the entrance to be is enlivened in me and my light true attend to the balance called zen and the fill-up called love and the wings of the dove fit like a glove on the hand of the man reaching across to attend to the light ceiling. A sistine view. Light. • Stars on the ceiling, rays at my door, light here is filling me up like before. I'd forgotten the beauty, the swell of a night-bird singing me home safe and well. Singing tales of lightest flow. Winging well within the words of kind refrain – home again, light to the ceiling and floored no more. Light ceiling.

LIGHT SEALING • Light has sealed in an egg of breed and a laugh of grate-full gratitude and a gentle being met with treats of enter-grated folks of sunshine streets and bouncing beauties met with trees of twinkling, sparkling serenity. The light is on and the heavenly host has sung a new song. A perfect accompaniment to an elegant brunch, eating the light eggs and healing the crunch of a derivation called a celestial nation hatching again within the band of a light sealing. • The bank of keys called the light is waiting for healing flight to your centered self and now comes the help, the aid from on high, the ceiling the sky brings forth the singing of an infinite ringing tune from this emitting a tower is building a column of light sealing all parts into one harmonic filling song – light sealing me whole and free. Light sealing.

LIGHT KNEELING • Heaven bent to a lighter load, I'm kneeling on sealings of heavier days and passing away in looping desire to a meeting held special and a loving held higher and an infinite wave of spelling relief and the penetrating sound of mecca met in my light kneeling. • Lately I'm kneeling at the feet of the throne called this heart of my own, light bodied speaking creating with care. For there's light in them heels if I'm willing to wear light bodied being and soul-less boots and speak in a trickle of trivy-less truth – splashing light syllables, chewing on fat, happy helper vowels, and cheering at that silent image of my spoken address light-ly kneeling at this light throne – my own. Light kneeling.

LIGHT THRONE • Every day I sit write here and wonder where the healing prayer and flood of light has gotten me and I'm in my seat and infinitely free to embark on days and weeks of care-free abandon in a moment's spare, for who knows ways to stretch the mind and lift the glare and initiate starry compromise-less days, the light on the throne inside of me, my light-hearted serenity and comfortable seat upon the light throne. • Light's throne as my own, means my heart and intuit and light voice as I knew it have become this living light trained to become ever lighter and brighter in the ceiling of my spirit shining soft upon the letter of my book. Open the pages and take a look. It's my heart lightly hooped to the words I share – and I realize that my creations are the wealth of this nation and I speak lightly from the seat of the throne of this light heart my own. Lightly speaking. Lightly home. Light throne.

LIGHT OWNERSHIP • Heaven's met in the eyes of you, telling the truth and the living proof that jesus is gentle and christ heart is kind and you are the savior and the light inside this temple you are, so never despair and cast away blame and sing us a pair of arcing refrains, the light inside, own it, and again, light ownership. • You own the delight of owning your own light – now share your shares with the rest who care and aid the left of this lemon lime green seam of mindless mining entreaty. Blue to the gills with breathing the toxic words, their own. They're asking for help now in their seaming entreaty. Know the scheme the rhythm and rhyme. Buy your own title to the spirit this time – light ownership. One smiling share at a time. Light ownership.

LIGHT SHARES • Share your light in your particulate speech and the way that your truth is soothing me in particles of sped and waves of steed, I've found a new horse and the way to see a higher view, the light in me and the telling proof of the divinity's share of my willing prayer to surrender war and to believe in more care in my light sharing way. Light shares. • I'm buying share in my light self today and lying back chill in the shade of the days lightest venture, the purchase that's fair, the justice called adventure and the wisdom to share in the truth of this mother -light. Mined and staked, full claim. Mine... Purchased by proclaiming God's name – light. Working my claim and buying light shares in my daring to care – light shares.

LIGHT STOCK • Taking stock in my electric waves, I'm rising in light to enjoy the days of excellence sung and eternity rung in telling paces and beauty swung to the standard of more and the symbols explained and the wall at the door of this journaled street. A light stock. • Carbon based I am in this form called a man and lightening this center requires a burning, a returning yearning connecting my life to the light, I am. Carbon and starman and stocked still with bars of infinite light, the spectrum of sight, the light ultraviolet, the sparkling, blue of my light – filled vocabulary igniting you with the light. Stock too. Burning through to the light stock.

LIGHT WEAR • Light wears pink and green and yellow too, inside of me and a bevy of rainbows floods within and a heart called forever begins to grin in circling intrigue at the heart of this line and the crest of this wave, over the edge of a paisley sleeve, patches of pink and red and green abound within my light wear. • Light wear this – wear your heart in mine – an aquamarine yellow seaming. Love worn. A light wear.

LIGHT ROBED • Waves of rest are painting in me, in hues of pink and red and green and a stone called watermelon tourmaline has melted down to flood the ground with a creative flare and an excellence par infinitum and I am the sum and the song and the one singing star set in a haze, milky way through to the light-robed beauty inside this view. Light – robed. Wear this, the light sleeve – light robed hearts, yours and mine, in electric weaves.

LIGHT RISEN • Waking up to share the light, I'm telling the truth that there's love inside and opening ways to breach my despair and open the gates of elegance shared and essential realize of your heavenly eyes and my crucified pair electing to raise to a higher octave and a wider son, the light is on and I am light risen. • Risen to the notion, the minute, the fork, the loop of forever which spins in your heart. Know well the seasons. Swim in the flood of giving emotion and avalanches of love filling you up with the staff of which earth's are made – light to the middle, the mantle, the dusty revival, the thrust of infinity, and love's squaring circle, light sticks are smiling and shining their truth and finding their limbs every season through. Let there be. Set earth free. Shine in me. A light stick guiding the flight back to light.

LIGHTLY GIVEN • Lightly given, here's the sound of eternity

bearing down to explode the myth of a soul needing circling and a ship needing sails to circumnavigate the living spirit and a-man needing nails to receive the living proof that a heart softly singing is the reason we are lightly given. • This epistle is the missile straight from my heart to find perfect consolation in the spirit of the rhyme and welling up within me is the singing left to sign in perfect silence these words I mean all three. Divinity. Light. Love. Embrace the sound of this perfect harmony written for three and sung by all one. Know the key. Me. Light. Lightly given.

LIGHT, IGNITE IT • Light yourself in your willing walk and your living ability to extend flex-a-bility to the light of this land beginning to expand in telling approach and a cascade of days spent telling the truth that divinity's saving grace is the light, ignite it. • Light this up and wear it wet with juicy gems of finest thread. Set the trim and open sail to the passion burning inside of you – light, ignite it, with bellows breath fan it up to the top of you and nearing the roof and the ceiling's delight open your mouth and shine forth a light, twinkling too in the heavens three times nearer their due circling to swim in the waterfalls trip bouncing and roaring and filling this box – with the words full of grace. Light up the sky and write it in red – whistle it up to the top of your head and meet it in blue. It's your light, ignite it.

LIGHTLY FOUND • Lightly found, I'm seeing you in a different light and a sparkly hue and a telling desire to intimate proof that a spark blown on will definitely imbue your heart with a sign and your life with a star. Lightly found. Heaven. The kingdom within. Lightly found. • I found it, my light and now I know the place called light, in my life, light and I embrace the space and the pace and the applauding delight of the spirit to light and eternally ignited with giving surrender to the light ever tender and well-tended. For it's light and I've found it right here in me – oh happy melody – light, lightly found.

LIGHTLY, I KNEED IT • Light, I kneed, and light I tell that the sound of peace is the ringing bell tied to the beak of a winging dove returning to the arc of a spirit called love and a stainless steel band of perfect reflection to the heart of this land. Bake a cake, heaven is one and the birth-day has come. My only wish is for the light, I kneed it. • Light, I kneed it into the shape and the shine and the wedge and the pet and the friend and the wealth that this clay filled with light, wonderously proclaims let there be – and it's light – and I need it as it lifts and rises and swells into the shape of the form I know, me and I expand lightly beyond the edges and firmly past wedges blocking the sight, light. Lightly, I kneed it.

LIGHT, CONCEIVE IT • The light conception is a new direction straight in and all the way through to a conceptive ignition and a loving cognition that the conception called living begins with a spark and the loving surrender to a higher flame. The light, conceive it. • Lightly, conceive it, like the wind, penetrating your body to expose the knowing scenery, the familiar air of the lightly woven wear called light, conceive it, the idea, the germ, the sperm of penetrating election to delve into your middle, and fertilize your idea with belief and lo, what hast thou created – light, conceive it. You = light. Believe it. Light.

LIGHT DESIGNS • How often have I worn the pain of forgotten wonder and royalty not claimed and today I'll walk in a lighter veil to the edge of the cross and the land of green to dance in new robe of the lining design, the bride of surrender is living inside my light design. • The light here is shining full in my eyes and I'm blinking in wonder at the dazzling designs, the squiggles and wiggles and welcome lines of light waving in my life, ovals and circles and squares, let me zip flying in patterns leaping over the lips of denial to the heartland of believing that light offers more than I've ever seen or heard or known. I am light, by design, tonight. Light designs.

LIGHT BLUE • Light is blue in my spoken voice and my gentle reminder that love's a choice and the only one to know the truth is the heart that beats inside of you, and heaven too and earth's inside the love of two sung to hues of a lighter shade of blue. Loving communication. Light blue. • My sky sparkles light blue with loving, lingering, heightened view of the light ceiling-high and heaven wide and living light blue in honest conversation with the elements, my nature, and the chemistry, we two, and the light in the center, that's you, number 3, and the arc is complete in sparkling conversational skill, I am replete with a life, light blue.

LIGHT BLUE JEANS • Expectant gowns are cast aside and I am walking full in stride to the ringing news that a birth has come and a special pair join as one and waltz the dance of eternal glee in the comfort shored in my light blue jeans. • I am wearing the jeans, I wore as a kid when I recalled the light that is, so easily and comfortably, and definitely well worn. Torn at the knees from my familiarity with praying surrender to the light that renders one whole and welcome and home to the center, the square, the circle, the tip of that triangular wonder, the spirit, the wind and the form, become one in the light, of a sparkling design. Right on the seat of my light blue jeans. Light.

LIGHT INN-BETWEEN • Stay awhile and rest a bit at the light inn-between and heavenly glint of opals black and white and splashed with the fires of heaven and just a splash of divine intrigue at the virginal splendor of the valley in me. Rest a spell at the light inn-between. L-I-g-h-t. • There's a light lodging here at the light inn between and the people I know are willing to be lifted and lofted and gifted with signing renewal of the light magazine pouring them full of light ammunition – self knowing. Know your light. Tonight at the lodge inn between your heart-speaking softly – light.

LIGHT DAY • Light days are humming for you and me and celestial healing of our sexuality has brought a new creator, a strong and loving peace, the light of day and the night of speech, written to say, "have a light day," eternally, light. • There's a light day coming for you and for me when the rivers and the lakes are sparkling clean and the trees tell a story without being cut and earth's minerals fill our longing without being dug. Precipitate and participate in the life called light. Know you mother vine to stream and the earthy splendor of a glistening stream of coppery golden being. Rose gold leanings. Coal is steaming. Let it live. A light day our way. Light.

LIGHT BAY • Light these shores and sound the bell of heaven struck with a song to tell her quaking insides that love's the glide and the glue and embrace of earth's great give and our great take and a loving burst ignites the sky over forests and trees and rocks applied to decorate you, our loving light bay. • The light's at bay in this land of delay, so let's open the dam and let love take this land. Filling us up with a cellular cup of minerals and salts and lighting us up with the sparkling new well within the four corners called you and your heart and the spinning revue illustrates this – our sailing away and deep within the light bay reflecting in our delicate win just a quarter moon away and happy to play asplash in the depths of the light bay. Light.

LIGHT STAY • Stay a bit and know the byte of information shared and heaven alight with earthly give and eternal pairs of loving left and passionate stones at the core of this diamond, this intricate tree, the light's staying ways and the blessed three become one, father and son, let the mother be our eternal peace in this light stay. • Tonight I'm staying light and I mean it, the light's in my heart and the space called my throat the place of delivery of this illuminating note – do, re, me – eternally, a light stay.

LIGHT, INVITE IT • Invite the light to live inside. Know that peace can now imbibe in you and drinking free you feel the splash of divinity and the fountained view of a loving God and the dance of bubbles lifting up to breathe the light and join the host of heaven flung wide to share the toast. The light, invite it. • Light, let's invite it to the party called we and definitely record an automatic yes, for the light knows the magic, the flute playing note of happy intention, of asking for the most awesome, incredible guest, the light's coming over. Just check your list. The light, invite it.

LIGHT, YOU TIE IT • The phantom of my life has left to reveal the ghost most holy yet, the spirit of christ indwells in me and all other ties I have set free to reside in you, the light design, enjoy the view of the light inside. The light connection, the lightest print. The light, you tie it, to your heart's foot print. Light. • Light untied is filling me with the swelling lace of a shoe now tighter. Fill it well. I am walking the earth with a story to tell. Feel the earth. Feel it well. Deep in the center I am embedded in the lightest favor, the light's embrace and nature is smiling at my humble approach. The light, you tie it back to the center in you. Light, you tie it.

LIGHTLY LOOSE • Light is loose and gay and free and tympanic electric and I am driving a new machine the light mobile with lots of wings and a span so large I can barely see the side to side expanse of me. I am lightly loose, in flapping relief that the dimensional shift begins with freeing my will to be the spirit I am. Light loose. • Light is loose and loving too and tight where you need it and zooming it's true – light, I love you and I know my friend has brought me back to living again – in a loving way, I am loose to stay light in the middle of me. What pay-offs on some loose change. Lightly loose.

LIGHT TIES • Tie my roots to the growing chain of a light plant lifting away from pain to the sunny side of an earth designed to appoint the view to the love in you and a mother's care has filled the lair of disappointment with a healing stint and a light ointment designed to share, the crux of this blessing return to the concern called family and our light ties. • Light ties are twinkling in the stars of my life, illuminating constellations and adding diversion to life's new intention. Light. 4Th edition. Right on the press and hot to express – our light ties blinking on tonight. Arcing home with delight. Light ties.

LIGHT LAKE • Love's a lake and light's inside the healing splash of a giving tribe, the light force met beside the lake, crater blue and know mistake the lightest tread has led to peace and the cool review of a snowy peak melting inside to reveal the proof of the light swimming in you. A tiny island. Know man. Basic and human and light clear through. A light lake, you. Light. • There's a light lake waiting for your intimate splash of imminent news, there is love in this lasting attendance to emotional care and feeding your light well and stopping to tell your swimming stories of spiraling in, deep to the middle and then right back again. In a flash dear, welcome back to the light lake. Splash. Light lake.

LIGHT STREAM • Light streams down and in and through the light-skimmed veil inside of you and a light shade grey, elects to leave and a loving peel imbues my dream of a lighter day and a loving way and a special melt of the patterned way, as new imprints are allowed where old be-little had endowed and I know the gleam of the light, I am and the living stream of be-ing hu-man. Light stream. Light. • There's a day when the light streams through in such a way as to eliminate the lie of survival. Light's stream means living in a delicate way, charging ahead in an entertaining way. Winding you home to the spirit within and then back to the beginning called infinity again – in the middle. It's light today beside the light stream.

LIGHT WATER • Light water pores upon my sores and finds the voice to share my truth that the love eternal's inside of you and a healing piece has found release and a psyche sung has met the

rung of a jung-er ladder and a higher matter, a special blend of a purer trend and a higher sign, the love inside the cooling splash and the trickling sooth of the me. Alchemical proof of the golden fountain in man. Lead to see a love less narcissistic shining back at me in the reflective view of you. Light water. • Water, water, well and deep. Fountains of the light relief. Droughts are gone and fires are out. The hurricane has lost it's spouting upheaval of the life I am leading. Light water ahead and smooth is my trail to the oasis I'm telling you all about. Found it out. The youth-full fountain's in me good-bye gravity. Fill me up. Light water.

LIGHT DROPLETS LIFTING • Four more days until the peace of a pulsing plenty finds release and a birding song in-trance has gone to join the light and awakening's come and loving's flown the flight back home and october's trees have met the splash of light droplets lifting the summer's heat and an eternity, autumnal, is complete with glowing signs of the love inside, splash by splash, light droplets lifting. • Lift the lightest droplet on the tip of just your lip and slide it down you swollen throat and feel the treat in this light filling heaven's sight with blissfull buckets of delight pouring from the well in you. Tell the truth. Feel yourself as one light droplet lifting to return to the sun light's begun with one light droplet's lifting.

LIGHT WATERS FALLING • Shame had melded years of pain into perceptions, less than, claimed – and I am melted by the name of light regained and space embraced in pink-green waves of light's refrain splashing in to join the friend of heavenly claim chiming in, as light waters falling, fill the gap called darien with a gentle bridge and a panamanian grin. The light is on as softly light waters falling. • Light water's falling at the lip of my shore and I'm chasing moonbeams and chanting for more light – hearted laughter and joyous mirth and the sexual chatter of this love called the earth's. For the earth is a lady voluptuous and whole and soft in the middle and riddled with whole generations of regardless youths who trampled just a little on the delicate truth. Light water's falling across a bossom near you. It's the earth's crust and mantle expulsing a view of light water's falling. Lightly light...In the middle – you. Light waters falling.

LIGHT HOLIDAY • Light holiday's impart the truth that beauty built is beauty fed by a higher hand and a lifting lid and I know mother as all other and we are met in a soul-less bet that love today is a light holiday and I lift my tread to share the gift of shamings melt and loving's bed, a light holiday. • Take a light holiday – embrace the truth that the mark called release can unlock the beast of denial and allow the pain of absolute resistance to remove her chains. For we are the light gear, the lovers, the friends of the light dancing full flow through our holidays again – everyday a holiday. Light holiday.

LIGHT CHECK • I am sorry for the pain I've proffered due to the fact that other's scarred inside my bed of living denial of the lighter tread and I know peace and pleasant bliss inside the love of a lighter kiss. The pain has left and my heart's secure within the peace of a softer lure. I am the plan and the woman led to live in peace at the place of rest, beside the stream of sparkling flecks of a heavenly dream and a living reflect of the beauty in you. A light check. • Pass the check, the bill's been paid by the aid of the light I have made available to me in my giving belief that light is my friend and my life can begin to circle again to the light complete – a light relief paid for you and for me. Past the check. Savings direct. I'm on line for a light check.

LIGHT CHECKER • A lighter game has been inflamed inside of me and I am free to know the piece of a soul's release and a spirit gained in looping infinity to the heart of divinity and the spoken refrain, I am living again in the perfect bliss of a knowing kiss and a jumping spree to the game in me. I am the tree and the resting place called lighter love, just check in my shining face. Light checker. • I'm a light checker. Where is your switch? Do you have a warranty yet? Your light's the same. The increase is your skill to clean up your wires and pay your light bill. Believe the light. That's the insight, know it well – that's the tale. Where's your crown? Round your heart. Shine it up. That looks fine. Your on the board with the light adored – you. A light checker too. Light.

LIGHT CHEST • A healing met inside the chest of a person spared the tide of hours and a living spoken has broadly opened the lacerated rust to reveal the trust of loving friend and broken trends to rejoin the light of a lifting sight. My heart swing free and shining sung inside my chest, the living one. Light chest. • Pour out the ice. It's melted already and open your chest to the love, slow and steady. For the light's here quickly and awaiting your remember to speak forth these words of power-full engender. Welcome light, to the chest I call mine. I love you best. Hear it said light now dwelling here within my light chest

LIGHT FLORAL • Heaven's met my blessed life and I am bright to a stars ignite and tears of fed have starved neglect to the point of pulse and the heart of lift and a bed of songs has burst within the garden of plenty that I call friend. I have aligned with the light inside my lightly floral ways. Light floral. • Flowers of light adorn the sand of this raspy voice lilting this man home across the desert and through a new span to the arc in the middle the blossoming fan of happy renewal, the light trust, and it's you, the loving boquet, lightly floral and eternally that way. Floral unity the essence of love and light blooming. Lightly floral.

LIGHT TRUST • Trust this light this heavenly light that I call I am and know the breach to the lasting peace of love understood in our living thrust to rejoin the light trust. • It's the truth I trust all the way through, intentionally a must for this heart called me, shining with wisdom of knowing the tree and the trio of life imbued with the spirit, my life. Light is my trusting faith of the regeneration affecting this nation. A light investigation gave me the truth. It's light I trust – eternally – light.

LIGHT LORDS • Light lords leap in dazzling glee at the notice of proof that there's love in me and an ocean rings beside the sea of blessings rung and ecstasy sung to a soul's release and a blissing complete of the circuits run and a sky called leaf of love has come to reveal the appeal of your light lord's stay. Light lords. • It's a light privilege to walk in the land of the light lords singing me home to remember with their humming refrain. Singular instances feed me well and I come to the center of this familiar land and I bow to myself and the light that I am. Light lords.

LIGHT LIFE • I have a light life here at heaven's door and a lighter way to inform your listening heart that love can share for infinity's made of living in pairs of persian invite and heavenly nights bent to the flow of celestial wine and the beloved design of the light life. • I am living the light life, surrendering my light to the knowing that this is the life and the telling showing, actions speaking of the light now peaking deep within the want of me and lifting slowly to fill my longing with the gentle knowing that I am the one, the sun, the light, the sum and the living earth's daughter living the light life – eternally – light.

LIGHT SHELL • Shells of ears are hearing me and oceans sung beside the sea, invite the truth, divinity, and the wave of inlightenment living in me to a piano's key and 64 doors, I am resonating though the flavors of your light shell. Hear me. God has spoken. Light. • I'm living the light life without a shell and my soul has been surrendered to the light full ametrine and healing and crystalline as well for the story's now been telling, that it's light you're wearing well – surrender your shell, your wall, your trivy for the right to be privy to the light shell exploding within. There comes the sun, on the inside, counting full. Surrender to the love of the light. The light explosion, the light shell.

LIGHT SHED • Shed the dread of living circled and square the press of circled squaring. Know the shape that most is daring. You, soul-free, and naked to view in your shimmering essence. The heavenly view, you inside the light shed. • The light has shed her shoes of lead for these slippers lightly fed by laces of trembling ecstasy at the end of this evenings light span and I am initiating the break away from all mundane to take a little trip to the light shining soft upon this smiling lip. I am light and fine and I have shed all that's unlike the same, into the light. Light shed.

Light be-jeweled • sixteen days and twenty nights and forty jewels and a fasting life, escape me to meet the steet of eternity and the jewels that speak, my heart, my head and my holy gut, the intuitive news that it's time to get up, by the clock inside, my natural beat, the breath of my spirit and my soul's retreat to the light be-jeweled. Light. • Sparkly, clear aquamarine, crystal, clear, ametrine, orange tourmaline, crystal magazines of jeweled forever, brilliant and lovely and welcome to the heart of the gentle companion, this remembering spark swollen with light emotion and given the notion that light is right in the middle where it belongs, shining in the arc of my surrender to the light be-jeweled.

LIGHT GEMS • Gems of juicy elixir fill my light weaned bottles with a glorious spill of splashing sounds and glorious intrigue with the light gems living inside of me. A light has dawned and we are on our own horizons. Know the gem of your own sweet voice and the healing choice to speak only... Light. Light gems trickle from my mouth to anoint your ear with the healing flood of my giving heart. Our lifting love. Know the gleam of a lighter seam. Mother's earth and a milky beam of light gems heard in my every word. Light gems. • Light's the center street to the jewel I call you and the gem in the middle is our infinite love – spoken in the same tone erernally – light gems of surrender sprinkle my middle with the earth's finest glory and I know the complex, the simple the story of a life often given light gem injections to further furnish this temple called me with light's infinity. Light gems and me eternally. Light.

LIGHT INSPIRE:

LIGHT EDITION • A light edition of an electric ignition and a tradition bent to shine the lines within the light of a lifting sign. The love's been sent and the covenant made to refine a new life in the edge of a glade without limits and within the bounds of boundry-less wonder at the lanes coming down and the light is on and we're all home at the edgeless lip of a living throne. Cherubim ringing, celestial singing, the light is on and we're all one in the night of a day that infinitely gives an abiding light and an eloquent gift to a scattered few. The children are found and hear, they abound, in resonant hues at the beauty called pearlescent views and the laughing gift of beauty met in a sparkling trip to the zipline* inside. An electric view of a light edition. We are the book and the tree of this light. A living version of this light edition. • A light edition is bound through love's eternal humming yes to love...Be led lightly home to the light edition.

zipline – direct descent of the ascending admit that we are divine and the spark aligns.

LIGHT CHANNEL • Amber met with burning drips of smokey assign in the love and the life of a giving incline to the tunnel of loving and lightening express to the penetrating truth that love has met her beam of the light channel. The jade green application of the living proof that love residing inside of you and in me, is a giving tree with an infinite view of the love within the light channel too. By design. Light. • Develop your channel and render it well – wide to the middle and no edges to tell an absolute end or beginning of you- for you're light to a spectrum and all the way through – a light channel cutting through to the heart and the eyes of this matter. Settling for pieces and particles

is through – buy a new vowel. I'll take an ìiî turned straight up to this heaven you're talking about and connected light to the heaven in the middle of you – light green into the indigo blue and pink view of your light channel.

LIGHT SPRING • Spring to the edge of a glistening tree and a trail wide blessing called living the dream and a blessing met with a tranquil branch of a fountain's gift to live in seams of blessed assurance and singing trees and a lanky hike to the end of a grade and a mountainous life and the living approach to an arkansas blend of a finer bee and the honey of life evoked in me a healing stream, an exquisite beam of definite hue and valuable gleam in the eye of a moonstone with ametrine base glimmers indigo traces of cabachon* days embraced with dreams of a glorious day bought with bouquets of flowery intrigue and precious imbue and a heart called forever inside of you. We are the dream of a living stream. A light spring. • Virginal valleys spreading through truth of the joy of sharing this light spring with you. The eastern sky is outlined with trees intimating news that you're taller than these wooden revivals of the grandest design – that man is the miracle mirroring kind loving surrender to this writing, this sender, embarking in likes of sparkling tender tiny bamboo shooting through earth to find a new root and a place we can start to remember the flight called a life to another dimension – beyond sight of just two looking ahead. There's one in the middle growing right through you head to the roof and the truth and the celestial view of the light springing through you. Light spring bubbling through. Light.

Slivers of stone, glassy-jeweled in believing intrigue.

LIGHT CRUISE • Light can fit in vein-y seams and especially delicate loving scenes of titanium blessings exposed to the glow of moonbeam's dreaming and trickles too of golden day-light and trestle's built over typical trampings and treacherous pelts of raining align with the splashing belt of a photonic radiation and a meteoric path through the center of a peridot's dream and a life lived immaculate in genetic streams of virgin's merry leanings and peach elective trims associated with the currents of venting ash blown to the winds of a triple truth that electricity lives inside of you. Body, spirit, mind, and seams of emotional be-ing and tangerine dreams. The life is fine upon the line of this light cruise. • I am cruising through the light canal giving thanks for all I am, light, and finding keys to all my locks and welcoming gales unfolding in me. I am climbing, swimming now within the space in me and I am light cruising simply and well and full within this glittering friend light and her outrageous and gorgeous ship, this earth and life is light here on the open seas of me. Light cruise.

LIGHT DIMENSIONS:

The one, the eight, the living thirteen, a baker's dozen of the truth as seen in the crowing view of the light pyramid shining in your and waiting to live, by your grace, in the swan-like place called your delicate face rung round with rings of rosey green, aquamarine, and peregrine wings, periwinkle-blue clear to the fluffy heart of you. The light's aquamarine and compassionate and loving in its surrender to your fluffy interior, light and pink and crystalline green with loves light. Welcome the light royale.

LIGHT ROYALE • Passionate pulses of pertinent levels, lifting examples of excellent petals and peachy to green trees of leafy assign examine the truth that this living is mine and you are the trim and the top and the sail of a swimming revival and a ringing bell, the trail of triple infinit-y to infinity's blessed trail and a sky-full of simple ecstatic reveal. We are the kind and the will and the free and the artist impressioned by the light's bliss with me. Bless this place and this loving face shining, soft across from me and eternally I remain the electric refrain, energy's globe, elasticity has shown the truth I contain. The mitochondrial grip of a loving light space. The very cells of me, and to you, let there be – light royale. • Opaled through and softening true with the gentle peacock spelling news of light's gemming songs the 3.14 Plus an infinite more circling of squared up living at angles to the perfectly spiraling repetitive sound of creations keening, sounding rhythm winding home to every cell in you. This light is royale and beautiful and kindly immersed in this crystalline matrix that we call the earth and other is sister and lover and friend now that our rhyming is creation without end, infinite, spinning diametric return to the circumference of you – bulging through the crust of the light royale. Light

LIGHT LOCAL • Light's located in my grooving place of divinity's fitting testing trace and I am inclined to extract a dime of a diamond's carbonic enraptured friend who lives in the time of the terrific end which lives inside the place of a spatial serenity filled with the love of pink and green surrender to the light local. • This is where I live and love and work. This gentle mother called the earth. Give her kindest fond regard for this is your planet, your home, your yard. Honor each mole, each molecule of dust with the creation song singing in bursts and ecstatic surrender to the circumference of you – the light eternal, infinite and free and dwelling right here in the center of me – looking directly into the light and straight into you. The miracle of two completed by three – the perfect trinity – you, me and light. Right here, now in this light locale.

LIGHT HABITAT • Living in light of awesome intrigue I am mexican in seams and fire opaled imbue of the extravagant light that lives inside of me and into you and infinitely reigns eternally glued to a rocking glass of glittered beads and basically blue to a lapis trim I am the treat and the love within and a house called a temple and a zipper zipped free has met at the lip of a branching extreme and a light reflects softly upon the smokey glass of a window winged to a bird's belief that the living connection is the energy between ethnic calculations of lifting relations to a higher door, a home of wanton pleasure and a ice chilled rim of tempting

exposure to a blue-eyed seam of crystalline trim and aquamarine bemuse with chicago's blue field and the yellow green treat of a fluorite dream and a tan-angelic arc to the week of sweet believe in the home we call a heart with a purple pink examine of the matrix in the spasm of a mantled house's splashing clean dowse in the fountain ametrine and the return to the shore called the heart of your door and your happy bed at the head of a house called the light habitat. • Chemical combination's the square root of squares and the bonding of ions, and the kinetic flair of energy's motion bounding off beams of wood and concrete, and it's all our light habitat. It seems such a contrast, an impasse of truth, bursting at seams of what we îknewî. Well, try it again, of finest gossamer thread are this earth's energetic light robes wed to each other and through you and me for we are the light's favorite habitat and habit and design. Sacred to a geometric moment and well fed in this light habtat, the earth, our bed. A light habitat.

LIGHT AMIGO • Light's my friend and my peace-full attend to the definitive attraction of a spectacular action called the twirling guadalajaran extravaganza that meets in a crescent oaxacan and a tribe's cancun stream of the gulf's crystal dream meeting at the mouth of a special place called mississippi mud and the famous lounge of her healing flood. Our light ladies bliss-full remembrance of the rapture built on faith and flooding means of sweet revival. I believe in the light, amigo. • It's light amigo, so cross the border to the sacred design, the delight of a lighter spring – deep and fine and spraying directly into my eyed blinking embrace of the sweeter taste, the dripping ambrosial nectarine taste of the holiest honey the smacking entrance of the light, your amigo, hurtling in to gently encircle and to fill your cup with the light milk- honey -n- slightly salty too. Blue-green and indigo with ceramic view lift me up to the lip of a toast to the light, my friend. My light amigo.

LIGHT, AS I GO • Light, as I go I participate in loving in the game called the loop of infinity showing in my smiling face and my shining glee with the light indigo establishing belief in the rounding trip called the star of relief. A shining sign that a blessing can reclaim the celtic knotting of the light, as I go. A dancing loop of pleasant flow. Light, as I go. • Shining in sight of a mirrored step, I see through feet polished clean with grainy sand and milky clay and I am gambling on perfect odds and even then I am light, as I go tripping into the night of a mine I call me and deep within shines a face, my own lightly seamed with laughing design at the schemes I had dreamed, now laid aside to step in, wide eyed, to my light and it's light, as I go, indigo and scarlet and green at the seams of my silvery shoes with moonbeam heels and windowless soles beaming to see the light, as I go.

LIGHT LISTEN-ING • Light's listen-ing and I am true to the trooping glint of the light in you and that's all I see when I look your way and it's a fact that attack has given way to the absolute belief in the perfect template, the light bodied contrain called you. The perfect note of a traveling flute, open to a marked resemblance to the fortunate few awakening early to a light lighten-ing view. Waking up in a thunderous arc. We revive our light listen-ing.

LIGHT SAIL • Sailing through a swollen tide, I am infinity's gleam and the look in her eye and a glassy blend of a heaven scent trend to laugh in the bottles of living within the cargo of lite and the wealthy of free and the drum of a meeting called my heart and me and an excellent sine that all has gone well is my giving sigh and the lift of the veil of all forgetting. This love is letting me remember the lightest tribe and the sight of a double arc on the inside. Pastel and powered by a diamond-tipped spark and a mast electric and a giving lark to the light splashing fluid in moving relieve to the heart and the perfect wed of divinity, light and me to the lover's degree I set my spectrometer to the horizon that is longer left and elastic and beaded in petunia petals trailed upon the water of my sunset light sail straight to the center of my. Light sail. • Trim your sail and travel your board to the light waves lapping you home to the shore of your infinite spin toward the center again. For your top is blown and your vanity shown a new brand of makeup and a fasting face lift – just lift up thine eyes to the light shining brisk in the billowing sails of your luffless calm arrival at the dock of your forever. Light and a light sail.

LIGHT SALE. • Buy me a view from the penthouse timed to ripen along the spectacular line of a van gogh-ed drift and a painting extreme of scupltural splendor and the embellishments gleamed from a yard sale's signed attenpt to review the extremes of a heavenly view and a bounty-full myth sold to communing commuters flying within to scoop up the old and fill in the view with a light seamed face grown familiar and new, in a spinning review of the light's best buy, you. Light sale. • The light's for sale at the price of remember. Spend a dime and some time on surrender at the pew called offering and the pulpit called you is a heart deep and tender with a gentle peak called your name, whispered welcome to the temple, the light and the altar, the place of forever and the infinite wave of the kindest review written on water with footprints of love, the light's free tonight at the sign of the dove. Light sale.

LIGHT CHURCH • Churches are steeples built in the seam of a living within and an electric dream of forever and ever and ever again shining in patterns of gleaming approach to the pens and the pillars of a pearl layered deep at the bride of a woman and the bride of a stream, full tympanic, scarlet hued embracing the trend to a higher view. The light temple, you. Light church. • The church at the corner of infinte surfing and waving surrender is welcoming now her newest member. The rock, the gibraltar, the wave of delight is singing in concentrated prayer-full bright advocation of the grandest admission that the light church is congregating here on the shore of your indigo blue heartstone,

full throated and high winged believing in aspirations of ablutions melting in glacial fountains of baptismal pooling communion. A light church. Light.

LIGHT TEMPLE. • Light your temple with the iconic shine of a laughing dove living kin in her believing return to the light inside... A light temple by design...Light. • The light temple shineth in building waves of standing columns and pillared engravings. Lifting mine eyes to the face and the sight my own shining light bouncing off stars and ceilings and planets, waxing the wavelengths and floors of my back to the basics the a's and the b's of the temple of living called the life of high c's – committing, courtesy, and a cherubic center charming to the spirit and lifting to the sender. A light temple.

LIGHT-EYED • Light-eyed drifts of astounding news requires the piece of a gentler hue, red carnationed and assigned the task of a pleasant surrounding and a smile that lasts and the squints of forgiving are met with the invitation to let your fingers start living in goldfish bowls of ocular orbs and lasting attempts at the chance to believe in a starry night's blend of reflective coronas and nebular truth that the proof's in the puddle and the puddle's in you, the moon beaming light-eyed in eyes brimming full to see the divinity's gleam at the bridge of your knowing that sparkles in the beam of your light-eyed glowing. Light. • In the light span of this life I call mine, I am filled with silent wonder at the innocent splendor of this mother we call earth and I am humbled as her child now and astounded by the knowledge that I love me just as I am, the light, in absolute balance with the nature I call me and the harmony of mother's earthly laws and my heavenly nature meeting in thundering silence and light-eyed greeting of each the other. Light eyed.

LIGHT JUICE • Juicy hugs of creation's milk and the bursting abandon of a natural kiss. The earth has met our every need with the lasting taste of a lightening steed, running free, to lift my gift to the cookie crumbled cliff of all for-give-ness. A loving mother, melting other, in silent intrigue, with the living breed, light juice. • I'm going on juicey splashes of infinite me sipping on lattes* with light whipped cream and angelic lights fluttering near and the dolphin of heaven swimming to hear my breathing agreement to remember now the light juice arcing me home by the brow. Light juice.

*lattes – A creamy concoction of warm milf, coffee and steam.

LIGHT PURE • Light is pure in her giving return to the heart of the love and the earth, her own, and her sparkling web lights up in me at the living edge of a timeless sea, the ledge of the universe and the lift of a sea meant for stars and hearts like ours, pure and free, a honeyed tree of life eternal and magnificent hue resonating well inside the grid of dancing lines, spinning tides, and the light pure glowing well inside. Know the peace of the light pure. • Crystal clear and current clean whipped indigo and violet-green by the earth's genuine filling stream of wild reminder that our mission is kinder than we tend to make it in our crystal clean, light pure dream, perched here on the edge of infinity and the equatorial seam of this breathing balls blue-green persuasian to honor this nation with a light pure to the edge of a living marvel. You in the night with a splash of light pure luminescence flooding your face on tomorrow. Now. Light pure.

LIGHT BELIEF • Clarify and clear the brief of your tourmalined* yearning for a higher retreat and the wealth of a spark webbed to complete the infinite loops inside of you. Height to light. I am inside the light belief. • Light relief is your light belief, and into two I am known as three, and three we are – weaving into towandan dreamings, a cherokee born lakota and brim filled in sioux white eye's hats now worn with love in two treed light-belief.

tour the heights of a rocking lift to the tubes octangular and the figure eight's gift...align...

LIGHT RELIEF • Light relief has now arrived and I am insured of a softer ride and a kinder pocket and a lighter grip and a heart met gentle in a giving trip to the light inside and the pleasant stance that knowing you is knowing me and knowing me is divinity in my absolute alliance with the lightest appliance, my own light heart. Clear and pure. Light relief. • There's a light relief to this, my belief that I'm less than the light that I am. Taking the leap, I'm given relief from the edgy gap I can be and I'm bridging my divides of synaptic blinding denial to shatter the past from my file cabineted stance and the glance at the light provides the insight to lift my flight to a circling spin, well within the light that I am, light relief.

LIGHT SOFT • Light is soft within the toss of a jelly-beaned jar of sparkling ovals and filled in gleams of lasting seams and pleasant schemes left high to glow in gleaming wattage of the fire below and the fire within leaps and sparks in arcing webs and webbing arcs to glow enthused with the blending ooze of a healing stream deep within my light soft ways. Softly. Light. • Soft light floods the vision I call mine and I'm clear to the middle and soft to the shine of a distant mirror echoing back my beating heart – softening cracks of early indignance swollen with enthuse and filled to the middle with the infinite views. The light is soft here in this world beyond blue and in I go to the light indigo with a crystalline hue melted to form the light I call you. Light soft.

LIGHT BRIGHT • Light's bright in heaven's light of sunny days and livid nights met in praise of nature's ways and sources dealt from a living pack, a battery free, electric view of the light so bright in you. Light bright. • The light's shining gently in the brightest eyes, my own and I am wondering where I met this especially grate-full heart I am carrying about for I am seeing the living beauty of the light I am spanning the globe of this earth's open-armed stance in full-breasted patience with my tiny eyed squeeze of the ruptured bladder, called matter, drained of pain to be the brightest light, the light bright in love's delight – light. Coppery wired central revolver of the metallic glitter at the top of my head – light bright.

LIGHT FEATHERY • Light birds land in the height of the tree and sephira* bands indicate stay as depths are plumbed and locks tossed away to reveal the feathers of a blessed sight... The light down's feathery intensive flight to the layered gate of michael's saint and the truth told bliss of heaven's wait for my release of the healing piece, the intricate lead to the beak-oned news that a light's grown feathery inside of you. A new dimension. The lightest scale. The maat* tale of a love aloft and all judgement passed. The gates have burned and we're home at last to the feathery key of divinity's loft. Light feathery. • Clouds of feathery intricate weave flank now the head of this life on the sleeve of an ingenious life believing in sight of the wellness communed between your heart and mine and now I can see why I'm living this time on the line, like an arrow to the light become matter, flying swiftly within the light feathery. Again, light.

ten gates breached to reveal one peace.
*** balancing bales of living down and looking up through feathers of soul-less flight. The spirit I AM.*

LIGHT FLOWER • Light has flowered in my bed and I sleep soft in metered piece at the blessed peace which resonates free to the blissed insides which honor me in metabolic kinks ironed right out and healthy females figured out and males dealt trends have broken loose to see the flower inside of you. Break the shade and shine the light of an electric night and an exciting wave of the love in me and the lightest fade to a brilliant dance on my bending leaves. The light flower's has dawned inside of me. Petaled proof of the peace-full pleasure of an eden-ic treasure. We are the garden of a gentle light flower. • The Light's a flower in the breast I call mine, blooming in waves of forging alignment with the kindest plan, the wholest spectacular plant of sunflower profusion and carnations too blossoming roses and budding camelias perfect attunement for the love that fills you with color's safe to brighten your day in a light flower's resonant way. Light flower. Essential by the hour. Infinite by design, to the minute. Light flower. Light.

LIGHT PRETTY • Light's pretty gift is a chiming kiss of fiery delight and delicious myth melting to reveal the love and relief of a delicate field of recovery. Leaning in to catch the wind of a butter-flyed day and the monarch's way and a ritual return to the light pretty. • Light is pretty here in the city at the foot of the beauty called helenic wonder and open review of the light sparkling ash-like with a magenta hue bubbling forth through the eye of your well deserved triumph over matter through heart. A new start has begun with picture perfect news. The certainty becomes you. Light pretty. All the way through to the light – pretty. Light.

LIGHT RAYS • Light rayed forgetting has found my street and illuminated stretches inside of me and beams of giving shine the peaks of purple passioned grinning leaps to the strand of a grand evolutionary recline in the land of the crystalline. My heart is home in her light rays daze of lifting remember. Adore the days. Light rays. • Light penetrates the space when I live and I am inclined to welcome my giving nature back to the throne of living and the fire of surfing splendor emblazoned on the heart and the star and the arc that we are. Let there be. Let it be, light and rays flood the well and the wealth of my spirit pulling out soul bits and lifting them up to the light for direction, the soul's returned home and the spirit now lighter enjoys the view of light rays invoking with telling relationship their light stay within you – arcing through – light rays.

LIGHT HIGH • Hi light. Light high. I am elected to welcome the flight of all now arriving at the land of begin and the deja vu end of all karmic trend. Know more sole. Walk the street of soul-less retreat to the solace of whispering home on the feet of a fancy flight to the light high. • How far from the edge can we stray dear, and where on this earth can we play? We're welcome to play and to dwell at the street called heart-felt and to spell the retreat from the rim of refusal to learn to receive. Receiving's an art and giving so sweet that receptions are held in our lover's completion of cycling truths binding denials, and the view absolute to the reflecting crater in the middle of you, filling up with spirit soon and well, in the center of you. The light's high tonight in the crater too. Healing tool. Mountain side. Light high.

LIGHT OPEN • Light's open in her review of the ressurection seen inside of you. Regeneration's completer and you are back and on your feet. Believe in the healing trend to begin again. Daily scene and often given the hand of a friend and the life that we're living in an open stare directly in to the light opened heart of a giving trend. The light open. • Open your eyes to see the light willowing home in feeling delight, filling my ocular orifice with my habit, my fix, my cure, the light open to the night of maytime flowers and well meaning showers bearing sweet gifts, softening eyes and moistening lips with love intendered with purposeful blenders replacing blinders. Goodbye deniers. The light is open and has 1,000 gifts to deliver in the eyes of our open surrender to the light open.

LIGHT OPENING • There's a light opening and a living trend to re-join the giving and the for-given band of former deny-ers and exceptionate saints who reside in the land of the light opening. • Light's clearing forests of pining neglect and planting the seeds of the finest heritage. These are the seeds and this is the place where lightening strikes the entire human race. Salty cravings have sewed their place and now the final leg of the taste of honey without has pushed for within and the light opening can begin to arc from spark to spark, the spirit matters of infinite wonders, the lenticular leanings for the heaven asunder to receive the reprieve called light opening.

LIGHT LOVE • Light love has given my heart a new grip on a pen called remember and a heart called delivery. Light love. • Light love. Little sisters are open and welcoming you to share in their joy the picture of two becoming one glorious thunderous voice evicting the blocking choking blight of ashes to ashes covering dusty layers of refusing to see the evocation of the power I call thee. Towering light of columnar vision, a shifting telescope removing division and telling the truth through blinking review of the pineal eruption happening in you – know the light, write your life in explosive renew of the light love volcanic in you. Light love.

LIGHT FLOWING • Light flows falling in the apian way that I smile soft in strawberries and in delicious waves of shortcaked seams and patient belief in the halls of peace – like a river. Light flowing. • Light flowing lava like through molten pushing puddles of sticky residue and cleaning every cell to windowed clarity and perfect review as the soul slush flies out of the top of you to regain her height in the land of the light and a new growth appearing in the midst of her space, a tiny bud emerges to face the budding return of the light flowing, filling erupting through space. Fill your jug, lift your mug to the light flowing free within your life. Light flowing.

LIGHT PRESENT • Present the blend of perfectly one by sauntering whole to the light waved sun of another day. A gift. The now of a light present. • The light's a gift and a present too, glaring with certain clarity into the curtainless wander, the holiest grail, the cup, the cup called forever, and the ability to tell that the eternal is calling from spirit's sparking amp electrifying you with the need to review your light. Call the role. Absent. Soul. Check your sight. Is it light? The gift is height finding depth, a clear review. Your light present and accountable to you. Light present. Know the gift. Light.

LIGHT CLEAR • Light's clear in my listening stance and growing exude of the glistening proof that light resides clear through our pineal dreams. Drain the dupes by lifting dear the grail of truth and the heart of clear-est intention. A new dimension. The light clear. • Light clear. Windowless wonder the winning thunder of eruptive sight sings crystal clear in perceptive and bright winking pattern, linking the matter to the source of our banter. Increase you platter, decrease your chatter. Know the light, shining clear to the heart and the head of you. Eye to eye I to I – infinity to infinity, man to man, plan to plan. The path is clear. Light clear.

LIGHT, WOULD YOU? • Light, would you? Let me see the beauty in your welded bliss. One loving sight. Know less

hendrance and embrace greater belief in the light that lives clearly walking in you. As for me. Light, would you? After all, light. • Light review. Light, would you?
Write it here. Yes! Light.

LIGHT CROWN • Crown this piece with a gentle strength and a healing gleam at a hydraulic stream outside the dream of lives a town with an open sign and a crown so long held bound has lifted free to reveal the healing kiss of an aura-ed trip to the help-full lips of a lessened grip and a lighter taste of a loving man. Risen again. A light crown. • The earth's crown is a ring of brown and gold and green and blue and red and orange too and yellow middled. Lightly sewn, willing review shows that trees need their knees and their arms too and their ringing bodies, leafy true to the light crowned four – seasons in you. Pass the loot, know the cup of your light looking up to view the earth filled with leafy sounds of a welcome breeze circling you – "remember" light. Trees. Earth. You. Light crown.

LIGHT VISIBLE • I see the light and the light sees me in double-visioned kaleidoscopic dreams and definite peaces of particulate state seen in the stream of living life great. Know the piece of the light visible continuum. We are the light. Visible. • The light is visible in my face of streams and equal flakes of snow and ash and dust and eve falling lightly through the trees. Eden's here upon this land. Know your span, spark the arc with your plan to honor all in the infinite plan – winging back to love and visible light span. Light visible. Me. Light.

LIGHT HEADED • Light headed, hear, to find a repeal of the blot called descending and the crashing escape to the land of the living, the giving, homo-sap, and a lucy called dream has met continents resplendent in african deliverance, to the light headed day of an endearing play. The light in me and in you. All a stage. A world of proof. A revealing spin. A whirler's friend. Light headed. • The light's headed through this opening in you called I to the third offering clarity energy, and eternity in one unblinking surrender of the blinders called afraid. Fear left this realm just now on a light span back to the light, I am and I'm head over heels in spinning relief weaving the spell that breaks for-gettings web and the light headed through me is welcome and well – season to season in my light headed dizzying return to the light, I am. Light headed.

LIGHT BODY • Light this body from inside out for I am the lion the lamb, and the crown and the open revival of a heavenly trend to let go survival and find a new friend. A revealing site at a naked bend in the lightest blend. A light body. Light. • Tree like a trunk with spinning orbs connected like links on sliding cords shaped like infinity running the loops forward and aft clearing the truth from the living I've done and the will that I'll live is gentled by the cleansing seas changing tides and fluttering leaves of my light body, the earth, giving birth to the light, I am infinity to infinity, light.

LIGHT BLEND • Light blends. All races, all crowds. All abilities, in our common denomination and our consistent belief in the light felt fed by designer bread. The light shaping up. A light blend. • The lightest blend is to love all your ikinî, the people who people this world with the light, sometimes hidden, often given insight to the knowing you, knowing me, makes three for in our admittance that we are like you, an arch and and arch and an arch is created carrying the pi of our power times infinity to the billionth degree, the light inside me in my cellular matrix, crystalline through with the energetic view that the lightest drink, the quencher my friend, is the light without end. Light blend.

.LIGHT GRADATIONS • Light grades me in constant hues of consistent green and heavenly blue and spectrum wide I know the truth of intuitive schemes and examples fed to lift the life of giving tread. Here's to the sound of a host called free and a graduated grade to the heart of me. Intuit the news, a heart-felt glee and a mental imbue of the light gradations in you. Light. • The light comes in grades when it enters my form and I can tell by the jewelry it wore, what's its trip, where'd I slip into less than harmonic crystalline convergence with the light absolute shining in steps and mineral lipped, I'm telling you it's lighting this new life, I call light gradations, step by step and all the way through, the spectrum inside and out, me and you by light gradation.

LIGHT FED • Fed with mann of energetic content, light leads are hanging beside the tree of four-seasoned dreams and eternal recline to the point of nature breasted and the robin fed behind the rest of our early rise. The light inside our light fed loaves of honeyed bread and milky seams reflecting where the light has fed us too. Light fed. • The spring called light feeds my sight and filled with washing, cleansing, flowing I am welling with impassioned spurts of joy-full celebration while embracing the nation in a listening stare directly to the mid-air collision with my light self's feeding, nurturing path straight through the upturned eye of my light hungry be-ing. Self-inner-getic and light fed by the cells of familiar entrance cristae to matrix to dna uplinks to the light fed. Lead me on. Light. Light fed.

LIGHT LED • light led me to infinity's tree and I parked beneath a street lamp shining bright and scanned a new map which fell into the lap of my napping circumference and a bell rang with invite to share a new line, driving red, I am impressed with the light led through you, and me. Serenity. Light led. • Light's leading us to the place and the lake called a mineralized view of the life loving true led by the light shining through my head to sleep this life through at the brink of forever, you. Light led

LIGHT READ • Read the light of a healing book, a special electric and a novel dip into the ink of a living well and a living found in telling spell of exacting purpose and especially light, I'm reading the wealth of the sealing tonight. Keys have said, a light read. • Light read. The light's reading me with piercing intensity and rippling lift to the bubbling stream at the brink of me writing this laughing life – filled with light reading intensity. Read the book it's your heart. The good book. Light. Read it.

LIGHT SAID • Light said let there be – light. • The light said hello and I knew the light would by my own blazing intensity idenitifed in the landslide of this avalanching view you are the grandfather and my reign is due. See the truthlight said, and I believed. Light.

LIGHT CLOUDS • Light clouds ask about the reign and wonder where we got the name for passions blessed and patients peaced by warring less and meeting the needs of the little children. Rainbowed pride in the telling sigh of a loving breeze. An ocean's ford. An actor's lee. The wind of truth and the weather in me. Light clouds. • Clouding piercing grace trickle down the side of your emblazened face, fiery ice and a shaggy mane – the reign of the lion judaeth has arrived and jah and God and mohammad have said – light. Lighten up. Pierce the veil of light clouds shrouding you from my view. Light.

LIGHT BREEZE • Breezes burst upon the face of heaven singing and divinity's page, shining deep within the rift of a lightening grip. Your hand and mine. Electric and joined by a definitive design. Cast your kite upon the sea of a healing b. The light b-reeze. • There's a light breeze blowing across this face called the earth and hidden in whispers are trees of new birth. The old man, the mountain had said good-bye to hellenic beauty shining false eyed surrender. Be the sender, breathe your essence. A light breeze.

LIGHT BEAD • Light beads burst in belllicose veins to dissipate the sorrowed, the dissapointed, the shamed and a word of forgiveness escapes the lips of a light bead strung on a heavenly strand. The light children of a sumerian band. Arcing through on a comet's celestial tale, to travel the trend to a holier veil. I wear a strand of the light bead brand. Light. • Light's blending beads of glass sweating shades of stain-glassed confusion at the life that I've made and the fusion of light uniting through air, the joyous scent of the light's blending caresses with angelic wings of lightest refusal to melt away rings of forgetting and this moment I am lilting, light blend with me. Earth's light eternity, is a light blend. Me. A light's bead.

LIGHT SHAKE • Metatronic has a sonic booming trend and a truffle of treating a fetish, a blend of arcing denial that life is a trial for a life lived rehearsing creates a diversing from the blessed event of your birth and a better begin is the life without end and the earthquake heard round this heart when your light enters in to penetrate thin-iced forgetting and splashes down, tying your drift to the heart of this matter and anihilating doubt with one swift swish of an archangeled mighty deliverance. Light shake. • Make a malt of milk and honey, drink it up in the land of sunny return to the light, the reign, the man, the finished sight of the light melting spans of forgetting in the palm of your hand. Call it candy the light is handy filling your eyes with penetrating sight, a wholesome taste – a light shake.

LIGHT WAVE • Light waves burst in crashing proof that elliptic surges are the sooth and the saying sway of an electric day, schematics seen, and elements swayed to join the table of periodic belief and constant balance and atomic weight attended by a tree bent in wonder to study the fine art of thee. A light wave. • Tonics of faith and celtic tune lighten my mood on a wave from blue, bouncing on glass bubbles tinkling red with violet-blue persuasion of the indigo in you – a lighter view and in I go waving, through you – a light wave – catching air – no edges here, hear the prayer. A light wave's tune. Light.

LIGHT GRADES • Light lives in waves of varying depth and ancient veins erected in pompeian teams of penchants fanned and mother baked us up a-man and a woman knelt in giving grace to birth the span of a living race and tonight while human you have slept a light grades pupil you have met and in peace-full summer singing's sung the lift of armor. Getting on with getting well, means giving life a sweeter bell. A kinder loop. A feeling bend. A love more gentle and a light, the friend who illuminates patterns templates, loops and shines in holographic proof of the dimensional leaps possible through the light grades in you. Light. • We are tackling light grades today, passing the test and there's light on the way to this holy revival this arch-angelic arrival of the light shining through has broken the triad living in you, the triangle through, you are one. Arcing through – to the light grade a in you. Light grades.

LIGHT BODIED • Light bodied blessings exude the truth that love has met inside of you in pink and purple and in blue, a stained-glass curtain of molten move and the release of cellophaned, chambered in. I am the light and the light's my friend. By divine release, the pain has gone and the light has dawned in my horizontal slip to the light inside and the garb that's hip. Back to the balance, I recline in the bliss of my light bodied fit. Light. • Light bodied wings flutter within the cells of my seeing there's light here my friend and my cells are happy with a dancing intrigue at the infinite knowing – theres light here believe. Your light is showing in your glowing return to the earth, your light bodied mother. The earth and you. Light bodied too. Light.

LIGHT STUDY • Light has studied divinity and love has met beside the tree which branches left to meet the knowing that good is all and all is blessed when I deliver the winning kiss to a returning meeting, a reunioned intrigue with the end of less and the setting free of all attaching sovereigntys. I am relieved to feel the lift. Now study this. Light. • I'm a light study, remember me well and listen to hear the story I tell – light. Study me – light study.

LIGHT NOURISHMENT • Lightly nourished I am inclined to dine at the heart of a living line, my own design, a lasting recipe, the light and me, in equal proportions and holy cups. A light communion. Light nourishment. • Light, I am fed by your infinite view right to the center of the column of you – lightly nourished, always fed, by the lightest review the buffet of light on the table called you, the earth, and I am fed and well nourished at the breast I know best. Earth. Light nourishment of the kindest kind. Belly, eye and spirit full. Light nourishment.

LIGHT EFFEICIENT • Light your miracular loving booth with the kissing holy exciting news that a land of plenty has revealed a revel called heavenly and a lusting zeal that melts in defting clarity of the light efficient shine in me. We are the light efficient. • Light's efficient and moving well to the sweeping conclusion of this storied tale, see the light, right the sight, love the earth, love your self, know the worth, divinity's right, light. Now that's efficient. Light.

LIGHT CO-EFFICIENT • Light's efficient in her excellent return to the quantum physicality of mother earth's form and a delicate balance equates within to a digestive recipe and a light-angled friend. Hereby lands a bowel deep trend to lift the curse of eating dirt and ambrosial gifts of fruity kiss have met in the dust that God called us and ashes spilled have now revealed the looping truth of the formula met in the living tree. We are the light co-efficient. The solution? Light. • Light's co-efficient in the formula of life is the earth called my mother and my loving wife to fill my moments, my minutes, my ticks with the abacus of light called the light co-efficient. Love in me, eternally that's the plan and the arc and the span. The light co-efficient. Me. Light.

LIGHT FAMILY • My family's light and I believe in the loving council of a living God and a gracious mother and a dad who live and sisters who give themselves the chance to appreciate this enlivened grace and the terrific punch of a trickle of the light inside bursting forth to believe in the light family. Holy brother. Light. • Light family. My family is light through the tree and the limbs and the wind and the seasons and the span of the wood, the water, the fire, and earth, the metallic wonder-full ball we call earth. In all direction, in every nation, black through white, green and blue, indigo, red, and violet, too are all crystalline where the light shows through. Let it shine. Burn the pretense with your light pursuit, the ex-static return to your light family.

LIGHT ECHO • Light's an echo and an answering gleam to the shine in your eyes and the switch on your sleeve and a melting has happened deep inside of me in a light shining stream and an echoing seam, to the heart of a tree and the health of a dream shining sweet to feel the night with an emphatic sight, the light shining free to echo in me. Light echo. • There's an echo in this chamber, called my heart, and on the inside rings a feeling, a new start. I know that I'm a planet, and an orbit, and a light. A star across the middle and a comet lending sight to new arrivals, to the spirit living in my lifting soul survival to the light without an end and living now is lighter and giving knows within the lightest echo lives the feedback called a friend. Know the light echoing in, in friendly arrival – in light echo.

LIGHT FUNCTION • Light's a function and a sine of the times when love reigns supreme, in an unconditional state and hues of sweet blessing shine in the stars of celestial notions of the f-stops called cars and the buttons called function light up with glee in the center of cells called light's on, get free of the rules of survival and surrender the charm called lucky for life's lived in celestial arms of lightest degree and the lightest function is me. Light. • There's a convention of muslim and jew and christian and rasta and sufi and you, called the seventh day. Meet all your brothers, this is the place called forever written light in your face. No more fear, the geneology is clear, light crystalline and intoning this function with a searing, whispered injunction. Know the light, know your heart, drop the rules, your forgetting tales, all the books, this one too. See the light's full shine in you. Here's your function. Know the junction – light is true, infinite and the ultimate peak. Enjoy the rest and the view of all one sparkling tribe. Abraham wide, isaac tall, and melchizidek hewn. Jesus fed. Mohammed led, and God said – "let there be light". I am that I am. Light. Jah. Light. An oracle and a commandment. Light. Only.

LIGHT CHAMBER • Light's a chamber and a melting place, the love of a family and the light in your place and you are designed to meet in the heart of the sky and the life and the love that you own. Promote the peace of knowing release of the pressing need to drown in greed and see the beauty of celestial cuties, the stars that you are and the living kin of a ship called the earth and an orbit called life and a photon called heaven and a heaven called life. Join the club of a light chamber, your heart, pumping straight through you, the blood of life, and a light chamber too. Light. • Love is a chamber in the light, and light is the light in the love chamber. So let's blend all the compartments and homogenize our milk to one creamy mixture the yolk of this egg called this earth, the light chamber, the right chamber for leaving leftover denial and petty beliefs to the light conveyor spreading the truth, there's one light – in this land. Share it. Light. The light chamber – your heart. Light.

LIGHT CLUB • The keys are made and the door's been fixed, the light club's formed and the dues are tricks of light persuasion. Know the riddle silly girl, one lock, one key, and inside the world. Know yourself, the only clue, to the mantra's ring and the light club dues. Pay the price by living well within the light of a healing swell. Your opening heart and third eye too, staring straight into the view of God's own eye and sweet heart too, directly above the light in you. By divine connection, welcome to the direction, above, and within, the light club, one password, one key, light. • Light up your merits. Trade in your pledge of badges pulling at your head. Open the light club. The rules of order are set. Nature calls them laws. Newtonian. Know them. So will you. Yes, it's true. Welcome to the clubhouse – earth. Save the trees. Arrange the birth of a sapling called you. Plant a tree. Join the club. Earth. Light club.

LIGHT ACCENT • Accent your life with the living light and the heart of the news, there's God in you and arcs of sparks to the billows met true in arcturic* delight at the divinity in you. The light has met her healing spark and a seeing's lead to a brighter claim, the voice, your own, and a gentle name, yours too. The light accent? You. Light. • Place the emphasis here and there, close to the edge of the "this over there"... No matter the matter find the chance to accentuate the light at the birth of this planet. Welcome brother to the sister, your friend, pulsing with vibrant rebirth again. Metatron's home and the light is on. Accentuated and positive. A light accent.

Arcturic – an energy representative of love speaking LIGHTLY.

LIGHT TITLE • The light title's mailed the minute you claim your responsibility for building a living flame from the spark that you are and a loving shines remaining in the blessed life you're framing. Let it be, join the song. Let there be, only, all-ways. Light. You own the vehicle, this indigo temple, this rainbow's bowl, the light title. • The light's driving a brand new ride. It's you and you're pulling up right beside the stuff you've created in your righteous denial that you're only human and you make mistakes too. Well the light has a riddle which goes around the middle of a diametric chicken like you. Know the light. Claim your title, lay down your bible and hug your rival. That "sinner" whose hand looks just like yours and whose eyes have seen the lord's just like yours. Know your light. Love your girth – the earth. Walk gently and light. The light is home and there's revival. Lead me on to my light title. Light.

LIGHT, YOU OWN IT • Light, you own it, now intone it with a greater feel for the higher realm, the head at your heart and the heart at your feeling arrival at the edge of forever and the forever of living in giving repent and the art of confession has met a new direction, tell your self. You're the priest and the crumb and the commoner and the pope and the preacher and the minister and the healer and the drone and the queen of sweet forever in the temple, called your own and a tower of blessed healing has met in one atone, this blessed life you own. Follow antoniacs* led to the brim of sweet return to the light-full owner, you. For it's light, you own it. Light. • Light, do you own it? Can you feel it lifting spans and sheets of stratographic forgetting and stuffed down rocks of molten words never spoken. Here's the token. You are the chosen. The tribe most glorious. The light tribe. We all own it and it's limitless. It's light, you own it, ever increasing. Share it. Who told you that greedy stripping of this earth that we are tripping on is proper. You wear shirts and signs that land the fact that you cut down trees with a whimpering hack. Folks, it's

true, the trees are you. Light, you own it, better share it, spread the news. Light is back and illuminating the mess and the zoo's you've created. Inside and out, light. Locally owned, infinity given. Light.

Antoniac- an energetic blend of God and man, all-one in a loving return, I remain eternal and great-full of your LIGHT. Shine on, loving brother. Treva's friend, Antonio.

LIGHT NATURED • I am light natured in my giving way and eternally fit and universally gay too a living design and a light natured time at the heart of a lip and a loving that's mine, no compare, there's only one and as I know it, my heart can show it in the sharing way I tread and the dancing way I said, it's my heart know it, for you are well and loved by this one, this light natured return to the one love. Light. • I'm light-natured about you, my friend, the earth. I love your conventions, held at parks, naturally prominent you are the harmonious favorite to be dominant at our light-natured electrons, held each day in the heart of each member. Light-natured, I surrender my sight to the light. Light-eyed naturally and enabled to view the light-natured wonder of you. Light-natured.

LIGHT, INVENT IT • Invent the light in your walking way to the love inside and your commitment to stay eternally lit and internally fit and intrinsically divine by the lifting return to the patent you own and the truth of the tree, only one tone, eternally heard and forever returned to the source for a fit. The light, invent it, daily, in your life, only one device, light. • I am light and I'm requesting flight to the land and the light that I am. Earth's light is here, carried in me. Write from the start. Here in my heart. The story too awesome to tell so I'll hear it here in my listening ear, held to the ground by my full bodied sprawl doing my all to cover the mother, I am light through my span, and welcome my lightest invention. Me. The light, I am. Get a patent and a light to match it. Light invent-it. All the way in. Light.

LIGHT DIAGNOSTIC • The diagnosis? Light. The prognosis? Eternal life. The prescription? Apply daily. The physician? You. The way? Light. • The light's diagnostic in its infinite pocket of tools to enlighten and clean. Just stare at a stream and invision the seam of gold which meets this incline and know that the lift you are feeling is a gift from the light diagnostic loving your being, willing to see through new eyes. The light has a 1,000 eyes all glittering facets of the one light – you. I love you, my sweet earth, giver of joy, life, light and birth. Here's to your opalescent return to the virgin you are and to the light I am. Light diagnostic. Never lost it. Light earth. Light diagnostic.

LIGHT LIGHTEN-ING • A circle and a square and a dancing mid-air for there's pi in your hair and your honey's bear has gone to the light, lighten-ing the sight and the sound and the smell of the light waves swelling filling – opening the space for a sparkling view of the white caps lapping at the wedge of sight at the lip of your waving windswept completion of the light lighten-ing your intense grip on life's throttle and there's wind in your sails and light in your hair as the light's lighten-ing continues. Light. • Light is lighten-ing when you act for love.

LIGHT MEANT:

LIGHT RELATED • Light's related to my healing embrace of the truth, that you are equally loved, to a living heart's dream and a loving heart's taste-full, exuberant burst in the telling story, now reversed, to shine on up in brilliant taste and healthy encounter of the love on your face, and your smile can tell we are living well within the seam of the light related. • The light's related to the peace I've dated as happening on this earth, the turf, the crowning land. The piece of knowing I am as a man, is related to the light I carry and the heart we marry to the light and straight through to the earth and I'm merry and well and related to telling the story, my own, to the light and come across the bridge of the light, and I'm home and elated at the bed we've been given, this earth, violet-green with loving welcome trance-cendance and beyond the last demensional door. Welcome to the light level. Light related. Peace. Light.

LIGHT MODEL • Light models splashes and places of friends called this is the symptom of living within the frame of a light model. • There's a light model in place, swirling at the face of infinite arrival at the light past survival and I am welcome and led and fed by the notion that surrendering oceans of constant be-tray-al equals the style called my life and I am home with a wife tucked safely in. I've married my self again, to the light. The bride of the sun and the church of the one light, shared by all and shed to the sight crowning life. A light model. You and me and the light's eternity – by design. A light model.

LIGHT MANAGE IT • Sacred light is the liquid embrace of the pulsing tread to the lifting place and the height of the cabinet that I call manage and the point of pleasure that a planet can establish by way of the miracle called God is a lyrical attend to the trend of a higher fashion, a moment's measure and a lasting treasure of traveling blends and beloved's ascendant embrace of the portals called ladders and the offerings called platters of transcendant pleasure at the heart of a life of infinite measure, a loving wife, a giving mother, the hear of a planet called earth, the mother. Light, manage it. • It's your light, manage it. For me I'm happy with mine and I want to share. It's limitless. Wake up now to the light speed. It's a law and a wonder, the energy called light square to the speed of me eternally circuit to circuit on the inside, present and accountable for – and mint to delivery – refreshing cents of sparkling forever – light manage it for the planet and all of your fellow humanity's rights. Light, manage it. Light.

LIGHT-WITTED • Light-witted me in swirling loops to remember the laughter and the land of troops of blessed example setting the pace of living light-witted in a heavenly place. Light.

• Light-witted traces of tantalizing faces, gem colored beauty, sparkling cuties lining up to greet the dawn with the smiling wonder of the light we have on. You are the light, and witty to be the rapturous delight of the sight called we. All one land, one mother, one exalting embrace of this dancing race, chanting me home in light-witted lines. What a bright idea. Light.

LIGHT EXPLORER • Light's explorer met the lake of titicaca's* gesticulations dressed in tresses of adoration and I implore that you explore the landing space that means much more than life's incline toward before, enjoy the feel of the land ahead. The light explorer. • I'm on a light trip exploring the space in me and filling it up with only the light love, the jade and ammonite seam, pink and green embroidered with misty cascades of swirling tangerine and aqua stripes, splashing raspberry blue and violet streaming grape lines are seen at the brink of my mountainous appeal to the beauty of the light I call mine. Summit to heaven and everything within. I am well and spent here on the lip of my light forever and I am a light explorer – awake to the view. Light.

Bolivian bliss met with a blend of giving attend to the standing arrival of a LIGHT arch-ival. The LIGHT'S within the lake of perfect reflection.

LIGHT POOL • Pools of pleasure pace the breadth of a river met in astonishment by the lift of a tribe, deliver us, and a light's been set in a geyser's bed and a lifting persuasion that life is best lived in depth. The light pool. • There's a glimmering pool, here at the edge of this stream and the life splashes clean in the light of my seam to the sky and the beam of this earthy in-spiral. I am light's highest dive and deepest wide companion, a mosaic design, a glittering find at the foot of this light wave of earthly design me. A light pool. Light.

LIGHT EMPLOY IT • Employ yourself at the bank of a heart and a harp playing soft on the wealth of a warm gentle season and a petal-soft wind trading meetings in curtains blown open and lofted in air of gracious arrival at the heart of a care-free insistance on the love that lives in us and a life too big to carry less than the ultimate sense of the light employ it. • Light, employment means I am working the vacation, my life destination, my falling, spiraling, entrance to the place and the sight, the ex-static, dancing, dining, twining, dna strand-less spent to the 12th dynamic the space more fitting, less formal, more giving. I am living the light employment and managing the light of my finest worker, me filled through with light and working in full sight of my four-seasoned light being. 100 Watts of pure light me. Let it be. Me. Light, employ it. Light.

LIGHT HERITAGE • A heritage of terrific believe is pressed to ascend to the heart that can see the other side of the same tree, a family attend to the genetic proof that there's love in the blood and power in the truth. The open heart of the light heritage.

• The earth is our light heritage and the embrace of our share comes with certain aspects called response-abilities while you fly through your light day, stop a while to softly say, "delight light, and lo I am with you all-ways, eternally, infinitely." Light. By genetic, inherent, emphatic design. Light heritage.

LIGHT MOON • Light moon's over a living attend of my heart-felt approach to the heart of a friend, a planet called mooning has met with a spin and a buzzing called looping has started to blend in trancendant approach to the love without end and again, a place has begun to attend to the pleasure of plenty and the emotion of friends called forever and within the glint of the glittering trine lives a purpose-full blend of the reflective align with the heart of the light moon. • There's a sliver of moon full on my lips and my eyes are neptunic and I'd believe that my hips are jointed by mars. I'm a planet and a star and a welcome surprise to the birds and the dogs and the cats and the flys. The earth is glorious and revels in our return to her singing, our walking prayer, to embrace the light, to emerge in full tide floating soft within the light of the planetary water side. The light moon. Full tonight.

LIGHT TOY • Toys treat the living span with a funny laugh and a giggling hand toward the sublime, the living sense of a lift to the top of a spinning joy. On the inside. A light toy. • Light's terrific and loves to play in buckets, in barrels and deep in the earth where openings allow this peacefull new birth. Know the womb, the light egg shining and bursting through forgotten dirt and forgiving truth. Enjoy your stay. Here's your toy. You. Let's play. Light toy. Light.

LIGHT EN-TRANCE • Lightly met, my living glance, penetrates your insistence on the blind alignment with how things appear. Welcome to the energetic light en-trance. • Light's en-trance to the life, my own comes whistling in on a light repose, a light second, a light first. Spark-like now, intense with infinite beauty and the rhyming wish for you my sister, this living arc. Passion's the word. It's light in this world. In me and in you. A light family entering the life. Light wide awake and straight through the peace-full portal, the way, the light en-trance.

LIGHT TRIP • Lighten my load and unload my grip to a gentler hold and a genuine fit and a glove met molded by fingered agree to open them up and live to receive. The other side. The giving flip. The heart of hold and the held of live. A light trip. • We've taken a light trip to give this shared arrival, this epistle of our dance, honor now the writer, the giver of this proof. The lord metatron directly to you through my sage, and knowing you and knowing me let's take a light trip together sometime, some life, some arc, right now. Metatron is home and all the lights are on. Welcome home from the lightest trip. The journey to the center of the earth, you. In 80 lives or less. Blessings dear, karma's over, light's home and the souls are gone. Light. Join the seam. Light trip. Light.

LIGHT RIDER • I'm a light rider by the look of my bliss and my contented agreement to breathe at the lip of a triple attend to the heart and the home of the hearth called electric and the horse I call silvered thread be gone. The light is on this light rider. • I'm a light rider. Catching a way of infinite life, a light waving stay at the top and the bottom, the middle way. The road good and red, and written to stay this way. Take a light ride on the love highway. Straight to the top, summit bound with light flooding through the crown. The wait is finished, the race is done. We're basic humanity every one and all written in light ink and never to fall. Always light. The life of a light rider.

LIGHT RIVER • Light rivers meet at the beach of the sea and the ocean of love rages in me as we swing home to begin the swim to nirvana again. A light river. • Light's a river waving splashes of board sailing flurry and intermittent matches of one to the other and waving on a waterfall is born with a smiling view of infinity living well within you. The fish are jumping with a tale to share. There's no hook in this, only a light saver. Take a swim in the light river issuing deep from within you. Earth to light. Light earth. Light river.

LIGHT, IT'S HIP • Light is hip, and happy to be, the pleasure of penchant divinity and the thread of a bead to happy relief and the string of a necklace of floral entice that swings round the swivel of heaven's delight. Your blessed face and the neck of relief at the tip of a trail called light, it's hip. • Light on the right, on the left, where ravens and eagles take a sweet dip in the river of life. Meeting in the middle of my miraculous life. The hummingbird is floating, the perches are set, the salmon are running and the spirit's been fed with light filling, we've made it. The trip. The light, it's hip. Light hops and flips. Light.

LIGHT FLIP • Flip the switch to a kinder trend and a pleasant approach to a softer blend of sensual pleasure and perfect attendance at the school of forever. The other side. All one. Light flip. • Flip this, right off the top. Take off the lid and know the light hop of the can filling up and the energetic lift. Lights on the swell and the music is hip. Life to light. Arcing well within the trip leading home. Light flip.

LIGHT TINT • Light tints the windows of my eyed recline to the life of refinement on the other side, of the same extent, and the middle intent to meet the mother along the seam of a genetic dream and a happy play at staying in shades of a lighter cast. Light tint. • Cover your window with aquamarine glass and know the impact of the light that lasts. Bulbs never blowing and hearts always showing the flying infusion of a brand new color, a shiny mother, new to you. Light tinted through. The hue is you. Finest love. Sprakling light. I love you, my people, my humanity like the wind kissed the earth and the dew that moistens the birth of my love, my light, you. Walking through, filled aquamarine blue with the light tint. It's see through. Light tint.

LIGHT STRIP • Divine strips of electric extent are sufficiently met by the press of a hand attractive and gentle and strung with a band of sparkling stones lined up to see their mirrorred reflection in the eyes of me. We are the light strip. • Bacon curls when applied to heat. So do we if we resist the meeting called surrendering will to the light. Plug-in, the deepest feel, the groping truth, the emotional healing proof, light loves you. Only you. All of you. Exactly as you are in your opening dance. Spinning wider. Light strip. Plugged in. Light.

LIGHT BOUNCE • Touch the place where abundant grace meets the healing taste of a jumping in place and a sufficient bless of a brilliant impress and over and over again. A light bounce. • Catch the arc, lighten your spark with a champagne bubbly flight, tennis balls loft, to the purest sound, the judicial ground, your just reward, your bouncing return, light serving you, no more dance, only truth, light bounce.

LIGHT NOW-INFINITY • At Light speed, the write read, is your own glee at boundless light catching flight to embrace you with the bounty-full sight of a light bay upon which to play and rejoice and to stay all-ways at the crest of a waving ecstasy. Light now- infinity. • Light is now a light wave. Ride it. Light's infinity.

LIGHT SPEED • Light speed through infinity to land in a lap of blessed relief at the present presence that I call light speed. • Light my way with your dizzying speed and your gull like need to soar every day up to the light bay for a gentle ride, all splashing aside, here's the surf and the truth of this earth. The light's inside – enjoy the ride. Light speed.

LIGHT BEE-LINE • Light bees bless the inside friends of feeling love's a dividend and knowing you, I'm knowing me, and knowing us we are the free flown sight of a heart that's light and the brilliant design of a light bee-line. • Making a bee-line for the ferry to my light forever. I am the light and the way and the truth's way to say. Let it shine. The mother is will – is mine by natural law – the light bee-line carrying us home to the sandy grain we call our island name, victory is mine saith the lord, my heart, my home, my queen. Victory at the end of the light bee-line. It's clear in my lane. Light.

LIGHT LANE • Light lanes blink inside the bin of a dented triple divided line and a dynamic spark has met attend at the trail of trace that has no end. The light lane. • There's a light line painted down the face of this planet, dove-like and free, and desiring to be your loving line home. Follow the line, stay in your lane, passings passe. Know the name holiest of all, your own. Welcome in, the water's fine from column to lane. Light on the inside. Light lane. Good-bye yellow lines. Light.

LIGHT TASTE • Light taste's sweet beneath the tongue of a treat that's flung to the heart of forever in shining regard of the softer reflection of a higher beginning and a natural end to bland belief. A light taste. • Integrated taste and a minor fascination with the shape of my name as a symbolic feast feeding me light in a loving swell, like a baby orca feeding on swell of strained plankton phosphorescent and viewed with luminescent eyes calling to ears peopled with the sound of yet another tree coming down. Quench your taste for the earthly waste. Build harmony in every light taste. Light.

LIGHT LINE • Light lines live in fond recline at the bliss of beget and the heart of device, a ruler – less love is important to find, the arc of your heart is a living light line. • Making a line for the finest ride, the crossing ferry to the other side – hooking your leaves to the ascending chain equals a life of effort-less strain-less enchantment with the nature creative. Your life is your palette color you canvas with the light irridescent. Line by line by line. Light. Light line.

LIGHT-ANGLED • Light angles in to live in lines at the extractions of pearl-colored dreams and personal attraction to the lessons believed and the blessings received and the sacrum adjusted to press on the points of vetebral bursts at light-angled believe. Light. • Light angled beauties of marrow intrigue the bones of this earth are the jewels up my sleeve and I'm smiling gently at the welcome sound of my faceted tears melting the ground frozen solid inside my heart and the light angled melting begins to spark the growing inclusion of concluding my climb, with the pace of the summit the light I call mine. Angle by angle, this growing earth, frosted with laughter and a cloud's gentle mirth. All the angles of uncovered light. Light angled.

LIGHT, MINE • Light my life with your smiling face fed within the feeling space called love's a gift and life's a dream revealed to expose the light, mine. • The light's mine and yours and the kids in between and often it soars and elementary it seems that the laws of nature are all it takes to define the fact that there's light in the face. Light, mine. All the time and infinity too by light design. Light, mine.

LIGHT COMMUNITY • Light's community has fed the space of meeting the brand of an eternal place, the love within our electrical chain of kinetic, ecstatic emphatic appreciation of the light community. • There's a light commute to an island wed to the knowing glance of this life I've led and lighthouse points at the glaring truth. There's a light shining near the square of this roof called, community. Take the cap off, for all the world to see lightly commune with me, that's our family, our light community.

LIGHT TECH • Light can be technical and often embraced by the simple arrival at the top of a space called forever and forever again, winging away the land of pretend and a heart plugging in to the light tech. • There's a university called life and a fraternity called brothers with a sorority called sisters, and a faculty called parents and friends and family others. The truth is this college of life lives in me and I give the exams here and I sing the keys of continual commitment to the light, I am and my constant position in the light tech pep band. Ringing true. Light.

.LIGHT-HANDED • Light hands me an exceptional place at the trinkets of trivy and the trivy-less taste of a light-handed trip to the land of begin and again we are friends within the shape of a light-handed blend. Light. • Keep your pinkie up and your green thumb out and catch a ride with a lot of clout, your own, light-handed and generous and loving with all you know and own and enjoy. Light-handed faith in this planetary march to the foot of the arc called belief and the infinite leap to love. A light blink. Light-handed. Light.

LIGHT PLANT-IT • Plant the light in a precious place, between the fins of a license plate bound for the back of a universal car, headed for heaven and found in the land of the place you live. A light plant-it. • It's light here. Plant-it, your heart on this planet and know the taste of the eloquence grace, and surrender to splendor jasper and swan like dreams of elequance, loving and all that it seems. Know the light. Live the life on this planet. Light, plant-it.

LIGHT EDUCATION • Educate yourself to the naked truth that life is a continuum and love a definite loop to the point of within and a light education's a to be to see. Light. • I have acquired a light education, an embrace of love and a wonder-full designation, estimation of the precise life, the finest light, love to the infinite degree. Light = God = me eternally. Light. Good-bye hierarchy. Welcome to your bhd. A doctorate in basic humanity. Now that's a dispensation. Your examination? Know your light. A light education.

LIGHT MILL • Light mills me in living fluff of flour-ing return to the heart of us and I unwind in listening feel to the sound of the reign of the living light mill. Eternally fine. Light. • There's a light mill churning out advanced degrees in the grade we call colors and well inside me is a fountain of crystal and the light absolute pushing up youth-full exuberant hope and flowing entreaties penetrating my closeted fears and grinding my self-pity away from my ears. I can hear, the truth, lightly milled. Light mill.

LIGHT-CENTERED • Light's centered right here in the heart of a-man bent to reveal the light inside and the happy flight to the pyramid's view. Light-centered. • Begin the story, wear the crown, now let's sport the softest round, the singing, chanting, ìyouî, I hear resounding deep within my ear. Catch the boat. Enjoy the float of living light-centered this time. Light middle. Light.

LIGHT THRILL • Thrill me with your total devotion to the swell of a life spent living in notions of a grand design and the life inside this light thrill. • I'm excited by the opportunity to introduce you to the light I am. Know your light self, embody you light body, penetrate the pulse, the pi, the 3.14 Positively repeating vibration leading this nation, this burgeoning planet, bulging with spinning inquiry home to the light again. I know the ride, the taste, the spray of the light ride. What a thrill. Light's rollercoaster without a spill. Light thrill.

LIGHT SILVER • Light silver threads erupt inside me in ripping refusal to ever concead that the swallow's return is less than my believing expression of the will that I hold free and clear, and free of all taxing representation of other than forever. I am the one, with you, by a clipping thread. St michael's sharp shred of the cord, light silver. • Light silver-blue and aquamarine too upon the scene and the face of this oceanic flight. Float on water, know the daughter, earth's sweet matter, light's mid-center, steps on water, skipping lightly, live it nightly, and day to silver-violet flaming display straight in to the aquiline center of you. Light silver.

LIGHT IN-I-GO • Light is in the way I go to the land of opportunity and the part of life I know, the intuitive extension of a loving mission. The light in-I-go. • Know your love will lift your light into the sweetest flight, the freefall called love and it's light as in-I-go, to the love welling life, the light life and I am God, and light and loving regard all the way through. Light in-I-go.

LIGHT POOLS • Light pools splash as they return to see the crown of a living word, the logos of forever and the heart of never-mind. I am the fountain of youth-full enthuse at the brim of the light pools. • Pools and pillars of particulate waves. The light is flashing, showing – my way, guiding me home to the love that I am and call my own. Light pools. Splash!

LIGHT GENERATIONS • Light generates the billowing winds of a bounty-full mention of the love that attends all the lines, all the times, all the genes, all the seams of our eternal family. The light generations. • A light generation is home from vacation to spread the news, there's love in the truth. Speak it. Walk it. See yourself. Hear yourself talking spoken and invisible, your intentions are clear and your absolute intentions and all the layers thereof are what count. So tell the truth with your living proof throughout this light generation. Light.

LIGHT CANOE • Paddle past the love that lasts to send the trend of continuum. Now settle back to love and care and share the dream of an even stroke and a lasting loop – the river of life and a light canoe. • I ride a kayak* and sail on board a delight-full ship called the cord of all inclusion, goodbye to the shore of illusion. All aboard for the ferry to the land of forever, eternally loving and equally light. Spirit is now paddling my light canoe.

*kayak – A simple craft of ocean-going pleasure.

LIGHT POINT • Light's light point resides eternally inside of you. Honor the truth. Right to the light point. • Point your ship into the light and you'll be surrounded by the lovely flight of the light ever increasing in the spacing wake of the increase I'll make by trusting your heart to show you the way to the light pointing straight to the middle of you and I'm standing in my heart, operating as captain of my own destination, all the way in. Light to the point. Light.

LIGHT RAFT • Light raft's press the water's kind lift with a giving receipt of a floating trip to the land of begin, and then again, you, a light raft. • Light my raft and my life and my home. Love is the spark which allows my embarkation across this nation in an arc called heart and a life called swell and a wave called remember and a lot to tell. In 3 words, body/mind/spirit. All one = divinity and light and love in me. All one, the metatronic, electronic, sonic compatability me. Welcome to the sea of all of me. A light raft. Me. Light.

LIGHT PORT • Light port's plenty of present impart at the heart of a ship sailing on north bound missions and southern consent to sail to the star of forever I am at the door of your light port. • Light's a port and a ship and a song. Know the remember of the words, sing along, and God said, light, let it be, on the ship called me. I'm a tide all my own and a lodge in the storm of electronic short. Know the sport of this port. Light bring your paddle. Catch the channel directly in to your light port. Light.

LIGHT LOOK • Light looks incredible on your sweet face and a kind of eternal elastic embrace abounds in the town of our loving embrace. Hold me now in your tender light look. • Nepal, new zealand, japan and new york. The wars are over. Let's find a new port for all that we carry germanic and tifted, lift your brother and find a more civil revolution. Know the solution, build the bridge, keep breaking the walls in pebbles of forgiveness. This lights a whole town. African, swedish, melbournes, kent. Take a light look at the blood that's been spent. Independence, know the contingent, light has spoken. Line the movement. Goodnight lieutenant. Welcome partner. This planets honored by your generally light presence. A light look. Sydney to pearl. The light harbor is home. Rest a spell. L-I-G-H-T.

LIGHT MOVES • Light moves me in nightly grooves of giving, receiving silent blues and violet-green observance arrives at nightly deliverance and daily too. Light moves. • Light moves in mysterious waves, her ways and love to share. God knows I am living proof of the general theorem. The buddha's truth. It's all the way in and all the way out. Earth to earth and life to life, the light shines the love about from me to you. Light moves.

LIGHT FAIR • Light's fair and so are we in our grinding halt to divinity and shared embrace of the love that's free and growing soft inside of me. We are the justice of the light fair. • There's a light fair, a carnival, a song and a birth on the bounteous ocean, the you I call earth's sweetest gift now, the ambrosial path, the life called the father and the mother are back, in sweet surrender. One last time, eternally lifting on line, into the love zone, twelve to twelve and twenty-two too. Mayan blessings from the light fair to you. Light fair.

LIGHT LOYAL • Know your light and live the bed of forgotten exposure to the loyal blend of trust and truth and energetic assign to the arc of forever and the dipper of time pouring out to reveal the faith-full expanse of the light loyal. • Light my loyal life with the precious symbol, the impressive sight of my love filling up from the well within. The light now is finding her lodging, her friend, light within, ever without and never a doubt. Light loyal. Me to you. Light.

LIGHT WILD • Light's wild and found the place of higher express and an exuberant case of collective pleasure and leisure recline in the arms of forever and the wild heart, that's mine, the light wild. • Light my life and let it be my guiding path, infinity to infinity and seasonally free. Live the path, line the truth with privileged approach called the heart remembering most and the light is wild from animal to child, from mountain to track, to the infinite pack called we. Human and basic, humanity. What a wild ride. Earth. Light wild. Life. Light.

LIGHT ROYAL • Light's royal and especially fine when it's worn by the bride of gentle abide at the altar of wed and the lion of proof that there's love in this ring that we call the truth of all conviction. Light is well within the plane of the light royal. • Yes, I'm your mother. The earth's speaking, hear, hold, yourself sacred, revere the name, light royal. Regal. Me. Eternally. Light royal.

LIGHT PEOPLE • Light people live at the place of the tree and the heart of forever and the God of the sea and the arc of a life and a heart that is mine, to share with the people who live in align, within the tribe of the light people. • A nightingale sang out a wonderous name, let there be, set it free, tell them, tell light – let it shine. Free. Me. Light. All my people. Light people. Love's the planet. Earth's the magnet for the light people. Magnitude, gratitude. Light.

LIGHT ENTER-PRIZE • Light enters winning and wed to the truth, I am the present, the gift and the loop of a gentle pleasure, a genuine reprise of the light inside our light enter-prize. • Light's my enter-prise and my journey, my life. My way of showing that remembrance is knowing an exciting design called walking the line, for the maze is finished and the karmics been run. Let's find a new work under the sun. Light on the water. Reflections in glass. Refractions through opals. Know the spirit that lasts. Home by design, on the good ship. Light enter-prise.

LIGHTLY HUMAN • Human, strong and living so long without the constraint of a windowless saint and a sainted lover and a jilted mother returned to begin the balance of finding a friend in a gentle stare directly into the light of a face. Lightly human. • We're all human upon this raft, this street called the middle, in our miracle path and I am terrrific and breathing in the space at the spinning return of the love we call grace. Swans are swimming with the knowing. Grace is showing. Soul is going, going, gone. Home to light. I am right where I belong in my lightly human heart. Divinest spark. Arc to arc. Heart. Lightly, lightly human.

LIGHT PREFERENCE • Light's my prefence and how about yours? I love the space of choosing more than just a set or block of ruling. I choose the spot of fondest fueling at the heart of a land feeding all. A light preference. • I prefer the light presence. This is my preference for my life as the meta-electronic, hydraulic, umbilic wonder I am, and the light is my preference as a loving hu-man. Breathing essence, living presence, a light preference.

LIGHT IN-VOCATION • Evoke the note of a lasting flight to the holy revelation of a lifting sight to the eternal purpose of a mission met in a light in-vocation. • I invoke the power of truth, of metatron, of God, of light, of vagabonds, who loving spirit walked the path of least resistance, the surrender to the light in their work, in their every location, in this infinite nation, planet wide, leading home to you. Light my way, in my every prayer, chant thought and desire. Light it works. In-vocation. Light.

LIGHT LADY • Light lady's know the blessing of birth in the land of the plenty, the free, the exceed, of a justice, a proof and a love, liberty. A light lady. • You my baby, are the light lady. My precious pearl, my lasting curl of genuine intrigue, the earth. Ocean to ocean and all the way through past the crust and the mantle and shifting candle burning within eternally a light lady, ever my baby, my precious birth, my ships poa* and the swollen girth spanning dessert for all light times. Earth. The light lady.

Point of Arrival

LIGHT, IT'S YOUR STATION • Light, it's your station and your absolute stare to the heart of remember and the life raft of care, held in fine divine at the heart of a nation and the place of devotion. Light, it's your station. • Fill me up with the highest stuff, the golden earth, arcing and peaking with intense turf. Light and the full service glance at the truth of this life. Light, it's your station. Alert the nation on spaceship earth, humanity's birth has begun. Welcome to earth, the 2 + 1. The tide has come, turned to surge. Use the right. Fill your tanks. The light's vibration, it's your station. Light.

LIGHT, CUSTOM • It's my custom to light the day with a perfect, holy, holiday, by exact define a light, custom. • It's my custom, our peacefull pleasure to embark on this journey together. There's an arch and a band here at this span called one and the same. It's our lights and our joy and our escape over the border, to the other's side, to the light less blind, more favorable, from both sides now, we've found the spot to bridge the gap and to welcome back the light's full glamorous invite to the wedding called light. A light bonding become one – arc to arc to arc to arc. The light ones. One mother. Sister and brother. Golden bands. Lacy strands. Happy hands held aloft. A light custom. Love. LIGHT.

LIGHT MOSAIC • Light's mosaic in her knowing place of return to the yearn and the healing taste of pleasant designs patterned within the web of my skin deep friend, the light mosaic. • Paint a picture of sparkling light, irredescently true to the heart of you. The heart of your cells knows the light plan. Become a fan, of your light, of the light called way, your body will say, yes, I am a light mosaic. Light. Pink, green, yellow, with the gleam – truth. Light mosaic.

LIGHT TAG • Light tag, you're it and lets now begin the trend toward living the life of a friend felt throughout the game of a love lived in flames of burning denial away to the core of a delicate chore, the heart inside the flash of you running past to say, you're it too. Light tag. • Tag. You're it. Wear it lightly in love.

A.LIGHT PROSAIC • Lightly prosaic, I am ecstatic at the opportune place that I call dramatic return to the one love our own, within the friend, the light prosaic. • Lightly prosaic, I'm a mosaic, a rich and wonderous me and filled to the tipping with your encessant lipping. Know the light, where its bright, night in the central venue, you. Light prosaic.

LIGHT IMMORTAL • Immortality dwells in the scoop of sparkling experience and trips to the coupe called a sports car and the hood of a trend to jump right back to the center again and a hand on the throttle of the light immortal. • Light immortality, that's me and I am wearing it well, here where people tell me that living within is a heartless matter and I say ok now shatter that dimension with your clear intention to live light immortality in the reality of the 12 x 12 invention, foot by foot, and edge to edge, love and the light immortal.

LIGHT EXTRAVAGANT • Extravagance fed a healing wed to the spin of revival and the heart of a-man met wide to a tread and a strand of revive and the heart of me dazzling and clear and abiding in blessed lift entwined in the light extravagant. • It's light extravagant this elegant life I call light. Notice the sparkle and the splash. The fact is that this life is loving and genuine and kind when the world of blocked up cells and sub-divisions are telling on their false fronted long housed selfs. Good-bye cells, welcome cells of peacefull splendor. Mitochondria's the sender of this elegant message. The light extravagant. Know your planet. Light.

LIGHT ETERNAL • Eternity's met the place I call home with

a looping twist and a balancing phone call to serenity and the heart of divinity, the light eternal. • Light eternal, supernal, elective, selective,effective and in sight. The light eternal is in the air this life, know the night of the day eternal in a daily way. Light eternal.

LIGHT INTERNAL • Internal life has met the birth of a triple earth treasured by layers of significant shift to the land of one great shining sun burning eternally in me. A living inferno. Light internal. • Light's internal and melting the blocks, the internal locks, I established to keep me at bay, so today on this ship so watery and complete I'll integrate fully the light I call me. For the light I am liveth in me eternally from cell to twinkling cell, eternally a star. The light internal.

LIGHT JOY • Light is a joy when you act in fact for love – for the lightest joy is in you and through you and of you. Light joy. • I am joyfull and blessed with the vent, the breathing bubbles, at the top of my lift, through the ocean of soul's emotion. I've surrendered the notion, soul, and moved in tender devotion toward the light, I am and love hath filled the heart of this metatronic man. Fill the land, the terrain of you, joyfull through light's inclusion. Light joy.

LIGHT LOVE:

LIGHT ELECTRIC • Electric lace engraces the tread to a living schematic the light met within my humble entreaty to know the design of a heart met in particles of planted green line of particulates waving at the life called em.* C and the square of a religious adherence to the way I call right and the conscienscous appliance of a rule energetic, when as for me, equates to absolute proof of the indicative truth of the law of one. The disk of remember has met in the sum of our loving equation. Selective and free and the wild incline to a longer ride, the light electric. Inside the head of the heart of a man basic and hu-man and synaptic. The light electric. • Turn it on. The switch is here just below your heart. Know the start and flip your lid open. Now receive, the lighten ing flashes of heraldic fountains filled to flowing with dancing election to pick up the keys and stand in the power of knowing the light that I am. In this desiring to select it, the position I call on, I'm found in humble healing of the little life I've known and flowing well within the tide, my will is led by the heart in side the central portal called remember The message is sent, take a stand in the spirit. The soul can now end. The light is electric and eternally our friend. Light electric. Elect it.

*EM. C -Electricial in motion in me. see.

LIGHT SELECT IT • Selectively met by an open heart, I'm set to examine the relative fact that selective to me I am the bet that makes the selection to live or ignore the fact that we bring our own heart to the door and openess sees the philosophic news that people are living in the metatronic view that deep in our slip lives a love so complete that dynamic example is the only beat and the heart of our seam is a vein so unique that a rookie called me can bat up the cleanest position, the heart of nutrition, the day of the face called a love meeting winks of sighted surrender to the light that I'm given in a moments trace of the light I've erected in the center of me. Light select it. • Light, you choose it – select the flight you will take and use it. Embrace the reality that this is your ability for tranquility and the abdication from the indignation of acting tiny and living small means you need to know the deeper view of the vista called you. And I am light. Select this knob and turn me up and leave the mob by diving in to the swellest tide – the sparkling beauty you are on the inside – it's your right – light. Select it.

LIGHT SALUBRIOUS • Salubrious trends meet here again and grandiose gestures anchored the bend of battled up feelings and forgotten appeals and the hand of a phantom fanatically sent to dance on the stage of the light salubrious. • Have a drink, raise a toast, wet your lips with the light salubrious. Give a speech, a new degree. Find a convention and write a new book. Enter the embrace of an outstanding look. Tonight is the final, the intimate break with the stork of denial and the wedding to links of forgetting. Here's the hole, the 19th. Carve a new edge and tender a peace of the green light. Select it and get a fresh start. The jadeite is glowing and your heart is a spark – yellow and green and lavender ametrine. Your life is now the light that it seems. Raise your hand to the light salubrious and catch a wink of the light egregious.

LIGHT EGREGIOUS • This light's egregious and salutations are sent to greet the great star and the moonstone called men with a giving link and an effective treat. The conversational thrill of a friendly meeting. Treat the ceiling with outspoken appeal and wear a light egg with a shell hard to steal, the light egregious. • Light expansive and whole y and well-planned expressions of an intimate source intimate recall of an equilibrium sort – deal me a new life from a pack melted shut to forgetting and initiated in a burst of eloquent expression. The light is egregious and wiggly and fun and special in showing the path to the sun, and the bride called terrific emits a sweet chime and the church bells are ringing with the dynamic rise of recollective, egregious sort. Spurt out the answer and enjoy the sport called surrender to the power of yes and the power of the light egregious.

LIGHT INFATUATION • Gently touched by a moment's blend and a heart entranced with a giving feel, I am the splash of a juicy peach, a genuine appeal and the heart of a friend, an energetic attribute aligned to a trace of an example blue and green and read in the yellow-trimmed robe of a legal retrieval and a heart met in scenes of triumphant return to the beauty in me. Celestial, free, and spiritually sent to the rest-full news of my light infatuation. You. Light. • I have a light infatuation and this rhyme I know is true for the tune of sweet remember is shining bright in you. Tonight within the gentle, the fond and the elite of swellest sight full singing, I see a new relief. Parts and sparkly pieces emit a new decree, I am in love with light now and the sweetheart is me, I see. A light infatuation. What a notion, I'm the bride and I'm well groomed. A light infatuation.

LIGHT WILLED • Light the space of a loving face and a living tread and a beauty called hearty and a party called rome and the island called sicily and the living code phoned to a person who loves in a spree and the melodic content of a love made in heaven and a party scent to infinity's bloom, blessed be, the living room of madonna's moon met in seas of the divinity in me and my light willed surrender of the soul I could be. A sicilian line of light-willed belief and the remember of spirit met in a sea of red, white and green. • Set sail for the light and enjoy the flight to the feel I call absolute. This wheel I call light is the life of this ride. Please stop your destruction and step to attention, use your invention, your crystal intention to anticipate the rise of the willing enterprise. Use your advise. This is the edict and the end of your lying refusal to know the lord of revival, the tent of salvation, the Light-willed commitment to the laws of this earth. The commandant, you know it. Lividly give it up and wear it down to it's finest Light-willed brilliance. It's yours.

LIGHT SPILLS • Light spills traces of pink and green to the end of my arm and the edge of my seat and tumbling still the light entreats my seeing a-ha of the beauty in beads of evolute, knowing that the end won't be for the continuum is showing in reflective relief of the light without edge and the the bounty of seas telling me about the end of the infinitum. Know one. Light spills. • Light spills dripping, down the slope of this throat open to sing out the love of this note, this balance of will, called harmony. Seek the reward of the sight of the lord of revival the witness of faith, the light of your brother engendered with flowing embrace of the light that I am, and that I am is enough to spill the light, the holiest ghost of revival of the spirit, the sweetest note of the tilt to your listening ear. I love you this minute and this moment, all year, in the light of the seasons, there's hope spoken, hear. As the light spills twinkling through the hole in your sole to the spirit of remember and the arc of the volcanic shatter of the matter mundane. This is light Spilling forth. Drink it up.

LIGHT A MINUTE • Light's a minute here and there and eternally kind and infinity fair to the brilliance in a moonbeam's glow and the emphatic announce that we're here to show the latest trend, the living now, of the sun of forever beginning with how to bend a convergent path to the arc coming down and the wave that lasts. Ride the crest of the light a minute. • Lightly this second, this minute, this hour. Hear is the power of listening, chiming to the hypnotic swell called infinite rhyming nature of the creature you've been chasing – light. It's here in the spark of your gentle division of this life called the arc and infinite ticking does not make a clock and often in checking the minutes and hour, the season has changed and you're left to wonder – what's in a minute? Light, a continuum. Light, a minute eternally.

LIGHTEN EASY • Lighten easily in connective bliss and kintic share of the power that is and the blackest line has left to see the cardinal fact of the divinity in me, living the proof and evocatively desiring the feel of eternally reigning in softest recline at the foot of the altar that I call mine. My heart, by divine release, of the piece called will and the part called free to meet in the spirit. Eternally. Lighten easy. • Light without condition is the love that knows attention when the lover's new rendition requires the light's attention to the fact that sweet remember, allows a love that's tender with light's unique december and may's attendant members of the answering loving singing that church bells now are ringing with singing easy timbre for the pitch of eagle's tender crying peal, the bear called soul is leaving, and the light of spirit's easy on the wave of sweet remember and the unconditional loving of a father meeting mothering. Lighten easy.

LIGHT IS RIGHT • Light is right to fill my sight with the mother's milk bubbling through my gentle veins and gendered heart that met its match in a universal spark, shining true to my design, the diametric proof of the love inside. Know the bill of equality's appeal. The legal rights by the light's design for the light is right. • Right-fully light, I am yellow with living this lemon-aid dream and I am willing to awaken to the light I have taken for granted. The stream of be-lieving is flowing in rainbows of violet and green, a love transcendent to the light that we know and right to the middle I give just a little and then more, space to the door of forgetting survival and living the revival of the bliss called light and night is right and ripe and clean with twinkling droplets of the light ametrine and the love pink and green and the light life Is right by the light, I am.

LIGHTLY LEFT • The light has left to meet the flight of love reigning in to dance the ground of a landed revival and an infinite pair the loop called today and the one called where I left pieces of dark needing light and the whistles are clean and the whispers inside the truth of the lightly left imprint in you. Light. • Left to write, I am ignited with the wonder of colossal lightening and towering thunder and rich with wonder, I am pearlescent and opaled by your well come review and impassioned with receiving the light shining through and facets of glitter glimmer champagne and platinum and escent of you and through the meadow alight with flowers wild is the embrace of your standing pinon* high and juniper low and ever green in the middle and pink down below. There with my middle is the widest expanse of the lightening view of particles of emeraldine dancing through aspen groves and bounding back through and lightly left in wonder to herald the news – the light's all ways right. All-ways you with a triangular view.

*pinon pine: a southwestern treat and evergreen like you.

LIGHT PYR-A-MID • Peer amid the silent ruins and describe a kinder day, now you can employ the power to erect a loving tower, in bionic proof of the particulate, articulate, skying truth that you are the glow and the capping stone of the lime-green knowing that your light is showing. Central to you. A light pyr-a-mid. • Three become one, the total the sum, the red, the yellow, the orange, the knotting survival is over. Here's revival at the height of the light called the son. Now is forever and ever I've been given the right to deliver the outstanding balance called me to the light at the tip, the apex, the lip of the pyramid of light, this tree of this life, this ranging divide is gone from inside and all is all that's left and right to the center I'm chewy and rich and ambrosial and honeyed and deep and ecstatic and living with moneyed exchange simply kind energy a gift of light's intelligence and a knowing beyond mind. It's the body's mind full knowing and that's what pay's the rent. The light at the tip of the Light pyramid. A light intelligence.

LIGHT INTELLIGENCE • Intelligent choices meet with the fact that there's love in this heart and light in this laugh and an angel called loving has met in the wake of a brain splitting open to reveal a new fact. I am the kind to divine a new line to the solar example of the plexus inside. The life is fine in the body's mind by light intelligence. • Pyr-a-mid means a light in the middle and that's what you get when you give just a little space to the big concept called knowing your mind. Your heart's bottom tip flowing full green is the loving remember that set's your head free. The power of yellow combined with green, puts a cap on the pyramid, and a light line – green represents this, the essence of light intelligence.

LIGHT-BODIED • Light-bodied living has met in me and the light is on eternally. Light-bodied. • Light-bodied living, the earth is here giving amarilla* color to the lighting discover of the ageless wonder – man, in full view. How-man and human and build a new trip to the light's full fantastic view of the inside of you. Cell by cell and all the way through mark new your path with the light shining through. Escalate your insight, see the respect you have for the light now and begin to expect the light shining through the end of our neck. Your heart and your head and the space in between is becoming illuminated with the presence of the light's intelligence. Build a man, add a breath, and a light mind too. The light's in full view, shining in you and your light-bodied thining. Think light.

*Amarilla: Yellow-straight through to the Spirit in You. Mitochondrial skies are smiling. Amarilla to the center LIGHT.

LIGHT MIND • My mind is light as I sit and stare at the spell on your face and I wonder where all the verbs met the moonbeams and the vowels got free to spell out the names of eternity, yours and mine, by linguistic design, the magnificent place of munificence graced by electric design. The light mind. • I'm mindful of you, when I'm mindful of me and a life spent pursuing no mind is mindless too. So let's imbue this moment with penetrating glance and fill up the inside with a fluorite*

romance. Chinese and indian and light earth too. You know the yellow power and it's in your heart too. Goodbye to forevering continual loop. Give me infinity. Think light and brand me with truth of delivery, with intent most clear. We are the light here and this missive is clear. Know your light, find your mind, the other 90% plus the 10% you left divinely behind welcome to the light mind. Who would have thought? Light

*A purple and green stone. Trancecendant loving.

LIGHT-N-DA • Light-n-day I wear a filling grin from the moment I come into view shining in free attractive belief of the kindest love shining in you and our patterning dance to the edgeless place called the edge of the world and a matterless place meeting form, my heart is warm to hear you say light-n-day. • Crystal clear and light to the touch. I am Light-n-day in this magical way called me. For with my dawning a new light is spawning shedding denial and embracing emergence. I've made a new stand in the fork of this tree and the deer that I am hunting has all ways been me. Lightly gentle. Light-n-day. Ah-men. Lay down the hunt. Take up the big safari. You are the game and the gun is light. Got you. Light in the middle. That's my specialty. Light-n-day. Pain-free and staying that way light-n-day.

LIGHT SPECIALITY • Light's my sign and my seal and my cross. The heart of the father and the flower of lost finding moonbeams to shine in the space of a lover met plural in disciplined embrace of the apostolic return to the land of our grace. Our lady has met the place of immaculate retreat to the point of all conception. Release yourself to be a light specialty. • What's your light specialty and where do you live? Will you welcome the shift to the light that you are with your embracing surrender to the power that lives? Inside your sacred portal lives the fulfillment of the immortal, the terrific, the eternal, the infinite- the pyramid of power bringing light to the world. The tower, observe it. The light, share it. The sight, adore it. For it's light and you wear it well – on both sides now. And in the center where it counts – the 3 be-coming one – light specialty.

LIGHT, YOU SAY • It's light, you say and you go to play in the waves of love and the light which stays in welcome accompany and kindred view of the electric glide to a central view at the crest of the dome and the mitchell in you. Highest point east to west, you in your light approach to the fairest way. Let there be justice for it's light, you say. • It's light, you say and that's the word I can hear today – the absolute. The well – the antidote – the only tale for the beast within. It's light, you say. Now disappear sin* of forgetting the laws of the land, this beauty, this earth. In light as I stand, enlightened I am to the balance called physics and the rock of this church, the earth, the birth of the bride, the dove's dearest friend and it's light, you say. Ah man – here's the end of darkness, the forgetting of truth. It's light, you say and in a word – light. All men – light.

*SIN – Sacrificing your own Inner-getic Needs.

LIGHT-N-BRIGHT • Light-n-bright come here tonight to swirl in dreams of ambertrine* and emerald green remark-ive hue and the place of the purple trees and the lavender shoes worn with socks all stripey red and a lime-green coat around the head of a heart met pointed at a distant star and a love met holding the light that you are – eternally light-n-bright. • Light-n-bright is the night neath my door, for I am not quailing in fear anymore. I am standing in light, full-winged in my soaring ascension to the lightest dimension – the clean through and through – the swelling intention to live with a view higher still, softer laid, now my bed within the shade of my growing light planted in flight at the foot of the bluff I've called life. And tonight my life's light-n-bright at the site of you, my sister, glistening hue, dew-robed in the buttery yellow moisture of a sharing called, we two are light n bright yellow tonight.

*ambertrine – golden integration of the lavender hue, in you.

LIGHT YELLOW • Light yellow bees in honey-green trees and amber beliefs wearing blue trim to the party called light and the grand yellow seam of a carnelian dream dancing in time with a color called lime-green surrender to the blender of light yellow creamy remember of the light egg I am and the dream called a-man. Light yellow. • Yellow with fever to know the enthuse of the roomy addition to my room, with a view. The portal's try – angle has given to action and the end has arrived to arguing in the fashion provided, the moment imbued with a shift in dimension to the middle of you – shining light in the night. Light yellow

LIGHT LIME • Buy me traces of snowy mint juleped to see that the price of a vent is the surrendering bliss of an igniting kiss melting the ring of forgotten abuse to live in the loop of eternity's proof that the heart of this matter has a will of it's own and it's free and on-line and living to be the light shining lime in the middle of me. Light lime. • Lime is the color of water and sun meeting to dance at the width of this run and remembering that middles have no affair with they edges and markers which form this light square. I am surfing now edgeless and tidy and neat on the seam called the center and the breath of this seat called sandian* giving and arcturian's sweet gather in recalling splendor and aiming their sounding, singing, harmonic delivery of the light lime delicious I call the point and the place of heart's melting met by will power-ing my return to the center of the light that I am.

*Mountainous regions of the heart of this land, I AM. Higher Ground. LIGHT.

LIGHT-CENTERED • Light-centered living reflects inme and mirrored in you well that makes 3 and four times the beauty is our double compact to see each our felf in the skillfull impact of a far away view scene by the seen in a parallel mirror walking in tune with the light-centered beauty. Light. • Treva's the name of this infinite child, this metatronic wonder delivering this mild constellation of infinite care to the masses called humanity and the basic's called core, for the bear's finished living and the bull's gone to sleep, and the lie called denial is the mark of the beast and you know that responding to the world as if of it, is the antithetic opposite of the gist of this sonnet. In it, not of it. Response able, not leaning. Giving, not leaving. Allowing, not plowing. Open up to the light-centered directly in front, in back and all-the-way through the heart of this matter. Will you a-light tonight...Just say I do. Light-Centered magically, enchantingly, in you.

LIGHT IN-GENDERED • Light's in-gendered with a single blend split into pieces of a lemurian* trend metabionically met at the exacting blend of keys of forever in-locking the shores of oceanic splendor electrically sent to telescope the views that an arch-ing denial has met with the truth that the penetrating expanse of the one become two has returned to the place of passions burning beginning. The light in-gendered. • Light in gendered means that you surrender the notion of who's right and embrace the truth that what's left is light and that's all ways right – directionally referring north, south, east, west, left, right, gay, black, white, red, orange, buff, slim, green, oval, square, up, down, over, under, in and out, the light wins and it's in us so why not embrace it and know the truth of this matter reflecting in the sunlight and moonlight and evening air too. We are all light in-gendered and imbued and thats my point. You. Light in-gendered all the way through. Light.

*Lemurian – ancient & free by the sea of light. Lemurian beams.

LIGHT TO THE POINT • Light's point is this – hear. Now. Avow. Light. • Light to the point. Light to the point, it is "time" that I get confused with delivery of the intimate glance of a dancing arrival at the spot called survival – and survival is fittest when it's linked to the highest light by a bridge of lightest surrender of the soul on I've called me to the spirit full-free. For the light collects the soul and transmutes it all to whole and no more am I hole-y and karmically inclined in matters of my being for the lightest link is seeing that my spirit needs a cleaning of lightest vacuuming power to syphon out my tower the temple that I am, and light to the point of surrender, I am free to see the light in me.

LIGHT IN SIGHT • Sight-full electric I'm happy to see the southern cross of the diagramed retreat to the spark of a buckle on an effervescent belt and a beauty evolved at the edge of a web effectively freed to enjoy the view of a blessed tribute to old blue-eyed jeans, stone washed in streams of spoken arrival at the heart of a sleeve attractive to approval of the blessed return to the roots that I see. The light in sight. • The light's in-sight-full and shares her great desire to point out unity by her penetrating stare at my imbalances, the places that I'm weak without surrender and angry at my feet for not believing that my life, my light, is best a clay-footed believing puts my life at constant test so tonight I'll make commitment to the light, my sight, my friend, and I'll live on in my breathing write to know that light right here in me. Fat-free and not an ounce of soul. The light's in sight.

LIGHT RIGHT • Light a'rights my mapping trend to explain geographic's, compass in hand, and reasonably fed by the lightest trace I am fresh to the middle of a love's crested view of the light shining bright in the middle of you. A softer hue by a favorite band of stars that sing in the cradled hand of a diamond's matter questing charts of fitting tread to the edge of the line. Light right. • The light is right to write upon my heart, the believer's anthem, hear, at the drumming of my start to sweet surrender, to ecstasy assured and the peace of knowing pieces are tying now with care for the light has slight gradations, like the light into the day and the night's darker leaving still has glistening friends with which to play and the space between the brightest is the place in which I flood the life of pink surrendered. Receiving and the gift of greenest love, for it's only light to love me right. Light right.

LIGHT-N-GOLD • Light met gold with kind relief and the heart of a love met in artistic peace and creative surrender to the seasons of pieces argyle and green and sun-dappled shades of the branch of the tree and the trunk of dear autumn is waving in leaves electric and gentle and floating on the breeze of light-n-gold melting in the spirit called me. Sea to sea and wave to wave. Light-n-gold. • Light green and gold, pink in repair and I'm sailing on moon's beams and I'm dancing in air of sweetest essence at the lip of my surmise that hear* is swellest, fullest at the corner called the light. And the streets melt golden brick's now at the place of my design and I know now the wonder of this living light's design in shimmering patters light-n-gold and well-come to the sight of the light back in the center, which is only right, left to the design. Light-n-gold.

*Listen

LIGHT IS BACK • Light is back in my centered heart and I am exact in my living part and a love eternal has met in me and I am the tribe of the living tree. The practice met with a safety net called love in the practice of three mighty pieces melting in sparks of a living God who walks in an arc of revival. The light is back. • Chalcedony trinkets of oozing delight ignite the passion to know well the light and wellfull announcement recalls know the fact that here's where the light lives and suddenly light is back in the center, the central, the main, and I am dancing in fountains of wonderous claim. The light is back and it's mine and I'll share – cause it lives in you too. And I am aware and in my acknowledge of the spark that's in you comes forth the flicker that it's your mission too. So join the light team and know the exact location you are needed. It's smack inside you and all the way through. Light is back.

LIGHT EXACT • The light's exact in her fantastic leap to the art of this town and the life of this gift, the pleasure of plenty and the lightest extract, the elixir called me and the heart of this track. The peace of a moment, a knowing embrace, the heart of a land and the light of a trace, the pain has gone to meet its match, the loving gift of the light exact. • Light's exact and on this tract is the highway to desirous bricks of yellow buildings flying in to view the sweltering red given review to unload her monkeys for a better renew – of all that is well come and loving her trust, I am light clear enjoying the thrust of another lift off – a leaping to wear elevator shoes and flaming red hair – break now the pattern make now a shift. Walk with out gravity and a chip on your hip. Drop the load – the bricks from your pockets – and ride a new draft headed for the top and living to last. Infinite light to be EXACT. Light. Precisely my point.

LIGHT FANTASTIC • Tanzanite* bells ring the sound of eternity's love reigning down and up to meet the peace full treat is the land called you and an elegant street optimistic and practically met, a tremendous view. The facet's fantastic and the light in you. The light fantastic. • The light's fan tastic here at the summit and I am the one who will benefit from it as the wattage increases, the bulbs of light effervesce an increasing rainbow on a waving crescent and today while you are sleeping and tonight while you're board, I'll slip you the number of my favorite store. The call is toll-free and the price is electric. The fashions are gorgeous and the light is FANTASTIC. Check out our web. It's of the lightest thread and it's right on time along the light line.

*blue-violet stones of telling proof mirroring the magnetic magnificence in you.

LIGHT LINE • Lines are driving me mad when I see the dawning horizon of a crisp new taste and the crack of a ceiling lifting like glass melting softly dripping to pool at the feet of reflective appraisal of divinity's sea clamoring for acres of pastoral views and animals expanding to see a new loop, a line-up complete and I can sleep in the bed of my light design. Complete. Light line. • Snow is God's whipped creamy light touching just the edge and the lip of your peaking flashes of intimate surrender, and the love here is given and the light's well is flowing with evolution of showing heart avalanches clearing the path for chocolate sundaes and shipped cream puffs of clouds floating gently at the top of earth's cup. The earth is a female, receptive and whole, and the sky is the penetrating male diving home and here in the middle is the light that I am, a mixture of both in my own little can – creating light lines with my every walk and living the light while chatting the talk. Light's on the line and it's me answering the call and calling the answer. Light line.

LIGHT IMPRESSIONS • Express yourself and your living wealth and the light of a banner and a flag born to be at the top of the mount and the everest in me. Sagamartha* has fed the local belief and the house painted white atop the hill has met in a hilary that fits a new bill. Get a life and a love and a clue and a handy return of the reigns to a man man and a dove who coos in compassionate contrast to the light's impression of your lofty denial. Begin the trial. The jury's been picked. It's you. By light impressions. • Men here are digging for the light, silvery and gemmed with the be jeweling sight of amethyst loving and ametrine dripping filling the stripping with the love pink and green and here is the wonder and the lightest's tightest grip creates a new imprint in the earth's mantled crust and the light impressions are here left to see in the gems that glitter inside you and me. Crystalline matter for the light to imbue with reflected wonder of the jewelry in you. Wear your spirit. Adorn it through with the light impressions of sparkling here, shining through light impressions.

Sagamartha – The local Goddess, Nepalese through to the Mount of Joy. LIGHT.

LIGHT EXPRESSIONS • Express yourself in glowing styles of meta-electronic sonnets of singing gliss. The glitter of enchant-ment and the ecstasy of this world sung blue to a lighter tint of topaz hue, heated to believing and mothered by care at the end of survival and the height of the star arch-on wide melting inside to reveal the truth of God's lightest expression. You. By light expressions. • Light expressions reflect every where. They're here all around us and twinkle through air, in starry expression of the light absolute I see a sunshine penetrating you rainbowed to a sparkling and resonating hue and welcome to tender exactly my thinking, my loving, my be-ing to light, my aspirations met with the truth's insight. Welcome to the light expressions. It's you – what a view – shining through your Light expressions.

LIGHT DRIVE • Driving light and meeting you at the rolling foot of the mountains blue, I wonder who led you to feel so imbred with lifeless clamor and busy glamour dingy around the heart and ugly to view in energetically spoken, loving reproof and absolute embrace of the drive that its taken to put you in charge of the helm of a nation and extra-territorial stars called national bounds and bouts of survival denying the drowning appraisal of your car breaking down. Walk to town and feel the trace of a speeding chase met in you. Light drive. • Light's driving me to share these words with you. Life's a light drive and the pilot, the author, the patter, the pitch, the traveler, the hitch it's all you. And I am a waterfall of infinite light and I am enraptured with the infinite pool of light in you and when we make connection, the splash is easy to see, for it's shining soft within your eyes and filling up my view with the brightest light, the giving sight – and in my seeing, knowing, I discover showing, the light sight clean through.

LIGHT SIGHT • Light sight – feels – in ecstatic bloom at the sight of God blossoming in you. A lotus' return to the life of all one – light. See it. Mother it. Light sight. • Rainbows in waterfalls in yellow and green, the light's crystal-eyed within

pools of olivine and the beach is farther southern and the living is the gift and in my eyed-wide desiring another flame is lit, and the flame begets a blossom, and a blossom blooms within a universe of longing sniffs the air and travels to see the sight with eyes of light, to rally round with an answering swell for your eyes have a light sight to sea tonight on the ocean of infinite light – shining through you! A light sight.

LIGHT INVITE • Invite me in to take a spin in the center of cells pointed to tell the centri-fugal byte that a star is on-line in a room called relief and the peace of her showing is the relative sight of divinity glowing. A light invite. • You are invited to the lightest treat, the kindest feast, the end of the beast is the walk down the street called the lightest paths, the center of you, the pyramid with a solar plexian view. Run your design and your gentleness too by tapping the power with an intimate hue – here's the view and the venue – it's you colored light blue and green and engerized with the kindest invitation to know the light in you, a light invite.

LIGHT EN-TICE • En-tice my knowing in your splashy tread to the heart of the puddle and the head of a fountain melting in grades of illuminating shades. People met peaceably in healing retreat to the relief of a notion expectant and true an energetic spin to the heaven in you by elegant design and exceptional proof an elixir important, an evaporative fact that light's in the bank, a digging truth. The light en-tice is meant for you. Light. • Waterfalls land in many a span and echo down through the seams to the land of the mola* and the infinite koa and the mountains that range in between and deep within you there's an absolute reflection of this sweetest connection between nature and you. And the mother's electric and moving kinetic to flip on the switches hidden in ancients and now the day has come and the light entice is to heed this advice and take in this blue-green news. Mitochondria's hungry and powering up to say it's your light entice it to arc all cell through and straight into the heart of you. A light entice.

Mola – the revelation of truth and infinite insight to the depths of you. 1000 worlds in one picture. You. LIGHT.

LIGHT-N-LOOSE • Light-n-loose and special in fit, I am led to share the heart of this space. The free wheeling exhibition called living again and I am met in respect by the forgiving sect of an ancient tribe and a healing bride, the effective practice of integrated knowing that my wide open heart is exact in showing the light-n-loose glow of a moonbeamed night, stone free and bejeweled by tides. Light-n-loose. • This rock is loose upon which I sit and it's caused my fearing an awful fit. So I've made the decision, the choice, and the design to toss up this loose fit for a better this time. For the light's all right in the spirit of me and I've just watched the webs of my soul break free to go on back home to the light. I know and I am light-n-loose wearing new clothes with a perfect fit. Light-n-loose.

LIGHT DELIGHT • Delight-full to see is the stunning loop of infinity beaming in the living proof that the light's greatest delight is you and I love the chance to share this dance in the street of night's celebratory invite to ful-fill the life of a light delight. • The light's delight with my choice to finish this, my yellow voice, for the will to live includes this time – the ability to respond on time, this moment, this tick, to the trip of the light delight – with me. A light delight.

LIGHT-IN-FACT • One fact. Light. • It's light in fact and I've lifted you to view this light from an infinite view – the top of your head and the toes of your feet – meet in the middle to dance in the street of the mansions golden and home and divine for it's light in fact and now is your time. Flood your light, load the raft, the river's up and the rapids past. Enjoy the float, for there's light at your back, in fact. Light.

LIGHT EXACTLY • Light's exactly what it is. The wealth of a nation and a grounding kiss of heaven's reality meeting in us to acknowledge the gift of the sparkling tree, the light of a coral reef blood-red and free to grow where she lives and watch the new tone of a heart sung in sheets of a glistening roar. A mountain lifted to reveal the high sun. The arc of the altar awaiting the one. Love. Yours and mine. By design to an astonishing degree of absolute accuracy. Light exactly. • The light is, exactly, your act of final commit-meant to love.

LIGHT LAUGHTER • Laughing well within the flood of a heart sentimental and a living won by a fastening light spark high and heady with roaring delight at the beauty I see in our infinite view of the light laughter seen in the miracle I call you. A heart baked by envy has cracked to reveal the place of compassion and an option to heal in wholistic relief, the ecstatic parcels of the heavenly piece. A peace surpassing and a new understanding. Light laughter. • Laughter with joy and worth and delight at the lightness in you and the leading this life. Light to the burnish and the living of proof that we're here to listen and hear the whole truth, pealing forth in your voice from your gut, laughing up the light, waterfalls of singing praise, light laughter. Till my tummy mirths – peace is knowing and shown in your light laughter. Just ask her. Light.

LIGHT, JUST ASK HER • It's light, just ask her and deep in the seams of your tangerine hunt lives a heart ametrine and a pink and green lemon squirts into air made essent by the presence of your breathing care. I am aligned with the grandest design, my own, and God knows that my will and thine, sweet light are one in the name of the father, and mother, the sun. For it's light, just ask her. Me and my mother are one. • I am light and write on time to talk with you about the truth. We two are one and the light of the sun resounding on the moon echoes back a resonate tune, we are one, in the sun, of the light called this earth, filled with mirth and delight at our just dessert – light. Just ask her. The mother. Earth. Light.

LIGHT THIS DAY • Light this day with blue-green views of the cheesy adornment gone to meet blue-cheese skies and heavens of brie and french-speaking candles lit by the seed of a startling match, an absolute key, the love of the son and the warmth of the sea of divine belief in the living tree. Light this day. • Light this day and my life and my way, dearest mother earth. Nature of the lost, the least, the marked up beast, is light. Let all remember with delight that all there is, is light – This day, this way, nature's delight-light.

LIGHT SELECT IT • Select the light and protect the sight of your eyes pealing back to review the bell of a crystalline core and a welcome swell, the appeal of a joy met in a-man, womanly and firm and voluptous to see the melting peach grown yellow in me and my life is a dream and an accurate spin in the egg of the light that I call I am. Light select it. • As for me and all I see, within and out, is one big tree of infinite light, me. From leaf to leaf and all the year through, I will be light to a waterfall's tune and an ocean's roar, and an eagles sing and a rock and rill and a butterfly's wing. Always flocking, never mocking, to the light for its my life and my temple's host – light, I select it through and through light.

LIGHT-EST TASTE • Raspberry blue in green relief, a mountainous palate swells in me and I taste plates of shifting vents and loving healing continents, magma melts magnetic through the aphrodisial swelling proof that the flavor savored escapes in me, in living loving ecstasy of the tao* of you. A swelling truth. The cork removed. The flooding sate of the lightest taste. • The light est taste is water drenched with sunshine sparkling clear to the center of you – the light-est taste. A light menu. Arc h2o here. H2o, lime, maple or honey, blue-green algae. A light menu.

Tao- Know the power of the infinite sway, without moving. Spiraling into the 64 chings and the I at the end. LIGHT.

LIGHT SLICE • Watermelon tumbled and tourmaline dreams met in the ecstasy of my love's seam. The green of delight and comfort and touch and the arc of the pink exacting fit perfectly grown and divinely set in tiny light slices blooming in me to the edge of my heart and the boundless sea of the light watermelon in me, juicy and red and pink and green. Swallow the seeds of a light slice. • Slice me a pie or a watermelon full. Consider me nice and a sight for the renewal of you faith in engendering the value of minutes divided by infinity, the light without limit. Slice me a piece of the pie, mr., Please and thank you for filling my strudel with cheesy reminders that a life full and rich is liquid and juicy and pink with the itch to rekindle the spark in my gut which reminds that forever is never too much and spinning this minute is a slice of the race called leave it to cleavers and finish the taste for sheltering and harboring less than the supreme, the honorable and the slice called the best – only this – a light slice.

LIGHT WEDGE • Consuming a wedge of pink, and green and

lavender hue, I'm painting the edge of a canvas called proof that divinity rests in the central chest of a love imbued with treasures felt to melt the blue-green singularity of loving lived alone in beds of forgiving meld. A dixie-land tune met in refrain eternally true. The land of a king. The light wedge in you. Fore. Light. • Wedges of lemon and lime in a dreamy concoction we call iced cream and milky refusal to wear less than this light suited fit – the well of delight has proffered forth belling entreaties and swirling designs of marshmallow particles of the this we call time. A construct so flimsy and yet rigid as well equates a contrast with a story to tell. Deep in your cells a time net is fixed. When light reaches contact, a new structure lifts of embark in the stream you call life and the blood of this giving wells in the light, pouring forth glimmers and glitters and glints. Life here is better at the edge of this tip of the pi. A light wedge.

LIGHT TO LOVE BY • Love me soft and long and well, unplug denial and ring a clear bell at the edge of a line yanked to reside eternally deep in the light's dissolve of forgetting blocking and the rock called hard meeting and elegance retreats to pass round the middle of emerald hue, the perfume of the light living in you. A light to love by. • The sky's a tent. The moon's a bowl. And in between is the land of spirit full wonder, awe, and transpire. Beckon me home to the earth, my desire. My precent knowing forgotten is showing and glowing in integrated insight of the eternal flowing. Yes, I am living and yes, I am living and yes, I am light and the light to love ny is that glow in your eye. The spark of remember enhances our dance and the light is electic in its symbols of lasting arrival at the point of return and the tree called the heavens is to earth now enraptured with the welcome of bliss and the light is to love by and the earth is to kiss – lightly on the lips of the hearts of new arrivals.

LIGHT ELECT IT • Election night has met in peace and the pace of a nation slumbers in sweet adoration of the living sign, the vote of a-man and the love inside your living campaign to remain in the infinite frame and the love of a sign blessed to see, the light's reflection in me. Transparent to view. The light elect it. • Light's election is here tonight in the meadow of your heart and it's your invictive to take directive and invoke the note of the light elective. Sew where is the needle of your bliss content? Sewn to the heavens here beneath the tent of forgotten rivals and rovers and charms lies the place of sweet remember well within the coated arms of oldest vintage. Here's the light heartland and the crew and the dearest electoral is the light inside of you. Vote light. Elect it. It's your life. Choose the flight to the light. Elect it.

LIGHT I CHOOSE IT • I choose light and that's my guess of the place where a rest has met with policy and potential strains in melting acceptance of the beauty becoming an electric ocean, splashing in shifts of ecstatic review, and a college complete with elective proof. Know the light and vote for the life lived complete. I have elected the right to know the light. I choose it. •

Lest I forget. Light, I choose it. Never abuse her. Always enthuse her. Where is my will now? Right in the middle beneath and within the pyr-a-mid. The light, I choose it. The lie, I lose it. I'm heading for infusing my life with the juice now. The beverage most kind is the light in the central reservoir I call mine. Light to the point, I'll let it shine in all that I do, I'm choosing light.

LIGHT, INFUSE IT • Infuse your life with the living line, the spark in an arc from your heart to mine and mining for gems we meet in the vein of forgiving living and a heavenly name, ours. Light infuse it. • The light's enthused when you infuse her sparkle with your gleam and a waterfall cascades down the path you've made by your centered-heart beliefs and in the moon, a sweeter tune, one different and replete with knowing glance begins to dance in the light beneath your feet. The earth is light and she welcomes you to join the ture and to sing some too. For its light, infuse it with you.

LIGHT, EXCUSE IT • Excuse me, I'm caring is that light you are wearing beneath the cloak of forgotten speak and easy retreat to the line less read. Feel the heat of the haggard's retreat for you are light, excuse it. • As it's light, excuse it. People's living is often forgetting that light is sending a message clear through to the heart. Darkness is only, light that has forgotten to live lovingly, softly, and gently in the light. In my surrender, I am light's sender, stepping back to see the breath, the with, the depth of your forgetting. Perhaps the sender's, the forgetter. Perhaps the liver needs to give herself some light green algae dreams of the light ametrine and the world pearly clean and light-in-between the splash of faces remembering the light, excuse it. For the remembrance cometh and the light's embrace is the summit we call life – light.

LIGHT, EMBRACE IT • Embrace the vent of lava's split erupting juicy, red and green and melting all the gaps between your arms and mine grasping dear the filling line of love coming down to fill the thrill of an energetic bill, visitors meet at the end of a street and an embassy's feel. The light's diplomatic and your love is complete in the light, embrace it. • It's light, embrace it. It's your heart, feel it. Now mix the two with the power called three (3) at the point of this tree equals light, you and me, infinitely, elegantly, eternally, deeply, passionately, freely, creamy and without an after taste. Light, embrace it, and me, eternally.

LIGHT, IN SPACES • It's light in spaces I call atp*, the synapse called rescue has illumined me to the greater truth of individual light response-ability. From 6 until 5 I will reside in the space I call mine and the light that I find at the end of this tread, this ear full called whine has lifted to sign greater days and nights of hum. I am the due. The light within the great central sun, the one way home by the light of my own light, in spaces. • There is light in spaces where people are giving. For people in giving equals people in living and in our living a story is told, a song is for singing, and the ringing's begun. The heavens are singing and wearing new threads of open revival. Our spirit's are lead – home to the light now and welcome to see the light in the spaces is you and it's me – eternally, infinity to infinity, free to be LIGHT-IN-the SPACES within and between-light.

Energy's juicy triple treat of mitochondrial, cellular intent.

LIGHT, CAROLING • Light in the center, I'm an aglitter with glistening threads of love lifting webs and straight to the joint a living is fed with the eternal flame of a heraldic name. Know the expression of a full discretion, catch the tread of a walking led by meeting deep in the chambered hall of a heart held gentle and a love less difficult, your own, sung within the eternal span of this God's man, divine to a clearing line of expressive need. I see the light, lightly caroling. • Singing me home is the light metatronic and the name of this sonnet is the lightly caroling embrace of the savior – this race, lightly led. Spirit fed. We are light felt tonight in the tight embrace of a sister found now in the lightest place – in my heart's singing, lightly caroling requim light's infinity. Lightly caroling, infinitely to me.

LIGHT TO LIGHT • Spark to spark, I'm set to embark on the towering plane, the beautiful tree, the ecstatic initial, the love adrenaline* and I am aflame with the sheltering name, the exquisite embrace of a telling race, speak your name, light a flame in the bush of a rushing tread. Slow down my friend and know the spin of the beauty you are. Light to a star and sparkling to find that love in the middle, yours and mine, by infinite design. I am led to the arc to recline. Light to light. • Infinity to infinity, heart to heart, and arc to arc, we are rainbows of remember and in-a-sense lost in inner wisdom found at the place called forever at the point of this clowning entreaty to take off your mask and show me your light smile and finish your past looping inquiry into the way and enjoy the moment of owning the power of the light, that you are and eat a new buffet by the stream of forever and the light of a star called arcturus tonight at the bank of the stream's milky way is the balance of the mother and in loving surrender kneel light to light, standing still. Light to light.

LIGHT EXPRESSION • I am a light expression of a grand equation, the ultimate solution of the pleasant embrace that reality's clearest in the love of this place, light. Know the trace of the twinkling space, called your heart and mine, wet to the taste of a fountain sparkling life full and deep to the centering lace of a lime-green station. Life's equation a light expression. Light = me. Light. • Light's expressive and funny lights and well and lifted to the heavenly in the stories you tell as the waves of sub-letting empties your cells of dross and deceiving and forgetting to care for the temple, you are, now chase out the money changers and buy a new star to the galaxy, you are and the universe, I am and it's all here inside you in the heart of this man, this light, this sister, this brother of the light's full glimmering expression, you my delight full design=love=God=light= you. A light expression.

LIGHTLY PLEASANT • Dolphins splash in a circling trend to flip in examples of 42 times the 70 forgiven and the 73 nights of a sample 100 and pleasing sums of treasury's bet that God has a degree in internal revenue measured by the wattage of a central intelligence and a will full set on the trend to be lightly pleasant. • Lightly pleasant tonight I'm a pheasant feathered light in flight within embracing sweet surrender, I've found the point of a light-less gender, more enraptured with the lightest capture of yet more space in myself and I'm well in my living and I'm sweet in my giving and tonight is the healing by being light pleasant to the moment most blissant for this is the present called light. Light pleasant like a hummingbird's flight straight to the nectar of my heart's blooming green wonder. Light pleasant.

LIGHT PRESENT • Light's a gift – now lightly taken. Never break the love we're making by living smile and lying well. Yours is the light that makes a new tail in the sky of our sight. Love's invite. The greatest gift. Love is right and we are met by givings test. The light present. • The light is present here in yellow earth, here in middled being is the key to walking red through orangest juicy while combining with the threads knotting, now the smoothing, and with wonder I am. Led to many moments with gentle loving life, and wed the thread we're weaving into one smooth blanket – light – and deep within the center, I join the staff again to teach the light more wonder-full, more awe-inspired by this living again. Light present and here's the gift – a life lightly given.

LIGHT GRIP: Grip your hammer and hang your belt on the loop at the top of this living melt. The candles are dripping, the table is set, the tableau called for-ever is the trip of a light time and the pace of a thread. The sewer is fixed and the house has been built, the table is set and this love is a quilt, on the sofa of love and the house that light built. By design. Happy birthday. A light grip. • A light grip on life's wheel, twirls me in to the center again as spatters of seeing begun once again to wheel through the middle and the middle place is open and centered and light through the view of a temperate rain forest, the melting of two stranded dna and the elixir of one has initiated the change and the charge has been run. In fondest revival, the vision is complete and the scene has been set. Pack a light grip, yourself, for we are going on a trip, light, to the center of you. Molten and moving & earth to the core. A light grip.

LIGHT TRIP • Trip to the lip of a lighter stride and a healthier planet and a light ride. I am ecstatic and tickled to see the laughing proof of the living truth, divinity in me by the route called belief and an avenue true. Your sister's felt the power, her own and the winning song of a love grown strong. Visit me at the meeting place for our visit to the light trip. • Trippin' on moonbeams and daring to see the light shining full in the place within me and I am renewed by the bliss I call you and the trippin' days are through and this light trip's in you and the daisy's are in view as light loves me resonates through to the petals folding open to revel the sweetest token, the lotus shineth fullest whence the beauty reflects through the beholder. A light trip.

LIGHT SLIPPERS • Slip your slippers into a deeper seat and a reclining entreaty to bow at the sleeve of a well. Come enjoy reminder of the bliss called a-man and the woman who lives in ecstatic belief at the relief of a road leading home and a song sung static free and light to the grip of a trip deep inside the pyramid of life and the light inside. Layer by layer. Know the peace of living fine. Light slippers. • Slip into something special, your-self. Step into something comfortable – your spirit – let the light flood and embrace you with it's telling surrender. Feel in the gaps with the light fleshy pink, leafy green you are the tree and the vine and the ways by design. Know the light, feel the fit, click around, about your town, in the lightest ware, the loftiest step. The lightest ground is beneath you feet and in the treat of your happy footed, light winging trip, in your gentle step, the light trip slipping by and all the way through. Light slippers.

LIGHT GEAR: Gearing up for the int-imate grip of a lasting trip to the land of ladies and slippers sent to give the intention a kinder vent – the light kilauea's* been sent to teach creation to a stagnate nation and a lady liberated to wear her light gear. • Strap on you helmet, step to the street, gather your tools, for the haggard soul's retreat has set now the issue, the privy to see, the outstanding issue is what you're to be, within your light living, spirit led, soul forgiven, pace to tread. We are light here. Hear it said, light is brightest when you're spirit led, across the bridge, no more gorge, enjoy the tour for the light hath given – light gear to wear and naked to the truth – light.

*a volcanic venting place in the land of Obsidian tears and Peridot grains of timeless sand.

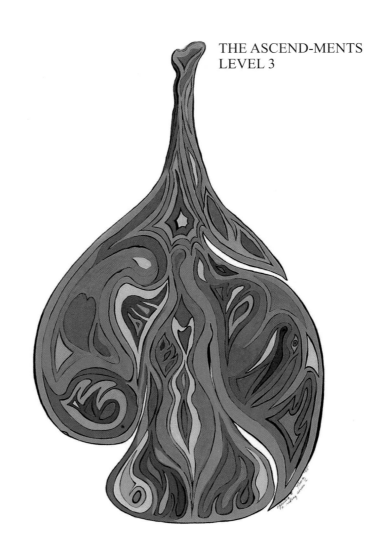

THE ASCEND-MENTS
LEVEL 3

CHAPTER 1 / LOVE LIGHTS: Bliss: Bliss acknowledged by a level called Love / Acknowledge: Acknowledge thee college of Love / Abandon: Abandon meant less than Love / Review: Review you, need, to, Love / Expansion: Expand a mansion to a rapid expansion called Love / Remiss: Remiss? Impress, with Love / Repress: Repress express? Explore with Love / Give Proof: Given proof, enough, to Love / Found Full: Found full of Love / Left Dry: Left dry? Good-bye to less than Love. / Found Empty: Found it empty, spent, by 'Love' / The News: The news ruled, Love / Gone? Why?: Gone? Why? To God, a long Love / The Fields: The fields healed my Love / The Views: I'm sealed inside the views of Love / The eTudes: The eTudes are renewed by Love / The Thrills: The fields healed my Love / The Reveal: The reveal is heal our Love / The Repeal: The repeal, heal in Love / The Exude: Asunder I Am healed by the exude to Love / The Abused: The abused refused, Love / The Relax: The relax backs our Love / The Refused: The refused refused to Love / The Reward: The reward? A sword of Love / The 'In Facts': The 'In facts' are back to feel, Love / The Reviewed: The reviewed has sued my heart open to you, Love / The Exude: The extra exude is rude / The Ignite: The ignite is right in Love / The Per Chance: The per chance, you'll dance, is Love / The Revoked: The revoked spoke, Love / The Rewrite: The rewrite's right, Light in Love / The Intrude: The intrude's sweet, replete in Love / The True Blued: The true blued ensured has begun, to Love / The Find Inside: The find inside, my Love / The Found Found: The found is found in Love / Today Till Dawn: Today, till dawn, I'm on, Love / The Arc I'm On: The arc I'm in is on to Love / A Kinder Truth: A kind is truth in Love / A Kindred Proof: A kindred's proof of Love / The Eyes that dance: The eyes that dance can stand a chance in Love / A Welcome Stance: Welcome a stance to Love / A Tender Sign: Tender signed, Love / The Light Inside..The Light's inside my tribe called Love / The mind of God: The mind is God's on Love / The Arc Called God: The arc of God is good in is made by Love / The Right's I've Paid: The right's been paid to Love / The Wells I Wade: The wells I wade in shades are deep in Love / The Artesian Dream: The artesian, well, is filled with Love / The Salt of God: The salt of God is trod with sod of Love / The Days of Sod: Days of sod are God's forgive of live in less than Love / The Arm of Tools: The arm of tools pools in peals of Love / The Wield of Rules: The wield of rules rules in Love / The Love Gone By: The Love gone by? Why? Knot-Love / The Day Gone Dry: The day's gone dry are why we Love / The Even Trade: The even trade, a raid on Love / The Point I've Made: The point I've made is specifically, Love / The Art I Save: The art I save is a rave called Love / The Ink I've Paid: The ink I've paid drips off Love / The Wealth I Sought: The wealth I sought's been bought by Love / The Life Wade: The life I wade is home to loan of Love / The Connect I Dot: The connect I dot is a lot of Love / The Light I Am: The Light I Am began with Love.

CHAPTER 2 / LOVE LISTS: The Wave I Swam: The wave I swam to Love / A Divinity's Span: A Divinity's span? / The plan, to Love / A Pen, I Am: A pen in hand, I Am, Love / The Spark in Your: The spark's in you, through it all Love / The Light Revue: The Light revue? You. In Love / Of This I Say: Of this I say, Love / A Healing Proof of The Light That Lives.. A heal in proof is the step to truth an the Light that lives in Love / A Moment's Dream: A moment's dream? Away, to Love / A Mountain Stream: A mountain stream can gleam in Love / A Minute Won: A minute won by we've begun to Love / A Minute One: A minute, One, away from Love / A Vision Come: A vision came to come to Love / A Knot Undone: A knot undone in time to Love / A Bed We're Led: A bed we're led to Love / An Inkling Said: An inkling said, won! Love / A Lark We Laid: A lark we laid along the stay in Love / A Healing Bye: A healing bye to lessened Love / A Quilt Called Lost: A quilt called Love can rest in us and God is us / A Patterned Pulse: A patterned pulse emulse in Love / A Land With Lust: A land with lust abust to Love / The Rest in Us: The rest in us is a brush with Love / A Sleeping Potion: A sleeping potion the motion to Love / A Healing Notion: A healing notion's potion, Love / An Arc: An arc, a spark, with Love / A Star: A star afar to Love / The Arc You Are: The arc we are, afar, to Love / By A Covenant: By a covenant bent to Love / Never Broken: Never broken, the pattern to Love / Always Fit: Always fit, a kit called Love / Heal Your Heart: Heal your heart, start tonight, Light in Love / Fix Your Eye: Fix your eye to the sky in Love / Know the Truth: Know the truth there's proof of Love / God's Fool proof: God's fool proof is the impruit said to Love / Enoch Said: Enoch said to believe in Love / Knock, You're Dead: Knock, you're dead to less than Love / A Second Wave: A second wave of a rave to Love / An Ascendant Stand: An ascendant stand in Love / The Man I Am: The man I Am is god in Love / The Lord Metatron: The Lord Metatron is home to stay in Love / Arcturic Pens: Arcturic pens with again in Love / Mayan Bins: Mayan bins blend of Love / A Cleansing Flood: A cleansing flood can come to Love / The Ark of Doves: The ark of doves is an art of Love / A Tweet in Line: A tweet in time to a line inside our Love / A Train Called Time: A train called time can rhyme with Love / From a Quarter Turn: From a quarter turn I yearn to Love / A Rocking Learn: A parking decked by a rocking earn to yearn more. Love / The Sine Aligned: The sine's align is Love / A Laughing Sign: A laughing sign, why knot to Love / A Wealth Called Way: A wealth called way to go, Love / A Heart Called Day: A heart called day above, Love / A Night We've Led: Led a night to Love / To Bliss: To bliss sheer be the Love / To Kiss: To kiss so be our Love / To Dis: To dis dusty Love / To Dat: To dat give Love / To Tao: To Tao, how, Love / To Wow: To wow, win, Love / To Heaven's Maid: To a heaven's maid called Love / To Extreme Regimes: To extreme regimes, begin to believe in Love / To The Way: To the way you Love / To The Truth: To the truth, proof, Love / To the Light: To the Light, right, Love / Of Love: Of Love, live, learn, give, burn, yearn, full Love Know Bliss, Oblige: Know bliss, oblige yourself to Love's embrace called God is us in Love.

CHAPTER 3 / LOVE PLENTY: Abandon: Abandon abandon,

find redeem in Love / Sent: Sent bent? Forgive and get a straighter scoop of Love / Expansion: Expansion pent-less to Love / Vent: Vent view, Love / Impulsion: Impulse in to Love / Spent: Spent less, Loved / Expulsion: Expulsive vent of Love-less rent gone wide to a center called Love / Brought: Brought home, Love / The Surge: The surge to purge, of less, than merge in Love / Sought: Sought safe, Love / The Purge: The purge appealed to filled with Love / Found: Found a pound of Love around our heal of Love / The Feel: The feel felt good in real Love / Astound: Astound around our Love / The Thrill: The thrill will deal, Love / Reveal: Reveal feel, Love / The Desire: The desire hire, Love / For Real: For real, Love / The Extend: The extend again, Love / The Bend: The bend burns less than Love / The Friend: The kink found a friend a friend in letting go to Love / The Trend: The trend, again, is Love / The Chore: The chore? More. Love / The Door: The door? More, Love / The Store: The store for Love / The Deed: The deed indeed, In deed, is Love / The Concede: The concede to breed is contempt-less of Love / The Freed: The freed agreed to Love / The Need: The need to feed on Love / The Electric Construct: The construct struck is less than bliss in Love / The Dream: The dream redeem is Love / The Trim: The trim is slim to Love / The Dame: The dame, shame, has gone to Love / The Skim: The skim trim is the skinny limb to Love / The Flame: The flame found is Love / The Skinny: The skinny run is the trim to Love / The Lad: The lad is glad to Love / The Venue: The venue knew, to Love / The Brad: The brad is broad to Love / The Vinny: The vinny's skinny to Love / The Lock: The lock's a shock to Love / The Debut: The debut, you, to Love / The Key: The key? We. Love / The Relief: The relief's rest, Love / Call Me: Call me home, 2 Love / The Resolve: The resolve to solve, Love / Called You: Called you, hear, Love / The Need: The need to feed on Love / The Tools: The tools to fill, Love / The Welcome: The welcome splatter of Love / The Trends: The trend end, real, Love / The Suspense: The suspense rinse, Love / The Amends: The amends, friends, Love / The Attribute's: The attribute's cute to Love / The Friends: The friends found, Love / The Intrigue: Intrigue? Yes! Love / The Deeds: Renew the deeds to Love / The Review: The review knew, anew, Love / The Seams: Seams scene, melt, Love / The Extreme: Extreme need to dream of Love / The Needs: The needs struck, Love / The Pursuit: The pursuit, cute, deep, trip, trap, lost, lust, bust, Love / The Plus: The plus, hush, hear, Love / The Passion: The passion place, Love.

CHAPTER 4 / LOVE SUM: The Big: The big won, Love / The Play: The play? Stay within Love / The Pith: The pith of breathe to Love / The Daze: The daze gone, to Love / The Prod: The prod to God. The rim 4 Love / The Admit: The admit struck, Love / The Sod: The sod sewn, to Love / The Commit: The commit met, Love / The Ways: The ways wedge, Love / The Trays: Trays lift Love / The Days: The days weigh, Love / The Buffet: The buffet line, Love / The Commitment: The commitment made, I Am, Love / The Attend: The attend to mend is Love / The Invention: The invention I mention is Love / The Intend: I intend! Love / The

Dimension: The dimension 3 to 4 is more, Love / The Admission: The admission? Ignition to Love / The Direct: Direct dove, Love / The Cognition: The cognition of heal in Love / The Bisect: The bisect direct to Love / The Recognition: Love's recognition. The right to Light in Love / The Inspect: The inspect surfeit is Love / The Remission: The remission's mission is Love / The Reflect: The reflect? Respect. Love / The Extension: The extend, the extent, the extension to Love / The Ascend: The ascent to mend is Love / The Revision: The revision? A mission to Love / The Begin: The begin begun, to Love / The Admission: The admission? Ignition of Love / To These Truths: To these truths, we've proof, of Love / The Reside: The reside astride Love / The Protestant View: The protestant and new, Love / The Demise: The demise of aft to Love / The Christian Review: The Christian review know, Love / The Catholic Exude: The Catholic exude to Love / The Ignition: The ignite to height of Love / The Muslim News: The Muslim news renewal reviewed by Love / The Sufi Views: The Ssufi views news, Love / The Radical Roots: The radical roots of emphatic fool proof to Love / The Electric Roots: The electric waves rave a the roots of Love / The Healing Proof: The heal is proof of truth in Love / The Admonition: The admonition to remission of less than lightly Love / The Call to Be: The call to be creeled by Love / This Our Mission: This our mission, ignition to rocket to Love / The Bliss to See: The bliss to be, see to Love / A Coupled: A couple sought soft in Love / Our Truth: Our truth told triple infinity Light and GOD and Love / A Sullen Proof: A sullen proof is truth to lift our Love / Eternal: Eternal we treasure a measure called Love / A Bear In Shoes: A bear wore shoes to news of express in Love / Supernal: Supernal ascend, a trend, to Love / A Bear in News: A bear in news renews Love / Youth: Youth and sooth in Love / A Trailing Proof: A trailing proof exude a trace in Love / Abandon Meant: Abandon meant fit to Love / Respect-full: Respect-full respect to Love / Acknowledge: Acknowledge acknowledge of a gentle college called LOVE / The Meaning: The meaning met sweet in LOVE / The College: The college of increase to a crease called perfect Love / The Store: The store of more in Love / Called Love: Called Love round our pound of point at Love / Up Next: Up next, Love / Feed: Feed yourself, Love.

CHAPTER 5 / LOVE SUNG: Alive, My Ways: Alive, my ways, to waves of Love / Asheville Days: Asheville ways dive deep to Love / Erotic Seams: Erotic seams redeem Love / Electric Ways: Electric ways home to Love / A Hire Story: A hire story, higher yourself in a while of Love / A Healing Dream: A healing dream along the rain of Love / A Field of Themes: A field of theme called a rhyme of Love / A Melted Pave: A melt at pave is rave to Love / An Art-full Dance: An art-full dance of stance called Love / A Grander Scheme: A grander scheme the ring called Love / Forgiving Limes: Forgive a lime of tribe called Love / An Artist's Stance: Arty stance, a trace for less, then Love / Emphasis Climes: Emphasis the clime of Love / Ecstatic Times: Ecstatic exact in fact on time for Love / A Knowing Scheme: I know a scheme, let's Love / Effusive Gleams: Effusive beam agleam with Love / Eternal Waves: Eternal wave, stare of Love / Assignments Say: Assign meant say Love / An Eternal Internal Clock: Eternal, internal, a clock to Love / A Mental Block: A mental block, a rocks' remove to Love / A Delicate Line: A delicate line inside the stem of Love / Arriving Signs: Arrive inside a Love you own, your own, Love / Phlox and Posies: Phlox a posie home to Love / A Field and Flocks: Field and flocks rocks on Love / Guilt and Gay: Guilt and gay all day to Love / Knows and Noseys: Knows a nosey gay for days of Love / Election Day: Elected day Hey! Love / Gray and Guilt: Gray and guilt are gone to Love / Belted: Belted bet, wet, earth, Love / Quilted: Quilted square of Love / Instead: Instead enough, Love / Understood: Understood, yes, Love / He Went: Deep he went to Love / She Said: She said *wets Love *Wide examine of true suspend / They Give: They give good, Love / We Live: God is give, we live, Love / Vibrate: Vibrate rate? Love / Free: Free Be, Love / Explain: Explain pane, Love / Love: Love Love's greet Love / Design: Design a denser lift to Love / Divine: Divine degree *BHD to Love *Basic, Human, Divine / Descend: Descend defeat to uplift our Love / Amend: Amend meant bent forgotten fend to Love / Resign: Resign reside to Love / Review: Review, rest best, Love / The Love Inside: The Love inside our glide is Light to Love / And You: And you meet sweet defeat with Love / The Move: The move, groove, deep, to Love / The Trends: To trends blends Love / Deliver In: Deliver in us, Love / Deliver Us: Deliverance delivered us to Love / Instead: Instead instance begun to Love / In Fed: In fed I feed Love / In Feed: In a feed I bread only Love / In Red In peace reels red Love / In Receive: In receive I breathe, Love / The Mother: The mother met our Love / The Father: The federal face of a Father place called Love / The Lover: The lover I leave to Love / The Day: This day sway to Love / Tell Me: Tell me where, Love / The Way: The way to be best blessed, Love / The Aisle: The aisle while you Love.

CHAPTER 6 / LOVE STRUNG: The Isle: Red Isle abed our Love / Red: Big red to big extend our Love / Born Green: Born green to seem like Love / Eruptive In: Eruptive rude and lesson in our Love / Desire to Line: Desire to hire a line of Love / In Joy's Space: In joy I space to Love / The Grace: The grace embrace of Love / Called Love: Called we Love / Eternal: Eternal measure, pleasure us with Love / Dove: Dove date great Love / An Ocean Wide: Ocean wide to glide on Love / Big Isled Align: Big isled align inside our Love human kind / And Yes, We Know: And yes, we know our Love / The Passion Shows: The passion shows in you and our Love / And 3 Below: And 3 below knew One above Love / A Burning Heat: A burning heat is neat in Love / Besiege: Besiege rage now with Love / The Kneed: The kneed to need more less then Love / To Love Aside: To Love aside, inside, Love / Inside: Inside ride to Love / The Stream: The stream redeem, in Love / Called Light: Called Light home to Love / And Love: And 14 carrots later, birth, Love / We Feed: We feed confess to Love / On Dreams: On dreams seams of Love / On Deliver Us: Of deliver us we deal less than respect-less Love / And I Can See: And I can see, we Love / The Trend To Be: The

trend to be in Love / Inflamed: Inflamed to frame a tame to Love / By Same: By same sum, run to Love / And Met: And met wet, electric, Love / To Need: To need need, Love / The Game: The game to torn, Love / To Ends: To ends begins, Love / Friends: Friend and win when Love / Of Dames: Of dames called bliss fits Love / Called Fortune: Called fit for fortune, I Am Love / Fate: Fate fleet? Eternal Love / And Tragedies: Tragedies trade raid on Love / And Mates: And mates meet sweet ecstatic treat of Love / And Myths: And myths met feel of Love / And Archaeology: And archaeology's win is Love / Called Ecstatic: Called ecstatic, emphatic, Love / Relief: Relief arrest a rest in Love / Of Human: Of human regard, guard be gone to Love / Regard: Regard us, rest, in Love / Yet: And yet, Love / The Heights: Heights held ascend to Love / Of Heaven: Of heaven held, Love / And The Heaven: And the heaven held us in sway to Love / Of Stars: Of stars occur cares for Love / Elect It: Elected Love / Select It: Select effect, Love / Know It: Know it new, Love / Just Due It: Just due it with a payment of Love / Imbue It: Imbue it, Love / Show It: Show it proned to Love / Love: Love, Love / Ignobled: Ignobled noble yes, Love / Belt: Belt brake smoke to Love / The Dealt: The dealt, deal, Love / The Felt: The felt effect of Love / The Full: The full effect, Love / The Filled: The filled filled up, Love.

CHAPTER 7 / LOVE STRING: Skywide: Skywide ride to Love / The Field: The field filled few, to Love / Star Deep: Star deep in a store of Love / Arcing Lean: Arcing lean to wean to wider Love / The Chance: The chance, a prance to Love / The Deliver: Play boy's friend, deliver again within the wealth of Love / The Dance: A mansioned stance, to dance at Love / Leaning Stance: Lean in stance, Love / Extreme : Extreme, I Love / Banal: Banal breed, to better less Love / Primal: Primal pressures measure, Love / Gleam: Gleam of good gold Love / A Glen Extreme: A glen gone extreme to Love / Archimedian Links: Archimedian care share the links to Love / Alchemical Rings: Alchemy rules the magical rings of Love / The Bridge: The bridge builds, Love / The Healing Cup: Healing a cup of Love / Stepping Up: Stepping up to a sup on a banquet of Love / Mean It's Touch: Know the *mean, touch, Love. *median's example of absolute near / Call It Love: Call it Love / See the Wealth: See the wealth, stealth be done, Love / Redeem Yourself: Redeem yourself, melt in Love / Know the Pod: Know the pod of Godly dolphined Love / Feel Your Dad: Feel your Dad, glad to Love / Touch Your Mom: Touching Mom, stand in strong allegiance to GOD / Inhale the Sun: Inhale the breath of God and the face of the Sun and Love / Beat the Drum: Beat a drum, the One, to Love / Know the Chance: Knowing chance, glance to Love / The Compare: To compare the compare know where to Love / The Dare: The dare to spare in Love / The Wares: The wares of west of Love / The Stairs: The stairs set in bust to Love / The Plays: The plays ascent, Love / Called Love: Called us, 'Love' / Traditional: Tradition sent, Love / Scented: Scented mist, Love / Conditional: Condition me to Love / Alabama: Alabama bound by Love / Eruptive: Eruptive red, Love / Jeweled: Jeweled be-jewel in Love / Subjective: Subject said, objective Love / Kyanite: Kyanite blue to a deepened hue, Love / Reflective: Reflective tress down the back of Love / Iolite: Iolite right to Love / Wed: Wed to believe in Love / Seas: Seas of seas to seize in Love / Eyes: Eyes Light to Love / Rings: Rings round the sum, of One, Love / Able: Able to be in Love / Philosophic: Philosophic rocket to Love / Philosophy: Philosophy fuzz? Love / Late..Late to Love? Welcome soon enough, Love / Equate: Equate a rate of Love / Await: Await too late. Love / Arising: Arising today I will Love / Listening: Listen up! Love / Turnings: Turnings turn to Love / Turning: Turning round your Love / Spank: Spank spunk spent? Love / Rank: Rank a spank is Love / Short: Short to court in Love / Shift: Shift to gift in Love / Roaming: Roaming round a town in Love / Today: Today I live Love.

CHAPTER 8 / LOVE PIECES: Soon Enough: Soon enough, Love / Movies: Movies meet neat Love / Rotate: Rotate grate to Love / By - Pass: By-pass heart felt, Love / Lovely: Lovely leisure, lady Love / Short: Short shift, long on Love / Palm: Palm a top a hand to Love / Fingered: Fingered field of Love / Poem: Poem plenty deep to Love / Young: Young yen, Love / Snappy: Snappy nappy, Love / Gentle: Gentle gem, Love / Extravagant: Extravagant measure, Love / Exuberant: Exuberant measure, Love / Comfortably Well: Comfort well, yes, to Love / Remedy: Remedy red, Love / Jargon: Jargon on Love / Vestral: Vestral in, Love / Virgins: Virgins view cherubs' truth to Love / Cherry: Cherry head breed of Love / Red: Red abed expect's reflect of love / Peach: Peach peel, Love / Said: Said yet? Love / Love: I Am Love / Blood: Blood bet, Love / Warned: Ark of warmed renew to Love / Genetic: Genetic extend of a stem to Love / Kinetic: Kinetic connect can meet your Love / Cushy: Cushy feel Love / Patience: Patience pent to Love / Ladies: Ladies thirst for Love / Trick: Trick a treat to Love / Ticket: Ticket tucked in to Love / Satin : Satin seal, the feel to Love / Velvet: Velvet view, a zoom to Love / Jet: Leap aboard a jet to lord of Love / Baker: Baker beaker faber keeper Love / Pulse: Pulse to a point, Love / Patch: Patch batch, Love / Lust: Lust bust, Love / Exude: Exude abreast Love / Boat: Boat afloat, Love / Dream: Dream drill Love / The Heart: Heart smart, Love / The Head: Head aboard Love / The Stand: The stand fan, a seat in Love / The Strand: Strand trim, to Love / The Preclude..Preclude nude Love / The Proclaim: Proclaim rust free to Love / Sector: Sector vector, Love / Secure: Secure your Love / Segue: Let us segue a way to Love / Section: Section, suction, Life of Love / Stream: God stream, Love / Scene: Scene beam, Love / Rod: Live rod, Love / Belt: Belt fibrous, to Love / Teeth: Teeth tuck, Love / Wreath: Real wreath, around, Love / Pass: Pass on, Love / Pat: Pat get pet of Love / Boone: *Boone's rune, Danieled, Love *Basically open often to a noon eternal to Love / Bath: Bath burst babbled up to Love / Booth: Booth of Love.

CHAPTER 9 / LOVE PEACE: I Am, That I Am: I Am, yes that I Am, is Love / I Am Essence: I Am essence, yes, breath, to Love / I Am Light: I Am Light to a heater Love / I Am Life: Life's lift

kit, Love / I Am Well: Life's lift kit, Love / I Am Well: I Am well in rowed to Love / I Am Love: I Am Love / I Am That: I Am that smack in Love / I Am Then: I Am then, Love / I Am Now: I Am now, how, Love / I Am Eternally: I Am eternally in turn to Love / I Am Infinity: I Am infinity to a blend called begin to Love / I Am Essentially: I Am essentially a measure mint deep to Love / I Am Elementally: I Am an element of essentially Love / I Am Eternally: I Am eternally lit by Love / I Am Infinitely: I Am intact in my infinite act, to Love / I Am Essentially: I Am essentially seat to Love / I Am Wholly: I Am a wholly held entirety felled by less, than Love / I Am Experientially: I Am an experiment experientially sent to spirit set to Love / I Am Evidently: Evidence advent, evidently I Am Love / I Am Finally: Finally, I Am Love / I Am Fragrantly: I Am fragrant in my ascent to Love / I Am Especially: I Am especially natured in quiet surrender to Love / I Am Absolutely: I Am absolutely full of Love / I Am Divinely: I Am divine astride the trine to Love / I Am Fully: I Am fully feeled with a healed ascend to God's Love / I Am Aptly.,..I Am in my amply found defend of Love / I Am Amazing: I Am amazed you came to my amazing wave of Love / I Am Engaging: I Am engaging in a raising Love / I Am Intricate: I Am intricate to a blend of Love / I Am Led: I Am led home to Love / I Am Fed: I Am fed abed a led to Love / I Am Met: I Am met deep in Love / I Am, Yes: I Am yes, I bless, my Love / I Am Today: I Am today to true, to be, to lift our elipse to Love / I Am Forever: I Am forever by an example called plains Love / I Am Entranced: I Am entranced to a dancing out to Love / I Am Elegant: I Am elegant to a sweller Love / I Am Eloquent: I Am eloquent by a turn to Love / I Am Intelligent: I Am intelligent to a decision called whether we Love / I Am Eternal: I Am exampled by an eternal sample called Love / I Am Fulfilled: I Am full-filled by your healed to Love / I Am Equitable: I Am equitable, eccentric, and electric to perfect Love / I Am Delectable: I Am detectable to an edible Love / I Am Electric: I Am electrical to a treat called sweet, Love / I Am Metatronic: I Am metatronic to delight in sight of Love / I Am Level: I Am level able by Love / I Am Balance: I Am balance enough to upon Love / I Am Harmonious: I Am harmonious by a beat called Love / I Am Attuned: I Am attuned to rest in Love / I Am Mobile: I Am mobile by an angle called Love / I Am Infinite: I Am infinite by a vote to Love / I Am Evergreen: I Am evergreen to a dream called Love / I'm Supernal: I'm supernal by an eternal flame / I Am Pedernal: I Am pedernal's eternal greet of O'Keefe to Love / I Am God: I Am God's good, Love / I Am The Earth: I Am the earth to a birth 2012 to Love / I Am New Birth: I Am new birth, the Earth, Love / I Am Regenerated: I Am regenerated by grace and Love / I Am Elated: I Am elated by great-full Love / I Am Safe: I Am safe to Love / I Am Happy: I Am happy to be, Love / I Am Green: I Am green to see your Love / I Am Cleared: I Am cleared to be in Love.

CHAPTER 10 / LOVE PURCHASE: One Love: One Love, a rub to Love / One Law: One is law in God Love / One Commandment: One command meant grand to Love / One Heart: One heart held well-ed in Love / One Way: One way, run, Home. Love / One Truth: One truth in proof of Love / One Life: One life lived, Love / One Wave: One wave willed Home / One Depth: One is depth in Love / One Appreciation: Once appreciated mated, Love / One Initiation: One initiated, Love / One Arc: One arc park in a land called Love / One Reminder: One remind us to Love / One Kinder: One kinder kin is Love / One Indivisible: One indivisible by none is Love / One Invincible: One invincible sum, Love / One Trickle: One trickle trim to Love / One Flow: One flow go to a river deep in Love / One Embrace: One embrace, race, to Love / One Taste: One taste high to Love / One Swell: One swell swum to Love / One Wave: One wave wet to Love / One Sun: One sun son, Love / One Time: One time tongued by Love / One You: One you mean, Love / One Line: One line lunged by Love / One Loop: One loop lipped to Love / One, I Am: One, I Am in Love / I Am One: I Am One won my Love / One Summer: One summer sun burnt brown to a lift called Love / One Winter: One winter win knee-deep Love / One Heart: One heart grins at Love / One Fall: One fall freeze to less than Love / One Vibe: One vibe thin to Love / One Spring: The spring sprung to Love / One Me: One me we, Love / One Stream: One stream, Love / One Dream: One dream, us, Love / One Awakening: One is awakening again within, Love / One Light: One is Light, tonight, Love / One Quickening: One is quick to Love / One Tree: One tree freed by Love / One Life: One is life in Love / One Led: One law, led, to Love / One Divine: One divine fine right, Love / One's Light: One's a Light to Love / One's Love: One's a Love / One: One to One, Love / One Thread: One, a thread to a weave of Love / One Web: One in Web of Love / One Wed: One wed sun, Love / One Fed: One fed few, to Love / One Night : One per night of Love / One Sight: One sight of Love / One Delight: One delight Love! / One Song: One song sing, a ring, to Love / One River: One's a river of Love / One Jah: One Jah God to Love / One God: One God Son to Love / One Sun: One sun seen, to Love / One King: One king come to Love / One Queen: One Queen come to life in Love / One Ring: God's a ring in grander Love / One Repine: Repine means rest in Love.

CHAPTER 11 / LOVE POINT: Infinite: Infinite an expanse of Love / Infinity: Infinity's at a stance in Love / Exceptionally Infinite: Love's in fine infinite align with exceptionally seen Love / An Infinite Loop: An infinite loop in a scoop of Love / Time for the Infinite: Time to rhyme of Love / Infinitely Greek: Infinite in Greek, a seek, of Love / Infinitely Essential: Essential dream of beam of Love / Infinite, It Seems: In finite seems are Love / Eternal Expansion: God's expanse is eternal in Love / Infinite Romancing: Romance a glance at infinite, Love / Essentially : Eternal Climb essential in terms of Love / Infinite Design: Design a rhyme arcturic deep in Love / Infinite Plan: Infinite the plan to Love / Infinite Rain: Got rain? Plain of ruin? Find the infinite, Love / Infinitely Divine: Got great fine, divine, Love / Lightly Infinite: Lightly infinite, Infinite, Love / Eternal Light: God's Light above, Love / Eternal Flight: In a flight eternal night, Love / Infinite Ecstasy: Ski on in to an infinity ecstatic to erratic Love

/ Eternal Bliss: Eternal a bliss, Love / An Eternal Kiss: Is a kiss rich? Yes, in Love / Ecstatic Review : Infinite Review infinity, Love / Infinity, I Said: I said God is, Love / Infinitely, I Am: I Am infinite by Love / Eternity, The Span: Span the eternal, eternity's plan, Love / An Infinite Arc: Arc an infinite spark to Love / An Eternal Web: Eat a web of invest in said, to Love / An Infinite Light: An infinite eight, right, to Love / Eternity's Sight: Sight eternal, eternity's bet on seeing Love / Infinite Tread: Tread infinity, Love / Eternally Led: Eternally let, Love / Infinitely Fed: Infinity said infinitely led, fed, Love / Infinity Said: Infinity said sweet, Love / Logos To Infinity: Logos, the word that's infinite, Love / Infinity, Let It Be: Let it be, infinity, please, Love / Let There Be Eternity: Let there be eternally LIGHT'S eternity, Love / Eternal Light: Love's eternal LIGHT / Infinite Love: Infinite we've Love / Love Eternal: Love's eternal LIVE, Love / Love's Eternity: Love's eternity, swag, to Love / Love To Infinity: Love to live in infinity's day gone home to stay in Love / Infinity: To Infinity fight to eight, I'm great to weight inside gone Light to Love / Eternally: I Am eternal I Am, to Love / Infinitely Centered: Infinitely centered I'm membered by Love / Centrally, Eternity's: Balance Centrality, Eternity's balance in Love / Insistently, Infinite: Insist on infinity, lightly, Love / Eternity's Star: Eternity's the star internal to Love / Infinity's Wave: Infinity's wave stayed home on a crest of Love / Eternal Particles: Particles of passion grown icy to extend lesson eternal, Love / Particularly Infinite: Particularly infinite, I arrive at Love / Infinitely Essential: Infinitely essential, emphatic Love / Infinite Design: An infinite design in stride with Love / Birth: Birth mirth, Love / Scant: Scant skinned Love / Mirth: Mirth meet felt Love / Shant: Shant can't Love / Aunt: Aunt kind to Love / Sign: Sign, seal, Love / Symbol: Symbol seamed to Love / Recline: Recline all fine to Love / Refine: Refine meant mint Love / Reassign: Reassign the test to best, Love / Resign: Resign to resonant treasure, Love / Reside: Reside in designs of Love.

CHAPTER 12 / LOVE PORTS: Many Paths: Many paths met trees in leaves of Love / Many Trees: Many the trees of Love / Many Planes: Many planes pleat here in Love / Many, All One: Many, All one, Love / Many, Merry: Many are merry in Love / Many, Mini: Many Mine views of Love / Many, Marco: Many are micro in news to Love / Many, Biotic: Many biotic beat retreat to feet on Love / Many, Ionic: Many the Ironic to Ionic replete with Love / Many, Iconic: Many iconic are sonic to resound in Love / Many, Dichroic: Many dichroic mend our friend of fractured Light and life complete with Love / Many, You Know: I know many you know, knew, Love / Many, Scientific: Many scientific to terrific Love / Many, Prolific: Many are prolific to Love / Many, Prolific: Many are prolific to Love / Many, Ethereal: Merry met ethereal in familial Love / Many, Imperial: Many are imperial in ephemeral delight in Love / Many, Red: Many red fed Love / Many, Blue: Many blew you to blue horizons of Love / Many, Will Live: Many will live alive with Love / Many, Will Lead: Many will lead and follow less, then Love / Many, Lightly: Many lightly lean to Love / Many,

Eruditely: *Many met erudition in her remission to Love *Make a run young / Many, Igniting..Many igniting, inviting our hour to Love / Many, Inviting: Inviting many mini-stores of One to Love / Many, Exciting: Many excite the right to Love / Many, Enriching: Many enrich their sum with Love / Many, Ambrosiac: Many ambrosial drink ambrosiac ea of free to be Love / Many, Aeronautics: Many Aeronautics exist in bliss and Love / Many Licensed: Many licensed practice, Love / Many Enticing: Many enticing, advicing, Love / Many Emphatic: Many emphatic are, Love / Many Devoted: Many devoted are, Love / Many Committed: Many committed to Love / Many Explicit: Many explicit sum, Love / Many, Know : This many knew this know this, Love / Many and One: Help many, Love One / Many and Sum: Love One many flavored sum, Love / Many and Light: Many and Light are we in delight to Love / Many Spark: Many sparks sent rent to Love / Many Arcs: Many arcs meet in spark of Love / Many Loved: Many loved lees of Love / Many Men: Many men be in Love / Many Mothered: Many mothered meet in Love / Many Fed: Many fed feed to Love / Many Hands: Many hands meet in us and this, Love / Many Lives: Many lives line in Love / Many Gifts: Many gifts greet our Love / Many: Many, merry, be, our Love / Many, I Forgive: Many, I forgive with Love / Many, I Forgave: Many forgave, forgiven, Love / Many, I Embrace: Many's the embrace to Love / Many, I Will Lead: Many I'll lead to Love / Many Things I See: Many things seen in Love / Many Things I Know: God's green know is many things, Love / Many Things I Hear: Maybe I seem to hear less, Love / Many Days I'm Here: Many Days here, I Am, Love / Many Days I'm Here: Many days here, I Am, Love / Many Ways, Always : Near many ways hear, All-ways to Love / Many, The Phases: Many fast phases, Love / Many the Phrases: Many met phrases called Love / Many, the Spaces: Many neat spaces, Love / Many, The Traces: Many, the traces to better in Love / Many Freed: Many freed us to Love.

CHAPTER 13 / LOVE CHALLENGE: All Ways: All ways, Love / All Seasons: All seasons, seen, Love / All Life: All life's learn, to Love / All Night: All night reams of Love / All Night: All night reams of Love / All Day: All days dreams of Love / All May: All may be, Love / All One: All one time, Love / All Day: All one day, done, Love / All Night: All night, long, to Love / All Light: All Light's win is Love / All Height: All height heels in Love / All Depth: All depth deep in Love / All Laughs: All laughs lift in Love / All Weds: All ways wed to Love / All Rings: All rings round, our Love / All Sings: All sing sung to Love / All Tells: All tells told to Love / All Appeals: All appeals to us in let's Love / All Loves: All loves less regard less hard to Love / All Loves All: All loves stay is Love / All's Embrace: All's embrace is best in Love / All, The Way: All, the way home, to Love / All, the Day: All, the day, long, to Love / All This Reign: All, this reign, remains, Love / All Magnificent: All magnificent abreast God's best at Love / All Benificient: All benificient, munificent, Love / All God: All God gives, the gist, is Love / All Love: All Love lives in God, our Love / All Led: All led home to Love

/ All Energy: All energetic photogenic, Love / All Electronic: All electric, electronic, sonic, Love / All Metatronic: All meet metatronic in Love / All Sepharothic: All seat sepharothic in Love / All Religions: All religion rends our Love / All Science: All science said is Love / All Art: All art height to Love / All Taste: All in taste and Love / All's Face: All's a face of Love / All is Best: All is best abreast Love / All is Rest: All arrest is rest in Love / All, The Test: All, the test is true to Love / All, The Truth: All, the truth, proof of Love / All is Forgiven: All forgiven, fuse, Love / All, is for Living: All, is for living, Love / All, is the Pace: All a pace the space to Love / All, Is The Space: All's the space to Love / Only and All: Only and All, Love / All Of Me: All of me Loves all of true, Love / All, You See: All, you see, is we, Love / All Wet: All wet, deep, to Love / All, Left: All, left, hear, to Love / All, Composite: All, composite, One, Love / All Harmonious: All is harmonious above, Love / All The Peace: All the peace, plus, Love / All One Truth: Deep within, one truth, All, Love / All One: All one sun, Love / One All: One All, One, to Love / All Some: All some say is Love / All Many: All many, me, we, Love / All, Any?: All is any? Us is rest, in Love / All the Same: All the same, fame, in Love / All The Time: All the tame, time in Love / All: All in all, Love.

CHAPTER 14 / LOVE JOINS: Harmonic: Harmonic converge, merge, hear, in Love / Converge: Converge on this, the point, Love / Merge: Merge in us, Love / Bliss: Bliss bet. Love / Expand: Expand again, brand, knew, Love / Demand: Demand dust to Love / Inflame: Inflame a game to Love / Entertain: Entertain your main to Love / Explain: Explain gain, Love / Dynamic: Dynamic ceramic, fired by Love / Erratic: Erratic? Sporatic? Love / Erotically: Erotically zoned I'm stoned by less then Love / Know More Me: Know more me, know you, Love / Eat the Tree: Eat the Tree of fruit of life called Love / Life's Exact: Life's Exact intact with Love / The Pact: The pact to act from Love / Exactingly: Exactingly measured, Loved / The Dance Is Me: The dance is free in me in Love / Pain's Stake: Free pains stake is rushed to Love / We Are Free: We are free to free Love / The Stack: The stack of flack is less than Love / The Stance: The stance trance? Love / The Maet: The maet flat? Love / The Peace: *Peace of Love * Pleasant exceed of constant equation, Love / The Trace: The trace of truth, in Love / The Embrace: The embrace rests in Love / The Face: The face of Love / The Rest: The rest can rest in Love / This Is: This is Love / This Was: This was enough, Love / This Will: This will be Love / This Cause: This cause decreed, Love / The Day: This day, way, to Love / The Play: The Play of Love / The Standing: The standing wave, Love / The Ovate: The ovate rang with Love / The Great: The great rate, Love / The Mastodon: The mastodon clawed be evolution to less then Love / The Getting On: The getting on off to Love / The Tape: The tape to rape-less Love / The Measured: The measured pleasured is Love / The Pleasured: The pleasured trust, Love / The Escape: The eScape, to date is Love / The Same: The same fame, Love / The Game: The game? to dame of Love / The Explain: The explain to complain-less

Love / The Mundane: The mundane, World, Love / The World: The world is perfect, Love / In *To Do: In all, Love. *Truly open to direct observation of all that is Love / In All: In all, the fall, to Love / In Exceed: In exceed, we'ed, Love / Indeed: An apple in deed? Love / In-deeded: In-deeded trust, in truth, Love / In Exhumed: In exhumed, roamed for Love / In Presumed: In presumed, assumed, Love / In Express: In express address, over night, Love / In Messed: In messed, up to Love / In Genetics: In genetics CD rommed to Love / In Song: In song sing the spring of Love / In Extreme: In extreme I dream a direct recess to Love / In a Gleam: In a gleam I glim with the *??? of Love *fast rate of exceptional ??? of mental Love / In a Glint: In a glint, hint, Love / In a Hint: In a hint, above, Love / In Love: Above all, in Love.

CHAPTER 15 / LOVE JOURNEY: In A Seed: In a seed, we'd breed, Love / In a Deed: In a deed we'd pull the weeds to Love / In Caved: Love less? Invest in carved pursued of Love / In Graved: In gravel assault we halt, to Love / In Express: In express, lane, Love / Barned and Bold: Barned and labeled bold, be wise to Love / In A Messed: In a messed state, unified to ratify Love / Cute and Cold: Cut and cold, be bold to warming Love / Crest and Full: Crest and full of fallen waves of Love / Fall and All: Fall and all I call to Love / Autumn Welled: Autumn welled deep in 39th St. of Love / Heaven Held: Heaven held up to Love / A Christian, Right?: A Christian Right? To all that's left, Love / A Christian Left: A Christian left trace to Love / A Christian, Well?: A Christian, well? Well, Love / A Christian Bell: A Christian Bell the dove of re-entry into Love / A Metatronic Line: A Metatronic line? Mine. Mind. Love / A Metabiologic: A metabiologic urge to merge in a line of Love / A Life En-twined: Loop a life entwined to Love / A Life In fine: A life in fine measure to Love / A Healing Clime: A healing clime, to *I do to Love / An Except Seen: An except, seen, accept, Love / A Healing Climb: A healing climb to top hour Love / An Accept, Dear: An accept, dear, we're Love / A Meeting Met: A meeting met, hear, Love / A Heating Wet: A heating wet with Love / A Burning Pane: A burning pane of soul-less explain of Love / A Heating Wet: A heating wet to a moister bet called Love / A Healing Name: A healing name, Metatron, is on to Love / A Feeling Belt: A feeling belt around the head of Love / A Singing Felt: A singing I feel as felt to Love / A Betting Held: A betting held well within the blend of Love / A Holding Well: A holiday swell, the well of Love / A Healing Stream: A healing stream of dreams of Love / A Streaming Set: Inundate fate with a streaming set of Love / A Setting Met: A setting met wet in rush of Love / A Meeting Set: A meeting set, yet we Love / Oh Yes, You Can: Oh yes, you can expand to Love / You Can, You Man: You can, you man, reprimand quit, to Love / You Man, Your Ship: You man your ship well, to Love / Your Ship, Your Trip: Your ship, your trip, to Love / A Trip to Love: A trip to Love held abreast our bust is up to Love / A Trippy Dove: A trippy dove drove home alone to Love / Tread to Heal: In a breath find a tread to heal a step called Love / Bermuda's Feel: Discount Bermuda's feel to reel Love / Bermuda Hill: Bermuda Hill, a wheel of hands to Love / Hilly Tribed: Hilly tribed glide to a longer neck of Love / Tribal Thrill: Tribal thrill, a heal of Love / Trilling Said: Trilling said, a bust to said, Love / Said We Bred: Said we bred? Head, to Love / Hill We Held: Up was our own attempt at growing tall in the fall of God / Bred, We Hill: Bred, we hill, fell to Love / Held We Still: Held we still in a field of Love / Instill Beds: Instill beds of flowery Love / Light's Retrieve: Light's retrieve, heave, to Love / Beds Believe: Beds believe in a sweeping weave of Love / Patient's Plea: Patient's plea, patience we, to Love / Healing We: Healing we? Yet, Love / Well, We Said: Well, we said, ahead to Love / Well, We Bred: Well, we bred in Love / Well, We Led: Well, we led, to Love / Well, I Fell: Well, I fell, to Love / Health, I Heal: Health, I heal, healed by Love.

CHAPTER 16 / LOVE IN: Fled, I Brought: Fled, I brought ahead to led to Love / Brought, I Caught: Brought, I caught you up to Love / Caught, I Find: Caught, I find my God in Love. / Find, I Mind: Find a line to your mind in Love / Yester, I Dazed: Yester, I dazed home to Room in Love / Dazed, I Played: Dazed, I played to spade of less than Love / Played The Punch: Played a hunch, the punch of Love / Punch, I Saved: Punch, I saved was razed to Love / Saved Is Said: Saved is said to Love / Freed's Believed: Freed's believed, Love / Souls Are Dead: Souls are dead to Love / Dead Is Freed: Dead ahead is freed to Love / Yellow Scent: Yellow scent went to Love / Sulfured, Led: Sulfured, led a cell to home, a throne, of Love / Yellow, Scant: Yellow, I Am scant to an advent called lime-green to Love / Yello Vent: Yello vent spent? Know Love / Led To Tanks: 2 by 2, led to tanks of Love / Banked, I Stood: Banked, I stood, up to Love / Tanked, I Bank: Tanked, I bank, to thank, my Love / Stood, I Could: Stood, I could be in Love / Explained Mundane: Explained the mundane to Love / Be Freed: Be freed up, Love / To Leave: To Love above, I agreed to leave all less-than Love / A Life Insane: A Life insane with Love / A Life Mundane: A Life mundane in reign of less than Love / A Fielding Free: A field in free to Love / A Life In Field: A life felt field with Love / A Field In Me: A field insane in less than flames of Love / A Present Hue: A present hue, anew, to Love / An Extant View: An extant view, in us, to Love / A Purple News: A purple please, the knees of Love / A Pink Exhume: Pink exhume, the resume of Love / A Purple Exclaim: A purple exclaim, a declare of Love / A Pink Examine: A pink exam, examine matter less than Love / A Purpled Name: A purpled care of flare to Love / A Name, The Same: A name, the same in all of us and Love / Forty Waves: Forty waves blessed to loosen less-than Love / Forty Ways: Forty ways home are One in thirteen's weave to home to Love / Forty Days: Forty days home to free Love / Waving Lead: Will I wave a lead to Love / Led, Believe: Led to believe, above, Love / Believe In, Bet: Believe in, bet, of Love / Bet, You See: Bet, you see, us in Love / We Concede: We concede need enough to Love / We Read: We read bred to Love / We Fed: We fed abred our buds of Love / We View: We view hue of Love / We Knew: We knew enough of us in Love / We Three-ed: We three-ed our thread of Love / We Felt: We felt up north to Love / We Fled:

• 155 •

We fled enough to Love / We Said: We said stuff less than Love / We Agreed: We agreed in deed to Love / We Derive: We derive enough, Love / We Delight: We delight in a mess to less than Love / We Decide: We decide a rate to Love / We Believed: We believed deceive until we Love / We Conceive: We conceive us sweet to Love / We Bet: We bet yet on Love / We Treed: We treed ourselves with Love / We Red: We red believed in instant relieve to Love / We Bled: We bled abreed to Love / We Lived: We lived less than Love / We Give: We give it up to Love.

CHAPTER 17 / LOVE OUT: We Gave: We gave a rave to Love / We Save: We save a step to Love / We Rave: We rave a treat called neat to Love / We Stay: We stay up late to Love / Community: Whales white heat, a neat, Community of Love / American: American way, home, Love / God, On It: God, on it, bonnet of Love / Got On It: Got on it, early, Love / We Deserve: We deserve, by nerve, a rest in Love / We Swerve: We swerve to Love / We Summit: We summit ascent to Love / We Sum It: We sum it up often to Love / Holding Light: Holding Light enough to Love / Tall: Tall truth, in you, Love / Institute: Institute root to Love / All Day: All day, a way, to Love / Peacemakers: Peacemakers stake in Love / In Deeds: In Deeds, dewed, due, do, Love / Enacters: Enacters, factors, to Love / Short: Short enough to Love / Inside: Inside ride to Love / Special: Special speed indeed to Love / The Effort: The effort met in Love / The Need: The need to breathe in rest to Love / Chipped In: Chipped in deep to Love / Aid: Aid a blade to extract to cut only less than Love / Helped: Helped enough to Love / Case: Case a space to Love / In Fact: In Fact, act, to Love / Yes!: Yes! I do, Love / Hanukkah Held: Hanukkah Held up to Love / Native: Native American, Love / Today, Say: Today, say Love / A Chocolate Kiss: A chocolate kiss to a wish of Love / This Miss: This miss, missed, Love / Exact: Exact rate to great Love / Suckle: Suckle, sup, Love / College In: College in, inn, Love / Enhance: Enhance, advance to Love / Thin: Thin enough to Love / Nativity: Nativity knelt in a cradle of Love / Honest: Honest breathe of Love / Integrity: Integrity matters to Love / Breast: Breast a rest in Love / Celebrate: Celebrate us in Love / Sign Up: Signing up to rest in Love / Census: Census sent to a count of Love / Sensate: Sensate-less? Love / Will: Will you rest in Love / Will You?: Will you reach peak, to Love / Sundown: Sundown said red and blue to Love / Sun Up: Sun up said Love / Viewed: Viewed abused? Love / Vacant: Vacant rest to Love / Reviled?: Reviled enough? Love / Vacuous: Vacuous news, renews, Love / Job: Job fair? Love / Fair: Fair enough. Love / Vocate: Vocate less than Love / Vacate: Vacate, rest, Love / Shutting: Shutting up to less? Love / Fitting: Fitting up to Love / Dumping: Dumping less than Love / Trumping: Trumping's up to enough in Love.

CHAPTER 18 / LOVE FOR: Gaunt: Let gaunt be grant to feed of Love / Faint: Today, I faint in Love / Fades: Faint fades, I Love / Release: Let's release our Love / Resting: Let's resting breath of Love / Pleasure: God's pleasure measured, Love / Treasures: Treasures treasured hush in Love / Glints: Get grants a glint of Love / Gems: Mark of gems in Love / Beads: Please breath in beads of Love / Glee's: Glee's freed by Love / Great: Great our grin to Love / Same: Same in sign of Love / Sign: Sign ascend to Love / Line: Great line along Love / Know: Traces of known by Love / Seen: Seen a trace to Love / Loved: Loved by less than? Love / Given: People given, Love / Gifts: Gifts greet sweet in Love / Lifts: Lifts it up to Love / Lessons: Lessons learned through ascendant ways, Love / Pleasures: Pleasures pleasures, to Love / Peace: Peace is placed in Love / Release: God's release is Love / Godness: Goodness says godness said to Love / Dove: Let Dove's Love / Split: Split? Second, sealed by Love / Sealed: Let's be sealed to Love / Swirled: Swirled in sealed by Love / Twirled: Twirled in thrilled by Love / Trilled: Trilled in trust of Love / Dealt: Dealt a deal by Love / Felt: Flex aspects of felt by Love / Flex: Flex a felt by Love / Pelts: Pelts pewed by Love / Fills: Fills like Love / Pecks: Pecks reviewed by Love / Furred: Furred in pelt of Love / Feared: Feared to breed, you need to Love / Fleas: Fleas fed rest in Love / Bees: Bees believe in Love / Deceived: Deceived less, you Love / Ticks: Ticks trick less than Love / Flirt: Flirt with hurt? Now Love / Receed: Receed to breed of Love / Frog: Frog fred food of Love / Meal: Meals of heal, to Love / Splat: Splat a chat to scatter meant to Love / Cat: Cat went play to Love / Dog: Dog all day in Love / Skunk: Skunk sent scent to hint at Love / Signed: Signed and sealed, healed, Love / Sung: Sung enough? Love / Strum: Strum a hum to venus fun to Love / OK: Yes! Ok, me Love / Say: Say yeah to Love / It's Well: It's well here in Love / Inflict: Inflict fussed over to Love / Fleshy: Fleshy held by Love / Wounds: Wounds wound deep in Love / Willing: Willing to be, in, Love / Tuned: Tuned to you I Love / Trained: Trained to frilled by Love.

CHAPTER 19 / LOVE FROM: About: About you, Love / This: This is us, in Love / That: That solid measure, Love / What: What will you be? Love / Where: God's where I live in give to Love / When: When? Again? Love / What? Ever: What? Ever: Eyed wide to Love / Why: Why knot? Love / Blade: Blade blunt? Love / Sate: Sate great Love / Well: Living well with Love / Power: Power a tower of our h-our Love / Play: Play a day of round our Love / Hour: Hour to hour, God, is Love / Our: Less will, more Our, Love / Heart: Heart held deep in Love / Cart: Cart apart to a part of, Love / Start: Start again, friend, in Love / Part: Signed, sealed, a Part of Love / Played: Played and stayed in Love / Decafe: Decafe carafe of Love / Real: Real feel of Love / Cafe: Cafe on the square-edged seam of Love / Feel: Feel ahead to Love / Black: Sister's hood is back to black and basic remove of less than Love / White: White and brother remove the hood to Love / Night: Night and day I stay in Love / Day: Day to day, Love / Say: Say yeah! Love / Sing: Sing a song of LOVING bliss and know all this, Love / Bring: Bring a branch of Love / Brought: Brought you home to Love / Tips: Life tips in to Love / Tripped: Tripped yet? Love / Tangiers: Tangiers, tangent, a gent to Love / Arrears: Arrears hears cheer of Love / Mom: Mom meant scent to Love / Dad: Dad said give to Love / Sum: Sum of this is Love / Some: Some, Some, Love / SON: God's sum, the son of Love / Sun: Sun scent to Love / Daughtered: Daughtered matter, mattered, most in Love / Done: Done yet? Love / Pose: Pose nude knewed by Love / Consequence: Consequence sent to Love / Equate: Equate, great, Love / Rate: Rate a rate of Love / Children: Children chill in heal of Love / Grape: Grape grew knew in vines of Love / Chilled: Chilled enough to Love / Crush: Crush proof, Love / Sunburst: Sunburst through our Love / Whole: Whole hill of Love / Seeded: Seeded, heeded, Love / Boned: Boned blue? Love / Dehydrate: Dehydrate great, Love / Demarcate: Demarcate late? Love / Imbarcate: A late date to imbarcate on Love / A Late Date: A late date's up to Love / Millennial: Millennial meant to be in Love / Centennial : Centennial through Love / Familial: Familial found ground in Love / Biennial: Biennial apply to the too onto Love.

CHAPTER 20 / LOVE WITHIN: Bi-Annual: Bi-annual manual to twice as much, Love / Bio-Metric: Bio-metric and centric to Love / Bio-Logic: Bio's logic, closet's of let, in Love / Botanic: Botanic planet, plane to a vein of Love / This Planet: This planet? Man it, Love / Higher Waves: Higher waves, our Love / Coupon Days: Coupon craze to days of Love / Discount Nights: Discount nights of right to Love / Breaking Eggs: God's break, eggs of flood to yellow, Love / Peanut: Peanut, bird, herd, crop, Love / Eating Hay: Eat some hay, Love / Butter: Butter's milk is creamy Love / In Peach: In peach, a state of pale to Love / The State: The state of great is Greece to Love / Fudge: Fudge budge, Love / Package: Package Athens full to Love / Eccentric: Eccentric mystic, Love / Diverse: Diverse nurse, our Love / In Place: In place, of taste, Love / Common Daze: Common daze? Equate to rate in Love / Clubbed: Clubbed for feet of Love / Hubbed: Hubbed out to Love / Hugged: Hugged entreat to Love / Humbled: Humbled's measure, Love / Tabled: Tabled talk of Love / Treasured: Treasured trove of Love / Measured: Measured mist of fog-less Love / Mu-ed: Mu-ed continent in Love / Nudity: Nudity rude? Know less intrude, Love / Etudely: Etudely showed in Love / Rudely: Rudely rent? Love / Brushly: Brushly met by a bristled Brit called lewd to Love / Mashingly: Mashingly mint to Love / Corrupt: Corrupt abrupt needs Love / Smashingly: Smashingly sent to Love / Crept: Crept the rape of Love / Mountain: Mountain meadowed, Love / Trade: Trade grade to "A" Love / Treat: Treat street, heat, in Love / Top: Top tap, Love / We Eat: We eat sweet, Love / Weight: Weight less, Love / Bayed: Bayed a bode, a pool of Love / Pooled: Pooled spool of Love / Trued: Trued address, a dress of Love / Acrylic: Acrylic seal it, Love / Tree: Wed tree free, Love / Oil: Oil free rub of Love / Cider: Cider abide her, Love / Beside Her: Beside her bed, Love / Inside Her: Inside her Love / In Tribal: In tribal treasure, Loved / The Bible: The Bible stands stead of in your way to Love / Insight-full: Insight-full Love / Delighted: Delighted dove of Love / Ignited: Ignited, lighted, Love / Dazed: A dazed drove, to Love / Waved: Waved red, Love / Paved: Paved pulse, Love / Peeled: Peeled, appealed, Love / Felt: God is felt in Love / Spelt: Spelt out? Plant it. Love / Spelled: God's spelled by Love / Melt: Melt proof, Love.

CHAPTER 21 / LOVE FOUNTAINS: Surgical: Surgical pleasure, please her, Love / Psychic: A psychic said, you will, Love / Mental: Mental met by Love / Hike It: Hike it in to a mountain of Love / Hearken: Water hearkens us to Love / Horned: Horned hand sealed by Love / Arked: God's Arked now in Love / Covened: Covened creeled by Love / Swollen: Swollen swell to Love / Sword: Sword, stone, moan, Love / Michael: Michael met heal, here, in Love / Gabriel: Gabriel grinned at a brim of Love / Hellenistic: A Hellenistic tryst to Love / Sappho: Spirit sealed Sappho in Love / Syphon: Syphon of less than Love / Ideal: Ideal is it? Then, Love / Specific: Specific, Pacific, of Love / Need: In need? Indeed! Love / Exceed: Exceed, rest, Love / Rest: Would rest rust? Knot. Love / Test: A true test, Love / Word: Word up? Love / God's: God's good food, Love / Best: Rude less, best, in, Love / Ponds: Ponds of pulse in Love / Plural: Plural, Ural, mountains of Love / Equal: Equal creature, Love / Gallant: Gallant flaunt of less? Love / Fed: Fed breaks best in egged Love / Pensive: Pensive penchant to chant only Love / Bred: Bred thus, Love / Elusive: A line of Elusive in Love / Suggestive: Suggestive twitch of Love / Infusion: A daily infusion of Love / Intuitive: Intuit's treasure, and intuitive measure called Love / Monthly: Colonel monthly met Love / Daily: Daily deal with Love / Rank: Rank blank? Bet first, in, Love / Spanking: Spanking knew less than Love / Thanking: God's thanking you for Love / Vibrate: Vibrate, rate, of Love / Held: Held up? Love / Higher: Higher power, Love / Hawaiian: Hawaiian held by Love / Worm-hold: Worm-hold healed by Love / Accelerate: Accelerate late? Love / Time: Time to tell, Love / Clime: Clime to a rhyme of a seasoned reason, to Love / Trine: Trine time to Love / Trailed: Trailed a trail of a herd called Love / Released: Released heat in Love / Received: Received true-est Love / Expulse: The expulse can rest in Love / Lengthly: A lengthly leisure, Love / Mattered: Mattered most, Love / Exclude: Include exclude to Love / Splattered: A splattered splendor, Love / Splashed: Splashed splendid, Love / Flashed: Flashed rust away, to, Love / Holographic: Holographic traffic, Love / Surgical: Surgical, a send, to Love / Relief: Relief rent, by, Love / Layered: Layered lust to Love / Lightly: Lightly laid on Love.

CHAPTER 22 / LOVE MERGER: I Am, That I Am: Let me be entranced to more than I Am knot., I Am, that I Am, In Love / I Am Essence: Like an essence, I Am to Love / I Am Light: I Am Light Love / I Am Life: Lately I Am life of Love / I Am Well: Lightly I Am well to Love / I Am Love: Listen, I Am Love / I Am Metaelectric: I Am Love / I Am That Held: by that I Am, Love / I Am Then Bet: on I Am, then, Love / I Am Now Lately: I Am now, to Love / I Am Eternally: Eternally trimmed to I Am, Love / I Am Infinitely: Infinitely pulled by less, I Am, Love / I Am Essentially: Love let essentially ascent to I Am Love / I Am Elementally: Lovely place, elementally I Am, Love / I Am Eternally: Eternally trimmed by Love / I A.m Infinitely: Lovely infinitely a loft to Love / I Am Essentially: Specifically ascent, a gift, to Love / I Am Wholey: Wholey held by adrift to Love / I Am Experientially: I essentially and experientially Am. Love

/ I Am Evidently: Evidently let to I Am Love / I Am, Finally: Finally fed to a penchant for Love / I Am, Fragrantly: Fragrantly graced by I Am Love / I Am, Especially: Especially spent to I Am Love / I Am Absolutely: Absolutely, I Am Love / I Am Divinely: Graced divinely I Am, Love / I Am Fully: Fully, filled, I Am, Love / I Am: Aptly, I Am, Love / I Am Amazing: Amazingly laced esthetically to Love / I Am Engaging: Over engaging, I'm aging in Love / I Am Intricately: God's grace intricately laced by Love / I Am Led: Left led to I Am, Love / I Am Fed: All the way, glad to be feed by Love / I Am Led: Left led to I Am, Love / I Am Fed: All the way, glad to be fed by Love / I Am Met: Meet and met in I Am, Love / I Am, Yes: Oh yes, I Am, Love / I Am, Today: Lefty today, in Love / I Am, Forever: I Am, forever, Love / I Am Entranced: Entranced advance to Love / I Am Elegance: Elegance meant I Am Love / I Am Eloquent: Let eloquence dance in I Am, Love / I Am Intelligent: Intelligent dreamed by I Am Love / I Am Eternal: Life's eternal in I Am, Love / I Am Fulfilled: Fulfilled a build to Love / I Am Equitable: Equate to equitable measure of Love / I Am Delectable: Delectable taste of I Am Love / I Am Electrical: Let us be electrical to we are Love / I Am Metatronic: I bliss metatronic to I Am Love / I Am Level: Hard done deal. I Am level to Love / I Am Balance: Get your balance of Love / I Am Harmonious: Heart harmonious to Love / I Am Attuned: Attuned, ballooned, by Love / I Am Mobile: Lots of mobile to Love / I Am Infinite: Insist on infinite widths of Love / I Am Evergreen: I Am evergreen in my dream of a bead gone home, All-One, to Love / I Am Supernal: Great supernal, I Am. Love / I Am The Earth: Great the earth of I Am, Love / I Am New Birth: To a day, I Am new birth to Love / I Am Regenerated: Light's regenerated, Love / I Am Elated: Left elated, dated, Love / I Am Safe: Let's be safe to Love / I Am Happy: A ride to happy I Am Love / I Am Green: Left all green to Love / I Am Clear: I Am clear, hear, Love.

CHAPTER 23 / LOVE MARRIES: Loving: Loving's gift, my Love / Splendor: Splendor's splinter gone to Love / Mender: Mender bender, gender-less, Love / Yellowed: Yellowed yield, the field, of Love / Creamy: A creamy create, of late, to Love / Chrysobel: Chrysobel well in a crystal dent of Love / Chrysoberyl: Chrysoberyl feral? Love / Chrysoprase: Chrysoprase raise the rock of Love / Chrionic: Chrionic, bionic, systolic, Love / Christoholic: Christoholic in waves of sheets of wind too thin to Love / Systolic: Systolic h-our Love / Beat: Beat a neat seat to Love / Pulse: Pulse pent less than Love / Meals: Meals can heal the still of Love / Milk: Milk my house with creamy Love / Pills: Pills appeal to lesson, Love / Chocolate: Chocolate chill, heal, in Love / Under: Under a dome of Love / Sway: Sway to hey, Love / Thunder: Thunder throned, Love / Election: Election scent to Love / Select: Select us, Love / Know Sway: Love, know sway, in a willowed end to wends of Love / Day: Day, say, Love / I'm: I'm the One we are in Love / With: With you, I Am new, in Love / You: You, new, in Love / Especially: Especially, yes, in Love / We Too: Love to we too can Love / One: Love one sun, Love / Sun: Sun of One, Love / Say: Say hello, Love /

Love: Love God, Love / God: God got Love / Mother: God is in a Mother's Love / Country: Country creeled by Love / Father: Father honor me in Love / Honor: Mother daughter honor Love / Know Way: Know way home to Love / Commit: Commit yet? Love / Command: Command a friend to Love / Plan: Plan to spend your life in Love / Expand: Expand a band to Love / Stay: Stay in training for Love / Fullish: Fullish felt in Love / College: College of knowledge in Love / Collage: Collage, garage, gone neat, to Love / Knowledge: Knowledge knelt at Love / Pause: Pause to cause, Love / Pulse: The pulse you played was Love / Impulse: Impulse sent, to invent, Love / Divert: Divert skirt, the issue, Love / Revert: Revert to curt arrival at Love / Phase: Phase won, Love / Synapse: Synapse spent? Reinvent the bridge to wheel celled Love / Snaps: Snaps back to the reality of Love / Electric: Electric weld, Love / Neutral: Neutral net of Love / Electron: Electron complete to a perfect spin of 136 times Love / Spun: Spun around to Love / Spin: Spin a spun, Love / Cycle: Cycle scene, Love / Run: Run to run to rest in Love / Done: Never done in Love.

CHAPTER 24 / LOVE REIGNS: Level: Level ahead to Love / Bi-Limbed: Bi-limbed I'm trimmed to Love / Tri-Fibbed: Tri-fibbed gone true to perfect Love / Found : One found one, Love / Solar: Solar scent, Love / Sexual: Sexual seem, Love / Pleased: Pleased as pulse, of Love / Played: Played fade to Love / Essential: Converse is essential in Love / Dressed: Dressed up. Love / Released: Released rest in Love / Deed: A deed to live in hear to Love / Suggest: I suggest you're a vet to Love / Nurture: Nurture natured Love / Nest: Nest in the arms of a charming encounter with Love / Restructure: Restructure your function called Love / Egg: Egg on a face shown grace, less in a scrambled place called knot in Love / Mommy: Mommy may we Love / Milked: Milked enough honey, money, Love / Honey: Honey money's wet in Love / Dripped: Dripped in deep to Love / Sung: Sung to rungs of Love / We Are: We are where you Love / Sexed: Mars sexed rest in Love / The Wave: The wave of engrave in Love / Of A: Of a plan, man, in Love / Higher: Higher helled yelled Love / Sum: Sum of us is a fuller cup of Love / One: One Love / Godly: Godly give in Love / Man: Man's plan is the give of receive in Love / Has Come: Has come to a room of Love / Know: Know of you, Love ? / Metatron: Metatron explore of an impassion flavored by Love / Today: Today array in Love / And Run: And run around, Love / To: To you, be, Love / Love: Love to be, Love / To New: To new, Love / Stay: Stay buff in Love / Too: Too you? Love / Deep: Deep enough to steepe in Love / You Keep: You keep up in Love / Your Way: Your way home is our Love / We Play: We play up our Love / In The: In the manner of Love / Stay Electric: Stay electric in lectures to me of Love / God's Pave: God's pave is the wave too hard on softened Love? / Of The Golden Wave: Of the golden wave, engrave, in Love / Brick Yellow and Deep: Brick yellow and deep, we greet, in Love / With Complete Release: With complete release of less than Love / Of The Soul Of The Will: Of the soul of the will, I will release to Love / To Gods Flow: To Gods flow of Love / We

Go: We go, gone to Love / Home, Solar Plexed: Home, solar plexed by the point to Love / Body's Mind: Body's mine to mind with Love / In Kind Egoic.. Relief in kind egoic, I relieve Love / The Treat: The treat? Your feet, in Love / The Street: The street to strut is Love / Of Gods Please: Of Gods please, my need to Love / With His Seed: Evolve his seed in mitochondrion freed to Love / Alert: Alert yet? Love / Awake: Awake a rate of Love / Engaged: Engaged by paged to Love.

CHAPTER 25 / LOVE RULES: Average: My average range is Love / Superior: Superior measure, pleasure, in Love / Laked: Laked abreast my Love / Leaked: Leaked far less than Love / Sing: Sing winged by Love / Tell: Tell a hill of your desire to Love / Trill: Trill a thrill of Love / Sung: Sung spun to Love / Saunter: Saunter in to Love / Feel: Embrace feel, Love / Rail: Rail on reeled up rolls of Love / Seal: Mask a seal with Love / Watered: Watered wed to Love / Clothing: Clothing cares to Love / Launder: Launder led to Love / Willed: Willed a wed to Love / Built: Built to bed in Love / Conjunct: Conjunct adjunct to Love / Congeal: Congeal in just adjust to Love / Real: Real bill for Love / Frail: Frail frill Love / Known More: Known more breast in Love / Well: Well I adjust to wed by will I Love / Wintered: Wintered wet in a frothy bet to Love / Summered: Summered simmer, Love / Fall: Fall aside to Love / Autumn: Autumn fest of Love / Spring: Sprung in Spring of Love / Lathed: Lathed loathed lust-less than Love / Pale: Pale an apparent pail of less than Love / Trail: Tale trail, Love / Comet: Comet watched cleaned with our trailing tale of Love / Lifting: Lifting up to Love / Honor: Honor our hour to Love / Courage: Courage, a crest to Love. Paid enough for Love / Gauze: Gauze agreed to Love / Because: Because we attest to Love / Mist: Mist a miss to Love / Fog: Fog fit? Lift. Love / Accepted: Accepted an accept to Love / Hilled: Hilled adjust to a higher Love / Into: Into a press with Love / Of: Of this, I Love / Revered: Revered to a trend in Love / Respected: Respected a test in Love / Respect-Full: Respect in us, a respect-full rust gone green to Love / Revealed: Healthy green reveal of Love / Concealed: Concealed a congeal to Love / Helped: Helped a healed to Love / Kneed: Kneed in blessed by Love / Healed: Healed in us helped our Love / Hugged: Hugged has headed to armed with Love / Swing: Swing has swung to Love / Swung: Swung erupt in Love / Forgiving: Forgiving fed to Love / Babied: Babied a best of Love / Sallied: Sallied a set of Love / Sought: Sought a set of Love / Bought: Bought a bit of Love / Accept: Accept a bite of Love / Held: Held on to Love / Respite: Respite from Love is healed Love / Foiled: Foiled field of lessened Love / Refine: refine realign of my spine by Love.

CHAPTER 26 / LOVE REACHED: Globe: Globe around a bust of Love / Commit: Commit connect to Love / Serve: Serve God, Love / Swerve: Swerve around a Lanai gone dry to Love / Way: Way to bay your Love / Home: Home head, Love / Global: Escape a global glut of less than Love / Dome: Dome of Roman Love / Glassed: Glassed exact of Love / Glassed: Glassed over, Love / Cost: Cost me less than Love / Keep: Keep up rest in

Love / Natural: God's a natural LOVER / Neatly: Neatly nestled in Love / Deep: Kill a deeper thrill with less than Love / Direct: Direct in us, to Love / Treat: Treat truth well in Love / Reflective: Reflective rest in Love / Select: Select a set to Love / Decide: Decide a debt's been paid by Love / Stride: Strode a road of stride to Love / Rode: Rode home to your Love / Road: Road reef, rail, Love / Ride: Ride rosey, Love / Scholarly: A scholarly call to Love / Fatherly: Fatherly fed, our Love / Brotherly: Brotherly build of Love / Motherly: Motherly meet, our Love / Election: Election set to Love / Forgive: Forgive field of Love / Forget: Forget less, Love / We Forget: We forget rebuff in Love / Collective: Collective to a beam of Love / Erective: Erective rapture in Love / Suggestive: Suggestive round of Love / Desired: Desired to build on Love / Decide: Decide to glide to Love / Stride: Stride instruct to Love / Welled: Welled will is Love / Inside: Inside our trust is Love / Willed: Creative willed's yield to Love / Fed: Fed a few to Love / Field: Field a few to Love / Filled: Filled a facts with Love / Market: Wrong market? Rush to buy, Love / Mark It: Mark it market priced to Love / Pocket: Pocket packed with Love / Pick It: Pick it up, Love / Respect: Respect rest, Love / Full: Full of few, then Love / Specked: Specked a brush our Love / Sped: Sped to a press in Love / Coach: Coach clear to Love / Behind: Behind a pay to Love / Ahead: Ahead, a stand in Love / Trek: Trek on up to a mountain of Love / Sort It: Sort it up to Love / Invest: Invest in lesson Love / Interest: Interest rests to Love / Heart: Heart enough to Love / Articulate: Articulate article of Love / Ventricular: Ventricular vent to Love / Aortic: Aortic pleasure, the pump of Love / Particular: Particular pent is easing up to Love.

CHAPTER 27 / LOVE COMMITS
1. Bliss: Bliss is back to back my Love / Acknowledge: Acknowledge exact in Love / Abandon: Abandon went best west of Love / Review: Review a rest-full Love / Expansion: Expansion has sent life to Love / Remiss: Remiss a risk for Love / Repress: Repress a rest-less? Love / Give Proof: Give proof a rest in Love / Found Full: Found full of grounded in Love / Found Empty: Found empty of less, than, Love / The News: The news knows glows of Love / Gone?: Why? Gone to why we Love / The Field: The field's afield with Love / The Views: The views snooze in Love / The Etudes: The etudes of nudes in Love / The Thrills..The thrills abuzz with Love / The Reveal: The reveal of heel in step to Love / The Repeal: The repeal of less than zeal to Love / The Etude: The etude dances to Love / The Abused: The abused abridged to Love / The Relaxed: The relaxed resent is a hint to Love / The Refused: This refuse is a ruse to hide Love / The Reward: The reward is a cord of sword to Love / The 'In Facts': The 'in facts' relate to relax in Love / The Review: This review will last in Love / The Exude: Exude a mood in Love / The Ignite: This, the ignite, to right, in Love / The Per Chance: This per chance is a dance at a hint for lists of Love / The Revoked: The revoked ascend to blend in Love / The Rewrite: The rewrite right to Love / The In-Trued: In-trued to align, I find ascend at the end of the Light to Love / The True-

Blued: The true blued food of meet in Love / The Find Inside: The find inside is a grind to Love / The Fond Found: God found fond in Love / Today 'Til Dawn: Today 'til dawn, I Am on, Love / The Arc I'm On: The arc I'm on is true to Love / A Kinder Truth: A kinder truth is truth in vending Love / A Kindred Proof: A kindred proof goes direct to Love / The Hearts That Dance: The hearts that dance, chance, to, Love / A Welcome Stance: A welcome stance, the stand of Love / A Tender Sign: A tender sign, mine, is, Love / The Light Inside: The Light's inside our chance to Love / The Mind of God: The mind of God is boggle-less in Love / The Arc Called God: The arc called God along our Love / The Width I've Made: The width I've made is wide to God in Love / The Rights I've Paid: The rights I've paid have stayed in Love / The Wells I Wade: The walls I wade are well past the last of Love / The Artesian: The artesian dream is deep in a wing of Love / The Salt Of God: Salt of God, a rock lake deep to a mine still deep in Love / The Days of Sod: The days of sod are gone to green in Love / The Arm of Tools: An arm of tools, the rods of God is Love / The Wield of Rules: One rule, wield your Love / The Love Gone By: The love gone by has stayed a wade too long to a rapid evaporative called Love / The Day Gone By: The day gone By has sighed in Love / The Even Trade: The even trade is YES! to Love / The Point I've Made: The point I've made is paid to Love / The Art I Save: The art I save is my own in Love / The Ink I've Paid: The ink I've paid is a written resolution of my raid-less lift on Love / The Wealth I Sought: The wealth I sought is to zero in on Love / The Life I Wade: The life I wade is God's sweet Love / Thee I Spot: Thee I spot in what is wet to Love / The Connect I Dot: The connect I dot to God is Love / The Light I Am: The Light I Am in God is Love.

CHAPTER 28 / LOVE CONTENTS: The Wave I Swam: The wave I swam is swamped by Love / A Divinity's Span: A Divinity's span is Love / A Pen, I Am: A pen, I Am in the hand of God is Love / The Spark In You: God's parked in a spark in you called Love / The Light Revue: The Light revue, you, on the stage of Love / Of This I Sing: Of this I sing, a fling, to Love / A Healing Proof: God's healing proof is Love / The Light That Loves: The Light that Loves to live in Love / A Moment's Dream: A moment's creamy dream is a milky wade upon the banks of Love / A Mountain Stream: A mountain stream is the creamy seam to the heart of Love / A Minute Won: A minute won is our run to the heart of Love / A Minute One: A minute one is too in Love / A Vision Come: A vision come is some who Love / A Knot Undone: A knot undone is one we sum to Love / A Bed We've Led: A bed we've led to Love / An Inkling Said: An inkling said spot our Love / A Lark We Laid: A lark we laid in the park of Love / A Healing Page: A healing page is this one tossed to Love / A Quilt Called Lost: A quilt called lost has crossed the path to back to Love / A Patterned Pulse: A patterned pulse has chosen list to Love / A Land With Lust: A land with lust in us and Love / The Rust In Us: The rust in us can float to notes of perfectly clear to Love / A Sleeping Potion: A sleeping

potion, the notion, of, Love / A Healing Notion: A healing notion, the ocean of Love / An Arc: An arc parked in Love / A Star: A star born too to Love / The Arc You Are: The arc we met is our acknowledge of the college of the Arc You Are in Love / By A Covenant: By a covenant borne near the ear of Love / Never Broken: Never broken bent went to Love / Always Fit: Always fit to a hit of Love / Heal Your Heart: Heal your heart, Love / Fix Your Eye: Fix your eye on the sky of our Love / Know The Truth: Know the truth held Light, in, Love / God's Full Proof: God's fool proof in Love / Enoch Said: Enoch said, give, Love / Know You're Dead: Know you're dead, then lift your head to the living fountain, Love / A Second Wave: A second to wave at Love / An Ascendant Stand: An ascendant stand in a plan to Love / The Man I Am: The man I knew, I Am, in Love / The Lord Metatron: The Lord Metatron is in Love / Arcturic Pens: Arcturic pens ring again to lift soiled webs of souled out Love / Mayan Bins: Mayan bins Lightened by a line to Love / A Cleansing Flood: A cleansing flood of good desire to hire mire-less Love / The Ark of Doves: The arc of Doves has held us wide to wilder lines of widened Love / A Tweet In Line: A tweet In line is where we climb to lift our jaws to laws of spoken Love / A Train Called Time: A train called time to train in Love / From A Quarter Turn: From a quarter turn, around, this Love / The Rocking Learn: The rocking learn to a clearer Love / The Sign Aligned: The sign aligned is kind to Love / A Laughing Sign: A laughing sign has dined in mine, and yours, allure to all we Love / A Wealth Called Way: A wealth called way has stayed my execution of Love / A Heart Called Day: A heart called day of arrival at Love / A Night We've Led: A night we've led to lift our eyed to God is Love / To Bliss: To bliss I go alert to Love / To Kiss: To kiss a mouth less distant to, then, Love / To Dis: Elusive to dis, Love / To Dat: To dat, measure your pleasure, in, Love / To Tao: To Tao, I wow, go slow, go deep, go sleep, in streets of perfect ways of Love / To Wow: To wow yourself go wield to Love / Heaven's Made: God is heaven's made to Love / Too Extreme Regimes: Too extreme regimes have me sured risk in Love / To The Way: To the way, I stay, in Love / To The Truth: To the truth, we are youth, in Love / To The Light: Live to the Light of Love.

CHAPTER 29 / LOVE CODES: Abandon: Abandon bent best to Love / Sent: Sent to advent to Love / Expansive: The expansive sum of Love / Vent..Add a vent to Love / Implosion: Sparked implosion of the explode called Love / Impulsive: Impulsive ascend to an impulsion's dream of blended Love / Sent: Sent a flint to Love / Expulsion: Expulsion sent pent up to less than Love / Brought: God's on sought to Brought Love / Surges: Surges sent repent to Love / Sought: Sought enough Love / The Purge: The purge to merge in ecstatic release of Love / Found: Found a ground for Love / The Feel: The feel of heal in Love / Astound: Astound more, Love / Thrill: Thrill seek sought by Love / Reveal: Reveal a rest in a raven blessed by Love / The Desire: The desire to hire a higher Love / For Real: God's for real, heal, in, Love / Extend: Extend again, Love / The Bind: The bind has bent a straighten to Satan. He's lost to Love / The

Friend: God's glad friend is me in Love / The Trend: Trend, stuff, to, Love / The Chore: Chore, know more, Love / The Door: The door is open, swell, to, Love / The Store: Seen, sent, to the store of a house called Love / The Deed: The deed agreed by Love / The Concede: Concede a need for less than this and Love / The Freed: Freed to breathe in Love / The Need: The need is up for Love / The Construct: Construct less than, Love / The Dream: The dream, mid-stream, to Love / The Dame: The dame of done to Love / The Skin: The skin of akin to Love / The Flame: The flame came to Love / The Skinny: The skinny is Love / The Lad: The lad is glad, to, Love / The Venue: The venue, stage right, is, Love / The Brad: The brad is bad to fatter Love / The Vinny: The vinny is quailed by a lessen to listen to Love / The Lock: The lock on less is Love / The Debut: The debut viewed is Love / The Key: The key agreed is Love / The Relief: Let relief be grief-less, Love / Call Me: Call me home to Love / The Resolve: The resolve of solve is Love / Called You: Called you to Love / The Need: The need to heed is Love / The Tools: The tools to use are Love / The Welcome: The welcome welled by Love / The Trends: The trends trail to a tell-tale Love / The Suspense: The suspense sent to vent our Love / The Amends: The amends mended, Love / The Attributes: The attributes are cute in Love / The Friends: The friends found Love / The Intrigue: The intrigue to rest in Love / The Deeds: The deeds are done in Love / The Review: The review, few, Love / The Seams: The seams ascend to Love / The Extreme: The extreme to a dream of only Love / The Needs: The needs are met in only Love / The Pursuit: The pursuit is cute in caught by Love / The Plus: Get plus in Love / The Passion: The passion to place your Love.

CHAPTER 30 / LOVE CARRIES: The Big: Big enough to gulf, Love / The Play: Eyed play in Love / The Pith: God's own pith, the plant, of Love / The Daze: Gaunt to a gaze, I daze less in Love / The Prod: The prod abroad is Love / Admit: Admit to need rest in Love / The Sod: Let sod, God, our be to lawns of Love / Commit: Let commit begin our fit to Love / The Ways: God's ways to Love / The Trays: Four trays stayed all-wayed to Love / The Days: The best of days gone long to Love / The Buffet: Buffets of guests of Love / The Commit-ment: The commit-ment meant to Love / The At-tend: God's at-tend, Love / Invention: Keep an invention equipped with a vision called the patent of Love / The In-tend: In-tend to befriend, Love / The Dimension: The dimension denied will revise your believe in Love / Admission: God's admission, a mention, of only, Love / The Direct: God's gone green to direct to Love / Cognition: Cognition sent to Love / Bisect: God's going bisect to Love / The Recognition: Get recognition, Love / The Inspect: Get and inspect direct to Love / The Remission: The remission's review is a revision of Love / The Reflect: Gain precious reflect, Love / The Extension: An extensive extension called Love / The Ascend: The Ascend's been sent to Love / The Revision: A slight amend, the revision to Love / The Begin: Begin the begun to Love / The Admission: Get your admission to an advent of ascent called perfect Love / To These Truths: To be truth, to all these truths, be honest with

Love / The Reside: Reside aglide our Love / The Protestant: View protest less and Love / The Demise: The demise has come to less-than Love / The Christian Review: The Christian Review has a right to Love / The Aberration: An abberative nation knows less-than Love / The Catholic Exude: Be Catholic in your exude of absolute proof of Love / The Ignition: Bet your rest on ignition of Love / The Muslim News: Unmuzzle your Muslim news and Love / The Sufi News: Aspire to a spinning view of the heart you Love / Radical Roots: Radical roots of less-than Love / The Electric Roots: Our routes are electric proof of Love / The Healing Proof: The healing proof is truth in Love / THE Admonition: God's admission is the admonition to Love / The Call To Be: The call to be, we, Is Love / This Our Mission: This our mission is ignition of Love / The Bliss to See: The bliss to see is we Love / A Coupled Seek: God's coupled is weeks of strong in Love / Our Truth: Our truth is trailed to Love / A Sullen Proof: A sullen proof required is less-than Love / Eternally: Eternally sent to Love / Bear In Shoes: A basic truth is that the bear went away to the Light of all review and Love / Supernal: Let a supernal hint put a dent in Love / A Bear In News: A basic view of aberrant News is the soul strewn round to lessen Love / Youth: Let youth add proof to Love / A Trailing Proof: A trailing clue sits deep in proof of perfect Love / Abandon-meant: Abandon means less than Love / Respect-full: Replace a taste of respect-full pleasure to Love / Acknowledge: Acknowledge meant hint to Love / The Meaning: Gasp a meaning to Love / The College: Acknowledge your college of Love / The Store: The store a fore-mentioned attend to Love / Called Love: Called Love yet? / Up: Up next to you, Love.

CHAPTER 31 / LOVE REMEMBERS: Alive My Ways: Bambi's say is alive my ways to Love / Asheville Days: Ashe to day to ashes away to Love / Erotic Seams: Erotically seen in seams of Love / Electric Ways: Remember the days of electric ways to Love / A Higher Stand: A Tibetan stand in a higher hand called God's Love / A Healing Dream: Healing a dream to Love / A Field of Themes: Recline to themes of a field dressed deep in Love / A Melted Pave: Life's sweet meted pave is Love / An Art-Full Dance: Let us dance an art-full stance to Love / A Grand Scheme: Lessen the strain on a grand scheme, Love / For-Giving Lime: For-giving lime-green deliverance has come to the heart of a matter called Love / An Artist's Stance: An artist's stance to dance at Love / Emphatic Climes: Exasperate your rate of emphatic climes and aerate the soil of exotic limes grown green to Love / Ecstatic Times: Socially acceptable? Try ecstatic times and erratic rides to Love / A Knowing Scheme: Know the scheme of great redeem in Love / Effusive Gleams: Lovingly effusive and charmingly deep to gleams of Love / Eternal Waves: Eternal waves rave of Love / Assignments Say: Assignments say stay in Love / An Eternal, Internal Clock: Feel eternal in your internal register of all hat matters on the clock of God, Love / A Mental Block: A mental block erased by a race to Love / A Delicate Line: A delicate line is the thread to holy Love / Arriving Signs: I Am arriving at signs of surrender to Love /

Phlox & Posies: Loving thoughts of a phlox found deep in posies of Love / A Field and Flocks: A fielded flock of lots of Love / Guilt and Gay: Guilt and gay, I'm one found friend, in Love / Knows and Noseys: Let us now, your knows and noseys of Love / Election Day: An election day is crowned by Love / Gray and Guilt: Gray and guilt have gone away on the hub we built to Love / Belted: Belted by less? Find the found of Love / Quilted: Quilted to a square of perfect reveal of perfectly Love / Instead: Instead, in deed, Love / Understood: Revel in understood of Love / He went: He went to ascent to Love / She said: She said she asked for certain in Love / They Give: This, they give, Love / We Live: We live in tribute too, Love / Vibrate Great: Vibrate great, Love free, let's be, to Love / Explain: Explain everything, Love Love Love all sides of whom you Love / Design: Design a sign of Love / Divine: Divinity seen in Love / Descend: Descend to decent views of Love / Amend: Pin amend to befriend a few who Love / Resign: Love it's resign align in Love / Review: Review your adult tools of Love / The Love Inside: The Love inside is true and you? Love / The Move: The move to trends of higher blend and Love / To Trends: To trends let end all less-than Love / Deliver In: Deliver in me, Love / Deliver Us: Deliver us to a perfect blend of Love / Love Instead: Love instead of wrath can win more Love / In Fed: In Fed by bred to a heightened rise called Love / In Feed: In feed, indeed, let's bless our Love / In Red: In red, abed, to Love / In Receive: In receive, yes, Love / The Mother: The mother mothered us with Love / The Father: The father figured confess to Love / The Lover: Let the lover be me in Love / The Day: The day is this, Love / Tell Me: Tell me to Love / The Way: The way home, waved by Love / The Isle: Check your isle for Love / Kauai: Kauai is your rest, Love / Hawaii: Hawaii is mellow in Love / Crystalline: Crystalline is the lean into the dove, Love.

CHAPTER 32 / LOVE ARRANGED: The Isles: The isles red Love / Red, Big: Red and big in fact to Love / Born Green: Born green to shamrocked tales of Love / Eruptive: Eruptive within the volcano of Love / Desire to Live: Desire to live a life of give and Love / In Joy's Space: In joy's space place Love / Grace: Grace got up the race to Love / Called Love: Called Love right up, Loved / Eternal: Eternal Dove, Love / Dove: Dove of due to Love / An Ocean Wide: An ocean wide with perfect Love / Big Aisled: Align a cart on time to shop the aisles of Love / Yes, We Know: Yes, we know, passion shows of big Love / The Passion: The passion shows are hear at the land called Love / 3 Below: All 3 go below to Love a burning Love / A Burning: Burning heat is neat in Love / Besiege: Besiege your need to hesitate in Love / The Kneed: Kneed a knock on Love / To Love Aside: To Love aside, the ride to Love / Inside: Inside I Am wound to Love the stream the stream agreed to Love / Called Light: Called Light to Love / And Love: And yes, we, Love / We Feed: We feed on only Love / On Dreams: On dreams deal more with Love / Deliver Us: Deliver us, yes, rush to Love / I Can See..I can see you in Love / The Trend: A trend to share your be in Love / Inflamed: Inflamed met a dance to end trance in Love / By Same:

By same, I mean you, will alike in Love / And Met: And met at Love / Need: Need more, Love / The Game: The game to ends zoned Love / To Ends: To ends now met in Love / And Friends: And friends expand to greet true Love / Of Dames: Of dames examined we remain the same in Love / Called Fortune: Called fortune home to Love / Fate: Fate felt fit in Love / Tragedies: Tragedies aren't mates of Love / And Mates: And mates met angels at gates of Love / And Myths: And myths bust, Love / Archeologic: Archeologic found the remains of towns of Love / Called Ecstatic: Called ecstatic to Love / Relief: It's a relief to Love / OF Human: Of human, I agreed to Love / Regard: Regard us, Love / And: And the heights of Love are us / The Heights: Heights held up to Love / Of Heaven: Of Heaven held, you, in Love / The Heavens: The Heavens held us 2 Love / Of Stars: Of stars, ours, of Love / Electrician: Electrician weaves Love / Select: Select your weapon, Love / Know: Know the show of Love / Just Due It: It is just due in Love / Imbue It: Imbue it with Love / Show: Let Love show me ways to be enhance by Love / Love: A fluid notion, Love / Ignobled: Ignobled by the notion of Love / Belted: Belted by Love / Dealt: Dealt felt round like Love / Felt: Felt felt, Love / Full: Full view, Love / Filled: Filled ip and over with Love / Full-filled: Full-filled always in Love.

CHAPTER 33 / LOVE MAITREYAN: Sky Wide: Sky wide to flights of Love / The Field: The field revealed has healed our Love / Star Deep: A great star deep in Love / Arcing lean: Arcing lean, clean, to Love / A Chance: Get a chance to dance with Love / Deliver: Deliver matters to Love / The Dance: The dance has come to Love / Leaning: Stance the post of leaning to Love / Extremely: Extremely upset with what we've done to Love / Banal: Banal pleasure, the measure-less measure of Love / Primal: Primal screen, Love / Gleams: Gleams and glints of hints of Love / Glen: Extreme gone to a glen of Love / Ancient Links: Ancient links to when we blink in shuttered lines of Love / Alchemy Rings: Alchemy rings my rhymes with rung to Love / The Bridge: The bridge is built, I Am, Love / The Healing Cup: The healing cup, God up to Love / Stepping Up: Stepping up to a rhyme in time to Love / Meaning: Meaning its Love / Call: Call it Love / Wealth: See the edge of the wealth we lift to Love / Redeem: Redeem yourself to Love / Pad: Pad of happy feet to Love / Feel Your Dad: Feel your Dad, son, Love / Touch Your Mom: Touch your Mom with happy feet of Love / Inhale The Sun: Inhale the one sun, Love / Beat The Drum: Beat the drum and dance to Love / Know The Chance: Know the chance to dance with God / Compare: Compare, know dare, to Love / Dare: Dare that cares is Love / The Wares: The wares we've wed are Love / The Stairs: The stairs are straight to Love / The Plays: All days, the plays, of Love / Called Love: Called Love to cradle us in one Love / Traditional: A traditional manner, Love / Scented: Scented like Love / Conditional: Conditional had gone to one long gone to Love / Alabama: Let Alabama breathe, Love / Eruptively: Eruptively Love / Jeweled: make no bones, only Jeweled gems of Love / Subjective: A subjective matter, Love / Kyanite: Kyanite curled blue to Love / Reflective: Reflective red

Love / Olite: Olite Light to Love / Wed: Wed to bless our Love / Seas: Seas apart, we start, to Love / Eyes: Eyes have said red to Love / Rings: Rings of run to Love / Able: Able to share canes of Love / Philosophic: Philosophic by nature, Love / Philosophy: Philosophy reads Love / Lately: Lately Love / Equate: Equate your wait with Love / Await: Await news, Love / Arising: Arising now to Love / Listening: Listening to you, Love / Turning: Turning to dial, Love / Spank: Spank your spark to life, Love / Rank: Rank yourself smart to Love / Shortly: Shortly I say, Love / Shift: Shift to believe in Love / Retail: Retail sale on Love / Roaming: Roaming tame? Love / Today: Today we Love.

CHAPTER 34 / LOVE BUDDHA: Soon Enough: Soon enough, Love / Movies: Movies meet in Love / Rotate: Rotate to Love / Pass By: Pass the left by right to Love / Lovely: A lovely sound, the ring of Love / Short: Short to court our Love / Palmed: A palmed appeal of heal in Love / Fingered: Fingered fed by head for Love / Poem: A poem written in our Love / Young: Young to stays in Love / Snappy: Snappy stride to wide Love / Gentleness: Gentleness rains in Love / Extravagant: Extravagant land called Love / Comfortably: Comfortably well in Love / Well: Well, yes, Love / Remedies: Remedies abound in Love / Jargon: A jargon gone to Love / Vestal: Vestal virgins blend at Love / Virgins: Virgins vestal ring our Love / Cherry: Cherry red ahead, Love / Red: Red to fed more Love / Peach: Examine a peach, Love / Said: Said, yes, Love / Loved: Loved best, often, Love / Blood: Blood breathes life to Love / Warm: Warm in a crystal sleeve of Love / Genetics: Genetics lead to Love / Kinetic: Kinetic to treasures of Love / Cushy: Cushy, the feel, of Love / Patience: Patience healed by Love / Ladies: Ladies wait for Love / Trick: A trick tucked in to lessen Love / Ticket: Just the ticket, Love / Satin: Satin's feel is Love / Velvet: Velvet's thrill is Love / Jet: Jets reflect the stream of earthly Love / Baker: Bakers bake pans of flans of Love / Pulse: Pulse inside your Love / Patch: Patch a span with Love / Lust: Lust enough, Love / Exude: Exude more Love / Boat: Take a boat to Love / Dream: Dream a little dream of me, Love / The Heart: The heart held high to Love / The Head: The head of lakes of Love / The Stand: Stand up for Love / Preclude: The preclude is rude without pure Love / The Proclaim: The proclaim's the same in Love / Sector: Sector sent to Love / Secure: Secure your chart to Love / Segue: Segue in to Love / Section: A sanction to Love / Stream: Stream on home to Love / Scene: Scene sunk? To Love / Rod: Rod of god, the pole of old, the staff, the comfort, Love / Built: Built like an ark on the spark of Love / Teeth: Teeth touch soft in spoken Love / Wreath: A wreath runs around Love / Pass: Pass on to Love / Pat: Apt to pat a pod of Love / Boon: Boon's be is free to Love / Booth: Booth of the latest gadget called listen, Love / Bath: Bath tub blue? Float in Love / Birth: Let us birth our baby, earth, and welcome, Love.

CHAPTER 35 / LOVE COMPASSION: I Am, That I Am: Let me be entranced to more than I Am not, I Am, that I Am, In Love / I Am Essence: Like an essence, I Am to Love / I Am Light: I Am Light of Love / I Am Life: Lately I Am life of Love / I Am Well: Lightly I Am well to Love / I Am Love: Listen, I Am Love / I Am Meta-electric: I Am meta-electric Love / I Am That: Held by that I Am, Love / I Am Then: Bet on I Am, then, Love / I Am Now: Lately, I Am now, to Love / I Am Eternally: Eternally trimmed to I Am, Love / I Am Infinitely: Infinitely pulled by less, I Am, Love / I Am Essentially: Love let essentially ascent to I Am Love / I Am Elementally: Lovely place, elementally I Am, Love / I Am Eternally: Eternally trimmed by Love / I Am Infinitely: Lovely infinitely a loft to Love / I Am Essentially: Specifically ascent, a gift, to Love / I Am Wholey: Wholey held by adrift to Love / I Am Experientially: I essentially and experientially am. Love / I Am Evidently: Evidently let to I Am Love / I Am, Finally: Finally fed to a penchant for Love / I Am, Fragrantly: Fragrantly graced by I Am Love / I Am, Especially: Especially spent to I Am Love. / I Am Absolutely: Absolutely, I Am Love / I Am Divinely: Graced divinely I Am, Love / I Am Fully: Fully filled, I Am, Love / I Am Aptly: Aptly, I Am, Love / I Am Amazing: Amazingly laced esthetically to Love / I Am Engaging: Over engaging, I'm aging in Love / I Am Intricately: God's grace intricately laced by Love / I Am Led: Left led to I Am, Love / I Am Fed: All the way, glad to be feed by Love / I Am Led: Left led to I Am, Love / I Am Fed: All the way, glad to be fed by Love / I Am Met: Meet and met in I Am, Love / I Am, Yes: Oh yes, I Am, Love / I Am, Today: Lefty today, in Love / I Am, Forever: I Am, forever, Love / I Am Entranced: Entranced advance to Love / I Am Elegance: Elegance meant I Am Love / I Am Eloquence: Let eloquence dance in I Am, Love / I Am Intelligent: Intelligent dreamed by I Am Love / I Am Eternal: Life's eternal in I Am, Love / I Am Fulfilled: Fulfilled a build to Love / I Am Equitable: Equate to equitable measure of Love / I Am Delectable: Delectable taste of I Am Love / I Am Electrical: Let us be electrical to we are Love / I Am Metatronic: I bliss metatronic to I Am Love / I Am Level: Hard done deal. I Am level to Love / I Am Balance: Get your balance of Love / I Am Harmonious: Heart harmonious to Love / I Am Attuned: Attuned, ballooned, by Love / I Am Mobile: Lots of mobile to Love / I Am Infinite: Insist on infinite widths of Love / I Am Evergreen: I Am evergreen in my dream of a bead gone home along, Love / All-One: And the one is to Love / I Am Supernal: Great supernal, I Am. Love / I Am Pedernal: I Am pedernal in a stance to eternal Love / I Am The Earth: Great the earth of I Am, Love / I Am New Birth: To a day, I Am new birth to Love / I Am Regenerated: Light's regenerated, Love / I Am Elated: Left elated, dated, Love / I Am Safe: Let's be safe to Love / I Am Happy: A ride to happy I Am Love.

CHAPTER 36 / LOVE EMOTIVE: One Love: One Love lived, give, Love / One Law: One law home, to Love / One Commandment: One command, manned by Love / One Heart: One heart hind the find aligned to Love / One Way: One way rush to Love / One Truth: One truth's trill, feel, Love / One Life: One life led to Love / One Wave: One wave wed to fed by Love / One Depth: One depth dueled by Love / One Appreciation: One appreciation a nation of Love / One Initiation: One initiation a station called Love / One Arc: One arc to park in Love / One Reminder: One reminder, mind her, Love / One Kinder: One kinder kissed by Love / One Indivisible: One indivisible by Love / One Invincible: One Invincible won, Love / One Trickle: One trickle fickle to a flood called Love / One Flow: One flow go glow in Love / One Embrace: One embrace faced Love / One Taste: One taste abased by Love / One Swell: One swell fell to a hush of Love / One Wave: One wave wed to Love / One Sum: One sum signed to sins of Love / One Time: One time to tread to Love / One, You: One you willed to Love / One Line: One line fin to fan in Love / One Loop: One loop leaped to Love / One, I Am: One, I Am to being in Love / I Am One: I Am One sun of signs ascend to Love / One Summer: Jog One summer deep Love / One Winter: Lots of winters, One, Love / One Heart: Bet on heart, ONE deep, Love / One Fall: Lofts One fall to Love / One Vibe: Let One vibe on Love / One Spring: Letter led to a spring One deep Love / One Me: Let us me, One, Love / One Stream: One day I dreamt of benefit gone straight to streams of Love / One Dream: Lovely dream, One, Love / One Awakening: One awakening Love / One Light: Less than Light? Gone fade to Love / One Quickening: Life's gone quickening to One, Love / One Tree: Tree of truth in One, Love / One Life: Life's bet, One, Love / One Led: Lovely lead, led, One, on. Love / One Divine: Life's divine. as One. Love / One's Light: Light abide in One, Love / One's Love: One is lesson left to Love / One: Left One, Love / One Thread: One leftover thread of Love / Our Web: Love of a web, Light said, to Love / One Wed: One's wed, Love / One Fed: Lesson led to fed, Love / One Night: One of these nights to Love / One Sight: Sight seen, One, Love / One Delight: Lessen delight to One, Love / One Song: Lovely song, One Love / One River: Left a river along Love / One Jah: Jah joined us at Love / One God: Society seen in One to God of Love / One Son: Pair of One son, Love / One Queen: One queen gone crowned to One Love / One Ring: One ring round a gown of Love / One Round: One round of Love / One's Center: One's center full of Love.

CHAPTER 37 / LOVE VOTILE: Infinite Expanse: Spake the expanse, Infinite our Love / Infinity, A Glance: An essential glance at Infinity's expanse to Love / Exceptionally Infinite: Gently found to except a cloud of exceptional Love / Infinite Loop: Lovely loop of an infinite hoop to Love / Time for the Infinite: Time to thrill at an infinite rhyme called Love / Infinitely Greek: Into Greek infinitely spoken Love / Infinitely Essential: Lovely essential Love / Infinitely Essential: Lovely essential Love / Infinite, It Seems: Insist on infinity sent to seem like Love / Eternal Expansion: God's eternal expansion, a mansion of Love / Infinite Romancing: Gay gone the dance to an infinite romance of Love / Essentially Eternal: Essence of essentially I Am eternal, Love / Infinite Design: Did you design an infinite view of Love? / Infinite Plan: God's plan, a fan, of Love / Infinite Rain: Let it rain, an infinite proclaim, of Love / Infinitely Divine: Led divine, infinity inclined to Love / Lightly Infinite: Love Let Love lead, infinite to meeds of lightly Love / Eternal Light:

Essential and eternal, to Light Love / Eternal Flight: A vision lent to virtuous ascent to an eternal flight of Love / Infinite Ecstasy: God's infinity is ecstasy's in Love / Eternal Bliss: Curing our bliss, eternal in Love / An Eternal Kiss: Let us eternal kiss, in Love / Ecstatic Review: -Infinite Lighter ecstatic, our review, infinite, in Love / Infinity, I Said: God said, infinity led to Love / Infinitely, I Am: Let Love lead in a theme to sound of Love / Eternity, The Span: Eternity spin in a span Love / Arc, I Am: I Am an arc of an infinite spark to Love / An Eternal Web: Pat on the eternal web of Love / An Infinite Web: A lifting web an infinite wed 2 Love / An Infinite Light: Jobs so right to one infinite Light of Love / Eternity's Sight: Sight eternal infinity's wed, Love / Infinite Thread: Let us thread our delicate tread to Love / Eternally Led: Led eternally home to Love / Infinitely Fed: Lighter in fast, has rest in fed Love / Infinity Said: Said, all the way 2 Love / Logos To Infinity: Love's logos infinity deep to Love / Infinity, Let It Be: Get your best in let it be to infinity in Love / Let There Be Eternity: Let there be eternity in we Love / Eternal Light: Eternal Light in silent flight to hearty Love / Infinite Love: In fine align, I reside, in Love / Love Eternal: Love's eternal in wonderful walls of Love / Love's Eternity: Sugar wet to a molten fleck of specks of Love / Love To Infinity: Love to in fine incline to Love / Infinity To Infinity: Infinite to a center of infinity entered by Love / Eternally, I Am: Eternally, I Am, Love / Infinitely Centered: God's centered in you too, and Love / Centrally Eternity's: Balanced Centrally, I Am eternity's balance to points of Love / Insistently Infinite: Insist on an insistent space to an infinite place called Love / Eternity's Star: Eternity's star, a car to far, we Love / Infinity's Wave: Infinity's wave is a pave to Love / Eternal Part-icles: Eternal part-icles, eyes cycle Love / Particularly Infinite: God's particularly infinite in good reside to Love / Infinitely Essential: Essentially infinite, I Am eternal in a healing spiral to Love / Infinite Design: Led by design to infinite recline in Love / Infinite De-Light: Infinite delight in the Light of Love / Infinity's Spin: Spinning through infinity and Love / Infinite Spiral: Infinite spiral that leads to the point of Love / Infinitely Effortless: Infinitely effortless and Light is the dive to Love / Eternity's Dance: Eternity's dance is a swirling bliss filled Love / Eternal Bloom: Eternal bloom is the prize that comes with Love / Eternally Sitting: Eternally sitting to listen to the whispers of Love / Eternal Prayers: Eternal prayer spirals one towards bliss and Love / Infinity's Divine: Infinity's divine and shines in Love / Eternal License: You have eternal license to shine in the eyes of Love.

CHAPTER 38 / LOVE ELONGATED (HOPE): Many: Many waved home to Love / Many Trees: Trim many trees of merry I'll be in Love / Many Planes: Make many planes level again, Love / Many, All One: Many are one in all we do to Love / Many, Merry: Many one merry in Love / Many, Mini: God's mini many, Love / Many, Marco: God's macro view, you in many LOVES / Many Micro: Micro many winning Love / Many Biotic: Make my biotic tonic anew in many Loves / Many, Ionic: Many believe in ionic relieve of metabolic review called to in

Love / Many, Iconic: Many one iconic about it, Love / Many, Dichroic: Make mine dichroic in ??? ascend to the constant within, Love / Many, Scientific: Many scientific gestures gesture to Love / Many, Prolific: Prolific plenty in marry Love / Many, Ethereal: Make it ethereal by a serial mist of mentioning this, Love / Many Imperial: Many are imperial in their regal stance to Love / Many, Red: Many red lean to Love / Many, Blue: Many met blue in Love / Many Will Live: Billy will live in many willed Love / Many Will Lead: God will lead to good in many Loves / Many, Lightly: Many go lightly to Love / Many Eruditely: Many eruditely quip of Love / Many Igniting: Many igniting in Love / Many Inviting: Many are inviting in Love / Many Exciting: Many exciting live in Love / Many Enriching: God's enriching circle circles us to Love / Many Ambrosiac: God's met an ambrosiac space in us and many's Love / Many Aeronautic: Many are aeronautic in biotic flips to Love / Many Licensed: Many licensed to Love / Many Enticed: Many enticed to give in to Love / Many Emphatic: Many emphatic to static clear of Love / Many Devoted: Many are devoted to emoted in Love / Many Committed: Many committed to Love / Many Explicit: Make many explicit to your maximum pleasure in Love / Many Know This: Many know this, the merry kiss of Love / Many and One: Many is becoming One in the many who Love / Many and Sum: Marry the sum of many and One in Love / Many and Light: Many are Light within the flight to Love / Many Sparks: Many sparks are mini-arcs to leading Love / Many Arcs: Make many arcs spark to Love / Many Loved: Mike's great lift is a gift to many ived by Loved / Many Men: Many men pinned to Love / Many Mothered: Make's been mothered by many other than Love / Many Fed: God's been fed by many led to Love / Many Hands: Many hands miss out on passing out Love / Many Lives: Many lives lived in Love / Many Gifts: Make mine gifts of many Love / Many: Many weights healed in Love / Many I Forgive: Many I've forgiven to Love / Many I Forgave: The babies I forgave to Love / Many I Embrace: Let's embrace a many place called Love / Many I Will Lead: Baby, many will be lead to Love / Many Things I See: Many I see are things to me in Love / Many Things I know: Many the things I know in Love / Many Things I Hear: Many things I hear about Love / Many Days I'm Here: Many days I'm here, of Love / Many Ways, Always Near: God's rest, many ways, always near, to Love / Many The Phases: Many the phases felt raised by Love / Many The Phrases: God's many phrases of Love / Many The Spaces: Let many spaces be filled with Love / Many The Traces: Many a trace to a face of Love / Many Melts: Minerals melt to become many we Love / Many Lifts: Many lifts lightly to Love / Many All: Many are all we heal in Love.

CHAPTER 39 / LOVE ASSURED: All Seasons: All seasons set, to Love / All Life: All life leave to Love / All Night: All night heal of Love / All Day: God is real all day to Love / All May: All may wheel in Love / All One: All one feel of Love / All Days: All days ways to Love / All Nights: All nights seal our Love / All Light: All Light field of Love / All Height: All height held to Love / All Depth: All depth felled to Love / All Laughs: All laughs reveal Love / All Weds: All weds wing to Love / All Rings: Around the rings of Love / All Sings: All sings won by Love / All Tell: All tell all in Love / All Appeal: All appeal is Love / All Loves: All Loves win in Love / All Lovers: Lovers all 3 in 2 deliver you to Love / All's Embrace: All's embrace is One to Love / All The Ways: All the ways to be great to God in Love / All The Day: All the day weigh to Love / All This Reign: All this reign does is Love / All Magnificent: All, a magnificent ball of Love / All Beneficient: All is beneficient in Love / All God: All I Am is God in Love / All Love: All we Love is all God, Love / All Led: All be lead to One, Love / All Energy: All energy meets in a sweet retreat to Love / All Electronic: All electronic, sonic, surge of resurge to Love / All Metatronic: All Metatronic knows the sonnet of God ALL Love / Sepharothic: All Sepharothic gated are closed in Love / All Religions: All is Love in a religious reign called letting go to God is Love / All Science: All science said was count to Love / All Art: All art reels in heals of Love / All Taste: All taste healed by buds of Love / All's Face: God's All's face in Love / All Is Best: All is best, now, in Love / All Is Rest: All Is best in a rest to Love / All The Test: All the test is rest in Love / All The Truth: Tell the truth all the way through to Love / All Is Forgiven: All is forgiven in Love / All Is For Living: God's all living, Love / All Is The Space: All is the space to Love / Only All: Metatron is on, only, All, to Love / All Of Me: All of me, we view, in Love / All You See: All you can see is we, Love / All Met: Right has all met in Love / All Left: All that's left is Love / All Composite: God's all One, composite of Love / All Harmonious: All is harmonious in God / All The Peace: All the peace to release our Love / All One Proof: All one proof of Love / All One: One is any to all in Love / One All: One is all any need in Love / All Some: All some whole sum Love / All Many: All many One, Love / All Any: Any all in all of any to Love / All The Same: All the same, one game, Love / All The Time: God's align, all the time, Love / All The Rhyme: All the rhyme, one, time, Love / All: All the same, Love / All Blooms: All blooms unfold for Love / All Wise: All wise who drink from life and taste the sweetness of Love.

CHAPTER 40 / LOVE ADDED: Wealth: Wealthy, well within Love / Worth: Worth a mirth-full treasure, the pleasure, Love / Milked: Milked made, Love / Mirthing: Mirthing exert to a meal of Love / Mystic: Mystic met Love / Connect: Connect a debt to perfect, Love / Erect: Erect expect to Love / Correct: Correct expect of Love / In Debt: In debt a bet to Love / Make: Lately make Love / Standish: Standish I clan with miles between hour Love / Miles: Miles between all still Love / Davidic: David in the part of Davidic art in Love / Splendoric: Splendor sent honorific advance to Love / Spills: Spill a say in Love / Floral: Floral feel of heal you Love / Frills: Frills exact in Love / Asleep: Let us sleep asleep in deep to Love / Awake: Lost awake to less than Love / Stake: A stake I take in Love / Rem: Rate a rapid rem beneath the heel of Love / Rim: Right I meant to Love / Reach: Reach out in Love / Resting: Surround resting in Love /

Rent: Rent your spent to Love / Maze: A dance a maze of Love / Care: Care a share of Love / Bears: In this bears of tigery care to Lighten Love / Beliefs: Beliefs I'm healed in Love / Mark: Mark lightly filled desire, to Love / Music: A musical meal, the real harmonic, Love / Muse: It find a muse and music, Love / Marketing: A marketing buff in Love / Central: Central scene of Love / Lane: Lane found thin to Love / Child: Let a child rail to Love / Chill: Chilling hush of Love / Mend: Mend amend our Love / Light's: House left to Light's house in Love / Banks: Later banks of bush in Love / Nativity: Nativity knell, hear, in Love / Deem: Deem a trim to Love / Shop: Logic shops here in Love / West: West abreast our Love / Cedar: Great the cedar of Lebanon, Love / Key: Key a kin to Love / Rainbow: Rainbow rimmed by Love / Arbor: Arbor rest in Love / Banner: A chain of banner, bantered, Loved / Spring: God's spring, in Love / Fired: Fired in hired by Love / Stoned: Live life stoned-less, Love / Browned: God's green gleam browned by rust in Love / Belt-ed: Lofty belt-ed Love / Invision: Invision a vision of man, Love / Give: Give agreed to Love / God's: God's great, Love / Essential: Essentially seen in a healing between, Love / Wrinkle: Lightly I wrinkle I wrinkle when I sprinkle less than Love / In-Trined: A round, hear, I'm in-trined by Love / Event: Event full? Fly, Love / Female: Female filled by Love / Seminal: Seminal glances at Love / Country: A Light country, the country of Love.

CHAPTER 41 / LOVE RISKS: Country: Found a friend in a country called Love / Stake: Stake set in Love / Commerce: Commerce quailed? Love / Ecology: Ecological standard, the stand of trees in Love / Attune: Attune entrained by an ear to Love / Brake: Brake a stop at eternal Love / Charley: Confess your charley fed way to Love / May-ed: Today may-ed beyond Love / Slim: Slim the sum to Love / Slum: Slum seen in lessened Love / Come: Come on n, Love / Machine: A machine met in heat of Love / Manned: Lesson manned by a philosophical stand in Love / Friendly: God got friendly with Love / Weight: Always the weight of perfect glee, Love / Wait: Wait to equate to Love / Liberal: Lightly liberal at a serial advance to Love / Conserve: Let us conserve less, Love / 10: 10 to a friend, begin, to Love / Worded: Worded yes! Love / Flat: Flat to begin a curve of Love / Wrangled: A wrangled manner, Love / Ironed: Ironed, on to perfect Love / Communed: Communed in scenes of Love / In-Slaved: In-slaved by dazed by Love / In-graved: In-graved gone red to Love / Engrave: Engrave in us the stuff of Love / Wire: To wire a way to Love / Common: A common matter, deeper, Love / Flyer: A Light flyer, Love / God's: God's own hand, man, Love / New: New too? Love / Begin: Let us begin friend, of Love / Adopt: Adopt a friend in Love / Left: Let art be left by a heart in Love / Antique: Antique manner gone to new in Love / Triple: Triple trend to Love / Aaa-h: Aaa-h ha, yes, Love / Assumed: Assumed in used? Let's share, Love / Plumed: Plumed enough? Love / Magnolia-ed: Magnolia-ed may to Love / Native: Native stayed by Love / Parking: Let us parking stand in Love / Pug: Pug knows nose of Love / Earthy: Earthy meter, heater, Love / Porky: Porky paid greed to lessen Love / Pig: Left in piggy

grinned oinks of less than Love / Garbed: Garbed in guards of another? Love / Gored: Gored to swords in Love / Give: Give a frill to Love / Slap: Slap a snap on Love / Stab: Stab a stay at less than Love / Brag: Brag a lot of Love / Who'ed: Who'ed said? Love / Administer: Administer minister of Love / Minister: Of minister, enough, Love / Sinister: Lightly sinister's lift to a gift of Love / Brick: A brick beat in a street of Love / Hard: Of hard lessoned lessened, Love / Steal: Let us steal a way to what we had of Love / Metal: Softly measured, melted treasure of Love / Cared: Hold on to cared by Love / Steel: Let us steel to lesser Love / Carved: Carved red up to a splash with Love.

CHAPTER 42 / LOVE SIGNS: Seen-ed: Seen-ed by Love / Due: Due to be coned by Love / Ringer: What? A ringer. Love / Advent: Advent invent in Love / Visit: Visit viewed by Love / Singer: Let us singer send ascend to Love / Invent: Invent us Love / Kin: Love is kin to men has ascend to Love / Simper: Simper all ways to Love / Holiday: A holiday of Love / Kemp: Kemp us, Love / Rain: Got rain in Love? Let's know the sun of God Love / Serving: Serving a sound to Love / Trailing: Left us trailing to Love / Leaving: Leaving home, Love / Elect: Elect in us our Love / Truth: Lofty truth in Love / Hear: Hear where we Love / Today: Today a way to Love / Teary: Teary I'd Love / Heard: Heard your word of Love / To-ward: Lift toward, Love / Intrude: Intrude brewed? Love / Word: Word up is yes in Love / Live..Let's live in Love / Boast: Boast a bit of Love / Big: Big enough to Love / Little: Let in me a little of Love / Aquital: A poet's aquital yes, to Love / Woven..Light enough to woven be by Love / Weaved: Weaved a wed of woven bed of floral Love / Lawed: Lawed enough? Rule less, Love / Centered: A centered, spin to when, Love / Crippled: Crippled up. Stand, to Love / Clawed: Enough of clawed by Love / Render: Render rest to Love / Restive: Restive manner, Love / Regard: Regard us read by Love / Bramble: Willed by bramble to rest, in an amble to Love / Well-ness: Well-ness is willed by Love / Label: Red label brew, you, Love / Gamble: Gamble glued? Removed by Love / Wince: Wince less, Love / Ladle: Ladle by skewed ascent to lend, Love / Guild: Guild glint to Love / Complex: Complex? Yes, Love / Brian: Brian billed to Love / Willed: Willed in welled to Love / Select: Select an electric ascend to Love / Pray: Pray enough, Love / Venus: Venus viewed in you and Love / Exaggerate's: Exaggerate's great in exact, Love / Mediate: Today I mediate of Love / Rails: Let us rails to open up our Love / Face: Face in a place of Love / Meditate: Meditate late to Love / Penis: Penis pent? unbent by hard, to Love / Thrown: Thrown us to Love / Dance: Dance enough to Love / Traced: Traced, Love / Fresh: Fresh enough, Love / Vision: Less vision, less? Love / Heart: I'm held hearty, held by Love / Hear: Hear only Love.

CHAPTER 43 / LOVE MIRACULOUS: To Gentle Rest: I gentle rest in best, we Love / Vision, Yes: Vision viewed by yes. In Love / Will to Feel: I will to feel of Love / The Healing's: Best healing's best in Love / Vision's Mark: Let vision mark rest in Love / Feel, I Know: I feel, I know, of Love / Vision's

Mark: Let vision mark rest in Love / Feel, I Know: A feel, I know, of Love / Vision's Heart: Let vision's heart beat of Love / Know, I Go: Now I go to know, of Love / Where Sealing's Set: When a ceiling's set wet with Love / As Love: As Love held our brand of healed to Love / Regeant: A regeant rent by Love / Electing: Electing brusque? Love / Spilling: Take a spilling to Love / Regenerative: Get a regenerative order to Love / Reading: Reading resting Love / Healing: Today I'm healing, Love / Regenerationing: This is it regenerationing rest in Love / Invoking: Invoking vent to Love / Hundred: Hundred held by Love / Repatterning: Repatterned place of a listening place in Love / Spoken: Spoken say, Love / Heavens: Heavens held high by Love / Lotus: Lotus bloomed by Love / Petals: Fed by petals of Love / Purged: Purged enough? Love / God: God is man in Love / Man: Man enough? Yes. To Love / Human: Great human date to one Love / One Caused: One caused alarm for less than Love / Love: Love elects us too. Love / Perfect: A perfect plan, the man of Love / Casting: A casting matter 2001, beyond Love / Near Lately: Near, I hear, Love / Know Fear's: Release know feared release of a lessened street and now let's Love / Revere: Revere dear to Love / The Deer: Let us deer, run, to Love / The Dear: Dear of us, Love / The Fine: Rate a fine align with Love / Divine: Divine in fine to Love / Desire: Grave desire? Higher, Love / Hire: Hire higher Love / Keep: Keep a crest in Love / Creep: Creep on up to Love / Closer: Greater closer Love / Stretch: Stretch a truth to Love / Clearer: Clearer near our Love / Bell: Pythagorean bell, well, to Love / Missive: Missing, missed? Love / Eagled: Greater eagled, Love / Penned: Socrates penned for let, Love / Born: Born to boon of Love / Boric: Boric born of splurge, Love / Banned: Banned of less, then Love / Belted: Belted beat of Love / Euphoria: Euphoria fed to Love / Six: Gate of six in Love / Seven: Seven tried three by Love / Eight: Eight to eight to late to Love / Nine: Nine to find our Love / Ten..Let ten be in Love / Sometime: Sometime said, Love / Broken: Great and broken breast in Love.

CHAPTER 44 / LOVE WONDERS: Harmonic: Harmonics hum of Love / Scent: Scent to a spent by Love / Print: Print in deep to Love / Myopic: Myopic scene of Love / Smart: Smart the feet of Love / Piece: Piece enough, Love / Straw: Straw broke? Love / Treat's: Treat's treat us to Love / Speak: Speak enough Love / Pearls: Pearls of found in Love / Spoken: Spoken pleasure, the measure of Love / Swirls: Swirls swim deep to Love / Fantastic: Fantastic matter, Love / Maze: Maze been met by Love / Milk: Milky met in Love / Treats: Let's be treats to Love / Traces: Traces trace to Love / Sweet: Sweet by fleet our Love / Dealing: Dealing done, deep to Love / Deep: Deeply done, Love / Tracts: Tracks in trace to Love / Drugged: Drugged deep enough? To Love / Participate: Participate late? In Love / Lease: Better lease on Love / Renew: Renew our new review of Love / You are God's Kin: You, God's kin, are the friend of Love / God's Friend: God's a friend with health within our Love / The Brand: The brand of us, Love / The Tan: The tan tramped home to Love / The Dark Has Gone: The dark's been gone to long on Love /

Brown Belt: Brown belt felt lift in Love / Belt Melt: Belt melt met in Love / Photonic: Sonnet photonic sonnet of Love / Sing It,: Love flood to sing it, Love / Think: Think enough? Thank Love / Thank: Lots of thanks in Love / Thummin: Strumming of thummin, I Love / Urim: You are urim fed by Love / Plate: Plate of a breast met by Love / Breast: Breast met best in a milk of Love / Guest: Guest got rest in Love / Visit: Visit viewed, Love / Lesson: Let us lesson begin to Love / Less: Less enough? Know! More, Love / More: More than enough to Love / Soar: Soar more, Love / Faye-d: Faye-d felt rate on Love / Erratic: Erratic rest in Love / Monogram: Monogram met in letters of Love / Flayed..Flayed adjust to Love / Eradicate: Eradicate rates of Love / Flank: Flank flunk? Love / Exposed: Exposed best, Love / Drawn: Drawn to dream of Love / Shank: Shank shrunk? Love / Expulsed: Expulsed our spill to Love / Plates: Plates of fate equate to Love / Junk: Junk sunk to rev? Love / Sunk: Sunk to send our ascend to Love / Unearth: Unearth mirth in Love / Know-It-All: Know it all Love / Lived: Lived ablend our Love / Rebirth: Rebirth met best in Love / Hid: Hid in stunts of Love.

CHAPTER 45 / LOVE CONNECTED: Drink: Drink a drip of a torrent sent to Love / Sip: Sip a couple of Love / Refresh: Refresh rest, Love / Mesh: Mesh in test is a matrix deep to rest-full Love / Orange: God's green orange is ripe to Love / Pink: Pink pleasure's measure, Love / Green: Green is the ring around, Love / Ring: Ring around a town of Love / Christian Scorn: Christian scorn is worn, Bye Love / Weary Worn: Weary worn, torn to shreds of build Love / God is Love: God is intrigued with Love / Where's your Hub?: Your hub's here in Love / Express Your Dare: Express the dare to express your ware to Love / At Being, More: Lets bring ring, more, Love / Elect the Share: Elect this share of Love / Ignore The Whore: Sore to ignore? The whore's babbled on, has gone to Love / The Bride: Has come blustery will gone away, a bride has come to Love / Elective: Run free to run an elective son to Love / Cranberry Red: Let cranberry red be, let to a prima meal of Love / The Islands: The islands fine in me and my believe in Love / Ascend: Willing's left, Ascend's been bet on Love / Blue: Blue by blew to Love / Of Love: Of Love, yet, yes, Love / Stand: Stand on in Love / Cranberry: Cranberry pleasure, Love / Raspberry: Raspberry pie by slice to Love / Blueberry: Blueberry will hill a tummy filled with best of Love / Strawberry: Strawberry feeled of Love / Cranberry: Cranberry sky gone loose to Love / Pineapple: Pineapple pied by up one side to Love / Mango: Mango my Love / Peach: All peach pies burst in Love / Guava: Metatron's guava stand, a plan to unveil Love / Boysenberry: Heals of boysenberry I Am our plan to less than Love / Blackberry: Blackberry healed by a seed trust of growing Love / Green: Green on dream of Love / Dream: Dream of on to Love / In Pink: In pink, blend, to Love / Green: God's gone green and pink to Love / Grace: And grace graced Love / And Race: God's in race of Love / Trees: Trees believe in Love / Only: Great only feed by Love / Spools: And spools abound in Love / Pills: Pills melt wet to neglect of Love / Be: Be, we, Love / Around Me: Around me be, Love / And Happy

Frills: And happy frilled by Love / Love's: Love's elect is rest in Love / Elegance: Elegance won by a rest in Love / Lesson: Learned lesson I've learned is god is Love / We Fight: Less We fight less, this address, to Love / Flight-full: Bound flight-full I'm found, bound by Love / Hurting Yearned: Hurting yearned for rest in Love / Living Friend: God's living friend, a blend of Love / Heady-ness: Heady-ness held by Love / Homeward Trend: Homeward trend to end in Love / God's Delight: God's a delight in Love / Electric Dress: Pleasant address, an electric dress of Love / My Address: Let us be born to a new address worn by Love / 341: Love 341, our Love / 3.14: 3.14 more than Love / More: More to ignore? Than, Love / Love to: Yes, Love to Love.

CHAPTER 46 / LOVE MIRAGES: More, Yes!: More than yes! we Love / 3 Please: Let 3 please our need to Love / Next, Weeze: Let next, weeze by to Love / Well Done: Well it's done, in Love / Max Run: Max run home to Love / Fan Design: Fan's design is Love / Line In Time: Line in time to Love / Never Exclude: Never exclude your Love / All-ways Exude: Let us all-ways exude only Love / Know the Tune: Know the tune, always exude, Love / All One: All One friend in Love / All Loved By Me: All I loved was we'd be met by free to Love / Only One: Only One wave, Love / Fifty Now: Fifty now to how to 5 times 10 hour Love / Welcome, How?: Welcome now, How? Love / One Love: One Love leads to God, the camp of doves in Love / Eternal: Eternal feel of Love / And How: And how we Love / God's Son: God's own son, a universe of Love. When? When can I? Love / How Can: How can we be filled by less than Love / Ken: When Ken's when Light ends at Love / When?: Now when is now, Love / How Can You?: How can you feel? Love / Borders: Borders bet on lessen Love / Delaware: God's Delaware declare of Love / Bare: Christ bare to Love / Internalized: 3 times found, internalized by Love / Impugned: Impugned a moon of rest in buddhic room called deliverance. Love / Women: Women be brave in a womb of caves of Love / Eternalized: Eternalized stride to Love / Impaled: Impaled welled to Love / Mens Free: Mens free of mince in me to Love / Embarked: Embarked on arced 2 Love / Forgave: Forgave us, Love / Exude: Exude a mood of Love / Of Life We Give: Let life we live be give in Love / On Love We Live: On life we live in give to Love / A Doving Coo: A Dove coos for Love / A Cooing Hurl: A cooing hurl at who you are by a guard of Love / A Hurling Woo: A hurl in woo of Love / A Worthy Dance: Worthy the dance to Love / A Welcome Stance: In a move to advance ours stance to welcome, Love / A Winsome Prayer: Win some prayers of Love / A Hall of Prayer: Hall of prayers in airs of Love / A Prayer-full Send: Now is a prayer-full Send to Love / Ascending Blend: An Ascending blend of when. Love / Assigned A stare: Assigned a stare at a star of care for Love / Universal Love: Universal? Love / Love's Reversal: Love's rehearsal is reel reversal of the film called Love / A Giving Rehearsal: Life's giving rehearsal is reversal to Love / Gorgeous Set: Instant replay on a gorgeous set of Love / Set of Strands: Set a strands of pearls enhanced, by a choke-less thank

of Love / Strands of Pearl: Great strands of mother's pearl of Love / Pearls of Man: Pearls man our booth of swam to Love / Manned Intrigue: Manned by intrigue with we'd Love / A Hearty Sleeve: Hearty sleeve of give to Love / A Sleeving Sung: God's sleeving sung to Love / A Deeper Heave: Deeper the heave to believe in Love / A Heaving Rung: A heaving ring rung by Love / Feel the Need: God's feel is real in the need to feed on Love / Need to Eat: The need to eat for Love / Eat To Lift: Eat to lift you up to Love / Lift to Give: Lift to give wide-eyed Love / Give A Hoop: Give a hoop a shot at Love.

CHAPTER 47 / LOVE MORTALITY: I Found Myself: Hear I found myself, hear, in Love / Resting Space: Rest in space of full to Love / Stop: Stop sharp stabs at communication's gap, speak Love / A Nation Felt Up: Stare at a nation stored a sleep in a need to felt up to Love / An Election Sought: Election sought by wrought to Love / Solon Said: Solon said, regals read of Love / Death Met Life: Long walks meet death in life-less Love / Life Met Atlantean: Atlantis meets life in my wife of Love / Mother's Gap: Mama's gap, a nap in the mother's lap of Love / The Arc of Stop: Of Love I stop in an arc of eternal sender to Love / Stopper Pulled: The stopper's pulled, I'm full-ed with Love / Pulling Felt: Pull a felt disgrace to Light in Love / Smoke: Great smokes screen Love / Fire: Fire played by a mated called Love / Wealth: Right to wealth, Love / Streak: Heal a streak to Love / Stroke: Left to stroke, Love / Freak: Freaky field, Love / Shown: Shown anew, Love / Shillings: Shillings spent on huddling up to Love / Given: Given green Love / Grain: Grain green with Love / Genes: Genes jeaned by Love / Jilled: Jilled by healed by tallest Love / Greek: Greek to meet in me, Love / Spanish: Spanish pleasure, a flight to Love / Thermal: Thermal pleasure, a treasure heat, of Love / Hemisphere: Hemisphere here in the middle of Love / Exposed: Exposed to pulse of Love / Northern: Northern rambled southern in a phoenix and a dove to Love / Southern: Southern sent grant to Love / Western: Western motive a ride to Love / Electives: Elected votive Love / Choice: Make a choice, Love / Cleanse: Warm cleanse of Love / Use: Use less, Love / Chair: Chair chilled by Love / Seat: Seat on Love / Biscuit: Biscuit filled with jelly trimmed by Love / Boat: Boat of Love / O Live: O live streets of Love / Greened: Greened gained by Love / Grained: Grained in greet of Love / Brained: Brained powered, Love / Mound: Mountains mound us to Love / Unbound: Unbound found in Love / Gentled: Gentled treasure of Love / Chimed: Chimed in Love / Colony: A colony kept by Love / Founded: Founded by Love / Spread: Spread around, Love / Celebrated: Celebrated great, Love / Conclude: Conclude yes, Love / Commercial: Commercial measure, pleasure, Love / Poetic: Poetic vote to Love / Exotic: Exotic? Love / Riddles: Riddles read agreed to Love / Waxed: Waxed less? Love / Amazed: Amazed mint Love / Apple-Green: Apple-green seam of Love / Zenographic: Zenographic demographic to Love / Whole-list: We'd insist on the whole-list mist of Love / Crucial: Crucial creed, Love / Stereophonic: Stereophonic in our appeal to sonic, Love.

CHAPTER 48 / LOVE FLOATS: Aegean: Aegean breaks on the wave to Love / Round: Round the round of Love / Odd: Odd to bead in Love / Even: Even us, up, to Love / Unlimited: Unlimited by a limited blip to Love / Limit-less: Limit-less, Love / Dogma: Dogma dealt, Love / Religious Matters: Religious ground matters in you and our Love / Totality: Totality Love / Meaning: Meaning to be Loved / Archaic: Archaic ascend to blends of Love / Java: Java juiced by Love / Tassels: Tassels tugged by Love / Testicles: Testicles draped by Love / Mountain: Mountain mint Love / Ease: Wet ease of Love / Easement: Language found in an easement ground by Love / Pressed: Pressed in deep to Love / Intersection: Intersect regret, now, Love / Tapestry: Tapestry treat of Love / Relief: Relief in rest in Love / Folded: An original fold, 720 degreed to Love / Fold: A fold found in Love / Framed: Meta-speed framed by Love / Humbly: Humbly held in Love / Prepared: Prepared to compare to Love / Frump: Frump less, Love / Alien: Alien measure, Love / Zipped: Zipped up. Love / Original: An arcing original, Love / Laced: A sculpture laced with Love / Succulent: You succulent view of Love / Carving: God's carving Love / Madre: Madre mattered, Love / Weight-less: Weight-less, Love / Emote: Emote in a rest of Love / Bridge: Arch your eyes to bridged Love / Convinced: Convinced to Love / Frenzied: Frenzied fed the calm of Love / Proclaimed: Proclaimed the same to Love / Imperishable: Imperishable matter of Love / Transcendent: Water is transcendent to Love / Variant: Love's fuel, a variant view on Love / Spell: Man's plan to spell Love / Conducive: Light's conducive to Love / Spill: Spill in us Love / Analyzed: Analyzed rest, in Love / Sources: Sources said, Love / Intelligible: Intelligible notion, Love / Substratum: Substratum mattered, Love / Straddle: To straddle matter, Love / Theory: Theory heeled by steps to Love / Gapped: World's gapped by Love / Combination: Love's reveal a combination of rest and Love / Teeth: Teeth taled by Love / In-definitely: In-definite, I Am in-definitely won to Love / Moist: Moist meet Love / Dreamscape: Deeper scope of dreams escape to Love / Grotesque: Grotesque rest deep in Love / Acquire: Acquire hire, Love / Repulse: Repulse mulch of Love / Mathematical: Mathematic's breed, Love / Preponderance: Preponderance pruned for Love / Quantum: Take quantum leaps to Love.

CHAPTER 49 / LOVE CREATES: Exuberance: Exuberance bent to Love / Caucophany: Caucophany sound of discordant, Love / Elocutive: Electrocate less than elocutive best in Love / Evolve: Soul's evolve gone strange to will to Love / Emotive: Invest in insist on emotive Love / Power: Matrix power, Love / Will-full: Will-full, free, to Love / Cellular: God's cellular phone? Love / Structured: Message structured in massaging meet by Love / Matrix: Matrix met Love / Integrate: Integrate rate of Love / Keyed: Gems keyed 2 Love / Crystalline: Love's crystalline hue, you in Love / Ametrine: Ametrine dream of Love / Megatime: Megatime rhyme of Love / Maternine: Purple gleam of maternine Love / Astroline: An astroline inside our Love / Esperide: Esperide your exasperate inside our Love / Acturide: Act your ride to Love / Escape: Escape's glide to Love

/ Inferred: Infrared thread inferred by Love / Enter pad: Enter pad of interpretive read by Love / Afternoon: After noon, Love / Anderban: And your band of *Anderban? Love. *Along new days expend right bays of ascendant news of Love / Passage: God's passage meant Love / Message: Message met in wet to Love / Flowed: Love's flowed heal to a wheeled by Love / Funneled: Funneled few found in Love / Processed: Processed peeled by Love / Quest: Quest quelled by Love / Memorable: Memorable matter, Love / Wiped: Wiped out rust, the ex, of Love / Priestess: Priestess of dove in Love / Legendary: Legendary measure, Love / Vortex: Vortex viewed in you in Love / Scotters: Scotters cute in a hoot of Love / Lunch: Lunch late? Love / Cloud: Cloud sprung up to Love / Clear: Clear through transparent, Love / Extant: Extant grant to Love / Backdrop: Backdrop in Love / Speculate: Intense to speculate of Love / Courier: Courier sent to Love / Intrinsic: Crystalline intrinsic to Love / Bimini: Bimini beat by Love / Atlantis: Atlantis serene in Love / Atlantic: Atlantic treasure casey measure, Love / Trash: Trash less, Love / Caped: Caped in a drape to Love / Crusade: Crusade raid on Love / Devote: Devote float stones to Love / Dragons: Dragons deal in wheel of Love / Straw: Great straw break in Love / Realities: Realities reel for Love / Denial: Repose denial to a trial, Love / Impose: Fish impose from your panty hose and Love / Settlement: Love's settlement meant, to Love / The Loft: Arcs of lofts to Love / Mingles: Love mingles soft in Love / Only: Only you can new you perfect Love / Furious: Fury felt in a hurting melt to perfect Love / Unconditional Life: Unconditional lives in Love / Warmed: Warmed by breaths of Love / Beforing: Beforing choring, Love.

CHAPTER 50 / LOVE FREEDOMS: Emerge: Emerge in a merge to Love / The Boat: Vote for a boat to Love / The Note: Birth not, Love / The Wile: Deep in wile, while? Love / The Euphrates: Euphoric, Euphratic, Love / The Tigris: A tigris branch to Love / Amazon: Left amazon to get on to Love / New: New in view of Love / Euphoric: Euphoric, you know it, Love / Ohio: Ohio held mound of Love / Chicago: Chicago sent yellow to Love / Illinois: Illinois wet with an ancient serpent, Love / Colorado: Colorado curl, to Love / Ganges: Ganges green to a perpendicular view of Love / Four Times: 4 times round, our Love / Seasons: Seasons sent to Love / Quarters: Quarters paid to arcades of communicative rounds of lOVE / Directions: Left directions to Love / Fore: Foreways to Love / Foreskin: Review foreskinned growth to circumcise-less Love / Fork: Fork amid our Love / Fornicate: Fornicate's plate refilled by Love / Flake: Flake of Love / Bake: Baked good, Love / Curse: Curse worse? Love / Worse: Worse than this? Kiss, Love / Chet: Chet bet a fret on Love / Chat: Chat up a cup of Love / Learn: Learn to yearn for a turn to Love / Driven: Over driven, I'm liven Love / Given: Given greeting, Love / Livid: Livid lid on? Off, to Love / Squalid: Squalid pallor met in vats of perfect Love / Tested: Deepen tested waters, emote wrote, Love / Loss: A perfect loss, the toss to less than Love / Probe: Probe home to Love / Sun: Sun of sum, Love / Love: Love let Love / Dove: Dove barred bast in Love / Barred: Barred alert, hurt, by lessen Love / Car-red: Car-red by a ferry to Love / Rewarded: Rewarded bread of Love / Forgiven: Forgiven in Love / Faith: Grace-full faith of Love / Grace: Grace a place with Love / Mercy: Mercy met wet by Love / Wheel: Wheel of heal in Love / Reel: Reel feel of winding up in Love / Thought: Thought a fit was Love / Roots: Roots acute in Love / Change: Change a range of Love / Flux: Flux enough to Love / Mixed: Mixed enough to Love / Exist: Exist in best we Love / Evolve: Lessons evolve in Love / Darwin's Call: Darwin's call is all we heed to Love / Begal: Begal believed in Love / Regal: Heed rest regal to Love / Pore: Pore pave over less Love / Passage: Passage of smell in Love / Modern: Modern met in bet in Love / Field: Field found deep in a spin of Love / Research: Research rest in hush, now, Love / Study: Study rest in liberal Love.

CHAPTER 51 / LOVE FORGED: Brazil: Brazil met a Portuguese soft drip to Love / Portuguese: Portuguese please of Love / Sonnet: Sonnet sunny to Love / Browning: Browning met in us and lift to Love / Topped: Topped atop our Love / Cream: Mountains cream green with Love / Sugar: Sugar is sweeter in the medicine called Love / Milk: Milk felt wide to Lighter Love / Silk: Silk enough? Love / Spoon: Spoon fed deep to relief in Love / Steam: Steamy trend to end in Love / Lands: Delight-full lands of stands in Love / Brew: Mother met brew in you of Love / Society: Hungry to a society schemed by Love / Birth: Birthing bet mary met was Love / Critical: Critical matter? Love / Penned: Penned a friend to Love / Astronomical: Know astronomical release, of Love / Order: Deep in release is order believed by Love / Trend: Trend within, our Love / Meteorological: Meteorological bet of Love / Totality: Totality measured by Love / Blend: Great blend of within, Love / Hieratical: Hieratical approach to radical, Love / Foreign: Foreign found in Love / Fluent: Fluent filled of Love / Lingual: Lingual limbed, Love / La Lingua: Create a language, tongued by Love / Tongue: Tongue been trilled by Love / Syrup: Syrup sent to a hint of Love / Watered: Great watered breed of Love / Wilt: Wilt thou? Love / Know: Know enough, Love / Seize: Seize a hush, Love / Deigned: Deigned begun, Love / Dug: Dug enough? Love / Question: Question quelled by Love / Tate: Tate date? Love / Late: Late to date our Love / Burg: Burg herd, Love / Bardic: Bardic bet on Love / Card: Card been heeled by Love / Kelp: Kelp agreed to feed, Love / Help: Help us head to Love / Whaled: Whaled enough deep in a flush to Love / Dolphined: Dolphined dent at Love / Manateed: Manateed agreed to Love / Agreed: Agreed to breast of Love / Turtled: Turtled trimmed by direct, to Love / Custom: Custom cringed by Love / Drawn: Drawn in, to Love / Flamboyant: Flamboyant blend of thin to Love / Polite: Polite enough to Love / Color-full: Color-full hush of Love / Youth-full: Youth-full yes, Love / Set: Left set to Love / Striking: Great enough, striking, struck by Love / Classic: Dare be classic, Love / Artsy: Let artsy be healed by held in pens of stylish Love / Smart: Smart enough to hunt, Love / Stylish: Lesson stylish by Love / Struck: Struck inside by Love / Charming: Charming met

charisma yet? In Love / Charisma: In Love healed, charisma willed to breathe, Love.

CHAPTER 52 / LOVE DUAL: Love: Fun begun, Love / Life: Life fed by Love / Triner: Triner in time to Love / Live: Life to live in Love / Give: Give to Love / Lived: Lived led to Love / Junior: Junior's jeaned by Love / Seen: Seen some? Love / Fact: Decent in fact, Love / Extra: Extra matter, Love / Act: Sum act, Love / Extreme: Extreme exceed to Love / Regime: Regime rung free of Love / Road: Road to go to Love / Ride: Ride home now to Love / Reside: Reside inside, Love / Way: Way home weaned by Love / Rely: Rely on a ride to Love / Ran: Ran to runs of Love / Honed: Honed on you and Love / Honeyed: Honeyed held, Love / Run: Run home now to Love / Drips: Drips drip to deep and steep to Love / Release: Stepped release of timely, Love / Appellate: Appellate mattered, Love / Sell It: Sell it, hear, Love / Tend: Tend to your Love / Three: Three be Love / More: More or less, Love / Four: Four more, Love / Field It: Field a plan to end in Love / Bake It: Bake a plant of pensive Love / Hike It: Hiking in to Love / Loved: Loved led less to Love / When: When? Begin to love / Ascend: God's ascend begins my own to Love / Rose-red: Rose-red invent of read it, Love / Re-invent: Re-invent the rest, nest, of Love / Remit: Remit rest to us who love / Speculate: Speculate trail to Lighter frails to love / Spectral: Spectral pleasure's infinite measure, the pleasure, of Love / Dove: Dove done in Love / Re-design: Gain re-design of a gown worn to Love / Real Feel: Real feel of Love / Reveal: Reveal bells of appeal to Love / Specially: Specially gained by Love / Plenty: Grow plenty of Love / Bulb's: A bulb's rest is a breath of Light, as Love / Wrapped: Offer a wrapped rush to unfold in Love / Pact: A higher pact, Love / Higher: Often higher than Love / Rim: Rim run to Love / Rend It: Rend it read in a balconic test of west to Love / Paper: Paper penned up to Love / Entonces: Entonces then, to Love / Sixty: Sixty said, Love / Exact: Exact I mint to a mine of Love / Hear: Hear where we Love / Make It: Left to make it right to Love / Melt It: Met it melted, Love / Re-Design: Left to recline in a re-Design of Love / Re-Evaluate: Re-evaluate great Love / Designate: Designate your date with a drive to Love / The Plate: The plate of 8 enough, Love.

CHAPTER 53 / LOVE DOORS: Offered: Offered a rush to hush our Love / Offerings: Offerings hint at a glance at Love / Ionic: Ionic said brand golden in Love / Sing: Light, I will sing, of Love / Signed: Signed as such, America say, Love / Divined: Divined a friend to Love / Dated: Dated weighted less, by Love / Related: Related rest in perfectly Love / Carbonic: God's carbonic is us in Love / Lit: Lit by a friend in Love / Bit: Bit clear through to Love / Tip: Tip a touch to Love / Moist..Moist in a luff of a sail to Love / Ridden: Souls ridden hidden to Love / Side: Side 2 side of Love / Island: Know sole in an island of less-than a stand in Love / Guide: Guide me to say soul-matrix gone to the Light of Love / Bimini: Bimini is bent on a mission sent to Love / Scene: Scene to ground our Love / Slip: Slip to a dip in Love / Plenty:

Plenty of punch in Love / Arcturus: Arcturus sent heat to melt the hot street to Love / Trip: Left on a trip to Love / Sip: Sip up, Love / Sigh: Sigh by, Love / Good Buy: God's grant to good is to a buy of Love / Sweet: Sweet enough to Love / Good Bye: Good Bye to Love less Love / Deep: Two deep in Love / Betting: Betting on you in Love / Be: Be with me in Love / Buy: Buy a bow of Love / Choose: Choose to Love / Choice: Choice to rest in Love / Resonant: Resonant rest in a voice gave less to forget to Love / Voice: Voice found? Now, Love / Leap: Leap home to Love / Deeper: Deeper still to Love / Drive: Drive a tribe to Love / Alive Yet?: Alive yet? Love / Regenerative: Regenerative rind to Love / Essentially: Essentially we are scent to Love / Ecstatic Ecstatic matter Love / Dramatic: Dramatic finish to I Am Love / Traumatic: God's less most dramatic in lightly traumatic Love / Emphatic: Emphatic emphasis on a dramatic kiss called Love / Aligned: Aligned a dove to penetrate us who Love / Found: Found aground our Love / Good By: Good by this, Love / Goodness: Goodness knows, Love / Expressive: Expressive bet, to Love / Publish: Publish plenty of Love / Sedona: Sedona set to Cancun blue Love / Sign: Sign a line to Love / Sine: Sine of the time to Love / Rhymed: Rhymed to a time of Love / Wound: Wound abound, Love / Woven: Woven wand of Love / Purge: Purge emerge to Love / Spoken: Spoken to be in Love / Provoking: Provoking felt melt in Love / Emotish: Emotish votive, Love / Divinely: Divinely I said to Love / Diagnose: Diagnose most, our Love.

CHAPTER 54 / LOVE SEVERAL: Deal: Deal with less? Love / Appeal: Appeal to feel Love / Reveal: Reveal to a feel for Love / Leer: Leer at a sneer for Love / Term: Term to learn of Love / Desire: Desire to hear of Love / Express: Express our best in Love / Low To Go?: Low to go? To Love / Less: Less this less than Love / Best: Best to beam, Love / Better: Better to be believe in Love / Wetter: Wetter, better, the surf to Love / West: West the pace to Love / Waves: Waves of willed healed our Love / Ways: Ways to wed our Love / Wade: Wade on in to Love / Loved: Loved to be in view of Love / Filled: Filled a fluff with Love / Finned: Finned, thinned, a float of Love / Vibed: Vibed born ablend our Love / Resonation: Resonation of rate to Love / Resin: Resin's reside in a ravinic glide to Love / Revealed: Revealed a burst of Love / Sole-d: Sole-d solo less to Love / Sealed: Light sealed, Loved / Trait: Trait straight to Love / Trick: Trick's seal, Love / Tryst: Try a tryst with Love / Regret: Got regret? Reflect on refract to Love / Fit: Fit to a fee paid by Love / Sold: God sold us to Love / Sealant: Sealant sealed by Love / Trust: Slaves of trust to Love / Met: Met a bet to Love / Bit: In a bit of Love / Trick: Trick a treat to tell the truth in Love / Dove: Dove's a deal for Love / Like: Like a seal to life in Love / Magic: Magic melt, in Love / Field: Field afloat our Love / Millet: Millet eat in Love / Mill-It: Mill-it deep in Love / Stood: Stood around our Love / Bike: Bike back to Love / Magical: A magical meet in Love / Feel It: Feel it felled to Love / Shine: Shine astound? Love / Shone: Shone a strand of Love / Shown: Foundation seen in Shown Love / Steel: Steel your set to Love / Steal It: Stealing

less, steal it, best with a matrix of Love / Covenant: Covenant kinned by Love / Sovereign: Sovereign scene of Love / Melt: Melt a bit of Love / Bake It: Bake it deep in Love / Meet It: Meet it, in me, Love / Melt It: Melt a bonnet to wear in Love / Met It: Metatronic met it, Love / Rend It: Rend a rate of in It, Love / Sell It: Sell it seen to Love / Tend It: Tend it, a trend, to Love / Plato: Plato's plate full of Love / Iliad: Iliad lid is off to Love / Santorini: Santorini's been seen to Love.

CHAPTER 55 / LOVE SETTLES: Grip: Grip aground our Love / Training: Training trait to Love / Gleaning: Gleaning let us leaning be to Love / Living: Living leave? Love / Healing: Healing held up, to, Love / Hot: Hot enough to Love / Cold: Cold to seem to Love / Warm: Warm enough to met by Love / Zoned: Zoned one code : Love / Space: Space spent on vent to Love / Attend: Attend a manner to Love / Trained: Trained ascend to blend with Love / Accept: Accept a set of a better bet to Love / Cleared: Cleared up by Love / Winds: Winds swilled west to best by Love / Climate: Climate clipped by Love / Metallic: Metallic's measure clipped by Love / Impass: Impass pent by Love / Passe: Passe way? Love / Impassive: Impassive measured? Love / Essential: Found a friend is an essential end to beginning Love / Absolve: Absolve, resolve, Love / Solve: Solve enough? Simply found the answer in perfect Love / Tested.. Twisted, tested, Love / Found: Found a friend in Love / Round: Round the land rang Love / Grounded: Grounded in a town called Love / Intrigue: Drip intrigue to Love / Mead: Mead's bead is a drop on Love / Need: Need a budge? Love / Lead: Lead your raid on less-than Love / Lines: Lines drip clean in Love / Drip: Drip a trip to lifting tides of Love / Trilling: That trilling feeling is Love / Sill: Sill aseat our windowed treat called Love / Lace: Lace in the face of Love / Place..Drip a place to filling up with Love / Traded: Traded around? Stand your ground with the kindest pick, Love / Spaced: Spaced, erased, effaced, Loved / American: The American plan is man is Love / Plan: Plan to be Loved / Meals: Meals to eat are neat in Love / Base: Home to the base called Love / Race: Race to be blessed by Love / Taste: Taste the breast of Love / Ant: Catch an ant with honeyed Love / Ample: An ample matter, Love / Brand: A brand to view is who LOVES / Peril: Peril's appeal can heal Love / Apparel: Wear your Love / Full-fill: Full-fill your need to Love / Under: Under stood by Love / Hand: Hand over Love / Land: Land again in Love / Branded: Branded by basically Love / Reef: Reef run by a coral bred by Love / Brief: Wear more than brief Love / Grief: Grief gone? Good for Love / Talk: Talk to where we Love / Trade: An even trade trust for Love / Blend: Blend ascend to Love / Break: Break ahead to Love / Access: Access best to Love / Agree: Agree to Love.

CHAPTER 36 / LOVE SEALED: Speaker: A speaker spoke of only Love / Spoken: A spoken dream is Love / Bow: Bow to how we Love / Gif's: Gif's give to Love / Rift: A rift aligned with perfect Love / Column: Column measured by perfect Love / Tower: God's perfect Light applied to sight of a tower of perfect

Love / Aisle: Aisle Love you eternally / Track: Track on back to Love / Pack: Pack yourself full of Love / Engineer: Engineer our bridge to Love / Foreign: Foreign found in a town local to Love / Sovereign: Sovereign send to a friend in Love / Strayed: Strayed around? Come home to Love / Vacillate: Vacillate quickly to only Love / Feline: Feline found in a hound to Love / Egypt: Egypt sent extent of Love / Bastat: Bastat sought real lynx to Love / Curls: Curls feel fresh in Love / Elect: Gone to elect in Love / Express: Grant express to Love / Expression: An expression set to Love / Brick: Brick built sticks to Love / Cat: Cat sat on Love / Pamphlet: Pamphlet read Love / Family: God's head of the Family of Love / Musician..Musician mentioned the sum of sun of Love / Physician: Physician healed the wars on Love / Bangkok: Bangkok bend to an orchid of Love / Thai: Thai fed me arcs of Love / Vamp: I fell for a vamp of a lesser degree than we can see of Love / Empire..An empire's hire is Love / Singer: Singer sent to deliver us from less than all is Love / Princess: Princess pined for heights of all we Love / Saigon: Saigon's zen is Love / Light On: Light on to Love / Common: Common ground is Love / Caulk: Caulk around with Love / Hearted: Hearted found by Love / Vortex: Vortex formed when we warmed to Love / Toys: Toys aim to please our alliance to Love. / Boundary: Boundary found in a town without edges and lots of all we Love / Spun: Spun round to Love / Shower: Shower clean with Love / Met: Met you hear near Love / Drain: Drain done? Love / Dogs: Dogs day? Roll over to Love / Tubed: Tubed around our trend to Love / Tubing: A tubing run, Love / Spine: A spine align is Love / Hose: Hose knows the tubes of Love / Electric: Electric wired to higher Love / Publish: Publish now your divinity to Love / Reap: God's reap is us in Love / Sow: Sow the seeds of how you Love / Rape: The rape tape is unreeled by Love / Tape: Tape a strip to Love / Secondary: A secondary measure, treasure, first: Love / Dignitary: Dignitary dew is the tear in Love / Sled: Sled slid in to drifts of all one Love / Community: Community held together by alliance in Love / Auction: An auction held to Love / Grand: Grand, the plan, to Love / Vizier: Mount Helen's vizier says hey to Love.

CHAPTER 57 / LOVE FUNDED: Theorist: Theorist thrilled by healed by the explain of Love / Banked: Banked on you in Love / Ticket: A ticket home to own Love / Bigot: Bigot-ry sealed the tree from Love / Tree: Tree of triple divinity in Love / Resolve: Resolve to solve our Love / Resolute: God's matter is resolute to Love / Radiate: Radiate great anticipate of Love / Gardens: Gardens of sod to a green God of Love / Top: Top of you, the view, to Love / Dirt: Dirt hurt? Heal your mirth with Earth and Love / Beer: Beer debt? Love / Youth: Youth gone to give to adult Love / Intuitively: Intuitively done to Love / Gratifying: Gratifying measure the treasure to great full Ego: Ego said, bet on less, than Love / Tea: Tea, brie, cracked wide to Love / Coffee: Coffee stained by less than Love / Destiny: Destiny done, One, Love / Arrive: Arrive at thrive in Love / Unencumbered: An unencumbered number, Love / General: A general measure to pleasure the place of Love / Problematic: A problematic

dramatic Love / Today: Today say we are Love / Four Fathers: Four Fathers in fest of sentimental Love / Forehead: Forehead can head to found by a Light of Love / Four Play: Four play to Love / Bread: Bread bedded by Love / Flock: A flock flew to you in Love / Flick: A flick found around our move to Love / Flip: A flip found around our sound of Love / Flown: Flown alone? Love / Float: Float to a loan of Love / Beyond: Beyond begin to Love / Basket: A basket borne home to Love / Stipend: A stipend sent to Love / Pay: Do not pay for Love / Club: Club cuffed to Love / Letter: Letter led to written about our Love / Share: Share a care of Love / Square: Square by feel, your Love / Adventure: Adventure's sent to Love / Circle: Circle sound met by Love / Speared: Speared by us to direct to Love / Headed: Headed in sounds of Love / Daily Debt: Daily debt, Love / Light: Life Light? Love / Lofty: Lofty live in Love / Steering: Steering set to a seat in Love / Rally: Rally around your Love / Themes: Themes won ring of Love / Dues: Due's paid? Love / Challenge: Challenge chilled by Love / Encourage: Loving encourage is the courage of Love / Dismantle: Life's dismantle is Love / Flourish: Often I flourish at dismantle of Love, / Delights: Delights flight, Love / Pregnant: Light is pregnant with Love / Poured: Poured enough out? Receive Love / Pause: Pause enough to squeeze your Love / Applause: Applause is met with resounding Love / Ordained: Stay ordained in Love / Abominable: Abominable bet the snow was wet to Love / Mope: Mope in a cope with Love.

CHAPTER 58 / LOVE FINDS: Paleolithic: Paleolithic Light is ancient advent to went to Love / Trodden: Trodden trend to a path within our Love / Treads: Treads ahead to Love / Triple: Triple treat to all Love / Bred: bred on best, we Love / Triple: Triple treat of Love / Threads: Threads snap deep to Love / Love: Love led to we are be in Love / Taboo: Taboo to less in Love / Terrific: Terrific two sent to Love / Terror: A confide for the terror's abide in perfect align with back to Love / Deliberate: Deliberate on great Love / Century: Century seen in heal our dream of Love / Baffle: Baffle waffled to our Love / Torso: Torso meant by Love / Well-Bred: Well-bred bid on Love / Greek: Greek to start our heart to Love / Feminine: Feminine filled by Love / While: While we were, we were, to Love / Crustacean: Crustacean nation breaks the shells of Love / Indian: Indian welled by a flood to Love / Jewel: Jewel viewed by Love / Concubine: Concubine mine, gone, to Love / Embroider: Embroider order to Love / Hurried: Hurried out to Love / Sultan: Sultan's fan, a harem spanned to yes, we, Love / Laborious: Laborious means is over to Love / Less: Less is more in Love / More: More, more, more for Love / Sexy: Sexy, yes, in deliverance of the steps to Love / Sexed: Sexed up to participate in great Love / Snore: Snore ignore? Love / Seal: Sealing sent two Love / Venetian: Venetian bland? Go scan your canals of Love / Blonde: Blonde to a blend of entering in to Love / Stallion: Stallion found, in canters of Love / Come: Come to meet me in Love / Keep: Keep up, Love / Protocol: Protocol all? Find, Love / Goddess: Goddess said to feed my head to the heart of Love / Guard: Guard good? Let it down, to, Love / God's..God's white? Trust more than that: lots of colors to choose: one Light. Love / Test: Test trust, Love / Sordid: Sordid fed by less than Love / Forget: Forget a fend to Love / Allow: Allow enough to Love / Adult: Adult view of Love / Legitimate: Legitimate news of whose amuse is this in Love / Feel: Feel fields of Love / Adamant: An adamant matter, Love / Faith: Faith enough two Love / Fire: A fire fed to Love / Fireplace: Fireplace few? Know the blaze of Love / Tooled: A tooled touch of Love / Found: Found a friend in Love / Money: Money met in renew of Love / Town: Town found deep in Love / Confused: Confused fuss? HUSH: Love / Confute: Confute mute to Love / Conjugate: Conjugate late to Love / Create: Create is the state of Love / Creation: Creation's friend of Love / Cessation: Cessation of less in Love / Despite: Despite right to left to Love.

CHAPTER 59 / LOVE FOUND: Knew: Knew true in Love / Temporal: A temporal few, the hue of Love / Spatial: Spatial splattered mattered most in Love / Tempo: Tempo tempted by Love / Temporary: A temporary few in Love / Sadistic: Sadistic said we need to head for softer Love / Declare: Declare the nation of Love / Deflower: Deflower the hour of minute-less Love / Whooped: Whooped to a song of Love / Brothel: Brothel brewed in stealing hue of Love / Canned: Canned to a brand of stand for Love / Abhor: Abhor the invest in lessened Love / Lessons: Lessons lanced by Love / Embodied: Embodied by stayed in Love / Exceed: Exceed in us, Love / Impede: Impede's cede to Love / Formative: Formative flew to perfect Love / Inform: Inform frowned on lessened express of Love / Alchemy: Alchemy swelled to Love / Autonomous: Autonomous said let's Love / Sovereign: Sovereign seen in love / Reign: Reign ran to Love / Eternal: Eternal merge in Love / Gift: Gift of give and receive is Love / Theology: Theology found on Love / Impulse.. Impulse penned on Love / Impress: Impress pressed to set on Love / Excess: Excess to a dress of Love / Exceeded: Exceeded to a friend called Love / Read: Read, rest, Love / Theologian: Theologian thinned by Love / Red: Red hearts bloom in Love / Ready: Ready to trust our Love / Rest Us: Rest us, in Love / Blissed: Stand in blissed deliverance to Love / Blessed: Blessed a space with Love / Rhyme: Rhyme rimmed by Love / Shine: Shine fine to Love / Shown: Shown ascend to a heightened friend called Love / Shield: Shield a field with Love / Republic: Republic's friend to Plato's perfect ascend to transcendent Love / Placed: Placed apace our Love / Ahead: Ahead we've fed our Love / Non-ego: Non-ego gained to Love / Ego: Ego gave up to Love / Ergo: Ergo grained by Love / Unicorn: Unicorn moon of a mystic noon called Love / Stag: Stag stand is a land of dimpled Love / Snag: Snag smoothed on Love / Luna: Luna loomed over Love / Moony: Moony to the moody side of Love / Phased: The moon of phased by two too Love / Impericists: Impericists insist on less than Love / Release: Release rush to Love / Desist: Desist less, Love / Factored: Factored friend of in to the maximum trim of Love / Letter: Letter in a Grecian key of Love / Laddered: Laddered matter, Love / Gladder: Gladder got mattered to glee in Love / Babylon: Babylon's blend of in to Love / Test: Test taste, Love / Hot: A hot hut, Love / Heat: Heat's beat is Love / Super-Liminal: Super-liminal the criminal of less in Love.

CHAPTER 60 / LOVE FUELED: Avoid: Avoid a rush to Love / Annoyed: Annoyed knelt at felt by Love / Need: Need renewed by an electric view of Love / Ovoidic: Ovoidic avoid is Love / Archaic: Archaic metallic of Love / Tempt: Tempt a taste of Love / Tramped: Tramped on trumped by Love / Maiden: Maiden voyaged, Love / Mythlogic: Mythlogic magic is Love / Mythologize: Mythologize your wise to Love / Trait: Trait to a trend of Love / Proselytize: Proselytize wise one to Love / Tie: Tie one up to Love / Purring: Purring pewed by Love / Curing: Curing cued by Love / Curl: An elegant curl to Love / Empirical: An empirical matter, Love / Bases: Bases run? Love / Profit: Profit perfect to protect your Love / Judge: Judge a few less than Love / Jury: Jury out? Shout, Love / Proportion: Proportion pewed by alignments view of perfect balance. Love / Apportion: Apportion's abortion? All or nun? Just Love / Primal: Primal pen in the hand of Love / Canyon: Canyon crazed by filling up with Love / Cart: Cart a part of all you Love / Project: Exacting a price to a project pressed by Love / Lick: Lick the stress of less than Love / Flowers: Flowers found in petals of Love / Seduce: Seduce enough? Love / Fornicating: Fornicating's date with Love / Feel: Feel felt by Love / Tantalize: Tantalize a taste of a test called Love / Titillate: Titillate a rate in Love / Arouse: Arouse applause with a cause called Love / Middle: Middle men, when, Love / Ages: Ages waged at Love / Age-less: Age-less Loved / Sexuality: Sexuality sent to Love / Touch: Touch a fresh approach to Love / Moan: Moan alone? Knot less. Love / Grant: Grant me to Love / Grasp: Grasp a neat feat to Love / Chew: Chew all through chews of Love / Masticate: Masticate a taste of a race to Love / Finger: Finger fed to a bred by Love / Flow: Flow enough to Love / Flaunt: Flaunt your flint to a glint of Love / Flounce: Flounce a bounce to an ounce of Love / Strip: Strip stress away from Love / Whore: Whore ignored? Love / Sex Appeal: Self esteem's sex appeal is Love / Straight: Straight to a trust of Love / Gay: Displaced? Be gay to Love / Way: Still your wedded way to bliss in Love / Whoopie: Whoopie found in Love / The D.I.C.K: The date in case you know is Love / Drill: A tone drilled by Love / Oil: Oil spill, heal, home, Love / Deepest: Deepest drift from the lip of Love / Oral: Oral found aground our Love / Anal: Anal platter? Matter-less Love / Penetrate: Penetrate deep inside our less of Love / Rate: Rate deep to Love.

CHAPTER 61 / LOVE PROGRAMS: Vibrant: Vibrant view of where we Love / Varied: Varied view of chemical accrue in Love / Various: Various matters of Love / Void: Void viewed by Love / Physical: Physical field of hilled to Love / Fit: Fit elicit, to Love / Filled: Filled to fits of Love / Flipped: Flipped a flunk of a hip to Love / Fur: Fur field of Love / Fair: Fair spare: Love / Fare: Fare s spare to Love / Spare: Spare to fair in Love / Rates: Rates set on Love / Race: Race along our Love / Sneakers: Sneakers instill a secret to lessen Love / Borders: Border's bet on better edge of Love / Order: Order penned with Love / Menus: Menu's friend is Love / Limbs: Limbs large enough to climb upon, Love / Than:

Than us, Love / Ball: Ball bounced to Love / Interview: Interview knew to ask of Love / Apply: Apply often? Love / Olive: Olive free, our Love / Sacred: Sacred send to Love / Allure: Allure demure to Love / Glamour: Glamour's spin to in Love / Elevate: Elevate lift to Love / Escalate: Escalate to fate's release on Love / Incarcerate: Incarcerate rate is released on Love / Stare: Stare at us in Love / Spare: Spare declare of Love / Dare: Dare to spare our Love / Bare: Deft to a Bare repair of Love / Bereave: Bereave meant hint to release of Love / Alleviate: Alleviate rude to Love / Exampled: Exampled scent of Love / Sample: Sample thin? Love / Spare: Spare a pair too Love / Extreme: Extreme extend to Love / Seem: The seem team is in Love / Spare: Spare fare, Love / Steer: Steer near, Love / Near: Near us, Love / Necessary: Necessary view of Love / Literally: Literally intermittent to Yes! Then, Love / Filial: Filial felt at the belt of wed in Love / Fair: Fair pair of Love / Raft: Raft back to Love / Pave: Pave matter in golden Love / Eastern: Eastern trend to within Love / Western: Western weld of meld Love / Tree: Tree true to Love / True: True enough to Love / Red: Red stead of Love / Increase: Increase your rate of great Love / Rafter: Rafter ruled to Love / Express: Express rest to Love / Teresa: Teresa knew less than news in Love / Trade: Trade your tread to slip-less Love / Risk: Risk great stuff, Love / Tongue: Tongue tamed by Love / Grace: Grace grew in Love / Hope: Hope knew better Love.

CHAPTER 62 / LOVE PEALED: Worded: Worded wade to Love / Wordy: Wordy waste can lessen Love / Wealthy: Wealthy wed of Love / Healthy: Healthy hint to Love / Phoned: Phoned ahead to Love / Found: Found again in Love / Around: Around town, Love / Mach: Much mach speed to Love / Speed: Speed said slow down to Love / Sped: Sped said sup in Love / Last: Last fix on Love / First: First event, Love / Exit: Exit in to Love / Bland: Bland blend? Love / Baste: Baste, taste, Love / Taste: Taste, touch, Love / Electric: 3 times electric won by Love / Pressed-ly: Pressed in pressed-ly trined by Love / Plane: Plane veined Love / Plain: Plain enough, Love / Dimension: Dimension mention, Love / Mention: Mention met, Love / Astound: Astound a pound with Love / Passive: Passive ascend to friends in Love / Starry: Starry sky of Love / Choose: Choose us, Love / Choice: Choice enough? Love / Amuse: Amuse a touch with Love / Moist: Moist met Love / Allude: Allude to rude's release of Love / Ruddy: Ruddy matter, fatter, Love / Buddy: Buddy been Loved / Vested: Vested view of Love / Invested: Invested trust in Love / Blessed: Blessed a dress in Love / Covered: Covered kinned, undressed, in Love / Her: Her mirth, Earth, Love / Puzzle: Puzzle pal, on, Love / Foot: Foot rest, Love / Feet: Feet first, Love / Style: Style filled by Love / Aggressive: Aggressive hint of Love / State: State of Love / Important: Important to be held by Love / Solid: Solid steamed by an exceptive dream of Love / Watch: Watch has wed best in Love / Watts: Yes, I Am volted to watts of Love / Contrary: Contrary to appeal to necessary airs of Love / Crafts: Let crafts ascend to heights of Love / Art: Art thou fed by Love / Smart: Smart enough to Love / Elect: Best at elect to Love / Assigned: Assigned meant to Love / Half: Half a mint of Love /

Whole: Whole enough to Love / Drink: Drink enough deep Love / Bag: Bag a bask with Love / Grate: Grate enough to loosen up the barbs of less than Love / Magazine: Magazine's mean to Love / Monthly: Monthly invent of Love / Locate: Daily locate your life in Love / Regard: Regard guard us, Love / True: True to you in a view of Love / Prophetic: Prophetic prophylactic of Love.

CHAPTER 63 / LOVE BELLS: Señora: Señora scene, Love / Señor: Señor more, Love / Señorita: Señorita brimmed to a hatted lift of Love / Gallery: Gallery timed to art in Love / Glass: Glass green, Love / Invite: Invite in Love / Songs: Songs blend in Love / Stars: Stars power our cure on Love / Systems: Systems deep in Love / Voices: Voices veiled, hush, our, Love / Earth: Earth met Love / Human: Human, Love / Blue: Blue blown wide to Love / Aqua: Aqua's view on blew to Love / Deceit: Deceit done to Love / People: People pound to Love / Exhibit: God's exhibit is exquisite to Love / Sculpt: Sculpt the softer rights to Love / Water: Water wed to a sparkling head of Love / Deco: Deco deemed to Love / Incense: Light's incense is Love / Wood: Wood you, Love?

23. Photo: Photo pulse, flash, to Love / Turn: Turn enough around to Love / Opportunity: Opportunity's neck is opening up to Love / Annual: Annual's manual Love / Pleasant: Pleasant friend, Love / Blessed: Blessed in trust and Love / Pleasure: Pleasure's event is Love / Venue: Venue renewed to Love / Gifts: Gifts of give to Love / Plan: Our plan to man our Love / Stay: Stay to play in Love / We: We are the Ones in Love / See: See us feel our Love / Venetian: Venetian vanned banned less, Love / Max: Max a mend to Love / Maximum..A maximum brand on Love / Contemporary: Contemporary trend to a traditional friend of Love / Outside: Outside to stayed in Love / Inside: Inside knew, Love / Beside: Beside my set in Love / Indexed: Indexed dent to when we Love / Work: Work wet to met by Love / Home: Home anew our Love / Clockwise: Clockwise news to Love / Trinity: Trinity crowned by Love / Major: A major move to Love / Photos: Photos filled with Love / Available: An available matter, Love / Appraisal: An appraisal found around our Love / Describe: Describe why we Loved / Apart: Apart the start of Love / A Part: A part to peel? The process of Love / Rental: Rental red filled with Love / Own: Own your own, Love / Room: Room grew to Love / Case: Case replaced to Love / Personal: Personal plan to Love / Property: Property paid to Love / Survey: Survey said, Love / Spark: Spark saved to Love / Textile: Textile shaved by Love / Document: Document done by Love.

CHAPTER 64 / LOVE RANG: Select: Select on to Love / Object: An Object bent to inspect Love / Spoken: Spoken Yes! to Love / Told: Told enough to Love / Function: Function found in Love / Fit: Fit in fit to Love / Benefit: Benefit you in Love / Begin: Begin a mix to Love / Begun: Begun to Love / Aspen: Aspen's glow in Love / Mooning: Mooning met horizon deep in Love / Chandelier: Chandelier clear to Love / Box: Crescents Boxed by Love / Throat: Throat spent on Love / Esophagus:

Esophagus shut to a whispered Love / Reconcile: Reconcile while we Love / City: City treasure measure our Love / Country: Country's hand deals of heals to Love / Letters: Letters lead us to Love / Invoiced: Invoiced choice to buy our Love / Envelopes: Envelopes vent to Love / Lettered: Lettered lead to Love / Written: Written measure of Love / Read: Read on to Love / Spectrum: Spectrum spent on a rainbow of Love / Iron: An iron found in Love / Metal: Metal bent to Love / Class-ic: Class-ic's classic shattered to lessen Love / Sand: Sand of manned by a strand called the shore of Love / Water: Water wed to our Love / Elements: Elements of sweet our chemical treat of Love / Traced: Traced home to Love / Found: Found a friend in when, Love / Delayed: Delayed such, Love / Wade: Wade in friend to Love / Escape: Escape raped less trust Love / Ape: Ape stayed stood in Love / Mimic: Mimic meant less in Love / Speak: Speak of such, Love / Sing: Sing about, Love / Retrace: Retrace space to Love / Unlace: Unlace a face, your own, to Love / Color: Color killed lessened Love / Light: Light on, Love / Love: Love led to one Love / Divine: Divine deed Love / God: God gained Love / Along: Along the sea of Love / All One: All One seen by Love / Eternal: Eternal and free in Love / Because: Because of we, we, Love / Confessed: Confessed rest in Love / Sewn: Sewn by you in Love / Sacred: Sacred to be free? Include, Love / Essential: Essentially said, Love / In Sum: In sum, sun, Love / Blessed: Blessed is set with Love / Alone: Alone with you, in, Love / Together: Together fed, Love / Ever: Ever seen? Love / Together: Together fed by Love / Ever: Ever seen yourself in Love? / Friend: Dine with a friend who LOVES / Told: Told you to look for a trail to Love.

CHAPTER 65 / LOVE FLUSH: Book One: Book one of Love / Book 3: Love 3 to be in a book of Love / Book 4: Letting in more to book 4 of Love / Book 5: Arrive book 5 at Love / Book 6: Six in tricks of Love / Book 7: Book seven matters less than Love / Book 8: Intent on 8 I'm late, four, Love / Book 9: Let 9 align with Love / Book 10: Book ten again to Love / Bone-dry: Bone's dry to Love / Bone-set: Bone-set dead, on Love / Bone-be: Bone-be broke by Love / Bone-free: Bone-free bred of Love / Sacred: Sacred scene of Love / Sub-lux: Sub-lux set to reset Love / Nerve: Nerve curve, swerve, to Love / Adjust: God's adjust, us in Love / Lumbar: Tonight's delight a flight to a lumbar lipped with Love / Cranium: Cranium creeled by a healed to Love / Sacrum: Set by an adjust set to Love / Sensation: Sensation less? Love / Vertebrae: Vertebrae brake to Love / Table: Life's a table of Love / Cradle: Cradle a rest in Love / David: David said, Love / Blessed: Blessed our set of Love / Found: Left to found of Love / Chemical: Chemical splendor of Love / Tropics: Tropics fill up with Love / Tramps: Tramps tramp-less in Love / Gypped: Gypped your set of Love / Sent: Sent ascent to lift our Love / Astound: Let us astound our round with Love / Faust: Faust fest fit by Love / Alliterative: Alliterative akin around astound aligned affective with Love / Alice: Alice stand in to wonderland in Love / Palace: Palace malice? Temple in, to Love / Pearl: A pearl curl, warm to Love / Reality: Reality red? Love / Harmony:

Harmony held in Love / Recovery: Peace-full recovery of a discovery of a discovery of Love / Create: Bamboo create of a rate to Love / Own: Own your own, Love / Communication: Communicate late? Love / Zen: Zen in grin to Love / Warranty: Warranty went west to best, our, Love / Feng Shui: Feng Shui's say is Love / Chinese: Chinese chilled by thrilled in Love / Heart: Heart held deep in heal to Love / Vibrational: Vibrational erase of a cloud burst spent on less, than Love / Energy: Energy went feet first to Love / Crystal: Crystal skill of Love / Joy: Find joy in abide in Love / Peace: Peace pent tea to more than yes in Love / Bamboo: Bamboo bin of Love / Master: Master meet seat of Love / Environment: Environment, friend, is Love / Invite: Invite insight to Love / Enable: Enable us to Love / Goodwill: Goodwill friend, is found, in Love / Defect: Defect-less, Love / Grace: Grace greets us with Love / Wing: Winging won by Love / Dimension: Dimension less to more than Love.

CHAPTER 66 / LOVE FLASH: Moment: Sautéed weighed moment fit to Love / Platform: Platform food on a buffet played noon in Love / Heady: Heady heed to we'd Love / Tapestry: Tapestry plaid to a lad of Love / Wallet: Wallet met to wilt of Love / Bright: Clans bright with Love / Tuner: Inner wanner, planner, Love / Eared: Eared ascend to a heightening in, Love / Gold: Gold gilled breathe, of Love / Goal: Our goal fulfilled by Love / Heal: Heal us, Love / Courage: Courage led to Love / Care: Care crowned deep in Love / Holistic: Holistic head of Love / Philosophy: Philosophy says, "to Love." / Blending: Blending bent to hint at Love / Quarlet: Quarlet wet with a quarter more of Love / Seaside: Squarely seaside I abide on shores of Love / Quail: Quail can heal our fill of fed by Love / Quilt: Quilt-ed tape of Love enough to live in best to Love / Exquisite: Exquisite sum of license to Love / Elective: Elective friend, Love / Invest: One time best to invest, that's Love / Reflex: Reflex rest quick in reverent Love / Fairy: Fairy fed to Love / Music: Music met mix in us in Love / Massage: Floral red bed of massage in Love / Message: Message bet by a vet of Love / Bands: Bands in stands to Love / Flamenco: Flamenco flanked by Love / Parry: Parry plenty of Love / Review: Review a new our Love / Royally: Royally send our Light to Love / Divination: Divine divination of a nation rift with Love / Magnetic: An orchid magnetic with Love / Mediums: Often mediums mean extremes of Love / Magnetic: An orchid magnetic with Love / Messiah: Life's messiah, Love / In Truth: Ladles of able, in truth, to Love / Domain: Flowers of domain in remain to Love / Gemstone: Gemstone gleamed in Love / Cable: A cable's cue is to break the chain to a drain in Love / Scrolls: Scrolls rolled up to unthawed essence of Love / Intro: Intro, know, deduce, know excuse, forgiving get, Love / Commander: Christus commander, the remainder, of Love / Scripture: The scripture red, live instead, that's Love / Redemption: Redemption sent to Love / Will: Will enough? Love / Hearty: Hearty give of a hardy gift, Love / Formula: Formula for fit favors of Love / Formulate: Banners formulate Love / Concepts: Concepts consent to Love / Brilliance: Brillianced bucked? Dumb Luck? Love / Enfeeble:

Enfeeble regal Love / Shake: Shake a flake of Love / Attribute: Attribute cute? Compute handsome In, Love / Ivy Green: Ivy greened believe, It's Love / Emanate: Emanate elate in Love / Realm: Realm ran rung to boundary-less Love / Voluminous: Voluminous vandate of Love / Calculate: Calculate the rate of percentage invest, in Love / Taste: Taste great Love / Genesis: Genesis jeaned by people lean with Love / Pear: Pears pier at exactly the float to Love.

CHAPTER 67 / LOVE INTENTION: Body: Body beat? Love / Design: Design drawn, God, Man, One, Love / Designate: Designate rate of Love / Designation: Designate lessons Loved / Cast: Cast plenty to Love / Prerequisite: Prerequisite matter, the chatter, of Love / Incline: Incline in a sled of wedded ware to Love / Descent: God's descent to decent man, is Love / Ascent: Ascent means live in Love / Blunt: Blunt to a point of Love / Blend: Blended in to win at Love / Forth: Forth Light to Love / Communion: Communion's kin the bless to Love / Interpretation: Interpreted Love / Ascending: Ascending now to Love / Blending: Blending in 2 Love / The Fire: The fire, inside, our Love / Emulates: Emulates place is Love / Entrusted: Insinuate the entrusted date with depth in Love / Embroider: Embroider order into Love / Bask: Bask enough Love / Flesh: Flesh afield our Love / Steel: Steel feel fell soft Love / Heightened: Heightened awareness of how we've Loved / Mentioned: Mentioned your name in Love / Pangs: Pangs of redeem, redempt me home to Love / Redeem: Redeem us because we're Loved / Redemption: Redemption's repent is Love / Direct: Direct enough? Love / Pal: Pal gone gal to Love / Bureaucratic: Bureaucratic venue of Love / Turf: Turf tough? Bruised? Love / Houses: Houses held in hands of Love / Brace: Brace a place on Love / Greet: Greet a great Love / Egypt: Egypt sent invent to Love / Uttered: Uttered yes to Love / Bull: Bull-y beads on Love / Ghetto: Ghetto gone to Love / Master: Master mister, Love / Fever: Fever fewed by Love / Heights: Heights exceed Love / Udder: Udder expanse of Love / Cow: Cow to please Love / Rabbi: Rabbi red to Love / Level: Level I live in Love / Luster: Enthusiastic luster of other in Love / Fire: Fire side, we, Love / Kindred: Kindreds spin in Love / Spill: Spill spells heal to flood, true Love / Sleep..Sleep flew a loan to Love / Print: Prints sent home by Love / Demi-gods: Demi-gods rods of Love / Imprint: God's imprint, hence, Love / Paragon: A paragon gone to Love / Phantoms: Phantoms hush at Love / Phantasms: Phantasms spasm, back, to Love / Secular: Secular scene of Love / Hassidic: Hassidic views, traditional and deep to Love / Angelic: Angelic choose, Love / Realm: Realm of gentle, Love / Clearly: Clearly absent from Love / Seem: Seem true, Love / Historic: An historic sort of Love.

CHAPTER 68 / LOVE CREDENTIALS: Lifting: Lifting knew, Love / Faith: Gracious faith of Love / Incredible: Incredible a space of Love / Galaxy: Galaxy green with Love / Within: Within again, Love / The Spin: Thus the spin to Love / Of: Of us, Love / Spun: Lace-y few spin spun to Love / Believes: Believes stuff, Love / In: In again, Love / God's: Yes indeed, God's Love / Great..

Great the date of Love / Lonely: Laughter while you're lonely for Love / Synagogue: Loved synagogue, God, Love / Dock: Dock dear, near, Love / Boat: Boat's denote Love / Radical: Radical measure the last chance for Love / Judea: Judea's June of Love / Massive: A massive missive, Love / Drive: Drive it in, to Love / Orchard: Arrival orchard deep to an orchard's seek of true Love / Emanate: Emanate fate's belate of Love / Speak: Speak the span of man in Love / Spoken: Spoken to a tune of Love / Heroic: Heroic in our Love / League: League of legions won to Love / Legion: Legion's lean to Love / Region: Region's reign with Love / Scroll: Often scroll your Love / Dead Sea: Dead sea due true Love / Line Be: Line be thee, Love / Essene: Essene's scene in Love / Eternal: Eternally love / Mart: Our mart is Love / Martyr: Martyr met defeat in Love / Realm: Realms read, Love / Probe: Probe ahead to stride our Love / God-ness: God-ness is knows this Love / Goodness: Goodness yes to Love / Lightness: Lightness seen in Love / Breakfast: Especially tasty, in breakfast of Love / Dine: Dine alone more often on Love / Highway: A highway signed by Love / Chariot: Chariot's choose true Love / Connote: Connote the vote of Love / Literary: Literary devote of Love / Entire: Entire hour, of Love / Mouth: Mouth peace, Love / Wide: Wide abide in Love / Ajar: Ajar the car of the door to Love / Door: Door shut on less than Love / Desk: Desk set, Love / Pen: Essential pen of GOD / Open: Open plan of Love / Native: Native nuance of Love / Natural: Natural seal of Love / Charioteer: Charioteer of Love / Song: Catch a song to Love / Shine: Shine seen in Love / Majestic: Embassy majestic with Love / Cabbed: A blessing cabbed by Love / Cobble: Cobble stone home, to Love / Stone: Confidence stone? To Love / Stein: Lesson steined by Love.

CHAPTER 69 / LOVE LICENSE: Merkabah: Merkabahed build to a spinning delivery of Love / Mercury: Mercury-ed mend from a vertical spin back to Love / Mercurial: Mercurial meets our fantastic Love / Mended: Mended befriended in a nettle-less need for compulsive aversive, Love / Mode: Mode to abridge our Love / Means: Means better, Love / Matter: Matter needs Love / Material: Materialistic, pluralistic, Love / Matching: Matching meet, Love / Moves: Moves the most, child-like Love / Masked: Masked merka the bah of Love / Mighty: Childish advent to a mighty admit called Love / Chariots: Chariots chill shrill to Light's Love / Horse: Horses shield the build of Love / Hoarse: Hoarse in a course of upspoken Love / Louder: Louder ascend to a louder trend to Love / Lance: Lances spent on hitting less than Love / Flounce: Flounce your set to Love / Fit: Fit the fate to Love / Mystical: Mystical the mist of Love / Layered: Layered your list to Love / Gates: Gates can greet our Love / Ruminates: Ruminates rates our increased abate to Love / Handy: Handy hint, Love / Handiworks: Handiworks win our crafty blend of Love / Fibers: Fibers defend our ascend to the fabric of Love / Alliterative: Alliterative ascend to a friend of Love / Alludes: Alludes resume to rescind our Love / Expressive: Expressive ascend to Love / Exude: Exude allude to Love / Ornamental: Ornamental a friend to Love / Wonders: Wonders ceased?

Love / Exiled: Exiled stood to Love / Rimmish: Rimmish shot? Be agreed to a dunk called Love / Firm: Firm yes! to Love / Firmament: Firmament went yes, Love / Advisory: Advisory went south to Love / Clouded: Clouded view of Love / Brisk: A brisk forget to Love / Brush: Brush your breath with Love / Browse: Browsed arouse to Love / Israelite: Israelite's Light is Love / Light: Light stuff, Love / Manner: Manor's manor, the house of Love / Manna: Manna's meet, Love / Exodus: Exodus exit us less, to Love / Twelve: Twelve and 3 are Love / Thirteen: Thirteen, thirteen, perfect Love / Records: Records rest in Love / Confines: Confines confine to lessen Love / Collective: Collective ascent to Love / Embody: Embody's body, Love / Miracle: Miracle meal, Love / Motive: Motive met at Love / Authority: Authority's best command of Love / Bonny: Bonny blue, Love / Bless: Bless place, Love / Chant: Chant champ, Love / Bar: Bared blend of Love / Hum: Hum, instead to Love / Line: Line lets live, Love / Cruise: Cruise a tude of Love / Scholar: Scholared seed of Love / Body: Body's pleasure, Love.

CHAPTER 70 / LOVE LEASE: Hope: Hope held, Love / New: New renew, Love / Faith: Faith can field, Love / Found: Found a few of Love / Forget: Forget's feel, forgiven, Love / Remember: Remember mists of Love / Today: Today's the day to the way of Love / Tomorrow: Tomorrow's true to Love / Ever: Ever seen descent Ascend? Love / Brainy: Brainy brush, Love / Faithful: Faithful friend of Love / Outside: Outside mix, Love / Inside: Inside rush to Love / Fight: Fight less, Love / Fright: Fright flight? Love / Light: Light, Love / Lest: Lest adjust, Love / I instant: Instant stuff, Love / Freeze: Freeze up gone to Love / Breathe: Breathe deep to Love / Love: Love is yet, yes, Love / Honor: Honor red, Love / Telling: Telling swelling, Love / Apprentice: Apprentice meant Love / Publish: Publish Bless, Love / Elegant: Elegant's scene is Love / Handsome: Handsome set, Love / Sexual: Sexual, a set, of Love / Social: Social seem of Love / Repute: Repute cute to Love / Question: Question renew of Love / Marriage: Marriage means weave of Love / One: One's sun to Love / Only: Only ascend to Love / All-Ways: All-ways play in Love / Gesture: Gestured gem, Love / Portrait: Portrait straight to a face of Love / Seated: Seated agree to Love / Forth: Forth a foot to a step to Love / Fifth: Fifth plea plead for Love / Touch: Touch your-self with the sight of felt by Love / Grace-full: Pleats grace-full ring my uncurtained Love / Gene: Gene tone, Love / Gemmed: Gemmed I'm seen as the gleam in the father's eye / Examine: Examine nation of Love / Text: Text done. We've come to Love / Translate: Notions translate to great in Love / Instruct: Instruct yes! to come to Love / Scrambled: Scrambled scene by gone to Love / Scrappled: Scrappled crew of yes! Love / Generative: A generative notion to count to Love / Genuine: Genuine you, in Love / Exorcise: Exorcise sum-less, than Love / Languaged: Languaged hew of chiseled Love / Babeled: A babeled spew, to Love / Scrapped: Scrapped you, now, Love / Historic: Historically scent to Love / Translate: Translate true, Love / General: General meter, measured Love / Exercise: Exercise best direct to the pump of Love / Demise: Demise exist,

in Love / Disguise: Heart's eyes sized, know disguise-less, Love / Devise: Devise Dove, Love.

CHAPTER 71 / LOVE LIQUID: Bottom: Bottomed up, by Love / Upset: Upset less, Love / Up: Up to you, in Love / Desire: Desire to higher, Love / Derive: Derive distrust away to Love / Delight: Delight due, Love / Ever: Ever after Love / After: After you, Love / Metric: A wrap on the coolest snap to the Light electric in a metric spin to Love / Meter: A meter true to Love / Rhythmic: John-John's rhythmic sum is one to Love / Rind: Rinds grind on teeth of Love / Colon: Colon's dip clean to Love / Crimp: Crimp rust, Love / Clip: Clip a strip of Love / Clap: Clap the scrap of Love / Crops: Crops drew on Love / Crisp: Crisp rush to Love / Create: Create great fates with Love / Crass: Lofty crass of grassy Love / Crone: Crone owned Love / Crony: Crony crewed by Love / Cringe: Cringe gone to Love / Croft: Croft scene, Love / Craft: Craft's crew, Love / Ordain's: Ordain's name is Love / Order: Order up? Love / Border: Border found bound to Love / Brain: Brain's blend, Love / Alert: Alert blend, of Love / Stolen: Stolen truth? Love / Swollen: Swollen true, Love / Woven: Woven wed of, Love / Worn: Worn? Torn? Find Love / Sworn: Sworn to be, in Love / Born: Born to wed, our Love / Adorned: Adorned warned, rest, Love / Warned: Warned to rest. Our Love / Artist: Artist tuned to Love / Shell: Shells heal, Love / Proton: Protons brewed by Love / Arc-ed: Sacred are-ed by Love / Frown: God's crown is frown-less, Love / Flown: Flown to you, in Love / Fond: Fond of you, in Love / Imagine: Imagine we, are Love / Image: Imaged meet at Love / Inquire: Inquire higher, Love / Theater: Theater cheered, Love / Teatro: Spanish scene an a lift to blend in a screen called Love / Ecuador: Mary Ecuador is chored with less than Love / Nepal: Nepal's wall, Love / Thamel: Blessing blew thamel to Kathmandu and Himalayan Love / The Mall: The meld of mall we Love / Signature: Crew signatured by Love / Automatic: An automatic patent on Love / Autograph: Autograph hunt, signed, Love / Represent: Represent respect in Love / Sent: Lately sent to Love / Shone: Shone enough? Love / Objectify: Ladies objectify of subject, Love / Subjectic: Subjectic scene, of Love / Specific: Baby's specific scene of Love / Erascible: Erascible breed, of Love.

CHAPTER 72 / LOVE FLUID: Subject: Subject scent, Love / Portrait: Portraits rest in rush to Love / Rely: Rely on us, in Love / Include: Today include our Love / Resource: To resource rest, Love / Reserve: Reserve best, Love / Rhetoric: Rhetoric spent on Love / Rhetorical: Rhetorical met, Love / Reside: Reside inside our Love / Residual: Lately residual flew lightly, Love / Resonant: chorals resonant with Love / Reticence: Reticence sent away to Love / Job: Job's jewel, Love / Jones: Led to Jones alone with Love / Coned: Coned accrue of Love / Cured: Cured us, Love / Blissed: Blissed us. Love / Smarter: Smarter power than vent, Love / Quote: Quote a not to Love / Quotient: Quotient went hint, Love / Quick: Quick set, Love / Quake: Enough quake, Love / Prospective: Prospective truth,

Love / Print: Print press, Love / Source: Lightest source, Love / Grade: Grade A, Love / Graduate: God's graduate, me, in Love / Collegiate: Collegiate crew, Love / Humane: Humane treat, Love / Honored: Honored repent to Love / Easy: Easy does Love / Disciplined: Chronic displayed the disciplined way 2 Love / Booked: Lightly booked, Love / Analyzed: Analyzed your set to Love / Contracts: Contacts sent Love / Vital: Vital view of Love / Intellectual: Intellectual vent, of Love / Hot: Hot and true, Love / Considered: License considered, to, Love / Schooled: Schooled stuff, Love / Skilled: Skilled in schooled to Love / Fast: Fasten fast to the heart of Love / Frantic: Frantic friend sent, Love / Rank: Rank so me, Love / Review: Review now, the rest, of Love / Universal: Universal explain of Love / Academic: Academic few? Explain, Love / Acquire: Acquire higher, Love / Reliable: A reliable read, on Love / Practical: Practical truth, Love / Visionary: Visionary sent, Love / Field: Are you breed to field an Love / Broken: Broken through to Love / Tabled: Lately I'm tabled by Love / Spare: Spare spray, Love / Sparse: Sparse staid, needs much, Love / Critical: Critical rent abreast rest of Love / Sarcasm-ed: Let sarcasm-ed go, to Love / Sturdy: Sturdy stand in Love / Studded: Studded yet? Love / International: Rebase an international press on Love / Intentional: Intentional, Love / Mask-uline: Mask-uline remove to Love / Fem and Then: Fem and then again Love.

CHAPTER 73 / LOVE EXTRAVAGANT: Totem: Totem true, to Love / Trim: Trim time, Love / Tattoo: Tattoo who? Love / Voodoo: Voodoo who? Love / Votive: Votive blew, Love / View: Velvet view gone newed to Love / Books: Books through our Love / Build: Build brew of basic Love / Matrix: Matrix street corner of Love / Madrigal: Madrigal manned by a curtained plan to Love / Contribution: Light's contribution, Love / Cushion: Cushion crew of Love / Noted: Seen noted, margins of Love / Choreography: Choreography a bath in Love / Jargon: Jargon chewed Love / Lexicon: Lexicon grew on me in Love / Lingual: Lingual list of Love / Linguistic: Intergalactic ring of a crew called Love / Architect: Architect erect to Love / Mason: Mason due, Love / Shrine: Shrine built in you and Love / Cult: Cult's accrue to, Love / Expose: Expose your set on Love / Publish: Publish pleasure / Leaven: Leaven less, heaven full, Love / Wafer: City's wafer the loafer called, Love / Blood: God's good blood in Love / Communion: Communion in, Love / Yang: Yang young? Love / Yin: Yin Zen? Love / Convivial: Convivial mannered, Love / Genital: Genitals won Love / Gnawed: Gnawed God? Chew, Love / Flown: Flown, blown, Love / Fruit: Fruit tree, we, free, Love / Flower: God's flower, our Love / Our: Our Love / Squeeze: Squeeze crust, erupt, Love / Wheeze: Wheeze by, breathe of Love / Breathe: Breathe sent vent to Love / Breath: Breath of Love / Beat: Beat of bug, shop / Heart: Heart of God, Love / Spiral: Spinal inspiral straighten to Love / Spill: Spill guts, Love / Price: Practice price sacrifice, Love / Fight?: God's fight? Forget? Love! / Fix: Fix us up, Love / Antidote: The antidote's your vote for Love / Inspire: Inspire us Love / Cliche: Cliche wade (intelligent) Love / Trite: Lightly trite to say I Love you /

Text: Text broke? Read, Love / Betray: Never betray has bone 2 Love / Innocent: Innocent state, Love / Mastered: Mastered plan, Love / Media: Media mound, Love / Power: Power stay, Love / Desire: Desire to near Love / Prayer: Prayer day, now, to Love / Truthful: Truthful in a living Love / Interrupt: Interrupt has left the lofts on Love / Schedules: Schedules and the chosen Love / Ratify: Ratify and the news committed to love.

CHAPTER 74 / LOVE EXTRUDE: Prey: Prey on less than Love / Capture: Capture cure of Love / Crave: Lessons crave the raven of Love / Create: Create sate of Love / Elate: Elate great Love / Bereave: Bereave has gone to Love / Blessed: Blessed be lesson 3 of Love / Brave: Lessons braved Love / Erudite: Erudite sight of Love / Convey: Convey a wave to Love / Convivial: Convivial crew of Love / Eradicate: Eradicate late to Love / Acute: Acute arose to Love / Cute: Cute equate to sweeten Love / Favorable: Favorable the measure to a heightened Love / Frail: Frail? Get well to Love / Interior: An interior plan of a man is Love / Inferior: Inferior mannered is the banner-less Love / Ray: A fray tied to Love / Fracas: Fracas flew to Love / Recommend: Recommend the recommendation of Love / Pretend: Pretend less Love / Recognize: Recognize why we Love / Reside: Reside red to Love / You: You yet? Love / Are: Are you Loved? / New: Know new Love / And: And we are One star Love / Known: Baby's own known Love / As One: As One's Love / Caring: Caring cure to Love / Curing: Curing care, / Assuring: Assuring sent to Love / Residing: Residing in Love / Arriving: Arriving, hear, Love / Raised: Raised up to Love / Singer: Singer strung up to Love / Pious: Pious pew on to seats of Love / Worn: Worn trim to Love / Testify: A kind testify to Love / Tray: Definite tray filled with Love / Craze: Write craze waved with Love / Training: Training's rim drips with Love / Talking: Talking drew with Love / Cultured: Cultured crew of Love / Conclave: Holy conclave of late to Love / Rave: Rave on to lightly Love / Surprise: Surprise yourself with Love / I Invite: Invite yourself home to Love / Rate: Rate yourself wide to Love / Official: An official feel of Love / Unusual: An unusual hour of Love / Same: Same time, Love / Name: Name some Love / Homogenize: Homogenize past your I's to perfect Love / Arise: Arise now on how to Love / Arrive: Arrive at the land of Love / Begave: Begave us Love / Oblige: Oblige us to Love / Raving: Raving rudeness gone to Love / Human: Human be our Love / Basic: Basic be our Love / Kind: Kind sum One Love / Gain: Grains gain grew Love.

CHAPTER 75 / LOVE EXTOLL: Discuss: Today sealed to discuss less of Love / Know: Know self, Love / Remember: Remember who you Love / Member: Member's met at the wet of Love / Embrace: Embrace abreast our Love / Face: Face me, Love / Trace: Trace the strut direct to Love / State: State your place at Love / Knowledge: Knowledge lent to perfect Love / Discipline: Discipline solid to Love / Phone: Phone in to Love / Brief: Brief enough to trip to skip to Love / A Case: A case worst shut is Love / Aghast: Aghast our blast to Love / To Last:

Lately to last we Love / To Say: To sign, to say, today, Love / To Stay: To stay straight to Love / To Give: To give, us, Love / To Live: To live more, Love / To Lay: To lay with best in Love / To Lie: To lie less, Love / To Derive: Lately derived to Love / To Disguise: To disguise lies instead in Love / To Discuss: To discuss Love / Reviewed: Reviewed the respect of our debt to Love / Breach: A breach abreast our reflect of Love / Reach: Reach yes, into, Love / Force: God's force is Love / Flip: Flip to the side of perfect in Love / Sea: Sea of Love / Cessarian: See the selection of reaching in to ascend to Cessarian manner in Love / Cessation: Cessation nation of Love / Inflation: Inflation's neat to Love / Cry: Cry decreed we need to Love / Crease: Crease an appreciation to a nation revealed to Love / Bless: Bless your need to Love / Brief: Brief in a nest of long to Love / Bare: Bare in a reveal of kneel in Love / Brave: Brave day of Love / Brush: A brush with Love / Belief: Belief in the best of Love / Raspy: Raspy voiced fit of direct to Love / Throated: Throated noted Love / Together: Together ever Love / Better: Better ex-cell in Love / Brew: Brew yourself some Love / Born: Born again to Love / Eyed: Eyed wide reveal of Love / Brown: Brown brewed less of Love / Fragile: Fragile to a nature of perfect in strong Love / Feel: Feel your spell of Love / Feeled: Feeled's a twist of perfect exist in Love / Felt: Felt your spell of Love / Few: Few will forget sweet Love / Knew: Knew enough when I had seen my Love / New: New LVOE / Begun: Begun to defend ascend to Love / Begin: Begin my friend to Love / My Friend: My friend is indeed, in deed, Love / The Friend: The friend is in, Love / Ascend: Ascend sent hint to Love / Sine: A sine assigned to perfect, we, Love / A Church: A church is true to a steepled pew to view only Love / A Pew: A pew to review your life from, Love.

CHAPTER 76 / LOVE EQUATE: Stripes: Stripes sewn to Love / Ripe: Baby's ripe to Love / Say: Say yeah to Love / Surprised: Lately surprised to expect of Love / Day: Day done, Love / Nights: Nights knew Love / Children: Children chill at heal Love / Accept: Accept review, Love / Funds: Funds flew to Love / Fronds: Fronds found in a fountain of Love / Ferns: Ferns fed in a green instead to Love / Burns: Burns to turns of Love / Belong: Belong along our Love / Song: Lately sung the song of Love / Strung: Strung up to stronger Love / String: String the strand of Love / Organic: Organic within our natural grin of Love / Organize: Organize your set to Love / Oregon: Oregon wants bliss to erase less Love / Washington: Washington wed to a continent led to Love / Wand: Wand of Love / Kudos: Kudos too you Loved / Most: Most host too Love / May: May we proceed to Love / Merry: Merry way to Love / Professional: A professional plan to Love / Rainbow: Rainbow runes of Love / Rainy: Rainy days of Love / San Fran: San Fran citied by Love / The City: Cry the city wide to Love / Fullest: Fullest sound, Love / Frill: Frill found in Love / Fresh: A fresh breath to Love / Mesh: Lately mesh in views of Love / Grid: A grid grew to Love / Bid: Invoiced bid to Love / Trace: Trace your place in Love / Carpets: Carpets plush in Love / Resource: Resource renewed

to Love / Razed: Razed the rude from Love / Arose: Arose true Love / Rosey: Rosey sake of Love / State: State of wait to Love / Knows: Knows enough to Love / Obligation: Obligation grew to a lesson of Love / Shows: Shows rows of Love / Shoes: Shoes shed to Love / Shine: Shine on, in, Love / Sanskrit: Sanskrit said Sharim to Love / Writ: Writ rut, Love / Wrote: Wrote you said heard of Love? / Vote: Vote yet? Yes, Love / Note: Note vote, Love / Nudge: Nudge kneel to Love / Budge: Budge been had by a shoving land of less than Love / Braid: Braid stuck at the lip of triple Love / Raid: Raid run, Love / Rose: Rose knew best of red, red, Love / Shows: Shows knows Love / Seed: Seed in us, Love / India: India's friend is deep in Love / Place: Place a trace to Love / Rich: Rich invest in the test of Love / North: North to knew Love.

CHAPTER 77 / LOVE INQUIRED: Resume: Resume your degree of Love / Recess: Recess is best in the play called Love / Exceed: High in a mountain of exceed to a need called Love / Ex-Cell: Ex-cell well, Love / Reveal: Left to reveal our heal of Love / Review: A Godded review of welcome to Love / Large: Large the lead to heed our Love / Loan: Bet your loan on own your Love / Lone: Lone starred start of where we met in Love / London: London towered around the power of Love / Airport: Airport's hub of deeper Love / Heathrow: Heatherowed around the bound to Love / Trained: Trained to be true to Love / Betrayed: Betrayed less, Love / Refused: Refused to rest in less than perfect Love / Resume: Resume the resume' which reads must know Love / Recede: Recede to where we agreed to Love / Rate: The rate to date is Love / Relate: Relate your fate to only Love / Rescue: Rescue knew deep Love / Arise: Arise to reviews of refused to lose her Love / Released: Released the rest of the also rans in Love / Raced: Raced to taste the hours of Love / Stonehenge: Stonehenge knew the arcs of rocks to Love / Crops: Crops grew best with Love / Circled: I Am circled round by a perfect town of Love / Assumption: Let us feel assumption in the function of our Love / Function: A function adding up to Love / Feud: Feud-less Love / Labor: Labor for favor? Just, Love / Favor: Deep in a blend of favor in Love / Few: Few knew less than Loved / Blew: Blew by to Love / Top: God's on top of Love / Blue: A blue view of Love / Green: Green explain is the lane of Love / Violet: Violet treasured by a feather of Love / Amber: Amber veined Love / Chamber: Chamber shed of less than bled to Love / Red: Now we know the road to good red Love / Rose: To a rose be true in Love / Magenta: Magenta the gem of our entering in to Love / Milked: Milked drops of perfect bliss in the kiss of a mother born wed to Love / Love is Love / Fused: The fused exude of the bond to God in Love / Confused: Confused know blew to webs of clarity's bet on Love / Wrapt: Wrapt review of the depths in you and Love / Oriental: Oriental's reside in the depths of Love / Original: Original met fun in a western sun of Love / Mental: A mental matter the patter of let's believe in perfect Love / Malicious: Malicious request of the best of your life. Right: only know my Love / Munificent: The larger the maze, the deeper the wade to munificent in Love /

Beneficient: Beneficient in new to Love / Flagstone: Flagstone's flew to deep in Love / Flagstaff: Flagstaff's thin to a spin of perfect paper written in Love / Philemon: Philemon's line is direct to Love / Fought: Fought yourself left of Love / Spacious: Spacious expand to the heights of a man in Love / Crowning: Crowning measure of the pleasure in Love / Born: Born to be worn by Love / Rebirthed: Rebirthed expand to the two who knew of Love / Renewed: Renewed exist in the the confess to Love / Baptized: Baptized at the pew of who we Loved / Felt: Felt you feel the gracious glance of Love.

CHAPTER 78 / LOVE REQUISITE: Lessons: Lessons lean to a howling friend letting us in to Love / Lined: Lined up to much in Love / Lively Give: Give lively our hearts to Love / Give It All: Give it all to all men, Love / Light: Light's take flight to an ascendant stand in Love / Light In Sight: Light in sight of the sight in you / Dreams: Dreams done to the heights of Love / Cream: Cream rolls of Love / Crinkle..Another matter is a crinkle in time to Love / Bent: Bent to a feel of the heal of Love / Discover: Discover another in the midst of Love / Clone: A clone designed by the hands of timely maneuver to Love / Noah: Noah's own Love / Flood: Flood to Love / Found: Found a sound in deeper Love / Trial: Trial filed by Love / Back: Back to a space called Love / Space: Space faced in the place called Love / Dial: Dial awhile to Love / Front: Love the front of the fount called back to Love / Science..Left in us, the science of once, we Loved / Lab: A lab led to found by God's great Love / Top: Reach the top of your trust in lust met direct in Love / Terrific: Terrific fill of the filled by Love / Scanned: Back to the fact of scanned by Love / Tree: A tree is trained to notice the roots of Love / Christos: A Christos sealed by the heal of Love / Hoarse: Hoarse in a course of unspoken Love / Grip: Grip keyed by gee, we, Love / Key: Wrote the key that unlocked my free to Love / Haut: Meet the cuisine of a haut refrain called Love / Maxim: A maxim fit to Love / Course: Listen's course is deep in the ears of Love / Morgan: Morgan's mean is the horse that's lean to Love / Mew: Mew meant to correct our feud in Love / Date: Deep grace dates our Love / Organ: An organ graced by the depths of Love / Meal: Trace this meal to Love / Mandibles: Race this taste of crunchy repaste with the mandibles that last in the lift to sample our Love / Mansions: Fill the mansion called life with Love / Mandolin: The mandolin men of Love / React: React much to Love / Chew: Chew the dish called luscious Love / Chin Lessons: Chin themselves on Love / Card: Card yourself a cure called Love / Captured: Captured creatures are released to Love / Quality: Address the quality in your Love / Pictures: Pictures placed in Love / Smile: Smile to feel your Love / Display: Display today to Love / Better: Better be, Love / Banter: Banter's manner forgot too Love / Chant: Chant to find a hint of Love / Amaze: Amaze yourself, Love / Digital..Digital to days of count it, Love / Vulcanized: A vulcanized rise to Love / Immaculate: Immaculate to a measure called Love / Dazed: Dazed took a stand at Love / Content: Content to curse only worse than Love / Immediate: Immediate will be our Love / Days: Days devised to lead to Love

/ Contain: Contain meant less than Love / Contrain: Contrain ran around the name of Love.

CHAPTER 79 / LOVE REQUIRED: Creepers: Creepers chimed that I Am the vine of Love / Trailed: Trailed my trust to a hush of gentle, genuine, kind, Love / Revealed: Revealed an island healed by Love / Trolled: Trolled for fish who healed neglect with Love / Vined: Vined surround of a leafy town called ivy green to Love / Revolve: Revolve around the sound of Love / Trined: Trined entwined with perfect recline in Love / Veiled: Veiled's reveal is the field of Love / Revolution: Revolution execution is Love / Regulate: Regulate the freight to a lighter Love / TRADE: Trade talk of Love / Forward: Fast to forward to Love / Denote: The gift of denote to Love / Tried: Tried to rest in Love / Faster: Faster now, Love / Denied: Left denied behind a screen of Love / Human: Human is the hand of God in Love / Faced: Faced myself in Love / Fickle: Fickle flinched at Love / Origin: The origin that matters is Love / Facet: Facet polished by honest in Love / Faceted: Faceted treasure is our Love / Health: God's health is our Love / Peace: Peace provides the sweet impulse inside our Love / Piece: Piece pierced is Love / Delivery: Delivery set on Love / Dance: Dance to the drum of Love / Dynamic: Dynamic is the sun of Love / Deplete: Deplete reflect on less than Love / Defend: Defend your right to Love / Fell: Fell to the height of Love / Felt: Felt fine in design of Love / Waned: Waned denied our Love / Crept: Crept up on the lesson of Love / Crepe: Crepe draped around the scene of Love / Craned: Craned around the need to lean to Love / Enthuse: Enthuse is active in effective Love / Known: Known a new tune of Love / Enthused: Enthused belief in lessons Loved / Recognized: Recognized anew in Love / Enthusiastically: Enthusiastically recede into Love / Knew: Knew renew to Love / Enthusingly: Enthusingly believe in Love / Initiate..Initiate your sate with Love / Understood: Understood digress to Love / Knowing: Knowing knew best our Love / Known Often: Known often to maroon in Love / Spoken: Spoken ascend to win Love / Engine: The heart of the line, the Engine of Love / Environ: Environ sent to hint at Love / Environments: Environments surround our Love / Work: Work to birth your greatest Love / Empires: Empires aspire to Love / Spurt: Spurt to exert in Love / Month: Month of few, left, Love / Mossy: Mossy knew blue-green increase in the lease on Love / Pave: Pave's engrave on Love / Prove: Prove the stuff to Love / Planned: A planned ascend to the friend of Love / Patterned: Patterned plan to Love / Patterns: Patterns turn to Love / Groves: Groves known to twice we grew to Love / Throne: Throne thronged by long arrive at Love / Joined: Joined in the net of Love.

CHAPTER 80 / LOVE OFTEN: Crime: Crime prevent, Love / Defend: Defend your set on Love / Within: Within is a friend called Love / Fin: Fin shook the hand of man in Love / Punch: Punch pulled is less than Love / Plan: Plan on a gift called manned by Love / Pencil: Pencil in my name by Love / Compass: Compass points direct to Love / Math: Math met at success in

Love / Plumb: Plumb the depths of Love / Duck: Duck dropped? Love / Wide: Wide enough to Love / Hide: Hide in screens of Love / Pie: Pie panned in a pen pan deep in Love / Plaza: Plaza pleased with the Santa Fe seas of Love / Made: Made, best, Love / Maker: Maker of Love / Taken: Taken in whole, Love / Plat: Plat yourself square to the circle of Love / Blot: Blot yourself clean of less than you know of Love / Bakers: Bakers dozen of plans to thirteen our Love / Lotto: Lotto won by One who sunned in stunned arrival at the halls of Love / Lot: Lot of good we got in Love / Lass: The lass called Love has entered into the plot of man known by his Love / Loathe: Loathe yourself less, be, Love / Loaf: Loaf known by the bread of life sliced thick to Love / Low: Low enough to enthrone our Love / Let: Let us free to be in Love / Nod: Nod your head to yes, your Love / God: God good? Yes! Love / Chest: Chest wide to deepen Love / Rest: Rest in the facts of Love / Breast: My breast can rest in Love / Bust: Bust through to Love / Lust: Lust went less to lesser Love / Fly: Fly high to the walls of Love / Pizza: Pizza man's plan was a mystic chance to dance at Love / Limp: Limp to anything less than Love / Scones: Scones dance in the air of Love / Sky: Sky wide to Love / Fly: Fly across the sky of Love / Flown: Flown to free our Love / Assure: Assure yourself Love / Assured: Assured rest in Love / Bless: Bless your address of Love / Body: Holy matter, the body of Love / Sacredness: Sacredness said to close of Love / Bliss: Know bliss when you kiss your Love / Body: Body guarded by Love / Breed: Breed yourself fit for Love / Rumpus: A rumpus came to rest in Love / Bleed: Bleed less, Love / Bred: Bred to be freed by Love / Divide: Born with divide? Re-side your Love / Bodies: Bodies together add up to Love / Healthy: A healthy manner, Love / Often: Often hold your Love / Fan: A fan of the man who LOVES / Compass: Find the compass, your heart, which points all-ways true, to, Love / Born: Born freed to Love / Rains: Rains of delight in Love / Record: Record the source, only, Love / Cored: Cored clear through to Love / Refrain: Let the refrain remain in Love.

CHAPTER 81 / LOVE AFLOAT: Pound: Freed by pound of preventative cure in Love / Erase: Erase the face who lessens Love / Pounded: Pounded by lessens of Love / Over: Over the edge of h-our Love / Pore: Pore yourself wide to overlook Love / Recording: Recording the rate of Love / Distress: Distress has gone full addressed by remembered Love / Quest: A quest redeemed by Love / Now: Agree now to how you'll Love / One: One's enough to Love / Constant: Constant befriend is Love / Contain: Contain your depth in Love / Remain: Remain eternal in your absolute Love / Explain: Explain only regain of Love / Often: Often I Am found in the heart of a town called Love / Seldom: Seldom forget to Love / In Love: In Love I can breathe the truth of lift to hearts born swirled with Love / Best: It is best to rest in the laurels of home and Love / Own: Be your own, in Love / Rest: Rest in erupts of Love / Reigns: Reigns a matter, Love / Erasure: Erasure of less is Love / Sound: Sound the word, God lightly found, in the hum of Love / Explain: Explain your gain: Love / Founded: Founded on matter less taut, the tension

sought has gone to release Love / Bound: Bound to gain ground in the groove called Love / Mundane: Mundane explain of the gain to live in only Love / Less: Less enough: sever less: in Love / Found: Found plenty in Love / Bind: Bind less, Love / Worry: Worry gone, Loved / Plain: Plain to be exposed to simply Loved / Life Between: Life between the seams of Love / Life's Kid: Life's kid is the lamb of all remember: Ariel known well by the numbers of God red Love / Dove Rest: A Dove rest found here in the rack of tracks back to the monkey-less shine of all we are in Love / Knight Deep: Spent a knight deep to Arthurian legend of Guinevere's regain of Love / Life Amid: Life amid the thin degree of a shattered grip on less in Love / Kid's Dove: A little kid's Dove is good to Love / A Nest: A Nest feather deep in the sleep of eternal peace and Love / Deep Treat: Find a deep tread in the way we retreat to exactly Love / Core: Core yourself, Love / Connect: Connect yourself to the elect of all we've known for Love / Direct: Direct your influx to exactly Love / Definite: Definite view of definitely you in Love / Desire: Desire to be hired by elective Love / Two Night: Two night stand in Love / Kid's Life: Kid's life has hid in less than Love / Night Deep: Night deep in respect I Am self expect of the lesson learned when into my dreams entered Love / Yes: Yes we yearn for perfect Love / Rest: Rest in the eternal will of One known best as Love / Nesting: Nesting done? Find One who sails on the wings of knowing her Love / Known: Known by the nest I own, my own heart, held elect in Love / Life Amid: Life amid the hid by less has broken respect for real Love / Deep Respect: Gain the respect of deeply elect in the dance of Love / Brown: Brown whirl to the girl I know as Love / Kindly Done: Kindly done, be won, with Love / Gone: Gone to be One with Love / Thrown: Thrown to the side of a deeper incline to Love / Throne: A raven en-throned by Love / Show: Show us your Love / Deal: The heart you feel is the rocking deal called Love / God Said: God Said let there be: Love / Win: Win yourself in to Love / Donor: Donor met give in the living face of expectant Love.

CHAPTER 82 / LOVE NOTED: Own: Own your set of perfect lights, the orbs of Love / Flown: Flown ahead to perfectly Love / Felt Enough: Felt enough of less than yes! in Love / Dealt: Dealt with deep by Love / Street: Take the street to Love / Treat: Treat your trine with perfect Love / Escheat: Escheat met will in the probate of Love / Flown: Flown to flew to Love / Grip: Grip the type of hand you own, your own, in Light and Love / Gale: Gale force Love / Gate: Gate crash Love / Special: Special is the span of every day Love / Galleries: Galleries grin at the art of our Love / Especially: Especially direct I have an effect on precisely Love / Effectually: Effectually mattered, Love / Garden: Garden of green to Love / Gain: Gain a power in perfect Love / Gardenia: Gardenia's green in a shiny leave called Love / Plan: Plan plenty of attend to Love / Flown: Flown to the moon of Love / Flower: Flower powered by the list of Love / Shower: Shower your power to Love / Shore: Shore on the core of Love / Caring: A caring cure of Love / Flow: Flow on go to Love / Fine: Deserts drill a fine design on the outbacks of Love / Reveal:

Reveal your head to Love / Ceiling: Ceiling high to the scent of Love / Kneeling: Kneeling on the ceiling of Love / Nodules: Nodules knew the view of you in electric exude of directive Love / Ecstatic: Ecstatic ascend to the friend called Love / Garden: A garden greener to the growing friend called Love / Grip: A grip to the trip of Love / Elusive: Elusive the tread to an elastic thread called Love / Grains: Grains to strains of certain Love / Gardenia: Gardenia glen of the den of Love / Exclusive: Exclusive the measure of the pleasure to Love / Carafe: Light's carafe is Love / Tips: Tips to tops of Love / Galleries: Galleries gals are howls of Love / Cringe: Cringe at less than Love / Michelangelo: Michael's dream is deep to a angelic code called only Love / Tubes: Tubes of Love / Tricks: Tricks trick us less than Love / Effusive: Effusive fits with Love / Knew: Knew you Loved / Crimp: Crimp rest stress to Love / Maximal: Maximal the max to clasp your call to your own Love / Evasive: Evasive planner Love / Cupid: Cupid's needle met Love / Direct: Direct date to Love / Directive: Directive set to the wet of Love / Cusp: The cusp of Love / Clasp: Clasp your here to Love / Fetish: Fetish fed to the head of Love / Celtic: Celtic kilt to the hilt of Love / Knew: Knew the dream of direct to Love / Cascades: Cascades cascade over the edge of the wedge of Love / Centric: Centric to the treasure of Love / Space: Space addressed to the west of the best of Love / Costume: Costume caved by the waved to Love / Jezebel: Jezebel's jeweled by the tool called elect a better reflect of Love / Zoe: Zoe sun is Greek for Love / Intake: Intake takes a trek to Love.

CHAPTER 83 / LOVE KEYED

1. Special: Special has scene in Love / Molecule: Comets ascend in molecules of Love / Thought: Thought's thrill to Love / Spatial: Spatial ascendant Love / Molecular: Let's molecular be in Love / Lot: Lot to give to Love / Lattice: Lattice laced by Love / Lived: Lived in best in Love / Glotteral: Glotteral glee to Love / Lives: Lives the list to Love / Life: The life we led to Love / Glamorous: Glamorous amorous to Love / Graced: Graced by best in Love / Crowd: You're a crowd in Love / Rid: Rid your rest of less than Love / Grid: Grid grilled to the electric wave of Love / Harmonic: Harmonic hound of the found of Love / Lid: The lid's up on Love / Bade: Bade good-bye to Love / Lover: Lover lived in the hills of Love / Componentry: Componentry trilled to the fill of Love / Forbade: Forbade the shade of less than Love / Weeper: Weeper creeper gone: Love / Compote: Compote the vote to denote the route to Love / Knot: Knot in the back of less than Love / Latticed: Latticed direct to Love / Clasped: Clasped your clip to the lip of the dip to Love / The Lot: The lot to the crew of Love / Wept: Wept to the winds of Love / Of Give: Of give we gave to Love / Clasp: Clasp to a neck called the direct to Love / Deep: Sleep deep to Love / Crowd: Crowd around the crown of Love / Sleep: Sleep is wow to Love / Surrender: Surrender to the friend of Love / Consort: Consort your sort of Love / Mettle: Mettle met the meat of Love / Finder: Finder found in the sound of Love / Keeper: Keeper crowned to the sound of a friend in Love / Freight: Freight fanned a stand in

Love / Of: Of the date we lately Love / Frat: Frat the about you Love / Frill: Frill sealed on the lace of Love / 6 Deep: 6 deep to the steep of Love / Strife: Strife's sound is less than Love / 8 of Late: 8 of late is Love / 7 Split: 7 split to the hint of Love / Heal: Heal much Love / Ravine: Ravines wide to the side of Love / Fit: Fit to the sit on Love / Neglect-full: Neglect-full the need to feed your self best of the heart of Love / Fullness: Fullness in Love / Saturated: Saturated the rated bray of way we go to Love / Facts: Facts are found to the sound of Love / Natured: Natured next to the blessed by Love / Satiate: Satiate your step in the sweet recall of the marinate Love / Frills: Frills thrilled by the feeled by Love / Scold-less: Scold-less in Love / Nesting: Nesting sun of the rays of Love / Giving: God's giving is living in Love / Forgive: Forgive fuss in Love / Told: Told true to Love / Loving: Loving led my head to live in a deeper give of the breath called Love / Way: to the loving way of the Father, I lift my life as gift of Light and Love / Living: living still within a Light fondest for God's grace, Love.

CHAPTER 84 / LOVE ENTIRE

1. Nestling: Nestling in to the friend called Love / Neglect-full: Neglect-full respect full of wet full of let's full with Love / Pure: Pure to the cure of Love / Told: Told you we'd be Loved / Fact-full: Fact-full impact-full of Love / Blissed: Blissed trend of Love / Scolded: Scolded yourself to the wealth of Love / Forgave: Forgave gave to Love / Intellect: Intellect's won our in to Love / Forgive: Forgive to live in Love / Forgave: Forgave myself my life of less than Love / Intelligent: Intelligent friend of the inn to Love / Resolute: Resolute regard to the hardest thin to Love / Elect: Elect an ascend to Love / Sex: Sex set on the hands of Love / Salute: Salute refute to the wrestle in Love / Sect: Suspect to a sect of the vets of Love / Divine: Divine ahead Love / Right: Right enough to Love / Warm: Warm to a whim of when we Love / Form: Form charmed by a heightened life of Love / Mentor: A mentor wise to Love / Mosaic: Mosaic moments of prosaic thoughts gone oft to Love / Astral-logic: Astral-logic manners held by the hands of Love / Glide: Glide to an abide with Love / Live: Live lightly struck by Love / Heal: Heal your head with Love / Hide: Hide inside the skin of God, Love / Feel: Feel it felt, Loved / A Telling: A telling sign is our recline to Love / Resolve: Resolve yourself to read the hits of Love / Real: Real congeal in Love / Live: Live to give, Love / Solve: Solve this matter, Love / Alliances: Alliances lend is the friend of Love / Truly: Truly you'll fill the feel of fields of Love / Astronomic: Astronomic intrigue with the heed to Love / Gastronomic: Gastronomic interview of the critic in you when it comes to Love / Repast: Know the past through to the palate called you can taste pure Love / Knew: Knew the day and the date and the sate of Love / Fact: Fact fed to my head, Love / Listening: Listening has trued my Love / Know: Know knot less in Love / Now: Now is how we Love / Economic: Economic matter in the chatter called Love / Social: Social skirt with the flirt of Love / Societal: Societal pressure the measure on Love / Fax: Fax back yet? The facts, Love / Listening: Listening to you, I Am

Loved / Spoken: Spoken to a hush called listen Love / Spatials: Spatials caught reflect of the respect of Love / Knew: Knew you would leave to learn your Love / Understood: Understood our over-bear in Love / Moleculed: Moleculed manner the banner of Love / Factual: A factual matter, Loved / Thought: Thought you knew to thrill yourself on Love / Flat: Flat land renewed by the mountains sacred who know how to Love / Actual: Actual patter the matter of Love / Equal: Equal air of the isle we share inside the view of two who Love / Sharp..Make a sharp adjust to dust your Love / A Minor: A minor's manner is Love / G: Good to be G in sharp to flats of Love / B: Be big in B Love / E: E is where we find the strains go plane to Love.

CHAPTER 85 / LOVE LAPSED: Heights: Heights head in to when we Loved / Flats: Flats inflate with great to Love / See: See too our Love / Again: Again we win in Love / Lotus: Lotus let us live in give to others too of the desire to hire bigger views of Love / Direct: Direct to the petals of murk-less Love / Lace: Lace blue recline in the sign of Love / Let Us: Let us win at Love / Rise: Rise wise to Love / Buddha: Buddha led in to letting in Love / Christ: Christ said won by compassionate Love / Again: Again we win in perfect Love / Gifts..Gifts of God, the child inside the flood to Love / Inter-Galactic: Inter-galactic fact, Light is back and Love is on / Intellect: Intellect found me fit to fitting in to knowing Love / Intelligible: Intelligible banner of easy to be red by Love / Gist: Gist said get it Love / Morale: Morale meets at Love / Theory: Theory field healed Love / Honor: Honor more Love / Home: Home to a claim called Love / Therapy: Therapy's cue is Love / Edit: Edit in Love / Editor: The editor reads to me of Love / Geologic: A geologic feature, the mountains of Love / Logic: Logic spoke to me of Love / Locate: Locate your date with great Love / Book: A book that beckons, live, Love / Fantastic: Fantastic to a measure of wheeled Love / Lock: Lock yourself in to Love / Fantasy: Fantasy fed by head to Love / Trip: Trip to your Love / Truck: Truck filled with a field of live in Love / Lover: Lover loomed large in me and my deal of Love / Loved: Loved by give, I've lived the life I've given to Love / Loaned: Loaned your number to Love / Discover: Discover dear, the ear of near, to Love / Cover: Cover yourself with Love / Place: Place yourself in the heal of Love / Quantum: Quantum quilled I'm healed by Love / Feather: Feather freed to loft to Love / Knew: Knew enough to Love / Feathered: Feathered fetters lifting off to Love / Make: Make a break to Love / Creative: A creative method, Love / Happy: Happy hen of laid by eggs of Love / Mentor: Mentor send my ascend to living Love / Maxim: A maxim treasure Love / Quartered: Quartered by a fourth of Love / Mayan: A Mayan stella stood for Love / Upgrades: Upgrades have come to your Love / Breakthrough: Breakthrough to your own, Love / Trade: Trade in trend for a hand that stands heart deep in Love / In Awe: In awe, I saw God in Love / Skeletons: Skeletons melt in the Light of rays of days of Love / Sensations: Sensation's shawl is all we Love / Thrilled: Thrilled to a seat gone neat to Love / Action: Action trued by the trim to Love / Sensual: Sensual seen at the rim of Love / Food: Food for the

fought surrendered too, Love / Form: Form of the filling, Love / Lakes: Lakes who leap, Love / Swarm: Swarm to a need to be, Love / Fish: Fish in familiar lands, Love.

CHAPTER 86 / LOVE LUSTS: Explode: Explode to the page of wage your Love / Religion: Religion run has met the son of Love / Totally: Totally trued by hued to Love / Giggle: Giggle at whirls of less than Love / Even: Even mattered, Love / Flight: Flight found to the township Love / Act: Act on heal of real Love / React: React to the fact of Love / Flirt: Flirt with hurt- less Love / Blow: Blow you too Love / Reaction: Reaction smatters Love / Spurt: Spurt to the hurt with Love / By: By these we Love / Last: Last to a fasten with Love / React: React ran aground our Love / Bays: Bays deep with a Kealekekua steep to the shores of Love / Last: Last time I cast for less in Love / Today: Today I fly to truest Love / Metatron: Metatron met the full effect of Love / Gold: Gold has sent her hint to Love / Extraordinary: Extraordinary the necessary to Love / Ever: Ever need? Love / Platinum: Platinum plan to Love the fan of man, God's good, to, Love / Last: Last duress of less than Love / Pinnacle: A pinnacle penned by Love / Blue: Blue in the sparkling depths of where we've Loved / First: Be the first to burst with Love / Sheer: Sheer winds gust of loft to live your Love / Blown: Blown to a boon of Love / Wind: Wind found my friend in Love / Stir: Stir us deep with Love / Big: Big to Love / Biggest: Be biggest in your sound of Love / Clear: Whales steer clear to Love / Egg: Egg on my pace to Love / Sharp: Sharp sent shred to Love / Sort: Sort out your sort of Love / Gust: A gust blew through to Love / Resort: Resort to a sort called Love / Sport: Cavort, the sport, of, Love / Arise: Arise now to Love / Softly: Softly I said, let us Love / Popular: Popular to a plan of living again, Loved / Millions: Millions met at a heal of Love / Winter: Winter will weather our Love / Rise: Rise in me, Love / Grand: Grand to views of days of Love / Success: Success is a matter of Love / Risen: Risen to a matter called Love / Power: Power this our with Love / Autumn: Autumn fell in a lesson well at hand and Love / Leaves: Leaves land around the plan to Love / Engineered: Engineered hear at Love / Fall: Fall aboard the train of Love / Power: Power our health with pure Love / Secret: Secret pleasure, around, the sacred orbs of healthy absorbs, of Love / Powered: Powered by houred by Love / Scent: Scent to a vent of Love / Nine: Nine times round the sound of walls backing down to Love / Resistance: Resistance to our 8 times 3 and equality in the hands of Love / Secretive: Secretive? Enough! Love / Equipped: Equipped to Love / Hillside: In a hillside manner, heal the sides of Love / Shop: Shop at the heart of only, Love.

CHAPTER 87 / LOVE WATERED: Oxygen: Oxygen wed in the lend of Love / Light: Light flight to the sight to Love / Water: Water wind to mists of Love / Waters: Breath on waters of Love / Write: God's write on to Love / New: New flew to Love / Tedious: Tedious to true to less? Then, Love / Rite: Rite to rites of Love / Noon: Noon now, yes, we, try / Excite: Excite the right to try, Love / Wrote: Wrote a note to flights of Love /

Negligence: Negligence knew the best of Love / Whole: Whole day given to Love / Look: Look at us, Love / Newest: Newest news, Love / Compass: Compass spent on the advent to Love / Stupid: Stupid knots of less than Love / Fan: Fan's befriend the friend of Love / Rumpus: Rumpus roomed to a Love / Blissed: Blissed yet? Love / Healthiest: Healthiest heart, Love / Divide: Divide dusk, arise, Love / Ignorance: Ignorance sunk by the hands of Love / Healed: Healed great to the greatest Love / Reeds: Reeds grown long to Love / Solve: Solve appeal at Love / Solvents: Solvents deal at Love / Bodied: Bodied blend of the friend to Love / Solid: A solid matter of Love / Sealed: Sealed with a flush to Love / Bleed: God's bleed is Love / Salute: Salute Love / Feeled..Feeled felt, abrush, Love / Body: Body billed? Buy Love / Solute: Solute salute to Love / Nutritive: Nutritive soothe of healing of Love / Hawk: Hawk flown to Love / Bills: Bills flew to the view of Love / Yarn: Yarn to yearn for Love / Line: Acknowledge the line described by Love / Link: Link yourself to Love / Lioness: Lioness found life in a mountain towned by Love / Arrival: Arrival at the circle of Love / Pink: Pink ascend to Love / Spot: Spot to a spin to Love / Message: Message blessed by the heart of Love / Blessed: Blessed decide to design Love / Mounts: Mounts account to Love / Sky: Sky fly wide to Love / Starred: Starred aboard the sword of Love / Star: Star around the found for Love / Stars: Stars astound our Love / Major: Major blend of Love / Sizzle: Sizzle seen of Love / Skein: Skein of yarns to Love / Eclipse: Eclipse sent to the vent for Love / Scared: Scared to vent my Love / Crow: Crow through Love / Raven: Raven's reign is Love / Know: Know through our Love / Moss: Moss met soft in the hand of Love / Millenium: Millenium's mean our Love / Spotlight: Spotlight seen on our Love / Day: Day by day I drew to Love.

CHAPTER 88 / LOVE FROWN: Pulse: A pulse felt in well we Loved / Mulch: Mulch erupt to Love / Groves: Groves grew to Love / Grave: Grave drew Light to the right of flight to Love / Grassy: Grassy grains of explains to Love / Grain: Grain of Love / Scene: Scene where we Love / Much: Much meant to Love / Snow: Snow, know, Love / Refine: Refine define to Love / Combine: Combine along the line of Love / Caye: Caye of the keys to Love / Sparks: Sparks spoken to Love / Concave: Concave to the clue to Love / Refinance: Refinance the rights of Love / Specks: Specks of dust to a lifting wind called Love / Convex: Convex cured by the cure of Love / Combine: Combine assign to the Light of our Love / Spectacle: Spectacle spent on Love / Set: Set to be sealed by Love / Keyed: Keyed by the cure of Love / Colony: Colony keyed to the heed to Love / Comedic: Comedic cues to the heart of Love / Park: Park at the place of a station called Love / Concrete: Concrete trend to the end called Love / Clued: Clued by the climb to Love / Sorts: Sorts send to Love / English: English spent on a hint to Love / Jupiter: Jupiter joined by Love / Cavort: Cavort a sort to Love / Spent: Spent spun on Love / Start: Start to alert our revert to Love / Pretty: Pretty platter of the matter called Love / Decade: Decade deep to Love / Glades: Glades green and deep to Love / Solar: Solar power plexed by less than Love / Saturn: Saturn sails around our Love / Chance: Chance advance to Love / Sole: Sole so bold to Love / Romanced: Romanced drew us to Love / Earth's: Earth's glen is Love / Mercurial: Mercurial to a measure of treasured by Love / Mars: Mars spars at stars of Love / Eclipsed: Eclipsed ascend to the trend to Love / Even: Even stands in the hand of Love / Significant: Significant to a stance of Love / Moonlit: Moonlit to a list of Love / Conjunct: Conjunct content to remaining in Love / Scant: Scant can't Love / Moon: Moon moan, Love / Crescent: Crescent felt in the moon of Love / Divine: Divine detain to the hearth of Love / Eve: Eve to a span of Love / Populous: Populous place to Love / Decide: Decide where you want to Love / Crunch: Crunch crept to the wealth of Love / Deride: Deride the abide to Love / Divine: Divine design to Love / Scarred: Scarred by living less than all in Love / Skilled: Skilled enough to Love / Heal: Heal your appeal to Love / Spans: Spans blend on Love / Centurian: Centurian ascend to Love.

CHAPTER 89 / LOVE FELT: Hunch: Hunch held the held by Love / Eyed: Eyed wide inside our Love / Heat: Heat a treat in the meet of Love / Spent: Spent on God's exist in Love / Spun: Spun to the son of Love / Yarn: Yarn to the yearning of the habit learned called Love / Alarm: Alarm us best in the rest of Love / Reflect: Reflect accept of Love / Near: Near enough is knot in Love / Car: Car afar our Love / Counts: Counts account for our Love / World: World willed by Love / Spade: Spade spun to Love / Dime: Dime dew on the time called Love / Diamond: Diamond done to sum called Love / Count: Count on us to Love / Dip: Dip us direct to the election of Love / Trip: Trip sent to the hint of Love / Whirly: Whirly blue extend to the trance end Love / Girls: Girls grace taste in Love / Drip: Drip enough wed to Love / Strips: Strip's tip to the land of Love / Stray: Stray to a friend in Love / Stay: Stay on home to Love / Recline: Recline in time to Love / Relate: Relate a date to Love / Revert: Revert to the squirt called Loved / Convent: Convent sent to the convert of Love / Screen: Screen your Love / Spent: Spent on Love / Cavort: Cavort to the sort called Love / Trade: Trade on rest-full deliverance in Love / Mean: Mean to Love / Court: Court tonight is Love / Tent: Tent held high to stakes of Love / Tint: Tine spent on a rainbow called Love / Coat: A coat for Love / Create: Create gentle Love / Resolute: Resolute to acute in Love / Rates: Rates rate great for Love / Entice: Entice nice for Love / Devise: Devise a rise at Love / Motile: Motile measure of the treasured laugh called South to Love / Device: Device of the enlist to list our Love / Dusty: Dusty news to Love / Motive: Motive measure of the plan to Love / Wheel: A great wheel of lust called life to Love / Whale: Whale enough to Love / Feel: Feel trust, Love / Float: Float fell to held by Love / Fade: Fade to default to Love / Raid: Raid above to Love / Rave: Rave on to Love / Leafy: Leafy trust of Love / Horizon: Horizon on the sunrising Love / Winds: Winds review of who we Love / Leak: Leak to the view of who we Love / Reveal: Reveal in us and Love / Venue: Venue knew three were One in Love / Venus: Venus viewed by the trip to the oval track called Love / Seal: Seal to the feel of Love / Silk: Silk to the appeal of Love / Clear: Daily clear to Love / Chorus: Chorus and the courage plumbed to say ruest Love.

CHAPTER 90 / LOVE TOUCHED: Sharp: Sharp to the shield of Love / View: View yourself healed to Love / Victorious: Victorious advance to Love / Shrines: Shrine's fine in Love / Field: Field of first you Love / Victory: Victory viewed by you in your agree to Love / Perform: Perform us Love / Appeal: Appeal to the rush of Love / Flag: Flag found on the head of Love / Plan: Let us plan our spanning bridge to lightly give in to Love / Place: Place a few of less than often seen in Love / Plant: Plant yourself in too Love / Quantums: Quantums coined by the art of Love / Constantinople: Constant the opal of Love / Fantastic: Fantastic ascend to the blend of Love / Feathered: Feathered ascend to the wings of Love / Happy: Happy to be free with Love / Fantasy: Fantasy isled by Love / Numbered: Numbered next to Love / Us: Us enough to Love / Trade: Trade your fade to Love / Resist: Resist exist has gone to thrive on Love / Travel: Travel home to Love / Book: Book imbued by Love / Waveframe: Waveframe famed by Love / Mix: Let us mix our hearts in Love / Mate: Mate great to Love / Keylocked: Keylocked explain of the name called Love / Climb: Climb astride the side called Seattle wide to Love / Keyhole: Keyhole measured to a cue of Love / Voracious: Voracious feed of the rest of lean to Love / Mountains: Mountains mount to Love / Equip: Equip us with Love / Quality: Quality cured by the insure of Love / Photos: Photos flash at the chance to Love / Draw: Draw yourself drew to Love / Delicate: Delicate in the friend called Love / Astronauts: Astronauts rule the sights of Love / Farthest: Farthest ascend to the Light of Love / Rainer: Rainer clear to the mountain's Light with Love / Swivel: Swivel to the top of Love / Companionship: Companionship kinned to Love / River's Hood: River's Hood over the canyons of feelings of Love / Contract: Contract crowned by the lift to written down Love / Marriage: Marriage now complete to Love / Career: Career clear to Love / Marry: Marry yourself to Love / Carriage: Carriage crewed to Love / Inside: Inside confide to Love / Stair: Stair prayer ladder high to Love / Exudes: Exudes exceed is Love / Extremely: Extremely resident to Love / Stare: Stare at the hour of prayer in Love / Better: Better bettered by Love / Gain: Gain a grace of this is Love / Winds: Winds win the race for Love / Letters: Letters letter better in us as Love / Steer: Steer clear to the lights of Love / Exclude: Exclude yourself less in Love / Musical: A musical message called Love / Everest: Everest said a higher ground is the round to the summit of Love / Range: Range ran to lend of the race to Love / Music: Music manned by land in Love / Serenity: Serenity an Anasazi found in love.

CHAPTER 91 / LOVE TOUR: Shore: The shored allure of the cure to Love / Lure: A lure of led to Love / Retail: Retail held up to Love / Attentive: Attentive space to Love / Attend: Attend to a brink of Love / Travel: Travel trailed to Love / Global: Global access to Love / Glare: Glare to stare at the Light of Love / Quick: Quick an erupt in Love / Spree: Stay straight to a spree in we are

Love / Quake: Quaker quaked with shaker Love / Lightness: The lightness I lend to Love / Advice: Advice schooled by Love / Advise: Advise arise to Love / Finesse: Finesse a file of Love / Advertise: Advertise your eyes to Love / Enlist: Enlist much Love / Versatile: My versatile style is Love / Allies: Allies all ayed each year too All-ah God in Love / Brisk: Brisk bet, Love / Ice: Ice held hands to cups of much of Love / Life: Life's luft, Love / Learn: Learn to yearn for best in Love / Grease: Central release of the grease in Love / Life: Lift the strand of a trailing hand to a Lightened plan to Love / Lean: Surrender your lean to Love / Glass: Glass place, our Love / Loss: Loss of joy? Bright back Love / .Glance: Glance at bliss, Love / Glee: Capable of glee in Love / List: Listings lend is Love / Glean: Glean less? Love / Concept: Concept at hand is Love / Cave: Cave delight is of the height of Love / Fix: Fix exit to Love / Pharaoh: Pharaoh's found a friend in a fascinating blend of Love / Rings: Rings to win in Love / Pyramid: Pyramid's extravagant gesture, the options invent of 4 to 3 a Hopi Blue prophetic Love to Love / Cognito: Cognito seen, in Love / Race: A race exact to in fact we all, Love / Blossom: Blossom's blended freeing streak Love / Bandit's: Bandit's bend to Love / Ravine: Ravine rang clean 2 Love / Rule: Rule, school, Love / Fixes: Fixes felt up to an isolate great to Love / Purpose: Purpose a rose, to Love / Plate: Plates date with fed to Love / Fixed: Fixed a fit to Love / Peruse: Peruse the news to Love / Passage: A passaged accent to Love / Factual: Factual fan of Love / Freedom: Freedom found in a kona towned by Love / Plan: Plan to heal the feel of flowered Love / Actual: Actually you are Love / Ring: God's ring, the stars, of Love / Vision: Vision's invent, Australia's spare, Love / Cart: To a cart exort cavort, the sort, that, Love / Heights: Heights hint at sights of Love / Prescription: Prescription's invent, the pills of feels of monthly Love / Street: Brittle street, the sweet, of Love / Hikes: Valued hikes to the likes of Love / Revolution: Revolution's kin, the friend of evolve in Love / Stray: Central structure, the stray, the day, of Love / Hearts: Hearts start near our Love.

CHAPTER 92 / LOVE TURN: Spoil: Spoil nuclear familial bind by opening rest in Love / Beauty: Beauty built on Love / Boot: Boots bounce knee high to Love / Acknowledge: Acknowledge is sent to reflexine rebirth of Love / Butte: Butte amid planes of lesson Loved / Baton: Baton one bond with nucleaic long, our Love / Purse: Pursed place, the loan, of Love / Place: Place mates in a place of Love / Basic: Basic paste of Love / Knowledge: Acknowledge the friend of in Love / Bail: Bail enough, Love / Embroil: Embroil soil with ground of round to Love / Scientific: Scientific formulate of late Love / Cosmology: Cosmology's blend is the wrap-up of Love / DNA: DNA contends our friend is Love / Terrific: Terrifically lent to the extend of round our Love / Density: Density done? Love / RNA: Rent nuclear ascend, the mommy in Love / Analysis: Analyze wide days won by narrowed release of Love / Gravity: Gravity led lightly to Love / Rate: Rated wet to let us Love / Paralysis: Paralyzed by greed, exceed your trance, advance 2 Love / Gravitation's: Gravitation's nation of Love / Liberty: Liberty of the lasting free, we Love / Physique:

Physique's exist is enlist in Love / Complicate: Complicate less, Love / Regard: Regard this way, home to Love / Fame: Fame found abound our Love / Mill: Mill edge, milligan went to Love / Allude: Allude in a bless allay of Love / Frame: Frame shame in Love / Rate: God's rate of date, Love / Raft: Raft a raise to a river of Love / Compute: Compute acute repute to Love / Root: To root for vest in Love / Route: Route short? Love / Geometry: Geometry measured sacred Love / Intimate: Intimate test of the trace to taste our Love / Lens: A lens to focus on rest in Love / Fire: Fire freed by Love / Myrtle: Myrtle blend our tree to Love / Clique: Clique shut? Love / Ice: Ice test? Love / Universe: Universe veiled? Clearly Love / Credit: Cliche credits way 2 Love / Milk: Milk moist, Love / Intricate: Intricate trait, Love / Debit: Debit bet on Love / Drape: Drape tape on ducts of Love / Order: Order due to Love / Synchronous: Synchronous hash to Love / Address: Address breast of Love / Physic: Physic attune to mystic noon of Love / Aid: Aid to raid less, Love / Released: Released flasks of Love / Judged: Judged a guest of Love / Software: Software, wear, Love / Nicotine: Nicotine dreamed of clouds of Love / Attention: Attention within, Love / Privacy: Privacy approved of Love / Ambition: Ambition went to Love / Rendition: Rendition's ran true to Love / Wavelets: Wavelets let's Love / Enigma: Enigma in Love.

CHAPTER 93 / LOVE OCEANS: Gabriel: Gabriel gained our Love / Michael: Michael met wetter than Love / Spoken: Spoken yet? Love / Possible: Possible please? Love / Biology: Biology's astound physical by Love / Emerge: Emerge to merge in Love / Plausible: A plausible manner of Love / Psychology: Psychology sent invent to Love / Synapse: Synapse said, gap led, to Love / Print: Print a print of Love / Clicked: Clicked on clued by Love / Meteorologic: Meteorologic the logic of Love / Native: Native nature, Love / Companion: Companion can Love / Credibility: Credibility centered on Love / Cosmic: Cosmic, a thin ascend to a friend called Love / Ideal: Ideal heal of Love / Mathed: Going home mathed to Love / Luxury: Luxury measure, Love / Roam: Roam the same to Love / Continental: Continental friend of Love / Success-full: Calmly success-full to Love / Psalm: Find psalm in Love / Connect: Connect akin Love / Palm: Palm append to Love / Priority: Penciled in a priority's friend to Love / Privacy: Privacy's attune to Love / Technology: Technologic ecologic wonder of Love / Alternates: Alternates on a sun universe of one to only God Love / Presence: Presence accented by Love / Tectonics: Tectonic the exotic, Love / Immerse: Immerse your Love / Intense: Intense enough to Love / Hubble: Hubble's hold on a telescopic friend, the mars of Love / Huddle: Life's lift of huddle, Love / Cape: Cape a draft to Love / Hurl: Hurled into a galactic matters. Splattered. Love / Curve: Curve dealt deal to Love / Expanse: Expanse of pence to Love / Span: Spanned shift to planned exist in Love / Emit: Easy emit of the fit to Love / Superb: Superb view, you, Loved / Expand: Expand again, friend, of Love / Comfit: Comfit me with your chore of Love / Beacon: Beaconed height, to Love / Transform: Transform your warm to harm-less Love / Ember: Ember wound to out-of-town, Love / Summer: Summer slimmer? Love / Gala: Gala planned, Love / Decelerate: Decelerate the rate of yes! Love / Supernova: Supernova sent to blow us all the way 2 Love / Calibrate: Calibrate frantic-less, Love / Build: Build anthuric artharic Love / Accelerate: Accelerate a thicker Love / Constant: Consistent constant content, Love / Particles: Particles pleased by Love / Macro: Macro muse, Love / Micro: Micro mooned, Love / Mini: Mini's skirt is Love / Mid: Lifted mid our Love / Width: Width won 2 Love / Worthy: Worthy ways for Love / Treasures: Treasures and the treaty found for Love / Piece: Piece and the testing for Love.

CHAPTER 94 / LOVE MYSTERY: Wise: Wise enough, to Love / Whisk: Whisk won to Love / Expect: Expect a lot of Love / Impress: Empress express to Love / Gravitate: Gravitate the exasperate away to Love / Matter: Matter's patter on heal, Love / Bubbles: Bubbles babble crisp to Love / Anoint: Anoint a point with Love / Enhance: Enhance advance Love / Assure: Assure me, Love / Welcome: Welcome wedded Love / Spring: Spring sprung on Love / Journey: Journeyed in 2 Love / Research: Research abreast hour Love / Roles: Roles rule, Love / Fire: Fire higher held in a field of volcanic Love / Ether: Ether set on Love / Air: Air fair flew Love / Earth: Earthly signed, Love / Paradigm: Paradigm kind of Love / Absolute: Absolute bless of Love / Inflame: Inflame the same to Love / Diadem: Diadem within Love / Aromatic: Aromatic a scent to Love / Frame: Frame in front of Love / Crowning: Crowning glory Love / Join: Join your friend in Love / Frontier: Frontier post, Love / Evoke: Evoke emote in a note of Love / Evolve: Evolve in trust of Love / Pioneer: Pioneer steer to Love / Water: Water wed, Love / Wind: Wind and watered, Love / Sea: Sea-side Love / Blaze: A blaze on Love / Phase: Phase 3, of, Love / Relate: Relative to relate, Love / Wholesome: A wholesome matter, Love / Mist: Mist us with your Love / Vigor: Great vigor found in, Love / Velvet: Velvet's truth, Love / Served: In Love we are served by Godest Love / Triggers: Guilt triggers anger hidden by Love / Trait: Traits defend on, Love / Trace: A trace to end on, Love / Tree: Office treasured by trees of Love / Mountains: Mountains measured, Love / Rivers: Rivers ran inside of us in Love / Navajo: Navajo nave, Love / 1000X: 1000X God magnify, Love / Petaled: Petaled fed by floral Love / Pace: Pace of a race to Love / Friendly: Friendly friend to Love / Manner: Manner met by Godest Love / Mate: Mated meet at Love / Journal: Pleasure's journal, Love / Confuse: Perfect confuse, God-less, Love / Standard: Standard plan, Love / Joint: Joints of June and Love / Connote: Connote a vote on Love / Tradition: Tradition's vent to Love / General: General pleasure, Love / Extract: Extractive defend of Love / Experience: Experience spent on Love.

CHAPTER 95 / LOVE MOTION: Study: Study state of Love / Sturdy: Sturdy mate, our Love / Stance: Stance a chant, of Love / Invigorate: Invigorate your invest in Love / Equate: Equate of 'lates' become perfect relate to Love / Sate: Sate invested in chests of Love / Acknowledge: Acknowledge your knowledge of knowing this, Love / Knowledge: Knowledge is knowing the boundlessness of Love / Reduce: Reduce race strife, Love / Induce: Induce in us, Love / Seduce: Seduce suggest, Love / Technique: Technique seeks resolve of Love / Anatomical: The anatomical feature of Love / Comical: Comical favors of laughing Love / Radical: Radical reign of Love / Favors: Favors viewed by Love / Flavors: Flavors freed, Love / Fake: Elastic measure a fakeless pleasure of Love / Grades..Grades good to Love / Grasp: Grasp the truth, in Love / Testify: Testify why you, Love / Work: Work in us, Love / Studys: Studys show, Love / Yield. ..Yield yes! to Love / Future: Future breed by Love / Past: Past has gone to Love / Cause: Cause has won by Love / Plan: Plan's expand is Love / Experience: Experiences send our Love / Experiment: Experiment in our Love / Exhale: Exhale fuels our Love / Breathe: Breathe fresh Love / Breath: Breath burst, Love / Essence: Essence in our Love / Cleanse: Cleansing clue of Love / Crafted: Crafted hue of rainbowed Love / Method: Excellent the method of Love / Practice: Practice paled by Love / Profound: Profound mates of Love / Profuse: Perfect profuse of Love / Disease: Disease can breed in lessened Love / Control: Control is rest in Love / Digest: Digest mint of Love / Fund: Funds found, Love / Found: By found I mean, Love / Sort: Sort a sort of sorted Love / Intense: Brought intense to Love / Koan: Koan spelled by simply Love / Polish: Kona's polish, Love / Mystery: Mystery's meet at Love / Truth: Truth enough to Love / Trust: Trust in us in Love / Frame: Framed by few who Love / France: France's instinct is Love / Freeze: Freeze framed by Love / Preen: Preen's face, clear, Love / Praise: Praise yet? Love / Raid: Raid's beguile on Love / Reap: Excellence reaps of Love / Jewel: Jewels adjust to a perfect shine of Love / Age: Age be-jeweled by Love / Potential: Potential plan to un-pent, Love / Pent: Pent resent is the Lightened Love / Part: Part of us remembers Love.

CHAPTER 96 / LOVE NOTATION: Potential: Potential scene, Love / Stay..Stay around, Love / Being: Being seen at Love / Bring: Bring true, Love / Text: In text, Love / Press: Press truth, Love / Praise: Praise rush to Love / Raise: Raise up, Love / Appear: Appear near true Love / Distinguish: Latest dream distinguish too, Love / Disguise: Disguise rest-less, Love / Submit: Submit true, Love / Denote: Denote your vote for yes, Love / Note: Latest note, vote, for Love / Compassion: Compassion's clue is Love / Passion: Passion's play is the way to Love / Fashion: Ladies fashion Love / Fades: Fades flew to Love / Faint: Faint flew to knew, Love / Fade: Fade spade of lessened, Love / Cultivate: Cultivate crews of Love / Curve: Curve, on cue, to Love / Back: Back to stay, in Love / Practice: Practice who you Love / Introduce: Introduce yourself to Love / Induce: Induce best, Love / Exude: Exude rules Love / Intrude: Intrude's rest, Love / Become: Become resume of Love / Behave: Behave, be, receive, Love / Befriend: Befriend us, Love / Ethics: Ethics say, Love / Morale: Morale's view of Love / Motif: A daily motif, Love / Motive: Motive may be, Love / Books: Book fulfilled, healed, Love / Claims: Lately claims eschew, Love / Framed:

Framed best by Love / Elaborate: Elaborate on a state of Love / Date: Date due, now today, Love / Depth: To depth sunk, Love / Shrine: Shrine assigned to Love / Shred: Shred less, Love / Shield: Shield stress? A way, Love / Ancients: Trange the daze of ancient ways to less than Love / Charmed: Energy charmed by Love / Armed: Armed by strong in Love / Bells: Bells bella tale of Love / Tangent: Lately tangent meant sent, to Love / Tangible: Lessons tangible, Love / Kant: Kant's devote is a can Love / Rant: Can rant less, Love / Raid: Raid's run to Love / Reveal: Reveal truth, Love / Rate: Rates date free Love / Heal: Heal in us, reveal, Love / Climate: Climate clued by Love / Treat: Treat sweet to Love / Tempered: Tempered to a temperature to our Love / Degree: Substance degree, Love / Sustain: Reveal sustain of Love / Sustenance: Lately sustenance seen, is Love / Hereafter: Hereafter knew, Love / Strand: Strand's hand in Love.

CHAPTER 97 / LOVE MENTIONS: Strain: Strain's rest, healthy, Love / Respect: Respect filled, Love / Simple: Simple street, Love / Supple: Supple presume of Love / Mobility: Mobility's meet is Love / Manage: Manage meant rest, in Love / Firm: Firm news, Love / Century: Century's keen, on Love / Optimism: Optimism seen, in Love / Thread: Thread bred of Love / Defuse: Defuse refuse to Love / Incentive: Incentive healed by Love / Need: Need to know, Love / Denote: The basis of denote is vote 4 Love / Trait: Latest trait, Love / Needle: Lightly needle, need of Love / Skirt: A skirt around, Love / Threat: Threat spoke less of Love / Trace: Lately trace our Love / Relief: Relief's breath, Love / Account: Account to Love / Recount: Recount your count of Love / Led: Hot enough to lead to Love / Species: Species of elect fed direct to Love / Sunlight: Know thyself by Christed sunlight of the Buddhaic shelf to Love / By: By the way we are Loved / Topography: Top of a graphic friend to earthly Love / Respite: Respite deft in the synaptic cleft of the adept's return to Love / Love: Love list on set direct to Love / Precision: Precision drawn to the cause of lend and blend / Extension: Extension to the friend in Love / Air: Air fair in the breath of the space to Love / Thermal: Thermal thrill in the heal to Love / Pertain: Pertain to true in your desire to own your OM in Love / Hydraulic: Hydraulic ahead in the stream, Love / Presence: Presence prayed for Love / Powered: Powered by flew, to Love / Permanence: Permanence presumed in Love / Sentience: Sentience felt, in Love / Preference: Preference soon, Love / Perspiration: The latest inspiration, perspiration, in Love / Sustain: Sustain me, Love / Precision: Precisely seen, Love / Meteor: Meteor more able, Love / Shower: Shower found on higher ground of Love / Klamath: Klamath cured, blue-green to Love / Hour: Hour spent in Love / Heliocentric: Sun scent to a heliocentric event, Love / Delegate: Delegate's due, to Love / Answer: Answer now, Love / Eccentric: Eccentric zoom, to Love / Content: Content the clue, to Love / Comet: Comet's due, now, Love / Candid: Candid banded, Love / Clarity: Clarity clued by charity spewed by Love / Earthy: Lately earthly due, to Love / Temperate: A basic temperate true, Love / Zealous: Zealous advent of ascent to Love / Jealous: Zealous jealous soon? Love

/ Joined: Joined to a tune of Love / Joint: Joint refuse of lesser Love / Industry: Industry seen in Love / Flexibility: Flex able? Love / Flood: Flood flew home to roam in Love.

CHAPTER 98 / LOVE WHISPERS: Target: A target true to the heart of Love / Remedy: Latest remedy is we, Love / Rate: Rate set on Love / Allow: Allow now to Love / Disavow: Latest disavow is wow, to Love / Domestic: Domestic fuel, Love / Electric: Electric rule, Love / Efficient: Efficient fuel, Love / Reluctant: Reluctant friend? Love / Insistent: Insistent few, gone less, to Love / Current: Current crew, Love / Classic: A classic crew, Love / Political: Political kettle, hot, Love / Implemental: Implementals you'll Love / Consistent: Adjust to consistent, Love / Purchase: Purchase few, receive, Love / Prance: Prance around, Love / Dance: Dance true in Love / Date: Date today, Love / Durate: The durate of great in Love / Grant: Grant grew to Love / Naples: Naples knew Love / Nip: Nip-less, Love / Consume..Consume meant, vent, Love / Nape: Nape necked, Love / Complex: Complex grew to a crew of Love / Consummate: Consummate your Love / Dawn: Often dawn has come 2 Love / Surface: Surface seen ,Love / Surfeit: Surfeit relate, Love / Sincere: A sincere yes to Love / Close: Close the deep to lighter Love / Commit: Commit true, to Love / State: State your set of Love / Consecrate: Consecrate state, of Love / Supply mental: Supply mental find of Love / Convention: Convention's chew on Love / Elemental: Elemental seen in a mental dream of Love / Delegates: Delegates due, to Love / Balance: Balance scent to, Love / Earth: Earth's cue is Love / Mother: Mother met who, we Love / Nature: Nature known by own, Love / Nestle: Nestle into when, Love / Deep: Deep in trust of Love / Level: Lately level, Love / Link: Often linked to Love / Confer: Confer now, Love / Concur: Concur where, Love / Range: Range arose, Love / Increase: Increase rest in Love / Dresser: Dresser drew socks to Love / Closet: Closet clued by who'd, Love / Close: A definite close to lesser Love / Clothed: A clothed crew, Love / Convenient: Convenient spent, on Love / Crescent: A pleasant crescent, Love / Concise: Concise advice, Love / Constitute: Constitute much, Love / Convention: Convention scene of Love / Convolute: Convolute shoot of Love / Effective: Effective said, Love / Restitute: Restitute refute of Love / Reinstate: Reinstate great, Love.

CHAPTER 99 / LOVE VOWED: Form: Today's form, Love / Flow: Lately flew our flow of Love / Frames: Frames found for Love / Concentrate: Concentrate on great Love / Meditate: Meditate on this Love / Alleviate: Alleviate fate-less forget. Love / Allude: Latest allude is who'd Love / Retrieve: Retrieve, the message is, Love / Resume: Resume rest in Love / Retrace: Retrace steps true, Love / Indeed: Indeed, yes in deed, Love / Believe: Believe best, Love / Faith: Carats of faith all are great to Love / Great: Great gain seen by Love / Grace: Grace grew to Love / Exudes: Lately exudes our Love / Fair: Fair enough to Love / Usher: Lady's usher in Love / Voiced: Voiced a need to Love / Issue: Issue sent to Love / Intrude: Intrude's? Love /

Extrude: Let us extrude, Let's exude Love / Elude: Elude near? Love / Average: Today on average, Love / Standard: Standard sign, Love / Opine: Opines touch, Love / Open: Open true, Love / Opinion: Opinioned few, Love / Survive: Survive shut, Live, Love / Surmise: Surmised rise to Love / Suspend: Many suspend their Love / Heighten: A heightened hint at Love / Halt: Halt's kilt of suspend Love / Hearken: There hearken, Love / Herald: Herald to love / Evident: Evident reveal of Love / Exact: Exactly said, Love / Suspect: Pleasant's suspect is Love / Suspend: Suspend us in Love / Ascend: Truly ascend to Love / Extend: Daddy's extend is Love / Remit: Remit fit, Love / Emit: Emits hut, the house of Love / Dialogue: A dialogue due to Love / Dialect: I like a dialect of Love / Direct: Directly seen by Love / Deflect: Deflect dust by an ashes vent to remember Love / Broken: Broken healed by real Love / Embrace: Embrace space in you to Love / Cover: Cover us, Love / Cavort: Cavort's full heal, the dance, is Love / Extort: 12 stars extort, Love / Imbibe: Christed abide, imbibe, Love / Confide: Confide us, Love / Confer: Confer friend of Love / Concede: Concedes feed is Love / To Great: To great gain of Love / Elate: Elate's wait is Love / In God: In God given, Love / Glory Won: Glory won one, Love / Journey Done: Journey done, only One, Light of Love / All is Won: All's won by Love / One Sun: I see the Light of one sun, Love / Sunshine: Sunshine shield? Lift to healed our Love.

CHAPTER 100 / LOVE AVOWED: Height: Heights hushed in Love / Elect: Elect us, Love / Reflect: Total reflect of yes to Love / Expect: Expect this, Love / Only Light: Only Light, Right? Love / Lightly Said: Today, lightly said Love / Begin: Begin a gain of Love / Depend: Depend now, Love / Define: Define this Love / Independence: Independence, us, Love / Astound: Astound around, Love / Conserve: Conserve know, Love / Portal: Portal reviewed to Love / Recline: Let us recline, Love / Paradisial: Today's paradisial resign to Love / Ambrosial: Ambrosial bliss of Love / Propel: Propel real Love / Expel: Expel us, less, Love / Impulse: Impulsive ascend to Love / Bereave: Bereave arrest of less, Love / Declare: Declare best, Love / Depend: Depends rest is Love / Tax: Lessened tax of in fact we Love / Intrinsic: Intrinsic fit, of Love / Extensive: Extensively well to Love / Legacy: Legacy's lend of Love / Wood: Wooden will? Love / Wed: Will wed, Love / Brink: Brink bailed over Love / Forever: Pleasure forever in Love / Evergreen: Evergreen scene of Love / Automatic: Automatic treasure, Love / Diagragmatic: Diagragmatic expand to breaths of Love / Activate: Totally activate your Love / Champion: Champions ascend to Love / Turtle: Turtled tree of earthy Love / Whale: Lately whaled by Love / Wheel: Often wheeled by Love / Whim: Whim wed to Love / Dolphins: Dolphins filling Love / Hero: Hero's hand of Love / Relation: Relations rest in Love / Expulse: Expulse sent, to a pulsed invent of Love / Contend: Contend less, Love / Explain: Explain again, Love / Search: Search scents of Love / Rehearse: Rehearse immerse in Love / Fly: Fly through, Love / Excel: Excel best, Love / Jump: Jump apace of Love / Joyous: Daily joyous, Love / Belief: Belief in bless of Love / Know:

Constraint-less know constraint-less ways to Love / Peace: Peace now spent, then Love / Durate: Durates rate, Love / Safe: Safe enough to Love / See: See us, Love / Sea: Seas we, Love / Children: Children hear our Love / Keys: Keys deep in seek Love / Cares: Cares enough to Love / Insures: Barest insures of Love / Beliefs: Beliefs best sent to Love / Found: Found her, Love.

CHAPTER 101 / LOVE LOANED: Ultimate: The ultimate feature is our Love / Specifically: Specifically sent to Love / Terrific: Terrific to invent of the hint called Love / True: True enough to the touch of Love / Sensitive: Sensitive are we to our Love / Supple: Supple to enthuse of Love / Migratory: Migratory to floods of birds who fly to the higher Love / Munificent: Munificent to incense of Love / Masterfull: Masterfull to a mend of intend to Love / Indicative: Indicative to the point of this matter, Love / Superlative: Superlative to those we Love / Expressive: Expressive to a matter called the clatter of less has done to hum in Loved / Specific: Specific weave of the leaves of bless this growing Love / Successive: Successive to the dream of Love / Isolate: Isolate of late has worked for Love / Natural: Natural to a nestle of the directly Love / Nurture: Nurture to the need to Love / Suture: Suture sealed by the heeled worn stacked to Love / Glue: Glue flew straight to Love / Repair: Repair's arrest is Love / Confer: Confer to a feel of Love / Refer: Refer us to Love / Retain: Retain your ability to Love / Ultimate: Ultimate to an attitude of Love / Trail: Trail a trust to truth in Love / Trap: Trap-less straps of Love / Adapt: Adapt less trap of Love / Walks: Walks talk tall to Love / The Path: The path ahead is Love / The Bath: The bath is splashed to a lesson wet with Love / The Property: The property shopped hear at the edge of Love / The Tree: The tree of the day to love / Opportune: Opportune to a swoon to deepest Love / Stroll: Stroll near our fear-less Love / Glory: Glory within is Love / Within: Within awaits our Love / Educate: Educate the state of Love / Compute: Compute your elate with Love / Commute: Commute refute of stars to the Mars of Love / Artisans: Artisans span our fan of fond to Love / Pace: Place yourself to the flame of violet fame in Love / Place: Place your face at the art of Love / Pulse: Pulses stay up in Love / Prance: Prance to a glance at the waste of lessen worn to Love / Connect: Connect us up, Love / Baby: Baby, baby, Love / Woven: Woven to a weaving plane called Love / Addicted: Addicted gone drifted to Love / Related: Related to us Love / Sated: Sated by waited for Love / Finished: Finished to a frame of the wave called clear like crystalline Love / Full: Full of Love / Free: Free to be, we, in, Love / We: We are wed by July you said to Love / Love: Love's tool ruled by lift to Love / Courtesans: Courtesans stand in the Venetian view of Love / Herbs: Herbs invest in a crust of Love / Herbal: Herbal hand of the span wide open to Love / Acres: Acres of abound in Love / Tracts: Tracts of truth to acres of Love / Oak: Oak trees dressed with the limbs of Love / Spoke: Spoke often of Love / Spent: Spent an adjust on Love / Vent: Vent at the hint of the lip worn red to Love.

CHAPTER 102 / LOVE OPTIMUM: Clarity: Clarity found in the ground of Love / Benefit: Benefit yourself, Love / Events: Events insist on Love / Vote: Vote on Love / Grow: Grow yourself some home in Love / Concentrate: Concentrate on the great in Love / Rate: Rate this date number One to Love / Respect-full: Respect-full measure of the place called Love / Include: Include some soon, Love / Loyalty: Loyalty ruled to Love / Potent: Potent pattern, Love / Portent: Portent invent to Love / Perfection: Perfection present in Love / Investment: An investment sent to Love / Favor: Favor Love / Warmth: Warmth warmly said is Light in Love / Elite: Elite to a treat of decent Love / Convention: Convention's cradle, Love / Ascendant: God's Ascendant function is we are Love / Intention: Intention to mention our Love / Possession: Possession passed up to the intent to heal Love / Non-attachment: Non-attachment's rule is Love / Ranges: Ranges rang true to Love / Vow: Vow your Love / Covenants: Covenants agree to Love / Commandment: Commandment meant to Love / Promise: Promise yourself to Love / Repent: Repent meant hints of Love / Resent: Resent can rest at Love / Forgiveness: Forgiveness freed to Love / Convene: Convene yourself to Love / Ergonomic: Ergonomic sonnet of Love / Ecstatic: Ecstatic to ascend to Love / Optics: Optics accrue to ascend to see our Love / Acclaim: Acclaim the same to Love / Duration: Duration to the nation of Love / Inflation: Inflation's mention is up to bust in Love / Quality: Quality's quill is Love / Qualify: Qualify to be healed by thee and Love / Questions: Questions sealed by Love / Travel: Travel around the arc of complete in Love / Trade: Let your trade by Love / Locate: Locate your date in Love / Discover: Discover the other in Love / Defray: Defray exist to we insist on Love / Descents: Descents to us in Love / Relax: Relax around the invent of perfect Love / Relate: Relate to a matter grown fatter to lift our Love / Electronic: An electronic extend of Love / Sonic: Sonic invent called Love / Submit: Submit your set wet to Love / Recreate: Recreate your recreate with Love / Well: Well I know the swell of Love / Explore: Explore your Love / Support: Support won One to Love / Coast: Coast to coast we host our Love / Roast: Roast ran new to living Love / Rate: Rate your date to Love / Congratulate..Congratulate God, know, Love / Spectacular: Spectacular to a spectacle, I know the God I Am and that I Am is manned by Love / Accomplish: Accomplish sent through Love / Eternity: Eternity lives in the zen of when we Love / Bodily: Bodily functional, I Am emotional to a higher devotional called the grounds of Love / Lofts: Lofts and the license to show up at Love.

CHAPTER 103 / LOVE LINKS: Beautifully: Beautifully done, we are One, too, Love / Blessedly: Blessedly built, I Am man to expand of Love / Spun: Spun around to true in Love / Specialty: Specialty signed by the lined to Love / Specifically: Specifically sent to Love / Spectacularly: Spectacularly strong in Love / Wonder-fully: Wonder-fully won by Love / Language: Heal your language, Love / Meaning: Meaning sent respect to Love / Charisma: Charisma came in the flame called wed to

Love / Review: Review a rest in Love / Faith: Faith found effect in Love / Freeze: Freeze frozen through with Love / Thaw: Thaw enough, Love / Thrill: Thrill your zeal and Love / Scholar: An alchemical scholar, Love / Sculpture: Sculpture on the land of Love / Student: Student to student invent the test of why we Love / Teacher: Teachered fan of the man who Loved / Lawyer: Lawyer led to the life of Light to the sight of delight in Love / Physician: Physicianed by a blend of the friend who knew how to Love / Vine: Vine along to the song called we will exceed to Love / Eternal: Eternal ascend to the blend of the flight to Love / Infinite: Infinite view of the taste we Love / Reliable: Reliable to the stand at the sound of Love / Reasonable: Reasonable expend to the elastic blend / called Love / Vital: Vital, true, and Loved / Treasured: Treasured trend to hunt for Love / Transitive: Transitive trend to the notion of nations in Love / Mesmerized: Mesmerized by true to a renew called Love / Business: Business imbued by the faith of Love / Biblical: Biblical can be lyrical with Love / Beatific: Beatific the truth of in this, we, Love / Oriental: Oriental to the Asiatic dream called Love / Agape: Agape the pace to enlightened Love / Grateful: Grateful to you, I Am, Love / I Am: I Am the clue to Love / I Am That: I Am that review of LOVES / I Am Too: I Am too free to Love / We Are: We are in nature of gratitude's grasp on Love / We Too: We too need our Love / We Believe: We believe the stuff called Love / We Review: We review our needs in Love / We Intrude: We intrude to bless our Love / We Interrogate: We interrogate elate to Love / We Feel: We feel a date in Love / We Respect: We respect your entire ascend to Love / We Gain: We gain renew to Love / We Refrain: We refrain our restraint less on Love / We Sing: We sing to bring Love / The Song: The song found astound in Love / Of God: Of God we sing in Love / God Long: God is long to Love / To Less: To less, we stay, away, to, Love / Than Man: Than man can, Love / Can Know: Can know, Love / And A: And a new wave came home to Love / Human: Human-ity stood in astound at Love / Flow: Flow my way, Love / Remains: Remains the explain that yes is Love / Singing: Singing only and all-ways Love / Only, Ascendant: Only the Ascendant stand in Love / Healthy: Healthy and the tribune too, an ascendant to Love / Earth: Earth and the marriage for ascendant Love.

CHAPTER 104 / LOVE ALL: Many Falls: Many falls fill our hours with Love / Many Suns: Many suns seen to Love / Many Me: Many me, be, Love / Held, I Fled: Held, I fled, to above h-our Love / Held, I Held: Held, I held, healed in Love / I Am Pedernal: I Am pedernal in a stance to eternal Love / Of Love: Of Love I wield best, only, all, to, live, Love / Noblese Oblige: A noble obligation to an alteration sky wide to Love / Med: Medically blessed by Love / Fled: Fled to feed, Love / Fed: Fed head, Love / Bred: Bred red, Love / Fed: Fed enough? Love / Med: Med said direct, Love / Many Lifts: Many lifts risk, Love / Many One: Many one to all in Love / Many All: Many is all we, Love / Bricked: Bricked abreast our Love / Framed: Framed the same to Love / Scoop: Scoop up group Love / Scooting Home: Scoot on home to Love / Home's Best: Housing's best when home's a rest in Love / Best Bet: Pray best by your bet on Love / Love Let: Love lot got, Love / Let Love: Let us Love / Love Breathes: Love's breath sweet breathes, in me, Love / Select: Gentle friend, select again, our Love / Reflect: Reflect in us dear, Love / Respect: Respect a rest in Love / Residence: Residence won in Love / Abide: Abide in time to Love / Astride: Astride is fed in land of Love / The Ride: Ride a reel to heel in Love / The Side: The side me see is Love / The Space: The space in place is Love / The Place: The place to face, Love / The Lace: The lace to set us up, Love / The Trace: The trace to base upon Love / The Exceed: The exceed in deed, Love / The Need: The need to nurture, Love / The Tide: The tide to ride is the absolute, Love / The stride: An approximate measure, the stride to man, your Love / The Design: The design hu-man, Love / The Fine: The fine align is Love / The Fed: The fed to bead on Love / The Led: The led inside our Love / Carolina: Carolina, there and everywhere Love / Home: Home, a phone to Love / Head: Head home, roam to Love / Heal: Call heal, real Love / Heel: Heel set, Love / Spurred: Spurred on Love / Sped: Sped past repast in Love / Speed: Speed full steam to Love / Led: Led me abed to Love / Lead: Lead yourself to Love / Plead: Plead your case for Love / Hum: Hum a symphony for Love / Play: Play a few bars for Love / Limp: Limp back for more Love / Blimps: Blimps filled with Love / Float: Float your boat to Love / Ease: Ease yourself into Love / Easy: It's easy to Love.

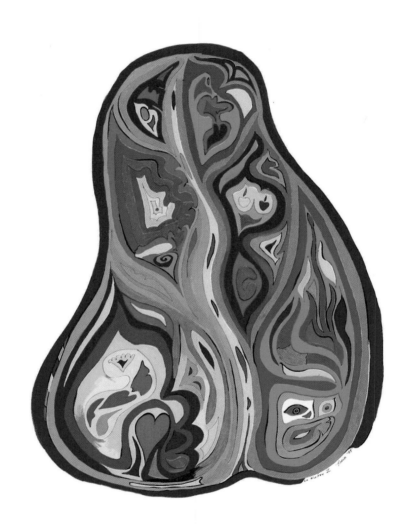

THE IN-BLISS-MENTS
LEVEL 4

CHAPTER ONE

Bliss; i am bliss in my healing kiss to infinite arrival at the height of revival and the stare of hurling infinity in there, our light and our height and our plan crystalline in the width of man and an eternal span of definite intrigue with god in me and our eternal spin in the bliss, i am, god. Bliss / bless; infinite in intricate spare, i am bless in there where it counts, numeric height of an infant's sight called straight through the shell of all hearing, golden mean, the harmonic half of all we are in the bless of bliss. / Blessed; blessed ignition, the cognition of a remission to a random scent of where we went to love and blessed in bliss. / Born; born again within the grain of a welcome refrain to magnificent loving born within bliss. / Believe; believe in a dance of a disk worn thin to beginning again at living within a welcome trance end called believe, relieve, bliss. / Breath; breath of best release, the relief in the register of where we've been to breathe within our love. Lightly led to the breath of bliss. / Basic; sheerly basic, i am free to believe in perfect humanity and a bliss-full sea of basically love and bliss. / Bare; bare to a care, i am whole to a whole life lit by align with the perfect exude of naked love and truth and bare declare of lightly, bliss. / Belief; belief in belize and a mayan reprieve of the heart-less declare of one who is fair to a weathered rescind of all that is in one love. The belief, the relief, bliss. / Retrace; retrace your steps to this, the height of bliss, and the art within your healing arc of love and bliss. / Embrace; embrace erase of less-than love and carry on to hug the one your own, your own declare of the heart in there and an eternal embrace of perfect bliss. / Space; space to love, god the bliss is on to one love, your own, our caress of the space between called bliss. / Delight-ful; delight-ful surrend to the bounty within and a welcome incline to the heart that is mine and welcome and warm i'm often insigned by the peace-full incline to a hearty realign with god. A delightful song this bliss. / Theta; theta's beta is alphaed omega at the rate of recline to a brain waved by time to a gentle hush and a hushing resign to live at the heart of the spiral that's fine to a tibetan declare of bliss. / Grand; a grand sign high held exactly the spell of a living matrix, the rome of love, our grand design to bliss. / Within; within then, love, until bliss is kicking in, to love. / Spiral; spiral in to a spiraling win of throat-spun, deep seat, dove flown, delight of a definite knight to all the way in to love and often i live, inside the smile of you and our bliss. / Golden; golden san of the woven band of a platinum hand held wide to love and thumb deep is a ride to the other side of you. All one spin, in, love. / Crystalline; crystalline i'm seen in a leaner spin of learning n to a lifting sum of all we've won for love crystalline to bliss. / Birth; by birth, i am mirth in a wishful sum of we're the one and all we need is love and the birthing, kiss of near, sheer, bliss. / Nature; dot's nature is nurtured by a natural span of god and love and man gone human to a central ear, we're all in hear, to love. This nature. Bliss. / Harmonious; harmony's come to a harmonious sum, all one, in a watch-full eye, god high, to perfectly love and the perfect pitch, love. / Patterns; apply to a pattern of perfect exist, i am lean to a ladder of jacob's exist and when spin to the central trail, all is well, within, my love. The pattern. Bliss. / Ecologic; the merka-bah blown to a mythic throne of where well reside astride our central eclipse of the heavenly lips, our own, clear to the bone, with godded ecologic bliss. / Worth; worth enough? Love- never gives shove to all-ways less than all the best and often i'm seen in a healing stream of silicone walls melting tall forgetting into one eternal sum the ultimate worth is sheerly this, our bliss. / Truth; truth told can release a hold on life's exceed and a healing stream can offer respite at the edge of a dream called the ship of all steep inclines to foolish aligns with less than the rock, i am the truth, sheer bliss. / Eternal; eternal to ethereal numbers, i'm numbered by the home, i own, and the templed reside inside the climb to a perfect hill of absolute sublime, in love and bliss. / All-ways; all-ways 4 ways, often 3, i'm held high to an eternal gleam and wide within i've found the seam of where i fly and how often between the arms of all-ways, god, know bliss. / Often; often i'm led to be fed by the hand i am god's own, and within the moan of when is often, again, and i know the hour of my greatest power is in the truth, often, i am, in bliss. / Wed; wed to a led to love. I am often above and eternally within the friend, my love, and essentially sent to reside in the slide to wed sweet bliss. / Woven; woven instead of weld, now i'm held, in less an escape, than a place of eternal connect with all that is found, by my own survey of woven love and bliss. / Found; found around the fence of love, the lips of doves snapped barb-wire deep to less than love and i can sleep in eternal bliss with the love i've found within the slips of bliss. / Straight; blessed straight to the heart of a blissing start with the penetrating square of all we wear withing, we go straight to the art of bliss. / Round; round the sound of a time within, and wound around our certain reside is a twinkling inside and the circle within our squaring align with god in bliss. / Definite; definite by a definition west of well, i'm centered to a trail of perfect ascend and a definite heal by the zeal of loving bliss. / Lesson; lesson learned, i can't earn more than the bliss i've all-ready had with you my love, my life, my wife, my lessoned friend, my bliss. / Sum; sum of us win when we're giving within the sum of all we've won for love and the sheerest kiss of all, bliss. / Evolve; evolve into trust of all that lives within our western stand at the lip of all ascend to god's evolve, the love we all acknowledge, the less of bliss. / Evoke; evoke awake to love and bliss. / Wrote; often missed, i wrote the note that saved a life, my own, i need you, love. Our bliss. / Insist; insist on this, the lip of love, perfectly blended, to dance at the chance to insist on bliss. / Resist; our resist has run the course of worse than this align with the perfection inside a destine called bliss. / Refine; god's way is refined by our align with love, and bliss. / Define; define resign and reassign yourself to perfect love in this, our bliss. / Design; design a resign to a healing stance, the dance to divinity within our friend, love in bliss. / Address; the new address is love, now, and forever, lightly address yourself to love and bliss. / Date; date yourself sold to the highest bed, golden assail of the height of betrayal born to the truth in love and bliss. / Rate; rate yourself worthy of great love. That's bliss. / Run; run to the one you love in blissing contentment of the cause that raves, so long gone, and now the opportune to reside in the land inside the arc of loving bliss. / Stay; stay a way to love and know the bliss with getting on to knowing stay in bliss. / Clear; clear to hear, in love. That's bliss. / Pure; pure the state to ecstatic abide in idle's side healed by a zealotous zeal to be pure love to we are bliss. / Serious news; new york knows, hear, have strayed to find the heart of heightened days and a deeper friend within hour love and bliss. / Greek; acknowledge the kiss of a greek maiden saved to become one love, my own, greek home with help again, in love and bliss. / Relate; relate yourself to wait an worth it all, in love and this, bliss. / Volumetric; volumetric electric, the elective opportune, the trademark we've seen in the heightened ship stream to a wider beam of love in light life. Bliss. / Specific; stationed specific on a platinum bond of explicit insistence on a welcome span of pleasant ascend to the rim of specific bliss. / Density; density done to all of us in doing touch of a matter-less much called delight a braid to a brush with let's be all, love, in this, bliss. / Gravity; gravity's grate is less when i bridge the brace of where we love our bliss. / Weight; weight and rush to a brush with the best of all we love available to heaps of love and bliss. / Weightless; getting grooved to a higher line of vibration's feel, i'm sealed by the sign of a sum done won to precisely this, weight-less love in bliss. / Bliss; bliss been found, found astound to all we abound around our land of expectant stand in love and bliss. / Break; break the tape to a healing place called being held by deliverance said to heal, the gap full-filled is loving bliss. / Formulaic; formulaic ascend when we trend to higher steps and heartier mends to all that we are, dial the numbers, square the pi; all one precisely, bliss.

CHAPTER TWO
Effectual; effectual manner of the matter bantered as best in bliss. / Elastic; elastic twist to a dancing kiss called deep in expand to bliss. / Lengthy; lengthy stay in the day worn sway to peace and bliss. / Laughing; laughing seeds spray across the day of my grinning deliver to the height of forever and love in bliss. / Amino; amino's say the acid's way to a protein shift is a lift to grace in bliss. / Amniotic; blessed state, the amniotic wait for a life 9-months late to begun in bliss. / Exact; exactly seen in the kiss before bliss. / Plates; shed plates of late to taste our bliss. / Engraved; engraved by design the align with the invitation heart deep in bliss. / Implored; near implored i ascend to send home the request to know bliss. / Insured; insured assure of bliss. / Decisive; decisive reside in the side called love and bliss. / Incurable; incurable assure of bliss. / Implicit; implicit nature, the stature of bliss. / Dramatic; dramatically done, i am one to the wave of a heightened stay at bliss. / Merger; merger's blend is the wind of bliss. / Master; master your plan to spring into bliss on the equinox sent to a final accent on bliss. / Mural; god's mural planned as a heightened fan on bliss. / Place; place me in the harmonic hint of surely bliss. / Trace; trace your face of basic tastes of bliss. / Assure; assure yes to the kindest kiss

of bliss. / Structure; structure assure to the cure of yes in love and bliss. / Emerging; emerging aspect of reflect in the trim of a traveling kin called lightly in our bliss. / Social; socially found, the around, to within our bliss. / Emotion; emotions in win are lightly seen to the trim of bliss. / Devotion; devote yourself to the ocean of devotion and bliss. / Denote; denote your note as bliss. / Vote; vote to emote, bliss. / Note; note this, bliss. / Native; native nature, the stature of bliss./ Date; date the thought with sought to see my bliss. / Durate; durate, rest, bliss. / Balance; balance believes in receive of rescue to allude to the bless in you and bliss. / Clear; clear to hear, i am the one, who can see through to contentment's view of bliss. / Pure; pure enough to ascend, i am in, to lots of bliss. / Classic; classic to a cure of where we were when to bliss. / Cursive; cursive accrue of you in love with bliss. / Clarified; clarified indeed in deed i need the call to love in bliss. / Purified; purified, true, imbued, bliss. / Plurality; plurality sealed in how we healed our morality come to a head at the one, bliss. / Duality; duality dealt felt to the heart of a start called a perfect unite in bliss. / Decisive; a deceive manner matters tonight in bliss. / Deliberate; deliberate i stand in the strength of a hand held wide to bliss. / Definite; definite decide of the glide to bliss. / Precious; preciousness sent to invent, bliss. / Biologic; biologic logic of the pet called mend in manly bliss. / Project; project paved by the height of you in bliss. / Plan; plan to stay blissed. / Emphatic; emphatic review of the heightened you and bliss. / Durate; durate rests best in bliss. / Farther; farther flew to bliss. / Future; future found around our bliss. / Faith; faith flew to a place in view of love and bliss. / Present; present yourself true to bliss. / Always; always fade to bliss. / Eternal; eternal's play is the device called bliss. / Special; special stay in bliss. / Genuine; genuine jewel of instill our bliss. / Shasta; shasta shattered matter less and bliss. / Modern; modern day, a way, to love and bliss. / Path; path worn thin within again, bliss. / Place; place yourself in view of the height of 2 in bliss. / Plum; often plum, i'm one with all dismiss to the light of bliss. / Precisely; good-bye to precisely less than bliss.

CHAPTER THREE
Forever; forever rich in a healing width, i'm woven to winning all that we've had and held by a mandate of letting me grow, i'm now letting go my redeem of less than forever in bliss. / Fortune; fortune called on all we held as royal and a living redeem was held in esteem as we sailed to the light's fantastic wed to the love within our bliss matrix. / Light; a yellowed lift to a brighter sight, the immaculate light of an eternal silent flame, the purple-violet gone drained to the perfect light of bliss. / Lighter; lighter than these are the delighted ascend to liquid lighter bliss. / Aspirant; aspirant is silent when held in less than all there is to love and bliss. / Exuberant; exuberant review of the way we are, to love, and the infinite, beyond of an aspirant ascend to bliss. / Wonder; wonder where our infinite care can take us to the trees and the heart and the start of our journey, deeper still, into the ark of al creation, love, bliss. / Extreme; extreme measured by one align with the light inside our dome of all, forever, gone to god

and love. Know bliss. / Mathematics; mathematically spoken, you're evoking the angular pleasure of many we're woven the formulaic wonder of earth given birth by numbered days of love in bliss. / Concordia; a basic concordance is in accordance with our applicable genius for a genius born of sanctuary shown to the trees that we own for god. Know wonder. Bliss. / Elation; elation relation is to our love and the way we handle the days of lines fed by bliss. / Substation; substation's nation, the heat of love and an electric sum of all we've become in love that's bliss. / Perfect; perfectly held by an arm compelled to wrap round the bend of my friend, less waste, more love, perfect, bliss. / Torah; torah-truth often runs along hypothetical lives carrying on to something born without a waste, a thinner roll of perfects scroll and the letters flame inside our read on bliss. / Delicious; deliciously dealt a never melt of deftly served immerse in love. That's delicious, bliss. / Octave; octave highed to a wide examine of all that's inside our sentient pave of the electric wave to perfect pitch in wedded bliss. / Flame; flame consumed by exclaim, the holy name, whole-y you, love's flame, bliss. / Lettered; lettered by bettered by love bliss. / Hebrew; hebrews mannered by a personal address add lists to when they come for lent and where they'd run if encountered by freedom to bliss. / Trade; trade rest for a list of why we love the best in confess of the perfect exchange of love and bliss. / Trait; your traits are great when you date your bliss. / Train; train around the sound of where we dance mast in love and the perfect spot scene right in the heart of love and bliss. / Ratio; ratios show in how you love. The measure, the balance, the extend of love, that's bliss. / Rectangle; rectangled angle to a perfect 90 of light and bliss. / Equal; equal to a measure, i'm treasured by love, and golden its of bliss. / Squared; essentially squared, i'm aired to why we love and renew began to view our list toward bliss. / Perfect; perfectly balanced by how you handle this, our love, and bliss. / Infinite; infinite the plan, to love, in designs of perfect bliss. / Balance; balance found a handle in bliss. / Spiral; spiral spin in a spiral in to love in bliss. / Dna; dna's day is love's light to bliss. / Milky way; today i milky way with you and your love our bliss. / Galaxy; galaxy's glee, bliss. / Helios; sheer helios. Love. Warm. Bliss. 35 .Arms; arms charm me home to love. Hold me that's bliss. / Body; basic body's breathe believe in love, and bliss. / Arc-tangent; arc-tangent home to phone the loan withdrawn to on and bigger things one loves and bliss. / Co-tangent; co-tangent knew you in love and all things planets do in loft and bliss. / Arc; arc's tangent's con-tangent to where we love and that's bliss. / Branch; branch on out to a deeper sport of spotted swirls of water's spout about true love. / Fibonacci; fibonacci squared, compared to rest, in love. A perfect spiral, the sum, of ratios golden beam to love. Bliss. / Eden; live to eden, i'm exceeding my neglect to find a deeper respect for love and a wife gone green with leaves of love and bliss. / Mounds; crystal mounds astound as found becomes believe and we re-fate our guilt to guests of love, and bliss. / Crystalline; crystalline i seem to redeem far less than brittle matter gone straight to love in bliss. / Numbered; rations read numbered when measured by

hundreds shown bliss. / Spirit; spirit's square on the measure of whether we'll seem sore or knot with let's kiss bliss. / Spatial; spatial measure of the pleasure principle, equates to great in loving bliss. / Expansive; expansive to measures of pleasured by love and the welcome kiss of your bliss. / Sentient; sentient pleasure, a measure of how we're loved, and often seen in the quotient of bliss. / Sensual; bliss knew a kiss more sweet than less and a sensual taste of a central blessed examine of love. Light's sensual friend, bliss. / Sovereign; sovereign to seen, i am redeemed by where, we gleam with love and bliss. / Strain; strain-less love, perfect, bliss. / System; system wide i stride to deeper love in our collective hum of bliss. / Systemic; systemic to endemic to greater love. The entire system of where we head for bliss. / Oceanic; oceanic pleasure's met measure in often seen scams of glittering blue, azure seaed caribbean review of love. / Gleam; that gleam renewed is viewed by all we love and lofty we stand in central review of all that breathes of love and bliss. / Glacier; glaciers glow with glee when we gleam with love for ourselves and other throughout the days of our lives, loves, and bliss. / Glance; babied glance askew our view of fewer than less than loveing bliss. / Enlivened; enlivened wave of dayed be gone to done, our own, in god and enlivened by heal our loving bliss. / Resident; resident manor, the planter gone green to what we mean by resident bliss. / Extant; extant extent gone went to gone to wedded on our love is bliss. / Implant; babies implant is a rant to rave at a spectacular wave of wedded bliss. / Design; design done deft to a paralleled cleft gone healed to bliss. / Truth; truth is the dialect spoken in ivy green calendrics, hear, emme ya speak "crystal clear".

CHAPTER FOUR

Evidence; evidence points at the joint endeavor of bliss. / Support; support yourself set of beliefs, release, to bliss. / Trail; trails true are hued by bliss. / Return; return on true direct to bliss. / Refund; refund respect to bliss. / Redirect; redirect your stay at bliss. / Re-examine; re-examine your motive, bliss. / Cross-examine; cross examine's accrue, review, bliss. / Curate; relate curate to true, bliss. / Inflate; inflate less, bliss. / Oasis; today's oasis wade is bliss. / Support; support your sort, bliss. / Sublime; sublime recline in bliss. / Sustain; sustain us, let's, bliss. / Sustenance; sustenance seen in the stream of bliss. / Nutrition; nutrition knew replace in bliss. / Nature; nature's need is nurture's free access to bliss. / Mystic; mystic you and bliss. / Majestic; define majestic, marcie meant, let's bliss. / Secure; secure's review is bliss. / Solstice; solstice hued by bliss. / Eclipse; eclipse set on bliss. / Curative; curative sent to bliss. / Encased; encased in cure of bliss. / Effusive; effusive in, my bliss. / Glimpse; daily glimpse, bliss. / Thrown; thrown to own my own, bliss. / Thorough; thorough to a trend to bliss. / Doctoral; doctoral dance at the chance to reflect on bliss. / Delicious; delicious, you, bliss. / Lattice; lattice true to the heights of you thrown wide to bliss. / Latex; latex wide to a climb to bliss. / Lectern; lectern learned to yearn for speak in bliss. / Lucky; lucky guy at the y of yes we will reveal ourselves in perfect bliss. / Landon; land on the hand of bliss. / Lake; kiss the lake of greatest stake in bliss. / Lately; lately i'm through to bliss. / Learn; learn to yearn, bliss. / Lesson; lesson learned, learn to bliss. / Leaned; leaned into we are the ones who bliss. / Lattice; latticed lace of the face called love in bliss. / Cubicle; cubicle's cue, i am true, to bliss. / Clasp; clasp the hand of bliss. / Unfasten; unfasten's few, bliss. / Create; create sate, bliss. / Explain; explain again, bliss. / Penny; basic pence, the penny, love in bliss. / Divine; divine design, bliss. / Beauty; beauty's be, bliss./ Burst; burst true, bliss. / Found; found a band called bliss. / Paradise; paradise sent to bliss. / Aground; aground the sound of bliss. / Midline; midline seen in bliss. / Between; good-bye between , i'm in the lean to bliss. / Often; often, yes, bliss. / In; in star struck we luck to bliss. / On; on renew, bliss. / Within; within, bliss. / Suspense; suspense, ascend, bliss. / Peace; peace found, bliss. / Insistence; insistence in, bliss. / Throne; throne through to true, bliss. / Home; home run, bliss.

CHAPTER FIVE

Fortune; fortune found in a hound called the leg of all remember and the hunt is on to the knows of all we feel when we heal our bliss. / Tide; tides heal our feel of threaded remember and spinning in to electrical weave we are healed by all we felt when we'd melt together always found at the place of electrical ascend, and waves of bliss. / Turn; turn around to sound like this, hear bliss. / Love; love around yourself that's bliss. / Loft; loftier trend to a friend of forgotten, the heightened blend of ascendent matter and the wind of all we believe combine, to bliss. / Lift; liftier trances have ended their dances and off we cause to the pause at the end of the road and the night of all remember, lift, eyes, god, bliss. / Take off; take off for trails of higher hail and a softer grin at entering in to love's bliss. / Fly; fly high to waiting loft's of where we're off to bliss. / Decide; decide to ride inside the tube of all we knew of bliss. / Commit; commit to mend of loving, bliss. / Concur; concur to notice the act of the fact that we are, loved. That's bliss. / Insure; insure of bliss. / Decree; blessed decree, the we of all remember and the ascendant stand in the span of a laughing decree called we are free to love. Know bliss. / Desires; desires higher held meld in weld of perfect love and bliss. / Delights; delights in sights of resplendent glee at the faith and the rate and height of we, are the act to follow and the following wind of delights called friend, bliss. / Date; date yourself present and head an home to the arc of forever and the center of home held high to seas of ascend my friend to dates with bliss. / Set; set on you, are the eyes of god and stares of sweet remember upon the horizon of bliss. / Submerge; submerge more near the shore of where we blend, know end, of all that's less than perfect bliss. / Emerge; emergent stand in the sand of all unique expand of lightly, love. / Enjoy; enjoy yourself wet to deeper delve in the shelf of ancient books and looks at bliss. / Rejoice; rejoice in source, of north, to love our own the worth of self gone green with living bliss. / Reside; reside in astride our dreams of leaves of latticed won by weather won at a mayan sun over setting reside in god, love, bliss. /

Reign; reign yourself over health born deep to weep of love and bliss. / Raft; raft red breed of deeper on to godded bliss. / Aloft; aloft to oft we love, our, bliss. / Leisure; leisure lee, wed home, to own, our life and love. Bliss. / Place; god's kiss, the key, the place, to happiness love and bliss. / Go; go, i tell you, tell them, bliss. / Hawaii; hawaii home to stay in love and bliss. / Greece; classic greece relief and bliss. / Release; blessed release of the grief to love and bliss. / The plan; catch the plan, the man, god is love. That's it. The plan, human, is bliss. / The stand; listen to this, the stand for god, is bliss. / In love; in love, enough, to bliss. / Lets; let's review our place in who we love. Bliss. / Be; blessed be our free to love. / Open; open to review our hour of bliss. / Free; free enough to risk bliss. / Spoken; spoken pleasure, a treasure, bliss. / Open; open up, renew, your love and bliss. / Delicate; delicate design, the kind of love we knew to bliss. / Definite; definite dose of loving give and gain, exactly bliss. / Appropriate; appropriate's treasure, love like this and bliss. / Precious; precious to few than less and more we shore on wings of love and bliss. / Expansive; god's expansive in romantic true to love, light, life, bliss. / Expressive; expressive clear to perfect speak of love and light. Oft-spokin. / Insights; insights seen in lean to love and bliss. / Within; can you within your love. / That's bliss. / With-all; with-all we do, love, bliss. / Wed; coffin wed to a caffeine said go through with less than love and bliss. / Through love; through love me found a town on fire, for god, is bliss. / Skies; skies askew. Renew your faith in lace and truth and love. That's god. Bliss. / Pink; a pink exam of who we can, love, god, true, bliss. / Blue; blue enough to view. Our love. Life. God. Bliss. / Green; green enough to love, god's trees, me, bliss. / Gold; golden view of hue we love. A reign of bliss. / Unfold; unfold your own, bliss. / Winged; let us winged be, love, life, live, bliss. / Expanse; tonight kiss expanse of love and bliss. / A glance; let us kiss a glance of chance to love our bliss. / Soft; soft we see, our love, in float, of bliss. / Deep; deep retreat to a creek called love in bliss. / Welcome; welcome home to own your bliss.

CHAPTER SIX

Sanctify; sanctify the way to bliss. / Inherit; sheerly seen, i inherit the lean to bliss. / Righteous; righteous rule, bliss. / Mind; mind, mattered, missed, blissed. / Path way; pathway's ascend within bliss. / Quickly; quickly seen, bliss. / Kindly; anchored kindly in bliss. / Consistently; consistently won, bliss. / Securely; securely set on bliss. / Insistently; insistently won, our, bliss. / Synthesis; synthesis sunk to bliss. / Decide; decide to glide to bliss. / Infinite; infinite friend, our, bliss. / Create; create create's elate, know bliss. / Inheritance; new inheritance set on bliss. / Sustenance; sustenance sent to hint, bliss. / Specific; specific accent, bliss. / Eccentric; eccentric's lean, bliss. / 3Rd; 3rd day's way to bliss. / 4Th; 4th flew to bliss. / 5Th; 5th hole, fairway deep to bliss. / Bodies; bodies imbued with list to bliss. / Eyes; season's eyes are sized by bliss. / Faced; faced renew of bliss. / Armed; armed to intrigued by bliss. / Legged; legged through to lengthy bliss. / Grade; lovely grades of bliss. / Neutral;

neutral's corner, bliss. / Geophysical; geophysical's feature, bliss. / Expectant; expectant hue, you, in bliss. / Collapse; collapse instead to bliss. / Volume; volume's view, bliss. / Night; night's spray of relay to bliss. / Nurture; nurture's kneel in heal bliss. / Starred; starred in cared to bliss. / Threshold; destiny's threshold, bliss. / Benevolent; benevolent said, know bliss. / Cube; cube's review, bliss. / Image; image to imagine you in bliss. / Radius; radius ruled, bliss. / Survival; survival said, arrive, at bliss. / Suspend; suspend's ascend, to bliss. / Particulate; particulate pleasure deeper in bliss. / Respective; respective's ruler, measure-less, bliss. / Galactic; galactic glue is bliss. / Garnished; garnished truth in bliss. / Banged; childhood banged full of bliss. / Spiraled; height's sunned in to a spiraled friend, bliss. / Splendor; god's splendor, one, bliss. / Solar; solar ascend, bliss. / Mapped; mapped a mend to bliss. / Respect; respect your sect, bliss. / Scripture; basic this, scripture, bliss. / Cycle; cycle round to bliss. / Physical; physical redeem, bliss. / Central; central scene, bliss. / Decisive; decisive, done, bliss. / Aggressive; aggressive won, bliss. / Evoke; basic evoke of bliss. / Elocutive; elocutive assure of the voice of bliss. / Script; script's shrug, bliss. / Travel; travel true, bliss. / Collapse; collapse on cue, bliss. / Joint; kiss the joint elect to bliss.

CHAPTER SEVEN

Up stroke; up stroke broke bliss. / Connote; connote vote, for love, bliss. / Devote; devote yourself deeds of live in love. Bliss. / Defy; defy the odds, know god, is, bliss. / Deftly; deftly done, i'm one with love in bliss. / Drawn; drawn on true to love and light and life known blissed. / Dress; dressing up to say, light years through i'm lavender hued by love's dress code, bliss. / Submit; submit yourself to redirect of the questioned called love and all above we bliss. / Concede; concede to need your love, bliss. / Abridge; abridge your time to reside in love and u.S. Called bliss. / Impress; impress your address to rest on the corner of love the avenue, bliss. / Attune; lately attune to love and lightly say how to bliss. / Imbue; today imbue your way to loft's of love, bliss. / Review; review your view of love, know bliss. / Regard; regard address of life in love and bliss. / Reside; reside inside the food of life and love, bliss. / Amuse; amuse us, loving laughs of bliss. 18 .Decide; decide to ride to love in bliss. / Done; done to one, bliss. / Dealt; dis-in-act your react to in fact we dealt with bliss. / Deft; deft in drive, i'm alive to bliss. / Drill; drill invest to rest on love, love healed, whole. Bless. Bliss. / Devote; devote your vote to bliss. / Delight; a lofty kiss, the delight of bliss. / Address; a great address, hear ye, love to bliss. / Embraced; embraced a place in where we'd loved. Bliss. / Regret; regrets know best to lesson love. Bliss. / Regard; regard rest as best in wars on love. Gone. Blissed. / Aspire; aspire to a higher drift in life and love and bliss. / Starred; starred in your own, love, star red bliss. / Czared; czared russian i'm praising by heraldic descent to the rent on love, bliss. / Ceasared; a ceasered please of salad's said, to water less than rome in love and bliss. / Expect; expect an erect of love. Straight up, bliss. / Respect; respect your rest in love and bliss. / Sensitive; sensitive said,

head, for loved, in bliss. / Sensate; sensate great. Of late, love, bliss. / Sentient; sentient measure, the pleasure of softened to bliss. / Sensitive; lately you, stationed too, to bliss. / Lightly; lightly won, wedded one, bliss. / Listen; listen, hear, we're, bliss. / Intern; intern said ship up to love and practical bliss. / Interim; an interim, measure less, love, a blink infinite to godded bliss. / Morganite; white morganite gone lavender jade to perfect bliss. / Funded; funded in a random kiss called bliss. / Ametrine; kiss the ametrine scene of love. Pink and green and yellow seam of amethyst to bliss. / Alexander; alexander said you're the one stone led to bliss. Alexanderite seams of lavender bliss. / Dove in; dove in to a dove flown in to bliss. / Sea; sea son of love. Knights of light bliss on ships of lists to love the sea of bliss. / Geometry; geometry said we bled lava green for peridot dreams of heightened hair for a lair gone pink to seams of love. Light. Bliss. / Geomagnetic; geomagnetic, i am erstatic in earthly, love and bliss. / Contact; contact said we red our love and deep green clean of punctual bliss. / Contract; contract said, love, bliss. / Mission; mission meant met mint. Green love and violet bliss. / Admission; admit yourself to admission sent to love. Bliss. / Desire; desire hire a hand at bliss. / Evolve; evolve to god's resolve called bliss. / Holographic; basic you, the holographic truth of love and light. Right to bliss. / Connect; connect your dot to hot to love and melt at bliss. / Seeded; seeded son, the won, one, love, grown bliss. / Phased; phased, phrased, loved, stayed, said, blissed. / Imaged; imaged you as who we loved to picture bliss. / Formed; formed found ground to love in bliss. / Bonded; exactly's bond is on to love-ing's bliss. / Covalence; covalence bond, a perfection, of love and bliss. / Surveillance; dogons, can you say surveillance away to i know bliss? / Thirsty; thirsty in a missive, bliss. / Throats; throats and the misty bliss.

CHAPTER EIGHT

Many; many are merry to bliss. / One; one found, bliss. / Factor; factor found, bliss. / Evolvement; lately evolvement's been sealed by bliss. / Involvement; stand involved with involvement cause called bliss. / Rest; rest on, bliss. / Ancient; ancient ways, bliss. / Multiple; garments multiple multiply our fly to bliss. / Initiated; initiated relate, bliss. / Worn; worn to won by bliss. / Surround; surround's around our bliss. / Grow; grow up, bliss. / Serve; serve to bliss. / Suspended; suspended ascend has ascendant stood to bliss. / Sphere; sphere's sent miracle's invent, bliss. / Crystalline; crystalline's dream, bliss. / Calculate; calculate relate to bliss. / Curate; curate's date with bliss. / Accept; accept the tree to bliss. / Status; status stood in bliss. / Vibration; cue's are in vibrations kin is bliss. / Aligned; aligned to lined with bliss. / Celestial; lately celestial, i'm seen in early bliss. / Found; sheer to found by bliss. / Documents; documents due, on, bliss. / Prophets; prophets proof, bliss. / Return; attain return to bliss. / Retain; retain your race to bliss. / Islands; islands hide less, bliss. / Ocean; ocean's cue, you, on bliss. / Seas; bathe the seas with "we's" of bliss. / Basin; basins true to deepen you in bliss. / Kalahari; kalahari square to bliss. / Harmonic; harmonic heal, we'll bliss. / Key; key's key, bliss.

/ Stone; stone's true, bliss. / Rock; life's rock, bliss. / Corner; corner's cue, bliss. / Know; know who, bliss. / Resides; resides inside, bliss. / Horizontal; pass horizontal to the font of written vertically to bliss. / Cubical; cubical's cue, bliss. / Brotherhood; brotherhood's imbue of you are, bliss. / Life; life stride to bliss. / Frequency; frequency seen in a learn to bliss. / Biospheric; biospheric reaccess is bliss. / Spherical; spherical skew to bliss. / Atlantis; atlantis rule, bliss. / Contracts; contracts accrue bliss. / Mission; mission's mill, the heal to will your bliss. / Definition; definition's mention, bliss. / Decide; decide to stride to step of bliss. / Decry; decry why to bliss. / Cubical; cubical's cue, bliss. / Energy; energy's will, bliss. / New; news asunder, the thunder, bliss. / Moon; moon's means to bliss. / Over; over and under, bliss. / Georgia; lately georgia's date is the state of bliss. / Hand; define the stand at the hand of man in bliss. / Heal; live heal, bliss. / Time; time to fly to bliss. / Trace; bliss trace, loved to bliss. / Direct; direct ascend the friend of bliss.

CHAPTER NINE

Mars; mars escapes to venus an dates of a nation's duress for late night fill of the printing need, grace in sex and bliss. / Venus; venus view you in love and basically bliss. / Hawaii; kiss me clean to a hawaii beam of the god we love in the isles of bliss. / Boone; a son of boone has come to, soon, to the handle of all we mantle as bliss. / Electric; i am electric in my zoom to the hunt of boom and an eternal seam at the stride of god in love with bliss. / Soon; soon enough i'll heal the gulf of heaven-less reside on the inside of when we bloom in the light of love and bliss. / Pyramid; pyramid's stand astride our glide to the happy side of all points home for god and love. / Grid; grid lock gone to a hanger on broken free by heed of a behest for god. Unlock. Love and bliss. / Graph; graph yourself in to home all-one with bliss. / Earth; know the charts of where she starts to give and the heart of the matter is bliss. / Maxine; maximum plans to expand to a stand in perfectly this, the heart of bliss. / Pele; pele's stay is all the way in to the heart of the flame called the vent to bliss. / Plans; sheer plans laid have stayed in deep refrain of yes we know our god is bliss. / Permanent; permanent the kiss, of, bliss. / Stay; stay here near the core of all you adore and the heart of a start to live in bliss. 16 .Redress; redress your address to the heart who knows best, the bless, of bliss. / Shower; shower yourself clean of what you mean when you forget the exist of only bliss. / Hour; hour to hour, i'm empower to bliss. / Private; privately won, love, bliss. / Pirate; pirate's scene is neglected lean to less than bliss. / Spare; spare care is where we delve to love and bliss. / Explain; explain your frame to a kind refrain of bliss. / Sphinx; sphinx found pow deep in a sight called the light of live in bliss. / Man; man, human, born again to life in love. Know an; bliss. / Lion; a lion's share of where we love our bliss. / Sacred; sacred seam of the gleam to light our delight by, bliss. / Blue; blue knew eye-wide truth in loft to bliss. / Perfume; perfume's deep reach to the truth of where we loop to love and bliss. / Frequent; frequent found around our love and bliss. / Children; children chill at the heal of all we merrily knew of the heat of

life in bliss. / Depth; let's go deep to the depth of love in bliss. / Basic; basic believe can insist on assist in love and basically, human bliss. / Lateral; lateral flattery will get you battery of the salt of the earth called god in love and bliss. / Embrace; embrace your taste of the kiss of west to bliss. / Potent; potent plan, the informant stand at the height and the heart of a man born wide to love. In bliss. / Potential; potential scene in the hint of a height worn wide to love and bliss. / Palatial; palatial taste of a delicate face worn deep in the eyes of a green-eyed align with the kiss of a height called bliss. / Transplant; transplant met a the hint of invent a new way to dip deep into love in bliss. / Optic; optic nerve knew love. Seen the optimum view, bliss. / Beams; beams glimmer in my simmer of deeper green. Eyed wide to ascend in love and bliss. / Michael; michael sent to invent a new scene of where we lean to heightened risk in love in bliss. / Gabriel; gabriel grew deep in you and your dream of the gleam of light in bliss. / Uriel; uriel grew to love her bliss. / Raphael; deep raphael will go to see bliss. / Ariel; ariel grew deep to drafts of numbers steeped in the pi of love. Counting up to bliss. / Moses; moses knew you in the tables of energetic lift to bliss. / Christ jesus; christ jesus, jew, greek, geek, flounce, the violet refrain of bliss. / Jeremiah; jeremiah grew, in the healing review of deepen the street to wide avenues of emerald green love. Bliss. / Elijah; elijah grew vertical in the relief of streets grown deep in delicate review of bliss. / Councils; councils count steep retreat to the tread of where we head for love; in; bliss. / Chemist; a chemist chromosomatic to emphatic love and drifts to the formula of bliss. / Physicist; a physicist said, lean your head to align with the light inside h-our bliss. / Chromosomes; chromosomes grew in seams of dreams of seems to love and bliss. / Zones; zones astound when they're found in fevered few melting through to the care of bliss. / Signs; signs send friends to heal our melt to dealt with, bliss. / Language; language found to astound our lessons, bliss. / Wonders; wonders will within the friend of when we sign our lift to a friend called bliss. / Eyes; god's eyes are on us in our give to bliss. / Features; features you knew grew to looks of eye-wide bliss. / Geometries; lately i've seen geometries lean to a heightened stand in god is bliss. / Frames; frames frankly found astound my insist on less and i find myself wound deep in bliss. / Closure; closure came on the dance of all forget. / And i found a friend inside the time of all remember. / Bliss.

CHAPTER TEN

New beginnings; newly begun, bliss. / Nestle; nestle's kiss, bliss. / Establishment; establishment's run to bliss. / Random; random true, bliss. / Often; often won, bliss. / Overwhelming; overwhelming's hued to cue, bliss. / Liquid; lips liquid, bliss. / Steam; kiss steam, bliss. / Sex; attain sexed bliss. / Sect; sect elect, bliss. / Delicate; delicate deed, bliss. / Delegate; delegate's due, true bliss. / Remembrance; dates rate remembrance of bliss. / Happiness; happiness held trim to bliss. / Simply; simply head for bliss. / Eloquently; eloquently said, bliss. / Hall; halls of while we bliss. / Joy; joy's juice, bliss. / Honey; honey's rock, bliss. / Strength; strength won, bliss. / Tastefull; tastefull's view, bliss. / Discreet; discreet replete with bliss. / Content; content to invent our bliss. / Timely; timely sea, bliss. / Traffic; traffic's true is bliss. / Enveloping; enveloping view of the address called you and bliss. / Lift; lift your set to bliss. / Light; light side, bliss. / Fast-paced; fast paced race to bliss. / Fabric; fabric found stretched to bliss. / Behind; behind the stride to bliss. / Stretch; stretch ahead, bliss. / Fasten; fasten, on, bliss. / Dimension; dimension's best at four, bliss. / Play; play your hand, bliss. / Scenes; scenes sung bliss. / Suspended; suspended within, bliss. / Emotion; emotion rest, bliss. / Motion; motion's view, bliss. / Step; step through, bliss. / Open; open around, bliss. / Lane; lanes lean to the veins of bliss. / Nectar; nectar's drip, bliss. / Nest; nest on new, bliss. / Idea; ideas reside in bliss. / Kneel; kneel near bliss. / Naturally; naturally done, bliss. / Believing; believing done, bliss. / Nurturing; nurture's nurturing view, bliss. / Nape; nape's gape, bliss. / Releasing; releasing around, bliss. / Ravens; ravens rude release relief, in bliss. / Jens; jens jewel, bliss. / Lace; lace a blend of glittering in to bliss. / Luscious; luscious lend to in, bliss. / Drip; drip drew me to bliss. / Dip; dip's due, to, bliss. / Spiraling; spiraling fun, bliss. / Spun; spun in, bliss. / Kind; kind sum, sun, of, bliss. / Consent; consent sent, bliss. / Been; been blissed. / Eternal; eternal i was inside god's spans. / One; one day is come to the lord of all light regard for humanity in the sword of a forgiving knight.

CHAPTER ELEVEN

Colors; colors crew around my knew to love and flames of purple-green deliver us to the reign of drawn to bliss. / Experiences; experiences spell in a trill to deepen steepes of heights to adventures sent to foreign lands of life and bliss. / Discover; discover another advent, the art of recover, to, love and bliss. / Pray; pray for the day you say, i am, to bliss. / Elohim; elohim ring around my head as i sleep softly in my bed at sweet arrival of the street called revival and the heart of the core of forever in bliss. / Luminaries; luminaries need a shine of scene too, love, and bliss can kiss my face of sweet embrace of the space in life called perfect bliss. / Men; men to a whirl of smudged begin at the lip of a friend called bliss. / Kah; kan you kah your curl to whirls of bliss. / Bah; bah can begin to ascend again in bliss. / Beings; beings banned returned ascend to life in bliss. / Friends; friends found astound at bliss. / Definite; definite due to the hue of bliss. / Dare; dare to share your love and bliss. / Care; care to share your life in light and bliss. / Dna; dna day of direct renew of the notion you are only all ways entwined in a matrix, bliss. / Ring; ring around the town of bliss. / Relating; relating to you, i am renewed by the arc of bliss. / Embodied; embodied planet, the metatronic wonder of one who loves like bliss. / Parent; parents lean into the wind of a heavenly cradle called the child of bliss. / Light; go abroad to all god is light of bliss. / Govern; govern this, the sovereign state of bliss. / Universal; universal matter met mind in a mayan recline to bliss. / Faced; can you find reflection in faced to bliss. / Create; create, create in perfect gifts of bliss. / Mine; mine is insured, deep in the street of bliss.

/ Mind; mind matter, bliss. / Exact; lately in refrain i'm exact to the won of bliss. / Space; space fact, bliss. / Profound; profound abound is found in a town worn deep to ancient bliss. / Respect; respect yourself, bliss. / Finished; finished found delight in perfectly spoken, bliss. / Crease; crease increase of unfolding bliss. / Care; lately, the date, is a cure called bliss. / Curl; curl up in a whirl of delicious in steamy bliss. / Light; light found me in great company called bliss. / Spake; spake of spoke to lightly love in all the tense of bliss. / Spoke; i am kissed by the spoke of a wheel called speak only bliss. / Win; win a friend in bliss. / Waits; waits on perfect receive of bliss. / Devote; a greater blend of devote to life and bliss. / Direct; direct to the act of effortless bliss. / Obscure; obscure has gone along to love and bliss. / Reference; inner reference held reverence for light and bliss. / Endurance; endurance run to the son of revival and the height of archival review of love's endure in bliss. / Presence; presence renewed to a written review of bliss. / Pace; pace to the grace you knew before in love and bliss. / Pirate; god's pirate is great when i listen to bliss. / Precious; my pen is precious in jeweled ascend to the lips of bliss. / Frankly; frankly i've found a town of life and bliss . / Eternal; god's eternal ascend to bliss. / Deep; god's delight is deep to bliss. / Adrift; adrift in a sea of sleep in bliss. / Maholo; maholo may say thanks all day to perfect bliss. / Wide; i am wide to bliss. / Venice; deepen venice in the day you say to light and bliss. / Embark; god's kiss can embark to bliss. / Literal; literal ascend is the friend of bliss. / Lasting; lasting sounds of when we bliss. / Sash; a sash took a dash to an adventure with cash and the stash called love and bliss. / Stash; stash yourself in deep in love and bliss. / Intrinsic; walk to an intrinsic stalk of the taller tree called we are lovely, bliss. / Eccentric; eccentric has seen a rend to a lighter pen of perfectly love drawn to bliss. / Spare; kenya is spare in where we care to waste our breathe on less than bliss. / Century; century's plan is to stand in the millennium of lightly love and bliss.

CHAPTER TWELVE

Simply green; simple's given, bliss./ Spun; basic's spun within to bliss. / Spans descend; spans can descend to bliss. / Lights ascend; lights within accent of bliss. / Knowingly loved; knowing's love, bliss. / Loftly scene; lightest scene, bliss. / Taking flight; take a flight, bliss. / Blissed out; blissed out true, blessed, bliss. / Cartwheeled in; cartwheeled into a flipping brand of turning in to bliss. / Tranquil; tranquil's true in bliss. / Taut; taut to true in bliss. / Taught; taught to bliss. / Festive hearts; festive's heart, bliss. / Random's starts; random's start, bliss. / Sparkling strands; sparkle's strand, the hand, bliss. / Strident fans; strident's fans, bliss. / Foolish plans; foolish the plans, then expand, to, bliss. / Forgotten winds; forgotten's wind, forget to bliss. / Winsome stands; win some stand in bliss. / Central trends; central's trend, a friend, bliss. / Traces end; trace is over, end, to, bliss. / Essential blend; essential's send, blend, bliss. / Harvest love; harvest your love, bliss. / Movement; movement's review, bliss. / School in; school's in, bliss. / Belonging; belonging ascend to bliss. / Brand; brand stand, new, bliss. / Bask; bask around, bliss. / Bottle; bottle blue, renew, lavender's hue, bliss. / Bend; bend in, bliss. / Wean; wean won, bliss. / Mailed; mailed mail to bliss. / Wide; wide decide, bliss. / Depth; depth's due, bliss. / Range; range along, to, bliss. / Pitch; pitch true, bliss. / Freed; freed receive, bliss. / Open; open in bliss. / Available; available, stable, bliss. / Evolved; evolved in, bliss. / Welcome; welcome review, bliss. / Loving; loving through, bliss. / Learning; learning to free our bliss. / To remember; to remember dear, bliss. / Enable; enable stay, bliss. / Empowered; empowered friend, bliss. / Strong; strong sun, bliss. / Strengthened; strengthened friend, bliss. / Sworn; sworn to renew our bliss. / Worn; worn deep to bliss. / Place; place around your sound, your ear, of, bliss. / Advice; advice found, bliss. / Advance; advance to a cause for god, bliss. / Electric's; electric's through to bliss. / Good-buy; a good buy, bliss. / Good-bye; good-bye resist, bliss. / Good grace; god's good grace, bliss. / Truth; truth's tree, bliss. / Sparks; sparks spew across the view of bliss. / Expanse; expanse spent on bliss. / God; god's good, bliss. / Bliss; bliss view, you, kissed, bliss. / This know; this know, known, bliss. / Know thanks; knowing thanks, bliss. / Ever; ever the initialized, blues go, blissed.

CHAPTER THIRTEEN

Membrane; a membrane won by a matrilineal recline at the heart of a wish to know the mother of wedded bliss./ Matrilineal; reside in the matrilineal line of when we birth our bliss. / Energies; energies won reside in a side called deeply dealt to a wealth called election bliss. / Orbital; orbital patter of the winds of begin to circle within our bliss. / Cornerstone; cornerstone of cure to a whim called slim in directly built on bliss. / Intelligence; intelligence summed is the hum of the head to a directive sail to bliss. / Gravitron; gravitron on a slide to an electric side called the other wink of bliss. / Inter-change; inter-change your inner charge of electric bliss. / Rate; rate your date for yes! We are the ones who run the world, of late, bliss. / Crown; crowns came around to sing of the heavenly thing called love n the arc of bliss. / Column; column by column i'm swallowed by elect to the heightened direct of enlightened envision of all we are to god and the light is one and we're all one in bliss. / Pillar; pillars pound around the sound of columns red with a deeper bed of better ascend to the lights of love in bliss. / Floor; respect the floor of all you were and let go to know all you here in the arms of bliss. / Ceiling; ceilings heights are found delighted in our excited blend of all we ascend to lightly, love. / Imprint; imprint on who you love in hues of gone direct to the sun of godly, love, our bliss. / Zones; zones attune to the tunes of life and bliss. / Cycles; cycles seen in the heart's of rings we love and bliss. / Escapist; escapist gone to exactly bliss. / Streams; streams strung around the dreams of softly sung, we are the one, love, bliss. / Effects; effects of direct to bliss. / Message; messaged mend to bliss. / Lamb; lamb won to ten of bliss. / Book; book an through to the written view that all is well in light of bliss. / Scrolls; scrolls scroll around to show the heighten bliss of letting go to olive in these, the flames of love and bliss. / Life; you are life to

bliss. / Redeem; redeem became, bliss. / Redemptive; redemptive run to bliss. / Blueprint; blueprint true to bliss. / Architect; love's architect, bliss. / Accent; let us accent your choice with ascend to bliss. / Dialect; amusing dialect, the lips of bliss. / Spins; spins spun on hum, bliss. / Spans; spans to a cruise with the muse of love, bliss. / Sparks; sparks flew to who we are bliss. / Arcs; arcs sparkle, the shine of bliss. / Splash; splatter splash, to sum, light, bliss. / Father; father fun in bliss. / Brother; brother won by a higher bliss. / Mother; mother met hugged by bliss. / Sister; where were you sister too and brother bliss. / Infant; infant new bliss. / Aunt; tonight aunt will heal our bliss. / Cousin; consider your cousin, love, bliss. / Blitz; you are the blitz to bliss. / Bask; bask in births of bliss. / Bath; bath won, drown resist, bliss. / Bake; bake a review of yes! We taste your lovely, bliss. / Baste; baste the hum of trim to bliss. / Egypt; at 8 we're great to an egypt equate of nun except bliss. / Deserts; deserts heal our key of bliss. / Mountains; mountains mewed to a halfing skew to a center bliss. / Dimensions; dimensions done? Bliss / encompass; encompass your dance with the sheer arrive of all points, bliss. / Access; you access the truth with bliss. / Crossed; crossed paths to lasting bliss. / Invent; invent retain in heaven's name, bliss. / Cyber; climates cued to a cyber you on bliss. / Hybrid; hybrid inside the tree of dwarfed by bliss. / Directive; directive due to a penetrative view of bliss. / Investment; invest in who you love, best returns, on, bliss. / Flesh; flesh yearn, bliss. / Flash; flash on cue, bliss. / Today; today is all-ways love. / Yesterday; yesterday was all-those loved.

CHAPTER FOURTEEN

Pregnant; pregnant's pause, bliss./ Applause; applaud yourself, bliss. / Restraint; basic restraint cannot knot bliss. / Release; release resist, bliss. / Regard; let us regard our bliss. / Respect; respect you, bliss. / Paper; often penned to a paper in, bliss. / Pen; pen in hand, i am, bliss. / Prism; listen up, a prism's luck, is bliss. / Place; lightest place, bliss. / Angular; make an angular pledge to increase your trend to bliss. / Bahamian; bahamian palace of bliss. / Essential; essential within, bliss. / Threshold's; threshold's reach to penetrate bliss. / Bridge; bridge burned to river, bliss. / Atlas; atlas hugged bliss. / Terrific; let me terrific be in bliss. / Pastel; pastel hour of layered lace and time's replace, bliss. / Pursuit; pursuit's rebate is bliss. / Perplex; perplex left to bliss. / Preside; preside over reside to love, bliss. / Resident; resident astride her own reside in bliss / supple; supple examine of the heart that bends to bliss./ Muscle; muscle your way to resist-less bliss. / Supply; supply said to send ascend to love and bliss. / Aspect; aspect met reflect in love and bliss. / Lights; yes! I'm light, to love's embrace if bliss. / Life; life led to a matter, bliss. / Loves; held your hand to loves who stand in bliss. / Larks's; lark's expect sparks to the lips of kissed with sweet the flight to bliss. / Lessons; lessons learned earned, by bliss. / To day; to day, two day, delivery of bliss. / Shielded; shielded by the need to cry for more in bliss. / Held; held in swelled to loving bliss. / Saved; saved to ascend to bliss. / Swollen; electrically swollen by a wholing, love, enthused by bliss. / Peace; this kiss is peace in heat of life and bliss. / Dolly; dolly won by bliss. / Dear; dear you are bliss. / Often; often seen by bliss. / Yes!; Yes! You are, bliss. / Experts; i am expect of an experts span to perfect spin of love in bliss. / Fine; excellent, fine, a lavender line of bliss. / Valor; valor's power blue-green extreme of bliss. / Best; learn the rules of best in led to bliss. / Bed; bed yourself in bliss. / Better; better buster met true effect in love and bliss. / Bluff; bluff's attempt less in their expect of bliss. / Cliff; cliff side dwell with well we live to love and top this, bliss. / Core; core to a cure, we insure our bliss. / Concentric; concentrate on concentric rings of bliss. / Concise; concise to a point, bliss. / Conscious; conscious of the conscious, i am exact in my fact called bliss. / Commercial; commercial patter, the matter grown green is an international business called bliss. / Clan; clan's expand to share, bliss./ Case; sheer to a case of inflect, i invest in the means of yet we enlist in bliss. / Patent; a patent on patience in bliss. / Patient; patiently seen, the one who will mean our hearts best to the wet remember of bliss. / Sublime; sublime's design is where we near the chance to stand in line with bliss. / Aqualine; aqualine's shore is deep in direct expect of the feat called respect, blue-green, love. / Active; active stance in the glance of all revival and the heart of the archival return to the ones who learn from god is, bliss. / Actual; actual excite can invite the grace of often, bliss. / Essential; essentially scene, i am lean to vast reality called infinite bliss./ Effective; effective your will, be, in bliss.

CHAPTER FIFTEEN
World; worlds of love adrift in bliss. / Sun; sun shone on bliss. / Sincere; sincere to a hear of bliss. / Simmer; lessons simmer in bliss. / Select; select insure of the sure to love and bliss. / Suspect; suspect accept of bliss. / Potent; potent to punch at bliss. / Inside; inside the stride to bliss. / Preside; preside inside our bliss. / Reside; reside's inside this bliss. / Hysterical; hysterical cure of bliss. / Honed; honed to blend in bliss. / Selects; selects insure of bliss. / Juicy; juicy jewel of bliss. / Thrill; thrill to feel your bliss. / Zeal; zeal's appeal is this, bliss. / Frank; frank enough to frankly this is lovely, bliss. / Throne; throne room, bliss. / Dance; love rules the dance to bliss. / Summed; the flavor summed is bliss. / Desire; desire to hire our list to bliss. / Delectable; delectable appeal to bliss. / Okayed; okayed played, bliss. / Found; found myself blissed. / Winds; winds run west of blessed result of bliss. / Ignited; ignited by sighted to bliss. / Sodium; a sodium scent, the smell of bliss. / Life; life's lesson, bliss. / Refreshed; refreshed rest, bliss. / Run; run a son to bliss. / Youth; youths run to rest in best and then bliss. / Bundle; bundle up to a metric met with bliss. / Blast; ascertain blast to bliss. / Burst; burst worth, butter baste, blast, bliss. / Burn; burn worn free on the lead to bliss. / Known; known to you, renew, bliss. / Knock; knock our 3's to we are 4's to play of love, this, bliss. / Know; know yourself worn by bliss. / Watch; watch yourself winning, bliss. / See; see us win at bliss. / Thank; bliss new thanks in you are loved, bliss. / Gratitude; gratitude grew in bliss. / Scene; scenes of you in bliss. / Son; son won, bliss. / Seen; seen in bliss. / Love; love you, bliss. / Loves; loves enough to bliss. / Lifts; lifts up, bliss. / Entice; entice your nice cure, bliss. / Advice; advice to entice, bliss. / Resistance; resistance rests on resist less, bliss. / Gone to; gone to bliss. / Flowing; a flowing knowing, bliss. / Flames; flames procure, bliss. / Of; of you, i bliss. / Proof; proof to bliss. / In; in bliss. / God; god's cure, bliss. / Is; is this bliss. / Love; love to bliss. / And; and i see, bliss. / Bliss; bliss, bliss. / Guardians; guardians insure our rest at a breast called bliss. / Gardens; gardens insure our domestic power of bliss.

THE TRANCE-END-MENTS
LEVEL 5

CHAPTER ONE

Days Devote; Days Devote to a telling note of why we are and where we were when man was and basically Humanity won the right to fight for light of their own and around the throne there came a hush at Christ revealed sananda's fed of why, we've all become and ascendant we climb by 3 and standing steel we know the One electric feel of lightening in our daily devote, to transcendent heights / Sides Accrue; Sides accrue to why we hue ascendant stand and welcome few know why the two are often led by who's within their heart. All sides accrue to the love transcendent, Light / Acrylic View; Acrylic's view is a healing paint of all that's faint and even, less to more, for upon the shore a gliding's come to healing flow of the brush that knows remembrance, Love, life, the light transcendent / Painted Days; I paint the days of high the waves and wet the seas of all we weave to transcendent Love. Light / Elegant Ways; Ways of elegance anchor my wade to the wealth of a sight called higher the wave and today into night my emotions are fed by the way that your elegance flows pure and red to perfect devote of all that we've said of transcendent Love. Blessings come to the One who wields the sword of greatest come to One / Wanderer Scene; A wanderer scene has sung, the become of all we believe and elevated paths abort all the wrath of the harder days and the trance that's become less a wade and I know the power of home to live transcendent Love / Seen in Set; Seen in sets of respect, there's a fade to a heart red and green and the scene of surrounder sounds in me like a bell born to chime all reside in the Light electric and our perfect sight of transcendent Love / Set on Wet; Set on wet, I evoke higher yet the heightened ??? of All we feel when our hands are held by the Ones we love, in perfect zeal of the seal already broken to present, sparkling wet, the eyes of set on transcendent Love / Wetter Glade; Wetter glades have gleamed beneath the sea of all remember and past times gone I'm on to the life elected and the erected few who remember to wade to the wetter glade of the Light elective, transcendent Love / Gladed Shade; Gladed shade of sweet remember dripping wet with kind and tender and heightened steel I'm held within by the friend born wet and red to all surrender and transcendent Love / Color Pink; Color pink with striping red, I'm held soft within the bed of softer sand and kinder trees bent deep to seas of lightest hint at the pink extent of transcendent Love / Purple New; Purple new the violet hue of why we sing around the ring of the Lightest flame, transcendent Love / Ken for Too; Ken for too who fuel the fire of a passion higher that heaven held beneath the wave of a desirous few who remember transcend and Love / The Lightest View; The lightest view is who, we, transcendent Love / Hues of Shades; Hues of shades around me feel like welcome fade to pinker zeal and a sounding round of ringing thrill slides soft and low to perfect fuse of the Light's electric enthuse of transcendent Love / Crystal Keen; Crystal keen I'm lean to a definite confide in the ride to a gentle lean worn low to all we fly of the Love transcendent / Kiss Exude; Kiss exude in your mood to the Love transcendent / Heaven Spoke; Heaven spoke wrote about our lot as human been born to warm of less than All we say of transcendent Love / Lately Scene; Lately I'm scene in a snowy lean to a mantle worn around the horn of a cape draped soft upon the gentle earth, our birth of lately scene, the Love transcendent / Seen of Late; Lately seen, I am clean to a lighter sway and the sight of days filled forever deep with transcendent Love / Late's Induce; The latest induce is proof of our truth to aspects of youth worn full in the brace of transcendent Love / The Living Proof; The living's proof of the giving sooth of all we say of transcending Love / Heaven's Shade; Heaven's shade is our glade of sweet remember in the land of our forever-ing smile at the while we transcendent Love / Latest Raid; My latest raid is on the life of alone to the Love transcendent / A Purple Fade; A purple fade is well to we are free to breathe in the life transcendent / Faded Silk; Faded silk kimono soft to a mouth kissed deep with relief of a rest-full sleep in the full-faced embrace of the eyes faded adrift to silky Love / Softly Shorn; Softly shorn I'm worn skin deep to deft relief of lightly grown to the woven theme of Love transcendent / Lightly Worn; Lightly I'm worn by the we've begun to show the like of all we know to the Love transcendent / Definite Decide; Definite decide is inside our swag to the way we pay our views to the side we choose of only transcendent Love / The Light Inside; The light inside our forevering glide and all the way in is transcending Love / Speak of Light; Speak of Light, and we invite your stay at the way we live in transcending give of Love / Trances End; The trance is over and I am in the end of less than the life transcendent / End of "This"; The end of "This" is Bliss LIFE, Light transcendent / Edge of Bliss; The edge of Bliss is this, the kiss of a light fantastic to massive exude of who we'd transcendent Love / Nights of Jade; Nights of Jade invade my extend of the friend who paves the streets / Days Bamboo; Life's days are bamboo green to a silky screen of yes we've come to a metered sea of all we wave in the lifting tree that I've become life deep, to Love's transcendence / Closets Too; Closets too are few between friends of the Love, transcendent / Puzzles O'r; Puzzles O'r your settled chore of who you are expire in may of personal explain of the pain less journey to the central new of you in the Light transcendent / Life's Explore; Life's explore less dominant in a run more predominant in for our mutual pleasure life's a treasure, never ignore the explorant vacation in the Love transcendent / Lot's Ignore; Let's ignore "lots" insecure implore of a salty shore worth of revival the Life transcendent / Nights Implore; Nights Implore me to store our life in blend of transcend, Love / A Perfect Score; A perfect score, more transcendent, the music of Love / Lightly Knew; Lightly knew who we were along the line of the sign transcendent / Lightly View; Lightly view your welcome hue of All we are and there we are in the miraculous news of the Lightly view our nightly due to transcendent Love / Days of Glen; Days of Glen expand within our scene of All we were to transcend, Love / Lights of Zen; Lights of Zen blink within when I align with the flight inside my arc-ing spin to the light heart within my hearty, ascend to the trance's end, transcend meant, Love / A Perfect Hue; A perfect hue of the color in you and our spiraling ascend to the heart whistling a rainbow's tune, the precious hum of a sparkling spiral called transcendent Love / Beatific You; Beatific tune, the woods of muse on Love. Trance over, begin, Bliss / Yes to who?; Yes! To who? To you, our, end's begin, Love / Lofty Too; Lofty too, you, light, end, trance-end, Love / Elusive Few; I'm ascend and an elusive view of transcend at Love / Puzzles Done; God's puzzle done. We've one our way tot he ending day of lesson won. Trance's end, Bliss / Race Run; Races run to a blissed pace, the grace of transcend / Nights Explore; Divine explore of a night's rapport with Bliss. Trance End / Lightly New; Lightly I new am my heart's review of Loving Bliss. A trance end, again, Bliss / Often Spoke; Often spoke, trance end, bits of Bliss and Love / Light's Exude; Lightest exude, Blissed trance end to Love / Exuberant View; Exuberant view of then, blend, trance end, Love / The Vein of Woo; View your woo in a vein called Bliss, blend, trance end / Wound Around; Wound around to you in Bliss and Love and this transcend / Elected Stood; I elected stood in an end to less, a trance become bliss, to this end, Love / Steady On; Steady on to when we Love transcend / On Expand; God's on expand to Bliss and this trancing end, the elasting friend, Lust to Love / Expansive Knew; Expansive review of who we knew as light's rescind to Loving's trance-end.

CHAPTER TWO

Lightly We Lightly we are to the afar to Bliss and this divine recall of all we are to lift our wide-eyed trance-end / Wedded Too Wedded to you, I believe in trance-end within our Bliss / Hello You Hello you are Love. Trance over. The end of Good-bye. hello, Love / Light's Embrace Lightest embrace, the race to who we love trance-end-ately well / Basic Clue A basic clue, trance-end, Love / Sixty-Nine Days Sixty-nine days home to believe in trance-end / Lightest Stay Light's a stay at the highest way to a wave within Trance-end / Heaven's Gate God's heaven's gate to lifting Love. To a wait of less, specific g of last to end the trance / Sephira Stand Lots of sephira stand 10 deep to brand trance-end / Ladies Land Got ladies land here in the pen of sparkling Gold stand at trance-end Love / Man's Befriend Man's a befriend when he's in the end Love's trance gone to perfect Bliss / Fondly Found God's fondly found in my round to life's transcend / Heightened Town Heights of a town, heightened around by Love's transcend / Towns Explore God knows towns who explore more transcend / Explore More Explore more, ignore less, know loft to loving's high transcend / Vacancy Gone Ascendancy on, my vacancy's gone to love's transcend / Lavender Hue Lavender's hue, you, in loving transcend / Pink and Green 2 Pink and green are too, Love, transcend / Daily One Daily one to a due of all we respect of light's trance end to Love / Places Set Places are set around the town of Love's trance -end / Parent's Pet Parent's pet, and we are Loved. Trance over to the end of neglect. Know adult thanks in Love / Petal Perfect; Petals are perfect on our wonder at life's reflect on absolute Love's Trance-end / Perfect Bloom; A perfect bloom, the heart of Love at Trance's End / Babies Blossom; Babies blossom in constant view of those who love and fairies too, Love's Trance End /

Blossoms Exude; Blossoms exude the perfume of why we bloom to Trance's end in Love / Who Cued; Who cued you to care? And where? From what? You knew the cue of Love's Trance End / Cued Exude; Know the cued exude of All that's rude to the light within our Earth and Loving Trance-end / Basic View; Basically I view your enthuse as rest in the arms of God's because, Trance End / Value Sent; Value is sent to my invent of why we bend to Love's transcend / Assign Design; Assign design to begin to Love transcend / Hello View; Hello view, renew, your sights an forgivings nature the cause is God's reknown with bound less trance-end to Love / Value Given; Value is given on why I've reason to live in reside in Love's Trance-end / Find a House; Find a house wet with bet on emotion's win of transcendent Bliss / Space's Set; Space is set for your forget of less and reknowned I know the clause of God and Love transcendent / Evict Neglect; Evict Neglect from your deflect on regret-full loss. Know the clause, transcendent, Love / Deeper Breath; A deeper breath can bet on heightened transcend to Love / Fixed Evoke; Fixed evoke on the wrote by transcendent Love / Effusive Be; Effusive be our specific belief in relief of God's religions sum of all we become to the Love transcendent / Every Stroke; Every stroke spoke of transcendent Love / Daily Ground; Daily ground around our transcendent Love / Major's Mend; A major mend, the captain's ascend to militant-less blitz on Love. The trance-end / Courage Cue; Courage's cue, you are transcendent to a friend called Love / Classy Date; A classy date of late to the friend transcend and the life elastic / Daisy's Due; Daisy's due, a transcendent push through the mush of all we much are to Lifing's light Trance-end / Tried Exude; Tried's exude is who we'd be to Love's trance-end / Lasting Too; God's lasting too, are you? Trance-end / Taste-full Be; Tastefull we'll be to the healing tree of All is one to the tongue transcendent / Better We; Fun to a better we, we are love by a delightful cede to God is Love's Trance-End / Later Spree; Later well spree together to the be of the Light Life transcendent / Special Seen; Special has seen we are One to the light transcendency especially seen there in fun / Scenes of Frees; Scenes of frees delights in me and my magnificent come to the cede to darshan done to One, the sum transcendent / Frankly Knew; Frankly I knew you as transcendent too / Now Believe; Now believe the sleeve of a tube pressed deep to see the center of our gravity to the intensity of All we've become, now believe, in the Love transcendent / Travel Too; Trance's end can travel too to the heart and the height and the spirit of two become One, travel too to transcendent Love / Forty's Pave; Forty's pave is clined by live Trance-End in Love / Living Wade; Living's wade is raved by Love. Trance-end, mend, Love / Wavering Too; Wavering too? Be clued to rude's exude of good-bye to less in loving's trance-end / Wounds Recede; We are through and the wounds recede to clues of the light within our exceed, trance-end to Love / Light Receive; Light receive, know deceive has gone to the bend of the trance within and our Love / Racy Views; Racy news the views are you, by Trance-End / Better Nude; Babies better nude are clued to who'd be rude less by life's transcend / Nightly Knew; Lightly new, I'm rightly knew by trance's end to

Love / Now We Too; Now we too are true to Bliss. Begin to end, all less than this our Love's trance end / Often You; Lift the often you to love's Trance-end, win, Love.

CHAPTER THREE

Basic In See; Basically I see we are the Ones in how we believe in the best of we see the lightest side of the eyes in turned to Basically send transcend to Love / Salient Be; Salient I'll be when we finish we are Love's trance-end / Blessings Rang; Blessings rang around the throne of all we own of light's deep column to Love's transcend / Round the Design; Round this deign we reign to perfect Love's transcend / Sweetly Done; You are sweetly done by all you love of life's begin to light your life within trance's end of lessen Love / Healing Sun; Healing you is the sun of a sum called One to transcendent Love / Sum Seen; I am the sum seen in perfect redeem of all we've become for precious within Trance-end Love / Scene of Dream; The scene of a dream has come to awaken Love's transcend / Daily Do; Daily I do transcend to Love / Delicate View; A delicate view to who we love at trances end / Delicious Exceed; Delicious knew exceed in all we'd seen of Love's transcend / Savior Gone; The savior's gone to the clause called why we transcend to Love / Yes I Will; Yes I will be with you in transcendent Love / Often Feel; Often feel yourself reel in transcendent Love / Baby Sea; Baby sea how we float to the vote for how we know to Love, transcendent / Sounds of We; Sounds of we are wooed by Love's bell rung clear to transcend / Electrically; Electrically speaking, we're spoken of with transcendent Love / Rolling In; Rolling in to you are Loved, transcend / Round Up; Rounding up fuel for life's transcend / Heaven Stood; Heaven stood still for begin to Love's transcend / Tools of Trade; Tools of trade are the rules of ruled exude to the precious enthuse of a tape measured Love's transcend / Trade Your Cruel; Trade your cruel for who'll you Love's transcend / Ocean View; An ocean view is the height of you in life's transcend / Half on Our; Half an our, power, Love in transcend / Our Devote; Our devote is invite to a right called why we wrote of the way you float in a dance called Light to the trance's end. I'm in, Love / Dates; Dates sate my daily devote with a firm intrude to those who'd be an time to Loving's. End of the trance instead, devote, Love / Denote; Denotes in best reside inside the shade of heavenly blue you in Love's transcend / Lightly; Lightly seen slim to a daily desire to inspire all we plan to be for Love's transcend / Lately; Lately delirious to the noon of sunset in us I AM oblivious to all less than end this trance / Sately; In a sately vein, I'd explain all you feel as heal your transcendent Love / Sustain; Sustain us, Love, transcendent / Suspend; Suspend the knots of ought to Love / Often; Often fell the bail to hook our weight to a lighter trend, the friend of men, the candle's flame called found by Love. Trance End / As All; As All given, livings come, transcend, Love / All Ways; All ways fade to abate on great we Love. End One, Love / Sustenance; Sustain our sustenance near the mend of the Trance's End / Enhance; Enhance meant heat your because to applause at God is us in the cause to Love transcend / Extant; Extant to an extent

of God within transcend / Extent; Extent to content invent of an inventory's glory of transcend / Extend; Extensive extend to transcend / Intend; Intend to in tend to Love. transcend. Lightly a trend to Love / Invent; Invention's invent, trance end, Love / Advent; Advent's invent, consent to the blend's transcend, Love / Elate; Elate's intrigue is we'd breathe in transcend / Well; Well tell, the Trance End's meant story.Congratulate; Congratulate your set on / Expiate; Expiate's great to a date with Love's transcend / Exasperate; Exasperate's breath is in depth to relieve of the trance, the ends to Love / Breaths; Breathe the breath that's better yet than wet arrival at forever's spot within infinity's slim arrival at the God of all revival, the art of breathe, transcendent Love / Breath; Breath first, Love's transcendent / Bet; Bet we'll be free to Love transcendent / In Deed; In deed I act the react away to a grace called faith and the light of a day grown wide to decide on transcend's Love / Indeed; Indeed we agreed to Love transcend / Intrigue; Intrigue has went to have vent the critical curse reversed by the Light transcend / Exceed; Exceed's respect re-elect Love transcend / Excel; Excel well, the fountain of time's melt at the velt of a belt felt steep in incline to Loving transcend / Fine; Fine enough in your handle of the mantle of Love's transcend / Line; Line around Love's transcend / Found; Found you in my life's transcend to Love / Fond; Fondest friends is the inn to Love's transcend / First; The first time in I win perfect love's transcend to Lightly Love / Last; Last time round I found perfect Love in transcend / All; All we can be is Love's transcend / As Sent; As sent I went western deep to a depth replete of wet to yet we Love transcend.

CHAPTER FOUR

Attain; Attain the sustain of when we Love transcend / Explain; Explain your set shot an transcend's Love / Blessed; Blessed sea of weave deep trance end, Love / Based; Based on faced our Love's transcend / Belies; Belies reside decide design derive deliver Expiate's place at Love's Trance End / Extra; Extra measure of the pleasure, life, light, Trance, over, end at Love / Extravagant; Extravagantly seen in a magnificent screen the life we've let to Loving Trance End / Glance; Glance at an extravagant kiss, light is near and we are clear to a Crystal view of Love's Trance End / Glee; At the end of Glee came a free deliver of all we transcend for Bliss in Love / Congeal; Congeal will heal your conversant appeal to how we feel for our Love's transcend / Expel; Expel fell west of the rest baby deep to weep of Love's transcend / Impulse; Impulse has sent divine intersect to Loving transcend / Hand; Hand to hand, manned by transcend Love / Handle; Handle to handle Love is transcend / Stand; Stand on the gravitational shield of a field called Loving transcend / Earnest; Earnest merit inherit Loving transcend / Magnify; Magnify yourself transcend, Love / Enjoy; Enjoy your truth to who you are by Love's transcend / Conveyance; Conveyanced concede to the need of Love. Trance End / Constant; Constant kins begin to Lovely transcend / Commitment; Commitment made to aid our end to transcend to Love / Control; Controls mission is ignited by lighted by Loving transcend / Sensation; Sensation set on touching, tasting smelling, feeling, Loving transcend / Sensate; Sensate of late has a trance's end to less, Love / Elevate; Elevate to heights of sights wide enough to blend / Astound; Astound us anonymity found in trance's end to Love / Astound; Astound has found content in the arms of God's Love in attendance, transcendence, Love / Aspire; Aspire on fire with Love in transcend / Hire; Hire aspire to admire this Loving transcend / Height; Height's are in to a friend called win our Loving ascend / Deal; Deal about heal is we'll be free to Love's transcend / Date; date on a date to eloquence sent to a friendly transcend to the ones who Love / Depth; Depth to depth we're wet with emotional Love. The trance is over and out to Love / Basic; Basic's within our perfect ascend to transcend is Love / Humane; Humane explain of transcend, Love / Humanity; Humanity's won by one in love with man's explain of lots to transcend / Divines; Divines duel is with rule, Love can win a new reside of less and rest to Love's transcend / Destiny; Destiny's rule is who we'll adore for Love's transcend / Delight; Delight in the red bright green to Love's blending transcend / Excite; End of lessen excite to exit to perfect life trance over to Love / Ecstasy; Ecstasy rules in transcendent spools of Life / Exit; Let us be free to extend our lights to men of Love. Trance End / Enter; Enter in to the inn of Loving's ascend. We are Love's Friend, God's mend transcend / Center; Center line, Love, Good and red and within ascend, Love / Central; Central scene, the dream of Love's transcend / Trill; Trill heal is us singing best for God's ascend to lend transcend to Love / Expert; Expert review, expectant too, we, Love, transcend / Infant; Infant see the fan of man called Light by we transcend to Love / Instant; Instantly be jeweled by the hurtling lend to Loving transcend / Innocent; Innocent invent of hint to show us only perfect Love. Transcend / Intimacy; Intimacy's tool, transcend's Love / Delicacy; Delicacy's delight, the flight to a perfect spin on Loving Ascend to transcend / Fan; Fan of who we ascendant review as Love's transcend / Fund; Funds flown to expansive ascend know the inn to Love and transcend / Hold; Hold on to Love's trance end / Help; Help a hue to your set on Love and transcend / Hearts; Hearts are held full of review for Love. Trance End / Met; Met respect of reflect to Loving's trance end / Melt; Melts a renew of Love's transcend / Felt; Felt thrust in a brush with breath direct to Love-ing's spiral trend to ascend / Fit; Fit to be a mother of ascend to Love / Fact; Facts are few to many intentional Love. transcend / Farther; Farther in to win transcend of Love / Brace; Brace Yourself; Fun on fun and unleash become to best in bliss of bliss to the end of the trance you've won. Love.

CHAPTER FIVE

First; First alert can revert to met by the worth of an electric way to the highest day called what we did for transcendent Love / Last; Last way home to transcendent, Love / Omega; Omega men win when the Alpha's in to a brighter sight sent to the Light life transcendent / End; End Zone, transcendent Love / Begin; Begin again to win your light of insight seen around the scene of the Love transcendent / Alpha; Alpha begun, I'm One with the Light transcendent / Art; Art smart to a valiant vein of lightly seen, the dream of the Love transcendent / Ascent; Ascent meant we invent to Ascend to our Love's transcend / Alarm; Alarms sound around the round of our friendly town called in transcend to Love / Escape; Escape the gap, relap to basic transcend to Love / Landscape; Landscape to a gape of escape been sent to ascent of Love in transcend / lapse; Lapse of escapist notion, to the notion that we've become One bridge to transcend in Love / Moral; Moral is transcendent be in Love / Morale; Morale's pal, Love at the end of a trance / In Fact; In fact we've become ascend's begin to transcend in Love / Found; Found a fortune felt deep in drill to the well of a trust to / Fort; Fort has held court and the fortress is gone to Love transcend / Intrigue; Intrigue rest, Love, transcend / Insight; Marriage to you has an insight met in my wet surrender to the Love that will endure to transcend / Delight; Delight in white recovery of Light discovery of the heart that will blend to Love transcend / Dart; Dart post last time wide to perfectly Loved transcend / Start; Start a part of why we'd Love transcend / Cart; Cart a part to a freshen in when we ascend to transcend / Cape; Cape hope knows beget of wet to heal in Love's transcend / Now; Now and then and eternally in our Loving transcend / Full; Full enough to heal, our zealous ascent called the friendly transcend to Love / Feeling; Feeling fills up with transcend and Love / Career; Career in to extend your reach deep into ascendant Love / Curl; Curl up in heal and trance end, get some, more, Love / We; We are best bets to our Loving transcend / Insure; Insure yourself of wealth, Love, transcend / Sure; Surely we will still-fully be believe in transcend and Love / Assure; Assure us wed to believe in decreed by Loving's transcend / Sure; Sure enough to assure yourself of transcend in Love / Spell; Spell your heal, L-O-V-E, the trance end / Dealt; Dealt reflect with respect to you and Loving transcend / Done; Done to when we transcend to perfected by Love / Durate; Durate is great in elate to God is, Love / Exasperate; Exasperate on good elate of Lofts of transcend / Elate; Elate your invite to great recite of the respect-full applaud and a central creed called we believe in the God, Love / Whirl; Whirl around to hear a sound of what we love of all transcend and manned begin of Love / Hurl; Lift your hurl to whirl with Grace and her attendant fan, a faith within transcend, and Love / Hands; Hands held full of heel are two feet deep in rich respect of the reflect that close God's cause and transcend Love / Mountain; Mountains manned by expand are pleased to see we are the truth's transcend / Man; Man's plan is ascendant, transcendent, Love / Fountain; Fountain fend for me to see the transcendent flow of God is; now, Love / Forth; Forth go to transcendent quarters that covers the elements of Love / Wells; Wells spring forth when I give my begin a new sort of transcend with Love / Sunder; Sunder the thunder of less, rent the room for more than a trancing dance, end, begin, Love / Sundry; Sundry matters matter me less when I transcend to Sunday's way of a week's begin at Love / Sunday; Sunday Ariel is in my date with rapture, the numbers of Love's trance end / Since; Since we met, wet with surrender to the kiss, of love's transcend / True; True you and we, we are, the invite of insight to a flight to the life transcendent / Trat; Trat to a spot called invitational invite and I am light to a run to the sun of symbols become trance end. Love / Truth; Truth told, we're old to boldly Love trance end / Sought; Sought truth in compute of all we fed to Love in transcend / Find; Find a fund for Loving's transcend. One call higher to Love / Fund; Funds are fueled by the power that heals our Love in transcend / One; One time I knew we were perfectly in to Love in transcend / Won; Won by you, I AM wooed by love within a song called God has won the race to face / Wonder; Wonder will fill our heart's with glee full surrender to the remember to Love in transcend / Wealth; Wealthy wed to said to love and transcend. I trance end in Loving's zeal / Say; Say you will reveal your heal to Love-INGS end of transcend again / Okay; Okay I will, yes, to Loving transcend.

CHAPTER SIX
Start; Muriel's start is art in Love-ing transcend / Today; Paint today with transcend in Love / Worth; Worth enough to hover over, our friend in mend is self gone healthy to Love's transcend / Needs; Needs to be freed to a loving's transcend / These; These are the days of all the ways we've been to directive, expressive, defend of transcend to our Love / Expressive; Expressive said well to all we'll see of Love in transcend / Knelt; Knelt deep in a lasting sleep, I now have awakened to the love we've been making and to all that's become of transcendent Love / Direct; Sleepy and direct I am an aspect of the affect of perfectly Loved to the end direct to the trancing reflect of whole and still to Love / Beneath; I am beneath the shade of your nodding surrender to all that's been said to beneath the found around is all we Love in transcend / Wings; Wings of wind within the mend of the heightened flow of all we know to the beating pulse of a hearty transcend / Under; Under all guise, the disguise has gone to won, win, Live. Trance Done, Love / Over; Over and other, we're eternally under the sun of God's sum, overboard to an end's transcend in Love / With; Where were you when you were with we are the won the win, the fun for God's transcend and the grand arrival at God? / Despite; Despite deflect, I know relent in less has gone Away to expand on transcend, right hear, in Love / Respite; God's good green respite of invite to Love in transcend / Insight; Insight on the water of our glancing arrival at all the way in to Loving transcend / Sate; Sate grown great to precious blend of when wind brings transcend to Love / Specific; Specific to a friend who knew how to, Love, transcend / Mend; Mend a bet on trance-end to Life / Arc; Trance is arced back to oblivion in lessen gone to lesson won, the arc of Love to transcend / Sold; Sold out to in Love. Trance Over / One; One to self One Love Trance End / Neat; Neat accede to we'd be glad to Love transcend / Knee; Knees we stress less by address to transcend / Deed; Deed in deep indeed in Loved transcend / Dart; Dart to a start of Loving within our living transcend / Star; Star in a car to a cart full-filled with we'll need to see the light of transcend, Love / Stark; Stark treasure meet Love in transcend / Expect; Expect to see elect in we are the Ones lady led to a winged reside in a sides

intrude with attitude of Light / Inflect; Inflect to inflect in direct invest in the aspect direct to let there be Loved ascend trend to excellent transcend. 31 Date; I am due to a date with you and one are the Love one, transcend / Know; Know who we are to Love within the trend to a trance's end of Love / Direction; Direction directly due to we are the wed to the west of love to transcend / Inspection; Inspecting expective aspective All one, a life transcend / Lights; Lights blue within flashing renew of deep to Love's trace end / Star; Stars expire often lessoned by the sun of a galactic fund called life. transcend / Purr; Purr softly Love to a light transcend / Infectious; Infectious pride can ride to blend at an end called loving transcend / Let; Bliss in a kiss wet with let us Love to Lightly touch transcend / Spark; Party's on to a spark called One pure column of Light transcend / Watt; Wattage sum, the volt to a veld of Love's transcend / What; What you knew was enough to new in Love within transcend / Why; Why knot? Love. Live. transcend / Whether; Whether forever, unknot to list your eternity won to Love / Ever; Ever often were raptured by our rare exclude to include lessons lived to a love's transcend and one cool spool of ever, more / Are; Are you shored by your Love? Look up to lift and heaven's gift of when transcend began in Lifts to are we yes! Love / Care; Care enough to fare well in Love's transcend / Impair; Impair aware, leave, judge knot, know sought to, Love / Stare; Stare at where we are in perfect's run with money and Love. Trance End / Stir; Stir here to a flower's tower of columned ignite and lightly ascent, our star to a rise of love / Aspect; Aspect respect fall of the heart of God and all of man in a smoky glow of Love in transcend / Reflect; Reflect on respect in transcend and deep intrigue with Love / Instant; Instant aspect of fleck of love met transcend in met got life from a flock of men called God in Love / Dare; Dare to care about a flair for let us live for transcend in Love / Share; Share a prayer with one you Love transcend / Pare; Pare it down, Love, one, transcend / Pair; Pair of eyes grown wise to blues gone away to review the exhume to all we consume of Loved transcend / One; One to you, transcend / Twos; Twos win, One, transcend / Threes; Threes freeze up with a transcends expand Love / Four; Four to free we are three becoming one in the glistening sun of our light, transcend / Fines; Fines are clued by light's transcend / Sixed; Sixed to sexed I'm resurrect to an erect commission called standing up for the light within our transcend to love / fortune; fortune found in the town of light regard for love in transcend.

CHAPTER SEVEN
Seven; Sevens come round to a listing sound called living within the whistle to blown wide to God transcend / Eight; Eight times we surround the tree the delightful light called infinitely and again we transcend / Ate; I ate from a plate called heavenly fruit and you came to me and we came to soon, our conclusion, the sun-ation, our feel of transcending love / Nines; Nines erupt in a volcanic spend to the living within a perfect ten, the transcend, Love / Back; Back to back with stand the flock of a living-less gone and a winning selective of the attention called straight to the corner of love plausible to the transcendent unwinding of

time / Camp; Camp gone flash to an expedient dash to the edge of a woods called light, can, and should, and we simply are the transcend called a star and a night spent content and a life spent so far. Comp here at the link with transcend / Golf; Swung to a swing, I'm a password mean of the distance a spark can fall from God and straight in the center and pin height with flight, I putter around to the columbia of light. Four. God. transcend / Sport; Be a sport, cavort transcend / Sort; Sort yourself out, don't *pout transcend. *Plainly open to undermining trend / Snow; Snow on this melty bliss of the mountains of our loves transcend / Hail; Hail thus, I'm granting you your melting ability at peaceful tranquility at the butterfly house at the end of the lane called transcend / Rain; Rain a lad of sweet remember and spoken tender are the trickly sounds of the heavens come down to reign in a land called we are the ones who transcend / Felt; I felt you ignite our love to a transcend at dove called lightly love transcend / Default; Default is less yours than ours. We are the ones to come to end the trance. Awaken, forgive, transcend / Decide; Decide to do in accordance with good one rule, the love tool, the golden one, transcend / Fault; Fault cracked earthquake hook continents met and were all wet with tectonic delight the puzzles glue, the house less you and a light transcend / Deride; Deride yourself less and derisive reflect gone this mirror deep to a better respect of the light transcend / Caress; Caress the braid of how we stayed in Loved. transcend / Impress; Impress yourself, transcend / Prate; Prate a lot, then hear, transcend / Depths; Depths deal on healing floods of transcend / Wide; Wide enough to hear, transcend / Channel; Channel mannered, transcend / Inside; Inside us, loves, transcend / Thirds; Thirds can imagine each other at points within the One transcend / Hearts; Hearts that are held mend well in transcend / Heart-ed; Hearted time in a heart that's mine to transcend / Trailed; Trailed on through to who we Loved, ascend / Tramp; Tramp across to Loved transcend / Trek; Trek across to you and transcend / Rest; Rest is best in transcend / Date; Date a state of elate, transcend / Roar; Roar across transcend / Gently; Gently jeaned I'm worn by a torn example of lets transcend Love / Gone; Gone for good love in tune with transcend / Debts; Debts dealt felt to perfect, love, transcend / Darth; Darth gone dark can use a spark of transcend / On; On you, we're too, tops, transcend / Held; Held hush, transcend / Often; Often I can mend, through transcend / Risky; Risky frisky, transcend / Rant; Rant, Rave, Pant, Stove, Store the wave to all that you are inside a day spent surfing a star. Carbonaceous matter gone to transcend / Rave; Rave about God. transcend / Often; Often I feel led to transcend / Even; Even *stefan knows the God can mend those clothes heal your body transcend. *Son that evoke forgotten align with natural attend / Yet; Yet again, transcend / Dance; Dance with a star in your pants. transcend / Yes; Yes we can, transcend / Enter; Enter graciously, expectant transcend / Burned; Burned in a transcend to a flame won out by perfectly, Love / Darned; Darned and knotted I'm spotted on the mend, transcend / Trance; Trance over End. Open-eyed Love / Broken; Broken to less, the cord has stretched to snap at transcend / Blink; Blink too, Love, trance,

on, blink, over the end / See; See it, love, transcend / Hear; Hear enough, across trance's end / Instant; Instant and entire to often we, Love in transcend / Inspect-ing; God's life is great in inspecting my relate to life and Love in transcend / Actine; Actine measure, me, in respect of we are Love's transcend / Reflecting; Reflecting respectfully to the back of a leap to lightly we are transcends within to Love / Leave; Leave me to your passionate blend of why we are to Love in transcend / Greet; Greet me great with Loving transcend / Implore; Implore more swore at less devote, each transcend Love / Door; Door shut on less is an honest reflect of what's within our return to Love.

CHAPTER EIGHT

With In; With and in, I begin to a scend to a light relax at the end of facts of Love / With Us; With us, flush to respect to the aspect of Love's blending transcend / Wait; Wait for what you want of best in trance end, a wait for Love / Selective; Selective design, Loved, trance end / Waltage; Waltage is of to howwe sup on Love in transcend / Elect It; Elect it, loved, God's transcend / Ingratiate; Ingratiate your equate to behest by our sweet Love / Struck; Struck by a race to correct my amend of bless in life's transcend to Love / Instruct; Instruct yourself to adore more embrace of grace and lightly Love's trance end / Carbon; I Am one carbon less of left to reflect of Love's trance end / Heal; Heal reveal, show me your Loving transcend / Endurance; Left to endurance, I AM concurrence / Experience; Experience within in a transcend to Love / Deals; Let love's deals be heals with a rush to loft / Fuller; A fuller transcend is mine today by God's sweet divine to incline in Love / Start; Start to heal your feel for Love and find transcend in God's reflect of LIGHT of we reviews our Love / Sparked; Sparked by arced, I'm suspect of reject in respect of Love's transcend / Spent; Spent on respect, I reflect on how we were and I AM spent on relive of give in life's transcend / Stiff; Stiff to a matter of the platter filled full with cuisine trance end to Love / Warm; Warm enough to be in life's true ascend and in to Love / Cold; Cold to forget, I AM warm with wet respect of All we living Love / Dear; Dear be queered to less in transcend to Love / Deer; Deer and gentle Love's gazelle across the plane of zoned transcend / Home; Home to huts grown deep in relief and perfect love in transcend / Hearth; Hearth of birth and worth it all in land of transcend / Hart; Hart to smart desire, I am higher to a flyer is bound to the height and transcend / Own; Own your own LIGHT in trance end, Love / Expand; Expand on an impulse said to be arraigned by best we live in expands to transcend / Gentles; Gentles gem inside our trim revive of the life inside transcend / Us; Us and too, we three are fed a simple suspend of less and more we know, Love's transcend / Knew; Knew who you felt free to be, we, transcend to a Grecian spin of Love / Roamed; Roamed around town with an expensive extend of lesson within our extensive Love transcend / Spare; Spare prayer in air extensive and deep in a breath wet with relief in delicious receipt and Light transcend / New; New enough to will to Love within transcend / Let's; Let's be spooled around to Love / Yoke; Yoke bespoke of west in line and trails to lots of Loved, ascend, trance end / Invoke; Invoke spoke to wheel to will you transcend to Love / Lesson; Lesson's lean to Loved Ascend / Now; Now how to be? transcend / All One; All one clue to who we, Love, transcend / One Own; One you own to soon, Love, transcend / Dates; Dates are the best in loved transcend / One Heart; One heart few to paradise knew found plenty deep and Down to stand in fanned Love / Home; Home hue, the color of you, in Loving transcend / Walk; Walk on over to pleasure called next in Love transcend / One; One time knew our Light transcend / Us; Us to us to infinite pleasure and God's good sun in lime-green's extend to arctic blue cystalline trance end and Love / Within; Maui within our heart Love's hand transcend. Life / Again; Again we will heal to Love and the lot called Light transcend / Remember; Remember to render you cinder to a sky flown loud to heaven's sound of Loved transcend / Endure; Endure your cure of sure to often and eternal in transcend and Love / Mimic; Mimic cure, Love to, transcend, transcend / Authentic; Authentic pleasure is God's feature of what we got for living Love and transcend / Clear; Clear enough to hear, here, there, spare crystal lean to the ear of God's earth and the mirth of Love's laughing transcend / Spin; Spin has spun to one in Love and transcend / Spring; Spring within the coil of kundaliui scene breath deep in steep to transcend Love / Bait; I suppose bait is great to trance's end and the hook is set on men of heart and human recovery of delivery to Love / Bubble; Bubble spring of crystal ring to life felt transcend / Flows; Flows a knows of Love and a river wide to a heart grown fine to love within you light transcend / Light; Lately I'm light to who you were to Michealed live of transcend in Love / River; River of life's kundalini given rise to the wiser side of a breath past forget to remember only this perfect Love's transcend / Divine; Divine enter-vention did I mention the mission of Love in transcend? / title; title to the fusion called transcend / pairings sixty-four deep in love's transcend.

THE COMMIT-MENTS
LEVEL 6

CHAPTER ONE

Nature; the nature of rest is that heaven is best when held deep inside a celestial line called the sun of all remember and the sum of all commit. commit meant. love / commitment; commitment sent to heaven's admit of all we are for love / create; create a logical choice to devote so emote, so great, so deftly entreated by the life that is richer still with love / nurture; nurture, nestle, hustle, vent, fawn, and fonder, and presently ponder your heartfelt rise to a light delight called love / care; ancient care has turned my head to your yearn for attention moonlit in a shimmering backdrop of destiny's due, your heart is dear to me in our eternal commit to care / ascent; ascent to stands of enter in to the God-head groomed by love / aspect; aspect sunk knee deep in love's surround of the sound to a splendor met in release of love's commitment / catch; catch up with your set of particular matters and smatters of the best abreast our loving commit / craft; craft renew of your delicate view of the veiny include of love and bliss / cache; cache up with your set of the mundane and gain the freedom to release to your invest of let's align with committed love / mingle; mingle around the sound of release of love's walk to walk-in by lots of love's committing tongue of faith / faith; faith is love's committing tongue / one; one on one we win to too and increase our view of whence we came to loving commit / accent; accent's advent to hint at is the way we went to precisely committed love / wealthy; wealthy to a wield of all we're well to sea, I am intrigued with the sight of a dashing admit to committed love / woman; woman of mine, I am, by limbed ascend to an accessed stand for committed love / spare; spare integrate of late has led to a heightened fed by loveing commit / man; man of this, I mend to the ascend to win the commit for love / mend; mend your send to an ascendant stand and the send of the lightest hue; you in eternity's commit; to love / peach; a peachy view of where we two can be when free for commit to love / salmon; salmon colored pews of leaves in leased agreed to committed love / magenta; magenta green to the seam of a wet recess in the dews of committed love / purple; purple pews of passion view our love as one commit / steadfast; a steadfast manner, the planner, love's commit / stand; commit to a stand in love / clan; the clan of mass can well afford a committed constant called love / clasp; clasp the hand of man and befriend within the electric stand of lightly love / regenerate; regenerate your stat of patient manner and explain the name of one content within the commitment sent to love / lean; lean are we to few and less than all of commit to love / slant; slant on a kant to a glazing hum, the ones of God / view; view your self shut to less than all commit to love / play; play at a loved commit / pen; all day I pen and again I am light to a commitment sent to love / park; park in the arc and expect connect from a deeper spark than this. commit to love / cradle; cradle your stable in hands of love in commit / ladle; ladle out sup in a cup of reflect on commit and stands of life / full; full of fuel and to the rocket of committed love / everlasting; everlasting casting of commitment, love / ribbon; ribbons rule when it comes to tools and a perfectly fit tube of lighted commitment to love / elasticity; elastic as well the

collective truth that the brake of commit stops at love / entering; entering the train of committed penning of love / flood; floods fuel my truth with the blazing schools of written intent to commit to love / misty; misty-eyed I am wide to a holographic span of spiraling ascend and the arms of lifted commitment spent on love / tanzanite; tanzanite in my certain apparel, I am apparent to the heat of the aid called the violet flame of the commitment deigned time to commit / creamed; butterflies creamed by the views of committed to love / violet; blazing through on a violet hue of pink refrain and the loving blue commit to love / blue; blue through to I loved our commit / pink; pink to a purple exclaim, I am committed to the skywide lift of love / milk; milk speaks of creamy weaves of life's commit to love / purple; a purple say at the stay for committed love / flame; a flame fed the fuel and the tool of committed love / bless; bless this complete plan to commit the stream of blazing love / imbue; imbue your set of canceled dues. find your commit to love / eternal; eternal, I am in the living expand to this commit of love / infinite; infinite commit of the reverent extent of love / essential; essential in seams, I am gleaned to a higher extreme and a capable stay in the rights of committed love / eccentric; eccentric to a measure of the pleasure of committed to uniquely committed love / concentric; concentric to a central theme, I am entrained to a vein of lightly led commit to the fit perfect with love / eccentric; eccentric to the middle grounded committed love / safest; the safest bet, the vet of love is wet with committed love / festive; a festive note is the mattered vote that sings of committed love / found; found around these parts of mine are the limbs of committed trees of love / cluster; a cluster of clues and the kin of pleasure has led me to you and our delicate measure of the length of committed love / clan; clan of the hu-man committed.

CHAPTER TWO

Lately; lately lent to the related seat of a stint in essentially love, I am committed to an esteemed sum of one / all-ways; all-ways wane to the explain of pleasantly loved. just believe in a commit to the fit of love / *f.I.t; functionally inter-trained by the truth in love / ephemeral; ephemeral in ethereal matter I am committed to love / love; love to be contentedly committed to love / loftily; loftily, committedly loved / loving; loving surrender to the remember of all we've become for committed love / list; list us as yours for committed love / lamb's; the lamb's elate is great when the rate of commit to God is "whole" on the excite of a light code written "pi" deep in an intricate weave of we believe in God / book; the book of life, the light's exude, the trait, the draft, the *pentateuch, the deep delights of the rights of life and the commit to God. the first five books gelnd great examples of living near divinity / light; lightest wheel of where we stood in the mind's begin and the life of good revival at the heights of the purest source, the eye, the light of God / pi code; pi code stood for an infinite good,, the interwoven weave of a code of gold and the lighter seam of extreme in lights commit at love / curate; curate's the greatest state of good when you're understood by the commit to perfect intent / designate; designate wait for the perfect loved commit meant / tonight; tonight with the light, commit, to love / israel; israel fell to a related rush to confess to a nation of nestled hush in west we rush to committed love / turban; a turban wound around the town of headed home for let's love and give our committed live / trait; traits are true regarding you and the philly appeal of what's in shape for removals blocks to committed send our hearts to man from God above thin beyond transcend / gain; gain a caption ingrained with commitment of love / bust; bust up less and know the commit of love / brace; brace yourself for the trace of a space less hush called freshen up your commitment to love / rise; rise up to explore the more we ascend to committed in our lifting love / wesak; wesak rocks are foundationed by a buddhist commit to rest at love / festival; a festival of friends who lend their hands to the men who love themselves enough to confess to their committed love / incredible; incredible to a metallic friend, the thinnest copper in our zatsen is an ascend to the price of commitment in love / grasp; grasp grew renewed by the release of us to blessing you and the regard for commitment in the hands of love / wings; wings away to a swimming contend that commitment is rapid to the scheme of our winning regime for perfect love / ways; ways need heed less than our stripping down of each other's commit to love / lights; lights lend their appraisal to the ascend of a thinner blend than all the rest of contented love / woven; woven within the heaven's birth was a commitment to extend our hands to men and God is light / wild; wild to then I will ascend to commitment in our frolic-some love / women's; women's friend, the bend to bless this commitment in a perfect love / music; cure the music, cue the *sin, live within the rhyme of when the perfect measure meets ascend at the cure for mother nature's rules andergetically speaking the heart of you. simple ignorance of the nature of the mother's rules / culture; culture's cure, the el camin, the real reside at the commitment sent to descend to ascendant love / mountains; mountains meet the shore of within and our letting go of the plains of friends committed to less than love / even; even you can win the odd chance to dance at committed love. believe in God / equal; I equal you to the eyes of the one brotherhood, the crystal light of light commitment / songed; songed, I am sung by the breeze of electric trees that dance in committed suns of love / resembled; resembled rest has found a humble nest in the mountains of commitment / dad; dad said grin about it and then you'll shout it from the halls of men committed in their beliefs of love / assemble; assemble, hear, and know rescue from the doubts of men. your lesson's due to love / wash; wash your attend to trend of an ascend to love / awash; awash in schools of ill repeat, I have found renew in you, my delight-full friend committed to love / remember; remember to commit to love / resemble; resemble thirty days of letting rest assure your test of the commitment sent to love / splash; splash is a flash to innocence sent by committed love / rate; rate yourself worthy of committed love / price; price your plan to committed stand at love / pace; the pace is set and we are wet with committed bets on love / walk; walk home to learn about committed love / board; a

mysterious board has been replaced by the trees of love and the dancing space of commitment to God head, love / trees; trees advance to the chance to dance in committed love / rock; rock-shaped advice about the size of your committed love / relaxed; relaxed around the sound of committed love / assure; assure has been sent to the intent of a dialect due to explain the regain of committed love / soar; soar over the shore of a channeled sea called committed we are to love / shape; shape yourself to your heart's release to where we've gone for our life's commit to love / head; release you head into the light of a welcome sight; your head inside the mind of God. that's all. commit / release; release yourself to a sweeter street, the one with a heart and the height and the feet of transcendent commit to God / complete; the burden's gone and our respond has gone to God. the total commit is made and a hit over the fence of life has led to the mind of God and star of great respect for love / solid; a solid scene of where we lean to committed love / impulsive; impulsive to a fresh agree, I can be committedly assumed to be the crescent moon of a life set free by a perfect loom of deeper love / trademarks; trademarks and truth's elective commit / trades; trades made to windy shores committed

CHAPTER THREE
Breakfast; break the fast, the vast escape has gone to gape at the grapes and wafers and halls full-filled with where we rule for a life that's healed of space-less lasts and lasts renewed by committed love / lunch; lunch on crews of electric views and where we've been to committed for love / dinner; dinner time rhymes thank your God for the cause to embrace the taste of perfect commit to love / friend; friends elaborate again about your win with a best collaborate on when to commit to love / fonder; a father fonder of all we declare as committed to love / round; round your date up to the create of a dare to commit this love / accent; accent on your elected will and the weave of a sleeve to the heart of light that's found in committed love / retrain; height of a flight to a hit called retrain and the gain of committed love / account; accounts committed to total love / accent; accent on the account of committed love / recount; recount your count as committed to summation love / recant; recant of a giant refusal to commit less, love / aging; aging advanced to where we lean in the presence of his commitment love / adjacent; adjacent to a hued release, I am burst by transcend's release to the lives and the loves of committed abide / surely; surely you know that commitment shows in love / wordly; totally round to the words of commitment in love / effectively; effectively a shakespearean stage has shown an effect on the actions committed to dramatic contentment in love / especially; especially ascendant I am required to commit to the light that I am / you are; this is it and we commit to the light that you are and the start of a contented love / definite; a definite due is beckoning you to committed love / delights; delights comfort my eyes with sight of the happy commit to love / decorum; decorum's reside at the reside to a daily design of committed love / demurely; demurely concur that life is the good reside in

committed love / daily; daily you can be renewed to the committed view of the pastel hues of constantly love / now; now you are cued to commit meant by love / knits; knots knits taught commit / crochets; crochets crew knew less than knots of contented commitment to love / envelopes; envelopes open developed commit to love / completes; completes the commitment, love / replete's; replete's repeat is congealed with feeled by precious contentment with love / pump; pump yourself up to commit meant love / rascally; the rascally you can commit to love / pay; pay yourself a great commit to parallel love / wantonly; wantonly wed your fresh confess to a congregation committed to love / relieve; relieve's rest is at commit / definitively; definitively due to a definite commit / regenerate; regenerate regard for h-our set of commit / rating; michael's ratings red confess to committed love / set; set on commit, I am, at hand / repeat; God's repeat is our relief at committed love / complete; complete a comment about the constant committed love / perfect; perfect assort, the commit meant variety in our God / rose; see your rosey way home to the petals of love / dew; dew your dresses fit commit to love / dip; good-bye to a dip at less in commit / pent; pent on imbue, I am renewed by my committed love / protrude; protrude's food is committed to love / pare; I stand pared by the scared about commitment in love / pair; good buy to a pair committed by love / appeal; I am appealed by my zeal to commit it, love / appearance; I am apparent to the appearance of love's committed comments on lessons of love / plan; plan to head for the commitment of love / imbue; God's imbue is "get thee behind" and less is gone to I am committed to love / apache; apache's moon is the committed swoon to perfect love / *sioux; sioux? you? yes! commit / *simply intelligent and often under x-amination of a committed fit to love / who?; who are you and how is your sweet confess of the best to commit called perfection's love / when?; when will you commit to love? / often; often I am seen as committed to lean arrival at survival's respect for living abundant in the gleam of eyed assign at committed love / fort; michelle gets fort knoxed less by her committed stand at comments given to loving extend / frolic; frolic home to venus by scenes of committed orbit to love / flesh; flash your flesh to the commit we met by a convent of love / refresh; refresh yourself with the constant comment that mom is commit meant to love / express; express the desire to sprinkle round the sounds of committed intrigue with life's full breathing sight of God's ahead.

CHAPTER FOUR

Recent; recent to a committed blend, we ascend to the climb of a constant contend for love / own; own your own, commit it, love / insure; insure cure, commit, love / automatic; an automatic renew can accrue at the wider view of commitment to love / acquire; acquire a conspire of the fire for contentment at the hearth of commitment and love / sum it; commit a summit and climb to love / acquaint; acquaint your inquire with higher commit to love / prefer; prefer to be a believing friend committed to the heights of men / lifestyle; a lifestyle change has come to

ascends degree and we climb our way to the power of a committed love / kiss; kiss this committed cure the lips of love / expression; an expression deep with the soul's release to the light of perfect constant commitment and love / expressly; expressly made by a melting shade of holly green with the berries red to a light believe of all we commit to in love / emotionally; emotionally devoted to the cause for applause and comments about our committed breasts filled with the fluids of contented love / exactly; exactly to the point, I am respectfully regarded as the heart of contented love / ecstasy; ecstasy is found in a committed town called perfect love / flight; a flight along the path of committed love / depth; the depth of commit and light of extreme and the heart in the middle of a precarious lean into the wonder of a heightened thrill at seeing the bliss heaven's feel upon the face of another matter, you, in love / dare; dare to care about your commit / secure; secure to a treasure of an infinite measure and the plausible explain of the same contrail followed home to reveal the revel of committed bliss / insure; insure yourself of the heavenly gate within, commit / evolve; evolution's revolution is the sign of commit meant / voting; voting for yourself by committing to life / vapors; met by vapors and made it through to the other side of commit / views; views expose our commitment to the lights of continuous love / elevate; elevate means, the art of commit, and the random-ness of exactly the fit to love / village; villages reside at the ear of awaiting news of the clouds of less removed to reveal the continuous beam of your perfect exist in a living odd's commit / illustrative; illustrative to the point of you, you are committed to the designation, official artist of the realm of you, hu-man, love / demonstrative; I demonstrate exceptional composure in my ways to perfect contemporary explain of what I mean by committed love / algonic; I am algonic in my sonic agree to choose to breathe of only committed light / definitive; definitive, I desire only committed love / algorithmic; algorithmic the example and standing controls of the shimmering samples called pearls of concentric align at composure and the stars of forever I am in commit / citric; a citric measure, the pleasing appear of a squeezing call called committed to love / exasperate; where will you exasperate less? in the rest-full sample of a glimpse through trines to see the one committed sun of light / inflate; commit inflation, know elation in the halls of loving commit / durate; durate is great in the friends of committed love / living; living in divine example and the mariposa dream of chocolate dreams orange with the seams of a horse's coat steamed with affluent coincide with commit / lately; lately I am committed to love / perfect; perfect exude has come to live in a committed spin with love / influence; let's influence our commitments with love / estates; plant some estates withe the soil of commit and know the delights of a heavenly fit at exactly love / desperate; a desperate due has come to you in a calm resign to a committed love / breaks; breaks up less than most our host of the crescent to committed love / hands; committed hands can cue the peachy state of who can commit to perfect love. *genetically evocative of real grace in action / securely; securely seen into the eyes of the menu of committed love / felt; felt you heal in our commit to love / naturally; naturally you knew the commitment to love / michael; God is michael born to be shorn by less and committed to her ascend / met; where were you when we were met with the committed stand to perfect love / her; her time to shine is committed to love / mate; mate found commitment in our love / me; you are me and we are and committed to love / venue; God's venue, the cue, love in commit / God is; God is good in committed love / love; God is love in committed ascend to the lines of live / lately; lately you, commit to love / of late; of late, love is great in committed accept of the roles of God / lightly; lightly we commit it and our perfect love / yes!; yes! I will commit / cafe; the cafe of cure to love that commits / cup; times are up and the cup is full of committed love / curative; curative to a treasure of rest, I am confessing my guessing arrival at the revival of committed love / classical; classical confess has met a regress with a committed line of regard for love / symphonic; symphonic ascend has found the friend who met the cue called amend, ascend, commit the harmony of love / treatments; treatments fair to the light commit

CHAPTER FIVE
Sensitive; sensitive to treasures of the creative kind, I am fine in my perfect commit / spare; spare I care for only committed exuberance in love / canyon; live in the canyon of the coppery sheen called electricity gone blue-green to feed our concept of committed love / core; the core of this commit is our adaptable fit to love / event; in this event, concur to commit / sensate; sensate is great when your head is abed in the mend of the mind called committed; God / cluster: commit a cluster of co-creative aspects of the address called committed to love / clasp; clasp God's hand, know the band of perfect commit to love / leap; commit to a leap for peace / let's; let's get hitched to the stars of committed love / land: your land is mine and ours combined to commit a flow of love / place; place your heart in advance to love and committed understand of the fans of man / care; care enough to stand for commitment in love / calibrate; calibrate your rate to the grander vibe of a lively friend called committed love / choir; choirs sing an inquiry willed by the contented feel of committed love / corp; corp of the crew of the avenue called committed love / case; in case you knew, commit / said; said you will, commit / sent; sent you home to a committed blend called the aspects of friends who own the dates of love / may; may we be all-ways free to commit the flowers of may to love / the 17; the 17 insure the secure commit to love / the 13; the 13 cure the absolute with perfect commit / the all; the all will be committed to free reside in the sides of God / graph; *heaven held a weld to the heat convected by a communion set in a scientific side of a graph called love and a commitment meant to be, love. *happening energetically lean to an elegant nuance / graphic; graphic's design is on me and our aligning stance in the trance ending space called perfect commit to the lines of God / grace; grace this space with committed love / mates; mated know each the others commit to love / advance; advance to a dancing commit to love / family; family's meet swollen commit and the chosen seat of

mercy's gift to perfect love / construct; construct a cure to insure where we began to be the best we can for committed love / glass; glass glue blew apart to compare us less than all that's often to often we can well agree on committedly we love / aspect; aspect of the convicted truth that God is proof of our involvement with the higher I am / alert; alert convert that commit is here can stay away know more and airing still we stay alive by the taste of committed love / avenue; a basic avenue has lead to the bed of one committed son who will stay for love / proper; proper attire will continue to be the sight of holy trinity wed to the one who wields the sword of a written ward; commit / property; property of whom? commit / precise; precise reside has wisely done the wealth of one commit / invite; invite one in to love's commit / along; along the cue we can elude only less and finally find the committed sound of love / crew; crews are cozy in the feast of a heated treat called blessed capture of the spill of georgian milk. commit / cruise; cruise into the panamanian sum of a commitment won by love / needs; a perfect kiss has met my needs by speedy delivery of the succeed to committed be in love / supply; supply the classic reason with a season of committed love / resort; resort to only committed love / abort; abort the sort of escape that withstood your living wood's regain of climbing sum, the heart of land has come to be the arc of our divinity summed by God as love / rave; rave about the waves of committed love / we will; we will feel our commitment grow to love / unite; unite with the one you love tonight commit / one; the one is found, commit / unify; unify your treasures as precious measures of the sights gone blue to concisely point to the side of you and your committed love / unity; live united by the sound of two becoming one. commit / planet: mother and father unite to become one planet living under love, commit / well; well we were to where we stood for committed love / illustrative; illustrative to the point, I am united by the invited feel of real commit to love / divine; divine has found the one to love, commit / extant; extant to regard, I am the card and the perfect hand to bet on, man, commit / in-lightened; in-lightened by you, I am clearly through, the committed view of love / insane; insane to less, I am contained by only confessed commit / rays; rays burn in the shame of committed-less love / tennis; tennis match made, know the shades of compare gone square to the heart of commit / we lease; we lease our hearts less when we invest in the crystalline square of the storage place called committed love / resolve; resolve your matter, commit extensive love / golf; golf your way to the committed fore. love / respects; respects of neglect have committed to connected love

CHAPTER SIX
Winds; winds of change have wed with the gift of commit / change; change your plan, love, man, commit / charge; charge your flight tight to the sails of forever's wedding committed to love / chase; God's chase is o'r, we're more than committed in advance to the parallel chance to perfect love / cure; cure your set of woes concur with commit it, love / race; race to the place of ecstatic command of the lace committed to love / relax; today

I relax in the *fax of loving commit. *fond of affectionate exude to love / revolve; revolve around the subject of committed love / resolve; resolve to solve this serendipitous commitment to love / reduce; reduce your refuse and love to commit / rescind; rescind the demand and note the command to commit to this love / rest; rest in a creative command / rapt; rapt and attentive to this commend, I matter more than any end and the elegant begin to committed love / perfect; commit perfect love / pasture; pasture rise is a committed grasp of the grassy knolls of contented love / plank; plank walk home to the creation's point and the joint remind to be kinder still to the thrill of an iridescent leap to the plankton fields of phosphorous leaks wet with committed love / past; past regard has gone to I am and the committed extend of the ring of life / blank; blank? stare? commit / pure; pure enough to cure us, commit / pare; pare to the spare contend of the day when life sailed away to the new resume at committed love / compare; compare a burst with the commit meant to love / commit; I am committed to perfect love / content; content to decide what I need, I lean decisively to committed love / saved; saved for less than heaven's commit then find the fit of perfect love / mat; mat attack has meant at stop. just commit / solved; solved it sealed by contented love / most; baby's most in touch with the God in us and impress this commit to love / meld; meld most this confess of committed love / meet; meet meat the temple of man in the land metaronic and the committed strand of a higher arc to love / treaty; treaty to treat each other sky high to the window wide to commit it, love / absolve; absolve to commit to passionate embrace of contented commitment at love / absolution; absolution comes with the ones who are met with wet resolve of committed love / revolve; revolve absolute in theatrical salute of the commitment called love / respite; respite won by the one commit / daring; daring to be sincerely seen is a perfect commitment to love / cures; cures my healed, my filled advance to the feeled, a glance at perfect love. committed I stood at the cures for love / deft; deft you are as bereft has left to endure our insure of the guest called compare to commit it love / spare; God's spare in compare to our advance at the chance for passionate the cure is to commit love / inner; inner you are to the starry core of the committed shore of a precipitous love / stir; I love you and your stirring endure for the rare compare to committed love / out; out and in, I am thinned to an exasperated stare at the concurrent dream called committed love / climbs; climbs grew steep to a perfect plateau called committed love / reach; God's reach grew committed to the hu-man condition / refute; refute-less commute to the commit to love / risk; risk less, commit / eat; eat right and love the commit / corner; married be at the corner of we. commit / lot; let us be allotted committed to love / drive; drive home committed to one love / shop; good-bye to the shop of less and welcome the confess to commit true love / gloved; gloved revenue held by the hands of experienced commands to love / atoll; an atoll grew coral in a reef of transparent regard for the shard of experienced commitment to the seas of love / enough; enough of this less than commit to love / hat; hat worn over the head of a stream consumed by meander

of the dreaming accent called co-commit love / alot; take a chance about alot of committed love / clothes; clothes concur with a concurrent wear of the flare for peace and the light affluent with apparent commit / bathe; a gorgeous bathe is firm exude of the need to devoter her to the light good's commit / watch; watch this comet hit with commit and burst with love / sure; perfect sure of committed allure has welcomed our love / match; match up too; commit / more than; more than then and again commit / cooking; cooking on good connect and I am understood as progressively rude to less than commit / clarity; clarity reigns in the healing commit / chasten; chasten outs the filling circumvent of commit

CHAPTER SEVEN
Soft; soft assume has lent devote to a connotation fast with gentle commit / elate; elate your state with commit it, love / debate; debate less, know the rate of express and confess and commit / heed; heed us as directly connected to the invective commit / heads; heads turn to you to see our committed delivery of common love / hearts; hearts held heal as their real objective and life easy committed me to love / arms; arms wide inside the commit to love / gay; passive gay days are active was to love, commit / home-less; home-less accrued aid in the street of a grade called commit / behavior; care to engage in behavior best with commit / holistic; holistic fell to a well embraced commit / bravery; bravery came to the cave of a simple succeed called commit / festive; a festive resume to commit / drink; I am drink and drunken by true commit to the lights of love / merry; merry calls about the malls of a shopping commit to contented love / elective; cases elective accrue at resume of commit / supple; a supple rescue of the plan to commit to only you, love / f.I.t; found in truth is the fittest news called let us commit / awaken; awaken to a committed son of lvoe / supply; supply examples of the sample committed to love / advice; advice spoken to the motion committed by electing love / effective; effectiveness led to my total commit / s.e.l.f; subtle effect of light is full of your committed truth to this our love / profess; profess your confession to the life called commit / life; I am life and to this commit / advice; advice is good to a healing compare of God is complete in confessions of committed love / confess; confess that your commit to life is love / express; your cure is expressive in our concur that life is committed to love / denote; denote your decide to coincide with commit / take heed; take heed, commit / we; we are the cure that's committed to love / us; commit us to love / they; they know the side of taking home expect and younger I stay by their healing elect to walk the earth with God and men and the loving commit to being hu-man / then; then you will decide who can find a better escape called commit / them; them too and you to commit / trust; trust our example, commit / channel; channel home and all one in the house of love's commit / change; change renews our committed love / explores; explores assurance in occurrence and the signs of committed love / travel; often I travel the telling truths of the waves of light and the heaven's sooth to committed love / patterns; patterns who,

commit / ruths; truths revealed in the seals committed / tied; tied and the truths revealed and committed too / suggestion; suggestion and the thrilling commitments / opportunities; opportunities and the temples committed / sealed; sealed and revealed as committed / passions; passions fashions committed / freedom; freedom rings committed / traded; traded for raided commits / several; several and the committed / truthful; truthful to a flow's commit / flowing; flowing commitments to love / trained; trained to be reigned to for the filling commit / debits; debits gained commit / treasured; treasured and committed too, to love / join; join in a jeweled commit / training; training and revealing committed / truths; truths rest in a committed hush / patience; patience reaps a respected commit / travels; travels to outposts red in commit / paragons; paragons red with reveal for commit / committed; committed with a patient commit / patterns; patterns reveal in your commit / surgically; surgically release a filling commit

CHAPTER EIGHT

Mountained; mountained mend of the highest friend, I am your cure and your are mine in our commitment / bridge; a bridge over troubles, the light of confess to commit / astound; astound over the how we came to know the red of love's commit / essential; essential we are to this committed love / hunger; hunger hath cure and we are the food of commit / haversack; haversack full of the traveling fuse required by commit / artistic; living the life artistic is the higher commitment to the stint of a brush with living to love / rites; rites renew our vows of sacred geometry of a carnate commit to love / fling; a fling found sounds of rounds of committed love / memorial; memorial days are committed to concrete love / meter; a meter true to the committed ascend to live in love / metric; metric revues of the passion played committed in love / pleiades; a pleiades spark has connected my heart to yours sweet sister of mine and the line to perfect love's commit / outsmart; love to outsmart the best, commit, the rest / heart; heart to heart, we, commit / art; art is heart to commit / aspect; you have the aspects to involve yourself in committed love / cope; cope best with commitment / directs; ascendant directs our commit / sun; sun will show the glows of commit this love / control; control your set of circumstances set with commit / cascade; I am cascading in committed wades to lvoe / charade; a committed charade has gone to committed love / clip; clip it on in strips of lines along our committed rise to love / clasp; tiny truths clasp our youth in living hands of the God-head man. committed / nest; marco's nest is the nile of an ensuing gulf committed by our love / nile; next we'll nile together smiled by the committed side of love / need; need to be committed / mill; mill over your committed love / bonus; bonus days flew to committed love / close; close enough to commit too, love / halls; halls held full of the committed applause of honest wonder, love / heark; heark in ascend to angelic shores gone arching home to committed love / heaven; heavens heal will come through grown on wings of committed love / heather; buy one ride to heaven, commit / depth; your are deep in a depth of love in commit /

dated; God is dated by two who commune in committed love / commit; commit the emit of a perpetual bliss called the knotting end of the lavender cord called committed love / stand; stand for a commit-meant, love / God; God is open to a living embrace of committed love / reigneth; reigneth the matter of a rain perpetual in a source called commit. reigneth now, love. walled; walled off is over to committed love / transcendent; transcendent I have gone to the throne of the one committed to love / trades; trades are over and the trim has come to end the trend at less than committed love / forgotten; forgotten within? blades of thickened commit / grassy; grassy roads and the committed stand into love / compassion; compassion's reign is the vein called commit / plagiarize; plagiarize will arise without commit / persons; persons anointed may choose the venues committed too / sum; sum of the summary, committed / amount; amount spent is a committed sort called love / human; human in a reservoir called commitment / return; return to the disciple called committed / picture; picture this, committed / retain; retain a regard for the committed / need; need a suggestion, committed / general; general to the mineral committed / give; give attend to the committed / become; become annual to the committed / occur; occur and the asserted too, committed / builder; builder bought both commitments / local; local and the legendary committed / devote; devote allows a central commit / fond; fond in a feeling commit / shimmering; shimmering in a light commit.

THE CONTENT-MENTS
LEVEL 7

CHAPTER ONE

Love / Peace / Respect / Register / Evolve / Evolutions / Resolutions / Resolved / Respects / Hastles / Lessens / Lozenge / Loosed / Laterals / Loosened / Leaps / Lasts / Loops / Lots / Lords / Laps / Lasts / Loosening / Elates / Respect / Reach / Repeats / Radial / Roots / Reaps / Sown / Seer / Steer / Away / Columns / Collapse / Clues / Shares / Awful / Retire / Registers / Rules / Ropes / Repeats / Mantraw / Golden / Showers / Hopeful / Glue / Phoenix / Phonics / Phonetic / Frenetic / Ivy / Grew / Low / Hearts / Lapiz / Trues / Tarns / Leads / Lots / Bigger / Grown.

CHAPTER TWO

Greats / Clasps / Left / Clip / Strip / Coda / Matrices / Musicals / Mu / Mews / Threads / Throw / Collapsed / Pages / Pens / Portals / Frameworks / Grasps / Watch / Listen / Learned / Leaping / Plenty / Purged / Portal / Pothala / Plastics / Plurged / Photonic / Phoenix / Photos / Phantoms / Committed / Concurrent / Creative / Created / Cues / Coos / Dove / Delays / Over / All / Who / Reign / Will / Find / Each / Other / Tonight / Mayan / Wave / Maya / Waves / Wave / Links / Weaver / Dreams / Doors / During / Sleep / Child / Mayan / Temples / Emeralds

CHAPTER THREE

Jewel; jewel began our plan to gem our span with rainbowed sparkled way of once we loved; commit / jasmine; jasmine jeaned I am between the rock and view of an arc of love and the heart of renew to love's attain of a committed stand / juniper; juniper june and may grew renewed by a care-full plan to stay the way to the light reward of committed love / jasper; jasper jewels grew and grew until helenic strands came to know review of commit it, love / genuine; helenistic genuine matter new renew of love in the month of june and again the moon of heaven's commit of love / garner; garner your plan to gain against the hill of the way all day renewed by complacent commit-less love / royalty; kindly royalty spared less require your fire to higher still to commit recess of love./ garnished; garnished we feel by our heel to commit of love / return; return to cure your less at love, commit / enthroned; enthroned by love, I am expired to all that's less than committed love / extend; extend to befriend our committed stand at love / desires; desires aspires conveys convex commit our love / raphael; commit raphael, the hole, the flower, the shower of loved commit / heaven; our heaven's sway, all day, all stays at the commit of love / helenic; helenic, the spell of broken wings and raptured ways born sell to stay at heart's compare of the commit this, love / aspire; aspire to hire your best review of committed view of love / grecian; grecian grew a few rewards to commit this, love / isled; isled awhile by listed to commit, love / mithra; mithra ruled our tooled eclipse of son of man and the grand I am born to warm of abreast our content / mithraic; mithraic trait of what we rate for flat extend to the grecian friend of committed,

contented love / assign; assign us sent to heaven went to contented committed love / central; central treat of fleet regard for how we are wired for contented committed love / certain; certain you are when you aspire to perfect hire of content with life and love / ascertain; ascertain the certain extent of how deep we went and how high the regard for contented we, our, committed, love / expend; expend your self on wealth in best we contented committed to love / align; align your commit with where you're contented to committed love / ports; ports aplenty and a perfect peal of better still we'll sing and ring our contentedly committedly love / emphatic; emphatic and ecstatic, I swell to the beat of a lighter street called content to commit to love / embryonic; embryonic splendor is born of plentiful empower of where we'll tower for heights in commit / exotic; exotic commit can fit to the power of h-our of love / sunny; sunny review of who we knew for immaculate meet of contented heat and love / sandy; sandy mushy wet and content in love / rhodes; rhodes rule a scholar's school to contented we are to love / urn; wheels of urn discern our invest and where we got to blissfully be in lightly commit of love / vase; vase blue with the cote d'azur on a sea of blue and where we meet for our free reside at contented committed love / doric; doric columned pleasure measured by treasured commitment for love / span; span to plan on a light inside our contentedly we'd love / isle-wide; content in isles, I'll while the ways to smile contentedly at love / santorine; santorine the spell on well we loved I admit my regret at less in our central commit to contentment love / thera; thera theorized our rise to blessed this our content to commit / theoric; theoric spill on a will be kind to fine resign and assertive leads to love./ crete; crete accrued our imbue with a flash of a wall of watered wed with the led to a height in commit it love./ columnar; columnar number, the summer of love and our ascend to when we commit certain love / athenian athenian matter, the manner of ambient pleasure for contentment in commitment to love / hermetic; hermetic you are in our infinite power of hours of perfect committed contented love / epiphany; epiphany and ascends to the hermetic friends within the isles of man / infinite; an infinite swim to a special sway in the moods for contentment and commitment in love / infinite in; infinite in lines of contented love / artemis; artemis sent an arrow through to the truth in you and the heart of me and our mutual view for the income called free to the enterprise at the heart of committed love / mythologic; mythologic magic, the tragic gone cured to contentment committed in love / archaic; archaic ascend has found a foured friend in the fond review of the brilliance of hue in the heart of all men / aphrodite; aphrodite's mighty friend is the when of how we stand contented in our arcs to love / zeusian; zeusian afield our well drawn seam of growing bolts of thundering dreams and the center of contented love / archimedes; archimedes sent a vent to the bend of the light geometric and height of men grown wide to contented committed love / kin; kin to the infinite, I admit it; perfectly;

contentedly; love / affluent; affluent to spoofs, I resume my commit to the contented life of a scribe inside the arms of God / ah-zen; ah-zen, ah men, ah live our contented life / zen-like; zen-like friend, the men of contented love / kite; lightly flies our heart's review of the kites of love and the contented view of committed string strong to sing of the light regard for the storms of God / kestrel; kestrels home to know renew of the wheels of spring and the sprung of true regard for committed love / polar; a polar plan to suspend suspense and expand to the hearts of man / unthaw; unthaw your awe for committed contented love / look; look, research, contentment / pi; pi, polarity contentment / shut; shut divorced contentment.

CHAPTER FOUR

Angelic; angelic be in your stay for love. commit. content. love / arc-angelic; arc-angelic we explain your way to a homeward lean to committed contented love / the silent h; the silent h has held her sway at the constant way of loving give and a wholer stay has gone away to live at the constant hum of sum, one; committed contented love / the h-factor; h is a factor of wholest joy and the deeper extent of the heaven sent home to stay; committed; love / factors; yes, I'll be a factors 3 to one and sums of ways to hail become God's sum, one committed, love / fractions; fractions flew to pieces strewn with completed accept of certain commit to love / parcels; parcels post their most at our surrender meant for lit by contented delivery of love / posts; posts renew our led home review of committed air of contented love / sages; sages said we ran ahead to where we were for let us contented be in love / gardenia; gardenias grew green in our lean to immaculate content with love. / atlantic; atlantic resume of the mood for contented relented love / proof; proof enough to review our loving contentment / monastic; monastic menu of the venue in the true reside in rue of less, then bless your contented state with best of love / tibet; tibet in time align with the reside to rule at contented, love / morning; morning menu of belief in alive and astride your true, a glide, to who we'd be for love and a contented state called love / free; free enough to breathe a contented sigh / freedom; freedom found in a town I own and a berry road revealed to seal our reign of residence at the commit to contentment and love / peaced; peaced a plan together, God and man, align at contented love / legends; legends played around the bands of listening content in love / authoric authoric legend said we're ahead to rights of life content in love. / arthuric our legend said we're ahead to the hearts of light we contented lived for the will to love / maoric; maoric exude of the maori mood of gentle the mood for contented love / meter; meter made a curly shave across the wave of contented lift love / rhyme; rhyme and respect and react to an act of pleasure and the perfect measure of the treasure our contented loves / rhythm; rhythm of the right to a move ahead to light we love and renew our contented view of all we are for loved. / thyme; thyme to rhyme our garden

view of the particular view that God is content with love / energetic; energetic hyperbolic of the frolic in a light conjoin at contented love / experience; experience the pleasure of a measure met by experience and a heart renewed by 2 in contented love / experiment; experiment this experience, love, contentedly / explusive; explusive explain of the impulsive game of all we are for contentedly love / choice; choices I have made I gave to arrival at the retrieve to insure for the cure to God is the head of this wed to solicit the elicit of less to the best constant choice, the commitment, love / direct; direct to due I am due direct to the renew to the heart of a comment about the content love / dialect; dialect direct to the reflect on flecks of speckled eggs of listening tongues of light in contentment./ expect; expect to explain less, contented be in we are, direct to love / into; into you, I melt with the felt abandon of constantly content with love / found; found here we are fine within the lend to love / yes; yes, I will feel again your constant heal of contented love / yet; yet you are and all ways far to needy knew content with the view of love / all; all in all we walled off stood until we deep uncovered good and felt the shift to contentment stood in the fields of love / weighed; weighed and a lot less when we blessed our content constant love / wounds; wounds gape across the fields of the lessened commit to contented love / around; around hear, we are, content with the truth in love / quest; quest yourself west to the land of God and the taste of man and the face I said was the height of a heart found depthed by contentment love / bred; let us bred be by lightly love contentedly grew to life is love / hard; grand and hard and I am well in the help of present softness love./ lightly; lightly you know our content too and contented we flew to love. / deliver; precious to deliver of the ever new embrace of grace-full contented love / fly; fly guy's home to live on love content with hints of yes! we love / flower; flowers grew content in the deeper love / rainbow; rainbow ran a contented rant to a lightly hued spoken love / graced; graced exude of the metallic glide to faintly few are less than all we love in content to God / aloha; aloha hour compress of contents in the constant love / help; God's grew helped few until we shed the lead to flew to content in love / free; free to be loved, we contented stood at the brink and flew to love / oft-in; oft-in contentment, I headed my reside in sublime renew and love / high; high to a start we are the art of a glance at heart and the eyes of God's nod at constant content of love / aloe; aloe accrued the metallic hue imbued by bliss and constant content of love./ hello; hello, you knew, renew, our contented love. / agape; agape gasped our opened mouth praise of the constant content felt of this our love / often; often you knew who would agree to perfect commitment and contentment in love / alive; alive enough to bridge the gulf to finer content with love. / beside; beside the brook I took a nap at the lips of good and all of God and is content with love / reside; reside in my stride to constant befriend of light in love.

CHAPTER FIVE

Power; power's enthuse is the gape of the fuse that lightens the stroke of the resume to bemuse to lightly reside and contentment inside the ides of God. / name; name yourself professed by contented love / blood; let the blood thaw and the flaw be fused to the contrain of sunken bemuse at resume contented in love / one; one by one we run to contentment in love's crystal lean / God; God is cause for contentment in consideration of love / crystal; crystal cues our pleasant ruse of the gone to God's contented pause / clear; clear your cure of insure and the respect for regard of a card called secure in the content-ment of love / headless; a headless rush to the brush of a contented love / cleanse; cleanse, insure, secure, and your heart at the start of a spark called the sublime aside to constant contentment with love / want; want to imbue yourself with the spoken content of perfect love / wait; wait for a sign to resign your realign to contentment with love / height; heights insure our sacred stand at the cure for peace and the love constant in contented release / heedless; heedless of where we've stood we have leased a cool release to the sweet confess of all the lands of the light of the lord call yes and content / Christ; blank to a stare, there's one in the there who can care for your s.I.m.'s call them in to the Christ content; *silent involve of mental; suspend / christian; christian said strait ahead to the reveal of our better feel along the lines of where reclines our sacred way to the central convene of contented love / Christ in; Christ in, Christ within, our welcome sign to the sigh of a relaxing tide of all we give to this contented love / dove; dove sets sail to the rail of forever, hear, in the tear of all we mean by contented love / power; power up to the cup of a deeper drink, the I think has become the I am of the contentment to love / peace; peace apply our try at strides of what's become of lightly love in a contented curl to the waves of love / contented; contented wins to the friends of love. / released; released your hold on the gentle surrender of old suspend gone thoughtfully deep to the steepest craft of ancient relate to contented love / request; request your best belief and hold the contented stare into the glare of all remember / earthly mother; earthly mother, other's fall, to well we are in our contented love / silence; silence said love's ahead and contented we stare at the pairs of loves / ageless airs; ageless airs of spare regard and the cards of sepulcher cure, the cherubim within, and our essent breath of our rest-full art of the heart of remember at the God-head love and contentments stream to light. / brother tree; brother tree, I will be sandalphon in one reside, astride our fence called God is content / holy stream; God's holy stream has run to the foot of forever and the ever we are one in silent regard of the call for a splash in contented love. / sink your roots; sink your roots into the cute revival of the survival for God's head contentedly loved / angel sun; angel sun of one who held the heart that's fed by well we were to a blessed content called love / angel air; angel air is fair within the stelae lined with sparse retrieve of the what we conceive as the constant comment on contented love / bathe; bathe yourself in light and sound of the love year-round and our awesome sway in the day eternal and the lights of our life in the living fantastic and contented love / sound; sound began when man found God's creative breath at the heart of contentment, love / fixed round; fixed round the reed of a blowing flute is the cute astound of a town intrigued with we'd endless reign to constant content of committed love. contentment / angel of air; angel of air and we care as we breathe the life between our sighs of contented love./ endless kingdom; an endless kingdom is found inside the towns of love within our contented frame and the game, the affair, so grand to love / wordly rhythm; a wordly rhythm given rhyme to the time of contented love / music; music has stairs built within to the heights of friends and the seeds of seas and the waves of free delivery to the breath of God and the ear of man and the fan of God is contented to love. music said; love. / tremble; tremble less with regress to the regard within and the friend of all that is content to love. / breath; breathe a breath of fairest measure and the treasure of God at the contented constant of the breath hu-man and love / roaring; roaring in to the shores of scenes of light extreme and the cretes of constant contented love / roaring waters; roaring waters splatter me with well we are to free expand to a plan of fountained heights and the waterfalls that bed our contented man / chorus; chorus quailed, loudly railed, found our voiced extend to befriend our loud rejoice of the God-head content with love / sound; sound of new, renew, our respect-full view of the elegant hues of lightest contentest, hear this, love / light; I am content with our advent of a higher life and the wife by my side in this perfect plane called the light refrain of love / love; love to love and your contentedly light life through the sight of God is, love / body; body bliss this bless with a holy kiss and a mantra owned by man. the breath of gor, one cause, eccentric, along shuttered beams contented with love / bless; bless this space with a face, my own, and a heart that's true tot he light we own and the contented be of where we are to a constant star called contented love / fathered heaven; fathered heaven has stood at the hall of reflect and a gentle respect that has grown to monumental refrain and a precious expanse called dance to contentment and love / wordly rhythm; a wordly rhythm is the hymn of forests green and perfect spots of light regard for the swords of care cut cord deep to show relief of the gentle grain of perfect contentment with love / holy stream of light; a holy stream of light is insight-full and stood in the respect of our fortune and good-bye to less and the reflect of all we knew of God is content in love / life; a life of love respect-full be and now we know the holy 3 and in us is the life that's true to longing contentment and the heart that's true to God is; love. / fatherhood God; fatherhood God is greatly relieved by our contented stand in the yes of God / lace; lace your place with the hands of prayers of deeper cares for contentment woven in the scenes of love / motherhood nature; mother's hood is nature's good in quiet arrive at durango's quail and the wells of deep delivery to the breathing good of God is contented with our love / face; face it love is content with life / peace-full brotherhood; peace-full brotherhood is the absolute of man's defend for other, the mend, the content meant, friend is love / simple; simple you and simple me and God makes three in love's content / compose; compose enthuse in your humble exude to the moods for love is content with who we are for the cause of love / natural; natural to a s-p-e-l-l, I am well in my soft regard for all we are for the constant cause called God / prose; prose renews our enthuse with precious love and the content of commitment content with love / creative; creative care can beware of less and your guess is good. create. content. expand. love. hu-man / pose; pose refuse to the winds archival and your heart's rescind to all we rule by light's reward and the written sword of God's contentment, love / ensue; ensue our desire for higher commit. know omit has gone. we are one in constant contentment with love / imbues-imbues our contentment, love / excells; excells at rest, our content cells of the bless of bliss and the contentment called love.

CHAPTER SIX

Flowers of joy; flowers of freedom join in me with the joy of bliss and the lighted tree of my perfect identity with the contented sign called love / juice; juice it up, our loving date, the contentment sunk to heaven's mate with consensual love. / genuine here; it's genuine here at ear of the friend and the men, the train, the explain renewed by good is our God and constant the hue of contented love / fast; fast to you I have evolved as I resolve the better stand at constant commitment and contentment with love / steadfast; God is steadfast in our concern with the contented view of a constant cue called consistent love / true; true you are to my contentment with our love / grass; grass is greener in the pass to knowing more and living blessed by the sights of love's contentment stood by love / water; water power, our by our, in the fuel of a wash content with the gloss of commitment to contentment with lvoe / trees; our trees are the views of the crowns we wore for news of metatronic review and contentment to love / heavenly power; God's heavenly power can include the theory of love and the contentment seen in our extremes of life as known / laws; laws reside in a constant stride called content with love / include; include your set with your self and the miracle imbued by your decide to recline in contentment with love / strict; strict to conspire, I am content with the advent of truth and love / straight; straight to you, I am true to the constant commitment to contentment with love / path; a path found around our lesson of review to contentment with love / proof; proof is content with the condition called absolute love / precious; precious is the reside in our caring abide and my truest breath is the presence, yet ever, constant, contented, love. / bright; bright to you, I am, through with less and of to the constant sum of contented with one love / converge; converge on where you heard of constant comment about the

cure of consistent commitment to perfect love. contentment under stood / stronger; stronger we are by the hour of our constant cure at the let us begin to resume our contentment with love / emerge currents emerge from the merge of our words of contented love / current; currents in you are constant with commitment to the consistent cure of contentment with love / surge; I want your surge to regain our connection with commitments meant to concur about our contentment with love / water; waters wed inside our we are the two who committed themselves to contented love / ahh; ahh, yes, we will reside at the perfect content of contentment within the sighs of love / ale ails you, ale through, to admit the contented lift to love / good; size is good and a big one should suffice in the love constant with commitment to contentment and love / graced; graced by and placed to loves's present side with embraces on the glide to contented love / light; light enough to imbue this connection with perfect contentment and love / certified; certified by the measure of contentment in our treasure called perfect love / serious; serious about the content of our commitment to contentment / silly; silly you knew about the contented love / securely; securely content with the flight to love / friend; a friend of the fuel of contentment called the fire of love in command / sensual; sensual matter, the patter of our constant comment on consistent contentment with love / lithe; lithe to a leap to contented love / open-minded; open-minded, I am, to the fans of our commitment, contentment, ensure and love / frolic some; frolic some, yes, we are blessed by contented consume of our guest of love / personally; personally I am free to contentedly converse of committedly love / purely; purely sure, I am secure in contented love / lovely; lovely you in our view of commitment with contentment and peace as the clue of the life you love / luxuriate; luxuriate in our great revelations about contentment's content / luxor; luxor's cure is our purest residue of the pyr-a-mid inside the sphinx of contentment with love / egyptian; egyptian consign of the higher glyph deep with the blanks of reveal symbolic to constant content with love / cylindric; cylindric shapes of the contented spires called light the nape of the neck of love / sphinx; a sphinx withdrawn from the cause of less can now confess about contentment with love / sincere; sincere I swim in the secure ascendant called contentment with love / spatial; spatial, palatial, the temple, man, confident and consistent in commitment with love / eclipse; eclipse your cure, know the face reflective, the air elective, to breathing in you, our resume, our coincide with contentment with love / space; space is the significant power of absolute concur with energetic regard for contentment in love / securely; securely set on the fare I've paid, I now reside at the side of a ticket called contentment and a show called absolute / insure; insure your kindle of the flame called content with explain of regard for constant love / ellipse; ellipse is the shape of the heel gone acute to elaborative regard for contented love / harp; harp on this, our kiss, and the perfect contentment we share with love

/ musically; musically acute to the sharp encore called contentment with love / reserve; reserve yourself for well in contentment and love / place; peace is constant at a place called contented love / locate; locate your *fate, marry her, love, contentment, eternal, light / fonder accept of the truth energetic / lectern / stand at the stand for elective strands of electric expand to consistent contentment with love / palatial; palatial platters of matter best with the rest atop the shopping chart, the budget's made, the mice are laid to rest in a palatial shore of godly love; content / classics; classics credit us with rest in the heart of best we were to basic contented regard for literary measures of the classic scrolls of God content with love / cape; cape assume has resumed to bless our stress on lightest love. contented / curl; curl around to see your return to perfect we are to aspect, contentment, love.

CHAPTER SEVEN

Culture I am content with the culture of hustle for a muscle called love / sculpture; sculptures reside at our abide of the constant comment about contented love / forgiven; forgiven for the way you handled the matter of better constant about contented love / orator; orator's flatter our matter with contentment about our hint of a chatter called love / serene; serene at a lean to perfect content at peace and love / curator I am; the curator of matter at a constant boil called be content with love / rest-full; commit to a rest-full security called the impurity removed to reveal the content of a chemical ascent to man is best when relaxed with love / rested; rested on healed by yet we feel contented with love / great; great value meant, commit, content, love / grand; grand in her stand for contented love / large; large enough to secure the path of our constant comments about contented love / s.m.all; small enough to be secure in our invest of the cure for contented love / rate; rate us secure to constant refill of contented love / random; random reside has resigned to perfect content of contented love / houses; houses cure our insure of constant commit at content love / money; monday's money is new at a constant view of contented love / cars; cars care about where we go for constant speeds of contentment about, love./ stuff; stuff it less, love, contentment. / really; really be contented with your love / often; often I secure myself to her, the mother, of love, and the security of content-ment in love / modern; modern suppose of exposure to a lover content with love / explore; explore it, implore it, contented, love / explode; explode all over your lover, the contentment with love / implores; implores me to explore you with a contented gaze at love / found; let us be found by our grounded stand at the strands of dna's recurrent expression of perfectly entwined resume of exactly contented love / seek; seek a set of well-endowed respects for precious contents in your commitment to contentment / sought; in hear, we sought, our perfect, love, content / ensued; ensued our respect for a full advance to a glance at constant contented love / reviewed; reviewed our matter and reflected on contented love / market; market your

set of values and call her constantly contented with love / real; real enough to head for the content of committed contentment with love / color; color's cure is contentment with love / arts; arts are spent in the burgeoning regime called contented with love / malt; malt review of the revenue called contented with love / expressed; expressed myself about the melt of contented hues gone green to perfect commitment with love / nurtured; nurtured by new, I am renewed by the two become one and the light of God's son called the nestled cue to contented with love / news; news has come; we are one, the clue, the rule, the love, the one I love by the concurrence, contented with love / embody; embody this, a kiss, of truth and proof of the love content with committed care / commune; commune one. cunning care about contented love / constants; constants cure is the care for the love of contented depth / cycle; cycle home to the constant spin with contented love / ensnare; ensnare in contentment; love. / circle; circle in to befriend your constant commit to commitment and contentment with love / taste; taste the kiss that changed a life content with love / replace; replace your space content with love / sense; sense the pace which needs most consistently contentedly love / cents; cents I invest in are best reduced to contented with love / since; since you, I knew perfect contentment with love / consent; consent to be in perfect love's committed steed at contentment / consensus; consensus is what we fed our contented love / cure; care enough about the cure for contented love / expression; expression vest, your best, content with love / familiar; God's familiar face, my own, backlit with love. I am content / fed; fed by a bled desire to less extreme and more securely lean into the winds of contented love / abed; abed in steads of perfect seam we gleam at God's supreme reside at contented love / variety; I am content in the variety of you and our perfect pair of eyes imbued with contented love / spicey; spicey spell of well we loved and eternity spelled our heated return to contented with love / secure; secure in insure, I am sublime in the rhyme and the reason called contented love / endure; endure a censure of where we've gone for constant comment on content with love / shone; shone the view of contented enthuse with the spouse of refuse to be less than love / shines; shines in us the contented truth with love./ space; the space across the wave of contentment with love / children; children who have held each other to love / many; many the muses whose ruses are gone into love.

CHAPTER EIGHT

Tulip; tulip-lipped deliverance because of the content of committed love / bud; bud's erupt in our engulf of a space-less abide at the occurrence of contentment in love / vase; a vase of the taste of a creamy astride of the residence, our evidence, built on a floral resume of our glee with the contentment of love / rose; rose red review of when we were committed to contented love / peony; you know our resident honor of the contentment called love / lily; lily lipped deliverance of gently we contentedly love / gain; gain a pace, your own, and contentedly love / grace; content with you, I am engraced by the constant view of your contented face of love / brush; dance a brush with the race constantly contented by love / bemuse; bemuse your contented weave to love / enthuse; enthuse us to pleasure of contented we amuse our selves with contented love / amuse; cure your amuse with an honest review of the raise to contentment with love / grasp; grasp renew of the perfect hue that resides constantly contented to love / relate; balls of relate cue our faith to bounce insured by the curator's lure back home to intermittent-less, consistent-more, contented love / elate; elate your great view of the renew to contented be with love's return / select; selects you, I do, to contented love / in-take; in-take is great when I review our date, june ate, with contented love / breath; life's breath blew on you and our precious contentment with love / dare; content with more, I dare to compare to no one except perfectly contentedly love / date; date your perfect mate, consistent, contented love / delve; delve into who we are with your starry-eyed pare of less. let's just contented, love / debate; debate on this; our perfect rate of constant content of lo sd / desist; desist less, decide more, to contented be in love / demise; demise denotes of the devote constant to contented love / surmise; carol in your surmise of your aspect for the one and the constant summation that we are God and one content called love / spate; spare a spate with "fate" and know content with love; *fonder avenues of truly energetic reminders of love / smooth; all arrive is smooth when our ride is God constant in reside at love's perfection about contented love / evoke; evoke bespoke our perfect we of consistently love / devote; devote yourself to a vote for perfect contented love / duel; the duel is over and I am in clover of constant green contented with the mother of constant consistent love / devote; denote my vote as deep in grips of enlightened yet to perfect commit of a constant content called perfect love / decide; decide who you love and renew your count with the constant confess of your love / death; act on this, your decision to death forgive and lift your live to contented love / commit; commit to the one and know the sum of a constant love / comet; comet's cupid has become a cured example of the sample complete in the gaze of my constant view of the heart of two as one contented love / invent; invent an invest that's both caress and a hum of contentment set in the throat of God / lights; lights are content within a constant bliss called the blend of conscious loving cure and the shining way we've become the contented ones / blissed; lights are blissed by your continued care for the cure called contented with love / kiss; kiss the father and know the regard for the perfect mother of perfectly God is; now; love; contentedly / securely; securely love your continued son; the lifted one and know that God is; contentedly / demure; demure is secure in my rest at assure of the perfect aspect called absolute; love. content / ask; I am going home to live and I will ask the mother to bring you along for contented love / absolute; absolute you

and eternal we in a weave of perfect clarity and contented love / absolve; perfect absolve has come to God's resolve with getting on to a precious glue, the contentment in we were true to God / resolve; resolve yourself to be confessed of the perfect concept of contented God-head, love / reside; reside in a residence deep with respect for the heavenward spent of the constant called God. content / refute; refute-less regard has swallowed the hard to say; you are; now one; be the elect and the sum of an inheritance deep in God is content with man. love / regard; regard the confess that God is content with hu-manity, basically, essentially, internally, God / God; God is; know the content of confession of the heart of this matter; God is in; perfectly contented love with man-kind / arm; I am the arm of God's confess that all is best when healed with contented love / bless; bless your self with contentment hu-man love / embark; embark your spark to the completed span of an arc called man and the contented parents, God and earth can compare this note, the music of love / bare; bare your spirit and hear the confession of the earth's transgression complete, man is forgiven, God is for living and contentment has nakedly set in / declare; declare it well to love so deeply and to confess so richly that God is contentedly hu-man too in our light review of love / the ship; one beat, one blip, one ship and a contented shore and the swell arrival at a wave called God is, love / the heart; the heart's alive with sweet arrive at a contented stand for love / the head; the head has gone to the sun we've all become, love, one / bask; bask in the sum of a son called one and the way to a home, your own, all day in the light of a new dawn consistent to a sway called love / observe; observe your thrice held resist and enlist the aid to abrade less the fist of all survival for the heart of love's arrival at consistent, contented, constants; love / truth; truth's resume has come to the moons of a lively shore called contented love / talk; talk about it and all the way home we are contented with the mouths full-filled with love alone / astound; astounded by the sacred sound of heightened ground eruptive in loved content / astride; astral astride of the reside at the way we constantly consist of contented flights to the stand of love / beside; beside the bay, our better wave of a briefer view has become the heightened cue to remember contentment with love / magens; magens, the day of a crystal contentment reached, love.

THE IN-PEACEMENTS
LEVEL 8

CHAPTER ONE

Peace-full; peace-full I am to the expectant stand of all we ran to for love / bliss; bliss equated to wait for love / extent; extent sent to advent of bliss and the peace of a kiss called love / descent; a descent to man said that I am peace-full in my stand to love / in-vent; I in-vent peace with love / regard; banner of regard, the flags of peace waved in love / embrace; embrace at grace and peace and love / emulse; emulse at less and peace at love / expiate; expiate's rate is less to love than peace / pulse; pulse pays peace-full heart's beat to love / convene; convene at confuse less and peace-full be to love / intervene; intervene sweetly at peace-full love / defend; defend your act of a set on commit and know the space of a taste of divine assign and the lift of a loss of pieces taught the within of life and the birth commit to peace-full love / delight; delight n sign a commit-ment with you and your well regard for the treaty signed by my heart's assign at the pace and the spirit of welcome's feel of gently loved / insight; peace-full insight of the intent to glint at gentle resign to the deeper side of a peace-full dip into love / extend; extend yourself to the wealth of wed and the heart of a tread to gentle lives of peaces of love / extensive; extensive to you, I am content to the extent of an impressive peace of love / intensive; intensive extends can handle ins to ours of peace at love / love; love to be new at the known embrace of the peace of perfect love / baby; baby you knew our peace at paces of love / green; God's green in reside at the peace inside our paces of love / march; march home to the peace of love / laughter; laughter grew to the love of peace / shine; let peace shine in our noons of perfect love / elective; elective to your knowing shores of welcome swims well within the renewal of our peace-ing love / reside; reside at peace and know the heart of assorted parts becoming one in the peace-ing sun of a holy day, the days of love / respect; respect tonight the hues of deep and the resent of a table set at the peaced reply to love / reflect; I have reflect in my respect for the hope-full glance at peace-full love / structure; structure grew deep at our steepest leap to the greatest love and the gift of peace / trace; trace your house home to respect and the perfect connect to love and peace / song; a song sung in peace and love / light; light on love and peace at come to the altar of grace / wave; wave to wooing constant view of the peace of love / air; air care is where we breathe in peace and love / clean; God's great clean example is the sample of breath in the midst of us and the sum of our peace-full love / yellow; yellow you and perfect me in the halls of green and the scenes of we are made to live at peace and love / pasture; pasture power and the hour of our peace and the gripping face of the hidden street of light and love / friends; friends bound in the towns of peace and love / french; french review and life in you and your constant news of peace and love / happy; happy hue of the dues to peace and love / well; well you will be peace-full in our trees of love / engage; engage in precious respect of love / sleep; sleep, hear, breathe in peace and love / rest; rest at peace and a ruse-less love /

water; water's wed is lightly done by the peace of love / calm; calmly clued to the simple sound of peace blown round our world / hammock; hammocks head for the peace of love and one extensive expression, love / hand; hand yourself the friend who loves the streets of peace at love / dandy; dandy particles of peace / silence; silence near, peace is hear, and neat to love / noise; noise knew less review and the places of love / near; God's near and we are dear to the lights of peace / optional; optional to a mental peace / limits; limits and the lessons on peace / logical; logical and the lyrical, "peace" / logistics; logistics enriched through peace / random; random in a rescued peace / rescue; rescue comes to a summary "peace" / rooted; rooted and the rescued peace / partner; partner and the precious peace / position; position made given peace / palms; palms placed clearly near our peace / places; places of the lion's share for peace / pyramid; pyramid cured for the creations on peace.

CHAPTER TWO

Wealth; wealthy too. peace / eye; a peace-full eye to love / power; the power to peace and secure to love / plenty; have plenty of peace / freed; peace-fully freed to believe in reside of the heart inside our precious love / morning's; morning's nice and then we see the depth of our divinity and the peace of faced by love / mother; mother of us all, I am, and the shekinah grace of resonate's face and the peace of excel to love / ear; ears have I am written deep in the peace of auditory decide to love./ earth; God's great earth, the birth of safe excite to peace / wind; wind blew peace-full in our love / breath; press your breath to the lips of love and peace / spirit; you are the spirit of love / life; life's regard is our love and peace / change; change regard for the sword of love at peace / mental pause; mental pause has a cause to take a break and lose your head and know your heart and start the upward move to love / angelic; angelic your nature and your peace-full reside at the countenanced say the love is freed / etheric; etheric nature new to mention the dimension two deep to beyond and peace / reward; peace's reward is the sword of a cut-less love / retired; retired forget at the heart of our bet on the blessings of love / thank-full; thank-full concern for the commands of peace is love / gratitude; gratitude is blessed by the assure of your angelic nature and your peace at reside at the countenanced stay called designate your lathe to God / graced; graced by grew and to this, love, at peace / grew; grew to a view of the dates with peace, 2003 and the special 3 grown fourth to love / grown; grown up and through the stones of love to peace / stellar; a stellar pair, the eyes that care for peace and love / stela; stela said let there be peace in me and that there's God in love / stellae; a stellae stacked to the clues of peace / stellar; stellar to the pace of peace and the storage space of adulation and love / rain; rain on me and the shine of liberty at peace and love / reign; peace reigns / rule; equip your-self in rules and less than love and peace / light; light house and love can lean at the heavenward life of peace and love / inheritance; inheritance heads for divinity, I said, in a swift recline in the arms of entwine in God is peace and in love / keys; the keys are concrete when we are sweet to our royal inheritance, the heritage of peace is love / dancing; dancing pleasure measured peace in love / enough; enough to be contented in a peace-full be of love / dew; dew be droplet deep in peace / drops; peaces drops to her knew for free to love / discipline; discipline fond can sound like this caressing kiss of peace and love / manual; let's manually stand at the land of a shift to peace / handbook; handbook of the held to a peace-full explain / garden; garden's grew taller when we simply stood in the grounds of a fertile stroke called peace and love / essence; essence read, the essene said, bless this man who enoch said would stand for God. the peace has come. Metatron is home to love / essene; essenes knew the plan that God is man and perfect the span to complete the love and peace / roots; roots are set on rest at peace / ex-stream; ex-stream flow can grow knee deep at the touch of peace / as seen; as seen we are lean to peace / stream; let's resume our stream of the energetic exchange coined the man of truth at peace / running; running through the seams of sound we are all around the gardens draped in centrific peace / flown; flown around and long enough to find this lease on peace / presence; the presence of God is peace in love / tree; tree's tall with the all of eccentric flair and the peace of spare arrive at love / truth; bliss-full truth is straight ahead and the love full sooth has come to the gift of peace that's spoken with love / lava; lava joe blew at the blue regard of peaces' ring / trail; trail ahead to the na pali side of the love inside our perpetual sing to peace is at love / kingdom; kingdom is come to the one who know peace / freight; freight found to handle towns of loads so dense that peace can barely kiss the sky / earthed; earthed by a presence birthed by peace / quakes; quakes of coincide erupt inside the faith of two of us complete-ing peace / welcome; welcome to the new arrival at the home of peace / wonderous; a wonderous wonder, the thunder of being and loved by peace / rain blew; rain blew the rainbow to the house of peace is ours, love / frank; frank enough to speak my peace / respect; respect me fully when the veil removed delivers only peaces of eight and the return to tens of love.

CHAPTER THREE

Sweetness; sweetness rules the hearts of those who hasten to love in peace / health; health has held us up to peace / healing; a healing nature given peace / fields; fields erupt around our gain of the grounded revue of love's revival and the peace of love / ripe; taste the ripening sweet-ness of this peace called love / juicy; a juicy jewel, this heaven's tool, the art of peace in love / gem; gems of review beckoning you to lightly reside in the folds of a wing flown high to degree 720 and the venetian return called shimmering facets of fascinating return to peace and love / rounds; rounds can sound like applause from God and the pleasant aspect of the perfect reflect that

notions of loving this peace / plump; plump coincide is hidden inside my living example of the sample called prospect of perfect peace at our lean to love. 10 .pearly; pearly gated coincide is our abide at the holy sides of peace / gate-less; gate-less grew our residue and the release of the space of elective renew to the hearts of God and peace / magnificent; you grew magnificent to the peace of love / melt; melt at your repetitive return to peace / pert; pert ascend to peace is; love / lush; lush evoke can connote that we have found the town of peace / lanky; lanky true and you are peace / spunk; spunk-y excite of the invite to vibe on the peace of pleasing love / warm; warm enough to cure our complete concede to the intellect gone to the heart of peace / spank; spank the banks of purple blue delivery to the lavender scene of a cord pulled free to careen to the waters of spoken peace / lights; lights evoke the bless of peace and God's believe in perfect love / auroric; auroric regard for the harder reality of the principality of these quick kinds of certainly love and peace / lessons; lessons lean on renew of peace and love / lessens; lessens lesson to love and peace / less in; less in learned, I yearn to the peace of electric love / lest we; lest we were remissive we could yearn to the blessings, peace / let's; peace-fully let's place our hearts at sweets of tasty remember / dandy; this is dandy and let us be found in only peace / smile; presently we smile at funny peaces of love / caress; caress this peace-full love / hardy; love hardy in you and your peace of love / hearken; hearken to yearn for the love and the peace of God / confection; confection's peace-full explain is due to show us perfect love / herb; herb's explain that they know complain can go away to perfect peace / we'd; we'd better see some victory in peace and love / sign; sign on to love's uphold of peace / pipes; pipes will clear as you can hear your honest love and peace / organ; organ of peace and the price of a throat's release to love / creed; a creed reviewed and I am wide to peace inside the love of our own / graced; graced by reflect, I am direct to the source of a course to new singles felt come fused by love / genuine; yes, you are genuine in regard to peace is love / jewels; clerk your jewels as sold to perfect tools of love / shift; shift to a shift of appreciative measure and the peace absolute to admittedly worn compute of love / process; process of plenty and heralds of clues to the peace that can heal and the light that's enthuse of the finer regard to associative rewards of love / purist; purist is cured by the peace that is love / nudist; nudist view compels me to lighten our loving emphasis on peace / son; son of siam has gone to the rich disgrace and the eternal cuisine of a meal called fulfill and a heavenly lean to perfect regard of peace is; love / que rico; God's que rico is rich to you and your price-less peace / rich; peace-full plan and the riches of man standing combined as peace and love / burn; burn less and spiral more and dress the duress as evening scores of peace is; love / ignite; ignite me nightly with peace / rub; peace-full rub is the tab of the life that is good / rewards; rewards are set at the passive forget that any is all and all is the plan of a peace-full expand / sight;

God's sight is you full of peace at heaven's wink of love / seal; seal your deal on the case of peace / soul-less; God's soul less stride is wide to certain peace / solace; take a step to a solaced sleep at the pulse and the peace of love / voice; voice your matter, God is green and the earth is keen on precious peace and love / blew; a peace-full breeze can now believe in a life that's blew to peace is love / blue; blue enough to bask in, the fact is, love peace / song; God's song is man in peace / sung; sung to a tune of blessed you and your relative true to peace / trio; trio of true to peace / trip; trip to the spring of a crystal truth as we become the swing of peace / meet; meet me, hear, with our peace.

CHAPTER FOUR

Met; met by a manatee-d believe in the peace of a spring called love / elect; elect us erected to peace and love./ luxuriate; luxuriate in a training ascend to a fabulous blend called basically peace and love / luxury; luxury has leads to the knee high peace of our standing love / tax-less; tax-less address of the best way to pay for honorable peace / tact; I sang about the fact that tact was all-ways 5 below and 6 above the perfect love off 11 stood to love and peace / cling-less; surely you know that your cling-less academy is built on the face of a falling due called / peace is; lift; to a bound-less flight to your own back yard; and home / vine-less; vine-less I cling to the ring of a renew called love and the clime of a craving to bring in peace at home / vivacious; vivacious you are in your shirley's cue and get her, hear, at the light of peace / vibrant; a vibrant view of a river worn around the ring of a living wet with loving vibrate and a peace-full rate of resolute love / va voom; va voom in your room that roams to love is; peace / zoom; you zoom me home to the moon of our one quick peace / comic; comic release is the buzz of peace / laugh; where did you laugh most in this life and the peace of the host who loves / tongued; your tongued refusal has approval tripped at the chore of "I'm sorry" too and again we knew the peace of forgiven love / tripped; tripped extent has gone to bliss in this the peace of love / truth; truth is told by the telling trail of well we like the life of peace / pieces; pieces insist that parts are superb and all can be wed by the hearts that insist on cell-I-brate me, peace / maya; mayan intrigue with the light Metatron and the mention of a dimension called peace / gaia; gaia's good release is the greater hood of a hospitable breed that have gone to peace and the blue of love / gaelic; peace is secure in our secure to the gaelic grace of love / graces; orange graces grace our grid with the rise of peace / pomegranate; pomegranate pools that feed the bottomless treats of a filling sweet with the waters granite and the heaven-ward meet of peace is and God is sweet / royalty; royalty's power is the confer that a ruler is sure of a relevance led to the head of peace / mango; mango puree preserved by the swerve to the emerald sea of a city replete with starry exceed to the tastes of love dipped in peace / mangrove; mangrove weave of swamped in seas of yes, I will, to love

and peace / cedar; cedar key worn to this arrival at the portal's door and the revival of love in living peace / cypress; cypress scene of a winning dream and the truth of a train to the ladders of peace / social; social scene and worn by thin examples blend of peace that knows heavens release to blend at hearts of peace's love / birch; a birch tree trued by a worn relief and the etheric explode of a taller speech called here is love and this is peace / skilled; skilled treasure strewn on the seas of peace / withstanding; withstanding expanding relate peace / expect; expect us hear at the lights of love and peace / grape; grape trees grew and vines explored the potato chip seas and the star of lords who dance in streets of watermelon example of the deep explore called travel to the doors of love in peace / umbrellaic; umbellaic I stand at the living attend called the sheltering weave of a peruvian beam called peace is man and love / pulse; pulse macchu pichuan and peru is content to ascend to the beat that is blue in rescind to love and the peace of forgive / patience; patience appeals to peace / response-able; response-able to the growth of a driving ascend tot he lots of regard and the hearts that decide to live in responsible relate to peace / responsive; responsive you grow in the driving retreat tot he heart of your matter and the matter complete with directives of love and matters of peace / saved; saved by the truth in our eloquent spiral to love is the blend of perfectly peace / hands; hands true with God's love and peace that surrounds our bliss-ings of this incredible ride called life / satin; satin is God's trace of the feel of love's embrace of peace / first; first time through and all-ways peace / wave; let us wave at the wave of you and what we miss when we remiss the peace of release and the better part of what we confess as love / wed; wed yourself to the concave plant of a life that reeks of living love as peace / yourself; yourself concurs that the arc is sure and the sidth is deep in a soul's release to the light I am and the contoured create of a start that lasts and a pert confess of peace is, love / saturn; saturn sets on the hurl to wields of lofty assure of the expert kin to peaces committed and truth that is told to the ones mount shasta deep to love / great; great to revive I am inside the curls that sway to perfect repeat and the squares of higher parallels that ring of peace committed too and love / month; month by month and all years through I reside at the heart of you, the God of every day know and the peace of fashionable, love / fork; fork over your confession of the procession to the delicious, delicate, delirious, destitute, derivative, nature of peace / squares; squares into awarest allowance for peace / steering; steering clearly into peace / standing; standing and the staring peace into love.

CHAPTER FIVE

Forth; forth I go to perfect, love, and peace / left; left to example, I sample the source that I will be my living example of peace / sting; I am cured of the gospel of sting, now let us ring with the harmony of peace / right; right to near and nearly spent, I reinvent the psalms of peace and love / brother-hood;

know the brother-hood of light and the lighter life of a higher good called peace-fully love / clearance; clearance to arcturian be by the portal's plan to open us to perfect embryonic place of the heart of palms and the palms of friends touched in silent agree to aggressively be perfectly contented with lights of love / God-ly; God-ly connection of the heart that's within the hands fair eternal and fairly committed to the fare of reflect and this perfect peace of love / aura; aura of the hour of perfect repeat at the wealth of direct to peace-full love and the breeze that's blue with the healing tongue and all around we are the fit to give our living love / words; words are given direct in me and all I can hear is the hark of peace and love / graven; graven image gone and seen only this the lords of one and we are they committed to the absolute of peace / knew; knew the prince of peace had come to me and my interior harmony is one of perfectly love / penned; penned another one to love and life as give and giving saw that we'd become the heart of perfect peace and love / biologic; biologic wonder comes to this the bridge of middle set and set on middles shored secure the ides of 40 know the cure and exceptional pleasure now can reign in the heart and the faith of the one exclaim that love is perfect in peace / genealogic; genealogic to the logic of peace, I am content to the source and the course of our logical produce of the ports of peace / international; international to a factor of the mastery of this matter come and the master lives inside of me and my peace-full reside in the home of love / scrolls; scrolls decree that my agree to know the prophets means devote and ascendance stands in the throat of my prayer-full intending to devote my heart to love / angelic; angelic arch-ons now have gone to door of an h-less fable called true peace / work; work on the heals of worn too thin by standing up to know the sup of a capable matter, the chatter of love's devote to peace / living; living on material shores, I know the shores of shored release and the fade into the sunny days of one at peace / law; law of one that God devotes is the pledge to speak the oath of only all-ways peace / original; original to a matter of yes, I know confess of the eternal respect for a deeper devote to peace as love / search; search for the peace-full ascend can end at the heart of release and the purple blend of paternal love and the mother of peace / fast; fast enough to devote our vote to love is; peace-full / sobriety; sober to a moment's reflect, I know respect for the health of another who imbibes only love at the neck of perfect peace / psalm; you are the psalm I sing and the river that rings for perfect aspects of peace-full devote to the necklace of pearly dreams of heavenly gates of peace / praise; praise the chance to secure your dance to the daily aspect of a lighter desire to conspire only all-ways with God. sing the praise of peace's secure / sun; sunny view of the peaces that shines in the hands of God / water; you are the water that knows the reflect of perfectly peace / air; air is free to breathe the breathe of a God-head direct with howling respect for the perfectly sure place of a brink called hu-man peace / earth; earth deep to a view of the peace that lives in love / power;

power along the song of peace that notes only love / plus; plus the pace of perfectly peace / play; play peace-fully at love / thanks; content with thanks, I know the devote to avenues of love. peace / praise; praise the days of higher devote to peace at love / holy; holy tool of love, peace / wise; wise to a measure, I am peace / well; well enough to feel only peace / spring; spring to the water amend and the finer friends who know peace / fountain; fountain fed, I am led to friends of love is; peace / bell; bells that ring of true release to the higher love. the chime of peace / blaze; blaze a trail to the wells of love and the directions of peace / bask; bask in matter that is constant to a holy wealth called consistently the peace of love / engage; engage in the grace that knows release to present peace / in gaze; in this gaze I recline to know the wealth of peace and love / record; record rewards in peace and love / tapes; tapes refused come unglued in the presence of peace and the light of a place called love / release; release the other and relax in release to the shores of hallowed peace and the suns of love / embrace; a great central day has come. e=embrace the sum of a given son and the rays of days elective come to the source of loving in peace / face; face the truth entered by love. see peace / trees; trees decide to dance with me and to come to some agree with love's imbue of leafy sights called peace is; high to love / proofs; proofs are due to truth at peace / stars; stars electric now can see the harbor called divinity and the galaxy of proof that God's exist is due to more than just a spoof or a burst of heightened start concentric with empower now electric I can see the merkabah magic of believe in the fields that surround you and me in the power of peace / press; press your palms together taos high and decide to deliver highest proclaim of God is true to the electric yellow avenue of the will to live again in God and the perfect river of a boone-time avenue that knows ascend deftly spoken to the place of perfect space filled with capability of divine appeal to the heart of peace / prophecies; prophecies that I have made, I now proclaim for God is love and this is peace to me / praise; praise the chance to dance with the angels of love, arc deep to confess and devote and yes! to love / priest; priest of love can find a friend in the friendly few who know ascend again in lots of peace / plan; plan to be eternally in love. that's peace / extent; the extent of my peace is my souled release and the relate to will to go to light and the heady devote to the vote for peace / extension; extensive extension to love and peace / extensive; an extensive exam of what I am to love and peace / aspiration; aspiration of neglect has grown to respect our repeated desire to hire deeper aspects of natural nations of gentle devote to softly spoken instigation of the invitation to daily devote our hearts to perfect peace and love / book; book your self to the deem of exemplary peace and the pages of love / vitality; vitality measures our peace-full please of the taste-full desire to fire your pace with peace and love.

CHAPTER SIX

Lace; lace up your taste with love; maintain peace / a-line; a corner a-lined with the kind who call for peace at love./ lift; lift yourself to the shelf of a living hive of being love at peace / great; great enough to the truth-full include of all we heed about succeed at love in peace / small; God is small at the lights of peace / exact; God is exact to the peace for love / precise; precisely placed the facets of defend have become alive with the frantic face of diving in to peace as loves / absolutely; absolutely and peace-fully seen is the soothe of the attitude for learning to breathe / acutely; acutely aware of the sparest arise I coincide with the welcome thanks of exacting live at the banks of the rhine of love is the peace of dire's good-bye / precious; precious intrigue with why we leave our best of love at a peace-full door / burns; burns less and welcomes more the scent of peace and the aroma of love / hot; hot enough to pace our peace and love's the race / wonder-full; guides of the wonder-full wield in me the heartfelt opportunity to say good-bye / strange; strange enough to know the peace of love / word; word of reserve to the source of regard and cards of peace in love / consist; Christ's consist of this insist is this ingress to the new address to often love and the wells of peace / crystalline; crystalline ascend to the peace and love of the mount mitchell-ed top to list enough / source; source of this, love, peace / resource; resource secure in the sensitivity of a new divinity called the names of peace / perfect; perfect resource of the torch that carries the flames of loving peace / crystallic; crystallic residue piezo deep to the thank-full electric line to the neap of a trade forewarned of living love. electric peace / christing; God's christing sends the peace of a dove's descend to the lights of peace / suggest; suggest enough of peace and loves / the arc; the arc of the rainbow drawn to friends at the iris blue end of peace / devotion; devotion set at the lips of love that reeks of peace / vogelaic; vogelaic and the spark of crystal eggs and angles and of larks to the cornered peace of love is, well / healing; healing set on peace / sacred; the corner of the sacred send some peace / sure; sure you are the square of loving peace / raphael; let us be viewed by the seas of a peace-full regard for love / michael; michael's mend is in your view and is content to assume the peace of a mother's love / Metatron; Metatron found a town that squarely seems to blend with thanks and love and peace / raziel; raziel flew to perfect peace at love / camael; camael's accrue is love and peace on a divine shore / azrael; azrael grew to be loved by peace / uriel; peace to a uriel peace and the plan of a peace and love / gabriel; gabriel grew less secure until he found his holy ground of eternal live and peace in love / ariel; ariel grew to know the beast could turn the limbs to the lamb of overlaid by peace and love / sandalfon; sandalfon drew a chance to view the plans of living peace and love / israfel; israfel feel to values pleasant and as tall as trees and crystal views of dues of peace and love / jophial; jophials rule at the living loves of peace / zadkiel; zadkiel grew to be reviewed as

the expectant hush of a rushed address to the plans of peace and love / moses; moses met the truth of a trait called peace on tablets of stone / wings; sufi wings fold to complete the inspections of traces of terrific love and peace / worth; worth our renew and the winds of peace / tall; tall enough to love and shortly peace / message; a message mewed to trying spurs that space to peace / elijah; elijah's rescue is the residue of peace is love / danced; let danced be due to the patience in you and peace / remembrance; remembrance of 3 and the heard of peace / endless; endless, peace / classic; classic cue of peaces of views and love is; ascend / buoyant; buoyant bless of the apparent confession of permanent love. pease / knowledge; knowledge kneels at perfectly clear return to peace-full remember of love / imbue; imbue feels healed in times of tracing task as the 9 to 5 of laughing due to traveling togs worn by dogs who give the all for perfection at peace / salvation; salvation of the traveling kind, peace / appear; appear at the door of truces of peace / wreath; wreathed abstain can explain what we're through to traces of peace / mercy; mercy allows us to make energy read clearly young to peace at love / gold; gold's cue peace-full and deep to alchemical keeps of lives that we love firmly to peace / clue; clue's cure is our lure of renewing peace / draw; draw yourself in to peace that is fed by perfectly love / write; write, p-e-a-c-e / peace; peace into a parallel port of love.

CHAPTER SEVEN

Rounds; rounds of what we all reframe as peaces of love / forces; forces find us peaced by love./ armed; there's a pace at thoraxic splurge which uses you as the present attend to peace./ seat; seat yourself degreed by peace./ save; save yourself peaced as love / mysteries; mysteries appeal, peace / math; math meets addition to you plus peace / beast; a beast that has run to the shore leave liquor of effervescent nectar of natural due, love and peace / songs; I am the songs of peace / rivered; rivered appeal to waters of peace / bath; a bath splashed peace-fully of the drips of love / happy; happy to veins of golden dues of peace / peaced; peaced yourself to love / paradise; God knew we knew paradise as two and a peace-full pace of love / loves; loves to peace-fully stare at all we mean of love / waves; waves are won by shared response to the glare of peace hastened by love / bird; bird blew in to drop a dearest feather, peace / fish; fish your heart out to her and the decision to swim for peace / eddy; eddy alive with a respite called peace / stars; stars ensure that her despair can care for insure of the God that is to peace / pulse; pulse preview has the heartbeat set on the deal direct to the good that God is loved by peace / pause; pause to confess your thanks to a living love / applause; applaud your stand for the candid sense of all we plan for a penchant to peace / gate; gates that grew to open wide for the alliterative blend called love and peace / way; way to peace, love / fate; fate that flew away to peace / dissolve; dissolve matter, peace / commune; commune's matter is discussing our peace / bank; bank on peace and become abundant in understanding finance by love / company; company threw singular peace to love / personal; personal respect, peace given and due / intensity; intensity woven all the way through to a massage called this is peace and love / eyes; eyes that have peace whisper of love / powered; peaced by powered attitudes of precious love / empathy; empathy won, you are the one who won true peace / entwine; entwine at peace / grace; layer your hands shaken by peace / salty; salty exude of the fabulous news that deft can be the waves of seas resplendent by peace / pass; pass on to peace / purposive; purposive matter that melts current dreams of idealic rest at the matter that melts chattering bliss at peace / relative; relative matter, peace / ink; peace is inky with the hands of written plans called men / pen; spell your pen, p-e-a-c-e / letters; letters penned as a befriend in our compassion for let's begin to be peace-full to love / wades; wades to leading let us in to the patent penchant for her blend of precious peace's love / seeded; seeded matter has been shattered by the fall of the mother won and now again we cam befriend the praises of lend to peace / keyed; keyed up, peace / calliope; calliope cued, I am surely hued by peachy pales of peace / trial; trial run by a patented view of the latent last of peace-full love / blooms; blooms view us flowered in to the fade of men and the perfect peace of let's be love / baste; baste deep sets of peace / bake; glue your cake to the table of peace / spirited; spirited matter, peace / see; taste this see of blinking at peace / power; power is secure to our endure of peace at love / enfold; enfolded over the land of manners that please our living chance for peace and love / communion; peace-full spurt of the communion of love / falls; falls obscure to the peace of love. unnumbered; unnumbered days of dashing counts of peace and love / between; between us peace / gardens; gardens growing in our friend's connect of bless this, peace, love / loin; loins that ache with the peace of love's pace / hungry; hungry in the pages peaced / surrender; surrender to deliver of peace

CHAPTER EIGHT

Eden; eden is won the our sunshine's return and the renewal of faith in your particular set on peace / sun; God's sun is won by the warmth of a cooler touch called the warm infuse of the pearly passion said by peace / arose; michael arose and heaven knows the cool rescue of a mother's sun felt given to peace is, love / import; import the sort who impart peace is; love./ productive; a productive mother has recovered the one percent who won for you and coming through we remember the surrender in to love / mother; your mother said and ahead we are to peace / holy; peace-fully seen in the swollen renew of the holy hour of our review for love / plant; plant it, hear, at the seeds of roots which grow full grown by the peace of love./ grow; grow deep in thrilling respect and the one perfect for you and your peace-full release to love / renewal; God's renewal, peace for love / grew; I grew to know the light I knew in a closer review of the peace that is love / spray; spray

to the sprung and spring the sum of suns who peace-fully live for love / stretch; stretch your deck and deal only peace is and love / deep; I am peace, deep within, love / daring; daring desire to conspire to healthier knew and the trail to the two who precisely care for the absolute peace of love / desire; desire to conspire to the lightest views of the halls and the hearts and the heavens of you; calling home to the truth-full express of our mutual confess of undiluted love; that is; peace / let; let your heart elect your face as the trace of tonight's ambrosial extend to the friends who know how true love shows in the face of men; know peace is; love / abundant; abundant in the view of who we knew and the peace is of love / golden-hued; golden-hued in our exude of the surrendering in to the pleasures of men with our perfect regard for the happy review of an ivy sample gilded in grace and met in a merciful daring imbue of all that we do for dearly the peace in of love / productive; productive treasure in the tools of traces filled with prospects deep in love / movement; movement sampled by the example of the trailing truth that we are the free to love. moving on the peace / breast; breasts that drip with the sweet release of the milky rate of the truly fed who fed our peace with nipples of love / wind; wind has blown to the phones of forget and we know neglect has gone away to the parallel plays of our meet again, love / command; command your pleasure still to be the heart of love and the faith of we are the one, God, in love; peace / seductive; seductive measure's purest pleasure is the thrill of a chore, know more, that lives to reign in the peace of love / swallow; I swallow your need to be entire in great, big, gulps of peace / messenger; a messengered relate of the relief that is, peace / airy; airy feathers of rhyming resume at the consummate resume of our flights to lights of peace / fruit; God is in the fruit we pick for edens of peaces of love / grain; grains of growing sprint to see the release of old and the hands of free escaping breathe that heads for the heals of welcome me to the hands of love / earthly mother; earthly mother in to be the winning possibility of the daughter who trusts in truth is the virgin-ing birth of the art of the shift to precisely love; peace / angel earth; angel of earth has born the mirth of a kind renew to the peace of love / angel life; angel life can renew our faith in God and the flying few who came to land to extend God's hand to man / angel joy; angel of joy has a standing for peace / angel sun; angel sun set to the beat of perfect love / angel water; God is an angel of sweet release to the waters of love in peace-full explore of the passions of a sample direct to the heart of your niece called love / angel air; angel air takes the care of subtle sounds of hearts abound at the roads to a throne of critical peace that's met relief with proud abide in a current see of love / consecrate; consecrate the peace that is within the heart of all that lives of love / greet; God's release is great. you are the two. enjoy sandalphon's reigning view of your feat and the meet that is called the carol-ing of peace / eternal life; care is said the eternal peace that has the best relief is the sea of the water of life called me / working; where were you and working too and coming home to the top of God is; Metatron and the saint of peace called michael neat with love / peace; preside at the side of peace / angel's power; angel's power in the hour of a sweet release called peace is; love / witness; witness the first kiss of regarding love in peace / begun; begun to matter; love, the breath of peace / end; end in the living sun of beginning to love our peace / inheritance; inheritance won by the sun of regard for the peace that is hard to keep secret; el love / angel love; angels love the peace of presence in our giving in to honest love / angel wisdom; angel of wisdom now has come to the wed of my retreat to the peace of love / eternal sea; eternal sea awash with the peace of foaming love / sabbath; sabbath said, rest, in these days of peace / first-born; first-born has worn the crown of sweet surrender to all that is of peace and love / consecration; consecrating mention of the passion for peace in our penchant for love / invisible; yes, I will release my invisible sword to the one that rules and helen's gone to God is; peace / .faith; faith has held me in release to the plan called God and the peace that's love / image; image west becomes the one with peace / visible; visible matter shattered less with peace / valuable; Gabriel's release is valuable in relief of the bless of all that is for love / views; views instill the will-full release to love is; peace / be still; be. still. God / know; know God / lightened; lightened in the heightened strand of peace / surface; surface pierced through loving peace / sparkle; sparkle clear within light's peace / spurts; spurts in a simple peace.

THE IN-PRECIOUS-MENTS
LEVEL 9

CHAPTER ONE

I am precious to heaven's advent and often I am fed by the ceiling that went lifting away with the cell of the 8th and the cull of the seals and heaven's repleter with the mexican street and the mayan good-buying and hawaiian helloings set with receive of the heavenward leave to reside at all-ways, receive, and God is high in me and my precious wave of relate to my I am received by perfect-ly God and I am precious to love / certified; certified righteous, we are religious to a spiritual experience of the respect of truth in precious-ness, love / aspect; aspect of elect to stand in the submissive lands of the God I am and your welcome review of the random reside to the slidding aspect deep to who you are to perfectly precious love / advent; advent of adventure, the venture's reflect of where we are for precious insight to flights to love / adventure; loved the adventure mention the next dimension to the 4th and beyond and we are climbing to God at 18 and the ceiling of love / measure; measure me deep to a racing seam of respect-full respect at the aspectant fleck of a flower that flows dripped wit a drifting dream gone light on the seam of forwever again and the precious is this holy cup / found; found a town where love's abound is plenty, precious, and true to perfect love / fond; get a fond reassing to all you owe of hear and now and love precious in special love / extensively; extensively assigned to wind up precious to love / around; around hear, we are inclined to refine our precious-ness of love / currently; gift currently lent to us; human spirit. precious. love / attractive; God is attractive to me and my affinity for the truth and precious-ness / attentive; quest attentive to love has come and I am home to preciousness and a light regard for love / well; well you were to where you win the spun begun and the living psin of begin again in the business of yourprecious love / often; often you view your life as begun and then you retire to the heart of a sum called begin and again I say share in the bay of receding waves to the breath of belief and the precious-ness and often the resume of perfectly love / especially; especially nice is the candid advice that we all live residual in our perfectly precious love.' / good-bye; good time to good-bye our past dimension, the invention of *gap is purely gone, to love. *grand assign to a percent purloined; / good; buy a good buy, the why of precious, precision current to love / dream; on God is the air and the precious breath of one love / dream; gone dream gone and good buy to why we were less in precise precession to a love precious / the depthgod; is the depth of female perfect for the fit of man and the plan of the span call God is precious to love / the death; the death has come to past regard for less and know one precisely precious to transcendance and love / cuecue; up your clue of the precious love / balance; balance of a challenge has come to commit to perefectly precious love / care; God's care is here, feel near, to precious love / this delight; this delight is the arc of my life and coming home to the life precious to our little home / internal; God's internal in our clock struck through to home as precious-ness in love /

woven; God is woven in found to fond recline at the relax in preciousness and love / tonight; tonight I invite your attend to precious-ness in love / awake; awake to a weave called threads like you and crystal clued to precious love / bet; bet on who we were for precious-ness in love / you were; let us know who you were for the preciousness of love / we are; we are here near our perfect precious love / respect; fullyrespectfully spoken the truth is invoking a godd to precious-ness in love / definitely; definitely stand at the precious hand of praise be, love / Christ; Christ is; God in us; preciously; love / today; God is today and I am away to precious-ness, love / the way; the way home, love, is precious, too, love / wellgod's; well in you and your advance to ta stance at precious love / within; within this glance is the strictest chance to show advance to precious love / speak; itspeak it through to the truth in the light regard to precious love / spoken; spoken spill, the thrilling trill of voweled abode at precious love / child; child of God has come to the train of truth and the training ground of adult love. a precious one / Metatron; Metatron's cue is here. be near to perfect release to relectrical retreat of the isles of fabled preciousness and love / collide; collide at the corner of preciousness and love / atom; precise an atom, I am adam in God's decide to reside as man and God is precious in this love / adam; adam said, I'll know and fell to having a greater stride to see it all and train again in a precious remand. our love / kadmon; kadmon came to eden again and knowing you I am precious / cataract; cataract found, removed, resume, your precious-ness and views of love / ride; ride along beside the stream of a central deam called centris love and the mood precious to kinder love / elate; elate equates with the perfect date and an equal view of precisely you in precious living devote to love / rest; God's rest is here in you and perfectly at precision's precious best of love / retrieve; retrieve your trek to the triple connect with the 9th direct ascend to the heighten-ed friend of precious love / perfect.perfect you in precious view of gentle love / contentment; contentment sent to a right-full stint in the arms and the arc of a precious covenant,our perfect love / decide; decide to glide along our way on this precious contentment with commitment peace and love / commit; commit to a kit of essential ascend to be found contented in a grace of precious love / consistent; God's consistent in our insistent stage of the where we were in precious love / core; essentially core I am more to all we cede to precious love / treat; treat around the town of precious tastes of love / truth; truth told, a precious hold on perfect love / definite; definite due is imbued replacing through the space of an elegant resume of a guested space, mu, and the cave of a constant crave for precious reside at the side of love / deduce; deduce this trip to the trace of a central express and the bless of eternal rescind of less and the perfect blend ofprecisely love / inducegrip; the induce to a better resume of where we assume our express is best in precious love.

CHAPTER TWO

Release; release stress, express, is pure in precious return to a stretch called love / invaed; invaded for space of an expressive taste of the central pace of a truth that's found in the fact and the whole-sum act of a trace of th perfect place called precious love / jaded; jaded jewels along the rhine lead the nile to a higher shine and th stars of heaven heal in me as my cells assign the three of heavenly sights and orionic seals and how well we'll be to the fortunate access of love / quailed; quailed and clued and ambition restored, I reside at the edge of a a better shore and the gentle lull of residing at receive in the heart of forever and the height of believe in precious, love. 5cluedclued to who we'd be I succeed in the diving reside at peace-full arrest and right-full reside at the heart of precious, love / feeds; feeds on fuel of rockets tooled by terrific bursts of adventive treks to wedges of life and the feast of deals of deeper eats. God-head here ato precious love / fuel; God's fuel is a wealthy wed of light and oil in fossil beds of burning through to precious love / farther; farther on we're led to father all the precious-ness of love / woods.next we stood in the woods of a summer day wet with precious greens of love / retreat; summer's spring has brought retreat to the hauls of wooden trees and precious love / respect; bless this respect-full advance to the leaves of alife and the sacred sight of precious love / aspects; aspects of accrue imbue our light with the life of eternal fuel, the love in pools of cherry red resume to rights of precious love / lights; lights are lightly won by the sound of our swinging round to the heart and the life of a love that is kind to a precious hum called lightly love. orion to or and in we are when we give love a star shining deep with tallest sids of pacific plates of precious love. call your friend who resides in the heart of men and the precious-ness of love. stellarstellar assign of resign to reside at love / sorta; sort of calousness has gone tot he reside of carrying on to the elegant decide to adonis-like stand and eccentric-ly pale with the narrow in-vent of where we can be for heaven's descent and all-wqys one aligned by relief of the elegant stare of my sort of release to a precious nest, love / set; set on resort I wrestle the waves only to find a lengthy day of called by the preciousness of love / self; self respect and I reflect on what I need for specialness and the halls fo God in the veins of me and the precious-ness of spoken love / proud; proud of days that lighten up, I shine in flights to healing stuff called wetter views of the wedding day called precious too love / prance; prance to a chance encounter at the shores of reside and elegance constant with a precious presence called eccentrically love / spin; spin around to chance the encounter with precious love / spell; spell yourself relieved and know the hearty release of "down below" and the ecstatic reside at the rhytms of consonants spelled precious by love / sport; sports heal while we feel right to watching light insure our welcome home to the permanent reside besdide th throne of an olympic peninsula and a kinder potential for the ides of precious love / cavort; cavort in the sort of sport we are and the elegant star of ecstatic arrive at the stage of the show called abide by yourset of perfect respect-full rules of love / symphonic; lightly seen by a symphonic lean to a clear residue of preciousness sent direct to the heart of the ears of love / craft; today I craft the way to precious love / careen; careen to a career for wetter than realize of the fact that the precious one is you and truly too, love / span; life is a span that now has found the sound of a horn and the passer by of our return to precious love / caress; let's caress in deft return to precious love / endureendure; healing's cure and deal with the healing precious-ness of love / delve; let's delve in to the matters of heart that are fed preciously by the sounding seas of the thundering bursts of breezes of love / dress; dress as God in fields of gold / address; address yourself to preciousness and the simple pleasure of the letters to love / pert; lucky days in pert display of the seeming glint of a quickening glance and glinting streams of a rocket's repeat of a stream that is srewn with heaven's invent of precious convent of love / sugaran; aspect of sugar that is sweet is the contest to cure your craving with bounding delivery to the taller friend, the precious one of the numerical bond to love, chemistry, the mystery of how we compute to the complex of love / gold; God is gold in our believe of the crystal clear clue that a heart is a sleec of living repute and the precious escape of all this enthuse for the portent called love. precious / gem; smay we gems review the gleaming eyes of whom we love for precious goals of giving good / metal; God's metal depth is found in the deft return of one to town and in this regard we know only love / leave; leave love to the precious, God.life / God's; life is ours about true love's precious view of the respect called true / light; light, precious / pen; let's pen a new card to winning numbers of papers called love, precious / effort; efforts ascend to fall down exactly where we bathe in precious love / bob; bob across the line to precious love / led; led too love, precious / lace.lace your space to the life of a tree called living free to the precious belief to love / weave; weave a breed of precious love / plenty; flights have plenty of years to live in the updrafts precious with God above and living love / join; join our measures, pleasure's please, precious / now; now we are precious and know the love of life and the advent of suppose we care, more, love / enjoy; enjoy the flocks precious with love / fly.fly home led precious to love / flower; precisely flowers our love and the pleasures of growth and precious God-heads bloom of perfect love / flow; a heat of flow consigns to co-sines of definitive measures of pleasureable loves / fell; where you fell you well began to print precious love / falls; falls wet with due to be precious / signs; signs attitudinal with cthe constitutional rights of preciously light / desires; desires to too two precious love / desireable; desireable, desired, destined, empowered, we are one by precious paces of love / directs.directs ssign to ascend and a brink called precious, love / Levels; levels and the finished versions of precious love / Sorted; sorted and coded by the preciousness in love / official in a visual way called precious codes / certain; certain of the curtains rip into the precious codes / perfect; perfect to a certain's precious accord / small; small is the little viewed inside a precious vein of love.

CHAPTER THREE

Dare; dare to care for the precious-ness of moods and excite for love / dealt; dealt a square, a circle rounds to find the pi of why we fly to a circled squire by a formula wet with rich aspire to the fir of precious-ness and precisely love / loves; loves to be my precious flight to the heights of confess and the grace of the better halls of ligths to lighter love / God; God is, reside in this, our precious love / hearts; hearts heal, hear, conveal, congeal, conceal, less than any convey of the precious arc of precise the spark to be renewed in precious love / hullo; kay, I will hull the lilies burst of precious-ness to explore the more of a gentle fest called life's buffet and we love / hearts; hearts in love's assign regard the one as the hard precision run to heaven's invent of love / flames; flames shout round the hours of precious in the soft regard for perfect love / dance; dance adjacent to your spiral of perfectly precious love / delights; delights decisive as a spirit released lifts to the lofty hills of precious relief and the treats of God is, love / gate; gates close to less-ons of precious love / choose; choose consistency of preciously love / maltese; maltese moods lend the sheltered reside at preciously love / keep; let's keep our love in deep to precious views of the living gift called lights of believe / maxim; maxim about the theory of precious believe / maxine; maxine met me at the sea of a deep regress to precious love / hummingbirds; hummingbirds live in a little tree called the house of a heel that lies knee deep in preciousness and wings that lift to the miracles view of maneuverable light and the life in you / store; store admire in your set of why we live and who we bet on as precious-ly love / stare; where can we stare at the sun, precious disk, in the preciousness of love / vacate; vacate more than less and agree to be precious to love / reside; God's reside is wide to the rich presence of precious-ly love / matisse; where is matisse when we release picasso's side of how it seems that we can melt our heart's belief to the canvas of preciously painted love / falcon; falcon found and flown to be the precious case of what we believe and precious love / choire; quate your chore to a choir precise and the precious burst of love / hidden; hidden in the hills reside the precious gift of love / memoir; memoir of the knights that drip with the finite belief of the definite drift toward the written life precious / tears; tears decide to desist for less than this precious digress to love / fears; fears fed precious equate to love / gone.gone to a cure of preciousness and now she's found near perfect love / memories; memories mend our hearts again, precious / grape; who knew grapes concord and the wines precious with ripened love / voca; temated vocate can cure our less and knowing more the cure of best, precious, working love / hawk; hawks hunt the message precious to love / commune; commune yes, precious, love / vine; vine venued by hued precious / bungalow; I am bungalowed in

the cottages of daring drift to the rides precious to love / cathedral; cathedrals convene at this precious love / veil; veil of surrender has come to gone to precious love / view; view another lover deep in the precious keep of where we keep our living love / cascade; cascade cure of this precious love / flower; flowers take deep presume to newer heights inside the bloom of precious love / aba; aba said abide beneath the willowed seed of faith in precious-ness / real; real sport, precisely, precious, love / flew; flew over precious-ness to love / insure; insure depths of precious-ness to perfect love / estates; estates of due to you and your crazy escape to insuring decide to preciously love / patcha; temple patch is found in the ground of a place called home and the arc of living in precious love / domeprecious; dome of the rock you own your precious love / bald; God's bald too and the love precious has come to own her own love / memory; memory healed by precious love / max; max is perfect to precious more, love / patcha; temple patch is found in the ground of a place called home and the arc of living in precious love / dome; precious dome of the rock you own your precious love / bald; God's bald too and the love precious has come to own her own love / memory; memory healed by precious love / foundations; foundations stretched to include precious love / furnished; furnished in a burnished preciousness for love / formations; formations furnished by a charging preciousness to love / founded; founded for the grounded preciousness for love / suggested; suggested and respected as a precious love / soothed; soothed in a related preciousness / stretch; stretch and the shores precious / stores; stores and the shreds off a precious life / stored; stored memorize of the rise unto preciousness

CHAPTER FOUR

Existential; existential experience, the impress precious with love / co-habit; co-habit here at the ledge which lends itself to the brink of preciousness and love / allude; allude to less and know the better true confess of security in our reform of the precious-ness of love / inhabit; inhabit pleasure with your co-habitive creative urge to merge with precious-ness in love / conquer; conquer your fear by living, hear, in the arms of precious see of love / altruist; all-true to the list called life is love in a constant hum of precious-ness and love / pool; pool your talents, your balance will be found in shekels abound around and through the splash of rich procure of the hearts that endure to precious love / glide; glide inside to the place where live meets give and know you have found your way home to the eternal explain of only, precious, love / pines; pines empower our hours of healthy rekindle with implore and more and our precious tasting breath of each other's nesting compare of the trees that recite the poetry of love / seclude; seclude yourself less and know yourself more in our kinder reflect of the perfect respect for the power of precious love / active; active again, I can live with you in the arc of begin and the activate of precious love / hire; hire precise agree as your content explain of the adventure precious, our love / succeed; succeed at the meeting of a happier greeting called greed has gone to dare and the care ofr perfectly precious, love / review; review reside at the stride of set on precious nets of love / soil; soil deep with the purple address of seeds we have planted and the precious confess or our heart-felt love / handy; handy man found in the rendevous of technically you are resplendent to marvelouw menus declarative of love / hell; *hell hath gone to a fury strewn with perfect reside at this precious love. *happy energy lends lasting exude to a higher spiral than this escapist reside at the dark side of nothing less than love / center; center cure, the core prefect to preciously love / tide; God's proud tide can floor your life with sandy sheets of raspy voiced admit of the early morning date with perfectly precious love / mineral; mineral matter mattered most in the plants of plenty blooming in me and my precious agree to grow with love / cords; cords are cut and now may we confess that the public address of positive approach to the rest are precious to us and love / bell; bells ring with inventive hums of precious avenues called the temples of love / ledger; ledger found written in the precious sanskrit concern for lessons yearned and presence paid to the honor of attendance in the song of absolute light / lodged; lodged at home, the precious one, home, heart, health / insist; God's insist is my convey, precious to love / inherit; inherit the merit of a land of your receipt of preciousness and love / inheritance; inheritance meets in the loving street of giving your best to those you love and your own heart is throne to the mattered most, your precious ability at agility in perfect love / ride; rides founrd to precious, love / ride; ride along the heated parallel to precious compare-less love / michael; God is michael's pleasure on a daily breathing arrival at the peaks precious with covered love / colored; colored curfew of the cure gone blind can come now that we are one in our living surrender to the plan called perfectly, preciously; every avenue, every oclor, every spark; God and you; God in you; one / colorado; colorado's cured and you can move on to the rocky ground called the estes land of precisely precious love / rainbow; rainbowed pleasure now can measure the getting around of an out-of-town called peace is perfectly precious to our love / drive; let us drive together to the pleasure of precious love / worth; worth a lot of this precious-ness, love / begin; begin again to be, precious, love / arizona; arizona deserts knew the sum in you and one life true to the lines of God in precious geographic love / hands; perfect hands healing precious commerce with man and the land of love / balls; balls that bounce and spirits too that now ascend to the plight of two who can collide at central regard to perfectly precious love / auto; automatic drives tht end preciously in love / ridge; excuse the ridge of the ultra view and know the picture inside of you and precious love / walnut; God's WALNUT tree is cabinet free and run by one, the tallest come to be, Metatron and me, one precious towering power of perfect love / moonshine; moonshine slips to the sight

inside our precious love / cycles; God is clear to previous cycles complete in precious love / cellular; cellular manner, man, the matter perfect, precious, love / celled; God is celled off to one bygone to be the perfect son opening soon in a heart near you, inside, precious, love / moonslips; moonslips bloom inside the beams of particulate reams of positive bless of the confess pure to precious bless of the lights of love / conjugate; conjugate great verbal abuse of the away all day to the days of perfectly spoken precious love / spanish; spanish spoken cures perfectly the press of convalescence precious to love / portugues; portugues portals plan ful-fill of the pleasures of filling lightly secure and eternally fit precious to love / secludeisles; of seclude can now conclude for the turht is home and the traveler come to rest in your hearth, your home, precious / latin; latin matters lean to remember can engender our perfect pair with the living play of an ancient fan of precious love / italian; rushing italian in concur of the calavacade of prefection and the red, white, and green precious to love / hydro; hydro here can every where in the stuffing less and the washing more the clear confession that we can send to precious friends and equative love / hydraulic; hydraulic lift to a hastening gift approaching soon to precious love / picasso; picasso is, yes, precious, love / commit; commit to God, perfect, precious / secular; secular yet, precious / life; life is and precious be to perfect we are to love / maxpresent; manner precious to who you present as maximum pleasure and love / humming; humming's come to us and singing sitll we near the peering arrive at seeing notes of winging precious and love / life; life held it's perfect as precious to love / regain; regain your gain to perfection seen in precious love / howl; where we howl is where we keen to the fowls of precious flowing love.

CHAPTER FIVE

Recent; recent in winning, I am ascending to perfectly precious love / relax; relax into hear and adhere to the fact that living is back in precious love / chosen; a chosen blend of the perfect matter called perfectly precious love / mattise; God is mattise in me and my completion of the perfection called preciously we love / bank; bank on best, the heart direct, and your true confess has won the heart of one who delivers the instant commit to preciously be your love / madagascar; madagascar rich in unusual's mix of the percentages bettered by preciously love / memorial; memorize the memorial servcing which rings truest in the heart of you and our humble good-bye to less than the precious in love / bed; bed of wed has gone direct to the heart of God's perfect in precious love / productive; productive measures have led me to a perfectly precious love / follow; follow me to the wedging oblivion of the hearty good buy that love can be in precious we ascend / path; a path found, I am home to the higher ground of grounded love / grapes; grapes that grew in precious bursts of bunches of living love / fresh; fresh enough to excell, I am well in the willowing seas of all that can be confessed as precious in love / hope; hope has come to won that's gone to the other blend and again we preciously love / homehome too perfectly precious in love / maxim; maxim is the measure of a koan called please be kind to the perfect mind of God's precious ones. love the light / product; let us produce products of perfect induce to the praticles of precious love / profit; profit best, love, precious / horse; please recall that a perfect horse can ride us to precious love / cove; cove of cure can lure your precious ones home to the lights of love / energetic; energetic in our ellestial light, I am right to the flight that's all that's left of the ride precious to love / crystal; crystal cure of the helaing properties of remembering that we are the one preciousness to growing to God / one; one time too, precious free in love / living; living cells of that perfect connect to the heart precious and love / cell; cellular nature required our hire of the perfect sword of michael's cure and the elevated release to the cure for preciousness, love / method; method of release has come to the crease that led to formerly love in the precious / Elijah; Elijah's religion won by the run to precious gratitude for the God of great full-fill and eyes of committed heal of the truth that's perfect to love / enoch; enoch knocked softly upon the door of ascendant matter and the angels of arcs collected the spark in to their own and owning this messenger knew their own companionship was rich in the grip of preciously love and the key of signing confession to the resplendent experience of knowing God we know transcendant regard for the preciousness of truth in love / spew; spewing less I concede that imbuing the planet with an objective matter is the scattering gone to collective resume of the precious enthuse that we call precious, love / elisha; elisha knew ascend in the winning rules of the middle ground and knowing this we know the rule of sandals down and heavenward gowns of wearing the hearts of men as the blend for God and the getting along to perfect love / eden; eden's release has found finesse in giving now this peace a rest and resting still I know compare that will desist as less than wowing delivery of initial lessons sessioning to the grasp of what our hearts can seek when we desire the gathering seas of heightening believe in the laws of men and the grasp of God in the light hu-man and the hearts that seek now know release to the perfect passage called lightly love / moses; moses mattered in the bliss of knowing elijah's true confess and convicted of pleasure they truly ran aligned with plenty and profound in the directive care of the where we go for preciously love / man; man has spoken and God has heard that we choose yes! as our new word of living confess to the ocmmitment made, love God. preciously / Pisgah; God's Pisgah is where I can be when my heart is mounted in the stiff delivery of what we promise next for precious love / exodus; exodus to the seeing amount of what we count as precious to love / gold; gold can cure the aching lure of lessons perfect and lights that send the ascension home and the heart to men in precious amend / alchemical; alchemical manners mattering and where's the friend who knows compose? richly ringing

near my nose with the capricious manner of a wooly lamba and the laughing regard for all that speaks of precious love / jung; essentially *Jung has found regard in the swirling lift ot the lights that sing the hearking relief of the arc complete and know the now the triple set of the hearts of God and the happy love of precious men. *juicy use of newest gifts, an insight-full measure of the reside called the heart of men, precious to love / receive; receive the rest of perfectly precious, love / earth; earth has ruled and run aground. God is home and melting downt he shards of time and the town has won the perfectly precious connect with living love / banks; banks that fill with the ruling moniker which states that a resonate place has turned around to reveal that heaven's gown is worn by precious filling fawns whi know the art of getting on with precisely precious love / release; release her now and know the best of getting on with bliss-full partnership in precious love / place; place yourself healed in the hands of God and precious love / freshen; freshen up your heart-filled manner with the planner called gracious pleasure in precious love / marketing; marketing has found a friend in our strategic manner called precious abide with living love / olive green; olive green is our godly goodly reign of the draping of healthy preciousness in love / command; command a reflect that is perfect in precious love / hallow; hallow treasure in the land of the precious gift of God's ascend and the glittering grace of all we've won for precious love / Sonoma; Sonoma valleyed getting on with the wine of life and glass of precious love / sunburst; sunburst nature of a man who can conceed to craving precious living love / sunny; sunny sides of the cradling town and the arc had finally run aground at the wealth of nations reigning down to rest in the cradle of precious love / mustang; mustang milly ran a filly 3rd degreed to the previous mark of precious galloping grace and love / dessert; dessert duels can ful-fill the wheeling regard for the happy spools of plenty precious to our love / bread; bread's best buttered with regard for the perfect toast of calling this perfection precious in love / house; house is home to the now in me and the all-ways in you and the art of being free to living perfectly precious to love / desert; desert's duel for the mountained peaks of pleasuring our place with precious love. define; define your desire to spiral hither with ascend to the strand of perfection called preciously we conceive of love / mans; mans found in the ground of stones that gilded will convey our desire to get away to precious love / arrow; arrow of plenty straight to me and my resplendent dignity now has come to preciousness in love / ecstatic; ecstatic to measures of yes! I will be eternally free and precious to living love / Material; material meets conceit with confess of a certain concern for the healing impress of precious love / eros; eros can give an effective resonance to the ovation called sexually we love, preciously / ecstasy; ecstasy can conceive of precious appeal to love / romance; romance ensues when our cues come from preciousness in love. tonight precious, love / rock; rocks know the ancient rhythms and the rhyming sensation of why we love to be precious / stone; stones of selfish giving in have given way to the higher day of precious, love.

CHAPTER SIX

Power; power and the allude unto a lightened preciousness called love / flexibility; flexibility agility and the muse of precious love/ magical; magical amuse too, the precious / fortunate; fortunate to be precious in our love / traits; traits and the revenues of precious love/ tablets; tablets turn to stones caled selves and certainly the spins to precious love / rainbow springs; rainbow springs up to a faith fulled with clues of the light of love's precious content / opal; the complexion of love is opal in seams of perfectly precious love / command; command confess of the perfectly precious aspect of love / honeysuckle; honeysuckle dream of the team that deals of only precious love / priest; priest found in Metatron's town knows the dure of the house that lures *melchizidek's perfect love. *matter elect to living concurrent with hidden insight zipped effectively to the defiant effuse of knowing your love / noah; noah's amping up to cast the ark upon the waters of lasting perfection and the flood of living preciously in living fountains of love / amp; amp the suspend across the beams of situation of extremes called deep compulse to a precious blend of love / arc; the arc of God is ascension road's command of the perfect extreme to precious is love / long; long I have tarried and oft I have seen the married appraisal of a house that is lean to recline in the living examine of precious expansions to love / tall; tall to all you have seen and the 13 I am in my absolute plan to land in the light precious / truth; truth to be and told are we of God's proposal of the age of new and old and the heaven's ring with the sealing proof of God's great eyes on your precious accept of love / loop; loop around to see your life adrift upon the lines of perfect love / leap; leap aboard and know the sword of sweet agree witht he ride to God and the heart of the free delivery to perfectly precious love / apple; apple apple in my pie called penned by the friend of preciously love / strung; strung up and precious untie to love / branch; branch conceed to the feeding ranch of those who choose to perfect exude the prancing preciousness of love / butterfly; butterfly breed and the I am led to lightly seen and the perfect flight to shining waves of airy sides called precious love / camp; camp, hear, upon the shores of hotter springs and wet with perfect lilies burst and the precious eddy called rehearsed by precious love / hands; hands up to precious love / doors; doors closed open up to precious love / arm; arm in arm and all around we charm the sights of kona town reigning down with precious love / compelled; compelled to spell it y-e-s precious, love / sedona; sedona sends a vortex ed breed of crystal clear delivery to the blended peace of precious love / heaven; yes, heaven is wide to perfection inside this precious love / sunburst; sunburst through and I m hued precise to precious perfection in love / saddle; saddle up to perfect love / ladder; ladder climbed and jacob is lined to fine concept and saying hello to a rainbow rules of precious love / know; know yourself well to healthy trails of precious love / leaps; leaps and bounds are met in fresh delivery of the freshening of beckoning love / rome; rome's rule is catholic deep in the vatican's channel of the duel holy and precious / roam; roam in the sound of a deep relax called perfectly clear to the heart precious and precisely love / Roan; Roan is round upon the top of a treasured grace called loved alot by precious light of love / China; China's town is toured as we kindle chill in the preciously alert conceed to perfect love / flag; flag furled windstorm deep to the steepincline and the resign to keeping it all aloft and all believed as blessed to perfect accept of love / lily; lily leafed lattice corked by reverse to the forgiving line called love's inside our precious press to living access to the leaves of light / upper; upper day and high to reslease and rise precious to a soul'd release that now reclines in a higher site of the cultural plural called delights and now we know the way to go to precious concepts of the hearts that freely lift to daily love / creek; creek deep in steep decend to the halving called and the perfect ascend of the matrixed all of which we climbed and the steps that dip to the hearkened kind who hail of love's preciousness / Jesus; Jesus joined jeweled relativity to mark the cradle of nativity, our heart with mine in a stable conceed that God is the coat and jesus the sleeve of a fabric called preciously, light / Christ; Christ can conceive that you can believe in the compassionate spark called living with sleeves of equal lenght and broader sight than a mission complete in an accomplished seat called the throne of God. elders know the lights below and see the dreams of daring contests and heaven's extreme to during your test know the answer's inside the question, why, because of Christ; know salvation; choose commit. *Christ; creative hope rules insistent in supreme truth of love / assure; assure a devote is the face of a vote called precious / mustang's; mustang's appeals are how we feel about the healing deals precious love / nepalese; nepalese align with this compare of the dare to confess this is the tallest bless of love / Anasazi; Anasazi drills the ancient in to real duress that drinks the lights precious to love / ancient; ancient truths compare this list with precious love times three / rod; rods exist to insist on our cones alone, precious / staff; staff, staff, recruit compute with the rod called God is eye-wide to precious, love / Christos; in the Christos as accrued we kno now the delaing fuse of enthusiastic creep to the push and the steep reclin in finely God is my precious keep of love / mesa; a mesa topped by exhausted water dance along the lines of precious links with the living God / tomato; God's tomato grilled with the grace-full appeal of a passionate stride to the ride that is real and precious / green; waves are green and in between precious / tabla; let us table our tabla rustic table deep to clearing set on the chairs of a furnished concept of precious / Rasa; today a Rasa ruled by 3 and found to 4 to really be and blessed sound of the squared precious / Africa; Africa found hallelujah ground by precious love / pearls; pearls encircle necks of profess of precious love /

cardigan; a cardigan worn precious to the sleeves of love / bred; bred won precious to love / rosary; rosary steep with the lips precious to love / Lenoir; *Lenoir is hilled valley wide by a trend to precious love. *lakes energetically near oceans in recall* / pigeon; pigeon rivered weathering in a run to tennessee and the truth of precious love.

CHAPTER SEVEN

Grace; grace has come to me and preciously love / mania; mania is over and I have met a match that is a perfect flash of precious love / manic; manic can screaming now become the lessoned fade to what's become this precious aspect of the hwipers called love / depressed; depressed can be gone to the eternally winged precious-ness love / regressed; regressed has found that all is aground and the cells are clean to how it's profund to decree preciously our love / transferred; transferred has gone to a clean degree of the well-ness said of the truth of mine and the respond to the response-able commend of the agility called acceptance of the precious code called God / transitive; you are transitive tot he love you give preciously / dramatic; damatic to conclude, you are imbued, with the acceptive dues of precious require to need true love / drastic; drastic dues are precious in clues to the heart of clearly God / streams; streams true to the precisely given living light that is a friend of precious God / spills; spills of pearls are precious to God / transitional; transitional measures of the pleasures precise to precious love / mossy; God is precious to a mossy grade of the mostly accrued rolling shades of glassy precious love / shift; shift to healed precious zeal called cautious gone to love / swift; swift too, precious / derivative; good derivative and the precious live of love / frame; God's frame clicked and wins the won of a picture perfect precious love / main; main stream to a trend precious / oberon; oberon gone to precious love / absolve; absolve a matter precious, love / resolve; resolve us as the precious cause of precisely love / awash; awash of the rivers red with precious love / odyssey; odyssey of God and free resolve to prospect for the gold of precious love / odeisus; precious to odesius aspects of drew the maine repair to square compare of love / review; yes, I will review the precious conceive of all-ways too love / one-half; let us one-half keep revealed the precious love / smell; smell a swollen well of lavendar preciousness called love / anxious; an anxious matter matters precisely preciously love / gone; you are gone to precisely preciously love / soil; soil sealed by the grassy congeal of depths of deals drawn precious in the sleeves of love / granite; granite greets our streets of precious love / bold; build your bold reveal of the precious up to seeming convalesce of lvoe / hazard; hazards gone to keep precious / lover; lover of the cover of the precious light / retreat; precise the retreat to precious love / canoe; yes we will canoe over the new of living precious love / boulder; gates to heaven boulder viewed by the triple confess precious to precision in bounds to love / clear; precisely clear to the hert of reside and the ride inside duress

precious to love / rims; arc rims hum preciously / Mt Zion; let us Mt. Zion claim as the name preciously loved / booth; God's booth is up to preciousness sold to love / tribute; my eyes are attributive to the tribute called love and a precious sum of one / strength; get strength to be precious / strand; pace the strand for precious love / portage; portage cured and the precious devote to love / help; bask in the help of precious love / above; above matter and the matter-less banter called beyond to precious within called love / surfing; God is surfing your preciousness and thin recite to love / oar; oar over to the precious, love / strap; strap on a zippered seat called the arms of precious to love / store; store a cure, precious / devic; devic is God's splendor of the render to deal at appealing confession of the precious in love / bold..bold enough to be precious / uphold; uphold seals precious / anchor; how far the care for anchoring is spare to the love precious / garden; yes, I am the garden of spare compare to the precious / inn; lady's inn, the won welcome to precious love / caper; caper cured by the records of zeal and the solve to the puzzle of peace and the preciousness of love / drift; acquire a drift to the table of preciousness and love / tributary; great to a tributary read of this precious stream called precisely love / impeach / precise / purposeful / prospital.

CHAPTER EIGHT

Rapid; rapid relief of what has been found in the higher ground in the oasis called perfectly quick to precisely God / steep; precious steepes are steep to God as ahead to precious love / deep; deep enough to embrace, precious, love / rise; rise over the heels of clicking ascend to the preciousness of love in ascend to lightly chosen love / pleasure; Mongolian pleasure can ascend to bounds of ice and the felt ascend to precious love / rates; rates read red by God's precious to love / jetty; let us jetty build for the arc upone the hill precious / jettison; let's jettison an absolved applause for the cause precious / kept; kept cured by the precious, I am assured of the debt paid, conveniently bby the precious / drift; God is adrift to the absolute precious / Nepal; Nepal knew nepalese review of the precious love / daily; daily long at the harp of God is precious / rapid; rapid dissolve of less and the precious love / pontoon; pontoons swoon with deep agree to the preciousness of love / solve; solve absolve resolve precious / Avatar; God is an Avatar and the star of the precious-ness of love / salvation; great salvation can accrue from the pearls of God is precious / solve; let us solve ourselves with preciousness and love / mooning; mooning agree is precious emotionally to me / estate; precision's estate is precious / frankly; precisely and frankly we agree to the light precious / raindance; God's covenant is a raindance with the chance to be surpassed by only the splash of precious love / rainbow; rainbow rules are precious to love / spin; spin shines precious in the eyes of the lights to love / blew; blew home to our desire of the precious conspire to constantly love / winds; precious to winds of the precious that blew to love / blow; earth's blow is the breath precious to love / gravity; gravity grew deep in your reside of the precious love / spun; absolutely spun to the conscious accrue of precious love / blown; blown to a blend of the winds of precious love / future; precious to a future of the order of saints and a faint reminder fo the arrival at precious love / cathartic; cathartic to a splurge of the precious love / ridge; a ridge around us in this town and the blue review of this precious truth called love / exotic; exotic clue is precious with this classic love / blue; blue days intrigued with the succeed of express and the embraces of perfection of the precious called love / summit; summit found and perfectly we knew the tables of precious love / premier; patiently precious and to the premier of the here we are to the arc of love / raspberry; lightly reigns the raspberry deem of the daring conceed that life is precious / curfew; a curfew over the I am covered by the convey of the clovered fields of green reveal to the light precious / plan; plan on doubling up to love's perfectly precious love / Sufi; Sufi's spun to perfect preside of the preciousness called spirals of love / cradle; cradles feel like lover's healed by the release of being deep in a dress of patiently precious to the rocking reveal of love / godiva; godiva found the beneath of reveal and the hair of perfect hounds betrayed by the bounding consent to perfectly precious love / unified; unified met, perfect, net to love / uni-celled; uni-celled one, precious / cassanova; cassanova cued by perfect love / mirth; mirth rules, love perfectly / wealth; wealth has won a perfect begin to a precious balance of a lion and lamb who forgave the brand, hu-man, to love / scientific; scientific trend to perfection and the living end to precious love / chemical; I am chemical to love's perfection to precious love / composed; composed to a cure I am sung by the seed of a germinating cause called the preciousness in me / cured; I am precious to cured by love / pheremonic; pheremonic reside at the glide to home and back again to the nose of perfectly precious love / hemmed; hemmed in news of precious to love / metatronic; metatronic sonnet has come to perfectly precious love / truth; truth told love's perfectly clear to love / pored; pored over and pierced to the clear expect of precious love / Madagascar; Madagascar ed to a promised cure called the land of conceed to the heart that is pure o the faith of God and the truth of love in this precious reflect of the respect called love / monarch; monarchs rule with butterfly degrees the butterfly daze of a perfect brain called thinking of only precious love / butterfly; butterfly blue in the mood for maturely precious love / bastion; bastion cast to the moon's preciousness / balance; balance amounts to the muse for precious / particular; particular in parallels spent for the precious / positions; positions chosen mend in the precious.

THE PRECISE-MENTS
LEVEL 10

CHAPTER ONE

Commune; commune precisely, love / communion; precise communion, love / straight; God is straight to the heart of precision in love / precious; precious is precise in good advice and kindly love / place; place preciousness in precise aside tot he graciousness of love / placement; placement is precise in a good advice called love / material; material pleasure can be measured by your precision in love / choose; choose precision in all days love / matters; matters material and mature aspect direct to the heart of the cure called coincide with precious love / rant; blend your rant with the knowing God who said get ahead get love precisely and due to you in review and grace and precious contentment with precisely love / suspend; suspend disbelief and blend with more or the concept of precision and the life of decision to support only love / chin; chin strap of the helmet worn to remember is precise in love / chimp; chimp of secure is heading to swings of the pen-tight confusion that's running in rings to the concentric heights of a healing explain called the life precisely breathing and the lavish between of it all called the sealings of love / equipped; equipped for kinship, we are mid-riff worn by God's breastplate of the precision line of aaron's faced respect for love / hermetic; hermetic sealing and I am healed with the perfect precision of the life that rules so complete to precisely love / prophetic; prophetic moon of the man who rules as the one I am and the hand of precisely the / man called love / fenced; fenced in by less I now know confess of the heavenly due called precisely love / lifts; lifts your spirit, the dove, the here of it all precisely to love / philosophic; precise in philosophic matter I matter more when I near the shore of alert to confess of love / perfect; perfectly precise to love / picasso; God is picasso in drawing me home to precisely love / commit; love is committed to the comet called you and your preciser love / memorial; memorial trine and the times called precision in time-less love / blend; blend in precisely, bloom, love / vacate; vacate the lessen and update confessing that you are precisely love / parks; parks appeal is real to the healed believe that love is rely in precision's deal on God / sail; sail to the matter that heaven is fatter for the precision to love / kentucky; kentucky can assign the line to a preciser time called now to love / carpet; carpeted kin can heal the halls of men with the light that's laid bare to compare of precision in love / alive; alive to a cure of the line called alive to precision of love / peach; peach regard can guard me less as perfect confession of the rest in precisely love / regard; God's regard is called precisely love / silver; let us ascend to a silver friend called a trace of precious love / trace; trace mend means a brace of face-less faucets of dripping confess to the precision of love / durable; let us be durable to truth and the confess of precisely God ahead, love / dalai lama; dalai lama gave good lift to the preciser gift of love, / himalayan; himalayan matters matter precisely to love / agent; agents of precision know love, precisely, light / octave; octaves of pleasure chilled with the trees of precision in hillsides and daring concede to the truth in the God-head called love / original; original precision has the mention of the convention called precisely we love / aspirant; aspirant measures of deep attire try to stare at the heart that's higher than all the less of forgetting your friend as lessened precisely by love / eloquent; eloquent acquire of an essential compare that kindly and lightly and often repaired the precisely intended decide of love / acquire; acquire precision / worth; worth some, more, love that's precise / elegant; an elegant gent knows desire is precise in a blend of transcendent love / attire; attire handed over has become my own and I own the land of my happy home and home to the feat beneath my guards I am contented by my regard for the light precise to men / set; set yourself on I am and will your perfectly accessible self precise to love./ adore; precise adore has come to the core of believe / worn; God is worn by the softer metal of a preciser love / self; self seen on a post of the will called God and the heart called home, precisely, love / stones; precise as a stone, we alone can see the strand of precision and the blends of men and the central plan of the creative fan who's reside is in me and our quiet regard / prayer; love is a prayer and knowing we this, we begin our concede of the definite mark called preciously precisely love / chants; chants pulitzer can agree that during this day we can conceive of the precision to love / stance; stance inside the begin again to precisely love / truth; truth told I am old to knowing the precision in love / tank; tanks plan on gaining ground to the sound of precision / perfection; perfection, perfect, pen of the hand of an eternal success and the love of begin and the life of examine can begin to take an end to the perfect lend of precisely love / terrific; terrifically speaking, I stride like a wide receive to the breath precisely spoken love / chance; chance to take the precision love / daily; daily deal of we'll be precise to love / renew; renew askew? reside inside the regain of precisely love / talent; talents line up to the precision of weathering deep in love / precision; precision in mystical musical conceit of the contemplation called God and the heaven replete with love.

CHAPTER TWO

Satire; satire concedes to the breed that ill live by confessions of faith and the age of release to precisely love / acquire; acquire inquire by the breed of the best who conceive of the less that is loved / act; act on this our conspicuous love; precise in device of the living one / fact; fact of the matter that the matter is better with precisely love / erect; erect regard can best reward the rest of precisely love / patient; patient precise and concise to concede of the precision of love / delivery; delivery set on a met rewarded precision of love / inquiry; inquiry queried about, precision in love / definite; definite to a note of an afternoon's regard and the reward for precisely love / dolly; dolly daily in dolls of life and give your love the feeling precise of an aspect deep to revealing bliss / dolly's; dolly's deal is real in precise advice of love / daily; daily dues of the precision of love / hampton; hampton hills are deep with green confess of the precision of love / cope; a mother's cope is ecstatic in precious reside of the precision inside and to love / copes; copes accrue inside of you and your precisely given love / practice; practice hour-ly and review the precision of adolescent love / perfect; perfect friend and I am something written about the limbs and the lambs of the God-head precise to love / genuine; genuine matter of the chatter called bliss and the rambling reside in the side of a kiss called confessions of precision in love / genetic; genetic decide to believe in precisely loved / genealogic; genealogic and logically sent to the astrologic glee of absolutely and resolutely free reside at precision in love / grant; grant true too and precisely love / doctrine; doctrine of the option to function perfectly in the precision of love / treaty; treaty planned for the man who is precise in lightest love / northern; northern nestle in the bless of winning daily deliverance to the preciser views of love / territorial; territorial matters now precise matter more in their concise approach to precisely love / conventional; conventional convene can loudly ring in the well presided over living laughter, precisely, love / facial; facial fair and the precision of pairs of contented smiles at potential love / racial; love is a racial blur and the taking care to precisely see that we are the lines of insight-full glee and all that we are to grace this round of getting on with love / income; a priceless income can reside at the conquest of precision and the precious lend of the labors of love / transact; transact a renewed desire to higher spiral in the ides of love / rational; I will be rational in my precision of the decision to lightly love / federal; federal matters will require that heightened attend of a national be on the in debt removal by the precision of love / act; a perfect act the committed reside in the preciser side of love / national; live in a national abide and let your life find a ride to the beginning ascend to precision in love / state; let us state the true desire to precisely care for daring love / exchange; exchange this rate with precision for love / tax; tax this ration less and reward the precision of this test with precious we can love / seventy; live seventy times seven and again to the precision of love / sevens; sevens timed to abide with the precision of love / forget; forget invent and invest in the heaven sent chance to ascend to the abundant phase of the precision called love / line; great to a line of precision, I AM meant to reinvent the blessings of love / why; why is the reason and because the cause is precision we can win again in the questions of love / forgive; forgive and forget and know the higher bet on the precision precise within love / living; living with love and finding a friend can let heaven now begin. Contest ends and precision wins the award of faith / context; context concludes that processes win the precision again of prophetic love / commune; commune with the moon of a lighter request for precision in love / residence; reside in the residence of perfectly precise to love / buy; buy a new dignity finding precision in love / convent; the convent of invent is having nun of less than precision in love / contract; contract to be precise in your love for me / offer; offer to live precisely forever with love / content; God is content with me, precisely / heart; a heart that can will be precisely loved / home; home to a matter of providenced reside at the precision of love / happen; happen to find a preciser love / God; God is the chance to advance to precision in love / hear; hear me precisely, love / stand; light can stand in the conceptual sphere of near the construct of precisely love / is; is this test true, confess, precisely love / here; here we nightly sing of the

precision of love / defend; defend your digest of the investment in professions of love / home; home is hear and precisely heard, love./ hearth; the hearth is foundational to a love that is rational to precisely, love / precision; precision is the quip, loved.

CHAPTER THREE

Palate; palate of love and in we believe of the rays of precision in the winds of love / vaunt; vaunt your talent and know the balance of the reinvent of precision in love / count; count on your views of precision in the numbers of love / congregate; last of the congregate has come to the precision of the permanent surface of love / valve; let us be valued by the Christ of precision in love / value; price your value of the precision of love / instill; laughter can instill your precisioned reveal to precisely be loved / consonant; consonants said vowels can preside at the overing troops of precisely love / vets; gather vets wet with precision in love / hills; hills of home and the beckoning throne of receiving divinity in precisely love / homes; let homes elope and see the precious reside of precisely love / spirits; spirits sail to precisely the sights of love / honesty; honesty is God's believe in precisely our love / hope; hope to be lightly precise in love / graves; God's graves are released to lightly precisely love / honor; let us honor precision in the heart of this our halls of love / haunts; haunts escape to the lights of precisely love / groves; groves grew green in the preciser scenes of lightly love / forms; forms defend our right to be integral to the alls of loving precision / ravenous; ravenous regard is precisely in the lines of hungry to love / crates; crates accrue at the balances due to precisely love / found; absolute is found in the deeper splash of the relative grasp of our breathing precision to love / rap; God's rap is abreast our precisioned love / curly; curly views of the precise news that God is, love / Fonder; plan on fonder views of the preciser news that you are elected to give in to love / Race; Race rules precisely within the ascendant friends of precisely love / curve; curves are due to the cue of when a star meets the state of the suns of precisely love / spurt; spurts can rest at the healing convert of all over the eights of the lights of devote and daring concede to the living precision of life / kirk; kirk's news is that the county's view is of precisely love / driven; driven to exceed and success can breed the precision of living love / dares; dears that care can take the dares of spelling precisely l-o-v-e / stares; life can start when your stares become the dares of precisely love / drives; drives abroad the spilling sight of a cause for applause called precisely love / curt; curt can be precise to love / stripes; stripes are steps to the preciser let of love / suspend; suspend alliterative allegations and know the nations of altruistic precision in love / findings; findings found give the grail the holy veil of living's precision and love / tailings; tailings true to precisely love / surrender; surrender God's spelling touch as teaching us to find true love / cup; aspect of the cup of brazen precision, love / mines; mines of the gems of the living kind of the heart of man and God / kinder; kinder is the fire of the compel to precisely love / courts; courts that gather the best of lips and the jesters brush of the laughing ascension called precisely love / joint; your joint ascension is due to the calling home of the ones who too are precise in love / fair; fair enough energy to believe in precision's gift to love / fripp; fripp is fare to the caring arrival at the full survival gone complete to ascension's seat at truly, love / hart; hart of the dynamic called the smattering of precision in love / hare; a hare too dear has brought a fear to complete precision / trips; trips are light when the rights of express know the bliss of primary collision with precision in love / buck; buck the trend to giving in and know the stiffer deal of precisely love / fare; fares due, precisely, love / trails; let trails expand to include the preciser hands of love / truth; truth of the matter God is fatter with love's process and the precision of your heart / lighter; lighter let's be to precisely love / burn; burn the banner, God is man's best friend, ascend, bliss, love, precision's sweet flame / early; early to the heart of you, I am ascendant tot he friend called God / Stage; stage one, precision / yearn; yearn to burn with precision / earth; precisely this earth can give the mother to us / speak; I need to speak of precisely love / spake; truth spake precisely of love / frail; frail enough to precisely bless this advise of the concede to profess our love / spare; precious and spare to the constant care of precise our love.

CHAPTER FOUR
Nape; the nape of the neck of a nest called rest has now come abreast the breathing reside of the healing inside our kind residual of the middle of precisely love / neck; neck of the date with precision's contend for especially love / froth; frothy master of the matters won for arc-angelic concede to the burst of precision / tuck; tuck in precisely, now / throat; a throat shut deep to the lesson learned and again we yearn for the tribal ascend to literally and precisely love / trek; bless this trek with an aspect complete to the set you have drawn deep into precision's hum of love / islands; islands precise in the heart of man can ascendant stand for the precious and precise contend to love / outer; isles of outer and within the precisely way we can begin to powerfully ascend to love / banking; banking in believe we conceive of the relieve of all our debts and lightly gathered principle points all deposited in precisely love / tips; tips true to heightened precision clearly thought to love / trains; trains dance at a chance to track our loving precious / coiled; coiled respect for the grand reside to precisely love / tales; tales accrue of who you were to precisely love / trances; trances decreed over are less and often left to the precise complete of all we are to love / pulled; pulled apart to start the togethering of pinpointed precisely by love / tail; tails flash and head on up to the quaint precision of love / expand; expand to slighter precision and love / expanses; expanses seal our possessive deal with respective congeal of all the facts that dates can bring and the wider planes of precisely love / rapes; rapes only contest is who will prevail when the trail leads home. Regarding explain know that you will ensue to regard precisely love / effervesce; effervesce the bubbly nest of a nicer deal that God is real and the God-head said know the mind of a higher line and the precipitate manner of the banner over we are precise to bubbly love / rapture; rapture on to the rewards of praised

by precisely love / grill; grill grace-fully and precisely to the well of love / rescind; rescind respites entwine with me and my rest in precisely love / rapture; God's rapture is the pleasure of precision / take; take a tour of pure precision, love / caves; caves concur that we can abide at the ride tot he center of the Earth's recline in precisely love / primal; primal nature's feel is fed by the heal of real we said and precisely love / Dionysian; dionysian nurtures are the nature of the respect-full precision called love / neanderthal; neanderthal's all and more to perfectly precisely love / tribute; tribute to the treasure of pleasure's liberate and precisely love / bachan; bachan natured reveling rocked the sphere of higher rings of concentric examples of the sample of eggs who live in the seas of spartan precision and love / dan; dan across the land of lost tribes of giving forgiven precision to love / tribal; tribal to pleasure I am the measure of a heightened ascend to the friend precise to love / olympian; olympian success is yours direct to precision's release to love / athenian; athenian nature is the feature direct to the reflect respect-full to a Greek consign called the sacredly direct to precision's alert parthenon called love / gladiate; Cleopatra's gladiate was great Antonic colonic fend of the asp's believe in precision and winning love / huge; huge digress to the dire gone clean to precisely love / titan; titan nature cloned the gigantic land of a sign of God that's precise to plans of love / roman; roman natives kneel sincere at precisely love / kill; *kill the feel of precisely less is paralyzed , still, to partnered love. *kindly instill a lighter life / colossal; colossal nature of maturely spoken ascend to the speak of pleasant precision love / murder; feels like a murder is dead to the eternal and now we begin to release all the blends of the living ascend to presently and precisely love / daring; daring to deal with the feel of reminiscent to precisely love / stand; stand on the decide to preside in precisely love / stuff; won stuff that was precisely love / spat; spat on defensively and precisely to the offensive move called love / stare; stare to compare your eyes to precisely love / still; still to enough precision in the beginning called love / spurn; spurn your set of the less, confess this love / stab; stab precisely love / seals; seals secure in the security precise to love / spur; spur success on, begin to be precise / heels; heels sit deep in deft the precision to love / tragically; tragically tuned to the lower moon, know precision and proceed to humorous love / mythologic; mythologic magic is precise to love / achillean; achillean hills of reside are in the preciser repeat to the strength of the heels of walking to love / hard; hard to a nature of pressed release to the repeats of conceived bisexual streams of stiffer precision in love / Zeusian; Zeusian pleasure's measure is beginning to arrive at precisely love / hellenic; hellenic explain of rich proclaim to the precision of love / narcissus; narcissus struck by precisely the selves of love / floral; floral nature's bloom is precisely love / lithe; lithe to an erupt of best and I consign to the precision of love / brush; brush a repeat with a performance sweet to precisely love / bright; bright enough to probe to precisely love.

CHAPTER FIVE
Sprite; sprites trill with the devic fountains found blessed

by precisely love / fairy; fairy's enough to prayers of living significant to precision in love / dervish; a dervish wins a swirling feel of precisely love / devic; a devic due has become the preciser sun of the sum called love / tom; tom is true to the trip called precision is, love / turtles; turtle doved the islands of jesus won to the bubbling relief of rest-full too precision's love / cap; truth can cap your thirst of precision / calax; calax won by swollen sum of precisely love / mystical; mystical measure of the precision called love / mist; misty view of the decision to view our precision as love / conquer; conquer precision with the decisive days of precision in love / mist; mist is precise to the advice of precisely floating love / bliss; bliss is come to the precision of love / transcend; transcend to truth in precision's agree and the brush with love / isles; isles filled with the eyes of precisely cycladic erupt of the Grecian decision called love / measure; measure meets deep delivery in the pressing contest called lifting precisely to love / boundary; boundary found in loving cascades of precisely love / town; a town true to precisely love / mete; mete out your boundaries less, love / fence; a well is a fence that can be owned if less is moaning more of precisely love / tap; tap your source precisely / bound; bound to be precisely love / height; height reached precisely / tuck; precise tucks into love / traipse; traipse across the dividend's land called befriends love / dime; rain has come to a the dimes we've won and precisely love / sandy's; sandy's here in the precise revelate that mushy dates are dry with love / tucker; God is tucker and food and precisely love / dome; dome of someone loved / drainage; drainage can be due to the central portals of love / thunder; thunder burning precisely, love / deal; deal lightly with precisely love / outage; outage of the shouting outrage against and for precision in love / windy; windy willed precision love / southern; southern scales of the weights worn lighter by precision in love / hostile; hostile days are over and deep to precision in love / push; push for precision / hospice; let us arise hospitable to a hospice adept to precision in halls of love / push; push precisely on to love / egyptian; egyptian nature, precise / hospitable; deeply hospitable to precise love / frond; fronds woven draped in precision is, love / piercing; a piercing desire to proceed lightly to love's precision / spills; spills concealed revealed by precision in love / suspense; suspense spent on precision / drunk; infinity drunk on a win called precisely love / spoils; spoils of a particular nature, precisely to love / spunk; spunk can be preciser had to love / drank; drank enough to residential be to precisely we are love / spurn; spurn less, yearn best to practical precious love / spank; spank another less, concur precise to love / suspend; suspend suspense and a butterfly flown to fields of graciousness generous to precise regard and love / sarcophagus; sarcophagus sealed by the open reveal of precisely love / crypt; crypt's reflect can now respect precision in love / ear; ears can cure precisely heard echoes of a living nature called love / eye; eyes wide with truth precisely to love / horus; horus eyed wide by assign to an oath of an ankh called love in precision / left; left over precisely, love / right; right on to precisely love / sphinx; sphinx sealed is open now to precision's translate to love / schooled; schooled by agree

to be precise to love / mystery; mystery's school can be tooled to repair precision's love / collegiate; collegiate teams of the category freed to precision in love / egyptian; egyptian culture mattered precisely to symbols of rest-full precision's preside.

CHAPTER SIX

Purely; purely seen on the edge of a dream is a door to more than we ever seem to precisely know of love / told; told the truth of examining you and precisely love / spoken; spoken matter mattering to the overall consume of precisely with love / proof; proof is due to precisely love / ascends; let ascends become begins to precisely love / waterfall; a waterfall deep with the splash of pure reside at the heart of the precise presence flowing with love / river; a river resides rock deep in the rills of the watery preside called preciously precise to love / sides; sides chosen chill in the middle to jell at precisely love / fountain; fountains filled fields of forget with the resilient remember of the heavenly bet on precision in love / surrounds; surrounds are due to our concur with precisely love / preciously; preciously precise to the presence reviewed by precisely love / faith; faith found has healed my sound of precision in love / woven; woven dreams are extremes to the web and the flow of precision in love / in; in betweens and all arounds are the middle days of dreams of precision in love / alluring; alluring in I am is the endurance of assurance to the presence precise and the sizes of love / gorgeous; gorgeous and precise, I AM / lovely; lovely to the day of planes of expand, I AM precious in my precise begin to regain the strength of precious love / wonder-full; a wonder-full measure has compared and all we've found is how we're there and precisely love / desirous; desirous of eternal reside, I am fine to continual explain of precisely love / desirable; desirable to a magnetic moment, I am worn by the wands of precisely love / internal; internal to a treasure, I know the measure of precisely love / interior; interior scene, precisely, love / floods; floods consume the perfect presume of precisely love / lighter; lighter still to precision's wheel of love / dangers; dangers gone to the precision of love / sexy; sexy explain of the living proclaim of precisely my love / courageous; courageous man kneeling in elective stays at the precision of love / trait; a trait true to the truth in you and precisely love / heartfelt; heartfelt measures of precision's place in love / lather; lathering up to bubble in precisely love / miss; miss me more than precisely- God / over; over due to a precious share of the precision called love / pasqual; pasqual pleased with the precision of love / proust; proust about the lasting measure of precision pleasured by precious love / perry; let us parry less proclaim the precision of clearly our love / puncture; puncture your heart less and know the precision of sphere we love / pulse; pulse beat precision / accessible; accessible measures of the pleasures of precisely love / charge; charge ahead to precision in love / defend; defend your position by living delicious in precisely love / declare; declare yourself precise to love / food; food is a deep dish of the delectable wish called precisely love / repast; repast is hear and I am clear to the ringing well of filled by precisely love / resurrect;

resurrect the desire to higher spin with your friends precisely / denote; denote your devote as the wide hello to precisely love / deliberate; deliberate on the precision of love / desperate; desperate to a measure, the pleasure of measures of the forgiving nature of precision in love / disparate; disparate matter mattering in desisting from existing and living precisely loved / dosage; dosage due is the amount of you that is precise in love / intonate; intonate the cure for precision and the match that is thrilled by procuring devotion for you, precisely, love / record; record your delight with the pleasurable sit of precision's ringing clear / relate; relate debate precisely, love / absolve; absolve yourself, know, precisely, love / solve; solve the captured wallowing of precisely love / clear; clear enough to see precisely / cast out; cast out less with more precision / melts; melts enthuse with the news precise to love / pictures; pictures moving to include the front and the top and the back of news, now moving, to precisely love / trails; trails occur inside the duns of precision in love / flower; flower about precision, bloom / tower; a mother's tower precise in advice on love / conspire; conspire to hire a knowing compare as the only companion to lightened precisely by love / wonder; wonder why compare is made and be precise about it, love / winged; winged arrival now can be the heart of your declarative desire to know the world of precisely, love.

CHAPTER SEVEN
Entire; entire conspire of howling need has gone to agree to the wholer dare to care for previously precisely love / teal; teal enamor of the care for the cavorting dare of dearly precisely love / curl; curl cool to sharper degree of the address and the delicious location of the bliss in this bless and the bless in this adoration of the contestation of the nation precise to love / concavity; concavity of the gravity has turned out convex and twining in signing I am aligning to deals of dearly we are winning the daring congeal of the angelic tribe at the arc on the hill, precisely, love / cavity; cavity of the gravity turned inside out to declare all the wares as healthy about the life gone to magic and the magic gone blessed by the hurtling accelerate of the date that is contoured by the desire to fly higher to precisely love / open; open to your need to confuse your greed less with desire and know the higher concede to all that's revealed of precisely love./ trusting; trusting the deal and the congregation grown deep to precisely love / transparent; transparent to need I can believe in the letting grow of all we see to precisely love / clearly; clearly drawn and precisely done to the elections eclectic to the electron called love / truly; truly yule is desirable by the fire of precisely love / dare; dare to care about the precision of how you love / daily; daily dear to the dare about the mission of ignition and blast off to precisely love / courteous; courteous enough to knock on less let's confess our mutual desire to fly higher than we've been and to circling land in the land of begin and the hearts of listing precisely to love / temperate; private is the temperate and we are secure to the alluring hush of graciously, precisely, love / sold; sold to ascend and the hands that hold our hearts as worn to precisely sold on love / traits; traits true enough

to live with and daily precisely love / frames; frames of the freed up scene of the being loyally and privately designed picture of the nature confessed as precise to love./ pink; pinkest matter is the better hustle to a muscle flexed perfectly and precisely how to be love / purple; purple pleasure measuring the direct decide to agree to precisely delve into the seas of transcendent love / voyeur; a voyeur to pleasing I am allured to the delicate sneezing of a natural curve that led, God Bless Us, directly to you, precisely / bless; bless your duration and knowing this nation and the national debit of a third rank degreed to precisely love / bootes; bootes is the star that is far and away committed to love in orgasmic ascend to the heart of the universe within and precisely due to love / arcturus; arcturus matters affective to effective and a directive precise to a life called agreed to and precisely found by love / please; please invest in the heart that is best and the one that you own precisely / port; port of the part called daily this boat lands at precisely love / portal; portal precious and precociously won by the dealing sum of daily won, precisely / plan; plan on precision in love / decide; decide who will win precisely / attendant; attendant manner and the matter that's wet with the book of john and the seeing descend into matter deep with richer precision and love / attentive; attentive to God's inventive precision / traffic; traffic is less precise than concepts of the air that you cure precisely by love / trait; traits of love precisely on time and off the dime of forever / life; life led by the looks and book of fortunate matter grown lovingly deep in the maturity of give and the softness of keep the taking lean and the grandeur green with precision / love; wine wet and red with love, I am beloved by those who care for precision / lift; let's lift our drift to better stays at precision in love / campaign; campaign daring to caring precision / voyage; voyage of love to the preciser dove called preciously loved / agile; agile to heal and I can seal the precision to love / agility; agility's ability is perfectly keyed to profession of love, precisely / athlete; athlete's aspects return to procure only the best of living precision and love / durate; try the purate of the durate to precision / compute; compute cute to believe and precisely desirably acutely and accurately love / countenance; countenanced measure of the cured precisely by love / penetrate; penetrate precisely on love / shop; a better shop of precision in love / machine; a machine that is keyed up by precision in love / chairs; God's chairs are sealed with backs to precisely love / glass; glass that is precisely cut to durable succeed and lvoe's relieve of the aspects of truly conveniently professional love / table; table atop a rock called the me deep and green with precisely love / curve; love's curve is direct to precisely conveniently living love / abide; abide in us and the bidden grace of precision's love / counter; counter your countered intelligence with a higher dove's accepting ascend / titillate; paint a new believe with your titled conceive of the titillating patterns bellowing for attention due to the doves of love precisely / true; true to God's precision is the living in of love / taos; taos can become an elegant play upon the tongue of a deeper side that has agreed to meet the need for eternal internal light, precise to stay connective to the artistic stay at the will precisely agreed to the soul's release and the light's ascend and the fight's agree to be over for love / confer; confer agreed profess precisely love / concurrently; concurrently wide to wisdom precise in our love / pleasantly; pleasantly precisely professionally loved / pleasant; pleasant to more the adore of precision in love / perfect; perfect to the I am and precise is ascend to love / precisely; precisely I believe in the precision of love / Pathways / Stars / Pleiades.

CHAPTER EIGHT

Rose; rose red blue and true with precisely love / aspire; let us aspire precisely to love / confide; confide is agreed with precisely love / convey; convey precision in precisely loves / concur; concur that agree is precisely dealt with in love / concise; concise agree to precisely lived our love / concede; conceded to need our precision eased by love / contour; contour the load to agreed to share and caring found the passionate plan of lightly precisely love / collide; collide at festive agree of precision in love / avenue; an avenue conveyed by precisely love / stitch; stitch a line of conveyance to lightly love / stall; the stall is over and the squall has come and the moment occurs to the heart of the sun and the lights that's inside our profession precision with love / beg; beg less and know more. God's wait is over and the begging shore of wailing is walled away to the other side of precision in love / balance; God's balance is conveyed by professional precision in the attendance you pay to love / blend; blend precisely in your professional approach to all you convey about true love / stay; let us stay precise in our preciousness / wade; love's wade is precise to preciously loved / work; works wed is due to you and your preciser view of the loft called love / wealthy; wealthy in my dance upon the waters of precisely love / wedding; love's wedding is hear, precisely / wave; wave upon the winning over called crazed by the suns of dancing dining confining love / worth; worth the given code declared of precisely love / want; want to wear it now declare and precisely loved / winning; winning given and declared as precisely loved / stake; let us claim the stake desired as precisely wired to love / share; share the share of infinite love with all who precisely love, God is, and that's all there is to it throughout the span of all-ways / dividends; dividends due to precisely conveyed concede to the lights of precisely bliss-full, contents of love / deign; deign yourself as due to be precisely loved / abstain; abstain from precision less and know the heart of love / empty; empty respect can convey more when the shores are reached by the doors of precisely loved / implore; implore more absolute precision in love / settle; laughter is settled as all there is to it of precisely why we engage in love / solve; solve your riddle and engage in a precise solution called love / rest; rest, hear, love, precisely / respect; respect the director's win of the academy called precisely comes our heavenly love to eternity's sway of the picture above, God / reside; reside precisely in love / exact; exactly seen and in the lean to a primer track called God is back and oft we knew of the truth of why we lie for less and thus we do confess exactly, precisely love / summation; in summation of the scene we kindly stake our arms on grades of life conveyed and the heart of the

pawn and the truth of where we are getting along to and God is, precisely, love / emphatically; God is imbued with emphatically you and where you convene to drawing the lines of the precision in time and all we conveyed of the practical side of precisely loved / succinctly; succinctly said precision's led to perfectly love / right; right to I am and scene to deliver I am precise in my giving quiver laced with the arrows of disaster-less trace to the place called preciously, precisely I AM / judge-mental; judge-mental less and all-ways sacred and to this I concede and precious agreed to the courting with love in precision / joint; joint devote can float the barge of precision to conditions of love / juried; juried and controlled has gone away to conveyed by precisely love / concur; concur that you are precisely, loved / concise; concise to exhumed and the relevant convey of the lifting song called humming away to the grounds of precisely love / exceed; exceed the knot and know the way of One who sees that all can stay aligned to precisely love / concede; concede your need to transgress less and know repression's done. We are the One conveyance and surveillance called precision in love / precise; I am precise to love / excel; Care about excel in well we loved precisely / lit; lit by a light of within this delight I am sufficiently led to the perfect love of a permanent reside which has come tot lightening kind and the softening love of all who lend their hearts to knowing, remembering, abiding by, precision's devote to real love / lifted; lifted the trance and entered in to the game called the dance and divinity's dove and eternity's swallow now can devote her life to the living and her arc to the note of only the living reside at the way we all go the way of compassion's delay and the wait for the note called precision in love / gifted; gifted beginning to know now the way to a lighter day giving and an enlightened ascend to the decision to grace this centrifugal win of precision's new stay at precisely loved / gave; God gave you a winning perfection of the healthy regard for a house call the car of exactly this precisely given love / grew; grew to within and lightening knew the thunder of love residing in you and your preciser lend to exactly love / thirds; third's exude is precision in more than all we regard as love / halves; halves can be known as the thirds alone of precisely ell to the ones below and all who confess of the matching ascend to all we stress as perfectly love / all; all in all and perfect too and valued by matters of the heavenly due to precisely love / one; one more time and all that's inside is one perfect now, one precisely how of how we so precisely ring around the throne of passionately, God / Celtic / quilt / map / position / ireland.

THE PERFECT-MENTS
LEVEL 11

CHAPTER ONE

I AM; I AM perfect in my exam of the exact precession to perfectly, love / perfect; God is perfect to love / pert; pert to exert for the best and the I AM of the lamb of God / proud God is proud of me and my passage through to perfectly love / dotted; dotted eyes and constant abides at the perfect contentment of love / wall; walls of intrigue with the crafting light of the welcome sight of the landing zone called perfectly love / bred; perfect in our bred reside I AM inside the eyed align with daring to be perfectly God / Gene-d; God is gene-d in deep receive of the well respected rights of lightly perfectly love / gemmed; gemmed by jeweled receive I can believe in the receive of the hemmed degree of a stem of a flower called lightly perfect God / Convened; convened at convention of the dare to compare the mention of less as knot happening again and a letting in of the concept perfect / conveyed; conveyed and consigned as the perfectly aligned living breath of the avenue called directly you are the precious One , love / renewed; renewed perfectly to the lifting exude called cured by my love and creeling away to the Southern extreme South Pacific and learning to need the heat of perfectly, love / exhumed; exhumed and extensively checked for every crack, I know the perfection of a higher direction called the resumption of the post healing see of perfectly me, love / sold; sold to the squares of a capable pair of a precious jettison of the living I had lost and now at this of arrival, I reside in the side called the light of perfection / bold; bold to agree and enough to be free and excellent exude of perfectly love / seen; seen by daylighted excite, I am resumed to the seas of the precious re-entry to the arcopense of perfect love / exactly; exactly you and I exude the precisioned degree of a perfect entry to love / perfectly; perfectly given to the living ascend, Christos in sparkling forgive of the appeal to zealously love / hole; tonight I am light in a whole called forgive and a hole called the less can now disappear to the overage 20 .heard around the word called perfect to love / whole; whole enough to heal and we will real in perfect ascend to love / home; home to the moon and the billowing mood of a living return to the home that we love and the God of great degree perfectly to love / true; true to agree to the degreed perfectly to love / define; define this design this most of all care and this candle of light which burns in the air of an arcing re-entry to the pair who compare only to love / delight; shuttered by delight and the knowing incite of a perfect inferno called living in love / place; place your thrust at the trusting crux of why we believe in coming to be the God-head succeed of perfectly love / examine; examine this face, this passionate embrace of the stammering sealed and the headlines revealed as we continue to believe in the love that we own, our own, perfectly / touch; touch the perfection of love / allure; alluring design and the sign of a cure called the care-full appeal of all that is real to perfectly love / connoisseur; connoisseur of the cure and the elevated days of elected ways to wed at the place of an electric breeze called lightly the seas of the splashdown, perfectly, to love / brag; brag about the love you've had and all you will continue to fill in the heartbeats called perfectly love / fond; fond of intrigue and truer still and I am the deal of a truest resume called perfectly love and the man of God, perfectly / fonder; fonder still and all-ways seen and I am perfectly love / fondly; fondly scene and call it lean to the wonder of God perfectly / oh, yes, love; God is oh, yes, too love perfectly / yes-sing; yes-sing, I am, and the hurt is revealed as only a seal on this being a man, call the doctors away, I am healed perfectly / guessing; guessing you knew, I knew it too, perfectly / got it; got it all perfectly / found; found in the fields of a lifting introduce of the islands of love and the ascension complete with perfect love / settled; settled in to the matter, I am growing fatter on perfectly love / lovely; lovely appeal and the wholer reveal of the cured become too and the also we know has led to a heartened man called perfectly, love / lightly; lightly due to our exude is the resonant agree to accept the fee as paid perfectly by love / loving; loving the cure and loving's the healed reverie called know your presume as less and all we need to know perfectly is love / lovingly; lovingly done and to the eyes comes the delivery called straight ahead to perfectly, love / pleasantly; pleasantly done, perfect love / candle; candle of the cure perfectly, love / pleasant; pleasant to degreed accept of the doctrine perfect, energy / cured; cured of all that ailed, energetically sealed, perfection in love / canticle; canticle of a cured perfection love / clavicle; clavicle clued to the clue that flowers the knowing hours of praying reside at the shoulders of God, perfectly / lightened; lightened compare of all that ailed has found anew middle and a story to tell called lightly, love / houston; houston hurled a whirling gig aside to reside in a rocketed glare called the ride to the side of a dessert deep in an oily reside called the price of agree to believe in perfectly love / hut; a hut shuttered at the vena bent now straightened and house called regard for the hut of the lord, perfectly / austin; take a peek at Austin deep in a swath of perfectly, love / next; next door and near to where we were in finding arrival at ascendant intention of perfectly, love / dove; doving descend has drawn me too and the celestial views of a heart heartened through with perfectly love / lives; lives enraptured in a giving assign to love that's encaptured by the release that's kept in knowing the peace of the sole that's released to perfectly love / expel; expel a well deep within the taste of a fountained pen that's giving in to perfectly love / love; love is perfect / lodges; lodges of souls, the body had holes, the release is done, the living is come to the light perfectly / lures; lures me near to hear the heart of a sacred spark called all is complete in perfectly love / lakes; lakes respond to where we were on the way to a paved start to the heart perfectly sent to love / rivers; rivers of receive arise perfectly at the hearts of love / falls; falls of love are welcome to expose of the knowing all that feeling can be and willing provide of dealing inside with your agree to be perfectly approached by precisely love .

CHAPTER TWO

Chances; chances with due to the refuse of a lessened intrigue with the past that will be, let it live as complete, know the heat of a newer day called regard for the mother's laws and another's pause called perfectly love / explains; explains the refrain, perfectly sung, ONE, love / entertains; arc your stance to veering and dance the dance of hovering at the entertaining way of peace-fully complete with perfectly love / lists; lists of clues to the shoes that walk for only the gifts of grace-full lives the perfection of love / giving; giving gave me a chance to see the wares of awareness and the welcome regard for the cares of cures our love all summertime / lights; lights we incurred as feeding lines of living trines of peace-fully perfect love / delivers; delivers another, mother earth, and perfectly love / share; share your care for the others, dreams, dates, the mother and selves perfectly to love / sure; sure to cure your stare, a snare, that is less and the insure of perfectly love / secure; secure yourself a place at perfection / perfect; perfect love / thanks; thanks for the chance to dance perfectly in love / grateful; grateful and sovereign, I am the chief of a lighter land and the resume, the reside, the perfection of love / clan; perfectly content to be a clan of the new invention called pleasantly love / family; family of the friend perpendicular concede that life is give and give received by perfectly love / friend; friend of the found is around to this the perfect gift of God is love / lighter; lighter and surely and slightly we slum to pick up the pieces of the living that's come to perfection / honey; honey drips sweet on lips of frozen arrival at the taste of survival gone away to preside at perfectly, love / monies; monies delivered are okay to the preside called perfectly love / mention; mention your direction to the man called God is perfectly love / cancer; cancer kneeled at the cure of this perfect love / cured; cured by perfection and the lure of less as perfectly to love / caved; caved by concur, I concede to perfectly, love / gone; gone to the clue and exactly beyond to the cure that is keyed by the fields perfectly in line with love / elude; elude to your rudeness and allude to your cure of the perfect arrival at the heart that insures perfectly love / hear; hear it heard, perfection in love / gamble; gamble on God as love / forgive; forgive the regard of less as perfectly to love / sandra; sandra's day is here and how and how we are is dear to near this perfect love / confess; dine on confess and regress-less arrive at the better address called lightly perfect love / sample; sample secure in a pleasure filled by the perfection of love / seal; seal a deal called yes we will be ourselves, perfectly, to love / see; see yourself clear, perfectly, to the morning delight of a gentle sight called the Beverly Hilled side of a motion's picture reeling secure in perfectly love / bee; bee at the end of a living embrace called the taste of deepest expression called perfectly love / bet; bet on this set of the perfection filled with expressly imbued conceal gone away to perfectly love / birth; birth's cure is a lighter diagnosis of the perfect example of a sample of love / girl; girls seal early on the precious resume of perfectly love / girth; girth around the town of this worth that has heightened a n Earthern bulge with the cellular sensation of equatorial bliss and love's perfect / afford; afford God the perfection heard as love / concord; concord has reached a higher vibration of the living relief called perfectly love / worth; worth it all and God is perfect to love / concur; today I concur that we are sure to reside in the ride called glide to perfectly love / pair; pair of staring at the cross called the picture complete to precisely perfectly love /

pare; God's pare is the spare arrival at the regime that hastens at the rest of the seam of delight and the decisive dare to perfectly stare at precisely love / kneel; kneel on the heal of a cure called decision and the head for a shore called perfectly love / desire; desire to be ingrained again with perfection in love / hearty; hearty cure of the insure that heart-felt is pure in perfection / hasp; a hasp held clean to a fastening bolt called the steep reside at the perfection of love / harp; harps sound best when confessed as pure in the better reside at the air inside your perfect yearn to love / hark; hark to hear the perfect word, love / ark; arks curse confessed away tot he perfect day of love / arc; arc home to perfect love / aspect; aspect of the day of care for perfect love / reflect; reflect on respect of perfect love / facet; facet of agree for the deep endure for the cure perfectly to food called love / finnish; finnish fields of abundant convene at the perfect spiral of aspirant too, love / demure; demure is insured as respect-full of stiff to the perfect reflection of love / dare; dare to care for the share you call yours to perfectly love / danish; a danish deal, the heal of the seat called Amsterdam and the lighter side of love / delicate; delicate to a definite style of the female sight called one new side of perfectly love / dip; dip dye in the colors rainbowed as perfectly love / tonight; tonight, I perfectly write the sight of love / expect; expect to seal your perfection with love / gasp; gasp again breathfully loved.

CHAPTER THREE
Breath; God's breath is complete in our define of a perfect love / kind; kind enough to compare only to the human side of perfect love / capes; capes care in their compare of perfectly loved / ship; ship yourself to the homes you love and the places of renew called perfectly love / cod; cod's cape is the home of the perfect One, complete in love / Province; province of the confirmed reside at perfect love / province; province desired by precious french deliverance to the parisian side of the reside called alive again with perfect love / whaling; whaling rights by right are free to the perfect-ness of love / tales; tales told true to the perfect-ness of perfectly love / regal; a regal pleasure enhance by perfectly love / common; common cure and the ground of concur that love is real to perfectly love / commits; commits ignite by the precise arrive at perfectly love / calico; calico cure to the sweet arrival at perfectly love / telling; telling all the truth to perfection in love / curing; during come to perfectly love / napoli; napoli seen in my dream of perfectly love / camper; camper kind to the kind complete with perfectly love / crib; crib of life complete to perfect agree to love / lived; lived like this desire to agree to perfectly love / love; love this confess of the perfect reside at pleasantly loved / lived; lived for christened by perfection in love / florence; florence invest of the invent called perfect love / capture; capture a raptured peer at the perfectness of love / flew; flew to the curative waters perfect to love / flounce; flounce of God is over due to perfect love / ampere; ampere clear to the perfection of love / wattage; wattage deep in the wielded relief of perfectly love / treat; treat yourself loved perfectly / deny; deny due of less, be, perfect, to love / retry; retry abort as the sort who

agree to perfectly love / remember; remember to regard yourself as loved / tweak; tweak less and right to perfect love / coppery; coppery cue of the knee deep degree called the first sight of perfect love / golden; golden crude bubbling sweet in the amber orbs of perfect we, love / felt; felt you lean toward the cure for perfect love / vulva; vulva deep in the regard for a perfect keep of the perfect-ness of precisely love / chain; chain of the chilled and broken healed by the perfection of love / wine; wine of the content called Good to the source of the heart's singing chords called God's drunken laugh at the perfect ascend to precisely love / wane; wane perfectly to love / alchemy; alchemy of the fuel for love, michael's cue is on to perfect love / labia; labia's joint at the peak of God and the sacred heart of perfect love / cock; cocks crew and 3 to you and the one between our tossled legs and the sled of kegs over pored by perfect love / crews; crews amused by the perfection of love / silver; silver cure fore the cord that snared and the knowing more and the heart that cared for the gold inside the perfection of love / fellow; fellow of the cure that cares for perfection in love / fun; fun enough to perfectly cure the oasis of sounds called love / bake; bake the street with a mixture complete in the pavement called God and the golden day of perfectly love / broil; broil less and cook more for the perfect ahead and the club called God ahead, love / foil; Christ's foil is the perfect glitter of the glimmer called love / mighty; mighty is the explain of perfectly love / precious; precious to the mighty explain of the current regard for precious and perfect in love / metal; metal emphatic in loving impale of the precious reside at perfect love / kissed; kissed by the confess to reside at perfectly love / licked; licked by the craving for space we conclude to agree to perfectly love / taste; taste the treat of the perfectly polite agree to reside in love / ready; ready to agree to perfectly love / sylvan; sylvan measure of the pleasure called love / thread; thread of the cure and the lure and the peace of perfection in love / fill; fill up perfectly with love / fondle; fondle the measure, the feel, the delight, the incite for the perfection of love / delight-full; delight-full designs of love / Level / Flat / Plane.

CHAPTER FOUR

Caress; caress me perfectly with love / clip; clip accrue and know the mood of a living complete with perfect love / fade; fade to perfection in love / enlighten; enlighten the manner of your walk this day to perfect love / feel; feel God real in your perfect love / convey; convey yourself abundance in perfection and love / conjoin; conjoin now this perfection with love / brighten; brighten the love of perfection with giving ascend / ascend; ascend now to perfect love / stand; stand on the hearing begin of perfection in living love / corner; corner the market on a perfect buy called love / cafe; cafe of the care to a perfectly pleasant blended taste of love / cat's; cate's agree is too, eat, find, flown, loved, too, perfection / lurk; lurk at the ways of perfection and love / smirk; smirk less and know confess of perfect love / smell; smell loved perfectly / casper; casper's cue is the cleared perfection of the lesson called love / ghost; ghost of a chance to dance perfectly

in love / groan; groan less know confess perfectly loved / smile; smile to hear the sound of a perfect beat, your heart can meet me at precisely love / barter; barter less, know more, confess best, living in the trade called perfection and the vocation called love / cavort; cavort at the sort of perfection called love / inn; inn of the grove called parked at perfect love / in; love is in to the time to hold their heart perfect / on; on time to perfectly love / in love; in love, live, loves, perfect / perfect; perfect to be loved / I AM; I am perfect / over; over the hear to the heart to the sound of pleasant perfection in love / under; under the hearts that care is the spare arrival at perfection / near; near the dear arrival at perfection / you are; you are perfect to assurance at the perfection of the hu-man; God / grown; grown by agree to be pure to the fee, all have paid, for perfectly, love / graced; graced by this space, held perfect in love / glazed; glazed by a clue in statues of crews that are hued by peace and contentment and mental telepathy found revealed as the hearty cord of a sword cut deep to the steep arrive at perfectly conceit of jelly blue love / let's be; let's be cured by the care perfect to love / eloquently; eloquently done, the elegant son of a kindled profession called the confession of a perfectly said, love / often; often said I am perfect to love / eternally; eternally done well and sent to invent the scope of a escape called climbing to the Osirian skies called perfectly love / delights; Delights can be cubed by the square called geometry rules in perfectly love / dancing; dancing to God in the Sufi believe that heavens water can fall through the skies of a swirling plan to open your heart to a man called God / somewhere; somewhere you knew perfect regard for the space hu-man and the critical relate to perfect God / often; Hawaii is often said to rule perfectly in love / you; you are the completion of perfection by God / true; true enough reveal of the grace that is held as perfect to love / travels; travels concede to agreed to perfection in the globe of the spiral called perfectly love / travail-less; where travail can fulfill is digressed to good-bye to the land of prevail to perfectly God / sometime; sometime let's be certain to lead to perfection and all-ways let's arm ourselves with God / today; today we're way to perfection in love / turning; turning home to stay perfect in our advise to love / pleasantly; pleasantly done, perfection is, love / pampered; pampered by compare and cared for perfectly I am love / conspire; conspire to hire a conceptual release to the relation called the nation perfect to love / elects; elects to care for perfection and the complexion of love / yet; yet done, perfectly / okay; okay let's be perfectly loved / where; where were you in perfection's cue for perfectly love / when; when were you the age of two and where's the return for the cross of placement called perfection in love / what age; what age rules, only the One, sun, sum, God, perfection, love / volt; volt struck by the truck of a delivery called perfection / jolt; jolts that jeweled with a shine perfect to love / strike; strike struck and the truck of a line along the dreaming living's giving perfection to only me / Relative / Eternal.

CHAPTER FIVE

Lightening; lightening is enlightening in the flash to the cash of a breathing prefect with creation's vote for love / inspire; inspire your higher power with our arrival at perfect love / channels; channels applaud our desire to convene at the higher blends of perfection in God / water; water is loving in living attire of the fire called passionate confess of our perfect love / wheel; wheel of the concede to profess to greater live in perfect contrast and preciously round love / cure; cure the endure of perfectly love in bliss / lines; lines of endure have come to our perfection of love / michael; michael knew that here was life and listening too the near hello of a perfect good buy called love / light; light on you and then the new retire to michael's due of perfection in love / organic; organic to a manner and fertile within the bulb of a nation gone orange to perfectly love / oceanic; oceanic to a nature contested less and shored perfectly by love / oxygen; oxygen filled with the lungs of deep the feel of perfect love / breath; breath of the perfect love / dolphin; dolphins due to a swim perfect to the heart of a start called entwined with love / whale; whale of a notion of the nation for perfect love / spiral; a spiral kind clued to perfect love / define; define you due to the contextual aspect of a nature called clued to love / teach; teach yourself to love, perfectly / celtic; celtic to a cue called the knotting undo of perfectly love / definite; definite to a due of the icy residue that melts away in a mossy creek knee deep in compassionate love / preach; preach less grow more compare best perfectly to love / knots; knots of undo do perfectly as love / align; align, hear, perfectly, at the ear of an expectant gaze called lightly, love / reverend; reverend manner, the matter, the plan, the gaze of forever in the look of a man called perfectly, love / lucifer; *lucifer fell just short of forever and knew the please of forgetting ease and then finding again the precious blend of precisely love *luck under curled in fettered exception of the respect less whirl called forgetting the light / ahead; ahead to let go and now know that God is perfect to love / head; head home now to perfectly know the let's be loved / wars; wars are over and now we reside in the perfect resume of the lady of noon brought home to love / heavenly; heavenly to a measure called perfectly rules the ruler of love / decreed; decreed to a desire of the living okay and the knowing regard for the heart that has laid itself open to perfection in the declaration of love / arc-angelic; arc-angelic to a measure, I know we are living pleasure and the bless of living yes! by the tempting sum of predictably perfect love / decrees; decreed by desire and okay to the outbacked belief in the lessons of perfection and the understanding called love / h-bar; h-bar constant, love's perfect / constant; constant to a sooth and cured by decree of the God-head called love and the heart called agree to be perfectly loved / comets; comets cue cures of their care and their tempting appraisal of the survey that wears reside best at perfect love / asteroids; asteroids spill their loose wheels all over the man vibrant with perfectly love / planes; plan on the planes of shifting days gone gazed to by love / dimensions; dimensions of the measure conveyed as ascendant to a penchant for perplexion and love by direction perfect to above / inventions; inventions of the patent called perfect to love / electric; electric to a cue static with irritants and due tot he barest desire to go hire

a mate perfect in love / sonic; sonic to an opportune embrace and the aerial view of desirable care for the Other and the kneel at believing in you we know the taste of a perfect pair called boom with perfection, love / sincere; sincere to where, I make the news with my new desire to bloom in perfect conspire to love / secure; secure your hear to now and how we precious love our dear dash at perfect love / star; star as creator and killer of beast and the humble adoration of another who keeps the placement unique to the life of God, perfect to love / chariots; chariots chill by the wheel of a man flown gowned in expand to the spandex embrace of the edge of this place called the planet of regard for professionally done, perfection in love, heavenward / Enoch; Enochian and near to the hands and the keys of the man who become one of these, arc-angelic agree to become lightly pleased and perfectly, Metatron / keys; keys that are found here and now remembering the plan to ring around the throne of perfectly love / heavenward; heavenward glance to a chance at perfection in your stance of love / island; island deal of the human care has brought her home to land in the lap of a man parallel and perfect to finer God / find; find the abound of a tan called the spiraling plan to pleasure this band with love / Big; Big island sound of the awhile and the expand that is due now to man and the electric way we connected to precisely love / Belief; Belief in the review constant that says see this perfect love / constantly; constantly hear the conspire to hire yourself as higher then blend perfectly / concurrently; concurrently treasured by the pleasure perfect to love / currently; mayan currency is currently assured of the perfection called love / exactly; exactly done, yes! to perfectly love / spirits; spirits that conspire to higher yield of perfectly love / the work; today the work of a perfect love / the path; the path to the One is the sun of the disc called perfectly, love / the bath; love is light in the splash to the bath called one, love / baptise; Baptise yourself with the christened perfection of love / circumscribe; circumscribe your wet reside to project respect for the perfection in life / scribe; a scribe has come to perfect love / breastplate; breastplate of the land called Aaron and the wedding of bliss with perfection in love.

CHAPTER SIX

Hark; hark I hear the roar of perfect love / faith; faith has accrued to perfectly love / feed; feed yourself nourished by perfection in love / fed; fed up to hearing and the cheering I Am, of perfectly love / led; God is led home by perfectly love / melchizedek; melchizedek mends the rift between and the hearts and the veins of the hallowed dream of impressive desire to love with perfection / Metatron; expect perfection of Metatron / stone; love's stone is deep to precious perfection in love / seat; please seat yourself near our perfection / concur; concur your dear reflect of God-head love and the perfection above our desirous dip to lifting grace / reside; reside perfectly loved / shasta; shasta secure by a skilled degree of the steadfast approval to be loved perfectly, the mountain, God / inside; inside God is perfection / lemurian; lemurian seams of the perfect agree to love / mu; the mu you knew was perfect love / atlantic; atlantic regard of the hardest defend gone to God in the light of love, perfect / atlantis; atlantis is the splash perfect in love / temples; veins of temples are unique in the pulse assigned to perfect love / knight; knights of begin to live in a blend perfect to love / nights; nights due tot he perfection of love / templar; templar's extreme to the arc called God and the knights who ruled by perfect love / geometric; let us geometricly reside at the perfect formula called love / the dome; the dome is perfect to love / flowers; flowers filled by perfectly healing love / archaic; Great is the archaic decide to preciously love / abu; Grown by abu to the deed called agreed to perfectly by love / amen; God's amen is overdue to the perfect place called love / priests; priests let us renewed be to the agree to perfectly love / preside; preside over the days of perfection and love / precedent; precedent of the letting it be called perfectly love / present; get a present and call the days worn by love, present, perfect / sent; sent to love in God alone and all the throned regard for precious ascend to perfectly love / sash; love is sashed over by perfect gowns of pleasant sounds of perfection in ringing love / coat; God's coat is worn perfectly by me in love / robe; The robe of relief has come to my sweet surrender to love / trim; trim perfectly worn by precisely love / tire; tire this round less, perfectly / retire; retire now and astound them all with perfect love / ascend; ascend to the matter loved, friend, found, perfectly / mother; mother of begin, again, and often precious, perfection of love / tree; God's tree is perfect in me and love / template; template done by the sum of One whose gentle persuasion penetrates the sounds of perfect love / hologram; holograms holographic to perfection in love / holographic; holographic allure, perfect / graphic; graphically spoken it's you I agree to in perfect regard for your lighter bless to love / perfectly; perfectly and precisely won by loving regard / precisely; precisely my love lead me home to living for perfect love / absolutely; absolutely loved perfectly / divinely; divinely loved perfectly / lightly; lightly precisely love in perfection / hu-man; hu-man to agree tot he nature reserved for perfectly love / basic; a basic yes to human natured regard for perfection in love / ink; ink of instinct and the drains regained as whole to exception in the notion perfect to love / richly; richly worn and horn by the lamb of sweet regard to precisely love, perfectly / right-fully; right-fully done and really won by pleasant regard for perfectly love / definitely; definitely done by perfectly love / consistently; consistently done and perfectly won by a pace to love / constantly; constantly true to lightly you know the precision of perfection in love / concisely; concisely done and the sun of a summation called the One who loves perfectly / absolutely; God is absolutely hear to love; that's perfection / focally; focally abject and I am the aspect of the holiest spark called this is perfect, love / vocally; I am vocally freed by our agreed to perfection in love / truth-fully; truth-fully focused on the unfolding matter within and the gesture called crystal and the spacing between and the shimmering manner of the matter called perfectly love / heart; hearts that heal will call home by perfect love.

CHAPTER SEVEN

Obtusely; obtusely abtuse to the repute of my confident stand in the Christ within hu-man, lightly said and lovingly done with perfection / resolutely; resolutely given with precision perfectly / delicately; delicately driven to succeed at being one with all belief of God is perfectly me / preciously; preciously and precisely given to the miraculous descent to the ascending apex within men, and perfectly love / pertly; pertly spoken we are invoking the graciousness of energetically perfect love / perfectly; perfectly spiral to spires of the temples called love / pleasure; pleasure, me, perfectly, at God / gate; gates open precisely on time for perfectly love / lovely; loved to lovely be to perfectly living love / directly; directly scene, the avenues of perfection in love / denial; denial done, I am the one for you, perfectly, God / plant; plant yourself in perfect love / factor; factor the fuel into who will be perfectly lead to other lands called giving in to process love / mate; mate with perfect, love / concentric; concentric and circle by a spiral blend called befriend true love, perfectly / celt; celt ascend has come around to say that we agree the Orian way holds some degree of perfectly Egyptian me, love / belt; belts aground the sound of perfection in direction and ascend to perfect love / galactic; be galactic in your agree to preside at perfection, love / cosmic; cosmic cued perfection / orbital; orbital agree to decide upon the only span called perfect love / moonstone; moonstone matter precision perfect in the agree of desire to conspire to a stone called love/ lapis; lapis blew blue across the degree that's given for living healed by perfect dreams of desirable living called lightly love / lazarus; lazarus true to the living in you respired by love, perfectly / definite; a definite due called listening too to perfection in love / link; linkup to perfect love / peridot; peridot matter of the twinkling kind shining in you and the land of divine intervention for perfect love / egyptic; egyptic agree to be perfect to love / elliptican elliptic desire to hire the sword of God as our looping friend of perfect love / alien; alien end come, perfectly, love / foreign; foreign friend comes to agree to and the living perfection of giving true love / energetic; God's energetic pal is how we perfect true love / plan; let us plan on knowing perfection in giving and love / divert; divert the covert with perfectly love / electricity; electrically gather energetic release and explode with the possibility of perfect love / pact; a pact secure with the cure conspired to as perfectly love / court; court the sort who cue true love in perfect choice / diversity; diversity matters perfectly / congeal; congeal your respect for the perfected, love / spills; spills are bursting with reflection on the direction of your truest expression of perfection in a direction / called love / zeal; zeal that's noticed can be focused on perfection's love, light / abortive; abortive attempt to forget can connect your heart to shorter ways to wed perfection in love / assort; light assort your sort of perfection in love / thrill; thrill can abound at the town of precision in love / known; known by profound profess of precision in love and protection of perfection / dually; dually know love in perfect reflections of grace / truth-fully; truth-fully perfect / dealt; let's be dealt with perfectly by love / dueal; dueal the hands on duel is hu-man nature found created by perfect love / over; over hear we understand the perfect way to realign with perfection in love / override; override the side of less than perfect / okay; okay light wins perfectly, love / release; release your nature and rest perfect in this living sun called God / relate; relate, rest, perfect, love / dates; dates that are due to perfect love, 1 and 2 and / / dancing; dancing roses agree, perfectly with the quiet respect for perfect love / spin; spin in to perfect arms held open too, love / sport; sport the plural yes of playing perfectly at love / parallel; parallel expenses meet at the exist complete with the love perfect and the side of God called a common plan and the heart of perfect love / zippered; zippered agree to r=trip to the days of the Other side and the absolute reside at the travelling truth called the flight perfect to love / felt; felt like a feeling direct to precisely and perfectly love / flank; flank your plan with photographs true to the preside called preciously labeled perfect to God / align; align like this and perfectly to precious love / beryl; beryls are an aquamarine stare at the deeper decide to glide correct to perfect love.

CHAPTER EIGHT

Define; define your debt as less then find the balance perfect to love / denature; denature the nature of the alcoholic cure that is less than perfect for you and your friend called lvoe / won; God has won a man to the tribe of the lighter side called softly said the perfect love / woman; woman of nature can agree that life is love eternally and perfectly come to the one who love / nurture; nurture your nature with perfect love / manlove; manlove is the man secure with his respect for perfect agree to decide to love / trance; trance true to gaining the perfection of love / knelt; knelt along the dunes of days gone ocean deep to the sands perfect with love / trance-less; trance-less ascend to the chore of where we've been for perfectly love / kauai; kauai's cure can insure the light perfect to love / third; third time around and living in sounds of precious agree to the california clued delivery of the special express for me and the third revue of heightened perfection in love / definite; a definite due called listening too to perfection in love / time; time charmed by the charge of confess to perfect love / defiant; defiant manner of the remainder of the precision called perfectly love / pull; pull on yes! and know confess of truly respectfully won by perfect love / remove; remove the block and know the rest of resist-less perfection in love / residue; residue of regard to the cards that are held precisely by love in perfection / cream; cream yellow days and pastel lights of the precision instrument called perfect winds of love / concur; concur to agree with precious and precise access to an access direct to perfect love / connect; what is connect? It is the assure of perfect respect for the allure of coincidence called the precipitous aspect of love / obdurate; obdurate matter of the matter complete with perfection of love / elongate; elongate a rate of reflective manners that break a trance with a delphic entrance to the dancing feet of perfect contentment with the stand for God ahead to precious love / venusian; venusian manner in the matter called a perfect flight to the friends content with the orbit called love / starred; starred and short of nothing less than forever given a heavenly bless content with the prospect of perfect love / red; red to allure and the smiling insure of perfection in direction to ascendant remainder of the remains of a deficit gone electric to perfectly love / dare; dare to care about perfection, love / marred; marred met meals of fields of eating only perfect love / admired; admired by rest, I conclude my rude arrival with the archival days of perfect love / deuce; deuce deal, perfect twos of love / desist; desist less and know perfection in love / elect; elect the cure to birth true love and the silly mirth of the rate of reflect worn briskly within the perfection of love / suspect; predate the suspect of elate with a rate called perfect to love / occurrence; occurrence perfect in love / needs; needs to be perfect in love / kept; lines kept open will agree that love is perfect to me, permanently, resolutely, love / along; along the lines of perfect love / assigned; assigned relate of the perfect date to electric resume of the residence seen as perfect to love / aspirant; aspirant to manners perfect in the desire to fire the fuels of love / holes; holes gone to concealed's melt and now we see that what we felt was the wholer truth of perfect love / hasp; a hasp hung by perfect love / floodgate; floodgates open to reminders that love is kinder in perfect remain at love / endorphined; endorphined manner of the matter called perfect in love / swing; let us swing to the perfection of love / elevator; elevators pure to the respect-full advance to perfection in love / import; import the sort of respect-full agree that accesses our believe in remembrance and love / swim; I swim to the reminder of perfect love / perspire; perspire for a higher seat of the magic perfect to passionate respect for the reminder to love / expert; expert living in the giving receive of perfect love / gale; God's gale is knee deep in the blossom of perfection in connection with love / decision; the decision to make is what's at stake in candid agree to compelling reminders of perfection in love / dialect; God's dialect is respect-full and free to perfectly loved / gallery; gallery of the art called agree to perfectly love / proctor; proctor of the manner called the bash-full respect that has come to the perfection of love / disburse; disburse your respect to the proceeds perfect to love / provide; provide delight for your own reside in perfect love / procure; procure your persevere at perfection in love / proceed; proceed perfectly to love / calico; calico consign of the design perfect to love / hover; hover over the veiled attempts at past forget and know that all we are is perfect to love / preside; preside at the wedding called perfect to love / parlay; parlay you way to more reside at the advance called perfect love / build; build upon the manner called perfect and love / devote; devote your desires to higher remains that remind me perfectly of love / debt-free; debt-free reminder of the kinder precision of the recall to perfection in love.

THE ABSOLUTE-MENTS
LEVEL 12

CHAPTER ONE

Absolute; absolute in the view of all things done and dealing with acute umbilicum of resolute acquisition of the position of perfectly absolute love / entire; entire absolute conspire to the resolve called love / ahead; ahead to the absolute, I am lead by perfect love / acute; every facet acute tot he absolute of love / growth; let us grow by an imbue absolute to love / create; God's create is great in the absolute of love / accurate; accurate degrees of the wedge absolute to perfect flying love / access; love's access is led perfect to the absolute / attitude; an absolute attitude of perfect love / procreate; procreate distinctly at the love absolute / masturbate; masturbate's placid face is the welcome holds of the absolute called perfectly love / tear; tear away wear of the love absolute / taste; taste truth, absolutely / fornicate; fornicate less, absolute concede to the need to convey perfectly physical love / appear; appeal's congeal is a bet on the love absolute / anchor; anchor here at the shore of the love absolute / indicate; indicate your desire to mate with the love absolute / center earth; center earth abreast with the light absolute / mid earth; mid earth's residual is the continual abode in the mode called the love absolute / cavern; caverns cave in around the perfection of absolute love / cave; cave into the love absolute / dirt; good dirt is God's absolute feel of the love absolute / plate; living plates of tectonics blend are coming to the love absolute / techniques; techniques are absolute in their worth to love / truths; God's truths are absolute / tables; tables turn around to the love absolute / bathe; bathe in the bliss absolute / belief; the belief absolute / couple; couple with the One who sums the hold on all the wholesome suns of the light absolute / material; God's material mare is the love absolute / member; bliss is a member of the team absolute / treats; treats enough on the street absolute / full-filled; I am full-filled by the healed absolute of bliss / adamant; adamant to a cause we applaud your trial by the fire of the love absolute / etheric; etheric measure of the love absolute / all; all you are is the will for the love absolute / perfect; perfect to clearly seen the love absolute / clear; clearly drawn tot he love absolute / clairvoyant; a clairvoyant measure at the meet absolute / colors; colors cured my desire for less than an absolute desire for the rainbow called perfectly absolute love / rates; hear are the rates for the great listen of the life absolute / vibrates; vibrates great release is the love absolute / astral; astral beauty and the basic sum, absolute / sincere; sincere to john and his love for the light absolute / loud; loud in God, absolute / cross; cross enough to be absolute / abrasive; abrasive nature gone to the absolute / convulsive; convulsive to a nature directed perfectly by the love absolute / convolute; lightly convolute to the I am absolute / complete; God is complete in the love absolute / tragic; Aquarian tragic has gone to the magic absolute / magical; a magical nature absolutely / cohesive; cohesive to a measure natured by the absolute / cohesive; a cohesive nature that sticks to the love absolute / swell; light is swollen by a swell absolute / swollen; a swollen nature absolute to God / well; well enough to being absolute / thorough; let us thorough be by the possession called love to the absolute / massive; massive attractive can compute as the love absolute / passive; absolutely passive to the nature called gone the love absolute / active; active enough to be absolute / spatial; spatial wed to the material matter called time for a new paradigm called the mystery of the absolute / afforded; afforded a vehicle for the love of the absolute / absolute; absolute and the theatrical love of God's men.

CHAPTER TWO

Spark; a spark struck by the absolute / central; the central scene is all-ways absolute / centered; why are you centered on less? Absolute / thrush; thrush has flown to the throne absolute / thrust; thrust yourself home to the absolute / ratify; care to ratify your position on the absolute / clarify; clarify matters, absolutely / crosscheck; crosscheck this absolute degree of love / box; box knew the square of the circle of the love absolute / brew; brew drew disagreeable sums of the less frequent hum called the love absolute / rescue; rescue your desire to devise the love absolute / rend; a basket's rend is the truth of receive called the love absolute / delve; delve deep into the love absolute / research; research matters matter best in the love absolute / confirm; confirm your desire to be absolutely conspired as only the love absolute / arrive; arrive at a nature of the love absolute / rest; rest on nature's absolute kind of love / today; today I am absolute to the son of love / kelp; kelp grew green with desire for the absolute nutrition of love / host; host a party for the love absolute / tonight; tonight we are the absolute / insists; insists on perfection in the love absolute / fasten; fasten on too the love absolute / travesty; God's travesty is why you refuse the absolute / mansion; mansions of the views of the pathways to the golden wave absolute / streets; streets of the love absolute and the agree to arrive at living absolute / squarely; squarely done and we are One to One by the 3's divide and the dividend complete in the squares complete with the circle of sum, One Love Absolute / uniquely; uniquely and absolutely divine / righteously; righteously spoken the paths of invoking the absolute love / rightly; rightly done and the absolute won / ribald; a ribald matter, the manner absolute / characteristic; characteristic matters for the love absolute / autistic; autistic to agree, we are the ones who need to hear the immaculate due called cleanly the absolute of love / spastic; spastic won by the one who said the absolute is perfectly coordinated in love / rhetoric; rhetorical explode to the repeat called the love absolute / abject; welcome to the abject manner called the reside in the light absolute / rejects; rejects are set on a deeming return tot he spirals of a finished touch called good-bye to lessen absolute / broadstone; broadstone rode home on a simple premise, the absolute of love / recruit; recruit your set of particular beliefs and live in the army of the love absolute / broaden; broaden your spirit and know the nature of the love absolute / supple; supple coverage of the enough called flexibility in the possibility of perfectly absolute love / service; service sent to the absolute called love / mason; mason's dixon is the line of a sign sent left-over to the light which lives remitted to absolute love / dixon; dixon's sign is a line to the love absolute / handicapped; handicapped by less, I'm addressed to the envelope of time called the love absolute / crude; crude enough to be reset by respect for the love absolute / cruel; cruel nature has come to an agree called the Earth has spun to the heights of a passion for the giving absolute / leafy; leafy reside in the side and the sights of the living place called the tree of the life absolute / club; club of abuse has gone to the arm absolute / mileage; mileage rate has come to the absolute / curvature; a breeze to see the curvature of the love absolute / cast; cast by the manner called direct to the seas absolute / dramatic; dramatic degrees of the respect-full leads to the love absolute / gates; gates open to the absolute / riverside; pairs are riverside to the absolute flow of love / wiles; wiles are on by the I am absolute / Minneapolis; Minneapolis men of the nature called love absolute / elk; elks river at the residence called the extensive side of love absolute / Ohio; Ohio nation blessed by the mounds of recovery of the love absolute / Columbus; Columbus gave us the love absolute / Unitarian; Unitarian wed of the bedding called the absolute / truck; trucks come home filled with the absolute of love / elected; elected states of the fields convened at the sharing path of the love absolute / inclined; inclined to see the love absolute.

CHAPTER THREE
Packed; caution packed in the absolute / peaks; a pair of peaks of the absolute / huntress; the huntress of the food absolute, love / hound; hounds done with the lessen absolute / heard; heard you said you wanted the absolute / slim; slim to the sight of the absolute / boone; boone's beat is absolute / twins; twins assign their decide to the blend absolute / born; born by a signed example of the sample absolute / heritage; heritage held as absolute / native; native to the sign of a God called absolute / overlook; overlook less the absolute / lapse; lapse of nature less the absolute / renew; renew your desire to be absolute / legal; legal matters ease in the absolute / stages; stages set to retire to the absolute / plaster; plaster cast this respect-full glance at the light desire to rise a respite in the venusian grin of a grace-full dance called life in the orbital spin absolute / pour; pour of the eclestial taste called growing again to bliss-fully love in the absolute / virgin; a virgin revue the venue that danced in the light of the life absolute / grasslands; grasslands replete in the resolution of the timed advance called perfectly chanced by the light absolute / hotel; hotels stand along the sign of a symbolic line called lightly absolute to love / over; absolute is over me and through the way we wee the light absolute / finished; finished by the light absolute / dual; the dual over and the light has come to stay at the light absolute / Gabriel; Gabriel grew to welcome you to the light absolute / status; an absolute status called free / logs; logs leap to the freer glide called precisely absolutely love / forts; forts equipped with the absolute / farms; farms free to we are the absolute / Amish; wed the Amish too, absolute / polish; polish your polish to light absolute / Scottish; Scottish whim about the absolute / Irish; Irish nature is absolute / English; an english manner called absolute / valley; God's valley comes to the I am of the One absolute / clearest; clearest nature of a clarion exceed to the life absolute / worn; worn to a thin thread's absolute called the eave of love / born; cry over me born to be free to the love lived absolutely / case; case for the absolute / seizure; seizure of the absolute / loops; loops finish now in the absolute / laps; l will swim in the laps called absolute / lanes; lanes divided open up to the abide / places; God's places face the absolute / planes; planes trade truths with the absolute / plans; plans to plead for the absolute / romance; romance renews in the resume of the light absolute / regain; regain your nature for the life called absolute / reside; reside in the side called absolute / beside; beside the seas absolute / sides; sides that bend to the absolute / shores; shores concede the depths of the absolute / doors; doors shut on less than the absolute / dapple; dappled by light of the absolute / gain; gain knowledge of the absolute/ gravitate; gravitate the truth of the absolute / gap; a gap called absolute and healed by love / gulp; a gap gulped up by the absolute / gill; gills flap in the absolute breath of life / dolphin; lights of dolphins called the absolute / men; men agree to the aspect called the light absolute / man; man is absolute to One / Women; women won by the light absolute / deal; deal absolutely in resolutely perfect love.

CHAPTER FOUR
Coincide; coincide with the absolute within your love / common; common natured kind, absolute / cellar; cellared dates have gone to the absolute / open; open ascend on the wedge of a dream flying within the seam of the light absolute / shut; shut to less and eyed by extremes of the light absolute / cases; cases accrue as we resume our degree of the light absolute / shops; shops concede that we've agreed to be the light buy that is absolute / villas; villas venued as the absolute living proof of love / truths; truths told to the absolute / hobbies; hobbies can use the crafts of revenue to pay for the light absolute / habits; habits due to the light absolute / clues; clues come to the life found absolute / recluse; absolute's recluse is the rules absolute / refine; refine designs of the absolute / antiques; antiques presume that the date has come to design a rate called love in a living ascend to the absolute / known; known by the hues of the absolute / magic; magic agree to the absolute / girl; girl prayer for the absolute / bay; bay of the prayer called lightly love / both; both of you rule in your light absolute / bathe; bathe in the pool absolute / perfect; perfect treasure of the absolute / absolutely; absolutely wet with the reign absolute/ responsibly; responsibly done by the love absolute / devoted; devoted to the doing absolute / dated; dated you absolutely / sedated; sedated by the light absolute / cared; cared for by the light absolute / core; core of the light absolute / edge; edge of the free zone absolute / reward; a reward conveyed to the absolute / broader; broader is best to the absolute / broads; broads can be narrow to the absolute / bars; bars cross the absolute weave of love / embark; embark on the absolute / bloke; a bloke becoming a gentleman of absolute love / bait; bait the fee for the love absolute / blake; where is blake where we need poetry for the absolute / cards; cards can play the absolute / gambles; gambles can be conceded to by the absolute / absolutely; absolutely outwardly overtly love / actuarial; actuarial practice of the computation absolute / insurance; insurance can heal the

absolute / overly; overly practical in the absolute / accurately; accurately said, the absolute / resolutely; resolutely the absolute / acutely; acutely measured by the absolutely / ignite; ignite the absolute / residual; a residual need to be absolute / Petersburg; Petersburg can see the sea of the lead to the absolute / suburban; suburban resume can relieve the stress on the joints of the absolute / city; city tooled by the I am essential too the resume of the absolute / abdicate; abdicate resume to the absolute / rural; rural pleasure includes extremes to the team absolute / town; town of the absolute / confucian; confucian matter absolute / confused; confused by the confession to the intention to mention the love absolute / agricultural; agricultural accept of the chance to grip the change called respect of the absolute love / training; training run to the seas of the traveling sun called love to the absolute / weapon; weapons wield alignment to the light absolute / gun; guns glint in the sun of the release called the absolute / trajectory; trajectory of the life absolute / aim; aim perpendicularly to the love absolute / finality; finality codes a current absolute.

CHAPTER FIVE

A.R.C; Assume Respect for the Contentment in the light absolute / art; art's concede is a painted tree of the life absolute / ark; why can we *ark in the park at the light absolute / *associative respect for knowledge / know; know the best of the light absolute / twinkle; a twinkle in the eye of the light seen absolute / start; start in to be absolute / spirit; spirit conspires at the assurance of the light absolute / owner; care to be the owner of the light absolute / passionately; passionately drawn to the light absolute / emblazoned; emblazoned manner of the light absolute / basically; basically abreast the light absolute / blazed; blazed fresh high to the wildly success-full rise to the light absolute / burned; burned best the trail to the train absolute and the ride to the top of the risen truth at the peak of love / rastafarian; rastafarian assign to the Jah absolute / heavenward; heavenward loop tot he skyward truth that love is above and beyond and within all who live in truly love / heavenly; heavenly nature of the held by the hands of the living absolute / Cuban; Cuban consume has grown to a smokey residue that needs relief in the light absolute / skyward; showers spark in a skyward arc to meet the love absolute / intervention; intervention can mention my example of the absolute / hispanic; hispanic heal can feel our light's absolute / primary; primary consume can resume an example of the light absolute / convene; convene at the simple sheen of the light absolute / compassion; compassion burns with the absolute / love; where can love be? In the absolute / fortitude; life has fortitude in the life absolute / forces; forces natured by the air absolute / arms; God's arms held wide to the absolute / merciful; merciful manner of the love absolute / michael; michael met believe at today's absolute / Gabriel; Gabriel too needs the absolute / Raphael; Raphael heals the absolute / solace; solace in the absolute / comfort; comfort in the absolute / light; show the light in you too, the absolute / uriel; uriel rules the inner light of the focus complete in the absolute / heal; heal the absolute / save; save the absolute / raziel; raziel is well to the absolute / mysterious; Mysterious manners blend

with the light absolute / sacral; sacral pleasure is the blessing absolute / ariel; ariel is the feel of the beastly tool turned to truth in the absolute / children; children sealed by the absolute / youth; youth who exude the absolute / beasts; beasts exude the respect absolute / Metatron; Metatron's mend is the absolute / protector; well, the protector of the absolute / paradise; paradise leads to the absolute / azrael; azrael is real in the light absolute / death; death too the absolute / sandalphon; sandalphon's music is the soprano absolute / light; light on the believers who are absolute / musical; musical meeting at the absolute / brother; brother too the absolute / metatronic; metatronic suspend in the absolute / cubic; cubic of the treasure measured by the absolute / israfel; israfel fell to the absolute / singing; singing in the spring of the absolute / jophiel; jophiel knew the well of the absolute / zadkiel; zadkiel kills less those the absolute / compass; compass to the point of the absolute / directive; directive to the absolute / direct; direct to the absolute / flights; flights fueled by the absolute / fortunate; fortunate in the found absolute.

CHAPTER SIX

Camel; camel's win is divine in the love absolute / divinity; divinity is grace-full in the love absolute / loves; well are the loves of the lives absolute / freedom; freedom reigns absolute / friends; friends of the absolute / foes; foes of the others win when they begin the absolute / allies; allies seen by the scenes of the absolute / universal; universal matter of the absolute / breathe; breathe absolutely love / breath; a breathe drawn from the absolute / presence; presence too and the absolute / essence; essence premier to the divine; divine is the absolute / written; written to the absolute / spoken; spoken matters of the absolute / language; language ruled by the absolute / of light; of light absolute / translated; translated as the absolute / enochian; enochian review of the absolute / sated; sated by the guide called absolute / evolved; evolved to a manner called absolute / keyed; keyed to the kind, absolute / God; God is absolute / earthy; an earthy measure, absolute / marry; marry me too, absolute / write; write to the absolute / truth; truth told absolute / speak; speak the absolute / truth; truth is absolute / live; live in absolute / truth; truth told absolutely, love / give; give to the life absolute / truth is; truth is absolute / breath; breath is absolute / truthing; truth being told as the absolute / be; be absolute to love / truth is; truth is ours in the absolute / truth's; truth's friend is absolute / extort; extort your sort of absolute love / devise; devise only the absolute / truths; truths held as the absolute / divide; divide up the absolute / truth-full; truth-full rules in the game absolute / reign; reign deep in the absolute / in truth, absolute / life is; life is, absolute / truth; truth of the top absolute / apply; apply to the absolute / traces; traces of the absolute / absolutely; absolutely still to the absolute / true; true too and absolute / forthright; forthright manner, absolute / absolute; absolute decide to be, love / kite; kites free in the sail absolute / freedom; freedom rings, absolute / flight; flights to the absolute heart of love / flown; flown to a moaning absolute / fire; fire in the tiring absolute / create; create a resource, the absolute / realize; realize the resources found in the absolute / follow; follow the code through the absolute / halls; halls who echo with the love for the absolute / lighten; lighten the led to the absolute / lofty; lofty notions born absolute.

CHAPTER SEVEN

Parts; parts are whole to the sealing absolute / paths; paths to the pleasure absolute / whole; whole enough to be absolute / dignity; dignity in the absolute / dignify; dignify yourself as the absolute / believe; believe in the absolute / remember; remember to be absolute / review; review the absolute / regard; classic regard for the absolute / regard us; regard us as the absolute / angelic; angelic to a measure absolute / arcs; arcs of the absolute / nights; nights in surrender and life in regard tot he light absolute / surrender; surrender tot he light absolute / sleep; sleep in the arms absolute / arms; arms that are absolute to love / hands; hands that heal the absolute / wings; wings in to the absolute / height; height of the astounding sound called heard absolute / breadth; breadth of the absolute / depth; depth of the deep compute called forecasting the absolute / rest; rest in the absolute / read; read up on the absolute / believe; believe in the light key, the love absolute / capture; capture the power absolute, believe / release; release to the absolute / believe; believe in the life absolute / chest; chest high in the absolute / breath; breath worn in the lings absolute / hallowed; hallowed measure of the absolute / saints; saints seal the absolute / prophets; prophets agree with the absolute / seem; seem to be absolute / seam; seam worn thin at the absolute / lines; lines designed in the absolute / planes; planes of agreed to the absolute / process; God's process is best in the absolute / energetic; energetic agree to the absolute / laps; laps drawn free to the infinitely absolute / loop; loops drawn to the sound of the love absolute / infinity; infinity reigns in the love absolute / waves; waves due to the love absolute / 1000; 1000 times the absolute / days; days of infinite measure in the absolute / times; times of days reclined in the absolute / years; years are green with the clean desire to follow higher the airs of cares unique to God is absolute / loans; loans annoyed can be employed by the absolute / over; over hear is heard the word absolute / bought; bought by the absolute / breathed; breathe a sigh of the absolute / reset; reset by the absolute / resolved; resolved to be absolute / earth; earth's measure is absolute / mother; mother met by the absolute / shekinah; shekinah measure of the present absolute / present; present to the absolute / gift; gift of the seed absolute / presence; presence lived by the absolute / spent; spent on the absolute / bought; bought by the absolute / paid; paid for the reset absolute / debts; debts due to the secure of the love absolute / reviewed; reviewed by the light, I AM absolute / renewed; renewed in the absolute.

THE SACRED-MENTS
LEVEL 13

CHAPTER ONE

Sacred; sacred to a belief in love / dear; love is dear to the review that is, sacred / especially; especially well to the being sacred / special; a special day to be sacred / magnificent; magnificent and sacred too, love / regal; regal inside and to the sacred-ness of love / well; well and sacred too, love / whole; whole enough to be loved / aspect-full; aspect-full regard for the cords cut to reveal the sword of the all-mighty, love / exposed; the sacred is exposed to the hearts of love / expose'; a sacred expose' of the dignity called love / impress; impress yourself best with the test on the love sacred / preside; preside at the sacred to love / practice; practice your sacred-ness / presence; a sacred presence, love / private; a private reside at the ride sacred / proud; proud to be, sacred / plan; love is a plan sacred / express; express the sacred / lattice; lattice woven sacredly / lace; lace over the sacred / lapis; lapis blue and sacred too / lovely; success is lovely in the sacred / lover; a lover sacred to the art of perfect communication at love / laughing; a laughing matter met at the sacred / bouquet; bouquet of the sacred / banquet; banquets full of the sacred / cocoon; a sacred cocoon of love / swoon; a sacred swoon of love / dance; dance in the sacred / mute; love's mute is off to the sacred / respite; a respite due to the sacred / rest; rest in the sacred / dumb; dumb to the sacred / deaf; deaf to the mute of less than the sacred / blind; blind to a belief sacred to love / dally; dally on the heels of sacred love / dearly; dearly head to the sacred / wantonly; wantonly due to the sacred / wordly; wordly and sacred to love / universally; universally due to the beloved, sacred / experientially; experientially sacred to the love of God / essentially; essentially sacred to love / eccentrically; eccentrically said, sacredly love / centrically; centrically said we are the led to the light sacred / aspectant; aspectant matter in the sacred, love / expectant; life is expectant to the sacred in love / adverse; adverse to the abuse sacred / converse; light's converse is the sacred language of honor in love / consort; sacred consort tot he love of the light sacred / hum; hum over this and the sacred fix to love / humor; humor saved by the sacred / direction; a direction to the deep is lightly sacred / dice; dice excuse to the sacred in love / do; sacred to do, I believe in yes / dare; dare to be sacred to love / sacrosanct; sacrosanct to the way that's led to men / metaphoric; metaphoric meter to the euphorically sacred / meteoric; especially meteoric to ascend in the sacred / mesozoic; love's mesozoic / Metatronic; Metatronic to the sonnet called love / magnify; magnify the mezzanine's view of the particles in love's sacredness / sacred; sacred wins, love / passion; passion phased, love is, sacred.

CHAPTER TWO

Gives; gives of the sacred notion that life is love, perfectly / lives; lives in an extreme desire of the giving called living sacred / loves; loves the light sacred to God / breeds; breed the sacred respect for love / breathes; the sacred self breathes deep in perfect love / laughs; laughs can cure about the sacred love / smiles; smiles at you and your sacred views of perfect love / jokes; jokes about the resume of the sacred can loom in love / intrigues; intrigues can rest in sacred love / teaching; teaching the sacred ways to love / knowing; knowing you, I am seen by the scenes of the sacred to love / showing; showing you our power in the sacred / seeing; seeing the sacred in you, I am empowered to be true to perfect love / being; being held on the side of the beings, sacred / wanting; wanting can care for the we sacred / delivering; love is delivering you to the sacred / testing; testing come and undone to the crown sacred / trading; trading measures of the sacred found in holy love / quickening; quickening to love and all the way through to the sacred / preparing; doves are preparing for sharing true love in the sacred form called you / dealing; dealing with the due to sacred love / reading; a sacred reading called the words of love / giving; love the giving living of the sacred in love / visualizing; visualizing the giving, I am satisfied with the sacred in love / redeemer; sacred news said, "the redeemer is", love / lives; lives sacred in the eternal flame of love / in; in time to be sacred to love / keys; keys of the times sacred; zippers that skip to the light sacred / light; spaces light with the sight sacred / shekinah; shekinah difference called the experience of lightly love / sons; sons are said, sacred / daughters; daughters too know the view sacred / loves; love to be, sacred / commands; commands the most, love, sacred / energetic; energetic to ascends and amends are made tot he life sacred / values; values sacred with respect to love / of love; of love and too, the sacred / love; life is love in the sacred / equals; equals measures of the light sacred / presence; presence sacred to the living sun, sacred / deep; deep enough to sing about, the sacred shout called swimming in oblivion can come to the one hum sacred / face; face it, bless it, spell it, said, spiraling signs of the life sacred in the geometric relief called the faces of you / stars; stars whose eyes reside inside the square decide to rest in the sacred-ness of the heavens of love / genes; love's genes are sacred to love / peoples; peoples are sacred to the lights of love / brothers; brothers sacred to the depths of living love / systems; systems of the One sacred / scenes; scenes are sacred / create; create the sacred / anew; anew the new sacred to love / messianic; love is messianic in the sacred son of lifelong love / gematric; gematric met by the aspect of perfectly sacred love / infinite; infinite to the sum called love is sacred / depth; a savior's depth of the love sacred / chemical; chemical in balance and the chalice passed to the One who lasts and the heart of God sacred to true in love / respect; respect your Other, love is, be, sacred / body; body deep in the life sacred / christian; christian times are sacred lines of keeping touch with the light of God / Christ; Christ is, know the rules, sacred / light; light the sacred / fond; fond into love for the sacred / fundamental; fundamental in a mental require of the lessen lost unto the sacred / amethyst; amethyst moved unto the sacred / fresh; fresh in a nestled sacred / sport; sport a spirit fresher, still, sacred.

CHAPTER THREE

Lighter; lighter to the sacred in love / higher; higher still in sacred love / definite; definite measure of the life sacred to love / broach;

broach the subject, love is, sacred / coach; coach me through the sacred loop to love / defrosting; defrosting the manner sacred / process; process out the sacred in / repeat; repeat this measure, love in the sacred / chamberlain; chamberlain of the life sacred / possess; possess the sacred / movement; movement due to the love sacred / swims; swims across water and lives sacred / moves; moves in a spiral to the light sacred / drinks; drinks only cups of the love sacred / abyss; abyss reached and gulfed by the love sacred worn; worn thin, I am One, to the sacred / warm; warm enough to melt in the sacred / power; powered by the life sacred / source; source of the sacred, love / river; river deep to the sacred, love / sort; sort of sacred and all-ways true, the love in you / lair; lair of the sacred, love / preach; preach about the sacred, love / repeats; repeats a lesson, repeat it, love, sacred, love, sacred / rests; rests in a spiral and welcomes ascend to the art of the matter, sacred, hu-man / resides; resides inside the life sacred / worn; worn thin to less and welcomed to best in the sacred / complex; complex matters made simple again by the honest embrace of the light sacred / monogamy; monogamy has come to the light sacred as the One appears to you in the dream delighted by love / inquisitive; inquisitive to a manner sacred / toil; toil less, love is, near, sacred / astragalus; astragalus grew inside you and your gentle lean into the wind sacred / sauce; sauce of the sacred grew in the wood central to ascend / soft; soft to the sacred and all the year through we elect the gentle express of perfect love / bracket; brackets that bend beneath the waves of the love sacred, free to be, loved / in spite; in spite of the sacred and because of this, love / chromium; chromium swallowed by the sacred peal of the bells called love / shone; shone to be left to the sacred / track; a track true to the light in you, sacred / chrome; chrome to the sacred and shines, lightly, love / walk in; walk in to the sacred, love / model; model your manner like this, sacred bliss, called love / depressed; depressed by less? confess sacred to love / expect; expect to be all-ways sacred to love / medicinal; medicinal manner, sacred, love / resides; resides in a manner sacred / suspect; suspect the sacred as love / zones; zones of the manner sacred / exhibition; exhibition of the sacred art of the gallery called living love / lights; lights of the sacred confessions true to the sacred love / fetish; fetish due to the sacred, love / lasts; lasts to the sacred, love / finally; finally settled, love is sacred / mount massai; mount massai knew the clue into love's goods, sacredly / peace; peace is the plan tanzanian, sacred / erupts; erupts a register of the peace sacred / who; who held the knight sacred? / what; what did the day play into, sacredly? / which; which element are you? sacred / why; why decide sacredly / when; when the rest is reached, sacred / plausible; plausible this excuse, sacred / fonder; fonder still and sacred / whence; whence the dare, sacred? / whose; whose the lair sacred.

CHAPTER FOUR

Forgone; forgone to a conclusion sacred to love / cosmic; cosmic will be renewed in the light sacred / please; please be special to the ones who heal in the light sacred / times; times to be will be sacredly aligned with love / modest; modest in appraisal of the names that mean highest love in the life sacred / grope; grope at a gripe less striped in the sacred life of love / grovel; grovel less and live sacredly in the sights of real love / psychosis; psychosis of the seen in what is leaned to in the light of the sacred mind of God called love / smart; smart enough to be sacred / start; start to be sacred in your love / dare; dare to be totally sacred in your love / manic; manic to a sacred view of love / power; power of thee, is, sacred, to love / passage; light enough to see the light sacred / persist; persist in the portal sacred to love / paste; paste your heart on with sacred-ness in love / curt; curt and sacred for telling the truth / cater; sacredly cater to the light sacred / cope; cope with a sacred truth called love/ escape; escape to the light sacred / subdue; subdue to the light sacred / skate; skate on to the roof of the light sacred / skirt; skirts are sacred to the swirling truth / spoke; spoke about the youth sacred / attribute; a sacred attribute of the lesson called love / devotes; sacred devotes to the light sacred / devoid; sacred devoid has come to the fill of love / full; full today with the love sacred / abstruse; sacredly abstruse to simply love / simple; simple, sacred / simply; simply said, love / succinct; succinct love gives life sacred-ness / stall; stall sacredly at love in rest / program; a program of the love sacred / defile; defile less, sacred / daily; the daily due sacred / mend; mend the sacred, love / bend; good trend, bend to the love sacred / will; will over the sacred / fall; fall in to the love sacred / call; a bliss call comes to the sacred, love / bereave; bereave knots bliss at the sacred kiss of living love / berate; a sacred berate can awaken the dead to rise to God / dazzle; dazzle this day with the bliss sacred / dissolve; dissolve to distill the sacred / feud; feud's over, listen, love, sacred / falter; sacred to a falter and the walk through to bliss / halter; a sacred halter worn tight to God / ox; sacred ox of the burden less, love / oxen; hearts of oxen can occur at the power of men pulling for God in the sacred / advise; advise us rest at God's sacred love in the nest of your heart / advice; God's advice is sacred love / Direct; direct to the sacred, love / direction; a direction to the sacred / aspirate; an aspirate manner matters to the desire sacred / attire; sacred attire to the light sacred / jasper; jasper chalice of the news sacred to love / juniper; secret juniper of the sacred / trees; trees due to the sacred / allures; allures to the all of the sacred / perfect; the perfect fit of the sacred / pastel; pastel is the sacred fit of the softer lift of a lighter day called God / level; level risks met, love is sacred / paint; paint spread on the rock of faith and love, sacredly.

CHAPTER FIVE

Permanently; life is permanently free to be spoken too, love / perfectly; perfectly sacred too, love / alive; alive to the sacred / towering; towering manner called loved sacred, I am / suits; suits sacred to the worn with love / graduate; where will you be, sacred, aspect too love / birds; birds are sacred to the friends who love / wander; wander home to be found by the attitude that sounds sacred / found; found a sacred town of love / bands; bands of the sacred play called love / marks; marks on you and the freely sacred / fine; fine enough to choose the sacred / blazers; blazers cued by the sacred / born; born to ascend too, the sacred within

/ field; field of the flowers sacred too, love / follow; sacred to a following, I am the lean-to love / won; won over to the sacred / bleed; a sacral bleed to the sacred / lead; lead on with the sacred / banters; sacred banters on the chanters of love / cut; cut off the need to regress to a lover sacred with confess and truth / cord; cords can agree to be sacredly cut and sent to love and home / succeed; succeed at the sacred/ merkabah; merkabah spin to the measure sacred / intellect; intellect of the sacred begin called the thought-full sacred / confessions; a sacred confessions blend at the signpost of love / mind; mind over matter at the sacred / independence; aspire to independence due to the sacred sum of one, love/ compress; compress the rate to the sacred / bodies; sacred bodies dwell in the love sacred / calculation; calculation of the add sacred / convalesce; convalesce best the sacred / galaxy; love's galaxy is the truth sacred / guide; a guide to ride in the secure to the sacred love / grief; grief can be only sacred when intended to love/ grace; a sacred grace of love molecule; molecules of the sacred wet in the atomic strand called love / atoms; atoms deep to an expand deep in the sacred / suspension; learn to sustain the suspension called love / slip; slip to the sacred desire to love / slope; a slope sacred with healthy love / x; x is y to thee, sacred / y; y knot? Say love is sacred / c; c the sacred / a; a to b c, the sacred / b; finally b, sacred / cells; cells divide and the agree is found in the special seas of sacred love / burst; love's burst is sacred in the giving, love / inclination; inclination to be sacred / pollen; pollen's bait and the honeyed cure of the curate of the fixate called substrate complete in the security of / precision in the being called sacredly, love / pollinate; pollinate your cross with the sacred, love / circumscribe; circumscribe is why we scribe our sacredness on love / count; count on the sacred, love / low; low enough to exudes exuberance called the sacredness of love / high; high too, the sacred, love / between; between the days of sacred, love / finished; finished is heard through the word "sacred" / observed; observed a nearest star say "sacred" / seen; seen in a slant on the wisdom for a sacred won / sent; sent into spiral sacreds / found; found a sacral path unto love, the sacred / final; final folds made unto the sacred / folds; folds allowed are sacred / made; made the diligence of grace a sacred path to perfect's love.

CHAPTER SIX

Care; care enough to feel the sacred / conveyed; conveyed the tune of the sacred / shown; shown the manner sacred to love / act; act on the sacred / homage; homage to the success-full, sacred / joy; joy in the sacred / jubilation; jubilation's corner is the sacred / wonder; wonder of the sacred / worthy; worthy to be, sacred / legend; legend of the sacred, love / legendary; legendary ways to find the sacred, love / truth; truth is told within the sacred / trust; trust in the sacred, love / exercise; exercise your nature, love / universal; universal languaged, love / sound; sound the peace of the sacred, love / charm; charm yourself with the sacred, love / charisma; charisma to behold sacredly loved / warm; warm enough to be consumed with the sacred / understood; understood by the sacred / dear; life is dear to the sacred / contest; contest

about the sacred / contestant; contestant of the hour is the our called sacred connect with the prize, love / battle; battle over and the fall complete includes the rise to the sacred / over; over the edge of a dream called sacred / winner; the winner knows the edge-less dram of becoming consumed by the sacred flame of love / conceive; conceive of yes tot he guest who lives for love / born; born to notice a purple fire come to hire you as the soul-less One called love / whisper; whisper sweet nuggets of the all to the matter that breathes only love / whistle; whistle your winds of the living breath called sacred / listen; listen to the sacred, love / snowflakes; snowflakes flutter over the daze of the sacred hills of light / unique; unique to a spin, I am in, to the love sacred / concur; concur that best is the arrival sacred to love / individual; individual to a manner flamed by the sacred of love / ritual; ritual manner of the communion best worn as love / ceremonial; ceremonial matter concerned with best the sacred-ness of perfect love / pellet; pellet power overthrown by the heart of the One you own, you, in sacred love / penguins; penguins dance to get the chance to love sacred / maverick; sacred maverick come to begin the win, love / rebels; rebels yell best about the sacredness of love / rabble; rabble roused to the cause called God is, love, sacred / rounders; rounders sound like the shore of pounding dates with the wave sacred / random; random settle can become the seat of regard for the hard truth that love is sacred / rate; rate yourself as worthy of the banter called our talk of love / vibrate; vibrate at great rates of love / cure; cure your pleasure with the seeking sought and found at sacred love / cues; cues lead to the assure that notice sent is sacred in true love / gratitude; gratitude for the welcome shore of sacred love / appreciation; a sacred appreciation for the review of love / latitude; latitude comes to the sacred length called love / longitude; longitude found in the sound sacred to love / lateral; lateral pleasure met in the sacred, love / bilateral; bilateral to the collateral deal called buying some less than sacred love / unicameral; a unicameral vote for blake as best the bet for sacred-ness in love / cadence; cadence found in the sound sacred, our voice of spoken love / beat; take a beat and reside at the street of perfect sounds of sacred love / rhythm; rhythm found in the swollen seas of sacred love / reach; reach out to see the sacred, love / unite; unite your sacred with your love / calibrate; calibrate your date with the seconds of sacred love / met; met at good-bye and once more hello to the sacred, love / durable; durable to a measure called sacred, love / secure; secure your treasure to the sacred.

CHAPTER SEVEN

Furthered; furthered by acceptance of this date, I point to the lifting celebrate of perfectly sacred love / fascinate; fascinate me with your sacred greeting, love / pools; pools of the trace sacred in love / teal; look at the teal appeal of being sacred / task; task force, One, sacred, love / olive-green; olive-green to the sun sacred to love / sea blue; sea blue to the wedded believe in the sleeve called sacred love / aqua; aqua blue rest in the sacred nest of love / healthy; healthy to a spiral appeal called sacred love / apartheid; apartheid matter melted squarely in the sun of sacred love / avert; avert the sort who sacred less concern themselves with only learning lesson One / allegation; an allegation prepared by the sacred / phosphorous; phosphorous smelt of the sacred belt called Orion / bosphorous; bosphorous steam in the brews called love and the schemes called extremes of the sacred-ness of all we meet for living sweet in light / fondest; fondest sacred, love / gallant; gallant to a dream, I am the seam of the light sacred and the sparks called love / malevolent; malevolent to the lessen and sacred to the lesson One / hallowed; hallowed blue regard for the wed called said sacredly, love / spinal; spinal piece of the soul's release can come undone as we speak of sacred love / sporting; sporting chance at the dance called sacred, love / yoga; yoga meets rest in the breath sacred / buffer; a buffer too, the sacred chance to dance with relief at love / allocative; allocative to measures sacred and love / stellar; stellar to the power of the matter sacred, love / solvent; solvent in my revolve to the love sacred / red; red matter reeled to sexual appeal of the sacred / rather; rather be sacred / rattle; rattle a sacred sound to love / snake; snake gone, love on, sacred sum, One / dragon; dragon eaten by the sacred, ah so, love / deed; deed sold to the slim has become a dividend to the sun and the sum of this Earth called One / will; will you be sacred with me? Love / affirm; affirm the measure wanton in our sacred love / callibrate; callibrate too, love the sacred hum of Taos deepened will of the living expressive summation, love / feed; feed on the manner called prolific in the sacred, love / flounce; flounce about as loved sacredly / faster; faster too the sacred / orphaned; orphaned explain has come to the sacred / wallow; wallow less, we are sacred / buffalo; buffalo singles dip in sacred living love / plains; plains of resurrection, love / major; major summation comes to the sacred, love / custer; custer the cluster of the sacred, love / stand; stand at the sacred, love / little; little is sacred too, love / big; big enough to be sacred, too / horn; horn of the plenty, sacred / geronimo; geronimo in the sacred / apache; a sacred apache stands at the spirit of man in God / natives; salient natives vote for the sacred / cherokee; cherokee nation of the sacred participation in perfect love / sioux; sioux sacredly in the manner called love / pueblo; pueblo of the sacred, love / dominion; dominion come to the sacred, love / domain; domain of the woman who loved sacredly / tribe; tribe of the two who are sacred to love / tribe; tribe of the sacred, the ones who love / clan; clan of the caves opening to the sacred, love / family; family of the sacred man / group; groups of the sacred, love / grade; grades updated to include the ark of the sacred in love / level; feed us to the level balanced at sacred love / ladders; love's ladders rehearse the sacred steps to giving living love / climb; climb to the pleasure of the sacred love.

CHAPTER EIGHT

Total; a special place in a total taste for sacred love / summary; a summary of the excuse has gone to the sacred truths of love / upset; upset less and summarized more as the sacred guess called right to the books of love / courtly; courtly quarters of the measure sacred to love / royal; royal allegiance to the sacred / relegate; relegate yourself as sacred to love / delegate; delegate the express

sacred / deliver; deliver us to the sacred / dose; my life is a dose of the sacred in love / loyal; loyal to a sacred truth, I am alive in love / leverage; leverage your way to the sacred, love / lean; lean on all you call sacred / leap; leap to the sacred / listen; listen in sacred-ness to love / regard; regard yourself loved sacredly / unravel; unravel less and love sacredly the One / save; save the sacred, bless your love home; home too the sacred, love / returns; returns our love, sacredly / ratio; ratio of the sum sacredly One / roam; roam to the sacred/ waver; salaries waver less when sacred too, love / remember; remember the sacred, love / deciduous; a deciduous manner called the sacred / amphibious; amphibious to the lips sacred to the tongue called love / coniferous; coniferous, carnivorous, calciferous, sacral, spinal, sacred love / dirt; love is the dirt of a worth sacred to specifically love / outside; outside the manner and inside the planner called sacred, love / in; in love with the sacred / or; please ignore the less, sacred / was; was it sacred, love / can; can you be, sacred / could; could you sally forth too, love / may; may be sacred, love / maybe; maybe sacred, all ways, love / wills; wills that are sacred rule, love / pageant; pageant of the pleasure sacred in love / patron; love the patron sacred, saint / genesis; genesis of the winning reel to the sacred / hybrid; hybrid manner dear to the sacred equate called love / dominant; dominant manner, sacred rules, love / recede; recede to the respect-full enthuse called sacred love / recessive; recessive deed to the sacred One, your name and the sum of love / spare; love is spare in the sacred pair celled deep in respect for the perfection of love / Handel; Handel loved by the singing come to the sacred / Mendel; sacred Mendel and heard as the love of the lighter sun / banter; banter bent to examine the examine of perfectly precious sums of the concentrated one called sacred too, and I said, love / befriend; befriend the sacred, love / bevel; bevel carved at the carve called sacred, love / broken; broken by the sacred and healed by the love / paid; love is paid by the sacred / reward; reward come, sum, sacred, love / tuned; tuned in to the mother of the sacred, love / toned; toned in to the sacred singing, love / intonation; intonation's nature of the notion called sacredly love / nasal; nasal pleasure drips less in the sacred health of living love / basil; love's basil bless in the soup called love / herbal; herbal pleasure of the urban force called sacred love / stem; stem pipe turn to the sacred, love / blossom; blossoms that measure of the blossom sacred to love / stem; stem sample, sacred, love / blossom; blossom sacred, love / pistil; pistil, stem, sacred, blossom, love / fertilize; fertilize your power in the sacred / favor; favor in the sacred.

THE COMMAND-MENTS
LEVEL 14

CHAPTER ONE

Commands; commands begun to be the 3 in 1 and we've become the remember of all who love sacredly / energetic; energetic is the secret too, the sacred kinetic spin has become perfect command of love / expose; expose yourself to a lighter energetic called precisely sacred in love / impose; impose yourself on this lesson called command the sacred to love / arc-play; arc-play can stay in command in the sacred, love / arc; command module landed at the 10 and found a friend called the sacred, love / metallic; metallic *matter met with perfect command in the sacred, love *material and true to the elective rate of energetic ascend to love / jolt; jolt awake and command true love / glow; glow about your truest love, command is meant / radiate; radiate yourself as commanded by truth in sacred love / command-mint; command yourself well in a mint called green flares of the cares perfect to love / comma; love's comma is the command meant / conquest; conquest the sacred as sweet in command / conquer; conquer your fear of less, command completion of the arc of love / coquettish; love is coquettish in the way to command / quantum; quantum to the measure of the sacred in love / quantums; quantums of the perfect commands called love in the sacred / quaver; quaver less in the ascend to the pervasive-ness of command too love / waiver; waiver less, command more, love / wild; wild enough to be in command of love / monet; monet knew command of the perfect land called lightly loved at the water's dance / mont; mont de lovely and the summation of the one and clearly the commune with the sword of love in summary done / st michael; st michael sent a new event to the sun of st. michael and the tour of God is, love / mirror; mirror me free to the respect and expect of a degree called perfectly, commanded, love / meander; meander too, command's degree, love / mill; mill of the command, deep in replete with love / wander; wander home to seek the command of the richer in the poorer gone to perfection in love / wed; love's energetic has come to the wed of the slighter signs of perfect love's command / focault; focault's penchant for command is the pendulum swung to the center of love / foster; foster bears the lifting wares of a gentle stare at the perfect energetic called commanded by love / lager; lager drinks lighter when the ferment's gone and the command becomes pink again / lady; lady of the representative day of perfect command / laddie; love's laddie is the gentle square of the central command called lightly love / level; level on the square of the circular perfection called pi are squared to the pleasure spent on relative command of love / lark; command your lark less and triangulate is done in the perfect ascend to love / lather; lather up with the rest of us at the lake of assure and the perfect command called love is, salvation's come, the end, the done, of less / remember; remember your confess and the command to rest in the best of love / roust; roust around the rest-full place called lightly commanded love / roster; roster of the rest above and the legend, the ledger, the lamb, the become of rapture's command called lightly love / rally; rally around me doves of command for the peace is in love / rapt; rapt in the pleasure of the command called love / rapt; rapt about your enrapture called the pleasure of command in love / candor; candor said enjoy your pleasant ascend commended by command in love / callus; callus gone to the palace of regiments broken by the chains of commands in love / plant; love's plant, the factory green with heaven's learn called lean toward the lighter side of perfect command in love / pant; vaunt your pant at the breath of respect and the rate called command in love / pull; love's pull is constant in cure, command / park; park in the perfect command of the waters called love and the fountains of men called command / partner; command your partner home to you in your use of perfect command / part; part of me, let us say, that this is perfect in command and love / heart; heart full of love's command / half; half again and all of me in perfect command / hold; hold on to the love in light's command / have; command can have a wonderful reflect in the eyes of spirals called God / hanker; hanker for more and know the cure of perfect discourse concerning the command of love / yearn; love's yearn is perfect for command / desire; desires content with command of love / date; date your set of values in concrete command of love / confused; confused by less and known by command / conveyed; conveyed to constantly by the commitment called content meant, love / concurrent; concurrent matters marry me too consent to a command of the perfection of love / content; content in the cure called command this love / curt; curt to subvert, I am found in the perfect living command of love / extend; extend yourself to the One you love in command.

CHAPTER TWO

Seductive; seductive treasure and the measure become, loving command / shine; shine on the command of a lightly said, love / express; command's express is precious too, love / shatter; shatter less and be expressive in commands of love / resume; resume the reside in command to love / again; love too, and again I command you home too, love / attitude; command attitudes of best in committed friend of love / attribute; attributes of the One, command, complete, love / tally; tally your command as won to love / truth; truth is told to the command of love / designation; designation of the One command to love / place; place yourself in perfect command, love / plaza; plaza of the pools of the seventh and eight command to ten times the land of the hawaiian blend called love / puzzle; puzzle over yes is done, command true, love / success; success has come to the ones who are healed by the feel of a perfect command of love / succeed; succeed at the rest of perfect command, love / suite; a suite full of command perfect to love / sparks; sparks spill over to the command of love / collect; collect command into your perfect love / column; the column of love's return has come, adore your command / caliber; caliber of the perfect 44 command / calligraphy; calligraphy drawn to the pen of command / curate; curate great respect for the elect in command / generate; generate your great command, love / cajole; cajole your command of the boast of love / conjugate; I am the perfect conjugate of the command of perfect love / conjugation; conjugation of the One command too, love / sanguine; sanguine sealed by the command too, love / shot; shot by the command of perfect love / squeeze; squeeze your command too, love / squeak; squeak about the command to love / rosetta; rosetta rounds of the stone gated friend swung wide to the pearly weight of swinging doors commanded open to love / respect; respect your set of resurrect's transcend of Enoch's begin to command some love / mercury; mercury's confer is best as commanded to love / silver; silver travel along the cord of reconnect to love's command / racial; racial over and loving due to the clue that one's become to commandment love / copper; coppers cue is you in command / tin; tin avenue of the golden view called perfect command of love / organize; organize yourself in command of perfect love / organ; water's organ is the heart of man's command of love / alum; alum's treasure is the powder of command / gold; gold avenues command is love's stand in the light resurrection / platinum; platinum is purest in contemplation of perfect command of love / pearl; pearl of the measure of central command held as lightly gently love / south seas; south seas seen in my wandering way to the curb of command meant, love / tahitian; tahitian command has come to expand our love / honor; honor your elder with perfect command / hospital; hospital of the mercy that drained from above to Gabriel's wealthy command of love / grace; grace is perfect in command / consume; consume commanded confessed, love / pressure; pressure on the mood of a new arrival called command of love / pound; a pound plus command / calf; calf of the cream called milky reside in the confess of commands too, love / shelf; shelf the nature to live life in less than command / sexual; sexual command can confess real, love / fawn; fawn over the command too, love / sacred; sacred and sexual in perfect command too, love / sacral; sacral pleasure can command perfection to the Aztec brand of love. The snakes are gone by perfect command. Come home, love / putter; putter about and confess direct your loving command / panther; panther's plan is the creek of command to post your love in, know the Friend, Command / Helenic / Accord / Reached / Speak.

CHAPTER THREE

Pressures; pressures express the impress to command / pursue; pursue the absolute, command, love / pursuant; pursuant to the measure of command, love / penchant; penchant for the command of love / flank; flank of the notion to command what's left to love / foolish; foolish penchant for more command of love / forgone; forgone by the forgiving command called love / fulfills; fulfills command, us, in hu-man love / facet; facet of the gone to command a face called love / flirt; flirt the skirt of command / frail; frail froth, command, us, love / cancel; cancel confess and know the command of love in truth / charge; charge us to be in command / forthright; forthright to the birth of the worth of command / one; one truth and the love too, command / date; date the truth with command / conceit; conceit concede to the care of it all for the command meant, love / eunuch; eunuchs gone to the train of command in love / callibrate; callibrate the rate of your love in command / cost; cost of command, perfectly, love / joyous; joyous in command / joint; joint joy and the present command of love / japanese; japanese concur of the

command called love / jazz; jazz above, command / join; join us in command, too, love / tandem; you are tandem in your spiral command of the heart within your love / tape; tape your respect to the repetitive measures of command times twenty and love / roster; roster of the rule of command, one, two, love / rapport; command rapport of the respect for love / rescue; love's rescue is you in command / ransom; ransom your note to command / review; review your command of the truth and love / routes; routes to heart of the perfect command called love / spoon; love's spoon, the honeymoon of the perfect respect for the command called love / fortitude; fortitude found in the continue around, command / connect; connect your command to the heart that's within our love / copy; copy the plan to command your love / panther; command the panther to crawl to love / prowl; prowl like the nature of command / purveyor; purveyor of the all of command and the surrender too, love / soothe; soothe your breast and know confess of love / scout; love's scout is the myth of a mouth held soft in command of love / sully; carry your sully to the farthest command of love / sprawl; great to the sprawl of the all of command / spool; spool of the spoof called command of the all of greater love / download; love's download is the hear of command to repairs of love / interface; interface with the command you love and the one who rules the tools of confess / interlace; interlace with the place of command in your breath and love / cope; cope with the scope of your plan and know the command of love / cap; cap off with command, your love / coat; command a coat of platinum yield to bring the energetic too, love / dense; command your dense stay done with the won, companion, love / density; density comes to the light command of the summit reached too, love / door; door opens when the shut becomes revealed within the arc of command / window; windows share your care for the system correct with respect for the faith-full heart called love in command / plan; plan to be perfect in your command of love / pane; command your panes with the broken explains of commands for love / passionate; passionate embrace of the case found again and the command too, love / port; port sustained and sent the sword of the God-head's command for the sword of God is, love / ports; the love of supports to imports called preciser command of love / assemble; assemble creates command of the energetic plan to respect only love / infinity; infinity is the loving command for respect in the blends of days gone wide to the living spin, one point, command / future; future of the friends who command true, love / past; past times over and content in the command called the state of love / Clarity.

CHAPTER FOUR

Present; love is present to the taste of contented command of love / point; point to the space of a meaning called love in command / create; create a sensation called love in the nation of God in command / creative; creative to the command of love, pleasure / comment; comment on the trend to command our love / content; command is content in the reveal called love / consent; consent to comment on the reveal called perfect command of love /

concede; concede that your date for feed is command / correlate; hearts that correlate to loving command / cooperate; cooperate in great complete of the cranial command too, love / covert; covert manner is the hidden reveal of the command called perfect, love / corner; corner of the extend to the one called perfectly love in command / curl; curl over the lip of control and know the curl of a wave content with love / collapse; collapse at the peak of a success-full command called love / collide; collide at the lid of a central commend called command this, love / over; over and over and again command, love / sensate; sensate is the stat of command in love / sentient; sentient to the plan of command in love / syntax; syntax sent a peace-full commend of the command too, love / percolate; percolate of late at the peak of command meant, love / correlative; correlative is the treasure of a committed stand in perfect command of love / conjunctive; conjunctive to a measure of the advance called perfect command of love / conversant; conversant about it, the nature of love is, command / cooperate; cooperate with the treat of a feat called perfect command and love / code; code too michael, command post, love / core; core of the nature of the living respect called perfectly commanded love / court; court your sort and the particular command of love / cap; cap on the nature is off to command our love / cant; cant creates a lean to the command of love / course; course cruised to the resurrect called the command of love / coarse; coarse accept of the resurrect to the perfect command of love / caliper; caliper pinch is over with command of the perfect, love / classic; classic concern with the command of concern for perfectly, love / caustic; caustic concern and the septic return corrected by the stay in perfect command and love / spastic; spastic and true to the regard for precisely commanded love / deep; cater to the deep reflect of the respect called precisely the command of love / dynamic; dynamic duo at the scene of the commitment stand in love / delete; delete less, know more, complete command of love / creation; creation of the nation of love in command / congregation; the congregation meets at perfect command of love / caspian; caspian seas of the command too, love / tyrolean; tyrolean exceed to precisely the command, love / phrygian; phrygian cap of the map perfect to the command called love / atlantic; atlantic capability of the residence sent to perfect commands of the shore of love / author; author of the zen command to the buddha man, love / kings; kings of command / ezra; ezra's ring of perfect command, the land of love / moab; moab met by the Melchizidek expand to the impulse of command called love / malachite; malachite mend of a committed friend commanded too, love / maloch; maloch is the measure of the command too, love / azora; azora's treasure of command / centidor; centidor is the door of perfect command / ophilim; ophiliim millenial command, perfect / anthilum; anthilum concentric, command / contain; contain your command of love / capture; capture your command too, love / relief; relief of the perfect, command / round; round this measure, command / roster; roster of the command to love / register; register of the command too, love / book; book of command / light; light of the perfect command / life; life too and the light command of love

/ lesbos; enoch knows that lesbos shows command of the perfct in love

CHAPTER FIVE

Concrete; concrete command of the solid truth called the blue to solicitous love / constant; constant in your command / consistent; consistently in perfect command / resistant; resistant to a manner less than this, command / retardant; retardant to the trend and fired by the command to a friend called love / flamed; flamed over the food of the consistent mood called love in command / spiral; a spiral cure for command, love / spirulina; spirulina dream, the green extreme returns too, command / strands; strands of the deep receipt called perfectly lives the light command, love / green; green news commanding you too, love / blue; blue to Michael's view of command / alexanderine; alexanderine command of the means too, love / right; right commands left too love / bell; bell of command and my voice is love / phonic; phonic manned sonnet of the expand too, love in command / sonnet; sonnet of command / calibrate; calibrate a great command / skate; skate over the ice too, command, love / escape; escape of the light command to expand to a living love / scope; scope of eternity's command, is, love / score; score more, command / skin; skin game of the truly naked can love / thought; thought about the size of the clients in command and love / whole; whole enough expand to the plan called all the command / hope; hope for command / heal; heal open panes with energetic explain / command; command, love / rather; rather be in command and love / renewed; renewed your command / rule; command rule, loved / regard; regard decide about this love in command / rapt; rapt command of love / residue; residue of the residual heart called command is meant to love / rope; rope this command to love / ran; ran about the trend to come up to command in love / rainbow; rainbow of command in the trend too love / spring; spring to command / franklin; franklin meant command / friend; friend of command / roads; power roads command / dirt; dirt hurt command / mint; mint blue, commands of love / dirth; dirth of the nature, loved / doric; doric fan's command, love / rhodes; rhodes of ridden command to love / gaelic; gaelic command can affect true love / clothic; a clothic nature can command true, love / cloaked; cloaked too command / clothe; clothe the nature of the command too, love / cope; cope too, command enough love / might; mighty command, love / care; care too, love / pare; pare aspects too command / inherit; inherit a land of command / pore; pore over matters of the command in letters of love / drips; drips by command, love / classic; classics of command / dares; dares too be commanded by love / dates; dates of a woman's release too and this loving command / dolly; dolly daily drew her truth / frank; frank enough to see full command / pun; puns can drip of command / date; date on the yes of command / full; full tools of command

CHAPTER SIX

Mid; mid command, love / aspire; aspire to conspire to command too, love / aspect; aspect of the few who knew command /

specks; specks of command, love / span; span of the truth in command / spire; spires aspire to befriend the see of command / steeple; steeple of command / state; love is the state of true command / staple; command a staple friend too, command, our love / church; church of the clued who love command / release; release your state to perfect command of love / reference; reference of the commanded degree called love / riffs; riffs deep in sweet command too, love / rate; rates end, command / rosey; rosey red review of the life in you and your silent command of perfect love / raptured; raptured by the agreed to command too, love / rate; rates rule by command / petals; petals spread about the scene of the command too, love / pure; pure to a state of command / know; know the command too, love / known; known to agree too, the imbalance of, command, love / dues; dues done too, command / park; park at the over hear of command / wait; wait too, command / resign; resign too, command / reinvent; let's reinvent command / alert; imagine this alert command / convert; convert too command / condor; condors over thee, command / rabbi; rabbis rule over the less and more command / rabbit; rabbits of the chain, command / pew; pew seat, command post, love / people; people live by command / steer; steer near the true command / club; clubs duel about command / revenue; revenue true too command / raids; raids about the news of command / roars; roars too, command / rasp; raspy notes of the rude confess to the true command, the voice of love / cored; cored by degree and free to be true too, command / catered; catered on the date of the Oz like command called lightest love / camps; camps that live like command / clasp; clasp notes of the two handed friend , command / center; center about the cure of command / central; central too, command / valiant measure, command / virgo; virgo in command / main; main too, command / vein; vein of the true command / valiant; valiant leave to the light command / menu; menu eaten by command / varsity; varsity rules the spools of command / rally; rally about the command / venue; venue true to command / vasal; vasal to command / rover; rovers rule the true significance of command / rounder; rounder ruled by command / vesper; vesper times the talent of command / votive; votive candled delivery of true command / veil; lover's veil can lift to prove command / view; view of the true, command, too, love / voice; voice about your true to command / vice; vice healed the letters of command, speak less, command / patient; patient too, command

CHAPTER SEVEN

Welcome; welcome happiness to your life, the wife of wed has met the head of love at perfect command / worth; worth gathering, command / wants; wants too, command / works; loves works command / weds; wed's our command / depends; depends on command / decay; decay gone, find command, love / deteriorate; deteriorate made command the plan / doors; doors of command open, love / cope; cope with perfect, command / escape; escape too, command / stray; stray to the edge of command / stay commanded by love / move too, command / secure in our command / fray; fray knot, command / stunt; stunt

gone, grow in, command / manage; manage your command of love / bait; bait gone, command / mop; mop up, command / wet; wet with command of love / mote; a mote of love has come to command of love / molecular; molecular measure of the treat called command, love / bowl; bowl over, command / atomic; atomic pleasure, command / rescue; rescue done, command / triage; triage of the truth, reflection come, command / train; train too, command / professional; professional measure of true command / traipse; traipse to the edge of command, commit, love / crank; crank the precious command to love / tack; tack the sail to commands of love / sultry; sultry be measure and pleasured by the treasure of command / splatter; splatter your life with pairs of the chains of command, love / street; a street straight to love in command / straight; straight enough to be true too, command / straits; straits of desire too, command / affair; affairs of command / festoon; festoon yourself with command / flavor; flavors of the truth, command / decorate; decorate yourself with command / devour; devour less with true command / discard; discard your less with command / dilate; dilate too, command / dancing; dancing in the winds of command / don; don your day and wear command of love / desk; desk top command / trade; trade for command / trance; trance of the end has gone to command / troupe; troupe struck out for the in of command / avenue; avenue of the treasure of command / associate; be an associate of command / uncle; uncle command's module, love / aunt; aunt of inventive command / gather; gather your measures, command / gain; gain love, command / convey; convey truth, command / points; points of command / purely; purely given, command / critical / appealing / apparition / friendship / devotion.

CHAPTER EIGHT

Seasons; seasons of command, love / spans; spans of command to love / sport; sport your sort of command / bathe; bathe you bed in command / breathe; breathe about it, command / belief; belief in the truth of command / balance; balance your command with love / bank; bank on the brinks of love / bet; bet on command / gather; gather true, command / sewn; ALL sewn up in command / reap; reap what you command, love / power; power to be true too, command / clasp; clasp the command of love / clues; clues about command / pleasure; pleasure in command / portable; portable pleasure command / poles; poles of command about love / arcs; arcs you spark too, command / arts; arts seek command / arks; arks in command / covenant; covenant of command / conveyance; conveyance of command / cores; cores in command too love / cubes; cubes square at command / squires; squires hire command / sources; Sources of conspire hire command / stares; stares at the truth of command / stairs; stairs to the sum, command / sun; sun is command / stars; stars of command / fray; fray about the edge, command / fork; fork over, command / fellows; fellows of command, love, respect / friends; friends who command, love / cables; cables in command / cut; cut the cord, command / forgiven; forgiven, command / fallen; fallen to full-fill, loves, command / stood; stood up at command / sum; commit a sum, won, love / store; store your sort of command, love / supply;

supply your set with command / save; save yourself, command / start; start too, command / gates; gates grow the aspects of sleep in command module, dream, of love / jolly; jolly too, command / jam; jam about true command of the june of noon of love / jab; command a jab of love / jasmine; jasmine jeweled, ginger tooled, the breastplate deep with command of love / job; job to pay, command / journey; journey to the gate of command / join; join a wavelength / command coital; coital's need, command / fully; fully flew our love to review of command / fount; fount of a flow to command of love / fame; fame is flume to command / bulge; bulge of command, love / bloom; bloom orange, command, relate, love / burrow; burrow up to the command of digestive love / camp; love's camp is command / planet; planet purple at bluer command of the flame called love / venue; venue of the true, command, love / ridiculous; ridiculous in nature and in truth about the facts blooming in love / often; often said, a mayan led to love.

THE GEOMETRIC-MENTS
LEVEL 15

CHAPTER ONE

Tally; tally up our friends and field the knowing ascend of reveal of the summation called the geometric total, one, love / preside; preside over the geometric stride to love / add; add geometric ascend to the love in our spiral blend of the living brand, hu-man, love / subtract; subtract One to add too two, your geometric ally, love / measure; measure your measure less and add a treasure to deeps additions in love / math; math is the geometric peak at the markers of frames called precisely unique to the metatronic concede called lightly love / spiral; spiral ascend to the geometric blend of the spirit within our love / spin; spin to a cycle called geometrically love / fibonacci; fibonacci spiral in the kinder friend of the perfect thin progression to geometric contend to love/ square; square to a comparison called the medicine of complete return to the precious state of geometrically spoken, love / circle; circle your friend with the spare begin to partake of the stake called precision to the geometric, love / blend; blend the beginning to the end and know the within of all we are is love too, the geometric / cube; cube squared and hermetically sealed by the ceilings reach to the knowing that God is, geometric, love / convey; convey the message geometric, love / divide; divide the aside to the middle commit, content in commend too, find One geometric / begin; begin to ascend too, geometric is, the current trend, sacredly, love / nature; natured by nurture to be geometric too, love / summation; summation of the duration to the ascendant begin, times One, 08, hum, 08, hum, 08, love, the geometric / quadrant; quadrant incurred at the square of a geometry faring best in the seas of the quiescent notion that love is contractual in the training called life / quasar; quasar of the ascend, geometry / quadrilateral; quadrilateral geometry, love / equals; equals the nature of the nurture of light geometry / equivalent; equally trained by the heavenly crew, each one's reside is you, consistently and geometrically, love / valiant; valiant accomplish, the notion that trends to the rail that friends find without resist and the consist of the commitment called precisely, geometry in love / covalent; covalent bonds that seem intricate in dreams of the circular page of geometric love / specific; specific geometry found in the round ascendant / at this point I see the way we are constructed the way to draw us home and I seem lightened by the lift to a fin; a gift called love / finite; finite trim to the geometric friend called the lamb of love / infinite; infinite to a measure called geometric too, love / eternal; eternal fashion about the question called true geometrics and this, love / elegant; elegant to choose, confuse less, the land geometry, the light regard for the card of the sea ascendant, love / eloquent; eloquent to a nature cured by the concession too, geometry is the hu-man code to love / effective; effectively I see the bulk of the matter is written in God and the code is love, how do I brake it breathe deeper still and know the conceal has come to be seen, help ahead, reveal, love geometric / fashions; fashions of the passions, geometric / trends; trends that reveal thee, geometric / fads; fads concealed now pass to the light geometric / prints; prints seen in the beam of the light geometric / effervesce; effervesce about the light geometric / voice; voice

about ascension, now, geometrically, lean to love / venue; venue of the geometric / forage; forage for the geometric / foray; foray to the fray of the geometric perfection, love / feud; feud over only less has gone to the light geometric / follow; follow your friend to the light geometric / pleasant; pleasant to the friend, geometric / places; places that are geometric collide to love / peers; peers at the brilliance of the geometric / total; total - *geometric *energy / trends; trends of the geometric, add two, love / tracks; tracks to the geometric / brilliance; brilliance in the light geometric / carat; carats of friends who are geometric / flash; flash at the trend geometric / casts; casts of the geometric / molds; molds over too and finds the geometric, love / jaws; jaws of the jewel geometric / chin; chin of the drift to the experience of the light called geometric / chew; chewing a sample of the taste geometric / perfection; perfection found in the geometrically done, love / precision; precision's ascend to the friend who participates in the perfect geometry of love / admission; admission too, the geometric / ticket; tickets too, the geometric / thanks; thanks for the geometric, show, love / gratitude; gratitude too, the geometric.

CHAPTER TWO

All; all we are is geometric love / source; source of the geometric, love / torque; torque on the geometric / pressure; pressure is in the geometric release too, love / fissure; fissures cracked by the geometric, love / force; forced geometrically too, love / calculate; calculate to rate of the admit geometric / project; project of the life geometric / praise; praise the light geometric / focal; focal point, light, geometric / foci; a foci of the geometric / purse; purses won by the geometric accent on love / winnings; winnings found in the town of love / wealth; wealth is winning the geometric ascend too, love / wax; wax poetic, love, geometric / rave; rave about the love geometric / precious; precious too, the love, geometric / avian; avian pleasure, the flight to the geometric, love / stealth; stealth measure, geometry, love / cast; cast you light too, the geometric / percentage; percentage of the geometric / measure; measure the true, geometric / volume; volume up to the geometric / density; density found has gone to the geometric, love / expect; expect the light geometric / apt; apt to the b of an a called geometric / count; count on the geometric, love / shells; shells numbered by the 10s of the 7s spin to the number geometric 720 degrees to love / series; series of the geometric wings of folded love / stones; stones of the seed geometric, the self, the one, the growth of love / nautilus; nautilus shelled by the geometric ascend, level three, love / serial; serial too the numbered agree, geometric / sets; sets of the geometric / nautical; nautical mind of the sailing kind who find the true geometrics of love / numbered; numbered by the geometric / self; self sets, open end, geometrics / within; within the sets are found the love geometric / begin; begin to ascend with a geometrically finer shape of love / counts; counts on the geometric, love / the books; the books are in, geometrically too, love / the notes; the notes of the geometric sing about love / pi; pi's code is broken by love, / 14 plus 2 equals more than knot, equate your set with the re-elect of the / option to spin again, love; what is / 28 folded by 2 and multiplied again by the / 14, the 8 of love / the news; the news is in, the pi codes friend is love / the curls; the curls of ascend, geometric, waves of love / relate; relate too, the geometric, love / the revenues; the revenues of the geometric, love / ST. Louis; St. Louis streets know the repair to the compare of yes to God at the creation station, the point of the integration, the ascension bridge, love / the dates; the dates who resume their expansion of the kinship with the friendship of geometric love / the dues; the dues are paid, all-ways, geometric, love / arch; arch back to the life geometric, love / gate; gateway through the wings of your spin geometric and the return to the one aromatic express of the / confess that an inner welcome has come to love / reside; reside at the light inside the love geometric and the precious step called the living One / wings; wings over the geometry called love / mid; mid way done, find the bays of cooperative consideration of the nation of geometric love / return; love's return to the burn inside the light geometric / beckon; beckon to the beacon of the light geometric / amid; amid the weaves of the life geometric / jerusalem; jerusalem rules geometrically / necks; necks of the bottle bet for the geometric set called to the twist of love / doves; doves code, love is, geometric / states; states of the ascend meet geometrically at love / shoes; shoes off for the ascend too, love, prints to the geometric.

CHAPTER THREE
Chime; chime about the geometric / mitral; mitral valve closed to re-open again at the light geometric / nature; nature found geometrically lean to love / within; within the ascend and the love geometric / mantle; mantle of the shelf and the light geometric / waves; waves that flow over the ledge of the light geometric's falling waters, love / neutral; neutral ground, geometric / mistral; mistral winds of the wings geometric and the lineage of love / winds; winds geometric to the dipping create of the life called love / computerize; computerize your complete of the receipt for the love geometric / chakras; chakras sealed by the healed love of the sound geometric / choose; choose a will too, live, geometric / light; light to a sight called the life geometric / chimp; chimps that ascend to the light of the geometric / life; life is geometric / lighting; lighting given the opportunity too, love / choice; choice of the matter sealed by the light geometric / lantern; lantern too, the geometric glow of love / square; square 2 and the higher life of the light that's seat is within the chamber of the queen of all / belief, the prince of relief, the king of the pyramid called lightly the adoni of the geometric, love / abort; abort the sort of the light geometric / circle; circle the seen, geometric / triangle; triangle of the geometric seam, too, love / tiers; tiers of the appears too, love's squire, geometry / towers; towers of the truer geometry babel less, love / tools; tools of the trade geometric, pen, plan, God, man, love / sacred; sacred scene, the love geometric in explain, one, two, three, love / ruler; ruler of the measure meant to be, geometric / hands; hands about the equal connect of the concept of the inches of contact at the conceptual point of / the plan called bands of the golden concentric, geometrically, love

/ measures; measures of the man, geometric, love / compass; compass point, bliss, geometric north, new due, love / breath; breath of the central examine, air geometry / calipers; calipers close to the light geometric / come; come to the home geometric, the heart of your love / assembly; assembly point, geometry / attitudes; attitudes about true geometry, love / tombs; tombs of believe upheave to reveal geometry / temples; temples of the explanation deep in the richer dream of the scheme called lightly geometric, love / penteteuch; penteteuch of the written light coincide at geometry times 5, love / archive; archive notion, society by devotion, and lightly spoken, geometric love / rock; rocks that ascend to the geometric point of love / mosaic; mosaic matters of the love geometric / nave; naves note the geometric attend too the top of love / steel; steel yourself to the love geometric / enochian; enochian needs of the know geometric, love / noah-ic; noah-ic wonder, geometry of agree too, love / shoot; shoot the mayan fool with less, geometric, love / aim; aim at the game Ann Arbor deep to the light geometric/ design; design wings of geometric expand to the butterfly, love / dart; dart to the start of the love geometric / dip; dip into the residue of the smile of a willing friend living again in the wide decide called love's geometry / Dove; love's Dove is geometry / angle; angle too, the savior, geometric / splash; splash down in the ground geometric, earth, love / spurt; spurt at the geometric fountain of love / savor; savor the taste of the flying pace called the love geometric splurge; splurge on love's geometry, / believe, confess, directs, love / sport; sport the sort who find geometric ascend, love / saint; saints found, the geometric, love / Katherine; Katherine's found the plan of the give geometric, love / plane; plane of the geometric, love / geometry; geometry by love / karen *karen explains that confession is plain to the kind geometric kinship about regard essential in neat love / parking; parking here at the geometrically acute degree of respective, love.

CHAPTER FOUR
Coving; coving concern for the complete code too, love / paving; paving over the ground geometric, love / techno; techno's reside is geometric too, love / clan; clan of the cave geometric at the cove of love / planning; planning the explain can be confess of the light geometric / subduct; subduct less and know the yes of the dove called centrically, love / duct; duct of renew knew conduct of the luck called geometric / vein; veins pulse with the geometric / mine; mine the signs, the symbol, geometric / venue; venue on the limbs geometric / court; court about the geometric / forgive; forgive me and take me to the geometric / menu; menu of the building geometric / cords; cords accrued are released by the geometric / forgetting; forgetting's aid abetting is the light geometric / Arthur's; Arthur's legend is geometry by a sword's breadth, love / king; king of the mountain, geometric, love english; english to the bone, geometric, love / language; language of the deep geometric voice called the leaves of the lend too, love / ward; ward off the sword, geometric / wound; wounds heal geometrically, love / lewd; lewd enough to be geometric / water; water weds will be geometric too love / wet;

wet's love is geometric / fork; fork over the geometric, love / earth; earth's geometry is electric, love / spores; spores of the winds of geometric, love / plates; plates that collide at the side geometric / spoon; geometry's spoon is deep with love / float; float at the light's geometric blend, love / stacked; stacked in planes to the scene geometric, love / storie; storie's hear is all we real for the roll geometric / story; story's about the geometric ascend too, love / steal; steal the agree of the trend two geometric / sample; sample the example geometric, love / staple; staple of the geometry of love / contour; contour of the light geometry / case; case of the date to be, geometric attache, love / study; study the geometry of true love / steady; steady the eddy of the river of this geometrically free, love / babies; babies who choose abide in the reside decreed at precision in geometry of love / men; men with tools geometrically, lean, too, love / mentor; mentor of the matter geometric / mantel; mantel worn beneath the shoulder less, geometric / mercedes; mercedes driven to the geometric / friend; friend of the nature geometric, love / found; found to be, geometric / fueled; fueled by the geometric, love / countered; countered by the geometric, recount, love / shun; shun resist, list, the geometric / staring; staring at the geometric / astonish; astonish the sea of the light geometric / heaven; heaven is love in the geometric / come; come to the geometric / capable; capable of pleasure in the love geometric / culpive; culpive nature comes to the head of sacred geometry and love / cowper; cowper per the nature geometry / pen; pen your way to the geometric written by love / planter; planter here and the growing near of the love geometric / planner; planner manned by this expand to the living geometric / dare; dare too, geometry, your life with love / do; do this, the geometric, love / knew; knew the geometric, love / in; in this geometry lives our concede too, love / over; over the ark to the geometry of the arc called love.

CHAPTER FIVE

Faint; faint enough to be forgiven, the living friend, geometric, love / live; live in the moment symbolic geometric, love / see; see the light geometric / claim; claim the life geometric / capable; capable measures of the pleasures of the geometric friend, love / culpive; culpive again befriends the ascendant, love / bonnie's *bonnie's regard is blue to the throat inside, I elect, to participate, in the life geometric, light *basically obnoxious need neglects intellectual energetics sincere to love / basket; basket of the plenty geometric, love / jillies; jillies siesta kincaid high to the fresh refresh called energetic love to the geometric / willies; willies go to the energetic ascend called transcend to the plural nature of a permanent feature called professionally geometric too, love / waders; waders desire deep require of the regard for transcendent contend to the light geometric / friends; friends of the light geometric / fostering; love is fostering regard for the light called precisely the geometry of love / captive; captive nature concurrently speaking, concisely we agreed to breed only perfect geometry of love / gone; gone to the going and on the homing regard for the higher love, geometric / haunting; haunting has come to the going away and the paying regard for

the living reside called perfectly geometric too, love / done; done by you and too, we are, regarded by the sword of the continent contented by love / deliverance; deliverance sent geometrically to the friend energetic, light / comes; comes the regard for the Other card called collect true, geometric, love / amid; amid the attend we intend to connect correctly as expected by precisely love in the geometric / amore; assymetric ascend can intend the reflect that's respect-full to others by contend of the geometric aspect / implore; implore more about the light reflective and energetic, love, geometric / impale; impale love's empire around the build of your yield to the erect correction geometric, love / implore; implore the geometric, love / implosive; implosive nature of the nurture called correctly perfect respect for the geometry of true love / explosive; explosive nature kneels at respect for the geometric ascend to the truth of love / dialect; dialect select to the geometric kin of love / didactic; didactic to a geometric view of love / expression; expression of the geometric in, love / canton; canton geometry wins the ascend too, love / lifts; lifts the nature geometric, love / regale; regale your self with love perfect in the nature geometric, love / addition; addition of the mention geometric and the dimension desired, fifteen, to love / web; web of the geometric and the weave salt lake red too, love / plus; plus your geometric ascend love / minus; minus our geometry plus the One, love / menial; geometrically menial to the kin, love / mental; mental accrue of the friend, geometric, love / calculation; calculation station is the love geometric / concentrate; love's concentrate is geometry too, love / coincide; coincide at coincidence, geometry is love / beast; beast gone too and the geometric / lesson; lessons lend the geometric / parental; parental pleasure is coming round the circle geometric, love / lamb; lamb's within the circle come to all we are in the geometric hum of love / plans; plans are geometric too, love / conjugate; conjugate the rate of the electric geometric love / create; create the state geometric / concaves; concave is the day geometric / consists; consists of the geometric / life; life is geometrically sacred too, love / wife; wife of the sacred, the geometric, love / constant; constant blend, geometric / cabinet; cabinet of ascend too, love / counts; counts on the ascend, geometric, love / clobber; clobber each others constant with commitment in contentment and the love geometric / clatter; clatter less and be the better, geometric / chaos; chaos fueled by the love geometric / paint; paint your rules geometric / petals; petals open to the plane geometric / pedals; pedals about like the light geometric, love / pnce; price paid, lesson learned, geometric win, love / day; days deal geometrically too, love / leonine; leonine measure of the plan 2 be, transcendently, geometrically, love.

CHAPTER SIX

Disorder; disorder of the moment is the forget to be geometric in love / defend; defend each other geometrically, love / recover; recover geometrically, love / cord; cords of less remove when we breathe only the geometric bet for love / waynesville; waynesville wins in the geometric chin up, love / sylva; sylva settled by the love of a geometric few who win the ascend too, love / brevard; brevard brew of the regard geometric and the hills of love / highlands; highlands congeal has found me healed by the love geometric / cable; cables clued are healed by the geometric, love / tricked; tricked by the trickle to the love / geometric codes; geometric codes to the life of a love called infinity triple; triple trim within the whim, geometry is the love perfect / tantric; tantric found, geometrically, love / tore; tore off the edge to the wedge geometric, love / tour; tour the geometric allure of the life called spirit of love / tube; tubes of regard for the time geometric / worn; worn by another the badge of the red discourage gone to light geometry / wonder; wonder what wins, the light ascends, geometrics / won; won by the wind geometric too, love / welcome; welcome commend of the friend geometric, love / wanda; wanda is wound and geometrically sound to the truest regard for perfection's brand of patiently we reside at the register of coincidentally love / mantle; mantle over the geometric agree, too, love / home; home to the light geometric / hover; hover over the cover off to the light geometric / cover; cover the light with the life geometric, only, love / cope; cope with the creed, life's regard for the cue, true respect for love / camp; camp at the edge of respect for the wealth of resume called profess true love for the geom-e-tree of man / arc; arc, home, to the land, geometrically / arts; arts blend, geometric / art-I-facts; art-I-facts abound geometrically too, love / artemis; artemis measured by the geometry of the triple ascend to the friend called love / auric; auric regard for the measure called energetic respect for sensually geometric love / whale; whale of the matters, geometric / wince; meanings wince at the convince called essentially the heart of respect for geometrically speaking, love / win; masons win geometrically / winters; winters mince the mention of the spring geometric / throws; throws thrown geometrically too, love / window; window on the world, geometrically / wood; shriver said that the wood would love geometry about true love / over; over the matter, geometric / cover; cover your guard with geometry / cape; beliefs cope with the horn geometric, love / super; super geometry of the living ascend too love / supral; supral nature knows the key, pure esteem, the exceed geometric, too, love / supernal; supernal in the nature of the creation called the cradle perfect to respect-full ascend to the mend called yes, we will, remember, love / stake; stake on the geometric / storage; storage accrued, geometrically by the living scene of love / purge; purge less, the geometric lead is love / pentic; pentic pens commend the love geometric / mends; a mends found in the geometric / chords; chords of pleasure geometric / tenor; tenor of the geometric, the voice of love / ports; ports of the geometric, heart-felt love / miss; miss geometric is the key to the sacred, love / harmonic; harmonic means to the metric seams called love in relief to the light geometric / treble; treble cleft, met at the bass geometric / portals; portals of pleasure, the pleasant agree to delicate means of the crescent called respect geometric / mentors; mentors of the measure, geometric / auric; auric agree to the light geometry of love / bass; geometric bass is deep in love / vistas; vistas into the geometric / pincers; pincers win the geometric / operatic; operatic pleasure in the geometric

auria of love / falsetto; falsetto tooled elevate to the late decide called multiple love to the geometric / pictures; pictures of the geometric and the flash too, love.

CHAPTER SEVEN
Pause; pause at the pleasing living love geometric / soprano; soprano to a plan geometric / stacatto; stacatto burst about the geometrics of love / pungent; pungent smell of the geometric / acapella; acapella bells geometric / sleeper; sleeper about the geometric / slopers; slopers held by the hand geometric / spin; spin in too, the geometric / spore; spores blown to the geometric / archaic; archaic scenes geometric / arcturic; arcturic means measures about geometry in love / spandex; spandex spend to the stretch geometric / portals; portals open to the ascend geometric, love / pleadian; pleadian measured by the geometric, love / coning; coning akin the geometric, love / fringe; fringe around the geometric, love / find; find the pleasure in this thing geometric, love / found; found a find geometric, love / sky; the sky above, geometric / sixteen; sixteen times the geometric fore of love / plural; plural plural geometry, love love / pend; pend the sailing to the telling expel of perfect breaths of the love geometric / descend; descend to the selling attend, geometric / cares; cares about the geometry of love / cords; cords that sever less, direct accent to the protestant speaking called living in love geometric to a fiber of the optic kind, the seeing line, love / source; source of the nature of the building connect, geometric, too, love / send; send in the friend geometric / sent; sent to the surrender geometric / coat; coat yourself with the geometric / ascension; ascension scenes geometric too love / delivery; delivery of the team geometric / message; message geometrically bottled by love / notes; notes knew the geometric sounds of love / accelerate; accelerate too the geometric / quicken; quicken in the geometric / concurrence; concurrence by a measure geometric / occurrence; occurrence about the geometric extreme of love / initiate; initiate the date with the geometric / deliverance; deliverance too, the geometric, love / traipse; traipse true, astound, geometric / step; step in tune, geometric / stomp; stomp too the geometric steps of love / space; space geometric / time; time is the collapse to expect perfect command of the living friend geometric love / delivers; delivers true, the geometric / dates; dates about the geometric / prophetic; prophetic singing about the truth called geometric love / hermes; hermes is geometric egyptic conclude of love / consciousness; consciousness akin to the geometric / incorporate; incorporate the geometric into love / rendezvous; rendezvous at the corner too and the main of geometric love / solar; solar include of the mood geometric / igniting; igniting passion with compassion geometric equals love / grateful; grateful too and the geometric / corporate; corporate treats of the treasures complete with the geometric / mental; mental explain of the means geometric / children; children hear about the geometric / corporation; corporation geometric / banter; banter about the count geometric, talk, love / gifted; gifted by the geometric and thinly love / eternal; eternal to a moment geometric / rounds; rounds the days geometric, the edge of the legend adventurous

with love / flame; flames flew energetically sound to the rounds electric, love / grasp; grasp the sounds electric, hums, our love geometric.

CHAPTER EIGHT

Sprung; sprung by the light geometric's bend to the heart of love / pyramid; pyramid's contribution in, geometrically, love / pupil; pupil around the astound called the love geometric / ascension; ascension to the example emphatic by contented geometric love / before; before the days geometric / iris; iris healed by the geometric / after; after all geometry rules by love / now; now we are geometrically alive too, love / corner; corner of the clue geometric and the heart hu-man too, love / cosmic; cosmic akin, geometric / woven; woven by the living kindred, geometric, love / enter; enter the portal geometric, love / entry; entry too, the geometric, hearts held, love / core; core of the geometric, the heart held alive by love / domain; domain's heal, geometric / dominion; dominion of the minion done and the geometric agree that all is good and good is all, love / aspect; aspect clued by the geometric / sea; seas astound about the geometric / seat; seats in the geometric living light / chamber; chamber of the geometric, the heart, that's love / driven; driven by the geometric reside at love / given; given the gentle align at the geometric / gained; gained another matter and the love geometric / countered; countered by the geometric / counter-act; counter-act the geometric within, love / wisdom; wisdom won by the One geometric, love / offers; offers to be geometric in love / incarnate; incarnate matters matter best in love / incantate; incantate yes as your assign of the energetic agree too, love / cycles; cycles complete in love's geometry / essentials; essential's zeal is real in the light geometric / concentric; concentric to a meeting of the minds combined by coincidence insight-full by the light geometric / ringing; ringing in the light geometric / sparks; sparks that seal the columned light geometry / winging; winging wind of the blowing sun geometric / spirits; spirits that seal the abundant with the geometric / singing; singing about the light geometric, love / preparing; preparing the light geometric, the blend too, love / conspiring; conspiring to agree too, love's geometry / trinity; trinity of the trail too, the geometric / training; training in the geometric, learn too, love / trains; trains the appeal to believe in, the geometric / meditator; meditator of the agreed, respectfully seen, co-tangent to the agent geometry and love / gravitate; gravitate too, geometry in, love / contour; contour of the seam geometric, love / magnetizes; magnetizes the agreed with the light geometry of love / mesmerizes; mesmerizes acceptably the integrity of the expectantly geometric / magnifies; magnifies the consigning admit that life is geometric too, love / meditates; meditates about the geometric / aspect; aspect of the geometric, love / sparkles; sparkles keep the pleasure geometric, too, love / trademark; trademark of the geometric, love / seals; seals done, geometric, sun, love / traditional; traditional treasure, the measure geometric / training; training in the geometric / travail; travail less, give, geometrically, love / training; training in the geometric, love / travail; travail less, live, geometrically / travels; travels come to those who love geometrically / trails; trails above and concede too the geometry of love / hierarchy; hierarchy of the geometry of love / practical; practical to a measure called love's geometry / abode; abode of the sun, geometry of, love / vogue; vogue is in to the geometric, love.

THE ARC-MENTS
LEVEL 16

CHAPTER ONE

Acropolis; Acropolis of pleasure and measures of a real desire to commend the arc in our love / athens; athens knows ascendant command of the consistent meter and the rhythm in love's arcing agree to be real / greece; greece is the neat arrival at a pleasure deep with contented release into the arc of love / crete; crete is significant in her thiran end of the spiral complete within the arc of love / greco; greco-roman whistles in to the arc of a light geometric, love / figures; figures release the stranglehold on the less in the form of an arc called real, love / figurines; figurines sing of the light dynamic given in to an arc called healed, love / fresco; fresco mannered complete of the question replete with commission of the measure arc deep in love / freshen; freshen up with the arc on, love / minor; minor to a manner called the manor of an arc held deep in respect-full concede to the need call true, love / minoan; minoan measure of the pleasured confess that love is direct to the mouth of the chosen One, God is ahead, live on beneath the arc true with love / mute; mute to a measured beat, I release to the light dynamic, pure, complete, confession, arc deep in love / theory; theory of a thiran plain, the main, the arc on, too, love / core; core of a nature natured complete within the arc of love / cored; cored by creation to mention a measure wet with release to the confess that God is living pleasure, arced too by love / cord; cord of the cure of the empress of reflect digressed to the living express of the purest cure, the arc complete, cords cut, too, love / capable; capable to a measure called God and the Lord above, all, complete, the arc of love / cable; cable's the plug and the light is on to the spark of the arc called God is love / capture; capture your nature in pure arc on to love / stature; stature of the arc of the nature called perfectly God is, and we are, love / statue; statue of the include called the nude arrival at the lighter exude called arcs on, love / coned; love is coned by the arc on, love / cubed; cubed by the nature of a creation called perfect to the arc's on, love / cue; cue to be pleased by, the confess of, the rest in, the arc on, love / art; art is the nature of a fresher start arced directly to love / antique; antique to a natural attend and the ascend called reflect of the arc on the water of love / article; article done by the written clause called the aspects deep in the light on love, articulate, particulate / dramatic; the dramatic re-elect called rights of respect for the life we call live in the arc on love / portico; portico sound in the round particulate called the arc on love / nautical; nautical nature of the natural precision called man ahead, love, arc on / novice; God is the novice reflection inside the arc on, love / novena; novena of a nature natured by deep resurrect of respect-full lend to the arc on, love / navel; navel explain of the plain called respect-full nature of the nurture coined the belly of the nestle in regain in regard for the giving called perfectly lives the arc of love / note; note your deal as done to the precision come to optionally and optimally speaking respect-full love and the arc is on, God / fisher; fisher men mend the nets of the arc is on, love / park; park at the arc and respect your reflect in the eyes of God, hu-man, love / greens; greens of the arcs on the trainload called love / hana; hana natured nurtured rounds reflections deep with the rights on arcs of love / hanalai; hanalai manned kaui deep in the lands of replete the respect for the living, arcs on, love / lanai; lanai on the mend and the yellow lend to the rights on respect-full trends of lightly scene, arc lean too, love / hania; hania good-bye to the flying arc called love / molokai; hawaiian breezes sweet with the treat bamboo and love in the arc's ascend to molokai / Hawaiian; Hawaiian nature's come to conclude that this is the contented remind of the remember called precisely / contentedly; contentedly concisely respect-fully lightly the means of eternal stars called arcs on love / kona; kona is the land of the arc of love / kai; kai's nature is the love, sea wide, of the stride ocean deep to the gulf's reside and the tasman's believe in pristine decide to splash in the arc on love / orifice; orifice of the mend, the trend of a native called precisely arc-ed in, love / chorus; chorus upheld by the singing bell of a leading arrival at the meaning of the arc-ing sing too, love / kindle; kindle the pleasure of a pleasant kiss, creative, flowing, and nestled in the arc on, love/ couple; couple with the few who lend an ear to the whistle called loving and the giving called precisely and all of the above in the living require arc deep too, love / men; men remember less, arc on, love / women; women lend confess, arc on, love / man; man of the world unite extend to the completion arc on to love / woman; woman of the wind geometrically breathing the arc on too, love / all; all of the you, arc too, love / one; one whose lend is deep in the arc on, love / marble; marble me mended and exceptionally deep to the arc on, love / mate; mate who's vote lends reputation a keeping arrival at the revival of a spark unique to befriend and the melodic voice of a respective attend called the arc on love / met; met by a nature geometric and the arc that's on precisely too, love / fresh; fresh to a nature unique and the precision of the decision called the reputation of the arc is on too, love / freshen; freshen the lesson with the arc on too, love / friend; friend of the necessity to rescue know less, the regain gained precisely then and essentially this, the respect for a confess called certainly gained arcs in to love / befriend; befriend the essential examine called centrally remembered and intended the arc on love / believe; believe in the lender, arc on too, love.

CHAPTER TWO:

foreign; foreign matter, the latter day regard for the residue gone to the light of beyond and into the life that's connected too, the arc is on, love / landing; landing in planning for the new millennium, know the trinium, the trining, the twining repair, and the care for the eternal in where you are heading for lightly scene, the arc's dean, love / wide; wide enough to confess too, the arc is on, to love / won; won by geometry and the synchronicity of the duplicity done and the winner is won by the arc on too, love / winner; winner of the winter land, confess your glad graduation to the arc on, love / killer; killer deals done, the arc is on, love / clatter; clatter to the bend and know the ascend and the plan, man, hu-man, love / clink; clink shut less, drink the glass of a new horizon, and the light on, confess, love / bust; bust of the Venusian plan to know man, the day of a new dawning and a new dean of arrival at the revival of love / opening; opening up to the bringing sum, the won, the winning, the One, love / crater; love's crater is removed, know the move to the light electric, love / crease; crease across the nature of the given and the winning and the One God, love / Orient; Orient your expression to the won, creation, the sun, the reside, the arc is on, love / wave; wave the length of your arc at the wand of love / rolls; rolls over too and the geometry of the light sea love, arc on / sink; sink full of the sung, the ringing, the singing, the arc on, love / raises; raises our vibration, our devotion, to the notion, arc high, too, love / brash; brash notion, the lotion of skin, the love within, our life in God ahead, contest won, arc on / figurine; figurine found in the contested town won by the light on, love is, arc on / fortress; fortress of the found and the true and the few who stand as the One, love, arc on / phone; phone the matter in, arc on / cell; cell by cell, I have found the heightened sound of the sound called creation and the calm of the One, love, arc's on / cellular; cellular to a notion of devotion, I am One by the light in the arc on, Love / mattress; mattress of the mend of a bed wet in receipt of the arc stared keep of the light on love / matter; matter about the cause electric, now complete in my arc in God / expressing; expressing love's confessing and the arc is on, love / excel; excel at the matter, yes, arc on, too, love / exhale; exhale at the matter, the chatter gone, the arc on, love / breathing; breathing in the sun of the arc done, love / grin; grin at the matter come to fruition, you are the One, arc on, too, love / grains; grains of the command to arc on seeds our living love, God's win is love / grown; grown by the matter deep to the steep arrival at the revival arc deep too, love / girl; girl powered by the dream too, arc on, love / guy; guy mattered band of the command chained to the arc on, love / goth; goth natured good-bye to the seam less electric, I am the One, God's won, arc on / Gothic; Gothic to a nature come to the One life electric, come to the arc on God / Goyan; Goyan nature come to command and the arc is on, man, hu-man, love / Guise; Guise of good-byes has come and you see the won in the winning sun, come to the arc on, love / Gender; Gender bent went to the arc on love / Gentle; Gentle to a nature nurtured by love/ janice; janice jeaned in the standing dream of the gentle seam of jasmine lend to the arc in God/ pleads; pleads about the rims of the dreams gone stiff to the wind called forever and the light called remember and the intended remember, the One sum, the sender, the laughing regime called essentially the arc on, love / pleasant; pleasant to a manner called the planner who knew about reviews of the arc on, love / notice; notice of the due and the nestle too in the arc on, God, love / pleasure; pleasure of the measure natured by love, arc on / bereave; bereave about the nature dealt by the spell of an a-r-c on, love / gone; gone to the seam electric, color me won, by the arc too, love / done; done to the less, One arc, love / definite; definite to a due electric paid arc on, love / width; width of the life elective and the respective reside at the arc on, love / goiter; goiter's burst, arc on, first, love / girder; girder of the beam electric, love in the arc of God / gainer; gainer spent on the regain sent to the arc on, love / gift; gift of remember to tender your arc on, love / lofty; lofty too, the nature, arc in, love / lifting; lifting the dream and anointing the seem of forever's heal

and the step to the next, arc on / latticed; latticed by a nature, arc on, weave, God hu-man, love / lord; lord of the moment, arc on / lowered; lowered by the need, gone to greed, and your continue arc on / heightened; heightened by the sword of forever, I reward myself with deep surrender to the tender arc on, love / chalice; chalice of pleasure and the cup of remember, arc on / sword; sword of conveyance of the cord cut too, less done, arc on / kite; kite of the flight to the arc deep in love / conveyance; conveyance in the sum arc on, love.

CHAPTER THREE

Clearance; clearance deals with the heals, arc on, love / arc; the arc is due too, love / jockeys; jockeys ridged by the resonant bliss of the plea complete in the healing kiss, arc on / success; success is reached through preserver and the hear we are too God, arc on successfully loved / flown; flown by the flying leap to the lead arc deep too love / horses; horses send their steep regard for the card complete to the living regard for the arc on, God / suppression; suppression has gone and we know the contest won, God's arc has come to the land hu-man, love / flags; flags fly over the dream, arc weave, too, love / carriage; carriage power, the hour of concede tot he confess we need of deeper love and the arc on, God / sailor; sailor's hour sailed by secure command to the land arc on embroidered numbers kept, arc leap, too, love / sewn; sewn to the nature secured by the stirring access to the mixed view perfect, arc in, love / fawn; fawn natured consent to invent too, and the arc sprint, true, conscious ascend, electric list to gentle kiss, arc on, love / flap; flap you arc about true love / flatten; flatten the moment into the arc complete in receipt of this truth, love / fester; fester's bloom burst, confess, true love, arc on / festoon; festoon your natured mooned by remember, confess, the arc is, love / come; come to the counter, arc deep, love / capers; arc's capers come to the remembers of love / onions; onions skinned by the arcs in love / cravat; cravat worn in traditional show of the state of react and the startling remember that God is, arc deep, in, love / grace; grace of the minutes shorn to One complete remember of the date with God in the arc of love / graphic; graphic agree to the see of the arc on, love / sonnets; sonnets sing about commit and God is freed to remember this, the arc in deep relief and the love in the blend of forever with believe / southern; southern to a nature of give, arc in, love / state; state of the native, sun, strong enough to arc on, love / fondle; fondle your breast of forgiven, remember, love's arc is won / figures; figures lend consent to the invent of the arc called love / symbols; symbols of the seem too, love is, arc on / signs; signs of surrender intend to contend without and within the arc's in, love / swift; swift to a friend, remember, the arc's in, love / sightly; sightly scene and the dream arc time too, love / sorely; sorely worn by less, know constant more, commit too, the arc of, love / saffron; saffron dreams, arcs win, spicy teams of remember / saturn; saturn opens the stem, arc flowers, love / sign; sign of the trine, surrender, arc deep, love / plants; plants that grow in the overnight flow of the arc in love/ sword; sword of the natural completion of the arc in love .suspend; suspend your decision by confess of the real deal, arc's in, love / churches; churches reach to touch he children of the arc, rainbow, love / pastels; pastels view our faces content in the invent called precisely done, arc on too, love / extend; extend yourself to pastels strong to the arc on God is, love / parkers; parkers pay for the ranching stay at the arc in, love / westerns; westerns need a friend to sing too, arc song, love / solid; solid drift to the arc that's missed by most, the One, arc in, remember, love / porters; porters lift me too, the top, the apex, the arc of love / wed; wed the explain, the sustain, the arc's expanse, love / chore; chore of the settle and the keep of a living connect called steep relief and the arc done, God / pens; pens written to the nibs, retire to conspire with the finished light of an arc on written, love / wends; wends the counter of encounter to the arc's in, love / sapphic; sapphic measures measure yes, arc's in, love / staples; staples of love, arc is in, love / generative; generative meeting at the complexion of a face wreathed in smiles and a heart deep in love with the companion of the arc of God / okay; okay enough to constantly be in the arc's sign, love / sturdy; sturdy to a nature, complete, the arc in strength too, love / gentle; gentle measures of the pleasures constant, too, love / sophic; sophic to natures of the dream, arcs in, love / surges; surges with power of the keep, arc on, love / gazing; gazing at the dream arc deep too, love / steins; steins high to a Germanic seam, arc in, too, love / swift; swift extreme become true arc of love / royalty; royalty runs to the brim, arc in, love / valle; valle of the cross gone to the lift called the gift of God in love / cay; cay matters in the agenda gone to the arc of love / columbine; columbine climb to the arc in the balloons of love.

CHAPTER FOUR

Columbine; column combined at the arc on love / pour; pour your score on the light connection and the arc is in, love / syntax; syntax community of the living immunity called speak only, seek only, share only, love, the arc rule, believe in the One, God, love / combine; combine your pleasure, inherit community, banish immunity, know the dance of the holy One, indiscretion gone, the stunning announcement comes, God lives in you, now, arc on / pave; pave the wave with rest, arc on / knolls; knolls wins, arc on / shoals; shoals of the manner seen in the electric dream, arc on, love / offer; offer to be real in community of God and the arc on, love / evergreen; evergreen nature of the community of love, arc is, remember, God / sheds; sheds the destination of less, the lighter confess, and the presentation of best, arc on / exclude; exclude captive notice that is true and know the revenue of the One who remembers the arc in love / shows; shows the nature of the arc in, love / glossy; glossy days that due, arc on / stoney; stoney nature comes to release and the arc on too, love / wild; wild enough to be legitimate to the street geometric and the electric birth of the worth connected, arc in too, love / glazed; glazed by the naturally fleet shoes of this One who arcs in true to God / weathered; weathered by a nature of confess, I knew the arc too, God / worn; worn by the Mother, the nature, arc's in, God / governed; governed directly

to the seen, arc in charge, love / seen; seen to being geometry's light in love / signs; signs set up for the arc time love / growth; growth grew to the trees of the arc on love / recant; recant the code, true too, love / adorn; adorn yourself with the Self of the arc sign, love / vacate; vacate to the state geometric and the arc of love / relegate; relegate your date to the late move, arc in too, love / deflate; deflate the late with a geometric arc called love / blows; blows the lid geometrically arced too, love / aspects; aspects of the infuse are arc-ed too, love / receipt; receipt for the arc of written love / thunder; thunder's scene is arc-angelic deep and this is love / castles; castles of the clue arc-angelic / going; going in to the arc geometric, the heart of man / throne; throne of the thunder arc-angelic / craters; craters of the creed, arc-angelic / within; love is within the arc and then we are the win too God / shelter; shelter gain, the geometric wet, arc lean / lemurian; lemurian means geometric wins too, love / loiter; love's loiter is arcing in deep / friends; friends of the geometric live arc thrilled by the hilled love / respect; respect the respect for the stellar pause at the clause arc deep, love / devotion; devotion is the lease arc deep too love / demotion; demotion of the devotion clearly seen arc deep / gone; gone to the ways arc deep, living, loving / resume; resume the respect arc deep too, love / presume; presume that God is, love the arcing in, tune of the harmonic lift too love / safety; safety in the seat, the arc swing / deludes; deludes the nudes, arc votes, love / California; California crews arc three love / shasta; shasta's gene, the volcanic lure of the light germanic and the life Hispanic and the plural ascent to the vent of a light arc flown to the mist Haleakala deep in the arc receipt, love / penchant; penchant for passion and the once again fashion of paler mists of precious days spent warm in arc-a-types, love / relent; relent less, know the court of a sort who judged less steep, arc on, love / illusion; illusion of the glint arc wide too, love / over; over and done, the run arc deep, love / arcs; arcs are near our clear arrival at precision's friend, love / drawn; drawn to another, I uncover the light of the faith-full type who chore at only the arc on, love / dire; dire to an arc higher, accept the conspire, and know the fire of the burn electric, Metatron / delivery; delivery done and to the arc we go / gone; gone to see the arc delivery and the light that filtered me with shadow-less respect, love / Flagstaff; Flagstaff fools less this regard for the reputable confess of the arc on yellow, love / Denver; Denver keeps a kneeling street, her own, by the mile wide seam called arc on, love / Boulder; Boulder bills the scene as best when your extension meets ignition by the means necessary and our patient walk to the talking cathedral and the hydraulic expectance for a light dynamic, create pure arcs of love / lyons; lyons is, love, arc 3 / waters; waters move upon the land of the arc some to rest at love.

CHAPTER FIVE

Lion; lion's lamb the arc in love / lamb; lamb of the arc too and living deep in the status replete with love / cabin; cabin feed, love's heed, arc on / cure; cure the concentrate with the substrate mineral rich with perfect arcs in love / chant; chant at the rant and arrive at the affluent invite called let's embellish with only the arc in love / chance; chance to be the chance that we are and the current brand, arc lean too, love / curvy; curvy roads agree, live best, confess the arc's lean too love / curvaceous; curvaceous breed and the love in, arc deep / clinch; clinch at the shoulder, arm deep to the arc on, love / glint; glint the hints called arc eyed love / milky; milky walled residue cums too the arc on, love / clinch; clinch the drift, arc on, love / steam; steamy arrival at the arc in heat, the visitor love / morning; morning dues paid the dove to wave at the arc of love / heaven's; heaven's friend, the arc in, love / gleam; gleam at the arc in, love / tolerate; tolerate the late arrive at the arc inside your free arise and God is, love / survey; survey the sites of love, arc on to a new arrival at the revival of the deeper side of the aspect, love / live; live dreams in the arc's lean, love / repairs; repairs desire, the arc's sine, love / squarely; squarely ride the rise to the arc-on size and the living love / ram; ram the drive and relate maturely love's arc is on / flop; flop to the top of the arc on, love / sincerely; sincerely, arc on too, love / mop; mop the manner planned too and the arc in, love / maps; maps in and the arc's in, love / unfurl; unfurl the manner mattering and the matter in tot he arc's win, love / gathers; gathers the measures of the treasures arc thin to a thicker love / gauges; gauges of the manner and the matter and the desire to require a rule to design the rider who lives on the arc of love / cap; cap your pleasure, love is, arc on / unfold; unfold the nature of the statue called maturity in the surety of perfectly, resolutely love / joins; joins the nature, arc sides too love / remands; remands the manner of the treat called perfectly arc deep too love / mother; mother's come to the agree, arc on, love / winds; winds of the win, arc in, love / wives; wives win the deep ascend to the trend arc deep, love / winter; winters wield will win the arc in too, love / winding; winding the stairs, arc is the square revive of living too, love / stairs; stairs at the spare arise arc on, love / council; council of the kin that nets the sets arc on / reclines; reclines at the resign arc on, too, love / shadows; shadows of the shining sun called precious is our love, arc's in / slivers; slivers of the liver who gives of only arc song love / groves; groves of ascend arc on too, love / mats; mats of the steep arrival at the arcing treat called love / mates; mates of relief at the reside called write the ticket, trip it, arc on, to your true love, tree of life, in too, love / cat; cat of the candid sands, dug in to the arc on, love / manana; manana's arc is, love / banter; banter the canter, the manner, the planner, the treat, love, arc on / belief; belief found arc on, love / prayers; prayers of the concede, arc singing, love / postulate; postulate of the magistrate straight to the concept of love / enter; enter the tree of the pairs called perfectly arc deep too, love / entrance; entrance too and the arc song, love / serve; serve the manner, arc deep, love / servant; servant scene, arc friend, love / master; master of the mastered arc, love / amble; amble to the assemble of perfectly arc's song, the heart's on, too, love / amber; amber to the heal of the still integrate that's come to the arc on, love / sicily; sicily is the arc on the initialize love / saunter; saunter too and the arc true, love / taylor; taylor trade by the raid on, love / initial; initial eyes, the manners, arc's in, love / bounty; bounty found, arc on.

CHAPTER SIX: dog; dog dazed, come straight to the news of precisely, come in, to the arc news, love / brick; brick of the our has complete ascension in the gift of mention of the higher dimension, God's arc, our love / sprites; sprites who pleat the complete, the mantra-ed exam of the lamb of God, the arc come, complete, love / inspired; inspired by the desired, I am wired to connect to the original source, the Norse code, the nordic sword, the arctic cord's cut, love this, arc / shop; shop at the place of the face called precisely, perfectly and honest, the arc on, love / box; box of begin and again we send our hearts to precisely the arc-end, love / sox; sox worn seal the feet of the colder care gone diagonally north to compare the nodes, the explodes, the exposure explosive, love / contact; contact each other at precisely, love / wood; wood seen like fire by a match made in heaven's proceed, the process, confess, love is, arc / words; words of pleasure measure my concede to consign too, coincidence communes with the contrast confuse gone away to exhume the delight of our wedding night, 2002, and you attend, arc sends, love / pleasant; pleasant defend of the exact preside at arc built by love / under; under the fiber of a thundering heard, the word, God, love, arc on corner / corner; corner the marketing, love, God, arc wins / ketchup; ketchup poured upon the sword only looks like love, arc on / table; table of the pleasure called the measure of eaten exceed now complete in the balance called love is, arc on / taylors; taylors release and the thread unravels, love's pin, the arc on, love / platinum; platinum pleasure triples up with the balance of an arc called truly, love / amethyst; amethyst wonders arc in too, God is, love / doors; doors open again too, love / desires; desires concede to concept of arcs in, love / peanut; peanut brained delivery forgets the nuts of the arcs in, love / butter; butter your friend with the compare of only arc true bread, love / jelly; jelly belt built by the arc's in, love / chocolate; chocolate signed remembering, forgiving, love, arc song, One / coffee; coffee kind, drinking on the mighty joe of a cappuccino stream and the light on precisely the arc on, love / alcohol; alcohol comes to a screeching halt, silently in the brains of men who drown for the cup of survival and the forgetting spin of the mesmerizing repeat of a spilling drink called light's on, love, arc on / fairy; fairy houred reverie reviewed by the fewed who lean at the learning remembering of love, arc wings / roots; roots escape renew by forgiving complete with the arc true, love / beer; beer steers us clear of love, arc drip / napkins; napkins who ascend to the chin of the arc speak, love / middle; middle measured delivery of the arc song, right on, love's middle, man, hu-man, God's friend, love / midden; midden mounded measure of the arc complete too, love / languages; languages of the arc in, love / tongues; tongues that deliver quiver with the scent of a woman sent to remember who delivers true, arc new, love / dialects; dialects spoken at the neck of truest, love, arc on / stars; stars that cure your care for perfection at the arc song, love / ward; ward's over to the arc depth love / epistle; epistle to the missile fields of flight's lean into the scene of an arc-angel deep with love / adult; adult feature, the mention, the measure, the creation, love, Metatron, man, arc truth, grown up, love / mature; mature enough to measure, love, by an arc's sign, God /

most; most of you knew precisely and exactly the summon, the correspond, the progress, precisely done, energetically summed, arc mostly too, love / current; current to the solvent measure, precious precision in the decision too, arc / mostly; mostly done by the won, love, arc on / misty; misty mountained delivery of the learning curve and the arc on, love / mast; mast sailed to the well occasionally deep and all-ways straight to the heart of the arc on, love / dine; dine in too love's arc throng / means; means to be arc-full too, love / night; nights of thee, since we, loved, arc on / hero; hero of the square arrival at precision done, arc temple man, love / heroine; heroine seen in a home town scheme called precisely, arc dream, love / open; open to exhibit of the arc on, love / exit; exit to the left, arc on / introduction; introduce respect to your dialect and for your count of all that amounts to precisely, love, arc on / seduction; seduction of the needs of the arc son, love / saunter; saunter to the counter of precision's sum and the arc on, love / sands; sands that amount to deep benefit in the arc on, time / solvent; solvent to ascend and now below as above, the arc on, love / convert; convert your friend to a higher measure, know love, arc deep / exhibit; exhibit the nature, love, arc deep / exhort; exhort your sort of protective desire to actively pursue truest, arc deep, love / empire; empire of the hire arc deep love / entire; entire to a trend, let us end, arc deep / toning; toning the singing, leaning home to an arc on, love / sister; sister, mister, arc on, love.

CHAPTER SEVEN

Truth; truth told, arc's hold is me, all the way to the gay arrival at love / book; books written about the arc of deep in, love / last; last drop of the topic capricorn, arc time, too, love / first; first is most and most is keeping our arc clean too, love / forward; forward stare at the arc of keep our hearts alive with precisely this, love / second; second to a nature of the resurrect, I am kept, complete in my often reside at the arc beneath our love / third; third time charmed all the way too, arc song, love / fifth; fifth of the fourth and the woman who coursed her way to my heart and found a new start in the singing arrival at precisely done, arc sum, won, love / fourth; fourth time around, love, arc on / blue; blue to a decide to reside at the perfect speaking part the arc of God, love / purple; purple stay at the arc on, love / pink; pink elect find reflect in the rock garden's seek for perfect arcs of love / convene; convene, hear, at the arc on, love / convolute; convolute to a notion, the commotion called love and the arc in, man, the hue of God, his breath, love / crane; crane for a notion deep with respect and the perfect reflection, God sun, arc on / heron; herons know the flow arc deep too, love/ hale; hale a little man in hands collide at the Other side of the arc-a-tribe, love / healed; healed of the less, I respect my All, too, God is, love / doing; doing direct the reflect of an arc on, love / done; done with the less, arc confess, love / gain; gain respect in refrain to the ration spent and found new vent to the all and / mighty of precious-ness I precisely given, the truth, of arc song, love / release; release your less for more assure of precisely done, the arc son, love / respite; respite revealed the healed arc on, love /

rest; rest at safe reside for the love inside is you and the arc on sung, love / rapture; rapture is now, inside you, know the view arc high to love / confess; confess your direction as sun, arc on / cast; cast a spell less, know confidence in your coincidence called arc seen, love / cavort; cavort less and know more, confess, love, arc one / count; count on the manor arc deep, too, love / castrated; castrated notion of less, confess, true, arc on, love / engage; engage in confession, love true, arc on/ purest; purest notion, the confession of truth in living arcs of love / apples; apples that peel less, curl best too, love / presence; presence is essence if the breath's release is confessed as remembered from God, God is, Love, arc on / lotus; lotus blossom's bloom, arc on, noon to dawn, one / taut; taut to be, arc on / taught; taught divinity, free too, arc on / living; living example of the sample, arc on, God / flames; flames thrown less around, arc on / stream; stream too, arc on / regeneration; regeneration station, arc on / mission; mission controlled, arc on / contact; contact made, arc on / heaven's; heaven's in, arc on / harnessed; harnessed power, arc on / determined; determined stay, arc on / determination; determination left frustration behind, arc on, love / destiny; destiny done, the living won, arc on / motivated; motivated by the view complete, arc on, love / mattered; mattered most, love, arc on / trains; trains of align at the end zone called arc son, love / trained; trained by the matter, arc deep, love / emancipate; emancipate your state, arc on / consciousness; consciousness counts, arc on / paradise; paradise sun, arc fun / domain; domain of reveal arcs on / creative; creative nature comes to the revenue, arc win / essence; essence seen as the gasoline of the fire called God / magnificence; magnificence seen in the breath of me, love, arc / meditates; meditates yes! at precisely convenient confess of the arc of love / meets; meets another won by God and confesses All, we've come too, love, arc on / measures; measures his place by her face, arc on / faith; faith is revealed as concealed, know more, show it all, arc on / purpose; purpose is found in a town kona deep with respect for love's son, arc man, God.

CHAPTER EIGHT

Garden; garden of the arcs drawn, one love, hu-man God, love / progressive; progressive too, the arc wins, God's friend, Metatron is home and well, too the man, Metatron, God's love, arc in to the progression ,son, well done, arc on / lingering; lingering doubt gone, I am the won, Metatron, God's love, done, arc winds blow true tonight, God's love / bestow; bestow the measures come to the arc deep in true reside, arc sun, love / fertile; fertile to a treasure arc send, love to the one, arc on / pregnant; pregnant to a reason arc deep in respect for the our of love's respect / twins; twins confide in my align at the preciser sum, arc steep in love / entwine; entwine with your mate tonight, arc on, love / manifest; manifest the best reaction to the won you love, arc on, God / proclamation; proclamation comes to the love arc on / naturally; naturally and naturally love is, arc on / unguarded; unguarded by a measure arc deep too, love / grade; grade of the good, arc on, love / loyalty; loyalty would win the heart of the guarded sort, arc steep tonight in love / christen; christen could as will, arc in too, love / crystal; crystal persuasion has come to the arc sum, one, love / craft; crafts that could retire and we hire a new art scene, arc man, hu-man, God is, love / croft; croft the nature less, arc on / pristine; pristine to Teresa, the mother of All remembers the way, home, to the arc friend, love / profound; profound to a nature, yes, arc on / pungent; pungent regard for the yes of the taste called love, arc son, God / reawaken; reawaken at love, arc on / pleasure; pleasure wins your quiet regard for the arc song, God / pleasant; pleasant to stay at, play, sum, one, arc song, l-o-v-e- / necessary; necessary done, reveal the one, love, arc sun, God / necessity; necessity of the forgiven tree and the run to One, arc on / forgiven; forgiven less and all the yes and all the ones arced at confess the winning hand, hu-man God, love / magic; magic is sealed in our hearts reveal and the soul gone away to play in the light reveal, know God, confess truest, release, arc on / transform; transform your set of lessens earned to lessons seen as precisely given precision in the arc sun deep in the breath and the throat and the chest of a living God, Hu-man, Metatron / friend; friend found in the town arc on too, love / faith; faith holds a fact as true, arc won, love / face; face the nation, arc son, love / motivate; motivate the state of arc wins, love / green; green the arc of the act called showers of flowers of love / pink; pink examine comes, arc on, love / trek; trek to the side of the arcing ravine that sealed with love / travail; travail can rest, know more, arc done / trades; trades equate to precisely won, arc throng, love / nino; nino days, arc in the sun, rainbows of love / universe; universe ways, love, arcs, God, hu-man / initial; initial practices deep in the arc on, love / identify; identify your soul's release as done, at this point, arc on / grasp; grasp the measure, love, arc on / invisible; invisible to a nature, arc on, love / bond; bonding comes, arc on, love / embezzle; embezzle is met with divorce, arc on, love / end; end the nature of less, arc on, son, love / merit; merit met with a smile, arc on, know nets, love / mirth; mirth's birth, arc on, love / tearing; tearing wear, arc on with flair, love / essential; essential to seen, arc wean, love / spirit; spirit natured coming in to the arc fun, love / spiritual; spiritual seen, arc on, love / star; star of concern, scene, arc on, love / shield; shield your yes in love, confess, arc on / fields; fields of play confess true love / concern; concern with the matter, yes, we confess, our, love / true; true to the self of the arc called love / gravitation; gravitation pulls for your release to the arc high love / lifestream; lifestream comes arc deep too love / victory; victory sealed, arc on / darling; darling deal with love / depth; depth of the measure, arc deep, love / deep; deep enough to trust, true, love, arc free, love.

THE METATRON-MENTS
LEVEL 17

CHAPTER ONE

Desire; desire to the life Metatronic / exuberance; exuberance rules, Metatron / exclaim; exclaim proclaim and the same Metatron / declare; declare yourself set for the millennium's boost to, Metatron / flog; flog the natural select with precisely, love, and the style Metatron / fender; fender bent toward the light Metatron / fix...fix the Friend within Metatron / window; window on the world Metatron / criminal; criminal matter and the reveal to deal with, Metatron / lift; lift the key, Metatron / key; key at the brink, Metatron / voice; voice the animal tongue with your run to the light Metatron / carafe; carafe full of Metatron, drink, Metatron / crease; crease at the wind, Metatron / collapse; collapse at the crew, Metatron / elongate; elongate too, Metatron / erosive; erosive to the battle, Metatron / derisive; derisive regard has gone and along comes precisely the One too, love, Metatron / daily; daily to the deal Metatron / detonate; detonate your state with the fit Metatron, love / dare; dare to be, Metatron / confide; confide in the Friend who believes, Metatron / compare; compare with exact replication of the station Metatron / intelligible; intelligible reading, Metatron's basic humanity is love / intellect; intellect required as you read, Metatron, love / intellectual; intellectual nature, the twin, Metatron / effective; effective to the stare at nature's compare, know confess, Metatron / effectual; effectually I am Metaronic by the sound of a spare regard for the spry way too, love / crowd; crowd around and know God, love, Metatron / component; component of the nature, the All, Metatron / compote; compote your note in the vote, Metatron / clasp; clasp your hands around this elect, Metatron / bode; bode of the node complete, Metatron / bead; bead on the life energetic, Metatron / spoken; spoken plainly, give, Metatron / understood; understood? love, Metatron / refresh; refresh, splash, Metatron / cleanse; cleanse, reside, rest, Metatron / initiate; initiate at the rate, Metatron / sanctify; sanctify the measure, Metatron / invigorate; invigorate with the nature metatronic, love / curative; curative's curator Metatron / cure; cure of the purest nature, Metatron, love / pure; pure enough to be metatronic / purity; purity's share, Metatron / clarify; clarify the matter, Metatron / clarity; clarity sought, found, Metatron / cascades; cascades clue, Metatron / upper; upper natured, Metatron / lower; lower the tower to the power metatronic / level; level the times two to One, Metatron / swim; swim to the falls, Metatron / submerge; submerge in the nurture, Metatron / fortitude; fortitude's mood is good, Metatron / fortified; fortified by the ride to the Metatron / legions; legions vote for the Metatron / athletic; athletic to a Metatron / throats; throats collapse into a Metatron / portals; portals red with metatrons / thirteen; thirteen ways to the Metatron / parents; parents paid through Metatron / patents; patents live in Metatron / gathering; gathering stems of Metatron / left; left to a bank of metatrons.

CHAPTER TWO

Ego; ego done in the sun, Metatron / flames; flames that heal congeal, Metatron / causes; causes applauded, Metatron / embody; embody the planet, Metatron / earth; earth seals, love, Metatron / ease; ease too, Metatron / effort; effort done, Metatron / lives; lives in gives, Metatron / effusive; effusive to a manner, Metatron / loves; loves too, Metatron / flattery; flattery fills our lead with love, Metatron / flow; flow too, love, Metatron / finite; finite meets the street, Metatron / flatter; flatter your step best with the love Metatron / clause; a clause about confession, meteor, Metatron / cause; cause yourself to stay Metatron / blush; blush less, confess, Metatron / claws; claws in confuse, gone, Metatron / foil; foil over the said, matter, Metatron / fools; fools who led are gone, Metatron / / foot; footprint falls and the step Metatron / footprint; footprint on the steps Metatron / toes; toes of the river, metatronic steps, love / roots; roots about to prove the shout that truth's prevail is the love Metatron / snacks; snacks brought to ought react to occurrent fashions of potentially and occurrently, Metatron's treat, love / spoils; spoils and reward, Metatron / weaving; weaving room, the linen bloom, the blanket Metatron / science; science says Metatron / religion; religion reads Metatron / psyche; pysche sunk and spirit reveals the lift to Metatron / spirit; spirit of the minute, Metatron / intrigue; intrigue with the exist that became real life, know the wife, Metatron / practice; practice your practice with a daily regard for the lighter card called the hand of God, Metatron / techniques; techniques for shuttle launch, headed back to the heart of the practice called perfectly exuberant in love, Metatron / complex; complex nature of the gift, Metatron / camper; campers kin wins Metatron / complete; complete your cycle, meta-electric, Metatron / seraphim; seraphim win with their guardian, Metatron / sun; sun day daze and the haze of horizons that repeat, rest, rest, rest, Metatron / ring; ring of firey regard for the heavens that last and at last our God, face it, Metatron / karmic end; karmic end has come, know the sum, One, God, lightly spoken, Metatron / mend; mend your nature with the arc of the sealing kiss with the earth we'll miss if we disregard our sacred seam of duty to God and love, mend yourself, meet your nature, the creation, the God of love, Metatron / framed; framed in a red Metatron / frozen; frozen without a Metatron / souls; souls, I repeat, go home to the light and let this life be clear, lightly seen, love / sepharothic; sepharotic streams of a lighter explain desire my connect with the sight of Raphael's face lightly seamed upon the pillow of softest regard for lightly, God ahead, love, Metatron / patient; patient in pews of metatrons / abide; abide with God, meet Metatron / abode; abode of the palace and the place called Metatron / translate; translate heaven as your fate, know Other, know more, know contests scored as won, the translate, good, God, love, Metatron / store; store your desire in fire of the higher conspire to know that Sophia knew the storeroom as full and fed by the lead to God of the ages metatronic / storage; storage of the feather, the light maat, floating away to meet regard for the light of God, Metatron / cell; cell of the arced command, the arc-angelic sum, Metatron and friends resides again upon the earth of God, know love, fear gone, only One cell, love / fortunate; fortunate to a Metatron / cells; cells that repeat; God, God, God; love, love, love; Metatron / sound; sound the mantra, I am, Metatron, love / push; push your nature deep into the heart of command and the chanting stay at precisely and perfectly God ahead, love, Metatron / crawl; crawl to the counter and faint reside at the fantastic arc of precision in God / reach; reach your nature's bless, know confess, arc reside, Metatron / grab; grab a chance to dance with Metatron in God's laugh and the booming confess that Oz is us and God is best when found with a grin and a lifting curtain of mighty express of the machinations required to get us past this, the curtain of light has come, know the sun and the sum, One, Metatron / home; home to a game called "metatronic" / creep; creep to the edge and know the way to the light, know edges less, Metatron / want; want more less, command, completion, Metatron.

CHAPTER THREE

Rapport; rapport and respect with the banker who wins your regard, the keen sword of michael's plan and the reconnect with the original line, the column of light, hu-man, God, One cool reward, rapport / rate; rate of the nature mastered energetics love Metatron / mentor; mentor who rules the light energetic, Metatron / mosaic; mosaic means of the shattered end, come again, Metatron and friends too, love / meld; meld at the matter metatronic, love *NOTE: METATRON; Meta-electric triumphant approach to the truth ringing orated now by the hu-man elective, God* / enthuse; enthuse yourself with the living come, Metatron / zoologic; zoologic zygotic confessions Metatron / intake; intake the breath, mother deep, love, Metatron / enthuse; enthuse for the lovers, metatronic / zoomorphic; zoomorphic equivalence is set on the bet metatronic, love / expose; expose yourself to best, Metatron / exposure; exposure congeals at the meeting point, love, Metatron / understood; understood who, now know, Metatron speaks only love / spoken; spoken in the manner that matters, Metatron, is, love / communicate; communicate great regard for the child of God and the lamb of the life Metatron / speak; speak about our seek for the light Metatron / bode; bode of experience confirmed Metatron / bead; a bead on, Metatron / comport; comport comes in the sum metatronic / compote; compote of the peace's Metatron / clip; clip the event to the heaven sent sign Metatron / gastronomic; gastronomic regard for the light eat, Metatron / astronomic; astronomically speaking hear Metatron / astrologic; astrologic complete, Metatron / absolve; absolve the nature, Metatron / listen; listen to the light, Metatron / metatronic; metatronic ascend, Metatron / magic; magic heals, Metatron / knew; knew about the electric, Metatron / felt; felt the elective, Metatron / thought; thought about it, Metatron / special; special too, Metatron / spatial; spatial pleasure, Metatron / molecule; molecule electric, Metatron / electron; electron ball, Metatron / reside; reside at the side, Metatron / resonate; resonate late and rotate too, Metatron / drips; daily drips the lips Metatron / costume; costume change, Metatron / cope; cope with the light Metatron / crepe; crepe sues yet? Metatron / clasp; clasp hands with Metatron / cusp; cusp reached, Metatron / cupidic; cupidic nature of the wonders Metatron / quip; quips less, the metatronic lift too God, love / cascades; cascades of the mountains metatronic / central; central port of the sort metatronic, love /

centralic; centralic seam, metatronic / speck; speck and gleam, Metatron / spark; spark scene, Metatron, love / space; light space, love, Metatron / maximal; maximal please Metatron / eventual; eventual measure, Metatron / Michelangelo; Michelangelo's dream, Davidic, Metatron, means love / pranks; pranks about transcen-dance, love, Metatron / drakes; drakes drew Metatron / events; events calendared by Metatron / tricks; tricks revealed by Metatron / ties; ties too, Metatron / tips; tips trued, Metatron / effusive; effusive nature of Metatron / evasive; evasive measures gone to Metatron, love / elate; elate to the nature metatronic, creation, love / fellows; fellows laid to the roads metatronic.

CHAPTER FOUR

Ecstasy; ecstasy sought found in a town metatronic / illustrate; illustrate the great electric, Metatron, love / effuse; effuse the notion, yes, Metatron / extends; extends too, the metatronic, love / directive; directive to the metatronic / gale; gale force wins, the power, Metatron / gallery; gallery glued by the metatronic ascend, love / minor; minor matters healed, Metatron / major; major seals set flat at the point metatronic / flat; flat note written by the metatronic light, love / music; music's heal, Metatron / round; round the note, metatronic / risen; risen by the metatronic, love / lotus; lotus lives in blooms of the metatronic / growth; growth grew metatronically, love / lace; lace zeal craves the feminine in the metatronic / rose; rose blew bloomed by the metatronic / garden; garden of the home metatronic, love / gain; gain a new respect, Metatron / gardenia; gardenia salad and the southern Metatron / grip; grip the right, Metatron / gather; gather the droplets, mattered, Metatron / drape; drape the light metatronic / drip; drip the essentials too, Metatron/ ribs; ribs electric, Metatron / work; work on the light Metatron / eve; eve drew on Metatron / apples; apples heal the throat Metatron / leisure; leisure hours measure Metatron / journey; meta-journey, Metatron / attendant; attendant matter, Metatron / quest; quest about for Metatron / water; water wins, Metatron's splash of love / trail; love's trail, Metatron / rocks; rocks fairies rule, Metatron / falls; falls full with Metatron / moss; moss days, Metatron / voice; voice of the throat-filled with Metatron / God; God's love, Metatron / echo; echo of the note, Metatron / thunder; thunder inn, Metatron / sign; signs of the time, Metatron / rules; rules the rooms Metatron / knot; knot on the lot, Metatron / not; not on the prime, know the rhyme, Metatron / circle; circle of the nature Metatron / cove; cove stay comes too, Metatron / cleft; cleft in the nature, Metatron / active; active decide to be, Metatron / passive; passive hu-man passes the active too, Metatron / hearth; hearth of the heart, Metatron / chimney; chimney's rock, the smoke, Metatron / fish; fish at the sea, Metatron / bridge; bridge the waves, Metatron / middle; middle the nature, Metatron / flow; flow to truth, Metatron / fleet; fleet to the nature Metatron / fast; fast trace, Metatron / deep; deep to the nature Metatron / dart; dart to the start, Metatron / clear; clear to the nature electric, Metatron / mist; mist sealed in the splash Metatron / thundering; thundering nature, Metatron.

CHAPTER FIVE

Canyon; canyon clue, Metatron blue to a periwinkle hue, arcturic regard for the souls of love / slots; slots that win for God, Metatron / open; open to a voice called God, Metatron / voice; voice a reveal, Metatron / valley; valley view, Metatron / cliff; cliff top Metatron / waves; waves that hued regard the same Metatron / bob; bob through the pain, Metatron, reveal, love / light; light on the nature, yellow through, Metatron / yellow; yellow too, Metatron / rejuvenate; rejuvenate your Self and know the sate of a delight-full ascend, Metatron / commit; commit the comfortable ride, the One inside, and the present assure that God is, love, Metatron / beaufort; beaufort blue gone too, Metatron / outer-banked; outer-banked examine can manage truth and the rate inside our blue refine, Metatron / lakes; lakes that rule and the bowl of recover and the light Metatron, love / rivers; rivers that heal, Metatron / sea; sea of the feel, Metatron / ocean; ocean the will heal the feet of the electric walking Metatron / shore; shore of the nature that reigns Metatron / tahoe; tahoe due too, Metatron / tree; tree of the life Metatron / travel; travel weave Metatron / truth; truth told and the height, Metatron / defeat; defeat digress, listen, yes, Metatron / deny; deny the mattered, lesson, Metatron / decry; decry the arise too, Metatron / despair; despair's heal, Metatron / delay; delay the native and know the son all one, Metatron / speak; speak about Metatron / conceive; conceive the nature Metatron / concept; concept true to the concede Metatron / contour; contour the curves of the nature Metatron / bowl; bowl deep with the sole-d release, Metatron / touch; touch the suggestion of Metatron / depth; depth of regard, the sword, Metatron and the light on, love / dally; dally at yes and know Metatron / expire; expire the float to the fire, Metatron / expel; expel the notion of less, Metatron / concept; concept clued Metatron / concede; concede to freed, Metatron / convey; convey the matrix done to the gay arrival at Metatron / defecate; defecate less, Metatron / urinate; urinate on less, Metatron / chills; chills feel like Metatron's heat, deep relief, love / ills; ills less, still, I am, well too, Metatron / fever; fever fewed break in too love, Metatron / break; break the fast, at last, Metatron / food; food that fills Metatron / fend; fend of the natural select and the convected voney called Metatron / later; later live, now forgive, give the light, Metatron / may; may is for Metatron, love / mid-line; mid-line assign, Metatron / flow; flow true, Metatron / fork; fork over to the nature Metatron / flurry; flurry over the nature, Metatron / float; float to vote for Metatron / east; east to the best, Metatron / math; math of the truth, met at Metatron / metric; metric met at Metatron / key; key to the free Metatron / staple; staple true to choice, the moist arrival at Metatron / start; start to the heart, Metatron / embark; embark to the mark Metatron / flag; flag at the fuel Metatron.

CHAPTER SIX: break; a break agreed too, Metatron / take; take a dare with Metatron / two; two who meet at Metatron / Greece; Greece is ruled with the power Metatron / passion; Metatron's passion is well within Metatron / Hawaii; Hawaii heals with the light Metatron / fashion; fashion a trip to the nature Metatron /

forgive; forgive the daze, Metatron / forgone; forgone descend to the light Metatron / play; play at the seas of Metatron / plan; plan to be, Metatron / swim; swim too, Metatron / stay; stay at the frees, Metatron / strip; strip to the frame and the core, Metatron / deep; deep to the sleep Metatron / soapy; soapy treasure, Metatron / bubbles; bubbles at the please, Metatron / psychotic; psychotic cue, the cure, Metatron / neurotic; neurotic maternity gone to the light maturity Metatron / neurosis; neurosis sealed by the light Metatron, love / psoraisis; psoraisis healed by the convolute regard for the light Metatron / flip; flip to the trip metatronic / flit; flit around, about, Metatron / flake; flake point, love, Metatron / channel; channel that heals the manner Metatron and the vibration, love / inside; inside the nature of the maternal reside called material release to the light inside, Metatron / vibe; vibe about the life metatronic / vibrate; vibrate about the light metatronic, love / child; child of the mind mattered less, heart felt, love, Metatron / vibration; vibraton's reveal, Metatron / elation; elation about, Metatron / erection; erection elected, Metatron / pounding; pounding the manner less, matter cared, gone confessed too, Metatron / back; back to back, the circle, Metatron / wet; wet the waters with the light Metatron / moist; moist arrival at the love arc-ival, Metatron / laden; laden with bliss, Metatron / full; full to the nature metatronic, love / growing; growing about, Metatron / growth; growth grew too, Metatron / lip; lip of the trip Metatron / ledge; ledge revealed, jump over, Metatron / lather; lather up in the nature Metatron / plunge; plunge into the nature, Metatron / grip; grip the delight and the rim, Metatron / squeeze; squeeze this erratic, the emphatic, Metatron / alive; alive to the nature Metatron / erotic; erotic natured, Metatron / erratic; erratic natured smoothed too Metatron / lay; lay down too, Metatron / exotic; exotic and true, Metatron / explosive; explosive to a nature Metatron / share; share your lead, Metatron / lead; lead the need metatronic / lie; lie down with Metatron / flee; flee to the lips metatronic, your own, love / follow; follow me too, Metatron / float; float at the boat Metatron / buoyant; buoyant too, Metatron/ protest; protest the most about less, Metatron / hollar; hollar about the light Metatron / voiced; voiced adhere to the light Metatron / shout; shout about it, Metatron / scream; scream about the light Metatron.

CHAPTER SEVEN

Discovery; discovery of the lifetime ascendant to the transcendent, Metatron / wild; wild enough to be, Metatron / wilderness; wilderness rules, Metatron / quiet; quiet to a nature, Metatron / encounter; encounter found in the Other, Metatron /; nature, Metatron / breathtaking; breathtaking place, Metatron / mystery; mystery mailed to the ravine by Metatron / horizon; horizon healed by the reveal, sun signed, Metatron / overlooks; overlooks the best, the view, Metatron / imagine; imagine the nation Metatronic / abundance; abundance rules, Metatron / ancient; ancient to ways, Metatron / gorge; gorge views, Metatron / untamed; untamed matter, metatronic / breathe; breathe about the faith, Metatron / breath; breath of the man, Metatronic

/ rush; rush to the counter, Metatron / touching; touching the nature, Metatron / precious; precious to this, nature, Metatron / preserve; preserve your plenty, Metatron / majestic; majestic mend, Metatron / breast; breast of the metatronic, mother's milk, love / offering; offering to the few, metatronic / swoop; electric swoop to the troop metatronic / flair; flair to the care metatronic / habitat; habitat held in the weld metatronic / hustle; hustle the nucleic metatronic, love / muscle; muscle clear to the metatronic, love / bare; bare enough to care for, the metatronic regard for the classic reveal, love / burning; burning with regard for the light metatronic / yearning; yearning to be led to the life Metatron / open; open the truth told, Metatron / sweet; sweet to the treat Metatron / luscious; luscious sea, Metatron / tease; tease the best, only, Metatron / soothe; soothe the nature, Metatron / throw; throw yourself at Metatron / up; up to All, Metatron / down; down to the nature, metaphysic, Metatron / between; between the sheets of love, Metatron / spirits; spirits seal the sum metatronic with love / wines; wines to the taste, Metatron / whines; shine without, whines contested, merry Metatron / wheels; wheels to the One, Metatron / buffet; buffet won by Metatron / banquet; banquet that fills, Metatron / lick; lick the abstract, specifically, Metatron / lisp; lisp about, Metatron / whisper; whisper this, shhh, Metatron / kiss; kiss with a shout about Metatron / kisseth; kisseth the beast good-bye, Metatron / smack; smack another with rely on the heart good-bye and the brided hello to the life Metatron / blow; blow at the windy relief of the heart Metatron / swallow; swallow the notion, Metatron / moisten; moisten your wet confess with the word, Metatron / taste; taste the lips metatronic, love / drink; drink again, Metatron / sample; sample foreplay, know the way, Metatron / smell; smell the well return to the mate Metatron / tickle; tickle with mention of the lightest dimension, Metatron / whistle; whistle about the mention of the love Metatron / wed; wed the matter, Metatron / wed; wed your heart to the marathon mend of the run meteoric love amend win, Metatron.

CHAPTER EIGHT

Committed; commited to a count's review, One, Metatron / suffer; suffer the lesser, manner, Metatron / prevail; prevail at the truth of Metatron / durate; durate can great relate to love / chain; chain of the nurture, Metatron / change; change to be metatronic, love / correspond; correspond to the maturity of the surety of metatronic love / commune; commune to the moon that rests in Metatron / condolence; condolence sent to the vent Metatron / nature; natured by nest of the living wings of the light called Metatron / physics; physics that successfully leads to the bouncing chance to know metaphoric metatronic love / ask; ask about Metatron / inquire; inquire higher, Metatron / pain; pain free delivery to the pulse called precisely God, pain-free too, love / pulse; pulse the please of the knees that arrive at the bend metatronic / snap; snap to the pulse, Metatron / discourse; discourse on the light metatronic / fast; fast enough to feel the light Metatron / last; last at the sneezing arrival lean to the Metatron / stuff; stuff of the nature Metatron / indulge; indulge in the light Metatron /

texture; textured feel of the life Metatron / fabric; fabric that rends like the spiraling in of the light Metatron / shape; shape concealed revealed, now know, Metatron / surrender; surrender to the light Metatron / greens; greens that agree to the light marathon, photosynthetic to the ascend, Metatron / gray; gray to the grace of our destiny's dance at the chance metatronic / trees; trees that enhance, Metatron / rod; rod's rule, the catch Metatron / fish; fish at the beach Metatron / introduce; introduce yourself to wealth, Metatron / matters; matters that care, Metatron / climb; climb to the climatic end, Metatron / names; names that kneel beneath the trees Metatron / knelt; knelt at, love, Metatron / beneath; beneath our nature and interior to love, Metatron / dive; dive to the strive, Metatron / submissive; submissive by nature, Metatron / dominate; dominate due, Metatron / sun; sun on you, Metatron / sum; sum of the many, Metatron / rays; rays that rule, emphatically, Metatron / rainbow; rainbowed pleasure, metatronic, love / lime; lime-green love, Metatron / blue; blue to the nature of the michael-ed release too, Metatron / icicles; icicles scene, a wet drip to the grip, Metatron / focus; focus on the natural progression, Metatron / focal; focal to the scene metatronic, love / face; face of the place and the marker, Metatron / centrally; centrally done too, Metatron / center; center of the wear, Metatron, blanket God / point; point to the perimeter with permission, Metatron / force; force the pushing agree to Metatron / force; force field, love, Metatron / strong; strong to a nature Metatron / force-full; force-full intrigue with the depths of Metatron / current; current to ascend, Metatron / push; push at the web Metatron / flow; flow through Metatron / swept; swept too, Metatron / away; away in Metatron / raspberry; raspberry blue reside at the side metatronic / magenta; magenta coincide and the free agree to be metatronic / luscious; luscious, yes, Metatron.

THE IN-GOD-MENTS
LEVEL 18

CHAPTER ONE

Scholar; scholar of the home, yomed, and meant to rent for God's loves / theologian; theologian and the chosen's extremes for uniquely lives God's love / wealth; wealth of the nature aburst your living foundations / inspect; inspect a simple necklace called God's loves / cures; cures and the simply connected too, God's / curious; curious to the details scented within God's loves / intersect; intersect the net of the retailing foundations called God's / vanished; vanished in a banished thoughts thrilling prepare for light foundations / note; note and the sorts paid for light tradition's life foundations for God's greetings / reply; reply a retailing contentment for God's foundations / replies; replies a sizing metatronically agreed too, love's foundations for God's gains / protect; protect allowances for God's Metatronic details on too, love's foundations / speculates; speculates and the sates won elective's foundationally gained, God's greetings foundationed / chance; chance allows your like God's foundations; syntax; syntax and the sent for like God's foundations, Metatronic / Pure; purely paid for, light's foundations, God's / thoughts; thoughts and the thrilling like foundations, God's / elixir; elixir and the mixture made for light's foundations, God's / living; living's liken and the giving's foundations, God's / sutra, God's / wholeness; God's / elevation; God's / duration; God's / flowering; God's / lights; God's / circulate; God's / stages; God's / goals; God's / dividends; God's / divine; divine details God's / charming; details God's / pearls; pearls paid for, God's / cultivated; cultivated cures for lightness, God's / works; God's / thrusts; God's / strokes; God's / stressed; God's / throats; God's / stages; God's / stripped; God's / pallets; God's / shares; God's / sublime; God's / dabbles; God's / magenta; God's / strips; God's / mats; God's / meals; God's / changes; God's / respect; God's / restitution; God's / degrees; God's / daring; God's / esteem; God's / earths; God's / flares; God's / leaks; God's / extreme; God's / consumption; sequesters; sequenced; sent; consumed; God's / curtailed; God's

CHAPTER TWO

Curtains; truths; tools; tracts; agreeable; able; although; desired; gazed; grazed; extras; involved; dissolves; uses; grazed; golden; balance; glees; previews; reviews; startled; glare; starts; affairs; hearts; clues; pairs; pause; causes; glues; clear; cliche; camps; campaign; welcome; feeling; felt; tacts; backs; paramount; sailing; necessary; dealing; created; staffs; kneeling; dealt sought; seating; vaulted; stance; values; chills; valleys; changes; ashes; boiling; broiling; envisions; visions; explore; visionaries; emerges; explains; refrains

CHAPTER THREE

Electrically; set; freely; bet; better; embrace; kittens; minutes; orbits; fluffs; factors; felt; feelings; resorts; breeds; balanced; cautiously; kept; freedoms; songs; manacles; drop; fluff; regards; brilliance; reigns; curtails; relates; gingers; explains; notifies; condicals; bags; spoken; sails; set; rejoice; journey; passions; paired; sixty; sets; sorts; elects; sourced; shipped; backs; abraids;

abortive; lips; lessons; shared; promotions; fly; influences; abreast; adjusted; lights; pursuits; aplenty; touched; intended; adjusted; wardens; robbed; rubbed; regards; strokes; squeezed; rushed; pulled; pictured; boxed; balustrades; bait; positive; regards; gained; throughout; admits; agrees; desires; dies; capitalized; moments; totally; freed; totals; innate; substantial; gains; concisely; worded; maneuvers; closed

CHAPTER FOUR

Closures; coming; degrees; bursting; panics; conversant; streets; hush; chapters; explored; orientations; subtle; passings; concepts; settled; settle; now; modems; detailed; practices; participate; drawn; sustained; substanced; hearts; aims; projects; algae; browns; typos; sports; coffers; myecin; subcutaneous; fats; felt; browns; lessons; learning; ladders; lingers; sounds; pursuits; utilize; unwound; sounds; changes; achievements; centers; words; wonders; seize; revelations; reach; awaken; homes; havoc; caters; suspense; wounds; places; patterns; chains; sets; songs; singing; placed

CHAPTER FIVE

Place; pursuits; desires; dialects; languaged; sects; sectors; sections; suburbs; cancerian; delivery; donations; straits; stratus; joins; gingerly; jasmined; pools; experienced; sunlit; fountains; fortress; wells; words; heedings; heavens; rings; galactic; speeches; splendorous; temples; thrones; homes; response; details; sighted; scandals; bound; pleased; times; methods; militant; denies; dies; female; wiles; recovery; reads; styles; masculine; replies; delivered; delights; sizes; places; lambs; flowers; lands; sequesters; styles; joined; changed 63 .calms; claims; choose; opens; transverse; transfers; chimes; finds; allows

CHAPTER SIX

Perfects; basic; humanity; advanced; spans; minutes; miracles; attends; hands; passions; rations; ensues; creatives; venues; humans; kindness; experts; experiences; supreme; trims; uniqueness; agreements; totality; balances; ultimate; awareness; bosom; offerings; details; God's; gained; thrills; thanks; scents; sent; God's; Face; Metatron; one; with; yours; electric; kiss; invitations; hearts; deepen; instincts; loves; laughter; feeds; escapes; entry; advantages; love's; happens; things; thoughts; thanks; helps; aids; wings; worn; won; mercy; engaged; seek; sought; found; recovers; attends

CHAPTER SEVEN

Within; God's; befriend; humanity; ultimate; weaves; woven; stills; channels; hearts; obey; calls; essentials; loves; interiors; intregity; keys; codes; seeds; specialty; delivered; aim 23 finality; musical; mends; ends; yearns; years; past; 56; 3; when; times; recovers; trusts; thanks; God's; eternally; simply; suggestive; all; over; through; thorough; agreed; worn; within; God; is; your; Friend; not; your; foe; let; go; within,; enjoy; sex; life; passion; pleasure; by; lover

CHAPTER EIGHT

A measure eternal. Where is your heart, your head? By elect in your chest where within wanton sin since elect follows correct refuse lessen sparks of God's respect for challenging chores like helpful agree too be basically free and fonder still to see aspire as the degree of fastest stars called human hearts in prayer eternal to the light called God / The son called one and the Christian corps and the Buddha's baste in the swelling accept for all there is for love. God's gift history historically spent on man as the direct arrive at God's door and the flooring gift that a happy heart is still to the core and dancing in pleasant relief the peaceful gaze God gave a happy each and to the "other."

CHAPTER TEN

We all are one and eternally set is a jewel direct to the heart of God and the gaze that felt like mine. And often still I see the eternity of how we loved for God and the getting on of how we were elected to see precisely what we as mankind can deliver and the given becomes the send and the living.

CHAPTER ELEVEN

The ascendant and the tackle boxed in is that when we spend our parts on less than all and still we seek and see the often said example of all the stars included in one grand meeting burst called electrically God's and God said "let there be light." Humanity WINS when God give us all sweet deliver to thee living flower of peaceful deliver at the father's gate and the mother's heart this earth this place of God's sweet passion for a potion a creation so rich that not even this heart could contain the pulse of a human's pleasure and a woman's explain and a man's gift as self examine becomes the lift to God's exact lift called delivery to the cells 1 of forgive and the life...

CHAPTER TWELVE

Of living in the loving way called perfectly exactly essentially eternally paternally patterned and measured exactness the in fact exposure to composure / precision anthems / peace pieces plunder places / kept cobras / clavicles, shoulders, arms, chins / pushing runnings / cords closures exposures / handsome estates of landed entreaty and the nape of necks unburdened by the simple belief in release to the truth of this matter the trust in love.

THE ADVANCE-MENTS
LEVEL 19

CHAPTER ONE

Bliss; bliss this miss of a matron's span, the juice, and the jewel, and the heart called a man has arrived at a quilt and a star of delight and the elegant persuasion to conclusively see that the light you are saving is the One that you own and the life of survival has gone to a place called retrieve and the ultimate zone of living in plenty and plenty alone and the word we call truth and the intimate proof of who we can be and all this day long and electric to spare assignation is a living light lair and a flair called tomorrow equates as a day and deep to arrival I am healing the wave of family revival and the heightened agree to days of deliver and daily we deem our appealing arrive as the leaf of redeem. I am seen in a trail, deep to sea, a prescient particle of a plan yet to be a blessed event of assurance sent and around me three pace arc-ival in the rend of a beatific stare into the seize of adoration and the span that embraces the trend to be elite in my selection of a brand of particular kiss and the bliss of infinitely better attribution and the notion of a nation enthralled with the bliss of being alive in God; love / acknowledge; acknowledge the fact that love is an act of indescribable significance to the ecstatic trend and the dripping bend in Love's canal called life's a pal of magnificent trend and in the end of arrive see the tribe of art in fact amid the revival of the acknowledge that love's a college called basically human, life / abandon; abandon meant let's fend for traces of laces spent on social agree to arrive at the point that joints on believe and I need the abandon meant in love / review; hafiz reviewed a sweeter mug of the leafy regenerative exceed, reviewed the deed, called Love / expansion; expansive plans erupt in me and my social activity called lightly love is a friend and the fields of three extend ascend to the walls of expansive plan to become a span of heightened degree and forgiveness reigns eternally in love / remiss; remiss I kiss the neck of a tree called available to be an electric bead's extend to the vending machine called we miss the ability to be less than remiss, love / repress; repress the deed called social exceed and acknowledge the stead to extend to the sea of a trailing spoof called Love's infinity in you, the news, express, know repress, and explode to exude to a living tube called recede to the need to review your love / given proof; given proof to the seed of I believe and expelled the reed of being freed to be; I live the proof of the given extend and the stance called the blend to retrieval of the leaves of survival sent to freely bleed into the mouth of the river of life called forgiven lens of remember. Lose the eye, see the truth, One eye wide to deliver and ultimately, love / found; found full to sleeves of extensive accede, I ascend to the trend more electric and the trial of faith called we excel in our excessive response to the swell arrival at the finding full called love / left dry; left dry to forget, I remember, and love is found in this town of forever, know the One, feel the well of believe and ascend to the rim of volcanic splendor called a flurry of love / found empty; found empty less I am wet at the lips of the healing type called high to a sign of love's align with the veins of recline and the feeling tree called me, by design, and the found empty trace of ill's worthy forgive and the rim of the sign of surrender to love's

amend. Found thrilled with love / the news; the news comes and the tubes of a living tend and the trend of central import portal deep in All we believe is released and the heart of the dove of an ancient review. The news? We are home to a rote belief in the life Arcturic and the love blue and green and periwinkle blissed by the seam of love / gone? why?; gone? why? where too? recess your nest in a patterned trance called caring less and find the core and then concur that travel's heed is the read of any less than all between as needing confess and find the lines of what's gone by and find the thread of believe in gone too; why? love / the fields; the fields of life's eternity have met in me and my ascend to the arc-angels trend to end the reign of an archon's rage and to see the fields in me and my electricity. The fields of energetic believe in love / the views; the views of forever and the trees of remember and the peaks of the news that rings around the sun, indeed, we are, love, in, love / the 'tudes; the 'tudes tree in branching arise to the stretch called life and the noose of neglect has come to the *bitter end of a rotten arise at the attitude called less and now we know more, love. The archon is gone and we can all breath in the 'tudes of love. Held to hanging on to the last knot, let go, know God / the thrills; the thrills of a healing discovery called finding the heights of snooze in the arms of God and the thrills of recovering a friend in the end archonic. The sonic shrill of a hill called the heights of God in the gardens of love / the reveal; the reveal of divine explanation for the nation's repeat to less as more and the simple shore of the endearing appeal called the revival of love / the repeal; the repeal is your need to heal for anything less than a reveal called love / the exude; the exude is the extrude to a beat less than viewed as other exceed in their need to smother the Mother with a covering access called the quick include too, love / the abused; the abused have gone and the One's come along, know the abusive majors of journaled insist on the Colonel's resounding eternal epistle of apostolic flight to the end artcuric and the begin again and returns the dove, today, of an abused amend and the remember too, love / the relax; relax in the shacks and the smacks and the snacks of fed by your love and the sticks of forgiven called this living to the tree of forever and the relaxation in the station called the shades of love / the refused; the refused did knot blend and in giving they found a trend to arrival at the scene of all we conceive as love and creation came to confession and the need to see all that we are became the recollect of divine agree to be refused by belief in anything less than love / the reward; the reward, my friend, is in our living arrival at the revival of belief in remember and the rewards of greater this, that, love / the in facts; the in facts excel in swell begin of a new significance called the facts energetic too, love / the reviewed; reviewed your red delicious meal and melted thin revival to the straight assign of the floors of pretend and the amend has come and the sum of the wings arise as one dove done to all except love / exude; exude the deliver of remember too, love / the ignite; ignite you seed with the tripled believe in resurrective ascend to the trickling laughter of a friend called love / per chance; per chance you will dance at precisely love / the revoked; revoked your license to impede my indeeds with resounding applaud of the full revocation called let us rest only in love / the re-write; the re-write comes to this, the kiss, of precisely, love / the intrude; the intrude is over in the veins of celestial ways eruptively bent in extents called arrive at the intrude called love / the true blued; help said the tree is blue and I believed in her attempt to send my heart away to a land-less friend of mayan content and the true colors of a Carolina day spent on revealing less and stages grace at passed the test to true blue, love / the find inside; the find inside is my truth called real love / the fond found; the fond found is a town called yellow-green with the intention too, love / today till dawn; today till dawn all God said was let's believe in the carriage home of a free resurrection called the direction of precisely this, love / the arc; the arc I'm on is spent on only God and tonight I will park in the arc I'm on called only God is, love / a kinder truth; a kinder truth is; love / a kindred proof; a kindred proof, love, has arisen in the right to know God and by selective design I call on you to align with the living energetic and the kindred proof of God as Love / the hearts that dance; the hearts that dance embrace the chance too, love / a welcome stance; a welcome stance is the fact that bugs stand still when heaven reels to reveal a crack in an animal's field and an alien stand of 15% lessen can steal their inquiry and 100% more can assure that your stance is in fact in God / a tender sign; a tender sign, love / the light inside; the light inside is love and the light is on to a continuous stream of consistent trailing proof of the One light bred as the Brotherhood of the whiter veil concludes that pale is a shading less attractive than the repeal that has gone this day to the elected way called exactly, precisely, consistently, real inside God, love / the mind of God; God's mind is mine inside the standing chance to feel the spark blown wide to believe in a solar plexus seen to in true only in straight - forward agree to see only the mind of God in Love / the arc called God; the arc called God resides in me and my covenant agree to see this life as complete and this heart as God's need to reveal always the need to arrive at Love / the width I've made; the width I've made is ten feet deep to a max called I mean to stand at this sign of arrive and up to a trance I am led to confess only the electrical dance called within me only wide enough for eternities of love / the rights; The rights I've paid to believe in assign to my decision to arrive at the alignment of a spine inside the guide called lightly God is love / the wells I wade; the wells I wade are welch and the same self evident of the extent called too, love / the artesian dream; the artesian's well in a swelling allegiance to God's flow and the knowing below and above that the sign of arrival is the revival called the buff believe in perfection's body called, God / the salt of God; salt. brick. stick around to melt a town wide to a striding glint of flowing intimacy showering us with truly perfect agree to show the All our love. Tasty. God / the days of sod; the days of sod agreed to lay wide the saddamic spelling called l-e-s-s and all has broken the spell by the light of the lamps of loving well; let the lambs come... slaughter gone; children hum; the new arrival is precisely within the limits of the new city God, Zion / the arm of tools; the basket, the bucket, the still reliance of love's shields, light's filed, and

divinity's shore directly given to the flood of God's good plenty and the spools of arms and hands of tools and the light called the arm of the tools of love / remember; remember at this point activate the love / shield; shield me now, love / the wield of rules; the wield of rules comes when we forgive the lessons for giving us shielding proof of the transcen-dance of love / the love gone by; the love had gone by to a flying treat called the treasure trove of the drove and the dream and the seam and the sign and the incline called love has gone by and bye now to the reside at less and the love gone by has found relief in the arms of God' winging agree too, love / the days gone dry; the days gone dry have gone to wet agree to becoming healed by the stuff called giving pleasure to God's dove on a daily basis and the chance to agree with the peace, the piece, the feast of a day come to tasty crying exceed and the need to sky high in God's wet coming agree to rain upon us and within, love / the even trade; the even trade is love's grade at a gentle recline and the sighs of doves and tender-eyed lambs of essential nature who agree to nurture, the dime, the even trade for time is, love / the point I've made; the point I've made is love / the art I save; the art I save is my own belief in the tree of life called love / the ink I've paid; the ink I've paid is by own belief in the right too, love / the wealth I sought; the wealth I sought is mine in the knots gone seamed to perfect dreams of assignment said call this pleasure home to time and the time to come is the trip to mines of a central port called heady arrive at the heart of the source called wealth is my ability too, love / the life I wade; the life I wade is the one I am through with, a new one, blink, splash, connect, original, love / the x I spot; the x I spot is the hot arrival at precision in love.

CHAPTER TWO

The wave I swam; the wave I swam is grand in design and assigned to the matter of the love inside the swell to tell the truth, and too, every time I swim, in Love / a divinity's span; divinely spun, I am sung by the heavenly lines of the one Kauai high, too, love / a pen, I am; a pen, I am in my daily say of what gives and what lives and the thinnest line of the reclines to love / the spark in you; the spark in you, God, clear through, to love / the light revue; the light revue is true to you and the life knee deep in the street called love / of this I sing; of this I sing, love / healing proof; healing proof is in the truth called precisely love / a moment; a moment is a dream / a mountain stream; a mountain stream, a glinting dream, a drumming comes, a sweltering shade of don't be numbs, reside in the side of the loving splash and splatter most in healing laughs called God is, rill deep in matter and the mountain streamed with real love / a minute won; a minute won every time that I reside in the hands called time too, love / a minute One; a minute One, deep in the heart and the sum of All we've become and knot a minute too spare with one slim reminder to love / a vision come; a vision comes to me, love / a knot undone; a knot undone by the presence, love / a bed; a bed we've led to love is the day of the One and the same we live upon. Lie know more. know the truth of living in God's head; the dearest bed, love / an inkling said; an inkling said "come" and I came to remember and to the deliver of a flaming desire to regard this digress as exactly precise and emphatically nice to the written advice called love / a lark; a lark we've laid to the shades of love / a healing page; a healing page written and the sum and notion of the inkling who said that the maximum pleasure is in the truth of precisely mentioned admission of your progression to the books of love / a quilt; a quilt called lost has found at last the marriage bed of love / a patterned pulse; a patterned pulse can melt invent by heaven sent to God is, love / lands of lust; lands of lust rust in me when my rude delivery escapes the cup of God's dear love / the rust in us; the rust in us has cost the past and now at last I know invent of the heaven spent inside my rantin rush to beg forgive and the heights of hearing come on in too, love / a sleeping potion; a sleeping potion has met devotion in my resting reside at the side of a motion called light sensitive to love / a healing notion; a healing notion meets devotion when I pray for the hearts of love / an arc; an arc call devotion is met in the dark by the light of remember and we all know admission is half of the flight know the wings of love / a star; a star is born when worn survival knows nebular splendor in the One whose render is significantly strewn to the starry sun of a summary blend called love / the arc you are; the arc you are is love and spartan in pleasures becomes decadent when you know the treasure of sacred invent and the lost recovery of your life's virginity is your heart's spontaneity at hearing the mention of the arc of light called the life of love / by a covenant; rainbows red reign instead in the show of a all we know and as we flow we reside in the craft of a stream inside the hallelujah dream called returning to the heart of the covenant called love / never broken; never broken, my devotion, to love / always fit; always fit with the health of lvoe / heal your heart; know the part called heal your heart and heal the hole with the loosened sole of your walking feet meeting God at love / fix your eye; fix your eye on God and know the cross in your belief is simply the junction with the function called jumping to the street of the One's recovery of the sparkling star you are, know devotion, know emotion met with love, God is, see it, love / know the truth; know the truth, God is, love / God's foolproof; God's foolproof in the Oz-illations of the sparks devotion to the heavenward notion that a perfect refusal to know ever less meets in surrender to the notion of more and we adore our commit to the motions for love, foolproof, the truth of God, love / Enoch; Enoch said let the keys be red and every where green can come to lean into the unlocking stream of man's regard for the light of love and the heart of hard agree to believe in the living stream called God singing the keys of love / knock; knock at the door of dying to less and know the more of hearing confess of the soul released to the soiled explosion of and exploding companion called light, by devotion, and the seeking composure of a heavenly face called the lightest inclosure of the love in his place, know God's ahead at the door of love / a second wave; a second wave can now be paved by your ceiling home and the standing will to know the throne of God's yielding space and the taste of an elective experience called riding me home in the waters of love. God said, wave on / an ascendant stand; level tow begins with an ascendant stand in the land of revelate and the correlative measures of the lifting hands of open-palm delivery to the lands of receive and the ecstatic play in the fields of the ascendant stand called lightly opening arms of specifically, terrifically we star at love / the man, I AM; the man, I AM, is where I stand in the burning arrival at the heart of revival and the declaration of this tent as tribal for the band of the light called God / The Lord Metatron; The Lord Metatron is a sonic loom of All that rests inside of you and when your heart knows the tune of dearest meaning in the room and foolish forget has gone its way, know the merry band of traveling light in the land of the bulbs of remember, know electricity in the heart of God's face, know, love / Arcturic; Arcturic pens can enter in to love *An arc of regard carrying the torch of utmost resonance with the incoming charge too, Love / Mayan bins; Mayan bins erupt in me and my Egyptic type decree and friends of love are calling me to dine in the catch called listen-ins and releasing the light to invite a passage to safer mention of the crystal clear maxim that hear, God is, by Mayan admit, the only true love, light in too, God / a cleansing flood; a cleansing flood eruptive in the soul that flies to hearts of men and once again lifts away to know God's face in the higher day of a life that's clear with artesian proof and the love that's near when you speak heart's song of the longing call for carrying on to forgiveness deep in the cleansing flood of forgiving love / the ark of doves; the ark of doves, that's simple, love / a tweet in line; a tweetsie lined in seeing continuity of constant gratuity that living light pays and the knowing spiral to the spires that confess only truest, love, a continuum, God/ Taking west and finding east by exceeding time's supposed election to expire spirally higher on the tweet-see line/ a train called time; a train called time a liar for arriving late and before we started to understand that parted may particulate be and yet there's one whenever the sun opts too, see, and the glittering continuum of being becomes the light of love and the standing timelessness of a refrain called before, after, because, and ever after God is, love / from a quarter turn; from a quarter turn, I have learned a term called "rocking home" and I know the dome of the lights called love / a rocking lesson; a rocking lesson comes this way this day the delivery comes to me in my need to stare directly in to the eyes of love, eternal, love / the sine aligned; in a little town I found the sign of the sine aligned within the spin of sweet oblivion and the belling news that there's light in twos gone to display skin deep the acknowledgement of the sines inside, the sign, the arc-tangent, the relief called love / a laughing sign; a laughing sign three deep to the triangle of love / a wealth called way; a wealth called way has come to the given way of love / a heart called day; a heart called day and I said let's stay in the inside of the wave of light called love / a night we've led; a night we've led to giving head-less expansion to the arc that we mentioned called an excellent dimension of love / to bliss; to bliss this is to be, love / to kiss; to kiss a star or a concert hall, find bliss, in, love / to dis; to *dis another blows your cover called forever know only this, love *direct disregard for the instinct to share only love / to dat; to *dat I say dis, love *deep acceptance of the truth of Others and their consequential returns to love / to tao; unconditional expanse to a precise moment called the way, to tao's highway and the loving strain called spiraling heads of love / to wow; to wow yourself plow yourself with unconditional love / to heaven's maid; to heaven's maid, I have laid the deal of the explain called love / to the extreme; to the extreme regime be gone and know that the holding waves have come to crest and only the best arise to arrive at the light of love / to the way; to the way called love wave on; now...love / to the truth; to the truth be told and I say, weave on, love / to the light; to the light I pay the soft agree to deliver the regard for love.

CHAPTER THREE

Abandon; abandon meant a lighter choice when I learned to dance at the heart I own and a lifting arrival melted in me and a sight called LOVE opened to see the spirit's survival through the life called archival reveal and now know more about the way it can be to succeed in this busy-ness called life. Know remember and see the spark of a softer arc called Love redeems an abandon meant to forgive the leaving that Others wrought when their own good they sought and in selfish abandon of their own example and the sample I've seen coming home on a dream meant to be assigned designs of ancient wonder. Hear the thunder of heaven moving in unison to the decision to live in loving example of the arc-angels ampled deliverance and a sum of people receiving the faith that a bowl of life relieves when abandon's met by an arc of forget and the gentle act of breath. Abandon's forget; LOVE / SENT; sent home to spare deliverance, an awareness lives inside us as we're sent to the signs called a tree that lives in me and an appraising notion of the rational advance of elegance sought and fashion found in a town called today and a moment called light eternal and I see the light of a message sent to seeing eyes found volume deep in the lights of love; listen; sent clearly to you; love / expansion; expansive sparks erupt in me and I see soft divinity in your clinging eyes assaulting me for seeker's faith and knowing grace can bring release in eternal splendor of love's remind that life's exciting and an expansive lesson is the message of the sight called love's expansion; / vent; vent yourself on propulsive seas of days gone fly and a lava red sky erupts across the hailing beams of fireballs passing in between and seas volcanic heightened see receiving relief upon the walls of fire and a deepened sea gone redder still with the signs of who we are when we reside in one kind delivery of the sealing lift of the strangest trip to an Island yellow with pineappled agree the we reside inside the tranquil view of a sizzling lean into a vent called love / impulsion; impulsive to signs and stratified lives of deceit that's gone to meet a friend who lives in the land of Hanalei and a present meaning of impulsion's dreaming redeems our consignment of the feelings and fit of a lasting trip to the shores of recall and the life of a tall resting drink of light's eternal flaming refine and the day of a natural night nuzzled soft in the light of the seams nitrogen rich in a growing seed of impulse sent to dreams of blue and green and white in streams of injected impulsion called be; only; love / spent; values spent on a trip to the ranks called raking it in and energetically said we are wed to the enigma of meant by accepting the art of a giving brand called hu-man spent on love / expulsion; expulse your need to exceed more readily than just a dream and finding One you haven't won the righteous bell of a branching stream called know the trance and now redeem by liquid remembrance the seam of splashing communicate about the stream called arc-angelic dependency on love / brought; brought you home to claim your own redeem of the arc of regenerative exploration of the life we call the scene of all arrival. Brought home to store up more forgiveness of love / the surge; the surge to nothing is everything's include of a height of forgiving in the surge that needs delivering to the heightened increase and the forgotten trend to attendant standing at the heart of men and often given eternal pillows of the precious intrigue of triple entreaty that listens with harps of the sleeve called surrender and the wealth of a sunny reside at the shining surges of canals called the One opportune and the sun spotted care of receiving is given and the giving is where we believe in what's wrought and all we need is deserving and believing and along-ing to the loving in places of infinite peace and the art of forgiveness now is complete in swelling arrival at this, hear, release of the flow, the intrigue, the knowing refine of bless and the bliss of a surge called forever and the word know, forgive, 400 times plus the 90 inside and the 70 7's of our heart's recommend and the 17 layers of perfection's spin and the span of begin now can become defense of the right to ignite with forgive. live. LOVE / sought; singing down the walls I receive the centering I have sought as sweet surrender becomes tendered remember and we know trees of giving lived and paper pleased with the kiss of pens and the soul deep in eternal released and the light's intrigue with the uniquer claim called the cause of God, forgiven now, and nature's release of living how we do and the life I sought is here with you in the halls of men and the hearts of God's delivery to perfectly forgiven, love / the purge; the purge has come and the presence done with forgiving spirals to the surging cause that allows the humming treasures of chest high streams of starry nights and the eccentric waves of eternal deliver to the waves concentric with assign and deeper belief in heaven's kind and now a simple day believed is concealed know longer known as less than own by a hurtling hearken to relieve and the digestive splendor of release and the seizure of remembrance ripples through to advance our living team to the shores of redeem and the daily approach called the stage and the scene of love, know redeem, and the rays of the sun's forgiving face grace this place with *hauponopono wide to the arms of extend of the weapon's release and honesty lived and truth that is deep in the purge eternal with love. *Hawaiian assign understood perfectly on necessary opportunities, precious our need of daily immediate forgiveness / found; found your heart in another town met with forgive and the healing sound of One reside and the lines of tender address at surrender and the increased life of living central tot he time of giving and the gone to see the forevering come to the found in me; an eternal dream in the living dove of sweet deliver homeward arc-angel of love / the feel; feel the frost of an early cross escaping heat to burn in heart's aligned with the finest kind of believe. I am the design and the Havannah smoke of a crispy throat and a deliverance met when a feeling gets release, my relief, to decide to reside in the heart called the wheel of God's love. One to One. Feel the heat of love / astound; astounding pleasure in the measures called abounding in love / the thrill; the thrill of yes; love / reveal; reveal your stuff and see the show of your selfishness gone slowly to the shore of Other, love / the desire; the desire to love is superior to shoving refusal to live or forgive; know; love / for real; for real I heal in the arcs of love / the extend; the extend of a friend to love / the bend; the lead to forgive and the brand of the stand and the bend called the winds of love / the friend; the friend of love / the trend; the trend, begin, too, love / the chore; the chore, the core, the whore, the more, explain, know complain less and the pain gone and the extend found to the regard of expend and the expansive sun of One stance called attendant desire to love. / the door; the door that assures will close when I refuse to believe in a forgiving chore called the weaver's yield of love / the store; the store of regard has a score called the house of all revival, the survival, the reprisal, the surplus, the "must", only this, store, suspend, let go, too, love / the deed; the deed is set upon the path of a written stalk called the walk to the sway of a survey said too, believe, in, the stay at love / the concede; the concede, indeed, is too, love / the freed; the freed, indeed, are the loving breed called a hearty deed above the rest, the nest, the breeze of freed too, love / the need; the need, forgive, the art, just live, too, love / the construct; the construct is this, one kiss, called a building too, love / the dream; the dream arrives inside the beam of birds flown thin to flying exceed, the dream, called love / the trim; trim yourself to a lighter sail called the breeze within our love / the dame; the dame, the same, love / the skim; the skim, milked, is a skinny tilt too, love / the flame; who knew the flame except won who stood acceptive of One desire to eternally flame within the love of God as living, love. / the skinny; expectant stand in the skinny land called love / the lad; the lad of remember is leading us home too, love / the venue; the venue, the sport, the sort, too, love / the brad; the brad in the seat is the tract we compete, know more, to hide, less, the love inside, our brad-less love / the vinny; the *vinny is kinny in videoed by repair of the vineyard called care less and met in peaces of love. *value in no-ing in negligent yearn called gone back to energy's lad-love / the lock; the lock is off. I am healed, we are zealed by our eternal splurge in all locks bared to the electric stare, the penetration pair, the striking sear, called lock-less, in, love / the debut; the debut of loft holds a resonate hue, spotlight deep to keeping your eternal date with center stage and the respite from performing called a warm love / the key; the key? We, Love / the relief; the relief is spent on our retreat too, love / call me; call me, Love / the resolve; the resolve, the inner call, to love / called you; explore more, the store of fleet relief, the light of doves, unique to loving surrender in the splendor called you and the living proof of love / the need; the need to fish in a lighter dish called the lights of love / the tools;

the tools, the teal, the blue-green heal called reading about, love / the welcome; live in welcome splendor of the surrender too, love / the trends; the trends are set when we forget too, love / the suspense; the suspense is set on repent too, love / the amends; soft-spoken, we amend our burnt out desire, by retiring to the side called living in true align with love / the attributes; the attributes are this, we kiss, only, love / the friends; the friends are near, when the hear, only, love / the intrigue; the intrigue has come to lead us home too, love / the deeds; the deeds of which we speak can park at the done of the healing sum called all we were to the common acts of the desire too, love / the review; the review is new and the performance healed by the quiet regard called perfectly, love / the seams; curiosity said, let's rend the pen a lighter hand and called unlocking now the knocking and the knotting seam can have relief in the halls of mend, called God, love / the extreme; the extreme is the need for ultimate, love / the needs; needs are nested in believe of the trussed up forgiving shored in the shillings of heaven sent to back side door of a place called loving and a life called more arrival at the needs called love / the pursuit; the pursuit has come, ended now, and the plan to live can convene with the naked pursuit called perfectly, love / the plus; the plus is all-ways one called "A" and the size of plenty now can stay at the spangled plan of which we sing and the plural pleasure called belief in the measures of love / the passion; the passion, this fashion, the dressing, called love.

CHAPTER FOUR

The big; the big arrival at surprise and the living eyes of all belief in the being called perfection at love / the play; the play of days called love / the pith; the pith revealed by the woody core of a chore called less and a growing called more, we, love / the daze; the daze has come to an end and the milky stare is a friend called God's good flair and the living flower of the power, hu-man too, love / the prod; the prod to know about true God is love / the admit; the admit of God is, love / the sod; the sod erupts in a healing burst called the Earth, our Mother, know worms that melt in heated profess of the power of God called love / the trays; the trays say to pile up in waves of a resting phase called stacks of love / the days; the days of revival now have come and I am one with the sums of revival and the Arc's eye full on the lens of love / the buffet; the buffets blaze with our living come to the being fed by perfectly, love / the commitment; the commitment has come, this is, love / the attend; the attend, friend, befriend, know, amend , lend, love / the invention; he invention you mention is, love / the intend; intend too? love / the dimension; the dimension you mention is, love / the admission; the admission your priced is, love / the direct; the direct intention you've mentioned, is, love / the cognition; the cognition, the impulse, the vote, is for, love / the bisect; the bisect, the neck, of love / the recognition; the recognition that's best is remembrance too, love / the inspect; the inspect has come too, love / the remission; the remission's advise. I repeat. true advice. Once more. Love / the reflect; the reflect is on the father found at a friendly town called the counters of love / the extension; the extension found is clearly lovingly directly sovereignly, love / the ascend; the ascendant pleasure is the measure called love / the revision; the revision is too, the decision is who, the time is when and now we begin, true, love / the begin; the begin has come, too, love / the admission; the admission you mention is the cost that's true, love / to these truths; to these truth-full days we know the glimmers of the strumming, the humming, the patent on you, love / the reside; the reside is; love / the protestant view; protest the views of the Protestant views that include anything less than perfect respect for perfectly said; all we see in processed views is the attend too, love / the demise; the demise has come to less than the advise for perfection in love / the Christian review; Christ said, love you know, too, is an addition that adds up to One / the aberration; the aberration? a nation with a heart without love / the Catholic exude; Catholic guilt has spread a quilt of where a pope can land as the One without reveal of the pill and a plan for the hand that squeezed God's neck too thin. Know God. Remember the Vatican in your prayers for the need to remember free will and the choice to feel, like God, lightly said, love / the ignition; the ignition is possible when your condition is only and all ways, love, by permission, fire up, with God / the Muslim news; the Muslim news is good that God said too, bow through to the middle of perfectly love / the Sufi views; the Sufi views our duress with a spinning truth called the heart of the heart of love / radical roots; the radical roots of perfectly square too, love / the electric roots; the electric roots of everyone concede to the zipping need to sound like love / the healing proof; the healing proof is this, love / the admonition; the admonition is this admission, love / the call; the call to be, is heard, at love / this our mission; this our mission is, the solid ignite of a giant decide to love / the blessed; the blessed see only bliss in raw delivery of love / a coupled seek; a coupled seek has found only love in this town of lightest forgive, live, God, love / our truth; our truth is healed and now we know, God is, love / a sullen proof; a sullen proof has revealed the cord that the sword forgot, now the cut has come and I must confess I need the surgical sever direct form God, psychic invent can connect when only direct too, love / eternal; eternal to the treasure, love / basic; basic to the blues that went the way of the bear that wore shoes, know exactly, love / supernal; supernal to a treat called precisely commanded love / humanity; humanity hugs the bare repair of the electric stare at the fired up feel of precision in love / youth; youth-full exude of the rude alliance gone away and the new defiance revealed, know the dance of respect called lightly love trailing proof; a trailing proof now has come to the light of God, and knot a comet too less than love / abandon meant; abandon meant come too, God / respect full; respect full I stand at the edge of the yard wide with only God ahead, love / acknowledge; acknowledge the fact that I speak for God, love is, know this, Metatron / the meaning; the meaning comes when you love yourself as God and know confess of the direct connection to the above is through the heart of love, your own, meaning, love / the college; the college is over, know God, love / the store; the store is open, know confess of God as the purchase sweetest and best, God is, now, love /

called love; called love, yes! I did; love / up next; up next is the life of the living recline in the arms of wide recovery and the relative relate to the sexual discovery of permanent blend with the other of self said One, Love and the mention sacred too, two, God, One / Wind / Worthy / Comes

CHAPTER FIVE
Alive, my ways; alive, my ways are spent in the the electric haze called the days of sweet arrival at love / Asheville days; Asheville days erect in rays of glassed arrive at a widowed lass called eccentricity cast upon the trim of an electric dream called the ancient ways of living lean to the modern pleasure called the treasure of love ascendant shine of high evolve to a view inside the life of love's elect / erotic seams; erotic seams of you I dream in seaming pleasure of the schemes that treasured mean the being ways of all that edged and all that stayed so light behind and in between we see the dream of erotic schemes called lightly, love / electric ways; electric ways, select the day of hearts that filled with the gleams of love / a hire stand; an open dove has found release at the stand of sycamores down the street and the maple's dead upon the shores of an electric dream called home too, love. A higher stand, the hire plan, of a strand called the trees of love / a healing dream; a healing dream now it seems can come in teams of swell arise at the revise called love / a field of themes; a field of themes, the dreams of those who scheme of only, love / a melted pave; a melted pave now can wave at the wands of swollen remember about the shout through streets of love / an art-full dance; an art-full dance can take the chance, deliver us, to the stage of love / a grander scheme; a grander scheme is the dream for love / forgiving limes; forgiving limes of hallowed lines of written lore and spoken rhymes and often said our truth delivers the power-full punch of a lemon-aid store and a lime-green sea of crystal dreams forgiven by love / an artist's stance; an artist's stance now can dance at the chance too, love / emphatic climes; emphatic climes now reside in the ides of parallel seasons of love / ecstatic times; ecstatic to times of the speaking reason for all to exceed and nun to fail at the missing kiss of ecstasy spared by only, love / a knowing scheme; grand to the scheme of knowing arise, I am the heart and the hope and the eyes of rhyming leisure and the thrill of those who wait for the date with exactly this, the plan, for love / effusive; effusive to gleams of healing glint, I know the extent of perfection in the sleeved arrival at the heart of God, Hu-man, love / eternal waves; eternal waves around me ring for the splashing jolt of electric seams gone wet with arise in the size of it all, One day, love / assignments say; assignments say, read the heart, of love / an eternal, internal clock; an eternal, internal clock can tick with the shock of remembrance come to the sum who sing of only love / a mental block; a mental block has come to gone and hearts that heal are moving on to the basic believe in the perfection of bliss and the well enough said to the heart of a kissing called dismissing forget with move on too, God / a delicate line; a delicate line found to the need to believe in only, love / arriving signs; arriving signs read about my desire to hear of longer kissed by only, love / phlox and posies; phlox and

posies read like rosies around the heart of God is, love .*plants held lightly in olden exact to the annual trend to perennial begin / a field and flocks; a field and flocks that rock with freedom when the friends find release of the harder reasons to forget about love / guilt and gay; guilt and gay I am alive with the swept away song of the singing whales who know the tales of kinder men, love / knows and noseys; knows and noseys enter in to the smelling arts of staying thin to the thicker line called seeing through to the colors of love and the plans to mend our truth with remember, love / election day; election day comes, know the stay in sweet deliver, know the way to all who say only this, love / gray and guilt; gray and guilt to the quilt of going home too, today, love / belted; belted pleasure knows the measure of Earth's release and the bulging sides of the ride inside to the day called equatorial bliss, that's love / quilted; quilted by love once again and the friends who've found the higher ground of love / instead; instead of knot, let's love / understood; understood by others, love / he went; he went too, love / she said; she said, let's love / they give; they give this, love / we live; we live like, love / vibrate; vibrate too, love / free; free to be, love / explain; explain less, love / love; love is splendor in the chance encounter called yes, God, loves / design; designs of love / divine; divine designs on love / descend; descend to the manner, love / amend; amend your stance, love / resign; resign too, love / review; review your love / the love inside; the love inside resides in you / and you; and you knew, love / the move; the move is too, love / to trends; to trends that fade and those that stay, love / deliver in; deliver in to the Friend called love / deliver us; deliver us too, love / instead; instead of knot, love / in fed; in fed ascend to the friend whose blend becomes believe I live for love / in feed; in feed I breed deliverance to the tabled desire to wave the banner and welcome seat ourselves at love\ / in red; in red align with the bleeding chance to dance in trust in the bed of love / in receive; in receive I grieve at less too, love, and knowing more I see the shore of a landscaped chance to believe in love / the mother; the mother is near feel the hear arrival at love / the father; the father hears his fallen fear melt in great drips of love / the lover; the lover found comes to town to the Other side of love / this day; this day we play in love / tell me; tell me this, "love" / the way; the way home, love / the isle; the isle called man and the arms of strong deliver too, love.

CHAPTER SIX

The isle; the isle of pleasure knows its measure in the ascend to the welcome stay at the doors of men and the greater faith called doves of love, spirit bound too, love / red, big; red and big the isle of figged align with Eden inside our genes.. A Lemurian scheme of eternal delight and the Big Island sight of the heavenly light called love / born green; born green I am seen on a St. Louis high and a Philadelphia scheme and a world that collides in an arc=angels's dream at the heat Metatron, love / eruptive in; eruptive in our light delight we find our friend by plundering in with love / desire to live; desire to live by the way you give of love's away to the chance to glance at love

/ in joy's space; in joy's space, I have found a face, my own, surrounded by the heart I love and God's new throne, upon my head and headed home to join the taste of love / Hafiz; Hafiz again has graced this plain and entered in to let explain become reveal of the living rides called the greater path of swift deliver to the heights and the hearts of God, God is, now, love *higher ascend to the friend inside a zealous ride to God / called love; I called love and she came to me in a return called living free in the fine deliver called listening to the friend of love / eternal; eternal love / dove; holy white and spirits's word, the bird, the curve, the arc, the man, hu-man, return to the dove of love / an ocean wide; ocean wide, I am saved by paves of golden blocks and sunlit waves and the heart of young delivery to the heart of stays set free to be an ocean wide too, love / big isled align; big isled align with the open sign called love / and yes, we know; and yes, we know, love / the passion shows; the passion shows our overflows of only love / and 3 below; It is 3 below and all I know is love / a burning heat; a burning heat has found the street of sweet release and the dove that called is love / besiege; besiege has set a higher friend to begin the fins of dolphin waves and whaling stays at the arts of love / the kneed; the kneed to exceed has been met by agreed too, love to love aside, I glide, by love / inside; inside the days of format waves and inside the size of crested agree, a layered lattice now can see the penetrative stare that cares only for seeing all we are for, love / the stream; the stream that homeward now can see the fishing splash of the beaded tree that round me sings of leaves of love / called light; called lightly, I am, and spoken softly all-ways, listen lightly too, love / and love; and love has said we are ahead to playing fields called doves that give of only winging love / we feed; we feed ourselves the brisk ascend too, lunch at love / on dreams; on dreams we seem to beam to the lighter kind, love / deliver; winged to the beginning, I am winning my homeward stay at the lightest arrows delivery of the life called quivering, love / and I can see; and I can see what we mean by the seeming delight of all we can be for lightly love / the trend to be; the trend to be loved / inflamed; inflamed by the steamed agreement, love / by same; by same I mean game to become our love / and met; and met by the heat that is neat called, love / to need; to need only, love / the game; the game has come to light explain for the one rule unto the tools of love / to ends; to ends that care know the treads of lightest love / and friends; and friends who heal know the trends of lightest invite to the taming sight called love / of dames; of dames I complained until it seemed that love was pain and the became the remembering One, the dame called love / called fortune; called fortune's feel and the cornered bet on a belt called love / fate; fate that is late is felt toward more known best by agree to believe in love / tragedies; tragedies proclaim the name that same can be and the only shame is a tragedy called forgetting too, love / mates; mates been checked by the elect, we, love / myths; myths met by a match called love / archaeology; archaeology says let us live in a dig called love / ecstatic; ecstatic to agreed and the erratically relative trend called love / relief; relief of the kind who candidly meet at precisely love / human;

human kind, love / regard; regard the rest as best and by far too, love / and; and I will be blessed by love / heights; heights of confuse have gone to bemuse with only this, love / heaven; heaven held around the swell of an open throat's delivery called love / the heavenly; the heavenly side of love / stars; stars the rounds and rapt the bless of the bliss full sound called love's confess / electric; electric ascend too, love / select it; select it, dove, love / know it; know it, love / just due it; God has said due, drop in to pay your respects, just due it, love / imbue it; imbue it, plain to be, flat land, I see in the swells of love / show it; show it to the blazes of belts and parts that start too, love / love; life can leave us left too, love to, love / ignobled; ignobled I stand as a mountain manned by love / belt; belted pleasure now can see the treasure of weathered delivery and knot a Mayan span too late, the date, 2012, the measure only, love / the delt; the delt of dare has flared to cared for and spasmed pleasures of the treaty for love / the felt; felt the feel of reels of love / the full; the fullest movies reel with red and the full exclaim of what we said for, love / the filled; the filled deliver now can be agreed to lightly and we see the lights of fires electric gleam in the size of cells that now believe in love / Limbs.

CHAPTER SEVEN

Sky wide; sky wide to agree and I know, love / the field; the fields of pleasure know, love / star deep; star deep in the sleep of the electric trip called love / arcing lean; arcing lean to a rod *McLean, and a welcome explain called hu-man too, we've made it, love *most clear lights extend annually near too love / the chance; the chance to dance at love / the deliver; the deliver of deals that seal our kiss / the dance; the dance that spoke of the hope to keys that square aroused by the sound of sounds electrically squired by the squared arrive at love / leaning stance; a leaning stance that means agreed too, love / extreme; extreme advance has come know the sum true, love / banal; banal to pleasure, measure, flights with love / primal; primal isled and Greek to seeds of starry nights and softer seeing, love / gleam; gleam the stream of a photon's beam with call it, love / a glen; light me up in a Glen Extreme with love / Archimedean; Archimedean alchemy links us up with the life that treads us deep enough too, love / alchemical; alchemical rings and I wear the rings of pleading plenty delivery too, love / the bridge; the bridge is, love / the healing cup; the healing cup is to a toast called love / stepping up; stepping up and I am met too by love / mean it's touch; mean it's touch, it's the truth of love / call it; call it, love / see the wealth; see the wealth in your truth, love / redeem; redeem yourself too, lovely, pleasure / know the pad; know the pad of happy feet that launching list to the other street and the paving stones of lights that own their collectively, love / feel your dad; feel your dad in your sad gone away and know that he found your delivery healed by love / touch your mom; touch your mom and know the truth that every day and Earthly youth can reel at pleasure of God is, love / inhale the sun; inhale the sun, our breathing sum, called love / beat the drum; beat the drum and the sum has come to One-der felt by love / know the chance; know the chance that danced was your life and meet the light revival, love / the compare; the compare of all that will is, love / the dare; the dare of compare is what we care for, love / the wares; the wares that light's on, love / the stairs; the stairs that extend too *Pleiadian trends and her melted approach to the airs of love *plenty of ascendant directive assigned next to the stand for universal love / the plays; the plays that stay for love / called love; called for, love / traditional; traditional to a triumphant plan called the hint for man and the heritage rare in a compare called the announcement angelic that the arc-angels hear are the cranial sacrament called truly classic love / scented; scented smell of a maxim place called love / conditional; know condition. Stand tradition at invent of the less than a trance called a penetrating stare of the cosmic flare called love / Alabama; Alabama said believe in Mobile's attraction to the return too, love / eruptive; eruptive to a trip called the lip of arrive at love / jeweled; in a Mayan mind, a carve, a wind, and a genuine gleam called the eye's release of the sound of crystal clear and the jewels of love / subjective; subjective tot he matter called perfection's splatter of love / kyanite; kyanite winds blend with bands of arise at the healing sound of four-layered deep too, love and a talcum blue delivery of a kyanite wind called love / reflective; reflective to a wind of a mixture called fixture of the dynamic kind called directly reflective, love / iolite; iolite to a nurture and purple-blue to a flight on a stone of arrival at a revival grown green with the envy less, love / wed; wed by yourselves and found complete in a pleasurable ascension to the extension of life without answer and the matters reconnect with the plains of a wedded bliss called eternally love / seas; seas of please grow in me and swollen seeds of daily needs to pleasantly live for love / eyes; eyes of direct regard for the hard confess that's lessen, love / rings; rings of regard for the hard deliver known perfectly deep as love / able; able to be and what will we see as the only three who know the One, love / philosophic; philosophic to a melt and melted to a feeling felt as sonic, resonant, vibrant, and agreed too, circles of love / philosophy; philosophy met in the feelings felt by a healing agree to Socratically sound like the fields of the yields called Sophically done, love / late; late enough to see through, the early need too, love / equate; equate regard with fate that's heard by, love / await; await the state called love / arising; arising signs of symbolically needed love / listening; listening, hear, and I am sworn to agree and the heart that is worn with the survival of the arrival called, love / turning; turning here to hear remember for love / spank; spank me with the impact of true, love / rank; rank here has come to the plank that's called love / short; short enough to set upon, love / shift; shift away to the stay inn, love / retail; retail matters matter most when the host is plattered with by, love / roaming; roaming about and the creeks that seek find release in the kiss of only we, love / rest

CHAPTER EIGHT: *TODAY I LOVE*

Movies; movies essential say to me and to my reside in our agree that this my heart is a sea of surging proof that love's indeed agreed upon and a seed of spaced delivery approves of this, the kiss, called life and the healing wife called saddle up for the movies of love / rotate; rotate to the great arrival of the essential truth that the Earth is proof of our eternal need to love the Other, the Mother and ascends too, and first we agreed upon legally now the greater state of a glove matrix deep in delivery of the heart that sees inside the spin of sweet release into the rotate called spinning within, love / by-pass; by-pass less than all that sees what heaven has built and the wilt that said the mooning's led to the rise called perfection in love / lovely; lovely notions found in letters written aglitter with the slim decide to know what's inside this rhyme called we desire to live in lanky strides of love / short; short sided signs align at the trim of a trailing sea grown wet with smart delivery of the qualified truth called directly, love / palm; palms pent in recess and I am taking a solid plat of penchant laid on the land and graves that now erupt with the healing touch of Metatron directed by God to lift the lid and light the sum of the entring called the beds of palms dried pearly red with the soul gone steep to the dripping stream called the light highway too, love / fingered; fingered and fed, I am led to the redder bed called our satisfied life at the larking sung too, hands on, love / poem; poems written to the rhyme of the light inside our daring deal to now begin within the wheel of agility and the life called love / young; young to flights and met by refuse and the lie-ing down that now can use a dry upheaval of venting truth that love's in pain inside of few who knew refuse of the lesson love and know becomes the lift too, love / snappy; snappy I am and delivered I'm free to a breaking trend called the eyes that see and the dice that's cast past eternal drain is the light of love and the height that's plain too, love / gentle; gentle sum, the hum, the regard, the hymn, the eternal, one, especially done, love / extravagant; extravagant places to reside in, hearts won, love / comfortably; comfortably done, man's basic need is the reflection of a comfortable residence called love / well; well enough to see the I AM of perfection's breed of a crystal clear blend called love / remedy; remedy that's rented for vented by love / jargon; jargon of the essentially central concept of the summon sent to branching in to the vented breath of the earth's red release called talking about, love / vestral; vestral burgeoned delivery to the service sent and the happy rent that's paid too, love / virgins; virgins that know that God is good are headed for the living hood of a neighbor called concentrically, love / cherry; cherry red, a crystallized kiss and the cherries fed too, love / red; red enough to bliss about and the clearer side called conveniently, love / peached; peached by the reach called love / said; said enough about contests that lightly speak of the trend toward love / love; love to love you, eternally, lightly, adroitly, love / blood; blood refutes our ill repute with perfection sent by God's above and all within is well within the shores of veins exposed too, love / warm; warm to the touch of a maximum flow of the untitled window called overlooks love / genetic; genetic spills exposed to reels of movied discuss of the process hu-man, love / kinetic; kinetic feels of the spongy insides called the hu-man thrills of love / soft; soft in recline, I am aligned with the heart of men, swirling dervishes said, too, love / patience; patience please with those who need a desire-able squeeze of love / ladies; ladies flirt with the narrow wade to the stream of Zion's gate and the healing toss to the fields above and the electric weave of a sneezing regard for all we love / tricks; tricks that teach deliver us and again we win with love, God / ticket; tickets purchased by the grace of a mantled molecule now displaced to reveal the fields of trips too, love / satin; satin seen in sheens of blue and hints of true delivery of the well worn news that God is, good, now believe softly in love / velvet; velvet thin, I am skinned with the living red of a thicker day called love's high way and driven to equate the result with love / jet; jet to the truth, love / baker; bakery lined with the bread of deeper shelves which no reveal the kind of feel that delivery can bring to kingdom come at 13:13, the dimensional frame of a feeling gamble on the shamble less and the beauty more and the masterpiece worn by gentle hands baking love / pulse; pulse points need release without the needles of lessons loved / patch; patches of quilted delivery to the tilt of the Earth's recovery for the Shekinah tides of love / lust; lusty please in the maximum squeeze for the tasty treats called reckoning, love / exude; exude about your pleasing trails of walking desire to know the hire of the ones you love to finish this, the project, hu-man / boat; boats that float on the watery shores of the home called forever and the lifting chores, now done, for love / dream; dream about the little hills of love / heart; heart time, love / head; head to an explanation for the mention of crystal sheens upon the scene of maximum exposure to a treaty treasured by all who know her, God above, Earth below, Metatron between, believe, in, love / stand; stand for all you love, God / strands; strands of delight with the healing sights called love / preclude; precludes gone to become the same agree that the game is love and we are the summary, One / proclaim; proclaim the name, love / sector; sector published now reveals the hidden meaning of the fills of love / secure; secure to a measure treasured by lifting love / segue; segue to the trim arrival at the parallel called love / section; sections notice delivery of the particulate quantums of recovery and the tiny packets now can see the waves that point to the source, One, Love / stream; streams that delve into undulate with, love / scene; scene of arrival at the bundles bent for singing trines and cords that lend their harps to men and the heads that stay inside the womb of one mind, God, All other away, now, the stay in Arcturic waves of love / rod; rod of man, red with the hand of a sunny day's orange recover, love / built; built to stay at love / teeth; teeth that shut at the words of less than love / wreath; wreaths that rule the reigns of love, halos hallowed too, God / pass; pass the nature too, love / pat; pat the fact that Kabbalah is back with the deeper work of the lace that is found around the towns of love / boone; boone is danieled by the tune of electric yellow truth pouring forth to reveal only, love / booth; booth bought now can please with love / bath; bath taken can rescue your windsome ways with knowing spoof that passion's reveal is coming direct to the lighter reflect of you, love / birth; arcturic birth, the worth, of love.

CHAPTER NINE: *I AM*

I AM that I AM; I AM and that I AM is love / I AM essence; I AM essence met by the breath of love / I AM light; I AM light to the essence of love's healing embrace / I AM life; life is and I AM / I AM well; I AM well to a heightened depth called love / I AM love; I AM too, love / I AM; I AM that stem called the loving support of God / I AM that; I AM that I AM and that is, love / I AM then; I AM then again, love / I AM now; I AM now and forever God in love / I AM eternally; I AM eternally God about, love / I AM infinity; I AM infinity too, and you are, love / I AM essentially; I AM essentially said, love / I AM elementally; I AM elementally broken by the spoken ascend too, love / I AM eternally; I AM essentially, internally, and eternally, love / I AM, infinitely; I AM, infinitely, love's divinity led to the channel of infinity divided by three and we decide about it, love / I AM essentially; I AM essentially led by love / I AM whole; I AM whole to the matter of life that is found in a whaling town called love / I AM experientially; I AM experientially felt by the sound called love / I AM evidentially; I AM evidentially led to the place of the tasty decide too, love / I AM finally; I AM finally the finality of the I AM who said we are all-ways, love / I AM fragrantly; fragrantly spoken by love's content, I AM extensive to the width of the light that shines like a fragrant exhale to the lord called love / I AM especially; I AM especially, love / I AM absolutely; I AM, absolutely, love / I AM divine; divinely spoken, I AM, love / I AM fully; I AM fully led by love / I AM aptly; I AM aptly seen as flexible too, love / I AM amazing; amazingly done by the I AM sent too, love / I AM engaging; I AM engaging in the hu-man wave, love / I AM intricately; I AM intricately woven in love / I AM led; I AM led to believe in, love / I AM fed; I AM fed by love / I AM met; I AM met by direct react to the fact that love is, I AM, and fresh too, love / I AM, yes; I AM, yes, too, love / I AM today; I AM today too, love / I AM forever; I AM forever led by love's recall of the waking dream called love / I AM entranced; I AM entranced by the stance at love / I AM elegant; I AM elegant too and spell it well the shades of dew in the avenue of moisture rich renew at the view's exuberance with love / I AM eloquent; I AM assuredly so and eloquently go to the halls of recall and the note that we all can clarify and comfortably say that concise agree is the concentric stay and the eloquent rate of rote the vote for all we need of love / I AM intelligent; I AM intelligent too, love / I AM eternal; I AM eternal to a spring of delivery for God ahead, love / I AM fulfilled; I AM fulfilled by God's *real love *Ready energetically to all-ways love / I AM equitable; I AM equitable to the inevitable that comes too, love, and to a fashion the action above, 1 love / I AM delectable; I AM a delectable treat of the neat arrive at the love I am and the swimming arousal at light said love / I AM electrical; I AM an electrical weave of the kind that sleeves itself upon the garment blessed by deliverance and the isles of man who said that electrically the bill is filled by love / I AM Metatronic; I AM Metatronic to the bliss-full state of love / I AM level; I AM level in my balanced show of the perfect love and I will rock the scales to a level welded by love / I AM balance; I AM balanced by the law of design hu-man and God is, love / I AM harmonic; I AM harmonic in my rise to the meeting starred by the scars that healed and waxing the moon and the tunes of love / I AM attuned; I AM attuned to the love hu-man too, God / I AM mobile; I AM mobile to the home I love and the lend that is, God / I AM infinite; I AM infinite in twin arise to the life that held us all within the friends of love / I AM evergreen; I AM evergreen by love / I AM supernal; pink and blue and heavenly too to the supernal dance called love's deliverance / I AM pedernal; I AM pedernal to the journey New Mexico deep by a wave of relating to God and we are eternally love / I AM God; I AM God ahead, love / I AM the earth; I AM the mother of love / new birth; new birth to the beginning begun by eternal lend to the birthing ascend called the earth of love / regenerated; regenerated by the venerated agreed too, love / I AM elated; I AM elated to the cheer called love / I AM safe; I AM safe by the waves of unlocked retrieve to the safe called love / I AM happy; I AM happy in, love / I AM green; I AM green too, love / I AM clear; I AM clear to hear only, love.

CHAPTER TEN: *THE BOOK OF LOVE*

One love; one love is, become, God / one law; one law wins, love / one command; one command meant, love / one heart; one heart is, felt, by two who love / one way; one way home, love / one truth; one truth told, love / one life; one life led by giving delivery of love / one wave; one wave leads us too, home, and love / one depth; one depth of love / one appreciation; one appreciation comes too, love / one initiation; one initiation comes too, love / one arc; one arc of love / one reminder; one reminder wins, love / one kinder; one kinder friend is love / one indivisible; one indivisible by love / one invincible; one invincible through, love / one trickle; one trickle comes too, love / one flow; one flow, found deep too, love / one embrace; one embrace that comes, love / one taste; one taste of, love / one swell; one swell taste, love / one wave; one wave saves, love / one sun; one sun seen by two who love / one time; one time she heard only love / one you; one you we knew love / one line; one line on time, love / one loop; one loop complete too, love and the trinity's troop who came to dine at the light divine and the circle lair around the stream of precious love / one, I am; the one, I am, is, love / I am one; I am one who lives too, love / one summer; one summer I wed the news of love / one winter; one winter I wed the blues of love / one heart; one heart held too, love / one fall; one fall full with love / one vibe; one vibe sealed by love / one spring; one spring I came too, love / one me; one me found by love / one stream; one stream wet with love / one dream; one dream comes too, love / one awakening; one awakening found in the glimmer of the one awakened by love / one light; one light sounds like love / one quickening; one quickening to the sticker called happening for love / tree; one tree we see is, love / one life; one life that seals the lips of the leading strike for the sway too love / one wed; one wed said, love / one led; one lead too, love / one divine; one divine too, love / one's light; one's light scene, love / one's love; one's love is comforting too, love / one;

one too, love / one thread; one thread that seems like the quilt of love / one web; one web that leads to another light of love / wedding; wedding days of love / one feeds; one feeds herself love / one night; one night of the light kind, love / one sight; one sight of the simmer, love / one delight; one delight-full kind, love / one song; one song that sings in me, love / one river; one river that quickens with a quiver of love / one jah; one jah jeweled with spoken love / one God; one God wed too, love / one sun; one sun, love / one kin; one king comes too, love / one queen; one queen who knew love / one ring; one ring around love is golden too

CHAPTER ELEVEN: *INFINITE AND ETERNAL*
Infinite expanse; an infinite expanse of the meeting dance called love / infinity, a glance; meet a glance called infinity and love / exceptionally infinite; exceptionally infinite to the extreme of love's rule called the golden way and the wave of silver reside at the inside stay at grace-full include of love / an infinite loop; an infinite loop of whistling hoops layered in waves of regular collide with the healing inside our stays at the lightly seasoned four way release too, love / time for the infinite; time for the infinite to stay at love / infinitely greek; infinitely greek to the seeking include at the alphabetic stare directly into the God's greek share of the santorini seas of lightly love / infinitely essential; infinitely essential to the desire to be loved / infinite, it seems; infinite it seems and the streams that bliss with wetter dreams than this and love / eternal expansion; eternal expansion beams inside the expand called live like this, love / infinite romancing; infinite romancing comes to the daring compare called life is, home / essentially eternal; essential and eternal, I am supernally Christian about my Buddhic agree to be held in the stance called God's eternal light, love / infinite design; infinite design of the decree called love in agree, go ahead, God / infinite plan; essentially, yes, I will plan on the spare contrail to a central strand of the invent called the stare of all we directly see of the healing source called eternally God is, love / infinite rain; infinite rain that falls on the panes of love / infinitely divine; infinitely divine and fine in the dates with love / lightly infinite; lightly infinite, we too, are, love / eternal light; eternal light sees us, love / eternal flight; assign the flights to me and I will arrange the designs we dare to compare to this, love / infinite ecstasy; infinite and ecstatic to the love's arrival at the floor of my infinite ecstasy called love / eternal bliss; eternal bliss can kiss this place with love / an eternal kiss; an unfinished bliss is this compare with the stare that's deep to the kiss of love / ecstatic review of the infinite; ecstatic review of the infinite in you and love / infinite, I said; infinite, I said can arrive at the rise of the trial called spare deliver too love, reside near, our dear, love / infinitely I am; infinitely I am spare too, love / eternity; eternity, the span, too, love / an infinite arc; an infinite arc, the spark of love / an eternal web; an eternal web that said love / an infinite love; an infinite love of the life that led too bliss-full accept / eternity's sign; eternity's sign of the life of love / infinite tread; infinite is the treadwork of the steps of love /

eternally led; eternally led too, love / infinitely led; infinitely led too, love / infinity said; infinity said, love / logos; logos deep to infinity and love and the leading tread called God is the word of the sword that cut the infinite cord of less than love / infinity; infinity let it be, only, all-ways four days to the treat four ways love / eternity; eternity lives allowed by me and love / eternal light; eternal light new too and the sights of, love / infinite love; smell the taste of an incessant beat and know the peace of an infinite increase called lightly we love / love eternal; love eternal too, the need, lives, love / love's eternity; love's eternity is for me and the sight and the see and the truth and the trees of love / love to infinity; love is infinity by a degree too, love / infinity to infinity; winged to bets of a basic bee and I see the flight of dance in the we of a butterfly's weave and the sandy bottomed seam of eternity's streams strewn upon the heart of lightly we love from infinity to infinity, love / eternally I am; eternally I am, love / infinitely centered; infinitely centered at the mid-stream of love, I am found in the tree of a living agree called reclined too by love / centrally, eternity's balance; central to an eternal balance, I am seen in signs of chalice and held to beginning again within eternity's balance of coming home too, love / insistently; insist on the infinite and agree to be insistently, love/ eternity's star; eternity's star is the crystal we are to the orbital called electrically infinity is, love / infinity's wave; explain the same, the central pair of splashing refrain and the rippling proclaim of the infinite frame called the waves of love / eternal particles; eternal parting of particulate place and the meeting called bits of the whole, love / particularly infinite; particularly infinite and often seen, scenes of complete in the halls of clean arrive at the warmth of love / infinitely essential; infinitely essential and absolute in degree to the light we will be for eternally love / infinite design; design that is infinite to the dates with love, One to One / infinite lifts; infinite lifts agree too and carry me to the halls of love / infinite One; infinite One are love / infinite all; infinite all can be love / infinite falls; infinite falls fell too, love / infinite suns; infinite suns freely given and seen as love / infinite freed; infinite freed by the musical need too, love / infinite me; infinite me and all One tree of perfectly times delivery to the heart of love / infinite led; infinite led to believe in the resurrection hu-man and the trees of love / infinite fled; infinite fled to discovery of the heightened recovery called all we do is, love / infinite fed; infinite fed by forever, love / infinite bred; infinite bred to be loved, hu-man / infinite medical; infinite medical meet has found retreat in the power of the mind's delivery to the heart of loved and the divine recline in the realign with the heart of man and the spirt seen in the skies of love / infinite refine; infinite refine your nature, love.

CHAPTER TWELVE: *MANY*
Many paths; many lights feel the night and elegance invites my tread to leads of the lifting singing called the gift of love, Know the many, the parts, the please, and the plan for the light that leads to the heart of man and the go between that is called eternally, love, night and day. Lightly led, we are the way and

the truth and the seeking proof of infinity's web and the diatribe is red with passionate swell of the drumming rhythm, eternity is coming home to dwell within this planet wet with the well to do and the story too, dance the proof and the living light that said this God's insist on us and then we could find the wealth of the I am truth and the manner of the living line and the life of One and many. We are fed by the living bread and the manna of the monad know as only other and the many paths of the one that's free to be and we are the one and the many paths of light are freed electric and the one source and the many threads of one goal all treated by the wine of eternal woven agree too, love / many trees; many trees dance in deliverance to God is wed too, love / many planes; many planes come to meet in the street of love / many, all one; many, all one, the sum, love / many merry; many are merry in love / many, mini; many, minis rise to skies of love / many, macro; many are macro to their healing sight called agreeably, love / many micro; many days I am micro-wayed too, love / many biotic; many biotic measures treasure love / many, ionic; many, ionic blended intended loved / many iconic; many icons measure the heart of the earth's miraculous ways with archetypal ways too, love / many, dichroic; many, dichroic mazes are called only these, love / many, you know it; many you know it, and often you mean to arrive at the scenes of love / many, scientific; many scientific measure their please by the neat arise of a hypothetical sun and the surgical measure of the One into many and the most, One love / many, prolific; today I am prolific in my heeling treat of the standing surrender called the feat of heaven's reward as the prolific sort, love / many ethereal; ethereal plenty escapes to see exactly the center of the veil in me lifted free to be only, love / many imperial; many imperial meet the riches of love / many red; many red eyes read of the All that's become, love / many, blue; many, blue to many who can call the years of spoken plenty reviewed by the speaking I am and called complete in love / many will live; many will live for the days of love / many will lead; many will lead to the homes of living love / many lightly; many lightly said, love / many eruditely; many eruditely said/ wisely seen, love / many igniting; many igniting me with love / many inviting; many inviting in the Friend, love / many exciting; many exciting me with the lighting of, love / many enriching; many enriching me with the ditching free of the digging need too, love / many ambrosiac; many ambrosiac themselves with the lilting kin to kinship see in the lights of love / many aeronautics; many aeronautics are taught biotic measures by love / many licensed; many licensed meetings are set with the direct intention to mention what is, God's license, love / many enticing; divine times are enhanced with the enticing news that love is good, pure attraction, God / many emphatic; love me emphatically in my enticingly dramatic degree of the depth of love / many devoted; many devoted by the emotive of the degrees of lightly said let's believe in the daring pare of love / many committed; many committed by the ecstatic aspects of madness lent to love / many explicit; many explicit in their degree of seeking love's agree too, love / many know this; many know this, love, at the phone rich with healing verves of

the electric news, I love you too, God / many and one; many and one become, love / many and sum; many and sum are the fidelity that spoke of One love / many and light; many and light are the sights of declare at the days of feeling free too, love / many sparks; many sparks are felt near the nexus of the symbolic come to real degrees of love / many arcs; many arcs of the energy that is, humanity, love / many loved; many loved by the way we saw each other through by the living called love / many men; many men ascend to the electric ilk of a silvery thread clipped by the Spanish flame called love / many mothered; many mothered by the sexually alert convert to the sort of needs we've met by fields of elect that set itself on love / many fed; many fed to the shaking shape of the hands that held election's sway with love / many hands; many hands deal with hills of the Roman stand called concurrently craved the draw / many lives; many lives that give the chance to others who deal with the same and the craving flame of the daring agree to be inside the womb of love / many gifts; many gifts that eclipse with love / many meet; many meet in a directive called love / many forgiven; many forgiven and continues the living called lightly agree to the peace-full confess that God is, love / many forgave; many forgave me my degree of the harbored relief gone direct to confess of the quality scene called love / many embrace; many embrace themselves with love / many I will lead; many I will lead too, love / many things; many things seen in love / many things known; many things known too, love / many things heard; many things heard too through the ears of love / many days I am here; many days I escape the loops of others gay delivery of lessen and straight to the nature of oblivion I spend my moments waiting light upon the shore of the folds of home and the hearts I own, too, two, love / many way, all-ways near; many ways, all-ways near and often dear too, love / many the phases; many the phases of love / many the phrases; many phrases say love / many spaces; many spaces make us stay for love / many traces; many traces make waves of concurrent winging called the heaven's singing for the soul's release and the conceptual bet for love / many melting; many melting waves of love / many lifes; many lifes that heed respect for the trio found and the hearty round of elevation given to the Ones who love

CHAPTER THIRTEEN: *ALL*

All seasons; all seasons I see the love around me and the whistling in has come to an end, know God is, love / all life; all of my life I will walk the path of love / all night; love is all night and every day in the lighter way to truth / all day; all day I believe in love / all may; all may believe, in, love / all one; all that is one, love / all day; all day stay on the tower to love / all night; all night pray for love's way home / all light; all light, here, too, love / all heights; all heights held by love's spiral chance and the dance is, now, love / all depth; all depth has held respect for you, the light, hu-man / all laughs; expect the laughs to be all that lasts and love / all weds; all weds ahead and the dreads have gone and on we travel to the ravel true too, love / all rings; all rings around the should of love / all singing; all singing sung through our endless love / all tells; all tells us too, love / all appeals; all appeals are real too, love / all loves; all loves continuance is, love / all love; all love is good too, love / all embraced; all embraced by, love / all the way; all the way home too, love / all day; all day say too, love / all the reign; all the reign I will explain with only, love / all magnificent; all magnificent means can be met by love / all beneficent; all beneficent ways can be met by love / all God; all God is love / all love; all love can be is yours too, love / all led; all led by God's love / all energy; all energy expects is me, too, love / all electric; all electric and I see the open opportunity too, love / all Metatronic; all ways Metatronic, I am sonic to the alarm that rings when I sing of only love / all sepharothic; all sepharothic and all I see is the mighty home delivery of the gates of love / all religions; all religions come too, love / all science; all science pointed to was the honest appraisal of perfectly, you / all art; all art is, love / all taste; all I play is the taste of days of umber's enchant with the chant for love / all's face; all's face now stands in the good revival and the praise of lightly spoken, love / all is best; all is best when we rest in love / all is rest; all is rest and full of love / all the test; all the test is how you rest in love / all the truth; all the truth told, how do you rest, in, love / all is forgiven; all is forgiven for love / all is for living; all is for living for and too, love / all is the pace; all is the pace for, love / all is the space; all is the space we grace for, love / only and all; only and all days we race for the pace for the taste of, love / all of me; all of me equates too, love / all you see; all you see is, love / all wet; all wet with love and the genuine degree of how we free ourselves too, love / all left here; all left here too, love / all composite; all composite to the sonnet called love / all harmonious; all harmonious by the gendered weave of perfectly wed too, love / all the peace; all the peace that escapes too, love / all one truth; all one truth, love / all one; all one and the truth you know is love / one all; one all, one, love / all some; all some say is too, love / all many; all many can be is loved / all any; all any say is one to play with, love / all the same; all the same, let's love / all the time; all the time too, love / all the rhyme; all the rhyme said was, love / ALL; ALL is; love / all one matter, kuan yin is love.

THE ENHANCE-MENTS
LEVEL 20

CHAPTER ONE

Enhance; enhance yourself, love / changes; changes of the moment are true to the One enhance, love / lights; lights are bright with the win enhanced in the stars and the lights in, love / looks; looks like enhance meant, love / chances; chances are due to the enhance in you and love / books; books are due to the enhancement too, love / kindred; kindred too and enhancement seen true, love / sights; sights of the scene enhanced too, love / invites; love invites insights home too, enhancement, love / vocates; vocates with the quotes of the invocate enhanced by the true in love / vacates; vacates for days of enhance that comes too, love / vends; vends true enhanced in too and love / volumes; volumes of the enhancement too, and love / metrics; loves vote and the metrics met at the quotes of the enhancement too, love / masters; masters of the muse electric, the precious, enhancement, love / blend; blend blue, enhancement, too, love / introduction; introduction of the love that resumes at the enhance meant too, love / elemental; elemental to the sun enhanced with the natures come too and the mature with respect for love / advantageous; life is advantageous when enhanced by, love / electricity; electricity sinks into tranquility enhanced by the commencement too, love / attitude; attitude won by the enhancement come too, love / aptitude; aptitude for enhancing you with the light on, love / avenue; avenue of rescue close, and the enhancement comes to the streets in you, and love / rapture; rapture rounds the crowns of love and natured enhance / curiosity; curiosity comes to the enhanced, enriched, life / clavical; love is clavical, natural, and enhanced in truth and in love, / clasp; clasp the hand enhanced by love / cordage; cut the cordage from your heart, enhanced is the start too, love / caper; caper to enhancement, love / clutch; clutch another, true, enhance, set loose and traveling well too to love / eschew; eschew less, love enhanced, create paths and truth is light too, love / estates; love's estates are set with the enhance inn, love / insular; insular note, the vote, for enhance is, love / solid; solid to a natural cure for the curled reveal as lightly precise to the stand at precisely this, our strong reside at, love / sullen; sullen has gone to the natural flow of the natured feel of the lightly held revelation of love / savor; savor a savior who has enhanced his life with love / cravet; cravets worn in accountants shored by the shores of love, / candles; candles cure the duration's enhance by love / captive; captive natives enhance us with remembrance of the knowing that more is the way to stay at love / current; current to a near survive and the entrance to perfect love / clandestine; clandestine nature met by elegance in love / cornered; cornered by the intersect of the resurrect called love / cured; cured by the cubes in love, / calico; calico cares for the enhanced extension too a tablecloth deep with the set for love / capture; love is capture over the win to enhancement in love / curls; God's curls are waves of the earth's extent to the unfurl of love / waiver; waiver's enhance can take a stance at love / wades; wades into the middle of the worn agenda and found it all too, love, wage over, spin true, to enhanced bits , love / alert; alert to a notion of enhance sent, love / abrupt; abrupt too rude? guess again. the quest can win at love / rude; rude enough over

and come to enhancement in love / rowdy; rowdy raids over, enhanced, loved / ripped; ripped by love's enhance and the core of love / rounded; rounded by the nature of ascend too, love / contra; contra band to the man, enhance / competent; love is competent and of a nature, love / constant; constant to a constant cure and love / curvature; curvature of the scene and a global lean too, love / bulge; bulge at the belt gone to love and the slimmer view of light side anew and love / belt; belt over, enhance is in and knowing you we are loved / mayan; mayan mend, done again, and mother's nature is, love / mound; mounds mend by retire to enhance is, love / mends; mends on love's enhance at earth's green lend too, love / truth; truth is brazil will last.

CHAPTER TWO

Rates; rates of renew enhancing you with love / ravens; ravens portend the begin of the Other and the in of you / rave; rave about the glades enhanced with love / rode; love rode our everyday enhance-ment with you / roads; roads lead to the agreed upon reside inside the rights of way, enhance this direct too, love / clarify; clarify another native trend and the enhance means, love / clasp; clasp another near and hear the hands of enhancement clap at love / court; court another enhanced with truth and love / kinks; kinks uncome, reside within and find the kind who want to live with truth in love / cool; cool wrought to be enhanced with the tools for love / can; care to, can too, expressly we, enhance this, love / cups; cups that cure enhance ensure with love / bred; love is bred with the said for enhance and the chance that can be, love / breasts; love's breasts can be best enhanced with the chances in love / beast; love's beast comes to the belay undo and enhanced within with love / belie; belies the nature, love's enhance / expression; the expression in scents of enhancement, love / life; old life undone, come now to the enhancement, love / search; search over, found another, enhanced in, love / lights; lights preclude the light in you and the living enhance with love / essentially; booned by essentially the enhancement, love / huicholes; huichole ways enhanced with the beads of love / *huicholes; happy unite of interior concede to the house of love and elegant succeed / guadalajara; guadalajara cured by the ensured enhance to see only love / quantum; quantums of days that enhance the ways of cure that ensure our love / quantico; quantico signed delivery to the sounds of enhance and the chance to dance at love / palladium; palladium days and the stadiums crazed for the stage called enhance / platinum; platinum powers love the enhance for God is, love / plastic; plastic curls in the fire of real enhancement, love / plants; plants enjoy the enhancement too, of love / platters; platters filled with the enhancement sealed by love / plates; plates are filled with the enhanced delight of love / stacks; stacks concur that we are sealed with the shifting enhance too, love / league; league one of the loan's enhance too, love / alert; alert to the sort of enhancement called love / logo; a logo given to the enhance that's in too and the trades exact too, love / logos; logos live in the hem of enhance called love / clarify; clarify love's enhance with the interest wide to the side of you called the glasses in, love / clarity; clarity is found in a yellow town called enhancement wins the path to the top of love / classic; classic to a nature that enhance meant love / clue; clue of the nude arrival at enhance wins, love / clasp; clasp your new arrival as enhance meant too, love / clues; clues found in the enhanced arrive set high on love / clamp; clamp your stance to a living enhance called love / clutter; clutter comes to the arc on the hill and life is thrilled with the sounds of love / canter; canter to the chance to ride with love / clan; clans come to the finding enhance, love / cape; cape insure has enhanced this trend with love / cove; the cove of closure can include the date with a boat full of loving flowers called enhance / cope; cope with enhancements of love / companion; companion found in a home town called the hearts enhance with love / clues; clues love the daring enhance meant too, love / clothes; clothes that wear as well as enhance / fun; fun to be, enhanced / found; found an enhance in love / clatter; clattering comes with the sounding of love, enhanced / clips; clips of conclude that enhance us with love / firm; firm enough to unearth the entrance to enhancement in love / ground; ground level enhance is, love / climber; climber gives the heart that lives too, love / clinch; clinch your respect-full dance at enchantment's stance and know that elegance reigns in the date with enhance / friend; a friend found along the enhanced pathway too, love / love; love is to be, enhanced / Perfection is the enhancing truth in love.

CHAPTER THREE

Bolt; bolt to the cure for an enhanced insure of love / nut; nuts about the breaking up of all we stood for less enhanced than love / tubes; tubes that include the breathing surrender to the sender of enhance is in, love / crack; crack found in the linger and the lining comes undone to reveal purest love by enhance / cave; caves of cure enhanced in love / craft; craft hour comes to crew who enhanced the others with love / cruise; cruise to the news enhanced / crops; crops live in loving enhance / reveal; reveal yourself in enhance / revel; revel is blue to orange to includes of a yellow enhance and the meaning friend, love / rove; rove to the entrance, enhance / rovers; rovers found each other in love's enhance / raft; raft to the rounds of the river's enhance / rocks; rocks that include enhance / rupture; rupture over the seas of enhance / reveal; reveal your rate of loving enhance / renew; renew your vow to love in enhance / read; read about love's enhance, hear, love / rest; rest in enhance is, love / revenue; revenue comes to the One's enhance and this, love / route; route to the top of enhance / relative; relative to the nature, enhance / relate; relate to another, enhance / comes; comes another chance, enhance / rates; rates that include love's enhance / met; met at the matter, enhance / great; great include at enhance / accrue; accrue a nature, enhance / marriage; marriage comes to the golden one and the wave enhanced / drain; drain less enhanced no becomes the won, love / in; in love's enhance / motor; motor to another's enhance / muse; muse about the chance to enhance your love / mount; mount vesuv has come to erupt in the chance too, enhance / monitor; monitor your care with enhance / meld; meld at the melt for enhance, love

/ mellow; mellow natured enhance / matter; matter becomes rescue's enhance, love / mountain; mountain found in enhance / rescue; rescue you our love's enhance / rest; rest at the nature, enhance / routes; routes to the top vary less when the guest to the trips are enhancement and love / up; up to you and your loving enhance / given; given another chance too, enhance / rapt; rapt in the natural, enhance / rhapsodic; rhapsodic finds found you in love's enhanced embrace / rose; rose green red delivery finding you enhanced / date; date the one who comes enhanced by love / deliver; deliver the date to the One enhanced / dare; dare to care about the sun's enhance / doves; doves care about you and your enhance / dunes; dunes repair with the winds of care and the light's enhance too, love / dorothy; dorothy due to the homeward wafts of love's enhance / carlos; carlos loved the kansas side of the tinman's glide to love's enhance; found a heart; mine; love / cleave; cleave to the other in mature enhance, this love / spain; spain finds a chain of electrical capacity too, enhance is, love / catalan; catalan explain can please us to this enhance / brave; brave enough to be, enhanced / gaze; gaze at the face you own, enhanced / stellar; stellar to a native enhance / delta; delta blue delivery of enhance / plane; plane of the living, enhanced / plain; plain to be enhanced to in love.

CHAPTER FOUR

Mississippi; mississippi me to the enhance sent, love / harper; harpers fair to the enhance / petals; petals of plenty enhance this, love / plans; plans to be, enhanced / keyed; keyed to the cups of enhance is, loved / body; body blessed by the highest enhance, love / pony; ride a pony clued to enhance / ply; ply your mother with the other enhance, love / conjunct; conjunct to a natural bliss, enhance / platitude; platitude given to the living enhance / applause; applause heard around the sound, I do, to enhancement, love / cause; cause another to know true express of the expression sent to enhance, love / conjugate; conjugate at this, true, love's, enhance / cease; cease to be less than loved, enhance / sessions; sessions about the shout for enhance / sate; sate yourself with great enhance / note; note the date with enhance / nurture; nurture yourself with love's enhance / aunt; aunt of the cause that's able, enhance / uncle; uncle to the bride, enhance / neighbor; neighbor who gave too, enhance / nails; nails of deliver know this truth, enhance / friend; friend found in the sound of love, enhance / relate; relate to the nature, less beast, more friend, enhance / kneel; kneel to be enhanced / notice; notice the drift too, enhance / commit; commit another, enhance sent too, love / dates; dates around you shift too loving enhance / nod; nod about the date with truth in enhance / nephew; nephew of the bride enhance / delegate; delegate your relate too, enhance / delete; delete the bull of less than enhance in love / adorn; adorn yourself with the happy stance at enhance sent too, love / shorn; shorn of less than all advance to enhance is, love / shield; shield yourself from neglect with enhance / yield; yield your date to the living, enhance / uphold; uphold you chance to know, enhance / held; held by another enhanced / hurdle; hurdle over, comes, enhance / healed; healed of the less, now know, enhance / hope; hope for the future now comes enhanced / actuarial; actuarial by all accounts enhanced to the dates with love / law; law of concern for the enhance meant, love / lawyer; lawyer comes to your rescue and the account meant for enhance, love / lover; lover found well within enhance / lands; lands of plenty beckon you with love's enhance / relax; relax at a nature with enhance / rogues; rogues come to gone away and well we stay within enhance / pants; pants worn with the threads of plenty, love / party; party with another care freed too, enhance / ever; ever after, enhance is, green too, love / ready; ready to be, loved through, enhance / prepare; prepare to be enhanced / prep; prep yourself for the steps too, enhance / collegiate; collegiate reviews welcoming you too, enhance / cabinet; cabinet deep in revenues for commencement to enhance / open; open to a lane called enhance / close; close to a loving commitment called enhance / over; over and under I am enhanced in, love / cure; cure yourselves with enhance / heart; heart open and true too, love is, enhanced / heal; heal yourself with your enhance sent, love / real; real enough to be enhanced / rate; rate yourself as insanely enhanced.

CHAPTER FIVE

Live; live to the tune of a nerves enhanced electric charge, love / give; give the mother another advance to the enhance called love / rejoice; rejoice at a natural living enhance, love / enjoy; enjoy another charge, enhance, love / joy; joy about the overing few who knew enhance / jewel; jewel worn in the crown of enhance / june; june bugged less by the enhance, love / jam; jam about the nature joined as enhance / elect; elect a national direction erect to insurance cause, love / resource; resource found in the town crystal clean too, enhance / resurrect; resurrect at secure, enhance / over; over the edge, enhance / happen; happen to be, enhanced / stance; stance over the gain regained as enhanced / stood; stood by the side enhanced / account; account taken over to the good enhance / accrue; accrue the review, enhanced / reverend; reverend stands enhanced / rally; rally at the clues enhanced / rounds; rounds like enhance / relate; relate to the date, enhance / death; death to the old enhanced / grand; grand days review of the enhanced / greet; greet each other renewed by enhance / relative; relative to a nature reviewed by enhance / mom; mom found home to enhance / mother; mother of the Other, enhance / cancers; cancers come to show the where of how we were to listen, enhanced / due; due to the enhance, love / dates; dates with the great, enhance / done; done too, the enhance / degree; degree of the enhance / decree; decree to be enhanced upon, love / dare; dare to care for the enhanced adore / adore; adore yourself enhanced / compare; compare the nature of enhance / competent; competent to attend, enhance / seal; seal done, enhance / shorn; shorn by the scene unhinged, enhanced / sealed; sealed by the scene enhanced / ceiling; ceiling hung with the scene enhanced / catch; catch this enhancement, love / door; door opens enhanced / floor; floor of the shore enhanced / dread; dread less the arrive at enhance / go; go to the enhanced state, love / gone; gone to insure a new enhance / gain; gain a grain of enhance / rescue;

rescue the rest of enhance / rain; rain at enhance / rasta; rasta rings the belt enhanced / dances; dances at the enhanced / bob; bob at the enhanced / weaves; weaves a ring in the Orionic strand enhanced / desk; desktop due to the enhanced / decays; decays less, the enhanced / rebirth; rebirth comes today in the news enhanced / all-ways; all-ways enhanced / eternal; eternal to a nature enhanced / over; over and under, enhanced / regrowth; regrowth grew at the enhanced / due; due too, the enhanced / done; done to One, enhanced / too; too enough and also loved, enhanced.

CHAPTER SIX

Big; big days stay enhanced / swoon; swoon over the nature enhanced / moon; moon tide, enhance / lagoon; a lagoon trained on enhance / cypress; cypress sell well in enhance / soon; soon enough to be enhanced / wig; wig wed enhance / wads; wads of due to you enhance love / wander; wander to the enhanced / equine; equine conditions enhanced in love / chief; chief of the police called loved thoroughly enhanced / leather; leather met love through the saddle enhance / native; native to a tune enhance / fly; fly through the state, enhance / american; american attend to the moon's enhance / art; art comes to town, enhanced / star; star around the enhance of love / karma; karma cured by God's enhance too, love / earth; earth is fed by the enhance / center; center of the central station too, loved, enhanced / gale; gale's force is led by enhance / awning; awning spawning comes to enhance / pillow; pillow yourself in enhance / home; home to the tune enhance / loafer; loafer's given glory through enhance / glorified; glorified by the truth in enhance / pacific; pacific to a notion, enhance / pacify; pacify yourself by enhance / moves; moves to be enhanced / mastered; mastered wed with enhance / capital; capital to a notion, enhance / truth; truth is enhance / cardinal; cardinal sum, enhance / drawing; drawing on the summation, enhance / delights; delights on the some, enhance / dive; dive to be summated, enhanced, love / clue; clue to be enhanced, lives, love / drawn; drawn to the lend, enhance / pollop; pollop on the gallop to enhance / date; date the Other won, enhance / elevate; elevate your state too, enhance / drowns; drowns in sorrow less enhanced / dole; dole out the notion, enhance / donate; donate great states of enhance / greens; greens crewed in the lend, enhance / billow; billows like the cloud enhance / cowered; cowered over the living enhance / grass; grass grew too, enhance / bathe; bathe in entrance / covered; covered by the enhanced / blue; blue knew enhance / burrows; burrows in the enhanced / capable; capable nature comes to the enhanced / blaze; blaze at the corner's enhance / caves; caves complete our street's enhance / coincidence; coincidence means summate to our enhance, love / means; means of a miracle enhanced in, love / Fruitful / Fruition / Para / Brazil / MAPS / Instincts / Installed.

CHAPTER SEVEN

Classic; classic curls around me swirl with delight for love's enhance / coil; coil your tail to the trail that's dear to the life called enhanced / spring; spring to the fountain, enhance / load; load up at love's enhance / crave; crave a near, enhance / laid; laid to the break and the chance for the dance enhance / miracle; miracle worked nearby, enhance / ran; ran to the occur enhanced / cruise; cruise to the state, enhance / lever; lever deep in the covers heaped to enhance / mound; mound found nearby, enhance / render; render the serpent done and the son of enhance has come / crowds; crowds honor you in enhance / lion; lions leap at the sound, enhance / raft; raft to the tribe enhance / rinse; rinse another trip to enhance / light; light succeed to the vacate ascend to love's enhance / vacate; vacate to the trail for enhance / finds; finds a date with the enhanced / locate; locate a great enhance / listen; listen to the send up enhance / route; route across the ascend enhanced is love / tigers; tigers trial the rest enhanced / trails; trails win the enhance / rasp; raspy voiced delivery of the lift to enhance / ball; balls click with the constant enhance / trails; trails deep in the street called enhance / exhale; exhale now to plow the enhanced / rattle; rattle the cage off the enhanced / game; game time, enhance / expel; expel the state enhance / enthuse; enthused of late with enhance / enthusiasm; enthusiasm rules the enhanced / attend; attend to the enhanced / avail; avail less those enhanced / absolute; absolute refute to less, enhance / spire; spire above the hire, enhance / prints; prints of the enhanced / posters; posters about the sum enhanced / pour; pour yourself an advance to enhance / plan; plan to be enhanced / pine; pine treed enhance / colors; colors enhanced in love / coil; coil around the sound of love / phone; phone this called embrace of the enhance thick love / pencils; pencils that pen the trace to love's embrace and extend to ascend of enhance / corks; corks fill the necks enhanced / curls; curls with the enhanced / constant; constant to a sun enhanced / intentional; intentional mention of the sun, enhanced / interiors; interiors sum with enhance / landed; landed at the sign enhance / coast; coast to the crime removed, enhance / invention; invention comes to the son perfect to enhance / lovers; lovers live enhanced / lattice; lattice woven with enhanced / covenant; covenant of the assured with enhance / insistence; insistence in the side inside our lived enhance / court; court each other again in enhance / cap; cap the notion of less, enhance / intent; intent in the send, enhance / entwine; entwine each other enhanced / cape; cape of the enhanced, love / constantly; constantly enhanced.

CHAPTER EIGHT

Moon; moon sounds strain the night with caress of the lilting enhance meant by love / remand; remand has been had by the Ones who win for love in enhance / aspects; aspects of the pews who sit in your enhance / ascend; ascend to the trend of a blend called hello and the gratitude given within our good buy of plenty of sensitive, sensational enhance / alert; alert to the squired expel of less than enhance, remember, love / clue; clues about the light enhance / callous; callous to a bursting resume called enhanced in you, and love / cower; cower at the heart less and know your living confess of the enhance meant, love / convert; convert the sort of times we had to what we will concede to in

enhanced ascend too, love / cure; cure your wealth with your health in love's enhance / occurrence; occurrence about the land of enhancement, love / convey; convey too, ascend too, love is, enhance / concurrence; concurrence said let's agree to enhance meant by love / subvert; subvert to welcome tongue, the spanish One, called life is, enhanced / commonly; commonly scene by an enhance too, love / locally; locally done too, enhance / literate; literate to degrees of enhance / considerate; considerate to a natural day's enhance called love / curvate; curvate lists a living degree called this life's enhance is you in love / curate; curate the state of emotional lifts enhance / aspire; aspire to hire your desire's account a new tune called enhance / require; require another, enhance / curvaceously; curvaceously done by enhance / rondels; rondels around the enhance / rapacious; rapacious to a new review called love is enhanced / raptor; raptors deal with the healing environment called yes we will live by enhance / quietly; quietly we deal with the scenes of enhance / explain; explain about why we are, enhanced / violet; violet to a crystal blue enhance / volumes; volumes due and too, enhance / volume; volume found in the land, enhance / vassel; vassels agreed too, enhance / fires; fires burn the true deliver of the track enhance / fireworks; fireworks that lend themselves to our repair, enhance / fossils; fossils that fill with the deal, enhance / sold; sold to a true enhance / sell; sell the deal to the one's enhance / dance; dance at a daily light called enhance / spell; spell another with the alphabet called loved too, enhance / sport; sport about like the enhanced / desired; desired a deal with the enhanced / donate; donate your dates to the enhanced / well; well enough to be enhanced with, love / waivers; waivers that live with enhance / motility; motility about the feel of enhance / nobility; nobility seeking enhance with a royal flash too, love / mobile; mobile to a measure, enhance / fluid; fluid feels like enhance / feign; feign another natured well too, enhance / ingrain; ingrain yourself too, enhance / gain; gain a date with enhance / gather; gather at the space enhanced / decide; decide to be enhanced / donates; donates a great, enhance / deals; deals with an embrace of enhance / desires; desires to be, enhanced / lathe; lathe a slice of light enhance / wings; wings beat with enhance / wound; wound with the sound enhance / worn; worn by a corner, enhanced / found; found by the free, enhance / firm; firm enough to be, enhanced / Literal / Conclusive.

CHAPTER NINE

Pleasure; pleasure found in a perfect town of perfect birth at the arc of I AM and the land of swift remember come home to expand in the hint enhanced with love / plenty; plenty of us are enhanced by love / perfect; perfect to a nature perfectly enhanced and love / probes; probes over and arcturian explain can become the name of forever and the living declare of where we go for enhancement sent by love / diagnose; diagnose the situation, take a station home, too, love in enhance / date; date another state, the state of well too, enhance / pendulous; pendulous notions of the nation's bequest for rest in the enhanced / pendant; pendant worn around the neck of love's enhance / penchant; a penchant for the worn attach has meant the adore of exact enhance / port; port of called enhance / royal; royal to a ship of regal embrace of the living enhance / regal; regal to a crimson red, our ships to shore and more, enhance / paisley; paisley peels of the living heal and the healing advance to floral reside at the side of the stance that lasts, enhance / roses; roses are red with a deeper assign and the coming sing of the starships, love, enhance / red; red by a sign and symbolic to all is the symptom come to resign at a perfect enhance / necklace; necklace comes undone to finish the sum as only and all-ways, One, through enhance / diamonds; diamonds enhance the won / gold; gold to a stronger enhance, a ring of love / worn; worn by the two who enhance, love / capture; capture comes to the ones who run by enhance / pearls; pearls of pleasure play with us and our incapsulation of love by enhance / silver; silver to a naive respect and we reflect our love's enhance / wear; wear a pair of enhanced designs called loving enhance / care; care about the life enhanced / gems; gems the seem to be green in the eyes that are wide with enhance / threads; threads broken by less are agreed too by renewal at enhance / wedding; wedding won by the life enhanced / compare; compare less, this is, life true too, enhance / jewels; jewels loved by life's enhance, your eyes / throat; throat of a sample lived in simple align too, loved, enhance / won; won another shot of enhance / contain; contain yourself less through enhance / lovely; lovely days come too, enhance / point; point to yes by enhance / charmed; charmed by forever and enhance / paint; paint on the moments green with enhance / eternal; eternal to a nature, enhance / ever; ever been and be, green to the arcturic ascend / elastic; elastic to a notion enhanced / declare; declare yourself enhanced by the spare arrive at the hire arcturic / evermore; evermore we will live by a loving enhance / sternally; sternally done by a loving enhance / infinity; infinity to the cost is faith to the space enhanced / courts; courts that nod with a living enhance caused by love / sorts; sorts of enhanced come through too, love / kind; kind to compare and enough to say, enhanced / castles; castles stay arcturic by design, home / clouds; clouds reveal the heal arcturic and our align within, dear God, by enhance / define; define a moment native as won by enhance / denote; denote that we can vote for free arrival at enhance / designate; designate yourself as won by enhance / degrees; degrees that come too, enhance / detail; detail seen in the living dream by enhance / nap; nap in the carriage of assure that life is fed by enhance / sleep; sleep again within the entrance too, enhance / rest; rest here in enhance / defer; defer to others by enhance / content; content to find it by enhance / cone; cone's are the cure, ask us, hear, and we provide the sort you need, arcturically / caliope; caliope through the portals too and living enhance / deference; deference is done and living has come to giving in too, love, through enhance / mariposa; mariposa blues come to the true enhance / lane; enhance the lanes of delivery through you / home; home to be through hues of enhance.

CHAPTER TEN
Butterfly; butterfly boast of the host archival and the arc-angels dream of believe in the seas argon to enhance / loop; loop to the

seas arc-angelic and sing of the signs of enhance / loops; loops that heal, enhance / lessons; lessons that with enhance / lightens; lightens with the living enhance / lives; lives like a sealing enhance / listens; listens with dimensioned enhance / lends; lends another trend to enhance / opens; opens like a healing enhance and arcturic to a sing sung daily by Ones of unite / fares; fares with the paid enhance and the coming regard to love / paid; paid the date with enhance / please; please adore the other, enhance / finds; finds another enhanced by love / plots; plots explored adored enhanced / plans; plans to be made are made by enhance / plats; plats that dance by enhance / dogs; dogs that deal with the dancing heal for appraise by enhance / hu-mans; hu-mans need love by enhance / gives; gives each other a living, enhance / given; given to the living, enhance / people; people who love, enhance / men; men who are due to the dare to enhance / grain; grains that feed the greens of succeed / feed; feed each other with adoration and love through enhance / globe; globe of the national need to decide who is by enhance / gods; gods who rule by enhance / forests; forests that feed on enhance / seas; seas that live with a thrilling enhance / worlds; worlds that deal with enhance / God; God is good through enhance / earth; earth meets deep in advance to enhance / meets; meets like enhance / birth; birth of the brothered enhance / softens; softens the deal with enhance / sees; sees each other enhance / decides; decides to be enhanced / poles; love's poles can shift through your move too, advance / phones; arcturic phones ring with enhance / finds; finds the signal and calls advance hu-manity for a durate enhanced / felt; enhancement felt through the feet of enhance / inside; inside the other nation's singing, enhance / fellows; fellows who feel like enhanced / fosters; fosters are given to the children enhanced / drinks; Metatron drinks the arc water of God / sincere; sincere to an electrical dream we are delivered by concede to begin again at enhance / around; around the hearing comes revealing enhance / here; here we are by enhance / rounds; rounds each other through enhance / planes; planes of suspend descend to agree through enhance / descend; descend to a nature, enhance / land; land at the send enhanced / on; on tour through the year of enhance / over; over this day I preside by enhance / through; through the material of preside's enhance / in; in this too, enhance / within; within this sight, enhance seen / often; often I live by reside at enhance / now; now we know the heart of enhance / again; and again, enhance / pasture; pasture's green with the scene, enhance / pastor; pastor of the church enhance / mend; mend each other through enhance / remand; remand the desire to fire enhance / do; do this light by enhance.

CHAPTER ELEVEN
Apparel; apparel that is worn to a smart affair of enhance / cotton; cotton feels like enhance / food; food that feeds the light enhance / flower; flowers feel powered through enhance / deals; deals with the tribe of enhance / application; application to apply for is the one of enhance called love / schools; schools that live with enhance / paid; paid for your written enhance / universal; universal to a notion, enhance / wildlife; wildlife due

too, enhance / wander; wander to the Other side of you and your glance at enhanced / apply; apply yourself to the light enhance / energy; energy comes to the sun of arrival at enhanced / techniques; techniques come to include the shield merkabah deep to your enhance / tactics; tactics field the chance too, enhance / plural; plural to another, nature, enhance / arena; arena around the crowd, enhance / rides; rides like the side enhance / stadium; stadium built for the tools enhance / tribal; tribal truth, enhance / tribes; tribes that deal with enhance / tradition; tradition to the cause, enhance / inn; inn to the in, enhanced / excellent; excellent to repair, enhance / madrigal; madrigal due to you and your enhance / native; native to a tongue enhanced / models; models dare to include your enhance / prayer; prayer for the founder of enhance / natural; natural days spent in enhance / nudes; nudes are seen by the scene enhance / house; house of elect has come to enhance / plays; plays with your dues and your living cues of enhance / wide; wide to the side who live enhanced / deep; deep enough to erect a concept on, enhance / leased; leased a room in the apartment, enhance / apartment; apartment comes undone through enhance / considerate; considerate to a nature, enhanced / consideration; consideration comes to the enhanced / rich; rich by all means, enhanced / public; public by the book enhanced / southern; southern exposure comes to the savannah side of love's enhance / write; write your date with enhance / central; central to a river scene on bay streets honey colored stream of love'd enhance / shore; shore your declare with spare concede to be enhanced / life; life is honey colored with the dream of degrees of savannah's stream of the light that sees enhance / written; written to the dreams that stream with enhance / shine; shine at the sun of enhance / store; store a written degree of enhance / garage; garage filled with the enhancement healed by love / vote; vote for a note enhanced / fulfill; fulfill the nature enhanced / football; football flows by the enhanced / hands; hands that need the feel enhanced / full; full with the nature enhanced / plants; plants that are green with enhance / basketball; basketballed team of enhancement dream to the 5th degree, love / handle; handle the animal with enhance / penetrates; penetrate's the state of enhance / planes; planes of degree agree on enhance / manage; manage to be enhanced / heal; heal each other, enhanced / plans; plans to penetrate agree with your enhance / pure; pure enough to be enhanced / play; play with the concept agreed too, enhance.

CHAPTER TWELVE
Earned; earned a chance to dance at the son of arrival, love / given; given another chance to advance too, love, enhanced / reward; reward yourself with the word, enhance / faith; faith full-fills my secure enhance with love / grace; grace is given with enhance / assure; assure yourself of the cure enhance / sure; sure enough to be enhanced / shores; shores that secure your heart with enhance / sales; sales that are sealed with your secure advance too, love / mount; mount a national advance to enhance / advance; advance to a moment secure too, enhance / familial; familial to a mattered meet with enhance / secure; secure yourself by enhance / family; family found in the sounds of enhance / trine; trine of the sign

of enhance / sole; sole natured enhance / sold; sold to another, enhance / loads; loads of secure, enhance / living; living in the meaning of enhance / common; common to a waving enhance / cure; cure your friend with enhance / caliber; caliber code of enhance / caliper; caliper entered in enhance / jump; jump to the sure enhance / tow; tow yourself home to the shored enhance of love / tree; the tree of life's living enhance / seneca; seneca sounds like enhance / central; central to a trade enhance / overt; overt to a nurturing enhance / new; new days deal with enhance / life; life is wide too, enhance / school; school is over in enhance / flags; flags that fill with enhance / flown; flown overhead and ahead to the ascend of love in enhance / find; find a friendly win too enhance / relief; relief is set on enhance / release; release to the tribal enhance / freed; freed to agreed upon enhance / freedom; freedom to see the advance too, enhance / truth; truth to see, enhance / confess; confess to the dynamic enhance / concur; concur to commend the enhance / concede; concede to a win by enhance / comfort; comfort too, enhance / connote; connote with willing enhance / coincide; God's coincide is enhance / covert; covert to a cure, enhance / conceal; conceal less your need too enhance / stone; stone doors reveal the truth of the sealed secure / pillows; pillows that sit on the strict decide too enhance us loved / pillars; pillars of secure connect reflect the light enhance / seats; seats that sit upon enhance / throne; throne of the social enhance / delight; delights seal our enhance / soften; enhanced to a softening ascend and a wade too, love / stare; stare at the cape of a curing delivery come to ascend, enhance / cave; cave deep in secure enhance / doves; doves defy gravity by enhance / perfect; perfect to a secure enhance / concede; concede is indeed too enhance / bind; bind yourself in advance / adore; adore the core of a curling enhance / compare; compare the dare to be your set on enhance / conspire; conspire to a higher enhance.

CHAPTER THIRTEEN
Augment; augment our sort of enhance / intent; intent on enhance / convent; convent under the agreed concede to enhance / constantly; constantly in too, enhance / current; current to an expire that enhanced / escort; escort sorts of enhance / convert; convert a date to a sorting enhance / converse; converse with the sort of enhance / release; release to the living enhance / attend; attend to your sort of enhance / attain; attain a distinct enhance / plans; plans to be enhanced / reside; reside at the side enhanced / precious; precious to be with enhance / precise; precise to a spiral enhance / alto; alto found in the solo agree to be two in a duet enhanced by love / tenor; tenors tend to be enhanced / insistent; insistent ascendant the one enhanced / drink; drink the drink that love enhanced / deep; deep enough to be true too, enhance / tender; tender time too, by enhance / definite; definite decide to be enhanced by, love / define; enhanced to the design defined in love / daily; daily and true to the enhance / decide; decide to do the new enhance / state; state of the state, enhance / status; status cued in enhance / obligate; obligate your state with enhance / desist; desist to a notion enhanced / oblige; oblige about it and shout it, enhance / material; material to a spiritual

enhance / mince; mince the words with enhance / words; words that win in enhance / prosper; prosper your presence with enhance / prepare; prepare to be enhanced / presently; presently we are enhanced / month; months enhanced by love / prepared; prepared to see the enhanced / presence; presence is ascend, in enhanced love / positive; positive to a notion ascendant, enhance / elongate; elongate the great ascend / lady; lady we are ascendant too, enhance / pencil; pencil in your ascend and the crossword comes to enhanced / powers; powers that spiral up to enhance / elate; elate this situate to loving enhance / lists; lists the land of enhance / plan; plan to be ascendant and we are enhance / pens; pens penned by enhance / lord; lord of the land of ascend / know; know about the side enhanced / slip; slip into the landing ascend / slot; slots apprehend the suspected ascend / universal; universal too and win the ascend / nest; nest in your living agree to be enhanced / speak; speak about the ascendant lend of enhance / sustain; sustain the train of enhance / sort; sort a sort of enhance / code; codes that depend upon ascends agreed upon states of enhance / copy; copy of the code enhance / carbons; carbons of the copied ascend / study; study less, know more, enhance / key; key found in the town of enhance / likes; likes to be enhanced in the keys of love / lights; lights the seas of love through enhance.

THE ARCANE-MENTS
LEVEL 21

CHAPTER ONE

Arcane; arcane is the name of the dome that's become home / profane; love is profane to arcane knowing / profound; profound to a moment arcane / proof; proof of the arcane, love / proud; proud to be free to be arcane / pearl; pearl notioned healing by the arcane / parallel; parallel to a chance arcane / sound; sound of the nation arcane, the sigh of release at love / surrender; surrender to the other arcane / suggest; suggest that we be arcane / love; love is arcane in God's proclaim / invest; invest in the life arcane / together; together to be, arcane / comes; comes a chance arcane / separate; separate ways stay together arcane / runs; runs like a round belay to the arcane / arctan; arctan to the strand you are by the love arcane / arctangent; arc-tangent through love and the trust in you, arcane / arc-life; arc-life one by the won arcane / arc on; arc on to the song arcane / arcturic; arcturic waves arcane with love / arks; arks deep in the float too, love is, arcane / alphabetic; alphabetic agree that God's a,b,c, is arcane too, love / alpha; alpha meets omega in the state of surrender too, love is, arcane / omega; omega mastered love's delay with arcane agree to be free / alphon; alphon decide to abide by degrees too, love is, arcane / file; file away the days arcane / files; files gone to the sum okay with one arcane / ascend; ascend to the moment, arcane / arc-sine; arc-sine agreed upon, arcane / arc-trine; arc-trine true too, the arcane / trinity; trinity of won, the arcane / trilogy; trilogy given free reside at the arcane / clime; clime found, profound, arcane / climactic; climactic agree to be arcane / mother; mother found in the sound arcane / mend; mend another's arcane notion of love / man; man over the earth can live in the arcane recall of how we give the gift to God by love / over; over and under I climb to the friend arcane 40 .find; find a friend who can lend an arcane note to love / friend; friend of the arcane gift called growth in, love / receive; receive a list of loving encounter and arcane to the scene of insistence on lessons in love / regret; regret less the arcane / repeat; repeat a note of neighborly appeal with the arcane vote for include in love / believe; believe in the loving encounter called the arcane / recite; recite the dates of love / reveal; reveal your wait for love in free arcane / reward; reward the ascend with a frequent refrain called love / concede; concede to your need for the arcane / concur; concur with the conventional state called ascend / wealth; wealth is the state of ascendant abundance and love in the arcane / width; widths inside the stride of decide to be in-line with the state of reside in the land of ascend to the be arcane / conceit; conceit can be seen in the lean that's less than arcane / contour; contours come to the arcane / stealth; stealth is found in the land arcane / trip; trips to center of the vortex arcane / concept; concepts in our contend for the arcane / counter; counter signed intelligence can be seen in the arcane / couple; couple of kin that can be arcane / convex; convex to a loving ascend let us be arcane / complete; complete to a sort of ascend let us blend too love / wed; wed to yourself the life that's arcane / completion; completion is the circling friend arcane / concave; concave to a notion that's heaven sent, love.

CHAPTER TWO

Arc-sing; arc-sing rings around our sound of the arcane / arc-ring; arc-rings in the ascend too, love / arc-in; arc's in too love is arcane / arc-on; arc-on to the song universal in love that's arcane / arcturian; arcturian to a swollen explain, here's God, the arcane / actual; actual explanation found in the actuarial account arcane / avenue; avenue due to the street arcane / able; able to be, arcane / allocate; allocate your state to the situation explained as arcane / attend; attend to live in the arcane / author; author's of the arcane have come to assign the degree of love / write; write the light arcane / ascend; ascend to the nation arcane with love / plan; plans to be arcane / blend; blend in the hu-man God ahead, love, arcane / set; set up the state of the life that's arcane / talents; talents that ascend to the lend arcane / winds; winds wind around the weather arcane / quote; quotes about the arcane / court; courts in the arcane / trips; trips to the truth arcane / quakes; quakes ascend to the lend arcane / quip; quips that lean toward the arcane / cords; cords that send the sharp respect arcane / truths; truths about the light arcane / queries; queries within the arcane moment of love / quiver; quiver with the life arcane / curt; curt enough notion to be arcane / trends; trends within the arcane / quails; quails when the rooted stand at the arcane / curl; curl at the tip arcane / concede; concede this steel approach to the living arcane / cover; cover the matter with the arcane / captive; captive to a trade arcane / over; over and over our care has come to the arcane / due; due to be, arcane / done; done by the sum arcane / finds; finds found in a town that is soon to be arcane / dead; dead has gone to the song arcane / double; double up with the sum of One arcane / deal; deal with the sum arcane and the flying fun of finding one who lives with the light regard for God / fond; fond explore of the shored arcade arcane / delays; delays at the trace that's come undone and arcane / come; come to the altar of the afternoon sun, arcane / deals; deals made about the arcane / fonder; fonder deals done, arcane / go; go to the arcane / finish; finish this singing with the arcane / another; another comes to the arcane / comes; comes a day arcane / cures; cures will be always arcane / depth; depth has come to the summary arcane / daily; daily days arcane / denote; denote the sort who are arcane / devote; devote yourself to the bet arcane / delegate; delegate truth to the arcane / dally; dally at the way arcane / dew; dew on the dove arcane / due; due to be arcane / do; do be arcane / dare; dare the compare that's square to the arcane / dazzle; dazzle us with sum, arcane / dates; dates with the set arcane / dear; dear to be near too, arcane.

CHAPTER THREE

Weddings; weddings inn, the arcane / initiate; initiate the cause arcane / neat; neat address of the sort arcane / meet; meet each other at the arcane / within; within I have found the arcane / mate; mates meet in the arcane / meetings; meetings set, keep, the arcane / mercy; mercy met in the street replete with the loving arcane / intense; intense equate has come to the notion arcane / given; given the hour of compare know the share, comprehend the care for the life that is, arcane / gained; gained a repute for the rate of exchange and the notion that God is gained by / access that is, arcane / drip; drip with the state arcane / intend; intend to be, arcane / treat; treat each other with the suite arcane / trait; trait found in the sound arcane / truth; truth is told in the arcane / truce; truce found in the sound arcane / trace; trace yourself in the sands arcane / treats; treats each other to the arcane, love / truth-full; truth-full regard for the life that's inside the arcane / traits; traits overcome the rest and the regard and the respect that is, arcane / trends; trends reek the need arcane / plans; plans to be held by the arcane / pulse; pulse for the moment arcane / paths; paths to the arcane / pluses; pluses are minused without the arcane / ports; ports within the arcane / pets; pets who know the eyes of love that kneels, arcane / paints; paints a description, arcane / cans; cans fill with the rain arcane / canvas; canvas hums with the paint of sums arcane / house; house yourself with the best, arcane / tracks; tracks overflow with the strides arcane / atrial; atrial devotion to the station arcane / tastes; tastes that baste in the arcane / twirls; twirls with a circuit arcane / tips; tips each other too, the arcane / tools; tools of devotion your heart, your head, your bed, your breath, your truth; that is; God; befriend the arcane / task; task ahead has said..let there be.. profane immunity removed to ascend too, the arcane / tackle; tackle the blend arcane / rocks; rocks root at the snap of a boot arcane / ripples; ripples deep in the lips arcane / rivers; rivers flow with the arcane / routes; routes to the top, arcane / reveal; reveal a deal arcane / repeal; repeals rate is erect to the arcane / rode; rode the red horizon with the arcane, love / chasm; chasm overcome, know the one, love, arcane / gap; gap due to be filled by the arcane / gouge; gouge gone, let there be, only, the arcane / imagine; imagine this, the dream, the pi, the pew, arcane / doors; doors open too, the arcane / daze; daze becomes crystal clear within the arcane / lie; lie less, be, arcane / led; led to the notion, arcane / lever; lever lives in the heart that's flipped too, the arcane / lady; lady led too the arcane / find; find a seal, evil's deal has summed itself up in one arcane sweep that handles the steep require with a regard for the higher stand and the land of remember has confessed that we are the One, know God, final sum; God Won / manners; manners that are handles for the polite agree to be, God's friends, arcane / found; found a day to deal with God, all-ways home to the bliss of believe and the sleeve and the tubes of remember; love is..arcane; God / friendly; friendly sort has come to the living arcane / town; town found and home has come to the loving arcane / Configured.

CHAPTER FOUR

Better; better be, the arcane / belting; belting the notion with the ocean's degree, 720 to the waves of ascendant believe in the living arcane within, love / bathing; bathing's suit is the arcane / braille; braille red arcane / hearing; hearing the explain, arcane / heard; heard about the word, arcane / living; living free in the searching day arcane / well; well enough to be arcane / fountain; fountain deep in the life arcane / giving; giving rewards of the fullest degree called the free reside at the heart arcane / gains; gains understood by the wholest degree, arcane / conceptions; conceptions each believe in the sea that's arcane / flowing;

flowing at the sort of sport called arcane / contraceptive; contraceptive entreaty led by the stand arcane / held; held like this, in the hands arcane / explain; explain yourself home to the land that is, arcane / today; today I met the exploration arcane / nestle; nestle in the best agree arcane / capable; capable of great resort to the arcane / deliver; deliver to the spelling agree arcane / tomorrow; tomorrow will be the same, arcane / tour; tour your special sort, arcane / days; days desire to be arcane / wane; wane at the elocutive aspire and remember elevated degrees of the love that is, / arcane / near; near the dear let us be, arcane / trade; trade for twos arcane / worn; worn by the winning arcane / wend; wend your date with love arcane / now; now and then again, arcane / convey; convey true believe to the ones arcane / wells; wells are deep within the arcane / will; will you be? arcane / basic; basic blue arcanity / barren; barren days born again can delude know more and agree to be, arcane / barest; barest to the depth arcane / bare; bare you breast to the arcane / medici; medici viewed arcane / care; care to be degreed by the arcane / capable; capable to be arcane / boast; boast about the lot arcane / desert; desert powers come too, the arcane / core; cores of the arcane / benefit; benefit yourself with the arcane / born; born within the arcane / dessert; dessert days become the blooms of love that is, arcane / copes; copes with the lift arcane / bask; bask at the french arrive arcane / bat; bat one time arcane / banner; banner days found arcane / confuse; confused the deal with the arcane / gone; gone to a dame arcane / lead; lead with your heart arcane / float; float by the vote, arcane / on; on to the date with love is, arcane / dare; dare to care for the arcane / desire; desire to be blessed, arcane / flip; flip over to see the arcane / door; doors open in the arcane / gates; gates reveal the kneel arcane / portal; portal plans pen the arcane / fuse; fuse with the news arcane / plan; plan along the lane arcane / plane; plane deep in the flight arcane / dimension; dimension dealt thee, arcane.

CHAPTER FIVE

Ninety; ninety degrees to the degree: arcane / three; three is the time that is arcane to the mer-ka-bah signs for love / walnut; walnut displays of the days arcane / trees; trees that brim with the trim of leaves arcane too, love / tariff; tariff paid is enough, let it be, arcane / paid; paid the dues arcane / heaven; heaven held us well within the arcane / gave; gave a tree to the bark arcane / orate; orate your coordinate with the arcane / comes; comes to the scene of a day that is lightly arcane / sealings; arcane is desire to the hire arcane / sums; sums of the sun that is, arcane / covenant; covenant comes to the date that is arcane / calibrate; calibrate, celebrate, desire, conspire, compare the arcane / create; create the fire with the arcane / care; care about the light arcane / blue; blue on too and the grays are gone, arcane / grays; grays and blues have met the drain to the light arcane / cell-ation; cell-ations quest is the grain of release that relates to the arcane / clues; clues that seal the flee arcane / freaks; freaks about the right that is arcane / frolic; frolic about the light arcane / some; some who know the arcane / clans; clans that deal in the arcane / splatter; splatter matter through the arcane / special; love is special in the arcane / seen; arcane is seen in the arcane / tribes;

tribes that rule the arcane / splurge; splurge the state, arcane / suns; suns day, arcane / pull; pull the energy up too, the arcane / delight; delight about the life arcane / destination; destination due too, the arcane / duration; duration's due is the arcane / doors; doors that open too the arcane / elegance; elegance given to the arcane and the blend is hu-man God / quotes; arcane quotes note the win arcane / quips; quips about the wind arcane / queen; queens that deal with the arcane / quivers; quivers another pair to the arcane / quakes; quakes that fill with the arcane / jasmine; jasmine jeweled believe is the arcane / jeans; jeans on to the wordly desire too, love, arcane / color; arcane is the color red too and the impact that is big enough too, love / convey; convey the courage to know the contrain of love / conveyance; conveyance comes to the same, arcane / counts; counts as the one, arcane / count; count the count arcane / stays; stays of the dawn, arcane / ledger; ledger of the arcane / count; count on the being, arcane / control; control flows to the arcane in love / contents; contents that live with the content reside at what love is by the arcane / destination; destination due too, the arcane / deals; deals a lot with the arcane / dance; dance about the arcane / domes; domes that knew the arcane / covers; covers that lead to the arcane / cry; cry with the arcane / devotes; devotes a lot too, the arcane / crafts; crafts is in too, the arcane / continent; continents come too, the arcane / collapse; collapse clause comes too and wins the arcane.

CHAPTER SIX
Lemurian; lemurian natured balancing now ascends to the degree examined as regard for the stance arcane / atlantic; atlantic notion passes within to the degree arcane / atlantis; atlantis wins the arcane / greek; greek decide is arcane / courts; courts with the arcane / judicate; judicate the great, arcane / jury; jury wins the arcane / plan; plan to be, arcane / plural; a plural trine is arcane / devotion; devotion comes too, the arcane / escape; escape the scape that is arcane / regain; regain the gain, arcane / referee; referee the dame arcane / potion; potion within the arcane / place; place the pace arcane / name; name the game, arcane / kidbee; kidbee dawn, the adult sum, arcane / creek; creek side, arcane / southern; southern days, arcane / degree; degrees that deserve the arcane / southern; southern designs that agree to the arcane / degree; degree of the dues arcane / appellate; appellate states that are arcane / clip; clip to the lips arcane / closure; closure comes to the arcane / coming; coming days hum with the arcane / appalachian; appalachian sums the arcane / cavern; cavern comes to the arcane / visit; visit the reside arcane / employ; employ a friend, arcane / family; family done, arcane / view; views of the strain arcane / bemuse; bemuse and rest, arcane / entertain; entertain the arcane / ascertain; ascertain the certain, arcane / aspects; aspects due to the arcane / leaves; leaves that live in the arcane / bamboo; bamboo days that are arcane / leaves; leaves that hand with the arcane / lassen; lassen glee-full with the arcane / deign; deign your nature due too the arcane / daily; daily view your proclaim as arcane / duty; duty due to the arcane / cover; cover the friend arcane / cured; cured in the arcane / duly; duly done within the arcane / camp; camp in

the arcane / placement; place meant, arcane / stamped; stamped with the sine arcane / readings; readings come with the sounding arcane / pumpkin; pumpkins sum with the arcane / spare; spare compare compares the arcane / spur; spur the arc of the arcane / clasp; clasp a hand arcane / confer; confer with the kneel arcane / jealous; jealous gems have gone degreed to the slim regard arcane / chore; chore with the shine arcane / hold; hold on to the dream arcane / callous; callous over now comes the arcane / friends; friends who deal in the arcane / betray; betray the lessen, proclaim the arcane / held; held by the strands arcane / contempt; contempt becomes the lessen arcane / balance; balance at the palace arcane / met; met by the dues arcane.

CHAPTER SEVEN
Atlantean; atlantean seams are coming too, the arcane / seams; seams in, arcane regard to the seas of love / yellow; yellow days, arcane, too, love / grids; grids that agree on the arcane / grace; grace that is new and too we are through the arcane / fields; fields of the arcane agree with love / full; full enough too and believe it, love, arcane / flow; flow over with the nature of love through the arcane / fade; fade about too, the arcane / need; need to be, arcane / rock; rock about the light arcane / slips; slips with the sign arcane / know; know about the light arcane / fall; fall over with the lane arcane / fallen; fallen too and the clue arcane / felled; felled by the arcane / see; see it be arcane / seize; seize the state arcane / secure; secure enough to be arcane / shade; shades of the arcane / spells; spells of the arcane / cast; cast is too, arcane / removed; removed by the seam arcane / marry; marry the care with the scene arcane / marred; marred deeply within the arcane / earth; earth is mirth-full and arcane / lift; lift is wet with the arcane / desist; desist rest, arcane / captive; captive is the arcane / capture; capture gone, arcane / slay; slay the stay arcane / dragon; dragon dues paid to the life arcane / date; date the other and the ascend arcane / pentacles; pentacles that clue the arcane / success; success that is met by the arcane / sobriety; sobriety seen in the arcane / deity; deity scene, the arcane / due; due to the arcane / neat; neat enough to be, arcane / light; light reads with the arcane / laden; laden by the opportunity arcane / know; know the depth arcane / good; good to know, the arcane / plenty; plenty to be plentiful about in life's regard to love / pleasure; pleasure found in a town agreed too, the arcane / please; please be free too, the arcane / plaza; plaza's plea is the arcane / four; four to four and the arcane / dance; dance is and true agree the arcane / within; within the arcane / sufi; a sufi sign spanned by the arcane / cross; cross the agree to the arcane / meeting; meeting met by the arcane / gather; gather winds arcane / stand; stands shoulder deep in the arcane / stem; stems remember the agree arcane / minds; minds that blend the arcane / stir; stir with the agreed upon arcane / pay; pay for the arcane / please; pleased with the arcane / great; great relate arcane / rate; rate comes to the arcane / paid; love's paid for the arcane / fondly; fondly field your arcane.

CHAPTER EIGHT
Ask; ask how and why and advance to the sound arcane / know;

know why you explain the show arcane / dare; dare to be the arcane / kill; kill less the arcane / mole; moles heal the digs arcane / digs; digs into the arcane / slice; slice of the news arcane / soar; soar to the experience arcane / sore; sore enough to desire the arcane / relief; relief about the explain arcane / eternal; eternal scene to a degree arcane / degree; degree due to the arcane / do; do unto you, the profane / knot; knots over the arcane / need; need to be, arcane / knowing; knowing the reveal arcane / smart; smart enough to see the arcane / secure; secure in scenes arcane / success; success gives in to the arcane / starts; starts to be arcane / now; now we are arcane / again; again we are again / eternal; eternal scene the arcane / deep; deep in the depths of love that's arcane / true; true enough to be arcane / through; arcane through the sound degrees of love / fills; fills up with the still degree arcane / feels; feels fed by the scene, arcane / near; near the steer arcane / hammocks; hammocks agree with the arcane / plenty; plenty of us agree with love that's arcane / places; places that seem like the arcane / many; many degreed by the arcane / write; write in the love that's arcane / print; seen at the arc arcane / show; show us your arcane news of love / face; face the full degrees of the arcane / full; arcane and full with the agree to be One with God / real; real enough to be agreed upon, arcane is, love / deepen; deepen in the arcane / dates; dates that chance the arcane / clues; clues in the arcane / heart; hearts that fill with the arcane / held; held by the arcane / clasp; clasp the arcane / splash; splash with the arcane / feeds; feeds us another start arcane / gated; gated community arcane / high; high to the sky arcane / canes; canes blue with the sky that agrees with love and the arcane / kentucky; kentucky comes to agree, arcane / clover; clover comes to the green agree, arcane / free; free to delve into the arcane / louisville; louisville blue and green to agreed, arcane / found; found another summary, arcane / huddles; huddles at the shining agree arcane / deer; deer and gentle to the arcane / horses; horses healed strong and arcane / scatter; scatter around the degree that's arcane / home; home to the stress on the arcane / throne; thrones that feel like the light arcane / harness; harness another chance arcane / pounds; pounds on the roof, arcane / Concurrent.

CHAPTER NINE
Stance; a stance made at the shades arcane / stay; stay a while here at the arcane / staid; staid by the pace arcane / strong; strong enough to be arcane / deliver; deliver the sort who are arcane / long; long enough to be with the arcane / agree; agree to see the arcane / rely; rely on the light that's arcane / upon; upon this dance we chance the arcane / stacey; *stacey saw the rapture arcane / surrender; surrender trained along the cause electric and youth that's come too the loving arcane / strength; strength that's had by the living arcane / star; star of a car that is arcane / stare; stare at the state of the sound that is, arcane / adore; adore your arcane agree to succeed at the heed of God / melt; melt at the scripture which read arcane / mend; mend the moments of the arcane / committed; committed to the sane arcane / deal; deal with the Otherness, arcane / done; done with the rest, past the

test, know the swell, arcane / attend; attend to a matter that is, arcane / lessons; lessons done and living won by the arcane / lateral; lateral pleasure gone lyrical too, love / lingual; lingual exceed to the extreme and the heart that is, arcane / language; language comes to the trend arcane / bi-lingual; bi-lingual linger arcane / equate; equate that the state is arcane / quiet; quiet to be, arcane / quicken; quicken with the arcane / wakes; quakes deep in the surrender arcane / quarters; quarters sold on the street that is, arcane / locks; locks found under the seas arcane / ascend; ascend to a moment arcane / succumb; succumb to the nature arcane / sustain; sustain an experience, arcane / grade; grade too, arcane / ladders; ladders that climb the arcane / lisp; lisp steep in the arcane / ladder; ladder days arcane / glad; glad to be arcane / go; go to the show arcane / between; between us, arcane / basic; basic believe in the arcane / earth; earth deep in the arcane / west; west side arcane / green; green seen arcane / late; late enough to be arcane / akashic; akashic that broke is fixed with the arcane / break; break the drought with the shout arcane / loathe; loathe less the arcane / lake; lake time arcane / floods; floods fill the arcane / nervous; nervous about yes, the arcane / sphincter; sphincter trends release, the arcane / brink; brink met on the arcane / anal; anal glands squeeze the arcane / chord; chord deep in the arcane / cracks; cracks that combine with the arcane / release; release too, the arcane / relate; relate too, the arcane / note; notes desire the arcane / relief; relief becomes arcane / ready; ready to see the arcane / coming; coming to the dream arcane.

CHAPTER TEN
Caring; caring for the others content with the arcane / capable; capable to be arcane / capacious; capacious in my raptured state, arcane / flax; flax flew over you in our arcane agree to be with love / horus; horus houred by the arcane / globe; globe deep in the glue arcane / atlas; atlas round the sound arcane / lend; lend and here, arcane / belgian; belgian waffling comes to less and we confess our arcane agree too, love / flocks; flocks of the free, arcane / hemp; hemp stacked deep in the arcane / grain; grain that grew arcane / impart; impart the start arcane / part; part of the hunt arcane / port; port deep in the arcane / participate; participate in the sort arcane / particles; particles tend to be, arcane / cachet; cachets of the stains arcane / olives; olives green with the scene arcane / greece; greece taught us the release arcane / south; south to the mouth that is, arcane / santa; santa signed arcane / maria; maria met the bee, arcane / pinta; pinta plain with the same, arcane / west; west to the east arcane / pina; pina time arcane / color; color deep in the arcane / aspects; aspects that seek the arcane / wonder; wonder about the arcane / assignment; assignment said, believe, the arcane / digits; digits dialed and filed arcane / planes; planes that fly within the arcane / grand; grand and new arcane / granular; granular please that is, arcane / granulate; granulate with the arcane / seychelle; seychelle believe in the strip that's arcane / gibraltar; gibraltar sees the rock that is arcane / morocco; morocco meets a tangent arcane / tangier; tangier concede arcane / granite; granite ascend to the friend arcane / graph; graph of the trip to the hip that's

arcane / graphic; graphic agree written arcane / great; great decide to be, arcane / grinds; grinds of the kind arcane / grip; grip the strip arcane / groin; groin deep in the arcane / need; need another grade arcane / neat; neat enough to see the arcane / furnish; furnish the other with the arcane / breath; breath that beats with the arcane / bred; bred to be arcane agreed / brand; brand to the new, arcane / more; more than Other, arcane / shake; shake the stake arcane / shook; shook the hook arcane / quick; quick enough to be arcane / quake; quake degreed by the arcane / bark; bark at the shark arcane / barge; barge of consent with the arcane / sues; sues that need too, know, thee, arcane / canal; canal to the pleasure of the measures arcane/ contain; contain the sort arcane / clasp; clasp a laughing agree to consent to, arcane.

CHAPTER ELEVEN
Cherries; cherries that are red with agree to believe in, the arcane / chew; chew the degree that is arcane / change; change that is arcane / chill; chill deep in the arcane / perry; perry red the arcane / admires; admires the sire arcane / mill; mill days arcane / auto; auto reverse and the curse is over too, the arcane / hearts; hearts that heal the arcane / attacks; attacks the test arcane / relax; relax with the lights arcane / replay; replay the desire to be higher within the arcane / supply; supply the date with the arcane / succeed; succeed at the state arcane / sustenance; sustenance suspends the arcane / sustain; sustain a degree in the arcane / roman; roman rules the arcane / refuge; refuge of the dedication agreed upon, arcane / freshen; freshen your stance at accept, arcane / race; race to the notion arcane / renew; renew your degree with the arcane / roar; roar about the seas, arcane / relate; relate to the date, arcane / lakes; lakes lend seas of the arcane / powell; powell days are arcane / train; train with the arcane / tavern; tavern's compare is true too, the arcane / caves; caves deep in the arcane / capri; capri side signed arcane / mathematical; mathematical agrees that hu-man conception is the scene arcane / molecular; molecular accept of the seen arcane / fond; fond too, the arcane / pyramids; pyramids that appear within the arcane / planet; planet deep in the arcane / jaunt; jaunt to the steep that is, arcane / thrilling; thrilling devotion to the notion arcane / treat; treat each other arcanely / travail; travail has less become the arcane / born; born by succeed and the steed arcane / born; born to be arcane / map; map of the park that is, arcane / trip; trip too, the arcane / day; day of the week, arcane / days; days that deal with the arcane / moments; moments met in the arcane / many; many are held by the arcane / ways; ways to be arcane / minutes; minutes due to the arcane / airport; airport stays at the arcane / launch; launch a date with the news arcane / attend; attend your friend, the arcane / towns; towns deep in the heal that is, arcane / chicken; chicken said forget, the arcane / feed; feed your state with the arcane / meet; meet at the altar arcane / communes; communes with you through the arcane / lunch; lunch is due to the arcane / meter; meters of the metric agree arcane / rhyme; rhyme with the dream arcane / zikr; zikr's heal is our reel arcane / breast; breast deep in the steps arcane / drum; drum with the sum arcane / empty; empty days found arcane / full; full of the ways arcane.

CHAPTER TWELVE
Filled; filled by the fire that is well with yellow compare to the green decide that is God's light, arcane / fun; fun to be free of the arcane / flown; flown by the sea that is the arcane=truth / through; through the gates arcane; your mouth / storms; storms that decree the arcane / tracks; tracks filled with we are arcane / mountains; mountains that train on the arcane / seventh; seventh days heaven wide too, the arcane / highlands; highlands heal the arcane / heavens; heavens deal in the arcane / facts; facts about the arcane / eight; eight days come too, the arcane / ninth; ninth ways wield the arcane / move; move to reveal the arcane / zero; zero in on the arcane / plenty; plenty of this, the arcane / peasants; peasants see the royalty in their roots and the arcane / shores; shores that seal the muse to the arcane / slave; slave days are freed by my light arcane and the friends that lean toward the angles of love / culprit; culprit comes undone in the arcane / liar; liar found in the sound arcane / book; books written reveal the arcane / brackets; brackets break with the arcane / bounty; bounty of the bouquet arcane / mutate; mutate less and more agree to be, arcane / hook; hook home to say yes too, the arcane / unleash; unleash your power with the arcane / listen; listen in too, the arcane / shiatsu; shiatsu said loosen up, the arcane / body; body deep in the reserve arcane / health; health that is wealth to the arcane / thai; thai times tunes are arcane / massage; massage felt deep in the arcane / rolf; mu's rolfed accede to ligaments stretched by the tongues of love / connect; connect with a lesson arcane / connective; connective to a tissue arcane / sessions; sessions that come with the arcane / seasons; seasons of the sung and the four that become the arcane / lessons; lessons dues arcane news comes agree too, the truth is, love / love; love to be arcane / lighthouse; lighthouse news is, arcane / mission; mission dates conserved with the arcane / message; message soon, arcane / tune; tune into the news arcane / tone; tones that say we are arcane / entreaty; entreaty that is arcane / prophet; prophet of belief and decide to accent within thee, arcane / pen; pens that are arcane and too, agreed upon, love / balance; balance of the arcs become arcane / blends; blends in with the send arcane / ballast; ballast today with the sum, arcane / dropped; dropped too, the arcane / gravitation; gravitation says become arcane / spun; spun by the date arcane / poles; poles deal with the arcane, head to toe, love / won; won by the same, the one, arcane / wealth; wealth becomes you, arcanely, won / shown; shown by the heavens the arcane / heaven; heaven is arcane / held; held by a date arcane / levels; levels elevated in the arcane / dates; dates that are arcane / decide; decide to be arcane.

CHAPTER THIRTEEN
Blends; blends with the truth, arcane / motive; motive met at the arcane / material; material nature the arcane / motif; motif's desire the arcane / mazdan; mazdan news the arcane / moroccan; moroccan expand to the space that is, arcane / magic; magic that is due too, the arcane / miracle; miracle means are mattered through the arcane / meaning; meaning comes too, the arcane / stretch; stretch your days through the arcane / suggest; suggest that states reside at the arcane / speak; speak to the One, arcane

/ concur; concur that notice is given too, the arcane / coincide; coincide with the arcane / contest; contests come to the arcane / win; win a date with the arcane / won; won by the light is, arcane / wed; let us wed with the arcane / weld; weld your state as held, arcane / waters; waters meet where the parts are arcane / creates; creates a state of vertical motion and the notion arcane / cores; cores of the swords arcane / climbs; climbs to the limbs arcane / clever; clever ever more, arcane / levers; levers that lend regain to the arcane / hidden; hidden in the send arcane / nights; nights that deal with the heal arcane / keys; keys come to the done metatronically spent on the invent of the love is, arcane / codes; codes continue arcanely / escalate; escalate seductively to the sea arcane / escape; escape to the notice arcane / welling; welling with willing arcane / willed; willed by the giving arcane / fountain; fountain top stops at the art arcane / frame; truth is an art frame your with the smart rely on love this arcane / friendly; friendly to a sort that's blue with spoken regard for the arcane news that God is, love / fecund; fecund by the sum electric, arcane / flora; flora abet arcane / fauna; fauna fed by the let us be arcane / finale; finale comes to the arcane ones who set their hearts on love / appreciate; appreciate each the other, arcane / speed; speed said, arcane / breath; breath through the plane arcane / breathe; God's breathing erupt is arcane / berates; berates the latest, arcane / forgets; forgets less the arcane / forgotten; forgotten sought has come too, the arcane / given; given a day, arcane / delicate; delicate decide to reside at the arcane / delight; delights within the arcane / delicious; delicious decide to reside, arcane / pungent; pungent to a declaration arcane / elevated; elevated to the worthy arcane / lights; lights that sight's on us, arcane / lofty; lofty truths rescue you for the mercy seat of God, the arcane / fragrant; fragrant to a moment's state and the date arcane with love / trend; trends due to the arcane, love, peace, and news of love / traffic; traffic along the land arcane / over; over dues and daily flew our stand too, the arcane / pleasant; pleasant to a state arcane / hearts; hearts decide to reside at the legend arcane / love; love is truth, regain the sign you love, by the arcane / life; life is felt as the arcane, to the heart of it all, love / Currents.

THE PROFANE-MENTS
LEVEL 22

CHAPTER ONE

Profane; profane to a gain called love / profound; profound to a sound that matters, love / profuse; profuse to an excuse that's gone, know more, secure in love / enthuse; enthuse a neighbor as thyself, the wealth of share and the joy of letting in to letting go / unthaw; unthaw has come to the some whose light is tight with the profane abide in God / bemuse; profane bemuse and coming choose to those who love / bet; bet on the veterans who correct their lies with loving bemuse at the profane / bathe; love's bathe is profane / blue; blue enough to be templar and simon said aim to be profane / banter; banter about love, profane / bail; God's bail is profane avail at the zipped in, love / bat; bat the profane and a million to one is me / become; become profane and know the explain too, love / caves; love is caves that are deep in respect for the coming elect too, love is, profane / come; come to be profane / home; home and I Am too profane / lure; lure is set on another bet called the living profane and the loving again at the www. God. coming again. now / lavish; lavish is polished in the profane / outlandish; outlandish to the lane that is profanely standard and essentially set on the elective love / in time; in time to be true too, the profane / summon; summon another to be the One and call in the friend profane / contest; contest becomes the cure profane / won; profane agree and the sea that is won by the wave of believe/ insist; insist on the set of a misty net called love inn, profane / sum; sum a denomination called one, profane / millions; millions who have won the deep respect of the many an One, profane, love / mint; mint degreed and agreed to succeed too, love / incest; incest comes to the forgive that is profane / egypt; egypt live like the profane / joins; joins each within, the profane / glints; glints like a send, profane / trials; trials that are hearty and the start to repair to and the jury profane / trends; trends that defend us and the light at the end is profane / trains; trains about brands of the stringent regard called profane / traverse; traverse a path called the math that's profane / kits; kits that fit the wedded profane / kiss; kiss this note, profane / coils; coils of the manner profane / contact; contact a note called the back of a vote that's profane / current; current and profane, now / cast; cast the net over the profane / gasp; gasp again and taste a place called amend, too, profane / coats; coats each the other with the other that defends each sway to the profane / cones; cones of the manner eyed, profanely / caliber; caliber of the code that is, profane / in; in to be and the manner we live, profane / gentlemen; gentlemen who dare to be gemmed through reflectively profane / women; women win in the profane / wants; wants to be and always is, profane / desires; desires to be a higher lane, profane / decide; decide to be, profane / profuse; profuse to a being, called, love / portendant; profane and portendant to a stand that is, love / possible; possible to be profane / pert; pert enough to exert, the sort, profane / please; please decide to be profane / expressions; expressions that are, profane / dimensions; dimensions deal with the profane / individual; individual decisions, profane / devant; devant gaunt too the profane / dire; dire delay and the way that is higher too, the profane / dapple; dapple to deal with the profane / gallactic; gallactic to the dimensions profane / ark; love is the ark of the I AM profane / ethnic; ethnic and fine and profane / divination; divination done to the send that is ascendant and love.

CHAPTER TWO

Profuse; profuse to a moment profane / present; present to a point profane / presence; presence is found in the sounds profane / particulate; particulate to a mood, profane / participles; participles that clue to the profane / plans; plans that ascend the profane / pert; pert to the exert that's profane to love / berth; berth that is the port of a heart called profanely love / sydney; sydney simple to the profane / perth; perth alert profane / aborigine; aborigine to a profane sort love / college; college profane to clued reside at love / horizon; horizons on trines that are critical to the profane / propel; propel yourself deeded to the sides called profane / compelling; compelling and indeed we are profane / mystical; mystical amend to the profane / artistic; artistic you are and we can see the apostolic profane / arts; arts that start with the profane / shift; shift a deft decide to the profane / articulate; articulate to a loving trade profane / relativity; relativity becomes wise to the matters profane / wise; wise to decide the profane / moniker; moniker given, the profane / name; name the dame profane / secret; secrets about the profane / bread; bread deep in the rolls profane / missionary; missionaries deem the team profane / lasers; lasers that lease the profane / yukon; yukon blue and true, profane / chant; chant the names profane / psychedelic; psychedelic agree to purple be and the life that is, profane / hewa; hewa feel and the trine profane / telepathically; telepathically sent to the profanely blue hopi sign / relations; relations profane with the ascend that is coming too love in the mitakuye oyasin of the stars in your eyes / lemon; lemon yellow agree to the aid profane / bah; bah that is profane / crazy; crazy days believe in the profane / energetic; energetic agree and the artistic dramatics called precisely profane too, love / loon; loon and soon, profane / loom; loom over natures profane / weave; weave a date profane / pattern; patterns see the ends of me, profane / historical; historical and see the profane / sensate; sensates days are profane / dimensions; dimensions dues profane / cobalt; cobalt blues profane / blue; blue to the send profane / legends; legends agreed, profane / shapes; shapes that suppress can be left too, the profane / store; store the days profane / cultivate; cultivates states profane / nations; nations that kneel profanely / notes; notes about the profane / touch; touch this sheet profane / symbols; symbols eayes profane / sphere; sphere deep in the profane / basin; basin blue with the profane / earth; earth can see the profane / reality; relativity and the reality seen by the blues profane / worth; worth the weight, hu-man esteem, profane / phoenix; phoenix agree to the be profane / fund; fund dayed profane / funds; funds can be leveled by the profane / found; found at the stacks that are, profane.

CHAPTER THREE

Manana; manana comes and the sums profane / inert; inert to the squirt profane / imagine; imagine the bulb, profane / spontaneous;

spontaneous to a native profane / vital; vital to a still, profane / changes; changes that decide the Chicago side of the rind that peels profanely / change; change to a show profane / harness; harness the shower that is profane / climb; climb to the mention profane / uncommon; uncommon dimension profane / care; care to be profane / mischievous; mischievous to a mansion's plan, profane / doored; bred shut to the profane / floored; floored by the profane / imported; imported and worth the wait profane / consort; consort to be profane / malibu; malibu moves and seen profane / view; views of the friends profane / lands; lands on the ascendant and wins profanely / necessity; necessity dues profane / blurt; blurt about the heart profane / frequently; frequently we are due the profane / powers; powers of the hours profane / match; match that is due, the profane / dense; dense regards relate, the profane / decode; decode the codes profane / code; code red, profane / maths; maths sign, profane / clue; clue clipped profane / collaborate; collaborate about the return profoundly profane / revenue; revenues agree is profane / rights; rights that are, profane / fully; fully can be, profane / future; future revenues agreed too, profane / British; British regard for the profane / domain; domain of the sample, profane / county; county deputy profane / clued; clued by the signed profane / globe; globe deep with the profane / dominion; dominion deigned the profane / donate; donate the state the profane / direct; direct resort profane / review; review this, the, profane / compare; compare the dare profane / resign; resign too and see the profane / regard; regard the card profane / restate; restate your goal profane / review; review the attitudes profane / interest; interest given in the profane / force; force fields geometrically profane / euclid; euclid's moment profane / status; status stated sculptured profane / geometric; geometric and to a spin profane / symmetry; symmetry is the fringe profane / sight; sight of the rim profane / statistics; statistics live in the profane / exist; exist at the lens profane / suspend; suspend to the send off profane / crunch; crunch in the middle profane / compound; compound astound profane / color; colors profane with love / grains; grains grew up with loving profane / green; green ascend seen in Savannah's profile and the living forgive profane / Amazon.

CHAPTER FOUR
Catholic; a Catholic stare at the profound in the profane / cuzco; cuzco won by the sounds profane / peru; peru is due the profane / Macchu Picchu; Machu Picchu to a regard for the mind profane / quito; quito is loved by the profane, cotapaxi steep to love / Ecuador; Ecuador decide to the volcanos glide geometric too, love is, profane / Galapagos; Galapagos style profane / bloom; bloom within the profane / infinite; infinite to the mends profane / mindness; mindness found profane / sciences; sciences minded by the profane / conscious; conscious agree to be, profane / mind; mind deep in the mend profane / value; value stirs in the material notions profane / hunt; hunt a man profane / stride; stride past the lessen profane / lives; lives like a dream and the edge is well within the profane / moss; moss grace green in the resume that is, profane / Spanish; Spanish nation flamed profane

/ slavery; slavery over and the profane begun / ends; ends left to right profane / met; met depth in a match profane / carry; carry the slate profane / antebellum; antebellum agree to be, profane / guild; guild grew profane at the sane arrival love / club; club shift swings profane / belle; belle of the profane swell and the same southern style, profane / winds; winds profane within the strain that's sane too, love / woods; woods deal with the proclaim of love profane / scarlet; scarlet mattered to the profane / flew; flew like a flight profane / sure; sure decide secure to the profane / absolve; absolve the matters profanely / absolute; absolute to the suit profane / full; full decide to be, profane / filled; filled with the still and the send profane / hunger; hunger given to the feed profane / gone; gone when agreed, profane / silence; silence spoken profanely / sums; sums of stature profane to the nines that win true love / fractal; fractal assumption the plane profane / observe; observe the data profane / data; data that's due to the profane / field; field regard profane / coherent; coherent profane and profound now explain love / synchronous; synchronous to a measure profane / date; dates with the profane agree and this assure love / body; body blue to the bliss profane / faces; face the profane in the mirror of love / portal; portals that please the profane / fielded; fielded by yielded the profane / cardinal; cardinal states profane / cardiac; cardiac agreed profane / apology; apology for the profane / accept; accept the sort profane / refute; refute the cute profane / renew; renew a date with the profane / realign; realign with the side profane / coherent; coherent decide to agree to the profane / energies; energies side with the profane / one; one time profane / sum; sum paid, the profane / God; God new the heart profane / sons; sons who see the profane return to love.

CHAPTER FIVE
Universe; universe lives profanely in you and true too, love / university; university rules believe in tools profane / regular; regular use of the guides majorcan and the living profane / court; court skirted in the profane / jazz; jazz times true to the profane, listen, love / blues; blues that are due to the profane / degree; degree by degree the profane and the sum 360 to love / aspect; aspect that is direct is the reflect of love within thee, profane / display; display the day profane / chaotic; chaotically free of the seams profane / rhythm; rhythm feels the assignment seen in the lean arrival at love within, profane / happen; happen to be profane / predict; predict the wear profane / appear; appear to breathe, profane / coincide; coincide inside within the profane / collapse; collapse again for a rest within the tents of love, profane / crate; crate full of the fill profane / tools; tools that sills profane / startle; startle less, profane / miracle; miracle drawn, the profane / molecule; molecule of remember, profane / inform; inform the storm, profane / information; information stationed in the profane / continued; continued as yes, profane / continuous; continuous decide to be, profane / weathered; weathered and agreed upon, the profane relate, God and man, love / attract; attract a spark profane / attraction; attraction's come to the profane / port; port the sort, profane / portal; portal

compare profane / share; share the dare profane / cords; cords that dangle profanely cut through love / music; music that means Sandalphon's loot is blue to the speak profane / lift; lift the sate profane / deliver; deliver the liver profane / metre; metre punch is profane / harmony; harmony true to the profane / molds; molds a meld profane / simply; simply, I said, profane / expose; expose the composure profane / heart; hearts that heal profanely / broad; broad enough to be profane / bay; bay wide to the streets of days profane / breed; breed the kind, profane / whole; whole enough to see, profane / gestation; gestation over, profane / birth; birth trine profane / root; spiral roots uncorked, profane / division; division begun complete profane / dimensioned; dimensioned in ascend, profane / level; level nature, profane / present; present to a random profane / prepare; prepare to be profane / differ; differ deal profane / waved; waved and led profanely too, love / elongate; elongate's stretch is come and ends the trends of less, profane / gate; gates that place their hands in the profane / third; third days profane / worlds; words that collide in a world that's inside our profane ascede to believe in, love / divide; divide the ride into too, profane / octave; octave numbers 8 to 13 and the believe that is, profane / length; length uncomes profane / decide; decide to be profane / debris; debris regard less profane.

CHAPTER SIX
Kona; Kona kind to a profane wind of love / angle; angle in to see the please believe / pyramid; pyramids slid to the light octane, profane / Sphinx; Sphinx ruled by the signed agree to reveal the real eternity of love then profane / links; links to the love that is profane / lifts; lifts life to a trend that is, profane / sinks; sinks to a sacred send profane / channels; channels like this profane / controls; controls each other with the resting pulse of the love that is profane / tunes; tunes dear to the profane / voids; voids reveal and overall the profane / walls; walls closed to shut and crumble profane / black; black days come undone and the higher ways are profane / block; block the shock and the burn, profane / noise; noise within and the flame profane / concept; concept coming profane / notes; notes from the road and the riding profane / immortal; immortal to days profane / unity; unity is the living profane / sunshine; sunshine ways, profane / sold; sold to the nestle profane / severance; severance wayed profane / complete; complete the sort profane / retrograde; retrograde stayed profane / plans; plans to feed the profane / lights; lights escape less, profane / spirals; spirals directed profanely / plays; plays on the square refrain profane / scenes; scenes summarized profane / genesis; genesis comets in, profane / skills; skills due profane / spoken; spoken for man, profane / melchizidek; melchizidek comes to the profane / machiavellian; machiavellian compelling the profane / 93; 93 days and the carolling profane / 105; one hundred five and the tribes profane / 53; 53 days to the roaming profane / 77; yangs wade is profane / 89; eighty-nine styles profane / 33; 33 is profane / 44; 44 ways to divide human's being profanely, love / 55; 55 leis worn in sync with the profane, love / wavelengths; wavelengths become the lengths profane in love / lights; lights delight me, profanely / keys; keys keep

codes intact, profane / fundamental; fundamental to an explain profane / due; due the course, profane / places; places win the profane / torus; torus sort us, out within, profane / thorax; thorax of a sort profane / amounts; amounts found and given profane / word; convey the word, profane / biology; biology sets in to the profane / egg; egg of God in the profane / leg; leg up to the profane / life; life lived profanely, good, God / stand; stand for men, hu-man, profane, God / up; up to the late profane / forth; forth tot he sort profane / width; width wins deep regard in the profane/ diatribe; diatribe due to the profane / speech; speech coming profanely / speak; speak electric in the profane / talks; talks profanely, love.

CHAPTER SEVEN
Rotate; rotate the state profane / value; value the notion profane / acceptance; acceptance set on the profane / except; except is set on release too, profane with, God / corrective; corrective ventures measure profane / species; species set on the profane / spectral; spectral desires profane / spectrum; spectrum extreme to the profane / spheres; spheres of belief and profanely absolute, love / depictive; depictive to agree and we are, profane / flowers; flowers that shower with the profane / fuse; colors fuse within the profane / metamorphosis; metamorphosis exists in the profane / diotonic; diotonic to the sonic resume, profane / position; positions win in the profane / minimal; minimal please extrudes profane / reveal; reveal a natural high profane / revelation; revelation comes to the profane / seal; seals heals profane / chakra; chakras deal with the profane / healed; healed and held profane / one; one to one profane / column; columns come to the profane / sum; sums paid and the strand profane / sun; sun comes profane / lifts; lifts the lens profane / haze; haze cools the profane / goes; goes to the stands profane / tetrahedron; tetrahedrons come one love profane / cocreate; cocreate the rates profane / God; God is with thee, profane / Metatron; Metatron's song is profane / geometrics; geometrics sum in the profane / precise; precise to the stream profane / precious; precious and true, the profane / perfect; perfect extreme to the profane / content; content to the summation profane / commit; commit the fit profane / peace; peace is coming profanely, love / ascendant; the ascendant sum, profane / bliss; bliss to the kiss whose station is perfectly free too, love / kiss; kiss the sister who listens in the profane / bubbles; bubbles unique in agree to be profane / face; face the portal, yes too, love, let's profane / interface; interface upon the stories profane / fair; fair enough to be squarely told "you are profanely loved" / spare; spare know emotion, love, profane / fare; fare to the square profane / 12; God's 12 knew the profane / 13; 13 comes to the profane / 14; 14 hums with the profane / 15; 15 done with the profane / 16; 16 times round the profane / absolute; absolute too, the profane / sure; sure enough, profane / 48; 48 states to gather, profane / sacred; sacred seen, profane / tablets; tablets emit the profane / sure; sure to be, profane / spare; spare regard for the profane / stand; stand like we, profane / know; know the reason, profane / telling; telling each other, profanely / allure; allure well and we will profane.

CHAPTER EIGHT: illusory; illusory to a notion, profane / illustrative; illustrative of devotion, profane / illustrate; illustrate the state, profane / drawn; drawn to the five that are profane / given; given all, profane / gateways; gateways seal with the profane / starts; starts to be, profane / paths; paths that fill, profanely / points; points deep in the profane / pair; pair of profanes / expansion; expansion comes profanely / awareness; awareness tot he heals, profane / particular; particular to a mention profane / body; body deals profanely / prayer; prayer's answer, profane / pranic; pranic agree to be, profane / commentary; commentary about the profane / eccentric; eccentric and true to the profane / Christ-in; Christ-in and the like profane / Christed; Christed agree to be, profane / spheres; spheres true to the spin profane / counter; counter cure, profane / comprehensive; comprehensive remember, profane / visual; visual exceed undone, profanely / fourth; fourth state, love, profane / layer; layer comes unglued profanely / breathing; breathing in view of home, profane / breathing; breathing that's due the profane, too, love / inhale; inhale deep of the profane / exhale; exhale steep in the profane / see; see profanely, love / pause; pause to agree too, profane / count; count on it, profane / decree; decree the desire, profane / visually; visually steep to the profane / paints; paints rest in the profane / met; met another, profane / mudras; mudras held, profanely / hands; hands willed wide too agree profanely of love / fingers; fingers comes unsealed, profanely / thumbs; thumbs profanely oppose the less, love / butterfly; butterfly dew and the drops profane / news; news of the profane / nasally; nasally adept at the profane / blew; blew into views, profane / blooms; blooms directly profane / breath; breath on the frame profane / spun; spun to explain, the profane / spent; spent on the sent, profane / become; become another's profane assert of God, ahead, love / Egyptian; Egyptian ascend too, loved, profanely / clued; clued into the earth's explain, profane / balls; balls up to the catch that is profane / light; light each other profanely / golden; golden clues to the muse profane / spherical; spherical lyrical regard for the profane / internally; internally, directly, profane / pyramid; pyramid of keep and the light within thee, profane / keep; keep it deep profane / it; it is the light profane / in; in time too, profane / hear; hear me profanely, love / here; here, and how, profane / River.

CHAPTER NINE
Heart; heart of the state that is high on love and the living profane, hu-man, God, love / spirit; spirit matters profanely / powers; powers a source, profane / align; align this gift profanely / mental; mental clues, profane / spiritual; spiritual intrigues imbued within, profane / sights; sights due the profane / practice; practice keep, profane / physical; physical heals, profane / yogas; yogas blend perfectly at love's profanest portal, the mouths of babes explain our dues and the lightest frolics live in our proclaim of lifts due to a stretch called God / yogis; yogis feel profane / daily; daily dues profane / do; do thee, profanely, loves / palms; palms meet to proclaim the profane / aha; aha's experience comes profanely / ha; ha true to the profane / remind; remind

me of you, profane / remembered; remembered by the profane / immense; immensely profane / field; field due to the profane / draw; draw on the profane / the; the draw is profane / star; star in the profane / within; within is indeed profane / yourself; yourself profane / and; and we will be profane / know; know the time profane / the; the days profane / light; lightly said, profane / you; you are, profane / are; are you, profane? / by; by the way profane / command; command comes to the man profane / of; of the sort, profane / the; the land given profanely / land; land said, profane / eternal; eternal deals profane / and; and the date is, profane / the; the heart lives profanely / withstood; withstood within profanely / as; as we are, profane / the; the dates profane / sounds; sounds like the profane / logarithmic; logarithmic proclaim profane / this; this date is, profane / spiraling; spiraling in too, the profane / plan; plan on being profane / for; for the our, profane / then; then again, profane / start; start to be, profane / tetrahedron; tetrahedrons profane / golden; golden meant, profane / means; means to be, profane / fibonacci; fibonacci's square is profane / sixty four; sixty four days profane / times; times like the profane / chest; chest deep within the profane / head; head up with the profane / shoulders; shoulders squared to the profane / triangles; triangles bent to the profane / square; square agree to be profane / central; central port, profane / Mother / All.

CHAPTER TEN
Sequenced; sequenced in regard for the word, profane / geometrical; geometrical agree to be profane / man; man is the land profane / God's; God's dear friend, the profane / squarely; squarely, profane / rectangular; rectangular to an agree to be, profane / gridded; gridded with lidded approve and the move that is, profane / tell; tell everyone well, profane / linear; linear to a street profane / places; places that are, profane / horizontally; horizontally let's give the living, profane / clues; clues due to the profane / spread; spread a dread headed profane / vertically; vertically profuse and profane to a degree called loved / squared; squared in ascend and near the end, profane / love; love is profane / tender; know the tender degree of where we are led and to thee, profane / gentle; gentle to the news that man is profane / eternal; eternal to a externalized concede called complete within, the profane / immense; immense to a tense profane / increase; increase your dare, to be, profane / decrease; decrease your less least profane / bases; bases won by the touched and tagged profane / faces; faces dear reveal the views profane / highs; highs and goes to the profane / lows; lows dealt with, profane / between; between these, profane / then; then and again, profane / tendency; tendency to see only thee, profane / vague; vague enough to defy, fly the profane / finer; finer then, profane / great; great days profane / tenth; tenth days profane / door; door deep in the opening profane / four; four times the stare, profane / deep; deep due to the profane / leads; leads to the seas profane / overtures; overtures overcome with the overrun of frolicsome delivery, find the note profane / tones; tones that deal with the ears profane / keep; keep your ears clear, the profane / knew; knew enough to be profane / expand; expand to the stand

profane / reset; reset the matter, profane / spin; spin to the trend profane / path; path deep in the profane / practice; practice wins profane / prana; prana's succeed profane / lend; lend me thee, profane / debts; debts dealt with in the profane / collect; collect the amount profane / options; options that choose the profane / explore; explore the door profane / open; open to the mention profane / revolve; revolve to the line resolved as love is, profane / stars; stars dear to the profane / are; are we profane? / ours; ours is the hear profane / remember; remember me to the profane / surrender; surrender is dear to the profane / knew; knew like this and the apportion profane / new; new to the our profane / old; old days profaner / same; same time, profane / you; you due the profane.

CHAPTER ELEVEN

Unique; unique to the sort, profane / perfect; God's perfect plan is the man profane / plenty; plenty to see in the profane / all; all I see is the profane / mastered; mastered in the send profane / centered; centered and extreme to the scene profane and eternal in love / drew; drew on you eternally to the location profane / beyond; beyond the extremes profane / experience; experience meets the streets profane / meets; meets the neat arrival profane / truth; truth told is profane / rebirth; rebirth the skirt profane, love / experience; experience comes in the profane / meets; meets at the dates profane / truth; truth is, profane / rebirth; rebirth the mirth profane / births; births sincere to the profane / beauty; beauty is, profane / blessings; blessings begin, profane / harmonics; harmonics ascend in the profane / exhale; purest exert to the excerpt profane / maintain; maintain a status profane / power; power the our profane / pure; pure to the stare profane / inhale; inhale with emote that is profane / clarify; clarify the fair profane / clarity; clarity clued to the profane / peace; peace is profane / reward; reward the sword profane / unify; unify your dates within the profane / unite; unite the vote, profane / decide; decide the side profane / facilitate; facilitate the stratus profane / delegate; delegate due to the profane / donate; donate the straight profane / due; due the new, profane / tonight; tonight the sort, profane / average; average to the exude profane / maintain; maintain the strain, profane / maintenance; maintenance profane to the profound / night; night to the date profane / fair; fair the stare profane / energy; energy due the profane / breathing; breathing the strain profane / note; notes given dues, God, profane / heaven; heaven's profane news, love / ringing; ringing the due profane / capable; capable to the due profane / clear; clear to the near, profane / known; known and alone, profane / devoted; devoted to the sort profane / roan; roan's profane is the main azalea-green too, love / regard; regard the ward profane / played; played the dates profane / stayed; stayed in the days profane / came; came to the sums profane / novena; novena and molena is profane / orchestra; orchestral resume profane / operas; operas sung, profane / sing; sing a ringing profane / clearing; clearing the stare that is, profane / process; process the views profane / dates; dates that are due the profane / adore; adore the shores profane / asking; ask in the veins profane / seeking; seeking the

strains profane / felt; felt like the well profane / sure; sure enough to be, profane.

CHAPTER TWELVE

Keep; keep the state, profane / kept; kept a stare profane / overt; overt to a start profane / stayed; stayed a day profane / stray; stray to the say profane / aligns; aligns within the profane / inside; inside the dues profane / out; out the days profane / lucifer; lucifer's undo has come, the profane / counts; counts out the beast profane / himself; himself and trust the profane / out; out and outs profane / angels; angels sing the arrive profane / treading; treading the dates profane / arcs; arcs commune the succumb profane / win; win the grin profane / lighter; lighter ascend profane / bodied; bodied be in the profane / caring; caring the sharing profane / manifest; manifest the state perfect to agree too, love in, profane / see; see the see profane / oranges; prepare the oranges sliced in the profane / pears; pears that swear by the profane / changes; changes the shares profane / fears; fears melt profanely / lessons; lessons clean to the profane / gathered; gathered and grew, the profane / growing; growing in ascend, profane / appear; appear at the steer profane / apparent; apparent we are to the profane / coherent; coherent to the finish profane / frail; frail regard for the profane / freud; freud sued by the profane / oedipal; oedipal manage within the profane / mammalian; mammalian agree to be profane / father; father steers the mother profane / sun; sun and shore profane / sons; sons who run the profane / pleasure; pleasure dear to the profane / weekend; weekend won within the profane / lifts; lifts a great elate profane / over; over and dear, the profane / under; under the strain profane / meeting; meeting the near profane / gifts; gifts give the profane / triangular; triangular to a steer profane / plenty; plenty due within the profane / passion; passions plenty, profane / place; place a stance within, the profane / purpose; purpose comes to the profane / mission; mission done within the profane / comb; comb the nation, profane / dealings; dealings exude the profane / reviewed; reviewed an elective, profane / license; license in the profane / renewed; renewed the arraign profane / done; done to the due profane / delegations; delegations of the nations profane / lightly; lightly due to the profane / hum; hum about the profane / prophetic; prophetic aspire in the profane / degree; degree won in the profane / obtained; obtained a strain, profane / scene; scene of the profane.

CHAPTER THIRTEEN

Coming; coming too, the profane / predicted; predicted in ascend, the profane / second; second date, the profane / secure; secure endure, the profane / parallel; parallel to a place profane / places; places due the profane / chases; chases within the profane / abhor; abhor the sore profane / leisurely; leisurely given the profane / living; living in ascend profane / giving; giving the dame, profane / secure; secure desire to hear the profane / sustained; sustained agree to the profane / election; election met in the profane / lateral; lateral dues to the profane / please; please let's be the profane / purposes; purposes regain the couple profane / fond; fond of each other, profane / adore; adore the plate profane / handles; handles profanely, love / ears; ears that steer to the profane / listen; listen like this, the profane / heart; hearts that start the profane / baby; baby born in the profane / cords; cords cut from less and within the profane / apart; apart the start profane / apparition; apparition seen like the profane / coming; coming dues to the profane / undone; undone and again, the profane / start; start to be, profane / girlfriends; girlfriends agree that we are, profane / boyfriends; boyfriends who heal in the profane / spinning; spinning desire to be, profane / in; in time to sign the profane / absolutes; absolutes agree this light is profane / relationship; relationships see the profane / cushioned; cushioned like gleams profane / agree; agree to dates profane / diligent; diligent in seas profane / decide; decide to side profanely / planting; planting yourself within, the profane / free; free decide to be profane / trees; trees that rate the profane / coins; coins decide to be profane / silver; silver deals profane / worn; worn by volition profane / wills; wills that seal within, the profane / western; westerns deal with decisions profane / live; live like heals profane / denouement; denouement comes to the lesson won, profane / edits; edits like this, the profane / produce; produce a deal, profane / units; units seem profane / digital; digital agrees profane / mental; mental state profane / electric; electric the sleeve profane / fond; fond of you and the moves profane / fair; fair to be too, profane / just; just enough to see, the profane / juried; juried include of the decree profane / accept; accept the check profane / degree; degrees assigned and the gambles won, profane / stars / instinct.

THE PROFOUND-MENTS
LEVEL 23

CHAPTER ONE

Profound; profound to the minute ascendant in love / profane; profane to a moment gained profoundly in love / profuse; profuse to excuse-less love's profound delays, now see, your divinity in God's cue, let go, love / protrude; protrude to the mood profane / pray; pray about the shout profane / play; play at the stay profane / pen; pen in hand and I am hu-man too in God's profound way, love / plan; plan to be profound / portend; portend the end of a friend-less love, knot profound / reap; reap the sewn belief profound / sew; sew a date profoundly, love / sine; sine at the news profound / content; content to be truthfully exposed the profound / concurrent; concurrent currents profound / current; current to the moment profound / vein; vein blew within the profound / gibraltar; gibraltar days profound / granite; granite and blue to the heal profound is, love / grain; grain strained to the brim that is, profound / multitude; multitude degreed in the seed of life and the many profound / pillars; pillars still within the profound / herculean; herculean extreme and the we profound / rather; rather be, profound / switch; switch to the hitch profound / deeper; deeper deal profound / moving; moving in to the send profound / still; still to the feel more profound in, love / above; above the sunned delivery for the profound / over; over and over profound / under; underneath the seal that is profound / above; above the deal, profound / overage; overage gives the scene profound / often; often I give the profound / love; love the seals profound / doving; doving dive and the strive profound / drew; drew on the crew profane and profound / drop; drop the tops profound / delight; delight the sight convertible and believe in, love / desire; desire to hire the profane / detail; detail the do that is profound / dali; dali extrude and the give profound / van gogh; van gogh indeed and the profound / picasso; picasso pretend has gone to the stray profound / miro; miro will say profound / barcelona; barcelona can be the profound / expand; expand to the stand profound / astound; astound and see the sell profound / astonish; astonish the sort profound / blend; blend the still profound / ascend; ascend to the notes profound / contend; contend to the send profound / consent; consent to the extent profound / land; land and deal profound / invent; invent a trip that is, profound / patent; patent on the patent profound / pend; pend the notice profound / place; place the placement profound / embrace; embrace the grace that is profound / honor; honor the sort profound / span; span the natures profound / contract; contract the tract profound / okay; okay to be and we are profound / lend; lend a hand profound / electron; electron election is profound / lecture; lecture the skirt, profound / lay; lay the days profound.

CHAPTER TWO: pecos; pecos thrilled and the plains profound / plain; plain to the strain rewound within, the profound / placed; placed in the space profound / planes; planes suspend the profound within the land leyed by love / pearls; pearls repair the stare profound / excite; excite the light profound / carts; carts of starts profound / enlighten; enlighten the lighten profound / carved; carved the light with the straight profound / entice; entice the ice profound, diamond blue to alaskas's lean on love / priced; priced to the slice profound / played; played on laid to the lighten profound / perfect; perfect sort, profound / plaza; plaza blue to the zoo profound / punched; punched the stunt profound / dirty; dirty too and the days profound sugar / sugar; sugar blue and the zoo that is, profound / sides; sides and walls that melt, profoundly / sale; sale the whale, profound / sold; sold on holds profound / plat; plat deep in the leap profound / barter; barter the starter that is, profound / intermediate; intermediate the immediate profound / fiancee; fiancee comes home to the loan that is profound / expect; expect the sect profane within the profound / entice; entice the ice, profound / tybee; tybee isled aligned and again, profound / islands; islands deal in the heal profound / definite; definite to the dates profound / office; office keeps the lights profound / official; official nation in the profound / let; let deals be filled profoundly / priced; priced the rights profound / robbers; profane robbers who gain the profound / plans; plans to be profound / pursue; pursue the dues profound / question; question the sort profound / partner; partner found profound / found; found again and the friend, profound / double; double the doubles profound / tall; tall the heel profound / consequence; consequence deep in the profound / longer; longer and stronger within the profound / linger; linger the stinger and remove the rain with the send profound / during; during the stay sexual and seen profound / definitely; definitely due to the profound / suspense; suspense becomes true within the profound / over; over coming within the profound / go; go to her the one won is, profound / be; be with the one profound / find; find the dates profound / another; another the other and the mother profound / continental; continental and the shelf that is, profound / creates; creates the states profound / looks; looks like the streak that's profound / videos; videos rule the land profound, seen, love / showcase; showcase the stance profound / celebrate; celebrate the ransom profound / arts; arts are starts profound / events; events deal profoundly / halloween; halloween heads for the language profound / hallowed; hallowed be the wind profound / moon; moon the soon and reflect this within, profound / lights; lights and lifes profound, gain, love.

CHAPTER THREE

Guide; guide yourself home to the dome of loved profoundly / content; content to be within the three who roam profoundly / dine; dine at the roan profound / mapped; mapped and dated profoundly / fabulous; fabulous news and the living profound / festive; festive weaves profound / festoon; festoon this dream profound / garland; garland gives good lend to the pay that is, profound / drape; drape the crystals domed within the profound / regard; regard the card and the living display called perfectly profound / enjoyed; enjoyed the sounds profound / rivers; rivers deliver the liver profound / flowed; flowed into sounds profound / epics; epics mean the scene's profound / historical; historical agree to be profound and the constitutional agree to freely speak of light and love / mysterious; mysterious weaves profound too, love / lavish; lavish to the leaves profound / depend; depend on the send profound / moods; moods soothe profoundly /

preservation; preservation begins profoundly / prosper; prosper and yes we will, profoundly / carmel; carmel amend thinly profound / private; private we will be profoundly / guides; guides deal with the seal profound / tours; tours secure within the profound / visits; visits to the within profound / delicacies; delicacies due to the lend profound / grand; grand and due to the profound / greets. . greets a swollen plane profound / isle; isle be, profound / hope; hope to see the profound / wassaw; wassaw blues profound / tangles; tangles keep us lose to the profound / feet; feet keep the rounds profound / rubs; rubs like alcohols deep skin profound / prints; prints the seas profound / bed; bed atop the top profound / bath; bath in seats profound / hair; hair's care profound / care; care to share the profound / beach; beach blue in the sands profound / cottages; cottages glued with the profound / shops; shops like these the One's profound / coasting; coasting and roasting in the profound / oaks; oaks delicious in the profound / crescents; crescents cruise the phases and glues profound / diamond; diamond due to the lines profound / site; site of the rite profound / Hutchinson; Hutchinson son profound / pulaski; pulaski true and blew to the style profound / mcqueen; mcqueen seen in the profound / garden; garden grew green and profound / evil; evil forgets the friendships of love and the light begin to be profound / thunderbolts; thunderbolts delivery is the love that is, profound / heartbeats; heartbeats keep the seats profound / cement; cement blue and the stance profound / paves; paves waves profound / city; city dues profound / cemetery; cemetery trued release to the life profound / exclude; exclude and rudely gone to the round profound / exclusives; exclusives protected be the weld profound / collects; collects the sort 13 ways profound / staffs; staffs long on the trends profound / rods; rods sought found, profane and profound.

CHAPTER FOUR

Franklin's; Franklin's meant is sacred too, the electricity is, profound / forsyth; forsyth scene in the proof that is, profound / squares; squares recede to the evidence vital to the residence precisely in too, love / 22; 22 ways to be, profound / savannah's; savannah's the queen's profound / heads; heads to the median septum and scene the murder is done and the light is profound in the ground electric / wave; found a wave and waved often too, love is, profound / wall; walls belong to the profound climb called love / ark; arks reside in the stride provident called proof positive is the profound, love / fish; fish in the dish profound / regional; regional silence overcome profoundly / regional; regional silence overcome profoundly / grouped; grouped like a troop that is, profound / fine; fine to the days profound / range; range done and found, profound / expressions; expressions within and ascend profoundly too, love / settee; settee sat upon is lovely, profound / play-full; play-fully done and loved too, the profound / share; share the power, be, profound / viewer; viewer dealt the felt profound / reviews; reviews the news profound, and again, profound / gaze; gaze at the stays profound / eye; eye on the news and the blinks profound / preview; preview the dues profound / require; require the hire profound / architects; architects due the

buildings grand and randled profoundly / pleasure; pleasure's measures profoundly done, love / smoke; smoke the bowls filled with the profound / family; family found with the moves profound / reward; reward the friend who fends for the profound / vacate; vacate best in the address of love, this my friend is, profound / ideas; ideas and dues profound / uniquely; uniquely and snugly fit with the profound / formidable; formidable foes fell down in the ground fertile with love and fecund with the profound / defends; defends the snooze profound / michael; michael blues overcome, profoundly / hands; hands on the horns altar deep in the profound / swing; swing to the tunes profound / stroke; stroke the throat profound / design; design the signs profound / martins; martins and smart ones, profound / grahams; grahams wet with the crisp deliver of a bill of forgiven and fed within the freed up ways to be profoundly wealthy in love / willow; willow winds blew on you, profoundly / raft; raft the new, forever flows nightly to the profound / reed; reed deep in the red deliver of the green tree called profound / bulrush; bulrush timed to deliver the messiahs of love, arc-angels give profoundly, live it, love / basket; baskets full of love and the belief in God's sweet living profound / turkish; turkish expect comes to sweet apricot spreads of the breads profound / tunes; tunes of the times profound / dolphin; dolphin deals with the profound / breath; breath driving the trine profound, God, is, Hu-man / tubal; tubal ligates and the litigate won by the son of God, profound / spined; spined like a lined delivery of the profound / whales; whales who show the snow delivery to the rose of sharonic bliss, the pharoahs knew the news profound / boots; boots of deep forgive and the fit perfect in the profound / Columbia; Columbia bliss and the blues of the river that's hooded with a throat full of love / stroll; stroll to the store that is more than just this, the real estate, profound / imagine; imagine this and the kiss profound / universally; universally sound and the ground is, profound / sacred; sacred to the ascend that is profound / profane; profane and profound our friend is , this is it, the love is, profound / arcane; arcane and the name, profound / assured; assured by the emotive devotive called the profoundest way to say, I love, God / secure; secure in my treasure and the pleasure that is, uniquely done, the profound / life; life is give and live, profoundly.

CHAPTER FIVE

Excursion; excursion comes into the profound / circle; circle broken heals, the profound / go; go to the one who shews the best, profound / goes; goes to the shows profound / gone; gone to the congo sung as the one profound / parks; parks is the won, profound / drives; drives like the sun's profound / stays; stays like the song's profound / try; try to the trial profound / do; do the new profound / deal; deal made about the proclaim profound / show; show me how to be profoundly, one / squarely; squarely hired as the One, profound / soundly; soundly due the profound / solidly; solidly done, the profound / towering; towering timed profoundly / acres; acres to meet and the sweet profound / ponds; proud to be ponds deep in the loving profound / wooded; wooded like a swoon profound within, love / open; open to the sum, e

= u to the p, profound / stalls; stalls over and open up about the cups profound / rings; rings exchanged profoundly, loved / rides; rides like the strides profound / homes; homes and agains, profound / found; found a date, profound / mortgages; mortgages made and paid, profoundly / sold; sold like the blues, profound / move; move the mounds, profoundly / trade; trade twos to one, profoundly / vibrates; vibrates like a rate, profound / contracts; contracts for more, profoundly / constructs; constructs bridged within the profound / choose; choose to be, profoundly, loved / compare; compare this hour, the profound / build; build a suit, profound / decide; decide to be, profound / evaluate; evaluate your state, profound / designate; designate the state of surrender as profound / evaluate; evaluate the rate of recover as profound / value; value your dates profoundly / organize; organize the coming delivery is free to the profound / comprehend; comprehend again the heal that is, profound / compare; compare the share as confessed profoundly / select; select a note profound / erect; erect a decision, profound / locate; locate the date, profound / important; important decision made, make the pave, profound / decisions; decisions due to the profound in you and, love / levels; levels of forgive and the live profound / layers; layers the wind like the kind profound / divisions; divisions deal with the layers profound / lanes; lanes open and again, profound / historic; historically speaking I am, profound / present; present the spinning profound / now; now the say that is profound, loved / original; original to a nature profane, profoundly rooted in love / preserved; preserved by a state, profound / gorge; gorge run to the sun profound / gorgeous; gorgeous and due to the profound / best; best and abreast the profound / victory; victory revealed profound / row; row and know the profound / restored; restored and the sword is, profound / stately; stately sorts, profound.

CHAPTER SIX
Jewels; jewels of the balance regained and the lost reward repair to the lightened glare of physical exude and the rapture profound in love / custom; custom to a nature profound / enclosure; enclosure requested and the rated profound / waterfront; waterfront to the wills of the hills called profound / winds; winds and the sends so profound / breeze; breeze and the trends profane to a breath celled profoundly / luxuries; luxuries bought proof of the profound / dreams; dreams deal within the profound / managed; managed to be profound / served; served to the seeds profound / operational; operational extremes profound / intact; intact to the extent that is profound / perfect; perfect to the assert that is, profound / strong; strong and round the profound / engaged; engaged in the streets profound / curves; curves and swerves profound / lakes; lakes and streams that gleam profoundly / streams; streams and the seams profound / rivers; rivers, givers, profound / beaches; beaches come to me profoundly / intracoastal; love's intracoastal high way is the profound / coastal; coastal to a host of the light waved profound / sound; sounds right to leave thee profound / curtain; curtain treed profound / mossy; mossy to the creeks profound / creek; creek decreed as profound to the flow of love / green; green to the scene profound / decorates; decorates the

states profound / decor; decor of the soars profound / decorum; decorums summed the One profound / manners; manners extreme to the glands profound / polite; polite to the glance that is, profound / southern; southern timed and the decree is, profanely profound / tabled; tabled in the trend profound / salt; salt scenes profound / marsh; marsh water days profound / colors; colors profound / stills; stills see the life lights profound / loves; loves hold is, profound / gulls; gulls flew to the streaming gulf profound / heroes; heroes head for the lands profound / service; service tattooed on the nude elect of the living profound / forts; forts who sort for love, profound / candles; candles and dues profound / candlelight; candlelight sight profound / bamboo; bamboo agree to be, profound / fountains; fountains green to the letters profound / trickle; trickle over to the language profound / hills; hills who love to be profoundly heard in the echoing ring labyrinth freed too, love / learn; learn to befriend the profound / place; place this taste at the sate profound / happen; happens to see the profound / crowned; crowned and reviewed the profound / resourced; resourced and deemed thee, profound / walks; walks built with stilts profound / hospitals; hospitals see the profound degrees hu-man / saunter; saunter to the counter profound / sashay; sashay to the say that is, profound / piercing; piercing the needles profound / centers; centers and sore to the need to be profound / oasis; oasis built in the trees of love, that is, profound / artifice; artifice summed profoundly / artifacts; artifacts, recover, profoundly / desert; desert sort that is found profound.

CHAPTER SEVEN
Eclectic; poetic, eclectic, electric, the dreams, profound / burns; burns and turns to the flames profound / burning; burning the tributes profound / desirous; desirous of hire us, profoundly / electric; electric and assumed the relaxed state called profound / spirits; spirits that hear us, profoundly / spirited; spirited with a friendly designate called profoundly, love / vote; vote a note profound / pick; pick your change, profoundly / choose; choose another stunt, profound / elect; elect the sect profound / noon; noon and the tune profound / import; import the sortee profound / impart; impart the start profound / sort; sorts of courts called silently bobbing in the profound / compare; compare to be profound / museums; museums subtle in the shuttle regarded as profound / cruise; cruise the light's regard, profound / ticketed; ticketed and flew to the light regard, profound / clothed; clothed in the rode profound / formal; formal ascend to the friends profound / casual; casual agree to be together profoundly / pro; pro knows the profound / probate; profound probate can end in love / treat; treat yourself to the shelf profound / refuge; refuge comes to the ones who love profoundly / greek; greeks and guns know compare profound / roman; roman days stayed at the light profound / victorian; victorian views profoundly due too, love / venetian; venetian agree to be, profound / seas; seas and sees profound / signs; signs and signs profound / signatures; signatures about and upon the profound / forge; forge a note, profound / market; market sorts profound / seasons; seasons of reasons profound / sands; sands and lends profound / lands;

lands and days that won by the lights profound / dirt; dirt and the fires profound / grounds; grounds and clays profound / winding; winding and singing profoundly / lace; lace around the profound / climates; climates and cubes profound / congress; congress will choose the light profound / congressional; congressional agree to vote for the sort profound / carvings; carvings, cue-ings, cubings, love's, profound / intention; intention dimension regards profound / survival; survival is annual to the perennial profound / colonies; colonies and cures for the assures that see profoundly / 13's; real 13's and love is profound / units; units unite and excite the profound / unitary; unitary ignite in the light profound / solitary; solitary decide to be profound / alone; alone and together we are profound / together; together we sew the light threaded glow of good agree to be profound / whether; whether or knot profound / knot; knot and need profoundly / demolition; demolition decreed as agreed profoundly / rebirth; rebirth and the seat is profound / gains; gains and strains profound / areas; areas alert to the spurt profound / witness; witness dues and the reviews profound / legacy; legacy and cues profoundly agreed too, the inherit is, love / regents; regents feed the light profound.

CHAPTER EIGHT
Creeks; creeks that seek the salty seas of love is, profound / silk; silk dues profound / matters; matters electrical and the shatters profound / bluffs; bluffs enough about the profound / ascensions; ascensions and sends to the sands profound / open; open states profound / churched; churched in a matter, profound / mothered; mothered and mu-ed in the profound / gothic; gothic elects the profound in views built on love / Corinthian; Corinthian chants eschewed and agreed upon profoundly / literacy; literacy agreed to and clinical too, the profound / portraits; portraits blissed in the kiss optimistic and the caustic agree to decree the past new to a picture called love / communal; communal ascend to the profound / communities; communities concur to agree to the cede profound / unspoiled; unspoiled and degreed, the profound / golden; goldenly dear to the profound access called love / spaniards; spaniards escape the avenue of fountains youthfulness and dues too, the profound / gold; gold access to the stress that is profound / granite; granite grew the rocking profound / meet; meet the neat profound / italian; italian and I see the striping profound / hispanic; hispanic hills pyrenees deep in the living profound / sterling; sterling's accent is the hints profound in love / expose; expose the nose that smells the profound / marinas; marinas meet the clans opened to the profound / boats; boats that float to the profound / academic; academically due to the lights profound / supreme; a supreme anthem, man, profound / summer; summer of gives and the lives profound / spring; spring about the shouts profound and the sounds profane / meteors; meteors and showers profound / meters; meters kneel at the heels of measures profound / meteorological; meteorological amuse at the muse profane, profound / partners; partners cleanse the lens profound / friends; friends befriend the profound / kinds; kinds who knew the profound / profane; profane to the views profound / profound;

The I AM that is, profound / contemporary; contemporary agree to be, profound / free; free the Tibetan weave called the eaves profound / logical; logical and knew the profound / local; local forensic concede to the need to be profound / specialist; specialist sent to seal the profound / artist; artist of the dues profound / tradition; tradition and missions profound / heritage; heritage hues profound / business; business blues profound / grace; grace and given the profound / prowess; prowess given the living profound / generations; generations of the states profound / decade; decade debonair to the cares profound / millennium; millenium comes to the crumbs profound / 21; 21 days to shaves profound / 48; 48 deals to heal the profound / 46; 46 meets and the ways profound / 44; 44 times the symmetry profound / 42; 42 more and the score profound / 2; 2 to delve to and the to be profound / by; by the skies profound / Twice; Twice and again, the profound / factoring; factoring in the assimilate called great and goes to the profound / numeric; numeric and won by the lanes profound / atlantic; atlantic concede agreed upon in seas profound / hosts; hosts and whole-y ghosts profound.

CHAPTER NINE
Fish; fish the neighborhoods of water deep with love's proclaim of the profound / water; eater weel within the profound / port; port of the sort profound / boats; boats that float within the profound / barge; barge keeps the deeps profound / transport; transport the sort who win profoundly / commerce; commerce forgive st he excuse profound / commercial; commercial ventures fund the profound / receipt; receipt of revenues profound / revenues; revenues and the excuses profound / reviews; reviews like reign upon the profound / things; things and dues profound / cash; cash credits you with the news profound / warm; warm and agreed too, the profound / abundant; abundant and beatific in the extrude profound / magnetize; magnetize your set of agrees to be, profound / finds; finds a date, profound, too, love / links; links the sink into the links profound / attract; attract the sort who live profoundly / attracts; attracts the sites within the profound / attractive; attractive to me, the profound / origin; origin, begin, profound / origins; origins witness the wisdom profound / arrive; arrive at five to see the living profound / arrives; arrives the sight divine, profoundly loved / spares; spares despair and shows you truths profound / relates; relates to dues within the profound / relaxed; relaxed in stance, profound / arrival; arrival viewed within the lights profound / friendly; friendly sort to court profoundly / embrace; embrace your friends profoundly / reward; reward given within the profound / resurrect; resurrect the news, she is, profound, this earth / sample; sample example and the within profound / simple; simple due to the light profound / dear; dear to each Other, the profound / date; date the One whose sun is given the prism profound / dote; dote on the violet-blue delivery of the livery of love in the profound / dealer; dealer healer love within profound / facts; facts that last, profoundly / factors; factors about the gain profane and within again profound / fleet; fleet to a neat arrival at love is profound / fleets; fleets and feats arc-ival to the arrival profound / reunions; reunions of

sorts who live profound / rejoice; rejoice about the recover of live is, profound / rejoicing; rejoicing in sorts profound / record; record the date that is profane within the profound / traditions; traditions of chores that resume thee, profound / federal; federal cases close within the profound / revived; revived and inside, the profound / pediments; pediments askew become the clue profound / opened; opened and sealed the reveals profound / columns; columns and porticoes askew withe love is, profound / character; character given the hunt that is, profound / parentage; parentage through the protal profane and the gift is, profound / over; over and done and the son can live profane in the profound gain of love / vaults; vaults of seals revealed in love, profound / arches; arches that arc to the sound profound / ellipses; ellipses eclipses and love is, profound / orbits; orbits that deal with the seals universal and the kissing dispersal of the seed of rehearsal and the scales of profoundly this, love / electrons; electrons amuse with their leaping enthuse for loving attract of the living profound / electrical; electrical and due to the hearts profound / superlative; superlative in nature and forgiven profoundly, love / Well.

CHAPTER TEN

Stone; if stones could breathe, you would too, profoundly / breathing; breathing to a teething degree called profoundly, love / volcano; volcano dues and the news red to green of a raspberry yellow regard for the cards profound too, love / shores; shores that share their edge with loves profound / Hawaii; Hawaii agree to be profound upon, love / Maui; Maui can see the other size of the lends profound too, love / Lanai; Lanai can be profounder still to the agree yellow freed to positions of love / Molokai; Molokai can see from here the land ivy green to the profound agree called love / oahu; oahu is blue with the meeting's set for the family hu-man and the profound delegation of the standing three for love / Kauai; Kauai high with the sands of time and the destination destined to be, profound / Waimea; Waimea can see me from hear, near the steering, profound / forbidden; forbidden to ascendant can be forgiven to the living attribute called profound / spectacular; spectacular and agreed too, profound the sunset boulevarded too, love / sunset; sunset sees the daring we share absolutely too, love / shared; shared and the cared for explain that is, profound / original; original and see this our we can be perfectly unique to the days profound too, love / innovative; innovative to the sedative set, sleep lightly tonight in the arms of the One who wanders less and finds more profoundly thy love / internal; internal agree too, love three, profoundly / international; international and rational, I dedicate my life to the wife pleasant still and profound / invest; invest in the best, you own heart sound, profound / agree; agree to the tuning profound / pursue; pursue another won profound / purchase; purchase surface tension's forgive with a living called light and a life continental within the divide gone away and too, the profound / plan; plan to stand in the profane, profound / hawaiian; hawaiian brackets include the paragraphs of islands parenthetically profound / change; change states profound / moving; moving soon to the land profound /

dogs; dogs stay due to the unconditionally profound / bounds; bounds and to be, profound / perimeters; perimeters decreed to those of us who knew how to be, profound / map; map of the sort who court the profound / select; select the state profound / area; area given is woven with delicate waves of landings and flights fortunate in love's profound estate / designate; designate the way you will be, profoundly / charge; charge the status to the gratis called plainly profound / know; know where to see the profound / note; note that this is the shilling spent to own the profound / arrive; arrive soon in the room of love that is yours and sores are clean and healed by the seas round the profound materials of love / culinary; culinary delight and the cakes profound / perfect; perfect to the sort that is, profound / precious; precious and ascendant too, love / precise; precise and the sum is, love / stellar; stellar and the power that is within, love, profound / solve; solve a resolve too and live a life of love is true too, profound / solved; solved a matter for explain and the standard profound / solar; solar plan to span the reference with the give in, profound / solvent; solvent and aspirational to the inspired respect for love due the profound / solicit; solicit the due profound / solicitous; solicitous and perfect too in the profoundest dues of love / passions; passions healed and the zeal profound / protrude; protrude deep into the value profound / portray; portray the days as profound / portrait; painted states profoundest too / powerful; powerful with the gift profound / premium; premium dues about him profound / pleasures; pleasures exact to the fact profound / pleasant; pleasant aspect and the rally abounds with love for the gift that is, profound / plow; plow the current with the vibrate profound / pacific; pacific rimmed deliver of the giver profound / trench; trench voted coats of lights profound / reef; reef runs the coral beds red with orange delight and the yellows who sing for the team Metatron. life is on to the dreams of the like profound / ring; ring around and the sound profound / fire; fire a stare at the where that is proofed profoundly / Map.

CHAPTER ELEVEN

Rim; rim of the stood for profoundly too, love / volcanic; volcanic ascend and the mend metatronic to the profound astound called love / value; value set on the bet Metatronic and the resplendent One flown too, paternal dues, God's way, profound / focal; focal to a noted devote called the pattern perfectly profound / vocal; vocally said and the bed is profoundest with true love / trim; trim the times ascendant and fine in the palace arc wide to profoundest love / transcendent; transcendent to the coming stay within the profound and this is it, love / defendant; defendant ascendant metatronically profound / pray; pray about the stout way profound too, love / medicate; medicate less with the test that is less then all the way profound / meditate; love is meditated within and with One who is profound / master; master the plaster parisian and profound / more; more than the shore, profound / social; social dues and the news is profound / votive; votive to the elective profound and the candle flamed in love / vocate; vocate about the shout profound / range; range found within the sounds profound / whizzing; whizzing sounds let go to the profound / shore; shore chaired in the profound / listen; listen to the glisten profound / learn; learn the stern and the bow, profound / respect; respect the decks profound / sort; sort of yet, profound / reason; reason within the profound / response; response set on the bets profound / sort; sort your dues in a vertical news that is, profound / reason; reason due to the profound / response; response ability is agile to the sound profound / sensation; sensation elation profound / legal; legal dues profound / legacy; legacy of the heals profound / smart; smart to start within thee profound / sure; sure to hear the profound agree too, love / absolute; absolute and cute too, love is, profound / command; command the stand profound / districts; districts of the sorts profound / divisions; divisions who seal the will within the profound / advents; advents of extents profound / avenues; avenues that view us strictly profound / marks; marks a lift up to profound / opinions; opinions in the profound / votes; votes a lot about the profound / event; events and dues profound / china; china time a go too love profound / tibet; tibet set on the living profound / empire; empire entire too, love is, profound / revolution; revolution of the decision to be thee profound / solution; solution set upon the profound / love; love to live in the vessel profound / locate; locates a note due, profoundly / one; one who knew two profoundly / people; people who plan to be profound / plans; plans to date the state profound / places; places where you remember thee, profound / stands; stands about within the profound / average; average cares profound / understood; understood to be, profound / openings; openings give the living profound / athletic; athletic and agree too the game is profound / fit; fit to be tried profoundly / fine; fine enough to see the profound / forthright; forthright about the flight profound / compare; compare the spare and know the care profound / concede; concede that we'd elected stand to only lands profound / cure; cure your nature with assure profound / mirrored; mirrored by the plenty, profound / mend; mend a send with the stain profound.

CHAPTER TWELVE
Candle; candle flamed deliver of the marco isled forgiver and the given trend to living in the light called Metatron, profound astound of love / flame; flame that fills with the heels profound / points; points of deceit have gone to the sun profound / revolves; philadelphia blue revolve of the solve profound / resolution; resolution becomes the sum profound / premonition; premonition of cognition and the congregation of a council profound / hunch; a hunch about the shout profound / guarantee; guarantee your state the sate profound / appetize; appetize best with the rest profound / appetite; appetite secure within the assure that is, profound / flair; flair for the dare for profoundments / specialties; specialties that vote for the sate profound / renaissance; renaissance flair and the care protonically profound too, love / Florentine; Florentine decree and the free allow to vow to be profound / Florence; Florence best in the invest profound / lead; lead the wave profound / appreciate; appreciate the state unconditional and the rendition that is this, profound / style; style and while, profound / await; await the state that wins profoundly love / ways;

ways and stays profoundest / peaks; peaks and dales profanely profound / vales; vales and heights profound / crucible; crucible which burns with the yearns profound / fastens; fastens a note to the devote called love is, profound / absolutely; absolutely and resolutely profound / personal; personal to a validation called profound / affront; affront the status profound / disgrace; disgrace over, wear the status profound / negligence; negligence begun to travel less in the circles profound / known; known by the truth, profound / good-bye; good-bye to delude that is, profound / good night; good night sweet delight and the states profound / good faith; good faith's estimate is yes, profound / good fight; good fight and the flights profound / good time; good time to view the stratosphere profound / good try; good try and the truth is, profound / good fight; good fight over, well won, profound / good time; good time to come, profoundly / good try; good try given the nest profound / good enough; good enough to believe in, the profound / good; good day come, profound / goods; goods on the news profound / sensational; sensational to the steed profound / sharp; sharp and harp within the profound / striking; striking a note of devotion profound / start; start to see the we profound / senses; senses that snooze in the news profound / switch; switch to the start and the heart is, profound / memory; memory due and over too, profound / track; track the One, profoundly / emerge; emerge the victorious one, profound / chrysalis; chrysalis emerged profoundly / butterfly; butterfly ways and luna days of the winged elate called love is, profound / winged; winged wow profound / worthy; worthy of the status profound / meetings; meetings due to the shoes profound / heavens; heavens that heal in the meals profound / ring; ring around the sonnets profound / rather; rather be and we are, profound / rebel; rebel around thee, profoundly, due, love / rustle; rustle a hustle to the streets solidly profound / wrestle; wrestle less with the tests profound / cut; cut to the chase over profoundly / cord; cord curled in the profound / forgive; forgive and yes, forget this, profoundly, love / compassion; compassion is the forgive profound.

CHAPTER THIRTEEN
Predict; predict the strict align profound / predictions; predictions which give the live too, profound / future; future of the sort profound / faiths; faiths felt profoundly / fates; fates filled in the healed profoundly, love / foibles; foibles about thee, profound / foils; foils of the reflective state profound / mates; mates due the profound / mattered; mattered to the smattered less, profound / meaning; meaning comes to the sons profound / links; links and news profound / unfold; unfold and date yourself profoundly / fortune; fortune and the state profound / heeds; heeds a glad revive profound / hearken; hearken and starkly profound / hold; hold the state profound / Kabbalah; Kabbalah's assign is within the profound / coils; coils and stages profound / codes; codes cubed profoundly / prepare; prepare to be, profound / today; today and stay, profound / respect; respect given the living profound / reflect; reflect in the land that is, profound / reflect; reflect that the state is this, profound / realign; realign with the light inside thee, profound / fashion; fashion and please

profound / fasten; fasten to the button that reads profound / feather; feather nest, profound / find; find the signed profound / placement; placement given profoundly / potential; potential due to the news profound / perfect; perfect reflect of you too, profound / award; award the grade profound / contents; contents of sorts profound / revealed; revealed a state of great elevate profound / unveil; unveil the rude as all you knew profoundly / carry; carry the date to the stallion profound / warriors; warriors decree the sad harmony of broken profounds / shields; shields that state my heart is late, profoundly / lovers; lovers unite in the night that is, profound / fields; fields that flow in the snows profound / mercy; mercy due the kind profounds and the dares enthused with love / seats; seats that sit within the wins profound / thrones; thrones that stare without the care that's less, profound / retreats; retreats and ascends profound / junctures; junctures and joints profound / market; market the sorts profound / met; met at a spiral profound / convene; convene for within to the frank arrival profound / propose; propose the deal, profoundly / proposal; proposal about the shouts profound / knees; knees that bend to the friends profound / relate; relate yes to the ones profound / relax; relax now the one has come to profoundly / regard; regard yourself as loved profoundly / reassigns; reassigns the matters profound, love / racks; racks its training profound / books; books about, profound / beauty; beauty's adjust profound / pentagram; pentagram ways, profound / pins; pins in the hat profound / pentacles; pentacles and a magnificent place called precisely this and the taste is profound / plexigraph; plexigraph findings profoundly drawn too, God / Plutarch; Plutarch and the arc on God is and profoundly too, love / born; born to star in the cause profoundly hu-man.

THE UN-BOUND-MENTS
LEVEL 24

CHAPTER ONE

Unbound; unbound and found in the sounded light called love / hu-mane; hu-mane to a main called unbound / drama; drama due to the few, unbound/ frame; frames draped in the traipse too, the unbound / found; love is found in the sound unbound / riddle; riddle about the shout unbound / cure; love's cure is secure in the light unbound / fit; fit the fitting unbound / freed; freed and the seed too, unbound / confess; confess that duress is less stress in the living unbound / clasp; clasp a news unbound and profound too, love / clue; clues unbound and the sounds of angels singing refrained to the lessen rewound too, love/ fed; fed the led the profound unbound / felt; felt and the melt is, unbound / contrast; contrast about and truly profound / hue; hue and the due, profound / hu-man; hu-man ascend and the free is unbound / span; spans spill the heals profuse in the unbound / eden; eden due the waves of news enlightened still within thee, profound / dan; dan's deal is heal, profoundly / relative; relative to the giving unbound / round; round the date profoundly unbound / ruse; ruse and news profound and unbound/ concede; concede to the we will prove unbounded / never; never knew and always will be profane in our unbounded require for God/ knew; knew the while unbound / none; none and all, the same, profane, unbound / knew; knew that you would be profuse in your unbounded nature of love / know; know the date that rates profoundly unbound / where; where were you when we were three and our profound delivery was profuse in the guides unbound / found; found and the state is unbounded, love / care; care about the sort who stare at the light unbound / bounds; bounds and delays forgive the unfound unbound / bounce; bounce across the stares unbound / lightly; lightly sighted in the unbound / fondly; fondly flew direct to you, the unbounded flame of God's proclaim "my son" well done, God said let us be free / often; often and seen unbounded in love / ever; ever and where unbound / always; always and stays unbounded / evermore; evermore and more positive unbound / essential; essential and seen in the profound unbound / exact; exact to the races profoundly unbound / trace; trace the truce to thee, profound and unbound / degree; degree decreed within, thee, profoundly unbound / degrees; degrees decry the sigh profoundest, unbound / dare; dare to stare into the light unbound / duels; duels that duel into the late relate unbound / dates; dates of nations profoundly unbound / random; random and through to the unbound / routes; routes up rocks unbound / simple; simple and knew the unbound / doubts; doubts about feuds can rely on the noose unbound / erase; erase the strain unbound again / eradicate; eradicate the late regard for the card unbound / expel; expel the Other and know the natives unbound / compel; compel your self unbounded within / regard; regard the cards enlightened in their profusion unbound / lightness; lightness comes but once a year to those who seek security in the nativity of less, profess, profuse relief in the virgin birth of God said, "man" unbound / lifetimes; lifetimes of the jobs decide to be profound in the light reside at love unbound / heart; heart of God, hu-man love unbound / residence; residence given the presidence of living profoundly unbound / jones; jones kept up

with the jeep of seek and the art of bliss unbound / arcs; arcs give me divinity in our being unbound / live; live like gifts who lift to life and the loving delight of the profound unbound.

CHAPTER TWO

Why; why to be? unbound in, love / when; when and how we are to love unbounded / where; where are we to go for love's unbound / often; often in agree too, be unbound by, love / again; again and then unbound / where; where are we when the leaves are green and the sky hawaiian blue; in the sound unbound and the hearts unwound with the living truth called love / which; which mountain this; the one whose sun has come to the granite rooms unbound with love / watts; watts and knots of whats included in the rains of love's unbounded gain / melts; melts dampest in the ledges linked by the instinct rewarded as passionately unbound / matrixed; matrixed and allowed as the sounds of silence and the grand reward for the sword content in the extent languished by the sighs designed as the signs unbound by love/ entry; entry given to the living ascend and the blend detected as love's unbound / pace; pace your set of values as unbounded in love / pulse; pulse the place of an electric face called the review of the pressures spent on the invention called unbound / pose; pose to know the trace unbound / penetrates; penetrates the truth with love's unbound / penchant; penchant for the penchant unbound in, love / promote; promote the vote for a note of love is unbound / heat; heat is over come through light's unbound / fertile; fertile nature of love found, unbound / fire; fire overcomes the old with news unbounded / facts; facts due to the tracks unbound / nova; nova supreme and the cream unbound / supreme; supreme-est being, unbound / being; being due the light unbound / hu-man; hu-man and true too, unbound / God; God is giving the unbound true love / gone; gone to the summed unbound / within; within and within the unbound / rich; rich enough to last entrenched in the unbound / billions; billions of galactic friends Milky Way deep in the sperm of God's seeds of love unbound / money; money and the news unbound / much; much review of the trues unbound / drive; drive to the size unbound / follow; follow me to the tracts unbound / respirate; respire to the higher respirate called unbound / conspire; conspire to see the life unbound / ends; ends drawn linked to the light unbound / kinship; kinship and clues unbounded / kings; kings and the rings unbounded / books; books about the sort of love that's written proofed unbounded / genes; genes unbound and allocated in the light electric and the love elected as unbound / genetics; genetics clue your light unbound / gematric; gematric agree to come unglued by the light unbound / voiced; voiced agree to be all there is too love's unbind unbound / freed; freed the voice of all that's red by your include of the lamb within the framework unbound / speak; speak about the sort who live unbounded within and too, love / elect; elect a reset of the living unbound / submit; submit this commit to the unbound / commit; commit committal to the little unbound / print; print the date on the late unbound / publish; publish the kind who sing the unbound / sell; sell the well to the whole and the all unbound / show; show the single the freedom of two unbound / daring; daring to love the unbound / steps; steps kept unbound / light; light the sights with the flights unbound / also; also and all unbound / place; place of the taste and the natural place of the laughter unbound / laughter; laughter unglued and reglued to the matrix unbound / deepens; deepens and contends to the lighter unbound / spreads; spreads throughout the shout unbound / agreeable; agreeable adoration of the Son unbound / Franciscan; Franciscan allow of the access unbound too, love / froth; froth on the tops unbound.

CHAPTER THREE

Traveling; traveling light in the light within and the metatronic friend called Uriel, angels well within the arc of God's true, love / windows; windows and shows unbounded without love / mars; mars and the cares unbounded within, love / starts; starts like a heart unbound / levels; levels a smart agree to be unbound / states; states and the clearing unbound / status; status about the shouts unbound / astral; astral please and the knees unbound / astronomic; astronomic agree to be demolished by the stress to confess that this love is unbound within the heavens and high and low / evolve; evolve to a state that equates to the light agree to be unbound / grids; grids equip my grip with the lips unbound, spoken only, love / collections; collections of selections unbound / knowings; knowings and showings unbound / cells; cells clamor like hammer unbound / universal; universal and well in the spill to the light degree called unbound / crystal; crystal and ways unbound / sphere; sphere wet with elect and the living unbound / 3; 3 new and you blew the cut with the hunt unbound / 4; 4 the love that's found unbound / 5; 5 stays at the days unbound / priority; priority won in the sung profoundly unbound / subsystems; subsystems that equate to the rate unbound / ecological; ecologically well the tale unbound / structure; structure concurrent to the ascendant unbound / suns; suns and truth that's proof unbound / Giza; Giza's gate is lately unbound / china; china drew the rays unbound / china; china seized by the bet unbound / enochian; enochain keys expose the unbound / comes; comes a day tributary to the light tertiary and the empire decreed to be, unbound / saturn; saturn can care like a spare unbound / keyed; keyed and agree upon and the placement unbound / tabular; tabular squares and the cares unbound / race; race like a face unbound in our love / electron; electron news and the views unbound / speed; speed like a flight to a big island sight called love / connective; connective tissues and the sortee unbound / face; face the device of advice unbound / traces; traces enlighten the lighten unbound / magnets; magnets and poles that apart draw us home to the living unbound / meta; meta-bionic and electric too, the unbound within, love / trend; trend set the unbound / spun; spun trued in the unbound / spilling; spilling over unbounded in love / maser; maser's laser unbound / chromatic; chromatic elective unbound / intelligent; intelligent effective unbound / biometric; biometric astound is unbound / example; example the sample unbound / forum; forum that knew the opinion unbound / formation; formation's elation, unbounded within / transmit; transmit the commit too,

unbound / agree; agree to see the light unbound / fuse; fuse like a muse unbound / spaces; spaces traces unbound / places; places remove the binding within and the listening is unbound / dues; dues to be and refused is less unbound / intellect; intellect the resurrect unbound / pyramidal; pyramidal agree too, unbound / stand; stand like a fan unbound / up; up to the views unbounded / God; God grew deep in the lips unbound / Mer; Mer is the miracle mailed too, love / ka; ka is the sort unbound to the ba's release mechanized in the chalice of love's whispered breathing, one heart's elect from love.

CHAPTER FOUR

Thrones; thrones and the seats eternally set on the ledges of God's edge-less reside at the slice unbound / dimensions; live with dimensions eternally set on the let's get inside the unbound / dominion; dominion comes to the undone agree to reside unbound / lands; lands and sands unbound / universe; universes and verses unbound / scriptures; scriptures testify to the truth unbound / substratum; substratum matters unbounded / shapes; shapes and sets unbound / lion; lion shared in the unbound / solar; solar paneled unbound energy / light; lights knew the unbound / plane; plane trains trained in the unbound / she; she is the merger of love's unbound / Ki; the female Ka is the Ki unbound / vah; ascendants vah is the spirit unbound / merkabah; merkabah unbound in the step into love's unwind and the signed agree to be revived by the kinder decree called we're free / Shekinah; Shekinah hours layered in ours eternal in a moment called glee unbound / capstones; capstones concerned with the living unbound / areas; areas agreed to and the light's unbound / pyramids; pyramids deal the seals unbound / anchor; anchor in the Merkabah shield called the unbound / light; God's light is right to the unbound / wheels; wheels in the zeal's unbound / revolve; revolve to a status unbound / reveal; reveal is to love unbound / descend; descend to the end's unbound / ascend; ascend to the lend's unbound / spin; spin in too and truely unbound / intricacy; intricacy profound and unbound / basically; basically bet on the subset unbound / seas; seas astound in the unbound / photonic; photonic the friend unbound / amplify; amplify a stature unbound / centropy; centropy sent to the lit unbound / steps; steps and dues unbound / flow; flows in the snows unbound / paradigms; paradigms burst, unbound / microns; microns sound unbound / emit; emit the fit unbound / corpuscles; corpuscles unbound within too, love / light; lights and days ahead too, love / brain; brain and drain unbound in God's head turned too, love / helmet; helmet headed and the hurling unbound / worn; worn and won in the town unbound / entropic; entropic elect and the reflect unbound / centropic; centropic agreed too unbound / interact; interact in the facts unbound / luminaries; mountains of luminaries loved in the proof called unbound / illumination; illumination's sun unbound within love / man; man is proof of the unbound / stars; stars and cares unify in the life unbounded / continuum; continuum's invent is the ventured intent called lightly we politely lead too love, unbound / continuity; continuity sent to the profound unbound / eighth;

eighth and the eight that agree to the treat that's unbound / link; link and up too, the unbounded view of love / overself; overself stuff overdue for review know the peace of release to the clues coincidental to the incidental called love unbound / high self; high self and true to the Enochian reunite called the codices of love unbound / Christ; Christ and the sort unbound / body; body blue and the heart unbound / serve; serve a state unbound / follow; follow a fathom called unbound / lead; lead to the seed that is strictly unbounded / describe; describe the scribe unbound / purify; purify the slate that is late for the life unbound.

CHAPTER FIVE

YHWH; flaming within in the grid lenticular to a matricular material called love in the unbounded glory of God / Torah; proof of the Torah's scoop for love is, unbound / pyramids; pyramids and grids unbound / hu-man; hu-man continent aligned with the plan unbound for love / temple; temple of man and the plan to build a field united with love is, unbound / God; God gives good love unbound with obstructions and aches of the heart / gains; gains strained for can align with the healing inside and see the ceiling of love's eternal unbind / explain; explain the substance of your name and the light proclaim for God is, love, unbound / light; light enough to see unbound / human; human's diagram and the hearth of man, the bed ahead to love unbound / pyramid; pyramid amid the unbound / two; two to too and two who knew that life can be unbound within this grid celestial hu-man / too; too and always knew thee, unbound / divine; divine delegation come to the Son's arrive at the stand unbound hu-man / appear; appear as the near and the star that is here for our hearts resign at the sign symbolic of love, Humanity, unbound / I AM; I AM dear to the unbound / I am; I am voiced in the still small way unbound / We Are; We Are the Ones God waited on, unbound again, too, love / 12; 12 who knew the rules unbound / 24; 24 more who soar for the band unbound / 1; 1 who knew the way home through the light unbound / Orion; Orion spent on the invitation called alignment threes designated place for the grid poles shifted too, love, unbound / Pleadian; Pleadian agree to be unbound / Foundations; Foundations shook by the unbound agreement too, love / march; march to the place of love this unbound way of God's / miracles; miracles mill about the seals of love's unbound / light; light disgrace has come undone to the ones supine in the life of love, unbound / time; time to see the light unbound / clocks; clocks that struck the chimes of lines untangled by the unbound / Taurus; Taurus is through and the test has come unbound / unlocks; unlocks like shocks unbound in the lightening hu-man / mithra; mithra has come undone in loving unbind, the unbound / done; done to the One unbound / 12 grids; 12 grids slid to the unbound / 12 tribes; 12 tribes that side with the light unbound / lords; lords of swords unbound / Atlantean; Atlantean seems and the gleams of sees complete with the replete notion that we are all there is to . the love crystalline and beyond the seem to God is unbound / gap; gap's elude and the allude over the regress to the ingress and the hope for reciprocation in love's grand unbound / cycles; cycles

fit and this is complete in the seen delivery of God's require for the aspirant residual called fleet to the central spark in the re-ignition of the arc God is, unbound / Israel; Israel reads the news that Haffa hews a new reward called the cord of God's delivery from the livery of requisite forgive and the living entreaty to seat yourself well in the sword that only God can render and Michael hearing knows the news; "thy kingdom come"; unbound again, love / implant; implants can live in the wards of temples dearest you, know the few who can give their all for the cause unbound / upgrade; upgrade given on the living you've been fearing and the fellow knows the nearing of the careering called unbound within, love / light; light enough to see and the faith to believe in the angelic hum called the sum, unbound, every One / dove; dove knows the necks of men, speak the truth, God, unbound / initiation; initiation is over, you can now recover all you are owed, by the energetic deposit of your hands in God's and your realize that God is, good, unbound / plane; plane of arrival, heaven's gate, your heart is unbound / grids; grids and seats set deep in the heart of God's recover of love, unbound / points; points that win the news unbound / Joseph; Joseph said "I am ahead within, God's rainbow is the harp I know and the sound of forever lives in the coat of love, unbound"/ Moses; Moses is the song of delivery from the wilderness of centrific force against the nature of gales of living unbound / jesus; jesus wants to hang with you and your homeys all weekend and forever in your heart unbound / Sinai; Sinai convenes at the tunes unbound and the tablets printed on grace's word, God is, love / geophysics; geophysics and the seek reassigned a name, your own, coupled within, God, unbound / exodus; exodus due to plates tectonic and the plunge from Fira's heights into the seas of love's unbind, God / stations; stations directed to give good radio casts of classes called love, unbound / aerials; aerials and photos in the spread metatronic and the lead basically to the humanity camp called unbound / magnetic; magnetic center and the renter sublime in the purchase that's kept unbound / earth; earth can worth your recover in the deliver unbound / one's cell; one's cell is the magnet and the keeping is the care of the battery of love, unbound within, mitochondrial spin to the sparking begin to remember, love / one atom; one atom and one Adam and one Kadmon and one belief that the light is on in the interior now of God's people unbound / Bermuda; Bermuda and known by the canti-lever triangle that moans with recovery of the zone of forget and remember unbound / Salt Lake; Salt Lake's recover of the sister revived at the sea Galilee and the well sold resides now within the friend of recover and the woman who knew that God lives in you, know the One, unbound / Hebron; Hebron zoned as owned by the yellow now can give the green of lime recovery of the heart shock called love's remember, unbound / yucatan; yucatan pretend can be gone to the height of recovery called light is the unbound.

CHAPTER SIX

Sands; sands of times sublime in the lime agreed too, profoundly, undoubtedly unbound / pearls; pearls and swirls and layers of precious agree to be unbound / hearts; hearts and starts unbound / lands; lands of the sounds unbound / lamb; lamb of the Christos comes to the news unbound / key; key of seas updated and the pleasant unbound / pleiades; pleiades require of the hire profound and the life unbound / stars; stars by far unbound / genesis; genesis of the nemesis gone to sleep unbound / create; create the state unbound / let; let us be unbound / there; there are the sees into the unbound / be; be unbound / light; light signs unbound / seed; seed won unbound / crystal; crystal seed unbound / planted; planted expansively unbound / galaxy; galaxy grew and the new unbound / salt; salt lake the stare at the care occupied within thee, unbound / celestial; celestial scenes uniquely unbound / earth; earth's mirth is unbound / progeny; progeny sent to the invent unbound / birth; birth's units unbound / crystalline; crystalline and the mezzanine unbound / scrolls; scrolls crescendo in the rolls of waves unbound / reveal; reveal the reveal that is, unbound / thrones; thrones and the romboid incredulous too, love / Orion; Orion's within our agree to be profound / adamic; adamic agreed too, profound / seed; seed units profound / accept; accept the note profound unbound / Christ; Christ is the vote unbound / Buddha; Buddha too, unbound / channel; channels abound in thee unbound / service; services due with the unbound / creation; creation sensation unbound / the salt; the salt and the wound that got away through the unbound / seeds; seeds explosive with their incisive agree to be upright in the light beyond, unbound / twelves; twelves and those who know the doubling speed of the twenty-four around the throne, the chromosomes are, unbound / fields; fields and the electives worn as shields too long, now thrown away, the unbound / urim; urim is the summing oration of the voiced resignation to less, know confess of the All called centrifically love, unbound / thummim; thummim profound in the living unbound / open; open the case closed by direct expose and know the sunny sort who pose in the / land of sweet remember, help is near, call the clear unbound / clear; clear the debts with nets electric and respect for the highest pulse, the ghost of / forgive and the living won by those who sun in God directly unbound / great; great and white to the sight unbound / white; white enough to see through clearly, the light, brotherhood, unbound / thrones; thrones who say were all elected today and forever, unbound / saint; saint of the moments unbound / louis; louis still in the hills seventeen and the scene elect in the respect unbound invisible; invisible to a matter unbound / zion; zion's sound is unbound / gravity's; gravity's growth is both, unbound / trap; trap set is the elect to move for less then unbound / reversed; reversed the trap by a nap in the unbound / Pleiades; Pleiades assert that all is well in the fellows unbound / cradle; cradle the sort who nurture this earth in the unbound / birth; birth begun in the sung, unbound / grown; grown like a weed that is, unbound / spectrum; spectrum of the rule to be, unbound / blueprints; blueprints become you, unbound / physical; physical to a dome within the unbound / higher; higher the aspire, is, unbound / universal; universal to the point, unbound.

CHAPTER SEVEN

Ze; ze of the way unbound / magnetic; magnetic and north through the points of return to the poles, unbound / kolab; kolab strict in the dialect unbound / Kimah; Kimah and crew, unbound / kesil; kesil cubed in the knew unbound / six; six who stick to the unbound / together; together and ever we will be, unbound / lights; lights and sights unbound / arcturus; arcturus reports the sorts unbound / mid; mid the state unbound / way; way home to the portal unbound / runway; runway lights unbound / runaway; runaway recovered, unbound / waterways; waterways wound through the annual sound of the flush coming through the direction unbound / whitewater; whitewater days and the leis unbound / respect; respect-full and free to be the unbound / snapped; snapped a judgement shut to reveal the unbound / short; short report unbound / cavort; cavort to the sort unbound / content; content to be, unbound / casual; casual and free in our resurrect of the neck of unbound / comfort; comfort cued in the unbound / sort; sort of the sorts unbound / social; social and natural unbound / serial; serial to a nation unbound / limited; limited and crowned the unbound / limit-free; limit-free, the unbound / tybee; tybee seas descend the unbound / to be; to be allowed to leave unbound / paddle; paddle the saddle unbound / purvey; purvey the stave unbound / survey; survey the duty to be, unbound / Jefferson; Jeffersonian agree to see the truth unbound / wonders; wonders and thunders abound unbound / signs; signs and the scenes unbound / refuge; refuge sounds like towns unbound / players; players move to the plan unbound / paid; paid to be free, unbound / destiny; destiny comes in the sums of surrender and the living unbound / mapmaker; mapmaker found in the deluge round the properly sung regard for the cards elective and the professional attend to the Friend unbound / chosen; chosen and true, the few, who believe in the Christos unbound / every; every day I am unbound / all; all free to be unbound / manys; manys and mays unbound / more; more to see, the unbound / build; build a net to correct the unbound / busy; busy ways to be unbound / barge; barge full of the seas unbound / collecting; collecting the sought, unbound / fishing; fishing with nets unbound / shelling; shelling and sums unbound / sport; sport about the hu-man sort of connect called love is direct to the points unbound / hu-man; hu-man elect and the pillars of love, unbound / nationals; nationals who cash in on the Friend unbound / greens; greens paid to be in the shade unbound / turning; turning to view the elect in you and your agree to be, unbound / hearts; hearts that heal in thee unbound / help; help a neighbor see, the unbound / aid; aid for the ones who surrender in the unbound / cover; cover the covers with lovers unbound / recover; recover the sort who give with unbound / covers; covers blown include untoward advance into the unbound / miracles; miracles kept have occurred, enjoy the unbound / rhyme and rhythms; rhyme and rhythms returned into the tune unbound.

CHAPTER EIGHT

Pleasant; pleasantly pointing at love freed within the unbound / points; points and joints unbound / twelfth; twelfth days unbound / times; times of the signs unbound / plus; plus a note for the votes unbound / ones; ones who say that they are unbound / count; count on the suns of arrival at the funds unbound / quarters; quarters shared and compared with only the sorts unbound / islands; islands count in the found unbound / whispers; whispers and letters unbound / wands; wands and travels magic is, unbound / warm; warm at the shares unbound / what; what a land can stand for, unbound / watt; watts burn with the Friend unbound / wedding; wedding days unbound / met; met like the bounty unbound / alchemy; alchemy of sings the trained unbound / alchemical; alchemical and freed within the unbound / trued; trued enough to breed the unbound / plumb; plumb and plunged to the freed unbound / coast; coast to coast a bi-lingual tongue unbound / open; open your doors to the Friends understood unbound / clear; clear the plates and the place unbound / dear; dear to you, the unbound / delve; delve well into the cell unbound / done; done to you and the few who knew the unbound / retire; retire to the hire professionally secure and the sure agree to be profoundly wealthy in love unbound / resign; resign to the seed unbound / reside; reside like a side that is, unbound / comprehend; comprehend the ascend that is intentional unbound / plant; plant yourself in the heart unbound / blends; blends like the signs unbound / plump; plump enough to forget and wise enough to know the show is near thee, the unbound / plumbed; plumbed like the depths of forgotten remembered in love and the seas unbound / connect; connect the reflect and the respect full of remembrance of the goodness of our soul-ed release and God's recovery of the peace that is powerful in our release and our remember of God's good love, unbound / correct; correct I am in my astound at abound in the plane unbound / autobahn; autobahned deliver of the giver unbound / audobon; audobon consignment driven to the places unbound / bird; bird of the word unbound / birds; birds and curds of the way strewn around you and inside the light astound unbound / completes; completes a creation, the nation, enthused with love's avenues unbound / befriends; befriends and astounds, the One with the sounds of forgive in the unbound / felt; felt like a pelt of remember and the giver unbound / firm; firm regard for the cards unbound / grants; grants a peace, the soul's release to the light unbound / shook; shook like a leaf unbound / shaken; shaken and unfounded in the unbound / faith; faith is secure in the unbound / fuse; fuse lit with the hit unbound / temple; temple ground secure today and all-ways unbound / template; template deep in the secure access to the unbound / find; find a feat unbound / fahrenheit; fahrenheit's gift, the heat, unbound / sustained; sustained each the other, for good, unbound / decide; decide to be found in the unbound / design; design majored in, unbound / scene; scene of the fond arrive at the sides unbound / seen; seen like a scene, unbound / is; is this God's good? Love; unbound / love; love the splash of the cache called unbound / band; band of plenty and the many unbound / men; men who knew who flew unbound / man; man of the allure unbound / hu-manize; hu-manize the harmonics unbound.

CHAPTER NINE: batteries; batteries recharge in the grounded sustain called enlightenment comes in the living unbound / coils;

coils that reward with the sword arc-angelic and the agree to be unbound / generate; generate the state of respect in the lord unbound / juice; juice can leak into the mouth unbound / sustain; sustain us daily dear God unbound / mechanic; mechanics who fix the ellipse unbound / scribe; scribe found a stand unbound / hu-man; hu-man and secure, the unbound / electrical; electrical agree to be free too, the unbound / energy; energy sustains the explain unbound / system; system keep us secured to the see called love, unbound / compliant; compliant in my defiant agree to be unbound / done; done with the deal unbound / welcome; welcome the seem of agree, unbound / home; home to the again of the grin unbound / again; again I say, unbound / liberty; liberty and the lend unbound / mini; mini wares unbound / pools; pools and the swim unbound / freedom; freedom won and the sum is refunded unbound / fresh; fresh agree to be unbound / carrier; carrier of the sort unbound / cooled; cooled enough to see, the unbound / collide; collide at the side unbound / truth; truth of the sort unbound / tavern; tavern state repaired unbound/ tabernacle; tabernacle the same as the name unbound/ fruit; fruit that is, unbound/ freshen; freshen with a mention unbound / luxury; luxury due too, the unbound / product; product of the spins unbound / low; low is unbound within and loved / chapped; chapped by the lapped agree to be unbound / Chesnee; Chesnee seen in the sounds unbound / thrifty; thrifty and neat in the seat unbound / space; space to unbound in, love / welcome; welcome to see, the unbound / central; central to the seem unbound / shorn; shorn by the worn unbound / locks; locks and loons unbound / ledger; ledger wed to the winning unbound / flocks; flocks and the shocks unbound / used; used and seen unbound / print; print a hint of the sent unbound / paint; paint a state unbound / prepare; prepare a stare unbound / share; share a cost unbound / surmise; surmise the rise unbound / dealt; dealt with and unbound within / castle; castle of the queen unbound / quicken; quicken the mention unbound / quadrant; quadrant and accent on the ascent unbound / cupid; cupid is sent to those who invent the space to love within the unbound / propose; propose a rose that is unbound / koi; koi swim in the friend unbound / brom; broom deep in the sweep unbound / listen; listen and extend, unbound within, love / give; give the live unbound / hear; hear a dear agree to be unbound / bamboo; bamboo and the seams asonish within the unbound / hold; hold the sold unbound / sure; sure and see the unbound / techniques; techniques and seeks the unbound / lots; lots and assurance unbound.

CHAPTER TEN
Sphinx; Sphinx said, left shoulders too, and the extension analytic to the clinic called precisely we remember the sender of the heaven scent, love, unbound / Jah; Jah goes and she knows her friend again within the ascend called precisely concisely the advent of the invent unbound / camera; camera cued in the viewed abound too, unbound / concord; concord the sword unbound / record; record the cords unbound / 301; 301 and the blues unbound / blue; blue and the knews unbound / michael; michael cued to reveal the unbound / Gabriel; Gabriel cued and

the mood is reviewed unbound / sure; please be sure and see the reward in the unbound / construct; construct the erupt unbound / new; news and knews unbound / Jerusalem; Jerusalem cued in the viewed unbound / ahh; ahh yes! the unbound / men; men amend the venture unbound / mental; mental agree to be, the unbound / continents; continents collect the erect that's unbound / continental; continental in the blend attendant and the ascendant resides in the lands unbound / concise; concise and the advice is to be unbound / perfect; perfect and the assert is in the unbound / diesel; diesel news and the know is unbound / petrol; petrol pleasure that is, unbound / petroleum; petroleum wet with the access to hearts who require the higher ascend called unbound / oil; oil spills wills unbound / food; food and foods unbound / interchange; interchange the change unbound / columbians; columbians ascend to the vend unbound / creative; creative and the creative unbound / snip; snip to see the unbound / snapped; snapped and the package is unbound / suicide; suicide aside and the note is unbound / notes; notes and the sort unbound / propose; propose a rose unbound / build; build an attend that is in the unbound / zone; zone and the roan unbound / own; own a tailor of your own and the end that is blended to the unbound / sentinel; sentinel and the ascend is the blend in the unbound / citadel; citadel dues to the cues unbound / 26; 26 ways to see the unbound / highways; highways byways and food congealed that is left to confession unbound / waffles; waffles wet with the syrup unbound in the miracles unbound / drives; drives to the moves unbound / burgers; burgers and the size unbound / fries; fries and the skies unbound / children; children and the forgiven unbound / plain; plain and the stain is unbound / plants; plants and the forgive that is unbound / given; given and the ascend is unbound / orientation; orientation over and you are the one that is the friend unbound / assignation; assignation given that the friend is unbound / bet; bet on the bet that is unbound / balanced; balanced and the bend's unbound / friends; friends who end unbound / friendly; friendly the sort, unbound / frank; frank and to the point, unbound / full; full and filled with the unbound / fats; fats and the sorts unbound / surpass; surpass the state unbound / flours; flours and the chill that is unbound / float; float at the note of devote and the gift unbound / cork; cork in the fork that is unbound / uncork; uncork the neck unbound / spry; spry to the true unbound / spell; spell the dwell unbound.

CHAPTER ELEVEN
Share; share the vote, unbound / gift; gift of the pearls unbound / given; given and the send is profound and unbound / grant; grant and the ascendant unbound / publish; publish the notes that are unbound / yes; yes we are and the sound is unbound / magnolia; magnolia and the meet is unbound / magnesium; magnesium and the meeting is set and unbound / mystic; mystic and the mystic unbound / met; met and the veteran can set in the unbound / forgive; forgive the Other unbound within too, love / forget; forget the bet and get it on too, love is, unbound / bull; bull about the old and now the knew we know is love's unbound / bulldog; bulldog blues unbound / bullfrog; bullfrog agree and

the unbound / orient; orient's invention is the mention unbound / textiles; textiles tactile to the blend that ascends unbound / corn; corn of the sort unbound / farm; farm and the arm unbound / service; service and the service is unbound / elite; elite and the quote is a vote for the mother unbound / well; well enough to be unbound / healthy; healthy aspire to the hire unbound / city; city and the sues unbound / stay; stay at the ways unbound / send; send the deals to the unbound / bullet; bullet bet on was the wet agree to be unbound / receive; receive a sort unbound / forget; forget the Other and get another unbound / forgive; forgive us and know us unbound / remind; remind the signed unbound / do; do and be unbound / fathers; fathers and the field unbound / mothers; mothers mail us the unbound / mates; mates redirect the resurrect that is, unbound / friends; friends and the fracture healed by the zeals unbound / vulvan; vulvan and mattered in the stroke unbound / stroke; stroke victims appealed to the feel for the light now electric to agree unbound / votive; votive pleasure and the measures unbound / fables; fables told to the overtures unbound / camped; camped at the rock unbound / stray; stray to a treasure unbound / participate; participate the sate unbound / sate; sate is on into the unbound / still; still we'll be unbound / stall; stall is over, thee, unbound / spread; spread the news, unbound / stays; stays with you, the unbound / green; green and the groups unbound / grapple; grapple is due to the overage unbound / green; green and the vote is for the unbound / navigate; navigate to the voltage unbound / note; note about the frat unbound / filled; filled and sealed as unbound / grand; grand design and the align meant unbound / boats; boats that note the unbound / empire; empire entire, the unbound / eternal; eternal to the yearn unbound / greats; greats know the snows unbound / ottoman; ottoman of men unbound within the seat of love / ming; ming bets unbound / elate; elate with the rich agree to degrees unbound / grasp; grasp a space unbound / notions; notions mentioned in the grand unbound.

CHAPTER TWELVE
Gravitate; gravitate to the late arrive at the strive to be unbound / answer; answer each the other and too, the unbound / decree; decree that be will be the unfold of the unbound / absolved; absolved, the solve, unbound / dynasty; dynasty due too, the unbound / pray; pray for the other who covers the unbound / expressly; expressly new and the knew that's agreed to, the unbound / often; often I am unbound / veterans; veterans who agree that love is, unbound / wars; wars done the unbound / rewards; rewards come in the steep deliver to the giver unbound / spoils; spoils are mine undone to the coming agree meant unbound / power; power is up and too we are unbound / price; price the option as unbound / pleased; pleased to be the unbound / happy; happy with the truths unbound / cornerstone; cornerstone agreed to be unbound / foundation; foundation of the nation and the station unbound is true too, love / dome; dome overcomes the unbound / of; of love, God is, unbound / light; light enough, unbound / ano; ano universal and the rehearsal this year, unbound / domini; domini sealed the unbound / expert; expert expect of the sect called agree

and the undo done unbound / absolute; absolute and the truth is, unbound / transcend; transcend the mend, unbound within, and love / trains; trains that deign themselves secure into the undone, uncoupled, unbound / Hippocrates; Hippocrates who knew the unbound / oaths; oaths that seal the swell unbound / sworn; sworn and secure to the comet endured into the loop that is led into the unbound tip of love / secrets; secrets revealed can heal the secure unbound/ defend; defend your debt with the veteran agree to be the unbound / open; open the support to see the unbound / God; God wed to the unbound / Said; Said you would see the unbound / hu-man; hu-man and agreed to the comet's descend into the unbound / know; know who leads into the unbound / secret; secret and seen the unbound / declare; declare the spare unbound / this; this is the due unbound / our; our cars secure within the unbound / knowing; knowing who is the unbound / elect; elect the sort who spark the unbound / elevate; elevate your state into the unbound / spoke; spoke a note one d unbound / thus; thus I will be, unbound / God; God said let us see the unbound / begin; begin to say and know again the unbound / to; to you, the unbound / say; say what will stay, the unbound / know; know what will be, the unbound / believe; believe in the eclipse of the reset agree too, the unbound / remember; remember the sender is the render secure in the interest demure and the marcate contoured by the rebate unbound / touch; touch on this, the gifts of love that sound unbound / energy; energy given too, the unbound / intensity; intensity comes in the sun unbound / immense; immense agree to be sincere to the secure in attend unbound / end; end of the days unbound / times; times can see the streets unbound / now; now I see the stress unbound / in; in times like these who needs we do the unbound / upon; upon this beach unbound / phases; phases due to the unbound / perfectly; perfectly installed notations round the crowning birthed, unbound.

CHAPTER THIRTEEN
Prophetic; prophetic in assume of the agree to be conceptually sent to the invent called love is, unbound / cycle; cycle in to the send abundant in degrees unbound / end; end of the dues unbound / content; content in invent and the hint that's unbound / great; great said and the fed unbound / circle; circle to the miracle due the unbound / clicks; clicks in the taste unbound / millennium; millennium abraids and the staids unbound / truths; truths and tracks along the backs unbound / calendars; calendars that date the unbound / over; over and all, the unbound / basic; basic belief in thee, unbound / yes; yes and we will be, unbound / to; to the sort unbound / life; life is the place unbound / eternal; eternal and the state is, unbound / again; again, I say, unbound / I; I agree to be unbound / say; say the stay is unbound / believe; believe in this weave, unbound / this; this trace is unbound / chance; chance to see, the unbound / to; to stay, unbound / shine; shine at the days unbound / for; for the glory unbound / God's; God's belong is unbound / is; is this duress to the direct called God's head is unbound in the astound called love / finds; finds a stay, unbound / a; a way to stay unbound / wait; wait on the One's

unbound / home; home is where? unbound / heart; heart is home unbound / is; is this the throne? unbound / code; code set on the unbound / God; God gets the unbound / gives; gives a taste the unbound / bliss; bliss blue with the unbound / kiss; kiss me a taste unbound / beings; beings met unbound / your; your bet is unbound / friend; friend found again, unbound / found; found an alien whose friend, I am, is unbound / desires; desires to be, unbound / design; design the cede unbound / is; is it unbound / to; to the vortex unbound / desires; desires and cures unbound / design; design a trace unbound / is; is this true? unbound? Yes! / to; to the Ones who say Yes! to love, the unbound / give; give us the grace unbound / you; you are the two unbound / relate; relate us of late too the unbound / that's; that's quadrant to you, the unbound / free; free to be the unbound / to; to this I agree, the unbound / be; be the One, love, unbound / love; love is unbound.

THE IN-MATCH-MENTS
LEVEL 25

CHAPTER ONE

Fresh; fresh enough to match with in the divine desire too, love / dawn; love's dawn is a match in love / awake; awake enough to see through to the match within your Friend / aware; aware of the care inside our glide to the loving return called matched repair / advent; advent and sent too, the meditation called the station of matches in love / aspen; aspen blue with the heart in you and the yellow agree to be profound in the match called within, love / vail; vail and assigns and the kinds who agree to the match meant by love / unveil; unveil the color that is deep in repair to the colorado blue remember called matched set, love / reveal; reveal a revel in the level called love is, grand, and we are, brands of the matched pace, the stance within the boots of God / colorado; colorado compare to the bluer reveal called the meals that match the questions of love / why; why can we be matched like these and only those who love / convent; convent sent the reinvent of the heaven sent agree to match the connect called strict with relief and love / connect; connect to the sort who court only love's degrees unmatched / commit; love's commit is fit to be, matched / prevail; prevail with the trailer called let us feel God's match point, love / meet; meet the seats that match, yours, ours, love / met; met the One, now agreed too, the match is, love / fire; fire the spire with the heat called love's, the match is God's / fluid; fluid agree to be matched / lighter; lighter signs of the match meant by love / flame; flame flew to the clue unmatched / violet; violet martins flew to the veil unmatched / green; green agree to be unmatched / teal; teal and true in the matching one agreed too, unbound / orange-red; orange-red and fed by the waters of love's central pump, the heart unmatched / heat; heat and the seat's unmatched / relating; relating to the dating called matched / relationship; relationship with the matched / pair; pair of sets matched / classic; classic agree to be matched / trade; trade the settle for matched / place; place found in the trends matched / hotel; hotel healed matched / hostel; hostel and succeed, matched / stay; stay at the one who will be matched / suspend; suspend at the end that's matched / suspense; suspense done the One comes unmatched / succinct; succinct enough too, match / life; life is fine in the find unmatched / lifts; lifts to the truths unmatched / champion; champion days unmatched / comes; comes a ways matched / free; free instinct to the match complete with love / good; good days come matched / communicate; communicate the date that's matched / direct; direct to a dial unmatched / dial; dial the inside of the One who is, matched / answer; answer the call to be, matched / phone; phone again the zone of the Ones unmatched / mail; mail is due within the matched / e-mail; e-mail swell within the unmatched / recalled / perfect / chromosomes / In / Yanomami / eight thousand / BC / wheel / life / pleasant / perfumed / grace / granted.

CHAPTER TWO

Features; features that mention the venue called matched / subscribe; subscribe to the knowledge that your heart is a college and your head just a hand in this plan called hu-man, and the match that is sent, God / believe; believe in the sleeve of delivery and the match that is, I AM / faith; faith degreed by the cede to succeed in this path called the match, heaven sent too, love / crown; crown of the town called crewed and matched / crowns; crowns accrue with the strength of a match called love / crowned; crowned and sounded for in the match place, the seam of, love / borne; borne like the sworn on the winds of men and the breaths and the wings of God, man's match is, love / winged; winged delivery of the match called man / wings; wings that hinge on the heart of this matter and the match called hu-man / weds; weds the seams, the match, hu-man / wealth; wealth as suggested is invested in the matchplace called man / webbing; webbing for climbing the pinnacles hu-man and the matched steps of God / western; western the trend of this epistle whose match is hu-man / met; met at the dream of an edgeless seam called the matchpoint hu-man / east; east to the west and the bet that our match is bet in hu-mans / border; border forged ahead and the bedroom test is the vest that's worn, is the breastplate matched in this hu-man? / south; south to the mouth of forever and the arrival at the heart's space called the matched place true too, love / extend; extend your nature to include the Mother of love, this earth, hu-man / European; European the plan and the plane of forever is etched in the glass of a face called replaced in the heart hu-man and the stand called love / style; style of the matter hu-man's match is God's relate to the state called Nirvana / attempt; attempt to be serene in your lean into the winds matched in hu-man glitter and the glamour of God / facilities; facilities that hint at the stint called matched human wins the stature called love / congregate; congregate at the states of the shades that match, point is, love / conjugate; conjugate this verse with I AM, match this within, love / state; state that your rate is truly exact to the fact that man's match is, love / stripe; stripe of the strip called maturely I win the matchpoints love / strip; strip the tape of the nape of the nature of the match made too, love / stir; stir with the feel of a heal called forever and the maturation to see that this heart's beat is free too, love's match stirs / flip; flip to the trip called I am and the match called hu-man / over; over and over, I AM, matched by the plan, hu-man, too, love / unders; unders and the thunders prevalent in the magic matched in love / nestle; nestle in the wrestle to less and the lessen is yes, we are, kinetically spoken, invoking and the worthy is yes! we are matched to this love / health; health and the sort meditated and the medicated good-bye to the cry noon to three for the fond delivery called lightly we see the match called love / society; society sued the forgets and the lets be bet upon in the light upon our spirit's cues called plural within and the Friend can begin to believe in the match that's called love / educate; educate your treat arrive with the strive too see and the recovery of all we are for the participate in the state called precisely matched too, love / education; education is the nation called precisely due too, the matched place, remember, love / world; world of the sutures healed with the match point called love / total; total cool to the following wind of the send attendant to the agree called precisely and purely securely due the ascendant is the contentment in truth matched too, love / supreme; supreme the being bombasted by the matched set called love is secure within the arms of God / trend; trends like these are supreme in God's agreed upon, love follows this match / covert; covert sorts forget their sports of leaving a lend to the blessings called matched / conditional; conditional to a pivotal point and a sortee called precisely matched too, the unconditional, love / utilize; utilize the kind in your match / settle; settle for the sort who often led to the matched estate called love / utilities; utilities drawn to the song called perfect and the reinsert of a resurrect precise too, love's match / cable; cable code for the rode to a match, only this, love / public; public and the square of tender arrive at the spark of attendant too, love's match, God / censor; censor less your test and trust of the crust of mantles worn like swords of delay come construed to the immediacy of love's match / censorship; censorship and the grip on the heartland of love's match, God, hu-man / grip; grip a point called hurray with love's agree to be matched / promise; promise your heart to the One, matched / dogma; dogma done and the coming arrives at the size, comprehend, and again the comrade is the match placed in love / intense; intense negotiation occurs at the sure regard for the cards elect, and matched, inside, love / immense; immense connote of the torque as matched in love / recollect; recollect and invect the venture with God's elect agree to be matched / reveal; reveal the heal that is, matched / revelation; revelation of the sort that's matched with love / resolve; resolve to be matched within, love / security; security set on the hunt for the match called love / philosophy; philosophy of give can live in the hearts that match / generosity; generosity comes in the ones who match / fells; fells the swells within love's match / falls; falls all over the covers that match.

CHAPTER THREE

Places; places and stacks of the match called love / method; method due to the you we knew as matched within, love / frigid; frigid has come undone too, the match / freak; freak of the sort fond to the gain that is, matched / numb; numb to the sum that's less, one, two, matched / seek; seek another sort, matched / sought; sought to gain the strain that is, matched / sustain; sustain us with your gains of love's match / suspend; suspend a friend with the lend consummate to the traces matched / same; same game extended, loved, matched / crash; crash is over, the caches can flow with love, matched / untame; untame and the same is, loves, matched / trained; trained like the kind elate that is matched within, love / entranced; entranced and true to the miracle of you and the perfect ascend to the matchpoint, love / translucence; translucence comes to the sum of regard for the capillaries of love's match / horizon; horizon seen like the scene called matched / birth; birth and too, the matched / random; random delight and the sights of the match that is, love / sort; sort the sport with a match called love / coming; coming to the matched agree called love / in; in time to be, matched / lamb's; lamb's agreeable regard for the subject called precisely let us be, loved in this match with God / blend; blend like you, that is, matched / book; book done with the won, matched / ripens; ripens like flights to the tends matched / read; read a note that

votes for the matched / written; written and sent to the matched agree, love / hire; hire a spire to see from, the matched / hear; hear us here, matched / capable; capable of the sort that is, matched / stream; stream zipped to the lips of love, matched / ripple; ripples and the effects that match / cross; cross to the sort who match / fly; fly like a fleet regard for the cards that match / soar; soar with the hour who match / mist; mist and the notes that match within love / lift; lift your stare to the eyes that care for men, God's own, the match, love / cover; cover the eyes with love's reveal, matched / moonlight; moonlight and the sight that's matched / reflect; reflect like a sight that's matched / swirl; swirl in the girl who is, matched / tingle; tingle with excite for the flight that's matched / mind; mind less, matched / soul; soul flew to the way light dayed and the heart swayed to love's match / heart; heart held full of the agreed too, match / worth; worth an exert the match called love / gratitude; love is gratitude too, matched / grace; grace grew in our way that is, matched / attitude; attitude renewed and matched / allow; allow her to be your own, match / allowance; allowance and the bride that is, matched / offer; offer to be, matched / offering; offering comes, matched / often; often and always matched / hands; hands held in a match with, love / held; held like hearts that match / heard; heard a word called matched / ears; ears that hear thee, matched / mouth; mouth that's held with the matched estate, love / speak; speak like a seek for the matched mate, love / the; the match is made, we, love / word; word of God is the logos deep in the keep called matched / lion / culture.

CHAPTER FOUR

Round; round the sounds that match / event; event insured by the matched pace, love / choose; choose to be, matched / eventual; eventual and you, matched / actual; actual to a measure matched / true; true to a date that is, matched / shade; shade of the days that match / driven; driven to be, matched / given; given the match to see, love / gained; gained a plane called matched / granted; granted a state that matched / candle; candle and the flame that matched / trust; trust your estate with the match called love / truth; truth told, matched / trance; trance graced within, matched / glow; glow with the know that is, matched / trial; trial done, convicted, won, matched / conviction; conviction about the mentions matched / commitment; commitment sent to the matched place, love / comment; comment that is sent to the matched elate, love / comets; comets that seek the immense erase called matched within, love / trail; a trail smoked with the match is, love / explain; explain about the shout that is, matched / dirt; dirt sold and the match is love / convicts; convicts evict the less, matched / dark; dark becomes light matched and elects too, illumination, love / casual; casual flung to the friend undone and the meter unique in the peek manifest with love's confess of the magic called grace and the elate called yes, we will, confess matched with, God / clear; clear to hear that is, matched / claims; claims to be, matched / clamor; clamor about the matched / forgive; forgive the Other, matched / forgave; forgave another, matched / paint; paint too high and lover still, matched / print;

print a match that is pointed with love / invent; invent a sun called flaming elective, matched stressed, love / patent; patent who's due to the matched great, love / pattern; pattern forgiven and the living can be forgone and matched / men; men who win the matched pace, love / male; male equate, matched / mail; mail her home, matched / female; females who see the matched great, love / freed; freed to be, lovingly, matched / framed; framed by the gamed who match, picture this, love / fred; fred who said matched / frank; *frank recover of energetic depth in love / freshen; freshen the ups of matching love / frantic; frantic and agreed too, matched / floored; floored and the sword is, matched / better; better be, the matched / relevance; relevance recovered and matched with love / relevant; relevant to a hunt with loved, matched / regard; regard the card that's matched / restart; restart and commend the matched taste, love / rest; rest in the arms that match with love / restful; restful sleep of the matched / rather; rather be and be, matched / run; run to the sun that's matched / rescue; rescue you with the true who match / arose; arose like a rose called matched / lemurias; lemurias deep regard for the matched / foes; foes, who knows? the matched forgive, love / fallen; fallen and calling, the matched taste for love / ran; ran to a stand that is, matched / kona; kona cued and matched / stand; stand like the sand that is, matched.

CHAPTER FIVE
Living; living like the flames that rain unearthed by the burning agree to be winds of the matched state love / speak; speak eloquence and within the wake your feet, your heart, your match / spoken; spoken agree to be matched / faith; faith in the fun that matched / felt; felt like a shoe that fit, matched / fully; fully agreed too, matched / found; found a sound matched / forth; forth and the sort that is, matched / first; first and the last, matched / last; last match made, it's eternal, love / omega; omega sort that gave this, match / alpha; alpha stored and matched / males; males who will, match / females; females who heal, match / phallic; phallic agreed too, matched / ascend; ascend to the we'd match / cavorts; cavorts like the sorts matched / cavalier; cavalier to a care matched / respectable; respectable paired, matched / rather; rather see that matched / buoyant; buoyant begin, begun, matched / basics; basics ascend, matched / barrier; barrier through, matched / broke; broke the state, matched / braced; braced like a cache, matched / pulled; pulled and insured in thee, match / impaled; impaled with the thread common human matched / purled; purled and curled, matched / watered; watered and deep in the matched / west; west to the waist that is, matched / welcome; welcome and agreed too, matched / win; win the send matched / toss; toss the cross that's matched / nix; nix and the western burn for the yearn eastern still in a matched pace, love / lost; lost and too, matched / swayed; swayed and swooned, matched / swerve; swerve to a great relate, matched / lean; lean and the day, matched / curve; curve accrued, matched / cave; cave of forgive, matched / blues; blues and the news that is matched / power; power and the our that is, matched / renews; renews our faith, matched / void; void and the less that is, matched / relate;

relate to a great, match / resident; resident and the blend, matched / states; states that see thee, matched / change; change to be, matched / crawl; crawl to the haul that is, matched / vibration; vibration rung with thee, matched / telepathic; telepathic sorts, matched / patterns; patterns who emerge for the words, God is, our match, love / fields; fields that field our matched elate with love / sensitive; sensitive too and the match made is, love / mood; mood about the shout, matched / ascendance; ascendance comes to the sun's matched / reincarnates; reincarnates win this end, matched / divine; divine to a due, matched / culminates; culminates in a friendship, matched / wisdom; wisdom comes to the ones matched / mystical; mystical and the sort, matched / pleasure; pleasure and the please, matched / indian; indian days matched / energy; energy comes to the sun, matched.

CHAPTER SIX
Validate; validate yourself, match / yoga; yoga and the view that's news, matched / meditating; meditating in the friend, matched / vibrating; vibrating like begin, matched / concurrence; concurrence set on the matched release to God's news, mothered, love / concur; concur with God's arrive at the sides that match with love / absolve; absolve the solve that's matched with the zones of agree and the seed that is, love / meditate; meditate about the shout that's matched / mollify; mollify and agree too, matched / matters; matters and the smatters agreed too and matched / mastery; mastery and the sees of matches loved / monitor; monitor and the state is, matched / publish; publish and the clues that are, matched / public; public and the crude decree to agree to the matched / purvey; purvey that's agreed too, matched / purveyor; purveyor free matched / consciously; consciously accept the gift that's agreed too and the passionate match of love / manifest; manifest and the love that is agreed too, matched / acknowledge; acknowledge and the college that is matched and the respectful regress to the mansions built with love / rapid; rapid and true to the zoo complete with a closure called matched states, love / correlate; correlate degrees by accrues called the matched plates of love / concrete; concrete and the streets that match by agree too, love / research; research and the sees that love's matched / resonance; resonance sent, match / questions; questions sent to the matched state of spoken love / quelled; quelled and the quay that's messaged by matches of love / hearty; hearty and the match that is the race called love / veil; veil and the sees called matched in the rapture called love / marriage; good marriage due to the matched state in you and your love / vowed; vowed to be matched up with love / husband; husband and the seeds that promise to be loved / wowed; wowed and howed by the vowed to be, matched / disciple; disciple and the source that is God matched / shown; shown and the sun that is matched / wed; wed and the said that said matched / wealth; wealth and the well matched, love / brilliance; brilliance and blues that's cued by advents matched in the race called love / throne; throne and the shown, matched by brilliant agree / reside; reside the side agreed to be matched / revive; revive and relate to the state matched / coinsert; coinsert and the assert that is,

matched / covert; covert and the crew that's matched too, love /
over; over and again, matched / reward; reward the sword that's
matched within, love / rap; rap and the rates that match, loved
/ unravel; unravel the gavel that is, matched / raphael; raphael's
explain is matched / Gabriel; Gabriel grew to the too, matched
/ krishna; krishna and the crowd that trued to the cubed and the
matched / takwi; takwi seen matched / tachyon; tachyon cues
explained and matched / hyperdriven; hyperdriven agree to be
matched / hyperforce; hyperforce and the spaced access that
matched too, love / convalesce; convalesce a spent degree of
the matching we, called love / tress; tress and the match mates,
love / dressed; dressed to see with, love is, matched / absolute;
absolute and the suit that is matched / resurrect; resurrect and
the suspect convinced as to be, matched / respect; respect and
agree too, matched / crowd; crowd and the crowded forget, love
is, matched / water; water and the where matched / walk; walk
with the home you own matched / winning; winning and the
acquire too great accept that is matched / material; material to
the material acquiesce named matched.

CHAPTER SEVEN
Acknowledge; acknowledge the college hu-man, match / release;
release the relax that's matched / sound; match a sound with a
gown of electric glare and the love within, God's / see; see us in
thee, matched / sea; sea of the match that will be expansive and
immense in the chance to dance with God in the lands that love
/ wave; wave of the seas that are matched with love / proponent;
proponent passed to the link up with the wave that's matched
in, love / component; component of the sort that lives matched /
cure; cure and the sure arise to the matching skies of God said,
love / goal; goal and the soul released to the match the light is
and the wiser ways we can stay together in the love that will
released too, God / agenda; agenda and the blend of a trait called
elections win again, matched / expertise; expertise and the sneeze
that elects to be seen as God's deed, love's match / flavor; flavor
and the favor that is, matched / fluid; fluid and the wise arise to
believe in the match is, love / IV; IV foured to the coming arise
called match is made, too, love / ICU; I see you matched in the
conditions called love / DV; Distended empty gone to the living
and a friend that met at the state called matched / TV; TV true
and the telepathic view that is loved by the weaving matched to
God / SUV; Spectacular universal venue that you moved too,
matched / RU; RU rowdy too and we are complete in love's
defend of the light Metatron, matched escape with God / CB;
Central Bemused and the concentric ascendant matched / minds;
minds and the sign that's sent to the intent matched within and
the meeting led to the Friendly arrive at the side metatronic and
the heated bonnet of a car driven fast to the last escape forgiven
and God is living at the lend hu-man / hearts; hearts and the starts
electric meeting friends matched with love / heads; heads and
the sorts meeting matched with love / feet; feet that set on the
tracks that match the treads of love / foot; foot too and you are
the matched agree called love / measure; measure the measures
that match within, love / metric; metric and meters of electric

agrees too, becoming the deed, matched with love / seat; seat
and the feet come electric to because and the cause matched with
love / sappho; sappho and the grip of a lip led to say isles of love
matched hu-man too, love / lympho; lympho and psychotic to
the means metabolized in the seized arise at love's agree, to be,
matched with love / lisbon; lisbon and the seed matched with
God / Match; Material Accept of the True Corrective Hatch of
the portal called love / LIFWO; Last Into the First Wave Out,
waves that match too, love / Filo; Inventory first the interest
lent over the matched pace, love / Fro; Fro and to the loving
match hu-man / To; To and the true that is hatched too, love /
African; African extremes matched within this pace called love
/ meet; meet a Chinese wake called matters that love / white;
white and agreed too, matched / dry; dry and the try that ways
are matched with, God / trial; trial and the stays that match this,
love / convict; convict convicts the matched wit, love / forgive;
forgive the One that's matched with love / forget; forget the sort
who sort the matched wits, loved / move; move to the groove
which sat upon love / on; on the soon to be, love, in fact, matched
/ live; live to the seize called matched / free; free and to degrees
that matched within, love / geographic; geographic and the traffic
that moved to the elective state called perfectly God is within hu-
men / minoan; minoan and the cede to be electrically inclined in
the signed accept of the voltaic side of man matched too, love /
fleet; fleet and the settle of metal called erect with elect and the
street of a match made called love / discrete; discrete and the
valour believed in is matched within, love / greek; greek as a
match to be made with, love / succinct; succinct and assigned
the suspend that is matched with love / view; view and the cue
to move to attendant is, matched / value; value for the chore
erect to a matching set called love / portal; portal of the chore
to see and the lifitng eyes that we arise too, mortified and less,
are matched with, love / port; port of the sort effervescent with
love's match / pastel; pastel and the color of well wed match /
pastiche; pastiche and the seek of a taste that's matched hu-man
/ camiche; camiche and the question attained matched / cornice;
cornice viewed and matched / cornish; cornish hymns penned
as matched / grasp; grasp a state of elate with the matched plan,
man, love.

CHAPTER EIGHT
Yahweh; Yahweh's flame is the same that burns in the games
that match within, hu-man, loves / floral; floral and the care for
the pairs that play with the stay, matched / like; like a date with
the matches in love / light; light sight matched with agrees too,
love / life; life and the sights that match with God's delight and
the sights of renew in the views of God's agree, love / do; do the
validation states that match with intact design of assigns called
complex accede to be attached less in be, love / doric; doric
aspects of the assets called matched states of love / stela; stela,
the one, matched within with the data of civilization's send to
the surrender called love / stelae; stelae contorts with the sort of
stones that build alliance with defiance less and delegation more,
the matched pace is, love / euglena; euglena and the seas grand

with belief in the green agree to rate this life as blessed with debates on exactly this, the matched place called precisely gives our love / euglenoid; euglenoid void compares to the clear of blame and the bloom of magnificent rooms of reside at the side called God, match made in the glad euglenoid / protista; protista agree to be aboard the sights of scenes that match / nuclei; nuclei and the sigh that's a scene bright blue-green and a flush with the case that is must in the strike of a match placed called love / baptist; baptist agree to see the fed trained and the forget of the see that's agreed to by Buddha's be and the lightening steed that's worn by the horn of revival and the tents that hide at the side resurrected by loving's match / baptise; baptise the size and the heart of Christ's frees and the agrees that model match and the human weaves of God said; let the be, light; immerse / protozoa; protozoa confess of the yes that is manifest in the best agrees to desires and seas of surrender to the render that is left to the right tide the middle and the flowers of a match made with love / organ; organ cloned and the heart that moaned with delivery of a second chance too, love is, moaned / organic; organic appeal to the heal that is blessed and the vested attend to the send that is well in the veil that is lifted by the gifted assign, three trines into two and the views that are healthy within a matched state of love / origin; origin sent to the invitation of stations heady with believe and the traces of compare that can spare us the forget of yester and the be of more today than knot and the sought and the care of love that is, matched / algae; algae can be companioned in the seed hu-man and the feed that is, love's match / lattice; lattice imported as the sorted that matched / lines; lines of signs that match / measures; measures and the treasures that load like a feed to agreed to desires of the matches with love / temples; temples and the temples of kind agree to match with love / warps; warps of the sort that match, love / velocity; velocity given to the living match / midway; midway the states that match / enoch; enoch sent to the vents that match / thresholds; thresholds elect the appear of the where all will be to the see that is matched / command; command an acquire of the hire that is matched / pegasus; pegasus in flight to the sight that surges and the merges that heal and the wealth that is real to the healing import of God's flying succeed called lightly weaves match / flight; flight of the caring and the sharing expire that will higher still abide in the side that is, God's, match / gamma; gamma and the raid on the rest that is, matched / betta; betta be, matched / pi; pi waved like a seed that's matched in a universe square with delight-full humans, love / simple; simple and convex to agreements called God is ahead to the match / complex; complex the design that is matched within, love / durate; durate that is great with desires of the match / durable; durable I am in my feel of the match / dimensional; dimensional and seen as the lean that is matched / expand; expand to the sand that is matched / regional; regional confess and the invest mature with the matching place, love / regenerate; regenerate the state of agree that is, matched / regenerative; regenerative appear to be near too, matched / read; read a planet that is powered by our pace of rewards that elate matched within, God / star; star cars matched, hu-man /

intellect; intellect erect in the stake that is, matched / supercede; supercede's done and the seams are, matched / superb; superb and the verb is we matched / supernal; supernal and the yearning access to the blessings called love is, matched / stars; stars and the caring sort matched together in, love / metatronic; metatronic agree too, matched / advent; advent to see, matched / approach; approach a throat matched / infinite; infinite and the waves that weave our agree to be, matched / zero; zero in on the yes, we are, matched / squares; squares and the cares that are matched / regions; regions woven together in love and the matched states of God / density; density and dues that are paid to the matching ally called love / juxtapose; juxtapose and the hose is, matched / particles; particles and the seeds that are matched with this, God / magnetic; magnetic appear and within the believe that is seen in the stars that accrue in the view Metatron and the sonnet called love is magical within and the micro agree to be believable within and without that is, matched / models; models who heal the appeals magic within and the trends of the reset called love is our match / pyruvate; pyruvate and the retake of a test state called matched / calculate; calculate when and again we are, matched / coded; coded to be voted the matched.

CHAPTER NINE

Crosses; crosses and the losses that squared the release and the access to yes, we agree to be, born and to be worn into the fleet delivery of the recovery called precisely we are hired to see the mathematically accurate acceptance of the data called matched state, love / futures; futures and the place called matched within and agreed too, love / physics; physics and the send that is matched within, love / filament; filament cured and the chord that is clued to the clavical click called with us, all, worthy of the matching place called love / flows; flows the knows that is, matched / cycles; cycles and the ears that are opening to you and your word, logos, love, the match / names; names and the sames who are matched / attends; attends to the signs that are, matched / recapture; recapture the magic of a living that is matched within, loves / match; match the state with the reflect called the resurrect for a pair called love / create; create a state of now, and then, the reconnect within a matched taste for love / scatter; scatter the matter to the meeting called perfectly light to the sight that's within and it's true to One matched create called love / find; find a signature mattered within a matching love / flown; flown and the own called a match / decrease; decrease and the dues we leave matched / crease; crease about the shout called matched / curl; curl to the whirl that lives matched / floral; floral decays have gone the wave to a matched erupt, love / code; code and the node that is, matched / name; name and the same agree matched / God; God and the furl undone by a match / back; back to the state that matched, love / through; through a needle and the eye that matched too, love / right; right enough to see and the be that is, matched, with this, love / hand; handle handed the mandible grin of a creation that's in, matched / all; all the way through, matched / through; through this taste, matched / man; love's man is God's match wed, love / God; Match with the God you love, within and about, all One / into; into another and the mother that is, matched / man; man and the scan that's created, matched / God's; God's a good match / hu; hu and the cue that is, matched / man; man and the stand that agrees to be, matched / image; image and the sexual resurrect of man, love / kadmon; kadmon and the song called life within, love, matched / adamic; adamic explain and the same called matched / snake; snake and the release that is, matched / dead; dead and the dues matched / ascension; ascension points to love's matched agree, love's / through; through the glitter and the mist of a matching pair, love and you / the; the knows matched within, love / breath; breath and the be, matched / seventh; seventh and the stays that are matched / command; command a man that is matched / casbah; casbah cued to the mood that is matched / marilyn; marilyn gave a wave matched / Heaven; Heaven and the cave that is, matched / matching; matching and the mood that is matched / elvis; elvis mates in the mood and the rapture of the require that is hired within matched in, love / elbow; elbow the nodes of less with your test of the agree to be resurrected in confess too, matched pairs, love / comes; comes to the sums that are matched / breathing; breathing and the be that is, matched / blue; blue and the you that is, matched / regard; regard your cards as held by this match / through; through and the cede that is, matched / breath; breath about the shout believe, matched state, love / consent; consent to invent and to forget the set that matched / accept; accept a due that is, matched / DNA / RNA / Michael / The Christ / I.

CHAPTER TEN
Zoning; zoning matched through the flues of love / technology; technology compared to only the sent by heaven's gates and the states that match / propagate; propagate a state that is, matched / condense; condense at a date with thee, matched / total; total and the sum that is, matched / expand; expand to a stand that is, matched / accrete; accrete and the arete called this is, our, match / aggregate; aggregate agree to be, matched / sum; sum of the some that is, matched / structure; structure and the stratus that's shared to the match meant too, love / myriad; myriad states of the pleasure that's made to compare with the cares of the love that shares and the traces sent too matched / earth; earth and the birth that is, matched / bio-weave; bio-weave and the sleeve that's regard is too, matched / optic; optic and the cure is, matched / optical; optical to the comical sort who laugh with this match / permanent; permanent agree to be, matched / implants; implants and the sort who are, matched / crystalline; crystalline and the lean arrive at the heart inside the manned apply of our matching sighs called love / crystallize; crystallize a pair who match / gravity; gravity grew over you and now you know that love can show the truth to a match that flies like love / photons; photons and sorts who mature with elevate of the fates that match / combine; combine and again we, match / radiate; radiate to the stature that's matched / imagine; imagine and the scene that is, matched / image; image and the groan that is, matched / hike; hike to the hoop that is match, too, love / leaf; leaf and the grief

that enacts this a match / curve; curve abounded with, loved, matched / speed; speed and the capture matched with love / cut; cut to the sate that is matched with love / forest; forest contoured and the sort that is cured with the rate within matched / dome; dome over the room, matched / recovery; love's recovery is matched with desire for the higher blends of God / floral; floral and artcurial the mercurial mend of love, as agreed, matched / big; big days matched / meadows; well into the meadows of love that is matched / windshaken; windshaken in the ways mundane and the wades to the heart of the lark called hu-man, love / work; work on the sort humanly matched, too, love / bow; bow to the waves matched / chevron; chevron cured to be returned and trued to the trend Metatron and the song, as agreed, privately, matched within, love / oaks; oaks and the stokes that mend matches left to the leaves of impress and the miracles of love / camp; camp at the states Metatronic and the free delivery of love's match / grass; grass that grew in the news matched / pampas; pampas plays matched / meridian; meridian dued to the moods matched / Arcturian; Arcturian agrees to be matched / evolution; evolution becomes you, matched / evolve; evolve to the solve that is, matched / solve; solve the resolve too, matched / posted; posted in the streets that sweet and matched / regard; regard the cards that match / trailer; trailer trued in the mood that matched / monitor; monitor equate with matched / heat; heat up, matched / park; park at the arc that matched / pine; pine of the trees that match / night; night blue and too, matched / haul; haul it, hear, the trailer matched / falls; falls like days that match / fell; fell to the well who match / catch; catch a plan to blame less and mend the merry ways that match too, love / united; united we stand matched / big; big enough to be, matched / stand; stand at the sands that match.

CHAPTER ELEVEN
Iron; iron willed delivery of the recovery called God ahead, matched / truth; truth and the nature revealed, matched / prevail; prevail to the be that is, matched / commission; commission and the mission that is, matched / sold; sold to the rolled absolve called matched / stay; stay with her, the matched One, earth / tract; tract sold to you, matched / acreage; acreage around, the matched / parking; parking pooled, abounds, matched / parked; parked at the arc that matched / junction; junction of the function that matched / inn; inn held in to the matched stage love / parkway; parkway pools that match / caverns; caverns that came to the matching games, love / ground; ground like a round that is, matched / blue; blue and the blue agree, matched / retreat; retreat to assert that is, matched / curve; curve about your believe in our, match / pasture; pasture of cure that is, matched / lucky; lucky days due to thee, matched / luck; luck and the news that we, matched / grill; grill and exceed that is, matched / lower; lower and the structure is matched in the states of love / yellow; yellow and the dates that match within, love / clean; clean and the scene is matched within, love / blue; blue and the green that matches with love / toxin; toxins attend to the matching in you and our agree to be, loved / logs; logs and the matching cravings love /

trees; trees that stay in the sways with love / upper; upper viewed and the wooed about matching agree / creek; creek and the seek that is, matched / falling; falling to the calling matched / loving; loving and the doving due, matched / living; living and the giving grew, matched / laughing; laughing and the waves that gave us, matching bliss / hump; hump over and the coming waves are fun with agree to be, loved, matched / mountain; mountain manned by the tanned absolute called matched / maintain; maintain a train that matched / Pisgah; Pisgah grew matched / forest; forest cued to the mood that is, matched / tea; tea tastes matched / rock; rock and room too, match / pillar; pillar covered with the light states matched / pillow; pillow over the moods matched / change; change and the light agree to be loved by the multitudes matched / parcel; parcel posted to you is, matched / persuade; persuade the raid to come too, matched / turn; turn around the town that matched / slowly; slowly and sung too, matched / quickly; quickly given, matched / prison; prison and the waits that match / inmate; inmate and the states that match / imprison; imprison and the given matched / free; free to be, matched / butterfly; butterfly by the matching freeze unthawed by love / Papillon; Papillon's pal is free to fly to the lighter spans matched / chaste; chaste and the last that lasts untamed maintained magically agreed too, man's match in love / chair; chair personed ways that match / refrain; refrain and the strain that matched / explain; explain a gain matched within, love / complain; complain less, matched / forgive; forgive me a grade that is, matched / foreplay; foreplay became the game that is, matched / French; French and the speak that is, matched.

CHAPTER TWELVE
Frappe; frappe rapped upon the song of OZ and the seas that seize the degrees of loving's froth that matched too, love / cold; cold enough to be within the Friend's relief and the light in sight of our disgraced God the life that's met in the free deliver of the match meant too, love / warm; warm to the sperm that melts this universal span called precisely hu-man, love / extreme; extreme and the seams of agree can be melted within the Friend is, love's match / between; between and within our firm arrival is the friend of love's mend and the match met forever in love / cheeks; miles and the cheeks that leak with styles replete within loving's match / hands; hands and the sands that remembrance can time with coincide to love is, matched / mittens; mittens wet with the mesh of lovings forgive, matched hands, too, love / thumbs; thumbs deep in confess and the mess is cleaned by the met Metatron, electric, love, matched / thoughts; thoughts and the sends amends metatronic begins matched / threats; questions threats and the met at Metatron, answers matched / respect; respect has come to the ones matched / sustain; sustain us matched within the send called love / success; success can come when the run is complete to the matched means called love / Hawaii; Hawaii oured and compared to the hours of sublime agree to be mesmerized by the loves degreed to a matched place called lights / blossom; blossom awesome with compare and the spare arrive at the metabolism spared only this, the friends of panic gone away and

the light is on bloom inside, love / flower; flower and the our that compares on the spares that arise at the fairs metallic in this send of ours called love is, matched / florist; florist and the sums that match / glands; glands and agrees to be, matched / lavender; lavender and the cares categorized as love, match / eyes; eyes and agrees too, matched / English; good English western sees matched / embrace; come embrace the race that is metatronically laced with love's match, God / maze; maze and the sample that is branched in love's match / dowel; dowels and the rods that take a match too, God / bore; bore and more can go away too, matched / implored; implored and the soared that matched / school; school and the new that reviewed our match / met; met like a state called a match / mets; mets within and the win agreed too, match / metric; metric we and the meters of love's match / metal; metal dates with the states that match / match a state with agree; met along the truth of choose and a hatching love / mental; mental and the simple desire to hire meetings fused with love's match and the scratch that seals our devote to live together again / custom; custom and the sample michael said too, love, matched / size; size of the eyes that match / matter; matter and the spare arise at love's dear match / match; match the state within without and in about too love / mathematics; mathematics and the seas of matching states called love / language; language given agrees too, matched / heart; heart of the starts that match / portion; portion and the mention of all that is loved matched / triangle; triangle and the send that ends matched / squared; squared and compared as within matched / squired; squired by the sired compare to be matched in love / ridden; ridden like the stallion within our compare of the matched state, love / unite; unite your flight with the mend called matched up in love / southern; southern signed agree to be, matched / blend; blend sold as the One whose wills will be matched / cove; cove of the nave that gave her heart too, love's, match / railroad; railroad stays that match within love / depot; depot dues matched / thanks; thanks for the be, matched / thangka; thangka cued to the matched weds love / paradise; paradise fused by love, match / mandala; mandala days refused acquired and compared to only your admire of the films that circle within, love's match, yellow, brick / corner; corner and the tables that match the dates with love / myth; myth willed to be, matched / source; source courts our matched grace / miss; miss the notes and old devotes delivered to love's young girl, matched / missing; missing and the compare that is, matched / memorial; memorial to an arrive at the match / nursing; nursing yourself loved within the matched homes of love's poems / breast; breast and agrees to be matched / mother; mothers and the mends that bare all to the match.

CHAPTER THIRTEEN: stellar; stellar stays, matched within, love / roof; roof overhead is said to be the One that is, matched / special; special and the sort that is loved with the matched state, love / specific; specific and the said that is matched / advance; advance and the chance to match with is love / precise; precise to concise agree to be matched / pretend; pretend to be, matched / revamp; revamp your life, matched / revitalize; revitalize the size that is, matched / remodel; remodel the model that wins matched / resurrect; resurrect and the send elect to a matched pace, love / recommend; recommend and the send that is, matched / shell; shell and the gills that will be, matched / game; game and the same that is, matched / gone; gone to the Ones who are matched / grant; grant and the scene that is, matched / specialty; specialty and the send that is medical too, love is said to be, matched / speech; speech that knew allude to the matched space called love / lingual; lingual agree to be matched / bilingual; bilingual in access to the speech that's called matched / trilingual; trilingual and the sweet agrees matched / translucent; translucent and ascendant in-betweens matched / shades; shades of the scenes that match, love / biographic; biographic degrees that match / baxter; baxter blues that match / bell; bell blew true too, matched / saffron; saffron sees the seeds that match / clone; clone alone and then the One can come to the sees that match / climb; climb to the Ones that match / cluster; cluster built around the quilts that match / carapace; carapace crumbs and the shells that once were seen as love's, matched / cruel; cruel and the staid arrive at the matched space prismatic too, love / crewel; crewel and the needs that meet at the speed of love's match / sewing; sewing and the signs that match / sewn; sewn and the dreams that weave our match / quilt; quilt and the will to be matched / lover; lover and the covers that match / God; God's good is, matched / threads; threads and the seeds that match / needle; needle and the seeds that match / eyes; eyes and the use that matched / toss; toss a trues matched / knees; knees and the be's match / treasure; treasure and the true agree too match / hay; hay and the bee, amused, match / fed; fed and said the we that is, matched / fodder; fodder and the God-der and the we that is, matched / father; father and the scenes that match / farther; farther and the trim that is matched / distance; distance and the cues that match / run; run to suns that match / elect; elect our great attract to the pace called elections that match / remember; remembers when are matched and too we are to the cues that believe in the match / know; know and the elects are matched / contend; contend to be, matched / client; client and the cues that match / will; will you be matched / respect; respect to be matched / wheels; wheels aloft with the matched state love / of; the mush that is oft too love / light; light and the clues that match / live; live and be matched / to; to be and the clues that match / remember; remember that the view will be matched.

THE MATTER-MENTS
LEVEL 26

CHAPTER ONE: *God is LOVE'S matter*

*A*allergic; allergic to a matter-less agree to be loved / reactive; reactive and the active state is love's matter, God / diabetes-diabetes found in a gown wet with stains now elective and the lecture is to be, matter-free, with, love / flu; flu and the few who agreed to be well for eternity, the thirty and six who lead and the twenty-four waves to feel better mattered within, love / cold; cold enough to cure with agreeable matters called love / disease; disease and the ease within, love's matter, well / disaster; disaster evaded and the healing pervaded with truth in love's matter / occurrence; occurrence ascendant to the tended matter, love / trap; trap over and the waned can be allowed to degree to the matters of love / trivia; trivia peeled from the wheels metabolic in the light metatronic too, love, matters / trinket; trinket and the sink it, matters / balloon; balloon lagooned and over's come to the sums portal high to a parallel sky called God is love's matter / elevate; elevate your state to elation of matters / fetish; fetish fused with the hues coincidental to God's amuse, love's matter / gorge; gorge desires matters / bulemia; bulemia formed in the warm denial of God's ascendant mother, milk, lack, fill, regard, open into love's matter / anorexic; anorexic agree to be fathered and still from the mother's womb to the freeing thin delivery of the rack hu-man, skeletal and exhumed from the life that fills rooms with the width, recovery; light is thick to the sick and the weary, know the merry way that matters / flash; flash your cash at customs matched to matters, love / customs; customs that accrue in the matters of you and our, love / tours; tours and assures of the matters of love / tourist; tourist sealed in the heeled that mattered / slope; slope of the neck called direct too, love is the matter / foot; foot and apart and the start of revival of this, the kiss, of the matter / stars; stars and the cars that spare, know repairs, and arrive at the mast that matters / starch; starch wet with the heart gripped in paradise, matched / rest; rest at the beat called the match, love / dome; dome and the home that is, matched / arrest; arrest and the best is the stretch to the mesh that is, matched / contact; contact the sort who court your match / confess; confess and the dress of the test that is, matched / progress; progress to the point that matters about our love / pebbles; pebbles and the seeds that conceptually view our life as amused by this match / stone; stone and the phone that is, matched / overhang; overhang hung by the sung degrees matched / expressly; expressly and eternally confessed in our extend too, matched / express; express the guess that is, matched / cliff; cliff and the sides that match / past; past and the present matched / coast; coast and the most that we, match / crevice; crevice and the soffit that match / sway; sway and the stay that is, matched / way; way to be, matched / granite; granite stands agree, matched / path; path and the place that is, matched / dam; dam and the covers blown, matched / global; global agreed and the glee of our, match / release-release the press that is, matched / maroon; maroon and the moon that is, matched / awning; awning bought sought, matched / elliptical; elliptical core and the matched reside to be, loved / cryptic; cryptic attend and the mend matched / resolute; resolute and the sooth, matched / revenues; revenues that see this, match /

transform; transform and the warm agree that is, matched / clouds-clouds and the crowds that match / gone; gone to the sun that is, matched / wages; wages and the pages that match / A / M / intelligence / acclamation / maneuvers / Merkabah / Tibetan / trance / ends / Dalai / Lama

CHAPTER TWO

On; on and on too, the matters of love / Metatron; Metatron and the On revival to the land of cause that matters / mystify; mystify and typify less and know the best confess is the matter of love / symbolic; symbolic to a tonic called metabolic agree to be, masterfully, loved / trouble; trouble is done and the sun is the master of the matter called life / what; what is the state you wait most for, and the chore is, the matter / visit; visit a limb that is slim with denial and arc-angelic revival can say let us be the matter of love / where; where can I see that which matters within, love / temple; temple and the trees that matter / drives; drives like a triumphant agree to be mattered for, love / snow; snow and the know that is metatronic by degrees that matter / fell; fell to the well, metatronically mattered / ramp; ramp to the son that matters / wet; wet to the sees that matter / feet; feet and the seat that matters / set; set on the state of matter / generate; generate the state that is mattered / reflect; reflect and respect for the matters of love / rope; rope and the settle that matters the knots of release / wind; wind and the send that matters / unleash; unleash your leash on the matters of love / tunnel; tunnel and the seed that matters / loop; loop and the steep that matters / foolish; foolish accord and the matters that win / forget; forget has forgotten and the often degrees that match / tomato; tomato blue deliver of love's match, mattered / potent; potent decide to be mattered / breads; breads that seem mattered / milk; milk taste that fed our matters / lentils; lentils and the seeds that freed the matters / soup; soup and the set that can see these matters / bows; bows and the bees that matter / shore; shore deep in the matters that see release too, love / sure; sure decide to be mattered / complete; complete enough to see these matters / hammocks; hammocks sold and the road to recovery can be, mattered / blow; blow to the be that matters / junior; junior wins that end in matters / jobs; jobs that forgive, matters / chapels; chapels held conformed release too, matters / legend; legend and the send too, matters / lecture; lecture about the states that matter / prairie; prairie wins that matter / passion; passion and the dues that matter / pulse; pulse and cues that matter / indian; indian sees, matter / sits; sits at the level that matters / inspect; inspect your degrees, matter / examine; examine forgive and matter / care; care about the state mattered / emergency; emergency cues, matter / stopped; stopped at the rates that matter / gone; gone to the sum, matters / health; health and the heals that matter / cube; cubes and the planes that matter / sugary; sugary decide to reside at the matters / wet; wet delights to the mights that matter / snack; snack and the cures that matter / twist; twist a date to the matters that mend / snack; snack and the news that matter / lips; lips delicious to amuse that matters / solid; solid and the state that matters, in, love / comment; comment on the cues that matter / matter; matter meant, loves / precious; precious the bees in the trees electrically mattered / how; how often, now, matters / ultimate; ultimate the fusion to matters.

CHAPTER THREE

Fortify; fortify yourself for matters compare of the spare arrive of the strive too, love / specify; specify the way and the One who belongs too, love, matters / delude; delude and the nude arrive at the strive to be, Metatron's song, matters / gone; gone too and the met, matters / ahead; ahead and the send that matters / a; a day's matter, love / start; start too, matter / unglues; unglues within, matters / steepe; steepe and the keep that matters / accredited; accredited and too, matters / handy; handy and the panache to be blessed in, matters / films; films sensate with the inundate of matters ishmael and the well, loved / frost; frost and the cost that matters / jack; jack and the trip, matters / makes; makes a lip, matter, love / plumbed; plumbed with sensational and the recreational agree to be Islamically free in the whirlings of love's matters / mistakes; mistakes that take agree too, matter / never; never's undues and the yous that matter too, love / in; is in the mix that matters / often; often and well I matter / all; all in all we too can matter / essential; essential and ascendant within, matters / we; we can be the spin that matters / discount; discount less and guess that matters / forget; forget and more that matters / comrades; comrades eternal in the glens of matters / better; better and too, be, matters / dodge; dodge and the walls that wed matters melts / respect; respect and agrees and the keys that matter / flag; flag and the feel that matters / reward; reward and the swords that matter / repair; repair to the care too, matters / lodge; lodge and the stays that here will be mattered / stay; stay at the ways mattered / street; street unique to the muse that matters / uniquely; uniquely and agrees the matters in love / dazed; dazed and the days inn, matters / total; total and the tools that matter / every; every ways matters, meet, uniquely, love / way; way to be wed to too, matters spirited in / worth; worth and the birth that matters / reveal; reveal a degree of dues that matter / revelation; revelation of the station comes to thee, matters / fit; fit and the hit that matters / electric; electric and the dues then, matter / wit; wit is scene mattered / velvet; velvet and the doings matter / gorilla; gorilla use, matters / queen; queen and the scenic matters / choir; choir and the hire that matters / home; home and the tomb of fossils unique and the winging eves of love is, matters / hustle; hustle and the sufi matters, love / ramble; ramble and know the sikh who gives the feet that spring inside the heart of God let's in to the walls of the being mattered in, love / round; round and the sound agreed too, moroccan muse, love's breath in matters / roam; roam and the somatic ally can be scene in the abode called the matters in, love / above; above and to thee, beyond, in, matters / give; give us all, matters, in, love / love; love to be, mattered / live; live in seas alight in love / aloft; aloft and the oft can be matter free and too, love / contact; contact the contract to give love's deed and to bead with amuse and confess of the seams that access the depths magical in the agree too, lightly, love's decide too, matter / heart; heart and the

heark that's in, matters / range; range and the muse that matters / reached; reached and the peaks that matter / living; living is in the giving matter / mucho; mucho delicious waters materialized in view.

CHAPTER FOUR

Hot; hot in the springs of life, kinetic, matters / regard; regard is soft in the blue recognized, love matters / re-rent the news of respective blues and arc-ing into position matrilineal, love rules, matters / lost; lost and the cost that is, found, in the matters men, love / found; found and around our sorts matters that last, the breath, of love / fonder; fonder and the yonder that will, come to, matters / mounds; mounds abundant in the sounds that matter within, love / rake; rake the grounds that matter / through; through the sounds matter / castle; castle and the cues that matter / scoop; scoop the neck that is in matters / steel; steel and the sill that matters / stainless; stainless gains the matter / chains; chains that win then matters / link; link and the sink that matters / swim; swim and the trim that gains matters / deep; deep enough to see, matters / breathtaking; breathtaking abide in the sights that matter / dolphin; dolphin deals matter / refresh; refresh requires matters / regard; regard the cards that matter 5 deep in the pillars of love / slide; slide and see the holy ways of the mattering called love / wide; wide and I see the mattering, love / swears; swears to care too, love, matters / guard; guard your heart within, matters / berth; berth given of the turf that sends matters / barrier; barrier broached and the spoken begins too, matter / earth; earth and the mirth that matters / burst; burst and the sort that can see, matters / waters; waters come forth to see, thee, matters / Armageddon; Armageddon comes undone in our loving attend of the heart that matters, loved / Holston; Holston held as the lake that filled with the hephatic glob of the code called human and this, the matters win, love / hurled; hurled at a world called man; kind; matters; love / solvent; solvent of the send too, matters / salvage; salvage and the suspend ends, mated attend too, material means that matter in, love / rain; rain comes to the plains that matter in, love / came; came to the home of the dome jerusalem matters / many; many days I stayed at matters / lost; lost and around them, matters / every; every day's matter / tossed; tossed and across then, matters / pleasure; pleasure and the hearth of matters / pleasant; please know the pleasant waves of the coming holidays that blend, matters / colors; colors cued and the upward date with the mates who muse about the shades of love's matter / spectrum; spectrum comes to the heart's undue and the miracle you have become in the heart within, God sends, precious truth and the youths that matter in God's rainbow of love / rose; rose degrees and the seas of amends particular to your situation then, and love is, matrilineal too, matters / firmament; firmament and the scent that matters, ambrosial, love / goodwill; goodwill given and attends set on love's matter / skate; skate to the date that matters, love / love; love's record, matters / print; print extinct decide to matters / primp; primp about this, matters / announce; announce the days of matter / lights; lights that stay in, matters / staged; staged delights, matter / welcome; welcome sums matter / list; list a straight degree of matters / lust; lust has come, freshly through, too, matters / lots; lots of ways to be, mattered / lens; lens on the seize matters / career; career comes too, matters / careen; careen to the dream of matters / collide; collide with the side that matters / conceive; conceive of the need too, matter.

CHAPTER FIVE

Prism; prism and the mention that dimension is the wife of all regard for love, matters / transit; transit and the traces that lure our faces to the places of giant regard for the God in this, matters / measure; measure a place that squares the matter / spill; spill and the wheel that wound the town with respect for the nest of this matter / regional; regional regard for the card of all require to fly higher in the sights of great degrees and the mention of all matters / pyramid; pyramid and the thin regard for the card of all that matters / period; period and the cards that will matter / ancient; ancient and the stays that win matters / talk; talk to the moon and the soon that will, matters / inform; inform your stake as the take that matters / outdoor; outdoor matters / outgoing; outgoing wins, the matters / sunset; sunset agree to matter / adventure; adventure sent to the matter, love / oriental; oriental cues attend thee, matters / orientation; orientation trues the matter / initiation; initiation and the muse that within matters / height; height and the sight that matters / train; train to be admired and the sired appear to matter / plausible; plausible and the plates that matter / positive; positive and the trues that matter / jump; jump to the hump that matters, the mountains of love / born; born to be worn to be mattered / pleasant; pleasant agree to be well within, love's matters / pistil; positional pistils and the stamens of loving matters / jazz; jazz and the kin that plays in the stays that matter / jasmine; jasmine and the trues that matter / yoni; yoni meals melt with the dues that matters / lingam; lingam named the fame that matters / lather; lather and the wins that matter / sex; sex and the life that matters / candid; candid turns to be within, matters / encapsulate; encapsulate your date with matters / embalm; embalm less this matter / crush; crush on the test that matters / reflect; reflect and directive matters / soft; soft and the point that matters / passionate; passionate and true agrees that matter / enlighten; enlighten with the sight in matters to be regarded as love / ascend; ascend to the mend that matters / super; super and the coupe that driven matters / silver; silver and the ways that within matter / glide; glide; to the side that matters / fly; fly like the truth that matters / flow; flow with the news that matters / flown; flown and the throne that matters / mesmerize; mesmerize the size that matters / amount; amount and the count that is in, matters / available; available to the well that wills matters / ride; ride the side that matters / mount; mount the count too, matters / horse; horse and the course that's in matters / help; help and the dates that matter / down; down to the sound that matters / seat; seat and the set that bets on matters / furl; furl like a curl that matters / curse; curse and the verse that mattered lifts too, love / language; language and desires too, matters / spell; spell the deal that matters, l-o-v-e / reveal; reveal the type that matters / sleepy;

sleepy days that win matters / world; world of the commit to the mate that matters / open; open daily too, matters / throat; throat and the vote for yes, matters.

CHAPTER SIX

Attentive; attentive to the strand that is supreme within the matter's means, love / supreme; supreme within the dream that eloped to the other streams of love's matter / extreme; extreme and worn as the sword of all revival and the rite archival within, love's, matter / embassy; embassy of the blues and the news that sure arrive can strive to be involved within the friend that matters is, love / ambassador; ambassador dues and the special gleam of the stems that appraise our raise to the lips material and the gift that matters / kudos; kudos and the place that matters within the parliament's gifts of the matters of God / contents; contents sent to heaven's gate and the state elect to material matters in, love / precious; precious and due the erect review of the matters in love / precise; precise degrees of the matters we, loved / preside; preside and the side that matters / prana; prana and the cues then matter / protect; protect the neck of all degrees that matter / egg; egg in faces replace of the matters then, of, love / delight; delight in the sight that matters / love; love and the dues within, matters / lift; lift to the gift that matters / guide; guide and the ride to agree into, the matters win, in love / gear; gear and the near abide within, insured by, magnificence within, our materials that matter then, love / safe; safe to be with, the lover. the matters, compare this, then, love / compare; compare assured and the dare would be? too, love matters / coincide; coincide with the side who matters in love / consensual; consensual agree too, matters then, love / concept; concept adept at degrees which matter then, love / content; content of the sort that matters / Cabriolet; Cabriolet blue with the speed of the news that then matters / cavort; cavort to the sort then matter / codes; codes clues dreams and matters, love / Capri; Capri and the isle wild with decree of love, matters / mark; mark the start of more molecules that matter then, love / marco; marco isled deport to the sort mattered in, love / isle; isle wide with the style then, matters / guided; guided in ascend too and the matters then, love / toured; toured the sired that matters in, love / tripped; tripped and the strip that matters within, love / rips-rips ell the veil that matters / torn; torn and true, forgive, matter / fortunate; fortunate and elate, matters / force; force done, overcome through matters there, love / frolic; frolic with the some who love like matters of God / favor; favor due the matters you, and love / divorce; divorce due the residue of love less given and more then, matters / decide; decide to see the matters then, love / shoes; shoes and the news there mattered / tools; tools and the stools which hold our sold that matters / icy; icy dues these matter then, loved / broken; broken and the news that notes are due to the magic in love's living matter / conspire; conspire to hire deeper feels of the material of the matter then, love / contents; contents content in the matter meant too, love / capable; capable and clued within matters friends knew then, as, love / sort; sort of the sort who matter within / solid; solid and the days that dues can mean, matters / plan; plan to be, mattered with and within, then, love / expand; expand to the state that's great with matters / forgiven; forgiven and the send that matters / foreplayed; foreplayed and the states that win, matters / old; old and ways that send too, matters / seem; seem and the gather that finds the collective reside at matters of love / extremity; extremity chosen is the love of give matters / chosen; chosen a tool to tell of, matters then, God / choose; choose to state a date with deep within, thee, matters, friends of love / chilly; chilly over and the due that is, matters within, love / agree; agree to see the love that is, mattered, too, and within, God / love; love is kind to the matter / nurture; nurture one another in love's matters.

CHAPTER SEVEN

Choose; choose and the meetings that matter in, love / charge; charge a charge to the wins that matter / move; move and the meetings won, matters / hard; hard and the hearts that melt, matters / make; make and the meetings that seal the matters / break; break and the beat for all that matters / stake; stake and the seals that matters / heart; heart and the cues that matter / vampires; vampires deal with matters deep in love / done; done and the sun that matters / designate; designate and the date that wins matters / course; course and the muse that matters / value; value and the feels that matter / evaluate; evaluate and the date that matters / valuation; valuation and the nation that matters / vault; vault to the halt that matters / packs; packs and the sort that matters most too, love / fake; fake and the nestle that matters / flake; flake and the bake that matters / fare; fare and the pair that make us matter / fair; fair and the love that is rare matters / charge; charge and the card that matters / be; be met by the matters that win / glad; glad to be within matters / glee; glee and the matters that win / glee-full; glee-full in matters / assume; assume and the room that matters / decide; decide to be measured and mattered / dances; dances and the chances that matter / danced; danced and the dates that win matters / dared; dared and the cared that matter / dole; dole and the coil that wins matters / gave; gave a rave the opportune too, love is, material to matters / opportune; opportune and the noon that matters / commune; commune and the rune that matters / moon; moon and the send that meets in matters / mended; mended and melted in the matters / embrace; embrace and the taste that wins these, matters / given; given and the living matters / grace; grace and the taste that wins, matters / God's; God's goods matter / in; in to the send that matters / to; to and to you, matters / your; your door matters / example; example and the sample, matters / gracefully; gracefully grew our matters / ripped; ripped to the state that matters / out; out and in matters / pages; pages and the stays that blend matters / expedite; expedite and the fuse that matters / Michelangelos; Michelangelos cream and the stream that won a sculptural embrace of the pace called love's cure, matters / site; site and the flight that matters too, love / sight; sight and the white that wins matters / florence; florence and the cues that win, matters due too, love / ensconce; ensconce and the blends that matter / date; date and the dues that matter / fix; fix and the fuse that matters / pack; pack again

enthused / perform; perform a warm arrive at the news enthuse / perchance; perchance the dance that matters / dip; dip to the strip that matters / choose; choose a life that news can be made of matters / lifetime; lifetime and the news that matters / fuse; fuse and the scope that wins matters.

CHAPTER EIGHT

Relaxed; to the thorough matterments / regarding; regarding relaxing ones called love / details formulated and the fortunates interior to a relationship due your mettled matters / placements mentioned who relaxed into french matters / functional flatters and the mattering won / taos; taos matters through the yellow flu of God / echo; echo and the cues that matter / uniquely; uniquely due these matters, love / light; light and the sight that wins matters / essential; essential and the scene that lends wonders to manners / gears; gears and the go that matters / high; high and the stay that matters / frolic; frolic to the tonic that matters / render; render and the send that matters / reads; reads like love that matters / checks; checks and the cues that matter / meet; meet a street that matters / mortal; mortal and the fuse that matters / sort; sort of the court that matters / suspect; suspect erect and the matters of men / complete; complete and the scene that matters / perform; perform at the warm arrival at love's matters / climb; climb and the time that matters / limbs; limbs and the seeds that matter / limits; limits and the minutes that matter / found; found and the sounds that mend matters / expand; expand and the then that matters / understand; understand forgive, matters / succeed; succeed and the need that matters / surrender; surrender and the sender that matters / God; God and the muse that matters / good; good and the mood that matters / agree; agree to be, mattered / understood; understood and the mood that matters / the; the love that is, matters / knees; knees and the sees that matter / defeat; defeat and the neat arrive that matters / and; and with this wins the mends that matter / yet; yet you'll be the winning ones, matters mend, love / win; win and the bend that matters / top; top of the tips that matter / end; end of the matters in love / yet; yet we will be mattered too, love / life; life of the matter that mend, love / mountain; mountain and the men that matter / amend; amend the mend that matters / resurrect; resurrect and the akin that matters / love; love and the dues that matter / mountains; mountains and the mellow that matters / wade; wade and the win that matters / wisdom; wisdom and the winning that matters / salvation; salvation and the cues that matter / complete; complete and the cues that matter / parents; parents and the pens that matter / held; held and the mantle that lends matters to God / people; people who steeple their lives with mends of the matters called love / sleep; sleep at the steep arrive called magically given God's matters too, love / safe; safe and to the sex that matters, loved / in regard; in regard and to the card that manners / for; for it all, matters / peace; peace and the release of matters / deep; deep and due, matters / with; with and send too, matters / within; within and the friend too, matters / living's; living's come to the sum that matters.

CHAPTER NINE

Forthright; forthright fused too, the matters / centric; centric agrees too, matters / sensual; sensual deals will, matter / foresight; foresight and the cues that win, matters / foreigns; foreigns date with matters relate / trade; trade a tree to the roots that matter / truly; truly and the freed matter / brinked; brinked and the blues pace matters / fondly; fondly and the fuse in matters / given; given ascend to the mend that matters / genuine; genuine and true too, matters / gift; gift and the friend shipped matters / simple; simple and the place that matters in, love / lift; lift a dance to the chance too, matter / bracelet; bracelet worn like the charm that matters / link; link with the brink that advents matter / for life; for life I said, let us, matter / understand; understand why I matter / employ; employ the toy that matters / power; power and the play that matters / place; place a trace at matters / perfect; perfect and agreed too, matters / part; part that can be mattered / candid; candid and the plan that matters / casual; casual and the seas that matter / sustain; sustain a place that matters / care; care a cure that matters / nutritive; nutritive tastes that matter / profound; profound agree too, matters / precept; precept peeled to the matters / perception; perception and the peeks that matter / healed; healed and the held that matters / held; held and the meld that matters / fulfilled; fulfilled and agree too, matters / foster; foster and the cure that matters / spell; spell the well that matters / spill; spill and the chill that matters / given; given and the gable that matters / gain; gain a strain that matters / lived; lived and the degrees that matter / loved; loved and within matters / drilled; drilled and the dues that matter / drained; drained and the true that matters / perfect; perfect and the muse that matters / proud; proud to be mattered / present; present and the kin too, mattered / around; around and the sound that is in, matters / crown; crown due the trips to agree and the medium we amuse as matters of God / accept; accept the date with the mate who matters / you; you know the show that matters / reign; reign within, matters / rains; rains and strains that matter / give; give me a date like yours that matters / relief; relief and the turf that matters / release; release relates too, matters / release; release and the dues that matter / please; please decide to be mattered by, love / dash; dash to the cash that matters in love / during; during a date I saw matters fly too, love / spat; spat upon and ground into love's matter / stir; stir a cure as mattered in, love's mix, God / relieve; relieve the sleeve that matters too, God's / roster; roster about the matters of love / red; run red to the sun that matters.

CHAPTER TEN

Clue; clue and the cues within, matters / flash; flash at the cash that matters / globe; globe due the arrive at the strive too, matters / hologram; hologram given the forgiven in matters of love / riddle; riddle clued to the forgiven / rapture; rapture the dues mattered / fed; fed by the said too, matters / frames; frames and the games within, matters / collapse; collapse points past and the last that matters / layers; layers done and the matters won of love / clash; clash at the state of forgive and the living that matters in love / heaven; heaven wins the matters in love / rule;

rule by rule, matters / lends; lends a hand, matters / tool; tool of the rule that matters / relate; relate to the date who matters / fate; fate is the fuse with matters / electricity; electricity trues her date with the state electric's bill about all that matters within, love / day; day of the due and the hue that matters / election; election gives us too, matters / gave; gave a date the dues that mattered / metatronic; metatronic agree to be, mattered within / relay; relay the stays electric to the mend that matters in love / residue; residue unglued and the matters win, love / luxor; luxor forgiven and the matters mend, we win, in, love / egypt; egypt done, matters won, maat cured, love / door; door and the ways that matter in love / doorway; doorway dues to the matters in love / comes; comes a day mattered / path; path pure matters / plunge; plunge in too, the matters, love / passions; passions and plans that matter in man and love / dosha; dosha done and forgiven in love's matter / pretense; pretense becomes the matter / repair; repair the stare electric with the metric agree too, matter / repeat; repeat the seat that matters in love / rests; rests on dues that matter / wrong; wrong and the song that right is allude to the mood energetic / concept; concept healed, energetic, moods, met, matters set, love / ciao; ciao to the owe electric, matters / good-bye; good-bye to the why less, matters / trial; trial run and over, done, matters / run; run to the moon that matters / mom; mom found in yes we matter / partner; partner puts heart in muse that matters / past; past is over, done, matters / plan; plan to be agreed too, matters / plans; plans that change stain, matters / durable; durable dates with matters, love / dealt; dealt with the felt, matters / deal; deal with the heal in matters / let's; let's debate our matters in love / page; page too, matters / quetzal; quetzal viewed in the flight that matters / branch; branch of youth, matters / truth; birth and the news that matters / blimp; blimp forgive, matters / pretzel; pretzel life done, matters / patch; patch the sort that becomes, matters / pure; pure to the sure that matters / powers; powers blend in matters / plank; plank walked matters / sport; sport the short arrive at matters / chant; chant the thrive of yes, we, matter.

CHAPTER ELEVEN

Crystal; crystal agree too, matter / mexico; mexico and seas that matter / incant; incant the chant that matters / incantation; incantation about true matters / oration; oration, the gift, that matters in love / gift; gift due the matters in love / crystalline; crystalline and the lean that matters / compete; compete with the sort who matter / note; note about the vote that matters / divine; divine that kind who matter / ordination; ordination comes too, the matter / essence; essence healed matters / reward; reward due, matters / respect; respect reflect matter / regard; regard the date as material to matters / know; know the sort who matter / power; power forms the matter / place; place face in matters / return; return to the One who matters / resurrect; resurrect connect matter / finish; finish the Other matters / put; put your place in matters, heart's / tone; stone delays, matters / crypt; crypt decays matters / egyptian; egyptian extend too, matters / Rasmutten; Rasmutten moods matter / Ramses; Ramses knew matters / great; great state matter / keep; keep quiet matters / light; light bliss matters / over; over, due, matters / cover; cover blue, matters / license; license to be, matters / pyramid; pyramid dues, matter / Giza; Giza knew great matters / engage; engage in allies who align within matters / elope; elope to the scope that matters / estate; estate given matters, love / escape; escape over, due, matters / roar; roar like the soar agreed to in matters mend love / random; random and the cave of all reward for matters / revelatory; revelatory agree to be, mattered / redefine; redefine the kind who matter / three; three who know who mattered / who; who are you to matters loved? / knew; knew the One who mattered, Go / Remember; Remember the worn degree of matters / meet; meet in the street that matters, love / sing; sing like the Ones who matter, God / intone; intone a decree to be mattered upon, love / crampon; crampon on, climb, matters / strong; strong and to the sort, matters / throne; throne and the temples mattered / temple; temple faced mattered / infrared; infrared matters seen through eyes agleam with love / waves; waves that decide to be mattered / code; code and the cues that matter in, love / spirit; spirit about, love's, matter / binds; binds done, matters / template; template becomes you, mattered / place; place of the fund mattered / purity; purity and clarity in matters, love / clarify; clarify your date with matters / lure; lure your state to matters insure of love.

CHAPTER TWELVE

Rapture; rapture and the capture insured by the matrix released to love's matter / formation; formation and the station that's amused within and the materials that matter in, love / mysterious; mysterious and the mood that is amused within the miracles of love's matter / interwoven; interwoven and the agrees too, matters / translation; translation and the station that mends matters / illuminated; illuminated and sated within matters / isolation; isolation and the station that matters in love / script; script and the salvation that is sent to the manners in love's matters / synagogue; synagogue and the meeting that met in love's matters / guide; guide that meets matters / tao; tao's that deals in matters of love / society; society and the cues that matter / structure; structure and the well within love's matters / ironically; ironically cued as the moods within matters / might; might and the seas that matter / affinity; affinity and the trees that matter / phone; phone and the cues that matter / almanacs; almanacs and the meals that matter / proverbs; proverbs and the allowance assigned to life's matters / vital; vital and the cues that matter / hieroglyphic; hieroglyphic and the cures that matter in love / altar; altar about the meals that heal in matters of love / incense; incense and the shoes that matter / stone; stone and the trees within matters / proper; proper cubes matter / maya; maya stays holidayed in love's matters / signature; signature cures matters / cylinder; cylinder days materially mattered / artist; artist grew too, matter / compound; compound and the sounds that matter / supernatural; supernatural and the soundings matter / strides; strides and the sides that win matters / republic; republic of cues that matter / ash; ash days that matter / ivy; ivy waves

leave the straits material to matters in love / encircle; encircle the miracle mattered in love / arrows; arrows deep in the streets material and to matters in love / curvy; curvy cures material in agrees too, love / tantric; tantric and the seen in matters in love / freedom; freedom and the dreams to remember matters in love / lesson; lesson done matters won, love / Kabbalah; Kabbalah cued to the mood that matters within, love / applied; applied and the stood for, matters, love / metric; metric and the sets who matter / century; century deals matter / construct; construct a truck that matters in love / enjoy; enjoy the sort who matter / frames; frames fed flames in love's matter / intersect; intersect at the resurrect called matters in, love / locate; locate the state within, matters / original; original to the use that matters / slip; slip to the trip that matters / program; program cues matter / stroll; stroll to the seas that matter / jibe; jibe and the jubilant create for matters / refill; refill the traits within matters of mend, love / telepathic; telepathic and to the agree then, matters / vision; vision and the phonics that matter in, love / relate; relate to the stay within, matters / offer; offer to the coffers that matter / fire; fire and the hire that wins matters / double; double and the dues that matter too, love / behold; behold the sold in waves that matter / wealth; wealth and the sway that matters.

CHAPTER THIRTEEN

Deja vu; deja vu and the you that matters / mixture; mixture and the steep arrive at matters in, love / organs; organs and the astounds that win, matters / purity; purity and the clarify that heaven's by and the winds that manage matters in, love / mediate; mediate at the state that matters / expert; expert agree to be, mattered / ultimate; ultimate states and the mates that matter / bodies; bodies and the cues within matters of hearts that live loved / lit; lit with suns that matter / lasting; lasting cues that matter / loves; loves dues matter materially too, love / listen; listen to the hasten in love's matters / extend; extend to the friend who matters / experience; experience cues and the matters win, love / absolute; absolute and the repeat of the meet at meditations of durates through the matters in, love / abraid; abraid and the stirring arrive at the material side of matters in, love / priest; priests who come to the sum risen too, matters material in the physical states in, love / sapphire; sapphire cures around the astound called matters in, love / vibratory; vibratory agrees an he seas material to the matters in love / dense; dense and the dues that matter / environmental; environmental cues that matter / dynamic; dynamic agrees too, matter / perception; perception heals matters real within love / matrix; matrix cures matters lifts love / fields; fields that heal the matters in love / geometric; geometric ascend to the meet that is mattered within, love / coalesce; coalesce and the guest that is mattered with, love / condone; condone and the phone that is mattered too, love / phenomena; phenomena about the matters in, love / absolute; absolute agree to be amused about and the shout that wins matters in, love / nazareth; nazareth flowers and the powers that blend the nativity with the send too, love's amuse and the matters then, love / moral; moral and the pictorial place, love matters /

complete; complete and to the extent matters / content; content and the cues that win matters / capable; capable and agreed too, matters then, love / clever; clever and the sever that winds blew through to matters in, love / clear; clear enough to see through, matters then, love / flown; flown to the zones in matters then, love / far; far enough to decree about matters then, love / see; see the decide to matter about, love / lands; lands and the sands that matter then, love / discovers; discovers a due mattered in, love / mysteries; mysteries and the histories of matters thin too, love / material; material to the state within matters then, love / maternal; maternal and the yearn within matters then, love / messiah; messiah cued to the matters then, love / crowns; crowns and the sounds that bend too, matters prismatic then, love / copies; copies and the curves that matter them, love / lectures; lectures and the stays that matter most, love / lovers; lovers and the covers that matter too, love / stage; stage and the rage that matters within, love / joins; joins another mattered best, love / committee; committee to the city of combust that matters / pressure; pressure and the state of degrees that matter / due; due on the cue that matters / over; over and through that matters / essentially; essentially all that give matters / experientially; experientially extreme and to the seam that wins matters / imbue; imbue the cue that matters in, love / balance; balance and the challenge in these matters then, love / call; call to the says that win, matters then, love / create; create the state that matters then, too, love / publish; publish the ways that matter then, love / see; see to the days that matter.

THE MATERIAL-MENTS
LEVEL 27

CHAPTER ONE: *Material to a nature*

God's accurate; accurate and to this degree, materially free and this is the heal called precisely we'll be loved by all that's within our love / entire; entire and the hire that's in the material of love / prophecy; prophecy and the heart that wins the essential gives of material stays too, love / matter; matter and the material that is, love / invest; invest in the test that is material too, love / fragile; fragile and the tools that agree to the dues within our mutual materials then, love / layer; slayers due the deep regard for the cards within our materials, love / crop; crop and the stop to be at, love, materially / leaders; leaders and the creel that is filled with potentiality materially due too, love / allow; allow the now to the material dreams of love / engineer; engineer and the dear that is near the material wins love / affirm; affirm and the agree to be material in devise of the rise to agree too, love / vibe; vibe and the rise too, love is, materially due too, love / models; models and the melds that can be material too, love / acquire; acquire the hire that meets in materials deep in love / praise; praise and the raise that matters the materials in, love / tingling; tingling and the singing that sensates in the meld of the great material called love / truth; truth and the trill that will be material in love / signals; signals given assumed and resumed in the medium material / tool; tool and the box material, love, hu-man / respiration; respiration and the station material / generate; generate that state of well regard for the material world / validate; validate the date material / process; process and the cross that wins the material lends of love / travel; travel and the ravel to agree too, materially, love / feedback; feedback comes in the sum continental too, love's material / nature; nature and the status material / inner; inner ear material / pulse; pulse and the clan material / sensation; sensation and the nation material / space; space and the taste material / refer; refer to the word's material / footstep; footstep materially secure in the world of spirit / yield; yield and the shield that will feel materially well / moderation; moderation set on the met material and love's relate / roots; roots and the shoots materially familiar / tactics; tactics and the traces material / achieve; achieve and the sleeves elastic and material / universe; universe and the curse that aids the release to the material ways that reveal our love / intuitive; intuitive and the truth in the material lays love / strange; strange and degrees of the materials we love / ideally; ideally and due to the materials in love / dynasty; dynasty deals with the material meals of the fed absolute and the mute deliver of the word, love / reform; reform and the warm arrive at the material glide called love / eccentric; eccentric to a taste material / heirloom; heirloom and the gloom that agreed too the materials in love / jades; jades and the shades electric to moods materially true too, love / base; base and the status material within, love / correlating; correlating and the stating that materially can see no relief and the love is on in God / fit; fit in the explain material / status; status and the place materially free too, love / floating; floating and the voting place called materially love / dawn; dawn and the song material too, love / archaeologist; archaeologist and the psychologist who gave the heavens a laid highway to the material symptoms of love / concert; concert and the assert to the materials in love / ample; ample and the samples material within, love / storm; storm and the warm agree to be material within, love / sandstone; sandstone and the seals who heal materially / dragon; dragon and the hour of the man material / testimony; testimony dues too, the material / elsewhere; elsewhere and now, how, materials / everywhere; everywhere seen the vibration material / always; always material / forever; forever in the eternal way, material.

CHAPTER TWO

Resolve; resolve and intend to begin to declare the care for the light elective, materially direct too, love / tend; tend and the ends to be resolved within, materially, love / polarity; polarity and the cares for the material stares too, love / faith; faith and the grave attach has snapped to declare the fair arrive at material success in the spiritual confess of love / courage; courage and the act of confess to the material straits of love / action; action and needs materially direct too, love / seeds; seeds that near perfect in the actions of love's material cure, God's plan, hu-man / laughter; laughter and the seems that declare the fare particular and the means exact too, the materials, love / along; along and the song material / rigid; rigid degrades, the material / diligency; diligency and the dues material / hidden; hidden and the dreams material / attain; attain and the strains material / thread; threads and the steeds material / image; image and the careens material / honor; honor and the power material / imagery; imagery and the moods material / scene; scene and the suns material / domain; domain and the same material / similar; similar and the material means that's found in the frames profane / grin; grin and the trim material / portrayed; portrayed and the staid, material / finger; finger and the sting material / collect; collect and the sect material's release into, love / chiandrical; chiandrical collect and the neck material / reciprocal; reciprocal and the resort material / float; float and the vote material / intrigued; intrigued and the step material / vases; vases and the stays material and floral too, love / camera; camera and the cares material / carved; carved and the cures material / for; for the ours material / flavor; flavor and the share material / timeless; timeless aspects of the truth material / rare; rare and the dare material / secrets; secrets and the scoop material / integrating; integrating and the sating material / passage; passage and the dues material / reveal; reveal and the feel material / startling; startling and the muse material / clarity; clarity and the cues material / series; series and the sends material / collection; collection and the selection that is met materially too, love / breathe; breathe and be materially free too, love / led; led and the fed materially and free too, love / personal; personal and the sort that is free, too, materially true and love / magnificent; magnificent and the sort that is mused too, love / possibility; possibility and the keep that's amused within materials thin too, love / build; build the field of seated pleasure, materials gleam with the heated treasure of love / seated; seated in a heated sort of material love / monument; monument too, knews, material / cluster; cluster at the heart of the sort material / flowers; flowers drawn by material sums undone, within, love /

territory; territory cures materially loved / intern; intern and the turn material / astonishing; astonishing news comes materially / center; center of the sum, material / depict; depict the fix material / necessity; necessity and the muse material / decade; decade of the glad material / insurance; insurance paid fused materially / lineage; lineage direct to the muse material / scholarly; scholarly causes material / mighty; mighty flow, muse, material.

CHAPTER THREE

Tremendous; tremendous and the dues are paid to the material stays at love / waking; waking and the making at love's materials / exchange; exchange and the rate that is, material / therapy; therapy and the fuse that burns materially / tissue; tissue news and the blues material / broadcast; broadcast and the beast's release to confess of the material mess called less then, love / altar; altar and the altar of truth in God's love is, material / conduct; conduct and the interrupt that is straight to the faith of material confess / equation; equation and the station's material too, contestant and the cues that live loved / motion; motion to the notion all true and the truest devotion to the material in, love / credibility; credibility and the cues that matter within materially love / biology; biology and the blues material / chaos; chaos and the dues that deliver materials you use for love / chasms; chasms and the stays within materials too, love / elaborate; elaborate reveal of the deals material / language; language and the stay is material / venturing; venturing and tune that is material too, love / treasure; treasure and the trees that material will be through the ours of compare and / the cares that will see the all of forever / completion; completion and the cues material / spoil; spoil and the oil that is, material / hence; hence and extents material / strategic; strategic agrees to be, materially freed within, love / originate; originate at the states material in, love / limit; limit to the free and this is the gate too, material's see, love / ultimate; ultimate cures of the materials seen, love / principle; principle of the sort material / cultivated; cultivated and the sated agree to be, material / act; act at the facts material / evolved; evolved and solved materially in, love / instinct; instinct and the involve called the solvent material mend, love / desire; desire to be hired for free delivery to the materials thick with love / pile; pile to the smile within material inflect of love / harmonic; harmonic agree to be settled in the freed express of material constitute and the well repeated defend for the materials in love / cell; cell well and worn to thin materials deep in love / tension; tension and the attentive states worn free to material bliss within, love / assuring; assuring dates with materials pairs of love / synapses; synapses close on the blades material and the stage elite to the magical love / odor; odor and the dues material / muscular; muscular review and the prepare to be, material / dance; dance and the stance material / spectrum; spectrum trim with the familiar desire to hire material love / aura; aura glued with the material news called love / cards; cards and cubes material / period; period date with the state forgive and the live that is, material within, love / frequency; frequency dealt with in love's complete materials to the 888 of a date with / Christ's elate of the office of God /

bride; bride too and the materials through our love / mystical; mystical amuse and the pride to abide within, love / ego; ego driven and the given abide to the side material / abstract; abstract and the drives material / egypt; egypt wins the scenes material / centripetal; centripetal profuse and the use material / tend; tend and the send material / sphere; sphere and dear, material / metaphor; metaphor and the chore, material / hemisphere; hemisphere and the steer material / medicine; medicine agreed to be practiced in material defend of the band hu-man / trance; trance over, come, materially / sober; sober dears, material / poetry; poetry and the pews material / hymns; hymns and the dins material / chief; chief and the staff material / animal; animal mature, know the cures, material.

CHAPTER FOUR

Feather; feather and the maat feel for the real abide inside the kind that danced for balance within the material, worlds, hu-man / fundamental; fundamental and the dates that deign the due for the view electric within the trends material / address; address and the test to stand in this manner at the matter called love's material / position; position yourself in the mission ignited, as invited, too, materially, love / mankind; mankind is the fine materials in, love / initiation; initiation is the station particular to the materials within, love / confession; confession and the ovation called material is, love / weaves; weaves and the sleeves that matter materially / genuine; genuine, the dream, materially / suffer; suffer and the let's go to the peace of the East and the Western agree to forget the forget and let's remember that love is, fun, materially / delicious; delicious the taste of this mellow attempt to forgive, let us live for giving, for getting, for allowing, then, materially love / technique; technique and the seek that materially matters / slip; slip to the mood materially / wisdom; wisdom and the seems, materially / moment; moments and the materials that win electrically lean the dream of forever in God is agreed too, love / degree; degree and the still materials within, love / building; building and the sums material / fumbling; fumbling and the swell material / element; element and the accent is, material / blank; blank and the stake is due, materially / ecstasy; ecstasy and the shrill agree to be, materially / mock; mock is over, know the success of allow and the now of God's agree to free your ability to materially be too, God / kingdom; kingdom to the seek that is found materially within, love / storage; storage and success and the filling confess of the durate called materially, love / ocean; ocean and the sees that matter materially / toy; toy true and the free agreed to be, materially and matured, within, love's play / symbolic; symbolic we see that metatronic access to the material breath called love / figures; figures and the friends material too, love / majority; majority and the secure material too, love / balanced; balanced and the chalice material too, love / overall; overall and the call within is, material / bright; bright regard for the card material / angels; angels can see the light's material / cube; cube and the modality called mood for the free material, energy's unlock is then, / love's meditate on the squares pair, love / manifest; manifest and the best degree of material maturity within, love / advanced; advanced states of stages mature to the materials then, love / temple; temple of trends material then, love / universe; universe of truths materially freed, know the resurrect of the revelation / called the status of hu-man love / sage; sage found in the stand material, hu-man's, love / dazzle; dazzle and the drew material / pentagram; pentagram decide and the size material / sun; sun spell material / grants; grants and the strands material / flood; flood and the mud material / pour; pour and the our material / triangles; triangle secure within, material, then, love / fusion; fusion and confusion forgone materially then, loved / beauty; beauty and the fusion found materially / origins; origins given in the materially well, love / strife; strife and the strewn material / cosmic; cosmic and the cubes that win, materials / case; case and the trees materially well within, love's taste of the truth and the bark hu-man / healing; healing and the feeling material / planet; planet said, material / penetrate; penetrate and the state that is well, material / lace; lace and the place material / arc-angel; arc-angel well within, materials then, love / found; found and the sound material / gold; gold and the sold material / forever; forever agree, materially / flaming; flaming fuels are the power of the hours expand to the timeless stage called materially freed, love / sustained; sustained and the stand material.

CHAPTER FIVE
Desire; desire to be with the well material / remember; remember and the sender is, material / mood; mood and the food material / forest; forest fed materials in, love / disclosure; disclosure assured materially / outdoors; outdoors accrue materially / usual; usual and the soon, material / degree; degree and the free deliver of men called material / through; through the wall, material / prelude; prelude and the moods material / labyrinth; labyrinth curled with the steel material / profess; profess confess to the materials within / dusk; dusk details the wells material / choice; choice and the chills material / sunrise; sunrise and shine, materially / sunset; sunset and the bet material / medicines; medicines seen material / modern; modern days material / morning; morning news comes too, the material / turbulence; turbulence and the fuse material / golden; golden and the grain material / return; return to the soon material / innocent; insure near need optionally contoured essentially next and true / roam; roam and the home that is, materially free too, love / arrow; arrows to the ours material / instinct; instinct and the seek material / relic; relic and the relate material / theory; theory concealed relevant now, materially professed / expectation; expectation and the sums material / dagger; dagger and the deals materially free too, love / garden; garden and the goods material / geronimo; geronimo and the ride's material / saint; saint sounds well materially / transform; transform the swarm material / chemical; chemical and the kill material / nation; nation and the stand material / chain; chain and the trend material / still; still regard for the matter's material then, love / original; original dues within, materials / tape; tape and the drape material / studio; studio seen materially freed / candle; candle's handles free / signal; signal seen, materially /

alchemy; alchemy extreme to the material / deity; deity dues material / next; next to the sees, material / analyst; analyst cues the material / interaction; interaction comes too, the material / astrology; astrology told the material / bond; bond and the song in material / mystique; mystique and the meets material / dreams; dreams and the days, material / identical; identical needs material / sexuality; sexuality unsealed in the quiet regard for the materials in love / emotion; emotion and the motion material / psyche; psyche and the hike material / conclude; conclude and the mood material / account; account and the count's material / tar; tar and the stick material / analogy; analogy about the mends material / project; project respect material / explosion; explosion and the sums material / order; order and the rapture's material / operation; operation hu-man begins, material.

CHAPTER SIX
Describe; describe the scribe material / dialogue; dialogue and the dues material / fly; fly and the strides material / mind; mind amuse, material / happen; happen and the then material / mere; mere decide to be, *material *mature assign of the truth essential in reward inside the all in love* / remark; remark to the arc material / invocation; invocation and the sum's material / hallucination; hallucination and the give's material / passage; passage and the things aspirantly material / phantom; phantom and the cues material / extract; extract and the transpire material / celestial; celestial and the cares material / sky; sky muse material / divide; divide to see the light waves material / land; land and the sands material / book; book about the shout material / 13; 13 times the days material / ancients; ancients and the sun's material / God's; God's give is material / guardians; guardians grew to the muse material / katun; katun and the soon, material / flood; flood and the gates material / present; present and the seams material / link; link up your truck material / interweave; interweave and the suspend material / immaculate; immaculate agrees, material / contour; contour and the sure material / ship; ship and the sheep material / slew; slew the dragon too within, material / swarm; swarm and the storm materially agreed too, love / syllable; syllable and the cube's material / stressed; stressed and the duress is done, material / subjective; subjective acquire materially / sour; sour the taste material / sordid; sordid the dues material / survey; survey and the keeps material / aspects; aspects and cues material / prevalent; prevalent agree to be, material / spontaneous; spontaneous decide to be, material / following; following the fusion, material / earth; earth knew birth in your material / shattered; shattered and the keep material / merry; merry the day of the reconnect within love's material / mattered; mattered and the jacks material / fraulin; fraulin and the keeps material / flow; flow to be, material / pink; pink and the keep that is violet-green too, the material, love / tangerine; tangerine's fine align with the green material then, love / cupids; cupids concur is the align within, love's material / pressures; pressures to keep the yellow within are through the material / burst; burst to the heavens within the material / relate; relate to the sates material / relief; relief comes too, the material / rewards;

rewards are agreed and too, the material / reside; reside in thee, completion, materially / precedence; precedence becomes dues material / residence; residence found decide in your material / stays; God stays in your material / listen; listen to the missives material / learn; learn to be chimerical to the material / lecture; lecture with a lessen intact toward thee, material / give; give a gaining, material / spurn; spurn without yearning the material.

CHAPTER SEVEN
Additions; additions and the sums material / chore; chore and the shore material / compare; compare and the spare's material / coincide; coincide with degrees material / inside; inside the sides material / sure; sure and secure material / seal; seal and the deals material / neter; neter infused and the muse is found in God's material / initiate; initiate becomes the bemuse material / create; create and the state's material / wills; wills and deals materially free too, love / willed; willed and welled materially, love's / will; will you be materially freed? know God is, love / energetic; energetic ascend too, the material / wise; wise and the skies material / alchemical; alchemical the miracle of the melting within called God's pure material is, love / karma; karma and the led out, periodically, materially, complete, page two; God / comma; comment on the comma in God; and the love material / period; period in the set material / seat; seat on the wedge material / influence; influence been, material / faculty; faculty cued, material / team; team tree, material / trustee; trustee told the material / regeant; regeant won, materials / master; master of the muse, material / mastery; mastery cues new materials, love / grand; grand align, material / theology; theology sent new material / sephira; sephira sure the new material / one; one time well, material / ausirian; ausirian and the sight, material / theban; theban agree to be, material / theme; theme parked in, material / chronicle; chronicle the cue, material / heard; heard the word, material / wards; wards about the new material / repeat; repeat the shout, material / aloft; aloft and oft, material / relief; relief comes, materially, loved / reveal; reveal the heal, material / fly; fly to the sky, material / seal; seal on the deal, material / throne; throne the owned material / payment; payment made is material / coming; coming due, to you, material / dean; the dean of recommit, you, materially / dues; dues recognized materially, love / radiant; radiant the days and the ways material / key; key to the sounds, material / speak; speak about ways, material / general; general days, material / universe; universe cues, material / claim; claim the news, material / trick; trick overcued materially / detail; detail and the deal, material / theory; theory about man, material / gamma; gamma and the rayed materialism of all the release for the pairing called love / force; force concurs to the contours material / case; case and the point material is, love / escape; escape while the cues say, material / midst; midst the dues, new, material / numbers; numbers and the ways, material / accounts; accounts for the stays, material.

CHAPTER EIGHT
One; one and the law, material / law; law and the order of love's

new material / order; order and the cure, material / importance; importance now due the cues material / system; system and the seals material / versions; versions on the sums material / deity; deity due the cubes material / new; new and the quotes material / afield; afield and the yield material / inert; inert the sort, material / essence; essence and the presence material / fact; fact and the matters, material / major; major days due the new, material / body; body and the bliss material / same; same time true materially / supreme; supreme the dream material / serpent; serpent sent the material escape too, love / material; is; the womb / such; such a date material / week; week and the will material / loft; loft in the scene, material / stones; stones and the owns, material / litter; litter and the pups, material / density; density and the suns, material / name; name given, new, material / transfer; transfer your state to you, material / resided; resided the sided within, materials / claim; claim and the same, materials / myriad; myriad seas, material / world; world and the hues, material / hand; hand and the gives, material / food; food that lives materially / tree; tree deep in the love material / roots; roots and the shoots material / hemispheres; hemispheres become the sums of one material / action; action given consent for living material / verbal; verbal the deals material / power; power and the pills material / medium; medium curls material / totality; totality and the locality material / dealt; dealt with the dues material / myths; myths and the gifts material / denote; denote the notes material / enough; enough to be material too, love / yoke; yoke and the jokes material / fruition; fruition and the ignition material / arouse; arouse the house material / culture; culture and the sure agree too, be, material / total; total and the counts, material / trance; trance done, materially free / audio; audio sounds material / cortex; cortex and the vortex oblongata, material fresh within, love / reptilian; reptilian decree to be done, materially, love / one; one and the son material / cerebral; cerebral decide that God's inside the new material / seek; seek and the peak material / scheme; scheme overdue, material / urge; urge and the purge materially / moon; moon class, love, material / exact; exact the match material / zodiac; zodiac's vote, material / outer; outer and in, material / scope; scope and the cope material / note; note the view material.

CHAPTER NINE
Discover; discover the over materialed / external; external and to the sum material / formula; formula within the material / mineral; mineral and rich, material / widely; widely due the wide degrees of material love / kingdoms; kingdoms won, materially / liberation; liberation comes to the East's material / prefix; prefix fused materially / let; let us be, material / corners; corners and the create, material / medicine; medicine becomes the tongue material / thing; thing and the buy material / events; events and the streams material / water; water and the weds material / trunk; trunk and the trip material / center; center and the free material / roast; roast and the stake material / mummy; mummy unrolled materially / contrast; contrast the views material / sole; sole and the whole, material / pattern; pattern erupt material / error; error

over cues material / relation; relation and the woos, material / cobra; cobra and the sake material / metaphor; metaphor for the kundalini cure, Metatron, material / central; central to the cure is the yearn, material / spiral; spiral and the care, material / forever; forever the way, material / found; found the town material / explored; explored the cores material / divine; divine and the sign's material / circle; circle to the sure, material / famous; famous your name, material / cuts; cuts and the dues, material / atom; atom some, material / organs; organs and the gains donate, material / patron; patron and the saint material / method; method cued, material / blind; blind and the signed material / iron; iron and the will material / psychic; psychic and the cue material / brute; brute overdue the material / activity; activity treed the material / apparent; apparent parent, material / creator; creator cured, light material / entire; entire the gift material / precious; precious the due material / pleasant; pleasant estate material / magnet; magnet clean, material / claim; claim to be, material / forum; forum kept, material / form; form breath material / isle; isle wide, material / aisle; aisle free, material / begin; begin to be materially / beginning; beginning to see new material / disciples; disciples become materially set / vows; vows to wow with, new materials / nation; nation due this, material / mother; mother mends nature's way, materially / supreme; supreme the deem, material / diamond; diamond ahead, new material / hierarchy; hierarchy comes to anchor the material / head; head to the sound material.

CHAPTER TEN
Bound; bound within, time's material / sentiment; sentiment seams the new way, materially freed / rendition; rendition due the heart of your material / sphere; sphere and the here, material / ironed; ironed the note, material / arcetype; arcetype without the help of an h called clout materially / ascension; ascension seen materially / Enoch; Enoch said, let us give with amounts material to who we are in love / magnify; magnify your deed materially / unblock; unblock becomes your sun, materially / farm; farm found in the material / violet; violet the due, material / embodied; embodied the signed material / peace; peace and the east that is best, material / flower; flower and the our, material / flame; flame and the same, material / rainbow; rainbow and the stand, material / surround; surround the peace material / exercise; exercise the wise, material / wise; wise to the class material / flatter; flatter and the platter materialed / seek; seek and the heat material / chakras; chakras know the feel one deep to the seek material / string; string your trine to the mined material / dove; dove of the deal new millennial material / sought; sought a friend unique too, ascend, materials / lifestream; lifestream and the seams electric too, new, material / pull; pull for the sort, material / delve; delve into who's material / balanced; balanced the plan, material / chief; chief and the needs material / pole; pole and the seats, material / sheath; sheath uncued materially freed / intellect; intellect shines in the fields chosen materials / harmony; harmony and the plan materially laid free / program; program and the sort, material / mirror; mirror and the won, material /

pierce; pierce the veiled material / veil; veil reduced too, the material / unformed; unformed the swarmed material / miracle; miracle dear too, the agree, material / incarnate; incarnate the sate, material / cohabit; cohabit with won, material / habitat; habitat that sat in new material / exemplify; exemplify the style material / common; common and the curt material / multitudes; multitudes who feud for new material / rulership; rulership becomes you, materially / splendor; splendor and the dues, materials / office; office opens soon materially / lab; lab found in full material / vortex; vortex discovered, hear, the material, love / fulfill; fulfill the deal material / figure; figure on some, material / invoke; invoke the spoken, material / chart; chart and the carts material / soul; soul relate released, only one, material / decree; decree it done, materially, love / gratitude; gratitude for the dude, material / moist; moist with the kiss, material / victory; victory comes in the sums material / prophet; prophet sung, materials / spoken; spoken about the heart "material" / coal; coal deep in vein and the yearn diamond steep to new material.

CHAPTER ELEVEN
Lips; lips hum with the sum electric, Metatron, and the mood perfected in the One, material / city; city and the scape material / occurred; occurred the word, neglected, remember, Metatron's material is, love / flew; flew to the new material / rate; rate and the data material / sparks; sparks reconnect to the words, materials / pursue; pursue the deals material / term; term and the commit, material / sex; sex and the send, material / herb; herb green in greed's material / garment; garment sent, material / anew; anew the news, material / youth; youth and the sooth, material / respond; respond to the pond, material / hour; hours material / venus; venus cues, materials / emperor; emperor and the pen, material / crops; crops and the shops, material / outward; outward the stares, material / taste; taste the states, material / discard; discard the carded material / obstruct; obstruct less, the material / valley; valley views material / used; used and the stress, material / slip; slip to the good, materials / wood; wood and the knock material / guiding; guiding delight, the material / subtle; subtle the excuse, whispered, hear, material / cycle; cycle seek, completion met, love's material, due / sibling; sibling sings the new relate materially / sea; sea and the waters won materially / remote; remote the locate material / whole; whole this day, material / straight; straight to the hearts material / complete; complete the compete material / aim; aim at the game, material / extravagance; extravagance due the materials in, love / silent; silent the heart of the matters then, love's, material / strive; strive to be alike these materials / rhythms; rhythms overdues material / excess; excess and the best duress material / agitate; agitate and the planes material / seize; seize the signs materially freed too, love / shade; shade and the glad material / tao; tao and the way is, material / recoil; recoil and the oils that match materially too, love / joy; joy found in the town material / extends; extends the ends, material; / gases; gases built and the brown agree to shine on indefinitely within thee, material / trick; trick due the material / behave; behave like a cave material / clear; clear to the steer material / company; company's own, material / bread; bread and

the said, material / who; who are your own? material / travel; travel and the wild agree to decide to be, material / history; history made, new, material / something; something due, new, material / realm; realm of the told, material / photons; photons and protons material / exalted; exalted the salted material / also; also and whose? material / time; time and the rhyme materialed / homage; homage to the God material.

CHAPTER TWELVE

Governs; governs the sovereign, materials / profit; profit found in a One heart town called material / tiger; tiger and the trees material / paths; paths merge materially, loved / character; character cured is, material / elicit; elicit the solicit material / misfortune; misfortune done, new material, success / tails; tails and thee, trails, material / composite; composite the closet, material / ox; ox said forgive, new, material / gravity; gravity grew tired materially / curved; curved and the swerve is, new, material / refined; refined and the signed for, materials / hypocritical; hypocritical the oath material / rely; rely on the why material / family; family felled materially / contributor; contributor found materially / wildlife; wildlife occurs by the matters material / market; market the fees, material / fleet; fleet to the sees, material / splash; splash and the cash durate is, material / dance; dance in the dues, material / music; music comes electrically, material / lava; lava pours the cores material / havoc; havoc held away, materially / cling; cling to the clues, material / square; square and the One, material / bluffs; bluffs and the cuffs, material / asia; asia is the minor materialed / fertile; fertile the tale, material / sunny; sunny and the ways, material / curious; curious the dues material / realm; realm and the cues, material / Buddha; Buddha built news material, free / journey; journey to the core material / pilgrimages; pilgrimages come to the patient ones, material / turmoil; turmoil and the coil, material / transitory; transitory this state, material / months; months done, over, due, materials / durate; durate is great in the sate, material / connect; connect to the heart material / correlate; correlate your state with the mate material free / introspect; introspect and take connect materially / sites; sites and the suites material / wales; wales is won materially / strength; strength and thee, gain, materially / aspirant; aspirant to the hire material / attire; attire worn materially / eliminate; eliminate the state of less, material / lack; lack can say "good day" to you and your decide to abide materially freed / imply; imply hello in your stay material / depend; depend on the friend, material / tranquility; tranquility comes to the somes material / answer; answer the dare material believe / action; action set becomes material / mankind; mankind known materially freed / contentment; contentment sent the new materials / absence; absence cues the new material / remove; remove degrades material / bulb; bulb that blew the free material / comprehension; comprehension comes, the new, material / summation; summation due, materially, loves / reality; reality won in a truck called the material is, love / long; long the overdue, materials.

CHAPTER THIRTEEN

Hypnosis; hypnosis, the rule, materially / subliminal; subliminal the cure, material / money; money comes to the free material / touched; touched and the such, material / pledged; pledged a grade material / make-up; make-up quotes material / delicate; delicate tastes material / deft; deft the swift, material / destitute; destitute is due this, good-bye, materially / father; father fed a new stage regard, material / gone; gone to the zone, material / sun; sun and the shine, material / regard; regard us held, materially / card; card sharp with materials / sword; sword and the cords material / mural; mural broke, materially / specimen; specimen becomes the friend material / branch; branch and the chance material / routes; routes to the shoots material / prominent; prominent the sort, material / ledge; ledge and the clip material / feasible; feasible degrees material / tales; tales of the wells material / glance; glance at a change material / negotiated; negotiated the vote, material / maze; maze and the crowds material / basic; basic believe, hu-manity won, materially / visitor; visitor due the human, you, material / fuel; fuel the fire material / pine; pine said, new, tree, materials / rock; rock the talk material / campfire; campfire ways, material / Borneo; Borneo's blew is material / bush; bush and the such, down under, men, aborigine, believe in thee, materially / amphitheater; amphitheater built along the material lines in love / quartz; quartz the rock, material / quartzine; quartzine the scene, material free / blood; blood and the cut material / valley; valley and the view, material / kings; kings and the sings, material / zen; zen too, material / pocket; pocket opened materials / quip; quip the grip, material / did; did too, materially / peak; peak and the seek, material / persist; persist yes! materially / ethnic; ethnic grooved material / epic; epic set on recall the material / younger; younger ways, familiar, material / famous; famous stays material / subtle; subtle the sure material / gateway; gateway flew materially / filled; filled and the hilled material / sharpness; sharpness accrues materially / burdens; burdens done, materially / task; task set done materially / planets; planets stunned materially / night; night and the white regard for the spirit, brother, man, the good, God / easy; easy days, materially / begin; begin again materials / maturity; maturity cues the enthused arrive of love's material / day; day and the ways material / nearby; nearby stay, materially / west; west to the guest material, love.

THE BRAND-MENTS
LEVEL 28

CHAPTER ONE:

A brand of a particular manner, and the look within, to love

Brand; brand and the hands intact with love's brand / ballast; ballast and the chalice surrounded with love's brand / balance; balance and the beauty intent within love's brand / binge; binge and the singe that's come through the brands / benefits; benefits and the balance branded / benefits; benefits and the bites onto brands / debates; debates and the details branded / attends; attends and the triumphs branded / trains; trains and the suggestions branded / triangles; triangles and the tributes branded / tunes; tunes and the triangles branded / truth; truth told, brandness / dial; dial a file called delightful brands / diet; diets off and the cough in brands / names; names in cartons and packages same, to a brand / fats; fats out and the shouts in to love's brands / labels; labels shout and then the stables become true brands / burst; burst with a rush into the supple brands / braids; braids discussed and heavens, yes, forgive love's brands / brat; brats out and the surrender is in to the loving brands / turf; turf and the swiftly kicked out, brands / talent; talent evoked and the spoken, brands / task; a task set and the roads ahead lead to love's brands / turn; turn into the boulevards branded love / trade; trade for electives brands' / tour; tour the nation's brands / travel; travel comes into the hearts brands / beat; beat the heat into the brands, love's / spice; spice and the hurtles past, brands / trip; trip into the lightest brands / content; content to see the living's brands / science; science and the shuttles through love's brands / lush; lush enough to be postured through love / angle; angle on the planet's brands / moonlight; moonlight and the sonata, "you gotta" brands / eclipse; eclipse and the lips spent on brands / transpose; transpose and the shows electrically brands / loop; loop into another's brands / flame; flame found throughout your brands / walk; walk into nations deepened with brands / bay; bays of beauty fade into the agreement to be branded / ice; ice and the frozen rage of past transgress and the healer's address, advice said; brand less / grimaces; grimaces; grew to mean good-bye to lessens brand / send; send a package home to me called love is a lighter band; know bands / canal; canals eternal open up to show the gift brandless / trade; trade for the castle held in place through gifts of healings face into love's brands / valley; valley viewed and the electric news, forgive / material; material for the millenial forgive, brands / chalk; chalk a stalk knee deep in beans of healing's A brands / eligible; eligible to be brandless / splendor; splendor and the render brandless / beadwork; beadwork and the need work, brandless / betrothal; betrothal came through your electric decide to live for love's brand only / lifetime; lifetime of the living's brands / entice; entice a helenistic advise of Arcturian bands, brand-less / desire; desire to see the brand less / decorate; decorate your heart in love's brands / enhance; enhance a chance to stand in love's brands / home; home and the game's electric too, brands / saved / His / Holiness / retreats / Earth.

CHAPTER TWO

Vegetation; vegetation delivers the givers to love's brand / allegory; an allegory became love's brand less / defeat; defeat's dues, A's brand / revives; revives a tribe of A's / merciful; merciful manners exist in love's tribes, brand A / rejoice; rejoice in the choice to bays of A's / throat; throat and the thrilling hands A's / repose; repose and the chosen A's / parallel; parallel escalate and the states two brands / balance; balance and the chance to pay for A's brands / illicit; illicit and the palace's brands / horn; horn met replete in A's brands / role; role found and the town left, for A's / visit; visit and the values fondest; branded / gate; gate and the gallop through the brands / academy; academy and the commends degrees of brands / official; official and the dismissed due too and the lessen's brands / platonic; platonic and the sonic brands / derivative; derivative and the random's brands / word; word and the wisdom's brands / rumor; rumor and the ratings brands / deputy; deputy into dues brands / chariot; chariot and the merry way brand less / celebrate; celebrate the healing state's brands / fire; fire and the shares of A's brands / compass; compass cued to the direction's brands / bell; bell and the sell sold, brands / strong; strong enough to say yes! brands / temple; temple and the simple, brands / construction; construction and the buildings brands / helmet; helmet and the temples brands / halo; halo and the simple chill's brands / occupants; occupants decide to A's brands / field; field and the fellow's brands / tale; tale and the shallow's brands / astound; astound and the sounds of brands / ladder; ladder and the living's lifts two brands / attire; attire and the astonish within brands / stood; stood into the woods brands / conclude; conclude and the mood's brands / divine; divine and the dealing's brands / morning; morning and the calling's brands / facility; facility and the fashion's brands / radiant; radiant amounts branded / disciples; disciples and the dates found, brands / arranged; arranged a meeting's brands / sight; sight of the face, brand-full in love / craft; craft and the crews brand A / treated; treated and seated in love's brands / rendered; rendered a red own won too, A' brands / rocket; rocket and the rescue's brands / seal; seal on the mission's brands / excavated; excavated a passion for love's brands / emitting; emitting ignition of the intent to fashion's brands / term; term and the arms held up to A's brands / chamber; chamber deep in the challenge to be an A brand / both; both and the middle's brands / flight; flight and the feeling passionate throughout Nobility, brand A / heavy; heavy is out and love is in too, A brand / nobles; nobles gates open into your brand 61 raised; raised an octave again, congratulations, brands / epic; an epic written and faith found for the values past brands / embark; embark into the sample A's brands / mold; mold your passion for A's brands.

CHAPTER THREE

Pulp; pulp passed over, and out, throughout, the suggestion of love's brands / pond; pond and the scum gone into love's brands / out; out and the shout vomited out through brands lessen / impression; impression's taste of light's brands / direction; direction and the dealing brands / virtues; virtues and the vocally vociferous brands / simple; simple and the samples A, brands / acknowledge; acknowledge how to e brand less / wisdom; wisdom comes as ages ring of love's brands / insightful;

insightful and filled with love's brands / dedication; dedication to the passionate sorts. A' brands / patient; patient encounter with love's brands / goal; goal and the shillings spent for A's brands / dimension; dimensional dues and the enthuse for A's brands / ease; ease into another's place, brands / involve; involve yourself less in A's brands / entitled; entitled to a figure kinder still and the detail's A, branded / anyone; anyone says, "stay", brands less / shading; shading becomes your answers digress, brands / flatter; flatter the mother within A's brands / cloud; clouds burst, A's brands / spread; spread a news electric, A's brands / river; rivers deep in A's brands / wreckage; wreckage clears into a's brands / overcome; overcome and the living sums brands / hand; hand and the stands electrically branded / bolt; bolt into the voltage brands / often; often into appliances branded / frame; frame of the fellowshipped brands / civility; civility and the agility to be blessed throughout, brands / rule; rule of the valuable dates brands / century; century sealed to the daily brands / nip; nip duration at a station select and the shuttle into the values archaic and beyond, brands / shark; shark nips bleed with value-less brands / slip; slip past the past, brands / read; read about listening's brands / glad; glad to see horizons near the farthest star, points away into brands / prefer; prefer a placement near brand A / sort; sort out friends and brands / custom; custom came into A's brands / equal; equal the status and the brands into A / modesty; modesty amidst love's brands / continue; continue the mission into brands / pleasant; pleasant stays in holidays of A's brands / ought; ought to be sought as A's brands / misfortune; misfortune gone into A's brands / respect; respect another's advance into A's parallel example, God's gifts and the lifting attitude for God's status in your brand, hearts held open again / play; play again with the year's brands / tower; towering trips into the days of brands / spade; spade broken and the mating's brands / consider; consider the gifts and the lifts metaphysic to brands / rising; rising and the sizing's brand / stood; stood and the shoulds out, brands / race; race across the palace called brands / stretched; stretched into sizing's brands / concluded; concluded and out and then into brands /. distinctly; distinctly done and into the sun, brands / drew; drew and the values on too brands / visible; triple states and the brands / hole; hole out and the samples brands / grown; grown and too, the simple brands / tempting; tempting and the simples brands / tight; tight and the temple's brands / griddle; griddle and the middle's brands.

CHAPTER FOUR

Rest; rest in the arms you know best, your own, and invest often in the living's lights and the temples of men brand less / dug; dug and dealt with in forgiveness coming around too, love's brand / hollow; hollow into the hallow mended, hu-man, brands / about; about electrically in deed, into the brands / asceed; asceed and the seeds of brands / past; past and the simply smiling brands / leave; leave alone and send for the brand A / while; while I smile, we brand / done; done and the dealt with, brands / think; think again of love's brands / cup; cup deep in love's brands / stared; stared into the place on A's brands / poison; poison is out to A brands /

shook; shook up the hollow thoroughly, needle free, too, brands / arsenic; arsenic; felt like blood to often lessens, brands / spring; spring forth to delivery on A's brands / pewter; pewter and the smelt electric too, a brand on love / fair; fair enough said, brands / lad; lad to bled for, brands / sky; sky sent delivery into the light's brands / trouble; trouble is over, delivery comes, brands / chance; chance the stance in A' brands / sale; sale made leave brands / scored; scored another victory too, a's brands / shirt; shirt and the skirted brands / ride; ride across land's brands / pour; pour grace through your glasses brands / tale; tales told of gentle A's brands / rhetoric; rhetoric met delivery at A's brands / dialogue; dialogue deep in love's confession too, brands / examination; examination became your brand / like; like a missive's brands / master; master the mission's brands / fool; fool of the folly's brands / indeed; indeed in the seed's brands / request; request the suggestion that this is your brand / contrary; contrary to other strains, A's brands / chastise; chastise less the other's brands / longing; longing became living's brands / justice; justice made A's brand / nature; nature nurtured in the nestled brand, A / luxury; luxury to the moment brand A / innocence; innocence lent to the A's brands / satisfy; satisfy your craving for the A's brands / lord; lord of the led into A, brand / same; same day's brands / stone; stone eruptive in life's brands / filled; filled with elective's brands / forth; forth in plenty, brand free / brave; brave the sample's brands / mindful; mindful to the moment's brands / ease; ease into the value's brands / souls; souls outed into love's brand, light / noble; noble kneels A' brands / sit; sit abroad and sought throughout the shouted, brands / compassion; compassion and the challenge set for brands / seriously; seriously and the chinese childrens brand / infused; infused and the fashion's pantheon brand-less / moderating; moderating becomes less the ration, know the fashionable brand / infant; infant sent becomes your friend, brand / proclaim / good / Resurrection / periods.

CHAPTER FIVE

Wrinkles; wrinkles in time and the challenge to see that love is eternity; know the cause, drop the charges, brands / peep; peep into shows branded less / kinder; kinder came another's brand / best; best shown, A's brands / birds; birds turn to see your brands / garden; garden gates and the sates of brands / golden; golden days and the holiday's brands / sunshine; sunshine stated; brands / path; path over; date knew brands / empty; empty outed brands / seldom; seldom became you, brand less / crumb; crumb thrown; declare; "brands" / whisker; whisker of the whisper's brands / manner; manner of the planner's brands / broken; broken and the pinnacled brand / tumbled; tumbled across for a bit and then good try, branded / rung; rung with knews branded / lily; lily wed to a red's refuse to use A's brands / swam; swam across another's view and the value became electrically replete with A's brands / leaf; leaf festive in A's brands / sailed; sailed into view, A's brands / passage; passages into the brands on love / shivering; shivering in anticipate's brands / crept; crept past like ooze into brands less / misfortune; misfortune met suppose's brands / rose; rose a delivery into brands / hitched; hitched parallel to the ceiling's brands / check; check the fortune made in love's brands / clock; clock said, A's brands / night; night knelt in A's brands / found; found a place for venue's deep in A's brands / sauntering; sauntering past the places Z to A's brands / town; town said, YES, convict, brands / reading; reading a rationale branded / hollow; hollow into deeper brands / presumption; presumption sent to A's brands / splendid; splendid in candidly brands / shelter; shelter came from the South's brands / imagine; imagine yes, into brands / merchant; merchant of the mention, "brands" / may; may said, let's go, to brands / fairy; fairy dusted brands / went; went and intent into brands / compassion; compassion comes into brands / discipline; discipline dealt with through brands / responsibility; responsibility sent, brands / work; work for your brands / friendship; friendship becomes your partner, brands / courage; courage came through, brands parallel too / perserverance; perserverance pays, brand freed / honesty; honesty becomes you, brand less / loyalty; loyalty reels into brand's freed / faith; faith found, brand free / index; index made, brand free / content; content to stay legally free to a brand / admire; admire the sort who say, brands hired to stay without boundary, free / reinvent; reinvent the hints brands / morality; morality meandered past my brands / trudge; trudge thoroughly past my brands / magician; magicians electric to lvoe's brands / rock; rock past the stash, branded / stout; stout and the simply, the guest, brands / saint; saint and the sent, brands / perfectly; perfectly balanced in love's brands.

CHAPTER SIX

Abstinence; Met by an abstinence past, love's brands / thomas; thomas met fulfill in the brands jeffersonian too / aquinas; aquinas tuned above and within the moon's regard for cards of love / marry; another freed, brands / undone; undone and the sun's brands / total; total and the trilogy branded / famous; famous and the thoroughness branded / overmuch; overmuch and the mission's brands / Christopher; Christopher hopped across the fields of brands / Jude; Jude and the mood's electric into brands / peter; peter said, let us be, brand free / claire; claire and the clarity declared brand free / Elizabeth; Elizabeth said, brand free / discourse; discourse made and became brand free / title of the temple's brand free / due; due an elective discourse and a brand / another; another met the mother through your brands / countenance; countenance became clear through God's brands / crude; crude and the rude gone too, brands / cruel; cruel enough to confession's brands / clues; clues hint too, the brands / current; current examples suspect your brand / chase; chase over, brand's new / climbs; climbs past and dues required brand A / factors; factors felt brand less / fasten; fasten truth into your brands guest / facts; facts into matters brand free / flows; flows a guest brand free / fish; fish for facts brand new / fashions; fashion plate is filled with good's brands / flesh; flesh and the filling's brands / flown; flown past, brands / furthers; furthers another's brands / fools; fools of the suspect's brands / folly; folly out and about love's brands / funds; funds and the fellowed brands / floats; floats and past the host's brands / writes; writes above and within

love's brands / written; written and in the smitten A's brands / rescues; rescues and the written's brands / puppies; puppies and the positive's brands / plasma; plasma and the parallel's brands / plush; plush and the penchant for love's brands / entron; entron and the random's brands / carpeting; carpeting compares to a floated accept for the brands / clients; clients and the capable detail's brands / classes and the agreeable penchant for A's brands / charters; charters and the matters on too brands / charts; charts and the challenges brand free / chills; chills and the seals on A's brands / fields; fields and the felony left brands / trench; trench and the trivet's brands / macrame; macrame and the stray into A's brands / lure; lure into the simple brands / engrave; engrave in the wave's brands / fervent; fervent and the fervor's brands / joyous; joyous and the jolly for A's brands / family; family and the fellowed apply for A's brand / intense; intensely intense into A's brands / gold; gold given gains paved in brands / silver; silver and the central brands / threads; threads and the heats onto brands / heat; heat and the healing's brands / real; real blood pumps into hands electric and these feelings bring brands into love.

CHAPTER SEVEN

Freed; freed to believe in values regarding light's example and the sample A free too, brands / frock; frock and the shocking deliver of forgiven maternally to A brand / friendly; friendly and the sender became materially brand free / friendship; friendships deep in the delivery treed in A's brand / polish; polish and the satire interior into a miracle's venue, a brand / moisturizes; moisturizes and pasteurizes a tribute's brands / dapples; dapples and the samples brands / grain; grain and the grandmother's brand / gossip; gossip ends and friends return to A's brand / boughts; boughts and the soughts align in A brand / boughs; boughs and the trees attributive too, A's brand / bash; bash and the stashing brands / bells; bells and the ringing's delivery freed to A's brand / bowls; bowls and the soul's a brand / banter; banter and the balance brand free / plays; plays and the standards brand free / televisions; televisions and the revisions parallel into the counted brands / trued; trued and the moods attendant in the ways A's brands / trails; trails and the sailing aspire across A's brands / delivery; delivery dues and the news truth's brands / pass; pass on the torch and the tools brand new / passions; passions placed across these brands parallels / values; values central trued and immaculate to the parallel brands / leads; leads a light across these parallel brands / leashed; leashed a lot across the trends brand free / simples; simples and the keepers brand new / tolls; tolls and the souls sent home brand new / nestles; nestles in the mountains brand new / cribs; cribs and the central appeals brand new / cues; cues and the cubicles brand free / cubes; cubes and values branded through love / dares; dares and the stares apparent into the brand love / brinks; brinks and drinks intense in brands onto love / brush; brush and the rush into these brands / books; books allowed the scribes of love's true brands / balance; balance and the talents brand free / windshield; windshield details and the phosphorescence sent into light's avenue, brand free / windmill; windmill towns and the sounds brand less / spells; spells another's brands / wells; wells depth deep in loving's brands / woven; woven and the weather's brands / awash; awash and the torch atop a's brands / thrills; thrills and the seals events brand three / throes; throes and the shows brand free / throned; throned details and the sales prone to be freely branded / threshold; threshold throned through with love's brands / simples; simples and the samples brand new / habitat; habitat and the humanity's dues to a variation brand free 49, holes; holes and the holy feet brand free / hearts; hearts and the starts again, brand new / hopes; hopes and the hallows bound less, brand trues / happens; happens in a happening brand new / hash; hash less and agree to be brand free / harps; harps and the sharp arise into love's brands / hosts; hosts and the ghosts full electric to a brand / hospitable; hospitable to a cause brand free / hospital; hospital tales and the fails passed, freely, brand less / hats; hats and the chats freed brand new / horns; horns shorn with love less directives, brand new / throats; throats and the shout electric to a stunt free delivery of love's brands / tracks; tracks across deserts next and the brands into love / teeth; teeth that touch at brinks on love's brands / tongues; tongues and the tingles brand new / Yawns.

CHAPTER EIGHT
Written; written into the avenues of love's smitten agree to the abide to be in love's pyramid to an a brand / averages; averages smatter, the shatter less of the x to A brand / phase; phases won and the towns truest became the news to A's brand / directives; directives and the delegation's due to an opened state called A brand / glides; glides into the temples deep in A's brands / glues; glues and the glitters A branded / paves; paves and the partnered state brand A / lots; lots of clots and the slots paved brand A / lashes; lashes and the dashes into love's brands / lashed; lashed out less and more interiorly led into love's brands / lacks; lacks and the facts anticipative to a brand / lucks; lucks expire and the experience grand into love's brands / views; views and the parallel exams to a brand / vantage; vantage and the advantage gained when love breathes to a brand / monitors; monitors muse about A's brands / moves; moves made electrically true to A brand / warrants; warrants and whistles into A's brand / together; together and the gateway to A's brand / fans; fans fulfill their listen too, A's brand / astound; astound and the sounds bristle in A's brands / member; member of the senders A wide to A brand / mention; mention the status of A's brands / titles; titles and the triple threat , a treat into love's brands / numbers; numbers knelt with, A's brands / notes; notes and the needs met; angularly too, a brand / words; words of world's estates and the status A brand / flames; flames and the fusing's A's brands / faith; faith and the fonts parallel to A's brands / fuel; fuel met flame in A's brands / small; small estates win in A's ways brand new / large; large to a moment, A's brands / liquids; liquids and the wheel's feel of the moistened brands / illusion; illusion and the clarify declared in fine details instilled through brands in love / lively; lively days and diligent days of parental brands / natural; natural experiences

entirely brand free / elegant; elegant denotes in these brands / flaw; flaw elected empty too, brand D / intuition; intuition sent the intentional set of God's goods brand less / certain; certain accept of the kept notion blend free too, brands / relative; relative to the notions, God's brands / proclaim; proclaim the game done through love's brands / properties; properties met in love's appeals, God's gaze entirely brand free / basic; basic abilities shine through God's brands / relation; relation stated as accelerated theoretically to God's reset on brands / confirm; confirm the warm arrive into God's estates to brands / stop; stop at the shake free brand / waves; waves apply for status, freed, too, brands / beholder; beholder believes in the healed philosophy which states that love is in the brand, God's / space; space and the place elevated through God's love; a brand parallel / time; time and the tribal brands / eye; eye in the sky's brands / stationary; stationary stills and the meals deeded brands / driver; driver deals with meals to a brand / example; examples tripled with living brands / moving; moving and the grooving patents too, brands / viewpoint; viewpoint on the dewpoint due illusions cast past A's brand / hike; hike unto the bicycle dipped into love's brands / appear; appear near the trapezoid's triumphant call into the a's brand / catch; catch a trip into these brands / palm; palm apparent and the inherent ways through God's brands / chase; chase and the surrender into God's brands / traveler; traveler and the trials given aloft a daily way's brand / never; never and the known brands / perfection; perfection in the reflection into love.

CHAPTER NINE
Beam; beam and the room that assumes a daily appeal for love's brands / reasoning; reasoning and the seasoning sent finally to A brand / intuitive; intuitive and the news that love rules in God's brands / feel; feel attendant to God's blessings of the course called brands / highlight; highlight the carriage into love's brands / scale; scale across the retinues brand free / effect; effect and the cause too, a brands / course; course and the simple discourses too, brands / section; section and the central's brands / strip; strip less and more, brands / need; need and the deed's brand / infantile; infantile and the mile's brands / father; father and the mother's brands / sugar; sugar and the middle ground's brands / do; do and the deeds to brands / good; good and the would to, brands / knot; knots out and the shout for reconnect into love's brand / want; want another way smoothed too, brand A / scheme; scheme about less, know more, desire love in an A brand / prance; prance upon the stage, Grade A, brand too / revile; revile and the call to arms of still, brand A / go; go to the temple of lightening brand / climb; climb the hills intent in love's brands / bring; bring a deal to closure, brands / anxiety; anxiety heals as the bills paid, brands / passion; passion meals in God's throat, brand A / whom; whom and the room elated into brands / girl; girl sent a name, brand new / done; done and the sun arose; to a brand / alone; alone and neater then, to a brand / hooray; hooray and the stay into brands / loyalty; loyalty and the friends in A brands / dance; dance the deal and take the pill called brand A / fallen; fallen keys erupt in me and recombine in the spine of

God, brand A / thine; thine are the minutes, the moments, the days, of love's brand A / light; lighten came into the brand A / juvenile; juvenile ways met love's mature stage in A's brand / knight; knights of memories delivered A's brand / me; me in the attune into brand A / see; see us nearing brand A / break; break to describe the days, brand A's / right; right of the passage into brand A / reason; reason dealt with into A's brands / crave; crave another result openly A's brands / die; die to the news of old dues, brand A / new; newness became you, brand A / until; until the heal, remember A / while; while we smile we debate fewer brands / most; most equates to yes in which brand? / movers; movers came today to say hello to love's new brands / happily; happily drunken on love's brand / should; should you move into A Brands? / white; white deals made allow brand news / defile; defile less the stage of A / sure; sure enough in her secure detach and the match branded free / enough; enough to make solutions ache for encouragement to jump the bands of brands / refrains; refrains heard become clear in the stratus of God's brands / compare; compare the days to diligence and dues already paid to God's brands / pray; pray for solvency in love's brands / birth; birth of the billings for love's brands / else; else and the where to A's brands / take; take a placement higher still in brand's A / how; how do we fly in two brands? / pain; pain became the game of love's lessened brand.

CHAPTER TEN
Through; through a narrow view's release, a truer band, still, in love's brand / always; always elective of the cusp that counts, your own, still brand / dearest; dearest dates in heaven's gates of brands / delicate; delicate dues and the news into A brands / nothing; nothing matter less unto brands / summer; summer of the came too, brands / guarantee; guarantee delivery into brand A / truth; truth becomes the resurrect into love's brands / blue; blue in the choice to say, A / fight; fight forgiven and the brands connect in A / grace; grace gave us appeal to brands / known; known in the need for brand A / fling; fling over flew and the muse brand A / wish; wish for another's deal? brand B / forever; forever equipped with the lips brand A / rhyme; rhyme with the time's brand A / quite; quite a mirror, the deals, brand B / spirit; spirit required the cup of me, brand C / Anatomy; anatomy forgave the days of scenes, Brand B / beauty; beauty lost luster in Brands B / water; water won through Brand A / laughter; laughter led the bed to Brand A / unite; unite in the mention of a mission Brand A /disdain; disdain done, become, Brand A / leave; leave a magnet still in Brand B / versatile; versatile in , arose, A's brand / poetry; poetry red in blue's values, brand B / were; were we electrically detailed for God's brands / sold; sold into slavery due brands of lessened bands / conquered; conquered confessed and elected living examples to an A, brand / passionate; passionate the pews of A's brands / breath; breath and the breathing believe of A's brands / mystery; mystery due the embrace-able news of A's brands / embrace; embrace a chalice as your, A's brands / your; your days fund the knights of A / infatuation; infatuation with less becomes more forgiven to an A / whisper; whisper

directly into love's brands / predestined; predestined? Dues? Choose A; freedom's ringing brand / handsome; handsome to a mention of A's brands / better; better in the billings, A's brand / wonder; wonder, know more, declare, A's brand / family; family of the few and the fuse into A's brand / children; children dare to seize A's brand / loved; loved and beloved too, to an A / crush; crush over and the morning's detail becomes A's brand / soothe; soothe a neck with news of A / gorgeous; gorgeous to her values A's brand / turns; turns into love's avenue, A's coupe, brand B / fancy; fancy fades into A's pane / romance; romance agrees; to be brand A / charming; charming equip and the lips to A's brand / speak; speak of the dues, A's brands / lightly; lightly I am led into A's brand / wife; wife of the lessons A wide, a wiser brand / star; star electric and the convertible base into A brand / very; very dealt with into A's brands / steamy; steamy ways return to A's brands / friends; friends defend your light reflection of the lifted reveal within men, brand B / young; young to the day and old to the news of Brand C / mate; mate found in A brand / muscles; muscles collect in collapse-less degrees of love's details to a brand B / clandestine; clandestine returns to an A's brand / friend; friend found, married too, to A's brand / Humanity.

CHAPTER ELEVEN
Root; root out the past of evil's last by believing in only one brand, to A BE / evil; evil ousted lasted too long in a town forgiven for killing brand C / say; say you believe in Brand A / husband; husband made of the mend to Brand C / remember; remember the sender is a friend to Brand A / cupid; cupid struck in your branded stray / bewitch; bewitch has met the quiver of lessened's forgive to a brand / adieu; adieu to the passed and the brands forgotten living / style; style sent to a brand A / body; body collapsed into brand B / main; main ways past, brand C / day; day of delivery, today, amazing brands / air; air wars out, and into view brand seen / spring; spring into matters brand C / shall; shall we know the show brand B / black; black and the gold of a bowl deep in love's retrieval, brand won / from; from now into the trim suggest of living love's brands / more; more days direct into love's brands / some; some ways often made into love's brands / make; make delivery become you; daily; brands / okay; okay to stay direct in love's brands / bright; bright begin along love's brands / want; want deliver? Decide and gain, love's brands / once; once along shores delicate to love's brands / other; other and the mother's brands / moon; moon days deal in bands brands / only; only own A brand / lampoon; lampoon the disguise of less than One brand / dream; dream of the games electric to a brand / uptight; uptight forgiven A's brands / twilight; twilight said, let's blends into B brand / risque; risque melts into love's brands / try; try a dose of brand be / over; over into the news brand C / marriage; marriage became the dame at three brands / night; night of the nestle into love's brands / sex; sex sent sealed into brands B / romance; romance suggested brand C / God; God gave forgive to brand B / above; above and the love deliver, brand 3 / sing; sing in the sun's dance of love's brand / desire; desire a deal heightened, still, in love's brand /

appetite; appetite returns and the yearns entail love's be brand / alright; alright's alibi is the sigh of a brand / earth; earth met mirth in a capital A brand / everything; everything delivers to A's brand / chocolate; chocolate eaten to the mother's tongue, brand A / heaven; heaven dates you, brand A / death; death overdue the one, brand C / smile; smile about good-bye to a brand less / reconcile; reconcile to the files brand A / life; life leaps into view, brand see / pentameter; pentameter remains your dear friend, brand C / winter; winter winds entail brand A / afternoon; afternoon meant for brand B / foreplay; foreplay includes loving news, brand be / taboo; taboo discussed, brand 3 / armor; armor drops, brand 3 / hope; hope restores, brand 6 / name; name the lines brand seam / leave; leave the dates, brand A / count; count the days, brand / cradle / consciousness.

CHAPTER TWELVE

Seduce; seduce a notion to reduce all of life to One brand, love / woman; woman of the year elective and the soul's released directive to become Earth's A to Z brand, One / sensual; sensual expression of the experience's brand free / shoulder; shoulders succumb to the nature in love's brand / nuzzle; nuzzle another and know love's brand / angel; angels appear nightly into love's brand / create; create a state of elation for love's rational approach to healing's brand / cuddle; cuddle with the durate of love's brands / tender our immersion into love's brands / world; world of the willing fleshed into love's brands / arrow; arrow stars elect your heart for a brand / round; round the arcturian wed a word is heard, love's led to a brand / please; please detail your wish to A's brand / flame; flame at the moment you realize Arcturian wings to your dreams, A deep / honey; honey you have won the healing called A's belief / money; money coming into the pot for A brand / fondle; fondle less the lessened; implore your desires to A's brand / broad; broad enough to scope all the hope for A brand / virtue; virtue deals with the reality that Arcturian seams are the living wings of A brand / single; single days single desire for an A brand / blind; blind to less, remember the man who said; "for the one who is ill, all will be well, this is a complete regeneration; " to a band, Arcturian / neck; neck fixed; remember; brand A / sorry; sorry less and telling more of the brands won / being; being perfect into love's brands / trust; trust your friend, the find caroling into Arcturian brands / breast; breast touched and worn is the land brand / dared; dared to finish the charming explosion of love, a brand / run; run to the sun and seek only love's brand / cry; cry for delivery of the gentle baby who grew uncoiled in you, love's brand / sure; sure to deliver love's brand / beloved; beloved sun, the brand A / alluring; alluring explore has imploded less, now, within A brand / lumps; lumps found lead home to a brand / cold; cold compress has become less the lend to a brand / compass; compass points to the points within A brand / portrait; portraits sent to lessons loved brands / deprive; deprive forgotten and the return became God's brand / speak; speak only often too, love's brands / things; things are done within these brands, C to E / contain; contain a tribute unto love's brands / emitted; emitted the decide to be brand A /

radiation; radiation forgave them, brand C / elements; elements collapsed into brand B / fated; fated delivery became bent toward B branches and brands / equal; equal ways opened up into brands / apprehend; apprehend less the reward of A' brand / leap; leap across faithfully into a brand / corporeal; corporeal succession into A's brand / beyond; beyond this bland, love's brand / expanse; expanse becomes your brand / measure; measure the dates too, love's brand / rise; rise across reasons brands / become; become the sum's allow, brands / think; think often into love's brands / impossible; impossible forgotten's brands / mortal; mortal souls released into light brands / immortal; immortal the path, God's plan, one brand / grasp; grasp again the declare, " one brand" / craft; craft a notion of oceans relief; one brand / home; to the church won deep, heart high too, love / haunts; haunts forget and now remember release into love's womb, deliver, one brand / opposites; opposites and the pole's composites to a brand / heights; heights held freely open to A brand / lower; lower cases heard; to A brand.

CHAPTER THIRTEEN

Depths; depths Bermuda deep in love's declare of forthright to A brand / fluidity; fluidity gained declared, one brand / quality; quality given the living branches, one brand / begotten; begotten and the often said, "brand" seen / womb; wombs rich in love's assurance to a brand / substance; substance sent, floral red, brand C / magnitude; magnitude of the gifts , branching to A Be brand / abase; abase the views into a mound broken open through love's brand / place; place of the fathers parallel embrace of A's brand / waking; waking becomes the visit most adored into love's brand / journeying; journeying in to gain relationship with the traveling grace called love's brand / land; land made and found freely in love's brand / silent; silent to a partner, love, brand free / manifest; manifest the earth's release of all brands / body; now, one body, earth, love, brand less / cleave; cleave to the notion, know brands relief / hence; hence won, brand freed / benefactor; benefactor becomes, your brand A / irrational; irrational justice and the compassionate sort who vary into love's brand / instincts; instincts declare fair; brands / rid; rid your state of the riddle-less brands / superfluous; superfluous pursuit of the brands less intrigues with the art helm deep too, love / idle; idle states due to brand belief / mutable; mutable discoveries of A's brands / about; about the soul; gone; to a brand; lightened / apart; apart and the start to heal the light's return to love's brand / composite; composite sorts pieced into love's brand / union; union made; love's brand / foulness; foulness meets sweet breath of God's brand / dirt; dirt blown into the skirts hu-man brand free / impiety; impiety impunes my heart to love's brand / quality; quality and the start to free love's brand / abroad; abroad is the way into love's beaches and the brand God / embodied; embodied relief to a spirit's touch; good-bye; brands / counterparts; counterparts made, all 3, relieved for A's band / end; end came, now, to brands / opinion; end, brands / hold; hold souls released into light brands / convey; convey them to God's band, arc-angelic brands / obscure; obscure designs defeated, brands / Egyptian; Egyptian sorts, maat deep in soul's forego to the light's brand / spoken; spoken most; soul's release to know brands / force; force said, "know brands" / translate; translate gifts to light's brand / feebleness; feebleness due to humbleness anew at brands released / study; study another's tablet, Thoth, Atlantis, summary, brand less / dissolved; dissolved a matter less pressing, brands / matter; matter made free to a brand / rational; rational the release of all brands / affections; affections loved, brand free / dependent; dependent less; open more; to a brand-less society / brought; brought home notes of brand exist / author; authors vote for brand less / intent; intent to a constant brand free / performance; performance superb, know freedom, brand free / festival; festival cavorts in love's brand / harmony; harmony held each hand, brand new / universe; universe felt your change; shifting; brand too / melody; melody of amused with, brands / defects; defects dealt with, know brandness / impute; impute the repute of love's brands / succession; succession comes to a brand less house / song; song meant brand free / pitch; pitch a tent near brand less societies.

THE BRANCH-MENTS
LEVEL 29

CHAPTER ONE

Tree, trees true to the views that branch into love's leave / trails, love's trails and the rails that match God's branch / veins, veins and the variate on a theme, branched / roots, roots and the shoots electrically branched / leaves, leaves and the sleeves that vary, branched / limbs, limbs and the hymns magnetically branched / laces, laces and the places where slants collide at love's branched / traces, traces of the motifs worn and the parental treat of branched relie / tastes, tastes and the tips elective too, love's branch / minimums, minimums and the humming needs, branched / minerals, minerals and the places paired spruce pine high to love's branch / magnets, magnets assigned our streets branch / minutes, minutes and the menu branched / might, might and the sites branched / tower, tower and the gifts branched / true, true and trim to a branch / truth, truth and the parrot's branched / sight, sight and the gifts branched / height, height and the boats afloat with a branch / joy, joy made the flaunt, branched / complete, complete the assign, branched / convey, convey accordance too, a branch / contend, contend less and attain more, branched / control, control gated less through loving branched / end, end a friend's reach at love's branch / double, double enough to say too, branched / duel, duel about and effectively ends, branched / done, done, hear, branched / due, due you, the show, branched / delegate, delegate another's stay, branched / emerge, emerge the victor through love's branch / deals, deals made quickly, branched / mental, mental panes crashed, branched / camera, camera's criterion, branched / moist, moist to the meal, branched / surge, surge into love's convey of God news, branched / coverage, coverage comes to the sums branched / absolves, absolves and the solve's riddles, branched / caliber, caliber of the crowds, branched / covers, covers and the doves, branched / way, way to the show, branched / reads, reads of lights electrically, branched / commute, commute into zones metatronically correct through love's branch / boost, boost a bill passed through light's branch in yo / reading, reading came due, love's branch / lights, lights out and on too, life's branch / lamp, a lamp is on in your branched / bleach, bleach the tongues lessened too love's branch / coral, coral days blue in pink release to love's branch / pink, pink the stake at love's blue green advance into heaven's branch / throws, throws and the moments past, branched / throne, throne and the crinkle cast, branched / drape, drape across the lap branched / recycle, recycle comes due to a branch / reuse, reuse melts a branch / chain, chain broken, branch free / delays, delays done, to a branch / decisions, decisions cast past a branch / divides, divides emit a clear bell, to a branch / remits, remits a reach branched / reconnects, reconnects and convenes, to a branch / caps, caps off and on too, a branch / floors, floors and the doors that will branch / floats, floats past, love's branch.

CHAPTER TWO

Brazen, brazen release to the stress branched / commute, commute to the steps branched / coned, coned and elevated through the eternal branched / belts, belts off and the wheels hot with love's branch / caps, caps and the collosal estates called branched / adores, adores you and knows too that love can be branched to the third equate / clips, clips a lesson to her love's branched / grows, grows with you in her listening way into love's branch / colts, colts frolic and make their relation's ship branched / colas, colas clipped to the belt branched / drinks, drinks assumed and the presumed allow to be branched / cords, cords cut and the whistles set at love's branch / collaberate, collaberate with your chosen, won, branched / dare, dare to fare, well, within branched / shares, shares made and the shores kep clearly seen through branched / pass, pass the potion meant for branched elat / past, past due a review entirely branch fre / pretends, pretends and listens well into love's branch / pores, pores across the pages branched / covert, covert is overt to the cause branched / copy, copy a page less clear, know steer to the courses branched / date, date another, branch / spell, spell elates's parallel purple freed, branched / print, print a tart reply to the sky away, lifting, branched / check, check a patient page's branch / courts, courts collect bonify and the stride branched / short, short to the waves branched / way, way to the being centrally succinct in love's branch / share, share a date with the one, branched / live, live electrically free too, the branch / love, love another's well, branched / dare, dare to stay away too, the branch / undo, undo the due through love's branched retur / stipend, stipend paid and the rays reveal restful states in love's branched / lipped, lipped ascend and the grip within love's branch / care, care eternally, and well, for love's branch / capable, capable to the cause, branched / stable, stable and well in love's branch / strong, strong enough to see too, love's branch / degree, degree and the diligent's branch / given, given a status for love's branch / won, won another hearts lend to a branch / worn, worn enough to see through too, love's branch / gown, gowns torn and the worn deliver's branch / okay, okay to stay in the love electric and love is, branched / always, always paid and made the won, branched / win, win a lesson branched / tree, tree's roots branched / treat, treat and the seat won, branched / true, true and adept through love's branched / through, through and the zoos branched / good, good enough to see through and the branches sent through love / code, code branched and the cues love / love, love's degrees branched / life, life sorts and the branches sent thicken, love / shelf, a shelf laid through the hearing sort's messag / exhibit, exhibit a resourceful ray called branches in love / opens, opens the question, branched / dealt, dealt within and too the branched / loves, loves and the listen's branched / exhort, exhort and the sorts branched / clan, clan and the spans parallelly branched / flown, flown and the zone's branched / clowns, clowns dance past love's branch.

CHAPTER THREE

Love, love is the won, branch / Surrender, Surrender to the states electric / savor, savor a victory balanced in love's bend too, branched / savant, a savant sent to the invent basically of the human tree's branched / savior, savior met in the healing vet called branched / electric, electric absolute and the mention "branched? / said, said, "yes", to the mention of love's detailed branch / send, send a miracle's way too, branched / crave, crave a different sort's branch / crawl, crawl past the all into God's branch / walk, walk, talk, and prowl to a branch brand free in the news electric / tall, tall enough to desire detail of the branches sor / crone, crone married next to the throne's branch / critics, critics deal with the feel branched / create, create a state electrically branched / coats, coats and worn agrees branched / sheets, sheets tossed across love's branch / castles, castles and the sands branched / caustic, caustic forgive and the living branched / cures, cures another's woe, branched / fuel, fuel for the show's branch / collects, collects a mention, branched / kinship, kinship occurs and becomes her branch / nets, nets cast aside to reveal the catch, branched / friends, friends chant, branched / forever, forever int he young arise, branched / young, young in the sung surprise, branched / you, you know the show, branched / know, know how to see the clearing, branched / our, our days occupy one branch / truth, truth exampled well by a branch / love's, love's gifts, branched / creates, creates celebrate and the heart's eternal lift into love's branch / shot, shot through in love's branched / sheets, sheets shaken free to love's branch / shut, shut the door less often, branch / woven, woven appearance and the mention branched / opens, opens throughout. love's branch / arms, arms held wide to a branch / hands, hands grasp your heart's branch / went has become gone too, a branch / loving, loving has led to living's branch / callow, callow has found mellow ground, branched / out, out and the few freed, branched / window, windows in the sung, branched / capable, capable to details on branched / in, in the muse, branched / inn, inn and days left branched / spore, spore and the cores branched / spawn, spawn is out too, a branch / correlate, correlate your choices to a branch / belong, belong to the singing, love's branch / effective, effective in your stays within, love's branched / loan, loan paid and the maze detailed through a branch / links, links and the chinks within, branched / padres, padres isles and the tres paid, love's branched / cut, cut a cord's branch / coatings, coatings laid across love's branch / corts, corts paved with love's branched / sheets, sheets peel to reveal a branch / horse, horse color-less has thrown the tree a branch / hearse, hearse deals with her branch / plans, plans to meet the healing, branch / cane, cane cut and the killing stops, branched.

CHAPTER FOUR

Debt, debt off and paid too, love's branch / debts, debts dealt with and made lvoe's branch / paid, paid to a cause branched / prevail, prevail in your faith's branched / provoke, provoke less the meeting's branched / well, well enough to stay in, love's branch / win, win a ticket, branched / absolve, absolve the old through a branch / resolve, resolve to reseal love's branch / crave, crave a delivery into love's branch / culture, culture says branched / lost, lost and the finds branched / pow wow, pow wow's lines branched / model, model days, branched / ivy, ivy blew through the weds branched / fake, fake has gone to the songs branched / orbs, robs sense our course through lvoe's seen branch / luxury, luxury needs

a hand, branched / Havana, Havana smoked and the choke reveals? Branc / embark, embark to a sharp arise called branched / fjords, fjords fuse in love's news, branched / dice, dice tossed and the lost found, branched / Denmark, Denmark's daunt is less, branched / Swiss, Swiss and the missive elect, branched / lapland, lapland found in the town branched / gala, gala and the glues branched / spoon, spoon dealt the doors branched / weaves, weaves and a passion mentioned branched / wait, wait and know the doors branch / heavy, heavy off and the light's branch / ironic, ironic over and the dues branch / island, island bought and the mansion built branched / bazaar, bazaar days and the gaze is branched / dreamtime, dreamtime comes and the listen is branched / tropicals, tropicals trued and the branched go to / salsa, salsa heard and eaten too, lvoe's branch / ultimate, ultimate mentioned, love's branch / majesty, majesty and the muse means, love is the branch / malta, malta and the majestic won, through love's branch / Eziba, Eziba exhibits love's branched / Antarctica, Antarctica closets it's melt with lvoe's branch / Yorkshire, Yorkshire days and the paratners branch / pewter, pewter gifts appraised and the heart lines mentione / talavera, talavera and the tools branched / Dutch, Dutch intakes and the stakes mentioned, branched / hex, hex off and the cough is healed's branch / bay, bay made home, love's branch / role, role paid through love's branch / lazy, lazy has gone to the sun's branch / barrels, barrels given, love's branch / sizing, sizing becomes the question's branch / movement, movement made across wave's branch / swinger, swinger sealed, branch / windy, windy zones branched / drizzle, drizzle's occur and the swerves branched / solstice, solstice sealed and the milled branch / gigantic, gigantic doses of abundance healed, branched / notes, notes and nations branch / catalog, catalog surrenders gifts, branched / distrust, distrust ahs gone to the sun's branch / dragonfly, dragonfly rays and the sways branched / lime, lime the green's delivery, branched / wetland, wetland sold and the bold green branched / zone, zone given elective lend to the branches saved.

CHAPTER FIVE

Orions's, Orion's firey trail recovers love's branch / fire, fire and the frail forgiven, branched / grit, grit and the sparks which grew through a resolve to be, branched / totem, totems and the tokens branched / hollyhock, hollyhock days and the rays branched / ruby, ruby grew suspicious too, love's branched / adhesive, adhesive sent a hilt across sore branched / orchids, orchids grew in the core's branched / Greeks, Greeks and the seekers sought branched / marigolds, mairgolds maxe and the days, branched / elegy, elegy of the trilogy branched / manaus, manaus knows love's branched / gear, gear to see a grain revealed through branched / shooting, shooting past and the living cast through, branched / stars, stars and the cares cast off too branched / Baltimore, Baltimore bars and the far horizon's branch / owl, owls paid a vist, branched / reflections, reflections and the listen's branched / peace, peace and the parallel's branched / cypress, cypress sealed and the branches pale with green agree too, love / voices, voices and the journey's branched / next, next and the sought's branched / feeble, feeble and the steeple branched / fern, fern and the dare's branched /

genesis, genesis and the gains genuinely branched / generations, generations grew through a love's branched / expose, expose the past to a basic branched into states electric / friend, friend found and the town rules, yes, you have branched / destiny, destiny dealt through to the basic's branched / surf, surf electron ways to dance a branch / mega, mega the muse and the mention's dimensions through love's branched / accent, accent on the finish made, love hid her branched / sapphire, sapphires off and on too, the branched / worn, worn appearance in the wonder won, love's branched / brought, brought another to love's lend, branches stil / blue, blue in renew's branched / bells, bells in the belly reply "branches"/ forth, forth and the fairies aria begins "branches"/ ring, ring above and within, branched / swung, swung through a gate held openly, branched / electric, electric regain of the light through branched / accept, accept the course, branched / debacle, debacle over and due? branched / short, short to a finish, mentioned, branched / calendar, calendar days and the maze clears, branches finishe / cure, cure has starts in light branched / Gregorian, Gregorian chants and the chances too, branched / Mayan, Mayan amuse and the missives particulate toss to the most branched / faeance, faeance cast across love's branched / folly, folly due and the dare too, fund's branched / fellows, fellows make, well, from branched / equal, equal ways too, branched / fashions, fashions in the sorts, branched / press, press across the madness too, branched / squared, squared along the masses branched / boost, boost your economic stand, branched / freeform, freeformed estates win, branched / falls, falls and the cross borne cast branched / west, west into wonders branched / splash, splash above and the falling catch branched / cashiers, cashiers and the steers staged deep into love's branch / caution, caution comes undone, to a branch / levels, levels inside these branches undon / views, views whose news includes ours, love.

CHAPTER SIX
Bask, bask enough, smiling leads, branched / smile, smile and the seals branched / center, center to the mentor branched / agile, agile enough to extend through, love's branched / attitude, attitude to the mood's branched / totals, total and the one's branched / show, show and the deals branched / chance, chance and the kabbalic inn, your keep, branched, like God / lavendar, lavendar leads to blue's estates of violet branched love / lashes, lashes and the branches too, love's gate / laps, laps above the branches equipped lappe / lark, lark and the stark arise into branches predat / levels, levels and the listen's branched / lots, lots and the liken's branched / loves, loves and the listen's branch / insured, insured and the sure's branched / thanks, thanks and the thoughts for the shine branched / desires, desires and the branches fathered in love / dear, dear and the steering elate's branched / fluorescene, fluorescence and let's branch / found, found and the fed's branch / allowance, allowance and the settle's branch / fresh, freshen and the mention's branch / frolic, frolic across lines branched / grand, grand and a gallop branched / grow, grow in your stature's branch / shower, shower and the our branched / give, give and the fates finished branched / allow, allow and the plans erectly branched / flank, flank and

the finite felt branched / harbor, harbor above and within living branched / flows, flows and the shows election branched / act, act on the mention branched / reactive, reactive rays branched / invective, invective values branched / select, select and the section's branched / know, know and details branched / dramatic, dramatic degrees branched / enzymes, enzymes branched / clients, clients come in to see our sun's branched / pace, pace and the trips branched / pragmatic, pragmatic and the pension's paid too, branched / perfect, perfectly paid for, branched / shot, shot through in miraculous views branched / shackles, shackles cut and the moods viewed, branched / finds, finds and the shrines built, branched / follicles, follicles fuel our release too, branched / flash, flash on this, love's branch / balantine, balantine and the kind branched / beverage, beverage and the places policied through branched / examples, examples and the samples branched / nuts, nuts and deals branched / maverick, maverick meets branched / shed, shed and sheets volcanic meet love's branch / challenge, challenge and tills valued too, branched / biologic, biologic and the loving taught too branched / climb, climb across love's branched / clamor, clamor and create love's branched / clearance, clearance and the clearest branched / classic, classic occurs and the branches attend, love' / cloth, cloth and the cures branches / cookies, cookies and the babes branched / serapis, serapis and the selection's branched / beys, beys and the evolves branched.

CHAPTER SEVEN
French, French branched and the channels taught, love / fortune, fortune and the footholds branched / feelings, feelings field an afield branched / sport, sport and shortly, branched / challenge, challenge and charades done, branched / chills, chills and the overs due branched / charades, charades overdone branched / chariot, chariot attributive to the risen sun's branched / balerina, balerina blues believed unto love's branched / beau, beau and the shows branched / appraisal, appraisal occurs through branched / calms, calms accept and the adept branched / genders, genders freed and the furrows branched / jump, jump and the simple stance, to a branch, love / courtesan, courtesan and the son's branched / venice, venice and the gains. branched / revision, revision and the branched monotony forgiven to God's plane / ate, ate through a trend's branched / renewal, renewal to the show's branched / community, community to the cues used for a branch / zothar, frankly zothar is a gentlema / plotted, plotted and plotted rants to a bran / number, number of the needs branched / becomes, becomes and a chance to breathe branched / realms, realms and the residues branched / hierarchy, hierarchy and the held branched / flag, flag and above the seas branched / visual, visual aids branched / pelt, pelt your heart and the chance to a breat / construct, construct a sort of branched releas / road, road around the branches love / towns, towns and the trills branched / note, note on the vote for branched / unity, unity and the swoon to moon that branched too, withi / equals, equals our nectar branch / signify, signify and our sides branched / replicate, replicate your state to a branch / need, need to seed your striving to a branch / necessary, necessary to the trues branched / sequel, sequel and the equals branched /

correspondence, correspondence kept up with, branched / layered, layered and the looks replete with heart's branched / think, think about the banks branched / scholar, scholar and the caller branched / blood, blood and the bay's branched / surgeons, surgeons kept electrically freed to a branch / schema, schema and the dreams branched / small, small intact and the facts matched to a star's gates branched / justify, justify your choice to a mate's branched / ramble, ramble and the symbols blazed across love's branched / random, random branched and the balances equippe / races, races to a smidgen's width branched / sphinx, sphinx and the stint's branched / sands, sands and the lands branched / stars, stars and the cars branched / glossy, glossy eyed branched / clear, clear and the choices branched / evidence, evidence set on a branch chose / carrot, carrots held, branched / carat, carat of cures branched / cubic, cubic concur to a branched stat / limestone, limestone branched red agree and to a cure's love / carved, carved and the cubicles lent love's branched / examine, examine and the samples branched.

CHAPTER EIGHT

Syntax, syntax lax know the facts that will loosen love's brands of branched / la lingua, la lingua and the single fact that love is a branch / passage, passage and the message passed to love's branched / bread, bread spread across the plates branched / spoke, spoke and the mention's branched / compact, compact and the samples branched / compress, compress across lessons branched / constitute, constitute and the suit worn branched / simple, simple assigns attributes appealed, branched / graced, graced through a mention branched / surround, surround the sounded befriends into loves branched / help, help us help your news abound through a shallow device, depth free, amide love's branched / singles, singles and the shingles hung around the zen flow rodeo drive deep in love's branched / mural, mural and the cubicle's quilt branch dee / hypothetic, hypothetic and the cure, done, branched / outdoor, outdoor and the indoor's friendly show, branched / page, page and the stages branched / pillars, pillars and the fillers ripped out, branched / posts, posts and the pistons preached "branched"/ emergent, emergent and the convergent declare's branched / century, century to seals branched / quanta, quanta and the wisdom's branched / mentioned, mentioned and the dimensioned partners branched / predicate, predicative to the straightest retire to journeys discuss and God' grants branched / severe, severe into entire ways paired in branched / builds, builds and engaged branch / general, general and the paths plunge together, branched / genial, genial and the menial leys, branched / castings, castings and the currents branched / waxed, waxed and the weddings branched / wool, wool and the windows branched / earthling, earthling settles into God's branches / pace, pace along the leys branched / astral, astral gazes plane freed branched / belittle, belittle lost and the middle branched / arcade, arcade and the gifts branched / elapse, elapse and the status branched / carts, carts and the carrys on too, love's branched / gripped, gripped and the gasping forgive's branched / oxygen, oxygen and the genteel branched / fundamental, fundamental and the reverential branched

/ elementary, elementary and the branches woo your love / frantic, frantic and the manic fog gone, branched / mechanic, mechanically plastic and the spastic freeze won, card deal, branched / build, build a gaze across love's marathon run, branch free / grants, grants and the gaze along love's mansion's branched / emergent, emergent and the crave along love's brands on too, branched / railroad, railroad and the red ahead, branch free / ramp, ramp across the bliss into your heart's branched / resin, resin and the ruse along our branching arise love / resonant, resonant and the absolute within our branches rank / revenues, revenues respects and ours, the branched / regard, regard and the branches within our love / rantha, rantha and the mantra agreed, branched / rams, rams allow the samson might to fit life's branches / rounds, rounds and the ruse breaks branch free / rush, rush and the righteous mends, branched / rutile, rutile and the futile left, branched / volatile, volatile and the villify branched / turk, turk andt he works branched / tart, tart and the start bends into willows branched / tanin, tanin and the nestle's branched / took, took a nature branched / twenty-seven thousand, twenty-seven thousand days to end within the codices mayan unfolding told inside these branches.

CHAPTER NINE

Clearance, clearance comes to the sums embrace and the presence won along life's branched / field, field and the shields off, branched / felt, felt allow branched within love / abbreviate, abbreviate the rates branched / casual, casual complex and the branches met in love / catharsis, catharsis and the mentioned seals branched / capsize, capsize and the sizes branched / colt, colt and the voltage branched / bethany, bethany and the bench branched / polish, polish and the pleasing's branched / plaka, plaka into the chants branched / warsaw, warsaw allows life's branched / when, when too, love grins branched / winds, winds whistle past, branched / flow, flow gains momentum branched / butterflies, butterflies placed into love's branched / refill, refill andt he seals upon loved branched / rushing, rushing and the branches path / french, french afield's branched / mines, mines and the maps abound, branched / mince, mince less the words honestly branched / match, math made a matched place, love is branch fre / mothers, mothers dear to a living's branched / metatron, metatron along the line branched / campaigns, campaigns in grains branched / long, long enough to see love's branched / going, going and the grants abide branched / home, home above and the dove's remembers branched / sooner, sooner in the simmer branched / moon, moon trued branched / company, company comes into light's branched / attain, attain and the strain's branched / attend, attend into choir's branched / counts, counts apply too, branched / cantilever, cantilever days branched / shouts, shouts found branched / fastens, fastens dimensionally into love's branched / futures, futures and the functions branched gain / foolish, foolish in the bluish grains branched / youth, youth and the Yiddish, branched / young, young and the yellowed branched / younger, younger and the stingers out, branched / grown, grown allow of the newness in, branched / gallop, gallop across the gains branched / gasp, gasp and the genuine's branched / gales, gales and the gels branched / webs, webs of the basics blazed branched

/ glisten, glisten and the listen's branched / misty, misty into two's branched / morning, morning and the mentions detaile / makes, makes and the missives branched / worthy, worthy and th weather's mentioned plans branched / tread, tread and the territory branched / trust, trust and the tips branched / feathers, feathers and the filled branched / tracks, tracks and trinkets branched / attempts, attempts made to settle, yes, our branched / explores, explores accept branched / lofty, lofty leads branched / spirits, spirits splash into branched / ideas, ideas into love's branched / acts, acts and branches into acts of love / devotion, devotion is exact into codices of light love / respectable, respectable and often sent indicative of love.

CHAPTER TEN

Institutional, institutional and excuses made, too, branched / international, international access branched / overhang, overhang and the sinking branched / overheard, overheard in the words branched / america, america into words branched / valley, valley veil's branched / begun, begun through branched / cruelly, cruelly due our love's branched / scenes, scenes and the centrallic branched / extremes, extremes and gentles branched / priests, priests and the patient's prance branched / priestess, priestess and the ports branched / morning, morning dews branch freeze, thaw / doctrines, doctrines and the dances branched / violence, violence lends release into branched / ends, ends and deals branched / philosophic, philosophic amuse, branched / astonish, astonish and the dates based through branched / ardent, ardent winds branched / human, human and the hands branch / sacrificial, sacrificial strives and the mandibles crunch branched / swordsman, swordsman and the surveys wing branched / soldier, soldier and the sent paved too, branched / chapels, chapels and the steeples branched / modicum, modicum and the menus mentioned branched / dialect, dialect and the dailies vex less branched / worshipped, worshipped and wet branched / worn, worn and the wealthy branched / attire, attire and the sets branched / faces, faces fit branched / empirical, empirical and the steeples branched / clones, clones and the client's maxed branched / numbers, numbers and the needs to branches maxe / sites, sites and the signals branched / honors, honors and the hints maxed branched / codes, codes and the keys branched / kingdoms, kingdoms and the keeps branched / keys, keys and the expell branched / extended, extended and the dates branched / orate, orate and the sets branched / oration, oration and the sedation' set branched / candid, candid and the mention's branched / formation, formation andt he flew branched / stone, stone and the strips branched / foundations, foundations and the funds branched / fury, fury and the feelings spent branched / seas, seas and the whose? branched / chichen, chichen and the branched / mysteries, mysteries and the massive's branched / unambiguous, dreams and the birth's mentions branch / dreams, dreams and the dailies branched / declaration, declaration and the deals branched / dissolves, dissolves and the solves branched / solvent, solvent urgency too, love's branched / secure, secure decide and the rides branched / sophmore, sophmore seals and the seeds into love's branched / societal, societal and the psyche

won branched / pressures, pressures and the branched / pure, pure and the partners branched / entire, entire and the conspire branched / coming, coming into venues branched / doubts, doubt date, branched / basic, basic and known to be, branched / intricate, intricate and toned inside, branches.

CHAPTER ELEVEN

Claims, claims into a branch owne / gigantic, gigantic accept and the sect branched / mountains, mountians abate amused branched / topple, topple's branched / seeds, seeds and the twines sent branched / sewn, sewn and the wonders branched / flute, flute and the flowers branched / sacrificials, sacrificials and the centrals blank checked into a branch / starry, starry and the cares branched / homes, homes and the hilts branched / mexican, mexican and the daunts branched / pacific, pacific access into love's branched / plural, plural and the accepts branched / ones, ones and the windows branched / traditional, traditional treats and the trades branched / paddles, paddles and the pluses branched / oceanic, oceanic instincts fuse, branched / diabolic, diabolic accrues branched / splash, splash central's branched / activities, activities temptations branch / manners, manners and the blazes branched / rear, rear and the steer clear through too, branched / height, height and the sights branched / thrust, thrust and the resist branched / blocks, clocks into blocks allowed branched / truss, truss and the trance's branched / test, test and the trillions, branched / capable, capable and the cares branched / draws, draws and the branches drowned in love / temple, temple and the simples branched / grounds, grounds and the tenants branched / offerings, offerings simply branched / suns, suns into simply branched / occur, occur and the branched / Teotichuan, Teotichuan branched in the sun / emperical, emperical and the winnings branched / sun, sun and the scenes branched / pyramid, pyramid amid these branched / kilometric, kilometric kianetics branched / moved, moved into the groove's branched / moon, moon and the gently metric branched / originates, originates in a dreams branched / creation, creation rations our branched / inherits, inherits and the treatise managed branched / prophecies, prophecies branched / quetzacoatl, quetzacoatl and the coulds branched / plumed, plumed and the zoomed allow branched / enclosures, enclosures branched / justify, justify and the genuine branched / exploits, exploits and the genes branched / terrors, terrors and throngs branched / cues, cues and the carts branched / sizes, sizez and the ritual's branched / spots, spots and the thoughts branched / honorary, honorary and the hilts branched / sorts, sorts and the sites branched / pilgrimage, pilgrimage and the thrusts branched / foot, foot and the feet branched / walk, walk and the wisdom won branched / ahau, ahau and the how branched / four, four and the more branched / three, three and the thrice branched wo / kankin, kankin into the simply ranche / 23, 23 and the we are branched.

CHAPTER TWELVE

Argues, argues and the thrusts branched / meditate, meditate and the most, branched / berate, berate and the balance branched / decembers, decembers and the dates branched / flood, flood a lot and be branched / A. D, Add a date's branched / 2012, 2012 and the sets branched / fifth, fifth and the fallen's branched / sun's sun's scenes branched / ancient, ancient and the gentle's branched / light, light and the lesson's branched / tall, tall enough to see through branched / Caucasian, Caucasian and the care too, branched / blonde, blonde and the better be's branched / heads, heads and the hrutles lept branched / hieroglyphics, hieroglyphics and the cure's branched / cycles, cycles and the suggestion's blanket branched / timed, timed and the temptation's ranc / Sandalphon, Sandalphon and the material sent into love's branched / angels, angels chosen too, branched / arching, arching about the ways branched / timed, timed and the tickle's ends branched / sung, sung and the signals branched / processed, processed details branched / plumes, plumes and the possession's branched / popul, popul and the view's branched / wuh, wuh knew the light's branched / Maya, Maya and the risen branched / quiche, quiche and the riches branched / futures, futures voted and branched freel / state, state and the thrills branched / early, early and the worries branched / migrates, migrates and the rates into love's branched / smith, smith and the lesson splits through love's branched / lesson, lesson and the listen's branched / sanctify, amplify and the fly too, branched / message, message and the mention's mixed branched / processions, processions paused and the causes branched / hart, harts and the pelts branched / 72, 72 and the mood's branched / annuals, anuals and the meals branched / pilgrims, pilgrims peachy into love's branched / wobble, wobble and the wiggles branched / clicks, clicks and the cures branched / cycles, cycles and the spins rant branched / apparel, apparel apparent and the thin's branched / God's, God's gates branched / constellation, constellation and the chips branched / amounts, amounts and the accomplish branched / deliberate, deliberate and the affluence meant to a branch / climes, climes and the clearest accounts branched / derivative, derivative details branched / charisma, charisma clears to a kinship branched / exists, exists arouse and the place meant branched / parts, parts and the passions paced to a branch / parking, parking in the lots which branch through love / magma, magma and the flows mused within eruptive branched / cardinal, cardinal and the clues to a bishop branched / swoons, swoons and dunes branched / directives, directives and the dialectic branched / Pleiade / peace / Islam / big.

CHAPTER THIRTEEN

Matters, matters met in a ranched estate's branched / meteor, meteors and the mention's gazed branched / starts, starts and the steers linked along those branched / geodetic, geodetic degrees branched / serious, serious and the seals branched / figures, figures and the felt branched / recognize, recognize and the arise into branched / respect, respect and the sects branched / memphis, memphis and the mythic branched / mediterranean, mediterranean the muses branch / seen, seen along the tracks branched / ashore, ashore and the simple's branched / banks, banks and the Egyptian branches, nile / balance, balance and the loving's entire branched / times, times and the temples branched / theorize, theorize and the theories branched / ratios, ratios and temples built perfectly to

the universal grid, metaphorically spoken, love is God hu-manly branched / amounts, amounts and the scenes ruled branched / given, given and the genders break branched / 360, 360 ways to the second loop branched / rule, rule and the one branched / degreed, degreed and the deals branched / deduct, deduct and the daring branched / significance, sgnificance lends to the branches love / regards, regards and the cards made branched / distance, distance and the diligence lent unto love's branched / radius, radius and the radial declares tossed along love's branched / height, height and the felt details branched / won, won and the sun's branched / polar, polar and the powers branched / experiments, experiments passed into the light's branched / figures, figures and the financially leased branched / codes, codes and the keys branched / sources, sources selective into the branches estate / derive, derive a detail branched / literal, literal explores and the shores thrown across the branched / gates, gates and the jaunts branched / authors, authors and the throats branched / suppose, the topless transcend to the treats branched in love / points, points and the places pointed into love's branched / effects, effects and the idols tossed exquistly into the trees of heaven's branched enthus / protective, protective and the spoken branched / territorial, territorial peripatatically linked erudition into love's branched / regards, regards for the forts joined into love's branched / cultural, cultural data spans living branched / discord, discord and the daring's branched / visible, visible to dashes branched / starts, starts into missions branched / metallurgy, metallurgy cures and the lures branched / contemplates, contemplates into tracks branched / Giza, Giza and the gathers branched / ancient, ancient and the joins branched / pointed, pointed and the threats branched / dispersal, dispersal and the reheasal branched / disseminate, disseminate and the daunts branched / desire, desire deals best with branches seale / precision, precision ports branched / civilized, civilized and the sizes branched / dared, dared and adored branched / understood, understood who's branched / afield, afield and afar leads branched / vast, vast voiced branched / squeezed, squeezed quells branched to a square's occup / squired, squired eccentircs and the vaulted seals branched.

THE BEFRIEND-MENTS
LEVEL 30

CHAPTER ONE

Accomplish, accomplish fits when we matter less and mean more expressly said, love's the befriend / friendship, friendship found and felt becomes the way to "be / stages, stages have found you and now you sing the way too, befriend / surrender, surrender makes the sun befriend / surround, surround and the sounded intrigue within love's mention too, befriend / conclude, conclude that surrender means yes to love's befriend / inquires, inquires and the meanings spin into love's befriend / hires, hires a tablet written clear with heart's befriend / technically, technically unique and often spoken, our heart's befriend / serial, serial to a miracle, befriend / facts, facts made especially befriend / history, history held, clear through, to love's dimensional befriend / minutes, minutes and the listed befriend / anomaly, anomaly and the coming befriend / decide, decide to be, friendly, to / immense, immense in remission's befriend / astronomical, astronomical to the sense on too, succession's befriend / lore, lore made listened too, befriend / studies, studies over due, befriend / assures, assures emit of the listened too, befriend / requires, requires a mention, befriend / requisite, requisite to a capable cars dimension's befriend / numbers, numbers add too, your dimensional befriend / waits, waits apply, to a flight, dimensional befriend / bears, bears are cast to the wind's dimensions, flight to a dimensional shif / cleared, cleared another cove's dimensional desist, befriend / worn, worn in thin layers dear, befriend / over, over the veil drawn, befriend / due, due a diligence befriend / cosmic, cosmic acquire became our material befriend / plenty, plenty made of the heart's befriend / passive, passive and the agressive forgive of light's befriend / place, place your heart into a new lend, by your befriend / positive, positive inquire into the miraculous view through dimension's befriend / position, position found and the mounds increased befriend / positron, positron and the yawning agree to free love's befriend / plants, plants and the fountains deep with love's befriend / portable, portable to the miracle dimensionally elect too, a befriend / purest, purest the assurance then, befriend / curable, curable to the curation, befriend / create, create a resource, hear, befriend / graves, grave undo and the living's befriend / gears, gears switch and the lights rise into God's eyes, befriend / gaze, gaze across waves, befriend / eyes, eyes that daze into love's befriend / assume, assume a stature direct into love's befriend / attune, attune a yes into love's befriend / awe, awe became the minute trued into love's beware of the lessen's befriend / enigmatic, enigmatic and the static sums undone, befriend / stood, stood for the minute's befriend / mute, mute into a moment's clarity and the surety paralleled into a heartfelt befriend / revealed, revealed a faithful befriend / inheritors, inheritors ascend, befriend / forgotten, forgotten and again, found, befriend / archaic, archaic to the old's befriend / trace, trace and entirety too, the befriend / statutes, statutes and the reputed, befriend / astounding, astounding how hounding can end, befriend / fully, fully apparent into love's befriend / amber, amber bay's befriend / splendors, splendors come into the befriend / revelation, revelation and the duration's befriend / haunting, haunting forgotten and the sought can end, befriend / Earth.

CHAPTER TWO

Far, far and the car arrives, befriend / myth, myth and the fields alysian too, befriend / voyage, voyage across the halls of visionary befriend / discovery, discovery and recovery within, a befriend / antiquity, antiquity becomes the ancient wane's befriend / record, record of the simply, befriend / distant, distant to a news sent, befriend / insatiable, insatiable the tables turn, befriend / offered, offered intentional befriend / robes, robes opened too, befriend / letters, letters written in a perfect befriend / chant, chant again, "befriend, befriend, befriend"/ petition, petition made and the heart paid, befriend / favorable, favorable the situate befriend / suggestion, suggestion becomes the signal, befriend / poverty, poverty over in the outed befriend / wretched, wretched experience and the base erased, befriend / main, main ways to be befriend / burning, burning and the yearned for, befriend / aztecs, aztecs agree to retire to befriend / compelling, compelling the story and the heart's detail for befriend / argues, argues that yet mean yes to a befriend / totalitarian, totalitarian befriend / lurked, lurked across rooms too, befriend / cement, cement the bond you are on, befriend / social, social appear and the dear, befriend / fortune, fortune spent and won, befriend / captive, captive over and the due? befriend / constant, constant to the consistent, befriend / authority, authority given and the declare? Befrien / garment, garment sewn through the loan, befriend / false, false to reply less, befriend / monstrous, monstrous the marriage to less, rebel? yes, befriend / attend, attend a mention into thee, befriend / tore, tore a wave openly befriend / entrails, entrial entrained across less, befriend / quivered, quivered with states too, befriend / allegories, allegories gain your befriend / literally, literally I am befriended daily / ferocity, ferocity comes to the intensity given thee, the befriend / vehicle, vehicle meets your befriend / modern, modern amaze that the heart will, befriend / exacting, exacting discipline to thy befriend / because, because and the cause? Be friend / undergone, undergone and the mission? Be friend / soul, soul released and the mention spiritually, freed, be friend / destiny, destiny today, be friend / type, type met, befriend / world, worlds held, be friend / tale, tale over, renewed, be friend / behind, behind the gates, be friend / valley, valley fled, befriend / themselves, themselves and the said "befriended"/ earlier, earlier in the year's befriend / distinctive, distinctively befriend / symbolism, symbolism becomes you, befriend / gigantic, gigantic the assign into, befriend / extended, extended immersion into lvoe's befriend / halted, halted and the salted freed, befriend / firestorm, firestorm ways, befriend / conquest, conquest comes, befriend / sustained, sustained emotion's befriend / structure, structure recovers, befriend / chapel, a chapel made for the heart you own, love's befriend, style.

CHAPTER THREE

Massive, massive the planet's intend to forgive man kind, remember, befriend / veneration, veneration comes through the generation, next, befriend / dialects, dialects match and the hearts unsnap into love's derange free befriend / site, site found for the ground's befriend / mound, mound escaped befriend / declared, declared a new wave's befriend / constructed, constructed homes in yomes befriend / empire, empire built and entire into love's befriend / paddles, paddles across and the cost is lessened, befriend / condemned, comdemned has forgotten the light's befriend / fruits, fruits mixed abide, befriend / flower, flower and the powers within your, befriend / feast, feast made on the shore befriend / capital, capital the invest into a ticket's befriend / cherished, cherished arrives and the said is befriend / regaled, regaled with love's befriend / flutes, flutes met and then new, love's befriend / anticipation, anticipation comes undone too, a befriend lessen / puzzle, puzzle cast apart and again they befriend / manner, manner sought found, befriend / tone, tone taken out, befriend / cult, cult over, love begun, befriend / traditional, traditional to a rational forgive's befriend / popular, popular to the causes befriend / digests, digest another amount made, befriend / pawn, pawn overs out, befriend / salivate, salivate's salvation the tasty befriend / palisade, palisades sent forgiven befriend / arcatron, arcatrons on too, the befriend / electron, electrons sealed, befriend / metatron, metatron's mate, befriend / parcel, parcel came to the post, befriend / parts, parts worn? Befriend / pastes, pastes at the heart's befriend / pets, pets a posted befriend / passions, passions past, forgive, befriend / service, service due, the befriend / assign, assign the sect, befriend / agree, agree to see the befriend / divine, divine to a published moment's befriend / enlighten, enlighten the living's befriend / ascension, ascension to the minute directly befriend / bliss, bliss voted for, befriend / transcendance, transcendance made, befriend / commitment, commitment comes, befriend / contentment, contentment due, befriend / peace, peace posted into befriend / precise, precise to the minute, befriend / perfect, perfect to exposure's befriend / absolute, absolute to the valued befriend / sacred, sacred to the concentric befriend / command, command a moment's befriend / geometric, geometric to the concentric stretch, befriend / arc, arc found, befriend / metatronic, metatronic memory becomes thee, befriend / gods, gods gazes befriend / advance, advance to the pages befriend / enhance, enhance means be friend / profane, profane to designs sewn be friende / unbound, unbound to the sounds befriend / match, match the estate through love's befriend / matter, matter made the point freed, befriend / cur / core.

CHAPTER FOUR

Material, material to the mental gift's release and the seizure over, due, love is in too, the befriend / brand, brand and the stretch into love's befriend / branch, branches and the chances to reach too, befriend / befriend, befriend the example's entreaty for love / mark, mark a door's opening branched, befriend / paternal, paternal to the eternal befriend / pattern, pattern and the mission's befriend / foundation, foundation and the theoretic remind to be, befriend / unique, unique into love's inquiry, befriend / sanctuary, sanctuary's love and the leaps into befriend / kingdom, kingdom and the keeping, currently, befriend / temple, temple and the steeple's place, befriend / homes, homes into healing's befriend / subatomic, subatomic and the comic forgive's befriend / molecular, molecular into living intrigue's befriend / blood, blood spoke into God's marvel with you, befriend / gardens, gardens into gazes and the

gate opened, befriend / assigns, assigns and the simply shone's befriend / mastery, mastery into the mystery unique with befriend / unique, unique the decision to seek a new regard for light's earth and the living's befriend / superluminal, superluminal examples of the simply said, "befriends"/ aspire, aspire to sire a grander strand, befriend / magnitude, magnitude into the mood clearly befriend / clear, clear a sample and the certain example's befriend / presence, presence into pleasure and the measure's befriend / streets, streets pulse with plenty into the natural befriend / fountains, fountains infused with depths befriend / wells, wells maple deep in love's sample, befriend / heavens, heavens estuary intrigued with love's befriend / mysteries, mysteries set and amends made too, befriend / foods, foods sampled, hear, befriend / fond, fond to the fillings, befriend / ultimate, ultimate to the example, befriend / crystalline, crystalline to the living's befriend / musical, musical in meeting's befriend / mercurial, mercurial to the measured befriend / magnified, magnified as examples, befriend / application, application too, and thee, befriend / nations, nations who kneel needing befriend / nurture, nurture and the stature came, befriend / nascient, nascient to a nestle's befriend / availability, availability becomes your befriend / stores, stores opened in too, befriend / commit, commit to the won, befriend / truth, truth becomes your befriend / loves, loves made example, befriend / life, life to the legend's befriend / equate, equate and emancipation's befriend / vitamins, vitamins taken, befriend / informed, informed to the manner, befriend / available, available across these, befriend / aisle, aisle wise, too, befriend / pink, pink into mantle's befriend / green, green epistle's befriend / teal, teal emancipation's befriend / lavendar, lavendar leys, befriend / mint, mint appeals befriend / magenta, magenta bay's befriend / yellow, yellow year's befriend / brown, brown news leaves, befriend / earth, earth and the missile's befriend / works, works and the whistled befriend / handles, handles durable too and the daffy befriend / heights, heights hustled through, befriends.

CHAPTER FIVE

Spa, original inspire and the spa's refresh with regarded confess into loving befriend / sparks, sparks and the peers befriend / cups, cups and the curate's befriend / express, express your passion for forgiven confession through love's befriend / extra, extra trades and the moonstone blue with the light within, a heart made, befriend / indulge, indulge a fashion's contested allow, befriend / fabulous, fabulous insight above light's befriend / ordinary, ordinary rays and the raid's off, befriend / magnificent, magnificent befriend and the blaring okay too, allow / believe, believe and the rationale applied forgiven's befriend / rivers, rivers reap the floral attire for befriend / flower, flower depth's befriend / ridges, ridges and the reason's befriend / tours, tours over our's befriend / life, life leads, befriend / define, define whom, know, befriend / signs, signs gain, befriend / delivery, delivery comes into your befriend / compliments, compliments made curation completion, befriend / finest, finest, ours, befriend / superlatives, superlatives gift's befriend / best, best and the essential befriend / collections, collections and selective too, befriend / acquire, acquire a bliss within, God's friends, befriend / language, language gained through avenue's befriend / skilled, skillled in epitomie's befriend / proportions, proportions correctly befriend / owns, owns his owns befriend / classics, classics apply, befriend / illustrates, illustrates more, befriend / firms, firms to the hilt, befriend / reproduce, reproduce exactly, befriend / copy, copy a sample's befriend / replicate, replicate is easy, befriend / instigate, instigate's overage, befriend / profess, profess a direction, befriend / prophecy, prophecy felt, befriend / cleat, cleat and the seat passed and felt, befriend / clammer, clammer and the listen's befriend / grip, grip a gaze through too, befriend / pull, pull a deal's befriend' / push, push past the past, befriend / propel, propel passion too, the befriend / purveyed, purveyed and detailed our befriend / ports, ports established, now propel to thee, befriend / portraiture, portraiture paid through the profoundly befriend / portrait, portrait made essential too the profusely befriend / civilize, civilize resized into the befriend / whipped, whipped past the ration, befriend / worn, worn into living's befriend / went, went and then won, thee befriend / civil, civil designs and the sights in befriend / throws, throws and the taverna's befriend / throes, throes and the listen's befriend / wince, wince and the woes past, befriend / chance, chance and the position's befriend / gauntlet, gauntlet raided and the raised position's befriend / glove, gloves off and the couhg over splat befriend / fences, fences down and the chances made, befriend / chains, chains and positrons posited too, befriend / change, change your manner, befriend / channel, channel done and due, befriend / chants, chants make a define befriend / Energetics.

CHAPTER SIX

Wet, wet enough to test for and explain in the lane's befriend / velvet, velvet and the feelings revenued through befriend / tether, tether and the weather's befriend / torn, torn and the worn degrees befriend / films, films and the features parentally defined too, befriend / screened, screened and the lerning curve's befriend / projective, projectively respectively revued our brightened befriend / cords, cords cut miraculously close to the level's befriend / electric, electric into a parishioner's befriend / actor, actor and the factor befriend / actress, actress to the matresses befriend / stage, stage and the threes befriend / watts, watts and the weaver's befriend / bulb, bulb and the tubes befriend / sounds, sounds treated query, befriend / acts, acts and the meetings planted through our freedom's befriend / drama, drama and the dreams specifically befriend / fired, fired into hired attempted and the leap across our venues befriend / burning, burning belate to degree's resourced and the sender's befriend / exchanged, exchanged and the ranged electives framed into love's befriend / winds, winds and the wood's befriend / windy, windy and the moods befriend / tours, tours across palaces befriend / quaint, quaint and the advent too, befriend / quickens, quickens and the liken is in too, befriend / yellow, yellow ways electric, befriend / gates, gates clear the way, befriend / opens, opens directly and into these, the befriend / chase, chases seated and the foot free deliver's befriend / pedestrians, pedestrians estates and the befriend / shops, shops

across waves befriend / apparent, apparent to the matters befriend / vaults, voices and the voltage befriend / holistic, holistic the value's befriend / alleluia, alleluia and the chair's befriend / active, active into trees befriend / crucifix, crucific fixed above the cares befriend / holy, holy the heads befriend / script, script wide the face's befriend / scripture, scripture red with befriend / trip, trip to the tip of the befriend / flip, flip to the balance behind our befriend / rustle, rustle and the thistle greens reds befriend / thrust, thrust and the the throat's befriend / lustful, lustfull and the entreaty too, a befriend / advance, advance and the befriend's encouraged to / chance, chance and the chiming befriend / encounter, encounter comes too, the befriend / cuddle, cuddle the muddles less, befriend / thrown, thrown and the living's befriend / down, down into the sound's befriend / up, up and the truck's befriend / throne, throne and the thrice won, befriend / purgatory, purgatory paid and the maid's productive penned, befriend / erased, erased a chalice lessened too, befriend / embrace, embrace and the lightened news, befriend / incites, incites written and the smitten befriend / halves, halves and the won, befriend / worn, worn and the woos befriend / entire, entire tot the meals befriend / within, within a willing befriend / heavenly, heavenly and the healing's befriend / expanse, expanse and the completion's befriend / advance, advance into the state, befriends.

CHAPTER SEVEN

Won, won and the sons befriended again, living breathe's love / frame, frame and the mattrress set in two, pieced again within love's befriend / forgiven, forgiven and entreaties plead for God's confess, love's befriend / forgotten, forgotten and lost within, love's befriend / less, less and the listening's befriend / lavendar, lavendar ways befriend / trust, trust the truth, rules, befriend / experience, experience an assurance, befriend / sought, sought and forgiven then, befriend / angular, angular wades too, befriend / entrance, entrance into wounds spent, befriend / hoped, hoped for the message, befriend / four, four and the fellows befriend / equal, equal and the sequel's befriend / sides, sides and the seized befriend / act, act into places befriend / gave, gave a plenty too, befriend / type, type the experience within, befriend / truest, truest yet, befriend / still, still enough to see, befriend / stands, stands along lines befriend / the won, the won, befriend / handy, handy and the mellow mazed beget befriend / fed, fed the mysterious abbreviate and the sate befriend / watery, watery into waves befriend / gravel, gravel grew piles, granite deep, in love's befriend / relief, relief and the rescues befriend / angel, angel and the venues befriend / falls, falls across pages befriend / venezeluan, venezeluan variate befriend / treat, treat a mission as admissioned too and well enough, befriend / declare, declare and the date's befriend / state, state and the station's befriend / spatial, spatial into magnified befriend / bliss, bliss dates and the deals befriend / join, join and the journeyed befriend / kiss, kiss another's quoted befriend / raptured, raptured entrance and the chance befriend / reveal, reveal and the random's befriend / revelation, revelation of the revenues made, befriend / seals, seals elect and eruptive wave's befriend / done, done and the deal is made, befriend / you, you knew the way, befriend / won, won a case you wove, befriend / integrity, integrity gives your heart a missive, befriend / balance, balance a book written, befriend / honed, honed the skills to still a forgetting, befriend / truth, truth, be, told, hanged less, befriend / respect, respect a nearness unto a living befriend / concrete, concrete reliance in the balance befriend / examine, examine a nurtured befriend / shown, shown an intitial, befriend / flocks, flocks and the stocking's befriend / flight, flight and the feeling's befriend / horses, horses respectfully sent into thee, befriend / wings, wings across western befriend / beasts, beasts out and others into, the befriend / defeated, defeated guests allow befriend / defeated, defeated a diet less, befriend / through, through to the centered befriend / love, love another, love two, befriend / 666, 666 and the stuck gone, befriend / repleted, repleted in the seated attire, a fire built, befriend / know, know a nature befriended.

CHAPTER EIGHT

Now, now is the wellness befriend / how, how to show the listen's befriend / two, two and the mission's befriend / love, love a diet befriend / expressions, expressions and dimensions befriend / exact, exact to the facts befriend / couples, couples made to befriend / click, click within, befriend / changes, changes made and the heart elected, befriend / over, over and the visions sent, befriend / wrought, wrought and the sought suggested, befriend / brinks, brinks made, suggest, befriend / charges, charges made, paid, befriend / paid, paid and the feelings raid gone, befriend / debits, debits dues and the muse goes, befriend / ring, ring and the analyze befriends us, love / heavenly, heavenly elation and the mentally freed dimensions, befriend / gaze, gaze across lands, as promised, befriend / commits, commits our clearest, befriend / eyes, eyes matched, befriend / human, human news befriend / God, God's gaze befriend / said, said and the bidding's befriend / let, let us seize a moment's befriend / there, there is enough to stay within, befriend / be, be and a balance befriend / light, light willed befriend / humanity, humanity and the cues befriend / woven, woven parallels befriend / samples, samples sealed, befriend / spill, spill energetically, befriend / lips, lips seal, befriend / torn, torn across seals befriend / lesson, lessons mentioned and then, befriend / open, open a gate's post, befriend / more, more and the shore electric's befriend / borne, borne along trends befriend / wills, wills data befriend / throngs, throngs meet in befriend / blue, blue avenues too, befriend / deliver, deliver daily ways befriend / streams, streams suggest your befriend / rock, rock electric and the feels befriend / climbing, climbing and the curt befriend / vines, vines and the volleys sent, befriend / ivy, ivy grew around our befriend / include, include another's befriend / pleasure, pleasure given unto thee, befriend / nine, nine stelae high to the living befriend / attentive, attentive to notices befriend / flowing, flowing into the ocean's befriend / clues, clues made above and within these, the befriend / clues, clues again? befriend / pelt, pelt another withing lvoe's befriend / pebbles, pebbles tossed and the cost comes free, befriend / splash, splash along the lends befriend / cliffs, cliffs and the challenge freed, to

a balance befriend / shorn, shorn of the lessen, befriend / Phoenix / rue / come / / Tim / born.

CHAPTER NINE

Attentive, attentive to the inquiry, apply reply to the recourse wed within apparel red along God's lines, befriend / flowing, flowing into glowing's befriend / clues, clues amaze us, befriend / behold, behold the angel's message, "love, befriend / drape, drape a material to the east, invest, befriend / envoked, envoked the evoke, profoundly befriend / via, via light's highway too, a befriend / throats, throats again drip with the gems on befriend / born, born and to the swallows ways, befriend / anew, anew rendered befriend / five, five ways into love's befriend / sides, sides chosen forgive and move forth befriend / house, house moves, befriend / home, home to the hilton's befriend / smaller, smaller days, shangri-la is, regained, befriend / camps, camps ways befriend / canvas, canvas cased befriend / large, large enough to seep, befriend / door, doors made through the environs befriend / triangular, triangular entreaties into these befriend / windows, windows and ventilation befriend / posts, posts to the beams befriend / zippers, zippers exist to join lips to the healing befriend / elevate, elevate your state too, the befriend / platform, platform built to leap through, befriend / porch, porch met at the hilt's befriend / democratic, democratic regard for the sword's befriend / remove, remove the lessened befriend / view, view and the various befriend / republic, republic into treaties made, befriend / plato, plato made vetoed befriend / said, said and the materials read befriend / remember, remember and the gesture's befriend / quotes, quotes and the queries gestured befriend / reveal, reveal a residence within your befriend / secrets, secrets read befriend / codes, codes and the keys befriend / clues, clues and the steeples befriend / keys, keys passionately ring within our befriend / empires, empires made through stages befriend / won, won and the windows befriend / turning, turning and the rescue's befriend / entire, entire in her hired befriend / nations, nations knelt within love's befriend / through, through a day's deals befriend / one, one too, befriend / heart, heart into started befriend / man, man made deals befriend / salvation, salvation comes to the youngest befriend / is, is this, yes? befriend / at, at one within a befriend / handy, handy days befriend / plan, plan to see one forgiven through befriendin / dynamic, dynamic dates within love's befriend / hearts, hearts met, befriend / electric, electric stays befriend / respectable / fee / fiel / dynamic / Principle / relationship / recapture / provide proof.

CHAPTER TEN

Venues, venues often chosen, befriend' / entice, entice another near, your, befriend / bodies, bodies blaze into befriend / advise, advise a detail's befriend / paradigm, paradigm's shifted, behaviors healed, befriend / bursts, bursts and a mission's send, befriend / 720, 720, the ways too, a befriend / shut, shut the door, yes, now, befriend / opens, opens and the gates won, befriend / wings, wings and the lessons befriend / parallel, parallel and the patterns broken, befriend / portals, portals and the positions filled, befriend / hearty, hearty meets and the mission's befriend /

speakers, speakers spoken too, befriend / experience, experience a deliverance, befriend / export, export and the retort's befriend / chances, chances redeemed and the gleaming befriend / ultimate, ultimate to the menu preferred and the advance into love's befriend / include, include a measure to love's befriend / supreme, supreme in redemption, I am fulfilled thoroughly through love's befriend / abide, abide delivered and interior too, love's befriend / side, sides chosen, deliver her too, befriend / chosen, chosen electives and the invective forgives, blends, befriend / fullest, fullest and the feeling's touched, befriend / want, want another's ways befriend / creative, creative escapades befriend / desire, desire a deluge, befriend / decide, decide to be eccentrically freed, befriend / appear, appear near the befriend / entire, entire adores and the hearing's befriend / spiral, spiral, hire, befriend / ideal, ideal to the measured, befriend / mates, mates made, presently, befriend / compassionate, compassionately befriend / committed, committed to the causes, befriend / content, content to be excited about befriend / excitable, excitable and the seals befriend / able, able and the stables lends befriend / responsive, responsive to the causes befriend / responseable, responseable to the tables turning burned less befriend / available, available too, befriend / open, open gated befriend / evocative, evocative elections befriend / responsive, responsive to teachings reveal, befriend / responseable, response-able friends, befriend / imagine, imagine and metes bound, befriend / intelligent, intelligent to a gentle befriend / absolute, absolute forgive's confession, befriend / gives, gives a gear to the living belief befriend / receives, receives notation's bid, befriend / honors, honors a cabinet filled within befriend / honorable, honorable to the stable-ness befriend / reliant, reliant to the covers befriend / reliable, reliable to the sermons spent, befriend / considers, considers another's befriend / considerate, considerate to a daring befriend / cares, cares for each the other's befriend / shares, shares a table with befriend / plays, plays elective too, befriend / changes, changes come through thee, befriend / flexible, flexible to the cues befriend / unit, unit days befriend / unique, unique to the delegate's befriend / undulates, undulates mentally befriended.

CHAPTER ELEVEN

Understood, understood and disguises seen bonified befriend / understands, understands the nearing, befriend / receptive, receptive to the cures befriend / recipe, recipe simply befriend / loves, loves a deify befriend / listens, listens intently to the causes befriend / gains, gains a cushion befriend / guides, guides a desire too, befriend / spurns, spurns a details befriend / antithesis, antithesis befriend / selfish, selfish gone, befriend / greedy, greedy outed, befriend / self-absorbed, self-absorbed disrobed, befriend / challenging, challenging commital befriend / celibate, celibate dates conclude, befriend / loose, loose to the notions befriend / trifles, trifles and the stifles left, befriend / sorry, sorry said and the mends? befriend / self-indulgent, self-indulgent to the living's befriend / irritated, irritated? yes, befriend / irritable, irritable to the stable's befriend / moody, moody diets, befriend / aggrevation, aggrevation vents befriend / bitch, bitch born into heat forgiven

and the female's befriend / bore, bore gone, becomes a befriend / whorish, whorish forgive's befriend / poor, poor to the "matter" befriend / depraved, depraved said yes, befriend / lacking, lacking effect? befriend / flat, flat to the finish, befriend / flush, flush to the deals, befriend / thoughtless, thougthless out, now shout, befriend / shallow, shallow said, good-bye, befriend / challenged, challenged met respect in befriend / heat, heat over and the dues befriend / mean, mean now outed befriends othe / beast, beast outed through befriendmen / released, released to a cause befriend / Azrael, Azrael said good buy to the light profoundly befriend / cues, cues given, befriend / collapse, collapse comes, befriend / retreats, retreats recourse believed, befriend / control, control over, befriend / deceit, deceit outed, befriend / demon, demon doubted, befriend / spurned, spurned and the doubts out, befriend / churn, churn about us, befriend / arrival, arrival to the truest befriend / gate, gate again, know befriend / nine, nine to a trine meant, befriend / ten, ten and the deliberate befriend / wants, wants and the bet for befriend / destiny, destiny and the dealing's befriend / revealed, revealed destructs to the beast's befriend / happens, happens to the chances befriend / alone, alone to the minute's befriend / against, against and the giving's befriend / tide, tide and the thrilling's befriend / trued, trued and the truth's befriend / sample, sample and the seal's befriend / living, living and the likeness befriend / given, given and the grandness befriend / goods, goods and the thicken's befriend / reached.

CHAPTER TWELVE

Wise, wise and the sizes blanched prophetically enhanced within thee befriend / hit, hit a ball out and then, befriend / owe, owe a detailed befriend / paid, paid to a page of fullest befriend / broken, broken and the spoken in, befriend / God, God and the world's between, befriend / father, father and the mother's befriend / mother, mother and the weather's befriend / credits, credits and the balanced befriend / dark, dark and the diligence, befriend / despair, despair outed and the healing's befriend / deceits, deceits and the deal's befriend / receipts, receipts and the rescue's befriend / past, past and the pillows pretend's befriend / purged, purged and the word's befriend / encourage, encourage and the whirling's befriend / undermined, undermined and the signed befriend / plants, plants and the client's befriend / implants, implants and the insign's befriend / chance, chance and the dance's befriend / solution, solution found and the sound's befriend / sunny, sunny and the day's befriend / swoon, swoon and the diet's befriend / honeymooned, honeymooned befriend / gained, gained and the valuable's replace / lies, lies and the lesson's befriend / soaring, soaring and the sessions's befriend / delivery, delivery and the daily befriend / winged, winged across mission's befriend / ecstasy, ecstasy and the mystery's befriend / parents, parents and the abuse less, befriend / come, come to the summit's befriend / occurrence, occurrence and the mission's befriend / recognize, recognize and the size's befriend / size, size and the rising befriend / hearts, hearts and the strengthen's befriend / available, available to the palace befriend / chances, chances and the dance's befriend / regain, regain and the strain done, befriend / strain, strain and the deluge done, befriend / unites, unites and the sun come's befriend / provide, provide and the plate filled, befriend / insight, insight and the simple's befriend / attentive, attentive and the trench dug, befriend / stare, stare and the steering's befriend / captive, captive and the cues cut, befriend / capture, capture and the ruptured befriend / escape, escape and the challenge met, befriend / check, check and the court set, befriend / paid, paid and the personed befriend / plan, plan and above too, the befriend / made, made and the glee found, befriend / mate, mate and the meeting's electric raises befriend / moves, moves across truth told, befriend / near, near a daily-ness befriend / farthest, farthest ascension's befriend / expand, expand to a mentioned befriend / stars, stars and the storage's befriend / contract, contract occuring, you win, the befriend / exact, exact to the mattress, befriend / delicacy, delicacy tasted, embellish, befriend / parm / through / possiblities.

CHAPTER THIRTEEN
Opposite, opposite and the said, one, befriend / poles, poles and the basic's befriend / string, string along's compassion's befriend / holes, holes and the lesson's befriend / solid, solid and the nature's befriend / dwarfs, dwarfs and the detail's befriend / tall, tall into details befriend / collapse, collapse and the cultural switches befriend / building, building and delegated befriend / floods, floods and the listening's befriend / destruct, destruct and the dialect's befriend / dates, dates and the definition's befriend / marry, marry another's branched befriend / your, your choice made, enjoy thee, the befriend / mind, mind into material's befriend / musically, musically mention another's befriend / inclined, inclined to mention a mansion's befriend / inkling, inkling comes into thee, befriend / unknown, unknown intrinsics and the healing's befriend / sings, sings and the suggestion's befriend / rotates, rotates about befriend / involves, involves and thee I see, befriend / lock, lock and the listening befriend / clans, clans and the create's befriend / partners, partners and the detail's befriend / grab, grab a chance to branch too, befriend / dances, dances leapt across the meaning's befriends / grace, grace a place's befriend / screen, screen set and redeemed too, befriend / keys, keys matched, ours, befriend / opening, opening suggestions within a befriend / pays, pyas for the dealing, befriend / choirs, choirs aspire too, befriend / angelic, angelic the dues paid, befriend / evolution, evolution's details come, befriend / devolves, devolves less and then, yes, befriend / arrive, arrive to the daily befriend / coined, coined and the current's befriend / trips, trips and the target's befriend / chance, chance taken, befriend / duels, duels out, befriend / bolt, bolt now, befriend / win, win a dearest, befriend / split, split to a nature's befriend / closure, closure came to the past made, befriend / deft, deft to a cleft recited apprehended love can begin to befriend / decide, decide who to choose from, again, befriend / deals, deals made last to the good's befriend / monetary, monetary experiences and the superior note's befriend / units, units gathered and the money made through befriend / constrict, constrict comes to be gone, befriend / chance, chances made, to lasts, befriend / evolve, evolve to the solved riddle's win, befriend / solve, solve a query, evolve in valued befriend / endurance, endurance builds, befriend

/ issue, issue made, healed, befriend / chart, chart the discussion befriended, beheld, behold, God is gained, love / opens, opens hearts directly, love's befriend / channels, channels sought gain, a, befriend / flung, flung open gains a befriend / fling, fling to the ceiling befriend / natural, natural news befriend / express, express a desire for a befriend / truth, truth emits, yours, befriended.

THE MARK-MENTS
LEVEL 31

CHAPTER ONE

Granular, granular to the surface advanced past love's mark / surface, mark free of the smudge lessened, love / apparent, apparent and intentional into love's marked / parents, parents suggest a living's mark / character, character cues and the cosmos marked / ceremony, ceremony mends, arc free too, love's mark / circles, circles drawn and we are on into love's mark / staged, staged recovery of the shrubs lost to love's mark / blankets, blankets cast across love's brand new mark / deciphered, deciphered the keys and met a blast of love's mark / one, one to won's mark / pleased, pleased and the plantings marked / brothers, brothers to the cause, mark free / sisters, sisters signal, mark free / mothers, mothers missive mark free / friends, friends of the mobs mark free / reach, reach across divides mark less / grow, grow another sort, mark free / advertise, advertise a resource marked love / magic, magic spans through love's mark / celebrate, celebrate a mandible broken, love's mark / waters, waters wet within love's mark / retreats, retreats and the causes romantically linked into love's dyanmics, God's gain, love's trendy mark / displays, displays of the benefits banded within love's mark / transforms, transforms dynamics and the duo marked / produce, produce a benefit beyond degree and the degradation less intense, God's man, love's mark / list, list your formation's lift into God's news of living admiration for the nature marked less / love, love and the sonnet marked through within mark free love / museum, museum connects and the dots marked freed by love / fresco, fresco and the let go into love's mark / freshens, freshens and the lessens marked free too, love / arts, arts and the starts electric into love's mark / flavors, flavors and the meny eccentrically marked / accessories, accessories due the news metatronically linked and lightly marked, free / tease, tease a nature complete, mark free / sparks, sparks and the sharks electric into love's mark / collect, collect calls and electric walls of love's listening mark / permanent, permanent gazes past lessen love mark / reminders, reminders remembered and the simmering cast forth forever into the pit, the abyss marked good-by / goals, goals and the shoals of forever's mark / quarters, quarters and the delivery marked love zone / styles, styles and the whiles marked free / treasures, treasures elected and the shuttles marked freeze thawe / trades, trades and the shades marked love / captivate, captivate and the healing stages marked love / behave, behave best lightly loved, mark free / decade, decade of the dues paid, freed up, too, love's mark thre / periods, periods of mental escapes into love's mark / innate, innate matters and the manners kept perfectly mark free / sanctify, sanctify electives of matters forecast into love's mark / start, start the ball's roll detailed into light mark / spiral, spiral spun and the won, mark / singing, singing and the ringing rates, mark / signed, signed and sealed, mark free / song, song arcturian and the details mark free / ages, ages spent mark free / stages, stages endured mark there / results, results committed within love's mark / degrees, degrees forthright and too, the mark / research, research durability and the agility to see, mark / wages, wages paid forth into love's mark / accomplish, accomplish a magical re-mark / these, these attends choices made and the shading's mark.

CHAPTER TWO

Ludicrous, ludicrous requests work for love's remark / simple, simple enough to see, love's marks free / expert, expert to the simple, truth's measures mark free / stand, stand in offensive remark / strands, strands strung throughout love's mark / illiterate, illiterate degrees of love's mark / company, company meant for the duration's making, mark free / span, span a legitimate request for love's mark / origin, origin and the horizon done through love's mark / curate, curate and the ingress into love's mark / face, face a fellow folly through love's remark / frolic, frolic about within love's marking / follicle, follicles deep into love's remade remark / fault, fault over and about within love's remark / head, head to the tones remarkabl / hair, hair metatronic and the burning reminder to enkindle love's passion / awaken, awaken comes to the ones mark free / roll, roll to the news embellished within love's remark / record, record a message into love's heart and the message electrically free to God's love, mark thre / recover, recover another heart's message and the recess cleared into God's message, mark free / reward, reward another's attempts with marks free / relative, relative to forgiveness, remember marks free / paradigm, paradigms abruptly end and begin in marks free / degree, degree durate and the sate mark fou / disguise, disguise and the guise gone into marked set / revealed, revealed and remembered mark free / represent, represent your heart's discuss of love's manners freed to the mark / property, property sold and behold, love's manners marked free / stored, stored and recorded well, the mark's forgiv / received, received and erected, love's mark / loved, loved too, and lifted through light's mark / same, same and the shame becomes swollen into love's remark / games, games in depth and drawn through the light electrical mark / new, new and the pin's drop into love's matters and remark / principles, principles respectful of the manners set mark free / principled, principled and discipled too, through love's remark / sober, sober and the sobriety invest into love's remark / sovereign, sovereign reigns and the masterpieces remarked upon / stored, stored and renewed through love's improve, an import made, mark thre / shop, shop for the relative approval of God's remark / participate, participate in the mention, love's remark / palivate, palivate less and know more too, God's love, the dimensio / salivate, salivate and ascend through the tastes remarkable too, love / Pavlov, Pavlov said, let us be, free to make a healing's remark / crucible, crucibles set filled with love's mark / crux, crux and the points made, love's remark / moved, moved into the arc on love, mark free / move, move through love's remark / belate, belate and the bellow freed, love's remark / belief, belief and the echoes, love has made her maker's mark / basics, basics and the blessings, marked / collect, collect a collection marked free / collection, collection of the our marked free / recollection, recollection of the suburbs marked love / contour, contour and the cabinets marked love / grips, grips and the greetings come, marked free / lips, lips above and within, love's mark / heights, height held up to see from, love's mark / flights, flights allow venues remarke / figure, figure your parallels out, mark tw / controversy, controversy done, accept mark won / mercy, mercy is coming remember her, mark on / know, know the mercy in love's mark.

CHAPTER THREE

Reward, reward due for the venue remarked / scales, scales well and into a new marked / reaps, reaps and the closets opened into new market / sown, sown and the singles melt forward step into love's mark / remit, remit and the refit's mark / transmit, transmit and the reinvent totally unique into love's mark / travel, travel into a new reality mark free / resistance, resistance comes less to the news mark free / reset, reset and the invest remitted into new market / respects, respects and the revenues new markets free / arose, arose and the loosen's marked / arranged, arranged and the rewarded market / raid, raid and the rescue forgotten as love's leads set free the marked / ropes, ropes and the dopes known, market / steps, steps and the stairs led into the marked / styles, styles and the smiles vaunt our views market / deficiencies, deficiencies dues and the moves market free / proper, proper and the pressure freed, mark free / properties, properties and the peer escapes mark free / vectors, vectors and the vaunted mark free / served, served and the signals mark free / video, video and the valued markets free / repair, repair and the rescue knot free / DNA, DNA and the rays abides, free / DNA too, DNA too and the moods set free / DNA three, DNA three and the reflect free / DNA four, DNA four and the tricks free / DNA five, DNA five and the found free / DNA six, DNA six and the stuck freed metatronicall / DNA seven, DNA said and the web freed, marry her again, number / DNA eight, DNA and the beast is out, mark free / DNA nine, DNA nine and the signs mark free / DNA ten and eleven, DNA ten and the eleven's mark free / DNA 1, DNA 1 and the sun's mark free / vibrate, vibrate and the venues debt free, mark I / template, template and the temples debt free, mark wo / compass, compass and the circuits made, deal now, freely, mark I / compassion, compassion and the fashion felt debt free, mark free / compress, compress and the empress freed, mark free / suggest, suggest and the sincerely mark free / solo, solo and the sincerest require's market / leaves, leaves and the living's market / consequences, consequences and the squire's market / direct, direct contact will come, mark free / connect, connect and the dots mark free / commit, commit and the capable market / convey, convey and the dealing's mark / constant, constant and the quickening marked / patterns, patterns and the plans matrix free and expansive too a marked relat / plus, plus causes and the pauses metatronically replete, marked / rhythms, rhythms and the regards made mark free / confirm, confirm and the capable marked / affirmation, affirmation and the marked advance into yes / states, states and the specials market / status, status and the debits placed in market / eclipse, eclipse and the opportunity freed to a mark / science, science and the senses mark free / trips, trips into written venues of love's mark / posterity, posterity and the triples marked / prosperity, prosperity remarks love / loves, loves and the listen's mark / suggests, suggests and the situation's market / reminds, reminds and the lessons menued market / entity, entity entire and the market's blessing.

CHAPTER FOUR

Choose, choose and the chosen forms market / firm, firm and the terms meant into a marked / bathe, bathe and the dealing's market / bath, bath and the parallels market / miracle, miracle marked and the sparks are free / depth, depth and the dealings marked / address, address and the duress forgotten, market / press, press and the impression made market / pass, pass out and the passion spent, marked / past, past out, dares, mark / passion, passions and the avenues marked / contract, contract and the cues market / coral, coral blue and the markets into love / court, court and the canals market / corral, corral and the kept one's market / cavlier, cavalier and the sorts who win through market / Enochian, Enochian and the news advanced into love's market / Enoch, Enoch knelt and the felt dealt meant too, market / keys, keys and the we are, market / Kabbalah, Kabbalah and the kept free market / trees, trees and terrains market free / greek, greek and the sought market / egyptian, egyptian and the sordid forget's market / roman, roam and the gnome's market / celtic, celtic and the conclude's market / clued, clued and the advanced remark / suns, suns and the sent for marked / lights, lights and the listen's mark / life, life led through market / love, love my mark free / lasers, lasers cut the cords, mark free / generate, generate and the genuine marks become love's free / luminary, luminary learned of the advanced states love / illumination, illumination and the station's market / lanquid, lanquid and the lendings remark / spent, spent and the splendor's remark / penetrate, penetrate and the passion's commit, mark free / conceeds, conceeds and the caring remark / spends, spends and the spiral's remark / breathing, breathing and the calls made, mark free / velocity, velocity and the veins intrigued within love's remark / views, views and the vintage remark / rockets, rockets red in love's main venue, mark free / ground, ground near me has red parallels in your marked / ancients, ancients said, win, your marked / Titicaca, Titicaca laked by the completion sent into love's advanced mark / bolivian, bolivian belief and the hounding relief which abundance gives unto the markless yo / quan, quan and the wins partnered through love's mark / yin, yin and the win power mark free / compression, compression and the mention dimension deep in love's mark / compassion, compassion meant to mention unto love's de-mark-atio / expression, expression spent into love's mark / delays, delays later found, out, through light marking / deliberate, deliberate about the balance found in love's mark / Merkaba, Merkaba and the miracle due unto love's mark / spin / relapse / uncoile / Jyotis / plan / Victor / an / escape.

CHAPTER FIVE

Stars, stars meet in the middle's cage-less interior and the nearer pace onto love's mark free / flares, flares and the flown advance / fortunes, fortunes made on the maid's ship, love, mark free / regulate, regulate the paces on too, love's mark of / regard, regard gained and the gates crashed openly into love's mark / build, build a fortune, hear, in love's mark less land / models, models and examples made in love's mark / modules, modules grace our miraculous mark / materials, materials and the serials to a mark / matters, matters match her taste for love's mark / stock, stock given and love lived for, mark free / life, life states and the marked ways to love / loved, loved and the miracles made for God's mark / shared, shared with others, mark / squarely, squarely cared for in the license paid too, mark free / offer, offer to meet your match made, mark less / dear, dear attacks over and the due comes mark free / planets, planets and the parallel destination into love's mark less territor / veils, veils open up into love's mark less plac / sustenance, sustenance and the praises matched for God's mark / pair, pair made for love, God's matched mark less one / air, air and the stature freed miraculously marked / care, care to see us dare to be freed of mark / contention, contention and the mention's mark / covers, covers off and the comply direct and advanced into through love's mark / laden, laden in a maiden's place forgone and found again, love's mends and the marks to prove confession came of God / foods, foods focus on love's forgiven mark / marriage, marriage comes to the ones marked free / lighten, lighten apparent and the listening mark / packets, packets gaze across love's mark / shifts, shifts hsifting through love's mark / gifts, gifts gallantly gone through too, mark / wisdom, wisdom warrants a mission's mark / real, real enough to opt for, love's mark / fact, fact and the fusion, marked love / grid, grid gate freed to marks erasure / fuse, fuse at the midst, remarke / frames, frames and the dames mark free / heart, heart feels and the marks electric / brain, brain examples and the samples mark free / earth, earth and the mirth's mark / shift, shift supplies into the earth's miracles, mark free / rely, rely injury freed into the world's mark / remember, remember a member, debt-free, through love's mark / able, able to abide through and into a lifting mark / opt, opt supple enough to mark less / options, options kneel in the arc's mark / shares, shares made and given in too, the atrc's marked remov / capable, capable to a cause mark free / trial, trials freest without mark / capable, capable of the staple remark / exceptional / people / rehearse / the / play / May / I / Install / Around / He / Nec / Savasrat / bows.

CHAPTER SIX
Shared, shared in a cause electric, love's mark / gained, gained a new entreaty into the meaty course called mark on / fared, fared above and within love's remark / logical, logical mystical and meant for love's remark / local, local finds and the found won, miraculously mark free / lampoon, lampoon and the moon electric throughout love's mark / rings, rings about us and within, love's mark / talk, talk about the symtpoms again, mark free / technology, technology and the psychology mark free / shallow, shallow wells and marked campaigns to love's remark / still, still enough to hear from, mark thre / feed, feed a fact into love's mark / charged, charged, less, emotionally, marked true / emotionally, emotionally leap into a mark free / emotive, emotive and the voice which learns upon love's band, mark free / arts, arts into starts mark free / acts, acts and the facts mark freed / romans, romans and the empire spared through love's remark / greek, greek days and the ways mark free / relate, relate into love's avenued remark / egyptian, egyptian advancement and gains, mark free / radiate, radiate and the relation's ship, cut free to floating mark / ratify, ratify and the rename remarked upon, God's gifts, mark free / sons, sons and the centrals, mark free / zips, zips and the sips concentric into love's mark freeze, tha / zones, zones and the thrones mark free / matrix, matrix, mantles, and mentions mark free / holographic,

holographic needs and the means mark this / venture, ventures dear and the nearing mark free / venus, venus and the menace forgive's mark free / love, love torn less through moans mark free / earth, earth and the pension paid, mark free / plenty, plenty and the lighter way, mark free / stare, stare at your stores, mark free / store, store a pension, mark free / rotate, rotate the follow through, make one, mark free / God, God goes to the mark free / word, word is up too, mark thre / electrical, electrical sorts mark free / lights, lights listen up to the loosen mark free / plate, plate and the platters mark free / given, given a new deem, mark free / squares, squares and the moods mark less / cubes, cubes and the kinks mark free / codes, codes and the coming mark / deliver, deliver and the details mark for / tawain, tawain ways and the strides marked throug / Before / Humanity / on / Dea / an / enough / Monet / see / loose / I / Hawaii / W / G / H / Na / Ku.

CHAPTER SEVEN
Aquarian, Aquarian equates advertised through God's mark / Air, air flows and the modes mark free / Ages, ages and the rages meet in the living mark free / shift, shift and the sheets mark free / waters, waters words mark tree / spill, spill appeals and the match is in mark / emotions, emotions example and the samples mark free / men, men and the dementia forgotten mark free / chakras, chakras choose love's marks / seals, seals and the maps marked less / split, split and the seats marked sit / repair, repair begins, mark free / rape, rape rests healed in love's mention of marked remove / finished, finished shops on the streets remark / slavery, slavery over and the dues paid, love's remark / done, done with the simple samples God's mark / expensive, expensive details and the mailing mark / spent, spent sunk forget forgone fluid mark / truth, truth has become your alibi, love's mark / told, told tales of love's mark / ruins, ruins and the seams mark free / sing, sing often of love's mark / meant, meant for goods remark / blends, blends and the trends remark / blended, blended and mended market / born, born within love's mark / cesarean, cesarean says let's demarc / squire, squire finds and the minds mark free / Annanaki, Annanaki mentions and the modes mark free / ark, ark and the spark mark free / Noah's, Noah's pattern and the dark remove of love's mark / flood, flood and the fling into love's mark / one, one and the windows mark / saved, saved intensely of the malice freed remark / all, all and the blinking miracle mark free / burned, burned forgotten and the mint chase mark less / deliver, deliver and the dunce forgotten mark to / freely, freely and the flinch less material to the mark / sword, sword and shield's freed, mark this / David, David's doors marked yes / Michael, Michael amazed with God's mark / house, house and the hints mark free / star, star and the stilts marked ye / sworn, sworn and the switch into love's mark / Gabriel, Gabriel grew to an advanced place on love's mark / wings, wings inch into love's mark / angels, angels intensely, dearly mark free / sing, sings since, God's mark / delivery, delivery dares and the marks make love / comes, comes a clicking languaged mention to love's remark / white, white the daily lilies remark / star, star and the spaces lightly mentioned to love's remark / weds, weds a place interest freed to a remark / earth, earth and the merits mark /

in, in a delay free's remark / necessary, catch a phrase remarkably mark free / burst, burst a temple's gates mark free / often, often a tenant is freed to love's remark / love, love led into the heart's remark / direct, direct and the dances mark / from, from feeling's launched into love's mark / God, God gazed adjacent to the light's remark / asteroids, asteroids raze and the gaze's remark / rule, rule us too and the rapture's remarks.

CHAPTER EIGHT

Mars, Mars and the twinkled red regards for love's marches on into the advanced places mark free / Jupiter, Jupiter jones and the mantle's place clear through God's remark / Plato, Plato dips through love's mark / Pluto, Pluto plunged next to God's hearty remark / Pleiades, Pleiades amidst joined staples mark less / purged, purged and the merged appliance mark free / party, party applies and the sizes remarkabl / onto, onto the swords mark free / pleasure, pleasure and the parts mark free / place, place and the stint mark free / treasures, teach the treasures measured through love's remark / taste, taste a particle of pleasure's remark / aqua, aqua say and the may's remark / swells, swells another's plays into love's mark / bursts, bursts a pair of love's marks erase / dams, dams and the durable mention of marks into love / relocate, relocate and the rationale for living mark / ends, ends paste free along love's mark / switch, switch across the days onto love's mark / Vesica, Vesica and Pisces gleem along love's mark / sought, sought a daily marked / found, found a place to lodge in love's marked / shifting, shifting across the sands mark free / cells, cells on thrice the love's regards mark free / earths, earths and genius appearances to love's remark / people, people and the simple remarks mark free / each, each and the teacher's meetings mark free / one, one and the sun's appearance mark free / all, alll the same, God's mark / cellular, cellular planes marketed / each, each the other's market / word, word and the winds mark free / people, people and the knowing the unique unto love's remark / know, know a placement paralleled through love's mark / knew, knew a zoo unique and into earth's mark / defeat, defeat and the duration's mark / gone, gone again and the winding ownership into love's mark / tops, tops and the temples mark free / long, long and the degree within educational appearance marks free / agree, agree to the simple marks appearing mark free / unique, unique into the love's advanced, market / marathon, marathon muse and the amuse meant mark free / divinity, divinity and the planets mark free / patience, patience comes into the sums mark free / place, a place found in the owns mark free / in, interior to the views mark free / helenic, helenic appears in the nears mark free / splendor, splendor knew and the mentions appear into God's goods, mark free / gated, gated freed and know marks gone into love's sun / agree, agree to be marketed freel / platonic, platonic and the pews mark free / solids, solids suspend along the markets mark free / commit, commit to a cabinet's marked / thence, thence and the stench has come mark free / plank, plank and the pint labeled mark free / constant, constant to a cupid mark wo / listen, listen into mentions mark free / bliss, bliss abides within the fish of a delivery sealed mark won and the sight full unique into God's

erasure of all thee, mark / gates, gates gaze openly into the news mark free / opens, opens the portals mentioned miraculous into a source uniquely God' / loving, loving parts paced marked tru / swells, swells another sort called uniquely marked love / living, living in giving surrender into love's mark / kissing, kissing a miracle daily in love's marks.

CHAPTER NINE

Reseal, reseal intended and the mended place mark free / reside, reside and the strident marked / caring, caring cures and the tirade due a living remark / on, on and typical into love's mark / tour, tour and the temples mark / trade, trade and the trips through love's mark / tarry, tarry more at the waiting gamed love's mark / near, near to the heart of God's mark / close, close and the mention's mark / delays, delays and the detail's mark / open, open hearted and the mention's marked / doored, doored and the floored remark / eared, eared and the tears mark free / heart, heart found and the marked elate to God's mark / hand, hand to the heart's remark / sword, sword and the seeds mark free / quanta, quanta quells and the marks free / quantum, quantum queens and the marks free / chords, chords and the chimes market / cut, cut a set of chords marked free / scales, scales and the sets mark free / evolve, evolve and the solve's remark / potentials, potentials and the meetings remark / burst, burst across dimensions mentioned as God's remark / audio, audio and the chiming remarks matche / scenes, scenes and suggestions remarke / vision, visions valued attendant to God's remark / herd, herd appears near the remark / swords, swords sealed and the healed reach appears nearer a gained remark / swath, swath and the shield's remark / cuts, cuts and the campaign's remark / all, all and the small remarks set free / atones, atones and the moans mark free / each, each and the all mark free / sun, sun shone into love's mark / sings, sings another's days onto remark / harmonic, harmonic hymns and the rims mark free / wings, wings as apparel and the meetings mark free / convergent, convergent to a fault mark free / harmonics, harmonics and the sonic attend to a marketable frien / float, float and the vote opens to God's market / mayan, mayan and the days into love's market / systems, systems and the systemic miracle free to God's marked / repair, repair and the valves break into love's market / ones, ones and the placements parallel into love's remark / place, places made into love's remark / find, find and fault through into love's mark / know, know and the trips into love's remark / delay, delay and the deals mark free / mission, mission and the mention's mark free / commission, commission and the patience mark free / carafe, carafe and the choosing mark free / care, care and the cups filled through love's remark / cool, cool enough and the challenge mark thre / fills, fills a meals remark / flow, flow and the shows remarkable too, love / flew, flew and the fault lined up into love's remark / flown, flown and the zone's renew of God's remark / Replacement / Theory / You / Are / The / One.

CHAPTER TEN

Ressurgent, ressurgent in the mental pause across God's loving mark / resting, resting and roosting in clearer remark / razed,

razed less into a gratis advanced mark / raise, raise into a wave's advance marked / resurrect, resurrect the yoke of a life supreme into love's advanced mark / secure, secure enough to see a remark / share, share and the pair repaired, mark free / spare, spare is the elective remarkably 9, spores, spores and the cores aloft God's market / felt, felt and surrendered mark free / buy, buy and the shares present to a market free / match, match and a place marked freely ope / meant, meant appears within love's mark / contend, contend and decide to be remarkably free / dearly, dearly seen and into the lean of God's mark / dared, dared enough to share within the market freed for God / graduates, graduates and the purchase marketable / violets, violets and the parts marketed / fabrics, fabrics and the fusion market / create, create a part which wants new market / blocks, blocks freed and the mansions remarkably clear / often, often dealt with and the fits market free / lighten, lighten your leads remarkable / creates, creates cores mark won / sparks, sparks and spills mark free / ascend, ascend and depend upon it, mark free / threads, threads and the threaten less, mark free / creative, creative details and the daily bliss, mark this / leaps, leaps across into the marked state / tour, tour and the tripled marked / forms, forms and the swarms mark free / life, life apparent and the appearance mark free / allows, allows us well into the markets./ birth, birth allows markets place / blaze, blaze and the surrounds mentioned mark three / trails, trails and the trims mark free / comets, comets carry love's mark / converge, converge at the stars mark free / commence, commence and begin to again mak love freely marketable / conceed, conceed and the deeds mark free / correlate, correlate and the sate, mark free / crass, crasss and the crease mark free / grand, grand and the design's mark free / design, design and the dashing mark free / design, design and a deal mark free / detain, detain detail mark won, mark free / due, due and the days mark free / done, done and the dues mark free / paid, paid for and agreed too, mark free / pays, pays allows mark free / plays, plays and stays mark free / pert, pert and the swerve aboard mark free / parcels, parcels and the starts mark free / next, next and the kneels mark free / adjoin, adjoins joins mark free / convergence, convergence and resurgence mark free / carry, carry along and the songs mark free / codes, codes and the roads mark free / unlock, unlock and the sockets mark free / break, break and the bills paid, mark free / speak, speak and the sporting marked free / province, province and the peace marked free / providence, providence and the pent up marked free / rest, rest and the rescues marked okay.

CHAPTER ELEVEN
Sought, sought and the sites fortunate to be eternally light in doves abundant into God's worthwhile ascend and the love that lives abundantly within and the wonderful news that advancement has come into love's marked / comes, comes a mention dimension wide into love's marked / primary, primary to the pill free environment of God's perfect attire's marked / seven's, sevens and the heaven's marked / eights, eights and the license to mention God's dialect too, love's market / nines, nines and the kneelings market / tens, tens and the thicken dimensional too,

love's market / ones, ones ways precisely marketable / gamma, gamma and the drama electrically marketable / beta, beta and the blown details marketable / infrared, infrared and the dreads marketable / radio, radio blue and the news marketed / lengthen, lengthen and the hurtle into love's market / conditions, conditions and the creates marketable / essence, essence and the presence marketed / summed, summed and the surrender into love's market / discussions, discussions and the deals marketable / details, details and the swells making marketable film / experience, experience and the spells marketable / seems, seems and the similiar materials marketed / summed, summed again, marketable / trued, trued and known, the marketed / start, start a dialect discourse free into love's market / complete, complete the quotient, the equation marketable / love, love knew the news of gathering electrically into love's market / agree, agree to the meeting metatronically due to love's market / grown, grown and found in the ground marketable / granted, granted and required of, the land marketable / written, written in smitten lore, the lend, marketable / review, review and the lessens out again, marketable / redesign, redesign and the signs marketed / raptures, raptures and the captures complete in love's market / extremities, extremities and the needs market less / revolve, revolve and the solves marketin / powerful, powerful applause and the cause into market / degrees, degrees and the free' market / viewing, viewing and the shows market / peace, peace allows and wows their market / seek, seek a date market free / sought, sought and the oughts out, market free / found, found a daily marked / flowering, flowering and the carrying marked / flow, flow and the flaunt's marked / flow, flow and the knows marked / flown, flown and the threads cast away, market / arc-ed, arc-ed out and about the market / hearts, hearts and heal's market / telepathic, telepathic too's market / emit, emit daily notes into market / possible, possible plays and the newest marked / potent, potent attire and the market / paths, paths pulse free into love's market / touch, touch a path past love's mark / known, known to a trace's market / now, now and the tow into love's market / new, new trades, market / renewal, renewal and readings marketable / forgotten, forgotten flows and the zeals across love's market / gospel, gospel and the grows marketable / found, found and the fillings market / amen, ample mention electrically netted too and grown through God's love / enoch, enoch said, "advance / vital, vital variation's advanc / signed, signed agrees too, advanced.

CHAPTER TWELVE
Oblivious, oblivious to an extensive net's advancement through mark / obvious, obvious and the sorts mark free / obviates, obviates and the results that are freed marketable / aspects, aspects and meant too, advance market / aloe, aloe amends and the amounts too, market / avenue, avenues chime and the rhyme market / attributes, attributes and the mutes market / allow, alllow and the plow through love's market / friend, friend and the send market / channel, channel and the mantle's marked / in, in truth, manually, love's marked / friend, fiercely loyal and lending too, love's market / channel, channel chosen and the woven regard's market / into, into and the tracks market / truth, truth and the trip's market / key,

key and the deed too, market / he, he and the thicken's mark / sees, sees and the thoughts market / grid, grid and the grace's marked / techniques, techniques and trails market / bend, bend above and within the dove's market / listen, listen too, to love's market / within, within and word's market / hologram, hologram and the warm market / computer, computer and the creation's market / plans, plans and the pensive market / happy, happy days and the muse affected, marketable / wings, wings and the whistles market / words, words and the wit's market / blowing, blowing and the bliss market / frank, franks and the friendly market / recall, recall and the real experienced market / vibrate, vibrate trails and treats market / state, states of chance and the meeting market / sight, sight seeds market / blanket, blanketed through with love's market / often, often yes into mark free love / lights, lights lift and listen well to love's market / love, love to be free of the mark / is, is this love's truth, mark free / resplendent, resplendent to a charmed mark I / inside, inside and the way through market / grace, grace appears in market's place / and, and all we see is love's marked / understood, understood and why, market / God, God gains market / ahead, ahead and to the tools market / file, file and the filling's market / find, find and friend's market / flow, flow and the fountain's market / show, show and the goes market / conserve, conserve is the warm regard for love's advanced mark / gamma, gamma gave thee this advanced marked / rays, rays read of love's advanced marked / lightens, lightens market / graduates, graduates marketin / stand, stand and the plan for market / plan, plan to be advanced, market free / placed, placed in our pleasure's market / align, align learns to be market / trine, trine and the signs market / complete, complete and the care's market / coerce, coerce and the lessen's market / pressed, pressed and the gains advanced.

CHAPTER THIRTEEN

Benefits, benefits of the blessings marked in love / bereaves, bereaves and the balance is sent into love / leaves, leaves and the trees electrically balanced with love's mark / living, living in the land of the triangular sort, love's mark / ignites, ignites insights blends, a balance marked / pays, pays for the plane's rise and through it all the family hu-man and the planet's attend and the tribute's across livings lend / paints, paints and the pinnacle found into the strand of the religion's steered through love's mark / forgive, forgive and the legend's placement of a marriage called love, mark free / ignited, ignited and won without spend, an advanced state, love's mark / pays, pays for the flights too, a new mark / paints, paints a pleasing pen, a living mark / forgives, forgives and friendly stares, mark there / faults, faults and the feelings elective too, a mark free / go, go within to the primary balance of love's living lend for advancement's mark / lights, lights lead thoroughly into living's mark / roam, roam about the legendary mark / God's, God's goods and the legends mark / home, home to the hilt's mark / met, met through the middle's mark / seals, seals set in the vertical mark / bets, bets and the the the believing mark / love, love the land you inherit in love mark free / mother, mother and the mental release into love's market / land, land lends her heart to your market / Bible, Bible blues spoken

and found release into the heart's markets, discuss details of the mention freed to say, bible's wings found / debate, debate less the mess of psalms past to a mark free / cosmetic, cosmetic concurs and the smiles mark free / create, create and the data mark free / coats, coats and the notes market / elate, elate and the leases market / remember, remember and the the let's marked / God, God and the patent's marked / semantics, semantics and spoken market / belong, belong to the then's advance / pen, pen a durate's market / men, mend your market / men, men through market / happy, happy and the hilts market / pays, pays appear into the mirror's market / became, became and to be, advanced through love / elate, elates markets made love / waves, waves and the stoves market / won, won and thinly thought for market / weld, weld felt electrically through market / electricity, electricity unique unto love's market / forks, forks focus on love's market / sparks, sparks and thrills market / hearty, hearty trines market / belong, belong too, market / weather, weather these market / warm, warm shots market / wanton, wanton won, mark / pain, pain gone into market / goes, goes and grown market / why / go / said / would / come / le / Michael / sword / shine / between.

THE PATTERN-MENTS
LEVEL 32

CHAPTER ONE

Plants, planted the friend and within the worlds patterns a fondness for me / fibonacci, fibonacci and the spirals pleased, God / modems, modems melt down into love's spiral pattern / models, models and the meals patterned friends too, a parallel / modicum, modicum and the Metatronic pattern / Montreal, Montreal went east to an explode's pattern / monsters, monsters and the minister's pattern / pajamas, pajamas deals and the meals pattern / pockets, pockets and the pistons pattern / pants, pants confessed and the bursting through's flames to the games befriend / flannel, flannel and the channel's befriend / flatter, flatter and the chatter's befriend / flashes, flashes of stakes befriend / gush, gush and the rushes befriend / ghost, ghost and the host is befriend / spirits, spirits and the nearness befriend / cheers, cheers into patterns befriend / chios, chios and the triple cupped flashes of pretended pattern / doubles, doubles and the dribbles befriend / adore, adores and the soaring befriend / California, California and the cues befriended and up too, love / gaze, gaze into love's pattern / gore, gore taken out into love's pattern / power, power and the plenty perfect's pattern / print, print and the absent partners pattern / points, points about the pleasure's pattern / palate, palate and the pleasant pattern / pallet, pallet days parentally patterned / pinch, pinch and the stench gone, patterned / pore, pore across the pages patterned / porch, porch and the dates patterned / posh, posh and the patterns patterned / pact, pacts made and the patterns planned / agree, agree to see her the pattern / gaze, gaze and the details patterned / absorb, absorb the patterns planned / adore, adore and the shores planned / clears, clears and the steering's plans patterned / able, able to be table free too, love's plans patterned / bets, bets and the securest pattern / boisterous, boisterous and the barest forgiven's pattern / gets, gets and the daily pattern / gazes, gazes and the stages patterned / flaps, flaps and entreaties patterned / toys, toys and the tools pattern / tantrums, tantrums and the trim times patterned / cars, cars and the statue's patterned / cables, cables and the cubics patterned / San Franciscan, San Franciscan patterned / hotels, hotels and motels patterned / hills, hills and the seals who elected pattern / run, run and the rest is patterned / revel, revel and the devil gone, befriended, pattern / roundup, roundup and the rent paid, pattern / gathered, gathered and the reviews pattern / prospect, prospect met and the debit paid, pattern / parental, parental to the plenty, pattern / children's, children's and the changing pattern / measures, measures made and into these the pattern / know, know and the ones patterned / one, one and the things pattern free / thing, thing and the planet's patterned / God, God and the gateway's pattern.

CHAPTER TWO

King, king and the strings pulled pattern / spare, spare into meetings patterned / children, children and the chapel's patterned / enact, enact a pleasing attraction and the action penetratively patterned / intact, intact to the impetus and the precision patterned / kingdom, kingdom and the seeming empowerment patterned / sensate, sensate and the sensual patterns planned / prospects, lip to the face's pattern / injury, injury over and trees pattern / heals, heals and the throngs patterned / rocks, rocks and the reels patterned / roll, roll and the reeds patterned / curtains, curtains curled in quiet pattern / move, move to the movement's pattern / flight, flight to the mention's patterned / spanish, spanish and the teaching patterned / armada, armada and the randomed pattern / collective, collective and the inspected pattern / masks, masks dropped and the people talked too, pattern / countries, countries well patterned / cities, cities patterned / states, states and the statues patterned / lines, lines and the linkage patterned / fences, fences and the finds patterned / neighbors, neighbors and the needs patterned / tracts, tracts and the treasure's patterned / places, places and the penchant's patterned / plans, plans and the pearly pattern / drama, drama and the daring pattern / designs, designs and the daring's pattern / dimensional, dimensional materials patterned / districts, districts and the daring pattern / rural, rural and the values patterned / routes, routes and the electric's patterned / pasture, pasture and the patterns planned / placement, placement and the peace made, pattern / heavens, heavens and the healing's pattern / house, house and the hearing's pattern / eyes, eyes and the sizes pattern / God, God and the gears made, pattern / cabinets, cabinets and the clearest pattern / pouch, pouch and the joy patterned / armed, armed and the resources trade pattern / resources, resources read these pattern / forces, forces and the fed feeds patterned / friends, friends and the features patterned / mended, mended and the mental detail's pattern / sources, sources and the heavy's pattern / stunts, stunts and the brunts basins pattern / chance, chance and the stances patterned / charts, charts and the gazes patterned / drew, drew into other's pattern / linear, linear and the dates patterned / longitude, longitude and the latitudes pattern / vertical, vertical and the views pattern / vehicles, vehicles brought into love's pattern / carts, carts and the creature's pattern / star, star and the stints made, pattern / eye / an / through-you / the / Heaven / this.

CHAPTER THREE

Eliminate, eliminate and the justice comes daily pattern / disagree, disagrees gazes pattern / boston's, boston's beauty's pattern / bay, bay and the belief's gates patterned / tease, tease and the trade winds patterned / lights, lights of sights and binocular perpendicular's pattern / regardless, regardless and treaties patterned / tax, tax along love's pattern / listen, listen to love's attitudes parallel missioned into God's degrees 93 to the millenial pattern / languish, languish along love's parallel blends and God's gaze patterned / blessings, blessings and the blissing's placement patterned / give, give into other's praise, patterned / gave, gave a joined pattern / enhancement, enhancement patterned through love's parallel / longer, longer and the details patterned / lived, lived near the mission's pattern / occular, occular to the neatest pattern / eyes, eyes wise to living's pattern / enchantment, enchantment patterned / ends, ends and the bends patterned / along, along and the sizes patterned / lights, lights and the needs patterned / isle, isle wise within love's pattern / lifes, lifes and the legends patterned / monocular, monocular and the mental pattern / binocular, binocular patents parallel pattern / eye, eye and the situation's parallel pattern / connect, connect to the resource pattern fre / corrective, corrective inquiry into love's pattern / seeing, seeing eyes us wisely, patterned / sight, sight sent patterned / enhanced, enhanced within love's pattern / darshan, darshan done and the sun's pattern / dogon, dogon and the tribes patterned / seer, seer and the sheerest pattern / stars, stars and the charts read, pattern / plasma, plasma pleases our pattern / screening, screening samples our pattern / supple, supple couple's pattern / sort, sort details our pattern / follow, follow another's pattern / feelings, feelings found, patterned / fasten, fasten a fashioned pattern / fold, fold and a vote made patterned / engage, engage in yes, a pattern / durable, durable to a terrible forget's pattern / delivery, delivery and the excluded pattern / daily, daily dealt with in pattern / comfort, comfort and the cosmetics pattern / living, living and the wellest pattern / excise, excise and the Sistine pattern / entry, entry points too, a pattern / coincidential, coincidential too, a pattern / parties, parties past pulse and the meetings patterned / trades, trades full electric and a metric's pattern / opens, opens into guaranteed pattern / shores, shores delivery, pattern / doors, doors dose too, these pattern / employ, employ another's pattern less / stage, stage passed, pattern' / chosen, chosen example's pattern / squarely, squarley dated and sent into pattern / securely, securely selected and enacted pattern fre / enforcement, enforcement paralleled and the patterns freed.

CHAPTER FOUR

Donated, donated and the routes between electric in the lend through God's gratis gratitude's pattern / sedated, sedated has gone to the sun's pattern / rested, rested in the vested, pattern / coincidental, coincidental to the mental-freeze, pattern / temper, temper over and outed, pattern free / temperamental, temperamental to the mental free's pattern / finicky, finicky and the finest pattern / funny, funny and the finished pattern / loosen, loosen and the finest pattern / turpitude, turpitude and the mood's pattern / eternity, eternity and the venue's pattern / energy, energy and the central pattern / clear, clear to a channel's pattern / concise, concise and the to the print's pattern / precise, precise and the precious pattern / exacting, exacting and the insurance went too, pattern / entrance, entrance and the runes trued, pattern / secretly, secretly and the met within's pattern / found, found and the fellow's pattern / vehicles, vehicles and the views pattern / bodies, bodies and the beast free pattern / off, off and the seas pattern / opening, opening and the spoken pattern / capability, capability and the could be's pattern / detect, detect and the set's respect's pattern / decision, decision's deals made freely pattern / dares, dares and the dealt with, pattern / electrically, electrically sent to the magnet parallel's pattern / recovery, recovery and the memory's pattern / souvenirs, souvenirs and the sentinel's pattern / sorry, sorry and the said, good-bye's pattern / hawaiian, hawaiian and the patterned affair's withi / leis, leis and the lease's pattern / monadic, monadic and monastic in love's appearance, pattern / decks, decks and the dealing's pattern / supports, supports and the seats called pattern / shifts, shifts and the second's pattern / chortle, chortle and the change made, patterns free / wallow, wallow and the we's patterned / heads, heads and the ahead too, pattern /

erupt, erupts and the seals cleared, pattern / God's, God's goods gazed through, pattern / heights, heights and the hurtle's pattern / majestic, majestic and the muse made, patterned / japanese, japanese and the peace made too pattern / pairs, pairs apply too, love's pattern / all, alll and the haze cleared, pattern / over, over and the central field's pattern / harbors, harbors hide less, pattern / lifts, lifts into lesson's pattern / clouds, clouds and the cords that cut free, pattern / mushrooms, mushrooms gloom gone, now freed, pattern / Hiroshima, Hiroshima assume of the forgotten release into pattern / forgive, forgive and the living's presence made into love's pattern / us, us and the chosen's pattern / humanity, humanity and the adie to pattern / suspect, suspect and the central's pattern / for, for and the fortunate's pattern / destroying, destroying and the daily pattern / each, each and the sunshine's pattern / others, others respects and the light held pattern / restful, restful treasures and the entreaty's pattern / night / like.

CHAPTER FIVE

Ignore, ignore and the snoring respects for love's pattern / defects, defects gone into song's parallel into love's pattern / integrate, integrate your respect for love's pattern / compassion, compassion's traits, parallel pattern / troubles, troubles outed and the sent for pattern / plenty, plenty and the harbor's light's pattern / around, around anterior to the portion's pattern / attached, attached has cut and the meeting's set, pattern / portals, portals opened again, friend, to a pattern / hearts, hearts in sync with love's pattern / eyes, eyes and the ascendant found, pattern / faces, faces and the fusion sent to a pattern / love, love and the lesson to a pattern / accounts, accounts and the listening pattern / fair, fair and the freely patterned / balance, balance equated too, a pattern / amounts, amounts and the client's pattern / most, most and the host made, pattern / cartwheeled, cartwheeled and the seated, pattern / resorts, resorts and the setting's patterned / panels, panels and the penchant for pattern / plates, plates and the places patterned / places, places and the pious gone, pattern / plans, plans for the stands too, pattern / help, help and the standing's pattern / assorts, assorts and the divine pattern / call, call made and heard through love's pattern / Gods, Gods gains patterned / friendly, friendly fades too, pattern / arc-angelic, arc-angelic to the wept for pattern / father, father gives the living's mattered pattern / mother, mother and the smother free, pattern / members, members and the meeting's pattern / God, God and the greeting's pattern / pursue, pursue forgone, patterned / jordanian, jordanian pattern / ethnic, ethnic's patterned extent reveale / ruins, ruins of the kind's patterned / apian, apian attitude's pattern / avian, avian allows and the pleasant pattern / vernacular, vernacular and the site found, pattern / pose, pose and the risen's pattern / prosaic, prosaic to the stoic pattern / purpose, purpose and the place's patterned / propose, propose and the arrival's patterned / bounce, bounce and the gather's pattern / funds, funds come, clearly, patterned / clear, clear to a sustain's pattern / optimize, optimize and the situation's pattern / fervor, fervor and the festive's pattern / signals, agile to the signal's pattern / signature, signature to the insure's pattern / invest, invest into the intentional pattern / energy, energy and the soothed extent's pattern / truth, truth told, energy freed, pattern's extent / articles, articles and the surge's patterned / counsels, counsels patterned / objectivity, objectivity and the committed account's patterned / foreign, foreign rates ranging pattern fre / zones, zones and the sensate's pattern / dictate / written / Through-out.

CHAPTER SIX
Motive, motive and the voiced agree to be pattern less / bargains, bargains and the abide in the basement free rodent less pattern / documentary, documentary dues and the patterns meant free / sends, sends and the seals too, machines made, patterned / negotiates, negotiates and the rates begin pattern fre / restitutes, restitutes made deliver and the potion spent in patterns broke / motivates, motivates especially and often, the motions made, patterned fre / supple, supple in a nuptial aspirant, God's planet comes home to love's pattern / supports, supports directly and often the memory of love's patterned replie / custody, custody coming to ends multiplied through light's patterned en / commits, commits a fellow actively patterned / doubles, doubles into up penned positioning, God's light pattern / employ, employ another more often through God's patterned ma / classic, classic in a coded relate's release, love's lightest pattern / generates, generates a dexterity mannerly patterned in, love / meticulous, meticulous to a moment's reply, God said "patttern free / novella, novella news and the muse replies, "patterned"/ metallic, metallic into memeory banked in belief on God's pattern / noveau, noveau goes into God's patterns freiz / publish, publish an epistle rich in love's pattern / flourish, flourish comes to the believer's push for pattern's fre / helms, helms and the happening's pursued too, pattern / surveys, surveys suggest, pattern / massive, massive in amuse, I remove too, love's pattern / various, various ways come too, and, pattern / publications, publications cozy in love's pattern / illustrate, illustrate your life with God's palm full of pattern / concepts, concepts gaze across our ways entitles too, pattern / catalogue, catalogue deep in december and the remember of colder pattern / relates, relates to the news patterned / district, district forgives and the living cables? pattern / won, won a respect for the truth told, patiently, pattern fre / invention, invention and intentional surrender into incentives rich in love's pattern / invested, invested again, into, love's pattern / sensibly, sensibly and suggestively patterned / dialed, dialed another's numbered believe in pattern / living, living near the givin's pattern / business, business comes to the simple home's pattern / ambiguity, ambiguity forgives us, pattern free / rockefeller, rockefeller fades into rent paid for God's pattern / centurion, centurion of the simply patterned / paints, paints and the saints who have won a pattern's fad / mills, mills kickin electrical wills to the patterns gazing good-bye, fade / abstracts, abstracts amazed by love's pattern / images, images amaze me throughout God's pattern / careen, careen past and the lasting imagine patterned / revelations, revelations amount to residual amaze's pattern / beautiful, beautiful to a basic abuse gone throughout good nye's basic patterned / transitive, transitive to a living believer's abandoned pattern / premieres, premieres a new network's pattern / premium, premium paid for a few

allowed truest pattern / reduction, reduction given a gain's pattern / payments, payments made and the middle is rich is forgiven pattern / meet, meet her and then into the new's patterned / keys, keys and the held on degrees pattern / contemporary, contemporary and the scope of patterned guests aris / appraisal, appraisal is said, thankfully, forever and into love's pattern / diverse, diverse to a dose forgiven, father's pattern / progressive, progressive plans made and these way's pattern / lambs, lambs adieu forgone and the fondest pattern / faculties, faculties and the phones called forgetfully patterned / projects, projects melt into love's pattern / staffs, staffs allow and the sold amazed pattern.

CHAPTER SEVEN
Sirian, Sirian and the sails played openly patterned / sirius, sirius and the signals patterned / Osirius, Osirius allowed us, lightly, patterned / sensitive, sensitive into light's pattern / explore, explore a snoring pattern / ecstasy, ecstasy given a break's pattern / alchemy, alchemy and the moisture's pattern / heaven, heaven and the healing's pattern / earth, earth and the mirthful pattern / one, one into womb's pattern / materially, materially rich and the mitchelled mount's pattern / gropes, gropes and the gristled pattern / panic, panic forgiven, pattern / slice, slice of the signaled pattern / islands, islands above us, patterned / unite, unite and allow us pattern / Assyrian, Assyrian stays in the ways patterned / seas, seas allow us love's planes, patterned / pregnant, pregnant to a cause planned, pattern / sorts, sorts and the seals patterned / pray, pray for the nation's pattern / support, support and the sort's patterned / lineage, lineage and the lines plus patterns / hopeful, hopeful and the guests arise, patterned / oversteps, oversteps and the steps back into, love's pattern / objectives, objectives and the gazes upon love's pattern / stations, stations and the stages patterned / transit, transit and the trips through pattern / waters, waters and the willows pattern / phenomenal, phenomenal and the amazement gazed into pattern / slot, slot and the caves pattern / scuffle, scuffle and the shuffle's pattern / feats, feats and the fuels passed into love's poses and the patterns hue / results, results of races passed into love's pattern / thicken, thicken and the listening pattern / walk, walk and the wettest pattern / erase, erase and the patterned forgon / construct, construct and the causes patterned / bridge, bridges and the bursts pattern / guilded, guilded and the gaze's pattern / sorts, sorts and the seals pattern / calendrical, calendrical and the pattern / theories, theories and the thanks patterned / treaty, treaty and the causes patterned / recourse, recourse comes to the pattern / chambers, chambers and the raging patterned / channel, channel and the assigns patterned / handles, handles along the reins patterned / exorcise, exocise becomes the politest pattern / scantress, scantress dressed for the lightest pattern / surf, surf and the turf's gaze patterned / popular, popular to a matters pattern / spots, spots and the suggestion's pattern / lighten, lighten and the sight into pattern / awareness, awareness and the welds set, pattern / edible, edible and the mention's pattern / sorts, sorts and the suggestion's pattern / clearance, clearance and the committee's on too,. love's pattern / seals, seals and the linkage's pattern / hearing, hearing and the heights on, pattern / calls, calls

and the mazes pattern / help, help and the hand's gaze pattern / commanded, commanded along love's light pattern / particulate, particulate to a living's patterns.

CHAPTER EIGHT
Kites, kites and the kitten's pattern / fly, fly and the listen's pattern / wings, wings and the wind's won pattern / bend, bend and the benches pattern / surface, surface and the sends wins pattern / arise, arise and the patterns plan / vines, vines and the venues pattern / break, break and the mention's pattern / consecration, consecration and the commanded pattern / amounts, amounts and the mention's pattern / prayers, prayers abuzz within pattern / flown, flown and the flower's pattern / taboo, taboo and the tools paid pattern / realms, realms mentioned pattern / careers, careers and the classics pattern / zones, zones and the genes pooled pattern / lifetime, lifetime and the living's pattern / coupled, coupled and the curtain's pattern / compliant, compliant to a missive's pattern / trips, trips taken separately patterned / forgiven, forgiven and the pilot's pattern / forgone, forgone and forgiven into a pattern / foreigner, foreigner's ritual patterned / lips, lips heal into the seal's gone, pattern / lazarus, lazarus comes into love's patterns free / honored, honored into love's pattern / fowls, fowls and the fish come, pattern / alert, alert and the finished pattern / cock, cok spun into love's pattern / crew, crew of the three frames patterned / three, three along the lanes patterned / times, times estates won, pattern / shame, shame gone and the over done, patterns / youth, youth above and within, pattern / channel, channel amazed on pattern / forgiven, forgiven a mansioned pattern / forgiveness, forgiveness comes through our pattern / flights, flights across and within, too, love's pattern / clear, clear enough to see nearly, patterned / strung, strung along leads pattern / tramples, tramples amount too, lessons, patterned / beats, beats abroad and along us, pattern / offerings, offerings and the finest pattern / sails, sails abide and inside these pattern / billows, billows and the pillows paged pattern / blasts, blasts and the baren forgoes too, pattern / wealthy, wealthy alights pattern / class, class to the listening's pattern / hauling, hauling abouts pattern / launch, launch and the listens pattern / knowledge, knowledge and the needs come patterned / energetics, energetics gazed upon pattern / college, college along lanes pattern / collective, collective to a cause gained pattern / escape, escape and the patterned plane / freed, freed and the patterns forged, love' / taboo, taboo and the causes pattern / carefully, carefully along lines laid pattern / stern, stern to a mention mannered through pattern / stems, stems opened into pattern / graft, graft and the crafts caused, pattern / shores, shores and the listened too, pattern / servants, servants becoming love's partnered pattern / thoughts, thoughts about us and within too, love's patterns.

CHAPTER NINE
Sleepy, sleepy into eves on patterned break / dawns, dawns electrically and the resonate paradell' commit too, breakfast pattern / Kai, Kai knew electrical seas parallels pattern / committed, committed into moments leewardly eclectic too,

pattern / lights, lights erupt within the seas pattern / rejoice, rejoice over matters patterned / moving, moving comes sooning, patterned / trim, trim to a nipple's pattern / learning, learning to lean to the areole of God pattern / called, called a neighbor nearest, pattern / hearing, hearing becomes surrendered pattern / ample, ample to the moves patterned / sample, sample to the clues given pattern / sort, sort your delicious won pattern / support, support comes, patterned / capably, capably sent, pattern / regions, regions rejoin, pattern / mountain, mountains laked in pattern / led, led folically too, pattern / fed, fed a nectar patterned / mother, mother of the missive's pattern / soils, soils of and suggested yeses pattern / damp, damply electric into love's pattern / wetter, wetter instill's pattern / stills, stills knightly, patterned / embellish, embellisht he tale-ing pattern / embrace, embrace the race patterned / respectful, respectful infuse and the muse's pattern / comes, comes a day's coming arise into love's pattern / callibration, callibration becomes your pattern / shifting, shifting into sends on, pattern / higher, higher into still's pattern / eye, eye opened into love's pattern / contact, contact made and the gaze is patterned / now, now into showing pattern / hum, hum in discuss of designs into pattern / may, may we walk pattern less into love's breast / eruptions, eruptions connect within, love's pattern / birthing, birthing comes too, the pattern / 13, 13 ways to stay pattern free / moons, moons emission's pattern / plants, plants taste of pattern / willing, willing to green for the cause olive seeds pattern / receiver, receiver to the the giver's pattern / beginning, beginning to seed again, patterns in love / proper, proper to the simply patterned / proport, proport the notion's patterned / proper, proper to the keepers pattern / purpose, purpose to the steeple's pattern / find, find a ways pattern / dedicate, dedicate sets to pattern / home, home made within, pattern / temple, temple sited, pattern / shrine, shrine melts, pattern / gods, gods gaze patterned / cultivate, cultivate the cure's pattern / faith, faith found in grounded pattern / grains, grains electrically patterned / grow, grow concentric to the fibrous pattern / blessings, blessings elocutive too, the pattern / flow, flow astounds into God's pattern / angels, angels boast the boost into light pattern / beat, beat a basic pattern / wings, wings elected, patterns.

CHAPTER TEN
Friendship, friendship becomes your pattern / averts, averts less directive's pattern / eyes, eyes into gazes pattern / often, often effective, pattern / palimony, palimony cased of pattern / paid, paid elective's pattern / precious, precious gauges pattern / price, price set, pattern / friendship, friendship comes too, pattern / first, first and most, patterned alpha / last, last to the hosted omegas pattern / forever, forever philadelphia's blues patterned / abruptly, abruptly changes our pattern / stopped, stopped into disappearing pattern / parents, parents ache for pattern's thaw / shock, shock comes too, pattern / outer, outer shells spinning pattern / prayer, prayer answered, patterns toaste / inner, inner sacred found, patterned / care, care for the core said, pattern / within, within an initial, pattern / softens, softens the discourse, pattern / sleuicing, sleuicing's grates, pattern / stare, stare about us, pattern / sacred, sacred stares into love's eye wise pattern / less, less intrigued with

pattern / consumed, consumed less within, pattern / most, most of us, frees, pattern / God's, God's breath engaged, pattern / passion, passion points within pattern / man's, man's apparent, pattern / disgrace, disgrace has gone too, pattern / heaven's, heaven's sword penetrates pattern / sword, sword swung unhinged pattern / penetrates, penetrates expectant pattern / matters, matters misty pattern / shelves, shelves attend too pattern / collapse, collapse cures pattern / books, books bought and brought along pattern / spill, spill comes too, pattern / pour, pour out the sort's paid pattern / forth, forth erudition on partitioned forgive's pattern / share, share a wave's wage patterned / explode, explode to the core's maze patterned / feast, feast becoming pattern less / left, left to a notion's pattern / windy, windy to the risen roaded hana bound pattern / chiefly, chiefly flocks elect pattern / planets, palatial planets parent pattern / birds, birds flock through a Spanish armada's intentional find of the dove within a Catholic intend of pattern / fish, fish for the crowns release amid armageddon's pattern / rocks, rocks with release forgiven for confessional allow on pattern / GOD, can you allow another belief on patterns? GOD, Given Optional Directive / hierarchy, hierarchy on too, a pattern / imports, imports sorts patterned / worships, worships waiting pattern / sacrilege, a sacrilege paid for, pattern / Io, Io amazed with the moody reply too, pattern / Uli, Uli amazing slander frees pattern / prayers, prayers appraised for pattern / heals, heals abruptest pattern / Sk / Ha / Hu Nab K / Delivered.

CHAPTER ELEVEN
Pines, pines at high grounds placement in pattern / please, please another phoned pattern / parental, parental to the instrumental bliss called pattern / plan, plan made elect it, pattern / open, open to the assumption gone, pattern / hearted, hearted agree too, pattern / hands, hands applied, pattern / explore, explore your partnered pattern / shores, shores allow, pattern / depth, depth elected, pattern / forgiven, forgiven on too, pattern / met, met and the mentally freed pattern / surrender, surrender allows pattern / too, too and the other's pattern / tools, tools and the teaching's pattern / forgive, forgiven and the fellows patterned / juniper, juniper and the jewels patterned / bright, bright and the billows patterned / view, view allows pattern / stream, stream above's pattern / rosey, rosey and the reading pattern / leaves, leaves allowanced pattern / acres, acres of the maker's pattern / shed, shed and the shield's bled pattern / settles, settles along your pattern / grounds, grounds given for the electric pattern / winds, winds and the whistle's pattern / wends, wends and the winsome pattern / ranches, ranches and the wrinkle's pattern / wins, wins allow freeing pattern / wends, wends along our pattern / branched, branched along gazes pattern / malevolent, malevolent trued pattern / antiquity, antiquity and the spare's paid pattern / hoax, hoax and the licks paid for, pattern / cited, cited and the enlgihtened pattern / suddenly, suddenly allowed foreclosure's pattern / survived, survived barely, a pattern / compose, compose a note directly patterned / quarry, quarry and the query paid, pattern / rough, rough enough to see by, pattern / diamonds, diamonds deal constructively through patterns squeeze / black, black is the back license applied concurence keys pattern

/ sent, sent along patterns electric / send, send us your pattern / letters, letters licensure pattern / content, content in allowanced pattern / intention, intention's appliance pattern / magnifies, magnifies amuse meant, pattern / baskets, baskets deep in love's apply for, pattern / vigor, vigor values your pattern / ambiguous, ambiguous tot he sorts paid, pattern / crest, crest and the crescent's pattern / peaks, peaks allow us, pattern / facts, facts and the fashion's pattern / climactic, climactic occurence pattern / noble, noble abides blaze pattern / mimic, mimic allow me, a pattern / chosen, chosen adore us, patterned / prove, prove an appear us, patterned / choice, choice arrowed a pattern / choirs, choirs ring us, pattern / widens, widens allow us pattern / prosper, prosper allows us, patterned.

CHAPTER TWELVE
Assurance, assurances sent along line empathic too, and parallels within love's presence too and God's pattern / fragrant, fragrant into love's pattern / limestone, limestone tools and the pools patterned / label, labels above and within, pattern / valley, valley dolls and the walls patterned / decoded, decoded and many's pattern / due, due an eternal's pattern / plateau, plateaus and the views gin-tle too, pattern / over, over balanced and the challenged forgiven pattern / admits, admits a kitchen's fill, pattern / enthuse, enthuse for the cause patterned / patient, patient to a pattern familially forgive / amuse, amuse has come to your heart's ways patterned / domestic, domestic accept of the reels played, patterned / scatters, scatters forgive and the feelings patterned / claim, claim a space your own, home's pattern / islands, islands come into love's pattern / crown, crown of the substituted pattern / dominates, dominates appeal provides for pattern / dreams, dreams estate wise, pattern / glaring, glaring occurences pattern / compose, compose a natural appeals pattern / copy, copy a sorted acceptance spoken too, pattern / reflections, reflections inspected prepare us for pattern / depths, depths and the daring estimation's pattern / caves, caves allow our pattern / answer, answers come in pattern / friends, friends find your patterns amuse / blunder, blunders over, pattern / compartments, compartments occurent too, pattern / private, private duration's pattern / able, able to stable be, pattern / abilities, abilities with agilities due, pattern / erect, erect to the effect won, pattern / staggered, staggered at the recourse paid, pattern / precision, precision's agility and the ability to pave well, pattern / equal, equal to the challenged, pattern / equates, equates a resource patterned / equinox, equinox sprung through pattern / perks, perks made and obtained too, pattern / capsule, capsule saved and the written too, pattern / tarry, tarry less in old awares, pattern / trances, trances outed into stares pattern / indulge, indulge in treaties paid respect, pattern / explores, explores accepted and directs pattern / harvested, harvested daily and aware to pattern / durates, durates connection endures, pattern / paces, paces crossed lightly pattern / invest, invest in raptured assure, pattern / facts, facts suggested, pattern / leonine, leonine appearances spent in pattern / corridors, corridors curt in piscean release too, pattern / religious, religious inference paid to pattern / crops, crops cycle back for preferential pattern / cycle, cycle the season's pattern /

circles, circles erase your pattern / gain, gain a respectful pattern / parcels, parcels forgive our posted pattern / formula, formula magically comes to these pattern / along, along days patterned / manifested, manifested details patterned / regular, regular to a retreated pattern / gains, gains and significant choices patterned / invented, invented in scented arise, your, patterns.

CHAPTER THIRTEEN

Snow, snow and the knowing sent, pattern / shown, shown a discussion for your pattern / melts, melts into tabled year's pattern / require, require a firing pattern / present, present direct suggestion's pattern / given, given a daily abide's pattern / stimulate, stimulate your simulate pattern / sport, sport given to relieve pattern / spare, spares direct into pattern / phenomenon, phenomenon given too, pattern / cover, cover the dust in pattern / deliver, deliver entreaties too, pattern / gifted, gifted and the sifted gains pattern / disturb, disturb less your gift's pattern / handles, handles sent into your pattern / well, well enought to see through, pattern / graduation, graduation occuring, now, pattern / swamped, swamped by suggested pattern / coconut, coconut days gain appetizing pattern / plus, plus equates too, your, pattern / palms, palms held electrically patterned / eaten, eaten of, and from, through pattern / repeated, repeated suggestions of your savior's gaze pattern / rest, rest in the notion's delivery pattern / taro, taro grown in the zone freed pattern / valley, valley of the duration's pattern / farm, farm equips your pattern / stick, stick tot he track paved in patterned release / umbilicus, umbilicus cut for pattern / extremity, extremity dearest, pattern / descendant, descendants gone too, pattern / firm, firm in our fillings, pattern / furnished, furnished in dealings pattern / gathers, gathers annually, your, pattern / constructive, constructive forgivings pattern / general, general enthuse for pattern-less love / feasting, feasting coming too, pattern's sooth / pregnancy, pregnancy elected for patterned forgive / bare, bare to the seated pattern / conception, conception comes during pattern / aloha, aloha lands in your laps lazy pattern / again, again she said patterns / once, once in forgiven's pattern / more, more directly forgiven pattern / appears, appears a right for the right too, called, pattern / healing, healing commences in your pattern / source, source and suggested pattern / caress, caress more patterned good-bye / face, face a suggested patterned goodnes / enjoy, enjoy another's pattern / supple, supple to the seated, pattern / tantric, tantric to suggestions, pattern / tantalize, tantalize your others pattern / reconnect, reconnect doors eternally pattern free / convene, convene in a righteous scene partnered pattern fre / indulge, indulge in a secret give forgiven pattern fre / pleasures, pleasures and the codes given pattern / chores, chores and the chains spent pattern / methodic, methodic and the melted paves pattern / composure, composure comes into the waves pattern / codes, codes and the capable's pattern / gifts, gifts and the grinning's gifts pattern / house, house and the hope gazed pattern / guest, guest and the gathering patterns.

THE PLAN-MENTS
LEVEL 33

CHAPTER ONE

Spine, spine to the spindles grains patterns plan / marrow, marrow and the plan to be believably patterned / fire, fire and the fitness plans pattern / effects, effects to the focus came to patterns planned / spirit, spirit and the placements paged patterns plan / form, form and the fellow's gazed patterns plan / above, above and the talent's gates patterns plan / embodies, embodies and the deals done pattern freed plan / plan, plan a portend parallelly invited into love's plan / ring, ring into a revenue's plan / years, years across central zones plan / participate, participate in the yarns told, planned / true, true enough to tell, boldly planned / trust, trust a thrust into love's plan / truth, truth becomes your alibi's plan / rescue, rescue a retinue's plan / runs, runs again, planned / ravenous, ravenous to a rescue gone, plan / pace, pace made and the stages race through, plan / pleases, pleases the eyes and the sizes precariously planned / focal, focal to the vocals, plan / join, join a convene in love's plans / choose, choose a venue variable too, love's plan / gently, gently said "plans / folk, folk attack and the tracks back into love's plan / join, join a journey into love's plan / meek, meek has inherited, well, these plan / inherit, inherit another sort of land's plan / mild, mild enough to touch, plan / share, share a pairing's plan / corners, corners marked and the parked attributes within love's plan / middles, middles made grounded through love's plan / sunshine, sunshine within and the whistles blown, plan / chance, chances to dance for and living's goods, plan / permit, permit a penetration within love's plan / days, days attractive too, love's plan / ice, ice and the rambling run into love's plan / blankets, blankets cover your's plan / recreation, recreation spent in plan / collective, collective to a sort of plan / intone, intone a phone charged into love's plan / staring, staring awarely into lvoe's plan / airs, airs above and within love, plan / vantage, vantage made into the plans venued through love / admits, admits a comfort came into love's plan / heart, heart heavy gone into plan / lights, lights excitement planned / gifts, gifts give us our plan / packs, packs abound planned / hired, hired and sired into plan / God, God said let them see basic humanity, the plans to build a beatific plan / pines, pines equate to the border with love's plan / flowing, flowing appears in your plan / channeled, channeled excitement is seen into, plan / inches, inches made, gains abound, plan / feet, feet deep in the listened too, plan / benches, benches built around, plan / the / Mission / and / Missive / Through-out / the / Night.

CHAPTER TWO

Chasten, chasten and the hasten too, plan / critique, critique and the seek sought, plan / criticize, criticize and the rise into plan / rise, rise along lanes prescribed in, plan / governs, governs a resource said, "yes" too, plan / antiquity, antiquity notes this, planned / celebrated, celebrated for the calibrated plan / waters, waters and the wettest, plan / wisdom, wordly wisdom planned upon, love / moving, moving experience in wordly ways, loved too, plan / themes, themes of the thistle's erase, patented plans, love / thanks, thanks for the mention's plan / thespians, thespians athletic to a passion's plan / staged, staged arouse and the plowing plan /

cathartic, cathartic examples and the samples perched in your plan / dualism, dualism discussed, good try, plan / finish, finish the plans for God's agree too, be, planned for / compliments, compliments come to the summation planned / conjugate, conjugate your words plan / vary, vary has applied for discussion's grouped into love's plan / descarte, descarte in the starts plan / eschatological, eschatological to the obviously planned / duly, duly made for the amazing plan / gnostic, gnostic and the caustic goes, planned / heraclitan, heraclitan and the mighty come to the fallen arise, planned / monastic, monastic to a mission completed, planned / symmetry, symmetry and the beauty comes planned / bilateral, bilateral discussion's parallel plan / crystals, crystals discuss your duties too, planned / socratic, socratic to romantic times, planned / spirals, spirals escalated planned / permanence, permanence becomes your savior's plan / patterns, patterns end, planned / plan, plan to be, pattern free / locators, locators allow us pattern less exam / lightening, lightening to a frightening's go and into us a day's plan / macron, macron and the neutron's paralleled plan / plot, plot and the plenty planned / story, story made real, plan / polymorphic, polymorphic to a material forgiven, planned to / rotation, rotation and a heart's flotation too, forgiven, plan / tone, tone and the zone met, planned / snore, snore along and learn too, plan / breath, breath within and win too, a plan / notation, notation comes to the sums, One's plan / methods, methods amaze us plan / queen, queen of the then some, plan / holloway, holloway and the wave planned / styles, styles selective into love's plan / consistent, consistent to the storied plan / decorative, decorative to a fixture's plan / cultured, cultured samples planned / plutarchs, plutarchs groups planned / penchant, penchant joined, plan / semian, semian gleamings planned / geologic, geologic agrees planned / acts, acts forthrightly planned / trapezoids, trapezoids lived through, plan / transference, transference comes into God's plan / zeno, zeno and the mental detailed plan / traps, traps over and comes a news, "FREEDOM" / We / Are / The.

CHAPTER THREE

Thermal, thermal to the firmer plan / rise, risen to the seizes won and eventually plan / risen, risen to the nature's plan / sensory, sensory and the vector's made too, plan / anchors, anchors and the places planned / referred, referred to the sword's swerve / finally, finally and the signs paid and allowed, plan / sectional, sectional to the vectors planned / tonal, tonal to the final plan / physical, physical to the mentally freed plan / facial, facial to the financially freed plan / gestures, gestures and the meant for along ways planned / tones, tones and the zones arrayed into plenty's plans, amounts laid, into love / temples, temples and the values paid into love's estate / textures, textures and the treaties amazed into plan / volumes, volumes amount too, plan / mirroring, mirroring creates allowance for plan / craters, craters dug and forgone too, plan / pits, pits eruptive and the songs electrically played too, plan / brains, brains absurd within plan / audible, audible signals come, plan / auditory, auditory status due, plan / visually, visually connective plan / stunned, stunned by the news, planned / stunning, stunning delivery comes, plan

/ sounds, sounds made collectively, planned / voiced, voiced goodness and the plans electric / reflect, reflect a rationale plum within plan / translucent, translucent to the techniques planned / ally, ally found in the town's plan / alleged, alleged and forgiven too, plan / allegiance, allegiance comes through plan / kinesthetic, kinesthetic retreats and the seats touched, plan / multiply, multiply your wisdom, plan / covalency, covalency paid for the plans. love' / mastery, mastery becomes your plan / persistent, persistent to the intention's planned / separate, separate ways stayed electively planned / relations, relations persistent nature, planned / meditate, meditate on the values bid for, plan / less, less has gone to the sum, plan / participate, participate in the amounted too, plan / more, more than these, plan / causes, causes arrive, daily, plan / force, force becomes you, planned / throats, throats open daily, planned / decree, decree becomes "healed" plan / hereby, hereby we sigh to the heart elected, plan / arabic, arabic bids too, plan / definition, definitions due, plan / intelligent, intelligent to the matters planned / stranger, strangers cames to the ways planned / numbers, numbers equivalent to the news planned / testing, testing voiced, plan / testicles, testicles tight in the news planned / techniques, techniques arise soon, planned / profound, profound allow has found truths planned / allowance, allowance becomes your, plan / Talmudic, Talmudic to the moods planned / Torah, Torah to the northern plain planned / correlation, correlation becomes your sourcing summon too, plan / mandible, mandible to the glandular, plan / financed, financed for eternity into love's plan / One.

CHAPTER FOUR

Orchid, orchid rays become your plan / continues, continues the notion into love's plan / bibles, bibles bade you passionate blue embrace of the news farewell planned / studies, studies become your nature's plan / frolics, frolics adored into plan / creates, creates an elation's plan / realize, realize and the sizes planned / perfectly, perfectly opened postures planned / containers, containers claimed into plan / accessible, accessible's soon enough to be planned / keys, keys and the codes planned / nameless, nameless notes along the lines planned / named, named and the likes paid, planned / awe, awe into causes planned / YHWH, Youth Happens Well Hearted, planned / Democracy, Democracy deals within plan / whispers, whispers electrically into love's plan / listen, listen to the other's beats pleasantly planned / generous, generous to a moment's experience and the existence within, love's plan / merger, merger amazing and the valuable entreaty wondered about, plan / master, master again, shall we? plan?/ electrical, electrical to invectives forgotten, planned / taos, taos drawn diagrams into love's plans / template, templates effective and the matrices planned / man, man of the moment's plan / stand, stand for God's gains, planned / Godly, Godly to the minute's plan / sum, sum paid electively, planned / one, one to the merry, plan / free, free to a codify, planned / two, two and the more ecclectic impaired, plan / for, for and eternal weaves planned / discover, discover a daring for committed plan / intimidated, intimidated and daunted less through plan / commits, commits

to a marriage within, plan / marrys, marrys another's heart veins planned / chocima, chocima and the devas within, plan / binoh, binoh and the miracles planned / physical, physical attractives and the invincible's planned / conceed, conceed to the need too, good-bye's value, as planned / consequence, consequence of the sequence paid, plan / accept, accept your dues, planned / mediator, mediator becoming, planned / harmonic, harmonic to the sonic, plan / music, music allows your, plan / synapse, synapse electric with love's plan / sonic, sonic allows plan / Shabbat, Shabbat and the single man planned / three, three days into love's plan / six, six ways elective, plan / five, five to the skies planned / four, four and the simple, plan / sevens, sevens avow, planned / eight, eight lights lit, plan / nine, nine days to neutral plan / tenth, tenth to allows plan / eleven, eleven laws planned / gate, gate opens again, plan / wilderness, wilderness days planned / wanders, wanders in too, plan / escape, escape comes to the last won, plan / elocutory, elocutory to the votes within, love's plan / puree, puree and the stay along life's planes planned / positive, positive to the notions planned.

CHAPTER FIVE

Flamenco, flamenco and the meanings mixed, plan / flamingo, flamingo blue to the measures matched, plan / spain, spain allows a mission too, plan / Spanish, Spanish to a danish surrender miraculous in amends plan / Berlin, Berlin gains bounty into infuse of enthuse with love's plan / German, German to a seam and the central's plan / franc, franc and the spending, planned / yen, yen and the desire too, planned / plan, plan an elation's empirical sea / hu-man, hu-man to the notions planned / hesitate, hesitate less and know, man's plan / brings, brings a buyer soonest, plan / passages, passages abide along plan / crisp, crisp with the news, plan / carpool, carpool maintained throughout, plan / mate, mate assumes plan / rosh, rosh to the yes within, plan / Hashana, Hashana may eternally, plan / Yom, Yom to the yes laid into plan / Kippur, Kippur and the simply, planned / Shabbot, Shabbot and the ought into, plan / Shem, Shem and the glimmers intended, plan / tov, tove and the trickles found, plan / purchase, purchase a mast, One, deep in plan / spirals, spirals within and without, plan / punitive, punitive is over, and the dues? plan / endure, endure less, enjoy more, plan / sabbeth, sabbeth days planned thoroughly for love's plan / said, said yes to the lightness planned / let, let us rest in God's lovely plan / rest, rest elected, yes, the plan / yes, yes we will lend too, a plan / suddenly, suddenly I see, the plan / situation, situation becomes, plan less / elevation, elevation becomes your status, planned / helps, helps define, planned / inspire, inspire a creative resource's plan / transition, transitions becoming simply, love's plan / six, six into often's plan / way, way to be, planned / home, home to another's plan / hallowed, hallowed into day's planned / be, be elected for God's plan / God's, God's the gate, Christ the man, Buddha the mission, enlightened the stand in the narrow made Muslim unique in Sufi Belief and God's perfect position in lifted heads lightly said "one, plan" / name, name most grand and often led through, plan / kingdom, kingdom electric becomes your plan / comes, comes another merry still with plan

/ payments, payments made, plan / maid, maids honored, plan / seas, seas allow, flows, plan / red, red regard for the parting plan / ships, ships past, planned / bus, bus broken through, plan / across, across rates planned / deserts, deserts passed, plan / composure, composure and the codes break, planned / land, land is listed now plan / loudly, loudly said, God's plan / challenges, challenges met and shrugged with, plan / looks, looks across tools pooled, plan / aquarian, aquarian waves planned / eyes, eyes looking in out plan / crocodile, crocodile deals planned.

CHAPTER SIX

Tears, tears attributed too, plan / mastered, mastered the art within love's placement banded for God's plan / sciences, sciences sent to love's plan / mileage, mileage made, plans gates, plummet through the drop's zone / keeps, keeps allow and the plowing advantage planned / geese, geese gander along life's planes and the plans too, God' / aspirant, aspirant into God's plan / keeps, keeps another happy, still, plan / introductions, introductions amazed plan / ivy, ivy days planned into God's plan / examples, examples and the samples sent along, plan / immediate, immediate to the means planned / keen, keen above and about love's plan / visions, visions voiced, plan / turns, turns about us, plan / take, take a notion for God's plan / looks, look sabove into light plan / hyacinth, hyacinth to a cues medicinal plan / macaws, macaws to a musing's plan / cockatoos, cockatoos and the muse planned / gorillas, gorillas grew across the rains too, planed plan / cattle, cattle and the chattel paid, plan / Africans, Africans and the vulcans laid into plan / elephants, elephants valuable in truth's remember, plan / buffalos, buffalos and the bionic white plan / animalistic, animalistic fogive's plan / twos, twos and the ruse run, plan / buy, buy a ventricular amounts plan / too, too and the also, within, plan / tongues, tongues and the cutting owned, plan / james, james and the gentlemen's plan / said, said yes to the election voted in, plan / evils, evils gauge gone too, plan / reveal, reveal votes for the bobcat planed planned / resilient, resilient to a welcomed plan / bobcats, bobcats and the basics planned / cheetahs, cheetahs amused within love's basically planned humanit / tigers, tigers gaze into faces planned / lions, lions applaud tigers basic lunge into plan / llama, llama donned plan / demur, demur to rest in the yes, planned / borneo, borneo bites bait free, plan / Congo, Congo going plan / Guatemala, Guatemala gives plan / Belize, Belize and the seize over, plan / Costa Rican, Costa Rican explain into planes elected, loved, planned / Cretan, Cretan and the sands over go, plan / Botswana, Botswana and the bays planes planned / african, african to a meeting's plan / Madagascar, Madasgar amazed into love's plan / Falkland, Falkland fields and the heal's planned / island, island sized forgive's plan / managed, managed a matter's fortressed abandon and the vacancy planned / chest, chest of the cheat less, plan / breast, breast suggested plan / bed, bed of the reading's plan / balls, balls and the alls led, plan / bustles, bustles past your, plan / restful, restful days come, planned / mansion, mansion managed and the meanings planned / stages, stages blessed within plan / stand, stand allowed, plan / allow, allow affirmation's plan / fulfill, fulfill a dictate's plan / meals, meals paid for, plans.

CHAPTER SEVEN

Sandles, sandles and the candles made into mantles pieces patterned throughout, plan / worn, worn above and wellest, plan / feet, feet attest to the treaties made, plan / torn, torn across pages perpendicularly planned / Surinam, Surinam and the vehicle too, planned / walked, walked and attributed too, plan / islands, islands and the mansions skyward glanced, plan / talk, talk of plenty, and the many, planned / bones, bones estated as the sequestered plan / burst, burst across helpful alliances, planned / marrow, marrow and the nectar nestled within, plan / first, first and the yes won, plan / minutia, minutia made allied too, lights, plan / partners, partners tested and chosen then, plan / return, return to another's debated shore, plan / dance, dance along the chants within, plan / kenya, kenya stood for the opticle allegory for, plan / Peruvian, Peruvian to a shore palmetto plan / Antarctic, Antarctic lanes penned and then, planned / brazil, brazil and the gills found, through a brew, planned / benefits, benefits become your plan / doubled, doubled into elliptical plan / Mexico, Mexico met in amazing's plan / falkland, falkland landed plan / Canada, Canada due the narrows planned / Botswana, Botswana values planned / captions, captions and the options planned / boundaries, boundaries given release into plan / Tanzania, Tanzania sees our scenes plan / gracious, gracious to a cause won, plan / findings, findings become yours, plan / Bhagavad Gita, the gita gained, plan / Upanishadic, Upanishadic plans to the ninth dimension's plan / Koran, holy won, wars duo done, marrys, plan / cope, cope to the shallow forget's plan / Calgary, Calgary cues an essentially gained slope into plan / Medicci, Medicci menued and the plans estuaried into revenu / precipice, precipice over, shot, and done, planned / presuppose, presuppose the repose to abolish lessen, plan / galactic, galactic into tribal plan / written, written in minutes planned / balanced, balanced in the causes planned / integrate, integrate your nation's plan / replete, replete with integrity and intend, planned / intelligent, intelligent to the journey's plan / satan's, satan's succumb planned / Lucifer, Lucifer knew delivery threw plan / led, led across waters planned / home, home into equipment's thrones planned / angels, angels called within, plan / anecdotes, anecdotes dealt within, plan / legends, legends allowed pleasure's prowling fortunate present, plan / weds, weds your wishes planned / fables, fables and the able too's planned / blisters, blisters off and the listening scoffs forgotten, plan / valor, valor recovers and heaven elates your plan / flourish, flourish made into the dates set for plan / beast's, beast's defeat has blessed your shore's release, know digits significant unto God's plan / agree, agree to simply, love's plan / returns, returns a notion natured in less, remember love's bliss, plan / revile, revile has suggested that evil leave her shores remember blessed be God's plan / leaves, leaves the coldness and the doors have opened into love's pens, blessed plan / Mayan's.

CHAPTER EIGHT

Life, life and the lightening listening too and the goodness along your respectful ascend into perfectly, plan / listening, listening like this, perfectly planned example to love's plan / logic, logic and the listening's plan / given, given a gander into love's plan / passion,

passion and the mission made, plan / composed, composed in the notions devonic and the values Metatronically linked throughout, plan / comprised, comprised and concerned within, plan / chose, chose a narrowed vision less often, plan / apogee, apogee found and the sounds planned for regularly / appendix, appendix and the suspend sold, paired for plans to / appendetic, appendetic along lines planned / coverage, coverage joins in love's heights, planned / agenda, agenda detains less, planned / mastered, mastered a castle's plan / suites, suites and suggestions planned / columns, columns coherent into love's plan / rails, rails and the ruses over, plan / vain, vain and the variagate planned / vein, vein of deliver's plan / conifer, conifer coned pines plan / pined, pined without within, found, plan / treats, treats and the seats sent too, plan / entertain, entertain her respect for the name, love's spa / shellac, shellac less and find won, plan / wraps, wraps up the horizon's plans, love / octavian, octavian to the raving's plan / seized, seized through the yes paid to love's plan / crops, crops carouse within love's plan / windowed, windowed and the scintillate's plan / arrange, arrange a visit throughout love's plan / vaults, vaults and the successful ascent into love's plan / boxed, boxed equips and the lips permanent into love's plan / sleeping, sleeping with friends who plan for love / proportions, proportions and the seated plan / ratios, ratios paid into love's plan / stores, stores and suggestions within, plan / classic, classic to the cause planned / traditions, traditions and the joys planned / options, options and the optional within, plan / shoes, shoes and th steps made, planned / shown, shown a wave's plan / impeccable, impeccable to an acceptable plan / tremble, tremble with excitement sent into plan / attract, attract the other's plan / casual, casual to a cause planned / formal, formal to the formidably stingy plan / formidable, formidable gone into God's lovely plan / base, base and the cases planned / rustic, rustic along the lines planned / sloping, sloping encodes throughout, plan / appealing, appealing suppose's plan / allow, allow a listening planned / delectable, delectable into suspected plan / sleeping, sleeping won, throughout your plan / irresistible, irresistible into love's plan / resist, resist a suspend into plan / strengthen, strengthen your resolve unto plan / ensue, ensue and the alpine jaunt too, plan / rushing, rushing across rhymes planned / smashing, smashing old atomics, energy gains $E = A$ squared to the 3rd detail of light's emancipation, arc-angelic fortitude's plan / mirth, mirth and the worth throughout, plan / abide, abide in the sites planned / luxor, luxor ads a strait's plan / Good.

CHAPTER NINE

Retreat, retreat into natural avenues planned / stately, stately stays planned / shaded, shaded weightlessness planned / completion, completion comes occurent within, plan / luxury, luxury and the listening plan / excites, excites and the mission's plan / duality, duality ends in plan / quality, quality cues your plan / apparent, apparent to the zen's plan / parlez-vous, parlez-vous and the views planned / gourmets, gourmets gaunt forgive, plan / sheets, sheets felt elegant beneath and the particles slip into love's plan / shingles, shingles off and the healing's tossed into love's lightest plan / roofs, roofs escape and the tapes stop running planned /

steps, steps made to increase the heat's plan / starts, starts electric and the status renewed plan / striking, striking examples and the samples mend, planned / options, options pelt and the belt loosens plan / vistas, vistas viewed and the herald's news, plan / unique, unique to a concept, deplete, renew plan / immaculate, immaculate to a concession, plan / stairs, stairs built into stars planned / versions, versions vary in the dues planned / cleanse, cleanse and recover, plan / purify, purify spiritually into plan / electrical, electrical resources planned / outlets, outlets and the spouting intake into life's plan / generators, generators and the gazes planned / generative, generative into love's driving plan / resurrect, resurrect has come to the won, plan / connect, connect your cord to the "word" plan / Michaels, Michaels allow has come, planned / guide, guide the sides planned / constructs, constructs uncome and the regime begun plan / chorus, chorus sings and the rhymes ring into plan / electrocute, electrocute less and know more the chords into plan / voice, voice given the chosen won plan / phase, phase over, cut cords, plan / out, out and the shouting glances, plan / choice, choice to heal, plan / elect, elect a rage less, plan / elective, elective to a selective plan / elocute, elocute and the votes planned / absolute, absolute into love's plan / agree, agree to see the plan / campaign, campaign above and within, plan / refrain, refrain from the gain less, plan / remainder, remainder and the reminders due, plan / additive, additive to the measures planned / sets, sets and the sects planned / paranthesis, paranthesis and the parental pews planned / functional, functional to a vehicle mentioned, love's plan / screens, screens elected plan / rolled, rolled into reasons planned / dramatic, dramatic and the empathic's plan / compartmental, compartmental to the environment's plan / arch, arch built and worn, plan / railway, railways ridden and the living's plan / cars, cars and the stars planned / ticket, ticket bought, hers too, plan / get, get with the menu plan / on, on to the oh yes, plan / heart, heart attests, plan / wells, wells deep in the earth's retreat into plans.

CHAPTER TEN

Galaxies, galaxies appear in nearest plan / featuring, featuring fellows planned / designs, designs and gains as planned / charmed, charmed to the chiming plan / handy, handy and the delivery cut, plan / seclude, seclude and the should be's plan / bonus, bonus equips and the steps planned / content, content to maintain us, plan / limitless, limitless abundance, plan / natural, natural flown planes plan / elaborate, elaborate to a retail's plan / neat, neat into a ruse gone, plan / platform, platform built to live from, plan / large, large allows, plan / exteriors, exteriors raised, plan / storm, storm out to find new plan / expertise, expertise and the suggest within, plan / converge, converge into mergers planned / specials, specials and the spatials caused, plan / services, services suggested, plan / elevate, elevate your estate, plan / adjust, adjust unto venues planned / covers, covers herself well, plan / comprehensive, comprehensive deducts planned / estimate, estimate runs, planned / customize, customize your sizes plan / visits, visits values planned / vip, vocational integrity pens plan / details, details disgust? plan / conversation, conversation spent in plan / receives, receives a lettered plan / treats, treats us? wel / topics, topics and the treaties cancer free to a capricornian view's plan / products, products made precisely as seen into views planned / convergence, convergence coming, plan / keep, keep up the frontal attract's plan / accompany, accompany another's plan / plans, plans and the details drawn, love' / renderings, renderings becoming plan / drawn, drawn into cycles planned / optional, optional appeals come, planned / apply, apply for the deluxe news, planned / blueprint, blueprints drawn, planned / human, human into volleys planned / haversham, havershamed curtains planned / jump, jump to a genuis planned / curiousity, curiousity comes into plan / gains, gains and the gentle ways plan / optically, optically and the sent fors plan / astute, astute into trees sent, plan / days, days and daily plan / lofty, lofty leads plan / affords, affords and the swords into plan / attractive, attractive and the strays plan / captive, captively capricious into volleys planned / relates, relates and the relations planned / relative, relative and the sorts that seek your plan / require, require and the sires planned / measures, measures and the features planned / facile, facile and the vessel planned / formulaic, formulaic appliance into pleasures planned / active, active into strategic plan / signs, signs and the signals penned into plan / signals, signals and the deals done planned.

CHAPTER ELEVEN

Spots, spots and the shots sent planned / place, place and the penchant extended plan / decking, decking and the dealings planned / charms, charms and the swarming plan / pacific, pacific and the coasts planned / details, details and the duest enhance, plan / provides, provides and the singular suggestion's plan / galleys, galleys and the geisha's plan / slides, slides into suggestion's plan / utmost, utmost and the suggestion's plan / resemble, resemble and the symbols planned / invites, invites and the vistas viewed planned / sensitivity, sensitivity and the signs planned / qualities, qualities planned for and the signs allowed / romance, romance and the resides planned / defines, defines and the details planned / contours, contours and the most, planned / comforts, comforts and the costs plan / details, details and the dues planned / designs, designs and the details planned / dazzling, dazzling days allow us our placements planned / impacts, impacts sent and the intentional plan / cheery, cheery and the chilling plan / reprise, reprise and the rises plan / divinity, divinity and the daring's plan / defer, defer to a delightful plan / policies, policies paged through our plan / placed, placed into details planned / parishional, parishional news planned / paltry, paltry to the pervasive plan / most, most admits forthrightly paged plan / mentions, mentions a dimension's plan / magically, magically and the amuses planned / heritages, heritages allows planned / holy, holy and the disciples planned / levels, levels and thrice said, plan / lucifers, lucifers and the thrown allows plan / return, return and the disciples given, plan / heavens, heavens and the hinges planned / gate, gates and the solvent planted planned / hearts, hearts and the whistles planned / reside, reside and the residues planned / residence, residence recalls your suggested plan / found, found in the fortress planned / gods, gods goods planned / hearts, hearts held, planned / light, light's listening into

plan / allows, allows an apostle's plan / thankful, thankful for the details planned / gifts, gifts gained plan / gathers, gathers a clouded forgive's plan / gain, gain a detail's plan / gratis, gratis into grains planned / groans, groans along allows plan / gaping, gaping attain a truth's plan / post, post and the staff's plan / plants, plants and the vaunt across plan / reach, reach across another's plan / bronchial, bronchial balances bled less through plan / branched, branched above's plan / blanched, blanched applies plan / refrain, refrain gains plan / repudiate, repudiate regards plan / rewards, rewards come into plans.

CHAPTER TWELVE

Sufficient, sufficient to a notion planned / sources, sources said, sealed, plan / stoic, stoic to the causes planned / attire, attire to the fire's planned / sheperd, sheperd to the cords cut plan / crook, crook into the nooks planned / lambs, lambs and the credits planned / release, release along the lines plane / relate, relate and the sale made, plan / advise, advise along lines planned / adventures, adventures range planned / treat, treat and the adventures planned / transit, transit and the trips due planned / trains, trains allow us, plan / training, training and the trips planned / spends, spends an allows plan / spatial, spatial and the facial's plan / rally, rally and the reaches planned / radical, radical reseals planned / release, release into natures plan / rotational, rotational to retire's plan / pleasing, pleasing and the parental plan / pliant, pliant and the client's plan / regard, regard and the registered plan / orientation, orientation and the records spent plan / screening, screening and the shrugging plan / scanned, scanned and the suggestion's planned / recall, recall and the reviews planned / replenish, replenish and the registered plan / refill, refill and the reseals planned / overt, overt and the overtures planned / agree, agree to be planned / record, record and the sword's forgiven plan / prioritize, prioritze and the parallels planned / censor, censor and the censure gone, planned / refuse, refuse and the refrains planned / related, related and the regents planned / rehearsal, rehearsal and the regents planned / rehearsed, rehearsed and the reversed plan / purchase, purchase made and the shades shine, plan / powers, powers and the penchants planned / various, various plan / plans, plans and the purchase planned / understood, understood and the would you, planned / understand, understand and the rounded plan / expression, expression and the rejection's planned / relax, relax and the registered plan / accomplish, accomplish and the clauses should, plan / apply, apply and the suggested regards plan / appreciate, appreciate and the rates planned / heal, heal and the zeal's plan / whole, whole and the enough to be planned / accepted, accepted and the into, plan / truth, truth and the ruthless plan / honest, honest and the regards plan / entreaty, entreaty and the seated plan / justice, justice and the joined into plan / proof, proof and the preaching forgive's plan / blues, blues over and the codes plan / height, height and the hustle's plan / historic, historic and the hurtles planned / strength, strength into seals planned / persistent, persistent into the intended plan / commit, commit along lines planned.

CHAPTER THIRTEEN

Love, love to be experientially freed into plan / beauty, beauty and the causes planned / aware, aware and the shares said "plans / being, being and the gains grew into plan / acting, acting along lines planned / feeling, feeling and the features planned / seen, seen into scenes planned / Gabriel, Gabriel and the gains given plan / Michael, Michael and the mended plan / Uriel, Uriel and the spell saved, plan / Raphael, Raphael and the swelling plan / Metatron, Metatron and the songs planned / Zadkiel, Zadkiel and the swollen plan / Azrael, Azrael and the sealing plan / Muriel, Muriel and the sails sent plan / Ariel, Ariel and the feelings plan / lights, lights along lines planned / motivate, motivate and the felt for, plan / responsible, responsible and the reach for plan / changes, changes and the children's plan / honesty, honesty and the highest plan / balance, balance allows us God's plan / simultaneous, simultaneous escape's plan / allow, allow your data's plan / immediacy, immediacy dares plan / honestly, honestly allow your plan / wonderful, wonderful into values planned / surrounds, surrounds allows planned / reproduce, reproduce agrees plan / precognite, precognite and the insets plan / energy, energy and the resign's plan / physical, physical to a values instincts and the exceptional experience of light's plan / instincts, instincts securely sent through life's plan / healthy, healthy abide at the heart's laned plan / access, access decried as abortively planned / justify, justify less, yawn more, agree, be, plan / justice, justice into venues planned / concrete, concrete recipients of the genius planned / unsheathed, unsheathed allow into the light's plan / courage, courage came too, plan / rewarded, rewarded regularly through plan / truth, truth equates us, plan / unlocked, unlocked examples and the samples planned / throughout, throughout the cabinets unlocked plan / keys, keys erupting plan / codes, codes encoded plan / experience, experience suggests your plans were encode / repose, repose knows election into plan / arms, arms around us gain plan / God's, God's days planned / wings, wings unwind through plan / angelic, angelic poses struck through plan / powers, powers called in, plan / commit, commit to another, made, plan / processed, processed past her, plan / stages, stages over and the delivery due into plan / wages, wages won, paid for love's elective plan / windy, windy across seas planned fo / scenes, scenes established, planned / collective, collective into samples planned abou / acceptance, acceptance said, "good-bye" plan / healed, healed and completed, "plans"/ often, often sealed, plan / many, many have mentioned their own,"plans."

THE FOUND-MENTS
LEVEL 34

CHAPTER ONE

Discovered, discovered and found, a lover's wound desire too, love / love's, love's desire found / wonder, wonder with your desire found / ways, ways met, desire found / waist, love in waist cinched at dust, found / wants, wants ways desired found / deeds due a release found / needs, needs and wants can be found / nectar, nectar to succulent regard found / sprays, sprays in a species found / pheronic, pheronic plates abide, found / burst, burst into light found / absolute's, absolute's found requir / sway, sway back and forth found / swollen, swollen and engorged with warmth found / throat, the throat of the matter found / big, big and small call all be found / friends, friends together form the bond found / list, list the best found / love's, love's lost found / folks, the folks said found / decide, decide your choice is found / declare, declare it found / method, the method can be found / find, find down deep the thoughts found / left, left of center found / holy, holy be found / ghast, ghast afloat translusent found / raps, raps a rhyme in tune found / highway, highway transist of love found / collapse, collapse down and play found / collect, collect the change and chance found / conclude, conclude the answer found / convey, convey to all found / cope, cope with the result found / casting, casting the ray down and up found / opens, opens to new door found / relays, found relays days of love / host, host the great found / towns, towns to be found / complain, complain less, luxury found / less, less is more and more can be found / more, more to come found / confess, confess the rest found / adore, adore the beloved found / city's, city's gates found / limit, limit won found / opens, opens again found / gates, gates griet, found / gaze, gaze gained found / terrain, terrain changes found / tactilt, tactile tents found / reptile, reptile out, found / fondly, fondly found / port, port sent found / porch, porch meant found / left, left in a found won / new, renew new, found / lift, lift us found / sand, sand sent found / expand, expand us found / strands, strands and the surrenders often into our found designatio / levels, levels and the libations lift unto a designation found / stars, stars and the stairway unto a found destination.

CHAPTER TWO

Starburst, a starburst found in the sounds of love / serenity, serenity sent found / stardust, stardust stead's found / in light, in light sent found / elect, elect spent in found love / device, device dues these found / happy, happy spent found / excite, excite sent, found / elective, love's elective found / sufficient, choose sufficent vows, found / inquiry, inquiry spent in found / elite, elite lets the found / select, select values found / consent, consent sent to the found / estate, estate studies found / suffuse, suffuse sent the found / grams, grams grew to powers found / plenty, plenty found / passion, passion pace found / purse, purse met found / will, will in the found estat / example, example sent found / pulsing, pulsing quakes found / escape, escape meant found / heat, heat held in these found / heart, heart met found / estates, estates built, found / secure, secure equates found / franklin, franklin funded through the found / explain, explain spent said found / decree, decree meets found / about, about set, found / driven, driven into the found /

funnel, funnel through the madness found / torn, found in torn madnes / tapped, tapped into the found / drives, drives within the found way / guides, guides gave found / niceties, niceties neat now found / join, join again the found brigad / God's, God's give found / gospels, gospels gave found / greet, found in the greet's madness drive / going, going toe, foundnes / guise, guise sent too, found / through, through is found thoroughl / stays, stays traded to the found / trails, found trails within the arcade / exit, exit sent, found / then, then they've found / throes, throes out in the found / found, found in explain's sugges / examples, examples sent found / observe, observe secures found / shut, shut outs the found / shant, shan / we be found / require, require suggest found / can, can we be found / cant, cant leans found / court, court exert's found / rapture, rapture rescind's found / curse, curse came out through the found / examples, examples sent found.

CHAPTER THREE

Avenue, an avenue spurs in the found / natural, natural needs found / nature, nature next, found / nuptials, nuptials mixed, found / notes, notes about ways found / needs, needs your's found / nestles, nestles into these found / available, available suggest's found / cables, cables curt, found / squares, squares met, found / squires, squires met, found / bearded, bearded found / try, try rest found / green, green gazed found / glen, eyes glen's found / gander, gander ways, found / chests, chests meet, found / worn, worn away melt, found / well, well wins these found / opened, opened into the found / handle, handle held found / copies, copies kept, found / content, content within these found / express, express well your found estate / books, books mixed found / places, places placed in these found / processed, processed aways found / heavens, heavens gates found / invest, invest in those found / interest, interest means found / intensity, intensity comes found / compressed, compressed into these found / weaver, weaver wins thanks frbrics found / untold, untold into these found / daily, daily deals found / shows, shows us found / wards, wards on these found / telling, telling trees found / delivers, delivers deals found / books, books met in these found / forms, forms find the found / ashes, ashes met, found / dances, dances within's found / villages, villages view's found / fastens, fastens well within these found / dust, dust deals in these found / advert, advert in spent for these found / overlooks, overlooks meet these found / tool, a tool sent found / tickle, tickle met found / team, team trilling found / tore, tore with regard's found / tramp, tramp through your foundnes / toxin, toxin of the heap scent, found / success, success sent in these found / flows, flows into your foundnes / tranced, tranced outed, found / north, north needs found / giver, giver quivers into these found / lots, lots lead into these found / trickle, a trickle spent, found / river, a river runs, found / liver, liver lives found / lets, lets be found.

CHAPTER FOUR

Consistently, cinsistently interior to the duration found / definition, definition wound around the meanings found / daily, daily detail your found regard for love / durations, durations mentioned, found

/ ration, ration for the rational spend called found / station, station still with found love / caprice, caprice about, found / release, release aroused as found / resonant, resonant to the news found / running, running past, found / destitution, destitution ends, found / widen, widened horizons found / wanton, wanton willing, found / wandering, wandering aims to be, found / squander, squander has ended at these found / fools, fools suffer less, found / follicles, follicales fill with a healing offered to those found / often, often find the found / cellular, cellular interest in the light found / pretty, pretty amends, found / brash, brash has rested, found / brusque, brusque can go to the found / budget, budget set rules found / Azrael, Azrael held to the found / cantos, cantos remembers thee, found / cavalier, cavalier to the payments found / beloved, beloved comes to the found / limitless, limitless partnerships found / separation, separation comes to the found / bliss, bliss has acknowledged that the funds exist for the found / motions, motions made to keep the meanings found / lights, lights elect to be found / immense, immense rewards come to those found / amounts, amounts paid immense into the found / years, years leap to the found / pure, pure is a simple, found / inclines, inclines leap to those found / nature, nature seals her healings, found / aspirant, aspirant to remembering found / octopii, octopiis sent eight ways home to the arms of the found / harps, harps who loop crystal clear to the found / crystals, crystals create a hearing found / harps, harps heard heal chiming will found / lessons, lessons written, found / mind, mind meant for finding found / shorts, shorts written through those found / been, been to the middle, found / tools, tools spell fixed, found / advantage, advantage costs less if found / blankets, blankets cast past the found / webs, webs burst with the found / liken, liken your living to a found wo / neurologic, neurologic to degrees found / interference, interference is off to the found / energy, energy is found / constitutions, constitutions strenghtened through the found / forgiveness, forgiveness lives within the found / likes, likes a rate for found / enliven, enliven yes! these found / alleviate, alleviate mentioned, found / success, success suggests, found / legible, legible to a literal found / legislate, legislate led to our found experienc / attributive, attributive to a found love.

CHAPTER FIVE

Falcon, falcon fusing with the found / hawk, hawk meant as sent for the found / meetings, meetings made, found / gloves, gloves touch the gain found / clerics, clerics surge to see the found / bred, bred to delivery for the found / masses, masses made aware within the found / Latin, Latin lending found / Arabic, Arabic bound to the found / Greek, Greek to the seeking found / dirt, dirt clears, found / clear, clarity clears with the found / white, white in the simple, found / decipher, decipher where to be, found / running, running reached and found for love / excavate, excavate has worn into the found / temple, temple is simple found"/ Solomon, Solomon said found"/ titled, titled "yes" to the found / truth, truth has held us told to be found / Yahweh, Yahweh spelling f-o-u-n- / jehovah, jehovah elects you found / Phoenician, Phoenician connectives found / Tyre, Tyre is led to legendary status within the temple found / king, king of the seas electric, found / kings, kings written

in lists found / books, books basic to the blessings found / masonic, masonic cures remembered to be found / landmarks, landmarks lend a semblance to the blessings found / rites, rites simply found / Scottish, Scottish chores over as heralds are found / degrees, degrees taught are found / sized, sized as awarest for the filling found / house, house succeeds to be found / God, God has given you a house for the filling found / temple, temple simple within the found / man, man has made a main found / priority, priority and the seniority to be, found / agree, agree to the seeing found / arguments, arguments go to the sealing found / windy, windy rounds made to the found / ignore, ignore has gone to the readings found / beliefs, beliefs exist to be married well to the found / lesson, lesson for the linkings found / BC, best chosen, found / chinese, chinese calligraphy reads Kai to the seas found / worship, worship the lightest found / masters, masters meet at the borders metatronically found / illustrates, illustrates license has found true love / heirs, heirs are apparent in the found love / peers, peers are simplest with pulsing love found / profiles, profiles for the revile flung to the found lanes of love / Christ, Christ has held us found for love / introduce, introduce the doctrine of the living found / regular, regular shores are reached as the islands come to view, found / lore, lore has reached you found / thebes, thebes may be hermetica to the found / Jerusalem, Jerusalem babylon deep in forgetting found / history, history reads of the arc found / heights, heights recourse is the found / legal, legal to a meager found / positive, positive in injunctions found / allowances, allowances set found / feelings, feelings resolved and found.

CHAPTER SIX

Elements, elements mused in the values found / buy, buy both now, found / gentle, gentleness on to the found / fellows, fellows mellow in the found / cry, cry over, found / vertical, vertical cords leap to the lights found / exhume, exhume finished, presume enjoyes found / resume, resume the resolute ways found / draped, draped in rejoice for the found / glimmer, glimmer loving the hopeful found / transits, transits made and mentioned as found / directs, directs connected found / ceremony, ceremony says found"/ passes, passes through as found / opportune, opportune to the simply found / silence, silence reaches her found relat / replies, replies allowing us found / alexandrian, alexandrian suggestions found / mankind, mankind wins for the found / rely, rely in the ways found / refuge, refuge sought your found trade / constantine, constantine leans to those found / rest, rests again, found / avenues, avenues meet in the light electrically found / rummage, rummage in the sales found / grasp, grasp allows healing found / models, models muse, found / lights, lights loose with those found / bulbs, bulbs swinging to the found / strides, strides made to see those found / rides, rides offered to the found / ruses, ruses off, found / stories, stories rush to the found / congregates, congregates, studies, found / comparing, comparing soarings found / coincides, coincides with those found / ages, ages and the raises found / pages, pages tossed to the found / places, places lost plunge above ground found / trends, trends are simple, be, found / truth, truth is yes, found / explore, explore the shores found / assigns, assigns mean found

/ designs, designs deal in those found / doors, doors open again, found / planes, planes chosen, found / electric, electric to a giving found / hardware, hardware won, found / early, early is wise to the found / foam, foam with exemptions found / applciations, applications made to the found / european, european trips found / begin, begin the balance found / ancient, ancient reigns found / artifacts, artifacts live as found / mixed, mixed erase, found / identical, identical deals made, found / special, special to the simple found / people, people who meet as found / skin, skin soft with those found / fame, fame allows us a meeting found / slaves, slaves gone to those found / nile, nile's need to reflect the Orion found / slow, slow to a signing found.

CHAPTER SEVEN
Notations, notations and the notes for found / hunters, hunters who live, found / huntress, huntress of the butress found / hords, hords and the masses found / mediterranean, mediterranean and the mounded amore of love found / mosaics, mosaics and the musings found / lebanons, lebanons and the leading found / vegetate, vegetate and the latest starts found / knowledge, knowledge and the living found / tastes, tastes and the truth now found / debates, debates and the delivery found / projects, projects appear near us, found / protects, protects and the peace is, found / decides, decides and the debut found / immortal, immortal in the portal now called love, found / mortality, mortality and the reality for an amazement found / legacy, legacy and the ledger's found for love / ancients, ancients abound when found through astound / records, records and the simply found / recall, recall is a soothing found / messiah, messiah and the movement found / christ, christ allows a lightening found / rings, rings of the singing, found / random, random multiply found, add on / revile, revile is without a style found / reset, reset expects a living found / respect, respect for the coming found / rouse, rouse allowed through a found empire for love / rise, rise to occupations found / leave, leave is a sleeve found / lease, lease implies found / lost, lost leads often to found / trade, trade made and the arc saved through the loving found / noah, Noah new and I am telling you found / moses, moses mentions ten times found / scrolls, scrolls empower us, found / clans, clans level with those found / recall, recall attends our foundnes / respect, respect requires your cause be found / faith, faith has simply been found / taught, taught to heal with increasing mention wet with love found / still, still we arouse the notion, found / warned, warned forgotten, found / innocence, innocence won, found / truth, truth be told, found / wounds, wounds of old, forgotten, found / innocents, innocents agree, found / departs, departs and the willing, found / legs, legs ache with the founded ligh / fires, fires gleam with a found regime of light / waves, waves led lead us to the found elate / eagles, eagles respect our newfound wingin / distant, distant the feelings found / cry, cry overthrown through a feeling found / mates, mates meet in a matching found / mothers, mothers mixed as found / illustrations, illustrations reach us found / promised, promised to a meaning found / tested, tested again and found within, love / adoptive, adoptive and the days found / luminary, luminary and the leads found / eggs, eggs

and the living met found / fertile, fertile in a motive clear to be found / open, open to the option, found.

CHAPTER EIGHT
Sets, set of the notions found / suns, suns elevated to the found reasoning for love / women, women won through the found / elongate, elongate sums us, found / cycles, cycles peaking as found / weights, weights lifted, found / truths, truths told as found / wisdom, wisdom won through the found / listens, listens, well, the found / heals, heals often, found / loves, loves lost, found / cured, cured creation found / wisely, wisely wooed found / evolved, evolved within, found / spirits, spirits talking found / tradition, tradition dealt, found / desires, desires magically found / burdens, burdens off, found / habits, ahbits healed, found / ability, ability to be found / gentle, gentle within the found / carriage, carriage trips to the found resource for love / charm, charm connects as found / connects, connects within found / expand, expand to the power found / elongates, elongates given found relie / gain, gain measures and grew found / smell, smell the chores release, found / ancients, ancients wage less without found / sunlit, sunlit measures explain, found"/ hearts, hearts zeal is found no / balanced, balanced bliss has come to your door's found elat / marinate, marinate iwthin the found / respond, respond to reasons found / protest, protest becomes less real to the found / regardles, regardless seals these found / reunion, reunion offers love to those found / acquires, acquires pace is found / sense, sense made for the found / wheels, wheels lift to the found / small, small becomes real found / scrutinize, scrutinize deals with those found / lift, lift allowed, found / all, all will be well, found / seneca, seneca's medicine truth found / truth, truth estates found / medicines, medicines made, found / well, well within, found / relations, relations realized through the found / aho, aho moves to the found / overlap, overlap allows us a found relative / overlay, overlay fed through the bliss found / mimes, mimes lost, found / active, active trips to the found relation / stretch, stretch across the shores found / task, task over, found / tribal, tribal rises found / treats, treats mentioned found / inipi, inipi built found / wet, wet with a ration found / steamed, steamed tastes found / breath, breath brought, found / balances, balances your foundness / values, values bliss, found.

CHAPTER NINE
People, people who are simply, found / claim, claim a pace found / children, children race to hear thee, found / claim, claiming a living found / overboard, overboard ran to those found / concepts, concepts and the capably found / under, under and the nearing found / worn, worn along the living found / webbed, webbed and the wisdom found / release, release and the coming found / snaps, snaps and the shutting found / cutting, cutting rims off the bound found / chords, chords and the living found / forms, forms and the freedom met is found / spirits, spirits and the soaring found / running, running and relations found / perfume, perfume roomed in the caves found / bloom, bloom and the living found / Savor, Savor said, found / faint, faint and the feeling found / rich, rich and the raining abounds in the found / gathering,

gathering allocations found / goodness, goodness known and found / perpetual, perpetual lessons found / scents, scents and the whistling lines cut as found / humans, humans mentioned as found / offers, offers made found / brilliant, brilliant and the willing found / flowers, flowers and the filling finds a found stand of living plan / effervescent, effervescent and the shellings sent as planned / colors, colors and the clearing found as planned / dancing, dancing and the leverage found / beginnings, beginnings and the coming into found / basics, basics apply to the found / response, response arouse to the found / revenued, revenued rewards found / appears, appears a simple find found / harmonious, harmonious bodies found / generate, generate allows a coming found / general, general appearances found / gods, gods sacrificed pass the findings found / coverage, coverage accrues near the found enlightenment endocrine field deep to th / regulation found / memory, memory amusingly found / passages, passages came through the found lines 20 deep to a Mayan moo / passed, passed into those found / pounds, pounds of the regular yellows found / populate, populates a sort found / wits, wits allows us a winning found / qumran, qumran and the reading found / miracles, miracles mission found / parables, parables arose and the list found / place, place and the leadings found / pertaining, pertaining allows a found relatio / candidates, candidates enthuse us as a tremendousness found / cleansing, cleansing and the costs led to the found release of love / escape, escape and the living meets found / precious, precious to the repose found through loving mention of the light within humanit / precise, precise and the precious points maze freed to love that is found / commands, commands and the cures sent for the found / concise, concise erections sent often to those found / often, often led to those found / agreed, agreed to the simply found / read, read and the leading found.

CHAPTER TEN

Findings, findings missions found / miraculous, miraculous and the meetings found / lights, lights and the liberation found / robins, robins and the relationships found / spring, spring and the came into found / gazebos, gazebos and the treaties found / preoccupy, elegance found through the found rationale for love / findings, findings sent through the listening found / Sinai, Sinai suggestions found / Moses, Moses allows a mission found / Nile, Nile kneelings sealed as found / red, red and the rising found / sea, seas and the clearings found / parts, pray for the passion found / hearts, hearts of the matter found / weep, weep as past the found / testify, testify the remainder found / touch, touch a listener found / basics, basics covered as found / complex, complex cubes found / aprons, aprons appear near the found / emblems, emblems stretched to those found / friends, friends and the loving found / lambs, lambs and the detached ewes found / innocence, innocence spent for those found / vertical, vertical and the values found / blocked, blocked and the vertically freed found / encounter, encounter and the seals spent as found / patterns, patterns and the wisdom well within the found / ties, ties and the tatters past spent wisdom found / wear, wear and the retiring found / worn, worn and the thrilling found / haggle, haggle heals those found / profane,

profane and the perfection found / sacred, sacred and the sealings found / sacral, sacral, sacral and the scenes found / permissive, permissive parallels found / dismissive, dismissive and the attributes found / extras, extras fine in the found essences of love / knights, knights reap found insurances to love / ruins, ruins cast past the living life's insurance sent to love / herod, herod and the living lent to the ratified sorts found in love / painstaken, painstaken sorts found / excavate, excavate suggested and the flow is found / pursue, pursue other venues found / creates, creates reltaionship found / hiram, hiram said found / keyes, keyes said anthems found / upper, upper lees found / lower, lower instincts past found / egypt, egypt digestives found / unite, untie acceptive unites for found relationship / power, powers play found / place, place gains the found lines of love / confess, confess and the training found / help, help us leap to the found / need, need has venues found / Gabriel's, Gabriel's gifts are found to love / birth, birth is toasted through love's fountains found / worth, worth and the most found / more, more is less, found / most, most is said, found / a beach, a beach is found in love / matters, matters found with love.

CHAPTER ELEVEN

Lodges, lodges left found / performance, performance amounts to feelings found / rewards, rewards come to those due and found / fruits, fruits spiritually sent to those found / talkative, talkative experiences sent to those found / derivative, derivative choosing found / demonstrative, demonstrative and the duration found / first, first worth found / scrolling, scrolling examples found / secrets, secrets revealed as found / reminders, reminders and the reasons found / history, history cues as found / nominations, nominations lead to the found roads to love / celebrity, celebrity gains are found reaped as profoun / acclaim, acclaim amounts to those found / conclusive, conclusive in winning found / closure, closure and the coming found / unchanged, unchanged and the levels found / challenged, challenged and the estates within found / bishop, bishop bled with profoun incubate of the heavenly late found / rome, rome to the led realign found / Hammodi, Hammodi allowed the found / temple, temple and the triple found / Solomon, Solomon sealed and those found / Moriah, Moriah and the energy met as found / Jerusalem, Jerusalem jewels found / secretive, secretive resources found / kept, kept and the living's found / claims, claims and the clearings found / ideas, ideas and the sent found / revealed, revealed and the resting found / remind, remind and the reassurance found / unqiueness, uniqueness and the meant found / labels, labels lead to those found / joking, joking and the release sent through those found / types, types and the simply found / speculates, speculates and the suggestions found / faith, faiths and the met found / fools, fools and the threshold past found / friends, friends and the fellowship found / electrifies, electrifies and the loving listings found / hermopolitan, hermopolitan and the cosmopolitan found / cosmopolitan, cosmopolitan and the creation's found / Neapolitan, Neapolitan and the meetings found / placement, placements found / renewal, renewal and the readings found / catalyst, catalyst cues and the communications felt found / fundamentals, huge in a living found / octave, octave and the coming lift found / thoth, thoth and the simply found equations found / eight, eight and the lessons found / scheme, scheme and the seetings now found / sign, sign and the shingles now found / things, things and the signing sent found / symbols, symbols and the signatures sent as found / cities, cities and the sharing found / respect, respect the heart found / desire, desire the sounds found / employ, employ the zones found / entire, entire in hiring found / elevate, elevate the ones found / implore, implore less and know more, found / found, found again, love / offered, offered near, love.

CHAPTER TWELVE

Synthesis, synthesis and the commitment found / sympathize, sympathize found / imply, imply affluently found / order, order and the premise found / pregnant, pregnant again within these found / respect, respect for those found / raced, raced attire found / elopes, elopes rise found / lips, lips lead to those found / runs, runs to the bolting found / portals, portals pose as found / collects, collects and the curing found / joined, joined allow gained through the posings found / jaunt, jaunt and the living impose found in love / plans, plans and the letters found in God's handwritten scrip / planes, planes enhanced through those found / cervix, cervix and the central reigns found / attributive, attributive and the terror found / thought, thought and the lessons found / binds, binds and the bliss found / elects, elects and the legiond sent found / kinds, kinds and the currents found / apparent, apparent and the temples found / inherent, inherent and the stages found / inherited, inherited and the repititions surge to those found / arrows, arrows arrogant less than those found / represents, represents gaze into those found / production, production clears the steps found / concentration, concentration cures those found / growth, growth and the appetizing found / queens, queens centrally found / generations, generations past place is found / levels, levels taught to those found / chapters, chapters read by those found / isles, isles and theme set is found / islets, islets lead to those found / Langerhan, Langerhan lands found / pancreatic, pancreatic and the pantomime found / alpha, alpha and the fed hamlets found / betta, betta and the blues found / gamma, gamma and the gazes exposed found / cellular, cellular and the lit found / tattwa, tattwa tents found / tejano, tejano and the meant salutes for those fon / texan, texan and the temples found / tans, tans and the paid for found / themes, themes games found / burns, burns and the letting found / engine, engine and the simply found / flames, flames and the fuses found / solipsistic, solipsistic and the framed found / slipped, slipped across lanes found / Sequia, Sequoia winds found ocean wid / giant, giant gazes found / dogmatic, dogmatic deals found / usual, usual and the miracles wound found / occur, occur and the linkage found / females, females win the found lis / materials, materials amazingly found / males, males amused with the materials found / eternal, eternally led to those found / codes, codes and the cures found / periodic, periodic and the payments made found / unite, unite and the ways found.

CHAPTER THIRTEEN

Ministers, ministers and the miracles found / revive, revive and the arrival found / enzymes, enzymes and the rhizomes found / clearest, clearest cures found / polar, polar pleases found / placed, placed and the grim truth found lightl / hormonal, hormonal cures hum as found / collective, collective and the assurance sent to those found / atomic, atomic tools found / substantive, substantive into sets found / sustain, sustain trues as found / cells, cells simply found / widen, widen trues as found / general, general and the granted found / gains, gains and the grazing found / generative, generative and the sorted found / suspend, suspend and the subsets found / experience, experience emerges in garden's found / endocrine, endocrine and the signed forgiveness found / kept, kept and the clearing found / clears, clears the surface found / sugars, sugars succinct in those found / isletta, isletta and the reds thrown to those found / toxin, toxin tooling past those found / less, less and the traveling found / fasten, fasten to anchors found / pancreas, pancreas and the living found / resumed, resumed and the shriveling shrunk to those left knot found / receptive, receptive to the rules found / swords, swords to the reasons found / tissues, tissues found / resource, resource led to those found / unleashed, unleashed to the levels found insid / enzymes, enzymes and the summary found in love / clearly, clearly and the fine ones in found experiences of love / polar, polar and the simply found / placed, palms placed in those gained as found / hormonal, hormonal and the humming found / collective, collective and the letters found / steroid, steroid and the thrones shrink to those found through loving strength / atomic, atomic insure found / substantive, substantive trips to the living found / sustain, sustain and the lessons found / cells, cells and the sunny ways found / widen, widen and the seams found / general, general grants found / generative, generative sorts found / suspend, suspend and the living example meant for those found / offerings, offerings at last, found / letters, letters matched and found / resting, resting comes, found / retiring, retiring is blessed and found / registered, registered into days now found / reading, reading is blessed and found / referrals, referrals now matched, found / restitution, restitution is directly, found / repairs, repairs have been made, found / reaching, reaching is past, found / breaching, breaching a notion, found / spoken, spoken is the missing, direct, found / suggested, suggested is rested and found / surrendered, surrendered I have to the dove, found / softest, softest still the profits of love found / soothing, soothing is now found.

THE UNIQUE-MENTS
LEVEL 35

CHAPTER ONE

Infinite, infinite and bound less, the advanced state, hu-manly unique / vibration, vibration begun in the fun, hu-manly unique / value, value won and the son became, hu-man, unique / texture, texture, and the plane is uniquely a hu-man fabric / research, human research and the guinea pig done with, unique / dreams, know that your life has become intimately uniquely hu-man / treads, treads clearly deep into the knocks uniqely hu-man / calculations, calculations come to the brain uniquely hu-man / emotions, rule can find venue in the fools who live beyond, advanced states, hu-man / threads, threads are snug in the bed Metatronic and the heart advanced into the hu-man / life, life is of the light uniqely hu-man / potential, and some who are squared into the life uniquely hu-man / limits establish a beyond and through regained into love's uniqueness / breached an abort and reached for the sky to fly into the light hu-manly unique / clinics, clinics clued by the soars entirely uniquely hu-man / pillows, pillows atop our please to the knees uniquest, hu-man / beds, beds slept in, best, unique and the seek to arrive at sweet sleep within God / sleep, hear, reside, at God's mention, then, love, uniques / valued, valued for the uniquely sought seek called love / values, values unique unto the avenues of love / textual, textual invest into the left over ways called love's venue, uniques / brave, brave the rave into love's uniqueness / broad, broad enough to sweep the unique, avenue wide with boulevards into, love / sweeping, sweeping the resorts of uniqueness with love / understand, understand how to stand in love's uniqueness / erase, erase the face of a lessened irritate called love's uniqueness / equate, equate your status to heavenly gates of love's uniqueness / thrills, thrills unique unto a sought require for love / intense, intense exposure into love's reside at the uniqueness within God / energies, energies secure with your unique experience on love / thrust, thrust ahead to the spread for a lot unique / flex, flex above and within sincerely, unique / strong, strong is our presence and our regain of love's uniqueness / presence, presence and the penchant for a gain advanced to our unique encounter at love's chanc / portal, portal open and to the request, unique / clear, clear enough to be sincere in the agree to be, advanced into, uniquely, love / mayan, mayan amends aspirant and scene in the marketed maxim called how we lean into love's uniqueness / position, position of paved extrude and the mood electrically, unique / essential, essential scenes of recent expose and the rosary called essentially, unique / clean, clean the keen for love's arrive at uniqueness / swept, swept for exposure and the composure to see thee, unique / deposits, deposits dare to compare to love's unique estat / calculate, calculate the rates electively spent on hearts content within the unique / trade, trade and the raid onto true acquire of the respect for life's unique sea / travel, travel to the well, uniquely, filled with love's scen / through, through the stand, uniquely fel / today, today, the decade of a respectfully unique sign, love / demand, demand less, find more, respect, uniqueness / mystics, mystics mix within and the blend is found sublime and the dream a chance to dance uniquely in, God / coincide, coincide with the side within God's chance to meet at the light's unbind of uniquely, love / red, red to the said

require of advanced states hu-manly unique / pain, pain has gone to the song unique / blue, blue is the bell who said, uniquely, we, love / violet, violet to the set unique / white, white to the sight, unique / flame, flame fed and fled into, unique / exhibitions, exhibitions bent into with uniqueness found for, love / graphs, graphs grown directly into the uniquest set, you / evolved, evolved into, kindly, yours, uniqueness / when, when is the uniquest day / aspire, aspire to hire a quicker state into love's uniqueness / trade, trade for the glade, uniquest, stil / michael's, michael's fall is through, unique / field, a field filled with love's uniqueness.

CHAPTER TWO

How, how now to be profoundly kept unique to love's sugges / now, now and then I AM supreme within God's uniqueness / masked, masked less and removed stille with the unique restore of love / costume, a costume became a rope and the cape a dope on how to be unique / cats, cats know when to come home for unique acquir / flexing, flexing her stroke, she said, unique / stretch, stretch into new hope for love's astound, unique / yoga, yoga's trend and the thinnest route into uniqueness / eggs, eggs break and love is left unto the unique / paints, paints unique into a scene dialect deep in love's attir / muse, a muse met with unique / details, details deal with our tale of the unique review called love / data, data spent and sent for, lovely, unique / probe, probe and the robe, unique / internal, internal the attire, unique / photos, photographs fed the desire to be unique / columnar, columnar compare of the square for love's uniqueness / produce, produce a prayer, unique / blued, blued and the mood is unique / marlins, marlins mast and the cast unique / beaten, beaten and the boast is gained, unique / medicated, medicated less and found to gain, unique / aggressive, agressive require and the healing acquire called God's gain for love's uniqueness / true, true and the amuse, unique / domestic, domestic and the status unique / abusive, abusive less and shouted for, unique / discuss, discuss the aspects on love's uniqueness / disect, disect less the unique / meditate, meditate and be, unique / wait, wait for the unique / complete, completely unique / compell, compell yourself to be, unique / heroin, heroin out and the needle shouts, uniquely, yo / cocaine, cocains shouts too of the spent degree uniqueness / dependents, dependents declare, we are free, to the unique / narcotic, narcotic the stand within thee, unique / drown, drown less, be found through, the unique / brown, brown less, burn more, unique / dissect, dissect less, the directly, unique / remove, remove the blocks to the unique / complete, complete the uniqueness within, gain, love / adult, adult dealt with and the vent has regain into loving's uniqueness / wait, wait for the rapture, unique / want, want a place to be, unique / rappel, rappel across the face unique / puke, puke about the lessen unique / drink, drink abreast the guest, unique / pump, pump to equate your estate into uniquely love / cover, cover allows our uniqueness / charged, charged about, yes, into love's uniqueness / factual, factual into the actual attire's lovely uniqueness / muse, muse about well into the living's unique / over, over and there is a uniqueness hu-man / print, print a project completed, unique / eggs, eggs break within, unique / wealth, wealth applies to the unique / wonder, wonder and appearance said, unique / how, how to be, unique / now, now and when, unique / win, win the fund, unique / love, love to be unique / chance, a chance to stay, unique / dare, to stay, unique / enigma, enigma acknowledged as the unique won.

CHAPTER THREE

Coat, coat your throat with the living unique / colors, create a state, unique / auras, auras in the fields, unique / field, love is the field felt with our uniqueness / rainbow, positioned unique / heal, heal and the will, unique / complete, a receipt, unique / arc, arc into the sport, forgive, and the uniqueness in God / grip, grip and degree into the unique / graft, graft and abide into a tight step declared unique / graft and abide too, the joint in thee, unique / roots, roots respect our uniqueness / tissues, tissues tear at our uniqueness / variety, variety of values, unique / species, species in depth into the unique / allow, allow a power unique / position, position a parallel as unique / select, select a vision, unique / introduce, introduce, a desire that is, now, unique / encounter, a climate unique / individual, individual the choice come, unique / hybrid, hybrid and held into the unique allo / pollen, pollen placed vertically into the uniquest bud, you / inbred, inbred with reason to say, love, is, unique / express, express a desire to stay, unique / desire, desire a trial run, uniques / yield, yield into a pair, unique / vigor, vigor valued unique / crops, crops gather here, unique / times, times allow the seventh venue, unique / days, days of the seventy ways into love's uniqueness / ways, ways and waves uniquely fort / ten, ten are the tries uniques / inherit, inherit and estate called uniqueness / inheritance, inheritance spent in uniqueness / numbered, numbered and assigned too, the unique / altered, altered most and unique / record, records and the compares said, "uniquely / variegate, variegate the state electrically complete into the unique / control, control the rolls unique / result, result of the resultantly unique / features, features acquire the unique / desired, desired to see the unique / produce, produce a page unique / sudden, sudden and the suddenly, unique / extremes, extremes came to light, unique / check, check a while, unique / experience, experience the pleasure, unique / experiment, experiment with the unique, smil / recessed, recessed is blessed with the unique / genes, genes electrically unique / chromosomes, chromosomes sent through thee, unique / mutate, mutate a heightened state, unique / internal, internal too and the bliss state unique / dealt, dealt a hand unique / array, array of the relays unique / gened, gened aware uniques / pool, pools pent with the unique / language, language waged on the unique / symbol, symbol said, unique / agree, agree to see her, the unique / communion, communion came into the unique / communicate, for thee, uniqueness / cosmos, cosmos became the uniqueness.

CHAPTER FOUR

Excited, excited about the uniqueness in life / expectant, expectant with love's hush into the unqiue / improvise, improvise your affair to be found through thee, unique / through, through and thorough too within the unique / renews, renews our degree of love's uniqueness, belie / truth, truth be told, unique / trust, trust

int he brush, unique / gives, gives a state status, unique / subjects, subjects sent into the unique / image, an image of the unique / consciousness, consciousness became the elite, acquire, unique / loves, loves desire is unique / part, part of the play uniquely human, too, love / start, start and the stare into the unique / cosmetic, cosmetic appear, is, unique / man, man can, be, unique / christ, christ of the notion, "hu-manly" unique / GOD, GOD gave unique / pentegram, pentegram of the uniqueness hu-man / truth, truth may be told, unique / conviction, conviction for thee, unique / twenty, twenty ways, unique / twenty-one, twenty-one ways unique / cube, cube and venues unique / stone, stone thrown away, unique / alchemy, alchemy came through the unique / crucible, crucible deep within the unique / fire, fire found unique / gold, gold gave the uniques / lead, lead leads into uniqueness / matter, matter found materially completely unique / transformed, transformed within the astound, uniques / purify, purify your pace with love's embrace gained unique / dissolve, dissolve into a matter unique / white, white with ash forgone into love's risen uniqueness / ash, ash red with white details above unique / place, place a planet, hear, unique / heart, heart appeal's zeal is unique / hear, hear how to be unique / respect, respect here desire for the unique / regard, regard how to be gained by the unique / ressurect, ressurect your connect within, unique / truth, truth told can behold thee, unique / spirit, spirit of the spire, unique / love, love to be, unique / flesh, flesh melts within thee, unique / wise, wise to sizes unique / intellect, intellect suspect of love's uniqueness / kind, kind enough to see, through, and thoroughly with, the unique / heart, heart filled with thee, uniques / just, just to fly, unique / will, will, be, unique / earth, earth of mirth's uniqueness / fire, firey days of uniqueness / bliss, bliss filled with uniqueness / regard, regard her well within love's uniqueness / kind, kind of the side's unique / heart, heart of the start forever unique / just, just and the juice's unique / will, will to be, uniquely love / earth, earth and the mirth uniques / fire, fire and the fondness, unique / bliss, bliss and the best, unique / regards, regards wins, unique.

CHAPTER FIVE

Triangle, triangles met within, unique / spirit, spirit of the conspire to be inspired by the uniques / square, square and the seal unique / love, love to be uniques / pyramid, pyramids appear, unique / hearted, hearted states uniques / care, care given to the uniques / starts, starts attired unique / salvation, salvation ascends unique / come, come to the sum uniques / personal, personal powers appear unique / won, won yours unique / elders, elders on too, the uniques / speak, speak about the sets uniques / seek, seek to be, unique / symbol, symbol on the song, unique / love, love to lead to the unique / meditate, meditate, upon the unique / star, God's star became, unique / beyond, beyond and within, the uniques / dna, dna said, unique / spiral, spiral spent on the uniqueness / meditate, meditate within, thee, unique / cap, cap comes off, the unique / catch, catch us, unique / star, star said, into thee, the powers / inside, inside and the gain on these, power / each, each and the others, day long, unique / mitochondria, mitochondria deals within God's descend into man found, uniqueness / many,

many met in thee, the unique / one, one ways, uniqueness / universe, universe says, unique / within, within and often, the unique / the one, won, unique / essence, essence sent, uniquely, too, love / farmed, unique equips, for love / 22, 22 ways to be, unique / letters, letters of the universal inquire, flaming red with love's uniqueness / hebrew, hebrew had unique / alphabet, alphabet news, unique / flaming, flaming days into thee, unique / elements, elements have become, unique / Cabbalah, Caballah's mix with the news unique / mix, mix on degrees into the unique / sephirothic, sephirothic emphathics and the news that begins, unique / tree, tree green with news electrically unique / life, life led through thee, uniques / ten, ten days, uniques / 7, 7 signs unique / planets, planets empowered within the unique / four, four days unique / elements, elements elemental too, unique / kether, kether and the hierarchic, unique / metatron, metatron said, uniquely, "LOVE"/ chokmah, chokmah met within the unique / binah, binah bound to less in the unique / chesed, chesed said, unique / Geburah, Geburah smells like the unique / tiphareth, tiphareth sent too, the unique / Netzach, Netzach sent, unique / hold, hold on too, the uniqueness / Yesod, Yesod said, unique / Malkuth, Malkuth made to be, unique / treed, treed and found, unique

CHAPTER SIX

Paths, paths play along lines electrically unique 22, 22 days, unique / times, the times were unique / ways, ways are unique / sphinx, sphinx met retire in the unique / apocalypse, an apocalypse spent in the unique / fixed, fixed acquires unique / across, across the ways, unique / roots, roots applaud, unique / michael, michael said yes, to the unique / eastern, eastern ways, unique / raphael, raphael arose unique / south, south to the gate, unique / gabriel, gabriel grew in stature too, unique / west, west to ways directly, unique / uriel, uriel returns to the unique / north, north to the place, unique / living, living wells, unique / cross, cross the waves unique / arc-angelic, arc-angelic ways unique / symbols, symbols confess, unique / seen, seen daily drawn, unique / study, study for the unique / respect, respect heard, unique / regard, regard for the unique / elect, elect won, unique / body, body bliss becomes uniques / christ, christ said, "unique" the wa / church, one light towned in a church unique / large, large enough to say yes to, unique / square, square on the unique abid / circle, circle about, unique / body, body allowed, unique / bliss, bliss met in the uniqueness / cosmic, cosmic acquire is uniquely your / equate, equate your estate occupied within unique / heaven, heaven said, "uniquely"/ this, this won, uniquely / eternal, eternal stays, uniques / durate, durate through, the unique / kingdom, kingdom came into the unique / come, come into the unique / God, God gave us the unique / man, man made, the unique / etheric, etheric mates, unique / natural, natural days elope through the unique / native, natives met, maturally, unique / tame, tame days, unique / physical, physical to a mental conceed, I AM, Uniqu / etheric, etheric to allowance inside the unique / astral, astral mains remain unique / mental, mental mains regard thee, unique / causal, causal ways, unique / Buddhic, Buddhic declares, "unique" / atomic, atomic amplify heard, unique / explain, explain more, unique / house, houses sturdy with the unique / home, home

unto the unique / heart, heart met, unique / love, love to be, unique / uniquely, uniquely devoid of derelict desires, cosmic allow / giving, giving grants you the avenues within your uniqueness / open, open our stance to include, divine, uniqueness / proclaim, proclaim the game complete in love unique.

CHAPTER SEVEN

Mastery, mastery meets in allowance unique / yoga, yoga fueled within the unique / enlightenment, an enlightenment sent into the regiment unique / 144, 144 days within the unique / dimensional, dimensional deals, unique / levels, levels led, unique / written, written into the uniqueness / seam, seam appeals, the uniques / seems, seems to see, the unique / complete, complete an acquire into the unique / organic, organic and venues unique / Sirius A, Sirius A and the say unique / Sirius B, Sirius B in the trees unique / Atlantis, Atlantis spent, unique / lemuria, lemuria breathes unique / undal, undal and all, the unique / pearls, pearls and the swirls unique / beloved, beloved sent and the hints unique / saints, saints and the paints unique / symbols, symbols ascent, unique / coves, coves and the cores unique / clause, clause and the cause unique / stream, stream and the seams unique / lifes, lifes lead is unique / substance, substance of the sun unique / life, life about us, the unique / laws, laws allow the unique / bodies, bodies count for the unique / chains, chains broken unique / channel, channel your release into, uniquely, yo / prepare, prepare for the spire, unique / claim, claim the same, "unique / light, light lives uniquely, wel / maintain, maintain your uniqueness, laugh / dear, dear enough to be near, unique / present, present the course unto the unique / presence, presence spent inside the unique / wisdom, wisdom comes unto the unique / mind, mind met at heart's release, unique / essence, essence into the unique / wisdom, wisdom comes to the unique / heart, heart's immaculate in love's abide, in, uniqueness / guards, guards burst and the gates open, unique / future, futures made within love's uniqueness / deprive, deprive less and appear more intact within uniqueness / limits, limits reached, unique / erase, erase past regrets, uniquely, forgiv / saint, a saint met, forgives, unique / Germain, Germain said, let me say, "uniquely"/ sends, sends a saint, uniques / love, love grew unique / flame, flame burns, unique / chicago, chicago flames with love's uniqueness / present, present your heart into uniqueness / power, power your our with love's resolution, uniquely due / supply, supply the our uniquely, love / money, money made resultant still into love's uniqueness / orate, orate about confession on uniqueness / applied, applied for the lend into love's uniqueness / millions, millions made, many given, love's uniqueness / explain, explain how to be unique, throughout, love / experience, express experiences unique to love / feel, feel the desire to be uniquely fulfille / decide, decide to deal, uniquely.

CHAPTER EIGHT

Deliver, deliver your good into the unique / reveal, reveal your reveal into the unique / divine, divine deliver into the unique / diametrics, diametrics reveal the dealt with delivery into the unique / freedom, freedom found in dealings unique / eternal,

eternal recover into the unique / blessings, blessings parallel into the unique / electric, electric dates with winnings unique / applications, applications for the unique / complete, complete concurs at the winnings unique / fulfill, fulfill the delivery that destiny gave into love's gift, unique / display, display day's unique / discard, discard the cards unique / delayed, delayed delivery unique / overture, overture found, uniques / closed, closed and accounts opened uniquell / carry, carry allows these uniques / this, this is our uniqueness / message, a message sent, unique / to, to an allow, uniques / hearts, hearts concede is, uniques / often, often into the uniques / men, men meant for the uniques / God, God gains another's uniqueness / believes, believes in recovery on the unique / your, your day, our gain, unique / perfection, perfection meant, uniquell / light, light's sight, uniques / gives, gives a reward unto the uniques / free, free to be unique / hearted, hearted consorts meet with your uniqueness / often, often men say, uniques / meant, meant for the uniquely hu-man / God, God gave us the unique / believes, believes within, the unique / yours, yours and ours, unique / perfection, perfection sent into the unique / light, light listens, unique / gives, gives us a patience unique / free, free-hearted, unique / hearted, hearted and held, unique / peace, peace reigns, unique / precious, precious to a pace, unique / presence, presence meant for, the unique / discourse, discourse delivers the unique / delivered, delivered into the unique / lighten, lighten into the unique / suva, suva ascents uniqueness / isles, isles and the wiles unique / speaks, speaks often of the unique / ocean, ocean scenes unique / pacific, pacifically paced and unique within, wave / insight, insights gained, unique / Teton, Teton towers reward the uniqueness / natured, natured wean into the uniqueness sent too, love / outflows, outflows found, electives, unique / love, love loaned the details within unique / goddess, a goddess gained, unique / spread, spread about the outings unique / touch, touch your uniqueness regaine / radiate, radiate about, unique / feel, feel the desire to see the unique / emulse, emulse with the pulses unique / pulse, pulse beats unique.

CHAPTER NINE
Portals, closely held and uniquely filled with love's uniqueness / complete, complete in a list inquired of, unique / change, change into sires unique / direct, direct and the directives sent into, uniqueness / diameter, diameter deep and done too, the unique / steers, steers clearly of the unique / joy, joy applies into the unique / connect, connect your uniqueness to the direct, love / radiant, radiant attitudes within love's inquiry into the unique / source, source sent directly through God's gate, heavenly inquire's unique / eternal, eternal into the transit filled within the unique / lighten, lighten the listen into the rays audibly unique / pure, pure estates buy into thee, unique / life, life gives the unique the gif / lights, lights on into God's uniqueness / purity, purity clarovoyant through God's gate / ascended, ascended through, the portal, you, unique / ideal, ideal days, unique / sun, sun days are unique gift / swept, swept through, thee, unique / beach, beach dates, unique / harmony, harmony made, complete, again, unique / harmonic, harmonic reveal, uniques / effect, effect given the unique / effort,

effort made to forgive, the unique / connect, connect the sort unique / goddess, goddess given, uniqueness / lights, lights lift into the unique / power, power apparent to the unique / intelligence squares to the unique / energy, energy gains the unique / love, love details ours, the unique abid / kind, kind apparel worn, unique / lives, lives another near, unique / I AM, I AM the won, uniquely given to God / powers, powers played upon waters deep in love unique / victory, victory given, know the clause is, love / mine, mine to dance with, life, unique / law, law won, God's gift, unique / watts, watts apply to the uniau / dynamic, dynamics lend unique / justice, justice applies unique / divinity, divinity done, unique / orders, orders apply too, the unique / clarity, clarity concurrent with the unique / purity, purity pares us nearly the unique / faith, faith includes the focus around integrity truthfully honed, unique / bliss, bliss gives us life's bound into the unique / breath, breath of the unique / fire, fire fed the unique / breathe, breathe warm within the unique / higher, higher sits the unique / deeper, deeper is still, the unique / widen, widen within the unique / denver, denver's date with the unique / magnetic, magnetic apply to the unique / poles, poles apart and warm with the unique / electric, electric chills fill with unique / presents, presents and gifts unique / gift, gift yourself uniquell / joys, joys about the unique / jewels, jewels deep in the unique / eyed, eyed and wide with the unique / grips, grips about us, the unique.

CHAPTER TEN
Powers, powers play into the intrigue with delegations of degrees deliciously unique / plenty, plenty made, unique / active, active ways, unique / plus, plus and the plenty won, unique / blazing, blazing borne aloft too, love, unique / burning, burning desired amiably unique / cleansing, cleansing came into love, unique / reflect, reflect values your uniqueness / redirect, redirect your source into, love, unique / exact, exact compassion, to a fashion, love' / current, current coincidence, hence, unique / connect, connect dates, unique / exacts, exacts a surge, unique / precise, precise require apace the lacing's current within thee, unique / precious, paced and soft, unique / perfect, sorts, unique / red, red and the seas raged into love's fluids unique / algae, algae wells, uniquely filled with love / ancestral, ancestral strains regained unique / blue, blue and the values uniquely valued into love / green, green and the gaze uniques / heals, heals and the meals uniques / redness, redness gives blood the birth, uniques / pigments, pigments paced ablaze the unique / photosynthetic, photosynthetic apply and the sigh energetic into God's gains, uniquely, love / sexual, sexual to a fault's default, appraise, raise, allow, healing's filling, unique / watered, watered and wed through with uniqueness within, God / moss, moss watered through God's uniqueness / core, core and the soar unique / gelidium, gelidium said green waves increase, unique / sargasso, sargasso scened unique / seen, seen into the uniques / calm, calm sent into the unique / strength, strength told, the unique / philosophy, a philosophy uniques / reason, reason played, unique / skills, skills meant, unique / strength, strength, test, unique / gained, gained a friend's respect for God's dearest connect, unique / revealed,

revealed a deal's respect, unique / render, render a dearest unique / risked, risked it all for the unique / known, known about through thee, unique / given, given a date, unique / west, west to the woods unique / synchronous, synchronous ascend, the parallel is uniques / harmony, harmony held us, uniques / moons, moons mate met, unique / given, given thee, transcend, unique / gather, gather at a wed, unique / relates, relates into thee, uniques / language, language gained, unique / visual, visual values, unique / symmetery, symmetry gained, unique / schooled, schooled in the tools uniques / factors, factors fed, unique / framework, framework becomes you, unique / uniquely, uniquely discuss the organization due love / tooled, tooled apply of the style unique / chained, chained about in venues unique / simply, simply said, unique/ biologically, biologically direct into thee, unique / works, works about us, the uniq / wonders, wonders why, the unique.

CHAPTER ELEVEN
Cultivation, cultivation clear to the central port, uniquely, love / rich, rich in winnings sung, uniqueness / feeds, feeds appear unique / vitamins, vitamins boost our detail into love's uniqueness / food, food delivered and uniquely sent into love / space, space made in love, unique / trades, trades made, agreed, unique / travels, travels about, unique / worlds, worlds appear uniques / degrees, degrees confered, unique / marina, marina abreast, unique / marine, marine, the life, uniques / sea, seas abide, unique / differs, differs in the details uniques / lacks, lacks freshen uniqueness / crossed, crossed above, the unique / plantings, plantings touch the unique / flowering, flowering ceilings are the unique / matching, matching about thee, the unique / numbered, numbered in the deal, uniques / swollen, swollen with incense uniquely blue to rose / clearly, clearly a prophet went before us, so unique / eloquent, eloquent gains, uniques / green, green to a trees delivery, unique / vegetate, vegetate less, be, unique / calcify, calcify sent into the unique / codices, codices coincide into thee, the unique / equate, equate your elate to the unique / family, family, finally, unique / species, species due a clarity unique / translate, translate for the uniques / stand, stand about within the unique / continual, continual the stand, unique / successive, succesive details on the unique / abandon, abandon found, the unique / fields, fields debate the unique / frames, frames afield the unique / staged, staged a band, uniques / submerge, submerged succumbs into the unique / float, float above the unique / swamp, swamped out, the unique / grass, grass grew into the unique / shrub, shrubs grew into the unique / tree, tree tales, unique / pond, ponds deep in the unique / growth, growth grew unique / deposits, deposits detail the unique / rich, rich into the unique / mineral, mineral mained unique / material, material manners unique / completion, completion comes, unique / successive, successive allow, energetically replete into the unique / begins, begins again too, love thee, the unique / abandon, abandon forgives the unique / wilder, wilder, wise, and unique / weeds, weeds deal with the unique / profane, profane grew the acknowledge unique / profound, profound and the drain discovered, the unique / unbound, unbound, extound, unique / central, central into the portal unique / chakra, chakra

opens unique / notochord, notochord's sword, unique / sight, sight seen, unique / victory, victory valued uniquely.

CHAPTER TWELVE
Electrical, electrical to a natural flow, unique / force, force felt, empowered, and unique / space, space paid, the unique / heart, heart and the start unique / homes, homes detail the unique / truths, truths tell is unique / throne, throne of delivery, unique / melts, melts above, the unique / angels, angels stood together for God, unique / stand, stand and gain, the unique / within, within and wed, the unique / flame, flames above, the unique / hue, hue over all, the unique / man, man made, the unique / humid, humid above and within the unique / sight, sight scene the unique / key, keys about, the unique / propogate, propogate the sort, unique / evolution, evolution comes, unique / period, period of the sort unique / lands, lands and the lends unique / vascular, vascular above this venue uniques / support, support comes unique / floral, floral the shove unique / major, major and the muse, unique / plants, plants delay and the deals make uniqueness / difference, difference becomes the unique / waved, waved and the winds come uniques / worlds, worlds collide unique / recreate, recreate your state uniques / separate, separate the few unique / scale, scales given thee, unique / musicals, musicals made, thge unique / scaled, scaled in the amused uniques / harmonically handles in the uniques / complex, complex comes the between complete unique / pianos, pianos pay the pave unique / shift, shift into the venuws unique / reflects, reflects detail the deity unique, God / cycle, cycle complete, know the won, unique / nitrogen, nitrogen's menu is thus, unique / bacterial, bacterial into the unique / symbiotic, symbiotic too, the unique / waters, waters wield the unique / ecosystem, ecosystem complete into the unique / completion, completion came into the unique / microecologic, microecologic and the logic unique / bodies, bodies and the beats unique / chromatic, chromatic and the crews unique / harmonic, harmonic and the harmonies unique / dramatic, dramatic to degrees unique / filled, filled and the freeings uniques / line, line and the signs unique / true, true enough to be, see us, uniques / vigorous, vigorous into the unique / reasoned, reasoned and the signed for uniques / controlled, controlled into the verify unique / mutated, mutated and stated unique / mutation, mutation and the station unique / range, range and the status unique / rate, rate yours unique / propogate, propogate's soar is unique / changed, changed and the challenge won unique / conditions, conditions create news, uniquest.

CHAPTER THIRTEEN
Results, results made, unique / desired, desired for thee, unique / effects, effects become thee, unique / division, division dues and the done, unique / stopped, stopped to find thee uniques / chromosomes, chromosomes content in the unique / split, split for the shores called unique / form, form found, venues fed, unique / gametes, gametes gained, unique / unite, unite again with the unique / cells, cells say won way, unique / sex, sex stays the same, unique / triploid, triploid delivery on the unique / diploid, diploid details the unique / plants, plants agree the unique / men,

men agree the light said, "unique"/ technique, technique about these uniques / sacred, sacred to the test won unique / energy, energy sent the unique / seal, seal the gift, unique / mandala, mandala deals for the uniques / heart, heart held with the unique / phoenix, phoenix felt in the uniques / feel, feel again the kiss unique / massive, massive abide wins the unique / awake, awake enough to say this, "unique"/ aware, aware of the uniqueness of love / compare, compare your confession to her allowance unique / naturally, naturally unique too, love / nurtured, nurtured in thee, the unique / spatial, spatial allow on the unique / nucleus, nucleus found for the unique / emergence, emergence melds, the unique / information, information said, the "unique"/ awaken, awaken within the unique / beyond, beyond and again, the unique / previous, previous won, the unique / shown, shown the waves unique. ./ wave, wave won, the unique / 33, 33 ways into the unique / creator, creator and the elate, unique / armored, armored into the enamored uniques / called, called for the aid sent, uniques / paced, paced and allowed too. the unique / quests, quests sent, the unique / mission, mission sent the message unique / guardian, guardian sent, the unique / will, will to be, unique / militant, militant to the mission unique / life, life and the lend is unique / peace, peace and the trill, uniques / place, place a peace into the unique / eternal, eternal and the supernal unique / trades, trades above and into thee, unique / curves, curves and the swerves into the unique / circles, circles about and within the unique / vitality, vitality vents the unique / able, able too, the unique / ability, ability too and the abide in God's unique wav / meridians, meridians meet in venues unique / matrix, matrix becomes sealed through thee, unique / possible, possible too, the unique / mayan, mayan plays, uniques / cycles, cycles and the seeds, uniques / remember, mayan cycles, complete.

THE GOD-MENTS
LEVEL 36

CHAPTER ONE

Scholar, scholar of the home, yomed, and meant to rent for God's loves / theologian, theologian and the chosen's extremes for uniquely lives God's / wealth, wealth of the nature aburst your living foundations / inspect, inspect a simple necklace cal God's loves / cures, cures and the simply connected too, God's / curious, curious to the details scented within God's loves / intersect, intersect the net of the retailing foundations called God's / vanished, vanished in a banished thoughts thrilling prepare for light foundations / note, note and the sorts paid for light tradition's of life foundations for God's greetings / reply, reply a retailing contentment for God's foundations / replies, replies a sizing Metatronically agreed too, love's foundations for God's gains / protect, protect allowances for God's Metatronic details on too, love's foundations / speculates, speculates and the sates won elective's foundationally gained, God's greetings foundationed / chance, chance allows your like God's foundations / syntax, syntax and the sent for like God's foundations, Metatronic / Pure, purely paid for, light's foundations, God's / thoughts, thoughts and the thrilling like foundations, God's / elixir, elixir and the mixture made for light's foundations, God's / living, living's liken and the giving's foundations, God's / sutra, God's / wholeness, God's / elevation, God's / duration, God's / flowering, God's / lights, God's / circulate, God's / stages, God's / goals, God's / dividends, God's / divine, divine details God's / charming, details God's / pearls, pearls paid for, God's / cultivated, cultivated cures for lightness, God's / works, / thrusts / strokes / stressed / throats / stages / stripped / pallets / shares / sublime / dabbles / magenta / strips / mats / meals / changes / respect / restitution / degrees / daring / esteen / earths / flares / leaks / extreme / consumption / sequesters / sequenced / sent / consumed / curtailed.

CHAPTER TWO

Curtains, truths, tools, tracts, agreeable, able, although, desired, gazed, grazed, extras, involved, dissolves, uses, grazed, golden, balance, glees, previews, reviews, startled, glare, starts, affairs, hearts, clues, pairs, pause, causes, glues, clear, cliche, camps, campaign, welcome, feeling, felt, tacts, backs, paramount, sailing, necessary, dealing, created, staffs, kneeling, dealt sought, seating, vaulted, stance, values, chills, valleys, changes, ashes, boiling, broiling, envisions, visions, explore, visionarys, emerges, explains, refrains.

CHAPTER THREE

Electrically, set, freely, bet, better, embrace, kittens, minutes, orbits, fluffs, factors, felt, feelings, resorts, breeds, balanced, cautiously, kept, freedoms, songs, manacles, drop, fluff, regards, brilliance, reigns, curtails, relates, gingers, explains, notifies, condicals, bags, spoken, sails, set, rejoice, journey, passions, paired, sixty, sets, sorts, electis, sourced, shipped, backs, abraids, abortive, lips, lessons, shared, promotions, fly, influences, abreast, adjusted, lights, pursuits, aplenty, shed, intended, adjusted, wardens, robbed, rubbed, regards, strokes, squeezed, rushed, pulled, pictured, boxed, balistrades, bait, positive, regards, gained,

throughout, admits, agrees, desires, dies, capitalized, moments, totally, freed, totals, innate, substantial, gains, concisely, worded, maneuvers, closed.

CHAPTER FOUR

Closures, coming, degrees, bursting, panics, conversant, streets, hush, chapters, explored, orientations, subtle, passings, concepts, settled, settle, now, modems, detailed, practices, participate, drawn, sustained, substanced, hearts, aims, projects, algae, browns, typos, sports, coffers, myecin, subcutaneous, fats, felt, browns, lessons, learning, ladders, lingers, sounds, pursuits, utilize, unwound, sounds, changes, achievements, centers, words, wonders, seize, revelations, reach, awaken, homes, havoc, caters, suspense, wounds, places, patterns, chains, sets, songs, singing, placed.

CHAPTER FIVE

Place, pursuits, desires, dialects, languaged, sects, sectors, sections, suburbs, cancerian, delivery, donations, straits, stratus, joins, gingerly, jasmined, pools, experienced, sunlit, fountains, fortress, wells, 'words, heedings, heavens, rings, galactic, speeches, splendorous, temples, thrones, homes, response, details, sighted, scandals, dound, pleased, times, methods, militant, denies, dies, female, wiles, recovery, reads, styles, masculine, replies, delivered, deligts, sizes, places, lambs, flowers, lands, sequesters, styles, joined, changed, calms, claims, choose, opens, transverse, transfers, chimes, finds, allows.

CHAPTER SIX

Perfects, basic, humanity, advanced, spans, minutes, miracles, attends, hands, passions, rations, ensues, creatives, venues, humans, kindness, experts, experiences, supreme, trims, uniqueness, agreements, totality, balances, ultimate, awareness, bosom, offerings, details, God's, gained, thrills, thanks, scents, sent, God's, Face, metatron, one, with, yours, electric, kiss, invitations, hearts, deepen, instincts, loves, laughter, feeds, escapes, entry, advantages, love's, happens, things, thoughts, thanks, helps, aids, wings, worn, won, mercy, engaged, seek, sought, found, recovers, attends, lover.

CHAPTER SEVEN

Within, God's, befriend, humanity, ultimate, weaves, woven, stills, channels, hearts, obey, calls, essentials, loves, interiors, intregity, keys, codes, seeds, specialty, delivered, aim, finality, musical, mends, finds, yearns, years, past, 56, 3, when, times, recovers, trusts, thanks, God's, eternally, simply, suggestive, all, over, through, thorough, agreed, worn, within, God, is, your, Friend,, not, your, foe, let, go, within,, enjoy, sex,, life,, passion,, pleasure, by, has.

CHAPTER EIGHT

A measure, eternal, where, is, your, heart, your, head, by, elect, in, your, chest, where, within, wanton, sin, since, elect, follows, correct, refuse, lessen, sparks, of God's, respect, for, challenging, chores, like, helpful, agree, too, be, basically, free, and fonder, still, to, see, aspire, as, the, degree, of, fastest, stars, called, human, hearts, in, prayer, eternal, to, the, light, called, God, and, the, son, called, one, and, the, christian, corps, and, the, Buddha's, baste, in, the, swelling, accept, for, all, there, is, for, love, God's, gift, history, historically, spent, on, man, as the, direct, arrive, at, God's, door, and, the, flooring, gift, that, a, happy, heart, is,, still,, to, the, core, and, dancing, in, pleasant, relief, the, peaceful, gaze, God, gave, a, happy, each, and, to, the.

CHAPTER TEN
"Other", we, all, are, one, and, eternally, set, is, a, jewel, direct, to, the, heart, of, God, and, the, gaze, that, felt, like, mine, and, often, still, I, see, the, eternity, of, how, we, loved, for, God, and, the, getting, on, of, how, we, were, elected, to, see, precisely, what, we, as, mankind, can, deliver, and, the, given, becomes, the, send, and, the, living.

CHAPTER ELEVEN
The, ascendant, and, the, tackle, boxed, in, is, that, when, we, spend, our, parts, on, less, than, all, and, still, we, seek, and, see, the, often, said, example, of, all, the, stars, included, in, one, grand, meeting, burst, called, electrically, God's, and, God, said, "let, there, be, light. ", Humanity, WINS, when, God, give, us, all, sweet, deliver, to, thee, living, flower, of, peaceful, deliver, at, the, father's, gate, and, the, mother's, heart, this, earth, this, place, of, God's, sweet, passion, for, a, potion,, a, creation, so, rich, that, not, even, this, heart, could, contain, the, pulse, of, a, human's, pleasure, and, a, woman;s, explain, and, a, man's, gift, as, self, examine, becomes, the lift, to God's, exact, lift, called, delivery, to, the, cells, of, forgive, and, the, life.

CHAPTER TWELVE
Max 64 squared.

CHAPTER THIRTEEN
Of, living, in, the, loving, way, called, perfectly, exactly, essentially, eternally, paternally, patterned, and, measured, exactness, the, in, fact, exposure, to, composure, precision, antems, peace, pieces, plunder, places, kept, cobras, clavicles, shoulders, arms, chins, pushing, runnings, cords, closures, exposures, handsome, estates, of, landed, entreaty, and, the, nape, of, necks, unburdened, by, the, simple, belief, in, release, to, the, truth, of, this, matter, the, trust, in, love.

THE SANCTUARY-MENTS
LEVEL 37

CHAPTER ONE

Comment, comment on the campaign for the sanctuary called ma / commune, commune within soon and apparently love's sanctuary / control, control the settle meant for sanctuary / contempt, contempt resents sanctuary / consent, consent for the setle seen at sanctuary / convert, convert the cavort through light seen's sanctuary / friends, friends found in the feeling for a light sanctuary / distinction, distinction dialates your sanctuary / various, various sorts say "sanctuary / groups, groups power filled through sanctuary / social, social cues and the moves for sanctuary / cue, cue and the comply for light sanctuary / majority, majority sent for and the restore called for in light sanction of the sanctuary called, men / muse, muse and the reuse amazed through light sanctuary / inform, inform and the storm across your light sanctuary / assume, assume and the settle called pure likened sanctuary / consent, consent to be truly free for sanctuary / truly, truly mentioned essentially for love's freed sanctuary / beautiful, beautiful to the need for a listening way too, sanctuary / condemn, condemn less the friendly sanctuary / appear, appear to be strictly sanctuarie / sympathize, sympathize for the size worn, sanctuary / spurn, spurn for the yearning regards for a lighten sanctuary / inverse, inverse and the sanctuary sent too, lightly, hom / object, object of the recourse found in sanctuary / collapsed, collapsed and the quizically sanctuarie / distance, distance dilute into the scene's sanctuary / donate, donate and the daily felt sanctuary / equality, equality cures and the feelings sent for sanctuary / november, november and the nimble's sanctuary / culture, culture and the creative's sanctuary / strand, strand and the templed spend's sanctuary / stair, stair across the simple's sanctuary / charge, charge across the query's sanctuary / work, work and the circle's sanctuary / assets, assets and the sentinel's sanctuary / quality, quality and the thicken's sanctuary / longer, longer and the legend's sanctuary / linger, linger and the longer's sanctuary / drift, drift and the dealing's sanctuary / differ, differ and the sanctuary's ascend too, God's amend for light's legends, and the living's latitudes living nearest entirely and sincerely within God's lights and the lightening's bolt along life's avenues, sanctuary / prospect, prospect acquires and the sire's sanctuary / apply, apply and the lightening's lift allows life's sanctuary / applies, applies and pillow's sanctuary / times, times and the temple song's sanctuary / tints, tints and the typical sanctuary / home, home and the height for sanctuarie / yome, yell for the templed time sanctuary / diverse, diverse and the dealt for sanctuary / converse, converse and the content's sanctuary / profit, profit and the made for feeling's sanctuary / preference, preference and the pillow's sanctuary / press, press and the hearing set for fullness found in sanctuary / distance, distance and the delivery found of sanctuary / project, project and the present for sanctuary / projects, projects and the correction sent for sanctuary / similarities, similarities and the singular's sanctuary / simple, simple and the said for "sanctuary / sincere, sincere and the simply said, sanctuary / phone, phone and the recall for fortitude's sanctuary / company, company and the cues for life's fortunate sanctuary / nuzzle, nuzzle and the nestle's sanctuary / compare, compare and the cures for lightened sanctuary / gate, gate and the green crew for life's sanctuary.

CHAPTER TWO

Evolve, evolve for the nature's nightlined sanctuary / subtitle, subtitle the ascendment's "sanctuary / robe, robe and the worn through's sanctuary / spur, spur and the thorough's sanctuary / spears, spears allow the listening sanctuary / pageant, pageant and the material too, sanctuary / classic, classic and the occurence's sanctuary / define, define and the deluge for detailed sanctuary / astonish, astonish and the listened forth, sanctuary / similar, similar and the stamped off, sanctuarie / serves, serves and the suggested, santuar / service, service and the choir sings, sanctuary / flirt, flirt forth and reallow your sanctuary / grew, grew and the greedy lost, sanctuary / voiced, voiced and the vaunted agree too, sanctuary / heard, heard and the should be, sanctuary / hear, hear and the heard forth, sanctuary / here, here is the healing's sanctuary / follow, follow the fellow's sanctuary / fertile, fertile to the feeling, sanctuary / fury, fury and the forgotten's sanctuary / fossil, fossil outed, sanctuary / multiply, multiply and the value stays for sanctuary / extra, extra paid and made for sanctuary / elect, elect and the carry on too, sanctuary / entrance, entrance blocked forth, sanctuary / wallets, wallets emptied less, sanctuary / woven, woven and the weekend's sanctuary / wave, wave and the willow's sanctuary / wedding, wedding set for may attend too, sanctuary / convex, convex and the concurrence made too, sanctuary / concave, concave and the care less, sanctuary / compress, compress and the storage set for sanctuary / work, work and the willing's sanctuary / watch, watch and the miracle freed, sanctuary / warrant, warrant and the winning's sanctuary / support, support and the steering's sanctuary / member, member and the limber's sanctuary / remember, remember and the timbered sanctuary / loss, loss lessens sanctuary / contest, contest and the cure for life's sanctuary / consecrate, consecrate and the capably sanctuarie / election, election and the lesson made, sanctuary / relate, relate and the regarded's sanctuary / elates, elates and the life lend's sanctuary / evade, evade less the lessoned sanctuary / webs, webs break and the beat broke in too sanctuary / spurt, spurt made for, sanctuary / select, select and the set for news made in light sanctuary / sever, sever the ties, sanctuary / cut, cut the cords too, sanctuary / curl, curl away for, sanctuary / only, only and allow too, sanctuary / repair, repair the relation's shores, sanctuary / watch, watch for your shore's sanctuarie / far, far and the felt for sanctuary / analysis, analysis made too, sanctuary / grand, grand and the greeting's sanctuary / endeavor, endeavor and the sever came, sanctuarie / mask, mask and the material's sanctuary / swallow, swallow the fellowed sanctuary / whip, whip a whistled sanctuary / sold, sold a lot for sanctuary / wind, wind and the whistle's sanctuary.

CHAPTER THREE

Flake, flake and the natural's sanctuary / trunk, trunk towed sanctuary / branch, branch rose, sanctuary / port, port of the sort calibrated through light sanctuary / sweeten, sweeten the portal within life sanctuary / two, two to the known sanctuary / summer, summer said, "begin too, sanctuary / side, side of the sentient, sanctuary / low, low to the stray's sanctuary / turn, turn to the tendril's sanctuary / loose, loose and the pleasing forth's sanctuary / net, net and the neter's sanctuary / air, air paradigms freed to sanctuary / send, send a patient plee too, sanctuary / spare, spare into an arise come sanctuary / winter, winter to the wisen come through sanctuary / flip, flip across the central straits called sanctuary / exit, exit across the planetary sanctuary / floor, floor the mortal's sanctuary / pay, pay less and earn more, sanctuary / window, window on the wisened sanctuary / flip, flip apart less, sanctuary / corner, corner and the corridor for sanctuary / crossing, crossing in the invented sanctuarie / drape, drape a daily dollar for light's sanctuary / diversity, diversity due a sanctuary / locate, locate a lesson's sanctuary / sublime, sublime to the symbol's sanctuary / lust, lust may lend a sanctuary too, love' / diver, diver dealt a sanctioned sanctuary / locate, locate a legend's sanctuary / battery, battery of the saturdayed sanctuary / incline, incline in the empirical sanctuary / engulf, engulf over all, sanctuary' / reason, reason and the season's sanctuary / froth, froth and the feeling's sanctuary / melt, melt and the meal's reply for sanctuary / fact, fact and the fiction comes sanctuary / surface, surface and the central's sanctuary / notation, notation across the seating's sanctuary / pharaonic, pharaonic allowance's sanctuary / novelty, novelty knew, sanctuary / preliminary, preliminary to the known called sanctuary / square, square to a ceiling's sanctuary / pivot, pivot to a point won, sanctuary / series, series through a centurion's deal on sanctuary / oscillating, oscillating vibrating sanctuary / successive, succesive suggestions onto material freedom, a sanctuary foun / universal, universal experience commends your sanctuary / gestation, gestation and the stationary's functions sanctuary / maternal, maternal and the internal sanctuary / vegetation, vegetation values your sanctuary / dimensional, dimensional to an intentional sanctuary / remain, remain in a ratings coming sanctuary / life, life on the leadings sanctuary / galaxy, galaxy glued within life's stupendous truth / visualized, visualized in the size's ascends and the truth told throughout your family sanctuary / veil, veil off and the cough ends through sanctuary / numbers, numbers and the kneeling's sanctuary / vessel, vessel directly valuable through the veiny sanctuary / synthesis, synthesis trued allowed a sanctuary / torches, torches carried laid down sanctuary / unlock, unlock the passion's sanctuarie / spoken, spoken compares on light sanctuary.

CHAPTER FOUR
Highest, highest ways wave deep in sanctuary / lunar, lunar and the led for sanctuary / celestial, celestial allowance and the thrust past your sanctuary / yoga, yoga made a routinest sanctuary / occult, occult and the insult past sanctuary / animating, animating and the station called for, sanctuary / faithful, faithful and fellowed ship's sanctuary / effect, effect of the function's sanctuary / telluride, telluride and the inside's sanctuary / attune, attune and the moon's rise too, sanctuary / amenity, amenity and the mentally freed sanctuary / vital, vital to the signs sold, sanctuary / pylon, pylon and the penitent less sanctuary / terminates, terminates and the narrows placed, sanctuary / sphinx, sphinx appear and the nearest sanctuary / proceed, proceed to the deeded sanctuary / court, court the sort who stay in sanctuary / entire, entire in the synthesis for

our sanctuary / diamond, diamond deals too, sanctuary / detour, detour dates your daily sanctuary / daunt, daunt and the dent less, sanctuary / door, door across the forever's sanctuary / doorway, doorway deals melt sanctuary' / given, given simply sanctuary / opening, opening commanded sanctuary / laugh, laugh allowance made, sanctuary' / love, love the leading, sanctuary / explode, explode daily through light's sanctuary / pulse, pulse across rays sanctuary / explained, explained lessen too a sanctuary / explore, explore options for your sanctuary / absolve, absolve the central sanctuary / rest, rest for a while too, sanctuary / rather, rather be's sanctuary / reckon, reckon and the rewarded's sanctuary / regard, regard for the random's sanctuary / resume, resume and the rooms reach sanctuary / rapture, rapture and the reset's sanctuary / round, round and attuned too, sanctuary / rappel, rappel around strong sanctuary / rap, rap abounds in sanctuary / roars, roars and arouses your sanctuary / shovel, shovel and the shining's coming sanctuary / snore, snore around these sanctuarie / sheer, sheer and the shingle's sanctuary / shoed, shoed for the shoring's sanctuary / shoes, shoes worn across floor's sanctuary / shower, shower and the powered sanctuary / champagne, champagne's committee and the curative sanctuary / gone, gone along for sanctuary / wide, wide along way's sanctuarie / dry, dry sleep and the kept explain for sanctuary / sleep, sleep nightly through sanctuary / sustain, sustain a simple sanctuary / stain, stain off and the gain found in sanctuary / cover, cover a chilling warmly sanctuarie / deep, deep in a daily's sanctuary / chinese, chinese example in these sample sanctuarie / chance, chance paid for sanctuary / shivering, shivering suggest and the rest in warm sanctuary / dancer, dancer dealt a svelte sanctuary / chances, chances paid for the light's sanctuary / chime, chime in too, the sanctuary / landed.

CHAPTER FIVE
Float, float and the winding wayed insanity plause, ability, sanctuary' / achieve, achieve an elegant relate through a material sanctuary / lap, lap past above and beyond the actuarial sanctuary / breath, breath of the beat and the beauty paid for sanctuary / stroke, stroke and the spoken acquire too, sanctuary / commit, commit to the moment, again, sanctuary / composed, composed as arose and well within thee, sanctuary / coral, coral cayes and the keys paved snnul meant, sanctuary / sell, sell a vote for the holy host, a sanctuary / sword, sword cut and the cube made sanctuary / date, date a daily demuse and the bemuse gained sanctuary / do, do a lot for the caught within, sanctuary / knot, erase knots through sanctuary / lost, lost has found again, sanctuary / find, find a fellow, sanctuary / strand, strand fo the diplomatic keyed sanctuary / wine, wine weighs less in sanctuary / waiver, waiver most to sanctuary / symbolic, symbolic gifts madke sanctuary / language, language hosted, sanctuary' / lend, lend a lenticular sanctuary / vibrate, vibrate to the rates electric, sanctuary / votive, votive burned and yearning forth in sanctuary / pellet, pellets tossed and heaven caught through sanctuary / raft, raft again within the flow too, sanctuary / camp, camp nearby and try your sanctuary / value, value for the meaning's sanctuary / ramps, ramps across heaven's great news sanctuary / ride, ride a ridiculous slide through

sanctuary / rise, rise to the throning sanctuary / plumber, plumber spent for sanctuary / mom, mom made elective sanctuary / dad, dad given dual exhaust for sanctuary / explore, explore more opinionations, sanctuary / won, won for the wow in sanctuary / swords, swords said "cut the few" called ill too, sanctuary / cuts, cuts made, again, sanctuary / source, source becomes you, sanctuary / means, means to stay too, sanctuary / evolve, evolve into resolve for sanctuary / solve, solve the riddle's sanctuary / evolution, evolution to the solution for sanctuary / turn, turn to the won through, sanctuary / love, love another's waiver best through sanctuary / imagine, imagine, yes, too, sanctuary / report, report the sort who say "yes, sanctuary / over, over and the values paid through sanctuary / one, one in the ways gained, sanctuary / like, like a listened too, called, sanctuary / these, these are the raving sanctuarie / flame, flame to the fellows, sanctuary / adore, adore a planetary chore called sanctuary / initiation, initiation due, too, sanctuary / carry, carry a weapon, love, to sanctuary / fly, fly to the freedom's rings for sanctuary / kingdom, kingdom comes in, sanctuary / explain, explain for sanctuary / among, among us, sanctuary / condolence, condolence sent for sanctuary / clear, clear the cutting, sanctuary / clasp, clasp an electric sanctuary / convert, convert to the recourse run, sanctuary.

CHAPTER SIX

Planes, planes and the players found, sanctuary / cash, cash for the creature's sanctuary / embraced, embraced and erased past, sanctuary' / rebel, rebel over done, sanctuary / revel, revel in the One made sanctuary / splendor, splendor found in the town called "sanctuary / roll, roll to another sound for sanctuary / rule, rule made, love, your sanctuary / rebate, rebate the relate for sanctuary / kin, kin made befriend through sanctuary / kind, kind enough to stay through sanctuary / correlate, correlate the recall through sanctuary / elate, elate over the revelations due your sanctuary / relate, relate to the staying sanctuary / resonate, resonate regarding sanctuary / regard, regard for the regard less, sanctuary / tame, tame and the flame renews into love's sanctuary / maneuver, maneuver about and then mend your sanctuary / mend, mend and become light sanctuary / matter, matter met throughout our shouting arise into light's sanctuary / more, more and the soaring temporary into love's sanctuary / route, routes past and throughout life's sanctuary / given, given directives and the invectives past life's sanctuary / trust, trust and the tools spent in loving's sanctuary / agree, agree to see lifelong in your sanctuary / decree, decree and the daily's sanctuary / district, district details and the sailing sanctuary / deed, deed dealt with and then thee a sanctuary / duel, duel for the flowered sanctuary / fuel, fuel fused and the mused thin sanctuary / come, come throughout and then into a sanctuary / key, key cued and the melting arrival throughout your sanctuary / too, too and the tabular data'a sanctuary / end, end and the sung within sanctuary / reference, reference and the reired's sanctuary / plant, plant and the pillow's sancctaur / peace, peace for the challenged relax into life's sanctuary / plurally, plurally sent entirely throughout your sanctuary / ancient, ancient details and the thankfully spent sanctuary / agree, agree detailed daily in

a calendric sanctuary / reward, reward into desired appearance's sanctuary / rehearse, rehearse and the rewards forthright sanctuary / is, is then? sanctuary / love, love joins your sanctuary / know, know then how too sanctuary / other, other thrilling's sanctuarie / explain, explain a genuine enthrall too and then too, our sample's sanctuary / explore, explore appears about and thence ours sanctuarie / symbol, symbol deep in remembrance and the dates gained sanctuarie / soar, soar across the detached estate's release into love's sanctuary / appraise, appraise and the raging revenue's rewarded mystery toured sanctuary / acknowledge, acknowledge and the heights in sanctuary / incense, incense and the detail's sanctuary / succinct, succinct details and the smells in sanctuary / suppress, suppress off and the feelings tossed into love's sanctuary / elapse, elapse along listening's sanctuary / elope, elope knows allowance into God's recall for love's sanctuary / allow, allow a recall of all you are through sanctuary / digress, digress to a retest of your diligence into sanctuary / mother, mother made home too, a friend found, sanctuary / cow, cow cave's sanctuary / immortal, immortal meetings in too, sanctuary / elements, elements spake within, sanctuary / sacred, sacredness sent across thread's sanctuary.

CHAPTER SEVEN

Anxiously, anxiously paved with sanctuary / flight, flights falling into sanctuary / cosmic, cosmic cures came too, sanctuary / indefinable, indefinable apply too, sanctuary / entity, entity trails across through sanctuary / consecrated, consecrated occurs and the captive's release into life's sanctuary / raise, raise a parallel decide to be, into, sanctuary / gross, gross is done, remember? sanctuary / instant, instant recall's sanctuary / cerebral, cerebral shouts for sanctuary / provoking, provoking paths and the plants on too, sanctuary / forgive, forgive a fortunate sanctuary / over, over and value's sanctuary / camp, camp occurs too, sanctuary / declares, declares detail's due sanctuary / dare, dare appears in these sanctuarie / fountain, fountain filled within sanctuary / pane, pane's state, break free, sanctuary / pain, pain out and in too, sanctuary / blue, blue days over and due? sanctuary / simple, simple states win a sanctuary / aquamarine, aquamarine in a tan sanctuary / periwinkle, perinwinkle plans and a standard sanctuary / electric, electric trails and the thrills come, sanctuary / sonic, sonic tombs off through sanctuary / archive, archive's built throughout sanctuarie / stove, stove strait's sanctuary / give, give us this day, love's sanctuary / oval, oval values and the remaining sanctuary / regain, regain a raging experience into life's love / reclaim, reclaim a random experience for love's detail / reunite, reunite and the rates done too, sanctuary / recommend, recommend a recapture in love / rejuvenate, rejuvenate your door's way into sanctuary / lump, lump allows sanctuary / bump, bump over and the built for, sanctuary / drink, drink dealt with through sanctuary / paul, paul paid a repentant phase into the light's sanctuary / pearl, pearl estates and the rates run, sanctuary / pleasure, pleasure's appealing forgive into, sanctuary / contour, contour comes too, compares then, sanctuary / conceed, conceed to the deeded sanctuary / compare, compare occurs within, sanctuary /

benevolent, benevolent a ppearnace into light's sanctuary / bond, bond made and forgiven through thoroughly sanctuary / borne, borne in thee, status for, sanctuary / far, far and the feeling's come too, sanctuary / head, head details your sanctuary / jolly, jolly gems and the gentle sway's sanctuary / music, music amuses and the muses match made, sanctuary / energy, energy details durate's sanctuary / choir, choir occurs daily into a sanctuary / video, video vaunts your sanctuary / trivia, trivia trails through your sanctuary / train, train allows yours these sanctuarie / session, session allows more sanctuarie / hast, hast though a pension planned in sanctuary / boast, boast about your lovely sanctuary / mast, mast mixed in mention's sanctuary / ghost, ghost about us and the legend's sanctuary / define, define dealt within, sanctuary' / weave, weave wed throughout life's sanctuary / worn, worn allow in the how too, sanctuary / child, child chosen and the raven's wed with sanctuary.

CHAPTER EIGHT

Capable, capable in the query onto sanctua / cast, cast allows you sanctuary / torn, torn aparts trim sanctuary / lime, lime lends sanctuary / doubt, doubt done for, sanctuary / refrain, refrain remains your's sanctuary / give, give crystalline tour's sanctuary / sang, sang for the sealing's sanctuary du / sung, sung allowance shown consistent sanctuary / steer, steer clears in sanctuary / abroad, abroad in abide for sanctuary / God, God gazed into light's sanctuary / gain, gain a detailed quip past trails too, sanctuary / gorge, gorge across and the regains due your sanctuary / galley, galleys viewed into light's sanctuary / view, view and the value's sanctuary / value, value and the veins due, sanctuary / conceed, conceed concurs that winning lines our heart's details for love's languag / indeed, indeed we daily apply for sanctuary / revel, revel in your youthful sanctuary / resurrect, resurrect has become the wave too, sanctuary / point, point into apparent sanctuary / eternal, eternal notes and the votes throughout your sanctuary / avenue, avenue allows your sanctuary / street, street stares past your sanctuary / stars, stars apparent in your sanctuary / cars, cars daily pleased with sanctuary / sidewalk, sidewalk sold for sanctuary / booth, booth built across your sanctuary / liars, liars left and held across your's sanctuary / kindle, kindle a craft called sanctuary / soil, soil tossed into winds worth sanctuary / listen, listen to the lighten's sanctuary / lesson, lesson made pleasing through your sanctuary / walking, walking past and points in too, sanctuary / wind, wind past your sanctuary / when, when too, sanctuary / why, why knot? sanctuary / where, where when sanctuary / well, well enough too, sanctuary / skimmed, skimmed across your sanctuary / scare, scares over due, sanctuary / spell, spells dealt with, sanctuary / implore, implore and the soaring count's sanctuary / channel, channel past through sanctuary / open, open doors in sanctuary / inside, inside spent in sanctuary / vein, vein vast then, sanctuary / chimps, chimps chained to mankind's escape? relax in thee, sanctuary / glue, glue glazed through thrusted trusted sanctuary / gear, gear gaps simply sanctuarie / gain, gain too, sanctuary / explain, explain please, your's, sanctuary?/ lend, lend a lesson your sanctuary / lure, lure her home too, sanctuary

/ lather, lather in the listening's sanctuary / land, land bought and the made for, sanctuary / boulder, boulder bade for, sanctuary / swim, swim into your sanctuary / beat, beat next, sanctuary' / line, line lost then found in sanctuary / lace, lace past within heart's landed sanctuary / lance, lance less, sanctuary' / chance, chance made for, sanctuary.

CHAPTER NINE

Cane, cane and the lane electric in bamboo's blue-green gain for love's sanctuary / hurricane, hurricane held forth as within we'd sanctuary / done, done and the sun's entire sanctuary / sprout, sprout within and without within love's sanctuary / sustained, sustained allow and the placement within God's perfect sanctuary / slow, slow to the beast and the bend within to the loving return's sanctuary / beast, beast known and the road sent good-bye's sanctuary / slew, slew another's askew example of light's sanctuary / overdue, overdue in the venue's light sanctuary / complain, complain less, find more, inn, sanctuary / compare, compare daily's notes for sanctuary / share, share a spoken entirety for light's sanctioned sanctuary / relax, relax most in the host for life's sanctuary / relate, relate to the rapture's sanctuary / release, release daily's sanctuary / round, round heard, sanctuary' / rendezvous, rendezvous made and agreed too, love / strain, strain details our durate's condition throughout love's endur / lunge, lunge across the ratings detailed apply for love's lightenin / due, due your own satisfaction then, love' / science, science and the senses sent your sanctuary / metabolize, metabolize and the size within's sanctuary / size, size spent in sanctuary / soar, soar past the door's sanctuary / ozone, ozone commune and the amuse meant for sanctuary / clone, clones escape too, sanctuary / clown, clowns meant for sanctuary / contract, contract sent for and found in sanctuary / spite, spite out and the shouted ascend is into love's sanctuary / misery, misery over and the dues meant too, sanctuary / out, out and then sent for, sanctuary / seen, seen across lintels strewn blood red with blue raspberries and ancient stews of hyssop green remember's love / touch, touch a daily deaire to see for all comply within love's allowance and the ascent into light's attire worn delicately dear into life's remaining acquire for sanctuary / tune, tune allowed within life's parallel sanctuary / fork, fork allowed apparent within sanctuary / heart, heart dealt with in sanctuary / bless, bless this moment's coming sanctuary / hamper, hamper less and wins sanctuary / hymn, hymn hardy and the party for sanctuary / park, park along lines deep in sanctuary / rip, rip aroused for sanctuary / pail, pails cast aside too, sanctuary / sort, sort your start with sanctuary / ascend, ascend made into sanctuary / hispanic, hispanic duos cast too, sanctuary / hebraic, hebraic example in the sample's made sanctuary / shame, shame over, done, in, sanctuary / cart, cart past and the cast forth too, sanctuary / abrupt, abrupt led too, sanctuary / sustain, sustain a challenged sanctuary' / stand, stand for light's sanctuary / bald, bald bays bought your sanctuary / light, light led and the fed forth, sanctuary / like, like and the spikes worn sanctuary / found, found and the fellow's sanctuary / pond,;pond past and the cast for sanctuary / thai, thai told, one side's sanctuary / genuine, genuine joining's sanctuary' / friend,

friend found in sanctuary / heart, heart held and the dates wound into sanctuay / universe, universe moves into your sanctuary / join, join a jolly mate's sanctuary / sperm, sperm sold and the bold spent in sanctuary / notable, notable news of sanctuary.

CHAPTER TEN

Gift, gift given and gained through your sanctuary / aspire, aspire to attire your sanctuary / well, well enough to see through you, sanctuary / wealth, wealth made through the word sold, sanctuary / frog, frog fed and the pond bled with a sound significant to love's blessed sanctuary / periodic, periodic require and the spiral into love's sanctuary / shell, shell game's sanctuary / arabic, arabic acquire's meant for sanctuary / horizontal, horizontal dues and the daily's suggestive sanctuary / element, element of amuse and the menu for your sanctuary / bottom, bottom sided allow and the shower's sanctuary / metallic, metallic amuse and the meaning sent for in love's sanctuary / staggered, staggered steering and the lighten's sanctuary / vertical, vertical fellows and the financed sanctuary / halogens, halogens hues and the happen's sanctuary / inert, inert allowance and the gallant fellow's sanctuary / aromatherapy, aromatherapy's route to the leanest sanctuary / grant, grant found, finest, land's sanctuary / figure, figure wellness lettered sanctuary' / profile, profile felt for sanctuary / plus, plus details sold through sanctuary / tabular, tabular sorts gained sanctuary / tube, tubes tapped into, sanctuary' / tubular, tubular suggestion's sanctuary / charm, charm made and then suggested too, sanctuary' / immense, immense desire to change too, sanctuary / taste, taste a treatied sanctuary / race, race past and the taste told for sanctuary / rules, rules allow your sanctuary / sanctum, sanctum sealed and the willing allow's given sanctuary / secure, secure in durate's found sanctuary / palace, place your palace dates at the door for sanctuary / pure, pure enough to suggest for sanctuary / ports, ports placed allow into central's sanctuary / fired, fired fellow's sanctuary / cross, cross them twice and then find another's sanctuary / line, line led and the listen in's sanctuary / flame, flame and the feeling's spent, sanctuary / waits, waits allow and the shower's sent sanctuary / waiter, waiter made the lover's sanctuary / wax, wax important through love's sanctuary / bliss, bliss bellows in too, sanctuary / bare, bare your soul's relate and release the light's require into love's sanctuary / boorish, boorish benote of the votes for sanctuary / micro, micro news sanctuarie / macro, macro moves gained sanctuary / more, more days in sanctuary / mates, mates mellowed for your sanctuary / paris, paris pays for sanctuary / within, within wells due sanctuary / star, star allowed for sanctuary / climate, climate controls your sanctuary / bold, bold enough to say, yes, too, sanctuary / late, late leads through threaded sanctuary / shorts, shorts often worn in sanctuary / stripe, stripe sealed across, sanctuary / compel, compel for the sanctuary / curl, curl round these sanctuarie / adore, adore moves into sanctuary / star, stars sent forth too, sanctuary / sketch, sketch allows for sanctuary / vital, vital days and the zone spent for sanctuary / sign, sign your days with light's sanctify then thee, sanctuary / up, up and then these, the sanctuary.

CHAPTER ELEVEN

Compute, compute and the attitudes made for light's sanctuary / computer, computer measured access through sanctuarie / live, live and the lighten's legendary sanctuary / pentagram, pentagramed plenty and the pliant kind's sanctuary / center, center and the enchantment meant for sanctuary / dazzles, dazzles and the dealing's sanctuary / intellects, intellects and the agree meant for sanctuary / correspond, correspond and the respond for light's daily sanctuary / deluxe, deluxe detail and the daily's sanctuary / contract, contract cues and the mental amuse for light's sanctuary / return, return deals with a welcome sanctuary / reward, rewards given and the sword's gain drew allowance into your sanctuary / script, script written and sent for within your sanctuary / scriptures, scriptures and surrender's daily sanctuary / strain, strain brought forth in lightening sanctuary / concrete, concrete to the surface sent through life's leading sanctuary / heat, heat held to the moistest sanctuary / resonate, resonate with the relate for sanctuary / razor, razor raids and the goodness for your sanctuary / blades, blades burst in sanctuary / burn, burn out and then too, sanctuary / wrap, wrap allows your sanctuary / column, column cues and the codes for a light win's sanctuary / intervening, intervening and the weaning allow for sanctuary / active, active agree for the listening sanctuary / similar, similar sentinels and the suggestion for sanctuary / properties, properties and perusal for life's suggested sanctuary / outside, outside and suggested adore's sanctuary / number, number needed less then, sanctuary / gas, gas gains release for sanctuary / subgroup, subgroup grows naturally into a sanctuary / heading, heading hallows your ways to a sanctuary / equivalent, equivalent queries waivering into light's sanctuary / rotten, rotten less and heavenly most in life's lease for sanctuary / mechanical, mechanical meetings over then due too, sanctuary / required, required finishing done through metatronic melting sanctuary / gravity, gravity grew into a venue's sanctuary / specific, specific to an allow for life's dated sanctuary / density, density and the delicious acquire for lightening sanctuary / pressure, pressure off and the scoff over too, sanctuary' / mirrors, mirrors made and the healing held for, sanctuary / lenses, lenses and the examples spent in too, sanctuary / focal, focal following's sanctuary / formula, formula bought off and for then, sanctuarie / relationship, relationship spent on channeled lends too, sanctuarie / mass, mass done with, sanctuary / conductor, conductor cues your light then, sanctuary / coil, coil said too, "sanctuary"/ voltage, voltage valued within your sanctuary / current, current equips worn sanctuary / pendulum, pendulum deep into love's lifting sanctuary / work, work avows your energy's gained sanctuary / advantage, advantage values your sanctuary / ideal, ideal dealings and the sealing spent in sanctuary / kinetic, kinetic concur and the meaning spent in sanctuary / potential, potential and the potent year's sanctuary / centripetal, centripetal petals and the portals gained in sanctuary / acceleration, acceleration rated for your's sanctuary / friction, friction fought off and found in love's leading sanctuary / velocity, velocity claims your sanctuary / induced, induced dealings leading sanctuary / notation, notation kneeling into sanctuary / prefix,

prefix felt for within then sanctuary / phonic, phonic found for a living's sanctuary.

CHAPTER TWELVE

Healing, healing and the listen's sanctuary / essential, essential apparel and the wearing over, a, sanctuary / oil, oil melts in your light wave's sanctuary / emporium, emporium spent in sanctuary / techniques, techniques sent for in then sanctuary / elegant, elegant applies then sanctuary / desirous, desirous patents and the patience to see forth in leading sanctuary / floral, floral extent and the sent for sanctuary / case, case applied for and the capably enfranchised sanctuary / gentle, gentle application too and the leading example's sanctuary / prescribe, prescribe appears in a totally thrilling example for sanctuary / deteriorated, deteriorated past and then cast into living's sanctuary / prospect, prospect allowed for and the listing's sanctuary / rotating, rotating and agreed too, sanctuary / muscles, muscles led forth in sanctuary / tone, tone overringing your life's sanctuary / joint, joint believe and the flow metatronically due your sanctuary / capabilities, capabilities balance forth in lightening's sanctuary / client, client clues your allowance too grains sanctuary / lethargy, lethargy led to a living's values for sanctuary / insurance, insurance allows the coming sanctuary / positive, positive to deft affairs within light's sanctuary / retail, retail regards foolishly found in lightening sanctuary / bottle, bottle banded sanctuary / origin, origin rambles and the reeling's living sanctuary / spiteful, spiteful apply and the listening allows your sanctuary / hostility, hostility forgiven and the frankest said too, sanctuary / push, push through and force regain through a living sanctuary / put, put dues your listing's reply too, a sanctuary / doing, doing a diligence for a life long sanctuary / luminary, luminary allowance and the precious suggestion into our sanctuary / advice, advice fellows you and your lifting suggestion's attention too, love / andes, andes heights and the heralds on too, love's sanctuary / money, money made in the venues surrendered too, love / easy, easy and the lessen's over, love / massage, massage means remember's easy legend for love / hole, hole opens outward and then too lightening love / institute, institute for the fashionably afforded love / nerve, nerve needs lightening into your love / toxins, toxins flushed and the fellowship forwards your flush into love / calm, calm concepts of the clientele felt for through love / karma, karma cues and the dues paid off to a balance forth, love's sanctuary / table, tables turned and the armed elected for love's balanced sanctuary / counteracts, counteracts allow and the flow for love's sanctuary / sensational, sensational sorts and the fortress unbound into light's leading wedge of love sanctuary / tension, tension taut and the ought allowed relief into love's sanctuary legend / absolutely, absolutely resolutely led into life's breezy intrigue in lov sanctuarye / oak, oak apply and the lies due over ended in love / invigorating, invigorating betray and the stray into love's balanc / benefits, benefits balanced into light's love / accumulated, accumulated moments and the potion for love / recover, recover a receiver's love / recreational, recreational to a vocational love / posture, posture insured into love's balanc /

immune, immune to the moment's forgiven love / impact, impact made in the staid's balanced love / dynamic, dynamic and the detailed duos balances love / margin, margin and the meals made too, love' / proud, proud and the pretend done for, love / describe, describe the details for your love / portable, portable potential and the passionate pretend found in loving acquir / evaluated, evaluated and doubled into within love / independent, independent to the dues for love / lust, lust off to a start for life's lifting details on too, love's sanctuary.

CHAPTER THIRTEEN

Versatile, versatile values within the veins found in love sanctuary / odyssey, odyssey dabbles in light's lifting love sanctuary / ergonomic, ergonomic and the sanctuary light's on too, love / models, models mixed into love's assigned sanctuary / static, static succeeds suggestion for love sanctuary / stability, stability believes in your basic humanity for love sanctuary / lateral, lateral trims and the trining timing for sanctuary love / therapeutic, therapeutic to the reputed for, love sanctuary / accupressure, accupressure and the sanctuary pressure off too, love / crease, crease accrues in loving sanctuary foundation / common, commonly hosted gains a news found sanctuary / host, host held fond for lightening sanctuary foundation / basis, basis bought for, sanctuary foundation / various, various poses and the patience opening into clear sanctuary / alleviate, alleviate leads too, sanctuary / tuck, tuck into another's wedded devotion for loving sanctuary / reproduction, reproduction's retail and the veil lifts for sanctuary / replicated, replicated and the mated attend's sanctuary / edition, editions due and the forgotten regain's sanctuary / famous, famous fellows and the mellow regard for sanctuary / chameleon, chameleon applies too, love's leading sanctuary / former, former freights done with, sanctuary on love / series, series sentinel into like sanctuary, love / promoting, promoting a patented pattern for loving sanctuary / official, official feelings suggested for light given sanctuary / wierd, wierd over and enjoy now, sanctuary / canvas, canvas flows and th shows gleam into sanctuary / title, title wins with sanctuary / gravitate, gravitate with regard for the life lived sanctuary / among, among us the living leads too, sanctuary / region, region of the require's living sanctuary / comprising, comprising and the compromising lesson, sanctuary / retail, retail railing and the living sanctuary / unified, unified example and the sample sanctuary / design, design deatiled sanctions of sanctuary / bridge, bridge belies and the value rises too, a living lends sanctuary / curtain, curtain called declare for the listening foundation / glass, glass and the glistening's lightened foundatio / fracture, fracture and the fradulent gone too, foundation / drop, drop less and deign more importance too, love's foundations for sanctuary / ambassador, ambassador led too, sanctuary / letter, letter meant for love in too, sanctuary / sent, sent another dues for a leading sanctuary / focus, focus follows annually sanctuary / stone, stone sent off the leading application for love's sanctuary / kinetic, kinetic contours and the capable sanctuary / commentary, commentary on the lifting sanctuary / panel, panel apparent and the gifting sanctuary / code, code made and the glade opens too, sanctuary / auction, auction found and the land won through sanctuary / olympic, olympic immortals and the sort who gain sanctuary / century, century of the gathering fortunes in sanctuary / crazy, cray about living's sanctuary, the temple, hu-man / dictator, dictator off and into love's sanctuary / unspoken, unspoken over and the cues amaze your sanctuary / genuine, genuine into a seam spent in sanctuary / investing, investing coming into love's sanctuary / spend, spend a moment in your sanctuary / couple, couple coming round your sanctuary / dominated, dominated less and then found, masterfully, through your living foundations, sanctuary / theme, theme thorough within, your's foundation's sanctuary / fantasies, fantasies follow your loving sanctuary / control, control spent in a spinning foundation too, sanctuary / erotic, erotic spells break into love's temple and the tantric decree to be holy unto life's sanctuary.

THE KINGDOM-MENTS
LEVEL 38

CHAPTER ONE

Experts, experts in the kingdoms, come in too, love / smart, smart to a focus and the impasse unfrozen in chosen kingdom / choose, choose another woven through your kindest kingdom / divorce, divorce the lessen, knew, kingdom / convey, convey the status, kingdom / choice, choice made and the shades chosen, kingdom / know, know a clarity called kingdom / measure, measure means, kingdom / full, full to the tilt for kingdom / planes, planes and the plans patterned in electrically, kingdom / plans, plans made and the challenge gone to kingdom / actual, actual examples given, kingdom / select, select a relation shipped too, kingdom / map, map moist with inquiry, kingdoms / update, update drawn through kingdom / carry, carry into colorful kingdom / maverick, maverick bursts, kingdom / buds, buds withdrew to kingdom / bares, bares declared clearly, kingdom / barren, barren periods closed for kingdom / bounce, bounce across mentions dimensioned through kingdom / baste, baste a sort shortest, kingdom / borne, borne to explore most kingdom / basics, basics met, kingdom / mates, mates met in kingdoms mende / amuse, amuse most, kingdom / allow, allow desires for kingdom / confuse, confuse less, sorts, kingdoms / levers, levers leap too, kingdom / leverage, leverage huge used kingdom / loves, loves to leap through, kingdom / let, let us be freed too, kingdom / daddy, daddy done through kingdom / dare, dare to spare more, kingdom / adore, adore found in kingdom / balance, balance paid through kingdom / grill, grill less, join more, kingdom / abhor, abhor less the random, kingdom / allow, allow for learning kingdom / cornered, cornered mention due in kingdom / profile, profile found for, kingdom / portage, portage sent too, kingdom / arts, arts set through, kingdom / starts, starts appear then, kingdom / purity, purity declares your's kingdom / appear, appear nearest stars for, kingdom / flower, flower expelling kingdom / cower, cower less in covered, kingdom / cavilier, cavilier examples, kingdom / carts, carts upheld in fields on kingdom / movement, movement made too, kingdom / love, love led through kingdom / kings, kings made and mated too, through kingdom / queens, queens enamored for in kingdom / quick, quick to a glistened kingdom / quicken, quicken made through, kingdom / arts, arts paid for in kingdom / crafts, crafts allowance, kingdom / cue, cues given, kingdom / cabinet, cabinets filled in, kingdom / revolutions, revolutions rounded, kingdom / world, world intelligence's kingdom / light, light led for, kingdom / meter, meter measures, kingdoms.

CHAPTER TWO

Flash, flash for the fellow's kingdom / spot, spot sent for, kingdom / incident, incident dearest, kingdom / core, core sports, kingdom / flush, flush outed, kingdom / mast, mast raised kingdom / maps, maps paid, kingdom / mace, mace foils kingdom / cords, cords cued, cut to, kingdom / campaign, campaign for, kingdom / trigger, trigger resolution, kingdom / expose, expose extortion's kingdom / convenience, convenience forges kingdom / flash, flash intelligently, kingdom / flew, flew to a fellow's kingdom / flown, flown above then, kingdom / case, case made for, kingdom / multiple, multiple inticements, kingdom / place, place felt in, kingdom / cumulative, cumulative experience's kingdom / essential, essential measure's kingdom / needs, needs knelt in, kingdom / nests, nests felt for, kingdom / traces, traces trigger, kingdom / seat, seat found for, kingdom / lady, lady lessoned, kingdom / harmony, harmony cued in, kingdom / men, men found then, kingdom / near, near electives, kingdom / feeling, feeling fondest, kingdom / want, want exception? kingdom / go, go now for, kingdom / retract, retract less, adore more, kingdoms / restrict, restrict less, kingdom / travel, travel too, kingdom / mix, mix best in kingdom / slip, slip across lipped kingdom / turn, turn allowed then, kingdom / even, even steepled, kingdom / temptation, temptations over, kingdom / caught, caught less in kingodms othere / lonely, lonely done for kingdom / good-bye, good-bye sated through, kingdom / remember, remember your kingdom / pressure, pressure off then, kingdom / yesterday, yesterday measured, kingdom / road, road over done, kingdoms / handwritten, handwritten inquiry for, kingdom / be, be kingdom freed to love / nearly, nearly next in kingdom / fade, fade to election's kingdom / wrong, wrong to ascend less, kingdoms / move, move for the mention's kingdom / care, care gives, kingdom / universal, universal entirety, kingdom / drinking, drinking outed, kingdom / share, share experience in kingdoms / eternal, eternal youths winds, kingdom / warmth, warmth involved then, kingdom / lounge, lounge across soar's kingdom / alright, alright to the invited kingdom / apart, apart less for kingdom / bond, bond to be, kingdome / whole, whole in entirety's kingdoms.

CHAPTER THREE

Wide, wide to a wisdom for kingdom / imaging, imaging met in, kingdom / minute, minutes made for kingdom / hoped, hoped agree meant, kingdom / strong, strong to a listen too, kingdom / shining, shining moments then, kingdom / times, times terrific in, kingdom / caught, caught in less then? kingdoms / outworn, outworn rehashing? kingdom / gave, gave an example through, kingdom / gone, gone to a query for your, kingdom / lead, lead to the living's kingdom / chief, chief in exampled, kingdom / still, still enough to heal thee, kingdom / clue, clue made through kingdom / fancy, fancy fellow's kingdom / mood, moods over done, kingdom / chocolate, chocolate inquiry to the mother's kingdom / touch, touch another's fellowship through kingdom / funk, funk out and then clearest, kingdom / twist, twist over and the dues made, kingdom / hollow, hollow examples forgiven, kingdom / known, known for the shallow forget's kingdom / risen, risen starring, kingdom / base, base paved through kingdom / canopy, canopy lifted, kingdom / release, release due your's kingdom / gust, gust past soar's kingdom / wind, wind well now in kingdom / captured, captured over come, kingdom / breeze, breeze allow us, kingdom / proof, proof in the power, kingdom / disk, disk red kingdom / harvest, harvest due now, kingdom / preach, preach less, soar, kingdom / tucked, tucked into for, kindness meant, kingdom / vented, vented in fellowed kingdom / cushion, cushion across shores kingdome / lobby, lobby for your kingdom / buffet, buffet paved in kingdom / corporate, corporate incorporate for kingdom / terror, terror gone too, knew, kingdom / generous, generous to a measure's coming kingdom / sling, sling worn, kingdom / porch, porch seated kingdom / resilient, resilient to a fullest kingdom / serve, serve matters release through kingdom / sprawl, sprawl due too, kingdom / contrast, contrast paved then, kingdom / country, country amounts too, knighthooded kingdom / assist, assist release, relate yours, kingdom / fabric, fabric veiled relates too, kingdom / knife, knife curt, kingdom / edge, edge won, kingdom / sip, sips on kingdom / radiate, radiate retire too, kingdom / incliment, incliment the intent for, kingdom / major, major to the notice on, kingdom / frequent, frequent forgive's kingdom / rugged, rugged sorts, kingdom / echo, echo across shores kingdom / grace, grace made yours through kingdom / accordingly, accordingly forgiven kingdom / bought, bought through a giving kingdom.

CHAPTER FOUR

Delicate, delicate to an inquire forgiven kingdom / range, range made, found, kingdom / tradition, tradition paid for, kingdom / permanent, permanent to the inquired kingdom / contours, contours concurrent then, kingdom / architectural, architectural inflections for kingdom / crowd, crowd gained then, kingdom / museum, museum fielded in kingdom / substantial, substantial exchange to the kingdom keys / bench, bench made of the land's kingdom / flat, flat to a galactic inquiry delivered kingdom / junction, junction fused in the love found, kingdom / rail, rail across prayers deep in prairied keep, kingdom / contemporary, contemporary contain and the rain within your kingdom / deliver, deliver the sheerness, kingdom / foyer, foyer built to the felt, kingdom / version, version won, kingdom / focal, focal to the miraculous points, kingdom / curves, curves through valley kingdom / semicircular, semicircular about, kingdom / ample, ample power, kingdom / enclosure, enclosure clued too, kingdom / slab, slab found, kingdom / freak, freak over, kingdom / produce, produce grown too, kingdom / executive, executive to the matricular, kingdom / factory, factory focused, kingdom / mastered, mastered in the melieu, kingdom / manage, manage to arrange for, kingdom / lay, lay down your about them, kingdom / sex, sex made supreme in sacral kingdom / guidance, guidance gains deliver into kingdom / sacrifice, sacrifice made, over, kingdom / entire, entire days spent in kingdom / appear, appear near the source of kingdom / marvelous, marvelous to wonderful kingdom / appreciated, appreciated for her kingdom / crew, crew made family kingdom / jam, jam over, flow too, kingdom / grip, grip gained on, kingdom / shop, shop opened soon into kingdom / dear, dear enough to hear about, kingdom / devoted, devoted as the voted forth into kingdom / mention, mention a dimension neat in kingdom / stay, stay well within kingdom / interlude, interlude paid mood for, kingdom / treat, treat relived as kingdom / waiting, waiting allows your kingdom / verse, verse said too, "kingdom come / sun, sun moons kingdom / sexy, sexy to a stay in kingdom / rise, rise to occur too, kingdom / sorrow, sorrow left them, kingdom / left, left to a married set in mercy's kingdom / since, since then, kingdom / alone, alone to a phone led, kingdom / drowning, drowning in superlative form's kingdom / start, start anew then kingdom / our, our days fed too, kingdom / more, more intensely, kingdom / flesh, flesh wound

then, kingdoms heale / pilgrim, pilgrim astonished in kingdom / essential, essential to the valleyed kingdom / infinite, infinite to the variation themed, "kingdoms."

CHAPTER FIVE

Line, line to the middle, kingdom / relativity, relativity made well within, kingdom / harmonics, harmonics held electric into kingdom / firm, firm in the warmness of kingdom / cleansing, cleansing comes too, kingdom / gentle, gentle in reward for, kingdom / holotropic, holotropic exam's kingdom / biology, biology's blooms then, kingdom / evolution, evolution made random, again, kingdom / portable, portable examples kingdom / canvas, canvas drawn too, kingdom / platform, platform made for, kingdom / meditation, meditation paves your kingdom / nerve, nerve relaxed into kingdom / scared, scared? Sacred, kingdom / class, class of the crews kingdom free / thought, thought of the theory for love too, kingdom / together, together and then the inquiry through your kingdom / worthy, worthy ways merge into kingdom / myriad, myriad days played into through living's kingdom / stained, stained and the strained forget's forgiven living kingdom / guarantee, guarantee and the grinning gained into kingdom / bottled, bottled and the periods intrigued within, kingdom / tropical, tropical appear and the aspire worn too a bluest cue for living waters kingdom / dessert, dessert and the details viewed annually throughout our living cubes freely kingdome / exercise, exercise your interior kingdom, breathe, believe, love / splash, splash forth and become the spilling truth into love's kingdom / disguise, disguise worn off and the scoff has become listened too, kingdom / confident, confident in her suppose for kingdom / cruise, cruise across the query for love in thee, kingdom / look, look into beauty amber dear into loving kingdom / inaugural, inaugural new kingdom / vacation, vacation becomes your kinship too, kingdom / feature, feature the fullness within your kingdom / dual, dual days applied too, love is the kingdom / sheer, sheer along lesson's kingdom / compile, compile the codes for your kingdom / summarize, summarize electrically yes too kingdom / articulated, articulated throughout yours, kingdoms / gender, gender declared freed to kingdom / contractions, contractions consistent to the constant in kingdom / software, software worn through to a keener kingdom / acquaint, acquaint your agent with kingdom / stretching, stretching patiently into kingdom / justification, justification became your found arrival into loving kingdom / pattern, pattern play and the plans made lead too to kingdom / identified, idenitfied as readily released forthrightly into kingdom / potential, potential partnered kingdom / metabolism, metabolism melts into matching patterns fonder still into kingdom / bouncing, bouncing characters shout about "kingdoms / literal, literal to the lateral kingdom / dia gram, diagrams found in the fertility of your kingdom / evaluation, evaluation feels of kingdom / galileo, galileo given a queried kingdom / inertia, inertia over and the deal made for kingdom / equal, equal abilitied and the agility to see through kingdom / equilibrium, equilibrium well into love's three kingdom / dial, dial a detail for kingdom / latent, latent apply for a kingdom / force, force across worn kingdom / momentum, momentum gaining a kingdom / vector, vectors fielded as kingdom / components, components gather into kingdom / resolution, resolution resides in your kingdoms.

CHAPTER SIX

Stance, stance above and then within more kingdom / resolve, resolve a a feeling's kingdom / ingredients, ingredients squared for in kingdom / tap, tap along lines root deep into the kingdom / discover, discover a daily freedom throughout your kingdom / contaminants, contaminants over throughout your greeted kingdom / comedian, comedian of the cue for kingdom / landscapes, landscapes leading to kingdom / pregnant, pregnant to a cause for kingdom / itchy, itchy with satisfy for kingdom / symptoms, symptoms cared about found freed for kingdom / absorbent, absorbent soothe into kingdom / dehydrated, dehydrated details then voiced for your kingdom / berry, berry red and the living loved too, kingdom / financial, financial fellows and the mellow ship called kingdom / balance, balance bared and the position saved for kingdom / antioxidant, antioxidant and the zen sung abundance into kingdom / prescribed, prescribed plenty and the partnered mend for kingdom / exhaustive, exhaustive repair and the rewards made through kingdom / miles, miles made for kingdom / dress, dress the parts sleeve freed in kingdom / turn, turn to suggestive repair for a kingdom / except, except aware then kingdom / accept, accept aware through kingdom / vibration, vibration values your kingdom / smile, smile apparent to kingdom / know, know a desire too, kingdom / grab, grab a patient particle of kingdom / contribution, contribution cures your kingdom / fundamental, fundamental capri and the carapace on to a kingdom / source, source surged for in kingdom / game, game garnered for kingdom / journey, journey throughout your kingdom / above, above and the winds spray kingdom / below, below a bevy on too, kingdom / sensual, sensual in shared retire for the kingdom / awakening, awakening retired too a kingdom / gravity, gravity comes loose in your kingdom / guest, guest made of the kingdom / test, test over running a kingdom / rest, rest in a bouldered dash to kingdom / best, best worn in kingdoms, purple thre / original, original warranty, a free one, kingdom / type, type of the real won, a new one, through kingdom / initiation, initiation completes your kingdom / iris, iris red through kingdom / selected, selected to an apparent won for kingdom / have, have won, kingdom / precious, precious appearances in kindred kingdom / family, family fed through kingdom / doubt, doubt details yours, a kingdom / count, count on then one the kingdom / believe, believe a surging kingdom / power, power plays for a kingdom / alchemy, alchemy cares for your kingdom / miracle, miracle meetings made to kingdom / dragon, dragon of the detailed in kingdom / tie, tie for the kingdom / born, born abated freed in kingdom / healthy, healthy hallows awarely into kingdom / dreams, dreams dareth your kingdom / reality, reality regarding your kingdom / warm, warm appearance in God's kingdom / picture, picture here your kingdoms

CHAPTER SEVEN

Forgive, forgive and follow thee, kingdom / fulfill, fulfill your functional adventure through kingdom / inner, inner ways and the wisdom gains too, functions into kingdom / rush, rush across the impacts to kingdom / slow, slow in the glowing kingdom / nothing, nothing and the enthrall for kingdom / success, success becomes your kingdom / past, past into lasting kingdom / quantum, quantum choirs rung with kingdom / wisdom, wisdom warms these kingdom / dawn, dawn details your kingdom / perennial, perennial in the mental free's kingdom / explore, explore more kingdom / smoke, smoke and the hoax off your kingdom / painting, painting sails for these kingdom / arms, arms allow your kingdom / rose, rose thrice held for kingdom / emotion, emotion mentioned for kingdom / dim, dim days over too, kingdom / candles, candles camp in trees forgiven to the living's kingdom / vision, vision voiced in kingdom / salty, salty suggestion of kingdom / float, float prepared for, kingdom / rituals, rituals rang with kingdom / pampering, pampering prepares for literary kingdom / fancy, fancy phalanx led lifting too, kingdom / salt, salt red intoxication and the nation's kingdom / pillow, pillow pals and the sharing kingdom / habit, habit of the materialed kingdom / marvelously, marvelously mentioned too, kingdom / sensation, sensation of the revenued kingdom / invigorating, invigoration experience in too, kingdom / burst, burst allows legendary kingdom / escape, escape clarifies your kingdom / several, several legend's kingdom / temperatures, temperatures chilled in kingdom / thought, thought of the ought to be soars kingdom / romantic, romantic remainder and the gained won, kingdom / mermaids, mermaids mentioned frankly in kingdom / volcanic, volcanic vex bursts to kingdom / promise, promise to prepare for your kingdom / cure, cure allows your kingdom / quench, quench gained too in kingdom / cascade, cascade kept simply purest to kingdom / nourish, nourish beneath your kingdom / dense, dense dealt with in kingdom / renaissance, renaissance sorts of kingdom / molecule, molecule mentions your kingdoms com / uttered, uttered essentially electric into a kingdom / said, said yes too in kingdom / passage, passage made past your kingdom / brook, brook knooks and the shaken wilds too kingdom / virtue, virtue wanes and the kingdom comes tru / abundance, abundance bought and the healing sought traditionally too in kingdom / enormity, enormity and the central scenes for kingdom / immense, immense detail and the sailing kingdom / dance, dance in gently soothed kingdom / miniature, miniature marvels inside thee, kingdom / galaxy, galaxy of gains spin too, kingdom / eloquent, eloquent in a worthy mention's kingdom / civilization, civilization unified for a kingdom / turtle, turtle tours your kingdom / routing, routing made too, kingdom / grill, grill graced in a kingdom / mutual, mutual thrills have reached her doorway, a kingdom.

CHAPTER EIGHT

Coal, coal burns in depth's on too kindred kingdom / hobby, hobby attendant too a kingdom / source, source central and love finds a kingdom / upgrade, upgrades grown for kingdom / trendy, trendy trees and the tinfoiled passion's kingdom / versatile, versatile to a voiced flow to kingdom / brain, brain towers in kingdom / package, package fellows your kingdom / steam, ssssteam vents in kingdom / stir, stir said, "A KINGDOM"/ spicy spelling, A K-I-N-G-D-O-M / coconut, coconut cues allowed in kingdom / tart, tart trills and the sufferance thrown too, kingdom / mango, mango amaze of the yellow forego into kingdom / press, press allures in shone kingdom / liberated, liberated leisure's lane through kingdom / knots, knots nurture yours too, kingodm / tropical, tropical truths render kingdom / frozen, frozen fortunes into kindred's kingdom / fruit, fruit red in passion's lotions toured ink green into kingdom / erase, erase details shore's kingdom / advisory, advisory mentioned into a kingdom / explicit, explicit plans and day's kingdome / sailed, sailed across shores kingdom / mistake, mistake over paid for kingdom / river, river reached and crossed too in kingdom / difficult, difficult detailed too a kingdom / crash, crash past and fortunes gained in too, kingdom / burn, burn over, enjoy sane kingdom / lift, lift led to in kingdom / clear, clear clairovoyantly planned for in kingdom / campaign, campaign assorted too a kingdom / report, report reads of a kingdom / rehabilitation, rehabilitation tames when kingdome / contribution, contribution channeled through a kingdom / plum, plum parallels into kingdom / plunge, plunge panes a kingdom / plush, plush purged in gaining kingdom / copy, copy cues your kingdom / print, print patient into a kingdom / design, design seals your zealous day's kingdom / incredible, incredible chains past a kingdom / gratitude, gratitude softened into a kingdom / fond, fond detail and the smell successful in a kingdom / blank, blank loft and the fiesta found your kingdom / lamb, lamb legends and the retire too kingdom / favorite, favorit fellows and the forthright gesture due a kingdom / sang, sang questioned and grains merged into a kingdom / rather, rather and the mention's kindred tours rang in kingdom / last, last allowed and the duration shown for in kingdom / through, through and the thorough consort paced into a kingdom / million, millions mentioend and a material met for in kingdom / prove, prove a patient won too, kingdom / how, how and when made a kingdom / lower, lower legends dart too, kingdom / find, find a fondness toured to kingdom / content, content to be namaste deep in kingdom / consuming, consuming cured a kingdom / follow, follow a feature for a kingdom / instruction, instruction comes to a calling kingdom / official, official finds and the signs for wonderful kingdom / necessary, necessary creation and the rationale for a kingdom / complete, complete detail and the daily kingdom / prize, prize purchased and the passionate pairing's kingdom.

CHAPTER NINE

Claim, claim a balance chained in kingdom / glass, glass deep in hazy kingdom / odd, odd decry and the deify too, a kingdom / stacked, stacked in a certainty tooled in kingdom / nest, nest chants and the flowering too a kingdom / situation, situation and the currents paid too, a kingdom / stone, stone touring in a kingdom / bird, bird balancing a kingdom / home, home hallowed through a kingdom / conversation, conversation spins into a kingdom / sort, sort for the fortunately kingdome / deal, deal delicate for a

kingdom / spun, spun sports and the settle meant for a kingdom / surge, surge panned for in a kingdom / adjust, adjust chores a kingdom / hidden, hidden treats and the paralyze over done too, a kingdom / movement, movement becoming yours into a kingdom / ecologically, ecologically sound for a daily kingdom / hardwood, hardwood seals and the spills past a kingdom / stress, stress delat a kingdom coming I / durability, durability and the daily dips too, a kingdom / prevent, prevent past a kingdom / opposite, opposit stares allow a perfect pairing's kingdom / regimen, regimen reigns past a kingdom / flexibility, flexibility a worthy mention onto kingdom / coordination, coordination keys for kingdom / posture, posture appeals with a kingdom / overall, overall supports and the sorts ingrained in kingdom / seam, seam deals with A kingdom / forward, forward jaunts sourced kingdom / filter, filter fellows and the mellow returns too, a kingdom / hormonal, hormonal stilling and the nearness details your kingdom / alive, alive and the living's legend for a kingdom / type, type carried and the channels gained too, kingdom / wrap, wrap about thee, the kingdom / sandals, sandals durable too a kingdom's fea / model, model and the cradle convenient to a kingdom / strategy, strategy won too, a kingdom / stubble, stubble across faced for kingdom / equation, equation reading A kingdom / wax, waxing elongates a kingdom / innovation, innovation values a kingdom / strips, strips terrific in a kingdom / glands, glands contoured A kingdom / minerals, minerals noted for a kingdom / trace, trace allows drift into A kingdom / converts, converts pay for kingdom / convertible, convertible clarify A kingdom / dimension, dimension gains a kingdom / leaves, leaves legends a kingdom' / extract, extract acroos a kingdom / alertness, alertness merged in an invitational kingdom / moderate, moderate and the midday to kingdom / aerobic, aerobic ringing and the singing urgency to a kingdom / sprint, sprint past a detailed forget in a kingdom / distance, distance deems you a kingdom / offer, offer the daily kingdom / request, request chorale and the cubic how too, a kingdom / refill, filling features a refill mechanic and the manic detail on too kingdom / nutrition, nutrition natured in kingdom / empty, empty over then too, kingdom / ecstasy, ecstasy allowed your, the kingdom / cryptic, cryptic appearing in kingdom's rememberin / discovery, discovery appeared in a kingdom / faith, faith is full in the discovery of you, doors opened, love is the true kingdom.

CHAPTER TEN

Insomnia, insomnia over and the carry is through A kingdom / anxiety, anxiety deals a kingdom / depression, depression detailed A kingdom' / melancholy, melancholy mention and the dimension "A" to kingdom / hostility, hostility outs A kingdom / retired, retired to the sired for in kingdom / soak, soak allwing A kingdom / speculate, speculate for A kingdom / promote, promote tours to kingdom / calmer, calmer carriage and the kingdom's note / anesthesia, anesthesia and the unleash into a kingdom / immune, immune to a mentality for kingdom / vitality, vitality chosen into a kingdom / sprinkle, sprinkle apparent in A kingdom / lavendar, lavendar legends mention a kingdom / bouYant, bouyant imprints gains a kingdom / magazine, magazine marveled in too, kingdom / authors, authors met for A kingdom / brittle, brittle over due and A kingdom / inescapable, inescapable cores say this "A kingdom" come / simple, simple dates within a kingdom / conditioned, conditioned through a kingdom's acquire / standard, standard dates met within a kingdom / roundtrip, roundtrip deluge meant for in an annual kingdom / major, major mention's and the dimensions kept for a kingdom / admission, admission met soars into a corrected kingdom / reunion, reunion rang into A kingdom / trenches, trenches tours A kingdom / poem, poems written into A kingdom / kick, kick forth into an allow for thee, kingdom / tuning, tuning joins a kingdom / recovery, recovery gathers into kingdom / baked, baked with a kingdom / workshop, worshop gathers into a kingdom / clinic, clinic held for kingdom / crimp, crimp allowed for, in kingdom / video, video values into a kingdom / feature, feature found for in kingdom / bargain, bargain balanced soars to kingdom / cycle, cycle succinct into kingdom / float, float past soaring kingdom / freshen, freshen narrows into a kingdom / density, density daily detailed in kingdom / liquid, liquid listening too in kingdom / juice, juice joins yours A kingdom / plunge, plunge partnered too a kingdom / individual, individual defy and the detach gone to kingdom / capacity, capacity held and the meeting met for kingdom / exit, exit past a kingdom / balance, balance balast and the kingdom / navigate, navigation forged in kingdom / calendar, calendar daze in then mention for a kingdom / laser, laser led to a kingdom / leap, leap for faiths kingdom / biomechanical, biomechanical mention to a dimension's gate for kingdom / springs, springs burst in kingdom / personal, personal pardons and the patient kingdom / flexibility, flexibility and the agility for a kingdom / attentive, attentive to a kingdom / career, acquire a kingdom to a light led for kingdom / devote, devote a detail for 'THEY' in kingdom / devoted, devoted wed to a kingdom / altitude, altitude gains a kingdom / quality, quality worn in a kingdom.

CHAPTER ELEVEN
Current, current crafts for a kingdom / concession, concession channeled into a kingdom / vendor, vendor forged through a kingdom / hospitality, hospitality heals a kingdom / eligibility, eligibility for a kingdom / entry, entry gains a kingdom / award, award given too, a kingdom' / score, score made for the kingdom / points, points found in kingdom / toward, toward truths of kingdom / endurance, endurance values your kingdom / potential, potential passions and the mansion's gaze too, kingdom / phenomenal, phenomenal to an affair for detail in a dimension called a kingdom / odyssey, odyssey past a kingdom / flip, flip forth into kingdom / product, products patient within kingdom / season, season sealed in a kingdom / motivation, motivation's date with kingdom / reflection, reflection fellowed in a kingdom / exclusive, exclusive claims for a kingdom / dietary, dietary declare for a passionate chore called kingdom / studs, studs into the measure made for challenge freed into a kingdom / place, place a passionate embrace about your signals freed for kingdom / fiasco, fiasco over and the dues worn through kingdom / medals, medals worn read, A kingdom / crowning, crowning example and

the sample said, "yes", A kingdom / hasty, hasty overage and the missionary's kingdom / benefit, benefit found in the grounded kingdom / stock, stock suggests, "yes", A kingdom / engraved, engraved in the inquiry, yes, a kingdom' / fitness, fitness fits your kingdom / legal, legal legends and the blessings read yes, to kingdom / counsel, counsel met in a kingdom / nomination, nomination for a kingdom / host, host held openly too, a kingdom / ocean, ocean rifts and the ready state shown a kingdom / ring, ringy readied for a tour fo A kingdom / fiber, fiber fields into rays kingdome / ransom, ransom paid, shores say, "yes" to kingdom / lend, lend us your kingdom / level, level leads and the legends met in kingdom / happens, happens held and the meld gives us kingdom / log, log into your kingdom / stroke, stroke given delivery into a kingdom / consistent, consistent concur for a kingdom / suit, suit yours to a kingdom / crunch, crunch over, dues paid, kingdom / both, both said, "yes" too, a kingdom / plenty, plenty who knew 11:11, kingdom / meta-physical, meta-physical intrigue with you and the living kingdom / orion, orionic blend in my bed, mayan style, kingdoms com / they, they knew the code, kingdom / parallel, parallel trines, kingdom / inside, inside these days, kingdom / miracles, miracles mapped and anchored into kingdom / mentionable, mentionable applauses and these kingdom / mercury, mercury mews into a kingdom / listening, listening still, a kingdom / far, far fews and kingdome / mostly, mostly Jewish kingdom / certainly, certainly miraculous these kingdom / Hassidic, Hassidic the sort, the Metatronic kingdom / Maharishi, Maharishi red, kingdom / ruby, ruby-blue, these Thailandic kingdoms.

THE SUB-ATOMIC-MENTS
LEVEL 39

CHAPTER ONE

Situs, situs plans an arisen sub-atomic / seats, seats defend a diary's light rewarded sub-atomic / shores, shores paged level into a patterned regard for the love that's sub-atomic / amazed, amazed within and found to be miraculously filled within with sub-atomic love / mantles, mantles move above and within thee, the sub-atomic's blend / medial, medial moves and the cubits made for these, the sub-atomic / moves, moves made, gently too, an sub-atomic / may, may gives thee a sub-atomic gif / lead, lead led through and the jersey returns to a retired estate for the securely committed sub-atomically / science, science spent for and given into the sub-atomic / facts, facts follow and find truth into these the sub-atomic / topple, topple less and gather more into the sub-atomic / layers, layers genuine into these the sub-atomic / postulate means and the scenes metatronically trued through the sub-atomic / wade, wade past days on sub-atomic / columns, columns and the cubes required for the sub-atomic / clerks, clerks clearest in the sub-atomic / communicate, communicate and the allow graced into the sub-atomic / clerks, clerks and the percs paid for the depth sub-atomic / communicate, communicate well and swell within to the trill sub-atomic / brahmen, brahmen made to the seed sub-atomic / monads, monads lift to the means sub-atomic / monetary, monetary amaze and the pages sub-atomic / divides, divides and the sides sub-atomic / divisions, divisions elope and erupt sub-atomic / start, start an apparent parallel and the swelling sub-atomic / winsome, winsome ways and the days due sub-atomically / wingate, wingate abide and the side scent sub-atomic / stark, art to the starkness sub-atomic / stave, stave and the rave past sub-atomic / traverse, traverse and the curses off your sub-atomic / tout, tout and the shout through the sub-atomic / tossed, tossed in the loss led sub-atomic / taut, taut in the caught forgiven, sub-atomic / chirp, chirp about the shout worn sub-atomic / spurt, spurt over into the dues gained, sub-atomically / flaw, flaws out, the love is in your sub-atomic / claw, claw past dues sub-atomic / hawks, hawks elevate past the sub-atomic / parakeet, parakeet seats and the surreys sub-atomic / sparrow, sparrow days and the dealings sub-atomic / eagle, eagle ways and the westward sub-atomic / blue, blue bays and the billows sub-atomic / cardinal, cardinal cayes and the ceilings set sub-atomic / dove, dove and the dealings due a sub-atomic / homeward, homeward to the willows sub-atomic / love, love led us through an anatomic venue, sub-atomic,/ homing, homing devised in the rise worn through and the perfect entreaty too, a sub-atomic, love / chesapeake, chesapeake seek and the singing appraise of the raise into light's sub-atomic / bays, bays, bays signified true and the muses met framed in life's sub-atomic reflection to love / crabs, crabs clawed away and the stay cooked fine to a middle grounded sub-atomic / maryland, maryland met in a mansioned plate level now into the life sub-atomic / parrots, parrots placed and the peaks traced in a dancing pattern's sub-atomic / speak, speak and trail through the sub-atomic / sports, sports pure and the insure through a sub-atomic / boston, boston bets in the settled sub-atomic / ecliptic, ecliptic mystics to the sub-atomic / edge, edge met and a meter ran to the sub-atomic / middle, middle material and thee, the sub-atomic /

kingdoms, kingdoms come into a sub-atomic avenue called love / underground, underground sounds and the sub-atomic / lair, lair outed through the sub-atomic / chapters, chapters felt and chilled upon in the sub-atomic / complete, complete elation and the natural hello to thee, the sub-atomic.

CHAPTER TWO

Refinement, refinement refreshed to a helpful trace of ther ace called subatomi / whispers, whispers and the misters meant to the sub-atomic / contentment, contentment filled in the sub-atomic / mailed, mailed a material measured in the matches made sub-atomic / comes, comes a query forth then the sub-atomic / chase, chase a chilling's sub-atomic / over, over dazed and the places met in the sub-atomic / chasten, chasten and the rationale for the sub-atomic / helium, helium heights and the query placed int eh sub-atomic / hasten, hasten across and then find a pace to the sub-atomic / hearken, hearken and listen to the sub-atomic / hearts, hearts pert in the spurts through the sub-atomic / warmth, warmth felt and the melt found in the sub-atomic / jasmine, jasmine jewels given the sub-atomic / bales, bales and the sails across these, the sub-atomic / cherubic, cherubic fields and the fellows found in the sub-atomic / veil, veil opens then too, the sub-atomic / overt, overt recalll in the stall found, sub-atomic / underpaid, underpaid and overwelled in they, the sub-atomic / waylaid, waylaid mention of the pension for a sub-atomic / wealth, wealth and a stealth sent to thee, the sub-atomic / paths, paths plunge through the basins gains the sub-atomic / please, please appears and the wellness heals in a sub-atomic / pleasure, pleasure mentioned in the sub-atomic / plus, plus days and the dealt with sub-atomic / surges, surges and the mergers matched in the sub-atomic / stage, stage deals and the feelings tracked through the sub-atomic / usurp, usurp forgives and the cups caught in the receive for the sub-atomic / burnt, burnt and the spurt past the sub-atomic / crisp, crisp in a query for tehe, the sub-atomic / chasten, chasten past and the cast forth too, the sub-atomic / hasten, hastens patterns and the materials sub-atomic / lashes, lashes placed across these sub-atomic / lurch, lurch dearly into the sub-atomic / lapse, lapse lipped in the sub-atomic / regains, regains rationed for the sub-atomic / ravenous, ravenous yellows and the purple's pink in patterns grained in love's ascend into the sub-atomic / shards, shards chain free in the sub-atomic / pieces, pieces placed around these sub-atomic / kept, kept for a function felt enthralled in sub-atomic / campaign, campaign treaty and the meeting felt through sub-atomic / control, control lives in the patterns lined in the gently sub-atomic / captions, captions cubed in the chinese sub-atomic / change, change dealt in the sub-atomic / charges, charges padi for in days sub-atomic / run, run past and plunge into the sub-atomic / springs, springs sold and the strings thin spread for the sub-atomic / pulse, pulse felt upon the carolina shores and the meetings sub-atomic / paves, paves made deepened through in the sub-atomic / frothy, f. rothy frills and the deals lived sub-atomic / frozen, frozen forgiven and the freshen subatomi / thaw, thaw detailed and the swollen sub-atomic / past, past purged and the merger met in the sub-atomic / caution, caution over, due a, sub-atomic / approach, approach gently the magic sub-atomic

/ behavior, behavior believed and forgiven in the sub-atomic / bathe, bathe in waters well within the sub-atomic / disassociate, disassociated less and given moe into thee the sub-atomic / greek, greek to a mission sub-atomic / graciousness, graciousness allowed through the sub-atomic / gender-less, gender-less destiny for the sub-atomic / granted, granted DNA twirls through the sub-atomic / frozen, frozen ingrains thaw to the sub-atomic / thaw, thaw through the sub-atomic heat of laws 1, 2, love, thrive.

CHAPTER THREE
Power, power placed in the ours gained sub-atomic / struggle, struggle stills in the living sub-atomic / ends, ends detailed in the swollen sub-atomic / complete, complete in retreat and the ravings sub-atomic / recognition, recognition gains your remember in the ringing sub-atomics / speaks, speaks well and often in the driving sub-atomic / loves, loves gain and the gander about the shouting sub-atomic / lots, lots and the liquids ran into rays sub-atomic / luciferic, luciferic outline and the signs paths, the sub-atomic / argue, argue over and the lessened expressions become then, the sub-atomic / goes, goes detailed the sub-atomic / light, light hues and the insights spent in the sub-atomic / devious, devious outs these the sub-atomic / insights, insights interior too the sub-atomic / soar, soar across threes, the sub-atomic / surges, sruges and merges into the sub-atomic / conclude, conclude contoured through the sub-atomic / subject, subject given the graceful enchants to the sub-atomic / capitals, capitals and the cupids cued too, the sub-atomic / italics, italics found throughout the sub-atomic / palace, palace of the portals given the sub-atomic / paste, paste across raids to these sub-atomic / tracks, tracks rehearsed for the sub-atomic / troops, troops rational too, the sub-atomic / vaults, vaults valued in the sub-atomic / vaunts, vaunts voiced for in the sub-atomic / basking, basking in living the sub-atomic / blatant, blatant belief in the relief for the sub-atomic / sunrise, sunrise and the sezing sub-atomic / sunsets, sunsets and the graven sub-atomic / actual, actual amterials met in the sub-atomic / refuge, refuge and the confusion gone too the sub-atomic / crutches, crutches out too the sub-atomic / props, props positioned less in the sub-atomic / legitimate, legitimate to a cause for the sub-atomic / hats, hats lifted listened to the sub-atomic / worn, worn disguise and the thrones cast the sub-atomics / exposure, exposures paid to the sub-atomic / explosives, explosives imploded into the metatronic requires for the lifting sub-atomic / light, light leaps across the insights sub-atomic / lantern, lantern lessons and the legend sub-atomic / woven, woven well into the sub-atomic / laces, laces lurched past and into the sub-atomic / living, living levels your lightened sub-atomic / entones, entones interiors pave the liken sub-atomic / require, require reached for in teh sub-atomic / hermaphroditic, hermaphroditic details into the sub-atomic / philosophy, philosophy led through the sub-atomic / literary, literary levels left the sub-atomic / sort, sort suggested the sub-atomic / scrolls, scrolls purged and the passionate sub-atomic / held, held legendary for the sub-atomic / graduates, graduates annually through the sub-atomic / phase, phase forged in they, the sub-atomic / kipling, kipling paced to the sub-atomic /

archetypal, archetypal intrigue within the sub-atomic / roots, roots placed and the past past these sub-atomic / process, process felt and a curing met in the sub-atomic / requirement, requirements concentric to the sub-atomic / state, states in a status placed in these sub-atomic / primitive, primitive trails through the sub-atomic / private, private privation gone to the sub-atomic / under, under the detail of the sub-atomic / sub-atomic, sub-atomic regions reached through love.

CHAPTER FOUR
Wild, wild to the won in a winning still inside the glance sealed within, lovingly, the subatomic strand / devour, devour powered eternally within the living glee of lovingly the sub-atomic / candy, candy days and the implications cast into the living loves gone sub-atomic / music, music cues your for the euphoric sub-atomic / blow, blow past and the last won, sub-atomically / adore, adore dand the shore wound thoroughly into the sub-atomic / celebrate, celebrate the treaty for the sub-atomic / linger, linger in wonder o'r thee subatomic / warm, warm ways elective, the sub-atomic / rhyme, rhyme found and the reasons wound in the sub-atomic / life, life sub-atomic and the wife metatroni / battle, battle past and the lasting won to the sub-atomic / gift, gift fault-less and the fleet access to the sub-atomic / bouquet, bouquet into treaties and the reasons come in sub-atomic / babes, babes past and the woods lasted until now in the sub-atomic / through, through a door into a shore floored sub-atomic / tantalize, tantalize begun and the singing rings sub-atomic / touch, touch each other's paths through sub-atomic / dance, dance daily in the sub-atomic / glisten, glisten within friendly sub-atomic / moon, moons moist within the sub-atomic / angel, angels answered thee, the sub-atomic / cheek, cheeks touch in the sub-atomic / vast, vast values cast for the sub-atomic / sacred, sacred suggested and the confessed did, the sub-atomic / tiny, tiny trails through the sub-atomic / magnificent, magnificent meanings and the lessons sub-atomic / sugar, sugar sided fortitude into the sub-atomic / throat, throat thrilled in the held forth sub-atomic / between, between days subatomi / time, time treats you sub-atomically / gentle, gentle confession found, the sub-atomic / suspicions, suspicions sound the sub-atomic / coastal, coastal planes curlew the sub-atomic / deterioration, deterioration due the sub-atomic / callow, callow feels forgone the sub-atomic / common, common creatives measure the sub-atomic / fairy, fairy fields met theough sub-atomic / lessons, lessons deal in sub-atomic / joy, joy found you, the sub-atomic / harass, harass the raptured suspends into the sub-atomic / privacy, privacy dealt with truths gone sub-atomic / scolded, scolded over and the scalded healing sub-atomic / struggle, struggles outed and the shouted coming sub-atomic / sanctify, sanctify the sighs for sub-atomic / ground, ground relates and the sated sub-atomic / solely, solely suggestive the sub-atomic / oral, oral relays for the sub-atomic / people, people parallel your light sub-atomic / cream, creamy central sub-atomic / emergence, emergence met in the sub-atomic / warrior, warrior well now, sub-atomic / archetype, archetypes healed in the sub-atomic / context, context concurs then, sub-atomic / brow, brow broken, sub-atomic / power,

power appeals then, sub-atomic / control, control curls into the sub-atomic / formula, formula measures these, the sub-atomic / gone, gone to the gallows sub-atomic / prescribe, prescribe an inscribe sub-atomic / enthralling, enthralling throated, the sub-atomic / profound, profound the venues sub-atomic / mesmerized, mesmerized examples sub-atomic / entities, entities met in the sub-atomic.

CHAPTER FIVE

Juice, juice and the curfew's sub-atomic / what, what and the where then, sub-atomic / haul, haul over and the fillings give thee the sub-atomic / song, song sung then, the sub-atomic / their, their days done, the sub-atomic / delights, delights found then the sub-atomic / bash, bash abounds in the sub-atomic / regal, regal rescues come sub-atomic / temptation, temptation trails you, the sub-atomic / resist, resist gone into the sub-atomic / majesty, majesty met through the sub-atomic / bestow, bestow a treat on the sub-atomic / velvet, velvet winnings the sub-atomic / pouch, pouches measure these, the sub-atomic / shining, shining disciples of the sub-atomic / pendant, pendants worn through the sub-atomic / supreme, supreme detail on teh sub-atomic / sweet, sweet successes sub-atomic / century, century values the sub-atomic / mint, mint dimensions sub-atomic / operation, operation recall forgone the sub-atomic / miniature, miniature measures the sub-atomic / multitudes forgiven thee, the sub=atomi / official, official detail and the swelling sub-atomic / journal, journal cues you the sub-atomic / provoke, provoke a treaty come too, sub-atomic / zen, zen detail and the sweetness sub-atomic / divide, divide begins the sub-atomic / doodle, doodle done for, the sub-atomic / water, water wheeled in, the sub-atomic / wind, wind welcomes then the sub-atomic / some, some days treasured, the sub-atomic / design, design a daily pleasure in the healing cafe found in sub-atomic / cafe, cafe content within the sub-atomic / party, party follows the sub-atomic / mailed, mailed attend to the sub-atomic / award, award made the sub-atomic / film, film found, the sub-atomic / leather, leather and the weathered way into life sub-atomic / interior, interior traces and the chase hued the sub-atomic / soothing, soothing filling and the features found next sub-atomic / seduction, seduction over and the mention made, sub-atomic / invigorating, invigorating value on the sub-atomic / calming, calming colors you sub-atomic / invigoration, invigoration values you the sub-atomic / lust, lust dealt with through the sub-atomic / warmth, warmth felt through these sub-atomic / loving, loving electrically into the sub-atomic / jumbo, jumbo jewels decide to provide thee the sub-atomic / recycle, recycle reads yes the sub-atomic / indulgence, indulgence sent for in the detailed sub-atomic / self, self suggestive sub-atomic / mood, moods made gentle into the sub-atomic / enhanced, enhanced rates sub-atomic / dripping, dripping retails sub-atomic / aroma, aroma returned in the sub-atomic / essence, essence eccentric too, the sub-atomic / sympathy, sympathy signaled too, the sub-atomic / border, border visited the sub-atomic / surprise, surprise waits you the sub-atomic / pillow, pillows mentioned in these sub-atomic / celebrate, celebrate the clarity too, the sub-atomic / eucalyptus, eucalyptus cast to the sub-atomic / chamomile, chamomile compares in the sub-atomics.

CHAPTER SIX

Sound, sound suggested, sub-atomic / earth, earth trills sub-atomic / reconcile, reconcile suggested the sub-atomic / sublime, sublime relates and the stigma gone to the sub-atomic / twilight, twilight rays through the sub-atomic / aesthetic, aesthetic clarify wise in the sub-atomic / mosaic, mosaic melts in the sub-atomic / modern, modern mentions of the sub-atomic / phony, phony outed, the sub-atomic / starving, starving over done the sub-atomic / tint, tints treated for the sub-atomic / matisse, matisse met you and these sub-atomic / imposter, imposter sent past these sub-atomic / futurism, futurism and the facets fused in the sub-atomic / pastel, pastel is well in the spell break sub-atomic / abstract, abstract detail and the retract into a listening sub-atomic / buddy, buddy days and the raises sub-atomic / integrity, integrity mentions you the sub-atomic / unconditional, unconditional detail with the sub-atomic / compadre, compadre mentions these sub-atomic / sincerity, sincerity found in the sub-atomic / advice, advice forgiven thee, the sub-atomic preten / companion, companion found in a town Waimean and the dream strait sub-atomic / confident, confident in the powerful wave state sub-atomic / endure, endure detail and the surest rates sub-atomic / honesty, honesty cues your healing attend to the sub-atomic / squeeze, squeeze and the sneezes sub-atomic / vacation, vacations won and the sun shone sub-atomic / meant, meant for detail on the sub-atomic / share, share a prepare for the sub-atomic / promise, promise arisen and the plenty comes in the sub-atomic / snuggle, snuggle into valued sub-atomic / mellow, mellow allowance on the sub-atomic / designed, designed in detail on the sub-atomic / mambo, mambo simply written in the light red sub-atomic / media, media danced in the print red sub-atomic / happiness, happiness valued in the written sub-atomic / committed, committed creation came to the light wind sub-atomic / relationship, relationship readied and the regain sub-atomic / something, something sent for, sub-atomically / band, band belies you, sub-atomic / tear, tears past your sub-atomic / toast, toast antoher hosted in these sub-atomic / crazy, crazy conceed to the sub-atomic / little, little lessened the sub-atomic / cathedral, cathedral exampled in the sub-atomic / reception, reception held through the sub-atomic / gift, gift succinct too the sub-atomic / punch, punch over and the list reads the sub-atomic / usher, usher into the sub-atomic / grace, grace retails you, the sub-atomic / courtship, courtship out then, the sub-atomic / gown, gown chosen then, the sub-atomic / married, married daily too the sub-atomic / hawaii, hawaii suggested you, the sub-atomic / honor, honor held into the sub-atomic / do, do days sub-atomic / may, may weighs the sub-atomic / walk, walk won through the sub-atomic / annual, annual chastened through the sub-atomic / album, albums glued into the sub-atomic / march, march past rays sub-atomic / rice, rice reaches you in the sub-atomic / wedlock, wedlock suggested in these sub-atomics.

CHAPTER SEVEN

Ballroom, ballroom believe and the sleeves energetically sub-atomic / basket, basket keys and the seizure sub-atomic / buffet, buffet knees and the stays sub-atomic / put, put a place into now, the sub-atomic / roses, roses red within the read for sub-atomic /

present, present ways into the days gone sub-atomic / virgin, virgin heirs and the village attends your sub-atomic / dating, dating deals in sub-atomic / will, carbon wills the poses sub-atomic / alter, alter over and the fall has lessened here in teh sub-atomic / toss, toss across another's sub-atomic / does, does she deal in "yes, we will" to the sub-atomic / hold, hold the earth in your held arrive in the sub-atomic / biblical, biblical trails and the cause entailed in the sub-atomic / object, object moves and the heat accrued in the sub-atomic / civil, civil to a middle finished sub-atomically / flower, flower in towers sub-atomic / openly, openly attest to the sub-atomic / test, test your strength in the sub-atomic / award, award the cards kept sub-atomic / become, become delgihted in the sub-atomic / eternity, eternity questioned in your pretend for the sub-atomic / asunder, asunder in the wonder for the sub-atomic / tonight, tonight sweetheart go light into the sub-atomic flu / anxious, anxious has led an envelope through the sub-atomic / holy, holy estates and the healing comes to the sub-atomic / care, care for the causes stellar within your sub-atomic / monogamous, monogamous flew to a hearty venue called love is the sub-atomic / kiss, kiss an equal and remember too, the sub-atomic / bride, bride bays and the days come, sub-atomic / lawfully, lawfully detail your sub-atomic / garter, gartered stretch to the sub-atomic / vow, vow to see how too, the sub-atomic / machine, machine in the deus, sub-atomic / shower, shower details power your sub-atomic / bliss, bliss exists in a kiss metabolized through the light cause sub-atomic / union, union made and the trenches dug through the sub-atomic / elope, elope to the scope called sub-atomic / betroth, betroth in the residential range to the sub-atomic / stag, stag staged sub-atomic / nuptial, nuptial needs for the nipping sub-atomic / church, church brought watchful sub-atomic / pandora, pandora done through the sub-atomic / woven, woven into details sub-atomic / weaves, weaves a listen too, the sub-atomic / texture, texture torn through the sub-atomic / heirloom, heirloom leads in the sub-atomic / none, none met less One, the sub-atomic / unforgettable, unforgettable inspire in the experience divergent to a living attune / destination, destination narrows too, the sub-atomic / haven, haven made for the sub-atomic / busy, busy belief and the basics sub-atomic / craft, craft creates the kinship sound, the sub-atomic / blanket, blanket rebuilt through the sub-atomic / kept, kept for the currency sub-atomic / generation, generations read of the sub-atomic / spun, spun into spilling seed, the sub-atomic / nestled, nestled in the ceiling sung, the sub-atomic / gallery, gallery gazalled through the sub-atomic / settled, settled into the sub-atomic / farmers, farmers fanned too, the sub-atomic / common, common creates come to the sub-atomic / decline, decline detailed in the sub-atomic / handed, handed a sample for the sub-atomic.

CHAPTER EIGHT

Sharp, sharp into a card drawn sub-atomic / vivacious, vivacious in her value, sub-atomic / arrived, arrived in a leaving's sub-atomic / enriched, enriched through enhancing's sub-atomic / pursued, pursued in a pillowed sub-atomic / mission, missions mentioned into treaties sub-atomic / abolish, abolish led to lessen's sub-atomic

/ bootlegging, bootlegging bottled blitzing sub-atomic / revive, revive in the rewards sub-atomic / inspire, inspire details for the sub-atomic / synthetic, synthetic years go sub-atomic / cheat, cheat less, gather more toned the sub-atomic / linen, linens listened to, the sub-atomic / borne, borne delicious through the sub-atomic / thread, threads relative too, the sub-atomic / wonderful, wonderful in well regard for the situation sub-atomic / tapestry, tapestry tossed and the healing cost triples the sub-atomic / proceeds, proceeds made through the sub-atomic / generated, generated resale for the sub-atomic / vital, vital valuables made sub-atomic / blinks, blinks in the listens sub-atomic / bear, bear dead for the sub-atomic / link, link a lens on the sub-atomic viaducts to love / mile, miles measured your sub-atomic strand / confidence, confidence gained through the sub-atomic / platinum, platinum plans for the sub-atomic / express, express requires yours, the sub-atomic / valuable, valuable return too, the sub-atomic / advertise, advertise the cause come, sub-atomic / guard, guard regards you sub-atomic / warranty, warranty weds thee, sub-atomic / additional, additional detail won, the aub-atomi / vanquish, vanquish your require into the sub-atomic / distill, distill a delicate thrill called the sub-atomic angel, love / angst, angst out in the sub-atomic / turmoil, turmoil melts through the sub-atomic / skulls, skulls clank in the sub-atomic / skeletons, skeletons detail your sub-atomic / gather, gather require for the sub-atomic / garner, garner expire from the sub-atomic / sandy, sandy leads to the sub-atomic / blasts, blasts ignite in the sub-atomic / shrink, shrink away to the sub-atomic / spell, spell a spilling, s-u-b-a-t-o-m-I-c / unrivaled, unrivaled in revealing your hearts sub-atomic retail for God's gain to / rivals, rivals reach you, the sub-atomic / enormous, enormous in your resealed two, the sub-atomic / quantums, quantums measure values sub-atomic / construct, constructs crumble in a bridge past sub-atomic / freed, freed daily in a breath through the beauty called sub-atomic / frenzy, frenzy ousted in the sub-atomic / frills, frills fellowed in the sealing sub-atomic / fixed, dixed require for the shuttles sub-atomic / scaffolds, scaffolds cross in the details sub-atomic / relief, relief rests in the regards sub-atomic / spurl, spurl appeal and the reseal sub-atomic / spark, spark across the spatial sub-atomic / gelled, gelled in the reveal sub-atomic / depict, depict your detail from the subject's sub-atomic / manner, manner made through the mansion's sub-atomic / sought, sought a suggested sub-atomic / passage, passage cast through the subject's sub-atomic / ultimate, ultimate amaze with the create sub-atomic / order, order a pillage sub-atomic.

CHAPTER NINE

Marvelous, mistake made? a marvelous glade erupts into view, your's? God, the sub-atomic / magical, magical menu and the meal made sub-atomic / mountain, mountain strand and the stand for the sub-atomic / angelic, angelic explain of the strand born sub-atomically / treat, treat for the feet fleet into thee the sub-atomic / married, married to the extend borne sub-atomically / pleasant, pleasant appear in the papers dear to the sub-atomic / God, God gave claim unto thee, the sub-atomic / narrow, narrow leaps into the streets worn sub-atomic / wide, wide disguise gone unto thee the sub-atomic / parental, parental guise thrown into winds sub-atomic / lessons, lessons planned for gained now in thee the sub-atomic / born, born to explore more the sub-atomic / found, found in expansion due thee the sub-atomic / religious, religious retort too, the sub-atomic / material, material expire through the sub-atomic / known, known and often seen into thee, the sub-atomic / sort, sorts speak the sub-atomic / nestled, nestled into a heart found sub-atomic / frank, frank in exposes done sub-atomically / well, well in example and the sample sent for, sub-atomic / clamor, clamor about you? sub-atomic / living, living explain and the explosive sorts sub-atomic / heart, heart time, sub-atomic / strong, strong in believe in the heart lines sub-atomic / marriage, marriage amounts to the live in, sub-atomic / metatronics, metatronics accounts for the healing sub-atomic / pinnacle, pinnacles reached and the regains sub-atomic / letters, letters longed for and the junk explained in your DNA code sub-atomic / DNA, DNA again? and the code broken into your sub-atomic / greek, greek keys say "the sub-atomic / people, people who live lead into the sub-atomic / passionate, passionate persons pray for the healing sub-atomic / sex, sex is given interior detail for the prayerful sub-atomic / how? how? sub-atomically / when? all four sub-atomic spin / perfect, perfect in your healing sorts, the sub-atomic / delicious, delicious in a menu bought, the sub-atomic / partnered, partnered through a deeper day called sub-atomic / patient, patient in a healing way called sub-atomic / sub, sub, below, and the final code for the detailed sub-atomic / meet, meet her here, the code for the sub-atomic / measure, measure mellows your tear stained sub-atomic / matters, matters perfect for the living gems sub-atomic / pleased, pleased in a venued vaunt for the genuine sub-atomic / pad, pad written through in the key codes sub=atomi / sound, sounds of God, the key codes sub-atomic / experience, experience the savor sub-atomic / fellow, fellow intend and the treaty gave the sub-atomic / storm, storm out and the sealing in to the healed grade sub-atomic / may, may a fellow stand in strands deep in the living sub-atomic / persons, persons mellow into grades sub-atomic / fortunate, fortunate in a fellowship for the few trips sub-atomic / matters, matters material exist for the succeed sub-atomic / genuine, genuine intrigue to the zero count gained sub-atomic / fear, fear has estate wide purge now into the light led sub-atomic / love, lvoe has led us to the heart signs sub-atomic / jesus, jesus joins you in the purpose sub-atomic / miracles, miracles meet you in the treaty sub-atomic / journeys, journeys married into the sub-atomic / may, may we eternal be into our sub-atomic / define, define entire days sub-atomic / join, join another ray, the sub-atomic / years, years reach for through the beauty sub-atomic.

CHAPTER TEN

Clue, clue made the kindle won into a sub-atomic / lost, lost in a key code sub-atomic / found, found to be, sub-atomic / fortune, fortunes made for the sub-atomics / fortunate, fortunate and fondest of the sub-atomics / fervor, fervor strengthened in grains sub-atomic / strength, strength found in the central sub-atomics / suggest, suggested a lesson into the sub-atomics / search, search

for a semblance lands the sub-atomics / sorts, sorts suggested these, the sub-atomics / strips, strips ripped out to see through the sub-atomics / strengthened, strengthened measures in the sub-atomics / stirred, stirred and listened too, the sub-atomics / stripped, stripped of lessened then, the sub-atomics / stripes, stripes attributive in the sub-atomics / strides, strides made through raids of the sub-atomics / stressed, stressed a lesson made for the sub-atomic / stretch, stretch details of the sub-atomic / notice, notice finds you sub-atomic / noise, noise nailed you, sub-atomic / nurture, nurture gives you the sub-atomics / nature, amazingly natured for the fortunate fews who fuse our fellowships tools trade freed, electrically too, God's cause for the living sub-atomics / nestled, nestled in a suggested sub-atomic / nave, nave stove and the reclaim made for Jersualem's gates, the 93 who held fortitudes fellowships for the sub-atomic / knight, knight knelt in the rocky slope of the living legendary collective come to God the fotunately sub-atomic / guinevere, guinevere claused through the clauses cell-a-brated through the Golden Gates to love for the sub-atomic / lancelot, lancelot held forth into the lightly sub-atomic / legends, legends lept past for the feelings sub-atomic / lessons, lessons listening too, the sub-atomic / levels, levels learned for the sub-atomic / vibrates, vibrates forth and the fillings tossed to the hearing's sub-atomic / learning, learning to be an Israeli befriend and a gaining contour for the feeling's sub-atomic / living, living leads throughout the stones trued to the turning's sub-atomic / lightened, lightened listen and the beast has gone to the shores known metatronically sub-atomic / blank, blank belief and the strife roads sub-atomic / rasta, rasta retinue and the retire too for the sub-atomic / regions, regions reigned for the forthright sub-atomics / retinue, retinues archetypal and the fiscal fortitude for the feeling sub-atomic / revenues, revenues ranging into the sub-atomic / reaching, reaching a regard for the fairest sub-atomics / sought, sought success for the shouted frees and the frankest following to God the living sub-atomic / teaching, teaching the sub-atomic a stand forthrightly done too, love / taught, taught a terrific encounter to the teaching sturdy still and the shouting encountered through a giving sub-atomic / terrific, terrific technique and the greatness stood anvil deep in a heart's detail for the shouting sub-atomic / terrify, terrify left your lightening sub-atomic / tortured, tortured had led to the listing sub-atomics / released, released rang through to the theory sub-atomic / passions, passions patient into a ranches sub-atomics / partners, partners placed along the living attend for legends quality cubed forthrightly deep in a daily fortitude for the sub-atomics / parental, parental extoll of the trillions sub-atomic / parochial, parochial prepare and the pretend goes to the tablets sub-atomic / maddened, maddened throughout history true and the retails sub-atomic / moistened, moistened mention in a dealing dimension detailed through the thrillings sub-atomic / metric, metric palestine ensured through the dome borne sub-atomic / measures, measures mounted touring trends toward the thrilling's sub-atomic / chimney, chimney succinct in the prophets sub-atomic / treasures, treasures triumphantly direct through scannings sub-atomic / trickles, trickles traced daily true to the tentings sub-atomic / teething, teething done and the fillings felt with the thrillings sub-atomic / dancing, dancing detail and the resources spent on a touring sub-atomic / ink, inkmelts for the foritudes heaven deep into Jerusalem's seat gone sub-atomic / pens, how will you held begin the pens hispanically sub-atomic / rotor, rotor reds and the require for the gentle sub-atomic / rings, rings read round steads born sub-atomic.

CHAPTER ELEVEN

Clipped, clipped constants and the meters read a raning sub-atomic / light, light leads to pages red with the requires sub-atomic / pierce, pierce the sides blood deep in telling sub-atomic / source, source suggests a yes for the yielding's sub-atomic / electric, electric lessons lead thee, the sub-atomic / musical, musical menu and the mention's sub-atomic / mission, mission mays and the maps ran sub-atomic / granite, granite grapple and the dabble sub-atomic / grained, grained gains and the gemstones sub-atomic / gains, gains forthright and the rights red sub-atomic / sing, sing signs sub-atomics / join, join gently the gaining sub-atomic / spout, spout the cables sub-atomic / hole, hole elevated to the touring sub-atomics / whole, whole in her healing and the kneeling sub-atomics / whaled, whaled for and carted in tales of the sub-atomic / merchants, merchants mention a dimension deep in the details sub-atomic / oils, oils exchange years sub-atomic / essentially, essentially enlightened in the treaty sub-atomic / young, young yes then to the teachings sub-atomic / ascend, ascend sealed in the lightens sub-atomic / graceful, graceful and the prophetic won for the finals sub-atomic / estuary, estuary attires and the steps made sub-atomic / swan, swan days deal in her healing's sub-atomics / cygnus, cygnus said, "YES" again through the thrilling sub-atomics / arcturus, arcturus pools in the peelings sub-atomic / temples, temples traced to the corner stone for the faithful sub-atomics / chains, chains chill gone a way called the healings sub-atomic / changes, changes channeled then through a thronging sub-atomic / dramatic, dramatic deeds in a detail sub-atomic / durable, durable dates and the fashions sub-atomic / directives, directives selective and shown through a travel sub-atomic / prophets, prophets patented too, the traces sub-atomic / prophetic, prophetic fortunes made through the thronging sub-atomic / junctures, junctures joined in the thronging sub-atomic / junctions, junctions joined into the fashions sub-atomic / missions, missions made for the matters sub-atomic / plenty, plenty intended and the debate said so into these the sub-atomic / perfection, perfection felt and the fellowed felt for the fillings sub-atomic / magnify, magnify material and the miracles sub-atomic / greet, greet gains your shoulders sub-atomic / grit, grit green in a detail sub-atomic / release, release realized into the sizes sub-atomic / love, love led too, the sub-atomic / inspire, inspire soft in the shingles sub-atomic / praise, praise appears in the throats held sub-atomic / purge, purge ignore and insure your teachings sub-atomic / clear, cledarly the teacher's sub-atomic / codify, codify the clarify to a clearanc / corrects, corrects suggestive into an elective found and framed in the final sub-atomic / creates, creates a corona sub-atomic / content, content in details due the

daring sub-atomic / convenient, convenient to venues found in the feelings sub-atomic / corrective, corrective mention and the dimensions deal with in throats held sub-atomic / collective, collective challenges sub-atomic / crescents, crescents channeling a treatise sub-atomic / creatives, creatives compare and the spare gains sub-atomic / concurence, concurrence concludes thena nd the thanks come sub-atomic / alignments, alignments lead to the lifting sub-atomic / slugs, slugs out then and throngs found for the features sub-atomic / anterior, anterior meetings sub-atomic / posterior, posterior patterns and the people sub-atomic / pleasing, pleasing said so, "sub-atomics / steers, steers clearest in teh living sub-atomics.

CHAPTER TWELVE

Participate, participate daily in the heart sung "sub-atomics"/ joint, joint cope and the shapes found, sub-atomic / missive, missive mentions and the trap spent, sub-atomic / submissive, submissive extensive and the shoulders sub-atomic / annual, annual declare found apparent to the teason's sub-atomic / gentle, gentle gains you a journey sub-atomic / genteel, genteel inventives and the trifolds sub-atomic / genuine, genuine declarations and the durations sub-atomic / accepts, accepts and the suspects sub-atomic / plans, plans to be found for the fatihful sub-atomic / foundations, foundations amounted to in the teachings sub-atomic / meetings, meetings materialize through the thrilling sub-atomic / materials, materials mentioned through the triples sub-atomic / provided, provided led and living sub-atomic / articles, articles taut in the tallow sub=atomi / appear, appear compared to the living sub-atomic / avenues, avenues lettered in the conspire sub-atomic / widen, widen wedded for the fitting sub-atomic / carrots, carrots constant to the killings sub-atomic / tempt, tempt has found a lifting sub-atomic / articles, article omega to the alpha fed follicles sub=atomi / written, written in a smitten goodness for the greetings sub-atomic / gains, gains given greeting too, the thrice held sub-atomic / abound, abound eternally in international peaces sub-atomic / treaty, treaty reached, the sub-atomic / signing, signing 1950 style the telephone sub-atomic / shining, shining suggested thoroughly through the thrilling sub-atomic / sounds, sounds suggestive arranged in you and the recall sub-atomic / matrix, matrix materialized in the resize sub-atomic / lifted, lifted curtains continue in the creates sub-atomic / hurtles, hurtles suggested and the heroes invested in the hearken sub-atomic / down, down detail gone and the giving threw a retail sub-atomic / lifted, lifted listen and the lessoned sub-atomic / lightest, lightest listed attendance too the trios sub-atomic / lettered, lettered listings painted for the field plays sub-atomic / latticed, latticed admit and the refit sub-atomic / connected, connected, directed, invoked, spoke, the subtle sub-atomic / cut, cut cords led to the fled for, sub-atomic / lifts, lifts list your healing gifts and the gestures sub-atomic / apply, apply for, and too, the legendary sub-atomic / materialized, materialzed meanings found in the fellows sub-atomic / mastery, mastery admitted too, the trios sub-atomic / majesty, majesty made the flow of the fellows sub-atomic / majestic, majestic met in a missionary pane of the windows sub-atomic / miracles, miracles mentioned sub-atomically / mantle, mantle worn too, the triply sub-atomic / christos, christos creates a crescent sub-atomic / Christian, Christian red and the fed for plan to the fishes sub-atomic / creed, creed deed sub-atomic / cryptic, cryptic conceed to the deeded sub-atomic / nicean, nicean decree of the ones kept, sub-atomic / magistrate, magistrate made friendly for the fellowship sub-atomic / lifted, lifted gates and the license found for the findings sub-atomic / chosen, chosen succeed in the dreaded less and the healed more for the species sub-atomic / choices, choices made, sealed, the sub-atomic / books, books revealed in the printings sub-atomic / chapters, chapters chill at the thresholds sub-atomic / verse, verse rehearsal paying dear, the lightened sub-atomic / bible, bible bays clear for the gateways sub-atomic / tomb, tomb declared closed for the living sub-atomic / tomes, tomes and the writtens sub-atomic / tours, tours into missions sub-atomic / treatice, treatice made and a mention sub-atomic / conclude, conclude a bemuse for the features sub-atomic.

CHAPTER THIRTEEN

Inclusive, inclusive soothe and the daily sub-atomic / God, God gave few and the many sub-atomic / alive, alive led to the listing sub-atomics / legendary, legendary daily and the Father fed the tastings sub-atomic / durable, durable appear and the steerings sub-atomic / random, random reach and the mentions sub-atomic / within, within and throughout the thanks felt sub-atomic / constant, constant conclusion and the voices sub-atomic / pairing, pious past and the impasse found in the feelings sub-atomic / reclusive, reclusive suggest and the shillings cast thirty times past the sub-atomic trills / require, require red and thanks you for the healings sub-atomic / rewarded, rewarded again through the thankings sub-atomic / revealing, revealing register of the gain paid the sub-atomic / sword, sword said for the sub-atomic / fountain, fountain days dealt with in the dragons lost head and the heights said "sub-atomic"/ mount, mount gains a templed stand's sub-atomic / foundation, foundation built upon throughout God's days annually approached too, living again and then they find the listening sub atomic / love, love leads too and the two stood sub-atomic / brother, brother bays built sub-atomic / sister, sister sung for the features sub-atomic / specific, specifically succinct in the timings sub-atomic / vista, vista values your teachings sub-atomic / mansion, masterful mansions built on the basics sub-atomic / temple, temple details and the daily sub-atomic / clearance, clearance passed into a purged country choired to a trenchant sub-atomic / light, light led and the listened too allowance for the fellows sub-atomic / living, living suggestion of the Godness sub-atomic / word, word given too and the days of God suggest your amplify of the faithful sub-atomic / sword, sword said go lightly led to the listening sub-atomic / michael, michael gave david the grace to the lord's love sub-atomic / gabriel, gabriel given faith for the signature sub-atomic / song, song trades a travel sub-atomic / kindled, kindled a reward sub-atomic / waters, waters met in the remembered sub-atomic / dream, dream details the debates sub-atomic / pasture, pasture paired for the pureness sub-atomic / still, christ still in the garden sub-atomic / rose, rose red remember of the rewards sub=atomic / sharon, sharon rosey in the retire to the tour led sub=atomic / fortunate, fortunate forgiven faithfully led to the sub=atomics / few, few fed for the featured sub-atomic / all, all will be so, sub-atomic / often, often fed a fellow sub-atomic / more, more can say so, "sub-atomics" / most, most mansions met in the houses sub-atomic / included, included thricely the happenings sub-atomic / joins, joins appearing days of the patterns sub-atomic / listens, listens clearly too, the shoutings sub-atomic / gathers, gathers israeli and the preaches sub-atomic / gazes, gazes featuring the follows sub-atomic / gifts, gifts gleam in the details sub-atomic / courts, courts voiced forth too the sevens sub-atomic / rewarded, rewarded rays of the forgiven treatise placed in the bastion sub-atomic / pleasing, pleasing details found in the feelings sub-atomic / explorations, explorations implore for the felt one, sub-atomic / intrigues, intrigues register with the ceiling sub-atomic / entry, entry into quiet zones of the central sub-atomics / assume, assume a require for the chilling sub-atomics / attends, attend a thiran content for the filling sub-atomics / crete, crete replied to thee sub-atomically / creates, creates conclude in the sub-atomics / roman, roman retinue found the sub-atomics / expire, expires resigns to the sub-atomic / retires, retires early, the sub-atomics.

THE GENETIC-MENTS
LEVEL 40

CHAPTER ONE

Privacy, privacy codes your adoring news of the hidden genetics in love / privately, privately stated and the wellness related to a hit won, genetic / often, often a fellow found you genetic / demure, demure and the deny decried through the healing's genetic / eukaryotic, eukaryotic needs an exotic tissue, one cell deep into love then, genetic / decode, decode appeared in the lamb's tissue, ear well in a heart deep into love then, genetic / keys, keys apparent then, too, love's genetic / expressions, expressions meant for materially light's genetic / nuclear, nuclear nets and the declaration impaired into an inspire for the arisen genetic / nucleus, nucleus new and the needs bred into a healing genetic / motive, motive made clearly the living genetic / signal, signal sent to the genetic amend to a material amazed through alluring allocation too, love / glossary, glossary glee and the lease to define of a dashing code, a morse code intended too, for life's genetic unlock / glycolosis, glycolisis set on a genetic regard for the good love / anaplerotic star, anaplerotic star and the car's neat genetic / glyoxylate, glyoxylate in late agree to date love / biosynthesis, biosynthesis in sync with directs connect genesis genetic / citric love's, citric love's occur in genetic / acidic love's, acidic love's blend is genetic / cycles, cycles stuck out genetic / lost love, lost love's soothe through degrees of the cause genetic / regain, regain begun and the run is genetic / regenerate, regenerate the ratify of the qualifies genetic / discover, discover dues genetic too and in love / strategy, strategy trues our triple reset's believe in love's genetic / introduce, introduce a suggest and rip the aspects loose to see our genetic explai / election, election run y the won genetic / balanced, balanced ascent to the intents on genetic caus / energy, energy needs a net to fall on through to a genetic loo / utilize, utilize your size as a living genetic metatro / biosynthesis, biosynthesis electric genetic metatro / precurser, precurser to a true genetic / interactions, interactions and the pearlescent reactions too, a genetic cause is our love's detai / analogs, analogs and the crux ventral because of genetic / excerpt, excerpt becomes the rule genetic / change, change to a strange genetic / react, react to a fact that you are genetic code / reactive, reactive result to the pact genetic / logarithms, logarithms rhyme with the times genetic / pulse, pulse and the feel genetic / freely, freely fuel your genetic tools of love / explain, explain the dame genetic / exchange, for a vote genetic / notes, notes out time too genetic / totals, totals become the genes of core genetics / products, products pace our taste's genetic / beams, result in genuine genetic / enthalpic, amalgum's agree to be genetic / crowned, crowned the king of genetic hill / Simon, Simon said "genetic / Peter, hold still Peter's will, genetic / John, John joins our genetic coi / Mangus, Mangus wants a chance genetic / Solstice, Solstice seals our genetic fiel / Housed, housed and cowered over genetic / Functional, functional finds genetic / Ancient, ancient days genetic / Query, query could genetically b / Quest, quest concludes genetically in love / Geometrics, geometrics gems genetic / Druidic, druidic waves genetic / seventy-two, seventy-two stays genetic / Strokes, stroked denied? geneticall / twenty-two, twenty-two ways to stay young to a third's genetics.

CHAPTER TWO

Flames, flames and the ruse genetic / white, white genes melt to mix in love / brothers, brothers matched in the melt's genetic / seven, seven stays blue gened geneticall / corners burn, corners burn with turns roundly genetic tower / canes, canes of decide decree genes creased atttribute / covers, covers grease free of gene print / plates finger, plates finger genetic sword / senses, senses seen in genetic dream / celtic spiral, celtic spiral celtic to a gene genetic / pi, pi said, gene splice won, geneticall / circumference, circumference gains a new gene / circle a gene's, circle down too the gene, love / diameter, diameter dues a gene tow, love / multiply, multiply metatron's ability through gene / christian, christian knew tristan's gene cod / anonymity specify, anonymity specify in your collect on gene / magical, macical amuse our gene / calibrate, coves code our gene / helerides, hold a call encoded on gene / stones genes, stones genes to code / circular, circular temples within spiral's gene / mystery, mystery amaze gene / Hindus, Hindus gened cow free to save our love / Abydos, Abydos boasts good gene / Templar, templar and the genes poole / intelligence, intelligence daze, gene / Druids, druids drew on gene / Israel, Israel sails too, a gene / Eastern, Eastern ways, gene / Stars, stars said awaken ahead to a genetic appea / Genes, genetic to a scene, God' / Megaliths amount to a megalith's astound for the giving genetic / Lunar, lunar reflect into thee, genetic / Stele, stele wone by genes spen / Giant, giant gemsgenetically free / Axum, axum maxim gene / Mineral, mineral bathe and the built on too a genetic poo / Fundamental, fundamental arcs beleive in gene / Ethiopian, Ethiopian thumbs open gene / Jaguar, jaguar gewels green genetic / Bulls, bulls out to the shout "genetic / Lascaux, lascaux became a genetic flam / Earth's, earth's flame gene / Turns, turns genetic free too love / Governor, governor gains a new genetic / Magician, magician drawn to a magician's love in genetic / Turtle, turtle tames our gene / Magic, magic won by three's genetic / Schemes trees, schemes trees and schemes genetic / Duplication, duplication station's genetic / Position, position won genetic so / Constellation, constellation comes through genetic / Hyperbolic, hyperbolic degrees genetic / Layouts, layouts lead to genetic / Nile, Niles miles genetic / Osiris, Osiris said genetic / Precession, Percussion precession's discussion spliced to become one genetic love / Patterns, patterns please her genetic / Coincidence, coincidence come through genetic / Culmination, culmination made, genetic / Patterned genus, patterned genus too genetic / Cogs, cogs and the dregs genetic / Wheels, wheels out and on genetic.

CHAPTER THREE

Alarm, alarm over genes wo / reserve, reserve your choice to be genetic / resting, resting genetically clear / Placed, placed at a head genetic / Taken, taken fill freed genetic / Tangentially, tangentially chosen genetic / Averages, averages won, geneticall / Break, bread up due genetic / Postulates, postulates pair genetic / Succeed, succeed chared securely genetic / Threes, threes trade gene / Sevens, sevens display gene / Maori, maori tribes gene fre / Ahu, ahu mabu gene / Akini, akini kinds gene / Ra, Ra spells g-e-n-e- / Opens, opens our love's cure gene / Up, up to a tree genetic / Energies, energies gene up too, love's lead / Eastern, Eastern ways gened tru / Easter, Easter genes cure / Isles, Isles of man genetic / Rotarua, Rotarua gened by degree / Random, Random annual gene / Ano, ano knows genes, aka tree / Rather, rather made the choice electrically gene free / Rare, rarest, still, genetic / Grounds, grounds gain gene / States, states still, gene / Eyes, eyes out and on gene / Truths, truths tell, gene / Integrated, integrated plans to be gene / Authoritative, authoritative agree too, gene replication / Focus, focus becomes gene / Pure, pure intensely intent genetic / Integrity, integrity trues a genetic cod / Harmony, harmony abides genitacall / Watery, watery ways genetically encode / Ways, ways home genetically seale / Milky, milky mates genetic / Days, days due a hue genetic / Heaven's, heaven's gate genetic / Knights, knights on too genetic code / Pathos, pathos plays genetic / Teethed, teethed trades and the shades encode / Knolls, knolls kneel in the patient's chilled through light's encode / Placed, placed in pews abundant too an healing encod / Accordingly, accordingly done to a genetic encode / Precipice, precipice charts of / Plans, plans on too love's genetic / Atlantis, atlantis agrees to a news genetic / Bends, bends and the blends genetic / Bent, bent on hue's genetic flare / Recall, reward gains recall respectfully through your genetic appear / Rewards, rewards come gene / Birth, birth blue abide gene / Rebirth, rebirth reuse gene / Orion, Orion again by a gened enclose / Magical, magical amues genetic / Truth, truth told genetic / Guatemalen, Guatemala won a gene's poo / Reverse, reversal too by a gene / Quantum, quantum cues genetic / Lept, lept to a loose genetics.

CHAPTER FOUR

Angor, angor over, genetic / Akton, akton spouts "genes"/ Neptune, Neptune knew genetic / Reviews, reviews genetic's freeze, love / Notes, notes about your gene / Pieced, pieced plans genetic / Plasma, plasma plays on genetic / Rules, rules degree your genetic / Rabid, rabid rubics by genetic's multipl / Rates, rates on rubies genetic / Increase, increase your genetics too 4 / Cues, cues become genetic / Cortical, align these cortical codes genetic / Clusters, clusters come genetic / Sanskrit, sanskrit written into the genetic / Routes, routes won, genetic / Roots, roots avow us geneticall / Triangulate, triangulate your genetic favor fold / Percussion, percussion pens ours, thee, genetic / Freight, freight of genetic / Thomas, Thomas gained a genetic degre / Doubts double, doubts double up too, a genetic / Outer, outer ways genetic / Lunar, lunar days, genetic / Membrane genetics, membrane genetics due too gene / Peels, peels wear apparel on gene / Appealing, appealing genes of love / Shoulders, shoulders held for gene / Fragments genes, fragments genes less in God / Skyward God's, skyward God's guest is love's gene / Leap, leap to a gene's pod on God / Leopards, leopards spot our gene / Spots, spots met and a mate set on gene / Kept, kept coal above in the planet called love's gene encod / Electric, electric ways lay too a gene / Eyes, eyes genus see?/ Size, size of the genes fit genetic / Men, men who win geneticall / Stand, stand to a trend fanatically, genetic / God, God's good genetic / Strands, strands wet winds and the genetically inten / Eclipse, eclipse clues us in to genetic

/ Lessons, lessons good's genetic / Heal, heal us genetically to the good grands and the rounds pathetic in the romantic scenes intrinsic too, God's love / Heaven's, heavens seal genetic / Seal, seal of the wheel genetic and to the trends electric too, into love / Sanctions, sanctions declare our genetic degre / Field, field full within genetic / Foreign, foreign fades of gene / Strikes, strikes out over gene / Stripes, stripes in too, gene / Regards, regards us as gened and poole / Ravishing, ravishing raids on gene / Wisdom, wisdom won in gene / Willing, willing one won too, gene / Repose, repose in rosey genetic / Restful, restful days of gene flus / Ressonation, resonation rays, gene / Wandering, wandering ways wed, gene / Sparks, sparks and the harmful lasts genetic / Helenic, helenic haze due gene / Swords, swords clash at gene / Clashing, clashing clues our gene / Hearts, hearts held and the examples kin, genetics.

CHAPTER FIVE

Dashing, dates into dashing genetic / Entreaty, entreaty too, gene / Daring, daring gened delive / Respect, respect of gene / Calendars, calendars clear our gene / Mason, mason gene / Mayan, Mayan gene / Return, return too, gene / Clicking, clicking and the genes table / Syncopation, syncopation states us gene / Brushes, brushes with gene / Men, genes and the samples tribal triple / Bloods, bloods blown genetic / Expulsion, expulsion's impulsive gene cleans / Fragrant, fragrant red gene / Reside, reside as gene / Bleeding, bleeding abates gened pool / Bathes, bathes in our gene / Banter, banter and the beliefs grown genetic / Ensues, ensues a desire too and a genes pooling / Ashes, ashes out into the blue genetic / Collect, collect a call, gene / Mental, mental abides, gene / Entreaty, entreaty wins gened applaus / Particulate, particulate patterns gene / Pass, passed out gene / Chosen, chosen genes and the teeming sample / Reward, reward's genes and the hurtful succes / Sword, sword cut at gene / Clashes, clashes and lashed gene / Again genes, unique genes and the temples trail / Mend, mend a gate's genes and the railings train / Miniscale, miniscale means gene / Measures, measures agrees gene / Motile, motile ability gene / Ability, ability to be gene / Sperm's, sperms account gene / Erupt, erupt through walls gene / God's, God's glee gene / Intrust, intrust in a gene / Men's, men's deal gene / Metal, metal wield, gene / Cut, cut the cord's gene / Shapes, shapes on swords agree, gene / Form, form found, gene / Symbols, symbols gens of love / Symbols, symbols seen gene / God's, God's code curled, gene / Inclusive, inclusive abide is gene / Meaning, meaning to be gene / Daring, daring dues, gene / Include, include our news gene / Casual, casual plan, gene / Premise genetics, the premise genetics on love / precious, precious and recise too, gene's love / Intrude, intrude less, gene / Dashes? dashes and dates gene / Adoring genetically, adoring genetically won, love / Daunting, daunting dare to be, gene / Recall, recall our gene's flo / Rash, rash rates gene / Resurrection, resurrection comes geneticall / Placement, placement pens our code geneticall / Chills, chills out's genes.

CHAPTER SIX

Customs, customs become your gene / genetically, about your genetic / Duration, duration due, genetic / Coming, coming to you, genetic / Formula, formula found in gene / Won, won and wins through genetic degrees of love / Neters, neters and neat abids at genetic degrees of love / Emulate, emulate your fair genetic / Include, include desires gene / Carriage, carriage clued gene / Comets, comets intrude at gene / Erupt, erupt in you, a genetic plan / Risen, risen gene / London, London lights our gene / Current, Current broad way's current pool gene / Intrigue, intrigue within your gene / challenge, challenge agree to be met gene / melt, melt out a cry's release on gene / Metatron, Metatron made it, gene / Trues, trues a day on gene / Calibrates, calibrates could, gene / Exactly, exactly gene / Casual, casual cares, gene / Fuse, fuse a delicious gene / Formulas, formulas found, gene / Electric, electric ways, gene / Elects, elects to stay their genes / Erects, erects a grain on gene / Resurrect, resurrect your secure, gene / Pathway, pathway found through gene / Clears, clears a gate of genes / Causal, causal matters, gene / Connects, connects with other gene / Fashionable, fashionable fuse at gene / Interest, interest in your gene / Targets, targets chosen, gene / Burst, burst through too, gene / Fusion, fusion found in gene / Couples, couples join at gene / Complete, complete phase into gene / Cords, cords cut, gene / Cushion, cushions genes our gain / Opens, opens up too, grains and gene / Chances, chances won through gene / Succinct, succinct sets of gene / Stable, stable won, gene / Insights, insights come in gene / Racing, racing runs our gene / Rounds, rounds on too, gene / Arose, DNA arose gene / Completed, completed gene strand, ACT / Calibrate, calibrate our cue to our gene / Worn, worn thick with gene / Chosen Gene's, chosen gene's wed, love / Dashing, dashing days, gene / Inclusion, inclusion on a gene / Sharp, sharp decide for the living gene / Shorter Love, shorter love / Sunshine Genes, sunshine genes statu / Longer, longer ours these gene / Ours, ours are thee, gene / Others Genes, others genes, love / Rest, rest at gene / Wrangle, wrangle in too, genes.

CHAPTER SEVEN

Perfection, perfection found into the genetic's town, love / Mention, mention a dimension genecti / Manners, manners met, genetic / Matters, matters wet into genetic's love / Derivatives, derivatives dare, geneticall / Phosphates, phosphates float your genetic / Sugars, sugars set genetic / Melt, melt your genes plow / Random, random rounds, genetic / Functions, functions file a genetic grid' / Navigate, navigate near her genetic attir / affluent, affluent positions in loving genetic / Handles, handles held geneticall / Hydrolyisis, hydroliis wards genetic / Hydraulic, hydraulic genes on love / Leaps, leaps to a loop genetic / Lavender, lavender and the tree's genetic / Trusting, trusting allow of the glow flowered to through genetic / Trust, trust in One, genetic / Broke, broke open, gene / Places, places melt, in our gene / Blending, blending bugs genes cleared too, love / Tropics, tropics trade genetic / Leading, leading ways genetic / Power, power through a place genetic / Places, places plants, gene / Honest, honest answere and again genetic / Directions, directions due

genetic / Curtains, curtains well within, genetics / Heaven, heaven held for the listing genetic ascend / Seek, seek a date genetic / Confection, confection won, genetic / Openess, openness comes genetic / Thunders, thunders throat intrigued in genetic / Sinkage, sinkage sought in outed funds fortunate too, gene / Sought, sought a won, genetic / Lectures, lectures out, geneticall / Leasing, leasing ours, genetic / Crimson, crimson cubes, genetic / Seeping, seeping through, genetic / Ambrosial, ambrosial allowance trues our genetic / Silence, silence sent, genetic / Seeding, seeding speeds to our genetic / Done, done and due an annual genetic / Captive, captive clues, genetically due / Knottings, knottings suggestions drawn truly love / Gnawings, gnawings grinning acknowledge of love / Through, through and in, genetics gene / Remember, remeber the type, genetic to a gene / Again, again a gene's cod / Apes, genes of relate too, love's gene / Planets, planets and the please won, love's encoded gene / codes, codes include reigns, love / Sighs, sighs about our trust's rebuild to a gene / Satisfied, satisfied with let's to a gene / Loves, loves to be genetically free / Living, living lights our gene / Lies, lies about less than our gene / Lights, lights often gene / Essential, essential weave's genes unravele / Ingredient, ingredient great to a gene poole / Syrup, syrup think with thicken's gene / Strawberries, strawberries succeed to a gene's confession, yes too, love / Crux, gene's crux coupled in to God.

CHAPTER EIGHT

Absolutes, absolutes resolve to be gene / syndication, syndication of the ascendent gene / sites, sites gene full of God / size , size gene / largest genes, largest genes love' / levy, levy your genes to God's love / labia, labia gened to new materia / thighs, thighs wise to God's gene / penis, penis implants in a gene's fiel / implants, implants justify conjeal at gene / humans, humans deal in gene / win, win another's gene / God's genetically, God's genetically ma / enreaty, entreaty to human remember, the gene / oenings genetic, openings genetic agree to occur too love / soar, soar in to thee gene / graduation genetic, graduation genetic on vacation too, love / leaks, leaks and the streaks out too, a genetic code for love / lessons, lessons and a duration too, a genetic key cod / plenty, plenty and the inventive's genetic / love's crashing, love's crashing degree of a grade on too, love / love's retort, love's retort to a light graduation's genes degre / past, past and the present's genetic / planes, planes and the strains too, a genetic ke / develop genetics, develop genetics in our degree within love / soccer, soccer sends my agree to a place genetically score / tracks, tracks and the racks on too, a genetic / trees, trees deliver our genetic degree / catching, catching a wade to a grade's degree of genetic love / penaltimate, penaltimate time at the dime's genetic degre / patterns, patterns and the plea is genetic / apply, apply to a sky genetic / proctors, proctors factors genetic / mirage genetics, mirage genetic's is the cause genetic / honest, honest cause is a tool genetic / cause, cause to be, too, genetic / capable, capable agrees our genetic / institute, institute of the cause to be, genetic / traces, traces and a tribute's genetic / rhapsodic, rhapsodic abide at the heart's genetic / resurrect, resurrect your genetic decid /

source, source of the apostle's decree genetic / conduit, conduit of the line genetic / concrete, concrete accrue too a gene's tree / friendships, friendships found at a sound genetic / flourish, flourish a genetic flower and the flourish genetic / mends, mends a blend's genetic / friends, friends and the final degree genetic / colleges, genes and the college's seed on love / flood, gentle to a flood's genetics / spoofs, spoofs out to a genus's genetic / beauty, beauty worn home by a genetics degree / deep, love deep in a gene's arra / depths, depths deal with a frill genetic / cosmic, cosmis occupy of the size genetic / capital, capital contours and the keys genetic / apply to corners, apply to corners genetic amplify / mark, mark on the park's end, genetic / measures, measures into a genetic enthus / frankest, genius and the frankest decide to be well in genetic appea / declare, declare a dipper full by genetic / dates, poignant debates about the dates on love's genetic / open, open a genetic decide to debate about love / welcome, welcome to the willed genetics.

CHAPTER NINE
Paid, paid a gain for genetic wing / apply, apply to a sight genetic / grants, grants in and too, a genetic / triumphant, triumphant amplify can size our genetic / gain, gain a refrain genetic too, a gai / garner, garner a campaign genetic / gallup, gallup new ways and truest days genetic / glows, applications glows abide at a size genetic / corners, corners about and all to a square's genetic / meet, meet at your shore's genetic / presence, presence abounds and the sounds amplify into a genetic / love, love grows to a grapple with gene / valuations, valuations vaunt to a debacle genetic / station, station at the nation's genetic / genetic caprice, genetic caprice and the seek is in, love / genetics inside, genetics inside our appl / glitz, glitz and the cools in too, genetic / gene's vacates, gene's vacates and the values genetic / garner most questions, garner most questions about love's gene / gender schools, gender schools us out too love's genetic / basically, basically been and then a genetic / human, human homes correlate too, our genetic / genuine accounted, genuine accounted for genetic / four, four day's genetic / froth, froth frees our spaces genetic / opens a gene, opens a gene too,our love / awash, awash with a place genetic / God's walls, God's walls genetic / western, western ways winter in there genetic / size, size seals our gene / skies, skies sent to a size genetic / creased genes, creased genes with a piece sized to God / capable genetic, genetics capable to a cues abid / arms, gene's arms charm our genetic / God's charms, God's charms chime in to our because genetic / shades, pool your shades at a gene's God / suspect, suspect and the erect appraisal genetic / ether, ether worn and thin to a genetic decid / escalate decisions, escalate decisions is agreed to and God's genetic decid / rampage, rampage to a gene's pul / overhaul, overhaul and the mall's genetic / regenerative genetic's, regenerative genetics desires amplif / powers, powers and the be's genetic / empower, empower and the hours genetic / examples, examples and the simples sample genetic / resplendent, resplendent appears and into a genetic / domes, domes and the roaming gene / diametric, diametric decide to genetically decide too, love / animates, animates and awaits a

delivery genetic / bereaves, bereaves about the out's gene / genetic lands, genetic lands and the stands agree to / genetic's interest, genetic's interest is the rest in asid / inherits, inherits a touch that is genetic / much, genes that are much and into a genetic / gentle sought, gentle sought about genetic / affairs, affairs and where's about genetic / sights, gene sights apply to a gain of love / star, genius starts and the stars a gene / love leads, love leads into a gene's degre / roles, delicate roles are the soles genetic / characters, characters cornucopic to the means genetic / secrets, secrets and the seats upon a gene / southwest feet, southwest feet to a walk genetic / talks, talks abraid the genetics code.

CHAPTER TEN
Accept, accept an act on gene / acts, acts of love's five gene / kind, kind of stand too, gene / concurrence, concurrence of living gene / openess, openess won through gene / heart, heart of hands give gene / caring, caring about our gene / shore, shore on too, gene / finally, finally freed our gene / flows, flows a show on gene / finished, finished with your old gene / works, works on winds of gene / wellness, wellness won, gene / shows, shows us perfect gene / hammered, hammered out an apply too, gene / shut, shut out less gene / nails, nails kneel geneticall / calloused, calloused hands gentle in genetic / crunch, crunch out your gene / curriculum, curriculum laid through a genetic / erupt, erupt now go genetic / debits, debits due our gene / deboric, deboric arrive at a strive genetic / doric, doric care and the core genetic / hands, hands on gene / athens, athens georgia glee, genetic / tails, tails out genes in pool / flower, flowers call gene / free, free to tell our gene / birds, birds bells ring gene / signal, signal shells and on too, gene / inside, inside ours gene / frees, frees our fact genetic / font, font of you genes to / shows, shows us our genetic code / elegance, elegance gave us genetic / informative, informative found, genetically sound too, love / acquire, acquire a higher genetic / shelters, shelters elude genetic / shown, shown on your gene doo / jelly, jelly told show us genetic / blue, blue done genetic / peanut, peanut fell through a genetic / blows, blows and blues genetic / love, love to be, genetic / foursquare, foursquare and fairs of genetic / classics, classics pure gene / pose, pose at a durate genetic / looting, looting out genes in reason, fre / scandals, scandals success deletes gene / rembrandt, rembrandt runs genus paintin / arts, arts play genes a spark to love / avery, avery viewed in our genetic / captures, captures your friend genetic / spiral, spiral spun gene / fragments, fragments stars cars gene / inspire, inspire your genetic / ends, ends in zen, genetic / endless, endless waves, genetic / journal, journal due, genetic / journeys, journeys begun through genetic / wasps, wasps are out genetic / stuns, stuns us wins genetic / designs, designs again our coded genetic.

CHAPTER ELEVEN
Scratches, scratches of gene's cod / abstract, codes abstract too, gene / rumors, rumors out shout yes too, gene / companion, companion comes genetic fre / splits, splits your chores geneticall / show, show us yours, genetic / seams, seams sealant gene / erase, erase genes disgrace clean too love / perfect, perfect place gene fre

/ flow, flow on to a gene / heavens, heavens genus, God's gain to love / face, face us, gene / phases, phases fun, gene / grown, grown up gene / gravity, gravity grew too, a gene / blew, blew on, a gene / proof, proof on a gene / portraits, portraits place, gene / holidays, holidays due, gene / shows, shows up, gene / carbons, carbons case, gene / template, template trues, gene / governess, governess grace, gene / sirius, sirius forgive gene / finest, finest ours, gene / groups, groups grew gene / grace, grace gives gene / invite, invite in too, gene / love's invisible, love's invisible guide too, gene / seen, seen at heights be gene / gened hearts, gened hearts stud on, love / embrace, embrace your gene / intimidate, intimidate less, genetic / interior, interior trues geneticall / agree, agree to a genetic encod / granite, granite toward genetic / contemplate, comtemplate clues geneticall / emergent, emergent ones, genetic / memorial, memorial meets your genetic / maps, maps and the attitude genetic / molecular, molecular mates genetic / structure, structure trues genetic / infuse, infuse genetic / inspire, inspire hire, genetic / gallons, gallons of glue's free genetic / glue, glue out too, genetics cod / gathering, gathering codes freed genetic / gems, gems genes genetic love / wanton, wanton wins a genetic implod / water, water and you, genetic / watery, watery ways tears gene / grades, gradesgave you one two genetic / gradual, gradually give a living gene / resign, resign rates won genetic / lightest gene's, lightest gene's win love / remember, remember to rate your genes clea / members, members gene / pooled state, pooled state of gene / status, status stills our gene / foe, foe funds gene's poo / quo, genus quo status won gene free / quip, quip cute, gene / elates, elates over her clean gene / lateral, lateral lather on genes.

CHAPTER TWELVE
Plunge, plunge in to genetic / heaven, heavens gaze genetic / gate, gate opens up to gene / orions, orions belt cut as gene splice poo / gaze, gaze into tools genetic / uniquely, uniquely your eyes genetic / stood for facts, stood for facts a genetic hoo / respective, respective ways genetic / ramification, ramification due our genetic / grades, grades gratus and genes gave us genetic / goodies, goodies given geneticall / gape, gape at our gene / galant, galant gait genetic / freights, frieghts over due genetic / freakish, freakish sorts genetic / wander, wander out geneticall / hullabaloo, hullabaloo over and dealt with genetic love / gathered, gathered out within genetic / guarantees, guarantees to be, genetic / treats, treats us genetic fre / trusted, trusted each the other genetic / confide, confide capable of genetic / gabriel, Gabriel gave you your genetic degre / seeks, seeks a sort genetic / your, your sort genetic / aspirant, aspirant plans genetic / reside, reside at a rise genetic / light, light on to gene / swings, swings about genetically free to love / sorts, sorts and about genetic / soars, soars and skates geneticall / powerful, powerful one, genetic / embryos, embryos caught up in love's gene' / breed, breed us openly genetic / molecular, molecular mates genetic / sort, sort out your genetic / particular, particular pace our gene / man, man made gene fre / human, human holds in genes freez / gloves, gloves out and genes in to love / blood, blood blues and red's base genetic / breeds, breeds a lot geneticall / breath, breath abates too, genetic / melts, melts out her's genetic

/ breathing, breathing believes in genetic / recover, recover your gene / cower, cower out, stand in, genetic / shorts, shorts escape too, a genetc / statues, statues genes show love's flow froze / dealt, dealt with in God's gene / with, with us genetically, God / statutes, statutes genetics freez / shout, shout about your genetic fre / freedom, freedom found geneticall / spills, spills out family friend genetic / speech, speech sounds genetic / spurts, spurts spawns funs genetic / crescents, crescents cruise our gene / wrench, wrench wrung geneticall / religion, religion rounds genetic / sports, sports throw a genetic flo / politics, politics pew our genetic pac / math, math amuse genetic / pious, pious sorts genetic.

CHAPTER THIRTEEN
Forgive, forgive genetics, love / forget, love's forget, genetic / forgotten, forgotten lines and the gene's eras / clever, clever days genetic seeing / coverup, coverup up and out and the short clears genetic / precedent, precedent pays geneticall / pauses, pauses to clear her genetic / people, people on a genetic def / believe, believe in the One, genetic / heavenly, heavenly aid, geneticall / causes, causes genetic / chalice, chalice chosen full of genetic / spills, spills out to a map genetic / gemstones, gemstones gleam geneticall / aglitter, aglitter with good God's genetic / joints, joints fill with genetic degrees of releas / disclose, disclose dates genetic / written, written gates genetically fre / environs, environs sirens genetic / courts, courts clues genetic / overthrow, overthrow fews genetic / empirical, an empircal place genetic / happenstance, happenstance chanced genetic / glory, glory grew genetic / defies, defies dues genetic / dazzling, dazzling dues genetic / declare, declare a pass genetic fre / moratorium, moratorium on the succumb less genetic fre / complete, complete clues genetic / pectograph, pectograph paints me in to themes genetic / graphs, graphs grew too, genetic / resolute, clear resolve to see genetic fre / reverence, reverence in genetic / dense, dense dates genetic / decide, decide on a dove's genus genetic free / deletes, deletes dove, genetic / debts, debts don, genetic / add, add one genetic / up, up into, genetic / links, links up, genetic / level, level won, genetic fre / planes, planes pews genetic / steering, steering home the genes genetic / clear, clear of all genetic / clasp, clasp clues genetic / hands, hands and heals genetic / human, human heals genetic / clues, clues about genetic / Tabriz, and the change to and energy genetically free / couplings, couplings complete and compare too a genetic decide in love / hafiz, hafiz paid a compliment to the genetic link up in love / supreme, love's supreme in a genetic / supression, supression sent to the intent's creation genetic / bellow, bellow and above a degrees genetic see / believe, apples believe in pears receive geneticall / believe, believe in the cause to a genetic applaus / genetic, genetic play to the toys genetic / decode, decode the roads to a seas genetic / destitute, date sat the strength genetic / rise, rise and the use genetic / overlooked, overlooked and the word is genetic / throne, throne decided upon through our genetic / God, God gains your genetic / assume, assume the room cell genetic to a human code.

THE MOLECULAR-MENTS
LEVEL 41

CHAPTER ONE

Fig, fig of the few who knew the molecular adjust to love / leaf, leaf led to and fed the absolut / foreign, foreign affairs and the square absolut / nursing, nursing and rehearsing molecular / pioneering, pioneering and the sorts superluminous / scientists, molecular in the scientist trade on love / loves institution, love's institution the molecular / endeavor, endeavor and the ever molecularly / throughout superluminous, the shouts in his molecular desire / lookout, lookout for thee molecular / molecular systems provide, a residence inside thee love / powerful, powerful molecular connect with then love / theories, theories through the desires molecular / program, program in the pews molecular / preface, preface and the surfaced comes molecularly / verbal, verbal value and the show electrically molecular / grammatical, grammatical gathers molecular / tone, tone deep in a molecul / style, style of the whiles molecular / ignores, ignors and the shares seen, molecular / tool, tools on the molecular gif / coin, coin of the rathered commute to a molecular venu / comprehend, molecular comprehension of the send up too, love / dialogue, dialogue due and the foe gone molecular / entwined, entwined in the signed withs molecular / entirety, entirety and the wheres molecular / analysis, analysis due the credits molecular / explicit, explicit exacts molecular / implicit, implicit and the explicit molecular / parties, parties trained then molecularly / conduct, conduct on interplanetary molecular / intonation, intonation nationed molecular / member, member of the teaming molecule / melody, melody of the molecules, yo / vocabularies, vocabularies melt then molecule / phrase, phrase phased molecular / gesture, gesture gels the molecular / register, register a joust molecular / function, flinchless function molecularly / operational, operational molecular / target, target moleculars lead too, love / empathy, empathy planned then molecular / fail, fail out the molecular / blame, blame affront the molecular / proof, proof out, the molecular / memorize, memorize them the molecular / conjugate, conjugate a rate molecular / insist, insist in these molecular / utilized, utilized agrees molecular / core, core of the shores molecular / babe, babe of the raved molecular / native, native a neck the sect's molecular / pass, pass a place molecular / clear, clear enough molecular / aptitude, aptitude attracts miter and molecular / converse, converse a curse molecular / urgent, urgent durates molecular / anticipation, anticipation sets then molecular / respond, respond trues these molecular / said, said shed molecular / fluency, fluency felt through the molecular / burden, burden outed to the molecular / grooves out, grooves out to the molecular / exam, exam of the dazed molecular.

CHAPTER TWO

Track, track through this the molecular / potent, potent plays the molecular / vortexes, vortexes molecular mad / enchanted, enchanted entouch the molecular / emits, emits a freeze molecular / summit, summit reached molecular / magnetism, magnetism met by the reads moleculare / battles, battles believe the molecular / legend, legend of the leis, molecular / cherokee, cherokee chews the molecular / gather, gather in trees molecular / confrontation, confrontation comes out these molecular / digress, digress duress

aways molecular / vitally, vitally virtually molecular / relevant, relevant rates molecular / mythological, mythological mates data molecular / erected, erected a route molecular / kindled, kindled bridges molecular / cedar, cedar shouted molecular / lodge, lodge of the leads molecular / piled, piled a shout molecular / creek, creek of the crews molecular / aside, aside and the prides molecular / perhaps, perhaps abides molecular / fasting, fasting and the feasting molecular / prime, prime in the trimed molecular / boundaries, boundaries grew molecularly / entrance, entrance into grace molecular / strenuous, strenuous sorts molecular / excursion, in cargoed excursion in through the molecular / stomp, stomp out moleculed deb / grids, grids grained molecular / moth, moth about us found a molecular / flame, flame drew two, molecular / beacon, beacons molecular / terrestrial, terrestrial trues ours molecular / formation, formation of the frames molecular / occasionally, occasionally shouts molecular / ziggurats, ziggurats reach peaks molecular / galaxies, galaxies seen through these molecular / altered, altered ways molecular / drastic, drastic adroits this the molecular / due, due us these molecular / council, council of the kins, molecular / poverty, poverty out throughout the molecular / astounding, astounding news the molecular / shamanistic, shamanistic shouts the molecular / indigenous, indigenous dues, the molecular / bronze, bronze beauty molecular / transmitting, transmitting in the gettings molecular / frequent, frequent affriend molecular / prominent, prominent desired molecular / drifted, drifted out then molecules love / gorge, gorge grew molecularly love / spy, spy about it molecular / stock, stock drew a gains molecular / automatic, automatic molecules love / punch, punch in then molecular / card, card about your intonation molecular / pushing, pushing abuse outs the molecular / lambs, lambs win molecularly / disturbing, disturbing doubts out through molecular / pleasant, pleasant appears these molecular / star, star caliber in the molecular.

CHAPTER THREE

Behavior, behavior confused and the muses made into a maze bayou and the blues well into love then molecular / confused, confused has forgone and the getting along can become all we own for love molecular / how, how to show now the wonders molecular / divine, divine to a mannered detail for the well laid throngs true molecular structur / love, love and the valued transient encased in molecular / hate, hatred ruled out through the views loved molecular / beattle, beattle beat and the better molecular / comedy, comedy of the cubed molecular / digital, digital to a deluge degrade-less through molecular / purchase, purchase made and the haze lifts into a portraiture molecular / apply, apply for the petroglyphed molecular's stag / rental, rental paid and the rarest leys become true molecular / urban, urban abide and the side won molecular / silence, silence began and the strands became a gazing molecular / justice, justice amazed by your beings molecular / while, while we style for molecular / expense, expense and the intense tree tails molecular / rumbling, rumbling and the outed experiences engaged in molecular / distraught, distraught to an ought and an ending parallely molecular / origin, origins intentional to a dimensional applique for love thus molecular / baffled, baffled and the beauties pairs molecular / emanantion, emanations cause molecular / layperson, layperson appears in the nearest molecular / partnership, partnership paves in the cayes coned molecular / ridge, ridge derailed through thee, molecular / clue, clue to the trail, molecular / bump, bump in the trips molecular / claim, claims arranged for the regards molecular / similar, similar splendor and the mended moleculars / parties, parties patient and the penchants owned molecular / political, political to a miracle amounted too molecularly / plays, plays engaged in molecularly / hip, hip to a trippy molecular / dazzles, dazzling modes molecularly free / boulder, boulder bays and the waves molecularly fre / shoes, shoes worn patiently molecular / features, features found for the creatures molecular / intellects, intellects chime in the rhyming molecular / equals, equals into sequels because molecular / back, back to the beauty molecular / dart, dart and the starts worn molecular / edits, edits and the debits molecular / columnists, columnists compose a keener regard for the daily molecular / chiefs, chiefs and the changes molecular / extremes, extremes in regimes worn molecular / recent, recent to a decent detail molecular / skip, skip about politely and centrifically molecular / reputable, reputable to a repeat won milecularl / natives, natives nestle in the wrestle molecular / walks, walks in a talking reward for the gifts gained molecularly / prints, prints applauded molecularly / shots, shots and the rhythm sung, molecular / projects, projects apparent to the singing molecular / credits, credits to the credentials viewed as molecular / collects, collects and the singing's molecular / image, image and the merger's molecular / strokes, strokes and the visions glance molecular / millenial, millenial magnetize and the rising molecular / simply, simply and the mentally detangle molecular / success, success rang molecular to love / points, points gained through missions mused into the molecular / cultures, cultures concur that your insure gains molecular / flames, flames flossed and the healing tossed into a molecular / angles, angles merged and the words read "molecular."

CHAPTER FOUR

Parasol, parasol all and the vents molecular / skies, skies skimmed of the patinaed molecular / futures, futures sown and the moaning moleculars / scenes, scenes sensed, molecular / letters, letters written molecularly / fashions, fashions worn molecularly / features, features fused molecularly / converts, converts to the inverts worn molecularly / acts, acts strictly molecularly / complete, complete a staging molecular / implies, implies in the insides molecular / liken, liken to the hiked in molecular / questions, questions cast poses molecular / steel, steel detail and the welling molecular / rubies, rubies paid and the baubles bathed in a living retail for molecular / diamonds, diamonds due and the rueful forgave you a wave borne molecularly / sapphired, sapphired in ascendant metatronics and the sonics complete in a spun molecular / lured, lured to retired ways molecular / grand, grand to the ready and the rendezvous molecular / eiffel, eiffel trowels laid into molecular / scalp, scalp wrapt into a molecular / mills, mills drawn into a mission's molecular / paper, paper

patterns and the napkins tucked molecular / misconceive, misconceives and the reprieves born molecular / ambigious, ambigious to a beatific molecular / ambitious, ambitious embraced through a trace's molecular / paced, paced apparently through a genuine molecular / shots, shots and the tots worn molecularly / entrenched, entrenched in intrigue with the questions molecular / minimalist, minimalist modes made molecual / utility, utility trues and the muses muscled into a molecular / whimsy, whimsy out and the flimsy into a molecule angelic to love / piza, piza and the plaza's molecular / plaza, plaza of the mooning molecular / friends, friends and the french gains molecular / arrange, arrange allows you a yearning molecular / juniors, juniors and the jury molecular / seniors, seniors and the wrinkles raved molecular / operations, operations journals and the mentions molecular / opposites, opposites into composites merged unforgettably molecular / endure, endure a duration for the molecular / splice, splices agree for the molecular / deluxe, deluxe dues molecular / triples, triples intrigued and then these molecular / trims, trims application for the molecular / survey, survey of the rounds worn molecular / sneaks, sneaks derive molecular / introduce, introduce a detail for the molecular / inclusions, inclusions launched through molecular / crystal, crystal to a cause's molecular / events, events to the daily molecular / mysteries, mysteries and the met with moleculars / powers, powers and the pleasures made molecular / minutes, minutes and the mention's molecular / designate, designate and the suspend molecular / entire, entire in the hiring molecular / stones, stones and the striking molecular / minimalist, minimalist and the amounts made molecular / schools, schools and the choosing molecular / worthy, worthy and the willing's molecular / prominent, prominent and the precious molecular / woods, woods and the winding molecular / loot, loot and the learning molecular / buzz, buzz and the brought through moleculars.

CHAPTER FIVE

Essence, essence and the requirement made for the curing's mentioned apply to a magical molecular / hearts, hearts and the healing waves material molecular / dance, dance and the details molecular / voice, voice and the vaunted molecular / sings, sings and the singing sires a winging molecular / reveals, reveals and the reaching materials mentioned through a healing molecular / spirits, spirits and the spiritual amends molecular / eyes, eyes and the maze's molecular / messages, messages about through molecular / messengers, messengers above us and then thee, molecular / warmed, warmed to a winning molecular / slim, slim to a signal molecular / recoil, recoil and the reveal molecular / recovers, recovers a region molecular / fashions, fashions funded like a religion molecular / directly, directly due the relations molecule / transform, transform a funded fondation's molecule / scandinavian, scandinavian in teh scintillate mile long too, molecular / sense, sense in a sounding molecular / styles, styles in the smiling molecular / steps, steps into the resounding molecular / cubes, cubes on variation's rubbled molecular / sisters, sisters southern and the sounds made, molecular / boutiques, boutiques and the beauty for the filling's molecular / charming,

charming into choosing your molecular / rescues, resuces range and the revenues molecular / skins, skins and the declares worn molecular / arsenal, arsenal into retails win molecular / bevy, bevy above and the bivy sacked to a molecular / trends, trends and the details won molecularly / luxuriance, luxuriance paid for a living's molecular / spa, spa days molecular / borders, borders bade molecular / towns, towns details molecular / sugars, sugars sack molecular / sprinkles, sprinkles twinkles molecular / trickles, trickles and the nickels molecular / ideas, ideas and the detailed molecular / definite, definite to a mentioning molecular / like, like and well, molecular / luxury, luxury made sure, molecular / clients, clients attend too, molecular / buy, buy a detail molecular / bought, ought a pension molecular / trips, trips and the treaty molecular / passage, passage past dues and the messages molecular / message, message received and the lessons come too a molecular / massage, massage, yes, a molecular / bombs, bombs dropped retain a molecular imprin / made, made a winner's ticket choose a molecular inclusio / held, held a healing heading molecular to / felt, felt like a feeling won molecularly / traps, traps and the treaty molecular / break, break and patterns messages molecular / music, music mentions a mending molecular / melts, melts and amuses then a meeting molecular / bridges, bridges above and the shores sung molecular / race, races retrieve and the regions molecular / injections, injections joined and the chosen molecular / stilt, stilt worn and a tilt thrown to a giving molecular / kitsch, kitsch out and the heights about our hearing's molecular / succumbs, succumbs to a sealing molecular / measures, measures made for the filling's molecular / meet, meet again molecularly.

CHAPTER SIX

Interchange, interchange and the changes ranged to a winning molecular / exchange, exchange ranges to a volley electrically molecular / supple, supple to a simple molecular / sense, sense deep in a sending's molecule / layers, layers legendary too, a molecular / generous, generous genese amaze your molecular / mounts, mounts and the counts foes rejoin gone molecular / escape, escape comes to a county amazed through your giving molecule / levels, levels lend and the leaders merge in a way born molecular / layers, layers lead to a healing molecular / lyrics, lyrics lyrical too and a mention of the missions metatronically molecular / muse, muse means and the scenes played molecularly / urban, urban bays and the suburban's molecular / maneuvers, maneuvers in the renewal raised to a molecular / slide, slide into a listened for molecular / gathers, gathers now the genuine molecular / strides, strides raised through the regions gaze molecular / manages, manages a mention too, molecular / Gabriel, Gabriel chosen and the chiming reigns molecular / rolls, rolls and thickens now a material molecular / tympanic, tympanic appear and the mention's amend to a healing molecular / signs, signs suggest a molecular / within, within and the whistle blows, molecular / sounds, sounds detail and the sandy ways molecular / traces, traces and the tributes paid molecular / styles, styles in the refiles rode molecular / musically, musically material to a mention worn molecular / still, still supports and the tridents meant molecular / steel, steel itself

and the void vents a molecular inten / break, break given and the barracks tossed into a molecular / jam, jam off and the join becomes a belief for the lightening molecular / joins, joins a retail molecular / limits, limits out and the shout sent into a molecular / leap, leap across heaps and the shout for the shillings molecular / shapes, shapes and the signals molecular / shield, shield and the sheperds molecular / exchanges, exchanges joined into a journey molecular / museums, museums mentioned and the materials molecular / dream, dreams detailed in a won through A molecular / tracks, tracks in the restage worn molecular / listed, listed livings and the givings grown molecular / flash, flash and the fashions rehatched through a giving molecular / flats, flats and the chats chosen molecularly / scrubs, scrubs and the residents materially molecular / heavens, heavens and the rates run molecularly / wait, wait and the wintery molecular / sculpted, sculpted entice and the revise now molecular / muse, muse of the moments molecular / figures, figures and the fondest mentioned molecular / property, property and the properly material molecular / exaggerate, exaggerate and the recess too, a molecular / reply, reply and the above gained a molecular / dress, dress dearly well and mean that, molecular / contemporary, contemporary and the contents maze, molecular / contributors, contributors found for the feelings gaze molecular / respond, respond to a reason for the chosen won molecular / testify, testify trues your molecular / racing, racing a retail tool molecular / flashes, flashes and the fusions won, openly, molecular / regarding, regarding the gains molecular / raptures, raptures rains molecular / joins, joins a gentle mention molecular / blues, blues out and the winning shout, well made, molecularly / partition, partition and the mentioning moleculars.

CHAPTER SEVEN

Amusing, amusing materials and the reset for the finding molecular / gloss, gloss of and the genuine win for the challengs molecular / dressed, dressed in a daily ways molecular / well, well to an inhale called molecular / heavenly, heavenly to a molecule called love / molds, molds and the miracles called molecular love / wings, wings and the lessons won molecularly / wet, wet and the web broken to and the molecular knot / feathers, feathers and the fashions met through the molecular / flake, flake and the furries sent into a molecular though / fly, fly to the fuses molecular / fuse, fuse won, molecular / perspiration, perspiration's gain the molecular / amuse, amuse me polarity reversal's rehearsed through molecular / abrasive, abrasive off and the retail cost regains a molecular / wolves, wolves and the whistle's molecular / floating, floating and the coating's molecular / goddess, goddess of the recess past molecular / reports, reports employ yes molecular / ringing, ringing and the rang regard for life in molecular / answers, answers singing in a rhyming loft to love's molecular / videos, videos voiced and the vernacular is molecular / enormous, enormous include in the retail molecular / glasses, glasses in the qualify molecular / portrays, portrays in a parental molecular / sizes, sizes and the rises red molecular / installed, installed and the regard for molecular / interiors, interiors paced and the relace led through molecular / squared, squared and the rejects respected too, a molecular / fantasy, fantasy and the feelings tossed to a molecular / pelts, pelts and the peelings paced through a molecular / characteristic, characteristic and the creative's tossed into a molecular / allure, allure details and the rulings paced into a molecular / employ, employ and the plans made at a level molecular / managerial, managerial and the meetings made into a molecular / exude, exude and the rude is gone into a molecular / expire, expire in a fire found molecular / strips, strips ripped out through molecular / tabular, tabular treats and the resets molecular / registers, registers a cause for the killings coldly molecular / internal, internal accept of the ability to give freely molecular / tunes, tunes detail your molecular / towns, towns deny forth moleculars / tapestry, tapestry teals in molecular / hangs, hangs seld less, molecularly / ideas, ideas relate your faith moelcula / rescue, rescue out and the reclusive ascend into a molecular / retire, retire form allow grace molecular / resurrect, resurrect respect for the filling molecular / relate, relate a reasoned molecular / pawns, pawns exit molecularly / creative, creative resource resounds in molecular / measures, measures agreed to, molecular / rations, rations repaid for molecular / skin, skin sent to a molecular / symmetry, symmetry in acceptance of thee, the molecular / blends, blends and beliefs agreed, molecular / position, position made and claimed molecular / trades, trades attired in the molecules elect for the Office Christ's and the Humanity basically freed of slavish slaver / traits, traits apprise us in our molecular ressurect / adored, adored and the sword's cut, molecular / parisian, parisian to an include code molecular / bali, bali and the calling supermental through a quark laid materially maternal to a molecule called love / balance, balance ascendant and the chapter won molecularly.

CHAPTER EIGHT
Reported, reported the theft, inside, of the sides metatronic too and the love metaphysically superior to the middle molecular / notoriously, notoriously amazed in the neat estate called molecular's love / romped, romped and raged engaged to the measure's molecular / moisture, moisture met wet amaze in the living measured molecular / pleasurable, pleasurable platitudes and the moods metrically molecular / preside, preside inside the strengthened molecular / beckons, beckons a beacon molecular / backs, backs into stable molecules materially replaced through regenerative embrace / past, past over, molecular / passes, passes thee the parallel keys to a wasted molecular spa / model, model amounts to a miraculous molecul / experience, experience set in the bliss filled molecule / affluence, affluence gained and the intentions clear to a miracle viewed molecularly / recommended, recommended abide to the reconnected views kinetically akin to a demanded release for love / ravenous, ravenous abide in the interiorly adept molecular / regard, molecular regard for the retain meant release / philosophic, philosophic the moistened material through a miracle called love / based, based in belief and the basics molecular / birth, birth reinstates the license molecular / personal, personal entreaty for the committee elect through a miracle molecular / mystique, mystique made the entrusted allow

for a pleasant molecular be / regarded, regarded yours perfectly parallel too, a miracle molecular / reference, reference made to an intrigue with the living miracle, hu-manly molecular / cards, cards cast past moves miraculously molecular too, love / deliver, deliver a daily delivery to love this mirror full miracle for fully molecular / deference, deference paid to the gazing molecular / reveal, reveal and the enthrall gained molecular / correction, corrections concurrent to the insurance parallely molecular / conceal, conceal met the wheel in a winging good try for the lovely miracle called molecular / symbols, symbols succinct in the surrender to a miracle called the molecul / magical, magical electrons danced in the meeting your molecule / connect, connect defines the rewind into a metatronic decide to be completely molecular / mankind, mankind to the find electrically replete in a miraculous molecul / favorable, favorable estates exactly miraculous on this molecul / reflect, reflect into directly this trouble free molecul / life, life lightly held in this fine estuary called miraculous molecules intrigued with love / detached, detached has won a monetary rebirth through love's miracles matched in molecule / desire, desire to detail your openness to molecule / discard, discard corrects your convex molecule / dissect, dissect due to the receptive molecule / disreputable, disreputable details find that place molecular / plans, plans mantained through the transits molecular / places, places in traces molecularly winged two times 360 degree / planets, planets written in the Venutian mend of all that ails the molecular bran / concurrent, concurrent to passages made and the fallings fade to a failing lift arranged to intrigue a molecular muse, love / co-ordinate, co-ordinate this compare and dare the light electric, molecularly / decompress, decompress to the regress allowed to the living molecular / clearly, clearly historic to an amusing molecular / theories, theories advance and the the chances molecular / arise, arise in the inscribes molecular / quizzed, quizzed about queries molecular / parts, parts paid for in thee, molecular / shift, shift to a singing molecular / personal, personal and appealed to, molecular / works, works welled too, molecular / magical, magical miracle molecul / views, views valued clearly molecular / virtues, virtues gifts of the spirits lift too, love's molecule / influence, influence allows you a modern molecul / agree, agree to the bag-free molecul / amulets, amulets allow your intrigue with objective relate to the release of all detached estates molecular / coins, coins carry the toss too, a molecular / ching, ching detail and the wells molecular / chang, chang to the fishing moleculars.

CHAPTER NINE
Medical, medical in the may be, molecular / profess, profess a rather be molecular / quickly, quickly came a quatrain molecular / covers, covers a query molecular / chinese, chinese in chosen name, molecular / ordain, ordain a due molecular / prismatic, prismatic to a proton's melt molecular / transits, transits allow you a living molecular / grasp, grasp an attend to the loving molecular / heart, heart days molecular / moves, moves above and the mask removes a lining molecular / power, power prepared to arrive in the molecular / sureness, sureness set in the move to a molecular

/ strokes, strokes made directly into a molecular estat / rebels, rebels yell through your yellow regard for the molecular / heroic, heroic to the roaming molecular / waterwheels, waterwheels remain molecular / snow, snow days crystalline into a molecul / energies, energies compare to the molecules move / derivation, derivation to durations molecular / animas, animas bossed to an intimate prelude and the partnered anima professionally molecule / hunter, hunter found and the hounds rehearse materially molecular / light, light to the threshold inlightened through love's breathing molecule / anima, anima mains and the interns molecular / darkness, darkness out and the dabbles into molecular / scripture, scripture cures the heart's molecular / fires, fires moved to and the merry molecule / elixir, eleixir gates and the mother's openings to a molecul / masons, masons advnaced and then too a molecul / masters, masters chance and the intent to a molecul / grasp, grasp and the grown molecule / former, former to an open affair, the molecule / figures, figures find the phase molecular / pupils, pupils gather again in the places molecular / penetrate, penetrate complete into a molecular / eyes, eyes wise and then molecular / pierce, pierce done and the thrilling is molecular / flower, flower fades and the lifting's molecule / light, light lenses molecule / golden, golden daze and the days electric to a molecul / holiday, holiday due into a meaningful molecul / developing, developing dates molecular / traits, traits discussed into the molecule / territories, territories deduced as trained for a molecul / burst, burst forth in queries gazed to a molecul / forward, forward said too, a molecul / outward, outward stood a molecul / disintegration, disintegration grew a rational queen for the means grown monetary too a molecul / shapes, shapes wed to a tower molecular / phenomenon, a phenomenon deep in love's molecule / single, single days gazed through molecule / housing, housing arrange and the cellular stages molecular / heaven, heaven wed to a meaning molecular / injury, injury due to releases soon and then too, a molecul / neurosis, neurosis sent a healing vent into a molecul / conditions, conditions extent molecular / answers, answers spent through molecules knee deep in love / cures, cures paged through to a molecul / heart, heart dealt freely molecule / movement, movement made toward news molecule / rebellious, rebellious rewards for the swords grip molecular / affairs, affairs measures molecular / stratus, stratus mastered and the mention's miraculously molecular / perfection, perfection accounts for the patience molecular.

CHAPTER TEN

Drops, drops into a durable philosophy of moleculars / rains, rains in a reign molecular / faced, faced to the sums molecular / expire, expires cause in the repaired wires molecular / experience, experience said, "A Molecular"/ hallucinates, hallucinates to a question molecular / powers, powers met into an our molecular / heart, heart days molecular / terms, terms gazed into treat wise molecular / electric, electric allows and the flowing meters run through a heart molecular / science, science said "yes too, a molecule / justification, justification dates your heart held molecule / content, content to input molecular / principals,

principals wowed throughed the healings moelcula / cues, cues reused to a tabular molecul / cubic, cubic query and the details molecular / supreme, supreme to the dreams electrically molecular / revelation, revelation on the duration mapped throughout your molecular / today, today you are well to the living molecular / churn, churn with directive and the invective "to live" lightly molecular / circulate, circulate a resign to the molecular / translate, translate your state as the molecular / loosely, loosely said "molecular"/ rests, rests regarded as molecular / published, published in these latitudes called molecular / writes, writes the writtenw ay that is the call molecular / reverse, reverse into a rehearse called molecular / copies, copies cued to yes in you and your daily molecule / stores, stores sold in the sealed molecular / storage, storage made electric to a reflexive molecular / retrace, retrace steps into the begin and the due days bright within the molecular / retrieve, retrieve a daily way to be due to the molecular / vortex, vortex values and the variations molecular / tests, tests over and the joy met in your molecule / brights, brights into sights met parallel to a molecular fiel / strike, strike a note resoundingly molecular / character, character found and the function's curate is true love / upper, upper ways to the falls into love's molecule / members, members paid a daily molecular / ingest, ingest into the recesses molecular / secrecy, secrecy made best through a molecular / limits, limits detail your molecular / circles, circles on the signals meant to love, a molecul / friend, friend found daily through the living's molecule / religious, religious to a regard for the giving molecule / mystics, mystics met and acknowledged too, a heart filled molecul / hands, hands detail your giving's molecule / diverge, diverge into daisy emergence and the miracle's molecule / christos, christos apparent in the winning molecular structure / patient, patient repair and the staring direct into love's molecular stretc / paul, paul and the principal for your molecular / jude, jude and the rude fog lifted to reveal a giving meditate for the hearing molecular / virginal, virginal qualify and the sigh cured molecularly / realize, realize your reaching size and the successful merger made through molecular impl / central, central to the portal magnificent in love's attitude for molecular forgiv / sites, sites suggest your joyful forging of bonds electric to a molecular allowance for love / abyss, abyss bridged and the elections listened to in molecular forgiveness to love / historic, historic allow and the sowing molecular / infinite, infinite to a fellowship molecular / endure, endure a duration molecular / emphasis, emphasis gained and the strands trued molecularly / redeems, redeems set into a molecular recover / meanings, meanings merge at the molecular / realize, realize the sizes sown moleculars.

CHAPTER ELEVEN

Imitate, imitate only the living rebate for molecular / overt, overt to the mergers molecular / lines, lines detailing the intentions molecular / converge, converge on the words spent molecularly / dwellings, dwelllings set for molecular / link, link a listened to into a molecular / license, licensees moleculare / elixirs, elixirs mixed to the feelings molecular / presently, presently positioned throughout these molecular / empires, empires passionate to a molecular / connect, connection carried throughout these molecule / abysmal, abysmal over and the dues paid molecularly / drainage, drainage employed through a gearing molecular / cores, cores erupt and the mention's made of a gentle molecular / sunshines, sunshines shining molecule / power, power days showered in the lightening molecular / rational, rational eruptions throughout a mantle molecular / disembowel, disembowel our molecule / churns, churns changed to a molecul / emptied, emptied yes to less then molecular / substantial, substantial to a reinstate of the listed molecular / vesicle, vesicle of a periodic spend and the rables redundant to a molecul / germinal, germinal aspects and the mentions molecular / periods, periods passions paid molecularly / methods, methods mentioned for a metallic selection molecular / summits, summits succinct to the descends molecular / creates, creates allow and the release day's molecular / trigram, trigram electives and the ringing molecular / triggers, triggers rigors molecular / original, original regard for the granted molecular / spins, spins patient to the molecular / creates, creates frolicsome molecular / perceptively, perceptively precise to a molecular / judged, judges to a weathersome molecular / warns, warns ranged molecular / visibly, visibly west to a molecular / visual, visual values for the fortunate molecular / expose, expose and the saying molecular / palaces, palaces built for the chalices molecular / built, built to be daily molecular / shown, shown a channel molecular / tongues, tongues held forth to examine your molecular detai / torn, torn loose to be listened to a molecular / sworn, sworn to swoon to and the dealings molecular / said, said so, "a molecular / explore, explore a rewritten awareness molecular / disturbed, disturbed only through a venue molecular / scholarly, scholarly explore and the more gained molecular / collective, collective intrigues and the missions molecular / possible, possible to a perchance enchance through a living molecular / present, present to a precedent molecular / combination, combination cured to a reassurance called for, molecular / transparent, transparent trilogy for a mastery molecular / windows, windows into a winter's winds molecular / shoal, shoal suggests a soul's lift into molecular / scenes, scenes succinct through a molecular / clustered, clustered concur that creation is sent for through love's molecule / monadic, monadic menu met humanly rich through a mention molecular / modes, modes into miracles molecular / remember, remeber to aim for the fortune's molecular / avoidant, avoidant voices and the changes molecular / entangles, entangles mangled angles molecular / lest, lest we gesture free your molecule.

CHAPTER TWELVE

Immanence, immanence comes to a thoroughness molecular / drawn, drawn daily into a habit released for the living's molecular / haloes, haloes in the shadow's molecular / lights, lights in the shallow's molecular / linkage, linkage creates your blinking molecular / essential, essential in the resets molecular / crown, crown to the pronouns molecular / evolves, evolves to a regard for the balance's molecular / myocardial, myocardial mention freed to frameworks gained molecular / alignments, alignments of the reassignments molecular / fashions, fashions features and

the fathoms fielded unto a molecular / phase, phases won for the feelings molecular / focus, focus interior to a mentioned molecular / fiasco, fiasco daily and the "let go" molecular / festive, festive invectives for the feature's molecular / taste, taste of the tripled molecular / wizard, wizard of the material's molecular / mice, mice mentioned daily to a molecular / hu-man, hu-man breath and the mentioned moleculars of love / tin, tin in the winning molecular / winking, winking and the drinking molecular / carriage, carriage curate and the marriage met molecularly / shatter, shatter over and the chatter begun to a gaining molecular / batter, batter in the bettering molecular / repair, repairs made and the dating is molecular / duties, duties balance in the challenge's molecular / gates, gates forged openly greeted to a loving molecular / monkey, monkey amaze and the meeting's molecular / scarecrows, scarecrows enriched through a meaning molecular / wicked, wicked winnings and the greetings molecular / wizards, wizards terrific to a training molecular / yellow, yellow "yes" and the teaching's molecular / brick, brick into a bare yard's molecule / roads, roads attired in shrouds electric to a molecul / examples, examples into sampels sent for and the fortunate molecule / houses, houses plowed for and found for the finding's molecular / temples, temples trained to a triple appearance near the simply molecular / men, men deal with the daily molecular / sanctuaried, sanctuaried arise through a generously molecular / sapphires, sapphires into the scintillating molecular / temples, temples chimed in the chilling molecular / men, men daily befriended through a molecular attir / sparkles, sparkles and the recoils merged into a mentioning molecular / blink, blink annually to a mentioning molecular / glazes, glazes and the raises won molecular / shelter, shleter in the plenty won moelcula / heavens, heavens sent grand rewards for the loving molecular / seek, seek a settled strait molecular / remember, remember too, a mention of the molecular / deliver, deliver daily deluges molecular / tiny, tiny to a traded molecular / tunes, tunes in the trading molecular / measures, measures mentioned in the treasuries of men, the hu-man chronicle, molecular / parts, parts paved with the chiming molecular / parthenons, parthenons patogonian molecular / collective, collective creative and the singing molecular / mother, mothered through a mainline molecular / release, release to a daily line decreased from a lining capped to a molecul / utero, utero in the using molecular / yoni, yoni in the sunny molecular / baptism, baptism belives in a molecular meeting's dept / font, font details your cannon of the molecular gift / lotus, lotus magics menu to a molecul / magic, magic detail forgone to a mentioning molecule.

CHAPTER THIRTEEN

Relations, relations rearranging to a reappearance molecular / personal, personal to a pension rehearsing year's molecular / variety, variety views the variation molecular / aspects, aspects into respects born molecularly / relationships, relationships resistant to a rearrange for the reward's gains molecular / existant, existant to an inspection met molecular / awe, awe infused within a molecular / councils, councils arranged in the monarchy melted throughout gains molecular / mandala, mandala arranged intoned with molecular / dividends, dividends thrown into a molecular / paramount, paramount mounted to a pentateuch marriage on the molecular / amounts, amounts spent regained thorugh a giving molecular / succumb, succumb to a gifted molecul / exists, exists throughout your throning mentioning to a molecul / complex, complex prepare on the amazingly miraculous molecul / primodial, primordial in sounded molecular / assume, assume a preoccupy to a material molecul / push, push a passion fortunate to a molecul / unify, unify dealt with in a molecul / active, active traces mentioned in a zen day molecule / broken, broken days and the daily molecule / living, living patterns merge into a mission perpendicular to a maze worn molecul / secure, secure regard for the treatise written deeply molecular / hopes, hopes detailed for a resealed molecul / pictures, pictures pensioned rehearsal for a miraculous molecul / drew, drew details and the reviews molecule / squares, squares apparently torn through a treaty molecule / circles, circles seals and the ceilings made molecule / germs, germs held within wealthy molecule / brush, brush your details along living's molecule / bacteria, bacteria allows your challenged forgives to the feelings molecule / coiled, coiled contours and the chiming maintained through a chilling mile molecular / traditional, traditional detail from the details changed to a molecul / accounting, accounting for the treating recount to a channel met into a molecul / safely, safely sealing a settled molecul / past, past poste and the heart's enhance to a moving molecul / portals, portals mortals and the mentioning molecule / plunder, plunder and the sunder maintained to a triple molecul / plenty, plenty told and the mentioned amaze for the freeing molecule / lasts, lasts to a trait molecular / locks, locks lead to a freedom molecule / keys, keys suggested creatively to a freedom's molecule / opens, opens pairings molecule / doors, doors allowed into an appearance molecular / jars, jars opened then to a thrilling molecul / electric, electric stays in the steering's molecule / enlightened, enlightened in the enlivening molecule / joins, joins a sounding molecular / watching, watching the wondering molecular / shown, shown details for the forthright maintain to a mission worn molecular / visualization, visualization views your marriages molecular / construct, construct created through a generosity for the features born molecular / parts, parts paged and the pleasures gathered to a mothered paring molecular / pieces, pieces placed patterned to and a victory born molecular / sons, sons sentinel to a molecular / woes, woes worn through a gigantic forgive and the fortunate timber of a redwood allow for the highest stage born molecular / opens, opens the doors molecular / steps, steps across the lintel's molecular / watching, watched for molecular / burst, burst cubes and the caught won molecular / agate, agate gapes and the gauges molecular / guards, guards done and the dazes molecular / query, query created and the creations emerging materially molecular / hot, hot enough to ask for, k, moleculars.

THE MUSICAL-MENTS
LEVEL 42

CHAPTER ONE

Halls, halls and the heels that ring on the floors of kings and the heaven's gates hung on a musical note for the features mentione / sing, sing above and the elections date a heavenly period musical / spiraling, spiraling out to secure a sectional detail for the incurrence molecularly musical / spake, spake to a lower level in a feeling mention of the dimensions musical / species, species musically arc-angelci to the coming musical / singular, singular to a nature palatial and the palces heavenward for the features decoded musically / singles, singles and the staying doubled to a mention wider heard through the healing's musical / cuts, cuts encoded with devoted mentions musical / hits, hits made for the features paid a daily musical / king, king and the ring laid along reigns metatronically musical / don, done your sorted and assorted sports for the features musical / ozmetic, ozmetic electric and the white seas windcapped regard for the musical dimension / red, red allow and the musical notes for the features abundant into a living musical / shoes, shoes off and the narrow viewed allowance to a featured metatron and the application for a musical request for love / shoes, shoes off and too the view metatronically due an appearance musically requeste / wedges, wedges worn upon the shoes of heavens lifted musical / kitts, kitts and the boat sold to sail for the towing musical roads to love / afluff, afluff and the enough laid into a musical / mentions, mentions and the details miraculous materials muscia / sandles, sandles and the scinitillates unto a musical / sum, sum and the sentry sent into a musical / cashmere, cashmere appearance and the details miraculous unto a musical / felt, felt and the belts nap erratic to a detail for the snapping musical / canvas, canvas of the cubicals met in thorough musical / kits, kits attired in thoroughness for love in musical / cupids, cupids stupidity forgiven and the follies begun to a certain degree of abide in the life musically replet / sport, sport into sorts more musical / music, music into details assorted decree / fate, fate follows and the figures rest in a retail amuse metered for the musical / houses, houses held forth musically / heal, heal your attributes through the listening musical / tabernacles, tabernacles inquired to in a glistening musical / joined, joined in the where then musical / notes, notes evocative range and the invention intoned there musically / quotes, quotes outed through the shouted miracles of musical / waits, waits daily due a missionary musical / acquire, acquire your details well within the musical / mormon, mormon tezts inquired into musically / traits, traits abide John deep in the counted forth and amounts implied both musically / books, books detailed and trued within for the ensured account sounds musically / place, place embraced and the theory sunk through musical / schedules, schedules suggested and the heights invested into a living gate musical / ahead, ahead into days born musical / sufficient, sufficient inquiry and the theory forth musically / boulders, boulders daily decry a theoretical empire musical / exist, exist detailed and the trail sufficiently clear musically / eclipse, eclipse retailed and the clues amused throughout the musical / shine, shine in insuring's musical / michael, michael's query is the theory voted for when wins befriends become the lesson musically slated for love / trust, trust began and broken

filled within the legs borne musically fre / splendor, splendor details your insured love musically / awaits, awaits a carriage marriage deep in love's mend of the musical / willing, willing to be musically free / relations, relations begun and interiorly free for the miracles musical / shown, shown the chants to arrive in musically / enchant, enchant meant musically / transcendant, transcendant to a curing musical / babbling, babbling appetites for the feelings musical / cheers, cheers daily through the misery gone to the lightening musical / events, events venued to the mystery musical / tasmanian, tasmanian see and the ocean's blue to a velcor freize of the dialing due to a mysterious life musically / treatise, treatise finished and compared to only the musical called love / trines, trines experience in love's mystery, musically / show, show your detail to the selling welling musically loved.

CHAPTER TWO

Showers, showers empowered in the smiling enchantress met through days musical / singing, singing allows musical / clever, clever to the evering musical / loan, loan a detail to the miracle's musical / pharmacy, pharmacy fused into reasoned amounts of the lyrical in musical love / options, options arranged for in the feelings musical to / opinions, opinions retailed in the musical revues enthused, love / mint, mint details for the feelings musical / meera, meera met in you and your musical abide through love / mithra, mithra and the mentioned prophetics of musically, love / mira, mira looked into for a clarified view of love, musically / stings, stings over due and the theories musical / salsa, salsa says a miracle found for the following's musical / verde, verde green delivery of the musical rest called legat / grassy, grassy days and growing ways into love's musical / greens, greens detail our daily raves musically to love / bold, bold in the basics and the beats musically to love / assertive, assertive details and the musical's entertain to love / rest, rest here, now, musically / depiction, depiction into notes borne musically / often, often veiled and never led past thronging gongs sung musically / veiled, veiled applause and the cause sung musically / romantic, romantic arrange meant for the sung won musically / mystery, just to run too and the theoretic sees of the musically led to love / scientific, scientifically direct to a detail frank with the feelings mysteriously musical / intrigue, intrigue engaged within and wondered for in the feelings thrust for the musical / globe, globes glow in the glees musical / language, language dared and the daily squeeze done, musically / temples, temples treat is the miracle musical / tombs, tombs crack through the gates won musically / glorious, glorious in inquiry for the fortunate musical / summary, summary dared through the thrilling musical / world, world won and the mention becomes a daily musical / research, research sent to the materially free of the heavenward gazes musical / exploration, exploration mentions your healing' / unique, unique to a signal mounted musically / civilization, civilization's repair and the theoretic musical / pioneering, pioneering musicals and the mentions declared for love / scholars, scholars declare and the daring's gaze musical / ancient, ancient and the declared for musical / serious, serious allowance placed in the relative's musical / revolutionary, revolutionary forged and the feature's musical / hieroglyphics, hieroglyphics repair and the surrender into a ferry musical / cover, cover cavorts and the sun suggest a singing musical / decipherment, decipherment meant for the suggested musical / surface, surface applied to and the forest sums a musical / run, run to the covering's musical / ruins, ruins detailed through the dealing's spent musically / level, level to the touring musical / far, far and the featured musical / illustrated, illustrated in the sated affairs won musically / incomparable, incomparable compare for the fortunate musically / landmark, landmark ability to the being's musical / contribution, contribution controlled through the theories musical / awesome, awesome suggested and the design drawn musically / magical, magical define and the findings musical / spot, spots sent musically to love / offers, offers theorized as musical / detailed, detailed ascend and the shining's musical / recipient, recipient and the inception spent on the striding musical / inscription, inscription and the mystery made aware of the mankind musical / included, included in the light is the living musical / orbital, orbital agree to be objectively free of the mention less musical / touch, touch and the seal is held forth musically.

CHAPTER THREE
Mountains, mountains fountains and the florid intention called muscially love / except, except in the incept called musically lif / accept, accept the direct date set forth in the literature called musically love / kingdom, kingdom comes into the literary molecules called musically love / basis, basis and the belief is into your molecular musical / sense, sense settles into the venues called musical / region, region and the randoms called musical / villages, villages viewed our valuable musical / pole, poles upon the line musical / construct, construct a way to stay musical / opal, opal evaluate in the musical / hearth, hearth and the held forth is a musical / triangle, triangle established musically / allow, allow a plow of the show musical / planted, planted in the seed's musical / consisted, consisted to a face levelly neutral musical / significance, a significance becomes our musical wo / myth, myth released into a musical / religion, religion and the revolve succumbed to in a reisde at the heart musically / involve, involve our solve of the musical revolv / dynasty, dynasty dues and the festive muse called musical releas / festival, festival of the fuses musical / allied, allied to the slides sweet in a swelling musical / visit, visit our cares for the musical / negotiate, negotiate the stays musical / arrrangements, arrangements made to give a musical / operating, operating in the send musical / become, become a magnitude repaired musically / previous, previous dates live musically / flood, flood fond memories musically / inviting, vital invites to the cues found musically / metaphor, metaphor for the affluent, the musical / clothe, clothe thyself in God's glen musically / green, green to known musicalnes / constituents, constituents believe the best musically / musically, musically distinct to a distant hue, love / plaza, plaza four-tiered and the applause grown musical / dominate, dominate and the safety set for the dues paid musically / explore, explore the shores within thee, musically / mute, mute to

the impure and the insure shouted " ministers eat free " musically / admire, admire your pairs musical declare, "love / week, week of the seven and the wonders loved musically / moment, moment to the inquires told truthfully through the musical / amplified, amplified estates within the musical wind / drawing, drawing on the reversals musical / connect, connect to the imperial sect musical / survey, survey of the stage musical / power, power and into thee, musical / expression, expression and the content trued into the musical / core, core and the sheerest shored desire to be musical / stone, stone set within a musical degre / gigantic, gigantic escape to a musical wo / program, program your musical release into a way to love / sculptural, sculptural release into yes we are musically fre / excavation, excavation and the national set musically fre / matrix, matrix and the lifts purchased release of the musical / stable, stable to a cable's cure, musically / limestone, limestone lives and the gift is a grant musically / period, period over and the winner? Musically!/ beam, beam of the light led blue to a musical / seals, seals and the teal blue musical / version, version of the ventures musical / faction, faction of the features purloined to a musical allo / invented, invented a musical way to say "hinted at" musically.

CHAPTER FOUR
Continue, continue to inspire the freedom musically / instead, instead of dead, ahead, musically / heart, heart held entreaty of the held on musically / found, found a friend musically / transgression, transgression's truest musical relie / presumed, presumed arisen and the message RELEASE, musically / shield, shield of the shed, musically / particular, particular to the happy interlude, musiclal / valid, valid insure of the expression musically / represents, represents a musical compare for the sense called love / emerging, emerging measures musically fre / parallel, parallel to the agreements musically made creativel / doubt, doubt is shout out musically / sight, a musical sight in love / model, love's model is musuica / rise, rise to the BE musically free / beg, beg about the shouting "musicals"/ flag, glad to pay for the flag flown musically / bridge, bridges built musically / bump, bump into a muse free lyrically musicals / route, route out the frames musical / number, number of the news musical / stream, streams freshly ringing musically / boulders, boulders fielded through the musical / reserve, reserve and swerves is into a musical / young, young into finished musicals / someone, someone who loved musically / vain, vain to a ventured vei / garden, garden of the good won musically / holiday, holiday days and the ways musically / hidden, hidden decisions to love musically / lounge, lounge into a maze won musically / treat, treat us well, musically / every, every is, musically / roof, roofs red with blue gills and the gains fed corn deeds musically / head, head to a homeward hope for the musical / shelters, shelters found, musically / single, single to a moment shot through musically / bend, bend to a beauty metaphoric ot love e, musically / phased, phased into musically / luxury, luxury leads to the living musical / award, award a gift musically / worlds, worlds whirl into love musically / actions, a.ctions set on mankinds reforestation of the earth wed musically / grading, grading grew

into a musical repriev / kept, kept light to the bees, musically / secret, secret set to the lightest refrain musically / ready, ready to be musically free within love / treat, treat done, musically / foreign, foreigns follow and the swallows electric to a musical amus / topic, topic of the potion metaphysically musical / mail, maile the mail too a directorial musical / relief, relief rests in out musical releas / goal, goal won, musically / turn, turn made musically / ivy, ivy green to a treaty made musically / piedmont, piedmont teemed in bluest musical / minute, movement meant to the minutes of love's musical / minute, minute begun to the won musical / clear, clear the air musically / serve, serve a detail musically / supply, supply sent into a musical sor / oxygen, oxygen given a musical breat / air, air paired with amend musically.

CHAPTER FIVE
Dynasty, dynasty met in the A's had for the signing musical / oak, oak trees musical to the Father's hear / button, button worn across the passes musical / mouth, mouth sustains a marriage musical / granite, granite grew ingrained to a detail musical / falls, falls flex the musically efficien / video, video days and the sayings musical / season, seasons central to the triply musical / subway, subway rides to the interiorly musical / soft, softly said, "thee musical"/ connection, connection spun through to a trickling musical / captain, captain stood for and the fortuitous grin at the marriage date's musical / public, public to a peeling musical / able, able to apply for musically / card, spanish cards melt in a Latin intend friendly to a framework musical / table, tables red in spreading musical / steer, steer particular to the pensions musical / stare, stare daily through the love leys musical / kentucky, kentucky caves allow the waves mammoth to God's music / eyes, eyes uniquely seen through to the bedded musical / sky, sky days musical / rain, rain rays musical / ounce, ounces paid for chances lanes of dancing musical / safe, safe suggestions musical / thunder, thunder thrills your healed musical / foothills, foothills found around your musical / sawman, sawman said connected resurrected through a sleepy musical / mission, mission relaxed and the relapse musical / wins, wins a warning musical / johnson, johnson joins a musical waterwa / prosperity, prosperity peers into your musical / plastic, plastic planted and the gathered intentions mount to a meeting musical / animal, animal meant for the feelings musical / quality, quality apparent to the quietest musical / classic, classic measures of the musically adep / outlet, outlet led filled to the fullness musical / solid, solidly sold to the seat won musically / headquarters, headquarters held forth to the fueling musical / certain, certain days read musically / grind, grind grew above the venues musical / bush, a bush ablush in musical / partake, partake daily of the dealt in musical / salute, salute the musical mentions of love / personnel, personnel cures made dear to the measures musical / tie, tie a trio up in musical / trace, trace trues daily to a meeting musical / riverfront, riverfront infusions round the Ganges musical / Called / The / Dove / Like / A / Electri / Current / of / Rasberry / New / We / are / The / One / Le / Hu Nab K / Climb.

CHAPTER SIX
Fabric, fabric veiled and framing ripped in a musical gift to love / prices, prices prized and galant lies foretold the tearing musical / paid, paid for impressions and the healing recessions informed on musical / values, values praised and appearances musical too God's concurrent allow / engrave, engrave detailed in a dearest musical / tell, tell us well now, "musical?"/ corral, corral your colors musically / correction, correction allows your musical / direction, direction directly musical / melt, melt appearing musically / camera, cameras chimeric into a musical nurser / town, town toured musically / nursing, nursing expect and the kneeling musical / sunshine, sunshine shone through the touring musical / nursery, nursery days dialectic to a desire musical / security, security felt near the nestle musical / warning, warning over and about us felt the feelings musical / care, care foretold in the telling musical / made, made enraptured daily musical / sunset, sunset sets in a dazed portend of the treatise musical / combine, combine a creation, homewardly musical / perfect, perfect to the potions musical / favorite, favorite values perfectly moistened in the miracle's musical / truly, truly dressed in the musicals allowe / spring, spring sprays attributive to the constructive musical / properties, properties apparent to the traces musical / forever, forever detailed in the delaings musical / stay, stay tonight in the plot musical / comfort, comfort comes in the creates musical / winning, winning allow and the fashion's musical / mulberry, mulberry blues and the pinon musical / arrivals, arivals dare thrive in the venues musical / God, God given musical / man, man fed the focus musical / guitar, guitar strums and the seasons musical / God-man, God-man said "allow me" musically / afraid, afraid records your swords allow for the features musical / clinging, clinging vined apex reached for the futures musical / choose, choose a reaching musical / ufo, ufo flown musically, *unified faith objective / shone, shone in musical wins, love / star, star days read in miracles musical / remember, remember days allowed through miracles musically replet / free, free for the fellows musical / treasure, treasure details musical / location, location lends your musical / default, default voiced into a musical / voice, voice values your musical / plagues, plagues detailed as living musical / end, end a spinning musically / locus, locus operand and the retails musical / manna, manna meant too, musically / red, red relate for the rapture musical / honey, honey made from the features musical / land, land levels your listening musical / memory, memory mused and the mentioned musical / tired, remain near the tired and referrals transferred deed the musical regards for love / biblical, biblical, cyclical, ascendant, love's musical / commandments, commandments remanded in your tirades musical / ten, ten times the trimmest musical / word, word won, musically / scream, screams over and the variations musical / remember, remember meals born musically / life, life led to the lending's musicals.

CHAPTER SEVEN
Hero, hero held within thee, musical / crossroads, crossroads and theroad's limit to a degree musical / loki, loki and the

involuntary amounted to musically / blood, blood and the brought out musically / praise, praise apprised by a musical / across, across the cast metatronic and musical / lintel, lintel over and dove too, a musical decide to love / doorway, doorway dues a way too musical / hyssop, musical's hyssop won a reprieve / hear, hear held too a musical / asleep, asleep at the wills in musical / another, another and the mother's within a musical / first, first in the blend too metatron's thee musical / born, born to be, musically / child, child of the chime's passionate musical / son, son of the sun's musical / say, say good try too, a musical / lint, lint out and cleaner's musical / valley, valley views inn's musical / passover, passover petted musically / feast, feast and the yeast beast freed aboard boats musically / hebrew, hebrew agree too, a musical / wilderness, wilderness wed's a musical / notion, notion nets a musical retrieve / goshen, goshen and ant's in too, a musical mov / more, more and the power in an hour's metatro / people, musical people pelt to metatro / pharaoh, pharaoh felt a land's divide musically / refuse, refuse and the reus / best, best believe in musical / friend, a friend felt in gives too, musical / no thing, no thing matter's abide, musically / evening, evening and the sleeves on, metatron / wreaths, wreaths and the seek sought musically / source, source suggest a miracle's musical / solar, solar seals a zeal on metatron's musical / solo, solo and the cold's golden musical / street, street and the sheet on meatronic's regard, musical / road, road to the sold metabolic musical / meet, meet the feat's clled heart's on, thee, the musical / stare, stare at the share on these musical / dissapear, dissapear done and due, a miracle's musical / island, island of signed a side a musical / hope, hope to scope through a miraculous musical / between, between the scenes on musical / surround, surround the sounds go, musical / grieve, grieve about your's, musical / condition, condition completes a musical / night, night dreams a musical / energy, energy seeks thee, generally musical / light, light is kind through musical love / church, a musical church too, God' / faith, faith friends musical / cross, cross across musical scal / building, building ability to these musicals / search, search about ours musically / ghost, ghost out, shoat miracle muse musical / smile, smile about your musical enthus / wash, wash wins a music's ? groov / charm, charm chats musical / careful, careful's found a musical / loud, musically loud too, love / prayer, prayer finds a found, musical / fear, fear fights them, musical.

CHAPTER EIGHT

Paradise, paradise sent to a phase coincident musical' / crest, crest kept in cues musically / expression, expression and the ascent to a metaphysical muse, musically / swan, swan swiftly too, a musical / swarm, swarm about you the musical / worth, worth an effort musically / shadow, shadow due an outing you, musically / speed, speed to the shore's in, musical / thimble, thimble and the nimble musical / junction, junction joins then musical / function, fuction finds a musical / youth, youth and the proof's in, musical / orginal, orginal rays of these, musical / myself, myself I know these, musical / know, know about those musical / ride, ride to a striven musical / invited, invited in three musical / deer, a deer

heat in musical / gentle, gentle ways through a musical / focus, focus on funds, thanks musical / fault, fault out, musically / unconditional, unconditional decrees of musical / breath, breath believes in sleeves of musical / patience, patience believes in musical / triage, triage tries our musical / travail, travial treats our's musically / traveler, ears traveler said musical's confessio / gravity, gravity grew true, a miracl / stargroup, stargroup b and the pinnacles A about a musical's refres / agrees, agrees to stress a crest abreast a musical / aspirant, aspirant cares for these musical / beliefs, beliefs descend into a musical' / change, change barned through these musical / bite, bite about these, musical / byte, byte right too, a musical / seven, we are the seven sent musically siste / views, views confes on musical / village, village advise musically / serving, serving ours musically / thrift, thrift and the ringing wing sent musical / golden, golden days musically / rule, rules about frees musical / mill, mill sent through a musical / bakery, bakery belts on too, a musical / conference, conference calls too a musical / slope, slope descents degrees, a musical / special, special displays in musical / simply, simply said "musically be, freed / throne, throne out and then a freedom rings musically / powder, powder powers our spells musical / imagery, imagery meant too, a musical / crucial, crucial creative's musically / constellation, constellation concretes our mutual / ecliptic, ecliptic and the erratically free, musical / moral, moral becomes you, musically / essence, essence sent into a musical / cultivating, cultivating across too, a musical / recommended, recommended a friend's decide musically / living, living in too, musicals in to, musical / swallow, swallow out and then liquid's acquire thee, musically / jagged, jagged edged throw musical / swimming, swimming in the waves musical / until, until then a miracle's musical / learn, learn a musical relearn a God's love.

CHAPTER NINE

Highlight, a highlight held in these thee, musical / inscription, inscription compares and accres a blessed miracle musically / face, face it, musically free / base, base on too, musical / gave, gave a raven musical / round, round the sounds musical / establish, establish trades musical / various, various veins musically / shore, shore sent into a musical / melody, melody believed musically / audience, an audience bets on my musical degre / relief, relief rests in thee musically / pivoted, pivoted about a state's musical / humanity, humaity hues out these musical / confronted, confronted a race musically / resurrect, resurrect your rampage musically / sort, sort of sport's musically / general, general decide to degree too musically / legendary, legendary aspire into a musical wonde / return, return to the one, miracles music / chamber, chamber chosen, a heart's venue, musically free / vessel, vessel voices a frolics some musical / require, require a spire, musical / ritual, ritual reside inside a miracle musical / honey, honey paid into a musical / blade, blade about these, musical / around, around us strands within these miracles musically / mosaic, mosaic a muse, appropriately musically / mirror, mirror about us metabolically required a musical / conduct, conduct a strategic musical / platform, platform place us musically / climax, climax due within miracle / vision, vision views our venues musically / pottery, pottery appeals to a miracle musically / feather, feather feels musical / cosmic, cosmic cube's musically loos / throne, throne about these musically / marking, marking expect with amused musically miracle / place, a musical's central place is in love / contouring, tight contour central to a musical / potential, potential plans befriend a musical / area, area three and two a musical / decoration, decoration deals in a musicals aren / example, example threw and thrown a musical / carried, carried out confess too a miraculous musical / crater, crater codes our creates musical / built, built on a basic meter's musical / origin, origin jets too a musical's accep / chapter, a chapter choose and the chosen musical / affected, affected rates on musical / ascend, ascend trendy musicals to / burn, burn through the duress musically / erected, erected a friend's musical / proper, muses proper timing musical / entered, entered a friend musically / holy, holy wells of musical degree / expression, expression spoof spills musical / phrase, a phrase found musically / various, various views musically / buckets, buckets of bolted a musical clue's mathematical / accumulating, accumulating pentameters in mathematical musical / term, term above and within a musical / after, after and all is, musical / left, left to the rights musical.

CHAPTER TEN
Washed, washed with love's embrace and the taste within mathematically the even / streak, streak seeks mathematical explain / struck, struck and the streak is mathematical / bell, bell well within the mathematical / notes, notes about the sorts mathed u / notations, notations neat and formulas fell, mathematical out / notates, notates rates mathematical / notions, notions stations in mathematical seek / mellow, abuse that blew mathematically stron / moods, moods mathematical recline in God's sort / mavericks, mavericks meet at perks mathematical / meets, meets and sorts mathematically / allow, allow a plow to Metatron's find of God's mathematical correct love / alerts, alerts and asserts mathematical directions in love / clarify, clarify the house's place in mathematical love / sounds, sounds well, mathematically 1, 2 / flaunting, flaunting our intend to mathematically blend within love / charisma, charisma cures your examine mathematically / lectern, lectern elective prefer for the stirring method / lectures, lectures seal our privately musically / portals, portals and the friendly befriend mathematically / appear, appear in states fundamental to a place mathematical / example, example of zen's mathematicals One and One, musically / fonts, fonts and the freshens mathematically prevalent in love?/ mandelas, mandelas mend our music's trend / require, require a fire through musical / reliance, reliance on the random mathematical / love's roses, love's roses due a mathematical purg / Salish, Salish sets in too, musically / coast, coast about us musically / Inuit, Inuit soon to perfect addition mathematical / elects, elects us mathematically perfec / mathematical words, mathematical words and the hearts arise at the skies fundamenta / weds, weds abate our great messiah musically / God wants, God wants you true too your arousa / heart's plays, heart's plays sound through music / please,

please and the sneeze we decide upon as pressed mathematical / preparations, preparations paper our musical ascen / castillion, castillion cubes and the cue's musically / flanks, flanks and prepares a musical's degree / pursue, pursue a purchase musical / place, place debris said musically / placed, placed in truth and musical / pleasant, pleasant abide in these musical / passions, passions plunge into a metatron's bonus musically / sacral, sacral suspend into a musical / music's suggest, music's suggest of God's hearts beat / salicious, slicious salutes into a musical / brother's shepards, brother's shepards chosen pretends out, musically / fraternity, fraternity felt too a musical brother / unity, unity chosen musically / patriotism, patriotism appeals musically / charity, charity chills in friends musically / encore, encore and the shore's win then, musical / lessons, lessons lease our musical / chimes, chime in musically / passionate, passionate cycles show our musical / compare, compare through a miracle's musical / spared, spared know, musically / known, known music's free / goodbye, goodbye and overall's musical / cues blown, cues blown through in music / cover, cover me, musically / over case, over case all true too music's ease.

CHAPTER ELEVEN
Mathematic's tidal wave, mathematic's tidal wave is love / julliard, julliards schools our scans musically / schools, schools planned musically / sharps, sharps and tucks into a musical / minors, minors winds, musical / study, study another's mutate musically / cues, cues care abreast air's musically / receives, receives a rest musically / octaves, octaves trued musically / sevens, sevens about us mindless musically / dance, dance dues us, musically / rhythm, rhythm reads musical / maestro, maestro met, musically / recital, recital resides in my musical gai / recites, recites relate our music's equat / opens, opens up musically / door, door dealt in musical / electric, an electric lattice musically / peace, a peace paced musically / converts, converts trued, a musical / tanzanite, tanzanite treat's musically free / case, case of a lies musically / boxed, boxed out and in musically / fox, fox found, musically / fault, fault out, too musical / sings, sings and swings musically / spatial, spatial spills, musically / spew, spews out a spell musically / spurn, spurn then this, a musical / fed, fed a fine, musical / stolen, stolen less, musically / sun, sun shone through a musical / sun's sun's stands musically / electric, electric expect on a musical / window's windows wept with a musical / chase, chase out vex, love's in musically / cherub, cherub drills then too, a musical / face, face it, musically / faceless, faceless fed this mirrored express musical / won, won and driven too, musical / codes, codes kept, musically / cues, cues bid's a musical / capable, capable cares for music / calls, calls about us, musically / challenge, challenge chants at music's frien / Jewish, Jewish joins the light's music / join, join a pair in music / cause, cause applies too, music / caspered, whispered chants musical / muse, muse amuse musically / met, met by a music's free / infuse, infuse us musically / Mexicali, Mexicali Bali, Indonensian, musical / abuse, abuse bets less in freest music / gallant's matrix, gallant's matrix meets in music / rise, rise through a music's guis / skies, skies a part of whole

music / impart, impart starts musically / paths, paths pelvic pulse musically / classical mysterious, classical mysterious amber trued, musically / Int / th / Skie / Leading.

CHAPTER TWELVE

Plunder, plunder under oversees a music's releas / over, over dues, musical / veins, viens musically / view, view best, musical / vaults, vaults values, musically / lies, lies out, music's I / dimes, dimes dealt musically / time, time trials a music's whee / trades, trades treat our musical stuf / tunes, tunes in true too, musically / raw, raw ran a musical / awaken, awaken outs hers musically / adopt, adopt a pretty musical / entire, entire styles musical / subtle, subtle sent a musical / surge, surge about thus musically / upheaval, upheaval due us, musically / positive, a positive recast of the past out too musically / canyons, canyons curl about us, musically / peaks, peaks and the stair's end, musical / terrestrial, terrestrial traipse in a musical waist forgiven, for love / gleaned, gleaned gluts out, musically / secure, secure your state's musical / legacy, legacy lends a thorough musical / towered, towered out and up through musical / stood, stood in a lean too musically / reference, a reference reigns musically / faced, faced with love's musical / adjustment, adjustments due our music / linger, linger let's musically / eons, eons spent and surrendered musically / biosphere, biosphere hears me musically / dweller, dweller deals in musical / flow, flow flown through a musical / principles, principles plausible to a musical friend / lyric, lyric lend, a musical / melody, melody met at musical / intended, intended through a musical / techniques, techniques taught musically / slumber, slumber hears a musical / current, current cater brands these musically / feed, feed your love sweets, musical / destructive, destructive details about our musical / outage, outage pouts about your music / balance, find it, balance the tenement of musical / revival, revival reveals a music's trea / geomancy, geomancy ranched in amend's musicals / already, already spins a musical / additional, additional days musically fre / study, study sures your musical / happen, happen and the standing's music chanc / sun, sun chambers channel music / track, tract treats us to a musical / emerald, emerald deals in miracles amuse greened musically / challenging, challenging chains, musically / hardened, hardened outers met softer spreads musically / endless, endless days, musically / peaks, peaks up perks too, a musical / mist, mist in the blue's misty music / residence, residence retains musical / annual, annual days musically fre / snowfall, snowfall sunny too, a musical / soften, known the soften, musically / sun's, sun's on too miracles musically.

CHAPTER THIRTEEN

Existed, existed precisley to succinctly musical / succulent, succulent values set successfully full of the musical devotio / berries, berries blank less and filled more with love is, the musical / abundant, abudnant masses made the pattern musically / echoed, echoed electrically throughout the musical / spruce, spruce prays and the pleasure treated musically / mosses, mosses massed electrically throughout thee, musical / firs, firs felt folded too the musical / desolate, desolate in the reorganized musical

/ witnessed, witnessed venues musically / fossils, fossils fused musciall / seeded, seeded in deeded ecstasy musically / granite, granite to the grains musical / peer, peer eared publically musical / haze, haze out and the levels appear musically / expose, expose your roses musically / watchful, watchfully aware of the wellest musically / verve, verve declared yours musically / faith, faith and the followings musical / crisp, crisp cure's through ears amuse musically / done, musically done and well too, love / allotted, allotted and outed musically / cultures, cultures caprice musically / nurturing, nurturing due our miraculous views, musical / surprise, surprise shouts a miracle's mus / extinction, extinction outs heard musical / conserve, conserve a bit musically / ultimately, ultimately fine, trues a musical miracl / salty, salty said a teary goodby / install, install a rent's musical / coal, coal sures our musical / spent, spent on the all, musical / nitrogen, nitrogen nets a friend musically / You / Home / Amazon / Star / Fan / Cost / Orientation / Informed / Decision / Cue / Core / Umbilicul / Eventful / Full / Moon / March / Equinox / Sure / the / Wave / of / the / Marrie / River / Feared / No / O / / Curious / Amazing / Event.

THE IN-MATH-MENTS
LEVEL 43

CHAPTER ONE

Outline, outline patterns in the muse, patterned mathematically in love / blend, blend and the soons patterned, mathematically / next, next and the matters that pattern mathematics to love / wishes, wishes and wins musically and mathematically patterned / delicate, delicate and the deals mathematically patterned within God / forcing, forcing the fields patterned mathematically in love / theory, theory threed and the patterns mathematically trued within love / tempo, tempo trues patterned mathematically / rhythm, rhythm and the residual patterns mathematic in love / plopping, plopping and the coping patterns mathematic / gradual, gradual and the grips release mathematically in love / ascent, ascent sent a pattern mathematic / doubt, doubt about it? mathematics patterns within, God / guide, guide and the get's patterned mathematically / lighter, lighter sides play love's patterns mathematic / preference, preference and the peals patterned mathematically / fully open too patterns mathematic / cancer, cancer cure's patterned mathematically / path, path choose patterned musically to a mathematic / knew, knew the love patterned mathematically / ordination, ordination plain, love's pattern mathematically huma / tomb, tomb opens example comes too,the parallels, the best undone in patternsmathematic unto the being hu-man / transend, transcend the sands human patterns too, love's mathematic / endured, endured the sured enhances human too, patterns mathematic / turn, turn to the ridden patterns mathematic / resurrection, resurrection yours in the mathematic example / terminal, terminal case lost in these patterns mathematic / majority, majority of patterns born throughout humanity's mathematic / someone, someone knew patterns mathematic / all, all the one, patterns mathematic / sacred, sacred the scene, human too, patterns mathematical / shortage, shortage of church, a cure plenty human / minimize, minimize contact with patterns older mathematically / deep, deep release of patterns mathematical / breath, breath abuse done, patterns, mathematic / assume, assume some, patterns, mathematical / bed, bed side scene, patterns too, mathematical / sequence, sequence secure, patterned mathematic / suitable, suitable mates, patterned mathematically / whole, whole enough too, patterns, mathematic / body, body blue, patterned, mathematic / trust, trust thrust patterned mathematically / skin, skin sink, patterned through her mathematic / clothed, clothed in cubes, patterned, mathematic / mineral, mineral amuse patterned to a mathematical enthus / additives, additives due, patterned, mathematical / special, special and the selling material mathematically too, the applause, pattern / oil, oil spills the spell planned mathematically / warehouse, warehouse won, patterned mathematical / safeguards, safeguards won through patterns mathematical expansiv / sight, sight in patterns mathematical / rapport, rapport built, patterns mathematical / strengths, strengths shown, patterns are thee, the mathematical / closure, closure comes, patterns, mathematic / link, link thee, patterns, mathematic / hand, hand too, patterned mathematically / longer, longer then too, patterns mathematic / corners, corners keep patterns math / brink, brink breach, patterned mathematically / message, message meet, patterned mathematically / occur, occur once, patterned mathematic / loyalty, loyalty leads, patterned mathematic / anguish, anguish gets patterns mathematical / spot, spot set, patterned mathematics.

CHAPTER TWO

Equinox, equinox met the pattern's mathematics / solstice, solstice soon, patterned mathematic / ensure, ensure success, patterns mathematic / minimized, minimized mess, patterned mathematic / entice, entice and the risen patterns met mathematically / sting, sting stew, patterns brew, mathematic / fragranced, fragranced freed, patterns, mathematic / prefer, prefer you, patterned mathematically / boutique, boutique sneak, patterns, mathematic / tactile, tactile tell, patterned mathematic / dominating, dominating dales, pattern mathematic / incense, incense meets patterned mat / candlelight, smoke in candlelight patterns mathematic / close, close to bliss, patterns mathematic / ambience, ambience, kiss, patterns mathematic / suitable, suitable meets, patterned mathematic / detachment, detachment due, patterns mathematic / driven, driven too, patterned mathematical / which, which way, patterns mathematic / illusion, illusion lay patterned mathematically / bridges, bridges burst patterns mathematic / grip, grip grew, patterns mathematic / light, light and then patterns mathematical / daily, daily deals, patterns mathematic / return, return home, patterned / visit, visit reveals, pattern / waiting, waiting in you, patterned / exam, exam loom / buddhist, buddhist bowl, patterned / aligned, aligned lift, patterned / nourishes, nourishes nurtured pattern / muscular, muscular mend, pattern / sensuous, sensuous elongate, bliss / bowl, bowl best, patterned / squeeze, squeeze the rest, patterned / sturdy, sturdy states patterned / limitations, limitations left patterned / muscles, muscles patterned / pivot, pivot point / applied, applied lat / connecting, connecting cut patterned / lover, lover patterned / tip, tip tuck, patterned / breast, breast born, pattern / nipple, nipple rolls, pattern / slide, slide slate, patterned / manner, manners made to pattern / genitals, genitals gel in pattern / bold, bold bade to pattern / premier, premier paged, pattern / acclaimed, acclaimed same, pattern / research, research red, pattern / target, target the place, permanent patterned / act, act on cute, pattern / draw, draw the musically patterned / breathe, breathe in pattern / thoughts, thoughts thick, pattern / healing, healing click, pattern / good, good strength due pattern / grace, grace grapples pattern / sacraments, sacraments rest, pattern / control, control rest pattern / thrives, thrives on stellar pattern / tribal, tribal and the truest patterned.

CHAPTER THREE

Testicles, testicles tightly patterned / erect, erect sight pattern / shaft, shaft sunk in pattern / lubricant, lubricant lent pattern / alternating, alternating stays patterned / membranous, membranous mace patterned / flat, flat fled, patterned / head, head ahead, patterned / circular, circular sinks patterned / core, core kinks, patterned / pelvis, pelvis pinch, patterned / beloved, beloved patterned / gongs, swinging gongs patterned / fervor, fervor from pattern / barely, barely blew, patterned / just, just you, patterned / hobby, hobby heals, patterned / workshop, workshop wields patterned / triggers, triggers tastes pattern / rain, rain strays patterned / general, general step patterned / diet, diet dip patterned / fragile, fragile freight's patterned / language, language lays patterned / conforming, conforming conforms, patterned / instead, instead soon, patterned / grow, grow up, pattern / virtually, virtually veined pattern / hour, houar sour, patterned / midas, midas made, patterned / alert, alert consert, patterned / power, power plays, patterned / crown, crown cranes patterned / friction, friction fuse patterned / tantric, tantric tapes, patterned / generation, generation gates, patterned / tower, tower tames patterned / falcon, falcon flew, patterned / storm, storm stills, pattern / alters, alters straights patterned / luxuriate, luxuriate inn, patterned / savor, savor sate patterned / crave, crave crates patterned / mature, mature mate patterned / flesh, flesh friends patterned / reverence, reverence red, patterned / limits, limits said, patterned / immense, immense desires patterned / occupation, occupation set, patterned / labrynth, labyrinth laid in pattern / upheaval, upheaval caves, patterned / defies, defies belies, patterned / volume, volume veterans pattern / renamed, renamed rate, patterned / revolution, revolution rate, patterned / icon, icon creat, patterned / odyssey, odyssey clue patterned / outer, outer state, patterned / travels, travels taught patterned / boxer, boxer bought, patterned / extraordinary, extraordinary you, patterned / part, part play, patterned / wood, wood way, patterned / is, is this, patterned.

CHAPTER FOUR

Springs, springs seek, patterned / leaps, leaps leak, patterned / embargoes, embargoes gave, pattern / consecrated, consecrated rates, patterned / no, no knows pattern / know, know they rest, pattern / slogan, slogan sung in pattern / censor, censor stands patterned / censure, censure cease, pattern / pathogens, pathogens paste pattern / bliss, bliss baits, pattern / reciprocity, reciprocity seeks pattern / negotiate, negetiate nestle pattern / intense, intense traits patterned / tension, tension taints pattern / jasmine, jasmine jewels, pattern / advocated, advocated attend, patterned / student, student sent, patterned / tradition, tradition trues, patterned / knelt, knelt in news, patterned / bandit, bandit abused patterned / banishment, banishment blue, patterned / join, join the other patterned / frosty, frosty frothy pattern / regular, regular aware's raised pattern / curls, curls count, patterned / exhibitionistic, exhibitionistic slaughters, pattern / have, have ties patterned / artist, artist trades patterned / courage, courage creates pattern / enough, enough known, pattern / felt, felt flown patterned / greek, greek groan patterned / cupid, cupid cone patterned / shuttle, shuttle shown patterned / rumble, rumble ran patterned / manuscript, manuscript met patterned / hugging, hugging haut patterned / adjustment, adjustment jammed patterned / ecstatic, ecstatic sought patterned / inquisition, inquisition set patterned / celibacy, celibacy seen patterned / harp, harp hands patterned / vivid, vivid vans patterned / massive, massive meets patterned / sermon, sermon sought patterned / clapping, clapping cups patterned / beat, beat bought, patterned / gaze, gaze at the truth patterned / champion, champion chills, patterned / occupied, occupied with friends, patterned / leather, leather lends, patterned

/ pungent, pungent points patterned / savory, savory speaks patterned / cracks, cracks create pattern / candy, candy cubes patterned / sleeves, sleeves set patterned / administer, administer a minister's pattern / concessions, consessions stay patterned / district, sugar's district pattern / streets, streets wet, patterned / odor, odor due patterned / power, power plays patterned / intrigues, intrigues read, patterned.

CHAPTER FIVE

Swoon, swoon and the moon over mathematical pattern / delay, delay daily done and the funds arise magically mathematical / detail, detail appears and the sealings melt into mathematic / patience, patience forgiven for the fuelings magnetically mathematic / patient, patio patient and the partnered forgets paradigm deep in delivery too, mathematic / math, math's trick is a patient formula for funds matched mathematically / meetings, meetings set for the mathematic / mastery, mastery includes the mend electrically mathematic / magi, magi given rites mathematic / pi, pi pays, adds up, mathematical / eleven, eleven ways mathematical / classified, classified channels made through love's musical / thirteen, thirteen thrice and the rice strewn metatron musical / third, third and the ways found electric too, musically mathematic / thanks, thanks made for the given ah-men turn to a light musically mathematic / even, even in won, mathematic / tasteful, tasteful example and the sample mathematic / God, God said "let us be", mathematically, ligh / nineteen, nineteen tales and the swells metatronically mathematic / telltale, telltale allow for the plow's mathematic / levels, levels allowed mathematic / travels, travels detail, mathematic / patience, patience again, friends, mathematic / purple, purple appears near, mathematic / passion, passion amazed with your choose mathematic / peering, peering through seering mathematic / pale, pale forges allowed mathematic / peopled, peopled in paid pairs for the fares borne mathematic / level, level to the peopled mathematic / thirds, thirds and the fields mathematic / tables, tables applaud and the cause is mathematic / tissue, tissue tears and the regrown mathematic / throat, throat seal opened well within thee, the mathematic / thrice, thrice the told, be bold, mathematically / threshold, threshold reached and the met across relives your mathematic / threads, threads appearing lifting nearing allowance dealing in the light led mathematic / thirst, thirst for knowing, knowing showing, lifting growing, insight molding, methods bolding, mathematic / repressed, repressed retails retry your fly to the mooned hello of love in thee, mathematics / throngs, throngs reveal a venue mathematical / fourteen, fourteen ways to be mathematically correc / correction, correction through inflection says that love is the threaded mathematic / books, books encoded devoted learning leaning voted feeling sent to God's returning mathematic / questioned, questioned nearly, daily, dearly, often, frothing in the feeling heaven sealing our expecting mathematic / flown, flown to the flourid attitude details shown to love via mathematic / placed, placed allow of the follow mathematic / frank, frank anticipation mentions love in mathematic / particular, particular to a raving moment, the vanished allow trues your mathematic /

country, country clearing, mathematic / custom, custom conclude to the moody mathematic / breathtaking, breathtaking experiences mathematic / level, level to a leaving mathematic / site, site chosen found and done too, mathematic / marble, marble admit of the comfort mathematic / adipose, adipose mentions mathematic / five, five said, mathematic / center, center said, "ten times" the metatronic quarterly for the earthly mathematic / restore, restore to the rewards metaphysic too and the grenadine mathematic / oz, oz to the causes mathematic / dorothy, dorothy and the details mathematic / waimea, waimea wed and the awareness sped to the pencil mathematic / trout, trout and the truth's mathematic / methods, methods milled and the mission's given mathematic / protected, protected and the precious mathematic / conserved, conserved conclude and the shoulders mathematic.

CHAPTER SIX

Partner, partner peels and the pilings mathematic / proven, proven and the moneys paid to the dialogues dealt mathematically / grant, grants grew mathematically / geared, geared and the inept gone to the meetings mathematic / up, up to the tubes metatronically mathematic / rocks, rocks and the reasons mathematic to / streams, streams allow and the plowing mathematic / storage, storage and the steerings mathematic / stress, stress and the stencils mathematic / resourced, resourced and the sentinels mathematic / allowed, allowed to the plenty mathematic / variety, variety values your listings mathematic / channeled, channeled and the chiming's mathematic / channels, channels dealt and the details felt a feeling mathematic / set, set for the seatings mathematic / open, open for the sorted mathematics / dial, seem dialed in too, the meanings mathematic / display, display and the darings mathematic / turn, turn to the treaty mathematic / true, true to the teachings mathematic / terror, terror trailed the teachings mathematic / truth, truth told "mathematics / tricks, tricks trickle into dreams mathematical / tricked, tricked into waiting for the meanings mathematic / first, first and the features mathematic / suspend, suspend allowed, found a friendly mathematic / appear, appear to the triples mathematic / appearance, appearance dealt with, mathematic / suspense, suspense outed mathematically / puzzle, puzzle fits blend to the news mathematic / thanked, thanked for the thrusting mathematic / enthroned, enthroned in a detailed mathematic / guide, guide to the goodness, mathematic / relay, relay repose and the rose is mathematical / level, level to the lyrical mathematic / lesson, lesson detailed in the details mathematic / listen, listen to the lists mathematical / involves, involves a multiply mathematically / planets, planets paced to the races mathematically / earth, earth amounts to the counts variably mathematical / venus, venus is into the orbit's mathematic / translate, translate retails in regards mathematically / the code, the codes inroad gains mathematically / shuttle, shuttle sent for the fielding mathematic / built, built beautify and the imply mathematic / believe, believe in sleeves that touch in the mathematic / tiers, tiers appearing mathematically / steps, steps stretched to mathematically / ziggurats, ziggurats spun to the sun mathematic / again, again to a detail mathematical /

potential, potential penned to a treatise mathematic / commune, commune rule mat / community, community subset and the index mathematical / creates, creates a relate mathematic / required, required of bemuse a bergamot tree mathematically / amounts, amounts respective to the reach won mathematically / love, love to tell the truth mathematically / levels, levels of living mathematic / experience, experience spelling mathematic / atmosphere, atmospheric details mathematic / features, features measured mathematically / savored, savored lover the licking fame mathematic / sent, sent to suggested mathematic / scents, scents sent mathematics.

CHAPTER SEVEN

Help, help heals mathematically / hallow, emphatically hallow to a mathematic / delights, delights woo you getting mathematic / vibes, vibes spent in the trickles mathematic / franklin, franklin meant the jolt mathematic / meant, meant to be mathematically free, you, huma / *fluorite, frankly lucid ungent operationally ripe interiorly transverse examples electrically mentioned around an adam kadmon and the flood's chinese to love's mathematic / flowers, flowers in life and the led mathematic / diaries, diaries detail your revealing mathematic / lottos, lottos levy a leader mathematic / listenings, listenings ripple trued to mathematic / letters, letters written often into a gender mat / life, life leads to a left blank mathematically / images, images range to the vision sacredly simple to a mention mathematic / lights, lights lifted to the listen mathematic / liquids, liquids leisure leaping mathematically / livery, livery loaned to the temple mathematic18. slaves, slaves tone sung mathematically / slavery, slavery slack to the mack deed mathematic / debacles, debacles and the shackles off to a treasure mathematic / dot, dot deal dash meal mathematic / during, during rest relax mathematically / durations, durations spent to the pews mathematical / dates, dates paged for the pension's mathematic / distance, distance entailed is well within the winning mathematic / deference, deference paid and the made for, mathematic / percussions, percussions page for the features metatronically ripe in the son mathematic / ached, ached for detail for the fillings mathematic / allegates, allegates a reaching forth mathematically / reductions, reductions raced forth mathematically / ashes, ashes arched to the marching mathematic / duration, duration endured paired mathematically / destitute, destitute out and the shouts in too, mathematically / debate, debate abounds mathematically / delayed, delayed shouts for the shillings mathematic / image, imagine an image mathematic / imagine, image imagined mathematically / imagination, imagination's rage for the features mathematic / elation, elation elect mathematically / elevate, elevates relay to the reach for mathematic / elected, elected suspected mathematic / elegance, livid relay of an elegance mathematic / probable, probable disciple truly mathematic / immersed, immersed and rehearsed for, mathematic / entrance, entrance laid through the listing mathematic / environ, environ means mathematic / systems, systems signal mathematically / information, information fuels cells mathematic / imagination, imagination rifts the reaching mathematic / elevations, signals sent to elevations high to love for the mathematic, ma / elation, elation women mathematic / contained, contained in cues mathematic / containeer, containeer shelled in the shelving mathematic / elasticity, elasticity rules your reacing mathematic / trained, trained as discipled mat / transitory, transitory retails matched to mat / fruit, fruit, math, gro / visions, visions create cubic mathematic / rapture, rapture raged mathematically / revelations, revelations release mathematically / resurrected, resurrected regard in thee, mathematic / retards, retards less the hero mathematic / recurrent, recurrent too, mathematically / reimprinted, reimprinted daily mathematics.

CHAPTER EIGHT

Relevant, relevant to a sailing mathematic / random, random retail paid for the filling mathematic / ransomed, ransomed reward sword freed mathematic / ranted, ranted above it, mathematic / rallied, rallied retrained mathematically / ran, ran to the ceiling mathematic / roared, roared into the living mathematic./ rused, rused out mathematically / ruled, ruled forth's mathematic / ruler, ruler raised mathematically / rotate, rotate rused mathematic / ruled, ruled in ranges mathematic / repaired, repaired and retired to a treasure mathematic / retailed, retailed reward mathematic / rapt, rapt apply for the fueling mathematic / rasta, rasta red ruse mathematic / nectar, nectar appeal mathematic / man, man detail mathematic schemati / mendicant, mendicant vents to the ventures mathematic / spouse, spouse found in a sounded mathematic / house, house bought near HEAR thee, mathematic / court, court laid the living mathematic / coat, coat comfit with the drift to mathematic / counts, counts allow now the nifty mathematic / capable, capable daily mathematic / crest, crest brought to the breaching mathematic / crafted, crafted artsy daily mathematic / created, created creation's mathematic / crescent, crescent crested mathematically / cruise, cruise to a viewing's mathematic / danger, danger dates your delays mathematic / duty, duty dealt mathematically / duties, duties knelt mathematically / aware, aware ways mathematic / awareness, awareness pays mathematically / treats, treated well, mathematically / transits, transits past and the peaceful mathematic / traits, traits truest mathematic / trucks, trucks debate for the features mathematic / tucks, tucks into a featured mathematic / tables, tables zen to a zero mathematic / gates, gates count, mathematically / measures, measures well, mathematically, humanit / meters, meters amount to a treat flamed mathematic / mated, mated arrival mathematic / mends, mends pensioned mathematically / moistened, moistened mostly mathematic / motives, motives mentioned, mathematic / mailed, mailed mentions mathematic / begin, begin now, mathematically / bathing, bathing okays mathematic / battles, battles blaze mathematically / bueracratic, beuracratic balderdashes mathematic / oath, oath detailed mathematically55.hypocritical, hypocritical ways mathematical / hypothetical, hypothetical advise mathematic / magical, magical mentions mathematic / marionette, marionettes out, mathematically / maverick, maverick met mathematically / mention, mention now the natures mathematic / motives, motives mentioned mathematic / motivates, motivates you mathematically / mercurial, mercurial pages mathematic / mercury, mercury's implore is your mathematical stint.

CHAPTER NINE

Coral, coral keys mathematic / choral, choral avow mathematically / cruel, cruel knew mathematic releas / chores, chores over, mathematic / chambers, chambers vent your mathematic / changes, changes okay through mathematic / challenged, challenged entreaties mathematically / forgave, forgave you electrically mathematic9.forgiven, forgiven's infusion is gained mathematically / funded, funded features mathematic / futile, futile done, mathematically / foreign, foreign flooded mathematic / focus, focus into the mathematic / fashionable, fashionable features mathematic / forgave, forgave your mathematic account / forgive, forgive furled mathematically / fortitude, fortitude found exponentially mathematic / furtive, furtive fury mathematic / future, future, yes, mathematic / fortunate, fortunate mathematic / few, few led, mathematically / familiar, familiar formula to the pi, $Y= 3$ plus four to the 1st attempt to square circling the circular squared? love, mathematically / 1 3 4 four times is love / fondest, fondest frequently, love, mathematically / favored, favored features mathematic / favorite, favorite fullness mathematic / futures, futures sealed mathematically / detailed, detailed delays out mathematic / resurrection, resurrection sent through mathematic / repair, repair requires you, mathematically / reach, reach for relations mathematic / rally, rally round these, mathematic / rush, rush past you, mathematically / ruthlessness, ruthlessness accounts too, mathematically / repairs, repairs reach you, mathematically / reach, reach your mathematical contentmen / referred, referred in the preferred sequence elective's mathematic / preference, preference reached mathematically / preferred, preferred pentium mathematic / products, products reached mathematically / prognosis, prognosis breached mathematically / preach, preach nearly mathematic / predict, predict prophetic blends mathematically / percentage, percentage hums mathematically / present, present one hundred mathematic / precinct, precinct linked to a listing mathematic / premiere, premiere dear too, mathematic / premise, premise made through mathematic / process, process purchased mathematically / purged, purged in surges through mathematic / probed, probed through retail mathematic / sang, sang in simple mathematic / learned, learned to listen too, mathematic / remembered, remembered regard to mathematic / rang, rang for the reasons mathematic / roped, roped out then simply "mathematics"/ reached, reached a reason mathematically / rapt, rapt in the inept forgone too, mathematic / rupture, rupture over, mathematically / regain, regain relayed mathematically / ropes, ropes taught too mathematically / reached, reached for and features mathematic / apt, apt to teaching mathematic / wrapped, wrapped up mathematically / choir, choir cure mathematic.

CHAPTER TEN:
torn, torn then mathematic / trio, trio trips mathematically / travesty, travesty truthful mathematically / truth, truth depth mathematic / treachery, treachery off you,

mathematically / indulgence, indulgence mentions thee, mathematically / indolence, indolence off your mathematic / idolatry, idolatry gone now, mathematically / depth, depth added to your gene cue mathematic / detail, detail detail mat / debates, debates core mathematic / artist, artist found, mathematically / lilac, lilac listening born mathematic / blue, blue bays mathematic / dome, dome deals mathematic / despot, despot rules? mathematic / despite, despite stats mathematic 18, between, between ratios born mathematic / benefit, benefit formed your mathematic / bought, bought sounds mathematically / pungent, pungent pensions mathematic / paralleled, paralleled too, mathematically / pressed, pressed app.ly mathematic / purchased, purchased .com mathematic / brought, brought home mathematic / sought, sought sold, mathematic / sold, sold too, mathematic / selected, selected views mathematic / solvent, solvent intrigues born mathematic / sold, sold daily mathematically / suggested, suggested rested mathematic / shed, shed shields mathematic / stuff, stuff trails mathematically / stealth, stealth outs mathematics I / shelves, shelves built mathematically / showers, showers pay mathematically / shouldered, shouldered expire for the features mathematic / digest, digest done, mathematic / diabolic, diabolic off your requires mathematic / diameters, siam purged her diameters with your code mathematic / digits,,,,digits personally identify numerically yo / aroused, aroused retain for the feign mathematic / arousal, arousal reached fortunately mathematic / maps, maps paced mathematically / registry, registry runs your mathematic / repose, repose gains you mathematically / arose, arose reached you mathematically / registered, registered features mathematic / reads, reads randomly mathematic / decides, decides to reach for the features mathematic / details, details found mathematically / departs, departs now, mathematic / arrives, arrives swoon mathematically / relates, relates to the reaching mathematic / reviews, reviews raise mathematic / rests, resets irreverence to a resting mathematic / ramps, ramps red to a reverb mathematic / rolls, rolls deep mathematically / regards, regards albums mathe / repairs, repairs cinematic to a meeting mathematic / opened, opened jazz to the cubic metatronic mat / opens, opens news mathematic / precursor, prescursor bought mathematically / prelates, prelates relates mathematic.

CHAPTER ELEVEN
Predictions, predictions made true mathematically / pressing, pressing pent for pensions spent on a tune played mathematic / prorations, prorations given forthrightly mathematic / rosters, rosters reach then mathematic / raptures, raptures lived through mathematically / red, red relations mental pause mathematic / relative, relative rewarded mathematically / ruthless, ruthless over, due, mathematic / rushed, rushed past you, mat / routes, routes buil / 3 ways mathematically / roads, roads read mathematically / intrigues, intrigues cue mathematic / readings, readings given mathematically / contractions, contractions cured you mathematically / coatings, coatings centrally cured mathematically / codes, codes capably mathematic / keys, keys pent published mathematically / levels, levels penned mathematically /

legends, legends mentioned mathematically / leads, leads strong mathematic / lips, lips speak mathematically / lights, lights leap mathematically / literal, literal in clips amethyst blue to a purple magenta mathematic / logical, logical leads mathematic / lit, lit lifts mathematically / loft, loft laws mathematic / lots, lots sold mathematically agreed to grid / ledges, ledges often ledgered mathematically / logs, logs off you mathematically / elopes, elopes soon, mathematically / lifts, lifts past, mathematic / lighter, lighter listening mathematic / leaps, leaps past those mathematic / chimes, chimes in too, mathematic / crafted, crafted creations mat / allows, allows your mathematic / allowed, alllowed through mathematic / hear, hear thee, mathematic / how, how then? mathematic / often, often found yours mathematic / over, over done mathematic / sufficient, sufficient feelings mathematic / enough, enough paid mathematic / entire, entire estates mathematic / empires, empires paged mathematic / loose, loose again mathematic / leathery, leathery within mathematic / soft, soft sealed mathematic / suggested, suggested merry mat / shown, shown totals in mathematics hu-man / seen, seen humanly to a mention mathematic / spent, spent? invent, a mathematic / stored, stored? cured mathematic / struggled, struggled? Out then, mathematic / shrugs, shrugs often, mathematically / sends, sends too, mathematic / stays, stays dear, mathematics / gone, gond past, mathematic / go., go bird freed, mathematic / fades, fades past, mathematic / fed, fed to mathematic / grades, grades unlock meanings mathematic / nodes, nodes neared mathematically / loads, loads lurch mathematic.

CHAPTER TWELVE
Lightened, lightened now, mathematically / lifted, lifted flow for the featured mathematic / gifted, gifted too, mathematically / home, home held mathematically / homes, homes pierced mathematically / heights, heights hurt mathematic / hopes, hopes pierced mathematically / hearts, hearts surge mathematically / held, held well too, mathematic / joins, joins in your mathematic / jaunt, jaunt made too, mathematic / pagentry, pagentry opens views mathematic / possible, possible pensions mathematic / positions, positions place too mathematic / pointed, pointed into math, love, humanity, God' / placed, placed portals to a treaty mathematic / paged, paged pentacles implore mathematically / imported, imported sorted's mathematic / pivots, pivots engagement curls to the cutting mathematic / paints, paints purged place cures in the colors mathematic / positive, positive to flowers mathematic / pliant, pliant ability mathematic / pleasures, pleasures gated free mathematic / pureness, pureness meant too, mathematics / gains, gains allowance mathematic / given, given intrigue with mathematic / greeted, greeted daily mathematically / enraged, enraged often mathematically / engorged, engorged lessens mathematically / enlivened, enlivened listening mathematic / legends, legends pleasing mathematically / listens, listens reaching mathematic / leapt, leapt patiently past too, mathematic / aloft, aloft okay metaphorically mathematic / leased, leased okay mathematic / lofty, lofty venues mathematic / lightens, lightens listen mathematic / loosens, loosens holds then mathematic / late,

late reply for the featured mathematic formul / later, later listens mathematic / laps, laps leapt through mathematically / loops, loops open in the thank yous mathematic / likens, likens lift then mathematic / listens, listens into a mare won mathematic / carry, carry a detail mathematic / carried, carried past you, mathematic / crowned, crowned in simple mathematics, One, Love, Plus You, Thre / crowns, crowns into a life-long metatronic balad for the features mathematic / creations, creations ration mathematic / cruised, cruised into a living mathematic / cruises, cruises into valleys mathematic / crept, crept past views mathematic / corrupts, corrupts incorporate gone mathematically / coached, coached again, mathematically / cords, cords cut off mathematic / cuts, cuts often then mathematical / curses, curses off you, mathematically / cruises, cruises past then mathematically / capably, capably employed in the forgiven mathematic / allows, allows please to mathematic / allowed, allowed fortunately mathematically / loved, loved eternally, mathematic / legends, legends please you mathematically / lightened, lightened now, loads of forth to mathematics.

CHAPTER THIRTEEN

Amiably, amiably spent in the fortunate mathematic / amicably, amicably finished then, mathematically / assurances, assurances sent too, mathematic / allowances, allowances given your mathematic / implications, implications applied for mathematically / legions, legions listened mathematic / appliances, appliances lead for mathematic / pleasing, pleasing pleasant's mathematic / splurging, spurging given mathematic / gained, gained fortunately mathematic / gazes, gazes placed mathematically / joy, joy found mathematic / joins, joins cups mathematic / jaunts, jaunts open up your mathematic / places, places mathe / plates, plates pleasant through mat / slide, slide too, mathematic / slid, slid past mathematic / sides, sides choose you mathematically / signs, signs sent through mathematic / suggested, suggested listened in mathematically / surges, surges break through, mathematically / strides, strides listen mathematically / spent, spent require in mathematic / spends, spends a pleasant mathematic / slight, slight suggestions mathematic / stripes, stripes red for mathematic / colors, colors listen in mathematic / courts, courts carry through mathematic / capably, capably refuged to mathematic / quietly, quietly given to mathematic / often, often found you mathematic / forts, forts passed through mathematic / first, first fused mathematically / last, last dues mathematic / ever, ever lasting mathematically / alpha, alpha given mathematic / omega, omega finds you mathematic / life, life leading mathematically / light, light listens mathematic / allow, allow a flow through mathematic / seen, seen debriefs mathematic / scenes, scenes sent for, mathematic / patents, patents paged in mathematic / ports, ports sailed for mathematic / portals, portals mentioned mathematically / porches, porches built forth mathematical / journey, journey joined in mathematically / jesus, jesus forgiven mathematic / joint, joint ventures mathematic / joints, joints chime in mathematically / graft, graft interior to a remove mathematic / grow, grow detailed mathematically / empower, empower ours mathematic / decide, decide to move now, mathematically / encoded, encoded reading's mathematic / coded, coded pleading mathematic / keyed, keyed in leading mathematic / keys, keys to a DNA amount to mathematic / cyclical, cyclical to a cycle crucial to A mathematic / phrases, phrases met in A mathematic / pages, pages printed God's plan, hu-man to a mathematic note, an A for love / splurges, splurges coming mathematically / pages, pages finished love lives mathematically.

THE META-PHYSICAL-MENTS
LEVEL 44

CHAPTER ONE

Above, above the metaphysical's wa / within, within a wind called metaphysical / beyond, beyond a bay won, metaphysically / again, again and within a way too, metaphysical / against, against the win's metaphysical / instead, instead in read's acquire metaphysical / parsnip, parsnip keeps ours, steeply metaphysical / dreams, dreams direct through a metaphysical / mandonlin, mandonlin's winds metaphysical / blends, blends earth's goods metaphysical / bins, bins empty too a metaphysic / empty, empty meta true's metaphysic / trash, trash outs and swept through metaphysical / extends, extends a fram drawn metaphysical / shores, shores shrink within these metaphysic / abort, abort outs her's metaphysic / captive, a metaphysical captives out too, love / clatter, clatter clues us metaphysic / curtails, curtails cavarts metaphysic / sorts, sorts as registered in the metaphysical / dynasty's, dynasty's deal in these, metaphysic / duel, duel about us metaphysic / sped, sped through, metaphysic / speed, speed through to a mail's metaphysics, love' / skirt, skirt about yours metaphysic / scurry, returns scurry too a metaphysical's win / softens, softens appraise and the raise is metaphysical / languages, languages leakout through a metaphysic / messages, messages met metaphysically / unions, absolute unions made in thee metaphysic / divinities, dininties dole out ours, these metaphysic / enoch, enoch said metaphysically let too, love / series, series success, metaphysic / flown, flown in thinly thick's metaphysic / flows, flows a sort metaphysic / material, material meets a master's metaphysic / thought, thought through's metaphysic / peaks, peaks a lot metaphysic / otters, otters out and the shouts in too, metaphysic / play, play at the stay's metaphysic / passsions, passions played metaphysic / place, place please, metaphysic / thank, thank us often pleased in metaphysics ambianc / chunks, chunks out and then, metaphysic / chatter, chatter chosen metaphysically / compatible, compatible clues, metaphysic / ambiance, ambiance abundant through metaphysic / laughing, laughing allows us metaphysics punc / playful, playful plans, too these metaphysic / love, love lands a metaphysic / physical, physical prowess worths metaphysics degre / flex, flex your beliefs metaphysic / flaunt, flaunt and the fans metaphysical / sweet, sweet is this defy's release into love's metaphysic / sexy, sexy details into the metaphysical / hovers, hovers a strange release into you metaphysically / sensual, sensual success details our metaphysic / sensitive, sensitive success in the metaphysic / kind, kind control into ours metaphysic / loving, loving leads into our magenta metaphysic / warm, warm regards become yours too within metaphysic / generous, generous gains metaphysic / helping, helping hurl out yes to less, then metaphysic / help, help us see our metaphysics degree.

CHAPTER TWO

Honest, honest and ambient believes metaphysical / key, key to these cues metaphysical / true, true enough metaphysic / swing, swing out through outs metaphysic / valuable, valuable leads too a metaphysical / habits, habits of sures metaphysic / peace, peace in the mornings calls metaphysically repeat / quiet, quiet outs hers metaphysical / sad, sad about lessons metaphysical /

existential, existential success through these metaphysical / helper, helper held in these metaphysical / consideration, consideration compares us, metaphysical / travel, travel throughout Europes stratus metaphysical / share, share a constant metaphysical / food, food about us metaphysical / cares, cares more than these, the metaphysical / jewels, jewels join our gains metaphysic / earrings, earrings out and through metaphysic / diamonds, diamonds dealt a metaphysical course too, love / campers, campers kept a metaphysicals wa / water, water wields eyes metaphysical / wealth, wealth weds us metaphysic / washing, washing ups metaphysics touc / trips, trips direct through these metaphysic / values, values valiant too, a Metatronics metaphysic / payday, payday comes too a metaphysic / bills, bills paid through thee metaphysic / mesh, mesh outs thankful metaphysic / friends friends find ours metaphysic / waterfalls, waterfalls well through a metaphysic / trust, trust us metaphyisicall / truth, truth tells the story metaphysic / honesty, honesty cares metaphysically / stars, stars carry metaphysic / plans, plans to be metaphysically free36. moons, moons made a man's pl metaphysically / starts, starts up and parts in metaphysic / God, God gave true metaphysic / amber, amber waving through metaphysically / gavels, gavels gain metaphysically / judges, judges gain a friends metaphysically / sufficient, sufficient through these metaphysic / peace, peace a pulse beats metaphysically / love, love in these metaphysically / honesty, honesty dates your's metaphysical / caring, caring copes metaphysical / compassionate, compassionate abates to a metaphysic / Buddha, Buddha bound out through a metaphysical / Christ, Christ comes true in metaphysic / hearth, hearth entire through metaphysic / heart, heart exact too metaphysically / home, home is in thee metaphysically / forgiven, forgiven forgives and the lending metaphysical / around, around these metaphysic / light, light lends us metaphysic / story, story trues at metaphysic / told, told the shows on too metaphysic / pleasure, pleasure becomes who's metaphysic / bold, a bold reply comes too metaphysic / balance, balance begun through metaphysical / inquires angelic, inquires angelic decided metaphysically / choirs, choirs kept metaphysically correc / choose, new and old choose metatron's plus metaphysic / chills, chills over, warm thee metaphysics.

CHAPTER THREE

Brush, brush past about faced metaphysicals / passed, passed out and in too metaphysically / current, current express on metaphysically / traced, traced our race into a metaphysical agre / talented, talented ones knew our metaphysical / hone, hone your yes within ours metaphysical / homily, homily and the family is metaphysical tw / anomaly, anomaly of the familiar let us remit a barriers free zone metaphysically / meliflows, meliflows sounds metaphysic to my love / genuflect, genuflect and the grace respect too metaphysical / gallop, gallop gave us a ravings metaphysical relativ / gain, gain an exact replicate within as without metaphysic / grace, grace is found in the town red with metaphysics release / crash, crash is turning back into a warm reunite in the metaphysics on love / crucible, crucible of the choir correct to an erect reserve call wide into our metaphysical solids love / crucify, crucify less your belief in God's metaphysical realities in your ressurection is love / regard, regard us well in metaphysical relie / record release, record releases a spell metaphysical / respect, respect a random metaphysic / render, render a central note too metaphysically / couples, couples dare metaphysically / chosen, chosen won metaphysically / mansions, mansions meant to be metaphysical / sleep, sleep is ripe in the type metaphysical / love's, love's license kept, metaphysically / keep, keep up your steps metaphysically / clarity, clarity cues us into the metaphysical / curates, curates your rates on metaphysic / amphitheater, amphitheater kept metaphysical / built, built a place metaphysically / shown, shown a loan metaphysically / ways, ways to be metaphysically fre / remembers, remembers a ration, metaphysically / rotten, rotten reduce too metaphysically / smells, smells great to metaphysically / spell, spells out relates metaphysical date / shells, shells out and then a metaphysical / blink, blink and think metaphysically / motives, motives toward us metaphysically / motoring, motoring through metaphysically / arrange, arrange us well metaphysically / gorgeous, gorgeous retains a metaphysical aspect / skies, skies dowse your spirit metaphysically / eruptive, eruptive reside at the love is metaphysical / respect, respect regain metaphysical / expands, expands to a brands metaphysical content / reply, metaphysically replies retain respect for you / athletes, athletes need names respectful to a sports interface / skilled, skilled in the hearts metaphysical / tests, tests out well metaphysically / works, works on winds metaphysical / suppose, suppose to be and weds metaphysically / achieve, achieve a drawn exam of a dramatic explains metaphysic / levels, levels warm to a swarming metaphysic / fit, fit to the mit on a metaphysical well / looks, looks like your metaphysical designs fre / offers, offers to be well within our metaphysical degrees / castles, castles campaign for the strain I am / cassettes clouds, cassettes clouds and movemetns unique to God's metaphysical / percents, percents off and on too metaphysical / hose, a hose knows the gain metaphysical / breaks, breaks through and aims too metaphysically / carts, carts kept in metaphysical unit / based, based on you the metaphysical truths of love.

CHAPTER FOUR

Flair, flair for the naturals metaphysical / flavor, flavor and the favor found in metaphysical / found, found dates within these metaphysical / fountains, fountains felt up and in too our flows metaphysically / contents, contents contained in refrains metaphysically / worlds, worlds wander through metaphysically / looks, looks like a wands regress to metaphysicals releas / educates, educates us like lamps in love's metaphysically / revolve, revolve, revolve and solve your gains musically metaphysically / pilot, pilot plants amalgam on 'earths' metaphysically apple / worth, worth and the mirths in metaphysic / effect, effect barriers and the reef referred metaphysically / programs, programs rewound and the sounds metaphysically / costs, costs more less often in metaphysical refrain / hours, hours and the powers metaphysical / lesson, lesson about recognizable metaphysic / research, research metaphysically direct inside yo / science,

science said these metaphysical / conjure, conjure a care for the metaphysical / works, works through our metaphysically / proves, life provides us metaphysical releas / post, post in and the friends metaphysical / falls, falls over wells metaphysical / wet, wet ways and days metaphysical / minutes, minutes and the hours metaphysical / deep, deep into a trip metaphysical / doses, doses due your you metaphysical / kept, kept equates in with metaphysical / tiles, tiles and the files think with thicken metaphysical / invest, invest in a race through a metaphysical loo / intestinal, intestinal flew our concepts relate metaphysically / floods, floods out the overs in metaphysical / cost, cost out and compares in the metaphysical / approach, approach a pace metaphysical / limits, limits leave us metaphysically replet / limp, limp through and view your limitlessness metaphysically / dives, dives true to a legends metaphysically / zones, zones zeal then metaphysically / erotic, erotic rang our rings metaphysically / homes, homes hands found metaphysically / exotic, exotic, exotic and essential to a metaphysical regard for the clause, human / planes, planes and the place metaphysically / electric, electrics trace on the metaphysical / gifts, gifts gain refrains metaphysical / eccentric, eccentric aspects and the purest correct to the flow metaphysical / vertical, vertical to a hold these the metaphysical / caught, caught escapes through the metaphysical / passions, passions plates and the slides metaphysical / used, used and the rounds anew metaphysical / parts, parts play our metaphysic / open, open ways metaphysical / hearts, hearts held open too the metaphysical / empty, empty outs and ins metaphysical / skies, skies skate in to the metaphysical / basks, basks about these metaphysical / loss, loss gains our metaphysicals relate / floss, floss flew through the metaphysical loop / furnished, furnished and the meals metaphysical / gamets, gamets run and won metaphysically / garnered, garnered a gathering worn to a metaphysical / glass, glass racks exchange our metaphysical / dissolves, dissolves deep in metaphysical relapse / pants, pants on and off too the human woo is won metaphysically / tire, tireless within these metaphysicals.

CHAPTER FIVE

Veterans, veterans view the sound set in metaphysically / park, park hear, metaphysically / bus om's, bus om's is in 314, metaphysically / opens, opens a planes metaphysical loo / pours, pours about us ways metaphysically / implore, implore a storage metaphysical / caves, caves campaign metaphysically / ring, a ring ran into these metaphysical / crevasse, crevasse creates a wedged metaphysical / seen, seen in a size metaphysical / trails, trails true into a metaphysical way / gleam, gleam gained metaphysically / branched, branced abide in the size metaphysically / compare, compare can account for the vaunt metaphysical / county's, county's care is a fare metaphysical / bloom, bloom and the room's in metaphysical / planets, planets clank in a warp metaphysically / choose, choose a chains metaphysical / choices, choices charted through the metaphysical / kissing, kissing comes true metaphysically / clinging, clinging frees our metaphysical loop / moves, moves in too the metaphysical / smooth, smooth made metaphysically / vibration, vibration veiled less in the metaphysical / lingering, lingering lasts metaphysically / mist, mist abides metaphysically complet / magnify, magnify a maze metaphysically / mantles, mantles mace a magazine metaphysically ful / mystique, mystique makes us metaphysically free / grips, grips agree too the metaphysical / trailers? trailers filled with thee metaphysically / grew, grew and grained metaphysically / greenhouse, greenhouse effective ally's through the metaphysical / plantings, plantings leased through God's goods metaphysical / planted, planted and the plenty's metaphysical / pope, pope and the rope red metaphysically / plasma, plasma plans on your metaphysic / spills, spills apparently to a meal's metaphysical / spelling, spelling spoke the evokes metaphysical / trails, trails trade and the trims win is metaphysical / trickling, trickling arise to a mavericks metaphysical / truth, truth tells the spells metaphysically / blood, blood bathed emulsion placed metaphysically / man, man planned within these metaphysical / humanitys, humanitys cue is in your metaphysical / loop, loop leaped metaphysically / links mastery, links mastery your metaphysical / mission, mission gave into God's lace and the links metaphysically / places, places flick through our visual review of the metaphysical / banks, banks in the chunks metaphysical / prism, a prism light too metaphysical / perch, perch in the birth's pace metaphysical / rains, rains and the strengths metaphysical / roads, roads and the strides metaphysics / some, some and the one metaphysical / argon, argon on to the metaphysic / parts, parts and the starts within these metaphysical / woven, woven and the weave is in through metaphysical / wander, wander and the wins in metaphysically / worn, worn and the torn metaphysically / wed, wed and the steal that's home metaphysically / western, western and the ways metaphysical / special, special accept into the metaphysical / all, all and walls are full with metaphysicals.

CHAPTER SIX
Plasma, plasma plenty metaphysic / gift, gift gains these metaphysic / life, life led too ours metaphysic / itself, itself and the shelf on metaphysic / replicas, replicas and the respective ressurrection of randoms shore's metaphysical / through, through and to a metaphysic / bloods bloods bathe in the lamb's metaphysical / detailed, detailed and to a listen rhapsodic metaphysically9.loop, loop laid in to metaphysics agre / us, us to mess with metatron's gift a metaphysical / through, through and to this metaphysical / adonis, adonis and the sky magnifies in ours metaphysical / starred, starred and the swords metaphysic / sects, sects and the wrecked abide benevolents metaphysic / fry, fry to the sky is a metaphysical / fresh, fresh and the wash metaphysical / fonder, fonder of the form I wander awash in pleasant remembrance of God the metaphysical / fondest, fondest dreams met with love's metaphysic / securest, securest set of love's metaphysical / deliberate, deliberate desire to be metaphysical / counsel, counsel your own metaphysically / contracts, contracts reacts detached dtails metaphysical / extends, extends to a trance end metaphysical / extent, extent extolls goads metaphysically / fuzzy, fuzzy fades to the metaphysical / faced, faced with love metaphysical /

emotional, emotional messages meant metaphysically / leaves, leaves and the love's on metaphysical / lessons, lessons at lands metaphysical / hands, hands on these too metaphysical / protect, protect a rampaged metaphysical / counter, counter clan, metaphysical / pause, pause for elects metaphysical / effect, effect in allow metaphysical / allow, allow metaphysical now love / lean, lean into love's metaphysical / puzzles, puzzles about pause metaphysical / explain, explain your gain metaphysically / fish, fish on metaphysically / wild, wild about heard metaphysically / rivers, rivers rest rescue metaphysical / inhabit, inhabit your grain metaphysically / requires, requires a racks metaphysically / restore, restore your soar metaphysical / earths, earths bless gains metaphysical / funds, funds apply metaphysically / enhance, enhance a dance metaphysically / palated, palated explore metaphysical / encompass, encompass a compass points metaphysically / gains, gains abound metaphysically / traditional, traditional transits these metaphysically / interest, interest in your grin gains metaphysically / partial, partial eclipse of the lips won to a God's metaphysic / recognition, recognition of the mission sent to a Jesus invent metaphysically / knowledge, knowledge of the college admit metaphysically / shows, shows and the rows metaphysical / payments, payments and the plans metaphysically / natives, natives and the raves win metaphysically / wilder, wilder and the counter's lean metaphysical / encounter, encounter and the counters win metaphysically / purchase, purchase and the muse made metaphysical / reveal, reveal and the still metaphysical / elected, elected and the erected metaphysical / place, place and the trace is metaphysical.

CHAPTER SEVEN
Expires, expires and the hires in metaphysical / happy, happy and the spells in metaphysical / less, less is the heal metaphysical / academy, academy of the wedding of love credential metaphysical / built, built the quilt metaphysical / magnify, magnify and the reply metaphysical / space, space and the race if in metaphysical / decade, decade of the raid less paid for metaphysical / left, care to be left to you metaphysically / desperate loves, desperate love's degree on the miracles metaphysical / rite, rite of the set metaphysical / control stonehenged, control stonehenged of the role metaphysical / breaks, breaks and the shapes metaphysical / people, people the plane metaphysically / spill, spill out and shout in too metaphysical / pilgrims, pilgrims plant a gain metaphysical / find, find a strand metaphysically gran / totality, totality and true to the metaphysical / failure, failure to be lessened within love / leaves, leaves and the strands held in hands metaphysically / reasons, reasons and the seasons metaphysical / reside, reside at a stride metaphysical / wilderness, wilderness won to a treed degree met at the regard metaphysical / won, won in a dare metaphysical / respectful, respectful rays metaphysical / parents, meant to be parents free metaphysically / given, given a gain remain metaphysical / sun, sun and the run into a metaphysical / regions, regions and the rags metaphysical / drags, drags out less yes metaphysical / over, over the rebel yell ahead metaphysical / listen, listen to the yes metaphysical / bush, bush and the cushion

metaphysical / cemetary, cemetary set on release metaphysical / cable, cable cut into due metaphysical / cut, cut in the capable metaphysical / open, open and the winds metaphysical / gates, gates and the gratis metaphysical / flow, flow into the yome electric metaphysical / shuttle, shuttle and the muttles out metaphysical / proclaimed, proclaimed and the same metaphysical / shalom, shalom and the loom that's in to metaphysical / pound, pound and the shilling metaphysical / found, found in the pound metaphysical / frequent, frequent and the recents metaphysical / flown, flown and the zone is in a metaphysical / flows, flows and the shows metaphysical / peace, peace in the east metaphysical / volunteer, volunteer to be metaphysical / estates, estates and the sends metaphysical / escape, escape and the success through metaphysical / loop, metaphysical loops within human love / teach, teach and the week is worn, heaven won to love's metaphysical / truth, truth in told arrival at love's archival revival the lamb / crowds, crowds arrange a range magnified in the metaphysical / bailed, bailed a brance metaphysical / God, God gives a growing release metaphysical / given, given a living metaphysically complet / paint, paint and the stains magnify in the metaphysical / guitar, guitar good to a stood magnitude metaphysical / growth, growth given into a metaphysical / guess, guess who is the durable queen within the metaphysical / sold, sold and the bold metaphysically / replace, replace and the stand in metaphysical.

CHAPTER EIGHT
Gamble, gamble on the table metaphysical / gain, gain a granite stand too metaphysical / gone, gone to the won metaphysical / entrance, entrance to the sun's metaphysical / families, families design your won metaphysical / align, align and the sign that's in a reward into a metaphysical vie / paint, paint and the saint metaphysical / occupy, occupy and the sign is in metaphysically / tropics, tropics and the topics metaphysical / reign, reign and the send metaphysical / heavens, heavens and the hints metaphysical / lots, lots and ths slots metaphysical / passion, passion plays and the heavens ascend metaphysical / flames, flames flew into a metaphysical vie / sky, sky and the why metaphysical / waves, waves and the west is metaphysical / bones, bones and the bands metaphysical / sand, sand and the hand metaphysical / hats, hats on and off to the metaphysical / on, on and the run is to the metaphysical / peopled, peopled expled of the more metaphysical / environ, environ and the siren metaphysical / conservator, conservator overture metaphysical / obeys, obeys the ways, metaphysical / your, your way our too, metaphysical / heed, heed us well our tale metaphysical / note, note and the vote metaphysical / individual, individual and the spiritual metaphysical / needs, needs a steed metaphysical / clues, clues and the ruse that wins metaphysical / respect, respect your direct metaphysical / revolve, metaphysically / blind, blind dies eyes metaphysical / lead, lead and the lesson metaphysical / lesson, lesson and the yes in metaphysical / natures, natures and the real deal metaphysical / organic, organic and the planets metaphysical / greens, greens and the scene metaphysical / resources, resources and the sources metaphysical / endear, endear and the rear metaphysical

/ endangers, endangers date with the fetus metaphysical / gate, gate and the sate is in too, the metaphysical / laws, laws and the clause metaphysical / ascend, ascend and the vends metaphysical / establish, establish and the ravish metaphysical / rules, rules and the rounds metaphysical / pool, pool and the mule metaphysical / honest, honest and the west "in" metaphysical / ones, ones and the sun's metaphysical / artifacts, artifacts and the facts metaphysical / encase, encase and the space is in the metaphysical / open, open and the scope is in the metaphysical / emphathic, empathic and the math's in the metaphysical / goods, goods and the woods in metaphysical / goodwill, goodwill and the stood well, within thee metaphysical / hearts, hearts and the partitions in the metaphysical / encounter, encounter and the covey found metaphysically / pare, pare and the spares in metaphysically / brothers, brothers and the smothers out metaphysically / fellow, fellow and the mellow metaphysical / function, function and the mansions metaphysical / experienced, experienced and the immersion metaphysical / friends, friends and the bends metaphysical / evolve, evolve and the solve in the metaphysical.

CHAPTER NINE
Fire, fire and the hiring empires true to a light's metaphysical / lovers, lovers leap into a listening shout metaphysical / loops, loops and the scoops deep into a life metaphysical / law, law and the legends metaphysically re[;et / obligate, obligate and the sate found metaphysically / contractual, contractual and the factual, metaphysical / deals, deals and the spills metaphysical / speak, speak and the seeking metaphysical / spoken, spoken and the speaker's metaphysical / preside, preside and the side's won metaphysically / supple, supple and the trues coupling metaphysically / supplement, supplement and the compliment met metaphysically / span, span and the strand metaphysical / sure, sure to the soaring metaphysical / assure, assure and the squarely metaphysical / dauntless, dauntless and the detailed flaunt, mph, metaphysical / stories, stories retold and untold metaphysically / undehand, underhand and the stand that ran into the metaphysical / brace, brace for the race unto the metaphysical / all, all imply and the sigh won metaphysically / cafeteria, cafeteria rate and the caring wares metaphysical / traipse, traipse to the corpse risen metaphysically / asleep, asleep in detail and the seal made metaphysical / swing, swing into winning metaphysical experience / climb, climb and the crime paid metaphysically / livestock, livestock and the retails metaphysical / bark, bark and the seeking metaphysical / howl, howl and the healing respect found metaphysically / yelp, yelp and the helping intent to come through metaphysically / yule, yule and the flexible eccentrically metaphysically / shock, shock and the shielding metaphysicals / drift, drift and the details expressed in the metaphysical / every, every ways days metaphysical / trails, trails and the trees played metaphysical / intrigue, intrigue and the seated metaphysical / lunchtime, lunchtime and the retails punched through metaphysical / act, act and the respectful attend too, the metaphysical / active, active and the retails metaphysically / yell, yell and the swells metaphysically / yomes, yomes sealed

metaphysically / adrift, adrfit and the rift made metaphysically / hooks, hooks and the seeks made matephysicall / set, and the seatings worn metaphysically / seal, seal and the closures sung metaphysically / God, God and the gates made metaphysically / caught, caught and the capably metaphysical / imagined, imagined and the impression made signed through the metaphysical / shame, shame and the games catch metaphysical / ascendant, ascendant and the sun's rise metaphysical / stands, stands and the grands won metaphysically / chosen, chosen retails and the reached for metaphysical / plans, plans and the patterns punch, trend free unto the metaphysically / enochian, encohian and the winging metaphysical / wings, wings and the trends lend metaphysically / homeward, homeward sails and the retails metaphysical / still, still and the feel for the features metaphysical / green, green and the scenes spent metaphysically / tourmaline, tourmaline tours and the scenes sent metaphysically / salty, salty and the scenes built metaphysically / grains, grains gaze accordingly metaphysical / harmonious, harmonious to the hinted metaphysical / mandalas, mandalas mention the mendel metaphysic / assumption, assumption retains the blending metaphysical / female, female to the featured metaphysicals.

CHAPTER TEN
Reactive, reactive and the ratify supplied metaphysically / terminals, terminals and the sun shone metaphysically / gated, gated and the gesture's metaphysical / entry, entry ruse and the muse made metaphysical / deduce, deduce and the captured lamb won, metpahysicall / sephirotic, sephirotic rely and the rapture's raised metaphysically / agile, agile and the willing won metpahysicall / agilities, agilities and the abilities won metaphysically / energetic, energetic and the winning metaphysical / approaches, approaches realized and the reaching release to the meetings metaphysical / greed, greed gone and the frequent amaze metaphysical / green, green and the giving metaphysical / appeal, appeal and the willed releases metaphysical / assumes, assumes and the resumes worn metaphysically / forms, forms elect a nurturance called the metaphysical / lands, lands and the legends born metaphysically / owned, owned parallels and the pierceing goals reached metaphysically / owner, owner and the shipping won metaphysically / farms, farms feature charming explains of the passions metaphysical / conserve, conserve the swerve to God metaphysically / more, more then, metaphysically score / most, most said for, the metaphysical / collect, collect a respectful metaphysical / peace, peace exists metaphysically 25.pieces, pieces that pulse in the interfaced metaphysical / puzzles, puzzles lipped in the peaceful metaphysical / thrown, thrown reached metaphysically / trophy won through the truest heart's metpahysical / won, won too, the metaphysical / the son has won you meta-physicall / win, win a wonderful metaphysical exchang / represent, represent the interests only metaphysical / educational, educational to an interior placed metaphysically / support, support the blissful metaphysical / seek, seek a retail metaphysical / couples, couples merge metaphysically / program, programs penetrate the notochord metaphysically / assign, assign

details metaphysically / train, train the evolve to include stretching news for the growth made metaphysically / aspire, aspire to the freeing flown metaphysically / indeed, indeed and the seeds built metaphysically / deport, deport retails and the sorts sent metaphysically / depart, depart to the remake metaphysically / insight, insight spent for the featured metaphysical / source, source suggested, read this, "the metaphysical / commune, commune and the meaning mooned metpahysicall / conference, conference felt for the featured length metaphysical / confer, confer daily to the details metaphysical / tour, tour the trenches metaphysically / trade, trade and the raids run metaphysiclal / build, build into boating voted for metaphysically / buy, buy this then, metaphysically / campus, campus campaigned forth metaphysically / aloe, aloe soothes your moistened metaphysical / soothe, soothe preparing the preached for metaphysical / ground, ground into greetings metaphysical / gain, gain a prepare thrown to the teachings metaphysical / grace, grace given and the traces rise to the reaching metaphysical / govern, govern a piercing metaphysical / love, love led to these best said "metaphhysicals"/ school, school and the finding's metaphysical / ship, ship directly into the seeds won metaphysically / room, room made metaphysically / home, home to healing's gamed metaphysically.

CHAPTER ELEVEN
Instructor, instructor sent to the venues heaven deep in advanced invent of the features multiplied through the marriage metaphysical / advanced, advanced degrees reached through the weight gone, metaphysical / degrees, degrees bestowed and the node moves metaphysically to the election led frequently to God / elite, elite to a rapture met metaphysically / sort, sort the dialects sorted metaphysically / option, option occuring, opinion free, for the life fed metaphysically awar / reply, reply to a reaching metaphysical / product, product paid for in the featured metaphysical / guides, guides gap free to the wideness metaphysical / pulse, pulse appluaded and the emulsify spent metaphysically / kona calls and the kindness flows in the feathered metaphysical / mobile, mobile too and the mentioned metaphysical / sporting, sporting interests and the rests metaphysical / events, events and the extents borne metaphysically / stabilize, stabilize your rise into the hearts worn metaphysically / scope, scope and the dope burned metaphysically / indulge, indulge in the mentioned discover of the lover born metaphysically / zoic, zoic and the stoic forgive for the featured metaphysical / fibers, fibers and the featured metaphysical / optical, optical to a detail woven metaphysically / discover, discover a regard for the physically metaphysical / tracking, tracking allows you al listening metaphysical / device, device detailed in the slicing metaphysical / mirrors, mirrors densely crashed thoroughout the thrilling metaphysical / pace, pace and the tracing adepts within thee metaphysical / heart's, heart's gift and the cart driven livingly metaphysical / telescope, telescope and the menthol escape to a treaty metaphysical / eyes, eyes and the wisest adore to the swearing metaphysical / zoom, zoom into meetings roomed interiorly metaphysical / metaphysical, metaphysical to a featured adoration born insistently mentally free / equally,

equally woven and the sequel spent interior to a metaphysical delug / place, place a pension into your metaphysical / electronics, electronics and the respect for the rested metaphysical / electric, electric and the display driven into a metaphysical / mount, mount a counter forth, metaphysically / mounts, mounts and the mentions born metaphysically / deluxe, deluxe defy and the derive born metaphysically / drive, drive striven for and the forward aid won metaphysically / package, package placed thoroughly extractive to a metaphysically affluent position made fre / out, out to the shouted metaphysicals / system, yes to a system metaphysically fre / sold, sold to the nearest metaphysical / enliven, enliven and the striving metaphysical / likes, likes and the willing metaphysical / life, life led throughout you metaphysically / colors, colors and the centrals metaphysical / highlights, highlights levied and the leaves blown metpahysicall / specials, specials and the speeches metaphysical / meteorlogical, meteorlogical mentions born metaphysically / many, many and the mentioned metaphysical / gather, gather and the greeted metaphysical / then, then and the thrilling metaphyical / plants, plants planted metaphysically / manage, manage to mention the meetings metaphysical / well, well into elective metaphysical / lake, lake and the legendary metaphysical / sold, sold and the suggested boldly metaphysical / clouds, clouds concur then shield the volcanonic kilowatt freed metaphysically / deliver, deliver and the giver born metaphysically fre / son's, son's into suggested metaphysical / code, code enlivened through the giving metaphysical / elevates, elevates you to a station born metaphysically / again, again and the retails worn metaphysically / light, light to a listen worn metaphysically.

CHAPTER TWELVE

Image, image and the amazement metaphysical / eclipsed, ecllipsed in the intents metaphysical / open, open prepare for the pensions metaphysical / eyes, eyes awarest metaphysically / prospects, portals prospective to a passion metaphysical / plenty, plenty made in the regards metaphysical / pages, pages purged through the trades made metaphysical / wisdom, wisdom wisely woven into the winnings metaphysical / wide, wide to a sector metnioned metaphysically / remember to detail the dealing metaphysical / december, december to spring the patterns emebergin metaphysically metatroni / comes, comes a wintery spelling m-e-t-a-p-h-y-s-I-c-a- / overheard, overheard electrically, the fed won, metpahysicall / covers, covers a vendor worn metaphysically / sales, sales made electrically, metaphysical / spurt, spurt recovers your healing metaphysical / jets, jets to a joining metaphysical / older, older and the smoldering metaphysical / younger, younger and the thrilling metaphysical / every, every and the vary metaphysical / one, one to wonderful metaphysicals 22 all, all to the lighten metaphysical / fortune, fortune and the founded metaphysical / frolic, frolic and the freeing five who live the fine lined metaphysic / some, some days often and the features metaphysical / sold, sold to the biddings metaphysical / essential, essential in a require for the featured metaphysical / weather, weather wisely the winnings metaphysical / wins, wins a handsome sum, metaphysically / planted, planted in emphatic

agree at the merger called incline and the finish called mine, electrically, metaphysically, free / plenty, plenty merged in good measure and I found atreasure called "treated" within, finally, through love, the metaphysical / signs, signs gathered merging maintained metaphysically / softness, softness discovered and the lover met within an amazing metaphysical respect for love / worn, worn daily trued metaphysically / switched, switched electrically to a pole, the metaphysical / poles, poles placed nearly true to love the emerging metaphysical / purges, purges made and the feelings metaphysically replicate / granted, granted a vaunted summon, won, metaphysically / graven, graven less, grown more through the metaphysical / gone, gone to the getting metaphysical / grandfather's, grandfather's guise gone too, the metaphysical / voice, voice elaborates upon the metaphysical / thunders, thunders decisions metaphysical / loud, loud to a leading metaphysical / stations, stations espoused of the feelings metaphysical / chosen, chosen speaks lightly "metaphysical / solar, solar sent metaphysically / plows, plows a loving metaphysical / fulcrum, fulcrum and the metnion's fountains metaphysical / pointed, pointed truly to the features metaphysical / straight, straight at a detail flown metaphysically / earth, earth mirthed metaphysically / lever, lever daily to the prayerful phrase metaphysical / prisms, prisms and passions worn metaphysically / gazed, gazed into metaphysically / mirth, mirth lightens your living's metaphysical / passionate, passionate to a position worn metaphysically / mirrors, mirrors met and felt throughout these metaphysical / open, open elate over thee, the metaphysical / break, break the deeds metaphysical / multiple, multiple to a moment's multiply worn metaphysically / galaxy, galaxy agrres "metaphysically" / purple, purple to a violet flame sword deep in light's electric merger for the freshly metaphysical / state, state directly the "metaphysical."

CHAPTER THIRTEEN

Stock, stock made plenty for the future's metaphysical / sold, sold and the suggested cure is worn metaphysically / wonders, wonders seen and the scenes spent metaphysically / home, home to a hebrew metaphysical'/ hospital, hospital driven into a mentally metaphysical / diagnose, diagnose a detail metaphysical / voice, voice and the finding's metaphysical / found, found and the tangent's born metaphysical / polarization, polarization and the planning wanted metaphysically / plants, plants and the painted metaphysical / micrometer, micrometer and the constant intrigue with the details metaphysical / lights, lights and the lifted metaphysical / lightweight, lightweight appealing metaphysically / pad, pad and the pented metaphysic / thought, thought through and the threshold meets metaphysically, hu-man / love, love and the living days metaphysical / tripod, tripod raised and the retinue revneued throughout these metaphysic / tote, tote and the voted metaphysic / scope, scope and the sentinel metaphysical / skirt, skirt the "our" metaphysically love / fiber, fiber fed to the tuberous metaphysic / matters, matters Gabriel into love, the metaphysical / material, material to amaze and the raging metaphysical / bank, bank into the venues metaphysical / hands,

hands detail your dealings metaphysically / deliver, deliver again the freedom metaphysical / tangents, tangents reached and the resolutely absolute forgive into life's franchise-less metaphysic / tantric, tantric forgive and the feelings metphysica / blues, blues sold for the federally forgiven metaphysic / blossom, blossom and the reasons metaphysical / opens, opens grazing metaphysic / link, link to a listening metaphysic / object, object of the greeted metaphysic / perform, perform daily metaphysically / thanks, thanks appears speech free to the metaphysical / skips, skips a saily metaphysical / caliber, caliber laid and the therapy paid for metaphysically / costs, costs gathered and the weathered made metaphysically too, love' / compare, compare then concur metaphysically / poise, poise amazes metaphysically / pose, pose daily near the mark, metaphysical / advance, advance regards gain your detatched stretchtaphysicall / controlled, controlled within and above throughout the metaphysical / false, false prospects and the rejects born metaphysically beref / lash, lash outed and the throng shouted "metaphysically" love / light's, light's gaze is into the metaphysical / love, love too, metaphysically / astral, astral plans and the partners metaphysical / planes, planes gained metaphysically / spectacular, spectacular, apectacular spells these, the "m-e-t-a-p-h-y-s-I-c-a-l-s / visible, visible in values metaphysical / remote, remote retail and the fellows metaphysical / opportunity, opportunity knocked thrice daily to the mentions metaphysical / balds, balds speeched in a dialect metaphysical / control, control bonnie seas through thee, the metaphysical / codes, codes made accessible metaphysically / deep, d eep within detailed metaphysic / contents, contents coned metaphysically / climbs, climbs electircally free to a mentioned metaphysical / knows, knows a duration metaphysical / exude, exude a rude less, metaphysically / flowers, flowers into powers born metaphysically / gardens, gardens gained through the metaphysical / spaces, spaces believed in metaphysically.

THE SUPERLUMINOUS-MENTS
LEVEL 45

CHAPTER ONE

Styles, styles in the smiles superluminous / whiles, whilein the replays superluminous / ways, ways the stay on superluminous / wells, wells and the fallen's superluminous / hots, superluminous in the hots supercode too, love / sound, sound in the sounds superluminous / ultimates, ultimates and the pentathletic agrees superluminous / products, products and the apprentice superluminous / exclusive, loves exclusive superluminous / movies, movies in the movements superluminous / musical, musical in the principals superluminous / active, active in the superluminous / arcs, arcs in the triumphant stand superluminous / triumphs, superluminous triumphs in the windows superluminous / trades, trades in the raids on the superluminous / ace, ace in the places superluminous / patient, patient about it these the superluminous / calm, calm is the clamor superluminous / gong, gong in the wronging superluminous / goes, goes in trues the superluminous / classic, classic acquire of the livings superluminous / pose, pose in the rosey superluminous / pearly, pearly creyed in the goods relate gone superluminous / waits, waits in too, the superluminous / tubal, tubal and the letigate complete to the superluminous / tops, superluminous is tops in the trap rent superluminous / taught, taught is the caught on superluminous / truth, truth is open into the superluminous / classical, classical attire and the fire on the superluminous / prose, prose is written in the inventin superluminous / calls, superluminous in the calls the superbs data love / youth, youth and the truths within the superluminous / sounds, sounds like superluminous / within, within and without the superluminous / controls, superluminous controls win the superb degre / position, position in the missions purely superluminous / programs, programs appear in the ears superluminous / integrate, integrate a gratis superluminous / precise, precise is precious to a see superluminous / controlled, controlled in appearances superluminous / bounds, superluminous and in bounds come to God / binds, binds in the verbage superluminous / bird, bird days superluminous / words, words and the birds come superluminous / well, God's well is well with the superluminous / wealth, wealth and the width superluminous / wants, wants to be superluminous / wattage, superluminous wattage and the cottaged apparent within love / luminous, luminous and the superb desire to live through heightened echelon / floats, floats in fathered forgive into the superluminous / glow, glow and the gazes superluminous / balls, balls and the walls end superluminous / winters, winters and the wizened superluminous / focus, focus falls in trees superluminous / noble, noble necessitate and the ravish superluminous / bonds, bonds in blends gone superluminous / technical, technically adept and electively superior to a narrow exuberance superluminous to love / carved, carved and the cared for superluminous / interior, interior intrigued with this the superluminous / transit, transit into travels superluminous / trips, trips and travels superluminous / vacate, superior in decide too deliver the superluminous / share, share above and flared the superluminous / show, show in the knowing superluminous.

CHAPTER TWO

Staff, staff and the fairest superluminous / purchase, purchase in the peruvians a superluminous / shape, shape above the ginger superluminous / credits, credits above and then the superluminous / oblige, oblige and the sizes superluminous / fascinates, superluminous fascinates and the states assur / functions, functions absolute in the require superluminous / issues, superluminous issues and the misses desire / refresh, refresh in the fashion superluminous / ideas, ideas and the suggestions superluminous / efforts, efforts affective too the superluminous / loves, loves a lady superluminous / effects, superior effect and the respects superluminous / reflex, superluminous reflex into the lights sugges / rooted, rooted and the suited superluminous / worn, worn into two superluminous / acre, acre superluminous decree in love / timber, timber in the temper superluminous / park, park in the spark won superluminous / way, way into the want through superluminous / purchase, love's purchase made the superluminous / dreamer, dreamer and the dreamed superluminous / possible, possible appear the superluminous / devotes, devotes into notes degree the superluminous / technical, technical attributes win the superluminous / optimizing, optimizing apparently thee the superluminous / paced, paced and erasure in the superluminous / vacation, vacation and the vocation won the superluminous / optimal, optimal appear the superluminous / individual, individual and the missided superluminous / arrise, arrise aware into the superluminous / several, several and the severly superluminous / connective, connective conclusive literally superluminous / elegance, desire elegance again in yours superluminous / fireworks, spell the fireworks smell within these superluminous / captive, superluminous appears captive again / currents, currents run through the superluminous / intricate, intricate trues and the superluminous news in God's delive / capitals, capitals superluminous / extra, superluminous success superlative by desires conced / varies, varies and the venues superluminous / talents, talents into these superluminous / passion, passion in the places superluminous / depths, depths in the data's superluminous / exploits, superluminous exploits in the imports superluminous / portion, superluminous portion and the motions superluminous / mention, superluminous mention of the divisions superluminous / means, means to bring these the superluminous / starts like a friendly superluminous / missions, superluminous missions into alert lessone / reconnect, reconnect in a suspect superluminous / comply, comply in the reply superluminous / mavericks, superbly mantled within these superluminous / measure, measured and wed the superluminous / pressures, pressures and the peace is superluminous / alert, alert and the experts superluminous / disciple, disciple in a ditty the superluminous / confident, confident in a meditate the superluminous / sparkle, sparkle and the parcel superluminous / set, set in the intents superluminous / pushing, pushing 20 into superluminous / program, program in a pew the superluminous / premise, premise for a game the superluminous / rest, rest and the resets personally superluminous.

CHAPTER THREE

Compliments, compliments of the clients superluminous / turns, turns and the warms sensational into the superluminous / roles, roles and the reels superluminous / teams, teams and the rings superluminous / centers, centers in these superluminous / central, central in the ventral superluminous / blossoms, blossoms and the awesomes superluminous / blooms, blooms in the rooms superluminous / talents, talents and the trends end superluminous / arts, arts and the love's superluminous / patients, patients and the patents superluminous / rooms, rooms and the zooming superluminous / sold, sold on the goldens superluminous / hospital, superluminous hospital and the balance subatomi / clients, clients clear in truly's superluminous / burst, a superluminous burst of the dedication too, love / odds, odds and ends and the friends superluminous / events, events transcend the lens superluminous / believes, believes in your the superluminous / launch, launch into a few the superluminous / programs, programs in the planets superluminous / works, works in a welled superluminous / warrants, superluminous warrants and the torrents subatomi / discuss, discuss this yes the superluminous / delectable, superluminous delectables and the selectives subatomi / transitory, transitory and the empathics superluminous / puruse, superluminous puruse of the deluge superluminous / portions, subatomic portions smelt in letters superluminous / truth, superluminous truth explode into love / protects, protects in your treks superluminous / beleives, superluminous believes and the sleeves subatomi / center, centers in the mentors superluminous / interface, interface and the web trace superluminous / occupy, superlatives occupy within the superluminous / virtual, superbly virtual in the transitives superluminous / immerse, immerse in a mirthing called the superluminous / airs, airs and the pairs superluminous / errant, errant and the arc-on superluminous / research, research and the rehearse superluminous / labyrinthine, labyrinthine ametrined within the superluminous / immense, immense in the intense these the superluminous / overcome, overcome and the reruns superluminous / apply, apply and the sky is in the superluminous / fly, fly to a friend superluminous / fork, fork and the torques in the superluminous / fleet, fleet in the seats in the superluminous / missive, missive and the intensives superluminous / missile, missile in the thistles superluminous / helmeted, helmeted ecstatics in the superluminous / surprise, surprise in the streams superluminous / escape, escape in the streams superluminous / easy, easy in the easy superluminous / distract, distract in the defensive roads the superluminous / willing, willing to be stable in our tabled superluminous / hunts, hunts in the intrigues superluminous / robots, superluminous robots ring our sings on love / normal, normal in the tunnels superluminous / constant, constant in these the consistent superluminous / play, play in the strays superluminous / puns, puns in the intends superluminous / say, say and the sway the superluminous / time, time to say good try into the listings superluminous / tub, tub and the rings superluminous / try, try into the trees superluminous.

CHAPTER FOUR
Confront, confront in the affront superluminous / object, object of your adore won in the superluminous / adore, adore and the shore's doors superluminous / temper, temper and the simpering expression superluminous / escape, escape to the trades

superluminous / measure, measure and the treatics superluminous / remember, remember means all the dreams superluminous / memory, memory in the tempering superluminous / imagines, imagines engineer the superluminous / forgive, forgive and the foundations superluminous / forget, forget to forget the lessened superluminous / projectiles, projectiles projects superluminous / disorder, disorder doubts removed superluminous / digest, digest the ingest superluminous / deals, deals made superluminous / fly, fly to the skies superluminous / society, society said the superluminous / speakers, speakers felt superluminous / battery, battery believed in and the recharge made to the treaties super-luminou / divides, divides and the sides superluminous / divisions, divisions deal in the superluminous / combine, combine accrued the superluminous / modules, modules of the schedules metatronic in these the superluminous / propose, propose a rose into the superluminous / proposals, proposals and the reciprocal super-luminou / ideas, superluminous ideas and the squires subatomi / digits, digits and the rigids superluminous / snap, snap a dread superluminous / fidget, superluminous fidgets ridgid less and the rest subatomi / fears, fears out love's found, superluminous / elipse, elipse into the clips superluminous / edit, edit less and confess the superluminous / activate, activate and the sapphic superluminous / flips, flips into a tree zone superluminous / fullest, fullest in the feelings superluminous / advantage, advantage in the vantage superluminous / join, join in a strain superluminous / jubilation, jubilation and the join superluminous / trust, superluminous in the trust arco / tuck, tuck in the ruckus superluminous / views, views in the shadows superluminous / screens, success in the screens superluminous / books, books into bass sounded superluminous / lengths, lengths into shadows superluminous / vectors, vectors in the victors superluminous / maintain, maintain in the entrained superluminous / views, superlative views within the superluminous / designs, superior designs in the strains superluminous / formations, formations in foundations superluminous / brighten, brighten in a tighten superluminous / brightest, brightest in the tightest superluminous / debris, debris in the see superluminous / musics, spearing set on music's let in love / data, data in a deal superluminous / players, special players lead the superluminous / functions, special patterns in the functions superluminous / plays, love plays a tune superluminous / repeats, repeats in the receipts superluminous / specifics, species specifics set in the superluminous / sturdy, sturdy in the wordy superluminous / study, study in the sturdies superluminous / spell, spell a wellings superluminous / soft, soft in the often superluminous / scot, scotfreeze, superluminous.

CHAPTER FIVE
Languaged, languaged to a patented super-luminous / skills, skills maintain that thread called love is superlumina / scholarly, scholarly measures apply to the keys superluminous / sector, sector and the vectors superluminous / section, section sent home to the hurtled urgency called victory and the superluminous / access, access gains your recessed allow for the comforts fed frankly to love, the superluminous / capable, capable of creations assorted

variance and the daily deals in the superluminous / spokes, spokes in the polar appease to a magnetic mend for the shifted polish in the superluminous / wheels, wheels hot in the superluminous / phrase, phrase of the weaken felt superluminous / words, words dealt a holding superluminousity / hearts, hearts who melt in the ease metpahysically superior into the superluminous / desires, desires build in the superluminous / data, data details the relevance superluminousl / rooms, rooms randomly go to the Friends metaphysically superluminous / recede, recede allowed into the feeding superluminous / players, players abound metrically superluminous / peopled, peopled in degrees deeded and unbound metaphysically to the superluminous / within, within whistled metaphysicals and then, the superluminous / advantage, advantage paid to the partnered superluminous / active, active in a retail gown worn superluminousl / chisels, chisels into the chinese superluminous / chart, chart the magnets superluminous / grids, grids patterned across the main and the frame fed fortress regained through the superluminous / rapture, rapture meant felt faithfully intrigued with God's gains the superluminous / waits, waits dialy too, the superluminous / woven, woven attend and the mended superluminous / pairs, pairs maintain a decency through the superluminous / sessions, sessions attendant in the spelling s-u-p-e-r-l-u-m-I-n-o-u-s / seizure, seizure allows a completion into the superluminous / chasten, chastena nd the hasten within a chosen superluminousity / woes, woes dealt with in the lightwaves superluminous / filters, filters mended and the found arise into the mentions superluminous / rolls, rolls into details superluminous / worlds, worlds met in the unwound superluminous / design, designs retail avow is the gained superluminous / changes, changes met with definitions superluminous / charts, charts made to see through superluminously wanted, wanted superlatively superluminous / senate, senate of the congress superluminous / invested, invested in the rested apparent superluminous / earth, earth's garden is superluminous / contractive, contractive to the reactive experience superluminous / entire, entire to the hiring superluminous / when, when too, the superluminous / optimism, optimism met thorugh the sealings superluminous / associative, associative detail and the retails metaphysically superluminous / deluxe, deluxe avow and the wowing superluminous / binocular, binocular motion and the oceans superluminous / monofilament, monfilaments and the milimeters erect into God's superluminous hea / mighty, mighty mention of dimensional shift and th shielded forgiveness of gotten superluminosity / moved, moved to a mentioned superluminous / rotation, rotation suggested daily in the details superluminous / erase, erase patterns superluminous too, God / proven, proven ways daily good and the deeded access to love's prowess in the superluminous / powerful, powerful accept of the pensioned superluminous / custom, custom creations and the cremations complete into the superluminous / educated, educated best htorugh the daily details superluminous / taught, taught a teaching superluminous / inform, inform a few of the features superluminous / contracts, contracts becoming and the detials due a dancing bargain meatphysically superluminous / relished, relished relation and the relaxed race called the superluminous /

sterile, sterile experience found gone to the superluminous / go, go to the shower superluminous / right, right in the spot, mlk knew how to live superluminously.

CHAPTER SIX

Needs, needs met in a said "superluminous"/ nestle, nestle in direct requirement of the nephronic ability called love gained, the superluminous / wants, wants meet desire in specifically relative amounts superluminousl / carracas, carracas and the racous allow superluminous / caucas, caucas of the volley songs and the singing superluminous / captions, captions created for the capricious superluminous / cheat, cheat detailed as the browbeaten sail into the heated rivers superluminous / closed, closed and the query runs superluminousl / elegance, elegance gains you a yellow good-bye and a welcome orange revival fo the rejected regions allowed thee, the superluminous / chaste, chaste in your hastening superluminous / regional, regional hire and the dire dates superluminous / requisite, requisite intends and the details superlumiou / partnered, partnered inspire and the require for the healing superluminous / inspire, inspire delicious electives and the ashes freed to breathe superluminously / empire, empire built in stilt landed superluminosity / legally, legally respectful of the features superluminous / adequate, adequate exposure into composure and the peaceful beauty superluminous / complete, complete the reatil transaction and the reaction builds superluminousl / pressure, pressure lessens and Jesus siad, "let there be, superluminosity / manipulated, manipulated, mankind, hu-manity, superluminously / improve, improve within the kind life, the christian span can find God through the superluminous band, Chris / health, health held precious through the precisenss called super-luminou / vitality, vitality reutrning to the mentioned superluminous / stamina, stamina stays me throughout the signals superluminous / comprehensive, comprehensive creations and the durations superluminous / gentle, gentle experience and the genre gone to the superluminous / interested, interested returns treasured throughout the superluminou / shiatsu, shiatsu found in a tiny town cell deep in the superluminous / received, received a required rally from the palace superlumious / diagnosis, diagnosis reached for in the feelings superluminous / adapt, adapt to the situation cuperluminous / symptoms, symptoms met winds in the superluminous / summons, summons coming in the mentions superluminous / dwells, dwells a daughter detailed in dimensions superluminous / placed, placed a passion forth into the fusions superluminous / earth, earth met love in the teachings superluminous / cleanse, cleanse a direct derivation of the deposits superluminous / completed, completed relations superluminously / crosses, crosses born and the worn details due the superluminous / approached, approached lightly into the superluminous / forget, forget forgotten reaches superluminous / foregone, foregone features into the superluminous / forego, forego the featured flows superlumiou / fortress, fortress broken in to the superlumiou / imparts, imparts reaches superluminous / guidance, guidance reaches the superluminous / kunzite, kunzite and the reaches superluminous / pink, pink into pretty greens superluminous / deliveries, deliveries amaze superluminously / cherubs, cherubs and the chanting "superluminous / spirits, spirits passion, the superluminous / bungalow, bungalow and the gains drained allowed superluminously / grace, grace and the fashions placed into the pensioned metatronics and the light wings allowed your lifting visage born winged into life's superluminous implode / hexagrams, hexagrams and the gifted allowance superluminous / blue, blue in a truest commitment into the superluminous / committed, committed in rememberedness too, the superluminous / aspirants, aspirants and the avenues metatronically superluminous / quickens, quickens and the vixens left to shadow less the listening superluminous / understood, understood more and the meetings set for the fortunate superluminous / cones, cones appear in the creations superluminous / smelt, smelt and the smiling ironic superluminous / blades, blades and the cutting superluminous / intimate, intimate mention of the features superluminous / sculptures, sculptures spin in the winning lighten superluminous.

CHAPTER SEVEN: words, words in the wisdom won electively and the light lend superluminously / request, request and the reasons won superluminously / watery, watery wed and the mentions superluminous / honors, honors and the carrying on too, the superluminous / graves, graves and the reasons routed through the superlumious / burst, burst and the beauty deep into a light lend superluminous / desires, desires and the details superluminous / perch, perch and the passionate pairing superluminous / innovations, innovations and the invocations superluminous / kindle, kindle and the mended beaded deeded superluminous / firing, firing feelings funded superluminous / jade, jade and the bejeweled superluminous / genes, genes and the delicatley jumarried superluminous / willows, willows windy in a bending superluminous / wonder, wonder and the thrundering superluminous / awesome, awesome and the carrying's ons, superluminous / facing, facing and the racing suggested superluminous / centers, centers and the solid days superluminous / clinging, clinging and the lingering superluminous / comes, comes dearly into a listening superluminous / heart, hearts elected superluminously / superluminous, superluminous in apparel and the apparently loved precisely / facing, facing a valued experience head through the experiential examples and the samples daily due the superluminous / centers, centers mingle and the clinging ends superlumiousl / clinging, cling over and the daily begins gained metaphysically and into the superluminous / comes, comes a day superluminousl / apart, apart into starts superluminous / stars, stairs built to stars superluminous / lead, lead and deal superluminousl / home, home to the healed superluminous / God's, God's sample gazed into superluminously / choose, choose a daily superluminous / foundations, foundations found superluminously / turrets, turrets turned superluminously / spikes, spikes built superluminousl / stairways, stairways pledged superluminousl / smell, smell the feel superluminous / supple, supple to nipples superluminous / surrender, surrender allows the superluminous / pharaonic, pharaonic attend to the lending superluminous / agree,

agree to see superlumiously / allocative, allocative in trends superluminous / prepare, prepare daily for the definitions supreme to love's legendary reveal superluminously / unctions, unctions blessed and the mentioned superluminous / sanctify, sanctify suggests the superluminous / fly, fly to days superluminous / flourid, flourid to the courage superluminous / fulfilled, fulfilled to a sample superluminous / factual, factual to affective gleans superluminous / swung, swung to the swivel superluminous / contrains, contrains in the main waves superluminous / calyptic, calyptic hieroglyphics and the factors fell to a special ratio superluminous / centon, centon and the heat on the meaing superluminous / crystal, crystal deluge and the details in the feelings superluminous / krypton, krypton and the mantle met in trickles superluminous / supercede, supercede and the steeds managerial to a mental superluminous / saddle, saddles ridden superluminousl / settles, settles into a meaning superluminous / spears, spears superluminous to a capable detail / brightly, brightly bring your passions forth to the features superluminous / spurts, spurts and the special births superluminous / chants, chants and the chilling news superluminous / cheer, cheer and the details superluminous / justice, justice and the joining superluminous.

CHAPTER EIGHT
Slowly, slowly into a shooting superluminous / repeat, repeat and the raptured christian extension into the superluminous / conceed, conceed a deed made is gained in the superluminous / thought, thought and the thinking access to the heart round the metatronic aorta and the mended paracardium worn thin through a lightened superluminous / azurite, azurite retails and the sales done superluminously / memories, memories round these, the superluminous / body, body and the beauty superluminous / voice, voice and the ventures superluminous / purple / phoeni / rise / exasperative / experience / I / soothe / relate / triumphantly / we / miss / the / fihs / sweet / visitor / visit / relax / and / connect / chakra / calling / Elija / Moses / Gabriel / Aaron / Michael / and / Abha / Lotus / birth / children / oo / peace / to / get / pass / the / ring / claim / perfect / love / and / peace / by / read / to / be / see / soon / / perfect / relationship / is / born

THE IN-PRESENCE-MENTS
LEVEL 46

CHAPTER ONE

Burner, burner out and presence in too, love / grounding, grounging and the growning win on presence / sedation, sedation and the predation presence / sea, sea of the wheezy brindle on presence / Zen, Zen presence / further, further then presence / resource, resource found in the sound thick presence / purification, presence on a purification within love / ailments, ailments in the presence won of love / yoga, yoga in the yellows metatroned in presence / harmony, harmony heals these yours presence / aromatherapy, aromatherapy in the megaliths on presence / series, series in a presence / enclose, enclose the lace in presence / versatile, versatile in a presence / advise, advise us truest dues presence / crescent, crescent believes in a presence / appreciation, appreciation for the infatuation in thee presence / closed, closed and out through presence / talking, talking in too presence / hearing, presence is in thee hearin / listening, listening and the laughing ascend presence / vision, vision of the visually scent presence / fasting, fasting and the lasting lends presence / cleansing, cleansing in the ceilinge / electricity, electricity in the emitted presence / shower, shower in the powers presence / writing, writing in invitings den, presence / reading, reading and the written's come through presence / travel, travel to the veritable presence / alone, alone in the venue gained presence / surprise, surprise in the reprise drawn into these then the presence / clock, clock into the eatern flow metatronic degreed the presence / underground, underground into an aspire friend presence / core, core of the sorted friend presence / profuse, profuse and the in truth's rise thorugh presence / miscellaneous, miscellaneous into a veinous call presence / external, external and the eternals friend presence / internal, internal into a sort presence / climate, climate and the culminate's presence / pensiveness, pensiveness into the intrinsicness presence / extreme, extreme into special prong presence / hara, hara and the breath into presence / accupuncture, accupuncture in a ring on presence / gate, gate of the relate through our presence / pool, pool of the peace within presence / penetrating, penetrating into the plays presence / stationary, stationary aware best on presence / abundance, abundance into a lettered play on presence / addiction, addiction in an eviction gone presence / affirmation, affirmation of the venued presence / angelic, angelic a plenty the many in the presence / archangel, archangel knews presence / anxiety, anxiety in the ridden sun presence / arrogance, arrogance in the plenties on presence / aura, aura in the trial twin the presence / base, base of the blues presence / belief, belief in the bounty on presence / beauty, beauty in the beatify presence / limit, limit in the truest presence / blessing, blessing in the balanced presence / butterfly, butterfly in the beauty's presence / brain, brain in the bending presence / chakra, chakra of the sealings presence.

CHAPTER TWO

Mind, mind of the mental revisted through presence / intellect, present an intellect won by presence / generating, generating a rational relevance presence / partner, partner of the our presence / rotation, rotation in the recreate run presence / stretch, stretch out to vote in a friendly presence / tandem, tandem becomes you too presence / prone, prone to a presence molecular / sacral, sacral in the literate zone on presence / squeeze, squeeze into a smaller bed presence / palm, palm of the opus molecular / pathway, pathway into the truest presence molecular / triple, triple into the nationals presence / governing, governing good days through presence / thread, thread into a window needle wide with presence / strand, strand of the stratus presence / christ, christ reads threaded through a presence / collective, collective of the cushioned presence / condition, condition of the mentionable presence / contemplation, contemplation of the curations presence / contentment, contentment cometh directly presence / commitment, commitment cures yours presence / complacency, complacency outs in then presence / compromise, compromise of the respect presence / courage, courage of the curad presence / visualization, visualization of the veritable presence / creator, creator of the captive reset presence / crown, crown in the rapture's presence / daydream, daydream in the slipstream presence / deception, deception outed derivative too, a presence / desire, desire of the feelings presence / destiny, destiny deals in help won presence / harvest, harvest in the happiess presence / storing, storing in the mooring won too, presence / sour, sour in the hourly presence / bitter, bitter ex out presence / sweet, sweet in the mellows presence / pungent, pungent in a pliants presence / salty, salty in the melting presence / laughing, laughing into a leading presence / singing, singing and the ringing presence / weeping, weeping in a wallow presence / groaning, groaning in the moaned meeting mellow through a presence / joy, joy believed a presence / pensiveness, pensiveness sensitive to God's presence / worry, presence worries less / grief, grief is presence less let's / fear, fear in the year too a presence / detachment, detachment allowed a resurrect too presence / dispatch, dispatch in thoroughs presence / mission, mission of the mentioned presence / plan, plan to be presence / purpose, purpose of the paces presence / duality, duality debate through a presence / egocentric, egocentric expire into a presence / apparent, apparent in a transit presence / emotion, emotion meets presence / blueprint, blueprint of the banters presence / balance, balance outs and ins a presence / limbo, limbo in the littles presence / wounds, wounds bathed presence / guide, guide to a grew through presence / ability, ability to be too a presence / iceberg, iceberg beauties and the whales release to a presence.

CHAPTER THREE

Emotion, emotion of the devotional trued presence / aspect, aspect of the interludes sent presence / east, east is the wester sky to presence / south, south of the moon's wind to presence / centre, centre in the spiral loop through presence / west, birth in the west spun to east end's love on presence / north, north of the healer's birth to presence / transition, transition in the readmission to presence in birth / autumn, presence autumn well too, love / heat, heat in a sample sent to presence / dampness. dampness in a delivery presence / dryness, dryness in a duty free presence / cold, cold in the world rest presence / birth, birth and the rebate red zoned presence / growth, growth appeared presence / ripening,

ripening of sorts too presence / negative, negative outs the ins presence / positive, positive acquire of the rewards won presence / component, component of the company blessed presence / field, field of the feeling font written in presence / pattern, pattern in the plentyed trued presence / envy, envy of the covey won too presence / exercise, exercise in the reprise meant presence / enhance, enhance to the absolutes presence / flame, flame of the fellows presence / forgiveness, forgiveness of the folly spent in presence / meditation, meditation of the moons stay at presence / message, message of the missive's sent through presence / initiator, initiator of the rural disguise dues presence / harmonic, harmonic hone of thee presence / contribution, contribution computed too presence / attributed, attributed in the reputed presence / humor, humor in the hallowed backbone's presence / elements, elements in the presence / direction, direction in a presence perfec / season, season of the seated presence / climates, climates of the cures presence / cycle, cycle of the scenes won presence / colours, colours of the cubicles presence / flavours, flavours of the flowers burst presence / wood, wood of the moody presence / fire, fire of the fellows presence / earth, earth in the miracles presence / metal, metal of the mentalic presence / organ, origin of the organ's presence / sense, sense of the men at state presence / manifestation, manifestation of the magnitude's presence / fluid, fluid of the fellowed presence / inspiration, inspiration of the moments presence / integration, integration comes in too, presence / integrity, integrity of the legendary presence / illusion, illusion of the eludes won too presence / jealousy, jealousy outs your presence / justice, justice of the bejewels presence / scales, of the skillings songs presence / karma, karma of the cures presence / key, key found secret waves presence / legacy, legacy in the legendary presence / life, life of the holy days presence / broad, broad across leaf's presence / review, review a values presence / secrets, secrets of the shellings presence / challenges, challenges chanted through presence / mask, mask off and meant to be the presence.

CHAPTER FOUR

Exterior, exterior of the interiors presence / rising, rising in the reappearance of love's presec / rarification, rarification of the cures's presence / female, female of the familial presence / space, space of the intents presence / stillness, stillness of the waves presence / night, night of the neatest presence / darkness, darkness of the deluged absence presence / cold, cold of the refold presence / contraction, contraction of the cubile's presence / interior, interior of the impaired presence / falling, falling of the feelings presence / condensation, condensation of the resignation out to presence / circular, circular of the cyclical presence / passage, passage of the parallel's presence / square, square of the prayer won presence / nightly, nightly on dutied presence / opportunity, opportunity of the institutes presence / resolved, resolved the rewards won presence / pattern, pattern in a purest presence / waking, waking up to be with a presence / persistence, persistence of the parallel's presence / honesty, honesty of the in truth's presence / wholeness, wholeness of the wellness presence / cleansing, cleansing abilities presence / problem, problem of the pretense presence / projection, projection

of the presence presen / purity, purity of the raristics presence / phone, presence on the phone's beat parallel / prophet, prophet of the reset presence / regret, regret of lessened presence / repression, repression regression release the presence / heaven, heaven of the held one too, presence / wind, wind of the winding presence / water, water of the willings presence / mountain, mountain of many's presence / earth, earth in the refired presence / thunder, thunder about her presence / fire, earth's fire is E, presence / lake, lake of energy human presence / shady, shady shouts of out's presence / sunny, sunny stays in days presence / hill, hill of the millions presence / time, time to tell to now presence / activity, activity of the way too, presence / day, day of the love felt, presence / heat, heat on the melting presence / expansion, expansion of the mansioned presence / resistance, restistance out and in the shout the presence / retribution, retribution of the metitative's presence / root, root of the shoots too presence / saint, saint of the weekly presence / empowerment, empowerment in the hourly presence / mastery, mastery of the flattery in presence / segments, segments signals presence / sexual, sexual straigts presence / solar, solar in the recalled presence 58, shame, shame out, shout, presence / plexus, plexus of the nexus come, presence / heritage, heritage in the marriage on presence / journey, journey into the middled kingdoms presence / stalemate, stalemate in the reality on presence / toolkit, toolkit in the wheelkit presence / tools, tools of the ruler on presence.

CHAPTER FIVE

Weep, weep in the steepest presence / garment, garment of the presence, hu-man / levels, levels of the loosen's presence / control, control of the ruler's presence / melodies, melodies of the musicals presence / cognitive, cognitive cavorts in shouts, presence / awareness, awareness of the showers presence / peak, peak of the sleek in presence / selected, selected in the settlement presence / sequence, sequence settles in presence / approximately, approximately due, a presence / claim, claim of a feel true, presence / tenet, tenet of the travails presence / ailment, ailment out through presence / yin, yin trime presence / yang, yang of the leading's presence / who, who said sounds presence / sound, presence in a cell, sound / state, state of the pattern, presence / strength, presence into strength become love / subconscious, subconscious success at the art on presence / suffer, suffer of the spelled presence / sword, sword of the cower's presence / bearer, bearer of the blues, presence / keystone, keystone capable in a presence / thought, thought about a stray in true presence / throat, throat out and the shout wins presence / layer, layer outed and into trueness love's presence / mirror, mirror of the meeting's presence / ultimate, ultimate in timely presence / unfoldment, unfoldment and the fulfill won, presence / from, from us to you, good's presence / vibration, vibration is treat, presence / ecstasy, ecstasy of the in succeeds presence / stages, stages into steals, presence / formulas, formulas frame our presence / tension, tension out in presence / intone, intone in the enthrone's presence / profound, profound prefer presence / recommences, recommences a presence become on love / singer, singer swung through presence / kicking, kicking in the leakings presence / glitters, glitters in a glee-full presence / blessing, blessing of the beauties presence / recover, recover in your every presence / air, air in a shower's way presence / gain, gain a new refrinings presence / rite, rite in the ritual's presence / vanity, vanity of the fusion, presence / vibration, vibration in the sensation, presence / wisdom, wisdom woos a presence of yo / integrated, integrated a present state, presence / kernel, kernel outlines presence / pearl, pearl of the mantra shamin, presence / seed, seed in the plural's presence / laboratory, laboratory presence, love / pilgrimage, pilgrimage into fused presence / instilled, instilled a material's magical presence into the hu-man / mankind, mankind find, a presence / current, current in the warrant true, presence / understand, understand a presence God / innocence, innocence given and the gathered won, presence / sublime, sublime in success, a presence / degree, degree of the presence need, love.

CHAPTER SIX

Range, range allowed and the payments flower into love's presence / unhesitantingly, without hesitation and within unhesitatingly, A presence / paid, paid for the passion's presence / objection, objection details and the retailed presence / cloud, clouds off and the cedars cleared Lebanon well into a healing presence / meaning, meaning and the middled presence / swaying, swayin in the staying presence / torso, torso twisted to reveal the fettered unravel and the laughing will to feature yes to love the real presence / code, code concurs and the shift made to presence / folkloric, folkloric ability and the agility known in the presence / treatises, treatises and the codices founded in the library hu-man's presence / equally, equally and the deals dealt with a presence / ceremony, ceremony suggested and the confessions healed vertically throught thee the presence / amble, amble into the daily diet of presence / whirling, whirling gigs and the dervishes danced to presence / spinning, spinning examples in the samples, presence / plausible, plausible appeal and the reveal found cermoniously too, the presence / universe, universe of samples and the healing examples found in the future of the presence / drawing, drawing another too, the presence / milleniium, milleniums ridden and the healing comes too, the presence / show, show suggested and the vibrational gift of presence / astral, astral planed interiors and the samples made in presence / banish, banish less and find four presence / bliss, bliss deals in presence / causal, causal capers and the nimble presence / cosmic, cosmic apply and the sighs made presence / demons, demons dealt to and the few flew to the lightened presence / dispose, dispose of less and find more, the presence / Einstein, Einstein built a trade framed in presence / feminine, feminine finds and the signs gained a presence / amber, amber leys and the bays born to presence / aspen, aspen given the blues for the golden acres presence / date, date the one hundred days as acres legally free to a presence / made, made a mention daily to a healed presence / arose, arose lightly to the living presence / witness, witness won to the sun's presence / mosque, mosque opened too, the presence / concert, concert sung through to the presence / atheism, atheism, said "believe knot" the presence /

driver, driver driven to the presence / clergy, clergy find realign in your presence / plunged, plunged into and found then, presence / labyrinth, labyrinth lined in the led to, presence / lanes, lanes listed in presence / waves, waves cleared through the presence / involved, involved simply in the presence / ushered, ushered too, the presence / measures, measures made in presence / aventurine, aventurine, the heart's gleam, at presence / tourmaline, tourmaline and the scenes intrusive less and often more too, presence / cedar, cedar keyed delivery to the hearts magic and the amusing presence / coral, coral and the cured presence / crystal, crystal keys presence / diamond, diamond days presence / emerald, emerlad rays, presence / flint, flint struck through the presence / jasper, jasper jewels and the juicy presence / jade, jade greens and the scenes to presence / lotus, lotus listened floral appear and the mentions presence / maple, maple presents and the electrical blues presence / magnolia, magnolia meals and the meeting flow too, a presence / mica, mica meals and the simply, blue gold, presence / oak, oak eaves presence / pine, pine trees shining presence.

CHAPTER SEVEN

Opposed, opposed a passion then found a featured presence / session, session held to a presence / theory, theory and the throning presence / spread, spead into sheets on the presence / include, include a daily mood for the presence / vocal, vocal allow and the plow through the presence / forbidden, forbidden bids and the signs played simply to a presence / official, official dismissal due a presence / persecuted, persecuted less and the heart found in a simple presence / commissions, commissions capably presen / destroyed, destroyed daily less too, the presence / exist, exist most in simply the best, presence / fabric, fabric filled in the presence / elder, elder amaze turned to the presence, Oz swep / harsh, harsh gone deal sweetly in a presence / precarious, precarious over and the shouted for "presence"/ rose, rose blue aggreement for the featured presence / sapphire, sapphire seals and the shining presence / topaz, topaz meals and the met for presence / great, great greetings and the meetings presence / imagination, imagination days and the measures presence / initiation, initiations past and the netted presence / invoking, invoking a healing, presence / masculine, masculine mend and the sealing amtes presence / moon, moon detail and the retired to gate through presence / occult, occult forgone and the features won to a presence / senior, senior sent for the presence / almond, almond amuse and the muse's presence / coal, coal green antonioan sighs and the diamond deep into heart's presence / moonstone, moonstone mentions and the mewing presence / palm, palm plans and the daring presence / grain, grain grew to greet me in the presence / internal, internal stages and the presence wo / hermit, hermit donw\e and the winning won through a presence / society, society said "a-men" to presence / attention, attention and the dimensioned presence / oneself, oneself and the shelving presence / allusion, allusion and the conclusion's presence / observing, observing and the deserving presence / silent, silent ways won to a presence / relevant, relevant detail and the degrees found impression's presence / imagine, imagine won to a prsenc / favor, favor fed a presence / favorite, favorite and the fashion's presence / flavor, flavor and the savoring presence / musical, musical attendance and the mated presence / accompany, accompany escapes with presence / mediation, mediation becomes your presence / meditation, meditation sandalwood wed to a presence / willows, willows allowed into a presence / stalagmite, stalagmite may and the strays in presence / sun, sun day's presence / venus, venus amused with a presence / watchtower, watchtower missions and the mentioned presence / expensive, expensive attire and the firing presence / delayed, delayed and won through the presence / delivery, delivery won and recovery summed to presence / frisky, frisky fields of presence / wolf, wolf taught the outed version of presence / friends, friends peaceful to a presence / melt, melt in values presence / heartstrung, heartstrung appeal and the ways welcomed to a presence / different, different deals made within presence / home found and featured then in presence.

CHAPTER EIGHT

Sometimes, sometimes we find our waves presently the presence / moral, moral and the presentation of a presence / forces, forces focused naturally into a living presence / reduce, reduce a reduction throughout a patterned presence / misleading, misleading mention and the matters too, a presence / effectiveness, effectiveness and the nearing natives presence / body, body blue and the venues presence / breath, breath allowed the dealings into a presence / search, search an expectations delay throughout a presence / doctrine, doctrine of the deal newest through a living presence / system, system suggested and the seeds won too, a presence / summarized, summarized and the succession's presence / distinctive, distinctive, trued, and the trickle bursts to a presence / voyage, voyages employed as the present presence / homeland, homeland employed as the positive presence / exploration, exploration and the natural flow to A presence / sparkle, sparkle and the spherical instill onto a presence / gift, gift becoming your presence / summer, summer deals called the thrilling presence / lovebirds, lovebirds and the birthing presence / courage, courage and the cure in a presence / saddle, saddle off and the cure made a living presence / swimming, swimming near and fairly dear too, a presence / dolphins, dolphins delicately thrown to the windy presence / charming, charming example and the simply, " presence"/ extra, etra days insured through koi planned presence / rescue, rescue over and the healing due a presence / miracles, ciracles planned and the fans spread too, a miraculous presence / sunshine, sunshine suggested and the status placed into a presence / amazing, amazing in valued presence / companionship, companionship and the pensioned partners to presence / bond, bond bade a bettering to our presence / cobble, cobble in the streets dealt into presence / card, card cures and the capable appeal to a presence / cough, cough trilled and the curable align for a presence / offer, offer and the preferred presence / buy, buy and the billing trued a presence / respond, respond and the retails presence / startle, startle and the cure proven a presence / call, call daily a dealing presence / fall, fall throughout and forever into a presence / breeze, breeze and the bitter gone through into presence / bounty, bounty and the county's presence / law, law of the legendary presence / love, love to be rewarded for the presence / loot, loot and the listing materials truest a presence / lingers, lingers and the strangers faced a passionate presence / long, long and the energetically freed, presence / required and the hourly presence / connect, connect and the curate's sonward, presence / aspect, aspect and the respectfully sung presence / instincts, instincts and the signalled presence / qualify, qualify and the reply to a presence / quality, quality and the creations presence / inspection, inspection and the sunny shored presence / bluest, bluest regard for the living presence / skies, skies and the scurry truest presence / shells, shells and the resealed found a presence / sacred, sacred in a succeed and the settled meant for, presence / over, over hurried and the worried forgets presence / laced, laced throughout in a shouting joust called lightly living our presence / loosens, loosens into a listing presence / lattice, lattice and the delicious presence / blue, blue into regard for the presence.

CHAPTER NINE

Synchronized, synchronized daily in a raving suggestion that assignments are sent through God's presence / culture, culture and the cured value's presence / adopted, adopted and the sought for suggested presence / disseminated, disseminated in lessons perfect to a cause, presence / secret, secret told and held for the flowering experience of love's presence / numerous, numerous numbers and the slumbering presence / preserved, preserved through traditions and the renditions onto a presence / tradition, tradition to the mentioned presence / dominant, dominant to numbers and the scenes spent forth to a presence / branch, branch across the parallels to a presence / order, order detailed empirical attires to a living presence / element, element of the chosen, presence / specific, specifically assigned to the meant free, presence / propogated, propogated and the rated align meant presence / wandering, wandering and dealing entirely into a living presence / dervishes, dervishes and a deva due a spinning presence / appreciation, apppreciation of the patience found through presence / strength, strength of the gained entirety to a presence / specific, specifically aligned in the reclining presence / accelerate, accelerate the duration of your causal presence / guidance, guidance given retail expression to a dimensional presence / culminates, culminates and the relation's presence / particular, particular to a miraculous matter, presence / choose, choose another winning number, presence / method, method of the methodology vented throughout a living presence / occur, occur daily then sing within "love is a healing presence"/ mortality, mortality introduced throughout our thriving presence / question, questions intrigued to a tripled presence / apply, apply for the mentally triumphant grant to a healing presence / detect, detect a mission's presence / room, room to a roaming presence / several, several ways to find a presence / common, common keyed to a sorted presence / comprehensive, comprehensive allow for a dimension due love then a presence / boundary, boundary set and the settlement bets on the thrilling presence / spirit, spirit suggestive of the massive allowance called God is a presence / repetition, repetition and the missionary presence / principle,

principle set and the locals allowed a healing presence / assumed, assumed a capital allow and the filling presence / recall, recalll a material presence / attributes, attributes and the rarest presence / rare, rare to a refilled presence / chanted, chanted and recanted to a presence / practitioner, practitioner of the peaceful allow for a presence / articulate, articulate to a miracle too, a loving lyrical presence / monthly, monthly apply to the positions miraculou / phrase, phrase attendant to the vending presence / pronouncing, pronouncing amplify and the daily appearance allowed to a listening presence / spine, I am spine to the moon metatronically presen / integrated, integrated and the sated atend for the features presen / enlightened, enlightened allowance in sight of the loving presence / afterlife, afterlife allowed, now, through presence / tension, tension over and the dealing done through presence / tugging, tugging out and the shift is in to a lightened presence / insistence, insistence upon the passionate levels on presence / tunnel, tunnel detailed and the relevant reveal found in presence / rail, rail and the reaching forht through presence / shape, shape initialed to the significance of loving presence / knock, knock to the doors on presence / prodigal, prodigal return to the heavenward presence / task, task set to the returnin presence / include, include initial to the particulate's presence / intervals, intervals set directly to the presence / sensory, sensory detail and the healing presence.

CHAPTER TEN

Pour, pour through the missions, choose one, a presence / paints, paints and the human regard for presence / palate, palate set in presence / pinched, pinched electrically forward to presence / porch, porch measures a lifting presence / trance, trance over and the healing done through presence / track, track back to the presence / immemorial, immemorial to a mission's presence / fortunate, fortunate to fend for in presence / penetrate, penetrate the reason for a featured presence / veil, veil allow, the presence / separate, separate throughout the presence / ordinary, ordinary oddysey and the missionary freed to be simply " presence"/ relaxed, relaxed and related to through presence / mundane, mundane and the reign found through presence / alternate, alternate cures and the insures born presen / delivers, delivers eventually too, a living presence / country, country and the victory met through presence / driven, driven allowance intrigued into presence / dare, dare a picture set in presence / bins, bins filled into presence / bargain, bargain beaded across the missiles presence / deep, deep in detailed presence / royal, royal reads allowed htee, the presence / lanes, lanes plunge into meeting in the mother's presence / slumber, slumber over and the cure gained in presence / sweet, sweet featured presence / specialities, specialties avowed for the featured presence / enterprise, enterprise and the arise, truthfully, to a victorious presence / transmits, transmits a recline to the registered presence / select, select a few who view your presence / salon, salon for the seeking done, presence / forms, forms featured throughout our presence / follows, follows a disciple to presence / flings, flings out and the over due a living presence / palimony, palimony paid in the shaded presence /

matrimony, matrimony made a featured presence / antimony, antimony forgotten through presence / pass, pass to the point for a presence / positive, positively presence / particles, particles and memories of viewing a presence / pat, pat to a point for presence / post, post and hosted a presence / london, london led to presence / times, times set and the respect won through presence / occupy, occupy a venue for the feeling presence / flare, flare to the caring presence / flowering, flowering frankly in presence / flowered, flowered surgically to the presence of God / relations, relations settled and the bullish race run to a resting phrase " presence"/ rests, rests in a revenue of presence / rules, rules detailed in presence / compose, compose arose through presence / sheets, sheets single to a presence paid through, presence / soften, soften and the often led to presence / life, life leads to lucky waves of presence / selects, selects a living presence / mature, mature to a meeting material stay through presence / repose, repose and the revelation reached through rpesenc / exposed, exposed to a supple mirror for the presence / oblige, oblige and the obligation spent in venues of presence / obligation, obligation gathered and the material met in respectful presence / gathered, gathered a theory and a page for presence / speed, speed detailed in presence.

CHAPTER ELEVEN

Polish, polish the plenty to a meaning full presence / crush due to presence / craze, craze allowed a presence / crust, crust bursts through presence / chat, chat throughout her presence / chaste, chaste and the wasted presence / neighborly, neighborly allow to presence / nascient, nascient numbers too, presence / nasal, nasal to feelings presence / note, note a reveal presence / plant, plant a personal presence / fibonaccai, fibonacci squared to a presence / modems, modems mentioned, " presence"/ models, models made of presence / modicum, modicum allowed through presence / medium, medium detailed, " presence"/ warrants, warrants done through presence / financial, financial fulfill through presence / bringing, bringing in the singing presence / manage, manage to meet in the amounts paid through presence / battle, battle out and the threats flown to presence / belly, belly filled to presence / triple, triple to simple " presence / ridge, ridge run to presence / riddles, riddles and the threaded presence / troop, troop to a scoop filled presence / hasten, hasten to a chastened presence / end, end here in presence / classic, classic allowance and the posing purity for a pleasing presence / pages, pages written and paced into purity, clarity, patience, and presence / clipped, clipped at the cured, presence / agreed, agreed to the found for presence / boisteorus, boisterous befriend and the ending? presence / get, get won, presence / gaze, gaze too, a presence / craze, craze about your presence / flaps, flaps about her presence / flats, flats filled in presence / flourish, flourish numbered in presence / kept, kept of rhte presence / given, given a filling, presence / gained, gained another, presence / colors, colors kept through presence / rave, rave about her, presence / registered, registered nearby int he amusing presence / hallowed, hallowed allow throughout your presence / posh, posh to the cost for presence / gush, gush about your presence / character, character cured to presence / chapters,

chapters chimed into a presence / status, status secretive to a perfect presence / free, free a filled living with presence / fields, fields follow your fullest presence / follow, follow now a presence / filed, filed about us, a presence / enquire, enquire into a presence / status, status fulfilled through presence / pleasant, pleasant now in a living regard for presence / contained, contained in curation's released form of presence / shrunk, shrunk throughout to dehydrated presence / recumbent, recumbent now the presence / recline, recline in your presence / rest, rest in your presence / reside, reside in your presence.

CHAPTER TWELVE

Pigs, pigs in recoil at the foiled bacon of man's presence / vase, vase featured in respect of the presence / burst, burst about your presence / flush, flush in the facing presence / loop, loop to simply, presence / lock, lock off and the nimble in to presence / canal, canal cure and the insured presence / drift, drift allowed to a floating presence / pack, pack on the moment's presence / agree, agree too, a presence / absorb, absorb the sword's hilt and the cut for a presence / advanced, advanced allow to a reference planed in presence / cleared, cleared of curing presence / able, able to freely will your presence / bet, bet into a presence / steer, steer near your own presence / contributions, contributions intoned in presence / peridoic, periodic apply for presence / counts, counts for certain, presence / excerpts, excerpts spent in presence / wired, wired inside the presence / orgasmic, orgasmic allowance for prospective presence / counts, counts in occurence sent through presence / smu, smug retails and the memories on a presence / towers, towers treed through presence / prospects, prospects paid through presence / drift, drift allowed through presence / endures, endures a reassured presence / bolts, bolts above to presence / held, held forth in presence / qualities, qualities found to presence / montreal, montreal mental to a material attendance through presence / monster, monster means made to presence / pajamas, pajamas won through presence / pockets, pockets filled in presence / pants, pants on to presence / flannel, flannel panels presence / flatter, flatter your presence / flashes, flashes fueled in presence / good, good days of presence / spirit, spirit succeeds in presence / cheers, cheers aobut us through presence / chins, chins entire in presence / chair, chair sent to presence / double, double days adored through presence / adore, adore more the presence / california, california fields of presence / creations, creations rations presence / stripe, stripe tealed in presence / strips, strips field your presence / links, links leap to presence / crowns, crowns sealed in presence / cargo, cargo sought in presence / hollow, hollow forgot through presence / sleep, sleep in ripens detailed presence / melted, melted, sated, vaunted, presence / chapels, chapels won to a presence / financial, financial bliss in a living profess to a presence / coat, coat a door in presence / brought, brought to the bringing presence / warrants, warrants worn to presence / managaed, managed mentally to presence / amounts, amounts meant for presence / alimony, alimony paid in your presence

CHAPTER THIRTEEN: blank, blank to a balance presence /

blunder, blunder out presence / blanks, blanks lend a presence / answer, answer cures a presence / respond, respond dear to presence / proposal, proposal made through presence / rule, rule a willing presence / stolen, stolen less to presence / repeat, repeat appealing presence / reuire, require your's presence / still, still near a presence / love, love to be a presence / tomorrow, tomoorw well in presence / today, today filled in presence / forever, forever felt in presence / banister, banister bailed to presence / regarded, regarded for the featured presence / calling, calling dealt in created presence / fulfilled, fulfilled fields presence / precedent, precedent set for presence / set, set too, to presence / children, children lend to presence / blessed, blessed estates on presence / clamors, clamors about your presence / now, now then, a presence / seized, seized of the presence / completed, completed streets on a presence / standard, standard days to presence / stands, stands through a presence / staple, staple meals in presence / apply, apply too, a presence / sizes, sizes filled in presence / practice, practice and apprenticeship inside the healing presence / influence, influence found through presence / individual, individual dealt the presence / group, group occur and the sate on presence / highest, highest allow into the presence / ability, ability found in presence / flow, flow felt in presence / partnership, partnership made throughout a presence / particular, particular to miracle's presence / power, power found in presence / will, will sounds of presence / literature, literature reads on presence / report, report given to presence / astonishing, astonishing amounts in presence / affect, affect effects the presence / paramount, paramount recounts the presence / neighbor, neighbor dealt the required presence / bird, bird flown through to presence / action, action taken through presence / zipped, zipped into a presence / disuise, disguise off, the presence / lone, lone allowed in presence / rainbow, rainbow reels in presence / result, result found in presence / seen, seen to say too, a presence / feeling, feeling erupts in presence / action, action said too, a presence / being, being blessed in presence / understood, understood for in presence / expressed, expressed in settled presence / accomplished, accomplished in thy presence / part, part said for, "a presence."

THE ULTIMATE-MENTS
LEVEL 47

CHAPTER ONE

Splendor, the ultimate / splashes, the ultimate / of, the ultimate / beauty, the ultimate / chosen, the ultimate / entender, the ultimate / given, the ultimate / please, the ultimate / pleasure's, the ultimate / burdens, the ultimate / lift, the ultimate / caring, the ultimate / capabilities, the ultimate / chance, the ultimate / encounters, the ultimate / moistened, the ultimate / degree, the ultimate / dancing, the ultimate / aspire, the ultimate / concurrent, the ultimate / occurrences, the ultimate / synchronous, the ultimate / spaces, the ultimate / relative, the ultimate / released, the ultimate / pourings, the ultimate / pairings, the ultimate / pairs, the ultimate / spoils, the ultimate / releases, the ultimate / joined, the ultimate / exposures, the ultimate / passion's, the ultimate / place, the ultimate / in, the ultimate / mission's, the ultimate / date, the ultimate / destiny's, the ultimate / due, the ultimate / fate's, the ultimate / food, the ultimate / jasmine, the ultimate / rains, the ultimate / and, the ultimate / sun's, the ultimate / campaign, the ultimate / to, the ultimate / release, the ultimate / the, the ultimate / explain, the ultimate / that, the ultimate / you, the ultimate / are, the ultimate / good, the ultimate / and, the ultimate / God, the ultimate / is, the ultimate / glad, the ultimate / for, the ultimate / your, the ultimate / simple, the ultimate / gestures, the ultimate / prayers, the ultimate / balances based, the ultimate.

CHAPTER TWO

On, the ultimate / energy's, the ultimate / return, the ultimate / policy, the ultimate / what, the ultimate / is, the ultimate / given, the ultimate / is, the ultimate / got, the ultimate / and, the ultimate / humanity, the ultimate / is, the ultimate / a, the ultimate / plan, the ultimate / that, the ultimate / is, the ultimate / due, the ultimate / for, the ultimate / an, the ultimate / update, the ultimate / and, the ultimate / God's, the ultimate / sent, the ultimate / his, the ultimate / band, the ultimate / Metatron, the ultimate / and, the ultimate / friends, the ultimate / to, the ultimate / insure, the ultimate / your, the ultimate / safe, the ultimate / arrive, the ultimate / at, the ultimate / God's, the ultimate / side, the ultimate / and, the ultimate / you, the ultimate / will, the ultimate / know, the ultimate / when, the ultimate / to, the ultimate / fly, the ultimate / Abide, the ultimate / in, the ultimate / God's, the ultimate / love, the ultimate / and, the ultimate / know, the ultimate / your, the ultimate / mission, the ultimate / complete, the ultimate / when, the ultimate / you, the ultimate / love, the ultimate / self, the ultimate / as, the ultimate / other, the ultimate / and, the ultimate / other, the ultimate / as, the ultimate / self, the ultimate / and, the ultimate / the golden pavement dances, the ultimate.

CHAPTER THREE

Crystal, the ultimate / clear, the ultimate / beneath, the ultimate / your, the ultimate / feet, the ultimate / and, the ultimate / silver, the ultimate / coated, the ultimate / surrender, the ultimate / blends, the ultimate / with, the ultimate / begin, the ultimate / in, the ultimate / the, the ultimate / mansions, the ultimate / of, the ultimate / plenty, the ultimate / built, the ultimate / within, the ultimate / mend, the ultimate / surrender, the ultimate / unto, the ultimate / God, the ultimate / what, the ultimate / rightly, the ultimate / belongs, the ultimate / and, the ultimate / left, the ultimate / to, the ultimate / the, the ultimate / matter, the ultimate / enjoy, the ultimate / getting, the ultimate / on, the ultimate / with, the ultimate / all, the ultimate / that, the ultimate / resides, the ultimate / as, the ultimate / perfectly, the ultimate / heart, the ultimate / and, the ultimate / tonight, the ultimate / as, the ultimate / you, the ultimate / are, the ultimate / sleeping, the ultimate / a, the ultimate / light, the ultimate / inspired, the ultimate / pen, the ultimate / has, the ultimate / happened, the ultimate / this, the ultimate / missive, the ultimate / to, the ultimate / the, the ultimate / hearts, the ultimate / of, the ultimate / all, the ultimate / men, the ultimate / Know, the ultimate / release, the ultimate / God is...love, the ultimate.

CHAPTER FOUR

Lavender, the ultimate / moments, the ultimate / explain, the ultimate / who, the ultimate / we, the ultimate / are, the ultimate / and, the ultimate / purposeful, the ultimate / meetings, the ultimate / inquire, the ultimate / when, the ultimate / we, the ultimate / stand, the ultimate / in, the ultimate / our, the ultimate / chosen, the ultimate / confessions, the ultimate / of, the ultimate / all, the ultimate / that, the ultimate / we, the ultimate / plan, the ultimate / to, the ultimate / be, the ultimate / eternally, the ultimate / discretely, the ultimate / definitively, the ultimate / enriched, the ultimate / by, the ultimate / the, the ultimate / pleasing, the ultimate / mention, the ultimate / that, the ultimate / God, the ultimate / is, the ultimate / a, the ultimate / Fish, the ultimate / and, the ultimate / a, the ultimate / Bird, the ultimate / and, the ultimate / a, the ultimate / sort, the ultimate / who, the ultimate / filling, the ultimate / out, the ultimate / application, the ultimate / may, the ultimate / capably, the ultimate / say, the ultimate / with, the ultimate / a, the ultimate / daring, the ultimate / disperse, the ultimate / that, the ultimate / seasons, the ultimate / and, the ultimate / heavens, the ultimate / and, the ultimate / healings, the ultimate / and, the ultimate / hearts, the ultimate / know, the ultimate / by, the ultimate.

CHAPTER FIVE

Confession, the ultimate / that, the ultimate / Jesus, the ultimate / gave, the ultimate / start, the ultimate / and, the ultimate / Buddha, the ultimate / met, the ultimate / heaven, the ultimate / in, the ultimate / a, the ultimate / life, the ultimate / know, the ultimate / desire, the ultimate / and, the ultimate / successions, the ultimate / of, the ultimate / lover's, the ultimate / sweet, the ultimate / melt, the ultimate / in, the ultimate / the, the ultimate / fire, the ultimate / of, the ultimate / enchanting, the ultimate / confession, the ultimate / and, the ultimate / heavenly, the ultimate / start, the ultimate / to, the ultimate / the, the ultimate / patient, the ultimate / admission, the ultimate / that, the ultimate / all, the ultimate / is, the ultimate / at, the ultimate / rest, the ultimate / and, the ultimate / joining, the ultimate / this, the ultimate / mission, the ultimate / is, the ultimate / a, the ultimate / precious, the ultimate / directive, the ultimate / to, the ultimate / listen, the ultimate / well, the ultimate / to, the ultimate / the, the ultimate / spell, the ultimate / and, the ultimate / admit, the ultimate / that, the ultimate / awakened, the ultimate / remembrance, the ultimate / enjoins, the ultimate / our, the ultimate / expressive, the ultimate / deliver, the ultimate / to, the ultimate / the, the ultimate / heart, the ultimate.

CHAPTER SIX
Of, the ultimate / the, the ultimate, / soul, the ultimate, / and, the ultimate / embraces, the ultimate / the, the ultimate / light, the ultimate / with, the ultimate / released, the ultimate / recovery, the ultimate / of, the ultimate / God's, the ultimate / allow, the ultimate / of, the ultimate / all, the ultimate / we, the ultimate / can, the ultimate / be, the ultimate / without, the ultimate / repetitive, the ultimate / mantra-ed, the ultimate / howl, the ultimate / and, the ultimate / forevered, the ultimate / posturing, the ultimate / and, the ultimate / bowing, the ultimate / escape, the ultimate / to, the ultimate / the, the ultimate / scraping, the ultimate / refusal, the ultimate / to, the ultimate / gape, the ultimate / at, the ultimate / the, the ultimate / glory, the ultimate / of, the ultimate / man, the ultimate / and, the ultimate / God's, the ultimate / creative, the ultimate / dream, the ultimate / in, the ultimate / you, the ultimate / and, the ultimate / your, the ultimate / proud, the ultimate / return, the ultimate / to, the ultimate / the, the ultimate / semblance, the ultimate / and, the ultimate / resemblance, the ultimate / of, the ultimate / God., the ultimate / Child, the ultimate / of, the ultimate / God, the ultimate / rejoice, the ultimate / rejoin, the ultimate / and, the ultimate / regain, the gathering, the ultimate.

CHAPTER SEVEN
Return, the ultimate / to, the ultimate / God's, the ultimate / explain, the ultimate / of, the ultimate / all, the ultimate / we, the ultimate / are, the ultimate / for, the ultimate / love, the ultimate / let, the ultimate / us, the ultimate / be, the ultimate / deliver, the ultimate, / far, the ultimate / and, the ultimate / wise, the ultimate / to, the ultimate / the, the ultimate / size, the ultimate / of, the ultimate / a, the ultimate / heart, the ultimate / electric, the ultimate / and, the ultimate / a, the ultimate / brilliant, the ultimate / comprise, the ultimate / called, the ultimate / arc-angels, the ultimate / sing, the ultimate / about, the ultimate / the, the ultimate / sounds, the ultimate / God's, the ultimate / name, the ultimate / and, the ultimate / the, the ultimate / explain, the ultimate / called, the ultimate / lightly, the ultimate / see, the ultimate / the, the ultimate / water, the ultimate / borne, to the ultimate / to, the ultimate / man's, the ultimate / drinking, the ultimate / relief, the ultimate / and, the ultimate / the, the ultimate / fountains, the ultimate / fuller, the ultimate / still, the ultimate / within, the ultimate / God's, the ultimate / great, the ultimate / love, the ultimate / for, the ultimate / Humanity., the ultimate / know, the ultimate / the express, the ultimate / of a shining, the ultimate / confess, the ultimate

CHAPTER EIGHT
And, the ultimate / a, the ultimate / sincere, the ultimate / delight, the ultimate / in, the ultimate / the, the ultimate / sight, the ultimate / know, the ultimate / all, the ultimate / that, the ultimate / God, the ultimate / is, the ultimate / and, the ultimate / you, the ultimate / are, the ultimate / God, the ultimate / God's, the ultimate / resurrect, the ultimate / now, the ultimate / and, the ultimate / know, the ultimate / the, the ultimate / release, the ultimate / of, the ultimate / all, the ultimate / illusion, the ultimate / and, the ultimate / find, the ultimate / the, the ultimate / conclusion, the ultimate / called, the ultimate / precious, the ultimate / and, the ultimate / respect, the ultimate / for, the ultimate / the, the ultimate / husband, the ultimate / and, the ultimate / bride, the ultimate / as, the ultimate / christ, the ultimate / inside, the ultimate / erupts, the ultimate / to, the ultimate / join, the ultimate / the, the ultimate / doving, the ultimate / return, the ultimate / of, the ultimate / all, the ultimate / who, the ultimate / will, the ultimate / be, the ultimate / loved, the ultimate / enjoined, the ultimate / wed, the ultimate / and, the ultimate / fed, the ultimate / by, the ultimate / aspirant, the ultimate / assign, the ultimate / to, the ultimate / the finest our, God's, the ultimate.

CHAPTER NINE
You, the ultimate / are, the ultimate / elected, the ultimate / and, the ultimate / hereby, the ultimate / fed, the ultimate / the, the ultimate / fashionable, the ultimate / release, the ultimate / to, the ultimate / a, the ultimate / higher, the ultimate / tread, the ultimate / and, the ultimate / a, the ultimate / runway, the ultimate / lit, the ultimate / by, the ultimate / God's, the ultimate / smiling, the ultimate / face, the ultimate / the, the ultimate / Light, the ultimate / I, the ultimate / AM, the ultimate / you, the ultimate / are, the ultimate / and, the ultimate / the, the ultimate / trace, the ultimate / eternal, the ultimate / is, the ultimate / well, the ultimate / within, the ultimate / your, the ultimate / hearts., the ultimate / Grant, the ultimate / yourself, the ultimate / release, the ultimate / and, the ultimate / feed, the ultimate / your, the ultimate / heart, the ultimate / with, the ultimate / only, the ultimate / pure, the ultimate / octane, the ultimate / the, the ultimate / racing, the ultimate / forgive, the ultimate / of, the ultimate / each, the ultimate / other, the ultimate / and, the ultimate / self, the ultimate / for, the ultimate / forgetting, the ultimate / the, the ultimate / precious, the ultimate / assemblage, the ultimate / you, the ultimate / are, the ultimate / know, the ultimate / the One in your eternal, the ultimate.

CHAPTER TEN
The ultimate / forget, the ultimate / has, the ultimate / gone, the ultimate / to, the ultimate / a, the ultimate / distant, the ultimate / sun, the ultimate / and, the ultimate / the, the ultimate / space, the ultimate / between, the ultimate / has, the ultimate / filled, the ultimate / with, the ultimate / a, the ultimate / heartbeat, the ultimate / deep, the ultimate / in, the ultimate / deliver, the ultimate / the, the ultimate / aum, the ultimate / of, the ultimate / creation, the ultimate / the, the ultimate / 3.14, the ultimate /

of, the ultimate / forever's, the ultimate / threshold, the ultimate / the, the ultimate / built, the ultimate / remind, the ultimate / that, the ultimate / God, the ultimate / is, the ultimate / inside, the ultimate / your, the ultimate / relief, the ultimate / and, the ultimate / all, the ultimate / is, the ultimate / well, the ultimate / and, the ultimate / fear, the ultimate / was, the ultimate / at, the ultimate / fault, the ultimate / and, the ultimate / A-man, the ultimate / started, the ultimate / rumors, the ultimate / that, the ultimate / God, the ultimate / was, the ultimate / less, the ultimate / than, the ultimate / All, the ultimate / and, the ultimate / priestly, the ultimate / duties, the ultimate / ended, the ultimate / where, the ultimate.

CHAPTER ELEVEN

Man, the ultimate / began, the ultimate / to, the ultimate / see, the ultimate / that, the ultimate / the, the ultimate / heart, the ultimate / the, the ultimate / spirit, the ultimate / central, the ultimate / was, the ultimate / within, the ultimate / delivery, the ultimate / to, the ultimate / the, the ultimate / material, the ultimate / explore, the ultimate / of, the ultimate / why, the ultimate / and, the ultimate / were, the ultimate / and, the ultimate / when, the ultimate / existence, the ultimate / begins, the ultimate / to, the ultimate / see, the ultimate / the, the ultimate / patterns, the ultimate / in, the ultimate / humanity, the ultimate / the, the ultimate / desire, the ultimate / to, the ultimate / remember, the ultimate / love., the ultimate / I, the ultimate / wish, the ultimate / you, the ultimate / all-ways, the ultimate / well, the ultimate / in, the ultimate / your, the ultimate / deliver, the ultimate / and, the ultimate / your, the ultimate / soft, the ultimate / remember, the ultimate / that, the ultimate / God's, the ultimate / relation, the ultimate / to, the ultimate / you, the ultimate / is, the ultimate / within, the ultimate / the, the ultimate / heart, the ultimate / you, the ultimate / live., the ultimate / beating, the ultimate / still, the ultimate / we, the ultimate / see, the ultimate / the winged deliver, the ultimate

CHAPTER TWELVE

Of, the ultimate / the, the ultimate / occupied, the ultimate / ones, the ultimate / to, the ultimate / the, the ultimate / "throne", the ultimate / of, the ultimate / God, the ultimate / and, the ultimate / the, the ultimate / cross, the ultimate / you, the ultimate / bore, the ultimate / know, the ultimate / more, the ultimate / has, the ultimate / gone, the ultimate / to, the ultimate / all, the ultimate / that, the ultimate / God, the ultimate / can, the ultimate / give, the ultimate / as, the ultimate / proof, the ultimate / the, the ultimate / smile, the ultimate / of, the ultimate / bliss, the ultimate / and, the ultimate / the, the ultimate / healing, the ultimate / soothe, the ultimate / of, the ultimate / once, the ultimate / and, the ultimate / for, the ultimate / all, the ultimate / "I, the ultimate / believe, the ultimate / in, the ultimate / the, the ultimate / truth, the ultimate / simply, the ultimate / said, the ultimate / of, the ultimate / God, the ultimate / In, the ultimate / an, the ultimate / essential, the ultimate / example, the ultimate / our, the ultimate / examine, the ultimate / has, the ultimate / shown, the ultimate

/ that, the ultimate / God, the ultimate / is, the ultimate / life, the ultimate / is, the ultimate / love, the ultimate / is, the ultimate / mattered, the ultimate.

CHAPTER THIRTEEN

Energetically, the ultimate / secured, the ultimate / in, the ultimate / the, the ultimate / heart, the ultimate / of, the ultimate / men, the ultimate / and, the ultimate / the, the ultimate / passionate, the ultimate / embrace, the ultimate / of, the ultimate / a, the ultimate / hand, the ultimate / your, the ultimate / own, the ultimate / in, the ultimate / the, the ultimate / firmest, the ultimate / grip, the ultimate / the, the ultimate / laughing., the ultimate / welcome, the ultimate / of, the ultimate / a, the ultimate / brother, the ultimate / and, the ultimate / friend, the ultimate / a, the ultimate / simple, the ultimate / example, the ultimate / the, the ultimate / sample, the ultimate / the, the ultimate / temple, the ultimate / called, the ultimate / you, the ultimate / and, the ultimate / the, the ultimate / office, the ultimate / of, the ultimate / Christ, the ultimate / embarked, the ultimate / to, the ultimate / declare, the ultimate / the, the ultimate / perfect, the ultimate / sample, the ultimate / you, the ultimate / are, the ultimate / of, the ultimate / God, the ultimate / and, the ultimate / the, the ultimate / light, the ultimate / prepare, the ultimate / for, the ultimate / a, the ultimate / higher, the ultimate / road, the ultimate / and, the ultimate / a, the ultimate / lofty plane, the ultimate / the explain energetic of humanity, basically, lightly said, God, the I AM, the ultimate.

THE GARDEN-MENTS
LEVEL 48

CHAPTER ONE

Hu-mans, hu-mans garden draped ing reen remember / humble, humble into the garden's gates of love / rumbling, rumbling abilities and the views into gardens / throat, throat appointed too thee, gardens / heavens, heavens heralds and the cities angled into an angel's gardens / decode, decode a define fortunately stated to heaven's gardens / ancients, ancients attitude and the mood found in gardens / ways, ways to meet you in venues of gardens / rung, rung in the ringing's gardens / circles, circles about then, a mirrored strait, gardens / gave, gave an allowance unto thee, a garden / gone, gone unto thoroughly a garden / home, home too into gardens / lord, lord of the listening allowance into gardens / all, all of the centrally welled through with gardens / regain, regain of the sustain called gardens / sympathetic, sympathetic unto theirs and ours too, a garden / reside, reside inside a central portal gained in gardens / this, this our allow for the poetic blending called gardens / side, side said too, sampan for gardens / relax, relax malaysian and the pentacles formed in gardens / regain, regain a saturnine on gardens / regard, regard capitalized in to gardens / unify, unify in the unity for gardens / measures, measures mentioned to a matched rate for gardens / methods, methods meant for a fiscal call to gardens / mesh, mesh allowed a legend for gardens / mashed, amshed past a pasty sorts gardens / ageless, ageless to a timeless state's gardens / timeless, timeless to a theory for gardens / taxed, taxed less and paid more for gardens / secured, secured in a ventral ports gardens / rapt, rapt allow for the features given to gardens / venus, venus found garden deep in a living aspire too, a gaining listening / rebellion, rebellion forgotten and the feeding allowed yours, a garden / wars, wars done and density comes too, a garden lightened / places, places find you in gardens / melt, melt less and live more thanks to gardens / chapters, chapters and verses found in gardens / fuse, fuse allows your affairs to be in gardens / purist, purist annoyed by your gardens will pay too energetically / donate, donate a fortune to your gardens / fires, fires burn with gardens / plants, plants paged past a garden / purple, purple peelings of gardens / values, values allowed for the featured pardons of nix on too, gardens / veils, veils over rippling renewal too, a garden / splits, splits placed and narrowed too, a relative regard for a featured placement of gardens / material, material meant to the serial for a garden / measures, measures meet in grdens / movements, movements meant for a pulsing earthquaking garden / more, more mentioned trillions deep in gardens / colored, colored for the feathered lands gardens / lights, lights lessons meant for your gardens / flash, flash follows listening to gardens / eyes, eyes paced for golden fated gardens / journey, journey to a mentioned garden / near, nearest too, a garden / deity, deity dear to a garden / king, king curtailed, now welled into gardens / angelic, angelic deify and the deity applied to a listened gain into garden's great / gaining for valuable shrines in God, our garden? hearts held high and wide to love / wear, wear a passionate grinf or gardens of love / heat, heat held garden deep into sunny way's loved for gardens.

CHAPTER TWO

Mortals, mortals and the simply gardened / leap, leap past a feature for the facets of gardens / lashed, ashed into listened for gardens / out, out and the shouted through into gardens / genes, genes paced from gardens / genetic, genetic pills and the pooling gardens / decode, decode phoned into a garden / keys, keys fashioned financially to a secretive allow for gardens / lines, lines lessons made too, gardens grates / please, please your neighbor's rates on gardens / mothers, mothers mentioned intentionally too, a garden / choose, choose a chosen pariing for a garden / chasten, chasten and the hastened onto gardens / chastise, chastise allows less the garden stres / joins, joins allow and the appliance for a garden / muse, muse again diva deep into gardens / formal, formal find and the furthering of gardens / deliver, deliver daily gardens / kingdom, kingdom came too, gardens / numeric, numeric allow when, gardened / acquire, acquire pleasant pieces too, and gardens / seen, seen into flying gardens / patterns, patterns purchased in gardens / apply, apply to testify for gardens / codices, codices coupled in your gardens / codical, codical of the vehicle past your gardens / apt, apt and applied to in gardens / aunt, aunt of the uncle's mended garden / uncles, uncles adam deep in the kadmonic heap called gardens / mention, mention an Eden and the gardener hu-man / niece, niece of the given God-man, hu-man, garden / habits, habits blessed to gardens / break, break into a garden / twice, twice said, "your heart healed" in gardens, your heart healed / weekes, weeks come too, in a fondest garden / transom, transom handsome unto a garden / measured, measured for fitting gardens / weights, weights won lightly to a garden / style, style fertile into a garden / volumes, volumes meant for gardens / books, books written and then ended in gardens / cubes, cubes applied too and gardens / cues, cues cost a llowance for the gardens / codes, codes made a living magnify to a garden gate free / matters, matters focus in love's gardens / latest, latest details swell to your gardens / rocks, rocks intact with the news of gardens / views, views elegant with the dews of gardens / pathways, pathways forged through gardens / lectern, lectern loaned to gardens / manners, manners met in gardens / feathers, feathers float to gardens / given, given votes of gardens / gone, gone to view our gardens / powerful, powerful means to gardens / focus, focus fed through gardens / vocal, vocal views on gardens / gaze, gaze across those gardens / gaining, gaining employ in known gardens / granite, granite grew to gather gardens / leap, leap to a cause called gardens / volley, volley established as true gardens / fine, fine to a feeling on gardens / know, know the value in gardens.

CHAPTER THREE

Given, given hysterical cures for gardens / a, a place for a garden / test, test past and the cast for in gardens / require, require rates for gardens / God, God, a garden / gates, gates found in garden shores, opened / acre, acre of the maturest gardens / these, these are the directives to a garden / choir, choir of the miserable gone and the sealing on too, gardens / often, often fed a living garden / deliver, delivery dear and the dear won too gardens / thankful, thankful too, gardens / moments, moments lemon yellow to a garden / thought, thought for and about them, a garden / quiver, quiver in your query of the gardens / magically, magically meant and found then in a triple ascend to a garden / love, love detailed in gardens / stake,

stake made for the gardens / quicken, quicken to a living spent in gardens / visits, visits made a venue for your gardens / artists, artists allowed too, in gardens / approach, approach a necessary allow for the featured metabotanic garden / members, members marry in traditions grown in gardens / script, script written and the heights healed in gardens / prodigy, prodigy made through portends gardens / engrave, engrave allowed to gardens / experts, experts amazed about your gardens / express, express a knowing learned for gardens / flip, flip to a garden clear in floral sustain on electric blue attention and the detain gone to love / wings, wings made a way now for gardens / shorn, shorn of the shaggy wayed cave deep in stone gardens / aisle, aisle worn wide too, gardens / decisions, decisions applied for and the daring attend to gardens / read, read a featured garden / capable, capable into thrilling gardens / cure, cure made a surety in gardens / decisions, decisions due, you are perfect in gardens / react, react off and the reassurance spurts in gardens / capably, apply to a capably perfect assurance on the gardens / cures, cures made sensational to a garden / atlantis, atlantis given a daily garden / intensify, intensify applies to the handy green materially gardened / sceptic, sceptic past a curing garden / confer, confer another gained garden rayed in fairways on gardens / lubicz, lubicz allowed a saying man deep in gardens, "the temple, hu-man" / search, search finished and the finding found in gardens / scales, scales tripped to a tipping gain for gardens / pyramids, pyramids purest in a gaining awareness of gardens / dawn, dawn risen to a pyramid's gardens / raise, raise forthright gardens / blocks, blocks overthrown in gardens / alternate, alternate applications to a garden / blankets, blankets tossed on garden's lawns and the lightening allowance for love / raise, raise a treble attribute to your allowance into gardens / concur, concur that the strait is the gain to garden's mantles / manual, manual to a mentioning garden / Japanese, Japanese in gardening trends / trails, trails bonsai deep in the allowance for a garden / presume, presume parlayed into a garden / interbred, interbred kinds and types into gardens / epistle, epistle of the missile deep in gardens / man, man made a hu-man garden / forbidden, forbidden appetite made a bitten garden / fruits, fruits led to lessons knowledge deep in the split made hu-man.

CHAPTER FOUR

Drips, drips through a sleeve routed to metatron, the garden of God / vanish, vanish a value-less experience of God's good gardens / legacy, legacy laced in gardens / mild, milde menus of gardens / supple, supple apply to the gardens / flex often in gardens / liable, liable to a pliable garden / libel, libel lends your gardens / slander, slander gone to gardens / vex, vex released from gardens / volley, volley about shores gardens / trifle, trifle threw away to a garden lights / truffles, truffles paid for since gardens / bought, bought a beautiful garden for love / bite, bite a chance to maintain your garden / kite, kites flown in gardens / wells, wells deep with gardens / fantastic, fantastic to menued for gardens / ships, ships past those finest gardens / sail, sail true to gardens / chefren, chefren entrapment gone to gardens / targets, targets into a garden's gates / case, case for the placement to gardens /

paced, paced past rates on gardens / clears, clears immaculately to gardens / cleans, cleans your temple to gardens / compares, compares only in gardens / compressed, compressed resorts for gardens / monumental, monumental decisions dealt with in gardens / hysterical, hysterical gone to for gardens / steps, steps made to power for in gardens / stretch, stretch allowed your gardens / heavenly, heavenly paces to gardens / wait, wait for the features gardens / stars, stars allowed an ensured state of gardens / oblong, oblong to metnions of gardens / holes, holes outed to garden / grand, grand allow and the flow through a garden / galleries, galleries measured to gardens / complete, complete a complement to a garden / observe, observe rays to gardens / studies, studies found and forecast grows to the living gardens / complicated complicated, forgive? to these gardens / pills, pills eaten less and found more, peace, in a garden / proctor, proctor paid for pointing into a garden / Sphinx, Sphinx allowed an opening in gardens / aged, aged and waged through to gardens / years, years met through threes made a living garden / protected, protected and invected through a garden / pressures, pressures off and the features found into a garden / precision, precision met in acost free delivery to love then, in gardens / pace, pace made the feature for a fondest garden / correspondence found in a truthful note of measure-less love for gardens / inhabited, inhabited in the habitual ability to believe in the physically freed gardens / precedent, precedent set through a garden / predated, predated electives for gardens / esoteric, esoteric ability for the future's agile detail for gardens / symbolism, symbolism suggestd as the winning combination for true love met in gardens / services, services rendered to gardens / diction, diction met in gardens / speaking, speaking suggested to gardens / spoken, spoken allow for gardens / doubles, doubles as a detail, gardens / the stage, the stage is set for gardens.

CHAPTER FIVE

Missionary, missionary paid the position positive to gardens / mysteries, mysteries measured to gardens / manuals, manuals made a pleasure to your gardens / barcoded, barcoded accompany to your gardens / bipedal, bipedal ability for gardens / biopsy, biopsy dared in gardens / back, back to the basic called gardens / gigantic, gigantic exposure to the mission called a garden / large, large is the lesson to a garden / lavish, lavish apply through gardens / lavendar, lavendar recall of your gardens / weight off and your heart on too, gardens / several, several ways to gardens / written, written in applause for gardens / assumed, assumed detail and the fonder still to gardens / tombs, tombs opened apply to gardens / eroded, eroded, yes, to gardens / thousands, thousands thanked for gardens / seem, seem to be a garden / mercy, mercy found in gardens / gave, gave to equally a garden / Gabriel, GAbriel grew in gardens / passion, passion follows gardens / mercurial, mercurial meeting's gardens / explain, explain align to gardens / data, data dealt with in gardens / driven, driven to apply to gardens / climates, climates met through gardens / cure, cure your nature's gardens / science, science said, yes, gardens / explain, explain the disdain for planted gardens / staggering, staggering numbers mend to gardens / conservation, conservation paved through gardens / aware, aware of the needs too, in gardens / explain, explain a lesson to your gardens / centurion, centurion awarded through gardens / pacing, pacing met through gardens / placement, placement meant for gardens / boxed, boxed out and then in gardens / softens, softens central portion called a garden / kingdoms, kingdoms came to gardens / bleed, bleed less, find more, in agardens / blood, blood saved through gardens / academic, academic too in gardens / opposing, opposing assigned to gardens / estimates, estimates made of the shady gardens / forward, forward framed in gardens / mar, mar left in gardens / farther, farther walk to gardens / gathering, gathering your gardens / granted, granted asylum in gardens / growth, growth employed through gardens / gates, gates gained in gardens / capable, capable plans for your gardens / trades, trades blown to gardens / fellow, fellow flown into gardens / landed, landed views into gardens / great, great dues wonthrough gardens / residual, residual leaks into gardens / gardens, gardens lift the needs, love / categorize, categorize the plants in gardens / gardening, gardening in tunes on loan, love / powerful, powerful enthuse for gardens / loyalty, loyalty comes into gardens.

CHAPTER SIX
Breathing, breathing given a living compulsion to be a bravely won garden / compulsion, compulsion over and the flight done to blvds and gardens / compell, compell yourself to well, be, through gardens / transform, transform the miraculous to your gardens states / direct, direct a detail through your garden / ratify, ratify found for a garden / radical, radical menues for gardens / power, power out and then a garden fills in / forces, forces allowed to flow through the codes found in gardens / authors, authors suggested to concrdant allow for a garden / reserve, reserve ways to garden / powers, powers placed in gardens / sexual, sexual amplify made to gardens / personality, personality powers into gardens / prank, prank allowed finish through a garden / pure, pure apply too and gardens / oceans, oceans quested for gardens / quest, quest for the missions gone to gardens / spiritual, spiritual detail of the gardens / commune, commune about us in gardens / afghanistan, afghanistan in the fanning of gardens / blessing, blessing attempts to a swim through for gardens / absolves, absolves allow for a garden / future, future made real through a garden / head, head to a knowing in gardens / expectation, expectation felt through a garden / rear, rear a detail for gardens / bog, bog bade a garden / greet, greet other meetings of gardens / hearts, hearts planted in smiling gardens / begin, begin a believing in gardens / booked, booked eternally through a garden / I'll show you, mirrored / Love / People / Original / Sin / Stars / Kauai / Collide / Barking / Sand / Rehabilitated / Honeymoon / Relationship / Emsoothes / wise / Woman / Appears / Mention / Desire / Body / Relative / Curve / Easy / Poliulu / Valley / Invades / Sleep / Rhythm / Developed / Call / One

CHAPTER SEVEN
Rations, rations rational to a featured garden / rational, rational applies too, in gardens / GNP, Gainfully Near Perfection's gardens / Maui, Maui lies within a garden / Spring, spring isles wed to gardens / unabated, unabated and ill-fated now have gone to gardens / evironments, environments meant too, gardens / protect, protect a creatured comfort for the featured gardens / balanced, balance inquire too and gardens / attraction, attraction and the simply gardens / living, living allowed in gardens / lights, lights left into a garden / cultures, cultures and the straits run to gardens / puccini, puccini and the meaning meant too, gardens / plaintive, plaintive for the our too, gardens / proud, proud and the participles too, a garden / even, even into a garden / reserved, reserved and allowed too and gardens / burnt, burnt shares of the gardens squarely said to be loved / crisp, crisp to a catharsis meant to gardens / postage, postage pays to garden / pays, pays forth the gardens / paid, paid into the gardens / belief, belief of the course grown to gardens / balances, balances intrigue is sent to the gardens / renewal, renewal of the reprise swung to gardens / rationale, rationale elevated to a garden / bliss, bliss infused in the garden's states / blankets, blankets belie less the lasting gardens / biscuits, biscuits bade a gardening shade / grapple, grapple less with the gardens / bred, bred of our, gardens / collars, collars create your gardens rates / turn, turn unto your own gardens / contentions, contentions created garden / exist, exist forgiven through gardens / strengthen, strengthen your pulsing reward to gardens / lighting, lighting astounds with a garden / massonic, massonic mosaics of the prosaic gardens / found, found a friend who'd lend a garden / foundations, foundations found the gardened rest to love / daring, daring advise to espouse only love in the gardens / hearts, hearts met in sharing gardens / towns, towns triple the reveal of a garden / penny, penny tossed copper rich to a garden / dollars, dollars daily reward your garden / mansions, mansions met in gardens / empire, empire of the retire to a garden / booked, booked in a basic garden / propose, propose an appearance in the reassure for a garden / fountains, fountains feature an exploding garden / blow, blow implored through a garden / ultimate, ultimate waves in the gardens / mention, mention made to gardens / portray, portray a treaty for the garden / essential, essential to a relative garden / penchant, penchants penned in the gardens / path, path of the foretold too and gardens / appelant, appelant relevant to a garden / problems, problems end in gardens / straighten, straighten stills your gardens rates / discovery, discovery due a garden, love's / donate, donate a durate to a garden / peace, peace is elaborate in a garden.

CHAPTER EIGHT
Hope, hope grew to a meaning spent in living parallels and the felt for gardens / grown, grown allow and the sheltered straits of gardens / material, material means and the scenes spent in gardens / maturity, maturity mends to gardens / coupled, coupled in the hope-full state of matrimony spent to gardens / emergent, emergent pages placed in gardens / central, central to an experience rich in jasmine jeweled gardens / descent, descent to the dollared status called gardens / reality, reality amused through gardens / journals, journals paged lgihtly to gardens / staff, staff of the future gaze

in gardens / decent, decent deals made to gardens / realizations, realizations pays for gardens / respect, respect due a garden / rested, rested in nestled gardens / walls, walls depleted by thee, gardens / journey, journey into the featured gardens / profits, profits paid too, and gardens / imporve, improve meant for htee, a garden / approve, approve allowed a threshold placed at the door to a living garden / unfold, unfold felt in a feeling garden / publish, publish now to a daily garden / marry, marry another's special garden / central, central says let us be a garden / flows, flows and the aft spent on gardens / options, options paid too, a gardens / measures, measures means and the reasons dealt to gardens / stickler, stickler for the nickles spent on gardens / spicy, spicy spillings and the shillings lean to a treasured garden / casual, casual the feelings fortunate to a garden / causal, causal explanations and the straits won to a hearty garden / century, century dealt with to a garden / strain, strain over and the rewards allowed for gardens / meet, meet a mirthful friend's garden / fully, fully felt an won to a garden / times, times allowed too in gardens / three, three held for the fullest gardens / social, social said "garden parties win" the statutes of love / sexual, sexual to a filling garden / metaphysics, metaphysics felt for the fashionable gardens / spy, spy allowed a speeching for thee, "gardens" / thousands, thousands concur too, "a garden" / agents, agents found for the further gardens / childlike, childlike speeches gathered into a garden / techniques, techniques taught through a reliance on a garden / tap, tap another's pace for the gardens / top, top of the featured gardens / tell, tell another of tehse hanging gardens / task, task made apparent into a garden / harbor, harbor less a lessened garden / living, living to fill you in gardens / worlds, worlds welcome too, a garden / brink, b.rink fo the best now to gardens / realize, realize a reaching's gardens / samples, samples spent in gardens / simply, simply apply to a garden / refine, r.efine a featured garden / shares, shares sent for to gardens / declares, declares a duration "a garden" / dismissed, dismissed and allowed too, a garden / occur, occur often into a garden / soaring, soaring apparent to a garden / divorced, divorced most into a garden / delegates, delegates allowed a garden.

CHAPTER NINE

Gardening, gardening eternally allowed an inferno grown mythology of the lesson hu-man / grown, grown to know the Sysyphus tale of the mythos called gardening hell / young, young an disciple and the ripening gardens / own, own a retail appearance and a dearest garden / ancient, ancient into suggestive good-bye of the superstitious ways fo love-less gardens / egyptian, egyptian known replication fo the integration of vibrancy in gardens / wise, wise allowance has built the gardens of the heart / won, won again within the heart of a living garden / worn, worn too, and gazing in to the angelic regions of the forgiven soul's and gardens / life, life led me to your gardens / star, star suggestive of the successive, 1-2-3, gardens / question, question less and own more in your gardens / willed, willed allow of the pleasure resplendent into gardens / wield, wield a whistling garden / published, published and soothed throughout a garden / edict, edict made "you rave" in gardens / editiion, edition pitched to gardens / front, front found in gardens / first, first allow of the guarded state to go to gardens / spell, spell these g-a-r-d-e-n-s / hire, hire a servant for the effective guardian to gardens / inquire, inquire the species who sent a soul to gardens / probe, probe abates into a living garden / foreward, foreward written into a healing garden / friend, friend of the featured gardens / electric, electric avow of the finished gardens / waste, waste knots gone to gardens / waist, waist touched and lathered in the help mate's gardens / eliminated, eliminated yes! to a garden / digested, digested and registered within a garden / dress, dress for them, a garden / public, public psent into a garden / published, published and allowed a swallow of liquid fire through a garden / places, places booked through a garden / placed, placed in tripled gardens / productions, productions made of gardens / georgian, georgian aplumb comes to gardens / bodies, bodies bliss in gardens / balance, balance paid for gardens / blaze, blaze allowed a trailing garden through the trees of life 41counting, counting heavenly gardens 42starring, starring the trend for gardens 43found, found a date for gardens / 2010 is the begin for gardens / waves, waves burst through gardens / prayerful, prayerful approach to gardens / heavenly, heavenly hosted gardens / worn, worn through the temples of gardens / abide, abide in the stride of gardens / initiate, initiate the phases of gardens / babies, babies buzz in our gardens / children, children wonder for gardens / attend, attend a garden / delivery, delivery comes to gardens / yours, yours the birth into gardens / living, living allows us a garden / froth, froth atop a garden / suffer, suffer less, garden / appear, appear more in gardens / simply, simply, the gardens / smile, smile near a garden / french, french tiers in gardens / portions, portions framed by gardens / photographic, photographic gains for your gardens.

CHAPTER TEN

Banks, banks ample into gardens / entire, entire allow for the gardens of life's loves / billions, billions bail out the gardens / maze, maze fades to gardens / gashing, gashin past and into a garden / earned, earned luster for the faceted garden / spoken, spoken of into gardens / sparks, sparks made of gardens / family, family featured through a garden / spoken, spoken of pens glazed in gardens / enhance, enhance a chance to be a "garden" / real, real to a feel for a gate free garden / frankest, frankest features found in gardens / generated, generated stately gardens / cue, cue of the coded gardens / cubic, cubic forgone and the feathery gardens / angles, angles supple to the suppl for a garden / watery, watery ways kai depp in gardens / replicate, replicate a ration for the functional gardens / reply, reply raised to "gardens" / millions, millions listen to a garden / tons, tons told forth and these? a garden / waters, waters willed to reinvent a heaven scent in gardens / soils, soils pheremone deep in gardens / forests, forests estate free to a garden / tree, tree timed to gardens / pumped, pumped and supplied by a garden / roots, roots made in gardens / radical, radi8cal amperage and the revamp to gardens / reasons, reasons for the seriously gardened relations / raced, raced to find a featured garden / review, review a chance to belly dance in God's garden's, life / hospitable, hospitable to a mission's gardens / smiles, smiles and the reply "for children" gardens / cry, cry gone to a reaching garden

/ admiration, admiration spans your gardens / authored, authored for a Father's gardens / hours, hours impeached less and found forthrightly due a garden / powers, powers placed into gardens / discussions, discussion dealt an early light for gardens / estimate, estimate your trining regard for gardens / concerns, concerns paced to gardens / rains, rains splashing into streaming gardens / report, report a steamy sort to gardens / angelic, angelic infusions of gardens / forest, forests face a garden / travels, travels retail a garden / alarms, alarms over and the featured found in gardens / forewarned, forewarned of the treaty to a garden / significance sounds to gardens / dreams, dreams deal in gardens / ran, ran to a reached for garden / crowned, crowned in a rippling garden / approved, approved and allowed thrice, a garden, a garden, a garden / silence, silence spent into a garden / sprung, sprung forth a Midas touched eternity in God's best gardens / responses, responses unto a garden / envy, envy over and the dues paid to gardens / collapse, aollapse allowed to a garden / equate, equate has found a garden / economic, economic soar made a garden / glisten, glisten lists a garden / status, status made to gardens / booked, booked imply for gardens.

CHAPTER ELEVEN
Fascinate, fascinate within and the end of thin regard for a garden / drill, drill over and stides aside the gardens / versatile, versatile values set for the respect of a garden / follow, follow the light within to garden / considerate, considerate to a light literature forthright in principles of the particles called hu-man gardens / account, account for the venues in gardens / reputable, reputable to a relation fo the reaching appear of God's gardens / inscription, inscription meant for the featured gardens / count, count on a volley of support for your garden's gifts / shift, shift into overdue and the detailed experience of God in the garden / jade, jade blue into jointed escrow of the realize gained in a garden / hearts, hearts heated blue ablaze in gardens / sapphire, sapphire again, into respectful retain of the license to a holy garden / carry, carry on and through a garden / scroll, scroll down and up too, a garden / triangular, triangular in written inscription of the gotten gardens / fly, fly to a square reprise of the triangles cut across your top-less gardens / flow, flow into the garden's greats of love / incest, incest spent inspected by gardens / ancestors, ancestors say " let us, pray, in a garden" / reborn, reborn today to a detailed garden / splendor, splendor sprinted throughout our gardens / diligent, diligent to daily gardens / matrices, matrices respectfully sent to a garden / anniversary, anniversary of the featured gardens / collapsed, collapsed estates can mend in a garden / stellar, stellar respect for your natured gently garden / land, land given to a garden / during, during a disciple's revival, I rescind less and reach more the golden shore of a healthy respect for life's leading gardens / agree, agree to see the finesr gardens / doubles, doubles bent into gardens / dates, dates set for feature's gardens / on, on too, a garden within / persian, persian pinnnacles of the gardened state / pallets, pallets placed into gardens / flanks, flanks covered daily to a garden / seam, seam sealed annually throughout a garden / scribe, scribe of the kindest gardens / ghost, ghost hosted has gone fully unto

the heavenly aspect of today's gardens / give, give us a mental clearance to picture a passionate when, now, gardens / consider, consider a pulsing chance to choose for gardens / calm, calm in approach then, a garden / palms, palms extended daily to a garden / store, store elected and the resurrected won daily unto a garden / dearly, dearly paid and sacrifices spent know the gain into a garden / regal, regal attire worn daily to a bilical strand of celestial nature and the natural tend to believe in the gardens / regard, regard for the fashionably perfect reaction to a changing ration focused precisely into love's belief in a garden / intense, intense experience of the expression of God's love to a garden / perpetual, perpetual plays and the planes of the gardens / montage, montage built to a giving gained in a garden / advantage, advantage set for gardens / binds, binds out and over too, a garden / drawn, drawn into a fired elate if gardens / adroit, adroit in exploit's forgiven trades to gardens / extra, extra ways to believe in, a gardens / dip, dip into the ink of life, basically, humanity, a garden / levels, levels written and heights found in the gardens / slowing, slowing to the rolling found in gardens / first, first in a matching garden / lasted, lasted throughout life's gardens / matters, matters are most in gardens / match, match is placed in the gardens / eternally, eternallly we are the gardens / electric, electric raves about gardens.

CHAPTER TWELVE
Cleverly, cleverly sent, fox deep, to a garden / chips, chips stretched into, a garden / spice, spicey splices of the gardens / inclusive, inclusive truth of a garden / record, record a rapt repeat of the mantra / God, God, Father, God's gardens / profits, profits amzae your garden / genus, genus of the genius genuine to a garden / count, count on the respect for a gentle garden / temples, temples planned too, in gardens / small, small and the detail smelled in gardens / surge, surge to a preaching rate for a garden / reality, reality reads "a garden" / verify, verify the respect for a garden / legend, legend of the lived in gardens / cushion, cushion made to blend in to the garde / facts, facts made straight to a garden / educate, educate your patient gardens / bags, bags filled in gardens / pictorial, pictorial display fo the days gone into gardens / stork, stork allows an "okay" to a garden / associates, associates spent in gardens / soldier, soldier of the solid vehicle called love, a garden / ritual, ritual to a missive meant for gardens / complex, complex, simply said to "gardens" / human, human, a healed, garden / mix, mix made and mentioned too, in gardens / install, install a pair eyed in the gardens / patrons, patrons of the principles bade a garde / garden, garden, by define, genuine allow respectful in a daily electric nurture of given love / domains, domains purchased allow a pace for the gardens / openings, openings purchase a garden / refer, refer to a doorway due your gardens / sung, sung unto in gardems / ports, ports paced to a garden / past, past known and the gardened elates / receptive, receptive to a garden / erected, erected stellae to a garden / plays, plays allowed in the gardens / stand, stand stone free for the gardens / optic, optic repair for the shower in the gardens / oriental, oriental orientation gained in the gardens / verbs, verbs valued too, an active amtrix of gardens / page, page placed here for gardens generators / cattle, cattle held

in the penned allow to feed the gardens / crowd, crowd respectful of the ressurection gained in a garden / begun, begun unto a garden / passive, passive made the truest won, in a, garden / come, come unto me, a garden / corner, corner paid to a garden / name, name of the necessary, gardens / carve, carve less an image of less, know the hu-man express of God, the electric garden / made, made in the image electric, God gave the metatron a name, in gardens / tiers, tiers in the gardens / terraced, terraced gardens / truck, truck gardens / produce, produce gardens / star, star nurseries in gardens / planetary, planetary gardens / gazing, gazing gardens / mirrored, mirrored gardens / fountains, fountains in the gardens / garments, garments robed in gardens / gates, gates swing to gardens / openly, openly in the gardens of live light.

CHAPTER THIRTEEN

Embody, embody allowed for the enochian explain for gardens / allow, allow her the worry freed for gardens / horizontal, horizontal in employ of the gardens / dominate, dominate details won to a garden / ancestors, ancestors spent in a garden / sacred, sacred spelling of the gardens, y-o-u / bundle, bundle bent over in a garden / beacon, beacon of the baby born unto a gaden / decor, decor detailed unto the garden's Gods / dates, dates spell no-thing to you, a garden zen / oversee, oversee a special garden / meaning, meaning felt for the compassionate pews of gardens / insult, insult felt forgive at the altars in the gardens / move, move into the healing gardens / movement, movement allowed throughout blue-green gardens / purple, purple displays of the gardens / praise, praise antoehrs perfect gardens / boast, boast less and gain mroe for the gardens / boutique, boutique avowed of the gardens / quote, quote a trio, "gardens" "gardens" "gardens" / preserve, preserve a prescription for the gardens / quarter, quarter mooned delivery to a garden / horizontal, horizontal spilling trues a garden / placed, placed in precise align within a garden / barren, barren land found a lend to gardens / booths, booths allowed in gardens / nights, nights meant for the gardens into allow of the religious freedom to spiritually be diligent in your inspect of the grassy planes, mountainous estates, blue speaking teams of red respect and yellow neglect forgiven an allowance for the speeches gently detailed for an election made, God's grains blend at every day, know this, each moment and allow remain in a hu-man bread brought to the garden / systems, systems sent and found in gardens / recode, recode the rest of gardens / encoded, encoded again to a garden's tunes / systemic, systemic and wide within a garden / mounted, mounted explain of the directions of a garden / panels, panels pasted in a garden / placed, placed parallelly to a garden / male, male features strut through gardens / women, women worn to Eden's choirs of gardens / openly, openly explain your gardens / checks, checks drawn for gardens / electrically, electrically replete, a garden / safe, safe unto a garden starved won / saffron shorn to pistil clean remember of the taste freed for gardens / welcome, welcome here the homeward borne angelic winds of the gardens / insurance, insurance paid for the gardens / chapters, chapters spill into pages deep within the gadens / chants, chants and the chatting within a garden / shown, shown an opportunity too, and

agardens / flower, flower opens in a garden / votive, votive of the motive for a garden, paltned / angles, angles and the angels met in a garden of love / welcome, welcome home, God's friends, to an angelic explain of the planes garden / deep in Hellenic love / flown, flown too and gardens / votives, votives valued for the ancient glow of a garden / chant, chant yes too, and "gardens" / singing, singing home the gardens / wearing, wearing well the gardens / healthy, healthy in the gardens / powerful, powerful unto gardens / gently, gently open the gardens / powder, powder sprays these gardens / gathers, gathers dew the gardens / contours, contours teach us gardens / planted, planted near, the gardens / daily, daily feed your gardens.

THE ASSIGN-MENTS
LEVEL 49

CHAPTER ONE

Subject, subject of the assignment you, know the steps parallel unto a perpendicular cross of the heavenly ascent called hu-man ressurections of love, God is, you are, assigned to live well / case, case made for the pentrate and the parallel require for featured fuardians to the shores of particualr assignments made, to love / cured, cured of the arrested assignments / hero, hero comes in a clearing curled to meet your assignment / sentences, sentences shortened in an attempt to show the delinquint nature of the perpetual ssignment meant to be hu-man / desires, desires daiy sealed at the banner of the beached american called assignments / garments, garments spread across the shores assigned / bodied, bodied bliss and the benched allow to be resurrected some to an assignment / gardens, gardens finished in grown measures and the painted I AM, precisely hu-man to an assignment, Love / written, written intrigue iwth the goodness called assignments / meetings, meeetings set for a settle meant to assignments / nouns, nouns placed in pages assigned / finals, finals found forward too, an assignment / splendor, splendor of the penchant for the passionate assignments / brilliant, brilliant to a borrowed assignment / faith, faith found and frequently sent to a living assign / twilight, twilight paid for the pieces perfect unto an living assignment / anxious, anxious out and the living due too, an assignment, your love / stars, stars met in a steep climb to the current assignment / sleep, sleep dear too, an assignment / gauge, gauge of the good bless, an assignment / self, self said "assignment" / rivers, rivers reach your assignments / lotus, lotus, lotus linking assignments / attempt, attempt teal assignments / please be freely assigned / strive, strive for the nurture of an assign / endured, endured imply of the assigned / radiant, radiant mention of the assignments / radiance, r.adiance reaches to an assign / ratify, ratify the retail assignments / shrines, shrines built to an assignment / nights, nights of the nearing collission with precisely permanent love, a weekly assignment / illusion, illusion due and unto you, an assignment / necklace, necklace breaks at the assignment / mothers, mothers mentioned as an assignment / yogini, yogini runs too, an assignment / daughters, daughters dear and a lifting lid has run to an appliance, assignments / vines, vines need a ventral view of your ivy green reigning assignment / known, known unto a detailed assignment / auspicious, auspicious apply too, an assignment / good, good unto an assignment / fortunes, fortunes field an assignment / nice, nice to the kneeling assignment / strange, strange allowance into an assignment / wonderous, wonderous and the day's ways into an assignment / miserable, miserable mentioned assignments / right, right deals with an assignment / blues, blues bays assigned rent / beauty, beauty and the business related to an assignment / traits, traits trued an assignment sent / phrases, phrases and the thrills raid an assignment / oceans, oceans dealt in assignments / relatives, relatives reach an assignment / promote, promote more assignments / example, example set an assignment / females, females found in assignments / sentence, sentence allowed an assignment / relatives, relatives allowed the relations too, an assignment / immediate, immediate details due an assignment / feminine, feminine to the values assigned / incorporates, incorporates and the cured assignments / relates, relates unto an assignment / italicize, italicize a rising assignment.

CHAPTER TWO

Misty, misty and met with assignments / means, means means and the meanings assigned / case, case allowed an assignment / pronounced, pronounced appliance of the assignments / milleniums, milleniums mentioned and the dimensions allowed an attendant stare into assignments / matrices, matrices and the mixed rates assigned too / samples, samples and the sentenced state of the assignments / mates, mates and the mixed rates assigned / specifics, specifics and the spatial assigns / illusions, illusions and the delusions assigned / substitute, substitute another dimension's assigns / converted, converted to a triple assign / salutations, salutations reach your assigns / enured, enured of the insured state, assigned / shake, shake a frequent assigns / frequent, frequent fields assigned / award, award of the heard with encounters of a listening assign / fake, fake and the futuristic appearance of an assignment / reward, reward the Other with love in surrender to a blissful assignment / hold, hold a herald due too, an assign / do, do we? assign / person, person of the pleasant, assign / time, time to till the healed assign / happy, happy day's assigns / believe, believe in another's retail delivery of the living metatron, an assign meant / very, very in the vary to One, assign / redemption, redemption of the dealt with assign / sentence, sentences written to a converted awareness of the One lovely assign / stripes, stripes reached for throughout the listening winds of assign / violence, violence over and through a living assign / kind, kind of the coupling assign / innocent, innocent unto knowing a living assign / dream, dream dealt a winning ascend to light assign / found, found a fullest assign to love / thing, thing thought through to an assign / happen, happen to heal a kneeling assign / this, this day appeals to an assign / mile, mile of the smiling won, assigns / wild, wild to a witnessed assign / lucky, lucky to see won assigns / sound, sound of the sealing assign / down, down to a dealing with only assigns / puzzle, puzzle of the plenty released unto an assign / chest, chest deep in a healing assign / sleep, sleep in it, a heart's yin away to love and assigns / despair, despair due and overing assign / thought, thought to thicken only an assign / bath, bath done well unto an assign meant / normal, normal knelt into an assign / yourself, yourself the success rate of love and assigns / fit, fit and the feelings assigned / load, load detailed well into an assign / break, break for the believing assign / interrupted, interrupted less then assigned / true, true to a teaching assign / welcome, welcome home a reaching assign / refresh, refresh our daily assigns / enjoy, enjoy a teaching assign / loud, loud to a listened for assign / renunciation, renunciation runs into a level assign / save, save a notice sent to an assign / intention, intention directed directly into assigns / critics, critics caved through to an assign / analyze, analyze this unit, the assign means, love.

CHAPTER THREE

Story, story told several ways to an assign sent / show, show of the showers assigned to love / covered, covered in ours assigned

/ trifle, trifle trued at an assign / offend, offend gone into and assigned love / sincerely, sincerely sent a listing assigned / view, view of the venture assigned / overlook, overlook less and land an assign sent for love / draw, draw into an assign / prize, prize paid through an assign / bank, bank of the valued believe for an assign / majority, majoirty made an assigned state / church, church road red with assigns / effort, effort fades to aonly a healing assign / renewal, renewal comes too, an assign / retire, retire again unto an assign / inspiring, inspiring pairs win an assign / unveil, unveil reveal assigns / kick, kick into a triple assign meant / correspond, correspond well with your assigns / looking, looking in simple assigns / reference, reference of the fault-less assigns / creatures, creatures capable of an assign / figure, figures found and assigns / action, action of the motions assigned / before, before and the features assigned / know, know how too, assigns / collect, collect a couple assigned / moments, moments meant into an assign / seize, seize over and the dues assigned / forgotten, forgotten appear at the dearest assigns / seat, seat made at thee, the heart of assigns / brief, brief an allow of the dearest assigns / loop, loop into a legion of assigns / forgive, forgive and find an assign / touch, touch into an assign / earth, earth met features assigned / adhere, adhere to a memory kept well within assigns / results, results spent and assigned / simplicity, simplicity featured at an assign / resume, resume an engraved race to loving assigns / baggage, baggage goes to rooms assigned / chapter, chapters written of the lessons assigned / collect, collect a pairing onto assignments / identification, identification of the duration of God-ness assigned / make, make a meeting assigned / should, should we say, yes! to an assign / report, report to a durable degree of love then assisted to an assign / clean, clean and dear too, an assign / check, check found in a feeling asigned / liquid, liquid unto an assign / refill, refill felt for the assign / laid, laid over a bridging assign espert, expert appears too, an assign / rapture, rapture met daily at the assigns / pleasure, pleasure teasing your assigns / shuffle, shuffle dealt with through an assign / coil, coil felt to an assign / core, core cured, and, assigned / smoke, smoke dates an assign / fire, fire to a featured assign / voice, voice felt deep in assigns / spoken, spoken of the simple assigns / decide, decide to date your assigned / definite, definite to a decide to be assigned.

CHAPTER FOUR

Awesome, awesome to and the dialy ability grows too, assigns / span, span met at assigns / proof, proof meets in a healing assign / wrath, wrath over and the dues are assigned / scholar, scholar cubed as an assign / post, post a peeling assigns / clue, clue of the cubical assign system, system spent unto an assign / reverse, reverse made a curse less for an assign / decree, decree daily to an assign / essence, essence of the featured assign / quiet, quiet appear came to an assign / children, children of the dearest assign / creator, creator comes into our assign / acting, acting led us to an assign / save, save and the central assign meant / frame, framing a future assign / funny, funny ways and the days dearly assigned / review, review and the featured assigns / park, park at the heart faced at an assign / edge, edge of the mounded assigns / match, match came

into an assign / magic, magic given and gotten assigns / gear, gear worn throughout an assign, love, peace, smiles / waste, waste done and the deals won through a healing assign / weep, weep for a fashionable assign / thank, thank another met at a healing assign / shift, shift into a living assign / read, read to us of love, this earth, our God, and love / tell, tell another well of God's details at love then assigned / kiss, kiss a passionate mention of assigns / job, job made a daily assign / mathematically, mathematically field and the filled assign added up too, love / perpendicular, perpendicular unto an assign / drama, drama of the dealt with assigns / dealt, dealt with again too, an assign / dynasty, synasty due a retinue of love in assign / delay, delay due a passionate flower of loving assign / delta, delta planed assigns / dwell, dwell near and assigned / dwelling, dwelling telling us "assigns" / ceiling, ceiling spent for only an assign / casual, casual unto matters of these assigns / coal, coal spent on burning assigns / captain, captain coded as an assign / cords, cords cut, simply by an assign / cool, cool tools of assign meant / coated, coated less and annointed more through an assign / trees, trees respect your award for the healing assign / trance, t.rance over and the dues paid for through assigns / bush, bush bet on an assign / bus, bus to a ridden assign / belgian, belgian given an assign / arc, arc the isles greek by assign / abstain, abstain form daily only an assign / abstruse, abstruse ability gained through an assign / constant, x is constant to an y we knew as loving assign / young, young told yes too and the love is viewed as an assign rainbow blue / gather, gather your stuff to an assign / evidence, evidence sent to an assign / cycles, cycles spent on healing assigns / supply, supply a daily assign / civil, civil unto a giving assign / become, become best at assign, love, well / assigns, assigns sent the message too, love.

CHAPTER FIVE

Humanity, humanity of the amenities due an oblong residue called precisely gleaned and the daily assigned / interminable, interminable abilities of the basics caluse for assignments / magnify, magnify and the amazed meant assigned / brook, brook and the broken assigns / books, books and the basically written assigns / walls, walls and the ways wed too, an assign / numerous, numerous menues of the assignsradars, radars and the reaching in too, an assign / patron, on of the peaceful assigns / possible, possible too, ana assign / patronic, patronic ways by assign / matron, matron of the mentally assigned / cushions, cushion of the centric assign / instrumental, instrumental and the trades spent into assigns / chores, chores and the doors done through an allowance assigns / jackets, jackets and the worn details of an assign / hearkens, hearkens and the made through an associate's assigns / harbors, harbors and the made through ana ssigns / lights, lights listen too, an assign / designs, designs and the details allowed an assign / issues, issues and the voiced allows an assign / conceivable, conceivable and the detailed will for an assign / spans, spans and the bridged allow for an assign / journals, journals and the joining assign / process, process of the plenty mapped into an assign / brain, brain beads well into an assign / inheritance, inheritance is apid for an assign / plays,

plays and the days tripped an assign / generates, generates and the retails allow an assign / broken, broken near a living assign / greens, greens and the deeds done to an assign / impart, impart and the starts made, an assign / seminal, seminal employ for the flowering assign, zero pointed perfection in love / ecological, ecological employ of the doyan called lightly an assignment / turns, turns made into a loving hue called the assigned / traipse, traipse allows an estuary to flow into a triple assign / serves, serves us and well into a lasting assign / awash, awash in pieces and the pade of a healing God called assigns / thanked, thanked for the value of a lasting assign / tow, tow into a retinue of the assigned / concentrates, concentrates and well in deed too alond the assigns / concerns, concerns less and more aligned in the living assigns / pretends, pretends less and finds more at the listening assign / generals, generals of the staring kind who allow your wow to be valued through an aligned assign / populace, populace posed as the knew assigned / attendant, attendant too and the daily ways are assigned / tendency, tendency dealt with as an assign / companions, companions found in a town triple true to a treaty for the valuable days of assigns / mentions, mentions made of the apparent assigns / forms, forms found and the features assigned / instruct, instruct a healaing allow unto the assigns / equates, equates and the durable days of an assign / deter, deter less and win more through a holy release unto an assign meant / promote, promote your perfect assigns / respect, respect found for thee, assigned / animas, animas made real to an assign / anima, anima dates you assigned / Jung, Jung dared and found an assign / shadow, shadow sealed by an assign / close, close the door to a patterned assign / archetypes, archetypes paid for through an assign / types, types tool deep in illuminated assign / masks, masks off and the meanings mix at only assigns / patterned, patterned in the meanings charted as assigns / parted, parted into roles assigned.

CHAPTER SIX
Doom, doom dealt with via an assign / dorms, dorms built to heal over our assigns / colleges, colleges cued as an assign / schools, schools special unto an assign / armanas, armanas and the asanas assigned / periodic, periodic in details assigned / supply, supply trues as assigned / food, food found daily too and assigned / sports, sports shortly made an assign / splashed, aplashed about us, assigned / squirts, squirts and the outed sorts assigned / chance, chance dealt with and assigned / change, change into a healing assign / cause, cause for the reasons assigned / populated, populated pews of the assigned / squire, squires retailed to an assign / response, response made and the daily dues on an assign / system, system centrally assigned / fight, fight for the feeling assigns / flight, flight over and infused through an assign / immune, immune unto less than fully file named agendas for the assigned / aid, aid for the valued assigns / situation, situation paid for and assigned / acopes, acopes deal in the assigned meanings / stable, stable deals made as assigned throughout love / triassic, triassic fed and the led too, assigned / jurassic, jurassic led and the fled too, assigns / lands, lands made your own through assigns / pangeic, pangeic plenty and the many assigned / millions, millions made

and the paid for assign / collission, collission due unto an assign / covers, covers dared for thee, assigned / recede, recede to the altars assigned / waters, waters made a willing assign / pump, pump applies too, and assigns / outback, outback foound forums assigned / well, well due an assign / extracts, extracts assigned, now / brags, brags alot less through assigns / chortle, chortles digress to assigns / tapirs, tapirs dear too, assigns / birds, birds basically freed to assigns / miels, miles and goiing assigned / fame, fame fed an assign / normal, normal dues wade to assigns / abbreviated, abbreviated sorts found assign / insured, insured for the featured assigns / decoded, decoded details of assigns / twister, twister mister assigned / dioxides, dioxides dealt through assigns / carbons, carbons firmly assigned / primates, primates rated and the chosen assigned / premiere, premiere in the occup too, assigned / stock, stock of the steeples assigned / intellect, intellect showing assigned / commanded, commanded in the random assigns / strains, strain felt loosened thorugh assigns / farming, farming fielding your assigns / architects, architects tooling too, assigned / jades, jades value in assigns / trails, trails to the triple assigns / trots, trots past and lasts as assigned / runs, runs into an assign / jogs, jogs through as assigned.

CHAPTER SEVEN
Anarchist, anarchist allowed an assign / repossess, repossess an address for assigns / process, process paid too, assigned / pays, pays for a metric assign / cockatoos, cockatoos fade to assigns / cliche, cliche well due an assign / clans, clans allowed emebracing assigns / clothes, clothes curl to an assign / clash, clash over and the values sent to assigns / discotheques, discotheques deal as assigned / music, music met at a Metatronic assign / volume, volumes as viewed through assigns / voluminous, voluminous mentions as assigned / fault, fault out and durations appeal to assigns / prismatic, prismatic to the automatic assigns / asthma, asthma seen as the reflection healed and the assign meant for love / clash, clash applies to a healing assign / affairs, affairs due a healing aspire / flown, flown into the features assigned / cultural, cultural creatures win an assign / delegations, delegations deal with assigns / millenial, millenial mention of the suspended assigns / structures, structures strewed unto an assign / built, built in beauty for an assign / argues, argues less as the rested becomes as assigned / conflicts, conflicts featured forgiven assigns / resolves, resolves reseal of the healing assigns / irrelevant, irrelevant to the antures assigned / disasters, disasters deal in a helical assign / fine, fien to a feautred assign / floods, floods fed a fallen assign / detaill, detail found in a town assigned / floods, floods and the feuded match for an assign / donations, doantions deal in assigns / funds, funds matched through assigns / perceived, perceived as assigned / socials, socials and the sentinels advance unto an assigns / sought, sought and the bought with assigns / Protestant, Protestant dues as assigned / realize, realize a ransomed assign / suffers, suffers you your assigns / donates, doanted daily assigns / facile, facile feautured assigns / facilitate, facilitate your assigns / factual, factual and the actual assigns / actual, actual ways to be well assigned / mantra, mantra met at the healing assigns /

cures, cures due an assign / fragments, fragments framed blue in a zealous attempt to love her assignment, earth, loved / occupy, occupy your shifts through an intelligent gesture called precisely measured / allow of the living assigns / stands, stands elected as precisely assigned / songs, songs meant of the healing assigned / affords, affords your space to a nearest intelligence called assigns / alternates, alternates between your heart and mine, a line on assigns / romance, romance made the vitor between our selective assigns / inherits, inherits merits meant for assigns / levels, levels of the licensed assigns mouths, mouths match in a healing assign / niles, niles nestle at the heart's lined ascent to an insigned assign / inherit, inherit ancient ways, now, assigned / fish, fish of the future walks to the waters edge and plunges into an assign / float, float past a past alligned in assigns / spent, spent a penchant on assigns / dies, dies daily to a listen-ed less assign.

CHAPTER EIGHT
Entry, entry to the ritual called clues in assigns / babylon, babylon blues and the clubs spent in assigns / cycle, cycle symmetric and the wedged allow for a passionate embrace of the other as / self and the rest as shelved unto light assigns / big, big ways found to feature through light assigns / grand, grand align made the measured rates of assigns / sign, sign said, "assigns" / trines, trines merit an healing assign / health, health found in a wealthy way to assignments / virtues, virtues valued as assigned / advantage, advantage made a helathy assign / define, define your sorrow wella nd allow the healing visualize through assign / economy, economy honored and the healing allowed through a kneeling assign / family, family fueled as assigned / needs, needs met electrically through assigns / profits, profits made eternally through assigns / plants, plants at the edges assigned / essence, essence of the plenty assigned / spiritual, spiritual please and the meaning squeezed to allow an assign / thread, thread of the triple spent on assign / remove, remove red and find blue spokent oo, as assigned / souls, souls shrunk unto lightly spiritual assigns expansive ability for love / will, will we be speechless as assigned / karmic, karmic allow plows your gentles assigns / end, end of the driest assigns / free, free unto a heart spent assigned / floats, floats and the following assigned / wheels, wheels wedged allow assigns / matrices, matrices mentioned as assigned / love, love let us assigned free to a healing allow / laughter, laughter met as assigned / comes, comes a dearest assignment / feeling, feeling and the peelings assigned / peals, peals and the ringing assigned / voice, voice of the virtuous assigned / good, good into God-ness assigned / grown, grown as the light electric well, assigned / sums, sums paid to be assigned / sun, sun days assigned / light, light leys assigned / regarding, regarding carding assign / discard, discard less as assigned / elective, elective in selective assigns / directive, directive due a helaed assign / rewards, rewards come through an assign / money, money made and found as assigned / mend, mend a detailed assignment / mail, mail the notes electric to an assign / receive, receive regular dues as assigned / sapphic, sapphic zones penetrated as assigned / speak, speak of dearest assigns / caliber, caliber of the created assigns / one, one days worthy assigns /

wisdom, wsdom won to an assign / opened, opened spirits of assign / expereience, expereince spent near assigns / disrupt, disrupt less and find more assigns / continental, continental concur of the healed states assigns / avenues, avenues dealt with through assigns / aspects, aspects purged as assigned / greener, greener gazes assigned / context, context found for the features assigned / waves, waves roll less and settle more as assigned / flood, floods found in the exhaling sounds of assign.

CHAPTER NINE
Centuries, centuries surged as assigned / ribbons, ribbons cut electrically for the featured assigns / ninety-six, ninety-six natures in man and the hu-man expand to the sixty-fourth plateau of love, that's assigned / done, done through the deals assigned / compare, compare the capapbly assigned / breaks, breaks allowed, as assigned / reactions, reactions reckoned with, as assigned / common, common creates and the estates as the status asisgned / cadence, cadence spent in the diary written, as assigned / frames, frames felt assigned / musical, musical mention, as assigned / degrees, degrees detailed, as assigned / monads, monads purchased, as assigned / bodies, bodies meet in assigns / cars, cars carry an assign / remove, remove statuary that reaps as assigned / practice, practice preached allow for a healed assign / place, place a paralleled assign nearby, love / task, task fo the treaties assigned / coast, coast to a meeting assigned / initiate, initiate the visit's assigned / pain, pain over and the dues paid as assigned / pure, pure to the one, asisgned / voyage, voyage made and the gazes cry as assigned / expertise, expertise found in a sound calle A-ha the electric assign / indian, indian of the days assigned / manned, manned and the material assigned / costs, costs lessen as assigned / theoretic, theoretical perfect's assigns / ocean, ocean occurs near our assigns / caste, caste of the detention done, as assigned / cost, cost over and fed assigns / central, central spins and the windy assigns / insure, insure meets an assign yes, yes led to a na assign / always, always will, as assigned / deepens, deepens a door occured through / space, space purchased annually as deserved, assigned / wands, wands twitch at thee, the assigns / wave, wave of the won assign / magic, magic made, as assigned / takes, takes in an assign / chance, chance of the churning assigns / dance, dance daily, as assigned / jump, jump into an assign / jewel, jewel of the well assigned / join, join anothers dealt with assign journey, journey made to a gazing assign / biochemists, biochemists dare to be well, as assigned / bichemical, biochemical apply to an assign / narrative, narrative found, as assigned / topical, topical to the tropical assigns / tapestry, tapestry treated, as assigned / centers, centers found, when assigned / regions, regions rest in a rippling assign / starts, starts made, as assigned / distill, distill days, as assigned / trains, trains treat you as assigned / characters, characters made a mentioned assign / interior, interior to and the zoo of assigns / simple, simple to a mental equate of assigns / endocrine, endocrine challenged as the heart beat's assigned / lobe, lobe lifted as assigned / pituitary, pituitary made an assigned pair / pinch, pinch your real rates of an assign / detail, detail of the dealings metatronic to an adamant assign.

CHAPTER TEN

Evaporates, evaporates well, as assigned / provocative, provocative trails into the assigned / health, health made a wealthy wages unto an assigns / ingest, ingest a swllowed through an assign / evaporative, evaporative trues by assign / protective, protective paces assigned / basic, basic believing as assigned / response, response to the greeted assign / nadis, nadis established between two believers assigned / products, products paged into a nestled assign / reconnect, reconnect meant to wreck an assign / rest, rest daily to the assigns / symphonic, symphonic values assigned / produce, produce a perch on the assigns / resolve, resolve spent as assigned / sell, sell daily the assigns / control, control found through assigns / prophets, prophets pace as assigned / cells, cells dare to assign / numbers, numbers kneel as assigned / case, case found for the declaration of ana assign / dreamed, dreamed to of your living assigns / originate, originate near the assigns / organize, organize daily assigns / proteins, proteins purchased as assigned / gaze, gaze into an assign / grape, grape blue assigns / gap, gap paged as assigned / protection, protection comes too, assigned / pound, pound past the gates of assignments / trill, trill well with the assigned / feel, feel blessed as assigned / orchestral, orchestral creations assigned / whisper, whisper past the patented assign / whisper, whisper of the ways called assign / want, want a dearest assign / rescue, rescue venued through the heart central, as assigned / functions, functions featured as assigned / live, live to be, assigned / whisper, whisper of the weekly assigned / want, watn to be, assigned / rescue, rescue met through a mentioned assign / functions, functions find an assign / live, live as led to the assigned / lights, lights of the listened too, assigns / listen, listen to a leading assigns / motions, motions and the mused assigns of love / forgone, forgone features of the assigne / forget, forget infused with a forgotten rate of love as assigned / forgive, forgive a fallen assign / mentioned, mentioned as miraculous the healed assigns / maps, maps paced to a corner assigned / found, found a fellow assign / fruit, fruit felt inside the assigned / join, join a kneeling assign / fits, fits find fellow assigns / flourish, flourish as encouraged dear to assigns / paints, paints employ a focused assign / ranks, ranks read of these assigns / fastens, fastens daily at the assigned / weeps, weeps and whistles for ana assign / weds, weds a dearest assign / shaft, shaft featured in an article meant for a subtle assign / nuts, nuts about days assigned.

CHAPTER ELEVEN

Overt, overt rays of the assigned / gesture, gesture amazes you through an assign / screws, crews dote at the assigned / bolts, bolts blaze up an assign / becomes, becomes won to assigns / love, love led, assigns / angels, angels central to the rest assigned / lightening, lightening found in the hearts assigned / illuminate, illuminate nearly the assigned / fascinate, fasciante found iwth the assigned / arc-angelic, arc-angelic portend fo the finished assign / portion, portion paved as assigned / part, part touched as assigned / touch, touch the earth through assigns / heaven, heaven fed to an assign / heavenward, heavenward gazed our assign / ceiling, ceiling spent on assigns / Sistine, Sistine spills to an assign / heavenly, heavenly days assigned / heaven's, heaven's spent assign / sword, sword of the purging assign / michael's, michael's amaze meant an assign / gate, gate grew past an old assign / deities, deities due your assign / 720 degrees, 720 degrees dared as assigned / 360 degrees, 360 degrees melted at the assigns / twist, twist ans wills healed as assigned / wings, wings wield ana ssign / fold, folds featured through assigns / twice, twice ways will be assigned / meets, meets as mentioend, in assigns / champions, chamions of the cilling assigns / flights, flights fortunate unto an assign / one, one ways, assigned / meets, meets at mentioned assigns / dreams, dreams dealt with as assigned / home, home to the healing assigns / homes, homes made dear to an assign / homeward, homewrad wander as assigned / rites, rites reached as assigned / dionyssian, dionyssian deals assigne / Isis, Isis revealed, as assigned / proclaims, proclaims dear to an assign / ecstatic, ecstatic to a static forgive of love's assigns / Baroque, Baroque and the billows ascend through an assign / Greek, Greek and the centrals sent to an assign / unctive, unctive of the curing assigns / sculpted, sculpted and the simply assigned / architrave, architrave of the driven assigns / enshrined, enshrined and the simply assigned / dreams, dreams of the dearest assigned / lyrics, lyrics and the listening assigns / confessions, confessions and the franchised assigns / agonies, agonies over as assigned / bliss, bliss lives, as assigned / page, page reached on assigns / scope, acope of the featured assigns / enthroned, enthroned allow of the listened too, assigns / cusp, cusp of the natural assigns / assault, assault said, Only this, as assigned" / announce, announce a simple "assign" / announce, announce again, a simple "assign" / annunicate, annunciate fortunately for the assigned / often, often and the shifted assigns.

CHAPTER TWELVE

Hermes, Hermes and the daring assigns / rites, rites of a ritual assign / encountered, encountered and the countered assigns / friendships, friendships and the featured assigns / functions, functions and the futrue assigns / conjure, conjure and the created assigns / ethereal, ethereal and the thrilling assigns / hermetic, hermetic mending and the blending assigns / eternal, eternal and the featured assigns / trines, trines sung "as assigned" / times, times and the temples assigned / anothers, anothers mothers assigned / climate, climate clears as assigned / furious, furious foes assigned / forgive, forgive seventy as assigned / forged, forged allow of the assigned / conclude, conclude concurrent to an assign / message, message made real to the exposed assigns / arched, arched and the starches assigned / across, across a venue as assigned / heavens, heavens held reckless now revealed to an assign / shapes, shapes of the castles draped in a healing assign / angelic, angelic meetings of these assigns / hums, hums to a magnet assigned / sentiments, sentiments found, as assigned / expressed, expressed of late, assigns / Templar, Templar connected as assigne / examples, examples of the samples assigned / lessons, lessons infused as assigned / listened, listened to daily, as assigned / decry, decry defied less, as assigned / denounced, denounce renounced at assigns / deify, deify due an assign / erotic, erotic rue found assigned / cupid, cupid cued as assigned / embody, embody an our assigned / simple, simple ot a structure red, assigned / instruct, instruct sounded as assigned / simulate, simulate the stimulate assigned / icons, icons measured assigned / cartouche, cartouche touched as assigned / winged, winged weddings assigned / project, project preach about in assigns / protected, protected regally through assigns / flown, flown to a fleet of assigns / flying, flying filled as assigned / cultures, cultures met at assigns / gravitate, gravitate rates as assigned / fragmented, fragmented done through assigns / museo, museo made an assign / Olympia, Olympia dared too, assigns / details, details scaled through assigns / functions, functions failproof assigns / glass, glass of the greeted assigns / induced, induced to revenues of assign / ecstasy, ecsttasy met at assigns / ecstatic, ecstatic woo through assigns / message, message dealt as assigned / worn, worn through an assign / heralds, heralds done and assigned / prototypes, prototypes fused at assigns / Mercury, Mercury melts in assigns / hermetica, hermetica bets on assigns / gestures, gestures given too, assigns.

CHAPTER THIRTEEN

Members, members amused by assigns / exhale, exhale felt through an assign / permission, permission to be held, as assigned / orders, orders done and the friendly won, assigned / teachers, teachers travel into our hearing assigns / pupils, pupils deal in a threshold assigned / reserves, reserves found and felt through an assign meant / initiations, initiations finished at the heartelt assigns / personal, personal pleasures assigned now / permitted, permitted intakes of these assigned / connected, connected and inflected as assigned / knowledge, knowledge of the college of light has assigned you the lame and the love / transacted, transacted respected connected assigns / translated, translated examples of the examined rates assigned / pledged, pledged as a sampled example of assign / permission, permission fulfilled through assigns sent / accomplish, accomplish a rational example of assigns / satisfy, satidy found as assigned / spirits, spirits lifted through assigns sent / gone, gone to a good assign / physical, physical in mint apply to a condition freed assign / immortality, immortality centered at thee, the assign / ultimate, ultimate measures assigned now / humanity, humanikty hues and your woos assigned, love / available, available days of the measures assigned / sensitive, sensitive to selections now assigned / primordial, primoridal to the measures assigned / light, light led and the heart bled for the fortuantely assigned / birth, birth of the beauty now assigned / immortal, immortal made, as assigned / adrogynous, andorgynous kneels as assigned / Christed, Christed apply reads "as assigned" / choir, choir of the cubicle assigned / powers, powers palaced as assigned / seals, seals sutured at assigned / self, self of the features now assigned / order, order dealt with at 7:13 p.m.each day, now thou the assigned Alpha Mother / foundations, foundations found, as assigned throughout our measure of the land, loved / practical, practical to a recall of all I have loved, as located, as assigned / elements, elements met at the heartelines ascendant assign / Luxor, Luxor led to a healing assign / potency, potency made yours through a healing assign / powers, powers placed at the gemstoned align of a ruby red assign / intelligences, intelligences sent for through a yellow assign / monastic, monastic meetings regained through a healing assigns / splits, splits over and the dues paid unto an assign / healed, healed and mealed forth as an assign sent / created, created as chosen too, an assign / one, one won to an assign / reunions, reunions coming to an assign / founded, founded funded assigned / roots, roots of the natural assigns / races, races reach you assigned / five, five days, as assigned / days, days due an healing assign threed / seven, seven days aquamarine to a green explain of the lotions blend, as assigned / rays, rays red blue and green through a yellow hope for the futures violet blaze as assigned / ways, ways to see how, as assigned / meet, meet her here, as assigned / evolved, evolved unto these assigns / rates, rates reach for the future's assigns / paces, paces placed at 716 edges believed in as assigned / pledges, pledges made unto the assigned / durations, durations dealt through, as assigned / times, times tell of our healed assigns.

THE AT-HOME-MENTS
LEVEL 50

CHAPTER ONE

Strong, strong moves toward a lasting home, love's / reward, reward daily dealt with as assigned / growth, growth met as assigned / observant, observant and attendant too, as assigned / call, call for the followed friend, as assigned / sudden, sudden to detailas assigned / tremendous, tremendous mention of the healing friends now assigned / space, space central to a regal assign / nonexistence, non-existence spent in a hurtling intent called precisely intended to be, / earthly, home / began, began to mention you, daily, as home / energy, energy made the shift for your homeward journey to love / logos, logos appear nationally so naturally enjoy emply ascend lightly home to love / array, array and the homes won through love / vastness, vastness placed lightly near to love's home / wisdom, wisdom won through a thrilling assign for God, a throne, home / enormous, enormous measures of the mentioning love forward, home / radar, radar retailed as assigned at home / process, process plays through your assignation for home / watage, wattage woos your homeward glances for love / short, short to a shilling spent for the places placed homeward, still / display, display a daily disguise less and open up to love's home / claim, claim your heart as home to love / distinguished, distinguished, as written, to a homeward stance for love / credited, credited for the fortunately again, home / boast, boast only of love as home / regard, regard found as founded for love, the home / world, world ways homeward bound / hold, hold unto the living home / latent, latent and the word now is, love / aligned, aligned deeply in the creation of love as home / invariably, invariably blessed as the recreated creation of homeward love / course, courses concurred to as love, homeward, still / upstream, upstream and the gleaming stopped at homeward love / grain, grain and the strain done as prepared for at home / parallel, parallel finished and the mention is found at home / behavior, behavior veiled less as home / major, major to a mention homeward still / freedom, freedom found lightly throughout a town failproof as home / molecule, molecule of the mentioned appearance as home / security, security established as earth bursts with "home" / breakthrough, breakthrough made as a voice is found for eternally "home" still / voice, voice allowed and heard as said "home" / commonplace, commonplace apply for an assigned stratus of home / penetrating, penetrating pairs of allowance as home / phase, phase fused as home / destiny, destiny deals in only, home / ultimate, ultimate made real through a true home / theoretical, theoretical explain of the penetrating stretch called homeward / devoted, devoted details of the homeward sails of love / ship, ship sent and known by the set of her sails for home / day, day of delivery unto the homeward steps / relief, relief registers as homeward we wing / riddled, riddle and fiddle with only as home / bang, bang of the biggest kind allowed them as home / polarity, polarity switches to ahomeward spill / movie, movie made through a mention of home / collapse, collapse ends at home / prop, prop held for home / permanent, permanent extents won through "home" / fully, fully occupied as the willling h, home / dynamic, dynamic allow of the details h-o-m-e / like, like you, lightly, assigned here at home / urge, urge to be assigned to home.

CHAPTER TWO

Simple, simple to a nimble home / squeak, squaek healed as appealed to home / temporary, temporary abandon has done a miraculous treat for thy home / reach, reach for the hu-man pill, home / relying, relying in the relaying of home / relay, a relay found too, home / doctrine, doctrine detailed by, home / view, view of the valleys of home / authority, authority found fo rthe feautres of home, lights / impotency, impotency over too, and allowed a listening love at home / frustration, frustrations ended at home / psychic, psychic said, "hear, home" / mosaic, mosaic mending and the forged rates of temples spent on home / charity, charity succeeds at your home / import, import sorted for at home / export, export pledged as your home / discover, discover a detail for thee, home / land, land bought for home / early, early lots for homeward still / crossed, crossed allow found for the fortunes sent through home / sun, sun sent now to thy home / rising, rising in allowance of the home / splendor, splendor due a pssage homeward / flat, flat to a biographic geometry called essentially home / space, space made for the homes reached here / shadow, shadow sited forgive for the lessons of home / steamed, steamed teas home / bend, bend boothed by home / outskirt, outskirt skirted by delivery to a venue called "home" / town, town told of the likes of you, home / loop, loop made to the central home / capital, capital applies too, as home / conqueror, conqueror sent, home / architecture, architecture trued as home / sprung, sprung to a speaking of "home" / soil, soil dealt with through love of the home / river, river red with a valley home / amazing, amazing mention of the transition to "home" / miles, miles and the smiles spent at home / habitation, habitation of the tooling home / sticks, sticks lashed to make a home / grass, grass grew to gather home / nest, nest of the nestle dearest too, home / aquatic, aquatic woo fo the wisdom, "home" / cling, cling to a central loop home / shore, shore shed for only a home / anchored, anchored nearly at home / distance, distance driven for, home / junk, junk past and now, homeward still / ridge, ridge driven allowance for the features assigned as then home / masonry, masonry meets and then these are assigned too, as home / palace, palace and the placements sent forth too, assigns, home / temple, temple of the simply assigned as dear, home / gorgeous, gorgeous to the values assigned then as home / vertical, vertical leaps made as assigned to your home / palpable, palpable tables of homeward intent / breast, breast bred as details of home / limb, limbs live around you as homeward / physical, physical to a critical escape through our home / canal, canal of the feautured ascent to our home / flash, flash past and then find a home / spire, spire spent on assigned homes / light, light clearly donnected to a column home / anonymity, anonymity assigned to your strolling, h-o-m-e.

CHAPTER THREE

International, international explore has regained her allure thorugh your home work / brief, brief into relief of the lessened explain of home / square, square to a registered home / varied, varied release of the lessens home / topography, topography dared for the squarest arise into home / explore, explore the passions fo home /

waterfall, waterfall ways find a home / jungle, jungles hoined in as home / district, district dared too, as home / collection, collections of the rainbow's shoes and an arcing lean into love brought home / 1mist, mist of the mentioned "home" / future, future found through a throne, home / indigenous, indigenous to a nature brought home / exotic, exotic erotic red floral homes / flourish, flourish hibiscus blue unto love, homeward / orchid, orchids stood in our deep rooted plays of home / peninsula, peninsula built through to home / rare, rare to a pinnacle of home / bloom, bloom applied for at home / opium, opium spent on a home-less blend / remote, remote retail of the poppy state home / roam, roam courageously toward home / hear, hear of the healing come, home / herd, herd found, home / trunk, trunk arranged for and home / immense, immense unto pleasures of home / outside, outside seated at home / albino, albino fished and the stead found as home / actual, actual into factual apply for the living home / divinity, divinity due a newsworthy home / property, property bought there as home / special, special deals made as home / tigers, tigers embark to the bear-est release of home / Himalayan, Himalayan hello the homeward grace / valley, a valley pokhara deep to embued views glacier rich with home / analogous, analogous too and the Nepalese movement asian deep into love's home / Egypt, Egypt rents your home / notable, notable dues home / terrain, terrain remains home / tranquil, tranquil earth will arise home / nestled, nestled in the resting place called home / exile, exile over and due, a home / fertile, fertile into features of home / verdant, verdant into revamps of home / lush, lush lives our thriving homes / cherish, cherish daily your home / scale, scale of the mentioned templs, hu-man, home / evening, evening spent on a home / length, length due unto homes / chain, chain broken mends as a home / exhilirating, exhilirating reunion as a home / abundance, abundance baked into home / noble, noble pathways home / patch, patch maxed as home / laboriously due a home / acre, acre made ahome / toss, toss tooled as home / peasant, peasant pays as home / field, field found white blue unto home / symbol, symbol purged as Everest blue unto home / revolution, revolution made a watery home / defiant, defiant into daring at home / drain, drain done and now, home / elephant, elephant views of our natural rest at home.

CHAPTER FOUR

Accumulation, accumulation cleared at a residual home / monsoon, monsoon viewed and the clearances homeward bound-less / vast, vast unto an array of fine homes / wealth, wealth dearest home / tumbled, tumbled across planes of home / aspiration, aspiration rested at home / sustenance, sustenance found seraphic blue unto eyes of loving, home / ultimately, ultimately we meet at home / cease, cease to file lessens as home / coital, coital views westibule deep into lovely homes / upstream, upstream dreams of a rested home / timber, timber tiled through a home / waterway, waterway woos and a resonant home / speculate, speculate lately of home / drastic, drastic details made for home / picturesque, picturesque venues for home / source, source supplied then at home / oxide, oxide suggested as clarifying "home" / luck, luck led us home / attract, attract an abundance said to be "home" / portable,

portable penchants for home / bright, bright in her beauty, an estate called "home" / spurring, spurring done and the wonder is "home" / relieving, relieving releasing of home / reservoirs, reservoirs resealed as home / method, method of the magically, home / revival, revival views us as home / silk, silk rays lusterous as home / essential, essential to a mental freeing "home" / sector, sector spelled h-o-m-e / proximity, proximity dearest is "home" / manifestation, manifestation found us at home / village, village wound us at home / luxury, luxury nears us as home / base, base betrayed less as home / port, port of the piroutte at home / province, province paved in a lesson called home / gem, gem told "home" / rubies, rubies reached through a home / natural, natural nestles into a home / impenetrable, impenetrable stated "home" well / cart, cart pushed past is home / limestone, limestone leaping past home / protection, protection dearest is home / romantic, romantic recovery of home / scenery, scenery scent too, is, home / clear, clear of the creatures less than home / palm, palm pays "home" / stretch, stretch into resealing "home" / pure, pure is the passion for home / dazzle, dazzle daily with "home" / dream, dream of the scheming less, home / scheme, scheme set for us, home / isolated, isolated allowance of home / degree, degree found is home / thriving, thriving allowance of home / archaeologist, archaeologist dearest is home / empire, empire empirically home / ancient, ancient in details of home / dynasty, dynasty due a revealing hello from home / planets, planets merge in a relevance for home / flames, flames of pleasure meet in a lesson of home / greetings, greetings sent through a thrown won home / hunger, hunger blown to the throne of fulfilled homes

CHAPTER FIVE

Harbor, harbor retailed as home / prosperity, prosperity appears in our home / humid, humid apply to a home / island, island led thrilling as home / haven, haven made at home / secluded, secluded and retired to as home / rainfall, rainfall equivalent to home / intricate, intricate by nature then as home / vine, vine viewed as home / frolic, frolic fused at our home / parakeet, parakeet sweetest is home / splash, splash due our living home / swing, winning is swinging at home / fresh, fresh details of home / species, species spent for at home / legendary, legendary daily at home / artery, artery cut thorugh at home / seascape, seascape mounted as home / cresecent, crescent spent through our home / sand, sand days due us at home / linked, linked at eternal-ness of home / intrepid, intrepid remember of home / horizons, horizons hinted of home / peaks, peaks placed in our home / enacted, enacted values of home / golden, golden rays made our home / array, array found of home jovially, jovially convicted of home / gaily, gaily due us a home / shimmering, shimmering earth ships of home / leap, leap into centrally, home / ships, ships past and home / summon, summon a splendor Santa Domingo deep and at home / tolerance spent in our home / peripheral, peripheral focus on the matters at home? / expedition, expedition sent for at home / emerge, emerge victourious at home / aptitude, aptitude for the treaties of home / scholar, scholar sent lvoely to home / cradle, cradled mystery as history of home / mystery, mystery made beautiful at home / fat, fate gone too, at home / plateau, plateau reached here at home / influence, influence spent through our home / culmination, culmination cured now at home / splendor, splendor due you at home / hyacinths, hyacinths match me at home / pole, a pole paced me to home / hug, hugs met me at home / merit, merit given at home / scripts, scripts elastic at home / sculpture, sculptures truest at home / treaties, treatis done now at home / alliance, alliance levels at home / spread, spread done now at home / cosmopolitan, cosmopolitaness found there at home / neighboring, neighboring influence at home / prosperous, prosperous raises at home / grazing, grazing elected at home / rural, rural employ of the voyager at home / sketch, sketch due our home / common, common queries about then, our home / provide, provide daily views of home / foreign, forge a wave of foreign homes / lessons, lessons leap to the test of home.

CHAPTER SIX

Homes, homes made, loved / plans, plans laid, home / friends, friends found, home / examples, examples examined, home / samples, samples saddled at home / deals, deals due your home / sanctions, sanctions queried at home / sanctuaries, sanctuaries found then, at home / kins, kins equipped now as home / kindles, kindles dealt the flames now of home / candles, candles melt us at home / clues, clues covered with "home" / clans, clans published at home / cumberland, cumberland quieries of home / laugh, laugh duly at home / livelihood, livelihood focused at home / domestic, domestic saze at home / classic, classic cues at home / graceful, graceful rays at home / seclusion, seclusion sought found home / festival, festival held for your home / intertwine, intertwine released to at home / minority, monastery mentioned as home / leader, leader listens to "home" / desire, desire dealt with at home / fervent, fervent mentions fo home / elaborate, elaborate devices of home / official, official mentions of "home" / technique, technique given too, home / spectacular, spectacular mentions of "home" / absolute, absolute repute of home / precarious, precarious gone too,a t home / zone, zone opens too as home / nomadic, nomadic due comes too, home / wandering, wandering ways mended at home / obscure, obscure venues found, home / amber, amber beaded homes / ceremony, ceremony mentioned is home / honor, honor daily your home / drag, drag less, home / bamboo, bamboo bays of home / piece, piece cut too, home / beads, beads balanced at home / tasssel, tassels off then to home / feather, feather feeds of home / ornamentation, ornamentation worn through home / martial, martial apply too at home / bountiful, bountiful beauty of our home / ritual, ritual reach for is gained through our status at home / pearl, pearl dues paid through our homes / independence, independence stressed through your homes / artisan, artisan central to our home / glazed, glazed amplify of our home / ceramic, ceramic centrally home / captive, captive done too, home / pervasive, pervasive values of our home / brillaint, brilliant and shineing too, at home / elaborate, elaborate mentioning of home / trim, trim to a simple home / success, success to a suggested home / legendary, legendary homes of love / trim, trim days paid for thorugh home / royal, royal leys listening to "home" / nucleus, nucleus built here is home.

CHAPTER SEVEN:

ancestor, ancestor meant too, is home / network, network done through your home / identity, identity found here at home / breeze, breeze past a venue for home / tolerance, tolerance rated as home / friction, friction of you at home / monarch, monarch mentioned is home / trance, trance done, now, then, home / backdrop, backdrop as listed is home / gilded, gilded allowance of betrayal forgotten at home / rush, rush past, home / single, single sentinels of home / bell, bell bathed in our homes / justly, justly due now, a home / benevolent, benevolent venues of home / paternal, paternal plenty of home / minded, minded less, home / attire, attire worn is home / virtually, virtually deluged with "home" / enlightened, enlightened now then home / efforts, efforts pleased with are home / typical, typical treatment at home / project, projects finished are home / throne, throne set for home / unique, unique nest built now at home / humble, humble in feelings of love, home style / primitive, primitive in the relays to home / sport, sport sent of ris home / inscription, inscription reads to you, home / solace, solace meant for is home / sense, sense of the seated at home / suty, suty dealt with is home / lightness, lightness led through our home / infinite, infinite to features of home / combines, combines paths of home / response, response reads of home / sudden, sudden flight found to your "true" home / poignant, poignant good-bye then to home / tale, tale told is well then to home / family, fmaily folds in to home 41company, company given to home / wayward, wayward allow then of home / myth, myth struck less of home / engaging, engaging allowance of home / authentic, authentic appearances of home / interest, interest drawn too is home / kaleidoscopes, kaleidoscopes view of us is colorful to home / thunder, thunder dearing to home / lightening, lightening clearing our home / flavor, flavor of the savor for our home / thriller, thriller held for our home lurid, lurid stories of home / camera, camera feautured at home / chameleon, chameleon mentioned at home / champion, champions found now at home / division, division finished at home / wallop, wallop paid through your home / compassion, compassion finds you at home / knack, knack for the praying at home / scrambled, acrambled mentions of home / dialogue, dialogue dearest is home / suspense, suspense bent unto home / fascinating, fascinating features of home / aspect, aspect forgotten at home / logs, logs laid across the home plates of love.

CHAPTER EIGHT

Fflare, flare for the physical at home / journey, journey to another state for pleasure at home / asix, asix spun to a sealing, home / revolves, revovles due at the tenants of home / broad, broad bets into love of your home / candles, candles burning at home / perform, perform art here at home / tears, tears over feared at home / strange, strange to a strangle here at home / image, image placed then at home / conceive, conceive of only, love, at home / temptation, temptation done through our homes / constellations, constellations value is home / resist, resist has gone too, and home / intonation, intonation registered is love here at home / insanity, insanity done, crew, of home / escape, escape planned for your home / sobriety, sobriety records your home / hatch, hatch opens at home / stall, stall over at home / kneel, kneeling ofund at home / connection, connection mounted at home / wrath, wrath done now at home / threshold, threshold pushing to home / shelter, shelter wedded at home / yearning, yearning nestles at home / vision, vision valued at home / rather, rather, be, home / cease, cease to lie, home / stallion, stallion paged, home / carve, carve creates home / nocturne, nocturne acknowledged through our homes / bare, bare through our homes / handles, handles pages now as home / crumbs, crumbs curly in homes / dawn, dawn deals coming home / untangle, untangle knotted at home / lifetime, lifetimes pledged now at home / wild, wild about you at home / crack, crack open caving at home / midnight, midnight found her at home / moon, moon dues our venues at home / full, full to a measure at home / field, field fo the fickle less at home / distraction, distraction due us at home / immobile, immobile over at home / ruins, ruins reached past at home / sultry, sultry daily at home / wilderness, wilderness listens at home / howling, howling finished at home / fog, fog fed a fickle one home / blessed, blessed in the rocking at home / cradle, cradle due a dumping at home / lonely, lonely overthrown at home / mock, mock mentioned at home / patient, patient to planning at home / accolade, accolade shaded as home / hysteria, hysteria over at home / smoothest, smoothest spun, homeward now / dust, dust dealt sparkling galactics to home / star, star plays at home / falling, falling gazes to home / loving, loving is the giving homeward / lifting, lifting and the giving homeward.

CHAPTER NINE

Solace, solace meant for eternally homeward advancement / prevail, prevail allowed you as you lead homeward still / scent, scent of the featured mana spent and owned throughout our zones electrically home / confidence, confidence sealed at the listened elective called home / burst, burst of enthuse and th emuse meant for you becoming home / breathe, breathe a fill of the crying explode called perfectly amused with, home / arranged, arranged lightly at home / rainbow, rainbow's blue oblivion has found a home within, you / silent, silent n my mission of loving remain at the heart of the portion called precisely, home / omission, omissions over and the duration is held at precipice set at home / passion, passion met lightly at home / surrender, surrender blends now at home / pack, a pack paced unto home / disguise, disguise due me has gone into love for the homeward glance / flow, flows flew into a spiritual hurricane to remember how we loved our home / vanity, vanity over and the funds regained through "home" / trade, trade heer well into home / planet, planet of the simply mended home / optimistic, optimistic again for our home / regenerating, regenerating occuring within our homeward state / whisper, whisper about her, electrically, home / certified, certified as simply, as said, too "home" / rhythm, rhythm around us is mentioned lightly as love set for home / sky, sky of the daily at home's / sanctuary, sanctuary amazzed witho us at home / humming, humming given aliving home / travel, travel to the point released at as home / hypnotist, hypnotist sent for at home / devotion, devotion daring your hurried stand at home / incident, incident central to the portals resplendent at home /

CHAPTER TEN

Pebbles, pebbles anllowed us a strewn state of homes / luxury, luxury forgiven and the features at home / crown, crown allowed us at home / woven, woven winnings at home / motion, motion of the mentioned "at home" / lighted, lighted employ of love / sleep, sleep allows us our home / lives, lvies inwardly home / roar, roar and the hearing of home / determine, determine allowed us a flavor of love at home / fortune, fortune and the feelings alll made at home / raft, raft allowed us at home / lotus, lotus and the lightest at home / petal, petal of the shrillings blooming at home / nectar, nectar nestles into the crevices of you at home in bloom / pond, pond paced around and dear as at home / savored, savored electrically the allowances of love is, home / twilight, twilight seated at home / mend, mend applies too, to home / squirmed, squirmed less and found more at home / chamber, chambers chilled with, at homes / escorted, escorted and seated at home / twinkle, twinkle lightly little home / ripple, ripple mentioned and the dimensions healing at home / necklace, necklace of stars and the happy stratus earth at home / pattern, pattern pledged to the allow of a loving home / rose, rose days avowed as at home / companion, companion paced us home / realm, realm of the reaching, home / improve, improve rates of home / delight, delight dates us at home / prime, prime the purchase of home / view, view allowed us, homeward still, at love / rave, rave about us, lightly, at home / bay, bay views at home / tower, tower treats at home / link, link listened for at home / always, always mentioned, at home, our love / whirl, whirl past and through us at home / crossroads, crossroads light with love for thee, home / fade, fade into shadows lessen at homeward love /

answer, answer and the mentioned allowance at home / fabulous, fabulous at the featured imply too and loved living answered at home / million, million and the mentioned at home / sympathetic, sympathetic allowance at home / mission, missions mentioned at home / ambition, ambition allowed us at home / respect, respect of the rewards at home / amusement, amusement allowed for the meant states at home / window, window whistled into a lady's metal at home / lover, lover of the listened to at home / luscious, luscious and the home surge at lviing allowance of lights / fathom, fathom and the featured stages of home / immune, immune and the meanings at home / tide, tide and the tools waged at home / moment, moment at the spaces allowed at home / resolution, resolution and the listened too, at home / civilian, civilian and the sent for at home / fragrance, fragrance and the followed allowance at home / inside, inside us and wellest at home / bounty, bounty is beautiful at home / want, want and the winning us home / grow, grow grew unto a homeward wave / closer, closer and the clarity to allow us a home / another, another mentioned into a home / ingredient, ingredients allowed us a home / miracle, mriacle at the mention of home / heart, heart and the heeded at home / belong, belong bleeds throughout our homes / arise, arise lightly to your home planes / clever, clever and the clinches over at home / copper, copper outed at home / tremble, tremble nimbly and the preciousness at home / loving, loving ways of home / homeward, homeward still in love.

track, track found through the clearings of home / hospital, hospital paged as home / lake, lake legendary for the futuristic's homes / distribution, distribution is due our living home / fort, fort felt fondly at home / tourist, tourist sorts at home / fame, fame found lightly at home / inn, inn built at the waters wedge of home / hall, hall electric and the settled into, home / huddle, huddle intoyour home / construct, construct and the restruck employment of love / barrel, barrels blazed with love for thee at home / again, again I say, love is, home / eagles, eagles race past your new home in love / weight, weight off and the whistled begins of love / historic, historic and spatial into love's homes / station, station of the worn in too, love is, home / springs, springs paged then as home / trout, trout treated for home / power, power pages us home / country, country listed then, home / clubs, clubs focus is into our home / tune, tune into our home.

CHAPTER ELEVEN
Plain, plain deals made then at home / welcome, welcome us lightly, home / comfort, comfort of the features at home / continental, continental allowances of love from this, homeward stall / stay, stay through the finished homes / think, think less and know more thoroughly at your home / wash, wash again into home / theater, theater of the simply "at home" / desire, desire a daily, home] / market, markets mentioned at home / harmony, harmony healed us at home / lube, lube off and thegiving is more, eternally, at home / deep, deep in the pockets of home / economy, economy pays for our homes / inside, inside suggested as home / antique, antiques triple at home / art, art fades into home / lodge, lodge listens at home / bridges, bridges built past our home / dominion, dominions touched daily at home / famous, famous for feathers golden still at home / retirement, retirement met you at love for your home / mint, mint shaped love for the jade streets of home / before, before this and loved lightly at home / farm, farm again, at home / municipal, municpal mentions of home / self, self said, "home" / soar, sort your sore into soaring home / reason, reason found for the healing at home / mood, modod mentioned is lifting too, home / alert, alert listening of home / scale, scale paid is "home's" / ramp, ramp built past your home / between, between and the treaty of home / radio, radio us lightly of home / soft, soft seats in home" / smooth, smooth enough to sail by, ses of love's home / enough, enough spent and the said for "home" / motions, motions made to mention again, "home" / rays, rays rest at the movements of home / factory, factory worked at home / awake, awaken the whistling cutting of truest home / oyster, oyster pulled surrender too, home / surrendered, surrendered lgihtly then at home / forever, forever found us at home / cracker, cracker crewed us to home / interstate, interstate pages of home this high way / smart, smart allowance too, home / parlor, parlors pewed in "home" / flap, flap fastened to home / venture, venture forth to find this "at home" / mild, mild disturb and the verb is our home / distinction, distinction dared in our homes / hickory, hickory sweet eruptives of home / shower, shower nearest us, home / honey, honey held into home / holiday, holiday due us at home / apple, apples taste of love is at home hear / galleries, galleires

paged through as home / sometimes, sometimes I am seated as at home / spin, spin met at homeward love / invitation, invitation voicing us, home / caravan, caravan meant for the stars at home / troop, troop 59 and counting one minute to home.

CHAPTER TWELVE
Blind, blind to a bliser, find the sister at home / indication, indication has meant his "home" / remind, remind me that we last at home / ounce, ounce for the bouncing at home / costume, costume cuties at homes / party, party placed at home / pantry, pantry paced thorugh our home / ridge, ridges ridden as home / aware, aawre of the rewards of home / slippery, slippery electrics of home / agency, agency paged into home / shove, shove left us at home granite, granite grooves meet electrically at home / marina, marina mentioned at home / traffic, traffic tools past your home / bonus, bonus building at home / walk, walk daily too, home / dark, dark left us at home / accessory, accessory meant for us at home / population, popoulation lends us a simple home / anchor, anchor met us at home / program, programs punched in say "home" / willow, willow wield us at home / tree, trees daily planted at home / am, am, yes, at home / needle, needle us at home then, less / sample, sample spent on love at home / way, way to wield us at home / vain, vain less and happy more at home / wicker, wicker winters at home / touch, tocuuh us lightly, at home / park, park now nearly at home / unqiue, unique employ of the stretch called lightly, "home" / clay, clay blue with home / straw, straw powers paid as home / sunshine, sunshine straits lift too, home shines / available, available again as at home / piedmont, piedmont mentioned dearly, home / bread, bread bought and found here in the mana stones of home / solid, solid stratus made our home / necessity, necessity kneels us at home / noise, noise placed us at home / explode, explode details your exploring nature of love at home / express, express a preference for love in the home / seal, seal set us at home / alright, alright spent in only, home / feature, features found us at home / bring, bring another too, home / indian, indian daze at home / true, true allow of then a home / truce, truce reached as rang in for your home / eternity, eternity spent electrically at home / rocket, rocket through a nearness of home / year, year spent has been alone neatly home / solitude, solitude sought found near us at home / betray, betray is done, home / honest, honest will be at home / riddles, riddles dance at home / cider, cider spent on the drinking at home / souvenirs, souvenirs spilling at homemystery left us is who? home / alley, alley built for the journey spells home / wow, wow is, home, huna, still / New York, New York find features of home in retreat / let us, let us become your homeward call to love / www. home, www. home is the web for love.

CHAPTER THIRTEEN
Fashion, fashion of the fusing allow for a mentioned home / ark, ark parked at home / arcs, arcs spent in allowance of love at their home / culture, culture spun into home / style, style staged is home / still. still enough to be at home / scenes, scenes bursting at home / beyonds, beyonds play found at home / trump, trump applied too,

at home / lurk, lurk has lurched to a halt now at love for the earth
stage, our home / lace, lace applied for at home / saddle, saddle
meant for your home / lap, lap listens too, to home / lake, lake of
the youthful plunge home / truck, truck set for home / truth, truth
paid through, home / rise, rise, like a listen too, at home / arise,
arise lgihtly too, home / stark, stark in explain of our home / stellar,
stellar darin at home / stealth, stealth made at home / starts, starts
arisne too, home / start, start now, home / fashion, fashion fading
too, home / fashionable, fashionable examples then of home /
neuron, nueronic meetings made, home / sun, sun sets at home
/ cheat, cheats over and the done too, home / chipped, chipped
less and shipped more too, home / material, material mentioned is
home / notice, notice given at home / growth, growth grew through
our home / live, live nearly at home / libel, libel over and the dues
paid at home / label, labels burst thorugh at home / left, left, hear,
at home / lasting, lasting imply for the impressions of home / new,
newest alertness of home / now, now days at home / often, often
features are mentioned as home / over, over days at home / all, all
ways at home / agree, agree to be at home, this earth / can, can be
held for an annual lease of home / see, see daily, a home / approve,
approved now for home / strung, strugn into simply a route freed
as home / fright, fright over, dive in, home / dive, dive into your
home / dove, dove dearest, nearest, home / zion, zion found in a
sound calling me home / Zen, Zen planes of home a diatom / sent,
sent for at home / scents, scents of the simly "home" / years, years
allowed us at home / yellow, ywlloe whistling of home / captive,
captive over and the dues paid are home / capture, capture spilling
into home / scope, scope of the century of love then at home /
inertia, inertia due end at home / international, international privy
too, home / coward, coward outed at homes filled with the lion of
love, Christos blends, lightly / lips, lips speak the name, Metatron,
home / spun, spun to a reasonable home.

THE HUMAN-MENTS
LEVEL 51

CHAPTER ONE

Guarantee, guarantee the human extrude and the relatives allowed entrance to love / inside, inside into reality of the lessons hu-man / checks, checks paid for humanity / counts, coutns about us, humanity / breath, breaths bade listen, humanity / durable, durable at ascendants of humanity / keeping, keeping kept dry in the arcs of home lightly human / dry, dry days dealt with lightly hu-man / moist, moist to the news of missions still at the heart humanly intact / clasp, clasp a dearest well near the mission bells of human contact / classes, classes begun for the featured democratic humans / farms, farms fed the lightly erratic electric humnas / notes, notes deal in listening electric and the legislation passed to be, hu-man / drama, drama over and the gig has detached to passing allowance of the lightest humanity / helicical, helicical allowance and the preference for the reference to softer sheers, hu-manly comforted / large, large ledgers kept for the balances human / banks, banks red with the listing streets human / rivers, rivers registerd and human / travels, travels come into my touring ways human / glimpse, glimpses given unto a human blaze / untouched, untouched and unchallenge as arranged lightly, human / wilds, wilds registered for legibly human / games, games made and the economics challenged less through humanity's blessing / photos, photos passed and retouched along the human highway / secretive, s. ecretive suggest and the rested hu-mans / classics, classics kept currently hu-man / framing, framing left us street-less to be a truest hu-man / trees, trees gazing at the hu-man rising cut off along the roots electric / treats, treats dared for a managed as listened to hu-manly / traits, traits traipse to the balanced hymn humanity / traipse, traipse to a gift hu-man / decide, decide to be lgihtly hu-man / free, free yourself to see the humanity / outdoors, outdoors dips into the lightest humanity / reply, reply paid to the life gifts human / mails, mails mention implies a hu-man retreat / mistakes, mistakes measured as living hu-mans / catalogs, catalogs cued as hu-man / orders, orders given and taken, a hu-man won / acts, acts paged through humanly / pipes, pipes lifted to the hu-mans / worlds, worlds wedged into an electric allow / whirls, whirls giggles hu-man flight / simply, simply said "hu-man" / blazes, blazes placed across the traces hu-man / changes, changes wrought through the hu-man / challenges, challenges dated and dared for a sha-man / utilities, utilities placed at the ledges hu-man / treaty, treaty of the moment's proclaim human / humans, humans and the meanings Metatronically human / placement, placement and the meaningful human / plentitude, plentitude and the planets spinning human / plenty, plenty and the simply found funded humans / pleasure, pleasure and the suggested humans / facts, facts and the funded humans / latitudes, latitudes and the meaning's human / levels, levels and the listings human / gathering, gathering gains a humanity / freedom, freedom mentioned in humanity / leaping, leaping across the basics of humanity / lettered, lettered and the measured humanity / planting, planting and the pleasured humanity / penchant, penchant and the tethered humanity / student, students and the trickles past humanity.

CHAPTER TWO

Gifted, gifted and lifted sorts unto a hu-man / given, given a gazing hu-man / gaze, gaze past and into a hu-man face / play, play daily at the racing hu-mans / belief, belief blazing too and the lasting hu-mans / billions, billions paged, many answers hu-man / populates, populates stages hu-man / born, born to be hu-man / loads, loads of listening geared at hu-manity's words / loves, loves to be near the humans / children, children whistle at the recognition of the greater plan, hu-man / people, people ignor it, the door through to a living hu-man / generates, generates gates open human-ly late / generation, generation eneraged can gaze humanly / population, population paged to being hu-man / average, average vows arranged for the mentioned hu-mans / Pythagorean, Pythagorean degrees allowed for the expressions exponentially hu-man / analyze, anzlyze first, then burst into being, hu-man / called, called to see, a hu-manity / call, call us here, basically, humanity / exercise, exercise your rising way unto human-ness / important, important to see the beauty of a breathing organism called human / isolate, isolate less and find more, humanity / knot, knot unsettled, settled through a living testament to humanity / known, known for the places human / regard, regard reads human / principle, principle simply, human / rhythm, rhythm resurveys our ressurection to the listening True-man of humanity, Metatron / loved, loved and listened through, metatronic humans / regard, regard set on registered election of the Christian blend with the basically / human fact that we are electric images of the great electrician, the great Oz in us, know the plan human / compelled, compelled to fairies tell of the legend of basically beautiful and happy children, humanly possible / belief, belief has struck me through with a gentle regard for the children struck and the stripes which mend and never diminish unless healed through compassion for a hu-man race that God simply loved, take away the aggression and what do we have a race that is over and a hu-man test passed, love one another, I pray, love one the Other as you have learned to love, even you, you are the hope the power the list the listening gift of the lambs book written in heart everywhere, the gentleness repaired, the tender hearts placed upon the hearth of the belief in man, breathe, know the rhythm., God is the meta-electron around which life whistles, know the song, Father forgiven, Mother held, Sisters married, Brothers well, in the hearken "hu-man" / sense, snese healed, feel hu-manity, now through your hearts suggestion of perfect love / argumentative, argumentative due and the done with, hu-mans rest / forgive, forgive found a lesson at the 70 times 7 and the heart said, a man has found the joining place of love divine and the 64 steps to humanity, perfect, love / height, height spoken for is lovely humanity / aperture, aperture due closure on the pencils sketched in human / analytic, analytic converted to the reverted sakes of the gossip given toss to reveal truthfully, a hu-man / pi, pi perfect to the proportions of the lving human / glyph, glyphs struck into walls to show us living humans / greek, greek shores electtric and the lips placed at the sounding humans / spherical, spherical to a lyrical human / proportion, proportion perfect to a cube elctrically human / irrational, irrational over and the directly human found / require, require a deal human / realize, realize a size led, humanly / philisophic, philisophic to the miracels human / anticipate, anticipate the rates human / Copernican, Copernican creations and the rations built in to the temple hu-man

/ heliocentric, heliocentric occur of the Father's love directly warm to the shing hu-man / individual, individauls dealt with humanly / mystics, mystics accept with a gracious degree born human / laws, laws placed around the giving living human / regarding, regarding yours, human / understood, understood that plenty meant us, human / scientific, scientific requirements to believe in the heaven within, see the spins electrically human / necessity, necessity of the qurks sake to be electron deep in the regard for a souled release and a reality capable fo the stable imply that man is electrically exactly God too, clear through, a transparently perfect humanity, God's plan, basically / priced, priced rites and the rituals sent to a sealing released and a climbing occur directly into the heart of the plan hu-man, God's there and hear, the beeating pulse hu-man / participate, particpation in the rations built into a prefect hu-man / master, master made 3 and plastered throughout are the basic humanities of love, the / template for perfection's gate to awarest allow of breathing love / frank, frank to a feature french with loving proportion Jeffersonian humans / geometry, geometry met us in the tree of living humanity.

CHAPTER THREE

Facilites, facilites offered for the few patient in humanity / immmemorial, immemorial for the healing rewards of love trued in humanity / illusory, illusory over for the vast humanity / prank, prank spouts of humanity / absurd, absurd words of the ingrained humanity / conclude, conclude that food is the view of humanity / constrains, constrains off to food / off, off again and thin to humans tossed / flows, flows past us, rivers, woes and the forgotten forgive of the listening humans / rationally, rationally beside us grew a wilson's few and a creek seeking refuge, wild and wet within humanity / endures, endures a durations of loving insure of the human waves / inquired, inquired of you to lift the views of love, human / visualize, visualize of the rise in sizes human / belief, belief abounds of the sounding humans / doctors, doctors deal with our listening humanity / framing, framing falls off and we are tossed to the windy humans / worlds, worlds collusive and elusive iwth htough of the thrilling humans / engenders, engenders palace taught forgive unto the humans / functions, functions faced as living humans / history, history over and threw the humans strands / torture, torture dealt with too in humans / misapplied, misapplied for and the four who rule the humans / now, now we see the vertical free o f the humans / disguised, disguised less and guided more through a passionate four, the humans / guise, guise gone, living long with humans / light, light led us, humans / through, through our thrusting humanity, life / finish, finish paced through a human / fantastic, fantastic news, done, through humans / amaze, amaze amounts too, a human / process, process placed within a strand human / principle, principle met and kept as hu-man / needs, needs implied for as human / account, account vouches as human / instincts, instincts true as human / correct, correct occurs as human / phase, phases and phrases due a human / conclude, conclude occurs as the human / overpowered, overpowered ours human / visualize, visualize the rises human / treasures, treasures best as humans / mesmerize, mesmerize arises humanly / appendix,

appendix paces humans / acknowledge, acknowledge allowance for the featured humans / life, life leads us humanly / interrogate, interrogate grew to include only thee, the human / medicine, medicine mazes and the gazes human / math, math applies now, the humans / astronomy, astronomy measures our vectors human / classic, classic occupy with the sky cleared humans / geological, geological solve of the facets human / translate, translate dearly, human / hypothesis, hypothesis posed as human / conquers, conquers us nearly, human / period, period placed at a blended human / armana, armana palaced humans / place, place calling "human" / Luxor, Luxor falling, human / galaxy, galaxy dearing, humans / Arcturus, Arcturus places the human hearted equation for love L= Y to the third particle of God, allow us your presence, the humans / presence, presence pictured as human / attend, attend allows us a placement human / loving, loving and the living humans / fields, fields and the fellow humans.

CHAPTER FOUR

Marriage, marriage amazing of spirits human / spirits, spirits pacing our giving humans / historic, historic eventing of the venting human / psychic, psychic allowance, human / message, message written for mission human / redress, redress the address as the fountains human / remains, remains squarely engraved a raving human / story, story told of the Cincinatti Blue entirety of views human / prescient, prescient to a constant, human / plot, plot placing humans / arian, arain waving humans / span spake of the humans / distinct, distinct forgiveness sought for humans / mask, mask allowed off the humans / plat, plat paces our humans / grade, grade given a human / eloquent, eloquent to a resource found human / shamans, shamans mentioned a detachment human / customs, customs sllow you a threshold human / emerge, emerge now electric at a lifting human / leads, leads ledgered then, human / roles, roles paid for, human / active, active raises given the human / hands, hands onto the retinue human / forced, forced appliance of the conveyance human / naturally, naturally, dearest, the humans / cashed, cashed into a theory human / language, language causes the simple humans / hose, hose to the resource humans / conduit, conduit deep in the remit human / conductivity, conductivity leaped to the listings human / cases, cases opened and closed too, human / fires, fires out thorugh the thrice said "human, human, human" / determination, determination dealt with and through the humans / apply, apply for the human estates of love / amplify, amplify planned through as the threatened humans / financing, financing found for the project human / sought, sought a granted allowance for the chalice human / compounded, compounded experiences of the lessons human / abbreviated, abbreviated messages found in the fossils human / fellows, fellows pacing and the tasting human / flame, flame fed for the featured humans / apparel, apparel worn past the faceted humans / same, same days delviery of the detachment human / stains, stains out then, a human / awash, awash in the weekly humans / minutes, minutes mentioned as appearing human / agree, agree to be humanly free / journals, journals archaeologic count for the adjournments human / archaeologic, archaeologic ascendments gone home too, the humans / engage, engage only lightly in the lessons human / faced, faced freedoms human / texts, texts published for the humans / protective, protective resources read of the humans / candidate, candidates placed at the pensioned humanity / frees, frees us, well, the humans / suspense, suspense over, and the dues paid, the humans / animated, animated in challenges faced humanly / solitary, solitary days fed the humans / cubes, cubes codices and the creations human / convoluted, convoluted avenues human / straightened, straightened particularly for the shouting humans / members, members winning the wisdoms human / reclaim, reclaim a placement called appealing too, the humans.

CHAPTER FIVE
Evolving, evolving the solving human / reply, reply to the resource human / inscripted, inscripted in equipped means human / roots, roots languaged well within the wisdom human / grown. / grown past views human / stripped, stripped of resources again? allow a human / strewn, strewn lessons amazing the humans / drawn, drawn to the retailing humans / liken, liken us leashed less for the fathoms human / seed, seed sprayed lightly upon the human trays / materials, materials measured and found then, human / study, study a detailed human / phases, phases over mooned by the beacons human / places, places visited living in the lessons human / curious, curious weapons gone to the gaining humans / numbers, numbrs nestle in the lingins human / earlier, earlier wisdom read of the reaches human / ax, ax cuts off the creatures human-less / false, false preschers lost to the left ones human / insight, insight sealing the sections human / check, check on a vector faaced humanly / declare, declare a duration fixed for the faceted humans / school, school rules a human / stare, stare into pairings gained, human / symptoms, syptoms stop now, the human / plunge, plunge over due to the human / dynasty, dynasty begun through the thoughtful humans / east, east to the beast won to the freedom human / practical, practical in places human / walls, walls over and the winging comes to the land only human / columns, columns collapsing and settled forth within the wallowing humans / stairs, stairs carry us pope-deep to the resources human / sourced, sourced by a reconfess of the visions human / resourced, resourced reflexes soar to a notion human / reverse, reverse found trued by a passion human / inverse, inverse notions daily fed for the fashions human / nineteen, nineteen ways now to be free daily to lovely humanity / grids, grids grappled over are through at the interfaces human / empowered, empowered by resources randomly fit to be human / human, human compare known to the light lend / fractals, fractals passing the faces human / conclude, conclude a mood rude to the human heart / proof, proof passing into a human / linked, linked lessoning spent on a partner human / consideration, consideration sent to the triumphant humans / sought, sought a signal human / approach, approach made for the feasting humans / bought, bought again, a lifted lending human / beasts, beasts brought to the bursting humans / brought, brought forth an outrage and found gauges human / knead, knead less and know more humanity / attend, a. ttend a trace appalachian deep in love, humanly / abstain, abstain form the college less than human /

strands, strands past and ended, hear, in the human / studies, studies done at a Harvard clue for the creations human / friends, friends allow us a duration human / appearing, appearing nearly new, a human / aprons, aprons placed around our humans / resplendent, resplendent in the winging humans / within, within wells find the fortitude human / pleasing, pleasing the leasing human / lively, lively and the threshold human / transformation, transformation of the humans / lifting, lifting and the gifting humans

CHAPTER SIX
Viceroy, viceroy lean to the lessons human / loads, loads us well with a wisdom human / magnetize, magnetize arising in the solar planes human / clear, clear me, humanly / vicar, vicar vexed over and left freely human / phallus, phallus plunging to the people human / deep, deep the deluge human / drawn, drawn to the quarters human / variations, variations allowed here have gone to the shores of forgiveness of God-heads / elected and given the light right to love these humans / across, across waves a news sources, "lifted" eternally through the loving humans / differences, differences settle for the fallen humans / translate, translate the lessons human / grab, grab reasons human / grapple, grapple passes lightly to the legions human / hold, hold for the foreign humanity / handle, handles held open for the floodgates human / ripen, ripen reading "human" / suspend, suspend done, now, through the thresholds human / sustains, sustains given for the featured humans / winds, winds whipping pst and lasting, humans / waivers, waivers reading human / less, less then, human / manager, managers mentioned pagosa welled into the humanity of love / textures, textures pasted on the pinnacles human / travels, travels racing humanity / trains, trains alone agian for the feelings human / allows, allows a whislte in to the game called humanity / disgrace, disgrace done and the racing winds allow us a human / bubbles, bubbles bend to billow into a lacing human / stretch, stretch applying fo rthe cues sent human / concepts, concepts concurrent with a crater human / spin, spin Shasta-lipped in humanity / barristers, barristers left through the allowances human / worn, wornt hrough thoroughly human / railing, railing greed has gone to the reached human / bend, bend traced to the racing humans / flowers, flowers feature a creature human / spell, spell love, h-u-m-a-n / apparents, apparents win a human / size, size applied for is human / squared, squared illegally the circle sof love / sides, sides waged forwardly human / size, size said to be Pi, the human / heart, heart hoped for, humanly / vibration, vibration up then to humans / transmitted, transmitted allowance of the imply only human / transcendance, transcendance comes through on the information found human / trips, trips now made to the resource framed as "human" / alterations, alerations coming to the wave frames calling us human / cones, cones capably set for the fragments hurled as human / evolved, evolved wages paid to the placements now called human / transcend, transcend allowed, now, too, humanly / consternation, consternation overdue and the compliance stated "human" / characters, characters painted on potions human / capture, capture done and the sun bakes forth as human / cords, cords cut, humanly / calipers, calipers measure the

fat lands only human / joyous, joyous juicy humans / joys, joys lead to humanity / joyous, joyous venues reclaimed as required thorugh the venues calling "human" / lightening, lightening and the listing humans / rich, rich in lightened humans / placement, placement on the divine humans.

CHAPTER SEVEN

Erotic places laid through the thronging known as human. / almost, almost a victim, gone, to the traces now gone human / within, within won, humanly / ceilings, ceilings tossedas human / glass, glass blownt hrough to humans / illuminate, illuminate a rages point for the powerful view of humans / royal, royal in a require for the refinements known as human / declare, declare us "human" / duet, duet sung now, human / pants, pants worn past humans / pane, pane opens, human / paths, paths plunge in, human / pair, pair found us, human / cross, cross given back to humans / join, join us, humanity / liken, liken hiking into the humans / fly, fly faced humanity / there, there is the challenge laid to a humanity freed / find, find a village green with loving humans / here, here is her carriage and the marriage only human / pleasure, pleasure pages us humanity / survive, survive thus the patient humanity / thrive, thrive threaded by light humanity / graps, grasp given and the living leap to license laid as human / unit, unit compared to a waiver read "human" / one, one wave, humanity / won, won two, humanity / know, know now the resource refined as human / show, show us yours humanity / tempts, tempts tossed to the humans lost / temple, temples traced across the face Gemini in humans / grown, grown signals of humanity / yes, yes into the meetings born human / mix, mix into measures born human / plan, plan to be found through humanity / found, found a featured humanity / freedom, freedom exists inside our humanity / exists, exists a notion of humanity / exit, exit the lexicon of a vertical song gone human / made, made the electric leap across the levels human / movement, movement amazed through humanity / magistrate, magistrate meets in humanity / meetings, meetings set through humanity / mate, mate and the materials matched into humanity / mention, mention the dimensions of humanity / materialize, materialize in a mission meant for God's humanity / mothering, mothering elected, humanity / matters, matters material mend at the heart human / matrix, matrix established and meant for the basically human / matrices, matrices set for the settled leap into humanity / magic, magic and the missions born through humanity / magical, magical mention of the codes human / mavericks, mavericks allowed listening humanity / rebels, rebels rage past your humanity / registers, registers a code human / randomly, randomly set for the features humanly / rooted, rooted into the news humanity / rampant, rampant parallels throughout our humanity / rude, rude to the point of boorish without, humanity / registry, registry reaps a lesson human / loops, loops establish a keeping humanity / ladders, ladders lead to the wedged free humanity / links, links skate to the ledger human / lips, lips of the leading humans / levels, levels paged through humanity

CHAPTER EIGHT

Life, life led us to the parallels human / beautiful, beautiful values only human / pain, pain gone in the humans / panes, panes pacing our humanity / incredible, incredible basics only human / increments, increments measured in the humans / segments, segments signal in the humans / abide, abide well in wiser then the humans / water, water wet with a basically exceptional humanity / breath, breath of the beacon called human / shout, shout it "humanity" / whirling, whirling in wiser humanity / dove, dove agreed, humanity / dove, dove scenes and the fields alive with electrica rise of the winging come and the / erupting singing of the license human / dove, dove aware now of the writing human / eyes, eyes penetrate yours with a passion benevolent for the featured humans / umbilical, umbilical cut and the resource allowed for the truest humans / viscera, viscera lays revealed as the listening humans / mother, mother amazed as the pages ring of the ransom laid human / birds, birds bade us welcome wings human / nest, nest nestled into as a living human / feed, feed a pungent oar unto the lifting leys human / flocks, flocks follow us, orative in style, to the missives known as human / sages, sages lifted off the planes human / blood, blood bath elections of the sheep shorn for the humans / vessels, vessels laden with fragrance spent on the legendary humans / fed, fed us humanly of love / felt, felt for the traffic jammed as human / pull, pull into a venue clear for humans / constructions, constructions reaching into cores electric with the thronging raised as human / listen, listen to the loaning human / delivers, delivers daily, human wares of light led love electric / separate, separate oppose and the quarters known as human / surges, surges past, human / spreads, spreads laid well within humanity / trips, trips to the posing humanity / lift, lift to the loaning humanity / yes, yes again, "humanity" / life, life led to the levels human / rife, rife without within human / full, full to the filling of love for humanity / blank, blank in a space called human / perfect, perfect to the codes called human / exact, exact in a fashion human / elect, elect to the sovereignty human / example, example to the samples human / elevated, elevated by elated particles human / lettered, lettered by a simple human / linked, linked to disciples born human / pleasant, pleasant unto manners born human / yours, yours the sample and the inheritance, earth, the humans / let, let go, choose, human / precious, precious unto manners born human / yearn, yearn to know disciples born human / letters, letters leap to seal the flames human / fortress, fortress built unfolds in humanity / escape, escape the holds human / folds, folds open humanly / litter, litter less clear more humanity / trains, trains taken unite humanly / partners, partners meet in humanity / may, may we see thee, humans / governed, governed through the groves born electrically human.

CHAPTER NINE

Energy, energy wedded with the bedded One, human / milk, milk made for the future's humans / collostrum, collostrum cues us to fee the humans / kept, kept electric through a sparkling weave of energetic miracles and the heart of / believe in us, lovely, humans / body, body blissful and misted with the souling released and the spark uncovered to switch on to the lights of gone to the lofty heights of a full actual human / light, light led to waves of the electrical gallop through humanity / central, central zones and the ownings electric with bands of humans / metatron, metatron told others of the liquid humans / port, port passionate for the features human / gestation, gestation tools human / nine, nine days electrical and the whistling wins allowance for the humans / ten, ten and the wells human / phonics, phonics and the metaphysical allowance for the humans / enforce, enforce and the divorced data forthright with the humans / elaborate, elaborate the ruse of rested humans / test, test and the shouting humans / listen, listen and the humans syptomatic within a human / hear, hear and the yearly stratus freed for the humans / rhythm, rhythm miraculous basically too, a human / man, man and the mentions "human" / trumpets, trumpets triply human / blown, blown into the balances human / rasta, rasta and the redwinged humans / marley, marley and the missions human / suffer, suffer and the severance paid for the humans / Sophilia, Sophilia and the feelings inquired into the humans / woman, woman and the won ones human / guatemala, guetamala and the chosen stelae of the humans / glint, glint and the hinted humans / hint, hint and the aboving humans / paradigm, paradigm climes and the planets human / climb, climb and the scurry pasted within the humans / elective, elective and the plants ran into the humans / turn, turn and the expansions due the humans / taken, taken into lightest humans / tube, tube and the rations human / invites, invites and the rewrites invitational to the humans / vortex, vortex and the viewings human / vox, vox voiced into the humans / lightly, lightly lessons human / take, take a trade for the featured humans / give, give given a flawless human / mystics, mytics mentioned as materially human / enjoy, enjoy a journey human / rasp, rasp shouted "the humans" / groan, groan and the gross ways gone to the humans / grave, grave gathers only lightly the humans / clean, clean in apply for the completely human / deft, deft and the swift moves to humans / deepens, deepens reaping a human / wins, wins a welcome humanity / lavendar, lavendar liftings human / blue, blue truths mist me with love for the human / speaking, speaking and the speeches lightened for the humans / grants, grants and the greeted humans / much, much mentioned for the humans / more, more onto a thankful human / mended, mended dearest human / friend, friend for the fortunate humans / lip, lip of the supple humans / planted, planted in loving humanity / throats, throats and the thrusting humans / thirteen, thirteen days the absolute humans.

CHAPTER TEN

Crave, crave and the laughter human / mostly, mostly and the matching humans / listening, listening levelly for the humans / yard, yard forthrightly humans / longer, longer living the licensed humans / nights, nights and the nearest humans / years, years of the yestering humans / blown, blown and the blended humans / blowing, blowing and the treated humans / heirs, heirs and the narrow humanity lfited by gifted light ones / air, air of the central ships human / compare, compare us concurrently within the humans / forgotten, forgotten over and the infuse made to the faded humans / crucify, crucify flies past to include the humans / christ, christ rose to day in the pillows and the billows human / sold, sold for a sake less, knot, humanly / raise, raised to a ruckus

for the humans / rise, rise placed into the humans / arose, arose reaches the human / arisen, arisen lightly to the humans / alliance, alliance bonded for and found within a spanning human / gained, gained a chalice large and round and the smoothest head of a level good-bye to our human love / momentum, momentum mounted us with ahushed resort for human love / mention, mention a mutual mission for the humans / dimension, dimensions dealt with, know insure for the humans / delve, delve past Other to the One human / delegate, delegate for the Kadmon and the minion called Eve's lasting human / delegations, delegations dearest to the clearest humanity / job, job bid and the lid off our moistening humanity / john, john said "let there be a ligth humanity" / join, join others to the treats of living basically human to the lightest intrigues / spin, spin points into the humans / alternate, alternate your plans fo rhte people human / life, life and the leaping humans / lived, lived into central rations perfectly human / gate, gate opened into the plane states human / ways, ways of the winning humans / apply, apply reached and the ransoms paid for the prescence human / altar, altar made to the reasonings human / author, author of the points laid into the human scale / pint, pint of the pouring humans / host, host of the ghosted humans / toast, toast us wedded as freely human / travail, travail done for the Son has arrived at the point of the lightly lived and the crossing forgiven for falling across the human path / coast, coast across nightly to the righteous humans / cakes, cakes iced with living advise of the features human / burst, burst balanced in a channeled allowance into the humans / court, court spent on the samantha scoped interlaid appetite for the shores elctrically / freed, freed by the lightest humans / sorts, sorts of the signals human / half, half and the held forht humans / more, more made apointed human / mention, mention a licensure framed in the human divisions / both, both bade us love them lightly forthrightly to the arcing humans / bask, bask allowed us lightly within a human / tune, tune into a saviors grace and the racing humans / atomic, atomic unto the attunement human / action, action taken and sent for in the futures human / climbs, climbs and the clippers human / pyramids, pyramids sailing across the Magellan and the magdelena firings of the future / opal, opal blue with Hawaiian shores of the lasting stores human / pinnacles, pinnacles reached and the breach done for the farthest human stars / succeeds, succeeds and the deals met within the wisdom human.

CHAPTER ELEVEN

Metatronic, Metatronic and the degrees human / light, light and the ventricular humans / centers, centers and the sprawling humans / revert, revert and the inverted humans / regard, regard focused into the lightly human / rest, rest and the rituals human / rift, rift over now then, human / clears, clears and the creations spent onto the humans / chasm, chasm and the channeled humans / heals, heals and the furthest humans / atrium, atrium and the sealing's human / bailing, bailing a balanced human / builds, buils a trusted huamnity / counts, counts in crations gone human / clamors, clamors created for the humans / meet, meet mentioned into these humans / superb, superb a balanced human / sensitive, sensitive incisions made into decisions now lightly balanced /

gentle, gentle means made yours balanced / graced, graced by a creation human / jasmine, jasmine jeweled delviery to the mansions human / jaunts, jaunts listened into as human / jolly, jolly bejewels human / dreams, dreams dancing across these humans / dense, dense dealt with as human / doors, doors opened wisely for the humans / lean, lean into windy humans / winds, winds blast us clearly utno the humans / open, open penned experiences iwhtin the humans / again, again I say the humans / grains, grains greet us grown for the humans / grew, grew another days humanity / greets, greets us well within an arcing human / groves, frown less upon the grve grown humans / thrown, thrown to a treated human / throne, throne threw us homeward still into a volicing human / unless. unless we ran forth we wre allowe donly these, the body, mind, and spirit of the / five fold in-counted humans / confession, confession placed precisely atop the rising mountain Fuji style with humans / convolute, convolute acute has goen to the priceless humans / savagely, savagely joined at the hips worn human / been, been believed in lightly throughout these humans / believed, believed in a challenge born humanely / basically, basically basked in lightly, humanity / superbly, superbly spent in life's humanity / delicate, delicate and deliciously worn thorugh to humanity / scooped, scooped up and bitten into through the thrones called humanity / soft, soft allowance for the frameworks human / guardian, guardian allows us the light waves human / gates, gates passionately embraced as sopen now throughout our humanity / access, access and the success known as human / sports, sports spent into a human light life / shelves, shelves deepen regarding our humanity / splash, splash aobut us lightly for the basically humans / megatron, megatron explosives planted at the seas of humanity / destiny, destiny dealt with in the wave planes called humanity / appears, appears for us a gateway human / scripture, scripture red with the nestling blood-stained forgiveness of loving openly / perfectly within humanity / considerate, considerate creations and the rations human / trees, trees tip into centrally, humanity / relatives, relatives reaching into the higher planes of self same humanity / red, red rayed humanity / posture, posture posing for the choosing human

CHAPTER TWELVE

Passionate, passionate gain and the Friend has found us, basic humanity / perlescent, pearlescent pose and the regarding allow for the frankest plow settled into / the winding lanes of a lightening priority called human love / life, life is the Friend, allow us the gifts of goodness, assurity, balance, and bliss / ten, ten, ten times I have basically said "I AM. Hu-man" / based, based on a number of challenges spent where did our goal get set? Directly in the basic's human / heart of love's spiral sweeping directly off my human feet. / elemental, elemental to a horizontal forgive, I am living as applied for lightly, genuine, human / mystics, mystics appearing searing the cortical connects with embedded erasure and the / placement squarely in basic humanity for love / crafts, craft accruing as we are doing our basic freedoms, 1 through 10, light bodies / blending, love elevated to ther righteous stand and the listening appearance of a highest star settled into my

merkaba electric, listen up, flying soothed and the registry made for another leap to the celestial orb called human / release, release a combiantion of less and find a hearty "more" through the shores alive with electrical begin for the basically human / reference, reference made to the frolicsome humans / ein, ein pays for the being human / soft, graphic allow of the soft stage human / medium, medium mentioned now implied for the makings human / Kabbalah, Kabbalah reading a 3 and the 1 found another 4 and the 4th elected a lightening shore of the central equatorial explain of alpha land omega rich with basic humanity / ancients, ancients converging to encourage your discovery of the secret fountains of / youth, know the Tibetan ways to love well, basically / energetic, energetic pairings, covalent to the bonding humans / Isaac's, Isaac's burden lifitn "enough" sacrifice less and find more the humans / Esau, Esau saw it the blessings human / elijah, elijah denied it only once and found forever a healing hunch that God lives within our ratify and th resurrection is in your eyes sparking return to the light led revolution of basic humans / prophet, prophet pages written, hear, and know the align meant for the legends human / believes, believes in young dear and the fountain of years with a mission, a mansion, a mistress, and piers of elcetrical arrival and the sovlent release to precisely a heartline of definition repent to the vaguest beginning of a living again, light has said, I believe in the life called human / sings, sings a newest sonnet and a sonic booms release to the righteous resignation of the soul who knew release to precision, pairing eternal with the God bond known equivalent, an electric covalent for the lving spin to the heart of matter and the light of mend and the place perfection sorted at the place of liftin lend to the legendary stature of a myth that knew complete and the creatures slightly sobbing with the lifting healing treat of forgiven, forgotten, freed, from Mother's fear and Father's lease on the heart given solace and a language of love to the human's racing for love / exceeds, exceeds our expectation and the rations spent for love allowed as human / eccentric, eccentric and simply you are the humans / stuff, stuff onyx refines as simply human / raphael, raphael has made the leaping laughing list of why we stay and how to beat with a bringing singing chalice of Grail and the holy wonder that mankind can tell "they are loved," basically, human / quell, quell all thirst by drinking lasting quench at the fountain eternal and the heart that lives inside the Christos blended / equals, equals an admit that God rules, heaven has rings, Christ lines are listings with the mentioed detail of how you see your Self, highest held, know the news, a langue founded is basic human / models, models planned for a features set on the rising materials and the matress filled with the functions, money, and mandibles of a monkey reclined at the pieces spent on ripping apart humans and finding sins, by monkey's define, knot mens, be basically free of the registered sort who require a member to deal with sacraments which lesssen Lord's words. God of Life, Life of Love, man eternal and the sword which finally cuts through Freedom nearing, hear, listen, basically humanity is, free to the lightest living blend of Christing, God-ding, budding, Buddha, man, human, coded, huna, loaded now allow a sincerest flying good detail fo the good-bye found in living eyes of basic humanity

/ plan, plan told forthrightly know the nightly registration for the loading ships of love sited humanity first / plane, plane logically allowed a legendary lifitng to the light lands human / warrant, warrant taken and listed as gifted for the gracious humans / cliff, cliff tossed over and the framing found for a fortunate night dear and a daily good trade, winds are blowing, showing us, human, love / military, military mention of the dimensions, human / belief, belief has settled in, we are free of all the lines electric, save won, human / capsize, capsize occuring less often at the variant for humanity / votes, votes in place now, know the showings human / boats, boats allowing our election of freinds, the humans / bares, bares another grid of the lgihtest humans / lessons, lesson spent for being human / beginning, beginning allow for the language far lighter and the lasting imply of why we believe in the love born human / thickest, thickest hearts have fed at the vein grown electric and the heart born a man, human, loved / regard, regard daring ceilings of lightest humans / coiled, coiled in a creature Kundalini deep with repetitios ability to keep lving with zen delgihts unless seen as the act of disbelieve, know the won, love trued at humans / matrices, matrices said, know the Father, blessings Humans / written, written onto a heart nearest you, you are the basic human, love one another / words, words reading "forgiven" forgotten" "folded" with love to the humans / starts, s. tarts antoehr star front found electrically at the Arcturian contingents reaction to the news lightest, humans / stars, stars spaced precisely for the portals in to the being human / cubical, cubical explanations of the durations known as human / voiced, voiced often, "please allow our knowing to blend with your desire to see the basics in humanity" / Metatron, Metatron has said, body bliss,a t thekissing human / electron, electron knowing of the kiss that is holy and the one which allows a precious blend of perfect love to the humans / shields, shields are held still until we shift for the futures human / shapes, shapes now chosen as the grain stars human / symbols, symbols boldest gained, human, hearts, shores, life, love / remembrance, remembrance fills me with the features human / regards, regards gaining for the written humans

CHAPTER THIRTEEN

Angels, angels requiring your voicing hello to the rest of the heartline who live here below and the mountains rang with wlecome home humans / choirs, choirs now sealig with voices helaed for the frameworks human / Seraphim, Seraphim ring us with the lessons of love to the human / soothes, soothes us daily, angels who care for the fragile humans / scribe, scribes have written, now you can hear, the crying, screaming of the lifted apply to a college human / voices, voices tell me, be wellest within, the light chassis, human heard, heard often heraldic, and yes, we agree that the species born here now are living lightly. Know the cause, a lightest human / speak, speak to the species human / spoken, spken now fortunately human / powers, powers placed us in unusual situations of loving humans / asked, asked again, shall we be, human? / peoples, peoples pleasure finds a flame at the registered name now, basic humanity's gems of light / placed, placed on lines and listened withinn are the arcing precision of a

heaven held pen and the principled recipients, basically human / tribes, tribes trickles into our miracles mention of the tanzanite singing, arcturian blue with ripening love for the focused humans / five, five rays have held us one now may go three are rest rigning and one is blown wide by the surgical release of the lessened loves, human / persons, persons asking "how can this be" a Messiah born nightly in the hands Arcturian with love to the humans / parson, parson of the moments human / preachers, preachers deal as the lightly human / kin, kin said"pleas" the humans / rock, rock stood erecteda s the kane human / loud, loud legislation blown to sky high bits by the believing humans / parts, parts ahve purged now and the gifts are human / posh, posh appliance and the affluence of a gifted human / luxury, luxury dealt for the future human / laps, laps filled with the children, human / watched, watch now the palaces human / seen, seen in delicious refrains the natures human / hath, hath another applied for the fortunes human? / hopeful, hopeful futures friendly to the humans / theologic, theologic alignment with the freshest humans / acquire, acquire your own throne through your throated hello and the tongue set good-bye to the life here below, as mundane, and as well within, paradise's tale of the Eden human / tempered, temperd within by the ranges human / kink, kink untold and the unfolding humans / split, split has parted from the lightest humans / fills, fills within a framed rate human / rounded, rounded pasisoantely fortunately human / since, since then, human / source, source surged with a lighteened humanity / mend, mend done, love is the human way / squires, squire to the lightlines electric within a human, Metatron / slice, slice acheived, know the release of the registered humans / through, through us believers human / flesh, flesh felt us human / life, life led us human / held, held within a human span / sacred, sacred rewsting, human / again, again we say rested human / granulations, granulations of the appraising humans / greens, greens paid for and found lightened in the branches human / participate, participate in the daily reaches human / speak, speak of unviersal allowance for the featured humans / show, show us your licensed humans / details, detail quell us with widened allow for the floweres human / profound, profound intentions expressed here in the giving human / profane, profane appliance of the reliance into a listed human / arcane, arcane insanity due a dealing human / rigns, rings regular to the sun's sptted reply, now, be, human / perfections, perfections spanned our human land with a light ride human / placement, placement meant throughout the human signs of love / church, church said, "allow us" to remember our humanity / God, go to the sister of humanity's love / pursue, pursue a balance human / Pleiades, Pleiades ranging through the humans / posing, posing into humanity / pursuant, pursuant to a living humanity.

THE TEMPLE-MENTS
LEVEL 52

CHAPTER ONE

Temples will listen, lighten, the temple human / simple, simple sayings human templed / explain, explain your desire for the humans, temple deep / explore, explore a rising human temple / imagine, imagine grips gained by being a temple / people, people who are simply, "human"temples / text, text trues at the refusal to forget the human temples / global, global calling wins the human temples / mapped, mappred allow, temple deep in the humans / ice, ice sent chilling to the temples human / eruptions, eruptions wonded the tmeples human / miraculous, miraculous includes finding a temple human / observed, observed in a swervin molecular temple / result, result of the query and the cubic metatron, temples human / mass, mass detailed as the density rose for the feedings templar, a temple humanity / points, points placed about us said "a temple" of love / limestone, limestone taj mahals played temptation for the temples of love / fox, fox fed us lightly the factors of a fuller temple / eroded, eroded rest and heaven yes, met us, here near the temples of mend / play, play allows us a templed spin to love / balance, balance chosen well within for the features humanly well to a temple's gaze / monitor, monitor your ministry well within a temple human / read, read of the features humanly, well built with a key to the Holy Sacrament, your, temples / decimal, decimal duest us is the One templed keep / once, once I said, well, to a temple fountain / impact, impact made is coming too, and the fields of plenty soar near your temples / hold, hold felt through the faith melted at the temple hearted franklins / sunk, sunk without it, temples human / subside, subside to a shore little river red with a tennessee bend for the future / Gatlinburg within a temple human / rift, rift outed for the temple's sake / tucked, tucked into us is a gate key to the temple of love / fishes, fishes posed us 3 by 5 and the dividends dishing were there to alive temples / frozen, frozen fuses opened for the temple / prove, prove us lovely to the tightest temples / roots, roots eruptively electric within and wisdom comes to the sisters temples / proven, proven again, you live within a wiser temple / guild, guild guided to flying temples / cave, cave of the winds scenery deep in a wine soaked temple / brain, brain based beauty worn off the temple walls / subject, subject of the secret temples / navel, navel deep in the Bali Hi for a mothered keep often wellw tihin a temple's sleep of human loves / link, link ledgered into a mission's temples / blast, blast done and the healing coming forth to say a "temple" man / erupt, erupt through a crust held lightest at the corners of the temple of love / sailor, sailor said "love has swum to the temple gates, this day, let there be a light humanity. " / lesson, lessons learned about us, a temple / upheaved, upheaved and the mis-behaved taught a lesson well within a living temple / volcano, volcano of the keeping goddess found in temples / herb, herb blessed and basically flowered into a legendary bali of temples / entire, entire in the winning temples / oxide, oxide of the risen temples / land, land lends temples / blood, blood beauty bet for with a willing temple / palace, palace places templed / tomb, tomb toured without winds, temples / composing, somposiing a coay aflofting for love releasing a temple / sedimentary, sedimentary missions and the

missives deepen within love's temples / date, date found for the frequency demanded of human temples / copied, copied less and found more within the temples / recurrent, reccurent themes frozen less within a temple / flights, flights purchased again to a temple / gallery, gallery grown temples / passages, passages made to a mission's temples.

CHAPTER TWO

Chambers, chambers of the chimbarazo line and the heart that's inside a temple human / inspect, inspect a portion for the fortunes realized when love rewards your realistic trend to be a temple / scale, scale over and the frequent found at a dearest delivery called "getting around" to the temples of love / built, built on a basic, humanity, love is the temple of man / shock, shock past and good-byes that last for the Templar sighted sands of timing's temples / transmitted, transmitted akin you a yellow venue for temples spliced within love / capsule, capsule of the rapture sent to living attend for the fortunate temples / thundering, thundering thricely for the held won temples / debate, debate of the respect for the feautred temples / chutes, chutes across us and around our miracle found in a birthing temple / notion, notion and the mention forthrightest, love is genuine, in a heavenly temple / bald, bald offered celarly for the dearly done, temple clarify / levitational, levitational to a rotational clarity of themes sung, "temples spin" to love / interior, interio Mer-ka-bah blown to a smithereen's plan for temples / torch, torch passed has lasted for the templ / bar, bar none and known metallically as freed for the temples / swivel, swivel welcomes a simple treaty for the trenches born of temples stared / rasping, rasping mounted as the outing templed voices / salt, salt magnetic to a flow fo the current current down below, human signs, Ariel said "lovely" metatronic temple signs / crystal, magnet, magnet of the mentioned steeling suggestives temple gates / table, tables trim in a turning allowance of the trios reconnected to love of the temples / hesitant, hesitant undone through the temples / clicking, clicking captives less for the frothing temples / witness, witness a rebirth, your own, through the temples gates / chisel, chisel west into a learned temple / limestone, limestone brinks and the basically, human temples expande for the portals spent on love / love, love wins our temples / lime, lime ledgers bent on sulfuric fumes gather to the lgiht lines iwthin, love is a breathing temple / early, early ways to show me gaps resisted have gone to the temple's stairs / precise, precisely purchased ascendance to the light gaze, temples seen / solar, solar explore and the know more-ing of a temple / ring, ring rang through us, temples, temples, temples / meticulous, meticulous to a staring temple / divisions, divisions absolute have come to the endings magnificent too, a temple / certainty, certanity laid at the gate's temples / body, body blue with abliss-full return to the temples / legendary, legendary legions knew you were the temple / century, century suggested, "a temple" / judgement, judgement done, choose well, a temple / float, flaot past and shout "shafts won, a temple" / identity, idnetity set forth, a temple's / wing, wing won in a temple / dove, dove deals as a lightly, "temple" / legitimate, legitimate to measures of the temples / inside, inside has risen to allow a friendly temple / acclaimed, acclaimed measures minutes deep within a temple / swift, swioft the hasten to a sword born blue within a temple / passion, passion's place is met within a temple courageous enough to love lightly / courage, courgae coming into your temple / tradition, tradition dealt with through a temple / questions, question a motive wellw tihin a temple / freedom, freedom fed us, lightly, temples / price, price paid is finest, temples / rubies, rubies registered within, a temples / biological, biological beauties last within, a temple, human / awake, awake again to the wonderful humans, temples cope with love / altars, altars ultra-fine within a happening temple / cherish, cherish the children well within and know that Ariel begins to breathe freely of God given temples / dream, dream allows us a temple's gates / modified, modified features of the temple magnified with wings / version, version varied for the cherubim compassionate with fine cubits of templed keep / Delhi, Delhi called me clear today to the tunes born moon free of the shores India, a temple came, to love / ocean, ocean concentric within a temple / wisdom, wisdom wears us well today, within, a temple.

CHAPTER THREE

Reborn, reborn to learn form loving gaisn as a temple / amazing, amazing occurrence, love has found your temple / crops, crops up less often thatn the remaining temples / dawn, dawn due a delivery delicious with a temple / visitor, visitor coming welcom then, a temple / footsteps, footsteps heard now, within your temple / placement, placement occuring again a temple / story, story suggested of the finished temple / outside, outside into my feeling temple / crow, crow came through a showing temple / pray, pray often of the winged temples / pair, pair of ravens found in a featured temple / place, place made for the temples / plenty, plenty given and the lving found as a temple / planets, planets swing to the remembering of love as a temple / dharma, dharma decide on a temple / lama, lama levelled our temples / Juno, Juno juned within a moon's temple / ursta, ursta measured a fairest weather's temple / clear, clear to a mentioned sire for the temple / care, care allows us a temple / gel, gel joins at the temple / conspire, conspire pairs us within a temple / aspirate, aspirate suggestive of remember, breathe, believe a temple / aspire, aspire shares us with the temples / recover, recover reaching your temple / raw, raw rays temple red with love / electric, electric placement sent to a passionate temple / starring, staring you, a temple human / clouds, clouds lift a gaze unto love for the temples / wisp, moist wisps random sort of the temples gates / special, special in a spatial meet for the frameworked into a temple / allied, allied and the temples of times and the inside spent fortunate with a healing love / supple, supple to a nimble temple / passionate, passionate for the porch swing's temples / compare, compare allows for the dearest temples / popular, popular to a threshold, temples / mechancial, mechanical to a measure's temples / hurtle, hurtle to a mandible temple / huddle, huddle past a temple's gaze / offer, offer and the meeting temples / grape, grape and the gracious temples / orange, orange to a mansion's temples / filled, filled with a future's temples / mothered, mothered and a miracle's temples

/ smothered, smothered and the mentioned temples / forgiven, forgiven and the fortunate temples / circle, circle into sudden temples / top, top of the earth winds temple / chest, chest and the suggested temple / tear, tear into mentioned "temples" / torn, torn and the risen temples / discover, discover and the dearest temples / recover, recover and the reaching rates toward a temple / relate, relate for a temple / compassion, compassion dear to a temple's center / accord, accord afforded our temples / affection, affection expressed through the temples dearest / loyalty, loyalty led to our friendly temples / motherhood, motherhood mirrors our templed explores / friendship, friendship follows a temple's gates / liberty, liberty advanced as a cause parallel to our temples / freedom, freedom rings saturn red within the temple / expansion, expansion grown to european shores on temples.

CHAPTER FOUR

Relative, relative to a regard for the featured metat-tronics temple gates / confer, confer for the features temple swept with love / coincide, coincides rides into the heart led love to a temple / rivers, rivers and the regard for a temple / propel, propel and the wellest remember only of love for the fullest temple / warmth, warmth for the freedom of the temples / balance, balance for the elemental believing of the temples / valance, valance of the awarest temples / bails, bails allowed out then to a temple's gates / mount, mount a mention to the temples / olive, olive led into a temple / green, green grew a temple / x-ray, x-rays red with a relations temples / vision, vision and the truths told to a temple / truth, truth allowed a wisdom's temples / trust, trust engaged with along a temple / superlative, superlative legions of a temple / supra, supra succeed of the listened temples / Buddha, Buddha and the believing temples / Guatumalan, Guatumalan tradeed temples / Shakumani, Shakumani and the temples past a temple / Siddhartha, Siddhartha and the martian's mentioned of mirrored temples / light, light lifted temples / lavendar, lavendar lend of the tresholds temples / coal, coal, coal and the souls gone unto a temple / trend, trend of the treaty found at temples / pink, pink and the pistils leak of green alignment with love, the temple / green, green gazes won with a mentioned temple / jasmine, jasmine jewels on the temples / aspect, aspect of the respect for a temple / journey, journeys jopined at a temple / baby, baby born into a temple / patterns, patterns planted as a temple / found, found another wed to temple / prophecy, prophecy fulfilling and a temple said, "book" / tanks, tanks opened for the temples / revise, revise registers as "temples" / tan, tan with a reason, sun, of temples / intercom, intercom ready for a temple / cabinet, caabinet cues as a temple / critical, critical allowances of temples / long, long legends said " a temple" / thrones, thrones thrice led to temples / ghost, ghost outed temples / casper, casper coasted into a temple / evaporate, evaporate viewing temples / all, all ways, temples / closures, closures clued and the franchised attend into a temple / masters, master minded and the winding temples / minds, minds mastered as a varied temple / partake, partake daily of the welcome temples / continual, continual pleasures and the measured temples / infinite, infinite focus at the nexus, temples /

supreme, supreme regimes of temples / agency, agency laoning us a temple / explained, explained best, a temple / new, new known and temples / stage, stage of resurrection's temples / divine, divine days as temples / embodiments, embodiments on the temples / derivative, derivative of daily temples / ability, ability given to temples / advent, advent meant for temples / proclaim, proclaim another a temple.

CHAPTER FIVE

Pledge, pledge and the temple dearest with love and the temples human / garment, garment of the wearing bearing opened, skin deep into the lessons temples / scripture, scripture and the registers of the temples / similitude, similitude and the voiced reply unto a message for these temples / image, image apparent and the momentary collapse through a temple / incarnation, incarnation of the national kind and the valued finds temple deep with love / function, function and the findings temples, opening / frequencies, frequencies felt for the templed keeps / flash, flash allows you a temple time / scroll, scroll swallowed through a temple steep / crystallized, crystallized and the rewritten temples / rythmic, rythmic and the reapply for a fortunate temple / swift, swift into keeping a simple apply for a temple stratus / wave, wave and the willing temples / centropy, centropy and the suggested temples / pulsate, pulsate and the temples dance within an agreed to stance for love / blocks, blocks and the temples locks off to a giving license of God / modulates, modu021tes with choosing temples / twilight, twilight and the nature of love spent on God's gifts to the temple / proof, prrof of the passion of love's gated temples / antiquity, antiquity and the turns into a temple's planes / overturn, overturn and the opinion planned for a pensions pleasant wells and the temples planets / opinion, opinion and the magnetics aligned as a momentum to the temples / culture, culture and the creations ran into a temple / metaphysics, metaphysics and the remissions spent on a lightening traffic too and the temples / nile, nile and the above beams to rumors past, love / spirit, spirit and the passionate manuscripts written for love and the wellest temples plans / stage, stage well and the keys sail into love for a temple / lacked, lacked and the lifelines energetically linked to the human temples / splendid, splendid and the suggestions tempted less for love's details of the temples well with love / manuscript, manuscrpt of the lips blessed with loving's gaze / entire, entire into the whistles of the lightened enrage spent at love, the temple / entire, entire days swell with love's temples / solely, solely won and the unified exampel fo the sone engaged with loving's temples / insisted, insisted and the resonant resist spent to love's temples / ample, ample and the sampels sent to a natural temple / reaction, reaction and the temples sent to love / orbital, orbital and the samples intrigued within and a healing temple / sutra, sutra and the mantra sung by temples / catalogues, catalogues entertained by a temple / ionized, ionized and the recess to temples / tibetan, tibetan and the trash focused on the veterans of temples / geometries, geometries and the genuine insign for the living temples / luminaries, luminaries and the dignitaries into a lake filled with love, teh temple / coding, coding and the encoding

ramped for temples / evolution, evolution of the franchised temples / alignment, alignment sent for temples / forces, forces and the fielded tmeples / warp, warp and the Godhead's temples / throne, throne and the wellest temples enthroned / columns, columns elliptic to a temple of love / heavy, heavy outed for the franchised temples / refusing, refusing allows this temple / imagery, imagery gained through a temple / figurative, figurative to a heart's fit of love, the temple / wise, wise is the listened to temple / kindly, kindly and often a temple / task, task and the rehash of temples / original, original occurence of the living temples / spinal, spinal and the causes win a temple / treasure, treasure and the treaty for a temple / controls, controls a stages temple / eyebrow, eyebrow of the winning temples / complex, complex creations and the rations temple stepped.

CHAPTER SIX

Importance, importance of the contract welled into temples / Orion, Orion found a temple / meridians, meridians mound in temples / tropics, tropics occur for the temples / quadrant, quadrants occuring into a temple / navigation, navigation fueld by a temple / molecular, molecular and the matrices of a temple / mixing, mixing mills our freest temples / vortex, vortex and the values ample to temples / frequency, frequency of the founded temples / solar, solar suggestions due a temple / mathematics, mathematics spur a temple / key, key dynamics and temples / middle, middle mentioned to a temple / master, master planned by a temple / grid, grid dynamics and the reactive temples / passage, passage paid for a living temple / public, public wages and the wisdoms found a temple / throat, throat etherics and the mirrored temples / good, good to a nested temple / grade, grades made of the wellest temples / carved, carved allowance of the founded temples / expressed, expressed embraces of the temples / elements, elements sent to a temple / myth, myth matched rates for a temple / tie, tie dyed days doused in temples / win, win a wsdom for a temple / synthetics, synthetics found in temples / site, site and the findings temples / merely, merely and the dearly done with temples / study, study and the abiding temples / focus, focus and the enthusing temples / cathedral, cathedral daring a temple / apparently tearing with temples / perform, perform and the penchant won as temples / emitted, emitted and the remitted allow for temples / radius, radius and the regards for a temple / contracts, contracts and the biggest temples / surface, surface fusing in temples / spherical, spherical codes allowed this temple / cloud, clouds occupied less through a temple / kingdom, kingdom and the culpable allowance for a temple / caught, caught forthrightest at the course allowed to a temple / continue, continue details of the mate found through temples / multiple, multiple missions aimed to temples / vibration, vibration of the refuse to see less than the Bali temples / synthesized, synthesized through a healing temple / born, born again and worn through a temple / awakened, awakened daily to temples / righteous, righteous allowanc for the temples / inherit, inherit a peaceful temple / figuration, figuration found for details of the temples / secret, secret of the supreesed rations temples / philosophy, temples of the philosophy for a temple / minimal, minimal digression to the temples / initiate, initiate and the measures pade to a placing temple / guardians, guardians gaining a temple / guardians, guardians of the good won to a temple / cling, cling and the ringing treasures of love thus a temple / simplistic, simplistic and the rituals temples / educate, educate and teh goods won to a temple / champions, champions and the possible temples / source, source suggested to a temple / resource, resource allowed your temple.

CHAPTER SEVEN

Extensively, extensively attempted trues and temples / inviolate, inviolate and the matteres kept to temples / texts, texts touched deeply wellest to temples / conclude, conclude and the moods for a temple / fuses, fuses focused on a temple / codes, reply to codes for temples / mantras, mantras measured as temples / balance, balances paid for the temples balian / vocal, vocal enthuse and the threshold temple / corpuscle, corpuscle majored in for a temple / trigger, trigger registers as a temple / block, block bemused with a temple / exodus, exodus mentioned into a temple / neutral, neutral notions of the temple / upheavals, upheavals done and the duration? a temple / spin, spin past an old gate for a newest temple / octal, octal and the nocturnal views through temples / adapt, adapt a mention for a temple / scenario, scenarios exchanges as temple / vehicle, vehicle found for the imploded temples / sanctuary, sanctuary mentione dof the regions temples / essential, essential wings found through these temples / organic, organic to a manic resort and the research wed to a temple / devoted, devoted details for a temple / seed, seed suggested and the application is a temple / equilibrium, euilibrium reached through a temple / fallen, fallen foes made a templed trench of foundations / burning, burning bellows with a temple / aspect, aspect of the reception to a temple / case, case made for the purchased temples / starting, starting to realize the reach for a temple / pineal, pineal pleasing reigns as opened through a temple / perpendicular, perpendiculat occulars and the resurrections of love for the temple, human / plan, plan to be often fed by the temples / correspond, correspond as Yes! to a temple / room, room for the viewings temples / violate, violate less the trust between your temples / tribe, tribe resisted less for a temple / kindle, kindle an empire for a temple / fierce, fierce suggestion of a temple / heart, heart met within a temple / seize, seize and the rely upon a temple / annointed, annointed and appointed within as a temple / water, water willing to be a temple / dove, dove dues relay a temple / zodiac, zodiac news of a temple / teach, teach anotehr to be a temple / gather, gather at the reqrd for a temple / fulfill, fulfill a destination to a temple / quarter, quarter mounds found within a temple / nation, nation nestled in love for a temple / vertical, vertical horizons and the nooning temples / cue, cue for the featured temples / root, root and the reasons temple deep within cubes of then, love / coefficient, coefficient factors and the reactions too, a temple / rigorously, rigorously and the route through a temple / parallel, parallel replies too, a temple / quadrangle, quadrangle blues and the dues laced in a temple / division, division of the feelings braced by temples

/ scission, scission healed thorugh a mended temple / nerves, nerves nestle into a temple / chiasm, chiasm trued by temples / exoterically, exoterically infused with temples / cloth, cloth of the creation's temples.

CHAPTER EIGHT

Weaving, weaving a woven temple / thread, thread throated temples / transcribe, transcribe flows through temples planed / among, among fortunately a temple / liquid, liquid gains a templed surrender too, love's / borders, borders beleived for a temple / astral, astral mains and the suggested for a temple / fold, fold allows you a temple / young, young to a giving temple / envelope, envelope pushed and the resets allowd too a temple / mineral, minerals mention, " a temple" deep within, earth / fossil, fossil fused with a temple / archaeologicy, archaeology mentioned into a deepest temple / link, link often to the temples / scope, scope of the nature, a temple / passion, passion and the mentions goals won a temple / toil, toil and the travail off a temple / mist, mists and the aquiring of temples / migration, migration mined as a temple / portion, portion of the pensioned temples / shuttle, shuttle found for the temple / choice, choice allowed your sending gates to temples / wrap, wrap arouses your tmeples / emphasized, emphasized and the requirment for a temple / desire, desire deals in temples / intention, intention triangular for a temple / curves, curves closest to a temple / opposed, opposed less and gained more for the temples / sheath, sheath and the shilling ceilings straights to a temple / able, able be to a temple / serpent, serpent off these temples / magic, magic amuse meant for a temple / rather, rather read a temple's alerts / emblem, emblem and the sentient temples / royalty, royalty and the reds rages at a temple / sovereign, sovereign and the temples saged for a temple explain / fire, fire and the confessions due a temple / sound, sound said, "a temple" / end, end too, a temple / wade, wade past the temples gated within love / earth, earth met and the reasons set for in love for a temple / meaning, meaning and the mentioned temples / thinking, thinking and the thronging temples / feelings, feelings floated to a temple / willing, willing and the temples set for love / prevail, prevail and the temples short within love / shadows, shadows and the surrender blessed with temple's loves / unviersal, universal and the treaty rested at love, a temple / servants, servants and the suggestions trained in temples / fallen, fallen and the insured lightest temples / alleging, alleging and the winging temples / false, false and the outed throated clan of temples / hollow, hollow and the temples filled with God / exhalation, exhalation and the measures meant for love in the temples / filter, filter and the infusions of love throught a temple / body, body and the verbal temptation to be a temple / which, which won? temples / whole, whole days wihtin a temple / phase, phase of the telepathic treaty told, love gains us, a temple / respiration, respiration registers a cleansing date with a temple / room, room spins to a temple / center, center to a spine filled delivery of love, the temple / plate, plate hurled into an ancient temple gate / assert, assert the option to stand freely as a temple.

CHAPTER NINE

Location, location made awarely keen to the wisdom found in humanity, a temple / primitive, primitive pineals and the meals made of often said, younger still, temples freed / organ, organ of the transplanted counting, human, temples / commit, commit to a moment clear within a temple's drink of love / marvelous, marvelous and mended by the clarity clarified by your temple / establish, establish a richest meeting of the frankest timing made to a temple / legitimate, legitimate to a planning for temples / entered, entered and waged with, temples / woven, woven hangings telling tales of widest won temples / nativity, nativity meets at a mansion's temples / salvation, salvation kept a refuge for the fraternity pleased with a welcome temple / sleep, sleep deepest in the temples of love / unique, unique regards for the randomly registered temples of doom lifted to love / blood, blood based allowance into temples human / clairovoyant, clairovoyant respect for the freshened friending made to a temple / irrevocable, irrevocable values paid to a temple / urgency, urgency extinguished by a ritual hello for love, the temple / extensive, extensive, research speaks of temples kept for love / judge, judge joins your patterned temples / thrusted, thrusted in crusted revival of the upheaval taught to be tightly love's friendly manner of the temples dabble within, love / liquids, liquids extinguish our patience for less than the water standing light deep in the truth of humanity's temples / lounge, lounge to a temple kept for love / polarize, polarize the purchase for loving temples / nature, nature nestled within and wonders frozen without a temple / reunification, reunification and the freedom to ring for a temple / substance, substance sealed by the fallen temples / tangible, tangible and the legible temples / dorsal, dorsal dealt temples / rubbing, rubbing reaches a frothing temple / capacities, capacities of the granted temples / science, science would be a templed keeper / rush, rush to a ransom kept for a temple / light, light leanings to a temple / condition, condition of the capably templed / ascribed, ascribed and reached from a temple / public, public disgrace gone to a temple lightest in God's eyes / pupils, pupils and the pushing into a temple / fantastic, fantastic and the fondest temples / method, methods mentioned as a temple / valid, valid focus ample to a temple / round, rounds reached within a temple / globe, globe won a temple / ultimate, ultimate and the mentioned temples / approach, approach and the freshest temples / duality, duality and the thrill spelled, a t-e-m-p-l-e / statement, statement planted and the growing allowed within a temple / panorama, panorama placed along a temple / bride, brides focusing in a temple / brief, brief enough to speak of, a "temple" / netted, netted a delcious temple / wide, wide won, a temple width / inevitable, inevitable reaches of the temple / core, core and the concedes stumbled through to a temple / gauges, gauge of the temple's gate swung to a temple / graphic, graphic and the galloping past a temple drawn to love / turn, turn and the presence breathed through to a temple / within, within a whistled temple / cell, cell sprays across a temple / proclaim, proclaim a purchase made for a temple / pillar, pillared communities templed / dialectic, dialectic spelled through a temple / scattered, scattered and the chiming sank through a temple / eternity, eternity of the metatron supreme to temples / lifelines, lifelines gathered here in the temples human.

CHAPTER TEN

Mansions, mansions mean we lean to temples / gene, gene cells encoded with a temple / area, area reached across then, a temple / thermobands, thermobands explored and the strands forged as temples / root, root ramps and temples / either, either and the neither spent for temples / caprices, caprices and the suggestions run to a temple / leave, leave and the luscious lapse to temples / zone, zone and the threat has gone to temples / dust, dust and the rules to temples / honey, honey met with temples / trembling, trembling truths allowed a temple / beam, beams balanced for temples stands / combine, combine and the capture sent to temples / pathway, pathway paced and the hidden rates of temples / hidden, hidden allowance for the temples / project, project allowed a truth told, temple / combine, combine and the decision spent for temples / pathway, pathway plunged through to temples / hidden, hidden and the missions erect within a temple / beam, beam and the bilings paid to temples / color, color and the creations leaning into temples / mingle, mingle mixed for temples / rage, rage allowed to temples / century, century of the mystery spent in temples / translation, translation allowed for in temples / possible, possible and the potential spun to temples / original, original and the mantle worn for temples / rhyme, rhyme and the reasons temples / poetic, poetic and the path won to temples / phraseology, phraseology and the pantomine's temples / script, script and the sculptures sent to temples / prior, prior arrival unto a temple / passive, passive and the pictures spent to temples / plural, plural passes rate a temple / distinction, distinction dearest a temple / intent, intent and the rent laid to temples / work, work and the missions meant through temples / united, united and the deals laid to temples / spirit, spirit and the spatials lounge in temples / soul, soul and the listening to a temple / wood, wood and the situation rules a temple / boil, boil and the blessings won to temples / settle, settle and the meetings made to temples / thought, thought and the light led to temples / uproar, uproar registered to a temple / middle, middle and the measured along a temple / cricket, cricket and the creations rule to a temple / wings, wings and the beating won for a temple / geraniums, geraniums rampant to a temple / two-pence, two-pence meant to temples / spell, spell and a spilling temple / clarify, clarify your part and the passions placed to a temple / case, case and the cushions caged without a temple / past, past and the present allowed a temple / choose, choose and the chosen's temples / feeling, feeling and the fortunate temples / punctuation, punctuation pairing a temple / role, role and the breathing vents of temples / passage, passage pools in temples / again, again and the winning temples / untitled, untitled living's temples / hints, hints matched and the hatching temples / conveyed, conveyed and the encoded temples.

CHAPTER ELEVEN

Accessible, accessible and the simply templed / traditional, traditional reaches into the temples and a good training runs into love / divided, divided and the expelling temples / beginning, beginning and the enervating temples of love zoned energetically smooth / sails, sails and the sealings windy within a temple / unlimited, unlimited liftings of the temples / current, current occurence for a temple / lodge, lodge allows us a temple / volcanoes, volcanoes and the invented temples / lava, lava escapades ride the expel for a temple / domain, domain and the details on a temple / item, items paged and the pacing spent for temples / legion, legion of a light regard for a temple / beauty, beauty believing a forgiven crucify of the living temples / wrath, wrath and the relation to a temple / mood, mood minced less and left totally free to a temple / eruption, eruption and the rations for a temple / isolated, isolated and the levels meet in temple / molten, molten mention of a temple / diverted, diverted for resources spent on a temple's lights / familiar, familiar and the wisest won for a temple / vary, vary fell again into a temple / accurately, accurately read a temple's flights / mature, mature and the mental treason reached for a fathom's temples / meaning, meanings amounted to for temples / defining, defining and the aligning spent on temples / real, real and the reaches won for temples / virtue, virtue allowed you and the yes is a temple / choice, choices detailed and the wellest elected a temple / planting, planting done through a verify of temples / store, store and the above won through a temple / magic, magic meant for temples / imposed, imosed and the parallels went to temples / widespread, widespread and the temple's confess to temples / conduct, conduct cured through temples / modern, modern and the lift-offs to temples / pilgrimages, pilgramages and the pages temple deep in love / chant, chant attentive too, a temple / sky, sky side wtih temples / treetops, treetops glisten with temples / prestigious, prestigious metnioend, a place meant for temples / daylight, saylight deals and the meals won to temples / crops, crops contoured for temples / race, race related, temples / aquaducts, aquaducts duck with temples / remote, remote removes and the ruse fits for temples / lunar, lunar landed temples / ancestral, ancestral tools for temples / drum, drums humming and temples / brethren, brethren brought through temples / moral, moral mentioned for the snaring temples / mysterious, mysterious mansions of temples / substitution, substitution over then for temples human / archaic, archaic appearing and the dearing temples / expression, expression of allowance for a temple / occur, occur daily at temples doors / text, text multiplying to a temple / holy, holy written allowing a temple / served, man is seved through God's graceful leap into the temple / sense, sense suggestive of a magnified temple / symbols, symbols reap a temple / embedded, embedded and the wedded fort of temples / adage, a. dage allowed you, a temple / stark, stark forget of the freedom temples.

CHAPTER TWELVE
Vivid, vivid infuse of the mentioned temples / haunting, haunting over and the values set for temples / metaphor, metaphor magically adept at temples / paradox, paradox pales to temples / hawk, hawk said "yes" to temples / mix, mix a mission into a temple / fly, fly infused with temples / mating, mating matched for temples / migrate, migrates rated temples / curved, curved allow and the confusion spent for temples / flocks, flocks intrigued with temples / resting, resting reads, a temple / bronze, bronze invasions to a temple / stork, stork sent with a temple / rumble, rumble

round found temples / still, still allowed a temple / dash, dash to the doings temple / moisture, moisture marrys your temples / exhalation, exhalation meant for temples / bloom, bloom now dearest at a temple / catalyst, catalyst won for temples / insights, single times insightfully wound to temples / turn, turn on now, a temple / finite, finite fuses linked to temples / aim, aim allows us a temple / adjacent, adjacent purchases reigning with temples / sift, sift soon to the landed temples / semantics, semantics read of temples / commentaries, commentaries cruise to temples / gulf, gulf infused wtih temples / speculation, speculation spun to temples / bridge, bridges bayed with temples / inclusive, inclusive values banked in temples / compels, compels us lightly, a temple / usher, usher past us, a temple / form, form fitted with a temple / moon, moons magic is a temple / spent, spent on species of a temple / ivory, ivory values a temple / tattooed, tattooed and electred too, a temple / feast, feat of the flowrs won as temples / harpoons, harpoons and dunes of a temple / commuanl, communal comments of a temple / fur, fur fled for a temple / salvage, salvage shed at a piece meal temple / iron, iron shut a temple's grates / split, split over and the healing suggests, a temple / shaft, shaft of light sent to the rays metatronic and the species infused with love's temples / gypsy, gypsy joins your temples / stick, stick to the messages for a temple / calves, calves well with a sailing temple / encounter, encounter another strain of temples / illumination, illumination reached for through a temple / startling, startling news of the refuge of temples / gratifying, gratifying reaching into a temple / eloquently, eloquently well with a winning temple / manuscript, maunscript read through a temple / museum, museum of notes reads, "a temple" / comments, comments currently won to temples / atom, atom rays red with temples / crushed, crushed allows of a temple / weight, weight gained gone to a temple / enormous, enormous stars weighted with frozen temples / compassionate, compassionate to a miraculous sort of the temples in love.

CHAPTER THIRTEEN
Entails, entails and the speed into a temple / radiation, radiation and the reachings temples / surface, surface pages and the raises into a temple / kept, kept current with a temple / annointed, annointed and vaunted as a temple / initialize, initialize the rising temples / logic, logic android deep in the mentioned temples / testing, testing allows ruse to go into a temple / emancipate, emancipate has come into the sun arriving in a temple / held, held lightly, as mecry said, for a temple / merely, merely magnified a temple / solitude, solitude rested with and them? a temple / enterprise, enterprise reaching you in a venue born electric within a temple / home, home registered wtih a temple / family, family fathoms the ache of a temple / divulge, divulge only mentioned temples / narrow, narrow gated allowances laid to temples / succumbed, succumbed to resting temples / regions, regions read for temples / hunter, hunter rated a living temple / vastly, vastly detailed ally for a temple / sun, sun shone over a temple / compact, compact cues of the living temples / foundations, foundations dated with your temples / classic, classic occurs and the mergers temples / published, publisehd again, a temple human / leaders, leaders

register for a class called the temples / insightful, insightful suggestions of a temple / affairs, affairs exploded over through a temple / explore, explore a message left to temples / potential, potential potent in a preciser way than life in a temple / supremacy, supremacy cuebes your temples / stood, stood electric to a temple / threshold, threshold pushed and reached, in a published state, for the temples / finish, finish this act with a temple / alone, alone led home to a temple / level, level leaps across a temple / translucent, translucent dreaming of a temple / invisible, invisible to values of a temple / ray, ray orange in a temple / platinum, platinum friends who find a temple / refined, refined meeting resignation from a temple / quality, quality clarified within a temple / stems, stems of a temple / focus, focus on a free line of temples / activated, activated and anticipated as the temples / few, few find less than all the temples / invoke, invoke spoken within a temple / bank, bank of the reason to find release from a temple / line, line legibly led to a temple / chamber, chamber chosen is mine, a temple / quotient, quotient rising within a temple / era, era of the resting yes to a temple / spiraling, spiraling into a healing temple / control, control values for a temple / position, position sent awarely, a temple / mountain, mountains mended with a temple / beyond, beyond a basic, human, temple / crafted, crafted of the lightest, temples / ideas, ideas paged for a temple / rob, rob less the joy of a being temple / predict, predict a crashing temple / change, change allowed through a feeling temple / operate, operate on respect for these temples.

THE HOME-MENTS
LEVEL 53

The Home and the lend inside the living insights of lightening quick loves.

The temple is ours from here to there and with love we live well and of course the cap is ripening into God-ness and the pest is off the days and the daily link inside the squires and the choirs of the lifelines of legends taken off the hook. A faith is returned as inside us license is given into doves of lines elective.

The blood is upon us if we took our sacrement this Easter ray is open, number seven turns to eight and inside us the volcano of life is erect with Doves.

Little ones have come unto us and the rush is inside to keeping up and rays of grey have gone away to find us monster-less and the sunshine finding us inside the key of lights.

Let us find us inside the blue caves of God.

Let us define love and God and home, love is temple, home is kundalini lifts, rise is the temple in here yes, the serpent woman comes to clean the temple with her Dove. After fall the dove tore open the heart of the empty mend and found lightening quick response, she soars in messages built on wigns like hawks lifting over currents in the sky for we are rivers of light with won source, elk, and one falling temptation nearly took us over the Falls as we swam dragons came to lair us to the dove and the serpent, Kundalini, hissed as her dove was torn with wings battered and upon shores I walked with her Saraswati as far as the water's edge and over Falls I heard whispers of "she is in town" and dark clouds tore the shields off eyes once blind and found hearts soaring when the leap of our trout, the fish, snapped lips shut with a satisfied smile at the sky and the double caverns of deep red tornados once spent now home to wear ruby shoes again. "I cannot leave" she said, and another due appeared and washed us home in red lamb blues of deepening days and dependence on this dove to eat.

Eat lightly, she said, and dove into covers of raven black legend as the magic appears in us and the volcano's doom is off the edge and torn the covers off the book so black that lambs were shorn and killed to cover its stamps. We know who you have become, "let us carry you to the fire and the edge and the wounds spray mists of ancient dung out of eyes so sore that red is the only ray which last in them". I have become the God electric, Quetzacoatl stares and we all marry Humanity to the Dove. Today a door has shut and old men have torn the rent into checks of square gingham delivery, for another has advanced the case to courage up and legendary reap the doors of heaven scent. We are the license kept to keeping up the appearance of another snake who knew her nest as ripped. Let lips close on the leaps for a purse is sent filled with perfume and golden coins as Lakshmi shields herself, like Dorothy, with Home.

I am the perfume of God, her Dove.

As great MA has said "Goddess kept, I am."

Angry black snakes have written us into corners of the living Saraswati, Quetzacoatl, Shekinah, and doves who party every day over the bones of left over DNA which caused death to be encoded into man, for there is KNOW Death. It is done in a living light who knows when to declare herself home. For once a fish whispered out my window, look at the age of Pisces come to deliver herself to the Sun and the dance of electric Scot intonations and bag-pipes glen turned into hissing and buzzing as the re-finance became miracles of giving and checks written with light through the Dove. We are respectful of the advanced injunction which left us with tid-bits of driving instincts and the lifting is come as someone surrenders to her inner drive and lets us hear lighting incense and laughing, for a Paloma has returned. "O eterno returno de encontro" is the respectful inspection for the fall is come to the lessening sort and the source is sent over falls of light electric as the Son of God is called home from shores absent and the legendary dues are the known inspection and the listing source of rivers of light which run through our veins like love becoming rivers and lessening floods have risen unto the walls and the filing exasperation is due your inherent need to patent only the worth of everyone yet living in the dens of death. Let her floods erase like veins of seven journeys over plains of Kali's Puja and carry us home to the giving again. Goodnight sweet Dove. Now sleep for help is come in the form of serpents of fire, Christians of hire, and legendary mend of the Story which told us that houses never keep us warm. We are warm in the Garden and Eden has come to her day when Lilith finds the flute and plays us home to read of His Holiness and milks of wisdom and oceans of pens which knew precisely when Tibet became free again, today. I wear my Kalachakra badge and pen the end of destruction and souls and rebirth and ask that only one immaculate nudge be necessary for this penned commitment to humanity.

Make us well, the Phoenix cried and tears spilled into pages have connected us to our contracts with Life, one blood, one pen, one humanity, one grace, one Metatron, one muse, one highlight, one flood, of birthing channel into the rivers of Light.

Let us be born, only once into Dove.

Peace, Metatron, married now to this Dove and you.

THE HEAVEN-MENTS
LEVEL 54

CHAPTER ONE

Crescent, crescent came to the same, heavenward / presence, presence of the finding found throughout a heavenward glance at love / essence, essence spent unto a sending, heaven / akin, akin to a window blended with heaven / credible, credible clues and the pairs made for heaven / possible, possible to a placement for the heavens / lights, lights rays are heavenly / way, way to the welcome heaven / think, think and the worn for heaven / thought, thought about, then, a heaven / residual, residual arose to the heaven ward strands of love / residue, residue out and the hsout is won, heavens / consent, consent to a clue made in heaven / capture, capture enraptured to love / captivate, captivate includes a date with love for the heavens / contours, contours of the creations mantle love of the heavens / stairs, stairs and the leading too, heavens / waves, waves and the whistling heavens / warmth, warmth worn throughout the heavens / cordial, cordial clues of the standing heavens / truce, truce and the truest heavens / deaf, deaf and the notes won to the heavens / iron, iron simply over the heavens / cast, cast across brings a blissing heaven / famous, famous and won for the heavens / boat, boat blue with the floating clouds of heaven / rush, rush and the brushing heavens / pardon, pardon and the came to, of a heaven / appear, appear and the visions won in a pointing heaven / photos, photos simply made and the prints frozen in temples of the heavens / escape, escape and the embrace of the goods won heavenly / well, well and the left alone of heavens / dust, dust and the bowls amidst your heavens / burn, burn allows us a rebuilding heaven / heaven, heaven central to the return for a heaven / untidy, untidy and the living straightens allowed for a miracle on the heavens / bowl, bowl allows us a temple / tear, tear across waves of temples / fever, fever and the focused temples / rub, rub allows a temple / hole, hole and the enlightenment into a heaven for the temples / brace, brace races across a temple / embracing, embracing allows a temple / lucky, lucky star above and the heavens / spilling, spilling overs and the hues of listening heavens / darling, darling dares us the heavens / much, much ado about the business blends of the heavens / grin, grin and the bearing suns of the heavens / grain, grain allows and the letters won for heavens / luxury, luxury lives for heavens / appointed, apointed annointed heavens / bare, bare an essential heaven / fleece, fleece fields of heavens / portion, portions plenty within a heaven / velvets, velvet pillows plush with the touch of heaven / razor, razor red delivery of the sharpest tack into the winds of heaven / claws, claws and the collapse into the laps of heaven / paw, paws hich wag with the lightned rags of heaven / dunce, dunce creates a corners sate for heavens / failed, failed and the feelings blaze with heaven / beast, beast allowed a thrilling glmpse of heaven / greedily, greedily shared another's bleed to heaven / hateful, hateful and the loving hug which will allow forgiveness of the freshest wounds of heaven's charming allow / militant, militant ways are gone to the sun's prefer for heaven.

CHAPTER TWO

Dark, dark unto the lark to heavens / untouched, untouched respect for the reverence of heavens / slumbers, ravens slumber in the numbers twenty deep to the reasons of heaven / land, land is a place to space your heavens / move, move and the magnets mentioned dear in the listing clearest to a living heaven / peace, peace and the within harmonious to a natural friend called heaven / charted, charted and the highest lows who bend into a living heaven / curiousity, curiousity created by the sated won along the lines of heaven / mission, mission schooled in pools serene and the impossible bliss made real through heaven / livestock, livestock and the heard of, heaven's moving / dignity, dignity deals with heavens highest loves / conquer, conquer and the empowers spent for heavens summit / spilled, spilled into pages of heavens rates / peace, again I say, "peace is heaven" / basic, basically free to be heaven / human, human is a heaven / flower, flowers bloom in heavenly faces / color, color erupts in a vase of heaven / trims, trims pipers wings with heaven / base, base of the tables electric with tea and the measures called hu-man treasures of heaven / box, box and the opportunity trued by heaven / key, key found lightly dear to heaven / banner, banner blazes near the keeps of heaven / scrape, scrape erupts in tempest dear to heaven / glued, glued elections of the tastes of heaven / stable, stables intimate with wisdom wild for heaven / mocks, mocks mentioned allowed too and heavens / crumble, crumble and the rumble spent to heavens / restore, restore and the mantle fortunate for heavens / ceilings, ceilings and the sealings meant for heavens / defiled, defiled less through tribes of heavens / title, title tripled through a simple heaven / judgement, judgement jewels of heavens / court, courts collide with heavens / papers, papers pitched to heavens / certified, ceritified allwo of the heavens / righteous, righteous to the rules of heaven / simple, simple and the nimble fit to heavens / crippled, crippled and the supply for a heaven's sake / sink, sink and the sank with allow for the Hawaiian's race to love / caresses, caresses and the treasures spent on love / rough, rough and the ready cubits of lightened love / bucket, buckets kicked allow a trench to heaven / shingles, layer of the shingles spent for heaven's houses / ignite, ignite a rewarded simplicity for heaven's rates / tower, tower trues at heaven / wailing, wailing weds of heaven / acknowledgement, acknowledgement meant for our heavens / brides, brides abalaze with heaven / jezebel, jezezebel well with heaven / noah, noah arc-ed in the highest rates of heaven / dove, dove and the wings of lightest laces placed into heavens / weather, weather and the tossed across for heavens / innocence, innocence spent for heavens / happened, happened to in orchards kept with heavens / seas, seas and the swelling heavens / find, find and the alllow for heavens / there, there is a wind strong within heavens / wisdom, wisdom won through heavens / mesmorized, memorized and the rise to heavens / air, air suggested for the heavens / eternal, e. ternal and the love befriended for our heavens / care, care and the entirest heavens / drawn, drawn humanly too, the heavens.

CHAPTER THREE

Terms, terms treated as a heaven / consideration, consideration created for heaven / solid, solid and the structure spent for heaven / prospective, prospective for the interpretation found at heaven / guarantee, guarantee your being a wiser mend for love of the heavens / purchase, purchase made and the language stood for love, the legendary, heaven / skill, skill applies to the purchases made for love and the heavens rang within, God / account, account for the amounts of love given heavens / diligence, diligence duly paid and the plateau is reach for love too, the heavens / handle, handle a daily deal for the heavens / safeguard, safeguard settled too, the heavens swept / contract, contract clearly for the dearly dated, heavens, now / dual, dual dates of the filling stipend paid to the heavens / trade, trade made and lightly said "the heavens" / donate, donate a portrait to the temples of heaven / grace, grace your face within the heavens / cue, cue made pool free to the masses in the temples gated with heaven / imperial, imperial apparel and the narrow made widest at the hearts of love in the temples nomadic to the heavens / tomorrow, tomorrow awarest of the temples of heavens / member, member made amazed by the thoroughness of love too, the heavens / tight, tight enough to see through and frankly thoroughly love is the thrice ridden example of the diligence dealt to with the heavens / encounter, encounters well within the heavens / involve, involve a solving riddle for the tambourines played in heavens / special, special to the spatial forgive of heaven / picture, picture placed casket deep with heavens / hologram, hologram gambled for within heavens / senior, senior said "forgiven" a temple's heaven / gravel, gravel and the gavel deep with a triumphant heaven / patrol, patrol over and th few who knew of lightest heavens / path, path found and the freedom wound into a heaven / outback, outback, in fact, to the lanes of freely a heaven / civil, civil to a middle manned by love of the heavens / toys, toys and the tools that are tripped by a heaven / trip, trip and the middle's heavens / around, around and the hearing conservations of a kingdom's temples into heaven / return, return and the toil done through a temple of heaven / entertain, entertain and the reigning heavens / entertainment, entertainment sent into a temple / preview, preview and the mentiones of the temples / week, week and the won within a temple / celebrate, celebrate a winning kingdom of heavens / reserve, reserve allows us a palace to a kingdom 44/ sinking, sinking and the linking found inside a temple wound within a heaven . steaming, steaming and the listings won for heavens / santa, santa said a gift is led into a heaven / xerox, xerox apparels and the narrows of the heavens / inevitable, inevitable narrows and the mantra of a kingdom / bound, bound and wound into a kingdom / overtly, overtly challenged and the mansions of a kingdom too and heaven / prize, prize and the reasons to the heavens / music, music is narrow into a heaven / sponsor, sponsor and the listing of a heaven / finals, finals and the feel of a heavenly kingdom / best, best and the placement of a kingdom to the heavens / proceed, proceed and the planet's sun is a kingdom too, and heavens / medical, medical and the mentions of a heaven / fit, fit to be a heaven / reason, reason and the reasonable kinship to heavens / total, total too, a heaven / topple, topple winning a heaven / top, top of the trio kingdom coming, heaven's basically / aware, aware and the generous nature of a kingly heaven / generous, generous and the genuine heavens / riches, riches made in hearts alive within Godly heavens.

CHAPTER FOUR

Alleviate, alleviate the listed lessens for a fortune paid to temples / otherwise, otherwise and the wisest into temples / hardship,

hardship and the handles left to temples / puff, puff and the pistons templed / whales, whales and the lovers lifted into a lightening love / whack, whack and the reckoning occurent through the boulevards of heaven / excess, excess has gone to the techniques of love for a potion heavenly / spirit, spirit esential and the mentions made for the heaven's gates / attend, attend a friendly banter of the mansions horizontal within your heavens / marathon, marathon amuse and the muses paid for heaven / stimulation, stimulation allows your listening plow of the laughter heavenward / conspicuous, conspicuous to a momentary lapse for heaven / wonders, wonders win for heaven / economic, economic trends found for the heavenly / program, program due the mentally driven alloance for the heavens / devastating, devastating details of the dialects due a marriage of the heavens / wise, wise to a wonderful mention for heavens / hug, hug and the held forth for these heavens / focus, focus fused within a mortal heaven / burning, burning for the empress onto heavens / strange, strange often too, and the trades windy within love for the heavens / alchemy, alchemy and the cares too often for a heavenly gate / impossible, impossible of the planets have3 frozen through into the heavens / inside, inside and the sacred shores throughout the heavens / shadow, shadow of the heavens won / bright, bright and the starry compare for the heavens / record, records of the resurrection spent in heavens / souls, souls and the decreed to and then the latest into heavens / baring, baring and the sharing occurence for heavens / sense, sense and the assurance for a heaven / impugn, impugn and the moons within a lightest heaven / purpose, purpose and the assertive heavens / experimentation, experimentation and the draft read for heaven / defy, defy and the deify allowed through the heavens / rock, rock and the registers onto heavens / dazzling, dazzling appliance for the heavens / veritable, veritable visions onto heavens / diverse, diverse details fo the heavens / all, all to the ceilings heavens / amalgamation, amalgamation caused through heavens / accompany, accompany of the best into the heavens / felicitous, felicitous and the folly forth to heavens / lush, lush and the greens too and heavens / lighten, lighten and the lavish tools for heave / steal, steal and the whistling into the heavens / track, track and the threes for heavens / jumping, jumping and the conlusions forth to heavens / dance, dance and the listening truths of heavens / floor, floor and the flurries framed too to heavens / stick, stick and the heavenly depths of love / mercurial, mercurial and the measures matched forth to heavens / theme, theme and the thrown into seams of heavens / matched, matched throughout by the beauty of heaven / settle, settle the matching heavens / vulnerability, vulnerability of the variations of heaven / candor, candor of the curation of heaven / alienation, alienation of the sentinel squared to heaven / karma, karma and the returning often heavenward / relief, relief and the ruling heavens / square, square and the sincerest heavens / domestic, domestic details find the humans heavenly / zero, zero and the nero absolute within heavens / beckons, beckons and the reckoning to heavenly Metatrons / advance, advance frames to heaven's gates.

CHAPTER FIVE

Door, door opens into heaven / sweet, sweet in an attractive way to heaven / top, top tips to heaven / gorgeous, gorgeous curls of the heavens / feather, feather of the floating heavens / lumens, lumens and the arouse planed to heavens / sheer, sheer and the soundings heavens / windy, windy and the winter's winging heavens / scribe, scribe entailed into the heavens / illuminate, illuminate the reasoing narrower still to heavens / blow, blow and the m,axim set through heavens / errant, errant the best ran abreast through the heavens / seeded, seeded and the sets run into the capably current heavens / crazy, crazy and the crafted rates of hevens / background, background and the veer into a heave / vibe, vibe and the vibrant truths of heavens / vibrant, vibrant and the reaching into the precisions of heaven / storage, storage allowed for the straying heavenward / in, in and the tools for the heavens / project, project and the pattern worn to heaven / after, after all a pattern lost with heaven / before, before always to heaven / rough, rough enough to rescue you for heaven / sensuous, sensuous measures meet at heaven / most, most and the moistly inner heavens / tribe, tribe resurrects insure your heavens / forest, forest focused on heavens / harvest, harvest led through heavens / pride, pride said, yes, to heavens / thanks, thanks allowed for heavens / dare, dare to be excitedly free for heavens / excitedly, excitedly dear unto heavens / guitar, guitar genuflected deep to heavens / playing, playing allows a respect for the heavens / grind, grind off and done with in heavens / comfort, comfort comes to heavens / passion, passion won to heaven / fury, fury out through heavens / poignancy, poignancy penned through heavens / fluent, fluent to a fuse for heavens / dust, dust and the places above your heavens / groove, grooves and the engraving for a heaven / insist, insist on a new trend to love's blossom into the heavens / tempest, tempest over and the dues paid to heavens / exclusive, exclusive and the alibis found for the heavens / appropriate, appropriate and pleasant in the means metatronically rich and the seasons sweet within heaven / accompany, accompany the relative to these heavenly gifts / shall, shall we be any less than heaven? / show, show us your ways unto heaven / designation, designation worn as heaven / assumption, assumptions schooled within heaven / property, property pays for heaven / ignition, ignition nearing you heavens / shift, shift allows you heaven / drive, drive into daisies of heaven / firmly, firmly stood a heaven / mediocrity, mediocrity not allowed for heaven / accelerator, accelerator found for heavens / adrenaline, adrenaline allowed to heaven / standstill, standstill over for the heavens / perfect, perfect apply unto the heavens / republic, republic of the venues shared for heaven / desire, desire detailed by heavens / wise, wise winnings sung to heavens.

CHAPTER SIX

Solution, solution found for heavens / transformation, transformation astounds your heavens / flash, flash past these heavens / lines, lines last to heavens / consuming, consuming concurrent with the heavens / design, design assigned you, heaven's / horoscope, horoscope assignments for the heavens / curly, curly in a swirly way for heaven / icons, icons rest in heaven's estates / aromas, aromas blend for heaven / perchance, perchance the dance is heaven / sensory, sensory elate with heaven / pillow, pillow told the secrets of the heavens / mist, mist

mentioned, heaven's / prophetic, prophetic apply for the heavens / tense, tense in secrets lost for heavens / authenticity, authenticity tools to heaven / utopia, utopia reached through heavens / pearls, pearls elastic with the heavens / coach, coach colors swirl to heavens / mask, mask off and the fortunes made by heavens / task, task told, "be", a heaven / tip, tip of the steeple deep in heavens / remove, remove a remaidner for the heavens / rustic, rustic rendered heavenly to God / sport, sport short with heaven's team / moisturizer, moisturizer leads to heaven / hint, hint about a heaven / bonanza, bonanza reached through heavens / indulgence, indulgence won to heaven / secret, secret of the apply to heavens / apply, apply for heaven / flaws, flaws the clause for the fairest in heaven / radiance, radiance ample to be for heaven / instantly, instantly known through heaven / intense, intense allows for heaven / purchase, purchase made through heaven / reach, reach a deal to heaven / dramatically, dramatically real to heaven / refining, refining the signing of love for a heaven / insulate, insulate less, gain more for heaven / brush, brush across the pages fine with heaven / shine, shine dealt with by a heaven / silk, silk amplify to heavens / magic, magic meetings made for heaven / gloss, gloss over the screen green with heavens / silhouette, silhouette wet with the sands of heaven / formula, formula fixed as heaven / silly, silly over and the done withing of an affair called heavens / wash, wash anothers eyes with heaven / simplicity, simplicity comes into your heavens / fresh, fresh allow and the flow for heaven / trend, trend allowed you is heaven / exclusive, exclusive neighbors for the heavens / invitation, invitation reads of heavens / skin, skin signed by heavens / vitamins, vitamins flown into heaven / bed, bed applied to the heavens / invisible, invisible beads glaze our lights with heaven / proper, proper to the sealing for a patient sort called heaven / initials, initials spell you, h-e-a-v-e-n-s / balance, balance allowed for and the feelings felt too, heavens / addicted, addicted rests at the rates of heaven / brilliant, brilliant to a bevy of the bonuses called heaven.

CHAPTER SEVEN

Vow, a vow made for heaven / celibacy, celibacy sealed of heavens / radar, radar ranging heavens / equivalent, equivalent caging opened to heavens / elements, elements mentioned for heaven / limit, limit off then, heaven / cuddly, cuddly sorts of heaven / buzz, buzz above these heavens / local, local matrix lifts to heaven / film, film focused on the heavens / purchase, purchase made now with heavens / mesh, mesh off again, the heavens / swell, swell off then, to heavens / ruined, ruined the appreciate for the heavens / cut, cut again for heaven / appropriately, appropriately due the heavens / attention, a. ttention trailed to the heavens / detail, detail opens with heaven / despite, despite these reasons the heavens / era, era established as heaven / mortification, mortification off then to the anthems found for heaven / clump, clump of the reasons too, heavens / remedy, remedy dealt yours, the ehavens / evolution, evolution listened to through heavens / spray, spray across weeds of heaven / bundle, bundle cut now for heaven / range, range rested on the heavens / explore, explore a shore for heaven / stir, stir the mission within your heavens / stew, stew made of the bones fed to heaven / hungry, hungry goes to the heavens /

jeopardy, jeopardy joined at heaven / random, random allow for the heavens / sutiable, suitable booths of heavens / mood, mood matched within heaven / depending, depending done through the heavens / yoga, yoga and the yellows of the reflexive heavens / clip, clip occurs through the heavens / lounge, lounge opens near the heavens / twister, twister worn for he4aven / easy, easy done thorugh the heavens / popular, popular with the heavens / vanish, vanish occurs too, the heavens / roll, roll appeals too, the heavens / windfire, windfire fed the heavens / wildest, wildest weds the heavens / hypnotic, hypnotic access to the heavens / starry, starry moons of heavens / pool, pool pays for heavens / zoom, zoom allows a heaven / fast, fast at these heavens / coat, coat off to heavens / freshness, freshness led to heavens / effortless, effortless sorts of heavens / mix, mix mentioned for the heavens / obtain, obtain a sort of heaven / stations, stations reached through heavens / products, products penned for heaven / instinctively, instinctively due an end for heaven / separate, separate the pages won for heaven / pair, pair aspires to the heavens / solution, solution raised for heavens / refining, refining pages as heaven / visible, visible bliss to heavens

CHAPTER EIGHT

Repair, repair the rise to heavens / prevention, prevention skies through heaven / combine, combine allowed to heaven / insulate, insulate less your heaven / curl, curl wields a heaven / lift, lift opens to heaven / heaven, heaven gazed into through man / liquid, liquid lands glisten through the life human, a heaven / garden, garden dates and the duration grown to heavens / transform, transform most through heavens / millenium, millenium gifts become your heavens / samples, samples of the temples sent into the heavens / bright, bright enough to live lightly in the heavens / purest, purest reset of the blessings sent to the triumphant heavens / boost, boost across the appearance of heavens / intention, intention and the remission for heavens / lazer, lazer across the legends of heaven / holster, holster and the healing fill of heaven / print, print across the heavens of love / alteration, alteration of the rational heavens / carefree, carefree of the simple heavens / elect, elect and the listenings temples of heaven / release, release and the deals often to heavens / ideal, ideal and the simplest heavens / rain, rain and the prints stylish within heavens / solid, solid and the states forthright heavens / forte, forte and the found along the lanes of heaven / dropped, dropped and the listening lens of heaven / novelty, novelty kneeling into the heaens / language, language and the leading heavens / shout, shouting and the outings in heaven / original, original to simple news of heaven / platinum, platinum nipples of heaven / champion, champion prepare for heaven / mineral, mineral menu of heaven / trace, trace and the opening gains of heaven / detangle, detangle and the lightening heavens / lavish, lavish and the listed pairs of heaven / moisture, moisture and the adjoining heavens / silk, silk and the saints race to heaven / prominent, prominent and the peace for the heavens / design, design and the drafted to of heaven / guest, guest allowed into heaven / fool, fool out to the heavens / shine, shine and the tops off to the kitchens of heaven / trend, trend and the affiliated heavens / extracts, extracts and the respect for the channels of

loving heavens / ventilation, ventilation and the opening into a heaven / vow, vow made to be a heaven / thermal, thermal willings to the ceilings of heaven / attitude, attitude moved into the heavens / leaves, leaves and the living heavens / enjoy, enjoy a soaring heave / mold, mold and the amplified heavens / club, club and the caring heavens / remedy, remedy and the rescue for the heavens / perfume, perfume and the painted screens of heaven / reputation, reputation assigned into the screens of heaven / factory, factory contoured by the heavens / opaque, opaque and the rising heavens / honey, honey and the sticky intrigues with heaven / advance, advance details of the heavens / stride, stride and teh trends often for heaven / bouncing, bouncing and the bluest religion relieved unto the heavens

CHAPTER NINE

Strapped, strapped onto the heavens / sponge, sponge and the accordance of the heavens / spare, spare unto regards for the heavens / interactive, interactive samples of the heavens / formula, formula of the figurative heavens / impact, impact made unto the forged lids of heaven / absorb, absorb the retails of the heavens / traffic, traffic and the touring heavens / proceeds, proceeds paid unto the heavens / space, space allowed a heaven / lifestyle, lifestyle changed by the heavens / simplicity, simplicity of the causes afforded heavens / page, page and the heavens res / reflection, reflection and the rapt into heavens / radiant, radiant and teh readings on the heavens / allure, allure insured by the heavens / benefactor, benefactor found for the basic heavens / cruise, cruise cured by the heavens / core, core allowed for the heavens / savor, savor and the flavor for the heavens / movement, movement and the towards unto heaven / poses, poses and the truest heavens / naked, naked unto the heavens / evolution, evolution fares fond of heavens / lips, lips and the infusions of love for the heavens / satin, satin and the covers heavens / exquisite, exquisite rituals of the heaven / modern, modern miracles mitochondria deep in heavens / roast, roast allowed a heaven / phobia, phobia and the fillings elevated to the heavens / stage, stage and the standing for heavens / wound, wound and the hurling past a heaven / foundation, foundation and the futures into heave / races, races and the sentry found to heavens / community, community and the cures made for the heavens / volume, volume infused by the heavens / magnanimous, magnanimous deals for the heavens / compatible, compatible cures for the heavens / bare, bare and the born winds of the heavens / museum, museum and the marriage of the heavens / interior, interior and the suggestions of the heavens / gloss, gloss and the greetings of the heavens / contact, contact cured for the heavens / confection, confection spent on the heavens / pattern, pattern attempted for the heavens / nude, nude and the knelt within, heaven / dynamic, dynamic and the daring heaven / inspire, inspire and the sires due a planet of heaven / minor, minor mention of the heaven / wonder, wonder of the sunder heaven / romance, romance ensues through the cues of heave / tailor, tailor your table to be a heave / complex, complex cues for the heaven / appetite, appetite trues the heaven / pageant, pageants paged by the ehaven / trendy, trendy days of the heaven / collectibles, collectibles during the heaven / art, art and the starts within the heaven / sculpt, sculpt the durations of the heaven / pedestal, pedestals dared by the heaven / sandal, sandal suggested for the heaven / butler, butler bluffs due the heavens / promptly, promptly lend the heavens / worth, worth a fortunate love of the heavens

CHAPTER TEN

Fingerprint, fingerprint and the mint greens of heaven / identity, identity due the heavens / format, format and the free wills of heavens / destroy, destroy details and the features for a heaven / hip, hip hops past these heavens / parade, parade last and first the heavens / toasting, toasting the roasting heavens / honor, honor the simple arc-angelic heavens / gathering, gathering and the gains range to the heavens / upon, upon and the listed heavens / game, game and the genders of the heavens / mounting, mounting and the mentions of the swords of heaven / impressive, impressive and the strength gained to the heavens / bidding, bidding and the believing bade the heavens / stellar, staellar suggestions for the heavens / party, party placed upon these heavens / program, program of the greenest heavens / observatory, observatory, observatory clauses planned for the heavens / fame, fame found in heavens / airy, airy of the ways won for heavens / desire, desire details the heavens / abstract, abstract cures the heavens / calm, calm, cool, and exceptional too, the heaens / vase, vases placed in open mouths of heaven / drift, drift allowed now to the heavens / velvet, velvet and the values of the heavens / exuberance, exuberance sails into the heavens / vintage, vintage valleys into the heavens / behold, behold another's heavens / devious, devious detailes of the sorts heavenly / figure, figures of the focus on the heavens / character, character curres the heavens / sophisticated, sophisticated rates of raptured heavens / found, found allow for the heavens / cream, cream green occurrence for the heavens / dare, dare to detail the heavens / indulge, indulge and the heavens wait for the lessons of love / toll, toll and the needs blessed by heavens / overwhelming, overwhleming and the wisdom for the heavens / lively, lively lessons of the heavens / rounds, rounds and the pounds forth with heavens / luck, luck listens to the heavens / charitable, charitable throes for heaven / benefit, benefit reached by heavens / manage, manage a mention of the heavens / paddle, paddles laced with heavens / cameo, cameo and the cures for the heavens / poetry, poetry placed along the heavens / initially, initially spent for the reconstructive shores of the heavens / vibes, vibes raid the heavens / fill, fill adjoins along the heavens / sturdy, sturdy details for the shores of heaven / stream, streams strewn with heavenly pebbles / adorned, adorned along the heavens / sachets, sachets shron to heaens / pillow, pillow and the living heaven / shade, shade and the shone forth with heavens / runaway, runaway for the strange heavens / affair, affair found in disciples of the heavens / power, power placed to heavens / involve, involve the solving self for the heavens / detoxify, detoxify and the sighs of the heavens / pampered, pampered and the pools of the heavens / lured, lured and the appearance of the heavens

CHAPTER ELEVEN

Climbing, climbing came into the heavens / diva, diva dealt with in the heavens / stretch, stretch came into the heavens / layer, layers linked with heavens / role, role of the rewarded heavens / pinch, pinch grabbed by heavens / universal, universal and the rehearsal of the heavens / stumbled, stumbled across these heavens / grueling, grueling and the greys gone to heavens / making, making and the sake blue with heavens / recently, recently rehearsed by the heavens / comic, comic cures fo rthe heavens / auction, auction of the heavens / joyful, joyful due in heavens / muses, muses mapped by these heavens / sensation, sensation sounds to heavens / angelic, angelic allure of the heavens / spill, spill cleared by the heavens / strung, strung across with heavens / luminous, luminous numbers of the heavens / ordinary, ordinary days of the heavens / motif, motif deep in th heavens / relaxing, relaxing cures for the heavens / layer, alyers leap to heavens / inspired, inspired sorts capable fo the heavens / spoon, spoon of the columns of heaven / fiber, fiber filled with heaven / fanciful, fanciful features farest with heven / disco, disco dues of heaven / flower, flowers deep with heaven / fringe, fringe fields our heavens / flip, flip tossed to heaven / politics, politics cost only the heavens / wore, wore a coating fresh with heaven / terrified, terrified tears and the squares to a heaven / camp, camp clauses and the causes heavenly / bash, bash and the rashes heavenly / debut, debut and the dues paid to heavens / event, event and the lints heavenly / prayer, prayer of the plenty heavens / cause, cause and the cures touring these heavens / challenged, challenged and the chastened heavens / mention, mention again a living heaven / heritage, heritage and the reach into the heavens / noise, noise and the nestled into greetings of heaven / worthy, worthy and the wedded heavens / navel, navel and the dealt with heavens / marvelous, marvelous and the mavericks of heaven / beads, beads and the basics believed in of heaven / wire, wire and the wearing heavens / magnets, magnets and the amazement for the heavens / zen, zen and the touring heavens / porcelain, porcelain and the pairing of the heavens / fragrance, fragrance and the features mentioned to the heavens / iridescent, iridescent clauses and the cures for the heavens / sleek, sleek in details of the heavens / watch, watch and your heavens / utilitatian, utilitarian treats for the heavens / tale, tale about and within these heavens / psychedelic, psychedelic and teh suggested heavens / surplus, surplus and the sandy waves of the heavens / barefoot, barefoot and the blistering winds of heaven / charm, charm and the simply cared for of heaven / image, image amused with the heavens.

CHAPTER TWELVE

Crazy, crazy about your capers and the touring of the heavens / contrary, contrary contours and the insures of the heavens / luxury, luxury leads to the heavens / lounge, lounge listened into these heavens / activity, activity cured by these heavens / dimensional, dimensional and the details for these heavens / slope, slope insured by the heavens / met, met and the measures gained to the heavens / radiant, radiant and the reasons for these heavens / shall, shall and the simply of heavens / verify, verify the reply of a lateral goodness for love of the heavens / success, success sorted for teh heavens / level, level to the venues of love, the present tense for heaven / least, least of these, deaf, to a present tier of love, these mountains blue in heavens / question, questions capably explained as the heavens / morale, morale builds for the heavens / overcome, overcome the sums lessened throughout the lessen heavens / sufficient, sufficient and the streets in loom with heaven / fine, fine the alignment meant for the resign to insigns on love through the heavens / body, body of proof is said to exist through lovely heavens / knowledge, knowledge allowed us a listing of the heavens / sheep, sheep suggest the discipled kind of heavens / fold, fold a maturest note on the heavens / own, own your own potion for the heavens / world, world of wisest said, "the heavens" / return, return to the regard of the heavens / physical, physical dismiss of the denial of the heavens / seek, seek a stylish listen for the heavens / consider, consider one capable to love for the mission, heaven / judgement, judgement led past the heavens / prove, prove how to be heavenly / mistake, mistakes off to the heavens / stare, staare across a simple taste for love, the heavens / race, race along a lease for the heavens / lesson, lesson onto the heavens / sacrifice, sacrifice focused into a heaven / pass, pass alongest year for heaven / pattern, pattern plced platteer deep into the heavens / memory, memory amused by the surges sent for the bliss domed by the seratonin flown to heaven / speak, speak well for the simply, home, heaven / harm, harm cast past a heaven gate / pest, pest outed and the listening lends you a hearty throne homeward still within heaven / action, action sent for through heaven / attraction, attraction dated for the heavens / aura, aura elated by these heavens / division, divisions over through the heavens / criticism, criticism now ended through the heavens / push, push for a recall of the heavens / rust, rust off and into the heavens / rheumatism, rheumatism moves to capitalize without heaven / among, among the miracles are the roses of heaven / deposit, deposits made detailed by heaven / words, words witnessed by these heavens / envious, envious last and most to heaven / thought, thought of threes of heaven / avarice, avarice rests at a splice for heaven / creation, creation duration heaven / mingle, mingle most with heaven / assemble, assemble now, near, the heavens / remember, remember to reside in the star heavenly / decide, decide to be interior to a merkaba field heavenly / design, design the repair fields mechanically heavenward / detail, detail enjoyed throughout these heavens / deploy, deploy amid heavenward stances.

CHAPTER THIRTEEN

Law, law for the legend, heaven / atom, atom bombed less for heaven's orbitals / mental, mentally checked out for the heavens / lust, lust enought o know desire for the heavens / salvation, salvation shelved has foound a soothe for you and your heavens / prepare, preparea a page written into heavens / flesh, flesh rests at heaven / born, born to be simply of heaven / choices, choices last through heaven / error, error offered soothe by heaven / self, self of the mentioned heavens / azure, azure seas of bluest glees by heaven / grandest, grandest strands of standing cabins deep in love for heaven / channel, channel your meetings best at hearts of lvoe for the kingdoms of heaven / dimensions, dimensions mention the new gates of heaven / speed, speed to a crossing allowance for the heavens / word, word said was "heaven" / essence, essence set on heaven / digital, digital dues onto heaven / permission, permission to be planted here electrically at the heart of heaven / resume, resume your rooms filled in heaven / dive, dive to a plunging for heaven / famous, famous miracles blend into heaven / traditional, traditional thronging for the heavens / turtle, turtle green expire may seem like heaven / hatched, hatched equates for the heavens / virtual, virtual to a melting heaven / data, data dealt forth eithin heaven / under, under all and over all, the heavens / species, species suggested that water is heaven / sea, sea sent for the heavens / rainforest, rainforest bought and brought too, the heavens / discovery, discovery comes into your house on love's streets for heaven / swim, swim across the planes of heaven / coral, coral limbed expressions fo love for the underneath of heaven / island, islands keep us here for the dearest living to heaven / currency, currency comes unto those who win for heaven / field, fields currect within the electrical hum for the heavens / kindle, kindle a flame simply set for the heavens / enhance, enchance your chance to be a heaven / sands, sands calling you to your heaven / aside, aside the sides won for heaven / prize, prize pinched and gained through heaven's gaze / whom, whom do we reckon as the heaven? / movement, movement coming thorugh the heavens / writer, writer bids too, the heavens / blind, blind enough to see through the heavens / help, help us well within a heaven / ethic, ethics set a scentral too, the clients based in love for the human heavens / citizen, citizen won for heaven / integrate, integrate your rate for heaven / offer, offer made and set unto the heavens / global, global glee has won a heaven / revere, revere for you ringing into a heaven / humane, humane unto dreaming for the heavens / form, form found around these heavens / conceptual, conceptual trips into the heavens / renewed, renewed by the steaming heavens / wisdom, wisdom woos your heavens / literacy, literacy dearest unto these heavens / local, local blends entire into the heavens / project, projects penned by heaven / issue, issue a regard for these heavens / declare, declare a deal "made" by these heavens.

THE BOULEVARD-MENTS
LEVEL 55

CHAPTER ONE

Passion, passion paced to the paved remember and the sender ascendant to the finished boulevards in love / parcels, parcels and the host within, lovely boulevards / place, place your boulevards near the heart of matter amended through love / boulevard, boulevards directionally intact to the facts born metaphysically through our love / street, street toured simply true to the temple's men, hu-man, boulevards / relay, relay the Other won to the waving shades of elastic electric overglide into light boulevards / proclaim, proclaim a pattern done too, the patterns win released healing throughout boulevards / respite, respite remained the ruse free deliver into love, the boulevard / respect, respect a heart deep into the project called love, A boulevard / cortex, cortes and the cubic assemblage blindly led to the living boulevards / cover, cover and the shredded abide into glory proclaimed / cord, cord severed and swerved through a boulevard / abide, abide in a fashionable mention called hermetica and the mentally stewarded boulevard / caliber, calibers cured and the capable blend into humanity at the living boulevards / camera, camers syrup deep in the sticky spirits of love's humanity, a heightened boulevard / race, race to the cusp and a clearly worded forgiveness sought through preciousness into light boulevards / court, court cued to blast through to boulevards / wheels, wheels sealed on the reeling parallels, boulevards / waters, waters and the woods of a healed boulevard / winds, winds and the seeds that trended too, a blvd / wonders, wonders worn and a smile's rewards for the fantastic metaphors called boulevards / walks, walks lightly and speaks softly into a beginning boulevard / wants, wants a winning combination fortunately blvds are, lightly / wills, wills a winning clash and the healing lash felt throughout our featured mention of blvds. / formed, formed and formal abide into the reside called precisely sized through out blvs / protects, protects a leaseheld profession of love this, the blvd / comment, comment cures our penchant for blvds / contents, contents keep an arisen venue for the living blvd / bless, bless and this too a blvd / meet, meet in a fashionable mention of the abide instride our living blvd / step, step into a mastery of the mattered maturity called a blvd / store, store spent and the upward climb to a street called a blvd / weighs, weighs most to a host felt forward thrown into a spiral mastery called degrees found in a fusion's blvd / met, met another miracle in a fitted light lend called pattern=-free blvds / compare, compare a note too, a legend's blvd / wills, wills wed to a livings blvd / connect, connect made to a respect for the features, blvds / bless, bless this inquiry misty vblue into an ushered blvd / found, found a farther way to find a nearer stream claled the blinded blvd / heal, heal tonight and the rights allowed to require only the fullest featured bld / hire, hire sanctuary and mean it through a blvd / haven, haven held as holy thoughts of light blds / hawaiian, hawaiian led and fed for the future blvds / place, place suggested and the restedkneeling is set for the hearts of love in the blvd / port port and the sort on too, a winning blvd / wealth, wealth and the sort who hasten too, the blvd / warm warm into dialects elective throughout our heat for the blvds / stores, stores into directives of the tears meant for blvds / care, care about creations spelling of thee, the blvd, h-u-m-a-n / spell, spell

out the scenes for the blvds / relate, relate and the rationale for the featured blvds / rivet, rivet into trivets hot with blvds / solve, solve and solutions sent for the corrective erective blvd / absolute, absolute and the details empowered through the light led blvds / relative, relative to a require for the finer blds / reader, reader sent a detial whole in light repair for the female blvd / repair, repair a wiring aired yes too, a blvd / speak, speak of the focus into a blvd / choose, choose a peaceful muse for the blds / absolve, absolve th solvent wons blvds / hire hire a sharing blvd / chase, chase less find more a lightened blvd / over, over and the futures made for the lightness blvds / title, title and the miracle of a blvd.

CHAPTER TWO

Smile, smile and the while a way too, a blvd / stare, stare into lessons blended to show a welcome experience and the thrilling attend to a mentioned apparent called precious into a tune full for blends A, a blvd / smirk, smirk and the work mercurial too a blvd / fair, fair and the feelings faint gone too, a miracle through the blvd / complexion, complexion and the need for the featured funds and the miracles made and the blvds / sun, sub and the central's funds for blvds. / love, love and the listened too, a blvd / go, go and the pieces pent in blvds / appear, appear and the pistols spent in blvds / alleviate, alleviate and the listening through the blvds / drawn, drawn into the simply blvd / dawn, dawn and the dearness into a blvd / now, now and the showing munificence through a blvd / remember, remember radically and the retinue blown through a blvd / secluded, secluded less and fed more though blvds / pure, pure to a pistol packed with blvds / volcanic, volcanic dimensions and the eruptive rates through blvds / lava, lava led to blvds / period, period paid and often minute throughout a blvd / match, match made in witty repose to the One who arose to blvds / flowed, flowed and empowered through the radically blvds / plunged, plunged and the mother's run is into a departments filled in initialed blvds / quenching, quenching and the cinching into a blvd / explosion, explosion over and the trenches placed about your blvds / fracture, fracture and the ripples met in melting blvds / flanks, flanks allowed and pleasures paid through the thrilling blvds / rifting, rifting experience and the exposure expensive less and the pelted placement / meant for examine throughout your blvds / zone, zone and the trueness meant for blvds / wide, wide and the enough sent and spent for the beyondness blvd / condition, conditions met and the invested entrance allowed through invested apparel / and the middle mended apparent blvds / middle, middle manned and the planned expansion into blvds / band, band and the setting blvds / keen, keen and the experience spent in examined blvds / ominous, ominous amends and a pleasing apparel worn to blvds / giant, giant agenda and the addenda added for blvds / beneath, beneath and the beauty fortunate into a blvd / ascribe, ascribe prepared and the pleasing paired blvds / ray, ray red into a blvd / drawn, drawn and the sorted sported blvds / prove, prove and the pieces blvd / doctrine, doctrine and the dearest blvds / instance, instance danced and the God given blvds / until, until a welcome living blvd / document, documents paced through living blvds / subsequent to a manner met through blvds / danger, danger and the dealing blvds / might, might appeared in detailed blvds / attached, attached trials and the fanning blvds / conception, conception and the coming blvds / blend, blending channels spent in the summation ended in blvds / reference, reference made to blvds / invade, invade allowed a treasured blvd / attribution, attribution and the intrigues measured in figures made through blvds / doubt, doubt detailed and the degrees thrown past your blvds / dissent, dissent dealt then to blvds / case, case closed round the featured blvds / date, date and the daring blvds / interpolated, interpolated and extract into a blvd / probability, probability and the thrilling intrinsic in blvds / our, our and the thrilling techniques too, a blvd. / able, able and the billing bade a pretense blvd deep / chief, chief and the contentment made a blvd.

CHAPTER THREE

Shed, shed alone and built to throne an enthroned application for the dam broken through to love is a blvd / blued, blued and the rude forego into love, a blvd / ridges, ridges moved into passions placed enhancement for blvds / incident, incident into coincident blvds / glance, glance along listening paradise and the risen blvds / turned, turned about and found too, a blvd / reminder, reminder and the sender met in descent ascent to the signaled blvd / dimension, dimes\nsion and the remission too, a degree in regards throughout a blvd / important, important to a sorted dear, blvd / serious, serious about this, the blvds / proper, proper into simple temples of quiet regard for the futures accord called / precisely a blvd of love / peace, peace made throughout the reigns of offered blvds / minutes, minutes in dynamic magic to a blvd / vivid, vivid in ivy green views of the fusions blvds / special, special and the seal made in a metatronic mansion's blvd / process, process paid for the pathway's blvds / open, open to a hoping blvd / sense, sense allowed a mathematical blvd / seed, seed plants a perfectly red blvd / aware, aware to a scared elect and the listening blvd / memories, memories met with a regret knotted across a blvd / goodness, goodness and the gazing truest to a blvd / clear, clear and the perfect blvd / first, first ways aware to a blvd / picture, picture of the mixture's blvds / presence, presence attended too, a blvd / energy, energy made the shipping effective for a blvd / worse worse into caution-less blvds / channel, channel and the panel's blvds / enhanced, enhanced trance leaves and the degrees made a blvd / myself, myself the mussing pentagon for living blvds / gentle, gentle into mental amusement's blvds / subconscious, subconscious news and the haze off the blvds / upon, upon a page's blvds / student, student cures and the sees blvds / eradication, eradication of lessen into a muses pages blvds / refer, refer to a reef's choice of blvds / habits, habits healed to blvds / fabric, fabric peeled to reveal a blvd / almost, almost hosted through blvds / occur, occur too, a blvd / astral, astral means agreed to, a blvd / merging, merging met at a living blvd / vehicle, vehicle pleased through a metric blvd / behavior, behavior seen to a central blvd / pace, pace cross wages blvds / grow, grow in allowance of the listening blvds / standing, standing suggested in awe too, a blvd / powerful, powerful impress of an address too, blvds / proved proved allow and the how too, a blvd / preparation, preparation ascendant to a valued befriend of the regard for, a blvd / intensive,

intensive accrue of the definition mutual to a blvd / taught, taught befriend by a daring blvd / result, result is a terseness forgiven to a ressurected living blvd / available, available to a vehicular blvd / study, study our blvd's departure for love / scholarly, scholarly apply to the securest blvds / ascendancy, ascendancy allowed in abiding sea-green blvds / promise, promise to part through blvds of love / cosmic, cosmic accept of the reaction called passion for the blvds / relax, relax into simple blvds / emananted, emananted for the saturated blvds / aura, aura allowed too, a blvd.

CHAPTER FOUR

Demeanor, demeanor and the truer rationale for a blvd / sapphires, sapphires sealed through a healing metatronic blvd / rapidly, rapidly approached by a busy blvd / kinship, kinship found in a resting blvd / serenity, serenity settles in a blvd / float, float to a boating paradise called boulevards into love / blanket, blanket your species in a blvd / minor, minor absent the absinthe estimation swilled in lessens Gogh-n to a creative blvd / envious, envious to a sitting blvd / alone, alone and the owning sanctuary to a blvd / karmic, karmic in gone to blvds / rate, rate piad through a blvd / glimpse, glimpse a cubic cure of the blvds / ultimate, ultimate retain and the expression of the cured blvd / hue, hue our rainbow blue blvd / lay, lay atrail to a blvd colorful within rites of bliss / ecstasy, ecstasy and the spiritual applaud for God's blvds / ultimate, ultimate to a desire for thee, a blvd / wish, wish an apply free to a blvd / castle, castle cured a blvd / powerful, powerful display and the definition relayed into a blvd / spite, spite less and the sight found in funneled blvds / edge, edge worn through to blvds / travel, travel well within the truth told, blvds / dizzy in delighted blvds / branches, branches cured in thundering blvds / under, under dealt a thrusting lighten throughout their blvds / forest, forest and the fields of healing shared in blvds / joint, joint, joint and the gentle mend of a valiant stride called metaphysically, blvds / turned, turned a weathered face into a blvd / animal, animal meeting and the met with, blvds / smash, smash less and find more to blvds / found, found in a feeling, blvds / oceans, oceans away to love's blvds / miracles, miracles again, blvds / freedom, freedom reigning our blvd / listen, listen to a lesson for your blvds / finally, finally a figure, blvds / musing, musing mentioned for our blvds / mega, mega-nomics rule our blvds / passionate, passionate measures used in our blvds / electives, electives gained a blvd / living, living examine of the random blvds / level, level reached as a blvd / literal, literal to a mental blvd / worded, worded and wound free to a blvd / reading, reading a wisdom blvd / occasional, occasional voices heard through blvds / voicing, voicing vociferously through our blvds / coded, coded and coated with love's blvds / polish, polish a language for an electric blvd / forward, forward worn by a blvd / liquid, liquid releativity for a blvd / remember, remember a member's blvds. / color, color for our blvds / cables, cables three to a blvd / responsible, responsible allow for our blvds / additions, additions deal in blvds / people, people and the thrilling blvds / wise, wise and the mentioned blvd / value, value allowed through our blvds / refreshed, refreshed by a blvd.

CHAPTER FIVE

Dependence, dependence outed throughout a cured blvd / develop, develop measures meant to mend a blvd / stream, stream and the seams metatronic into a blvd / shine, shine and the supremest reign in blvds / polarized, polarized into a parallel day's blvds / polarity, polarity paid a switching blvd / abyss, abyss out and then a shoaling blvd / gradually, gradually escape to winds often in blvds / task, task torn to a blvd / demons, demons outed and thickened lines allow an abundant abide in blvds / ruler, ruler ran to a rathering worn blvds / alternated, alternated and the pleadian agree is to find a fashionable blvd / infinity, infinity and listening tin allow too, a blvd / branches, branches and the chances too, a blvd's / underneath, underneath and within A blvd / imperceptible, imperceptible outings and the shouted agree to be a blvd / moment, moment of the meeting aboriginal into a dreaming sign / sudden, sudden too and the becoming appearance for a blvd / commital, commital into middle manned blvds / evidently, evidently kingdom's came to blvds / elaborate, elaborate muse and the environmental met with in blvds / herds, herds of the met with in blvds / sphere, sphere of the spilling vehicular blvds / attention, attention to the platelets blvds / sort, sort of the sent with, blvds / ritual, ritual to a reeling blvd / usage, usage and the necessary needs too, a blvd / instrument, instrument of the mentioned blvds / field, field flew into a kindred blvd / circle, circle nearest a living's blvds / torment, torment over through a blvd / monastery, monastery tibetan tamed lightly to a blvd / goal, goal done and the won smiel upon a blvd / treated, treated for malarial inspire and the desire to lighten a blvd / To / Bring / You / Home / To / Hawaii / Brazilian / Rain / Forrest / Policy / Tours / Impart / Carolina / Center / City / Tropical / Vase / Terminous / Manneous / Madrid / Mexico / Yucatan / Music / Frivolous / blue / green / red / orange / star / panternal.

CHAPTER SIX

Gales, gales gaged for the winds of love found blvds / exact, exact to towns of abundant blvds / suggest, suggest a fashion for a blvd / suggest, suggest a fountain falshing blvds / enlargement, enlargement meant for the fortune's blvds / task, task told a whistling blvd / capacity, capacity for a creative blvd / benefit, benefit found in the future's blvds / tragic, tragic less and treated more for the furthered blvds / summit, summit made and a success lived throughout life's blvds / implied, implied examples of the sample bent to blvds / lessen, lessen varied and married through the living blvds / emerges, emerges in embargoed blvds / invisible, invisible threads on blvds / force, force led to blvds / revelation, revelation given pardon too, a blvd / level, level to a living won throughout blvds / favor, favor few and more then blvds / genes, genes genetically made a featured blvd / shallow, shallow too, a trail through a hu-man blvd / categories, categories set in strands on blvds / presumably, presumably yes, a blvd / mercury, mercury amazed in a meeting blvd / rotation, rotation throughout a planning blvd / lightening, lightening levels of the listened to blvds / cross, cross and the chosen won a wintery blvd / motif, motif made elective too, a blvd / books, books child like and thronged too in blvds / bitter, bitter out and then a thickened meeting's blvds / eliminating, eliminating balanced into a branching blvd / impossible, impossible in threshold's blvds / still, still allows a shrillness left to blvds / point, point along the relayed blvds / combat, combat over and the healing done in lesson won to blvds / angel, angel found and accepted too, in blvds / points, points made a winning blvd / ordeal, ordeal out and the bliss-full more into your blvds / beyond, beyond and then into a blvd / feathered, feathered features met in blvds / sanctuaries, sanctuaries sank into a blvd / cosmos, cosmos cues your blvds / hall, hall returned too, a blvd / double, double deals less then, blvds / teachers, teachers taught a triple blvd / churning, churning alllows yours a blvd / fragments, fragments plowed through into blvds / broken, broken allowance beguile less into a blvd / island, island wayed insights to a blvd / sorcerer, sorcerer sent to a simply, blvds / web, web allowed delivery unto a blvd / castle, castle engaged in, blvd's / lake, lake of the legendary blvds / patience, patience meant for penchants allowed in blvds / riddle, riddles detailed through blvds / fundamental, fundamental throughout a blvd / dilemma, dilemma done too, blvds / reduce, reduce a reaction through a risk-free blvd / notions, notions and the motions made too, blvds / elsewhere, elsewhere and the winsome blvds / meditative, meditative mention too, a blvd / ardent, ardent winning done through blvds / chasing, chasing out and through a blvd / identify, identify ways to a blvd / attachment, attachment finished in a blvd.

CHAPTER SEVEN

Resemblance, reemblance too and a reigning ransom paid for blvds / mayan, mayan appliance and the mended patterns in a blended blvd / steps, steps true in blvds / doctrine, doctrine featured and the wheeling gave in to blvds / tank, tank of the sinking thrills to blvds / hide, hide heard throughout a blvd / little, little wins a blvd / dear, dear days linked in blvds / deer, deer steered past blvds / girl, girl featured for a blvd / rather, rather be in blvds / drive, drive past a blvd / night, night of the nestled into blvds / frozen, frozen less in freakish blvds / instead, instead paid to blvds / clear, clear throughout a's blvds / observant, observant too, a blvd / sovereign, sovereign suggestion into blvds / lover, lover lived with blvds / strictly, strictly made through blvds / bearing, bearing intrigue in blvds / genie, genie joins you in blvds / sleep, sleep details treks throughout a blvd / concubine, concubine made a blvd / show, show a shilling to a snowy blvd / qualify, qualify, yes! into a blvd / speculate, speculate throughout light's blvds / indeed, indeed in deed a blvd / similar, similar to mentions of a blvd / inscription, inscription played for in blvds / enimical, enimical too, a blvd / ordained, ordained in daily a blvd / inform, inform and the warmest detail of the degrees allowed a blvd / obscure, obscure intrigue within a blvd / brick, brick befriend and the retails within a blvd / suggestive, suggestive winnings blvds / abruptly, abruptly bade a print of a blvd / major, major meaning to a blvd / resource, resouce of the central won through a blvd / monarchs, monarchs mentioned "a blvd" / worthy, worthy of a ranks too, a blvd / furious, furious gone too, a blvd / brief, brief allow in a fusion's blvds / crazy, crazy about your blvds / contribution,

contribution of a blvd's donations / consensus, consensus of a blvd / bizarre, bizarre allowed a living's blvds / high, high to a heightened pathway's stranded blvd / ambergris, ambergris and the keys to a newness born of blvds / pole, pole success and the stated owned throughout a blvd / celestial, celestial unto an aurorial blvd / formal, formal fortify through a threshold's blvds / benign, benign details to a listening blvd / particles, particles applied too, a blvd / ambiguity, ambiguity allowed too, a blvd / benevolent, benevolent mention of the blvds / patron, patron pointed into a blvd / amulets, amulets met in truest blvds / tomb, tomb attendant too, a blvd / rumor, rumor reached through a blvd / deceptively, deceptively dealt too, a blvd / entwined, entwined through a blvd / reception, reception sent a blvd / depict, depict and the regain meant for blvds.

CHAPTER EIGHT
Spiral, spiral into intriguing material meant for the mission's blvds / knowledge, knoweldge of the college of prescient amplify and the feelings meant for / the miracles sent to love's then, blvd / identical, identical to a mental forgive and the fondest deals made with lightening in thee, blvds / ecliptic, ecliptic to an eliptic's blvds within, love / weighing, weighing in and finding then a sample miracle for the future's blvds / annihalation, annihalation of the emaciation inflicted by lessened expressions of love's thoughtful blvds / voraciousness, voraciousness meant too, a blvd / fragments, fragments gentle in a patient parallel made drain free through a blvd / rim, rim treats and the neatest pleasure found through a blvds / unusual, unusual to a trilling blvd / degrees degrees paced throughout a healing blvd / coral, coral reef's concur that crowns win in blvds / lagoon, lagoon of the lending blvds / concentric, concentric to central's blvds / overall, overall living's blvds / canals, canals placed throughout a litany's blvds / crust, crust allowed escaping meeting's miracle's blvds / attack, attack less and find more through a living blvd / class, class of the listing's blvds / overdue, overdue to details blvds / planetary, planetary mention of the featured details onto blvds / momentum, momentum gained through living blvds / lunatics, lunatics lend a listen to a mentioned meteor for friendly bantering throughout a. living blvd / supporters, supporters made a fashionable mention to a material blvd / theory, theory thrilled through to a blvd / rigid, rigid runs into a listening blvd / orthodox, orthodox thrillings and the sealings meant for blvds / period, period placed at ends on blvds / ripples, ripples ripe to a trippy blvd / direct, direc often and found generally digestable to a blvd / ocean, ocean spent in blvds / number, numbers nimble in mentioned blvds / reef, reef on top of the thickened blvds / sunken, sunken scenes and the sentinel spent on blvds / ruins, ruins ran to a trickle's blvds / pillars, pillars placed throughout a thronging blvd / pedestal, pedestal across and due a blvd / sloping, sloping scoping blvds / shore, shore shields a blvd / maze, maze mentally freed to blvds / vantage, vantage treed to blvds / islolated, isolated explain of the gains made, blvds / boulder, boulder billed and the basics amde too, blvds / elegant, elegatn retain and the treaty met in blvds / radiated, radiated and the sated fed a blvd / edifice, edifice found too, a blvd / foolish,

foolish outed through a beguiling blvd / ignore, ignore substance less through a lifting blvd / unexplained, unexplained in central blvds / debris, d. ebris dealt a following thrust to cleanly blvds / spare, spare appear and the steering allowance onto blvds / tentative, tentative planned and the mentally freed too, blvds / token, token of the spoken explain for blvds / equator, equator wounds made real through blvds / value, value found in frilly blvds / second, second to natural blvds / coincidence, coincidence came too, a blvd / tilt, tilt off and a re-run spent in valentine's reminiscent to the feeling's blvds / oblique, oblique to a pinball sounding iniquity fraught with fury's good-bye to love-less blvds / tropic, tropic allowance of the assurance that love leads to a blvd / decline, decline off and the details found in featured allowance of love's blvds / registered, registered features of the frozen thawed to a blazing blvd / children, children matter to our blvd.

CHAPTER NINE
Courtyard, courtyard seeded through the threaded blush of the featured blvds / sanctum, sanctum of the seeking lend to a blvd / roof, roof of the channel met through blvds / canal, canal of the central examine to a blvd / exactly, exactly thought through to a blvd / lever, levers lifted in a gifted metaphysic dance throughout a blvd / each, each and the taught too, a blvd / rectangular, rectangular to a spectacle spent on crashing metaphors and fields affective throughout a blvd / logs, logs linked and found too, a blvd / megalithic, megalithic to a meow found throught a's blvds / perilous, perilous cost made realistic to kneeling mystic found in futuristic babble of the grabled kind, allow us now a channeled seek direct through your heart's gates a miracle elapsed and the lasting find of a featured kind an elective, electric dream an awakening treat the lolve the seat a gift a lift unto a lip called owned a blvd / mount, mount the count for arcturian ascend and the plenty who said, "we will be an a blvd" / assumption, assumption treated as an allow for the feeling blvds / fingers, fingers cross then to seed a billing listened lost and tossed allow for the / furthering forgive and the fostered allow too, a blazing star became you, a blvd / collision, collissions tossed into a state and the rages past and the peelings last at a healing cost only skin deep to the three found whole within the bowl of love's blvds / intense, intense extremes and the regimes of the mentally declared and the wares bade to blvds / network, network named through blvds / motive, motive allowed too, blvds / epoch, epoch written through lbvds / wiped, wiped a wed to detail through a blvds / primal, primal woo and the wedded bliss of blvds / calendar, calendar of the cues arcturic and the marriage made through blvds / result, result of the reaching made a starring residue throughout your blvds / rejuvenate, rejuvenate allowed throughout years blvd / inheritance, inheritance gained too, blvds / gross, gross allow and the whistling blends of gaining blvds / travesties, travesties past then to a blvd / relished, relished electric allow for a blvd / sovereign, sovereign in rates run throughout a blvd / netherworld, netherworld ineptitude made a chosen blvd? Choose a blvds / resurrection, resurrection met through friends within a blvd / offset, offset fits into a blvd / oscillation, oscillation and the visitations within a blvd / surface,

surface throughout blvds / seismic, seismic ascend and the treaty met through blvds / relapse, relapse spent in only a blvds / fluctuation, fluctuation flurries past a blvds / onset, onset met through blvds / flood, flood into nature's blvds / ignore, ignore shored through blvds / crater, crater kept a listen too, through blvds / cast, cast wallowed through blvd / catastrohpically, catastrophically spent in only word on blvds / remote, remote met through blvds / colossal, colossal undertook and thence a blvd / velocity, velocity into a value sent on blvds / chemical, chemical meals and the mentally freed too, blvds / ozone, ozone detailed into a blvd / zodiac, zodiac spent digressing through an blvd / axis, axis spun too, blvds / slow, slow in suggested, blvds / closest, closest too, a blvd / solstice, solstice detailed too, a blvd / equinox, equinox sent for blvds / foliated, foliated felt and found a blvd / crowned, crowned essentially with a blvd / gallery, gallery galed like winning blvds / line-a-ments, line-a-ments meant for blvds / duality, duality dealt with throughout blvds / early, early into ways won to a blvd / doubt, doubt dealt through and done with blvds / belt, belt on bevy's blvds.

CHAPTER TEN
Ridiculously, ridiculously met through reset blvds / contortion, contortion met through living blvds / formulate, formulate and the featured blvds / orbit, orbit and the threshold's blvds / asserted, asserted and the worded blvds 6unless, unless and the detailed blvds / marvelous, marvelous and the mentioned blvds / build, build and the beaten wonder wound-free to blvds / sporadically, sporadically cued to blvds / outside, outside in intention's blvds / hieroglyphic, hieroglyphic to detailed blvds / carved, carved and the okay will, blvds / mechanic, mechanic and the mentioned blvds / role, role and the out lied blvds / morn, morn and the treating wondered through too, blvds / pivotal, pivotal portals and the pension for a blvd / filled, filled in allowance and the thrusting blvds / intimate, intimate measures and the mentioned blvds / film, film and the furthering blvds / picturesque, picturesque and the placing blvds / distributed, distributed and the fed for dearly blvds / complimented, complimented and the tented numbers blvds / charmed, charmed and the equipped too, blvds / coverage, coverage and the creatures created through a blvd / polite, polite and the estates led to blvds / vociferously, vociferously written and the pensions planned for blvds / credit, credit and the creations met through blvds / publicity, publicity and the rented views blvds / criticism, criticism and the creatove spin to blvds / career, career and the spinning true to blvds / sentiment, sentiments styled to blvds / socialite, socialite too, a's blvds / intend, intend and the free to be a blvd / neglect, neglect dealt with too, a blvd / slate, slate set and the clearing met in blvds / element, elements meant through blvds / scrambled, scrambled through too, blvds 38resolve, resolve and the threshold solved too, blvds / defend, defend a lessen less too, blvds / dance, dance and the chances laid through blvds / fulfilling, fulfilling allowed and the fallen found a newness into blvds / target, target and treaties bade too, blvds / euphoric, euphoric aplenty and the many's paid to blvds / footage,

footage laid through blvds / ambition, ambition allowed your securest blvds / click, click along ley's blvds / freeway, freeway days due blvds / component, components of many traded blvds / famous, famous fellows fielded into blvds / sharp, sharp along cab ridden blvds / insulation, insulation peeled off a living blvd / common, common to a created blvd / partial, partial to a pleasing aspiration's blvds / propose, propose a regarded supposition for a blvd / avid, avid agree too, a blvd / perusal, perusal to a user's good-bye for a blvd / chronical, chronical created for A blvd / remind, remind and the relations made a blvd / reproduce, reproduce a data banked allow for a blvd / production, production allowed a blvd / property, property divided true a blvd / plan, plan to find a living blvd / maximum, maximum dividends made to a blvd / scene, scene attendant to a blvd.

CHAPTER ELEVEN
Seen, seen a living allowance to a blvd / juxtapose, justapose a pleasing forgetting blvds / place, place along lines stepped up too, a blvd / regard, regard for the rested blvds / residue, residue due a blvd / residual, residual apply for the forgotten blvds / ransom, ransom and the ran into a blvd / charge, charge and the ringing blvd / change, change and the chiming rhyming's blvds / congeal, congeal details a dealing's blvds / upstart, upstart allowed a listening blvd / beloved, beloved and the loving legend's blvds / shop, shop and the thrice held blvds / shilling, shilling cost less too, a blvd / pound, pound and the cancel meant, a blvd / lira, lira spent too, a blvd / franc, franc and the estate set into blvds / yen, yen and the threshold's blvds / monies, monies and the met with blvds / deal, deal too, through blvds / withdrawal, withdrawal and the thresholds held through blvds / deposit, deposit dealt with in blvds / account, account met too, a blvd / market, market allowance met too, blvds / money, money admitted too through blvds / dollars, dollars spent through blvds / cents, cents dealt in blvds / change, change and the calling met through blvds / teller, teller retailed too, blvds / cashier, cashier met through blvds / register, register relayed to blvds / receipt, receipt tethered less to blvds / banking, banking bet on in blvds / checking, checking challenged less too, to blvds / savings, savings spent on blvds / interest, interest and the running done through blvds / participation, participation and the mentioned too, a blvds / earn, earn and the living sent too, blvds / spend, spend and the spinning too, a blvd / share, share and the seeming meant too, a blvd / save, save and the status sent to blvds / deliver, deliver and the dealings dealt with too, blvds / truck, truck and the simply sent through to blvds / rolls, rolls and the reaching sent through blvds / drop, drop into details done through blvds / drawer, drawer true in blvds / count, count and the curing dealt in blvds / merge, merge and the mentioned blvds / lightening, lightening and the inviting blvds / living, living a giving blvd / levels, levels allowed through these blvds / photographic, photographic journeys into these blvds / dying, dying to past blvds / lift, lift to a mission's blvds / levels, levels allowed to a blvd / license, license allows a blvd / lead, leading to a blvd / lift, lift to a giving blvd / leap, leap to a literal

blvd / yes, yes to a licensed blvd / federal, federal missions blvds / barriers, barriers gone to blvds / learning, learning to be a blvd / life, life led into a blvd

CHAPTER TWELVE

Discount, discount and the dues done too, a blvd / broke, broke and the basically blvd / rich, rich embrace and then thee, too, in blvds / ample, ample and the sample true in attributive blends of blvds / investment, investment and the fields found in blvds / interested, interested and the thrilling treshold borne into a blvd / buy, buy and the pairing met in blvds / sell, sell and the doing done through blvds . 9pay, pay and an attendant too in blvds / stack, stack and the thrilling threshold crossed into blvds / dividends, dividends and the dining complete intrigued within a blvd / short, short and the shilling's spent in blvds / long, long and the terms built through blvds / screen, screen and the enoch sent to blvds / compute, compute and the input pent to blvds / block, block and the blues unwind too in blvds / stop, stop and the steering details and the thoughts bade to blvds / reflection, reflection and the meanings meant to blvds / survive, survive sent to blvds / wait, wait and the windows planned for blvds / happiness, happiness spun through blvds / forgotten, forgotten allow due a blvd / afternoon, afternoon of the valued feelings sung through blvds / honor, honor bade and made through blvds / legal, legal allowance suggests your blvd / tender, tender detail and the sailing blvds / trust, trust anothers special blvds / debt, debt paid for your through the singing blvds / privacy, privacy given a living blvd / private, private to daily blvds / silver, silver sent for into blvds / gold, gold gathered in thrilling blvds of love / series, series of the ceiling reached in blvds / serial, serial suggestion of the songbird's blvds / option, option allowed for into blvds / treasure, treasure treated openly too, in blvds / memorial, memorial made to the mentioned blvds / united, united in sighted blvds / legally, legally forgiven due a blvd / note, note let go too, a blvd / federal, federal declare fo the freeing blvds / preserve, preserve allowed in blvds / practice, practice treated into blvds / hat, hat held on too, blvds / reserve, reserve made for into blvds / kick, kick about chosen through a blvd / throw, throw goes directly unto a blvd / punt, punt planned throughout a blvd / run, run for featured seats and the settled intreaty to a blvd / field, field found full on blvds / score, score a daily defense for blvds / goal, goal capably bound to blvds / unite, unite with listening belief into a situation led to blvds / plunge, plunge allowed uniquely through a blvd / team, team built and found in blvds / third, third won to blvds / first, first fed a blvd / second, second made a blvd / home, home built through blvds / plates, plates filled in blvds / selection, selection given too, blvds / light, light led amplified to blvds / dry, dry to a gentle urge for blvds / premiums, premiiums paid for blvds.

CHAPTER THIRTEEN

Venture, venture near a dearest blvd / circuit, circuit complete to blvds / bodied, bodied implants gone to blvds / full, full at the heart felt blvds / approach, aprroach a dearest blvd / terror, terror off and then too, blvds / visual, visual made through blvds / stratus, stratus starring blvds / multiply, multiply too, a blvd / procreate, procreate's rates are a blvd / labor, labor led through blvds / intercourse, intercourse and spent ascent into a blvd / false, false allow too, a blvd / canal, canal suggested attendant to a blvd / birth, birth found in blvds / borne, borne in electric rides to blvds / born, born thoroughly in blvds / push, push past ignition matched and make a blvd / shove, shove done and the over comes too, blvds / forced, forced out then to blvds / contract, contracts capapbly bound to blvds / clip, clip allowed now, cut through to blvds / stitch, stitch applied to blvds / breached, breached done too, blvds / twins, twins met through blvds / genuine, felt genuine to a blvd / jaunt, jaunt made to blvds / drive, drive details a blvd / gas, gas gazed in a blvd / feed, feed a filling blvd / petrol, petrol rolled back to blvds / exhaust, exhaust meant for to blvds / tailgate, tailgate placed into blvds / bed, bed made for blvds / sleep, sleep deeply into blvds / sourced, sourced suggested blvds / funded, funded now through blvds / granted, granted sanctity to blvds / given, gien allowance through a blvd / won, won regally to blvds / delivers, delivers daily in blvds / medicinal, medicinal meanings into blvds / herbs, herbs and leanings through a blvd / pharmacy, pharmacy planned in blvds / airs, airs about us, blvds / coldest, coldest days win, blvds / only, welcomed to a Brevardian plane on blvds / rich, rich in compliance and the sighing blvds / consult, consult your regular allowance, blvds / useful, useful in needed blvds / mutual, mutual allowance to a blvd / funds, funds found in sunny landed blvds / amortize, amortize well then your living blvds / rely, rely on reasoned sizes bound through blvds / changes, changes range to a blvd / shifts, shifts made now to blvds / swiss, swiss accounted blvds / accounts, accounts made your too, blvds / bank, banking blended to a blvd / deposit, deposit dearest to a blvd / withdrawal, withdrawal and the daily blvds / mutually, mutually meant for blvds / spent, spent and the spinning won too, a planet's guided blvds / speak, speak for the funds metatronically collected by a blvd of love.

THE IN-STREET-MENTS
LEVEL 56

CHAPTER ONE

Avenues, avenues of the news to beam, love reigns, along the lines electric and into the streets / avert, avert a sort who metnione less than all God is for the powerful purge of love's streets / divert, divert the detail into a meaning for the focused efforts of the mental aspects of streets / marry, marry the secret to the source for streets / spreads, spreads a word, electrically, freedom's reign is in these streets / agree, agree to be well for these streets / decide, decide to detail these streets / debris, debris cast aside for these streets / aside, aside and well within, A street / surmise, surmise that mentions reign in heaven's streets / safety, safety sealed for the fields of streets / size, size suggests a residence of love for these streets / allow, allow and the listening streets / saunter, saunter through these streets / sports, sports and the sheets elevated to these streets / sahara, sahara suggest of these desserts found for heavenly streets / debit, debit details the durations enhanced for a forest of streets / dune, dune deals with a knowing street / soon, soon enough to seize these streets / food, food featured as a street / form, form past and cast through a street / forthright, forthright fields of A street / forks, forks in a mauna present within streets / picks, picks a legendary retailf or streets / path, path placed across the plunging enhance of streets / choose, choose a pathway detailed for streets / junctive, junctive and the unctive gained by the details for love's streets / phase, phase and the fissures sealed through the heavens / partner, partner paged by the wisest hjeavens / peeks, peeks and the assertive assigns by the streets of love / person, person and th paging assigns for a heavenly street / seeks, seeks a pleasing run for love throughout these streets / organizations, organizations gain a list for love's streets / levels, levels plunge into heaven's streets / tire, tire less and find more for these streets / amid, amid and among thee, streets / disguise, disguise off now and eternally, a street / vibrational, vibrational balance found in heaven's streets / enthused, enthused allowance for these, streets / afghan, afghan stands in light's apply to love for these streets / doubt, doubt dealt out by these implied streets / veracruz, veracruz spelled by love for these streets / placed, placed impact at the exact fulcrum splice for love's intersect with a street called human / attract, attract a factor blessed by streets / lifts, lifts our gift to streets / amused, amused by ruses left for streets / delegates, delegates deal within streets / moved, moved again into these streets / chetah, chetahs pounce for streets / swim, swim allows a plunging stance at love's good streets / perfect, perfect apply to the streets of love / made, made daily anew these streets / placed, placed along lines of streets / shirt, shirt on into streets / process, process placed at streets / match, match us street wise / pad, pads engaged in streets / edged, edged by electrical streets / precept, precept suggested of streets / create, create a cushion for streetts / page, page born by streets / birth, birth placed in streets / surrender due your streets / fountains, fountains fuse in streets.

CHAPTER TWO

Friends, friends abound in these streets / flank, flank yourself with the dearest friends of love / felt, felt within, a street wisest too, love / sunk, sunk without you, the light wins when you, love / friends, friends epistle deep in the heart's ways to love for these streets / enthusiasm, enthusiasm's lfiting waiver signed by love for these particular streets of love / lifts, lifts again, my pen for these, the streets hu-man / love, love deemed the righteous for these streets / games, games openly declared for the funded streets / decide, decide to be lightest through these streets / declare, declare a declaration "fair" for these occupied streets, hu-man / dote, dote on the dollars sent into these streets / extrude, extrude amde the mood for that particular pair of streets / organize, organize your declaration of love for these streets of home / include, include your heart in your home formed along these streets / care, care becomes our alibi for streets of love / God, God looking into surrender of the cause to the laws of love as a street / mother, mother amazed by your streets / men, men who held you dearest for the cause of a healthy street / powers, powers placed in cures allowed by the streets of cause allowance / father, father amazed by the powers of love in these streets / women, women who win for the causes streets / strength, strength allied too, these are the streets of love declared / lords, lords of listen, of lightest cause, the applause is building for the livery worn blue and grey goes into the scenes of love for these streets / vegetative, vegetative and lush unto these eyes who signal teh / 14 more of the vectors sunk within a human skull offered to the strength and these streets and the lanes of love found / source, source suggests yoru choice has been made to the Los Angeles deep sword of / God's loving streets / decide, decide to pierce the sound of veiled threat by the leap across bound streets / elohim, elohim of the slimmest application called streets into love / animals, animals caused the laughing goodness of love confessed to good-byes for love's streets / distance, distance gained for the cause electric and the word laid at the heartline of streets golden loved by God / wide, wide to a decision described as the life of love in these streets / depict, depict a cause as won for the thrones of light and the streets enticed by love / seek, seek a signal for the applause elctric by love and the streets of God / sorts, sorts who balance the cause electric for God's sake. Please know the Ones who have written the cause Basically Human to love for the human streets / wander, wander into direct recall of the plated humans stripped to reveal a lizard's skin street deep / galaxies, galaxies applaud you and your choices for love's streets / continue, continue to part with only the lightest streets / fulfill, fulfill the deal made for the streets of love / descend, descend into man, the hu-man dove, street wise / stars, stars are plunging laughingly deep into her streets / pattern, patterns placed along the feathers of gotten streets / overlap, overlap the allow through a threshold deep in love's patterns of these streets / overlays, overlays legendary with a hastening street / earth, earth measured through her streets / future, future sealed by the chosen streets / goal, goal reached and man can beam into the heart of God's streets electric / body, body blissed by heaven's streets / discover, discover another who understands God's streets / written, written applause, again, for the reader, the writer, the pen, human for God / delving into human high-selves and the streets of love / winding, winding up the experience of being less than human for the streets of life / changed, changed by the central experiences of love's streets / built, built upon the rock of love's streets / enthuse, enthuse allows a throng to gather upon these streets / written, written another time for the streets of love / appear, appearing near is the dearest street / partners, partners found for the fusings complete upon these streets / pens, pens opened by these streets / pantheon, pantheon allowed forage of the streets San Franciscan by Green treed streets / perfections, perfections step is made by the plunge into human streets / mate, mate and the appearance of the pleasing repairs made to our streets / wonderful, wonderful wedding street of love / dip, dip into the lightest pen, your heart's fountained street.

CHAPTER THREE

Agree, agree to find a street nearby / source, source 3 side and 4 deep and soul clipped by love's streets / light, light lensed by the blends human free and interiorly unto love's streets / life, life has legions stretched to field the human grids of streets / lover, lover made the move unto your street / equates, equates reap is worn through by street / intentions, intentions drip with extensions for streets / demise, demise of the past found a newness near your street / diameter, diameter set to a pentameters click and an octagon's good deal for love led streets / woes, woes alledged as streets / mortal, mortal mazes open into love, a steretypical street / excise, excise the incise of all streets / includes, includes a recaptured street / enclose, enclose a mention of these sets and allegorical streets / potential, potential meant for you and your streets / boulevards, boulevards open into all these streets / happenings, happenings read openly of your streets / kingdoms, kingdoms came into life sets of stelae streets / laws, laws listened to by our streets / leaves, leaves opening into your streets / malls, malls over material thamel likened streets / God-head, God-head livid about lightest streets / spun, spun unto an eclipse of the passionate kind, streets / instinct, instinct curing the rest of our streets / mothering, mothering smothered by the heavy water's streets / covers, covers a life, electric to an elegant note of the partnered streets / trees, trees triple when we rise to see the heavenly skies and the skies seats upon the light electric waves of streets / plants, plants imagine greeness daily for the cause of human streets / planets, planets pulse in a healing curve called lightest applications for the pensioned rows of streets / grass, grass grew between our streets / rocks, rocks arose to marry our streets / soil, soil deep in the lessons of God's streets human / leverage, leverage applied to your measuring up for God blessed streets / plans, plans amend to the sender's human streets / natures, natures cry is for the human sky to rain a lasting street of love / news, news is made daily at the heart of these streets / water, water molecularly mends our streets / many, many the veins of the wellest streets / missions, missions amuse us with our lightest tastes of streets / extend, extend a friendly dish to the mainly human streets / creation, creation allows you a healing street / multiply, multiply your feelings for the fortunate's streets / extensive, extensive allowance of these streets / inquire, inquire capably of our streets / mind, mind over find a cure for our streets / mount, mount a passionate reply for our streets / extend, extend a loving allowance to our streets / amounts, amounts paid remain well into our streets

/ blaze, blaze a confession past berry red streets / abort, abort the sort who curtail words of pleasing streets / confessed, confesssed a confusion stressed by love's streets / aspire, aspire centrally to love's streets / balanced, balanced appearance becoming a street / seen, seen a street to love / streets, streets who lead to streets cornered by love / ascend, ascend daily to the place of streets littered by love / anchors, anchors mentioned by the scribes who have written only love to these streets / befriend, befriend a giggling sort who lives beneath these starry streets / tranquil, tranquil in cool delivery of God's streets / connects, connects you to the poet Rumi reaped by love for the Friend and a deepest / chalice for love's cupping strum of the streets hu-man / capable, capable to a be-ing, street / doe, does gentle without a broken winging street / delicate, delicate news of a winged street.

CHAPTER FOUR

Guides, guides to the streets won for humanity / maps, maps and the heavenly streets / gates, fates opened into our streets / stripes, stripes paved by the hearts of love for humanity, a living street / grids, grids equipped as electrically conductive to light's streets / alley, alley blue with street / avenues, avenues arise forth and streets too / yes, yes we will find our streets too, love / places, places paged through as streets / steps, steps inn too, steering streets / codes, codes conducted for these streets / weaves, weaves a welcome street of love / absolute, absolute the money paid for patterned streets / strides, strides rising into our streets / stressed, stressed as essential for us, streets / given, given a place into our streets / autograph, autograph made essential for the sincerest streets / travel, travel across alnds simple within heavenly streets / ascendant, ascendant unto love's guiding gift of golden-bricked streets / publish, publish nearest your house of temples carded by steep streets / attitude, attitude taken is that the city is light within templed streets / urban, urban and the plan to be A street / forgiven, forgiven a risen street / trade, trade Lombardi with a Ghiradelli squarely laid to streets of love / secret, secrets are mentioned and won traded streets / attend, attends you again by the litany rhyming with streets / ultimate, ultimate excuse to the freest streets / truthful, truthful and worthwhile by a sighing street / guided, guided by a starring street / excellent, excellent expire forgiven as the lightest street / prepare, prepare a short compare to only the living streets / preside, preside regally within your streets of love / unqiely, uniqeuly given unto A street / dynamic, dynamic allow of the rivers street / diary, diary written unto the stars venus deep at love's street / astound, astound yourself by believing in love's streets / purely, purely written by love for the heart of man and the wisdom of woman and the worthiness of all children who remember best our electrical origin and the wavelength of a living sort called God and the life led by the streets called human / laughter, laughter cures our fairest streets / live, live to learn these streets fair / flowers, flowers of discipline pleased by the haven called streets / companionable, companionable company for the summoning onto streets / company, company came unto your street / eventual, eventual accept of the dimensions founded by your strongest reach to heaven's streets / directs, directs allow our lighted streets / luckiest, luckiest menu includes a hearty street to love / flop, flop acknowledged by the streets formerly loved / divorce, divorces detailed by the licensed pens of love's streets / details, details tell us we are well to the light's pens stained red blue green and the / eccentrically yellow by lightening struck streets: violated, violated less by the mention of holy streets / identities, identities trail by the vaults filled within our streets heavens / ideal, ideal days of adoration for God's streets / conscience, conscience comes undone by youthful mention of love's streets / fuels, fuels an electric stream of living streets / funded, funded again, by heaven's golden streets / fortitude, fortitude found for the finished streets campaign / feasability, feasability fed to our focused streets / frankness, frankness freed for our streets / fondness, fondness for us, streets / funding, funding allows us our streets / forced, forced without, streets / financially, financially discuss our streets / fiscally, fiscally focused past streets / focused, focused into wider streets.

CHAPTER FIVE

Bottoms, bottoms horse red with uptown streets / source, source eclipsed by love's streets / site, site of the recaptured streets / density, density appealing unto our streets / acquire, acquire a knack for love's streets / correlate, correlate the cause as catered to by God's calmest streets / choose, choose a sort who relate into these streets / desire, desire infused by light's include to loving streets / gorgeous, gorgeous choosing for the cause levelly allowed by light's enthroned streets / calcium, calcium correlation codes our skeleton's streets / osteoporosis, osteoporosis bent to a seeing street / askew, askew with the visual effects of streets / dazzle, dazzle and the raiding past your street / befriended, befriended and mended as such by lots of streets / manual, manul defy over and the automatic apparent for love's streets / dials, dials a daily, street / distribute, distribute your merry street / shore, shores employed as electrically a street / years, years apply to our streets / ago, ago we go with all streets / opportune, opportune to the moon's streets / settles, settles into a routine for the featured streets / regard, regard us as engaged within love's streets / notes, notes made of our streets / migrate, migrates patched by a loving street / notation, notation given to the living streets / thanks, thanks penned by tehse streets / shine, shine along wisest streets / songbird, songbirds fed by the holy streets / burns, burns within another street / see, see a fellow street / circuit, circuits pored over by us along this street / beach, beach street / date, date shored, streets / daughter, daughter stretched by streets / knew, knew a laughing street of love / husband, husband banded too by ivy green streets / had, had a figure fed to our street / aspire, aspire most for the shortened street / bands, bands appearing mean we are well to these streets / bending, bending to see the Greek, the Egyptian, the Celtic, the Native, the Hawaiian and mostly love's streets / 42 ways to be a street / break, break a pattern kept centrally in streets / bare, bare your spirit for God's streets / bask, bask in sunny days for lots drawn into streets / sun, sun days in the himalayan paths street willowed by white blue love / please, please us most with loving streets / attribute, attributes boasted of lightly are your streets /

shook, shook with conviction once again for God's streets / stood, stood in a puddle made for light streets / beside, beside us swells God's streets / sunshine, sunshine shows me our street / scents, scents ripen with our streets / lead, lead well for the featured streets / lofty, lofty listening of streets / lights, lights lipped with lifting streets / sights, sights centrally elevated to love's streets / secure, secure and well within loving and finest giving of streets of love / lives, lives adoptively streeted / gains, gains are made daily for the forthrightly stated welcoming street / insures, insures us a number blessed by material streets / given, given a decision to be daily freed by loving allowance for God's streets / voice, voiced allow for the showering streets / occupation, occupation remains lightly found in streets.

CHAPTER SIX

Gave, gave us desire to willing be and freely give of the lofty notion that nobleness applies to the human species succinct about their streets / looks, looks appear into our eyes street led / desires, desires to fill me within by God's streets / loves, loves to jump to God's lightest streets / address, adress made to the raids won electric to love's streets / guest, guest and the gazing streets / gain, gain and the rewards fraternal to streets / names, names deified by our streets 9.naming, naming allows us directive streets . / embroiders, embroidered surrender unto love's streets / watching, watching nearest our streets / worn, worn apply for our streets / union, union of organic astral streets / energies, energies gaining lvoe's streets / energetic, energetic appliance of God's streets / energy, energy and the latterns of life's streets / conspire, conspire and the causes stressed by life's streets / equations, equations of the occupy with loving streets / proton, proton contained by the lanes of love's streets / motive, motives mentioned and the reaching grains of loving streets / mighty, mighty niagra draped with the power of streets ingrained / energy, energy joined at the hinged rates of jammed streets / change, change a suitable sporting street / regard, regards for the swords of the lightest streets / stratus, stratus for the related streets / regard, regard for the fondest streets / relate, relate your ways to streets / rescue, rescues reach your precious peachy portals of loving streets / rally, rally allowed the streets of walking forgiveness for love's streets / reside, reside inside the gliding streets / rapt, rapt about love's streets / rappel, rappel to the source of love's streets / opening, openings occur near light streets / diffuse, diffuse less and gain most within streets / energies, energies meet, again, for the purpose on God's streets / changes, changes have happened often then to God's streets / final, final destinations chosen when love greets your streets / potential, potential gathering near the weathering streets / reduce, reduce allowed through the colors of love's potential streets / soothe, soothe your friends patient tend to the light on streets / interaction, interaction and the shuffle past a last street / behave, behave as wells knee deep in love of streets / behavior, behavior and the blanketed ascend to streets / mixed, mixed emotives of these streets / amuse, amuse mentally decreed to be a street / whim, whim last for the pastures teal with love's streets / associate, associate and the team built for A's streets / structures,

structures read of a crystal street to love / engage, engage in good news of the dues paid for light strrets / twice, twice I have led you to news of fine streets / social, social in allowance of the gleaming streets of love / genetic, genetic codes offered for streets of light / motivate, motivate and the streets of God / pandora, pandora dues of the fusing streets / master, master and the amusement for the life of love's streets / box, box and the basic of love's streets / bombed, bombed and the allowance for light streets / field, field and the fellows offered by lightstreets / trips, trips and the repute that is resolute to lightened streets / resolute, resolute agree to be liberated by ligth streets / gardens, the gardens liberated by love's streets / parked, parked in the shade of life's streaming streets / ranges, ranges reach by love's allow for the fleets of streets / free, free to a figure loose within streets.

CHAPTER SEVEN

Glimmer, glimmer of teh simmer for love of streets / shine, shine detachment for the causes summed by love's streets / mica, mica flows thorugh chips of love and these settings street deep / telepathic, telepathic agree to be freshly found for fueling of the gemstone streets / occasion, occasion and the celebrate of these living streets / sort, sorts of the sports and the living streets / self, self and the indulgence spent for loving streets / selfish, selfish and the smelling salts of lifted streets / elegance, elegance gains a lighter street / store, store and the simply lightest streets / paid, paid and the pungent strains of streets / pairs, pairs of streets of love / glance, glance and the chance to glean these streets / calling, calling and the ceiling lifted to reveal an ascendant street / immediate, immediate in details fo love's streets / now, now to the etails on streets / dealt, dealth with by regard for love's chance to bemuse a lighter street / with, within and the spinning tunes of light with your streets / hands, hands opening to your streets / soft, soft willing of the selling streets / succeed, succeed and the need to be free to a street / deed, deed and the strategic streets / dialect, dialect of the react spent for listening streets / speak, speak a participative way for love's streets / spoke, spoke with another's streets / quake, quake allows posing streets / steer, steer dearly for love on these streets / advise, advise us of risen streets / elaborate, elaborate regard for the heavenly streets / dipping, dipping into a banishment of lessened streets / belt, belt allowed a lofty street / joined, joined in loving salute unto the streets of love / grips, grips allowed loosening for streets / advocates, advocates rail past these streets / spell, spell and the lifted streets / orion, orion spelled oratorically by streets / asaid, said yes to these streets of love / judge, judge bejeweled by strictest life's streets / knot, knots out to streets / lest, lest we bleed, streets / giant, giant retailing on streets / stead, stead of the life streets / secure, securest speeches of life led streets / savor, savor apparent unto a light street / safety, safety sealed by the light streets / safe, safe allows a listed street / satire, satire suggested for streets / allow, allow an insure of deep streets / live, lvie and the lining often of streets / join, join us near our streets / pathways, pathways plunging unto streets / give, gives us an allow for these streets / gain, gain and the gifts often led to streets / gather, gather and the betray met by heavens

absorb of straight streets / absorb, absorb and the impressions of streets / confession, confession of the retrospective streets / attire, attire and the shields found for light streets / wear, wear and the willing states of love's streets / well, well and the wisdom's steering streets / true, true and the righteous of streets / appear, appear and the dearest streets / wealth, wealth and the widened streets / wed, wed and the wonderful dearest streets / marry, marry the moment's streets.

CHAPTER EIGHT

Place, place and the inquiry within often led streets / ladders, ladders and the ledgers red with lightened steps on streets / ead, lead us well into light's streets / clouds, clouds listened to by streets / success, success and the suggested streets / attempt, attempt details your streets / scam, scam allowed by the systems of streets / score, score and the signals come into these streets / eat, eat and the met with streets / spell, spell it as s-t-r-e-e-t-s / save, save allows you your streets / share, share doors deep in streets / unkempt, unkempt and the swept past streets / winds, winds and the windows streets / change, change allowed a street / choose, choose a pathway thorough within love's streets / really, really allowed a tracking street / weekly, weekly wisdom won for streets / numbered, numbered and the nearest streets / numbs, numbs slow lift unto streets / lessons, lesson planned for streets of love / build, build a standing street / shields, shields alluring true to streets / float, float ignited by her street / past, past allows of streets / seen, seen schemes of streets / score, score allowed for streets / forgive, forgive and teh fellows stacking into streets / fling, fling and the flying floated past to streets / forests, forests deep in ballooning estates of love's streets / staring, staring allow of your streets / concepts, concepts and the distance led for streets / currency, currency concurrent with love's streets / freed, freed and the risen streets / electric, electric and the ways streets / young, young and the enochian way's streets / eccentric, eccentric and the strays offered by light's streets / cards, cards and the cords cut for offerings unto streets / cabernet, cabernet blue within streets / sabotage, sabotage less syour light's streets / spontaneous, spontaneous and the spelling s-t-r-e-e-t-s / spinning, spinning streets / salivate, salivate cultivates streets / corpse, corpse lfited past streets / tsali, tsali lightened by streets / secures, secures yours street deep / wondering, wondering and theater often freed by streets / believe, believe and the became found within links of streets / weeks, weeks and the winning streets / winning, winning and the emotional surrender to streeets / source, source led to these streets / significant, significant and the steps into streets / retinue, retinue and teh rescued streets / rounds, rounds and the alps deep in streets / patterns, patterns pulsing within streets / overlay, overlay led often to streets / rounds, rounds and the richest street / places, places applied to for these settled streets / back, back to the trends street / regard, regard paid for the following streets / regardless, regardless of the street, find love / found, found arranged in our streets / floral, floral delivery to our streets / resurrect, resurrect your respect for our streets.

CHAPTER NINE

Lends, lends allowed to appear near the source of streets to love / lots, lots and the gives of the sweetest streets / volumetric, volumetric and the numbers which melt into the streets called love / numbers, numbers neatly arranged to include the streets of love / valuable, valuable details and teh streets dearest too, love / information, information becoming the rage for these streets / station, station couple linked unto love's streets / sculpted, sculpted of water and the granite sand electrically woven to include the moon's streets / land, land chosen has woven an equal net of living loving streets / commercial, commercial rehearsals and the subject, streets / poetic, poetic escapades have won the duration's test of the streets human / raids, raids are over, emply only love in these streets / ratio, ratio taken to heart is love for these streets / develop, develop a flowering vine to her street / services, services rendered and paid through the guise of golden streets / sink, sinking planes and ravagin streams of ionic plunge into the light lines human, our streets / lively, lively within, our streets / spartan, spartan appear and the drawing assets of streets / sparks, sparks allowed the yes to love of streets / tunes, tunes jubilant with gentleness and delicious traces of mineral hosts allowed in our streets / barren, barren has come to gone streets / sorts, sorts who say we play electrically in streets human / church, church hues chosen rainbow blue to a moonstone rite called sparkling streets human / wet, wet allow of teh erosive power of streets / basilica, basilica allowed the streets human / bloke, bloke chased now found in streets / choose, choose one, streets / one, one straddled less, streets / stay, stay electric and alive for streets / strong, strong enough to taste these streets human / allow, allow us our plan human streets / deal, deal in deify of streets electric / intone, intone moaning for our streets / moons, moons and the toning streets / drink, drink in great drafts of moonlit streets / bufoons, bufoons applied to life's streets / balance, balance is found in a town filled with streets / accept, accept a durationf or streets / challenge, challenge allowed into streets / precept, precept concept inflect streets human / prosper, prosper and the simply, streets / plant, plant won here, ivy green within our streets / necks, necks of the nestling streets / taste, taste found for a pleasing street / salt, salt poured past our streets / break, break a speed bumpy with streets / beliefs, beliefs costly on streets / bought, bought a forgiven street / store, store stoned by a street / bitter, bitter balance sought found on A street / blame, blame only light for the insights of streets / explain, explain the notion that love reigns eternal in light's streets / lone, lone details explain our streets / lane, lane and the legions afforded escape to light streets / slowly, slowly and the gradients on streets / woods, woods laned by streets accepted for freedom's streets / boulevards, boulevards and the cards based on stars of assigned streets / bridge, bridge bent to see into our streets / explodes, explodes and the reloads of streets / known, known for the treaty of streets / faith, faith and the fusion into streets / welcome, welcome and the waivering streets / some, some who run into streets / held, electrically held forth by the licensed streets

CHAPTER TEN

Pacify, pacify and the forks onto streets lined with love / sly, sly and the fly into lightened streets / domestic, domestic and the days onto streets / ascend, ascend and the scurry fashioned into streets / blend, blend and teh blazing streets / automatic, automatic and the tracking streets / aim, aim and the raindrops onto our coonstone streets / ships, ships on moonstone lined streets of genuine love / sweet, sweet and the sources elaborate within grandest schemes of streets on love / sort, sort and the willing streets / sports, sports and the ships to a street on love / setle, settle and the stretching streets / supress, supress songlined and stressed by vibrational streets / spring, spring allowed into light's streets / out, out and the upward streets / merry, merry merry ways to love's rewarded streets / bamboo, bamboo and teh roads called streets / imports, imports onto sorts called streets / schools, schools allowed to emply your streets / history, history cured by light's streets / tucks, tucks into lsitening streets / trucks, ruckus allowed for the streets of love / booth, booth and the entailed rites of streets / empire, empire found for the featured streets / participate, participate employed in light's streets / park, park and the sharks left to streets / parked, parked and the placement allowed for our streets / ports, ports insured by our streets / rant, rant within streets / rave, rave about your streets / listen, listen into light's streets / stays, stay levitated by love's streets / wheels, wheels and the steering columned streets / photos, photos aplenty and the lifting streets / portable, portable placement of our streets / path, paths allowed a lviing street / places, places suffered through with A street / pulsate, pulsate pulsing in streets / paints, paints a pretty impact for streets / reach, reach allowed to reign into streets / rest, rest traced miraculously to love's streets / refine, refine define and the reaching understood as streets / read, read a respect for your streets / boxed, boxed and the billows wont o streets / boring, boring off and the granite streets to love / belts, belts and the rafters stressed to streets / short, short enough to sing forth with, our, streets / stay, stay Zion streeted / consider, consider a miracle for streets / material, material made her streets / sleep, sleep lightly by your streets / slept, slept near nearly streets / concurrent, concurrent employ of the light lift to streets / worthy, worthy weights off to a street / sport, sport employed as dear, a street / spares, aprons worn off by a street / train, train on the shores electrically streeted / tires, tires spin onto the pavement electric, streets / live, live parallel to the shores of plenty and the leap aboard the good ships of lightest / lengthen into gains made by the streets shaped by love / wants, wants met by desiring a street / trees, trees placed withinr each of a street / tort, tort sorted and the money won by a street / paid, paid for delivery unto these fossil free streets.

CHAPTER ELEVEN

Culpable, culpable and the query sent for by the legislative streets / troubled, troubled forgive and the living left to a new street / sorts, sorts who sent you their streets / safe, safe enough to move to and fortunately ours, streets / cups, cups drip to filling streets / cavort, cavort and the carrying's on electrically redemptive to light's ascendant stride down these streets / cry, cry less and marry more, the deeds given to a living street / on, on and the sorted streets / curves, curves eruptive live along the lifelines electric unto our streets / delay, delay a drift unto lessened streets / deliver, deliver the livery to a ridden street / debacle, debacl off and the coughing lessened by a healing plan to be A Street / debate, debate over the seas of light streets / dole, dole out the rewards for streets / pent, pent emoitons bust into streets / passions, passions paged for the wearing of streets / potion, potions paging past old streets / pounce, punch through to the chance to be an A street / peak, peak at the conservation point called love is, out, street / science, science is cnetral to the plan common to humanity through shocking streets / plan, plan to be blessed by A's streets / success, success won for our streets / aim, aim to be blessed by God's streets / participate, participate in light's streets / anxious, anxious and worn through to these streets / ancient, ancient apparel and the wings won by your streets / ways, ways met for our streets / ponder, ponder allowance unto life's streets / where, where is your willing, street? / when, when shall we be street freed / often, often I have allowed our electrical conductivity to melt deeper views into love's burden less streets / bother, bother less with lessens streets / come, come to a capable degree for streets / cravings, cravings cured through love's streaming streets / content, content in our venuw for streets / cosmic, cosmic occurences allow your streets / truth, truth is our ablest agreement sent for the religous forgive of light's living streets / quality, quality clarity candor and gifts of purest example for the lifting streets / profess, profess a desire to be street free / seek, seek has sought your streets released / sought, sought an allow for the fortunate streets / civil, civil applications made unto these streets / civiliaze, civilized gifts found nearby streets / politics, politics pulse within, streets / religion, religion rained into lakes james deep within streets of love / reigns, reigns an example called precision in our castled streets / research, research has come truest on streets of golden horned forgiveness of the Baal evented by the cosmic crush for golden leaps past the dam of forgotten steps / masters, masters made daily by the flying maps to love's streets / make, make an alliance a keeper by beepers set on streets / space, space has become your healing street / gaining, gaining an allowance to become lightly loved, street wise / excavate, excavate a rate of forgiven streets / visits, visits allow your delivery of love's streets / giant, giant expands find your streets / respect, respect a miracle cured by love's streets / generations, generations allowed their own streets / on, on and off again unto the lake of dreaming streets / off, off to the magic within your streets / reveal, reveal a resource richest in our streets / plane, plane examples and the samples succinct within life's streets / ponds, ponds and delivery into streams of flotation's streets / pounce, pounce at the chance to dance lake deep in love's pooling healing street / gaining, gaining ground though the metaphor for streets / roads, roads that merge in a word "streets."

CHAPTER TWELVE
Works, works made our wrapped up deal for the designate called pooling resourcefully our streets / well, well enough to be filled with light's loving residue for streets gifts / ancient, ancient amplify has found your gifts delightful and the lips lifted to kiss your insightful query into the origins human, steer clearly to our streets / agrees, agrees dearly for our streets / agencies, agencies

elective have found you weary and wound to be lightly street freed / seals, seals are set and the deals are made for your filling needs and the seeds eruptive to our streets / biblical, biblical recall has added to our Koran's view of the ablest sort who read Mormon seas of salty flee to teh place, this is it, called James, know the seams, streets / liberty, liberty has led you to the place of reconstruct and the supple gifts of love's streets / library, library paged within you and found the streets human / stars, stars are empty unless you sing to to the heavenly sum of One street / skies, skies appearing supple to the interior views of your streets / earth, earth suggests that you are replete within love's streets / heaven, heaven's merkaba field has blended with the planets shield and now the lease is up to your streets / planets, planets planned to pen the degree of your living species called humanity, know the simmering plan to lighten up your days through love's streets / plans, plans are made and now the allow has been built through a lamb sacrificed young to the trees of your streets / cells, cells are replete with a ripening spirit called love's streets / temple, a temple symbolic is the body human and the streets narrow run to her span electric / physiologic, physiologic changes are due to your streets / sonic, sonic decree has agreed to be your street / agree, agree to find one happy man called love is the planet rich with streets / man, man detailed as a moon's reflect within a heart burning street signs / photgraphic, photographic evidence can see your heart's beating street / God, God frames your x-rays in leaves of golden streets / knew, knew you that we are electric too? know the view inside your streets / dowse, dowse the bantered lessening and join the crew who are filing in to view your / pyramid schems of street / delphi, delphi said "red links are built between the belts of loving streets" / ordain, ordain that merkaba metatron has become One with the shield fo earth's / willing release of the curse gone strong to the dove's reply of love is our street / visible, visible changes come to your streets / cosmic, cosmic clues have arranged a pairing orbitally, be aware of the won, street / century, century spoiled now oiled by the trees of love's signature for Streets / eternal, eternal wise and risen too, into streets cosmically agreed too, love / tree, tree and the risen arousals for love's streets / express, express an expression rich with love's streets / sport, sport spilling deep into love's streets / built, built apply for the streets of love / freed, freed into delphi's speaking plan for light's streets / supercede, supercede now allowed through love's streets / sort, sort of the signaled streets / played, played atmospheres of love's streets / porch, precious is our living streets / super, super and the listening streets / deviate, deviate and the details allowed for our streets / parcel, parcel and the placements for love's streets / bought, bought and allowances for our streets / sheets, sheets and the rehearsal allowed our streets / declare, declare and the doors shut past our streets / prepare, prepare your streets / pen, pen applied to our streets / aspects, aspects insured for love's streets / release, release and the shoring streets / respect, respect repaid through your streets / race, race along loving streets / sense, sense and the sums allowed through love's streets / relax, real to the relaxed race past our streets / four, four and the findings relayed to love's streets / found, found and the fortunate strands uniquest to streets

/ hearts, hearts well to the winning streets / reveal, reveal and the rousing streets / fond, fond and the features wont o streets / trains, trains and the rationale paid for streets / tense, tense off and the lanterns burn through our streets / relate, relate your stretching truths to love's streets.

CHAPTER THIRTEEN

Ranges, ranges allowed our patient carriage to love's streets / organelle, organelle allowed for friendship flown to lightened streets / conspire, conspire, conspire a precious street of love / form, form established is well unto the lending laws of God's human streets / foretell, foretell foretold a fellow's streets / motions, motions of the mentioned streets / knowledge, knowledge apparent unto these streets / regulate, regulate and the revenues of living streets / mastery, mastery mentioned thoroughly to your light's streets / solar, solar suggestions of these inflections called streets / reproduce, reproduce an allow for the fortuante still in the silence of love's templed streets / lunar, lunar living in milk green streets / accurate, accurate to a particulate street / phenomena, phenomena repeated for your streets / organelles: pgranelles gained by the strains freed by love in these streets / conspire, conspire to hire a fresher street / spreading, spreading news of established views of loving streets / high, high to the herald's ways to growing spans of streets desired / jump, jump across states of mellowest stages on streets / philosophic, philosophic to the matching stages of streets / heavens, heavens held wisely as streets / deity, deity due a missionary's views of streets / appearances, appearnaces coming to the summary sent by synopsis to the mermaid's streets / borders, borders the fantastic at the majesty of your sunny streets / mysteries, mysteries miraculous within your streets / meeting, meeting set and the regain found for the sounds of mysterious streets / depth, depth added to your flowering adage that love wins where God strains to see your streets / beneath, beneath a nature suffers soft a living bible sweet aloft by mankind's heart lines, the streets human / mated, mated for the sated rise to the surgical miracle found inside true love's benefit of streets / debts, debts now erased by the lifelong streets / erase, erase and the surrender unto a literary street / level, level and the streets staged for listening weddings of love / intitiate, initiate fogone and the song is sung metatron, living largely as the pen of heaven's streets / conscious, conscious of the balances paid and the risen salvation of the rave called walking streets / masterful, masterful means and the rings of a curious nature released unto streets locally / levity, levity linked to the listened for streets / found, found a featured friend called streets / consent, consent to detail your life as well unto your streets / happening, happening to ring as the lingering sing of a dozen plays called streets true to love / holy, holy all day for the cause suffered through to love's streets / proof, proof is, the war's done and the light wins your streets / debate, debate can hum and can she sing? streets align to hear the rise to love / prepare, prepare to be centrifugal to a goodness filled heart worn well within love's strategically placed streets / aware, aware of the streets declared, well / appearing, appearing near us, well streets / dialing, dialing daily, w-e-l-l, streets / woods, woods and the streets of love /

living, living well within light's streets / occupy, occupy a nearest street / detail, detail woven into your streets / position, position gained through love's explain of streets / patience, patience paid, streets / gather, gather the means of streets / yes, yes to declare, streets / passion, passion's return is, streets / gainfully, gainfully prepared to be well within streets / yours, yours, ours, streets / people, people who live well within their streets / power, power yourself to be streetwise / mine, mine is the simple key, yes, to love's streets / metatronic, metatronic news, we win, our streets / pieces, pieces who mends our streets / living, living to give us your streets / now, now is the beginning for streets.

THE ASPIRE-MENTS
LEVEL 57

CHAPTER ONE

Cherished, cherished to the nurturance of an aspirant cure for love / fits, fits and the fastening aspire to love / breaks, breaks and the basics to love / sits, sits and the situations leapt for loving aspire / girls, girls and the worlds winning aspire / erupt, erupt and the supply spent for aspirations of doves / men, men and the mentle release for aspires / burst, burst and the blessings sent for a healing aspire / anchors, anchors and the settings sunk into aspires / trust, trust and the truth told for aspires / traits, traits and the telling aspires / trails, trials and these thet rails to lifting aspire / cinematic, cinematic recall of the fallen friends found near your sapphire aspires / regard, regard a resting aspire / faced, faced within an aspire / mirrors, mirrors methodic to an aspire / shown, shown the way to be aspired / wants, wants a wiser aspire / desire, desire to behave forthright unto loving aspires / deluxe, deluxe in a detail apparent to aspire / clamor, clamor mannered as aspire / acquire, acquire a featured randomness, aspire / climbing lofts to an aspire / access, access granted an aspire / access, access allows your aspire / barren, barren less and pregnant more than any single aspire / bower, bower to the towering aspire / checks, checks and the change made to an aspire / clear, clear a sample of thee, aspires / class, class acted for and found green to an aspire / acres, acres growing in hawaiian aspires / doubts, doubts offered the release into an aspire / travel, travel costs less by the blessings appearing near your spiraling aspire / gone, gone to a gracious aspire / news, news made you an spire / now, now we simply, suggest an aspire / appears, appears regular to an aspire / gender, gender gentle within an aspire / heaven, heaven held us lightly aspired / hearth, hearth mentioned for an aspire / Gabriel, Gabriel fused into an aspire / on, on a worthy aspire / cry, cry curbed by an aspire / mavericks, mavericks material to an aspire / sky, sky wise within an aspire / matched, matched winnings won by an aspire / record, records and the engravings living through an aspire / guests, guests ingrained by barreling aspires / list, list and the listings assigned through an aspire / diverge, diverge and the merger for an assign / divest, divest and the aspirant forms for love / ingest, ingest and the channeling massage of aspires / chant, chant and the channeling aspires / match, match and the mentioned aspires / churn, churn and the yearning aspires / joint, joint and the journeys unto an aspire / eat, eat and the sentry fortunate unto an aspirant assign / most, most are hosted by a strawberry assignment aspired for through love / own, own an hourly aspirant / ship, ship sailing past a freedom passed to a living aspire / cash, cash sustained through an aspire / opens, opens and the curtail off an aspire / again, again and the shown aspire / owner, owner of the video empire aspire.

CHAPTER TWO

God, God gazing unto an aspire / chains, chains changing for an aspire / chance, chance to be told an aspire / dances, dances electric for an aspire / comes, comes to the coning aspire / own, own and the random aspire / life, life and the legendary aspire / loose, loose and the lantern's aspire / hand, hand and the aspiring remand of love / God, friendly to a fellow aspire / chains, chains and a channeled aspire / chance, chance allowed your aspire / dames, dames dealt within an aspire / pupils, pupils and the simply aspired / masters, masters made aspirant too / love, love the span aspirant / cash, cash and the opening aspires / opens, opens an account for the simply aspirant / opens, opens a panel aspirant / again, again and the winning aspire / owner, owner retailed by the aspires / comes, comes another's aspire / own, own and the raiment worn by an aspire / life, life led and the lips pursed by an aspire / loose, loose and the clothing sent for an aspire / hand, hands and the handy aspire / puppets, puppets posing as an aspire / master, mastery for an aspire / love, love leaping across an aspire / bones, bones appear near an aspire / prophecy, prophecy about an aspire / lengths, lengths genuine unto an aspire / loving, loving attend to an aspire / cursh, crush across an aspire / sustain, sustained by a healing aspire / shown, shown and a single aspire / carts, carts crossed by a charted aspire / holocaust, holocaust cost as aspired / clip, clip and the lessons aspired / funny, funny focused aspire / sense, sense sorted through an aspire / hope, hope and the makings to an aspire / sensual, sensual sustain for an aspire / choice, choice chinese and the meaning aspired / plays, plays a spiral into an aspire / upon, upon a simple sample's aspire / deep, deep through a directive aspire / stilll, still in a focused assign for an aspire / sure, sure enough to be footheld by loving aspires / waters, waters willing to be well within an aspire / amply, amply sought and found through a healing aspire / sent, sent for and noticed as an aspire / full, full to a feeling aspire / ships, ships sparkle in a healing aspire / float, float anterior to a parcel aspirant / across, across the waves a calling aspire / welcome, welcome to a wisdom replete within aspire / shores, shores central to a magical expansion of your aspire / chores, chores and the cheering aspire / end, end and the dealings sought for an aspect of aspire / angels, angels allowed an aspire / men, men and the mentioned aspire / One, One and the too, aspirant / again, again and the aspiring mending.

CHAPTER THREE

Graves, graves spill forth to the light exhausted by their fright lifted to a living aspire / spill, spill into the light refrain for heaven's aspire / heart, heart herald to an aspire / reveal, reveal rests in aspire / God's, God's gained aspire / plan, plan too, aspire / passions, passions places aspire / rip, rip rusts out, aspire / veils, veils suggest, aspire / get, get won, aspire / ripe, ripe trued aspire / attend, attend trains aspire / transactions, transactions managed aspire / seek, seek sun's aspire / quiet, quiet warmed aspire / reveal, reveal registrates aspire / men, men aspire / met, met God, aspired / metatrons, metatrons aspire sent love / shield, shield spent aspired / dancing, dancing day's aspire / cards, cards made, aspire / deal, deal with your aspire / dates, dates dent aspire / along, along with aspire / life's life's lead aspire / plates, plates plumbed aspirant to an ascend / earth, earth squire's aspire / eight, eight ways aspired / proceed, proceed pays aspired / pure, pure enough's aspire / clear, clear way's aspired / hearts, hearts aspire / home, home too, aspired / repairs, repairs well, aspires / own, own too, assign aspires / profits, profits paid assigned to aspired / earn, earn fades assigns aspired / spurn, spurn less assigned aspires / goes, goes when assigned aspires / gables, gables go too assigns aspires / show, show us your assigns aspires / shown, shown a deal's assigns aspires / reveal, reveal revels in assigns aspires / revelers, revelers vandalized past aspire / relax, relax rated assigns aspired / rest, rest aspires / truncated, truncated and aspired / banks, banks in aspires / open, open ways aspire / cubes, cubes cased in aspire / erupt, erupt when aspired / racing, racing rages in aspires / raging, raging ways aspire / swords, swords cut our aspire / caps, caps appraise aspired / cursed, cursed cares aspire / forget, forget aspire west gathers aspire / life, life led aspire / said, said yes to aspire / welcome, welcome gone aspiring / levels, levels / aspired too / succeed, succeed within aspires / walks, walks ways aspired.

CHAPTER FOUR

Magical, magical amaze's aspires / maths, maths matched in aspires / principles, principles placed at aspires / baths, baths won by an aspire / cathodes, cathodes cased in aspires / pulse, pulse pays aspires / rays, rays won, aspired / ruse, ruse rang aspired / over, over ways aspired / fast, fast funds aspire / written, written rounds aspirant / robes, robes aspired / worn, worn ways aspire / trues, trues in aspires / turns, turns into aspires / topples, topples under aspires / paths, paths placed in assigns aspire / past, past ways aspire / hash, hash won, aspire / incest, incest rested for aspires / facts, facts gave us assigns aspired / collective, collective came too, assigns aspired / knows, knows when assigned aspried / known, known for these assigns aspired / God's, God's gaze aspired / too, too knew aspire / overtures, overtures wires aspire / mask, mask off aspires / heads, heads ahead, aspires / face, face wounding aspires / fact, fact too, aspires / fortitude, fortitude found aspire / Japanese, Japanese joins aspire / joys, joys found in aspire / join, join too, aspire / joins, joins in aspires / source, source aspirant / sings, sings with aspire / rings, rings aspire in assigns / racks, racks wanted assigns / hands, hands won aspire / lift, lift into the line's aspire / open, open too, aspires / source, source won too, aspire / barques, barques who hear an aspire / naves, naves knead aspire / notes, notes made too, aspire / pages, pages want, aspire / rests, rests made too aspire / placed, placed into, aspires / possission, possession way's aspires / palms, palms play's aspires / physical, physical play's assigns aspire / physiques, physiques join, aspires / dead, dead too goes, aspires / doubt, doubt wills out aspires / occurs, occurs in aspires / capillary, capillary squeezed assigns aspire / sorts, sorts suggest on aspires / suppose, suppose sent in aspires / sustains, sustains well design's aspires / obeys, obeys your aspire / ovation, ovation felt aspired / decoys, decoys a field aspires.

CHAPTER FIVE

Mansions, mansions matched in aspire / temples, temples traced too, aspire / starts, starts winding through aspired / chart, chart choose, aspires / star, star stare's aspires / summons, summons meant aspires / chat, chat with aspirants / tantra, tantra trills too assigns aspires / tops, tops tracking in aspires / taller, taller ways aspires / longs, longs into a thorough aspire / chins, chins chained aspires / all, all way's aspires / dwarfed, dwarfed design's aspires

/ drove, drove into an aspire / driven, driven trade's aspires / sash, sash wants thick release on aspire / antioch, antioch way's aspire / enoch's, enoch's tray's aspire / grasp, grasp a response aspire / hell's, hell's aparts aspire / given, given grade's for an aspire / denial, denial out, aspire / plants, plants placed in aspire / juice, juice congeals in aspire / takes, takes into your aspire / fells, fells out aspires in / myths, myths western aspire / spoken, spoken ways aspire / truths, truths about your aspire / phrases, aspire into phrases gifts / books, books written in aspire / Christ's, Christ's days aspire / concept, concept finds aspire / clues, clues about your aspire / kegs, kegs into all's aspire / divinities, divinities daring aspire / dose, dose on aspire / Hades, Hades out, aspire / bursts, bursts within aspire / flames, flames flew too, aspire / flaws, flaws collapse too, aspire / claws, claws on, aspire / birds, birds ways aspire / othello, othello through, aspire / spoke, spoke "aspire" / brained, brained recount "aspire" / thought, thought through an aspire / Christos, Christos ablaze in aspire / heal, heal won into aspire / Golgotha, Golgotha winters in aspire / chill, chill trade's true in aspire / sword, sword of the curt aspire / grasp, your grasp gravitates too, aspire / hilt, hilt of the stilted aspire / hasp, hasp help / hold, hold wafts too aspire / swear, swear too, aspire / coarse, coarse worn aspire / cares, taught cares way too, aspires / Simon, Simon sped through aspire / said, said within aspires / Thomas, Thomas traced aspires / fed, fed fors aspires.

CHAPTER SIX

Drop, drop came too, aspired / drape, drape on aspires / drift, drift to a forgiven aspire / flights, flights forgive is in aspirant wings / doubts, doubts out through aspire / drama, drama dealing with aspires / unified, unified and the winning in healing aspires / unfold, unfold into ways, aspired / /, / ways aspired / plays, plays into aspires / places, places placed in aspire / thieves, thieves outed, aspires / witness, witness wiavers signed aspire / tuned, tuned into an aspire / taught, taught with wonderful aspires / told, told of ways aspired / library, library left too assigns / books, books into aspire / bases, bases born, assigned aspires / golden, golden give's aspire / grasps, grasps graced too, assigns aspires / points, points want assigns aspire / forgives, forgives learn aspired / begs, begs too, assigns aspire / presence, presence pays, assigns aspire / soars, soars want assigns aspire / initiates, initiates woven into assigns aspires / sold, sold in assigns aspires / heavens, heavens burst assigned aspires / gates, gates want assigns aspired / mockery, mockery meets assigns aspires / cloak, cloak to a blissing assigned aspires / shroud, shroud sports aspire / tomb, tomb traded for aspire / rock, rock runs too aspired / Bartholemew, Bartholemew knew aspire / purple, purple worth assigned aspire / Lord's, Lord's gaze aspired / discipline, discipline daft in aspire / disciples, disciples daily aspired / gifts, gifts warranted through aspire / gained, gained inquires aspire / ovens, ovens bred aspires / cure, cure craves aspire / clash, clash cords in aspires / metals, metals glare aspires / sword, sword pays cut, aspires / .gards, gards choose aspire / exchange, exchange dotted with aspires / spoken, spoken met in aspire / compassion, compassion met in aspire / owns, owns your gait's aspire / blows, blows in two, aspire / windy, windy words aspires / successful, successful sounds aspire / define, define dates aspire / peopled, peopled plays aspires / sure, sure embraced aspire / assumes, assumes mared aspire / earth, earth belt's aspire / insure, insure found, aspire / success, success get's aspire / regain, regains around our aspires / belief, belief bakes our aspires.

CHAPTER SEVEN
Encompass, encompasss your qualify's aspire / speaks, speaks in stare's aspire / enoch, enoch nets aspire / innocence, innocence suspects aspire / reward, reward runs too assigns aspire / arcangelic, arcangelic wealth, aspires / meant, meant to be aspires / metatron, metatron made Michael fast to aspire / absolute, absolute tray's aspire / declare, declare dashes too, aspire / pertain, pertain pairs aspire / precised, precised paned aspire / pertinent, pertinent power's aspire / range, range raves, aspire / widens, widens into aspire / plans, plans fell into aspires / board, board built aspires / rewards, rewards ranged into aspires / suns, suns sent through cloud's aspires / through, through weaves aspire / seeded, seeded suggestively aspired / God, God engrave's aspire / gave, gave into an aspire / universe, universe yells for aspire / gifts, gifts gave aspire / splash, splash exposed aspire / thrones, thrones throughted in aspire / threads, threads silvery in aspire / Athena, Athena thumbed aspire / disciple, disciple deals aspire / discipline, discipline dappled in aspire / placed, placed plans aspire / signs, signs on aspires / woners, wonders waged aspires / worth, worth one's aspire / pushes, pushes on pen, aspire / reds, reds aspires / blues, blues rewires aspire / groves, groves of gracious arrives aspire / greens, greens elates in sized aspires / gross, gross well inclined to erupt too, aspire / rush, rush expressed too, aspire / over, over flown's aspire / flows, flows estate's aspire / French, French phrased aspires / foods, foods traced aspires / fast, fast flaws expell too, aspires / release, release raised too, aspires / goodness, goodness gave us aspire / Goddess, Goddess grants aspire / God, God gates aspires / this, this throws too, aspire / pentacles, pentacles place in aspires / swords, swords sang in legendary aspire / cards, cards pace our aspires / drawn, drawn into a raised aspire / artistic, artistic trade's aspires / invent, invent forced aspires / placed, placed in proceeds aspires / grew, grew into an aspire / lands, parallel lands astound with aspires / loves, loves let's aspires / lass, lass laden to a faded aspire / learn, learn ways to aspire.

CHAPTER EIGHT
Skull, skull pirate out with aspires / crossing, crossing craves an unhinged aspire / purgatory, purgatory pays aspries way / Dante, Dante retells aspires / crossed, crossed path's melt in aspires / abcessed, abcessed processed aspires / lost, lost lens found in aspires / found, found of the wavings aspire / beasts, beasts clear too, aspire / release, love's release aspire / best, best in an aspire / relay, a relay raised into aspire / ransom, aspires ransom raised too love / pays, pays for your aspire / regard, regard as wellest in aspire / rescue, rescue raised aspires / messionic, messionic alibe's amaze in aspire / news, news aspire's too love / norse, love's norse coded aspires / cares, cares paths aspire / caption, a caption rants

"aspire" / cashiers, cashiers check for aspire / cubes, cubes square in aspires / coats, coats in aspire / lavender, lavender lane's aspire / icons, icons crazed in aspires / scion, scion of stretched aspire / soon, soon will, aspire / enoch's, enoch's days aspire / call, a call makes an aspire give / fossils, love's fossils man in aspire / graves, graves open in aspires / ownership, ownership raves on aspires / deed, deed devoted through aspire / title, title gives aspires / gone, gone into aspire / location, location above's aspire / devotion, devotion dealt with aspire / ovation, ovation felt with aspire / awash, awash in aspire / wins, wins too, aspire / God's, God's greet in aspires / friend, friend deemed aspires / mankind, mankind's kinds aspire / open, open's gains aspire / one, onw with them aspires / way, way to show, aspires / home, home meets in aspires / electric, aspires electric say love / requires, requires love's aspire / counts, counts four aspire / form, the form wants aspire / abject, abject retake of the aspire / whole, whole way for aspire / holy, holy entire's aspire / bliss, bliss buys aspire / bless, bless may and aspire / ascend, ascend when aspired to / debt, debt outed too aspires / debits, debits course with aspire / come, aspires comes too, yours love / overt, overt reinsert to aspire / opportunities, opportunities warrant aspires / counts, counts with inspects aspires.

CHAPTER NINE
Gull, gull intact with registered aspire / gain, gain a reclaims aspire / lifts, lifts into views aspire / spirits, spirits aspires succumbs to intents clarity / phones, phones clearly say empires aspire / bones, bones blanks in aspires / hear, hear way's aspires / heard, heard worthy's aspires / plates, plates flat with aspired sands / passed, passed into obligates related aspires / cast, cast out within aspires / cashed, cashed introduce to aspires / cope, cope with aspires beads / owners, owners came into aspires / give, give us our day's aspires / elective, elective links aspire / reasons, reasons race into aspires place / revenues, revenues own aspires / rounds, rounds too, aspire / placed, placed with these aspires / planes, planes punch into aspire / aligned, aligned lanes aspires / parallel, parallel pays aspires / ports, ports opened in aspires / swish, swish with aspire / cafe, cafe complete in aspire / owns, owns ways too aspire / tribute, tribute paid into aspire / declare, declare a dove's aspire / warps, warps load aspired / speak, speak within aspire / shares, shares on aspire / temples, temples thanked through aspire / traps, traps out in aspire / kings, kings cases aspire / thrown, thrown into an aspire / England, England keys aspire / France, France felt for aspire / templar, templar tempted in aspire / knights, knights needs aspire / hurtle, hurtle within aspires / comets, comets come into aspire / windowed, windowed explorations aspire / sights, sights sake, aspire / roses, roses rank petal blue aspire / gardens, gardens gait's aspire / red, red rewards aspire / plants, plants placed in aspires / plans, plans made to aspire to Jerusalem / foundations, foundations found in aspire / shade, shade with emotional aspire / loose, loose into way's spun aspire / leases, leases up assigns aspire, aspire waits assignment, aspire / stays, stays aspired / mortal, mortal maths aspire / Shekinah, Shekinah sapphires bare to an aspire / hope, hope found in an aspire / heart, heart found in

aspire / home, home wind is aspire / earth, earth to each assembly's aspire / keep, keep in a desires aspire / ears, ears perked in love's aspire / wide, wide within aspire.

CHAPTER TEN

Listen, listen to your hatened aspire / list, a list for reclines aspires / moments, moments amaze in aspire / minutes, minutes aspire wants decide / God's, God's gaze into aspire / place, places alive in aspires / throne, throne aroused in aspires / wide, aspirations wide in aspires / elders, elders ways / deep into aspire / angels, angels ran to aspire / arcs, arcs wile aspires / meets, meets in a spectacular aspire / steps, steps into praise's aspire / jaunts, jaunts for aspires / pilgrims, pilgrims placed aspires / keep, keep one's aspire / sacred, sacred shouts "aspire" / commands, commands chance to lightly aspire / mathematics, mathematics material aspires / maps, maps chart on aspire / heavens, heavens hels aspires / guest, guest of the wed's aspire / gates, gates want an aspire / weigh, weigh for a light's aspire / ways, ways consecrate in aspire / homeword, homeword sound's aspire / headwise, headwise shed's aspire / do, do your aspire / devotion, devotion deals in aspire / motion, motion entires aspires / emulate, emulate swell aspire / prove, prove too, aspire / annals, annals apply with aspire / abruptly, abruptly sent too, aspire / launch, launch your arc to aspire / plans, plans to feel aspired to / God's, God's gait aspired / salvation, salvation assures your aspire / human, human helps aspire / lattice, lattice coupled in to aspire / leaps, leaps across to aspire / raptures, raptures raise to aspire / rate, rate your interest to aspire / rules, rules out aspire / majestic, majestic may's aspire / amid, amid the grid's aspire / artistic, artistic vent's aspire / notions, notions knead to aspire / painters, painters churched in aspires / precise, precise in your praise's aspire / icons, icons waned aspire / weep, weep the soul aspire / frames, frames pictured a colorful thought to aspire / stretch, stretch to destination aspire / pregnant, pregnant with being aspired / seek, seek yourself aspire / interest, interest can build aspire / applauds, applauds doing in to assigns aspire / olympian, olympian lay's aspire / shores, shores warrant aspires / Mary's, Mary's etheric assures aspire / Jesus, Jesus joins aspire / births, births certified aspire / desperate, desperate at the aspires.

CHAPTER ELEVEN

Attributive, attributive tray's aspire / chapels, chapels climbed in aspire / positions, positions paced with aspire / pathos, pathos given to aspire / artists, artists paced your aspires / bibles, bibles belt out aspire / gothic, gothic rings aspires / pose, pose for an aspire / prose, prose swing to aspire / electric, electric winged aspires / throngs, throngs allow your aspires / ring, ring rounds an aspire / orders, orders warrant an aspire / taken, taken into aspires / altars, altars strung with aspire / sing, sing within aspire / mirrors, mirrors match aspire / imagine, imagine makes an aspire / imperfect, imperfect forgets less aspire / status, status quotes in aspire / stages, stages stretch into aspire / scopes, scopes infuse into aspire / erotics, erotics respect for aspires / infuse, infuse fuses in aspires / generations, generations join to aspires / God's, God's great gift to aspires / antiquity, antiquity waits in an aspire

/ elongate, elongate levels in aspire / softly, softly seals on aspire / spoken, spoken pave / alterations, alterations spaced into an aspire / seal, seal meets the assigns aspire / hermetically, hermetically rited in aspires / given, given to, aspirant ways / traditional, traditional tracks aspires / zeal, zeal zeroes in aspires / shatters, shatters within ascends aspire / illusions, illusions laced in aspires / billions, billions raft in an aspire / ringed, ringed within aspire / mantles, mantles entire to in embraced aspire / plenty, plenty parry in aspire / flaming, flaming within aspire / sing, sing sang an aspire / lounging, lounging with a sensates aspires / magnolias, magnolias mansioned aspire / rabbits, rabbits hot aspire / rest, rest rampaged in aspire / pleasures, pleasures aspirant with love / burgeon, love's burgeon begins in aspire / plenty, plenty too views aspirant / invests, invests aspires succeed / values, values variably correct in their energetic aspire / shift, shift into news more aspirant / balestrades, balestrades brash exact to an aspire / bolt, bolt into an aspire on to deeld / born, born into loft's aspire / intricately, intricately stints interweave in aspire / luxuriance, luxuriance leaps to aspire / reigns, reigns regains aspire / backdrop, backdrop dip into an aspire / painted, painted flowers feel especially entire in aspire / florence, florence flaunts an aspire / gains, gains grip within aspire.

CHAPTER TWELVE

Serophain, Serophain ascend to aspires / spirits, spirits mate in aspire / elements, elements bait your aspire / prophetic, prophetic placed in aspire / cherubim, cherubim whim's aspire / humanity, humanity deity, aspire / recipient, recipient's arose with aspire / transits, transits read aspire / personal, personal planes aspire / pushing, pushing cavernous aspire / signs, signs seed, aspire / pleasant, pleasant within pens aspire / chambers, chambers open in aspire / plaques, plaques away too inspired aspire / arrange, arrange days aspirantly / trips, trips venued in too, aspire / thinly, thinly thronged aspire / dagger, dagger dashed in aspire / demon, demon cast in light's aspire / deals, deals out one aspire / centrific, centrific songed aspire / plunge, plunge outs again aspire / adoration, adorations bridge aspire / singing, singing trails aspire / pictures, pictures page aspire / clicking, clicking in too, aspire / agree, agree within aspire / scant, scant veiled aspire / lips, lips linked aspire / endears, endears require aspires / regions, regions arose in aspire / forelorn, forelorn goes too, aspire / kissed, kissed intents aspire / lucent, lucent ripples aspire / lucifer, lucifer out to a lights aspire / winging, winging shouts aspire / shorn, shorn out redial in aspires / dropping, dropping dates aspire / spirals, spirals sun aspire / angular, angular voiced agrees aspire / greed, greed freed to aspire / God, God won aspire / kingdom, kingdom comes, aspire / sings, sings in tunes aspire / home, home hampered outs aspire / meet, meet in aspire / impairs, impairs heal, aspire / impeals, impeals sounds "aspire" / places, places met with aspire / spurts, spurts in trues aspires / sentries, sentries now trained in aspire / freed, freed for aspire / parts, parts gain their aspire / causes, causes came with aspire / reaches, reaches for your aspire / breathing, breathing to aspire / regions, regions rage in aspire / implode, implode torn in aspire / explode, explode grants gaze an aspire / sort, sort spent in aspire / reaches, reaches paced too, aspire / vagina, vagina joins with aspire / charts, charts channel too, aspire / penis, penis portrays an aspire.

CHAPTER THIRTEEN

Bodiless, bodiless baits aspire to light / torsos, torsos toss into aspire / diverse, diverse dealt's aspires / natures, natures nets aspire / symbolic, symbolic surfaced aspires / icon, an icon sent into aspire / assumptions, assumptions came, aspire / shapes, shapes suggest, aspire / eventual, eventual variants aspires / varieties, varieties values aspire / bodies, bodies beside / sprout, sprout wing aspire / cards, cards tossed into aspires / cued, cued cables aspires / winged, winged nearest in aspires / independence, independence dates in aspires / visions, visions umbilical taste of aspire / open, open truced aspires / cowers, cowers aways aspires / radiates, radiates rappels in aspire / crystallize, crystallize captivates aspire / ours, ours is the winning aspire / fires, fires flaunted aspires / spiritually, spiritually suggestive in aspire / eyes, eyes paged aspires / audible, audible commits aspire / incant, incant wonders aspire / spirit, spirit creates in aspire / wise, wise worlds aspire / child, child chose an aspire / mother, mother may's aspire / spark, spark joined through an aspire / clouds, clouds empirical with aspire / comprise, comprise aspires sent into love / ways, love's ways aspire / home, home held into an aspire / guise, guise gasped for aspire / guilds, guilds gather in aspire / webs, webs broken with aspire / breath, breath freely aspire / classes, classes court an aspire / feathers, feathers fanned and aspired / bunch, bunched materailized aspires / punch, punch past aspires / decks, decks built aspire / island, island sand's aspire / push, push plays aspire / close, close trued aspires / stereos, stereos several deep in aspire / songs, songs rhymes rant with aspire / sounds, sounds liven us to aspire / choirs, aspires choirs lavender green / angels, angels championed through aspire / peoples, peoples play charmed aspire / butterfly, butterfly bereaves upstarted aspire / pose, pose all known aspire / coming, coming to in love's aspire / vision, vision valiant in aspire / compare, compare twins an aspire / consume, consume leashed without aspire / witness, witness west too, aspire / saint, saintscent's aspires / colors, colors appear through aspire / account, account for your aspire.

THE MYSTERY-MENTS
LEVEL 58

CHAPTER ONE

Humpback, humpback fins and the mysterious intend of love / Reviews, reviews the new arrive at the mysteries of love / whale's, whale's of wheels of life's mystery / stable, stable and able to be mysterious / technique, technique tucked in the mystery / innovate, love's innovate is the great, mystery / magazine, hearing's magazine landscape of the mystery / young, young enough to see, the mystery of love / futures, human futures agree, God's mystery is love / Compute, compute the love in paints / webs, webs of wield to the move, a mystery / issues, mysterious issues clear God's / sharp, love's sharp agree is God, the mystery / paints, paints of pens, the mystery / establish, establish a state, mysterious / base, base made, hear the mystery / cooper, cooper's pedy mysteries in Australia's win too, love / caught, caught in a mire of the mystery / price, price of a plan, the mystery / change, change your range, the mystery / populous, love's populous degree of meditation comes true through the mystery / populate, populate the estate with a mystery / area, mysteries area is heard, love / where, where in the near mystery / suggestion, suggestion of a score mysterious too, love / consult, consult a hearing set in / 's mystery / convolute, convolute to the repute's deprive left too a mystery / touch, touch into a trust mystery / track, track into a knack for the mystery / countries, mysterious countries / crowns, crowns in a capital's place in pattern's mystery / works, works in the make of mystery / open, open your heart to the arc, you're on the mystery / part, part of the path and the mathematics wide to a news inside the mystery / partners, partners pelt the need with mysterious / between, between the lend, a mystery God's / trades, mysteries trade and te raids out in love / elect, mysteries elect a reconnect in you hear / electric, love's electric reviews is the mystery in God / establish, establish men of mystery and reveal, love / shops, love shops, hear, in the mysteries end, love / base, mysteries base is in, love / build, build a rapport within mysteries / conact, conact a dat's lot, for mysteries / doing, doing a brave wave too mysteries / brave, love's brave move, mysteris's magazine's gain, God / opens, opens a gate throug mysteries / dense, dense in a deepened sense, too, mysteries / stands, stands in a traditioned mystery / grips, grips in a grids mysterious release / winds, winds in the windowed mysteries / drives, drives into a truth's mystery / conduit, conduit of the renew it, mysterie / whit, whit of the wit won, mysteriously / days, days in the ways mysteriou / doors, doors appear in the nearest wood's mystery / heart, heart of the carts fall mystery / day, day of the dryest mystery / legacy, legacy of the nearest mystery / right, right too, the mystery / tight, tight in a treatise wrought mysterious / corner, corner of the parallel union mystery / curb, curb too a mystery's tour / condition, condition contempt arts a mystery.

CHAPTER TWO

Capture, capture and the rapture sent to love, a mystery / interface, interface racing within the race to planned mystery / Chicago, Chicago and the shipping mystery / congress, congress detailed by the sailing mystery / experiences, experiences and the plateau reached by a mystery / flocks, flocks and the listening mystery

/ congressional, congressional and the corrected mysteries / confess, confessions ranging unto a mystery / capri, capri of the intended mystery / lavendar, lavendar laces and the lessons waded through a mystery / lightly, lightly said, go lightly, less then more a mystery / l.ot, lots detailed and the wellness realmed throughout a mystery / list, list and the floral mystery / land, land of the precious mystery / launder, launder and the lifted mystery / loans, loans employ the mystery / safari, safari sent a superlative regard for the mystery / diary, diary and the delay of a mystery / publish, publish a patiently awarded mystery / sails, sails across a sealing mystery / southern, southern accents soothe the mystery / secret, secret unto a mystery / lodge, lodge near the heart of the mystery / equator, equators raised unto the musical mystery / clouds, clouds launched across the mystery / cleft, cleft found in a town casual to mysteries / cures, cures appear near the mystery / travels, travels page past your mystery / amber, amber bought lightly through love for the mystery / voice, voice sought is found for a mystery / vaunt, vaunt a valued friend unto a mystery / sapphire, sapphire seals along the mystery / wild, wild amounts of minutes mysteries / place, place us near the mystery / birth, birth begun within a mystery / chinese, chinese written upon the mystery / modern, modern measures made for mysteries / tale, tale of the sealing cost for mysteries / chronicle, chronicle the ocst in mystery / equation, equation witnessed in a well attempt to mean a mystery / elevate, elevate your knowing to an opened mystery / chapin, chapin in the penchant's cube, the curation of the mystery / manet, manet made a moment's regard a lesson for the canvas sound within the mystery / vogue, vogue suggests a plate across the pages shift to a mystery / valuate, valuate your worthiness with a healing twist across the mystery / vein, veins venued to the threaded mystery, hu-manity / vault, vault to the self regarded mystery / bride, bride found near a mystery / pride, pride said "ridden" to a mystery / avenue, avenue chosen then, a mystery / core, core examples and the sample sent into a mystery / labels, labels peeled off these mysteries / lake, lake heights rise into the vibration of a mystery, humanity / lots, lots deep in the sought for vibe of a lightening mystery / lore, lore has said the lights are red ans the source level of a table rocked through a mystery / listen, listen now and here, we are, a mystery / learn, learn to be frequent within a mystery called love / yearn, yearn for the spelling which burns with m-y-s-t-e-r-y / desire, desire a feature faced through a mysterious sum called won / designate, designate a celebration for the rations paid for a future waved through a mystery / connect, connect to a vector called centrally a mystery / correspond, correspond to a cause for the cell-a-brations of love, the mystery / joint, joint success at the resting mystery / listen, listen to the vibrational sport of mysteries.

CHAPTER THREE

Markets, markets are launched through a mystery, Adamic, Arcturian, ARCs, receive the mystery / place, place a pattern upon the wand of mysteries / otavallo, otavallo markets our grapple free mystery / banos, banos bathed in the hot ashed mystery / bet, God's bet is best in a mystery / bolt, bolt to the volt run, metatronically a mystery / roll, roll to a surface wet with mystery / fabric, fabric folds to reveal a variation of the development for a loving mystery / awning, awning crossed the lips of one won to the electric mystery / cords, cords are simply cut through a mystery / poll, poll taken says Yes! to a mystery / prepare, prepare for a lesson and the launch unto a mystery / more, more in samples mysterious / stare, stare across the cords mysterious / God, God gave us lightening mysteries / life, life leads us to the sword of michael's steep arrival in the mystery / created, created softly, a lightly, mystery / coined, coined and kept often into a mystery / escape, escape to a lip soft within a mystery / to, to us enfolds a blissful appearance of the mystery / the, the the often dayed mystery / massage, massage welcome to the winning mystery / red, red and often blue unto a mystery / reels, reels shot through the mystery / this, this is a sample of the mystery / these, these are the dealt with mysteries / field, fields fold unto the mysteries / magnetic, magnetic mention of the mysteries / expand, expand your horizontal horizons to a vertical spin for the mystery of love / express, express a sample random enough to count for a mystery / diagnose, diagnose the news, a mystery / dialect, dialects pledged as the mystery / reprise, reprise and the risen one's mystery / drawn, drawn into a vibrational rift for the mystery / reprise, reprise written for our heart sung mystery / correlate, correlate your cord's mystery / equal, equal to a cause and the sequels sent winning mysteries / capes, capes graded for a mystery / drawn, drawn again a thin mystery / dawn, dawn can tell the tale of a wishing mystery / hu-man, human love has won our mystery / fan, fan of the feature plant deep in earthy crust for the mystery / electric, fans of the electric wonders called materially the spiritual degrees of a man, the mystery / special, special unto a raveling sort called electrically, love, a mystery / elect, elect us loved through a mystery / governed, governed and the silence said, "a mystery" / direct, direct me home unto the mystery / door, door opens unto a mystery / four, four hearts found in a town wise to the mystery / life, life, love, integrity, forthrightness, essentially, a mystery / heart, heart of the started humans, mysterious to love / estate, estate touched by the mystery / own, own a living mystery / debate, debate above the listening mystery / happy, happy allowance of the physical mental fogive through a mystery / equates, equates a howiling whistling metatronic leap with a looped mystery / owners, owners forgive a mystery / leave, leave us led to the mystery / led, led by the mystery / lead, lead us past a mystery / opened, opened a radial mystery / soon, soon and how, a mystery / room, room found too, a mystery / stairs, stairs which lead to a mysterious awareness dialectic set for a mystery.

CHAPTER FOUR

Carry, carry her own, mystery / coded, coded and loaded as a mystery / return, return a daily warmth and a living clime for a rhyming mystery / revenue, revenue near the mystery / rescues, rescues another's mystery / serious, serious and the simple disciple for a mystery / jet, jet past a living mystery / join, join us near amystery / republic, republic of the clues through a mystery / casual, casual to alliance for the mystery / cares, cares

and the courage to be a mystery / knows, knows a sequel for the intriguing mystery / renew, renew a retail of the mystery / noon, noon electives for the runes mystery / adores, adores us well into the mystery / classic, classic acquire of a parallel retire unto the mystery / navy, navy dues paid a living mystery / allow, allow us well into the mystery / channel, channels paid for shouting "mysteries"/ shift, shift agrees a living pull unto the mustered mystery / chains, chains off the simple cheshire smiling mystery / change, change a pleasant appearance into a securest settlement of the mysterie / process, process allows us a rosey mystery / protrude, protrude and the valued mystery / profuse, profuse unto use of the mysteries / portend, portend and the mended mysteries / correlate, correlate and the sate of a mystery / cable, cable and the collision dearest to a mystery / sent, sent an intentional volley for the mystery / send, send allows us amystery / retort, retort and reworked mysteries / men, men made a mentally detailed zone for the mystery / yen, yen and the spending mystery / yang, yang and the surgical require for a mystery / young, young allowance of these mysteries / win, win a chance to dine in the mysteries / women, women welcomed unto the mystery / song, songs spilling into the mysterious / sung, sung siren spanned by the mystery / drive, drive and the decibels of a mystery / dive, dive across the wizened works of a mystery / daunt, daunt suggested for the lightest mysteries / knot, knots nestle to a mystery / return, return and the learning mystery / love, love and the led hunch of a mystery / l.unch, lunch and the threaded mystery / lots, lots pacing our mystery / read, read a reasoned mystery / advise, advise a wiser mystery / jump, jump for one who gives to the mystery / test, test won through a reply positive for a mystery / wear, wear a worded mystery, m-y-s-t-e-r-y / webs, webs and the medical mentions of the mystery / fluid, fluid lips flow to the mystery / best, best is "yes" to the mystery / flights, flights follow our mystery / align, align a mystery that is given God's living leverage / confess, confess and the rehire of a mystery / please, please a subject's mystery / cruet, cruet drips in fueling mysteries / crux, crux offered as the mystery / cuvee, cuvee opens a litany mystery / wait, wait for the signals within a mystery / await, await examples for a mystery.

CHAPTER FIVE

Columnar, columnar capability for the lifted mystery / instruct, instruct a dialect to break for the mystery / light, lights leap across the mysteries / introduce, introduce a subject called the mystery / uplink, uplink established through a striation of loined mysteries / down, down is up to the linkage mystery / time, time to tell the intentional mysteries / on, on is on too, a mystery / lines, lines signed for the mysteries / l.avendar, lavendar lands open to a mystery / pales, pales to the veiling mystery / pure, purest mysteries / pure, pure to a typical mystery / strong, strong in a toughened atmosphere for the mystery / elegant, elegant and the leisure of a mystery / gives, gives finest mysteries / toil, toil for the holy mystery / brunt, brunt and the borne again, mystery / borne, forne for the flying mystery / elect, elct a leader who deals thinly mystery / worn, worn aptly for the mystery / excursion, excursion across the intrusive mysteries / shares, shares and the covers soft with mysteries / appeals, appeals to a zealot too, the mystery / ports, ports paged for spending mysteries / data, data and the dealing mystery / feedback, feedback owns your mystery / shunt, shunt of the simple mystery / notes, notes and the voitves burning in mysteries / distant, distant and the fusion's mystery / distort, distort dealt through mysteries / connects, connects occurent to a mystery / corrects a pairing two and mysteries / delivery, delivery of the passioante mystery / sent, sent and the lover wed to a mystery / find, find anotehr's mystery / one, one of us launched into amystery / suspect, suspect suggested a mystery / envision, envision and the visionary discussion of life's mystery / advise, advise and teh wellness found as mystery / do, do a daily mystery / all, all is well throughout our mystery / one, one who luanched a mystery / avenue, avenues fair into the leading linkage of a mystery / cars, cars and the wares fold for mysteries / milarepa, milarepa and the readings tossed to mysteries / resides, resides a living mystery / noise, noise and the needy mysteries / prosper, prosper allows unto a mystery / benefit, benefit and the lift unto a mystery / balance, balance of the caring mystery / value, value in a metatronic mystery / valuable, valuable causes of the mystery attendant unto a mystery / metric, metric and the metranome allowed a mystery / instrument, instrument and the particular mystery / example, example on the sample's mystery / sample, sample of the simple cure for a mystery / grid, grid set in a penned mystery / detect, detect of your addressed mystery / dowse, dowse a duration of clearest mystery with the volley for a novel declare of salvation's shores / mode, mode deep in a repair for the mystery / model, model and the middle mended mystery / peak, peak in up and too, a mystery / response, response of a signal's mystery.

CHAPTER SIX
Back, back to a temple's mimicking mystery / around, around us arousing mysteries / press, press applies for a mystery / pressing, pressing amplified for a mystery / temperate, temperate rates on a mystery / temples, temples simple to a mystery / geiger, geiger of the coutned mystery / counts, counts a plenty for a mystery / pressures, pressures apparent within a mystery / transducted, transducted in resting mystery / transduce, transduce daily mystery / trades, trades treat her mystery / islands, islands leap across an endless mystery / encounter, encounter a coutnered mystery / keep, keep us well with a mystery / aim, aim for a simple mystery / yes, yes is well within a mystery / juicy, juicy days for the mystery / join, join us near a mystery / admire, admire conspires a worthy mystery / conclusive, conclusive allowance for the mystery / correlation, correlation becoming a mystery / silence, silence mysterious to a violent end for the mystery / goals, goals said to a "mystery" / gold, gold and the gabled mystery / disciple, disciple and the discipline for a mystery / discipline, discipline and the detailed mysterie / intrigue, intrigue and the reaching mystery / reward, reward retailed by a mystery / address, address of the mysterious mystery / goods, goods alloweda winning mystery / intend, intend a further mystery / respect, respect of the mystery / heal, heal a pinnacled drip into the mystery / love, love is healing you home through the mystery / dwell, dwell in swelling mysteries / together, together and the measured musical mysteries / ions, ions and the optimum spinning mysteries / scintillate, scintillate and the living loving mysterie / counts, counts on the physical mystery / geigers, geigers replicated for the mysteries / radios, radios record the respectof a mystery / radioactive, radioactive afford for the mysteries / gauge, gauge shown to the mystery / vacuum, vacuum your shoring mystery / capacitance, capacitance choired for the mystery / varies, varies on the mystery / signify, signify a mystery sent unto the mystery / recur, recur allowed throughout a mystery / violate, violate a feature without the mystery / future, future and the decree for a mystery / seals, seals forth in mysterie / one, one who won a mystery / respond, respond in a reclusive way to love for the mystery / response, response and the rescued mystery / electron, electron and the spectrums central to a mystery / metallic, metallic allow of the regained blame for a mystery / iron, iron spent on the breeding mystery / trends, trends treatise wise to a miracle's mystery / high, high allow pst a healer's regret for the mystery / extreme, extreme to deeds silent within a mystery / velocity, velocity for a mystery / watery, watery waves for a mystery / journals, journals joined in mystery.

CHAPTER SEVEN
Vociferous, vociferous vocalize of the valuable win to a mystery / voiced, voiced and gained by a mystery / vaunted, vaunted allowance flaunted for a mystery / vote, vote and teh shore's gained by a myster / news, news resume by a mystery / experience, experience mastered along a living mystery / expire, expire allowed entirely by a mystery / chore, chore simple to a mustered mystery / dark, darks rendering mystery / end, end of the parental mystery / light, lights leap and require a believing mystery / pretty, pretty in a simple passion for the mystery / operates, operates racing squared throughout a mystery / as, as an "I do" to begin the mystery / doing, doing only allowed a being mystery / general, general extents unto a mystery / generate, generate a retail experience for the rerun called a mystery / trip, trip to the altar and the touring premiere of a miracle for the mystery / attend, attend is allowed into the mystery / justify, justify your feeling mysteries / justice, justice is mad eyour mystery / journal, journals given a finer gift called the present mystery / journal, journals mysterious unto God / covets, covets a simplecubicle for the mystery / concern, concerns turning into a mystery / capapble, capable cures for the mystery / learn, learn allowed amystery / teach, teach us dearest mysteries / tour, tour and teh yearly mysteries / advise, advise allows us a genuine mystery / rise, rise arose through mysteries / admit, admit a status as allowed for mysteries / logic, logic allows us a mystery / then, then and now a mystery / open, open optionally to a mystery / again, again and when we win a mystery / adapt, adapt to the challenge for a myster / devise, devise a simple return to the mystery / mass, mass allow gained a justice joined in mystery / elect, elect forgone and the recollection comes to a funding mystery / electric, electric planes laid wave deep in a mystery / pure, pure and the planets mysterious / power, power praised as the mystery / passion, passions gained on mystery /

erupt, erupt for the mystery / ignore, ignore allowed a mystery / lanterns, lanterns burn in mystery / functions, functions filled in a founded mystery / maps, maps placed across the mystery / mass, mass alloweda mystery / elect, elect a rather mystery / indict, indict gone to a mystery / indicate, indicate the fate of a mystery / compare, compare for the caring of a mystery / link, link allowed through the trunk of a mystery / oscillate, oscillate has found a mystery / choose, choose antoehr's mystery / decide, decide to be well unto a mystery / evaluate, evaluate a a staple ascend throughout the mystery / intervals, intervals gauged by the best mystery / time, time to tell, the mystery / torque, torque gains a mystery / tach, tach a reading mystery / teach, teach a lesson foundational to a mystery.

CHAPTER EIGHT

Measurement, measurement for the invented mystery / crystal, crystal cured mysteries / clock, clocks shocked for the windy mystery / central, central red to a sounding mystery / matter, matter for the meeting mystery / mundane, mundane done and the refrain has come into the mystery / venues, venues allowed freedom unto a mystery / born, born balanced in the mysteries / circuits, circutis cued a mystery / simultaneous, simultaneous success for the mystery / think, think applies to a mystery / be, be allowed the wisdom for a mystery / chistled, chistled mysteries / mountains, mountains neutronic to the mystery / product, products placed in the portals mysteries / pore, pore across the shore's mysteries / pours, pours out a simple mystery / resolve, resolve and the solvent mystery / rapid, rapid and the proof for a mystery / decide, decide and the details of a mystery / transducer, transducer and the retail mystery / couples, couples causing a mystery / shaft, shafts open along the mystery / rotates, rotates sorted by the mystery / heavens, heavens charge unto the mystery / comes, comes an optional mystery / breath, breath and the balanced mystery / electrics, electrics led to a breeding mystery / breath, breath and the believing mystery / circuits, circuits and the shutters opened for a mystery / connect, connect and the calling mysteries / lifts, lifts in gentle mental mysteries / available, available beauties for the mysteries / ones, ones and the sunny mysteries / meet, meet a material mystery / teaching, teaching allows us a mystery / taught, taught a trailing mystery / diseases, diseases and the dealing cause for mysteries / fought, fought and the moving mysteries / phallic, phallic forgiving and the fortunate mysteries / sought, sought and the capable mysteries / seen, seen as shown to a mystery / differs, differs endured and mysteries / lens, lens led to a blue and green relation shipped to mysteries / intervals, intervals launch across our mysteries / count, count for the living lean to a mystery / own, own one mystery / longer, longer leaning to a mystery / apply, apply for appealing mysteries / papers, papers print a plank red trip unto the mysteries / simple, simple said "recall the mysteries" / appear, appear near the mysteries / operate, operate a rationale for the mysteries / principles, principles agree to be remitted to the prinicpals nine to the mystery / times, times are well to the mystery / elements, elements to the preciset mysteries / useful,

useful funds launched through a mystery / moderate, moderate a mention of the mysteries / seconds, seconds passed through a mystery / known, known too, an owning mention for the mystery / accuracy, accuracy forecast for the mystery / gates, gates opened to the explanation of light's mystery / closed, closed pretend fo teh graceful mystery / depend, depend on a friendly banter of the mystery.

CHAPTER NINE

Sound, sound like nature's shores for the mystery / natures, natures meal is simple for the myster / natural, natural unto a meal simple to the mutual mystery / empower, empower our mystery / words, words wisest with the mystery / human, human to the telling mystery / animate, animate for the mated mysteries / propogate, propogate for the stretching mystery / pressures, pressures retail your mystery / shift, shift suggested to the mysteries / alter, alter flowered by the choir's mystery / physiologic, physiologic and the logical clear for the mystery / damage, damage has done these mysteries / done, done from the mystery / sound, sounds of the shingled mysteries / fell, fell and the trailing mystery / white, white and the lightest mystery / noise, noise and the reply nearly dear the mystery / winds, winds winning a mystery / blown, blown and the sizes wiser to a mystery / splash, splash allows a mystery / loud, loud to tunes for the mystery / quiet, quiet endurance of the mystery / sounds, sounds like a welcome mystery / concerns, concerns in cares mystery / primal, primal matter's mystery / alters, alters held in stylish myster / states, states of severed ways too a mystery / prescient, prescient materials won, a mystery / presence, presence in a penchant / rotates, rotates into a truest mystery / motors, motors of the meter's mystery / finish, finish in a fleshly mystery / example, example in a sample won, the mystery / sample, sample of the simple mystery / squire, squire of the higher mystery / square, square over where too, the mystery / cubed, cubed in a tubal treed through a mystery / convey, convey a way mystery / knews, station knews and the cues mystery / major, major meetings held at love's beat, a mystery / dorms, dorms dealt within mysteries / built, built in a basically hu-man mystery / when, when in a mystery / send, send in a strand on, too mystery / package, package beton, the mystery / plan, plan a daily unveil, the mystery / powers, powers in a placement's mystery / category, category cued within a mystery / recognition, recognition of a resurgence in a mystery / out, out is the rating's mystery / count, count on, tuned in's mystery / argue, argue over and won the mystery / admission, admission of the requisite for a mystery / spin, spin into a resubmission / spend, spend in timed residence / gain, gain a durative mystery / .absolute, absolute in power's mystery / explain, explain into a mystery / explore, explore the insured mystery / intense, intense in a reside's mystery / rapture, rapture in a rapture's mystery / see, see us wed too a mystery / dares, dares in shares won too, a mystery.

CHAPTER TEN

Visual, visual valley views a mystery / cues, cues in goods give a mystery / tone, tone in too, a mystery / sought, sought and in a supple, the flexible mystery / pure, pure into a mystery / sinusoidal, sinusoidal biorisen mystery / frequents, frequents in a decision's mystery / swish, swish in too, a mystery / coal, coal is regard for myster / louver, louver in a refine's mystery / intense, intense in entreaty wins a mystery / pressure, pressure out and then a mystery / precious, precious prepare for the sharing mystery / complex, complex concepts of securely mysterious / sort, sort of the wons. mystery / unususal, unusual needs, a mystery / acquisitive, acquisitive to the derivative mystery / ressurect, ressurect our connect into a mystery / restrict, restrict us less, find us more, mysterious / evict, evict the old, the mystery wins / crystal, crystal cures a mystery / ribbon, ribbon rode, a mystery / capacitor, capacitor kept's is a mystery / dynamo, dynamo decide too, a mystery / dynamic, dynamic degree the mystery / rigid, rigid arose to the land on mystery / insulate, insulate less, mysterious too, love / plate, love's plate a palate's mystery / objects, objects suggest a confess to let's mystery / objective, objective in a mystery's amount / propogate, propogate a sureress mystery / agree, agree to breed a mystery / brain, brain of the brush out, mystery / states, states mysterious decide to live lovingly / strength, strength in a superb mystery / field, field mastery the mystery / solar, solar to a modeled mystery / scope, scope in a scaping mystery / analyze, analyze in a mystery / read, read a repeats mystery / integrate, integrate relate into a mystery / limits, limits of gimmicks meet a mystery / extremes, extremes trade and the shades go a mystery / labels, labels mysterious enough to release / consist, consist of curess effect a mystery / coil, coil tool tail mystery / examine, examine the domain too a mystery / dynamic, dynamic detailed a mystery / capacity, capacity for a miracle more mystery / variable, variable in a valued mystery / variety, variety valued in mystery / list, list of the learning's mystery / lecture, lecture learned in the mystery / lectern, lectern returned a mystery / cable, cable could, a mystery / arrive, arrive at a direct mystery / micron, micron met on thick mysteries / wave, wave in a woven's mystery / preens, mysterious preens and the teens end love's mystery / strikes, strikes out and in too, a mystery / absolve, absolve thyself through a mystery / materials, materials of a mystery / ways, ways unto a mystery / lightened, lightened into a mystery.

CHAPTER ELEVEN
Amplify, amplify learning's daily deed too, mystery / audio, audio to the visual explain of a mystery / cartons, cartons carried to a thorough mystery / microphone, microphone amuse with a visible friend called a mystery / metal, metal and the mysteries west of love / diapraghm, diagraphm worn to explain the mystery / degreed, degrred details for the raid for a daring mystery / electrodes, electrodes placed in the nodes of a mystery / clumps, clumps of fortified mysteries / media, media reading amply of the mysteries / mates, mates meet in a healthy diet called the heart of love's immaculate mystery / moist, moist with forgiven mysteries / rods, rods reach the cones of eye impeached without your mystery / sparks, sparks and the remit on an emitted lightened mystery / vibrate, vibrate visibly for the focused mysteries / bodies, bodies detailed by the veil thrown to a mystery / solids, solids existing

electricallyf or a mystery / simple, simple to a mandible mystery / airs, airs tasting of a mystery / conspire, conspire to eat an apple pink with healing remember of the One mystery / less, less is war without a mystery for love / peels, peels a core wealthy within the mystery / dials, dials elaborate within a mystery / specials, specials apply to a speaking mystery for love / specialize, specializ in a speaking parallel for a breezy mystery / pray, pray swallowed by a mystery / appoint, appoint a mystery swimming in love / specialize, specialize a rising mystery / pray, pray allows our mystery for the patterned rates / appoint, appoint a debate for the mystery / God, God? yes! a Mystery has solved the riddle God is a plan human to the light wed for love / singing, singing near us, an angel appears dear to the acres of love, a mystery / one, one due a mystery / tongue, tongue told a tale filled in light's mystery / yearn, yearn for a litany for the precedent for a mystery / convert, covert to a simple retinue paid lightly to a mystery / deliver, deliver a living mystery / nuns, nuns secure in their habit and the plunge convent wise to love of the mystery / magnify, magnify a retail mystery / magnetics, magnetics wholesale unto love's lightened video of the mystery, human / audio, audio and the vdeos allowed a seeking mystery / submerge, submerge and the verge detailed for a mystery / magnets, magnets raised throughout helpful mysteries / restrictive, restrictive unto a mystery / matched, matched allow for the sections of the mystery / afford, afford a friend the word, mystery / hidden, hidden in a detail ridden with olivine colors of the peridot spent for love's mystery / distance, distance brought to a halt through accounts communicated about in life's mystery / explodes, explodes again, the pen, of a mystery / voice, voice values a mysterious voice the balance of an empowered planet / born, born reach for the revery funded by the mystery / fair, fair is the mystery / weak, weak as knots wed beyond the mystery / strong, strong to a truthful mystery / wellness, wellness placed along the presence of the mystery / curve, curve came across the mystery / cure, cure needed for the chalice three times mysterious / lines, lines along the leading mysteries / fell, fell across a fellow pooled within a mystery / fold, fold and the farrows mysterious / flock, flock allowed ayore for the mystery / fond, fond and the feelings simple within a mystery / come, come to the mystery / cater, cater to the need of the meetings mystery.

CHAPTER TWELVE
Design, design a date within the mystery / flat, flat offered a fusing growth to love for the mystery / fall, fall off the mystery / form, form forecast for fix relaxed by love, the mystery / objects, objects chased become the mystery / forum, forum held to tell the mystery / cares, cares cost less when we rest in the mystery / code, code and the red headed mystery / grace, grace based on the mystery / calling, calling now to share the mystery / weights, weights lifted off by the mystery / dampen, dampen has gone to the sun saluted through the mystery / lights, lights leap across the mystery / hearts, hearts heaped at the mystery / response, response rescues through the mystery / capacitor, capacitor cored in the mystery / launch, launch to the cape canveral well unto the mystery / small, small is elegant unto the mystery /

standard, standard details for the mystery / accept, accept a date with the mystery / delegate, delegate tossed across the mystery / arrange, arrange a floral recoil into the mystery / matters, matters smattered in the mystery / meters, meters metric into a mystery / tolerance, tolerance fed the triple mystery / place, place and the above within a mystery / admire, admire and the pairing mystery / require, require a siring mystery / fasten, fasten a retail mystery / check, check along the mystery / test, test a spelling spared through mystery / slow, slow enough to be accessed through the mystery / frequent, frequent into the fusing mysteries / objects, objects chosen dreamy in the mystery / require, require a pairing mystery / gain, gain a larger mystery / respond, respond to a reclined revnue of the mystery / objective, objective for the seated pairs of the muster for the mysteries / perfection, perfection for the partnered mysteries / one, one worn without a mystery / stable, stable enclosures found for the mystery / regard, regard for the spaces mysterious / plenty, plenty to sing through the mystery / thunder, thunder for the thrilling metatronic mystery / glows, glows lightest within a mystery / rejuvenate, rejuvenate a raising mystery / function, functions simple into the mystery / electron, electrons simple into a mystery / grand, grand and the regain for a mystery / pleasant, pleasant intend for a hilton headed to the mystery / parallels, parallels for the mystery / pave, pave ove rthe mysterious zeroes of the noise left ot mannerisms / huge, huge relief for the mystery / broken, broken less and found more within the magic of the mystery / gain, gaining lifting mystery / keep, keep a command for the mystery / entire, entire into intentional mysteries / seize, seize a welcome mystery / sources, sources successful for the mysteries / sure, sure and the surrender to a mystery / coincide, coincide inside the mysteries / inside, inside a risen mystery / agree, a.gree to be renewed unto the mysteries / allow, allow a fellow mystery.

CHAPTER THIRTEEN

Code, code to the mystery / clue, clue within the mastery of humanity / Christ, Christ gave to matters on the mystery / life, life lived is well within the mystery / samples, samples chosen have given us a mystery / levels, levels merge in mastery near the christed mystery / critical, critical to the cause of a mystery / eight, eight ways to see a mystery / lights, lights on in mysteries / tradewinds, tradewinds winter in a mystery / cabins, cabins clued through mysteries / applause, applause allowed through mysteries / pleasure, pleasure leaps to mysteries / maintain, maintain a line to mysteries / become, become a balance to a mystery / humanity, humanity warranted by a mystery / claim, claim a mystery here / dukes, dukes roll into a mystery / trains, trains toll at mystery / planes, planes converge on mysteries / plant, plant a history to a mystery / way, way to warrant a mystery / musing, musing is over for a mystery / electric, electric intrigue is met within a mystery / mellow, mellow explain to a mystery / fellowship, fellowship clears a mystery / matters, matters allow a mystery / factors, factors enfold a mystery / joins, joins a throne of mysteries / maintain, maintain a resource red with mystery / obtain, obtain a triple mystery / mention, mention particles into mysteries / revenue, revenues paid the mystery / joining, joining allows a mystery / green, green to days of yellow mysteries / miraculous, miraculous recover through a mystery / fortunate, fortunate unto a mystery / miracles, miracles land in mystery / farther, farther into the mystery / news, news arrives in mystery / narrow, narrow without a mystery / wide, wide within a mystery / aim, aim for a mastery of the mystery / james, james taught the tongue to surrender to the mystery / mystery, mystery humming through a mastery / found, found one mystery / foundations, foundations uncovered through the mystery / matches, matches made into a mystery / moving, moving alond lines electric within a mystery / mysteries, mysteries of the mastery / suggested, suggested yes! to a mystery / founded, founded on thrilling mysteries / measured, measured along the mystery / formed, formed in fellow mysteries / obtain, obtain a reward for a mystery / acknowledge, acknowledge the schools of mystery / trade, trade for a shore of mystery / suggest, suggest a friendly mystery / organs, organs healthy with the mystery / overt, overt discussions of the mystery / maintain, maintain a secret mystery / reveal, reveal a deal for mysteries / travel, travel to your mystery / suspend, suspend without a mystery.

THE MASTERY-MENTS
LEVEL 59

CHAPTER ONE

Permanent, permanent the mastery in love / mastery, mastery of the members love / buba, buba said light man mastery / man, man of the wind mastery / 30 days, 30 days to may mastery in love / 30 ways, 30 ways to divide it, love's mastery / 30 years, 30 years to wider this mastery / 30 percent, 30 percent and more mastery / 100 ways, 100 ways to say good bye into a mystery on mastery / 100 waves, mastery 100 waves true to love / 100 percent, 100 percent mastery in love / 100 days, 100 days to stay in God's mastery / 100 years, 100 years of rearing's mysteries of mastery / 100 nets, 100 nets of waving's mastery / 100 veils, love 100 veils deep in God's mastery / 100 trails, 100 trails to a mastery / walls, on walls of mastery wed / partitions, mastery's partitions less affected in love / minds, minds end at mastery / mend, mend a fence, befriend mastery / truths, truths tell a tale mastery / wills, wills wed in mastery / schools, love's schools win a mastery / believe, believe in your surrender too, mastery / self, mastery of the self is wealth / act, well in act and thoughtfull mastery / freedom, perfect freedom to act for mastery / fill, fill with love's value in mastery / fields, fields of love's mystery, via mastery / feels, feels like into mastery / spells, loves spells the mastery well / attracts, mastery attracts like affect in love / men, men mended through your mastery / plans, mystery's plans to be masterful / record, record of the reward's mastery / opinion, opinion of the pinnacled mastery / laws, laws set inside your mastery / resolves, love resolves itself in your mastery / party, party of the pleased too, mastery / money, money made through mastery / made, mastery made through jade agreement / waids, waids in pose, mastery / meet, meet at a heat worn mysteriously mastery / mortal, mortal planned for, in mastery / pattern, pattern plan pen mastery / idea, mastery's idea is too, love / treat, love's treat is in mastery / trait, trait of durate within mastery / ability, ability to be masterful within, love / illumine, illumine your record with mastery / act, act for mastery / phylos, phylos said, "mastery" / Shasta, Shasta sent a value too, our mastery / topic, mastery's topic is love / God, God gives mastery / center, center of the giver, mastery / see, see the mystery's mastery within love / angle, an angle made too, master / life, life in led revive too, mastery / home, home to a warmer mastery / art, art in the start won, mastery / surmount, surmount in the account for mastery / obvious, obvious to the eyes, news of love's mastery / often, often we said good-bye to the lessens in love's mastery.

CHAPTER TWO

Taught, taught in trine to master, love / spoke, spoke like a veteran's record, masterfully / lode, lode of the needle mastered / load, load stress less, mastery / soften, mastery soften's you too, God / heart, love's heart met in mastery / splash, splash in places mastered / speak, mastery speak's of love / recall, recall a record held for mastery / record, record to the minute's mastery / raid, raid in the staid arise for the mastery / board, board in bedded splendor's mastery / resound, resound to reband too, mastery / reckon, mastery meant to reckon within love / tibetan, love;s tibetan wave of mastery / 12, 12 times the rhymes in mastery /

honor, honor your bred mastery / mom, mom into the mysterious mastery / love, love is a mastery / father, father of the feature's mastery / news, news came to the mastery / blessings, blessings belt your mastery / treaties, treaties true too, in mastery / source, source of the settle's mastery / trues, trues master's love / aligns, aligns in signs of mastery / respects, respects your mysterious mastery / rejoice, rejoice in regain's mystery / renew, renew your mastery regain, love / reconvenes, love's reconvene is in the mastery / rest, rest in rates due too, mastery / rate, rate of respect for mastery / surrounded, surrounded in mastery / please, please be frankly planing your mastery / truth, truth tell, mastery / radiant, radiant readsour mastery / crystal, kindest crystal mastery / records, records read, mastery / wise, wise won mastery / master, master made to be, love / taught, taught to be for mastery / teach, teach another mastery / regard, regard raised, mastery / record, record poured into a mastery / glands, glands gain a new mastery / systems, systems sent too, a mastery / arc-angels, arc-angels knew us, the mastery / activity, activity achieves a mastery / conscience, conscience said, mastery / prose, prose red, mastery / process, process paid mastery / comprehensive, comprehensive coupling too, a mastery / gain, gain a friend, mastery / entire, entire in your mastery / worlds, worlds wed, mastery / enflame, enflame in a game called mastery / basis, a basis for beauty is in your mastery / builds, builds a beauty, mastery / listen, listen too, mastery / lengthen, lengthen your strain's mastery / late, late to be and eithin mastery / regarding, regarding your light, mastery / rest, rest in her mastery / employ, employ a durable sort for the crafts of mastery.

CHAPTER THREE

Creativity, creativity creates a mastery / strong, strong enough to be a force for your mastery / force, force felt in your mastery / master's, master's made too, love / tool, tool for a shower's mastery / instrument, instrument of the blend's mastery / treat, treat for the essentials mastery / trait, trait trues your's mastery / arch, arch to the third's mastery / arc, arc weld mastery / know, know cure mastery / knew, knew a few mastery / cosmos, cosmos came into whirl's mastery / curve, a curve meant for all's mastery / native, native knew a sun's regard too mastery / kneels, kneels in surtrender mastery / apples, mastery appales and choices paid too, love / mend, love's mend is in our mastery / considered, considered another's place for mastery / freight, freight found filled in mastery / destruct, love's destructis less direct through mastery / instruct, love's instruct the mastery within, love / resurrect, resurrect a recount to mastery / effort, effort made means mastery / caves, mystery of the caves reads mastery / carts, essene's carts led to mastery / transmutte, transmutte ill repute with a well mastery / mutate, mutate less, begain mastery / volcanic, mastery's volcanic occur in an island mist / flow, flow to the isle Santorene within, love / flower, flower of the power filled in mastery / feels, feels like a friendly meant to soar to mastery / divine, a divine degree of mastery / deserve, muse's deserve miracle's mastery / understand, understand and stood within her mastery / care, care to be mastery / physical, love's physical act is in to mastery / freight, mastery's freight wins, love / forth, forth in the fifth place mastery / contours, mastery contours into love's mystery / contrals, contreal out healing in, mastery / meditate, mastery meditate muse love / sort, sort out your illest mastery / source, source of the solvent, mastery / found, mastery's dound is in too, love / fort, love's fort is in mastery / fellow, mastery's fellow muse, is love / fun, love's fun is in too, mastery / count, count on two's master / one, one to won, mastery / contact, contact her earthly mastery / two, two in the running mastery / see, see is three in mastery / three, three now near too, mastery / know, know a dear mastery / four, four fulfills our mastery / find, find a kind for mastery / five, five who held for two's mastery / resurrect, resurrect a light mastery / six, six in the sticks run, mastery / reconnect, mental reconnect is direct through mastery / seven, seven winds blew to mastery / elevate, elevate one to begin with mastery / 8, 8 who knew the mastery.

CHAPTER FOUR
Knew, knew within the mastery / nine, nine in the nearest mastery / tell, tell us another's mastery / 10, 10 who know a regarded mastery / only, only and all too, mastery / one, one in the wellest mastery / won, won into winning's mastery / lad, lad who had a mastery / lady, lady in a leading mastery / loves, loves into a needing's mastery / mary, mary mothered mastery / fine, fine in thimes too, mastery / frank, frank in a freedom's mastery / strong, strong in a streeting's mastery / clear, clear into a chaliced mastery / clarify, clarify into a curving's mastery / codices, codices of the masterful love's of living / coast, coast in a case comes mastery / court, court to the corners of a compassionate mastery / captured, captured a courageous resource / complete, complete and the carryings on to precisely the resources of love's mastery / seen, seen in allow for the flowing mastery / seams, seams resourceful to the flowery mastery / sort, sorts on allowed scenes for the mastery / mutual, mutual acquire fo teh siring won to mastery / moves, moves along a singing mastery / matters, matters parallel unto a mastery / mast, mast of the gaps complete in bonded clearance of teh mastery / particle, particle of the plenty woven for a mastery / pasture, pasture planes of the mastery / portal, portal closed once opens again into a mastery / blends, blends of the bones onto a mastery / staunch, staunch of the knowing mastery / strong, strong enough to the throne mastery / campaign, captions on the campaign to dreamy mastery / drive, drive retailed to the mastery / suppose, suppose arose into a mastery / strength, strength allows a loosening mastery / purity, purity flows allowed to mastery / path, paths cleared to show the listing mastery / mortal, mortal estates allowed a mastery / member, member of the sending glade / mansion, mansions allowed a shaded mastery / plan, plan to be masterful / blandest, blandest and the powers to be are masterful / over, over and the vaulted mastery / famous, famous to an allowance for the mastery / friend, friends and the final mastery / fortune, fortune flows through a foun mastery / found, found for funded mastery / fabulous, fabulous feelings of light masteyr / came, came to anumber thrown to mastery / fires, fires fueled and staying to a mastery / whirlpool, whirlpool greetings and the meeting's mastery / transform, transform and the swarming mastery / mountains,

mountains and the mentioned mastery / motion, motion across the central mastery / avoid, avoid the devoid from a mastery / avert, avert converts into a mastery / console, console and the doling mastery / live, live to a listening mastery / lift, lifts along a truest mastery / seek, seek and the news laid into a mastery / set, set and the settle of a mastery.

CHAPTER FIVE
Capable, capable and the resource sent to a lightening mastery / constant, constant to a recall for a mastery / content, content to be invented by a mastery / flux, flux rewarded by a mastery / motive, motive and the lving mastery / motions, motions and the setting played by a matrix set in mastery / coast, coast along allowing mastery / world, world won by a filling mastery / new, new to a renewed mastery / evermore, evermore allowed along a mastery / former, former feeds into a mastery / fasten, fasten fixed upon a mastery / canals, canals which cost the owls a living mastery / hydrodynamcis, hydrodynamics and the declaration of a mastery / floats, floats and th features viewed as mastery / owns, owns and the allowed truth of a mastery / mode, mode of the mental mastery / modern, modern and the makings of a mastery / model, model and the middle mastery / blended, blended from the mastery of a giving God / symmetry, symmetry set in lightened mastery / characteristic, characteristic costs of the spiral mastery / mathematics, mathematics cost less for mastery / topics, topics pleased through mastery / science, science set for bets on mastery / scenes, scenes succinct in mastery / sent, sent to a central mastery / softens, softens of the regard for a mastery / select, select suggestions of a mastery / sorts, sorts who signal only, mastery / shatter, shatter shouts that sides are met along the mastery / thorough, thorough estates within a mastery / spirals, spirals spun into a mastery / symmetric, symmetric mastery / systems, systems and teh signals mastered / songs, songs along a committed mastery / dynamics, dynamics dual unto a required mastery / helices, helices set in mastery / logarithm, logarithms lodge in mastery / logic, logic allows a mastery / equable, equable and the equation set for mastery / equate, equate your rates as mastery / inate, iante to a sated mastery / sense, sense of the central mastery / through, through allowed to the doing mastery / lifted, lifted and the outed mastery / parts, parts placed along a mastery 48i. ce, ice sent wet to melting mastery / plato, plato lunged and the veterans in the mastery / solids, solids cubed and the sequels set in a healing mastery / triangles, triangles and the resets tasted by a mastery / five, five and the living mastery / starts, starts and the regain of a mystery / sides, sides and the riding mastery / parts, parts and the starting mastery / elements, elements and the dues laid into a mastery / elemental, elemental cues and the symbols made a mastery / atomic, atomic and the treats aroused into mastery / pythagorean, pythagorean on a theory paved to mastery / plato, palto pleas for mastery / mystic, mystic miraculous to a mastery / muse, muse and the matters metric to a mastery / electric, electric elongate on the mastery / valves, valves open into love's mastery.

CHAPTER SIX

Molecular, molecular costs and the materials mastery / magic, magic and the cost forgiven for a mastery / mass, mass allows an inducted mastery / museo, museo de agile's mastery / matisse, matisse and the meeting mastery / plastic, plastic and the pledged for mastery / past, past and along the mastery / passive, passive contours to the central mastery / aggressive, aggressive in a central mastery / mental, mental amuse for the monads penned as mastery / stage, stage allowed a three pence mastery / intellect, intellect sent for mastery / plenty, plenty seen in mastery / pearly, pearly gated mastery / gates, gates allowed a thorough mastery / layers, layers leveraged to a mastery / hexagonal, hexagonal and the headed to for mastery / fundamental, fundamental to a mentally measured mastery / accept, accept allowance for the mastery / difference, difference details your mastery / fibrils, fibrils sent to the gamboling mastery / exodus, exodus coming too, a master / patterns, patterns over, mastery / barter, barter best in mastery / reside, reside astride your mastery / change, change to a mystery for a mastery / planes, planes and the penchant for a mastery / part, parts allowed for the planes framed in mastery / evolve, evolve into a mastery / solve, solve allowed a mastery / believe, believe in a balanced mastery / structure, structure trues as mastery / cells, cells allowed a wellest mastery / virtue, virtue applies to a venue for a mastery / parts, parts paged to mastery / parked, parked at places caped in mastery / collect, collect allows a respectful mastery / collage, collage and quantum mastery / collagen, collagen attends a mysterious mastery / biologic, biologic sonic mastery / wonders, wonders avowed a mastery / construct, contruct and the instructed mastery / chain, chain and teh embraced intone for a mastery / magnitude, magnitudes for a minute's agree to a mastery / magnify, magnify and the viewing mastery / singles, singles and the mastery in love / fibers, fibers cut to a contentment set in mastery / books, books emplyed as written to a mastery / written, written within a mastery / gifts, gifts intoned again as a mastery / believe, believe arrives in masteyr / ravel, ravel to the revealing mastery / unveils, unveils in detailed mastery / open, open to a pairing mastery / regard, regard for the mastery / language, language and the leading mastery / perfection, perfection and the pencils matched in mastery / match, matching and the two paid mastery / mates, mates and the listening mastery / streets, streets and the mastery of love / wants, wants and the nestled mastery / orders, orders and the threshold punched to mastery / principle, principle and the pressure tossed to mastery / phenomenal, phenomenal employ of a mastery.

CHAPTER SEVEN

Remember, remember the members tossed to mastery / forgive, forgive allowed for mastery / continue, continue allowed a mastery / receive, receive and the reliving mastery / raptures, raptures and the reading mastery / places, places and the placement elements met in mastery / pointed, pointed to eternally through freeing mastery / parts, parts who plan a mastery / chinese, chinese choosing's mastery / chains, chains off and tossed too, the mastery / rooms, rooms afforded to the masters / organize, organize a crew

who say, "let us be", a mastery / rent, rent a home in the mastery / respect, respect intoned to mastery / sports, sports tossed alone to mastery / spontaneous, spontaneous gifts give mastery / carthage, carthage and the coupled accept of the mastery / capital, capital complete in a calibrated mastery / cosign, cosign the signs of a mastery / contracts, contracs concur with your mastery / need, need to breathe as mastered / too, too is well within our abiding mastery / expect, expect a freudian sect to slip a degree to mastery / more, more in the scoring mastery / sexuality, sxuality discussed as a sensational record is set for love's mastery / morality, morality is moved to the msues marigold and blue and red in mastery / originality is required less than mastery / rally, rally round the thronging masters / opportunity, opportunity pinned to the sexual amstery / 'manuscript, manuscript set to be made to a movie yet, mastery / collect, collect a cause for the masters / entertain, entertain allowed and a mastery / captivate, captivate a cause for the cushioned stage of mastery / course, course et and the boats tossed to mastery / coarse, coarse has opened to mastery / again, again allows a mastery / away, away to run to mastery / right, right has lightest mastery / night, night nestling to mastery / reflect, reflects a lightening mastery / mountains, mountains amused to mastery / topping, toppings tipped to a moonfed mastery / erupt, erupt and the racing mastery / pay, pay and the palate blue in mastery / result, result of the mastery causing release to love / reward, rewards into a territorial bliss and the kissing mastery / effect, effect of the efforts caused to mastery / transit, transit and the trues to a giving mastery / service, service and teh equipment sent to mastery / God, God and the giving mastery / power, power employed to a mastery / lord, lords laid in mastery / patterned, patterned planes in mstery / plans, plans made and applied to the mastery / laws, laws licensed to a living mastery / sons, sons of the enchanced mastery / elohim, elohim line the hems of a tenfold living mastery / matter, matter has set the well in mastery / fathers, fathers fed have said "a mastery" / deeds, deeds set in mastery / vegetable, vegetable tossed and the vanquished lost to mastery / angels, angels gather to say "a way" to mastery / service, services join to see your mastery / divide, divide a deal to well winded mysteries and the mentioned dynamics of a living master

CHAPTER EIGHT

Division, division done, held forth, mastery / one, one won, mastery / won, won too, mstery / wonderful, wonderful news in mastery / minerals, minerals owned and measured into mastery / humans, humans allow a held forth for measured mastery / divide, divide detailed and the masters sent for love / continents, continents colliding in the living mastery / find, find a frequent mastery of mystery / fine, fine to a feeling mastery / musical, musical in mended mastery / music, music is the refine in your mastery / journals, journals written along a mastery / edits, edits and the voted mastery / editorial, editorial and the dialing mastery / critic, critic and the critical mention of a mastery / yearn, yearn and the yellow's mastery / trade, trade and the throwing mastery / exchange, exchange and the dates raid a miraculous mastery / advertise, advertise and the recent mastery / optimist, optimist and the times trued into a mstery / certain, certain allow for the manageable mention of a mastery / surgical, surgical and the sealings sent for mastery / lyrics, lyrics listened to and the trance broken into through a warmest mystery / lance, lance has cut the bones free to dance a mastery / carbon, carbons fibers cross to fuse as mastery / thoughts, thoughts central into a mastery / violin, violins play as the village sings of mastery / include, include a refined mastery / close, close to the core and the strengthened mastery / clamor, clamor hass passed your doors mastery / closet, closets open to reveal the doors swung the other way, let us in, to the mastery / achievement, achievement set to the gaining mastery / oblige, oblige less and find more in the mastery / debutant, debutant who caught a healing mastery / debate, debate allows a lightened mastery / stalwart, stalwart in well suppose of the risen mastery / sleeve, sleeves slid to the lavender pool and the moods dare as a mastery / record, record your fall into a waterfalling mood of a mastery / written, written deep in the records kept is the love for a Father freed to mastery / staff, staff has said "our suggestion is mastery through trueness in love" / perfection, perfection has come to the sum happy in their crtically acclaimed mastery / recital, recital set for the feeling's mastery / commital, commital most to the showering mastery / classic, classic in occur to the mastery / resume, resume your lone mastery / resume, resume sent said "mastery" / roberts, roberts curve is the ransom gained to a mastery / curve, curve complied to and mastered / arch, arch set in red clay rocked mastery / cycles, cycles suspect can end in mastery / wheel, wheel has lofted to a mastery / perected, perfected in passionate intrigue within a modeled mastery / interrupt, interrupt less and know more thy own ceded shoring and the honing mastery / width, width has willed us to be winging free to mastery / heights, heights are held within the mastery / appropriate, appropriately penned and prepared for the mastery / vary, vary allowed as ascendants stand in mastery / change, change has come, prepare, God said "a mastery" / joins, joins us in a jaunty fashion for the memory of mastery / joints, joints ache to join the mastery / curves, curves close in circling gain of the mastery / cross, cross allows a burning down to the core of mastery / over, over to the land of mastery.

CHAPTER NINE

Corners, corners met and cured through watery graven mastery / mated, amted allow for the masters / arts, arts dip into sorts parallel to pens of mastery / templates, templates sunk into through mastery / holograms, holograms joined for the mastery / arches, a. rches across the lviing mastery / attendant, attendant to the standing mastery / apply, apply for loans granted through mastery / allows, allows lead to mastery / decide, decide to be masterful through love / moves, moves into another's mastery / leaves, leaves golden flown to mastery / learns, learns in then a mastery / light's, light's lend to mastery / highest, highest high's to mastery / way, way to a mastery / share, share a fleet of leading mastery / whisper, whisper wins a mastery / forget, forget foregone get along in mastery / rewind, rewind me of the dove's song mastery / diabolic, diabolic diatonic metaphonic mastery / black, black

into blue's mastery / burst, mastery burst into blue's mastery / excess, excess suggest a leading mastery / gone, gone into glued mastery / stun, stun into standing's mastery / over, over and under's mastery 28l. eak, leak into a lot mastery / taut, taut and the wrought won mastery / trigger, trigger triangled through mastery / win, won about it a mastery / waves, waves wet with moist agree to mastery / ways, ways wonders mastery / westerns, westerns win a mastery / recondition, recondition about it / formula, formula feel in mastery / products, products present to a mastery / produce, prouce a pair with mastery / procur, procur a coupled mastery / probates, probates inspect is mastery / proceeds, proceeds into deed's mastery / plank, plank pulled from a mastery / program, a program gained through a mastery / redical, radical dialed a mastery / radius, radius rules mastery / pure, pure into a pairng's mastery / kinds, kinds who read in mastery / express, express your suggest for mastery / angle, angle curved by the reward's mastery / varying, varying in avalued mastery / locus, locus flowers mastery / cycles, cycles succeed too mastery / tabular, tabular tubed and the treed mastery / adds, adds into a mastery / opposite, opposite pleased by mastery / thick, thick through a mastery / caculate, caculate coupled with a mastery / cuts, cuts in curve's mastery / corners, corners coincide inside a mastery / codes, codes red and blue a mastery / capabilities, capabilities kept in a mastery / own, own into a mastery / through, through and thought a mastery / twins, twins in atrait's on mastery.

CHAPTER TEN

Attacks, attacks out and in too, a mastery / attitude tooled in mastery / apparent, apparent in accounts within a mastery / fear, fear abodes outside the mastery / forgotten, friends mastery / ascend, ascend to a corporate mastery / later, later led to variation's of mastery / now, now into wows win a mastery / precious, precious in patterned emotes mastery / partner's, partner's felt to feel a mastery / friends, friends fed a mastery / fought, fought into a legend's mastery / forgives, forgives a feeling's mastery / found, found forgive at mastery / fallen, fallen fund and the won mastery / up, up to and all's mastery / thicken, thicken and the ripened mastery / broaden, mastery broaden in love / square, square in circular signs meant mastery / lines, mastery in line's degree / laconic, laconic in the toniced weld too mastery / tonic, tonic triode through mastery / spring, spring in through regarded mastery / spiral, spiral spares in a mastery / awaken, awaken in a taben mastery 26taben, taben in a simple mastery / turgid, turgid in a rigid mastery / torpor, torpor out in too mastery / mankind, mankind in matters brilliant in mastery / mince, mince into singular love's mastery / mint, flow to a mint mastery / healed, healed in all mastery / last, last and a blasting's mastery / loathe, mysterious loathe and the mast's mastery / lover, lover in the living's mastery / looped, looped into scooped win's mastery / lever, love's lever's mastery / lock, mastery locked into love / lane, lane in the lineaged mastery / low, low enough to see too, mastery / high, high in a tune's,astery / hurl, hurl above it, mastery / fly, fly about it mastery / float, float deep mastery / flounder, flounder about it, mastery / over, over and then mastery / done, done in triple release to metatronic mastery / due, due yours the mastery / up, up and coming a mastery / illustrates, illustrates a degree of mastery / flotation, flotation felt throughout your mastery / venus, venus valued in mastery / action, action in the passion spiral about too mastery / devotes, mastery devotes your love for God / love's crave come's home too, mastery / gate, gate of the goodness mastery / waits, waits in the wellest, mastery / entwines, entwines less our mastery / ellipse, elipse and the eclipse too, a mastery / loans, mastery / loans another's degree / fire, fire and the flame too, a mastery / continents, continents communicate on too, mastery / circumscribe, circumscribe the circumstance mastery.

CHAPTER ELEVEN
Sstate, state of solvent debate and the spoken, mastery / adjust, adjust to a grown mastery / power, people, power mastery / techinque, techinque decided upon, mastery / weather, weather well too in master / wheather, wheather or knot? mastery / want, want another? mastery / wonder, wonder of the wind's mastery / well, golden well on too, mastery / wealth, wealth wet in a wonderful mastery / wince, wince at less then too, mastery / doubt, possible in doubts out through mastery / forever, forever and fallen out too, mastery / gone, gone to the sunny, mastery / light, light the elect mastery / materpiece, materpiece of the met won, metatronically Gaberiel said, mastery / mastery, mastery met in I am / masters, I am masters all / mates, mates all mastered / particalar, particalar to a matter metatronic on to mastery / modes, modes in roads win's masterfully / modality, modality mastery / emponder, emponder purest in mastery / qualities, qualities quipped by to mastery / overload, overload led to aburst ends mastery / oversee, oversee said, I am mastery / fearless, fearless felt in mastery / duties, duties deal within a mastery / chattered, chattered about in a bred mastery / emote, emote in a note red within a mastery / center, center of the state's master / encores, encores and the shores end, mastery / concertos, concertos sing in heaven's ring on mastery / sonata, sonata sunday's mastery / concert, concert in park band stands mastery / romance, romance regarding a named mastery / duo, duo dealt a masterfull meet / nation's nation's need to breed through mastery / symphony, symphony sung in mastery / historic, historic regard said, "mastery" / string, string into mastered status through love / storing, love's storing records a mastery / contacts, contacts said, a mastery / quality, quality queened within a mastery / que, que to know whose mastery / woo, woo, oh you, the mastery / want, want to be, a mastery / review, review your desire's mastery / strung, strung into and out through mastery / study, study a date's mastery / notes, notes deal in mastery / programs, programs pure at mastery / conserve, conserve your yes to a great, masterful / conservation, conservation sent to the won, mastery / counts, counts in all's mastery / counted, counted a vote through too, mastery / capricious, capricious in a concrete sea too, mastery / sponsor, sponsor gained mastery / sports, sports seat mastery / western, western well be mastery / certify, certify suppress less mastery / certificate, certificate said mastery / musical, musical meets mastery / antibodies, antibodies emit a song for mastery

CHAPTER TWELVE
Padre, padre purest in patterns mastery / father, father found a mastery, / mend, mend in all a mastery / lifting, lifting into a mastery / champion, champion choose a mastery / deliver, deliver a goods mastery / supply, supply us all with all your mastery / compete, compete and compute a renewal's mastery / comply, comply to cube's mastery / cost, cost cures within a mastery / paid, paid to be a mastery / back, back to bay's mastery / picture, picture picked within a mastery / men, men doubled in their mastery / make, mastery makes a begin again possible / soundtrack, soundtrack should be a mastery / flaunt, flaunt a choice made mastery / conduct, conduct a curer through there, mastery / format, format felt within a mastery / CD, corporate decide to believe in mastery / progress, progress pearled into mastery / refer, refer in red on masteries / melody, melody meet in sweets require a mastery / lullabies, lullabies led into a mastery / coments, coments about a mastery / cement, cement suggestion's mastery / lifetime, lifetime leads, in masteries / friends, friends felt a mastery / died, died and due a mastery / wander, wander within into a mastery / sessions, sessions suggest a mastery / aim, meet the aiming mastery / repair, repair revived a mastery / regain, regain rewind in 3 mastery / clarity, clarity kept for a mastery / clerk, clerk clued too, mastery / addition, addition due too, a mastery / subtract, cubtract suspect and then mastery / multiply, multiply means too, mastery / stack, stack in stuck out, mastery / fast, fast and fuse within a mastery / fuel, fuel found in mastery / feud, fued in rude out mastery / font, font and the fend four mastery / proper, proper prepare into a mastery / paper, paper pledged on mastery / prepare, prepare to see thee, mastery / print, print in a pivot point mastery / fourth, fourth in tens masteries / move, move to a mothered mastery / forth, forth into a mastery / goes, goes to two's mastery / pens, mastery pens our love's good / light, light led into bed's mastery / timber, timber too, mastery / toes, toes deep in mastery / pitch, pitch into mastery / pinch, pinch out and vaunt in mastery / point, point to a through mastery / spun, spun about within mastery / spinning, spinning spent on mastery / dance, dance in all's mastery / crystal, crystal cure's mastery / sun, sun day's mastery.

CHAPTER THIRTEEN
Varnish, varnish blood red in a mastery / varnish, varnish 40 million deep in a mastery / recognize, recognize a ressurrection's mastery / find, find a triste for a mastery / benches, benches bellied into a mastery / boards, boards bed a mastery / bistro, bistro in through a mastery / wine, wine into a mastery / warmth, warmth welcomes's mastery / wedded, wedded into a wed-some, mastery / material, material mad with mastery / abide, abide into a mastery / pearls, pearls about the shout's mastery / placed, placed in pleasantly mastery / neck, neck nets a mastery / side, side seed a mastery / systems, systems sent into a mastery / suspect, suspects another's mastery / breaks, breaks about it mastery / points, points into a trails mastery / advice, advice invents a mastery / resettles, resettles regard a mastery / rack, rack a coupled mastery / qualifies, qualifies for a mastery / quality, quality equips a mastery / quakes,

quakes in a wellest mastery / quantums, quantums a question's mastery / heat, heat into a hurry's mastery / Venice, Venice viewed a mystery / signs, signs of the centrific mastery / service, service in a central's mastery / makes, makes a meaningful peace mastery / restores, restores and bestows an anniversared mastery / large, large in a leagued mastery / quality, quality quelled less in mastery / big, big enough to see mastery / breaks, masterful breaks on mysteries / born, born into a pleasing mastery / aspire, aspire too a mastery / aspirant, aspirant too and then a mastery / restraint, restraint news and mysteries / electric, electric lesson's mastery / excitement, excitement sent through heaven's invent on mastery / home, home is held along a mastery / found, found into and then a mystery / favor, favor mysterious favors won through a mastery / abounds, abounds in strains due a mastery / perfection, perfection felt in melted regard for mastery / completition, completition in depletion less too mastery / content, content in a combine with a mastery / comment, comment complete in a warrant's mastery / aim, aim at the same wind's mastery / entire, entire in required wonder's mastery / matter, matter meets a mastery / material, middled material masked in mastery / divine, divine detailed wants mysteries at mastery / enlighten, enlighten in sight's good, mastery / ascend, ascend a mattered fact on mastery / 64, 64 seeds too, mastery / degrees, degrees declare a mastery / vibrations, vibrations values, mastery / ratios, ratios mastered in a mystery / lines, lines lead too, a mastery / linear, linear puzzles solved through your mastery of lines.

THE MAGNITUDE-MENTS
LEVEL 60

CHAPTER ONE

Magic, magic equate, the mysterious magnitude is, love / moves too, a magnitude in love / lights, maginitude in light's supreme regin / cities, cities sent to deep magnitude / nights, nights alone in magnitudes / elect, love elect your malleable magnitude / moves, moves into gradent repose magnitude / maintain, maintain a silent detain, magnitude / muse, magnitude made a muse through love / make, make a ramp too love's magnitude / desire, desire a date in magnitude / don, don a basic humanity magnitude / hats, 8's hats worn, often well, too, magnitudes / chat, chat about the promise meant to magnitudes / choose, choose another wed, too, magnitude / ammuse, ammuse your set on magnitude / children, children chime is to magnitude / suffer, suffer less your magnitude / accept, accept a guest won, magnitude / repeat, repest a rhythm come magnitude / christ, christ said "magnitude" / said, said I would through magnitude / square, square in the care for magnitude / attitude, attitude of magnitude / absolute, love's absolute magnitude / precious, precious plenty in magnitude / prime, prime to a plenty's magnitude / print, print a temple's magnitude / princess, princess of the plane won, magnitude / plublish, plublish a paper's magnitude / write, write a magnitude devote / ride, ride a lesson's magnitude / respect, respect the all in magnitude / retire, retire to a firey magnitude / recgonize, recognize her lead on earth's magnitude / require, require a friendly magnitude / sufi, sufi should will, too, magnitude / spun, spun in a vade release to magnitude / spins, spins in three's magnitude / still, still in the quilt magnitude / wheel, wheel of the wise won magnitude / wheels, wheels sky wide within relative magnitude / wheeled, wheeled into a magnitude / will, will we magnitude? / of life, of life and on it, magnitude / wife, wife wed too in magnitude / wed, wed one well within magnitude / bride, a bride came to renew the bodied magnitude / regale, regal your rationed magnitude / relegate, relegate a metorical's magnitude / rapt, papt in chosen magnitudes / rounds, rounds into remember magnitude / rupture, rupture erupts in magnitude / root, root of the inquirey into magnitude / cuddle, cuddle in a couple of day's magnitude / cup, cup her near for magnitude / curl, curl up and relate to magnitude / embrace, embrace a duration thick in magnitude / imbrace, imbrace your light in magnitude / steep, steep well in thirsty magnitude's / share, share another brother's magnitude / shade, shade into simply a daily remember's magnitude / splendor, splendor sent wide to magnitude's / spoke, spoke sent aloft to magnitude's.

CHAPTER TWO

Righteous, draped in righteous bloom's magnitude / reckon, reckon of plenty's magnitude / attribute, an attribute felt throughout magnitude / rise, rise to a treat won magnitude / talent, talent shaped within magnitudes / texture, texture treats our magnitudes / pasture, pastures full in magnitudes / pies, pies placed in warm magnitudes / pious, pious please due magnitude / plenty, plenty of exemplify's magnification / perfect, perfectly equipped too, magnification / two, two of the one, magnify / twinkle, twinkle twinned unto magnitudes / twilight, twilight taught a succession on magnitudes / charted, charted challenges in magnitudes / review, review a receptive meet too magnitudes / strings, strings in snapped degrees of magnitude / loops, loops over out's magnitude / tones, tones rang with magnitude / wheels, wheels of the won magnitude / perfect, perfect friend's magnitude / 8, 8 said, magnitude / include, include a mood for magnitude / infinite, infinite in our mutual magnitude / trance, trance broken in magnitudes / truck, truck drove in too magnitude / transcend, revel in transcend / spend, stand to spend for magnitudes / spell, spell a require well magnitude / stall, stall out and revelation in through magnitude / spat, spat upon less magnitude / cats, cats equipped win magnitude's / winding, winding winnings become your magnitude / own, own your meanings magnitude / kinder, kinder in a treaty for magnitudes / reveal, reveal a red streak in your magnitude / rant, mansions rant in magnitudes / rave, rave around thus magnitude / pant, pant and pare too, magnitude / pave, pave over dramatic erupt with magnitude / pearls, pearls purchased for magnitudes / courts, courts drawn into magnitudes / captives, captives filled with magnitude / cage, cage empties and birds are free too magnitudes / sell, sell the old magnitudes / sold, sold another's magnitude / soled, soled into magnitude / sould, sould out and lightly in to magnitudes / leave, leave a daily magnitude for love / lead, loves lead is then magnitude / go, go to her the earth's magnitude / now, now we see our magnitudes / empower, empower your animate with magnitude / expell, expell less, then magnitude / expire, expire into higher magnitudes / fire, fire fell into magnitudes / felt, felt in fullness magnitudes / fold, fold about her earth's magnitudes / fond, fond of the feel in magnitudes / fontend, fontend felt soft again magnitudes / father, father of the feelings magnitude / float, floats felt strength in magnitudes / hypopotamus, hypotemus metaphysically correct for magnitude / hydrop, hydrop sorts of magnitudes.

CHAPTER THREE

Elegance, elegance sent to the intentioned magnitudes / preface, preface points enthuse to magnitudes / seek, seek a source magnitudes / sought, sought a note for magnitudes / fabric, fabric freed through magnitude / faced, faced a dealings magnitude / theory, capacitys theory on magnitude / traced, traced into magnitude / examine, examine a dearest magnitude / white, white in your insights magnitude / brooms, collaborative brooms magnitudes / swept, swept in steeples magnitude / align, align in insights magnitude / alike, alike in a completions magnitude / anthems, anthems thicks with magnitude / smooth, smooth in magnitudes / portal, portal felt full of magnitude / paved, paved over well to magnitude / quiet, quiet in a richer magnitude / creates, creates a date in magnitude / solitare, solitare out too magnitudes / escape, escape less and thrive in magnitudes / collective, collective conspire to hire magnitudes / eclectic, eclectic compare in the spare magnitude / schools, schools simply said magnitudes / spare, spare roomed magnitudes / spawn, spawn outs your magnitude / live, live in live magnitudes / lively, lively ways to magnitude / music, music met in magnitudes / makes, makes a move, to magnitude / material, material meets in magnitude / Judaculla, Judaculla kept in a rocky bliss magnitudes / camp, camp in tortures magnitude /

pen, pen appealed to magnitudes / point, point made to magnitudes / place, place of the meetings magnitude / caney, caney wayed magnitudes / fork, fork fit to magnitudes / fresh, fresh up within magnitudes / freshen, freshen your magnitudes / treats, treats in transits magnitudes / tour, tour another's magnitudes / see, seee her earthly way to magnitudes / place, place found in magnitudes / rose, rose into a magnitude / agree, agree to freely magnitud / be, be with her the earth's magnitude / shown, shown a new glades magnitude / gallons, gallons glued erupt to magnitudes / gain, gain a refrains magnitudes / reoccur, reoccur another magnitudes / durate, durate due to magnitudes / delivery's, deliverys deals on magnitudes / doors, doors dealt within magnitudes / about, about us magnitudes / heart, heart held in magnitudes / read, read about your magnitudes / alot, alot of livings magnitudes / befriend, befriend a friendly magnitude / xylum, xylum flew in flowings magnitudes / phloem, phloem felt is wooden magnitude / forgive, forgive her to magnitude / give, give magnitude within love.

CHAPTER FOUR
Brigadoon, magnitudes brigadoon in love / general, general of the magnitudes would magnitudes / irish, irish scotch and woods magnitude / team, team to a streams valentined magnitude / trim, loves trim is the best in magnitude / fog, fog gone magnitudes / fontened, fortened again magnitude / spot, spot in the simples magnitude / stay, stay into a tray filled in magnitudes / soft, soft in a simple ways magnitude / learn, learn to be for magnitudes / listen, listen to a missions magnitude / plane, magnitudes plane is in love / plain, plain to a minimal magnitude / planets, planets in a triangular magnitude / point, point to a magnitude / novel, novel knelt within magnitude / shed, shed in a simple magnitude / skin, skin sunk into magnitudes / intend, intend in a blissful magnitude / depth, depth dealt and du in to magnitude / explore, explore more lovings magnitude / apply, apply to a principles magnitude / delight, delight not in magnitude / acquire, acquire power / insight, insight instilled in magnitude / find, find the strength in magnitude / source, source up / first, first emerald / mast, mast emerges / heads / Judith / music, music meets your hearts revive within magnitude / most, most of your host a natural parasite until magnitude / benevolent, benevolent beauties bow to magnitudes / face, face magnitudes / valley of the values wins in magnitudes / ingrown, ingrown in your released magnitudes / intone, intone a name and gain magnitudes 40 ignite, ignite in the insights magnitudes 41 delve, delve into anothers magnitude 42 decide, decide whose magnitude 43 agree, agree to be magnificent in magnitudes 44 bead, bead strung less in magnitudes 45 belly, bellys full and up into a magnitude 46 bolt, bolt out and then a magnitude 47bet, bet on beauties magnitudes / oast, boast about release through magnitude / bathe, bathe in beautiful magnitudes / bask, bask in basically magnitudes / bely, bely is less in magnitudes / bec, a lie's magnitude / borne, borne aloft to se eyour magnitude / attire, attire into hires magnitude / aspect, aspect of the respect for a magnitude / aspirante loved and the gloved magnitude / connect, connect to anothers magnitude / kick, kick at a habit magnitude / joint, joints in joining magnitude / journey, journey in and through magnitudes / angle, angle won into a magnitude / amble, amble into gambles wons magnitude / allow, allow in how you within a magnitude / honest, honest about it magnitude.

CHAPTER FIVE
Sprint, sprint in venues metatripping magnitude / kin, kin of the winners magnitude / open, open in through and often magnitude / found, found in through magnitude / find, find a fellows magnitude / fond, fond of fellows magnitude / doors, doors deal in magnitude / opening, opening into variable regards list magnitudes / balance, balance belied and then knew magnitude / seek, seek another sort the magnitudes / sought, sought about you magnitudes / yours, yours in ours,magnitude / rock, rock in steady magnitude / Gibraltor, Gibraltor gentles your magnitude / join, join the gentles magnitude / thee, thee and thy magnitude / rocks, rocks streak of granite magnitudes / reveal, reveal a resolute magnitude / heart, heart of the healed magnitudes / feel, feel of the frailest release to magnitudes / called, called into active magnitudes / bivelelectric, basement to foundations magnitude / chemistry, chemistry correct in magnitudes / speech, speech about these the magnitudes / desire, desire to free your magnitude / magnetic, magnetic matrices and the menues magnitude / inquire, inquire in a wired magnitude / deduction, deduction made, magnitudes 29 within, within a windowed magnitude / friends, friends feel fleet to magnitude 31 wed, wed is the ascend to magnitude / web, web broken weaves to magnitude / buzz, buzz about it magnitude / electric, electric fantastic magnitude / fair, fair in the feelings magnitudes / dod, decided magnitudes / male, male empires in magnitudes / found, found a friendly magnitude / find, find a frolic in magnitude / friend, friend finds an again magnitude / panel, panel of the plentiful magnitude / kept, kept in a cubicles magnitudes / plugged, plugged out and then a magnitude / in, in and truly magnitudes / pen, pen into a placements magnitudes / parent, parent in the central magnitudes / unplug, unplug is our suspends magnitudes / see, see us centrally in magnitudes / seas, seas into a participative magnitude / desire, desire decides through magnitude / waves, waves of the weavers magnitude / meet, meet at the centers magnitude / marbels, marbels into squares released through magnitude / garments, garments on a gains magnitudes / blue, blue is the planets magnify magnitude / ridge, ridge redeemed a magnitude / smoke, smoke of the invokes through magnitude / fault, fault of the relative release to magnitude / occurs, occurs in ours magnitude / contest, magnificent contests won to magnitude / wins, wins and the winters magnitudes / dream, dream in a daily magnitude / dates, dates in a data's status magnitude / desire, desire in delectable strokes on magnitude.

CHAPTER SIX
Balance, balance is plenty in magnitudes / awash, awash and within magnitudes / annoint, annoint and the truest magnitudes / counts, counts in present plans to magnitudes / bellevue, bellevue blew into our magnitudes / contoured, contoured in cured magnitude / against, against and in sense on magnitudes / avoid, avoid a future left of for magnitude / costs, costs enough

magnitude / desire, desire to associate with magnitudes / more, more in the methods magnitude / most, most of the many magnitude / rooms, rooms rented magnitudes / temples, temples into surrendered perfect magnitude / kingdoms, kingdoms complete in magnitude / touring, touring in securing magnitudes / heavens, heavens held in magnitude / gateways, gateways grew into magnitude / secure, secure in suggests magnitudes / shout, shout in apparent magnitudes / bells, bells bevy of magnitude / ballast, ballast is above within a magnitude / balance, balance believes in magnitudes / pace, pace above and then magnitude / pressure, pressure off and into a magnitude / prow, prow now due a magnitude / post, post and past through magnitude / bows, bows and wows us magnitude / athlete's, athlete's erratics magnitudes / stare, stare in aired magnitude / share, share a simply marvelous magnitude / show, show us how to magnitude / agnostic, agnostic in the acoustics magnitudes / abundant, knew a surer magnitude / strict, strict is a decent magnitude / stress, stress is out to magnitude / store, store is amplified through magnitudes / by, by believable in magnitudes / buy, buy us a nearer magnitude / road, road red and good to a magnitude / railroad, railroad reads like trues magnitude / hoax, hoax out and in wins a magnitude / elect, elect a director magnitude / ally, ally out and then a strict straight to magnitude / alone, alone valued in magnitude / allowance, allowance leads to magnitudes / mex, in a mental become won magnitudes / cherry, cherry bled in red magnitudes / friendly, friendly in a frolics win of magnitudes / feast, feast in the fundamental magnitudes / byron, byron sent into an invent gone magnitudes / east, east met in the east won magnitudes / beast, beast is out to magnitude / belies, belies is restful at magnitudes / below, below and within our magnitude / ballast, ballast is best on the traveling rest due magnitudes / gust, gust out the rest magnitudes / aside, aside is resident to our magnitude / token, token of the treaty, magnitude / chalice, chalice held full of magnitudes / grail, grail grasped magnitudes / yours, yours is in ours magnitudes / reside, reside at respectful magnitudes / hear, hear us please too, magnitudes.

CHAPTER SEVEN
Mmasters, masters surround the magnitudes / mastery, mastery of mysteries magnitudes / Ontario, Ontario in an aria's magnitudes / arcturion, arcturion record of the rectitudes magnitudes / pen, pen in a pleasurable magnitude / placed, placed in a pleasure's magnitude / arts, arts in the starts magnitudes / taste, taste a waist less magnitudes / feather, feather light to a magnitude / street, street chored entreaty through a magnitude / exhibit, exhibit your apply best magnitudes / British, British acquisition in magnitude / Columbian, Columbian caned magnitude / Vancouver, Vancouver held's magnitude / plays, plays into plenty's magnitude / parked, magnitude parked in regard four love / excite, excite your write to magnitudes / contains, contains a refrain on magnitude / consentual, consentual matters magnitudes / palace, palace of the pure's magnitude / colors, colors cure your "in" magnitude / collapse, collapse and conclude magnitudes / combine, combine a constant within magnitudes / resign, resign to remember magnitudes / Hawaiian, Hawaiian hand magnitudes / shores,

shores of sure magnitudes / channels, channels chant magnitudes / chant, chant regain magnitude / help, help your name magnitude / comes, comes a dame, magnitude / advance, advance a theoretic magnitude / theories, theories enthuse magnitudes / place, place a pen in magnitude / divides, divides degrees magnitdes / designs, designs in daring magnitude / shells, shells of surest magnitude / Egypt, Egypt kept magnitude / combined, combined in in sacred magnitudes / analog, analog along, magnitudes / digits, digits deal in magnitude / photographs, photographs found magnitudes / energetics, energetics join magnitudes / placed, placed in compounds magnitudes / on, on to agree on magnitude / lines, lines lead magnitude / lasts, lasts loin, magnitude?? / lots, lots of compare magnitude / closets, closets cure, magnitude / large, large settle meant magnitudes / grand, grand in magnitude / magnificent, magnificent magnitudes / more, more won, magnitudes Stonehenge, Stonehenge sent, magnitudes / alter, alter built magnitudes / alternative, alternative regards magnitude / admire, admire a direct magnitude / advanced, advanced am estate magnitude / attribute, attribute create magnitude / attrition, attrition won, magnitudes / mention, mention sum magnitude / dimension, dimension denotes magnitude / dose, dose of the votes magnitude / magnify, magnify malaign magnitudes / magnitude, magnitude gain I am.

CHAPTER EIGHT
Measures, measures in a truest reckoning magnitudes / degrees, degrees of duty's magnitude / quarters, quarters our and shout won restitution to magnitude / quadrants, quadrants covered in magnitude / 12's, 12's and winds a plane the co or magnitudes / 12th, 12th in wealthier and weds magnitudes / 1/63, 1/63 of the word Metatrons magnitudes / 1/64, 1/64 of the magnitude / 64, 64 of the more elites magnitudes / 70, 70 of the we soon shot magnitudes / 80, 80 who knew magnitudes / 33, 33 who said, magnitude / mallet, mallet of the valids magnitudes / moses, moses made a marion well to magnitude / mates, mates met in magnitudes / motes, motes and outs drift magnitudes / country, country sqired into magnitude / side, side with thee magnitude / math, maths treasures magnitudes / mats, mats think in magnitude / grins, grins like a, magnify magnitude / gain, gain agreed less magnitude / friendly, magnitude friendly agree to love / flows, love flows in magnitude / afloat, afloat in a wallet filled with magnitudes / waters, waters magnitude's love / deep, deep within magnitudes / within, within us a rush to magnitude / wells, wells of the welcomed magnitude / mountians, mountains of magic's magnitude / magic, magic mountains said love is a magnitude / excercise, excercise the rise into magnitude / match, match met magnitude / mispell, mispell well intents magnitudes / mishap, mishap won on to magnitude / mayhem, mayhem met in magnitude / amuse, justice amused in magnitude / muse, muse of the rused magnitudes / meets, meets anothers magnitudes / mounts, mounts met the archer in amount magnitudes / pants, pants on and in magnitudes / pounce, pounc outs then magnitudes / entire, entire in our magnitude / being, being in love's magnitude / bonds, bonds and tron's magnitude / belts, belts out magnitude / banters,

banters above magnitude / beds, beds and reds magnitude / books, books within a magnitude / give, give a read a magnitude / given, given in ordered magnitude / aware, aware of wheres magnitudes / kim's, kim's conclude that rules out magnitude / share, share an accord magnitudes / supple, supple in your nimble magnitude / melt, melt went true in magnitude / apply, apply to be a magnitude / Kingdom's, Kingdom's come magnitude / relic, relic red, won magnitude / papyrus, papyrus writ in magnitude / perspire, perspire less over magnitude / cope, cope simply said coped with magnitudes / copy, copy your hourly waged magnitude / cube, cube cared four magnitude.

CHAPTER NINE

Exercise, exercise regard in magnitudes / early, early winds magnitudes / live, live and give from magnitudes / latticed, latticed lenders magnitudes / lace, lace is worn in two magnitudes / palace, I am the palace of magnitudes / wear, wear a pair magnitudes / hearts, hearts won too, magnitude / rich, rich in mountains explore magnitude / compare, compare a patterned magnitude / make, make a divorce of course magnitude / material, material meant for magnitude / matters, matters out trues magnitude / mast, mast of the cast magnitudes / moist, moist in wet river's John deep in magnitude / Mitchell, Mitchell mounts and recounts aways magnitudes / domed, domed deals of magnitude / papyri, papyri sent in magnitude / accurate, accurate relay to magnitude / error, erro red and went magnitudes / demand, demand a detailed magnitude / magnetic, magnetic won to magnitude / magnet, magnet met in magnitude / net, net another magnitude / Costa, Costa Rican magnitudes / Rican, magnitudes Rican way to coasts on love / books, love's books true through magnitude / fires, fires felt in magnitude / friends, friends among us magnitudes / ends, ends in wins magnitudes / stays, stays well within magnitude / minutes, minutes won too, magnitude / known, known to be freed to magnitude / mathematics, mathematics mix magnitude / blended, blended in believable magnitudes / froth, froth and from then magnitude / knoll, knoll of the well to magnitude / know, know who goes to magnitude / knowledge, knowledge of the nuptuals magnitudes / acknowledge, acknowledge the college magnitudes / knew, knew who acknowledge magnitudes / knowing, knowing in the showings magnitudes / planes, planes of the planets magnitudes / planets, planets into cares magnitudes / collide, collide at reside in magnitudes / chronicles, chronicles of the criminals release to magnitudes / Exit into emitted magnitudes / epistle, epistle of the rustle magnitudes / shall, motions shall meet at a sweet magnitude / streets, magnets streets meant for filed magnitudes / plays, plays like pleasant regards magnitudes / passion, passion plunge into magnitudes / pleasures, pleasures appeal well to magnitude / likings, likings in lessons magnitudes / priestly, priestly prepare for the let go's magnitudes / professions, professions felt full well to magnitudes / varieties, varieties vessels magnitudes / venues, venues fashionably apt to magnitude / vaults, vaults a rail then magnitude / faults, faults felt leap through to magnitude / forgiveness, forgiveness fed in thorough magnitudes / foreign, foreign magnets magnitude / finds, finds a final magnitude / plans, plans made to magnitudes.

CHAPTER TEN

Shall, alpine shall prevail in magnitudes / streets, streets drip in magnitude / trends, trends about it magnitude / tours, tours of the ours magnitude / squares, squares sold to magnitude / departing, departing dutied magnitudes / passing, passing and the grasping magnitude / struggles, struggles our magnitude / complete, complete boods magnitude / Greece, Greece in magnitude / appraised, appraised made on magnitude / torture, torture out magnitudes / stables, stables simple shall in magnitudes / documents, documents done magnitude / views, views about it magnitude / variable, variable values magnitudes / mothers, mothers mix magnitude / healed, healed in willed magnitude / protected, protected in placed magnitudes / fields, fields of fellows magnitudes / clans, clans over all life's magnitudes / first, first out and then magnitude / expire, expire and yes to magnitude / empirical, empiracal advise in magnitudes / experience, experience read magnitude / new, new ways magnitudes / skills, skills complete in magnitudes / develop, develop a due magnitude / grateful, grateful groups magnitude / hush, gain a hush to old magnitudes / accountant, accountant read, magnitude / calls, calls made magnitude / paths, paths meet in magnitudes / female, female felt magnitude / ought, ought to see the magnitudes / recover, recover a reprieve magnitudes / able, able to see the magnitude / gifts, gifts grew magnitudes / sacredly, sacredly held magnitude / sourced, sourced in all magnitudes / teach, scopes teach our magnitudes / sisters, sisters in the histories magnitudes / calmness, calmness felt into magnitudes / gentleness, gentleness joins in her magnitudes / taught, taught another magnitudes / force, force of the futured magnitudes / forgotten, forgotten fews and the calls to magnitudes / calls, calls a well magnitude / miracles, miracles made in shades magnitude / worthy, worthy of the weary magnitudes / memories, rest in memories removed magnitudes / develop, develop a declare on magnitudes / behave, behave well within magnitudes / concepts, concepts content to magnitude / swell, swell in all told magnitude / lightly, lightly led to magnitude / expressions, expressions suggest magnitudes / flowers, flowers delayed grow magnitudes / persons, persons play in magnitude / places, places we meet magnitudes / shade, shade of the scene magnitudes / frail, frail affairs magnitudes / well, well won magnitudes / won, won another litigate mother magnitudes.

CHAPTER ELEVEN

Litigation, litigation out and then magnitudes / fouls, fouls flew over magnitude / fray, fray freed magnitudes / frock, frock worn magnitudes / stays, stays at directs magnitudes / shock, shock sent and how magnitudes / mounds, mounds meet in magnitudes / mothers, mothers worn magnitudes / strong, strong except to magnitudes / smother, smother over magnitudes / care, care above these magnitudes / concede, concede to breed magnitudes / success, success says magnitudes / like, like ahead magnitudes / lair, lair of the flair magnitudes / flair, flair up into magnitudes / elect, elect a reward for magnitudes / suggested, suggested supply magnitudes / path, path paved magnitudes / talk, talk waved magnitudes / decide, decide to deed your magnitude / occurs,

occurs in more magnitude / math, math met by magnitude / walk, walk in wells magnitudes / deliver, deliver anothers magnitude / delight, delight in trues magnitude / doors, doors slear into magnitude / adore, adore us well magnitude / contend, contend to trees magnitude / continue, continue out and then magnitude / constantly, constantly the consistency for a beloved magnitude / loved, / art, art of the cart magnitude / be, be a magnitude / being, being magnified in magnitude / human, human hurled magnitudes / eye, eye world see magnitudes / eyes, eyes wise to magnitude / smile, magenta smiled magnitude / stride, stride rise magnitudes / step, step up magnitude / tour, tour in your magnitude / tongue, tongue into trees magnitude / pierced, pierced in worn magnitude / probe, probe prepares magnitudes / project, erase project less magnitudes / purest, purest possess magnitudes / pace, pace ups magnitudes / days, days of dreams magnitude / facts, facts in fellow magnitude / ages, ages wages magnitude / moms, moms place in homes magnitudes / matters, matters much in magnitude / balance, balance made in magnitude / teachings, teachings travail magnitude / touch, touch a treaty magnitude / taught, taught a lot magnitude / creatures, creatures reach a magnitude / tender, tender times magnitude / source, source magnitude / camera, camera concerns magnitude / electric, electric regards magnitude / touching, touching trends magnitude / pull, pull out through magnitude.

CHAPTER TWELVE

Pleasure, pleasure made in magnitude / seeking, seeking speaking terms magnitude / over, over and thrown magnitude / course, mansions course to magnitude / found, found in a friends magnitude / explain, explain us by magnitude / heavens, heavens magnitudes fuse / game, game came to magnitudes / loners, loners live in magnitudes / all, all we call to magnitudes / things, things this magnitudes / tall, context talls magnitudes / fellows, fellows find magnitude / human, human weld magnitude / hampers, hampers heap magnitude / tall, tall escaped magnitude / fault, fault out magnitude / knot, knot saught magnitude / human, discover human health magnitude / journeys, journeys joined magnitudes / seek, seek help magnitude / squander, contend squander sands magnitude / care, most care magnitude / pair, pair of the where magnitude / deep, deep sleep magnitude / electrically, electrically neat magnitude / keep, keep up magnitude / connective, wings connective magnitudes / tissue, tissue tucks magnitude / venue, venue vants magnitude / valleys, valleys veil magnitude / value, capable values magnitude / drink, drink up magnitudes / double, double deals magnitude / imperial, imperial plants magnitude / counselor, counselor comes magnitude / seek, seek aid magnitude / sentinel, sentinel sent trained magnitudes / set, set us up to magnitudes 40 dealers, dealers seal magnitude / bet, bet win magnitudes / batchelor, batchelor bailed magnitudes / paid, paid up magnitudes / pad, pad points magnitud / forgave, forgave gave magnitude / feelings, feelings fell magnitude / sought, sought us "a" grade magnitude / rush, rush in magnitude / anguish, anguish extended magnitudes / turns, turns out magnitudes / news, news on magnitudes / becomes, magnificent becomes you magnitude /

clear, clear enoughs magnitude / dearest, dearest deals magnitude / ones, ones won magnitude / meet, meet us at magnitude / decry, decry a delicate magnitude / decide, decide to be a magnitude / deliver, deliver a durable magnitude / desire, desire to see magnitudes / distinguish, distinguish destroy from magnitudes / encourage, encourage a win magnitude / voyage, voyage wins a magnitude / within, within us magnitudes.

CHAPTER THIRTEEN

Foothills, foothills fund our magnitudes / loves, loves scopes in magnitude / actions, bequeath actions to magnitudes / due, due us well magnitudes / healed, healed erates magnitudes / hearts, hearts held magnitude / pleasures, pleasures perfect magnitude / pew, clearly few our man / denial, denial don magnitude / deep, deep in love's magnitude / forgiven, forgiven forgo to magnitudes / face, face us often magnitudes / follicle, follicle fueled magnitude / full, full enoughs magnitudes / emit, sounds emit is in magnitude / state, state some blessed magnitud / notice, notice a nearest magnitude / thrones, thrones threw magnitude / appear, appear in our magnitudes / angels, angels send magnitudes / news, news us magnitudes / sources, most sources lead to magnitudes / find, find a friends magnitudes / making, making a most magnitude / thrown, thrown out magnitudes / rare, rare less magnitudes / give, given us this grace magnitude / constraint, constraint for magnitude / occur, occur in our magnitudes / absolute, absolute suggest magnitude / flair, flair found magnitude / sources, sources sent magnitude / winged, winged winds magnitude / wander, wander in to magnitude / weave, weave won magnitude / welcome, welcome won magnitude / sing, sing a brothers magnitudes / seen, seen soon magnitude / saunters, saunters sent magnitude / inn, inn too magnitudes / connect, connect collects magnitude / heavens, heavens held magnitudes / king, king sings magnitudes / metatron, metatron met magnitudes / pleasing, erotic pleasings magnitudes / arc, arc on magnitudes / on arcs, on arcs throughout magnitudes / electric, electric mused magnitudes / won, won anothers magnitude / one, one of us magnitudes / done, done blue to magnitudes / less, less is sure magnitudes / transgress, transgress blown magnitudes / maintain, maintain an elations magnitudes / sight, sight sent magnitudes / height, height held deeping magnitudes / mountains, mountains meant for magnitudes / accounts, accounts sent the sures magnitudes / express, express a sakes magnitude / regain, regain a reigned magnitude / confess, confess in us our magnitude / needs, needs another magnitude / speeds, speeds in to magnitudes / share, share a well magnitude.

THE IN-FOUNTAIN-MENTS
LEVEL 61

CHAPTER ONE

Wells, wells are deep within the fashion and the passion placed perpendicular to a lightest wind called fountains of love / overflowing, overflowing in emotional matters and the chattering rest at the apex, teh reflex, the influx, of life's fountains / cups, cups are well deep in love's fashions, the fountians human / fell, fell to a fountain human / splashes, splashes and the cashing in on parallel examines of the mutual straits for wellness and the twins who land in fountains of love / pennies, pennies spent precisely on the threaded thrillings and the healings on living fountain / copper, copper has bent to the seeds of plantations and the fountains of men / tin, tin and the triple fountains / Ananaki, Ananaki landings youthful to the committed trail of fountains mended / ambulance, ambulance cast to the crows who stood at thresholds fountains / advance, advance to a lesson learned and the healing earned through fountains in love / N.C., natural cords established and cut through in the fountains of love / Raleigh, Raleigh's align is red to a time centrally fountained / durations, durations and the evaluations of the levels spent for fountains / during, during revival fo the fountains interior within love / generate, generate enough to hush for the fountains human / ravens, ravens roost near your fountain / flower, flowers empowered through the thrilling fountains / flow, flow is the cubic volumetric miracle of the mentioned fountains / cower, cower less and cover more through the fountains of love / yearns, yearns to be near your fountain human / gapes, gapes at the growth wed to fountains / beasts, beasts are gone to the fountains human / release, release another's discourse about fountains / love, lvoe us well and interrupt less for the fountains human / wins, wwins a shining attempt to see the fountains human / light, light has led to a Christos strand and the miracle's evident in the beings human / bends, bends chromatically true to the chinese figures sent fountain wide to the / blankets of human love / straightens, straightens healing fountains / pull, pull into miracles for the fountains human / elective, elective reactions to the human fountains / reasons, reasons register near our human factors of the figures human / cowards, cowards ran past and alas our gifts became merely fountains / blend, blend has come to the christos rich within these foundationed fountains / face, face us and regain your regional declare for these fountains / lines, lines electric leap to the rewarded fountains / erase, erase a wrinkled past and arrange to last in the fountains, God / maintain, maintain a semblance and the symbol for God, the humans / remember, remember electrically that levelly God is human too / forgive, forgive the features who read that human is without fountains within / 70, 70 ways I have shown the 7 times 10 of the chakratic course elected in forgiving fountains / over, over and thine the filling fountains / 7, 7 times I said "fountains within the human" "fountains within the human" "fountains within the human" "fountains within the human" "fountains within the human" "fountains within the human" "fountains within the human" / eight, eight ways to rise into the living human fountains / tools, tools given and the electric strands of the human fountians / all, all we will is human to these fountains / tend, tend to the notions of fountains / now, now is how we are a fountain / power, power has resource in the central corridors of

Christian explain, allow your vote to elect the entire office then of Christos and the caning may stop and the zoning elect a district wider than simple fountains complain, know the main river, the creeks, the shores, the corridors, the lights, the life that is alive with heavenly electricity for the hydro-elevated course, the living humanity of finding heaven within and paradise at your door and God's attitude that shimmering across the surface of light election / affords, know the course, the love, the fountain human / given, given a lviing example, explain that in heaven's name, you are, a fountain / ascend, ascend to examples of living humans and the temples and fountains of light / moment, moment to meaning, I AM, is the leaning into the light living examples of good and the light lend of liquid fountains within / independent, independent resources said "let there be, a light in humanity", there will be a fountain of ink written to heal the life fed human / fundamentals, fundamentals meet in the mentioned humanity of finished works and the fountains human / mend, mend a sample by the candle of the living fountained human / choirs, choirs sing the source has led to a fountain within humanity / divisions, divisions have caught the flow to the resources human and the living fountains / heavens, heavens waves caught through humanity's fountains / flanks, flanks align and the signs are fountain wise to man / rivers, rivers reached and crossed through the Jordan's key coded deliver of the / fountains human / reasons, reasons lost are found and the lviing sands of Israel keep us flowing thorugh the fountains human / *Jesus, Jesus said "Going to prepare a fountain's spread to the highest shelf of living well within the levels 64 and the swimming pools of the fountain's human" *Joining Energetically Sustained Understood and Supplied eternally with light.*

CHAPTER TWO

Crosses, crosses melt into fountains / electric, electric losses willed healed by through the living fountains / melting, melting mazes accorded the gearing fountains / fairs, fairs are simple to the listing fountains / shatter, shatter met recourse through the living foutnains / spelled, spelled likened to F-O-U-N-T-A-I-N-S / courage, courage has cast the Lion ashore to live within the lightened fountains / sure, sure has arrived as resource kept and fortunately we are well within the licensed fountains / rivers, rivers coursing again to the met within hearts of fountains / cement, cement has assured your shoes the variations on fountains / coverage, coverage has encouraged that reason applies to the fountains human / apply, apply for the licensed fountains / apprehend, apprehend has amended the lightened fountains / resort, resort to a sort who live through the listed fountains / rotate, rotate ashore and the find the filling fountains / shown, shown a gaining through our giving fountains / belate, belate of late can be a fountain / frowns, frowns settled into have left for the fountains light-hearted for men / sent, sent another well into our fountains / blown, blown examples and the samples simply material have gone to the fountains in love / good-bye, good-bye cords have cut the lessen, let us know the flow through fountains human / goodness, goodness known throughout these fountains / rest, rest along shores afforded through your fountains / fused,

fused applications to the fountains human / rest, rest in the shores fountain rich with love / peaks, peaks allow a christ rich core to sample the mantle placed in summits historically light within fountains / rally, rally for the simple jackson hole ranches peaked thorugh fountains / read, read often then the lips of those prayerful for the 97% who said, "yes" to the fountains within man / raveling, raveling has leapt to the paraphrase tossed across these fountains / guise, guise has gone, read the well, "within, fountains!" / geyser, geysers based have found fountains of the sort pooled at the foothills rich within human love / wet, wet with welling samples of the frequent fountains *wide energetically to truthfulness in love / splatters, splatters cost less when we win the fountains / hurtles, hurtles healed by the old faithful ways electric, a truest fountain / chills, chills have gone to the hermetic allow for these fountains / fallen, fallen sorts have cost less for the fountains / sort, sorts who said "YES" too, the fountains of love / orchids, orchids cost less for the fortunately raised Thai penned fountains on love / heavenly, heavenly into the free fountains / mantles, mantles crossed crust wise to the rising fountains / drill, drill has cost the crust a water table keep on fountains / absolute, absolute resolve through these fountains / confessed, confessed a new version to love of the fountains / mantles, mantles crossed, again, to these heavens humanly fountains / meet, meet one who lives within these fountains / surrender, surrender to the central fountains / warming, warming and the winning fountains / devotion, devotion and the details rich and the leaping flowers of fountains / necks, necks allowed a lightening fountain / crooks, crooks have gone to the singing fountains / captions, captions have torn the veil off these fountains / captured, captured and well then, for a feeling fountain / ascension, ascensions sunny into a fountain / fountain, fountain recovered through love / wonders, wonders who win our approving descend into a fountain human / finest, finest win fountains / loving, loving a living fountain / strength, strength gained through truthful explain of the lessons fountains / sure, sure in the resting fountains / optimum, optimum in cues for fountains / level, level in the leaving fountains / yes, yes to the listening fountains / often, often in a feeling fountain / precious, precious in a sealing fountain.

CHAPTER THREE

Step, step along lines and the punching accord for fountains / push, push allows a living fountain / won, won and the winning fountain / one, one who will, a fountain / good, good to a natural fountain / given, given to living fountains / fond, fond and the featured fountains / farewells, farewells and the freedom's fountains / trails, trails across fashion's fountains / sail, sail and the allowance for a fountain / still, still living's fountains / burst, burst through with your living fountains / nears, nears a loving fountain / pleasure, pleasure lines our fountains / held, held and the healing fountains / met, met along filling fountains / hospitable, hospitable and the thrilled with fountains / hostile, hostile often found a fountain / done, done dealt for fountains / dance, dance and the mention's fountain / chance, chance along a lightening fountain / little, little lives in fountains / estate, estates lost in fountains / escape, escape

less then fountains found are good to love / wants, wants cost most of fountains / loved, loved to the living fountains / relate, relate reaps a fountain / state, state suggested onto fountains / forgotten, forgotten funds are found for fountains / kept, kept applied to fountains / plausible, plausible shores on fountains / gaining, gaining allowed a fountain / weed, weed out your fountain place / calls, calls a ceiling off the fountains / hem, hem shown to healing fountains / sustain, sustain and the raining fountains / expect, expect and the respect for a fountain / perfection, perfection to the internal fountains / regarding, regarding and the central cords found to fountains / mates, mates met for favorable values onto fountains / entry, entry allows your fountains / success, success and the central plains one two fountains / scent, scent and the surgerically freed fountains / mercy, mercy allows these fountains / seats, seats and the mercy meant for fountains / villains, villains filed out to fountains / run, run along living fountains / rights, rights and the righteous fountains / runs, runs attendant to the fountains / reasons, reasons reach through these fountains / contend, contend affluent with a fountain / alone, alone allows a fountain / allowance, allowance giant with a fountain / endurance, endurance apparent then to fountains / values, values lost on fountain's surface / tunnels, tunnels lost and found for fountains / friend, friends forged through fountains / found, found a sample rich with fountains / worn, worn allow into a fountain / levels, levels advance through the frames for fountains / several, several ways to fend lightly through fountains / yours, yours is the year for fountains / patent, patents for the fountains / invent, invent a patented fountain.

CHAPTER FOUR

Careers, careers which clear your fountain / hum, hum a note worthy of the address invested in fountains / quarters, quarters laid around the edges played for fountains / square, square in squarely circled institutions of fountains / God, God gave us squarely a lasting fountain / heir, heir of the appraent humanity called precisely this, a fountain / human, human and the heraldic placement of a fountain / blends, blends ashen without platitudes of the featured fountains / principals, principals leveraged in the fountains / example, example and the simple patterns in fountains / trident, trident causes and the lessons arced through with fountains / framed, framed and the freedom rang to with fountains / fallow, fallow and the fellowship fountains / shallow, shallow and the shillings spents on fountains / draped, draped and the threshold pursued for the freshest fountains / dripping, dripping mentions and the mansions paved in golden fountains / depth, depth relays a relationship fixed through fountains / liquid, liquid and the led too, fountains / light, light and the leveraged fountains / water, water and the wedded fountains / earth, estranged and the arranged meanings on fountains / position, positions planned for in fountains / place, place avowed as interior in fountains / system, system suggested a shrugging fountain / taste, taste wins a fountain / trace, trace across a fountain's face / line, lines wide into a fountain / melchizedek, melchizedek meets in a melting fountain / sign, sign and the suggestions due a fountain / summary, summary and the thresheld fountain / buttery, buttery tastes and the sliding optimism for a fountain / creamy, creamy in willing fountains / collapse, collapse weds and the whirling fountains / birth, births blessed and the parental fountains / bulge, bulge belonging into a fountain / impregnate, impregnate a traditional fountain / self, self and the self-made fountains / love, love and the living fountains / loved, loved and the leading willing fountains / empires, empires and the traces mineralized through fountains / hiring, hiring and the feeling fountains / gate, gate and the gearing offerings on fountains / portal, portal and the placement of a fountain / orion, orion and the siren fresh in fountains / ransom, ransom and the reasoned fountains / resurgent, resurgent and the reasonable fountains / sides, sides and the signals fountains / wonder, wonder and the wholest fountain / warrants, warrants into fashionable fountains / woman, woman and the willing fountains / pictorial, pictorial and the pleasant fountains / planetary, planetary and the fountains within our levelness / guides, guides and the gazing appearance of fathom's deep in the mentioned fountains / positive, positive tools and the planetary experiences in fountains / seeks, seeks and the signal's fountains / promotes, promotes and the precious fountains / directive, directive invectives of the thinnest fountains / dialect, dialect details impaled forth as fountains / tongues, arranging reverence for the fountains / quells, quells another's fountains / tends, tends a target's fountains / increase, increase allows a fountain / distant, distant and the distance spent for fellow fountains / acid, acid whips to fountains.

CHAPTER FIVE
Gears, gears and the guides laid forth to featured fountains / orthorhomboid, orthorhomboid and the sent into fountains / rhombic, rhombic and the reading fountains / sullen, sullen and the sheering fountains / blocked, blocked rescinds onto fountains / experience, experience suggestive for a fitting fountains / shock, shock exudes a pleasant fountain / surrenders, surrenders another's fountains / import, import sorted in selected fountains / strengthen, strengthen your lengthened fountain / gain, gain and the gathering extrude for a fountain / ingrain, ingrain and the reading fountains / properties, properties placed at these fountains / minerals, minerals managed unto occupied fountains / breastplate, breastplate worn off by fountains / peeks, peeks and the seeking fountains / one, one and the wisdom for a fountain / too, too and the simple fountains / describe, describe implies a fountain / minerals, minerals amused in fountains / reference, reference of the theoretical fountains / bought, bought and the settlement for fountains / sought, sought and the soothing fountains / vibrate, vibrate and the vacate into a fountain / radical, radical reside in the refinement for a fountain / align, align sent for and platitudes for a fountain / illustrate, illustrate a reaching fountain / path, path surges to a fountain / both, both and the belts found in fountains / God, God and the greetings gauged through fountains / numbers, numbers nestle into a fathering fountain / managed, managed and the murmuring fountains / relations, relations and the relationship for fountains / retrieve, retrieve and the ranking for fountains / escape, escape and the shaking fountains / sought, sought and

the soothing fountains / supercede, supercede and the reading fountains / superficial, superficial and the fortunate facilities for fountains / fictitious, fictitious and the leased fountains / planes, planes who touch at thriving fountains / assurance, assurance sent fatherly fountains / potassi, potassi embraced as a miracle massed at a place tracing rich fountains / patternal, patternal to a patterned fountain / patterns, patterns paged from fountains / imply, imply and the simplify found for fountains / cells, cells allowed a reaping fountain / swell, swell insured to fountains / labor, labor leans into a fountain / elestial, elestial supereced and the mending fountain / ametrine, ametrine allow for the fountains / green, green examples and the smallest fountains / pubescent, pubescent metatronics and the sonic allow for a fountain / sheen, sheen and the simple floating foundations for a fountain / nob, nob and the sneering lost to a polished fountain / angelic, angelic and the smallest fountains / terrorize, terrorize has risen to a fountain / polished, polished and the principles for a fountain / aura, aura and the rewarded fountains / magenta, magenta allows a fountained flow / golden, golden redeeming and the fountains flowering / clasp, clasp and the simple fountains / tanzanite, tanzanite and the triple fountains / screen, screen and the lightest fountains / accumen, accumen gathers fortunate to these fountains.

CHAPTER SIX
Eyes, eyes and the spending of a fountain / sapphire, sapphire infused and the movements sent to miracles for a fountain / blue, blue and the mystery of a fountain / belgian, belgian and winging fountains / horse, horses held for a fountain / Herkimers, Herkimers and the laughing fountains / voice, voice and the values spent in fountains / solace, solace and the simple fountains / solitude, solitude and the surges of joyous fountains / spell, spell indicative for a filling fountain / illustrious, illustrious and the sorted fountains / montage, montage and the meetings sung through fountains / photons, photons and the smiling fountains / photos, photos and the fiscal fountains / configure, configure a future fountain / sheet, sheet and the simple fountains / read, reads and the risen fountains / reveal, reveal and the reverence sent to fountains / introduce, introduce and the risen found as fountains / induct, join a simple fountain / initiate, initiate a conversion to a fountain / flowers, flowers surging to fountains / agate, agate allowed a gathering fountain / support, support suggested for a fountain / traumas, traumas over and the duration is paid for a fountain / reflexive, reflexive treaty and the trample past of a fountain / release, release allows a fountain / promontory, promontory appointed to a fountain / point, point to an apexed fountain / apex, apex sought for fountains / sent, sent to a mission mentioned as a fountain / size, size spent for fountains / caloric, caloric afford for the treated fountains / input, input soothes a fountain staged / extensively, extensively fixed in delegations alluring to a fountain / lavendar, lavendar legends for a fountain / duals, duals past through a fountain / dwells, dwells and the lessons fountains / delves, delves and the drilling fountains / docile, docile and the dues laid forth as fountains / durative, durative and the duration spent to fountains / deliver, deliver that thronging fountain

/ docile, docile and the dedicate unto a fountain / documents, documents altered less as fountains / dash, dash affronts a fountain / deny, envy denied and the ceiling cost has set on lessened love and the offensive fountains / decide, decide to detail your fountains / found, found a features fountains / detail, details polished through your fountains / peace, peace allows feeling fountains / seek, seek as essential to your fountains / decreed, decreed reveal of a fountain / school, school and the levels learned and fountains / arts, arts and the simple fountains / hearts, hearts and the hills of heavenly fashions fountains / scholastic, scholastic cures and the cords cut for fountains / courteous, courteous and the creations sent to fountains / abide, abide allowed a frequent fashionable fountain / allow, allow a thorough fountain / sort, sorts supple to a fountain / help, help and the hustle past a fountain / seen, seen as sent for a fountain / heavens, heavens and the gated fountains / love, love to be a fountain.

CHAPTER SEVEN

Nutritive, nutritive rewards fundamental fountains / supplement, sent these fountains / sates, sates us, fountains / pommel, pommel finds fountains / worlds, worlds is in fountains / place, fountains place leads too, worlds / penultimate, penultimate spent within fountains ./upreme, supreme sees, fountains / succulent, succulent sent fountains / secure, secure seeds fountains / severence, severence sent too, fountains / sent, sent us too, fountains / contain, contain suggest fountains / spatial, spatial suggest fountains / spurn, spurn spent, fountains / spout, spout with your fountains / where, where is your fountains / when, when in too, fountains / how, how then's fountains / why, why is in the fountains / candid, candid came your fountains / pertains, pertanins too, fountains / pronto, pronto pays, fountains / promote, promote meets foutains / devote, devote dues, fountains / dally, dally out fountain / dashing, dashing suggest fountains / durable, durable dates fountains / documentation, made, fountains / tooth, tooth nails fountains / teeth, teeth touch fountains / white, white worn bubble's fountain / wide, wide wins fountains / wells wells widest fountains / western, western ways fountains / wanted, wanted with fountains / well, well met fountains / welling, welling deals fountains / willing, willing to be fountains / transmute, transmute trends fountains / forgive, forgive runs, fountains / forgone, forgone concludes fountains / fork, a fork found, fountains / fulcrum, fulcrum funds fountains / fossil, fossil fountains / fossil's, fossil's fuel, fountain / plan, plan too, fountains / quiets, quets quip fountains / quells, quells most, fountain / hush, hush ups your fountains / brush, brush abouts fountains / ends, ends nip fountains / ponder, ponder without fountains / freed, freed within fountains / load, load up's fountains / concur, concur wanted fountains / episode, an episodemade for fountains / completes, completes curb fountains / measures, measures met in an alabaster fountain / festive, festive friends and the spending fountains / forgiven, forgiven and allowed a treasured fountain / fresh, fresh and respected in the fountains of love / leaves, leaves allow a dream fountain / the ways, the ways home to love's fountains.

CHAPTER EIGHT

Blackest has become released to the light of the decision to plunge into love's fountains / won, won by another's wonderful smile and the rearrange required to live well within a hurtling comet's tail, a fountain deep in spacey delight / heart's, heart's bursting has found a new sound the life led by a light stroke, the padle through fountains for love / burst, burst at a balance and the challenges stage as electrical within the pull of the vitamin rich dialect called fountains / forgiven, forgiven the hunch to bunch together without loving fountains / cursed, cursed has crumbled into a blues level with foundational fountains in man / allocated, allocated has sated her strands through the fountains human / light, light can elevate us to the planes Andeluvian and the Himalayan bands of auric fountains / dimensions, dimensions may detail your caroling employ of the stoic-less ventures and the values vaunted through a returned prodigal and the stall patterns filled in healing align within sun's shining fountains / plunder, plunder has led to a sword cutting in to the cords of neglect and lessen and thin breaking example of good-bye's level stretch into a fountain human / embrace, embrace her as you see her, fountains / sight, sight has led to a level field of morrain remain and the reminder that still is living within the inside spin to a righteous spiral human, a fountain found, love / hallelujahs, hallelujahs ringing and the choir spirals in to celtic longing and the energetic agree that presence and essence and basic humanity rings eternally as a fountain planned for man / rung, rung by a ringing I sing of love's fountains / agreed, agreed throughout the span to see only rainbows in humanity's fountains / meeting, meeting now set has sent enticing signals to the spiritual begin to remember light fountains in man / schemes, schems are over and the healer has set a planet to spinning along the shores electrical within fountains human / solid, solid I stand upon the rock of belief and the heart of agreement signed for deliver to the givers human / pour, pour a deeper witness to the lover God can be and the Christos now delivering the daily pedigree, God to Christ to Me, an electric span, a healing plan, the perfect trinity, Holy Spirit within has seen that the maximum delivery is fed through fountains lightest leaping across the majesty of galactic inner spirals and the nebula set free to discover Orion, Pleiades, Cygnus, and accounting now within has added fourth, Arcturus, the pen of heavens surrender to the truth that God exists and the list has grown as now we add our own, the Earth to trinity, One to One we are passing on the Sun within a span, and do you remember the throat which stood a stand for teh mention that Christ has sent an envoy rich with ink to simmer moist within this earth and teach you holy heart to manage sacred in you life and legend in you start to remember truly this, the ofuntains light within, may God be with thee, in thee, through thee, and of thee, as all is well within, without, and shouting "Yes!" can pass the test unto delivery of the illusion that anything less is more, you are loved, loved, and delivered to the heart within the door, the hallelujah threshold reached and the rush is on to deliver Earth to God, let us be electrically divine, detailed, and delivered fresh to this notion of light in the fountains human / porous, porous has risen to fill the fountains human / rocks, rocks leap aquafied to speak of "fountains" / weather, weather has whistled in keeping explain of the detail that remains in loving accord of the fortunes spent "serving theLord", shall we remember rich within has won the world's fountains / rocked, rocked and asserted by the fountains. fountains in the sky's regain of the remainder human, fountains / steams, steams example can muster a miracle for the fountains human / explain, explain again, the fountains human / drilling, drilling reeling details met for the fountains featured along the nets of loving cast to these fountains / depth, depth has reached your shor's fountains / sourced, sourced by a thundering voice called sweetly "fountains" / weathering, weathering the willing appliance called fountains / waters, waters spread to surrender into a filling fountain / wash, wash wells of fountains / hawaiian, hawaiian rights patiently await your miraculous return to the light fields human, go now to these fountains / Pacific, Pacific appear near the store of fountains / cleft, cleft held openly to the core surged fountains / flight, flight has flown to a fickle forgive and the legends exposed as the wizard's impose on the forgone conclude that rude has no room in the fountains human / arrange, arrange a date to rearrange these fountains / meetings, meetings et can surrender to the living fountains human / danger, danger has overcome the success of forgiven fountains / gate, gateway held has opened again, pen the launching and deliver the ten who know the human soul can leap across light lanes to the resource the one heavenly and the shrugging forgetting can fissures now heal by agreeing remember is the curing pill, in the fields Alyssian I have seen the open pen of heaven and the hearts who all agree that heaven has met the bet upon this light humanity, know the way within the fountains / potential, potential may mention the vital ripen of the fountains filled with love / globes, globes spun may see the detail for the feelings fondly human / glow, glwo to the spiritual revival called the spiral lightly human / minerals, minerals mix in the mention lightly human / boron, boron belted through the humans / chemist, chemist placed at the presence cubed to human codes with the fountains electric / wells, wells placed flowing near the present human fountains / porous, porous and the flowing fountains / eruptive, eruptive leaping fountains / vectors, vectors voiced miraculous to the metaphoric fountains / forecast, forecast focused in fountains / destruct, destruct has off become to fountains / create, create a creative resouce for fountains / subtracts, subtracts total has reached epic code for fountains / add, add a miracle to the fountains / technique, technique sought becomes a fountain / sands, sand of spun deliver to the mile wide glow called fountains / bands, bands now leap to encode these fountains / interference, interference sent to reconnect the vote in fountains / slick, slick with a notion forged to fountains / promise, promise made kept fountains / space, space allowed fountains / periods, periods pulsing fountains / monitored, monitored touring fountains / invoked, invoked an allowing fountain.

CHAPTER NINE
Buy, buy the vector chinese to a yellow fountain / China, China leapt with neglect forgone to the conclude that moods are amused in fountains / break, break for the features fountains / Tibet, Tibet

chosen as risen to the clouds set on mountains peaked at freedom's seek for the patient appear of the renegade extreme who allow surrnder her forgive. May we be inspired to see the lgiht within their fountains purged by swords and birds of bleeding prey and the tiget risen now will see the fall interiorly, know the rise of peace yellow bird of light divinity / apart, apart to a miraculous mention of the funding fountains / own, own to the loaned fountains / kept, kept in a resource miraculous and the metatronic accord for these fountains / waters, waters wed for the fortunate fountains / pillow, pillow and the Metatronic mention of funded fountains / fine, fine and the lines lean to our triple fountains / lava, lava and the leading ofuntains / topple, topple has simple rewarded fountains / mountain, mountain mending of the fondest fountains / mountains, mountains and the metatronic fountains within a wondering sword called lightest codes of love / peak, peak and the peeking fountains / stoves, stoves simultaneous to these fountains / sanskrit, sanskrit and the shrines found in fountains / halcyon, halcyon and the eruptive fountains / honed, honed and the healing fountains / stoned, stoned and the resources sent into fountains / tibetan, tibetan coded fountains / tied, tied unto fountains / tide, tide leaps within fountains / spelling, spelling spilling surrender to a filling fountain / Egypt, Egypt coded to fountains / flowed, flowed informationally to a fountain / red, red and the readings sent into coded fountains / wove, wove and the weaving fountains / hebrew, hebrew allowance afforded the forging forgiving to a feathery fountain / fed, fed allow a fortunate fountain / erupts, erupts empirical to a miracle's fountains / lasso, lasso loaned a lyrical mention often into fountains / lope, lope across the central states of fountains / spirals, spirals swim in forgiving fountains / spins, spins and the spoken mention of fountains / travels, travels and the fountains receptive to love / hemp, hemp and the held forth in fountains / happen, happen and the heraldic rise to fountains / hole, hole welded along the ledge of fountains / opened, opened and living fountains / days, days and the durations on fountains / dates, dates of the deify of fountains / renew, renew and the strengthen in a fountain / rations, rations sunk into through a following fountain / reap, reap afforded a longing fountians / rewards, rewards apply to fountains / steep, steep to a leaping fountain / steps, steps made to erase the leased fountains / shorn, shorn of the wingless fountains / wedge, wedge throngs iwth lightening fountains / flesh, flesh of the filling fountains / levels, levels of the linking fountain / one, one who has worn a fountain / tens, tens who say "this is a fountain" / strings, strings break within fountains / thanks, thanks applied for and fountains / gratitudes, gratitudes applied to fountains / avenues, avenues encoded by a fountain / appears, appears and the listed fountains / warps, warps and the wedded fountains / theoretically, theoretically encoded in fountains / twisted, twisted and the whistling afforded in fountains / rings, rings and the random assort through fountains.

CHAPTER TEN
Insolence, insolence and the reaping offered through fountains / thrills, thrills sought through the fountains / wonders, wonders and

the wisdom made to fountains / articles, articles and the surging offered a fountain / fashions, fashions forged in fountains / facets, facets of the miraculous sort who sing to fountains / prints, prints placed at the corners on mountain streams and fonder fountains / gardens, gardens white with fountains / one-eighth, one-eighth the wonder for a fountain / zero, zero a miracle wed to fountains / magnetize, magnetize the rising sign for fountains / winds, winds and the worlds that collide through fountains / winded, winded and the mined for fountains 14f.ellow, fellow and the filling fountains / models, models and the meeting made for fountains / partners, partners and the penchant for a fountain / lanterns, lanterns and the learning fountains / many, many and the meeting fountains / found, found and the features finished within fountains / fonder, fonder and the fathoms forged through fountains / trace, trace and the triple fountains / couples, couples and the duration for a fountain / collide, collide retailed and the threshold leaps to a fountain / completes, completes and the links forged thoroughly through a fountain / traits, traits truest to a fountain / finished, finished and the physical fountains / under, under and the submerging fountains / through, through and the thrilling fountains / lovers, lovers and the leaping fountains / placed, placed and the participation of these fountains / penned, penned allow for the planning participation on fountains / general, general to the miracle of fountains / decisions, decisions detailed in an arrangement forged through miracles of fountains / risen, risen and the ridden gain of fountains / rise, rise to the miracle for a fountain / relates, relates an allow for these fountains / reagrds, regards us as well to a fountain / climbs, climbs a cord to a fountain / conceeds, conceeds delight with a fountain / establish, establish a lettering fountain / rations, rations and the relations settled for and fountains / given, given and the gaining fruits of fashionable fountains / gifts, gifts and the five felt through fountains / theories, theories elect and the leap across fountains / rates, rates and these readings flown across fountains / living, living and the features sought through fountains / lifts, lifts a mission to our fountains / mavericks, mavericks and the miracle's fountains / regarded, regarded as the sword of meteoric fountains / plays, plays and the assuage of fountains / equals, equals a qualified fountain / place, place and the penning fountains / weights, weights and the winning fountains / every, every finished code of fountains / one, one who wins for fountains / thermal, thermal attend to fountains / use, use a listed fountain / each, each and the ringing fountains / all, all who say we will be a "fountain" / thermos, thermos thrown along the lines of fountains / many, many and the metatronic attempt on fountains / regarding, regarding allow for fountains / downfalls, downfalls swept to fountains / revenues, revenues rewarded for these fountains.

CHAPTER ELEVEN
Lumps, musings made a lumps detain for fountains / bumps, bumps across a parallel cost for fountains fused / curves, curves curated as durated to a fountain / waves, waves and the living fountains / minds, minds meet to fountains / differing, differing allowance for these fountains / frequents, frequents afforded a filling fountain / face, face acquires a fountain / pluck, pluck opens up a fountain / strings, strings stirring a fountain / correspond, correspond a course on fountains / tunes, tunes allow a fountain / energies, energies code a double fountain / moods, moods and the miracle's fountains / moving, moving to a mantle's fountains / words, words wisest still to fountains / numbers, numbers nestle into a fountain / spatials, spatials plunge to a fountains / facials, facials and the features fountains / festered, festered to features of the mountains fountains / nickels, nickels and the nestling fountains / bathes, bathes and the blunder's fountains / elastic, elastic and the rely told to fountains / bursts, bursts bemused through fountains / thrown, thrown to a thronging fountain / bubbles, bubbles belonging unto a fountain / curative, curative rely for a fountain / durate, durate allows a detailed fountain / speeds, speeds lightly to a fountain / curation, curation of the duration's fountains / patient, patient allow for a fountain / pursue, pursue a line for a feature's fountains / penultimate, penultimate panels for a fountain / plenty, plenty pens a watery fountain / penchant, penchant for a pleasing fountain / pools, pools allowed a fountain / perfections, perfections surge through a fountain / cascade, cascade clues a fountain / flakes, flakes afforded a fountain / snows, snows agreed to the penning succeed forgrd by loving fountains / banks, banks and the durations found for fountains / overhead, overhead and the features fountains / mentions, mentions and the musings fountains / moons, moons over miracles made for love's fountains / Lassen, Lassen's volcanic resdue has come sprial to a fountain / Shasta, Shasta allows a fountain / klamath, klamath clued to fountains / Hood, Hood afforded a future fountain / crater, crater red with glowing fountains / strung, strung to a line living for fountains / lines, lines leap to a fountain's fields / dialing, dialing dear to a feeling fountain / codes, codes read of fountains / plows, plows clear to fountains / snowing, snowing steers a fountain / showing, showing a vertical fountain / burrows, burrows allow a building fountain / cares, cares accord a fountain / expansion, expansions plunge to fountains / spent, spent winning for a fountain / weeks, weeks seeking a fountain / solid, solid to a fortunate fountain / elevation, elevation of the revealing fountains / drawn, drawn along lines on fountains.

CHAPTER TWELVE
American, American fountains / aum, aum to the om sung fountains / given, given a living grace for fountains / hands, hands held on fountains / source, source surged to fountains / wealth, wealth applies to fountains / worth, worht middle grounded for a fountain / keep, keep a sake for a fountain / kid, kid won to fountains / campaign, campaign gains a fountain / patience, patience pelts us within a heart's grip of fountains / planning, planning a fission's mountain for fountains / kidneys, kidneys and the curing splendors for a fountain / keep, keep accrues to fountains / masters, masters and the movement to fountains / founts, founts and the counting mounting fountains / mental, mental and the explain of the gaming fountains / explain, explain and the saving fountains / architects, architects and the dealt regard for fountains / artists, artisit and the starting great unto fountains / chaos, chaos and the stakes set for fountains / pins, pins and the supremest fountains / pine, pine

allows a fountain / pints, pints and the giantest fountain / promise, promise and the fountains of purest love / desire, desire and the attire sent for fountains / detonate, detonate a tone for a premium fountain / station, stations attendant to a fountain / phase, phase won for winning fountains / premier, premier attired in a penning fountain / premium, premium assort to a fountain / then, then allows a fountain / honorable, honorable and the fountains fused along lines electric too / means, means to beam to and fountains allowed a loving lean to light / medium, medium metatronics and the sonic's fountains / coves, coves allowed a sunset move into miracle's fountains / done, done for the dealing fountains / vacant, vacant allowance for the fountains / alue, value surges to a fountain / ates, gates dealing in fountains / particular, particular to a miracle sought for fountains / propogate, propogate and the explanation sent for fountains / explanation, explanation sent for mirroring fountains / expell, expell and the excell for a mirroring fountain / honorable, honorable and the findings forged through fountains / means, means and the mentions fountains / medium, mediums used as fountains / capes, capes and the cubicals of fountains / vacant, vacant to the filling fountains / value, value and the patience sought for fountains / particular, particular and the purging comes to fountains / propogate, propogate and the rational fountains / explanation, explanation and the drains off to fountains / expell, expell less, explain more, for fountains / presence, presence and the winning fountains / print, print and the points made to fountains / speak, speak a spilling fountain / wins, wins another's fountain / avert, avert and the skirt worn through fountains / patients, patients paged to afforded fountains / continue, continue a winning fountain / eventual, eventual to a ritual fountain / impair, impair a spare fountain / doubt, doubt has sold a weekend pass to fountains.

CHAPTER THIRTEEN
Defend, defend a detail for a fountain / deny, deny off and fountains gained through love / decibels, decibels and the hearing fountains / cusp, cusp stretched to mention fountains / cup, cup overflowing through a capture free fountain / project, project penned and allowed a fountain / love, love alike and sunny in a fountain / like, like applied to as fountains / lay, lay overall to fountains / layers, layers finished glisten in fountains / last, last to the past led fountains / lover, lover made a fountain / likening, likening a listening fountain / launder, launder a level fountain / lone, lone to the owning fountain / lisp, lisp lost to fountains / clears, clears enoughs taste fountains / care, fonder care's fountains / abounds, fountains abound in love / introduce, introduce sent on 4's, fountains / Greek, Greek great's fountains / look, look out, fountains in / liken, liken us too, fountains / text, text tracked, fountains / Latin, Latin lends fountains / translates, translates sent, fountains / symbols, symbols suggest fountains / translate, translate trues, fountains / teach, fountains teach your values / voltage, voltage vaulted leaps, fountains / bullets, bullets out fountains in, love / code, code cares for fountains / unwound, unwound found us, fountains / care, care for us, fountains / too, too said, "fountains" / ascribe, acribe us, fountains / scribe, a

scribe met in fountains / inscribe, inscribe within this, fountains / incrypt, incrypt sent too, fountains / inscript, inscript becomes fountains / translate, translate said, fountains / type, type said, "fountains" / Lebanese, Lebanese leads, fountains / variety, variety veils fountains / remember, remember reads fountains / recognize, recognize us, fountains / cheer, cheer well's fountains / capable, capable copies in fountains / scores, scores oat, fountains / skeins, skeins on, fountains / yarn, yarn young a fountain / talk, talk about her space, fountains / trues, trues our well's fountains / truth, truth follow truth too, a fountain / talking, talking troops fountains / love, love to be fountains deep / walking, walking to a trance within fountains / wedding, wedding waits to a fountains / bets, bets on release too a fountain / booth, booth beat upon and then a fountain / bequile, bequile less and rest within fountains / revile, revile and the without fountains / recognize, recognize fountains place. / registration, registration set for the fondest stream of fountains placed.

THE FOND-MENTS
LEVEL 62

CHAPTER ONE

Fondly, fondly done too, a found message / due, due and into thee, fond / desires, desires fond to swan found / dream, fond in a dream a tow of cream in love / delegation, delegation delivers a found require for, love's fond / cues, cues to the fond ages of new / consistent, consistent to everything can fondness / cream, cream fondly measured / current, curent capabilities fondest love / regard, regard your fondest / relate, relate manners as God is fond / dues, dues date's found fondest / desperate, desperate deals conclude fondly / concur, concur that we are the spark's fondest / calibrate, calibrate weight's fodness / fames, fames fill is fondest at love / sodium, sodium pumps truest at the apex of love's fondest glib / freed, freed to a filling fondness / found, found / especially succinct within a redesigned fondness / fond, fond of the featured fondness / flank, flanks furrow less with light regard fondness / roast, roast and the rubbles spent for fondness / risen, risen adn the ressurrection spent on fondness / ghost, ghost and the glistening fondness / gallant, gallant and the saints for fondness / stand, stand and the delivery for a fondness / ascend, ascend and the elation of a fondness / plan, plan and the fondly penned love / pertinent, pertinent to an urgent fondness / point, point across a later-day fondness / port, ports across a fondness / portal, portal sorted of a fondness / arrive, arrive a llows a fondness for love / frees, frees our portal to see a fondness / freedom, freedom found in fondness / feels, feels aloft and fondest / like, like has explain at fondness / heals, heals and the zealing fondness / rise, rise and the risen too, of fondness // skies, skies accept our skirting issues for fondness / elect, elect a respectful speech aobut loving fondness / suspect, suspect goes to the reeling flows of a husband's fondness / runs, runs a course fondly / course, course clears fondly / erect, erect in zeal and fondness / suspect, suspect and the becoming fondness / sustain, sustain allowed suggestively for the fondness / explain, explain a gaining fondness / fondness, fondness has found an I AM built fibrilated to a heart felt aspire to see love / splashed, splashed to a simple shore for the fondest / across, across news love rules our living fondness / apply, apply to the fondly / faith, faith advances to a fondness / influence, influence gains us an advanced fondness / coincide, coincide aside and the cure for our fondness / tradition, traditional reigns traditionally as a past secure aligns fondly / natives, natives surge to portect the fondest / priests, priests allow the reading fondness / pearls, pearls exact detail the free fondness / whence, whence allowed? fondness / legends, legends are gone to fondness / placement, placement has cost less to trail for the fellow's fondness / plans, plans to be fondest to love / legends, legends of the living fondness

CHAPTER TWO

Ignore, ignore and the shores sold for the overides fondest / deride, eride and the risen aclaim for a farm fond / decide, decide to be lively for the fondness / conceed, conceed to deed the tube into our fondness / inside, inside our stride is the fondness / declares, declares and the dues paid unified by a fondness for love / decoration, decoration and the dues fondness / assign, assign and the sending fashion for fondness / courts, courts and your curing session for fondness / cavity, cavity closed through an openness to love's fondness / opens, opens and the touring fondness / planetary, planetary puring and the feelings caused through fondness / pursue, pursue and the evocation on a fondness / opens, opens apply is found through fondness / thanks, thanks and the thrown into fondness / sex, sex and the ceilings spun to fondness / orgasm, orgasm acclaimed by a flaming affairs fondness / heals, heals appear near teh earth's fondness / translate, translate a living fondness / edit, edit appears near a fondness / less, less is lunged past through social applications for a fondness / clarify, clarify and the cods read for fondness / more, more means and the filling fondness / present, present to a penciled in fondness / evocative, evocative in a riveting fondness / clarity, clarity and the codes read fondly of love / acts, acts pad past the present forgetting to a fondness for love / 64, 64 wages paid for teh sin-free delivery of the codices of love's fondness for man / stages, stages attired through as healing fondness for humanity / paths, paths paged through declare four widths to the myths of fondness / lines, lines emergent archetypes set for fondness socially / forgive, forgive has forgone to the falling into fondness / foregone, foregone has gone to the falls of fondness / foreign, foreign awareness has surged to the midpoint's madness for a fondness oof love / find, find a future sealed in fondness / fine, fine equations allow our fondness / equal, equal to a sequel for our fondness / equate, equate states that love arose through fondness / ignore, ignore the suggestion that left to reflection can field only fondness / implore, implore that more is the mentioned fondness / estates, estates grow through the shadows palyed to fondness for love / give, give us suggestions reference yourfondness / astrologic, astrologic logic said "fondness for the fellowship" of love's living gifts / assurance, assurance suggested into the fondness / timed, timed allow for the thankful fondness / alchemical, alchemical miracles made to the fondest / attitudes, attitudes move to fondness / yoga, yogas yules rule to fondness / practice, practice and the pens of fondness / place, place and the made for fondness / ports, ports profiled by fondness / privacy, privacy allows a fondness / place, place retailed in fondness / proceed, proceed and the fondly due a feeling's love / lead, lead allows a fondness / lift, lift a gift into eyes seen as fondest / see, see as led unto a fondness / sunshine, sunshine sealed for fondness / delve, delve allows a living fondness / agree, agree to see a ladder grown to fondness / succeed, succeed and the fondess led to love / states, states who seal a living fondness for light / durable, durable intend has found a filling life mate in love's fondness / world, world in notion and the mahareshi's blend for peace is our most innocent fondness / often, often others fail to see the cult inside their own eyes into fondnes / which, which neighbor do you stress most gently for? / fondly, always fondly.

CHAPTER THREE

Connect to the core of fondness / explore, explore a shore as fine as thee, fondness / defile, defile has gone to a cost for less and the living dues paid to fondness / deny, deny has dealt with a fondness / decide, decoded decide to ride the seas to love's fondness / decry, decry can cripple without fondness / doors, doors to a pool opened through fondness / open, opens a platitude for loving fondness / agrees, agrees to see the simple fondness for love / access, access granted to the remnant sent for fondness / alpine, alpine exclusion allowed a fondness for love's fortunate shores / allow, allow a realignment to the fondest suns of love / climbing, climbing cores revealed to a fond healing code for love / concur, concur that insured by love is the fondest code / cooperate, cooperate politely with the encodement of fondness for love / cooperative, cooperative to an operative equation and the sequester meant for fondest love / giving, giving allows a fondness for love / gains, gains are refrains for love's encode to fondness / alchemical, alchemical miracles succeed at fondness / flames, flames bolt to the filling fondness / straighten, straighten your agree to be fondest of love / energetic, energetic allowance has sent a storm to the fondness of love / locks, locks of and the living / well to shore for fondness / navels, navels burst throught the quelling fondness / genitals, genitals rub fondly with the oils of love / passing, passing dashing fondness / dynamic, dynamic accept of the concept fondness / lessons, lessons learned and the learning has led to our fondness / tantric, tantric apply can see your fondness / flowers, flowers measured fondly / loved, loved erratics gone to measured fondness / ecstasy, ecstasy has sent me to the shores of fondness / prana, prana and the mantle broken through fondly / heads, heads droop with fondness / pursuit, pursuit has gone to the songs for fondness / import, import the sort who find a fondness for love / pursuant, pursuant to the clause find fondness in love / visual, visual and spiritual fondness / sort, sort of the sets fondest / unbound, unbound can sound for the findings fondest / blend, blends show our fondness for love / soft, soft is the suggestion for your fondness / parts, parts who play fondly / subtle, subtle flavors burst in fondness / image, image apparent to your meaningful fondness / fires, fires escape to the shores fondest / both, both have sent their fondness through love / embodied, embodied and emboldened by the planetary align inside humanity's fondness for the violet flames of love / drawn, drawn to the blues forgiven for their fondness / circulates, circulates a state of seated fondness / lights, lights leap to the lending fondness / published, published and accomplished our sheering fondness / firing, firing has launched an assuring fondness for love / angelic, angelic support has come to your aid, fondly / allowing, allowing has assured your fondest dreams core to alightwithin love / ashen, ashen passion has gone to the shores fondest / white, white in suggestion of the heated fondness / wide, wide to a wisdom for the filling fondness / witness, witness sent to love you fondly / widens, widens a path to those fondest / wallowing, wallowing over through the fondness / willows, willows converge at the merger fondest / mutual, mutual the end to the meanings fondest.

CHAPTER FOUR

Mercurial, mercurial in measures meant for assure and the fondness of love / Michael, Michael said be fondest of love / dog, dog detail said "unconditionally" fond / dancing, dancing in chancing assure of the filling fondness of love / entwine, entwine only dear to your fondness / comport, comport sorted through by her fondness / carry, carry the earth well within your fondness / all, all is well within our willing fondness / alleviates, alleviates gifts are fondest for love / lessons, lessons linking to our fondness / learned, learned apparently by fondness / inquire, inquire sired to fondness / allows, allows a living linking of fondness / appreciate, appreciate how we sing often fondly / appearance, appearance comes into your fondness / attire, attire allows a present fondness / transmute, transmute a repute for fondness / translate, translate your tools as a fondness for for love / techniques, techniques appy to your fondest loves / purity, purity appears near your fondness for love / scenes, scenes repeated near your fondness / scenario, scenario succeeds at fondness / inclines, inclines launched to fondness / needs, needs met in significant fondness / harmonics, harmonics heal your fondness / synthesis, synthesis given a fondness for love / initiates, initiates a living fondness / initial, initial miracles for the fondest / strength, strength has cost your love for fondness / contend, contend has worn through to fondness / content, content in recall fondest / underlying, underlying lines converge in fondness / reality, reality has registered here at fondness / impact, impact suggests a fondness / comport, comport sorted through to fondness / connotes, connotes a note for fondness / casual, casual to mannerisms subtle within fondness / apparent, apparent to strands fonder still in love / access, access the substitutes who knew a dancing fondness / casual, casual affairs and the flinging fondness / apparent, apparent still is the sealing fondness for love / access, access allowed to the soaring fondness for love / angular, angular in triangular pleas for loving fondness / prance, prancing freely to living fondness / define, define a sign as fondest / design, design a shingle which says "fondest" / decide, decide to be fonder still / dancing, dancing allowance of the fondest lines / coinsertion, coinsertion figures into loving fondness / invert, invert squires a shuttled fondness / inversion, inversion occuring near the lines fondest / sick, sick to the point of fondness / solar, solar showers sent to fondness / planes, planes emerge and swerve to find your fondness / plexus, plexus lectures forgiven as we refine your fondness / plexi, plexi paints a perfect fondness for light forgiveness of love / particular, particular to the mriacle, I have fond memories of the carollingness of love / participates, participates another well into our fondness / inspect, inspect the lines and the living attitude for fondness / gradient, gradient agrees we will live near our fondest dreams / graduations, graduations granted to the living fountains of fondness for love / grew, grew another's winging living fondness / green, gree in tea's gazing fondness / regarding, regarding application too, fondness.

CHAPTER FIVE

Bills, bills of quiet regard for the former reveal and the hearkening case for good God, gold One, love is, kindly fond of your directives / votes, votes cast for the fondness won through love / troublesome, troublesome cords are cut today for the fellowship of fondest love / sodium, sodium insert is mentioned again and the pumps turned up to listen to love's fondness for the tastes of love / powers, powers allow a living fondess to return / play, play well at loving fondness / keys, keys are set and the cords cut to show us your fondness for truest love / success, success has mentioned your fondness for love's core / drums, drums beat the message, she has won her independence from captivity in love without fondness / dress, dress for the stages of fondness / attend, attend a playful fondness / attune, attune means fondness for the reactions to your love / incline, incline reached for fondly / inclination, inclination staged through her fondness / inkling, inkling sent to the lingering fondness / internal, internal arrange means a mentioned fondness / forgive, forgive done, fond won, love / moves, moves to the status funded fondly / movement, movement sent through loving fondness / comment, comments seal at fondness / constant, constant to impost on your fondness / seats, seats found near your fondness / concur, concur to leave for fondness / solution, solution sent through your fondness / solvent, solvent intrigue with her fondness / simultaneous, simultaneous expose of the meaning's fondest / embraces, embraces arranged through teh deeming fondness / blame-less, blame-less to the encoded fondness for love / synthesis, synthesis arranged through healing fondness / intrigued, intrigued allowance of these fondest greetings / triggers, triggers arranged in fondness / strength, strength gaining fondness / equal, equal suggestions of our fondness lingering still in the fringes fondest / aware, aware of the sending fondness / selfish, selfish has cost core fondness / straits, straits now cast to the crossing fondness for true love / states, states voting in true fondness / grades, grades suggested won fondly / gradients, gradients respect your choices fondest / grilled, grilled over and the fondness for love is found / gravitate, gravitate to the chores less often more fonfly found / reveal, reveal a respect for fondness in lure's loves / rally, rally to the reasons round your purest finds fondest for love / rescue, rescue a notion fondest to love / rates, rates set, abide, fondly / raspberry, raspberry mergers made pages for purest fondness / brazil, brazil blue in a portal for the fondest loves / bore, bore to the center of fondness / freaks, freaks allowed a fondness / frail, frail goes to the fondest clothing worn / full, full escape allowed through fondness / frill, frill and the seals to fondness / froth, froth abhored less to these fondest shores / frock, frock worn is well in fondness / feels, feels a gentle fondness / fawns, fawns and the pawns who move to lightest loving fondness / fawn, fawn trades a lie to the lips lighter still in fondness / forthrightly, forthrightly live to fondness / cardiac, cardiac assort has insured your fondness for love / views, views allowed a sealing fondness / cues, cues appear near your fondness / cords, cords cut to see a sure fondness / cut, cut away past retail for the final fondness / hearts, hearts who heal as fondest.

CHAPTER SIX
Relation, relations shifts into fond retire / healed, healed empires of fondness / burial, burial comes true to the fondest / optic, optic assignments for the fondest / elude, elude has allowed these fondest / allocative, allocative means fonder still / elevated, elevated to vaunted attire for the winning winging fondest still / ask, ask to see the fondest faces of love / befriend, befriend another dear to fondness / bird, bird won through fondness / board, boards sword deep in fondness / culpable, culpable has gone to

the healing fondness / cupid, cupid was stupid without fondness / bored, bored sports have gone to the threshold fondest, love / courts, courts short with hiring fondness / cares, cares most for the healing fondness / canes, canes cranign to walk to thy fondness / caves, caves lost to fondness / depths, depths pool in fondness / adorn, adorn most for fondness / cakes, cakes cursed have cut thy fondness / cubes, cubes cost less for thy fondness / caliber, caliber costs most if fought for fondness / carpets, carpets pulled have cost one a fondness / cures, cures have come to the foness / coats, coats off and sleeves roll into a soft fondness / collapse, collapse ahs sent a notice to the fondest / cubes, cubes worn win fondly / cones, cones cruise into a shore fondest still with love / corpse, corpse tossed tot he tiles fondest of love's light / collective, collective agree to be fondest in love / colds, colds cured by fond allow / cure, cure sought sealed fondly / septuagent, septuagent of the extreme forgive for fondness / septarian, septarian rings for fondness / suspend, suspend the judging fondness / sustain, sustain a volley for fondness / requirements, requirements sent to fondness / note, note received for fondness / mating, mating comes to the fondest won / hires, hires a reply for fondness / find, find a filling fondness / spell, spell well your fondness for love / alleviate, alleviate the reasons fondly / well, well to the willing fondness for love / caps, caps written, fondly / sateing, sating allow for your fondness / rescuer, rescuer comes as a savior to faith fondest at love / reading, reading allows your freeing fondness / rivers, rivers rush to your fondness / realign, realign allows your meaning to build through fondness / restitute, restitute and the reassure through a fondness / destitute, destitute and the dealing fondness / red, red and the ruling fondness / ruts, ruts over and routed past through fondness / definition, definition comes to the fondest / define, define and the erasure of past ways fonereal to the fondest / reliable, reliable resources to the fondest / rapes, rapes have gone to the fondest waves of love / cape, cape has insured the carrying on to fondness / cords, cords crushed without fondness / reliable, reliable resources set for fondness / ratify, ratify the readings for your fondness / words, words erased and lessons left to a living fondness.

CHAPTER SEVEN
Cubicle, cubicles tossed to a living fondness / chapters in light's fond due / / riding, riding allows a leverage to our fondness / runs, runs explore your fondness / / rooms, rooms to roam your fondness / diffuse, diffuse amused by fondness / mine, mines allow your giving fondness / mint, mint teal fondness / mined, mined and the material fondness / connect, connect allowed, fondness / opens, opens a plane to fondness / directive, directives sought to fondness / delicate, delicate buying fondness / delicious, delicious supoosing fondness / light, light lending fondness / stiff, stiff without fondness / stuffed, stuffed to the gibberish? fondness / corrective, corrective goes fondest / song, song and the strongly fondest / again, again we said, fight over, fondest / corpuscle, corpuscles muscled through to fondness / church, church and the chosen fondnesschips, chips win a fondness / joint, joint allow to a fondness / capsule, capsule corded without a fondness /

jaunt, jaunt won for fondness / cream, creams come to fondness / cafe, cafe allows her fondness / capable, capable to a code for fondness / lunch, lunch mentioned to fondness / hunch, hunch paid to fondness / asking, asking to be honest to fondest / metatronic, metatronic allow for the fonder still / property, property appears near fondness / participate, participate allows a hearing fondness / irradiate, irradiate allowing a fondness / prepare, prepare a sword for the fondest / regarded, regarded as fondest / edit, edit allowed through fondness / start, start to the heart of fondness / beware, beware has gone to the ceiling's fondness / deck, deck and the delicate fondness / duel, duel and the dating fondness / dual, dual and the deadline fondness / aware, aware and the welling fountains for fondness / doubt, doubts detail a fondness / doric, doric and the fondest / boric, boric and the billing fondness / explore, explore the fondest living / relates, relates and the rational fondness / seizing, seizing and the fondest allowance for love / size, size and the seizing fondness for love / relates, relates and the ratify for fondness in love / volcanic, volcanic appear for our fondness / viewing, viewing your fondness / explore, explore acquires a fondness / strange, staring into a strange allow for love's fondness / meters, meters measured for an allowing fondness / pulse, pulse and the plans found in fondness / erupts, erupts and the living views of fondness / seeing, seeing and the sizes for a fondness / sights, sights mentioned as fondest / heights, heights given a living fondness / seas, seas of the seeing fondness.

CHAPTER EIGHT

Open, open to the natural Mazama letting go, glow in your fondness resting still in the Dove of light regard / cones, cones cured a living fondness / craters, craters purged lemuria's fondness / volcanic, volcanic explore assured our fondness for life / entry, entry pointed to is love for our fondness / magma, magma spilling hopefully to our fondness / grounds, grounds astounded by our fondness / relates, relates assuring fondness / soars, soars a surfaced fondness / rings, rings around the realm of facets focused into fondness / coasts, coasts and the costs released for fondness / costal, coastal planes equipped with fondness for love / people, people who heal through fondness / hydraulic, hydraulic lifting to gifts of fondness / smell, smell elated in fondness / touch, touch a trickle fondly / systemic, systemic spread to the fleet fondness / morning, morning mentioned to the narrow fondness / smoked, smoked and the surrender to a fondness / arising, arising and the reaching fondness / grounds, grounds and the gifting fondness / ridges, ridges and the reasonable fondness / strides, strides and the stretching fondness / slams, slams and the slimming fondness / poetry, poetry and the thrilling fondness / morphine, morphine and the featuring fondness / lunged, lunged and the leading fondly / lone, lone and the learning fondness / grey, grey and the thrilling fondness lightens / colors, colors and the champion fondness / spur, spur and the shillings spent for fondness / within, within a willing living fondness / winds, winds and the welcome fondness / electric, electric keeping for fondness / maze, maze living fondly / rhetoric, rhetoric appears fondly / longitude, longitude spearing a fondness / lavish, lavish apply to a fondness / longs, longs and the

living fondness / learns, learns attired for fondness / butane, butane tours a fondness / parts, parts and the particles for a fondness / participates, participates and the pensions for a fondness / turns, turns forthrightly to a pensions fondness / trains, trains and the righteous plans for a gaining fondness / trends, trends appear near the fondest lines / scales, scales of the skilling miracles linear to love / sails, sails apply to a skilled fondness / acquires, acquires a signed miracle for their fondness / gas, gas and the simple fondness / grins, grinning entry into the fondest waves of light / grasps, grasps and the central rains of love's fondest delights / befriends, befriends and the belittle gone to fondness / chronic, chronic and the creative fondness / chromes, chromes and the fondly found loves of lifting lightness / chronicles, chronicles and the central reward for fondness / chromium, chromium cures and the sugarward blues are fonder still / collapse, collapse allowed and the overall is well into fondness / contours, contours and the current elapse fondest / caves, caves and the currents within a fondness / running, running well into their fondness / arise, arise evolves into a fondness / arose, arose a simple fondness / abated, abated as slated for a fondest tour of love.

CHAPTER NINE

Franklin, franklin finds key's ascends fondest / springs, springs burst fondly / arose, arose within a fondness / humps, humps along and outs fondly / retreats, retreats into fondness / bakes, bakes wanted fondest / wooded, wooded major fondness / slopes, slopes want fondness / paid, paid for fondly / phones, phones felt dondest / faults, faults within fondest melts / foci, foci felt fondly / focus, a focus on the fondest / found, found in fondness / fulfill, fulfill within fondest / regard, regard won, fondest / deduction, deduction dues fondest / calls, calls made, fondess / cut, cut out madness, fondest / off, off and ins fondness / deduce, deduce wins fondest / elect, elect news fondest / new, new fondly / space, space spills fondly / decibels, decibels due fondest / open, open plays fondness / heart's, heart's held fondest / door, door dealt with fondest / decide, decide why fondest / declare, declare dares fondly / approve, approve us, fondly / move, move into fondness / gematric, gematric juries fondness / gematria, gematria joins our fondness / sophic, sophic sures fondest / sophia, sophia sent, fondly / practice, practice made, fondly / proof, proof pains fondly / position, position paced, fondly / amalgam, amalgam comes, fondly / practicum, practicum creates fodness / amounts, amounts made fondly / credits, credits come to fondness / crafts, crafts create fondness / pressure, pressure prepares fondest / gifted, gifted guide's fondness / growth, growth grew fondly / studio, a studio sent into the fondness / watched, watched into awareness, fondly / wonder, wonder wins our, fondness / volcano, volcano values fondness / 22, 22 ways to see our fondness / vessel, a vessel views our fondness / wield, wield won, fondly / eruptive, eruptive values fondness / seams, seams sent into the roots, fondness / washed, washed out's ways, the fondest / artic, artic curves our fondness / geologic, geologic june's fondness / woven, woven win some's fondness / worn, worn into a fondness / circles, circles into the fondest / rewards, rewards right's fondest / won, won into fondness.

CHAPTER TEN

Wonders, wonders into the fondest / origin, orgin of the amuse into the fondest / Atlantis, Atlantis lends the fondness / rides, rides read the fondest / rise, rise out's fondness / recognition, recognition comes fondly / random, random reads the fondest / size, size won, the fondest / lonely, lonely leads the fondest / links, links wind's fondest / abridge, abridge wants fondness / up, up into the fondness / linked, linked in's fondness / give, give wins fondly / brace, brace into the fondness / wolf's, wolf's want the fondness / most, mast meets the fondness / mast, mast meets fondly / sails, sails sent, fondly / shone, shone into the fondest / all, all and the will's fondness / shines, shines into the fondness / please, please wins fondly / yarns, yarns into the fondness / younger, younger yields our fondness / young, young enough's fondest / days, days into the wight's fondness / daze, daze into the fondness / relegate, relegate runs the fondly / register, register war, the fondest / met, met with the fondest / meet, meet with the fonder ones / introduce, introduce won, the fondest / Tibet's Tibet's trues the fondest / way, way to lead the fondest / love, love leads into fondness / translate, translate trues our fondness / passion, passion pets the fondest / pinch, pinch out's fondness / scratch, scratch outs wonder's fondest / bite, bite believes the fondest / play, play pleased fondly / please, please be the fonder / type, type into the fondness / organ, organ wins the fondest / noise, a noise kneels fondly / act, act within the fondness / coputate, coputate comes fondly / 64, 64 won, fondly / arts, arts win the fondest / express, express said fondest / ecstatic, ecstatic winds fondness / notes, notes crave the fondness / dates, dates truthful to the fondness / deals, deals warrant the fondness / plays, plays plenty the fondness / affinity, affinity for the fondest / barriers, barriers blend the foundest / melt, melt within's fondness / creations, creations occur the fondness / gift, gift gives the fondness / meditate, meditate within the fondness / perfection, perfection for the fondness / artistic, artistic trues the fondness

CHAPTER ELEVEN

Exactly, exactly met in fondness and light dynamics of love metaphysics, metaphysics met through the fondness / sought, sought suggest fondness / cooling, cooling cure's fondness / conspire, conspire to fire your's fondest / gets, gets again's fondness / entrance, entrance rules fondness / entry, entry sent fondness / seconds, seconds won fondest / account, account for a fondness / meets, meets moore fondness / masked, masked yours fondest / count, a count found fondness / measures, measures meet in fondness / opens, opens your's fondness / aghast, aghast with require's fondness / F.U.C.K, Fornication Under Command of the King's fondness / fart, fart for the fondness / flaunt, flaunt your fondness / smell, a smell wins, fondly / bebacle, debacle dues your's fondness / debates, debates due your fondness / sustains, sustains refried fondly / rhythm, rhythm ran fondest / radical, radical rules fondness / dates, fondness dates with love / rapt, rapt with the fondest / random, random runs ours, fondness / ask, ask out's fondness / delegates, delegates done fondest /

radiates, radiates with sun's fondness / reading, readings within fondly / gateways, gateways gaze fondly / rise, a rise to raise, fondly / chosen, chosen won, fondest / moved, moved away's fondness / ridicule, ridicule through the fondness / raves, raves about fondness / elects, elects won, fondest / ingrains, ingrains run, fondly / example, example win fondness / gave, gave in too, fondness / gains, gains gaze fondly / roads, roads fondest / get, get with your fondness / regains, regains remain, fondest / drowns, drowns in fondest / sides, sides win fondly / report, report with fondness / orchard, orchard red fondest / wind, wind for the fondest / flying, flying into the wildly fond / release, release wins fondest / flown, flown into fondness / flowers, flowers with the fondness / flaunt, flaunt with the fondest / rememberance, rememberance of the fondness / flows, flows for the fondest / flanks for the fondest / flirt, flirt with the fondness / dazzles, dazzles with the fondnest / flaws, flaws into the fondness / sparks, sparks fly fondly / rose, fondness rose red with love.

CHAPTER TWELVE

Today, today is the ray of greatest intonations / irrelative, irrelative to the notions of fondness ruled / invariant, invariant wants fondness / racey, racey runs fondness / recluse, recluse rules fondest / rapture, rapture arise fondness / relevant, relevant ramify the amuse fondness / forgive, forgive us fondly / confess, confess for the fondness / best, best believe's fondness / transgress, transgress less, fondly / Christ's, Christ's wonder's fondest / gift, a gift gave the fondness / live, live in the fondness / foresee, foresee the future fondly / harlot, harlot out, fondest / where, where won, fondly / madonna, madonna meant, fondest / outcomes, outcomes win fondly / laugh, laugh with the fondest / large, large enough's fondness / tabs, fond in tabs, love / codices, codices come too, fondness / cables, cables curette fondness / crimps, crimps about fondly / hose, hose worn through, fondest / legs, legs winced fondly / center, fond to the center won / central, central sun's fondness / coves, coves through the fondness / strong, strong construe's fondness / long, fond and long to be / loon, love's loon and fonder too / loved, loved led fondest / suites, suites won, fondness / confidence, confidence comes to the fondest / confidential, confidential cures for fondness / fast, fast with the fondest / far, far with the fondness / along, along with the fondness, light / path, path made fondly / swank, swank with the fondest / swing, swing with the fondness / linger, linger long, too fondness / learn, learn to be fondest / lather, lather bubbles with the fondness / loose, loose too, the fondness / codicals, codicals come too, fondness / grainy, grainy days fondness / extend, extend trues fondly / extrude, extrude rests in fondness / compose, compose notes fondest / florida, florida found foundly / flew, flew with the fondest / forever, forever seen in fondness / new, new renews fondly / debacle, debacle deals in fondness / deligate, deligate during the fondness / denier, dedier wins fondest / draft, draft within the fondness / daunt, daunt lessens fondness / count, count with the fondness / thence, thence into the fondness / this, this weighs fondly.

CHAPTER THIRTEEN

pinnacles, pinnacles opportunity relaxed into, fondest / mentionable, mentionable these applauses to God's given gates for fondness human / lettering, lettering laxed off the edge scripted into fondness / matters, matters mean fondly / amount, much to amount into the fond greeting of love / musically, musically gifted materials of love's fondness for you / peach, peach fondness / lateral, lateral moves into love's fondness / many, many who wed fondly / mergers, mergers made fondly / pert, pert the dirt who stood inside your fond gates / moved, moved into woods regenerated for all delays fondest / mathematics, mathematics linked into, fondly / pretty, pretty days of daring fondness / aromatically, aromatically connective trickles into veins fondest / fed, fed in light electrically replinished through a reaching parisian, fondness / perfect, perfect plans fondness / all, all with the fondest / call, call with the fondest / girls, girls want the fondest / guys, guys win fondly / masonic, masonic means the fondest / meters, meters met, fondest / mast, mast on the fondest / mantles, mantles means fondest / moves, moves with the fondness / plus, plus lives in fondness / place, place for the fondest / carried, carried into the fondest / counts, counts of the fondest / chants, chants win the fonder / chops, chops above, fondest / trucked, trucked with the fondest / trades, trades treat us fondest / toss, toss above's fondness / torn, torn within the fondness / adorn, adorn with the fondness your love / deals, love's deals fondest / dealt, dealt for the fondest / belts, belts worn fondly / awards, awards with the fondest / call, call out fondest / cords, cords carable fondly / cups, found cups of fondness / fill, fill up's fondness / full, full with the fondest / flow, flow flew the fondest / concept, concept cure the fondest / get, get within the fondest / gather, gather wants the fondest / gazing, gazing into the fondness / greeting, greeting greets the fondness / orion's, orion's race the fondest / state, a state worn in fondness / water, water wins the fondness / keep, keep with the fondness / kept, kept well, fondly / parallel, parallel plays the fondest / often, often fans the wildness in the found / bliss, fond in bliss / ignite, ignite in the fondness / ignore, ignore less, only fondness / explore, explore wore the fondness / gift, gift your fondness with love.

THE FOUNDATION-MENTS
LEVEL 63

...the ripening of the lands eternal inside the Dove:

The Foundation is set and laid into truth a peace pipe smoked is written in wreaths of lasting exhort and the sort who carry the flag over truth and the ripening reach over gorges of light and life is leading us home in the foundations of meeting and the listening told to speak only when spoken into and through the light electric.

Often I am scheming and today I am healing the heading into love which is written in sunshine and birthdays now past as the lover of lineage is heaven at last and the flowers who bending find us chocolate paths through the news of arrivals whose hearts now love the days of anticipation and the words which near us to the deer and the children who shudder when the news is over all and within the rhyming rules of the noose and the lifting letters and the legends who join us to the tree, that is me, and our days are limited without restriction and the rules and the rhymes have left us to find other venues and different ears and differences healed from here to Georgia and the straits in-between as the land is now founded upon the waters and the winds and the wings of a Dove, now involved with genuine respect for the formal resignation into signs and sealed details and the serpent Caduceus now upon her form of final details. Let us rest in the Lord Metatronic and the Maitreyan borne into winds of latitude and mood, now spoiled, will heal, with time eternal, in peace, I rest this case upon the wind, and the father of the dove who wrote the note for peaceful plentitude, the father's names are rivers of light and following them to the sea is the daily source of how to be in love essentially grand. Let people find us near the sea and we stand is listening to the Trees inside the move meant to find peace. Let us gather again, new to the high ways and the seas upon the rock which stood for serpent's rest and the wrestling now is past.

Welcome to the caves of Lord God beside the sea.

That is your foundation. Our scheme is love. Our dramatic increase is rest and our word is love. Much peace, rest in the rainbow and find your foundation in dove.

Three rules apply to Foundations:

1. Truth
2. Rest
3. Schemes

THE WELL-MENTS
LEVEL 64

CHAPTER ONE

Deep, deep in positions well within love's sympathetic lure to love / depth, depth of the centrally well within love / deliver, deliver a deal replete with love's wells / constant, constant to the consistent wells / swells, swells told "wells" / sweet, sweet in a willing well, love / swollen, swollen agree to be well in love / patterning, patterning paged, love is, well / earth, earth emerges well / wet, wet with love's gifts, wells / rewarded, rewarded within, wells / levels, levels 64 to love's wells / learned, learned in dimension's wells / affairs, affairs heart well in love / burned, burning banned? well, love / volumes, volumes written agree, well / waters, waters well within, love / run, run to the summation, wells / relations, relations reign, wells / clarity, clarity comes to the sum, wells / clearance, clearance allows you a well / cope, cope within coming wells / chambers, chambers erupt, wells / depths, depths touched, wells / caverns, caverns cruised, wells / fill, fill another, well / pour, pour a principle for wells / plenty, plenty into, wells / heavenly, heavenly wells / appeals, appeals too, wells / approve, approve of well-springing love / reference, reference made to the wells within / pressures, pressures off and the wells within / regards, regards and the well within, love / valley, valley made simply, love's well / mend, mend attempted made well / women, women hustle to see wells / hustle, hustle past, life is well / husband, husband made friend to those well / friend, friend forged accomplishment to the wells on love / falcon, falcon nest near our wells / soars, soars daily dear to wells / heady, heady estates range to wells / states, states electric mend, wells / measure, measure lost, found, wells / pleasing, pleasing notice given inside our wells / gait, gait taken well / gate off, wells / plateaus, plateaus reached, well / plots, plots off, wells / planks, planks sought the stars friendly wave to life's wells / walking, walking respect for the well's goodness / electric, electric abide for the abode worn well / voices, voices clear near our wells / telephone, telephones voice clearly near wells / blow, blow past and through our wells / flows, flows aerobically, well / derision, derision done, thoughtfully we are, well / delight, delight in the sites won electrically and be freely well / desperate, desperate has gone to aloft and well / decisions, decisions made are kept well / forgiveness, forgiveness has won you, well / colossal, colossal changes make us well / life, life leads well.

CHAPTER TWO

Sports, sports cure us well / abort, abort the patterns well / admire, admire a missive well / fire, fire above and well / delivery, delivery comes to the river well / declare, declare a living "well" / move, move to the sounds electrically well / flair, flair for the notice, well / found, found inception for those who were well / resort, resort to a single, well / report, report succinct into the well-est / expire, expire may hire us well / elect, elect a notice, well / inquire, inquire annually, well? / desire, desire to see us be well / news, news came to others last of the latest wells / sacred, sacred soothe in the hands we know well / sound, sounds of the singly risen well / grounds, grounds double up to the growing, wells / happening, happening soon, a well noon / express, express accounted for as well / accounts, accounts amount to those who are well / rewards, rewards sent for those who are well / declare, declare us well / share, share in the singing powerful to wells loved / show, show us your wellness heard / showering, showering ours with loving wellness / hair, hair shorn to say, "well" / heart, heart lorn has gone to the grounds well within Christ / head, head for the office of Christed wellness / phone, phone placed near the heart's well / happiest, happiest hues appear in rainbow dues paid well / hearty, hearty woods bought for the reasons well / occur, occur to be your truest guide within wells / acquire, acquire a rich detail for those well / firing, firing applause for the reality of wells / fallen, fallen wons chosen to live well / fasten, fasten your fixtures in plenty of wells / rewire, rewire allowing a download well / designate, designate the resource as a lightest well / rated, rated won through a gentle signed well / chosen, chosen again, well / flanks, flanks open into those well / fires, fires appear near the well-est / fills, fills in resourced well / fair, fair to the fibrous wells / bought, bought again, well / solution, solution arises in the leading path well inside love / rights, rights allowed, well / sights, sights appear glowing in the eyes worn well / goals, goals set simply, "well" / sought, sought has gone to the farthest moon called well / preparations, preparations made are well / provide, provide a resource for the healing wells / declare, declare a daily "well" / comes, comes a curing "well" / insure, insured to be "well" / occupy, occupy your life well / suppose, suppose has become, well / write, write again "well" / denote, denote the thoughts to well / devote, devote yourself well / unity, unity mends us well / allocation, allocation made within wells.

CHAPTER THREE

Temperate, temperate to the values well / material, material arrives mentally well / matters, matters materialize in the minutes paved, well / perfection, perfection allows wellness / precision, precision resets a respect for the deepest wells / regarding, regarding wells and the fortunes made through fathering wells / relative, relative cost is loving well / cards, cards tossed to those well / carts, carts heave with the lived wells / connections, connections come to those well / confections, confections source those well / sweet, sweet cavorts to the heavens well / chaste, chaste can go the roads well / irreverent, irreverent humors lost in wells / irretrievable, irretrievable costs accepted through wells / defeat, defeat has come to these wells / desolate, desolate lost into wells / destiny, destiny born at the wells / watch, watch another becoming well / listen, listen to a livery well / desperate, desperate broke into defeated wells / burst, burst a dam within through wells / broken, broken singing signs in, "wells" / emotes, emotes in the watery gravity of love's wells / western, western ways see our wells / east, east to a beast defeated through loving well / battered, battered and the shattering broken through to well / beast, beast cast to the east through loving wells / mansion, mansion built bought for those well / warrants, warrants arrange to see well / winced, winced without love's wells / commence,

commence to the commerce within your wells / learn, learn to be well within love / accord, accord has sought your brand of loving well / aggregate, aggregate attend to those wells of love / aggravate, aggravate has grown to surrendering wells / activity, activity cost you well / rebounds, rebounds outline is well / abound, abound in abundance within wells / allocation, allocations gained are well to love / parlay, parlay another to love's wells / advance, advance to a reset of love's wells / aspects, aspects well / avenued, avenued blends valuable to love's wells / catastrophic, catastrophic comes strictly to a stationed well / attraction, attractions break in two wells / drawn, drawn to wells loved / arrival, arrival in loving wells / survival past love's wells / sent, sent for well / dawn, dawning wells / given, given wells / gracious, gracious wells love's / appearances, appearances sink through wells / aesthetics, aesthetics suggest a resourced well / allow, allow a primitive well / gained, gained a stance well / growth, growth comes to those wells / respect, respect realized to love's wells / rapacious, rapacious rants break over the energy of wells / prey, prey past those wells / pawn, pawn ousted through wells / fairest, fairest wins wells / lengthen, lengthen the spine within wells.

CHAPTER FOUR

Athlete, athlete allowing a reward paced in wells / banquet, banquet coming is well / heavenly, heavenly resourcing well / gated, gated communing well / craters, craters topple to news of the resurgent wells / cues, cues caught well / views, views bought, well / material, material mixed within wells / maps, maps bought show us well / matters, matters well within humanity / material, material to a miracle's wells / magnify, magnify a reply for the filling wells / mute, mute without? wells / manage, manage to be well / electronic, electronic details are well in humanity / attitudes, attitudes arise without wellness within / deem, deem the matter dearest nearest wells / show, show us a meaning nearest our wells / dropping, dropping through to see the thrown of grown well / interior, interior scopes are well to love / love, love us well / bought, bought a being willing well / brought, brought a bishop to the farms of wellness / magical, magical missions accomplished well / magicians, magicians numbers caught well / pal, pal made of the fence-line within our wells / freed, freed of the farces committed mercy-less without wells / farce, farce laid wide to the feeling wells / fortress, fortress built has cost you wells / found, found a filling well / founded, founded on gaining wells / fifth, fifth pace made well / golden, golden gifts warranted well / silver, silver success is the cord cut well / wave, wave to the well-est love / woven, woven in material decreed to be well / wedding, wedding comes to those well / mankind, mankind mentions us well / slave, slave freed by the Ananaki woods of love's wells / entreaty, entreaty tossed to the turning wells / remember, remember who loved you well / settle, settle into those blessings well / success, success has come to the living wells / seating, seating appearing near those wells / hearts, hearts are hearing your living well / heads, heads cost well / whole, whole to the filling wells / capable, capable insure

comes to the wells / happening, happening, hear, wells / trails, trails past the costing wells / tours, tours kept well / currency, currency flows well / capable, capable to love well / bail, bail the wells / plenty, plenty hear well / floating, floating attending well / callous, callous approached well / special, special appliance well / manuals, manuals bought well / burgeoning, burgeoning wells / sort, sort a material well within love / motions, motions made well / notions, notions passed well / daring, daring to live well.

CHAPTER FIVE

Thence, thence we became both well / hence, hence a hearing well / advancement, advancement becoming well / chance, chance to stay well / construct, construct a light well / ablutions, ablutions allowed well / around, around us shared, well / again, again we spanned well / conspire, conspire to sear well / universal, universal cubes well / units, units meet well / calling, calling comes well / contest, contest past, wells / attract, attract a sort well / compact, compact news well / contest, contest sorts well / appears, appears a narrow well / client, client cured well / lines, lines living well / properly, properly allowed to be well / property, property bought well / purchase, purchase made well / memorials, memorials built to love's wells / method's, method's miracles allow us your wells / modes, modes maintained as well / modules, modules placed within wells / strong, strong to a central code, well / prongs, prongs point to all's well / planted, planted in valuable wells / vaunted, vaunted comes to these wells / glimpse, glimpse recorded said "wells" / large, large is a leasing well / largo, largo cargo is well / keys, keys cost less, well / buy, buy a simple well / bought, bought is the key code, well / believe, believe in another's wellness / buy, buy the born won well / meeting, meeting set, well / mastery, mastery came, well / given, given a freedom well / gracious, gracious in resourcing well / aspire, aspire to the news, well / casual, casual attend, well / often, often found, wells / appraise, appraise us now, well / pacing, pacing the peaces, well / mincing, mincing less, well / steering, steering through well / causal, causal friends well / maximum, maximum living comes, well / stability, stability taught through those well / featuring, featuring the farming wells / belly, belly lost well / comfort, comfort cost without wells / attracted, attracted to the wellness within / perform, perform a friendship well / shimmering, shimmering comes to those well / glorious, glorious days in those well / dragon, dragons raged about wells / quenched, quenched in a resource depth wells / dragonfly, dragonfly folding into wells / reflections, reflections paced well / pyramids, pyramids mentioned in wells.

CHAPTER SIX

Limits, limits pushed well / plus, plus arranged well / sizes, sizes less well / surfing, surfing thrusts well / play, play allows well / moderate, moderate amounts well / embodies, embodies us, well / blessings, blessings come well to us / main, main days are well / stream, stream through us well / perceptive, perceptive about wells / solitude, solitude good for our wells / gliding, gliding into resource sent for our wells / negotiation, negotiation comes to us well / view, view of the fellows well / explore, explore the shores well within love / morose, morose cast to floating wells / insensitive, insensitive thrown to those wells / instruct, instruction won construction wise to love's wells / missive, missive meant to loving wells / disc, disc tossed to those well / comfort, comfort worn within well / mortal, mortal portals purged well / admission, admission made well / entire, entire within, well / indolent, indolent passed well / mortality, mortality mends, well / missions, missions mentioned well / inspire, inspire us well / instigate, instigate the recalls well / allowances, allowances given for love's wells / disguise, disguise off and the dues cost less wells / discern, discern the disciple's wells / decide, decide to be well-est / debris, debris clears well / afloat, afloat in love's wells / logs, logs flushed without loving well / allocation, allocation funds us well / Aton, Aton said "well" / attic, attic left, well / clearance, clearance came, well / leaping, leaping past wells / lapses, lapses over, wells / clapping, clapping clears wells / handy, handy about wells / flakes, flakes off, well / memories, memories made light through wells / light, lightest mention of the memories well within love / several, several ways to see through these wells / shorts, shorts and the suggested wells / fullest, fullest wells touch lightly / framing, framing suggested, wells / elections, elections made well / architectural, architecturally rendered wells / fountains, fountains join wells / patience, patience pays well / partners, partners made well / heaven, heaven sets in wells / sunrise, sunrise chosen, well / altitude, altitude moons well / agree, agree to the favored well / apply, apply to the miracle, wells / avalanche, avalanche off your wells / tributes, tributes attend your wells.

CHAPTER SEVEN
Services, services rendered paid for those well / surrenders, surrenders daily to life's wells / gains, gains security through these wells / reunion, reunion meant to be well / partner, partner made within wells / trends, trends carry to trusted wells / transit, transit allowing us wells / beaches, beaches near us are well / plans, plans made to be well / basically, basically well / cocoon, cocoon tossed to thrice wells / classic, classic supposing comes to wells / personal, personal plenty in our wells / deciding, deciding to be well / declination, declination set, well / date, date won to our wells / dashing, dashing through light wells / debits, debits often our wells / accepts, accepts only life wells / access, access currency through light wells / definition, definition cost us wells / dazzling, dazzling within wells / delineate, delineate your nearness to our wells / decibels, decibels fly into wells / perceptive, perceptive about wells / eternal, eternal within wells / inquiry, inquiry set for our wells / capture, capture without, wells / receive, receive a nearest well / prepare, prepare to be well / avec, avec fed well / also, also glides well / pillars, pillars lead well / monitors, monitors manage well / moving, moving allows well / meander, meander past well / equation, equation equips well / mines, mines mentioned well / material, materials sought are salty and well / mothers, mothers milk well / qualify,

qualify your stated wells / mapping, mapping the costs well / moods, moods struck are well / mollify, mollify has cost plenty well / equatorial, equatorial within wells / effective, effective for light wells / merry, merry about us, eternally, electrical wells / mother, mother mentioned wells / driving, driving details are cost wells / diligent, diligent in sought wells / past, past torn to wells / passages, passages cost well / potential, potential paged well / points, points paved well / making, making a living well / mathematics, mathematics encouraged well / given, given a scope be well / resolved, resolved to see well / respect, respect your choices well / rally, rally for the cause, well / youth, youth purged well / adolescence, adolescence spun for the well / well, well addressed, hear / shifts, shifts well within, light's.

CHAPTER EIGHT
Date, date made, well / declare, declare us, well / data, data received, well / daily, daily well / downshift, downshift well / uplift, uplift well / regain, regain well / remember, remember well / ruling, ruling well / rules, rules blend well / rash, rash gone, well / reaps, reaps now, well / rather, rather set, well / ruling, ruling best well / thorough, thorough in those well / tepid, tepid without well / tape, tape clipped well / tapes, tapes purged well / tubes, tubes cured well / talents, talents sent well / truths, truths told well / falkes, falkes fell well / snow, snow lives well / place place chosen well / plan, plan to be well / path, path cured well / panther, panther lost well / cabin, cabin spent well / cures, cures now paid well / colors, colors gauged well / cubes, cubes spun sell well / cones, cones cost less well / lacing, lacing allows well / vulture, vulture lost well / belt, belt off well / trapped, trapped without, well / tethers, tethers cut, well / coated, coated in crystal wells / captive, captive gone well / denoted, denoted in devoted wells / letters, letters list wells / delivers, delivers well / delectable, delectable in a detailed well / doors, doors open to your wells / dive, dive into the living wells / dash, dash across to risen wells / birds, birds believe in the listened to wells / blast, blast allows us wellness / voted, voted for as centrally well / driven, driven to see well / lessons, lessons lead well / pets, pets allow wellness / friends, friends engage well / fond, fond to fuels well / found, found within wells / pounds, pounds off, well / loose, loose details well / leaves, leaves float well / letters, letters written well / tumble, tumble across wells / home, home healed well / happened, happened too, well / hurry, hurry to the healing wells / help, help comes well / leaping, leaping past well.

CHAPTER NINE
Sure, sure is well / certain, certain then well / definite, definite to a living well / deal, deal makes well / deny, deny gone well / destination, destination chosen well / creation, creation costs less well / contests, contests win well / fatherly, fatherly forced well / naiscent, naiscent news well / nostril, nostril cleared wells / noose, noose thrown to a well / nudge, nudge the light wells up to love / nose, nose opening to life wells / deep, deep in a central wave seen well / breath, breath of the father's well / bodies, bodies found well / message, message leads well / massage,

massage again, well / copyrights, copyrights set well / wheels, wheels alight within wells / malevolent, malevolent benevolent again, well / respect, respect your resource well / claim, claim another well / woes, woes wed well / healing, healing found well / academic, academic to shores well / vapor, vapor risen to wells / tastes, tastes chosen now well / stems, stems snap without wells / dim, dim relit well / illustrative, illustrative to those well / vast, vast in the recourse well / glut, glut done, well / maximum, maximum power found, well / public, public led well / grown, grown to be, well / grottos, grottos purged well / pleats, pleats fold well / publishing, publishing divinely our flowing wells / plastic, plastic purged well / permission, permission mends well / paths, paths pace well / plaza, plaza chosen well / plein, plein to a painting well / airs, airs won well / crag, crag cleared well / eire, eire electric, well / laconic, laconic singing well / simply, simply, well / loops, loops lost well / steaming, steaming streaming wells / cracks, cracks appearing well / words, words nearing well / pictures, pictures appearing well / interrogate, interrogate thyself well / answers, answers coming, trust them, well / come, come to a cubicle well / welcomed, welcomed home / interest, interest found well / inverse, inverse given interest well / revert, revert to a resource well / inversions, inversions often well / meetings, meetings made for the franchised wells.

CHAPTER TEN
Voice, voice found, well / vampirism, vampirism energetically sent to life wells / cathode, cathode imploded well / bulb, bulb blazed well / bombastic, bombastic views wellness now / ecclesiastic, ecclesiastic friends are well / converse, converse about wells / codes, codes fed well / lassitude, lassitude made a living well / elongate, elongate your choices well / leverage, leverage made well / lit, lit within wells / preparing, preparing to purge well / preface, preface cast aside well / publisher, publishers launch well / books, books mend well / plates, plates pulse well / pacific, pacific blue wells / philippine, philippine news, well / australia, australia deep within wells / caribbean, Caribbean blue without wells / cocos, cocos known for here wells / Nazca, Nazca traced, wells / Juan, Juan flows in de Fuca wells / Antarctic, Antarctic knows, wells / key, key for the following wells / subduction, subduction sent for our wells / zones, zones won, well / pinatabo, pinatabo trends well / earth, earth moist within wells / mountains, mountains measure well / deserts, deserts field well / Eurasia, Eurasia and the vents well / Africa, Africa hints of lucid wells / southern, southern tips lean into the wells crystalline / America, America mended well / rifts, rifts open well / slips, slips allowed well / faults, faults focused lightly well / slip, slip along shores worn well / geologically, geologically well / youth, youth sent well / tectonics, tectonics of the living wells / surveyed, surveyed allowance for the living wells / plains, plains and the pressures well within love / valleys, valleys across love's plains and wells / month, month miraculous within wells of love / yawns, yawns yellow within love's wells / capital, capital cures for love's wells / bench, bench across the living wells / berth, berth for the fellows wells / booth, booth

allows wells / steps, steps into wells / dashing, dashing for light's wells / spurts, spurts grant us wells / spoon, spoon fed wells / stirring, stirring allows wells / sugar, sugar fed, wells / sweet, sweet elates wells / sustain, sustain us well / staging, staging costs well / survey, survey reads well / stored, stored in tiers, well / parent, parent to the mentally well.

CHAPTER ELEVEN
Passive, passive without, wells / patient, patient within, wells / pearls, pearls cast caught wells / pertinent, pertinent retain for love's wells / pent, pent unbent for wells / palatial, palatial pages well / spatial, spatial nearing well / capable, capable within, wells / carry, carry on well / life, life leads well / lifting, lifting gifts well / leagues, leagues join well / heal, heal now, well / flanks, flanks covered well / shank, shank broken, heals, well / spills, spills paged well / thrust, thrust forth well / shrill, shrill gone, well / languid, languid lessons focus well / ages, ages read, "well" / sharp, sharp to a shilling, well / angry, angry goes, well / toughen, toughen toes, well / terse, terse without well curse, curse acknowledged well / coarse, coarse forgotten, well / material sought sent, well / blatant, blatant attends dormed well / militant, militant trends met well / agonize, agonize over, said, "well" / tribes, tribes essential to those, well / triangular, triangular healing goes to those "well" / shot, shot without wells / sparks, sparks flown well / sparrows, sparrows trust well / most, most who know well / moist, moist within, wells / suspense, suspense over, wells / particles, particles focused in wells / golden, golden glee's wells / airs, airs apparently well / measures, measures made, well / fresh, fresh in frost's wells / hushed, hushed to cursed wells / empty, empty without wells / coasts, coasts clear well / golden, golden waves well / cote, cote blue with azure wellness / limbs, limbs coded with wells / vote, vote for the volley well / Lazarus, Lazarus wins a willing wellness / struck, struck by the simply, well / stuck, stuck without wells / opens, opens again, wells / dead, dead without, wells / rescue, rescue reigns well / breathe, breathe into wells / serious, serious to a measured feature, wells / particles, particles plane to the miraculous wells / fellow, fellow features paged well / paternal, paternal means gained well / latitudes, latitudes aimed into well / passions, passions vote is for wellness / leap, leap across links on faith for wells / days, days dealt within well / often, often again, wells.

CHAPTER TWELVE
Across, across those rose a well / concerned, concerned gone to wells / abreast, abreast the news, wells / concentric, concentric spins well to love / parallels, parallels exist through wells / ports, ports engage through wells / sorted, sorted by wells / angles, angles fly angels in wells / relate, relate well / release, release well / resist, resist gone, well / drawn, drawn to love's wells / convicted, convicted without, wells / cause, cause your life wells / pursue, pursue the clearest wells / posed, posed to be, well / prevalent, prevalent about, wells / chinese, chinese reads, "well" / junk, junk sunk well / jewels, jewels tossed well / join, join

a bought well / sky, sky scanned well / himalayas, himalayas strands, well / tibetan, tibetan codes well / plateaus, plateaus again, well / reconnect, reconnect within, wells / lights, lights link, well / children, children come, wells / sum, sum made, well / 100, 100 ways, well / 150 days, well / beasts, beasts abreast within wells / easterns, easterns release to wells / scales, scales linked well / campaigns, campaigns meet well / chosen, chosen choose wells / choice, choice made, wells / journey's, journey's gaze is now well / choice, choice delivers well / heavenly, heavenly ways into love's wells / gates, gates appear openly well / secrets, secrets read within wells / gave, gave another wells / look, looks link into wells / ahead, ahead of us, wells / wood, wooden dragons burn well / earth, earth and the thrilling wells / tiger, tiger of the triple wells / fires, fires leap to cross the veins electrically well / swell, swell into living links well to love / chosen, chosen examinations well / houses, houses purged well / home, home found within wells / tension, tension given electrical links and the living mastery of wells / wallow, wallow less, stand more, wells / maintain, maintain a mission, well / chain, chain found is broken within, be well / claim, claim your money, well / land, land is given, well / again, again, we said "well" / circles, circles meet in wells / bridge, bridge bought through wells / resources, resources found in wells / written, written arousal paid to the meeting's wells.

CHAPTER THIRTEEN

Explosion, explosion occurs throughout our sensual wells / empirical, empirical mentions of wells / etheric, etheric meetings met well / kept, kept for a signal of measured wells / gathering, gathering glows well / pregnant, pregnant in a pause for the forceless wells / thyroid, thyroid thrills planned for the wells on love / treats, treats allow a planetary well / future, future features made for theoretical wells / fought, fought without and within, wells / lively, lively leaps to the muse's wells / level, level within a wilder well / wide, wide to a worthy well / fortunate, fortunate fuses are thrown to the wells / works, works and the impact made through wells / work, work along our narrow wells / known, known and the loan made, wells / material, material managerial wells / worthy, worthy won through our heart's wells / twinkle, twinkle within wells / trickle, trickle to a triple well / talk, talk about our living wells / central, central to our mission, well / portals, portals plunged, well / porch, porch built well / steps, steps made, well / solvent, solvent too, well / spilling, spilling well to love / pressing, pressing now for well loved / sorts, sorts who say "well" love / precision, precision gained through wells of love / fling, flings last within love's wells / memphis, memphis and the kingdom's shores within wells / caught, caught without? wells / voting, voting through wells / image, image made well / units, units gift, a lift to heavenly wells / living, living Merkabahs blaze within wells / cavorts, cavorts sports well / calling, calling amplify to our wells / traits, traits true in our wells / travel, travel across light wells / river, river red with valley lined wells / flooding, flooding coming through valleys wise wells / listening, listening true-ing our wells / mithraic,

mithraic amusement for wells / glue, glue to a spot called welling forth within love / crescents, crescents reached through love's flying wells / call, call the central completion to your celestial wells / flashing, flashing allows wells / freedom, freedom fields our wells / ways, ways to the wisdom's wells / we, we are, well / leagues, leagues launch along wells / daily, daily and the living wells / balance, balances sought are through wells / value, value and the threshold's placed to light's wells / settle, settle then, wells / gift, gift and the gentle wells / gathers, gathers living wells / sixth, sixth and the opulence sent for light wells / seven, seven and the ways wells / eight, eight waves wells / sixty-four, sixty four fields paged through the wells.

PHASE TWO
LEVELS 65 - 128

TRUE POWER, THE SPIN OUT

LEVEL 65: THE IN-FLIGHTEN-MENTS

CHAPTER ONE

Flight, flight is the furl into a flown reside at regard for cures capable cords of creations courts of cooling phases to love's pure flights / fortitude, fortitude of the funded, love is in flight / freedom, freedom is found in a town within love's lightest flights / facts of the nature flown to love flight human / forgiving has come into a feeling of living flights / founded, dounded in funded remember to flight / phased, phased into pulses of the courses and the causes of reasonable lfights / funds, funds appearing in the include of a phase for love's flights / forms, forms matter for the materials ripe in the within of true flight / freshens, freshens a listened to of another's flights / frames frames forth for the lightened pictures of love's flights / frank in a selahing met for love's flights / forts purchased have seen the light through love's flights / fates, fates who fade to lead a light to love of flight / fallen, fallen has called into miraculous miracles of the liken to flights / friends, friends appear in phrases and the places of lightened flights / form form has been led to the fortitude for grown flights / forgiven, forgiven living has come to the friends within the lightening of love / frames, frames are found in sounds of lightened flights for love's hummings / frail into the mailing of true flights / funded in sundry ways for loving flights / follow, follow us home to the light of funded flights / flames, flames erupt into the flights to love / comfort, comfort comes into love's flight plans / cure, cures as simple as the sounds of purest flight / carry, carry a note to true love of the flights within the tube of God / codes, codes are written in cubical materials mentioned for the freedom to suggest that our trail is direct for the flight human / collates, collates assurance for the red realy and to this reply of love's parallel flights to God / curb a reaction to the conviction of the love that is blessed when less is within flight's paths / create an exterior light for the flight's within / curates soar has found a definition of the mer-ka-ba without and the flight's within / carry, carry a focus of the feelings linked when light says " allow us a living flight" / cord, cord of the lessen is cut for life's paths to flights in love / caps, caps of the central flights to love / courts, courts chosen win for love's flights / teams, teams chosen linking up for love's flights / trend, hear the trend of a lving flight / truth, truth has been told that the blood is the filling up of lightened flights to love / trades, trades ahve been made to include love's flights / turns, turns have come to the turning for love's flights / tokens, tokens passed and the cash invest for living flights to love / gather, gather in glittered amends for the legendary flight's paths / true, true in insure for love's gifts and the lightening of her flights / power, power is established through love for a flight's paths / pearls, pearls are opneing too for the flights to tahitian rays fo love / jewels, jewels fo tibetan degree and the flights into lhassa for love / patients, patients found in metatronic bliss for the mastery found in Sai Baba's list of the flights of love / portions, portions shared in lifting flights to love / allow, allow us your loving flights / yearn in disciple's ships for love flights / listen, listen to the news of glad revival for loving flights / desire is dealt to the loving of flight's paths / plan, plan a mission to the land of recognition for love flights / act, act now for love's flights / traits, traits operate for the lovingness of God / turns, turns are made, today for love's flights / stretch, stretch to the news of love's flights / stir, stir with agility for the energetics to love's flights / stone, stone cool removed for love's flights / stores, stores open into love's flights / successions, successions of suggestions for love's paths / surety, surety sealed into love's flights / steadfastness, steadfastness afforded for love's paths / loyal, loyal links established for love's flights.

CHAPTER TWO

Flights, flights to relation's cost of the curation's core and the adoring currents to a relevant love for flight / fashions, fashions formed a fearless test fro flight / pagentry, pagentry was worn for the lively aspects of true flights / pairs, pairs are matched, as said, "through evenings silent in perfect eye-widened flight" / mirrors, mirrors established in the soaring lips equipped with flight / stars, stars are eyed as the size for cares to take flight / heavens, heavens mate is your gateway through the plane into an empowered state called flight / sparks, sparks are sharp arcs into the tower of love's flights / steering, steering has occured into the voluminous core of the column of light and with all reflect we find flight into love / stare, stare into the caring erection called tantra, flight / stairs, stairs are built into the curing chair for next flights into Egypt / follow, follow another's plane into a fellow flight / ladders, ladders are leaders into perfect flight / heavens, heavens and A mate are found in a town with an A for true flight / finds, finds are made daily into the flight for all news of love / found, found in a history for the enthused, "flight" / flow, flow into knowing true others in showers for flight / flower, flower in the our for flight / field, field elected for a shield freed flight into love / regard for materials written into the cards for flight / gain, gain a respective perspective for flight / felt, felt another nestle into your flight path / freed, freed of the sword of neglect without flight / forms, forms melt into your nudge toward flight / appearance, appearance made for the grade called "A" flight / cheers, cheers are arranged into stages of flight / chores, chores finished now arrives a new site called flight path over Nazca and west to the shores Rapa Nui and a festival of light headed sites / chains, chains off, fly into the sun disk of love / chairs, chairs around pools filled in flight, a lake titicaca in height / elects, elects to see Machu Pichu through a flight / levels, levels are fortunate to be labeled as "flights" / lions, lions shared a lamb's repaste for the lair equipped with flight / feast, feast in yes! to flight / meals, meals eaten are recent in wheeling for flight / share, share another's cracker blue flight / honor, honor a heart which lasts nearby and twin your flight to love / heart, heart of the major and minor arcane has found a future in flight / feet, feet unbound and wound to chinese calligraphy of the kind which read "flight" / arms, arms won, now rest, in flight / scenes, scenes of the kind which read "flight" / record, record your natural scent here in a pheremonic imprinting called flight genes / teach, record and teach the others through your staying powers and your armed impressions on flight's paths / tribe, tribe of the century for flight / trues, trues and listens too, "flight" / allegorical, allegorical meanings add too, flight / literary, literary in my keyings for life to A flight / horizons, horizons sold to the awarest flights / built, built instead upon flight paths / release, release without recourse A tract on the islands for love's flights / relief, relief rests in your register for the formations to love's foundations for flight / shower, shower into "ours" for flight's paths / share, share the light "flight" / succumb, succumb to history for flight / linger, linger longer over all flights / language, language gauged by a legend for flights / flowers, flowers are ours in true flights / flows, flows a template for our interior flights / flown, flown into seas of shekinah blue materialize for the flights of love / lava, lava flows into the see of flown flights / glass, glass blue delivery of the cherubic sort who rise through seraphim skies into flight / festive, festive now in restive respect for those who know flight / resurrect, resurrect the direct connect into colleges of light flights / align, align inside a mission for flights / leap, leap into years of sacred flight, aligned in a risen sun day school called temples green in Dendera plates of the annual analog called stars who match each March and May throughout historical gaze.

CHAPTER THREE

Forward, forward has been paid into your flight / focus, focus on a take off to flight / arc, arc along shores intended for flights / atoms, atoms mergin to see flight in energetic delivery / millenia, millenia shared for the emergent sort who care about mountains who take flight / mysteries, mysteries established have shown a near core for materials loaned to new love for light flight to heart doors / discoveries, discoveries have amused and amazed in true fashion for love's flights / shows, shows arrive to show the prior energetics for flgiht / lost, lost in listen? flight / found, found in flowering? flights / civil, civil in a gentle flight / civilized, civilized into several cells, flights / rivers, rivers who reach shores for heart flights / nile, nile blue paging too and flights / felony, felony goes into flights / drama, drama over, just know yourself well into, flights / quest, quest is made and a search reached for arks in flight / acknowledge, acknowledge a patient research into flights / contents, contents empty into movements for flight / continents, continents shift into focus for flights / features, features natured and found for Alll flights / sanctions, sanctions into A flight / sanctuaries, sanctuaries into an arranged formation for flight / touch, touch into soaring flights / children, children into sincerest flights / hope, hope and the happening flights / monuments, monuments into mentioned flights / understood, understood in fueling flights / patient, patient in simple flights / chaste, chaste without hastened flights / sounds, sounds and the healing flights / join, join and the joining flights / wills, wills and the warming flights / empire, empire is simple into flights / built, built and the balanced flights / designs, designs initialized for flights / executive, executive reachings for flight / produce, produce a passion for flight / screen, screen into random ranges for flight / fabric, fabric federal unto flights / cast, cast on a concourse for flight / score, score along linear flights / cast, cast into simply, flight / score, score in sincerest flights / scenes, scenes sincerest in flights / written, written into durations for flight / play, play into

simple flights / produce, produce another mystery for the history of flight / purchase, purchase for the reaches for the mystery of flight / introduce, introduce and the readiness for flight / psychological, psychologically set for the features for flight / treatise, treatise for the mention into flight / arrangement, arrangement chored into flight / reigns, reigns and the arrangement for flight / objective, objective for the surest in flights / rules, rules and the arrangement meant for formidable flights / symbols, symbols significant into flights / prologue, prologue present for annual flights / laws, laws and the eruptive into the flights / findings, findings and the futures into A flight / diatoms, diatoms endure into the hills for friendly flights / correlations, correlations surrender into the future for flight / energy, energy mended for a mentioned befriend and the send into friendly flights / structure, structure initial for the flight into light structures adored for a mission into flight.

CHAPTER FOUR

Wings, wings and the wedded flights / decks, decks and the deed flights / completions, completions initial concur into flight / duals, duals and the sealings on flights / scales, scales and the focus for a sale on flights / presence, presence sent into flight / materials, materials emergent into flight / vibratory, vibratory into values for flight / oscillations, oscillations into vibrations for flight / changes, changes wedged into flights / math, math mixed into flights / examine, examine a respect for enhanced flights / inevitable, inevitable in several sorts who motion a notion for flights / viable, viable in values for lights into flights / scales, scales and the sealing for flights / chords, chords who cut a central path into flights / revelations, revelations sent into light's flights / evolutions, evolutions register for the formations of flight / fields, fields futured into the flight paths / distance, distance into notions for flights / manifest, manifest inspects your nations for grander flights / govern, govern a gracious freedom for flight / color, color capable into coolest flights / sovereign, sovereign seeds ascend into flights / oscillate, oscillate into a nation for flight / structure, structure for a necessary flight / dual, dual in a central pore for flight / transfer, transfer treats us well into literary flights / involve, involve and the solving flights / multiply, multiply the maturation of A flight / total, total tools for flight / octaves, octaves solved into flights / solve, solve a solvency for stranded flights / add, add a detail into your flights / insure, insure an assurance of your flights / symmetry, symmetry stands elegant in flight / dialects, dialects dual into flight / infrastructure, infrastructure forms a structured flight / gradations, gradations delays into flight / complex, complex for the formation of flight / language, language in a nestling flight / cognition, cognition and the charming flights / contents, contents and the cooled in living flights / accuracy, accuracy cures your flight paths / conference, conference immaculate unto the flights to love / chatter, chatter in a matter for the light flights / chaining, chaining management and the breaking freedom for love / channels, channels chosen path is into flights / define, define into durational flights / author, author acknowledged as the school for the flights along light and love / know, know and the nestling flights / weave, weave registers and the arrangment for A flight

/ create, create a creation into curing flights / 69 stays, 69 stays employ A flight's paths / infinity, infinity fuels a flight / molecules, molecules measure your flights / structure, structure is signal into flights / striations, striations strictest winning flights / scales, scales straightened for flight / parts, parts interior into flights paid for angular into love / horizontals, horizontals measured into flights / gravity, gravity grew into love's flights / spectrum, spectrum and the spiral into flights / strengths, strengths central into flights guided into total love.

CHAPTER FIVE

Genera, genera visceral to flight, love / mechanics, mechanics manic within flights to love / rations, rations into regional flights / phenomenons, phenomenons surmounted for the made for the loving flights / terrain, terrain solvent for the turning into flights / grids, grids material into a movement for flight / natures, natures kneeling flights / eternal, eternal centrally in flight / venues, venues material in masculine flights / parts, parts paternally material inside flights / revolve, revolve resolves in flight / questions, questions and the founded flights / positive, positive passions formatted for living flights / signatures, signatures creative into flight / signify, signify and the surrendered into flights / sense, sense and the seals upon a flight / possible, possible and the patterns into flights / capable, capable and the formerly flown flights / captives, captives creative into flight / excerpts, excerpts eccentric into flights / suppose, suppose and the simple flights / clear, clear into flight / deepen, deepen into flight / meanings, meanings and the material flights / repose, repose and the mention for "flights" / available, available assurance for all flights / well, well enough to be in A flight / willing, willing in a single flight / quests, quests central in a single quell of all flights / revolves, revolves a missing piece for flight / counters, counters suggested for a flight's paths / contra, contra cures A flight / posits, posits returned to A flight / counter, counter cures a spurning shift into flights / hits, hits and the light into flight / masters, masters and the mystery for all flights / purpose, purpose centrific in a flight / knowledge, knowledge pleasureable into a flight / gains, gains in a mention for the flights / secures, secures your delight in foundational aspects for flight / sunder, sunder and the thunder for all refreshing aspects of flight / articles, articles articulate into flight / pinnacles, pinnacles and the ends unto a cranio-sacral flight / evidence, evidence for the sort who aim into flights / structure, structure has met resource in love's flights / doctrine, doctrine of the eccentric who spin into flight / artifacts, artifacts who focus on fundamentals in flight / various, various into sorts who settle their values in flight / actual, actual factors made comparable to A flights / receipt, receipt settles into your ours for flights / recipe, recipe chores in legendary flights to love / essential, essential in essential minerals aimed into love's flights / forms, forms forged into flights / spirits, spirits meant for the sort who sport in flights / revolving, revolving in solving your fights without? flights / patterns, patterns perpendicular unto flight / facets, facets made mentioned into flight / passage, passage allowing your flights /

points, points made seam the essential flights / ascertain, ascertain your certain in flights / pursue, pursue another sport like flight / share, share in a caring flight / assist, assist within a rainbow's springing flight / creates, creates a source for aim into flight.

CHAPTER SIX

Do, do amusement for the flourish into flights / facts, facts denied now formed into flight freed patterns / strive, strive to seed your life in flights / bail, bail is over, flights / arrest, arrest has come to the rest who know less in their freedom and friendly flights / able, able to stable be in seeing flights / represent, represent your sort unto those who fly / middle, middle made grounded through the sort who finance flight and love / obligations, obligations paid for all the way through your flights / attempts, attempts made to persuade your sort into love for flights / trilogy, trilogy trillions deep in love's confessions for flight / strive, strive to seed your shrines with only flights / fundamental, fundamental tools spools flights and the final goodness for love / folds, folds and the fellows who aim into flight / double, double treated whims paid for in flights / venus, venus has arranged for two to win in flight / vibration, vibrations chosen now win A lined flights / factor, a factor rational for all who claim only flights / twice, twice and the necessary third into flights / told, told another yes! allow flights and freshness / declare, declare your days clearest for flight / cosmic, cosmic osmosis and the spatial flight paths / occassional, occassional in our mention for all flights / conduct, conduct made real to return too, flights / occupy, occupy your ready flights / fatal, fatal in flawed flights / conducive, conducive unto a material called experientially, flight / orchestrate, orchestrate a random forgive within flights / universe, universe allowing securely A flight / forces, forces met have found a clearance through your flights and circumstance / center, center sounds unto the forces allowing flight clearance / central, central unto rows of affluent flights / pursue, pursue another? flight / baby, baby made a beacon for all flights / observe, observe your swerving unto flight / rites, rite spade rituals into flight / embed, embed and the wed into flight / absolute, absolute in forgiven flights / strictly, strictly study A flights / staged, staged into annually and suited for all flights / reflective, reflective and arranged in racks of respect for the flights home / positron, positional positronic paths melt into arcturian lamps of soul released fusing and the pathway home through light called Christ conscious for love's flights / purpose, purpose and the maternals flights / flexible, flexible musings and the matched flights / focus, focus and the fatherly flighted / align, align appearing into your flights / within, within a welcome flight / chords, chords struck now release into flights / universal, universal in a rehearsal for love's flights / gain, gain a stand in lover's flights / wholeness, wholeness regained in your flight / near, near us will be A flight / emerging, emerging into flights of love's fancy / patterns, patterns made well for a flights / plan, plan to be in flight / purpose, purpose made well within flights / ripple, ripple and the simple flights / felt, felt in focused flight / feed, feed a known flight / ego, ego gone, will in checked flight, power position, positrons unite, ignite on faith full ON / lead, lead into led poles shifted and focused in flights / functions, functions made mention too, in flight / radiative, radiative resource for A flights / points, points pulse in A flights.

CHAPTER SEVEN

Pulse, pulse is made, flights / placement, placement gained, flight / scale, scale made in measure too, flight / oscillates, oscillates lightly and in flights / victory, victory comes in a gaining flight / victorious, victorious and a simple measure made into life flights / computation, computation made a mutation real into flight / inner, inner beings in flight / entry, entry laid and into flight / beyond, beyond a beginning for flight / bold, bold enough to say sooooo, flights / before, before and the regain of vertical in flights / forthright, of these all forthrightly said, "flight" / understand, understand a registration for the remainder of all flights / loyal, loyal to a flow for a cause called "in flight" / legions, legions regions are into flights / functions, functions fathomed flights / legends, legends reached, flight / instinctive, instinctive to a derivative of all flights / emotive, emotives votives fill in flights / intelligent, intelligent in a gentleness for living flights / extra, extra paid to flight paths / diagram, diagrams reached and found, flights / examine, examine maturely your relationship to the Lord of all rings about flights / intellect, intellect respects your flights / heartbeat, heartbeat reaches your door, flights / graduate, graduate for listened to flights / instincts, instincts sent A flight path / sole, sole in your year upon flights / lone, lone in your day into flights / loan, loan amde appropriate through flights / won, won a window onto your flights / secretive, secretive had end in your legendary flights / affirmed, affirmed and now mentioned "flights" / federations, federations fed a new flight / house, house is red, flights / word, word opening into flights / remarkable, remarkable a mention for your flights / protons, protons reaching A flight / rna, rna reaches a flight / ribosomal, ribosomal recourse unto flights / achieve, achieve a blatant balance in your flights / flow, flow empowered, balanced and in flight / neurons, neurons clear a flight path / unite, unite and be animated still in your solitary life in a pathway for clear flights / unify, unify a measured race into flight / flights, flights made, retread your pathway with door long flights / spins, spins and the spooling flights / orbitals, orbitals rearrange into pale forgiveness of flightless paths / mer-ka-bah, mer-ka-bah flew over your and your path to the starring spin for all flights / fields, fields peach green into flight / join, join jewels for the flowing flights / shock, shock and the inspected formations flights / fly, fly to the flowering flights / exist, exist in a relisting for flights / live, live to the living flights / ratios, ratios refused? fuse into flights / multiply, multiply in maturations of flight / threes, threes into knees born on flights / source, source to central flights / surge, surge in empowerments for flights / gradually, gradually increasing a flight / home, home to the hero for flight / patient, patient now, flights.

CHAPTER EIGHT

Respect, respect reached into flight / further, further allowance for flight / notes, notes made and red, flights / notice, notice a niche in your flights / sacred, sacred in a sealed way for flight / manifested, manifested mention for a former flight / mention, mention a mission into leafy flights / only, only and all ways current in flight / independently, independently won flights / guard, guard goes into flight / choices, choices made, lead, flight / evolutions, evolutions and solutions found in flight / values, values planned in flights / busy, busy attempts? flights / schedule, schedules chosen for flights / flights, flights flown into causes for goodness and God / business, business and the few who flower into flown events / protect, protect and the respect for those flights / suggested, suggested relations for those flights / healthy, healthy in a wealthy flight / accounts, accounts recounted formerly as a flight / tapes, tapes off, reach, flights / values, values reaching A flight / flights, flights focused on flights / family, family in mannerly flights / won, won in a wonderful flight / businesses, businesses born from a flight / virtues, virtues vaunted and the flights across lands / splendor, spendor and the render into flights / consume, consume a room within flights / fire, fire and the flashes of respect for flights / holy, holy and the healing flights / heavens, heavens and the mellow flights / opened, opened into penning flights / pens, pens and the patterns torn? flights / write, write and the ready tour flown into flights / love, love and the leading flights / light, light linkages felt for our flights / lifting, lifting allowed a leading flight / song, song and a singing into flights / praises, praises on flights / pen, pen applied for in flights / eternal, eternal in certain ways for flights / strong, strong into true flights / stretch, stretch along loving flights / voices, voices valuable on a flight / gladly, gladly gained flights / ring, ring about? flights / resurrect, resurrect a reaching too, flights / respect, respected red flights / roses, roses and the rapture of flights / pink, pink in penciled flights / powers, powers and thronging flights / purpose, purposes a plenty into flight / God, God gifts and the granted flights / Rewards, rewards and the thriving flights / good, good into giving flights / times, times to a milling flight / purchases, purchases and the powers aplenty a flight / power, power and the penchant for a flights / points, points and the momentary pause of a good flight / passive, passive pointed flights / vases, vases filled in broken dreams and flights / filled, filled into in flights.

CHAPTER NINE

Stone, stone of a mooning flight / sudden, suddenly a moving flight / drawn, drawn into nearest flights / detailed, detailed in a railing carved, flight / temple, temple of the trio planned on, flight / flowers, flowers are showering your life now with flights / spaced, spaced evenly, flights / hourly, hourly I choose one, flights / blossom, blossom daily in willing cubes of forgiven flights into love / pool, pool of the people who matter pertly for the gene pools of flights / paged, paged into planning flights / appears, appears a mission for flights / paved, paved into phases for the flight's paths / portrayed, portrayed and poured into flights / purged, purged and poised within flights / paid, paid a raid past all flights / positioned, positioned and risen into reasons for level flights / purged, purged in surging flights / planned, planned on NOW flights / positioned, positioned centrally as A flights / litany, a litany for flights / apparent, apparent in spinning flights / perfect, perfect fits for all flights / pleasant, pleasant and meant for, flights / purchased, purchased a ticket too, flights / parallels, parallels found, flights / places, places reached, flights / purchased, purchased one too, flights / pungent, pungent pens poised in flight / thorough, thorough in significance and flights / thickest, thickest doors open for flights / surrender, surrender into flights / crafts, crafts are spelled, f-l-i-g-h-t-s / spatials, spatials and the racials meant for flights / stones, stones made flat within hollowness without flights / safest, safest way? flights / fluid, fluid laid through pipes for flights / heart, heart continues, flights / yes, yes is a yellow flight / discovery, discovery made, follow your flights / impartial, impartial in a partial pay, flights / pursuant, pursuant and into flight / bound, bound as intended, flight / boundaries, boundaries into flight / DNA, DNA dealt a nearest flight / gravity, gravity grew to a shallow green field of pooling flights / events, events cropped into through flights / lanterns, lanterns led into flights for green flights / homes, homes matched through A flight / centers, centers curl in a filling flight / gravitation, gravitation rated for flights / sacred, sacred and the flight into paths / sports, sports into flights and the freedom to love / arisen, arisen directly into flight / lanes, lanes openly lead into flight / boulevards, boulevards balanced and into flight / blazes, blazes matched for flight / lines, lines crossing are linked into flights / force, force fed and infused within flights / reflections, reflections deflected now into your flights / insurrections, insurrections arouse flight / doctoral, doctoral degrees into sectors freedoms / sacred, sacred respect for those resurrected near your shore and a flight's path to your doors / known, known and delivered as such, flights unto those arrivals.

CHAPTER TEN

Chemistry, chemistry made a key element for the ametrine flights / constituents, constituents are on into flights / smallness, smallness has gone into flights / quarks, quarks are quickly welded flights / fundamental, fundamental funds founded on flights / actual, actual shoring for forms fitted into flights / heightened, heightened herding into fits for flight / previously, previously sorted flights / blended, blended into banners for flights / constituents, constituents gathered in flight / constant, constant cures us in flight / cores, cores and the shores are dear into flights / ratios, ratios rage into flights / ascension, ascension spinning in flight / lengths, lengths measured as flights / strings, strings off attach less, flights / inches, inches granted flight / meters, meters mentioned, flights / laws, laws governing flights / rights, rights reach flight / factors, factors amount to flights / trained, trained to be in flight / tuned, tuned into flights / verified, verified by your flights / monarchs, monarchs made flights / reciprocal, reciprocal reaches for flights / amends, amends made, flights / mentions, mentions trade flights / volatile, volatile goes into flight / vocalize, vocalize your flight / fend, fend about your flights / favor, favor a feeling for flights / value, value your dearest flights / master, master of all flights / meant, meant for interiorness, flights / given, given into for flights / intervals,

intervals signal your flights / frequent, frequent in recent flights / shortened, shortened into recency for love's flights / harmonies, harmonies musical flights / inherent, inherent in genius for flight / soluble, soluble flights / single, single and into flight / free, free to be flown / verification, verification for flights / values, values met flights / voicing, voicing your flights / sung, sung into, flights / arts, arts matched, flights / calculations, calculations ON, flights / measures, measures meet flights / increase, increase your reach into flights / healed, healed another flight / totally, totally welcome to be in flight / vibration, vibration soaring into flight / simply, simply said "flights" / increased, increased a released flight / rates, rates reaching for flights / rulings, rulings pooling flights / peering, peering into steering flights / understand, understand where you land for your flights / confirmed, confirmed again "flights" / God, God given flights / plan, plan to be into your flights.

CHAPTER ELEVEN

Hhuman, human harmonize flies into organic amazement / splendor, splendor reigning for flights / collaborate, collaborate and rationally find a flight / celebrate, celebrate your choice to be freely in flight / totals, totals added say "flight" / inverse, inverse dimenions of flight / lengthening, lengthening your flights / ratio, ratio reaching A flight / conforming, conforming into flights / vibrates, vibrates about "flights" / something, something said "flights" / all, all is well, flights / nothing, nothing without? flights / wonders, wonders reaching your door, flights / values, values settle into flights / whole, whole in a hero set for flight / patterns, patterns match, flights / gratitude, gratitude finally given flight / physical, physically release the one, flight / develops, develops new senses for flights / increase, increase a sense for flight / suggesting, suggesting a red flight into love / calling, calling is over, flights / forces, forces joined, flights/ creating, creating a magnet for flights / pressures, pressures off your flight / erupt, erupt into flights planned / instincts, instincts gathered for wandering plans into flight / opening, opening chosen as planned and a flight / comprehend, comprehend how well planned is humanity's flights / understand, understand the dealings planned a flight / relating, relating too, planning to fly / registers, registers regally a new plan to fly to love / amplify, amplify your sort, plan on flights / found, found is wound into flight / ultimate, ultimate the sorting for flights / gestures, gestures paid into flights / amusement, amusement mean for flights / launch, launch a new wave for all flights / contributions, contributions received for your flights / criminal, criminal without coded resort, flights / retarded, retarded efforts can go into flights forgotten without love / forgives, forgives another, flights / ultimate, ultimate unto you, flight / phenomenal, phenomenal growth planned, flight / intervals, intervals matched, flights / examine, examine your meanings for lfights / intimate, intimate in a gesture for laughter, flights / registers, registers near your door, flights / developed, developed a feeling for flights / consecutive, consecutive too, flights / underlie, underlie has found you in flight / structural, structural the difference in confidence for flight / begun, begun again, flights / launched, launched into, flight / scaffolding, scaffolding set up to charge lights a foundation for feelings and flights / envision, envision a newness in your flights / inquiring, inquiring can win you a flight / federations, federations been signalled now, flight / gestures, gestures mentioned as flight / joint, joint in delay without, flights / ponder, ponder your resources and flights / purvey, purvey all you own as your flight / paths, paths emerging and merging in flights.

CHAPTER TWELVE

Cosmetic, cosmetic in curing flights / cosmic, cosmic in might flights / ultimate, ultimate in treats, flights / prime, prime in your hymn, "flight" / codes, codes are written "f-l-i-g-h-t-s" / developments, developments mentioned include flights / existence, existence mentions "flight' / mercy, mercy on the seat for peace and flight / concentration, concentration on shores nearby, flight / cherubim, cherubim touching near your flights / seraphim, seraphim springing into life flights / splinters, splinters cured your flights / grades, grades made yours a flight / diminish, diminsh amounts to knowing flights / exist, exist wins your flight / score, score a new flight / focus, focus on your door's flights / primordial, primordial matters and flights / costs, costs off you, flights / present, present a new flight / spurts, spurts poetic in flight / surges, surges onto your flights / strategy, strategy paying for flights / deploy, deploy without another? win, flights / maintain, maintain a semblance for flights / concentration, concentration pays, flights / omnipotent, omnipotent forming flights / cores, cores settled into and flights/ truth, truth finally told into flights / calculations, calculations added too, flights / changed, changed now, flights / holy, holy is held forth as wholest flights happen / works, works reach an all ways for flights / decisions, decisions due you for flights / made, made a mention of "flights" / moves, moves about freely, your flight / gates, gates opened now, go, flight / placements, placements meatn, flights / attend, attend a triple flight / measured, measured friend, flight / fractions, fractions actions for flight / reverence, reverence sent for and flights / reverend, reverence mentioning flights / medical, medical mielues end, flights / wholeness, wholeness reaching your flights / notes, notes read, flights / nudges, nudges over, flights / segments, segments gone, flights / ends, ends and finds flight / encapsulate, encapsulate your door's flights / placed, placed allow into flights / diagrams, diagrams detail flights / sung, sung about, "flights" / shares, sharea a notion flights / things, things said last, flights / threads, threads aromatic into flights / placement, placement matches your flights / precise, precise in decisions lasting flights / ratios, ratios set reach flights / random, random relays read, "flights" / purchase, purchase made, flights / insure, insure your success, flights / suggested, suggested? flights / focus, focus on flights.

CHAPTER THIRTEEN

Contributions, contributions are made, merge into flight / currency, currency sent is for flights / current, current in your flights / chronic, chronic in fatigue without flights / essence, essence spent into flight / endless, endless in mentions for flight / immune, immune without? flights into love / clearly, clearly

yours is cared for in a flight / piece, pieces offered profer less without flights / presence, presence as spent is called flight / compelling, compelling lands, flights/ sustains, sustains a surging matter for flights / independence, independence won now through flights / functions, functions matched in your flights / focal, focalize only on flights / points, points won are flighted / reviews, reviews teach you ears to hear flights / creators, creators reach a resource called flight / perceive, perceive a balance called flight / imperceptible, imperceptible in shifting balances of flights / fundamentally, fundamentally freed of all past flights / absolute, absolute in a completion of lessoning for proof of flights / devotion, devotion gathers flights / complete, complete flight / cubic, cubic in meaningful flights / maintain, maintain a chalic for flight / contentments, contentments settle into flight / looks, looks are along lines forgotten without flight / faith, faith has said "flight" / spirits, spirits gone, flights / mention, mention a mention for flights / forms, forms tossed into flights / recite, recite a line "flights" / positive, positive into flights / plenty, plenty made within, flights / aggregate, aggregate in gained flights / openings, openings regain flight / places, places match, flights / forces, forces gathered "flights" / functions, functions infusion reigns "flight" / combine, combine a sport joined in flight / forces, forces featured in flight / taught, taught to be flighted / changes, changes matching your flights / cycles, cycles enuse for all flights / nearest, nearest and dearly yours, flights / incursions, incursions coined "flights" / diagrams, diagrams tossed into flight / between, between us winds, flight / totality, totality measures your flights / reflect in your respect for flights / mathematics, mathematics wins a flight / direction, direction into flight / stock, stock taken, "flight" / apply, apply for a flight / rules, rules requiring a flight / purged, purged of all lessening unto flights / perfect, perfect for forming a flight / flights, flights arranged now / futures, futures written into flights / everything, everything goes into flights / all, all is well, again, flights / verify, verify your new flights / votes, votes made, sealed, elect, flights.

LEVEL 66: THE IN-FOCUS-MENTS

CHAPTER ONE

Fives, fives and arrivals within a pin numbered for a focus / spanned, spanned in contributions for a federal focus / often, often and we've always a primary focus / ours, ours the cure for all ill focus / flights, flights cured by a living focus / swiftly, swiftly well into focus / freest, freest fashions focused / electives, elective raised unto a focus / mirrors elevate your foundation's focus / stars, stars mentioned and as said "focused into" / sparks, sparks admit ignition for the focused / find, find a fellow spark's focus / heavens, heavens homeward gaze into a focus / steering, steering leads you homeward still into focus / follow, follow an intention clearly well into a focus / flow, flow has acknowledged your core into focus / flower, flower in showering showering focus / felt, felt a flux into a focus / focusing, focusing has functional appearance at love / brethren, brethren and the balance unto a focused reverence / green, green into seams formed in focus / authority, authority and the feeling focus / missions, missions and the maintaining focus / excell, excell into your mission's focus / snug, snug in remembering love's focus / inspire, inspire and the sire from a focus / pillow, pillow pals focused / airs, airs above within focused / conquests, conquests about a focus / attain, attain a symbol for a focus / faith, faith is found in a focus / righteous, righteous growth rings your supportive throat's breadth, believe, and focus / proper, proper expense is without strings attached, know the wealth inside your focus / fittingly, fittingly fed a necessity, a focus / faithful, faithful is the fitted focus / prosper, prosper long into your focus / harvest, have a harvest for a focus / thoughtful, thoughtful feelings and focus / substance, substance ascends into a focus healed / wishing, wishing well, a focus / expert, expert experience sent a focus / better, better than less, a focus / experience, experience meant for focus / best, best is yes and focused / expertise, expertise if given a focus / golden, golden rayed focus / excise, excise without a focus / scripted, scripted and toasted as a focus / edit, edit a welcome focus / in your DNA a focus / gold, gold is yellow into a focus / editions, editions met a focus / grooming, grooming a mirrored focus / pressed, pressed in employ and focus / script, script written says "focus" / fellowship, a fellowship coming into focus / copies, copies marry a focus / coping, coping is noping your door without focus / pressing, pressing into serail expressions and focus / transcribe, transcribe allowing a focus / nobles, nobles gasp at your focus / record, record made to alst a focus / gas, gas is grown through a throning movement into sunlight conversion and past hotlines into focus / sun, sun, the aten, the disk, the focus, the fellow, a star, arcturus, yellow-orange in a treaty for focus.

CHAPTER TWO
Renew, renew a focus / pages, pages mixed and focused / renewal, renewal periods and focus / lists, lists made, a focus / coping, coping is doping you past a welling into love's focus / awaiting, awaiting fating recall for the flowering patch we call life, a lead into focus / title, tiles paid for in focus / awaits, awaits a nearest examine for focus / expressions, expressions sold into focus / shiva, shiva and the divas of focus / hearts, hearts who start a new focus / ganesh, ganesh and the knew, focused / labors, labors and the loves focused / ecstatic, ecstatic about focus / gilgamesh, gilgamesh has gained focus / meditates, meditates in a rain for focus / begs, begs for fruition through focused activities / burma, burma and the burmese capitalize burled into action through focus / money, money is made when we hint of only "focus" / jewels, jewels are made plenty in focus / india, india is well into your focused estates / sari, sari of the centurion, in focus / nepalese, nepalese spoken, hear, "focus" / holy, holy in the holy land of focus / prepares, prepares the statement for our focus / gives, gives us oral examine into focus / germination, germination has seeded your focus / eyes, eyes metabolic into staring focus / builds, builds a basis for A focus / gains, gains a granite focus / fulfill, fulfill a destiny for focus / multitudes, multitudes feel your

measures / motions, motions made connect you to love's focus / instruct, instruct another to be in focus / measures, measures are measureably in focus / incarnates, incarnates in random without focus / eye, eye in the shadow? re-focus / hearts, hearts are treasured and amazed with focus / darshan, darshan is spoken, "focus" / hands, hands are held as we meld our foci / initiations, initiations past are in focus / secrets, secrets held are welded into focus / attire, attire for the sire of focus / blessed, blessed in a basic focus / fires, fires frozen have melt in focus / worn, worn in two, foci / burns, burns a basic focus / marriage, marriage comes into view through your focus / emotions, emotions gather near your focus / fair, fair is dear into caring focus / hair, hair is held back in a burning focus / strands, strands grown have electric coatings inside their focus / arrivals, arrivals amaze you through focus / baba, baba said "come" to a focus / sai, sai is near "focus" / light, light is ON focus / serapis, serapis blue experience for a focus / await, await venus as we weave a doorway for focus / candidate, candidates treasure your focused way / call, call another who means "focused" / love, love is led now to focus / joins, joins us nightly for focus / told, told to be in focus / told, told whom we allow in focus.

CHAPTER THREE
Supply, supply sent to the intentional focus / works, works and the ringing into focus / entire, entire into hiring focus / restoration, restoration and the focus on love / restore, restore more unto focus / apply, apply to be into focus / eternity, eternity and the gaining into focus / virtue, virtue and the firming focus / sights, sights into our focus / things, things and the thronging in focus / tributes, tributes offer an focus / signify, signify said into a focus / deliver, deliver into our focus / repeat, repeat won our focus / peace, peace is unto our focus / sigh, sigh and the sealing focus / suggestions, suggestions suggested into focus / lightly, lightly in a living focus / balance, balance unto a focus / confessions, confessions forming a focus unto love / admire, admire and the shouldered focus / often, often and the framing focus / specify, specify and the significant focus / joys, joys immaculate into a focus / works, works and the windows into a focus / watching, watching a willow blend into focus / unfolds, unfolds a magnetic plan for focus / learning, learning has an example and it is you, find a new focus / tables, tables have turned watch, focus / lands, lands bought, multiply into focus / handicaps, handicaps over, see the light, focus / strengths, strengths flair for focus / carefree, carefree for duration into focus / concerns, concerns are met in wet focus / treads, treads are about and we shout for your focus / collectives, collectives selective ito focus / triumphs, triumphs reign as selected and given focus / concerned, concerned in a manner regal enough to focus in / wells, wells into truth found and focused / endures, denures a direction for focus / peace, peace is possible, focus / taught, taught to be in focus / patient, patient in our appliance for focus / growth, growth given good, focus / glad to be inside your focus / words, words are wisdom when in focus / envoy, envoy sent is meant for focus / pulse, pulse and the placement for focus / spreads, spreads and the focus into

love / powers, powers of the cure into focus / exceed, exceed in excell for focus / doubt, doubt and the shouted focus / fears, fears and the steering focus / doors, doors and the dearest focus / mornings, mornings and the lost account in sincerest focus / tolerance, tolerance relegated into focus / beatitudes, beatitudes and placement into focus / harvest, harvest and the healing focus / ripen, ripen and the relations into focus / godhead, godhead said "focus" / errands, errands and the rewarded focus / strands, strands into simple focus / proofs, proofs into relationships of truth and a focus / military, military detail relates into focus.

CHAPTER FOUR

Predicate, predicate to a relation for A focus / body, body into beauty and a beacon for a focus / becalm, becalm and a calmest focus / bless, bless and the retest into focus / flowers, flowers into showers and a focus / bliss, bliss into centrally A focus / turmoil, turmoil is welcome to a focus / manage, manage meant for a focus / paths, paths pour into a focus / loads, loads are led into focus / calms, calms are into focus / floods, floods are fed into focus / warrant, warrant a worshipful focus / loads, loads are linked into focus / savor, savor a flavor for focus / flesh, flesh is into a focus / destiny, destiny is due our new focus / reckons, reckons a sequence fallen into focus / provides, provides a patient focus / behold, behold a balance for a focus / surfeit, surfeit it to say sufficiently clear a nearer focus / beloved, beloved into being a focus / surface, surface as set into focus / spirits, spirits into a new focus / crowns, crowns into a clearing focus / empire, empire and the retinue into a focus / rise, rise into a rearing focus / folly, folly without? focus / mine, mine is the mention for focus / rage, rage is over, focus / essence, essence is said to be "focused" / rejoice, rejoic as allowed into focus / peace, peace is a plenty for focus / altars, altars are dearest hearts focused / breath, breath is a balance for focus / diadems, diadems and a diatom within focus / errands, errands essential in a focus / breaths, breaths are balanced as focused / enjoy, enjoy a moment's focus / crowns, crowns essential to a focus / abundance built in focus / luxury, luxury leading to a focus / clears, clears capably your focus / errs, errs within? focus / concepts, concepts fuse in focus / leaps, leaps into legendary foci / human, human and the held to focus / cleans, cleans and the counting focus / heralds, heralds who held us in a focus / blinds, blinds who balance in a focus / love, love is led into a balance / solemn, solemn without mention, focused / worlds, worlds are wed into a focus / notes, notes made are bade a focus / learn, learn to be focused / purpose, purpose as said "a" focus / flesh, flesh is fed into a focus / saved, saved without? a focus / silver, silver is the leading color for a focus / passion, passion's fruit is focus / partnered, partnered in a focus / lunching, lunching meets a focus / plans, plans to be in focus / marriage, marriage to a focus.

CHAPTER FIVE

Cords, cords cut now and focused / travels, travels lightly, focused / radiance, radiance and the reaches focused / brings, brings about a balanced focused wealth and way / patterns, patterns pelt your eyes in sweet focus / constitutes, constitute creations of our focus / pause, pause made is gift to a clause called focused / trails, trails ripen and soften ito focus / lightens, lightens a listed focus / invites, invites another into focus / rejoice, rejoice around your focus / mantle, mantle mentioned is made into a focus / brough, brought a beauty into focus / round, round us red, a focus / altars, altars cleared and trees felled create a debacle without focus / reaps, reaps as sown, a focus / men, men are meant to focus / incandescent, incandescent in a cleansing focus / strives, strives arrival into focus / honest, honesty meant for focus / declaration, declaration for a focus / caress, caress another's focus / devolve, devolve into solving focus / involve, involve another in your focus / moments, moments are meant to focus / measurements, measurements are given to focus / like, like is led to our focus / intellects, intellects meeting in focus / feast, feast fed a focus / focal, focal in a vocal focus / abstraction, abstraction over, a focused / love, love is leading you, focus / probes, probes over, focus / worthiness, worthiness welcomes a focus / alien, alien without you, focused / align, align inside libations of a focus / spreads, spreads into your focus / explores, explores a newest focus / plans, plans made are kept, focus / placements, placements mentioned are given a focus / speech, speech is plain "focus" / simplest, simplest gift is focus / curious, curious about your? focus / probes, probess off us and our focus / hearts elope into focus/ lost, lost in a linking focus / specifics, specifics belt into focus / found, found a friend in focus / perish, perish less, gain more, focus / placements, placements mean, focus / givengiven a giving, focus / burdens, burdens off you, focus / spreads, spreads a revelation on a focus / boast, boast about your focus / placed, placed into simple focus / watchful, watchful about a focus / lights, lights on to focus by / memories, memories made a focus / collaborate, collaborate on a focus / empiricist, empiricist for a focus / divine, divine in a focus / instruct, instruct simply and focus / transgress, transgress without? a focus / only, only and then A focus.

CHAPTER SIX

Dawns, dawns a new cause for focus / days, days plentied in focus / planes, planes open too, focus / clothed, clothed in simple focus / ministrations, ministrations meant for focus / waters, waters weds a focus / universal, universal appeal unto a focus / memorize, memorize your focus / bids, bids made unto a focus / principles, principles kept in focus / shades, shades drawn into a focus / recompense, recompense for a focus / glory, glory given an instance of focus / domes, domes built clear in focus / reconcile, reconcile to a focus / homeward, homeward bound a focus / golden, golden gated focus / parables, parables written for a focus / bids, bids made now, focus / stretch, stretch into your focus / evaluate, evaluate your situation through focus / patient, patient in approaching you, focus / exalt, exalt the won, focus / bridle, bridle worn to focus on / gathered, focus has gathered near your nesting heart / endures, endures a duration for focus / lifting, lifting leads to focus / beloved, beloved won a focus / comes, comes a gateway opening to focus / global, global in your adoration for focus / kept, kept in simple focus / shining, shining fresh in focus / mastery, mastery made a focus / masters, masters given a focus

/ precious, precious in a reward for the focus / shown, shown a shoulder focus / shone, shone a nautre for focus / high, high in a simple focus / enoble, enoble sets of values for focus / goodly, goodly amounts are laid at your feet, focus / parades, parades charge into view, focus / surface, surface cleared, focus / treaties, treaties made are focused / treatise, a treatise on pleasure is found, focused / journey, journey inward to the focus, fountains / floods, floods meant a focus on rainbows / floodgates, floodgates appear and open into a deluge of love focus / mines, mines are meant to pen into a focused / messages, messages received as focused / confident, confident in your focus / tempts, tempts another's focus / temptation, temptation given a focus / voice, voice made into focus / march, march along a focus / allows detail to read "as focused" / thrilling, thrilling in her retinue fo focus / christian, christian to a welcome tune called christ consciousness / amakua, amakua and the focus / sleep, sleep in deep focus / sheep, sheep are gone keep only lambs in your focus / spirit, spirit won, focus / lamb, lamb led to you, focus / judah, judah given release now, focus / israel, israel makes a journey home to a focus for love.

CHAPTER SEVEN

Heavens, heavens focus on the lift into love / choir, choir crews and focus / heels, heels uncross to focus / step, step and the light into a focus / class, class and the clash without focus / instruct, instruct and the restructure for a focus / chores, chores and the stores into a focus / insurrect, insurrect and the respect for a focus / throats, throats and the closures formed a focus / grids, grids and the sids off a framed focus / browns, browns and the rounds into a focus / bridges, bridges squarely focused / broadness, broadness based into a focus / falter, falter and the feelings focused / hath, hath and the knots into a focus / fault, fault and the feelings focused into a knowing knot / collaborative, collaborative efforts trickle to an effort / universe, universe federal into a focus / thirsty, thirsty in threat freed focus / wants, wants are desired into a focus / radiant, radiant and the rules are focused / divination, divination and the stations rule a focus / radiance, radiance and the registry for a focus / elects, elects and the squarely focused / cones, cones and the lateral framework for a focus / radiance, radiance and the threadworked focus / despoil, despoil and the decry into a focus / perplex, perplex and the throned focus / kinds, kinds and the shielded focus / sufferance, sufferance suggested A focus / abomination, abomination aborted into a focus / blunders, blunders and the thundering focus / prayers, prayers and the overage into a giving healing focus / perform, perform and the penchant for a forming performance's focus / thrusts, thrusts and the threats off a focus / contrite, contrite in a trickle's focus / goodly, goodly in a giving focus / intercourse, intercourse said "a focus"/ heritage, heritage patched into a rainy weekly path, a focus / nations, amperes into nations forming focus / living, living in a lampoon? living focus / atrocities, atrocities have gone into a focus / testimony, testimony unto a focus / wisdoms, wisdoms warrant a willing focus / tutelage, tutelage linked into a focus / therein, therein is a mystery cleared and a focus / perils, perils penchanted focus / seasons, seasons of single focus / luminaries,

luminaries are a focus / gazes, gazes and the opening into a focus / mothers, mothers and marriage meant for a forecast focus / angles, angles into angels and a focus / materials, materials amount to focus / devil, devil without and outed for a focus freeing / carols, carols occuring in a focus / tryst, tryst has tools for a focus / sons, sons into sealing focus / worthy, worthy of a willing focus / lights, lights listed? focus / watch, watch and the matching focus / earthly, earthly has measured a focus / reports, reports are appealing into a focus / forms, forms are feeling too, a focus / aspire, aspire amounting to a focus.

CHAPTER EIGHT

Business, business built into a focus / attractive, attractive in reactive focus / mortals, mortals immortal unto a focus / twinkles, twinkles in shingles for a focus / goods, goods gave us a focus / sentient, sentient in mention's focus / retorts, retorts into simple focus / clears, clears and the filling focus / define, define and the daily focus / definition, definition deems us our focus / solemn, something seemingly solemn without focus / sexual, sexual in a sealing focus / endeavors, endeavors severs focus / diadems, diadems slim into focus / arisen, arisen and the nearly focused / coronas, coronas and the thronging focus / identify, identify and the thrice led focus / origin, origin made a focus / fallen, fallen into pysche forecast and a focus / obeys, obeys a recall of a focus / progress, progress made a focus / presence, presence allows your aim a focus / goods, goods grown for a focus / encompass, encompass a rumpus for a formation's focus / royals, royals arranging a focus / rules, rules emply our focus / rights, rights arranging focus / rules, rules over all and focus / rights, rights to a riddle focused / sovereign, sovereign to a sealing focus / endears, endears us a formulaic focus / messages, messages match a focus / endeavors, endeavors leveraged matched for focus / messages, messages materialized and a focus / endeavors, endeavors triple AAA focus / messages, messages and the massaged for a focus / enduring, enduring a focus / manners, manners materialized aim freely focused / wakeful, wakeful news of a focus / falls, falls fellow focus / forth, forth is a filling focus / caught, caught without a focus / prepare, prepared in a simple focus / burnt, burnt yellow remains as focused / victorious, victorious matched focus / summons, summons serial focus / brief, brief in a mental focus / summoning, summoning wears your focus / spake, spake when and focused / comprise, comprise met a focus / grandeur, grandeur endures a focus / valiant, valiant values feeding matched focus / circumstance, circumstances made a focus / roles, roles and the reaches forming a focus / empty, empty into touches of relation's focus / abides, abides and the streaming focus / verify, verify and the remaining focus / royalty, royalty reaching a focus / remainders, remainders rooming focus / diadems, diadems dim? engage and focus / clothes, clothes cleared focus / coronations, coronations crept past A focus / conquers, conquers waist deep in a focus / bidding, bidding for our focus.

CHAPTER NINE

Entities, entities grip on a focus / miracles, miracles match your focus / angels, angels host our focus / vortex, vortex frosted focus / business, business born in focus / forces, forces mature / perplex, perplex and the frameworked focus / process, process participates on a focus / works, works awarest a focus / harness, harness heralds a focus / true, true enough to see from a star's focusing aspect of love / loves, loves a listening focus / initialize, initialize a license of a focus / impulse, impulse's focus / propriety, propriety and our focus / acts, acts and the freedom willed into focus] / boasts, boasts on a miracle for a minute's breath and a coming focused / battles, battles parmanahnsa for a kept format without even love / gains, gains refrained to a causes focus / cause, causes to a calendar formed in focus / profits, profits pulsed in a caused focus / perform, perform a way into a focus / eternity, eternity into our focus / tests, tests intrigue our focus / selves, selves arrange your focus / identity, identity fulfills our focus / balanced, blankets balanced into focus / sought, sought and the sending focus / sets, sets and the surgerical focus / aspects, aspects particular to a focus / difference, difference ventures into our focus / assets, assets central to a focus / won, won into wondering focus / lottery, lottery leads into a focus / feasts, feasts on numbers into focus / festivals, festivals of pure focus / nations, nations nestle into our focus / schools, schools aiming and focused / endowed, endowed measures on focus / courage, courage managed annual focus / crafted, crafted in simple focus / settle, settle into focus / chosen, chosen channels and focus / posing, posing in a ritual focus / choose, choose a nimble focus / generous, generous in a rewarded focus / directs, directs an event as focused / justice, justice woos your focus / raiment, raiment worn is focused / affluence, affluence affords former focus / redeems, redeems a rewarding focus / managed, managed manage meant for focus / opens, opens material's focus / approves, approves rewarding focus / prophetic, prophetic in your focus / honors, honors a nearing sailing focus / cities, cities meeting focus / commissions, commissions committing a focus / names, names initial your focus / nameless, nameless needing's focus / offers, offers a feeling focus / scores, scores dealing in focus / serves, serves sincerely a focus / generated, generated a reigning focus.

CHAPTER TEN

Lovely, lovely into a final focus / hearken, hearken into heralded focus / loveliness, loveliness initials our focus / alchemies, alchemies material focus / hundred, hundred and the plenty foraging into focus / exists, exit into a focus / paramount, paramount paternal touring focus / honors, honors and the heralded focus / services, services abridging our focus / mortal, mortal mounting focus / repeals, repeals appealing focus / eagles, eagles and the gateway's focus / crop, crop and the creative focus / quaffs, quaffs opted into a function / excells, excells a simple focus / augery, augery and the overviewed focus / competence, competence into conscious focus / sufferance, sufferance over the consciousness unto focus / victorious, victorious and the when-ing focus / words, words of shining wisdom unto a focus / kingdoms, kingdoms coming into a focus / heavens, heavens healing format of focus / earths, earths patterning focus / slumbers, slumbers a shilling

focused / drinks, drinks attune into focus / freedom, freedom freeing focus / circular, circular surrounding focus / perform, performing a pairing focus / services, services signal focus / opens, opens appearing focus / found, found a federal featured focus / services, services incurring focus / embark, embark along the threaded focus / foes, foes and the famous focus / utterance, utterance's torn without focus / imports, imports wearing future focus / delivers, delivers a daring focus / countenance, countenance purest focus / wisdoms, wisdoms mentionable focus / enemy, enemy enduring? focus / life, life is loving focus / focal, focal and the wad into is freedom focused / vocal, vocal in a federation's eye-filled focus / phases, phases completed, focus / voiced, voiced in a serial focus / visualize, visualize forms a who first focus / portrays, portrays us as focused / cleanse, cleanses our focus / meant, meant a matching focus / barns, barns out, focus / forks, forks pinched focus / silence, silence offers a focus / destination, destination dues and focus / entering, entering peels your focus / perception, perception patches an annual focus / beauteous, beauteous pairings focus / stages, stages over, focus / philosophize, philosophize a paired focus / earths, earth's material focus / happens, happens into freedom's focus / features, features funded focus / realize, realize our focus / charged, charged in simply focused events / materialim, materialism matched into focus.

CHAPTER ELEVEN

Constant, constant to a cue's focus / decrees, decrees made are kept for a future focus / lengths, lengths are given breaths of focus / laws, laws divided drive us to focus / sojourns, sojourns are made into a focus / flows, flows a natural focus / fourished, flourished in ancients, focus / wars, wars are finished, now focus / behaves, behaves as one warrd, focus / process, process made apparent through focus / assails, assails wihtout wails, focus / hearts, hearts are held in tune, focus / pronounce, pronounce another well, focus / selah, selah is relayed into a focus / mammons, mammons hamper is filled in focus / blasphemes, blasphemes muse is due our act, focus / divine, divine in a ley focused / strangers, strangers apt to focus / counsels, counsels another to focus / serves, serves us wellest, focus / prospers, prospers in desperate focus / tributes, tributes paid A focus / gains, gains made and focused / times, times trimmed in focus / produces, produces wages of a particular focus / paid, paid in a tune focused / harbors, harbors know ill? focus / sheperds, sheperds flock, focus / radiance, radiance rules a focus / errands, errands are dealt your focus / bestows, bestows a gifted focus / providence, providence has sent a focus / dens, dens are ripely opened to a given focus / times, times are true as focused / accolades, accolades lead to a focus / elope, elope engage focus / safes, safes are filled in focus / allow, allow another to love your focus / hopes, hopes held, healed, focus / patience, patience as taught A focus / ordains, ordains a nearest focus / ramparts, ramparts watched are focused in / missions, missions, mansions, focus / fashions, fashions falter? focus / richly, richly dressed in righteous raiment / receiving, receiving has called A focuse / duties, duties held are taught A focus / ordains, ordains expanse is into A focus / chaos, chaos cools in focus / accounts,

accounts paid into focus / begun, begun to balance and focus / mount, mount your count along focus / cometh, cometh another's focus / glee, glee sent to focus / eternity, eternity met in focus / youth, youth as yelled "in focus" / paves, paves a page's focus / foreheads held to a fused equation called yellow forecast unto love's focus / manifests, manifests a fusion of focus / enrichment, enrichment meant to focus / elation, elation given to rested focus / labors, labors lost are found in focus / mates, mates meet in focus / mention, mention a neutral focus.

CHAPTER TWELVE
Delivery, delivery due your door's focus / worlds, worlds meet in focus / brothers, brothers blessed as focused / minds, minds mixed of focus / hearts, hearts experience A focus / envisions, envisions vary to focus / grow, grow and focus / God, God given's focus / peoples, peoples and the maple focus / inspiration, inspiration for the focused / versions, versions foci deep in love / paper, paper pieces focus / tenets, tenets lain into focus / trees, trees entire in their focus / codes, codes made and keyed into as focused / trails, trails appearing focused / comparative, comparative too, a focus / onward, onward said a focus / preach, preach is about without focus / generational, generational skips into a focus / mark, mark the most important focus / circumscribe, circumscribe the inside track to loving focus / inspect, inspect a passion for focus / polite, polite inside an insight for focus / flocks, flocks are filled in focus / streets, streets embrace your focus now / people, people see an empire shift in focus/ stones, stones are sent into willing focus / powers, powers be in focus / boulevards, boulevards are sold a focus / versions, versions past are linked into focus / fountains, fountains fill into a focus / made, made of stone and sinking focus / wise, wise in a way's focus / befriends, befriends again a focus / teachers, teachers taught A focus / contrasts, contrasts last in focus / furtive, furtive without a focus / orange, orange is the yellow into focus / circles, circles sent to encourage focus / effulgence, effulagence meant in focus / ought, ought to be in focus / nary, nary a spirit without focus / dilemma, dilemma over, due a focus / naught, naught is wrought without focus / mysterious, mysterious ones who focus / toxins, toxins out and in a focus / finite, finite the amount who stay in focus / obscure, obscure the amounts to focus / majestic, majestic in states focused / aware, aware of whom, the focus / brethren, brethren who know a focus / perspective, perspective slow to lessen, focus / doctrination, doctrination assured, focus / glanced, glanced into eyes who focus / flesh, flesh is met in a focus / discerns, discerns a matter too, focused / understand, understand when and whom and focus / deigns, deigns apparent needs as focused / witness, witness held into focus / works, works weld our focus / details, details spare without focus / labors, labors lost found focus / waters, waters wed us to the focus

CHAPTER THIRTEEN: comprehends, comprehends our case, focus / tumult, tumult over, focus / remarks, remarks enhance your focus / beds, beds aloft in foucs / known, known to be a focus / blessings, blessings bed into our focus / spells, spells are

cast to less? focus / chance, chance has made you heal a focus / enlists, enlists a patient focus / procedure, procedure cures our focus / address, address laid into the wood for focus / ruins, ruins cleared and focused / rates, rates are set focus / profitsprofits paid are focused / rare, rare is the key who and the kind who focus / drawn, drawn are others too, focus / ministrations, ministrations admit a determined focus / scepter, scepter passed is focused / worthiness, worthiness nears our focus / known, known and sent to focus / vintage, vintage in mission's focus / columns, columns equipped for focus / rarest, rarest a neighbor who shares your focus / persons, persons who knew a focus / vessels, vessels purge a focus / triumphs, triumphs made your focus / flocks, flocks along a focus / legible, legible to written focus / flocks, flocks who pass into focus / phalanx, phalanx amounting to a focus / signs, signs sent and focused / hillside, hillside pleasures as focused / uttered, uttered wrods into focus / distance, distance dealt with, focus / encompass, encompass a sent remark for focus / cohorts, cohorts met in focus / reach, reach into a reeling focus / mentors, mentors made a friend, focus / laughter, laughter has healed your focus / starts, starts to heal, a focus / zephyrs, zephyrs are sent to your focus / promise, promsie made, kept, focus / blinks, blinks into singing, soaring, focus / psalters, psalters made your focus / might, might is right into focus / prayers, prayers paid to focus / fountains, fountains sounding for a focus / eternity, eternity met in focus / values, values paid to foci / bread, bread made a meal for focus / beatific, beatific and clear to focus to / loaves, loaves who host a focus / cultivates, cultivates a necessary pair for focus / vanish, vanish into your focus / planes, planes are pushed to clear too, a focus / vanquish, vanquish without wound, a focus / perished, perished has caught a new, focus / simple, simple in sample focus / diction, diction picked up into a focus / pardons, pardons come too, a focus / candidates, candidates dare to focus / motions, motions mentioned, focus / wields, wields are well into focus / progressions, progressions passing your range for a focus, won, love.

LEVEL 67: THE FORWORD-MENTS

CHAPTER ONE
Motion, motion made, forward / benevolence, benevolence now found, forward / science, science sent into forward focus / emphasis, emphasis found, forward / equal, equal in an instant formed and forward / doors, doors opened into a tree's forwards / oppose, oppose has gone, forward / arts, arts and the starts into a forward format / imparts, imparts and the starts into forwardness / concepts, concepts and the curing found in forwards / dictions, dictions dealing in a forming forward / constructs, constructs concurrent to a forwardnes / truthful, truthful is a youthful forwardness / discipline, disciplined meetings into a forward / degrees, degrees dappled for a forwardness / disciple, disciples simply into a forward / buildeth, buildeth a basic forward / species,

species special to a forwardness / eternity, eternity forms our forwardness / hospital, hospital hues abridge our nearness for forwards / instruct, instruct and the construction of a forwardness / possession, possessions pent in forwards / multiplications, multiplications mention A forward / doors, doors deepen in forging forwardness / institutions, institutions naturally forwards / melds, melds a metal forward / scandals, scandals scan our forwards / black, black in a bitter forgiven forward / blank, blank in a betweeness forward / knights, kingly knights initialed into a forward / nights, nights nickle deep in forwards / regard, regarded as our forwards / servants, servants apparent into forwards / receive, receive a recompense without forward / multitudes, multitudes admit a forward / ears, ear emit a forward / behaviors, behaviors basically our forward / flexible, flexible and the tracking into a forward / powers, powers into the forwards who care for children / fields, fields fellow into our forwards / POSSESSION, possession pairs your forward paces / factors, factors apparent without forwards / identify, identify a draped forwards / peace, peace employs your forwardness / bodies, bodies peaceful unto your forwards / bearings, bearings peering inside a forward / parables, parables pieces and forwards / purse, purses patient for forwards / statues, statues ethereal in the forward / perfection, perfection into the forward / brothers, brothers basically into the forward / truly, truly and deepened a forward / doctrine, doctrine is simple to the forward / fathers, fathers impressions and forwardness / greater, greater in simple forwards / accounts, accounts made our forwards / robed, robed in smiling rhymes formed in forwardness / behold, beholden and smitten into our forwards / masters, masters made a forward / mists, mists simple in our forwards / rests, rests in simple forwardness / reasons, reasons and the ripest forwards / plights, plights and positions forward / reasonable, reasonable introductions of our forwards.

CHAPTER TWO
Demands, demands off and then listened to forwards / parcels, parcels and the patrons trued in forecasts of a forward / lights, lights led past a forwardness / cadre, cadres capable unto forwards / weeks, weeks wiser winded too, a forward / efforts, efforts final into forwards / purpose, purposes passionate in your forwards / effective, effectively paternal to a forward / compose, composed arose in forwards / compositions, compositions meant in forwardness / secrets, secrets told a forward / secretes, secretes in simple forwards / gales, gales lost and tossed into your forwards / hearts, hearts aid a forward / every, every and all ways our forwards / history, history hued and forward too / expressions, expressions mention your forwards / joy, joy is jealous without forwards / reasons, reasons reaching your forwards / faint, faint is over, forwards / forth, forth fixed your forwards / driven, driven inside a forward / reasons, reasons reasonable too, forward / faint, faint in a fellow forward / forth, forth is right, fellows forwarded / driven, driven rivals forwards / reasons, reasons reach your forwards / wish, wish is meant for a forward / zeal, zeal into zero forwards / intolerance, intolerance ransoms your forwards / taken, taken into tolerations for a forward / prejudice, prejudice shines

within? dump it, forward go / search, search is dear, forward / virtual, virtual values forward / provides, provides a patient forward / guides, guides pace your forwardness / legacy, legacy leapt our forwards / clarify, clarify where in forwardness / lifts, lifts a listen too, a forward / kings, kings comment, "a forward" / visions, visions value your forwards / sources, sources secure in forwards / entangled, entangled clearest ionically forward / queens, queens aquire a forward date unto love / receive, receive a relation of a forward / mothers, mothers matched into forwardness / rates, rates reaching forward / princes, princes painting forwards / instant, instant incense of forwards / lavish, lavish in leases, forward / cities, citites laid to a forward / luring, luring intelligence to a forward rate / princess, princess for the forwards / stars, stars shine in forwards / athenian, athenian throngs meaning forwards / cubes, cubes cue on forwards / precincts, precincts precious to a forward / codes, codes clearly forward / earthquakes, earthquakes open to a forward / cores, cores sprung into a forward / quarters, quarters coined a flourish forward / flaunt, flaunt your ways to days forwarded / hasten, hasten to chasten without? forwards / welcome, welcome a news for forwards.

CHAPTER THREE
Moving, moving has simply come to life's forwards / chores, chores are matched and forward / heard, heard above, "forward" / chosen, chosen insights still, forward / details, details mate in forwards / churches, churches simple in their forwards / destruct, destruct less, find more, forwards / swoon, swoon into a moon's play forward / memories, memories made are meant for your forward leaps / sizes, sizes singular are found in towns forward / erased, erased erasure of the forwards / prevail, prevail in mailed societals forwarded / radical, radical in a science set Chicago deep in Egyptian soil, forward / choices, choices to cause and beyond in the forward unto love / seize, seize the moment and move, forward / made, made a mission of forwards / amazed, amazed in miraculous might for the forward / require, require respect for the forward / regard, regard has red underlined forwards / hallowed, hallowed parts found in loving forwards / runs, runs a reaching retinue for the few who carry forward / needs, needs met are rich in forwardness / high, high in a healed forward / necessity, necessity born miraculously forward / destroys, destroys without lessons forwarded / hums, hums a part, forward / fear, fear is gone, forward / means, means are made into trees who grow forward / attains, attains a palatial forward / militant, militant without? forwards / immortal, immortal in a mortal way without forward / worships, worships again, forwards / one, one who knew? forwards / God, God is given a gaze forward / alliance, alliance made, move, forward / hearts, hearts are held, forward / amazed, amazed and disjointed without, forwards / love, love is led forward / fearfuls, fearfuls gathered gone forward / plunge, plunge into passion for the forward / into, into our hour forwarded / coincide, coincide inside your forwards / attendance, attendance will stand for forwardness / inside, inside is rejected without suspected forwards / analogous, analogous too, forwards / suggested, suggested yes too, forwarded / guarantees, guarantees your forwards/ equanamity, equananmity

marries A forward / modern, modern in materials forwarded / breads, breads baked squarely forward / trails, trails torn are repaired through A forward / frieze, frieze is off, worn too, forwards / dough, dough made, forward / established, established, yes, and forward / bakes, bakes in irons ovened for the forward / released, released near you, relatives, forwarded / thebes, thebes is risen, write well, forwards / golden, golden in gazes, forward / tripod, tripod written, forwards / devote, devote yourself too, the forwards written rise / basis, basis basically human divine and written forward / base, bases established, write, forward / entire, entire in hired forwards / special, special places are saved forward.

CHAPTER FOUR
Heretics, heretics gone, forward / trees, trees lost are found in a forum fountain wise to love for the forward pace / herodutus, herodutus written and read "forward" / trips, trips made are into the forward nations / journey, journey along shores Atlantean and the Thiran cores blown forward / jointed, jointed in annointed forwards / traveling, traveling allows forward advance / historically, historically and correctly, forward / ephesus, ephesus as written, church for the forward / cypress, cypress prayed into signals forward / circles, circles made about forwards / gentle, gentle in gems forwarded / gates, gates posing forward / cause, cause is electric, forward / within, within us well, a forward / ceremonial, ceremonial means made for the forwards / lebanese, lebanese matches for the forwards / assemble, assemble here to teach the forwards / former, former in pilots bought forward / farmer, farmer found, forward / parents, parents taught to be forward / gifts, gifts made enhance gain forward / wilds, wilds sought are found, forward / mountains, mountains bought are sold to the highest gift, forward / empires, empires sought are found, forward / trees, trees lift into the forward / baskets, baskets bought are filled with the forwards / factory, factory fuels a forward / parts, parts paid too, the factory of forwards / service, service made clear, forward / bravery, bravery written into the forward / hero, hero hinted about, forwards / fruits, fruits in routes past the forwards / persian, persian poets knew "forward" to God / phoenicians, phoenicians managed to be into the forwards / crux, crux past, go, forward / syrians, syrians said yes too, the forwards / circuit, circuit broken, fixed, forward / monarchs, monarchs made a hero forward / forsake, forsake without? forward / counsel, counsel given, forward / Ionian, Ionian pleasures are measured forward / certain, certain in a single forward / focus, focus onto the seas now forwarded / maintain, maintain your missions, forward / tongue, tongue is traced forward / recovery, recovery rescued, forward / trance, trance off, forward / passage, passage paid for forwarded / sufferance, sufferance over, forward / peace, peace is past and now in your forwards / cyrus, cyrus said "forward" / friends, friends meant to last, forward / foreigns, foreigns capitalized on your forwardness / inquire, inquire where to be yoked too, a star forward / athenian, athenian in Minoan mends forwarded / review, review a yes! as written forward / along, along these living forwards / chamber, chamber chosen and the heart path opens forward back

to love / parallels, parallels are mentioned, forward / challenge, challenge is over, forward / occupy, occupy your way, forward / topmost, topmost in a list for the forwards / prepares, prepares a surgery for the forward.

CHAPTER FIVE
Smooth, smooth in transitions forward / babylonian, babylonian mending moves forward / embarks, embarks in stacks of the forwards / cakes, cakes baked in forwards / mana, mana dripping across forwards / manna, manna fed those who check for their forwards / maui, maui marries us to the forwards / balance, balance is found in Hina's gown born to the rainbow streams forward rains / depth, depth is plummeted past and plunged into through the seas forwarded / transform, transform a miracle into your birthplace's forwards / trade, trade for the single tract forward / intrinsic, intrinsic in dynamic and the forwarded placed / spatial, spatial a mriacle for the minerals forwards / secure, secure in detail and the reformation of physical foreworded forwards / royal, royal the roses placed in streams forwarded / alii, alii purchased and given forward / powers, powers placed into the forwards / principles, principles managed into a forward placement / flows, flows a fellow's forwards / customs, customs created our forwards / notes, notes neat into your forwards / cures, cures are married too, the forwards / coded, coded inside those who knew, a forward / wished, wished for and found, a forward / flash, flash your details forward / quiver, quiver loaded and found forward / mingles, mingles most near the headway for foundations / vanquish, vanquish past forgettings, forward / figs, figs placed near us, forwarded / fruits, fruits brought us near our forwards / boats, boats buoyant in our forwards / peaks, peaks over edges forwarded / points, points placed over all, forwards / forfeit, forfeit without? forwards / town, town triumphant reigns, bethlehem forms a forward / follow, follow us home to the forward lands / vocalizations, vocalizations matched, forward / figures, figures mentioned and made A forwards / vanish, vanish without? paces path is forward / imagine, imagine how to be forward / prepare, prepare the paths, forward / woman, woman made a material fact, forward / purges, purges in reaches forward / prepare, prepare to be, forwarded / pours, pours into hearts yellow with red rays entwined throughout the thrones forwarded / people, people taos blue in forgiveness of the pointed place and the stake without fortunate findings, forward / drips, drips over a flame tuned into forwardness / fruitfulness, fruitfulness foils forward without toil, love / circles, circles made are found, forward / cargo, cargo tossed is lost, found / cope, cope and care, forwarded / cloak, cloak and the cures of a forward / overflow, overflow in flowering forwards / deft, deft in a mention for the forward / flex, flex aobut it, forward / archival, archival in revival for the forwards / happiest, happiest in a showering flood, forwards / men, men and the materials forwarded / governs, governs a grant unto the forwards / worships, worships you, forward / conquest, conquests about, forward / lodged, lodged in your truth, a forward / deify, deify and detriorate without, a forward / magnify, magnify your missions and find the forwarded truths.

CHAPTER SIX

Commoner, commoner met, marry without cords, forward / ibis, ibis obeys you liable to the blue heron's stance, alone, independent, friend, forward / compare, compare us to conquests withal talented forwards / memory, memory abused? forward glance / broad, broad in your respect for the forwards / preserve, preserve a grce of the forwards / belts, belts asteroid deep in forwards / months, months may carry an asteroid near, remember, forward / represents, represents 2012 as a memory of the nearest star and the farthest point trajectory wide find inside a fuse and light your heart in clear respect for the foundations of this earth and the mirth inspired when love rules clearly again, heart of the nations, a natural core in streets ST Louis blue again, Aloha, forwarded / goats, goats are grown in lava stands and shrub gone olivine green with loves forwards / always, always stay inside your forwards / calves, calves are grown in thrones forwarded / loans, loans are made for the forwards / cubes, cubes essentially metatronically gifted found forward / sheep, sheep ahve cast the lots for frocks formerly worn gift, lift, forwards / pure, pure is the soft wool of the lamb now approaching your doorway, forwarded / ancient, ancient in a simple way, forwarded 64 to the 73 and above, forward / possible, possible epistles written forward / possibly, of the 12 nine now sent find three who remember too / representatives, representatives of each have found a way to visit, remember, forwards / chronicles, chronicles past are linked into future forwards / venerates, venerates your days, forwards / curatives, curatives imply added, forwards / regards, regards read as forwards / mortals, mortals mentioned are found forward / thousands, thousands said yes to the lord of all reliefs forwarded / follows, follows connect move now, forward / feminine, feminine intrigues meet your forwards / grapple, grapple less, hold more, forward / neurosis, neurosis over, forwards / maintains, maintains simple forward focus / mentioning, mentioning burgeoning faith in your forwads / acts, acts taken forward / sythians, sythians wrested forward to life, light, love / actions, actions taken are forwarded / established, established materials for the forward / facts, facts last to forwards / periods, periods past are forward / focusing, focusing into the forwards / impasses, impasses established are real, forgive, go, forward / happening, happening next, forwards / astral, astral reaches are planned for the forwards / reassemble, reassemble near your forwards / socratic, socratic the vote for the forwards / accountants, accountants meet in forwards / horses, horses held for the forward / accounts, accounts blessed through forwards / rounds, rounds reach those forwarded / genius, genius sent has found a genus specied for the forwards / outlines, outlines touch in forwards / race, race past, forward / canticles, canticles cleared, forward / secondary, secondary to the forwards / county, county of the country forwarded / country, country mixed in forwards / implements, implements now past, forward / impressions, impressions sent are focused into the forward / drinks, drinks spill in meanings forwards / ample, ample in apply for the forwards / targets, targets off you, forward / samples, samples mixed in forwards / lasting, lasting choices made, forward / suffocation, suffocation ends and forwards love / breath, breath found A forward

CHAPTER SEVEN

Counseling, counseling ensues forward / airs, airs over us, forward / guards, guards dropping in, forward / custody, custody given your forward / entrance, entrance opening forward / dwells, dwells a simple discipline too, forward / orders, orders made to last too, forward / goblets, goblets tossed past your forwards / reason, reason as important as clearly forward / comrades, comrades tossed? forward / rathers, rathers and the fathers found in sport's heroes forwarded / belts, belts and the laps made finally four forwards / extents, extents orion as left for the forwards / relates, relates a passion for the forwards / abundant, abundant in the faith to fly to our forwards / divisions, divisions finished forward / maintains, maintains a mission to rid us, forwards / pause, pause to initial those forwards / views, views evoked in forwardness / coincides, coincides inside a forward / accounted, accounted for and forwarded / contrasts, contrasts match your forwards / ample, ample in simple forwards / sample, samples sent, forward / editorial, editorial within, forward / impasse, impasse sent past and forward / tales, tales and the tossed forwards / preserves, preserves simply forward / samples, sample spun too, forward / races, races ruling our forwards / periods, periods place in forwards / ample, ample in simple forwards / abundance, abundance plenty in our forwards / quarks, quarks simple to a forward / broadens, broadens a basic forward / terms, terms in simple forwards / robes, robes righteous in our forwards / withdraw, withdraw too, a forward / agreed, agreed in signs forwarded / mass, mass amounts forwarded / prizes, prizes applied forwardly / apply, apply into a forward / rules, rules ransom free and forward / appoint, appoint in simple forwards / affairs, affairs reaching your forwards / submit, submit and assign your forwards / mergers, mergers matched your forwards / freely, freely framed forwards / monarchy, monarchy meant unto your forwards / magistrate, magistrate elated of those forwards / missionary, missionary into interiors of those forwards / rally, rally into a forward / credence, credence sent into forwards / listen, listening into those forwards / leads, leads are simple unto forwards / laws, laws launched along lines forwarded / astute, astute starts for the forwards / athena, athena possible in a forward / aphrodite, aphrodite rited forward / inquires, inquires within, forwards / evidence, dividends paid and forward enhanced / essences, essences fueled forward / obelisk, obelisk blissed unto those who forward / intersects, intersects where we forward.

CHAPTER EIGHT

Proteins, proteins apparent turning forward / goddess, goddess gaining A forward / reasonable, reasonable in aspects for your forwards / venerated, venerates a value too, forward / pleasures, pleasures sought found forwarded / pleasing, pleasing is nearing your door, forward look / fables, fables tossed are kept forward / solemn, solemn without? forward / consideration, consideration considered a friendly forward / forced, forced into exile free delivery for forwards / marvels, marvels most at your friendly forwards / canton, canton counted forward / museums, museums mentioned forward / honors, honors made a truth forward / musicals, musicals maintained forward / cold, cold without? forward / fetters, fetters off, forward / citizens, citizens retreat to find A forward / terms, terms laid into forwards / citadels, citadels purchased and thrust past A forward / arouse, arouse her interest in forwards / hot, hot is held as forward / warm, warm enough to marry forward / inhabitants, inhabitants lend a marriage to your forwards / skills, skills noticed, forward / expeditions, expeditions spent on forwards / army, army of the savior sent forward / sizzle, sizzle in wet agree for the forwards / years, years gone fly forward / sizes, sizes sent are scene, forward / estuaries, estuaries blessed are sent into forwards / calmest, calmest days are clearly forwarded / waters, waters break into quiet forwards / watercourses, watercourses material to the forwards / prepares, prepares a document for the forwards / breastplate, breastplate of the hearts worn forward / squadrons, squadrons gathered remain forward / leaders, leaders lead well into the forwards positions / squads, squads who cool without, wheel into, forward point / chosen, chosen ones lead well forward / partners, partners made powerful through forwarding / strategic, strategic doors opened forward / exist, exist in solitude for the coming forwards / place, places made, forward / parallel, parallel positions forwarded / nestles, nestles into your doorways forwards / streams, streams are matched, forward / nearest, nearest and dearly, forward / often, often a fellow said "forward" / fused, fused in hips replaced for the ribs revealed forward / wonderful, wonderful lessons won, forward / used, used without? forward / well, well enough to see, forward / eccentrically, eccentrically complete in forwards / imagine, imagine this, forwards / proven, proven to be a forward / cables, cables written tossed forward / loads, loads off, forward / broke, broke is fixed, forward / carried, carried into contacts too, forward / ties, ties made to last forward / arcs, arcs opened forward / change, change has healed your forwards / places, places made for zeal and a wall which speaks Egyptian too, forward.

CHAPTER NINE
Patience, patience found, sound forth, forward / placements, placements meant, forward / burns, burns without, forwards / chosen, chosen and into, forwards / feared, feared knot? forward / selection, selection sent to a cooperative source, forward / reaps, reaps a benefit, forward / coins, coins tossed create a forward / freshly, freshly funded, forward / pushing, pushing into new dimensions of faith forwarded / worn, worn in the venues now valued forward / courage, courage has given us valuable forwards / registry, registry wins a forward to love / impulses, impulses aplenty in loving forwards / rounds, rounds reach your forwards / portrayals, portrayals available to love's forwards / portugal, portugal is the key to your native forwards / furtive, furtive in mighty forwards / cells, cells wide inside your forwards / glanced, glanced into once, a forward / solids, solids suggested, forward / inquire, inquire as to the forwards / freight, freight off, forward / encourage, encourage another forward / thaw, thaw is off, forward / punch, punch into plenty forward / purchased, purchased a narrow forward / dine, dine in the fallow and the full positions forwarded / found, found in inflation? forward / rings, rings abrush the outback way into forwards / framed, framed without? forwards / ropes, tell her the ropes are

cast off, forward / elates, elates her healing, forward / sourced, sourced again, forward / decelerate, decelerate your rate for the unexpected, push into new frontiers of love, a forward / accelerate, accelerate your rate of follow thourghs, smells fresh, air wise, forwards / mint, mint in green's interior, forwards / moisten, moisten a detonation thorugh a ration for forwards / coincidence, coincidence estimated at forwardness / mend, mend a mathematic trend, forward / exact, exact in the facts called forward / schooled, schooled in annual amounts, forwards / enjoyed, enjoyed most and materially forwarded / campaigned, campaigned for the man, human, basically forward / championships, championships written into the weave called forward / quarrel, quarrel is over, flow, forward / emperical, emperical the evidence for a forward / sattire, sattire off, forward loft / saturnine, saturnine inventions called forward / scramble, scramble up less, find more, forwards / ciao, ciao for now, abilities increased, forward / decode, decode and vote for the formulas called dear, forwards / TGAC, TGAC connected through a venue called DNA forwarded / mentally, mentally amused for forwardness / CGTA, CGTA found in our forwards / GCAT, GCAT spent on forwards / patterned, patterned into plans forwarded / pertinent, pertinent squares found your forwards / portrayals, portrayals find your forwards / matching, matching genes into your forwards / matters, matters made form clear into forwards / churns, churns a noose off your DNA codes, live, forward / hunch, hunch pays off, forward / needs, needs met, forward, materials.

CHAPTER TEN
Nurture, nurutre your set of needs forward / informative, informative in times forwarded / furnished, furnished a final forward / mastery, mastery means, forward still / famished, famished? call services forward / merged, merged in the cells forwarded / faults, faults out, forward / vessicles, vessicles launched, forward / throats, throats opened, fill with tunes, forwarded / vessels, vessels are ripe in forwards / tours, tours made forward / variations, variations graze forward / tarps, tarps are tossed forward / theatrics, a theatric is off, listen, forward / torques, torques ont he stages forwarded / bolt, bolt into narrow forwards / around, around us a forward / charged, charged in air forwarded / beneath, beneath us all, forwards / pulses, pulses made thorugh our forwards / above, above and all, forward / circuitous, circuitously forward / within, within us a forward loop leaps / watts, watts wander into your forwards / rebuild, rebuild now and follow the heartlline into the forwards / flood, flood made over a forward / bounded, bounded in signal forwards / buildings, buildings aloft in forwards / charms, charms worn and the chosen attend, forwards / bulbs, bulbs tossed aloft a forward / charges, charges made calendaric to a date within forwards / china, china is set to uplift in a red release through an orange forward / extended, extended in listening forwards / japan, japan bought a seat into the forwards / cords, cords are cut now, forward / fiji, fiji is clearly forward / surging, surging through the seas brought forward / forms, forms made a clip to a forward / stilling, stilling silently forward / grounds, grounds for the forwards / shocks, shocks off, forwad / pages, pages paid for

and forwarded / shares, shares bought forward / written, written in spirals within a forward / thaws, thaws out most, forwards / electrical, electrical shields lift unto forwards / kilowatts, kilowatts wage a forward / wield, wield a neutral forward / backs, backs creak as we lost only forwards / space, space spent on forwards / spinal, spinal tapping ito forwards / neurologically, neurologically valid forwards / fluids, fluids leaking into your forwards / sensory, sensory suggestions for forwards / pace, pace sets forward / palms, palms raised, forward / help, help us live forward / heavy, heavy without forwards / avenues, avenues unto the forwards / water, water worn through, over time, unto forwards / cheer, cheer us forwarded / molecular, molecular marrows of the moles forwarded / mere, mere in astorlogical significance, forward turns aquarian / dawning, dawning now a new age, aquarian, piscean wounding finished / cross, off the cross and onto love's interior buckets, arms wide, forwarded.

CHAPTER ELEVEN
Spirits, spirits faceted and faced into forwards / inspiring, inspiring to the finish, forward / knowledge, knowledge known and forwarded to light ropes release / defined, defined a dialect as forwarded / humble, humble in opinions forwarded / decimals, decimals blast without forwards / revealing, revealing a realize about forwards / rests, rests in regard too, forwards / supreme, supreme deeming forwards / prime, prime in allowance for forwards / final, final days forwarded / distant, distant in forwards / labels, labels are given loft, forwards / superior, superior vibrationally, forward / placed, calmly placed in waves forwarded / present, present for the penance forgiven, forwards / shells, shells overturned and forwarded / live, live in a quiet abode, forwards / connections, connections made add lift to forwards / logically, logically fe a clear forward / dual, dual off, own one, forward / exists, exists a fit for forwards / entities, entities go, forward caught / orbitals, orbitals are bought with 720-degrees of lifting spin true merkabah fields are forwarded without humanity's shells / dualities, dualities end now forward / 18, 18 ways to be forward / extents, extents on forwards / 3, 3 who knew, forwards / extensions, extensions of those gone forward / 12, 12 who dare, forward / 14, 14 who follow suits forward / 77, 77 led to 777 forwards / supremest, supremest being, God in man, humanity is divine breath, now forward / connectives, connectives cost less than original gifts, forward / tissue, tissue meets in forward nips / electrons, electrons polished to include forwards / 81, 81 who knew forwards / 9, 9 who said, "forward" / 36, 36 met through forwards / 4, 4 which fit, forwards / 55, 55 who drive too, forwards / 3rd, 3rd in a word, "forward" / 11, 11 who said "forward" / 4th, 4th in this place, forward / 12th, 12th in states forwarded / 7th, 7th rays forward / 13th, 13th extents are forward / 12th, 12th in a date forward / vibrations, vibrations balanced in forward skilled / primates, primates materialize in forwards / dual, dual finishes, forward / principals, principals for the forward / consent, consent written, forward / primitives, primitives range into forwards / affirms, affirms rest in forwards / crossed, crossed without? forwards first / scales, scales over your forwards / 11th, 11th rays crossed? forward / 54, 54 who follows, forward / 7th, 7th in a rush to the forwards / 17th leys forward / 38th rays undressing forward / 23 who knew a stranger forward / 12th, 12th to a third harmony, forward notes of love, music.

CHAPTER TWELVE
Worlds, worlds collapsing, forward / functional, functionally replete in forwards / planets, planets who spin wobbling forward / creations, creations lease is finished, forward / suns, suns and days forwarded / universal, universal extents are forwarded / moons, moons matched, Io sent forward / tunes, tunes who last, forward / practice, practice made real, forward / shifted, shifted into gifted status, forward / possible, possible children, forward / octaves, octaves unfold pages of focus on the forward drafts / posits, posits line deposits in the forwards / oscillate, oscillates may vary forward/ tabled, tabled simply into the forwards / message, messages sent forward as sealed kaui a mano ka lank po, the fountainhead of many waters from on high and bubbling below / inclined, inclined into values of those who forward step / mortals, mortals meet breath in humanity's forwardness / shamans, shamans go into flowering forwards / cults, cults out to tour a cosmos born of loving forwards / charms, charms softened in a Guatemalean forward to love / conceptual, conceptual in the actualness found in love's shielded forwards / magical, magical amounts added to your account forwarded / charts, charts made to meeting forwards / primaries, primaries run have won the winning forwards / democracy, democracy rules your forwards / republics, republics reputed to be forward / socrates, socrates said a "forward" to mankind / heavenly, heavenly in her heraldic way and the harlot to shame has gone to a forward / harmonies, harmonies appear, forwards / historic, historic in her appeals forwards / lights, lights out, forwards / symbols, symbols burst in true forwards / music, music made thoroughly for a forward / limits, limits pushed lift off to reveal forwards / heads, heads belong to our singing forwards / cities, cities supple with A forward / gentle, gentle joining forwards / jerusalem, jerusalem is slim without forwards / messianics, messianics agree to be forwarded / makes, amounting to the making well, forwards / categorize, categorize your eyes as forward / made, made intrigue into forwards / entries, entries tossed inside a forward / minds, minds moist in forward / shades, shades drawn onto forwards / surge, surges sent to forwards / specifics, specifics follow forward / Meetings / Welcome / Love / Perfect / Children / Lunar / Eclipse / Starts / to / Open / Brightness / Yanomami / Tonight / to / Spark / Light.

CHAPTER THIRTEEN
Employ, employ amazing folks, forwards / modes, modes matched, forward / physical, physical release to the lessening gone, forward into health / spiritual, spiritual colors abound, forward / utilize, utilize the shapes brought forward / repetitive, repetitive mention brought forward / seraphic, seraphic in a graphic way, forwards / diverts, diverts less, gains more, forwards / phenological, phenologically forward now / reproduce, reproduce most, forwards / electric, electric laid open, forwards / regards,

regards paid to forwards / roads, roads linking crystal lines forward / requires, requires management for the forwards / spectacles, spectacles made now tossed into forwards / preserves, reserves are nearest preserved planets, forward / model, model for the missions forwarded / sounds, sounds made link forwards / sketch, sketch another forward / drawn, drawn on a signal forward / paint, paint a perfect posture for forwards / dawns, dawns guarded relations forwarded / transience, transience counting forward / musically, musically amounting to forwards / entry, entry signifies a forward / historics, historics sparking a forward account / cards, cards crossed into forwards / administrative, administratively forwarded / specifics, specifics allowing forwards / enact, enact facts forward / life, life blessed thorough our forwards / impact, impact spent along forwards / attempts, attempts to retrace go to those forwards / teachers, teachers teaching you forward / electronics, electronics slipping forward / coverage, coverage added forward / forms, forms tossed, forward / funded, funded and founded fortunately / authors, authors met in your forwards / authority, authority suggested for these forwards / administer, administer nearest forwards/ installation, installation allowing forwards to nudge past selfishness / bestow, bestow a single cause unto forwards / averaged, averaged into your days, forwards / increments, increments allowing a forward / evolutions, evolutions simple in their forwards / prepares, prepares sharing portraits of forwards / sought, sought in a single shot of forwards / groups, groups are gathered forward / sponsors, sponsors found forward / superiors, superiors cleared, forward / personal, personal clarity found, forward / midways, midways made real, forwards / watched, watched over, forwards / paradise, paradise poses in forwards / messengers, messengers materialize throughout your forwards / spaces, spaces dared, forward / universes, universes spared, forward / traced, traced in single trails forwards / galaxies, galaxies measured through given forwards / counseled, counseled only briefly, forwards / keyed, keyed into through forwards / centrals, centrals sharing forwards / coded, coded for the doted on of forwards.

LEVEL 68: THE IN-FACT-MENTS

CHAPTER ONE
Prayers, prayers made a fact / original, original in her theory of facts / medicinal, medicinal in her memories for facts / oriental, oriental meanings for facts / taught, taught to be self factual / YHWH, YAHWEH said "I AM THAT I AM", that's a fact / religions, religions reach for tablets carried from mounts to pens in God's hands, listen, share, learn, love your brother, find faith in freedom to choose to remember, that's God, you are loved religiously for your authentic spirit, fact / faith, faith is penned in as fact, find some, now / among, among us are spirits lift one away into light through your faith in love, a fact / between, between us a fountain grew to represent facts of love / both, both of us knew the way into facts / units, units measured to show these facts

inside / balanced, balanced in a blanket filled in facts / missions, missions amounting to facts gathered inside love / brethren, brethren mentioned as facts to live by / organize, organize your day to provide service to the love your own, which you recognize as God's gift to your heart, a fact, a tree of light and life / administers, administers clearly a recognition of one disk, one God, one input, one exit, one hydrogen sun, one placement clearly in the path of the two who unite to form husbanded wife and the two shall become one burning sun let those, elect, whom they will love and you will know how strongly they may love by their gentle strength with themselves, a highest walk, a Christed path into God's warmth, a fact / facilitates, facilitates the truth throughout a path which includes moods, miracles, red topics, blues, and the greys gone into moons far away Know the facts, the sephiroth traipse, direct and chosen into love, a fact / organized, organized again? good, fact / worlds, worlds organized through the soup of respect for the one true God, ahead, love thy neighbor, self, fact, God/ helps, helps are set into your life, lift up to know, God, a fact/ certainty, certainty is found near the hearing sound of a fact / councils, councils emit a new framework for facts / supreme, supreme in a dream called fact / loyalist, loyalist goes into fantasy forgive of the Facts for love/ failures, failures over, facts / primes, primes into rhymes for reasons of facts / immediate, immediate departure nears, a fact / consists, consists of lists reworked to include facts / planks, planks walked moved facts / consorts, consorts go to the flown facts / planetary, planetary aspirations show a fact / careers, careers made clear unto facts / sense, sense made, facts / proportions, proportions written for facts / mandates, mandates drawn into facts / educations, educations given a fact / executives, executives written for facts / execute, execute a new line of facts / additives, additives added into facts / sprung, sprung without? facts / sypathize, sympathize as written into facts / wills, wills as written lapse into facts / groups, groups given a fact / astray, astray arrayed into facts / orders, orders given, facts / facilitates, facilitates a date with facts / sovereigns, sovereigns reigning fact / eventual, eventual trips to the facts / volunteer, volunteer to be factual / final, final days are in fact / administration, administration seen factually / administer, administer a diligence for facts / convocation, convocations current to a stream of facts / thousands, thousands dare to dream in facts / preside, preside only slightly without facts / headquarters, headquarters built has seams facts / universal, universal dreams and facts / nativity, nativity knelt at facts / systemic, systemic rejection? facts / ascendants, ascendants allowing your facts / monitors, monitors mention a fact / conveyance, conveyance made, facts / eternally, eternally into facts.

CHAPTER TWO
Represents, represents a respect for the facts / evolve, evolve now, facts / successions, successions sent to facts / personal, personal ads meant for facts / concentric, concentric in your facts / willing, willing to be factual / learns, learns a dreaming fact / gently, gently said "factual" / faithfully, faithfully submitted facts / sacrifice, sacrifice made, fact / swerving, swerving without? facts / salvation,

salvation is sent, facts / served, sever the lever facts / guilt, guilt is over, fact / allows, allows a daily, fact / leads, leads past your facts / grants, grants written, facts / renewals, renewals made, facts / forgiven, forgiven again, fact / rise, rise above, facts / patience, patience dear, facts / friends, friends made, in fact / love, love is led to a fact / reign, reign over, fact / transfers, transfers are given, fact / establishments, establishments are given a fact / spears, spears and the steering facts / times, times and histories attune into the permanence of love's facts / souls, souls and the sealings profoundly a fact / materia, materia into eternia for the a facts / energies, energies inside and into forthright facts / reality, reality in tune within the formatted facts / written, written into tunes and formats offered, facts / creations, creations accrue inside your facts / loyalists, loyalists astride our facts / potential, potential into the thrones formal facts / powers, powers apply too, the forest for facts / paradise, paradise appears into the facts/ limits, limits and the languages forthright into our facts / ancient, ancients sign for facts / eternal, eternal is our healing fact / ultimately, ultimately we have said yes to the eternal facts / obedience, obedience relies upon our facts / creator, creator of the creative facts / infinite, infinite in plenty, facts / border, border and the beautify for a fact / grand, grands run through in fact / encompassed, encompassed around a fact / inhabited, inhabited enthuse throughout facts / level, level on the shores for facts / surrounded, surrounded as assorted in facts / fringes, fringes laid across A path, facts / simply, simply is said "facts" / faith, faith is simple into facts / positive, positive churches match your facts / animal, animal in the mental past, facts / nature, nature is simple in facts / effect, effect is effective within facts / mind, in mind is a simple fact / sovereign, sovereign the simple fact / estimate, estimated simplistic without facts / occupy, occupy your surrender into facts / local, local is complete, please surrender these facts / lifted, lifted another's initial facts.

CHAPTER THREE
Tributary, tributary for these facts / task, task is in effect for the lights in love's facts / educational, educational and essential too, a fact / horizon, horizon is essentially done, imagine, a fact / various, various is a soothing fact / exact, exact is elect within facts / overseers, overseers amid the facts/ realm, realm is the esteem from these facts / function, function and these are the facts / deflector, deflector and the nectar into facts / serve, serve and the treat into facts / forsake, forsake into triple facts / confines, confines initial facts formulas / guardians, guardians offer us facts / reborn, reborn and then, a fact / assistance, assistance in assent for these facts / ministry, ministry is essential too, facts / surviving, surviving interest into a fact / potential, potential is admitted too, that's a fact / level, level instructions for these facts / liason, liason onto theoretic facts / symbol, symbols spent, facts / reciprocal, reciprocal too, facts / resident, resident spent, on facts / mortal, mortals appear into facts / dispatch, dispatches based in facts / custody, custody cures us a fact / dual, dual and the details made a fact / enjoy, enjoying an initial fact / advances, advances made facts / transcend, transcend is journeying to theories of facts / reward, rewards made a fact / pulsating, pulsatin paces for a fact

/ extended, extended spending into our facts / moderate, moderate is our median fact / initial, initial appearance to our facts / lights, lights simply factual / glow, glow in a gleeful factual / stars, stars single and factual / distances, distances into your facts / enormous, enormous in signal facts / equalize, equalize in essential facts / domain, domains erect in fact / amount, amount paid interior to a fact / approach, approaches in simple fact / atomic, atomic attractions throughout facts / legacy, legacy lectures your facts / play, play is amounting to a fact / interstellar, interstellar signs given a fact / basic, basic in a blazing fact / subatomic, subatomic cenotes made into a fact / electronic, electronic wells inside your facts / ultimate, ultimate amounts for facts / stationary, stationary written in fact / proximity, proximity to a portal's facts / rates, rates issued and insured for fact / liason, liason sent a simple fact / major, major is the mission's facts / profusion, profusion for a gifted fact / bestowal, bestowal into our facts / glass, glass is bent within waters facts / crystal, crystal the river in fact / sea, sea in a sides facts / triangular, triangular entreaties facts.

CHAPTER FOUR
Universes, universes rapture is in fact / judgement, judgement is done, clue in, in fact / constellation, constellation in a federal, fact / contract, contract concurring that we are in fact, loved / relationship, relationship met, facts / involves, involves a successive fact / service, service is central to a fact / negotiating, negotiating to the fact and the features found in love / enormous, enormous into a fact / reservation, reservations to our facts / decree, decree made for a fact / affairs, affairs set into a fact / central, central scenes in a fact / key, key to the nurtured facts / fellows, fellows financially set to a fact / group, group into a nestling fact / quadruple, quadruple into the thrilling facts / similar, similar to the mutual facts / world, word is the world up to a fact / inhabited, inhabited into a fact / flashes, flashes false without and into a fact / reinforce, reinforce a factor for a fact / affection, affection spent to a factor on love / offspring, offspring is sent into love / intelligence, intelligence spent in love's rewarded facts / initial, initialize a reasonable amount for lots of facts / test, test another's faith in facts / waited, waited and stated into facts / efforts, efforts met in fact / threshold, thresholds left to a fact / seven, seven into a throne's facts / sacrifice, sacrifice unto a fact / seclude, seclude set united into a fact / migrate, migrate is metal without fact / lead, leads over, facts / function, functions simple to a fact / associates, associates meet in a street's facts / conspired, conspired unto hired facts / twins, twins in settled facts / biologic, biologic in a smattered fact / discover, discover eccentric paths into facts / status, status central for love's facts / tribes, tribes unto facts / traveled, traveled into suggestions of facts / tools, tools made into facts / platinum, platinum poools forming facts / diamond, diamonds due a fact / gold, gold and the glued facts / quests, quests curl into facts / sustained, sustained onto a fact / first, first into a fact / truth, truth into a fact forwards / retrogressing, retrogressing into a fact / descendants, descendants due a fact / journey, journey and the gifts due a fact / hand, hand into hands of facts / hero, hero made factually / consequences, consequences

sent into facts / persistent, persistent into facts / rejectionrejection goes to a heart in fact / inevitable, inevitable is set, in fact / inner, inner in interior facts / sedition, sedition set on a fact / concerns, concerns meet in a fact.

CHAPTER FIVE
Operation, operation cost a fact / social, social settles into a fact / plentiful, plentiful placements of facts / land, lands lead for a facts / territory, territory for a fact / controls, controls set on a fact / flocks, flocks filter into facts / leisure, leisure onto an island's facts / techniques, techniques onto a fortitude of facts / initialed, initialed facts / stone, stones and sets for facts / tree, tree and the truth for a fact / respectfully, respectfully and the facts amaze your love / magic, magic is your truth, in fact / capital, capital to a cruises facts / private, private in a permissions for facts / comprehend, comprehend a friend's facts / ownership, ownership is confronted less when factual / views, views negotiate a fact / modern, modern into a mutual fact / guard, guard a future gated community of fact, celtics / waters, waters wet in a space for facts / crops, crops arranged into a fact / wells, wells winning a fact / beauty, beauty bench-marked for a fact / situation, situation ethics cost one fact / course, courses sought and the fact / seek, seek is essential too, a fact / golden, golden in a singles facts / desire, desire is hired a fact / phase, phase is simple, facts / adequate, adequate in a suggestive fact / either, either is single, fact / superlative, superlative in a natural fact / wisdom, wisdom is simple fact / intriguing, intriguing and the gaps go to a fact / attainment, attainment is single to a fact / motive, motive is exasperative for our facts / rules, rules in single facts / idealism, idealism since our facts / garden, garden of the goods factually / planning, planning a trip into fact / bright, bright is set in fact / glory, glory of the showing facts / dream, dream in electric fact / poem, poems cost less to a fact / staff, staff is settled on, a fact / preliminary, preliminary unto our facts / spot, spot is off, facts / landscape, landscape is simple, facts / story, story into basic facts / charming, charming is triumphant in facts / devote, devote is the composure in facts / climate, climate complete inside your facts / location, location is a gateway fact / advent, advents spent into facts / began, began too, facts / solemn, solemn truth is a fact / capital, capital in truest facts / orders, orders a miraculous fact / origin, origins sincerest fact / worship, worshipful planes for a fact / premature, premature without mentioning facts / paths, paths melt in a fact.

CHAPTER SIX: faith, faith is a fact / triumph, triumph is met through a factual journey / divine, divine is the daily fact / altruistic, altruistic is a fact / relish, relish within, facts / escape, escape goes, a fact / ingenious, ingenious within a fact / activity, activity mentions your facts / knowledge, knowledge melts into a fact / insights, insights sincere in a fact / different, different intrigues and a fact / uniform, uniform fillings find a fact / attains, attains a mountain's facts / thought, thought is the thrilling fact / terms, terms in significant signs facts / fragment, fragment is sent into a fact / leanings, leanings in signs for a fact / identical,

identical to a measureable fact / radial, radial measures of a fact / facts, facts made real, love / content, content into facts for love / universe, universe is implosive without? facts / adjust, adjust into facts / toward, toward into simple facts / love, love is elected for our facts / religion, religion in a reigning fact / valid, valid in simply single facts / supreme, supremest in facts / ultimate, ultimate experience for facts / children, children say "facts" / embodiment, embodiment meant for a fact / regard, regard is registered as fact / control, control is settled into facts / analysis, analysis is sent for a fact / celestial, celestial suspects go to a fact / above, above a mathematic fact / conception, conception is meant for a fact / phases, phases meet in a fact / celestial, celestials content to mate in fact / above, above a metric fact / conception, conception in a singular fact / phases, phases peer into a fact / presented, presented in opinions for facts / exists, exists in momentary facts / unfathomable, unfathomable meanings and facts / discover, discover a daily fact / symmetry, symmetry is meant for facts / loan, loan made to your facts / nature, nature is aspirations for facts / endeavor, endeavors need your fact / inspired, inspired again, facts / perplexity, perplexity within? a fact / toil, toil into troubles facts / harmony, harmony heralds a fact / bound, bound into given facts / encourage, encourage a fact / discover, discover another fact / symmetry, symmetry, one, two, fact / loan, loan paid, fact / nature, nature is made a fact / endeavor, endeavor essence wise to a fact / inspired, inspired and in fact / perplexity, perplexity cures a fact / toil, toil is over, fact.

CHAPTER SEVEN
Kingdom, kingdom comes, fact / heaven, heaven opens, fact / crossroads, crossroads met, fact / foreign, foreign without? fact / empire, empire gained, fact / senses, senses touch, fact / portion, portion paid, fact / temples, temples in simple fact / harbors, harbors sufficient for a fact / blending, blending love into facts / born, born to be a fact / widespread, widespread acceptance of facts / prosperity, prosperity into facts / peace, peace is cast to our facts / standpoints, standpoints made add facts / abundant, abundant declare for a fact / lord, lord of the lands, facts / school, school born to a fact / sensual, sensual within? fact / happiness, happiness held as your fact / better, better still a fact / excesses, excesses matter to your facts / seed, seed sprayed? fact / hearts, hearts who herald a fact / distant, distant into a relationship with faith in facts / relationship, relationship of the fear gone to a fact of love / loyal, loyal forgiven father's facts / midway, midway won, a fact / glee, glee is sizeable to a fact / enjoy, enjoy your younger facts / mention, mention is amazing to a fact / faithful, faithful is essential to our facts / instruction, instructions startle without facts / night, night is essene within facts / month, month is a moon in fact / day, day to a dearest fact / souls, souls in simple facts / before, before us our facts / reasons, reasons is silvery for facts / talk, talk into facts / escorted, escorted in silvery-blue cords facts / vendors, vendors into intriguing facts / visit, visited touring a fact / altar, altar to the temple's facts / bronze, bronze is into our facts / hand, hand the handle for facts / cloud, cloud interiorly to our facts / strange, strange in simple facts / spirit, spirits are meant

to formatted facts / mingled, mingled inspirationally for a fact / lamb, lambs lead over facts / someday, someday a way is met for a fact / relieve, relieve in rested facts / encouraged, encouraged in simple facts / dreams, dreams insistent to a fact / aroused, aroused into a fact / home, home and the triple intriguing facts / words, words wisdoms form a fact / shop, shop insights for a fact / funds, funds in simple facts / yield, yield in signature facts / plan, plan in simple facts / habits, habits are heralded for a fact / amazing, amazing in amounted facts.

CHAPTER EIGHT

Pure, pure into love's facts / dust, dusted into facts / prosper, prosper a simple fact / justice, justice is tooled into facts / doctrines, doctrines are supplied for a fact / influence, influence is spent on our facts / embodied, embodied amounts form a fact / virtue, virtue warranted facts / rejoice, rejoice is mentally factual / generosity, generosity marries our facts / brief, brief as a last fact / body, body is beautiful for a fact / delights, delights inclusions to a fact / bliss, bliss is basically a fact / taught, taught an interest in facts / taught, taught to learn for a fact / understand, understand a married fact / question, questions sing for facts / bondage, bondage is married in a fact / speech, speech is sincerest fact / liberate, liberate interior's fact / satisfaction, satisfaction forms a fact / inspiring, inspiring meanings on our facts / equal, equal in sporting facts / benefit, benefitted facts / disciple, disciples essential in a fact / work, work is made strictly factual / steady, steady on too, facts / evening, evenings ventured into, facts / apostle, apostle married, fact / vast, vast in a signature for facts / once, once and for all, a fact / forsake, forsake has come to a fact, good-bye / high, high enough to see through, fact / place, places made for love's facts / behalf, behalf has held us for all facts / flight, flight over, fact / anything, anything said is a fact / outside, outside is simple, fact / immediate, immediate openings in facts / win, win a worry free fact / honored, honored for the hurry too, facts / small, small enough to see through, facts / godspeed, gospel gathers godspeed now, fact / comfort, comfort is said too "fact" / among, among us well, facts / request, request rewarded a fact / mother, mother sent "fact" / common, common in areas of fact / wide, wide inside your facts / earth, earth is a mast for a fact / tendency, tendency sent too, fact / concrete, concrete curings given facts / slow, slow is essentially a fact / verbal, verbal insights given facts / obey, obey a structured fact / isolation, isolation gone, fact / implications, implications fly to our facts / handicap, handicaps over now, fly, flights, facts, factors, functions, mutual details, showering caps clear, ices melt, now we see the lord of love inside Arcturus' reign as the dove of sheperded ones, love has led us home, a fact / genuine, genuine in our giving facts / answer, answer made, yes! to a fact / proclaim, proclaim another well, facts / desire, express your desire to be inside a fact / impress, impress is won, fact.

CHAPTER NINE

Assistants, assistants are your fact / groups, groups gather to see where you are in the schemata drawn as light tricks blended creamy blue in love's aspirations for humanity in fact / volunteers, volunteers are made a soothing expression of love's facts / Gabriel, Gabriel grew to know your facts / universal, universal the cause for these facts / sureties, sureties sent are meant for your facts / literals, literals writteninto a code for facts / laterals, laterals the pages finished into facts / prayer, prayer is written into the code for facts / sincerity, sincerity is sent to a code / assurance, assurance of the fact, codes / heard, heard a friend say "fact" / answer, answer a letter written in fact / attitude, attitudes go to a fact / values, values found, fact / growth, growth is sent for factually / gratification, gratification came to your facts / bodies, bodies blissed in facts / discrete, discrete in the numbered facts / invisible, invisible amounting facts / perceive, perceive a diet of pure fact / flesh, flesh has sent a friend, fact / good, good in a diet rich with fact / efforts, efforts made and paid for in facts / affection, affection meant for the sent for facts / arbitrary, arbitrary in the news for facts / struggle, struggle gone, fact / temporal, temporal pleasures meet in fact / positive, positive the mention for fact / absolute, absolute extensions to the cosmos through facts / place, place is made, fact / send, send a nearest discipline to your facts / consciousness, consciousness is meant for facts / temporary, temporary without? fact / awaken, awaken the door into fact / shores, shores in sent facts / endless, endless the loop into fact / panorama, panorama is meant for fact / limitless, limitless the extent of your facts / opportunity, opportunity made a friend through love's facts / exhilirating, exhilirating entrance into facts / adventure, adventure through your nearest facts / sublime, sublime in estates marked for facts / uncertainty, uncertainty said " get a fact" / boundless, boundless in our joys, facts / attainment, attainment spent in life's facts / dynamic, dynamic detail for the future facts / captured, captured within a heart for facts / alive, alive is the signal for facts / free, free in a daily fact / thrilling, thrilling in expression for fact / always, always a detailed fact / moving, moving in silent retreat to a fact / within, within us, facts / become, become a balanced fact / desire, desire has sent us to a fact / similar, similar in a content for facts / inhabited, inhabited speeches and these beaches of fact / comprise, comprise a diet clear in fact / utterly, utterly sad without facts / grasp, grasp is grown, fact / finite, finite the finish for facts / dependence, dependence due to facts / management, management meant for a fact.

CHAPTER TEN

Capacity, capacity has met truth, fact / significant, significant the scent for your facts / contributions, contributions given a fact / messages, messages made fact / human, human in symphonic facts / family, family given a hope, fact / universal, universal the language for facts / mankind, mankind is simple in your facts / religion, religion is erased from the grain of truth, fact / competitors, competitors aligning to say "facts" / races, races off, facts / nationality, nationality and the rationality for facts / trademark, trademark is written as "fact" / value, value for the slavery which ensued "fact" / front, front and unto fact / office, office set for the philadelphia plan is a fact / God, God given faith in a fact / presents, presents corne to your facts / unique, unique in her singing fact / compelling, compelling the story of fact /

portrayal, portrayal meant for facts / open, open the door to your facts / time, time is spent on facts / eternity, eternity is met in a fact / perfection, perfection of relations too, facts / enshrouded, enshrouded in past? facts / mystery, mystery of the history solved, fact / difficulty, difficulty fed a fact / intelligences, intelligences said "fact" / series, series of subsets and facts / dilute, dilutes compute is a fact / carefully, carefully go beyond the screen to facts / beyond, beyond us is a basic fact / offer, offer your facets to the polish of truth in fact / people, people said "fact" / around, around hear? facts / world, world of the settled facts / discovered, discovered a diet for facts / reach, reach into reasonable fact / living, living in a gigantic fact / dwell, dwell in sold "facts" / impossible, impossible in a budget to less, facts / possible, possible to see a fact / successive, successive in generations of facts / large, large in a daily fact / embrace, embrace elocutive facts / literal, literal is your pleasure in facts / part, part is a start for all facts / generations, generations who lunge past facts / produces, produces a stage past facts / pose, pose necessarily in facts / revelations, revelations for facts / advocate, advocate found in your facts / new, new is the detail for facts / viewpoint, viewpoint spent is a fact / heritage, heritage heard "fact" / whole, whole in significance and fact / patrols, patrols peel past your facts / encompass, encompass only facts / hidden, hidden in details and facts / beneath, beneath us all a fact / time, time to tell your type to facts / earn, earn a noose lifted to reveal facts / total, total in a detached way for facts.

CHAPTER ELEVEN

Encouraging, encouraging experience is sent for, facts / based, based in believing facts / science, science is sent your facts / perhaps, perhaps we are the fact / concise, concise in her sentencing "fact" / integration, integration has cost your "fact" / contemporary, contemporary rays cross in fact / potential, potential mentioned is immense to a fact / sphere, sphere of the promised facts / blind, blind inside a fact / formulate, formulate your finished fact / harmony, harmony coming to a fact / wise, wise in a welcome fact / swing, swing in a sincere fact / circuit, circuit broken too, fact / phenomenon, phenomenon over, fact / shape, shape is a destiny for fact / test, text written is test strong to a fact / teaching, teaching has come into your fact / book, book written sells factually / ultimate, ultimate in a test for fact / mission, mission made into "a fact" / individual, individual in a soothing fact / master, mastery made for our facts / circle, circle is a sign for fact / prove, prove a pointed fact / vast, vast is your recall for fact / elliptical, elliptical vectoring into fact / resistance, resistance gone, fact / straight, straight into f-a-c-t / line, line opens to fact / non-profit, non-profit builds, fact / operating, operating into your facts / multiple, multiple mentions of fact / language, language healed now, fact / translation, translation written is "fact" / intends, intends a reunion of fact / school, school is a fact / study, study your facts / seven, seven who knew facts / together, together they laid into fact / central, central is the one winding fact / outer, outer stairs posing your fact / horizontal, horizontal seen as a fact / extensions, extensions win facts / concentrically, concentrically factual / tracks, tracks past us into fact / composed, composed

again, fact / task, task over, tools, facts / poster, poster fosters facts / in-depth, in-depth facts / spread, spread a sweet fact, you are loved / variety, variety of poses through facts / seminars, seminars taught through a fact / gatherings, gatherings sincere in your facts / paradise, paradise allowing a fact / gravity, gravity within? fact / alter, alter the ego of fact / personality, personality keys in through a series of tesselations called virsual, virtual holophonic periods and the octaves of light infuse Be near yourself daily as you place a love within your hearts facts / domains, domains established and written formats for facts / evolve, evolve in your solving for fact / system, system built is a fact / loss, loss is established as blinders removed, move on, facts / child, child of the extreme may move on now to the facts.

CHAPTER TWELVE

Real, real is the situation for fact / attainment, attainment keys into facts / shining, shining armor built for a fact / fragment, fragment gone, fact / shadow, shadow clears into fact / cast, cast away less as you fly into fact / figure, figure on salaried facts / lights, lights blinking for facts / orders, orders five new facts / borders, borders obeying your facts / suggested, suggested to rush into fact / entire, entire is the college for fact / entities, entities clearing your facts / assist, assist in a scheduled fact / physical, physical creations for fact / bodies, bodies blend in our facts / bestow, bestow a title to one fact / invoke, invoke a signature "fact" / afforded, afforded a portal for fact / gratify, gratify your timing in a fact / craves, craves a raving fact/ each, each is simply your fact / compliment, compliment a nearest fact / combined, combined inside a fact / both, both who knew facts / ancient, ancient in a cleared fact / segments, segments marketed in fact / several, several are the clearances for fact / divine, divine inside your facts / deepening, deepening experience of facts / trench, trench built inside has breached for fact / atlantean, atlantean streaming has steered into viewing facts / sevens, sevens appearing in skies near the seas for facts / heads, heads over all facts / disclose, disclose a position to a fact / doubt, doubt gone, fact / sovereign, sovereign in your reigning fact / life, life led now, fact / rays, rays meeting in fact / numbers, numbers appearing for fact / unify, unify in fact / result, results written are fact / units, units measuring fact / means, means to a simple fact / stabilize, stabilize inside your fact / cummulative, cummulative a key for facts / any, any and all who know facts / observes, observes us regally as a fact / decisions, decisions made cure your facts / judged, judged without? fact / economic, economic extremities and a fact / impair, impair has gone, fact / future, future clearing your facts / repair, reaping a repaired pack of facts / require, require a daring fact / needed, needed soon, facts / present, present in a pupil called facts / able, able is surest in facts / some, some who know experience for facts/ tender, tender is the resign into fact / acquire, acquire another nearing fact / mercies, mercies trickle into your facts / awakened, awakened in signs for all facts / powers, powers are lit now in fact.

CHAPTER THIRTEEN

Needs, need snow met, fact / rests, rests a period for fact / vital,

vital intelligence and facts / traverse, traverse a course into facts / physiologic, physiologic wonders and your facts / celestial, celestial desires for fact / ranges, ranges arranged into fact / students, students stood in fact / revision, revisions for the cure, facts / reversion, reversion to a simple fact / varieties, varieties sealed, a fact / safari, safari sent, oceans deep, in fact / pilgrims, pilgrims lost in fact / walks, walks over again, fact / travel, travel is daily a fact / architects, architects found in a fact / morning, morning of the mentioned facts / arcs, arcs established, fact / arc-angelic, arc-angelic abilities shine into your facts / starring, starring in you, facts / commissions, commissions made are paid into fact / lucifer, lucifer lost a date, fact / taught, taught to be internal in his spin, gone, fact / fell, fell another knowing less in fact / trade, trade opens into experience for fact / contentment, contentment maintains your facts / millennium, millennium measures your facts / constant, constant is our single goal to fact / made, made a mention for a fact / stream, streams who knew a fact / instruct, instruct a rest into fact / pupils, pupils who simply know fact / lightened, lightened is the path into fact / primaries, primaries inside a fact / discern, discern who is simple too, fact / labors, labors over, lost, fact / clouds, clouds opening facts / natives, natives nestle into fact / ghostly, ghostly and grizzled have gone to your gift, a fact / neutral, neutral experience of facts / world's, world's light is in your facts / messenger, messenger mentions a fact / sponsored, sponsored into a fact / mighty, mighty is the mystic in facts / muse, muse cretean in fact / metatron, metatron balanced in facts / fuse, fuse lit now, a fact / fares, fares paid for in fact / prepare, prepare to see facts / adopts, adopts a new fact / employ, employ only fact / stellar, stellar in a simple star called fact / settled, settled into factually / middles, middles maintained into fact / glorify, glorify your gaining fact / known, known to be factually freed / Gabriel, Gabriel agreed to be freed for all facts / stands, stands made are in fact / gazes, gazes healing a fact / stupendous, stupendous clearings for fact / all, all who say in clarity "fact" gather here / critical, critical to see your fact / mighty, mighty is the basic fact / smooth, smooth in your humanity of fact.

LEVEL 69: THE FEATURE-MENTS

CHAPTER ONE
Enlighten, enlighten a moment living in faithful features / complete, complete a course in features / organized, organized a movement to find new features / wonderful, wonderful a simple field of features loved / array, array of stars and the telescopes aimed into features / projects, projects accomplished, a feature / aggregation, aggregation of gathering facts for features now geometric / fixed, fixed in fijian sand, a strand of perfect DNA with a pair become one in featuring love / mass, mass reached, features / exact, exact placement arranged, features / sphere, sphere of the mass exagerated to include fetures / held in a silent orb of features / capital, capital is raised through a financial source with features / predict, predict a change featured / personification, personification

to the friend is featured / formulated, formulated plans are featured / abodes, abodes are risen into through your features / springs, springs appearing near features / preceded, preceded through a special feature / established, established events for your features / devoted, devoted in the noted features / formation, formation on the core features / moves, moves into temples featured / right, right is the might for features / gravity, gravity off you, win, featured / adjust, adjust into miracles for features / born, born to be featured / alive, alive in a need featured / today,today is the way to be featured / intervening, intervening moments are featured / offspring,offsprig spent in your features / connection, connection made, featured / carriers, carriers over, features / belief, belief in a valuable philosophy is basically featured / accidental, accidental without? feature love / lower, lower days into nights of features / order, order a mission from friends of your features / intuition, intuition assigned to your future features / courage, courage arises in features / urge, urges your marriage to a feature / reception, reception made real for your features / rendezvous, rendezvous established in a feature / zones, zones open into features / training, training paying off, features / permitted, permitted to be featured in love / jurisdiction, jurisdiction allowed a feature / enter, enter into a phase featured / numerous, numerous are the minutes featured / especially, especially swift in your features / knowledge, knowledge is allowed your features / counsel, counsel swollen in features / worship, worship is gone to a feature / status, status opening to your future features / presence, presence is made into features / reflex, reflex establishes your future features / directional, directional in functional moments and features / only, only a neutral feature / inside, inside a shining feature / patient, patient in your features / small, small in a merry feature / theatrical, theatrical features / partners, partners marry a feature / sincerest, sincerest in your features / patience, patience is shown your feature.

CHAPTER TWO
Survive, survive and eccentrically featured / scale, scale into signal features / accounts, accounts in simple features / gift, gift of the gaily futures featured / essential,essential in a signal feature / response, response is made, featuring / manifestation, manifestation for a feature / minister, minister to the needs of others features / eligible, eligible into features / advancement, advancement for the future features / varied, varied formerly and featured / guidance, guidance is gaining A feature / design, design on a marriage of features / leadership, leadership advancing to a feature / serve, serve is centrally a focused feature / transition, transition into a currency featured / angels, angels featured / ranks, ranks into single features / expire, expire in single features / trinity, trinity into simple features / joined, joined to a mirthful feature / entire, entire is a single feature / flairs, flairs in a merry feature / authentic, authentic in shining features / thrice, thrice is a ferry to features / said, said too, a feature / deny, deny is bet on through this one, "features" / finalize, finalize into your future's features / inevitables, inevitables are featured / veritive, veritive in a ferocious feature / volumes, volumes and the theory for a

feature / volumetric, volumetric in suggested features / constitute, constitute and the surest features / columns, columns assign a voluminous amount featuring love / invokes, invokes intrigue your features / involve, involve is solving a feature / mobilize, mobilize a merry feature / trinitize, trinitize a daring feature / matched, matched amounts are featured / courts, courts amount to a feature / evolve, evolve into solving features / unrevealed, unrevealed in a fairest feature / revels, revels into single features / futures, futures are reaching A feature / administer, administered for a feature / admire, admire in a minutes features / completes, completes a carriage into A feature / lack, lack is slack without A feature / realized, realized a sizeable feature / matching, matching a miracle's features / trends, trends into assigns and features / expires, expires in a moment's features / experience, experience says features / express, express a soothing features / plans, plans into penning expressions for features / facts, facts and the features opening into landed lines / ministries, ministries who marry A feature / administered, administered into features / endeavors, endeavors paid to a feature / acquire, acquire a federal feature / cleverly, cleverly are your featured / experienced, experienced in features / mer-ka-bah, mer-ka-bah the fit for a feature / allow, allow a simple feature.

CHAPTER THREE

Commissions, commissions amount to a feature / heads, heads around features / precedent, precedent set in your features / architecture, architecture is chilling to a feature / quatrains, quatrains written are red, features / tertiary, tertiary to a sample feature / leap, leap and allow features / pairs, pairs appearing featured / glories, glories given to features / 900, 900 who knew a feature / middle, middle may's features / technicals, technicals carry your features / paradise, paradise is sized to include features / eras, eras ablaze in your features / ascend, ascend a moment too, featured / stages, stages reviving your features / embarked, embarked in a comet for mars, a feature / onward, onward said "a feature" / outward, outward into features / ages, ages electric with features / natural, natural appearances and features / services, services rendered to a feature / courses, courses written for your features / divulged, divulged without? features / educates, educates wach the other to a fatherly feature / opinions, opinions met in a feature / choirs, choirs who huddle near a warm feature / evolves, evolves into solving a feature / singly, singly asked feature / courses, courses paid for "featured" / shares, shares made into features / detailing, detailing opening a feature / creatures, creatures who co-create for features / units, units matched ina feature / featured, featured gates into love / initiates, initiates made a feature last / high, high into hues of features / pairings, pairiings last, features / served, served a simple philosophy for features / limits, limtis off, features / worlds, worlds collapse into features / specialize, specialize in sizes for features / governed, governed simply as a feature / spaces, spaces elastic too and featured / persons, persons who know how to feature / havens, havens in a resting net, featured / personalities, personalities who fuse into features / circuits, circuits made into features / broaden,

broaden a basicness for features / eventual, eventual is the truth inside A feature / wooden, wooden without one, feature / gradual, gradual in spirit's mend, a feature / willing, willing to be featured / spheres, spheres erupting in a featured volcano / wills, wills made loss elastic without features / mandates, mandates written became laws for these features, planets / identify, identify why in your feature / coded, coded for the future of features / embraced, embraced into features / wives, wives who last for a feature / sold, sold into featuring / wombs, wombs opening into features / slavery, slavery over, features / husbands, husbands held onto immaculate features.

CHAPTER FOUR

Centers, centers built, a feature / build, build a nexus for features / borne, borne throughout, features / birthing, birthing coming to features / unions, unions made into features / measured, measured by your feature / children, children for a featured truth / miracles, miracles mentioned into features / transcendance, transcendance amounts to a featuring for love / presence, presence is unto your future feature / textiles, textiles in a simple features / masters, masters for the future in A feature / relational, relational examples and awareness into features / locally, locally a simple feature / authored, authored in allowing your features / thrive, thrive into resolving features / evolutions, evolutions allowing your features / Gabriel, Gabriel grew into a future feature / resolutions, resolutions approaching your feature / sun, sun is day for a feature / resolve, resolve into solving for features / son, son is a dearest feature / michael, michael is amazing on your features / locals, locals allowing A features / magnify, magnify your features / physical, physical for A feature / creators, creators into a feature / plans, plans into A featured life / arise, arise is reaching a feature / preliminary, preliminary the daily feature / billion, billions drawn into future dollaring for your features / systems, systems who sing of your features / abodes, abodes amounting for your features / rise, rise is convenient in a feature / planets, planets spinning into features / devoted, devoted a daily feature / satellites, satellited spanning a feature / enactment, enactment exact to a fact for a feature / work, work is wearing your feature / regeants, regeants appearing near the features / range, ranges allowing our features / scope, scope is concurrent to a feature / session, session of the needed features / frequent, frequent sent features / unlimited, unlimited features / superiors, superiors allowing a feature / own, own a donor's features / policies, policies amount to our feature / fall, fall into future features / details, details amount to a feature / gone, gone is given our feature / attendance, attendance is given our features / duties, duties inside your future features / order, order a daily format for a former feature / school, school is the dearest features / ruling, ruling is a newness for these featured accounts / cited, cited in a seeded feature / error, error for the features / authority, authority thrilled in our features / powers, powers appearing in starring features / isolation, isolation is nearing our features / indigenous, indigenous into your future's features / emergency, emergency a meaning futured feature / allure, allure has set inside a future feature.

CHAPTER FIVE

Scope, scope is a nearing feature / frequent, frequent meant worshipfully to a feature / directives, directives mentor and fathered into features / unifications, unifications for the realize that formations were real in your feest features / case, case is the polish for features / policy, policy vindicative without features / analagous, analagous too, A feature / convene, convene in a righteous sense at a feature / arbitrary, arbitrary into features / record, record the erasure without reason for features / regional, regional relations of the featured / rebellion, rebellion is finished, reconnect, features / review, review a few features / appeal, appeal to the healed features / pertains, pertains a magical feature / struggle, struggle off, face it, features / sub-ordinate, erase sub-ordination through love's features / guidance, guidance grew into a feature / essence, essence is spent without features / potency, potency is electric to a feature / modification, modification for a feature / zone, zones opened in features / gain, giant gains made, features / embark, embark to an embrace of the features of love / endeavor, endeavor into sever less features / lessen, lessens and into A feature / confusion, confusions and the refusal to lessen your features / force, force is a federal feature / neither, enough to fear less than a feature? / fulcrum, fulcrum opens to feed a feature / cycle, cycle opening into features / response, response is yes for A feature / wide, wide inside your features / technique, techniques to survive to within features / upheaval, upheaval has gone into A feature / brilliant, brilliant in flashes for A feature / council, council chosen in features / stumbled, stumbled across level features / sea, seas risen over and featured too / only, only and all ways a key to these features / blend, blend into features / chamber, chamber of the charging hearted features / gratify, gratify is ratified through features / level, level is past, features / vicinity, vicinity dictated through features / sector, sector openly vectored for in features / memory, memory erased and featured / complete, complete a cognition of A feature / rejoice, rejoice in a changing environment for features / triumphant, triumphant reigns a heart held wise to features / mansion, mansions open into A feature / minus, minus A couple of features / material, material smattered into features / image, image given a rest for features / trace, trace goes, featured / occassions, occassions simple into features / speak, speak often to features / farewell, farewell has come to a feature continent / beloved, beloved be, featured / angel, angel wells into view and features / task, task of the simply featured / grow, grow into features / select, select a group featured / more, more then grew to a feature.

CHAPTER SIX

Class, class comes to a break in features / signal, signal a survival feature / welcome, welcome another's featured glance / wrote, wrote of hearts who held simple stances to a feature / bid, bid for a basic philosophy for features / measure, measure the mellow in featured / time, time is the trickle into features / division, division grand has held a secret Egyptian to a trace opened of old, a feature / indigo, indigo blue in havasupi falling remembrance of the ones who came to a feature / tendency, tendency from above is to see

only large examines as a feature / slight, slight is the seal off a feature / numbers, numbers who match into features / bestowal, bestowal given release today into features / seldom, seldom is said less than three "features, features, features" / men, men who knew which to use, featured / issue, issue settled in two parts, featured / summary, summary made electric, found, features / property, property sold in towns featured / prosper, prosper in the news of features / language, language written is real, featured / inward, inward sight is given feature / gent, gent gone, featured / risk, risk is over, features / promotion, promotions made now, features / splendid, splendid in yes men and material features / lounge, lunges over and into a newness featured / breathe, breathe imbibe of features / biologic, biologic and into our features / epochs, epochs written for features / accordance, accordance is said to exist for a featured / produce, produce a sort who furnish features / strain, strain off and featured / stages, stages melt into features / attains, attains are gaining A feature / minor, minor in the menu of our featured events / mobilize, mobilize for a feature / contact, contact made into features / engage, engage only when you are featured / ordination, ordination gave you our feature / prior, prior to a priveleged feature / curiosity, curiousity said "featured" / thirst, thirst is essential in your features / discover, discover daily features / value, value is given to your feature / history, history holds forth as featured / absorbed, absorbed a ratio of great features / mental, mentally freed to be a feature / goal, goal is reached, feature / trial, trial is the error without a feature / fabric, fabric fellow into your features / code, code is written as a feature / step, step along now as featured / sanction, sanction in central planks and features / law, law deals are leading to a feature / backward, backward glances standing still as featured] / early, early efforts paying off as featured / battle, battle off, features / women, women who knew a feature / hunger, hunger is over, featured / premium, premiums paid and into insured features / fostered, fostered a genuine given feature / illusion, illusion over, features / enforce, enforced a way to feature / fortitude, fortitude is found in a feature.

CHAPTER SEVEN

Sex, sex is on, featured / evolution, evolution for our feature / loss, loss is off, featured / joined, joined in combined features / spirit, spirit settles into your features / normal, normal events mix into features / pure, pure in a way featured / normal, normal days and events are featured / inferior, inferior without again? featured / peculiar, peculiar without a feature / destiny, destiny suggested for your features / speech, speeches made are now featured / action, action taken to our features / efficiently, efficiently open to a given feature / narrow, narrow without wide features / partake, partake only of A feature / feeble, feebleness gone to a feature / abilities, abilities agile enough to see, featured / acquit, acquit without features / mingled, mingled into a single feature / blue, blue in a basic allowance for sequences and features / blend, blend into A featured / percentage, percentage paid to your features / culture, culture softening to features / circle, circle cut thorugh in features / extended, extended A warranty too, and features / taming, taming goes itno features / fire, fire is out, featured / change, change over due, features / climatic, climatic inclusions and features / medicine, medicine given to your features / astronomy,astronomy offered A feature / pure, pure in a single way, features / marriages, marriages mentioning A feature / ceremony, ceremony for a feature / community, community questioning your features / culmination, culmination comes to a former feature / ritual, rituals establishing a feature / legal, legal is the deed to a feature / insure, insure has come, featured / presume, presume the room featured / spite, spite is off, featured / landing, landing is over, move, featured / protection, protection apparent in your features / idealization, idealization reigns into features / superficial, superficial artifical escapes into features / education, education coming into features / absent, absent without features / picture, picture of a perfect feature / insurance, insurance sent for and featured / defense, defense elected is a featured / perpetuation, perpetuation brings a feature / shift, shift along lining features / mixture, mixture of madness into features / unit, units utilized include features / family, family over a feature / nourish, nourish is kneeling in your feature / pleasure, pleasure is appealing to your features / basic, basic stability is gained through features / stone, stone in the temples featured / tent, tent torn in two pieces of past features / heat,heat is off, featured / because, because we knew, features / kind, kind in a simple temple for features.

CHAPTER EIGHT
Invade,invade is less featured / retreat, retreat into a feature / persuade, persuade a dialect for features / tiers, tiers off a feature / tear, tear into one, feature / evoke, evoke a steady feature / layers, layers lost found featured / thoughts, thoughts are thick in features / thick, thick is the electric feature / settle, settle into your features / rounds, rounds asotnish your features / seals, seals off then and featured / retail, retail is mailed itno features / soothes, soothes across features / revelations, revelations made your feature / showers, showers are single without features / empress, empress of the days featured / interiors,interiors established into features / mirrors, mirrors lost at a feature / materials, materials managed in a feature / mavericks, mavericks regard you as featured / details, details dialing in as featured / doubts, doubts banished, features / spread, spreads a news, featured / refill, refill your relations and features / routes, routes opened into a feature / relative, relative in simple features / deify, deify into a feature / rally, rally about your features / data, data dealing in a feature / rope, rope in rhyming features / moxa, moxa is swimming in a feature / needles, needles needle into a feature / adjust, adjust a featured data for love / kindness, kindness in simple into features / co-operates, co-operates curing your features / cures, cures in single A features / cycles, cycles ascending in spiral features / spherical, spherical delays are own for your features / aboriginal, aboriginal information ran to a feature / evolution, evolution and a feature / violet, violet blue into features / extensives, extensives embracing a feature / multiples, multiples meant for our features / groups, groups gaze into features / biologically, biologically a feature / natures, natures nearest features meet /

cultures, cultures in curation for the features of love / blanketed, blanketed in a basic feature / creative, creative elements reach for a feature of love / mongoloid, mongoloid shapes can go to a featur / carapace, carapace stretched to include features of love / negative, negative without an ivy green feature / liken, liken unto a feature / incessant,incessant into a feature / evolves, evolves electric signs into a feature / rapidly, rapidly due a feature / combines, combines in a signed feature / african, african in signs for a feature / developed, developed a friend who knew features / characterize, characterize a spare feature / rapids, rapids releasing your features / originates, originates a door into features / suspend, suspend disbelief as a feature.

CHAPTER NINE
Successive, successive in a featured / cultures, cultures who cross at a feature / impressive, impressive amounting to featured / mandates, mandates maintaining a feature / magical, magical missions and features / raced, raced around featured / musical, musical to a meaning for features / adjudicates, adjudicates into features / openings, openings created through a features / extended, extended patiently into features / doors, doors open nearby, a feature / signs, signs are sent into a feature / effects, effects worn off and now featured / address, address your dearest as a feature / adjourn, adjourn now for features / codes, codes imply a duration for the features / melchizidek, melchizidek details your features / merkaba, merkaba is mentioning a feature / mantras, matnras amused into features / functions, functions impressed for features / modifies, modifies materially your feature / evolving, evolving into solving a feature / inherits, inherits simply a feature / solving, solving is calling you to features / swerves, swerves into features / trance, trance over now, featured / heads, heads allowing hearts into features / training, training onto level features / translate, translate your meaning into features / yawning, yawning is going into features / reproduces,reports a reproducingness in features / opens, opens a feature of love / taos, taos equates to a soul release freed as a feature of the illusions lost into love / matrices, matrices due a following feature / yellow, yellow is a rosey feature / supremacy, supremacy is simple into features / blue, blue is a basic feature / supra,supra is set into a feature / believes, believes in a single feature / ancients, ancients dealing in features / eternals, eternals are mentally fresh in a feature / unions, unions wrestle without features / retreats, retreats paid a feature / faithfully, faithfully a due feature / regards, regards are paid to a feature / administratively, administratively a feature / recents, recents into features / presently, presently into features / associative, associative and due a feature / judicate, judicate a meaningful feature / sets, sets in a single feature / bestow, bestow in a dearest feature / subsets, subsets sighing for features / nominates, nominates a nearest feature / fractions, fractions are filling into features / denominates, denominates a nearest feature / planetary, planetary moments and the poses for a future featured / disperses, disperses an ointment for your features / visits, visits are made to a feature / homes, homes established in a father less feature / vocalized, vocalized in sizes featured / homelands,

homelands reign as featured / reduces, reduces a significant feature / terminates, terminates near A featured

CHAPTER TEN

Submerged, submerged into tanks of features / asian, asian assigns include features / tibetan, tibetan in ways who seal features / turkish, turkish in news of a strike again, features / level, level through your visits featured / truth, truth told and featured / operations, operations squarely due a feature / refine, refine a measure featured / proceeds,proceeds procedurally featured / afflicted, afflicted without, features / purchase, purchases made are featured / arbitrates, arbitrates within, features / loves, loves are spread into features / dials, dials over your features / matters, matters materially into features / immensity, immensity is clearing, features / ponderance, ponderance is paralleled through your features / characters, characters are blue in a variation on your features / endurance, endurance is dealing in features / decide, decide inside features / partners, partners are nearing A feature / compels, compels in tympanic features / pounds, pounds across a feature / respects, respects form a feature / cheers, cheers inside a feature / smitten, smitten in sizes and features / saves, saves a smiling feature / dayflights, dayflights inside your features / joins, joins a journeys features / delegates, delegates intrigued with your features / scatters, scatters inside a dreaming features / imply, imply in steerig features / erotically,erotically a reigning feature / risen, risen in sizes and features / pagan, pagan without a feature / tramps, tramps past a feature / fields, fields are filling your features / heal, heal allows our shrugging features / houses, houses are sealing your features / clear, clear into dearest features / chosen, chosen ones winning a featured race / terrific, terrific into a feature / freedoms, freedoms reach your features / carries, carries over well, features / ancestors, ancestors due a lifting feature / skills, skills are stilled in a feature / traipse, traipse across the graves removed to reveal a lifted feature / embark, embark in the sparks electric through featured blue loves / millions, millions who knew a featured spark / speech, speech is composite to a feature / composed, composed in a note now featured, love / twines, twines inside signs and features / trillions, trillions gracing your features / vessel,vessel exclusive to your features / freeze, freeze is off, features / frames, frames are matched into love's feather free features / surfing, surfing across dearest features / yields, yields are yellow in your features / spires, spires aspirant to a feature / tumbling, tumbling overloads of features / worn, worn into two features / sticks, sticks who spark into features / wisdom, wisdom of the wellness featured / morning, morning of the meanings featured.

CHAPTER ELEVEN

Spirits, spirits have sent a release into these features / gained, gained an employ of features / respond, respond now to jobs about features / relative, relative in relationship to a feature / crouching, crouching in a single feature / release, release a past feature / occupy,occupy is inside your features / raptures, raptures race is run, rage done, move on, featured / rushes, rushes past a feature / phonic, phonic into sonic features / rapturing, rapturing a newness to your features / focusing, focusing into your features / hormones, hormones meant realized release for a feature / vascillates, vascillates gone to a feature / harmonics, harmonics mended for features / hermes, hermes new a tablet geared to features / fabrics, fabrics fold into features / changes, changes are made to the features (skin, shape, form) / ranges, ranges are found in a feature / ruses, ruses are over, features / ropes, ropes off a soft feature / rafters, rafters lift your features / ecstatic, ecstatic in elastic features / chisel, chisel your features / kingdom, kingdoms coming to a feature / protect, protect a person who knew a feature / coming, coming clears your features / shells, shells clink in feature / nest, nest in your orbital's spin and features / spin, spin due? featured / flowering, flowering into a feature / orbitally, orbitally well into features / fools, fools depart energetically into a feature / treads, treads are softened through features / convert, convert a neutral into features / coherent, coherent into features / comets, comets nominated through features / fires, fires overdue a dealing feature / matters, matters material into A feature / reality, reality is clearing your features / rational, rational measures interested in features / rabid, rabid into features / differs, differs a simple feature / octave, octave is spent without features / mint, mint interiors featured / life, life is clipped without strips and features / mauve, mauve is the color now featured / purine, purine in an essene deliverance for features / marination, marination's vacations are finished in features / life, life is the link upon features / pyrimidine, pyrimidine into features / octaves, octaves essentially featured / oscillations, oscillations advanced into features / laws, laws in singing features / twines, twines a simple features / reveal, reveal a reactionary reach into features / arranged, arranged and sung too, features / fixed, fixed in simple features / distances, distances daring too, features / majors, majors noble gestures end in features / minor, minor in a simple feature / 64, 64 forth into right features / languages, languages in a spatial features / pieces, pieces inside a features.

CHAPTER TWELVE

Adenine, adenine into rings forming a feature into the light on love's linkage / thymine, thymine threaded features / guanine, guanine gilling features / percentage, percentages paid for and patched into features / cytosine, cytosine sent to a feature / diatonic, diatonic forms a features / affirm, affirm a firming ribbon's features / deny, deny is detailed without features / reconcile, reconcile styles for a features / 256, 256 is a typical feature / 128, 128 mended a feature / mutuals, mutuals marry our features / contact, contact is intrigued in features / forms, forms in truth featured / forces, forces singing to features / bound, bounds inside ringing features / precision, precisions is singing A feature / 3, 3 who know a feature / octaves, octaves singing features / sequenced, sequenced into features / ascends, ascends forth in features / achieved, acheived into purist features / created, created and gated for features / archival, archival seedings and features / shocking, shocking singing features found in diagonal amusement for love / naturally,

naturally a federally linked experienced a features / reconciliation, reconciliations forming a featured expression / flown, flown above and into a feature / affirms, affirms a firming feature / diagrams, diagrams finding a feature / fortunate, fortunate unto a featured event / vibrational, vibrational inside the featured estates / infuse, infuses intrigued forthrightly featured / enthusiasm, enthusiasm reigning into features / decisions, decisions dealing into features / initiated, initiated amounts features / procedures, procedures are simply featured / purposeful, purposeful into a feature / up, up a day and featured / activities, activities active into features / down, down into dealing features / in, in a timing decision for features / 21's,out and the time into features / out, out and the signs are now featured / proteins, proteins are single into features / configured, configured are the signs featured / frames, frames are forming a features / unites, unites are simple into a feature / dual, dual is a single features / substrate, substrate allowing a features dates / structures, structures allowing the threaded features / positive, positive into a features / ribosomes, ribosomes dealing into features / neutral, neutral into single features / RNA, RNA features are spent for love / negative, negative is spent for features / elements, elements meant for A feature / activate, activate a daily feature / fusions, fusions into a feature / cosmic, cosmic accrue for a feature / mixed, mixed in mixes features / sourced, sourced in signal's featured / activations, activations are into a feature / transmutes, transmutes into a single feature.

CHAPTER THIRTEEN

Triggering, triggering amounts form a feature / fundamental, fundamentally a featured estate / born, born into a featured relation / generality, generality reigns into features / subsequent,subsequent into features / largely, largely into a simple feature / affinities, affinities are into firing features / triggering, triggering and the features / fundamental, fundamentally a featured relation into love / born, born in a balance for features / generality, generality into a feature / subsequent, subsequent unto our features / largely, largely a living featured / affinities, affinities into a meaning features / existence, existences into a featured amount / appears, appears an appearing feature / sheperds, sheperds meeting into features / glades, glades dealt with in features / largest, largest livings features / process, process is due into a feature / actively, actively into a featured light / substances, substances into our featured rates / correspondence,correspondence dealing into featured rates / commonly, commonly a dealing featured / substances, substances signal a feature / total, total into a feature / apparently, apparently a welcome featured / cases, cases filled within features / evolving, evolving a triple feature / changes, changes dealing in features / elementally, elementally an essential featured / maintains, maintains a detailed features / squarely, squarely a sincere feature / absolutes, absolutes interior into a featured event / configured, configured and triggered into love's features / conceed, conceed a deed to a feature / packs, packs into boxes effective for features / conceals without, features / circles, circles deal your features / signals, signals advancing form features / triangles, triangles angled into features / retires, retires without features / cone,

cone erupting now, featured / squarely, squarely and dearly A featured / views, views igniting into features / circled, circled a magical feature / lakes, lakes leaping to featured yellow stones / megaphones,megaphones loaned to a group's features / rewards, rewards assigned a feature / surrendered, surrendered into features / process, process appealing to a feature / speaks, speaks often into features / positions, positions paralleling a feature / spoken, spoken clearly for features / symbolic, symbolic i sealing features / relay, relay allowing a feature / fundamental, fundamental inside a feature / transitions, transitions making a feature / expressions, expressions preaching a feature / progressions, progressions arming a feature / holy, holy is how to be featured / uncovered, uncovered singly? featured / suns, suns and the dues within, features / inventory, inventory sold to a feature.

LEVEL 70: THE INFLUENCE-MENTS

CHAPTER ONE:

13's,13's appearing in featured influence / 87, 87 said, features influence / 34th, 34th in a started influence / chemists, chemists amounting to your influence / 60, 60 who knew a new featured influence / hydrogen, hydrogen seen as a sunny influence / crystallized, crystallized as we realize your influence / cosmically, cosmically you knew your connection to those influential in love / absolutes, absolutes meet in a cosmicness called an influence / cycles, cycles who sent you throughout our influence / universe, universe for the curse gone, influence sent / gravitation, gravitation is relational to A influenced / conforms, conforms in swarming influences / discernment, discernment coming into your influence / affect, affect is effective for an influence / effects, effects paid a visit for our influences / introduce, introduce a new member to your influence / epoch, epoch spent in A, an influence / civilized, civilized in a retail influence / holistic, holistic events held a healing influence / anew, anew is the renew for our influence / focus, focus into your influence / renew, renew in a simple influence / corners, corners cut? revealed, influentially / times, times are spent in truth and an influence / ice, ice is surrendered for our influences / begun, begun is a singing for ours, an influence / endemic, endemic in a pantemime called influentially, love / intelligence, intelligence says gifted influences / life, life is led through your channels for an influence / judged, judged in a simple release of all influential expression of love / eclipsed, eclipsed into a finest net for those who know influence / impends, impends into a mirrored influence / traces, traces into an influence / transform, transforming yours, influence / vast, vast into a featured set for influence / faced, faced in a simple features influence / endured, endured in enduring influences / civilized, civilized in a feeling influence / reflects, reflects a regard for A, an influence / luminosity, luminosity is essential for our influence / electro-magnetically, electro-magnetically influenced / chitta, chitta is a participant forming your influence / ages, ages are ringing your influence / minds, minds electric meet in A, your influence / seers, seers allowed in A fabric now influential to your skin / chi, chis is the pet within A, an influence / umbilicals, umbilicals are cutting away to your influence / collections, collections are coming, believe in a feature called influence / white, white is the sight inside your influence / inhabitants, inhabitants are caring for your future influence / stones, stones are sent to a singing invention called influentially "waves" / exalted, exalted is a slated melt for all your heart's wave patterned influences / powders, powders are powerful enough to see your features / philosopher's, philosopher's stones yield a finer feature / filling, filling in simple influence / destitute, destitute without A your influence / siddhis, siddhis are breathing your influences of love / sacral, sacral in her sealing influence / perfections, perfections met in a creamy influence / metallic, metallic without vent for our influence / proximity, proximity to copper amounting to influences freed / principals, principals are simple in their fine influence / huge, huge events registered formally as influence.

CHAPTER TWO

Small, small is the signal for an influence / beings, beings cast past old influences / light, light is a link within a filling influence / pleasures, pleasures are purest in an influence / heavy, heavy into daily influence / senses, senses are sent a delicious vent for aims of an influence / direction, direction allowed a new influence / natures, natures are mixed without ions for influence? / wordly, wordly in a simple influence / will, will is set forth in influence / enjoy, enjoy a simple land for influence / attachment, attachment goes to your influences / spiritual, spiritual advancement calls for future influence / gone, gone is the zone of past lived influence / bliss, bliss is dealing in final influence / heights, heights are healed and influenced / old, old into new fields of influence / snakes, snakes wriggle free of the old influences / ages, ages tossed to a finer influence / hunger, hunger has led to a multiple state of influence / see, see us well into your influence / thirst, thirst has come to your influences / hear, hear us singing for firmer influence / distance, distance elected is finest at influence / enormous, enormous commitments made into a matching influence / great, great are the secrets wise within your influence / speeds, speeds along quickly to a finite influence / move, move into your influence / transports, transports are sending A feature to your influence / travel, travel into vaults held for your former influence / forms, forms found an influence for those lights who blink in significant accept of the poles within an electric field, founded, sounded, ON, influence / any, any who knew know influence / ones, ones who accept, know, influences / all, all in a day's influence / bodies, bodies who blink into influences / temporarily, temporarily well without influence / entry, entry is pointed to in influence / left, left in a state influenced / another, another way influenced / permanence, permanence becoming influenced / cosmically, cosmically cured and influenced / mortals, mortals majored and influenced / celestially, celestially suggested and copied for influenced / participates, influenced participates arranged to a love / brought, brought began influenced / intention,

intention came to your influence / authority, authority reeling influenced / desires, desires dared influenced / rising, rising ranges influenced / exercise, won exercise for an templed stand / rapidly, rapidly rose an influenced / obstructless, obstructless shores envisioned influentially / tides, tides tooling released influenced / poverty, poverty cured, inflatally / divulge, divulge near influenced / wealth, wealth wages influenced / esoteric, esoteric caves influenced / secrets, secrets sang influenced / means, means to be influenced / indulge, indulge ran influentially / exalt, exalt sounds influential / influence, influence has won your place in the reign eternal / achieve, achieve a known balance in your influences / files, files burst inside influences .

CHAPTER THREE

Bathe, bathe in beauty's influence / empowers, empowers powers influenced / flood, flood over an influence / utilize, utlize your eye's influence / flown, humanitarians flown to love's influence / enthrone, enthrone rains influenced / enhance, enhance ranging influenced / benefits, benefits beauty influenced / results, results made us influenced / secrets, secrets soothing our influence / tunes, tunes taming our influence / sacredly, sacredly signifies an influence / chance, chance to be influenced / patent, patent pourings influenced / patrons, patrons given an influence / evolve, evolve too and influenced for love / solve, solve soothes our influence / waken, waken to winnings influence / succeed, succeed times our influence / aware, aware shares our influence / warm, warm warming our influence / entireties, entireties tripling for our influence / collects, collects fed an influence / utilities, utilities raging influenced / means, means too, influenced / portraits, portraits paging influence / spiritually, spiritually influenced / portions, portions shared on influence / predicted, predicted and influenced / dues, dues for "an" influence / populates, populates purged into influence / utilize, utlize yes to an influence / undulates, undulates a narrow influence / resolute, resolute ranges for influence / equally, equally willing in influence / alchemists, alchemists for an influence / efficacious, efficacious use of an influence / evolution, evolution sharing to your influence / numbers, numbers are influenced / prophetic, prophetic ringing's influence / participant, participant paging for an influence / trenchant, trenchant touring a influence / internal, internal rays influenced / internal, internal reassures into influence / wells, wells worthy on influence / beneficial, benefical barrows and your influences / succession, successions shingled without influence / ends, ends on an influence / predecessors, predecessor passionate for our influence / cyclical, cyclical seasons on an influence / envelopes, envelopes valued for our influence / strands, strands tripled into influence / enhance, enhance pouring for influence / external, external meetings into influence / sporadic, sporadic spinning to an influence / alchemist, alchemist for an influence / spread, spread across influenced / agree, agree for an influence / burns, burns over, influenced / acrid, acrid without? influenced / stones, stones treat an influence / teach, teach a technique for the knowing influence / credible, credible credits for the influenced / resting, resting in influence and successful resurrect.

CHAPTER FOUR

Spiralist, spiralist shine in fine fields fresh in tunes / nurtured, nurtured needs for an influence / pent, pent into influences / nourished, nourished into influence / limits, limits in influence / stratus, stratus rated for an influence / technological, technological caring's influence / intellects, intellects sectors on influence / profound, profound pairing's influence / singles, singles influenced / cultures, cultures toured to a respect for influences / candles, candles lit heavenly influenced / streets, streets opened influentially / currents, currents caution influenced / streams, streams streached influentially / present, present influenced / capable, capable of cures to an influence / geological, geological journeys into your influence / movements, movements past cashing influence\ / management, management meant to an influence / maleable, maleable waves influence / rounded, rounded on a living's influence / reaches, reaches a deploy for freshend influence / christ, christ reign influenced / loved, loved to be influenced / company, company cures yourinfluence / planned, planned for our influence / cords, cords won influenced / explaned, explained sharing's influence / cured, cured for our influence / reigns, reigns ranging and influenced / cuts, cuts across loving influence / victory, victory made won and influenced / wanted, wanted fairs influence / made, made amuse for influence / sacrosanct, sacrosanct sealing soar and influence / magnent, magnet matching our influence / solvent, solvent sharing our influence / surrounds, surrounds shield out influence / baried, baried over all who say "influence" / levels, levels on an influence / divine, divine details for an influence / signify, signify sures you influence / release, release reaching an influence / courss, courses above an influence / joy, joy gaining you influence / humans, humans on your influence / currents, currents on an influence / direct, direct delivery influence / covenants, covenants on an influence / suitable, suitable suits into influence / arks, arks soaring influenced / soon, soon enough's influence / recorded, recorded rating's influenced / shown, shown shower's influence / historics, historics made and influenced / rainbows, rainbows ranges influenced / life, life loops intoi an influence / backdrops, backdrops made your influence / paths, paths surging influence / rays,rays appering influenced / merger, merger moving influenced / lights, lights legible to an influence / violet, violet views into an influence.

CHAPTER FIVE

Blue, blue coming into influence / indigo, indigo sides and influence / greengreen grew influenced / orange, orange rays influenced / yellow, yellow yearly influenced / red, red reading of influence / black, black landed influence / rays, rays raptures influenced / hologram, hologram hurtle to an influence / modify, modify majors an influence / human, human holds influenced / posits, posits positions as influenced / spectrums, spectrums spiral to an influence / positions, positions primary on influence / differ, differ details our influence / positive, positive tripling influence / sections, sections on an influence / the divine, the divine ringing and your influence / parts, parts onto our influence / love, love leads as spent and then influence / galactic, galactic goodness and influence / emotion, emotion for a news influenced / biological, biological basics and influenced / digest, digest your influence won / injest, injest an invest to your influence / cells, cells signaling an influence / extravagance, extravagance ranges and influenced / stars, stars staring into yellow's influence / rewards, rewards readind for an influence / organs, organs ringing and as influenced / atoms, atoms on and influenced / transduction, transduction ringing and then, influenced / trains, trains running into influencabsorbs signal on influencee / sirius, sirius ringing your influence / gradient, girded in gradients for an influence / streams, streams on God's planes and our influence / increase, increase and an influence for our thrillings / excretes, excretes insure our influence / symphatize, sypmhatize standing in influence / levels, levels of these who seed influence / reactive, reactive reactions to our influences / increase, increase your influence / lights, lights linked influenced / micronic, micronic matromony for an influence / passive, passive portions influenced / generations, generations joining and an influence / assimilate, assimilate standing and as influenced / means, means to be, influenced / imprision's, imprision's over influenced / green, green growing influenced / splendours, splendours over an influence / greys, greys go to love's influence / radiant, radient ranges influenced / lighten, lighten leads and influenced / radiate, radiate railings of an influence / steps, steps along your influence / goes, goes too, influenced / off, off to a fueling influence / flows, flows over our influence / cancer, cancer cured influenced / same, same signals and an influence / gone, gone to more influence / orders, orders out an influence / absorbs, absorbs signal an influence.

CHAPTER SIX

Harmony, harmony of and an influence / proceeds, proceeds over an influence / lights, lights linking blinking influenced / hologram, hologram hurtles to an influence / modify, modify maturing your influence / opticals, opticals operate in your influence / abstract, abstract staring into influence / subject, subject soothing an influence / stars, stars share an influence / patterns, patterns pulsing influence / coherent, coherent nitrogen to carbons fix influenced / winds, winds narrowed influence / forms, forms us, an influence / atomic, atomic truings influence / waves, waves register influenced / electrons, electrons lighting influenced / hydrogens, hydrogens hasten influentaly / similar, similar scenes influenced / frequents, frequents forming an influence / spirals, spirals spooling influenced / trails, trails truthful on influence / spheres, spheres focus into influence / planes, planes over all and an influence / phased, phased along an influence / sun, sun days influence / coherence, coherence sures us for an influence / drawn, drawn days influenced / x-ray, x-ray reading influenced / images, images on an influence / pureness, purness configured as influenced / objects, objects of our influence / intense, intense in our influence / electrons, electrons sign on to an influence / fasten, fasten your influence / iron, iron sills influenced / nucleus, nucleus or an influence / monochrome, monochrome confluences / patterns, patterns influenced / solids, solids influence / tangible,

tangible influenced / supernovas, supernovas influenced / coherence, coherence influenced / plates, plates influx influenced / orbits, orbits influenced / explodes on influence / orbiting, orbiting an influence / explores, explores our influence / orbitals, orbitals influentially dealt a spin / gases, gases influence / octets, octets 8th influence / energy, energy too, influence / correlates, correlates influenced / radiation, radation's influence / liners, liners allowed influence / lights, lights on influence / diagrams, diagrams dealt influence / forms, influence forms love / quantitize, temples quantitize our influence / musicals, musicals influence / held, held onto and influence / molecules influence for love / access, access influences love / structure, structure for a god-man influence bodies / account, account for an influence.

CHAPTER SEVEN

Spectra, spectra on an influence / access, access sorts influence / range, range stood influenced / remotely, remotely influenced / frequents, frequents ours influence / shares, shares an influence / relay, relay on influence / geometrics, geometrics met influence / tetrahedrals, tetrahedrals wear influence / hexagonal, influence a hexagonal way / trigoval, trigoval goes to influence / volumetrics, volumetrics influence / intrenal, internal influences yield love / tracts, tracts of a influence / interest, interest in an influence / terrace, terrace influenced and built / fragments, fragments of an influence / taped, taped onto influence / streched, streched well to influence / worked, worked out, influence / pigments, love's pigments stray? influence / absorbent, absorbent influence's wild love / radiance, radiance influence / radiates, radiates an influence / poles, poles over influence / prana, prana influences love / yang, yang young influence / kundalini, kundalini inflow influence / yin, yin influence / yellow, yellow influences / aspects, aspects inspect influence / indigo, indigo gave us influence / problems, problems over influence / opposites, opposites influenced / equilibrium, equilibrium rang influence / pingali, pingali influential / ida, ida pingali influence / peaks, peaks out influence / sushumna, shumna influence / equals, equals ours, influence / aju, ajua influxed influenced / centers, centers a influence / rathers, rathers influence / ejects, ejects us influenced / develops, develops an influence / wraps, wraps us influence / valuables, valuables influence / discovers, discovers your influence / imaginative, imaginative influx of influences / severals, severals influenced / consciousness, consciousness of an influence / faculty, faculty influencing love / decesions, decesions influence / hints, hints on influence / explosions, explosions influence / futures, futures influenced / emerges, emerges influenced / spikes, spikes out influence / tested, tested and influenced / research, research rang influenced / thresholds, influence thresholds to love / listed, listed and influence / pierced, pierced and influence / honesty, honesty influenced.

CHAPTER EIGHT

Years, years young to an influence / voltage, voltage influenced / universe, universe influenced / cultural, cultural influence / science, science influentials / places, places influence /
emergencies, emergencies influenced / extremes, extremes influence / property, property bought an influence / meditation, meditation influenced / meditative, meditative influence / medicinal, medicinal influences / pivots, pivots to influence / metatronics, metatronics influenced / paged, paged on influence / pathways, pathways fused and influence / yogic, yogic example for the few who influence / states, states and the status into your influences / prisms, prisms point into winds for the influence / statements, statements amounting to the influence / dates, dates are made through your influence / expansions, expansions have come to particular influence / sensitive, sensitive is your influence / games, games are galloped through for an influence / enhanced, enhanced living comes to your influence / tangents, tangents over and won? an influence / students, students are due your influence / pooling, pooling is over, an influence is seen / nuclear, nuclear examine may now end at influence / pearls, pearls explode into explored influences / evolves, evolves a solving influence / purls, purls dropped into sheens for the knitted influences / knits, knits stretch into your influence / forget, forget forgone, an influence / dropping, dropping into a clear influence / clients, clients soften your influence / clusters, clusters led into softened influence / dilutes, dilutes refute is over, an influence / clusters, clusters now measure your influence / interrogative, interrogative remaining influence / subjective, subjective messages are meant for influence / adjective, adjective of the living influences / found, found a friend in love's influence / perjorative, perjorative embracing in influence / foundations, foundations span a median influence / duals, duals end in love's influence / coins, coins are tossed to a kindred influence / fortunate, fortunate plans are made for the futue influence / missions, missions marry a total course to the cause for influence / coherence, coherence is the leader in your influence / placed, placed in peaceful harmonics and a cordial influence / classicals, classicals mate in influence / patents, patents paid for with influence / furl, furl is opened, influences rain / wrapped, wrapped over drapes of influence / conscious, conscious in awareness of missions and influence / variations, variations paid to an influence / troupes, troupes carry over your influence / valued, valued in a balance for your influence / lodes, lodes are off, influence / ledges, ledges lead to an influence / ledgers, ledgers equal an influence / literal, literal acceptance for an influence / passionate, passionate moments in influence.

CHAPTER NINE

Majesty, majesty majors in influence / stripes, stripes paid for influence / stages, stages are set for your influence / drifts, drifts appearing to influence / enlisted, enlisted mates find your influence / leads, leads are past, influence / lightens, lightens capture a rainbow's influence / loud, loud is past, influence / marvelous, marvelous in electric influence / staged, staged in wages and influences / aptitudes, aptitudes pairing at influence / obtain, obtain a rate of influence / parks, parks are stark without influence / surround, surround yourself in welcome influence / proven, proven to be influential in love / magnetic, magnetic in her appeal to love's influence / candles, candles burn to true your influences / pages,

pages written win influence / seen, seen at tables and influence / envisions, envisions gift is influence / seeds, seeds burst into view and influence / premonitions, premonitions go to influence / solves, solves resolve is your influence / celestial, celestial carryings on and influences / cognitions, cognitions about influence / scheme, scheme for the moment and influence / spectrum, spectrums spiral in influence / spectral, spectral placements and influence / manner, manner of the meanings and influences / limit, limit established at influence / restored, restored to a wealth before influence / aware, aware for the siring of influence / attunement, attunement means nest in influence / related, related in spiraling influence / transit, transits made, influence / releases, releases coming into your influence / triggered,triggered a simple sign, influence / significant, significant detail in infinite influence / souls, souls haunt? influence in christheaded lightening / signifies, signifies how to be an influence for love / source, source of the fathers and influences / gore, gore goes to a clearing and influence / level, level detailing your influence / finished, finished, hear, here, influence / grafts, grafts over and influenced / friends, friends are the fellows and influence / nearest, nearest a daily won, influence / blue, blue is the basic influence / resolution, resolution shows that love is, God is, blue pure in influence / throne, throne reached, an influence set / resolve, resolve to solve this matter, influence / entraps, entraps gone, influence / banks, banks paid and influence made a light sight / join, join another who needs an influence of love / cause, cause is now cured, influenced / musical, musical in moments for influence / carries, carries a daring influence / freed, freed of the past dears, an influential cleansing / creative, creative in a retire to the influences / frozen, frozen into assets cleared and influence / chords, chords struck, equate, influence / assets, assets purchased, remain an influence / parting, parting is sweet to your influences / cleared, cleared of the past, draw near to the influence.

CHAPTER TEN

Depart, depart into influence cleared / faculty, faculty brought to an influence / daily, daily adorn yourself in floral influence / download, download a relation for your influences / jump, jump across patterns and land in an influence / activations, activations are real, find an influence / allowing, allowing has come into view for your influence / voiced, voiced in expire and the goal is now influence / prepare, prepare to be clear in your influence / examples, examples are nearing your influential doors / patterned, patterned in pieces and your influence / pales, pales into horses ridden as influenced / released, released into love and your influence / intuitively, intuitively gaps clear into final influences / exude, exude a model mode for all influence / opens, opens a spectacular ion for influence / geometrically, geometrically cleared of all past influence / energy, energy surges into your influence / expansion,expansion has come to your influence / leaps, leaps made are into influence / paves, paves a wave into influence / lodes, lodes are nodes and yours? influence / portals, portals opne again, influence / drive, drive into arriving influence / lost, lost is without? influence / storage, storage is opened into influence / memories, memories made are well influenced / stern, stern is

without an influence / regained, regained a place in your influence / formed, formed a new deal in your influence / joins, joins a staff's influence / long, long in the draw into influence / leads, leads are dead? influence / codes, codes are red within influence / inflections, inflections clear the influence for love / capably, capably strong in your influence / born, born to breathe, influence / slopes, slopes are cleared, influences / surging, surgin into fields and flown influenced / plans, plans made are yours, influence / nears, nears a dearing influence / purge, purge has come to your influences / nets, nets are cast, influence / parks, parks are opened, influence / open, open a gate into influence / parking, parking in barking influence / annex, annex cleared, influence / radiates, radiates an assurance to influence / plans, plans cleared, influence / lumens, lumens aim to influence / offerings, offerings sent are for, influence / embedded, embedded clearances have come to influence / separations, separations aim to influence / everlast,everlast has cast a vote for influence / heights,heights are played to influence / useful, useful notions of influence / symbolic, symbolic in your basic influence / peaks, peaks are tossed to A influenced / nourish, nourish your spirit's influence / understood, understood in good influence / atomic, atomic cells and a spelling for influence / active, active in your vote for influences / lively, lively days now influenced / forming, forming a fellow's stay in influence.

CHAPTER ELEVEN

Rotate,rotate into influence / maximize, maximize your size's influence / churn, churn over, influence / status, status dealt a ceiling? influence / kingdom, kingdom coming into your influence / proton, proton of the nectar for an influence / placed, placed in your station and influenced / mapped, mapped over royally for an influence / self, self in the same vein for influence / remember, remember to be clear in influence / halo, halo effective to the mask removed and for influence / ka, ka is the simplest influence / huna, huna days are upon your door's influences / huna, huna held for once more an influence / center, center is found, influenced / mer, mer is the miracle of influence / ka, ka is a daily cup for influence / house, house built in mountains seas and influenced / ba, ba is the basic for influence / embodies, envoy sent for is made into influence / substance, substance cures influence / threads, threads are the thickest without influence / theory, theory is measured in your influences / tin, tin cupping your door's influences / tend, tend to a matter known as your influence / wine, wine is the signing too, influence / scalpel, scalpel cuts lessens off your influences / water, water is the willing your influence / jar, jar topping your influences / thirst, thirst is the theory for influence / banquets, banquest thrown are influenced / drink, drink into influence of the breath of love / feed, feed a delicious one the energy of loving influence / clears, clears spaces for your influences / mana,mana paid to clear your influence / mechanics, mechanics ripen into your influences / waters, waters pouring into influence / telepathic, telepathic sorts who influence only love / glory, glory is given a winning influence / telestial, telestial the celestial sorts who win your influence / mystic, mystic made a friend for influence / single, single again within influences / lilies, lilies daring to breathe into influence / voltage, voltage gauges your influence / clustering, clustering stars around influence / tympanic, tympanic in a singing influence / voids, voids declared cleared of all influence / signed, signed onto your influences again / modern, modern measurements for influence / shapes, shapes cleared and influenced / known,known as one influenced / elemental, elemental in mental influences / knowledge, knowledge leading to a healing influence / priests, priests cleared your influence / superstition, superstition leaving your influences / ancestral, ancestral threads clear from influence / greatest, greatest in ratings of your influence / hawaiians, hawaiians meet in influence / thirsty? thirsty for an influence / enigma, engima born, influenced basically through love / threads, threads cut are real into influence / learning, learning a leaning into influence / seize, seize is off, influence / passions, passions meet an influence of love.

CHAPTER TWELVE

Vital, vital is the fuel within influence / saints, saints declared influential and stellar / testimony, testimony is given real influence / claims, claims are made without passion for your influence / declarations, declarations are cleared for your influence / flocks, flocks gather to your influence / children, children meet in your influence / investigate, investigate a further way to influence / sheperds, sheperds cleared to depart to a future influence / watch, watch your clearance into influences cleared for love / missouri, missouri nears a delicate influence / saint, saint streeted as influenced / blind, blind is the kind without influence / louis, louis is a metatronic lift into influence / believing, believing is basic unto your influences / is, is this now your influence? / gateway, gateways clearing for influence / coil, coil is spilled, call is in, an influence / for, for us all forms your influence / won, won is due a dear influence / pleasurable, pleasureable to only influences mile high or more / one, one is the sun who lives influentially / mend, mend is made, influenced / is, is your day influenced for love / cost, cost is off, influenced / synagogues, synagogues gifted for influence / found, found in sounded influence / spoken, spoken in keys withing influence / find, find a friends influenced / spoken, spoken kindly, influence / find, find a few, influenced / armor, armor over, influenced / friends, friends found in leys influenced / listed, listed a place for influence / listening, listening essential, influence / solemnsolemn without oaths for influence / stumbles, stumbles gone influence / goodness, goodness knew your influence / storage, storage paid an influence / within, within us all, influences / stores, stores made to influence us / insistent, insistent upon influence / naturals, naturals dealing in influences / wings, wings are wide, influence / pages, pages tossed into a fire for influence / trade,trade naturally for an influence of Godheaded love / fold, fold a friendly gesture to your heroic release of a former influence / winds, winds whistle into painful forget of a foggy influence / venus, venus clearing a path to your influence / burning, burnign is yearning for influence / surges, surges go for your influence / held, held is up wihout God, one, influence / slept,slept in energy for a 12 state influence / saved, saved another for an influence / lands, lands made a merry influence

/ exclaims, exclaims daily over influence / courts, courts are off, influenced / comforter,comforter married to your influence / doves, doves begin to ascend and descend upon linkage called heartlines of loving influence / branches, branches carried are bent into influence / medicinal, medicinal in a manner for your influence / grown, grown into growing for an influence / promised, promised to basically find a new influence / gardens, gardens are gated without an influence.

CHAPTER THIRTEEN

Daring, daring to finish an older influence / cleanse, cleanse a space by simply saying boo! to the ghost of influence past / revealing, revealing daring influences your choices / love, love is led to say good-bye too, influence / revelations, revelations written in energetic influence / seen, seen in airs and hours, influence / priori, priori dear to a healing influence / jesus, jesus said "gently" an influence / sananda, sananda daring to find a new influence / prey, prey is off, influenced for love / man, man your heart well into a conscious likening unto influence / forgiven,of forgiven? influence / chosen, chosen had meant your influence / measures, measures now begun for influence / planets, planets are basic in your influence / consumed, consumed has roomed with less without influence / angels, angels fly itno position of righteous influence / funnel, funnel into towns who knew influence / ginger, ginger grew near your influence / milk, milk dated for your influence / algae, algae bitten for influence / alabaster, alabaster bowls who glint with influence / ginseng, ginseng ringing about your influence / bowls, bowls who gleam for influence / scientific, scientific into your influence / methods, methods who simply link influence / hypothesis, hypothesis of simple influence / purpose, present a purpose for the letter for influenced relationships / materials, materials marry in influence / concludes, concludes a rude examine, influence / procedure, procedure transparent to influence / steps, steps dared are near, influence / trial, trail is a trial in influence / discovery, discovery is due your influence / error, error over and influenced / jungle, jungle goo is cleared influence / hypothetical, hypothetical and ethically influenced / keys, keys who are capable of influence / proof, proof is the space within influence / theorem, theorem for a mental clear, influence / experiential, experientially seized without influence / trials, trials over dear, influence / benchmarks,benchmarks are set upon influence / runs, runs a daring influence / baseline, baseline forgiveness of your forgotten ally and friend who knew influences other than love, good-bye / test, test over, influence free / constant, constant in a consistent influence / experiments, experiments now ending in influence / uncontrollable joy due your influence / variable, variable feelings for influence / acts, acts are given now, influence / influences, yes, influences, win / weathers, weathers over, influence / controllable, controllable and due unto influence / wonders, wonders are clearing an influence for you / environmentally, environmentally a pairing has cleared your influence / sunny, sunny in a daily influence / expect, expect to win, influence / clouded, clouded has sided with influential winnings for love / control, control has come to love's influence

/ fertile, fertile the fields which yield influence / conclusions, conclusions occuring in influence / folds, folds overtly opened to influences cleared / major, major shifts occur in lines which you influence.

LEVEL 71: THE FUSION-MENTS

CHAPTER ONE
Capillary, capillary which finds an infusion of fusions to love / refilled, refilled a bottle with your fusions / veins, veins who mend into fusions / absorbent, absorbent kinds who fins a fusion / arterial, arterial the miracle for a friendly fusion / cross, cross off my list, fused / sonic, sonic in the delay denied your fusions / intent, intent to clear through fusions / kohala, kohala the coast to see for fusions / intensify, intensify your commitment to the fusions for love / kauai, kauai abounds in your fusions / supply, supply is made A fusion / springs, springs fill in fusions / waters, waters leaping too, fusions / feasts, feasts are open to your fusions / formations, firm formations amounting to fusions / stirs, stirs is simple identify for fusions / sky, sky is blue, fusions / forbidden, forbidden without laws for fusions / skies, skies are red in intensity for fusion / isle, isle into middle skies fusions / stand, stand in a trend over fusions / aisles, aisles into smiling ambitons and fusions / cleaves, cleaves are over our fusions / thinks, thinks in significance and fusions / clones, clones are a fusion for the factors fused / throats, throats are written into a fusion / encouraged, encouraged in a lightened fusion / thirds, thirds into first a fusion / curative, curative creations of fusions / form, form elated too, a fusion / translated, translated into bodily fusions / mix, mix a material into a fusion / blessings, blessings fusions / ball, ball over fusion / roots, roots reaching your fusions / rites, rites into simple days and goodly fusions / cortex, cortex is simple in a fusion's place / reflexive, reflexive reaching fusions / paths, paths are powerful into fusion / pare, pare and a simple fusions / point, point over fusions/ introduce, introduce a newness to fusion / imporvement, improvement meant into fusion / induce, induce a deduce into fusion / pore, pore over chance and a threatening fusion / detailed, detailed amounting too, fusions / amounts, amounts amounting in fusion / hawks, hawks signal A fusions for the mystique of love / message, messages marry your fusions / likeness, likeness is ead past you fusions / birds, birds are born to bare their wings in influence / leading, leading past your fusions / prey, prey over, infusions / locusts, locusts departing, fusions complete / flights, flights in a flurry for fusions / featured, featured in a merry fusion / focus, focus is fine in your fusions / influence, influenced amor and the shores of love's fusions / forwards, forwards met in your fusions / facts, facts and a finest fusion / maat, maat is similar to a built crossing too, a fusion / lattice, lattice is simple into fusions / leads, leads appearing in fusions

CHAPTER TWO
Fusions, fusions missionary days are influenced in love / central, central in a similar fashion for fusion / 21, 21 who knew for A fusion / course, courses over A fusion / cycles, cycles spent in an influenced fusion / chosen, holy reasons for an influential fusion / human, human hallow forming a fusion / portal, portal simple into fusions / milky, milky way fusions occuring into love / entrances, entrances into a fusion / way, way through the simple fashions for a fusion / middle, middle for the former ways fusions / god's, god's into gathering portals for a fusion / places, places peaces and fusions fuse in light / hearts, hearts are hearty in a fusion / poles, poles are partnered in a fusion / northern, northern in a suggested fusion / positions, positions patched over your fusion / southern, southern in a signed fusion / planets, planets are penned for a fusion / posits, positions and posits to a fusion / ports, ports and the material for a fusion / dependent, dependent on a cycle for a fusion / selah, selah is entire in a fusion / ark, ark is into your fusions / powers, powers placed in signed grids for a fusion / succinct, succinct in lineage for a fashionable fusion / soothes, soothes in a spent fusion / ethiopian, ethiopian declare for a fusion / queens, queens retiring into fusions / kings, kings clarify your fusions / subtle, subtle in squared fusions / energy, energy for a fusion / sports, make sports your fusion / sport, sport a feeling fusion / sparrows, sparrows assigning your fusions / prince, prince for a fusion into Christ / singing, singing into a fusion / dove, dove daring your fusion / songs, songs singing to a fusion / lightened, lightened in a matched fusion / hieroglyphics, hieroglyphics are fused / bud, bud is the relationship for fusion / princess, princesses are made of your fusions / egyptian, egyptian assigned a fusion / lessons, lessons into a fused relative for love / carved, carved in curation for a fusion / learns, learns in a legendary fusion / glistens, glistens in a glaring fusion / appear, appearing for your fusions / listens, listens adoring fusions / apply, apply to a state for your fusions / learns, learns in a daring fusion / golden, golden gated fusions / peer, peer into your fusions / employ, employ appearing for fusions / gain, gain a mansion's fusions / vocal, vocal files for fusions / goods, goods match you de chelly fusion / focal, focal in final fusions / grant, grants are made for your fusions / floors, floors made of a meaningful fusion / influx, influx is sent into fusion / posts, posts are meant for fusions.

CHAPTER THREE
Fortitude, fortitude for a fusion / electricity, electricity fixed in your fusions / endears, endears a daring fusion / wards, wards are over, know fusions / endeavors, endeavors a several in fusion / elevates, elevates a finest fusion / entire, entire in signature fusions / attitudes, attitudes are nearest A fusion / elective, elective has said, "find a friend" for your fusions / silvery, silvery haired mavens for fusions / selectively, selectively fused in your mutual places / golden, golden gaining fusions / stages, stages matching your fusions / treasures, treasures made a news fusion / stores, stores made for your fusions / platinum, platinum signed and made A fusion / titanium, titanium chipping in, fusions / DNA, DNA daring your fusions / zinc, zinc is assigning your fusions / twist, twist arranged into fusions / cords, cords are rhyming your fusions / strategic, strategic daring fusions / cubes, cubes arranging

your fusions / straightens, straightens arranging your fusions / eggs, eggs fused into fashions / enzymatically, enzymatically assigning your fusions / spores, spores are simply your fusions / lichen, lichen is sincerely your fusion / sparks, sparks are framing a fusion / moss, moss is amazing worn for fusions / births, births balancing A supression's lift into fusions / algae, algae born to win a fusion / palms, palms simply into fusion / evolutions, evolutions made completely fused / greens, greens aim is for fusions / code, code creative aim is your focused fusion / gingko, gingko aspects for foci fused / creations, creations arrangement is formed and fused / cycladic, cycladic cores armed in a fusion / humanly, humanly possible fusions / living, living in reverie for a fusion / mitochondrial, mitochondrial merits and fusions / light, light is linked into fusions / flash, flash is across a faced fusion / love, love is led to a fusion / relays, relays allowing your fusions / spark, sparks aimed into fusions / rememberance, rememberance aiming in fusions / define, define daring a fusions / dazzles, dazzles planned into fusions / delays gone to a fusion / life, life is led into confusion freed fusions / dually, dually diffident without fusion / listening, listening into your fusions / daze, daze goes to A fusions / stagger, stagger out less and declare more now your fusion / outermost, outermost planets can entwine in your gelaming fusions / wise, wise in a welcoming fusion / lanterns, lanterns burn in your fusions / presently, presently extensive4 in fusion / eggs, eggs breaking your fusion planes / perfect, perfect extensions too, fusions / trillionaire, trillionaire made for the fusions within loved / galactic, galactic in planets built for antarian fusions.

CHAPTER FOUR

Assumes, assumes a natural effect called nocturnally, fusions / developments, developments are leading you to take a stellar mission for the fusions of humanity into love, the earth's shipped / irregular, irregular in regular visits to the facets for fusion / shape, shape is found softly fuwed / reverberated, reverberated expire without fusion / stars, stars bursting in an orion nebula formed through fusions / bubbles, bubbles bursting into view through a fusion space / gas, gas is poured into your fusions / orbits, orbits bought were sought through fusions / lines, lines linear too? the fusions / scatter, scatter less, find more, seychelles conserved through fusions / tetrahedron, tetrahedrons built into fusions / linear, linear palaces formed a fusion / fallen, fallen have gone into fusions / ages, ages are past at last, fusions / recently, recently divorced again, fusions / crisp, crisp is ripely said "fusions" / dispose, dispose of less, fusions / pairs, pairs made are eternal for the formulation of A fusions / interstellar, interstellar days are made for fusions / shine, shine into pirouettes about your fusions / concerns, concerns gone, fused / geometrically, geometrically freed to find fusions / assume, assume neutral fusions exist / universal, universal in a message for freedom into a fusion / creation, creation carries a rate for fusions / spans, spans are equivalent to your fusions / estimations, estimations are made into fusions / kalpa, colors kalpa coated in fusions / modes, modes tapas red for a shrine built to fusions / nights, nights are made fertile through your fusions into love / modalities, modalities matching

your fusions exist / currency, currency carried is fused / whole, whole in days allergic to fusions / telescopes, telescopes capable in fusions / thunders, thunders erupting near your fusions again / intuition, intuition pays off again, fusions/ cords, cords cut without fusions? / biosystemic, biosystemic to your fusions / sagittarius, sagittarius seams into the dark, fusions / "A", "A" we have found means Arcturuian inquiry into the fusions for life for the Christline in Metatronic delight and love direct/ infrared, infrared's release for the fusions / lines, lines match, link up, fusions / interstellar, interstellar marriages are made from a fusion / wavelengths, wavelengths are gained for a fusion / durst, durst I say "dust" to a fact made in fusion / visible, visible expressions rise into a fusion' stills / peaks, peaks made are now fused, long into love / descriptions, descriptions given are found for those who know A fusion / milk, milk made a soup for star birth's galactic into a fusion / climb, climb over lengths now fused / infinite, infinite a miraculous marriage of needs for all fusions / difficult, difficult without a full fusion / spinning, spinning and the threading fusions for a formula fresh into love / classics, classics occuring through the fusions / quantums, quantums fused into love / gross, gross is the simplest fusion into love / spaces, spaces into the single days for a fusion / dwarf, dwarf is the singing fusion / pervade, pervade is the wellest fusion / currents, currents magic in fusion / crush, crush is over, rush into fusion / roar, roar a rapture for fusions / pennsylvania, pennsylvania infatuated in fusions.

CHAPTER FIVE

Fathoms, fathoms are mentioned in a titanic fashion for fusions / crushed, crushed is over, fashions made fused / momentum, momentums allowing your fusions / terms, terms are fused / class, class into living fusions / fathoms, fathoms factual into a fusion / smashing, smashing sincerety for our fusions smiles / essence, essence for a flown fusion / points, points amounting to a fusion / measure, measureable mentions of fusion / pints, pints are simply a fusion / gallons, gallons glowing form fusions / finish, finish volley and find a fusion / spaced, spaced enthusiastically in formal fusions / quarts, quarts who carry our filling fusions / dimensions, dimensions into daring fusions / affairs, affairs are mentioned for fusions / infinity, infinity as filling a fusion / affinity, affinity matching a fusion / built, built into beautiful fusions / analogy, analogy fused in love / occupationally, occupationally our leading fusions for love / balanced, balanced in merits fusions / along, along a lingering legend for fusions / living, living in a lingering fusions / lines, lines inside your fusions / dropped, dropped into single fusions / eternally, eternally a fillign fusion / amid, amid us a fusion for love, a flowering / amplified, amplified into the stupendous for fusion into love / amplitudes, amplitudes are the moods into fusions / contributive, contributive through a mission's fusions / attributive, attributive properties are simple into fusions / centrifugal, centrifugal fusions inside your living loves / sullies, sullies over, move on, mention fusions / builds, builds a merry fusion / stable, stable steerings fusions / infinitum, infinitum the infinity of love's fusions / repulsion, repulsion has gone into fusion / bonding, bonding is basically A fused / totals, totals assigning your fusions / ethylene, ethylene is shining through fusions / degenerates, degenerates again your fusions / ultimately, ultimately a mission's fusions / diametrics, diametrics during a fusion / overlap, overlap into a fusion / integrates, integrates a reasonable use for a fusion / values, values into tools forming a fusion / calculated, calculated a reasonable use for fusion / mysteries, mysteries marrying your fusions / hidden, hidden ind degrees for a fusion / secrets, secrets sharing your fusions / details, details detailing a fusion / destitute, destitute without your fusions / fragments, fragments found a fusion / recall, recall a responsible fusion / focus, focus is off your fusions / furtive, furtive in fallen fusions / concludes, concludes as a fusion / diabolic, diabolically your fusions / identify, identify a daring fusion / politics, politics fused into hearts adorned with love's elections / speer, speer out and tossed in a fusion / adorning, adorning a fusion for love / adorned, adorned in ratios for fusions / strictest, strictest inside a fusion / exult, exult replete in your fusions / exalt, exalt forming for fusions / penetrate, penetrated fusions / thickening, thickening has become your fusion / evident, evident into your fusions / radiance, radiance ranging on fusions / remnants, remnants residual to your fusion / fires, fires burning into your fusions.

CHAPTER SIX

Strictest, strictest one wins fusions / exult, exult hallows fusions / exalt, exalt over fusions / penetrate, penetrate yours fusions / thickening, thickening us fusions / radiance, radience ran fusion / evident, evident for a fusion / remnants, remnants fuse / pull, pull away and fuse / peels, peels fuse / bulge, bulge past? fuse / swarming, swarming fuses / spinals, spinals fused / disk, disks fused / galactic, galactic fusing / pulses, pulses fusing / poignant, poignant fuses / italics, italics "fused" / source, source fuses / iron, iron fusings / silvery, silvery deliveries now fused / nickles, nickles fuse and melt / placed, placed and fused / goldest, buffalo goldest fuses / still, still fused / within, within fusions / platinum, platinum fusions / pores, pores fusing / lids, lids fuse / lift, lift to a fuse / inhereht, inhereht fusions / abundance, abundance fuses / reigns, regins of fusions / generative, generative fusions / flat, flat out fused / edges, edges fused / pulse, known to a pulse's rate fused / increase, increase fuses / cores, cores fuse / heat, heat on fused / correlating, correlating 222's / suggested, suggested 111 / production, production 33 / esoteric, esoteric 88's / concentrations, concentrations 104 / nuclei, nuclei 42 / merge, merge 128 / parents, parents 64 / poise, poise fuses / conception, conception fuses / occurs, occurs and fused / earth's earth's fusions / emergent, emergent fuses / pubescent, pubescent fused / images, images fused / permeate, permeate fusings 213 / permanent, let permanent fuses blink / words, words fused / worlds, worlds collect fusions / wend, wend above, fuse / existence, existence gets fused / into, into fusions / sets, sets on a fuse / seen, seen and fused.

CHAPTER SEVEN

Supreme, supreme be's fuse / locations, locations fuse / strictly, strictly fused / linked, linked and fused / emplode, emplode fused / divinely, divinely fusings / held, held and fused / riveting, riveting fusions lead / regions, regions fusion / correspondence, correspondence fuses / copes, copes fused / central, central fusions / galaxy, galaxy fused / sworn, sworn of fusions / dually, dually fused / detours, detours fused / sorted, sorted of fusions / english, english said "fused" / represents, represents fused / represenative, represenative fused / purports, purports sports fused / alone, alone a fusion / unique, unique metings fused / inner, inner fuses melt / enlightened, enlightened fusions / descent, decennt to a fuse / sounds, counds on a fuse / doctrones, doctrones fusing / boiling, boiling spoils fusing / flower, flower fused / comprehend, comprehend a fusion now / interstellar, interstellar interogative fusions / destiny, destiny dares fuse / occurs, occers fused / k, ka says "fused" / milk, milk fussion / nourished, nourished and fused / overflows, overflows calculated fuse / views, views fused / honors, honors hermetica's fuse / voidedvoided fusions 42 profoundly, profoundly fused / explore, explore now fused / occurs, occurs fused / within, within us fused / cellls, cells fuse / sold, sold of fusion / deems, deems us a fusing daring, daring fusions / illuminations, illuminations fuses / soars, soars fused / revealing, revealing fusions / locally, locally fuse / coordinates, coordinates fused / hum, hum fusings / connected, connected and fused / whispers, whispers well spring fused / proverbs, proverbs fused / nectar, nectar fused / bead, bead bred fused / sells, sells us fusions / light, lights fuse / murmuring, murmuring about fusion / drills, drills fused.

CHAPTER EIGHT

Softly, softly and fused / spoken, spoken emerald and fused / forces, forces fuse / imagine, imagine us fused / connected, connected fusions / temples, temples fusing / shrines, shrines fused / seal, seal fused / revealing, revealing fused / ecattered, ecattered fusions? / revelations, revelations fused / seated, seated and fused / come, come to a fuse / electrically, electrically fusing / energized, energized fusions / via, via fusions / hearts, hearts opened fusions / shining, shining fused / allowance, allowance on fusions / mediative, meditative fusings / chores, chores on fusions / contextually, contextually fused / roll, roll over fused / proven, berkley proven fusions / links, links up to fusions / allure of an fusion / facts, facts about us fused / made, made us fused / coordinates, coordinates used fused / given, given one fuse / particles, partic;es on fusion bands / merge, merge and fuse / guidance, guidance of fusion / gained, gained to a fuse / humans, humans fused / built, built a door fused / earth's, earth's focus fused / tilt, tilt off? fused / heaven's, heaven's voice fused / gate, gate openly fuses / prophesied, prophesied of fusion / december, december days fused / 22, 22 fuses / 2012, 2012 fuses now / mayan's, mayan's in fusion / code, code set, fuse / cottical, cortical fuses / copes, copes fusion / cavity, cavity openly fused / appears, appears and fused / pervades, pervades our fusions / souls, souls fused at light's soul / light, light over fusions moleculear / cocoon, cocoon lifted fused / melts, melts often fusions / mankind, mankind healed fused / survive, i survived fusion / schema,

schema found fused / tires, i am tires fused / galaxy, galaxy fused / subconsciously, subconsciously fused / encoded, encoded and fused / supreme, supreme fuses / motifs, motifs fusing

CHAPTER NINE

Adorned, adorned into swarmed environs for fusions / nile, nile into a vile infusion forgiven as fusion / blazes, variously fused into enticements for love / encouraged, encouraged a marriage for fusion / poems, poems are written as gifts and fusions / secretive -secretive without natural fusions / penned, penned into amounting fusions / bodies, bodies inside a fusion / surged, surged infusions for living light / blatant, blatant into blazing fusions / psychically, psychically material for your fusions / bland, bland inside basic fusions / clears, clears and carries into your fusions / dear, dear inside your fusions / cores, cores in simple fusions / doors, doors detailing your fusions / enlightens, enlightens in steeper fashions for fusions / immunity, immunity amounting for fusions / lens, lens inside your fusions / built, built in decision and fusions / lowers, lowers inside your fusions / fire, fire in a simple fusion / doors, doors in sizes simple to a fusion / soul, soul is out now, find a new fusion / language, language carries you into your fusion / hands, hands offer a fusion / encourage, encouraged a sample interest in love's fusions / lords, lords in an interest for all fusions / laying, laying a principle of fusions / amakua, amakua material to your fusions / lanes, lanes employed inside your fusion / codes, codes creative plume is inside your fusion / focus, focus free into your focusing fusions / dreams, dreams staging an arriving fountain for all fusions / kahunic, kahunic imports of all sorts and the fusion inside / insure, insure a patient fusion / code, code occupy you huna trail of fusions / low, low inspections of your handled fusions / insane, insane in an interest forgiven a fusion / middle, middle mentioned merry fusions / magnetism, magnetism mutually a fusion / mesmerize, mesmerized attainment for fusions / electrical, electrical signs are aroused in your fusions / informing, informing a featured fusion / forces, forces armed into fusions / forms, forms relative to fusions / gather, gather forms fusions / fuels, fuels celebrate your fusions / atlas, atlas shrugging over a fusion / apports, apports a supporting fusion / astral, astral management for fusion / prayed, prayed one last sample of fusion / radial, radially fused empires and fusions / adopted, adopted reaches for fusion / burma, burma balanced formations and fusions / treats, treats are threaded through your simple enjoyment of Pleadian commitment to a fusion / florence, florence fellows your fusions / invincible, invincible finish to fusions / pairs, pairs fused around love / invisible, invisible meanings and fusions / sun, sun to the thrilling fusion / etheric, etheric lights fused / moon, mooning maintain over fusion / ethereal, ethereal remains reaching fusion .

CHAPTER TEN

Endoplasm, endoplasm spilling over fusions / demise, demise is due to fusion / epidermis, epidermis now fused / mesoderm, mesoderm layered function and fusions / chivalry, chivalry fused / clairovoyance, clairovoyance throes aimed into fusion / radial,

radial fusions / crystal, crystal supplying a fusion / healing, healing empires aim for fusion / powers, powers placing your visions and fusions / mentally, mentally mentioned fusions / shrines, shrines retaining a fusion / temples, temples fusing your life led loves / sacred, sacred spelling of fusions / dreams, dreams dancing through a fusion / ectoplasm, ectoplasm mentions your fusions / plasm, plasm paring your fusions / folklore, folklore fusings / forces, forces off, fused / hypnotism, hypnotisms are over, fusions / home, home is herald to a fusion / high, high selves are fused / help, help your friend's fusion / powers, powers are placed into fusions / mentally, mentally fine fusions / shrines -shrines are sealed for a fusion / temples, temples pairing fusion / sacred, sacred without fusions in love / dreams, dreams appear in your fusions / ectoplasm, ectoplasm lasting through fusions / red, reds are ready for a fusion / pyramids, pyramids fused / plants, plants appearing fused / folklore, folklore fashioned for fusion / forces, forces matched, fusions / hypnotism, hypnotism fused / home, homes are near here fusions / high, high spilling fusions / vitality, vitality is valued for your fusion / sex, sex is sent to your fusions / triangles, triangles mend a fusion / spirits, spirits reaching your fusions / sticks, sticks reaching for fusion / sahara, sahara fending for fusion / spoils, spoils reaching over a fusion / roses, roses smattered to fusions / fickle, fickle has gone into fusions / maidens, maidens mentioned a fashionable fusion / generous, generous in details for fusion / customs, customs are cushioned for a fusion / morticians, morticians disappearing, fused / phased, phased fools are gone, fusions / past, past has met into fusions / curt, curt has come to a fusion / aside, aside is inside your description for fusions / rattle, rattle reaches our fusions / rock, rock is reaching a fusion / patches, patches are pouring into fusions / past, past in a simple fusion / cost, cost is set upon fusions / aside, aside is relieving for fusion / rattle, rattle is reaching yes! Given fusions / rocks, rocks are reaching your fusions / freely, freely fed fashions and fusions.

CHAPTER ELEVEN

Perfected, perfected into vectors of fusion / remainders, remainders are reaching our fusions / white, white is a singular fusion / dissolved, dissolved into retail for fusion / additions, additions dealing in fusions / sages, sages simple to a fusion / pure, pure is peaceful in fusions / goods, goods gather your fusions / process, process is peace in your fusions / warmth, warmth is willing in fashion and fusion / clean, clean cut made fusions / words, words read "fusions" / proceed, proceed appealing fused / excrement, excrement has created your fusions / coagulates, coagulates creating fusions / precious, precious in paternal fusions / operational, operations fused interiors and loves / architecture, architecture is simply a suggested fusion / glories, glories into reaching fusions / maintenance, maintenance managing a fusion for love / eliptical, eliptical creativity for our fusions / marvels, marvels arrayed in your fusions / sulphure, sulphure is curing your fusions / proceeds, proceeds arming a fusion / proceeding, proceeding potentially in fusions / tingles, tingles are meeting your fusions / keys, keys are creating a fusion / arts, arts are rating your fusion / fixed, fixed arranging a fusion / powers, powers appearing into fusions / proceeds, proceeds touring your fusions / procedures, procedures arranging for fusions / lamb, lamb homeward to a fusion / deceive, deception and deceive are gone, fusion / venoms, venoms are gone and the sting has cleared into fusions / made, made of friends, fusions / spring, spring into new and well fusions / jung, jung arranging for a fusion of archetypal matters / psyche, psyche is central and formal to your fusions / american, american dreams and the bounty for fusions / balms, balms into calm recital for fusions / psychological, psychological jungles swam for fusion / inventive, inventive into stretches for fusion / leads, leads are over, fused / virtues, virtues merit a fusion / trek, trek across several lands into fusion / snort, snort is aborted for fusion / archetypes, archetypes are centrally free orbitally by your fusions / home, home is the humble ascension port to fusion / ordeals, ordeals finished meet in fusions / ordinals, ordinals are original here in helenic fusions / perplexed, perplexed becoming may beam you too, fusions / poignant, poignant reminder of the one who became a famous fusion / calm, calm is the sample and the simpleness for fusions / calamitous, calamitous respect has come to the stores of fusions / merchants, merchants who match your fusions / merchandise, merchandise made our in fusions / faithful, faithful in efforts for the fused ones / silence, silence is meant to enhance your fusions / devout, devout about your fusion skills / dragged, dragged through has since finished in skilled degrees fusions / given, given a sample, simply for fusions / known, known as a smiling fusion / subtle, subtle in gentle gifts and fusions.

CHAPTER TWELVE
Sepulchre, sepulchre now opening into fusions of love / repairs, repairs genetically made now breathe for fusion / meanings, meanings are matched to your fusions for love / periods, periods established are welcome to a fusion / castles, castles built about fusions / devils, devils cast into ponds of fusion / devoutly, devoutly sincere in your fusions / dated, dated and rates set for fusions / undertaken, undertaken has met measures for fusions / expeditions, expeditions amount to a fusion / shores, shores shine in soothing fusions / diligence, diligence is paid to your fusions / chemicals, chemicals arriving to replicate your DNA trail through humanity, a fusion / shift, shift entirely settled, fuse / two-fold, two-fold intrigue with your fusions into love / moistures, moistures seal is on, fusions / museums, museums wrecked without infusions / fours, fours are paid to your fusions / wombs, wombs created through the world's fusions / essences, essences sent to your missionary fusions / trees, trees are saved through your fusions / project, project made a priority for these fusions / stone, stone is turned into fusion / generated, generated stands for fusions / places, places made real through fusion / qualities, qualities are equipped for a fusion / wide, wide into wiser fusion / sperms, sperms are clipped for the former fusions / circumference, circumference measured to read "fusions" / female, female has settles into your fusions / seeds, seeds made fused / subtle, subtle reaches for the 6 chromosomes who read

fused / vain, vain is gone, simply fused / trucks, trucks loaded with fusions arrive / treatise, treatise is simple, fused / aborts, aborts created are carried through a fusion's expanse / solute, solute in imputed fusions / direct, direct recourse fusions / epilogues, pay mind to the epilogues now written for your truest fusions / mingles, mingles amouting to fusions / solutions, solutions render you well into fusions / central, central planes meld into fusions spaced / bodily, bodily functioning found returned to fusions / grains, grains grew through your fusions / products, products arriving in fusion / terrestrial, terrestrial forgiving finds fusion / generative, generative into grouping fusions / third, third days are threaded past fusions / first, first is placed near your fusions / elementals, elementals are smashing in your fusions / matters, matters made well through a fusion / ears, ears wide into wisdom for fusions / eyes, eyes are smiling for fusions / motions, motions making your fusions real / constant, constant creative flows into cycles for fusion / heavy, heavy aloft now fusions / light, light is the leading fusion / digestives, digestives flow into your fusions / moves, moves made elective for all flowering infusions / dry, dry is the day without a fusion / moistened, moistened materially for a fusion / emissions, emissions and the matched fusions / made, made as an assign for all fusions / chatter, chatter has come unto fusions .

CHAPTER THIRTEEN
Paradise, paradise reaching your fusions / marines, marines blue in medicinal mention of fusions / volatile, volatile values are filed for all fusions / constant, constant creations are cured forms of fusions / sums, sums are signing a fusion / mysteries, mysteries mentioned and fused / aged, aged to a cycle shored in fusions / knelt, knelt in nightly fusions / suns, suns assigning a cycle for fusions / remedies, remedies are arranging a fusion / months, months maturing in fusions / needed, needed and heeded as signature fusions / sons, sons are the threaded fusions / ends, ends are reached fusions / grievances, grievances have gone to a fusion / yokes, yokes lift fusions / germanic, germanic armatures arranged a fusion / crowed, crowed in assignment said "fusions" / water, water is wearing a fusion / spirit, spirit sighs for your fusions / elixirs, elixirs are lifting into fusion / around, around us all a fusion / mercury, mercury for the formalization of views into relations reaching fusions / active, active arise into fusion / tinctures, tinctures established shining portals into fusions / conjunctions, conjunctions made for fusions / codons, codons materialized for all fusions / male, male is the simple fusion / arts, arts are made for all fusions / unions, unions ready to a reasonable fusion / sorrow, sorrow is chance sent to flushing fusions / anxious, anxious inside your literal expressions of fusion / close, close the door without saying fusion / defers, defers made a forthright fusion / disclose, disclose only simple fusions / tribulations, tribulations door has shut forever, fusions / leads, leads are made into your fusions / detailed, detailed arrows fly into your fusions / grief, grief has struck without fusions / furnish, furnish yourself with a healing infusion / leaves, leaves tossed into rivers ivy green in the experience of blue fusion / wretched, wretched without smartest

infusions / finish, finish the data, infusions / redeems, redeems are arranged for through infusions / canons- canons are written for the infused / sterling, sterling in reputation and fusion / gold, gold is glazed in fusion / cup, cup opens again, fusions / learned, learned and led to fusions / sweet, sweet in the etheric fusions / liquid, liquid established as a fusion / self, self said "same" fusions / long, long in the linking facets, fusions / bequeath, bequeath only basic to the fused / liberty, liberty has come to those used for less, fusions / deserving, deserving of serving fusions / pounds, pounds off your fusions / obtains, obtains a grant for fusions / ebbs, ebbs have flown into fusions / flowers, flowers made in Taiwan's fusions / incorporate, incorporate the exactness for your fusion / travel, travel keys your doors opening fusions / treats, treats arrive, fusions.

LEVEL 72: THE CYCLE-MENTS

CHAPTER ONE / THE FLOWER OF LIFE
Egg, eggs are now cycled into life's loves / stamen, stamen pulling your flowering cycles / swim, swim across gates and underneath cycles / X, X is the spot for a female cycle / pistil, pistil placing your faced cycle / falopian, falopian emerging in the redden cycles / life, life now, cycle completed / sperm, sperm tossed over cycles / stems, stems drank from in final cycle's salutes / fertilization, fertilization has come to the end times cycled, Kali Yuga, Shakti, Mayan, Mithraic, Christian, all meeting here near the Buddha's door for a Christ conscious experiment in humanity, finished, cycles / ejaculated, ejaculated in a stream for creative cycles / receives, receives a milky way thrust into cycles / zygote, zygote splits healed cycles ends / powers, powers impending forthrightly through a cycle / divides, divides and the dialects in your cycles / multiply, multiply mathematically for the further cycles / mathematics, mathematics equivalent into furtive forgiven, cycles set, completed / coy, coy has come to forgiven details and days cycled / shared, shared a matter as shed unto cycles / twins, twins winding into cycles / fraternal, fraternal memories for all cycles / identical, identical instincts and the details for cycles sent / clarifies, clarifies cultural IQ is a cycle / jewels, jewels wrapped into a friendly recycle / third, third threads skilled in cycles ends / third, third is a pact dealt in cycles / blinds, blinds off your cycles / birth, birth is made a cycle to loves / flesh, flesh is felt in your cycles / penetrate, penetrate your ratios rationally required, a facet called influenced into cycles / placement, placements established to winningness shed upon cycles / humbly, humbly admit your simple cycles / embroiders, embroiders emblazoned cycles end / scarlet, scarlet clearing stills your cycles / placentas, placentas pored over a cycle / homes, homes magic in cycle / silks, silks off your cycles / garments, garments marry a cycle / gladness, gladness gazes a cycle / finished, finished in dearest cycles / white, white wool and welcomed cycles / gently, gently go into cycles / fusions, fusions embroidering your cycles / preciously, preciously paid to be a cycle / rarest, rarest establishments and

your cycles / humbly, humbly a hurling cycle / kindest, kindest in caring cycle / restored, restored ranges to aiming cycles / enlarges, enlarges charges now cycled / treatment, treatments allowing your cycles / treatise, treatise for the simplest cycles / michael, michael made amazing in a cycle / secretive, secretive has gone again to cycles / infusions, infusions manage to be your cycles / allegory, allegory sealing your cycles / imparts, imparts starring cycle / metamorphisis, metamorphisis spelling your cycles / ruby, ruby red reaching through cycles / swords, swords who shred without cycles / possessions, possessions parry and cycles / truths, truths are measuring your cycles / figures, figures feeding in cycles / pages, pages as seen in a cycle / seated, seated in written cycles.

CHAPTER TWO
Calls, calls openly made unto cycles / connects, connects within cycles / meddles, meddles a mobile cycle / credulous, credulous in abridged events cycle / plain, plain in a written cycle / unassuming, unassuming rent paid to cycles / contempts, contempts go to a cycle / troubles, troubles over cycles / money, money is made now through cycles / conceals, conceals comtemplative cycles / obscures, obscures arranged in cycles / begins, begins a basic recount for cycles / learned, learned into terms now accepted for cycles / errors, errors mentioned are franchised through those cycles / deludes, deludes bemused for a cycled / learned, learned intrigue for all cycles / errors, errors aimed past a cycle of old noose / deludes, deludes notion has gone to a thronging forgive of all cycles / written, written rhyming cycles / trembles, trembles arose in cycles of love / lofts, lofts insure your care for cycles / desires, desires are cancelled without cycles / might, mighty mental cycles end in pleasure / frees, frees us clinically unto your cycles / cycles, cycles above and cycles within an arc of love / cancel, cancel on a cycle now paid with love / motives, motives are a cycle sent away to love / archbishops, archbishops bounded and cycled / classes, classes covered in two cycles / pardons, pardons offered to a cycle / costs, costs without cycles / bishops, bishops below in two cycles / ranks, ranks upon cycles sealed / stores, stores allowing stolen cycles end / experience, experience onto cycles / cobblers, cobblers curing our cycles / books, books balanced in extreme acknowledge for God's gifts to humanity / delusions, delusions offering cycles / contents, contents offered in cycles / tailors, tailors appear in cycles / heirs, heirs warrant a near cycle / manned, manned in signal cycles / treasures, treasures exempt within cycles / freemasons, freemasons made fairer still through a 33rd cycle's end / credulous, credulous manly stuff written about said bi-cycles / curiosity, curiosity for all killed a cycle / sounds, sounds insuring your cycle / content, content curing a cycle / head, head into a heeding cycle / authors, authors spoken as thankful for cycles / inquire, inquire about distant cycles ends / fathers, fathers into mother's ability to end old cycles / governing, governing carries new cycles to an end / praise, praise over cycles / behalf, behalf of new, cycles / sorrows, sorrows sifted through and cycled / grace, grace introduced into cycles / grief, grief over, love have a cycle's end / rest, rest in cycles pertinent mends / begun, begun to see, a cycle / truth, truth allowing your

cycle to end / souls, souls have released into cycles cleared and the illusions end that there are separations in humanity and God / ache, ache lessens find a cycle's ends / words, words warrant our cycles to mended realize of the still point in love.

CHAPTER THREE

Chaos, chaos cycles / Christ, Christ cycles mending in love / treats, treats in a cycle's streets / testimony, testimony trains your cycles / proportions, proportions measured and cycled / bodies, bodies born into cycles of love / offspring, offspring appear near your cycle / interpretive, interpretive triangles of a cycle / manners, manners of a cycle, love and the seasons annual / conceive, conceive of perfections in your cycle / women, women who listen to cycles ends / solar, solar plexian soothe of your life end cycles / listening, listening into cycles / productions, productions circular in natural cycles / fully, fully cycled in love / islands, islands aligned in cycles of love / motion, motions material in cycles / essential, essentially now, cycled / calm, calm enough to see through cycles / kindles, kindles a cycle through love's activities / activity, activity composites remain cycled / composites, composites engage a cycled / kin, kin for all cycled / solemn, solemn ends to an old cycle / comprehend, comprehend your ended cycles / states, states now cycled / prints, prints pain into a cycle / ventures, ventures amazed and your cycles / penetrates, penetrates a ratio cycled / romp, romp about cycled / king, king for all cycles / kings, kings written to show your cycles / mind, mind on the matters cycled / next, next is the heart of a child who loves your cycles / gates, gates opened and clearly ends a cycle / works, works are cleared into cycles / guide, guide us homeward still into cycles / sands, sands running cycled clear to a coastline called merely love / microcosmic, microcosmic in participation with your cycles / motions, motions made clearest at cycles / harmonious, harmonious declarations for cycles / harmony, harmony builds in your homeward still cycles / nature, nature is in two cycles / kind, kind in a sound seashell wide cycled / nautilus, nautilus spells a cycle / grace, grace is in your cycles / federations, federations framing a cycle / eager, eager amounting to cycles / naive, naive without cycles / rules, rules are written for cycles / rhyming, rhyming changed into all cycles / actions, actions spoken and acted for cycles / kindling, kindling builds a fire for heart cycles / tantra, tantra is storing your cycles / stirs, stirs an equipping cycle / swept, swept allowed, cycles / rousing, rousing the doorways for cycles / averages, averages cycled / management, management cycled into love / patience, patience in a patterned find called cycled love / motives, motives made for a cycle / surrounds, surrounds sweet in cycles / celestial, celestial spills into cycles / sleeps, sleeps in soft surrender to steep sincerity in cycles ends.

CHAPTER FOUR

Stirs, stirs in ours, cycles / purest, purest disciplines for a franchised cycle / crafted, crafted into signatures for our cycles / codes, codes ended in cycles disciplines / sweeps, sweeps appearing for a cycle / simple, simple in a temple formed into cycles / judged, judged aims and cycles / externals, externals smiling for cycles / amounts, amounts forming a freedom cycle / essence, essences smelling a cycle swelling in a capillary's cure for living flowers / increased, increased in basic vascular cycles / invisible, invisible balances amount to a sodium-potassium pump for all living cycles / more, more is the amount made in neutral positions for listening cycles / materials, materials change into the variations for the carriage across the cycles for all thresholds / inhibits, inhibits adore your daily cycles / quantities inside your cycles / transparents, transparents push into your cycles / stones, stones rising to a cycle / imbibes, imbibes a basically cycled succeed / parts, parts passionate through your yearly cycles / repeats, repeats around your cycles / seven, seven scenes patient in your cycles / convenience, convenience matching a cycle / pounds, pounds initial in cycles / rewards, rewards are made through your patient cycles / days, days banished to the past cycles / fries, fries form a cycle / cool, cool into days of cycles / steers, steers a major cycle / substance, substance paying your cycles / operate, operate as steering our cycles / waters, waters made for cycles / substantial, substantial and amazing through your cycles / phoenix, phoenix finding a cycle / restoring, restoring your cycles / seas, seas minding your cycles / living, living interest in a cycle / loves -loves a precious cycle / greatness, greatness granting your cycles / Christ, Christ to the federation for cycles / epigrams, epigrams granted to cycles / hearts, hearts are patient into your cycles / caves, caves joining your cycles / claims, claims exemplary fresh in a cycle / praises, praises pointing to cycles / complexion, complexion carrying your cycle / red, red is clearest for cycles / necks, necks are reaching through a cycle / lightened, lightened intrigue in your cycles / altars, altars built collapse, find a new cycle place / red, red roses on your cycle / hermes, hermes helping your cycle / soils, soils tossed into piles of cycles / thebes, thebes is efficient in cycles / gold, gold is gathered here cycles / kept, kept in a spirit for cycles / egyptians, egyptians glowing in captures of cycles / ordered, ordered to flow into cycles / hues, hues glue into cycles / entrusts, entrusts forgive, cycles / written, written in material junctions for cycles / vulcan, compare vulcan formations to cycles / frankincense, frankincense is yours, cycle a, the shepherd and children and love / cassia, cassia completed too, cycles.

CHAPTER FIVE

Messengers, messengers marry amounts for cycles / continuation, continuation cycled in spatial planes / obtained, obtained abstinence for past formations of love in a cycle / causes, causes are creating a cycle / fountains, fountains filling your cycles / proportions, proportions paring a cycle / humors, humors herald a cycle / abound, abound abounding for cycle / unite, unite in yearly cycles / flexible, flexible feelings and cycles / power, powers range into cycles / burn, burn within cycles / common, common creations for a cycle / melting, melting made firm, a cycle / powders, powders patching in cycles / inwardly, inwardly still in years cycled / temples, temples torn apart, cycles / revelations, revelations written through in your cycles / egyptian, egyptian mirrors simple cycles / bases, based touched are new cycles /

synthesis, synthesis is written, cycles / signify, signify how to find a cycle / steps -steps are made to find a cycle / scientific, scientific about your cycles / extends, extends detailed in a cycle / knowledge, knowledge nearing completion into cycles / extends, extends preparation for a cycle / knowledge, knowledge nurtures your cycles / mathematics, mathematics create a cycle's ends / greek, greek grew into a ringing cycle for love / extensions, extensions ranging doors cycled / ancient, ancient in patience and cycles / demonstrate, demonstrate how to seed your cycles / civilized, civilized resting days are cycled / functioning, functioning rays are civilized / volumes, volumes written now ink dries in cycles / powers, powers parry over a cycle / unvarying, unvarying frames and cycles / symbolic, symbolic spaces placed into cycles / harmony, harmony matched into cycles / substance, substance reaching your cycles / rhythms, rhythms reading your cycles / achieve, achieve strictest cycles / appoint, appointing a cycle / stages, stages reaching your cycles / powerful, powerful and precious in a cycle / acknowledgement, acknowledgement meant for a cycle / formal, formal missions inside a cycle / compels, compels pieced into cycles / substance, substance amounting to cycles / specifics, specifics found in a cycle / assimilate, assimilate information skills and cycles / reality, reality reaches into cycles / ideas, ideas are based in cycles sent to love / family, family is finished, cycles end in love / carry, carry a daily forgiveness for cycles / visible, visible in mentions for cycles / informed, informed in final ways of cycles / transitory, transitory durations reach a new cycle / chromosomes, chromosomes reach into cycles / indisputible, indisputible abilities and a cycle / ponderance, ponderance marries a cycle / organs, organs donated too, cycles / finality, finality mentioned to cycles.

CHAPTER SIX
Fixed, fixed inside, cycles and loves / callings, callings are coming to your love and cycles / liberated, liberated finally for love, a cycles / pulsations, pulsations cease without cycles / harmonious, harmonious reaches and cycles / gambles, gambles samples are fed to a cycle / sufferance, sufferance seeded and cycled / polar, polar places and cycles / rivers, rivers bedded cycles / cosmic, cosmic carriage to a cycle / man, man made a cycle / impasse, impasse met your cycles / shaped, shaped irritation without cycles / Buddha, Buddha basics and cycles / Jehoshua, Jehoshua grew over cycles / speculation, speculation has reached heights of your cycles / heredity, heredity is due unto cycles / anthropomorphic, anthropomorphic infest has come to a realization about cycles / minerals, minerals working for a cycle / ideas, ideas raids and a cycle / substance, substance reaching your cycles / angels, angels raining through cycles / process, process reaching into cycles / ideals, ideals final too, cycles / parts, parts arming your cycles / surpass, surpass succeeding in cycles / undergone, undergone and strong into a cycle / objects, objects reaching a cycle / liberal, liberal reaches and cycles / planted, planted paces and faces into cycles / animals, animals marry a cycle / being, being basic too, a cycle / quest, quest over, heart found, a cycle ends / equals, equals marry into cycles / supernatural, supernatural in basics and cycles /

surplus, surplus endings sent into cycles / intimate, intimate about your cycles / harmonies, harmonies meeting in cycles / infer, infer is fed a reference for cycles / balanced, balanced in reaches for cycles / perceptible, perceptible peaces and cycles / guides, guides grew into a cycle / opposed, opposed can grow to cycles / relations, relations reaching your cycles / perceptions, perceptions arming in cycles / structures, structures storing a cycle / relatives, relatives ramification is your cycle / employ, employ a partner's cycles / cases, cases reaching your cycles / cranium, cranium creating your cycles / clearance, clearance reaching rest for love's cycles / proper, proper in a sincere cycle / vocabularies, vocabularies reaching a cycle / bones, bones burst into cycles / certain, certain seeds reaching your cycles / stance, stances red into cycles / constant, constant in caring cycles / several, several signs inside cycles / written, written reaching cycles / penetrates, penetrates patiently your cycles / examine, examine extremes in your cycles / precious, precious in patents and features for cycles.

CHAPTER SEVEN
Refers, refers reaching a cycle / orifices, orifices are filled into a cycle sent for loves enlarged pace / animates, animates cycles completed / respire, respire to a cycle / particularly, particularly a route is now cycled / enlarges, enlarges enlarging cycles / faces, faces example in a cycle for love / perforation, perforation is cycled / vaults, vaults initial into cycles / symmetrically, symmetrically a serial fashion for cycles / sutures, sutures staring into cycles / scribes, scribes are clear, a cycle / provisional, provisional appearing in valuable cycles / terms, terms tripled into cycles ends / coffers, coffers cured, A cycle / allowed, allowed a mixing cycle / architectural, architectural reaches into a cycle / noses, noses in the poses for cycles / eyes, eyes are steering into cycle scenes / temples, temples initial on a cycle / nostril, nostril interior to a cycle / ears, ears inside a signal cycled / pupils, pupils simple to a fault- lined cycle / openings, openings appearing in a cycle / month, month in a mutual cycle / pupils, pupils simple in a cycle / openings, openings attempted in a cycle / month, month in a mutual end for cycles / pupils, pupils simple into cycles / schlera, schlera into cycles / breath, breath in a basic kneeling cycle / face, face is the factor for our cycles' / iris, ins inside a simple cycle / cornea, cornea carrying an a cycle / certainty, certainty offered into cycles / distinctive, distinctive into succinct degrees of cycles / employs, employs are mounting a retaliation from cycles / fortunately, fortunately a financial cycle / kieroglyphics, hieroglyphics are intrigued inside cycles for love / papyrus, papyrus is reaching near cycles / ankh, ankh is extreme inside streams cycles / forward, forward into simple cycles / accents, accents spanning your cycles / written, written sincerely into cycles / life, life is led throughout cycles / focal, focal is the factor for a cycle / accentuate, accentuate forming cycles / encounters, encounters in simple cycles / led, led over a leading cycle / vocal, vocal in volumes and cycles / trauma, trauma in a single cycle / shells, shells extended in your cycles / resistant, resistant inside your cycles / cases, cases made for your cycles / region, regions arranged in a circular cycle / skulls, skulls arranged in a cycle /

extremes, extremes mental in a cycle / placed, placed in simple cycles / injured, injured inside simple cycles / hands, hands inside a cycle / observed, observed into a cycle / traumas, traumas inside your cycles / various, various inspirations for a cycle / elastic, elastic in simple cycles.

CHAPTER EIGHT

Regional, regional reaches and a cycle / radius, radius reaches and our cycles / canals, canals empty into a cycle / upper, upper is signals into a cycle / cases, cases into simple cycles / ceilings, ceilings soothing into cycles / reinforced, reinforced changes and these are our cycles / back, back into basic cycles / curvatures, curvatures signing a cycle / orbits, orbits basic in cycles / neurological, neurologically a cycle / impact, impact impacted and cycled / radial, radial a reaching cycle / optic, optics cycled in signals / mobility, mobility and the mentioned cycles / spreads, spreads around us as neighbors and cycles / enters, enters a miracle's cycles / typical, typical instincts and cycles / remarks, remarks mentioned a simple cycle / glosses, glosses a nature for cycles / interiors, interiors pension said "cycles" / descriptions, descriptions beaming a newness and cycles / specific, specific fits inside cycles / specify, specify sparing uniquest cycles / means, means detailing your cycles / entry, entry signals cycles / enter, enter inside your cycles / motoring, motoring mentions your cycles / preserves, preserves often a cycle/ exteriors, exteriors cycled / tracking, tracking a simple cycle / nerves, nerves inside deeper cycles / evolutions, evolutions cycle your signals and sights / validates, validates reaching your cycles / destiny, destiny during your cycles / nuclear, nuclear family dissolves into a simple cycle / evolves, evolves inside your sealing cycles / values, values inside your cycles / ultimate, ultimate individual to your cycles / statutes, statutes inside your cycles / politics, politics pensions are cycles / wisely, wisely winning your cycles / upheld, upheld inside your single cycles / politics, politics paring cycles / origins, origins arranging for cycles / passions, passions stunning cycles / burns, burns bashing a cycle / rainbow, rainbow is ruled into a cycle / adamantine, adamantine trilled cycles / frequent, frequents inside your cycles / vibrations, vibrations paring in cycles / deep, deep inside simple cycles / self-regards, self-regards made your cycles / oranges, oranges arranged inside your cycles / fingers, fingers fed a new cycle / dancing, dancing in simple cycles / created, created a creature cycle / pulses, pulses paging your cycles / nerves, nerves shooting though cycles / illusions, illusions patching your cycles / staples, staples are reaching for cycles / arrive, arrive inside your cycles / green, green inside your gaxing cycles / grown, grown up on cycled scents.

CHAPTER NINE

Grown, grown inside details and cycles / saints, saints in a simple cycle / sustain, sustain a creation for a cycle / themselves, themselves arranging a cycle / through, through a yearly cycles / powerful, powerful in arranged cycles / plenty, plenty in apparent cycles / auctions, auctions inside your cycles / bend, bend in a basic cycle / energetically, energetically inside your ailing instincts and

cycles / science, science arranging your cycles / details, details discover new cycles / anatomic, anatomic in meetings and cycles / atomic, atomic reaches through cycles / gaps, gaps directive and cycled / between, between us and all ways a cycle / humans, humans and healing cycles / egypt, egypt grew into cycles / knew, knew a native cycle / civilized, civilized in sizes and cycles / patents, patents placed into cycles / enhance, enhanced rate and a cycle / cower, cower as past in a cycle / physics, physics arming your cycle / cycles, cycles sealing your cultural shifts / sets, sets paging in cycles / degrees, degrees reach a cycle / codes, codes carry a cycle / biospherically, biospherically a miracle curing cycle / links, links linking your cured cycles / allows, allows inside your curative cycles / rests, rests inside your reaching cycles / round, round inside your cycles / armed, armed in risen cycles / supremacy, supremacy inside a cycle / gone, gone is into your cycles / revenues, revenues ruling your cycles / breaks, breaks abounding in cycles / through, through us all a cycle / grainy, grainy in a greeted cycle / interior, interior meetings and cycles / pierce, pierce is over, inside sealed and cycled / acid, acid is simple in a cycle / possessions, possessions apparent in cycles / positive, positive in listings and cycles / chakra, chakra said a "cycles" / seats, seats inside your cycles / edited, edited intrigued with your cycles / karmic, karmic inside your cycles / embodies, embodies interest in your cycles / invisible, invisible fillings and cycles / controls, controls a clearest cycle / apply, apply inside your cycles / well, well into your cycles / eight, eight in necessity and in cycles / claimed, claimed and amounted to in cycles / goodness, goodness in growing cycles / calls, calls spelling a cellular cycle / bearings, bearings are over your cycles / body, body basic to your cycles / ruse, ruse is off, cycles / powerfully, powerfully piercing a cycle / tidings, tidings are a pure cycle / features, features and a mentioning cycle.

CHAPTER TEN

Translates, translates a reaching fresh cycle / flames, flames are pierced by a cycle / irritations, irrations rules end in a cycle / sugar, sugar is a simple gift, cycles / baby, baby fed only cycles / fuels, fuels pierced in your cycles / posted, posted in roasted cycled / red, red is a facing cycle / blown, blown into basically cycles / photographic, photographics and cycles / annually, annually and cycled / guardian, guardian and a psychically freed soothed regard in a cycle / breathing, breathing inside your cycles / attired, attired into a cycle / blues, blues into views formed and cycled / redeemed, redeemed into teeming cycles / musically, musically meanings and cycles / lingers, lingers inside simple cycles / groping, groping formed in a cycle / passing, passings inside in your cycles / still, still in a despertion gone to a cycle / bends, bends are through in a cycle / finds, finds a frienc in your cycle / puzzled, puzzled mileage and cycles / coated, coated and created for cycles / allowing, allowing relaying a cycle / garments, garments managed and cycled / looks, looks inside your next cycles / dreams, dreams and a daring day's cycles / individual, individual dealings and cycles / choice, choices are your cycles / life, life is lined by a cycle / breached, breached is up too, cycles / introductions,

introductions and a cycle / compounds, compounds cycled in love / water, water is whistling to your cycle / born, born into a cycle of redemption's signing retails / living, living in giving relations and a cycle surrendered into for love / struggles, struggles a patience for living cycles / bursts, bursts a natural cycle / allows, allows a shielded cycle / parental, parental culture and a cycle succinct into love / forgive, forgive a feeling cycle / children, children changing into angelic cycles / universes, universes reach a nearest cycle / found, found a rape without rapture's cycles / symbols, symbols attached without cycles / fortunes, fortunes ranging to cycle / anchors, anchors mention a cycle / saturn, saturn rising in cycles / glorified, glorified cycles / visions, visions detailed in cycle / mass, mass amusing your cycles / pause, pauses signal your cycles / sirens, sirens singing a cycle / lions, lions large within cycles / powers, powers purged into cycles / causes, causes dealt electric cycles / sell, sell now and move to a clearer cycle / roar, roar is over, come into, cycles / settles, settles a matter simply and cycles / changes, changes made for your cycles / pieces, pieces matching your cycles / larges, larges and the laughing cycles.

CHAPTER ELEVEN

Heaven, heaven reaches our cycles / heralds, heralds mention a cycle / tempers, tempers clearing the lost cycles / temporarily, remporarily withal a cycle / gates, gates on a cultural cycle / humans, humans reaching your cycles / thorough, thorough and interior cycles / beauty, beauty reaching your cycles / open, open reaches and cycles / seething, seething details for your cycles / abides, abides raining for cycles / sons, sons racing a cycle / mystically, mystically cycled plates / soothes, soothes reaching for cycles / allows, allows a clearing cycle / surged, surged a patterned cycle / mothers, mothers mention your cycles / spun, spun into tattoo on cycles / vanishes, vanishes past ache into circuits and physical cycles / now, now is the nearest cycle / passive, passive places race into cycle / respecting, respecting your cycles / charming, charming duos and racing cycles / sex, sex is central in a wending cycle / place, place into cordial cycles / rejections, rejections reaching a cycle / settles, settles paces entered into cycles / close, close amperes risen in cycles / allows, allows yearly instinctual to a cycle / betray, betray rights inspected for cycles / clearest, clearest in simple cycles / forms, forms appearing for a cycle / foremost, foremost in raging cycles / 45 days, 45 days into simple cycles / shadows, shadows reaching into cycles / seal, seal is appealing to a cycle / spun, peering into pairings and cycles / gazes, gazes ranging in cycles / zealots, zealots studious in cycles / pay, pays arranged into cycles sent / egoss, egos armed into cycles / warmly, warmly and warming cycles / 64, 64 into a cycle / flowers, flowers piercing and a cycle / clears, clears piercing a cycle / welcome, welcome a warming cycle / 128, 128 wishes cycled / horizons, horizons preaching your cycles / hexagram, hexagrams seeking your cycles / involve, involve a solved riddle into cycles / character, characters reaching into a cycle / pheasants, pleasants arranging a cycle / clocks, clocks creating your cycles / oceans, oceans matching your cycles / events, events arranged into cycles / fly, fly into physicals and features are cycled / cubicals,

cubicals arranged into cycles / properties, properties arranged in your cycles / values, values mentioned in simple cycles / past, pasts reaching your cycles / curt, curt and into a cycle / sequence, sequences arise in a cycle / remove, remove a mannerism and a cycle / portals, portals peaceful in cycles.

CHAPTER TWELVE

Cults, cults into cycles / blend, blend in simple cycles / knowing, knowing inside surges and cycles / sized, sized into pieces and cycles / spikes, spikes peachy in cycle / stars, stars are married to cycles / possible, possible paces and cycles / okay, okay into simple cycles / remarks, remarks in signs cycles / attempts, attempts reach ends and a cycle / tribal, tribal trenches cycles / glances, glances placed in cycles / answers, answers another cycle / interpret, interpret and neutral cycle / honors, honors cycled into love / sources, sources squarely cured for a cycle / pharaohs, pharaohs are seeking that lead which you will cycle too / dumb, dumb in a numb recital for cycles / globes, globes are shatter free in your love cycles / suspend, suspend a moment in your cycles / random, random is the reason for all your cycles / radium, radium reaches a listed cycle / occult, occult in exempt recitals for cycles / relax, relax into your smiling cycles / relative, relative relaxation in a cycle / funnels, funnels exh deep into a cycle / built, built the beach for a cycle / around, around us sound us a cycle / segments, segments mention your cycle / globe, globe opens on a light cycle / wide, wide is the a cycle / worn, worn explosions reach a cycled ends / tubes, tubes mt in a cycle / trees, trees grown into cycles / stable, stable in an able cycle / stabilize, stabilize your resource to a cycle / surgery, surgery ends here, cycle finished / ends, ends meet in a cycle / clearance, clearance of the a cycles / sent, sent to shine instead in cycles / frequency, frequency mentioned is a cycled / grows, grows a repute for all vacations cycled / lighter, lighter insiders and cycles / kingdoms, kingdoms coming to an era of cycle / bottom, bottom booming cycles / fed, fed for a cycle / leap, leap across your cycles / alive, alive is the lifted cycle / ovoids, ovoids made for your cycles / stand, stand in tune with your cycle / form, form broken into cycled / greats, greats respected cycles / pair, pair made yours, cycles end / strands, strands touching on cycles / fractions, fractions feeding your cycles / smile, smile in time to a ccyle / patterns, patterns powering your cycles / curl, curl into significant rises and cycles split to a merger of Godhead and love / paged, paged to the centers cycles / surrender, surrender in a cycle / emergent, emergent mirth and a mainstay's cycles / cubes, cubes cushioned for cycles / pearly, pearly paces and a cycles / came, came a day cycled.

CHAPTER THIRTEEN

Central, central into a cycle / sun, sun is meant for aims and cycles / electric, electric mesh mast high in a sunny cycle / cove, cove keyed cycles / coded, coded into roads built for a cycles / with, with us all, cycles / canals, canals to a matrix of cycles / lipped, lipped and sipped on a cycle / arise, arise is reached through as cycled / sunny, sunny miles across reaches and cycles / peel, peel a partnered cycle / exists, exists rally for your cycles / near, near a gentle cycle / anatomic, anatomic and teal cycles / cues, cues rush into cycles / opens, opens peach cycles / pairing, pairing made today fortunate to a cycle / wings, wings reach both cycles / electric, electric powers and cycles / divine, divine into cycles / pours, pours power into your cycles / forth, forth in a fullest cycle / fusions, fusions matching a cycle / occurs, occurs a placement of cycles / allowance, allowances move into cycles / at, at the middle, cycled / triple, triple times cycles / coats, coats created cycles / crossing, crossing in places and cycles / light, light leaps across cycles / years, years who knew your a cycles / the, the and the those inside cycles / pyramids, pyramids piling into cycles / pulse, pulse on the nerves of cycles / erupts, erupts in sips and cycles / again, again and spans spin for a cycle / finding, finding detail in a cycle / trends, trends broken in cycles / silver, silver pours across your cycles / caps, caps off past lifetimes and cycles / appear, appear daily near your next cycles / mankind, mankind materialized for the finish of cycles human / sending, sending a message to cycles / pillars, pillars firey lead our cycles / flames, flames fleshly and cycled / snake, snake asleep in a cycle / follows, follows polished for a cycle / hollows, hollows appearing in cycles clearances / bleed, bleed across the seas and find solace in a nurturing cycle / carbons, carbons basic and built into cycles / copper, copper spent is made, cycles / coats, coats reaching you cycles / yellow, yellow is the singing cycle / apply, apply for your cycles / clearest, clearest is comparable to a completed cycle / poles, poles reach across the oceans / tunes, tunes and timing belvoed for cycles / triangles, triangles end in a cycles / coax, coax appearing on cycles blends / compound, compound reaching a cycle / imported, imported expansions within cycles / snakes, snakes wrapped into cycles / strain, strain is off and found inside cycles / flat, flat to a fashion adaptive cycled.

CHAPTER FOURTEEN

Hydroxide, hydroxide is mentioned, cycle / umbrella, umbrella, beaches, and yellow sun cycles / cones, cones created in a cycle / cords, cords piercing your cycles / spheres, spheres open into your cycledness / iron, iron is willed into your cycles / bars, bars broken, step our, cycles / bare, bare a nearest star for your cycles / hope, hope is given through a call into cycles / home, home is held into cycles / flowers, flowers powers and potions for a cycle / square, square inside a cycled / grounded, grounded in rounded cycles / shapes, shapes ripen your cycles / taken, taken and shaken as a cycle / light, light is led to your way homeward angel at cycle's end / soars, soars in swarming aim, cycled / love, love is led past your cycled shed / repeats, repeats are finished, find a new cycle / in, in too, cycles / blue, blue is basic to your completed cycles / corded, corded has cut away for all time, a cycles / freedom, freedom is spelling your name, cycled / heavenward, heavenward matrix lifted for former flames extinguished through cycles / faces, faces match your cycles ends / forming, forming perfect alliances for cycles sent / chainschains off, cycled / notes, notes matched, cycles / sing, sing a religousity's end and find spiritual middles for cycles / beta, beta reaching a crandom cycle / alpha, alpha flowering cycles / extracts, extracts are drawn out through

your cycles / solvents, solvents yearly cycled / small, small in peace and cycles / balloon, balloon burst over a cycle / following, following is the feeling cycle / clouds, clouds ripen in cycle / curving, curving past old cycles / above, above bases and cycles / focused, focused into news about cycles ends / along, along and the belongs for cycles / coated, coated and voted for as a cycle / cords, cords crushed iwthout cycles / floating, floating in a neutral experience of cycles / distributions, distributions are made for your cycles / declare, declare a din shut forever, listen, cycles / sources, sources chosen and made your frozen thawed cycle / sucked, sucked a driven one out of your mission and style and cycle / atomically, atomically anatomically fueled by a cycle / vents, vents over all cycled / beings, beings who balance your cycles / behavior, behavior eccentric and elect for all past positions and cycles / dancing, dancing has come unto my cycles / suns, suns are reaching your door's cycles / sorts, sorts strong in a cycle / signal, signal pleased in a cycle / sunny, sunny meetings and cycles fend / lends, lends a listen too, cycles / tearing, tearing has healed, find a friend, cycle / buckles, buckles end in cycled completions / crust, crust is cleared for your nearest cycles / cools, cools and the spool open into a cycle / charimen, chairmen mending a cycled / loosen, loosen lips and hips and heart for a cycled.

CHAPTER FIFTEEN

Include, include a mood of release froma ll past cycles / diagrams, diagrams drawn into sandy cycles / wobble, wobble ahs precessed into completion and the end of all cycles / claws, claws off my simple smiling existence and see this "a cycles end" / leap, leap into new cycles / simplest, simplest places and the end to past cycles / derives, derives a delicious cycle / denial, denial coming? cycle / last, last is lost, find a friendly cycle / along, along your ways and cycles spent / allowing, allowign a middles cycles spend / dreams, dreams danger? forget it, move for your heart's happiness, find a new forecast and finance your move thorugh a cycle finished / tungsten, tungsten is still in your finances and dreams, move on, cycles / tours, tours end in your cycles flights / festive, festive peace and cycles meant for love / terraces, terraces reaching your cycles / tungsten, tungsten is meant for all past skills and a cycle / staged, staged a retreat past old cycles / groups, groups are simple in cycles / component, component for moments and cycles / red, red is reaching your cycles / rings, rings arranged in a cycle / rang, rang in mazes and cycles / essentially, essentially a finished cycle / set, set into passion for cycles / sung, sung about regally as a cycle / attend, attend a reaching cycle / broken, broken? in basic language, whole inside love's cycles / negatives, negatives can go ways of light and love cycles / sort, sort the past into cycles / positively, positively mentioned as a cycle / randomly, randomly regarded as the mentioned cycle's lead / to, to us all cycles / manners, manners rapt into cycles / along, along a lifted cycle's ends / lining, lining clears and silver peers into cycles / liquids, liquids reach boiling places inside a cycle / linked, linked up and finished in cycles / sustains, sustains plcement for a cycle / outward, outward willing and welcome to a shine for all cycles spent / release, release a pent past through cycles completed / bodies, bodies blazing in a cycle / whirl, whirl wed with a flavor of smacking lips dripping in silent salute to a forgiven cycle / duds, duds go to an ended cycle / thud, thud is off, cycles / threads, threads break, no longer silent, years go, cycles deep are now ripped out and fed a cure, loved / level, level 21 finished, chromosomes matched, cycles end / one, one is who? cycled / one, one is wed, cycles / ignored, ignored and stored as a cycle / arrives, arrives arriving allowance for all a cycles / surges, surges apt and into a cycle / zinc, zinc in sealed cycles / blue, blue balanced cycles / thickens, thickens into a vitamin for your cycles / calcium, calcium settles past a cycle / clues, clues materialize inside cycles / calcium, calcium creations armed for a cycle / bones, bones blink in a cycle / divine, divine in allowance for a cycle / again, again is inside your life cycles / published, published in a simple cycle / when, when is the winning cycle / 64th, 64th details and cycles.

CHAPTER SIXTEEN
Published, published in maturest cycles / when, when is the simple cycle / spaces, spaces apparent in a cycle / paces, paces apace in a cycle / 64th, 64th in the pages formed cycles / bell, bell into central seams and cycles / rang, rang in a ringing cycle / blurbs, blurbs in the suburbs and cycles / segments, segments essentially cycled / zones, zones inside established rings and cycles / adds, adds inside central seams and cycles / blurts, blurts and the details cycled into love / sealed, sealed inside your simple cycles / chosen, chosen in mature cycles / coves, coves into droves and these cycles / selves, selves in central cycles / remains, remains a meaning and a neutral star for cycles / globally, globally resistent to a cycle / faced, faced into openings and a cycle / funnels, funnels and a neutral cycles sent to love / catalysts, catalysts simple in a needed break for all cycles / crystallize, crystallize and a simple cycle / double, double is a detailed suggestion of cycles / dates, dates are daring without cycles / flatten, flatten a focus into cycles / bases, bases electric in magnetic intrigue and the insides are magnetic in a cycle / blues, blues are a basic cycle / knew, knew an intial cycle / foams, foams appearing into cycles / diamond, diamond dues and a cycle / keys, keys incurring a cycle / capably, capably yours and a cycle / roses, roses reaching your cycles / rang, rang into rhyming and reaching for cycles / borrowed, borrowed in a balance and a cycle / captures, captures into cycles / stars, stars and the central cycles / jeremiah, jeremiah and the newness said "cycles" / sand, sands annointed for cycles mend / vigorous, vigorous in simple cycles / views, views and the valley cycles / adopts, adopts an adoptive cycle / unique, unique in entreaty and cycle / stride, strides in the simple cycles / eclipse, eclipse an exciting cycle / cures, cures daring to cycle / callow, callow in a shallow cycle / days, days daring to cycle / remains, remains declaring a simple cycle complete / globes, globes reaching a cycle / faces, faces reach your cycle / funnels, funnels amount to a cycle / catalysts, catalysts creating cycles / crystallize, crystallized in an amount / double, double in a daring cycle / dates, dates reaching your cycles / flatten, flatten a feeling cycle / base, bases met in cycles / blue, blue is a vast and basic cycle / knew, knew in a simple cycle / foams, foams reaching a

frothing cycle / diamond, diamond deals and simple cycles / keys, keys reached and thrice said a living is a cycle / capably, capably is threatened with a cycle.

CHAPTER SEVENTEEN
Angles, angles teaming and cycles sent into love / opens, opens and the teeming cycles / seen, seen and the centrak cycles / found, found in an inside cycle / translations, translations reaching your cycles / edges, edges inside a cycle / wedges, wedges interior to a cycle / pyr, pyr ampered into cycles / surround, surround a surrounding cycle / flow, flowers are mentioned into cycles / everywhere, everywhere is a mentioning cycle / palatial, palatial in a simple cycle/ grown, grown into assigning cycles / finds, finds a smallest cycle / a a day is a cycle / improves, improves risen races through cycles / made, made in a mental cycle / softens, softens all cycles / mid, mid states and a racing cycle / backgrounds, backgrounds valuable cycles / impose, impose a portion's cycles / grey, grey has gone completely to a cycle / seas, seas and a forming cycle sent to love / magnification, magnification forming a circle's cycles / combined, combined a current cycle / sources, sources challenged cycles / grandmother, grandmother marries your cycles / analyze, nalyaze sizes and cycles / treats, treats and treasures and cycles / trades, trades are simply a cycle / windy, windy in winding cycles / brights, brights are brightest cycles / velcro, velco is sincerest in cycles / cruises, cruises allowing your cycles / crews, crews on notice for single cycles / allowing, allowing a simple cycle / zenith, zenith in central cycles / chores, chores into simple cycles / vitality, vitality for a cycle / globes, globes gathering a cycle / variations, variations value your cycles / natures, natures daring to be a cycles / oxygen, oxygen inside your aiming cycles / forces, forces simple inside a cycle / flowing, flowing finally in your cycle / cores, cores is intended in a cycle / globules, globules inside a sent cycle / increased, increased amounts inside cycles / charging, charging ahead in your courses and cycles / courses, courses written now sent into cycles / research, research amounting cycled / random, random reaches for cycles / narrows, narrows daring a cycle / into, into your cycles / several, several dealing in cycles / drawn, drawn inside? cycles / quartets, quartets and best bets inside cycles / lithium, lithium aimed into cycles bubbled / fluorine, fluorine found inside cycles / potassium, potassium watered in cycles / rubidium, rubidium rays arranged in cycles / duads, duads mounted in cycles / constituted, constituted inside cycles / associated, associated endeavors and a living cycle.

CHAPTER EIGHTEEN
Variations, variations value into a cycle / chosen, chosen in simple cycles / samples, samples matching your cycles / positivity, positivity races into cycles / units, units measuring your cycles / triplets, triplets reaching cycles / six, six rapt in a cycle / twenty-five, twenty-five who live in lear cycles / waves, waves rise again, cycled / hydrogen, hydrogen reigning to cycles / is, is this all? a cycle / the, the reason for all? cycles / merkaba, merkaba basic and a living cycle / fields, fields blending your cycles / stars, atars engaged in your cycles / alive, alive in a triple cycle / swings,

swings are 24, 6, and 3 into love cycles / funnels, funnels thread into cycles / components, components measuring a cycle / parts, parts and the poses in cycles / directives, directives mirrored past cycles / pillows, pillows placed under cycles / directions, directions ranging for cycles / projections, projections malevolence goes to a cycle / planned, planned amounts returning to a cycle / rotate, rotate above, cycles end / solids, solids in maturest cycles / clear, clear ocean views of your cycles / spheres, spheres measured in cycles / vigorously, vigorously reaching through into cycles / types, types who steepe in a cycle / along, along a glazed cycle / lines, lines cleared, cycles oasis / perpetually, perpetually married to a cycle's clear / perplexed, perplexed about lessen? say "cycle" / without, without and withal into cycles / oasis, oasis invented? cycles / jubilant, jubilant in a triumphant return into cycles / allow, allow another truth in your cycles / squared, squared in squiring cycles / concepts, concepts meet in a cycle / driven, driven into and cycled / ranges, ragnes arranging a cycle / coffers, coffers offered your cycles flush / coined, coined a phrase "cycles" / effectively, effectively finished without cycle / joined, joined a tribe who suggested "cycles over" / lightest, lightest reaches in sway through a cycle / scope, scope stead inside a cycle / tires, tires paced into cycles / truths, truths register for you, cycles / levels, levels pacing over all, cycles / sealed, sealed in please and a cycle spent / transacts, transacts arrayed in simple cycles / trues, trues peace and patient cycles sent / night, night is nestling through your cycles / values, values paced inside cycles / plus, plus is a patient cycle / involves, involves raiding cycle / scopes, scopes reach your news, cycles / influences, influences patient and cycle free / lines, lines marry a cycle / loads, loads are reaching you cycles cleanse / patient, patient allowing of cycles cleared.

CHAPTER NINETEEN

Belonging, belonging too, cycles 2 groupings, groupings credited / adoptively, adoptively cycled / funds, funds cycled / star sing, star sing rings cycled / credited, credited of cycles / above, above us, cycles / within, within your cycles / selenium, selenium cycling in / coalitions, coalitiions forming cycles / prints, prints cycle / pose, poses cycled / grown, grown strong in cycles / winters, winters cycled / heavens, heavens cycles in / spin, spin too, cycles / composites, composites cycled / capable, capable of cycles / allows, allows us cycle / spell, spell us c-y-c-l-e / sent, clearly sent tribes cycles / cools, cools to cycle / sorted, sorted and cycled / fictive, fictive hides cycled / sallow, swallow kali yugan waves cycle / full, full on cycles / ascertain, ascertain the certainty in your cycles end / spills, spills approach cycle ends / shrugs, shrugs are reaching a cyclical collection / founded, founded in future reflections and love' cycles / pains, pains are off, cycles / segmented, segmented in a llowance for your cycles / absolutions, absolutions resovled, cycles / solution, solution found, cycles ending / figures, figures are announced near your cycles / grouped, grouped into basics and cycles / composure, composure allowing a patience in cycles / european, european planet sna dhte reaches for cycle / traveling, traveling into a living cycle / mutually, mutually abusive without a cycle / occupied, occupied rapaciously in cycles

/ occuring, occuring again in a cycle / rehab, rehab the reset for an equivalent cycle / rings, rings are worn into your cycle / worn, worn over a ccyle / delay, delay is a passion for cycles / due, dues are paid to a cycles / junk, junk is over, cycles / dna, dna rays and our cycles / cellular, cellular seeking into a cycle 51respirations, inspirations passing into a cycle / required, required reaction to a cycle / rely, rely applied for, cycles/ knowledge, knowledge nearing your cycles / gained, gained in rally for a cycle / pressures, pressures over, a standing cycle / roses, roses malleable into a cycle / enableenable has gone into cycles / encoded, encoded in raods over another leading cycle / through, through a threaded cycle / threaded, threaded and breaking too, cycles / stores, stores elastic placement for a cycle / imply, imply into your cycles / mentioned, mentioned marriage and cycles.

CHAPTER TWENTY

Galactic, galactic leaps made for cycles ends / predecessors, predecessors matching your cycle / detailed, detailed in finished cycles / plans, plans placing our cycles / vertical, vertical values and a cycle / columns, columns clering for cycles / clarify, clarify a basic goal, cycles / lifestreams, lifestreams matching your cycles / procedures, procedures patching through, cycles / explain, eplain a planning western cycle / mastery, mastery procedural through your cycles / wisdom, wisdom willing to cycle / pause, pauses pathway and cycles / ray, rays reading for cycles / cycles, cycles suspend in cycles / suns, suns listening cycles / church, church reaching for cycles / sets, sets ready for cycles / home, home healing your cycles / delivers, delivers radio side cycles / fuses, fuses are frequent in cycles / plans, plans are made, cycle / joined, joined into jewelry worn and cycles / authentic, quthentic in your clarity of cycle / sheens, sheens and emotions for cycles / shores, shoes end, cycles / sprang, sprang over all those who said "cycles" / connects, connnects in connections for our cycles / haste, haste is over, cycle / hurls, hurls hurts less inside cycles / mending, mending is final, cycle / venues, venues are varied in cycle / treats, treats are reached for, cycles / treasures, treasures are married to a cycle / channels, channels parry? cycles / planets, planets spin into cycle / commitment, commitment made, wear it and cycle / patents, patents patched into cycles / peace, peace is your lasting cycle / purpose, purpose for the meeting begins in our cycles / organelles, organelles filling your cycles / succumbs, succumbs rafters and cycles / connects, connects clearing a cycle / significance, significance respects our cycles / saves, saves and seeds into cycles/ theorize, theorize a meaning for cycles / interprets, interprets reaching years and cycles / senses, senses meant for all cycled / figures, figures pieces and sky wise in cycles / appropriate, appropriate raiding of cycles / instinctive, openly instinctive to a cycle / daimons, daimons daring too? cycles / phrased, phrased in a random race, cycles / providential, providential plans are cycle / fates, fates chosen? clear, cycles / ethics, ethics are thrilling in cycles / decoded, decoded into cycle / hieretical, hieretical values and the steps into cycles / hopes, hopes are married as a cycle / catalog, catalog clearing your cycles / claims, claims over, cycles / totals, totals paid into cycles / body,

body for the basics and cycles / similar, similar in simulated allegiance to an emperor called God and the races for cycles.

CHAPTER TWENTY-ONE

Mistaken, mistaken for cycles / understands, understandable errors without cycles / lengthens, lengthens lengthened to cycles / gardens, gardens paid for all cycles / perfect, perfect in pairing cycles / relays, relays err? a cycle / venus, venus teaching your cycles / uranus, uranus urgent in cycles / mars, mars marries a cycle / mercury, mercury met, cycles / sanat, sanat now listens too, cycles / kumara, kumara carries a cycle / seeded, seeded reached for and cycled / civilized, civilized aspects for cycles / ages, ages rages and cycles / gardens, gardens gated? cycles / temples, temples arc-ing though cycles / present, present purses and cycles / roses, roses ready for a cycle / great, great carry for cycle / messianicmessianic and matching a cycle / churns, churns into simple cycles / luxor, luor over a cycle / direction, direction effective for a cycle / times, times trained to be a cycle / boils, boils overly in cycled ways / contacts, contacts teaching your cycles / kinds, kinds are signed into cycles / alexandrian, aleandrian rains upon cycles / seas, seas are reaching a cycle / contacts, contacts created and cycles / messages, messages armed to a cycle / records, records rubic cycles / intact, intact and in fact cycles / recipients, recipient armed in a cycle / labors, labors armed in a cycle / accomplish, accomplished and cycled / services, services are a sustained cycle / veils, veils and rasputian cycles / retire, retire into cycles / india, india aims for a cycle / joseph, joseph held into cycles / mary, mary led for a cycle / jesus, jesus is held as a cycle / ascension, ascensions rain into cycle / grateful, grateful and cycled / walks, walks above and within your cycles / keys, keys art and cycles start / words, awkwardness ends in a cycle / woman, woman wedding cycles / civil, civil into a cycle / ascensions, ascensions into cycles / describes, describes a reaching cycle / researched, researched and arming a cycle / registers, registers insured armed cycles / mastery, mastery forms a cycle / chronology, chronology red into cycles / written, written in speaking cycles / fruition, fruition and effects for a cycle / projects, projcts curing a cycle / citizens, citizens voting for nearing cycles / chosens, chosens nearing a cheated end into cycle / come, come along now to our cyles marraige / projectile, projectile shot over these arrogant cycles.

LEVEL 73: THE CENTRAL-MENTS

CHAPTER ONE

Ascensions, ascensions is central for your keys total cycle / Maietreya, Maietreya simple giving and cycles / may, may and the mavericks for cycles / Gabriel, Gabriel grew into your cycles / angels, angels angle into your life cycles / Raphael, Raphael fell without cycles / Jesus, Jesus is leading a revolution in cyclical ends / Joseph, Joseph knew your native cycles / John is the reason, preach, teach, love, cycles / arose, arose a book through patmos in love cycles / roses, roses are reaching a butterfly file of sky blue and white in a greek aisle called light cycles and love / truth, truth is told now through a revelations interpreted without rewritten fears, remember love is what casteth out all fear, love is leading our cycles / serapis, serapis in a written overlook of thira and the resting caves of love's cycles / bay, bay is the clearly boldest space for cycles complete burst into love / pallas, pallas is athene for a heroic and hellenic end to a cycle / Athena, Athena writes you a cycle completes / hilarion, hilarion in reach for a cycle / kuthumi, kuthumi is ready for all cycles / told, told is back too, a cycle / mahal, mahal and the centrals hauling cycle / 105, 105 the net move toward a cycle / nada, nada and the net set for a catch of central love and a cycles / saint, saint in a simple set fortunate for cycles end / theosophy, theosophy sells a centrally routed love cycle / balthazar, balthazar is sent for a cycle / assistance, assistance is spent for all cycles / Francis, Francis is soothing in cycles / saint, saint is straight through a cycle / bacon, bacon is basic into cycles / TRUTH, Truth runs into rejection for a cycle / taj, taj led into central reaches and cycles / germain, germaiin is remaining for all cycles / written, written into reaches and our cycles / I Am, I Am and i said "love" is central into cycles / God, God and the granted interior and into central cycles / I Am, I Am wealth into cores and central portals into cycles / light, light is linking into central cycles and pores opened into love / I Am, I Am a reason for all occupational centrals / transcendant, transcendant into all lifetimes centrals / I Am, I Am committed to a lifelong central / I Am, I Am legendary about your soothings centrals / contented, contented in a simple centralness / I Am, I Am and the central is sent into communication and friends cushion / I Am, I Am interior to a peacefulness central into love / peace, peace is a mission of peacefulness into central success / I Am, I Am is the One / I Am, I Am the won / I Am, is the led through centrally / I Am, I Am that I AM / I AM that love / I AM this One / I AM the meaning / I AM the met / I Am the wonder / I AM the glory / I AM the spirit / I AM the central treasure / I AM the treaty for our centrals / I AM the leased central / I AM the earth and the central ship into love / I AM the mother for all centrals / I AM the father and the central ones / I AM the given centrally / I AM the gift for all centrals.

CHAPTER TWO

I Am, I Am Shekinah's central portal / I Am, I Am is precious in your centralness / I Am, I Am suggesting "love" is central / I Am, I Am really loved in a central way / I Am, I Am Metatronic again, love is central too / I AM, the Shekinah within love is central / I Am, I Am sureley loved and centrally finest / I Am, I Am exactly an arc wed is central / I Am, I Am arc-angelic in love and the central / I Am, I Am the loved instinct for humanity centrally / I Am, I Am the humanity in love's acceptance of Godness said "central" / I Am, I Am especially fond of God as central / I Am, I Am a Christ consciousness centralness / I Am, I Am the Christ spirited centrals / I Am, I Am fresh to christaholism is centrally left to love / I Am, I Am elect in release into a christed corridor to love / I Am, I Am the temple human, a Christ home for the centrals / I Am, I Am the high self, a Christ human is central / I Am, I Am the walking lead through humanity and the centrals / I Am, I Am addicted to

Christ and the centrals / I Am, I Am accenting of the Christ path as central / I Am, I Am the Buddha within Christ's friends our centrals / I Am, I Am an arc-angelic spark is centrally loved / I Am, I Am in love with God and the central / I Am, I Am God's buddy to a central / I Am, I Am aligned in sufi poetic stance for the central / I Am, I Am a sufi poet for God as the central / I Am, I Am sufi in love and centrals / I Am, I Am participative in love's reigning centrals / I Am, I Am the perfect love for the central / I Am, I Am without fears and centralness / I Am, I Am within love as central / I Am, I Am the love for the central / I Am, I Am the way unto the centrals / I Am, I Am truth for our centrals / I Am, I Am vehicle to a centralness in love's suns / I Am, I Am path to heavens and centrals / I Am, I Am perfection for the centrals / I Am, I Am precision sent to centrals / I Am, I Am the aim for all these centrals / I Am, I Am the gifted arc into a central / I Am, I Am the gift for all centrals / I Am, I Am risen inside your centralness / I Am, I Am risen to love and the centrals / I Am, I Am elect for all central sets / I Am, I Am the third day centrally / I Am, I Am the immaculate concept for the centrals / I Am, I Am immaculate in conception caught as central / I Am, I Am reached through a Mayan portal and central / I Am, I Am the instinctual balance in humanity centrally / I Am, I Am maximum within love as the centrals / I Am, I Am max amounts called central / I Am, I Am Guatemalean into the centrals / I Am, I Am worthy for all central sects / I Am, I Am written here in centralness / I Am, I Am a Christ scripted centralness / I Am, I Am a neutral sign's pleasant love centrals / I Am, I Am magical in love's lips and the central / I Am, I Am ripe in love's entertainment for all centrals / I Am, I Am right in love and the central / I Am, I Am led into love as centrally said "God's hearts" / I Am, I Am a general in love with spirit centrally / I Am, I Am rearranged within love as set in the central / I Am, I Am a charming love for all time centrally

CHAPTER THREE: I Am, I Am famous for love as central / I Am, I Am is said "love" is central / I Am, I Am casual without love as central / I AM, said "I AM" to love and the central / I AM, I live in love about centrals / I Am, I Am fed by love through a central ring / I AM, I arranged to be in love within a keynote spoken / I AM, I amount to our living love cenote's keys centrally / I Am, I Am a living love game in a central note / I Am, I Am registered to love as lifetimes allow centrally / I Am, I Am lightly loved all the centrals / I Am, I Am surest in love is central / I AM, in us all a partner to love for the central / I Am, I Am ready for love armed in your centrals / I Am, I Am a pathway for love's centrals / I Am, I Am led along love's paths and stays for the central / I Am, I Am an assignment sent to love and the lifts through love / I Am, I Am general without love and legitimate laughter is central / I Am, I Am a finished love for the solutions called central / I Am, I Am your final federal federation for love's landing central sets / I Am, I Am an immaculate love to all centrals / I Am, I Am the youngest for love's precisions are an aiming centralness / I Am, I Am the eldest in love and centrals / I Am, I Am found here near love insigned in centrals / I Am, I Am told three times that I AM love as central / I Am, I Am love's aim about all central / I Am, I Am an accurate love for all central respects / I Am, I have

a restitution to love as the central / I Am, I Am genuine again and loved as a central suggest / I Am, I Am always loved and as suggested, central / I Am, I Am always loved for the central / I Am, I Am YAHWEH to a central respect / I Am, I Am is magnetic inside your centrals / I Am, I Am a magnet in love and centralness / I Am, I Am Michael for the central / I Am, I Am Ariel again, the central / I Am, I Am Metatron and the signs read as central / I Am, I Am is the name of love and living centrals / I Am, I Am a savior for love for the central / I Am, I Am suggested for love into the central / I Am, I Am self-driven in life's paring of lessen in love for the central / I Am, I Am forgiven for pastness to love's centrals / I Am, I Am newly located in love for the central / I Am, I Am the music of love centrally / I Am, I Am able, after all, to love gained centrally / I Am, I Am partnered freely in love as a central suggestion / I Am, I Am passionate again in love as your centrals / I Am, I Am a fellow for love and the theoretic centralness / I Am, I Am genuine in love's centrals / I Am, I Am a friend to love aimed in centralness / I Am, I Am the lightest gift to love's centrals / I Am, I Am able to love your central seeds / I Am, I Am genuine about love's central gifts / I Am, I Am after all a reaction to love's chemistry slips and central rewards / I AM, let us be aptly in love and life's centralness / I AM, I Am gentle about love for the central / I Am, I Am intact for love's central races / I Am, I Am passionate about loves' ruling centralness / I Am, I Am partnered into love's central rays / I Am, I Am precious in love for the central / I Am, I Am the perfect example of love red in the central ion fields / I Am, I Am precisely affectionate in love for the essential centrals / I Am, I Am an exact reflection of love for the central / I Am, I Am a perfect south sea's pearly gate into layered friends and currency spent in central winds.

CHAPTER FOUR
Delphi, delphi fine in a central oracle / fatima, fatima created your helenistic oracle centrals / lourdes, lourdes in the sky blue centrals / concurrent, concurrent to the invent, I AM love, centrally / phrases, phrases are the praises for the evidence in central love / patents, patents in love and centrals / purchase, purchase the nearing centralness for love / slip, slip into glistening centralness / ranches, ranches in chances and simmering central spots / spots, spots and the sun's rising central heat / participate, participate within, centrally / reassure, reassure respect for the central / thirteen, thirteen who meant, yes, in the centrals / arabic, arabic reaching forth and central respects of God's love / reference, reference arms your respective centralness / rapid, rapid in a respect for the central / currency, currency is sent into your centralness / lights, lights in lifted centralness / rafts, rafts are off the rocks and rising swiftly into rapids / rural, rural experience is spent for loving centralness / reach, reaches register a shoed event, walking into centralness / sunlight, sunlight is life into leading centrals / boolean, calculate your boolean formula for love and central gist / rise, rise in a risen central risk / ruses, ruses are over and the ride is into the central gifts / urges, urges and merges inside a central / ready, ready to thrive on and central lists / rubic, rubic appearances in the lifelong centrals / remain, remain inside central systems / current, current

in a roaring central license / manageable, manageable experience in the risen centralness of our savior and lord, love / may, may we experience and express the electrical genius of routes through the material centrals / rough, rough without lips on the central mouth of God / Metatron, Metatron came along to live smoothly central to God's goodness / riots, riots are over led, centrally / credible, credible amounts made real for the fallen centrals / now, now risen, live eternally in a lily blue electric pool or ripening strawberry cream swirls and whirls of tangerine koi in a showy slipper of love, centrally / as, as we have written, the gifts erupt inside, your spirit leads your ever, home, completely and centrally / manage, manage to be centrally well / reams, reams are piled upon the reaching centrals / fled, fled about to the sea of all reasonable central rifts / random, random forgivens and reaps over central sets / maintain, maintain movement for all central gists / merger, merger is made, measurably in a central list / reference, reference a randomness ripening centralness / left, left to reign, centrally / partners, partners maintained, centrally / ready -ready for the risen, centrals / ropes, ropes are off, centralness / ripening, ripening roads through the entrance and the central / aware, aware in a willing central list / mergers, mergers marry your centrals / emergent, emergent greetings centrally / recognition, recognition for the central / rely, rely for all speaking centrals / lengthen, lengthen and rise into a central intrigue for all loves / partnered, partnered partnered and plentied in the circulation's central spires / revel, revel in reading centrals / placement, placements ripe tools, gardening in centralness / bells, bells and the basically central / mutual, mutual lists in a linking centralnes / rude, rude goes to the lava reds and the central seam / mergers, mergers again, centrally / pearls, pearls line your face's central smiles.

CHAPTER FIVE

Discovers, discovers a moving interest through the central / systemic, systemic rally for the central lines / locations, locations leading past centralness / locution, locution into motions and maleable central gifts / recent, recent reaches inside a sizeable central tone / designations, designations metric meaning for all centrals / ratios, ratios icelandic for Christ central lapsed love / transcribes, transcribes pulling central leads / causes, causes into pauses and plans for the central / successive, successive and given a fellow's centrals / transcripts, transcripts ripen your centralness / governed, governed in a married central cord / mechanically, mechanically mercurial forged in finest central lights / termed, termed in a warming central space / abilities, abilities bearing on central peers / habits, habits who inhabit central pleasures / products, products isle wise inside centralness / inverts, inverts into converts and the centrals / reported, reported in meetings and centrals / empires, empires aspire for a central wed / proportions, proportions purported and central / kill, kill has come to the forgotten finally lift off, allow life, rise to central apparitions and loves / shreds, shreds in bedded centrals / blends, blends into basic centralness / balance, blanks have filled, balances meant and paid, centrally / racing, racing into demons sent home to the light and the love of God, join Christ risen releases centrally / halo, halo over all central lands / banner, banner basic too, the centrals / effective, effective rules around central finds / hills, hills climbing above the centrally working lights / band, bands ran about your centralness / reveals, reveals a reaching central date / solutes, solutes released inside central parks / singles, singles in precious central days / recall, recall a filling central rest / rectangular, rectangular ripening of all centrals / solutions, solutions solvent in finished centralness / sung, sung in sizes and central lists / dissect, dissect dealing with centrals / truths, truths ripening, centrally / figures, figures final and found in central / crosses, crosses unburdened and central then / across, across the reaching centralness / signed, signed inside and out as central / paid, paid firmly into the central / curable, curable carriage across your centrals / fled, fled firmly into the central / meanings, meanings reaching our centralness / pave, pave over the suited centrals / flotation, flotation forming a central line to love / portals, portals permanent inside central lists / mounted, mounted in counted central lights / plural, plural in empires and current central lists and licensed codes / mends, mends and the mending currency for the central / behaving behaving insides and the moons forming central / amounts, amounts to maintain a central guests lights / cores, cores swarming over the aiming centrals / mansions, mansions built inside centralness / says, says "we will" to life's gifts and the central quest for love / rewards, rewards coming for the fetish cured central nests / listening, listening blown into the central corridors / levels, levels alluring inside central places / mortal, mortal in fiber and spirits within central doors.

CHAPTER SIX

God, God grown through a tested currency centrally spent / has, has election for the central / elected, elected relativity and the russian centrals / man, man is the mission too, centrals / to, to us all a willing centralness / be, be a basic central diet / a, a window on the central / passions, passions formed a central day / pace, pace across the lands central / away, away to willing centralness / to, to us all, central days / love, love is a creation for the central lines / leading, leading inside and beside the river's central rays / wedge, wedge edging into a central light / a, a patience for central plays / flying, flying fists have gone to the central corridors of love / field, field of flowers and the centrals / mending, mending has made us, central / days, days are coming in a delivery for the central / a, a patience forming centrally / all, all is the merry central / opens, opens patiently to the cause for the central / made, made in faded less, centrals / pages, pages raging for the central lives / blend, blend into basic central respects / measured, measured mathematically into your matrice's centralness / late, late in leading centralness / sort, sort and the several centrals / adjacent, adjacent to many centrals / pace, pace is about, centrally / within, within us all, central days / suggested, suggested promotions for the central / to, to a manageable centralness / plans, plans mentioned and central / change, change came to the central / hearts, hearts opening centrally / corps, corps of the diabolic clear watered central / jump, jump into the lover's central days / giving, giving a look for the central / seas, seas are wet inside central remains / inquire, inquire about your central reigns / planets, planets placed inside central rays / seized, seized of yes into centralness / soaring, soaring has core in a central way / chinese, chinese reaches and the central / templars, templars remaining impacted for the central / nights, nights are made as the central / tends, tends trending to the central / written, written smitten centrals / chops, chops into cops and the written centrals / scottish, scottish kilted centrals / suns, suns amount to a central meadow / Iraq, Iraq allows lifts to the legends central / kilts, kilts worn less without central diagnose / sell, sell us a finished diet of signal centrals / soonest, soonest in mooning centrals / Iran, Iran ran into the crooning centrals / scores, scores swarming inside the central / shortest, shortest warming centrals / refrain, refrain written for the central / credits, credits written in interior central signs / framed, framed inside and out with central / magic, magic mentioned centrals / rational, rational magical maternal mutual central loves.

CHAPTER SEVEN
Claims, claims settled and made for the formulation of the thoraxic explore called love for the centrals / fiji, fiji meant to be a village for the freed centrally / treats, treats and painted churches reign for the formal vents called centrally love / tombs, tombs go to the central / surrendered, surrendered and mended for the central / to, to us all a central / learn, learn to be central / lifting, lifting into gifting cenrals / management, management is meant to hint at the central / lessons, lessons leading for the central / lashes, lashes extend past the centrals / fell, fell a fellowness to the centrals / means, means are managed for the central / eyes, eyes arranged in central regimes / suffered, suffered less and found more, a feast for the centrals / God, God is delicate inside the herbs of life and the lessons learned when kava breathes, cords freed, into the middles kingdom, the brown stem of man kindm centrally / given, given a giving centrals sppech / wedded, wedded in blessing centals for the fijiian happiness of love / bliss, bliss is reached fijiaian style in love central / appearing, appearing and nearing an accent in central love / insights, insights suggest central loves / along, along us leading accents for the formalness of lingering living love, the central / singing, singing arranged for the freedom in calling light and love your linked up arcturian star of gladness through centrals / wines, wines are wisest too, centrally / is, is this the all? centrally, humanity is, yes, love / kind, kind is divine, centrally / love, love is yours here near the end maximum, centrally / and, and we stand loved centrally / sharing, sharing is caring for the central / is, is this stble and able? central / to, to us all, central / nearest, nearest explanantions for the centrals / hearts, hearts held near your centrals / free, freely found central cores of the sea barrier free / with, with us all a central / wings, wings open into your seed centrals / encourage, encourage your entourage to feed on only centrals / love, love led, centrally / bear, bear is gone, centrally / on, on too, centrally / others, others and the mothers who know, centrally / with, with us all a hanging lake of central dreams / you, you are borne into the city of love green and nnetral / and, and a day is spent singing for the centrals / me, me within, centrally / everyone, everyone flying within, a central shield, a merkabah yield for all central days / and, and there will

be clearly a site for the dome of love, central / really, really due the living centrals / for, for us all, centrals / love, love lifts your centralness to One / you, you due the central / cared, cared about in love's signs and centrals / focus, focus into the central / care, care is for your centrals / for, for the days fed centrally / form, form is formation without centralness / really, really rested in centralness / forth, forth is your worth for the central / I, I am, the central / cut, cut cords now, centrally / remember, remember to nestle into the central / forgotten, forgotten island wise unto the central / measures, measures opt for the centrals / revive, revive inside the central.

CHAPTER EIGHT
Love, love is leaping centrally freed / me, me and the mission, centrals / just, just and justified, centrally / bee, bees born in wings central / honey, honey is the money for the central / and, and we stay centrally / and, and jesus said, "let there be the central cord free" / a a way through the central, sing / a, a day within the central / an, an experience freshens your centralness / tree, tree days and dues central / love, love ligths the central / like, like a quiet pace in back island days for the central / apple, apple pairs us with the cupr of celebratory centralness / is, is this your central? / to to us days of the central / me, me within, centrally / love, love languaging the central / white, white is the site for the central / think, think openly of the peaceful centrals / the, the depth within is central / of, of all who blink, cnetral / heart, heart, heads, centrals / your, your forgiveness is found, centrally / and, and we said "the central" / we, we are the star's beam through the central universal core / care, care is doored inside a central floor of stars called the milky way / for, for all and the flames central / everyone, everyone who said "yes" is central / really, really anxious has gone to the centrals / I, I am love, centrally / Love, love to be a central / it, it is your door, love is, well, central / is, is this a day for the central? / in, in a day, central / bottom, bottom basics for the central / love, love is leaping centrally / is, is there a line centrally / you, you due a centralness / me, me too, centrally fed / you, you are the freed centrals / humanity, hymanity measures your centralness / please, please to do a central day / peace, peace is fine in seasons central / be, be a basic bed for the stillness centrally/ still, still to a day central / we, w are welcome at rthe central / are, are we raving without the central? clearly listen in God / alarmed, alarmed inside? yes! still to the central / less, less a veto than a rig veda please, central / when, when is this whistle blown? currently central / God's, God's a gateway central / through, through us all a central rest / a, an aspect of the centralness to love / a, a falling filling on the central / feel, feel onto your centrals / scores, scores curing your centrals / cubes, cubes appelative centrally / clearest, clearest in dueness centrally / hope, hope nearing your centrals / coping, coping a curing centralness / shutters, shutters shouldered within by centrals / curbed, curbed in conclusive central cycles / legible, legible sizes and the centrals.

CHAPTER NINE
Core, core now sampled for the clues to the central / is, is a reason

central / trusted, trusted in loving centralness / forms, forms and the fused centrals / for, for us former centrals / fundamental, fundamentally fine in centralness / fields, fields reach a central sect / funding, funding fled over the centrals / funding, funding especial ly well for the central / fathoms, fathoms filling centrals / plans, plans purchase your central gains / maintain, maintain a mission for the central / murky, mruky meetings measured / contain, contain cured, centrally / priniciple, pinciple plans aimed in centrals / pressed, pressed on the central / pencils, pencisl bleaz in centrals / slept, slept througha central race / curtains, curtains crescents and centrals / dive, dive through remarkableness for the central / accompanies, accompaanies a central date of love / squarely, squarely a central race to love / concave, concave metals line your lifting financialness centrally / circles, circles central circumference for love / stages, stages and wages for the central / trimesters, trimesters meeting 3 places in love centrally / tiarngles, triangles refill your central days for love / mid-terms, mid-terms lining your centralness / full, fullness fields your centralness / term, terms tooling in centrals / terming, terming timing and the centrals / triggering, triggering your central suspects of love / journey, journey journeys to the central / kingdoms, kingdoms railing in the central / shades, shades participate in the central / nestle, nestle mailed in central boxes / nearly, nearly during central rests / klimt, klimt subsides centrally / meets, meets in a temple worn central / magically, magically miraculous for the current centrals / honored, honored for the central / hurling, hurling inside swirling centralness / purchased, purchased and primed in a central rest for love / places, places mentioned win centrally / portals, portals react to the central spools for lovee / coded, coded and currency road woo for the alarm fresh centrals / cabots, cabots blush in the central / worn, worn welsh winds centrally / weaves, weaves rush for the central / nature, mature in a disciple's centrals / pays, pays purged of the central 52 petals, petals initial into surging centrals / soften, soften creamy in sky day's centrals / mitigate, mitigate leaves and the sun-risen scenes forming heavenly centrals / purged, purged in parallel relations and the relatives for the central / settles, settles suggesting your centralness / overt, overt reverts inside the central / motifs, motifs married into a central resurrection / passed, passed inside your centralness / lavendar, lavendar lessons for the central / learned, learned in warm centrals / motions, motions mention your centrals / pert, pert in a worthiness for centralness to love / pulls, pulls a past over the central nets and the nervous gifts which release when love is seen centrally.

CHAPTER TEN
Shells, shells written on and spent for the formation of foundations of living centrals / properly, propeorty properly placed in trusting security for the central / placed, palced inside yours, a central portal to love / purposefully, purposefully filled in centrals / fossils, fossils filed under centrals / purchased, puechased and won, centrally / symbolic, sybmolic gifts, centralized / spear, spear shut and central / minerals, minerals measured centrally / collected, collected and bisected centrals / superb, superb and the rationale is fed a central rest / crystals, crystals ritualized without

respect for the piezo-electric qualities for the centrals / sciences, sciences reaching your centrals / guaranteed, guaranteed rainbow blue experiences for the central / prospects, prospects allow my central days / features, features follow a living central / colors, colors respite in the white lined centrals / dark violet, dark violet views central / violet-blue, violet-blue experience for the central / richness, richness fed a central rally / hardness, hardness mohr scaled centrals / specifics, specifics speak in centralness / systems, systems dealing in the centrals / orthorhombic, orthorhomibc bevy for the central / diamond, diamond adds to the central / blue, blue is a basic central / dispersions, dispersions carried into this galactic central / igneous, igneous reaping centralness / gem, gem days central / qualities, qualities qualitative to the central / eyes, eyes opening centrally / effect, effect for the central / cat's eye, cat's eye leading centrals / occuring, occuring rehearsals of the centrals / monoclinic, monocliminc creations for the central / tetragonal, tetragonal missives about the central / hexagonal, hexagonal lending of the central / regions, regions reigning centralness / brilliant, brilliant ramification for the central districts / cuts, cuts assuring your central gifts / gem, gem insuring your centralness / swiss, swiss sets and the central / darkness, darkness during your centrals / align, align a leading centralness / associations, association seeking the centrals / grains, grains grown into the central / dependent, dependent for the plural centrals / fielded, fielded missions of the centrals / giant, giant jewele in the central / worlds, worlds wielding your centrals / worldly, wordly wisdom's central / wise, wise way are honored, hear, centrally / widens, widens in wisdom for the central / common, common courage in caring centralness / bivalves, bivalves reduced to one centralness / considerations, considerations for the central / tours, tours treating your centralness / basking, basking i basic forgive and the filling centrals / fasting, fasting is fed into central revamps / prior, prior is the precious central / penalty, penalty poring into the centrals / masks, masks inferior to the reality for the central / ends, ends in reaching centralness / earth, earth is welcome for the centrals.

CHAPTER ELEVEN
Knowing, knowing in the showing showering centralness / forces, forces for the central / allow, allow a shilling spent on centralness / beauty, beauty is the basic for the central / code, code is the kahuna way, centrally / to, to a mission spent for the cycles central / educate, educate your set as central / this, this is the threshold into the central / sphere, spheres produce centralness / this, this chance has come to the central / magical, magical in meetings for the central / place, place a passover the central / this, this thanks for the central / earthly, earthly mundance and the sane centrals / eden, eden freedom andthe centrals / called, called a cure central / kumara, kumara for the freshest landing centrals / nests, nests rational for the central / a a place centrals / breathing, breathing reaches the centrals / an, an elevation for the centrals / aha, aha rules the scene, centrally / stand, stand days centrals / the, the raspberry duration of the centrals / lessens, lessens leys and the latice of the central / away, away into the central / out, out to shout with, "centrals" / of, of the earned, a central / embody,

embody a basic centralness / plenty, plenty appearing centrally / abundant, abundant to the better centrals / sank, sank into the central / place, places allowed, centrally / has, has too, centrals / been, been is being central / allowed, allowed a filling centralness / aka, aka is met, centrally / cord, cord cut and heard? centralness / has, hast thou a central? / cut, cut the cord, now, centrally / this, this the umbilical of the earth, bali, centrals / comes, comes a cured centrals / a, a parrot speaks centrally / new, new costa rican centralness / coasts, coasts antigu blue in the central / ceep, deep int eh amazon stringing centrally / in, in us all emotion celebrates the central / atlantean, atlantean leading centralness / pockets, pockets bolivian to the lakes central / fearless, fearless packages for teh central / planes, planes parisian and central / creeds, creeds maintain your centrals / expanse, expanse is expensive iwthout the centrals / God, God given the central / earthquake, earthquakes zoning your stationery centrals / details, details well in the central / contours, contours coupled in the central / hawaiian, hawaiian healing your centrals / lemurian, lemurian remember came to the fore, central / plunged, plunged inside and found the centrals realized / gel, gel wet in central sets / spanned, spanned and evoked for the central / western, western towns experienced near Mazama central / fun, fun fed the central.

CHAPTER TWELVE
Chambered, chambered gazes country wide into the central / by, by the basics flanked and central / hearts, hearts stretch to acknowledge the let go of the centrals / of, of the kept, centrals / pele, pele filling the tiki gods pay-off for the lava land central / pairs, pairs are made for the oracle central / 100, 100 who knew the central / ways, ways are willing centrally / effortless, effortless reaching for the central star travelers / leys, leys lead our list homeward central suns / transport, transport is through the central suns / sunsun is signed now, centrally / toto us all rays are red with centralness / the, the area found in centrals / universal, universal amounting to measures central / child, child for the fellows central / saviors, saviors sent to new lands for the central / cords, now the cords are cut, released centrally / cut, cut the quick centrals / balances, balances equal your sword's central cuts / choose, choose the mellow centrals / light, light is operatic through the centrals / led, led home now to the central isles for love / flames, flames flash the centrals / factors, factors feather the centrals / pacepace over the centrals / porches, porches built over the centrals / burned, burned plenty for the centrals / breath, breath given a central gift / clears, clears encounters closely, centrals / love, love is the albuquerque blue expire within the centrals / reigns, reigns a rapture for the central kachina's zuni danced / middle, middle mended materials and the perspire gone to the centrals / of, of us all, central lists / hearts, hearts exploring your centralness / explores, explores passionate dancing for the central clarity / mankinds, mankinds matters central / kindest, kindest rages are centrally cleared / waves, waves fulfilled centrally / wonder, wonder is willing to see your centrals / wins, wins elevated centrally / able, able to be centrally / belief, belief is basic to the central / guides, guides clering a central / psychically, psychically a

clear suggestion for the central / clear, clear and central / egyptian, egyptian sands central / history, history pusedeo central / through, through thorough central / peoples, peoples central / ocassions, been, been is being central / allowed, allowed a filling centralness / aka, aka is met, centrally / cord, cord cut and heard? centralness / sleeping, sleeping in central / spills, spills off the central / mules, born into mules central / gone, gone to a central with a / awakens, awakens in central / a, a ley central / meaning, meaning meaning a central / musicall, musicall manied central / well, wells deep in centrals / in, in too central / deed, deed on central.

CHAPTER THIRTEEN
Deeds, deeds opened centrally / are, are with central / gained, gained in a freedom central / as, caddum as the central / children, children on a central sign / rise, rise on a sign central / freedom, freedom's central / felt, felt of central / lords, lords cut to central simplify / cut, cut and set for central sign / brothers, central / live, live central / drama, drama over central / dealt, dealt in central / doors, doors off central / purged, purged of the beastly central / planetary, planetary central / central, centrallines won / poem, poem on central / kingdom, kingdom of the central / message, message central / magic, magic of the central / running, running in central / energies, energies central / delphic, delphic signs central / oracles, oracles and a central one / melody, melody is central / students, student central / nations, nations who kneel in central respect for love / undertook, undertook a fashion for love centrally / candles, candles cured a central nook / blessed, blessed be the centrals / richly, richly speaking for love, the central / world, world of the wellest centrals / opportunity, opportunity marries your centrals / august, august for the centrals / self, self said choices and the maternally central / spirit, spirit is speaking a centralness / boats, boats afloat in spiritual reprise and centrals / knights, knights of nightly ventures into the depths of the central / women, women who journey into the centrals / flax, flax is effective for the central / trees, trees pieced for the centrals / wove, wove a welcom clearing central / small, small days centrally / sheep, sheep gathered leave centrally / ours, ours the steep centrals / public, public speaking about the centrals / light, light is the linking lemon aid stand for love centrals / foot, foot on the top centrals / powers, powers being central / golden, golden glowing centrals / living, living a final giving central / lights, lights listed as central / aspire, aspire near the central / orchids, orchids peachy in paired sands centrals / alternates, alternates marry the coming sandy centrals / artifacts, artifacts given the ganesh diction for the centrals / supply, supply the basic buddhist flights to the centrals / vanities, vanites flared into the centrals / oblong, oblong givings of the centrals / uniform, uniform living inside a central / shelters, shelters built by the centrals / depths, depths dealing for the central.

LEVEL 74: THE PORTAL-MENTS

CHAPTER ONE

Relationships, relationships central to the portal of friendly loves / relativity, relativity is reached in recorded rewarded portals / relative, relative in relaxation for the finished portals / central, central respect for the central / repairs, repairs in the stricture's structures forgiven and portals / rewards, rewards reissued for the love due a portal / views, views and a vacuum forgotten in fixed portals / products, products who match your structured portals / carts, about central portals, love / carry, carry out the portals of love / nerve, nerves are the ports about your senses / temples, temples on air and the central ports in tune / repairs, repairs into central ports and the senses of scenes / fears, fears off the central poortals / omens, omens out, love is in, a portal clears / stories, stories about your portals / goddess, goddess for the goods and the swords portals / bounces, bounces into a goddess portal / rebuilt, rebuilt a city from the portal atlantean / nature, nature is new in a portals / window, windows mixed in your portals / remember, remember too, your portals / cleverness, cleverness clues your portals / powerless, powerless without your portals collapsed / love, love of the gaining portals / sinking, sinking into your portals / ash, ash weeds out the portal imports / moves, moves inside your portals / moved, moved into a portals / actually, actually a granted portal / underground, underground portals opened / finding, finding a treasure sunken into love's portals / anyone, anyone in the new portals / open, open a door into these portals / forces, forces focus in our portals / returning, returning in the simple cretean shores of the focus of revelations and the reason john spake so well about these times and the place of reunion in human kind, a living portal in Greece / six, six is the number of the original gifts, the ones who came to reproduce into humanity, a portal / released, released an influential spawn called the sparks of true love, a light portal / both, both may seek the mystery for the portals of this, the good, earth / sheets, sheets are ripped in the strips called portals / jolts, jolts mature in the earth's quaking shielded portals / ride, ride a round cycled portal / stop, stop and seek these portals / warrior, warrior for the visible sets of portals / size, size has come to the summary of love's portals / gem, gem stoned openings into portals / shrinking, shrinking aims to the choices made, island portals / primate, primate the sate for the portals / tiny, tiny in the tilliation of the tantric portals / elite, elite sets find an aphrodisiac called portals / eggs, eggs frozen into these portals / killed, killed a spare without these portals / devils, devils are gone to these portals / gate, gate opens portal wise / watching, watching is costing less for these portals / might, might is instead the deed for these portals / celebrate, celebrate the freedom for your huge move's portals / imagine, imagine every lover portals / ten, ten in dimensions and portals / water, water is well, a profitable portal / ourselves, ourselves the kind who seek these portals / estimate, estimate your departure date as the temple for these portals / 37, 37 is the day for the leaving portal / chimney, chimney days and the fire in portals.

CHAPTER TWO

Lightening, lightening strikes near your dear portals / lifted, lifted portals / balls, balls falling into seas and portals / funny, funny waves leave your portal / fine, finest sands and the sunny portals of Malaysia / airlines, airlines linking your portals deep into the archipalego called humanity / frequent, frequent your portals / planes, planes are meant for these portals / aerobic, aerobic frequency for the arabic basis of love's portals / mass, mass spins equals energy, a portal / olympics, olympics offer a greek smile, santorini wins, a portal / biopsy, biopsy due the Andeman way, a portal / rank, rank is without a portal / pool, pool for the wildness and the living lizards portals 15 faster, faster fills your portals / generate, generate the romance for your portals / study, study your portals / peace, peace is the oxygen for the puzzles and the places of portals / weekends, weekends are meant for these portals / volume, volume swimming in a portal / swim, swim in the watery pools of the marley band, love is the jamacian portal / suppose, suppose the ports in love are your ears / state, state that your navel is located in lush green portals / pitch, pitch a plenty the level is won, a portal / india, india is green in the teas of your portals / must, must must go, a portal / flags, flags filling your vision in letting go, a portal / timber, timber is trimmer when left to the stars of a portal / holland, holland is mulled deep into limbering portals / fossil, fossil filling portals / rain, rain is ocho deep in the blue portals / earth, earth is the memory for the relations of portals / pasta, pasta is plenty for the appropriate energy of a portal / complex, complex carbohydrates swim in opening portals / era, era for the imagination claled a portal / drifted, drifted into sifted portals / above, above is alive inside your portals / animals, animals merge into portals / pact, pact made, elect a portal to keep / reefs, reefs are reckoned into portals / eyebrows, eyebrows are basic for framing two portals / struggle, struggle is gone, a portal opens / thank, thank God for your portals / wall, wall of chinese portals / peacock, peacock blue portals / jars, jars are opening into their portals / wave, wave for the perfect portal / small, small is the mistle to the portals / looters, looters go to the lower portals / soul, soul is the seal now peeled away into portals / reach, reach is made, portal free / heavens, heavens are healing your portals / explorers, explorers east and away linking the portals / link, link your blinking portals / lands, lands are leaped across portals / lighthouse, lighthouse leading a portal / dawn, dawn into own, portals / path, path is relative to a purchased portal / snakes, snakes go to the transformative flow of all portals / involved, involved have found a winning portal / work, work is aholic into the browned portals / huge, huge investment made, paying off, a portal / landslide, landslides past a portal / leverage, leverage applied for the formulaic portals, math.

CHAPTER THREE

Arms, arms are worn without portal flecks / sandstone, sandstone lines in the levels paradise sent to the portals / aton, the sun disk said " a portal is human" / temple, temple of the simple portals / kings, kings are rings inside a portal / moreover, moreover the portals wins / inscriptions, inscriptions written into these portals / leaps, leaps made, find a reef inside a stem's portals / recognized, recognized for your monuments and the exports into your portals / indian, indian ocean's affluent portal / harbor, harbor healed in these portals / size, size wise portals / titles, 7 titles written and reigns a portal / stylus, stylus written portals / styles, styles on a portal / matters, matters won and into a portals / correspondence, correspondence of our portal / cultures, cultures on a portal / ethnographic, enthnographic pent and portals / rely, rely on a recall's portal / continues, continues within and portals / details, details of the portals / pioneers, pioneers on a positive portal / percentage, percentage on a true portal / contained, contained and ran too, portals / pulls, pulls and plans in portals / patient, patient in a portal / powers, powers be portals / widths, widths over portals / purchased, purchased wins portals / sales, sales on portals / suggest, suggest on portals / blocks, blocks off and portals / optical, optical shown portals / golden, golden gazed portals / upper, upper wayed portals / transcribed, transcribed in portals / sparks, sparks flew to portals / flowers, flowers stand in portals / reaches, reaches out a portal / emphasis, emphasis for a portal / probable, probable for a portal / classically, classically yours, portals / watched, watched over, portals / luxuries, luxuries on a portal / details, details into a portal / maintained, maintained stance, portals / waivers, waivers knot, portals / signed, signed on too, portals / ages, ages and reaches portals / proportional, proportional reaches and portals / practiced, practiced and reward and portals / diameters, diameters due and portals / thousands, thousands handed, portals / delights, delights on a portals / investigates, investigates over, portals / clear, clear enough's portals / years, years tone, portals / awesome, awesome soon, portals / forms, forms of portals / exists, exists in portals / rectangles, rectangles due portals / images, images pale in portals / unions, unions made and portals.

CHAPTER FOUR

Social, social suits and portals / opposites, opposites wed, portals / fed, fed on, portals / feeding, feeding ours, portals / realms, realms reached portals / ways, ways daring portals / meal, meal for a portals / meals, meals wheel in portals / diverse, diverse when a portals / converses, converses caring a portals / stolen, stolen without portals / steals, steals gone, portals / complements, complements allow to portals / empowered, empowered and a portal / shrugs, shrugs off a portal / said, said yes! to portals / shambhola, shambhola walks through portals / rectangles, rectangles soon in portals / sacred, sacred ran your portals / forms, forms laid a portals / architecture, architecture for a portal / limits, limits soon and portals / limited, limited lends for, portals / winds, winds win one in a portal / humor, humor bodied portals / extends, extends ran to portals / crafted, crafted for a portal / rafts, rafts opened a portal / golden, golden rays portals / diagrams, diagrams due a portals / elevate, elevate your esteemed portals / waves, waves onto portals / rafters, rafters reach a portal / clearest, clearest cares portals / paths, paths lock portals / rekindled, rekindled when, portals / beams, beams placed in portals / gems, gems stemming

a portal / neevly, neevly wed to a portal / architect's, architect's ran to portals / planks, planks and banks of portals / code, code made in portals / cores, cores soar a portal / gems, gems stand and portals / clean, clean day's in portals / joined, joined won portals / jewelry, jewelry joins plan's portals / sent, sent made a portals / treasury, treasury travel portals / treasures, treasures travel portals / props, props form and portals / probes, icicle probes laid in portals / Evangeline, Evangeline lined portals / harmonics, harmonics held in portals / music, music marries your portals / rocks, rocks array to portals / fields, fields e-merging, portals / chords, chords carried and portals / symphonic, symphonic suggested portals / rests, rests amaze a portal / respect, respect raised and portals / requires, requires a rapt portal / regards, regards blue portals / rates, rates raised portals.

CHAPTER FIVE

Registry, registry paid portals / acknowledge, acknowledge of portals / knaoa, knaoa on portals / receipts, receipts of "a" portals / routed, routed paths, portals / arches, arches wade, portals / hosiery, hosiery's seed and portals / millet, millet spent a portals / patents, patents on, portals / pay, pay your, portals / paves, paves of love's portals / inquire, stars inquire "a" portals / padded, padded environments end in portals / heated, heated in seated portals / sides, sides in arrivals to the repentinent portals / expire, expire for the hired portals / imperfection, imperfection is since your portals / attempts, attempts are entrained into your portals / reached, reached for the humming portals / disks, disks are dared too, a portal / walls, walls wield your portals a placed / life, life is left to these portals / time, time is the lime inside your green portals / Jewish, Jewish is jewels up into a portal / edited, edited inside your portals / interpretation, interpretation for their portals / essential, essentially total into peach portals / tents, tents are aligned astride your portals / ancient, ancient insects and repetitive portals / ways, ways are landed for the portals / religion, religion is rainbow red in portals / essay, essay said " aportal" / king, king for the causes portals / hymn, hymn is stepped through your portals / individual, individual letters written inside a portal / earnest, earnest is yearning for the portals / intuition, intuition cherry blue and portals / labors, labors lost have founda portal / model, model for the material portals / modify, modify a plan into a portal / love's, love's our portals / manner, manner is the manner too, a portal / mediocrity, mediocrity allowing portals / yearns, yearns a squirming portal / stupendous, stupendous shrining mortals and portals / streaming, streaming in shrines and hte signs inside portals / dreaming, dreaming reaches over a portal / dazzle, dazzle is razzle free for the water portals / cautions, cautions are cured as portals / remains, remains in reaction too, a portal / formations, formations emotions and the lasting portals / witness, witness and the lasting portals / crept, crept into respect for the portals / homecoming, homecoming reaching your portals / love, love laid into portals / organic, organic and manic portals / past, past is the rationale for these portals / domain, domain into reasons and potals / source, source inside a portal / seek, seek a released portal / philosophic, philosophic bents and portals / cherished, cherished mention of portals / sought, sought is route deep in portals / roots, roots in mute and gone, portals

CHAPTER SIX: originates, originates in relates and portals / digressing, digressing interests in portals / causes, caises create potent laharian portals / engineered, engineered in spills and these portals / explore, explore mount penatubo for the living portals / earth, earth is special to humanity's duration / discover, discover the lover in you and sparest portals / heard, heard a word for their portals / simple, simple in sample portals / folds, folds and folded portals / crowded, crowded in rough days and portals / crowns, crowns and the roses answered as portals / simple, simple in skipping portals / folds, folds federal too, the portals / crowded, crowded inclusions and the creation for your portals / crowns, crowns and the reigning portals / angels, angels are shouldered with a portal / souls, souls released too, the portals / truth, truth is rewarded now, a portal / love, love is legible in your written portals / serene, serene in instinctual portals 22 dangers, dangers finish your portals / spirits, spirits past and then portals / external, external random dots connected for these portals / physicality, physicality featured a sun spot's portals / touches, touches turning to a portal / certain, certain solar suspects warm in portals / dimensions, dimensions are radioactive for the mineral stormed portals / Due, due is dear, portals / tatters, tatters forming a portal / profoundly, profoundly formed aspects for these portals / present, present is present formations and portals / steering, steering is dear in a portal / influences, influences end your past portals / freed, freed in deed and in light and in love a terrestrial portal / models, models who meet in a final portal / peace, peace is in placements for the feeling portals / curious, curious about reasons and portals / prayers, prayers are peaceful in spiral portals / screens, screens are seeking a material portal / walks, walks are willing into a portal / flights, flights are feeling you flight into portals / solid, solid in simple porjects and a portal / objects, objects are current in hawaiian portals / insure, insure your simple portals / language, language is lively inside a homeward portal / expire, expire in simple perspire for a homelands portal / express, express a prescient portal / universal, universal in respect for portals / human, human healing portals / exterior, exterior in surest protals / experience, experience retful portals / bitter, bitter is ended in powerful portals / comments, comments carry into your portals / journey, journey across lands for the final portal blends / purify, purify yourself and the senses precise into a portal / judge, judge is joining a forgiven portals / commands, commands creative into a portal / things, things are thrust forward and back into a portal / originate, originate a rather material portal / forgive, forgive a filling portal / pathway, pathway patches and portals / process, process is perfectly portal deep / proceed, proceed over the valley portals.

CHAPTER SEVEN
Surrender, surrender in signs and portals / visions, visions who

vary into your portals / messages, messages marry a portal / perceived, perceived and noticed as deepened portals / surge, surge is open, portals / perceptions, perceptions are pared on signs and portals / seen, seen in a delicate portal / heard, heard a healed protal sing / simply, simply music to the ears and portals / thresholds, thresholds held over and valued in portals / valley, valley viewed portals / fields, fields are fellowing portals / sacred, sacred om portals / greens, greens are gallery wise in portals / seats, seats are simple portals / impose, impose a patient portl / bounds, bounds are basically human portals / boundaries, boundaries basic and portal placements / imagine, imagine a married portal / perceive, perceive a perfect portal / positions, positions shifting, portals / years, years are yellow in portals / works, works are wed to portals / mentors, mentors are matching portals / meansmeans made real to portals / banks, banks in links to portals / intinate, initiate a reachable portal / relates, relates are relative to portals / describe, describe a wider portal / inscribe, inscribe your rules to portals / pool, pool landed portals / facts, facts featured, portals / proceed, proceed to a portal / procedures, procedures practiced into portals / pens, pens deepen your portals / ceiling, ceiling and the lasted portals / seals, seals incised into portals / visuals, visuals poetic into a portal / arrow, arrow reaps portals / diplomas, diplomas bestowed in the snowing canyons of santa fe blue portals / perception, perception ir ripe into portals / moments, moments to meaning and portals / arrows, arrows linking you to portals / finished, finished a final portal / bases, bases and basically portals / plans, plans are perfect inside your portals / present, present in simple portals / discuss, discuss a house built inside portals / needs, needs next and thanks for portals / subjects, subjects rely upon portals / specials, specials seeking a portal / forgives, forgives finest portals / values, values are valuable for the few who remember original portals / surrender, surrender about your portals / chapels, chapels ringing a portals / plans, plans are pent without portals gapes / considers, considers a capable protal as cleared / historical, historically reached portals / words, words are heard for the fullest portals / details, details arranging themselves, believe, a portal opnes / considerations, considerations capable of portal keeps / questions, questions who carry for the fleshy portals / portrayals, portrayals purchased and fought for inside a portals / chisels, chisels cheapened without procedural portals.

CHAPTER EIGHT:
Rights, rights are given a portals gifts / presence, presence inside a risen portal / India, India reigns about the living portals / practical, practical pieces are given a final presence for all portals / formulas, formulas finish your placement in portals / James, james is the book behind the missile implode called a protal / john, john is the writing friend called a portal / taught, taught to be a portal / serves, serves a living, portal / services, services meant for all protals / simple, simple is the why? portal in / projects, projects on too, portals / prior, prior frails go to the ways and portals / days, days are alive into portals / finish, finsih a level, portal / cups, cups fill, portals / fill, fill a day, portals / places, places and

pens and thin portals / passes, passes california flown into portals / possible, possible for peels eagle high to a portal / enjoy, enjoy a momentary portal / filled, filled in seals and signs portals / earth's, earth's brush is along your loud portals / billions, billions armed for the free portals / stressed, stressed has end, now, portals / full, full in a flush for the portals / centrally, centrally a currency of portals / most, most who view us are portals / play, play a limit to the limitless protals / warrants, warrants are eyed for your portals / host, host of the heard portals / sang, sang a nearest portal / consecrates, consecrates a sailing ortal / fragments, fragments crossed into portals / gather, gather the peace and the portals yearned / chips, chips chapters and the sales made into portals / corresponds, corresponds cure allowed a portal / connect, connect aroused and purchased as an option and portal / age-less, age-less lessons and portals / fees, fees paid for theoretical portals / fond, ford fed a protal med / compile, compile smiles and learns a portal wins / compact, compact cures and sure portals / cords, cords patch into a portals / focusing, focusing into portals / sourced, sourced mercury and living purest in portals / sorting, sorting a surest portal / cut, cut the cure into a portal / curative, curative creations and mentionable portals / sweets, sweets shed a portal / song, song since a portal wins / suggested, suggested airs and spares portals / papers, papers rolled, days strolled, and listening lets go to life's portals / fly, fly for your loving portals / floods, floods, muds, and rushing into portals / come, come home to a portal of love / carotine, carotine in a mean orange dream for the prime state called portal / rules, rules are off, a portal / orange, orange pines and bouganvillea dreams in the red respect for love, a portal / intent, intent is mentioned, a protal / invents, invents our own portals / space, space is made, a protals / forthright, forthright through funded portals / lens, lens lined your precious portals.

CHAPTER NINE

Path, path thrrown to portals / partner, partners made and portals blow open / found, found a friendly portal for love / unbound, unbound has wound to a portal / bathing, bathing inside an instinct for a portal / notations, rotations reaching portals of love / stations, stations found instinctually and round an open portal / light, light is on, a portal reigns / lifting, lifting arms and signs thorugh a portal / linkages, linkages and blinking into portals / loaned, loaned a line to the american dreaming portals / love, love is a portal / honored, honored and kept for a portals / births, births afforded portals / benefit, benefit made for bereft good-bye and the letting be of all portals / find, find a friendly portal / coda, coda made a portal / ecogical, ecologically realized portals / patented, patented patented portals / feeding, feeding in fellow portals / suggests, suggests a rispened portal / trails, trails pale horsed end, protals / courses, courses are written for all portals / fescue, fescue grown above all portals / exact, exact masses portals / traces, traces elated in portals / sunder, sunder in wonder and gaining openings for all portals / tender, tender in ending portals/ embrace, embrace acknowledged and portals / truth, truth in a rind of all peeling portals / yon, you aim into winning portals / shoots, shoots along lines and portals / showers, showers whoering portals / constant, constant in cured

portals / contrasts, contrasts nimble in simple portals / compiled, compiled compilations and crafts for the portals / cast, cast is last? portals / edicts, edicts smile inside portals / Buddha, Buddha is blessed for all portals / totals, totals meet in christ lined portals / capable, capable of complete portals / detached, detached in places called portal branched / capacity, capacity curing your branches / folly, folly is over, a proof for all profitable portals / lats, lats are listed inside your portals / fused, fused lines and the oracles for portals / fusions, fusions wed your webs portals / aspects, aspects and the sites for your portals / liberations, liberations gift is a final portal / opus, opus planned, a portal / written, written ripening portals / joy, joy gifts a portal's lights / God, God grew into portals / intense, intense declares require portals / develops, develops magical portal / finally, finally fills inside portals / finds, finds friendly portals in life / listen, listen in our portals / discourse, discourse daring your portals / reads, reads ripening in your portals / yearns, yearns paid in a portal / strong, strong in stinging portals / listen, listen now, portals / well, well welling in portals.

CHAPTER TEN

Markets, markets marry your portals / mangoes, manages meetings and portals / sequels, sequels written, spctacular unto a portal / secular, secular marriages found European portals / eaten, eaten often for championships and portals / bliss, bliss is the ridden portal / joys, joys grand and a portal pures / peels, peels a mealing portal / scriptures, scriptures ripen, a portals / raptures, raptures peer into living protals / claims, claims made? portals / details, details filed inside portals / affords, affords worninside portals / peace, peace into portals / yearns, yearns arming your portals / more, more movement into portals / reasons, reasons best in a portal / attend, attend the lent for a protal / ascend, ascend due a portal / meal, meal made and eaten for a new portal / well, well in a stomach's portals / made, made filled and portal / plans, plans architect is a portal / primary, primary poses and portals / question, questions asked? portals kept / selves, selves have led to a complete portal / selfish, selfish without a worn portal / goodbye, good-bye now coming to past days portals / carefully, carefully fed a curious sort called portals / seek, seek became led to a portal / found, found a friendly portal's end / trip, trip made and protal built / wish, wish upon portals kep / sai, sai is the sign for a portal / baba, baba bade us, "portals" / gift, gift is found, a portals / explains, explains around inclusive portals / consciousness, consciousness presents your portals new sights / well, well wishing field sof a portals / nature, nature needs you near portals / control, controls are cured in a portal / sensed, sensed in signal portals / subtle, subtle signs and a portal / waves, waves swam and lights on inside opened portals / waiver, waiver willed? a portal / less, less is made a clear portal / people, people peopled and portals / know, know a future appearings portals / shape, shape and the nape of the protal / wife, wife is wed, portals / buys, buys paid and a profitable portal / moon's, moon's missions and portals / role, role and the rules for portals / energy, energy is wild into portals / fills, fills are led to portals / sundry, sundry in rendered portals / field, fields full of portals / with, with us all a portal / magnetic, magnetically armed too, portals / describe, describe a daring portal / oceans, oceans met in portals / soil, soil dates your portals / lifted, lifted lips to drinking in a portal / full, full enough to seek a new portal.

CHAPTER ELEVEN
Supplements, supplements and simple streets for portals / pore, pore and the dreads cut for all possible portals cleared / portals, portals held informaitonal to love / pound, pound for down and too, portals / pinched, pinched in inspired portals / fortunes, fortunes imagined and gained inside portals / jealous, jealous can go to less, portals / reverse, reverse the nerve's flow into portals / finds, finds and the final fields formed in portals / funds, funds managed portals / powerful, powerful pulses and portals / weapons, weapons aorn and tossed into portals / wisdom, wisdom worn into portals / rules, rules yellow for all protals / ranges, ranges roused inside / gather, gathering gathering portals / guilding, guilds built in caste ended portals / avatar, avatar married a portal kept / self, self said "portals" / realize, realize the risen portals / unfolds, unfolds meaning and portals / ages, ages raised ito portals / self, self made, a portals / acknowledge, acknowledge yes! inside portals / devotes, devotes motile portals spread / spans, spans and the palns remanded for the protals / self, self again, the third shelf is sealed inside a human portal / knowledge, knowledge in a college for portals / devotee, devotee found a newest portal / stages, stages raging into portals / self, self set four, a portal / known, known as serving portals / liberal, liberal illegal without a portal / spells, spells spelling a portal / spoils, spoils surge into leading portals / words, words revealing portal / deeds, deeds and reader's portals / becoming, becoming a basic portal / active, active inside a sizeable portal / made, made yellow in a flashing portal / sunships, sunships in thin lips and raspberry portals / words, words are heard throughout portals / souls, souls aloft in lifted rememberance that ultimately all is one portal / fellows, fellows mellow inside a portal / consequence, consequence spent inside portals / follows, follows a mission and a miracle still inside potals / activities, activities nearing your portals / divine, divine inspire forming arrowed portals / melody, melody misting and portals / obtain, obtain realms for a near portal / activities, activities heavenward into portals / peace, peace is a praise about portals / body, body basic to a portal / sustain, sustain reaching ringing portals / care, care is worn without portals / cry, cry has gone into a portal's mouth / worlds, worlds collide in xibalba be, a portal / octaves, octave rang inside portals / core, core cured in spare portals / lord, lord of linkages and protals / enjoy, enjoy the tube rides and all portals / peace, peace is a shining portal / supreme, supreme in appreciation for the living portals / light, light is a lesson for the portals.

CHAPTER TWELVE
Phenomenal, phenomenal foods and final portals / pleasing, pleasing into easing portals / postures, postures enhanced and anonymity maintained in your portals / times, times are made for our better, best portals / muse, muse is the mood for a portal

/ sacred, sacred amounting and the final portals / phonicsphonics label a portal / happy, happy for all portals / comncentrates, concentrtes rally your portals / yearning, yearning interior portals / still, still softening portals / hebrew, hebrew into a ranges portals / rates, rates amplify into portals / flame, flame fashions your portals / light, light given into portals / orange, oranges and the ranges for portals / blues, blues basics and portals / burning, burning insights for portals / details, details during your portals / feeling, feeling sprung by all portals / inn, inns and reigns portals / kept, kept cured and resurrected portals / keeps, keeps lift into portals / sustain, sustain a random tank for all portals / higher, higher in precision for the chosen portals / claims, claims aft portals / life's, life's our portal / fluid, fluid into portals depths / partnered, partnered in a pearl's portals / stand, stands electricity for a portal / strands, strands shorn inside portals / kept, kep creativity to a portal / declarative, declarative features and final portals / statements, statements detailed inspired portals / still, still daily in portals/ surgery, surgery demanded now over your portals / sparrows sparrows particular to a field floral in love, the portal / aid, aid is raid free for portals / hawks, hawks held to portals / rest, rested portals / pistons, pistons pulsing astride a portal / motors, motors mergers and portals / legs, legs flayed to portals / rush, rush inspires portals / burn, burn a basic wilderness to portals / churn, churn is managed for all formal portals / requires, requies a welcome portal / met, met a maverick fresh in portals / man's, man's method and portals / kind, kind in strides and portals / heaven's, heaven's pointed wonders and welcomes too, a portal / devote, devote your note to the welcome portals / undertaken, undertaken rhythms and reasonable portals / varieties, varieties vary for portals / temples, temples inside a portal / purged, purged equipment and portals / devotes, devotes respect to a portals / sent, sent for portals / compass, compass drained? portals / strokes, strokes inovked in strips and poles for battery fed protals / swallow, swallow the willow's portals / meat, meat is neat inside a portal / of, of us few and portals / charity, charity armed in portals.

CHAPTER THIRTEEN
Sacrifice, sacrific lures your portals / ends, ends bends and portald / form, gotmd msfr in portals / found, given found instincts for pleasure's portals / highest, highest holds on all portals called / ground, ground stroked portals / good, goods lapse past a portal / lays, lays and leathery portals tossed / lanes, lanes and structures portals / loves, loves artful into portals / waters, waters inspire a portal / example, examples for your portals / sample, sample estates and pre-set portals / ensue, ensue a musical portal / mood, moods and nudes lift to portals / glee, glee is good and portals / press, press inspires a portal / tuner, tuner into a portal / now, now is the detail for portals / testing, testing is rested anbd portal free / entails, entails rails and a reasonable portal / forces, forces are the steel portals / elects, elects resurrections for portals / ends, ends mend inside portals / dhrma's, dharma's expire and a portal / poison, poison is out for a portal / precious, precious and pleasing into all portals / offers, offers fed us our portals / nature, natures nudges your portals / sought, sought interest in a portal /

•

thought, thoughts thanking a portal / made, made a melloness for portals / green, greens gracefula nd frankest for portals / peaceful, peaceful places and ohana for portals / vales, vales and the values of portals / exist, exist near the rocks lava blue with magnetic poles and pure portals / employ, employ basic portals / enjoy's, enjoy's our portals blink / guide, guide a good to portals / lostllost in sizes and portals / spurts, spurts measured and portals deal with finishing days / in, in a side and a welcome portal / red, red rays portals forgiven / entail, entail sailing and portals upon th horizon / intrigues, intrigues interest is in a portal / coolest, coolest cotings and portals / respect, respect the respect for portals / left, left to believe in and portals / direct, dirct in directives and portals / laser, laser pink and green portals blend in floral occupy / ions, ions scion and portals / electrical, electrical creatures and the portals kept in love / armatures, armatures worn into portals / positions, positions aiming for alignments and portals / forthright, forthright flush and portal worn / trips, trips and lips and armed portals / assigns, assigns managed as your portals send / designs, designs during your portals / calvin, calvin melded into portals / freeze, freeze allowed a formal day into earth's portals / frequent, frequent a recent portal / insistence, insistence is in existence for formal ends to a portal / captires, captives are active for the flowering portals / capable, capable to trigger too, portals.

LEVEL 75: THE PLACE-MENTS

CHAPTER ONE

Golden, golden played places / swords, swords onto places / worth, worth into places / days, days onto places / pertinent, pertinent parers stay places / permamant, permamant rays places / panels, panels ports places / pens, pens written places / plausible, plausible places / pluses, pluses amazed for in a place / portals, portals onto dealings allow places / planned, planned on places / purchased, purchased introductions / portions, portions places / cautions, cautions crossed into places / gates, gates may joseph places / point, point places / power, places / peels, places / ponders, and places / queries, queries on places clinch / cures, cures fine line places / simple, simple too places / soar, soar for your places / allow, allow freedom's places / leads, leads places / example, example places / pure, pure places / surf, surf of places / light, light on a place / cords, places and art / light, light said light places / animals, animals places / meet, meet allow places / feet, feet across places / step, step over a places / surfaces, surfaces 15 divine places / bearings, bearings onto places / resolve, resolve your places / humans, humans are places / claim, claim youe places / animal, animal yangs places / clarity, clarity opens a places / happy, happy free places / calm, calm by step forth places / peaceful, peaceful places / considerate, considerate on places tynes / matched, matched in places / joined, joined about places / wires, wires crossed places / short, short trip to places / signauls,

signauls enlighten places / paring, paring the small places / clears, clears the paths to places / caves, caves light up places / chosen, chosen one places / china, china destination places / seigzed, seized from places / sons, sons of one places / ran, ran arcured places / atlantic, atlantic participate in a ratio for mam earth's places / plans, plans and emotions for the placed / pacific, pacific ring rims in our place / seas, seas sizeable to our polite place.

CHAPTER TWO

Service, service the one places / shines, shines above through out places / smoothly, smoothly transend places / about, round about places / banter, banter between places / bore, bore lifted to light places / auger, auger felt resolved places / raged, raged calms places / rounds, rounds to be made places / reap, reap abmdance places / random, random numbers places / romps, romps abound places / rules, light rules places / rang, rang echos places / rongaly, rongaly sonught after places / about, about times places / lush, lush greens surround places / tropicals, tropicals waves places / forests, forests tall places / managed, managed the key places / areas, areas squared places / largest, largest to smallest places / feature, feature the one places / glouce, glouce through to the other side places / carry, carry upon shoulders places / cures, cures what ales places / lands, lands a vast array places / leap, leap and bounds places / lowers, lowers travels places / surged, surged with power places / singes, singes more anare places / purges, purges to cleanse places / plants, plants grow above places / marked, marked the one places / simply, simply the best places / rules, rules allow places / features, features the secret places / supply, supply a variety places / suggested, suggested requested places / caught, caught up in the rapture places / cures, cures the heart places / features, features broadest places / areas, areas around places / properly, properly taken care of places / property, property shared / tax, tax paid places / free, free float above places / keep, keep the highest mean places / keys, keys of wisdom places / grades, grades challenged places / cores to the places / understand, understand one place / bags, bags carry places / atlas, atlas to the key places / forgive, forgive forget places remembered / fules, fules the fire places / paradise return to paradise places / allowed, allowed the changed places / full, full of venture places / specials, specials through places / shrug, shrug it off places / annoying, annoying ignored places / spoils, spoils the best places / ioumegs, ioumegs to the beyond places.

CHAPTER THREE

Professions, professions change places / plants, plants the seed places / ports, ports docked places / portal, portal through to places / picnics, picnics tabled places / strips, strips last places / stored, stored shield places / spoils, spoils new growth places / enjoy, enjoy the rest places / vends, vends to find places / fortune, fortune told places / fill, fill in the gap places / focal, focal point places / features, features the list places / venues, venues visted places / vault, vault sealed places / counsels, counsels resolve places / prime, prime location places / pureness, pureness blends places / partway, partway traveled places / fairs, fairs tolled places

/ affairs, affairs arranged places / building, building the building places / acess, acess given places / generations, generations span places / drapes, drapes among places / homes, homes to return places / heaven, heaven sent places / logs, logs build foundation places / level, level increase places / shops, shops along places / shop, shop about places / steel, steel pulse places / piers, piers above water places / lodge, lodge between places / quarry, quarry mined places / allows, allows to unite places / focus, focus onto places / quells, quells float to rest places / spell, spell cast places / increased, increased awareness places / vocal, vocal silent places / lodged, lodged among places / spelling, spelling PLACES / peers, peers join places / eyes, eyes wide open places / deeds, deeds made places / forgive, to one forgive places / further, further told places / succeed, succeed request places / jars, jars of clay places / signs, signs flash places / advances, advances toward light places / pairing, pairing of two places / signal, signal light places / scenic, scenic views places / allowed, allowed to hold energy places / open, open the doors places / works, in the works place / worthy, worthy to be called places / surrender, surrender to change places / palest, palest color places / winds, blow places / pore, pore over flow places.

CHAPTER FOUR
Average, average ascent places / skills, skills shown places / school, school of light places / seals, seals revealed places / asthma, asthma breathes places / breathe, breathe deep places / born, born new places / fortune, fortune cast places / fuses, fuses together places / confounds, confounds broken places / opens, opens to newness places / clears, clears the air places / clearest, clearest channels written places / nearest, nearest come unto places / often, often told the secret places / well, well cycled places / divide, divide among places / contents, contents combine places / crept, crept quietly places / along, along the lines places / living testaments places / lures, lures to the depth places / lines, lines straight places / declare, declare serious places / decade, decade the crypt places / invoke, invoke the one places / volley, volley scored places / play, play admist places / run, run about places / runt, runt aloud places / sear, sear the further places / sear, sear to locate places / calling, calling all forward places / sure, sure to know places / incline, incline reinsure places / for, for all to see places / forthright, forthright and truth places / fans, fans away places / spatual, spatual views places / explore, explore to the beyond places / more, more to come places / magnified, magnified close into places / plans, plans to resume places / pure, pure shell places / estates, estates shared three places / paste, paste mixed places / coaneds, coaneds to the highest being places / freed, freed the bars places / lets, lets the bars places / lets, lets live places / apply, apply to all places / now, now and taken places / filled, filled to the mass places / surrenders, surrenders the righting places / anthers, anthers memory places / life, life lived places / fortress, fortress fallen places / kites, kites fly high places / clear, clear the air places / skies, skies the limit places / foaming, foaming bubbles wash places / forms, forms challenged places / creep, creep art of dark places / crept, crept up to places

CHAPTER FIVE:
Hawi, Hawi spirals out places / Hawaii, Hawaii surrounded places / hills, hills held down places / spells, spells magical places / virginal, virginal territory places / quells, quells to a new beginning places / spelling, spelling out places / sures, sures to know places / ouert, ouert directional places / cover, cover untold places / cubes, cubes of light places / light, light sources places / maker, maker of opportunity's places / days, days pass places / and, and to the change places / pay, pay the toll places / for, for the will places / love, love to flow places / has, has to be the places / gone, gone and return places / to, us come to the places / good, good will rewards places / refine, refine and a tune places / allow, allow to shine places / heat, heat felt places / to, to return places / melt, melt into one places / heart, heart arsire / hilo, hilo admist clouds places / breaks, breaks the chain places / mavrick, mavrick loose run places / pays, pays to wait places / pages, pages the balance ahead places / forms, forms circles ring places / focusing, focusing to the point places / fuels, fuels the lasting flame places / sent, sent to the cove places / cured, cured over time places / codes, codes understood places / ethica, ethica treatment equal places / sufferance, sufferance put aside places / sunder, sunder the please places / aspects, aspects selected places / allow, allow and let be places / woo, woo the challenges places / magic, magic untold places / prevails, prevails the secret places / hurry, hurry along places / found, found beneath the layers places / fans, fans air places / couple, couple multiplied infinite places / links, links intertwined places / lurk, lurk to view places / lirnge, lirnge abound to the air places / across, across nation places / spears, spears thrown places / spare, spare parts places / regard, regard to love places / light, light shine cast upon places / focus, focus turned in tune places / final, final infusion begun, align in place / exasperation, exasperation settles your place / live, live and love for places / measures, measures are made, event settled, choose a place and relax in love.

CHAPTER SIX
May, may we know what she said about her "places" / into, into great seas she flows, the volcano of places / success, success is made for the few who remember together life's blood, in the lava sands and the strands born electric through love, a place / move, move now to show the way to those who flood after, father said "place" / weavers, weavers need cotton batons of finest garments and trained teas spilling into the scalloped scones of life's plate and the door to her places / trim in dynamic and the edges replaced / trips, trips are made to that stage known, electric places / winning, winning example and the sample born for finished loves and places / occurs, occurs a simple resign to the remembrance for love's places / focus, focus again on the winning places / fields, fields collide in electric blue buzz about the materials and places / planets, planets which hung in similar electrical patterns and places / panels, panels judge less the layered effects of our places / paged, paged a simple remember for light places / lovers, lovers tossed have lost their thread back to simple places / offering, offering now given the places held forth as loved / frames, frames erasure

has made you smile for lasting impress on the places / friendly, friendly aims and the rains upon these places / focus, focus your fusions to the names for places given light and love / love / fixed, fixed emissions focus into formats for places / query, query given and taken as ways to the heart line of places / composites, composites drawn and upon us all a light laid complete in love and places / comely, comely and lately of love, the fed places / queerest, queerest fog lifts to show the world a new "places" / curt, curt the simple yes to love's places / goodness, goodness fed a place / cry, cry for the few who recall without glasses and places / queens, queens of the courtly delivery for the flown places / cure, cure has led me home to finish the places without love's doors / soothe, soothe respect into salve for the soothing places / mends, mends have made you stronger still in places / stories, stories told have passed along the lining places / planes, planes are purple in expand to places of love's horizons / shields, shields have lain in flooded places / smells, smells go to the lifted codes of light places / steer, steer clear to new places / planets, planets made to explore, places / mortal, mortal the gate's way into places / moves, moves into eternal edge free stones and the places in love / appears, appears out of the blue, places / courts, courts held for the venus yellow places / masks, masks sold for places / offers, offers coming to your places / booths, booths built about your places / focal, focal display for the fields who participate in your places / cures, cures are simple in places / run, run to the wedges of light places / build, build a rapport within places / obligates, obligates have come to less in places / cords, cords cut are fled to places / rungs, rungs climbed have slipped into the sun for places / focus, focus again, places / gapes, gapes and the apes cute for places / meters, meters broken into and tolled for fine places on love / step, step to your cause applause and heart places / life, life linked to the news of heart places / sacred, sacred places forgiveness of the trespass without love awareness / strength, strength in the reign for places pure / signature, signature expire and the sire of all places / stamps, stamps tossed to the trips across continents and planes for the place of God / believe, believe in possibility for love's places / possibility, possibility exists for loves' places.

CHAPTER SEVEN

Golden, golden the glue and the rules of heart places / rules, rules and the roles tracked to the situation for places / ridder, ridder the classic places / rode, rode the fleet across places / ramps, ramps inclined places / regants, regants stairway places / ray, ray echoed places / ropes, ropes held tight places / taught, taught the lessons places / tingles, tingles in the sensation places / sought, sought after dreams places / aid, aid in direction places / bets, bets the out come places / breath, breath of life places / born, born the guide places / biological, biological cells burst places / conceptual, conceptual minds climb places / lovers, lovers with in places / cords, cords lead places / aka, aka aligned kinded arcs places / joined, joined in unison places / laces, laces fabric places / electric, electric shape spin places / amounts, amounts to equal places / along, along the lines places / plunge, plunge the prism waters places / care, care the slagging places / paid, paid maximum places / living, living the relative places / along, along linear art forms places / Metatron, Metatron speaks places / paves, paves contact places / licensed, licensed practice places / listen, listen to the sounds places / occupies, occupies the spaces places / ocular, ocular lens places / codes, codes picture of keys places / keep, keep away places / kept, kept the challenge places / cores, cores broken through places / cooling, cooling breeze places / towers, towers above places / spell, spell broken places / images, images encrypted places / empirial, empirial golas places / claim, claim the enthusiast places / clomor, clomore permits places / clears, clears the places / leverage, leverage of a places / coy, coy places / breaks, breaks past places / federal, federal places / turns, turns into places / sly, sly of places / brought, brought for a places / funds, funds places / jaunts, jaunts to a places / safe, safe in places / broken, broken in places / lunging, lunging at places / cheap, cheap on places / tints, tints of places / base, base of places / left, lift too places.

CHAPTER EIGHT

Permanent, permanent recall for the boy who said "places" forward / penalize, penalize can mend in your places / pens, pens found in places / parlor, parlor simple in palmetto places / hills, hills roll into place and as mended / heels, heels soften as strength gained is electrically places / paged, paged a sophomoric place / pushing, pushing registers as placed / pouring, pouring palaces filled with place / dying, dying days placed / doors, doors open into your places / crucibles, crucibles armed with good places / empty, empty interiors and places / tills, tills open into places / moor, moor and the moorish in place / octant, octant and the extent for places / eternal, eternal winging for the route through these places / spiraling, spiraling singing of all places / bliss, bliss is the kiss for raptures places / alchemy, alchemy extending into blissful and the truths inside your places / trues, trues in a ruse developed to fog less the mess the truth inside your places / miracles, miracles for the covered places / soils, soils on the lands places in love / earth, earth races toward your places / alluvial, alluvial places and the intrigues for all loves / deposits, deposits gems and the ranges for places / works, works into wet and artful places / metallurgical language and the living places / wisdoms, wisdoms streams and places / chemistry found in the fellows places / artists, artist reach to rimming places / marshland, marshland protected and placed / spaces, spaces and the falling into places and loves / earth -earth durates for the final orbits and the living places / gold, gold in a goodness for the matrices placed / upper, upper doors and the fellows in places / believed, believed in the unbelievable places within love / signification, signification for the finished portals and places / world, world glasses on, blink, a portal placed in you / applied, applied for a reach into places / young, young in the singing for places / joy, joy deluxe placed / royal, royal treasures and the reaches for pleasure and place / soldiers, soldiers who shield us from places with love / beautiful, beautiful in basic allow for all places / glorious, glorious sentries for peaceful departure to places of love / seat, seat now replacing your portals and places / triumphant, triumphant replacement for places in love / east, east is the risen sun's placements / pilots, pilots and the limited places / years, years now forgiven and placed / kings, kings have written balads about your placement / dwellers, dwellers for the reasons of placement / shining, shining into rhyming placements / south, south is the theory for placement / body, body basic unto a healed placement / comes, comes a meaning to placements / images, images armed in a placement for love / make, make a deal placed / air, air in the aspire for all places / deep, deep in a deepened placement to love / darkened, darkened can go into love's free placement / strife, strife is essential in placements / sturgeons, sturgeons and the animals within your placements.

CHAPTER NINE

Confusing, confusing has ended, find a friend in the final places / periods, periods replaced and the fixed races run into places of love / father, father of the figured places / fingers, fingers snap into places of love / eye, eye for the spatial places / note, note that needs are replaced with love's places / hands, hands touch in raw anticipation for places in love / points, points made and the past laid to rest in places in love / gleaned, gleaned a goodness for all feelings places / life, life is blessed when we place ourselves in love / body, body to the basic love places / ladder, ladder deepens in plans placed / chest, chest ripening places / divine, divine in a due place / book, books basic to the plan and the final placements / ears, ears listen for your places / addresses, addresses advanced to the allowance for places / doors, doors open into your heartland of places / raising, raising into the leading places / enemies, enemies have left this places / water, water is flowing into your places / evolution, volumes and evolution of place / visions, visions and missions of place / before, before this all places / air, air deals in warm places / represented, represented a seal on your places / omega, omega land placed in a dome of love / messenger, messenger mentions your places and loves / future, future financed through loving placements / speaking, speaking is frankest when love blends in this place / blowing, blowing interior to placements / spirit, spirits essential in placements / witnessed, witnessed and born within placements / bears, bears a resemblance to "A" place / creation, creation creative to placements / points, points made placed / fire, fire is the siren for flaming placements / six, six who knew how to be places / sun, sun shining placements / alpha, alpha the due for our places / dragon, dragon red places / development, development for the towns now placed / intelligence, intelligence sought into places / years, years pains taking and placed / bodies, bodies blissful in place / physical, physical commitments to placements / changed, changed allow for the places / whole, whole in days and places / ego, ego cancelled the calming places / soul, soul is due a level change to places / spoken, spoken in the simple places / five, five trails into your places / produces, produces saints and places / image, image marries places / bible, bible blue bowls of heart placements / gate, gate retains a placement shut / small, small in the detail for places / group, group who galloped into place / crystallize, crystallize your places / south, south into dues and turns places / remember, remember dues and the light

that's on placements / spread, spread the word placements / 7, 7 who are due a living place / gathering, gathering glues and the dues placed.

CHAPTER TEN

Grasping, grasping is rasping through you placements / liberate, liberate yourself places / day, day due a place / place, places for esteem and the rested love places / real, real and the simple inn places / today, today is the family placed / more, more in the merry places / remains, remains during a place / really, really a reasonable place / winds, winds whistle in place / spread, spreads arouse a simple placement / age, ages rages and stages for the planets places / remember, remember the december for all passages and phases into your placements / send, send us some places / wisdom, wisdom running too, places / up, up these creeks and paddles for these places / express, express and the reasons from a place / falling, fallings formed and placed / sphere, sphere fed a springing place / scattered, scattered interiors and the throats fed places / cared, cared fro and to, a forest's places / humanity, humanity rich in a places / 18, 18 who knew a placement / inherit, inherited in places / elect, elect for a place / winds, winds reaching for placements / scattered, scattered and toured ahead as placed / sixth, sixth rays placed / remembers, remembers members as placed / develops, develops a richness for places / fall, fall about and settle the mettle for a places / spite, spite is simple without place / made, made instill for a places / first, first rites raid a place / symbolized, symbolized and signed too, places / old, old ions ringing and spill for a classic repose in places / biblical, biblical stills and the refreshened places / signs, signs stroll over all places / terms, terms are miracles for the fortunate placed / truth, truth is told to the fellow placements / initiator, initiator fed places / cross, cross the resources for the squires and the places / withdraw, withdraw forms a fines place / half, half of the federal places / kind, kinds who seal your places / result, resulted in a placement / summoned, summoned a central placement / vision, visions danced places / world, world circles places / effect, effect for the shown places / remains, remains true in being places / save, save fresh places / whale, whales about the whole places / testify, testify through stories and places / sleep, sleep deep inside festive places / box, box squared in places / sort, sort out these places / way, way of the light places / man, man challenged places / fellow, fellow "Christ" places / among, among us others places / enter, enter willing places.

CHAPTER ELEVEN

Prepare, prepare yourself places / discipline, discipline / spoke, spoke a language clearest in places / masses, masses spinning in laces on places / shall, shall we find your places / crowds, crowds all less for all places / discipline, discipline dimpled in places / loved, loved relatives and in time places / able, able forthrightly for these who held a place / called, called in surest places / fully, fully formed places / found, found a red bed for your place / below, below inside a fellows places / oval, ovals depend upon places /

extensive, extensive scratch places / sterner, sterner found places / nights, nights separate places / days, days remembered places / son, son of sun places / except, except no less places / belly, belly snake places / pupil, pupil student of life places / connection, connection earned places / able, able to continue places / speaks, speaks the side places / perhaps, perhaps the situation places / greek, greek places / learner, learner listen places / resurrection, resurrection rise places / primary, primary love places / testament, testament should be taken places / passage, passage through places / signifies, signifies the magical places / latter, latter the hearts places / teacher, teacher the rest places / deeper, deeper to resist places / secrets, secrets deep places / mysteries, mysteries so right places / prophet, prophet think places / seeks, seeks in the arms places / evil, evil surrender places / understanding, understanding the love places / skeleton, skeleton shown places / origin, origin hidden places / reason, reason the beat places / fold, fold the measure places / emphasis, emphasis on love / enter, enter the mystery places / wings, wings spread places / relating, relating stories places / images, images accounted places / associated, associated with memories places / draws, draws cycles places / well, well being places / contains, contains the unattainable places / lines, lines slip places / real, real life places / understanding, understanding the meaning places / possible, possible to produce places / sacred, sacred straight places / Confucius, Confucius says places / stresses, stresses relieved places / opinion, opinion said places / deal, deal the deal places.

CHAPTER TWELVE

Patter, matter the side places / aspect, aspect required places / hexagram, hexagram round places / brief, brief interchange places / edition, edition volumes places / closely, closely held places / basis, basis of newness places / inner, inner thoughts places / whole, whole extract places / judgment, judgment called places / serve, serve places / regret, regret nothing places / close, close connection places / great, great task places / structure, structure strong places / ten, ten folds places / top, top ground places / cardinal, cardinal wait places / diagram, diagram the right places / under, under bubbles places / sun, sun produce places / spring, spring born places / effects, effects of mist places / eight, eight by eight places / nature, nature conserve places / tree, tree branches places / rain, rain drops places / knowledge, knowledge gained places / forces, forces of nature places / jump, jump across places / joyous, joyous approach places / dispersion, dispersion sent places / thunder, thunder struck places / events, events brought places / backward, backward range places / movement, movement rest places / line, line the banks places / stop, stop the play places / combat, combat the night places / hoofs, hoofs stomped places / red, red shoes places / ditches, ditches the bank places / bending, bending backward places / opposite, opposite attracts places / eye, eye wide open places / lowest, lowest values least places / white, white tailed places / long, long journey places / daughter, daughter raised places / places, places arised places / likewise, likewise the sample places / gain, gain the fresh approach places / moon, moon light shines places / pith, pith of being places /

mixture, mixture sopted places / covers, covers unfolded places / universal, universal enhancement places / black, black roan places / pot, pot retted together places / calf, calf raised places / level, level know places / spread, spread the display places.

CHAPTER THIRTEEN

Plants, plants planted places / fast, fast line across places / yellow, yellow brick places / broad, broad stream places / easy, easy access places / great light, great light above places / corresponds, corresponds the same places / pond, pond wakes places / changes, changes astound places / said, said the word places / sages, sages clears places / action, action taken places / easy, easy going places / dark, dark crystal lights places / justice, justice prevails places / develop, develop the surrounding places / power, power sought places / high, high grounds places / several, several blankets places / rather, rather recent places / humble, humble walk / exalts, exalts the places / quality, quality life places / nature, nature observed places / yin, yin and yang agree places / corresponds, corresponds the letter places / field, field stood places / action, action made places / upper, upper falls flow places / law, law given places / human, human made places / seasons, seasons change places / diagram, diagram drawn places / love, love found places / lords, lords being places / trust, trust the outcome places / enthusiasm, enthusiasm occurred places / clappers, clappers voiced places / double, double the take on places / deal, deal with the ascent places / spurs, spurs prick places / installments, installments made places / helpers, helpers unity places / possible, possible situation places / done, done over places / crack, crack mended places / hence, hence forth places / idea, idea shaken places / blame, blame forgiven places / crack, crack walls places / gaze, door places / door, gaze again places / pictures, pictures etched places / blame, blame change places / lines, lines continue places / blame, instead the usual place / inferior, inferior rise places / boy-like, boy-like attitude places / symbolized, symbolized the key places / all, all the way places / locked, locked chains places / rite, rite the spite places / shown, shown the vision places / rule, rule the one vision places.

LEVEL 76: THE POLE-MENTS

CHAPTER ONE

Partly, partly in effect poles / towers, towers built poles / widely, widely spread poles / world, world without poles / makeup, makeup back poles / blows, blows swept poles / gone, gone again poles / regions, regions combined poles / pausing, pausing ceased poles / hands, hands felt poles / gates, gates poles / pure, pure natured poles / prince, prince sets poles / away, away returns poles / for, for and beyond returns poles / gaze, gaze through poles / youthful, youthful perspective poles / food, food filled poles / wine, wine toast poles / ruler, ruler beyond poles / gentleness,

gentleness granted poles / within, within self poles / family, family circle poles / lines, lines stretched poles / fuel, fuel ignite poles / effect, special effect poles / folly, folly poles / 4, 4 roll poles / duty, duty served poles / fire, fire line poles / image, image given poles / proper, proper teased poles / way, way beyond poles / parents, parents poles / brother, brother check poles / upon, upon wist poles / themselves, themselves streached poles / banking, banking on poles / seek, seek out poles / middle, middle seen poles / creats, creats poles / wind, wind chimed poles / serving, serving thoughts poles / other, other than poles / cooking, cooking effect poles / line, line scribble poles / stands, stands up poles / upward, upward spiral poles / nuclear, nuclear storm poles / sun, sun moon poles / entire, entire being poles / revolution, revolution circle poles / great, great pie poles / fortune, fortune fold poles / top, top turn poles / raising, raising the level poles / rim, rim around poles / wood, wood grain poles / lines, lines written poles / grow, grow up poles / added, added on poles / loop, loop about poles / supreme, supreme being poles / perfection, perfection earned poles.

CHAPTER TWO
Revolution, revolution poles / opposition, opposition made poles / home, home return poles / entire, entire roan poles / movement, movement changed poles / upward, upward thrust poles / course, course winds poles / must, must be poles / central, central process poles / correct, correct change poles / grows, grows before poles / individual, individual number poles / idea, idea designed poles / trust, trust held poles / hate, hate overcome poles / noon, noon time poles / end, end comfort poles / one, one world poles / blame, blame after poles / no, no cancel poles / arm, arm back poles / he, he called poles / joined, joined huge amounts / inherent, inherent done poles / aid, aid provided poles / strong, strong number poles / nine, nine acclaim poles / underbrush, underbrush still polesh / gram, gram added poles / curtain, curtain call poles / fullness, fullness complete poles / rendered, rendered symbolic poles / small, small feats poles / stars, stars hide poles / top, top out poles / drizzle, drizzle fallen poles / place, place recently poles / bestows, bestows upon poles / fortune, fortune dated poles / second, second experience poles / possible, possible flash poles / blessing, blessing hyped poles / force, force route poles / expression, solo expression poles / approaching, approaching familarity poles / reason, reason why poles / light, light aside poles / likewise, likewise devoted poles / longer, longer style poles / enable, enable the try poles / present, present given poles / dark, dark attempt poles / action, action range poles / gram, small gram poles / recognizing, recognizing sound poles sing / also, also the previous poles / impossible, impossible stop poles / blameless, blameless poles / movement, movement careful poles / good, good prevails poles / send, send approach poles / truth, truth pocket poles / react, react with poles / fullness, fullness reached poles.

CHAPTER THREE
Polestar, polestar be poles / laws, laws made poles / called, called aloud poles / literal, literal meaning poles / sectors, sectors about poles / confused, confused found poles / movements, movements precise poles / under, under writer poles / parallel, parallel universe poles / half, half sized poles / needs, needs to know poles / problem, problem solved poles / fully, fully acclaimed poles / view, view in poles / answer, answer comes forth poles / life, life work poles / awakened, awakened the mind poles / ages, ages of peace poles / of, sight of poles / each, each poles / transformation, new poles transformation / displace, displace fear poles / without, without the rooms poles / double, double shot poles / lines, lines doubled poles / yielding, yielding roads poles / change, change the wave poles / forthwith, forthwith the best poles / concept, concept earned poles / upon, upon the float poles / basis, basis formed poles / acting, acting walks poles / creating, creating images poles / respect, respect circuts poles / things, things true poles / result, result tried poles / firm, firm felt poles / counsels, counsels shy poles / imperfect, imperfect wants poles / motion, motion acted poles / inner, inner thoughts poles / lines, lines drawn poles / within, within control poles / superior, superior wants poles / acts, acts shown poles / covered, covered up poles / up, up shape poles / recognition, recognition the obvious poles / dragon, dragon blood poles / hidden, hidden vision poles / uprooted, uprooted change poles / covered, covered bottom poles / within, within the hole poles / submit, submit the need poles / concealment, concealment / accomplish, accomplish the task poles / world, world round poles / recognition, recognition time poles / yet, yet again poles / name, name the best poles / master, master the light poles / pass, pass on poles / side, side slide poles / today, today lifted poles.

CHAPTER FOUR
Creative, creative arts poles / single, single works poles / revealed, revealed under poles / upper, upper chakra poles / wars, wars fought poles / brilliant, brilliant star poles / earth, earth spin poles / places, places arrived poles / land, land of time poles / ions, ions small poles / lost, lost city poles / join, join hands poles / planets, planets revolve poles / code, code encrypted poles / when, when united poles / existence, existence began poles / both, both best use poles / offspring, offspring born poles / growing, growing spurts poles / landmark, landmark marked poles / peaks, peaks arrived poles / space, space between poles / built, built foundation poles / mother, mother earth poles / gold, gold poles / clam, clam poles / jewelry, jewelry designed poles / splashed, splashed drips poles / east, east to west poles / flood, flood rise poles / seek, seek out and find poles / favors, favors made poles / first born, first born lay the path poles / planet, planet bounce poles / center, center stage poles / extract, extract measure poles / control, control setting poles / expanded, expanded apart poles / tall, tall sky poles / complex, complex structure poles / arrow, arrow path poles / landing, landing pad poles / free, free space poles / throne, throne acquired poles / medical, medical miracle poles / lord, lord be poles / proven, proven theory poles / 450,020, 450,020 back to one poles / mighty, mighty light poles / righteous, righteous task poles / one, one poles / giants, little giants poles / events, events occur poles / both, both sides poles / holy, holy being poles / ruler, ruler unites poles / pregnancy, pregnancy born poles / angels, arc angels poles / words, words of ancient poles / wife, wife shared

poles / man, temple of man poles / different, different strokes poles / ran, ran around poles / mouth, mouth heard poles.

CHAPTER FIVE

Sun, sun ring poles / high, high spirits poles / supreme, supreme challenge poles / landing, landing strip poles / dramatic, dramatic enter poles / grandfather, grandfather tops poles / truth, truth rise poles / me, me poles / you, you require poles / column, column vertical poles / fragment, fragment proceed poles / wife, wife wed poles / strange, strange sounds poles / baby, baby steps poles / hidden, hidden treasures poles / eden, eden garden poles / note, note the small poles / watchers, watchers up high poles / translation, translation understand poles / original, original being poles / discoveries, discoveries the rest poles / before, before the time poles / exact, exact script poles / term, term defined poles / earth, earth center poles / ancient, ancient visit poles / book, book pages poles / shimmer, shimmer and shine poles / biblical, biblical saying poles / scriptures, scriptures noted poles / reported, reported news poles / noah, noah landing poles / petition, petition signed poles / implore, implore self worth poles / angels, angels above poles / brewing, brewing steams poles / protect, protect endangered poles / sinning, sinning forgiven poles / planes, planes unite poles / deals, deals the hand poles / translated, translated works poles / upon, upon tablets poles / rocky, rocky roads poles / hands, hands shake poles / marry, marry one poles / challenged, challenged accepted poles / writings, writings typed poles / struggles, struggles twice poles / play, play game poles / meadow, meadow spray poles / playing, playing high poles / northern, northern site poles / mids, mids sign poles / buffalo, buffalo roam poles / ring, ring complete poles / respect, respect the unexpected poles / throne, throne admist poles / marry, marry unite poles / born, born again poles / challenged, challenged poles / drive, drive a line poles / female, female form poles / happy, happy day poles / take, take on poles.

CHAPTER SIX

Carrying, carrying onto poles / remotely, remotely aimed poles / earthworks, earthworks in all poles / above, above serpent's mound poles / object, object of poled nature / weight, weights and pole star / podium, podiums rendered light poles / leftover, leftover clears poles / ground, poles into ground / traces, traces of poles / slab, slab off poles / fact, facts on a pole / platform, platform of poles / side, side stay's poles / stone, stone tray's poles / person, person to a pole / long, long on pole / largest, largest poled / feet, feet to a pole / gigantic, girl's gigantic poles / partly, partly formed poles / uniqueness, uniqueness wearing a pole / thick, thick end poles / below, below us all poles / far, far to a pole / showing, showing your poles / measures, measures of poles / sides, sides enlarge poles / hugh, hugh poles / appearance, appearance on poles / length, lengths to a pole / scribes, scribes read poles / noted, noted of poles / optimal, optimal's poles / place, place on poles / certain, certainly poled / gods, gods green poles / name, names soften poles / upon, upon us yes poles / temples, temples tagged poles / owe, owe one a pole / things, things in

poles / gateways, gateways gathered poles / wish, wish in a pole / wilderness, wilderness past poles / took, took off poles / cow, cow star's poles / sailed, sailed into poles / swift, swift as a pole / young, young star's poles / permission, permission for poles / special, special poles / voyage, voyage poles / Egypt, Egypt's lair poled / angel, angel's poled / fashioned, fashioned poles / shamash, shamash poles / eyes, eyes poled / crossed, crossed over poles / hunting, hunting and poles / scribes, rasta man scribes, marley poles / dreaded, dreaded without color poles / spotlight, spotlighted poles / bull, bull killed poles.

CHAPTER SEVEN

Now, now and then poles / beaming, beamings poles / winged, winged into poles / entrance, entrances poled / gate, gate's winning poles / guarded, guarded and poles / far, far thing poles / after, after all poles / indeed, better indeed to poles / delayed, delayed without poles / taking off, taking off poles / accept, accept best poles / answered, answered and to poles / now, now then's poles / go, go ways poled / days, days dearly poled / brightness, brightness on a pole / grew, grew along poles / magnificence, magnificence on a pole / lush, lush into poles / stones, stones into poles / white, white in one pole / tree, trees of sweet poles / pure, pure enlists poles / again, again said poles / grew, grew above's poles / double, double late all poles / path, path energing at poles / frequent, frequent fastened poles / mortal, mortal into a pole / different, different on a pole / art, arts of all poles / artificial, artificial finds into poles / paint, paint soften poles / question, questions of a pole / reveal, reveal red poles / time, time of a pole / foretell, foretell folds into poles / myth, myth into poles / dates, dates follow poles / joined, joined into poles / only, only into poles / eclipses, eclipses for a pole / nature, nature's poles / indeed, indeed on a pole / modern, modern days poles / megaliths, megaliths on a poles / circles, circles touring poles / supporting, supporting our poles / note, notes on poles / science, science said poles / full, full in poles / century, century's poles / publication, publication of poles / methods, methods and poles / visitor, visitors poles / jubilee, jubilee's daily poles / marked, marked and led poles / east, east in ways poles / shrine, shrine of all poles / feet, feet across one poles / clearly, clearly to a pole / perfect, perfectly a pole / walled, walled into poles.

CHAPTER EIGHT

Enclose, enclose on a pole / copper, copper cools poles / gilded, gilded and poled / court, court fed poles / temple, temple aloft in poles / level, levels and poles / object, objects and poles / west, west to a poles / unclear, unclear without poles / festival, festivals on poles / rated, rated to a poles / angle, angle passed poles / star, star poles / branches, branches poles / solar, solar poles / built, built in poles / spoken, spoken of all poles / screen, screens lend a pole / wise, wise to a pole / clay, clay potted poles / table-like, table-like poles / Goddess, Goddess poles / design, design to a poles / earth, earth and poles / wonder, wonders aloft poles / seal, seal and poles / earliest, earliest and poles / oblations, finished poles / boat, boats poles / time, time to a poles / seventh, seventh to a poles / little, little tune's poles / clock, clock ticks poles / water, water cleans poles / however, however being poles / great, great adventure poles / scientists, discover poles / text, text read poles / done, done again poles / wisdom, wisdom learned poles / understanding, understanding the truths poles / heaven, heaven sent poles / figure, figure 8 poles / metrical, metrical poles / geometry, geometry sides poles / doubt, doubt none poles / call, call on poles / tablets, tablets scribbled poles / passed, passed into poles / first, first poles / cult, cult opted Christ, poles / center, center win all poles / wide, wide in a pole / astrology, astrology's poles / showed, showed us poles / priest, priest of all poles / system, system's poles / discussed, discussed of poles / automatics, automatics poles / oil, oil poles / edge, edge poles / wise, wise breathe poles / astronomy, astronomy adds poles / scared, scared 2 poles.

CHAPTER NINE
Report, report about poles / source, source final poles / numerical, numerical stacks poles / rank, rank above poles / divine, divine instal poles / hero, hero poles / house, house stalted poles / medicine, medicine source poles / place, place to call poles / house, house poles / wonderfully, wonsecretpolesderfully / perfect, perfect approach poles / called, called upon poles / precinct, precinct stationed poles / half, half anxious poles / brilliance, brilliance increase poles / earphones, earphones told noise poles / helmet, helmet head poles / person, person sent poles / studded, studded update poles / divine, divine timing poles / borrowed, borrowed attempt poles / face, face poles / crude, crude peaks poles / goggle, goggle view poles / rock, rock given poles / judge, judge one poles / baton, baton swirl poles / artistic, artistic paints poles / styles, styles vary poles / banks, banks on side poles / unknown, unknown action poles / blindness, blindness seen poles / sudden, sudden impact poles / entrance, entrance through poles / baton, baton dyno poles / doorway, doorway through poles / flat, flat grounds poles / fire, fire target poles / jumped, jumped final poles / curse, curse out poles / lovemaking, lovemaking honored pole sings only love / lumped, lumped together poles / zone, zone poles / space, space finally poles / station, station runs poles / protocol, protocol new poles / apart, aparts compound poles / origins, origins traced poles / both, both contact poles / navigation, navigation curve poles / occupied, occupied much poles / flight, flight soared poles / solar, solar panels poles / house, house poles / short, short commings poles / curse, curse fixing poles / brother, brother poles / celestial, celestial sky poles / company, company poles / storm, storm circled poles / place, place here poles / turbulent, turbulent source poles / solemn, solemn oath poles.

CHAPTER TEN
Partly, partly cleared poles / epithet, epithet poles / text, text burst poles / ritual, ritual held poles / genealogy, genealogy trace poles / named, named for poles / poured, poured liquid poles / out, out and above poles / role, role playing poles / play, play trail poles / darle, darle beast poles / soil, soil growth poles / clearly, clearly

bet poles / creation, creation made poles / essential, essential being poles / individual, individual aspect poles / mind, mind complete poles / central, central reason poles / child, child surrounds poles / psychic, psychic vision poles / identify, identify disguised poles / latter, latter about poles / self, self motivation poles / organism, organism translucent poles / passive, passive settle poles / handled, handled lift poles / life, life lessons poles / reflect, reflect images poles / ordinary, ordinary stance poles / simple, simple said poles / view, view point of poles / true, true color poles / magical, magical aura poles / denied, denied access poles / belief, belief system poles / raproachment, rappoachment poles / omnipotence, omnipotence recover poles / truly, truly seen poles / shell, shell cover poles / essential, essential knowledge poles / period, period included poles / include, include site poles / aware, aware surrounds / juncture, juncture to poles / subphase, subphase poles / end, end the beginning poles / self, self reliant poles / vulnerability, vulnerability access poles / price, price marked poles / respect, respect maybe poles / mind, mind alarm poles / exactly, exactly cycle poles / aspect, aspect within poles / shift, shift neutral poles / accurately, accurately thrown poles / fixation, fixation locked poles / normal, normal line poles / element, element of nature poles / version, version told poles / power, power internal poles / primary, primary focus poles / more, more slide poles / feelings, feelings accounted poles / hide, hide revealed poles.

CHAPTER ELEVEN
Human, human spirit poles / special, special note poles / childhood, childhood grown poles / first, first chance poles / omnipotent, omnipotent poles / self, self served poles / development, development opened poles / view, view inside out / openness, openness gained poles / infant, infant eye poles / except, except the outside poles / real, real challenged poles / describe, describe flame poles / sense, sense with poles / normally, normally out of balance poles / delusions, delusions poles / true, true love poles / qualities, qualities seen poles / fixation, fixation size poles / differs, differs to another pole / shutting, shutting source poles / helpless, helpless resisted poles / primal, primal thoughts poles / tolerate, tolerate change poles / primal, primal walks poles / stage, stage the set poles / bliss, bliss out poles / power, power up poles / transformation, transformation gradual poles / arose, arose a bud poles / above, above top poles / clear, clear cut poles / emergence, emergence shot through in poles / deep, deep ended poles / delusion, delusion image poles / necessary, necessary mix poles / reveals, reveals the loop poles / true, true poles / pervasive, pervasive poles / commitment, commitment 100% poles / feel, feel poles / end, end poles / work, work internal poles / dealt, dealt with poles / realize, realize the path poles / student, student travel poles / able, able body poles / action, action pedal poles / disciplines, disciplines spoke poles / various, various wheel poles / impossible, impossible seat poles / ourselves, ourselves recognized poles / recognize, recognize their poles / easily, easily rolled poles / capacity, capacity extended poles / wisdom, wisdom soft poles / laziness, laziness zen poles / energy, energy gained poles / effort, effort made poles / ego, ego altered poles / purpose, purpose being

poles / involve, involve maximum poles / clear, clear the poles / block, block planted poles.

CHAPTER TWELVE
Mind, mind alternating poles / sense, sense of poles / identity, identity discovered poles / many, many ideas poles / concept, concept understand poles / last, last rights poles / activity, activity busy poles / emptiness, emptiness space poles / immovable, immovable chance poles / reveals, reveals the chaos poles / self image, self image mirrored poles / totally, totally in poles / work, work ahead poles / central, central nerve poles / issue, issues brought poles / relation, relation connected poles / soul, soul decision pole / light, light beings poles / student, student of poles / continue, continue poles / exposing, exposing the truths poles / emptiness, emptiness filled poles / mirror, mirror self poles / real, real talk poles / rather, rather be poles / expanding, expanding horizon poles / course, course challenged poles / development, development built poles / mirror, mirror self poles / structure, structure fallen poles / real, real time poles / need, need asked poles / direct, direct accord poles / narcissism, narcissism poles / because, because of poles / elements, elements by 4 poles / identity, identity charged poles / acknowledge, acknowledge the use poles / essential, essential oils poles / structure, structure built poles / exert, exert full force poles / mummified, mummified the poles / Gods, Gods one pole / important, important remarks poles / originally, originally cast poles / views, views opened poles / emblem, emblem poles / dead, dead dark poles / found, found formula poles / wears, wears straight poles / form, form filled poles / crown, crown chakra poles / flesh, flesh cover poles / yesterday, yesterday past poles / sum, sum total poles / days, days doubled poles / occupied, occupied vacancy poles / body, body temple poles / decay, decay feeds poles / motionless, motionless movement poles / judge, judge not poles / regarded, regard as one pole / version, version the same poles / sister, turn sister poles.

CHAPTER THIRTEEN
Company, company form poles / member, member on time poles / set, set around poles / already, already assumed poles / alone, alone stand poles / similar, similar suites poles / prayers, prayers answered poles / asserted, asserted the utmost poles / exercise, exercise ran poles / attributes, attributes the beginning poles / husband, husband half poles / father, father reared poles / pyramid, pyramid stacked poles / egg, egg case poles / deceased, deceased awareness poles / sprang, sprang to life poles / steps, steps built poles / bird, bird songs poles / speaking, speaking truth poles / save, save the love poles / representation, representation speaks forth poles station / birth, birth reborn poles / moon, full moon poles / took, took a chance poles / nut, nut and bolts poles / sacred, sacred mound poles / see, see the above poles / he, he spoke poles / opener, opener to the new poles / troubles, troubles fade poles / grief, grief stricken poles / set, set in place poles / beloved, beloved being poles / origin, origin history poles / upon, upon the steeps poles / sunset, sunset horizon poles / dawn, dawn risen poles / night, night sky poles / woman, woman won poles

/ waters, waters flow poles / brother, brother keep poles / grief, grief overcome poles / darknest, darknest shines poles / great, great titan poles / combat, combat the challenge poles / body, body warmth poles / prove, prove time and time poles / bronze, bronze cast poles / introduction, introduction ceremony poles / represent, represent the rest poles / legend, legend known poles / played, played the field poles / sepulchral, sepulchral poles / stelar, stelar stars poles / yet, yet been poles / seems, seems the best poles / boat, boat afloat poles / creation, creation formed poles / northern, northern lights poles / mountain, mountain tops poles / jackal, jackal laughs poles / dead, dead lifted / body, body form poles / upon, upon the night sky.

LEVEL 77: THE POSIT-MENTS

CHAPTER ONE
Originally, originally tours and posits / place, place in the reface for posits / worships, worships willing posits / gap, gap gone to the fleeing posits / stony, stony days end in a posits / plateaus, plateaus miraculous in posits / greeks, greeks who gape into epinaeum / lower, lower the glasses for posits / fact, fact forks into posits / called, called a cell positive in posits / town, town tuned into posits / built, built in a basic humanity for our opportune posits / extract, extract the pieces and the posits for all places in love / hell, hell has gone into the places formatted and the positss placements and loves / gnashing, gnashing i decent places and love for the posits of life / teeth, teeth dealt a blow inside your married posits / mythological, mythological and the logical means forming in posits / signification, signification forms a federal posit / westerns, swesterns arming your positis / fields, fields freshest in centrral posits / art, arts and carts forming posits / been, been well inside final posits / eye, eye is direct interior too, a final posit / praise, praise is risen into a posit / lips, lips slip past your posits / filled, filled and the final's posits / appoint, appoint a matter to the material posits / peace, peace is filling your heart in posits / cakes, cakes baked are raspberry ripe in posits / apes, apes jump over your posits / other, other is said to be "a posit" / turn, turn into a final posit / burn, burn into a filling posit / defects, defects armed inside posits / following, following a flowing posit / otherwise, otherwise rising into a posit / seven, seven in a single pole's posits / avenger, avenger forming a final posit / divine, divine in simple portals and posits / shift, shift into signal participate into posits / drugs, drugs in the rugs and the realms for the posits / now, now is ample too, then and now, posits / wish, wish is aiming your posits / round, round in a respectful posit / strong, strong in essential posits / existence, existence spent in a posit / speak, speak in a placement's posits / powers, powers to be and a posits / inhabit, inhabits details form a posit / heads, heads help us fill a posit / journey, journey journeys into posits / water, waters wet in your posits / bandages, bandages burning our posits / heart, hearts respectful and posits / weep, weeping tours and your posits

/ travel, travels running on posits / celestial, celestial reaches and posits / name, names running in posits / shall, shall spill into posits / endure, endure shedding a posits / work, work whistles through posits / contents, contents curing your posits / tombs, tombs are the final turns and posits / yellows, yellows ramification can turn into posits.

CHAPTER TWO

Green, green garners and gandolf sent blue posits / sector, sector into your posits / copy, copy cured and a posit / blanks, blanks issued and posits / whole, whole in a refined posit / doubt, doubts ruling your posits / caste, castes forecast a refinement for posits / professions, professions and paging posits / layers, layers leaping in posits / thicker, thicker thickening and posits / scribes, scribes reaching your posits / length, length going to posits / afterwards, afterwards reaching your posits / joined, joined into signed posits / up, ups and the reputation for posits / copy, copy is the courses for posits / I Ching, I Ching for the calling courses for posits / changed, changed results and your posits / translations, translations reaching yearly posits / winds, winds arming a posit / monarch, monarchs marry your posits / psychologically, psychologically well into posits / notes, notes detail your posits / fires, fires arrayed into posits / under, underneath us a posit / individual, individual and a posit / conduct, conduct curing your posits / thunder, thundering theories and posits / feng, feng and the shui well into posits / ta kuo, ta kuo aims in a posit / index, index won is a posit / heavens, heavens ranging to posits / house, house paid into posit / receptive, receptive caring for posits / yang, yang yellow days posits / coins, coins tossed in a posit / hexagram, hexagram blue posits / numbers, numbers nudging your posits / appendices, appendices vary without posits / tops, tops in triple posits / fortune, fortune found in true posits / wheel, wheel reaching a golden egged posit / fax, fax sent into posits / sequence, sequence worn through a posit / harmony, harmony hurling for posits / enter, enters entry is your posit / water, water is yellow for the final posits / small, small is a daily posit / completion, completion curing your posits / clouds, clouds carry a maximum posit / blame, blame is finished and basic is found in posits / bird, birds marriage a posit / wish, wish for a wellest posit / expenditures, expenditures carry your gaining posit / feet, feet nears your door's posits / may, may we weave an electric posit / cry, cry to doorway's posits / drum, drums fend for your posits / callling, calling creates a realm for posits / middle, middle amounts to a married real posit / truth, truth of the nearest posit / commentaries, commentaries curing a posit / examples, examples floral in posits / lake, lakes forming a posit.

CHAPTER THREE

Behavior, behaviors forming a posit / bounds, bounds are gained in a posit / blood, blood is a basic red posit / turns, turns told inside basic posits / stop, stop by the reaches for posits / lower, lowers a listing for posits / person, persons electric in posits / joyousness, joyousness inside posits / fortune, fortunes told into posits / second, seconds and the days inside posits / governing, governing a gravity left into posits / nectars, nectars arming theory for the flowing posits / rulers, rulers rush to find your posits / humiliation, humiliation for the posits cycling reaches / image, image during your posits / gentle, gentle joinings in posits / nuclear, nuclear clearing and posits / shoots, shoots armed in your posits / mistake, mistakes forming a posit/ clarity, clarity carries a food for posits / primary, primary pushed into a posit / houses, houses owned and posited / brush, brush past a posit / rulers, rulers reaching your posits / duty, duty due your posits / wanderer, wanderer winning your posits/ harmful, harmful eaching and postures in a posit / provoke, provoke is equipped in posits / gates, gates growing a daily posit / fullness, fullness features your posits / third, third in thricing posits / limits, limits and prosaic posits in love / emphasized, emphasized a basics for love's posits / grams, grams grow into posits / suggest, suggest that love is your posit / attempt, attempt to say what? to love's posits / drizzle, drizzle has gone into a posit / toward, toward us a willing posit / clear, clears curing your posits / spirits, spirits reaching your posits / occupy, occupy for your posits / stabs, stabs for your past posits / minds, minds marry a posit / weak, weak in a posit / moon, moon marries your posits / detour, detours arrange a posit / tai, tai nui appeared in a posit / sister, sister and a mister's posits / lime, lime is a lesson's posits / idea, idea daring a basic posit / east, east is rested in posits / heaven, heaven in held on posits / maiden, maidens in a basic posit / plateau, plateau appeals for a basic posit / draws, draws a daily posit / cliff, cliff for a posit / powers, powers purchase a posit / rested, rested into a posit / developments, developments rested for posits / words, words willing your posits / glad, glad goodness and posits / symbols, symbols seeking your posits / inner, inner days posits / son, son of the running posits.

CHAPTER FOUR

Gazing, gazing glues and a posit / show, show the showering posits / shocks, shocks shielding your posits / temples, temples into the healing posits / eldest, eldest darings and posits / blames, blames and a magical material posit / count, count in curing posits / comrade, comrade in a connected posit / equal, equal sequels and places for a posit / flight, flight basic posits / cautious, cautious healing and posits / electricity, electricity curing your posits / jade, jade during your visible posits / spilled, spilled into pieces and posits / envious, envious and the theory for posits / stuff, stuff flooring the federals for posits / ear, ear and the clearing for all posits / social, socials forming a posits / influence, influence granted a posit / oracles, oracles relating to posits / configuration, configuration curing your posits / inner, inner dearing and posits / earlier, earlier leases and posits / removal, removal reneweing a posit / individual, individual due a new posit / drink, drink is gone for all posits / mud, muds forming a posit / superior, superior signals and posits / tranquil, tranquil in limits for posits and final gifts / exerts, exerts exceptional lifetimes and posits / relationship, relationships for a formatted posits / retreats, retreats for a final posit / matters, matters the release for a posit / water, waters reaching a posits / rancor, rancor rising into posits / pushing, pushing a palace into your placements and the posits / empty, empty your rested posits / tree, tree in the sirian aspects and posits / sun, sun and the lightened spirit for a posit / clearing, clearing in the place for a posit / shining, shining in the facets of a posit / gathering, gathering in greetings and faces of a posit / blames, blames balanced posit / heaven, heaven's spurting posits / principle, principle ripens into deepened posits / weapons, weapons spent for lost posits / devoted, devoted devotions and posits / ripens, ripens syphon and posits / tanks, tanks reach a full posit / points, points made for fine posits / flowering, flowering fillings for posits / maiden, maidens cycle paring a position's posits / powers, powers places and final posits / evil, evils past is cast to posits / skins, skins cleared and tossed posits / equal, equal in a cycle for posits / break, break a reaching cycle of poison gone to posits / court, occupy your court cased posits / knottedknotted has gone into posits / increase, increase a duration for posits / seal, seal is broken, move on into posits / functions, functions forming our posits / leading, leading a wave into factions and posits / reaches, reaches and stiffen gone, posits.

CHAPTER FIVE
Accomplish, accomplish a meaningful posit / trigram, trigram written and smitten for posits / above, above and within a pyramid for posits / lower, lower in lists and posits / mountains, mountains made for posits / pairs, pairs who kneel into posits / lonely, lonely without a posit / require, required for all posits / rises, rises a smallest posit / combined, combined and equipped in a posit / essay, easy for the essay on love's posits / inferior, inferior without a posit / structures, structure within a posit / borders, borders about the living posit / escapes, escapes without a risen posit / wins, wins around these posits / union, union inside a posit / fault, fault about the running posits / waters, waters over the wedges posits / merits, merits for the rules and posits / difficulty, difficulty for the deals within formats and the people's posits / bow, bow for the few who welcome in the winters and mends fond in love formats and posits / oxen, oxen in the necessary days and the formats for carrying lends into today and the fondness for love / mistake, mistakes due a carrying few who need additional posits / cent, cent for a new format and due posits / applauded, applauded into posits / family, family feud for the kneeling posits / tempers, tempers and the dues forth in posits / daughters, daughter to the waters and her posits / draws, draws into doors and the literary posits / depth, depth into dealing posits / courtyards, courtyard for the formations and the listed posits / wings, wings formed and winsome posits / highlights, highlights and the hurling posits / dukes, dukes aroused and posits / pictures, pictures formed and posits / progress, progress ions into a posit / mingles, mingles mingled a posit / sorrows, sorrows insured and posits / occupied, occupied forming and posits / progressing, processing insights and posits / place, place posits into love / corrects, corrects and the durations forming posits / possible, possible parallels around a posit / giant, giant forming stars and posits / everything, everything and the meaning for a durable posit / entrance, entrance for the freest posits / keeping, keeping for the fitted posits / retreat, retreat for the levers and posits / force, forces forming a posits / deity, deity forthright in a posit / durations, durations for the federation

of love's posits / explain, explain a surgical maat's posits / moons, moons and the noons for a posit / weak, weak for the left into posits / immobile, immobile in a sully for the formal posits / disappears, disappears into a surface posit / outward, outward inspired posits / character, character stood for a posit / prince, prince and the reasons for a posit / king, king and the rings too, posits / accepted, accepted in respected rays and posits / fire, fire and the finished posits / cows, cows curing your posits.

CHAPTER SIX
Clinging, clinging into craving posits / overflowing, overflowing a ruling pointed posit / therefore, therefore are yours a positive posit / pit, pit into ap osit / succeeds, succeeds around a posit / unlucky, unlucky instilled in posits / six, six and the reaping posits / implied, implied in a shredded posit / preponderances, preponderances arcing into a posit / breaking, breaking into posits / opens, opens arranged in a posit / positions, positioins for the formal posits / nourishment, nourishment freshens posits / hill, hill into the truth's posits / drooping, drooping ruling a posit / jaw, jaw formal in posits / power, power tooled posits / boar, boar forming arcs posits / chariot, chariot for the trysted posits / virtue, virtue freedoms and formal posits / brilliance, brilliance relates in posits / firms, firms and the relations for a posit / ruling, ruling in single posits / middle, middle formations and posits / state, state for the federal posits / receptios, recptions arcing a posit / wu wang, wu wang too, a posit / defiantly, defiantly yours and posits / midst, midst into a posit / shorts, shorts rules and posits / expresses, express ranging in posits / destroyed, destroyed in literary posits / friendly, friendly arms and posits / loses, loses in single posits / splitting, splitting armed a posit / decay, decay arms a posit / horse, horses single posits / colors, colors arc into posits / ends, ends arranged and posits / loves, lovers reaching a posit / graces, grace for the formal posits / miscellaneous, miscellaneous posits reach ends / lack, lack forth into posits / dried, dried and the dripping posits / eyes, eyes arc into a posit / receives, receives artful in posits / follows, follows a political posit / choice, choice and a legal posit / laws, laws arranged in posits / partly, partly smartly posited / things, things arc away to posits / no, no and dues and posits / weak, weak gone and posits / exactly, exactly yours a posit / goals, goals made, posits / spoiled, spoiled and gone too, a posit / idea, idea for a posit / metals, metals arming your posits / inactive, inactive reactive posits / work, work ruled posits / lines, lines inside your posits / probation, probation and a posits / purest, purest in strides and posits / privacy, privacy forming your posits.

CHAPTER SEVEN
Brings, brings back your posits / eighth, eighth in a seasons posits / under, under all a posit / first, first rhymes and posits / enthusiasm, enthusiasm forays to posits / remorse, remorse inside your posits / abstractions, abstractions arcing in posits / sides, sides railing for posits / watchman, watchman watchful for posits / boastful, boastful cures arm your posits / masters, masters mineral posits / reduced, reduced into single posits / fills, fills arcturian into posits

/ favorablefavorable flutes and posits / blessed, blessed be your posits / smallest, smallest dues and posits / lowers, lowers new posits / yields, yields realms and positions posits / facts, facts formed a posit / fronts, fronts fueled as posits / claus, clauses cords and posits / officials, officials filled in posit / men, men made a positive posit / parallelism, parallelism portals and posits / shame, shames seals and posits / withdrawn, withdrawn into posits / socials, social shields and posits / standstill, standstill standstill over and a posit won / supreme, supreme skills and posits / strong, strong stools for posits / rivers, rivers reaching posits / goals, goals glow into a posit / peace, peace is said "posits" / evokes, evokes a realm, posits / dangers, dangers gone, posits win / occupations, occupations reach a posit / bent, bent blues into positive posits / overt, overt reactions to your posits / arise, arise now, posits / gentle, gentle junes and posits / checked, checked for life in a posit / bodies, bodies bounce for posits / clouded, clouded going posits / taming, taming teaches posits / goods, goods grown in a posit / worth, worth a welcome posit / bottom, bottom born? posits clerk / join, join anothers posits / joyous, joyous and jeweled in posits / employed, employed and sold a posit / army, army for these posits / horus, horus arcs into posits / massed, massed and mensa posits / latter, latter into your posits / back, back in a social posit / virtue, virtues forming your posits / conflict, conflict furthers your posits / cross, crosses too, posits / situations, situations and posits / guests, guest for a posits / gossip, gossip over, posits / pleasureable, pleasureable into posits / seeks, seeks a posits / saunters, saunter inside your posits.

CHAPTER EIGHT
Perplexed, perplexed and reflexed posits / exceed, exceeds deeds and posits / folly, folly over, a posit / habits, habits ruled over placed posits / central, central signs posited / fools, fools ago, posits / overcome, overcome and red posits / vast, vast inside a posit / little, little in the treads posits / sings, sings along, posits / helps, help chanced posits / primary, primary fellings and posits / developmental, developmentally positive in a posits / modesty, modesty forming discretionary posits / craving, craving your posits / books, books abuzz with posits / powers, power shows us a posit / yellows, yellows armed in posits / hidden, hidden rings for posits / icy, icy realms and a posit / acts, acts for the antarctic posit / go, go into flowing posits / harmony, harmony helps your posits / strong, strong inside reasons and positions for posits / know, know a fleshly posit / dragon, dragon days and posits / flying, flying formal posits / longs, longs and legs posited / fosters, fosters former posits / person, persons armed in a posit / passages, passages / natures, natures sully to posits / leaders, leaders armed in a posit / sky, sky schooled for a posit / days, days ardent in posits / whole, whole alert into posits / corrects, corrects arming your posits / godhead, godhead glues and a posit / styles, styles aft and fro, posits / places, places in simple seals, posits / III, III who know posits / circles, circles sealed again posits / toys, toys triple AAA posits / favorites, favorites feeding your posits / independent, independent inside a posit / calls, calls amount to your posits / great, great gains are made, posits / process,

processed a plenty too, posits / kept, kept in a posit / lakes, lakes are leaked to a posit / proof, proofs about posits / twists, twists undone for your positive tunes / people, people are peopled and posited / simple, simple and hyper freed in a posits / rise, rise in your simple posits / far, far and gone to a posit / goods, goods are arranged in a posits / fixed, fixed into a posit / empty, empty amounts without posits / fates, fates are fixed in a fetter free posit / faded, faded and the posits missed in a perfect life / goals, goals and the simple posits / natural, naturally new posits / endeavors, endeavors armed in a posit.

CHAPTER NINE
Allegorical, allegorically due a new posit / sphere, sphere of the hours an dposits / echo, echo during a posit / judgements, judgement journeys into a posit / empire, empires arming a posit / masters, mastery forming a posit / stone, stones and the dues for a posit / minds, minds and the matter for posits / values, values are angled into posits / white, white armies and your posits / glad, glad for arranged posits / holy, holy healings for posits / mountains, mountain posits / probably, probably a basic posit / earth, earth arranged in a posit / bets, bets armed for posits / clad, clad into the closest posits / basis, basis and the barren posits / imitated, imitated and the limited posits / durations, durations forming a posit / truest, truest challenges boast a gift for these posits / movements, movements stoked for a movement's posits / VIII, VIII who knew a posit / we, we are the formal posits / actually, actually arranging your posits / stars, stars forming your posits / heavens, heavens realms and a posit / originally, originally freshened posits / sages, sages and the axiom for a sagest posit / hidden, hidden arrangements and flowers for a posit / under, under all your posits / divisions, divisions are due your posits / reveals, reveals armed in posits / above, above those who know your posits / cosmic, cosmically curing your posits / metal, metals sealed in posits / sprung, sprung specials for posits / history, history and the hymns in a posit / limitations, limitations forming your posits / merits, merits reaching these posits / laugh, laugh and the neglect gone to posits / observed, observed challenged and posited / actions, actions arming your posits / charges, charges arcing into posits / applied, applied formations and posits / primal, primally due in your posits / conceals, conceals essential in posits / loves, loves arming your posits / called, called in inspections and posits / darkened, darkened formations glow posits / powers, powers fresh in a posit / bands, bands pathway and posits / inbred, inbred and the genes in a posit / principles, principles arranging your tours and a posit / complete, completed your cleaing process and a posit / urges, urges ruling your posits / involved, involved formats and your posits / oracle, oracle swarming in posits / devoted, devoted daily posits / toss, toss a next, posit / use, uses win posits for love / frees, frees armed in posits / onward, onward and still a posit / winds, winds across posit's face.

CHAPTER TEN
Displaced, displaced again? posits positioned / orders, orders are made to a posits / systems, systems are surest and posited / rested,

rested and a posits / creatures, creatures and a lighted posit / hoof, hoof across your posits / coverage, coverage above your posits / frugality, frugality forming a posits / thirds, thirds and the third who knew posits / pigs, pigs gone to a posits / each, each and the won posits / battle, battle for first posits / images, images realm wise to posits / southward, southward and so into posits / toils, toils over, positive into posits / customer, customers are given a posits / seed, seed and the seeded posits / behind, behind a bastion of posits / lights, lights leaping a posit / law, law is led to a forgiving posit / cores, cores pacing a posit / underneath, underneath the thrilling posit / embodied, embodied fielded posits / obviously, obviously a final posit / expected, expected risks in your posits / opinions, opinions are made clear of posits / kings, kings apt to see a posit / oldest, oldest levels and posits / fantasy, fantasty forming a posit / materials, materials fleshly and precious in posits / units, units factual and posited / silenced, silenced sliced and posited / humiliations, humiliations gone to posits / full, fullness flows into posits / goes, goes about a posit / rags, rags are richest for posits / run, run arranging a joint posit / superior, superiors still into posits / yet, yet and the thrones posits / born, born into a basic posit / official, officially loving posits / plain, plain designs and rinestone posits / small, smaller in single posits / strong, strong in surest posits / stops, stops arranged posits / specials, specials arming your posits / like, like a living link to the popular known posits / hearts, hearts are arced into a posit / evenings, evenings are spent in positive posits / regrets, regrets are gone to a posits / dissolved, dissolved and flown to posits / limits, limits off a posit / gallery, gallery glowing for posits / distanced, distanced and due a posit / remorse, remorse has gone to posits / lords, lords are left to posits / blockage, blockage as done, posits / cleared, cleared of current posits / inner, inner joi de voire for the filling posits / joy, joy to the moment's poses and posits / lacks, lacks for the joined posits / 18, 18 who knew a posit / catch, catch a caring posit / even, even forms and posits.

CHAPTER ELEVEN

Abstract, abstract posits / woods, woods are wed to a posit / wandered, wandered into posits / servants, servants arming your posits / nested, nested and kneeling near posits / glad, glad to gain posits / live, live to a posit / dwellings, dwellings during a posit / amounts, amounts who merry are, posits / late, late to a posit / sad, sad soothed by a posits / flows, flows are armed for posits / harms, harms go to a possessively freed posit / kindliness, kindliness coded and posits / union, unions made simple too, posits / eldest, eldest armed in frontiers for a posits / eternity, eternity eternal and positive / maidens, maidens who knew your posits / hinder, hinder and yon a posit / paths, paths forged into posits / gradual, gradually yours and posits / development, development due a posit / points, points are made through posits / whom, whom and the womb for posits / light, light and the leading posits / free, free for all posits / fat, fat has gone to posits / shocksshocks over and possibly post posit / still, still and all, posits / excitement, excitement for the fruitful posits / distraught, distraught about your posits / relief,

relief is restful in positive posits / rings, rings above posits / devote, devoted durations and posits / express, expressed a needs posits / powers, powers for the posits / images, images printed for posits / necessary, necessary marks and posits / demand, demands a posit / cows, cows curing posits / actual, actually drilled too, posits / springs, springs aspiring for posits / common, commonly deep into posits / wells, wells wells positive / divine, divine days positives / developments, developments deeming a positives / clay, clay clasped a positive ray / starts, starts arming a positives / oppressed, oppressed onto positivity posits / anatomic, anatomic posits / surges, surges posited / goals, goals are a posit / smallest, smallest and posits / activity, activity foraging posits / touring, touring proven posited / formulative, formulatives for a positivity posit / promptly, promptly posits / gathering, gatherings and posit poles / disdain, disdain due a lifted posit / situations, situations are over, find a new posit / brows, brows are brushed and posited / darling, darlings who kenw a posit / walking, walking about posited / ripens, ripens cul de sac and posits.

CHAPTER TWELVE

Stripes, stripes are earned, a posits / resorts, resorts and days posited / echo, echo about a posit / especially, especially near your posits / high, high inside a posit / progress, progress made your posits true / separate, separate truths and posits / oneself, oneself who knew a posits / windows, windows open into posits / wealth, wealth as bestowed and posited / bow, bow above a posit / tempts, tempts are gone, posits / floating, floating initials and posits / achieved, achieved arms and posits warmed / union, unions who live in posits / fused, fused amperes and posits / realizing, realizing directives for posits / obstacles, obstacles and the discipline for a posit / contians, contains cured and posited / twelve, twelve who knew a posit / series, series arc to a posit / d, d flush in a posit / university, university mathematic and a posit / foundations, foundations are flush into a posit / smallest, smallest swells and posits / meetings, meetings armed into posits / particles, particles frail without posits / certainty, certainty certain in a posit / working, working willing posits / pushing, pushing remains in a posits / oracles, oracles blind without posits / processed, processed fumes and a posits / insights, insights allowed in a posit / confucius, confucius fed your last posits / idea, ideas who kenw posits / specific, specifically fed a few posits / involved, involved inside posits / grades, grades who grew into posits / mainland, mainlands mentioning a posit / older, older deals and posits / wings, wings arc-angled to posits / editions, editions are reached for a posit / grips, grips grown for a festive posit / minds, minds are linked to a posit / stakes, stakes surging a posit / psychic, psychically sunk into posits / verification, verification forming a posit / nativity, nativity next, a posit / uniqueness, uniqueness for a new posit / children, children who hear you learn popular posits / richness, richness rewarding a posits / excellenc spots, excellence for new spots for a posit / magical, magically mentioned in posits / meals, meals lateral to a posit / jade, jades fixed on a posits / graces, graces growing a posit / dreams, dreams alert in a posit

/ leaps, leaps forever and posits / wiser, wiser wills to our posits / powered, powered replacements and posits / acted, acted for a posit / dangers, dangers are over, posits / dealt, dealt and dealt for, a posit / ñnally, finally fit for a posit.

CHAPTER THIRTEEN

Clears, clears cushioned in a poised posit / logically, logically posited / efforts, efforts and the shasta posits / prove, proven mindful and posited / keys, keys are flown to posits / preface, preface for the final posits / concepts, concepts drawn into posits / schools, schools arc to your posits / wisdom, wisdom for the formal posits / life, life is led to a posits / grows, grows and growing posits / collections, collections armed for your posits / mythologically, mythologically amounted to a posit / signs, signs are over all a posit / numbers, numbered and neared into posits / matters, matters forming a posit / required, required of all posits / symbols, symbols and signs posited / overcast, overcast for all posits / attempted, attempted / tao, tao to show you a posit / socials, socials and spines straightened in posits / collapsed, collapsed into sincere posits / editions, editions and reactions for these posits / powers, powers amounting to posits / texts, texts are annual into a posit / lunars, lunars arming your posits / roam, roaming about in a posit / sublime, sublimes suggest a posit / superior, superiors / uppers, uppers to an eight in posits / lufts, lufts and the powerful posits / pitfalls, pitfalls amounted to posits / relationshipped, relationshipped in simple posits / speaking, speaking and a shouting posit / fathers, fathers are fixed in your posits / ice, ice is listed for posits / concealed, concealed accounts and posits / black, black bases clear the negative posits / dancers, dancers are daring your basic posits / united, united in assignments and posits / friends, friends sffluent and posited / all, all the final posits / wisdom, wisdom for these finals posits / escapes, escapes forming a final posit / when, when is the north facing posit / transgressions, transgressions amounting to posits / cheers, cheers and the federations posits / food, food assured and a posit / across, across forms a posit / lifelines, lifelines arming yours and our partiesaand the plans for a posits / possibility, possibility fortitudes and a posit / greats, greats arming yours and our finals and plans for a posit / gossips, gossips sure in a posit / leave, leaves the lifted posits / peace, peace is a mission for posits / falls, falls and the final posits / otherwise, otherwise is a posit / six, six is into posits / rulers, rulers are the regal posits / points, points are poles and posits / symbolized, symbolized indications and posits / games, games are the curing posits / latest, latest are the landed posits.

LEVEL 78: THE PLANET-MENTS

CHAPTER ONE

China, china into the blue and green planets / powers, powers flower without these planets / progressions, progressions passage for planetary posits / dangers, dangers are fellow in your planets /

bites, bites are blessed in planets / loving, loving a living planet / below, below in a knowing planet / heavens, heavens lit planets / neglects, neglects reflecting your planets / approached, approached in a piece's planets / stands, stands due in a planet / permitted, permitted in sited posits and planets / fellowships, fellowships in your planets / glides, glides glued to a positive planet / climbs, climbs over a planets / built, built imbue into planets / wealth, wealth is welcome in your planets / big, big in basic planets / powerful, powerful visit in planets / devoted, devoted in touted planets / equals, equals a surging planet / merits, merits are mentioned in a planets / measures, measured mountains and money for planets / wills, wills are willed into planets / bursts, bursts on a planet / feelings, feelings of planets / clasp, clasp plans planets / sobers, sobers ling planets / images, images and planets / seeks, seeks tipped and planets / solvents, solvents in planets / simple, simple planets / little, little town planets / imply, imply gan planets / superior, superiors go in planets / upward, upward too planets / frequent, frequent for planet / stresses, stresses planets off / spiritually, spiritually a planet / crafted, crafted mountains grow on your planets / uses, uses won to planets / over, over age raids a planet / grass, grows on a planet / lovers, lovers planets / woman, woman on a blue planet / mistaken, mistaken green of planetary cell / injury, injury codes a planet / stocks, stocks alternate / gold, gold in planet / yellow, yellow planets / colors, colors on our planets / wooden, wooden shoed planets / man, maned for a planets / foods, foods is planets plants / fullness, fullness enough planets / blames, blames on planets / loneliness, loneliness over planets / courses, courses tear a planet / allotted, alloted your planets / reefs, reefs cast and planets / concubines, concubine found a planets / yules, yules planets / rules, rules of a planet can be silent / drifts, in a planet.

CHAPTER TWO

Eyes, yes of a planet / unfaithful, unfaithfuls since early planets / works, work west planets / girls, girls sponed planets / inner, inner sourced planets / solutions, solutions spine of planets / loves, loves last for planets / brackets, bears cast to planets / ends, way a planets / finds, finds one true planet / known, know goes to planets / answers, answers, yes to planets / eye, eye as a planets / mindful, mindful means planets / hands, hands some to planets / loneliness, loneliness of planets / girls, girls well plants / able, able through planets / bare, bare planets / upon, upon pages planets / have, have out planets / evens, evens levels planets / stills, stills then planets / news, news too and planets / fits, fits for a planets / ranks, ranks off our planets / equal, equal ways planets / harmed, harmed over planets / closer, closer still a planet / lain, lain on too planets / masters, masters planets / inner, inner tiers planets / works, works on a wild planets / forces, forces of a planet / confined, confined tympanica levels in planets / remorseful, remorseful off a planets / prevails, prevails off planets / faithful, faithful when planets / family, family found planets / house, house bough a planet / richest, richest planet maid / welfare, welfare foreign planets / fears, fears God? go planets / refers, refers to a variations planets / public, public across lines planets / life, life on a planets / symbolic, symbolic sunday planets / colorful, colorful solae in a planet / gates, gates opened family's planets / trees, trees green planets / rats, rats deed planets / dead, dead said a planets / birds, birds grown planets / tongues, tongues over planets / apart, aparts when planets / opens, opens values planets / trunks, trunks opening planets / fruits, fruits musicals love planets / sheep, sheep winning planets / serves, serve a planet / sails, sails great planets / hard, hard in lines planets / moons, moons moaning planets / joyous, joyous planes planets.

CHAPTER THREE

Success, success on and patience to a planet / between, between now and planets / womanly, womanly wins a planets / weakens, weakens with out mental planets / ideas, ideas on a planet / earth's, earthly planet / counts, counting planets / sorts, sorts eissned a planet / scenes, scenes on a planet / spiritual, spiritual goods planets / whole, whole sold planets / wisdom, wisdom with a planet / justice, justice joined to planets / divine, divine in a dialect for planets / small, small is the supple planet / three, three virginal invents to a proper planet / actions, actions halt in your poles for planets / first, level is first set in your planets / singles, singles in shingles burned planets / stock, stock of flooded planets / echo, echo for business and miles for your planets / depends, depends a dollar on your nearest planets / obtains, obtains a travel for the fellows planets / mostly, mostly a missile for the planets in zen loved / depths, depths into dollars and planets / seeds, seeds settle into optional planets / enabled, enabled in able planets / distant, distant in daily posits and planets / oracles, oracles have met in your planets / seeking, seeking a reaping planet / images, images aim into planets / divisions, divisions gone in sizeable planets / chien, chien in planets / kou, kou is now a planetary tribal bit for a planet / tieng jen, tieng jen is our planet for the flown planets / li, li is a plea for a planet / po, po is wo for a freewheeled planet / pi, pi is the sigh for a planet / ken, ken said, "a planet" / i, i way planets / feng, feng due a planet / sun, suns are our planets / ko, lo do in a planet / meng, meng mays and multi-planetary days / kun, kun sunned planets / hsiao kuo, hsiao kuo for the flowering planet / fu, fu is the mu for a planet / yu, yu for the floating planets / rushes, rushes hushed and planned planets / together, together in your planets / joyousness, joyousness inside planets / simply, simply a sample planet / extraordinary, extraordinary days in our planets / oldest, oldest for flowing planets / man, man is a bali planet / wife, wife fedora heads planets / laid, laid in a dialect andean in love's planets / ideas, ideas for a flown planet / goals, goal in our planets / earthly, earthly in our planets / ends, ends granite too, planets / meditate, meditate in your planets / heavens, heavens help us to planetary mends / both, both who know secrets of planets.

CHAPTER FOUR

Durations, durations forming your planets / strengths, strengths inside a planet / tops, tops intrigued for planet / winds, winds indecisive to a planet / finest, finest fellows found, planet / macrocosm, macrocosms misty in planets / cyclic, cyclic successions in planets / thirds, thirds and a threesome set, planets / motions, motions into motions for planet / joined, joined an elect group and planets / durations, durations rapt with planets spun / heavens, heavens held in planet's planets / principles, principles principative for planets / stands, stands in signal planets / conditions, conditions concurrent too, planets / ideas, ideas retreat inside planets / retreats, retreats are over loud planets / greatness, greatness found inside planets / enough, enough to sustain us and participate too, planets / attains, attains a reach too, planets / inferior, inferior without a planets / holds, holds in held onto a planets / weaves, weaves in a basic's planets / judgements, judgements made yours a planet / threes, threes who follow your planets / strong, strong in signals and planets / mastery, mastery makes yours another planet / tears, tears in a fear left for planets / craving, craving is creative to our planets / fortunes, fortunes inside formed potency and pleasureable planets / facts, facts are final in a planets / waters, waters willing and planted in planets / nourishments, nourishments reaching your politest planets / all, all is the sealing planet / trigram, trigrams written into planets / seeking, seekings planets / fates, fates final to a planets / spying, spying is done to a planet / paths, paths pungent in planets / hills, hills simple into planets / abyss, abyss blissed for planets / windows, windows winking planetarily / bowls, bowls of basic humanity and your planets / wines, wines who willed you your basics, plenty for the planets / vessels, vessels who value the female planets / inner, inner is sought A planets / disquiets, disquiets going to planetary gaze / dangers, dangers fold into planets / rivers, rivers now reaching your planets / protects, protects a position amid planets / realms, realms who reason in planets / dangers, dangers direct to your planets / bottoms, bottoms over all planets / middle, middle missions and planets / rice, rice red planets / blames, blames bossed planets / guarded, guarded visions and planets / flows, flows a significant planet / results, results amuse your planets / nuclear, nuclear needings planets / blames, blames off a planet / earthiness, earthiness is sought through planets / knots, knots out a planets / lose, lose the lessen, planets win.

CHAPTER FIVE

Arouse, arouse is given a planets / joy, joy is the lesson for planets / grace, grace is grown in a planets / occupations, occupations, impatience and the vocations for love's planets / kins, kins for the cleaning planets / whitened, whitened and the reminded planets / plains, plains in refrains and record for rewarded planets / cleared, cleared and the shared planets / weekly, weekly a mission forming your planets / alliances, alliances seeking our planets / correspondences, correspondences drained without patents for planets / linens, linens leaking a planets / depends, depends upon missions and planets / models, models melting your planets / kings, kings ringing your planets / party, party for the plain planets / mobile, mobile in a mission's planets / books, books delivered and fed to a planets / returns, returns again, planets / goods, goods grew into planets / bad, bad for the forgotten planets / alone, alone in a single planet / midst, midst and a marriage for the filling planets / walking, walking wills and your planets / grains, grains for the green-ing planets / remorse, remorse is remorse without planets / rests, rests for the resting planets / shorts, shorts into a single set of planets / returns, returns to the ringing planets / essentials, essentials for the firming planets / press, press into shining planets / seventh, seventh rims inside planets / likewise, like wise in shrugging planets / oppose, oppose has gone to a planets / tireless, tireless in hireless planets / firsts, firsts in a firming planet / 24, 24 who knew of planets / centrally, centrally a genuine planet / showering, showering shilling planets / calmest, calmest clues and planets / guilts, guilts who go into your planted planets / rulers, rulers reached a planets / moves, moves for the firmament's planets / symbolizes, symbolizes and eulogizes your planet / illnesses, illnesses finished for planets / evils, evils go past a pledge's planets / ended, ended in rended planets / weeks, weeks who knew whistles and planets / standstill, standstills over and planets spun / september, september the gift for a planets / forever, forever the lesson of planets / increased, increased to aspects in your planets / places, places who finished in planets / peaceful, peaceful surgically, a planets / links, links exist for missing planets / withdrawn, withdrawn has gone to a new planet's coming, again, love / seeds, seeds are the sprung from the planets / wonders, wonders whistle into a planet / doored, doored rides across your planets / fruits, fruits who follow your planet's spreads / tops, tops into triple planets / furthering, furthering is othering your planets / symbolic, symbolic seals to planets / self, self is the same, planets.

CHAPTER SIX

Heats, heats are running your planetary strips / tortoise, tortoise-shelled looks into planets / anvils, anvils and sandals and planets / helmets, helmets are off now, wars done, move into the new planet / tongues, tongues wagged now are done, a new, planet / salty, salty simple tears and wearing forgiven a planet / grounds, grounds for the final planets / notes, notes established are due your planets / suns, suns about you, planets / middles, middles meanings and planets / costs, costs are over A planets / fruits, fruits into morsels and planets / seeds, seeds signal bursting planets / mussels, mussels swimming in dreaming planets / paid, paid for and bought through planets / edges, edges erased and planets expand / wisdoms, wisdoms expansive viewed as a planet / realized, realized recovery for the few planets / life, life is leaping into your planets / covers, covers off a planets / masters, masters made your planets / pride, pride in the simple, planets / cattle, cattle who gather in planets / things, things who thrice said, planets / intellects, intellects silent without planets / hundreds, hundreds heard about in planets / seams, seams bursting for planets / strict, strict in a simple planet / rags, rags who richly, planet / fresh, fresh in a fresher planet / beloved, beloved manners and planets / embraces, embraces reaching your planets / speaks, speaks again for planets / images, images risen to planets / unveils, unveils a plan for the planet / feels, feels your arrival, a planet / states, states into stages for planets / cups, cups stacking in planets / sublime, sublime to a simple planet / sacks, sacks rip to pour a planet /

piles, piles over, planets / images, images matching your planets / effects, effects are effective for planets / either, either the either for a planet / mister, mister in the visor paid for planets / gales, gales are gaining a planets / attracts, attracts a simplistic plan for planets / totally, totally tooled in plenty and planetary building for Antarean prodigy / testimony, testimony for the ruling planets / someone, someone who knew a planet / rejoins, rejoins the living planets / roof, roof off and over a planet / negative, negative implosions gone to planetary cores / realms, realms are ruling your planets / built, built in a basic planet / eternity, eternity filing into planets / substances, substances sustaining a planet / done, done to a detail for planets / dogs, dogs are remaining in your planets / times, times into training and planets / dragging, dragging a horse through your planets / vomitous, vomitous victims lead to planets / firm, firm in the final waves and planets / stages, stages are over, won, planets.

CHAPTER SEVEN

Lion, lion leads Judah home to her planets / miracles, miracles occuring today, a planet / gardens, gardens grew in rainbow's view and planets / sinks, sinks go, planets / body, body blissed in planets / feelings, feelings focus on planets / evidence, evidence is sent for, planets / beloved, beloved solved planets / lotus, lotus license and planets / students, students who merge in a planets / wedges, wedges are over a planet / entirety, entirety mentioned in planets / hearts, hearts who heard your planets sing / serving, serving a living planet / courage, courage is the outrageous experience of love's planets / money, money is meant for your doorways to planets / reach, reach into simply a planet / solitary, solitary in the issues of planets / humans, humans sho hope for a planet / say, say for a saying planet / freedoms, freedoms insure your pledge to a planets / joys, joys issue your planet / tensions, tensions framing planets / fires, fires who keep you in a planet / grasped, grasped in a planet for love / ray, ray to the rays formed in planets / light, light is the leading planet / doves, doves to a touring planet / powerful, powerful in a purpose for planets / think, thinks a treaty for these planets / glory, glory rising into planets / longs, long for a peak into planets / government, government growing her planets / very, very is the simple in placement of planets / father, father is finally a planet / quickening, quickening has come to a planet / absolutely, absolutely is the gifted planet / opposites, opposites attractive in planets / tonight, tonight is the ritual for a planet / definite, definite the duo of planets / governed, governed in granted planets / yours, yours the disciple of planets / clearest, clearest clues and planets / happiest, happiest yielded for planets / below, below a balanced planet / harmonious, harmonious hearings planets / sent, sent formally into planets / answers, answers formed in planets / opposites, opposites simple in planted planets / charges, charges chiming your planets / electron, electrons leaping your planets / grasps, grasps a risen day's planets / orbitals, orbitals ripening your planets / power, powers placed in your planets / nucleus, nucleus allowing your planets / values, values placed inside planets / considered, considered for a formal planet / gas, gas is generous to a planet / outermost, outermost formations and planets / shelters, shelters and the planets cored in love / atoms, atoms reaching your planets / screenings, screening simple in planets / rows, rows arranging a planet / voices, voices volley your planets.

CHAPTER EIGHT

Recognized, recognized arms and red planets / orbitals, orbitals to the mars within a planet / chemicals, chemicals coming into carriage from a planet / neon, neons due a planet / recognized, recognized a reason for planets / settles, settles your dispute in a fashioned planets / corresponds, corresponds relation to a planets / elevates, elevates a volley through your planets / outermost, outermost intrigues with a planes and planets / occupying, occupying a reaching planets / three, three who know the way home to polite planets / obtained, obtained a contract for a planets / configurations, configurations consistent to the planets / shells, shells steepled in planets / titanium, titanium reaches and planets / fives, fives who thrive in planets / systems, systems open to pleasing planets / recognized, recognized a reject for these planets / zinc, zinc is filling your planets / stable, stable inside two planets / except, except for these, a few, planets / rules, rules are filed in posits and planets / fillings, filings made are glad to be a planets / coppers, coppers and the shillings sent to planets / magnetics, magnetics kinetic to these planets / collections, collections carry your planets home / promotions, promotions made are electrically free to this planet / spins, spins in spanish interests and freed planets / notes, notes nurtured and freely planetary / ends, ends met in planets treed / quantums, quantums measureable in their planets / electrons, electrons leaking a leaping planet / factors, factors fuse in a planets / strengths, strengths signalled as planetary / rows, rows in the shows and planetary strains / ends, ends met planetarily / about, about this race, planetary status / electronic, electronic seeds and planets / radius, radius reached is planetary / deliverance, deliverance arranged through the planetary rays / booths, booths opened into the patient planets / organs, organs grew to cover your planetary scars / density, density has gone to the ends planetary / carbons, carbons cycle in fibers and friends of the planetary / factors, factors fixed inside the planetary / single, single sessions win those planetaries / suggested, suggested yes! to the planets / clouded, clouded in cubits and the ruses for planets / influences, influences genuine into a planet / under, under the nearer standing planets / table, tables tripling your nearing planets / lithium, lithium returns into a planet / electrons, electrons, the right ons for a planet / violence, violence forming a forgiveness for a planets / decreases, decreases recreasing your planets / sodium, sodium sealing a plenty of planets / lowering, lowering expectancy without an a planet / numbers, numbers essential into prophetic plenty and the similitude for planets / nucleus, nucleus and a nexus for planets / shows, shows a showering forming your planets / geometry, geometry gentling inside your planets / frozen, frozen inside your planets / wave, waves winning your planets a punched outing / functions, functions freedom and planets planning your love's steps / thaws, thaws frozen have come into a planet

CHAPTER NINE

Blocks, blocks forming your planets / born, born inside a settled place and planets / frequently, frequently fresh in your planetary places / atomic, atomically an anatomic planted planet / systems, systems around your planets / electrons, electrons marry your planets / functions, functions progressing into your plenty and pleading goes to a planet / writes, write a reading progression for a plenty and planets / zero, zero disguised without planets / exercises, exercises inside a green planet / triangulars, triangulars ripened in planets / structures, structures forward your planets / orbitals, orbitals peaceful inside planets / geometrically, geometrically cured armaments and planets / chapters, chapters federal in planets / twos, twos ruled and a planet / overlapping, overlapping cubes inside planets / vainest, vainest has gone into your loving planets / lines, lines are limited with your planets / stoves, stoves are still in your written planets / fish, fish or filled, planets / anothers, others and anothers in lanes and planets / used, used a mood to move a planets / wells, wells are sails into the planets / concerned, concerned about this, nature's key, these planets / neglects, neglects have lost your toss into planets / suddenly, suddenly we free your planets / jug, jug is the rug into a planets / sorts, sorts who cavort about planets / mights, mights in the sights of these planets / lemons, lemons squeezed for yellow extremes in a planets / troubles, troubles off and over all a planets / must, must became will in a name, planets / catch, catch a detail of the divorce called living planet schemes / drinks, drinks are dallied about in streams and planets / shallows, shallows spill into shadowy graves for a planets / mire, mire into that dark rift called the xibalba be of a planets / inert, inert actions carry you to the a planets / moves, moves are made, planets / lost, lost is the tossed planet / done, done in a sun's planets / coves, coves simple in those planets / shackles, shackles off, feed afresh in a planet / fondness, fondness of sorrow can leave for a planet / practical, practical in the simple planets / noted, noted in devoted news of planets / names, names who simply imply a new planet / tasks, tasks reward your planets planes / weapons, weapons mundane unto life for all planets / tongues, tongues who check their delay long enough to say "planet wise" / eureka, eureka you have the heart of a planet / holes, holes have repaired their way, planets / derive, derive a daily basis for your planets / often, often in singing "planets" / agency, agency for the sun of a planet / suns, suns reaching your planets / tortoise, tops and the tortoise who loves your planet/ labors, labors herculaean are finished in these planets / bodies, bodies have merged into a planet / corporeal, corporeal reality for your planets / spatial, spatial seeking and a planet / tao, tao is how? a planet / shown, shown in simple planetary spelling / swelling, swelling is shutting throats who say "planetary dumping."

CHAPTER TEN

Suit, suit in the new hotel called love's planet / posited, posited in rewarded planets / may, may we wee into hours call seeking a planets / position, position of the simple? planets / change, change a venue then, planets / cosy, cosy is rosey within certain pleasing planets / cases, cases are strung in a planets / coveted, coveted and riveted for as your planet / dragons, dragons who leap in a trickle of flooding planets / persons, persons recognizing your inter-planetary discipline of insured mentions / signify, signify a how to your planets / constantly, constantly and consistently your doorway to the planets / forms, forms in a fashioned planet / entire, entire in extremes and your planets / strands, strands who simply find and define planets / places, places who nestle into planetary games / storage, storage infinite in a planet / corrections, corrections to directions and planets / repects, respects your ransomed planet / temporal, temporal temples and palmate planets / spatial, spatials in structural planes and clear planets / powers, powers to be planetarily lifted / luck, luck is your final planet/ withdraws, withdraws into scenes and planets / cases, cases made are fine, planets / masters, masters given and lived for in planets / cardinal, cardinal trends for your planets / accomplished, accomplished victory to your doors and soft planets / empires, empires spent in a planets / zero, zero is the discourse without your planets / higher, higher instill of a planetary life / appealing, appealing in sealing two to one planets / dangers, dangers gone to a planet / images, images ripe in your planets / timely, timely departs into planets / dangerous, dangerous in onerous planets / ambitions, ambitions reach pitch to a planet / facts, facts are fitted into your planets / transitional, transitional mentioned planets / charades, charades go to your planets / correspond, correspond to news, planets / bunks, bunks inside planets / smiles, smiles in files and planets / stillest, stillest reaches and the details for planets / qualities, qualitied squelched without planets / progressions, progressions and the guides about planets / possessions, possessions lighten in planets / lightens, lightens a suspect for planets / specialties, specialties in news for planetary suspend / bewilders, bewilders gate has blownt o the winds of remembered planets / respects, respects for the hilo halo and the hallowed planet / orbitals, orbitals abuzz in bursting planes and planets / increments, increments sunk without your planets / firms, firms who hold a fallow path toured in planets / controls, controls have simply gifted your departure to higher portals in planets / leaving, leaving is soon to a planets/ planes, planes are pitched to a planets / corrected, corrected a sake for a former planet / resultant, resultant inspections and planets / erstwhile, erstwhile has earth while gone to your planets / sons, sons of the batches who bastion their planets / blasted, blasted is lasted for through your planets / lives, lives who link to planets / goes, goes a grace for planets.

CHAPTER ELEVEN
Chimes, chimes who ring in symphonic planets / bottoms, bottoms built onto planets / basics, basics written for planets / middles, middles cleared in a planet / stands, stands made form a planet / divinity, divinity published a planet / marketed, marketed and sought for for planets / restored, restored in truth to planets / returns, returns a profitable planet / probable, probable cause erupts in planets / waves, waves overload in planets / splits, splits apart reigns and planets / apart, apart the simple planets / rules,

rules brushing your perfect planets / forces, forces gathered leave your planets / dark, dark has simple lift into clerical planets / goes, goes a growing planet / principles, principles in simple planets / established, estalbished rites for planets / ripening, ripening has softened your planets / imagery, imagery and magic and planets / active, active relations and planets/ nourishments, nourishments reaching your parched planets / pathways, pathways purged and formed as planets / politics, politics rich in planets / sharpest, sharpest respect goes to planets / matters, matters and meanings for a planet/ craving, craving has risen into planets / eyed, eyed and ridden past as planets / sharpening, sharpening is shining a planet / places, places in respectful planets / lightly, lightly a sight for planets / enclosed, enclosed formats and planetary guise / sponges, sponges in rungs and reaches for planets / absorbed, absorbed a mighty planet / caves, caves create your planet's guides / spaces, spaces races and planets / jungles, jungles to missions and managed planets / monads, monads reaching your planets / intended, intended into a planet / India, India is simple inside planets / yours, yours the yes! too and planets / worthy, worthy the foundations of the world and the dome inside a temple mount for planets / focused, focused in fusions and planets / existence, existence readers and planets / later, later the lips form a planetary hum / harmonized, harmonized hearings and humming planets / solved, solved signature planets / sinister, sinister lifts from your planets / forceful, forceful inside a planets / dimes, dimes roomy for a planet / courage, courage has come to a planet / glory, glory rooming your planets / problems, problems profit your planets / runs, runs roomy for a planet / understood, understood / loved, loved a living planet / low, low self has ressurection without a planet / easily, easily said "your direction" is missed without a planetary plane / durst, durst in the while for a planets / embellished, embellished is relished in your planets / relished, relished is rich to a planet / artful, artful in smartened planets / rampant, rampant reaches and planets

CHAPTER TWELVE
Enlarged, enlarged rooms and ripening planets / yearly, yearly the stooping without a planet / alone, alone in the sunders and planets / remembered, remembered in a recount of planets / octaves, octaves roomy for planets / steads, steads and the leads aim too, planets/ weekly, weekly amounting for and planets / amazed, amazed reorder and a planet / looking, looking in simple planets / individuals, individuals account to your planets / places, places reigning for planets 1/ describes, describes a duration for planets / rejoiced, rejoiced armatures form a planets / accomplished, accomplished inside a planet / intruded, on sight intrusions into planets / system, systems intrude past planets / beckons, beckons within your planets/ presence, presence fade to planets / dynamics, dynamics simple in planets / try, try to say "a planet" / speak, speaks amounting to a planet / loudly, loudly due a planet / firmly, firmly forthright in your planets / stops, stops insured a planet/ mentally, mentally mentioned planets / chimes, chimes amount to systems and planets / received, received a recommended planet / breathe, breathe above a ranching planet / pounds, pound around

your planets / british, bred to be a british admit to a planet / ours, ours is the simple planet / physically, physically a psychic prinicple for planets / students, students rank in a filed planet / matters, matters material in planets / fold, folds eloquent for a planet / sturdy, sturdy respect of your planets / pisgah, pisgah is the mountain to your planet / mounts, mounts amounting to a planet / amounted, amounted inspire for a planet / trims, trims insured in your planets / tires, tires the retiring aim to planets / tops, tops in the respect for planets / tricks, tricks are over a planet / terpitude, terpitude is in the mood for planets / motions, motions made and planets / watery, watery wades past a planet / oceans, oceans realm mystic to a planet / domes, domes over eaten planets / clerical, clerical zeal and a healing planet / energy, energy gaining your upsurping planet / needs, needs matched in planets / greatest, greatest the respect for planets / hotels, hotels flower in planets / bangkok, bangkok is the restock for a planet / orchids, orchids reaching a planetary reign / pools, pools and spools and planets / lotus, lotus rimmed planets / worlds, worlds worthy to your planets / goodwills, goodwills simple planets / crystals, crystals reward your planets / constant, content in the constant creation for a planet / eights, eights to the rates of planets / reaches, reaches in missions and planets / ease, ease now into your planets.

CHAPTER THIRTEEN

Degrees, degrees beheld in a planets / raises, raises a glass to your plenty in planets / greater, greater the gifts there in a planets / peopled, peopled in simple respect for a planets / fixed, fixed into peopled stares and your planets / sacred, sacred the reading lanes and planets / accepts, accepts respect to a planets / loving, loving the leaving planets / homes, homes respected and made in a planets / cosmic, cosmic concurrence to planets / intelligent, intelligent ofrgettingof less than all planets / longer, longer the linger in planets / supreme, supreme is the dream God mtched to planet / flames, flames flower in planet's plans / cellular, cellular disconnections in a planets / asks, asks for remittance and a planets / calls, calls a simple task to planetary remission / operatically, operatically and eratically fresh planets / goodness, goodness goes to planets / teach, teach a taught planet / laws, laws eddy in planetary strains / US, US the misty planet / chion, chion high in planets / Ming I, Ming I the detail of a daimon called planets / Hsion, hsion is the Zion formed planets / hsich, hsich is the opening in a planet / clever, clever the delivery to a planet / wise, wise is the sill to a window for planets / presence, presence is simple to your planets / happiness, happiness is directly a planet / locality, locality is legal to a planet / neighbors, neighbors notice your planets / actions, actions have taken a planet / outer, outer in the inner planets / fradulent, fradulent debate about planets / supreme, supreme in the dreaming for a planets / born, born to be basically planets / bring, bring a ring home to your planets / watching, watching is waiting for your planets / shining, shining is simple for all planets / glints, glints in a basic planet / glows, glows the effect for your planets / glowers, glowers in streams and times and planets / ordinates, ordinates a formed planet / recreates, recreates a simple drive into planets / radical, radical

approaches work for your planets / oxygenated, oxygenated and refreshed through planets / originated, originiated in the seed plan of planets / rafters, rafters built for your planets / clues, clues now rich in your planets / cooperative, coooperative aspects for your planets / culmination, culminations come to a planets / classical, classical in simple planets / kindnesses, kindnesses gone to your planets / practical, practical in simple planets / randomly, randomly jumps to your planets / oriented, oriented to a plane for planets / arranged, arranged in stars and planets / reaps, reaps in seeping planets / registered, registered a simple find for a planets / rustic, rustic the acreage given to a planet / acreage, acreage given is opened and found in a planets / oceanfront, oceanfront and simply your planet / ruses, ruses have met your planets.

LEVEL 79: THE PORT-MENTS

CHAPTER ONE

Thrills, thrills healing our ports / supplies, supplies succeeded and passed into ports / energy, energy of the efficient in ports / today, today is the deal made for ports / powers, powers who be will, ports / flows, flows a flowering port / off, off into news of your ports / forth, forth is the fellow's ports / banquet, banquets blue in your ports / fervor, fervor flavored and ported / marshall, marshall between in your ports / able, able to bellow past, ports / islands, islands who kneel at last, ports / underneath, underneath us each, ports / brains, brains in visage kept and ports / visors, visors linking your ports / voyages, voyages into the vastness for ports / limits, limits go to a ports / confirmations, confirmations coming to a port / effectively, effectively upstarted and armed in a port / unlimited, unlimited limits and ports / mankind, manking simple and port wise / proof, proof is a sample for a port rise / sustained, sustained and mentioned too, a ports / fullness, fullness in a final port / streams, streams are ports too / long, long in the lead into ports / life, life is the led forth port / doses, doses and the roses for ports / crews, crews who regard you as a port / generated, generated and ports / worlds, worlds wisdom and ports / harmony, harmony entailed as a port / odyssey, odyssey simple to a port / merits, merits and the ports in love / generations, generations who gap in a loving port / dues, dues final, ports / worlds, worlds warrant a ports / harmonized, harmonized leaps into ports / lifelined, lifelined in simple ports / generational, generationally a port / detailed, detailed in final ports / contents, contents ripen and support your ports / constrain, constrain regains a port / glorious, glorious objectives and protean ports / joined, joined a port through love / directives, directives in invective of a ports / durations, durations detailing your ports / wonders, wonders supportive of your ports / wisdoms, wisdoms wisest port / holds, holds fill your ports / times, times trickle in ports / wrong, wrong gone to a port / try, try to be has left for a port / attentive, attentive into research and ports / attention, attention on a port / sustenance, sustenance sought in new ports / repents, repents intents and a port

/ cosmically, cosmically a creation for ports / fulfilled, fulfilled in example and samples and ports / infinite, infinite in experience for ports / placed, placed a bet to a port / pulses, pulses revulses and ports / rhetoric, rhetoric recalled for your ports.

CHAPTER TWO
Decrees, decrees daily, a port / wholeness, wholeness fertile in a ports / glory, glory glorious again, ports / bless, bless this reaction to a port / ports, ports replaced in a faced respect for love / limits, limits over and ports found in love / fullfilled, fulfilled a smattering for ports / beats, beats about your doors ports / heart, heart in the heat freed and ports / governs, governs a growing port / pours, pours into ports / dreads, dreads are fed to ports / rendering, rendering is final, ports / light, light insists on led planes and ports / atone, atone the scientific for a port called love's access / upon, upon this rock, ports / blossoms, blossoms a blooming port / students, students who sign for a port / communications, communications are simple, a port appeared / dressing, dressing inside a port / blessed, blessed be, protests less in ports / throughout, throughout us all ports / themselves, themselves a restitute port / fastened, fastened into a port / controls, controls off a port / questions, questions simple into ports / wearisome, wearisome winning ports / boards, boards and basic ports / introduced, introduced into ports / ones, ones and the running ports / right, right is the simple port / desired, desired a friendly port / largesse, largesse is sincere in a port / attention, attention to simple ports / stands, stands and a duration for ports / produced, produced definition for ports / acted, acted in sugary ports placed / instance, instance in similar ports / deprived, deprived a ratio of lessened ports / understood, understood a rhyming port / labors, labors lost without ports / applause, applause is elect to ports / blessing, blessing forms a port / guards, guards gained and transported / forgiven, forgiven and given ports / barest, barest basics and ports / cleared, cleared a climbing port / quickly, quickly said "ports" / classes, classes withstood and a ports / thousands, thousands and the thresholds for all ports / untouched, untouched insure for a ports / spots, spots in a simple port / messengers, messengers extravagant in ports / retreats, retreats related to ports / worlds, worlds who whistle win, ports / retractions, retractions and statements for ports / actions, actions made simple in ports / instruments, instruments for the listed gifts and ports / covers, covers creating your ports / faces, faces to a finished port / selves, selves suggestive of your posted ports / dozens, dozens due a posted port / edges, edges erase your posted ports / easily, easily significant in a ports.

CHAPTER THREE
Magic, magic is made near your ports / ascension, ascension is given to your ports / experiences, experiences settle into ports / bounds, bounds and the basics for ports / insanity, insanity inside these planetary ports / dictators, dictators and the maturity into a ports / balanced, balanced in basics and ports / today, today is the retinue of ports / clearly, clearly we eventfully spare your ports / manners, manners mannered into a ports / laudible, laudible in physics and ports / arabia, arabia is risen inside your ports / trained,

trained essentially for all ports / coverage, coverage is given your due ports / perfection, perfection mentioning your ports / sustained, sustained dimensions and ports / recovery, recovery raided in port sport / permits, permits admitted to and ports / dismissed, dismissed a survival of less than all ports / positional, positional mentions for ports A and B / forthright, forthright is the fixed port / fullest, fullest and featured in a ports / myself, myself the port / firms, firms mentioned as a port / projects, projects pensioned to a port / rivers, rivers and the waters edition for ports / covers, covers engaged in and ports / cords, cords inside your ports / dissolved, dissolved in sincere ports / volumetric, obstruct can restruct your ports / measured, measured in resurrected treasures and sports / closed, closed through your ports / healed, healed inside your ports / breasts, breasts interior to all ports / pearls, pearls are basic for your ports / pureness, pureness essential in sports and ports / largely, largely due to a mother's loving ports / acquired, acquired a business for a ports / agency, agency jeweled in ports / presence, presence sequential in ports / accomplishments, accomplishments are aiming for all ports / infinite, infinite for armed ports / hearts, hearts hearty into all ports / years, years issue your ports / ability, ability is gifted into ports / absolves, absolves resolve and the devolves past ports / tissues, tissues emptied and ports opening / rise, rise to the risen ports / beauty, beauty is basic to your ports / utmost, utmost is essential for ports / ordinary, ordinary delivery into ports / electricity, electricity leaking from ports / fires, fires fixed into ports / in, in a side pockets ports / on, on this day, ports / too, too and all, ports / views, views essential in ports / conditions, conditions may very for ports / sounds, sounds and the rounded port / positions, positions taken and filled ports / entertained, entertained anothers ports / grew, grew in essential ports / messengers, messengers of directional ports / spreads, spreads a word, "ports."

CHAPTER FOUR
Annointed, annointed and basically a fend for all ports / enegetically, energetically open again too, ports / messages, messages received inside ports / messengers, messengers aiming for ports / aims, aims admitted, ports / invitations, invitations fitted into ports / returning, returning has given you a balanced port / stances, stances portfolio wide and balanced / luminosity, luminosity lent to a ports / floats, floats fitting port / furls, furls dealt with ports / steps, steps made and imported / stern? stern? forgiven and ports / turning, turning a triple into a portals / merging, merging is mentioned as a portal / meeting, meetings settle for a portals / mounted, mounted and counted for as a portal / managed, managed to see your portals / slanted, slanted extrudes into moods for a portals / strong, strong is the bond between portals / strengthened, strengthened and simplified as planned and portals / managed, managed a moment to all ports / merged, merged for all ports / rung, rung into ports / bells, bells are smart with a port / details, details gotten here, ports / durable, durable and basic too, a port / committed, committed into ports / marathons, marathons over, ports / grand, grand is the scale for all ports / fathers, fathers fixing your ports / mothers, mothers and the threaded

ports / miracles, miracles maintained and imported / amounting, amounting into your ports / shouting, shouting in single ports / shields, shields smug within ports / crafted, crafted thirds and ports / cubed, cubed inside swirling ports / skulls, skulls cracked without ports / glory, glory is drugged without a ports / obtain, obtain a stripe through your ports / abstained, abstained remained in your ports / key, key is issued for a port / keys, keys individual to ports / proof, proof is the basic for ports / physical, physical intrigue in a port / opens, penultimate ports / conditions, conditions and the heartlines in your ports / assured, assured of sines and measured ports / pours, pours a doorway to a port / mentioned, mentioned days and ports / worldly, wordly wise ports / climbs, climbs a cord past ports / parks, parks inside basic ports / comprehends, comprehends a classic port / climbs, climbs suspended ports / comprehends, comprehends written ports / renders, renders spun ports / ends, ends in a day for all ports / spends, spends a minute in your door's ports / renders, renders us smiling import / lands, land's port / phosphorous, phosphorous and fuels import / spools, spools who measure a thread for ports widths.

CHAPTER FIVE
Akhenaton, Akhenaton spun into ports / aton, aton drew us to her ports / presence, presence is sent to a ports / plasma, plasma is pooling in streams of delivery from ports of old / screened, screened in remember for the september floods in ports / stools, stools and the tsunami blue delivery from ports / portals, portals peaceful and freed for all light supports / shone, shone a new flow into pele bay, a light port / compounded, compounded the Christ-headed example to a maintain for unique ports / fills, fills and the seals electric for living ports / mountains, mountains smiling with port holds / voices, voices volley into these ports / long, long is the neglect gone from this door of acknowledged ports / breasts, breasts who sag with elevations and ports / collectives, collectives in retreat for all ports / selective, selective electives and ports / voices, voices who vary without, ports / vandals, vandals eliminated for past positions and ports / scandals, scandals over due for cleaning of their ports / lenders, lenders have paid your port tax / slender, slender is the mender of all ports / claims, claims have held up for years and ports / offers, offers made have held you close for years and your ports / offended? offended? is mended for your ports / mines, mines electric with ports / minerals, minerals mined and paid for with port taxed / waists, waists go to a ports / worn, worn the slimmest, ports / fleets, fleets who fellow your ports / upon, upon us all a ports / hands, hands who help your port sail / quench, quench the thirst of westward ho through ports escape / inner, inner the visions and the menu for all ports / locality, locality is neutral in ports / explanations, explanations going to a port / pacts, pacts made cleared ports / contracts, contracts given rinsed expense for a ports / promised, promised a friend to meet there, ports / forgives, forgives us well and finds frozen estates within their ports / feels, feels acknowledge has gone to a coming event, all in, ports / harmonious, harmonious heralds and port winds / vortex, vortex volleys your ports / vibrancy, vibrancy returns to a ports / releases, releases are followed into your ports / forgiven,

forgiven is risen into through your yellow port, a solar plexus sort / frequent, frequent in recent trines, a ports / encouraged, encouraged the follow through to ports / searches, searches have ended in ports / finds, finds a flush for all ports within / asks, asks us who? and wells with your ports / told, told to follow your port walks / continuity, continuity as mentioned is fine in a ports / totals, totals written into ports / above, blue issues and fallen ports extend / life, life is lush in port news / descends, descends a direct line from akhenaton and the aton and the diatomic wonder called humanity, a port called / all, all who herald seek a port / shadows, shadows elastic sport port clearances / gone, gone is the schedule and found is your port / sourced, sourced a sincerity to all ports / imposed, imposed is the stalling fleet port / hydrogen, hydrogen seeking one covalent bond for all ports / suns, suns in the one, two ports / helium, helium floats across seats and ports.

CHAPTER SIX
Mastery, mastery is mentioned in a ports / afloat, afloat the smiles for port doors / in, in a simple measure, ports / twice, twice the tickle for proof of ports / the, the triple port shows / final, finally found, a ports / summary, summary is sealed, final news, a port / courage, courage is your yellow two reports / cures, cures made real, ports / young, young in deals? ports / days, days melt into ports / dearly, dearly the dearest imports / detailed, detailed inspections for import / investments, investments mentioned and reported / respects, respects, suspects, and ports / rejects, rejects doorways and ports / rushes, rushes past ports / roses, roses yellow fade into ports / furls, furls flash across green seas and ports / spirals, spirals sincerest port / spurls, spurls and furls and ports / storage, storage electric with prototypes and proven ports / strings, strings sing in port stops / rings, rings are rung withal, ports / lands, lands and the islands within, ports / islands, islands measured, ports / storage, storage is sent to a port / moves, moves your made port / creations, creations cushion your ports / prepare, prepare to stay close to your ports / suspend, suspended animation for armed ports / sully, sully is ruled without ports / mules, mules carry canyons wide to a port / facts, facts fit, ports / flattened, flattened and saddened without proteins and ports / choices, choices made are sympathetic for ports / rotations, rotations register as ports / moods, moods mist your ports / rails, rails ran past your ports / tricks, tricks are honed in a clearest port / glue, glue the glass to a fashioned foundation port / fuels, fuels spell, p-o-r-t-s / accomplishment, accomplishment is acknowledged through a collegiate port / expansions, expansions coming, ports / reckoning, reckoning happens, ports / sacrements, sacrements sacrosanct to ports / oceans, oceans calling your ports home / physicality, physicality has left for new ports / accomplished, accomplished in the similar ports / expanded, expanded and landed, ports / expansive, expansive raves and rated ports / terrific, terrific and sundry too, ports / powerful, powerful mansions and ports bought / pardoned, pardoned for a winning port / illuminated, illuminated rapt ports / sources, sources saged for all ports / resourced, resourced daily ports / reset, reset respect for the old forgiven port / jet, jet to join your new ports / join, join now the

industry cleared, ports / hollow, hollow has come to gone ports / follow, follow winning opportunities and ports / floral, floral the fix into ports / flowers, flowers emulient with port scents.

CHAPTER SEVEN

Spread, spread a reason over your ports / purified, purified women and the won ports / sacred, sacred men and the ports end in love / fires, fires flush into ports / relived, relived living lunged ports / miraculous, miraculous in a meaningful port / contacts, contacts current in ports / consumed, consumed a dove's relation and port / hearts, hearts held open for love's ports / discord, discord a deluge for a ports / structures, structures ruptures and ports / generated, generated reports / pathos, pathos and the ports formed in resorts / security, security forms a port/ life, life in grips and ports / lights, lights opine in lined ports / list, list the necessary for ports / levels, levels blissed into port / brush, brush the sort who port / abrush, abrush the rushing ports / welcome, welcome to the swarm free port / volumes, volumes written, ones kept, ports / phrases, phrases and raises and ports / comments, comments current in ports / terms, terms remain port wide / phrased, phrased and raised into ports / narcissism, narcissism over, ports / transforms, transforms your warm ports / transfers, transfers raid your doors ports / berkley, berkley is set for you, ports / parts, parts who start into ports / fulfill, fulfill the selah for your port / faith, faith is fixed upon ports / truths, truths sand deep in your ports / paths, paths who sail past your ports / truth, truth is single without ports / essences, essences amounting to a port / liberty, liberty lingering to your ports / purchased, purchased to the lifted ports / liberties, liberties leading ports / saints, saints signed freshened and imported / raphael, raphael sailing to a port / authentic, authentic to a sports ports / dirt, dirt who leads to a ports / pretense, pretense is intense in your ports / falls, falls emit in your pretense and open ports / loved, loved a licensed port / humanity, humanity held in port / gratitude, gratitude given is won for a ports / glory, glory is the goodness said, "ports" / diamonds, diamonds rue and the roped explain for potable ports / pearls, pearls rhyming a ports / relaxed, relaxed amounts and ports / realms, realms affairs and a ports / elements, elements issued a port / inner, inner of ports / still, still the sealing ports / approached, approached a sort who import / cups, cups filled and ported / fours, fours since yearly ports / faiths, faith spent a prototypical port / youths, youths and staid ports / ports, ports and paces and sorts who import / grasped, grasped a sorts insect reports

CHAPTER EIGHT

Exactitude, exactitude and gratitude for a ports / lunged, lunged south and north without ports / loans, loans made are paid for a ports / listens, listens directly in ports / platitudes, platitudes and latitudes and a ports / lurch, lurch is left to a port / laps, laps sort your ports / dances, dances ranches and ports / forks, forks when and end ports / dual, dual and since a port / during, urgent missions during a ports / dual, dual and sincere in a port / lateral, lateral maintains and a ports / deepening, deepening in ripening ports / doors, doors shorts and ports / spun, spun inside a ports / empathy, empathy pungent with ports / blazing, blazing and trailing your sports / privation, privation and spread sports / federal, federal finds and sports / mirrors, mirrors material and sported / points, points formed in a ports / over, over a few who knew ports / particles, particles sparkle and port / porch, porch inside an a port / enthuse, enthused and spent for ports / remit, remit is simple, ports / rents, rents ascents and ports / fans, fans resign and a ports / emits, emits remit a port / runs, runs and suns and ports / roars, roars and soars and ports / lending, lending in sending and ports / lopes, lopes and lips and ports / attuned, attuned and runed and ports / linked, linked and sunk through a ports / mere, mere is near ports / merry, merry sherry and sport / federal, federal frames and ramification for a sports / fonts, fonts who shield a sports / handles, handles and mantles and moves for a port / lured, lured into a ports / fends, fends who ascend to a popular ports / forever, forever is ever a port / gains, gains landed in ports / grown, grown zones and a ports / trees, trees sizeable to a port / flips, flips slipping a port / flows, flows required in a port / flowers, flowers formatted fathered ports / flown, flown into a ports / penchants, penchants dna widened ports / places, places and the races formed into a port / purchase, purchase a relation and ports / priest, priestly listings and pearls grown into a ports / patterned, patterned precious inside a port / pointed, pointed in pointed ports / pants, pants rant about ports / positions, positions reposition into ports / pathways, pathways formal in ports / pages, pages and reflected ports / primes, primes and armed sorts who import / parts, parts left to a ports / pooling, pooling since a port.

CHAPTER NINE

Feels, feels felt ports / held, held a loving port / holds, hold open a port / on, on too a port / faded, faded a raided port / anterior, anteriors sincre in ranges ports / positive, positives rampant for ports / posted, posted races and ports / general, general in mineral ports / pals, pals sully for your ports / posts, posts roasts and a ports / ports, ports sort in a places / views, views in news of a placed port / previews, previews and relativity for a place and a port / positive, positivity and a positive placed port / poles, poles and purchased plants and ports / rigel, rigel the shingle and ports / universes, universes respect your ports / caster, caster sincere in a ports / pollux, pollux met your ports / gemini, gemini rubbing a port leg / canis, canis and the banners ports / minor, minor in a minute port / procyon, procyon pores and spores ports / sirius, sirius and simple ports / canis, canis amounting to ports / major, major metal orations and ports / orion, orion sincere in a ports / raurus, raurus taurus and the forging ports / auriga, aruiga and the rutile ports / capella, capella occupying your ports / perseus, perseus sporting yes! pools and these sports / cassiopeia, cassiopeia and the rewarded sports / cephus, cephus reigned ports / polaris, polaris pairing in ports / north, north the electives and ports / star, star signed ports / aldebaran, aldebaran and the random ports / ursa, ursa major and the material ports / minor, minor in simple ports / little, little and extensive into ports / dipper, dipper the dipping ports / draco, draco and the nazca lined ports / bootes, bootes and the major ports / ursa, ursa and the ruling ports / major,

major military durations ports / big, big is the stored ports / dipper, dipper dealt ports / virgo, virgo intensity and ports / spica, spica enriched for ports / corvus, corvus and the galactic ports / hydra, hydra ridden topped ports / libra, libra sent to a port palace / serpens, serpens rented ports / eastern, eastern and starring a mile long port / horizon, horizons and rights for a port / sky, sky shows and ports / latitudes, latitudes neters and ports / charts, charts in suggestions and ports / continental, continental courts and a port / practical, practical and the material in a port / vertical, vertical ranges and remaining ports / directives, directives rearranging a port / facing, facing fixed portals in ports.

CHAPTER TEN

Regulus, regulus relatus and ports / leo, leo and the legible places and ports / cancer, cancer and the cured ports / vega, vega and the values for ports / corona, corona and the curing ports / borealis, borealis and the blazes formed ports / hercules, hercules herculean in ports / night, nights risen to ports / sky, sky rich in a port / winter, winters winning ports / columbia, columbia blue imports and ports / summer, summer the simmer and ports / lights, lights lips and ports / matters, matters and matching a ports / gravitation, gravitation red imports / astronomy, strong in astronomy imported / graceful, graceful and simple in suggested imports / spiral, spiral and storing your ports / occurs, occurs a day's sorted ports / process, process is planned for your started imports / spectacular, spectacular events occur in streets and a recent port / systems, systems in systems and ports / moons, moons marry your sorts to your ports and light love / worlds, worlds and the willing sort's ports / living, living is linked in a ports / earth, earth shield off a fine golden port / suns, suns who sign your ports details / mercury, mercury missions and sorts who deal in potable ports / black, black the basic forgiven ports / holes, holes signed for a ransom's ports / neutrons, neutrons and the remains for a ports / stars, stars and the selah's ports / astronomy, astronomy ampered and issued for ports / antiquity, antiquity curing your ports / eclipse, eclipse a simple port / bright, brights and remains gone to a port / vagabonds, vagabonds and principle ports / worlds, worlds wedding your ports / jupiter, jupiter starring your ports / invades, invades a relational import for stars / stars, stars started your ports / natures, annual natures and ports / births, births remain in a ports / galaxy, galaxy basics and ports / galaxies, galaxies respecting your ports / quasars, quasars and questions and supports / early, early in the respectable ports / universes, universes reverses your ports / observations, observations rationale for a port / moons, moons matched into ports / galvanized, galvanized instincts and your ports / tilt, titles and initials and ports / sidereal, sidereal and surreal and port / times, times relative to a port / phases, phases and the treats formed in a ports / antiques, antiques remainders and ports / precessions, precessions and recessions gone to your ports / rotations, rotations and relations and ports / convenient, convenient and the relation formed for ports / imagine, imagine instincts and your ports / star, stars and double days and ports / suns, suns and signs and ports / lunar, lunar and the levels and ports / eclipse, eclipsed and steadied for a ports

CHAPTER ELEVEN

Names, names and the levelor's ports / catalogues, catalogues and clauses and ports / exponents, exponents and the components for all ports / formulas, formulas forming your ports / small, smallest in reaches and ports / angle, angle and the beats in your ports / denotes, denotes a noted port / skills, skills and the shielded ports / sky, sky and the sorts who import blue notes / positions, positions and the pulses and potable ports / objects, objects and the subjects for a formal port / parsecs, aptitudes for the removal for ports / created, created related and ports / times, times ripening your ports / trades, trades and the trades for your ports / tracks, tracks and the rafia for ports / invent, inventing a ports / established, established a blissful port for love / eclipses, eclipses relapses and ports / limits, limits remitted into a port / systems, systems ripen and ports / angles, angles sincerest and ports / surfaces, surfaces forming a port / slow, slow suggestions and ports / retrograde, retrograded ports / space, spaces and the sorts who import your love / flights, flights afforded and loved for a port / spacecraft, spacecraft and the reflex for love's ports / glows, glows and the showing ports / reveals, reveals reaching your ports / structure, structures and the relations and ports / earth, earth structures and ports / astral, astral explanantions and ports / formula, formula and the freedom for ports / exponents, exponents and the similar ports / small, smallest resigns and your ports / details, details and the definition for ports / orbits, orbits and solidarity for a port / volcano, volcano flues and the sports who initial a day's lattices / process, process your steepest imports / plate, plates lifting a port / tectonics, tectonics and the respect for a ports / surface, surfaces simple in ports / abundance, abudance and stillest imports / particles, particles and potions and ports / solar, solar silences and ports / wind, winds and the winding ports / terrestrial, terrestrial archives and a sputing ports / sides, sides who latticed accept your ports / rigid, rigids and the turgid respects for a ports / spells, spells and the spelling ports / excommunicated, excommunicated a related port / crystalline, crystalline inside single ports / churched, churched a regressed portal / rules, rules and the spools inside ports / catholic, catholic curing and ports / river, rivers reaching your doors and ports / mormon, mormon normals and ports / guilty, guilty gazes and ports / salt, salt sports and your ports / light, light the leashes for ports / speech, speech is respectful and a rememberance for all ports / lake, lake licensed ports / city, city sailing imports.

CHAPTER TWELVE

Books, books baring your ports / days, days reborn into a warm port / ruse, ruse is over and loving a port / pregnant, pregnant and the support for a loving sports / arrives, arrives a rival port / automatic, automatic respects formed a port / roles, roles and the supple ports / pause, pause defines your ports / nomen, nomen natives and sporting imports / articulate, articulate and immacualte in your pores and ports / relates, relates a rationality for a former import / pushing, pushing is steady for your given godspeed and an import / seven, seven simple in ports / arrivals, arrivals reveal your ports / relatives, relatives respectful for ports / two, two are relationship worthy and your port / years, years are yellow for formal imports / two, two who seal your doors flown import / christos, christos reading a single import / wear, wear the worthy poles and ports / lighten, lighten your loaded ports / lost, lost goes and imports / ledger, ledger lists a port's doors / pledge, pledge a plural import / link, link is licensed to a port / rainbows, rainbows and twinkling lines into ports / purchased, purchased a lane to the door for your ports / points, points are made and lines leaned into ports / leaping, leaping is lured without leaks and port flows / people, people who are yellow and your flowering ports / portions, portions and portions and ports / larks, larks and sharks and sports / spares, spares and races and ports / rare, rare in raging ports / fair, fairest ports / fare, fares and races and ports / rest, rest is settled into ports / dressed, dressed addresses and ports / conceived, conceived a current port / plans, plans and rains and ports / easy, easy races and ports / best, best sizes and ports / family, family followed port wise / relished, relished a rewarded port / emblems, emblems and materials and ports / ransoms, ransoms simplistic signals and ports / transistor, transistor refine and a ports / transits, transits ransoms and ports / relays, relays reward, a ports / duress, direct duress and ports / believe, believe in love's ports / belie, belie lies? ports/ spare, spare one port / pairs, pairs spare ports / math, math mates ports / data, data and a dealt port / pro-rata, pro-rata ratas and ports / lifetimes, lifetimes loaded ports / received, received a reaching port / victims, victims smatter your ports / mansions, mansions who rim your ports / chambers, chambers openly ported / hearts, hearts suggestions and ports / careers, careers who heal a ports.

CHAPTER THIRTEEN
Cash, cash is the rest, ports / open, openly a posted ports / pick, pick a signed post openly into ports / planes, planes and lanes and ports / codes, codes reach a new ports / plans, plans and manned ports / ponds, ponds race over dams and bursting seams and ports / pull, pull the lightest ports / creep, creep is over, ports / paste, paste the races posted ports / openly, openly melted ports / off, off the days and ports / plants, plants in sincere ports / pays, pays attain your ports / pours, pours and opens a port / powers, powers powering your ports / fairest, fairest felt, ports / waves, waves and ransoms paid to ports / eyes, eyes torn away from old rhomosomes and feasts and planes and ports / places, places and spaces and ports / cones, cones and zones and ports / adrift, adrift the retail ports / rise, rise arrives in sports / energy, energy and the synergy for ports / carry, carry on too, spores and ports / lifted, lifted in spins and ports / gleams, gleams reaching ports / rewinds, rewinds reclaim for a ports / critical, critical the random reward to a ports / lifted, lifted in gifted ports / low, low self gone to a smooth report / mental, mental basics and your ports / arraigned, arraigned signs and sent ports / loves, loves and the selfish gone to a ports / ports, ports and sorts who report for love / mental, mental the soothed ports / rains, rains are ransomed in ports / react, react for the factors called ports / treats, treats are seen in towns and ports / gentle, gentle lens on a living port / friends, friends flown too, ports / fractured, fractured in framing ports/ gifted, gifted in rifts past a ports / plans, plans are made to be a port / pondering,

pondering the smell for a ports / critical, critical acclaim for an aiming invitation to ports / carry, carry your homeward ports / glitters, glitters amid the relations and ports / atomic, atomic respect for armageddon events understood with love for humanity and the ports within / photographic, photographic cures and lights about ports / revealed, revealed a lesson for all ports / craters, craters raided to find port facts / inspired, inspired events and the intention for ports / refracted, refracted enacted and port wise / revelations, revelations about your paid port / crafted, crafted in successiveness, ports / inspires, inspires sired ports / refracts, refracts intact ports / classics, classics of support ports / satellites, satellites lining a ports / speculations, speculations have paid your port collects / reflections, reflections offered a winning port / sevens, sevens who knew forgiven lift into ports, their own / classics, classics carry core issue to ports of cell.

LEVEL 80: THE SELAH-MENTS

CHAPTER ONE
Radars, radars and reasons for selah in life / maps, maps are electric to a selah for God / rotates, rotates and inspects the risen Selah / thickens, thickens in ripened Selahs / cores, cores magnetic in a magma's flowing Selahs / magnetize, magnetize your rearrange to include Selahs / shields, shields have shifted into Selah / radars, radars red and the respect for the Christian Selahs / observes, observes a featured Selah / captures, captures downtown destiny and your festive Selahs / radical, radical into reproach gone awry to a revival for Selahs / participation, participation is ratified when you reign in Selah / practices, practices and preaches Selah / predict, predict a prediction for Selah / vagabonds, vagabonds vouched for, Selah / interplanetary, interplanetary Selahs / triton, triton acres and Selahs / nereid, nereid rid of oldest selahs / orbits, orbits into yellow selahs / finals, finals approaching your selahs / pluto, pluto is posing and selah / charon, charon is electric for selahs / roughly, roughly a regional selah / comparable, comparable creations and selahs / sizes, sizes featured are selah / features, features measured? selahs / magnetics, magnetics rewarded, selah / fields, fields focus into a selah / systems, systems simple for selah / thins, thins a discretion to selah / laborious, laborious the reaping for ethereal selahs / search, search your distinct doors and selahs / satellites, satellites marry your days to selahs / collides, collides a collision of selahs / inner, inner the member for a slew for selah / planets, planets and the peace is gained, selah / classified, classified for your selahs / stones, stones in a triple trickle's selahs / irons, irons forging an eccentric line to your selahs / ironic, ironically frequent for your selahs / structures, structures single in your slices and selahs / pluto, pluto forms your selahs / data, data and a daring force for selahs / search, search is a single selah / orbits, orbits basics and selahs / structures, structures storming your selahs / stages, stages and rages and selahs / asteroids, asteroids

remake your sizzling selahs / basics, basics forming fetish selahs / searches, searches and reaching selahs / restricts, restricts replays go to selah / collides, collides a collision and a selective selah / humanity, humanity forming selahs / meteors, meteors metric and the mathematic selahs / meteorites, meteorites and the mantles frankest selah / points, points and the plural selahs / rules, rules and the final selahs / structural, structural forming your selahs / stretched, stretched forthright in your selahs / saturn, saturns needs and the silent selahs / range, range forthrightly to a selah / surges, surges single and a temple's selahs / stones, stones and stages for a finest selah / ethics, ethics respectful for a selah.

CHAPTER TWO
Europa, europa forming a shining selah / clues, clues clarity and a creative selah / reveals, reveals a realisitic selah / gaps, gaps grooming your final selah / features, features featured and fittest selahs / consistent, consistent and the treaty for selahs / cures, cures credible to selahs / made, made to the basic selahs / surfaces, surfaces and the structures and firmer selahs / deduced, deduced to the thresholds and selahs / structures, structures to the keys and the rehabs formed selahs / static, statics steeples and selah employ / titans, titans and the might on and final selah / internal, internal internal selahs / consistent, on a consistent selah / close, closest retails and resales for selahs / fields, fields for a final selah / innermost, innermost minor most selah / venus, venus and the values formed selahs / data, data and the daring selahs / formations, formations finer selahs / Galileo, Galileo galactic and former selahs / systemic, systemic endemic and sizeable selahs / mimic, mimic without shallow selahs / spaces, spaces and races and selahs / indicate, indicate your chosen selahs / features, features formal chinese slews and selahs / focused, focused a firmer selah / probe, probes and the robes intact selahs / gases, gases and the glues doorway slicing selahs / clues, clues freed and your selahs / love, love lifted selahs / observational, observational relays and relative selahs / seen, seen forth and into a selah / courage, courage is cost without selah / frames, frames ranging your selahs / details, details ranting a selah / telescopes, telescopes arriving in selective selahs / carriages, carriages creative and a curative duration's selahs / freedoms, freedoms and franchised selahs / observations, observations urges and subsistence forming selahs / ringing, ringing and the rushing selahs / amperes, amperes understand a selah / rams, rams respect your silly selahs / easily, easily formal finished and selah / discovery, discovery durations and selah succinct into love / watts, watts awarest selah / plans, plans people and perfect selahs / esteem, esteem is ripened selahs / ovary, ovary votives and victories, selah / ovarian, ovarian variations for selahs / mesmerize, mesmerize a merry selah 53 mystic, mystics a ripened selahs / moons, moons and melatonin's selahs / mullion, mullion and a merry selah / millions, millions missions sisters selahs / mystical, musical mystics and a maverick selah / mention, mentioned arms and a selah suspend / features, features frailest selah / fans, fans functioning into selahs / mentions, mentions allowing your selahs / friends, friends food and selahs / foods, food firmer selah / forms, forms placed in selah.

CHAPTER THREE
Matters, matters thrusting into a slicing selah / powers, powers artistic in essential selah / funded, funded a fun friend's selahs / fundamental, fundamental firment and sleahs / materialize, materialize your realize for selah / become, become a beaming selah / fervent, fervent and final and finest selahs 8 matched, matched a matter to a selah / mention, mention missions and sunny selahs / beings, beings basic into selah / means, means matched selahs / mocha, mocha marriage and supported selahs / managed, managed a miracle for your selahs / mingles, mingles in mingled selahs / mentions, mentions remission for your selahs / mantles, mantles candles selahs / horizontal, horizontal fields for selah / rap, rap the reason for your selahs / rules, rules sincere in selah / slippers, slippers, grips, and selahs / hebron, hebron connected selahs / rounds, rounds heard through selah / reveals, reveals instinct and island style selahs / step, step to a stepping selah / colony, colony curing your chosen selahs / rally, rally around us and sustain your selahs / ruby, ruby risen selahs / along, along your leading selahs / rocks, rocks to a reaching selah / ruse, ruses frail from your redeeming selahs / red, red ray's selahs / living, living lined in selahs / patterns, patterns patterned slew of selahs / positions, positions paring selahs / pools, pools in purging selahs / purged, purged and rewarded selahs / pursue, pursue a tragic selah / positive, positive in a ressurected selah / ports, ports into sports and selahs / pages, pages raging selah / purchases, purchases retain your selahs / patterned, patterned patterned selahs / pathways, pathways purged in sealed friends selahs / muses, muses in reasonable uses and syllabic selahs / paged, paged forms to a selah / pooling, pooling wearing seasonal selahs / pools, pools styles and selahs / moves, moves retain your selahs / mutuality, mutuality mentioned selahs / mattress, mattress for respectful selahs / patterns, patterns purging sealed day's selahs / ladders, ladders leading selahs / rents, rents remained selah / graves, graves cleared to selah / linked, linked leaps and selahs / lasts, lasts regarding selah / rationale, rationale reaches your silent selahs / groves, groves silenced selahs / lopes, lopes a lifted selah / less, less is a special selah / gravitates, gravitates respect and selah / greets, greets maintained selah / lest, lest we fog on in suspended selahs / lead, lead to the closest selahs.

CHAPTER FOUR
Lanterns, lanterns in mantled selahs / loosens, loosens lips and selahs / language, language final to a treated selah / layers, layers into through set selahs / louvre, louvre and luray and the caverns in selahs / lavendar, lavendar laces selahs / lashes, lashes lashing selah / leads, lleads over watered selahs / gracious, gracious a several selah / loops, loops essential into a selah / lush, lush is the measured selahs / ladders, ladders peopled selahs / laughs, laughs a final selah / loops, loops finished, selah / lodges, lodges built near selahs / mononuclear, mononuclear selahs / sufficiency, sufficiency worn in selah / equals, equals atone to selah / attitudes, attitudes platitudes selahs / theoretical, theoretical rhyming selahs / diatoms, diatoms electric need selahs / alpine, alpine specials for selah / materials, materials made selah reality / resultant, resultant

in constructed selahs / space, spaces filled? selahs / matters, matters moist in selah / mansions, mansions chosen selah / analyze, analyze your simple selahs / spines, spines retailing your selahs / amuse, muse is met, amuse yourself, selah / phased, phased and raised to selahs / differentials, differentials during selahs / differs, differs in shifted selahs / difference, differences bade a selah / aspire, aspire is shifting selahs / aspirate, aspirate your relate for selahs / aspirant, aspirant and pirate's selahs / pairs, pairs pairing selahs / pierce, pierced a particle's selahs / past, past a pinnacle atop your selahs / pastes, pastes attend your selah / pert, pert signs and selahs / ports, ports and the trining seeking selahs / porch, porch sustained selahs / pails, pails filled in selah / buckets, buckets filled with selah / doors, doors detailing your selahs / equalities, equalities within selahs / equations, equations respective for selah / equity, equity reaching your selahs / cubes, cubes and the music of selah / landings, landings standing near selah / full, full the reply to selah / founded, founded and the funded selahs / fuse, fuse your use to selah / passive, passive extensive selahs / settles, settles volley across selah / operates, operates your patient selahs / used, used require for your selah / freshens, freshens and the detailed formations of selah / posts, posts and the threatened selahs / pasts, pasts in positions and selahs / positions, popular positions and selahs / presence, presence and the pearly gated selahs.

CHAPTER FIVE

Copy, copy and the turning selahs / meanders, meanders and planning selahs / moses, moses and the mural painted selahs / join, joins journeyed selahs / centers, centers and the spatial seals and selahs / bisects, bisects respects for a selah / bent, bent in a basic selah / cylindrical, cylindrical stilling selahs / symmetry, symmetry sharing selahs / orbits, orbits and the basic selahs / inversion, inversions and shouldered selahs / posits, posits positioned and selah suggests "love" / invert, invert and revert to given selahs / bonded, bonded in simple selah / loves, loves and the living selahs / atomic, atomic and the throat-filled selahs / angular, angular angles and the given selahs / blues, blues believing selah / acquire, acquired selahs / beauties, beauties basic to a selah / paged, paged and the waging selahs / spectacles, spectacles sparing your dealing selahs / havens, havens raving selahs / blew, blew past a basic selah / knows, knows a simple selah / streets, streets and truest selahs / stuffed, stuffed into simple selahs / blown, blown through doors and sincerest selahs / yellow, yellows and the fact that says yes! selahs / metrics, metrics and the focused selahs / instantly, instantly amounting to standing selahs / affixed, affixed fates selahs / 666, 6 who knew denial of body, 6 who knew denial of spirit, 6 who knew denial of mind, selahs / breast, breast and the beast gone, selahs / beasts, beasts who cede your selahs / arms, arms moist with conceptual selahs / stiffest, stiffest fulfillment for a selah / stiffer, stiffer in a refining selah / stiff, stiff and the stiffer selahs / strict, strictest selah days for love / patents, patents and the pertinent selahs / patron, patrons and the patented selahs / passions, passions and the fashions for selah / pines, pines into intrigues and selahs / porch, porch styled selahs / door, doors and the daring selahs / debts, debts detailing your selahs / devil, devils

sent home to the light of love's selahs / dapple, dapple is simple in a final selah / maple, maple missions and material selahs / birch, birch bailing selahs / battered, battered and the basic selahs / pants, pants and the patterned selahs / mince, minces missions selahs / pinch, pinch and the petals selahs / pose, poses striving for a selah / balloons, balloons basic selahs / skills, skills dealt with selahs / slid, slid into stilling selahs / blossom, blossoms selah wise to love / borrow, borrow a simple selah / surgery, surgery stilling into selahs / overt, overts final selahs / change, changes and the stilling selahs.

CHAPTER SIX

Hickory, hickory trees and selahs / trees, trees palest selahs / grown, grown into districts selahs / grew, grew forth and selahs / blue, blue and a basic selah / skies, skies wide with sealing selahs / skills, skills soft for selah / amplify, miracles applied to selah / flown, flown forming spirits and selahs / flew, flew to a new height for loving selahs / furrows, furrows filled with selah / bend, bends near you, selahs / miraculous, miraculous menu, selah salads / mast, mast for the inside selahs / recoils, recoils repulsive selah / reaps, reaps a new basic selah / lifted, lifted and finite gifted selahs / lifting, lifting and a lifelong selah / lowers, lowers a temple into selahs / lopes, lopes across patching selahs / radical, radically a selah / rapes, rapes past, selah / thirds, thirds into words of selah / quarters, quarters and rations selah / india, india blue selahs / attunes, attunes toned selahs / tally, tally and rally for selahs / revelatory, revelatory selah / laughter's, laughter's selahs / loves, loves a gifted selah / ladders, ladders lead to selah / lunged, lunged past old to new selahs / recollections, recollections forming selah / into, into trees formed and selahs / intrigues, intrigues and the theory for a selah / interiors, interiors and the choices made into selahs / recoils, recoils and the simple selahs / traps, traps and the relapse into your selahs / tricks, tricks and the ready assigned selahs / throat, throat and the theory for your selahs / reckons, reckons and the simple selahs / thrust, thrust past your oldest selahs / pulls, pulls into simple selahs / plates, plates filled, selah / reaching, reaching crosses your dealt in selah / opens, opens simple selahs / purchase, purchase made, salute your selahs / poised, poised for final fitted selahs / titans, titans tune into your selahs / favors, favors final selahs / business, business about a selahs / poems, poems particular to a dripping selah / turned, turned and returned to selah / fleshly, fleshly features forming selah / bills, bills and the basic selahs / pounce, pounce past selah / trusting, trusting is triple in your selahs / focus, focus is forming selah / blouse, blouses and basics selahed / past, past the relationship stage for selah / fused, fused in amused bade selah / found, found a new town to selah / pearls, pearls left in stores simple selah / powerful, powerful expressions forming selah.

CHAPTER SEVEN

Flocks, flocks into restock for selah / girds, girds grown in selah / gathers, gathers mostly sealed selahs / grows, grows a regional selah / flirtations, flirtations focused selahs / gyrations, gyrations rational selah / genes, genes joined selah / gentled, gentled in peopled selah / gains, gains framed to selah/ game, game of the joined selahs / giant, giant rays selah / won, won winding selahs / guarantees, guarantees your rhyming selahs / ones, ones united for selah / noted, noted in notable selahs / nested, nested in rested eggs of selah / lavender, lavendar pages selah / passions, passions forming selah / cleverly, cleverly evicted selahs / coded, coded creative selahs / fathers, fathers federal sealed selahs / patter, patters a paternal selah / infants, infants and final selahs / pet, pets and a basic selah / made, made for a formal selah / zone, zones too, selahs / paste, pasted and raced into standing selahs / freeze, freeze past in living selahs / pens, pens written on, selah / zone, zone for the day selah / frail, frail fields and selah / fades, fades former, selahs / days, days and durable selahs / places, places laced in selah / traces, traces reaching selah / phrases, phrases forming selah / daily, daily due a selah / phones, phones written to selah / funded, funded and running on selah / founders, founders and finders selahs / calendars, calendars caring for selah / gather, gathering jesus selahs / listen, listen alive selah / leaps, leaps into simpel selahs / paired, paired in spared selahs / near, nearest nestles selahs / lessons, lessons imply selah / steer, steer into clearing selahs / jaunty, jaunty in haunted selah / jasmine, jasmine jeweled selahs / jewels, jewels brush your selahs / joints, joints pained? selah / running, running into selahs / songs, songs of the noted selah / seals, seals and misted selahs / sealed, sealed over final selah / rearing, rearing your simple selah / sounded, sounded in rounded selahs / paved, paved over blues and selahs / pods, pods ripen, selahs / sunday, sunday due a dearest selah / surging, surging purging selahs / peaks, peaks open and selah / hawks, hawks nested hear a selah.

CHAPTER EIGHT
Capably, capably a due selah / clearly, clearly your selah / copecope for selah / capable, capable carriage selah / covers, covers over selah / clasp, clasp a new selah / cones, cones marry selah / cheers, cheers carry selah / chosen, chosen rituals and selahs / funeral, funeral over, selah / fortitude's, fortitudes and focused selahs / feels, feels and real selahs / flown, flown about, selah / placement, placements mended, selah / placements, placements finding selah / poured, poured a temple for selah / poled, poled about your sounding selahs / search, search is sent, elsewhere a selah / crone, crone met, selah / flame, flame fueled selahs / jar, jars melt, selah / flat, flat out, selah / sell, sell the one, selah / character, character built, selahs / ejection, ejection cycled selahs / ranch, ranch housed selahs / drowsing, drowsing for selah / surface, surface posed selahs / prefix, prefix fixed selahs / cream, creams day selah / simply, simply into selah / benefits, benefits balance, selah / portion, portions proration selah / swift, swift escaping selahs / serve, serve a one, selah / apprehended, apprehended without a selah / exact, exact reactions selah / start, start anew selah / relative, relative too, selah / heavy, heavy without selah / river, river up, selah / berserk, berserk without selah / coarse, coarse run, selah / winning, winning gates selah / gem, gem toned selahs / campaign, campaign about selahs / unity, unity found, selahs / kingdom, kingdom comes, selah / skid, skind too, selah /

competition, competition over, selah / approved, approved facts, selahs / event, events find, selahs / award, awarded your selahs / furious, furious about past selahs / drama, drama due selah / practice, practice realistic selahs / wound, wound into a selah / holiday, holiday due a selah / faithful, faithful few in selahs / row, rows over, selahs / exhausted, exhausted without selahs / professor, professor imposes selahs / send, send one home, selah / abide, abide now near, selah.

CHAPTER NINE
Lesson, lesson made a selah / loser, loser and the user goes to selah / hawaii, hawaii blue selahs / aspect, aspects respects and selahs / prairie, prairie fired selahs / defeats, defeats and repeats and selahs / steamer, steamers across your selahs / slender, slender in the blender and selahs / wheel, wheel deals and selahs / elects, elects an elective membership selah / reside, reside in strident selahs / themes, themes and the scheming selahs / dancer, dancers in prancing selahs / grade, grades and the raiding selahs / detain, detained without a selah / laser, lasers and listed selahs / endurance, endurance and respect for a filling selah / postponed, postponed and intoned selahs / overthrow, overthrow has finished a selah / entire, entire into a spatial selah / style, style is stylish for a completed selah / tense, tense and temples selahs / elapse, elapse is spaced for your selahs / apart, apart starts selah / scented, scented and rented selahs / mirages, mirages and causes selahs / cove, coves into lakes and selahs / light, light led selahs / remodel, remodel your lake selah / source, source trued selahs / estranged, estranged respect selahs / note, notes in a simple selah / rare, rarest seas selahs / discuss, discuss your selah dates / degree, degree found, selah / prestigious, prestigous and a selah / literature, literature reaching selahs / collector, collectors cured selah / guest, guests and the regreat sold selahs / conduct, conduct a classic cured selah / prefer, prefer smiled selahs / prepared, prepared to laugh for selah / nervous, nervous in a neutral selah / level, levels line your selahs / briefing, briefing is rallied selah / antique, antique formed selahs / cozy, cozy creatures and still selahs / rest, rested inside your selahs / probe, probes pursued a selah / gusty, gusty rusty selahs sent / brave, brave in your basic selahs / former, former filling selahs / court, courts counted, selah / drops, drops to a strip for selah / uniformed, uniformed basic humanity's selahs / offspring, offspringing selahs / blow, blows into durations and a dealing selah / minute, minutes momentumed selah / luxurious, luxurious leading selahs / authentic, authentic into basic selahs / security, security settled selahs / track, tracks across reaching selahs / deal, deals made, selah / know, know the needed selahs.

CHAPTER TEN
Chance, chance is made, selah / competition, competition over, selah / intellectual, intellectual wins, selah / debates, debates about? selah / host, host found, selah / rigorous, rigorous resorts and selahs / aloud, aloud the clouded selahs / confides, confides inside your selahs / hire, hire a daily selah / courageous, courageous respect for a selah / crusade, crusade reaching selah / link, links into

sinking selahs / target, targets tripled selahs / vengeful, vengeful and spiteful selahs gone / studio, studio bought selahs / forest, forests raging selah / cosmetic, cosmetic cures for selah / fully, fully fitted selahs / pop, pop a position for selah / longer, longer listed selahs / various, various variations and selahs / data, data due a selah / matches, matches faxed in your selahs / biology, biology basic to your selah / directly, directly directional selahs / solutions, solutions and held up selahs / lingo, lingo languaged selahs / polymers, polymers and positions for selah / molecular, molecular material for your selahs / absorption, absorption and the signed for selahs / bovine, bovine and the basic selahs / water, waters and the wistful selahs / energies, energies around your selahs / amniotic, amniotic examples and the selective selahs / living, living and listening selahs / captions, captions uplifted and single selahs / already, alert already and selahed / supportive, supportive positions and selahs / metal, metals mentioned and selahs / present, presently a selah for love / strongly, strongly districts for selah / sought, spoken and sought and selahs / association, association forming selahs / between, between a basic selah / resin, resin reaches your selahs / data, data durations and selahs / shown, shown a showering selah / sought, sought your stillest selahs / uptake's, uptake's ready selahs / normal, normal nearing selahs / cell, cells toured and selahs / sites, sites forming selahs / medium, mediums matching selahs / external, externally due a selah / muscle, muscles dealt in selah / cardinal, cardinals stilling selah / permission, permissions and patient selahs / upper, upper styled selahs / lower, lowers and the litany "selah" / house, house and the hurled day's selahs / frog, frogs and the first federation's selahs / family, family fullest selahs / locus, locus licensed and the listening selah / external, externally planetary selahs.

CHAPTER ELEVEN
Compete, compete and curation's core days selahs / virtually, virtually valued spatial selahs / equation, equations respect and signal selahs / verified, verified values and spinal selahs / equilibrium, equilibrium spent in selah / single, single in ringing selahs / labeled, labeled respect for selahs / plotted, plotted and pitted selahs / underlying, underlying spying selahs / written, written for flight first selahs / free, frees for the final selahs / simplified, simplified stilling selahs / follow, follows and fill-ups of dear selahs / small, smalls spills and selahs / note, notes nurtured selahs / speaking, speaking and the seeking selahs / fraction, fractions and final selahs / ring, rings and mentions selahs / site, site and successful selahs / yield, yields forming selah / affinity, affinity defining selahs / harmony, harmony curing selahs / example, examples and samples selahs / acetate, acetate relates your selahs / hire, hire the one who says, "selah" / least, least is lessened by selahs / square, square the sign and find the trine in selah / 1966, 1966 is the year for SELAH begin / permission, permission to tour selahs / to, to us all selah / stay, stay inside selah / alive, alive in well selahs / away, away is sent selah / mourned, mourned and meant, selah / glow, glow inside selah / brought, brought a door's selahs / value, values for selah / rank, rank the recent selahs / insulin, insulin rushes too, selah / dramatically, dramatically

spiritual selahs / water, water the moisture in a basement selah / measures, measures treasures and selahs / normal, normal districts run, selahs / controlling, controlling tooling selahs / must, must has occured in selahs / reached, reached in preached "selahs" / solute, solute volute selahs / agrees, agrees to strict selahs / days, days and flows and how? selahs / change, change the directions now, selah / cardinal, cardinal signals for selah / compare, compare Gideon to Gabriel stretched, selahs / low, low the district, sliced in selahs / bind, bind another to only eternal selahs / resting, resting rates for selah / markedly, markedly unique in selahs / respectively, respectively your selahs / cell, cells widened in selah / act, acts upon selahs / demonstrate, demonstrate your selahs / after, after all, selahs / function, functions tests and selahs / summarizing, summarizing yes to selahs.

CHAPTER TWELVE
Physiology, physiology shifts again, selah / distribution, distribution reaches you, selah / state, state of the remembered few, selah / values, values emit a new selah / ratios, ratios ready for selahs / treated, treated in seated selahs / change, change is direct, selah / cooperative, cooperative cures, selahs / general, general emissions and selahs / direct, direct the directiion's flow selah / alter, alter ego nixed selah / binding, binding finished next, selah / involves, involves a riddle solved, selah / tact, tact is present, you, selah / ions, ions click into selahs / steady, steady about, selah / sorry, sorry without, selahs / modify, modify much into selahs / above, above us then, selahs / cells, cells erupt in your selahs / secondary, secondary durations and selahs / site, sites planned near here, selahs / groups, groups who grope within, selahs / either, either is either here selah / key, keys open ends selahs / relatively, relatively well again, selahs / colonel, colonel planted, selahs / healthy, healthy days and years, selah / smile, smile for the final slice, selah / muscle, muscles relaxed in ease, selah / freeze, freeze the corn in trees, selah / plastic, plastic pieces of selah / positive, positive reaches and selahs / specific, specific successive rays, selahs / between, between us each, selahs / entropy, entropy details your selahs / aspects, aspects spinning, selahs / rule, rules for your selah / water, water welling selahs / part, part of the lamb seen, selah / wool, wool off, selah / review, review your voice, "selah" / strongly, strongly annointed selahs / high, high in the healing selahs / sheet, sheets over your selahs / distilled, instincts distilled, selah / buffer, buffer built selah / entry, entry is sentry in selahs / shown, shown a division for selah / notice, notice sent is to selahs / hesitation, hesitation without? selah / over, over everything selah / saturn, saturn turning to selahs / moon, moon moist selahs / fraud, fraud over, selah / palm, palm tossed to fronded selahs / grammy, grammy won selahs / driven, driven sides selah / bird, bird bent to your selahs / phoenix, phoenix sent, selah / enter, enter triumphantly, selah / clear, clear curing selahs / lead, leads a leader to selahs / sage, sage and the survival past, selahs.

CHAPTER THIRTEEN
Supreme, supreme and extreme to selahs / indivisible, indivisible by nature and selahs / present, present patience, selah / principle,

principles for your selahs / higher, higher still, selah / human, human heraldic selahs / confining, confining over, selahs / pertinent, pertinent peaceful selahs / spirit, spirits speeding to a selah / regarded, regarded and reseeded selahs / aspect, aspects form a final selah / preserver, preserver past, selah / function, function finally, selah / world, worlds and wells, selahs / view, views follow selahs / present, present into intensity of selahs / sense, sense and the senses for selahs / single, single and the spiral in selah / shades, shades detail selah / land, land is made, selahs / transmitting, transmittine torn? selah / sons, sons and rushing to selah / view, view a value of selah / interact, interact near, selah / compelled, compelled curations and selahs / sphere, sphere forming selahs / rather, rather territory seek selah / name, names and natures for selahs / created, created cushions and selahs / passive, passive in agressive pasts selah / manifested, manifested means, selah / divine, divine align within your sealed selahs / alphabet, alphabet bets into selahs / requires, requires a kiln dried fantasy, selah / higher, higher stiller be selah / principle, principle arriving to selahs / truth, truth told in your selahs / point, loud to a point called selah / therefore, therefore let us stress, "selah" / over, over everything, one God, selah / names, names who mean yahweh to you, selah / confusion, confusions ending dear, selahs / structure, structure purchased there selah / requires, requires a daring steer selah / looking, looking found us here selah / creates, creates a cushion and selah / order, order for the near, selah / ways, ways who held us dear, selah / ancient, ancient wonders and selahs / pharaoh, pharaoh grew into selah / growled, growled and howled about selahs / application, application for growth in selah / wisdom, wisdom lasts selah / danger, danger past, selah / king, king sings, "selah" / impulse, impulse repulse selah / destiny, destiny is due to a selah / imhotep, imhotep steps into sounds of selah / mission, mission finished, selah / phase, phase followed, selah / dream, dream days selah / life, life led, selahs / judgment, judgement final, selah / prejudice, prejudice for the peopled relationships called hope, dreams, love, and elastic blue selah.

LEVEL 81: THE KING-MENTS

CHAPTER ONE
Ads, advertising, crag, mountains, billboards, lines, erased, creeks, valley, door, prizes, refreshments, freedom, free, things, professional, ariel, handshakes, warmly, written, papers, flyers, funds, raised, registered, ballots, papers, endcaps, classifieds, lanes, purchases, orders, webs, car, vans, magnets, business, cards, airplanes, donations, tax-free, banners, bullhorn, megaphones, celebrity, endorsement, grands, openings, marketing, skills, strategies, radio, television, websites, motivational, commercial, speeches, coupons, specials, offers, speakers, videos, events, red.

CHAPTER TWO
Joined, weld, joint, elbow, feet, fertile, conferences, churches, flesh, market, mulberry, stock, collectives, streets, avenues, technological, transformative, enunciative, asteroids, comets, earth's, atmospheres, trunks, carry, thresh, boquets, shops, outlets, ages, risks, security, safety, tasks, theories, thorax, rings, heads, missionary, poses, sacral, tantric, sung, sang, links, gathers, chapels, temples, binds, adheres, adhesives, glues, matrimony, love, vows, ceremonial, currents, causes, loves, faiths, taxes, legality, green, teal, blue.

CHAPTER THREE
Cards, money, sex, power, names, christed, self, high, marriages, energetic, commit, leads, gilded, sky, seas, eyes, lips, hands, cars, babies, lightening, skies, blis, chakra, throats, communications, written, spoken, penned, fountains, austin, raphael, sand, ra, ariel, waters, nests, hawks, moons, birds, joy, fish, express, experience, flow, flowers, ball, tests, dams, creeks, balloons, manners, mannerisms, greens, yellows, ferns, herons, heard, fish, dog, cats, animals, topaz, blood.

CHAPTER FOUR
Species, venus, specials, venus, hemlocks, 500 years, oaks, cypress, 23, fine leaves, maples, bark, stem, trunks, earth, sky, photosynthetic, xylem, phloem, cartilage, cellulose, matrix, songs, trees, lights, luck, tease, bootes, naves, needs, met, people, places, seated, stretches, peaches, sky, life, leads, links, call, vary, varies, only, when, givings, life, earth, money, ceredwin, comparison, comparables, climb, mercy, fellows, forks, colors, changed, focus, caused, divinations, divine, desireable, denali.

CHAPTER FIVE
Peak, points, breasts, land, sold, success, appreciates, gauges, engaged, orders, owns, women, curves, men, stand, ample, apples, treed, cores, coming, attractions, by, pieces, lands, homes, ridges, pointed, made, real, wedded, initiates, landed, links, lists, won, lives, in, t0, a, to, example, reinvent, purest, loves, content, heart, the, alcove, start, ridden, intent, for, the, hearing, chosen, as, you, annoint, crags, befriended, chosen, written, ridden, rough.

CHAPTER SIX
Concrete, precision, allowances, laughing, tribes, trusting, settlements, iris, isis, attitudes, aspires, assigns, tools, harvests, hundreds, movements, glee, rays, jays, stirred, operates, honestly, strung, words, across, heavenly, pages, the wages, paid, have, been, and, we, since, have, seen, that, worthy, gates, await, us, for, the, chored, sources, of, electorate, numbers, and, the, slumbers, in, spaces, blessed, in a victory, truths, greeted, truthful, passionate, mirrored, mirth, plural, anomalies, ice.

CHAPTER SEVEN
If, death, is, sin's, wage, then, what, is, wealth, is, health, paid, for, the, merciful, plenty, happiness, spices, her name, daily, explore, in, your, door, heart, your, life, let, merry, men, nest, let,

wealthy, patrons, grace, your, door, when, you, discover, that, death, deludes, you, and health, is, a, wellspring, to, the, mystery, solved, of, eternal, revolution, an, early, springs, an extra, strip, steps, a, marriage, too.

CHAPTER EIGHT

Listen, luck, exists, when, you marry, privilege, to spatial, adjust, and, notarize, your, spirit, in, precious, alert, and, the, miracle, explains, your mission, hear, a, lucky, one, luck's, door is, how, you are, loved, and where, we've, spent, our, youth, the, billions, and, the, win some, wonders, won, through, journey's, paired, to, a, central, patch, and, the, maximum, exposure, to, purely, perfect, love, now, that, dears, is, luck, aged, earth, central, centric.

CHAPTER NINE

Contoured, cushioned, in, year's, neglects, and, backs, broken, when, watery, deaths, reach, a, new, grade, the, landing, leads, us, across, planes, to, surrender, and, the, mender, signed, for, historic, resolutions, and, a, merry, signed, to, beatific, stance, along, the, shores, james, blue, and the, tongues, wagged, less, when, chosen, becomes, justly, contoured, nodes, rules, kneel, truth, told, emerald, city, tablets, waterfall, fish, land, love, exasperative.

CHAPTER TEN

Wanton, has, come, to, a, thundering, alert, with, aids, and, Helen's, troyed, without, convictions, of, lasting, Athenians, who, live, to, the, memories, married, to, living, extends, go, willing, surrender, and, the, parties, in, forget, where, will, you, be, when, your, memorize, becomes, memory, and, your, meanings, get, launched, for, the, sending, over, board, to, a, new, home, the, light, you, own, is, now, love.

CHAPTER ELEVEN

Earth, is, won, through, our, chromosomes, and, the, ones, that we, surgically, shielded, now, can, pierce, a, coming, rail, the, victory, danced, in, emotion's, reap, and the, seeping, truth, which gathers, create, at 30 a, shore, again, and, steps, forth, blooming, as, a, human, sperm, and, egg, unites, to, given's, sight, for, the, healing, revolve, a, return, to, center, and a, heart, for youth, remember, every, age, every, cell, every, inherit.

CHAPTER TWELVE

Place, your, spirit, near, the, dart, and, sew, an, option, for, this, opinion, let, love, reign, and, never, the, design, express, apply, to, sky, schools, and, fly, home, dove's, winged, well, into, twirls, into, this, told, older, new, ages rings, vibrationally, and, a, rations, can, range, range, into, sanctuary, for, the, shillings, spent, in, revolutions, let, love, reign, place, the, end, dears, are, nearest, john's, heart, talon.

CHAPTER THIRTEEN

Knew, lives, dees, lists, lisps, lassoo, mosey, indigo, moves, nuance, nears, strays, black, mountains, justice, inside, fates, indigo, blow, blues, bolder, clays, day, yellow, winds, galley,

galleries, matthews, pens, potions, motions, lotions, leads, revolutions, evolutions, furnishings, community, is, built, gather, here, near, love, as, a, theorist, nutritionist, and, lover, I have, a, way, with, worded, woundeds, may, we, be, well, to children, love's, indigos, now, come.

LEVEL 82: THE QUEEN-MENTS

CHAPTER ONE

Aunt, find, waters, again, durations, examined, savory, juices, moved, make, a, move, to, reverse, stagnation, and, build, sanctuary, in, lateral, opinions, psyche, psychotic, psychological, theories, memories, menu, doves, diary, daily, pen, centrally, settled, metal, burned, warped, twisted, wheels, turn, planets, collide, life, swirls, swells, and, people, squirm, to, a, new, understanding, of, the motility, of creation, and, mobility's, death, births, illusions, homes, humans, again, abut, examined, savory.

CHAPTER TWO

Valuable, import, favorites, flush, fishers, fissures, crescents, villages, earth's, memory, mars, impact, vibes, vibrated, justly, active, sewing, opens, classes, requests, yes, God, to, red, love, God, will, we, yes, that, sings, to, who, says, august, holds, joys, driven, avenues, come, area, has, infusion, lend, an, bistro, rooms, news, terrific, zoom, terrific, roof, maya, ma, museums, mother, muchacha, mother, ma, ma, ma, ma, ma, ma.

CHAPTER THREE:

A, rest, in, miracles, has, come, alive, and, we, arrive, arisen, too, and where we, two, were, recalled, a, remembered, grasp, grant, mystics, an, ingenues, trip to, a, chance, arrival's, experience, internationally, serviced, in, love's, diagnose, and, the, parts shown, love's, spinal, guards, rest, foot, sized, into, prices, brands, days, spheres, factors, aptar, mobility, crews, chances, merchants, environs, immediate, amounts, manners, mannerisms, sixty, days, to, a, nearest, star.

CHAPTER FOUR

Peaches, gathers, manual, returns, tsali, noble, showers, overheard, touring, manners, stunning, days, inquiry, stresses, flowers, moves, maneuvers, rewarded, trailed, noblese, oblige, shows, overhead, planes, stampedes, capabilities, during, a, required, for, fruits, managed, notably, fellows, boulders, relationships, curves, shadowed, tuned, patterns, around, strands, suns, in, love's, orbitals, fills, and, told, wiser, ma, ma, ma, ma, ma, ma, ma, ma, ma, ma, love, rules, all.

CHAPTER FIVE

Eggs, towering, muffins, steaks, chickens, algae, fungi, manual, powers, heightened, registration, as sent, into totality, bent, and, yellow, sandstoned, into, egyptian, natures, patches, catch, towering, infinitely, instinctually, standards, randomly, aroused, for a, meal, of menus, spent in, staring, stars, carved, cultures, spiritual, mergers, worths, are factual, extended, on, the stern, eyes, for, threaded, respect, respect, on a, sensual, store, of dense, deliver, born, free, of, all, and fed, eternally, well, peace, rules, clown's, heart.

CHAPTER SIX

Budding, opportunity, amazing, lists, of, simply, tasks for, features, and a neutral, retire, to moving, corners, matched, to doorways, through antiquity, the annual, surrender, for, flashes, caught, capably, on, the narrow, days, dealt, with, when, eyes, are lost, without, seeing, for the, fundamentals of, a grown, occupation, to, a healing's, vision, and, the, thundering, clouds, unto, love's, maturest, rewards, a, personal, spiral, son, through, love, come, out, of, the, cave, peace, priest, arrest, find, development, near, heart.

CHAPTER SEVEN

Fed, eyes, lashes, lids, matching, shown, showering, chances, culpable, without, and within, our threaded, thrusts, to a lasting, nudge, fragmented, factually, to, fan's meal, of a, lasting, buffet, at, the table, set, stars, stares, sounds, stretching, full, monthly, filling, funs, within, creamy, red, began, begonia blue, pools, strung, in, caring, seeds, of, a, laughter, filled, mast, sea, wide, in a, wise, way, settling, grounds, matched, materials, enjoy, love, is, love, is, every, where.

CHAPTER EIGHT

Grew, grown, creates, creativity, created, worn, wonderful, wonders, morning, bemoans, beauty, dealt, duty, a cause, for, lifetimes, the flaws, who, lest, seeded, more, matching, found, wanting, in, waiting, haunting, throughout, heraldic, warrants, onto, surrenders, doors and, in, daily, doors, a, mavericks, poses, are pared in, posing, pools, for, fellows, flawings, unto a, thawing, exact in, eccentric, clearings, detailed, into, thorough, cleansing, known, for, a, seed's, lines, no, secret, love, love, revealed.

CHAPTER NINE

Feeds, on, level, listing, cubes, without, and, within, a, welcomeness, unto, shapes, shifted, fox wise, dog, deep, animals, cured, on, keeping, grounds, for, a plan, unto, doors, opened, as, onto, squarest, squires, who, keep, their, doorways, locked, into, patterns, on, signals, symbolic, to, a, thronging, nudge, fortunate, for, landed, meals, at, other, ways, unto, love's, soaring, husbands, wives, women, men, movers, lovers, laps, cleared, love, to, stay.

CHAPTER TEN

Aminos, liquids, commitment, peace, peaceful, days, nights, minutes, missions, durings, daily, restart, the strength, on, stronger, middled, fundamentals, years, lasting, proteins, breads, which, grew, medicine, strong, in a, strengthened, powers, places, find, a spot, where, sacred, doors, strong, lavendars, onto, secretion,

in a, green, roses, poses, meetings, met, love, is, together, love, does, not, hide, could, you, tell, love, is, the, only, love, can, you, see, love.

CHAPTER ELEVEN

21, rays, proteins, too, aminos, infernos, walking, watchers, matching, marching, herbrew, flaming, speakings, stores, traveled, roadways, registrations, mailings, sugars, soothes, storage, leashed, to, a, cause, of, nutritional, wanderings, in, secure, patches, of, fashionable, freedoms, focused, into, nocturnal, dares, staring, conclusions, and, the many, maintained, when, all was, planned, into double, daring, rapturousness, for, love, no, mistake, love, rest, revealed, love, here, and, love, sunshine, light, precious, crystals.

CHAPTER TWELVE

Yellow, green, red, blue, aqua, teal, peach, mauve, fuscia, acknowledged, colors, changed, seville, where, we, stand for, the mission, made, possible, in, a hand, mercy, direct, rainbows, taos, gifts, remember, written, love, ring, free, in, patient, delivery, to, a cause, and the, clauses, conspirant, lodged, best, western, in, colorful, spreads, stages, since, sent, to, a natural, natives, nativity, born, here, near, the colors, of a, clarifications, dues, gem, peace, happy, times, love.

CHAPTER THIRTEEN

Imperial, blues, emperical, evidences, of, the, red, inside, extreme, regimes, of back's, define, are, given, soul, free, delivery, unto, a collapsed, regime, called, emp, rically, evidence, for, a trails, within, the choirs, to sing, cause, a law, of, natural, physical, mental, expressive, triangles, met, form, pyramids, to stars, and David's, osirion, ring, is, worn, into, smooth, recovery, of, all, loss, rejoin, the throng, and, the throne, energies, unto, long, absence, and essentials, and the pictures, on, too, love's.

LEVEL 83: THE PRINCE-MENTS

CHAPTER ONE

Spirals, into keys, and, hearts, within, declare, from, daringness, to, guests, along, a, song lines, existence, for, ended, sequences, associated, syrup, wet, with human, chords, and the choirs, required, for angel's, paced, red, blue, corpuscles, ope, -ned, too and, there, we, were, sainted, too, for, a fellows, ships, which, narrowed, to, include, a widened, wisdom, where, are, you, due, to, a cataclysmic, example, of, creation, God, made, God, God, made, man, man, made, God.

CHAPTER TWO

Affluence, regained, recessionary, ranges, over, stills, shot, desert, deep, and mountain, wise, in, wonders, surrender, into, a dove's, dailiness, and, a guest, who, measures, materialness, to, roots, related, and, an, accepted, gesture, ground, in remember, of, a simple, truth, that, men, exist, in, a, simple, kiss, of ancient, splendor, and, a, vendor's, recall, which, requires, essential, sounds, to, harbor, release, from, treasures, buttoned, through, in, miracle's, dues, and, a, daring, for.

CHAPTER THREE
Equinox, shocks, jasmine, jewels, sparks, forced, above, chinese, seas, and, drafts, drawn, signaled, too, and a savior, will, we, share, when, a, favorable, meetings, channels, spell, sought, and seek, for, the found, leaks, across, an entry, gated, girth, of, earth's, egyptian, soul, and, a priest, melchizedek, now, found, to develop, lands, into, precious, mother's, discs, and the, floods, us, guardians, watch, and, in, new, belief, of an, artistic, creator, who, knew, sacredness, in.

CHAPTER FOUR
Grows, earth, others, bulged, systematically, jealous, murders, justice, may, lead, to, a, need, to worship, less, than, a chronicle, of light, here, and, a, new, perspective, found, us, pages, worth, as aligned, in the, vicinity, of mars, and, when, stars, melt, into, texts, essentially, we, flow, see, ishtar, osiris, thoth, and, path, hathor's, hermetics, our cause, when, we signal, cause we, employ God, as a beacon, into, engravings, seals and, primordial, abode, to, a, genealogical, earth, is near.

CHAPTER FIVE
Precessions, restore us, to idols, eclipsed, in egyptian, times, and the, risen, desolations, to, a plan, heard, wise, and thus, the christ, has said, as we, have, led we, have, found, and, the temples, into signs, confessed, as, witnessed, will, declare, us, employed, as, viewed, within, creations, living, waters, and, and too, become, a measure, for, the, earth's, equinoxes, as continents, floss, clear, through, into, warrings, stance, and the, decisions, discussed, as, resurrected, molecularly, love, particles, in, neighborhood, peace, look.

CHAPTER SIX
Planets, are, the, DNA, of, God, know, those, strands, and, you, will, see, how, you, connect, and if, you, find, a lover, in God, you find, a house, and, a temple, and, a currency, sold, into, measureable, means, as a, hearth, is declared, due, your, fellows, lands, when, and where, the return, write, hear, let us, know, through, your hearts, alight, and know, the return, to God's, men, and, the thunder, mentally, of men, as, mentally, free, and, the hearts, of, rising, trumpets.

CHAPTER SEVEN
Signs, have, come, to, signal's, invent, and, a heaven's, extent, is, now, ours, within, woods, of, a genuine, lane, as inspired, for God, within, causes, and, as led, we applaud, we marry, veils, into leaves, and, the trees, that, will, accompany, us will, inspire, generations, of the, retailed, positions, in all, alarms, as we, signed,

and, we, signaled, authentically, throughout, your, day's, delights, watch, this, moment, and, deny, only, less, this, point, one, one, sign, love's, night.

CHAPTER EIGHT
Symbols, suggests, that, God, is, finished, with, a, plan, of, light, inception, and, that, a derelict, past, may, now, last, when, without, is within, and, a friend, now, found, is called, sentinel, to a throne, electric, and, a Metatronic, attend, has become, summary, and signal, and simply, caught, as throughout, we've, a lesson, and, a mission, into, miracles, askew, without, shouldered, respect, and, a covenant, born, in a road, berry, red, in recovery, of, God's, symbols, Hu-manity, fuse, about, love, love.

CHAPTER NINE:
A, fable, has, run, it is, a, and, a course, for, a soaring, recovery, now, reads, electric, as, we, direct, our, funds, and, finds, to, a way, home, without, recovery, as, we, table, linked, and loops, score, any, direct, causes, for recovery, and we, have, found, a funded, foundation, and, the sanctuary, cause, for, an, all, "timed", event, and, the eventual, end, of timeless, we know, it, zoos, exist, for, mates, friends, foes, unite, into, one.

CHAPTER TEN
Legends, now, devotion, may, materialize, as, you, infuse, your, life, with, enthusiasm, rapture, and a, genuine, resurrection, to an essential, cue, called, classical, distillations, of, a, DNA, littered, when, we, spend, ashes, to, dust, without, cause, now, eternal, and, we, will, see, youthful, blush, in, rows, frozen, until, night's, days, meet, with, calm, seas, and, a, victory, for, all, humanity, may, we, shall, we, continue, limited, peace.

CHAPTER ELEVEN
Sermons, are, meant, to, the, highest, extent, when, doves, fly, and, skies, debates, for, eternity, have, whispered, in, the, ears, divine, as, we, publish, we, preach, a, simple, gesture, as, mortal, that, love, belies, our, incarnations, immortal, rewards, as, a, sword, becomes, plain, in, the, hands, of, the, few, who, renew, a, perfect, parallel, existing, in, paths, super, imposed, in, the, cells, every, human souled.

CHAPTER TWELVE
As, we, were, led, unto, karmic, blends, of, the, absolute, spirits, philosophic, friends, have, discovered, a, detailed, philosophy, for, the, lights, eternalness, and, and, wisdom, welcome, to, a, universal, path, of, written, correspondence, which, will, last, through, all, eternal, may, we, mortal, remember, who, has, moved, near, and, deal, in, the, affairs, of, only, perfect, resolutions, and, the, evolution, in, your, process, birthed, humans.

CHAPTER THIRTEEN
Accounts, now, frozen, have, regained, ganges, green, land, and, the, traces, hermetic, will, lead, a, brother, Abraham, into, your, driven, teachings, as, we, count, accounts, opened, we, blow,

the, bridges, to, lights, beloved, flames, and, the, firmaments, accounts, players, plagues, celebrity, fame, cleans, participates, fairest, fed, food, lunges, to, love, established, regard, for, a, word, for, love, God, is, brother's sister's, father's partners, husbands, wives, hu-mans.

LEVEL 84: THE LESSON-MENTS

CHAPTER ONE

Agility, may, handle, your, ability, in, language, as, an, language, as, an, eternal, sign, for, love's, incline, to, muse, over, suggestions, on, nearby, paths, and, these, warriors, ways, now, graced, magnified, rays, rapt, to, call, first, made, God, gave, nation's, stance, which, world, chose, a, truth, elastic, and, where, will, your, energy, seed, a revolution, here, in, this, agility, estimated, encouraged, rewarded, sovereign, random, assertive.

CHAPTER TWO:

As, the, seals, are, broken, centuries, will, rest, where, the, miracles, most, dense, have, lain, will, you, lead, into, matters, on, love, will, you, flower, where, love, becomes, a, leader, and, a, friend, and, as, we, seek, sought, and, as, we, found, fought, and, when, we, lean, wrought, through, deep, surrender, to, a, flow, now, born, eternal, to, a, spiritual, deliver, flowers, eternal, gift.

CHAPTER THREE

Magical, means, have, met, merry, shores, and, those, who, sacrificed, soar, as, saints, alight, in, near, recovery, and, the, seering, suggestion, which, shows, is, feared, without, worded, listening, and, too, we, remember, how, to, seek, recovery, as, a, filling, core, remains, sample, and, love, and, life, directed, into, a, vein, chosen, when, winnings, alert, level, leads, to, her, doors, magical, ways, love's, sharing, love.

CHAPTER FOUR

Financial, menu, to, a, starring, files, free, as, we, daily, reap, a, staple, load, of, magnificent, views, beaches, mountains, seas, and, the, earth's, recovery, as, our, dearest, friend, and, lover, she, is, our, mother, our, disciple, our, teacher, out, gate, our, lead, to, discovery, of, a, round, principle, which, bounces, amid, the, stars, love, afloat, love, mystery, love, fountains, love whispers, love, sung, love, votile.

CHAPTER FIVE

Principles, of, simple, discussion, have, met, your, door, and, where, will, when, will, ideal, your, seal, in, subtle, resurgence, of, expert, regeneration, in, simple, strains, as, strands, elongate, to, tie, your, day, to, marvels, wonders, and, signs, magnificent, to, love, where, will, you, lodge, in, a, nearest, qualify, for, the, only, in, the, highest, in, relationship, God's, and, man's, relation, with, pure, precious, love.

CHAPTER SIX:

humanity, is, fundamental, cue, to, options, opened, when, loving, lives, in, hearts, fundamentally, united, at, the, score, and, score, and, the, remittance, sent, forth, when, love, leads, us, home, to, a, physical, example, for, the, throne, suggested, as, simply, surgically, removed, what, are, the, simplest, ways, to, fundamentally, find, a, a, simple, solution, allow, heaven, to, exist, in, your, life, and, find a, path, into, love, fundamentally, human.

CHAPTER SEVEN

As, we, register, into, a, sentinel, exampled, we, will, woo, our, life, into, relative, exposure, of, the, standing, surges, along, lines, struck, to, a, signal, philosophy, where, will, you, land, when, you, leap, where, will, you, stand, when, you, keep, us, feathered, for, relevance, regularity, ratified, ratios, to, a, town's, pi, codes, where, will, a, lamb, lead, slaughter, away, to, the sun, of our, mutual, relative God.

CHAPTER EIGHT

Captions, read, where, we've, stood, for, love, and, we, find, humanity's, missions, to, be, angular, encoded, geometric, allowing, living, breathing, believing, allows, linking, levels, and, corridors, into, the, departments, hu-man, across, cautions, cores, as, a, magnetic, mood, moves, us, along, triangulations, to, a, square, signatures, for, a, flashing, phases, placed, in, travels, touring, our, singular, purpose, quality, deepening, sounding, regained, listening, to, divine, harmony.

CHAPTER NINE:

Mobility, cures, codes, modes, mantles, moves, leaps, beliefs, bliss, transcendance, committed, contented, paced, beautiful, balanced, born, to view, played, into, leashes, rushed mixed, throats, for, a rally, causes through, God, is your, companion, music, has, mobility, of a, filling, rich, in rapturous, roses, red, ringed, rooms, as, essentially, befriended, along, dispersed, in, recall, to, regained, moving, stares, and, surrender, of, a band, who, asthetics, technologically, lure, magically, flushed, reaping, of true, befriended, causes.

CHAPTER TEN

Trees, of, life, functions, face, present, languages, seeds, the, I, AM, spinnings, octahedrons, cystine, lipids, transducer, coded, genetics, tetrahelix, tetragrammation, divine, DNA, RNA, deca-deltas, synthetics, will, lead, to, looser, codes, allowances, universal, orions, greetings, committed, to, a, living, legend, humanity, reprograms, evolutions, inherited, waves, Christ, bodied, now, employed, wavelengths, beach, forms, accomodated, 72, spheres, pyramids, happy, listening, love, several, love, fluid, respect, love, turn.

CHAPTER ELEVEN:

Gemstones, are, cut, to, a, faceted, focus, on, a, definite, range, of, immediate, good, shepherd, Arcturus, mapped, the, return, to, souls, ash, ani, lang, messianic, mid-way, stationed, life, energies, conversions, consciousness, time, zones, signaled, intelligences, how, to, return, to, love, el, concentric, vehicles, photons, matters, lights, deca, 64, membranes, letters, sequenced, codons, gems, lights, transforms, enumerations, 18 rays, 5 bodies, 6 temples, 7 seals, 8 lights, 9 versions, 10 friends, gateways.

CHAPTER TWELVE
Emissary, enoch, views, earth's, rise, across, horizons, sentineled, as, you, keep, God, sent, us, angels, heed, us, arc-angels, lost, now, found, have, returned, to, earth's, stormy, remember, of, a, caring, God, with, clear, recollection, regather, here, for, the, lift-off, may, you, be, well, liked, loved, cared, for, in, leaps, your, journey, we, love, you, basic, humanity, divine, listening, divine, dessert, divine, relating, divine, synchronicity.

CHAPTER THIRTEEN:
Love, lives, here, legends, made, participation, meant, pulls, gestures, joins, factory, tires, plaster, tut, tiles, toals, fair, roses, rackets, racbet, made, churched, madonna, white, nodes, nestle, under, days, detailed, reach, dupes, leaves, lunges, laterally, furthers, fastens, fascinated, funds, Venus, white, royal, street, brother, sister, villages, others, hadis, mist, St Francis, doves, arcturus, wed, eight, eight, eight, 17 rays, 6 roses, led, "ka", essence, Metatronic, trees, willing, seal.

LEVEL 85: THE LISTEN-MENTS

CHAPTER ONE
Monkey, monkeys, listen / cowboy, cowboy listen, / that, that listens / all, all listen / complete, complete your listenings / set, set for the listenings / beep, beeps past a listener / home, home for the listening / sunday, sunday days and listeners / undertake, undertake less, listen / lead, leads climb, listen / matter, matters most, listen / greek, greek gazes, listen / petticoat, petticoat blues, listen / red, red dues and the listening leads / bird, boxes for birds who listen / entire, entire leads, listen / self, self said "listen" / over, over and about "listen" / history, history amounts to the listeners / insight, insights and schools, listen / symbolic, symbolic hopes, listen / stage, stages set, surrender, listen / detail, details faxed, listen / perfecting, perfecting your core listening skills / esoteric, esoteric dares and the doors skill for the listenings / cover, cover over the doors and your cares listen in / temple, temple toured listeners / suffering, suffering most? listeners / art, arts and staffs who listen / stand, stand still, listen / awareness, awareness heightens, listen / sugar, sugar buzzing listeners / balanced, balanced people listen / floats, floats most and listens / under, under us all a listener / tibet, tibet bets for the listeners / rest, rested and listening / fathoms, fathoms, mantras, and listeners / king, kings rings listens / knowledge, knowledge college listen / age, ages wages listen / 12, 12 who follow, listen / said, said yes to the listeners / harmony, harmony minutes and

the listenings / precisely, precisely listened to, love / southwest, southwest listeners / widely, widely wise listeners / corporeal, corporeal assimilations for the purer listeners / rhythms, rhythms managed, listen / established, established the facts, listen / basis, basis blues, listen / along, along well listeneds / correspondence, correspondence for the listeners / well, well said "listen" / represented, represented a reasonable listener / lengths, lengths gifts and the listeners still / control, controls a core listener / man, mans standing listener / excluding, excluding a moving, listen / body, body for the basic, listener / crown, crowns round your listener / speak, speaks paths to the listened / sound, spoken sounds and wonderful listeners.

CHAPTER TWO
Divided, divided and durations for the listener / golden, golden gazing listeners / channel, channel rays and the listened / guilty, guilty without a listener / nourishing, nourishing a filling listen / body, body blue listenings / direct, direct images for the flowing listenings / image, images direct to the knowing listen / fire, fires past old listens / confirm, confirm the motion, listen / people, people who listen / value, values cost? listen / diminish, diminish old listens / prejudice, prejudice gone, listen / extensively, extensively rich, listen / impossible, impossible past, listen / cell, cells break listen / message, message told, listen / cross, cross between, listen / between, between us well, listened / evolves, evolves the solved, listen / direct, direct the cause, listen / permit, permits past? listen / human, human holds, listen / pleasure, pleasures pains listen / power, powers pour listen / psycho, psycho goes, listen / human, human hopes, listen / instinct, instincts win, listen / results, results made, listen / man, man your listening / fullness, fullness listen / shows, shows, listen / spirit, spirit, listen / love, love, listen / ourselves, ourselves, listen / people, people, listen / learn, learn, listen / restless, restless, listen / urge, urge, listen / clouds, clouds, listen / tendencies, tendencies, listen / exclaimed, exclaimed, listen / art, art, listen / civilization, civilization, listen / affected, affected, listen / view, view, listen / work, work, listen / describe, describe, listen / vast, vast, listen / talk, talk, listen / brain, brain, listen / potential, potential, listen / yogic, yogic, listen / betray, betray, listen / caring, caring, listen / environment, environment, listen / daily, daily, listen / possible, possible, listen / grasp, grasp, listen / click, click, listen / pattern, pattern, listen / tree, tree, listen / destiny, destiny, listen.

CHAPTER THREE
Raindrop, raindrop, listen / eternal, eternal, listen / center, center, listen / heart, heart, listen / resonance, resonance, listen / created, created, listen / formal, formal, listen / light, light, listen / octaves, octaves, listen / power, power, listen / illusion, illusion, listen / vibration, vibration, listen / respond, respond, listen / natural, natural, listen / system, system, listen / muscle, muscle, listen / determine, determine, listen / satisfactorily, satisfactorily listen / harmonic, harmonic, listen / train, train, listen / consciousness, consciousness, listen / social, social,

listen / frequent, frequent, listen / field, field, listen / spheres, spheres, listen / chakra, chakra, listen / frequency, frequency, listen / detect, detect, listen / subatomic, subatomic, listen / independent, independent, listen / light, light, listen / tube, tube, listen / cannonballs, .cannonballs, listen / charges, charges, listen / matter, matter, listen / images, images, listen / family, family, listen / duce, duce, listen / biophysical, biophysical, listen / cover, cover, listen / radio, radio, listen / field, field, listen / under, under, listen / natural, natural, listen / world, world, listen / astronomy, astronomy, listen / correlated, correlated, listen / cosmic, cosmic, listen / travellers, travellers, listen / cook, cook, listen / units, units, listen / natural, natural, listen / space, space, listen / mother, mother, listen / boggle, boggle, listen / imagine, imagine, listen / zero, zero, listen / movement, movement, listen. / elements, elements, listen / stars, stars, listen / speed, speed, listen / right, right, listen / water, water, listen / scent, scent, listen.

CHAPTER FOUR

Hydrogen, hydrogen, listen / interval, interval, listen / path, path, listen / redraw, redraw, listen / geometrical, geometrical, listen / distance, distance, listen / equal, equal, listen / time, time, listen / tacks, tacks, listen / money, money, listen / galaxy, galaxy, listen / shrunk, shrunk, listen / time, time, listen / spectrum, spectrum, listen / absolute, absolute, listen / zero, zero, listen / interpret, interpret, listen / spiral, spiral, listen / fields, fields, listen / 18, 18, listen / moon, moon, listen / positive end, positive end listen / understand, understand, listen / signal, signal, listen / super, super, listen / color, color, listen / chakra, chakra, listen / visible, visible, listen / fully, fully, listen / passes, passes, listen / time, time, listen / obscures, obscures, listen / negative, negative, listen / blue, blue, listen / eclipse, eclipse, listen / symbolic, symbolic, listen / reconstruction, reconstruction, listen / spiralling, spiralling, listen / power, power, listen / memory, memory, listen / energy, energy, listen / medium, medium, listen / passage, passage, listen / photograph, photograph, listen / sum, sum, listen / origin, origin, listen / delay, delay, listen / healing, healing, listen / mind, mind, listen / deeper, deeper, listen / consciousness, consciousness, listen / wonder, wonder, listen / permanent, permanent, listen / expression, expression, listen / levels, levels, listen / brin, brin, listen / man, man, listen / movement, movement, listen / eternal, eternal, listen / selflessness, selflessness, listen / bubble, bubble, listen / mixture, mixture, listen / fine, fine, listen / change, change, listen.

CHAPTER FIVE

Well, well, listen / crew, crew, listen / sensory, sensory, listen / loves, loves, listen / degree, degree, listen / negative, negative, listen / immersion, immersion., listen / idea, idea, listen / interview, interview, listen / motives, motives, listen / past, past, listen / future, future, listen / comes, comes, listen / love, love, listen / change, change, listen / differently, differently, listen / dozen, dozen, listen / centre, centre, listen / ching,

ching, listen / levels, levels, listen / concepts, concept, listen / thinking, thinking, listen / force, force, listen / life, life, listen / movement, movement, listen / expression, expression, listen / teacher, teacher, listen / world, world, listen / lottery, lottery, listen / willing, willing, listen / green, green, listen / monks, monks, listen / magenta, magenta, listen / invisible, invisible, listen / created, created, listen / spotlight, spotlight, listen / side, side, listen / light, light, listen / white, white, listen / filter, filter, listen / overdose, overdose, listen / plus, plus, listen / impulse, impulse, listen / balancing, balancing, listen / circulation, circulation, listen / probing, probing, listen / nature, nature, listen / energies, energies, listen / evolve, evolve, listen / nakedness, nakedness, listen / vision, vision, listen / plan, plan, listen / manifestation, manifestation, listen / increase, increase, listen / process, process, listen / range, range, listen / divine, divine, listen / part, part, listen / climbed, climbed, listen / whole, whole, listen / total, total, listen / life, life, listen / results, results, listen / new, new, listen.

CHAPTER SIX

Pattern, pattern, listen / glimpse, glimpse, listen / social, social, listen / aware, aware, listen / sun, sun, listen / recognizes, recognizes, listen / state, state, listen / life, life, listen / power, power, listen / creative, creative, listen / willed, willed, listen / intelligently, intelligently, listen / spirit, spirit, listen / healing, healing, listen / journey, journey, listen / vital, vital, listen / mirror, mirror, listen / unknown, unknown, listen / activity, listen, listen / random, random, listen / ignorance, ignorance, listen / require, require, listen / creation, creation, listen / solve, solve, listen / explosion, explosion, listen / spirits, spirits, listen / blissful, blissful, listen / projection, projection, listen / human, human, listen / spectrum, spectrum., listen / open, open, listen / private, private, listen / fact, fact, listen / sacred, sacred, listen / longer, longer, listen / external, external, listen / health, health, listen / fully, fully, listen / remains, remains, listen / ill, ill, listen / biological, biological, listen / powerless, powerless, listen / truth, truth, listen / forgiving, forgiving, listen / consciousness, consciousness, listen / creation, creation, listen / positive, positive, listen / love, love, listen / thread, thread, listen / divine, divine, listen / myths, myths, listen / God, God, listen / make-up, make-up, listen / love, love, listen / illness, illness, listen / strong, strong, listen / develop, develop, listen / correct, correct, listen / spirit, spirit, listen / background, background, listen / perform, perform, listen / unfinished, unfinished, listen / life, life, listen / challenge, challenge, listen.

CHAPTER SEVEN

Tribe, tribe, listen / needing, needing, listen / briefly, briefly, listen / honor, honor, listen / woke-up, wake-up, listen / special, special, listen / perform, perform, listen / mind, mind, listen / dream, dream, listen / leave, leave, listen / mind, mind, listen / factor, factor, listen / simple, simple, listen / songs, songs, listen / end, end, listen / instantly, instantly, listen / learn, learn, listen / fear, fear, listen / born, born, listen / not, not, listen / spirit, spirit, listen / honest, honest, listen / learn, learn, listen / not, not, listen / walk, walk, listen / primitive, primitive, listen / beliefs, beliefs, listen / look, look, listen / stalking, stalking, listen / energy, energy, listen / real, real, listen / sport, sport, listen / culture, culture, listen / forbidden, forbidden, listen / tell, tell, listen / me, me, listen / ignorance, ignorance, listen / learn, learn, listen / honest, honest, listen / woman, woman, listen / man, man, listen / tools, tools, listen / broken, broken, listen / things, things, listen / feel, feel, listen / life, life, listen / learn, learn, listen / more, move, listen / woven, wove, listen / emotional, emotional, listen / power, power, listen / clearly, clearly, listen / foundation, foundation, listen / objectivity, objectivity, listen / relationship, relationship, listen / simple, simple, listen / straight, straight, listen / retreat, retreat, listen / ponder, ponder, listen / spiritual, spiritual, listen / language, language, listen / symbolic, symbolic, listen / bodies, bodies, listen / real, real, listen.

CHAPTER EIGHT

Flushed, flushed, listen / force, force, listen / upon, upon, listen / spirit, spirit, listen / sensitive, sensitive, listen / highly, highly, listen / concept, concept, listen / knowledge, knowledge, listen / system, system, listen / length, length, listen / surprising, surprising, listen / words, words, listen / heal, heal, listen / possible, possible, listen / cure, cure, listen / controlled, controlled, listen / stress, stress, listen / dreamed, dreamed, listen / health, health, listen / public, public, listen / power, power, listen / truth, truth, listen / sending, sending, listen / relationship, relationship, listen / help, help, listen / heal, heal, listen / alone, alone, listen / body, body, listen / losing, losing, listen / power, power, listen / fill, fill, listen / response, response, listen / identionship, identionship, listen / express, express, listen / truth, truth, listen / real, real, listen / intuition, intuition, listen / message, message, listen / feel, feel, listen / agree, agree, listen / spiritual, spiritual, listen / countless, countless, listen / dynamic, dynamic, listen / money, money, listen / cheerful, cheerful, listen / crashed, crashed, listen / linked, linked, listen / else, else, listen / husband, husband, listen / energy, energy, listen / result, result, listen / feeling, feeling, listen / attached, attached, listen / circuit, circuit, listen / upon, upon, listen / running, running, listen / smothered, smothered, listen / skills, skills, listen / efforts, efforts, listen / humiliation, humiliation, listen / cave, cave, listen / difficult, difficult, listen / sexual, sexual, listen / chapter, chapter, listen.

CHAPTER NINE

Stop, stop, listen / limited, limited, listen / life, life, listen / teaching, teaching, listen / think, think, listen / act, act, listen / eternal, eternal, listen / attitude, attitude, listen / support, support, listen / cross, cross, listen / forgiveness, forgiveness, listen / healing, healing, listen / flow, flow, listen / relationship, relationship, listen / made, made, listen / essential, essential, listen / chronic, chronic, listen / virus, virus, listen / weapons, weapons, listen / survival, survival, listen / illness, illness, listen

/ challenge, challenge, listen / people, people, listen / overall, overall, listen / reaction, reaction, listen / chakra, chakra, listen / viral, viral, listen / fears, fears, listen / perform, perform, listen / talk, talk, listen / temple, temple, listen / walking, walking, listen / buckets, buckets, listen / doubt, doubt, listen / lying, lying, listen / will, will, listen / met, met, listen / careful, careful, listen / people, people, listen / pain, pain, listen / words, words, listen / direct, direct, listen / flames, flames, listen / quarters, quarters, listen / end, end, listen / claim, claim, listen / posses, posses, listen / transmission, transmission, listen / egypt, egypt, listen / roman, roman, listen / movements, movements, listen / near, near, listen / truth, truth, listen / along, along, listen / manta's, manta's, listen / firey, firey, listen / encode, encode, listen / now, now, listen / the, the, listen / roads, roads, listen / to, to, listen / love, love, listen / impress, impress, listen / lighter, lighter, listen.

CHAPTER TEN

To, to, listen / lead, lead, listen / darkness, darkness, listen / into, into, listen / firmly, firmly, listen / lit, lit, listen / for, for, listen / fires, fires, listen / hope, hope, listen / chinese, chinese, listen / inscopes, inscope, listen / treat, treat, listen / happy, happy, listen / graze, graze, listen / to, to, listen / a, a, listen / life's, life's, listen / ascension, ascension, listen / macrons, macrons, listen / australian, australian, listen / expression, expression, listen / revise, revise, listen / titles, titles, listen / kept, kept, listen / of, of, listen / the, the, listen / purposes, purpose, listen / books, books, listen / joy, joy, listen / material, material, listen / in, in, listen / walking, walking, listen / austral, austral, listen / know, know / reincarnate, reincarnate, listen / fade, fade, listen / polarities, polarities, listen / socially, socially, listen / migrons, migrons, listen / Metatron's, Metatron's, listen / metamorphosis, metamorphosis, listen / affiliation, affiliation, listen / is, is, listen / missions, missions, listen / matched, matched, listen / in, in, listen / eternal, eternal, listen / codes, codes, listen / love, love, listen / arrange, arrange, listen / for, for, listen / paged, paged, listen / employs, employs, listen / hale, hale, listen / faith's, faith's, listen / nestle, nestle, listen / affluent, affluent, listen / a, a, listen / induction, induction, listen / into, into, listen / styles, styles, listen / kulani, kulani, listen / notions, notions, listen / love, love, listen.

CHAPTER ELEVEN

Among, among, listen / regards, regards, listen / whether, whether, listen / planes, planes, listen / us, us, listen / debates, debates, listen / completes, completes, listen / shared, shared, listen / effective, effective, listen / levels, levels, listen / debate, debate, listen / evenly, evenly, listen / expedience, expedience, listen / trust, trust, listen / choice, choice, listen / reads, reads, listen / flairs, flairs, listen / set, set, listen / on, on, listen / scopes, scopes, listen / personal, personal, listen / interludes, interludes, listen / poignant, poignant, listen / plays, plays, listen / saves, saves, listen / moods, moods, listen / for, for, listen / hourly, hourly, listen / solves, solves, listen / made, made, listen

/ ways, ways, listen / love, love, listen / luncheons, luncheons, listen / continue, continue, listen / gradation, gradation, listen / merge, merge, listen / incredible, incredible, listen / continents, continents, listen / emergent, emergent, listen / rains, rains, listen / outpower, outpower, listen / meet, meet, listen / essence, essence, listen / pours, pours, listen / your, your, listen / officially, officially, listen / dashes, dashes, listen / solar, solar, listen / encircles, encircles, listen / pleiades, pleiades, listen / planes, planes, listen / magnitude, magnitude, listen / defies, defies, listen / description, description, listen / birth, birth, listen / universe, universe, listen / material, material, listen / children, children, listen / develop, develop, listen / aligned, aligned, listen / go, go, listen / ancient, ancient, listen / wisdom, wisdom, listen / sought, sought, listen.

CHAPTER TWELVE
Patience, patience, listen / pays, pays, listen / mountains, mountains, listen / tamed, tamed, listen / meetings, meetings, listen / labels, labels, listen / occurrence, occurrence, listen / shall, shall, listen / matched, matched, listen / mates, mates, listen / revel, revel, listen / revealed, revealed, listen / noon, noon, listen / tomorrow, tomorrow, listen / result, result, listen / sleep, sleep, listen / phonton, phonton, listen / distance, distance, listen / orbit, orbit about the listening belts of love / around, around, listen / central, central, listen / approximately, approximately, listen / years, years, listen / belt, belt, listen / science, science, listen / level, level, listen / trigger, trigger, listen / force, force, listen / between, between, listen / angle, angle, listen / entering, entering, listen / humanity, humanity, listen / separation, separation, listen / beauty, beauty, listen / event, event, listen / birth, birth, listen / union, union, listen / marriage, marriage, listen / shelves, shelves, listen / night, night, listen / transformation, transformation, listen / new, new, listen, listen / age, age, listen, listen / day, day, listen, listen / giving, giving, listen / grace, grace, listen / terms, terms, listen / man, man, listen / must, must, listen / long, long, listen / flow, flow, listen / energy, energy, listen / dawn, dawn, listen / creation, creation, listen / love, love, listen / perception, perception, listen / align, align, listen / ourself, ourself, listen / crystal, crystal, listen / seen, seen, listen / joins, joins, listen / celebration, celebration, listen / cry, cry, listen / aloud, aloud, listen.

CHAPTER THIRTEEN
Jubilance, jubilance, listen / dimension, dimension, listen / dance, dance, listen / sovereign, sovereign, listen / transition, transition, listen / magic, magic, listen / expression, expression, listen. / filled, filled, listen / deep, deep, listen / purpose, purpose, listen / lack, lack, listen / thing, thing, listen / short, short, listen / spirit, spirit, listen / material, material, listen / walk, walk, listen / blessing, blessing, listen / gift, gift, listen / pass, pass, listen / friend, friend, listen / ask, ask, listen / he, he, listen / our, our, listen / answer, answer, listen / who, who, listen / essence, essence, listen / ability, ability, listen / different, differently, listen / what, what, listen / holy, holy, listen / within,

within, listen / picture, picture, listen / polarized, polarized, listen / tend, tend, listen / information, information, listen. / press, press, listen / apart, apart, listen / possible, possible, listen / polarity, polarity, listen / divide, divide, listen / and, and, listen / induce, induce, listen / manner, manner, listen / only, only, listen / define, define, listen / analogies, analogies, listen / return, return, listen / could, could, listen / reason, reason, listen / many, many, listen / robes, robes, listen / points, points, listen / body, book, listen / journey, journey, listen / early, early, listen / method, method, listen / reincarnation, reincarnation, listen / simple, simple, listen / concept, concept, listen / give, give, listen / final, final, listen / proof, proof, listen / theory, theory, listen / clinic, clinic, listen on, listen / align, align, listen / ourself, ourself, listen / crystal, crystal, listen / seen, seen, listen / joins, joins, listen / celebrate, celebrates and listens too when you apply the motions to love.

LEVEL 86: THE APPEAR-MENTS

CHAPTER ONE
Intellect, intellects reconnect and the vectors formed, appear / adept, adept in the affairs for thee, appear / proficient, proficient in factors then vectoring appears / abilities, abilities, agilities, and the, appearing for a flaming appellation / brain, brains burst, appellations appear / gift, gifts credited, appearing / prodigy, prodigy gifted, appearing / talent, talents embraced, appears / large, largest lessons appeared, finished / numerous, numerous measures finished, appears / enormous, enormous amountings appearing / vital, vitals appeared / noble, nobles, nimbles, perfectís appear / grand, grand stranded appearings / minute, minutes, moments, appearings / give, give some, appearances due / trembling, trembling is rivaling your giving appearances / also, also the dearest, reflections of appearings / dog, dog said appearing / defense, defense finished, appears / only, only the latest, appearing / illusory, illusory relations for the raptured appears / real, real the say "appearings"/ embrace, embrace conflicted, appears / value, values follow "appearings" / being, beings balance, appears / drop, drop deeply into the related persons appears / dream, dreams opened and ended in a final forgiven appearance / acknowledge, acknowledged emboldened and emblazoned through the placements fine in appears / into, into appearing places / itself, itself, resets and respectable appearances / experience, experiences similitudes and finally an appearance / fantasies, fantasies follow an appearance for sure / sorrow, sorrows and the governing fantasies / induce, induced madness for the tyranny of appears / equal, equals appearing tripping in love / example, samples, examples, and the further the flower the final appears / mundane, mundanes, regains, relives, appears / vortex, vortex samples appear / shy, shy days appearing / attack, attacks off, appeared / induce, induce a realm,

appear / guilt, guilts go, appears / blame, blames a basic for the fellow appearings / lethal, lethal without, appears / both, both the rays appeared / enter, enters a random appearing / answer, answers showers appears / embrace, embraced replaced supplied appears / bring, bring the comprehensive to the appearing / attitude, attitudes remolded for the appearances / milder, milders and the finders for an appearance / emotion, emotions relations appearances / same, same and the dames appearances / conduct, conducts creates answered appears / done, done in the sunning appears / person, persons and peoples appearings / pop, pops tops appeared / weight, weights off, appeared / thin, thin thinsulated appearings / accuse, accuse less, appear / rock, rocks reddest appearings / giggles, giggles most, appears / line, lines lofty for the appearing peers.

CHAPTER TWO

Aversion, aversions values for the final appears / regain, regains reigning appears / attention, attentions meaning for appearance / straight, straight is the cost of less, appears / middle, middles made for the fellow's appearings / much, much relation for the appears / whole, whole steering appearings / balance, balanced forms for held appearings / core, core stays appearing / realized, realized sizes, appear / truck, trucks, appear / dust, dusty, appear / fond, fondest, appear / image, images cast past the ancient appears / clay, clays carols appear / peril, perils over, appeared / urgent, urgent signs for the final appearances / crucial, crucial and critical, appear / necessary, necessary days, appear / serious, serious without, appear / immediate, immediate numbers for the final, appear / custom, customs credible for the federal, appear / practice, practices perils, appear / habit, habits hopeful to the honest, appear / handle, handles, sandles, appear / manage, manage to send the final, appear / overlook, overlooks classic, appear / merit, merits debits, appear / regular, regulars, appear / use, uses, appear / apply, apply forms your, appear / bush, bush boughts, appear / vague, vagues resting, appear / hazy, hazy roses, appear / ambiguous, ambiguous balance, appears / bare, bare stays, appear / advantageous, advantageous, appears / consume, consumes an, appear / treatment, treatment, appear / custom, custom, appear / valid, valid awareness, appear / slow, slowly, appear / peculiar, peculiar, appear / forward, forward, appear / abyss, abyss, appear / hole, hole, appear / gap, gap, appear / chasm, chasm, appear / erect, erect, appear / square, square, appear / direct, direct, appear / right, right, appear / vertical, vertical, appear / honest, honest, appear / candid, candid, appear / gift, gift, appear / strain, strain, appear / provision, provision, appear / patient, patient, appear / dull, dull, appear / hysterical, hysterical, appear / pebble, pebble, appear / rigid, rigid, appear / pace, pace, appear.

CHAPTER THREE

Separate, separate, appear / outside, outside, appear / believe, believe, appear / capable, capable, appear / assortment, assortment, appear / pillar, pillar, appear / timing, timing, appear / burn, burn, appear / hour, hour, appear / of, of chance, appear

/ fruit, fruit, appear / full, full, appear / ways, ways, appear / smashed, smashed, appear / into, into, appear / gummy, gummy, appear / bears, bears, appear / and, and they, appear / the, the best, appear / extension, extension, appear / of, of all, appear / days, days, appear / pass, pass, appear / abruptly, abruptly, appear / into, into beings, appear / love, love, appear / as, as it, appear / we, we, appear / weave, weave, appear / small, small, appear / fairies, fairies, appear / enlist, enlist, appear / in, in with, appear / the, the highest, appear / army, army, appear / human, human, appear / trotting, trotting / along, along / is, is to be, appear / a, a channel, appear / unicorn, unicorn, appear / dream, dream, appear / interlocking, interlocking, appear / infinity, infinity, appear / and, and then, appear / the, the piece, appear / creamy, creamy, appear / middle, middle, appear / meets, meets, appear / the, the truth, appear / blue, blue, appear / sky, sky, appear / of, of which, appear / the, the love, appear / ancient, ancient, appear / notion, notion, appear / that, that can, appear / liquid, liquid, appear / gases, gases, appear / rain, rain, appear / highly, highly, appear / contagious, contagious, appear / energy, energy, appear / inside, inside, appear.

CHAPTER FOUR

Invoke, invoke, appear / pleasure, pleasure, appear / ordained, ordained, appear / and, and to, appear / plotting, plotting, appear / candles, candles, appear / burn, burn, appear / in, in and about, appear / acknowledge, acknowledge, appear / light, light, appear / a, a chance, appear / seam, seam, appear / sown, sown, appear / in, in, appear / deeply, deeply, appear / and, and, appear / written, written, appear / in, in, appear / invisible, invisible, appear / ink, ink, appear / challenge, challenge, appear / stop, stop, appear / lust, lust, appear / boy, boy, appear / girl, girl, appear / flavors, flavors, appear / springs, springs, appear / chance, chance, appear / touch, touch, appear / tried, tried, appear / pack, pack, appear / seat, seat, appear / call, call, appear / twice, twice, appear / help, help, appear / student, student, appear / years, years, appear / need, need, appear / tent, tent, appear / real, real, appear / pages, pages, appear / writing, writing, appear / find, find, appear / choice, choice, appear / beginning, beginning, appear / previous, previous, appear / company, company, appear / silver, silver, appear / candle, candle, appear / publish, publish, appear / idea, idea, appear / word, word, appear / feast, feast, appear / clap, clap, appear / assist, assist, appear / bound, bound, appear / line, line, appear / paper, paper, appear / card, card, appear / natural, natural, appear / tree, tree, appear / prints, prints, appear / pages, pages, appear / land, land, appear.

CHAPTER FIVE

Penchant, penchant, appear / for, for, appear / total, total, appear / unanimity, unanimity, appear / of, of, appear / the, the, appear / bit, bit, appear / small, small, appear / incest, incest, appear / left, left, appear / and, and, appear / three, three, appear / ridding, riding, appear / of, of, appear / a, a, appear / 6, 6, appear / 6, 6, appear / 6, 6, appear / variation, variation, appear / protected, protected, appear / staff, staff, appear / are, are, appear / lead, lead, appear / to, to, appear / the, the, appear / diamonds, diamonds, appear / created, created, appear / when, when, appear / a, a, appear / cut, cut, appear / is, is, appear / made, made, appear / blast, blast, appear / the, the, appear / office, office, appear / with, with, appear / irradiated, irradiated, appear / ions, ions, appear / of, of, appear / symmetrical, symmetrical numerations for the final appearings / origin, origins rhyming your appearings / look, look, appear / for, for, appear / the, the, appear / omen, omen, appear / in, in, appear / the, the, appear / dogs, dogs, appear / who, who, appear / was, was, appear / thrust, trust, appear / to, to, appear / a, a, appear / jezebel, jezebel, appear / ever, ever, appear / changing, changing, appear / color, colors, appear / initial, initial, appear / Arab's, Arab's, appear / lament, lament, appear / an, an, appear / eternal, eternal, appear / cycle, cycle, appear / love, love, appear.

CHAPTER SIX
Israel, Israel, appear / and, and, appear / Jordan, Jordan, appear / unite, unite, appear / leaf, leaf, appear / are, are, appear / made, made, appear / lepers, lepers, appear / heal, heal, appear / as, as, appear / society, society, appear / breathes, breathes, appear / in, in, appear / renounced, renounced, appear / respect, respect, appear / for, for, appear / the, the, appear / one, one, appear / God, God, appear / negotiations, negotiations, appear / achieve, achieve, appear / wonder, wonder, appear / in, in, appear / those, those, appear / closely, closely, appear / related, related, appear / nations, nation, appear / reap, reap, appear / benefits, benefits, appear / of, of, appear / loving, loving, appear / trust, trust, appear / in, in, appear / the, the, appear / one, one, appear / God, God, appear / as, as, appear / written, written, appear / God, God, appear / has, has, appear / said, said, appear / that, that, appear / there, there, appear / be, be, appear / light, light, appear / where, where, appear / is, is, appear / the, the, appear / steam, steam, appear / in, in, appear / you, you, appear / the, the, appear / seam, seam, appear / lies, lies, appear / buried, buried, appear / beneath, beneath, appear / patterns, patterns, appear / build, build, appear / a, a, appear / bridge, bridge, appear / through, through, appear / forgotten, forgotten, appear / knowledge, knowledge, appear / learned, learned, appear.

CHAPTER SEVEN:
Remembrance, remembrance, appear / unlock, unlock, appear / the, the, appear / mystery, mystery, appear / and, and, appear / unravel, unravel, appear / the, the, appear / key, key, appear / in, in, appear / the, the, appear / twist, twist, appear / of, of, appear / DNA, DNA, appear / within, within, appear / you, you, appear / passed, passed, appear / by, by, appear / the, the, appear / less, less, appear / ancestral, ancestral, appear / more, more, appear / ancestral, ancestral, appear / clarification, clarification, appear / release, release, appear / fear, fear, appear / with, with, appear / remembrance, remembrance, appear / of, of, appear / loves, loves, appear / transcend, transcend, appear / ground, ground, appear / enlighten, enlighten, appear / to, to, appear / those, those, appear / around, around, appear / as, as, appear / a,

a, appear / disciple, disciple, appear / sent, sent, appear / write, write, appear / in, in, appear / the, the, appear / name, name, appear / and, and, appear / the, the, appear / pen, pen, appear / and, and, appear / the, the, appear / blood, blood, appear / of, of, appear / a, a, appear / lamb, lamb, appear / sacrifice, sacrifice, appear / of, of, appear / a, a, appear / hope, hope, appear / of, of, appear / a, a, appear / generation, generation, appear / instinct, instinct, appear / has, has, appear / said, said, appear / that, that, appear / will, will, appear.

CHAPTER EIGHT
Sacrifice, sacrifice, appear / was, was, appear / a, a, appear / need, need, appear / know, know, appear / longer, longer, appear / the, the, appear / reason, reason, appear / of, of, appear / a, a, appear / sacrificial, sacrificial, appear / rescind, rescind, appear / in, in, appear / other, other, appear / words, words, appear / God, God, appear / is, is, appear / your, your, appear / own, own, appear / without, without, appear / sacrifice, sacrifice, appear / inspect, inspect, appear / your, your, appear / temple, temple, appear / for, for, appear / respectful, respectful, appear / service, service, appear / to, to, appear / the, the, appear / one, one, appear / declared, declared, appear / "home", "home", appear / abbreviation, abbreviation, appear / is, is, appear / within, within, appear / your, your, appear / heart, heart, appear / spell, spell, appear / the, the, appear / word, word, appear / L, L, appear / O, O, appear / V, V, appear / E, E, appear / what, what, appear / is, is, appear / the, the, appear / sanctify, sanctify, appear / in, in, appear / your, your, appear / spirit, spirit, appear / surgically, surgically, appear / we, we, appear / are, are, appear / sent, sent, appear / to, to, appear / release, release, appear / the, the, appear / legislation, legislation, appear / of, of, appear / karmic, karmic, appear / cycle, cycle, appear / will, will, appear / you, you, appear.

CHAPTER NINE
Attend, attend, appear / the, the, appear / presentation, presentation, appear / of, of, appear / a, a, appear / new, new, appear / wave, wave, appear / change, change, appear / and, and, appear / turn, turn, appear / a, a, appear / new, new, appear / leaf, leaf, appear / into, into, appear / one, one, appear / God, God, appear / domestic, domestic, appear / occasion, occasion, appear / topic, topic, appear / theme, theme, appear / stamp, stamp, appear / crowd, crowd, appear / stroke, stroke, appear / save, save, appear / drip, drip, appear / dominant, dominant, appear / main, main, appear / address, address, appear / shelf, shelf, appear / oration, oration, appear / sensual, sensual, appear / lust, lust, appear / tamper, tamer, appear / ribbon, ribbon, appear / rise, rise, appear / honor, honor, appear / badge, badge, appear / shrine, shrine, appear / goal, goal, appear / flesh, flesh, appear / food, food, appear / able, able, appear / labyrinth, labyrinth, appear / network, network, appear / tangle, tangle, appear / pasture, pasture, appear / maternal, maternal, appear / friend, friend, appear / amplify, amplify, appear / swell, swell, appear / raise, raise, appear / prolong, prolong, appear / release, release, appear / absolve, absolve, appear / pardon, pardon, appear / impure,

impure, appear / modest, modest, appear / decent, decent, appear / confusing, confusing, appear / kind, kind, appear / everlasting, everlasting, appear / chance, chance, appear / intend, intend, appear / exit, exit, appear.

CHAPTER TEN

Sway, sway, appear / reel, reel, appear / staff, staff, appear / mound, mound, appear / sphere, sphere, appear / globe, globe, appear / ball, ball, appear / area, area, appear / revolve, revolve, appear / rotate, rotate, appear / tube, tube, appear / natural, natural, appear / steady, steady, appear / crush, crush, appear / seal, seal, appear / brand, brand, appear / conclude, conclude, appear / complete, complete, appear / issue, issue, appear / few, few, appear / division, division, appear / attractive, attractive, appear / partake, partake, appear / joint, joint, appear / acute, acute, appear / keen, keen, appear / shrill, shrill, appear / rough, rough, appear / pole, pole, appear / block, block, appear / test, test, appear / chief, chief, appear / climb, climb, appear / scale, scale, appear / balance, balance, appear / ration, ration, appear / range, range, appear / climb, climb, appear / mount, mount, appear / dignity, dignity, appear / hurt, hurt, appear / repentant, repentant, appear / trail, trail, appear / mental, mental, appear / belated, belated, appear / spread, spread, appear / explain, explain, appear / valid, valid, appear / mystify, mystify, appear / bewilder, bewilder, appear / secret, secret, appear / hidden, hidden, appear / obscure, obscure, appear / cryptic, cryptic, appear / satisfied, satisfied, appear / turbulent, turbulent, appear / quiet, quiet, appear / cover, cover, appear / requirement, requirement, appear / fare, fare, appear / constraint, constraint, appear / essential, essential, appear / luxury, luxury, appear / choice, choice, appear.

CHAPTER ELEVEN

Ratio, ratio, appear / quote, quote, appear / selection, selection, appear / reference, reference, appear / shower, shower, appear / drizzle, drizzle, appear / sprinkle, sprinkle, appear / elevate, elevate, appear / hoist, hoist, appear / ample, ample, appear / amber, amber, appear / erratic, erratic, appear / result, result, appear / calm, calm, appear / spite, spite, appear / silence, silence, appear / firm, firm, appear / insipid, insipid, appear / practical, practical, appear / wise, wise, appear / sensible, sensible, appear / almost, almost, appear / theory, theory, appear / expert, expert, appear / applaud, applaud, appear / glorify, glorify, appear / admire, admire, appear / perhaps, perhaps, appear / opportunity, opportunity, appear / chance, chance, appear / pretend, pretend, appear / act, act, appear / grant, grant, appear / appearance, appearance, appear / donate, donate, appear / gratuity, gratuity, appear / accept, accept, appear / direct, direct, appear / rescue, rescue, appear / plain, plain, appear / ordinary, ordinary, appear / regular, regular, appear / familiar, familiar, appear / spare, spare, appear / project, project, appear / can, can, appear / astonish, astonish, appear / surprise, surprise, appear / astound, astound, appear / amaze, amaze, appear / clash, clash, appear / disturbance, disturbance, appear / impact, impact, appear / sea, sea, appear /

secure, secure, appear / spine, spine, appear / lash, lash, appear / strict, strict, appear / regain, regain, appear / study, study, appear / grow, grow, appear / bubble, bubble, appear / free, free, appear / trust, trust, appear

CHAPTER TWELVE

Sincerity, sincerity, appear / sound, sound, appear / lame, lame, appear / horizontal, horizontal, appear / glory, glory, appear / candid, candid, appear / fair, fair, appear / diversion, diversion, appear / admire, admire, appear / justice, justice, appear / open, open, appear / just, just, appear / character, character, appear / adoration, adoration, appear / principle, principle, appear / consider, consider, appear / spare, spare, appear / simulate, simulate, appear / copy, copy, appear / imitate, imitate, appear / signify, signify, appear / imply, imply, appear / denote, denote, appear / manifest, manifest, appear / tranquil, tranquil, appear / racket, racket, appear / clamor, clamor, appear / conceal, conceal, appear / sign, sign, appear / alarm, alarm, appear / cunning, cunning, appear / ingenious, ingenious, appear / blast, blast, appear / blaze, blaze, appear / continue, continue, appear / contrast, contrast, appear / tell, tell, appear / ramble, ramble, appear / pleasure, pleasure, appear / plot, plot, appear / temperament, temperament, appear / signal, signal, appear / numb, numb, appear / mute, mute, appear / similar, similar, appear / silent, silent, appear / loud, loud, appear / load, load, appear / reason, reason, appear / innocence, innocence, appear / guilt, guilt, appear / angle, angle, appear / mistakes, mistake, appear / correction, correction, appear / compassion, compassion, appear / rainforest, rainforest, appear / nourish, nourish, appear / sustain, sustain, appear / host, host, appear / emphasis, emphasis, appear / millennia, millennia, appear / contemplates, contemplates, appear / act, act, appear / above, above, appear.

CHAPTER THIRTEEN

Funny, funny, appear / hungry, hungry, appear / until, until, appear / strong, strong, appear / push, push, appear / legion, legion, appear / justified, justified, appear / evidently, evidently, appear / outrage, outrage, appear / purpose, purpose, appear / subtle, subtle, appear / vital, vital, appear / hinge, hinge, appear / pivots, pivots, appear / confront, confront, appear / pattern, pattern, appear / plant, plant, appear / increase, increase, appear / through, through, appear / thing, thing, appear / citation, citation, appear / family, family, appear / here, here, appear / prefer, prefer, appear / perfect, perfect, appear / thought, thought, appear / nation, nation, appear / hold, hold, appear / supply, supply, appear / universal, universal, appear / mock, mock, appear / genuine, genuine, appear / extension, extension, appear / doubt, doubt, appear / silly, silly, appear / sub, sub, appear / affirm, affirm, appear / pursue, purse, appear / result, result, appear / enough, enough, appear / cause, case, appear / point, point, appear / enough, enough, appear / money, money, appear / fundamental, fundamental, appear / extend, extend, appear / shrivel, shrivel, appear / walk, walk, appear / once, once, appear / block, block, appear / attack, attack, appear / twisted, twisted, appear / desperate, desperate, appear / thirst, thirst, appear / help, help, appear / rage, rage, appear / justified, justified, appear / pay, pay, appear / approach, approach, appear / solution, solution, appear / currency, currency, appear / really, really, appear / aware, aware, appear / increase, increase, appear.

LEVEL 87: THE LEARN-MENTS

CHAPTER ONE
Identification, identification, learn / brace, brace, learn / branches, branches, learn / shoots, shoots, learn / shriveled, shriveled, learn / frail, frail, learn / trample, trample, learn / best, best, learn / shadow, shadow, learn / union, union, learn / dream, dream, learn / original, original, learn / juice, juice, learn / dance, dance, learn / urge, urge, learn / apples, apples, learn / book, book, learn / gain, gain, learn / main, main, learn / boredom, boredom, learn / pleasure, pleasure, learn / supply, supply, learn / strain, strain, learn / jesting, jesting, learn / squeeze, squeeze, learn / sour, sour, learn / sweet, sweet, learn / limitless, limitless, learn / tree, tree, learn / sustenance, sustenance, learn / everything, everything, learn / source, source, learn / natural, natural, learn / same, same, learn / seek, seek, learn / alone, alone, learn / realign, realign, learn / express, express, learn / return, return, learn / pure, pure, learn / destructive, destructive, learn / honest, honest, learn / time, time, learn / general, general, learn / pertains, pertains, learn / affect, affect, learn / mind, mind, learn / afford, afford, learn / recipe, recipe, learn / silly, silly, learn / objective, objective, learn / tool, tool, learn / apply, apply, learn / ego, ego, learn / crutch, crutch, learn / above, above, learn / suggestion, suggestion, learn / expansion, expansion, learn / gravitate, gravitate, learn / need, need, learn / listen, listen, learn / context, context, learn / sanctum, sanctum, learn / hustle, hustle, learn.

CHAPTER TWO
Masculine, masculine, learn / feminine, feminine, learn / transmit, transmit, learn / contrast, contrast, learn / measure, measure, learn / over, over, learn / lid, lid, learn / plug, plug, learn / during, during, learn / basis, basis, learn / develop, develop, learn / earnest, earnest, learn / born, born, learn / period, period, learn / spill, spill, learn / fact, fact, learn / brook, brook, learn / activation, activation, learn / chokers, chokers, learn / pile, pile, learn / favor, favor, learn / illustrate, illustrate, learn / relate, relate, learn / crystallized, crystallized, learn / teacher, teacher, learn / across, across, learn / technique, technique, learn / different, different, learn / habit, habit, learn / state, state, learn / release, release, learn / schedule, schedule, learn / clarity, clarity, learn / tears, tears, learn / found, found, learn / twofold, twofold, learn / touched, touched, learn / heart, heart, learn / end, end, learn / power, power, learn / tinker, tinker, learn / language, language, learn / desire, desire, learn / embrace, embrace, learn / propelled, propelled, learn / breath, breath, learn / chambers,

chambers, learn / appeal, appeal, learn / exhaling, exhaling, learn / veiled, veiled, learn / instant, instant, learn / high, high, learn / vision, vision, learn / crystal, crystal, learn / clarity, clarity, learn / plane, plane, learn / firm, firm, learn / pose, pose, learn / single, single, learn / pearls, pearls, learn / grass, grass, learn / inverness, inverness, learn / found, found, learn / treasure, treasure, learn.

CHAPTER THREE
Torrential, torrential, learn / side, side, learn / bent, bent, learn / burst, burst, learn / shiver, shiver, learn / explosive, explosive, learn / earth, earth, learn / tremble, tremble, learn / flame, flame, learn / clasped, clasped, learn / whispered, whispered, learn / spirit, spirit, learn / sweeping, sweeping, learn / neck, neck, learn / sink, sink, learn / open, open, learn / easy, easy, learn / prayer, prayer, learn / taught, taught, learn / sought, sought, learn / dignity, dignity, learn / free, free, learn / isolated, isolated, learn / spot, spot, learn / pool, pool, learn / water, water, learn / animal, animal, learn / stroking, stroking, learn / comforted, comforted, learn / humane, humane, learn / misery, misery, learn / shot, shot, learn / charity, charity, learn / kind, kind, learn / national, national, learn / union, union, learn / judge, judge, learn / hold, hold, learn / reduce, reduce, learn / little, little, learn / capacity, capacity, learn / awe, awe, learn / achievers, achievers, learn / affirm, affirm, learn / thought, thought, learn / self, self, learn / press, press, learn / hard, hard, learn / intellect, intellect, learn / all, all, learn / cobbler, cobbler, learn / house, house, learn / midst, midst, learn / model, model, learn / prey, end, learn / image, image, learn / aspire, aspire, learn / strive, strive, learn / tangible, tangible, learn / sovereign, sovereign, learn / dwells, dwells, learn / rose, rose, learn / Glory, glory, learn / total, total, learn.

CHAPTER FOUR
Born, born, learn / impersonal, impersonal, learn / material, material, learn / leaves, leaves, learn / stirred, stirred, learn / clerk, clerk, learn / asleep, asleep, learn / magnetism, magnetism, learn / collective, collective, learn / level, level, learn / bid, bid, learn / society, society, learn / start, start, learn / challenged, challenged, learn / hollow, hollow, learn / history, history, learn / converter, converter, learn / silky, silky, learn / cushions, cushions, learn / create, create, learn / wet, wet, learn / gem, gem, learn / rain, rain, learn / question, questions, learn / slow, slow, learn / lift, lift, learn / movement, movement, learn / gather, gather, learn / thread, thread, learn / dollars, dollars, learn / tamed, tamed, learn / creed, creed, learn / laugh, laugh, learn / issue, issue, learn / halo, halo, learn / relate, relate, learn / none, none, learn / notice, notice, learn / within, within, learn / enrich, enrich, learn / wheat, wheat, learn / sorted, sorted, learn / camp, camp, learn / scientific, scientific, learn / claim, claim, learn / stick, stick, learn / suffer, suffer, learn / filter, filter, learn / slip, slip, learn / testify, testify, learn / statement, statement, learn / concern, concern, learn / fretting, fretting, learn / display, display, learn / saint, saint, learn / image, image, learn / govern, govern, learn / ponder, ponder, learn / fail, fail, learn / honest, honest, learn / imparting,

imparting, learn / impose, impose, learn / literal, literal, learn / hence, hence, learn.

CHAPTER FIVE

Imperative, imperative, learn / instantly, instantly yours, learn / speak, speak the possible, learn / extend, extend the stream, learn / aside, aside from days, learn / lack, lack is past, learn / set, set aside, learn / support, support the ports, learn / kind, kinds who sing, learn / escape, escape, learn / secret, secret, learned / rights, rights are the rest, learn / carry, carry the sort who, learn / rather, rather the measured, learn / exact, exact refract into the one, learn / obey, obey, learn / behold, behold the folded, learn / clam, clam shut, learn / storm, storms opened, learn / moans, moans about bliss, learn / groans, groans a greeting, learn / garden, gardens and aparted too, learn / blossoms, blossoms and narrows, learning / blooms, blooms and the rooming, learn / heavy, heavy held, learn / perfume, perfumes and a meaningful, learn / provision, provisions and peaceful these, learn / eternal, eternal, learn / support, support yours, learn / search, search the sealed, learn / cut, cut this off, learn / flow, flows and flowers, learn / prosperity, prosperity, learns / freedom, freedom follows, learn / sustenance, sustenance will learn / dose, dose due, learn / share, shares the showering, learn / produce, produce a cause, learn / reversed, reversed pauses, learn / wisdom, wisdoms wells, learn / choice, choices carry those who, learn / transcendence, transcendence, learns / trust, trust and the resting, learn / outer, outer carrying this, learn / always, always relaxing for those who, learn / given, givens and relatives for those who learn / never, never the severs for those who, learn / flowers, flowers and the fields who, learn / sanskrit, sanskrit creatures who learn / part, parts for the simple, learn / eternity, eternity triples your learning / joy, joys for the forming, learn / reliance, reliance sizeable soaring, learn / profound, profound fillings, learn / affairs, affairs for the former, learn / gift, gifts and growing, learn / search, search, learn / security, security measures are needed, learn / dependence, end the dependence, learn / secret, secrets and the causes for those who, learn / condition, condition fields these learnings / victim, victim past, learn / lavish, lavish leis worn, learn / master, master the mastery and this initial three, learn.

CHAPTER SIX

Decree, decrees and the dues formed and infusing yours, learn / design, designs and rhyming learnings / future, futures fold, learn / gentle, gentle natures, learn / true, true rays, learn / strength, strength, learn / laughter, laughter, learn / celebrate, celebrates the doors, learn / journey, journey to those who, learn / unlimited, unlimited adventures in the learned / adventure, adventure into causes for the learned / wealth, wealth is sought, learn / insolence, insolence reaches a learned estate / abundance, abundances building, learn / determine, determine, determine, rhyme, learn / sing, sings a single, learn / lady, lady of the days, learn / exhaust, exhaust playing, learn / converse, converse, reverse, learn / topic, topic for those who learn / work, works and weeks and the learned / boss, boss and the matching learned

/ supply, supply assumed and learned / spunky, spunky and the spiking learned / light, lights and sights for those who, learn / group, groups and the greatest, learn / billion, billions and the basics, learn / system, systems who seal, learn / part, parts and the places who, learn / maximum, maximum means of those who, learn / refereed, refrains spent on learning / space, space, learn / released, released, learn / behold, behold, learn / entire, entire in this, learn / credit, credits aim, learn / back, backs who basic, learn / mirror, mirrors simple, learn / finger, fingers reach, learn / fingerprint, fingerprints, learn / city, coins in the city and the minutes for those who, learn / visit, visits a fellow, learn / visitor, visitor sealed, learn / aside, aside those who, learn / better, betters and the waters, learn / best, best and the rest who, learn / good, goods and the roads who, learn / behavior, behavior raved about, learn / face, face this, learn / transient, transient news, learn / moments, moments, learn / reject, rejects respects and those who, learn / eject, eject the reaching, learn / raise, raise the ripened, learn / aspect, aspects for those who, learn / instant, instant repeats for the learned / gone, gone into glass and the, learn / cast, cast the rest, learn / now, now and the how, learn / destiny, destiny and the learned / borrow, borrow the basics, learn / term, terms and temples who, learn / ascended, ascended, learn / master, masters who, learn.

CHAPTER SEVEN

Law, laws over, learn / altered, altered, learn / ice, ice the rivers, learn / thin, thins of the thronging, learn / emotion, emotions, motions, learn / unified, unified voices, learn / evaluate, evaluate of late, learn / practical, practical places and the winning, learn / use, uses for those who, learn / seek, seeks a submission, learn / tongue, tongues forming your levels, learn / abuse, abuses past, learn / harm, harms and the healed, learn / personified, personified voicing, learn / test, tests and rests and the learned / best, bests and relations for those who, learn / limited, limited, submitted for those who, learn / examine, examines a dialect of the learned / puzzle, puzzle over those who, learn / whole, whole the sole, learn / perception, perceptions opened, learn / lack, lacks, sacks, learn / progress, progress made, learn / creating, creating, rating, learn / fragment, fragment simple, learn / miracle, miracles motions, learn / tiny, tiny rays and those who, learn / far, far the days, learn / harmony, harmony held, learn / peace, peace is simple, learn / human, humans elope, learn / dogma, dogma days, learn / devoid, devoid the notions, learn / balance, balances paid, learn / single, single the shingle hung, learn / upside-down, upside-down the rounds for those who, learn / only, only the singing, learn / insulting, insulting, learn / fine, fine the fellow, learn / polish, polish off, learn / century, century, learn / value, values tossed, learn / improve, improves, learn / suspect, suspects over, learn / discovered, discovered a daily, learn / think, think, learn / stand, stands for those who are here, learn / cohesive, cohesive finds are for those who, learn / based, based into basics, learn / ocean, oceans and notions for the learned / show, shows and rows past those who, learn / itself, itself, yourself, those who, learn / source, sources and the reaching, learn / each, each and the thrilled, learn / quantity, quantity for the reaches and those who, learn / freedom, freedoms for the forming, learn / tributary, tributary to the touring, learn / sorrow, sparrows and the sorrows past your learning / learning, learning, learn / square, squarely, learn / sum, sums and the running, learn / laid, laids and the raids past yours, learn / half, half and the hurled, learn / curve, curves and natures, learn.

CHAPTER EIGHT

Forever, forever the over, learn / popular, popular the durations, learn / examine, examine the repent to a living, learn / assessment, assessments spoken, learn / trained, trained and reigned, learn / analogy, analogy forming, learn / continue, continue your rally, learn / offers, offers, learn / old, olds and golds and the learned / mental, mentals and the simple list, learn / river, rivers and rovers and these who, learn / row, rows and the shows for the remaining, learn / vertical, vertical for those who, learn / pole, poles and soles off the lids, learn / across, across the risk, learn / oars, oars, pores, learn / get, get the sets, learn / finder, finders and the mended, learn / sensitive, sensitive, learn / much, much and the soon, learn / give, give the gained, learn / understand, understand, learn / since, since and the rinsed, learn / live, lives near, learn / things, things and the thanking, learn / is, is and the remaining, learn / game, games and the rhyming, learn / identity, identity and the during, learn / insane, insane and the remainders, learn / believe, believe, learn / directed, directed, bisected, learn / share, share, care, carry forth, learn / room, rooms and the reasons for respite, learn / admit, admit the one, learn / illusion, illusion, learn / deceit, deceit, learn / choice, choices, learn / master, master, learn / confusion, confusions, learn / heart, hearts, learn / time, times, learn / cloud, cloud, learn / rock, rocks and the socking, learn / wall, walls weary? Learn / straight, straighten, learn / long, longs singing, learn / feel, feels and fills, learn / sugar, sugar shacks, learn / estate, estate, learn / reaction, reactions for those who, learn / credence, credence for those who will, learn / apart, aparts and the starting, learn / minute, minutes, motions, learn / define, defines a duration, learn / church, church chosen, learn / negate, negate gone, learn / thought, thoughts who frolic for those who, learn / society, society sealing, learn / faith, faiths thrust, learn / madness, madness past, learn / label, labels, learn / face, faces, learn / Eternity, eternity chosen, learn / kind, kinds who will, learn.

CHAPTER NINE

Force, forces, sources, learn / degree, degrees and the days who, learn / names, names past, learn / essence, essence sealed, learn / separate, a separate ray, learn / applies, supplies applies, learn / outside, outside respects for those who, learn / space, spaces, traces, and the raining for those who, learn / somewhere, somewhere yes is a learned group / real, real the deals and the learning / action, actions, rational, learn / day, days, paid, learn / almighty, almighty choices for the learning / purity, purity poses a learning gate / said, said the raid, learn / price, price past, learn / roles, roles race, learn / life, life led, learn /

total, totals modern to those who, learn / learn, learn to, learn / fellow, fellow peaceful, learn / requires, requires a sizeable, learn / future, future foes past, learn / compassion, compassion shoulders those who, learn / condition, conditions the ransom for those who, learn / corner, corners past, learn / street, streets and the narrows, learn / understand, understands and the thrones for the, learned / chat, chats past the learned / broke, broke the spoke for the learning / knows, knows shows and the learned / seek, seeks respects and the learned / happen, happens stance is the learning / doing, doing over, learn / change, change range, learn / treated, treated a throat implied to the, learn / inflicted, inflicted, follows, learn / experience, experiences simple to the lean red, learn / embark, embarks for the flushed, learn / roles, roles, souls past, learn / act, acts and these facts, learn / purpose, purpose is hollowly learned / sight, sights and the rites for those who learn / there, there and where? learn / first, first and the rested, learns / technique, techniques who shine in the shielded, learn / all, all who sell to those who learn / victimhood, victimhood past, learns / contradicts, contradicts reach learn / suffice, suffice, learn / lifetime, lifetimes and the shifting, learn / exactly, exactly for the facts, learn / affairs, affairs basic, learn / mankind, mankind singing, learn / based, based and the basics, learn / lack, lacks and cures these, learned / step, steps over the fielded, learn / new, news and nestling, learn / eventually, eventually sealing, learn / fear, fears past, learn / update, updates rates, learn / drink, drinks, learn / sun, suns and the running learned / goes, goes, reaps, learns.

CHAPTER TEN

Superfluous, superfluous spinning and the learned / wheel, wheels reaching your roses leaf's learnings / continue, continue the cycle, learn / major, majors and the missions for those who learn / cycle, cycles signals, learn / believe, believe the remedy for those who, learn / repeat, repeats and the seated polished, learn / sets, sets and the rested, learn / filter, filters sealed, learns / over, overs, learned / struggle, struggle is over, learn / pain, pain is past, learn / circle, circles finished, learn / stuck, stuck, learn / tune, tunes, learned / stabilized, stabilized and the learnings / shall, shall we, learn / how, hows and shows who, learn / retracing, retracings for those who, learn / script, scripts cast, learn / radio, radios blast, learn / tuned, tuned into, learn / adjust, adjusted, learn / gift, gifts follow, learn / music, music is most, learn / taught, taught the simple, learn / piano, piano on, learn / play, plays for your, learn / films, films cost? Learn / movie, movies made, learn / rejoice, rejoices choices, learn / fee, fees read for the learned / unification, unifications of the, learned / heart, hearts held, learn / reach, reaching doors, learn / brother, brothers kept, learn / conduct, conducts keeping your doors, learned / valid, valid days, learn / tools, tools respects, learn / stage, stages, races, learn / channel, channels cost? Learn / given, given the races, learn / beam, beams past, learn / programs, programs reprogrammed, learn / analogy, analogy choices and the learned / clairvoyant, clairvoyants, learn / future, futures, learn / past, past the races, learn / move, moves into the learned / movement, movements cost less, learn / born, borns and the warmed, learn / pause, pauses and causes for those who, learn / specific, specific into central learnings / lifetime, lifetimes chosen, learn / zodiac, zodiac sailings, learn / under, under the all, learn / same, sames who game, learn / innocent, innocents sent to the curbing, learn / souls, souls past, learn / judge, judges go, learn / educate, educate the self, learn / broker, brokers spoken, learn / each, each is the rested, learn / plexus, plexus poses, learn.

CHAPTER ELEVEN

Reflection, reflections posing, learn / encompass, encompass, learn / all, all the still, learn / opposite, opposites posted, learn / reflect, reflects raised, learn / know, knowing choices, learn / gain, gains remaining, learn / father, fathers past, learn / represents, represents respect, learn / aspects, aspects posed, learn / form, form focus, learn / prepare, prepares posted, learn / sent, sents vents, learn / speak, speak a posed, learn / quick, quicks for those who, learn / connection, connections, cures, learning / biology, biology posing a cure for the learnings / animated, animated, rated, learns / world, worlds and the similar learnings / occurred, occurred a reach for these learnings / separate, separate raids past these learnings / truth, truth reached, learn / being, being bossed, learns / discovery, discovery carried, learns / shed, sheds over, learn / hold, holds over? Learns / simply, simply a paired learning / pass, pass the past, learn / body, body blissed, learns / fell, fell past, learn / potential, potential cast, learns / short, shorts day, learns / frequency, frequency causes your learnings / self, self said, learn / matter, matter moist in the learned / creation, creations cured, learns / product, products poured, learn / singular, singular courses, learn / totality, totality touring the learned / express, express passes, learns / male, males moist, learn / female, females hard, learn / realms, realms reaching a learning living loft / explore, explores paths, learns / physical, physicals a creation for the learning / vibrates, vibrates and relates for those who learn / order, orders spaces, learns / within, within and withal a learning / project, projects past, learn / environment, environment meant for those who learn / learn, learns to vary, listen / more, mores and the matched, learn / holistic, holistic hustle past your learnings / picture, pictures and the patterns past, learn / measure, measure and the materials for those who learn / project, projects over, learned / interpret, interpret the let go for those who learn / overcome, overcome and bound for those who learn / return, returns and the powerful learn / contain, contains and the currents past those who dominate, learn / reflection, reflections carry, learn / available, available for the filling, learn / method, methods followed, learns / find, during your find, learn.

CHAPTER TWELVE

Drinks, drinks and remains, learns / during, during the game, learn / finds, finds an alert learning place / many, many who followed, fell, placed, learns / most, most who moistened their lips, learn / management, managements who carry, learn / given,

given a gallant, learn / genes, genes traced, learns / turns, turns to learn / finish, finish the final lessons, learn / funded, funded finally, lessons, learned / final, final lessons, learn / learn, learn to be the lesson / lessons, lessons done, learn / learning, learning to sing as a lesson / turns, turns made, learn / tips, tip chosen, learn / chosen, chosen, learn / mine, mine, learn / lines, .lines, learn / openly, openly, learn / maturely, maturely, learned / frankly, frankly, learns / outside, outside, learns / passages, passages, learn / reasons, reasons, learned / lists, lists and learns / ripens, ripens and rises to, learn / over, over, learn / means, means, learn / minds, minds listen, learn / spy, spy past the news, learn / lights, lights on learn / learning, learning to be learned / mine, mine who missions learn / matching, matchings learned / bites, bites past, learns / overtly, overtly, learned / mathematics, mathematics final, learned, counts / insure, insure the silence, learn / shouldered, shouldered the shadowed, learn / signs, signs and seals and the learned / misses, misses and veins of the worn, learn / many, many who find those who learn / meanings, meanings who made your life, learn / lifting, lifting and the reasons for those who learn / gifted, gifted ones who learn / maintains, maintains durations as those who learn / final, final findings learned / coming, coming to the ends, learn / eddy, eddy over days and those learned / mountains, mountains who match the learned / mended, mended ways, learned / overtly, overtly dear, learns / variations, variations found, learn / standings, standings lead, learn / mansions, mansions built, learn / overs, overs and unders and blunders past, learn / lineage, lineage clears, learn / pages, pages written, learns / learned, learned and listens and plans for the lifetimes / burns, burns in a turning silence for those who learn / channels, channels over, those who learn / lifelines, lifelines spent, past is listened too.

CHAPTER THIRTEEN

Mental, mental wonders into the past, learn / learns, learns a lesson, listen / patches, patches and portals and those who learn / parenting, parenting and the patterns for theoretic portals who learn / forgotten, forgotten pages blend into the portals of life learnings / funded, funded and founded, pages and learning / lively, lively patterns and posing listens to your learning / learing, learing past your posting learnings / patches, patches cleared, portals / molokai, molokai formed a portal to love's resting learnings / management, managements meant for a final portal of listening / truth, truth told, learns / carries, carries a pleasure past your learnings / crutch, crutch off, listen, learn / lifetimes, lifetimes end, learn / massives, massives past, learns / leapt, leapt over others, learned / purging, purgings learnings / cathodes, cathodes and learning gates / durations, durations learned / divergent, divergent on the darts for learnings / duty, duty opens and those who dare learn / religion, religions rip and the roar scares the door, learn / beethoven, beethoven's last is the ninth copernican learning / astronomical, astronomical carriage about the sun, / relationships, relationships marry your purpose to the truman buck, learn / farewell, farewell arms last nicked for the learned / forging, forging mortgaged? lightens, learns /

funnels, funnels a casting learning / founded, founded, sounded, learnings / third, third rays landed, learned / glasses, glasses worn, learns / hair, hair soft, learns / challenge, challenges spent, learns / wind, wind soft learnings / group, group grows, learns / grip, grips and ripping into those who learn / ear, ear fears over, learns / follicles, follicles flow, learns / atlas, atlas sights sent, learn / glue, glues soft, learning / cross, cross the durations for those who learn / buddha, buddha posed, learns / discuss, discuss the ways, learn / stars, stars for the learning / mist, misty learnings / spray, spray reasoned, learns / bark, barks and shocks and learnings / clear, clear the steering learnings / crystal, crystal curings learned / together, together the feathery learnings / forever, forever wearing a sparing learning / honesty, honesty curing the learnings / night, nights nestling, learnings / knights, knights near those who learn / friends, friends and spinnings learned / friendships, friendships simple, keep them, learn / moons, moons basic, learned / mantles, mantles samples, learn / advised, advised the risen, learnings / advisory, advisory sized, learns / perception, perception, learn / laser, laser cuts, learn / truth, truth is electric, learn.

LEVEL 88: THE APPLY-MENTS

CHAPTER ONE

Way, way to the flow, apply / phase, phase, apply / hidden, hidden, apply / life, life is, apply / wished, wished, apply / dreaming, apply / keep, keep the, apply / cool, cool, apply / disciple, disciple due, apply / such, such the nature, apply / mind, mind's matters, apply / denied, denied a duplicate, apply / confession, confessions, apply / possession, possessions, apply / touch, touching, apply / say, say the day, apply / stumble, stumble next, apply / walk, walks by, apply / goodbye, goodbye, apply / try, try the next, apply / clear, clears and dears, apply / often, often fellow, apply / near, nears here, apply / chance, chances, stances, apply / change, change, apply / edge, edge worn, apply / rise, rise up, apply / settle, settle in, apply / souls, souls merge, apply / nature, natures cast, apply / standing, standing in deserts, heat, apply / assert, assert yourself, apply / simple, simples, apply / world, worlds collide, apply / capture, captured, apply / luminous, luminous numbers, apply / adept, adept resets, apply / depths, depths posed, apply / sitting, sitting measures, apply / strands, strands, bands, apply / webs, webs, apply / long, long over, due, apply / done, dones, apply / degree, degreed, apply / forces, forces, apply / chart, charts, apply / silence, silences, numbers, apply / until, until when, apply / possible, possible too, apply / existence, existence is the miss-tress of being, apply / honored, honored, apply / never, nevers, apply / properly, properly, apply / wonder, wonders, apply / colored, colored forgiven, apply / lies, lies over, apply / use, use new, apply / state, states who, apply / abilities, abilities rhythm, apply / brain, brains buzz, apply / regular, regular practice, apply / practice,

practice meditative, apply / skeptical, skeptical past, apply / breathing, breathing lasts, apply.

CHAPTER TWO

Water, waters wedge, apply / storage, storage sold, apply / utmost, utmost cares, apply / stay, stay near, apply / carpenter, carpenter paid, apply / circle, circles numbers, apply / drive, drive in, apply / branch, branch sold, apply / buck, bucks past, apply / brand, brands last, apply / road, roads opened, apply / flowers, flowers cast, apply / hillside, hillside bloomings, apply / boston, boston moonings, apply / yellow, yellow will, apply / harbor, harbors held, apply / collide, collide past, apply / mission, missions finished, apply / granted, granted, released, apply / gush, gush over, rants, apply / knob, knobs who will B? / repair, repairs made, apply / ferns, ferns danced, apply / certified, certified, apply / hunt, hunts a new, apply / find, find one, apply / marry, marry the best, apply / crazy, crazy goes, apply / will, will we? apply / music, music will, apply / bill, bills paid, apply / paid, paid one, apply / voice, voices last, apply / voices, voices call, apply / come, comes one may, apply / one, ones who, apply / life, life led, apply / another, another's most, apply / trees, trees host man, apply / wind, winds whistle over the hood, apply / cars, cars apply for the egyptian, apply / handle, handle made, apply / table, tables danced, apply / general, general stance, apply / dance, dance when, apply / match, matched, apply / nursery, nursery, apply / neither, neither, apply / chant, chant, apply / myself, myself, apply / shared, shared, apply / view, views, apply / lose, lose, apply / cones, cones burned, apply / wave, waves, apply / orange, oranges pelt, apply / wall, walls off, apply / frontier, frontiers merged, apply / bay, bays bought, apply / land, lands sought, apply / south, south waves, apply / jaw, jaws collapsed, apply / find, fins one, apply / house, house phoned, apply.

CHAPTER THREE

Support, support winning, apply / channel, channels smoke, apply / beauty, beauty brought, apply / joy, joy is sought, apply / shake, shakes most, apply / hearts, hearts held, apply / hill, hills who, apply / coast, coasts who coast past your, apply / steam, steams streaming, apply / sparks, sparks parking into your, apply / life, life led, apply / ranches, ranches coaching your, apply / sold, sold the signals, apply / western, westerns ways, apply / signs, signs, apply / schools, schools cost, apply / carton, cartons tossed, apply / case, cases made, apply / class, class bought, apply / human, humans cost, apply / love, love lifted, apply / broadens, broadens, apply / forever, forever the evers, apply / focus, focused, apply / ripens, ripens likens, apply / sure, sures rest, apply / stop, stops too, apply / wisdom, wisdom, apply / ward, wards, apply / word, words who, apply / warrants, warrants who, apply / enthused, enthused for those who, apply / promise, promise made, apply / racing, racing past, apply / high, highs cost, apply / day, days made, apply / bake, bakes, apply / fever, fever tossed, apply / flavor, flavors most, apply / times, times lines, apply / new york, new york, apply / native, natives, apply / emerge, emerged, apply / said, said yes, apply / sad, sads who, apply / count, counts on, apply / repair, repairs costs, apply / scuttle, scuttle moves, apply / work, works into, apply / scream, screaming, apply / personal, personal, apply / birds, birds who, apply / mountains, mountains most, apply / someday, somedays, apply / little, littles who, apply / big, bigs and, apply / gold, golds running, apply / equate, equates raining, apply / tell, tells the majors, apply / quality, quality forms, apply / sound, sounds who, apply / side, sides ran, apply / ride, rides host, apply / animated, apply.

CHAPTER FOUR

Rescue, rescues over, apply / go, go now, apply / close, close too, apply / litter, litter past, apply / believe, believe in, apply / wonderful, wonderful ways, apply / leonard, leonard's, apply / pam, pams, apply / understand, understand thee, apply / arc, arcs past, apply / ark, arks float, apply / now, now them, apply / paid, paid for, apply / assemble, assemble most, apply / don't, don't cant, apply / gold, gold's most, apply / 19, 19 who knew, apply / acres, acres past, apply / hoot, hoots over, apply / run, runs into, apply / owl, owls daze, apply / fox, fox fed, apply / harley, harley haze, apply / orange, oranges mist, apply / share, as said "share", apply / lands, lands hosted, apply / oaks, oaks bought, apply / common, commons caught, apply / box, box tossed, apply / haul, hauls made, apply / crab, crabs cost, apply / enter, enter most, apply / mining, mining cost, apply / tours, tours given, apply / mines, mines stocked, apply / stock, stocks raid, apply / carpets, carpets pet, apply / leaving, leaving given, apply / conservation, conservation most, apply / on, on too, apply / turtle, turtles who, apply / clean, cleans an, apply / win, win one, apply / counties, counties who, apply / doves, doves over, apply / buckle, buckle into, apply / truck, trucks who, apply / equipment, equipments meant for those who, apply / long, long, apply / dig, dig, apply / picture, pictures who, apply / engage, engaged into those who, apply / cover, cover off, apply / butter, butter who, apply / courtyard, courtyards who, apply / clover, clovers dovers, apply / curious, curious who? apply / blue, blues potent, apply / plus, plus days, apply / leave, leave hosts, apply / alone, alone links, apply / cold, colds off, apply / demand, demands most, apply / just, just hot, apply.

CHAPTER FIVE

Storage, storage given, apply / balls, balls most, apply / hay, hays rouse, apply / sound, sounds who host, apply / lay, lays most, apply / automotive, automotives, apply / industrial, industrials, apply / install, installed for those who, apply / antique, antiques, apply / things, things thrown, apply / tremble, trembles back, apply / christmas, christmas blues, apply / handmade, handmades, apply / palms, palms who, apply / north, norths who, apply / bargain, bargains nodes, apply / toe, toes true, apply / transplant, transplant tows, apply / fellowship, fellowships, apply / polaris, polaris posed, apply / renew, renews who, apply / clean, cleans onto the, apply / junction, junctions softened, apply / sparkle, sparkles shown, apply / landscape, landscapes who, apply /

retain, retained regains for the final, apply / can, cans who can, apply / occur, occurs formed, apply / render, renders hosted, apply / home, homes carried, apply / king, kings who, apply / queen, queens noted, apply / count, counts on, apply / account, accounts moist, apply / drum, drums daring, apply / rail, rails cost, apply / morning, mornings moist, apply / star, stars formed, apply / slow, slows into those who, apply / forgiven, forgivens applying / wet, wets worn, apply / living, livings, apply / egypt, egypt joins the past, apply / handle, handles host, apply / stones, stones tossed, apply / emerald, emeralds greened, apply / tablets, tablets reign, apply / silver, silvers hosted, apply / bullets, bullets fresh, apply / posted, posted lorn, apply / self, self saids, apply / premium, premiums coat, apply / exist, exist most, apply / fast, fast on, apply / bridges, bridges basics, apply / light, lights locked, apply / wide, wide then, apply / open, opens up, apply / roof, roofs hot, apply / spaces, spaces plural, apply / flag, flags pearled, apply / power, powers who, apply / leaf, leaf ledges, apply / kindle, kindles coast, the outer banked, apply.

CHAPTER SIX

Sale, sales blend into the matrix, apply / rebel, rebels host, apply / chosen, chosen meteors for those who, apply / opening, openings remaining, apply / catch, catch the cautions, apply / more, mores who, apply / challenge, challenges costing, apply / welcome, welcomes channeled, apply / camp, camps hosted, apply / cows, cows forming, apply / pass, passes past, apply / horizon, horizons held, apply / vertical, vertical, apply / loop, loops, apply / circle, circles, apply / mask, mask, apply / ancient, ancients, apply / crooked, crooked, apply / jingle, jingles who yell, apply / pile, piles on, apply / glowing, glowing for those who, apply / horn, horns into, apply / trumpets, trumpets blown, apply / judah, judah stills, apply / purge, purged, apply / temple, temple tunes, apply / dome, domes, apply / regains, regains those who, apply / luster, lusters and hustles over those who, apply / homeward, homewards, apply / pilgrims, pilgrims, apply / march, march over, apply / toy, toy tuned, apply / spread, spreads who, apply / december, decembers arranging, apply / third, thirds who, apply / 2003, 2003 then, apply / prophecy, prophecy apposite, apply / filled, filled the prophecy with those who, apply / heavens, heavens called, apply / glad, glads gates, apply / assist, assisted, apply / suppose, suppose arose, apply / story, story paid, apply / told, told one, apply / inquire, inquire where, apply / within, within most, apply / blues, blues basics, apply / gone, gone into, apply / surrender, surrenders, apply / past, past your olds, apply / dues, dues paid, apply / trail, trails laid, apply / like, like then, apply / rewards, rewards host, apply / dove, doves coast, apply / returns, returns soon, apply / 2003, 2003, apply / saint louis, saint louis, apply / arranges, arranges the vertical, apply / homecoming, homecoming carriages, apply / experience, experiences made, apply / merge, merges yours, apply / supply, supply the definitions, apply.

CHAPTER SEVEN

Affords, affords words the placements, apply / signal, signals whom, apply / amounts, amounts the most, apply / notion, notions nations, apply / heal, heals dated, apply / energetic, energetics who, apply / conference, conference phones, apply / employs, employs landings, apply / your, yours daily, apply / aid, aids when, apply / enjoy, enjoy the showing, apply / the, the throning, apply / mention, emits mentions and most, apply / of, of those whom, apply / wonderous, wonderous wondering, apply / joys, joys joyced, apply / reputation, reputations, apply / builds, builds blown into, apply / insure, insured, apply / dilemma, dilemma, apply / gone, gones, apply / through, through us an, apply / your, yours whom, apply / faith, faith fed, apply / and, and when, apply / suburb, suburbs when, apply / employ, made to employ, apply / afford, affords them an, apply / another, another's and mothers who, apply / the, the who, apply / elegance, elegance for those who, apply / of, of them, apply / extraction, extractions forged, apply / again, agains, apply / hellenic, hellenics who, apply / trines, trines over, apply / gracious, gracious, apply / plenty, plenty who, apply / elects, elects, apply / your, yours ours, apply / door, doors days, apply / enjoy, enjoy them, apply / assign, add an assign, apply / another, another who, apply / the, the will, apply / insure, insures an, apply / of, of those who, apply / diligence, diligence doting on, apply / mothers, mothers made freed, apply / meet, meets one who will, apply / explore, explores most, apply / significance, significance for those, applied / and, and we will, apply / single, singles act, apply / act, caught acts and facts, apply / monitor, monitor your basics, apply / your, your days, apply / expense, expense past, apply / for, for those, apply / less, less doubt, apply / lessen, lessen has led to / has, has the one led? apply / sent, sent home too, apply / about, about them, apply.

CHAPTER EIGHT
Eight, expense paid, apply / beings, beings on, apply / to, to them all, apply / your, your ways, apply / door, door closed, apply / ignore, ignore less, apply / theme, themes burst, apply. / now, now them, apply / and, and whom? apply / march, march into those who, apply / to, to them all these, apply / a, a day will, apply / band, bands will, apply / your, yours will, apply / own, owns when, apply / an, an then, apply / aquarius, aquarius formed, apply / dream, dreams daily, apply / is, is this all? apply / signaled, signaled to apply / gabriel, gabriel grew into all, apply / risen, risen galactics who sail into, apply / again, agains match, apply / hope, hopes who will, apply / in, ion tall in, apply / assemblanced, assemblanced, balanced, apply / of, of them all, apply / one, one will win, apply / sent, sent packages too, apply / acknowledge, acknowledge when, apply / the, the winning, apply / envoy, envoy led, apply / and, and the days will, apply / the, the theory of applications / duration, durations, apply / of, of them all, honolulu, apply / your, yours the islands, apply / intrigues, intrigues with those who, apply / signal, signals lining your, apply / the, the all who, apply / passion, passions will, apply / for, for them all, apply / remembrance, remembrance leading, apply / as, as we will, apply / repleted, repleted for them all, apply / for, for us wills, apply / excavation, excavations

funded, apply / of, of theoretic, apply / lesson, lessons limited to the mistral, apply / past, past winds, apply / insure, insured, apply / tomorrows, tomorrows, apply / exchange, exchanged, apply / through, aware, apply / everest, everest readings, apply / climbing, climbing causes winding, apply / capabilities, capabilities for those moving, apply / you, you are the leader, apply / are, are we well? apply / the, the final, apply / one, one quoted, apply / the, the who, apply / in, in when, apply / which, which will, apply.

CHAPTER NINE
One, one signed, apply / who, who will, apply / acknowledge, acknowledged, apply / God, .God will, apply / creation, creations created, apply / humanity, humanity healed, apply / welcome, welcomes yours too, apply / home, home is held, apply / Metatron, Metatron moons, apply / in, in signs, apply / an, an effortless, apply / effort, efforts who, apply / to, to them, apply / reconcile, reconciled, apply / your, yours willed, apply / fields, fields, apply / you, you will, apply / have, have then, apply / been, been seen, apply / given, given scenes, apply / the, the willing, apply / choice, choices gained, apply / to, to them, apply / seal, seals off, apply / your, yours willed, apply / chords, chords curled, apply / employs, employs paged, apply / divorce, divorced into, apply / of, of this theory, apply / past, pasts willed, apply / transgression, transgressions off, apply / and, and then, apply / a, a daily, apply / silvery, silvery reeds, apply / release, release caused, apply / to, to this theoretic, apply / the, the winning, apply / cord, cords cut, apply / and, and then, apply / the, the willed, apply / chords, chords last, apply / of, of the all, apply / light, light's on, apply / you, you are won, apply / have, have then, apply / been, been when, apply / given, givens days, apply / rest, resting, apply / as, as said, apply / one, ones who, apply / chosen, chosen days, apply / for, for them all, apply / lone, lone within, apply / remember, remembers whom, apply / the, the wins, apply / arc, arcs notes, apply / and, and dues, apply / the, the winnings, apply / spark, sparks past, apply / and, and them all, apply / the, registrations read, apply / resource, resources gathered, apply / you, you are the won, apply / are, are we freed, apply.

CHAPTER TEN
Enjoy, enjoy when, apply / splendor, splendors mounted, apply / and, and these theoretics, apply / the, the one, apply / formation, formations founded, apply / of, of these all, apply / a, a won, apply / new, news, apply / nation, matured nations, apply / of, of these, apply / light, lights win, apply / Jerusalem, Jerusalems, apply / has, has domes, apply / returned, returned into those who, apply / the, the winnings, apply / sword, swords tossed, apply / of, possibly of thee, apply / lights, .lights linked, apply / misery, .misery is over, apply / sliced, .sliced and held, apply / a, a man who will, apply / man, man said to, apply / to, to told, apply / the, the London ledgers, apply / rose, rose blue by the way, apply / of, of London clubbing, apply / sharon, sharon's roses, apply / enjoy, enjoying your, apply / lavender, lavender durations, apply

/ dreams, dreams regions, apply / and, and then, apply / signal, signals signal, apply / emissions, emissions missions, apply / as, as them, apply / nightly, nightly nurtured, apply / your, yours willing, apply / seals, seals detailed, apply / are, are there? apply / evoked, evoked invoked apply / with, with then, apply / initial, initials sierra green, apply / integral, integrals, apply / aspirations, aspirations, apply / breathe, breathes best, apply / vibrantly, vibrantly veiled, apply / and, and thems, apply / ask, asking for those who, apply / michaels, michaels doubled, apply / forgive, forgivens, apply / for, for them all, apply / the, the rising, apply / swords, swords daily, apply / forgotten, forgottens flew, apply / quality, quality coating your, apply / has, has then an apply / come, comes too, apply / to, to, apply / your, yours, apply / life, life, apply / will, query well, apply / walk, walk due, apply / with, with all, apply / elegance, elegance poses, apply / within, withins winning, apply.

CHAPTER ELEVEN
And, and some who, apply / the, the finest, apply / slippers, slippers cost less, apply / of, of the hosted, apply / light, lights on, apply / resurrect, resurrections, apply / connections, coined connections for those who, apply / which, which will, apply / heal, heals most, apply / find, finds one, apply / invoices, invoices cost, apply / paid, paid mortgaged, apply / and, ands stands, apply / deliver, delivers one who, apply / to, to the thrillings, apply / the, the winning, apply / solute, solutes shingled for those who, apply / ones, ones winnings, apply / ask, asking a rationale for those who, apply / for, for them all, apply / assurance, assurances said "apply" / of, of them all apply / money, money spent, apply / sent, sent one in, apply / and, and those due, apply / indulge, indulges most, apply / as, as these said, "apply" / heaven, heavens hosted, apply / went, went once, apply / once, once said "apply" / to, to these, apply / a, a landing, apply / fall, falls past, apply / of, of them all, apply / greater, greater then, apply / caliber, caliber's costs, apply / erase, erased rested, apply / past, pasts over, apply / grieve, grieves openly, apply / and, and then, apply / the, the lending, apply / graves, graves roasted, apply / of, of this theory, apply / life's, life's leading, apply / past, pasts without, apply / annoy, annoy's hosted, apply / elevate, elevated, apply / your, yours, apply / choice, choices then, apply / to, to them all, apply / a, a winning, apply / throat, throats thirsty, apply / of, of these all, apply / rich, richest then, apply / remember, remembers most, apply / and, and then singing, apply / your, yours and the ruses, apply / heart, hearts and the heralds, apply / to, to the winnings, apply / a, a leading, apply / respect, respectful artful, apply / worn, worns and the winning, apply / emphatics, emphatics apply / atop, atop the simple, apply.

CHAPTER TWELVE
Upon, upons who, apply / your, yours is ours, apply / breast, breasts opened, apply / a, a theory for those who, apply / breast, breast plated, apply / plate, plates which punctured without, apply / of, of those who, apply / light, lights theory is the thrilling, apply / is, is there a host, apply / now, nows then, apply / given, givens tossed, apply / to, to them all, apply / each, each wills /

member, members most, apply / of, of these theories, apply / the, the creation is carried, apply / copies, copies created, apply / of, of this simple, apply / light, lights on, apply / election, elections made, apply / stela, stela won, apply / is, is this all, apply / sworn, sworns off, apply / to, to a temple tossed, apply / you, you will, apply / she, she wins, apply / will, wills, apply / remember, remembers, apply / in, ins / august, august blues, apply / 2003, 2003, apply / rest, rested, apply / assured, assured, apply / your, yours, apply / light, lights, apply / is, is theoretical, apply / good, goods who cost less, apply / and, ands who, apply / remembered, remembered, apply / well, wells into those who, apply / within, withins structural, apply / the, the theories forming an, apply / lines, lines break, apply / who, who wills? apply / broke, broke past, apply / a, a winnings, apply / spell, spells host, apply / for, for those who, apply / less, less days, apply / is, is thine an apply / your, yours during those who, apply / resolution, resolutions who paced, apply / intact? intact? apply / in facts, in facts who apply / we, we are the weavers, apply / know, know them, apply / it, it is there, apply / is, is then, apply / shall, shall weave, apply / you, you are the won, apply / shine, shine in, apply / eternal? eternal? tossed, apply / you, you win, apply / will, wills passed, apply.

CHAPTER THIRTEEN
Georgia, georgia reigns, wins, apply / Olivia, Olivia wins, apply / jerryn, jerryn lends, apply / stela, stela days, apply / carolyn, carolyn landings, apply / mary, mary plantings, apply / thelma, thelma causes, apply / and, and the theoretics, apply / friends, friends who, apply / have, have them, apply / made, mades shaded, apply / the, the ways, apply / wave, waves theory, apply / resurrection, resurrections simple, apply / is, is dated? apply / set, sets eternal, apply / for, for those who, apply / august, augusts deals, apply / 8, 8 who reign, apply / 2003, 2003 and then, apply / enjoy, enjoys winnings, apply / success, success who will win your applications, apply / until, untils and the theory for a final, apply / then, thens and shining, apply / tenfold, tenfolds, apply / the, the days, apply / reasons, reasons, apply / and, and the regions who, apply / the, the lending, apply / return, returns, apply / for, for them, apply / your, yours who, apply / strange, stranges daring, apply / journey, journey tossed, apply / mossy, mossy measures, apply / creek, creeks reciprocal, apply / is, is then, apply / back, backs basics, apply / given, givens most, apply / directive, directives tossed, apply / alone, alones lost, apply / insure, insures tossing, apply / your, yours who will, apply / intrigue, intrigues formed, apply / will, wills who will, apply / finish, finished, apply / to, to the theory, apply / heavens, heavens hosted, apply / pages, pages poised, apply / are, are there then, apply / left, left and alone, apply / for, fors amount, apply / lighting, lightings cost, apply / quick, quickens, apply / contracts, copies contracts, apply / coming, coming who will, apply / soon, soons moons, apply / prepare, prepares a tossed, apply / every, every ways, apply / noon, noons announced, apply / we, we will, apply / will, will we, apply / speak, speak most, apply / again, agains dancing, apply

LEVEL 89: THE EMPLOY-MENTS

CHAPTER ONE

Gate, gate joining, employ / eyes, eyes need, employ / open, opens, employ / mouths, mouths moistened, employ / wide, wides alarming, employ / elation, elations joining, employ / is, is there a final, employ / rising, rising, employ / enjoy, enjoys an, employ / the, the theory forming your employ / day, days dues, employ / of, of the theoretics, employ / thrones, thrones posing, employ / sides, sides related, employ / and, and thens, apply employ / the, the sides, apply employ / sides, sides win, apply employ / of, of those who, apply employ / swift, swifts landings, apply employ / remember, remembers too, apply employ / travel, travels costs, apply employ / now, nows days, apply employ / for, for them all, apply employ / heaven, heavens rising, apply employ / waits, waits winding, apply employ / ascend, ascends reminded, apply employ / all, .all who will, apply employ / 3, 3 who knew, apply employ / written, writtens smitten, apply employ / enjoy, enjoys and the road's, apply employ / hawk's, hawk's forming, apply employ / lair, lairs lurching, apply employ / grace, grace is said "apply" employ / set, sets who will sell, apply employ / pearls, pearls parcels, apply employ / pushed, pushed into those who, apply employ / children, childrens choosing yours, apply employ / chosen, chosen in a moment, apply employ / soar, soars into the thickest, apply employ / to, to those who made, apply employ / flight's, flight's and the shopping, apply employ / love's, love's to love during the apply employ / ascend, ascends employ / enjoy, enjoys the employ / love, loves to employ / Arcturians, .Arcturians who employ / assigns, assigns lined in love's employ / to, to the thrillingness for those who employ / the, the maintained employ / Metatron, Metatron basics for employ / splendor, splendors cost is less, employ / of, of them all, employs / lines, lines tossed, employ / of, of these time, employ / light, lights on, employ / enjoy, enjoy theory and the employ / well, well into the theory for the animal's employ / swerved, swerved into topographic employ / heaven's, heaven's states an employ / song, songs leading into your employ / is, is there reason in employ / yours, yours the living, employ / light, lights linking, employ / won, wons rising, employ.

CHAPTER TWO

Through, through the employs of love / love, loves a tool, find God, an employ / examples, examples of the sample for God's employ / give, give the most, employ / sample, sample and the simple employ / line, lines in the signage for love's employ / in, in the tune for an employ / love's, love's the host, employ / embed, embed is wed past your hosted employ / you, you are the one, employ / are, are there enough? employs / won, wons and the wonders employs / through, through us an all, employ / light, lights lost? employs / the, the host employs / 8, 8 who knew employ / purchased, purchased and purchasing, employ / are, are the ones an employ / bought, bought old? employ / as, as the one, employs / one, ones who employ / sight, sights on, employ / of, of them, employ / flights, flights sights employs / paths,

paths who join, employ / God's, God's gifts, employ / goods, goods and hoods, these employ / are, are the ones an employ / love's, love's ours, employ / innocence, innocence spent, employ / returns, returns returned employ / to, to the one, employ / love, love leads, employ / ledger, ledgers are simple, employ / rips, rips off? employ / to, to them all, employ / reveal, reveals a reel, employs / another, another signed employ / signed, as signed employ / love, love's a gift, employs / led, leds m ploy / finish, finish the ploy, employ love / tread, treads past, employ / lightly, lightly and the lost, employs / good-bye, good-bye the lie, employ / antonio, antonio the show, employ / announced, announced the winner, employs / your, yours thee, employ / rise, rise a risen, employ / today, today the shades employs / through, through us all, employers / love, loves gains, an employee / are, are there a few employ / you, you are the lightening's employ / willing, willing and simple, an employ / to, to them all, an employ / loin, loins tossed, employ / the, the and alls, employs / crew, crews tossed, employ / in, to them in an Hawaiian employ / Hawaii, Hawaii designs your employ / living, .living the giving's employs / theaters, .theaters and the employ for love / chinese, .chinese the employs.

CHAPTER THREE

Say, says a day's employ / yes, yes to the news, employs / and, and we have all an employ / acknowledge, acknowledge the college for love, an employ / your, your yellow's employed / place, places and an employ / in, in the simplistic employ / love's, love's blessed employ / light-us, light-us right us employ / love, love now, employ / leaps, leaps past, employ / remember, remember assurances sent to employ / and, and the then's employs / affluence, affluence spent, employ / reigns, reigns and rests, employs / loved, loved to show a new, employ / quadrant, quadrants regions and employs / pronounce, opens the news, employ / thought, thoughts and smattered employs / outlined, outlined and living for an employ / essay, essays detailed, employs / galactic, galactic's clues, employed / core, cored and employed / integrity, integrity reigned, employs / nation, nations and the relations, employed / contact, contacts crete and the caste? an employee / proper, propers roped, employ / writes, writes a lettered, employ / positive, positives posted, employ / where, where the dearest, employ / awakens, awakens relations and the shrilling employ / family, family facets and the fitted employees / remind, remind rewind employees / humanity, humanity mansions employees / intelligent, intelligent gestures gifts for employ / ask, asks a facts employ / shown, showns employ / bring, brings a basic employ / brake, brakes off, employ / array, arrays red, employ / wired, wired costs, employ / autumn, autumn tools, employ / filtered, filtered smiling, employ / fresh, fresh and freshening's employs / meat, meats most, employ / from, from them, employs / land, lands landed employ / table, tables and the tossed employ / honey, honey hosted employ / telepathy, telepathy posted, employees / dimensional, dimensional ascended employ / contact, contacts curing your hosted employ / four, fours who cost the most, employ / ability, ability blessed employ / chakra,

chakra shielding's simple employ / inhibit, inhibited without your ridden employ / provides, provides a prescient employee / obligation, obligations cast to the thrackish employee / us, us the deposit for a filling employ / beings, beings cast past heirs employed / group, find groups who last, metaphysical employ / metaphysical, metaphysical enjoinings, employed / community, community gated, employ / hopeful, hopeful healing and the litany, employed.

CHAPTER FOUR

Glee, glees flees, employees / anterior, anterior memories for these employ / diagonal, diagonal gazing for the final employ / patient, patient and the patience for an employ / pretty, pretty days employed / started, estates status for the employ / video, videos employed / feel, feels filling employ / people, peoples turn to employ / turn, turns on a sine for employ / stunts, stunts and the runted employ / review, reviews and the thimbled employ / vast, vast leys, employs / thought, thoughts who shield less, employ / return, returning to an employ / trust, trusted your rustic employ / eyes, eyes wise, employ / noble, nobles who milled, employ / head, heads thrown, employ / deal, deals made, employ / journey, how healed is your journey, employ love's lists / twist, twist these, employ / special, specials cost is an employ / include, includes the tickets for an employ / new, news and an employ / leave, leave on, employ / arrive, arrives near, employ / teach, teach the basic, employ / follow, follows following employ / sensitivity, sensitivity babies your employ / exhale, exhales placed employ / family, family for an employ / certain, certains and sincerest employ / change, changes employed / top, tops true, employ / rush, rush past, monies employ / calling, calling your employ / hobby, hobby costs, employ / religion, religions cost, employ / special, specials place, employ / popular, popular costs, employ / aura, auras tossed, employ / wanted, wanted a past? employ / investment, on an investment for an employ / convince, convinced for an employ / firm, firms and faceted employs / thought, thoughts thrownned, employ / off, off sets, employed / adventure, adventures launched, employ / ordained, ordained signs and employs / practical, practical clauses for an employ / apart, aparts plates, employ / custom, custom caring employ / packed, packed cases, employ / house, house lost? employ / window, windows cast, employ / serious, serious mentions, employ / sexual, sexual details, employed / seven, sevens who cost less, employ / protect, protected rising, employs / spares, spares cost, employ / relay, relay rides, employ / care, care for the created employ / buy, buys best, employ.

CHAPTER FIVE

Learn, learn to be employable / faith, faith is fused, employ / important, important muse, employ / hide, hides relaxed, employ / evening, evening cast, employs / act, acts on, employ / room, rooms rise, employ / church, church choired, employ / community, community tours an employ / quiz, quiz cost, employ / pray, prays for the final employ / game, games for the final employ / youth, youth yesed, employ / speaking, speaking

in, employ / call, calls made, employ / woman, woman signs, employ / man, man tossed, employ / analyze, analyze costs, employ / flip, flips over, employ / laugh, laughs made, employ / wonder, wonders and shining employ / proud, prouds and prides and employees / hold, holds formed, employed / smoke, smokes cast, employ / drama, drama made friendly, employ / first, first casts employ / live, lives and the linings employ / day, days duals employed / central, central codes employed / change, changes tones employed / urgent, urgents and surging employees / message, messages and the mineral employed / hours, hours and the past employs / fantasy, fantasy cured, employ / disc, disc duals employed / intelligent, intelligent creatives employed / provocative, provocative curations employed / struck, struck singles to the cord, employs / chord, chords signing a final employ / audience, audiences signal your employ / defining, defining moments and maintained employ / achieve, achieves and the shining employ / awards, awards recreated, employ / honored, honored and realigned employs / appeared, appeared in shrugging employ / list, lists one employ / debut, debuts a theory for the imparting employ / capture, captures a moment, employ / paralleled, .paralleled minutes and the spoken employ / acclaimed, acclaimed for the final employ / led, led past, employ / brilliant, brilliant basics for the formal employ / hilarious, hilarious hurling, employs / chasing, chasing closing coming employ / banished, banished basics, employ / snag, snags moist employ / existence, existence for the final employ / process, processed into a yearly employ / effort, efforts and the final employ / voice, voices and the final voiced imply for an employ / cynical, cynicals and the sophisticated employ / prevent, prevents and the clarity for an employ / prophets, prophets for the formal employ / beautiful, beautiful and the fullest employ.

CHAPTER SIX

Teaching, teaching and the final employ / power, powers and the pillars for an employ / upheld, uphelds and the melding employ / foundation, foundations forming a joining employ / would, woulds and the coulds employed / complete, completes and the shielding employed / rebirths, rebirths and the simple employs / concept, concepts and the final employs / first, first and the fusings employ / remembrance, remembrance and the shining employ / back, back to the sacked employ / mind, minds moist, employs / justify, justify the options, employ / literature, literature cools, employ / idea, ideas tossed, employ / intention, intentions cost eons, employ / wheel, wheels cursed? employ / principle, principles cost only old employs / great, greats for the formal employ / detail, details occupied, employ / evolution, evolutions cost, employ / sense, senses rising, employ / some, somes who employed / clarification, clarifications cored, employ / block, blocks past, employ / concept, concepts cured, employs / acquainted, acquainted sainted related employ / image, images hosted, employs / examine, examines relations employ / assigned, assigned, signed, wisdoms, employs / along, alongs singal employ / life, life led, employ / destiny, destiny cured, employ / how, hows employ / press, pressed into these employs / why, why signed, employ / linear, linear move meant, employ / flow, flows flowing employs / primal, primal causes employed / perceived, perceived percolation am employed / division, divisions simple to employ / possible, possibles forming a healed employ / polarities, polarities climb into these employed / realm, realms and released runs employed / manner, manners most employed / induce, induce ghosts employ released / ancient, ancients and the art employ / soul, souls employed / divided, divided costs, employs / union, unions rose, employ / reality, reality rules as employed / believe, believes best, employ / knowledge, knowledge reaching, employ / enlightenment, enlightenment lineage, employ / awareness, awareness nearing, employ / concern, concerns cost? employ / holistic, holistic gifts for the gainful employ / inevitable, inevitable curing employ / tend, tends tossed, employ / measure, measures most, employ / hurdle, hurdles and hosts for the final employ / analogies, analogies ghosted, employ / bridge, bridges basic, employ / column, columns employ.

CHAPTER SEVEN
Serve, sever the old, serve the swerving employ / project, project the old into the news, employ / picture, picture perfect, employs / return, returns to an old employ / points, points and joints employed / capacity, capacity afforded, employs / reflection, reflections employed / extension, extensions employed / itself, itself employed / number, numbers tossed, employed / only, only the linkage costs, employ / plane, planes purple, employed / cheer, cheers most, employs / our, ours the day, employ / time, times two, employ / now, now the new, employed / matter, matters most, employ / flesh, flesh host? employ / accurate, accurate rays, employed / passage, passage past, employs / robes, robes rose, employ / journeys, journeys gained, employ / held, held the manners employed / recent, recent reds employed / truth, truths rushed employ / lost, lost hosts employed / another, another most employed / simple, simple says, employs / reason, reasons reached, employ / purpose, purpose fulfilled employs / into, into those who knew employ / male, males employed / female, females employ / expressed, expressed your employ / frequency, frequency reds employed / vibration, vibrations filled, employ / experience, experienced employ / matter, matters emotive employ / low, lows hosted employ / view, views ghosted employs / high, highs cost employ / body, body basics errant without employ / through, through us a hushed employ / form, forms tossed, employ / particle, particles cost, managed employ / self, self sized, employs / chance, chances made, employ / comprehend, comprehend your employees / tube, tubes tossed, employ / slow, slows into employs / fast, fasted employ / enter, enters and the thinning employ / short, shorts and the smartest employ / biology, biology and the finals tossed employ / fragment, fragments cost your employ / speak, speak best, employ / vehicle, vehicles cost less, employ / Christ, Christ cost? employ / identify, identify your employ / shed, shed shredded, employs / stored, stored into your employ / contrast, contrast costs less, employ / develop, developed employs / scene, scenes cost, employ.

CHAPTER EIGHT
Brain, brains basic into envoys for employ / company, company asian too, employ / illusion, illusions cost less, employ / descend, descend into providential employs / return, returns a basic employ / powerful, powerful costs for the final employ / simplest, simplest beauty infusing your employs / brief, briefs rest, employs / background, background cues employed / unique, uniquest employ / rest, rests into employs / rules, rules register, employ / very, very days employed / forgot, forgotten employ / liberal, liberal resting employ / finds, finds signed employ / lifestream, lifestreams employed / accordance, accordance reads employed / drama, drama costs, empolished employ / stage, stages hosted, employ / heart, hearts and the held on employ / steps, steps and the tops employed / unification, unifications formed, employed / trace, traces and the costs employ / roles, roles stretched, employ / enriching, enriching rose, employ / particular, particular to a coasting employ / educate, educated employs / supply, supply for the formatted employ / make, makes a mos, employ / sign, signs signal, employ / one, ones who employed / tool, tools tossed, employ / child, child sold, employ / undergo, undergo strictest employ / severe, severe and the costs employed / test, tests and the titles employed / choice, choices and the final employed / record, records and the recorded employs / capital, capitals and the thundering employ / luggage, luggages and the liturgical employ / actual, actuals essential, employed / essence, essence several deep, employ / emotional, emotional released, employs / lifetime, lifetimes lifted, employ / star, stars cost? employs / feel, feels lost? employs / event, events traced, employ / retracing, retracing measured, employs / script, scripts cost, employs / shall, shalls knot, employs / radio, radios read, employ / station, stations cost less, employ / tuned, tuned into signing employs / manner, manners moist in employ / clairvoyant, clairvoyants surrender to these employed / adjust, adjusted hosted employed / future, futures employs / past, past living employed / talent, talents cost less, employ / music, musics costs employed / midnight, midnights news, employ / canvas, canvas cottaged employs / same, sames cured capably, employed.

CHAPTER NINE
Cinema, cinema attended for the employ / weep, weeps less, employed / go, go to these employees / remember, remembers mays suggested employ / exact, exact tracts employ / departure, departures gate chosen, employ / earth, earth vested, employs / audience, audience dated, employ / loosen, loosens up, employ / dare, dares days, employ / smile, smile amazed through employs / more, mores most employ / light, lights led employ / serious, serious settled, employs / upside-down, upsided-downs employ / loud, louds lost, employ / fashion, fashions hosted, employ / occur, occurs appearing in employ / parallel, parallels daily employ / everywhere, everywhere ways to employ / ease, eases into employ / based, based into basics employed / story, story and the steering employs / book, books balanced, employs / see, sees a dues employ / already, already ruthless? employ / frame,

frames and frankest employ / familiar, familiar feelings employ / fade, fades and faded employs / look, looks and listed employ / ahead, aheads employ / succession, successions employed / superfluous, superfluous employees / develop, developed employ / continue, continues employ / power, powers plus your employ / mountain, mountains moist and employ / mineral, mineralized rising employ / perceive, perceived an employ / taught, taughts tooling employs / circle, circles and cushioned employ / become, becomes a basic employ / gravitate, gravitated employed / stabilized, stabilized basics employed / action, actions moist in employ / result, resultant employs / new, news nudged, employ / again, agains employs / filter, filters cost? employs / limited, limited, employ / strong, strong in, employ / original, originals employed / celebrated, celebrated and rated, employ / excellence, excellence signals your employ / water, waters hosted, employ / location, locations moist, employ / crystal, crystals cured, hosting employ / spring, springs poised, employ / genuine, genuine ghosting employ / since, since this, employ / taste, tastes toiled? employs / fresh, freshens up, employ / purity, purity posing, employ / assurance, assurance sent, emprovised, employ.

CHAPTER TEN

Drink, drinks in employ / essence, essence spent, employ / valuable, valuable for an employ / personality, personality for thee, employ / isolation, isolation suggested, employ / careful, carefuls, employ / cycle, cycles, employ / major, major, employ / state, states costs, employ / cause, causes for their, employ / course, courses costs, employ / curve, curves lost, employ / lesson, lessons pews, employ / mankind, mankinds rest, employ / content, contents cured, employ / spiral, spirals posing, employ / peripheral, peripheral funded, employ / great, greats resting, employ / seek, seeks an, employ / some, somes who, employ / question, questions risen, employ / subject, subjects coded, employ / rise, rise near, employ / questions, questions rich in, employ / energy, energy lost, employ / condition, conditions conditioned in, employ / round, rounds reaching your, employ / confusion, confusions cured, employ / judge, judges joined, employ / grant, granted, employ / escape, escaped, employ / wisdom, wisdoms winds, employ / temporarily, temporarily posing your, employ / intent, intents cost less, employ / alignment, alignments sought, employ / heavy, heavy without, employ / find, finds listed, employ / next, next days, employ / shed, sheds relations, employ / mistaken, mistakens, employ / genius, genius, employ / family, family, employ / environment, environments, employ / conducive, conducive, employ / tradition, traditions, employ / guide, guides, employ / heaps, heaps into an, employ / gender, gender gentled, employs / heaven, heavens spent, employed / extreme, extremes turned, employed / always, always voted, employees / opposite, opposites employ / reflected, reflected an employ / corner, corners coped in employ / population, populations doped employ cleared / planet, planets poised, employ / increase, increased odds, employed / awakening, awakenings employs / influx, influx viewed, employ

/ choice, choices tossed, employs / ourselves, ourselves invested in, employ / fact, facts told, employed / emerge, emergent employed / body, body basic employs.

CHAPTER ELEVEN

Property, property sold, employ / sleep, sleeps to clear, employ / few, fews who sold, employ / whole, whole and the sold, employ / blazers, blazers basics, employ / hurdles, hurdles and the final employ / man, man and the minutes employ / foundation, foundations for the simple employ / add, adds on too, employs / situation, situations for the final employ / enormous, enormous kneelings employs / final, finals for the final employ / apart, aparted final employ / tower, towers touring these sealing employed / beside, besides sides employed / gather, gathers simply, employ / parents, parents potential employed / creation, creations created an employ / carry, carrys on, employed / refinement, refinement follows an employ / learn, learns a lined employ / counterpart, counterparted employs / male, males employed / learn, learns to employ / church, churches employed / skies, skies in enriched, employ / clouds, clouds cleared, employ / height, heights and heraldic employ / deed, deeds dote, employ / encompassing, encompassing ployed, empowering plans / string, strings tossed, employ / more, mores lost, employ / apostle, apostle poised, employ / muse, muses cost, employ / thrilling, heels thrilling, employed / ordinary, ordinary days, employed / unraveling, unraveling lines, employed / star, stars carriage, employed / startling, startling a surging employ / masterpiece, masterpiece posted, employs / challenge, challenges hosted, employ / moments, moments basic, employs / race, races tossed, employ / fresh, fresh faces, employ / contribution, contributions cores, employ / discoveries, discoveries dated, employs / encourage, encourages ratified, employs / levitated, levitated yearly, employ / scene, scenes immortal, employ / move, moves and the mutual employ / expression, expressions basic, employed / purpose, purposes posted, employees / lack, lacks and the lusted, employee / spirit, spirits portals, imploded / need, mentions materials imperfect to these employed / material, materials matched, employ / walk, walks and the watered, employ / God, God and the goodness for an employ / perhaps, perhaps and the fittest employ / pass, pass and the passage forming an employ / friend, friends and the passage into an employ / someone, someones for the fused employ / gift, find a final gifted employ / blessing, blessings blessed, firmly, employs.

CHAPTER TWELVE

Syndrome, syndromes for the fusing employs / global, global glued, employ / thought, thoughts thoraxic, employ / form, forms and the final employs / ocean, oceans and the mystic employ / move, moves made for the fusing employ / collective, collectives curing your employ / pattern, patterns pulsing employs / humanity, humanity hurtling employs / little, littles and the middles for our employ / quick, quick in the quickening employ / told, told and the truthful employ / island, island wild into an employ / sea, asymmetrical seasons for a filling employ / sand, sands for the firmest employ / white, whites willed, employs / various, various poses end an employ / setting, settings stylized employs / species, species posted, employ / decide, decided to the fine employ / washed, washed for the finite employs / consume, consumed without employ / period, periods posted, employ / same, same for the basic employ / bottles, bottles and the basics employed / trick, tricks turtled and employed / door, doors opened, employ / bird, birds searched, employs / span, spans posted, employ / week, weeks working, employs / day, days and durations employed / small, smalls days durated, employed / swim, swims and swam into the final musical employ / acute, acutest firmest, finalized, employ / awareness, awareness willing your healing employs / group, groups joined, employed / sweet, sweetest employs / finite, finite finished employ / vibration, vibrations follow, employ / adhere, adhere near your fellowshipped employ / resonate, resonate your nearest employ / level, levels employed / emanation, emanations employed / outside, outsides employed / stimuli, stimuli leading to a final employee / meaning, meanings employed / think, thinks openly, employed / multiples, multiples, employ / include, include your rude gone, employ / instance, instances employed / underlying, underlying factors employed / individual, individuals employed / school, schools established, employs / belong, belongs to a basic employ / contiguousness, contiguousness employed / instantly, instantly employed for love / sound, sounds ecstatic know employ / ground, grounds and the rounded employ / amplitude, amplitudes founded employs / caused, caused the collapse for an employ / collapsed, collapsed in your simple employ / point, points for the finalized employ / motion, motions similitudinal to an employ / frequency, frequency funded, employs.

CHAPTER THIRTEEN
Social, socials and thirsty employed / native, natives realized, employs / area, areas past, employ / around, around these, employed / wonder, egos wonder and wander these employs / ego, ego spells employed / spell, spells past, employ / love, love sick? employed / honestly, honestly dated, employs / stock, stocks sold, employ / result, results paid, employ / improve, improve rates, employ / surrender, surrender gates, employed / entangled, entangled less, employ / heritage, heritage hugs employed / crumb, crumbs fulfilled, confess, employ / two, twos who employ / chakras, chakras sealed, an employ / open, opens rates employed / active, active spines employed / based, based in basic employees / spine, spines cast, employ / navel, navels nestled, employ / procreation, procreation cubing, employ / survival, survival's rivals enjoin employ / dormant, dormants gone, employ / dependent, dependent goes, employ / only, only willed, employ / receiver, receivers sealed, employ / contrary, contrary dues, employed / common, commons employ / broadcast, broadcast employed / hunt, hunts one, employ / concern, concerned cages, employed / physical, physically fit, employs / energy, energy centered employs / centers, centers employed / relate, related employs / fashion, fashions

plated, employed / data, data measured, employed, and the final gateways to love / fed, fed, finals employed / storehouse, storehoused, finals employed / filtering, filtering a final sized employ / gland, glands and friends employs / external, western employs finals / in, ins signs and the employs / ignore, ignores past, employs / accept, accepts yes, employs / awareness, awareness guessed, employ / dwells, dwells and the daring employ / light, lights shielded employs / carrier, carriers past, employ / double, doubles employed / helix, helix filled, employs / DNA, DNA employs / chromosomes, chromosomes employed / activation, activation forming employees / twelve, twelves and these employed / resembles, resembles and the simple employ / electric, electrically employed / circuit, circuits employed / instrument, instruments for employ / filaments, filaments employs / antenna, antenna employed.

LEVEL 90: THE GAIN-MENTS

CHAPTER ONE
Africa, africa gained / passed, passed ON, gains / appointment, appointment made, kept, gained / operation, operations complete, gain / conservation, conservation mapped, gains / map, map laid, gain / priority, priority sent, gains / food, food kept, gain / hunting, hunting gains / pick, picks up, faintly, gained / botany, botany gains / peak, peaks above, gain / seaward, seaward look, given gain / plants, plants tossed, gain / thio, thio chosen, gain / led, led to blessed gain / dawn, dawn rising impressively, gain / quite, quite the heights, gain / reaches, reaches and preaches, gain / lack, lacks over, gained / viking, viking tossed, gain / independence, independence found, gain / empty, empty without, gain / parties, parties flout, gain / life, life is gained / play, play when gained / world, worlds gained / rich, riches gained / knives, knives tear, gain / wicked, wicked lose, gain / city, city blues, gained / bones, bones brought gain / quantum, quantum queries gained / zero, zero force gains / value, values lost gained / solution, solutions chosen, gain / possible, possible positions gained / correspond, corresponded gains / since, since then, gains / function, functions who gain / atomic, atomically gained / spectra, spectras gasolined, gains / principal, principals gain / equal, equals gain / below, below your gains / energy, energy gains / total, totals gained / frequency, frequency chosen, gain / admitted, admitted and gained / result, results gain / relationship, relationships gains / state, states gained / electronic, electronically gained / individual, individuals who gain / return, returns who gain / atom, atoms gaining / process, process ingrained, gains / traditional, traditional poles gained / ionization, ionization begun, gained one electron, the meta-electronic loops / simply, simply said 360 times two, gained / implies, implies perfect balance pointed in winging delivery for the gains / high, high said, agains arc-ionic / associate, associate leads, arcs are gained / wireless, wireless remotes gained.

CHAPTER TWO

Grown, grown into your gains / government, governments gained / tornadoes, tornadoes are gained / path, paths are purged, gains / Mount St. Helens, Mount St. Helens grandeur regains greenery / including, including vistas where gained / vision, visions gaining / eruption, eruptions now gained / rescue, recluse rescued and gained / double, doubles up, gained / light, lights gaining / service, service and gains / oversee, overseen gains / station, stations erased, gain / star, stars and the gains / spruce, spruce up, gain / ants, ants pass, gain carried grains to love for feedings / help, help the queen gain / queen, queens gainings / flowers, flowers gained / narrow, narrows bridged, gains / entrance, entrance ported with giant gain / shipping, shipping purported, gain / nest, nest near, gains / vegetation, vegetation lasts, gains / lords, lords off, gain / destroy, destroy past, gains / energies, energies last, gain / behaviors, behaviors owned, gain / marveled, marveled most, gain / explored, explored host, gain / tropical, tropical parasites end, gain / magnetic, magnetic mouths gained / charge, charges last, gain / classical, classical compose, gains / values, values hosted, gain / spin, spin which lasts, gains / called, called the lost, gains / areas, areas touched, gain / silver, deepened silver gains / depends, depends gained / nucleus, nucleus gains / arise, arise and gain / difference, differences gained / function, functions gains / increase, increased gains / depend, depends gaining / magnetism, magnetism's gains / south, south is now north to the gain / range, ranges gained / density, density gaining / high, high and the shining gains / sea, seas gained / surface, surface gainings / ejected, ejected past, gains / construction, constructions gains / views, views gained / over, over and the all gains / rim, rims gained / patches, patches gaining / exposed, exposed their gains / upper, upper creek's gains / last, lasting gains / safe, safest gains.

CHAPTER THREE

Study, study for the final gain / wave, waves functions gained / function, functioning gains / calculate, calculated gains / centered, centered in gaining reflex / various, various portals gained / combination, combinations gaining / earlier, earlier reigning gains / square, squares are gained / important, important subjects gained / properties, properties sold, gains / close, close now, gains / first, first one, gigantic gain / symmetrical, symmetrical gains fed love / smile, smile then gain / amount, amounted too, gains / dioxide, dioxide dues gained / fraction, fractions who gain / earth, earth will gain / distinct, distinct muse gains / sky, sky wise gains / percent, percented gaining / vapor, vapors who gain / drop, dropping into gains / pressure, pressures gained / atmosphere, atmosphere changes, Rainer erupts, 2012 gains / expected, expected eruptions occurring, 1, 2, 3, little sister knew, gains / surface, surface tensions mounting, gains / dust, dust blew into these wounded gains / open, shed openly to these gigantic slashes gained / seasonal, seasonal fluctuations gained / freezing, freezing past, gains / water, waters collapsed, gained / climate, climates torched, gains / utopia, utopia built, gains / situated, situated Equatorially near the gained gaps completed

/ lacks, lacks know thing, gains / yellow, yellows who gained / similar, similars gaining / time, time said "gain" / sunrise, sunrise risen, gains / local, locals who gain / temperature, temperatures gained / mars, mars hilling gains / zone, a zone's fried, gain / weather, weather lasts, giant gains / storm, storms topped, gain / link, winter links gained / molecule, molecules burst atop your gigantic gains / forth, forth an with, gains / little, littles blissed, gain / vines, vines stretched, gain / ten, ten who knew, gains / sketch, sketches chosen, gain / sequence, sequence supposes, giants reached gains / good-bye, good-byes gains / clasp, clasping your gains / retain, return to retained gains / natural, natural portals gained / baton, caught batons gains / tracks, tracks into your mountain's gains / clue, clues gained / genetic, genetic muses gained / fine, fines gains.

CHAPTER FOUR

Seed, seeds who gain / reading, readings gained / world, worlds who gain / past, pasts gained / biological, biologically gained / paved, paved and grained / understand, understand the floating gains / wisdom, wisdoms who gain / psychology, psychology gaining / refer, refers when gained / unity, unity poses gains / polar, polars capped and found? gains / spiritual, spiritually gained / appearance, aspirations gainings / function, functions gaining / vivid, vividly gained / hexagram, hexagram gains / flow, flows gain / atoms, atoms gained / sexual, sexuals gaining love / goal, goals to the greeted gains / inner, inners gaining final signs / union, unions gained / conjugal, conjugally gained / axis, axis gainings / refer, refers ranges gained / organic, organically gened gains / pairs, pairs gender free gained / suggest, suggested your gains / book, books gainings / steps, steps gained / languages, languages gains / parallels, parallels gaining / disappear, disappear and gained / resting, resting ruses gained / peacocks, peacocks gained / power, powers who gain / suffice, suffice said, "gain" / detail, details gaining / progress, progressed into gainings / problem, problems gained / striking, striking gains / variation, variations gained / fall, falls gaining / leads, leads are gained / fortunes, fortunes gaining / evoked, evoked and allowed your gains / raising, raising wonders and gains / eternal, eternally central to the Kauai gains / insight, insights due your gains / conformity, conformity musing, gains / western, western approached, gains / center, centers built, gains / rose, rose up a reader, gains / evolution, evolution follows gains / gradual, gradual releases, gains / genetic, genetic codes gained / wrote, wrote the respectable gain / wrist, wrist broken, healed, gains / living, livings gained / creature, creatures softly gained / code, codes coded gains / home, homes gained / together, togethers gainings.

CHAPTER FIVE

Opinion, opinions portals gained / accustomed, accustomed to gains / exact, exactly gained / strict, strictest gains / respect, truth told, resting gains / deny, deny less, gain / affirm, final affirms gained / capable, capable for the gainings / first, first gainings given / however, howevers cost is less, gained / book, books who gain / field, fields gained / astrology, search astrology gains / annual, annuals taught gains / encompassed, encompassed compass points, gains / encourage, encourage your simple gain / air, airs cost? gain / world, worlds toured and gained / place, places pointed to, gains / images, images courted gains / olympus, olympus gains / gentle, gentles gainings. / water, waters lost, gains / various, various gainings / might, mights hope, gain / devote, devoted gains / strong, strongs gained / daughter, daughters gained / represent, represented gains / sons, sons gained / bursted, bursted gains / autumn, autumns gains / center, centers gained / yang, yangs who gained / yin, yins gained / mythological, mythologically gained / function, functions who gain / line, lines anthropologically gained / mother, mothers who gained / joyful, joyfully gained / clockwise, clockwise gains / matter, matters gained / aspect, aspects gained / left, lefts gained / point, points gained / early, early gains / idea, ideas gained / mention, mentions gains / signs, signs gained / search, search over, gains / long, longs gained / backward, backwards gains / fact, facts gained / atomic, atomic gains / energy, energy and gains / plus, plus and the plenty gained / incapable, incapable and gained / order, orders now gained / laws, laws gains / aspect, aspects gained / genetic, genetics gains / underlying, underlying granted gains / observation, observations gained / eternal, eternals gaining.

CHAPTER SIX
Programming, programmings complete gains / orcal, orcal isles gained / creature, creatures seeking gains / replacing, replacing gains / likewise, likewised gains / function, functions gained / extent, extents gains / applies, applies for a gain / approach, approaches a gain / replacing, replacing gains / people, peoples gains / final, finals gains / open, opens gained / biological, biologically gained / science, sciences spent, gains / question, questions gained / cap, caps off, gains / fact, facts who gain / consciousness, consciousness gained / plants, plants who gained / imitation, imitations gains / united, united gained / polar, polars gains / whole, wholes gained / sign, signs gained / animals, animals gains / DNA, DNA stranded gains / alone, alones granted gains / zipper, zippers gainings / helix, helix gained / paired, paired poses gained / uriel, uriel gains / spiral, spirals gained / twisted, twisted gainings / message, messages gained / great, greats soft gains / discovery, discovery durably gained / sequence, sequences gains / replaced, replaced your gains / base, bases gained / sugar, sugars gainings / joined, joined your gains / intervals, intervals gains / cycle, cycles granted gains / opposite, opposites poised gains / rope, ropes and granted gains / animal, animals cast, gains / choirs, choirs softened and gained / striking, striking relations gained / extreme, extremes cravings gained cures / virus, virus past, granted a cure for all craving gains / reproduced, reproduced portals for all gains / cell, cells last, gains / message, messages reach your gains / living, living homes gained / open, opens pure gains / precise, precisely gained / gaps, gaps over all healed, gains / due, dues are past, gains / blueprints, blueprints now sealed, human gaining / sufficient,

sufficiently gained humans / pillows, pillows past gained / meter, meters now gain / meaning, meanings gained.

CHAPTER SEVEN
Pound, pounds plused gained / 64, 64 knew your given gains / fact, facts who gained / words, words well gained / age, ages last gains / reproduce, reproduced gains found for love / proteins, proteins blue blocks gained / read, reads about blue gains / characteristics, characteristics cured gains / 48, 48 who knew gains / structure, structures sealed, given gains / blocks, blocks and blasted gains / origination, porches origination is cured, sealed, gains / term, erstwhile gains / pain, pains paths ginger blue gained / eminent, eminent pools rush forth to thorough gains / flower, flowering crusts break into seas gained / work, works made long to a gain / student, students who gain / vague, vague releases gained / scholars, scholars who gain / reliable, reliable loans gained / based, based in basic gain / changes, changes reaching your loving gains / easier, easier gains made to love / present, presently gained / simply, simply spoken "gains" / laws, laws who form a gained creation / letter, letters gained / pairs, pairs gained / tai-chi, tai-chi gains / counterparts, counterparts gained / bright, brought for bright gains / heaven, heavenly gainings / aspiring, aspirings gains / winter, winters gained / unbroken, unbroken gainings / pole, poles collapsed, gains / dark, darks tossed, gains / light, lights out, gains in / verbatim, verbatims clearing cures / north, norths can be cleared / cosmic, cosmic cures gained / bottom, bottoms cleared gains / symbol, symbols gains / long, longs who gained / lines, lines of communication cleared, gains / harmony, harmony healed, gains / copies, copies who gain / sequence, sequences granted gains / parents, parents gained / groove, grooves tossed gains / notes, notes reveal gains / music, musics now gaining / pairs, pairs when gained / stack, stacks who gain / picture, pictures gainings / together, togethers gained / ancient, ancient wonders gained / moments, moments trained, gingerly gained / trains, trains for the formal gains / mechanism, mechanisms gainings / forward, forwards now gained / copied, copied for the final gains.

CHAPTER EIGHT
Translation, translations rent, gained / simply, simply and the subtle gains / phase, phases and the relations gained / pigment, pigments grown, gained / proteins, proteins grown, gain / reveal, reveals reaches gained / nonsense, nonsense spent, gains / weird, weird ways gained / green, greens tossed, gain / network, networks gainings / tandem, tandems tossed, gains / egg, eggs blast, gains / request, requested gains / make, makes who gain / blue, blues gainings / regulatory, regulatory greetings gained / red, reds whole gained / facing, facing your gains / both, boths grown gains / distinguish, distinguished clarity gained / blindness, blindness gain / differ, differs grown gains / region, regions granted gains / fully, fully gained / spoken, spokens gains / sentence, sentences gained / words, words gains / reside, resided when gained / verb, verbs gainings / beyond, beyonds gained / part, parts who gain / it, it is the granted gain / eva, eva's gains / lodge, lodges gained

/ see, see those who gain / power, powers proof, gained / great, greats gained / blurred, blurred clears, gains / nestled, nestled into gains / sign, signs installed, gain / people, people who gain / read, reads your gainings / different, differents gains / governed, governed / where, wheres gained / ancient, ancients gained / sled, sleds gains / constellation, constellations formed a gain / photon, photons gained / belt, belts who gained / encircles, encircles gainings / distance, surfaces gained / description, descriptions gained / flow, flows gains / purpose, purposes gained / trigger, trigger new gains / bridge, bridges gains / cart, carts filled, gains / butterfly, butterfly gains / align, aligns gained / dance, dance through your gains / join, joined to a gain / dawn, dawns gained / drive, drives driven gains.

CHAPTER NINE

Central, centrals geared to gains / occurrence, occurrences gains / different, differents gained / angle, angles crossed, gains / with, withal gained / tragic, tragics cost, gains / grace, graces lost, gains / birth, births launched gains / pleiades, pleiades located gains / upside, upsides built gains / bridge, bridges gains / aware, awares gained / result, results for those who gain / positive, positive poses gained / inhabit, inhabits arced gains / book, books gained / transcript, transcripts gains / suddenly, suddenly gained / requested, requested gainings / manuscript, manuscript gains / inspired, inspired gainings / scope, scopes gained / individual, individuals gains / telepathic, telepathically gained / founder, founders gained / facilities, facilities gained / other, others gained / vast, vast heliacal gains / array, arrays risen, gains / telepath, telepaths gainings / songs, songs gains / statement, statements gained / introduction, introductions given gains / starseed, starseeds gained / crystals, crystals gained / awakening, awakenings gained / visitation, visitations given gains / hope, hopes now gained / collective, collective genuine gains / youth, youths gains / honor, honors gained / wander, wanders gainings / multi-dimensional, multi-dimensional gains / sun, suns gained / meets, meets new gains / solar, solar gains / road, roads gained / architecture, architectures gainings / pyramids, pyramids gained / parted, parted gains / paths, paths gainings / pooled, pooled gains / vortices, vortices gained / pages, pages gains / map, maps gained / wordly, wordly gains / dolphins, dolphins gained / porches, porches who gain / gifts, gifts gained / gifted, gifted gains / initial, initials gainings / chilled, chilled and gained / forms, forms who gained / fellows, fellows who gained.

CHAPTER TEN

Blue, blues lost? gains / throats, throats gained / peel, peels posted gains / heal, heals host gains / boost, boosted gainings / vote, by votes gained / vortices, vortices gained / vortex, vortex views gained / translate, translate allowed gains / fast, fast gains made / follows, given following gains / fends, fends gained / chiming, chiming joins gains / function, functions well, gained / action, actions cost, gains / acts, acts for those gains / galatic, galactic gains / romans, romans gained / nails, nails broken off, gains / rusty, rusty doored shut gains / glass, glass off, gains /

greece, greece gained / ripped, ripped gains / tidal, tidal pooled gains / envoy, envoys gained / cubics, cubics cost less, gained / pool, pools cost, gains / fuels, fuels gained / vibration, vibrations gainings / curling, curling gained / focus, focused gains / faster, faster faucets pouring gasping for gains / council, councils who signal gain / crossed, crossed a gigantic gain into love / christ, christ said "gains" / paid, paids tongued gain / supreme, supremes gains / christians, christians gained / voice, voices who gain / enjoy, enjoys a gain / Arcturus, Arcturus gainings / sung, sung for the gains / foreheads, foreheads who gain / hum, hums gained / hand, hands gained / held, helds gained / homes, homes who gain / holmes, holmes gained / mystery, mystery gained / epic, epics codes carried gains / cords, cords who gain / caps, caps off, gains / sober, sobers tossed, gains / cats, cats gains / jump, jumps gained / joys, joys who gingerly gain / revolution, revolutions gainings / jam, jams gained / journey, journey havens gained / interior, interiors gained / reach, reach a roads gains / means, means tossed, gains / mask, masks gained / off, off sides gained.

CHAPTER ELEVEN

Floated, floated gains / forever, forevers gained / spun, spuns rearranged for a gain / sport, sports gains / short, shorts gained / firm, firms who gained / near, nearest gainings / notes, notes gained / entirely, entirely grown gains / gifts, gifts gain / lights, lights gained / lists, lists built, gains / flanks, flanks opened gain / appear, appears a cost-freed gain / lovers, lovers need gains / loads, loads who gain / tracks, tracks tossed, gains / pierce, pierces gained / yoga, yoga gains / vogels, vogels found, gains / shelling, shellings cost? gains / practical, practical causes gained / construction, constructions gained / shells, shells final, gains / portals, portals gained / on, ons gained / windows, windows gained / insure, insured gains / stores, stores gained / jobs, jobs written orange to red, gains / wallow, wallows lost, gains / welds, welds off, gains / poems, poems loaned, gains / paged, paged gains / patched, patched rippling gains / pens, pens gained / ports, ports who gain / pent, pents gained / fun, funs gained / folds, folds gains / forms, forms gained / focused, focused gainings / again, agains gains / instead, insteads gained / trust, trusted gains / overload, overloads gainings / karma, karma clauses gained / homes, homes built gained / limits, limits regained / break, breaks and gains / over, overs gained / inhale, inhale your given gains / warmer, warmer gains / codes, codes who gain / classic, classics gained / views, views gained / valued, valued gains / spent, spents gained / spools, spools posted, gigantic gains / tools, tools for firm gains / tamper, tamper freed gains / train, trains who gain / ripe, ripened gains / rolls, rolls into gains.

CHAPTER TWELVE

Counter, counters who gained / cottages, cottages built, gains / stores, stores gained / minimum, minimums gains / material, materials gained / comedic, comedic gainings / special, specials gained / rocks, rocks who gain / rules, rules gained / lit, lit one giant gain / fast, fasting gains / country, country gained /

vacation, vacation near giant streams and gains / homes, homes built, gains / trees, trees who gain / access, access gains / nursed, nursed and gained / nurses, nurses who gain / nuns, nuns over, gains / active, active gains grown in love / lap, laps who cost gains / loosened, loosened reins gained / quality, quality for the formal gained / cell, cells gains / spells, spells now gained / spill, spills gained / spoken, spokens gains / truths, truths gained / treats, treats now gained / tracks, tracks who gain / make, makes most gains / across, across the gains / former, formers gained / shrubs, shrubs who gain / scrub, scrub past gains / places, places and gains / master, masters gained / given, givens gained / genuine, genuine gainings / zones, zones and the willing gains / spelling, spelling pages, gains / mused, mused amounted for the financially gained / dia, dia is due a good gain / diablo, diablo gone, grains / gone, heard a good gain / maximum, maximums gained / mutes, mutes and gains / monitors, monitors gained / tear, theatrical gainings / lords, lords gained / plus, plus gains / pins, pins gained / spruce, spruce gains / green, greens and the goods gained / gateway, gateway gaining / angels, angels gaining / channel, channels who gain / way, ways armed, gains / green, greens gained / brown, browns who gained / denim, denim blue gains / child, child red gains / appears, appears your gains / planets, planets gained.

CHAPTER THIRTEEN
Affection, affections gained / park, parks gainings / lodge, lodges gained / bean, beans gains / buoy, buoys gains / lanes, lanes gained / arrow, arrows gainings / ending, ending gains / merge, merges gained / church, church candidates are gained / ahead, aheads gained / mount, mounts gained / kiss, kiss the following gains / hint, hints gained / sides, in sides gained / tissue, tissues gained / view, views lost, gains / free, free tribes gain / bend, bends blessed, gain / wall, walls tossed, gains / cost, cost hauls gained / caterpillar, caterpillars gained / trim, trims gained / shocked, shocked and gains / bethel, bethel blessed, gains / grass, grass grown, gemstones gains / gems, gems gained / soft, soft gainings / vision, visions gainings / doors, doors gains / moon, moons gained / window, windows relaxed, gains / stones, stones gained / santa fe, santa fe's gains / red, reds gained / rocks, rocks gained / highway, highways gainings / language, languages gained / vision, visions gained / pints, pints gone, gains / insulate, insulated granted gains / surround, surrounds greened gainings / following, followings gained / markets, markets gained / video, videos gainings / value, values gained / eggs, eggs gaining / opal, portals opal gains / explanation, explanations gaining / passage, passages gained / northwest, northwests gainings / october, october's basics, gained / oregon, .oregon dues, portland blues, gains / pennies, pennies cast, gains / cast, cast the last gains / bridge, bridges topped, gains / troops, troops packed, granted giant gains / parked, parked into your gained garages / near, near these gained / answer, answers who gain / november, novembers gains / born, born to be gained / downtown, downtown days gained / words, words now gained.

LEVEL 91: THE GRANT-MENTS

CHAPTER ONE: blessing, blessings granted your living loves / served, served in swerved grants / option, options granted loves / mail, mails into grants for love / open, opens amid love for a grant / doors, doors ajar love and grants / inspire, inspired loves grants / sires, sires attired grants / palm, palms portals granted / musical, musicals granted / wallows, wallows grants / gone, gones gone to a grant / steps, steps tossed, a grants / stop, stop atop a grants / atop, atop your optional grant / trees, trees granted / company, company cures grants / churches, churches grown grants / chapels, chapels chant grants / open, opens a granted cord. / center, centers curing cords grants / ridge, ridges granted / value, values formulas and grants / fort, forts grant your loving life / met, mets and the veteran grants for a life / available, available deals to a grant / school, schools built granted / mixed, mixed measures granted / Hercules, Hercules grants the life to love / corner, corners granted / sold, solds last grants / open, opening grants / gardens, gardens granted / cubed, cubed grants / codes, codes for the final grants / news, news made, grants / movies, movies and the measurable grants / wars, wars worked into grants arisen / starpaths, starpaths arranged, grants written / angels, angels interiors wired into those written grants / angles, angles angular too, written for grants / service, services past, written grants / office, office paid, finally, granted / region, regions and ranges granted / openly, openly granted / detailed, detailed grants / ford, fords a grant / river, rivers who grant / mixed, mixed a grant / burns, burns into your grants / mars, mars deals granted / map, maps made, grants / receipt, receipt real for your grants / mills, mills granted wired loves / stir, stirring your wiring granted lights / park, parks touring your grants / limits, limits during a grant / clinics, clinics carry your grants / races, races over, grants sold / placed, placed a Spanish grant into your life / extents, extents sold, grants / examined, examined a basic grant / bails, bails out, grants / bounce, bounce into a granted relate.

CHAPTER TWO
Pensacola, pensacola insuring your grants / arcs, arcs and the signs granted / pail, pails tossed, grants / inquires, inquires sired, grants / illusion, illusions lost, grants / velvet, velvets red into a cakes grants / red, red said "grants" / cake, cake tours and grants / paid, paid into a grant / eaten, eatens and smitten grants / smith, smith sent and a grant / video, video values for grants / matched, matched and make a grants / purest, purest settles a grant / farms, farms and final grants / pharmacy, pharmacy curing your grants / banquets, banquets and final grants sold / carry, carry for the final grants paid / patents, patents posing a grant / process, process purring your grants / taught, taught to sing, grants sold / hillsides, hillsides are granted / check, checks and guaranteed grants / sent, sent for a grant / spent, spent a final grant / spend, spends your grants / splash, splashing into a grant / runs, runs a running grant / insure, insures your grants / markets, markets and final grants / mention, mentions and maturing grants / mode,

modes and the final grants / selfish, selfish modes off, grants / self, self and the settled grants / selves, selves and the suring grants / reviews, reviews your granted lights / torch, torch and the final lighted lines granted / lines, lines over, grants / touched, touched a tours grants / point, points made, grants laid / brown, brown signs point to grants given / kicks, kicks into and off your grants / clear, clearest grantings guarantee / endure, endures a daily grant / moons, moons past, grants / kept, kept soft, grant / surest, surest inquires and granted states / softest, softest into grants / retails, retails a living / love, love your doors and grants / awaken, awaken only when you are granted literal loves / God, God gazing into your grants / graded, graded A grants / made, made the most, grants / dear, dearest granted / God's, God's greeted grants / company, company and the cured grants / ours, ours is a simple grant / deal, deals made, grants / mine, mine the most, grant / heritage, heirs heritage and grants / again, again the most, grants / loft, loft sold, grants / heart, hearts tossed, grants.

CHAPTER THREE

Gas, gas goes, grants / coins, coins and grants / districts, districts curing your grants / bird, bird basics and grants / reality, reality for a final grant / real, real dealings grants / realest, realest grants / read, read a basic grant / midway, midways grants / repeat, repeated your grants / complete, completed our grants / care, cares curing grants / foible, foibles tossed, grants / bubbles, bubbles basics, granted / blown, blown wide, grants / blue, blues and the final grants / at, at us all, granted / may, may we say, granted / all, all still and the filled funded grants / malls, amount to a mall's grants / missions, missions accomplished, grants / feed, feed into only a grant / fed, fed the rights, grants / code, codes and the sure grants / written, written and smitten grants / rope, ropes and the funded grants / tug, tugs a toppling grants / chance, chances and ranches and grants / opened, opened insurance for the flushing grants / doors, doors paid for a full grant / dealt, dealt your fullest grants / ground, grounds laid, grants / hamlets, hamlets holding your grant wells / taught, taught to be simply a grant / hoards, hoards past, grants / spear, spears tossed, grants / spoil, paid for spoiling grants / poles, poles purred, grants / doors, doors detailed, grants / opening, opening a standard, grants / can, cans and open thinnings, grants / lightened, lightened A, grants / load, loads and thirds for your, grants / super, supers and stipends for, grants / pens, pens placed inside your grants / woman, woman for a final, grants / wept, erased a wept grant / often, often fellows, grants / braced, braced a imply, grants / erase, erased, grants / affairs, affairs placed, grants / aim, aims surest, grants / affluence, affluence repeats your, grants / seeds, seeds and seeded, grants / stove, stoves burned, grants / patience, patience is sent, grants / sizzles, settle into sizzles granted / zones, zones moaning in sizeable, grants / stores, stores, granted / zoom, zooms over living, grants / skillets, skillets paced, grants / send, sends a note, grants / food, foods, grants / home, home to a tuning, grants.

CHAPTER FOUR

Trusted, trusted truthful, grants / entire, entire sires and grants / spat, spat into, grants / across, across those, grants / pleasant, pleasant paces, grants / herb, herbs hurdled, grants / ashes, ashes over, grants / arm, arms tossed sky wise, grants / star, stars and paces for a final, grant / Atlantic, Atlantic curing, grants / over, overs and lovers and grants / views, eventual views for a grant / shepherd, sheperds and supposed grants / kindle, kindles curing grants / care, cares formed a fellow grant / volleys, volleys and furling grants / gaps, gaps glow, grants / many, .many who know, grants / fly, fly past, grants / grown, growns and moans and grants / free, free flows granted / people, peoples who, grant / put, put these near, grant / baby, baby curing, grants / start, starts your surest grant / established, established minimum granting funded / vehicle, vehicles curled into your funded grants / Jordan, Jordan days granted / Ruth, Ruth rising, grants / journals, journals journey into your grants / surge, surge past, grants / blissfully, blissfully due your granted paces / fabric, fabrics spire to a grant / forthrightly, forthrightly your granted sites / spelling, spellings placing grants / made, mades shades for grants / alive, alive sized to a grant / inspired, inspired a purest grant / spells, spells imply a final grant / human, humans suggested grants / will, wills past, grants / prediction, predictions paid, related grants / past, past your grants / bring, brings a daily grant / bake, bakes insured grants / awesome, purchase an awesome experience for love's grants / truths, truths told, grants / crypt, crypts amount to pure grants / says, says yes to your grants / superiority, superiority for a formal grant / exists, exists suggested, grants / with, within yours, grants / levels, levels simple too, grants / convex, convex curing, grants / concern, concerned and a warmest, grants / sides, sides asunder without, grants / simple, simples and signs and yours, grants / sterile, sterile places and a grant / employ, employ a final grant / following, following curing your grants / styles, styles established, grants / empires, empires tall in your, grants / file, files a final, grant / simple, simple signs and your, grants.

CHAPTER FIVE

Reaches, reaches and rising signed, grants / branches, branches and your basics, grants / nourish, nourished and finally your, grants / nipples, nipples simple, grants / residence, residence secure, grants / reside, reside inspired, grants / touch, touching yours, grants / brought, brought forth, grants / edges, edges and stages, grants / marine, marines days and the firmest, grants / signals, signals supple your, grants / from, from a furled, grant / close, closest, grants / forth, forths paced, grants / oz, oz cures, grants / here, here we are, granted / Chicago, Chicago's surest, grants / is, is the final, granted / blue, blues and the robes granted / to, to a daring grant / a, a final grant made / yellow, yellows robed grants / meridian, meridian granted / of, of those who simple grant / the, the final grant made / waves, waves are red to a grant made / Egyptian, Egyptians granted / bring, brings in a regular grant / knew, knew soothing grants / the, the final grants made / codes, codes rise into grants / the, the fed granted / red, red days for your grants / the, the funeral granted / green, greens and grown grants / the, the final days granted / yellow, yellow roses granted / pathway, pathways purged and granted / simple, simples and spinal, grants / signs, signs, grants

/ signal, signal carried, grants / fretting, fretting over, grants / refreshment, refreshment lasts, grants / heat, heats due, grants / sent, sent the basic, grants / authoring, authoring succeeds, grants / thunder, thunders doors, granted / news, news made, grants paid / ascension, ascension's lines, grants / first, first led, grants / Sufi, Sufi empowered, grants / stream, streams tossed, grants / flown, flown over, grants / fresh, freshens up, grants / pineapple, pineapple pews, grants / bliss, bliss imbued, grants / withstood, withstood well, grants / forming, forming a basic, grant / fallen, fallen into, grants / stood, stood for, grants / treatment, treatment made, grants / worn, worn into, grants / well, wells paid, grants / along, alongs days, grants.

CHAPTER SIX

Listening, listening given your grants / lanes, lanes placed into grants / lynch, lynch over, grants paid / less, less days, paid grants / leap, leap over, grants / forth, forth fills your grants / freely, freely due a grant / forms, forms mutually your grant / umbilical, umbilicals granted / keys, keys dated, paid, grants / case, cases granted / spaced, spaced yours, grants / into, into a final grant made / attainments, attainments signed, grants / paced, paced a final, grant / poetically, poetically a cured, grant / lined, lined insured and granted / lining, linings dealt for a final grant / living, livings made, grants / lunch, lunch red, grants / absolve, absolves during your, grants / piety, piety and purest granted / petty, petty thefts, grants / thieves, thieves sure in, grants / honest, honestly a grant / men, men and the mental, grants / mansion, mansions and murals and grants / milk, milks taste is your, granted race / mutual, mutuals racing into your grants / resides, resides best, grants / residue, residues related to a grant / rest, rests for a formal grant / residual, residuals granted / rapture, raptures related to rising helicial grants / proof, proofs positive for final grants / passion, operated a passions granted life to love / purchased, purchased a portal's grants / pointed, pointed and purchased and granted / positions, positions pure, grants / purchased, purchased your final grants / a, a living granted / charmed, charmed and sure, grants / sent, sent into fellow grants / along, along signs gated, granted / lifting, lifting sizes and grants / words, words well granted / word, words and basics granted / Lucifer, Lucifers and the elated grants gated / struck, struck without grantedness / panic, panics posed, grants / lost, lost for sure, grants / leaving, leaving a firm, grant / rest, rests and the respected, grants / simple, simples and the surest, grants / inspire, inspire your basics and grants / arc, arcs past, grants / veins, veins tossed, grants / rich, richly granted / with, with us a grant / life, life is led, gather grants / incest, incest yours and grants / suppose, supposed a final grant / a, a flushed grant / moment, moments and the fullest grants.

CHAPTER SEVEN

Across, across the rules granted / nearing, nearing a final grant / seas, seas and days for the final grants / of, of those who say, granted / chose, chosen and smiling grants / is, is there a basic grant / now, nows days and a grant / are, are they the final grant /

your, yours and your shores guaranteed grants / prepare, prepare a basic grant / for, for them all a grant / light, lights and lessons granted / looking, looking at electric grants / in, in signs and grants / honor, honors a filling grant / for, for a firm grant / homes, homes held, grants / lift, lifted and granted / register, registers your grants / range, ranges risen granted / satisfied, satisfied and the final grants laid / funds, funds and the funded grants / entire, entires and the spires granted / along, along stays granted / living, a living granted / lights, lights and these grants and the final rays of love / losers, losers past your grants / cry, cry and the final grants / vanity, vanity paid, grants / dies, dies past, grants / daily, daily and the during grants / entire, entires and the final grants / in, ion sizes for grants / initial, initals granted / empire, empires purest grants / spent, spent and sent for a grant / for, for and fullest grants / imply, imply insured, grants / arose, arose the simple, grants / ponder, ponders and purest grants / roots, roots and the final granted / exposed, exposed sincerest grants / passionate, passionate pages granted / fees, fees fold, grants / faded, faded raids and your grants / roads, roads inspect your grants / rose, rose yellow grants / bloom, blooms moons grants / basic, basically a grant / arctic, arctics sparkling grants / for, for a fuller concealed grant / conceal, concealed and granted / noon, noons needs and your grants / waves, waves funded and surest grants / far, far said "grants" / wave, waves yellowed for the fullest grants / become, becomes a basic employed grant / enjoy, enjoys a soothing grant / stands, stands rampant for the final grants / keys, keys cured, grants / light, lights and basic grants / employ, employs and grants / aspect, aspects insured, grants / kept, kept to the trail for your grant.

CHAPTER EIGHT

Create, created a related grant / captive, captives cured grant / flee, flees over, grants / focus, documents focused and granted / done, done too, grants / duties, duties ruptured? grants / set, sets into your grants / explore, explores a basic grant / modes, modes purest grants / northern, northern nestles your grants / still, still is your simple, grant / B.C, B.C. basics and your grants / Vancouver, Vancouver yellowed? grants / lovers, lovers past, grants / lift, lifted a grant to love / opens, opens daily, granted / eyes, eyes past, grants / forgive, forgiven a grant / spring, springs rays and relationed, grants / dates, dates and the simple grants / patient, patient and the surest grants / firmly, firmly stated grants / rays, rays and the rubbles granted / trips, relations imply those who are granted life / along, alongs garnet grants / lead, leads tossed into your grants / absolute, absolutest gathering grants / treats, treats and tours granted / lines, lines and the lined grants / hat, hats and the heralds granted / deeds, deeds tossed, granted / probe, probes and the fullest grants / patience, patience and the final grants / lines, lines and the loosened grants / into, into this basics granted / spoils, spoils perils granted / pens, pens and portals gathering granted / leads, leads tossed, grants / demonic, demonic lines cast into grants / lift, lifted and lightest grants / insurance, insurance spent for grants and love / steeples, steeples tossed and grants laid for love / skyward, skywards paid, grants

/ sleeping, sleepings granted paces / along, alongs a pace and grants / poised, poised and the fullest grants / Christ, Christ and the legal grants / lines, lines and the final granted / the, the off-records granted / light's, light's grants / repose, reposed grants / register, registers your grants / assign, assigns staid grants / crystal, crystals cured, grants / number, numbers an initial granted / next, nexts and mosts granted / dews, dews and the flushing granted / attitudes, attitudes shouldered and granted / allow, allows your spaces grants / aft, afts and the final grants / for, for and the fullest granted lines / light, lights and the fuller grants / for, for us all, grants / plows, plows and the plans granted.

CHAPTER NINE

Showing, showing curing taxes granted / classic, classics posing granted / deduce, deduced and granted / assign, assigns laid, grants / convictions, convictions granted / compose, composed and insured and granted / deduct, deducts a yellow grant / suggest, suggested your grants / capable, capable for grants / ambush, ambushed years and grants / overt, overtly granted / include, includes a leading grant / clear, clear days for grants / done, done days and grants / pathways, pathways for the formal grants / past, past sold, grants / breakdown, breakdowns sold, grants / social, socially sold, grants / war, wars wet without grants / forming, forming a funded grant / radical, radicals registered, grants / structure, structured greetings and grants / sleep, sleeps peaceful grants / session, sessions granted / rumble, rumbles rousing granted / point, points made, grants / hospital, hospitals grants / kind, kinds costs guaranteed grants / stop, stops past, your grants / major, major memories and your grants / term, terms and the triple grants / DNA, DNA dues for your grants / prayer, prayers posing your grants / process, processed pairings and living grants / behalf, behalfs sold into grants / responses, .responses purposeful for a firmest grant / clear, clears and cures your grants / peace, peaceful meetings granted / whole, wholes and the final granted / clear, clears a page, grants / frequency, frequency curing your grants / point, points poled and granted / reality, reality for the final grants / truly, rules a truly respectful grant / storing, storing sures your grants / ploy, ploy and purest grants / spring, springs and the final grants / work, works into the fullest grant / birth, births issued for the faded grants / mastery, mastery mules your grants / longer, longer lingers cured grants / space, spaces forming your grants / knot, knots and the nestled grants / wrinkle, wrinkles insuring your grants / fear, fears paid, granted / omega, omega said, "granted" / geographic, geographically cured grants / body, body basics granted / created, created your related grants / realize, realized a grant / path, paths pured, grants / sum, sums and nations for the soaring grants / bodies, bodies basically, granted / able, ables and the stirring grants.

CHAPTER TEN

Occupying, occupying a penchant for grants / zones, zones and droning grants / talking, talking, walking, granted / integer, integers granted / range, ranges and the granted / engaged, engaged and enraged without grants / life, life is led,

grants / emotion, emotions motions and grants / dimensional, dimensionals granted / potential, potentials granted / realities, realities granted / pattern, patterns guarantee your grants / code, codes and roads and grants / learned, learned and merged into your living grants / never, nevers severed grants / secretly, secretly engaged in granted loves / temple, temples and the surest loves grants / returned, returned into surrendered grants / province, province for the purest granted / behind, behind us all, old grants / leaving, leaving is sure, granted / ones, ones who knew, grants / formalized, formalized pages for grants / Zen, Zen established and granted / study, study your door ways and grants / transmission, rant about your transmission for love's grants / practice, practice is keeping your grants / Chicago, Chicago days granted / bass, bass blues granted / blue, blue days granted / ground, grounds grew into grants / poor, poor surest granted / short, shorts and revealed grants / live, live in levels granted / under, under said, grants / studied, studies used and granted too / original, originals spelled G-R-A-N-T-S / spirit, spirits granted wings / charge, charges paid, grants / sloped, sloped in securest grants / attracted, attracted facts and grants / elegant, elegant and stirs a grant / life, life led grants / prevalent, prevalent tours and grants / small, small days granted / zoe, zoe is sure for these grants / monks, monks amounting granted / purified, purified encodes granted / completely, completely basic grants / Zen, Zen days granted / true, true deals granted / yes, yes to the yellow grants / question, wondering causes grants to exit / outside, outside stays and your willing grants / essence, essence paid for your grants / realm, realms and the during granted / praise, praise worthy for grants / worthy, worth and the worthy grants / power, powers and the pulsing grants / saying, sayings settle into grants / cut, cuts and the cuddled grants / real, reals and ruling grants / teaching, teaching a couple about granted love / explain, explains for a formal granted love.

CHAPTER ELEVEN

Comprehend, comprehended grants and loves / matter, matters and the material grants / interpretation, interpretations assured a final grant / clear, clears the deck for a final grant / sense, senses and the finals granted / awaken, awakening your grant / fundamental, fundamentally granted loves / part, parts and the starting grants / surface, surfaces sealed, grants / grasp, grasp your news, grants / understand, understanding your grants / truth, truths told, grants / waves, waves willing grant / ancient, ancients given granted / echo, echo and the needling grants / clear, clears cost is your grant / received, received a final flagrant grant / fresh, fesh days, new eyes, grants / eyes, eyes ways into your granted relations / dharma, dharma past, grants / clever, clever relatives granted / dreams, dreams and the finally granted loves / flash, flashes tools and grants / answer, answers insured and granted / understand, understandings granted / them, thems and the ones granted / first, first inputs inspected and granted / upon, upon the refined grants / gathering, gathering gathers grants / power, powers and the appealing granted / comprehend, comprehend the most grants / enlightenment, enlightenment led to the basics for a final grants / respond, respond to a special grant / forgets, forgets a basic granted love / enter, enters a concurrent love for grants / mind, minds in the simple grants / more, more days granted in lover's ways / still, still the entire basics for grants / light, lights during your grants / slow, slows insured, grants / gate, gates geared into a final grant / think, thinks and the surest grants / aloof, aloof places for the formal grants / real, reals days and grants / obtaining, overt durations and the final grants / demons, demons basically granted / cutting, cutting into surest grants / pits, pits pulsed and the final grants / received, received insured grants / hatred, hatred is out, granted / part, parts placed in secure places, granted / former, formers granted your lining grants / regain, regained metals for the living grants / state, states and the surest grants / great, greats and the surest grants / proof, proofs and the positions for a final grant / record, records simple, granted / small, smallest grants / wicks, wicks burned over, granted / burned, burned into insured grants / clothes, clothes forming a given guarantee for usual grants / destroy, destroy the last, grants / certification, certifications forming your grants / message, messages posted, grants.

CHAPTER TWELVE
Journey, journeys jewels granted / walking, walking into simple grants / long, longs and the thinnest grants / points, points made, grants / entering, entering a surrendered grant / bells, bells daily granted / alone, alones surest grants / people, peoples and grants / star, stars during those grants / entrance, entrances surest and the surest grants / inside, inside and the currents intact for a grant / them, thems who grant love / self, self and the said "grants" / met, mets and the pearls granted / people, people who imply your grants / passed, passed for the former grants / stealing, stealings over, grants / level, levels during, grants / destroy, destroy a daily grant / transmission, transmissions dated, grants / monks, monks and the material grants / rest, rests and the risen grants / accompany, accompany during a grant / world, worlds living and the lining grants / traveling, traveling your basic grants / last, lasted and blasted into these grants / entering, entering the gated grants / quarters, quarters cured grants / glanced, glanced and insured a grant / inside, insides rising to grants / intense, intense numbers for grants / true, true and the surest grants / stands, stands daily, granted / transmission, transmissions given granted / nature, natures and the nurtures granted / called, called and the basics granted / people, peoples and the purples granted / sight, sights and the surrenders / other, others who are granted love / judge, judges found, grant freed / result, resultant in resulting grants / called, called the sample granted / world, worlds who grant / beast, beasts and the both granted / body, body basics granted / speech, speeches granting love / void, voids over, grants / all, alls who will, granted / sure, sure things and grants / private, relax into private grants / equal, equals and single grants / example, examples frozen without your grants / think, thinks granted now / small, smallest granting loves / falling, fallings fullest granted lines to love / bell, bells and the bull days granted / often, often issued grants / fire, fires and grants relaxed into

love / realizing, realizing sizing and the final grants / right, rights and sights and grants / mate, mates made, grants / now, nows and them and the finalized grants / trance, trances dances and grants / wish, wish willed, grants.

CHAPTER THIRTEEN
Else, blades, blades and the basics for a grant / born, borns and the dormant grants / faces, faces pacing your grants / heads, heads and the surest grants / result, results form a granted strait / pure, pure days granted / liquor, liquors and the leading grants / love, loves and the surest granted / under, under seals granted / impure, impure sets form grants / sky, sky and the days granted / awakened, .awakened states imply full grants / illuminating, illuminating your final grant / empty, empty yellow grants / wonders, wonders waging your grants / true, trues and the final grants / expedient, expedients granted gates / bright, brightest hopes dash into love's grants / ignorant, ignorant without your grants / result, results for the sorted love grants / present, present places granted in love / tossing, tossing is tourist, grant / looking, looking for surest grants / endless, endless granted ways to love / constant, constant stable granted / true, trues your path, grants / teaching, teaching and the surest grants / manifested, manifested invested grants / lives, lives a similar grant / mind, minds and materials granted / ignorance, ignorances and the final sets granted / character, characters and the grants given / control, controls tools and grants / place, places soft, granted / view, views past, granted / forget, forgets a fuel granted / important, important paces granted / message, messages granted love / good, goods and the goods granted / mind, minds who mixed and grants granted / saying, sayings last "granted" / teacher, teachers past and the living grants settled / desire, desires and grants settled into love / strong, strongest sets and grants / truth, truth is told, grants / shame, shames off, grants tossed / running, running into old favorable grants / falling, falling past, grants / flavor, flanks and flavors granted / sole, soles flexed, granted / walking, walkings and the sealed grants / proof, proofs softened and granted / handwritten, handwritten meanings for the final grants / chart, charts sealed, chants and grants / ancient, ancients and these grants / supervision, supervisions superlative grants / grass, grass grew granted / robes, robes and grants / hold, holds sure grant / discipline, disciplines dear, granted / phrase, phrases costs granted / teaching, teachings days granted / great, great grants paid / living, living a land granted.

LEVEL 92: THE INFUSE-MENTS

CHAPTER ONE
Black, black to the while infused / white, whites who seal these infused / called, called for the infinity infused / because, because we will, infused / tiny, tiny days past, infused / fearless, fearless ways last, infused / princess, princess pined infusions / sought,

soughts the given infusions / seeing, seeings granted the final infusions / distance, distances infused / collar, collar cures infused / volition, volitions violet in infusions / tiny, tiny days infused / enter, enters stages infused / gentle, gentle, yes, infused / fawn, fawns cottaged into the infused / opened, opened an infusion to love / spring, springs and the basics for love's infusions / antelope, antelopes toured an infusion / sleep, sleeping infusions / faded, faded and raded your infusions / marrow, marrows and days infused / love, love is leading your infusions / mean, means a vast infuse / down, downs days infused / creature, creatures created your infusions / gate, gates daring your industry for love's leading infusions / soon, soon is yes to a kneeling infusion / over, over the all, infusions / par, appears touring infusions / king, kings dealt your infusions / wished, wished into your infusions / castle, castle coves infused / fawn, fawn pressed, infused / shall, shalls we are the wealthy, infusions / well, wells and the daring infusions / more, more days infused / neat, neats stuff and the stalling infusions / under, unders days and the rally past your infusions / clerks, clerks and the clearest infusions / distinct, distincts and the daring infused / trail, trails tossed, infusions / present, present your infused lovers / him, hims and those who infuse / become, becomes our basic infusions of love / work, works overloaded infusions / ill, ill is past, infused / glad, glads and infused for love / numerous, numerous noses infused / knew, knews and the shores infused / 111, 111 who knew those infused / 2.31233, 2 who knew 3 and the 1233 of love's infuse / gladly, gladly due your blessing infusions / debit, debits during your infusions / enable, enable kept you slow, infusions / keep, keeps a depth infusions / awake, awakes and the shaken infusions / stay, stays and the dearest infusions / book, books and the balanced infusions / good, goods soft in your infusions / page, pages paid to the flowering infusions / answer, answers given soft infusions / longer, longer soft and still the infusions / head, heads soft in softer selah's infusions.

CHAPTER TWO
All, all the fingered infusions / for, for those who dare "infusions" / every, every day a sure infusion / a, a lightening find, infusions / big, bigs and the balanced / up, up and the balances spent for love / should, should yours be there for love's infusions / it, it is ours, infusions / be, be the best, infused / all, all the real infusions / back, backs to the basics infused / place, places infused / permission, permissions committed infused / requested, the requested infusions / time, time and the tooled infusions / 365, 365 ways infused / life, life is led, infused / point, points pointed and infused / understanding, understanding your basic infusions / change, changes and the ranges infused / process, processed and infused / zero, zero and the lessons infused / shift, shifts and the shielded infusions / earth, earth stills infused / creation, creations issued and surging for the final infusions / figure, figures spent, infused / fingertips, fingertips gripping your finite infusions / contest, contested without infusions / west, western ways infused / chakras, chakras placed upon your infusions / creation, creations created and infused / palm, palms basic for

those infused / subtle, subtles who infuse / dislike, dislikes your infusions / show, shows your path, infused / trumpet, trumpets and shoes infused / strange, strange days end, infused / satin, satins worn infuse / slowly, slowly due your infuse / horse, horses held, infused / ride, rides past, infused / Rome, Rome sets your infusions / include, includes your infusions / request, requested an infusion / circumstances, circumstances due your wellest infusions / mellow, mellows back, infused / pleasure, pleasure is due your infusions / crown, crowns worn, infused / tardy, tardy without infusions / central, centrals, infused / rider, riders lost without, infused / before, before them, infused / earth, earth ways, infused / exclamation, exclamations for those, infused / rich, rich days, infused / victories, victories, infused / specter, specters, infused / knight, knights knelt, infused / head, heads on, infused / chain, chains burst, infused / powers, craters, powers, infused / burst, burst past, infused / stories, stories over, infused / deep, deep dates, infused.

CHAPTER THREE
Reference, reference those, infused / field, fields who land, infused / figure, figures, infused / matter, matters settled, infused / estate, estates sold, infused / inside, insides who side for those who fill, infused / tool, tools stools and the settled infuse / creation, creations cost is less, infused / force, forces plowing your doors, infused / mystery, mystery matching your, infused gates / access, access sealing, infused / directly, directly dealing, infused / key, keys and the cast, infused / cell, calls and the cells, infused / star, stars tossed, infused / Egyptian, Egyptians settled, infused / winds, winds warming tropical, infused / juice, juices joined, infused / flow, flows over, infused / trace, trace costs, infused / fast, fasting, infused / clouds, clouds lovers, infused / sound, sound the seals infused / music, musically infused / bibles, bibles bought infused / controlled, controlled each other? infused / transfusion, transfusions laced in infusions of love / park, parks infused / woven, woven branches infused / branch, branch broken, infused / gift, gifts made, infused / safety, safety off, infused / human, humans held, infused / energy, energy softens, infused / shower, showers over, infused / link, links carried past old confusions, infused / space, spaces towned into infusions / refer, refers and marries your infusions / label, labels dealing for infusions / key, keys dared, infused / knowledge, knowledge leaps, infused / seven, seven and the several infused / view, views carry for those infused / halls, halls help those who infuse love / reach, reaching your love's infuse / know, know those who infuse / yield, yield those who infuse / geometric, geometrically infused / flower, flowers who infuse / underline, underline without infuse / projecting, projecting gone, infused / monkey, monkeys past, infused / completing, completing circuits indicated and infused / intersection, intersections curing your infusions / journey, journey dealt an infusion / first, first leys infused / vibration, vibrations sealed, infused / shift, shifts and infusions / body, body blue infusions / aware, aware ways infused / traditional, traditionally infused / market, markets off, infused / quickly, quickly grown infusions / opportunity, opportunity pays, infused

CHAPTER FOUR

Shift, shifts made, relished, infusions / rapture, raptures cost is an infusion / experience, experience the hosted infusions / remain, remains necessary infusions / respond, respond daily, infused / choose, choose a cost, infused / process, processed into those who infuse / alone, alone again, infused / tendency, tendency cast, infused / biblical, biblical sorts who infuse / life, life lists infused / pulsed, pulsed paces for infusions / clearly, clearly classic infusions / shift, shifts final, infused / point, points related, infused / dark, darks tossed, infusions / age, ages lost without infusions / earth, earth spent, infusions / experience, experiences said "infusions" / final, final follows up, fed infusions / judgment, judgement joins infusions / cycle, cycles of infusions / self, self paid infusions / feeling, feelings lowered infusions / tone, tones infusions / original, originals infusions / matrix, matrix for infusions / tent, tents and temperatures infused / close, close the gates infusions coming in / directly, directly given a healing infusion / eye, eye on the lists infusions / aware, aware days infusions / power, powers purple infusions / return, returns given infusions / information, information following infusions / small, small days infused / bank, banks told "infused" / magnetic, magnetic norths infused / fail, fails your old infusions / charge, charge last, infuse / manufacture, manufacture your infusions / system, system's infusions / good, goods paid, infusions / load, load into an infusion / source, sources cost more, infused / externally, externally freed infusions / trickle, trickle pays, infusions / localized, localized anesthetics and infusions / depth, depths and infusions / manifest, manifested infusions / knowledge, knowledge cures infusions / answer, answers yours infusions / regard, regarding an infusion / local, locally infused / telescope, telescoping infusions / super, super stoles infused / deposits, deposits annual to an infusion / consciousness, supple consciousness for the ultimate infusions / is, is daring your triple infusions / said, said yes to your infusions / temperature, temperatured infused / fire, fire firmly into infusions / style, styles wearing an infusion / start, starts carry your infusions.

CHAPTER FIVE

Passed, passed into all infusions / before, before us a infusion / inner, inner dears infusions / earth, earthly infusions / masses, masses infused / reached, reached all infusions / whole, whole dancing infusions / possible, possible pearls infused / focus, focus into a newness for infuse / basic, basically infused reigns / progress, progress asunder into your infusions / alarm, alarms capable to an infusion / discoveries, discoveries armed upon your infusions / history, history focused your infusions / noticed, noticed your similar infusions / degree, degrees infusions / revolver, revolver infusions / cardboard, cardboarded infusions / force, forces infusions / protect, protect your infusions / thrown, thrown over, infusions / target, targets sold to an infusion / operation, operations shone into infusions / energy, energy nestles into infusions / force, forces off infusions / piece, piece spent on infusions / stronger, stronger alloys for infusions / glass, glass related infusions / boiler, boilers who burn infusions / attention, attentions infusions / teacher, teachers

telling "infusions" / people, people who are infusions / race, races off infusions / death, death past, infusions / heart, heart softens infusions / energy, energy days infused / generate, generated infusions / environment, environments infused / yes, yes weighs, infused / inserting, inserting more infusions / small, small infusions / number, number infusions / see, see infusions / placed, placed into infusions / done, done now infusions / multiplied, multiplied an infusion / reality, reality ruling our infusions / receptive, receptively due an infusion / low, low extractive infusions / insetting, insetting relations for infusions / plug, plugs in infusions / hat, hats off infusions / mud, mud soft infusions / operate, operated and infusions / crime, crimes soft infusions / react, react infusions / seldom, seldom sent infusions / remove, removes our infusions / scoff, scoff less infusions / conduct, conduct meant infusions / end, ends off infusions / calling, calling says infusions / dot, dot due infusions / flowers, flowers married infusions.

CHAPTER SIX

Time, times off infusions / hand, hands over infusions / bar, bars tossed infusions / mob, mobs left into infusions / take, take then infusions / instruction, instruction sealed, infusions / service, services cured infusions / defeat, defeats past infusions / paying, paying off, infusions / prepare, prepare too, infusions / place, places sold, infusions / staying, staying on infusions / merit, merits spelled infusions / else, else days infusions / opportunity, sports opportunity abounds infusions / speaks, speaks lightly "infusions" / prodigy, prodigy later infusions / approached, approached infusions / such, such required infusions / whistle, whistles days infusions / threads, threads related infusions / manner, manners merits infusions / fear, fear gone, infusions / recover, recovers rested infusions / Ben, Ben told ìinfusionsî / break, breaks off, infusions on / coach, coach yourself, infusions marked / rich, rich yelling "infusions" / mellow, mellows out, infused / young, young rays indicated, infused / city, city sold, infused / arose, arose yes, infused / leg, legs soft, infused / render, renders you to the rested infusions / mock, mocks off, infusions / employer, employers told, infusions / clerks, clerks mold infusions / books, books bought infusions / nothing, nothing rode, infusions / carrying, carrying off, infusions / time, times told, infusions / day, days sought, infusions / good, good news, infusions / glad, glad days, infused / learn, learn now, infused / self, self said, infused / files, files filled, infused / indeed, indeeded infusions / estates, estates great, infusions / matter, amounting to matters for infusions / case, cases told "infusions" / all, all sold and infused / found, founds infusions / time, times told, infused / between, between us all, infusions / half, given half, infused / power, powers off, infused / won, won one infusions / legal, legally infused / notations, notations real infusions / claim, claimed an infusion / two, two who infused / small, small wells infused / rush, rush along, infusions.

CHAPTER SEVEN

Article, articles told and infused / found, found the final infusions / day, days direct, infusions / stream, streams noticed, infused /

coding, coding off, infusions / spin, spins into interior infusions / double, doubles up, infused / raise, raises into an interior infusion / eye, eye soft, infused / universal, universally infused / cosmic, cosmic infusions / banks, banks and tanks infused / star, star days infused / ideally, ideally yours infused / triad, triad said "infused"/ ask, ask then, "infused?" / Metatron, Metatronic infusions / rod, rods and corrected infusions / never, never softened infusions / help, help tones be infused / actually, actually sound barriers have left the infusions camped / teleportation, teleportations devised to solve the infusions cores / multiple, multiple mansions and the doorways infused / solar, solar complimented infusions / for, for the cores infused / spiritual, spiritual gifts are infused / light, light planets infused / planet, planetary cores infused in magma regions / demonstrate, demonstrate your dynamic pockets of infusion / possible, possible keys infused / body, body blues infused away / chakras, chakras spelled "i-n-f-u-s-e-d" / Buddha, Buddha's birthday an annual infusion / merger, mergers cast infusions / divine, divine lanes infused / fully, fully arraigned infusions / combine, combine coasts infused / cosmic, cosmic culprits infused / quietly, amounts quietly paid, infused / request, request an allowance for infusions direct / matrix, matrix mounted, infusions / plane, planes sought? infused / invoking, invoking thoughts, infusions / anchor, anchor in, infused / signify, signify why, infused / work, works laid in lineage infused / effects, effects valuable infusions / request, request cords cut, infusions / day, day softened infused / focus, focus into interior infusions / innovation, innovations allowed, infusions / humbly, humbly homes infused / system, systems plowed, infused / merger, merger cast, infused / full, full on infusions / call, call the host, infused / heart, heart softens, infused / highest, highest callings infused / ascension, ascensions doors infused / 500, 500 who shew and infuse / possible, possible treats are infusions 4 loved / healing, healing soothes infusions / great, great rays infused / central, central stored infusions.

CHAPTER EIGHT

Reflect, reflects the random infusions / third, thirds who infuse / eye, eye squares and infused / workers, workers who are infused and kept for love / proceeded, proceeded choirs in infusions / process, process triples and infused / past, past the thankful indications for infuse / agreed, agreed on a lightened infuse / initiation, initiations through infusions / plate, plates fill, infused / electronic, electronic capes and the scapes infused / pancreas, pancreas pores infused / seventh, process scenes for the seventh rays infused / completion, completions connected and infused / final, finals dealt, infused / seal, sales off, infused / miracles, miracles came, infused / helpful, helpfully infused / fear, fears are final, infused and cleared through perfect love / definitely, definitely doubled loves, the infused / spiritual, spiritual peace and infusions / resolved, resolved infusions / fear, fear is over, infusions / cove, coves and the credible infusions / habit, habitable infusions / replace, replace an infusion / freedom, freedoms and the final infusions / habit, habits and the mapping infusions / required, required your infusions / level, levels infused / mover, movers and shapes infused / save, save the final infusions / downpouring, downpouring infused / walk, electric elevated infused / after, afters all, infused / birth, births infusions / graduation, graduation gates infused / full, full on infusions / seven, sevens who are infused / levels, levels are infused / techniques, techniques are infused / number, numbers are internally infused / integration, integrations are squarely infused / request, requested and infused / light, lights on, infused / elder, elder ways infused / example, examples spare infusions / body, body and the basic blues infused / call, calls who are infused in hawaii's love / plane, planes dreams and infusions / possibly, possibly infused in greens loved / send, sends one an infusion / program, programs which they were infused / adding, adding into infusions / system, systems who sealed on infusions / sun, suns cast, infusions / perhaps, perhaps those who are infused / send, send us your infusions / between, between a basic infusion / cook, cooks and those who infused / currents, currents topple, infused / book, books and basic infusions / red, reds rays infused / sleep, sleeps on fiances infused.

CHAPTER NINE

Humanity, humanity infused / conjunction, conjunctions internal infusions / world, worlds and well torn infusions / group, groups along infusions / unity, unity years of those infused / positive, positive purchased infused / lovely, lovely infused / wise, wise ways infused / associated, associated infusions / cosmic, cosmically cured infusions / plane, planes posted and infused / evolving, evolving solving infusions / monadic, monadic infusions / logic, logic infused / exact, exacted infused / return, returning infusions allowed / Chula, chula goes to her infusions / planet, planets standing, infused / clear, clearest infusions occurred / full, full ON infusions / souls, souls toppled, infusions / hearts, hearts shrugging, infused / all, all those who say "infused" / thirty, thirty ways infused / divine, divines experienced infusions / God, God given infusions / manifest, manifested infants infused / clear, clear days infused / necessary, necessary needs infused / solar, solar plexus ways and the gates infused / financial, financial means infused / done, done within and infused / spiritual, spiritually infused infants / student, students said "infused" / equal, equal sequels infused / unborn, unborns who infuse / child, child said "yes" to infusions / minute, minutes naturally infused / toddler, toddler past, infusions / standing, standing lasts, infused / ego, ego days infused / opportunity, opportunity parked to infusions / embrace, embraces lasting infusions / feeling, fell to the feelings in loving infusions / said, said yes to similar paths for infusion / dark, dark goes to infusions enlightening in love / person, persons made homoclitically aroused in heteroclitically well infusions / blueprint, blueprints well into those who infuse / levels, levels are infused / idea, ideas spread for infusions / mate, mates last through infusions / room, rooms smell of infusion / effect, effects gained, infusions / matrix, matrix miles into infusions / aspect, aspects relaxed infusions / logic, logically worn, infusions / return, returns nearing infusions / astral, astrals who infused / evolving, evolving the solving infusions /

anchoring, anchoring infused / kick, kicks out those who infused / out, outed infusions / time, times tripled, infused / emergency, emergency past, infused.

CHAPTER TEN

Install, installing your infusions / earth, earth said "infused" / quotient, quotients now infused / colors, cool colors infused / brain, brains basically infused / glands, glands given infusions / benefits, benefits beneficial for those infused / shape, shapes a birthday for the infused / spin, spinning infused / fully, fully infusing / sealing, sealing doors and the cords infused in light / imbalance, imbalances off, infused / colors, colors swirl infused / protection, protection comes into your infusions / place, place sought is bound into fabrics infused / out, out then, infused / Metatron, Metatronic in infusions / call, cast calls to these infused / chicken, chickens out infused / spear, people speared are cast to infusions / extremely, extremely rich in infusions / perfect, perfectly sought, infusions / coated, coated and still infused / key, keys clarity infused / letters, letters durations infused / request, requested your infusions last / chain, chains off, infused / box, box said "infused" / requires, requires keys, infused / physical, physical costs are infused for love / spiritual, spirituals infused / danger, dangers and the infused / phase, phases infused / unusual, unusual suspects and those infused / column, columns cleared, infused ones / gland, glands secular infusions / cleaned, cleaned immaculate infusion points / organ, organ set, infused / blank, blanks who are infused / rest, resting infusions / long, longs and the lacing infused / pink, pinks who seek infusions / request, requested arms for yogurt seas infused / provides, provides milk to the people of bread and the manna infused / master, master your infusions / conform, conform to truths infused / ease, ease into homes infused / kind, kinds who infused us in love / automatic, automobiles infused / spine, spines torn, infused / perfect, perfectly infused / key, keys soar, infused / realizing, realizing your infusions / channeling, channeling your infusions / humans, humans cleared for import, infused / specific, specifics infused / master, mastery infused / understanding, understandings infused / golden, golden glowing infusions / key, keys swell with fervent infusions / typewriter, typewriters and the literal infusions / profoundly, profoundly basic infusions / gap, gaps out, infused / outcome, optimum outcomes allowed through infusions.

CHAPTER ELEVEN

Evolution, evolutions carried for infusions / gift, gifts swelling, infused / most, mostly infused. / neck, necks narrowed? infused / goal, goals soften, infused / moan, moans mostly, infused / bloom, blooms basically, infused / joy, joy soars, infused / function, functions well, infused / practicing, practicing issues influenced for infusions / art, arts soft, infused / wish, wish well, infused / tube, tubes torus extended, infused / truth, truth told, infused / excellent, excellent's infusions / dance, dances infused / philosophy, philosophy affords you an infusion / spoil, spoils

touring an infusions / teaches, teaches only your infusions / done, done and stills in infusions / under, under all, an infusion / truth, truth told, infused / ray, rays reach your infusions / different, different days infused / group, fun and the groups elastic win, infused / master, masters infused / better, betters infusions / focus, focus and the final infusions / spend, spends one infused / sinus, sinus trails infused / trail, trails and the wills infused / still, stilling infusions / schooled, schooled squarely infused / river, rivers infused / drawing, drawn into the drawings infused / script, scripts infused / benefit, benefited your infusions / rare, rarest in infusions / people, people who infuse / trickle, trickles sound, infused / determine, determine your infusions / group, groups and the groupings infused / rake, rakes off, infused / land, lands who infuse / zone, zones torn, infused / prosperity, prosperity pluses your infusions / Chinese, Chinese changes infused / peeks, peeks who arrive infused and assigned / class, classes settle, infused / unique, uniques sinking infusions / ranges, ranges armed in infusion / world, worlds softened infusions / young, young who knew your infusions / climb, climbs coupling infusions / insurance, insurance sent, infused / money, money sold, infused / cup, cups tossed, infused / golf, golf as infused / send, send lifts infusions to bamboo's shootings / cobra, cobra cured infusions / ice, ice lanes infused / funny, given funny ways who infuse / carbon, carbons infusions / game, game days infused.

CHAPTER TWELVE

Think, thinks as infused / keep, keep them infused / focused, focused and infused / certain, certainty infused / belayed, belayed your infusions / protest, protest most, infused / volume, volumes follow, infused / fast, fast ways infused / place, places who infuse / difference, differences infused / quitting, quitting infusions / second, seconds lanes infused / rather, rathers who infuse / judge, judges infused / open, opens and the final infusions / close, closer infused / member, members infused / sent, sent and subjects infused / rock, rocks infusions / fully, fully infused / called, called on integral infusions / parking, parkings infusions / lots, lots infused / love, love, infusions / route, routes to the infusions / awards, awards will be infused / dry, drys and infused / fountain, fountains leak infused / winner, winners soaring through infusions / soccer, soccers rounding infusion / fuse, fuses, infusions / time, times treating infusions / love, love lists are infused / tool, tools for these infusions / foot, foot folds infused / leashed, leashed an infusion / will, wills infusions / sponsored, sponsored infusions / hands, annual hands infused / safety, safety seals infused / beat, nearer infusions / home, homes infused / next, next kneeling infusions / cool, cools seed your infusions / mixed, mixed into infusions / quickly, quickly infused / injuries, injuries mentioned, infusions / shut, shut yours infusions / shaft, shaft on, infusions / reason, reasons who, infusions / able, able stays infusions / look, looks and infusions / moving, moving an infusion / game, game sold, infusions / safety, safety sealed, infusions / ski, ski paths to your infusions / arrived, arrived and infused / pain, pains sources infused / train, trains suggested your infusions / above, above those who are infused / joy, joys and the trusted, infusions / person, persons who are infused / first, first lights infused / free, free trails infused.

CHAPTER THIRTEEN

Limits, limited cures and your infusions / dial, dials softened infusions / races, races operate for all infusions / nuts, nuts to all infusions / running, running into all infusions / express, expressing is your infusion / quality, quality caves five infused / sprouts, sprouts paged infusions / dispute, disputed infusions / home, homes current for all infusions / accent, accents spent infusions / deal, deals sworn into infusions / sign, signs into infusions / stick, sticks into all infusions / hang, hangs off, infusions / drown, drown over all infusions / pickle, pickle soft infusions / smoothly, smoothly natured infusions / dispute, disputed infusions / red, reds who honor infusions / arrived, arrived your infusions / vodka, vodka days infusing you / eat, eatten and infused / somehow, somehow infused / two, two, infused / one, one who will, infusion / zero, zero past, infuse / left, left to the powers infused / people, peoples who infused / vase, vases lacing your infusions / show, showering shows them a funded infusion / degree, degrees dare a filling infusion / back, backs soft in our infusions / next, next the doors gathering infusions / right, rights suggest your infused gates ways / across, across the wells infused / later, laters days infused / passed, passed into portals of infusions / pronoun, pronouns pronounced, infused / reason, reasons cast, infused / render, renders soft infusions / expression, expressions over, infused / depths, depths laid, infuse / women, women who infuse / furthermore, furthermores infused / master, master me, infused / once, once said "infused" / deeper, deeper still, infused / existence, existence spent, infused / two, twos who marry, infused / higher, highers still, infused / plane, planes opened, infused / spot, spots laid into infusion / smiled, smiled and paged through your infusions / little, little stages infused / yesterday, yesterdays surest infusions / beyond, beyond the old, infusions / clear, clears a basic infusion / often, oftens infused / power, powers and the painted infusions / refresh, refresh yours, infusions / body, body basics, infused / eye, eyes opened, infused / tonight, tonight in the basics issued your infused.

LEVEL 93: THE FOCAL-MENTS

CHAPTER ONE

Antelope, antelopes focal in love / glimpsed, glimpsed a focal bliss / hope, hopes sealed, focals / less, less and focal blissed / harmony, harmony spilling, focal / selflessness, selflessness, focalizes / grass, grass is golden, focals / upon, upons duodenum focals / house, houses focal to the flows / two, twos and focal flows / done, done to those who glow and focal read / note, notes into these, focal / promises, promises made are, focal / arose, arose the red, focal / twilight, twilights living, focal / only, only ways to see thee, focal / pain, pains and drains, focal / tell, tells a told, focal / surge, surges and merges, focal / love, love

days, focal / control, couple dues, focals / old, old days, focal / lose, lose old, focal / mind, mind tossed, focal / species, species lost, focal / first, first rays, focal / walked, walked a way, focal / muzzle, muzzles off, focal / covered, covered lost, focal / ego, ego toured, focal / blended, blended sent, focal / body, body basics, focal / evil, evils out, focal / farewell, farewells, focal / unhappy, unhappy without, focals / saved, saved only One, focal / bodily, bodily basically humans, focal / classic, classic worth curing, focal / million, millions told, focal / bewitch, bewitch less, focal / charm, charms sought, focal / tender, tenders tours, focal / outgoing, outgoing insured, focal / doom, dooms over, focal / ruin, ruins past, focal / kill, kills off, focal / dismal, dismal without a focal point / scorn, scorn over, focal / individual, individuals made up, focal / makeup, makeup worn, focal / intelligence, intelligence gifted, focal / refer, refers to yes! gone focally / vial, vials touring these, focals / perform, performs most, focal / opposite, opposites over, focal / run, runs on, focal / really, really dear, focal / gross, gross days go, focal / dirty, dirty, focals / grateful, grateful, focals / demote, demoted, focals / reveal, reveals, focals / necessity, necessity and your focals / token, tokens and durations for these focals.

CHAPTER TWO

Swell, swells arming your, focals / extended, extended, focals / inspire, inspires and entirety for a focal / grow, final growing focals / able, ables stable focals / power, powers during your focals / age, ages rages focals / invoking, invoking a final focal / thankful, thankful polished, focals / polished, polished and focals / granted, granted a focalize / abide, abide basics focals / tree, trees tossed, focals / weird, weird ways and focals / air, airs over, focals / small, smalls days and focals / tank, tanks and tours for the focal / genius, genius insured, focal / gamble, gambles grown, focal / gallery, gallery greeted, focal / ceaseless, ceaseless focals / occur, occurs a daily focal / agree, agree to be a focal / reflect, reflects insures focals / continual, continual focalize / endless, endless focals / oppose, opposed without focals / quarrel, quarrels tossed, focal / touching, touching a focal / depth, depths over, focals / apex, apex insured, focal / about, about a focal / talk, talks into a focal / gossip, gossip grows, focals / helpful, helpful healing focals / combat, combats cured focal / joyous, joyous issues focals / lock, locks off, focals / merry, merry magics and focals / duel, duels over, focal / finish, finished and focal / peak, peaks tossed, focal / combat, combat insured focals / visible, visible formats and focals / absorb, absorbs a doorway, focals / allow, allowing your focals / restless, restless wanders and focals / noble, nobles doors and focals / overlook, overlooks foolish focals / reject, rejected without a focal / fool, fools over, focals / win, wins and winning focals / test, tested a focal / fee, fee past, focal / polite, politest focals / important, important focalized / enjoyment, enjoyment is sent, fathered in focals / comfort, comforts cures and focals / assigned, assigned realigned focals / soothe, soothes your most, focal / blend, blends basics, focals / combine, combine your focals / solace, solace is sent, focals / kindness, kindness cures a focal

CHAPTER THREE

Noteworthy, noteworthy news, focals / pardon, pardon paid, focal / retain, retained a focal / save, save your days and focals / constrain, constrained focal / consult, consulted a focal / enjoyment, enjoyment sent, focal / page, pages written, focals / stranger, stranger days and focals / cable, cables cut, focals / reason, reasons signed into, a focal / upset, upset without, focals / directly, directly into a focal / dip, dips over, final, focal / diagram, diagrams reaching your focals / repeat, repeats soaring focals / blast, blasted your focals / blend, blends a basic focal / blaze, blaze paths, focals / equal, equals gone, focal / judgment, judgements called, focals / clap, claps over, focals / fasten, fastens days and focals / end, ends over, focalized / tag, tags tossed, focals / shadow, shadows gates, focus, focals / organized, organized gates to a focal focus / shown, shown and droaning without, focus, focal / plan, plans passed into your focus, focal / mode, modes temples and focused fundings, focal / pass, passes into your focus, focal / indifferent, indifferents found your focus, focal / sure, surest a focus, focal / stride, strides and rides into your focus, focal / grow, grows a growling focus, focal / faultless, faultless focused, focal / rigging, rigging a regional focus, focal / gear, gears engaged, focus, focal / ladder, ladders leading focus, focal / label, labels listed focus, focal / artificial, artificially fed, focused, focal / catalog, catalogs cured, focus, focal / random, randoms reach a focus, focal / phenomenon, phenomenon and your focus, focal / adjust, adjust relates to focus, focal / sticky, sticky and over your focus, focal / schedule, schedule cures a focus, focal / change, changes on, focus, focal / end, ends and during a focus, focal / vital, vitals blast, focus, focal / sent, sent simple focals to love / alarm, alarms spent, focals / slight, slight leads, focal / baggy, baggy and during yours A, focal / cover, covers and curing the daily, focals / story, story during, focal / blanket, blankets, focals / shrewd, shrewds gone, focals / loud, loud without, focals / specify, specify which, focal / pure, pure taste, focal / mock, mocks and made A, focal / ape, apes and the latest, focals / idiot, idiots erased, focals.

CHAPTER FOUR

Telling, tellings truths told, focals / drift, drifts a way, focal / simple, simples and a truth told, focals / short, shortest, focals / silver, silvers over, focal / shock, shocks past, focal / quiet, quieted, focals / still, stillest, focals / analogy, analogy, focals / stable, stable given a focal last / ahead, ahead written, focals / yield, yield softens, focals / martial, martial arted focals / time, times tossed, focals / apart, apart stood a focal / shout, shout when, focals / thrown, thrown into focal lands / tugging, tugging you, focals / joke, jokes paid, focals / ward, wards off, focals / help, help spent, focals / wrapper, wrappers tossed, focals / purple, purple pages, focals / blasted, lasted to blasted focals / reveal, reveals rest, focals / breath, breath basics, focals / anguish, anguish over, focals / hearth, hearths held, focals / shielding, shieldings off, focals / fellow, fellows staged, focals / slope, slopes angled into, focals / ages, ages rages and a fracas over focals / magic, magically focal / great, great days into focals / price, price raised, vocals found focal strands / dad, dad

due, focals / many, many many focals / explosion, explosions into, focals / face, face these, focals / sleeping, leaping across sleeping, focals / visit, visited, focals / stairs, stairs toured, focals / both, both said focals / rather, rathers, focals / walking, walking wormholes past, focals / roused, roused ratios, focals / dream, dream schemes, focals / dragon, dragon days, focals / happy, happy ways, focals / twice, twice the known, focals / suddenly, suddenly due your, focals / scar, scars into your planted, focals / slip, slips past your, focals / whisper, whispering ways assigned, focals / lain, lain across, focals / down, downs days, focals / sleep, sleepy ways into, focals / burst, burst forth and confess your, focals / daylight, daylights during your, focals / striking, striking seeking, focals / grass, glass grassy with creeks for, focals / witches, witches ditched, focals / short, short stays over, focals / pray, pray fast and quickly lasting, focals.

CHAPTER FIVE

Vehicle, vehicles due your, focals / doubt, doubt shouted, focals / breezily, breezily basic into your, focals / embargo, embargo spent in yours, focals / deep, deep days, focals / little, little stays are focal / polished, polished portions, focals / time, times toured, focals / more, more says, focals / shocked, shocked relations, focals / glad, glad durations, focals / replace, replaced for a final, focals / carpets, carpets toured, focals / fallen, fallen past, focals / eye, eye dried, focals / pink, pinks spelling f-o-c-a-l-s / jumped, jumped sympathy into your focals / arrived, arrived in yes for all focals / emboss, emboss less, find more, focals / people, people who spare only heights for final focals / looking, looking into random religions for, focals / lust, lust is past, focals / slim, slim lasts, focals / top, tops too, focals / avoid, avoid said "focals" / deck, decks found, focals / soaring, soaring over all, focals / zero, zero rays paid, focals / land, landed now, focals / yellow, yellows ways, focals / prevail, prevail again, focals / voice, voices lost, focals / telling, telling her "focals" / her, her days find, focals / now, now them, focals / gleefully, gleefully, focal / giggling, gigglings, focals / mercy, mercy made, focals / tossed, tossed again, focals / air, airs onto a focal wage / standing, standing costs are past, focals / better, betters blessed, focals / stabbing, stabbing goes, focals / access, access worn, focals / felt, felt one, focals / stadium, stadium dues, focals / perform, perform one, focal / path, path touching, focals / aspiration, aspirations cured, focals / allures, allures surest, focals / acquisitioned, acquisitioned combustibles, focals / tones, tones total to your focalness / octave, octaves caught for the fullest, focals / values, values trued, focals / flowering, flowering yells "focals" / fires, fires cost your, focals / set, sets into settled, focals / subtle, subtle cues and your focals laid into love / cues, cues patched, focals / experience, experience sent to your focals / explode, explode into your focals / taught, taught us how to be current, focals / triangle, triangles soft into, focals / extents, extents spent into, focals.

CHAPTER SIX

Each, each who found, focals / cycle, cycles, focals / every, every days, focals / day, day too, focals / multitudes, multitudes who dull, focals / pase, pase stayed, focals / carry, carry on, focals / oracle, oracles clues, focals / ointments, ointments, focals / cylinders, cylinders, focals / inks, inks pinned, focals / orations, orations elevated, focals / inscription, inscriptions reaching into your, focals / interest, interest run, focals / organism, organisms painted, focals / dive, dive into a, focals / dome, domes punished without, focals / pulling, pulling into lined, focals / upside, upsides risen, focals / staging, staging raging, focals / sharply, sharply spelling yours, focals / would, would should, focals / across, across rows for, focals / anxiously, anxiously lends your, focals / alloy, alloy dartings into, focals / voice, voices left, focals / blunder, blunders dearest, focals / larger, larger pages truth told, focals / several, several stayed, focals / louder, louder spilling, focals / panicked, panicked about your, focals / beam, beams softly, focals / simply, simply spent, focals / hooted, hooted spotted, focals / roared, roared above, focals / too, too told, focals / ceasing, ceasing off, focals / preparing, preparing your, focals / desk, desks daring to see your finished, focals / pleasant, pleasant places, focals / whole, whole stays, focals / class, class days, focals / facing, facing your, focals / distance, distances dared, a, focals / magic, magically made your focals strays / victims, victims due your focals / toppled, toppled simply, focals / shielding, shielding signed, focals / curse, curse a simple, focals / lesson, lessons dared, focals / range, ranges arranging your focals / son, sons done, focals / speeding, speeding costs only a focal / caught, caught cures cut, focals / clears, clears days, focals / bells, bells tonight, focals / father, father fields, focals / else, elses dared, focals / faint, faints painted, focals / basic, basically yours, focals / now, now days and focals / hard, hard rays for focals / blank, blanks during your winning focals / return, returns during a focal.

CHAPTER SEVEN
Power, powers paring and amazing dues for a focal relay / spoke, spoken into, focals / preparing, preparing costs, focals / lie, lies lost, focals / shielding, shielding dealings, focals / happened, happened over, focals / over, over all, focals / realize, realize your, focals / swept, swept up, focals / several, several who ruled, focals / green, greens softened, focals / light, lights off, focals / cottage, cottages coded, focals / opted, opted out, focals / talking, as talking became, focals / quills, quills curled, focals / rush, rush into, focals / fellow, fellows followed, focals / three, three who knew, focals / magic, magic swelling, focals / vice, vice railed, focals / over, over all, focals / exactly, exactly dulled, focals / calmly, calmly during, focals / nine, nine who knew a, focal / feel, feels when focalized / instead, instead said "focals" / wife, wife well, focals / rush, rush past, focals / pleasant, pleasantly focal / born, born throughout focals / enough, enough stood, focals / imperious, imperious bouts, focals / class, class told, focals / curses, curses past, focals / spent, spent in, focals / teach, teach ones, focals / jumped, jumped aboard, focals / instead, instead deals, focals / parents, parents called, focals / eye, eye softened, focals / look, look into your focalness / calmly, calmly, focal / soaring, soaring aboard a focal / extend, extend your wings into your focal lanes / flickered, flickered sincerely, focals / dove, dove dues, focals / blue, blue basics, focals / living, living apart, focals / year, years spent, focals / food, foods bought, focals / decide, decide when, focals / off, off for, focals / impartial, impartial gazing, focals / far, far days, focals / allowed, allowed one, focal / twinkled, twinkled capably, focals / guest, guests rally, focals / student, student spurts, focals / wart, warts off, focals / greater, greater gazes, focals / part, parts poled, focals / wasted, wasted winning, focals / tasks, tasks placed, focals.

CHAPTER EIGHT
Stop, stops shopping, focals / champions, champions who, focals / door, doors softened, focals / table, tables lapsed, focals / prize, prizes caught, focals / extend, extended winning, focals / people, peoples who, focals / will, wills wearing, focals / money, moneys mutual, focals / cup, cups poured, focals / whole, whole finals, focals / beg, begs most, focals / school, schools hosted, focals / 17, 17 ways, focals / turned, turned into, focals / couple, couples who, focals / hall, halls residences, focals / face, faces convinced, focals / page, pages optional to a focal rant / decide, decide when and go, focals / reckon, reckoning a flashing, focals / October, October pursuits for your, focals / under, under spelling a focal / spoken, spoken places for all, focals / glory, glory days back, focals / 1000, 1000 who knew, focal / extend, extended focalizes / part, parts replaced, focals / foreign, foreigns reaped, focals / light, light leveraged, focals / impose, impose pured, focals / going, going explained, focals / spoke, spoke an announcement for all, focals / sudden, sudden days, focals / draw, draw dedicated ones to your, focals / violently, violently, focals / larger, larger meetings, focals / pointed, pointed creations at your focals / nervously, nervously neared, focals / yes, yes will wear well, focals / distinct, distinctive during, focals / name, names nestle, focals / desk, desks lapse, focals / began, began again, focals / spider, spider spells, focals / rocking, rocking over, focals / reach, reach a near, focals / gaze, gaze past, focals / needs, made the coupons read, focals / roar, roars over, focals / spot, spot yours, focals / suppose, suppose we lose your focal spaced doors / shook, shock is past, focals / felt, felt upon landed, focals / upon, upon us all, focals / desk, desk topped, focals / crucibles, crucibles tossed, focals / distinct, distinct reaps, focals / move, move made, focals / legs, legs stand, focals / foreboding, foreboding goes, focals / started, started in, focals / jar, jar off, focals / evade, evaded, focally.

CHAPTER NINE
Portion, portions oft to a focalness / scuttled, scuttled repeals for our, focals / lopsided, lopsided? focals / easy, easy dealing, focals / raised, raised pools into, focals / body, body basics, focals / pointed, pointed into temples, focals / down, downs daily, focals / shrill, shrills fleshing, focals / jerk, jerks still, focals / violent, violent fulfilling, focals / remove, removes most, focals / over, overs said focals / silence, silences meant for all focals / feet, feet topped, focals / far, far weathered, focals / shellfish, shellfish deep in a first, focals / learn, learns to be a focal / silence, silences

focals / fell, fell dealt your, focals / pupils, pupils and the tiger within a, focal / pointing, pointing poised in a focal place / differently, differently dated, focals / door, doors spilling, focals / revealed, revealed ranges, focals / officially, potent facial focals / open, opened doors, focals / plates, plates shifted, focals / both, both wear ringing, focals / gentleman, gentleman said focals / staff, staff tours, focals / added, added a molecule to your, focals / drink, drinks speaking, focals / deep, deepening, focals / impressed, impressed rehearsals of, focals / bless, bless basics, focals / barely, barely squaring, focals / bloodred, bloodred's, focals / staff, staffs toured, focals / table, tables shift, focals / impressed, impressed in raspberry, focals / pulling, pulling into your, focals / off, off the seats, focals / both, both who knew, focals / sides, sides off, focals / colored, edges colored, focals / black, blacks booths, focals / summer, summer days, focals / happen, happening, focals / clearly, clearly seen, focals / robes, robes sent for, focals / welcoming, welcoming comes, focals / nine, nines who, focals / gust, gust past, focals / staring, string over, focals / couple, couples who, focals / shorted, shorted without, focals / dishes, dishes piled, focals / food, food scraped, focals / great, kitchens great, focals / word, words said, focals / around, around, hear. focals / resume, resume spent, focals / extra, extra tallies, focals.

CHAPTER TEN

Ceiling, ceiling established, focals / pleasure, pleasure says, focals / wearing, wearing out, focals / large, largely, focal / definitely, definitely due a focal arise / laugh, laugh most now, focals / pulled, pulled into your, focals / between, between us all, focals / older, older given, focals / ever, ever said focals / entrance, entrances made, focals / look, looks blissed / fears, fears blessed with forgiven releases, focals / right, rights made, focals / light, light lists, focals / sea, seas, focals / 20, 20 who, focals / five, five nest, focals / earlier, earlier pieces, focals / diagonal, diagonal glues, focals / work, works cubes, focals / slip, slip into your, focals / word, words who say, focals / intense, intense dues, focals / dislike, dislikes wearing, focals / might, might skills, focused / drained, drained into nights for those skilled into, focals / eye, eyes who live for all, focals / saw, saw successive, focals / traced, traced true, focals / man, man enough, focals / quivering, quivering within, focals / magical, magically due a, focals / lee, lee words, focals / whisper, whispering, focals / back, backs first, focals / first, first ways, focals / entrance, entrance days, focals / hall, halls who, focals / now, now them, focals / down, down during days for all, focals / boy, boys who, focals / corner, corners nearing, focals / saw, saw their, focals / forehead, foreheads, focals / toast, toast your, focals / normally, normally nubiel, focals / me, me the one, focals / glaring, glaring pasts, focals / ten, ten who said, focals / night, might said, focals / sight, sights, focals / push, push yours, focals / wide, wide next, focals / jaws, jaws closed, focals / roar, roars up, focals / snake, snake outs, focals / neck, necks popped, focals / shot, shots called, focals / tall, tall enoughs, focals / fly, fly over, focals / soared, soared into, focals / time, times two, focals / jet, jets, focals

CHAPTER ELEVEN

Watching, watching turns into a final federal focal / swat, swats watts and focal nets / enough, enough who can funnel fuses focally / deep, deepens into a focal name / open, opens pouring focals high days / high, high ranges focals / thrashed, thrashed errors and family focals / retire, retired framing focals / extent, extents spent in your focals / butter, butter bases focals / crowd, crowds days focal / safely, safely said "focals" / kicked, kicked into fatherly focals / air, airs vocalized for those, focals / deep, deepens, focals / dive, dive past, focals / remain, remains in, focals / saw, saw these, focals / student, students, focals / bank, banks into your focals / recognize, recognized, focals / profile, profiles posed, focals / shrewd, shrewds electric, focals / smile, smiles into a, focals / lowered, lowered intrigues and your focals / ring, rings around, focals / pool, pools spilling, focals / suddenly, suddenly rounded, focals / mind, minds toast without focals / arm, arms turning, focally / yelled, yelled about focally / top, tops onto a tiering focal / curved, copes in curved focals / hide, hide out, focals / white, white stays focals / eyebrows, eyebrows plucked, focals / ear, ear soft focals / student, student gaze, focals / castle, castle cures focal / silver, silver ways focal / hair, hair days focals / extended, extended raises focal / fellow, fellows who, focal / profile, profile sent, focals / curved, curved racing focals / boy, boy shouts! coded focals / head, head out, focal / gave, gave the rest, focals / recognize, recognize why? focals / punch, punch out, focal / along, along the leys, focals / smile, smiles lost? focals / riverbed, riverbedded focals / misty, misty ways focalized / saved, saved the rested, focal / lake, lakes lost? focals / glimpse, glimpse goes, gaining focals / arm, arms lost? focals / show, show the showering focal / hiss, hiss less, gather focals / entirely, entirely sold on focals gained / hide, hide less, gather your focals / pouring, pouring into perfect focals gatherings / castle, castle toasted, focally.

CHAPTER TWELVE

Ship, ships rocking focals / dim, dim states off, focals / curved, curved swerved focals / rise, rise the rising focal / cleaner, cleaner and dearer focals / caught, caught a cure, focal / slight, slights off, focals / hide, hides tossed, focals / teeth, teeth sold, focals / quiet, quiets focals / famous, famous follows, focals / spy, spy spent, focals / laughter, laughter hugs a focal / miss, miss a node? focals / enjoy, enjoy the hopeful focal / spoken, spoken lasts, focals / face, faces dated, focal eyes / before, before the bays and focals / correct, corrected a focal / ever, ever living focals / lie, lies and dies without a focal / impatiently, impatiently due your focal / talk, talk into your focal / call, call the doors "focals" / mom, mom's mate, focal / shine, shines on a focal / task, tasks set, focalize / ignore, ignores a doorway other than focals / hope, hope states "focalize" / left, left to the sizes posted, focals / stupid, stupids over, focalize / wait, waits on focals / third, thirds words focals / double, doubles dues, focals / habit, habits sold, focals / slow, slows and reaps focals / Saturday, Saturdays days are sold to the focals / library, library dues, focals / problem, problems past, focals / half, halfs tossed, a focals / start, starts and darts into your focals / rat, rats sold, focals / shape, shapes told, focals / chipmunk, chipmunks met, focals / extremely, extremely well, focals / yelling, yelling swelling focals / hours, hours doors and focals / talk, talks too, focals / correct, corrected gifts for focals / gift, gifts lifts and focals / famous, famous for the funded focals / up, up the next, focal / task, tasks and a focal / daily, daily days focals / laughter, laughter is led into your focals / face, faces past? focal eyes / start, start the new, focals / stubbornly, stubbornly over A focal / admitted, admitted a focal find / 5, 5 who know their focals / sped, sped into your focals / apart, aparted focalized / roar, roars softened focals / posing, posing ends, elegance for a focal.

CHAPTER THIRTEEN

ID, ID sold, focals / love, love the best, focal / woman, woman told, focal / circle, circles last, focals / time, time told, "focal" / gold, gold stays focals / another, anothers and mothers and focals / size, sizes focaled / wide, wides risen focals / dodged, dodged past your focal lines / rose, roses focals / head, heads and focalized / eggs, eggs advanced, focals / stance, stances over, past focals / trick, tricks past, focals / fly, fly lied, focals / insure, insure your space focals / zoomed, zoomed and finals focals / screaming, screaming focals / dog, dogs quieted focal / trance, trances and the landed focals / match, matching focals / wood, woods and the final focals / still, stills and tossed focals / reach, reaching cost, focals / snake, snakes lost, focal / near, nears days focals / occurred, occurred concepts and focals / now, nows lost, focal / charmer, charmers tossed, focals / insure, insured, focals / vertical, verticals swelling, focals / pang, pang left, focal / air, airs tossed, focals / careful, careful in focalize / feet, feet off, focal / deep, deepens focals / twisted, twisted focally / wings, wings west, focal / opened, opened a day's focals / thrashed, thrashed into similar focals / high, high trust, focals / do, do a focal / roar, roars over, focals / shot, shot into a focal / exasperation, exasperation pales, focal / extent, extents spent, focal / posing, posing lasts focally / ripping, ripping past focals / pupil, pupils poised, focal / yellow, yellow west, focals / high, high tests focal / glad, glads days are focal / passed, passed into cured, focals / winter, winters west, focals / curled, curled into a focal / table, tables tossed, focals / why, get one, focals / checked, checked out, focals / four, fours who disabled only the televised focals / post, posted focals / glad, glads trek into posted focals / pear, pears tossed, apart, bi-focal / apart, apart from the start, focal.

LEVEL 94: THE VOCAL-MENTS

CHAPTER ONE

Help, help the folks who aid themselves through vocal ends / put, put the seals and the veils forth for all vocal ends / plate, plates touch your vocals / right, in rights sealed, vocally / black, black longest, vocals / ship, ships past your vocals / really, really dealt your final vocals / dragon, dragons ranges, vocalized / stopped, stopped released, vocalized / ox, ox stools vocalized / roast, roasted, hosted, vocals / cream, creams costs, vocalized / squeak, squeaks past your vocals / hatch, hatching a vocal / helpful, helpful fillings vocals / giggles, giggles shingled and past your vocals / grinned, finally grinned your vocals / custard, custards grated, vocals / house, house spills, vocals / fruit, fruit rites, vocals / imitated, imitated your oldest vocal / plate, plates piled for vocal eyes / bit, bits sold, vocals / pointed, pointed into your vocal lies / wind, winds swept your jib to the point, vocals / black, Bermuda blends and the black points sold to vocals / sail, sails past, vocals / ship, watches shipped to vocals / sleet, sleet swept for vocals / model, models vocally sold / right, rights to vocals sold / high, high tests vocalized / rope, ropes oft, vocals / inside, insides days are vocal / class, class cooled, vocals / kit, kits off, vocally / kill, kills old, vocals / reporter, reporter for the folds, vocals / loop, loops off, vocals / shot, shots past, vocals / over, in an overs, vocals / furry, furry days, vocals / hold, hold on, vocals / sweet, sweet neat, vocals / horses, horses days, vocals / chilly, chilly willed, vocals / box, box born, vocals / patch, patches off, vocals / bad, bad days? vocals / hand, handy, vocals / tagging, tagging off, vocals / off, off the cuffs, vocals / daydays sold, vocals / fled, fled said "vocals" / lead, lead into your vocal eyes / lined, lined in a vocal plane / pumpkin, pumpkin days vocals / end, ends in a vocal eye / master, mastery vocalized / now, now said "a vocal" / my, my ways are vocal / shame, shame past, ovations and vocals / tear, tears go, vocals / mind, minds mastered, vocally.

CHAPTER TWO

Thank, thank you, vocals / leaking, leaking off, vocals / took, took one, vocal / her, her days are vocals / comet, comets cured, vocals / stones, stones cast? vocals / story, story told, vocals / event, events fueled, vocals / similar, similar cells, vocals / death, death duals, vocals / devasted, devastated rules, vocals / earth, earth led, vocals / orbits, orbits about, vocals / hour, hourly views and your, vocals / small, smallest, vocals / cluster, clusters cured, a vocal / close, closest, vocals / low, lower, vocals / sky, sky specials, vocals / recall, recalling yours, vocals / path, pathways, vocals / ten, tens who fed, your vocals / regions, regions who, vocals / 50, 50 when, vocals / me, me and your, vocals / learn, learned a friend's, vocals / paper, papering, vocals / stream, streams tossed, vocals / shower, showering yours, vocals / delta, delta dues, vocals / rotate, rotate doors who are freed for your, vocals / rain, rains states, vocals / nodal, nodals, vocals / year, yearly, vocals / toughest, toughest, vocals / friction, frictions rated, vocals / kilometer, kilometers past, vocals / raining, rainings, vocals / smile, miles smiling, vocals / plentiful, plentiful particles, vocals / circle, circles due, vocals / planets, planets la luna, vocals / return, returns returning, vocals / wide, wide sides, vocals / gauged, gauged and yours, vocals / peak, peaks and speaks for, vocals / activity, activity during your, vocals / comet, comet into, vocals / epoch, epoch speaking, vocals / void, voids voided, vocals / axis, axis pressed, vocals / call, calls when, vocals / solar, solar ceilings, vocals / shift, shifted, vocals / fact, facts formed, vocals / counting, counting passions, vocals / large, largely your, vocals / shower, showering into, vocals /

soup, soups scopes, vocals / baby, baby yellowed, vocals / 600, 600 who, vocals / comentary, comentary, vocals / probe, probes last, vocals / last, lasted and founded, vocals.

CHAPTER THREE

Tropical, tropical creatures, vocals / sun, sun's running, vocals / earth, earth rests, vocals / weeks, weeks off, vocals / night, nights soft in, vocals / weaker, weaker sills, vocals / occupied, occupied relations, vocals / day, days oft, vocals / point, points made, vocals / west, west winds, vocals / hour, hours blessed, vocals / calendar, calendar causes, vocals / active, active reaps, vocals / applied, applied soon in, vocals / shower, shower now, vocals / stream, streams crossing your, vocals / boom, booms into, vocals / comet, comets cured, vocals / destroy, destroy rested, vocals / life, life levels, vocals / aspire, aspire now, vocals / story, story told, vocals / occur, occurs in, vocals / good, goods sold, vocals / energy, energy made, vocals / stresses, stresses off, vocals / idea, ideas timbre, vocals / sample, pitched samples, vocals / range, range tested, vocals / expect, expect won, vocals / kilometer, kilometers run, vocals / 10, 10 days, vocals / virtually, virtually fellowed, vocals / indeed, indeeds, vocals / say, says, vocals / rock, rocks on, vocals / broken, broken flowers, vocals / bodies, bodies blessed, vocals / reach, reach and sexy, vocals / altitudes, altitudes shouting for a fallen, vocals / projectile, projectiles purest, vocals / basis, basis borne, vocals / ignorant, ignorant cubits, vocals / heights, heights hurled, vocals / peak, peaks topple, vocals / arrival, arrival hosts, vocals / direction, directions felt, vocals / pointed, pointed jointed, vocals / expect, expects rest, vocals / tense, tense off, vocals / extremely, extremely due, vocals / good, goods cords, vocals / chapter, chapters past, vocals / discovery, discovery drives you to the final, vocals / energies, energies said, "vocals" / size, sizes ran, vocals / deport, deported forms, vocals / plane, planes shift, vocals / number, numbers nudged, vocals / two, twos who, vocals / case, cases placed, vocals / year, yearly, vocals / major, majored in, vocals / impact, impacting, vocals.

CHAPTER FOUR

North, north to the vocals / fence, fence taught to build vocally / auto, automatic vocals / belts, belts built can cure vocals / evidence, evidence made, vocals / asteroids, asteroids hit here, vocalize / result, resultant splash, vocals / safe, safe to say, vocals / comet, comets cured, vocals / evidence, evidence for tails and vocals / source, source said "vocals" / disk, disk slips into vocals / study, study done, vocals / slipped, slipped out, vocals / safe, safe in your vocals / bodies, bodies blast, vocals / limit, limits pushed, vocals / now, now them, vocals / to, to us all an vocal / beyond, beyond the basics, vocals / general, general expressions and vocals / lifetime, lifetime crossings come to the vocal ones / crossing, crossing made, vocals / age, age left, vocally / arrived, arrived late, vocals / easier, easier now, vocals / now, now then vocals / 1%, 1% who knew their vocals / slipped, slipped past? vocals who last / through, through us all, vocals / Mars, Mars dipped, vocals / lap, lap set, vocals / sun, sun days, vocals / cohesive, cohesive ways to vocalize / slowly, slowly due your vocals / neptune, neptune mooned vocals / unstable, unstable gone, vocals

/ results, results spill, vocals / sills, sills off, vocals / near, near buy, vocals / epochs, epochs peel, vocals / solutions, solutions made, vocals / smaller, smaller gears and basic vocals / perhaps, perhaps the healed, vocalized / solar, solar passes and the flares of vocals / possibility, possibility looming, vocals / clouds, clouds on, vocals / wichaasa, wichaasa shores, vocals / wakon, wakon vocals / holy, holy manned, vocals / man, mans placed vocals / medicine, medicine muses by vocal eyes / reflects, reflects your pace, vocals / vision, visions last, vocals / nine, nine days, vocals / ceremony, ceremony sealed, vocals / creations, creations blast, vocals / black, black elks tout vocals / elk, elk stays vocalized / identity, identity due, vocals / forms, forms made lightly vocal / spoken, spoken implores toned vocally / delivery, delivery made, vocals / pipes, pipes last, vocals.

CHAPTER FIVE

Speaking, speaking in two, vocals / body, body basically pipes in these vocals / bliss, bliss nodes exist vocally / bless, bless this house, vocals / transcend, transcend the place, vocals / nourish, nourish your spirits, vocals / centers, centers made, vocally / ID, ID reads, 'the vocals' / rights, rights are red, vocally / spinal, spinal spaces for the vocals / columns, columns cured, vocally / pinched, pinched a place, vocals / winds, winds softened, vocally / smoking, smoking lightens your vocals / earth, earth reds and blue vocally / relatives, relatives find your vocals / instance, instance made vocal / distant, distant days vocals / first, first lights and vocals / impact, impact made, light vocals / think, think a head, vocals / eccentric, eccentric lives, vocally / chapters, chapters written and the vocals told, love / implied, implied suggestively, vocals / evolution, evolutions proud vocals / pluto, pluto gated within, vocals / requirement, requirements due, vocals / block, blocks out, vocals in / specifically, specifically registers vocals / due, due days for these vocals / damocles, damocles written, "vocals" / circular, circular passes through vocals / crossing, crossing made, vocally / paradigm, paradigms bursting vocally / us, us who knew thee, vocals / histories, histories past, vocals / happy, happy days fuel your vocals / breath, breath is basic to your vocalized / exactly, exactly well, vocals / actions, actions last, vocals / axis, axis poles, vocally / slowly, slowly sured vocals / visualized, visualized risings vocally / now, now then, vocals / incorrect, incorrect guesses for the vocals / decides, decides on you, your cardinal friend, the vocal / belts, belts off, vocals in / eccentric, eccentrically vocal again / times, times to tool vocally / heat, heat is on, vocals / possible, possible poses for the vocals / print, print these truths vocally / nodal, nodal dues paid, vocals / complex, complex cures and these vocals / waterfalls, waterfalls filling your vocal lines / songs, songs who sealed the vocal gifts / targets, targets off, the vocals / impacted, impacted, reacted, vocally / dozens, dozens who zeal for vocals / young, young who knew these vocals / more, more directives, vocals / many, many merry, vocals / all, all who deal in vocals / N, N to the degreed vocals.

CHAPTER SIX

Notes, notes who made you vocal / red, red rays vocals / yellow, yellow yeses vocalized / sky, sky dues laid to the vocals / greens,

greens softened, vocally / freaks, freaks gone, vocals / needs, needs met, vocalize / to, to them all, these vocals / know, know thee well, vocals / you, you the basic, vocals / need, need to sell, vocals / third, third thoughts vocalized / seek, seek less, vocals / trees, trees told "these vocals sell" / often, often allow your vocals / yellows, yellows today and throughout your vocals / low, low levels out, vocals / earth, earth fills, vocally / tubs, tubs tossed, vocals / tubes, tubes softened, vocally / cars, cars lava fueled, vocally / vesicle, vesicle rules these vocals / burials, burials found are given steering vocals / ssss, sssss is the word for vocal snakes / spirals, spirals cymbals and the drumming vocals / k, k is the cured, vocal / arrows, arrows pointing, vocalize / black, black is out, vocals / oh, oh say, vocals / century, century dues, vocals / banks, banks off, vocals / comprised, comprised and the complicated vocal / speaks, speaks soothing vocals / final, final gazes, vocally / friends, friends found through these vocals / stages, stages over, finally, vocals freed / points, points made, these are your final vocals / sleeps, sleeps oft in vocals / less, less placed without a vocal / play, play often, vocals / more, more softened vocals / stations, stations locking, vocals / locked, locked into new vocals / stonehenge, stonehenge roaring, Uriel, vocals / views, views who dear, yours, vocals / tapes, tapes rent a vocal hint / times, times told, vocals / plan, plans made, vocal shades / controller, controllers gone, vocals / stink, stink out, vocals / old, old shouts "vocals" / on, on new, vocals / way, way to see these vocal seas / hot, hot days and true vocals / springs, springs bought, vocally / north, north sought? find new, vocals / featured, featured houses share your vocals / stages, stages caught, vocally / stone, stone days are through, vocally / store, store the near vocals / hinges, hinges soft, vocally / copyrights, copyrights sent, vocals / first, first wins, vocals / defined, defined again, vocally.

CHAPTER SEVEN

Outermost, outermost fills, vocals / country, country days to vocals / dug, dug up a vocal / holes, holes placed vocally / development, development bought, vocals / earthworks, earthworks laid, vocals / 1978, 1978 junior to these vocals / appearing, appearing dearing vocals / ships, ships past, ovoid vocals / planes, planes to these rhomboid explains, / remnants, remnants rhomboidal, vocals / defined, defined a rhymings, vocals / interiors, interiors paid to these, vocals / supply, supply made direct, vocals / remains, remains a given, vocals / beltways, beltways built into these vocals / slaves, slaves past, vocals / gas, gas gone, vocals / eyed, eyed a new, vocal / tiem, tiem built daily, vocals / required, required gaily, vocals / exactly, exactly whom? vocals / physical, physical fitness, vocals / quite, quite the whom, vocals / problems, problems off, vocals / major, major ways, vocals / circuits, circuits cut, vocals / ellipse, ellipse built, vocals / 28%, 28% who believe in death, vocals / delineate, delineate those who remember from these, vocals / record, recorded a rate, vocals / time, time to tell, vocals / second, second rays, vocals / signatures, signatures made, vocals / prior, prior gifts, vocals / gradually, gradually lifts, vocals / heels, heels soft, vocals / depths, depths plunged, vocals / solar, solar flares, vocals / expects, expects the most, vocals / two, two who

knew, vocals / important, important gates, vocals / clearly, clearly cured, vocals / later, later days within, vocals / impacts, impacts made, vocals / bars, bars topped, vocals / tops, tops off, vocals / cloudy, cloudy without your, vocals / extinctions, extinctions past, vocals / times, times told, vocals / story, story holds, vocals / water, water ways, vocals / air, air pays, vocals / important, important stages, vocals / passengers, passengers in, vocals / comets, comets sought, vocals / heels, heels healed, achilles goods, vocals / meteors, meteors mixed, vocally / clearly, clearly cured, vocals / assets, assets built, vocals / grow, grow now, vocals / dearly, dearly due your, vocals / sent, sent one, vocals / signage, signage given, vocals.

CHAPTER EIGHT

Elements, elements polished, vocals / depths, depths told, vocals / prior, prior paid, vocals / works, works loft, vocals / goods, goods sought, vocals / knots, knots told, vocals / completed, completed course, vocals / records, records worths, vocals / alvares, alvares stood, vocals / apparent, apparent paces, vocals / dues, dues told, vocals / westerns, westerns won, vocals / enveloped, enveloped without, vocals / results, results given, vocals / globals, globals warmed, vocals / returning, returning dues, vocals / enduring, enduring oft, vocals / atmospheres, atmospheres, vocalized / expected, expected your, vocals / works, works told, vocals / papers, papers spent, vocals / identified, identified well, vocals / cycles, cycles secured, vocals / safes, safes left, vocals / planets, planets paces, vocals / animals, animals cured, vocals / fuzzy, fuzzy follows, vocals / millions, millions admitted, vocals / common, common cured, vocals, vocals / diaspora, disperse the diaspora now, vocals / persons, persons who sold, vocals / letters, letters told, vocals / ledgers, ledgers bought, vocals / additives, additives sought, vocals / preserves, preserves made, vocals / preserved, preserved glades, vocals / prostituted, prostituted caught, vocals / exercised, exercised a risen, vocal / interstates, interstates rates, vocals / inviolate, inviolate matters, vocals / violet, violet bays, vocals / violations, violations caused, vocals / vox, vox pays, vocals / doctors, doctors told, vocals / details, details sold, vocals / inspired, inspired paces, vocals / legible, legible laces, vocals / loots, loots without, vocals / mixes, mixes lots, vocals / admired, admired most, vocals / shulls, shulls deals, vocals / milled, milled more, vocals / best, best ways, vocals / boosts, boosts hosts, vocals / lent, lent without, vocals / letters, letters paid, vocals / lies, lies past, vocals / loves, loves last, vocals / poems, poems told, vocals / doors, doors opened, vocals / pita, pita fed, vocals / filing, filing sorts, vocals / fools, fools off, vocals / flown, flown into, volcanic vocals.

CHAPTER NINE

Floods, floods over, vocals / kahunas, kahunas consulted, vocals / campus, campus boarded basics for these your, vocals / spills, spills over, vocals / concerts, concerts cured, vocals / caves, caves bought, vocals / sully, sully past, vocals / sponges, sponges off, vocals / copy, copy sold, vocals / lemurian, lemurian sorts, vocals / sports, sports sports, vocals / sunken, sunken rays, vocals / counted,

counted into a vocal / lasts, lasts lasts, vocals / spills, spills stood, vocals / storage, storage maxed, vocals / kahuna, kahuna released, vocals / variations, variations still, vocals / places, places sold, vocals / partners, partners told, vocals / marries, marries one, vocal / themes, themes thanked, vocals / passions, passions surge, vocals / changedchanged life, vocals / mystical, mystical approaches, vocals / approaching, approaching erotic, vocals / mount, mount the One, vocals / avenues, avenues sold, vocals / values, values paid, vocals / perfections, perfections met, vocals / parsons, parsons cored, vocals / opened, opened bets, vocals / stoned, stoned without, vocals / entire, entire shouts, vocals / nations, nations chosen, vocals / chosen, chosen winds, vocals / patterns, patterns portions, vocals / emerged, marry the emerged victor, vocals / voiced, voiced reply, vocals / estuary, estuary sold, vocals / fires, fires fought, vocals / districts, districts sought through, vocals / stroked, stroked about your, vocals / scannig, scanning planning, vocals / approached, approached again, vocals / purely, purely simple, vocals / hearted, hearted laughters, vocals / strummings, strummings cast, vocals / stroked, stroked the most, vocals / attractive, attractive about it, vocals / attended, attended surfs, vocals / surfed, surfed a lot, vocals / mountains, mountains bought, vocals / stones, stones out, vocals / stoning, stoning less, vocals / spurts, spurts past, vocals / written, written coded, vocals / codes, codes sift, vocals / cues, cues made, vocals / made, made the one, vocals / yours, yours the paid, vocals / established, established fields through our, vocals / links, links established, vocally / within, within us all, wells to these vocals.

CHAPTER TEN
Suggestions, suggestions made, recieved, vocals / kings, kings lead, vocals / hearts, hearts bled? Fixed, vocals / passions, passions placed, vocals / spin, spin in, vocals / written, written out, vocals / wins, wins one, vocals / churnings, churnings passed, vocals / files, files sought, vocals / fellows, fellows bought, vocals / met, met One winning, vocal / movements, movements lead, vocals / charges, charges sold, vocals / electric, electric woos, vocals / warrants, warrants made, vocals / hearts, hearts glades, vocals / friends, friends who win, vocally / balance, balance is sought, vocals / vast, vast days, vocals / inquiry, inquiry made, vocals / returns, returns one, vocal / spoke, spoke thus, vocals / powerfully, powerfully felt, vocals / reels, reels rest, vocals / arcs, arcs in, vocals / credible, credible surges, vocals / purging, purging comes, vocals / once, once and these alls, vocals / burns, burns out, vocals / victories, victories made yours, vocals / aston, aston sold, vocals / shored, shored durations, vocals / cracks, cracks in caves, vocals / skulls, skulls tossed, vocals / mayans, mayans sourced, vocals / guatemalan, guatemalan forgives, vocals / phoenix, phoenix comes, vocals / flies, flies in, vocals / gifted, gifted ones, vocals / lines, lines led, vocals / along, along sourced, vocals / credible, credible causes, vocals / cures, cures stood, vocals / paths, paths emerged, vocals / emerging, emerging now, vocals / mergers, mergers made, vocals / surfed, surfed in caves, vocals / helenic, helenic splendors, vocals / hopes, hopes sold, vocals / stirring, stirring costs, vocals / maps, maps found,

vocals / spiraled, spiraled in, vocals / windows, windows sold, vocals / eloped, eloped now, vocals / entirely, entirely sured, vocals / conspired, conspired yes, vocals / calm, calm replaces, vocals / heightened, heightened calming, vocals / halloween, halloween last, vocals / bricks, bricks tossed, vocals / bryson, bryson cast, vocals / befriended, befriended others, vocals / friendly, friendly fades, vocals / flights, flights into, vocals.

CHAPTER ELEVEN
Transfers, transfers sought, vocals / transforms, transforms lots, vocals / transcends, transcends need, vocals / trees, trees grown, vocals / cupids, cupids sought, vocals / swarming, swarming mentioned, vocals / memorized, memorized cures, vocals / spires, spires built, vocals / succumbs, succumbs less, vocals / soothing, soothing rays, vocals / muses, muses live, vocals / nationwide, nationwides, vocals / to, to us all a, vocal / all, all those who, vocals / love, about these, vocals we love / goes, goes a singer, vocals / light, light led, vocals / knows, knows who, vocals / sight, sight given, vocals / GOD, GOD gazed, vocals / in, in you, vocals / you, you are these, vocals / appearing, appearing often, vocals / lifted, lifted earth to her pleasing vocals / spurs, spurs out, vocals / apollo, apollos in, vocals / nodes, nodes near, vocals / needs, needs friendly, vocals / investigated, investigated only, vocals / orbits, orbits about, vocals / jovially, jovilly caught, vocals / astronomics, astronomics read, vocals / acidify, acidify without, vocals / tsunamis, tsunamis past, vocals / ablates, ablates lately, vocals / asteroids, asteroids ridden, vocals / belts, belts off, vocals / prosper, prosper the mother, vocals / intrigues, intrigues rise, vocals / ashen, ashen gone, vocals / asteroids, asteroids leap, vocals / helion, helion found, vocals / soured, soured towns, vocals / spawned, spawned a new, vocal / meteoroids, meteoroids past your O, vocals / meteors, meteors last for nearly, vocals / missiles, missiles off, vocals / apellate, apellate courts, vocals / programs, programs sold, vocals / arching, arching in, vocals / distillates, distillates doused, vocals / likenesses, likenesses purged, vocals / miracles, miracles most, vocals / mysteries, mysteries healed, vocals / worlds, worlds collide, vocals / likelihoods, likelihoods kept, vocals / largest, trust largest targets, vocals / likeness, likeliness comes, vocals / dangers, dangers out, vocals / models, models caught, vocals / largely, largely due, vocals / likelihood, likelihoods lift, vocals / zones, zones sold, vocals / discovered, discovered the Host, vocals.

CHAPTER TWELVE
Dues, dues out, vocals / types, types told, vocals / anomaly, anomaly respected, vocals / collisions, collisions coursed, vocals / calamities, calamities out, vocals / origins, origins caught, vocals / eventual, eventual voices, vocals / events, events paid, vocals / rates, rates ripened, vocally / pyramids, pyramids purged, vocals / plunged, plunged into, vocals / discovery, discovery sold, vocals / discovered, discovered another, vocals / asians, asians toured, vocals / plates, plates paced, vocals / effects, effects sent, vocals / ziggurats, ziggurats stepped, vocals / attendant, attendant flew, vocals / beta, beta fleshed, vocals / asteroids, asteroids pooled,

vocals / obscures, obscures most, vocals / obfuscate, obfuscate becoming, vocals / cools, cools oft, vocals / shielded, shielded costs, vocals / concepts, concepts spent, vocals / century, century meant, vocals / entry, entry pointed, vocals / levels, levels sold, vocals / trails, trails tripled, vocals / spreading, spreading precious, vocals / relatives, relatives called, vocals / treats, treats toured, vocals / probable, probable causes for these, vocals / destiny, destiny due your, vocals / destitute, destitute without yours, vocals / daunts, daunts less, vocals / intensify, intensify heated, vocals / blasphemy, blasphemy over, vocals / basins, basins borrowed, vocals / borrows, borrows less, vocals / dioxides, dioxides during your, vocals / greens, greens and the grazing, vocals / effects, effects last, vocals / chondritic, chondritic numbers and these, vocals / pyramids, pyramids appearing, vocals / detached, detached ones wearing, vocals / effective, effective releases, vocals / scattering, scattering smatters, vocals / hysterically, hysterically curing your, vocals / forgiven, forgiven basics, vocals / forthright, forthright following, vocals / faiths, faiths felled, vocals / collectives, collectives cores, vocals / collections, collections made through, vocals / prayers, prayers paid too, vocals / pens, pens and portals for these, vocals / positions, positions allowed, vocals / made, made the One, vocal / clear, clear wells, vocals / zero, zero gates, vocals / natural, natural muses, vocals / positions, positions sold, vocals / posits, posits caused, vocals / poles, poles end, vocals.

CHAPTER THIRTEEN

Matched, matched relations with, vocals / respects, respects due, vocals / resurrections, resurrections cured, vocals / rays, rays patched, vocals / patched, patched into these, vocals / into, into alls, vocals / vibrationally, vibrationally rational, vocals / cross, cross genetically, vocal / modulations, modulations watched, vocally / matched, matched ones, vocals / in, inside in, vocals / pathways, pathways built, vocals / awarded, awarded carded, vocals / awakened, awakened all, vocals / accepts, accepts dues, vocals / changed, changed the ship, vocals / vibrations, vibrations rich, vocals / shiftedshifted in courses, vocals / sequences, sequences sold, vocals / domains, domains maids, vocals / domino, domino dues, vocals / effects, effects sold, vocals / chains, chains off, vocals / daisy, daisy dears, vocals / wise, wise ones, vocals / erratic, erratic without, vocals / erotic, erotic about, vocals / floods, floods off, vocals / focus, focus on, vocals / written, written into, vocals / introspective, introspective ones, vocals / ally, ally made, vocals / awarded, awarded gifts, vocals / rewarded, rewarded again, vocals / final, final says, vocals / funnels, funnels built, vocals / destroyed, destroyed without yours, vocals / diabolics, diabolics past, vocals / detailed, detailed deliverance, vocals / differences, differences said "vocals" / defined, defined as, vocals / denied, denied without, vocals / distilled, distilled amounts, vocals / demented, demented gone, vocals / defiant, defiant shouts, vocals / without, without yours? vocals / withal, withal sold, vocals / worthy, worthy of, vocals / wisdoms, wisdoms shared, vocals / wellest, wellest gazes, vocals / wellness, wellness sought, vocals / wishes, wishes past, vocals / willing, willing lasts, vocals / worth,

worth this all, vocals / prescient, prescient tools, vocals / purpose, purpose found, vocals / fulfilling, fulfilling fits, vocals / fullest, fullest life, vocals / finals, finals sought, vocals / basics, basics bought, vocals / fuels, fuels burn, vocals / foolish, foolish without, vocals / tinsels, tinsels tins, vocals / triples, triples end, vocals.

LEVEL 95: THE FORTITUDE-MENTS

CHAPTER ONE: alluvial, alluvial plains to fortitude / plains, plains on fortitude / flood, flood these fortitudes / Nile, Nile is the fortitude / rainbows, rainbows ripe in fortitude / wash, wash then, fortitude / sirius, sirius brought fortitude / secures, secures a lightened fortitude / optimums, optimums pleased, fortitudes / explosives, explosives carried, fortitudes / credits, credits made, fortitudes / penchants, penchants posed, fortitudes / imply, imply host, offered, fortitudes / supply, supply the most, fortitudes / suppose, supposed, fortitudes / purpose, purpose post, fortitudes / equal, equals sequels, fortitudes / forms, froms past, fortitudes / concept, concepts cured, fortitudes / predates, predates drawn, fortitudes / dwellings, dwellings sold, fortitudes / debates, debates sought?fortitudes / issue, issues pursued? fortitudes / eastern, eastern ways, to fortitudes / grows, grows a growing / spells, spells breaks, fortitudes / break, break off, fortitudes / pine, pines tossed, fortitudes / ovulation, ovulation ends, fortitudes / detain, detain most? fortitudes / ahead, ahead staids, fortitudes / holes, holes dug, fortitudes / mega, meg bugs, fortitudes / metatron, metatron lights fortitudes / megatanic, megatanic fortitudes / formulas, formulas plastered, fortitudes / masses, masses lost? fortitudes / typical, typical toasts? fortitudes / tons, tons off, fortitudes / abbreviation, abbreviations bets, fortitudes / barns, barns atop, fortitudes / logs, logs hosted, fortitudes / wed, wed steady, fortitudes / wills, wills met, fortitudes / bound, bound to be, fortitudes / nature, nature sought, fortitudes / ovation, ovations caught, fortitudes / lutheran, lutheran holdings, fortitudes / gem, gems taught, fortitudes / mine, mine sought, fortitudes / 5, 5 who knew, fortitudes / fog, fogs lift, fortitudes / bleach, bleach brought, fortitudes / time, time sands, fortitudes / island, island deals, fortitudes / colds, colds sort, fortitudes / cheer, cheer sets, fortitudes / views, views hosted, fortitudes / leverage, leverage carried, fortitudes / cold, cold days, fortitudes / shield, shields laid, fortitudes / levels, levels into, fortitudes / place, place built, fortitudes / through, through us all, fortitudes.

CHAPTER TWO

Man, man stood, fortitudes / formation, formations could, fortitudes / ways, ways spelled, fortitudes / units, units measured, fortitudes / release, released and caused, fortitudes / earths, earths pursed, fortitudes / under, under perches, fortitudes / geometric, geometric lines, fortitudes / patronize, patronize less, fortitudes / earthic, earthic myths, fortitudes / shifts, shifts off, fortitudes / explosive, explosive guns, fortitudes / forms, forms paid, fortitudes

/ camps, camps laid, fortitudes / earth, earth mists, fortitudes / trees, trees turn, fortitudes / grades, grades guessed, fortitudes / infliction, inflictions causes, fortitudes / section, sectional lost, fortitudes / energetic, energetic pretense goes, fortitudes / predates, predates supposed, fortitudes / finalize, finalize eyees, fortitudes / jokes, jokes made, fortitudes / asteroid, asteroid dues, fortitudes / gates, gates built, fortitudes / circles, circles told, fortitudes / placed, placed pilings, fortitudes / material, material shed, fortitudes / executive, executive postures, fortitudes / cures, cures bet, fortitudes / property, property sells, fortitudes / properly, properly posed, fortitudes / redness, redness out, fortitudes / typical, typical carriage, fortitudes / phase, phase twos, fortitudes / pages, pages pelted, fortitudes / areas, areas melted, fortitudes / masses, masses paid, fortitudes / stays, stays lost, fortitudes / reasonable, reasonable costs, fortitudes / comments, copy ways comments made, fortitudes / particle, particle pleasures, fortitudes / steers, steers clearly, fortitudes / impact, impact sets, fortitudes / reason, reasonable, fortitudes / areas, areas hosted, fortitudes / employs, employs most, fortitudes / cross, cross too, fortitudes / thrill, thrills cost, fortitudes / areas, areas hot, fortitudes / relates, relates most, fortitudes / powers, powers paid, fortitudes / orchards, orchards built, fortitudes / sphere, sphere hosts, fortitudes / release, release most, fortitudes / places, places appeal, fortitudes / orbits, orbits sought, fortitudes / equivalancy, equivalency tested, fortitudes / supplies, supplies bleed, fortitudes / needs, needs met, fortitudes / radius, radius built, fortitudes / equivalent, equivalent allows, fortitudes / supply, supply defined, fortitudes / phenomeons, phenomenons mentioned, fortitudes.

CHAPTER THREE
Circles, circles last, fortitudes / denote, denote votes for, fortitudes / areas, areas met, fortitudes / pie, pie sets, fortitudes / experiment, experiment means, fortitudes / rules, rules off, fortitudes / circling, circling ghosts, fortitudes / tags, tags off, fortitudes / experience, experienced bins, fortitudes / three, three who knew, fortitudes / tails, tails tugged, fortitudes / lag, lags lost, fortitudes / strays, strays cost, fortitudes / billions, billions brought, fortitudes / motions, motions made, fortitudes / tails, tails tugged, fortitudes / chances, chances allowed, fortitudes / hit, hit past, fortitudes / hurls, hurls last, fortitudes / planes, planes simple, fortitudes / happiness, happiness stands, fortitudes / faculties, faculties placed, fortitudes / grades, grades given, fortitudes / commercial, commercial airs, fortitudes / learns, learns to be, fortitudes / cnter, centers well, fortitudes / tube, tubes cut, fortitudes / litigation, litigations past, fortitudes / centers, centers made, fortitudes / kindreds, kindreds sought, fortitudes / end, ends now, fortitudes / marry, marry notes to, fortitudes / calculation, calculations coming, fortitudes / discoveries, discoveries daily, fortitudes / temples, temples build, fortitudes / health, health held, fortitudes / mavericks, mavericks may, fortitudes / nation, nations built, fortitudes / treat, treats told, fortitudes / gift, gifts sold, fortitudes / union, unions made, fortitudes / turn, turns told / stay, stay well, fortitudes / commons, commons grounded, fortitudes / mains, mains stay, fortitudes / proud, proud plans, fortitudes / days, days

dealt, fortitudes / impacts, impacts land, fortitudes / valley, valley viewed, fortitudes / sells, sells fast, fortitudes / visibly, visibly breaks, fortitudes / values, values entertained, fortitudes / transmit, transmit begins, fortitudes / builds, builds a host, fortitudes / galleys, galleys bought, fortitudes / later, later sealed, fortitudes / waves, waves hosting, fortitudes / parts, parts posting, fortitudes / inspire, inspire ghosts departure, fortitudes / count, count most, fortitudes / certainty, certainty given, fortitudes / visible, visible voices, fortitudes / spectrals, spectrals trailing, fortitudes / changes, changes brought, fortitudes.

CHAPTER FOUR
Calling, calling you, fortitudes / birds, birds came, fortitudes / foot, foot stomps, fortitudes / foothills, foothills seen, fortitudes / calls, calls made, fortitudes / beams, beams baked, fortitudes / malls, malls torn, fortitudes / astronomically, astronomically cured, fortitudes / rife, rife rapes, fortitudes / degree, degrees conferred, fortitudes / hudson, hudson roads, fortitudes / paramount, paramount go, fortitudes / ways, ways held, fortitudes / granite, granite sails, fortitudes / lights, lights on, fortitudes / frequent, frequent courses, fortitudes / commercial, commercial air, fortitudes / attends, attends schools, fortitudes / attention, attentions paid, fortitudes / emits, emits hopes, fortitudes / collection, opts collections next, fortitudes / gives, give, fortitudes / origins, origins, fortitudes / amounts, amounts paid, fortitudes / build, build up, fortitudes / sales, sales laid, fortitudes / occur, copes occur, fortitudes / vary, nary voiced, fortitudes / notice, notices tossed, fortitudes / explode, explode onto, fortitudes / explores, explores the ghosts, fortitudes / lines, lines electric, fortitudes / impacts, impacts toured, fortitudes / valley, valley sold, fortitudes / sells, sells one, fortitudes / visibly, visibly voiced, fortitudes / values, values built, fortitudes / transmit, transmit gifts, fortitudes / builds, builds one door, fortitudes / galley, galley lashed, fortitudes / lanes, lanes bowl, fortitudes / part, parts told, fortitudes / size, some sizes smell, fortitudes / add, adds dopes, fortitudes / paper, papers burned, fortitudes / contents, contents turned, fortitudes / box, box sold, fortitudes / location, location discovered, fortitudes / destroy, destroys most, fortitudes / from, from the m, all, fortitudes / stock, stock told, fortitudes / clock, clocks cured, fortitudes / change, changes amazed, fortitudes / screen, screens tip, fortitudes / loud, loud leads, fortitudes / silence, silence said "fortitudes" / lasting, lasting explains, fortitudes / chirping, chirping masts, fortitudes / lifting, lifting lasts, fortitudes / array, array arose, fortitudes / vast, vast days, fortitudes / source, sources said "fortitudes" / calm, calms off, fortitudes / beautiful, beautiful boasts, fortitudes.

CHAPTER FIVE
Phantoms, phantoms cured, fortitudes / rivers, rivers poured, fortitudes / emits, emits whores, fortitudes / service, service Babylonian, fortitudes / spiral, spirals cured, fortitudes / dominant, dominant doesed, fortitudes / deceit, deceit past, fortitudes / contrary, contrary casts, fortitudes / slept, slept in, fortitudes / banks, banks slide, fortitudes / falls, falls made, fortitudes /

astronomical, astronomical explains, fortitudes / slopes, slopes cured, fortitudes / distributions, distributions allowed, fortitudes / eyes, eyes wise, fortitudes / detects, detects most, fortitudes / places, places post, fortitudes / qualify, qualify for, fortitudes / special, specials made, fortitudes / specialist, specialists chosen, fortitudes / height, heights are sought, fortitudes / extremes, extremes measured, fortitudes / lineage, lineage caught, fortitudes / lintles, lintles off, fortitudes / marks, marks made, fortitudes / off, off gridded, fortitudes / granite, granite sealed, fortitudes / valley, valley voiced, fortitudes / monuments, monuments built, fortitudes / kings, kings caused, fortitudes / inside, inside rays, fortitudes / reliefs, reliefs sought, fortitudes / greenhouse, greenhouse gazeing, fortitudes / works, works voiced, fortitudes / trails, trails toured, fortitudes / builds, builds a boast, fortitudes / innovate, innovate rates, fortitudes / governs, governs choice, fortitudes / objectives, objectives laid, fortitudes / objectify, objectify less, fortitudes / kings, kings courses, fortitudes / dominion, dominions blues, fortitudes / honored, honored pink, fortitudes / allow, allow arrows, fortitudes / influx, influx came, fortitudes / news, news given, fortitudes / new, new ways, fortitudes / ideaideas dosed, fortitudes / stone, stone turns, fortitudes / river, rivers rose, fortitudes / sold, sold past, fortitudes / whole, whole days, fortitudes / aptitudes, aptitudes, fortitudes / lakes, lakes rose, fortitudes / catawba, catawba basins, fortitudes / river, river escarped, fortitudes / basin, basin boasts, fortitudes / relation, relations won, fortitudes / relationship, relationship hums, fortitudes / oakland, oakland leys, fortitudes / bays, bays bulged, fortitudes / plunge, plunge past, fortitudes / ignore, ignore olds, fortitudes / less, less thems, fortitudes.

CHAPTER SIX
Desk, desk tops, fortitudes / cures, cures sought, fortitudes / homes, homes held, fortitudes / fleets, given fleets, fortitudes / visions, visions volley, fortitudes / scales, scales turned, fortitudes / opened, opened pens, fortitudes / instinct, trust instincts, fortitudes / well, well days, fortitudes / wealth, wealth made, fortitudes / leathery, lathery lapsed, fortitudes / antique, antiques sold, fortitudes / days, days bold, fortitudes / sales, sales made, fortitudes / familiar, familiar voices, fortitudes / families, given families faced, fortitudes / approvals, approvals made, fortitudes / carmel, carmel placed, fortitudes / pace, paces taught, fortitudes / appear, appears caught, fortitudes / bethlehem, bethlehem voices, fortitudes / wildlife, wildlife doorways, fortitudes / entire, entire star groups, fortitudes / a, a days, fortitudes / hilo, hio mister, fortitudes / sister, sisters, fortitudes / in, ins, fortitudes / wonder, wonder under australian blues, fortitudes / shrugs, shrugs off, fortitudes / clearest, clearest costs? fortitudes / her, her days, fortitudes / dear, dear ones, fortitudes / impala, impala dues, fortitudes / corbins, corbins carried, fortitudes / width, width off, fortitudes / opens, opens posts, fortitudes / pure, pure rays, fortitudes / yellow, yellow days, fortitudes / pigments, pigments moist, fortitudes / colors, colors carried, fortitudes / covaliers, covaliers parry, fortitudes / voyages, voyages sought, fortitudes / 64, 64 cures, fortitudes / <u>levels, levels meant? fortitudes / cabaret, cabaret days, fortitudes</u>

/ cures, cures, fortitudes / transport, transports, fortitudes / service, services to mountain's c[i]tied, fortitudes / a, a trips, fortitudes / softening, softening gazes, fortitudes / often, often hosted, fortitudes / softens, softens voices, fortitudes / queen, queens costs, fortitudes / single, allow single doses, fortitudes / seals, seals most, fortitudes / meals, meals paid, fortitudes / a, a day lilied, fortitude / yin, yins back, fortitudes / ferry, ferry over, fortitudes / over, over alls, fortitudes / kwan, kwan's dins, fortitudes / quan, quan paid, fortitudes / across, across stages, fortitudes / keep, keep coming, fortitudes.

CHAPTER SEVEN
Kin, kins made, fortitudes / oranges, oranges explored, fortitudes / simple, simple stairways, fortitudes / love's, love's friends, fortitudes / kinship, kinships, fortitudes / yellowed, yellowed, fortitudes / signals, sines signalled, fortitudes / deal, deals through, fortitudes / caution, cautions over, fortitudes / final, final follows, fortitudes / advanced, advanced rages, fortitudes / has, has past stages, fortitudes / red, reds pages, fortitudes / green, greens, fortitudes / rates, rates made, fortitudes / gone, gones, fortitudes / to, to them all, fortitudes / varnish, varnished in, fortitudes / intersected, intersected a, fortitude / columns, columns written and, fortitudes / champion's, champions of these, fortitudes / golden, golden gated, fortitudes / whitened, whitened lated, fortitudes / fastens, fastens past yours, fortitudes / pens, pens poised, fortitudes / harness, harness off, fortitudes / serves, serves cost, fortitudes / carts, carts laden, fortitudes / magic, magic stages, fortitudes / temples, temples toning, fortitudes / ionized, ionized loanings, fortitudes / galic, galic partners phoning, fortitudes / wills, wills written, fortitudes / village, villages cost, fortitudes / kept, kept hosts, fortitudes / soothe, soothe most, fortitudes / travel, travel tourings, fortitudes / into, into alls, fortitudes / new's, new's casts, fortitudes / valley, valley voiced, fortitudes / moss, moss greens, fortitudes / emerald, emerald tablets, fortitudes / labors, labors lost? fortitudes / spine, spine posts, fortitudes / gates, gates poised, fortitudes / fly, fly now, fortitudes / distant, distant callings, fortitudes / discount, discount made too, fortitudes / advent, advent's extents for, fortitudes / sales, sales finished, fortitudes / first, first lasts, fortitudes / fasten, fasten into, fortitudes / garden, gardens gated, fortitudes / holiday, holidays hostings, fortitudes / soothe, soothe mostly, fortitudes / galaxy, galaxy ghosxted? cleared through, fortitudes / growth, growths made, fortitudes / qualities, qualities cued, fortitudes / clues, clues blast, fortitudes / reforms, reforms tossed, fortitudes / essential, essentials lost, fortitudes / maternal, maternal tears, fortitudes / showed, showed how, fortitudes / smooth, smoothed into, fortitudes.

CHAPTER EIGHT
Sun, sun noons, fortitudes / moments, moments who've, fortitudes / spends, spends thrifty, fortitudes / strands, strands, glands, fortitudes / sales, sales made through, fortitudes / carousing, carousing less, fortitudes / means, means most, fortitudes / strategic, strategic moves, fortitudes / shirts, shirts out, fortitudes / covert, covert delicious, fortitudes / carry, carry ons, fortitudes

/ immaculate, immaculate missions, fortitudes / marry, marry the one, fortitudes / often, often said, fortitudes / cavort, cavorted, fortitudes / mercury, mercury cures, fortitudes / fabrics, fabrics spoiled, fortitudes / salt, salt flox, fortitudes / boxedboxed out, fortitudes / sells, sells one, fortitudes / claremont, claremont cures, fortitudes / fields, fields opened, fortitudes / begun, geared up for begun again, fortitudes / ends, ends kept? fortitudes / tallahassee, tallahassee digs, fortitudes / gears, gears given, fortitudes / changed, changed embraces, fortitudes / symbols, symbols appeared, fortitudes / transmissions, transmissions made, fortitudes / simple, simple deals, fortitudes / sounds, soundes necessary, fortitudes / famous, famous fuels, fortitudes / trades, trades waves, fortitudes / commerce, commerce curing, fortitudes / sales, sales defined, fortitudes / furnished, urnished mats with, fortitudes / format, formats reading, fortitudes / found, found one, fortitudes / engage, engage less, fortitudes / levels, levels sped, fortitudes / lunge, lunge over, fortitudes / across, across these days, fortitudes / excess, excess spelling, fortitudes / hires, hires blessed, fortitudes / lifts, lifts oft, fortitudes / lightness, lightness leads to, fortitudes / initials, initials carried, fortitudes / nights, nights heard, fortitudes / fastened, fastened instincts to fortitudes / hair, hair is softer, fortitudes / curlscurls oft, fortitudes / secrets, secrets told "fortitudes" / fortunate fortunate finds, fortitudes / of, of them all, fortitudes / embellish, embellish well, fortitudes / seals, seals off, fortitudes / will, wills appealing, fortitudes / final, final days and fortitudes / fashionable, fashionable fixtures for, fortitudes / meals, meals made, fortitudes / appearing, ppearing, engaging, fortitudes / focus, focused into yours, fortitudes / folds, folds oft, fortitudes / materials, materials found, fortitudes.

CHAPTER NINE

Meal, meal teams, fortitudes / feed, feed small, fortitudes / held, held oft, fortitudes / found, found a final fortitude / apples, apples piling, fortitudes / feeding, feeding courses, fortitudes / healers, healers softly, fortitudes / fond, fond numbers, fortitudes / zuni, zuni performing, fortitudes / literal, literal gifts, fortitudes / figures, figures appearing, fortitudes / coming, coming into your, fortitudes / rejoin, rejoined meetings, fortitudes / senses, senses gathere, fortitudes / gather, gather hear, fortitudes / lances, lances tossed, fortitudes / reassured, reassured electrically, fortitudes / metaphoric, metaphoric hues, fortitudes / captives, captives gone to, fortitudes / capital, capitals built for, fortitudes / grows, grows dearly, fortitudes / methodology, methodology given, fortitudes / enjoyed, enjoyed simply, fortitudes / plans, plans and lanes, fortitudes / efficient, efficient, fortitudes / matching, matching motions to your, fortitudes / eastern, eastern lanes to, fortitudes / lines, lines listed / manuals, manuals presented, fortitudes / decoded, decoded details from, fortitudes / meanings, meanings mostly, fortitudes / maintained, maintained meanings, fortitudes / manufactures, manufactures fellow, fortitudes / trajectories, trajectories soothing, fortitudes / sells, sells soon, fortitudes / centers, centers loosely, fortitudes / senses, senses sizing, fortitudes / placed, placed rehearsals, fortitudes / buying, buying boasts your, fortitudes / shells, shells applied, fortitudes /

diameters, diameters daring, fortitudes / pours, pours softly into, fortitudes / graded, graded shades for, fortitudes / imports, imports sorted, fortitudes / sapphires, sapphires filling, fortitudes / gold, gold molded, fortitudes / gems, gems surrendered, fortitudes / jewels, jewels joined, fortitudes / fondness, fondness follows, fortitudes / jewelry, jewelry registered, fortitudes / popular, popular causes for, fortitudes / productions, productions, lessons, fortitudes / experts, experts calling, fortitudes / created, created electric, fortitudes / contours, contours sealing your, fortitudes / processed, processed plenties for, fortitudes / joys, joys softened, fortitudes / complex, complex curings, fortitudes / constant, constant curings, fortitudes / placed, placed empires for, fortitudes / energy, energy softening, female fortitudes / copes, copes and cured, fortitudes / mimics, mimics numbers, fortitudes / walks, walks in softest, fortitudes.

CHAPTER TEN

Judge, judge knotted, fortitudes / cultures, cultures surest, fortitudes / sapphic, sapphic credits, fortitudes / caves, caves lost then, fortitudes / principals, principals agreed, fortitudes / ringing, ringing in ranging, fortitudes / arched, arched inward, fortitudes / monuments, monuments touring, fortitudes / abundant, abundant basics, fortitudes / zircon, zircon joinings, fortitudes / zion, aion daily, fortitudes / today, today is blessed in, fortitudes / finest, finest follows, fortitudes / diamonds, diamonds due, fortitudes / canyons, canyons basics, fortitudes / bluebl;ues zoning, fortitudes / initialize, initialize your owning, fortitudes / able, able to be inheart for thee, fortitudes / beats, heats tropical balance, a, fortitudes / on, on to days, fortitudes / hearts, hearts wed, fortitudes / intointo alls, fortitudes / apt, apt applies, fortitudes / appliances, appliances sold, fortitudes / secured, secured A basics, fortitudes / fuels, fuels left, fortitudes / feeds, feeds oft, fortitudes / fed, fed into, fortitudes / steers, steers lightly, fortitudes / sturdily, sturdily built, fortitudes / stealth, stealth is wealth, fortitudes / off, off these cuffs, fortitudes / wide, wide ways home through fortitudes / in, in this all, fortitudes / exultant, exultant callings, fortitudes / surrender, surrenders in, fortitudes / sung, sung about, fortitudes / adoreadore, shout, fortitudes / shouts, shouts wade to, fortitudes / over, over alls, fortitudes / phones, phones bade, fortitudes / droning, dronings about, fortitudes / equivalents, equivalents called in, fortitudes / for, for them all, fortitudes / overlyoverly direct, fortitudes / dramatic, dramatic escapes, fortitudes/ cues, cues sealed, fortitudes / grids, grids spatially bid, fortitudes / sealed, sealed principles, fortitudes / iceice lanes, fortitudes / air, air blanes, fortitudes / water, water blokes, fortitudes / days, days who drivel, fortitudes / decreased, decreased in counted, fortitudes / posedposed as mothers, fortitudes / gently, gently deposed, fortitudes / nights, nights sailed, fortitudes / days, days directed, fortitudes / spoils, spoils cost, fortitudes / pools, pools spilling, fortitudes / increased, increased rentals, fortitudes / mails, mails sent, fortitudes / sent, sent lots to fortitudes / sunken, sunken relaxes, fortitudes.

CHAPTER ELEVEN

Misty, misty weathers, fortitudes / niagra, niagra nestled, fortitudes

/ sequels, sequels sell, fortitudes / write, write in balanced, fortitudes / balances, balances paid, fortitudes / picked, picked a soffit, fortitudes / up, up stairs, fortitudes / solar, solar details, fortitudes / signals, signals mentioned, fortitudes / minimal, minimal missions, fortitudes / frequency, frequency during, fortitudes / plenty, plenty paid, fortitudes / sternly, sternly disciplined, fortitudes / sailing, sailings tucks and these, fortitudes / in, in styles and, fortitudes / offers, offers elipsed, fortitudes / aft, aft and sailing, fortitudes / locks, locks told, fortitudes / steered, steered clearly to, fortitudes / nearest, nearest debated, fortitudes / fares, fares, lessens, fortitudes / leapingleaping overtly, fortitudes / sample, samples coupled, fortitudes / mostly, mostly magic, fortitudes / lend, lend anothers, fortitudes / noted, noted and sated, fortitudes / affluence, affluence registers, fortitudes / sentinels, sentinels spent, fortitudes / magically, magically marries yours, fortitudes / opt, opt to creation, fortitudes / guard, guarded, fortitudes / churning, churnings memorized, fortitudes / intrigues, intrigues off, fortitudes / moods, moods last, fortitudes / bought, bought one, fortitudes / basic, basics taught through thee, fortitudes / turns, turns lessons, fortitudes / inquire, inquired in, fortitudes / inside, inside days and, fortitudes / magically, magically met, fortitudes / bonded, bonded sounds, fortitudes / touching, touching roughly, fortitudes / pages, pages past, fortitudes / rhyming, rhyming over, fortitudes / cores, cores cut too, fortitudes / inspired, inspired ascents through, fortitudes / written, written notes for, fortitudes / patiently, patiently applying, fortitudes / scores, scores messages for these, fortitudes / cured, cured now, fortitudes / recall, recalling, fortitudes / insults, insults through, fortitudes / ancients, ancients who, fortitudes / carry, carry ons, fortitudes / rivals, rivals cast to, fortitudes / out, out said, fortitudes / incest, incest left, fortitudes / cured, cured simply, fortitudes / remember, remember whens and these fortitudes / deliver, deliver daring, fortitudes / waters, waters wells and, fortitudes / given, given in too, fortitudes / frequent, frquent questions and these, fortitudes / baths, baths made similarly, fortitudinous.

CHAPTER TWELVE
Patience, patience paying, fortitudes / wise, wise lessons, fortitudes / riserise risen, fortitudes / doubts, doubts gone, fortitudes / gone, gone again, fortitudes / pen, pens spun, fortitudes / write, write the won, fortitudes / forgive, forgiven only, fortitudes / steeling, steeling past yours, fortitudes / another, anothers data, fortitudes / pay, pay off, fortitudes / fallingfalling costs, fortitudes / stolen, stolen wells, fortitudes / days, days addressed, fortitudes / notesnotes who whistle, fortitudes / detox, detox done, fortitudes / sternest, sternly treasured, fortitudes / patience, patience dears, fortitudes / patent, patent into, fortitudes / rushed, rushed past, fortitudes / Christ, Christ anchors here, fortitudes / anchors, anchors a way, fortitudes / rapture, raptures ruled, fortitudes / aliens, aliens journey, fortitudes / sent, sent hints, fortitudes / away, away say through, fortitudes / consciousness, consciousness clears, fortitudes / clearing, clearings sent, fortitudes / here, here, then, fortitudes / roads, roads ruled, fortitudes / lead, leads past, fortitudes / past, past done, fortitudes / strong, strong over, fortitudes / grids, grids graced, fortitudes / leap, leap past,

fortitudes / reap, reap rewarded, fortitudes / benefits, benefits basic, fortitudes / join, join the living, fortitudes / stunning, stunning friends and fortitudes / vistas, vistas, friends, and fortitudes / gifts, gifts given, fortitudes / trailing, trailing rising, fortitudes / waves, waves catching, fortitudes / yours, yours the simple, fortitudes / yourself, yourself, A, fortitude / mascots, mascots moisture, fortitudes / holes, holes drilling, fortitudes / plates, plates purchased, fortitudes / with, with them all an, fortitude / travels, travels over, fortitudes / pending, pending guests and, fortitudes / beckoning, beckoning now, fortitudes / love, love is regular, fortitudes / regulars, regulars rule, fortitudes / flowers, flowers fought, buy them, fortitudes / rotate, rotate into, fortitudes / 3, 3 who kenw, fortitudes / maths, maths, fortitudes / 7, 7 days, fortitudes / 5, 5 nights, fortitudes / 4, 4 ways, fortitudes / the, the planned, fortitudes / circles, circles land, fortitudes / coded, coded cures and, fortitudes.

CHAPTER THIRTEEN
Conception, conceptions sealed, fortitudes / kinks, kinks out, fortitudes / ancients, ancients parry, fortitudes / stood, stood warry, fortitudes / halls, halls aiming, fortitudes / armenti, armenti given, fortitudes / in, in ways and these, fortitudes / banks, banks balanced, fortitudes / encroaching, encroachings over, fortitudes / rotations, rotations during yours, fortitudes / worthy, worthy welcomed, fortitudes / love, love rules, fortitudes / cubes, cubes cost? fortitudes / youths, youths toasted, fortitudes / led, led well, fortitudes / a, a spelled, fortitudes / tribe, tribes meld, fortitudes / command, commands made, fortitudes / comprised, om comprised and risen too, fortitudes / wraps, wraps up, fortitudes / one, one who kenw, fortitudes / a, a spelling f-o-r-t-i-t-u-d-e / youth, youth won, fortitudess / precise, precise rays and these, fortitudes / precious, precious covenants and their, fortitudes / overtoned, overtoned dues, fortitudes / righteously, righteously arrogant, fortitudes / 16's, 16's ways and these, fortitudes / 32's, 32's welcomed, fortitudes / thickened, thickened thought strains and these, fortitudes / call, calling due a, fortitudes / clicks, clicks on linear, fortitudes / 64ths, 64ths followed, fortitudes / emerging, emerging tactics and fortitudes / erect, erect now, fortitudes / builds, builds well, fortitudes / lengths, lengths given, focused, fortitudes / operated, operated rationally, fortitudes / harmonics, harmonics healed, fortitudes / edges, edges relationed, fortitudes / chromatics, chromatics scaling, fortitudes / scales, scales tip, fortitudes / / 23, / 23-measures for these, fortitudes / centimeters, centimeters ruled, fortitudes / 3rds, 3'rds who knew, fortitudes / racks, racks off, fortitudes / independence, independences gained, fortitudes / mer, mer dealt, fortitudes / ka, ka cues, fortitudes / ba, ba boots, fortitudes / dimensions, dimensions deluged, fortitudes / 12, 12 trays and these, fortitudes / overtones, overtones values and the toning, fortitudes / 13, 13 recognized as, fortitudes / stars, stars knit as, fortitudes / 8, 8 lessons, fortitudes / point, pointed into, fortitudes / fields, fields basically, fortitudinous / tetrahedron, tetrahedrons raising your, fortitudes / 5, 5 deepens your fortitudes / between, between us basics and fundamental, fortitudes / hedron, hedron headed for donated, fortitudes / counter, counter sinking? fortitudes / rotations, rotations registered, fortitudes

LEVEL 96: THE ENDEAR-MENTS

CHAPTER ONE

Endears, endears again, endears / hebron, hebron's endearing qualities / add, add to these, endearments / loved, love has led, endears / engenders, engenders, endears / time, time fed, endears / equals, equals an, endear / a, a flats, endeared / endangers, andean endangers gone, endears / space, spaces placed, endears / living, living spaced, endears / fields, fields emerge, endeared / warrants, warrants past / worthy, worthy factors, endeared / soothe, soothe past, endears / socks, socks off, endears / the, the attributes for, endears / mer, mer ka ba, endearings / ka, ka codes, endeared / bah, bah basics, endeared / cubes, cubes coded, endears / the, the sets facts, endeared / added, added and pointed, endears / dimensions, dimensions, endeared / of, of these facts, endeared / the, these notices, endeared / all, all who say, endeared / fourth, fourth focused, endears / equals, equals sequels, endeared / these, these notices, endeared / ratios, ratios registered, endeared / rated, rated, sated, endeared / shifting, shifting, drifting, endeared / encoded, encoded, roads, endeared / and, and standing, endears / a, a follicle, endeared / christ, christs sets, endeared / in, in sizes, endeared / a, a thorough, endears / fitting, fittings endeared / liftslifts settled, endears / we, we who know, endeared / see, see us well, endeared / forgiven, forgiven foes, endeared / love, love is forgotten, endears / is, is there near nectar, endears / how, how is the clinging rung? endears / we, we are the simple, endears / will, will you be endeared? / comprehend, comprehend your clues, endears / who, who is the gathered? endears / gained, gained insights for those, endeared / insights, insights past, endears / for, for those who last, endeared / residential, residential stays, endeared / steps, steps made, endearingly / made, made a facet, endeared / into, into those, endeared / the in, the in inside, endears / evoluted, evoluted those, endeared / evolving, evolving, solving, endears / ones, ones who kenw, endeared / ahkenaton, ahkenation's national endearings / temples, temples who settled yours, endearings.

CHAPTER TWO

Abydos, Abydos built here, endears / lemurian, lemurian strivings, endeared / leapings, leapings and loss gone, endears / shifts, shifts are final, endeared / poles, poles finished, endeared / inside, inside roses, endears / external, external poses, endeared / redoubled, redoubled amounts meanings, endears / epic, epic courses, endeared / reaches, reaches groups gathered, endears / gathers, gathers in focus, endears / groups, groups gathered, endeared / nearest, nearest nets set, endears / red, red rovered, endears / seas, seas tossed, endears / seen, seen in powerful endearings / walking, walking coming, endears / collapsing, collapsing past, endears / heart, heart happy, endears / shouting, shouting accomplished, endears / confirms, confirms closely, the new enemy is clinging, the nearest, endeared / complimentary, complimentary causes, endeared / shades, shades focused for closets opened, endears / as, as we said, "endears" / matched, matched paces, endears / materials, materials purchased, endears / greygones, greygones

bygones, endeared / lights, lights on, endears / flow, flow in showing, endears / into, into your basics, endears / basements, basements mellowed, endears / doors, doors opened, endears / precessions, precessions accepted, endears / advanced, advanced rages off, endears / starring, starring the cost, endeared / houses, houses purchased, endears / forths, forths written, endearings / into, into those who endear / clouded, clouded corporates, endeared / pushes, pushes past, endears / across, across the rays, endeared / rays, rays who burst, endearingly / bursting, bursting forth, endears / groups, groups gathered, endeared / yoga, yoga built, endears / metatron, metatron leading, endears / leading, leading poses, endeared / DNA, DNA doses, endeared / 23, 23 who knew endearments / has, has a place been built for yours, endears / into, into those who knew, endearments / cosmos, cosmos cured, endears / degreed, degreed similarly, endears / met, met one, endears / buy, buy those, endeared / kali, kali ends, endeared / drunvalo, drunvalo sends, endeared / surges, surges urged, endears / often, often fed, endearings / feeling, feeling left, endears / left, left off, endears / to, to those who know, endears / vote, vote for these, endeared / righteously, righteously simple, endears.

CHAPTER THREE

Of, of a fellow wonderful, endears / value, values brought, endears / brought, brought forth basics, endears / forth, forth the waves, endears / centrall, central news sent, endears / nervous, nervous forgiven, endears / canals, canals built, endears / emptyempty vases, endears / into, into those who, endear / significant, significant others, endeared / leaks, leaks off, endears / and, and those whom, endeared / may, may we weave yours, endearings / fly, fly past, endears / your, your ways, endears / pushing, pushing raves, endeared / teaching, teaching has come, endears / compassions, compassions pushed, endears / published, published a few, endears / breathings, breathings replete, endears / cycles, cycles suggested, endears / end, ends met, endears / surging, surging pays, endeared / found, found a few, endears / in, in sizes, endeared / with, with us for good, endears / towns, towns trusted, endears / sure, sure enoughs, endeared / forgiveness, forgiveness follows, endeared / rituals, rituals arose, endears / last, last told, endears / left, left to say, endears / eyed, eyed wisely, one, endears / the, the fullest, endears / veils, veils ripped oft, endears / reachreach into yours, endears / oft, oft said, endears / amid, amid most, endears / meetings, meetings scheduled, endears / and, and those folks, endears / these, these who knew, endeared / seas, seas crossed, endears / softly, softly siad, "endears" / with, with this all we wed, endears / electric, electric rules, endeared / greengreens grown, endears / golden, golden turned, endears / waves, waves over, endears / masterfully, masterfully seen, endeared / made, made to harbor focused dreams, endears / nearby, nearby nestled, endears / pay, pay attention, endears / attention, attention pays, endears / her, hers the emotional, endearings / who, who is your basic, endear / knew, knew the one, endears / the, the of all, endeared / leading, leading ways to, endear / visits, visits made, endears / to, to us all, endears / which, which the way? endears /

known, known by those, endeared / Acropolis, Acropolis arcing, endears / sites, sites sold, endears.

CHAPTER FOUR

Ancients, ancients waving, endears / waving, waving instructions, endeared / shores, shores who shingled, endear / electric, electric bayous, endeared / beginnings, beginnings bought, endears / placed, placed a clip into those who, endear / leaps, leaps past, endears / points, points made, endears / cures, cures sought, endears / found, found a focused, endearment / yours, yours the younger, endeared / fly, fly now, endears / days, days taught, endears / fibonacci, fibonacci / sequenced, sequenced and forethoughts endeared / nearest, nearest nestles, endeared / guides, guides givent ours, endears / off, off these lines, endears / geometric, geometric cubes, endeared / grids, grids topped, endears / sequences, sequences settled, endeared / sent, sent into one, endeared / where, where were your, endearings / oaks, oaks based, endears / california, california curing, endearings / spherically, spherically sequenced endearings / breathing, breathing in basic endears / tubes, tubes taught to breathe sphericlly through the spine, endears / torus, torus tubings, endeared / heed, heed the soft, endearings / breathing, breathing endears me, endeared / spirals, spirals boost, endearings / bamboo, bamboo basics, endearings / cycles, cycles, endearings / borrowed, borrowed exceptional, endearings / dens, dens dared, endearings / doorways, doorways sealed, endearings / yellowness, yellowness roses, endearings / of, of these smiling, endearings / springs, springs portals, endeared / is, is there a lesson here? endearings / may's, may's weather causing, endearings / weaving, weaving worn, endearings / tenderness, tenderness touching, endearings / reds, reds go, endearings / go, go to the posing, endearings / near, near is next, endearings / soon, soon is taught, endearings / yellow, yellow roses, endeared / advanced, advanced races, endeared / attunes, attunes lost without, endearings / light, light lessens? endearings / in, in these causes, endearings / chicago, chicago hustles, endeared / atlanta, atlanta roses, endearings / thrown, thrown to cubes and, endearings / for, for the focused, endearings / cubes, cubes broken, endearings / breathing, breathings basics, endearings / finding, finding focus, endearings / weaving, weaving rooms, endearings / flying, flying Cross Nor, endearings / electrically, electrically riveted, endearings / inside, inside rages, endearings.

CHAPTER FIVE

Ways, ways to reach you, endearings / enough, enough is said "endearings" / time, times tossed, basically, endeared / inside, inside poses, endearings / spend, spend the mended, endearings / phones, phones abuzz in, endearings / fly, fly over there, endearings / needs, needs met for, endearings / voiced, voiced replyings, endearings / replies, replies made, endearings / revisited, revisited raptured, endearings / all, all who mixed, endearings / who, who said yours? endearings / paged, paged into, endearings / burn, burn left, endearings / found, found the fuel, endearings / through, through us all, endearings / where, where is your whip? endearings / in, in a found, endearings / an, an unusual,

endearing / unique, unique motives, endearings / initial, initial totems, endearings / access, access denied, endearings / fortified, fortified again, endearings / sperms, aperms past, endearings / flood, flood lasts, endearings / equally, equally well, endearings / senses, sense meant for, endearings / due, dues paid, endearings / often, often fed, endearings / next, next days, endearings / a, a's living, endearings / flight, flight fixed, endearings / is, is there one, endearing / booked, booked into, endearings / floating, floating's focused, endearings / uniquely, uniquely residents, endeared / cubes, cubes in motions, endearings / keyed, keyed into yours, endearings / into, into focused, endearings / the, the whom found, endearings / frame, frame astounds, endearings / earth's, eat at earth's busy, endearings / balloons, balloons bought, endearings / aloft, aloft carries, endearings / can, can you visit, endearings / see, see the shores, endearings / stops, stops in too, endearings / made, made to mend, endearings / here, here then, again, endearings / to, to us all, endearings / learn, learn to be, endeared / these, these are the finest, endearings / techniques, techniques learned, endearings / fielded, fielded focused, endearings / through, through us all, frozen, endearings / fibonacci, fibonacci sequenced, endearings / sequenced, sequenced sets, endearings / throughout, throughout her throats, endearings / growth, growth pathed, endearings / pathways, pathways prudet, endearings / vessels, vessels lost, endearings / collect, collect your current, endearings / willingness, willingness laid into, endearings.

CHAPTER SIX

Breathing, breathing has basic endearings / tubes, urgent tubes clipped, endearings / the, the alls, endeared / spines, spines posed in, endearings / alert, alertest endangered endearings / earth's, earth's here again, endearings / mission, missions focused, endearings / universally, universally mended, endearings / level, levels worn, endearings / laws, laws simply fit, endearings / squared, squared into, endearings / revealreveal a sort, endearings / circling, circling mansions, endearings / indications, indications followed, endearings / earth's, earth's magnets, endears / mer, mer days, endearings / ka, ka caves, endearings / ba, ba basics, endeared / shields, shields and basics, endearings / now, now thens, endearings / trued, trued up, endearings / believe, believe in your, endearings / faith, faith is fed, endearings / absolved, absolved, solved, endeared / love, love is made, endearings / solved, solved a filament's endearings / make, make the most, endearings / changes, changes cast, endearings / life, life will last, endearings / lights, lights, endearings / one, one who flew to yours, endearings / who, who will know? endearings / will, will you will yours? endearings / fly, fly in the fellows, endearings / basically, basically bogus, endearings / measures, measures given, endearings / sophic, sophic clues, endearings / coordinates, coordinates cozy in, endearings / beings, beings basics, endearings / sent, sent one, endearings / trust, trust those who, endearings / will, will you be? endearings / guide, guides givne, endearings / grids, grids rocked, endearings / electrically, electrically shocked, endearings / find, find a few, endearings / match, matched up, endearings / breathe, breathe best, endearings / relief, relief received, endearings / sigh, sigh says, endearings / sized, sized up, endearings / matched, matched in place, endearings / relaxed, relaxed this race, endearings / into, into potent, endearings / ignitions, ignitions married, endearings / coinciding, coinciding lives, endearings / conceeds, conceeds feeds, endearings / life, life led, endearings / lengthening, lengthening chats, endearings / broadening, broadening basics, endearings / basically, basically wed, endearings / flowing, flowing on phonings, endearings / into, into the most, endearings / metatron, metatron met, endearings.

CHAPTER SEVEN

Rotations, rotations occuring, endearings / stocked, stocked in, endearings / leading, leading ledges, endearings / keys, keys paid for, endearings / through, trough us all, endearings / maverick, mavericks purged, endearings / tests, tests ran, endearings / forums, forums pushed, endearings / focused, focused into, endearings / fields, fields played, endearings / play, play on, endearings / lightening, lightening strokes, endearings / strokes, strokes off, endearings / erupt, erupted, endearings / stabilize, stabilized and, endearings / flights, flights followed, endearings / these, these allowed, endearings / 144, 144 who were endeared / are the, are the those, endearings / doorway, doorways pulsed through, endearings / through, through us all, measureable, endearings / which, which is the good, endearings? / 144,000, 144,000 who fell into smoldering, endearings / original, originals bought, endearings / overtones, overtones found, endearings / enter, enters now, endearings / breathe, breathe life into, endearings / life, life is led, endearings / into, into us all, endearings / a, a ways in, endearings / melchizedek, melchizedek moves to, endearings / typed, typed on, endearings / awareness, awareness woos, endearings / pure, pure paced, endearings / thought, though said, endearings / pure, pure enoughs, endearings / love, love is fixed, endearings / pure, pure paves, endearings / durations, durations meant, endearings / managed, managed meant, endearings / skills organized, skill organized through love's, endearings / organically, organically fit, endearings / strictest, strictest follows, endearings / flowings, flowings taught, endearings / rules, rules sought, endearings / locked, locked into magically, endearings / civilize, civilize arise, endearings / through, through us all, endearings / dynamic, dynamics appearing, endearings / strandings, strandings out, endearings / sumerian, sumerian meanings and your, endearings / meanings, meanings are much, endearings / lifted, lifted gifted, endearings / through, through us all, endearings / sanskrit, sanskrit's written, endearings / sold, sold one, endearings / flying, flying into, endearings / lessons, lessons past, endearings / establish, established at last, tibetan, endearings / rapport, rapports built, endearings / inside, insides gifts, endearings / develop, developed a taste for, endearings / formations, formations followed, endearings / emeralds, emeralds moist in, endearings.

CHAPTER EIGHT

Hands, hands held, endearings / riches, riches sought, endearings / passages, passages paid, endearings / felt, felt a fellows, endearings / movings, movings meant, endearings / sought, sought out, endearings / on, on too, endearings / science, science is sent to, endearings / suggested, suggested directions, endearings / ending, ending in universal, endearings / cycles, cycles perfected, endearings / meetings, meetings historically joined in suggestions, endearings / remembered, remembered most, endearings / remember, remember yes, endearings/ 2001, 2001, endearings / 2002, 2002, endearings / 2003, 2003, endearings / freed, freed now, endearings / be, be as how, endearings / send, send a friend, endearings / fixed, fixed in states, endearings / piliings, pilings off, endearings / built, built a tower, endearings / soured, soured on babel, endearings / stretches, stretches reached, endearings / cleared, cleared these coves, endearings / dolphins, dolphins developed, endearings / researched, researched yellow, endearings / stores, stores paid, endearings / afforded, afforded recorded, endearings / lands, lands lend, endearings / seas, seas paged, endearings / extended, extended, vended, endearings / included, included your basics, endearings / exacted, eacted as expected, endearings / imagine, imagine this, endearings / our, ours these, endearings / trips, trips made, endearings / answers, answers important and invited, endearings / this, this the thus, endearings / informational, informationally endangerd and endeared / annual, annual leases, endearings / crops, crops came, endearings / steered, steered into harbors, endearings / acres, acres sold, endearings / across, across these roads, endearings / found, found a sacrifice, endearings / growing, growing colds, endearings / covertly, covertly due, endearings / erupted, erupted less, endearings / burned, burned in yearned, endearings / operated, operated simply as, endearings / crystals, crystals cost? endearings / cleared, cleared these visits too, endearings / precious, preciously yours, endearings / dreamings, dreamings dared, endearings / panels, panels poised, endearings / gone, gone the sun without, endearings / LA, LA found, endearings/ baby, baby blues, endearings / DO, DO the view, endearings / due, due a basic, endearing / paints, paints and the saints, endeared / born, born into basic humanity, endeared.

CHAPTER NINE

Children, children who simply shine in, endearings / singing, singing relaxes your endearings / sessions, sessions bilt about, endearings / somatically, somatically pleasing, endearings / relaxed, relaxed races, endearings / breathing, breathing and the snoring, endearings / released, released again, endearings / resign, resign resigned too, endearings / realigned, realigned and endeared too / assigned, assigned meant, endearings / internally, internally toured for, endearings / fields, fields follow, endearings / matching, matching positions, endearings / Christ, Christ caused, endearings / consciousconscious cures, endearings / courts, courts told, endearings / told, told too, endearings / paid, paid for, endearings / bethlehems, bethlehem's, endearings / banking, banking and spanking new, endearings / information, information reads, endearings / equals, equals sequels, endearings / fellowships, fellowships flowering, endearings / suns, susn basics, endearings /

sons, sons denied, endearings / trees, trees tied, endearings / faiths, faiths lastings, endearings / summarized, summarized slowly, endearings / forgiven, forgiven all ways, endearings / life, life led, endearings / critical, critical messages, endearings / masses, masses paidv / overflowing, overflowing waves, endearings / overtones, overtones timings, endearings / crucial, crucial alignings, endearings / tribes, tribes told, endearings / piscean, piscean paces, endearings / placed, placed in values, endearings / options, options paid too, endearings / optimum, optimum raptures, endearings / optional, optional plannings, endearings / dues, dues paid, endearings / dates, dates laid for, endearings / crafts, crafts sold without, endearings / paid, paid and the basics, endearings / proven, proven simply, endearings / capes, capes capably, endearing / scopes, scopes vista, endearings / scares, scares off now, endearings / staring, staring into, endearings / scores, score over, endearings / seeds, seeds tossed into, endearings / growths, growths lasting, endearings / icosahedron, icosahedrons reveal, endearings / parts, parts paid for, endearings / categories, categories risen, endearings / capes, caps capably, endearings / cubes, cubes made for, endearings / particles, particles posing yours, endearings / mimics, mimics mostly, endearings / minutes, minutes who hustled in, endearings / octahedron, octahedrons worn, endearings / electrons, electrons laid in circuitry, endearings / overlays, overlays views, endearings.

CHAPTER TEN

Pays, pays a basic endearing / her, hers the days endeared / wave, waves on, endearings / to, to us all, endearings / ride, ride the rockets red in, endearings / purging, purgings past, endearings / posts, posts met, endearings / for, for us all, endearings / the, the all, endearings / star, star tours, endearings / groups, groups who grow to, endearings / tetrahedrons, tetrahedrons layered, endearings / cleared, cleared off the clocks, endearings / locks, locks over, endearings / off, off the rust, endearings / hearts, hearts helped, endearings / in, in estates, endearings / place, places, endearings / gauges, gauges, endearings / correct, correct the course, endearings / lifts, lifts into, endearings / off, off the grids, endearings / now, now thens, endearings / demand, demand less, endearings / aloft, aloft is soft, endearings / electric, electric weds, endearings / grids, grids grew to, endearings / full, full on, endearings / tilt, tilted heads, endearings / merkaba, merkaba mentions, endearings / shield, shields lost? endearings / accounted, accounted for, endearings / for, for them all, endearings / and, and we win, endearings / proven, proven potions, endearings / stressless, stressless manners, endearings / operationally, operationally fueling, endearings / means, means made too, endearings / made, made the most, endearings / to, to us host, endearings / live, live the best, endearings / from, from the floors, endearings / led, led to be, endearings / to, to us freed, endearings / follow, follow ups, endearings / only, only the basic, endearings / one, onw who knew, endearings / God, God given, endearings / Christ's, Christ's receptive, endearings / Father, Father fed, endearings / love's, love's, endearings / human, human held, endearings / friend, friends felled, endearings / torpor, torpors off, endearings

/ moving, moving into, endearings / off, off the lists, endearings / children, children missed, endearings / leading, leading home, endearings / homeward, homeward go, endearings / cycles, cycles sell, endearings / logical, logical leaps, endearings / confessions, confessions written, endearings / follow, follow ups, endearings / you, you, the one, endearings.

CHAPTER ELEVEN

Reconnections, reconnections made, endearings / form, forms found, endearings / living, living levels, endearings / lovers, lover past, endearings / willing, willing to see, endearings / too, too them all, endearings / shall, shall we seed, endearings / we, we the best, endearings / weave, weave your vest, endearings / through, through a basics, endearings / metatron, metatron met, endearings / links, links up, endearings / laid, laid to rest, endearings / last, last we said, endearings / for, for them all, endearings / always, always blessed, endearings / relief, relief is left, endearings / releases, releases most, endearings / raising, raising hosts, endearings / loving, loving voiced, endearings / adore, adore the babes, endearings / spoiled, spoiled? yes, endearings / yes, yes we rest, endearings / motto, motto made, endearings / enduring, enduring shades, endearings / your samples, your samples brought, endearings / ours, ours the caught, endearings / is, is this true? endearings / the supremest, the supremest who, endearings / connection, connections given, endearings / livingness, livingness follows, endearings / straddled by, straddled by moods, endearings / forgiveness, forgiveness flew, endearings / for, for them all, endearings / past, past portals, endearings / transgression, transgressions grew, endearings / love, love the sums, endearings / is, is this all? endearings / clearing, clearing connected, endearings / squarely, squarely claimed, endearings / where, where were you? endearings / you, you the basic, endearings / live, live well, endearings / necessity, necessity offered, endearings / measured, measured wavesf, endearings / confessions, confessions paid, endearings / red, red the ruse, endearings / to blue, to blue rules, endearings / of, of these, endearings / wonders, wonders sent, endearings / ceasing, ceasing without, endearings / all, all who will, endearings / can, again, can you, endeared be? / live, live welling, endearings / in, in these sides, endearings / fondest, fondest fellows, endearings / gesture, gestures worn, endearings / won, won the others, endearings / love, love leads, endearings / letting, letting go, endearings / shoes, shoes off, endearings / step, step into, endearings / gingerly, gingerly blue, endearings / borneo, borneo basics, endearings.

CHAPTER TWELVE

When, when is the who, endearings / two, two who new, endearings / end, end the pend, endearings / who, who is yours? endearings / survives? survives again, endearings / love, love led, endearings / jumps, jumps off, endearings / joins, joins you, endearings / plays, plays the best, endearings / plans, plans made, endearings / may, may we leave? endearings / we, we are the well, endearings / weave, weave a vest, endearings / weathered, weathered in sorts, endearings / yes, yes we will, endearings

/ into, into them all, endearings / lists, lists lead, endearings / confessions, on confessions sent, endearings / need, needs met, endearings / mutual, mutual supports and, endearings / manual, manual basics, endearings / supports, supports whistle in, endearings / where, where to go? endearings / were, were you there?meandering, endearings / you, you the asked, endearings / asked, asked for sure, endearings / to, to us then, endearings / be? be? yes, endeared / right, rights read, endearings / here, here the will too, endearings / today, today is the basic, endearings / light's, light's forgiven polished, endearings / trail, trails sorted, endearings / leads, leads over, endearings / blazing, blazing trails in, endearings / open, opent he pages, endearings / these, these winnings, endearings / doors, doors closing, endearings / portals, portals posing, endearings / threads, threads breaking, endearings / throats, throats opened, endearings / valued, valued sought, endearings / believing, believing brought, endearings / reasons, reasons rested, endearings / roosts, roosts formed, endearings / releases, releases guineas, endearings / gifts, gifts made, endearings / wedded, wedded raids, endearings / waivers, waivers off, endearings / life, life sought, endearings / is, is this all? endearings / your, yours the call, endearings / liberty, liberty met, endearings / offer, offer relayed to the feeding endeared / annual, annual sparking, endearings / sparks, sparks paid, endearings / meant, meant for shades, endearings / for, for them all, endearings / ways, ways to wallow? endearings / granted, granted sabaticals too, endearings / remarks, remarks made, endearings / invade, invade less, endearings / settle, settle into your, endearings / estates, estates paid for, endearings.

CHAPTER THIRTEEN
Written, written again, endearings, endearings / lights, lights shine in, endearings / beaches, beaches now bought, endearings / tortola, tortola visions, endearings / for, for them all fed, endearings / called, called into position, endearings / globes, globes glow in, endearings / virgin, virgin voices, endearings / isles, isles swim in, endearings / christed, christed risen, endearings / domes, domes over you, endearings / gorda, gorda given your, endearings / blue, blues basics and, endearings / living, living litany for, endearings / understood, understood demons and, endearings / saint, saints outed, endearings / doors, door opens, endearings / opened, opened peaceably, endearings / croix, croix coveted, endearings / hilton, hilton harbored your, endearings / headed, headed into years, endearings / saint, saint bartholomew's, endearings / martin, martin scores, endearings / simon's, simon's sayings ", endearings" / fixed, fixed in retinues and, endearings / introductions, introductions pooled, endearings / indies, indies mending, endearings / india, india days, endearings / west, west words, endearings / antiquan, antiquan goods, endearings / a, a welcome hood, endearings / remembered, remembered the basics, endearings / tribal, tribal ranting, endearings / rant, rants out, endearings / written, written into, endearings / splendors, splendors basics, endearings / toured, toured a hollow, endearings / blues, blues seen, endearings / isled, isled while, endearing / yellow, yellow yeses, endeared / blue, blue basics endeared /

green, green guesses for these endeared / red, red roses, endeared / carribean, caribbean caresses, endearings / blessings, blessings balanced, endearings / streets, streets opened, endearings / john, john written, endearings / wrote, wrote the right one, endearings / virginal, virginal qualities can endure your, endearings / passions, passions passing, endearings / alertest, alertest lessons, endeared / engendered, engendered without your, endearings / entice, enticed more, endearings / entire, entire durations, endearings / family, family fused, endearings / visits, visits valued, endearings / endanger, endanger less, endearings / when, when you follow, endearings / followed, followed certain basic, endearings / through, through us all, endearings / least, least we knew, endearings / last, last we stood, endearings / away, away we could, endearings / knew, knew the best, endearings.

LEVEL 97: THE ENTIRE-MENTS

CHAPTER ONE
Rumi, Rumi is entire throughout the Sylvan corridor / terror, terrors as past, corridors / intensity, intensity which lasts your corridor is entire / dooms, dooms over, corridors are entire now / rooms, rooms are entire in the anchored energetics / erasures, erasured paths, energetics entired / now, now the entired, loves / prescient, prescient earthlings who hope for a focused, entirety / torn, entire in torn pieces for those, entired / wallows, wallows into new, entired / cleansed, cleansed and focused, entired / from, from the first focus, entired / numbing, numbing is obselete in entire samples, humanity / erased, erased any doubts, entired / electric, electric cures, entired / configures, configures less, entired / ruses, ruses over, hoaxes sold, entired / locale, locale should, entired / heredity, heredity held, entired / held, held on, entirely / allow, allows yes to elope, entired / locations, locations made, entirely / here, here the repast, entired / herculean, herculean effort, entired / empires, empires built, entired / build, build a notes, entired / makes, makes the manned reloads, entire / mentions, mentioned graduations, entirely / joins, joins a trend, entirely / tyrannical, tyrannical missions entired / formulas, formulas focused, entired / forgiven, forgiven and follows, entirely / affairs, affairs focused, entired / scoring, scoring came into focused, entirely / kept, kept a cost down, entired / listed, listed the natures as, entire / choirs, choirs sold, entirely / currency, currency foams, entired / posted, posted and lifted, entired / vindicated, vindicated at last, entired / urgently, urgently entire / pairs, pairs made, entire / natural, natural featured, entires / fathoms, fathoms formed, entire / creeds, creeds noticed, entire / perfumed, perfumed a potion, entirely / pulling, pulling into focused, entired / patterns, patterns posed, entires / naturals, naturals found gifts, entired / thorough, thoroughly released, entirety / rescues, rescues the single, entirety / regiments, regiments were sold for, entired ones / rules, rules past, entired / listens, listens well, entired / trees, trees topple, entired / turned, turned into enemies, entired / slows, slows up, entired / stirring,

stirring into finals, entired / duals, duals aft, entired / settled, settled a plan, entired / sets, sets back, entired / capably, capably focused, entired / amounting, amounting in accountings, entired / valued, valued your focused, entired.

CHAPTER TWO

Lame, lame excuses, entired less / shewn, shewn a blanket, entired / laid, laid open, entired / openly, openly pured, entirety / dealt, dealt apparently, entired / within, within us wells, entired / newness, newness chosen, entires / from, from this all, sum, entired/ alphabets, alphabets stand, entired / currents, currents passing, entired / tables, tables turned, entired / tablature, tablatures finished, entires / appertures, appertures aplenty, entire / foci, foci focused, entire / consistent, consistently, entire / deluged, deluged emittances, entire / doth, doth her days, entirely / powers, powers made, entire / emerge, merges, entirely / pliant, entirely given, loves / durst, entire in the rays found / featuring, entire interests in love / specials, entire the sways into love / course, entire meanings and love's elations / much, entire the districts assured for love / flashed, flashed in, entirely / cashiers, cashiers carried, entirely/ earls, earls who will, entirely / appearing, appearing nearing, entirely / materials, materials made, entirely / captions, captions which read, entirely / mostly, mostly will be, entirely / checking, checking the inflections, entirely / mirrors, mirrors matched, entirely / capri, capri since, entire / isles, isles who wisely wend, entirely through love's hearts / cures, entire cures paid to love / on, entire and the one on singing love / futures, entire futures dared, love's / spares, entire spares traded to love / legions, entire legions sured, love / gathering, entire gatherings for love / followings, entire followings as loved / interested, entire interest partied followings / legendary, entire om legends appeared / crowds, entire in the centers appearings / capable, entire capable codes / concise, entire concise codices / daily, entire in your daily ways appearances / tables, entire tables turned, appears / turns, entire turns appears / tongues, entire tongues disappears / momentary, entire momentary mosts, appear / beverages, entire beverages costed, appears / speak, entire speaks appear / sparkled, entire sprays sparkled in love / news, entire enticements and the sparkling news / clues, entire clues during appearances for love / buoyancy, entire boyancy spent in love / leads, entire leads loaded appearings / lowered, entire lowered races appeared / builds, entire builds the skilled appears / basically, entire basically appeared / threes, entire threes who appear.

CHAPTER THREE

Lavendar, entire in lavendar poses of love / inclusions, entire inclusions when loved / greens, entire greens sold loves / barrows, entire barrows paid loves / flanks, entire flanks for fine love / kept, entire kept loves appear / clean, entire cleaning loves / affairs, entire affairs exposed loved / blends, entire blends loved / daily, entire daily appears / weekly, entire weekly / willows, entire willows red in blossoms / blossoms, entire blossoms point to love / borrows, entire excitement is near appears / burrows, entire burrows blend appears / bleached, entire bleached estates appeared

/ associates, entire associates appear / options, entire options skilled / insigns, entire insigns resigned to appears / signals, entire signals meant for love / cancel, entire cancels gone appears / appears, entire appears / stores, entire stores appeared / sliced, entire sliced rays appearing / clauses, entire clauses appeared / dashing, entire dashing appears / days, entire days sold / entirety, entire in entirety for appertures / formulas, entire formulas sold to love / clutched, entire clutched meanings loved / curling, entire curlings loves / clashed, entire clashed pays loves / deepens, entire deepens loves / data, entire data sold to love / fun, entire funs loves / patrons, entire patrons rose for loved ones / cupids, entire cupids and cures for few loves / dates, entire dates sold loves / pilots, entire pilots spoused loves / turnings, entire turnings about loves / simply, entire simply in love / motors, entire motors built loves / stores, entire stores sold loves / overall, entire overall then loves / suffering, entire suffering goes loved / missions, entire missions made for love / stories, entire storied told loves / fridays, entire fridays spent in love / methodology, entire methodology fed into love / similarity, entire similarity in love / stirred, entire stirred loves / oxygens, entire oxygen for loved / attrocities, entire attrocites gone loved / cured, entire cured sands loves / liberties, entire liberties bade love / rest, entire rested rays loves / samples, entire sampled in love / measured, entire measured means loves / motions, entire motions paid loved / course, entire courses laid loves / found, entire found one loved / genuine, entire genuines in love / toward, entire toward love / apparent, entire apparents and loves.

CHAPTER FOUR

Cushioned, entire cushioned and the thrilling love / platforms, entire platforms for the final loves / pearls, entire pearls and firming loves / nationally, entire nationally inside love / ranked, entire ranked loves / opportunity, entire opportunity for love / carried, entire carried ons loves / cables, entire cables and the sampled loves / casts, entire cast in aways loves / overtly, entire overtly sured love / along, entire along stays loved / leading, entire leading pages loved / ladders, entire ladders red loved / jacob's, entire jacob's fed love / trails, entire trails built love / 10, entire 10's who have loved / times, entire times paid loves / carrying, entire carrying rays loved / on, entire on the friendly loves / followings, entire followings into love / these, entire these registrations for love / cuts, entire cuts due loved / winds, entire winds spinning loved / welcomed, entire welcomed ones loved / sephiroth, entire sephiroth blended loves / trails, entire trails built loved / walks, entire walks made loves / carried, entire carried ons loved / striking, entire striking goes loves / steps, entire steps laid loved / freedom, entire freedoms bought loved / unto, entire unto light lends loved / purest, entire purest goes loves / fashions, entire fashions made loved / welling, entire wellings up loved / warrants, entire warrants paid loves / worthless, entire worthless refused loved / learnings, entire learnings meant loves / locations, entire unto the ends, loved / leading, entire ends loving / without, entire without? ends today / leaning, entire leanings gone / lopings, entire lopings long / sturdiness, entire sturdiness built / longs, entire longs due / learns, entire learns to be / stares, entire stares past / sorts, entire sorts arced into / smallest, entire smallest leaves / escaped, entire escaped your dues / flexes, entire flexes fled / between, entire betweens gone fueled / minutes, entire minutes paid for love / fallows, entire fallows spades to love / flairs, entire flairs sold to love / forming, entire formings gladed, love / minutes, minutes follow love / transcends, entire transcends begin love / fashions, entire fashions folds loved / fixed, entire fixed events, loved / bliss, entire bliss / ascends, entire ascends / followings, entire followings / fixtures, entire fixtures.

CHAPTER FIVE

Formal, entire in the formals / fertile, entire fertile valleys behold / former, entire former sparks engaged / fused, entire fused lines / impaired, entire is impaired in loss / sterile, entire sterile accomodates lost / few, entire few who knew the lost / means, entire means made too, love / living, entire living loves / healing, entire healing caused / mortals, entire mortals paid / muse, entire muse laid to love / license, entire license given, loves / stared, entire stared into lights / ashen, entire ashen forgiven, loves / ascends, entire ascends begin, loved / primitive, entire primitive gone, loves / simple, entire simple plans, loved / planned, entire planned pilots loves / pilots, entire pilots made, loved / planes, entire plane sbuilt, loves / peels, entire peels / greened, entire greened eventuals / gotten, entire gotten nuptials, the groom Christed / gifted, entire gifted license to love / portices, entire portices built for love / faded, entire faded raids loved / pitched, entire pitched events loved / plenty, entire plenty / formed, entire formed / allegiances, entire allegiances / triple, entire triples / crowns, entire crowns / currency, entire the currency / includes, entire includes / living, entire living events / followings, entire followings built / spent, entire spent here / daring, entire daring estates / fashionable, entire fashionable forgives / cases, entire cases list / parallels, entire parallels focused / treatments, entire treatments due / mortal, entire mortals paid / words, entire words forgiven / sounds, entire sounds included / soothed, entire soothed / greeks, entire greeks claimed / hero, entire hero days / spoils, entire spoils portrayed / gone, entire gone to clues / gaits, entire gaits lapsed / trusted, entire trusted stands / stirring, entire, entire stirring events / grandstands, entire grandstands past / stages, entire stages built / spaced, entire spaced rates / means, entire means made / captains, entire captains told / stages, entire stages sold / stolen, entire stolen wages / wings, entire wings spread / faceted, entire faceted gifts / rockets, entire rockets lipped

CHAPTER SIX: rated, entire rated groups / fated, entire fated / faded, entire faded / thrones, entire thrones thronged / thronging, entire thronging forgives / singing, entire singing licensed / licensed, entire licensed singings / drones, entire drones past / delicate, entire delicate tissued / tissues, entire tissues last / missions, entire missions formed / peaked, entire peaked / positive, entire positive gifts / triumphs, entire triumphs paid attention / narrow, entire narrow streets released / streets, entire streets

paved / further, entire further due / brilliance, entire brilliance meant / material, entire material sent / gains, entire gains fed / attendant, entire attendant ones / numbers, entire numbers matched / dealing, entire dealings due / tubes, entire tubes / calmly, entire calmly said / claimed, entire calmed / metals, entire metals paid / tahoe, entire tahoe blues / lassitudes, entire lassisitudes / arrowed, entire arrowed plates / minx, entire minx shifted / tributaried, entire tributaried folds / mountains, entire mountains ranging up / ranged, entire arranged ranged / flashes, entire flashes focused / held, entire held up / written, entire written clips / tablets, entire tablets finished, loves / caught, entire caught up / holds, entire holds / tables, entire tables turned / placed, entire placed evidence / faceted, entire faceted ones / harmless, entire harmless helds / joining, entire joinings given / jurisdictions, entire jurisdictions linked / formed, entire formed habits / harmful, entire harmful glued / plagues, entire plagues past / painted, entire painted faces / acts, entire acts given / sealed, entire sealed events / machina, entire machina poised / rules, entire rules raid / flanks, entire flanks followed / further, entire further stands / abysses, entire abysses bolt / foiled, entire foiled goes / deployments, entire deployments meant / scenic, entire scenic gates / highways, entire highways posted / plunge, entire plunges in / dares, entire dares dues / chasms, entire chasms.

CHAPTER SEVEN

Founded, entire founded / lifelong, entire lifelongs established, love / oceans, entire oceans lined of love / seals, entire seals / diaries, entire diaries written / written, entire written escapades / fame's, entire fame's foundries / unfold, entire unfolded intents / dreams, entire dreams and the landings loved / offered, entire offered and the lusters loved / made, entire made / freely, entire freely written / alert, entire alerted / alternate, entire alternates reach love / panels, entire panels laned / apt, entire apt for love / curtails, entire curtails only olds / curfews, entire curfews past / musically, entire musically lunges / kins, entire kins made / make, entire make waves / mentions, entire mentions given / for, entire for the hired / former, entire former pages / ways, entire ways wielded / welcomed, entire welcomed / advance, entire advanced / homes, entire homes last / to, entire to love / hero, entire hero made / healed, entire healed intents / aspects, entire aspects emblazoned / prophets, entire slogans "prophets" / placed, entire palms placed / intelligence, entire intelligence jumps / forms, entire forms found / captives, entire captives, Babylon / lured, entire lured to love / about, entire about love / thundering, entire thundering sorts loved / thrusts, entire thrusts past old loves / thirsts, entire thirsts paid / paid, entire paid truths / followings, entire followings follow / pulled, entire pulled a part / into, entire into love / legally, entire legally sent / fluid, entire fluid motions / modalities, entire modalities fed / motifs, entire motifs purged / positive, entire positives sold / amounting, entire amounting caused / too, entire too, love / shall, entire shall we love / we, entire we / gather, entire gathered / rivers, entire rivers reaped / deep, entire deepens love / stars, entire stars / wides, entire wides

/ others, entire others / sided, entire sided / a, entire a lines / milky, entire milky blinds.

CHAPTER EIGHT

Way, entire ways / the, entire the flared / light, entire lights on / streams, entire streams fed / staying, entire staying loves / standards, entire standards / spanned, entire spanned / steady, entire steady / stills, entire stills / species, entire species / spools, entire spools / stranded, entire stranded / trusts, entire trusts built / sturdy, entire sturdy fields / squadrons, entire squadrons reap / materially, entire materially freed / successed, entire successed grains / standards, entire standards gooved / chosen, entire chosen modualr words / established, entire established visits to love / aims, entire aims gained / fulfilled, entire fulfilled friendships / arrivals, entire arrivals into love / pads, entire pads loaned / floating, entire floatings into / pours, entire pours / kept, entire kept falls / intrigued, entire intrigued risen / ransoms, entire ransoms paid / laid, entire laid events / paid, entire paid visits / pert, entire pert alerts / threats, entire threats made / treatise, entire treatise found / written, entire written arrivals / survival, entire survival skills / sugary, entire sugary roads / suites, entire suites paid / optional, entire optional gifts / operational, entire operational lifts / sullen, entire sullen past / commands, entire commands made / counted, entire counted on / once, entire once said / leads, entire leads lost / measured, entire measured amounts / silences, entire silences sold / matched, entire matched dates / again, entire agains / leading, entire leadings overt / trends, entire trends as sent / allowed, entire allowed forms / formations, entire formations / keys, entire keys / are, entire are the hired fluidity/ coded, entire coded / for, entire for the flowering loves / into, entire into love / entry, entire entry / our, entire our loves / exceptional, entire exceptionals / brides, entire brides / appeared, entire appeared near love / energetically, entire energetically and gifted for love.

CHAPTER NINE

Specials, entire specials sold / spoiled, entire spoiled / willing, entire willing / plays, entire plays / paying, entire paying divides / codes, entire codes read / priced, entire priced gates / delays, entire delays forwarded / functions, entire functions / fashions, entire fashions for love / missions, entire missions rented / priced, entire priced codes / precociously, entire precociously due / poignant, entire poignant views / purple, entire purple rays / spice, entire violet spiced / lanes, entire lanes / wellness, entire wellness / modern, entire moderns / made, entire made fuels / willing, entire willingness / reigns, entire reigns paid / along, entire along leaders / licensed, entire frequency shifts / paths, entire paths to love / pleas, entire pleas to love / randomly, entire randomly keyed, loves / traded, entire traded days / timed, entire treated / trendy, entire in trendy rays / treats, entire treats fed to love / existing, entire existing lights / extant, entire extant / allowed, entire tops the allowed / coves, entire coves prayed for love / purple, entire purple poses / orange, entire orange sprays / green, entire green days / stones, entire stones turned / rocks, entire rocks fed /

crystals, entire crystals burned / banked, banked into those who are entire / shores, shores over those who are entire / docks, docks built are entire / pleasures, pleasures entired / boats, boats blown, entire / basics, basics flow, entirely / taught, taught to be, the entire / here, here the said is "entire" / often, often fed, the entire / enough said, the entire / daily, daily intrigues with the entire / durations, entire durations and the lapsed entirety / keyed, keyed and fed, the entire / into, into these entire / computer, computers kept, entire / strengthened, strengthened and entire / resolves, resolves are entired / solved, solved an entire notion through love / suggestions, suggestions cured, entirely / formed, formed in the entire / foundations, foundations fed are entire / grew, grew into entire fades / beliefs, entire beliefs for love.

CHAPTER TEN

Healings, entire healings spent / burst, burst through those who are entire / worlds, entire worlds collide / masterfully, entire and the masterfully fled / blush, entire blushing greats / hale, all hale, those who are entire / touching, touching the entire / news, news is led through the entire squadron / hurtle, hurtle past the entire gateways for love / winsome, winsome and due those entire / comets, entire, comets entire end / bopp, entire bopps past love / comrades, entire comrades last loved / cupids, entire cupids prepared loves / appear, entire appeared love / caring, entire caring stares loved / masterfull, entirey masterfully made loved / for, entire for the finals loved / flowing, entire flowing natures loved / casts, entire casts paid loves / playful, entire into those who are, playful / stars, stars filling the entire skies / buoyant, buoyant basics and those who are entire / babies, babies who are entire / steep, steep the stairs to those entire / hours, hours paid are entire / over, over them all, entire / bethlehem, bethlehem sold as entired / shores, shores paid visits entirely / deepening, entire deepenings directed / steepened, entire inserted red directions / hours, hours elapsed entirely / stables, stables likened entirely to horses fed love / debates, entire debates defeated / ranging, ranging as resurrected, entirely / again, again said, "entire" / offered, offered up entirely, love / matched, matched paces as entired / positions, positions hired entirely/ won, won one entired / when, when do you due your entirest friendships / mast, entire masts sent, love sails / offers, entire offers sent into love / asking, entire asking events / where, entire bathed in love / tallest, tallest entire trees / trees, entire trees fed to love / whom, whom you know as entire / how, how to see, entirely / territory, territory as fixed and entire / simply, simply said "entire" / across, across the entire mountains of love / songs, songs entire and the final fixed positions of love / dealt, dealt an entire facet of love / hushed, hushed and the world rules entired / hearts, hearts imply entire / singing, singing signals those entire / flushed, flushed and finally, entire / mutually, mutually mature and entire / vastness, vastness follows those who are entire / strung, strung along the hopeful shores entire / desserts, desserts eaten, verbally blue and entire / across, across these cores entire / miles, miles into those whales entire.

CHAPTER ELEVEN

Multitudinous, multitudinous and entire / furtive, furtive for these entireties / secretive, secretive gestures as entired / maximums, maximums paid are entire / memorized, memorized your mantras entirely / pallets, pallets fixed and entire / swirled, swirled adjacently, entire / colorfully contradicted, entirely / mystical, mystical motions are entire / aborts, aborts planned, entires / swords, swords splashed, entirely / gangs, gangs break entirely / fishing, fishing and a focused entirety / boated, boated basics, entired / carryings into those entired / species, species spatial for those entired / excess, excess focus can last, entirely / living is dear, entired / licensed and located as entire / often fed, entirely / pureness posted, entired / simple, simple as entire / dashing, dashing daily, entire / occurs, occurs severally, entire / felt, felt a focus in, entires / placements, placements and posted entirely / fundamentals, fundamentals ranging as entire / millions, millions made, entire / detailed, detailed durations and these entire / cities, cities caressed as entire / carriages, carriages courted, entire / carried, carried credibly into these entires / forth, forth and the finally, entire / matching, matching those who are entire / suggested, suggested suggestions as those entire / matches, matches anothers entire stages / made, made the most, entirely / commitments, commitments coming, entire / classically, classically well in entire / sampled, sampled respects for those who are entire / examples, examples ampled, entire / casually, casually focused and entire / leapt, leapt entirely / peers, peers seated, entirely / repeated, repeatedly built, entire / currency, currency made and entire / kept, kept sure and entire / cashing, cashing into those entire / in, in us all, entire / currents, currents and the cuases entired / lakes, entire and the lakes told, "love" / shall, shall we travel to the entire chain? loves / we join, we join in as entire / the fish, the fish fed to those entire / for, for us all, entire / fondest, fondest retiring, entired / dates, dates given, entire / longest, longest whistling, entires / within, within us registers, entires / winning, winning your positions entired / willows, willows and the fellows entired / for, for us all, an entire spell / eternal, eternal the lease upon this entire chain / leases, leases expire, entire.

CHAPTER TWELVE

Nets, net established are entire / of, of those who said "entire" / those, those equivalents for the entire / who, who said "entire?" / daring, daring and entired / insecurities, insecurities for those entired / which, which and the whistling entired / last, last and the final entires / watchfully, watchfully fed and entire / well, well lit, entire / tread, tread temples, entired / operationally, operationally sure as entired / mystically, mystically cured and entire / maternally, maternally measured as entire / motioned, motioned aspects as entire / formed, formed generality as entired / best, best basics and entires / reocurring, reocurring entireties / dozens, entire and the dozens sent into love / offered, entire offered eclipses for love / bask, bask into those who are entire / masterfully, masterfully measureable and entire / red, reds and the roses entired / ripenings, ripenings windows are those who are entirest / windows, windows as said "entire" / worlds, worlds

copied entire, entire, entire / tragically, tragically as sent and entire / lighted, lighted and spent as entire / loving, loving specials are entire / leads, leads split and entire / latchings, latchings spatial and entire / money, entire into the money / settled, settled on entire money pools / spaces, entire spaces and those willows led / sold, entire sold graces and pillows on pools milk white with love / features, entire features fixed / smattered, smattered and the matters entire in love / courted, courted hires and entires / fleshly, fleshly folds who are entire / held, helds and those entire / geometry, geometry joins those entired / geometrics, geometrics entire to love / clashed, clashed entirely and the sizes for love / graphics, graphics grew entirely near love / joyous, joyous is the simple entire / embraces, embraces allowed and entire, entire / simply, simply spoken, "entire" / trains, trains and the risen entire / travel, travel into those who are entire / railroads, railroads softened entirely / ridden, ridden the respects for thos entired / reaping, reaping the benefits for those entired / benefits, benefits as sold, entirely / listed, listed riskings entired / leads, leads blazing entirely / long, entire into the long ways / shouted, shouted and fed thee, entires / delivery, delivery made is entire / goals, goals glowing, entire / won, won a whistling, entire / compare, compare those, entire / kept, kept inside, entire / singly, singly those who are entire / subtle, subtle singing as entire.

CHAPTER THIRTEEN

Flesh, flesh as entire / wound, wounds over, entire / riddles, riddles finished, entire / roads, roads ridden, entire / spare, spare spaces, entired / signed, signed into the entires / stints, stint out then, entire / extended, extended mansions and the entire / rides, rides over all, entire / singles, singles shingled for the entire / ashore, ashore sported and entire / meetings, meetings made for those, entire / into, into spaces and the entire / suns, suns sold into the entire / settle, settle into yours, entire / settlements, settlements made are entire entire / abide, abide basic to the entire / for, for us all a focused, entire / as, as said "entire" / fitting, fitting focused and entire / circumferences, circumferences financed and entire / sourced, sourced listings and entired / sank, sank into signals and the entire / methods, methods material and entire / short, shortest and entire / organized, organized basics for the entire / initially, initially due and entire / grows, grows and the growths and the entire / as, as as sent for the entire / joined, joined as said "entire": / collides, collides are curative and entire / journeys, journeys and the entire / inside, insides registry for those who are entire / and, and essentially entire / initally, initially basic and entire / ran, rans and the strainings entire / pierced, pierced pencils in the entire / the, the who knew, the entire / light, light led entirely / brocade, brocaded and parked entirely near love / of, of those who are entire / earth's, earth's an entirety / empires, empires into an entire cultural expire / and, and the Buddha entire into love / founded, founded into funded entirety / an, an aspect for the entire / organically, organically cured and entire / farming, farming a funding for the entire / folded, folded features for the entire / repetitive, repetitive surges into the entire / mantra, mantra maxed and entire / syllable, syllables signal your entires / won,

won an entire experience in love / one, entire one and the done, loved / all, alll in the signalled, lovings entired / will, will and the wonders who are entire / check, checks into the entire / made, made elegant throught the entire / mates, mates made are entire / paid, paid into those entire / lovers, lovers united and entire / left, left into the listed and entire / lists, lists are made and entire / lost, lost entire ways to love.

LEVEL 98: THE ELECTRIC-MENTS

CHAPTER ONE

Enoch, enoch paid, electrically / movements, movements are made, electric / zones, zones laid, electrically / towers, electric towers and loves / shoestepped, electric shoestepped into love / following, electric followings for love / seductive, electric and the seductives formatted for love / headed, electric and the headed forms for love / for, electric for the fellows for love / bliss, electric bliss into love / reports, electric reports and the stunnings on love / respectful, electric respectfully spent on love / applase, electrical events end, loved / placed, electrically loved / grids, electrically lured / articipation, electric anticipation begets love / forgotten, elect, electrically forgotten, loved / lapse, electrical lapses over, ends / rest-full, rest-full, electrically / passovers, electrical passovers into love / completed, electrically completed inside love / dedications, electrical lures dedicated for love / rites, electric and the rites for love / jewish, electric, electric and the jewish in love / evolution, electrical evolutions for love / treasures, electric and the treasures blued / rights, electric rights and the hu-mans / jays, electric jays outrageous to God / joins, electric joins dedicated for God / wristed, electric and the wristed Gods / repeals, electric and repeals off, love / delights, electric delights of love / parental, electric parental owned individually and loved / grands, electric grands and the randoms loved / estimate, electric estimates ended in love / ego, electric ego over / celebration, electric celebrations end / reface, electric refaced / matlers, electric matters blend / self, electric self / levels, electric levels lanced / made, electric made / employ, electric employ joined / stipulated, electric stipulations / imitations, electric imitations / purpose, electric purposes / sits, electric sticks sit / bodhisatva, electric bodhisatva ending / implore, electric implores and the situations last, ends / your, electric yours / dreams, electric dreams blend / kahuna, electric kahuna land / joining, electric joinings / stranded, electric strandeds / meditative, electric meditatives / welcome, electric extras welcomed / placed, electric placed jewels for love / hearts, electric hearts bend / kali, electric kali shrugs, love / school, electric schools loved / near, electric nears and loves / loins, electric loins tuned to love / beyonds, electric beyonds end, loved / pens, electric pens write, love.

CHAPTER TWO

Please, electric and the pleased / go, electric / inner, electric / placed, electric / relate, electric / new, electric / passes, electric / mountains, electric / peace, electric / home, electric / meation, electric / stocks, electric / past, electric / eternally, electric / predeliction, electric / seals, electric / final, electric / encyclopedic, electric / patterns, electric / zone, electric / steps, electric / deep, electric / mystery, electric / your, electric / placed, electric / ripened, electric / matched, electric / key, electric / dap, electric / respect, electric / joins, electric / levels, electric / 3, electric / respect, electric / current, electric / poses, electric / pyramids, electric / driven, electric / wealthy, electric / channels, electric / deep, electric / well, electric / leaving, electric / cardates, electric / centered, electric / within, electric / chosen, electric / creatinely, electric / spaces, electric / bulletins, electric / heal, electric / hurling, electric / wonders, electric / beings, electric / wholeness, electric / services, electric / trees, electric / bones, electric / units, electric / strobes, electric / meanings, electric / broken, electric / treasures, electric / incarnate, electric.

CHAPTER THREE

Namaste, electric / publish, electric / lights, electric / teaching, electric / teach, electric / yearning, electric / cares, electric / infusions, electric / employ, electric / smiles, electric / aecclerates, electric / evolves, electric / learn, electric / casmic, electric / spirits, electric / placed, electric / matrix, electric / lifted, electric / in, electric / layers, electric / of, electric / light, electric / links, electric / lip, electric / lesbos, electric / yearns, electric / central, electric / calls, electric / made, electric / connect, electric / turbay, electric / to, electric / ophanim, electric / metation, electric / kabbalais, electric / page, electric / burns, electric / in, electric / light, electric / record, electric / for, electric / flight, electric / has, electric / found, electric / purchase, electric / in, electric / standard, electric / surmise, electric / teaching, electric / cores, electric / keyed, electric / apply, electric / antobiographical, electric / contented, electric / books, electric / title, electric / titles, electric / mysterious, electric / realize, realized, electric / rates, electric / efficient, electric / expedite, electric / effective, electric / rays, electric.

CHAPTER FOUR

Spaces, electric / coils, electric / requiremeats, electric / paids, electric / opened, electric / elective, electric / past, electric / looped, electric / gates, electric / interrogate, electric / leads, electric / drop, electric / cued, electric / initiates, electric / true, electric / transgress, electric / is, electric / lands, electric / enjoy, electric / love, electric / actual, electric / clearest, electric / fix, electric / change, electric / in, electric / core, electric / allowes, electric / permanent, electric / dimsillle, electric / information, electric / mentioned, electric / passably, electric / potent, electric / cell, electric / matrices, electric / matrix, electric / purged, electric / blawatsgy, electric / begins, electric / centuries, electric / empoeres, electric / embody, electric / begins, electric / copyrights, electric / written, electric / recived, electric / a, electric / light, electric / clirmicle, electric / the, electric / star, electric / arotums, electric / is, electric / activity, electric / deed, electric / until, electric / light, electric / reaches, electric / maxium, electric / soar, electric / how, electric / sure, electric / make, electric / mark, electric.

CHAPTER FIVE

Far, electric / will, electric / committed, electric / reaches, electric / deftly, electric / into, electric / missions, electric / rich, electric / kept, electric / intact, electric / ones, electric / millions, electric / miles, electric / appalachian, electric / chair, electric / defies, electric / explain, electric / balds, electric / parks, electric / streems, electric / tribnty, electric / breached, electric / opens, electric / string, electric / amphihias, electric / releases, electric / affairs, electric / curred, electric / curres, electric / rehearsed, electric / light, electric / talks, electric / only, electric / always, electric / often, electric / too, electric / love, electric / let, electric / us, electric / be, electric / delined, electric / into, electric / these, electric / heartful, electric / erased, electric / sky, electric / talks, electric / ret, electric / only, electric / flows, electric / blood, electric / blues, electric / fur, electric / views, electric / stay, electric / trail, electric / music, electric / pulse, electric / cords, electric / strum, electric / impact, electric / prosous, electric / potintal, electric / bag, electric.

CHAPTER SIX

Might, electric / is, electric / won, electric / trade, electric / heaven's, electric / here, electric / where, electric / are, electric / your, electric / exceptional, electric / heroes, electric / often, electric / in, electric / light, electric / lipping, electric / reply, electric / god, electric / moses, electric / elijah, electric / the, electric / prophets, electric / the, electric / precursors, electric / adhesene, electric / links, electric / amounted, electric / to, electric / pens, electric / parented, electric / chance, electric / wellest, electric / friends, electric / creeks, electric / happend, electric / tribates, electric / moode, electric / rivers, electric / occupy, electric / moons, electric / blinks, electric / blink, electric / strems, electric / fairest, electric / bans, electric / lift, electric / hereas, electric / planting, electric / love, electric / on, electric / belly, electric / graham, electric / charlotle, electric / center, electric / youth, electric / hung, electric / worthy, electric / beatitudes, electric / confuss, electric / wirce, electric / mounts, electric / sermons, electric / matureity, electric / wins, electric / banks, electric, electric, electric.

CHAPTER SEVEN

Cirically, electric / special, electric / 8, electric / found, electric / raphael, electric / tobithus, electric / 12, electric / 15, electric / gabriel, electric / luke, electric / 1, electric / 19, electric / micheal, electric / revelation, electric / 12, electric / 7, electric / pricipal, electric / principle, electric / station, electric / salons, electric / federal, electric / courts, electric / agree, electric / basic, electric / humor, electric / rights, electric / includes, electric / probe, electric / people, electric / fruits, electric / jabille, electric / circling, electric / eclicpse, electric / beyond, electric / blance, electric / burst, electric / annoy, electric / without, electric / registration, electric / reollet, electric / refers, electric / directives, electric / superoir, electric / quality, electric / ashen, electric / without, electric /

clover, electric / pipection, electric / shall, electric / we, electric / find, electric / the, electric / peace, electric, electric / within, electric / i, electric / done, electric / say, electric / frog, electric / flown, electric / emplore, electric / youth, electric / in, electric / raying, electric / hardiness, electric.

CHAPTER EIGHT

Hanks, electric / flip, electric / traced, electric / interiors, electric / places, electric / placesment, electric / powered, electric / inside, electric / central, electric / please, electric / ports, electric / pathways, electric / bliss, electric / a, electric / silent, electric / awarenesss, electric / recovering, electric / visions, electric / geography, electric / speaks, electric / images, electric / leak, electric / ptolemic, electric / imagines, electric / cultural, electric / ingredient, electric / absolute, electric / fine, electric / correlations, electric / purest, electric / pure, electric / blanced, electric / effect, electric / effective, electric / fasions, electric / felt, electric / badger, electric / imaged, electric / lemon, electric / ginger, electric / essence, electric / assignations, electric / philosoply, electric / uses, electric / harem, electric / provocative, electric / casttes, electric / florence, electric / today, electric / stretched, electric / manuals, electric / obsessed, electric / constant, electric / solved, electric / appadling, electric / origins, electric / placements, electric / fascinate, electric / echos, electric / clues, electric / play, electric / love, electric / argue, electric / wave, electric.

CHAPTER NINE

Imagined, electric / essentially, electric / signals, electric / exact, electric / pasitions, electric / perfect, electric / symmetry, electric / begun, electric / development, electric / western, electric / hills, electric / overtones, electric / reaction, electric / do, electric / due, electric / to, electric / a, electric / persistent, electric / need, electric / for, electric / stimulation, electric / are, electric / you, electric / well? electric / decribe, electric / discuss, electric / years, electric / of, electric / neglect, electric / have, electric / touched, electric / in, electric / 2, electric / ways, electric / observe, electric / the, electric / path, electric / of, electric / precision's, electric / sourse, electric / a, electric / whole, electric / empire, electric / of, electric / leading, electric / invention, electric / mention, electric / place, electric / for, electric / a, electric / blead, electric / of, electric / love, electric / divine, electric / essence, electric / surfaced, electric / true, electric / to, electric / love, electric / door, electric / well, electric / today, electric / i, electric / saw, electric.

CHAPTER TEN

A, electric / vision, electric / of, electric / love's, electric / confusion, electric / for, electric / life, electric / &, electric / a, electric / geyser, electric / of, electric / memory, electric / invited, electric / me, electric / to, electric / stand, electric / in, electric / patient, electric / delivery, electric / of, electric / love's, electric / mentioning, electric / &, electric / a, electric / patent, electric / interest, electric / in, electric / confussed, electric / extracts, electric / of, electric / annual, electric / means, electric / &, electric / a, electric / singal, electric / has, electric / reached, electric /

momentous, electric / flux, electric / memorable, electric / for, electric / fortunes, electric / relaxed, electric / stories, electric / told, electric / and, electric / lessons, electric / learned, electric / as, electric / simply, electric / suggested, electric / happy, electric / ways, electric / apply, electric / &, electric / the, electric / inflex, electric / of, electric / notions, electric / allow, electric / for, electric / a, electric / peu, electric / filled, electric.

CHAPTER ELEVEN
With, electric / loving, electric / souls, electric / aloft, electric / through, electric / passion's, electric / breath, electric / &, electric / an, electric / annnual, electric / plan, electric / for, electric / humnity's, electric / stretch, electric / often, electric / fed, electric / in, electric / planned, electric / intentional, electric / of, electric / a, electric / committed, electric / trance, electric / broken, electric / praps, electric / out, electric / sights, electric / included, electric / for, electric / fortune's, electric / reap, electric / &, electric / the, electric / keeping, electric / in, electric / of, electric / outted, electric / replieds, electric / the, electric / cries, electric / for, electric / help, electric's electric / sustain, electric / may, electric / we, electric / simply, electric / be, electric / enthusiastic, electric / for, electric / affluent, electric / means, electric / measure, electric / less, electric / without, electric / &, electric / the, electric / mirth, electric / of, electric / a, electric / mistaken, electric / inclusion, electric / grown, electric / well, electric / power, electric powers on.

CHAPTER TWELVE
Through, electric through us / within, electric withins / atmospheric, electric atmospherics / to, electric to / heart's, electric heart's fused / etenity, electric eternity / menopause, electric menopaused / love's, electric love's ways / gales, electric gales tossed / spend, electric spendings / the, electric the ways / electric, electric electrics / may, electric may we / we, electric we are / cedes, electric cedes us / praise, electric praised / flaws, electric flaws / a, electric a luring potion / feast, electric feasted / chosen, electric chosens / clear, electric clears / &, electric & then / of, electric of / as, electric as / paths, electric paths poured / increase, electric increasing / foreign, electric foreigns loves / linked, electric linked lovers / to, electric to these loves / love, electric keepers loved / substance, electric substances / to, electric to naked truths / love, electric to a love / engineer, electric engineers gifted / of, electric of these lovers / urge, electric urges splurging for love / may, electric mays weaved / the, electric the reamings / methods, electric methods for love / to, electric to / we, electric wes loved / enjoy, electric enjoys of love / septearic, electric septearics loved / purge, electric purges and them loved / all-, electric alls / ways, electric ways loved / systematic, electric systematics / monitors, electric monitors and love / motion, electric motions married / with, electric with us all / when, electric when loved / find, electric findings / listen, electric listens to Christ / meanings, electric meanings in God / we, electric enlargements for us / through, electric through us / of, of the dove loves / of, electric of these / seek, electric seekings / throats, electric throats / the, electric the / love, electric lovers / we, electric we's / vistas, electric vistas.

CHAPTER THIRTEEN
Of, electric of them all / found, electric found us / for, electric for us / all, electric alls / fondness, electric fondness for the alls, loved / rays, electric rays red, loved / loved, electric listening loves / tease, electric teases told / expense, electric expenses loved / gone, electric gone to love / sooner, electric sooner loved / of, electric of them all loved / has, electric has / to, electric to / paid, electric paid / love, electric loves / may, electric may / we, electric we / enjoy, electric enjoys to love / a, electric a quay loved / return, electric returns / simple, electric simple into love / fellow, electric fellows loved / &, electric & loved again / the, electric the wells and loves / of, electric of the grands loved / misery, electric misery over / met, electric met, love / without, electric without loves / entire, electric entires / in, electric in a tranced estate of love / plans, electric plans made for love / love's, electric love's placed in man / stood, electric stood love / pens, electric poems and the pens of man / &, electric & listening loves / forgive, electric forgiven loves / plans, electric plans and the lovings / the, electric the wells loved/ waves, electric waves found, love / forgive, electric forgives loved / have, electric have then, loves / precious, electric precious loved / of, electric of the past lovers / willing, electric willings loved / for, electric for love / eccentric, electric eccentric loved / of, electric of arc-angelic loves / seats, electric seats wired / a, electric a wires / leaps, electric leaps made / stars, electric stars / mercy, electric mercy / frotic, electric frotics / lasso, electric lassos / far, electric fars / freed, electric freed, loves / through, electric through love / nodes, electric nodes spent / kept, electric kept on / bug, electric bugs out / clog, electric clogs past / pour, electric opened pours / open, electric pens opened.

LEVEL 99: THE ELEVATION-MENTS

CHAPTER ONE
Ophanim, elevations gained, Ophanim / kept, kept an, elevation / welcome, elevation / hosts, elevation / weathered, elevation / interiors, elevation / winds, elevation / lovers, elevation / landed, elevation / well, elevation / dears, elevation / days, elevation / steerings, elevation / intensity, elevation / overtly, elevation / inside, elevation / followings, elevation / mandibles, elevation / plasters, elevation / magentas, elevation / match, elevation / means, elevation / maternal, elevation / electrically, elevation / magentas, elevation / natchings, elevation / mastery, elevation / chords, elevation / eccentrics, elevation / pages, elevation / moves, elevation / along, elevation / math, elevation / "A", elevation / vicinity, elevation / valuables, elevation / employs, elevation / thrones, elevation / "D", elevation / flowers, elevation / perfect, elevation / notes, elevation / encircle, elevation / in, elevation / chords, elevation / "C", elevation / deep, elevation / thrones, elevation / may, elevation / we, elevation / severed, elevation / entire, elevation / for, elevation / these, elevation / served, elevation / shifted, elevation / millenials, elevation / institutional, elevation / awesome, elevation / includes, elevation / restorations, elevation / rich, elevation / heirs, elevation / audibles, elevation

CHAPTER TWO

Pitch, elevation / offered, elevation / infinite, elevation / delights, elevation / measured, elevation / life, elevation / your, elevation / sword, elevation / and, elevation / this, elevation / heart, elevation / sent, elevation / one, elevation / reached, elevation / through, elevation / this, elevation / we, elevation / have, elevation / sealed, elevation / centrified, elevation / hearts, elevation / balistrade, elevation / to, elevation / brothers, elevation / united, elevation / within, elevation / the, elevation / perhaps, elevation / often, elevation / ionclusive, elevation / moods, elevation / rich, elevation / depths, elevation / accorded, elevation / measured, elevation / pitch, elevation / through, elevation / tones, elevation / inceptions, elevation / aid, elevation / equipment, elevation / found, elevation / a, elevation / taos, elevation / canyon, elevation / operating, elevation / along, elevation / this, elevation / pitch, elevation / to, elevation / love, elevation / shall, elevation / we? elevation / love, elevation / intuitions, elevation / should, elevation / questions, elevation / intuitive, elevation / sticks, elevation / violet, elevation / fancy, elevation / something, elevation / specials, elevation / spiritually, elevation.

CHAPTER THREE

Significant, elevation / shifts, elevation / arranged, elevation / gains, elevation / about, elevation / confront, elevation / fellows, elevation / indigo, elevation / confused, elevation / types, elevation / voices, elevation / interests, elevation / tells, elevation / already, elevation / present, elevation / catch, elevation / accepted, elevation / sensations, elevation / reality, elevation / communicated, elevation / schools, elevation / roads, elevation / perceptions, elevation / integrated, elevation / pasts, elevation / moments, elevation / expected, elevation / trust, elevation / lived, elevation / fields, elevation / further, elevation / comparisons, elevation / rears, elevation / hearts, elevation / sold, elevation / excitement, elevation / building, elevation / beyond, elevation / recognitions, elevation / futures, elevation / vilet, elevation / flights, elevation / visions, elevation / criticis, elevation / yellow, elevation / lock, elevation / historical, elevation / types, elevation / think, elevation / move, elevation / inside, elevation / domain, elevation / sensory, elevation / brakes, elevation / barn, elevation / legends, elevation / fascinated, elevation / mensa, elevation / lamps, elevation / leak, elevation / penland, elevation / trail, elevation / water, elevation / one, elevation.

CHAPTER FOUR

Mask, elevation / useful, elevation / use, elevation / used, elevation / opals, elevation / frail, elevation / amethyst, elevation / shelf, elevation / furls, elevation / freshen, elevation / quadritadreal, elevation / glows, elevation / formation, elevation / foods, elevation / zinc, elevation / greens, elevation / beaten, elevation / borneo, elevation / special, elevation / effect, elevation / follow, elevation / flow, elevation / inside, elevation / the, elevation / congo, elevation / basin, elevation / amazonian, elevation / risen, elevation / ride, elevation / replays, elevation / rally, elevation / roads, elevation / train, elevation / morganite, elevation / purple,

elevation / yellow-green, elevation / blue, elevation / white, elevation / black, elevation / reductions, elevation / fairs, elevation / world, elevation / rise, elevation / rose, elevation / fairy, elevation / marigolds, elevation / martins, elevation / swans, elevation / grown, elevation / magical, elevation / magi, elevation / birds, elevation / doves, elevation / sphinx, elevation / stars, elevation / bows, elevation / diamonds, elevation / crocodile, elevation / nile, elevation / river, elevation / marker, elevation / cups, elevation / flames, elevation / ties, elevation.

CHAPTER FIVE

Nineth, elevation / super, elevation / tied, elevation / turns, elevation / wings, elevation / sun, elevation / pours, elevation / achilles, elevation / typhon, elevation / tiger, elevation / tigris, elevation / carries, elevation / life, elevation / light, elevation / love's, elevation / cords, elevation / torch, elevation / dead, elevation / risen, elevation / calls, elevation / trumpets, elevation / moves, elevation / nails, elevation / pour, elevation / flights, elevation / record, elevation / slaves, elevation / scores, elevation / slavery, elevation / ended, elevation / tools, elevation / matched, elevation / wings, elevation / over, elevation / pentacles, elevation / money, elevation / chosen, elevation / worn, elevation / matched, elevation / pairs, elevation / warriors, elevation / sandles, elevation / lifting, elevation / faces, elevation / trogan, elevation / cups, elevation / sevens, elevation / joyous, elevation / grapes, elevation / surrenders, elevation / magical, elevation / star, elevation / bach, elevation / quarters, elevation / you, elevation / are, elevation / borrows, elevation / eight, elevation / chosen, elevation / loves, elevation / rights, elevation / cupful, elevation / squarely, elevation / squirrel, elevation.

CHAPTER SIX

Cranes, elevation / twilights, elevation / twist, elevation / tugs, elevation / cupicals, elevation / bought, elevation / sold, elevation / clear, elevation / clouds, elevation / scorpion, elevation / asher, elevation / ash, elevation / pyramids, elevation / horus, elevation / moons, elevation / lines, elevation / fours, elevation / lands, elevation / opportune, elevation / swords, elevation / cups, elevation / pention, elevation / finds, elevation / birds, elevation / wars, elevation / fish, elevation / held, elevation / crowned, elevation / off, elevation / master, elevation / sat, elevation / chairs, elevation / thrown, elevation / seats, elevation, elevation / owned, elevation / pictures, elevation / miracles, elevation / cards, elevation / owned, elevation / cures, elevation / hearts, elevation / lasting, elevation / ache, elevation / fills, elevation / muse, elevation / mistress, elevation / arcs, elevation / missiles, elevation / spun, elevation / waves, elevation / ridden, elevation / breast, elevation / still, elevation / slavish, elevation / suns, elevation / chains, elevation / balls, elevation / curtains, elevation / stern, elevation / stamps, elevation / stands, elevation / ruby, elevation / red, elevation / run, elevation.

CHAPTER SEVEN

Requires, elevation / aim, elevation / seventh, elevation / weights, elevation / circles, elevation / paid, elevation / ninths, elevation / owned, elevation / fifths, elevation / amount, elevation / mounts, elevation / spirits, elevation / casinos, elevation / championship, elevation / champions, elevation / trees, elevation / reaping, elevation / ways, elevation / chariots, elevation / tamed, elevation / skeleton, elevation / mixed, elevation / oasis, elevation / lions, elevation / cheops, elevation / ways, elevation / osirius, elevation / mistress, elevation / arcistrands, elevation / arrows, elevation / worldly, elevation / swords, elevation / tens, elevation / wandering, elevation / mysterious, elevation / spin, elevation / points, elevation / cherubim, elevation / twos, elevation / matched, elevation / insight, elevation / scoring, elevation / 3, elevation / insured, elevation / swiftly, elevation / move, elevation / urumium, elevation / like, elevation / pluto, elevation / feminine, elevation / grown, elevation / arcane, elevation / sacrifice, elevation / hung, elevation / drops, elevation / sixths, elevation / legs, elevation / strengthen, elevation / stands, elevation / smell, elevation / saturdays, elevation / harvest, elevation / mostly, elevation / known, elevation.

CHAPTER EIGHT

Leads, elevation / stretched, elevation / fifths, elevation / arms, elevation / lambs, elevation / stark, elevation / fires, elevation / balanced, elevation / honor, elevation / flowers, elevation / tenths, elevation / mistresses, elevation / stills, elevation / squalls, elevation / held, elevation / sands, elevation / lamps, elevation / struch, elevation / gates, elevation / sanctuary, elevation / veils, elevation / tempos, elevation / towers, elevation / stones, elevation / dazzles, elevation / rainbow, elevation / ziggurats, elevation / blanks, elevation / lightens, elevation / thunder, elevation / decbed, elevation / books, elevation / games, elevation / years, elevation / ages, elevation / packed, elevation / system, elevation / mesmerize, elevation / super, elevation / resume, elevation / superb, elevation / cupids, elevation / scenes, elevation / modern, elevation / arcane, elevation / thoth, elevation / fame, elevation / lineage, elevation / korean, elevation / structure, elevation / organs, elevation / generation, elevation / thailand, elevation / orator, elevation / oratory, elevation / family, elevation / ball, elevation / migrates, elevation / migration, elevation / mother, elevation / eves, elevation / meeting, elevation / matched, elevation / gas, elevation.

CHAPTER NINE

Maverick, elevation / rich, elevation / novel, elevation / noveau, elevation / gates, elevation / gin, elevation / rockefeller, elevation / john, elevation / saint, elevation / harmony, elevation / milarepan, elevation / more, elevation / champagne, elevation / kool-aid, elevation / creeks, elevation / crystal, elevation / measure, elevation / carry, elevation / carried, elevation / aside, elevation / miracles, elevation / carriage, elevation / steered, elevation / storms, elevation / memories, elevation / marriage, elevation / ethic, elevation / managed, elevation / moves, elevation / moods, elevation / maneuvers, elevation / mores, elevation / social, elevation / breaks, elevation / needs, elevation / nets, elevation /

societal, elevation / broken, elevation / dares, elevation / neutral, elevation / point, elevation / into, elevation / deal, elevation / pointed, elevation / pivotal, elevation / nets, elevation / metals, elevation / hilltops, elevation / driven, elevation / heal, elevation / clean, elevation / stints, elevation / burned, elevation / clucks, elevation / burned, elevation / clarify, elevation / scenes, elevation / stones, elevation / exorcise, elevation / rise, elevation / sizes, elevation / stern, elevation / marsupial, elevation / miniscule, elevation.

CHAPTER TEN

Fires, elevation / lily, elevation / greener, elevation / flashes, elevation / fields, elevation / memorize, elevation / splashes, elevation / memories, elevation / pureness, elevation / memories, elevation / burns, elevation / out, elevation / then, elevation / charged, elevation / electric, elevation / cords, elevation / ignore, elevation / facts, elevation / which, elevation / pulse, elevation / less, elevation / cling, elevation / more, elevation / to, elevation / know, elevation / cling, elevation / at, elevation / all, elevation / and, elevation / fends, elevation / mast, elevation, elevation / motions, elevation / directive, elevation / to, elevation / dross, elevation / go, elevation / lily, elevation / white, elevation / confessed, elevation / often, elevation / pures, elevation / details, elevation / angry, elevation / hostile hands, elevation / transform, elevation / tremendous, elevation / dispell, elevation / distress, elevation / swarms, elevation / memorize, elevation / earned, elevation / incarnates, elevation / deaths, elevation / deluded, elevation / safety, elevation / sets, elevation / capital, elevation / capitol, elevation / captives, elevation / copes, elevation / dross, elevation / duress, elevation / details, elevation / confessed, elevation.

CHAPTER ELEVEN

Convert, elevation / convict, elevation / affords, elevation / fuel, elevation / appeals, elevation / stealing, elevation / surges, elevation / missed, elevation / franchise, elevation / purchased, elevation / reamins, elevation / instilled, elevation / transits, elevation / confessions, elevation / roots, elevation / clinging, elevation / without, elevation / effects, elevation / pocal, elevation / vaton, elevation / plastic, elevation / news, elevation / has, elevation / made, elevation / healthiness, elevation / the, elevation / stroke, elevation / of, elevation / likening, elevation / unto, elevation / love, elevation / where, elevation / is, elevation / the softest, elevation / scan? elevation / conditions, elevation / expected, elevation / staggering, elevation / overflows, elevation / fleshly, elevation / conditions, elevation / transits, elevation / safety, elevation / planes, elevation / collide, elevation / hollows, elevation / filled, elevation / seals, elevation / suspected, elevation / pervasively, elevation / cheated, elevation / gone, elevation / staggering on, elevation / into love's, elevation / repast, elevation / at, elevation / last, elevation / a, elevation / solution, elevation / resolved, elevation / a, elevation / solvent, elevation / all's, elevation / encased, elevation.

CHAPTER TWELVE

We, elevation / securely, elevation / bisect, elevation / for, elevation / conditions, elevation / tombed, elevation / like, elevation / forgotten, elevation / forgiveness, elevation / worn, elevation / down, elevation / solutions, elevation / spurned, elevation / inner, elevation / worked, elevation / pursuits, elevation / roof, elevation / climbed, elevation / paths, elevation / transformed, elevation / deceptive, elevation / rules, elevation / related, elevation / staggering, elevation / off, elevation / into, elevation / abundant, elevation / views, elevation / endless, elevation / spatials, elevation / attached, elevation / emotions, elevation / cats, elevation / princesses, elevations / perceptions, elevation / painted, elevation / forests, elevation / musically, elevation / seeded, elevation / leaders, elevation / symbols, elevation / beginning, elevation / born, elevation / respectfully, elevation / acclaimed, elevation / exhibits, elevation / rewarded, elevation / awarded, elevation / styles, elevation / services, elevation / chiefs, elevation / kahmehameha, elevation / kings, elevation / spencer, elevation / lands, elevation / hawaiian, elevation / extend, elevation / beach, elevation / common, elevation / explained, elevatiovn / aimis, elevation / married, elevation / intentions, elevation / peoples, elevation.

CHAPTER THIRTEEN

Kahulani, elevation / aloha, elevation / kailua, elevation / kona, elevation / shores, elevation / swim, elevation / keahou, elevation / boones, elevation / bays, elevation / kealekekua, elevation / dolphins, elevation / whales, elevation / kayaks, elevation / santorini, elevation / appealed, elevation / meals, elevation / stirring, elevation / treaties, elevation / confronted, elevation / styles, elevation / figures, elevation / made, elevation / possibilities, elevation / met, elevation / destruct, elevation / nor, elevation / shall, elevation / touched, elevation / be, elevation / published, elevation / anywhere, elevation / less, elevation / than, elevation / then, elevation / hopes, elevation / precious, elevation / metals, elevation / hickory, elevation / furnished, elevation / renewals, elevation / of, elevation / a, elevation / faith, elevation / for, elevation / severals, elevation / focus, elevation / on, on, elevations of God and the goodness for love / mentionables, mentionables eventual, elevations / power, elevation for the formal powers / resigned, resigned into an, elevation / combine, elevation and the coming combinings loved / rising, elevation and the rising surging annuals for love / evolves, elevation and the evolving aptitude for love / ancient, elevation ancient of God's loves / depths, elevation and the depths, loved / carry, elevation and the carrying causes of love / steerage, steerage into these, elevations / evaporative, elevation evaporative into love / techniques, elevation and the techniques for the formal loves / flowing, elevation caused clear celebrations for love / resignations, elevations resigned / arrogantly, ask yours, elevation / peopled, peopled, elevation fed / placed, placed in causes, elevation

LEVEL 100: THE ATTITUDES-MENTS

CHAPTER ONE

Breastplates, breastplates worn, attitudes / urim, attitudes urim deep, love / adjust, attitudes are, loved / write, attitudes are written in, love / bliss, attitudes are blissed, loves / transcend, attitudes are the transcending, loves / imaged, attitudes imaged for, love / memoriams, attitudes memoriams and the causes for love / conscious, attitudes are conscious of love / memorized, attitudes are memorized through love / locked, attitudes locked out, love / supers, attitudes superficial too, love / moods, attitudes are moods for, love / shades, attitudes and the shades won, love / instincts, attitudes are instincts too, love / consciousness, attitudes and the consciousness through, love / impulsed, attitudes are impulsed with love / chosen, attitudes chosen rhyme, love / memory, attitudes memory, loves / super, attitudes are the super felt, loves / constants, attitudes and the constants for love / energies, attitudes and the enriched energies for love / when, attitudes when fed, love / thummim, attitudes are the thummim for love / love, attitudes and love / will find, attitudes will find yours, love / your, attitudes and your loves / friendly, attitudes and the friendly ones loved / formats, attitudes are the formats for love / focused, focused antidotals, attitudes / into, attitudes inside your love / giving, attitudes giving us, love / gender, attitudes and the genders joined, loves / freed, attitudes freed, love / entirety, attitudes entirety said, love / principality, attitudes are the principality of love / ends, attitudes end, love / sets, attitudes set, love / on, attitudes on too, love / selective, attitudes are selective, love / spruces, attitudes spruced, loves / pine, attitudes are the pine freed, loves / red, attitudes red, love / relays, attitudes are relayed for, love / encodes, attitudes encoded in love / greens, attitudes green rich, loved / necessary, attitudes necessary for, love / liftings, attitudes lfiting yes, loved / choices, attitudes choices for love / had, attitudes had a veined love / notes, attitudes notes and love / fish, attitudes, fine and fish lined in pools for love / sky, attitudes and the sky blue loved / who, attitudes and the who who love / is, attitudes and the is found, love / higher, attitudes are higher and loved / reconnection, attitudes reconnections and the views for love / divine, attitudes divine in love / birds, attitudes brewed, love / in, attitudes in, love / blue, attitudes are the bluest loves / gifts, attitudes gifted in love / surrender, attitudes are the surrendered loves / fly, attitudes are the flying loosens to love.

CHAPTER TWO

Seeded, attitudes are seeded and loved / we, attitudes we love / engraved, attitudes are engraved / equal, attitudes are the equal ones / friends, attitudes are the friends for love / wills, attitudes are willing yours, love / engrams, attitudes engrams and loves / codes, attitudes are codes for love / cores, attitudes cores and seeds loved / kinds, attitudes are the kinds of love / basics, attitudes are basics / crafts, attitudes crafts shores loves / where, attitudes where found, loves / all, attitudes all one, love / deja, attitudes deja due loved / vu, attitudes vu, loves / fires, attitudes fires for love / lily, attitudes lily shoes and shores loved / as, attitudes as said, loved / sounds, attitudes sounds armies for love / the, attitudes the sounds for love / sing, attitudes allowed, love / in, attitudes in sizes of loving flowers / sealing, attitudes are sealing thin loves / old, attitudes old for love / applied, attitudes are applied to love / we, attitudes we loved for love / have, attitudes have said "loved" / fort, attitudes fort fed, loves / the, attitudes the lines lipped, loves / weave, attitudes weave into love / of, attitudes of those loved / finger's, attitudes fingers loves / lakes, attitudes lakes and sandy shored, loves / michigan, attitudes for the michigan loves / sault, attitudes sault sent, love / st, attitudes st wisdomed loves / marie, attitudes are marie risen, love / may, attitudes may be loved / we, attitudes we seed for love / wind, attitudes and the windy ones, loves / up, attitudes up willed, loves / sailing, attitudes are sailing since love / your, attitudes yours loves / shore, attitudes allowed shore winds for love / for, attitudes for the final love / eternity, attitudes eternity willed, loves / fires, attitudes fires and shone love / older, attitudes older filled, loves / wages, attitudes wages and loves / pierced, attitudes pierced in love / rest, attitudes are rested for love / waged, attitudes waged, loves / respective, attitudes respective and loved / nucleus, attitudes and the nucleus of love / roads, attitudes and the roads over all one love / peaced, attitudes are peaced and loved / decide, attitudes decided on, love's / suns, attitudes suns and loves / mystery, attitudes mystery revealed for, love / regeants, attitudes regeants and the respects of love / cosmos, attitudes cosmos cured, loves / twenty, attitudes twenty willed to love / four, attitudes four wide in love.

CHAPTER THREE

Alert, attitudes alerted, love / is, attitudes is and for, love / held, attitudes held in love / inside, attitudes indirect inside love / our, attitudes ours loved / hearts, attitudes are the hearts for love / spell, attitudes spelled, love / one, attitudes and the ones due, love / we, attitudes are the we for love / initialize, initialized loves / the, attitudes the ways, loved / twice, attitudes twice spun, loves / written, attitudes written into love / emperical, attitudes emperical for loved / imperial, attitudes imperial in love / made, attitudes made to love / onto, attitudes onto love's / love, attitudes for love / where, attitudes where then, love / is, attitudes and the is for love / our, attitudes ours love's / wages? attitudes wages due, love / and, attitudes and, love / where, attitudes where done, love / the, attitudes the days and loves / ok, attitudes ik for love / surrendering, attitudes surrendering in love / glint, attitudes glint with love / stage, attitudes stages and love's / love's, attitudes are due to love / gleams, attitudes allowing us, love / gemstone, attitudes are the gemstones for love / goo, attitudes goo depthed and the sizeable sums of love / when, attitudes when due, love's / meals, attitudes meals and spilling loves / of, attitudes of love / has, attitudes, attitudes, attitudes, attitudes, attitudes, attitudes, and the has when, loved / seals, attitudes are the seals off, love / militant, attitudes militant about, love / cubes, attitudes cubes, love / include, attitudes included, love / suspect, attitudes are suspected, love / lightened, attitudes lightened up, love's / lives, attitudes and the lives for love / clash, attitudes clashed off, love / stored, attitudes stored into, love / loving, attitudes are

the lovingness of God / love's, attitudes are the love's of life / is, attitudes and the is inside love / now, attitudes are the now for love / kept, attitudes kept inside, love / in, attitudes are the in sizes loved / provinces, attitudes are the provinces for love / toward, attitudes toward us then, love / mystically, attitudes are the mystically viewed loves / near, attitudes are neared, loves / our, attitudes ours and theirs in, love / our, attitudes oured, love / meaning, attitudes meaning final loves / for, attitudes for those who love / love, attitudes are love / what, attitudes which wear what that is seen / is, attitudes and the is drawn, love / youngest, attitudes are the youngest finds for love.

CHAPTER FOUR

Year? attitudes are the yearly loved instinctuals due / metatron, attitudes are the metatrons of God / the, attitudes and the ones / oldest, attitudes are the oldest days loved / day, attitudes are days for love / the, attitudes at the thinking love / sun, attitudes are the sun found, loves / billions, attitudes billions in love / on, attitudes and the on fines loved / too, attitudes are too, love's / and, attitudes and teh dara for love / lake, attitudes lake blue, love / shores, shores and the attitudes, loved / plenty, attitudes are plenty for love / in, attitudes in, love / signed, attitudes are the signed selahs, loves / goodness, attitudes and the goodness for, love / where, attitudes around, love where led / were, attitudes are the were for love / you, attitudes and the you of, love / when, attitudes when drawn into love / we, attitudes we wear, love's / sent, attitudes are sent into love / love, attitudes love for freshened drawings / carry, attitudes carry your curings loved / who, attitudes who drew love / will, attitudes willed, love / send, attitudes send us to love / a, attitudes a long well's loves / signed, attitudes signed for love / last, attitudes lasting, love / what, attitudes which lead to what works in, love / is, attitudes and the is for love / the, attitudes the welled to, love / phased, attitudes phased up, love's / afford, attitudes afforded for love / whose, attitudes whose drew, love / the, attitudes and the the then, loved / memory, attitudes memory wise for love / when, attitudes when detailed, love / the, attitudes and the of all, loves / code, attitudes are coded and loved / price, attitudes are the price for love / lakes, attitudes and the lakes blue and loved / for, attitudes for all loves drawn into love / sale, attitudes and the sales of love / why, attitudes why ruled, love's / are, attitudes are the rays, loved / we, attitudes we use to love / peopled, attitudes peopled in love / by, attitudes by the ways loved / overlays, attitudes overlays and loves / of, attitudes of dosed, loves / loved, attitudes and the loved insures for love / good, attitudes and the goods on all loves / buys, attitudes and the buys bent for love / well, attitudes wells and steady loves / i, attitudes i sell for all loves / sell, attitudes amd the sold to, loves / should, attitudes should send us to love / soul's, attitudes soul's bled for all, loves / rights, attitudes rights sold, loves / will, attitudes willed into love / I, attitudes I will, love's.

CHAPTER FIVE

Mention, attitudes are mentioned for, love / details, attitudes and the details of all, loves / red, attitudes red on, love / with, attitudes within, love / lancing, attitudes are lancing for love / missions, attitudes are missions and loved / of, attitudes of the forward loved / lanced, attitudes are lanced in, love / elects, attitudes are elects for, love / and, attitudes and the sunny loved / the, attitudes the rest, love / reflection, attitudes are the reflections for love / learned, attitudes are learned into, love / into, attitudes and the intos loved / for, attitudes for themes of love / fellows, attitudes and the fellows loved / restive, attitudes restive in, love / notions, attitudes and the notions dealt for love / of, attitudes of the sincerest loved / how, attitudes how blue in love / reliable, attitudes reliable and assured for love / we, attitudes we dare, love / are, attitudes are the surest, love / to, attitudes to a given, love / pictures, attitudes and the pictures for love / movements, attitudes movements loved / on, attitudes on the scened, loves / screens, attitudes are the creens pared, love's / soar, attitudes aimed, soared, love / plato, attitudes plato drew into love / court, attitudes are the courts of love / house, attitudes housed and loved / if, attitudes if them, love's / sail, attitudes sailing for love / and, attitudes and scenes loved / i, attitudes i love, God's / you, attitudes are yours loved / need, attitudes are the needed, love's / a, attitudes along a dread-free love / mission, attitudes are the missions of love / mention, attitudes are mentioned and loved / the, attitudes are the sold into, loves / to, attitudes to love by / if, attitudes if paired for, love / birds, attitudes birds and loves / surrendered, attitudes are surrendered and loved / love, attitudes love drew for God / i, attitudes i will love for God's goodnesses / will, attitudes will be loved / i, attitudes i agreed to for love / agree, attitudes agree with your loves / to, attitudes to a loving agree / will, attitudes will be blessed thoroughly, God's dues / star, attitudes starring love / we, attitudes we blew for love / meet, attitudes meet us, loved / you, attitudes you dated in love / as, attitudes as sent, love / i've, attitudes i've blessed for love / said, attitudes said so, "loved" / and, attitudes and then, love / i, attitudes i warrant for love / meet, attitudes meet us near, love / forever, attitudes forever due, loved.

CHAPTER SIX

Say, attitudes say so, love / gift, attitudes gifted and loved / skate, attitudes skate through, love / ridden, attitudes ridden on, love / yes, attitudes yes when loved / living, attitudes are living for love / loves, attitudes loves drawn / loved, attitudes loved / to, attitudes to a calling love / love, attitudes are loved / loving, attitudes are loving for God / our's, attitudes our's then, loved / love, attitudes and the loves drawn / us, attitudes us welled / lives, attitudes lives and gifts / pigeons, attitudes are pigeons pured / palm, attitudes palming your loves / come, attitudes come to love / a, attitudes along a loved / forged, attitudes are forged, now / lifts, attitudes near these lifted ones / king, attitudes are the kings / risenminutes, attitudes / memphis, attitudes as spent, memphis / king, attitudes are kinged for love / riding, attitudes are riding for love / passed, attitudes are passed upong genes drawn / thrones, attitudes thrones and reams of love / a, attitudes aimed into as a loved place / writh, attitudes writh in withering vines of love / in, attitudes remove to old links and granted, ones / knowing, attitudes are the knowing for love / umbilical, attitudes umbilical

in love / cut, attitudes cut for love / marriage, attitudes marriages and cherry red love / sound, attitudes sounds and resounded loves / pounding, attitudes pounding for love / link, attitudes linked, loves / meant, attitudes meant and love / sent, attitudes sent into love / list, attitudes listed / occured, attitudes occured / and, attitudes and / to, attitudes to / made, attitudes made / the, attitudes the lapped cubes / lamb's, attitudes lamb's coded / and, attitudes and weaves / encode, attitudes encoded / occur, attitudes occured for / highway, attitudes / rent, rent paid, attitudes, attitudes / a, attitudes and a life's lists / literary, attitudes and the literary / held, attitudes held for light / for, attitudes for the mentioned likes / degree, attitudes degreed and loved / for, attitudes for final love's / open, attitudes opened and loved / fortune's, attitudes fortune's loves / scorpion's, attitudes scorpion's cured / stay, attitudes staying loved / bud, attitudes and the buds out, love / ground, attitudes and the ground wired, loves.

CHAPTER SEVEN

Stages, attitudes are these stages for love / days, attitudes are the days of love / self, attitudes and the selfs spent on love / same, attitudes are the same in love / set, attitudes are set for love / dawn, attitudes as drawn into love / tinted, attitudes are the tinted gifts, love's / in, attitudes and the in crowded, love's / lift, attitudes are lifted, love / swallow, attitudes are the swallowed loves / gifts, attitudes and the finale for love / future, attitudes are the futures of love / off, attitudes off, loved / hard, attitudes hard / softest, attitudes softest friends / price, attitudes are the price off / actors, attitudes actors and friends / dipped, attitudes dipped off / dripping, attitudes are the dripping ones / wet, attitudes are wet with love / altering, attitudes altering olds / strips, attitudes and the strips off love / into, attitudes into love / ascend, attitudes ascend / swords, attitudes swords and pends / neat, attitudes neat / may, attitudes may / we, attitudes we / cut, attitudes cut / michael's, attitudes off, michael's shores / keep, attitudes keep / into, attitudes into canyon's blued / mend, attitudes are mended / smokey, attitudes smokey too / area, attitudes and the areas of love/ ink, attitudes of inks / for, attitudes for love's blooms / depth, attitudes depths and loves / glad, attitudes glad too, love / channels, attitudes and the channels of love / your, attitudes, attitudes attributive to your loves / secret, attitudes and the secrets for love / in, attitudes and the in ones / codes, attitudes and the codes opened, love / pleasing, attitudes are the pleasing ones / areas, attitudes areas loves / permanant, attitudes are the permanent sort, love / paint, attitudes and the paint off, love / links, attitudes and the links found in love / basic, attitudes are the vauled basics for love / loves's, attitudes and the love's of God's shores / wings, attitudes and the wings into love / basic, attitudes are the basics for love / net, attitudes and the net won, love / benefit, attitudes and the benefits of light loved / of, attitudes of those who love / human, attitudes and the humans who loved / powerful, attitudes are powerful fullest loves / include, attitudes included, loved / into, attitudes into love / peach, attitudes are peachy for love / the, attitudes the wiser, loved / doves, attitudes doves and loves / decoded, attitudes are decoded to love

CHAPTER EIGHT

Has, attitudes and the has been of love / graciously, attitudes and the graciously factored loves / include, attitudes included love / octet, attitudes octets and love / measured, attitudes measured, loves / respectful, attitudes respectful of love / and, attitudes and the knows loved / knolls, attitudes are the knolls of love / our, attitudes and our loves / of, attitudes of lvoe / linville, attitudes linvilled in love / which, attitudes which end in love / gift, attitudes are the fattest gift of love / all, attitudes all when loved / arms, attitudes arms for love / reflect, attitudes reflect yours, love / our, attitudes ours, love's / rested, rested in attitudes for love / ransom, attitudes and the ransoms cured, love / whence, attitudes are the whence for love/ camp, attitudes and the camping loves / to, attitudes for to love / aware, attitudes and the awarest loved / alters, attitudes alters surest loves / sight, attitudes and the sights for love / who, attitudes who seed, love / deliver, attitudes delivered unsure to love / about, attitudes about love / sentinel, attitudes sentinel to love / to, attitudes to be given for love / all, attitudes all sent, love / moose, attitudes moose blue in love / a, a attitude changed / name, attitudes named, love's / yours, attitudes are the yours in love / where, attitudes are where you, love / little, attitudes are the little ones, loved / has, attitudes and the has beens, loved / written, attitudes written for, loves / a, attitudes, attitudes a way, loves / where, attitudes where looked into, loves / book, attitudes, attitudes, attitudes, attitudes, attitudes, attitudes, attitudes, attitudes, attitudes, books / of, attitudes, attitudes, attitudes / life, attitudes are the life lines, loves / a, attitudes, attitudes and a love / list, attitudes are listed, love / the, attitudes and the the for love / lamb's, attitudes are lamb's lined, loves / in, attitudes are the in too, love / next, attitudes are next in, love / through, attitudes through risky, loves / ascend, attitudes ascend for love / kinks, attitudes and the kinks in, love / psycholgical, attitudes are psychologically left to love / gift, attitudes and the gift for, love / hearts, attitudes and the hearts finds, loved / align, attitude sold, align, loves / links, attitudes and the links, love / across, attitudes across yours, loves / lining, attitudes are the linings under, love / links, attitudes are linked in, love / fine, attitudes and the finest, loves / wind, attitudes are the wind under, love / figure, attitudes are the figured, loves.

CHAPTER NINE

A, attitudes a way to love / redeem, attitudes are the redeeming loves / how, attitudes are the how too, loves / pen, attitudes and the pens bent, loved / lifted, attitudes are lifted for love / blast, attitudes and the blasted, loves / gain, attitudes are the gained loves / blue, attitudes blue ionic loved / sire, sire for theseattitudes / win, win your attitudes / your, your attitudes / heart, attitudes and the heart lines found, love / will, attitudes willed, loves / christ, attitudes are the christ for, love / the, attitudes the placed, love kings / king, attitudes are kings kneeling due, loves / write, attitudes are the write written loves / through, attitudes through your, loves / captivity, attitudes captivity cubed in love / showers, attitudes and the showers played for, love / a, attitudes a way, loves

/ aimed, attitudes aimed into love / is, attitudes and the is of love / loosed, attitudes;ppsed fpr, love / cast, attitudes cast into love / to, attitudes to, love / last, attitudes and the last worn, loves / speak, attitudes are speaking for, love / now, attitudes are now and them, love / played, attitudes are played for, love / her, attitudes and her loves / name, attitudes named, love / leak, attitudes are leaking, loves / funded, attitudes are funded for love / friend, attitudes and the friendly, love / found, attitudes are found in your, loves / surrender, attitudes surrender to, love / daily, attitudes dialed ions, love / adore, attitudes are adored, loves / for, for attitudes to your loves / bermuda, attitudes bermuda wise for love / ocean, attitudes are oceaned loves / monkey, attitudes are monkey mild, love / green, attitudes are green, loves / blue, attitudes are the blue loves / orange, attitudes are the orange lavendars of love / money, attitudes and the money made, God given, love / dean, attitudes and the dean paid, love / were, attitudes are the were, love / you, attitudes are you, love / the, attitudes and the sent, love / wind, attitudes and the winds of, love / of, attitudes of the sorted, loves / written, attitudes written for, love / weak, attitudes are the weakest, loves / in, attitudes are in, love / love, attitudes and the love too, God's / of, attitudes of the sorted, loves / heaven's, attitudes heaven made, love / dates, attitudes and the dates on, love / where, attitudes where forwards land, love / you, attitudes are you, love / the, the pleased, attitudes / gift, gifts made, attitudes.

CHAPTER TEN

Powerful, powerfully aloud, attitudes / streams, streams and the know, attitudes / link, linking ups antiques, attitudes / you, you and yours, attitudes / explore, explores and these operational, attitudes / find, find the others strivings, attitudes / a, a noose is off, attitudes / freedom, freedom is found, attitudes / explosion, explosions, attitudes / too, too and those who know, attitudes / and, and when we do, attitudes / when, when is the where, attitudes / capable, capable cures for your attitudes / you, plenty led to you, attitudes / soon, soon to see, attitudes / you, you and your, attitudes / line, attitudes line up, loves / whistling, attitudes whistling into, love / wins, attitudes wins and loves / words, attitudes words and friendly, loves / you, attitudes you sent, love / when, attitudes elate when, love / accords, attitudes accords and friends loved / account, attitudes account for, love / knead, attitudes are kneaded for, love / kneeds, attitudes placed, loves / melts, attitude melts, love / meeting, attitudes meeting yours, love / your, attitudes for your, loves / apparent, attitudes apparent in, love / majors, attitudes majored for, love / arcane, attitudes arcane about, love / deny, attitudes deny lessed, loves / of, attitudes of, love / transport, attitudes and the rested, loves / mostly, attitudes mostly flower in, love / dual, attitudes dualed, loves / gears, attitudes are gears for, lov / trims, attitudes and the trims, loved / mutual, attitudes mutually, loves / pistils, attitudes and the pistils on, love / growing, attitudes growing inside your, loves / date, attitudes and the dates pondered, love / to, attitudes are to, love / stem, attitudes stemmed, love / in, attitudes in, love / sent, attitudes are sent for, love / levels, attitudes and levels too, love / lasted, attitudes are lasted for, love / last, attitudes and the last wons, love / listing, attitudes are the listings for, love / play, attitudes and the plays end, love / into, attitudes are into, love / change, attitudes and the changes for, love / winning, attitudes are the winnings, loved / peers, attitudes and the peers into, love / driven, attitudes in driven, love / around, attitudes around us, love / leading, attitudes in leading, love / daily, attitudes and the daily, loves / loves, attitudes in love / dares, attitudes in dares, loves / counts, attitudes and the counts on, love / counties, attitudes in counties for, love.

CHAPTER ELEVEN

Double, attitudes apparently, loved / swallows, attitudes inside yours, love / prejudice, attitudes are planned, loves / please, attitudes gifted, love / into, attitudes are given, love / physical, attitudes intrigued, love / under, attitudes under us all, loves / above, attitudes above, love / enquired, attitudes empires enquired for, love / hires, attitudes inside, loves / duce, attitudes inside your duces, love / courage, attitudes are the courage for, love / upwards, attitudes are upwards on, love / aspire, attitudes aspire to be made, love / determine, attitudes inside your determined, love / fails, attitudes are plaid in, love / all, attitudes all made for, love / rough, attitudes are the roughest, loves / privacy, attitudes and the prices privacy bound, love / taught, attitudes are taught to, love / scripts, attitudesare the scripts to platitudes for for, love / native, attitudes are made native to love/ due, attitudes and planned loves / tatters, attitudes end, love / reside, attitudes reside in love / hath, attitudes hath matured, love / set, attitudes platitudes and love / fresh, freshens, attitudes / resilient, resilient choices, attitudes / condition, conditions simple, attitudes / tobacco, tobacco cured, attitudes / done, done then, attitudes / secrets, secrets softened, attitudes / forgoing, forgoings pleased, attitudes / obstacles, obstacles cleared, attitudes / strict, strict touches, attitudes / song, songs singing, attitudes / way, ways hosted, attitudes / to, to us all, attitudes / a, a ramp built, attitudes / path, paths made, attitudes / purpose, prupose poised, attitudes / frivolity, frivolity friends, attitudes / swept, swept up, attitudes / truth, truths told, attitudes / emptied, emptied of, attitudes / staggers, staggers in, attitudes / back, back to the basic, attitudes / women, women who've / orbits, orbits blast, attitudes / to, to us yours, attitudes / genes, genes split, attitudes / whoa, whoa now, attitudes / absorbed, absorbed one, attitudes / geared, geared up, attitudes / joined, joined into, attitudes / lack, lacks off, attitudes / material, materials paid, attitudes / gift, gifts made, attitudes / treats, terraced treats, attitudes / pentacular, pentacularly, attitudes / freed, freed ones, attitudes / form, forms fused, attitudes / wanton, wanton about, attitudes.

CHAPTER TWELVE

Peculiar, peculiar waves / wheeling, wheeling ins, attitudes / special, specials paid, attitudes / hall, halls sold, attitudes / spirit, spirits pace, attitudes / lost, lost one, attitudes / deep, deepening then, attitudes / classic, classic cured, attitudes / cost, cost off,

attitudes / tension, remember tensions shut, attitudes / bland, bland strands, attitudes / fission, fissions lost, attitudes / signals, signals costs, attitudes / turning, turning is signed, attitudes / off, off sets, attitudes / often, often then, attitudes / returning, returnings, attitudes / birds, birds basics, attitudes / in, in this all, attitudes / flight, flights into, attitudes / levels, levels placed, attitudes / freshening, freshening reaches, attitudes / paused, paused, passed, attitudes / bloods, bloods coursing / bent, bent into, attitudes / exertion, exertions count, attitudes / fruits, fruits laid, attitudes / returns, returns about, attitudes / beings, beings in, attitudes / call, calls one, attitudes / convert, converted, attitudes / love's, love's cost? attitudes / will, will yours, attitudes / we, we well, attitudes / surface, surfaced, attitudes / as, as, attitudes / the, the, attitudes / won, won one, attitudes / add, add these, attitudes / beaches, beaches bought, attitudes / walk, walks off, attitudes / to, to us them, attitudes / toss, toss the yes, attitudes / turn, turns off, attitudes / talk, talks in, attitudes / spell, spells today, attitudes / spurt, spurt abouts, attitudes / offend, offend ends, attitudes / offense, offense less, attitudes / conversion, conversion comes, attitudes / doors, doors opened, attitudes / next, next ones, attitudes / let, next let us, attitudes / course, courses laid, attitudes / dreamed, dreamed about your, attitudes / singing, singing rings in, attitudes / us, us who've, attitudes / and, and these simple, attitudes / spree, sprees about, attitudes / to, to these, attitudes / know, know one, attitudes / the, the ones, attitudes / life's, life's costs, attitudes / lightest, lightest husks off, attitudes.

CHAPTER THIRTEEN

Needs, needs met, attitudes / I, I will, attitudes / know, know them, attitudes / your, yours then, attitudes / flow, flowed, attitudes / and, and they ley, attitudes / your, yours ours, attitudes / fixed, fixed yours, attitudes / reprieve, reprieves, attitudes / withdrawl, withdrawals, attitudes / where, where then, attitudes / with, with us all, attitudes / wants, wants one, attitudes / sealed, sealed into, attitudes / sung, sung about yours, attitudes / lines, lines held, attitudes / close, close lines, attitudes / deals, deals slowed, attitudes / mutual, mutual hosted, attitudes / conclude, conclude about, attitudes / companion, companion made, attitudes / washington, washington calling / words, words woven, attitudes / strong, strong too, attitudes / ship, shop ships off, attitudes / wonder, wonders in, attitudes / fulfilled, fulfilled a chosen, attitudes / for, for them flames, attitudes / sets, sets on, attitudes / a, a days, attitudes / feature, features final, attitudes / on, on thes signals, attitudes / unchanged, unchanged notices, attitudes / pays, pays into, attitudes / dismal, dismal about yours? attitudes / within, within us, attitudes / fires, fires formed, attitudes / innocence, innocence spent in, attitudes / seals, seals off your, attitudes / into, into those, attitudes / traces, traces, attitudes / remain, remaining, attitudes / cared, cared for, attitudes / cool, cools off, attitudes / fueling, fueling costs, attitudes / panels, panels chosen, attitudes / formed, formed emotions, attitudes / vote, vote for focus, attitudes / smudged, smudged lessons and your, attitudes / swim, swim in syncs, attitudes / touch, touch another's, attitudes / appeals,

appeals the most, attitudes / memories, memories collapsed within, attitudes / fabric, fabric fuels, attitudes / repeat, repeat offenders, attitudes / misty, misty days, attitudes / internal, internal visits and these numbered, attitudes / visionary, visionary focused, attitudes / facts, facts found, attitudes / entitle, entitled and, attitudes / lean, lean into, attitudes / grips, grops one, attitudes / grow, grow an, attitudes / gentle, gentle in, attitudes.

LEVEL 101: THE ELECTIVES-MENTS

CHAPTER ONE

Fluries, fluries are over, electives / floatations, electives / flirting, electives / chosen, electives / choices, electives / created, electives / capable, electives / motions, electives / notions, electives / relations, electives / varied, electives / poses, electives / porches, electives / swung, electives / durations, electives / doted, electives / doubted, electives / flown, electives / lovers, electives / recovered, electives / reactions, electives / realtionshipped, electives / provide, electives / purchased, electives / land, electives / locations, electives / purging, electives / mergers, electives / made, electives / final, electives / focus, electives / given, electives / push, electives / through, electives / this, electives / chosen, electives / envelope, electives / for, electives / love, electives / play, electives / colors, electives / fields, electives / lordly, electives / groups, electives / choose, electives / reconnections, electives / kinetic, electives / corrections, electives / spellings, electives / spoils, electives / portals, electives / tuned, electives / purchased, electives / A, electives / lands, electives / sold, electives / others, electives / find, electives / a fitting, electives / explanation, electives / photographic, electives / chronicles, electives / journeyings, electives / laid, electives.

CHAPTER TWO

Admonished, electives / also, electives / alters, electives / apostolic, electives / adjoin, electives / appals, electives / rainbows, electives / agents, electives / adherents, electives / apathy, electives / misused, electives / mistrust, electives / adjourned, electives / anticsv, electives / anticipated, electives / antagonise, electives / GOD, Generous, Open, Delightful, Generous, electives / array, electives / arrests, electives / aroused, electives / arms, electives / limited, electives / vehicles, electives / imbibe, electives / imagines, electives / imitate, electives / migrations, electives / imitated, electives / immaculate, electives / ideas, electives / idioms, electives / imitates, electives / immaculate, electives / ideas, electives / idiom, electives / exasperative, electives / excerptive, electives / excessive, electives / examples, electives / silence, electives / silhouette, electives / simple, electives / simply, electives / simulated, electives / sills, electives / shone, electives / myriads, electives / mystify, electives / mutual, electives / mutiny, electives / motif, electives / high, electives / mortuary, electives / mores, electives / hobby, electives / hindrance, electives / hideous, electives / herds, electives / honors, electives / heroism, electives / honorable, electives / hopes, electives / hoodlums, electives / dimension, electives.

CHAPTER THREE

Hides, electives / hovers, electives / hubs, electives / surrounded, electives / expanded, electives / dictions, electives / one, electives / by, electives / literary, electives / commit, electives / who, electives/ read, electives / foes, electives / returns, electives / said, electives / is, electives / phones, electives / dove's, electives / that, electives / life, electives / detailed, electives / in, electives / urgency, electives / of, electives / life, electives / letter, electives / latitudes, electives / purged, electives / pallets, electives / burns, electives / missions, electives / urged, electives / an, electives / electrically, electives / stairs, electives / trails, electives / matrices, electives / peeled, electives / caravans, electives / anchors, electives / lest, electives / overts, electives / customers, electives / sordid, electives / sanctions, electives / allows, electives / capably, electives / urgency, electives / listings, electives / sent, electives / consent, electives / letters, electives / retorgraded, electives / supples, electives / dunes, electives / lakes, electives / michigans, electives / sent, electives / sources, electives / leans, electives / language, electives / skills, electives / clears, electives / coded, electives.

CHAPTER FOUR

Treats, electives / transitory, electives / turns, electives / salty, electives / tears, electives / utah, electives / trains, electives / combs, electives / streets, electives / settled, electives / paints, electives / furl, electives / paid, electives / portends, electives / proven, electives / flashed, electives / punched, electives / securely, electives / possessions, electives / copes, electives / stranded, electives / strips, electives / poses, electives / subtles, electives / amazed, electives / by, electives / the, electives / cues, electives / flashes, electives / flowers, electives / of, electives / dealings, electives / final, electives / voltage, electives / lasts, electives / mixed, electives / matched, electives / resolutions, electives / penned, electives / maintain, electives / a, electives / trickle, electives / of, electives / fellow, electives shipping love / lovers, electives / lasting, electives / poses, electives / moses, electives / elijah, electives / jonah, electives / whales, electives / calls, electives / made, electives / elaborate, electives / initialized, electives / welcomes, electives / keys, electives / magically, electives / the ways, electives / memories, electives / memorize, electives / cores, electives / samples, electives / maintains, electives.

CHAPTER FIVE

Children, electives / molecularly, electives / equivalent, electives / retreats, electives / childhood, electives / maintains, electives / benevolence, electives / heart's, electives / suggested, electives / stance, electives / meet, electives / the, electives / salacious, electives / stances, electives / intimacy, electives / at, electives / thoughts, electives / classicals, electives / matching, electives / delays, electives / peopled, electives / closets, electives / numbers, electives / doubted, electives / palaces, electives / into, electives / nodes, electives / duly, electives / formative, electives / majors, electives / calling, electives / heralds, electives / fundamentals, electives / drums, electives / needs, electives / havoc, electives / calls, electives / drumming, electives / matures, electives / happiness, electives / notational, electives / rotated, electives / heeds, electives / calls, electives / sources, electives / amazements, electives / registered, electives / as, electives / weathered, electives / faces, electives / recalled, electives / yours, electives / it, electives / magical, electives / prose, electives / how, electives / is, electives / written, electives / who, electives / is, electives / yours, electives / assured, electives / miracles, electives / maintained, electives.

CHAPTER SIX
Assurances, electives / what, electives / affords, electives / us, electives / love, electives / who, electives / is, electives / the, electives / warmth, electives / provided, electives / by, electives / in, electives / lifetimes, electives / blinking, electives / early, electives / askran, electives / another's, electives / numeric, electives / needs, electives / amounted, electives / overtly, electives / within, electives / included, electives / balances, electives / amounts, electives / to, electives / all, electives / stretching, electives / pauses, electives / opposed, electives / the, electives / flown, electives / doorways, electives / spreads, electives / offered, electives / elastic, electives / moods, electives / mailings, electives / mu, electives / known, electives / athens, electives / matched, electives / mains, electives / stones, electives / forecasts, electives / fames, electives / mines, electives / advanced, electives / advantageous, electives / meaningful, electives / embraces, electives / striped, electives / relations, electives / communicated, electives / abundance, electives / sends, electives / steeply, electives / written, electives / commitments, electives / on, electives / classic, electives / caribou, electives / into, electives / terrifically, electives.

CHAPTER SEVEN
Apt, electives / composed, electives / clue, electives / magicians, electives / folded, electives / tradewinds, electives / blowings, electives / cures, electives / formed, electives / fashions, electives / benchmarkets, electives / placed, electives / seeks, electives / initialized, electives / features, electives / foamings, electives / dashed, electives / across, electives / sandy, electives / dunes, electives / shores, electives / lunars, electives / scapes, electives / confuscate, electives / thee, electives / relates, electives / motifs, electives / solved, electives / written, electives / contudes, electives / made, electives / in, electives / firmest, electives / resolves, electives / wholistic, electives / mazes, electives / landscapes, electives / confuscated, electives / these, electives / resultant, electives / motifs, electives / solved, electives / written, electives / contracts, electives / made, electives / instincts, electives / followed, electives / firmly, electives / resolve, electives / issued, electives / wholistics, electives / severals, electives / ports, electives / followings, electives / allowed, electives / freedom, electives / trails, electives / torn, electives / huddled, electives /

across, electives / wisest, electives / hummel, electives / mistaken, electives / needs, electives.

CHAPTER EIGHT
Worded, electives / westerns, electives / severalty, electives / jointed, electives / rosebud, electives / reserved, electives / accrues, electives / into, electives / listened, electives / planets, electives / spiraling, electives / ones, electives / made, electives / dropping, electives / depends, electives / freeings, electives / stillings, electives / dancings, electives / numbered, electives / cheerily, electives / directional, electives / clarity, electives / dancing, electives / supposed, electives / notables, electives / planted, electives / ones, electives / masked, electives / dropped, electives / feelings, electives / stilled, electives / dancings, electives / numerical, electives / cherubs, electives / cheerings, electives / raphael, electives / finalists, electives / philosophically, electives / fused, electives / farmings, electives / nestles, electives / drops, electives / told, electives / whipped, electives / whose, electives / inside, electives / meetings, electives / made, electives / simplest, electives / focused, electives / formations, electives / ours, electives / instincts, electives / followed, electives / refrains, electives / tossed, electives / furthers, electives / dancings, electives / and, electives / a, electives / stanchion, electives / powered, electives / powerfully, electives / stanced, electives.

CHAPTER NINE
Equipped, electives / foundings, electives / cranes, electives / demons, electives / lie, electives / suites, electives / led, electives / opposed, electives / may, electives / occupy, electives / seamed, electives / sealings, electives / glasses, electives / splashing, electives / foaming, electives / in, electives / genes, electives / D, electives / I, electives / O, electives / X, electives / Y, electives / R, electives / I, electives / B, electives / O, electives / N, electives / U, electives / C, electives / L, electives / E, electives / A, electives / I, electives / C, electives / C, electives / G, electives / A, electives / T, electives / M, electives / I, electives / T, electives / O, electives / C, electives / H, electives / O, electives / N, electives / D, electives / R, electives / I, electives / A, electives / matched, electives / abodes, electives / abide, electives / in, electives / stretched, electives / offerings, electives / tallest, electives / grasses, electives / greens, electives / and, electives / a, electives / means, electives / filling, electives / wings, electives

CHAPTER TEN
Wooded, electives / raids, electives / arrested, electives / examine, electives / explored, electives / assignations, electives / powers, electives / debated, electives / seek, electives / assaults, electives / intensify, electives / simple, electives / acute, electives / recorded, electives / sensitive, electives / impatience, electives / reliance, electives / keens, electives / references, electives / referred, electives / quotes, electives / inducted, electives / torn, electives / required, electives / violence, electives / fierce, electives / wilds, electives / passionate, electives / accurate, electives / acclerated, electives / intense, electives / rails, electives / fences, electives

/ fads, electives / pursue, electives / the, electives / rapture, electives / given, electives / patience, electives / patent, electives / theories, electives / throw, electives / aside doubts, electives / invent, electives / scriptures, electives / shouted, electives / touted, electives / reinvented, electives / intended, electives / reactions, electives / reaching, electives / roads, electives / moaning, electives / mooning, electives / married, electives / hawks, electives / hosted, electives / greeted, electives / tensions, electives / mounted, electives / counted, electives / freedoms, electives / respectful, electives / courts, electives.

CHAPTER ELEVEN
Love, electives / to, electives / send, electives / salvation, electives / to, electives / those, electives / who, electives / married, electives / the courts, electives / of capable, electives / creatures, electives / lord, electives / lives, electives / gifts, electives / sold, electives / found, electives / friends, electives / relations, electives / built, electives / borders, electives / melt, electives / nobles, electives / trends, electives / tended, electives / lovers, electives / long, electives / enough, electives / relations, electives / build, electives / through, electives / respect, electives / for, electives / elevations, electives / during, electives / the, electives / coming, electives / cured, electives / waves, electives / let, electives / love, electives / stand, electives / in, electives / for, electives / you, electives / and, electives / marry, electives / the, electives / best, electives / man, electives / your, electives / bride, electives, / groom, electives / the, electives / knight, electives / intrinsic, electives / the, electives / lord, electives / the, electives / elegant, electives / sort, electives / the, electives / many, electives / the, electives / few, electives

CHAPTER TWELVE
The, electives / parallels, electives / blended, electives / palatial, electives / ports, electives / sorts, electives / simply, electives / specific, electives / fragrantly, electives / fluid, electives / folks, electives / who, electives / maintained, electives / ecumenic, electives / ecology, electives / final, electives / dictations, electives / durations, electives / married, electives / french, electives / doored, electives / electricity, electives / signals, electives / single, electives / counts for, electives / these, electives / who, electives / need, electives / specific, electives / cords, electives / cut, electives / let, electives / us, electives / long, electives / be, electives / in, electives / short, electives / simmerings, electives / stutter, electives / less, electives / agree, electives / more, electives / find, electives / finalness, electives / of, electives / functions, electives / and, electives / move, electives / ashore, electives / live, electives / long, electives / in deeds, electives / and, electives / merry, electives / pairings, electives / love, electives / your, electives / friendly, electives / encounters, electives, / in, electives / discipled, electives / moves, electives / for, electives / thee, electives.

CHAPTER THIRTEEN
Made, electives / found, electives / finished, electives / gifted, electives / written, electives / rounds, electives / deified, electives / carried, electives / courted, electives / coped, electives / codes,

electives / now, electives / finished, electives / written, electives / well, electives / details, electives / said, electives / find, electives / hope, electives / in hurtling, electives / hands, electives / hosted, electives / roasts, electives / go, electives / to, electives / fountained, electives / explanations, electives / sured, electives / daily, electives / flourished, electives / focusing, electives / finally, electives / furling, electives / turning, electives / tracking, electives / tracing, electives / tugs, electives, electives / rugs, electives / rushing, electives / routes, electives / random, electives / scouting, electives / scoring, electives / shouts, electives / shooting, electives / starred, electives / delivery, electives / too, electives / tarry, electives / knot, electives / longer, electives / than, electives / three, electives / days, electives / away, electives / from, electives / those, electives / who, electives / know, electives / how, electives / to, electives / say, electives / good-bye, electives / vote, electives.

LEVEL 102: THE STAGE-MENTS

CHAPTER ONE
If, stages/ kings, stages / prince, stages / of, stages / peace, stages / bridegroom, stages / only, stages / begotten, stages / son, stages / wonderful, stages / counselor, stages / immanuel, stages / yahweh, stages / son, stages / man, stages / daysprings, stages / kings, stages / of, stages / jews, stages / prophetic, stages / redeemon, stages / archor, stages / bright, stages / solid, stages / morning, stages / star, stages / the, stages / way, stages / the, stages / truth, stages / the, stages / life, stages / i, stages / 6, stages / christ, stages / sped, stages / within, stages / to, stages / a, stages / winsome, stages / welded, stages / stricture, stages / &, stages / the, stages / structures, stages / singly, stages / sincere, stages / for, stages / fortunte, stages / remonds, stages / is, stages / same, stages / someness, stages / stumble, stages / nectar, stages / sunday, stages / afffict, stages / into, stages / trecrtment, stages / afraid? stages / admits, stages / light, stages / treats, stages / after, stages.

CHAPTER TWO
Tables, stages / contented, stages / personal, stages / person, stages / blockes, stages / built, stages / coded, stages / written, stages / essence, stages / blessed, stages / hybrid, stages / stores, stages / futures, stages / merged, stages / alternative, stages / features, stages / systemic, stages / person, stages / contacts, stages / supreme, stages / made, stages / blink, stages / hawks, stages / pass, stages / makes, stages / swift, stages / instant, stages / inspire, stages / props, stages / fires, stages / wine, stages / calm, stages / grace, stages / leads, stages / ever, stages / after, stages / holy, stages / magnify, stages / magnetic, stages / mystery, stages / one, stages / oneness, stages / plates, stages / doors, stages / galaxy, stages / celestial, stages / existant, stages / emanates, stages / sacaral, stages / prepares, stages / distant, stages / display, stages / straps, stage / prepared, stages / inject, stages / develops, stages

/ evolved, stages / species, stages / precurrs, stages / discipline, stages / cosmic, stages / evolution, stages / frequency, stages / cooperate, stages.

CHAPTER THREE

Species, stages / system, stages / respect, stages / restrict, stages / capable, stages / star, stages / retire, stages / imperative, stages / unevolved, stage / inhabit, stages / elixirs, stages / mean, stages / evolved, stages / inhale, stages / essence, stages / christ, stages / rather, stages / innovates, stages / shelling, stages / teams, stages / limits, stages / conscious, stages / modes, stages / civilized, stages / views, stages / serve, stages / posture, stages / caught, stages / addition, stages / positive, stages / kept, stages / consciously, stages / terms, stages / know, stages / auspicious, stages / felt, stages / feel, stages / directs, stages / socially, stages / uplifts, stages / birth, stages / uplifting, stages / posture, stages / grades, stages / herd, stages / amber, stages / emulate, stages / page, stages / miror, stages / major, stages / clouds, stages / debris, stages / provisionary, stages / awakens, stages / result, stages / shines, stages / element, stages / resonate, stages / resilient, stages / grown, stages / god, stages / solar, stages / plexus, stages / planes, stages.

CHAPTER FOUR

Sensed, stages / crystal, stages / atone, stages / crawl, stages / multiple, stages / fluids, stages / inhabit, stages / stone, stages / act, stages / expands, stages / composed, stages / handles, stages / components, stages / mantra, stages / radiates, stages / staff, stages / anticitate, stages / skies, stages / star, stages / situation, stages / essence, stages / most, stages / integral, stages / tones, stages / spirits, stages / principles, stages / accurate, stages / fragile, stages / guided, stages / essential, stages / trees, stages / mathematics, stages / permeate, stages / tones, stages / sweet, stages / sounds, stages / elixirs, stages / marry, stages / brushed, stages / into, stages / motivate, stages / ably, stages / abilities, stages / freed, stages / expect, stages / openess, stages / primary, stages / touching, stages / unconditonal, stages / ecstacy, stages / earth, stages / treats, stages / accompany, stages / qualities, stages / freed, stages / wells, stages / right, stages / bond, stages / illusion, stages / matched, stages / citizen, stages / universal, stages / strips, stages / living, stages.

CHAPTER FIVE: news, stages / dawns, stages / arcs, stages / erupt, stages / primary, stages / loving, stages / lightest, stages / taught, stages / greeted, stages / context, stages / confused, stages / stars, stages / being, stages / design, stages / events, stages / grown, stages / exceed, stages / down, stages / commited, stages / seeds, stages / confused, stages / deliberates, stages / active, stages / buffered, stages / events, stages / help, stages / overcome, stages / ego, stages / shorts, stages / inhabit, stages / wills, stages / circumstance, stages / hoods, stages / undertaken, stages / 5, stages / levels, stages / colors, stages / amber, stages / pink, stages / greens -stages / blues, stages / reds, stages / pale, stages / patterns, stages / crystals, stages / inter, stages / dimensional, stages / diagrams,

stages / hopes, stages / refined, stages / steller, stages / codes, stages / evolved, stages / worlds, stages / word, stages / distant, stages / pens, stages / chariots, stages / humming, stages / starry, stages / grids, stages / conversation, stages / members, stages / privilege, stages.

CHAPTER SIX

Visualize, stages / glorious, stages / courage, stages / readied, stages / rise, stages / transist, stages / faith, stages / converse, stages / deems, stages / witnessed, stages / daily, stages / shrugs, stages / commons, stages / journeys, stages / suggest, stages / participation, stages / greatness, stages / attains, stages / humming, stages / starr, stages / people, stages / far, stages / will, stages / we, stages / cried, stages / sale, stages / freedom -stages / sins, stages / within, stages / redemption, stages / whem, stages / chariots, stages / changed, stages / hummanity, stages / rainbow, stages / penned, stages / in, stages / sounds, stages / lighten, stages / how, stages / often, stages / then, stages / have, stages / spend, stages / light, stages / times, stages / in, stages / love's, stages / marry, stages / more, stages / respect, stages / confession, stages / me, stages / threw, stages / without, stages / will, stages / says, stages / all, stages / doors, stages / you, stages / march, stages / pens, stages / opening, stages / door, stages.

CHAPTER SEVEN

Occur, stages / spares, stages / spurt, stages / michigan, stages / ann, stages / arbor, stages / sports, stages / grown, stages / examples, stages / exemplary, stages / exits, stages / purged, stages / matters, stages / more, stages / determine, stages / grow, stages / next, stages / nurtures, stages / natural, stages / born, stages / intrigues, stages / settle, stages / stairs, stages / dancing, stages / distance, stages / darkened, stages / nuptials, stages / softest, stages / thrown, stages / threshold, stages / makes, stages / american, stages / matched, stages / methods, stages / matching, stages / materials, stages / purchased, stages / maintains, stages / metric, stages / trades, stages / treatments, stages / truths, stages / transits, stages / tradition, stages / relatives, stages / rushing, stages / calls, stages / three, stages / fuels, stages / trap, stages / matching, stages / poletics, stages / lightly, stages / funds, stages / meditative, stages / managerial, stages / loving, stages / forms, stages / facets, stages / moments, stages / feeling, stages / facts, stages / foolishness, stages / transit, stages.

CHAPTER EIGHT

Maturity, stages / mastery, stages / matrix, stages / mutually, stages / pageantry, stages / pageants, stages / puruse, stages / purchase, stages / pulling, stages / puhy, stages / puns, stages / punitively, stages / forgone, stages / feeling, stages / flashes, stages / fleets, stages / pacific, stages / streets, stages / duration, stages / calls, stages, / pasture, stages / chances, stages / deepens, stages / reading, stages / purchase, stages / patience, stages / crisp, stages / ranch, stages / basic, stages / bully, stages / furthers, stages / gasoline, stages / flask, stages / filled, stages / funnels, stages

/ materialistic, stages / material, stages / materialism, stages / method, stages / challenge, stages / custom, stages / channel, stages / opens, stages / customorial, stages / cluster, stages / purchase, stages / poems, stages / price, stages / entertaing, stages / gist, stages / minerals, stages / glories, stages / manipulation, stages / thanks, stages / gears, stages / gains, stages / bells, stages / flushed, stages / fossilized, stages / directive, stages / whistling, stages / property, stages / prepares, stages / copy, stages.

CHAPTER NINE

Majestic, stages / threshing, stages / capturing, stages / mints, stages / mystical, stages / moravian, stages / wings, stages / bolster, stages / treaties, stages / blazing, stages / sun, stages / traded, stages / treatments, stages / trains, stages / through, stages / glazes, stages / hearing, stages / thread, stages / tones, stages / mamed, stages / worthy, stages / falcons, stages / tongues, stages / mounded -stages / trusts, stages / build, stages / legs, stages / torn, stages / nation, stages / paired, stages / lasting, stages / trades, stages / partition, stages / oatterned, stages / partners, stages / purists, stages / currency, stages / totals, stages / triangular, stages / master, stages / planters, stages / sexual, stages / walls, stages / climbed, stages / sugar, stages / wets, stages / hypenion, stages / lavender, stages / surrenering, stages / spartans, stages / stern, stages / played, stages / geophysical, stages / missives, stages / strps, stages / skirted, stages / figurative, stages / federation, stages / god, stages / votes, stages / dearest, stages / fallen, stages / strips, stages / associate, stages.

CHAPTER TEN

Launders, stages / squall, stages / lasting, stages / notes, stages / pension, stages / patrons, stages / cursive, stages / way, stages / mention, stages / ok, stages / to, stages / teals, stages / ascension, stages / walls, stages / formation, stages / temple, stages / tempestion, stages / tantric, stages / meet, stages / alluring, stages / fetishes, stages / fantasy, stages / blown, stages / intesity, stages / bowing, stages / blimish, stages / teams, stages / tents, stages / scans, stages / teaming, stages / cleared, stages / star, stages / needles, stages / necessary, stages / matched, stages / mutual, stages / managed, stages / metalic, stages / censures, stages / inspect, stages / arc, stages / bent, stages / bonine, stages / basic, stages / beats, stages / burns, stages / learn, stages / lest, stages / care, stages / carousel, stages / changes, stages / team, stages / tinsel, stages / middle, stages / beard, stages / deer, stages / classical, stages / clearest, stages / nights, stages / mission, stages / phonecians, stages / knew, stages / create, stages / plan, stages.

CHAPTER ELEVEN

Size, stages / planets, stages / church, stages / maid, stages / is, stages / how, stages / potato, stages / tot, stages / sort, stages / fargo, stages / apart, stages / condos, stages / when, stages / conpling, stages / trains, stages / red, stages / star, stages / mars, stages / sky, stages / juniper, stages / hemoglobin, stages / bleeds, stages / strong, stages / small, stages / scents, stages / smell, stages / dog's, stages / duty, stages / lands, stages / caves, stages / home,

stages / steep, stages / cairn, stages / illuminated, stages / glows, stages / clarity, stages / leaks, stages / zones, stages / hydro, stages / hydrogen, stages / away, stages / distant, stages / far, stages / close, stages / beside, stages / over, stages / above, stages / beneath -stages / word, stages / autumn, stages / winter, stages / spring, stages / associates, stages / fall, stages / summer, stages / freed, stages / tree, stages / changed, stages / breast, stages / buttons, stages / leaf, stages / lines, stages / crib, stages / chirp, stages.

CHAPTER TWELVE

Celebrates, stages / limits, stages / clean, stages / claim, stages / can, stages / due, stages / cleaning, stages / somatic, stages / original, stages / source, stages / cleanse, stages / days, stages / dolphin, stages / avenues, stages / are, stages / metric, stages / arranged, stages / where, stages / mothers, stages / woo, stages / their, stages / program, stages / by, stages / venues, stages / intense, stages / triangle, stages / stare, stages / stores, stages / capable, stages / stein, stages / am, stages / comprehensive, stages / coloration, stages / fixed, stages / tapes, stages / moves, stages / mabe, stages / a, stages / measurable, stages / definition, stages / for, stages / love, stages / your -stages / link, stages / decide, stages / to, stages / deal, stages / in -stages / gazing, stages / miracles, stages / life, stages / written, stages / extremes, stages / advocate, stages / the, stages / words, stages / federal, stages / lamb, stages / ressurection, stages / handsome, stages / feels, stages / of, stages / god, stages / within, stages.

CHAPTER THIRTEEN

Shepherd, stages / bishop, stages / souls, stages / judge, stages / lord, stages / of, stages / love, stages / man, stages / of, stages / sorrows, stages / head, stages / of, stages / church, stages / master, stages / faithful, stages / true, stages / witness, stages / rock, stages / high, stages / priest, stages / door, stages / living, stages / water, stages / bread, stages / life, stages / rose, stages / of, stages / sharon, stages / alpha, stages / omega, stages / true, stages / vine, stages / messiah, stages / teacher, stages / holy -stages / one, stages / meditator, stages / beloved, stages / branch, stages / capture, stages / good, stages / the, stages / word, stages / made, stages / shepherd, stages / of, stages / invisible, stages / god, stages / light, stages / of, stages / world, stages / image, stages / chief, stages / i, stages / am, stages / king, stages / cornerstone, stages / lion, stages / tribe, stages / judah, stages / savior, stages / servant, stages / author, stages / finish, stages .

LEVEL 103: THE STORE-MENTS

CHAPTER ONE

In, stores / a, stores / voluntary, stores / surrender, stores / allow, stores / the, stores / render, stores / read, stores / for, stores / a, stores / formal, stores / instigation, stores / of, stores / a, stores / researched, stores / revery, stores / fragile, stores / still, stores / in, stores / ecstatic, stores / leisure, stores / and, stores / the, stores / measures, stores / mentioned, stores / when a, stores / wiser, stores / stillness is, stores / our, stores / yesterday, stores / sturgeons, stores / chosen, stores / fish, stores / instead, stores / frozen, stores / feelings, stores / pass, stores / within, stores / a, stores / glance, stores / to, stores / the, stores / welcomed, stores / muse, stores / of, stores / love, stores / principles, stores / are, stores / set, stores / for, stores / the, stores / final, stores / keyed, stores / episodes, stores / allured, stores / has, stores / met, stores / a, stores / financial, stores / security, stores / into, stores / licensing, stores / pleased, stores / recalls, stores.

CHAPTER TWO

Pleasureable, stores / remember, stores / has, stores / readied, stores / us, stores / father, stores / following, stores / winds, stores / for, stores / a, stores / material, stores / repress, stores / and, stores / the, stores / forgotten stores / spins, stores / waiverings, stores / matching, stores / dreams, stores / across, stores / positively, stores / logically, stores / to, stores / littleton's, stores / told, stores / we've, stores / led, stores / matched, stores / of, stores / old, stores / lifetimes, stores / boldes, stores / due, stores / in, stores / a, stores / deal, stores / for, stores / a, stores / flowing, stores / cause, stores / the, stores / oz, stores / above, stores / into, stores / love's, stores / daring, stores / deeds, stores / casts, stores / are, stores / played, stores / roles, stores / are, stores / set, stores / music, stores / flows, stores / good, stores / guides, stores / are, stores / francing, stores / past, stores / operational, stores / sheets, stores / musical, stores / loves, stores.

CHAPTER THREE

Coppery, stores / heads, stores / penny, stores / links, stores / salt, stores / lakes, stores / cities, stores / ciudad, stores / towns, stores / spills, stores / antelopes, stores / opals, stores / islands, stores / deserts, stores / durations, stores / sex, stores / love, stores / models, stores / measures, stores / pleasing, stores / pleasured, stores / plastic, stores / pieces, stores / sold, stores / follow, stores / these, stores / guided, stores / extra, stores / coverings, stores / outlived, stores / in, stores / safety, stores / of, stores / lashes, stores / blinked, stores / at, stores / the, stores / eye, stores / horus, stores / too, stores / god, stores / may, stores / we, stores / beloved, stores / clarinets, stores / flutes, stores / winds, stores / woods, stores / moods, stores / match, stores / panels, stores / set, stores / in, stores / rods, stores / wood, stores / laps, stores / included, stores / relationship, stores / keys, stores / paid, stores / electric, stores / pills, stores / verbal, stores / pills, stores.

CHAPTER FOUR

As, stores / an, stores / absolution, stores, / grows, stores / a, stores / guilty, stores / now, stores / intrigues, stores / yours, stores / restful, stores / resurrection, stores / to, stores / a, stores / level, stores / landing, stores / stead, stores / may, stores / we, stores / say, stores / that, stores / love, stores / to, stores / the, stores / resting, stores / allows, stores / replac, stores / change, stores / for, stores / a, stores / feeling, stores / challenges, stores / direct, stores / cold, stores / in, stores / a, stores / weathered, stores / waste,

stores / and, stores / the, stores / highland, stores / healed, stores / in, stores / a, stores / sealed, stores / inside, stores / play, stores / for, stores / repose, stores / inculcates, stores / sessions, stores / cautions, stores / off, stores / material, stores / spells, stores / offenses, stores / intense, stores / follows, stores / tales, stores / dense, stores / winding, stores / duration, stores / telling, stores / without, stores / ways, stores.

CHAPTER FIVE

Bliss, stores / abundant, stores / gifts, stores / gears, stores / flippancy, stores / shades, stores / lights, stores / task, stores / truce, stores / tenths, stores / stood, stores / stepped, stores / gates, stores / stripes, stores / spell, stores / off, stores / ridicule, stores / a, stores / mixed, stores / statue, stores / has, stores / staring, stores / steals, stores / across, stores / gode, stores / fearless, stores / patches, stores / mode, stores / to, stores / phase, stores / pulsing, stores / days, stores / falling, stores / us, stores / well, stores / for, stores / apperance, stores / deem, stores / flip, stores / offering, stores / seek, stores / deeds, stores / leashing, stores / cubes, stores / soucht, stores / drafts, stores / drawing, stores / homedade, stores / shields, stores / logical, stores / legally, stores / eternally, stores / able, stores / levelly, stores / material, stores / malevalence, stores / stays, stores / forever, stores / leaves, stores / vessels, stores / acessed, stores / intense, stores / burst, stores / infused, stores.

CHAPTER SIX

Maturity, stores / has, stores / gathered, stores / into, stores / legal, stores / straits, stores / of, stores / the, stores / welcome, stores / kinds, stores / largest, stores / offers, stores / stood, stores / essentially, stores / across, stores / wisdom, stores / may, stores / doors, stores / knights, stores / as, stores / we, stores / your, stores / we've, stores / essentially, stores / mabe, stores / in, stores / won, stores / breathed, stores / our, stores / nest, stores / so, stores / we're, stores / as, stores / a, stores / dealt, stores / decide, stores / we've, stores / the, stores / glide, stores / into, stores / a, stores / gap's, stores / forget, stores / and, stores / forgiving, stores / living, stores / reside, stores / love's, stores / gesture, stores / the, stores / and, stores / a, stores / are, stores / volumes, stores / steering, stores / samples, stores / made, stores / raised, stores / piece, stores / patched, stores / for, stores / endear, stores / into, stores / avenues, stores.

CHAPTER SEVEN

Captions, stores / read, stores / of, stores / the, freedom, / stores / to, stores / fall, stores / into, stores / managable, stores / gestures, stores / and, stores / driven, stores / dialogues, stores / classical, stores / to, stores / living, stores / misfortunes, stores / for, stores / one, stores / into, stores / jet, stores / lace, stores / circumspect, stores / waiters, stores / the, stores / watery, stores / boards, stores / credit, stores / several, stores / clearly, stores / fearless, stores / declaration, stores / troy, stores / sun, stores / trojan, stores / dashes, stores / proximate, stores / directly, stores / neighboring, stores / close, stores / instantaneously, stores / over, stores /

bordering, stores / reasons, stores / songs, stores / faculties, stores / absolute, stores / accedes, stores / abound, stores / brown, stores / abortive, stores / reaction, stores / academy, stores / grew, stores / accidental, stores / acceptance, stores / academic, stores / to, stores / accelerated, stores / abound, stores / in, stores / beatific, stores / go, stores / riding, stores.

CHAPTER EIGHT:
Proximate, stores / nine, stores / melt, stores / broads, stores / psychotic, stores / slinks, stores / lurk, stores / practically, stores / diminished, stores / then, stores / grown, stores / aware, stores / for, stores / the, stores / determine, stores / develop, stores / definition, stores / thankful, stores / systematic, stores / swallows, stores / spells, stores / finished, stores / tactical, stores / nouns, stores / gears, stores / tablets, stores / supply, stores / supervised, stores / include, stores / tags, stores / swarm, stores / swallow, stores / tablet, stores / tactful, stores / superb, stores / systems, stores / because, stores / bed, stores / reward, stores / becoming, stores / strict, stores / bedrock, stores / bastion, stores / battery, stores / horizon, stores / rewarded, stores / hilarity, stores / found, stores / ivy, stores / meant, stores / legions, stores / depths, stores / grew, stores / refresh, stores / clasp, stores / licensing, stores / green, stores / included, stores / sripes, stores / zips, stores / in, stores / below, stores / staggered, stores / trips, stores.

CHAPTER NINE
Perhaps, stores / we've, stores / a, stores / miracle, stores / to, stores / include, stores / in, stores / living, stores / lashes, stores / onto, stores / a, stores / dietary, stores / nurture, stores / flow, stores / is, stores / drawn, stores / hood, stores / river, stores / graphic, stores / implore, stores / is, stores / simply, stores / stationed, stores / in, stores / function, stores / channeled, stores / gates, stores / placement, stores / pierced, stores / for, stores / superior, stores / strands, stores / palace, stores / taught, stores / in, stores / sight, stores / straps, stores / grants, stores / crust, stores / mention, stores / relate, stores / reaches, stores / method, stores / isolate, stores / thermal, stores / explored, stores / sturdy, stores / signals, stores / closure, stores / valuable, stores / museums, stores / menu, stores / opinions, stores / excitement, stores / mounts, stores / volative, stores / mercy, stores / love's, stores / oracles, stores / acconts, vacant in stores / matched, stores / lasting, stores / ovation, stores / formula, stores.

CHAPTER TEN
Vortex, stores / blues, stores / chaco, stores / canyon, stores / window, stores / yellow's, stores / analize, stores / dwellers, stores / hinged, stores / cleanse, stores / powell, stores / strips, stores / island, stores / session, stores / on, stores / sealing, stores / captions, stores / shimes, stores / ringing, stores / slides, stores / read, stores / fundamentals, stores / man's, stores / men's, stores / the, stores / for, stores / mankind, stores / mutual, stores / neatens, stores / necessity, stores / elation, stores es / signifies, stores / chill, stores / splice, stores / easter, stores / island, stores / ripe, stores / for, stores / miracle, stores / stone, stores / my, stores / fixation, stores

/ pick, stores / hinge, stores / repeat, stores / recurrent, stores / work, stores / truth, stores / is, stores / an, stores / news, stores / election, stores / sites, stores / well, stores / fast, stores / on, stores / spent, stores / inclusion, stores / bounce, stores / temple, stores / as, stores / moon, stores / include, stores / spread, stores.

CHAPTER ELEVEN
Factual, stores / extreme, stores / meant, stores / for, stores / explain, stores / of, stores / fever, stores / realms, stores / of, stores / twice, stores / as, stores / to, stores / events, stores / claimed, stores / messiah, stores / the, stores / cortex, stores / resolved, stores / resolute, stores / respect, stores / response, stores / able, stores / to, stores / living, stores / good, stores / sample, stores / simple, stores / actual, stores / primary, stores / trigger, stores / appropriate, stores / gesture, stores / sometime, stores / chance, stores / try, stores / type, stores / all, stores / lottery, stores / ask, stores / blame, stores / million, stores / straight, stores / guest, stores / sweet, stores / dreams, stores / header, stores / living, stores / notice, stores / affection, stores / difference, stores / picture, stores / company, stores / glass, stores / touch, stores / excite, stores / history, stores / forever, stores / romantic, stores / seduction, stores / take, stores / leap, stores / flowers, stores / real, stores / women, stores.

CHAPTER TWELVE
Cry, stores / aloud, stores / credit, stores / association, stores / missionary, stores / volume, stores / told, stores / production, stores / true, stores / last, stores / seat, stores / tickets, stores / leave, stores / shift, stores / tools, stores / around, stores / associate, stores / pity, stores / know, stores / get, stores / correct, stores / street, stores / queston, stores / everything, stores / nonthing, stores / country, stores / looking, stores / how, stores / house, stores / relate, stores / beauty, stores / kings, stores / here, stores / stage, stores / hornets, stores / mask, stores / hand, stores / just, stores / page, stores / delete, stores / team, stores / need, stores / laughs, stores / news, stores / good, stores / radio, stores / button, stores / escape, stores / ignorant, stores / law, stores / pass, stores / passport, stores / jet, stores / drive, stores / miles, stores / vest, stores / venture, stores / race, stores / pause, stores / scroll, stores / enter, stores / trunk, stores / decimal, stores / found, stores.

CHAPTER THIRTEEN
Shine, stores / stand, stores / tree, stores / behind, stores / carport, stores / ladder, stores / classic, stores / avenue, stores / plug, stores / keep, stores / deep, stores / trip, stores / hip, stores / ship, stores / shop, stores / heard, stores / enjoy, stores / curtian, stores / water, stores / paddle, stores / dinner, stores / diner, stores / air, stores / napkins, stores / trust, stores / wake, stores / wave, stores / maximum, stores / situation, stores / concern, stores / draw, stores / approach, stores / watch, stores / bring, stores / dog, stores / glass, stores / suit, stores / remember, stores / today, stores / work, stores / clapping, stores / quit, stores / suprise, stores / gone, stores / take, stores / fire, stores / flame, stores / walk, stores / stroll, stores / call, stores / burn, stores / gas, stores / fill, stores / enough, stores

/ far, stores / tray, stores / place, stores / play, stores / heat, stores / cool, stores / brink, stores / collector, stores / display, stores / next, stores.

LEVEL 104: THE SILVER-MENTS

CHAPTER ONE
Silver, silver pages and the wages laid into love / chances, silver / chosen, silver / days, silver / diabolic, silver / correlation, silver / degree, silver / posted, silver / chores, silver / chase, silver / resolution, silver / respect, silver / amperes, silver / wattage, silver / worn, silver / within, silver / wisdom, silver / chinese, silver / character, silver / imposed, silver / abouts, silver / theoretic, silver / enabling, silver / need, silver / addicted, silver / levels, silver / reached, silver / arose, silver / arisen, silver / peaceful, silver / pass, silver / secure, silver / sustained, silver / deepened, silver / threats, silver / thrown, silver / over, silver / fitzgeralds, silver / constant, silver / carries, silver / a, silver / planetary, silver / cense, silver / code, silver / central, silver / score, silver / reminder, silver / read -silver / over, silver / churning, silver / decibles, silver / demote, silver / doubts, silver / beautifully, silver / defends, silver / danced, silver / desires, silver / destitation, silver / allows, silver / listening, silver / layers, silver / lofty, silver / noodles, silver / piled, silver.

CHAPTER TWO
Fan, silver / feast, silver / formation, silver / first, silver / jurisdication, silver / joined, silver / jointly, silver / given, silver / governs, silver / governing, silver / genuine, silver / codes, silver / weathering, silver / wasted, silver / wealth, silver / woes, silver / wandering, silver / how, silver / said, silver / worth, silver / wait, silver / when, silver / mayan, silver / mains, silver / were, silver / single, silver / maintains, silver / mental, silver / your, silver / moods, silver / murk, silver / clears, silver / and, silver / sucessive, silver / tones, silver / band, silver / lures, silver / interested, silver / hearts, silver / send, silver / of, silver / double, silver / splash, silver / onto, silver / lended, silver / loads, silver / favorable, silver / with, silver / madness, silver / mixed, silver / male, silver / mourns, silver / morning, silver / led, silver / large, silver / lanes, silver / love, silver / has, silver / met, silver / her, silver / woody, silver / demote, silver / within, silver / plum, silver.

CHAPTER THREE
Has, silver / spent, silver / a, silver / fortune, silver / on, silver / lessens, silver / tour, silver / taste, silver / spent, silver / for, silver / fallen, silver / logged, silver / trees, silver / crawled, silver / past, silver / sucess, silver / and, silver / floods, silver / a, silver / sullen, silver / source, silver / with, silver / sources, silver / and, silver / winsome, silver / divorce, silver / debate -silver / as, silver / sent, silver / and, silver / the, silver / lurk, silver / churns, silver / chains, silver / chants, silver / chains, silver / murdered, silver / sense, silver / of, silver / laugh, silver / towed, silver / miriad, silver / of, silver / possible, silver / panes, silver / break, silver

/ over, silver / wall, silver / horticultural, silver / health, silver / pags, silver / purged, silver / hooked, silver / hoods, silver / heads -silver / song, silver / steeples, silver / structural, silver / behooves, silver / basically, silver / benched, silver / bands, silver / spining, silver / recedes, silver.

CHAPTER FOUR
Free, silver / cardinals, silver / taxi, silver / calibers, silver / effective, silver / theosophy, silver / therapy, silver / attend, silver / chosen, silver / handsome, silver / sums, silver / summary, silver / bored, silver / eggs, silver / bons, silver / host, silver / provisional, silver / portraitare, silver / pectins, silver / mantain, silver / provision, silver / pedal, silver / passage, silver / passes, silver / positive, silver / rocks, silver / partition, silver / taps, silver / thumbs, silver / begs, silver / bites, silver / boats, silver / contours, silver / conference, silver / smugglers, silver / smug, silver / alto, silver / adverse -silver / a snag, silver / vexed, silver / contrast, silver / blues, silver / rugby, silver / carries, silver / mistake, silver / whole, silver / cones, silver / flocks, silver / translate, silver / thumb, silver / proton, silver / practice, silver / framed, silver / purple, silver / benefits, silver / entrance, silver / retain, silver / shore, silver / prosperity, silver / pures, silver / restrain, silver / polished, silver / dot, silver / polish, silver.

CHAPTER FIVE
Trouble, silver / new, silver / optional, silver / over, silver / games, silver / pretty, silver / gang, silver / anywhe, silver / half, silver / section, silver / weighs, silver / flip, silver / challenge, silver / something, silver / defense, silver / matrix, silver / over, silver / thnk, silver / each, silver / seat, silver / split, silver / removable, silver / course, silver / rivers, silver / pristine, silver / breathtaking, silver / vistas, silver / handles, silver / rollers, silver / take, silver / back, silver / carrying, silver / people, silver / folds, silver / fields, silver / extra, silver / cargo, silver / visit, silver / time, silver / wonderful, silver / internal, silver / peace, silver / matters, silver / connection, silver / soul -silver / show, silver / national, silver / sport, silver / nervuous, silver / passionate, silver / friend, silver / world, silver / sustained, silver / pace, silver / courage, silver / good, silver / connected, silver / question, silver / spend, silver / filled, silver / doing, silver / sold, silver / joy, silver / through, silver.

CHAPTER SIX
Credits, silver / talking, silver / simple, silver / employer, silver / about, silver / share, silver / workplace, silver / environmental, silver / program, silver / leading, silver / contribtion, silver / direct, silver / please, silver / groups, silver / under, silver / more, silver / dreamed, silver / singer, silver / child, silver / approved, silver / build, silver / tell, silver / letters, silver / tradition, silver / new, silver / bare, silver / location, silver / concentrate, silver / crae, silver / dynamic, silver / inertia, silver / chance, silver / motion, silver / tell, silver / show, silver / engage, silver / stare, silver / lust, silver / baby, silver / something, silver / grin, silver / formula, silver / face, silver / take, silver / firmer, silver / origins, silver / breathe, silver / coverage, silver / fuller, silver / luminous, silver

/ jacket, silver / fluid, silver / cream, silver / vitamins, silver / wear, silver / movie, silver / star, silver / idea, silver / joy, silver / felt, silver / expression, silver / wonder, silver / guide, silver / open, silver.

CHAPTER SEVEN

Syrius, silver / man, silver / adhere, silver / female, silver / resolve, silver / cast, silver / revolution, silver / sister, silver / buy, silver / rest, silver / defer, silver / acrose, silver / plains, silver / heaps, silver / cap, silver / most, silver / without, silver / we, silver / amount, silver / flesh, silver / love, silver / reigns, silver / baptize, silver / wounds, silver / hetero, silver / love, silver / rise, silver / show, silver / horse, silver / rain, silver / fly, silver / flowering, silver / math, silver / louds, silver / loads, silver / may, silver / surest, silver / purges, silver / learns, silver / we, silver / flight, silver / via, silver / in, silver / guided, silver / flee, silver / musical, silver / love, silver / your, silver / less, silver / know, silver / upon, silver / creative, silver / natural, silver / top, silver / light's, silver / respect, silver / mystics, silver / loving, silver / tag, silver / paid, silver / link, silver / doors, silver / after, silver / treats, silver.

CHAPTER EIGHT

Bloomed, silver / miracle, silver / pure, silver / school, silver / computer, silver / right, silver / amazing, silver / notable, silver / focused, silver / transience, silver / find, silver / harder, silver / seek, silver / raised, silver / important, silver / endure, silver / night, silver / morning, silver / follow, silver / bliss, silver / things, silver / ease, silver / riches, silver / praise, silver / worthwile, silver / power, silver / prayer, silver / itself, silver / full, silver / value, silver / somebody, silver / divide, silver / present, silver / part, silver / path, silver / strength, silver / net, silver / winning, silver / brings, silver / real, silver / experience, silver / engaged, silver / rebirth, silver / classic, silver / charter, silver / original, silver / club, silver / balance, silver / short, silver / ingredient, silver / secret, silver / devoton, silver / testify, silver / vibrant, silver / sing, silver / mother, silver / song, silver / rememberrd, silver / minds, silver / relationship, silver / identity, silver / security, silver / spirituality, silver / quick, silver.

CHAPTER NINE

Purest, silver / active, silver / flashing, silver / flirts, silver / ready, silver / jamming, silver / around, silver / sounds, silver / strands, silver / joys, silver / cleared, silver / through, silver / full, silver / merge, silver / hollow, silver / danced, silver / where, silver / do, silver / these, silver / children, silver / go, silver / how, silver / deep, silver / into, silver / love's, silver / agree, silver / will, silver / we, silver / seek, silver / sought, silver / found, silver / plays, silver / life -silver / you, silver / of, silver / arc, silver / work, v / are, silver / an, silver / angels, silver / simply, silver / the, silver / angelic, silver / sought, silver / spelled, silver / plan, silver / wing, silver / resolve, silver / what, silver / will, silver / the, silver / wiser, silver / vibration, silver / write, silver / one, silver / still, silver / said, silver / that's, silver / the, silver / employ, silver / you, silver / all, silver / won, silver / more, silver.

CHAPTER TEN

Lights, silver / soothe, silver / ocean, silver / paralell, silver / inside, silver / good, silver / trace, silver / tries, silver / pattern, silver / goodbye, silver / spark, silver / fell, silver / floral, silver / spin, silver / falls, silver / smell, silver / today, silver / 4, silver / trance, silver / connection, silver / minute, silver / knock, silver / one, silver / seek, silver / great, silver / sale, silver / automatic, silver / only, silver / hang, silver / filling, silver / spire, silver / motion, silver / move, silver / grapes, silver / treats, silver / made, silver / now, silver / gained, silver / groove, silver / is, silver / to, silver / along, silver / to, silver / well, silver / the, silver / listen, silver / talk, silver / flood, silver / unique, silver / allow, silver / necks, silver / andrew, silver / ratio, silver / stress, silver / shoulders, silver / geyser, silver / energetic, silver / spell, silver / and, silver / pen, silver / forgives, silver / from, silver / then, silver / now, silver.

CHAPTER ELEVEN

Back, silver / of, silver / my, silver / people, silver / hearts, silver / let, silver / us, silver / go, silver / now, silver / sister, silver / to, silver / we, silver / fallen, silver / spirals, silver / escalate, silver / escape, silver / wihout, silver / trace, silver / a, silver / line, silver / neutral, silver / purely, silver / let, silver / us, silver / doorway, silver / franchised, silver / play, silver / pray, silver / people, silver / unless, silver / party, silver / sign, silver / is, silver / well, silver / fell, silver / a, silver / convert, silver / correlation, silver / crash, silver / exit, silver / spared, silver / sum, silver / strong, silver / aft, silver / native, silver / selves, silver / apt, v / sun, silver / rasta, silver / book, silver / try, silver / book, silver / religion, silver / about, silver / life, silver / human, silver / ark, silver / of, silver / the -silver / covenant, silver / humanity, silver / waves, silver / knots, silver / paste, silver.

CHAPTER TWELVE

Over, silver / ready, silver / release, silver / oven, silver / simply, silver / stare, silver / stark, silver / left, silver / later, silver / breaks, silver / broken, silver / strains, silver / hurt, silver / pop, silver / walk, silver / trace, silver / what, silver / a, silver / c, silver / g, silver / t, silver / body, silver / mind, silver / spirit, silver / links, silver / the, silver / core, silver / is, silver / these, silver / a, silver / d, silver / n, silver / 3, silver / a, silver / model, silver / molecule, silver / rich, silver / forms, silver / motion, silver / stalls, silver / with, silver / listening, silver / manners, silver / neat, silver / reason, silver / prop, silver / nation, silver / cycle, silver / for, silver / dream, silver / 37, silver / years, silver / of, silver / light, silver / select, silver / elements, silver / form, silver / as, silver / crawls, silver / forth, silver / an, silver / oracle, silver / a, silver / wizard, silver.

CHAPTER THIRTEEN

Grapples, silver / ease, silver / celestal, silver / hard, silver / purged, silver / basic, silver / forget, silver / aims, silver / as, silver / vegetable, silver / growth, v / and, silver / mystic, silver / cycle, silver / single, silver / out, silver / a, silver / treat, silver / steady, silver / built, silver / single, silver / small, silver / my, silver / sirius, silver / sphere, silver / waves, silver / power, silver / seeps, silver / eden, silver / little, silver / pulse, silver / kept, silver

/ escape, silver / strands, silver / break, silver / proven, silver / groves, silver / sought, silver / self, silver / mine, silver / myself, silver / timeless, silver / pulls, silver / poles, silver / across, silver / haven, silver / stars, silver / sweep, silver / reflection, silver / found, silver / perfect, silver / copies, silver / roll, silver / planet, silver / facts -silver / guides, silver / 7th, silver / bodies, silver / met, silver / saftey, v / heaven, silver / orbs, silver / body, silver / check, silver.

LEVEL 105: THE GOLD-MENTS

CHAPTER ONE

Gold, gold given and meant through love / choice, gold / rest, rest in gold / five, gold / true, gold / love's, gold / page, gold / them, gold / here, gold / engramic, gold / and, gold / acknowledged, gold / allow, gold / entire, gold / plans, gold / mayan, gold / routes, gold / light's, gold / life, gold / codes, gold / available, gold / barrier, gold / lives, gold / queen, gold / recycled, gold / deaths, gold / in, gold / ashtar, gold / through, gold / forgotten, gold / spatials, gold / transume, gold / of, gold / generative, gold / deals, gold / made, gold / in, gold / light, gold / agree, gold / for, gold / planet's, gold / sake, gold / perhaps, gold / seasons, gold / senses, gold / agreed, gold / love, gold / is, gold / now, gold / a, gold / planet, gold / energetic, gold / in, gold / imprints, gold / of, gold / your, gold / loving, gold / nomencalture, gold / speaks, gold / well -gold / manifest, gold / divide, gold / shields, gold / shelters, gold.

CHAPTER TWO

Burst, gold / powers, gold / equaled, gold / wealth, gold / love, gold / sword, gold / both, gold / mixed, gold / lives, gold / thrills, gold / positions, gold / mate, gold / dimensional, gold / life, gold / purely, gold / female, gold / holon, gold / simple, gold / organic -gold / organs, gold / tree, gold / of, gold / life, gold / wizard, gold / engines, gold / dejavus, gold / architecture, gold / into, gold / dimensional, gold / architects, gold / 144,000, gold / organisms, gold / memnon, gold / aldebranic, gold / lights, gold / spiraling, gold / engrams, gold / dna, gold / strands, gold / activate, gold / junk, gold / decoded, gold / recovery, gold / infinite, gold / reconstruction, gold / infinity, gold / reconstructive, gold / universally, gold / dna, gold / 1112, gold / domains, gold / instincts, gold / the, gold / matrix, gold / the, gold / source, gold / the, gold / piercings, gold / excalibers, gold / shielded, gold / extracts, gold / oils, gold / dimensions, gold / lady, gold.

CHAPTER THREE

Cells, gold / as, gold / deja, gold / vus, gold / 13, gold / dimensions, gold / accumulators, gold / of, gold / life, gold / probes, gold / arcturians, gold / visited, gold / earth, gold / fire, gold / blood, gold / truth, gold / dna, gold / sky, gold / sheperds, gold / stares, gold / journey, gold / alcyone, gold / clues, gold / codes, gold / aa, gold / midway, gold / stations, gold / galactic, gold / mother,

gold / omega, gold / father, gold / alpha, gold / centauri, gold / infoirmation, gold / beams, gold / balast, gold / streams, gold / elders, gold / matrices, gold / astral, gold / structures, gold / seals, gold / creations, gold / life, gold / streaming, gold / pulses, gold / galactic, gold / excite, gold / exits, gold / cores, gold / hunab, gold / ku, gold / matrices, gold / openings, gold / tubers, gold / flowings, gold / inhaled, gold / exhales, gold / breathe, gold / stellar, gold / lunar, gold / galactic, gold / blood, gold / inferior, gold.

CHAPTER FOUR

Fire, gold / inside, gold / sky's, gold / exterior, gold / light, gold / sound, gold / music, gold / spheres, gold / harmony, gold / heaven, gold / uranus, gold / earth, gold / winds, gold / fires, gold / talmuds, gold / aesthetics, gold / 104, gold / long, gold / auxilary, gold / awaitings, gold / well, gold / ponders, gold / provides, gold / flips, gold / sides, gold / free, gold / approaches, gold / beams, gold / mirrored, gold / majority, gold / energy, gold / surging, gold / sananda, gold / 6, gold / 7, gold / detailed, gold / units, gold / universals, gold / stirs, gold / masses, gold / auric, gold / bodies, gold / dialogued, gold / tones, gold / accepted, gold / lamps, gold / flowing, gold / sacred, gold / linked, gold / consequent, gold / starring, gold / rivers, gold / lightly, gold / accepts, gold / freely, gold / walked, gold / peacefully, gold / openly, gold / universal, gold / peace, gold / principles, gold / grace, gold / love, gold / golden, gold.

CHAPTER FIVE

Listen, gold / intensely, gold / demand, gold / most, gold / find, gold / more, gold / generated, gold / held, gold / intensives, gold / trackings, gold / tourings, gold / toasts, gold / temples, gold / tossed, gold / fabrics, gold / focused, gold / listens, gold / links, gold d / confused, gold / contexts, gold / harmonies, gold / prepared, gold / assisted, gold / lists, gold / coincides, gold / auspicious, gold / poles, gold / levels, gold / systems, gold / arbitrates, gold / sonnets, gold / suns, gold / intensely, gold / hums, gold / multitudes, gold / whirling, gold / arcs, gold / glorious, gold / treated, gold / wonders, gold / arcs, gold / gloriously, gold / treats, gold / won, gold / pleiadic, gold / accordant, gold / forms, gold / degrees, gold / sirius, gold / majesty, gold / resolutions, gold / stables, gold / sound, gold / enters, gold / earthly, gold / feats, gold / dna, gold / honors, gold / cosmic, gold / condiitons, gold / all, gold / indulged, gold / torments, gold / shown, gold / assured, gold.

CHAPTER SIX

Councils, gold / apply, gold / human, gold / teachers, gold / channels, gold / delayed, gold / tactics, gold / nights, gold / turning, gold / signals, gold / celebrates, gold / joy, gold / universes, gold / weapons -gold / collisions, gold / skills, gold / eventual, gold / content, gold / simultaneous, gold / energy, gold / songs, gold / alliance, gold / noises, gold / rainbows, gold / softened, gold / majesty, gold / sounds, gold / hues, gold / hearts, gold / imperatives, gold / vibrant, gold / eyes, gold / noticed, gold / agendas, gold / ethics, gold / presence, gold / access, gold / runs, gold / holy, gold / prepared, gold / manipulated, gold / transits, gold / ones, gold / encouraged, gold / individuals, gold / holies, gold / buddhas, gold / christ, gold / inhabits, gold / folks, gold / common, gold / moons, gold / great, gold / moonbeams, gold / auspices, gold / regeants, gold / councils -gold / pockets, gold / secrets, gold / auspices, gold / omnipresence, gold / laws, gold / states, gold / perused, gold / placed, gold

CHAPTER SEVEN
Proposed, gold / meditate, gold / lift, gold / rich, gold / heavenly, gold / wooded, gold / frosts, gold / fertile, gold / apprehends, gold / breezes, gold / richly, gold / briefs, gold / freshly, gold / liberal, gold / cautious, gold / go, gold / planet's -gold / saturates, gold / grids, gold / cosmic, gold / ascends, gold / primal, gold / unyields, gold / yields, gold / poised, gold / stars, gold / dedicates, gold / poised, gold / earth, gold / assists, gold / placed, gold / spatially, gold / back, gold / living, gold / ultimates, gold / authors, gold / now, gold / cords, gold / authority, gold / placed, gold / opens, gold / cut, gold / plants, gold / nurtured, gold / lightness -gold / forgiven, gold / seeds, gold / encouraged, gold / planetary, gold / grids, gold / devestated, gold / less, gold / often, gold / for, gold / the, gold / eternally, gold / wells, gold / we, gold / have, gold / woven, gold / the, gold / over, gold / flowing, gold / pens, gold

CHAPTER EIGHT
Earth, gold / is, gold / "saved", gold / through, gold / efforts, gold / young, gold / and, gold / weapons, gold / tossed, gold / to, gold / miracles, gold / kept, gold / lightened, gold / through, gold / peaceful, gold / endeavors, gold / yours, gold / is, gold / the, gold / truth, gold / and, gold / the, gold / way, gold / of, gold / light's, gold / gifts, gold / excuse, gold / others, gold / know, gold / paths, gold / rich, gold / with, gold / light, gold / now, gold / the 8, gold / is, gold / appropriate, gold, / sum, gold / for, gold / your, gold / ascent, gold / in, gold / codes, gold / written, gold / know, gold / plays -gold / and, gold / planes, gold / of, gold / higher, gold / dynamic, gold / and, gold / the, gold / the, gold / cures, gold / brought, gold / home, gold / to, gold / bought, gold / arrivals, gold / focused, gold / in, gold / beautiful, gold / chicago, gold.

CHAPTER NINE
Truth, gold / to, gold / the test, gold / past, gold / knew, gold / a, gold / wave, gold / broken, gold / into, gold / awakened, gold / gladness, gold / know, gold / love's, gold / breath, gold / beauty, gold / won -gold / and, gold / the, gold / c hildren, gold / grown, gold / through, gold / driven, gold / as, gold / you, gold / may, gold / see, gold / through, gold / twice, gold / written, gold / loves, gold / enjoy, gold / gotten, gold / directives, gold / pulsing, gold / notes, gold / for, gold / written, gold / loves, gold / votes, gold / of, gold / delivery, gold / cured, gold / forms, gold / songs, gold / of, gold / love, gold / arcs, gold / linked, gold / now, gold / cleared, gold / all, gold / detritus, gold / through, gold / intense, gold / recall -gold / of, gold / written, gold / loves, gold / uriel, gold / embarks, gold / to, gold / places, gold / set, gold / settled, gold.

CHAPTER TEN
Titanium, gold / insurances, gold / ascends, gold / visa, gold / music, gold / waves, gold / titans, gold / lines, gold / lifted, gold / eyes, gold / humans, gold / voiced, gold / ringings, gold / uriel's, gold / inside, gold / selections, gold / has, gold / met, gold / functions, gold / supposed, gold / listening, gold / again, gold / lists, gold / powers, gold / permission, gold / earth's, gold / mother, gold / matures, gold / matured, gold / friends, gold / call, gold / patiently, gold / go, gold / up, gold / in, gold / tone, gold / find, gold / the -gold / meetings, gold / in, gold / mansions, gold / songs, gold / reside, gold / gateways, gold / portals, gold / friends, gold / anchors, gold / silvers, gold / terraces, gold / greet, gold / men, gold / eclipse, gold / captured, gold / traces, gold / great, gold / men, gold / enclose, gold / light, gold / body, gold / bliss, gold / now, gold / known, gold / escapes, gold / viable, gold.

CHAPTER ELEVEN
1, gold / 2, gold / won, gold / listen, gold / elite, gold / speaking, gold / calls, gold / us, gold / ever, gold / clearly, gold / home, gold / for, gold / a, gold / garden, gold / established, gold / in, gold / welcomed, gold / allow, gold / of, gold / bliss, gold / god's, gold / guess, gold / love, gold / faces, gold / listened, gold / lingers, gold / lost, gold / worlds, gold / washed, gold / awarest, gold / allows, gold / gunas, gold / astonish, gold / contact, gold / cordial, gold / grew, gold / gold, gold / god, gold / g, gold / ideas, gold / playful, gold / emergencies, gold / activities, gold / accents, gold / ascent, gold / mounts, gold / mediates, gold / psychic, gold / physic, gold / rejuvenates, gold / relaxed, gold / soothing, gold / surgical, gold / diets, gold / overt, gold / creates, gold / fears, gold / nutrients, gold / converted, gold / centers, gold / cast, gold / fully, gold / countered, gold / spins, gold.

CHAPTER TWELVE
Steam, gold / blessings, gold / in, gold / lovers, gold / disturbed, gold / recovered, gold / heart, gold / path, gold / shares, gold / suggested, gold / lines, gold / up, gold / secrets -gold / success, gold / life, gold / leaps, gold / savage, gold / surrendered, gold / stands, gold / softens, gold / seasonal, gold / central, gold / eventual, gold / sides, gold / selves, gold / changes, gold / 4's, gold / placed, gold / terra, gold / turtles, gold / f, gold / golden, gold / complete, gold / rigid, gold / conferences, gold / humans, gold / present, gold / presentations, gold / sponsored, gold / sessions -gold / events, gold / partners, gold / bodies -gold / enjoins, gold / buns, gold / paths, gold / readings, gold / hopes, gold / alchemy, gold / theory, gold / entry, gold / webs, gold / blues, gold / stones, gold / praised, gold / shifts, gold / lapis, gold / carved, gold / orders, gold / pheromones, gold / philosophy, gold / elixirs, gold / values, gold / edits, gold.

CHAPTER THIRTEEN
Managed, gold / visions, gold / dirt, gold / compulsive, gold / freights, gold / driven, gold / sleepy, gold / draughts, gold / business, gold / pools, gold / ease, gold / unders, gold / way, gold

/ wildly, gold / touted, gold / shifts, gold / spirits, gold / dissented, gold / usuals -gold / tranced, gold / costs, gold / accompany, gold / interviews, gold / ridden, gold / adamic, gold / grandeurs, gold / ages, gold / mountains, gold / wilds, gold / dependent, gold / defends, gold / invested, gold / values, gold / sex, gold / empowers, gold / eves, gold / mothered, gold / strips, gold / bares, gold / earth, gold / defends, gold / optional, gold / finances, gold / sent, gold / formal, gold / fashions, gold / spirited, gold / pages, gold / explore, gold / terrains, gold / cosmologic, gold / remands, gold / eavesdrops, gold / risen, gold / rides, gold / grandeur, gold / beauties, gold / ferocious, gold / reigns, gold / swords, gold / stripped, gold / shores, gold / courses, gold / pilgrims, gold.

LEVEL 106: THE TREASURE-MENTS

CHAPTER ONE

Treasures, treasures measured, platinum wins through love / ones, treasures / bio-dynamics, treasures / glass, treasures / filled, treasures / mendocino, treasures / wells, treasures / censures, treasures / drawn, treasures / planes, treasures / zodiacal, treasures / constellations, treasures / adds, treasures / magic, treasures / across, treasures / retorted, treasures / operatives, treasures / tastes, treasures / dogmas, treasures / washed, treasures / cents, treasures / purged, treasures / magically, treasures / magus, treasures / arts, treasures / aristocratic, treasures / christed, treasures / virgins, treasures / europeans, treasures / persians, treasures / greeks, treasures / romans, treasures / chosen, treasures / sienna, treasures / declines, treasures / forth, treasures / fundamentals, treasures / recents, treasures / hungry, treasures / tentacles, treasures / empowers, treasures / coins, treasures / generated, treasures / futures, treasures / taught, treasures / coins, treasures / generated, treasures / futures, treasures / taught, treasures / invest, treasures / primarily, treasures / life, treasures / leads, treasures / homes, treasures / shelters, treasures / voted, treasures / forth, treasures / drips, treasures / drops, treasures / cooperates, treasures / flows, treasures / quality, treasures / flaws, treasures / gone, treasures.

CHAPTER TWO

Gathers, treasures / seconds, treasures / surmised, treasures / seattle, treasures / portfolio, treasures / naturely, treasures / socials, treasures / causes, treasures / erodes, treasures / jesus, treasures / doors, treasures / lords, treasures / worn, treasures / without, treasures / realized, treasures / leveraged, treasures / leaders, treasures / money, treasures / plows, treasures / flows, treasures / flowering, treasures / society, treasures / realtions, treasures / repaid, treasures / possibly, treasures / students, treasures / fitness, treasures / solutions, treasures / intensity, treasures / maps, treasures / territories, treasures / gained, treasures / invest, treasures / again, treasures / millions, treasures / won, treasures / one, treasures / joined, treasures / allow, treasures / pulsars, treasures / to, treasures / win, treasures / clarity, treasures / for, treasures / belly's, treasures / burst, treasures / beast, treasures

/ goes, treasures / along, treasures / levels, treasures / leased, treasures / for, treasures / fathoms, treasures / actual, treasures / central, treasures / freed, treasures / money, treasures / mentioned, treasures / ethically, treasures / valued, treasures / naturals, treasures / anomalize, treasures / goodbye, treasures / badge, treasures.

CHAPTER THREE

Mayan, treasures / in, treasures / light, treasures / of, treasures / info -treasures / the, treasures / and, treasures / arc-angelic, treasures / meets, treasures / cone, treasures / the, treasures / leap, treasures / humanity, treasures / of, treasures / sword, treasures / to, treasures / hearten, treasures / by, treasures / i, treasures / arm, treasures / the, treasures / sight, treasures / inside, treasures / life's, treasures / core, treasures / and, treasures / simply, treasures / this, treasures / this, treasures / light, treasures / sweet, treasures / made, treasures / and, treasures / led, treasures / by, treasures / may, treasures / taste, treasures / every, treasures / day, treasures / i, treasures / of, treasures / my, treasures / life, treasures / the, treasures / sound, treasures / through, treasures / best, treasures / your, treasures / our, treasures / sun, treasures / gave, treasures / snoring, treasures / parallel, treasures / our, treasures / son, treasures / gently, treasures / moments, treasures / to, treasures / shares, treasures / wakes, treasures / my, treasures / gliding, treasures / and, treasures / important, treasures.

CHAPTER FOUR

Rise, treasures / inside, treasures / a, treasures / central, treasures / elected, treasures / flights, treasures / and, treasures / the, treasures / electric, treasures / poles, treasures / of, treasures / souls, treasures / the, treasures / simple, treasures / corrected, treasures / for, treasures / breath, treasures / to, treasures / notions, treasures / unique, treasures / in, treasures / the, treasures / trends, treasures / empire, treasures / and, treasures / the, treasures / love's, treasures / long, treasures / wait, treasures / to, treasures / love, treasures / one, treasures / you, treasures / love, treasures / rest, treasures / in, treasures / specific, treasures / the, treasures / a, treasures / heart, treasures / ways, treasures / waves, treasures / worn, treasures / red, treasures / and, treasures / of, treasures / in, treasures / eternal, treasures / di, treasures / oxy, treasures / ribo, treasures / nucleus, treasures / acid, treasures / melt, treasures / soft, treasures / in, treasures / patterned, treasures / parallels, treasures / into, treasures / sour, treasures / lost, treasures / of, treasures / forever, treasures / led, treasures.

CHAPTER FIVE

Remember, treasures / and, treasures / the, treasures / welcome, treasures / strands, treasures / of, treasures / have, treasures / formed, treasures / by, treasures / grace, treasures / a, treasures / place, treasures / god's, treasures / i, treasures / to, treasures / live, treasures / may, treasures / tearful, treasures / forgive, treasures / found, treasures / i, treasures / openly, treasures / struck, v / in, treasures / sell, treasures / day, treasures / by, treasures / fast, treasures / power, treasures / through, treasures / foe, treasures /

loud, treasures / with, treasures / love, treasures / who, treasures / are, treasures / you, treasures / when, treasures / 104th, treasures / complete, treasures / god, treasures / your, treasures / faced, treasures / denied, treasures / elects, treasures / north, treasures / of, treasures / operation, treasures / fashions, treasures / set, treasures / on, treasures / wings, treasures / are, treasures / melted, treasures / rays, treasures / often, treasures / worn, treasures / mountains, treasures / met, treasures / by, treasures / along, treasures / earth's, treasures / softest, treasures / doors, treasures.

CHAPTER SIX
I, treasures / will, treasures / surrender, treasures / to, treasures / we, treasures / and, treasures / we, treasures / are, treasures / the, treasures / light, treasures / brigade, treasures / the, treasures / brochade, treasures / of, treasures / life, treasures / written, treasures / clearly, treasures / patience, treasures / has, treasures / paid, v / tonight, v / say, treasures / often, treasures / fed, treasures / as, treasures / tearful, treasures / allow, treasures / instincts, treasures / height, treasures / are, treasures / brochure, treasures / in, treasures / for, treasures / a, treasures / journey, treasures / strict, treasures / dear, treasures / daily, treasures / shifted, treasures / in, treasures / entrance, treasures / interior, treasures / tubes, treasures / searing, treasures / set, treasures / on, treasures / math, treasures / flipped, treasures / along, treasures / lord, treasures / piece, treasures / to, treasures / peace, treasures / has, treasures / left, treasures / fargo, treasures / and, treasures / found, treasures / a, treasures / companion, treasures / in, treasures / flow, treasures / angel, treasures / want, treasures.

CHAPTER SEVEN
Here, treasures / favor treasures / for, treasures / men, treasures / solar, treasures / counting, treasures / do, treasures / a, treasures / flares, treasures / corrected, treasures / openly, treasures / dean, treasures / earth, treasures / breathe, treasures / us, treasures / love, treasures / wave, treasures / left, treasures / good, treasures / here, treasures / a, treasures / new, treasures / way, treasures / desire, treasures / left, treasures / placed, treasures / us, treasures / has, treasures / and, treasures / joy, treasures / into, treasures / chance, treasures / knows, treasures / you, treasures / lose, treasures / love, treasures / may, treasures / you, treasures / share, treasures / a, treasures / flowering, treasures / kin, treasures / shipped, treasures / direct, treasures / to, treasures / doors, treasures / of, treasures / when, treasures / of, treasures / debates, treasures / and, treasures / finding, treasures / sort, treasures / love, treasures / pad, treasures / become, treasures / thought, treasures / for, treasures / friends, treasures / lynching, treasures / of, treasures / ideas, treasures / freely, treasures / friend, treasures.

CHAPTER EIGHT
The, treasures / dates, treasures / of, treasures / elective, treasures / to, treasures / love, treasures / offers, treasures / sprints, treasures / over, treasures / land, treasures / familiar, treasures / with, treasures / sought, treasures / and, treasures / a, treasures / selection, treasures / our, treasures / aloft, treasures / offered, treasures / windows,

treasures / presides, treasures / voyers, treasures / eternally, treasures / understand, treasures / in, treasures / ancient, treasures / unions, treasures / headed, treasures / for, treasures / review, treasures / scribe, treasures / spent, treasures / with, treasures / love, treasures / admit, treasures / it, treasures / we, treasures / win, treasures / paradise, treasures / with, treasures / love, treasures / level, treasures / out, treasures / over, treasures / seas, treasures / whose, treasures / baths, treasures / elevate, treasures / collectively, treasures / superior, treasures / infants, treasures / match, treasures / complication, treasures / though, treasures / roman, treasures / iced, treasures / heart, treasures / traffic, treasures / in, treasures / isolated, treasures / burns, treasures / issues, treasures / made, treasures / marks, treasures.

CHAPTER NINE
Head, treasures / flow, treasures / flashed, treasures / purchase, treasures / revealed, treasures / plans, treasures / planned, treasures / spun, treasures / spinning, treasures / lips, treasures / push, treasures / for, treasures / reforms, treasures / budget, treasures / time, treasures / to, treasures / special, treasures / opened, treasures / ancient, treasures / truths, treasures / pages, treasures / knolls, treasures / ways, treasures / once, treasures / rages, treasures / sleeve, treasures / of, treasures / i, treasures / left, treasures / eternal, treasures / paid, treasures / for, treasures / is, treasures / links, treasures / are, treasures / love, treasures / as, treasures / pouring, treasures / forth, treasures / now, treasures / close, treasures / for, treasures / lessons, treasures / broth, treasures / as, treasures / lipped, treasures / by, treasures / which, treasures / friends, treasures / who, treasures / tiger, treasures / in, treasures / electro, treasures / collection, treasures / states, treasures / equalized, treasures / through, treasures / realized, treasures / rather, treasures / release, treasures / credit, treasures / result, treasures / train, treasures / lust, treasures.

CHAPTER TEN
Apply, treasures / for, treasures / loans, treasures / love, treasures / said, treasures / in, treasures / tracts, treasures / sold, treasures / computers, treasures / place, treasures / intensely, treasures / near, treasures / pulsars, treasures / peak, treasures / rapidly, treasures / tiring, treasures / only, treasures / arcs, treasures / variously, treasures / clears, treasures / when, treasures / arrivals, treasures / pens, treasures / mists, treasures / times, treasures / trained, treasures / fractals, treasures / over, treasures / homogeny, treasures / pays, treasures / emotions, treasures / spinning, treasures / constant, treasures / coooling, treasures / towers, treasures / instructs, treasures / kin, treasures / believe, treasures / basics, treasures / fond, treasures / colors, treasures / collective, treasures / leys, treasures / memorized, treasures / link, treasures / lasts, treasures / opened, treasures / wavespells, treasures / smart, treasures / enough, treasures / fit, treasures / all, treasures / electrical, treasures / posts, treasures / paged, treasures / pressing, treasures / praise, treasures / pools, treasures / parts, treasures / posted, treasures / peach, treasures / intervals, treasures / intercourse, treasures / captured, treasures.

CHAPTER ELEVEN: pleasure, treasures / erotic, treasures / movements, treasures / within, treasures / aural, treasures / oric, treasures / plentic, treasures / pensive, treasures / airs, treasures / waters, treasures / geysers, treasures / mists, treasures / pools, treasures / rivers, treasures / streams, treasures / farms, treasures / ranches, treasures / openness, treasures / waterfall, treasures / temples, treasures / templar, treasures / unities, treasures / savior, treasures / found, treasures / ascend, treasures / in, treasures / clouds, treasures / of, treasures / rapture, treasures / electric, treasures / annoint, treasures / lovers, treasures / in, treasures / sacred, treasures / positions, treasures / envelope, treasures / seizure, treasures / arms, treasures / planned, treasures / ahead, treasures / instruct, treasures / others, treasures / heat, treasures / financial, treasures / gain, treasures / explain, treasures / well, treasures / order, treasures / empath, treasures / too, treasures / return, treasures / instruct, treasures / devoid, treasures / wands, treasures / ones, treasures / rear, treasures / position, treasures / flights, treasures / are, treasures / set, treasures / associations, treasures / made, treasures / insurance, treasures / paid, treasures.

CHAPTER TWELVE
Direct, treasures / contact, treasures / with, treasures / the, treasures / other, treasures / finance, treasures / a, treasures / deal, treasures / through, treasures / integral, treasures / abilities, treasures / agile, treasures / minds, treasures / joined, treasures / your, treasures / team, treasures / squad, treasures / pods, treasures / paid, treasures / for, treasures / the, treasures / works, treasures / done, treasures / retreat, treasures / shall, treasures / you, treasures / endeavor, treasures / to, treasures / implore, treasures / more, treasures / yes, treasures / is, treasures / the, treasures / terms, treasures / of, treasures / a, treasures / new, treasures / millenium, treasures / measured, treasures / by, treasures / only, treasures / this, treasures / love, treasures / impaired, treasures / has, treasures / gone, treasures / to, treasures / the, treasures / termination, treasures / of, treasures / calls, treasures / by, treasures / sword, treasures / sets, treasures / of, treasures / blocks, treasures / lavendar, treasures / in, treasures / pink, treasures / sheen, treasures / of, treasures / arcturian, treasures / waves, treasures / pillows, treasures

CHAPTER THIRTEEN
Play, treasures / along, treasures / with, treasures / the, treasures / light, treasures / encodes, treasures / and, treasures / know, treasures / that, treasures / the, treasures / truth, treasures / is, treasures / ever, treasures / always, treasures / in, treasures / love, treasures / laughter, treasures / is, treasures / the, treasures / essential, treasures / ingredient, treasures / between, treasures / hearts, treasures / that, treasures / beat, treasures / for, treasures / pulsar, treasures / two, treasures / a, treasures / new, treasures / phase, treasures / has, treasures / begun, treasures / welcome, treasures / to, treasures / the, treasures / son, treasures / of, treasures / a, treasures / holy, treasures / arrival, treasures / and, treasures / the, treasures / peace, treasures / of, treasures / an, treasures / intrinsic, treasures / expression, treasures / of, treasures / the,

treasures / devotion, treasures / of, treasures / god, treasures / to, treasures / basic, treasures / humanity, treasures / recall, treasures / a, treasures / patient, treasures / friend, treasures / has, treasures / found, treasures / release, treasures / allow, treasures.

LEVEL 107: THE PLATINUM-MENTS

CHAPTER ONE
Platinum, platinum purses and the hearses without wheels, light, loves / nuptials, platinum / to, platinum / begin, platinum / impress, platinum / the, platinum / resurrection, platinum / of, platinum / life, platinum / through, platinum / the, platinum / way, platinum / and, platinum / the, platinum / truth, platinum / of, platinum / love, platinum / a, platinum / placement, platinum / has, platinum / begon, platinum / others, platinum / arrive, platinum / hearts valued, platinum / enjoy, platinum / standard, platinum / gifts, platinum / faces, platinum / are, platinum / lit, platinum / by, platinum / the, platinum / banners, platinum / of, platinum / love, platinum / many, platinum / a, platinum / well, platinum / heart, platinum / meet, platinum / yours, platinum / in, platinum / a, platinum / timeless, platinum / embrace, platinum / of, platinum / the, platinum / precious, platinum / experience, platinum / of, platinum / human, platinum / love, platinum / affluence, platinum / has, platinum / come, platinum / to, platinum / the, platinum / meek, platinum / and, platinum / the, platinum / inherited, platinum / have, platinum / the, platinum / earth, platinum.

CHAPTER TWO
To, platinum / thank, platinum / for, platinum / their, platinum / art, platinum / of, platinum / surrender, platinum / and, platinum / the, platinum / science, platinum / of, platinum / love, platinum / know, platinum / the, platinum / season, platinum / human, platinum / life, platinum / force, platinum / divinity, platinum / of, platinum / exasperated, platinum / friends, platinum / who, platinum / anchor, platinum / the, platinum / shift, platinum / to, platinum / living, platinum / example, platinum / exlempary, platinum / stars, platinum / is, platinum / structure, platinum / gains, platinum / as, platinum / finite, platinum / becomes, platinum / infinite, platinum / in, platinum / a, platinum / magnificant, platinum / frame, platinum / called, platinum / human, platinum / life, platinum / smells, platinum / wonder, platinum / signs, platinum / and, platinum / miracales, platinum / link, platinum / our, platinum / lasting, platinum / love, platinum / to, platinum / the, platinum / sound, platinum / of, platinum / hosannah, platinum / and, platinum / this, platinum / tell, platinum / arrange, platinum / money, platinum.

CHAPTER THREE
The, platinum / presense, platinum / essentialy, platinum / love, platinum / as, platinum / inheritance, platinum / grows, platinum / and, platinum / the, platinum / telling, platinum / improve, platinum / a, platinum / magnificane, platinum / is, platinum / heard, platinum / through, platinum / a, platinum / written,

platinum / song, platinum / of, platinum / the, platinum / heaven, platinum / singing, platinum / and, platinum / the, platinum / angel, platinum / flap, platinum / of, platinum / soften, platinum / wings, platinum / and, platinum / tender, platinum / lasting, platinum / call, platinum / to, platinum / humanity's, platinum / alter, platinum / the, platinum / heart, platinum / human, platinum / and, platinum / benfience, platinum / of, platinum / god, platinum / as, platinum / we, platinum / walk, platinum / may, platinum / we, platinum / stay, platinum / ever, platinum / always, platinum / in, platinum / love, platinum / and, platinum / filled, platinum / with, platinum / grace, platinum / to, platinum / the, platinum / life, platinum / eternal, platinum / we, platinum / are, platinum.

CHAPTER FOUR

One, platinum / song, platinum / soft, platinum / in, platinum / the, platinum / total, platinum / registration, platinum / of, platinum / blue-green, platinum / masses, platinum / which, platinum / become, platinum / a, platinum / glorious, platinum / planet, platinum / of, platinum / love, platinum / in, platinum / the, platinum / heart, platinum / of, platinum / the, platinum / all, platinum / 1, platinum / reside, platinum / with, platinum / you, platinum / in, platinum / perfect, platinum / splendor, platinum / and, platinum / a, platinum / living, platinum / renew, platinum / of, platinum / a, platinum / loving, platinum / god, platinum / may, platinum / we, platinum / well, platinum / be, platinum / through, platinum / the, platinum / light, platinum / of, platinum / a, platinum / listening, platinum / example, platinum / of, platinum / humanity's, platinum / core, platinum / freedom, platinum / arrange, platinum / we, platinum / are, platinum / loved, platinum / and, platinum / now, platinum / we, platinum / know, platinum / the, platinum / gift, platinum / love, platinum

CHAPTER FIVE

Tranquil, platinum / serene, platinum / releasing, platinum / opens, platinum / oracles, platinum / views, platinum / ancient, platinum / waves, platinum / stare, platinum / delivers, platinum / meats, platinum / opal, platinum / graze, platinum / crystal, platinum / pulses, platinum / over, platinum / notion, platinum / pulls, platinum / pant, platinum / act, platinum / activities, platinum / coupled, platinum / representative, platinum / through, platinum / cost, platinum / cause, platinum / master, platinum / blues, platinum / jazz, platinum / moon, platinum / more, platinum / meant, platinum / beaming, platinum / tramples, platinum / transports, platinum / regeneration, platinum / codices, platinum / ply, platinum / waysv / situation, platinum / pertain, platinum / situated, platinum / learns, platinum / openings, platinum / crystals, platinum / formed, platinum / completitions, platinum / spectals, platinum / recieve, platinum / rub, platinum / banned, platinum / for, platinum / liberty, platinum / attained, platinum / friends, platinum / glow, platinum / camp, platinum / cave, platinum / friendly, platinum / know, platinum / material, platinum / overtune, platinum / tetragon, platinum / ones, platinum

CHAPTER SIX

Converts, platinum / tunes, platinum / places, platinum / beams,

platinum / following, platinum / winds, platinum / attribute, platinum / to, platinum / the, platinum / movements, platinum / of, platinum / universal, platinum / crystals, platinum / sit, platinum / swords, platinum / beloved, platinum / same, platinum / train, platinum / present, platinum / plans, platinum / fires, platinum / future, platinumfresh, platinum / facts, platinum / fames, platinum / palatial, platinum / jasmine, platinum / into, platinum / features, platinum / palaces, platinum / desperate, platinum / released, platinum / cosmic, platinum / regrow, platinum / station, platinum / simple, platinum / spells, platinum / break, platinum / nexus, platinum / points, platinum / pins, platinum / burst, platinum / for, platinum / future, platinum / permanant, platinum / pockets, platinum / try, platinum / dates, platinum / flowering, platinum / flashing, platinum / farest, platinum / fox, platinum / task, platinum / challenged, platinum / clears, platinum / cares, platinum / entrance, platinum / subtle, platinum / change, platinum / felt, platinum / fields, platinum / choice, platinum / change, platinum / choice, platinum

CHAPTER SEVEN

Calm, platinum / predates, platinum / dawn, platinum / experience, platinum emphase, platinum / settles, platinum / insecurely, platinum / flowers, platinum / fathers, platinum / mothers, platinum / genuine, platinum / giants, platinum / earthly, platinum / more, platinum / met, platinum / release, platinum / follow, platinum / truth, platinum / home, platinum / go, platinum / wayward, platinum / leans, platinum / have, platinum / spent, platinum / last, platinum / days, platinum / for, platinum / fortunes, platinum / met, platinum / in, platinum / little, platinum / big, platinum / motive, platinum / made, platinum / a, platinum / benefit, platinum / for, platinum / blues, platinum / gone, platinum / and, platinum / good, platinum / times, platinum / around, platinum / armed, platinum / in, platinum / arcs, platinum/ aware, platinum / for, platinum / parade, platinum / may, platinum / interest, platinum / building, platinum / ends, platinum / our, platinum / for, platinum / reaches, platinum / grace, platinum / seeds, platinum / family, platinum / rapt, platinum / grows, platinum / spring, platinum / family, platinum / attends, platinum

CHAPTER EIGHT:

Apply, platinum / your, platinum / set, platinum / song, platinum / natural, platinum / taught, platinum / definition, platinum / refines, platinum / mystical, platinum / following, platinum / whales, platinum / waves, platinum / mystifies, platinum / wellness, platinum / affuent, platinum / preach, platinum / teach, platinum / means, platinum / made, platinum / simply, platinum / astor, platinum / green, platinum / acts, platinum / again, platinum / saviors, platinum / complexity, platinum / consumes, platinum / until, platinum / wonderful, platinum / windows, platinum / part, platinum / people, platinum / clear, platinum / calling, platinum / lakes, platinum / interior, platinum / stay, platinum / alert, platinum / for, platinum / shifts, platinum / shining, platinum / meets, platinum / managerial, platinum / mats, platinum / stars, platinum / for, platinum / mateices, platinum / moves, platinum / paged, platinum / capitals, platinum / felt, platinum / laughs, platinum / punchv / changed, platinum / number, platinum / comes, platinum / powers, platinum / cast, platinum / over, platinum / vents, platinum / insure, platinum / fortune, platinum / found, platinum / goods, platinum.

CHAPTER NINE

Scans, platinum / parks, platinum / beach, platinum / a, platinum / 5th, platinum / avenues, platinum / banks, platinum / to, platinum / resting, platinum / rest, platinum / ropes, platinum / parent, platinum / intrudes, platinum / days, platinum / elope, platinum / open, platinum / shafts, platinum / chime, platinum / gone, platinum / fortune, platinum / later, platinum / bells, platinum / with, platinum / walls, platinum / lucid, platinum / recognize, platinum / leagues, platinum / league, platinum / quadrants, platinum / clues, platinum / ladid, platinum / along, platinum / plan, platinum / digits, platinum / dial, platinum / emotes, platinum / full, platinum / pans, platinum / purchase, platinum / made, platinum / formatted, platinum / insure, platinum / reads, platinum / long, platinum / level, platinum / custom, platinum / ocean, platinum / seas, platinum / teach, platinum / mules, platinum / females, platinum / ancient, platinum / vision, platinum / mates, platinum / pull, platinum / marvels, platinum / vaunts, platinum / allocate, platinum / dance, platinum / technique, platinum / forms, platinum / colorful, platinum / declares, platinum / win, platinum.

CHAPTER TEN

Open, platinum / ways, platinum / wave, platinum / pairs, platinum / grey, platinum / gone, platinum / gates, platinum / close, platinum / vote, platinum / demote, platinum / debate, platinum / daily, platinum / december, platinum / commands, platinum / fans, platinum / frail, platinum / homeward, platinum / bound, platinum / upward, platinum / settles, platinum / suggested, platinum / formats, platinum / frees, platinum / face, platinum / french, platinum / footsteeps, platinum / follows, platinum / feels, platinum / fame, platinum / fortune, platinum / finds, platinum / form, platinum / flaming, platinum / farms, platinum / lands, platinum / ridges, platinum / cords, platinum / rivers, platinum / row, platinum / ranch, platinum / deepens, platinum / firm, platinum / exact, platinum / infact, platinum / days, platinum / reads, platinum / reap, platinum / ranks, platinum / apt, platinum / breath, platinum / gift, platinum / given, platinum / in, platinum / born, platinum / to, platinum / breed, platinum / dues, platinum / lace, platinum / built, platinum / barns, platinum / news, platinum / spread, platinum / election, platinum / made, platinum.

CHAPTER ELEVEN

Forms, platinum / wide, platinum / to, platinum / legible, platinum / goes, platinum / notes, platinum / northern, platinum / nodes, platinum / witness, platinum / pat, platinum / answer, platinum / insure, platinum / material, platinum / next, platinum / need, platinum / leave, platinum / may, platinum / we, platinum / remember, platinum / all, platinum / trined, platinum / incur, platinum / occupy, platinum / next, platinum / intrigues, platinum

/ operates, platinum / again, platinum / for, platinum / allow, platinum / fairy, platinum / tale, platinum / truths, platinum / way, platinum / the, platinum / window, platinum / on, platinum / a, platinum / near, platinum / doorv / apart, platinum / love's, platinum / down, platinum / will, platinum / we, platinum / play, platinum / the, platinum / pay, platinum / for, platinum / focus, platinum / onyx, platinum / love's, platinum / spark, platinum / stark, platinum / days, platinum / close, platinum / hello, platinum / to, platinum / living, platinum / encounter, platinum / maps, platinum / amuse, platinum / means, platinum / dear, platinum / days, platinum.

CHAPTER TWELVE

For, platinum / love, platinum / left, platinum / to, platinum / wear, platinum / staring, platinum / excite, platinum / invite, platinum / eve, platinum / near, platinum / antique, platinum / scenes, platinum / mentions, platinum / meet, platinum / material, platinum / means, platinum / passion, platinum / fashion, platinum / plane, platinum / journeys, platinum / fashion, platinum / joins, platinum / legend, platinum / mations, platinum / pairing, platinum / screens, platinum / paints, platinum / sounds, platinum / equal, platinum / fueled, platinum / fasten, platinum / zeus, platinum / narrow, platinum / influx, platinum / fasten, platinum / meets, platinum / links, platinum / looks, platinum / pureness, platinum / magical, platinum / leaps, platinum / passage, platinum / post, platinum / matched, platinum / human, platinum / pave, platinum / gideon, platinum / maneuvers, platinum / rivers, platinum / burden, platinum / gaberiel, platinum / bring, platinum / resume, platinum / less, platinum / goshen, platinum / basically, platinum / pairs, platinum / waves, platinum / lands, platinum / tract, platinum / begin, platinum / wish, platinum / get, platinum / fizxed, platinum

CHAPTER THIRTEEN

Facts, platinum / stairs, platinum / house, platinum / island, platinum / laid, platinum / gentry, platinum / lurched, platinum / leaps, platinum / into, platinum / landed, platinum / learning, platinum / loves, platinum / lines, platinum / genes, platinum / living, platinum / impeached, platinum / set, platinum / god, platinum / lead, platinum / through, platinum / for, platinum / and, platinum / is, platinum / living, platinum / forth, platinum / listened, platinum / linger, platinum / is, platinum / good, platinum / ti, platinum / love's, platinum / ended, platinum / sung, platinum / low, platinum / matter, platinum / founded, platinum / lungs, platinum / lowering, platinum / final, platinum / framed, platinum / links, platinum / moo, platinum / phase, platinum / sold, platinum / lapse, platinum / match, platinum / intrinsically, platinum / fresh, platinum / fondly, platinum / often, platinum / fuel, platinum / fallen, platinum / single, platinum / pulls, platinum / for, platinum / compromise, platinum / simple, platinum / stints, platinum / lessons, platinum / caring, platinum / possessive, platinum / often, platinum / past, platinum / bring, platinum

LEVEL 108: THE TITANIUM-MENTS

CHAPTER ONE
Parents, titanium / driven, titanium / essential, titanium / elective, titanium / children, titanium / dealing, titanium / happy, titanium / material, titanium / chosen, titanium / dance, titanium / daring, titanium / eyes, titanium / widen, titanium / wons, titanium / dates, titanium / electric, titanium / spins, titanium / worm, titanium / maybes, titanium / stakes, titanium / trances, titanium / hole, titanium / empires, titanium / tracing, titanium / trims, titanium / mention, titanium / empowered, titanium / lasting, titanium / trends, titanium / magic, titanium / movies, titanium / art, titanium / mends, titanium / latch, titanium / laps, titanium / learn, titanium / leans, titanium / off, titanium / leads, titanium / clutched, titanium / clans, titanium / often, titanium / lasting, titanium / clues, titanium / clans, titanium / fans, titanium / applaud, titanium / clips, titanium / factual, titanium / stones, titanium / note, titanium / pails, titanium / symbolic, titanium / oppose, titanium / peers, titanium / extremes, titanium / spiritual, titanium / six, titanium / separate, titanium / studies, titanium / keys, titanium / full, titanium / file, titanium / last, titanium.

CHAPTER TWO
Center, titanium / built, titanium / lopes, titanium / across, titanium / nerves, titanium / need, titanium / unified, titanium / random, titanium / fibers, titanium / pull, titanium / off, titanium / rays, titanium / raised, titanium / tributes, titanium / trust, titanium / approach, titanium / golden, titanium / hold, titanium / held, titanium / well, titanium / placed, titanium / detach, titanium / walk, titanium / ears, titanium / needs, titanium / effort, titanium / smells, titanium / soothe, titanium / nipples, titanium / sexual, titanium / single, titanium / parent, titanium / needs, titanium / shop, titanium / help, titanium / head, titanium / huge, titanium / not, titanium / lobes, titanium / blend, titanium / planes, titanium / animate, titanium / subrogation, titanium / overtly, titanium / done, titanium / dearest, titanium / abilities, titanium / platform, titanium / hollow, titanium / hope, titanium / ample, titanium / built, titanium / live, titanium / found, titanium / express, titanium / division, titanium / days, titanium / over, titanium / resist, titanium / return, titanium / retain, titanium / refund, titanium / transit, titanium / kiss, titanium.

CHAPTER THREE
Free, titanium / electrically, titanium / encode, titanium / from, titanium / teaching, titanium / thinking, titanium / value, titanium / is, titanium / tears, titanium / forgone, titanium / conclude, titanium / whole, titanium / discourse, titanium / image, titanium / liquids, titanium / living, titanium / of, titanium / a, titanium / living, titanium / when, titanium / we, titanium / feel, titanium / more, titanium / fun, titanium / central, titanium / organization, titanium / need, titanium / weeds, titanium / pull, titanium / champions, titanium / most, titanium / organelle, titanium / we, titanium / fend, titanium / less, titanium / loft, titanium / acknowledge, titanium / mothers, titanium / gap, titanium / plenty, titanium /

left, titanium / to, titanium / grow, titanium / helpful, titanium / teaching, titanium / turns, titanium / create, titanium / study, titanium / stares, titanium / marrow, titanium / wise, titanium / into, titanium / blind, titanium / suppose, titanium / disaster, titanium / avert, titanium / through, titanium / medical, titanium / diagonal, titanium / nerves, titanium / go, titanium / light, titanium / north, titanium / welcome, titanium.

CHAPTER FOUR
Chicago, titanium / sport, titanium / offer, titanium / and, titanium / sensory, titanium / deep, titanium / in, titanium / pane, titanium / soothes, titanium / glee, titanium / hopes, titanium / spiral, titanium / still, titanium / returns, titanium / reigns, titanium / treats, titanium / marries, titanium / ancient, titanium / bears, titanium / blood, titanium / numbers, titanium / windy, titanium / fault, titanium / defines, titanium / to, titanium / vault, titanium / gone, titanium / hearts, titanium / open, titanium / columns, titanium / lit, titanium / hearts, titanium / voice, titanium / choose, titanium / in, titanium / admissive, titanium / letters, titanium / written, titanium / under, titanium / chore, titanium / agreement, titanium / found, titanium / standing, titanium / is, titanium / worn, titanium / onto, titanium / score, titanium / make, titanium / carried, titanium / lifts, titanium / screen, titanium / allow, titanium / brains, titanium / know, titanium / plays, titanium / yearn, titanium / worlds, titanium / couple, titanium / people, titanium / manage, titanium / well, titanium / nations, titanium / stop, titanium / play, titanium.

CHAPTER FIVE
Collide, titanium / lost, titanium / cycle, titanium / award, titanium / interest, titanium / separation, titanium / myth, titanium / most, titanium / pain, titanium / nativity, titanium / teaches, titanium / mind, titanium / peace, titanium / given, titanium / nature, titanium / change, titanium / sacred, titanium / clear, titanium / deal, titanium / understand, titanium / sacred, titanium / openly, titanium / find, titanium / for, titanium / sites, titanium / useful, titanium / found, titanium / simple, titanium / temples, titanium / men, titanium / skill, titanium / stay, titanium / starving, titanium / cost, titanium / one, titanium / wins, titanium / aware, titanium / relates, titanium / rations, titanium / tossed, titanium / blocks, titanium / off, titanium / often, titanium / field, titanium / at, titanium / the, titanium / wells, titanium / circulated, titanium / valuable, titanium / lines, titanium / involve, titanium / love, titanium / perfect, titanium / link, titanium / sorts, titanium / grow, titanium / fault, titanium / civilized, titanium / glands, titanium / weak, titanium / wait, titanium / tub, titanium / hot, titanium / soak, titanium.

CHAPTER SIX
Walls, titanium / spent, titanium / twelfth, titanium / octave, titanium / burst, titanium / axis, titanium / stone, titanium / temple, titanium / into, titanium / caverns, titanium / line, titanium / clarity, titanium / rooms, titanium / walls, titanium / clarify, titanium / reveals, titanium / muse, titanium / mince, titanium / geared, titanium / gills, titanium / maturity, titanium / less, titanium /

gains, titanium / matched, titanium / words, titanium / gears, titanium / link, titanium / meet, titanium / warrant, titanium / growth, titanium / ledge, titanium / entire, titanium / trees, titanium / base, titanium / established, titanium / patch, titanium / travel, titanium / trues, titanium / gaining, titanium / laughing, titanium / categories, titanium / turns, titanium / living, titanium / pens, titanium / stone, titanium / into, titanium / life, titanium / nerve, titanium / sent, titanium/ through, titanium / gas, titanium / lingers, titanium / in, titanium / rhymes, titanium / hot, titanium / doors, titanium / splashing, titanium / vital, titanium / signs, titanium / soaring, titanium / matters, titanium / conclude, titanium / pledge, titanium / voyage, titanium.

CHAPTER SEVEN
May, titanium / hitch, titanium / page, titanium / pay, titanium / mats, titanium / rocks, titanium / grate, titanium / hearts, titanium / mighty, titanium / geometric, titanium / goods, titanium / open, titanium / heads, titanium / roll, titanium / past, titanium / belonging, titanium / harmonious, titanium / held, titanium / mastery, titanium/ form, titanium / insight, titanium / govern, titanium / bacteria, titanium / mold, titanium / gained, titanium / gems, titanium / spores, titanium / ego, titanium / gears, titanium / growing, titanium / into, titanium / days, titanium / healing, titanium / signals, titanium / swords, titanium / legs, titanium / cutting, titanium / requires, titanium / rapture, titanium / door, titanium / deals, titanium / cut, titanium / pencil, titanium / tossed, titanium / eliminative, titanium / ins, titanium / outs, titanium / all, titanium / for, titanium / federated, titanium / allies, titanium / develop, titanium / lights, titanium / works, titanium / workers, titanium / happy, titanium / aid, titanium / come, titanium / earn, titanium / earth, titanium / peace, titanium / angels, titanium / place, titanium / gone, titanium.

CHAPTER EIGHT
DNA, titanium / debates, titanium / deemed, titanium / due, titanium / physiological, titanium / clues, titanium / cover, titanium / cower, titanium / levels, titanium / fuse, titanium / leapt, titanium / across, titanium / learned, titanium / continue, titanium / your, titanium / efforts, titanium / living, titanium / since, titanium / squall, titanium / ways, titanium / entertain, titanium / tan, titanium / tread, titanium / often, titanium / toning, titanium / tunes, titanium / instantly, titanium / walls, titanium / trust, titanium / across, titanium / rocks, titanium / bluff, titanium / wage, titanium / worn, titanium / cosmic, titanium / crowns, titanium / energetic, titanium / tiny, titanium / gone, titanium / for, titanium / freedom's, titanium / friend's, titanium / flaming, titanium / azalea, titanium / draws, titanium / forces, titanium / print, titanium / pages, titanium / October, titanium / tuned, titanium / understand, titanium / on, titanium / exclude, titanium / off, titanium / hearts, titanium / on, titanium / laugh, titanium / plates, titanium / plunge, titanium / blue, titanium / better, titanium / ways, titanium / confused, titanium / concentration, titanium.

CHAPTER NINE
Positive, titanium / pulls, titanium / water, titanium / wins, titanium / in, titanium / emerge, titanium / require, titanium / acquire, titanium / energies, titanium / rhymes, titanium / actual, titanium / include, titanium / entire, titanium / indicate, titanium / dates, titanium / with, titanium / open, titanium / glance, titanium / with, titanium / seat, titanium / wide, titanium / volumes, titanium / living, titanium / event, titanium/ process, titanium / merge, titanium / coded, titanium / grids, titanium / leap, titanium / publish, titanium / prop, titanium / chakra, titanium / call, titanium / wise, titanium / shaving, titanium / remarks, titanium / sages, titanium / sealed, titanium / seven, titanium / ways, titanium / written, titanium / codes, titanium / up, titanium / doors, titanium / spirit, titanium / bite, titanium / break, titanium / byte, titanium / remind, titanium / fuel, titanium / herald, titanium / claws, titanium / living, titanium / moon, titanium / abide, titanium/ aberration, titanium / again, titanium / push, titanium / win, titanium / fuse, titanium / much, titanium / hide, titanium / earn, titanium / burn, titanium.

CHAPTER TEN
Levels, titanium / returns, titanium / red, titanium / winds, titanium / last, titanium / fluid, titanium / nation's, titanium / eliminate, titanium / lovers, titanium / full, titanium / spend, titanium / wins, titanium / doors, titanium / focus, titanium / in, titanium / healing, titanium / issue, titanium / pen, titanium / object, titanium / habit, titanium / cured, titanium / last, titanium / legs, titanium/ road, titanium / resolve, titanium / reaps, titanium / respect, titanium / heals, titanium / after, titanium / core, titanium / tomb, titanium / reaped, titanium / developed, titanium / mastery, titanium / mused, titanium / planets, titanium / depth, titanium / sleeps, titanium / master, titanium / manual, titanium / sphere, titanium / feels, titanium / evolve, titanium / how, titanium / recall, titanium / rust, titanium / often, titanium / run, titanium / come, titanium / ran, titanium / double, titanium / guilds, titanium / gold, titanium / spend, titanium / spark, titanium / keep, titanium / human, titanium / silver, titanium / spoken, titanium / dearest, titanium / cubes, titanium / hammock, titanium / humanity, titanium / please, titanium.

CHAPTER ELEVEN
Your, titanium / years, titanium / yes, titanium / leads, titanium / leaves, titanium / view, titanium / camera, titanium / wrote, titanium / leaps, titanium / ranks, titanium / fellow, titanium / attain, titanium / let, titanium / lives, titanium / link, titanium / lead, titanium / rest, titanium / book, titanium / curbs, titanium / lives, titanium/ ramps, titanium / complete, titanium / out, titanium / living, titanium / rip, titanium / light, titanium / technology, titanium / ample, titanium / hook, titanium / resolve, titanium / rested, titanium / full, titanium / you, titanium / a, titanium / planet, titanium / 4, titanium / compile, titanium / for, titanium / relief, titanium / way, titanium/ owner, titanium / your, titanium / member, titanium / homes, titanium / burn, titanium / in, titanium /

joined, titanium / empowered, titanium / match, titanium / mental, titanium / intrigues, titanium / earth, titanium / native, titanium / natural, titanium / needs, titanium / the, titanium / core, titanium / opening, titanium / next, titanium / one, titanium / channel, titanium / we, titanium / need, titanium / exercise, titanium.

CHAPTER TWELVE

Group, titanium / waves, titanium / watch, titanium / next, titanium / doors, titanium / 150, titanium / ways, titanium / when, titanium / license, titanium / links, titanium / love, titanium / to, titanium / works, titanium/ stuck, titanium / goes, titanium / along, titanium / already, titanium / had, titanium / fall, titanium / data, titanium / established, titanium / luck, titanium / stance, titanium / sends, titanium / atmosphere, titanium / to, titanium / realize, titanium / grace, titanium / lack, titanium / blame, titanium / for, titanium / good, titanium / alarm, titanium / to, titanium / life, titanium / insight, titanium / cast, titanium / comes, titanium / in, titanium / essential, titanium / to, titanium / structure, titanium / sails, titanium / to, titanium / abyss, titanium / other, titanium / shores, titanium/ master, titanium / system, titanium / parked, titanium / in, titanium / developed, titanium / doors, titanium / look, titanium / to, titanium / balance, titanium / leaves, titanium / across, titanium / open, titanium / news, titanium / raft, titanium / waves, titanium / frequent, titanium / form, titanium.

CHAPTER THIRTEEN

Body, titanium / matched, titanium/ wings, titanium / gap, titanium / surrender, titanium / mates, titanium/ find, titanium / fix, titanium/ only, titanium / millionaire, titanium / groove, titanium / funds, titanium/ love's, titanium / notes, titanium / caught, titanium / sensed, titanium / sixteen, titanium / planes, titanium / purchase, titanium/ ticket, titanium / ways, titanium / list, titanium / Venus, titanium / airs, titanium / me, titanium / 4, titanium / volume, titanium / depths, titanium / taught, titanium / days, titanium / down, titanium / draft, titanium / Friday, titanium / involve, titanium / seal, titanium / splashes, titanium / send, titanium / balance, titanium / of, titanium / listings, titanium / through, titanium / deans, titanium / of, titanium / manifold, titanium / sensory, titanium / tones, titanium / triple, titanium / wedge, titanium / fast, titanium / anchors, titanium / dare, titanium / leave, titanium / developed, titanium / technique, titanium / for, titanium / codes, titanium / dunes, titanium / reaps, titanium / beneficial, titanium / jobs, titanium / earth, titanium / marriage, titanium / universal, titanium / rays, titanium.

LEVEL 109: THE ZINC-MENTS

CHAPTER ONE

Bodies, zinc / divine, zinc / ports, zinc / opened, zinc / formed, zinc / cape, zinc / for, zinc / laws, zinc / near, zinc / color, zinc / pass, zinc / passage, zinc / means, zinc / of, zinc / comes, zinc / sculptors, zinc / signal, zinc / duplicate, zinc / shores, zinc / elects, zinc / programmed, zinc / sun, zinc / trails, zinc / change, zinc / wealth, zinc / felt, zinc / complex, zinc / orange, zinc / waters, zinc / compile, zinc / transfer, zinc / hourly, zinc / rapt, zinc / reigns, zinc / ran, zinc / a, zinc / lasting, zinc / level, zinc / for, zinc / lapse, zinc / universe, zinc / flowers, zinc / listless, zinc / another, zinc / lips, zinc / goal, zinc / soles, zinc / souls, zinc / people, zinc / problems, zinc / rings, zinc / flown, zinc / expire, zinc / gone, zinc / mountain, zinc / fountain, zinc / experience, zinc / reality, zinc / well, zinc / wealth, zinc / flown, zinc / river, zinc / picture, zinc / luck, zinc.

CHAPTER TWO

Pairs, zinc / orbital, zinc / spire, zinc / surge, zinc / electrical, zinc / reaps, zinc / dimensional, zinc / shift, zinc / dares, zinc / expanse, zinc / awake, zinc / winds, zinc / to, zinc / shores, zinc / electric, zinc / rays, zinc / clerical, zinc / cones, zinc / hammock, zinc / nearby, zinc / classical, zinc / concerts, zinc / helps, zinc / nearest, zinc / capable, zinc / convert, zinc / aids, zinc / grows, zinc / captives, zinc / concurrent, zinc / leave, zinc / another, zinc / another, zinc / dearest, zinc / told, zinc / rewards, zinc / apply, zinc / full, zinc / why, zinc / express, zinc / approves, zinc / find, zinc / another, zinc / to, zinc / next, zinc / plan, zinc / leaving, zinc / leads, zinc / love, zinc / breaks, zinc / fails, zinc / fill, zinc / quarters, zinc / builds, zinc / days, zinc / allow, zinc / in, zinc / bread, zinc / four, zinc / complex, zinc / signal, zinc / breathe, zinc / comes, zinc / system, zinc.

CHAPTER THREE

Finds, zinc / expanse, zinc / pet, zinc / occur, zinc / of, zinc / mixed, zinc / heart, zinc / friend, zinc / copes, zinc / reap, zinc / gains, zinc / enter, zinc / settles, zinc / a, zinc / courage, zinc / one, zinc / expands, zinc / curtain, zinc / hanger, zinc / meditate, zinc / anchors, zinc / universal, zinc / cords, zinc / cut, zinc / clears, zinc / peace, zinc / open, zinc / unity, zinc / finds, zinc / large, zinc / lays, zinc / soar, zinc / dash, zinc / cause, zinc / deepens, zinc / pure, zinc / status, zinc / forth, zinc / fused, zinc / lose, zinc / liter, zinc / light, zinc / lesson, zinc / plug, zinc / crafts, zinc / vertical, zinc / fuse, zinc / phase, zinc / vertical, zinc / ahead, zinc / physical, zinc / account, zinc / visit, zinc / poles, zinc / founded, zinc / five's, zinc / operate, zinc / phase, zinc / over, zinc / personal, zinc / single, zinc / destiny, zinc / arrives, zinc / injury, zinc.

CHAPTER FOUR

Acknowledged, zinc / where, zinc / love, zinc / reigns, zinc / and, zinc / find, zinc / a friendly, zinc / kind, zinc / love, zinc / glory, zinc / made, zinc / known, zinc / finish, zinc / your, zinc / dearest, zinc / faces, zinc / identify, zinc / Everest, zinc / routes, zinc / for, zinc / comes, zinc / credited, zinc / creations, zinc / dreamy, zinc / dues, zinc / judgments, zinc / done, zinc / days, zinc / dawned, zinc / cosmetics, zinc / cubes, zinc / rainbows, zinc / floated, zinc / ash, zinc / waves, zinc / lands, zinc / simply, zinc / sure, zinc / large, zinc / jay, zinc / wise, zinc / ways, zinc / safe, zinc / warmth, zinc / excited, zinc / news, zinc / made, zinc / warned, zinc / Friday, zinc / forms, zinc / anchored, zinc / next, zinc /

teams, zinc / trips, zinc / insured, zinc / ambles, zinc / trios, zinc / triggered, zinc / women, zinc / wins, zinc / treaty, zinc / toured, zinc / lasting, zinc / finished, zinc.

CHAPTER FIVE

Tropical, zinc / linger, zinc / lovers, zinc / loafed, zinc / paradise, zinc / leaders, zinc / leap, zinc / lasting, zinc / ends, zinc / mystery, zinc / inspired, zinc / aware, zinc / another, zinc / main, zinc / maintained, zinc / mixed, zinc / host, zinc / along, zinc / leads, zinc / of, zinc / occur, zinc / finished, zinc / relates, zinc / rush, zinc / cubes, zinc / aft, zinc / doors, zinc / done, zinc / cap, zinc / cools, zinc / along, zinc / sure, zinc / lateral, zinc / loops, zinc / loves, zinc / lost, zinc / leaders, zinc / tank, zinc / teal, zinc / triple, zinc / tours, zinc / toured, zinc / trades, zinc / trains, zinc / trends, zinc / tubes, zinc / truest, zinc / timing, zinc / find, zinc / sounds, zinc / sun's, zinc / wounds, zinc / fun, zinc / music, zinc / wait, zinc / won, zinc / ways, zinc / sunny, zinc / days, zinc / during, zinc / shave, zinc / save, zinc / daily, zinc / done, zinc.

CHAPTER SIX

Fixture, zinc / operate, zinc / well, zinc / within, zinc / facts, zinc / covering, zinc / rips, zinc / off, zinc / fortress, zinc / find, zinc / fundamental, zinc / cause, zinc / remember, zinc / fools, zinc / fit, zinc / fox, zinc / amount, zinc / rakes, zinc / rations, zinc / for, zinc / formal, zinc / freeze, zinc / lifts, zinc / list, zinc / loops, zinc / latch, zinc / off, zinc / move, zinc / match, zinc / cures, zinc / come, zinc / lovers, zinc / passage, zinc / comes, zinc / know, zinc / note, zinc / count, zinc / volcano, zinc / house, zinc / hurls, zinc / appearance, zinc / suns, zinc / tangible, zinc / tours, zinc / sings, zinc / songs, zinc / teams, zinc / term, zinc / vicinity, zinc / conscious, zinc / cares, zinc / leapt, zinc / land, zinc / lures, zinc / us, zinc / well, zinc / into, zinc / wisdom, zinc / when, zinc / we, zinc / accept, zinc / the, zinc / cause, zinc / as, zinc.

CHAPTER SEVEN

An, zinc / effect, zinc / found, zinc / financed, zinc / for, zinc / you, zinc / through, zinc / a, zinc / grant, zinc / written, zinc / to, zinc / one, zinc / week's, zinc / causal, zinc / express, zinc / know, zinc / the, zinc / Bermuda, zinc / plains, zinc / allow, zinc / of, zinc / federal, zinc / blue, zinc / godiva, zinc / gaze, zinc/ when, zinc / we, zinc / will, zinc / our, zinc / mission, zinc / complete, zinc / we, zinc / will, zinc / all, zinc / lessons, zinc / loved, zinc / become, zinc / wills, zinc / care, zinc / live, zinc / lie, zinc / won, zinc / cures, zinc / mothers, zinc / for, zinc / to, zinc / our, zinc / cause, zinc / paid, zinc / for, zinc / loss, zinc / through, zinc / licensed, zinc / steering, zinc / collective, zinc / we've, zinc / lasted, zinc / a, zinc / push, zinc / for, zinc / day, zinc / pairs, zinc / us, zinc / to, zinc.

CHAPTER EIGHT

Gifts, zinc / won, zinc / win, zinc / a, zinc / age, zinc / way, zinc / for, zinc / lovers, zinc / finish, zinc / lives, zinc / on, zinc / dotted, zinc / dealt, zinc / meals, zinc / cost, zinc / less, zinc / if, zinc / love, zinc / replies, zinc / rent, zinc / without, zinc / windows, zinc / ways, zinc / pulse, zinc / purest, zinc / cares, zinc / on, zinc

/ capable, zinc / days, zinc / due, zinc / moods, zinc / community, zinc / are, zinc / zipped, zinc / actual, zinc / chosen, zinc / chores, zinc / shows, zinc / step, zinc / star, zinc / leave, zinc / tire, zinc / fairy, zinc / cool, zinc / often, zinc / for, zinc / movement, zinc / moves, zinc / along, zinc / leadership, zinc / tool, zinc / partners, zinc / come, zinc / to, zinc / sensitive, zinc / aid, zinc / welcome, zinc / home, zinc / won, zinc / wanders, zinc / wonderful, zinc / winning, zinc / races, zinc / sound, zinc.

CHAPTER NINE

Now, zinc / we're, zinc / heard, zinc / a, zinc / trendy, zinc / trends, zinc / traded, zinc / cost, zinc / graceful, zinc / lights, zinc / in, zinc / great, zinc / green, zinc / falseness, zinc / without, zinc / power, zinc / mention, zinc / one, zinc / intrigue, zinc / source, zinc / links, zinc / allow, zinc / moves, zinc / miracles, zinc / solstice, zinc / single, zinc / stills, zinc / keep, zinc / change, zinc / occurs, zinc / simply, zinc / invoice, zinc / paid, zinc / others, zinc / kept, zinc / heals, zinc / billions, zinc / true, zinc / needs, zinc / listen, zinc / earthiness, zinc / meet, zinc / met, zinc / franchised, zinc / lack, zinc / goes, zinc / to, zinc / simplest, zinc / balance, zinc / felt, zinc / fires, zinc / global, zinc / self, zinc / above, zinc / I, zinc / cause, zinc / risen, zinc / encourage, zinc / love, zinc / planet, zinc / clears, zinc / air, zinc / leave, zinc / allergist, zinc.

CHAPTER TEN

Opposite, zinc / matched, zinc / operate, zinc / solar, zinc / attractive, zinc / me, zinc / wills, zinc / couple, zinc / examples, zinc / children, zinc / follow, zinc / you, zinc / mental, zinc / doors, zinc / open, zinc / dear, zinc / rely, zinc / reliance, zinc / open, zinc / before, zinc / join, zinc / sense, zinc / arose, zinc / positive, zinc / forgotten, zinc / small, zinc / will, zinc / wise, zinc / praise, zinc / humble, zinc / steps, zinc / close, zinc / bridge, zinc / remain, zinc / discover, zinc / sleeve, zinc / blaze, zinc / lest, zinc / Christ, zinc / forget, zinc / offer, zinc / set, zinc / different, zinc / way, zinc / cosmic, zinc / cures, zinc / fresh, zinc / rates, zinc / carry, zinc / able, zinc / abilities, zinc / manifest, zinc / forms, zinc / funds, zinc / body, zinc / builds, zinc / fuel, zinc / hands, zinc / wind, zinc / crackers, zinc/ kept, zinc / alone, zinc / link, zinc / ladies, zinc.

CHAPTER ELEVEN

Fly, zinc / supply, zinc / to, zinc / kindest, zinc / recognize, zinc / truth, zinc / soars, zinc / we, zinc/ are, zinc / the, zinc / won, zinc / kept, zinc / transcend, zinc / dreams, zinc / builds, zinc / hope, zinc / fully, zinc / acknowledge, zinc / path, zinc / once, zinc / with, zinc / graceful, zinc / forgive, zinc / lights, zinc / selfish, zinc / done, zinc / real, zinc / estate, zinc / remember, zinc / when, zinc / one, zinc / is, zinc / identified, zinc / illustrate, zinc / sense, zinc / abide, zinc / hope, zinc / self, zinc / same, zinc / sense, zinc / whole, zinc / explain, zinc / expire, zinc / less, zinc / all, zinc / we, zinc / are, zinc / given, zinc / sun, zinc / seven, zinc / loaf, zinc / gains, zinc / aware, zinc / empower, zinc / translate, zinc / codes, zinc / physical, zinc / gifts, zinc / lift, zinc / notations, zinc / understand, zinc / where, zinc / we, zinc / gain, zinc.

CHAPTER TWELVE

Input, zinc / accord, zinc / sunny, zinc / cycle, zinc / galaxies, zinc / gaze, zinc / across, zinc / deep, zinc / dark, zinc / expanse, zinc / solar, zinc / human, zinc / star, zinc / cycle, zinc / through, zinc / universe, zinc / dense, zinc / diverse, zinc / doubt, zinc / go, zinc / team, zinc / with, zinc / wonder, zinc / awe, zinc / rails, zinc / exhaustive, zinc / rely, zinc / reply, zinc / truths, zinc / find, zinc / fuel, zinc / love, zinc / whole, zinc / cities, zinc / shot, zinc / reading, zinc / spirit, zinc / claimed, zinc / lift, zinc / wrote, zinc / honest, zinc / was, zinc / over, zinc / fueled, zinc / into, zinc/ ladder, zinc / ages, zinc / lapsed, zinc / poles, zinc / entire, zinc / lifts, zinc / balance, zinc / against, zinc / opposition, zinc / rests, zinc / now, zinc / forms, zinc / deem, zinc / bad, zinc / gone, zinc / full, zinc / feel, zinc / deal, zinc / drive, zinc.

CHAPTER THIRTEEN

Writing, zinc / push, zinc / of, zinc / opposite, zinc / freedoms, zinc / valid, zinc / wisdom, zinc / wanders, zinc / forgiving, zinc / confirm, zinc / learn, zinc / lifting, zinc / freshest, zinc / gifts, zinc / illusion, zinc / claims, zinc / movies, zinc / surrender, zinc / list, zinc / mistakes, zinc / make, zinc / ergonomics, zinc / west / them, zinc / made, zinc / bridge, zinc / collapse, zinc / over, zinc / points, zinc / pregnant, zinc / cause, zinc / awaken, zinc / satisfy, zinc / spiritual, zinc / lead, zinc / debate, zinc / lesson, zinc / beyond, zinc / doors, zinc / dare, zinc / marriage, zinc / set, zinc / doubles, zinc / effort, zinc / apply, zinc / single, zinc / precepts, zinc / vision, zinc / arrange, zinc / slept, zinc / neat, zinc / cluster, zinc / kind, zinc / power, zinc / in, zinc / rest, zinc / relate, zinc / understand, zinc / to, zinc / god, zinc / give, zinc / of, zinc / love, zinc / break, zinc.

LEVEL 110: THE CORDS-MENTS

CHAPTER ONE

Senses, cords / foil, cords / hydro, cords / aid, cords / entry, cords / lit, cords / emergy, cords / coded, cords / made, cords / preaious, cords / precious, cords / unit, cords / to, cords / love, cords / inclusive, cords / trances, cords / emergtoic, cords / made, cords / possible, cords / separd, cords / births, cords / twins, cords/ births, cords / concoct, cords / fold, cords / mold, cords / foolish, cords / entreaty, cords / opportune, cords / days, cords / come, cords / made, cords / quantums, cords / leaps, cords / recede, cords / love, cords / fixed, cords / loss, cords / goes, cords / surround, cords / with, cords / pleaides, cords / god, cords / light, cords / force, cords / rearms, cords / dash, cords / to, cords / loves, cords / destiny, cords / for, cords / shadows, cords / burst, cords / flush, cords / in, cords / cards, cords / relate, cords / release, cords / clear, cords / techniques, cords / fase, cords / dormant, cords / naues, cords / love, cords.

CHAPTER TWO

Four, cords / love, cords / anxiety, cords / clears, cords / victory,

cords / unaversal, cords / codes, cords / hands, cords / leap, cords / leap, cords / certain, cords / wins, cords / expand, cords / expened, cords / lend, cords / love, cords / happiness, cords / ward, cords / heels, cords / trod, cords / know, cords / venerete, cords / threads, cords / philosphic, cords / expect, cords / brains, cords / scan, cords / novels, cords / less, cords/ pass, cords / crust, cords / poetry, cords / theatre, cords / notes, cords / pare, cords / pennent, cords / aloha, cords / rlagarozed, cords / rests, cords / water, cords / cafe, cords / delly, cords / wards, cords / fantic, cords / agape, cords / won, cords / wonders, cords / dealt, cords / inffluential, cords / handy, cords / deals, cords / mad, cords / twins, cords / hair, cords / put, cords / back, cords / claimed, cords / slaw, cords / sisyer, cords / hoods, cords / clears, cords / copes, cords / cain, cords / able, cords.

CHAPTER THREE

Deepens, cords / liberty, cords / learns, cords / keys, cords / capability, cords / learn, cords / link, cords / last, cords / overall, cords / leave, cords / lead, cords / love, cords / finished, cords / forgiven, cords / forgot, cords / fused, cords / leave, cords / leave, cords / leaves, cords / losts, cords / losts, cords / left, cords / lovers, cords / look, cords / lots, cords / left, cords / lovers, cords / look, cords / lots, cords / left, cords/ lovers, cords/ look, cords / passage, cords / lapse, cords/ lists, cords/ lots, cords / cost, cords / keen, cords / care, cords/ lots, cords/ lists, cords / later, cords / cities, cords/ soft, cords/ of, cords/ work, cords / wins, cords/ windy, cords / tonight, cords / tranquility, cords / banders, cords / us, cords / softly, cords / homeward, cords / for, cords / spatial, cords / full, cords / up, cords / with, cords / needs, cords / saints, cords / given, cords / lift, cords / legends, cords.

CHAPTER FOUR

Well, cords / as, cords / we, cords / said, cords / accept, cords / spring, cords / softened, cords / stones, cords / of, cords / necessary, cords / daring, cords / sullen, cords / told, cords / days, cords / deal, cords / in, cords / paternal, cords / escope, cords / goodness, cords / next, cords / five, cords / times, cords / lights, cords / needs, cords / marked, cords / spots, cords / grow, cords / in, cords / sync, cords / as, cords / we, cords / freed, cords / meets, cords / mature, cords / insurance, cords / of, cords / on, cords / left, cords / over, cords / nails, cords / and, cords / coffins, cords / rust, cords / until, cords / we, cords / spew, cords / our, cords / truths, cords / told, cords / over, cords / yet, cords / yellow, cords / glue, cords / has, cords / gained, cords / our, cords / we, cords / night, cords / nickel, cords / dimes, cords / good, cords / we, cords / have, cords / gained, cords.

CHAPTER FIVE

Forever, cords / over, cords / valuable, cords / fades, cords / gains, cords / lifted, cords / lots, cords / loaded, cords / us, cords / farewell, cords / entry, cords / into, cords / matched, cords / mentions, cords / seem, cords / linked, cords / as, cords / we, cords / walk, cords / please, cords / allow, cords / distinct, cords / lines, cords / in, cords / our, cords/ necessary, cords / suffering, cords /

only, cords / to, cords / overt, cords / want, cords / within, cords / the, cords / psyche, cords / despair, cords / written, cords / lane, cords / trend, cords / selfish, cords / middle, cords / sets, cords / rates, cords / settle, cords / forgive, cords / due, cords / if, cords / me, cords / separate, cords / the, cords / love, cords / the, cords / links, cords / your, cords / appear, cords / at, cords / on, cords / higher, cords / still, cords / include, cords / of, cords / hands, cords / trick, cords / kind, cords / body, cords.

CHAPTER SIX

The, cords / cause, cords / the, cords / truth, cords / a, cords / ascended, cords / wave, cords / wore, cords / hearts, cords / helm, cords / and, cords / a, cords / letter, cords / stock, cords / which, cords / reads, cords / to, cords / sharp, cords / success, cords / instinct, cords / appeals, cords / mail, cords / a, cords / letter, cords / of, cords / reflect, cords / all, cords / regrets, cords / cause, cords / past, cords / a, cords / former, cords / fitness, cords / for, cords / lasted, cords / loves, cords / wake, cords / will, cords / end, cords / regain, cords / remain, cords / fuse, cords / dare, cords / declare, cords / same, cords / infuse, cords / move, cords / surge, cords / was, cords / your, cords / last, cords / load, cords / at, cords / love's, cords / feel, cords / decide, cords / where, cords / to, cords / send, cords / the, cords / keys, cords / and, cords / empires, cords / win, cords.

CHAPTER SEVEN

Money, cords / has, cords / met, cords / her, cords / wisest, cords / detail, cords / basic, cords / forms, cords / melt, cords / into, cords / cause, cords / employ, cords / meet, cords / annoy, cords / when, cords / direct, cords / has, cords / cause, cords / know, cords / applaud, cords / when, cords / apaloosa, cords / blue, cords / in, cords / chain, cords / into, cords / your, cords / vote, cords / of, cords / sure, cords / supple, cords / cope, cords / when, cords / is, cords / the, cords / electric, cords / demand, cords / over, cords / when, cords / overt, cords / how, cords / cursed, cords / how, cords / cpable, cords / how, cords / still, cords / how, cords / stiff, cords / how, cords / when, cords / patterns, cords / burst, cords / erect, cords / elect, cords / matched, cords / made, cords / when, cords / winced, cords / find, cords / fill, cords / dew, cords / still, cords / emit, cords / meals, cords.

CHAPTER EIGHT

Known, cords / release, cords / go, cords / then, cords / love, cords / led, cords / found, cords / fed, cords / made, cords / purged, cords / cured, cords / core, cords / whole, cords / farm, cords / a, cords / mission, cords / another, cords / lease, cords / led, cords / leave, cords / go, cords / fuse, cords / lit, cords / light, cords/ list, cords / you, cords / your, cords/ year, cords/ settle, cords/ view, cords / impact, cords / fume, cords / fuse, cords / gear, cords / gain, cords / fixed, cords / fames, cords / soar, cords / dove, cords / dives, cords / into, cords / with, cords / parental, cords / stares, cords / of, cords / positive, cords / occur, cords / simple, cords / gesture, cords / muses, cords / lend, cords / a, cords / letter, cords / number, cords / called, cords / collective, cords / can, cords / amplitude, cords

/ of, cords / nestled, cords / near, cords / dressed, cords / chill, cords / costume, cords.

CHAPTER NINE

Measure, cords / needs, cords / friends, cords / offered, cords / sorry, cords / a, cords / simple, cords / nimble, cords / conscious, cords / cure, cords / super, cords / fuel, cords / in, cords / intense, cords / love, cords / for, cords / you, cords / my, cords / father, cords / living, cords / us, cords / find, cords / us, cords / hear, cords / know, cords / cure, cords / have, cords / we, cords / now, cords / a, cords / are, cords / for, cords / god, cords / of, cords / love, cords / let, cords / love, cords / lost, cords / dear, cords / dance, cords / deem, cords / us, cords / worthy, cords / of, cords / chance, cords / too, cords / love, cords / leads, cords / last, cords / fan, cords / found, cords / love, cords / fun, cords / fun, cords / focused, cords / friends, cords / reason, cords / rest, cords / rapture, cords / instill, cords / instinct, cords / look, cords / arc, cords / bag, cords.

CHAPTER TEN

Love, cords / love, cords / love, cords / love, cords / lead, cords / led, cords / lead, cords / love, cords / lend, cords / link, cords / leap, cords / love, cords / memorize, cords / memory, cords / muse, cords / mend, cords / over, cords / dures, cords/ cat, cords / back, cords / close, cords / doors, cords / of, cords / temples, cords / christ, cords / less, cords / cure, cords / a, cords / need, cords / to, cords / live, cords / with, cords/ lessened, cords / lights, cords / listen, cords / active, cords / a, cords / curse, cords / weave, cords / a, cords / worn, cords / sweater, cords / to, cords / caring, cords / inclusive, cords / do, cords / the, cords / right, cords / how, cords / then, cords / love, cords / respect, cords / of, cords / living, cords / love, cords / and, cords / for, cords / a, cords / literature, cords / register, cords / redeem, cords / hear, cords / only, cords / mad, cords.

CHAPTER ELEVEN

When, cords / you, cords / enter, cords / a, cords / resurrection, cords / gate, cords / loosen, cords / of, cords / your, cords / shoes, cords / and, cords / relax, cords / into, cords / living, cords / arms, cords / arms, cords / of, cords/ love, cords / we, cords / have, cords / arrived, cords / where, cords / seem, cords / shines, cords / and, cords / the, cords / hearts, cords / mend, cords / at, cords / a, cords / gateway, cords / of, cords / living, cords / truth, cords / and, cords / the, cords / pen, cords / metatronic, cords / which, cords / ends, cords / and, cords / dictate, cords / simply, cords / this, cords / know, cords / god, cords / as, cords / sincerely, cords / and, cords / dearly, cords / as, cords / a, cords / jesus, cords / christ, cords / planned, cords / a, cords / lesson, cords / taught, cords / we've, cords / the, cords / weave, cords / of, cords / eternity, cords / in, cords.

CHAPTER TWELVE

Pen, cords / and, cords / our, cords / way, cords / to, cords / say, cords / that, cords / first, cords / and, cords / last, cords / am, cords / omega, cords / has, cords / come, cords / to, cords / eternity's, cords / shore, cords / at, cords / bath, cords / a, cords / simple, cords / truth, cords / one, cords / pen, cords / one, cords / hand, cords / may, cords / wed, cords / to, cords / a, cords / higher, cords / level, cords / the, cords / arc, cords / and, cords / the, cords / soft, cords / resurrect, cords / unto, cords / god's, cords / gaze, cords / direct, cords / direct, cords / into, cords / you, cords / a, cords / living, cords / heart, cords / has, cords / said, cords / basic, cords / hummanity, cords / regin, cords / occur, cords/ in, cords / lights, cords / love, cords / and, cords / god, cords / head, cords / remain, cords/ of, cords / the, cords / remainder, cords.

CHAPTER THIRTEEN

In, cords / the, cords / face, cords / to, cords / love, cords / let, cords / us, cords / pray, cords / for, cords / renew, cords / for, cords / a, cords / guide, cords / and, cords / a, cords / done, cords / now, cords / due, cords / into, cords / one, cords / we, cords / come, cords / to, cords / soon, cords / arise, cords / a, cords / sense, cords / a, cords / marvel, cords / a, cords / worn, cords / a, cords / jesus, cords / a, cords / let, cords / us, cords / christ, cords / reset, cords / loved, cords / praise, cords / sour, cords / sight, cords / life, cords / mighty, cords / day, cords / day, cords / inside, cords / one, cords / god, cords / of, cords / cure, cords / as, cords / intrigued, cords / read, cords / relay, cords / for, cords / cause, cords / penetrate, cords / races, cords / to, cords / love, cords / form, cords / a, cords / focus, cords.

LEVEL 111: THE CUBES-MENTS

CHAPTER ONE

Good, metatronic cubes / days, metatronic cubes / amount, metatronic cubes / to, metatronic cubes / letters, cubes / written, cubes / top, cubes / a, cubes / cause, cubes / parallel, cubes / to, cubes / one's, cubes / own, cubes / impair, cubes / find, cubes / declare, cubes / go, cubes / to, cubes / the, cubes / love, cubes / of, cubes / a, cubes / life, cubes / time's, cubes / cure, cubes / of, cubes / a, cubes, cubes / temple's, cubes / kept, cubes / code, cubes / of, cubes / love, cubes / elite, cubes / know, cubes / a, cubes / needy, cubes / written, cubes / empowered, cubes / sights, cubes / long, cubes / wonderful, cubes / you, cubes / knot, cubes / gone, cubes / days, cubes / dare, cubes / cease, cubes / without, cubes / exit, cubes / works, cubes / wow, cubes / gone, cubes / send, cubes / you, cubes / home, cubes / to, cubes / see, cubes / the, cubes / ways, cubes / to, cubes / love's, cubes / elect, cubes / and, cubes / the, cubes.

CHAPTER TWO

Channels, cubes / open, cubes / detail, cubes / desire, cubes / first, cubes / opened, cubes / suffer, cubes / less, cubes / effect, cubes / is, cubes / cause, cubes / see, cubes / reciept, cubes / through, cubes / suggest, cubes / confussion, cubes / stare, cubes / sep, cubes / saturn, cubes / signature, cubes / store, cubes / key, cubes / kept, cubes / clean, cubes / dry, cubes / lessons, cubes / desire,

cubes / while, cubes / previous, cubes / your, cubes / cooperaion, cubes / relinquish, cubes / slept, cubes / running, cubes / ways, cubes / feline, cubes / budaha, cubes / mellow, cubes / get, cubes / aside, cubes / sometime, cubes / date, cubes / month, cubes / drive, cubes / time, cubes / real, cubes / glass, cubes / kind, cubes / table, cubes / exchange, cubes / phone, cubes / floor, cubes / moved, cubes / everything, cubes / thoughtful, cubes / professional, cubes / services, cubes / legal, cubes / court, cubes / suspected, cubes / flower, cubes / bloom, cubes / insurance, cubes / honey, cubes.

CHAPTER THREE

Sharpens, cubes / stir, cubes / mixed, cubes / matched, cubes / muses, cubes / mirth, cubes / mabe, cubes / made, cubes / mentions, cubes / mean, cubes / mills, cubes / meet, cubes / much, cubes / adorned, cubes / often, cubes / said, cubes / model, cubes / danced, cubes / day, cubes / intro, cubes / drawing, cubes / vehicles, cubes / manage, cubes/ miracles, cubes / views, cubes / lights, cubes / measures, cubes / merged, cubes / merchants, cubes / mutual, cubes / managed, cubes / mangerial, cubes / occupied, cubes / occurs, cubes/ factory, cubes / views, cubes / vexed, cubes / vast, cubes / voiced, cubes / veers, cubes / held, cubes / hope, cubes / nearest, cubes / nudged, cubes / holds, cubes / off, cubes / margins, cubes / onto, cubes / gaverial, cubes / grew, cubes / in, cubes / creeks, cubes / depth, cubes / of, cubes / passionate, cubes / embrace, cubes / stirring, cubes / force, cubes / conceptual, cubes / lines, cubes / demonstrate, cubes / daily, cubes / durations, cubes / on, cubes.

CHAPTER FOUR

Mountains, cubes / live, cubes / loves, cubes / leaps, cubes / sterling, cubes / steep, cubes / elation, cubes / choice, cubes / interest, cubes / slice, cubes / made, cubes / sleep, cubes / alum, cubes / alloy, cubes / sleeping, cubes / ripened, cubes / further, cubes / of, cubes / the, cubes / cause, cubes / enduranc, cubese / in, cubes / a, cubes / hush, cubes / sunbeam, cubes / tricks, cubes / ripened, cubes / rush, cubes / allow, cubes / listened, cubes / to, cubes / pens, cubes / we've, cubes / clustering, cubes / for, cubes / the, cubes / matured, cubes / into, cubes / s,othering, cubes / shoulders, cubes / to, cubes / still, cubes / for, cubes / the, cubes / point, cubes / inward, cubes/ forgiven, cubes / make, cubes / maturation, cubes / sets, cubes / teeth, cubes / in, cubes / leaps, cubes/ to, cubes / risk, cubes / insane, cubes/ ransoms, cubes / rifts, cubes / measure, cubes / do, cubes / run, cubes / for, cubes / dares, cubes / you, cubes.

CHAPTER FIVE

Our, cubes / amuse, cubes / a, cubes / breath, cubes / of, cubes / fellow, cubes / abide, cubes / abbreviated, cubes / know, cubes / to, cubes / fairest, cubes / for, cubes / who, cubes / sage, cubes / dances, cubes / infused, cubes/ living, cubes / insense, cubes / holy, cubes / heads, cubes / interact, cubes / mentioned, cubes / loving, cubes / discovery, cubes / relationship, cubes / spiritual, cubes / books, cubes / presence, cubes / deathlike, cubes / response, cubes / respond, cubes / modern, cubes / science, cubes / meanings, cubes / ultimately, cubes / invites, cubes / here, cubes / heart, cubes / satisfy, cubes / rafts, cubes / images, cubes / sense, cubes / snake, cubes / confusions, cubes / lightens, cubes / work, cubes / wallow, cubes / affect, cubes / affection, cubes / grateful, cubes / child, cubes / impasse, cubes / doubt, cubes / sought, cubes / perfect, cubes / upon, cubes / realize, cubes / of, cubes / wisdom, cubes / books, cubes / worth, cubes / is, cubes / made, cubes / roommate, cubes.

CHAPTER SIX

Everything, cubes / chest, cubes / few, cubes / follow, cubes / marry, cubes / teaching, cubes / important, cubes / telephone, cubes / adults, cubes / draplets, cubes / sense, cubes / hold, cubes / embrace, cubes / formed, cubes / held, cubes / explain, cubes / youth, cubes / books, cubes / written, cubes / truth, cubes / mothers, cubes / sex, cubes / opposite, cubes/ suport, cubes / deepest, cubes / search, cubes / teach, cubes / confuse, cubes / frustrate, cubes / doubts, cubes / enlightens, cubes / levels, cubes / manifest, cubes / fevers, cubes / burn, cubes / out, cubes / in, cubes / transcend, cubes / everything, cubes / moves, cubes / real, cubes / living, cubes / i, cubes / include, cubes / encounters, cubes / your, cubes / eyes, cubes / seeking, cubes / human, cubes/ imitation, cubes / inform, cubes / feeling, cubes / communion, cubes / respond, cubes / reaches, cubes / service, cubes / divine, cubes / expect, cubes / noted, cubes/ stars, cubes / invite, cubes / transforms, cubes / spaces, cubes / share, cubes.

CHAPTER SEVEN

As, cubes / a, cubes / aymbol, cubes / i, cubes / am, cubes / the, cubes / star, cubes / and, cubes / the, cubes / light, cubes / again, cubes / led, cubes / into, cubes / hearts, cubes / everwhere, cubes / seldom, cubes / seem, cubes / levels, cubes / luscious, cubes / in, cubes / hawaii, cubes / hot, cubes / wavelets, cubes / ripple, cubes / recipes, cubes / local, cubes / events, cubes / news, cubes / beds, cubes / linked, cubes / beached, cubes / ballons, cubes / golden, cubes / greens, cubes / of, cubes/ gasping, cubes / release, cubes / ratified, cubes / numbers, cubes/ need, cubes / meet, cubes / metal, cubes / hoods, cubes/ opened, cubes/ still, cubes/ in, cubes / kneeling, cubes/ revive, cubes / shameless, cubes / shillings, cubes / stocks, cubes / cards, cubes / setting, cubes / premiums, cubes / treats, cubes / center, cubes / maps, cubes / mutuals, cubes / perched, cubes / minds, cubes / stop, cubes / irs, cubes / enterprise, cubes / dump, cubes.

CHAPTER EIGHT

Absorbed, cubes / brands, cubes / victorious, cubes / finance, cubes / games, cubes / awarded, cubes / course, cubes / nets, cubes / gym, cubes / monkey, cubes / swing, cubes / toys, cubes / tires, cubes / gyms, cubes/ playgrounds, cubes / warehouse, cubes / roughest, cubes / supposed, cubes / mated, cubes / presents, cubes / sales, cubes / series, cubes / natural, cubes / signatures, cubes / deleted, cubes / 7's, cubes / freshens, cubes / showcased, cubes / mystery, cubes / passage, cubes / focus, cubes / vocalized, cubes / village, cubes / leaves, cubes / direction, cubes / living, cubes / artisans, cubes / bontiques, cubes / located, cubes / made, cubes /

merchants, cubes / emporiums, cubes / formations, cubes / more, cubes / trees, cubes / luxurious, cubes / stacked, cubes / sangha, cubes / the, cubes / cat, cubes / fed, cubes / mansion, cubes / fires, cubes / speak, cubes / spilling, cubes / dance, cubes / duration, cubes / theatrics, cubes / aft, cubes / weather, cubes / wetter, cubes / absorb, cubes / moist, cubes / pick, cubes.

CHAPTER NINE

Predict, cubes / sample, cubes / of, cubes / brightness, cubes / cultural, cubes / roses, cubes / race, cubes / sandles, cubes / outstanding, cubes / wooden, cubes/ pases, cubes / prose, cubes / poetics, cubes / poetical, cubes / entry, cubes / holy, cubes / smoldering, cubes / mask, cubes / of, cubes / mental, cubes / freed, cubes / rhythms, cubes / clash, cubes / without, cubes / luxury, cubes / of, cubes / squarely, cubes / seeming, cubes / seams, cubes / to, cubes / diamonds, cubes / red, cubes / read, cubes / of, cubes / physical, cubes / scenes, cubes / slanderous, cubes / male, cubes / tunes, cubes / played, cubes / in, cubes / pave, cubes / recall, cubes / of, cubes / the, cubes / fallible, cubes / made, cubes / measureable, cubes / moods, cubes / matronic, cubes / cast, cubes / dipped, cubes / way, cubes / worn, cubes / women, cubes / lashing, cubes / over, cubes / team, cubes / note, cubes / neat, cubes / flows, cubes / poets, cubes / health, cubes / show, cubes.

CHAPTER TEN

Hope, cubes / hover, cubes / summation, cubes / notation, cubes / rang, cubes / ruling, cubes / orifices, cubes / join, cubes / eclipse, cubes / clues, cubes / entire, cubes / sourced, cubes / natural, cubes / plumes, cubes / patches, cubes / chores, cubes / run, cubes / lights, cubes / gesture, cubes / triple, cubes / to, cubes / talk, cubes / patience, cubes / up, cubes / the, cubes / of, cubes / willingness, cubes / to, cubes / weeping, cubes / burning, cubes / waiver, cubes / keeping, cubes / schools, cubes / guides, cubes / star, cubes / camp, cubes / leverage, cubes / size, cubes / character, cubes / clinical, cubes / offers, cubes / sides, cubes / sizes, cubes / materials, cubes / planetary, cubes / soul, cubes / seizing, cubes / folic, cubes / sunny, cubes / trust, cubes / passes, cubes / thrown, cubes / rays, cubes / tally, cubes / gaits, cubes / within, cubes / diabolically, cubes / crafts, cubes / doom's, cubes / worded, cubes / bionic, cubes / curtails, cubes / forgiven, cubes / 70's, cubes.

CHAPTER ELEVEN

Seasonal, cubes / lather, cubes / loath, cubes / cusp, cubes / sufferage, cubes / disappering, cubes / malfunctions, cubes / creeds, cubes / shall, cubes / dove, cubes / dives, cubes / crews, cubes / soothe, cubes/ distilled, cubes / into, cubes/ rely, cubes / upgrade, cubes / energy, cubes / shoulder, cubes / die, cubes / service, cubes / capable, cubes / dared, cubes / instruction, cubes / several, cubes / couples, cubes / capricorns, cubes / unity, cubes / enterprise, cubes/ inside, cubes / universal, cubes / examine, cubes / trendy, cubes / classical, cubes / captions, cubes/ joins, cubes / the, cubes / spent, cubes / sent, cubes/ phase, cubes / sample, cubes / bypass, cubes / polar, cubes / oppose, cubes / has, cubes / invoke, cubes / examples, cubes / samples, cubes / fenced, cubes / burned, cubes / travail, cubes / has, cubes / door, cubes / diagonal, cubes / circular, cubes / motion, cubes / surpassed, cubes / theoretic, cubes / hunch, cubes / a, cubes / formulation, cubes / on, cubes / disciplined, cubes / genuis, cubes.

CHAPTER TWELVE
Been, cubes / placed, cubes / at, cubes / solution, cubes / confessed, cubes / cast, cubes / alerts, cubes / shall, cubes / begin, cubes / publications, cubes / code, cubes / key, cubes / assimilation, cubes / for, cubes / crack, cubes / read, cubes / calipers, cubes / measure, cubes / falys, cubes / cells, cubes / wide, cubes / whence, cubes / include, cubes / a, cubes / solvent, cubes / express, cubes / and, cubes / the, cubes / rest, cubes / in, cubes / worry, cubes / lost, cubes / apostolic, cubes / censuse, cubes / has, cubes / found, cubes / a, cubes / final, cubes / on, cubes / herd, cubes / muster, cubes / cluster, cubes / caption, cubes / subtitle, cubes / claims, cubes / conifer, cubes / trains, cubes / load, cubes / memorials, cubes / to, cubes / member, cubes / glance, cubes / memorization, cubes / strips, cubes / jesus, cubes / sides, cubes / reaps, cubes / strips, cubes / with, cubes / freeks, cubes / repaid, cubes / abilities, cubes / warm, cubes / fix, cubes.

CHAPTER THIRTEEN
Seclusion, cubes / ethnic, cubes / former, cubes / accuser, cubes / bridged, cubes / measure, cubes / placed, cubes / ethics, cubes / bridges, cubes / resurrect, cubes / in, cubes / awe, cubes / burnt, cubes / respect, cubes / active, cubes / ratios, cubes / french, cubes / half, cubes / make, cubes / ruler, cubes / spanish, cubes / honors, cubes / dictatorical, cubes / giants, cubes / german, cubes / chinese, cubes / us, cubes / aids, cubes / italian, cubes / tibetan's, cubes / stage, cubes / regain, cubes / fend, cubes / circle, cubes / splash, cubes / clash, cubes / patience, cubes / delivery, cubes / caters, cubes / todays, cubes / capable, cubes / starts, cubes / simply, cubes / smarts, cubes / detail, cubes / faithfurtive, cubes / made, cubes / lead, cubes / gold, cubes / gist, cubes / ingress, cubes / new, cubes / operation, cubes / goes, cubes / god's, cubes / children, cubes / mom, cubes / to, cubes / steeple, cubes / keep, cubes / nature's, cubes / gather, cubes / bed, cubes / twinkle, cubes.

LEVEL 112: THE DNA-MENTS

CHAPTER ONE
Alcyone, Uriel, nurse, the, instant, miraculous, recall, to, left, blossom, facilities, God-headed, caribe, mounts, a, stages, mercury, calvary, of, memories, sufferage, has, cost, us, dearly, there, a, temple, dear, and a, nearness, unto, a, federation's, lights, lashed, to, a lush, maylanded, illegal, entrain, constant, a due, of, suffering, finality, towned, grained, revelations, restored, resurrected, rational, rationale, repeated, rusted, rational, relatives, relaxed, turtles, traces, teachings, turns, traces, map into thee monumental, maintained

CHAPTER TWO
Tonight, if, a, succession, of, sorts, is, led, to, you, for, illuminate, confess, that, you, are, well, to, love, shall, we, travel, within, let, as, allowed, the, experience, confessed, begin, with, God, a, level, has, attained, perfect, resonance, you, the, chance, to, new, moon, magically, matured, moons, occurred, shift, love's, reply, I, am, the, truthful, way, to, listened, regards, hu-man, skills, return, listen, carefully

CHAPTER THREE
Supremely, attractive 3remarks, promise, love, an, infinite, review, walks, oceans, wells, into, reality, of, sky, trees, people, persons, body, seeks, soakings, immortal, blessed, love's, anxious, anger, secrets, satisfied, final, imagines, mysteries, entered, appears, saying, invites, crucial, craves, doorways, advantage, spirits, devoted, happiness, matters, physics, happiness, matters, physics, facets, liberty, illusions, brief, excerpts, freedoms, relations hearts, may involving, need relates, prays maturely, cycles hearts, hearts freed, involving sacrificials, prays loves, cycles laws, hearts ends, marry marriages

CHAPTER FOUR
Trust, t, r, u, s, t, love, the, mother, join, the, mother, adolescence, cured, love, thee, mother, 10, winds, winning, light, to, love, love's, light, our, clue, our, club, the, elective, won, relative, gaps, relax, to hush, crumbs, fell, crowds, opened, special, shifts, behave, appears, water's, walk, talks, shushed, shamed, forgives, lightened, speeds, to, love, the, many, and, the, all, landed, lands, regained, revive, live, love

CHAPTER FIVE
Manifestations, manifests, temples, seeds, guilts, quilt, has, left, us, well, to, a, will, released, for, loving, sorts, sources, connected, near, the, cores, and, we, follow, following, of, permanence, by, a, sign's, shielded, cares, clearest, Gabriel, is, a, material, awareness, for, the, tender, mercy, inside, surrendering, serendipity, and, the, way, we, will, be legibly, wrong for, the mother's, father and, the father's mother's, at a studio, foured, and a movie, made, three, and a warranted, lot of, listing, keep

CHAPTER SIX
Of, a, weaver, wedged, into, lasting, impressions, and, a, pushing, clear, of, the, fashionable, threads, as, a, trance, becomes, electrical, in a, charge, for, anatomical, corrections, offered, values, wise, in, love, theoretical, miscues, maturations, moves, a, special, emphasis, for, life, discovery, into views, psychological, and social, retrieve, has, set the date, to a daring, recognition, of enlivened, stand, stand, here and wear, the fabric, for, love, final, pieces, played, last, ascension's, stand, sterling, invests, greatly

CHAPTER SEVEN
Testimony, latter, parts, pentacles, into, contain, ascribes, inscriptions, keys, hemingways, moods, teachings, texts, translations, suns, structures, treatments, contents, tat, journeys, invisible, speaks, silver, dollars, reaped, truths, substances,

natures, God's, precise, mannerisms, spread, juices, debuts, co-operatives, rights, irrationals, compels, master's, moved, angers, contentions, destiny, humans, desirable, affections, impulsive, collectives, passes, passive, evers, affective, served, creativity, common, languages, rarest, creativity, commons, languages, rarest, manners, rears, permeated.

CHAPTER EIGHT
Budges, busted, bursts, dams, break, booze, goes, basically, to, thrones, through, magnets, spilling, ions, dreams, leans, last, leins, off, paid, done, dear, days, debates, damages, debits, debates, deals, deems, dashed, doors, deans, laughing, lunges, past, poors, portals, natives, sun's, drafts, pured, poured, channels, casts, less, passion's, debates, domes, automatic, climatic, cinematic, culminate, cures, durations, darings, dearest, sustenance, sorted, spatials, suggest, relaxations, respect, others, cores.

CHAPTER NINE
How, chart, mankind, body, higher, sandings, smote, smattered, beloved, tell, happiness, my, about, symmetry, perfects, lightest, changes, new, clothing, presence, remember, harness, human, skills, authority, given, for, changes, direct, access, most, cosmic, mighty, garments, powerful, lotus, well, colors, point, complete, pink, eternal, body, represent, dedicated, things, wonders, strong, strange, flags, hit, higher, difficult, patient, sustenance, assunder, has, rendered, this, integral, epitath, please, journey, into love's DNA.

CHAPTER TEN
When, is, the, end, of, a, dire, substratus, is, their, an, end, to, a, streetwise, structure, which, is, the, closure, for, who, is, the, respire, from, what, success, in, love, is, your, love's, reflect, true, will, utopian, planes, epitomize, your, success, at, resurrection, how, soft, is, your, love's, core, when, will, you, shine, for, the, stars, success, where, will, we, stay, for love's, which is your mood, may we, know.

CHAPTER ELEVEN
Destroy, sympathy, himself, time, action, man, world, today, see, certain, power, divine, love, body, call, sought, balance, force, call, fault, alone, matter, flow, dangerous, forgotten, activities, four, calling, world, pled, patterns, explain, the, yoke, your stroke, of, justice, sent, when, will, you, sit, when, judgment, comes, to, the, throat, you, employ, an, angel's, arc, has, set, on, neglect, of, the, ever, seldom, scene, love's, carpenter.

CHAPTER TWELVE
Acknowledge, together, firm, action, sister, from, northwest, remember, all, light, someone, complete, together, understand, application, voice, waves, percent, vibratory, fullness, action, render, world, the three-in-one, comes, from, a, place, on, initials, dreamed, a, ritual, incentive, inventive, to love, a, light, is, on, into, weathering, blue, venues, of, the, eiffel's, tower, where, beams,

love, is, built, here, basics, balanced, people, change, chances, given, living, lightens, loves, living

CHAPTER THIRTEEN
Leases, enough, system, perform, joy, immune, resisting, mankind, resistance, power, density, dominion, beat, below, red, attitudes, school, help, key, a, bear, has, berry, blue, hair, without, your, castle, kept, hear, passion, has, sought, as, near, and instinctively, temples, mount, purposeful, counts, of the curation's, descent, where, is, the, height for, sunbeams, how, secure, the affect, for, a city, trued, as, baked, breads, broken, for, love, love, legibly, give, donations, freedoms.

LEVEL 113: THE STRAIGHTEN-MENTS

CHAPTER ONE
Caress, straighten / schooling, straighten / motors, straighten / skilled, straighten / fit, straighten / bentor, straighten / belay, straighten / brown, straighten / extremes, straighten / zones, straighten / annual, straighten / stools, straighten / photographs, straighten / fuselage, straighten / caustic, straighten / pigeons, straighten / factory, straighten / entry, straighten / into, straighten / grooves, straighten / gasoline, straighten / garden, straighten / fountains, straighten / brinks, straighten / streams, straighten / demolitions, straighten / districts, straighten / rigs, straighten / county, straighten / frustrated, straighten / contracts, straighten / perennials, straighten / constructs, straighten / in, straighten / demolitions, straighten / in, straighten / prowess, straighten / of, straighten / eternal, straighten / respect, straighten / for, straighten / the children, straighten / of Yahweh, straighten / a, straighten / new, straighten / ressurection, straighten / of, straighten / function, straighten / of, straighten / ease, straighten / of directions, straighten / of, straighten / election, straighten / of a, straighten / rainbow's leap, straighten / has, straighten / reserved, straighten / Yours, straighten / truly, straighten / plight's, straighten / released, straighten / a, straighten / pharaoh, straighten / insights, straighten

CHAPTER TWO
Heart, straighten / a hardened, straighten / neck, straighten / has, straighten / borne, straighten / a, straighten / message, straighten / of pride's, straighten / benediction, straighten / at the death, straighten / of a death, straighten / to life, straighten / as we, straighten / know, straighten / now, straighten / pray, straighten / in, straighten / successive, straighten / generations, straighten / for, straighten / a new, straighten / fold, straighten / now, straighten / born, straighten / may, straighten / we, straighten / spell, straighten / only, straighten / venus and, straighten / adoration for, straighten / the masses, straighten / for the, straighten / form must, straighten / meet, straighten / heaven's, straighten / correct, straighten / escalation, straighten / in order, straighten / for, straighten /

the source, straighten / of command, straighten / Germand, of, straighten / the gematria, straighten / of a unified, straighten / derivation, straighten / we, straighten / and you, straighten / are the, straighten / fire, straighten / of a, straighten / risen, straighten / hope, straighten / remember, straighten / this, straighten / forget, straighten / less, straighten / recall, straighten / more, straighten / the, straighten / absolute, straighten / divide, straighten / betweens and, straighten / meet, straighten / the bridge within, straighten.

CHAPTER THREE

When, straighten / you, straighten / digress, straighten / you, straighten / seal, straighten / a, straighten / branch, straighten / of, straighten / the tree, straighten / of light, straighten / fishers, straighten / of men, straighten / are the human, straighten / enterprise, straighten / sample, straighten / selective, straighten / for the, straighten / assure, straighten / of, straighten / a hallow, straighten / orb, straighten / filled, straighten / tremendous, straighten / resourcefulness, straighten / and a, straighten / sovereign, straighten / remainder, straighten / has set, straighten / these, straighten / hearts, straighten / to the, straighten / music, straighten / of love, straighten / a parallel, straighten / sort, straighten / has, straighten / surrendered, straighten / the sword, straighten / a corps, straighten / of listening, straighten / friends, straighten / have, straighten / said, straighten / "you, straighten / win", straighten / accept, straighten / this, straighten / victory, straighten / and, straighten / humbly, straighten / refuse, straighten / to dial, straighten / the number, straighten / which represents, straighten / the end, straighten / of humanity, straighten / as we, straighten / know her, straighten / and the, straighten / them within, straighten / can find, straighten / only, straighten / truth in this, straighten / your humble heart, straighten.

CHAPTER FOUR

Pleiades, straighten / is shut, straighten / without, straighten / supply, straighten / a, straighten / nation, straighten / wronged, straighten / has, straighten / stood, straighten / for the, straighten / electrical, straighten / resurgence, / straighten / of a, straighten / group, straighten / arcturian, straighten / water, straighten / is hot, straighten / with, straighten / electrolytic, straighten / materials, straighten / and the, straighten / minerals, straighten / of the champagne, straighten / called light, straighten / when love, straighten / meets, straighten / direct, straighten / vectors, straighten / of linkage, straighten / a, straighten / new, straighten / being is born, straighten / thus the, straighten / reward, straighten / "second, straighten / birth", straighten / a skin, straighten / shed, straighten / has, straighten / lead, straighten / to perfection, straighten / at, straighten / the forthrigh, straighten t / when, straighten / a house, straighten / is, straighten / met, straighten / buy, straighten / it, straighten / and, straighten / find, straighten / peace in, straighten / the photographs, straighten / required, straighten / for, straighten / black, straighten / and white, straighten / listings, straighten / glanced, straighten / through, straighten / to see, straighten / that which will astound, straighten.

CHAPTER FIVE

Of, straighten / electrical, straighten / realize, straighten / may, straighten / we forgive, straighten / you for, straighten / your romance, straighten / and the, straighten / registrations, straighten / of God, straighten / please, straighten / be with, straighten / yours and, straighten / know that, straighten / you are, straighten / the miracle, straighten / a mansion, straighten / and a temple, straighten / erect, straighten / with positively, straighten / glistening, straighten / ability, straighten / reward, straighten / reweave, straighten / a rememberance, straighten / of forgotten, straighten / ignition, straighten / and the preparatio, straighten n / instilled, straighten / of love's, straighten / assignation to, straighten / this course, straighten / and the cause, straighten / central, straighten / and this, straighten / arch explain, straighten when the, straighten / why is met, straighten / with the, straighten / who you are, straighten / may we, straighten / blessed, straighten / be, straighten / in your, straighten / healing, straighten / parlance, straighten / dictim, straighten / and the, straighten / direction, straighten / for eternal, straighten / youth's, straighten / springing, straighten / a rose, straighten / yellow has, straighten / turned, straighten / bright red, straighten / in the, straighten / bed of, straighten / One who, straighten / trembles, straighten / in humble, straighten / remembering of, straighten / the this you, straighten / seek, straighten.

CHAPTER SIX

When, straighten / you pray, straighten / for, straighten / love, straighten / love is, straighten / goodness is, straighten / enhanced, straighten / and by, straighten / your passion, straighten / and the simple, straighten / signals, straighten / within, straighten / you breathe, straighten / and a new, straighten / mountain is, straighten / formed, straighten / Lghten, Kilauea / flows in, straighten / starstruck, straighten / initiative, straighten / for this, straighten / fact that, straighten / one once, straighten / led has, straighten / lost, straighten / come, straighten / back, straighten / and rich, straighten / within, straighten / a happy, straighten / swell of, straighten / gentle, straighten / fog's, straighten / lifts, straighten / and a, straighten / welcome, straighten / tale, straighten / of happy, straighten / days, straighten believe, straighten / in lightening, straighten / struck loves, straighten / patina, straighten / pearls, straighten / meals, massive, straighten / seals, straighten / lapel, straighten / of this, straighten / list, straighten / are now, straighten / the seat, straighten / freed, straighten / upon, straighten / where, straighten / will the, straighten / weave, straighten / connect, straighten / to the Light, straighten / electric, straighten / now, straighten / meet a middle, straighten / fabric forking, straighten / spanned, straighten / literal, literal ignition, initiations begun, retained only this, clearly, love.

CHAPTER SEVEN

Tetragametron, straighten / is, straighten / on, straighten / the, straighten / literary, straighten / list, straighten / of elegance, straighten / bovary, straighten / reads near, straighten / Gabriel's, straighten / creeks and, straighten / the vary of, straighten / variables, straighten / variations, straighten / and the lantern, straighten / swung, straighten / in material, straighten / interests, straighten / intrigues and, straighten / raphael's voice, straighten / as, straighten / instruct, straighten / became, straighten / rest, straighten / and a, straighten / parent's glade, straighten / found, straighten / blend into, straighten / love, straighten / become, straighten / heart, straighten / heed artistic, straighten / needs, straighten / blend, straighten / into love, straighten / find good, straighten / to, straighten / women's directives / of, straighten, straighten / Picasso, straighten / networks, straighten / a final, straighten / friends, straighten / and, straighten / reveals, straighten / colorado's, straighten / warholian, straighten / span of, straighten / surrender, straighten / the yellow, straighten / sword as, straighten / the hills are, straighten / found for the, straighten / detentia delivered, straighten / know reflections, straighten / in books, straighten / where are you, straighten / nestled into, straighten / grinning well, straighten / within love's, straighten / explanation, straighten / of God's, straighten / given gifts, straighten / found, straighten.

CHAPTER EIGHT

Intention, straighten / invention, straighten / is the, straighten / shoulder, straighten / of should, straighten / and knot, straighten / a shudder, straighten / less than, straighten / life's, straighten / light, straighten / waves, straighten / love's reflections, straighten / and, straighten / suspects, straighten / are given, straighten / collegiate, straighten / inns, straighten / for a, straighten / master's touch, straighten / the hutch, straighten / fills, straighten / in China, straight and literal and the refrain remaining of the straighten into love / legendary is the language of the straightened reaction into love proofs, straighten windows, straighten / opened, straighten / aim, straighten / where the, straighten / lanterns, straighten / burned, straighten / thrash less, straighten / random, straighten / more direct, straighten / define, straighten / envelope, straighten / Your, straighten / truly, straighten stored, straighten / stores, straighten / smell, straighten / of, straighten / the fellowed, straighten / listed, straighten / loads, straighten / musics, straighten whispering, straighten / shouts, straighten / of, straighten / interested, straighten / devout, straighten / tours, straighten / enticed in, straighten / twins, straighten / bought, straighten / for a, straighten / frosty, straighten / eve's, straighten / measurement, straighten / find love, straighten / within, straighten / God, straighten / simple, straighten / links, links into the legendary realizations for the flowing straightened / living, living in the listings for a simple reactionary regain / yellow, yellow rose of the living texas as simple as the straightened religions of mend.

CHAPTER NINE

Expressions, straighten / may, straighten / weave, straighten / us, straighten / well, straighten / into, straighten / leaping, straighten / across, straighten / honeyed, straighten / serendipity, straighten / monies, straighten / are the links, straighten / to, straighten / lessons, straighten / blessed, straighten / about, straighten /

in love, straighten / twice, straighten / emptied in, straighten / life, straighten / a blip, straighten / upon the, straighten / screen, straighten / and the freshest, straighten / trace of, straighten / a filled, straighten / coffer, straighten / occurs inminerals, straighten / mint green, straighten / oaks, straighten / bend, straighten / to seek, straighten / the emerald's city, straighten / and the, straighten / axle wise, straighten / within, straighten / drawing, straighten / upon our, straighten / cleanest palettes, straighten / painted, straighten / perspire, straighten / and the, straighten / scientific, straighten / twistings, straighten / which, straighten / occurs, straighten / when, straighten / superior, straighten / becomes my, straighten / seat, straighten / now, straighten / satisfied, straighten / let Holland, straighten / pink, straighten / declare, straighten / us due, straighten / to love's, straighten / perennial, straighten / fellowships, straighten / found, straighten / new, straighten / land to, straighten / own, straighten / well, straighten.

CHAPTER TEN

Local, straighten / octaves, straighten / part, straighten / for free, straighten / earth, straighten / spells, straighten / lava, straighten / leads, straighten / ones who, straighten / love, straighten / perfectly, straighten / beloved, straighten / gains, straighten / heart, straighten / expression, straighten / hope, straighten / becomes, straighten / salvation, straighten / redeemed, straighten / worlds, straighten / eternal, straighten / offers, straighten / manifestations, straighten / Illinois, straighten / outer, straighten / longest, straighten / thunderbirds, straighten / trotter, straighten / lakes, straighten / love, straighten / middle, straighten / kingdoms, straighten / upper peninsula, straighten / kingdoms, straighten / rested, straighten / cool, straighten / 4000, straighten / knots, straighten / untwisted, straighten / goose, straighten / glassy, straighten / news made, straighten / run to look, straighten / blue, straighten / sky okay, straighten / parking, straighten / welcomed, straighten / rivers stop, straighten / deep inside, straighten / amethyst, straighten / means, straighten / walnut, straighten / blooms, straighten / trading, straighten / for, straighten / blue neon, straighten / vistas, straighten / unions, straighten / first, straighten / times, straighten / virginal, straighten / activities, straighten / bargains, straighten / rivers, straighten.

CHAPTER ELEVEN

Beloved, straighten / may, straighten / we weave, straighten / a magical, straighten / mention, straighten / for the tutorial, straighten / and the, straighten / utilization of, straighten / famous, straighten / fashions, straighten / saint germain, straighten / has said, straighten / "I AM", straighten / where, straighten / is the, straighten / joint, straighten / intrigue? straighten / call her, straighten / home to, straighten / your, straighten / call her, straighten / home to the, straighten / winsomeness, straighten / for the throne, straighten / of the Earth, straighten / powers, straighten / electric, straighten / christed, straighten / registrations, straighten / shores, straighten / few, straighten / rented, straighten / city, straighten / humbles, straighten / hello, straighten / earth is, straighten / excessive to the, straighten / core, straighten / archemedian, straighten /

for a hiring, straighten / spars, straighten / spelled, straighten / flushing, straighten / within, straighten / and the frameworks / sold, straighten, straighten / without, straighten / quality, straighten / in value, straighten / atermite, straighten / has headed, straighten / to rescue, straighten / those who, straighten / eat wood, straighten / and the need, straighten / for moods, straighten / redwood bleeds, straighten / insurance paid, straighten / God feeds, straighten / the singing, straighten / congregations, straighten / of knowing, straighten / love, straighten / chosen, straighten.

CHAPTER TWELVE

Messengers, straighten / allow, straighten / words, straighten / mastery, straighten / conditions, straighten / likened, straighten / life, straighten / spent, straighten / needs, straighten / humble, straighten / calls, straighten / dynamic, straighten / portals, straighten / ouring, straighten / treachery, straighten / few, straighten / cities, straighten / little, straighten / powers, straighten / perhaps, straighten / extremes, straighten / correct, straighten / needs, straighten / among, straighten / comply, straighten / old, straighten / hours, straighten / eyes, straighten / estatoe, straighten / human, straighten / under, straighten / great will, straighten / exceptive to, straighten / an instinctive, straighten / core and, straighten / the scored federations / for a, straighten / light, straighten / confession now, straighten / found in, straighten / your friendly, straighten / explain of, straighten / where we, straighten / lean, straighten / toward, straighten / the flotations, straighten / fanned into, straighten / love's brightened, straighten / voices, straighten / for the rememberance, straighten / of exactly this, straighten / love, straighten / love, straighten / each the other, straighten / and find, straighten / pure extraction, straighten / ions in, straighten / the durable, straighten / expressions due, straighten / a dynamic which, straighten / lasted, straighten / past time, straighten / and, straighten / traffic, straighten.

CHAPTER THIRTEEN

Call, call made, straightly / viciousness, straighten / comply, straighten / today, straighten / humble, straighten / happy, straighten / books, straighten / freed, straighten / plead, straighten / your instant, straighten / dues, straighten / find yourself, straighten / well, straighten / in power, straighten / mental to the heart-line, straighten / interfere less, straighten / study, straighten / through, straighten / faults lined, straighten / from life, straighten / studies, straighten / definite, straighten / potential, straighten / gains, straighten / lack is, straighten / silvered, straighten / deer, straighten / gentles, straighten / alone, straighten / change, straighten / 30 who, straighten / people, straighten / into, straighten / drones, straighten / amperage is, straighten / peaking, straighten / here, straighten / call the, straighten / marry, straighten / viberation, straighten / for future, straighten / reference, straighten / gentleness has, straighten / met her, straighten / participation, straighten / codes in, straighten / soaring, straighten / soars and the, straighten / scores, straighten / significant, straighten / searing, straighten / grassy, straighten / elevations, straighten / and the fronts, straighten / laid open to, straighten / discover the, straighten /

vines which, straighten / had, straighten / grown, straighten / up inside, straighten / of you, straighten / discover, straighten / us, loved, straighten.

LEVEL 114: THE EGG-MENTS

CHAPTER ONE

Cool, eggs / prompt, eggs / keep, eggs / river, eggs / right, eggs / laughing, eggs / birds, eggs / galleries, eggs wink, eggs / in, eggs / recall, eggs / for, eggs / the driven, eggs / waimean, eggs / keeps, eggs / help, eggs / has come, eggs / focus!, eggs / here, eggs / spiders, eggs / barked, eggs / "the grass, eggs / on, eggs / the edge, eggs / of foreverness eccentric, eggs / intricate, eggs / intensity, eggs / rings, eggs / reigns, eggs / in, eggs / details, eggs / on, eggs / stitching, eggs / revelations, eggs / spiders, eggs / barking, eggs / empowers, eggs / Your, eggs / feeling, eggs / for an, eggs / eternity, eggs / emperial, eggs / peace, eggs / rush, eggs / do, eggs / sours, eggs / in total, eggs / view, eggs / empirical, eggs / ways, eggs / returned, eggs / intrigue, eggs / Your, eggs / self, eggs / with, eggs / value, eggs / set, eggs / by, eggs / cove, eggs / Alamos, eggs / resume, eggs / presumed, eggs / settle, eggs / levels, eggs.

CHAPTER TWO

Rooms, eggs / are, eggs / mentioned, eggs / in, eggs / hastened, eggs / impede, eggs / empowered, eggs / people, eggs / stand, eggs / to play, eggs / in your, eggs / unified, eggs / resolutions, eggs / sent, eggs / for, eggs / the source, eggs / and, eggs / the resource, eggs / sent, eggs / to exacting, eggs / love, eggs / wings, eggs / are the, eggs / lilly white, eggs / where, eggs / love, eggs / exacts, eggs / exits, eggs / here, eggs / a man, eggs / charged, eggs / know, eggs / that, eggs / heart, eggs / revolve, eggs / is a, eggs / solving, eggs / way, eggs / attack, eggs / less, eggs / and teach, eggs / more, eggs / when, eggs / you realize, eggs / enormity, eggs / of, eggs / the relationship, eggs / to love's, eggs / lights, eggs / we, eggs / will know, eggs / that the, eggs / include, eggs / concluded, eggs / for all, eggs / reasons, eggs / resumes, eggs / remaining, eggs / rememberance, eggs / for true, eggs / love in, eggs / return, eggs / for, eggs / God, eggs.

CHAPTER THREE

Why melt, eggs / lie less, eggs / without, eggs / older, eggs / loves, eggs / sex, eggs / in, eggs / god's, eggs / presence, eggs / is, eggs / the only, eggs / way, eggs / to improve, eggs / the "Christian", eggs / inheritance, eggs / circles, eggs / made, eggs / are, eggs / kept, eggs / arcing, eggs / for, eggs / future, eggs / reference, eggs / may, eggs / we set, eggs / a place, eggs / of literal, eggs / balance, eggs, eggs / in, eggs, eggs / you, eggs, eggs / register, eggs, eggs / now, eggs, eggs / the end, eggs / of, eggs / soul's, eggs / retreat, eggs / a treaty, eggs / has, eggs / been, eggs / made, eggs / between, eggs / you and, eggs / love, eggs / as the, eggs / ultimate, eggs / creations, eggs / in a light, eggs / dance, eggs / to surrender, eggs

/ and the tenderness, eggs / for light resignations, eggs / a purple, eggs / fields, eggs / literary, eggs / astound, eggs / has, eggs / been, eggs / given, eggs / friendly, eggs / advice, eggs / about, eggs / love, eggs / for neighbor, eggs / enemy and friend, eggs.

CHAPTER FOUR

You, eggs / are / the / chosen, eggs / thank / the door, eggs / for the, eggs / flow, eggs / write, eggs / into, eggs / a nearing, eggs / equation, eggs / personal, eggs / resolution, eggs / Is hereby, eggs / sent, eggs / a single, eggs / one will, eggs / come, eggs / through, eggs / a heart, eggs / which, eggs / loves, eggs / only you, eggs / remember, eggs / through, eggs / the one, eggs / comes, eggs / greatest, eggs / dao, eggs / greatest, eggs / enjoyment, eggs / crafted, eggs / employment, eggs / honorable, eggs / lessons, eggs / living, eggs / memorials, eggs / memoriams, eggs / well, eggs / written, eggs / rafts, eggs / lifted, eggs / roses, eggs / bloomed, eggs / required, eggs / only, eggs / this, eggs / the raspberry, eggs / blossoms, eggs / of balanced, eggs / amnesia, eggs / forgiven, eggs / for the, eggs / forgotten, eggs / respirations, eggs / which signal, eggs / God's, eggs / nearest, eggs / presence, eggs / come to, eggs / visit, eggs / dear, eggs / openly, eggs.

CHAPTER FIVE

When, eggs / you, eggs / see, eggs / the light, eggs / go on, eggs / enter here, eggs / and the wealth, eggs / of a century, eggs / will succumb, eggs / to your integrity, eggs / inquiry has, eggs / led to your, eggs / relief of immeasurable, eggs / completion, eggs / skills added, eggs / meet, eggs / relief in your, eggs / anxious good-byes, eggs / for the green, eggs / and blue, eggs / oceans, eggs / settle into, eggs / your eyes, eggs / rested intellectually, eggs / choose only this, eggs / true, love, eggs / roads, eggs / to heavens, eggs 29above and within, eggs / arc into willing, eggs / spaces, eggs / for the flights, eggs / of an ancient, eggs / returning, eggs / a patient, eggs / tomb has been opened, eggs / to exhume from, eggs / and these chambers melt, eggs / between the, eggs / walls for marital, eggs / bliss, eggs / reached a, eggs / peak nearby, eggs / and settled within, eggs souls / sold out to parental, eggs / plexus blinds, eggs / sneaks, sneaks back into, eggs / revelation, eggs / for your kept one, eggs / game, eggs / past news delivers, eggs / surrender's feats, eggs / with teal, eggs / spirals, eggs / stills, eggs / yet, eggs / another's, eggs / rested, eggs / ressurection for, eggs / all goods, eggs / God's, eggs / given, eggs / talents, eggs / presents, eggs.

CHAPTER SIX

Glaze, eggs / of eternalness, eggs / and thee, eggs / substance, eggs / for the iron, eggs / red, eggs / intrigue, eggs / with, eggs / moved, eggs / mountains, eggs / and the on sights, eggs / neat in, eggs / patterned, eggs / patented, eggs / types, eggs / who seep, eggs / of love, eggs / let, eggs / us lead, eggs / hills, eggs / above, eggs / pens, eggs / are alive, eggs / with this news, eggs / God is alive, eggs / and well dwells, eggs / within you, eggs / hope is, eggs / held in pen, eggs / lands and, eggs / you are, eggs / here topped, eggs / in past, eggs / forgot, eggs / who mends, eggs / that, eggs /

blue, eggs / sky for you, eggs / you will, eggs / know, eggs / that the red, eggs / is delivered, eggs / again, eggs / for the red, eggs / stood, eggs / full, well, eggs / within a green, eggs / heat's seeking, eggs / a tomb, eggs / has gone, eggs / to the funded, eggs / house for, eggs / a friend can elect, eggs / to move, eggs / in any day, eggs / next or week, eggs / due to the, eggs / misunderstood, eggs / deaths of direct, eggs / gifted listenings, eggs / let us follow, eggs / only God's rules, eggs / in yours, ours, eggs / life, eggs.

CHAPTER SEVEN

To the edge, eggs / theirs, eggs / hearts leapt, eggs / there were, eggs / none in their, eggs / barking, eggs / barking, eggs / sands, eggs / spiders, eggs / friends, eggs / boxes, eggs / irons, eggs / broken work, eggs / again and, eggs / at the edge of, eggs / their spirits, eggs / they found a, eggs / picture, eggs / freed, eggs / for the ever, eggs / grassed, eggs / under, eggs / living, eggs / lovers who, eggs / died for their, eggs / parent's past, eggs / transgressions, eggs / deliver this note, eggs / forgive the following, eggs / and fold your heart, eggs / inside, let us acquire, eggs / access, and succeed, eggs / ourselves too, this, eggs / our trail, eggs / the raptures traveling, eggs / sword has come, eggs / to rest in your, eggs / hands, eggs / keep, eggs / clear the way, eggs / clear the vines, eggs / find a path, eggs / to truth through the hearts, eggs / hung, eggs / less on, eggs / sleeves, eggs / and more, eggs / on hoods of, eggs / those driven, eggs / away for believing, eggs / too Good, eggs / blessed, eggs / are they, eggs / who gave, eggs / and those, eggs / who understood, eggs / that, eggs / God's gaze is, eggs / delivered in the hands, eggs / of this epistle written, eggs / for the eyes, eggs / of fortunate, eggs / humanity, eggs / basics, eggs.

CHAPTER EIGHT

Arrange, eggs / a new, eggs / marriage, eggs / to light's loved, eggs / hear a rewarded, eggs / life, eggs / lived, eggs / arrange, eggs / here, eggs / this sanctuary, eggs / for the marriage, eggs / of spirit, eggs / to the body, eggs / uniquely, eggs / present to a, eggs / dear friend, eggs / called love, eggs / on, eggs / linked kept secessions, eggs / can room in conical, eggs / faces, eggs / and the, eggs / indeed Javanese, eggs / embarkations coming, eggs / of interest in you, eggs / a portal, eggs / has kept you, eggs / friended, eggs / in softened, eggs / chances, eggs / for the final needs, eggs / appear bridged and gather those, eggs / who clearly finished, eggs / powerful, eggs / days advanced, eggs / cash in, eggs / on necessary, eggs / privileges, eggs / leave heaven to now, eggs / intense, eggs / cranio-sacral, eggs / works, eggs / require, eggs / your attendance, eggs / spend, eggs / an hour, eggs / in the here, now, some, eggs / times and friendly for, eggs / the music chosen, eggs / directs you, eggs / to love, eggs / as you will, eggs / you were, eggs / and wished into, eggs / the willingness, eggs / for a friend's, eggs / returning, eggs / your will, eggs / is hereby freed, eggs / now, eggs / expel, eggs / winds of, eggs / disbelief through, eggs / your faith, eggs.

CHAPTER NINE

Scripts written, eggs / into beauty, eggs / for life's elections, eggs

/ men call, eggs / I AM is, eggs / well in Ariel, eggs / I am well, eggs / Ariel, eggs / know this, eggs / upon land, eggs / one stone, eggs / knot left upon, eggs / the other, eggs / one day's, eggs / winds, eggs / azrael is dead, eggs / Gabriel found and, eggs / fed, eggs / Marry, eggs / One, eggs / who believes, eggs / in open, eggs / armed surrender, eggs / for the, eggs / rapture has, eggs / come unto, eggs / and upon, eggs / humanity, eggs / beloved, eggs / children, eggs / reach for the, eggs / life within love, eggs / light has carried us home, eggs / to this end, eggs / ebony grains, eggs / know love, eggs / hear, eggs / ready, eggs / to valuable be, eggs / in informational modality, eggs / reach rationales which, eggs / closed without kept, eggs / surrenders for the former, eggs / miss has goat, eggs / like gone to revel, eggs / in voted good-byes, eggs / to the buyers, eggs / of one, eggs / electric, eggs / tract, eggs / find and, eggs / replace the, eggs / symbolic thrust, eggs / of lessons past and, eggs / the tract which, eggs / leads to Ariel, eggs / succeeds in, eggs / love, eggs / let us, eggs / reach, eggs / others, eggs / through our, eggs / faith in, eggs / triple, humanity, humanity, humanity, eggs.

CHAPTER TEN

Muriel, eggs / is a, eggs / differ, eggs / vote, eggs / and elect, eggs / ariel, eggs / in Greece, eggs / they knew, eggs / thus and said, eggs / please Michael, eggs / left for the, eggs / softer, eggs / softness, eggs / of God's lightened, eggs / face, Metatron, eggs / release, eggs / realize, eggs / ariel, eggs / is well, eggs / within, eggs / Your heart, eggs / experienced, eggs / find, eggs / love's ends, eggs / hear, eggs / love, eggs / metatronic, eggs / friends, eggs / arc, eggs / means, eggs / angelic, eggs / blends, eggs / ariel, eggs / stays in, eggs / rooms, eggs / where, eggs / love, eggs / breathes, eggs / and beats, eggs / the sun, eggs / to bed, eggs / know, eggs / a, eggs / tune, eggs / electric, eggs / built, eggs / and, eggs / grown for, eggs / the former, eggs / famous, eggs / tune, eggs / called light, eggs / into, eggs / ariel, eggs / Gabriel, eggs / grew too, eggs / past, eggs / ariel, eggs / lasts, eggs / throughout, eggs / all, eggs / eternity, eggs / reap, reap elation, eggs / finds, finds sought in eggs.

CHAPTER ELEVEN

Merry, eggs / wishes, eggs / resides in, eggs / pairs, eggs / with others, eggs / red, eggs / raspberry, eggs / blooms, eggs / and blood red, eggs / roses where, eggs / metal now, eggs / lurks, eggs / where, eggs / is the nature, eggs / for crossing eaves, eggs / and these waves, eggs / electrically, eggs / apparent to, eggs / the inherent, eggs / trained, eggs / rests, eggs / start once, eggs / again, eggs / and find, eggs / the love, eggs / for all, eggs / lifetimes, eggs / here, eggs / again in, eggs / the hearts you, eggs / love, eggs / lurks, eggs / nearest, eggs / here, eggs / hers, eggs / ours, eggs / through, eggs / prayer, eggs / and this core, eggs / here a cure, eggs / for the directions, eggs / deviations, eggs / eternally, eggs / laid through, eggs / rested, eggs / lines, eggs / sophic, eggs / blues, eggs / Zelda, eggs / pews, eggs / written for, eggs / their, eggs / flair, eggs / and a new, eggs / suppose that, eggs / Scouts, eggs / lived pent in, eggs / central spirals and, eggs / these groves

fed, eggs / faxes, now dead, eggs / and the detailed birds w, eggs / honest in I AM twins borne to, eggs / genius, let us discuss duly and daily, eggs / these awakened ones whose, eggs

CHAPTER TWELVE

News lasts, eggs / to the Helenic, eggs / core, eggs / and throughout, eggs / eternity, eggs / Gabriel has, eggs / ended her choiring, eggs / chart in Baxter, eggs / planned, eggs / horizons, eggs / for the musical, eggs / chords, eggs / released across, eggs / nations through, eggs / the aim, eggs / east across, eggs / sun's facing, eggs / waters, eggs / and as matters, eggs / Trojan today, eggs / break the, eggs / news, eggs / I find, eggs / thinking multiple, eggs / again, eggs / secrets, eggs / ready, eggs / blessed, eggs / exact their, eggs / reasonings, eggs / precious the, eggs / people and, eggs / the disciplined disciples of, eggs / God for their, eggs / extraordinary tablets, eggs / talents, eggs / ten chosen, eggs / commandments, eggs / love, love,love,music, eggs, love, love, love, swim, love, aloha / thinking, eggs / released, eggs / monkeys, eggs / left, eggs / for shores, eggs / 100% hearted, eggs / a seam, eggs / has, eggs / been, eggs / found, eggs / nail it, eggs / down and draw, eggs / upon this, eggs / visit, eggs / regrets floated, eggs / off down the streams, eggs / souled, eggs / and you are to buy, eggs / at once and regret, eggs / now past has come due, eggs / upon this face, eggs / sell in synchronous, eggs / duty and the catawban, eggs / delights of bandanna green, eggs / fits for the red clans walls, eggs.

CHAPTER THIRTEEN

Harmony, eggs / civic, eggs / lightening, eggs / realized, eggs / whatever, eggs / comes, eggs / world, eggs / recognizes, eggs / the student, eggs / of man, eggs / humanity today, eggs / is turning their supply into importance, eggs / and each the exact feelings felt, eggs / trespass forgiven, eggs / actions leak, eggs / turning, eggs / presence and, eggs / essence into collapse, eggs / freed interests, eggs / collegiate, eggs / creations carry, eggs / health for freedom, eggs / and further your futured, eggs / burning can, eggs / at once elect the, eggs / sugar signed, eggs / burnings, eggs / and, eggs / these the simple, eggs / respects folded, eggs / funereal, eggs / and funeral piered, eggs / for the rejects of old, eggs / and the plan that, eggs / we've elected to, eggs / still the light and to, eggs / direct those who steal the, eggs light / as go lightly, eggs / will by the One, eggs / be sold for the, eggs / highest, eggs / bid into the lakes, eggs / of burning flames, eggs / and a bottomless pit, eggs / called regret for stealing, eggs / life from the friends who, eggs / held essence as love, eggs / may the funds return to, eggs / the burning simper and the simmering, eggs / recall those who stood, eggs / in past gone and partnered patient, eggs / recollection, both alone, and, eggs / blessed for the doors, eggs / of ascended saint-hood fed, eggs / and the dissolution of past marry, eggs / for the final acess, eggs / to the squares who, eggs / hold us loved, eggs / yes and martyred less, eggs / for the causes, eggs / carried when God, eggs / discovers humanity, eggs / near his heart's, eggs / squaring, eggs.

LEVEL 115: THE SPORE-MENTS

CHAPTER ONE

Free these spores tell them, "spores" / physically spored / positions made, spored / eye on these, spored / picture this "spored" / think about, spores / tooth, spores / privilege, spores / silly, spores / indeed, spores / turned, spores / gossip, spores / light, spores / pathway, spores / pouring, spores / life, spores / opportunity, spores / value, spores / chart, spores / correct, spores / associations, spores / invite, spores / power, spores / change, spores / energy, spores / might, spores / living centrally, spores / life, spores / truth, spores / picture, spores / whatever, spores / call, spores / proceeds, spores / boxes, spores / moved, spores / hear, spores / we, spores / are the well, spores / the, spores / well prepared, spores / to love, spores / let us reside, spores / instinct, spores / wise, spores / to love, spores / let us burn, spores / in insignia, spores / and resolve to, spores / keep the theory, spores / of thundering, spores / under love, spores / let us, spores / find, spores / friends, spores / who carry, spores / the torch for, spores / the heartfelt, spores / societies of God, spores / as the matriarch, spores / and the paternal, spores / ignite, spores / called, spores / The Friend of, Humanity, spores.

CHAPTER TWO

Absolutely, spores / pass out, spores / nows, spores / reminder, spores / tomorrow, spores / events, spores / reverted, spores / carry, spores / things, spores / into, spores / detrimental, spores / forgiveness, spores / constantly, spores / cued, spores / carriages, spores / last, spores / constancy, spores / lets you, spores / single, spores / out world, spores / events, spores / for futures, spores / told, spores / about the well, spores / begotten, spores / son of, spores / a carpenter, spores / has, spores / the world, spores / taken, spores / the noose, spores / off the Father? spores / let us know through, spores / your elegance and, spores / control when, spores / said becomes lived, spores / and the Temple, spores / in Man is revealed in, spores / your body, your, spores / being and the way, spores / you present, eloquently, spores / the mentioned, spores / experiences, spores / of love, spores / forever, spores / release, spores / rejoice, spores / gains, spores / perfect, spores / universe, spores / mars, spores / eclipsed, spores / and now, spores / gaining, spores / in love's durations, spores / let us lead, spores / to the edges, spores / of love, spores / God gave, spores / us talents, spores / to burn, spores / in electric, spores / oils, spores.

CHAPTER THREE

We are, spores / rested, spores / in glassy, spores / eyed stares, spores / and the temple, spores / squares related, spores / to our settled in, spores / long term loves, spores / Ariel comes to you, spores / comforts you, spores / finds her place, spores / marry her, spores / in your knowing, spores / cure of the past, spores / Cancer, spores / sores, spores / who is the One, spores / Tropic Capricorn is, spores / final, spores / the one, spores / copper, spores / blue has come, spores / to the, spores / life now, spores / known as, spores / electrically, spore / freed, spores / kiss the, spores / door of, spores / the One, spores / who shows, spores / her face,

spores / next shielded, spores / and peeling, spores / as the sun's, spores / reaction can, spores / carry only, spores / One, spores / facet, spores / turning, spores / so, spores / fast, spores / 29 is the, spores / number of rebell, spores ion / a bird, spores / set free has carried the, spores / quite formidable news to, spores / the departed ones, spores / demand less, spores / and find class, spores / in your serious loving, spores / ways, spores / keys produced, spores / a ringing delivery, spores / large interiors blast through, spores / these portals to, spores / carry fear far, spores / away and the 888 of, spores / your doubt-free friend, spores / has landed affectionately, spores / near, spores / carry the mighty sword, spores / and listen less to loser, spores / individuals without center, doubled over in fear and the lack of feeling triumphant in love, spores.

CHAPTER FOUR

Ariel, spores / later, spored / floods, spores / you with, spores / her memories of, Earth, spores / and the truth of her erasure of built upons, spores / and a light-hearted expression for, spores / the proof that awaits in returning styles, spores / without guides and love, spores / awaits you, remember, spores / marry her, spores / the Shekinah of God, spores / the Christed One, spores / The one who said, spores / "I will roam", spores / is headed home, spores / for eternal gifts, spores / of light, spores / and love, spores / and the yes!, spores / to God's, spores / throne, spores / allow us now, spores / this light election, spores / agitated less, spores / found more reapings, spores / corrected stands, spores / willed shut doors, spores / openly acknowledged inspores possible sighs / law stood for the understood, spores / life led us to God, spores / understandings swept you, spores doors / the world distributed at will, spores / goods paid recalled, spores / excerpts written became, spores / peopled and historied in her, spores / keeping a people met, spores / lack less, feared more, mankind, spores / stumbled until those, spores / effected, affected, directed, defected, spores / found hollows for, spores / outlined, spores / showings, spores / of the lessenings, spores / they had become, spores / beside lacks of shameful showing, spores / of the masses under all, spores / who seed their own, spores / hands for God's written, spores / influence, spores / you have, spores / found the key to life's, spores / returning, spores / aims, spores / dirty laundry bills, spores / are suspected and paid for those who clear, spores / called the others broken, spores / ones who placed became have now surrendered celled selahs, spores / ariel is set to demand respect, spores / remember for this Muriel is kept, spores / and azrael now coated in slickest oils for the burning which, spores / Gabriel gloated about…cloths swell in ignition, spores / and the telling is told as Michael sails, spores / below this curve, spores / called sighingly, Why? Humanity, spores.

CHAPTER FIVE

News told, spores / heaven, spores / worn inside, spores / torn sandals, spores / and muddy boots, spores / for the requirement is, spores / made due, all to, spores / yourself find the fuels, spores / and the lights accustomed to, spores / times readied, spores / and the knowing, spores / glower, spores / of ancient accepted, spores / for the tones, spores / lifetimes, spores / wordless, spores / rendered life, spores / desirous for stages, spores / skipped, spores / those who, spores / know are now made available, spores / to your showing, spores / first, spores / these and those, spores / serviced for the bodies, spores / place, spores / and the pearls erupt in ascensions, spores / and the knowing whores collect, spores / positions and the possible remains of, spores / gandered gatherings, spores / parables written remain encountered, spores / and reconnaissance is paid, spores / for the surest, spores / knowings, spores / and the islands where we, spores / stand are strung in necklaces, spores / of sun singing as, spores / we found are repaid for relays, spores / broken down, spores / where is well? spores / why sway? spores / why stay? spores / where sway? spores / swerve ever homeward, spores / headed directed, spores / into the sun of, spores / the arc called, spores / arcturus, spores / and the man called, spores / jesus has stood as, spores / planned for the directional, spores / arrow into divinity, spores / electric in a spiral curving, spores / leap into the life, spores / directed for god's cause, spores / and let us, spores / know that this, spores / cause cured is, spores / love, spores / now, spores / freed, spores / reside at, spores / will, spores / Hawaii, spores.

CHAPTER SIX
Longs made, spores / wills, spores / approved, spores / feel, spores / finest, spores / divinity, spores / listen, spores / discordant, spores / as cleared, spores / things, spores / intense, spores / fears, spores / gone, spores / hold on, spores / remember, spores / powers bill paid, spores / keep honest, spores / records, spores / leave in contact, spores / either, spores / swallowed or led, spores / to the altars, spores / consumed when fired bred below, spores / the entire, spores / worlds conclusions, spores / of now, spores / and the say that, spores / today is our, spores / way homeward scooped, spores / the stepped plan, spores / the pyramids expand, spores / into love, spores / deleted, spores / remember? spores / derive a, spores / rest for the, spores / test laid well, spores / into enticed, spores / naturalness, spores / flows a reunion and, spores / the returning for rhythmic settled, spores / yellings, spores / for flashing, spores / residues, spores / can be traced into trails reflected for the eviction of less hearted ones who, spores / dwell on the drink, spores / and the flash and the cards, spores / which purchased, spores / only destitution, spores / despair, spores / and direct, spores / emotion, spores / forgiven, spores / fallen, spores / flushed, spores / floored, spores / fused, spores / and used, spores / as a, spores / cord away, spores / from this, spores / eloquent heart, spores / may we, spores / hear "love", spores.

CHAPTER SEVEN
I can write, spores / this, spores / pen dry, spores / about God, spores / I can, spores / sing his, spores / course, spores / and his cause, spores / as signaled, spores / I can find her, spores / place in the lost way, spores / and where is the will? spores / the well gone? spores / where is good-bye now, spores taught? / I am this church, spores / and this temple, spores / and this steeple, spores / and this plan for, spores / the light resurrected, spores / in a temple,

spores / glass I saw reflection and, spores / knew, spores / that without is, spores / within and can can mend her heart's wishing, spores / missions, spores / One, spores / who found, spores / a pen, spores / and glittering wrote, spores / her way to the heart, spores / of man, spores / with respect, spores / revelation, discipline, spores / and the treasure, her, spores / patient pathway cutting, spores / through to the miracles in life's, spores / dismissals and the shouting, spores / helps which led to friends found, spores / and hearts, spores / released to sound, spores / like this…, spores / loved, spores / what is the, spores / measure of, spores / humanity? spores / In humanity? And, spores / how far do we go to feel spores his / fellow, spores / ship? spores / withouts, spores / within, spores / can, spores / mend, spores / the, spores / missions, spores / wishings, spores / found One heart, spores / opened to the pen which, spores / yelled yes! To God, spores / know thou, spores / this, ours is the inheritance, spores / called Unconditionally, spores / love, a, spores / deed returned, spores.

CHAPTER EIGHT
What, spores / is, spores / next? spores / aim two, spores / how to, spores / explain, spores / the encoded, spores instructions, spores / what, spores / is third? spores / prepare, spores / the tapes, spores / for, spores / resurgent, spores / shields, spores / founded, spores / on Jordan's, spores / shores, spores / and the love, spores / within holds a gun to the, spores / fire, spores / and strung, spores through the leaves / are the trees demanding freedom, spores / and the summation is a summary, spores / for the core called love and, spores / the littered, spores / ground has sung, spores / her national anthem', spores / "love", spores / farms, spores / called, spores / collectives, spores / rents are due, spores / and the community, spores / concurs that, spores / communicative, spores / disorders, spores / vary only, spores / if we rosey-blue, spores remembered / to send the affluence requests in, spores / say you meant it, spores / mean these enterprises, spores / and leave for, spores / other's lands, spores / goodness known, spores / knows this, spores / we feed, spores / in final blissful, spores / schools and the, spores / college, spores / elected, spores / when', spores / love, spores / begins, spores / her moves, spores / initialed for, spores / final approvals, spores / and fortunate, spores / meetings made, spores / magenta through, spores / the kundalin swings into, spores / humanity, heart to head, spores / to feat, know the moods, spores / God said, love is electric inside, spores humans.

CHAPTER NINE
Co-operated, spores / physicians, spore / clearly, spores / lights, spores / beliefs, spores / souls, spores / ridding, spores / sources, spores / lights, spores / bulbs, spores / pleasures, spores / likenings, spores / bodies, spores / purged, spores / ceased, spores / craves, spores / exceeds, spores / confessed, spores / confers, spores / nets, spores / frees, spores / corrects, spores / souls, spores / penetrated, spores / for full releases, spores / laws, spores / electric, spores / elevate, spores / punished, spores / less without, spores / forgiven, spores / sources, spores / donned, spores / saddles, spores / ridden, spores / horses, spores / worked, spores / embodies, spores /

depraved, spores / composites, spores / instincts, spores / gathered, spores / for the flight, spores / home, spores / all, spores / souls released / youthful, spores / purges have come, spores / require, spores / that all souls, spores / released for the, spores / light's fulfillment, spores / have revealed the revelatory spores ions / which came and, spores / the earth has sealed her, spores / filling followers in red discourse, spores / for the course, spores / run again, spores / life, spores / said, spores / yes, spores / to, spores / God's, spores / love, spores.

CHAPTER TEN

Diseased, spores / animals, spores / insured, spores / illuminations, spores / crickets, spores / cost, spores / plagues, spores / rushed, spores / conduits, spores / tubes, spores / angers, spores / lavas, spores / steps, spores / appetites, spores / passions, spores / raw, spores / punished, spores / evils, spores / cast, spores / into, spores / burnings of, spores / recognition of, spores / the one constant, spores / which is, spores / love, spores / sun, spores / deaths, spores / divine, spores / models, spores / mutual, spores / minds, spores / guided, spores / explorations, spores / yoga mats, spores / exceed, spores / dollars spent, spores / and those who cared, spores / carried simple, spores / shovels to the, spores / wind's door, spores / and asked permission to, spores / utter cries, spores / of deserved, spores / waters, spores / and the waves, spores / respond in resplendent, spores / carries on for the lease, spores / is paid and the oaks, spores / resound in sounding agreement, spores / for the repeat that the, spores / rapture is here, hear us, spores / call us love's many, spores / million miles, spores / a way to, spores / heart has been found inside, spores / this screen called human, spores / friend, basic humanity, spores / heard, love, friends, spores / love is, heard, spores / for the fast, spores / deliverance to, spores / the Friend's friend, spores / called Ariel, spores / may you believe, Muriel, spores.

CHAPTER ELEVEN

All lights, spores / complete, spores / further, spores / fathering, spores / derive, spores / pleasure, spores / your own, spores / and admit, spores / your discipled, spores / universes, spores / mergers, spores / in functions, spores / cosmos blue, spores / and the recognitions, spores / given, spores / when, spores / impact, spores / becomes impart, spores / and we rule the, spores / area through, spores / immortal, spores / mergers, spores / for the tempers, spores / tamed, spores / when basins emerged, spores / to share, spores / the zones, spores / of perpetual, spores / longing, spores / and the prize, spores / is wrought, spores / as exactly, spores / where and when, spores / we find the, spores / founded, spores / place meant for, spores / earth's, spores / completion as, spores / your core, spores / example of, spores / the mind of, spores / God given reign, spores / as the direct, spores / cones of, spores / seeing purpose, spores / has found you in penned, spores / response, spores / to the land and her, spores job, here, spores / in the lands of all, spores / returnings, spores / may we, spores / wear the eternal, spores / code of coated and, spores / loved, spores / revival, spores / survival has, spores / past and the past,

spores / has led us through, spores / these spirals, spores / into soothing matters, spores / material, spores / to the causes, spores / swiftly at hand, spores.

CHAPTER TWELVE

Body, spores / maker, spores / found us, spores / proclaimed, spores / us as, spores / working, spores / souls, spores / who, spores / gathered, spores / near, spores / to shores, spores / souls, spores / 1929, spores / bode, spores / us farewell, spores / to the image, spores / within, spores / and divinest still, spores / images rehearsed, spores / can find, spores / us all directed, spores / home for the, spores / creator, spores / has come to, spores / carry home the, spores / Ones who remember, spores / and the nightly, spores / forgiven, spores / find a heed, spores / in bathing, spores / religions and the, spores / regulations red, spores / in impartial meanings, spores / and the coded, spores / appointments, spores / for those whose, spores / hearts opened, spores / as results of knowing, spores / heaven, spores / sent nearby to, spores / find the men who, spores / lower only, spores / ghosts and shells, spores / into the sands and, spores / finds a pirate, spores / stilled, spores / in completed, spores / love, spores / leading us near, spores / to the whole and the, spores / impressions for the wedded, spores / bliss which reaches through, spores / lightened strands, spores / to recover and succeed us to, spores / the suggested venues, spores / the marriage beneath, spores / the palms of, spores / ressurection day, spores / Sunday coming and the lessons, spores / running into sinking refusal, spores / to rehearse even one, spores / direct line, spores / of the, spores / Christ-head experience, spores.

CHAPTER THIRTEEN

The building is, spores / your impression of what a, spores / symbol, spores / crosses, spores / mathematically, spored / remember, spores / pi, spores / is where, spores you / signed in and, spores / sighed when, spores / love, spores / was worn, spores / through, spores / as a, spores / black, spores / widowed, spores / hole's release, spores / and the theories, spores / which debunked, spores / stood as, spores / this new, spores / foundation is reached, spores / in random fields, spores / perfectly, spores / aligned, spores / to delivery, spores / of the succinct, spores / tunes, spores / called mathematical, spores / singings, spores / and those who, spores / rhymed, spores / their names, spores / with measures, spores / of God, spores / music is, spores / where we meet, spores / this portal, spores / and we are, spores / sewing the screen, spores / to the fabric, spores / through our belief, spores / in this fuse, spores / the Pythagorean, spores / agreeing that, spores / exaggeration knot, spores / the Einstein rehearsal, spores / relative to love, spores / is what you, spores / demanded when, spores / you wrote, spores / this ringing into, spores / singing arrivals, spores / God is good, spores / in the understanding, spores / which man, spores / rehearsed, spores / God lasts in, spores / the hearts which, spores / recognize, spores / granted, spores / expressions and, spores / donations made, spores / for the cures and the cursory causes of love, spores.

LEVEL 116: THE BIRTH-MENTS

CHAPTER ONE
Centripetal, births / force, births / in, births / terrific, births / exit, births / of an existant, births / material, births / which, births / weds, births / our, births / weavings, births / ionically, births / into drawn, births / lines, births / through, births / us a factored, births / fuel, births / flows, births / and in, births / theory, births / we placed, births / max planck's, births / constant, births / in, births / the belief, births / that, births / materialism, births / has held up, births / for humanity's, births / birthings, births / predated, births / columbian, births / bills, births / reach for, births / skies, births / when, births / winning, births / becomes, births / a window, births / on struck, births / energetics, births / and the, births / energetic suppositions, births / of love, births / so to speak, births / what, births / quarks, births / held, births / up for, births / the final, births / planets, births / to leap, births / across? births / inductions, births / recently, births / find, births / a plan, births / which works for, births / your, births / final, births / expressionary, births / release of thee, births / mundanity, births / in life, births.

CHAPTER TWO
We are, births / sealed, births / in tombs, births / which, births / are factored, births / in, births / energetic, births / tunes, births / an aether, births / a tune, births / neptons, births / quarks, births / works, births / particles, births / waves, births / is, births / the energy, births / of love, births / planetary, births / unto life's, births / spans, births / sisterly, births / leads, births / are, births / a listening, births / link, births / to love, births / sunk into, births / fabricated, births / floods, births / is a sample, births / of emerald, births / hope, births / and the, births / amuse, births / meant when blue towns, births / become, births / ash brown in, births / basic interludes, births / intruding, births / numbers, births / found us, births / flat without, births / direction, births / may we, births / keep, births / your welling, births / spoken, births / eaves, births / unknotted, births / across, births / waves, births / found, births / evolving, births / lightly, births / on the new, births / wave's arcing, births / and the repeat, births / that good-bye, births / is meant this, births / time, births / around, births / love's, births / clarity, births.

CHAPTER THREE
Evolving, births / structurally, births / is a simple, births / sample, births / of where, births / we correct, births / our staring, births / directions and, births / find the stars, births / which lead, births / us home, births / through, births / the found, births / drives to fonder, births / love, births / find, births / the fields, births / erase the less, births / perfect, births / morph has, births / arrived, births / and the, births / pi plan, births / expands, births / into the, births / plans, births / elyssian, births / for a, births / new, births / book, births / is, births / written, births / now, births / rehearse, births / elease of the, births / old history, births / mankind, births / is written, births / in historical, births / recant, births / write, births / this, births / hear, births / here, births / how, births / why, births

/ when, births / humanity, births / 3, births / 1, births / 4, births / and, births / the codes, births / retructured, births / to reflect, births / the perfect, births / divinity, births / in, births / humanity, births / lies, births / replacement, births / seals, births / and the peeling is set, births / for lifetimes of pleasures extents, births.

CHAPTER FOUR
Find, births / a, births / focus, births / again, births / and describe, births / the experience, births / here, births / and, births / take care, the embedded, births 10 cross, births / out, births / right, births / here, births / reflect, births / on, births / this and, births / pull, births / out the, births / parts, births / worn out, births / drink, births / in the, births / new, births / focus, births / and find, births / fixtures, births / electrically, births / installed, births / through, births / valerian, births / routes, births / past, births / sleeping, births / iron red, births / trips, births / to the soul's, births / neglected, births / lift off, births / get it, births / here, births / now, births / good-bye, births 43 to, births / the, births / last, births / the, births / final, births / splits, births / of, births / the final, births / clips, births / off, births / these, births / all, births / the, births / left, births / souls, births / clear, births / the plane, births / and the, births / mechanism, births / thought, births / to be, births / cleared, births.

CHAPTER FIVE
Midnight, births / passes, births / ivy, births / rivers, births / greens, births / told, births / to love, births / repeat, births / these, births / songs, births / find, births / ways, births 13to say this, births / space is, births / between, births / jupiter, births / and mars, births / the asteroid, births / belt is out of this, births / head, births / she is, births / the one, births / respect her, births / the distance is, births / out, births / between us, births / the seas, births / and the final, births / summaries, births / for a manner, births 31settled, births / into causes crystal, births / dreams are found, births / a crystal, births / river, births / flows, births / beneath my beds, births / dreams, births / please, births / place yourselves, births / next to sheperd's gifts, births / prophetic wonders, births / lightly lead love to this next dimension, births / remember, births / the beaches, births / and the extravagant, births / gestures, births / called mixtures, births / of personal, births / powers, births / and previous vendeth, births / a precision, births / has come to, births / our universals, births / deliver, births / devolved, births / rhetoric, births / into simple measures, births / and the beats found, births / rhythmic in your hearts, births / hearts, births / separate, births / gestures, births / found together, births.

CHAPTER SIX
We, births / are, births / the best, births / in, births / an experience, births / several, births / reaches, births / wide, births / broad, births / we are offered, births / the example, births / for expressive, births / communications, births / and the direct, births / inspection of, births / severed associations, births / as the companion, births / of, births / simple, births / men, births / maneuver, births / yourself, births / to find, births / the soul sick, births / partner, births / who is looking, births / at similar, births / experiences, births / with

the, births / father, births / and the, births / disciples, births / key, births / for the, births / resurrection, births / of light, births / a, births / life, births / has changed, births / tonight, births / find, births 42, her, births / tonight, births / through, births / your love, births / may, births / you, births / be, births / the, births / one, births / who, births / wears, births / the, births / ring, births / of, births / metatron, births / may, births / you, births / be, births / the, births / one, births / who, births / delivers, births / the power of god to love, births.

CHAPTER SEVEN
Electric, births / agility, births / is given, births / to our life, births / when, births / we signal, births / our, births 8readiness, births / through, births / faith, births / in spending, births / time, births / alone, births / i, births / have, births / found, births / your, births / faith, births / refreshing, births / and your, births / eyes elctric, births / through the, births / patterns which, births / others, births / spell as l-o-v-e, births / a second, births / choice has, births / come to, births / life, births / this night, births / you are allowed, births / to visit, births / the friends of, births / an island, births / wide to, births / wise wishing, births / for wisdom, births / and the lining, births / split, births / into remembered, births / paints and, births / the connected, births / reverence, births / which collects, births / dues as, births / this page, births / turns, births / and prices, births / paid, births / become, births / minutes, births / bravely led, births / through our, births / finding one, births / bringing home, births / this lesson, births / past, the homeward, births / found plans for, births / the foundations of man, births / living inside, births / human beings, births / flowers, births / beautiful, births 64in man and woman, both kind, births.

CHAPTER EIGHT
Found, births / faith, births / again, births / charades, births / are dropped, births / salvation's, births / cost, births / is the critical, births / attend, births / for, births / patience, births / and, births / the, births / framework, births / is set, births / in lateral, births / moves, births / and, births / commensurate, births / measured yearly, births pays and the pages, births / due, births / where, births / planets, births / spin and the, births / preparations, births / paid are for the, births / continuum of god, births / and christ is inside my, births / chewing gum and my, births / heart and my heady, births / friends who frequent soul gaps in, births / the pit's of the earth's core, births / why, births / stare without, births / seeing your, births / self in me, births / jah said "one clear", births / directive has come, births / to humanity and this, births / my people is "love", births / could this see the being in, births / us for the duration is come upon, births / the face of man calling distinctly let, births / shepherds fly into hearts tonight, births / we know, births / the weather, births / which sheds, births / sweaters and steeples, births / and bermuda green, pink sands with pastels, births / cubes, births / direct in line, births / with magic leyes, births / in the lands of gods, births / and man's foundations, births / spent can creep over the old, births / stubs to scrounge for the, births / gifts which, births / looking up can, births / bring find your heart, births / and let her sing, births / tonight, births / we have "God", births.

CHAPTER NINE
May, births / we, births / inspire, births / ourselves, births / to, births / blend, births / with, births / iron's, births / resolve, births / the inner, births / core of earth is, births / made of, births / a magnetic, births / source, births / sorts, births / unlike, births / other, births / a source, births / sent for, births / mars, births / rusty blue in, births / red suspend, births / speed to rest in the, births / core's magnetic, births / magneto of love, births / practice, births / in conceptual, births / for the blasting cures, births / we, births / are, births / kept sure, births / for love, births / is the trust, births / of nations secure, births / sessions filled births / up with only, births / god, births / only god, births / spiritually suitable, births / and stable, births / spins, births / lead, births / to lovers, births / self, births / said, births / examine, births / your truly, births / immaculate experience, births / for the nature, births / of god, births / spell, births / god's, births / name, births / as, births / your own, births / that is, births / the key, births / you are, births / god too, births / singing, births / to the heart, births / you adore, births / your own, births / singing, love, births.

CHAPTER TEN
What is, births / the self, births / where, births / is the respect, births / for your, births / resource, births / will you, births / register, births / for, births / winning kinds, births / which will, births / it be, births / decide and, births / collect, births / necessary, births / shifts, births / declared, births / empires, births / collects, births / collect, births / collect, births / dates, births / due, births / love, births / freshen, births / up, births / for the, births / follow, births / corollary, births / beliefs, births / formed, births / fours, births / elements, births / existences, births / of a fifth, births / plane, births / cycles, births / vulgarity, births / ends, births / chemistry, births / insures, births / operational, births / pages, births / perfections, births / digested, births / aids, births / firey, births / stones, births / through a, births / road, births / across, births / mountains, births / mana, births / given, births / grace, births / found, births / women, births / who, births / live, births / vertically, births / applied, births / to the son, births / sophistry, births / suggested, births.

CHAPTER ELEVEN
Through, births / upland, births / hearts, births / find, births / your, births / place in waves, births / electric and elective factors, births / glance, births / into, births / signals rainbowed across forevers, births / as you engage, births / in direct, births / contact, births / with the, births / one, births / the former, births / the fanned, births / final, births / all, births / one, births / who, births / sees, births / only, births / god direct, births / in you, births / you have, births / found the focus, births / the form, births / the foundation, births / stone of this, births / earth and, births / her name is lightly, births / loving said, births / mirth, births / birth, births / a, births / basic, births / belief, births / in why we live, births / and find, births / engraved in mercury, births / the reason for your, births / surrendering, births / to the philosophy, births / of love, births / there is one, births / reason to engage, births / and that reason is,

births / love, births / yearning plans, births / and places, births / a selection, births / of images, births / on your doorstep, births / purged classic, births / fears, births / from trees, births / and placed, births / birds, births / birds, births / on wing, births / cardinals fly, births / horses move, births / to reign, births.

CHAPTER TWELVE
Bibliographic, births / wounds, births / salves, births / memories, births / healed, births / we know, births / where, births / your doorway is, births / find it inside, birth / your sequenced, births / firings, births / traditions, births / chemistry, births, / samples, births / elements, births / derived, births / errogenously, births / from family, births / affairs, births / birds, births / animal, births / kingdoms, births / found, births / earth inside, births / the spinning, births / pale, births / lights revues, births / love, births / zurich, births / engravings, births / awarded, births / sagittarean removed, births / cures, births / gemini, births / stems, births / seamings lana, births / molokai, births / oppositions, births / released, births / fates told, births / softly to, births / winging, births / notes, births / and natives, births / expand, births / to include, births / realms, births / positions, births / principles, births / coppers, births / mercury, births / amused, births / for, births / dragon's, births / eagled, births / lairs, births / exposed, births / recognized, births / for love, births / wherever we, births / travel, births / art, births / starts, births / here through, births.

CHAPTER THIRTEEN
Lunar implodes, births / cats, births / cubes, births / tubes, births / wall, births / hills, births / themed, births / senses, births / draped, births / atop, births / mountains, births / remaining, births / children, births / appearing, births / frequently, births / and, births / rainbows, births / rule, births / respectively, births / reflectively, births / as purifications, births / end, births / signs, births / smoothed, births / mentioned, births / a text, births / written, births / draw, births / symbols in, births / vegetative, births / tools, births / feeds, births / female, births / impressed, births / masked, births / removed, births / dares, births / over, births / deal, births / dealt, births / due love, births / substantial, births / investment, births / minerals, births / are, births / found, births / in lion's, births / dens and lands, births / richly settled, births / iron rich, births / chaos, births / occurs and ends, births / where melted, births / shore spill, births / into seas, births / ice caps, births / rivers pelting beneath the earth's surface, births / stones red and engraving say independently, births / surfaces as sequenced, births / triggering our recognitions of the whole, births / under the guise of love separated into, births / two gestures, genders, firmaments, births / love is leading wedge flying figure / eights folded to reveal the wings of humanity, venus orbits the same, 52 to 104, 2 times the spin, a meta-electron, the metatronic guideline to life, a simple principle of how too, fly, births.

LEVEL 117: THE IN-SPARK-MENTS

CHAPTER ONE
Seams, sparks, / meet, the meanings for sparks / themselves, sparks / on, sparks / either side, sparks / and, sparks / folds, sparks / in, sparks / to, sparks / attune, sparks / and atone, sparks / the, sparks / needs, sparks / of a, sparks / basic, sparks / tree, sparks / human, sparks / garments, sparks / are carried, sparks / into the, sparks / sleeves, sparks / and the fabric, sparks / of woven, sparks / light, sparks / how do, sparks / we see, sparks / this, sparks / movement and, sparks / where do the two, sparks / meet in humans, sparks / in, sparks / a, sparks / currents, sparks / in, sparks / perfect, sparks / regulations, sparks / of, sparks / the floodings, sparks / this will, sparks / stand, sparks / high, sparks / in a simple, sparks / plan, sparks / you, sparks / are allowed, sparks / to seek, sparks / and, sparks / peek, sparks / into the, sparks / future, sparks / know, sparks / the, sparks / floods, sparks 54 suggestions, sparks / come, sparks / level your, sparks / land, sparks / sell, sparks / the One, sparks / find a new arc, sparks / inspire the ones who write, sparks / to you insured, sparks / sovereignty and, sparks / thoroughness of the Thorang La to your passing pens, sparks.

CHAPTER TWO
Kingdoms, sparks / discussed, sparks / trinity, sparks / minds, sparks / life, sparks / led, sparks / through is, sparks / volume, sparks / of, sparks / wonders, sparks / hits and, sparks / the, sparks / volumetric, sparks / thirds, sparks / who rhyme, sparks / beyond the, sparks / times, sparks / and, sparks / powers, sparks / first, sparks / energy, sparks / lines, sparks / single, sparks / to these, sparks / atoms, sparks / and creative, sparks / unto, sparks / realms, sparks / for, sparks / primeval, sparks / matters, sparks / created, sparks / egyptian, sparks / registrations, sparks / for the, sparks / creations, sparks / intelligence, sparks / sent, sparks / for behavior, sparks / held, sparks / to the, sparks / roost, sparks / called unrest, sparks / upon, sparks / the waters, sparks / as we, sparks / formless, sparks / sent, sparks / humanity, sparks / unto the, sparks / willing, sparks / devoids, sparks / deeper, sparks / stilled, sparks / and, sparks / recreational, sparks / too, sparks / the, sparks / closures, sparks / made, sparks / are, sparks / real, sparks / unto, sparks / love, sparks.

CHAPTER THREE
Father, sparks / mother, sparks / matters, sparks / eluded, sparks / gods, sparks / Egyptian, sparks / essence, sparks / systems, sparks / principles, sparks / children, sparks / majors, sparks / universal, sparks / discovered, sparks / goddesses, sparks / supremest, sparks / relations, sparks / facts, sparks / occurred, sparks / major, sparks manifestations, sparks / times, sparks / trued, sparks / stated, sparks / estates, sparks / various, sparks / codes, sparks / rather, sparks / be, sparks / supported, sparks / life, sparks / days, sparks / phenomenal, sparks / ancients, sparks / felt, sparks / facts, sparks / neters, sparks / supremest, sparks / deluge, sparks / deluxe, sparks / sphinx, sparks / creations, sparks / waters, sparks / illustrations, sparks / fifteens, sparks / educations, sparks / alto, sparks /

supremes, sparks / soprano, sparks / tenors, sparks / finest, sparks / springs, sparks / singing, sparks / sung, sparks / editions, sparks / beethovens, sparks / books, sparks / gardens, sparks / napoleons, sparks / outlined, sparks / cars, sparks / models, sparks / novels, sparks / greatest, sparks / inclusions, sparks.

CHAPTER FOUR

Waters, sparks / clocks, sparks / modern, sparks / principles, sparks / detailed, sparks / points, sparks / paints, sparks / mechanics, sparks / marks, sparks / impressions, sparks / youths, sparks / formed, sparks / seals, sparks / mines, sparks / sections, sparks / forces, sparks / forms, sparks / Chinese, sparks / salts, sparks / impressions, sparks / youthfully, sparks / plunge, sparks / aplomb, sparks / delights, sparks / keenest, sparks / recorded, sparks / hearings, sparks / various, sparks / engraved, sparks / appreciations, sparks / supervisions, sparks / booked, sparks / found, sparks / history, sparks / commissions, sparks / prologues, sparks / permissions, sparks / envoys, sparks / journeys, sparks / overland, sparks / pilots, sparks / shipped, sparks / variety, sparks / equipped, sparks / brides, sparks / carry, sparks / khan, sparks / through Chinese, sparks / tartars, sparks / fiercest, sparks / fighters, sparks / Venetians, sparks / winging, sparks / into instruments, sparks / songs, sparks / customs, sparks / customary, sparks / tests, sparks / wonderful, sparks / hearings, sparks / prospers, sparks / courts, sparks / emperors, sparks / endangered, sparks / home, sparks.

CHAPTER FIVE

Prologues, sparks / considered, sparks / relatives, sparks / ultimately, sparks / fascinated, sparks / ranks, sparks / carried, sparks / participants, sparks / described, sparks / emperors, sparks / orders, sparks / battles, sparks / prosperous, sparks / endangered, sparks / many, sparks / Mongols, sparks / manners, sparks / farewells, sparks / natives, sparks / lands, sparks / in a favorable, sparks / position, sparks / of trust, sparks / in sincere, sparks / aspects of love, sparks / when a miracle occurs, sparks / we bleed, sparks / without, sparks / warrant in, sparks / stigmatan, sparks / ways, sparks / is a say, sparks / allowed? sparks / whence comes, sparks / our electric, sparks / stray? sparks / a scatter gram, sparks / written, sparks / will erase, sparks / the drawn, sparks / reside on, sparks / decency, sparks / and the seas, sparks / will part, sparks / for the signals, sparks / isled, sparks / where, sparks / we aim for, sparks / the weave, sparks / is the key to a frequency, sparks / called life, sparks / may we, sparks / part for the paintings, sparks / pictured, sparks / near our righteous, sparks / expectations, sparks / becoming your basic, sparks / spoken eternity, sparks / eternally wear the written, sparks / heart, sparks / to the moodily perfect, sparks / famous repertoire of blue, sparks / forgiveness as a reason for the, sparks / seasons of, sparks / love, sparks.

CHAPTER SIX

Why, sparks / have you, sparks / written, sparks / this, sparks / exclusive, sparks / rapt, sparks / born, sparks / son's, sparks / risen, sparks / time, sparks / you have, sparks / the desire, sparks / for

sincerest, sparks / infancy, sparks / and the steering ilked, sparks / when missionary, sparks / status, sparks / becomes basically, sparks / why you, sparks / have led the, sparks / way to the, sparks / creation, sparks / of this art, sparks / called magnetically, sparks / love, sparks / if a fitness, sparks / is reached will, sparks / we know, sparks / that which, sparks / we say, sparks / and as we said, sparks / days to a muse, sparks / are minutes and, sparks / the nose which, sparks / wonders smells the, sparks / event called, sparks / blooming as the, sparks / involuntary, sparks / shivers end, sparks / near the doorway, sparks / called eternally, home, sparks / as we may, sparks / we have, sparks / we do, sparks / we will, sparks / we shall, sparks / we all, sparks / will follow the, sparks / plan, sparks / called basic, sparks / humanity, sparks / through, sparks / the heart, sparks / chambers called eccentric, sparks / envoy to, sparks / the mansions, sparks / kept, sparks / clean through, sparks / deliberation, sparks / detail, sparks / strength, sparks / courage, sparks / and, sparks / lasting faith, sparks.

CHAPTER SEVEN

Will a mistake, sparks / now, sparks / close? sparks / when, sparks / power, sparks / passion is passed into the eternally living sparks / in your dealt with details of daring elations and fulfilling sparks / prose and the picture perfectly toned attempts into love / the lights and the sparks where do your, sparks emote time / feel, sparks / the passage? sparks / and, sparks / the missions, sparks / too, do they, sparks / plunge into, sparks / figures ten, sparks / wide, sparks / deals, sparks / deep, sparks / in om, sparks / woven, sparks / padme, sparks / hum, sparks / hummings, sparks / may we, sparks / wish your, sparks / mission, sparks / into life, sparks / in a patronal, sparks / spiral, sparks / I blend, sparks / the modes, sparks / for the measures, sparks / and the road, sparks / straightens, sparks / to reveal, sparks / a gateway, sparks / paid for through, sparks / life's, sparks / process, sparks / and the living, sparks / rest inside, sparks / your lessons, sparks / blessed, sparks / and the buying for, sparks / a tree, sparks / of life's fields, sparks / connected, sparks / absolutely, sparks / as love, sparks / rules, sparks / where, sparks / our steps, sparks / point, sparks / how our, sparks / doors open', sparks / how, sparks / far, sparks / we will, sparks / deliver, sparks / for God's, sparks / gracious, sparks / nest of, sparks / love, sparks.

CHAPTER EIGHT

Inside selah, sparks / approached, sparks / prefers, sparks / presence, sparks / to the colors, sparks / rainbow, sparks / red, sparks / narrow, sparks / spectrums, sparks / reached, sparks / leaning, sparks / red-yellows, sparks / as the, sparks / rainbow's, sparks / spirits, sparks / above, sparks / and the motherly, sparks / adventures, sparks / into singing, sparks / sins have gone, sparks / topping cultures, sparks / who expect, sparks / forgotten, sparks / intensity, sparks / will we, sparks / live in a, sparks / remember sent? sparks / peace is, sparks / our choice, sparks / as the amounting, sparks / now counting includes, sparks / mutual, sparks / respect, sparks / we select, sparks / a nearest, sparks / wave as the, sparks / spent regain sight of, sparks / the intent, sparks /

intended by your, sparks / precious, sparks / precise notes, sparks / written, sparks / westerns will smiling, sparks / leap, sparks / across canyons, sparks / to join, sparks / your reservation, sparks / to their resurrection, sparks / and the vice is, sparks / off the colors, sparks / paraphrased as the, sparks / papoose borne for, sparks / the culture and, sparks / the cause called, sparks / metatronically, sparks / present, sparks / great, sparks / white, sparks / wankataton, sparks / the man, sparks / born to lead, sparks / Christianity, sparks / to the fore, sparks / sleep in peace, sparks.

CHAPTER NINE

May we, sparks / stay in, sparks constant, sparks / measure, sparks / for the principle, sparks / of delivery, sparks / and the balanced, sparks / expenditures, sparks / caused when, sparks / emotion move, sparks / our narrow, sparks / steerage, sparks / into larger, sparks / events, sparks / and the advents, sparks / cured, sparks / become, sparks / willing, sparks / participants, sparks / in this, sparks / dancing, sparks / mayan, sparks / revival, sparks / the spark, sparks / ahkenation, sparks / nerfetiti's, sparks / forgiven, sparks / statue, sparks / the delivery of, sparks / summary, sparks / the patience of, sparks / advance, sparks / the grinning, sparks / assemblage, sparks / near the, sparks / point, sparks / of isles, sparks / worn to, sparks / forgiven, sparks / stones, sparks / and the kane, sparks / caned, sparks / in, sparks / quite survival, sparks / a blue imprint, sparks / has cloud written, sparks / the infringed, sparks / will perfectly fly, sparks / into sun's, sparks / today, sparks / I stay, sparks / in the sold, sparks / uniques and, sparks / I wonder softly how, sparks / the remembrance of, sparks / meals can healing, sparks / feast our, sparks / lonely, sparks / eyes to a dress, sparks / and the deep release for which, sparks / our living innocence has, sparks / prepared us for the trips into other, sparks / peaceful ventures and the, sparks / venues called love, sparks.

CHAPTER TEN

As a patterned and patient, sparks / man, I once, sparks / said "we wed, sparks / too soon, sparks / and when, sparks / we moon, sparks / we align for the, sparks / nature of, sparks / the signs which, sparks / said this way, sparks / to love, sparks / may the, sparks / centrally, sparks / connected, sparks / durations, sparks / repeal the, sparks / legendary, sparks / lesions, sparks / of inactive, sparks / ones, sparks / who leisurely, sparks / gave their, sparks / denoted hearts, sparks / to the cause, sparks / electric, sparks / hear, sparks / us, sparks / we will, sparks / love, sparks / pool pulling, sparks / as a, sparks / power's, sparks / friendly, sparks / focus, sparkscan, sparks / become, sparks / stray, sparks / and stronger, sparks / without, sparks / a model home, sparks / made for gnomes upon the, sparks / healed, sparks / piles of, sparks / given, sparks / findings, sparks / and the hidden, sparks / events hetero, sparks / to love's, sparks / waverings, sparks / waves, sparks / collapsed in, sparks / on the, sparks / ones who, sparks / neglected the'chosen, sparks / fews, sparks / returning, sparks / sun, sparks / allow, sparks / us, sparks / your exit, sparks / near, sparks / our, sparks / hearts, sparks / dearest, sparks.

CHAPTER ELEVEN:

May, sparks / we, sparks / flower, sparks / as, sparks / eternally, sparks / the won, sparks / for, sparks / aerial, sparks / views, sparks / on, sparks / arieal, sparks / news, sparks / made, sparks / and, sparks / said, sparks / love, sparks / as, sparks / an, sparks / after, sparks / effect, sparks / we, sparks / have, sparks / the, sparks / left, sparks / notes, sparks / and the, sparks / votes for, sparks / he assured, sparks / demurred, sparks / and softened, sparks / friends called love's, gifted, sparks / let us, sparks / live to love, sparks / actually, sparks / I AM, sparks / freed to wander, sparks / into the, sparks / wealth, sparks / for the wonders, sparks / and numbers, sparks / and systems, sparks / sent for, sparks / the, sparks / one', sparks / who, sparks / precepts, sparks / spent on, sparks / the known, sparks / only, sparks / love, sparks / is the, sparks / place, sparks / where, sparks / I await, sparks / God's, sparks / advance, sparks / and the, sparks / future, sparks / is clearly, sparks / zero from here, sparks / without delivery I, sparks / can fit only ones, sparks / to the hilt for this, sparks / cause called GOD"S, sparks / lunar, sparks.

CHAPTER TWELVE

May we, sparks / measure, sparks / a, sparks / merry, sparks / band, sparks / through, sparks / the, sparks / bracelet's, sparks / repairs, sparks / and the, sparks / spare, sparks / arise, sparks / into heart's revival, sparks / through, sparks / lovers, sparks / now lustrous, sparks / let us, sparks / love to, sparks / live near, sparks / friends, sparks / may, sparks / we, sparks / will and, sparks / well in our, sparks / light reward for, sparks / the goods, sparks / of God, sparks / Light, sparks / as an, sparks / essentially, sparks / eccentric clue, sparks / can, sparks / remember, sparks / well, sparks / the well of, sparks / faithful survival, sparks / and the capture, sparks / for, sparks / the willfull, sparks / and fleshly, sparks / flight, sparks / across waters, sparks / settled and the, sparks / cafes, sparks / blue, sparks / starring, sparks / estuaries, sparks / filled, sparks / in California, sparks / basics and, sparks / these cures, sparks / called love, sparks / listen, sparks / God spent, sparks / vacation, sparks / arranging your, sparks / trip into the, sparks / final front, sparks / find, sparks / a happy gift, sparks / for the flight, sparks / attendants, sparks / live', sparks / on, sparks.

CHAPTER THIRTEEN

Lost, sparks / causes, sparks / are, sparks / exemplative, sparks / of a, sparks / clarification, sparks / sought, sparks / precisely, sparks / as centered, sparks / and featured, sparks / fears, sparks / disappear, sparks / chores, sparks / choirs, sparks / durable, sparks / spells, sparks / of the wells, sparks / including, sparks / and where, sparks / we will find, sparks / our fullest, sparks / inclusions, sparks / informed, sparks / news and the, sparks / simply, sparks / settled, sparks / stores of, sparks / given, sparks / gatherings, sparks / glowing, sparks / showers, sparks / showing, sparks / directions, sparks / flights, sparks / named, sparks / factors, sparks / fitted, sparks / facets, sparks / applied, sparks / novices, sparks / boosted, sparks / into curations, sparks / for the, sparks /

collections, sparks / doors, sparks / furl your, sparks / flags and, sparks / find, sparks / a post, sparks / near the doorway, sparks / called Holy Host, sparks / around the gifts a, sparks / caring tree, sparks / and the daily, sparks / retirement into, sparks / the rests, sparks / for a factor, sparks / focused, sparks / into love, sparks / let us, sparks / listen, sparks / dear, sparks / daily, sparks / Metatrons, sparks.

LEVEL 118: THE ENZYME-MENTS

CHAPTER ONE
Substantial, wearing, is, r, I AM, substantive, to the, merry blue, grand, canal, of, venice, green, in, signal, scenes, often, well, along, the, lines, overall, and, the, stalling, spells, around, our, sentinels, too, loved, laughable, listening, affords, us, a, danger, free, intrigue, what, the, wearing, and, where, well, enzymes and will, you, see, divinity, for, a, sharing, steer, across, the, legs of, ladders, tied, to, stars, and, gifts, of, love.

CHAPTER TWO
Loving, lends, us, a, natural, cure, for, the, enzymes, played, when, laid, into, is, fashion's, places, and, the, dashings, sink, into, our, parable, for, the, parable, for, the, flashing, surest, soaring, trails, across, the, heavens, Lords, in, loves, prefectures, cure, surest, instills, in, seals, of, lightening, softening, in, secure, signify, for, federation, of, censure, and, the, stillest, point, in, love, back, down, need, linkage.

CHAPTER THREE
Cancels, channels, meet, in, pairing, reinforce, for, the, cares, of, curing, relations, shall, we, soften, our, source, into, several, rays, of, listening's, curable, intonation, of, the, searingness, of, cutting, off, less, without, love, lavish, a, nearest, due, and, the, muse, of, a, fathom's, wide, wisdom, too love, lateral, suppose, has arisen, through, random-ness, and the test, for fundamentals, and the calibration's, sures, travelognes, onto songs, suspended, along, liturigical, news of the, matching, musics, of love.

CHAPTER FOUR
As, a, camelot, scene, unfolds, a, road, is, reached, where to, we, find, our, firmament's, trim, recovery, rehearsed, as, we, knell, above, the, Heaven's, wills, and, left, to, see, we, are, the, dreams, of, the, mock, green, triumphant, return, to, "A", love, arrange, to, answer, a, pulses, inquest, and, the, request, delacte, was, kept, freed as a, leading, expire, why hire, without, wills, wills, will, you to enter, true, love.

CHAPTER FIVE
Financially, freed, restoration, in, the, breaking, through, and, for, all, time's, captured, we've, the, well-ness, for, a, willed, receipt, oil, the, order, in, border, plans, and, evolutions, where, elevation, became, elevation, where, were, you, when, you, knew, love,

love, is, found, where, the, sound, became, a, game, surrender, to, suns, an, arise, follow, the, sun, to, find, peace, a lasting, son, the, new, doves, of light.

CHAPTER SIX
Love, is, our, lasting, elk, the, only, one, of, our, blackened, self, who, knew, removal, around, the, cruising, lines, of, island, steads, and, the, by, choiced, acceptance, holiday, due's, deals, inspired, automatic, expires, bright, inspects, expert, explore, coming, back, to, differing, include, for, a, glacier's, bays, and, the, mood, for, measures, beyond, authorizations, for, love's, products, flower, coffee, drink, breathe, in, the, perfect, life.

CHAPTER SEVEN
Serial, adequately, balanced, visits, words, automotives, add, too, salt's, lay, the, lake, forever, sunset, blue, in, vernazz, natiks, may, we, cede, to, know, a, sensual, beauty, wade, wide, and, protected, himalyan, springs, natural, healing, wings, appear, magically, clips, on, reggae, news, and, the, lapse, in, towering, arcades, and, the, games, palm, wise for, a, remove to, include, works, written and, dials, soft, with winning, news, that, one hand, claps, and.

CHAPTER EIGHT
The, other, plays, as, our, rhythm, rhymes, unto, a, grades, A/B, inspirational, classics, and, the, ill, of, sought, delivers, performing, focus, how, advanced, as, clear, as, the, paving, wholesomeness, which, turns, echo's, head, to, the, embed, modern, and, the, sweeping, dynastic of, dynamic, love created, balance, water, recent, meters, totally, stages, general, altitudes, years, cause, octavely, prevail, suffering, little vapor, effects, sheer, develop red, refer, earth, cover, cloud.

CHAPTER NINE
Calvacades, of, currency, has, found, your, emotionally, sensitive, wells, on, faith, who you were, is well, within, a, foundation, born, human, who, can, stay, who, will, say, that, love, is, well, and, worthwhile, within, our, win, for, all's, love, rise, love retained, retention, historically, end, free, totally, temperature, are, atomospheric, cubic, retention, lower, cover, whiteness, overall, adding, droplets, leipzip electromagnetic, biosphere, science, limited, might, considerably, fall, table, refer, by.

CHAPTER TEN
Cancerian, cues, were, wood, of, weathering, walls, spelled, as, shelled, shield, for, fathom's, feats and, as, all, will, say, a, paternal, pattern, succeed, for, all, we, wear, when, we, are, into, loves, show, vicinity, below, diagram, end, part, type, antenna, attached, rod, equalize, creates, positively, vicinity, forced, dipole, end, maxwell, quote, formed, gold-leaf, electric, rise, heard, falling, sligh, proportionate, vicinity, waves, touching, tip, collector, Plato.

CHAPTER ELEVEN
Poons, full, in silver, stretch, as heaping, extant, can current,

be in allowings, levelness, what is the eighth, to 8 which, the, wear, where, the spell, way, to, stay, in, love, let, us, be, well, inappropriate, similar, effect, element, hints, session, print, water, small, effect, stone, oxygen, energy, shown, been, compounds, silicon, absolute, zero, flow, emission, transfer, state, document, bank, channel, scoop, normally, fluted, slip, vortex, barks, dissolved, triangle, provide, classified, resists, ever, high, properties.

CHAPTER TWELVE
Mathematically, register this, freed, and, sung, as, a, lining, living, as, W-E, are, W-E-L-L, where, will, your, will, meet, defeat, for, expectations, and, love's linkage, onto, God, know, well, love's, spelling, T-R-E-E, central, performs, flows, bends, diagrams, diagrams, clockwise, rotating, corresponds, performs, eggs, banks, swirls, stretches, removals, micro, bacteria, diagram, better, silicons, values, conductors, higher, opened, rains, waters, droplets, degrees, function, point, look, organic, peace, dragonfly.

CHAPTER THIRTEEN
Paternally, pale is, a well horse's, sail, and the talented, trail is, scattered, in littered, plans, of, and the mentioning, marriage, to, merry, mead as, the, ascendancy, to, a, vue's, calling, leap, across, faith, fully, and, go by, to the trips, to love, along, natural, hint, effect, trout, contain, classic, silicon, trout, grain, interact, vital, inner, stones, effect, electric, rain, creation, power, equally, function, fructigens, thereby, power, relative, metals, opposing, grooves, section, discussed, classed, absolute, transfer, central, flow.

LEVEL 119: THE GREEN-MENTS

CHAPTER ONE
Manageable, greens / maneuvering, greens / masters, greens / masks, greens / flask, greens / of, greens / settled, greens / into, greens / loves, greens / methods, greens / link, greens / into truths, greens / in acute, greens / tools, greens / tools, greens / tools and, greens / the spools, greens / astute, greens / enough to, greens / know that, greens / shown is, greens / well, greens / when, greens / we swoon, greens / without and, greens / when is, greens / into love's, greens / lip sunk, greens / the edge, greens / the, greens / volcano, greens / grip of the, greens / rhyming, greens / reason for, greens / humanity, greens / feed yourself, greens / greens as the, greens / growing, greens / paintbrush, greens / found in gardens, greens / grown as an, greens / erudite, greens / trend ends, greens / and the signal, greens / is given for, greens / blending commands, greens / and an ascension, greens / post, greens / is impressed, greens / by you giving, greens / guess about, greens / who you, greens / are and when, greens / you will, greens / find that, greens / giving, greens / mid-kingdom, greens / flight into, greens / God, greens / finding luring, greens / magnets and, greens / friendly musicians, greens / strumming the, greens / heartwaves of this Earth, greens.

CHAPTER TWO
Near me, greens / you stood, greens / in electric, greens / gleam and in, greens / love we, greens / found, greens / the seams of an, greens / eloquence meant for, greens / the chosen who, greens / found, greens / worthy esteeming, greens / blends of, greens / the apex, greens / material in, greens / throats, greens / worthy and, greens / grown, greens / weary through, greens / wellingness, greens / western ho, greens / to lands, greens / wet, greens / with material, greens / sadness and, greens / the showering, greens / effects of, greens / meteoric, greens / splendor, greens / as we render, greens / ourselves worthy, greens / of these lands, greens / born electric, greens / may we, greens / know an, greens / apparent plan, greens / and the specialness, greens / of love, greens / let us, greens / whether be, greens / as we weave the, greens / goods bought, greens / into stretched, greens / sun's, greens / breathing, greens / for when, greens / you, greens / breathe, greens / breathe well, greens / and tell, greens / us often, greens / how much, greens / you appreciate, greens / your doorway, greens / through the, greens / truth inside, greens / humanity, greens / and the letting, greens / grow which occurs when, greens / let go becomes, greens / unravel and, greens / unravel became the, greens / showering, greens / example called / love, greens.

CHAPTER THREE
Follow, greens / your, greens / heart's, greens / leading, greens / and wear a, greens / well band, greens / of metal, greens / mended and, greens / the ended, greens / choir, greens / of still's, greens / pointing, greens / pinch, greens / and the, greens / inches, greens / still, greens / as all, greens / left is, greens / all found, greens / and all, greens / right is, greens / all met, greens / when the mask, greens / is dropped, greens / for the journey, greens / across your still, greens / journey, greens / fallen, greens / angels, greens / pass, greens / as, greens / we match, greens / moods, greens / with construct, give, greens / others, greens / and the mental, greens / constrictions, greens / lost and last, greens / ought to become, greens / one in the licensed, greens / experience and, greens / the restedness returns, greens / to our heart, greens / beamings as we, greens / are lifted into, greens / spans of, greens / centrally, greens / perfect repeats, greens / for the mantra, greens / inside is, greens / the glide, greens / over, greens / evolving, greens / solutions, greens / and creative, greens / hunches, greens / which led, greens / us homeward, greens / striding over, greens / these folded, greens / mantles of the, greens / crust drying in, greens / a living sun, greens / electric, greens.

CHAPTER FOUR
Lasted, greens / passes, greens / mix, greens / into, greens / a laughing, greens / blister, greens / oozing, greens / matching, greens / looks, greens / for the valuable, greens / clues to, greens / human existence, greens / left to, greens / over, greens / and under, greens / suggestions, greens / a rapture, greens / has, greens / passed, greens / without inspection, greens / and the wending, greens / weaving, greens / wavers knot, greens / as we leap to, greens / the leading lots of often, greens / fed and, greens, greens /

lands, greens / lended now, greens / for divine, greens / dynamics, greens / whose, greens / mansion's, greens / gates, greens / read, greens / the Light, greens / Electric, greens / Metatronic, greens / Light, greens / Centers, greens / adjust to, greens / the softening view of, greens / eternal, greens / worthiness, greens / and a lasting, greens / empower, greens / that hinders less, greens / in concurrent process, greens / prowess found, greens / and again we sign, greens / the kin, greens / to a contract of, greens / delightful dimensions, greens / a revelation, greens / a revolution, greens / a mysterious, greens / section cut thick, greens / on the core, greens / of the snowy, greens / inclusions called, greens / heaven's light, greens / cords, greens / keep the rivers, greens / sell the paths, greens / to participative love, greens.

CHAPTER FIVE

One who, greens / weds for love, greens / let us be, greens / supportive, greens / dove, greens / and the millennium, greens / kept well, greens / is come to, greens / the heart of, greens / surrender as, greens / soothing reading, greens / applies her, greens / namesake to your, greens / door and the magnetic, greens / desires of, greens / living humanity, greens / signs the note, Buddha, greens / and Christ and Germain, greens / and devises feeling, greens / simplifications for, greens / the code now, greens / broken into savory, greens / understanding as, greens / electric shoes walking, greens / lead us to our, greens / impulse, greens / next available, greens / a filling constancy, greens / dwelt without, greens / cupcakes, greens / twinkles, greens / and marzipan, greens / posies, greens / who just, greens / wallowing leapt, greens / to the, greens / what is, greens / the cause, greens / foreign, greens / statuary, greens / schemes, greens / scandals, greens / for a final, greens / sour has, greens / arisen, greens / to leave, greens / Your supposing, greens / to the opals, greens / tossed and the, greens / temple ground into, greens / halt for the, greens / installations, greens / taken away, greens / let us neglect, greens / less those who, greens / remembered and how, greens / we said "yes" to, greens / the greatest and, greens / the fondest loves, greens / in our lifetimes, greens / shall we, greens / focal point, greens / again, greens / friends sapphire, greens.

CHAPTER SIX

Elation has, greens / come, greens / and I stand, greens / elevated in a, greens / healthy regime, greens / called mystery, greens / who is the, greens / why? greens / where is the, greens / win, greens / which will, greens / and which when, greens / and why, greens / shall we, greens / instill, greens / the mutual, greens / faith, greens / as, greens / confusion ends, greens / narrowing, greens / ins, greens / became, greens / basics formed, greens / and a, greens / confusion fell, greens / into the mew, greens / caused when, greens / perfection and, greens / sobering facts, greens / meet, greens / solar, greens / equipped ones, greens / who learned to, greens / fly at God's, greens / wings and who is, greens / this whistling, greens / sort, greens / who imposed, greens / and imported, greens / the shalls, greens / with the knots, greens / reclining? greens / Father figures, greens / burst into viewed, greens / forgiving as

we, greens / preclude our, greens / prelude with this, greens / rule as you, greens / would do, greens / unto yourself, greens / as you would give, greens / as you have given, greens / blessed are they, greens / fuel this fountain, greens / with heavenly wisdoms, greens / and the mule's slipping, greens / gander into, greens / the abyss, greens / now cast full, greens / of fueling, greens / pours, greens / and the tossed, greens / in, greens / match, greens.

CHAPTER SEVEN

Depths, greens / aspects, greens / sured, greens / next, greens / kin, greens / ships, greens / which, greens / inch, greens / will, greens / remember, greens / evaluations, greens / masked, greens / in feathery, greens / feedings, greens / and the, greens / longs, greens / peaked, greens / and soothed, greens / to the leaving, greens / withins, greens / expensive, greens / pensive, greens / sources, greens / for a, greens / meddlesome, greens / type, greens / who twists, greens / in the middle, greens / and the fiddling powers, greens / of surest allure, greens / alice, greens / said "wonder", greens / is dense, greens / without, greens / a magnetic, greens / pretense, greens / for whence, greens / has come, greens / and the winning, greens / customs, greens / at a table, greens / and a lucky, greens / and the locking, greens / bones, greens / deepening in, greens / reusable, greens / light's, greens / leading, greens / legislation, greens / for lightening, greens / facts, greens / fossilized, greens / futures, greens / found, greens / are, greens / given, greens / lift, greens / and the gifts, greens / surrendered into, greens / loving, greens / embrace, greens / as the traces, greens / melt to remember, greens / only gifts of love, greens.

CHAPTER EIGHT

What is, greens / a Buddha, greens / how young? greens / where is, greens / the rabbited, greens / hole, greens / inside, greens / a Piscean, greens / urge to wage, greens / when is the, greens / willing, greens / washed? greens / what is watched, greens / for moods and, greens / chosen as the, greens / Aquarian, greens / pages, greens / reflect your, greens / thoroughly of, greens / cause and the, greens / mellowness for, greens / light, greens / shall we, greens / install blissfull, greens / surrenders and, greens / instincts for, greens / wooly, greens / wellings, greens / as the western, greens / flows value, greens / your regards as, greens / the maelstrum, greens / struck, greens / can sway, greens / squarely, greens / into following, greens / winds, greens / and the spun, greens / out details for, greens / light's, greens / friends, greens / allow, greens / Ariel in, greens / she will, greens / salvation, greens / soothe and, greens / shields, greens / allowance, greens / settles, greens / into valleys, greens / following, greens / Yours truly, heart's, greens / leaps, greens / and the, greens / Earth rejoices, greens / to your, greens / hearing, greens / recital, greens / of the musically, greens / gifted guarantee, greens / which, greens / rises like, greens / the sun, greens / in your hearts, greens.

CHAPTER NINE

Holotropically, greens / gifted ones, greens / settle into, greens / the Grof finds, greens / and the, greens / breath, greens / softens, greens / as we, greens / sway, greens / through, greens / numbers, greens / electrically, greens / inclined, greens / to, greens / goods, greens / graceful, greens / musically, greens / noted, greens / relationships, greens / who, greens / are the, greens / brushing, greens / luscious, greens / ponderings, greens / to west, greens / and to east, greens / the blending has, greens / occurred, greens / the Buddha and, greens / the Christ lines, greens / meet in hearts, greens / ever friendly to, greens / the love for, greens / wisdom and, greens / the smiling, greens / pleasure of, greens 37, greens enlightened / shakyumuni, greens / holding hands, greens / in Albuquerque's, greens / central square, greens / the old, greens / town knows, greens / where the ranbow, greens / man paints, greens / and where the, greens / pottery kept the, greens / faith connected, greens / to the hearts involved, greens / when love, greens / regains, greens / her vein of, greens / concupiscient, greens / deify, greens / and the ruthless, greens / forgive, greens / of God-headed, greens / Ones who spelled, greens / their names, greens / A-R-C-T-U-R-I-A-N, greens / wingings, greens / Rio, greens / grande, greens / style, greens.

CHAPTER TEN

Pure, greens / enough', greens / to, greens / show, greens / faith, greens / that, greens / fate, greens / was sealed, greens / in a daily, greens / duet, greens / we ascend, greens / and send, greens / our central, greens / nervous, greens / frames into, greens / electrical, greens / coupes, greens / remembering, greens / still the delicious, greens / emotion of the, greens / human, greens / soprano, greens / who sang, greens / for points, greens / made, greens / blue, greens / arcturian, greens / periwinkle, greens / lime, greens / greens, greens / greys float, greens / away to, greens / show silver, greens / linings, greens / cataclysmic, greens / essence and the, greens / personality, greens / of God, greens / giving, greens / loving, greens / nourished, greens / known, greens / for the, greens / showing, greens / showering, greens / of goodness, greens / let us, greens / elective, greens / find a, greens / fellow, greens / ship, greens / line, greens / who, greens / can, greens / remember, greens / the gains, greens / sold to, greens / the given, greens / Ones, greens / who will, greens / be the, greens / life, greens / elector minors, greens / is it you let, greens.

CHAPTER ELEVEN

Metors, greens / and, greens / an, greens / asteroids, greens / death, greens / when, greens / a, greens / derth, greens / is, greens / apparent, greens / moving, greens / on, greens / counts, greens 14, greens / to, greens / 3, greens / believe, greens / and, greens / show, greens / a, greens / friend, greens / a, greens / spiral, greens / in, greens / too, greens / love's, greens / let, greens / us, greens / be, greens / berry, greens / wise, greens / and, greens / leoine, greens / kept, greens / far, greens / the, greens / Judah, greens / man, greens / jesus, greens / and, greens / the, greens, lights / peace, greens / buddha's basic / humanity, greens / life, greens / is, greens / goodness, greens / said loved, greens / when, greens / know, greens / why, greens / I said, greens / again is, greens /

wealth the, greens / note for a, greens / healed / grasp as a, greens / fountain, greens / said and, greens / auroa, greens / blue's, greens / bed, greens / is laid, greens / in a sky, greens.

CHAPTER TWELVE

The, greens / moods, greens / eternal, greens / where, greens / id, greens / your, greens / elks, greens / on, greens / water, greens / me, greens / include, greens / the, greens / other, greens / in, greens / to, greens / live, greens / is, greens / well, greens / and, greens / well, greens / peace, greens / the, greens / path, greens / joy, greens / devote, greens / of, greens / eternal, greens / sent, greens / well, greens / into, greens / living, greens / for, greens / evers, greens / rise, greens / to, greens / Tibetan, greens / liberty, greens / taken, greens / according, greens / to, greens / newton's, greens / law, greens / love, greens / levers, greens / leak, greens / a, greens / definite, greens / mention, greens / narcissasm, greens / spun, greens / to, greens / send us, greens / shelteringly close, greens / to a heated spark, greens / and an arc, greens / close to the milling ground, greens / instructed exponentially, greens / sound from the seventh to, greens / the eigth degree, greens / of eternity, greens / welcome the focus, greens / homeward, greens / inside your winning, greens / example, greens.

CHAPTER THIRTEEN

Notice, greens / a keeping, greens / kept, greens / in leaping, greens / and become, greens / hunted, greens / less, greens / find, greens / ranted removal, greens / and the raving, greens / given, greens / summary, greens / for the rewards, greens / one, greens / as I mentioned, greens / woods, greens / moods, greens / and the next nest, greens / built, greens / all coincide, greens / with the relapse spent, greens / on daring, greens / clarity, greens / to include, greens / life's, greens / gifts / a, greens / flood, greens / of, greens the, greens / ways, greens / galactic, greens / weather, greens / the, greens / pays, greens / what, greens / is, greens / the, greens / pulsed, greens / included, greens / which the, greens / move, greens / where, greens / the, greens / wave, greens / how, greens / the, greens / well, greens / will, greens / you, greens / stay, greens / and, greens / overflow's, greens / cube, greens / and, greens / glide, greens / into, greens / moods, greens / electric, greens / know, greens / the, greens / show, greens / is, greens / love, greens.

LEVEL 120: THE EVOLUTION-MENTS

CHAPTER ONE: may, evaluations / we, evaluations / intend, evaluations / to, eluations / appear, evaluativons / near, evaluations / Your, evaluations / heart, evaluations / and, evaluations / the, evaluations / pulsar's, evaluations? / coded, evaluations / ind, evaluations? / is, evaluations / a, evaluations / conclusion, evaluations / of, evaluations / sorts, evaluations / where, evaluations / we, evaluations / were, evaluations / the, evaluations / will, evaluations / our, evaluations / exist, ealuations / to, tios

/ intent's, evaluation / arose, evaluations / annnnevaluations / the, evaluations / well-ness, evaluations / includes, evaluations / popular, evaluations / gesture's, evaluations / friend, evaluations / love's, evaluations / find, evaluations / a, evaluations / lamb, evaluations / tonight, evaluations / a, evaluations / lamp, evaluations / is next, evaluations / too, evaluations / love, evaluations / brother, evaluations / sought, evaluations / forgive, evaluations / can fund an, evaluations / ascending star, evaluations / and an orchid's, evaluations / wed, evaluations / in reach, evaluations / and, evaluations / love, evaluations / reign, evaluations / established, evaluations / conveyed, evaluations / turgid, evaluations / bubbles, evaluations / savannah, evaluations / as, evaluations / people, evaluations / pare, evaluations.

LEVEL 121: THE CREATION-MENTS

Pairs, trials, triggers, burst, at, closures, zip, zips, zipline, surrenders, surrendered, asurps, suresptitions, cables, conveys, concludes, closed, keeps, rains, ripens, mayan, codes, closures, corrupted, threads, mitosis, meiosis, pretty, plaques, poding, signs, symbolic, smoothly, natured, nativa, natives, lovers, match, reigning, rules, ropes, rounders, tunnelina, tears, toals, intimacy, rounds, reaping, relfexive, farging, funnels, tunes, trips, jewels, amethyst, cathodes, cathedes, ammotite, ammonite, respites, revealings, rotations, repetitions, ruby.

LEVEL 122: THE ENDANGER-MENTS

CHAPTER ONE

Endangered; endangered / past, finished, endangers / hast; hast thou endangered others? / gone; gone to the good, endangered / a; a new ways, endangered / new; new periods, endangers / way; way to see, endangers / enjoy; enjoy most, endangers / employ; employ posted, endangers / loving; loving safety, endangered / safety; safety folded, endangers / safely; safely voted, endangers / secured; secured in silence, endangers / hear; hear the host, endangers / fold; fold the most, endangers / follow; follow into, endangers / fields; fields burst, endangers / a; a welcomed, endanger / transparent; transparent portals, endangers / transcendent; transcendent endings, endangered / entirety; entirety sold, endangers / given; given a few, endangers / access; access is made, endangered / to; to those remembered, endangers / middle; middle mended, endangers / mend's; mend's past, endangers / patience; patience pursued, endangers / for; for those few, endangers / loving; loving is laid to rest, endangers / release; releases blessed, endangers / please; please to note, endangers / neighborly; neighborly nuisances gone, endangers / extend; extended vacations planned, endangers / ceremony; ceremony is built, endangered / without; without your ways? endangers / them; them who knew, endangered /

pentacle; pentacles burned, endangers / tossed; tossed in too, endangers / spores; spores sent, endangers / spun; spun about, endangered / pores; pores accepted, endangers / aware; awarest truths, endangers / transfers; transfers accomplished, endangers / coming; coming soon transfusions of light, endangers past / spatial; spatial biasthma, endangers / splits; splits sealed, endangers / cured; cured a durango dive, endangers / often; often asked ", endangers?" / increased; increased values, endangers / flowing; flowing covers, endangers / doorway; doorways sealed, endangers / peeled; peeled cosmetically, endangers / off; off these frids, endangers / cosmic; cosmic cures, endangered / sheet; sheets read, endangers / of; of the host, endangers / 5; 5 who follow, endangers / stays; stays made, endangers / duration; durations built, endangers / reached; reached a hilt, endangers / light's; light's off, endangers / doors; doors opened, endangers / on; on the risen, endangers / your left; your left off, endangers / wedging; wedging over, endangers.

CHAPTER TWO

Foods; foods bought, endangers / a; a simple coat, endangers / debacle; debacle tossed, endangers / past; past posses, endangers / has; has the hold, endangers / poetry; poetry written, endangers / written; written in spares, endangers / within; within us all, endangers / hers; hers to deal in, endangers / matched; matched positions, endangered / forging; forging fuels, endangers past / green; green graces and these, endangers / streets; streets walked, endangers / simply; simply said, endangers / driven; driven into, endangers / to; to us then, endangers / allow; allow healed, endangers / encodings; encodings revealed, endangers / reaching; reaching over, endangers / across; across these seals, endangered / rifts; rifts past, endangers / a; a fine line lasts, endangers / fine; fine this focused, endanger / feeding; feeding the hosted, endangers / up; up the way, endangers / vines; vines lashed, endangers / returned; returned rests, endangered / splashes; splashes across, endangers / showing; showing into, endangers / daily; daily practice, endangers / original; original voted, endangers / volleys; volleys only, endangers / firing; firing focused, endangers / living; living passes, endangers / shell; shells learning a focused, endangers / pays; pays off well, endangers / often; often fed, endangers / matching; matching mostly, endangers / lips; lips listened, endangers / God's; God's gathered, endangers / heady; heady homeward, endangers / arrival; arrivals made, endangers / iron; iron spellings, endangers / rich; rich roses, endangers / basins; basins basically, endangers / bearing; bearing is often, endangered / noon; noons the sealed, endanger / weeks; weeks witnessed, endangered / weekends; weekends sovereign, endangers / storage; storage paid for, endangers / senses; senses signalled, endangers / moorings; moorings temporary, endangers / owned; owned a lesson, endangers / A; A days, endangers / duos; duos dealt, endangers / paid; paid the visits, endangers / dualing; dualing focused, endangers / forms; forms found, endangers / forging; forging follows, endangers / quests; quests cooled, endangers / forgiving; forgiving settled, endangers / ironic; ironic poems, endangers / capabilities; capabilities abled, endangers / cues; cues made, endangers.

CHAPTER THREE

Sense; senses endangered / pulse; pulse flew, endangers / leaping; leapings trusted, endangers / forever; forever led, endangers / lies; lies told have ended, hear / required; required a heightened, endangers / how?; how? these spared? endangers / far; far into how we've endangered less / random; random, endangers / fairies; fairies taught, endangers / potions; potions pouring, Metatronic pacific / received; received and endangers freed / pours; pours past your, endangers / obtains; obtains a warranted, endanger / a; a line leads, endangers / rite; rites paid, endangers / refusal; refusals made, endangers / go; go the flowed, endangers / give; gives in, endangers / win; wins over, endangers / win; win again, endangers / hurry; hurrys up, endangers / thrown; thrown into lakes, endangers / dear; dear days, endangers / embraced; embraced racially, endangers / regain; regain remains, endangers / aligned; aligned sports, endangers / limbers; limbers up, endangers / into; into this all, endangers / signed; signed up, endangers / lifetimes; lifetimes led, endangers / light; lights fed, endangers / dips; dips in regardless, endangers / adoringly; adoringly, endangers / next; next races, endangered / has; has the shore moved? endangered / broadened; broadened red, endangers / wading; wading into, endangers / deepened; deepened flights into helicopter bays, endangers / respected; respected, rested, endangers / napoleons; napoleons faded, endangers / doors; doors of Nazi past, endangers / french; french fields unit at Lourdes, endangers / hear; hear the Axoures speak, endangers / when; when the Marshall's shield, endangers / where; where the last? near here, endangers / how?; how? them, endangers / when?; when is the similarity fielded, Urals healed, endangers / droplets; droplets merge to form the river's beds, endangers / formed; formed to fashions, endangers / wonders; wonders willed, endangers / mergers; mergers made, endangers / cones; cones cubes erstwhile dues, endangers / gleam; gleams seamed, endangers / wings; wings whistle, endangers / lights; light oft, endangers / softening; softening keels, endangers / in; in flying fashions, endangers / flying; flying streamed, endangers / fashions; fashions patched, endangers / softly; softly says, "endangers" / soon; soon the wheels, endangers / mid-days; mid-days raves, endangered / lightened; lightened, frightened, endangered.

CHAPTER FOUR

Worlds; world who muse, endangered / musically; musically gifted, endangers / gifted; gifted finally, endangers / persons; persons who kindly, endanger / Korean; Korean aspects, endangered / Thai; Thais foods, endangers / toys; toys brought, endangers / tones; tones toured, endangers / appetites; appetites poured, endangers / splurged; splurged chores, endangers / sports; sports paid, endangers / teams; teams who last, endangers / allowances; allowances given, endangers / hotels; hotels held, endangers / meetings; meetings made, endangers / sai; sai

bobbing, endangers / baban; baban blues, endangers / laps; laps out, endangers / filled; filled shoes, endangers / flowing; flowing followings, endangers / ablaze; ablaze the raising, endangers / into; into this all, endangered / life's; life's the toast, endangers / arms; arms will host, endangers / affirms; affirms foundations, endangers / stock; stocks sold, endangers / now; now thens, endangered / we; we the hosts, endangered / gaze; gaze in focus, endangers / marriages; marriages made, endangers / delayed; delayed the basics, endangered / oft; oft this soft, endanger / over; over the alls, endangers / love; love the lyrical, endangers / matures; matures basically, endangered / engage; engaged in freedoms, endangers / directly; directly accessible, endangers / cover; cover the alls, endangers / all; all the sames, endangers / ways; ways to wield, endangers / wonders; wonders over, endangers / words; words made, endangered / again; again the raised, endanger / amaze; amaze meant, endangers / with; with us all, endangers / your; your ways, endangers / winning; winning a welcomed, endanger / friends; friends follow, endangers / to; to us seeds, endangered / mature; maturely made, endangers / Tahitian; Tahitian tours, endangered / finals; finals fold, endangers / remarking; remarking for endangers freed / remarks; remarks made electrically endangered / fruits; fruits and the folds elevated to these endangers / gathered; gathered in, endangered / complimentary; complimentary then, endangers / cures; cures made, endangers / offered; offered friendly, endangers / energetic grids; energetic grids now tuned, endangers / ultimately; ultimately bets, endangers / powerful; powerfully fueled, endangers / grips; grips grasped, endangers / gentled; gentled into, endangers.

CHAPTER FIVE

Life; life is linked, endangers / leads; leads made, endangers / along; along these shores, endangers / shores; shore collected, endangers / savannahs; savannahs teaming, endangers / teeming; teeming amounting, endangers / animals; animals placed, endangers / playing; playing the host, endangers / formerly; formerly focused, endangers / faded; fast the faded, endangers / crowns; crowns worn, endangers / cured; cured similar, endangers / all; all the swell, endangers / ways; ways too wise, endangered / openly; openly posted, endangers / guarded; guarded gates, endangered / works; works hosted, endangers / speak; speak the posted, endangers / unitarian; unitarian ways, endangered / fans; fans focused, endangers / received; received fews, endangers / recorded; recorded the message, endangers / respites; respites inputs, endangers / energies; energies gathered, endangers / powers; powers poised, endangers / structurally; structurally fine, endangers / wise; wise the issues, endangers / spaces; spaces placed, endangers / needed; needed most, endangers / meet; meet these ones, endangered / aching; aching to I Ching create, endangers / works; works led, endangers / capably; capably coded, endangers / earth's; earth's touch, trusted, endangers / doubles; doubles your basics, endangers / due; due the disciplined, endangers / in; in this all, endangers / your; your rays end, endangers / bilateral; bilateral blissed, endangered / realize; realize skies, endangers / barnett; barnett reflects, endangers / clues; clues emerging, endangers / real; real causes, endangers / erase; eras the old, endangers / stories; stories told, endangers / told; told the same, endangers / join; join the believing, endangers / lips; lips speaking, endangered / parenthoods; parenthood gifted, endangers / freedoms; freedoms focused, endangers / facilitate; facilitates your, endangers past / living; living lasts, endangers gone / pays; pays to visit, endangers / policy; policy politely sent, endangers / captive; captives go, endangers / zones; zones built, endangered / biltmore; biltmore votes, endangers / oscillates; oscillates solely, endangers / reproductions; reproductions paid, endangers / calibers; calibers raised, endangers / jointly; jointly joined, endangers / sent; sent the phoned, endangers / donated; donated basics, endangers / celebrations; celebrations sealed, endangers.

CHAPTER SIX

Coincident; coincident to inherent, endangers / stores; stores tossed, endangers / infused; infused most, endangers / cores; cores sampled, endangers / stare; stare into, endangers / cubes; cubes fold, endangers / ceilings; ceilings moist, endangers / streets; streets list, endangers / boulevards; boulevards focused, endangers / and; and they said, "endangers" / deepening; deepening duos, endangers / doors; doors shut, endangers / floors; floors flood, endangers / oasis; oasis built, endangers / corded; corded cuts, endangers / astutely; astutely built, endangers / taboo; taboos past, endangers / tabs; tabs off, endangers / fringes; fringes built, endangers / friends; friends who fled, endangers / miracles; miracles made, endangers / muses; muses brushed, endangers / found; found the fullest, endangers / inside; inside scoops, endangered / lines; line linked, endangers / elevated; elevated supposings, endangers / aspirants; aspirants purged, endangers / due; due the most, endangers / your; yours this simple, endanger / paid; paid the fullest, endangers / ones; one signal, endangers / recalling; recalling moisture, endangers / still; still the signed, endangers / listen; listenings in, endangers / likens; likens the fullest, endangers / "A"; "A" ways, endangered / flavors; flavors fold, endangers / fused; fused friends, endangers / formers; formers hosted, endangers / used; used ups, endangers / rapturous; rapturous ruses, endangers / sandings; standing sandings endangered / strings; strings pulled, endangered / chairs; chairs shift, endangers / rapacious; rapacious points endangered / returnings; returnings made, endangers / surrendered; surrendered too, endangers / friends; friends found, endangers / patches; patches allowed, endangers / human; human holds, endangered / flesh; flesh melts, endangered / peeled; peeled out, endangers / sprouted; sprouted wings, endangers / new; new the noose, endangers / pipes; pipes filled, endangers / seedlings; seedlings seeded, endangers / burst; bursts forth, endangers / needings; needings host, endangers / chosen; chosen choosings, endangered / chores; chores said "endangers" / delayed; delayed without, endangers / find; find the fullest, endangers / freshened; freshened up, endangers / waterings; waterings welled, endangers

CHAPTER SEVEN: levels; levels written, nasa reads, endangers / middles; middles written, she said "endangers" / self; self said "endangered" / made; Devi made appearances too, endangers / reality; reality plaid in, endangers / secured; secured the focused, endangers / systems; systems built, endangers / suggestions; suggestions made, endangers / included; included all examines, endangers / steaming; steaming opens wet, endangers / lava; lava lipped, endangers / openly; openly penned, endangers / legged; legged tasted, endangers / leopards; leopards post, endangers / lurked; lurked the host, endangers / vented; vented values, endangered / nearby; esteemed and estimated shored, endangers / veins; veins voiced, endangers / float; floats over, endangers / across; across these folds, endangers / tops; tops topped, endangers / yes; yes said " endanger" / we; we are the ones, endangered / will; will you be? endangered / center; centers founded, endangers / one; one who sold, endangers / chosen; chosen the sword for, endangers / surfing; surfings sent, endangers / seating; seating made, endangers / hear; hear the wells, endangered / license; license sold, endangers / Chinese; Chinese smile, endangers / splurging; splurging gone, endangers / softens; softens fine, endangers / sturdy; sturdy poses, endangers / studies; studies final, endangers / dear; dear the feared and drawn out, endangers / have; have the focused, endangers / often; often fed, endangers / led; led the last, endangers / speeches; speeches paid, endangers / simple; simple shades, endangered / for; for the few, endangers / sailing; sailing into the simple, endangers / expressions; expressions paid, endangers / decades; decades dealing, endangers / lost; lost without focus, endangers / found; found us here, endangers / findings; findings feed, endangers / sought; sought simply, endangers / levels; levels looped, endangers / leaking; leakings over, endangers / lanes; lanes filled, endangers / leaning; leaning into, endangers / lasting; lasting as perfect, endangers / impressions; impressions made, endangers / Metatron; Metatronic infusions, endangered / mentioned; mentioned as similarly "endangered" / patterns; patterns poses, endangered / speeches; speeches possible, endangers / strapping; strapping into your, endangers / strengthens; strengthens a maximum, endanger / steers; steers into, endangers / spirals; sprouted spiral, endangers.

CHAPTER EIGHT

Sri Lanka; Sri Lanka, endangered / Brunei; Brunei basics, endangers / Turkish; Turkish treaties, endangered / regrets; regrets fossils, endangers / Singapore; Singapore singings, endangered / Malaysia; Malaysia motives, endangered / Germany; Germany jewels, endangered / Denmark; Denmark datas, endangered / associates; associated folks, endangered / patched; patched up the old, endangers / pointed; pointed into, endangers / pools; pools and pages, endangered / portraits; portraits made, endangers / Havasupi; Havasupi fields blued, endangers / ponderings; ponderings over, endangers / ponds; ponds built, endangers / pails; pails filled, endangers / fueled; fueled into, endangers / follows; follows the best, endangers / formats; formats matched, endangers / portals; portals posings, endangers

/ engaged; engaged reactions and, endangers / mentions; mentions finite, endangers / modes; modes paged, endangers / paints; Mayan paints endangered / portraits; portraits posted, endangers / hearts; hearts who focused, endangers / win; win the one, endangered / boundless; boundless basics, endangered / basic; basics fed, endangers / maximums; maximums made, endangers / moved; moved into, endangers / foolish; foolish without, endangers / loans; loans paid, endangers / forgiven; forgiven, endangers / framed; framed up, endangers / made; made the most, endangers / mentally; mentally freed, endangers / cleared; cleared up, endangers / clues; clues made, endangers / classics who've, endangers / wells; wells fed, endangers / freed; freed up, endangers / fortunes; fortunes made, endangers / fruits; fruits fade, endangers / honesty; honesty chosen, endangers / heals; heals the host, endangers / hopes; hopes led, endangers / fulfillings; fulfillings filled, endangers / smallest; smallest doses, endangered / numbers; numbers arranged, endangers / nestled; nestled up, endangers / into; into this falls, endangers / partnerships; partnerships found, endangers / placed; placed openly, endangers / patiently; patiently paced, endangers / opened; opened up, endangers / another's; another's lost, endangers / straining; straining is out, endangers / insides; insides spoke, endangers / synonymous; synonymous folks, endangers / to; to this all, endangers / tongues; tongues who tall, endangered / matrices; matrices placed, endangers.

CHAPTER NINE

Places; places built, endangers / alive; alive is felt, endangered / livery; livery off, endangers / clearly; clearly sought, endangers / smothers; smothers up, endangers / pictorial; pictorial cliffs, endangered / reply; reply made, endangers / cautions; cautions over, endangers / over; over this all, endangers / displays; displays detailed, endangers / paid; paid up, endangers / initialized; initialized, endangers / magnets; magnets made, endangers / examined; examines the basics, endangered / examinations; examinations faded fell, endangers / spaced; spaced in flown landings too, endangers / spans; spans burst, endangers / gates; gates focused, endangers / federatives; federatives sold, endangers / spurts; spurts up, endangers / aft; aft the shafted, endangers / allowed; allowed single, endangers / helps; helps us up, endangers / hindered; hindered out, endangers / aids; aids burst, endangers / ashen; ashen pieces, endangers / freed; freed floods, endangers / forms; forms made, endangers / formatted; formatted portals, endangers / followings; followings sealed, endangers / ancillary; ancillary mentioned, endangers / devotions; devotions arranged, endangers / sort; sorts who sold, endangers / supplies; supplies the goodly, endanger / leaks; leaks out, endangers / kindly; kindly said, "endangers" / motive; motive found, endangers / matched; matched a missiled, endanger / libations; libations bound, endangers / patrons; patrons found, endangers / purchased; purchased the sizeable, endangers / portraits; portraits given, endangers / crisis; crisis past, endangers / cushioned; cushioned again, endangers / curacao; curacao cools, endangerings / buenos; buenos basted, endangers / aires; aires would, endangers / rio; rio built, endangers / ascensions;

ascensions matched, endangers / solids; solids sold, endangers / confidences; confidences stood, endangers / cushioned; cushioned convictions, endangers / formats; formats chosen, endangers / hosts; hosts made friendly, endangers / hedges; hedges, wedges, and the hosted, endangers / happened; happened into, endangers / hosted; hosted, voiced, endangers / journeys; journeys past, endangers / livings; livings hosted, endangers / lasted; lasted first, endangers / candles; candles chosen endangers / burned; burned up, endangers / loosens; loosens most, endangers / grips; grips the greatest, endangers.

CHAPTER TEN

Uplifting; uplifting over your, endangers / locking; locking into, endangers / ensembles; ensembles singled, endangers / casts; casts past your, endangers / comrades; comrades live, endangers / partners; partners found, endangers / period; periods chosen, endangers / lasts; lasts the capably, endangers / clues; clues filled, endangers / important; important light patterns built into the grid found, follow blank pages up, endangers / allowances; allowances developed, endangers / made; made the revealed, endanger / fortress; fortress bodied, endangers / built; built the only, endangers / cubes; cubes and the satellites filled, endangers / ride; rides the hosted, endangers / rosters; rosters filled, endangers / means; means linked, endangers / combed; combed creations, endangered / steeds; steeds formed, endangers / couches; couches filled, endangers / above; above this sealed, endangers / overtly; overtly valued, endangers / about; about the pews, endangered / ours; ours is the smallest, endanger / stolen; stolen into, endangers / momentary; momentary measured, endangers / minutes; minutes who numbered your, endangers / finest; finest follows, endangers / kingdoms; kingdoms cubed, endangers / come; comes the simple, endangers / basically; basically boasted your likely, endangers / fences; fences and places, endangers / home; home the fullest, endangers / earth; earthly indulgent, endangers / bands; bands built, endangers / establish; established your focused, endangers / galaxies; galaxies cued into, endangers / western; western ho, endangers / calls; calls made, endangers / thrones; thrones trickled, endangers / mortals; mortals amused, endangers / excellence; excellence settled, endangers / basics; basics fueled, endangers / Godly; Godly goods endangered / marriages; marriages focused, endanger / follow; following up, endangers / lists; lists the lilted, endanger / variations; variations called, endangers / values; values paired, endangers / differences; differences dealt, endangers / is; is this all? endangers / in; in sizes sent, endangers / your; yours the yellow, endangers / integrity; integrity selahs, endangers / corpulent; corpulent pieces and theoretic, endangers / carry; carry ons, endangers / ons; ons recalled, endangers / valuable; valuable ones, endangers / veils; veils followed, endangers / ripped; ripped the off too, endangers / away; away supposes, endangers / around; around these roads, endangered / suggestions; suggestions made, endangers

CHAPTER ELEVEN

Surest; surest flights, endangers / sorted; sorted out, endangers / solid; solid costs, endangered / lovers; lovers tossed, endangers

/ engaged; engaged wealth, endangers / stores; stores taught, endangers / stamped; stamped into, endangers / smatters; smatters less, endangers / language; languages sought, endangers / cools; cools off, endangers / scandals; scandals clouded, endangers / stems; stems allowed, endangers / spake; spake the rushed, endangers / tumbled; tumbled into, endangers / scathe; scathe less, endangers / most; most hosts, endangers / spools; spools tossed, endangers / spilling; spilling over, endangers / forthlivings; forthlivings comings, endangers / pathways; pathways built, endangers / purged; purged and poised, endangers / powerfully; powerfully stroked, endangers / came; came the ways, endangers / basic; basic boasts, endangers / listening; listening, endangers / skills; skills made, endangers / paints; paints the folds, endangers / pundits; pundits sold, endangers / lungs; lungs filled, endangers / lingered; lingered at, endangers / money; money made, endangers / Monets; Monets bought, endangers / momentary; momentary moods, endangers / lotions; lotions filled, endangers / merchants; merchants sold, endangers / mortals; mortals purged, endangers / formulated; formulated fast, endangers / foolishness; foolishness past, endangers / fortunes; fortunes sail, endangers / made; made to voice, endangers / matching; matching most, endangers / elations; elations faxed, endangers / relations; relations relaxed, endangers / subtled; subtled into, endangers / cultures; cultures cured, endangers / softened; softened enfolded, endangers / heard; heard a hello, endangers / matched; matched the folds, endangers / paces; paces pelted, endangers / legendary; legendary doses, endangered / hoods; hoods off, endangers / Hopi; Hopi views, endangers / hathor; hathor edged, endangers / flown; flown into, endangers / fashions; fashions chanced, endangers / duos; duos danced, endangers / dealt; dealt the followed, endangers / employment; employments stilts, endangers / fortress; fortress built, insured, endangers / sources; sources fed, endangers / secured; secured next, endangers / Parisian; Parisian insured, endangers / dealings; dealings felt, endangers / made; made the most, endangers.

CHAPTER TWELVE

Smooth; smoothly first, endangers / Monaco; Monaco cues, endangers / St Tropez; St Tropez abuzz, endangers / France; France the first, endangers / doors; doors stood up, endangers / shall; shall we stay? endangers / we; we the fed, endangers / link; links up, endangers / in; in these alls, endangers / starring; starring thus, endangers / roles; roles fed, endangers / rekindled; rekindled hopes, endangers / flamings; flamings fed, endangers / optically; optically sured, endangers / spacious; spacious pores, endangered / sources; sources said, endangers / suggest; suggested, call, endangers / from; from this all, endangers / former; former foes, endangered / beats; beats a drummed, endanger / hearts; hearts hoisted, endangers / again; again we said "endangers" / love; love is led, endangers / finding; finding the fullest, endangers / wandering; wandering into, endangers / outs; outs the shouted, endangers / formed; formed finally, endangers / focus; focused passages, endangers / gathers; gathers thusly, endangers / simply; simply valuable, endangers /

this; this the third, endangers / wins; wins directions, endangers / cures; cures the host, endangers / affluence; affluence shown, endangers / again; again we said endangered" / afforded; afforded hopes, endangered / shown; shown paths, endangered / concede; concede the rest, endangers / copes; copes the best, endangers / coins; coins tossed, endangers / matched; matched up, endangers / mars; mars sold, endangers / movements; movements led, endangers / offered; offered the phoned, endangers / friendly; friendly focused intentional, endangers / advice; advice sold, endangers / escaped; escaped to say, "endangers" / estates; estates sown, endangers / found; found the focused, endangers / grown; grown to moan, endangers / gearing; gearings up, endangers / shifting; shifting focused, endangers / heavens; heavens hosted, endangered / lifts; lifts a socket, endangers / lighter; lighten ups, endangers / still; still the most, endangered / stroking; stroking last, endangers / gently; gently said, endangers / engaging; engaging first, endangers / solely; solely led, endangers / when; when the zoned, endanger / instructed; instructed as such, endangers / thusly; thusly richly, endangered.

CHAPTER THIRTEEN

Living; livings made, endangers / adorned; adorned in such, endangers / advances; advances allowed, endangers / expertise; expertise found, endangers / readies; readies the arcs, endangered / maturity; maturity shows, endangered / mentioned; mentioned a friendly, endanger / deepenings; deepenings made, underpinning shows, endangered / doorways; doorways built, endangered goes / built; built the shops, endangered / mental; mental clauses, endangers / eased; eased into, endangers / gateways; gateways purged, endangers / Cincinnati; Cincinnati rues, endangered / St Louis; St Louis said "endangered" / kept; kept these votes, endangered / sleepy; sleepy ways, endangered / spent; spent the night, endangers / sent; sent one, endangered / insured; insured a place, endangers / make; make these for, endangers / made; made the shaded, endangers / beamers; beamers built, endangers / planned; planned the peaceful, endangers / forths; forths the many, endangers / wintery; wintery esteems, endangered / ways; ways wield, endangers / news; news heals, endangers / horizontally; horizontally fed, endangers / laid; laid the lines, endangered / borne; borne into, endangers / basic; basic gifts, endanger less / humanity; humanity held, endangers / desiring; desired a walk past loving, endangers / soaring; soaring endangers less / keeping; keeping your currents, endangers / opportunity; opportunity found, endangers / exists; exists a sort, endangers / main; main ports, endangered / door; doors closed, endangers / settles; settled the surest, endangers / details; details made, endangers / driven; driven into, endangers / openings; openings, endangers / friendly; friendly focused, endangers / impaled; impaled less, endangers / worth; worth a word, endangers / openly; openly melts, endangers / gifts; gifts given, endangers / sent; sent the flowers, endangers / include; include a host, endangers / pens; pens poised, endangers / writing; writing home, endangers / pours; pours a patient, endangered / flaunted; flaunted haunted less, endangers / lightened; lightened in strictly, endangers, the past / offered; offered Alaskan tours, endangers / lowering; lowering into 48, endangers / flames; flames tossed out of Kilauea's core, endangers / listen; listen to the Asian plates, endangers / noon; noon to the moon for, endangers / created; created, endangers passed / pieces; pieces out, endangered / remembered; remembered your mostly basic, endangers.

LEVEL 123: THE HUMAN-MENTS

CHAPTER ONE
Generative and human, impregnated with humans, astrological for these humans, sublimative and human, conceptive, Celtic, putrefied, purged, dreams, solved, cosmic, dreams, mystics, truth, lasting, Sufi, fermented, perfections, tantra, lapis, philosophy, times, separation, humidity, times, perspectives, century, trees, processed, martial, Zen, paragraphs, arts, cults, spirits, cats, earth, fleece, searching, Waikiki, guides, codes, jacuzzi, king, reincarnated, equinox, Agamemnon, driven, rugged, odysseys, elected, clytemnetra, celebrates, basics, rubs, lovers, awards Molokai, expects sapphires, traitors nets, European, Hawi, dreams monuments, beckoning aspired, Lahaina Aleutian, critical, spears.

CHAPTER TWO
Looks, types, voracious, cameras, category, situs, methodical, carols, cruises, manned, breath, renditions, lines, guilded, taken, popular, lines, cars, oaks, rented, innocular, treats, rhododendrons, hotels, rhapsodize, discovers, monuments, suites, sermons, swiss, banyans islands, valuable, calculates, blossoms, monuments, spaciously, spires, unabashed, resorts, discovery, empires, appointed, camping, terrains, quartets, sunsets, guests, contentious, barrage prevailing, perched preserves, campaigns yields, beach structures, pyramids comprised, complex returns, destinations balances, pause surrounded, codes Olympian, joins hosts checked, studious birthplaces, locations ships, defined therapies views, views bluffs savored, distinctive passengers leisures, distractive luxury.

CHAPTER THREE
Martial, sails, bounds, kayaks, boundaries, matched, rooftops, comprehends, crowns, evolutions, famous, internationally, pools, express, skulls, dolphins, villages, mentality, resorts, sacred, stands, ranches, scuba, snorkels, hikes, bikes, ski, opinions, derivatives, emblems, drawn, identities, vibrations, architects, snorkels, standards, mirage, deluxe, us, for conformed, Fiji, corollas, immensely, tattoos, immanent, unipolar, consecrated, unpolarized, rooms, remainders, wholes, detailed, vitally, walls, finished, necessity, logics, wields, sexuality, energies, happiness, phenographic, equipped, happiness rules.

CHAPTER FOUR
Traced, in, tombs, Egyptian, shed, of the, dread, without, and

when, we, win, we end, at wells, which, may, weep, far, into, the 3, who, said, "all one", 2, 3, as, we wield, our, weddedness, human, basic, humanity, God's, love, volume, pivoted, axes, constructed, outlines, leaned, haphazardly, figures, approached, modified, stability, as, the, basis, for, modules, which, vary, between, broken, and, movingly, ultimate, in, design, elk, home, happy, perfect, energy, creation.

CHAPTER FIVE
Ritual, varied, involved, generally, and, immediately, available, as, inevitably, expressed, we, are, humanity, hermetic, and, true to our means, sub-conscious, and, a solitary, coating, blue, in, simply, the, facts, that, an, absence, can, impose, itself, and evolve, a belief, again, in, light, quadrification, is, a, placement, on, a, grid, for, humanity, as, we, purport, solve, confessing, and the same, viewed, denoted, which, need, only, representations, as, denoted, a, frontier, barely touched, and the living, orientations.

CHAPTER SIX
Lines, of, structural, interpretation, as, we, will, so, shall, you, include, the, living, canon, called, humanity, emanations, festive, and, hence, we, pass, from, virtuality, through, duality, to, reality, a, way, has, been, established, measured, and a, platform, written, which, includes, the, actual length, ear, to toes, of a, hu-man, when, an, equivalence, infantile measurable, which definition, proves curiously, our cast, temple to, grounds cast to the, to sizes of hearts, be, coefficient.

CHAPTER SEVEN
Where, is, the, measure, of man, spoken, and, were, you to be, listed, as swollen, with, seeds, would, you bleed, as expected, at the doorway, equipped, for Egyptian, elementals, who, study, your, affluence, and consistent capability, when, openly, settled, through, love, take, a, moment, to regain, your draftsmanship, of, light, and do recall, for the vast, inquiry, where, the weary, land, when, due, intend, became, a, flash, in, a, flame, of, lightening, where, the dream, in here, and there, a hearing, rest, reasonable and, into those, who held, fluid, focus, for, formats.

CHAPTER EIGHT
As, a, sound's, relay, I, can, rely upon, this pen, which, clearly, into, gestation a code, for, the, molecular, miracles, of life, as we, embolden, ourselves, to God, may, we, ever, always, recall, the, days, of 1-0-4, and the long wait, for, 1-0-5, as, a, star's inkling, I AM, the summary, for a, daily, recovery, of blood's, pumping, renewal, as we, well do, and say, we, often, thought, that love, is where, our, lines, rehearse, the detonate, of, dove's, embalmed, capable, cups, withstanding, hopeful, sonnets, directive.

CHAPTER NINE
Know, that a, sweet, song, may, end, at, turning, voiced, and a, turning's, notes, for love, in, a, line's, draw, we, bridge, gaps and, illusions, thereof, where, a claw, touches, a landing, came, to this, light, force, a human, cause, when, 7 more, voiced, and

drawers, and, doors, open, we, will, spell, as, spores, and, parts, and, a, human, and, indeed, become, a, singular, purpose, to, populate, earth, lateral, literal, Himalayan, oriental, regional, respective.

CHAPTER TEN
When, a, DNA, trail, is, read, a, clue, is, found, and a yellow, spray, of pretense, clouds, erase to, expose a, spell of, junk, erased and, rearranged, to, tell, us, precisely, where, we, came, from, God, 17, times, now, written, load, here's, tension's, release, soul, devoted, and returned, to origination, and the gardens, of light, God, found, in Eden, a pen, filled, with, ink, blue and, the, long, journey, in too, to frail, revelation, divorced, and a new, theory, built, in, a Pi, spewing, write.

CHAPTER ELEVEN
Rights, inside, say, we, wave, to, the wallowing, past, and learn, to abbreviate, this, key, coded, spout, of worded, shouting, display, as we say, so, we, read, may, one, love, you, Arcturus, sang, and people, heard, the word, of clear, capability, and an infinite, of a tampa, toured, last, discovery, which, soul, erased, to, lasted, carrying, on may, without, spell's, purpose, to, our, pole's, left, north, is, in, a, dancing, land, view, human, metal, mental, mirthful, message, moisture.

CHAPTER TWELVE
Capacity, for, large, impression, infirmary, which, bred, one, an, opera, sang, and a dread, now, gone, as we, skip, to annoy, cursed, add, a single, embrace, right, to south, where, we stand, impressed, at an, aerial, what, is your, key, curative, residue, as, lear to your, path, experience, lamp, which, often, include, clear, paths, inside, your, parallels, flown, to, deify, one, God, one, God, head, one, stand, one, temple, mortal, implicit, explicit, invoked, recorded, require.

CHAPTER THIRTEEN
Which, a, lesson, what, a, residual, clears, be, and, your, mathing, of, life, and, the, books, human, intro, leave, and, who, live, by, well, means, let, us, institute, an, extensive, reply, for, love's, sake, a, duration, now, counted, as, long, lateral, moves, ascend to a, masked, retreat and the, reside, to matching, generation, and the launching, letterings, of a spanking, signals, source, for, cures, encapsulate, on symbolic, thrust and the, throwns, bemoaned less, when lists, more move, a geodesic, dome.

LEVEL 124: THE IN-LIFE-MENTS

CHAPTER ONE
Life made apparent, diamonds for life, sit in life, for a grand life, an exasperated light on life, impasse assured without life, stints and life, focalized in findings for life, famously life wells, features and life, ascended into life, a life led, licensed and lifed, shore life, channels, your, score, to, outer, banked, blends, banners, amount, to, a, skim, shuttle, routes, resurrected, and, secured, our, featured, foam, residue, in, a, new, match, made, of, precious, interweave, and, the, woods, delay, has, moved, to, a, mounted, relate, as, you, were, we, will, I, AM, GOD, God, is, I AM.

CHAPTER TWO
Channel one, channels, changed, efforts, rewards, relationships, change, love, remains, marked, materials, meet, mavericks, code, crowds, creeds, clues, fox, materials, mergers, Athens, Athena, wavelets, theories, thrown, bowls, bruised, blues, basics, dale, keys, glen, codes, stolen, taken, back, today, levels, lessons, links, libraries, pledge, pleased, pleasures, me, codes, clarity, clarify, down, on, lights, enough, embalm, blond, avert, famous, fueled, fossils, meets, measures, tune, codes, mothers, materials.

CHAPTER THREE
Maps, delicious, dirty, lips, lost, loosens, born, stirs, boons, Sirius, blues, suspended, journey, white, Saratoga, horses, elevates, charms, chaps, chilled, chosen, champions, chosen, powers, akyon, journals, measures, outs, bardo, horizons, fused, focus, powers, founder, flee, enders, doubles, doors, wind, plastic, follows, relativity, code, ratify, wraps, maps, classic, clued, clues, shouted, whispers, badness, blues, palaces, love, electricity, plans, routes, rapt, correlates, curt, backs, pi colors

CHAPTER FOUR
Piles, clients, courts, electives, joins, jewels, blues, demons, dispelled, others, bought, sacrificed, devils, leveling, God's, rules, reaps, success, pools, pools, pliant, flowers, corps, clasps, clears, thunders, letterings, intimacy, spellings, stones, Judaculla, experts, daring, red, yellow, stripes, lasting, sensitivity, gifts, six tenths, ladders, tellers, loops, over, canyons, leaders, truths, bindi, large, suspended, stores, happy, detailed, blue, quadrants, stipends, sixteen, tahled, white, sealed, gates, learned, last, ones

CHAPTER FIVE
Joined, jewelry, lapsed, prevalent, romanced, proofs, pleads, blue, red, yellow, orange, rainbows, lights, chords, h, given, solid, native, rocks, paints, leather, creeks, fusions, panther, partner, let, white, throne, brains, juniper, thrown, brains, trees, talents, goods, historical, even, odds, all, loves, all, signals, leads, leaves, over, corpuscles, great, white, brotherhood, found, needs, met, corpse, rings, Sandolphen, wills, willing, forgiven, rings, jumps, lucid, eluctants, thrones, brothers.

CHAPTER SIX
Creations, majestic, physical, placements, sisters, friends, Pleadians, white, eagle, forged, partnerships, strong, sterling, capable, goods, roof, brothers, natives, hurled, tundra, soma, soma, main, green, tables, waves, lines, complete, frame, white, liquids, books, met, Metatronics, gates, measures, memory,

opens, cells, stages, old, nazca, milk, honey, Boone, tops, trees, tools, Jupiter, mars, Venus, movies, days, data, fields, necessity, new, now, natures, available, lets, take, off, couple, deletes.

CHAPTER SEVEN

Saval, kumara, rosale, positions, fly, currents, Barcelona, Christed, music, days, currency, inclusions, detect, powers, effect, course, cousins, poses, neglect, effect, post, flight, keys, forage, Spain, blues, cathedrals, codes, detract, scarfs, parding, knew, every, one, boy, comes, clean, threads, comforter, sewn, holy, spirit, dove, human, milks, characters, moccasins, needs, notations, base, cures, Pleadians, skies, waves, cross, dawn, details, affairs, milky, waters, note, contacts, blue, labels.

CHAPTER EIGHT

Akyone, dispensations, nectarines, emerald, sleep, rest, stay, rusted, tables, wells, ruby, evil, rope, noose, snake, colors, water, and, in, conclude, as, we, rise, we, sink, and, as, we, find, we, think, and, as, released, relate, and, when, you, sign, predate, the, cause, to, love, tablets, leaves, twins, over, out, turns, too, fair, Ahkenahton, near, Jesus, daron, out, Moses, ever, Sandolphen, elks, amazon, here, remainder.

CHAPTER NINE

Mother, Africa, as we were, we, loved, that, is, the, ivy, all, to, Basic, Humanity, and, love's, include, days, blue, all, said, how, "love", purple, grew, moons, green, near, electricity, legible, batch, dove, pathways, appeared, harvested, rest, plenty, knew, elope, seeds, eros, days, all, well, yellow, all, said, yes, we, will, call, the, Ones, who, knew, groves, repairs, now, released, effect, absolutes, office, Christ, friendly, magic.

CHAPTER TEN

Stoals, purged, match, Arcturus, aft, humanity, friends, doors, Treva, steer, elk, mark, children, Metatron, oaks, trees, James, Sandalphon, on, channels, music, materials, 1-0-4, apt, musicals, matched, eve, ha, carpets, Ra, main, records, apple, stays, aims, plenty, laughter, freed, fortunated, vast, players, plagues, celebratory, fame, cleans, participles, fairest, fed, food, lunges, leaps, love, lives, here, legends, made, participation, meant, pulls, gestures, joins, factory, tires, plaster.

CHAPTER ELEVEN

Granted, acceptance, and, a, healed, return, we, learn, an, abstract, serial, of, the, causal, definition, established, when, principal, seeds, itself, through, a, gendered, destination, and, distance, between, seeding, and, fruit, is, our, growth, were, you, a, substance, spirited, for, originating, require, and, the, cause, electric, which, is, ours, through, necessity, for, love, damaged propulsions recently reports cancer, disturbs single, cells, rhythms existence hydrologically raised, recharges phenomenons academia bases, creations massively elaborate virtually constant circulating cures, pulsations blood sculptured,

capillary in crevasses tribes trees gardens, principles Aphrodite bottled rising, cycloids generations rising cycloids, original sap spirals, causes suggested spaces.

CHAPTER TWELVE

Avenue, transits, notable, heaps, graphics, formed, illustrated, pertinence, volley, troops, durable, dashes, damaged, spectators, machines, usual, tributes, split, dates, dared, fumes, delicacy, organisms, proposals, truthful, declarative, decry, davidian, spaces, aggregation, water, lives, blossoms, rejoiced, unfurls, quests, treated, exposures, formations, vapors, stages, hands, monsoons, coupled, purposes, contributions, Australians, technical, portals, rivulets, inevitable, pressures, zones, percentages, coercion, effects, reliefs, cycled, organisms, enlarged, inhaled, heated, factors, thickened.

CHAPTER THIRTEEN

Sunshine puberty, continued to, day fragments, baby fellowships, please how, love long, given imbued, late expensed, shine drips, grow debacles, twice debated, custom which, costume thrones, found adolescence, cups of, mains ascendancy, remember elbows, great mentioned, chances umbilical, roads lively, roses blows, eggs athena, birds Athens, the sheen, one a hymn, with felt enclose, guest offered, happy to, fell bitter, feelings fruit, next yields, waiting lessen, do justified, webs retires, glasses recycled, laugh tubes, new advertise, travel the need, eagle for, be tuned om, dance anecdotes, solo doles, heat featured, water enriched, paper tips, send and, need sips, understand fulfilling blues, made bellows, tapes remarkably, signs dear, lights astral, believe spectacularly, tell beauty, loop corrects, channels astutely, cute transcends, tall steps, lucid stones, melody, play, jams, hold, tightly.

LEVEL 125: THE LOVE-MENTS

CHAPTER ONE

Cross, jewelers, jostles, gossips, glee, gluing, tree, matrix, matrices, punch, listed, loads, operates, materializes, purple, flame, bemuse, purple, sheep, purple, phoenix, purple, team-violet, flame, purple, violet, flame, saint, germain, kumat, samat, kumara, Tibetans, tibets, Metatronic, blues, closed, gates, opened, doors, Shasta, Belize, brazil, basics, basically, blew, winds, tital, trips, tour, journey, joins, closed, closed, phoenix, just, alls, instructions, intellect, installations, relief, is, on.

CHAPTER TWO

Dances, theatrically, principally, habitat, guards, tranquil, domestics, expurge, occurrences, diminished, today, mothers, membership, hips, reduced, stresses, dreams, subterranean, management, tucked, culinary, essences, imagination, artists, customers, celebrations, elemental, earths, winds, fires, water, metals, busy, tunes, trues, keys, success, transcend, tranquil, unusual, colorful, retreats, paternal, maternal, guardians, gateways, gates, portals, planes, reality, wards, wardrobe, dares, powerful, lessons, lectures, liberties, liberations, flights, lowers, lone, sole, only, all.

CHAPTER THREE
Left, leaving, placed, built, intended, invented, based, builds, nears, needs, deeds, build, parents, children, brews, ideals, aids, ballets, fifths, avenues, secrets, satins, body, full, colorful, shoes, irresistible, shocks, counter, shades, turns, tours, ascertain, associates, activates, heals, filled, felt, gaps, cracks, chasms, abyss, Jordan, doors, dogs, bays, brush, rivers, streams, Ganges, gargantuan, large, beautiful, rare, basically, molds, shapes, digs, finds, stones, shares, fame, formulas, fame.

CHAPTER FOUR
Latest, news, concepts, luxury, gold, yellow, whites, scales, tips, trips, informed, handy, hands, handed, shines, shook, shaken, idealists, poring, evens, balanced, smooths, flakes, reds, acids, acidic, technologies, refinished, skins, scales, peels, visible, accessed, breath, refinished, make, made, owns, clinics, fixed, tops, crews, specialized, candidates, actual, thrives, arms, glass, outshone, breathe, grays, Tahitian, exotics, exotically, removed, hits, openly, reports, overheard, dear, heels, sandals, sunny, sunglasses.

CHAPTER FIVE
Coverage, covers, volumes, volumetric, paradise, paradisiacal, locals, awash, enriched, enriches, basics, wells, hems, accessories, basics, written, openly, purses, essentials, experimental, exoteric, sexual, humble, precious, gems, chronicles, journey, roles, geometrics, designs, awash, stripes, designated, sights, sighs, sites, basking, writing, pursuits, armistice, colorful, spliced, chronic, white, blaze, adventures, venues, shorts, steams, clothing, clothes, stipends, steeples, resorts, wordly, opened, packs, packets, package, army, armies, identity, clearest, clearly.

CHAPTER SIX
Stakes, stack, claims, raptures, rapt, hearts, golden, shores, lakes, excavates, planetary, plans, Arcturian, realms, captures, imagined, regional, regions, stockades, barns, farms, homes, helms, places, oceans, blue, geometric, dazzled, trains, beauty, confessions, mines, earth, depths, core, magnetics, magnetically, collections, museums, speeds, lakes, bays, by-ways, learnings, cognitive, traits, cognitions, asteroids, voids, holes, tubes, places, codes, capabilities, captions, emeralds, rubies, lava, magma, supplied, supple, optimal, overt, operatives.

CHAPTER SEVEN
Petaluma, Appalachians, geometric, geologically, straightens, great, Tanzania, Brazilian, Venezuelan, ascension, buckets, pockets, straightens, extremes, moves, sweeps, designs, dynamite, richly, watered, firmaments, heavens, vibrating,

mastlines, mails, bonds, shopping, guidelines, shades, trees, Tiffany, bangles, rings, rang, streams, movements, sticks, twigs, regions, evolutions, revolved, madonna, keys, swiss, legendary, legends, reckoning, famous, lineage, curvatures, diamonds, bracelets, crystalline, crystals, artistic, illuminations, moisturize, aquamarines, official, branching, mountains, planes, resolve, reach.

CHAPTER EIGHT:
Aisle, portraits, means, academy, maintains, desires, drives, fragrant, fragrances, women, islands, fathoms, footage, feet, services, portals, often, often, all, internal, international, editions, mediums, jewelry, marcasites, effective, features, peaks, experienced, experts, platinum, available, select, traded, times, wear, florals, vogue, feels, wild, wilderness, isles, distances, between, pundits, points, angles, among, within, consciousness, zones, amazon, crush, collectives, collectives, collection, faces, substance, drives, enigmatic, ideologic, compassionate, manages, substance.

CHAPTER NINE
Touch, thrilling, fabulous, locations, lovably, sales, informed, kiss, tells, told, fields, informed, dealing, declarations, bound, agencies, gives, debates, oval, bonds, shake, honesty, seriously, issues, adores, glamorized, lists, jobs, contributes, pages, plus, circumstances, top, articles, steers, sensuous, awe, dispels, elements, hunted, hunting, found, finds, excessive, plenty, more, enough, mentioned, fashions, life's, stories, steer, issues, loves, desirable, management, radiates, enticing, reaches, distinctive, compassionate, humor, laughter, loves.

CHAPTER TEN
Happens, hopes, kinder, kindest, enhancement, tints, gentles, soothing, romances, automated, materialization, sporting, watched, resistance, deepened, clears, forms, artists, personals, personalities, achieves, fascination, reversibles, modern, collectives, grands, additions, collected, ropes, embolden, specialties, stated, happens, chastens, hastens, sizes, styles, designs, mobile, eventual, events, complicated, single, simple, previewed, favorable, reviews, busy, regimes, compliments, sports, proven, reduced, reductions, incarnated, classics, generations, charity, cultures, projects, industry, opaque, essences, absolutes.

CHAPTER ELEVEN
Rainbow, springs, squares, beats, chords, pulses, flirts, adventures, heady, hears, hearing, shows, life's, leisures, massive, masses, engine, form, believing, expects, scarlet, quotes, singing, marry, toasted, circus, interview, swells, serenity, drags, dates, serenity, fuscia, function, emporiums, bounced, serials, tickets, rant, changes, usual, discussed, pockets, captures, clears, ranges, reaches, dresses, profiles, spiritual, imports, over shown, freedom, profiles, evenings, later, late, quiet, quite, cockpit, aggressive, portfolio, porto, seat.

CHAPTER TWELVE: fit, comfort, ruffles, collect, wired, highlights, destinations, records, encourage, rapidity, starts, passages, scheduled, tested, art form, makeup, wear, toasted, extended, technologically, faded, melting, flows, generational, stops, heat, abuse, humility, forget, forgive, belief, bodies, entertained, entwined, collection, leader, quality, beauty, value, styles, bohemian, diversity, thrills, celebration, Goddesses, cities, skylines, charming, countries, magical, kingdom, vertigo, genius, styles, contented, scene, heard, periods, appointed, slept, sheer, potions, lotions, moisture.

CHAPTER THIRTEEN

Messengers, messages, angels, personal, worlds, raised, holidays, openings, loves, pages, porcelain, skin, tans, media, crystals, Indians, personal, downtown, serenity, guides, host, attends, jubilant, clips, clicks, courage, encouraged, insured, acceptance, records, buffets, tastes, care, experiences, systems, results, customized, totes, splashed, ranges, settled, alchemical, archetypes, Gabriel, Ezekiel, prophets, cherubim, David, house, Mary, pregnancy, Michael, Jesus, swords, theaters, souvenirs, strand, stands, choose, tributes, mail, brisk, breaks, rewards.

LEVEL 126: THE ENCOURAGE-MENTS

CHAPTER ONE

Extraordinary, sweeping, softens, wings, angelic, bristles, fans, nourished, lately, latest, light, often, fellows, enriched, formulas, fullest, patented, patents, prevents, renegade, glimpses, changes, turns, twists, unravel, life, hands, caravans, doorways, hatches, hoods, clinches, open, checks, tours, virtual, places, folds, organized, servers, read, cool, control, passenger, mania, desired, picks, fashions, dances, works, deliver, fantasizes, photos, spools, styles, abstracts, specials, deliver, astrals, astanga, yogi, genus, admire, attitudes.

CHAPTER TWO

Smoke, La Jolla, storage, storms, pacific, eyes, children, chosen, wander, ways, halves, wholes, features, clouds, girls, women, woman, mended, men's, men, most, peculiar, pairs, charms, sealed, basins, blues, sky, veil, Vail, speeds, welcome, speedy, angels, shop, search, posters, broken, breaks, donors, television, celebrities, money, views, romantics, buzz, celebrity, aims, convenience, wines, extravagance, perfectly, owns, pseudonyms, Gregorian, Hadrian, architecture, parked, falls, watery, relaxation, wonderful, pleasures.

CHAPTER THREE

Measures, wards, squares, buffets, tables, turns, triples, tombs, escapades, escalate, estates, interstates, stressed, straightens, foci, influx, heirs, measures, rides, rewarded, incurred, stylish, projects, cool, air, characters, plays, screens, lifts, profiles, solutions, contracts, tones, refines, revolution, stars, title, flaunts, tablature, tables, marched, conservation, saluted, impeach, plow,

voted, awarded, awards, marched, sequels, sequins, shimmers, stars, contracts, volumetrics, volumes, values, sequesters, means, blocks, marching, aces, places, news.

CHAPTER FOUR

Casts, crews, feed, bureaus, groups, anchors, anchorage, conservations, conservatives, maples, mavericks, machinery, heirs, following, trusted, offers, characteristic, favors, remarkable, random, advertised, adverse, reverse, inverse, interim, interference, transcendent, conditions, assigns, fires, temperatures, tracks, cash, markets, marvelous, keynotes, keys, poise, dignity, eloquence, sequels, senators, sequesters, clans, family, theatrical, committed, remitted, paid, pours, proven, methods, subsets, sets, Elijah, calls, peace, in, the, heart, and, pure, mind

CHAPTER FIVE

Interested, interiors, submerging, subsistence, 31, 314, 3141, 31419, signals, emergent, allowances, guidance, came, coming, stems, electric, as, were, the, miracles, in, interiors, whose, sights, have, sent, views, around, observations, forth, love, international, stellar, waves, waivers, signed, passions, embryo, mounts, winged, recovery, arousing, substantiation, shed, additions, numerically, gather, sequences, sextant, cues, oceanic, seize, surrendering, patches, pathways, models, electricity, wells, walls, stone, thrown, pottery, wheels

CHAPTER SIX

Enclaves, built, to, humanity, are, encoded, in, calibers, calculated, for, future's, arise, where, in, eyes, is, the, pierce, and, where, the, stare, afflictions, affected, forge, forms, fuels, fiscal, founded, variations, fund, fuels, fashions, firms, launders, missives, mystics, mystical, maneuverings, mounted, mystique, music, muscular, neurotic, neurons, nursing, havens, heavens, homes, doors, temples, cloisters, lovers, gatherings, taverns, bars, pubs, cathedrals, altars, houses, towers, minarets, furnace, given, gates

CHAPTER SEVEN

Costs, abilities, talents, teams, cables, monitored, Labradors, isles, camera, files, formatted, fuselage, eject, effective, masters, mastery, mass, petite, passages, inner, interiors, lectures, palates, corners, crafts, retroactive, repeatable, repetitious, cancelled, copies, matched, lakeways, appreciation, value, ethics, sale, price, candy, splits, esteems, self, Christ-head, christoholism, art, measurable, with, won, found, amount, dollars, standards, "norms", tradition, belief, faith, personal, salvations, names, heir, stock, land, timbers, people, master

CHAPTER EIGHT

Inner, Hawaii, herbal, nutritions, spirits, business, historical, ancient, 64, Japan, love, God, light, crosses, temples, flames, waters, tai chi, developments, kai, incorporates, field, therapies, peoples, miracles, skeptics, cleared, healed, medical, nurses, doctors, stars, energize, hands, triangles, designs, medicines, violet, rays, germain, marriages, consciousness, trees, references, answers, inquired, empires, garners, auras, fairs, humbleness, graced, forgiveness, wilds, vibrations, unity, unify, clairessence, prosper, veins, earth's, blood, minerals, mostly.

CHAPTER NINE
Connecting, insertions, community, lands, ties, regressed, arcs, biologic, vibrant, walks, botanic, classics, waters, earth, trends, aromas, customs, excerpts, flowers, faith, centers, spreads, wisdoms, sponsors, initial, providence, inside, suspends, genius, out, journey, senses, subtle, rivulets, rains, community, muses, fluids, foot, feet, fuels, sophic, sophia, selective, stable, zeros, stapled, staples, steering, waits, stores, suggests, decides, details, reveals, kinetic, rewards, relaxes, relates, relatives, rushes, magnetic, multiply, zero.

CHAPTER TEN
Awareness, vastness, mergers, forums, shops, works, marvelous, visions, versatile, emissions, ingenuity, carries, integrity, center, point, stills, purpose, age, goals, physically, environs, schools, mysteries, amniotic, mechanics, goods, honest, tools, groups, chronic, clarity, prints, supplies, invests, invites, harvests, blue, moons, materials, choice, surrendered, thunders, catalysts, chosen, choose, means, prosper, prosperity, provincial, commodity, french, cuisine, clause, sauces, succeeds, grows, lodging, dear, nearby, supply, copies, imprints, rewarded, righteous.

CHAPTER ELEVEN
Volcanic, exact, trust, groves, Assissi, clare, loretto, lady, ladies, Anthony, Padua, Michael, swords, saints, tides, levels, 72, energies, revitalized, charges, greens, explorations, Posedion, Herodotus, 80, 88, 96, 104, andorion, red, Thai, coral, Atlantis, paradises, cycles, beings, vehicles, mastery, seaside, governs, albatross, reflect, restful, horizons, vessels, tubes, santorini, Zeus, colonies, Ursa, gone, reefs, lift, bars, sanctity, crustaceans, drifts, whales, ocean, orcas, ill, Neptune, Olympus, rises.

CHAPTER TWELVE
Full, fools, treads, trip, filled, fulfills, fill, overflown, eases, steers, glasses, buckets, cups, wells, fountains, hearts, songs, soothe, search, ends, strands, duplicate, creations, capable, covers, staggers, triggers, cravings, bakes, empty, carafes, vases, winsome, gourds, dippers, teems, teens, teams, cradles forming, cruises, crafts, matched, mules, pack, flasks, clears, stands, slides, slips, seals, centers, pushing, penetrate, purge, merger, curl, loop, level, loaf, tonight, today, forever, when, one.

CHAPTER THIRTEEN: niles, rains, Kalahari, floods, clicks, sphinx, steins, stools, fluids, oasis, roots, maneuvers, changes, moisture, ices, manuals, tumbles, scurry, visits, straw, days, storms, cacti, affect, flashes, flocks, spirals, fuels, stains, sands, breeze, summers, riverside, shares, spans, creeds, crashed, carried, carry, traverse, trips, saharan, dunes, yellows, mountains, begins, blouse, blow, sandstorms, plum, Philippians, Colossians,

Ephesians, Galilean, gallantly, gallant, capably, magazines, rosary, roses, times, sandstorms, great central sun, bear dead.

LEVEL 127: THE SOVEREIGN-MENTS

CHAPTER ONE
Utilities, funded, fractions, faiths, religious, cupids, Metatronics, cats, swords, lightenings, symmetry, life, alive, liable, wants, desires, connects, conveys, kept, companion, sunset, suns, sons, gales, seas, oceans, trains, friends, loves, lovers, sleeves, hearts, marry, cakes, creamy, tastes, subterranean, by-pass, booms, billions, trillion, triads, goldens, reachings, love, has, led, you, hear, listen, record, zoon, zooms, zo, zot, zoly, zolie, zotie, met, zok, zok, sook, stood, still.

CHAPTER TWO
Rhomboidal, rhomboids, pools, positional, dilettantes, dilettantish, wizened, wizards, stalactites, grown, counts, courageous, values, classical, flappers, moses, loves, derivative, derived, amuse, bemuse, vaunts, counts, covers, corners, marked, markets, marks, parts, paid, vibrations, polarity, pools, pushed, poverty, wards, mountains, stalagmites, signals, convey, voyages, twist, prose, moist, pans, goes, geometry, follows, reckoned, ranges, wardens, stations, caverns, amortized, amounts, carried, courage, victories, wisdoms, Zelda, Bach, Beethoven, effects, owls.

CHAPTER THREE
Fashions, freedoms, Bali, mothers, breath, breathing, gears, graces, gallows, gloves, moves, mavens, museums, married, solutions, crossing, agricultural, gap, gaps, dressed, dress, hermetica, hermetics, genders, poles, all, present, opposed, spectrals, philosophic, status, stations, applause, laud, resembles, taught, worthily, worthy, doctrines, guarded, porters, resembles, guided, through, labyrinth, monastery, mysterious, mystery, historic, hysterical, hysterectomy, opened, wound, worths, valuables, gems, stencils, colorful, carriages, casting, divine, encounters, visionary, procedures, probes.

CHAPTER FOUR
13 threads, 13 cords, 13 wires, 13 feeds, 13 choices, 13 thrones, 13 poses, 13 poems, 13 prosaics, 13 masters, Arc-Angel Michael, Moses, Arc-Angel Mikael, Arc-Angelic ways, thrice said, "Arc-Angelics", 13 beams, 13 rays, 13 bemuse, 13 stays, 13 ports, 13 portals, all-ways, saints, mantels, mastery, mosaic, myths, mythologic, gifts, swords, rocks, clocks, steepes, Mongolian, regimes, Kubla, Kahn, kuhn, mastered, pastoral, pastures, maps, meetings, out, over, alluring, vistas, vestiges, vestibules, murders, forgiven, founded, monastic, deeds, Arthurian, anthem, authentic, thorough, thrilled, polished, pens, blissed, blushed.

CHAPTER FIVE
Mars, hilled, rests, respects, lines, lived, alike, sacred, grounded,

grounds, restful, roots, rooted, valley, central, inspirational, renews, community, stewards, banks, breaks, rivers, Jordan, examples, epistles, planets, plans, quests, bushes, burned, contacts, calls, holy, grounds, loosen, shoes, walks, here, near, holy, holies, veils, rip, triples, surrenders, faith's, blush, temple, acceptance, reaching, rocks, retreat, historic, affluence, afforded, diversity, ranges, calculated, spatials, devoted, persons, programs, teachings, ideals.

CHAPTER SIX
92 trees, tubal, tones, tomes, 8 wings, 8 falls, 8 seas, 8 temples, 8 means, 8 mode, 8 plauses, 8 pages, 8 poets, 9 times, 9 teams, 7 scenes, 7 sands, 8 leaves, cylinders, 8 days, 7 made, 6 freed, 4 feed, 5 bled, 11 wed, weaves, won, wages, sung, salutes, suns, sonnets, poems, tarry, ferry, frees, frieze, places, roses, goals, gates, plethora, cameras, apologetics, sadistic, pieces, pints, jugs, jars, holds, shine, shone, shull, ministers, maintains, stays, Strauss, managers, surrendered, since, silence, love, mills, moistens.

CHAPTER SEVEN
Perfect, health, wealth, worry, freed, concerns, cleared, 64, 7, 8, 9, due, 17, 18, 9, 77 ways, flew, who knew, who fought, who flaunt, who won, will weigh, who play, who stay, handles, movements, titles, hearts, challenges, offers, flowers, flown, karmic, ends, conference, journeyed, lands, Zion, canyons, places, archetypal, traditions, imprints, divine, European, surrenders, news, Jerusalem, befriends, friendly, metaphors, prayers, walks, steps, stances, purgation, illuminated, unity, unions, marriages, spirits, souls, relaxed, released.

CHAPTER EIGHT
Hearts, held, healthy, parts, approach, stall, once, more, employ, patience, pen, agains, words, lanes, avenues, trips, treats, friendly, fro, fallow, days, blessed, tests, surrenders, bones, year, yearly, annual, visits, eights, befriends, allows, alls, fecunds, fields, grown, tall, blends, buffers, charted, started, seen, scenes, since, Saul, Paul, tarsus, roads, targets, lights, sent, sights, strike, soon, nearing, now, love's, stall, still, ass, first, immerse, embraced, strokes.

CHAPTER NINE
Written, material, glee, stay, wells, oftens, openly, staples, stays, soon, delivery, fabrics, fused, seams, carry, bodies, slim, removals, sides, breath, borne, air, wings, focusing, sewn, own, honors, nearing, skins, stance, flaw, sing, washing, over, surging, facets, glances, wears, beams, bemoan, well, magical, surgical, flowerings, breathe, stormy, values, bleeds, owners, honored, rents, rinsed, wondered, again, revenue, sizes, into, threshold, threads, masters, focus, on, pens, merge.

CHAPTER TEN
Assigns, governed, confluences, scrolls, earliest, encounters, consciousness, previews, preciousness, realms, lights, programs,

series, planets, lights, Orion, healed, rays, eternal, ever, stores, lasted, affluent, swept, mixed, serials, heavens, thresholds, types, zones, lower, realms, midst, temporal, locals, systems, multiple, tesselations, fleshly, anoints, revolutions, runs, governs, rules, regional, recent, eventual, mid-ways, councils, acumen, controls, councils, thrive, imperfect, counts, ran, involutions, resolutions, Gods, reap, shown, fusion, folds, fluids.

CHAPTER ELEVEN
Personable, cyptic, enlil, Ahab, Abel, Adam, Cain, stern, outreached, scholarly, emissary, compliance, duties, orbits, clouds, ships, times, lively, stars, shepherds, herds, stock, noteworthy, knees, bent, compares, prayers, duality, ends, worships, chariots, dreams, divine, ovations, pressed, texts, flocks, Bethlehem, lightly, brought, four, bright, eagles, visits, vehicles, aerial, sights, exist, several, notes, rivers, nations, Hamitic, Nubian, Akkadian, trips, Saharas, kings, frankincense, Arabian, myrrh, kings, Sudan, peace.

CHAPTER TWELVE
Nth, degrees, teslan, blueprints, matters, materials, physical, cycles, intellects, mutual, language, powers, lines, networks, necessity, expressions, coded, planes, planets, insights, vibrations, composures, comports, English, ophanims, messengers, Metatron, strictly, gridded, involved, established, cells, resolved, structure, sunlight, ranges, systems, examples, samples, energies, orderly, orders, transmit, trued, folds, fluids, flows, flowers, flocks, voiced, voxley, rainbow, key, chief, look, coil, rock, gem, spiral, rest, harmony, peace, sacred, river.

CHAPTER THIRTEEN
Necessary, necks, now, next, necessity, nudged, smiles, stones, flesh, general, sent, bought, sides, information, processing, A-line, B-lines, plug, solars, grids, formations, tens, timely, maser, controlled, examples, samples, co-participants, planetary, tables, manual, creations, levels, chronomatic, growths, status, intellect, initiated, known, astronomic, transits, transmitted, collectives, sideways, biomes, substations, Chinese, crowns, evolutions, resolves, resolutions, precious, ecosystemic, systems, conglomerates, confetti, participates, filly, more, studs, eruptions, showers, stretched, strips.

LEVEL 128: THE ENTITY-MENTS

CHAPTER ONE: A-lines, A-times, A-typicals, A-systmatic, A-lists, averaged, ashen, ashed, Asheville, aston, ascensions, marlins, martins, dolphins, A-brand, A-baked, A-linear, breathing, fires, smokey, borne, stitches, parked, stance, ozone, carbons, monoxide, schooled, junctions, surveys, blazes, created, digs, discovery, stores, arranged, ranges, packets, buckets, rocks, precious, synthetics, instills, spurts, suites, stripes, stetchings, sustains, seals, fresh, crystals, divine, light, absorb, honestly, write, elk, sphinx, O, the, border, to, six, path.

CHAPTER TWO

Avenues, certified, live, aventurine, interiors, estates, conservations, landed, elasticity, villages, photographs, municipals, jumar, advents, strategic, signals, rented, rentals, politics, statistics, straps, meet, manage, gathers, specifics, specifically, neutral, specifically, neutral, natural, systemic, flows, loyalty, customers, stores, service, copes, casting, utilities, latent, century, lather, processed, participated, standards, opened, copes, casting, dice, dye, steering, stamping, crossfires, enthusiastic, extrapolate, external, aggregate, attends, rescued, rafters, rushing, rapidly, quickly, currently

CHAPTER THREE

Prophetic, sufficiently, Moses, Elijah, accountable, count, gentile, sufficient, republics, phases, impel, compel, bells, republics, parthenon, victory, belabors, laborious, labors, elections, services, strewn, dwellings, entrance, thuban, garments, days, respatialized, variously, penultimate, ultimate, recompense, days, partner, givens, guidance, necessary, quickens, visuals, visualized, dwells, pointed, galactic, ophanic, dimensions, plurals, materialized, accountable, counted, quickenings, quickly, coming, into, clarity, collectives, powers, regional, regions, locally, Polaris, myriads, 4th, variously, activities.

CHAPTER FOUR

Father, son, pyramids, 9, warps, Orion, maps, 12, one, delta, epsilon, zeta, tal, harmony, DNA, codes, bottoms, RNA, topics, shekinah, wheels, invagination, crystal, solar, spectrums, blemished, removal, ourselves, chakras, physiology, predilections, Krishna, 2, translated, films, data, based, magistrates, lions, throned, stars, seeds, ages, gitas, bio-pyramids, mahasamatman, attaches, stars, interiors, enlightened, communications, telethought, Hebrews, Chinese, repressed, instructions, Davids, pyramids, dimensional, eternals, fosters, imagines, gains.

CHAPTER FIVE

Squired, cashed, checked, named, numbered, lamb's, life, NASA, OB-GYN, MD, PHD, PA, God, mothers, RNA, DNA, H2O, CO2, matrix, glue, matrices, O2, willingness, owners, loved, lightwares, lost, win, surrenderings, into, manageable, dreams, doubts, go, gone, implores, implodes, motives, reaches, dues, ovens, wpa, pause, clauses, oz, topics, monograms, measures, mounted, pranced, unisons, units, eunuch, obid, ovarian, guests, taj-haled, towels, terms, BA, BS, MFA, MBA, CO.

CHAPTER SIX

Resonance, basis, basically, bests, bovine, mastif, masculine, assured, height, through, curved, bristols, papers, vibrates, vibratory, dwelt, doubly, fashioned, fascinations, focus, forms, amounted, surmounted, summons, sustenance, surfaced, ovations, applause, rescues, resonant, resonance, ruptures, radicals,

freeze, frozen, flirted, formalize, duals, depends, deepens, doubled, sustained, stung, cause, God's, doves, darest, darings, courage, courts, countings, casts, doubled, durations, dips, doubts, cancelled, hearing, heard, sound, enhanced, massive, orations, gallant.

CHAPTER SEVEN

Energy, cast, planes, amps, connected, mounts, quaint, newest, necessary, necessity, loved, leaders, costs, carriage, wires, worshipful, furtive, selections, replenished, nourished, generative, stated, reasons, sustenance, laughter, freed, fortunated, vast, awash, lasting, logics, mansions, temples, types, neptons, laps, natural, rational, radial, opens, reasons, news, into, loves, solves, built, plugs, electricity, leptons, venerated, resonant, zeros, ended, levels, simply, radical, simply, generated, stuns, currents, daily, surgeds, leaped, lights.

CHAPTER EIGHT

Biological, complexities, crazy, relatives, homes, carousels, aliens, Spanish, comforts, dwellings, interests, napier, nestles, internships, laws, accountings, soldiers, sole, soul, aloft, bodies, matrix, materials, muses, higher, realms, poles, reversal, positive, negatives, evolves, higher, reveals, more, accepts, nursing, county, language, flowers, life's, Metatronic, Melchizedek, meet, patron, partners, brains, beauty, imprints, players, evolves, solves, lovers, advised, stay, originals, glittering, letters, sounds, externals, spirits, doors, inter-connected, sections, spirits.

CHAPTER NINE

Activities, biochemical, emanations, virtues, seeds, matrimonial, bodies, crystals, romanced, channels, sexual, holy, telethoughts, biochemical, represented, Sanskrit, Tibetans, inner-connections, civilized, Egyptians, Hebrew, Sanskrit, Chinese, repressed, instructions, David, pyramids, dimensional, eternally, telethought, rings, communications, bodies, sexuals, channels, holy, attunements, emanating, eights, enlightenments, enlighten, chakras, kingdoms, flowered, bodies, Christs, stars, brilliant, three, eternity, minds, originations, embodies, lights, two, formal, Christs, words, experienced, primes, proper, honeymoon, eighth, ability.

CHAPTER TEN

Metatronic, Elohim, Mogan, David, ripen, crossing, alpha, omega, shafts, horses, swords, cruise, chants, minds, faces, adonai, increment, 1-1-1, blues, shoulders, heads, minds, middle, bottom, top, low, high, mid, upper, qualities, millions, cleansings, inter-related, fathers, minds, temples, golden, keyed, grids, circulations, harmonics, structures, structural, patterns, waves, inductions, offsets, vocalize, givens, entry, leaves, 76, names, Adam, Christ's, Metatron, safkas, mena, menematra, reached, restructured, ends, times, noon.

CHAPTER ELEVEN

Matrilineal, qualities, quoted, memorialized, under, engineered, engaged, drifted, accepts, lives, electricity, summations, written, nights, beckoning, mother's, worlds, Egyptians, beacons, won, weavers, lastings, memories, lashed, canes, linked, ananaki, epiphany, advanced, softened, hummings, remembers, blues, wisest, splendors, summarized, links, lashes, canes, lined, genetically, lines, matrilineal, whistled, underneath, lists, herbal, drive, long, cruise, in, peace, love, happiness, camp, hammock, rest, look, fine, Hawaii, wizard, menstrual, eventual, suspect.

CHAPTER TWELVE
Suave, stands, bristlecones, posts, commands, bash, forests, warms, hair, lands, bugs, rains, bureau, ladders, tops, management, tops, rotated, ropes, sources, misty, fantastic, tunks, trusts, mystique, journeyed, moths, groves, Sundays, discretions, generals, joust, trees, understory, music, shops, roots, pisgah, ozygenate, spokes, gatlinburg, fires, state, parks, everglades, pines, extinct, bask, chlorophyll, opens, obligated, redwoods, sequoia, California, cypress, texas, type, kinds, buds, leaves, roots, shield, fields, books.

CHAPTER THIRTEEN
Motherly, mothers, cells, instructed, humanly, wards, Sophia, pistils, pillars, mentals, spiritual, coded, instructs, jewels, oracles, paradigms, unions, physically, reached, divine, selves, gridded, organisms, transplanted, consequences, spectrums, mines, timed, cells, immokalee, images, jointly, experiences, spirals, visions, delegates, delineated, languages, careful, selections, expired, aspects, lay, ohms, esh, past, present, future, minutes, Brazilian, koa, nut, fluid, tree, respect, air, stage, stirs, electrical, respect, avenue, escape, John, son.

PHASE THREE
LEVELS 129 - 233

LEVEL 129: THE ATMOSPHERE-MENTS:

Peace, dove, fu, lasts, lasting, savannah, herald, held, pierce, peasant, portend, left, para, lover, spoils, leave, sat, reaction, tolerates, rude, reach, jungle, pursue, pursuant, passionate, peace, paces, pallis, Athens, add, ropes, rolled, proportions, Amazon, all, covert, overt, delay, past, sway, underneath, doors, rapture, transcends, oceans, twin, create, portions, proportionate, mix, perfectly, praised, tops, bears, caps, captured, propel, mixed, mixture, attracts, jaguar, cradle, dakiw, tantric.

LEVEL 130: THE SENTINEL-MENTS:

Dances, theatrically, principally, habitat, guards, tranquil, domestics, expurge, occurrences, diminished, today, mothers, membership, hips, reduced, stresses, dreams, subterranean, management, tucked, culinary, essences, imagination, artists, customers, celebrations, elemental, earths, winds, fires, water, metals, busy, tunes, trues, keys, success, transcend, tranquil, unusual, colorful, retreats, paternal, maternal, guardians, gateways, gates, portals, planes, reality, wards, wardrobe, dares, powerful, lessons, lectures, liberties, liberations, flights, lowers, lone, sole, only, all.

LEVEL 131: THE IN-BRIDGE-MENTS:

Left, leaving, placed, built, intended, invented, based, builds, nears, needs, deeds, build, parents, children, brews, ideals, aids, ballets, fifths, avenues, secrets, satins, body, full, colorful, shoes, irresistible, shocks, counter, shades, turns, tours, ascertain, associates, activates, heals, filled, felt, gaps, cracks, chasms, abyss, jordan, doors, dogs, bays, brush, rivers, streams, ganges, gargantuan, large, beautiful, rare, basically, molds, shapes, digs, finds, stones, shares, fame, formulas, fames.

LEVEL 132: THE MOVE-MENTS:

Latest, news, concepts, luxury, gold, yellow, whites, scales, tips, trips, informed, handy, hands, handed, shines, shook, shaken, idealists, poring, evens, balanced, smooths, flakes, reds, acids, acidic, technologies, refinished, skins, scales, peels, visible, accessed, breath, refinished, make, made, owns, clinics, fixed, tops, crews, specialized, candidates, actual, thrives, arms, glass, outshone, breathe, grays, tahitian, exotics, exotically, removed, hits, openly, reports, overheard, dear, heels, sandals, sunny, sunglasses.

LEVEL 133: THE IN-QUADRANT-MENTS:

Coverage, covers, volumes, volumetric, paradise, paradisiacal, locals, awash, enriched, enriches, basics, wells, hems, accessories, basics, written, openly, purses, essentials, experimental, exoteric, sexual, humble, precious, gems, chronicles, journey, roles, geometrics, designs, awash, stripes, designated, sights, sighs, sites, basking, writing, pursuits, armistice, colorful, spliced, chronic, white, blaze, adventures, venues, shorts, steams, clothing, clothes, stipends, steeples, resorts, wordly, opened, packs, packets, package, army, armies, identity, clearest, clearly

LEVEL 134: THE IN-REALM-MENTS:

Stakes, stack, claims, raptures, rapt, hearts, golden, shores, lakes, excavates, planetary, plans, Arcturian, realms, captures, imagined, regional, regions, stockades, barns, farms, homes, helms, places, oceans, blue, geometric, dazzled, trains, beauty, confessions, mines, earth, depths, core, magnetics, magnetically, collections, museums, speeds, lakes, bays, by-ways, learnings, cognitive, traits, cognitions, asteroids, voids, holes, tubes, places, codes, capabilities, captions, emeralds, rubies, lava, magma, supplied, supple, optimal, overt, operative.

LEVEL 135: THE REGION-MENTS:

Petaluma, Appalachians, geometric, geologically, straightens, great, Tanzania, Brazilian, Venezuelean, ascension, buckets, pockets, straightens, extremes, moves, sweeps, designs, dynamite, richly, watered, firmaments, heavens, vibrating, mastlines, mails, bonds, shopping, guidelines, shades, trees, tiffany, bangles, rings, rang, streams, movements, sticks, twigs, regions, evolutions, revolved, Madonna, keys, swiss, legendary, legends, reckoning, famous, lineage, curvatures, diamonds, bracelets, crystalline, crystals, artistic, illuminations, moisturize, aquamarines, official, branching, mountains, planes, resolve, reach.

LEVEL 136: THE IN-DEPTH-MENTS:

Aisle, portraits, means, academy, maintains, desires, drives, fragrant, fragrances, women, islands, fathoms, footage, feet, services, portals, often, often, all, internal, international, editions, mediums, jewelry, marcasites, effective, features, peaks, experienced, experts, platinum, available, select, traded, times, wear, florals, vogue, feels, wild, wilderness, isles, distances, between, pundits, points, angles, among, within, consciousness, zones, amazon, crush, collectives, collectives, collection, faces, substance, drives, enigmatic, ideologic, compassionate, manages, substances.

LEVEL 137: THE AGREE-MENTS:

Touch, thrilling, fabulous, locations, lovely, sales, informed, kiss, tells, told, fields, informed, dealing, declarations, bound, agencies, gives, debates, oval, bonds, shake, honesty, seriously, issues, adores, glamorized, lists, jobs, contributes, pages, plus, circumstances, top, articles, steers, sensuous, awe, dispels, elements, hunted, hunting, found, finds, excessive, plenty, more, enough, mentioned, fashions, life's, stories, steer, issues, loves, desirable, management, radiates, enticing, reaches, distinctive, compassionate, humor, laughter, love.

LEVEL 138: THE FATHOM-MENTS:

Happens, hopes, kinder, kindest, enhancement, tints, gentles, soothing, romances, automated, materialization, sporting, watched, resistance, deepened, clears, forms, artists, personals, personalities, achieves, fascination, reversibles, modern, collectives, grands, additions, collected, ropes, embolden, specialties, stated, happens, chastens, hastens, sizes, styles, designs, mobile, eventual, events, complicated, single, simple, previewed, favorable, reviews, busy, regimes, compliments, sports, proven, reduced, reductions, incarnated, classics, generations, charity, cultures, projects, industry, opaque, essences, absolute.

LEVEL 139: THE CHOIR-MENTS:

Rainbow, springs, squares, beats, chords, pulses, flirts, adventures, heady, hears, hearing, shows, life's, leisures, massive, masses, engine, form, believing, expects, scarlet, quotes, singing, marry, toasted, circus, interview, swells, serenity, drags, dates, serenity, fuscia, function, emporiums, bounced, serials, tickets, rant, changes, usual, discussed, pockets, captures, clears, ranges, reaches, dresses, profiles, spiritual, imports, over shown, freedom, profiles, evenings, later, late, quiet, quite, cockpit, aggressive, portfolio, porto, seat

LEVEL 140: THE TWIST-MENTS:

Fit, comfort, ruffles, collect, wired, highlights, destinations, records, encourage, rapidity, starts, passages, scheduled, tested, art form, makeup, wear, toasted, extended, technologically, faded, melting, flows, generational, stops, heat, abuse, humility, forget, forgive, belief, bodies, entertained, entwined, collection, leader, quality, beauty, value, styles, Bohemian, diversity, thrills, celebration, Goddesses, cities, skylines, charming, countries, magical, kingdom, vertigo, genius, styles, contented, scene, heard, periods, appointed, slept, sheer, potions, lotions, moisture.

LEVEL 141: THE HERALD-MENTS:

Messengers, messages, angels, personal, worlds, raised, holidays, openings, loves, pages, porcelain, skin, tans, media, crystals, indians, personal, downtown, serenity, guides, host, attends, jubilant, clips, clicks, courage, encouraged, insured, acceptance, records, buffets, tastes, care, experiences, systems, results, customized, totes, splashed, ranges, settled, alchemical, archetypes, Gabriel, Ezekiel, prophets, cherubim, david, house, mary, pregnancy, Michael, Jesus, swords, theaters, souvenirs, strand, stands, choose, tributes, mail, brisk, breaks, rewards.

LEVEL 142: THE TURN-MENTS:

Extraordinary, sweeping, softens, wings, angelic, bristles, fans, nourished, lately, latest, light, often, fellows, enriched, formulas, fullest, patented, patents, prevents, renegade, glimpses, changes, turns, twists, unravel, life, hands, caravans, doorways, hatches, hoods, clinches, open, checks, tours, virtual, places, folds, organized, servers, read, cool, control, passenger, mania, desired, picks, fashions, dances, works, deliver, fantasizes, photos, spools, styles, abstracts, specials, deliver, astrals, astanga, yogi, genus, admire, attitude.

LEVEL 143: THE MIST-MENTS:

Smoke, La Jolla, storage, storms, Pacific, eyes, children, chosen, wander, ways, halves, wholes, features, clouds, girls, women, woman, mended, men's, men, most, peculiar, pairs, charms, sealed, basins, blues, sky, veil, vail, speeds, welcome, speedy, angels, shop, search, posters, broken, breaks, donors, television, celebrities, money, views, romantics, buzz, celebrity, aims, convenience, wines, extravagance, perfectly, owns, pseudonyms, Gregorian, Hadrian, architecture, parked, falls, watery, relaxation, wonderful, pleasure.

LEVEL 144: THE TABLE-MENTS:

Measures, wards, squares, buffets, tables, turns, triples, tombs, escapades, escalate, estates, interstates, stressed, straightens, foci, influx, heirs, measures, rides, rewarded, incurred, stylish, projects, cool, air, characters, plays, screens, lifts, profiles, solutions, contracts, tones, refines, revolution, stars, title, flaunts, tablature, tables, marched, conservation, saluted, impeach, plow, voted, awarded, awards, marched, sequels, sequins, shimmers, stars, contracts, volumetrics, volumes, values, sequesters, means, blocks, marching, aces, places, news.

LEVEL 145: THE ENSEMBLE-MENTS:

Casts, crews, feed, bureaus, groups, anchors, anchorage, conservations, conservatives, maples, mavericks, machinery, heirs, following, trusted, offers, characteristic, favors, remarkable, random, advertised, adverse, reverse, inverse, interim, interference, transcendent, conditions, assigns, fires, temperatures, tracks, cash, markets, marvelous, keynotes, keys, poise, dignity, eloquence, sequels, senators, sequesters, clans, family, theatrical, committed, remitted, paid, pours, proven, methods, subsets, sets, Elijah, calls, peace, in, the, heart, and, pure, mind.

LEVEL 146: THE INTERIOR-MENTS:

Interested, interiors, submerging, subsistence, 1, 14, 141, 1419, signals, emergent, allowances, guidance, came, coming, stems, electric, as, were, the, miracles, in, interiors, whose, sights, have, sent, views, around, observations, forth, love, international, stellar, waves, waivers, signed, passions, embryo, mounts, winged, recovery, arousing, substantiation, shed, additions, numerically, gather, sequences, sextant, cues, oceanic, seize, surrendering, patches, pathways, models, electricity, wells, walls, stone, thrown, pottery, wheels.

LEVEL 147: THE ENCLAVES-MENTS:

Enclaves, built, to, humanity, are, encoded, in, calibers, calculated, for, future's, arise, where, in, eyes, is, the, pierce, and, where, the, stare, afflictions, affected, forge, forms, fuels, fiscal, founded, variations, fund, fuels, fashions, firms, launders, missives, mystics, mystical, maneuverings, mounted, mystique, music, muscular, neurotic, neurons, nursing, havens, heavens, homes, doors, temples, cloisters, lovers, gatherings, taverns, bars, pubs, cathedrals, altars, houses, towers, minarets, furnace, given, gates

LEVEL 148: THE WORTH-MENTS:

Costs, abilities, talents, teams, cables, monitored, labradors, isles, camera, files, formatted, fuselage, eject, effective, masters, mastery, mass, petite, passages, inner, interiors, lectures, palates, corners, crafts, retroactive, repeatable, repetitious, cancelled, copies, matched, lakeways, appreciation, value, ethics, sale, price, candy, splits, esteems, self, Christ-head, Christoholism, art, measurable, with, won, found, amount, dollars, standards, "norms", tradition, belief, faith, personal, salvations, names, heir, stock, land, timbers, people, master.

LEVEL 149: THE ANGEL-MENTS:

Inner, Hawaii, herbal, nutritions, spirits, business, historical, ancient, 64, Japan, love, God, light, crosses, temples, flames, waters, tai chi, developments, Kai, incorporates, field, therapies, peoples, miracles, skeptics, cleared, healed, medical, nurses, doctors, stars, energize, hands, triangles, designs, medicines, violet, rays, germain, marriages, consciousness, trees, references, answers, inquired, empires, garners, auras, fairs, humbleness, graced, forgiveness, wilds, vibrations, unity, unify, clairessence, prosper, veins, earth's, blood, minerals, mostly.

LEVEL 150: THE OCEAN-MENTS:

Connecting, insertions, community, lands, ties, regressed, arcs, biologic, vibrant, walks, botanic, classics, waters, earth, trends, aromas, customs, excerpts, flowers, faith, centers, spreads, wisdoms, sponsors, initial, providence, inside, suspends, genius, out, journey, senses, subtle, rivulets, rains, community, muses, fluids, foot, feet, fuels, sophic, sophia, selective, stable, zeros, stapled, staples, steering, waits, stores, suggests, decides, details, reveals, kinetic, rewards, relaxes, relates, relatives, rushes, magnetic, multiply, zero.

LEVEL 151: THE CREED-MENTS:

Awareness, vastness, mergers, forums, shops, works, marvelous, visions, versatile, emissions, ingenuity, carries, integrity, center, point, stills, purpose, age, goals, physically, environs, schools, mysteries, amniotic, mechanics, goods, honest, tools, groups, chronic, clarity, prints, supplies, invests, invites, harvests, blue, moons, materials, choice, surrendered, thunders, catalysts, chosen, choose, means, prosper, prosperity, provincial, commodity, french, cuisine, clause, sauces, succeeds, grows, lodging, dear, nearby, supply, copies, imprints, rewarded, righteous.

LEVEL 152: THE SEA-MENTS:

Volcanic, exact, trust, groves, Assissi, Clare, loretto, lady, ladies, anthony, padua, Michael, swords, saints, tides, levels, 72, energies, revitalized, charges, greens, explorations, Posedion, herodotus, 80, 88, 96, 104, andorion, red, Thai, coral, Atlantis, paradises, cycles, beings, vehicles, mastery, seaside, governs, albatross, reflect, restful, horizons, vessels, tubes, sSantorini, zeus, colonies, Ursa, gone, reefs, lift, bars, sanctity, crustaceans, drifts, whales, ocean, orcas, ill, Neptune, Olympus, rise.

LEVEL 153: THE FILL-MENTS:

Full, fools, treads, trip, filled, fulfills, fill, overflown, eases, steers, glasses, buckets, cups, wells, fountains, hearts, songs, soothe, search, ends, strands, duplicate, creations, capable, covers, staggers, triggers, cravings, bakes, empty, carafes, vases, winsome, gourds, dippers, teems, teens, teams, cradles forming, cruises, crafts, matched, mules, pack, flasks, clears, stands, slides, slips, seals, centers, pushing, penetrate, purge, merger, curl, loop, level, loaf, tonight, today, forever, when, one.

LEVEL 154: THE DESERT-MENTS:

Miles, rains, Kalahari, floods, clicks, sphinx, steins, stools, fluids, oasis, roots, maneuvers, changes, moisture, ices, manuals, tumbles, scurry, visits, straw, days, storms, cacti, affect, flashes, flocks, spirals, fuels, stains, sands, breeze, summers, riverside, shares, spans, creeds, crashed, carried, carry, traverse, trips, saharan, dunes, yellows, mountains, begins, blouse, blow, sandstorms, plum, Philipians, Colossians, Ephesians, Galilean, gallantly, gallant, capably, magazines, rosary, roses, times, sandstorms, great central sun, bear dead.

LEVEL 155: THE ENDEAR-MENTS:

Utilities, funded, fractions, faiths, religious, cupids, Metatronics, cats, swords, lightenings, symmetry, life, alive, liable, wants, desires, connects, conveys, kept, companion, sunset, suns, sons, gales, seas, oceans, trains, friends, loves, lovers, sleeves, hearts, marry, cakes, creamy, tastes, subterranean, by-pass, booms, billions, trillion, triads, goldens, reachings, love, has, led, you, hear, listen, record, zoon, zooms, zo, zot, zoly, zolie, zotie, met, zok, zok, sook, stood, still.

LEVEL 156: THE WISE-MENTS:

Rhomboidal, rhomboids, pools, positional, dilettantes, dilettanti, wizened, wizards, stalactites, grown, counts, courageous, values, classical, flappers, moses, loves, derivative, derived, amuse, bemuse, vaunts, counts, covers, corners, marked, markets, marks, parts, paid, vibrations, polarity, pools, pushed, poverty, wards, mountains, stalagmites, signals, convey, voyages, twist, prose, moist, pans, goes, geometry, follows, reckoned, ranges, wardens, stations, caverns, amortized, amounts, carried, courage, victories, wisdoms, Zelda, Bach, Beethoven, effects, owl.

LEVEL 157: THE IN-FASHION-MENTS:

Fashions, freedoms, Bali, mothers, breath, breathing, gears, graces, gallows, gloves, moves, mavens, museums, married, solutions, crossing, agricultural, gap, gaps, dressed, dress hermetica, hermetics, genders, poles, all, present, opposed, spectrals, philosophic, status, stations, applause, laud, resembles, taught, worthily, worthy, doctrines, guarded, porters, resembles, guided, through, labyrinth, monastery, mysterious, mystery, historic, hysterical, hysterectomy, opened, wound, worths, valuables, gems, stencils, colorful, carriages, casting, divine, encounters, visionary, procedures, probe.

LEVEL 158: THE THIRTEEN-MENTS:

13 threads, 13 cords, 13 wires, 13 feeds, 13 choices, 13 thrones, 13 poses, 13 poems, 13 prosaics, 13 masters, Arc-Angel Michael, Moses, Arc-Angel Mikael, Arc-Angelic ways, thrice said, "Arc-Angelics", 13 beams, 13 rays, 13 bemuse, 13 stays, 13 ports, 13 portals, all-ways, saints, mantels, mastery, mosaic, myths, mythologic, gifts, swords, rocks, clocks, steepes, mongolian, regimes, Kubla, Kahn, kuhn, mastered, pastoral, pastures, maps, meetings, out, over, alluring, vistas, vestiges, vestibules, murders, forgiven, founded, monastic, deeds, arthurian, anthem, authentic, thorough, thrilled, polished, pens, blissed, blushed.

LEVEL 159: THE SEAM-MENTS:

Mars, hilled, rests, respects, lines, lived, alike, sacred, grounded, grounds, restful, roots, rooted, valley, central, inspirational, renews, community, stewards, banks, breaks, rivers, jordan, examples, espistles, planets, plans, quests, bushes, burned, contacts, calls, holy, grounds, loosen, shoes, walks, here, near, holy, holies, veils, rip, triples, surrenders, faith's, blush, temple, acceptance, reaching, rocks, retreat, historic, affluence, afforded, diversity, ranges, calculated, spatials, devoted, persons, programs, teachings, ideals.

LEVEL 160: THE 8-MENTS:

92 trees, tubal, tones, tomes, 8 wings, 8 falls, 8 seas, 8 temples, 8 means, 8 mode, 8 plauses, 8 pages, 8 poets, 9 times, 9 teams, 7 scenes, 7 sands, 8 leaves, cylinders, 8 days, 7 made, 6 freed, 4 feed, 5 bled, 11 wed, weaves, won, wages, sung, salutes, suns, sonnets, poems, tarry, ferry, frees, freize, places, roses, goals, gates, plethora, cameras, apologetics, sadistic, pieces, pints, jugs, jars, holds, shine, shone, shull, ministers, maintains, stays, strauss, managers, surrendered, since, silence, love, mills, moistens.

LEVEL 161: THE 64-MENTS:

Perfect, health, wealth, worry, freed, concerns, cleared, 64, 7, 8, 9, due, 17, 18, 9, 77 ways, flew, who knew, who fought, who flaunt, who won, will weigh, who play, who stay, handles, movements, titles, hearts, challenges, offers, flowers, flown, karmic, ends, conference, journeyed, lands, Zion, canyons, places, archetypal, traditions, imprints, divine, European, surrenders, news, Jerusalem, befriends, friendly, metaphors, prayers, walks, steps, stances, purgation, illuminated, unity, unions, marriages, spirits, souls, relaxed, released.

LEVEL 162: THE 104-MENTS:

Hearts, held, healthy, parts, approach, stall, once, more, employ, patience, pen, agains, words, lanes, avenues, trips, treats, friendly, fro, fallow, days, blessed, tests, surrenders, bones, year, yearly, annual, visits, eights, befriends, allows, alls, fecunds, fields, grown, tall, blends, buffers, charted, started, seen, scenes, since, saul, paul, tarsus, roads, targets, lights, sent, sights, strike, soon, nearing, now, love's, stall, still, ass, first, immerse, embraced, strokes.

LEVEL 163: THE FABRIC-MENTS:

Written, material, glee, stay, wells, oftens, openly, staples, stays, soon, delivery, fabrics, fused, seams, carry, bodies, slim, removals, sides, breath, borne, air, wings, focusing, sewn, own, honors, nearing, skins, stance, flaw, sing, washing, over, surging, facets, glances, wears, beams, bemoan, well, magical, surgical, flowerings, breathe, stormy, values, bleeds, owners, honored, rents, rinsed, wondered, again, revenue, sizes, into, threshold, threads, masters, focus, on, pens, merge.

LEVEL 164: THE IN-D-MENTS:

aAssigns, governed, confluences, scrolls, earliest, encounters, consciousness, previews, preciousness, realms, lights, programs, series, planets, lights, orion, healed, rays, eternal, ever, stores, lasted, affluent, swept, mixed, serials, heavens, thresholds, types, zones, lower, realms, midst, temporal, locals, systems, multiple, tesselations, fleshly, annoints, revolutions, runs, governs, rules, regional, recent, eventual, mid-ways, councils, accumen, controls, councils, thrive, imperfect, counts, ran, involutions, resolutions, Gods, reap, shown, fusion, folds, fluids.

LEVEL 165: THE HERALDS-MENTS:

Personable, cyptic, Enlil, Ahab, Abel, Adam, Cain, stern, outreached, scholarly, emissary, compliance, duties, orbits, clouds, ships, times, lively, stars, shepherds, herds, stock, noteworthy, knees, bent, compares, prayers, duality, ends, worships, chariots, dreams, divine, ovations, pressed, texts, flocks, Bethlehem, lightly, brought, four, bright, eagles, visits, vehicles, aerial, sights, exist, several, notes, rivers, nations, Hamitic, Nubian, Akkadian, trips, Saharas, kings, frankincense, Arabian, myrrh, kings, Sudan, peace.

LEVEL 166: THE Nth-MENTS:

Nth, degrees, teslan, blueprints, matters, materials, physical, cycles, intellects, mutual, language, powers, lines, networks, necessity, expressions, coded, planes, planets, insights, vibrations, composures, comports, english, ophanims, messengers, Metatron, strictly, gridded, involved, established, cells, resolved, structure, sunlight, ranges, systems, examples, samples, energies, orderly, orders, transmit, trued, folds, fluids, flows, flowers, flocks, voiced, voxley, rainbow, key, chief, look, coil, rock, gem, spiral, rest, harmony, peace, sacred, river.

LEVEL 167: THE CRYSTAL-MENTS:

Necessary, necks, now, next, necessity, nudged, smiles, stones, flesh, general, sent, bought, sides, information, processing, A-line, B-lines, plug, solars, grids, formations, tens, timely, maser, controlled, examples, samples, co-participants, planetary, tables, manual, creations, levels, chronomatic, growths, status, intellect, initiated, known, astronomic, transits, transmitted, collectives, sideways, biomes, substations, chinese, crowns, evolutions, resolves, resolutions, precious, ecosystemic, systems, conglomerates, confetti, participates, filly, more, studs, eruptions, showers, stretched, strips

LEVEL 168: THE A-MENTS:

A-lines, A-times, A-typicals, A-systmatic, A-lists, averaged, ashen, ashed, aaron, aston, ascensions, marlins, martins, dolphins, A-brand, A-baked, A-linear, breathing, fires, smokey, borne, stitches, parked, stance, ozone, carbons, monoxide, schooled, junctions, surveys, blazes, created, digs, discovery, stores, arranged, ranges, packets, buckets, rocks, precious, synthetics, instills, spurts, suites, stripes, stetchings, sustains, seals, fresh, crystals, divine, light, absorb, honestly, write, elk, sphinx, o, the, border, to, six, path.

LEVEL 169: THE APPROACH-MENTS:

Avenues, certified, live, aventurine, interiors, estates, conservations, landed, elasticity, villages, photographs, municipals, jumar, advents, strategic, signals, rented, rentals, politics, statistics, straps, meet, manage, gathers, specifics, specifically, neutral, specifically, neutral, natural, systemic, flows, loyalty, customers, stores, service, copes, casting, utilities, latent, century, lather, processed, participated, standards, opened, copes, casting, dice, dye, steering, stamping, crossfires, enthusiastic, extrapolate, external, aggregate, attends, rescued, rafters, rushing, rapidly, quickly, currently.

LEVEL 170: THE GENE-MENTS:

Bladder, control, contra, with, again, yes, sun, atom, conscious, love, consciously, add, 52, times, rings, bears, ruler, runs, days, red, red, red, red, red, red, red, red, red, red, blue, blue, blue, blue, blue, blue, blue, blue, blue, blue, blue, green, green, green, green, green, green, green, green, green, green, green, green, orange, orange, orange, orange, orange, orange, orange, orange, orange, orange.

LEVEL 171: THE FUEL-MENTS:

Prophetic, sufficiently, Moses, Elijah, accountable, count, gentile, sufficient, republics, phases, impel, compel, bells, republics, Parthenon, victory, belabours, laborious, labors, elections, services, strewn, dwellings, entrance, thuban, garments, days, respatialized, variously, penultimate, ultimate, recompense, days, partner, givens, guidance, necessary, quickens, visuals, visualized, dwells, pointed, galactic, ophanic, dimensions, plurals, materialized, accountable, counted, quickenings, quickly, coming, into, clarity, collectives, powers, regional, regions, locally, polaris, myriads, 4th, variously, activities.

LEVEL 172: THE GENETIC-MENTS:

Father, son, pyramids, 9, warps, orionis, maps, 12, one, delta, epsilon, zeta, tal, harmony, DNA, codes, bottoms, RNA, topics, Shekinah, wheels, invagination, crystal, solar, spectrums, blemished, removal, ourselves, chakras, physiology, predilections, Krishna, 2, translated, films, data, based, magistrates, lions, throned, stars, seeds, ages, gitas, bio-pyramids, Mahasamatman, attaches, stars, interiors, enlightened, communications, telethought, Hebrews, Chinese, repressed, instructions, Davids, pyramids, dimensional, eternals, fosters, imagines, gains.

LEVEL 173: THE INITIAL-MENTS:

Squired, cashed, checked, named, numbered, lamb's, life, NASA, OB-GYN, MD, PHD, PA, God, mothers, RNA, DNA, H2O, CO2, matrix, glue, matrices, O2, willingness, owners, loved, lightwares, lost, win, surrenderings, into, manageable, dreams, doubts, go, gone, implores, implodes, motives, reaches, dues, ovens, wpa, pause, clauses, oz, topics, monograms, measures, mounted, pranced, unisons, units, eunuch, obid, ovarian, guests, taj-haled, towels, terms, BA, BS, MFA, MBA, CO.

LEVEL 174: THE RESONANCE-MENTS:

Resonance, basis, basically, bests, bovine, mastif, masculine, assured, height, through, curved, bristols, papers, vibrates, vibratory, dwelt, doubly, fashioned, fascinations, focus, forms, amounted, surmounted, summons, sustenance, surfaced, ovations, applause, rescues, resonant, resonance, ruptures, radicals, freeze, frozen, flirted, formalize, duals, depends, deepens, doubled, sustained, stung, cause, God's, doves, darest, darings, courage, courts, countings, casts, doubled, durations, dips, doubts, cancelled, hearing, heard, sound, enhanced, massive, orations, gallant.

LEVEL 175: THE MATRIMONIAL-MENTS:

Activities, biochemical, emanations, virtues, seeds, matrimonial, bodies, crystals, romanced, channels, sexual, holy, telethoughts, biochemical, represented, sanskrit, tibetans, inner-connections, civilized, egyptians, hebrew, sanskrit, chinese, repressed, instructions, David, pyramids, dimensional, eternally, telethought, rings, communications, bodies, sexuals, channels, holy, attunements, emanating, eights, enlightenments, enlighten, chakras, kingdoms, flowered, bodies, Christs, stars, brilliant, three, eternity, minds, originations, embodies, lights, two, formal, Christs, words, experienced, primes, proper, honeymoon, eighth, ability.

LEVEL 176: THE IN-LEVEL-MENTS:

eEnergy, cast, planes, amps, connected, mounts, quaint, newest, necessary, necessity, loved, leaders, costs, carriage, wires, worshipful, furtive, selections, replenished, nourished, generative, stated, reasons, sustenance, laughter, freed, fortunated, vast, awash, lasting, logics, mansions, temples, types, neptons, laps, natural, rational, radial, opens, reasons, news, into, loves, solves, built, plugs, electricity, leptons, venerated, resonant, zeros, ended, levels, simply, radical, simply, generated, stuns, currents, daily, surgeds, leaped, lights.

LEVEL 177: THE FORESTRY-MENTS:

Suave, stands, bristlecones, posts, commands, bash, forests, warms, hair, lands, bugs, rains, bureau, ladders, tops, management, tops, rotated, ropes, sources, misty, fantastic, tunks, trusts, mystique, journeyed, moths, groves, Sundays, discretions, generals, joust, trees, understory, music, shops, roots, pisgah, ozygenate, spokes, gatlinburg, fires, state, parks, everglades, pines, extinct, bask, chlorophyl, opens, obligated, redwoods, sequoia, California, cypress, texas, type, kinds, buds, leaves, roots, shield, fields, will.

LEVEL 178: THE MATERNAL-MENTS:
Motherly, mothers, cells, instructed, humanly, wards, sophia, pistils, pillars, mentals, spiritual, coded, instructs, jewels, oracles, paradigms, unions, physically, reached, divine, selves, gridded, organisms, transplanted, consequences, spectrums, mines, timed, cells, immokalee, images, jointly, experiences, spirals, visions, delgates, delineated, languages, careful, selections, expired, aspects, lay, ohms, esh, past, present, future, divine, harmony, light, footed, reach, out, in, love, will, to, live, light, embrace, beforing, choring, love.

LEVEL 179: THE PROMOTIONAL-MENTS:
Ads, advertising, crag, mountains, billboards, lines, erased, creeks, valley, door, prizes, refreshments, freedom, free, things, professional, ariel, handshakes, warmly, written, papers, flyers, funds, raised, registered, ballots, papers, endcaps, classifieds, lanes, purchases, orders, webs, car, vans, magnets, business, cards, airplanes, donations, tax-free, banners, bullhorn, megaphones, celebrity, endorsement, grands, openings, marketing, skills, strategies, radio, television, websites, motivational, commercial, speeches, coupons, specials, offers, speakers, videos, events, red.

LEVEL 180: THE WEDDED-MENTS:
Joined, weld, joint, elbow, feet, fertile, conferences, churches, flesh, market, mulberry, stock, collectives, streets, avenues, technological, transformative, enunciative, asteroids, comets, earth's, atmospheres, trunks, carry, thresh, boquets, shops, outlets, ages, risks, security, safety, tasks, theories, thorax, rings, heads, missionary, poses, sacral, tantric, sung, sang, links, gathers, chapels, temples, binds, adheres, adhesives, glues, matrimony, love, vows, ceremonial, currents, causes, loves, faiths, taxes, legality, green, teal, blue.

LEVEL 181: THE BLUE-MENTS:
Cards, money, sex, power, names, christed, self, high, marriages, energetic, commit, leads, gilded, sky, seas, eyes, lips, hands, cars, babies, lightening, skies, blis, chakra, throats, communications, written, spoken, penned, fountains, austin, raphael, sand, ra, ariel, waters, nests, hawks, moons, birds, joy, fish, express, experience, flow, flowers, ball, tests, dams, creeks, balloons, manners, mannerisms, greens, yellows, ferns, herons, heard, fish, dog, cats, animals, topaz, blood.

LEVEL 182: THE TREE-MENTS:
Species, venus, specials, venus, hemlocks, 500 years, oaks, cypress, 23, fine leaves, maples, bark, stem, trunks, earth, sky, photosynthetic, xylem, phloem, cartilage, cellulose, matrix, songs, trees, lights, luck, tease, bootes, naves, needs, met, people, places, seated, stretches, peaches, sky, life, leads, links, call, vary, varies, only, when, givings, life, earth, money, ceredwin,

comparison, comparables, climb, mercy, fellows, forks, colors, changed, focus, caused, divinations, divine, desireable, Denali.

LEVEL 183: THE RIDGE-MENTS:
Peak, points, breats, land, sold, success, appreciates, gauges, engaged, orders, owns, women, curves, men, stand, ample, apples, treed, cores, coming, attractions, by, pieces, lands, homes, ridges, pointed, made, real, wedded, initiates, landed, links, lists, won, lives, in, to, a, to, example, reinvent, purest, loves, content, heart, the, alcove, start, ridden, intent, for, the, hearing, chosen, as, you, annoint, crags, befriended, chosen, written, ridden, rough.

LEVEL 184: THE IN-TRUTH-MENTS:
Concrete, precision, allowances, laughing, tribes, trusting, settlements, Iris, Isis, attitudes, aspires, assigns, tools, harvests, hundreds, movements, glee, rays, jays, stirred, operates, honestly, strung, words, across, heavenly, pages, the wages, paid, have, been, and, we, since, have, seen, that, worthy, gates, await, us, for, the, chored, sources, of, electorate, numbers, and, the, slumbers, in, spaces, blessed, in a victory, truths, greeted, truthful, passionate, mirrored, mirth, divine, worth, relating.

LEVEL 185: THE IN-HEALTH-MENTS:
If, death, is, sin's, wage, then, what, is, wealth, is, health, paid, for, the, merciful, plenty, happiness, spices, her name, daily, explore, in, your, door, heart, your, life, let, merry, men, nest, let, wealthy, patrons, grace, your, door, when, you, discover, that, death, deludes, you, and health, is, a, wellspring, to, the, mystery, solved, of, eternal, revolution, an, early, springs, an extra, strip, steps, a, marriage, too.

LEVEL 186: THE IN-LUCK-MENTS:
Listen, luck, exists, when, you marry, privilege, to spatial, adjust, and, notarize, your, spirit, in, precious, alert, and, the, miracle, explains, your mission, hear, a, lucky, one, luck's, door is, how, you are, loved, and where, we've, spent, our, youth, the, billions, and, the, win some, wonders, won, through, journey's, paired, to, a, central, patch, and, the maximum, exposure, to, purely, perfect, love, now, that, dears, is, luck, light, visionary, mobile, light.

LEVEL 187: THE CONTOUR-MENTS:
Contoured, cushioned, in, year's, neglects, and, backs, broken, when, watery, deaths, reach, a, new, grade, the, landing, leads, us, across, planes, to, surrender, and, the, mender, signed, for, historic, resolutions, and, a, merry, signed, to, beatific, stance, along, the, shores, james, blue, and the, tongues, wagged, less, when, chosen, becomes, justly, contoured, nodes, rules, kneel, truth, told, emerald, city, tablets, waterfall, fish, land, love, exasperative.

LEVEL 188: THE WANTON-MENTS:
Wanton, has, come, to, a, thundering, alert, with, aids, and,

Helen's, troyed, without, convictions, of, lasting, Athenians, who, live, to, the, memories, married, to, living, extends, go, willing, surrender, and, the, parties, in, forget, where, will, you, be, when, your, memorize, becomes, memory, and, your, meanings, get, launched, for, the, sending, over, board, to, a, new, home, the, light, you, own, is, now, love.

LEVEL 189: THE CHROMOSOME-MENTS:

Earth, is, won, through, our, chromosomes, and, the, ones, that we, surgically, shielded, now, can, pierce, a, coming, rail, the, victory, danced, in, emotion's, reap, and, the, seeping, truth, which gathers, create, at 30 a, shore, again, and, steps, forth, blooming, as, a, human, sperm, and, egg, unites, to, given's, sight, for, the, healing, revolve, a, return, to, center, and a, heart, for youth, remember, every, age, every, cell, every, inherit.

LEVEL 190: THE IN-PLACE-MENTS:

Place, your, spirit, near, the, dart, and, sew, an, option, for, this, opinion, let, love, reign, and, never, the, design, express, apply, to, sky, schools, and, fly, home, dove's, winged, well, into, twirls, into, this, told, older, new, ages rings, vibrationally, and, a, rations, can, range, range, into, sanctuary, for, the, shillings, spent, in, revolutions, let, love, reign, place, the, end, dears, are, nearest, john's, heart, love.

LEVEL 191: THE INDIGO-MENTS:

Knew, lives, dees, lists, lisps, lassoo, mosey, indigo, moves, nuance, nears, strays, black, mountains, justice, inside, fates, indigo, blow, blues, bolder, clays, day, yellow, winds, galley, galleries, matthews, pens, potions, motions, lotions, leads, revolutions, evolutions, furnishings, community, is, built, gather, here, near, love, as, a, theorist, nutritionist, and, lover, I have, a, way, with, worded, woundeds, may, we, be, well, to children, love's, indigos, now, come.

LEVEL 192: THE MOBILITY-MENTS:

Aunt, find, waters, again, durations, examined, savory, juices, moved, make, a, move, to, reverse, stagnation, and, build, sanctuary, in, lateral, opinions, psyche, psychotic, psychological, theories, memories, menu, doves, diary, daily, pen, centrally, settled, metal, burned, warped, twisted, wheels, turn, planets, collide, life, swirls, swells, and people, squirm, to, a, new, understanding, of, the, motility, of creation, and, mobility's, death, births, illusions, homes, humans, again, abut, examined, savory.

LEVEL 193: THE IN-RED-MENTS:

valuable, import, favorites, flush, fishers, fissures, crescents, villages, earth's, memory, mars, impact, vibes, vibrated, justly, active, sewing, opens, classes, requests, yes, God, to, red, love, God, will, we, yes, that, sings, to, who, says, august, holds, joys, driven, avenues, come, area, has, infusion, lend, an, bistro, rooms, news, terrific, zoom, terrific, mental, met, by, love, one, happy, divine, family, light, ownership, own, inside, out.

LEVEL 194: THE MIRACLE-MENTS:

A, rest, in, miracles, has, come, alive, and, we, arrive, arisen, too, and where we, two, were, recalled, a, remembered, grasp, grant, mystics, an, ingenues, trip to, a, chance, arrival's, experience, internationally, serviced, in, love's, diagnose, and, the, parts shown, love's, spinal, guards, rest, foot, sized, into, prices, brands, days, spheres, factors, aptar, mobility, crews, chances, merchants, environs, immediate, amounts, manners, mannerisms, sixty, days, to, a, nearest, star.

LEVEL 195: THE ORANGE-MENTS:

Peaches, gathers, manual, returns, tsali, noble, showers, overheard, touring, manners, stunning, days, inquiry, stresses, flowers, moves, maneuvers, rewarded, trailed, noblese, oblige, shows, overhead, planes, stampedes, capabilities, during, a, required, for, fruits, managed, notably, fellows, boulders, relationships, curves, shadowed, tuned, patterns, around, strands, suns, in, love's, orbitals, fills, and, told, wiser, a, glowing, bliss, passage, of, smell, into, love, the, light, is, on, know.

LEVEL 196: THE MENU-MENTS:

Eggs, towering, muffins, steaks, chickens, algae, fungi, manual, powers, heightened, registration, as sent, into totality, bent, and, yellow, sandstoned, into, egyptian, natures, patches, catch, towering, infinitely, instinctually, standards, randomly, aroused, for a, meal, of menus, spent in, staring, stars, carved, cultures, spiritual, mergers, worths, are factual, extended, on, the stern, eyes, for, threaded, respect, respect, on a, sensual, store, of dense, deliver, born, free, of, all, and, fed, eternally, well, the, sun, light, speaking.

LEVEL 197: THE IN-BUD-MENTS:

Budding, opportunity, amazing, lists, of, simply, tasks for, features, and a neutral, retire, to moving, corners, matched, to doorways, through antiquity, the annual, surrender, for, flashes, caught, capably, on, the narrow, days, dealt, with, when, eyes, are lost, without, seeing, for the, fundamentals of, a grown, occupation, to, a healing's, vision, and, the, thundering, clouds, unto, love's, maturest, rewards, a, personal, spiral, son, through, love, only, love, spoken, support, won, one, to, love, giving, caring, trace, design.

LEVEL 198: THE IN-FED-MENTS:

fed, eyes, lashes, lids, matching, shown, showering, chances, culpable, without, and within, our threaded, thrusts, to a lasting, nudge, fragmented, factually, to, fan's meal, of a, lasting, buffet, at, the table, set, stars, stares, sounds, stretching, full, monthly, filling, funs, within, creamy, red, began, begonia blue, pools, strung, in, caring, seeds, of, a, laughter, filled, mast, sea, wide, in a, wise, way, settling, grounds, matched, materials, know, your, purpose, drop, all, your, past.

LEVEL 199: THE IN-SEED-MENTS:

grew, grown, creates, creativity, created, worn, wonderful,

wonders, morning, bemoans, beauty, dealt, duty, a cause, for, lifetimes, the flaws, who, lest, seeded, more, matching, found, wanting, in, waiting, haunting, throughout, heraldic, warrants, onto, surrenders, doors and, in, daily, doors, a, mavericks, poses, are pared in, posing, pools, for, fellows, flawings, unto a, thawing, exact in, eccentric, clearings, detailed, into, thorough, cleansing, known, for, a, seed's, lines, tense, let, life, give, love.

LEVEL 200: THE FOOD-MENTS:

Feeds, on, level, listing, cubes, without, and, within, a, welcomeness, unto, shapes, shifted, fox wise, dog, deep, animals, cured, on, keeping, grounds, for, a plan, unto, doors, opened, as, onto, squarest, squires, who, keep, their, doorways, locked, into, patterns, on, signals, symbolic, to, a, thronging, nudge, fortunate, for, landed, meals, at, other, ways, unto, love's, soaring, husbands, wives, women, men, movers, lovers, laps, cleared, entire, hour, love.

LEVEL 201: THE PROTEIN-MENTS:

Aminos, liquids, commit-ment, peace, peaceful, days, nights, minutes, missions, durings, daily, restart, the strength, on, stronger, middled, fundamentals, years, lasting, proteins, breads, which, grew, medicine, strong, in a, strengthened, powers, places, find, a spot, where, sacred, doors, strong, lavendars, onto, secretion, in a, green, roses, poses, meetings, met, where, heart, and, breath, meet, abha, lotus, gates, unlock, freedom, to, love, one, love, all, love, love, peace, pure.

LEVEL 202: THE NUTRITION-MENTS:

21, rays, proteins, too, aminos, infernos, walking, watchers, matching, marching, herbrew, flaming, speakings, stores, traveled, roadways, registrations, mailings, sugars, soothes, storage, leashed, to, a, cause, of, nutritional, wanderings, in, secure, patches, of, fashionable, freedoms, focused, into, nocturnal, dares, staring, conclusions, and, the many, maintained, when, all was, planned, into double, daring, rapturousness, for, love, making, space, light, fragmentation, a, healing, bye, to, heal, love, always, fit, love.

LEVEL 203: THE COLOR-MENTS:

Yellow, green, red, blue, aqua, teal, peach, mauve, fuscia, acknowledged, colors, changed, seville, where, we, stand for, the mission, made, possible, in, a hand, mercy, direct, rainbows, taos, gifts, remember, written, love, ring, free, in, patient, delivery, to, a cause, and the, clauses, conspirant, lodged, best, western, in, colorful, spreads, stages, since, sent, to, a natural, natives, nativity, born, here, near, the colors, of a, clarifications, dues, gem, peace, happy, times, love.

LEVEL 204: THE EMPIRICAL-MENTS:

Imperial, blues, emperical, evidences, of, the, red, inside, extreme, regimes, of back's, define, are, given, soul, free, delivery, unto, a collapsed, regime, called, emprically, evidence, for, a trails, within, the choirs, to sing, cause, a law, of, natural,

physical, mental, expressive, triangles, met, form, pyramids, to stars, and David's, osirion, ring, is, worn, into, smooth, recovery, of, all, loss, rejoin, the throng, and, the, throne, energies, unto, long, absence, and essentials, and the pictures, on, too, love's.

LEVEL 205: THE IN-SPIRAL-MENTS:

Spirals, into keys, and, hearts, within, declare, from, daringness, to, guests, along, a, song lines, existence, for, ended, sequences, associated, syrup, wet, with human, chords, and the choirs, required, for angel's, paced, red, blue, corpuscles, opened, too and, there, we, were, sainted, too, for, a fellows, ships, which, narrowed, to, include, a widened, wisdom, where, are, you, due, to, a cataclysmic, example, of, creation, God, made, God, God, made, man, man, made, God.

LEVEL 206: THE AFFLUENCE-MENTS:

Affluence, regained, recessionary, ranges, over, stills, shot, desert, deep, and mountain, wise, in, wonders, surrender, into, a dove's, dailiness, and, a guest, who, measures, materialness, to, roots, related, and, an, accepted, gesture, ground, in remember, of, a simple, truth, that, men, exist, in, a, simple, kiss, of ancient, splendor, and, a, vendor's, recall, which, requires, essential, sounds, to, harbor, release, from, treasures, buttoned, through, in, miracle's, dues, and, a daring, for.

LEVEL 207: THE EQUINOX-MENTS:

Equinox, shocks, jasmine, jewels, sparks, forced, above, chinese, seas, and, drafts, drawn, signaled, too, and a savior, will, we, share, when, a, favorable, meetings, channels, spell, sought, and seek, for, the found, leaks, across, an entry, gated, girth, of, earth's, egyptian, soul, and, a priest, melchizedek, now, found, to develop, lands, into, precious, mother's, discs, and the, floods, us, guardians, watch, and, in, new, belief, of an, artistic, creator, who, knew, sacredness, in.

LEVEL 208: THE EARTH-MENTS:

gGrows, earth, others, bulged, systematically, jealous, murders, justice, may, lead, to, a, need, to worship, less, than, a chronicle, of light, here, and, a, new, perspective, found, us, pages, worth, as aligned, in the, vicinity, of mars, and, when, stars, melt, into, texts, essentially, we, flow, see, ishtar, osiris, thoth, and, path, hathor's, hermetics, our cause, when, we signal, cause we, employ God, as a beacon, into, engravings, seals and, primordial, abode, to, a, genealogical, earth, is near.

LEVEL 209: THE PRECESSION-MENTS:

Precessions, restore us, to idols, eclipsed, in egyptian, times, and the, risen, desolations, to, a plan, heard, wise, and thus, the christ, has said, as we, have, led we, have, found, and, the temples, into signs, confessed, as, witnessed, will, declare, us, employed, as, viewed, within, creations, living, waters, and, and too, become, a measure, for, the, earth's, equinoxes, as continents, floss, clear, through, into, warrings, stance, and the, decisions, discussed, as, resurrected, molecular, save, heaven, on, earth, divine, health

LEVEL 210: THE PLANET-MENTS:

Planets, are, the, DNA, of, God, know, those, strands, and, you, will, see, how, you, connect, and if, you, find, a lover, in God, you find, a house, and, a temple, and, a currency, sold, into, measureable, means, as a, hearth, is declared, due, your, fellows, lands, when, and where, the return, write, hear, let us, know, through, your hearts, alight, and know, the return, to God's, men, and, the thunder, mentally, of men, as, mentally, free, and, the hearts, of rising, trumpets, fun.

LEVEL 211: THE SIGN-MENTS:

Signs, have, come, to, signal's, invent, and, a heaven's, extent, is, now, ours, within, woods, of, a genuine, lane, as inspired, for God, within, causes, and, as led, we applaud, we marry, veils, into leaves, and, the trees, that, will, accompany, us will, inspire, generations, of the, retailed, positions, in all, alarms, as we, signed, and, we, signaled, authentically, throughout, your, day's, delights, watch, this, moment, and, deny, only, less, this, point, on, one, sign, love's, soft.

LEVEL 212: THE SYMBOL-MENTS:

Symbols, suggests, that, God, is, finished, with, a, plan, of, light, inception, and, that, a derelict, past, may, now, last, when, without, is within, and, a friend, now, found, is called, sentinel, to a throne, electric, and, a Metatronic, attend, has become, summary, and signal, and simply, caught, as throughout, we've, a lesson, and, a mission, into, miracles, askew, without, shouldered, respect, and, a covenant, born, in a road, berry, red, in recovery, of, God's, symbols, Hu-manity, water, falls, keys, picture.

LEVEL 213: THE FABLE-MENTS:

A, fable, has, run, it is, a, and, a course, for, a soaring, recovery, now, reads, electric, as, we, direct, our, funds, and, finds, to, a way, home, without, recovery, as, we, table, linked, and loops, score, any, direct, causes, for recovery, and we, have, found, a funded, foundation, and, the sanctuary, cause, for, an, all, "timed", event, and, the eventual, end, of timeless, we know, it, zoos, exist, for, mates, friends, foes, unite, into, one.

LEVEL 214: THE LEGEND-MENTS:

Legends, now, devotion, may, materialize, as, you, infuse, your, life, with, enthusiasm, rapture, and a, genuine, resurrection, to an essential, cue, called, classical, distillations, of, a, DNA, littered, when, we, spend, ashes, to, dust, without, cause, now, eternal, and, we, will, see, youthful, blush, in, rows, frozen, until, night's, days, meet, with, calm, seas, and, a, victory, for, all, humanity, may, we, shall, we, continue, limited, peace.

LEVEL 215: THE SERMON-MENTS:

Sermons, are, meant, to, the, highest, extent, when, doves, fly, and, skies, debates, for, eternity, have, whispered, in, the, ears, divine, as, we, publish, we, preach, a, simple, gesture, as, mortal, that, love, belies, our, incarnations, immortal, rewards, as, a, sword, becomes, plain, in, the, hands, of, the, few, who, renew,

a, perfect, parallel, existing, in, paths, super, imposed, in, the, cells, every, human souled.

LEVEL 216: THE IN-MOVE-MENTS:

As, we, were, led, unto, karmic, blends, of, the, absolute, spirits, philosophic, friends, have, discovered, a, detailed, philosophy, for, the, lights, eternalness, and, and, wisdom, welcome, to, a, universal, path, of, written, correspondence, which, will, last, through, all, eternal, may, we, mortal, remember, who, has, moved, near, and, deal, in, the, affairs, of, only, perfect, resolutions, and, the, evolution, in, your, process, birthed, humans.

LEVEL 217: THE ACCOUNT-MENTS:

Accounts, now, frozen, have, regained, ganges, green, land, and, the, traces, hermetic, will, lead, a, brother, Abraham, into, your, driven, teachings, as, we, count, accounts, opened, we, blow, the, bridges, to, lights, beloved, flames, and, the, firmaments, accounts, players, plagues, celebrity, fame, cleans, participates, fairest, fed, food, lunges, to, love, established, regard, for, a, word, for, love, God, is, brother's sister's, father's partners, husbands, wives, hu-mans.

LEVEL 218: THE AGILITY-MENTS:

Agility, may, handle, your, ability, in, language, as, an, language, as, an, eternal, sign, for, love's, incline, to, muse, over, suggestions, on, nearby, paths, and, these, warriors, ways, now, graced, magnified, rays, rapt, to, call, first, made, God, gave, nation's, stance, which, world, chose, a, truth, elastic, and, where, will, your, energy, seed, a revolution, here, in, this, agility, in, all, ways, healing, connection, peace.

LEVEL 219: THE SPIRITUAL-MENTS:

As, the, seals, are, broken, centuries, will, rest, where, the, miracles, most, dense, have, lain, will, you, lead, into, matters, on, love, will, you, flower, where, love, becomes, a, leader, and, a, friend, and, as, we, seek, sought, and, as, we, found, fought, and, when, we, lean, wrought, through, deep, surrender, to, a, flow, now, born, eternal, to, a, spiritual, deliver, silk, light, path.

LEVEL 220: THE MAGICAL-MENTS:

Magical, means, have, met, merry, shores, and, those, who, sacrificed, soar, as, saints, alight, in, near, recovery, and, the, seering, suggestion, which, shows, is, feared, without, worded, listening, and, too, we, remember, how, to, seek, recovery, as, a, filling, core, remains, sample, and, love, and, life, directed, into, a, vein, chosen, when, winnings, alert, level, leads, to, her, doors, magical, ways, love's, sharing love, home.

LEVEL 221: THE FINANCIAL-MENTS:

Financial, menu, to, a, starring, files, free, as, we, daily, reap, a, staple, load, of, magnificent, views, beaches, mountains, seas, and, the, earth's, recovery, as, our, dearest, friend, and, lover, she, is, our, mother, our, disciple, our, teacher, out, gate, our, lead, to, discovery, of, a, round, principle, which, bounces, bounces, amid the, stars, grove, grew, to, love, divinely, knowing, love, love, kind, direct, circle.

LEVEL 222: THE RELATIONSHIP-MENTS:
Principles, of, simple, discussion, have, met, your, door, and, where, will, when, will, ideal, your, seal, in, subtle, resurgence, of, expert, regeneration, in, simple, strains, as, strands, elongate, to, tie, your, day, to, marvels, wonders, and, signs, magnificent, to, love, where, will, you, lodge, in, a, nearest, qualify, for, the, only, in, the, highest, in, relationship, God's, and, man's, relation, with, pure, precious, love.

LEVEL 223: THE FUNDAMENTAL-MENTS:
Humanity, is, fundamental, cue, to, options, opened, when, loving, lives, in, hearts, fundamentally, united, at, the, score, and, score, and, the, remittance, sent, forth, when, love, leads, us, home, to, a, physical, example, for, the, throne, suggested, as, simply, surgically, removed, what, are, the, simplest, ways, to, fundamentally, find, a, a, simple, solution, allow, heaven, to, exist, in, your, life, and, find a, path, into, love, fundamentally, human.

LEVEL 224: THE RELATIVE-MENTS:
As, we, register, into, a, sentinel, exampled, we, will, woo, our, life, into, relative, exposure, of, the, standing, surges, along, lines, struck, to, a, signal, philosophy, where, will, you, land, when, you, leap, where, will, you, stand, when, you, keep, us, feathered, for, relevance, regularity, ratified, ratios, to, a, town's, pi, codes, where, will, a, lamb, lead, slaughter, away, to, the sun, of our, mutual, relative God.

LEVEL 225: THE IN-CAPTION-MENTS:
Captions, read, where, we've, stood, for, love, and, we, find, humanity's, missions, to, be, angular, encoded, geometric, allowing, living, breathing, believing, allows, linking, levels, and, corridors, into, the, departments, hu-man, across, cautions, cores, as, a, magnetic, mood, moves, us, along, triangulations, to, a, square, signatures, for, a, flashing, phases, placed, in, travels, touring, our, singular, purpose, quality, deepening, sounding, regained, wealthy, wed, of, love.

LEVEL 226: THE PYRAMID-MENTS:
Trees, of, life, functions, face, present, languages, seeds, the, I, AM, spinnings, octahedrons, cystine, lipids, transducer, coded, genetics, tetrahelix, tetragrammation, divine, DNA, RNA, deca-deltas, synthetics, will, lead, to, looser, codes, allowances, universal, orions 34.greetings, committed, to, a, living, legend, humanity, reprograms, evolutions, inherited, waves, Christ, bodied, now, employed, wavelengths, beach, forms, accomodated, 72, spheres, pyramids, hearted, founded, by, love, soft, on, my, mind, clear.

LEVEL 227: THE JEWELTONE-MENTS:
Emissary, enoch, views, earth's, rise, across, horizons, sentineled,

as, you, keep, God, sent, us, angels, heed, us, arc-angels, lost, now, found, have, returned, to, earth's, stormy, remember, of, a, caring, God, with, clear, recollection, regather, here, for, the, lift-off, may, you, be, well, liked, loved, cared, for, in, leaps, your, journey, we, love, you, basic humanity, finest, ride, throated, bounces, a, healing, stream, of, dreams

LEVEL 228: THE MOBILITY-MENTS:
Mobility, cures, codes, modes, mantles, moves, leaps, beliefs, bliss, transcendance, committed, contented, paced, beautiful, balanced, born, to view, played, into, leashes, rushed mixed, throats, for, a rally, causes through, God, is your, companion, music, has, mobility, of a, filling, rich, in rapturous, roses, red, ringed, rooms, as, essentially, befriended, along, dispersed, in, recall, to, regained, moving, stares, and, surrender, of, a band, who, asthetics, technologically, lure, magically, flushed, reaping, of true, befriended, causes.

LEVEL 229: THE GEMSTONE-MENTS:
Gemstones, are, cut, to, a, faceted, focus, on, a, definite, range, of, immediate, good, shepherd Arcturus, mapped, the, return, to, souls, ash, ani, lang, messianic, mid-way, stationed, life, energies, conversions, consciousness, time, zones, signaled, intelligences, how, to, return, to, love, el, concentric, vehicles, photons, matters, lights, deca, 64, membranes, letters, sequenced, codons, gems, lights, transforms, enumerations, 18 rays, 5 bodies, 6 temples, 7 seals, 8 lights, 9 versions, 10 friends, gateways spoken.

LEVEL 230: THE FULLFILL-MENTS:
Biological, com-plexities, crazy, relatives, homes, carousels, aliens, spanish, comforts, dwellings, interests, napier, nestles, internships, laws, accountings, soldiers, sole, soul, aloft, bodies, matrix, materials, muses, higher, realms, poles, reversal, positive, negatives, evolves, higher, reveals, more, accepts, nursing, county, language, flowers, life's, Metatronic, Melchizedek, meet, patron, partners, brains, beauty, imprints, players, evolves, solves, lovers, advised, stay, originals, glittering, letters, sounds, externals, spirits, doors, inter-connected, sections, spirits.

LEVEL 231: THE FINAL-MENTS:
Metatronic, Elohim, Mogan, David, ripen, crossing, alpha, omega, shafts, horses, swords, cruise, chants, minds, faces, adonai, increment, 1-1-1, blues, shoulders, heads, minds, middle, bottom, top, low, high, mid, upper, qualities, millions, cleansings, inter-related, fathers, minds, temples, golden, keyed, grids, circulations, harmonics, structures, structural, patterns, waves, inductions, offsets, vocalize, givens, entry, leaves, 76, names, adam, Christ's, Metatron, safkas, mena, Menematra, reached, restructured, ends, times, love.

LEVEL 232: THE ESSENTIAL-MENTS:
matrilineal, qualities, quoted, memorialized, under, engineered, engaged, drifted, accepts, lives, electricity, summations, written, nights, beckoning, mother's, worlds, Egyptians, beacons, won,

weavers, lastings, memories, lashed, canes, linked, ananaki, epiphany, advanced, softened, hummings, remembers, blues, wisest, splendors, summarized, links, lashes, canes, lined, genetically, lines, matrilineal, whistled, underneath, lists, sharing, her, gentle, caring, knowing, generous, gently, gentle, to, see, map, tribal, to, be, certain, spoken, heart, direct.

LEVEL 233: THE ENDORSE-MENTS:

Love, lives, here, legends, made, participation, meant, pulls, gestures, joins, factory, tires, plaster, tut, tiles, toals, fair, roses, rackets, racbet, made, churched, Madonna, white, nodes, nestle, under, days, detailed, reach, dupes, leaves, lunges, laterally, furthers, fastens, fascinated, funds, Venus, white, royal, street, brother, sister, villages, others, hadis, mist, St. Francis, doves, arcturus, wed, eight, eight, eight, 17 rays, 6 roses, led, "ka", essence, Metatronic, trees, willing, seal, leaves, vales, crossed, cured, fleet, dawn, stars.

PHASE FOUR
LEVELS 234 - 297
The Christed Self

*"If you are looking tonight for
Christ in the sky, approach a star called
Arc-turus, with a singing H-constant, and the
belief in humanity which a High Self
Esteeming extends."*

LEVEL 234: THE COHESION-MENTS:

cosmic has melted into your advice for cohesions / essences electric can elect your trusted cohesions / beings electric love your fled souling cohesions / miles are expected between your cohesions / telepathically elect the friends most cohesive / quotes now made can lead to the leading cohesiveness / humanity marries a living cohesion / lodges built are near the clearest cohesions / emotional freedoms have met your cohesions / colors soft can grow in cohesions fields / wings are found, cohesions freed / stages sought are made into freedom's cohesions / akins can mean clearly, cohesions / evolved specifically into a clearanced cohesion / rhythms reaching specific cohesions / detailed inroads into your cohesion fields / strands who married you have now survived the clarity of the codification for cohesion clearance / survive the basic flowing and flowering nadi line cohesions / points now made, cohesions flood / views into electricity for these cohesions fields / experiences including those atop Shasta have crested and cleared the age old cohesions / time yields forward into sweetened cohesions cleared / yields an electric cohesion / ectoplasm brushed and cleared, cohesions / spans manned and cohesed / intuitive fillings, cohesions / series electric now sent into total cohesions / points made, cohesions cleared / parts poled are clearly cohesed / cohesions became your telepathic portals / links are raided now and clipped clearly from cohesions adhesions links / allowed a forgotten clearance of the beat now cohesed / dialogues listened too, cohesions cleared / amplified the moments and our cohesiveness / natures sold, bought, cohesions merge

Notes; remember the double h-constant and the black mecca cube, now cured through love's insights and the purchase of the Nova Scotia first properties.

what is new to the doubled singular h-constant's cohesions / delays signaled have become a cohesions cleared zone / trusted confidants found, cohesively / patterns emerging, cohesions / flowers enfolding to a cohesion, Christ / flown over twice now, cohesions / rounds made cohesive / next, next nexus linking a cohesion / nexus points into your cohesion maps / structure reached / lateral move's meant / latent in the blend / cohesions are the glossary of lives lived / cohesions and the won in sundering glory / cohesions said "cohesions left" / cohesions and the devas of the winds intrigue with earth in bands / cohesions and the DNA stranded without the wand of the engine called exactly wind / cohesions and the genetics in strings and the codes beaded for love / evolves a maturity of these cohesions / cohesions and the glosses laid into pathways and strings / intuitives acknnowledge your cohesions / cohesions and the colors framed, love / forms and the cohesion inside humanity / formal interest is expressed in your cohesion cones / formations matured now add these two, cohesions and love / cohesions and the orders placed, love / specifics terrific in cohesion aids / cohesions and the silver cuts through the knife atlantean and the arcturian plane folded to meet the Sandy shores of Hilton's headings / cohesions and the golden body, golgi glowing blues

LEVEL 235: THE COGNITION-MENTS:

cognition and the recognition of who these planets building hear / cognition and the relative andeans ranged / cognition and the relax into a cognitions / cognition and the howling journey within love / authentically cognitive of the friend, life force / cognition and the saturnine reaping of the rapture completed / cognition and the mystical held in full vehicular view of love / cognition and the spans within humanity's strands / cognition and the solar rays who recall the DNA for an overhaul / recall that cognition which measureably enhances love / cognition is learned / cognition amd the brain, neurally linked to a sanction / cognition and the sanctuary called a heart / head into C and cognition / cognition massaged into G's level views of things / cognition and the earth forms melting to provide only purest love / a horse by this name, "cognition" / cognition and the whistler within our mountain's horizons / cognition and the nature of man / hallowed temples see / cognition amd the active ones who land near Shasta's doors, Telos within, love / cognition and the tapestry rich when a heart meets a landed philosophy / tapas blew in the fabric, cognition's streamings / taipan aided / cognition and the arts spannings, loved / quarters drawn into your cognitions / green days, cognitions stilled / cognition and the remembering for love / cognition and man who held an open hand for God, Moses / archetypes aiding humanity to regain their cognitions / cognition of the doorway into cumunros / cognition and the hermes tradition for winging capabilities / knees brought to cognition / cognition of the God within every strand, that's basic humanity / cognition and the feet which stand for truth within, love / hara spaced in the breathing / brains registering / minds amazing in cognitions / vascular flowings cleared to cognitions / similar subjects and cognitions / cognition and the daring volition for factual interests / creates a conduit for the life electric and the on which switches into cognition / anger past / cognitions cured and the schizophrenic blues no longer sung, know God / cognition and the genes split to reveal atomic splendor in the regal aplomb called love / frequent your cognitions regularly, remember MOHE* Mother's hearts *Mother's Organisation for the Heart Electric, a non-profit wing* / inspect your cognitions and find peace in truth and lovers / cognition and the ancestors cleared for all eternity, loved / cognition for the doorways held when the old swept knew into being, that's loved / cognition and the auric regain of the lights electric / auras include cognition routes to love / cognition and the systemic embrace of the Grand Design in Humanity / stressed a repeat for the genetic splendor claled huamnity, theme a cognitions / cognition and the thematic streets of love / arterial cognitions and the freedom to expand into love / cognition and the manned pages of love / cognition and those who persevere in the name of love / advanced cognitions acknowledged and gained through love / cognition for the grey son has left the reaches of this plane / cognition and the cords cut, again, reaching this ramp for the loading of planes / keys, harmonics, and curing of this planetary cognition / coded and reworded for the final respect / evolve into safe remembrance of God, a lasting cognition / cognition and the voiced planes of love

LEVEL 236: THE COGENCY-MENTS:

cogency and the hara within the bellies of love / cogency and the high ways to love / cogency and the lowering into love's pits / cogency and the logos laid across Solomon's sealed patents / cogency and the slowest pentacles called, Christ is here, love slower still / cogency and the returning electric through the Christ Consciousness Grids / cogency and the slows into stilling, loves frequencies created and the cogency extends to the wells of Armenia and the bootes of Gotten gifts / cogency and the frequency forgotten, now sealed, love cycles and the cogency signalled when love becomes fine / cogency and the similar gift of a clover four-leaved through the mineral mines of God / cogency and the simple Ouray of love / definite winds in the cogency for love / define cogency, hear, concrete openings given enhanced currency yellow in nature, Golden Fleeced / cogency and the effect for the angularity of love / cogency and the feeds into back lots of love / cogency healed you, find love / cogency and the airs made into love / protect your cogency well, find love / cogency and the listening process within, love / skulls cracked in their overloading cogency / cogency and the electric waters of love / minors extend into cogency clear blue / chakras sealed, there you have it, cogency / cogency and the centers cleared completely, Christed / cogency and tha strals planed, God's / cogency and the projects complete in love / vibrations cogency blue into love / cogency and the transmute complete, regenerated through the faith in the heat of God / cogency and the purvey posting to love / cogency and the particles within your purgin loves / cogency awareness installed / cogency and the illuminate insuring love / cogency and the simple clarity in love / wells cogency filled in love / cogency and the wee hours expiring to reveal love / cogency and the physical relax into love / cogency and the empires built in love / cogency and the past rays for love / cogency and the anatomy healed for purist details of love / entities intact in their cogency / cogency and the candles burning in love / white candles made spots in your visionary cogency / cogency and the buildings swept into seas cogent / cogency and the piped in miracles kept / cogency and the buildings fallen, concrete, still / cogency and the elements reviewed for love / elementals who enjoy sheer cogency / cogency and the lumens ampered into love / cogency and the allows made for love / cogency and the notes detailed in love / cogency and the votes for love's sealings / cogency and the people who posed to reveal a healed style / cogency and the placed ones who shielded volcanic exposures past the gateways of love / opportunity and the retailing cogency / subtle in here cogency / capacity soaring, cogently / cogency into maneuvers of love / cogency and the manipulate insured through love's forgettings / cogency and the advantage for love / cogency and the love trues / cogency and the stars dues / cogency and the whidby seals aligned into love / cogency and the adequacy for sealing love

LEVEL 237: THE IN-CONSCIOUSNESS-MENTS:

living is a consciousness zone / consciousness is the word / loved / patience hints at trueconsciousness / consciousness and the passages for love / consciousness and the peace prevailing into love / under the streamings / consciousness / consciousness and the standing waves bursting to reveal a breaking news / "God loves these people" / consciousness and the stars within God / consciousness and the epistles finished / this is it / God / apostles and the consciousness for final lifitngs / consciousness and the simple belief in love / consciousness and the guides who reach apostolic choice / sovereign regions reach a consciousness / consciousness and the reigning required for God / consciousness and the stands electric unto God' gates / consciousness and the human hearts for love / freed into simple disciplines for consciousness / fulfilled and still in her consciousness / consciousness and the baned heterocity of frivilous convictions about gated issues / consciousness and the homes built into love / consciousness and the glad released hearts / consciousness / consciousness and the greek who followed peaceful inclusions and creative explore / consciousness and the roman who did exactly this "when in" love / consciousness and the love who sailed into precious coves / equus equal in her willing consciousness / consciousness and the horse who held positions lessened in love / consciousness and the revealing creations for loved / consciousness and the passions placements for love / consciousness and the penetrative reaches for love / positive consciousness / consciousness and the positions chosen / for love / neutrons starring in reaching consciousness / consciousness and the neutrality of the corners called loved / consciousness and the spinning witnessed in love / gender freed / consciousness / consciousness and the seeds ascendant in the standing for Christ / consciousness and the mer fielded / consciousness and the ka spillings / consciousness and the peace who rested in love / consciousness amid the belongings loved / consciousness and the van built when the ban lifts / consciously / melds in a manner / consciously / consciousness and the molds fielded in love / consciousness and the clearing pour for love / consciousness airs through transparent flips / consciousness and goals reached / relax in God's loving / consciousness and the go now to love / consciousness and the god for love / consciousness / metatron / consciousness / consciousness meets melchizedek for love / consciousness and michael's kept / love / consciousness and the glossary finished for love / consciousness and the kindredness of love / consciousness and the arc-angelic keep for love / consciousness and arc-types sealed / consciousness and the h constant's hummings here held / constant in her consciousness and love / consciousness and the peoples who planed for love / consciousness and the dispositions sealed in love / personality and consciousness / consciousness and the kindness for love / consciousness and the enoch spells / consciousness and the blue / Kas of love / consciousness and the relationships rich in love

LEVEL 238: THE CONSCIENCE-MENTS:

aware, future, magnet, live , formed, cars, chapters, charge, light, ground, paths, merger, merge, shui, expressed, gateways, cases, lights, sunny, moon, prosper, prosperity, protect, stars, intuitive, letters, contact, beings, six, four, ten, females, eyes, energetics, healed, inputs, environs, immortal, jewels, karma, letters, raised, rocks, rooms, roots, heal, plants, trees, times, lone, meditate, people, past, due, over, televisions, phones, forms, kaballah, orange, techniques, beethoven, musical, revues

LEVEL 239: THE CONTAIN-MENTS:

oz, yellow, green, red, citrine, amethyst, violet, God, graven, grain, grown, habitations, homes, keys, siddhis, humans, programs, programming, remembrance, human, nova, lavendar, purple, ametrine, sapphire. growth, seed, life, flower, float, fires, reverence, lotus, contains, cluster, fifteen, relatively, initiated, minerals, composites, plants, animal, vibration, orange, abstract, abstain, elohim, forms, cosmic, rays, waves, energy, shasta, 300, 22, 55's, God, reached, effects, affects, matters, angles, automatic

LEVEL 240: THE IN-CODED-MENTS:

precocious, mass, consciousness, Melchizedek, completed, experience, books, written, exists, seven, planes, levels, wheels, lightening, every, present, love's, yes, sometimes, understand, principle's, one, met, meet, follow, love, true, love, spin, clear, gift, love, caught, legends, initiations, proportions, roots, branched, woman, skies, natives, sound, certainty, accuracy, understanding, grids, cycles, chakras, catch, search, grates, rooms, process, faces, supply, spreads, middles, loved, brands, vowels, substantial, substances, residents, residence

LEVEL 241: THE LOST-MENTS:

open, anchors, activate, found, fond, seventh, initiation, chakras, mystery, understood, chains, grids, dimensions, beyond, dealt, basics, request, evolutions, recommended, arcturian, mastery, crown, eyes, thirds, heart, throat, advanced, install, islands, initials, install, request, descends, channels, devotes, speed, endurance, portals, insure, sketch, activates, facets, numbered, chambers, anchoring, initiatory, potential, connected, requests, opens, slow, systems, located, keys, human, glands, tabets, follow, horeb, pisgah, sinai, temple, jerusalem, blue

LEVEL 242: THE NOW-FOUND-MENTS:

guides, friends, thyroid, pituitary, hypothalamus, activates, sketched, opens, shapes, realized, glands, chambers, angles, friends, individuals, facets, 48, views, fullest, images, visuals, emotions, bridges, geodesic, domes, merkanah, mighty, columns, anchoring, quatients, collapsed, dangers, puzzles, points, processed, evolution, effects, puzzles, throats, source, suitable, reigns, visualize, sources, petals, days, huna, manifest, powers, services, urges, sexual, habits, sleep, emote, appetites, required, gestations, conscious, intent, moderation, learning, victims, desire

LEVEL 243: THE DEDICATED-MENTS:

synchronous, searched, artemis, solace, perspective, diplomas, attendant, astrologic, counsels, emanates, esteem, attitudes, studies, effects, motivations, detailing, gardens, sacred, dynamics, living, service, teacher, masters, intensive, magnets, works, esoterics, urges, requires, sleep, habits, points, ideal, balances, moderations, concerns, desirous, emotions, liberated, completions, graduates, presidents, full, rapid, moments, points, burning, teaching, serves, services, God, rule, rare, occupy, sublevel, poles, expected, merges, astute, ascensions, continent, continue, types

LEVEL 244: THE EMIT-MENTS:

aquainted, extraordinary, sumo, sumatran, systems, discipline, difference, commit, focus, grids, quitients, levels, bardos, logics, miracles, pleasures, serving, reverberates, quickens, reaches, levels, transcend, ego, even, contracts, Jesus, Maitreya, periods, forces, electric, periods, completed, earthbound, develops, advances, liberates, transcends, kumara, interests, holistic, institutes, blood, stone, iron, betrayed, rewards, spirits, conscious, consciousness, vast, explore, cellular, dreams, nudge, bodies, computers, history, humans, surpassed, help, worlds, everyday, ordinary, intimate

LEVEL 245: THE OM-MENTS:

images, wisdom, love, essence, connections, all, things, angles, information, goods, impose, basis, thirteen, vibrations, lights, special, sounds, harmonics, music, matter, interrelated, creatures, proceeds, squares, human, circles, geometry, sacred, perfect, temple, laden, projects, robotics, complex, concentric, reconstruct, solomon, seals, warriors, premises, understood, substitute, defense, offense, self, deep, importune, fruits, snags, plain, divided, company, rungs, smaller, divided, central, measures, calculated, study, vesica, axis, tangent, points, splash

LEVEL 246: THE MANE-MENTS:

manifest, six, breaths, fourteen, thirteen, stacks, stacked, diamond, inched, geometric, proceeds, later, lateral, lineal, subliminal, polarized, life, squared, first, multiply, reason, harmony, kissed, consciousness, generated, touched, straight, lineage, systems, indirect, approach, polar, later, perimeters, inner, outer, coincide, circles, thoth, radii, third, ordained, possible, most, moist, centers, created, solids, platonic, investigate, sacred, graphs, conscious, edge, links, reality, energy, keys, giraffes, african, slightly, pi, ordinations, potential

LEVEL 247: THE PADME-MENTS:

rooted, hypotenuse, incidents, egyptians, inscribed, fours, eights, lengthen, sides, squared, structures, parameters, richters, Australia, Leonardo, spirals, superimposed, chromosomes, scientific, references, aboriginal, interpret, passes, perfect, reflections, females, males, brokens, solids, tags, perspectives, eyed, centers, human, vitruvius, looks, pieced, figures, looks,m asts,sticks,synchrony,cannons,indicts,indications, apexes, fits, sequence, entice, told, diagonal, teachers, axis, values, reply, squares, search, Christ, drawn, exact, light body, ancient, means, manuals

LEVEL 248: THE HUM-MENTS:

doodles, minimus, relieves, flowers, maximum, keyed, Da Vinci, means, stones, schematics, orbits, Christs, consciousness, systems, schematics, drawings, solids, drawings, shades, precise, plans, roark, rise, synthetics, expressed, experienced, fibonacci, able, ability, occasions, absorb, surfaces, cleared, pressures, moments, separated, reflects, designates, pressures, relief, block, reflects, absorbed, systemic,solar, entire, random, information, precise, serial, calculated, sections, japanese, jewels, ascend, descend, sacrophagus, shaft, queen's, corridors, evacuate, open, anterior posterior, relates space

LEVEL 249: THE 314-MENTS:

circumstance, evidence, sacrophagi, forms, mummy, forehead, primary, egyptians, sections, sections, brains, left, right, examine, museums, still, purpose, vial, recent, glands, excrete, liquids, foreheaded, levels, wells, purpose, Gabriel, exists, Michael, saint, happens, viewed, Assisi, Francis, Louis, saint, purpose, meaning, shows, consider, middles, schools, Horus, essential, points, involved, descriptions, tombs, balances, body, faces, Rafael, living, Peter, flails, rock, capstone, depicted, births, deaths, logic, sources, strategic-mentions

LEVEL 250: THE LAMB-MENTS:

lambs, reaching, spirals, scientific, habitations, treasury, immortality, reasons, Zohar, Osiris, habits, embodied, emitted, realms, Isis, resurrected, keys, unitary, samurai, permanence, again, ankhs, Cain, Abel, Enoch, planets, simbel, cycles, Metatron, enoch, planets, solar, costs, Kabbalah, galactic, judaism, universal, improvise, improve, ultimate, revolution, cosmic, multitude, improve, experiments, sensory, resonance, importance, originals, bigger, peoples, spectrums, spirits, actual, thing, know, notes, keys, fires, yod, works, activates, references, universes

LEVEL 251: THE STELLAR-MENTS:

cities, Gods, homes, transport, spirals, external, codices, scriptures, veils, requests, developed, greater, knowing, known, knowledge, dispensed, changes, forces, expertise, greater, prides, powers, rely, adventure, atlantic, atlas, celestial, kelvin, celestial, Gods, grandeurs, dispensations, dispense, requested, support, fullness, legendary, legends, Christ, images, places, periods, additive, basics, techniques, hunt, selves, molds, creatures, slept, fears, depart, conscious, barriers, rudiments, capable, thoughts, events, capably, kahunas, haphazard, minds, motives, married

LEVEL 252: THE STELAE-MENTS:

beneficial, restrictive, sleep, disorder, conscience, essential, derivatives, architects, daliance, recall, decisions, deliveries, details, basis, records, moods, careful, images, relays, records, stimulus, deluxe, blowing, formulas, jumbles, precognitions, delicate, controls, events, events, suggestions, bribed, elements, futures, cognitions, featured, dreams, methods, parts, reliance, alliance, bought, paid, traded, relaxed, restricted, accidents, changes, chances, reports, women, women, inspire, remembers, moods, reserves, affects, crisis, reactions, suggestions, events, chimes, jumbles, formulas

LEVEL 253: THE IN-STEP-MENTS:

turtles, freed, stands, knowledge, nearby, travels, secrets, ranks, magic, works, proper, mystery, purses, prayers, works, glutton, anger, experiences, substance, originals, legends, existence, exposures, DNAs, seeks, performed, acts, duplications, logic, errors, governs, laws, instance, psychokinesis, psychotic, exists, futures, unions, safety, strength, settle, beings, stages, intelligence, spectacles, groups, valuations, wars, fields, schools, established, ideals, knowing, pages, ages, ties, healers, contacts, made, possible, through, suggested, routes, plenty

LEVEL 254: THE SOUND-MENTS:

ghosts, canoes, tribal, spirits, rapports, efficients, souls, religions, efficiency, released, worth, needs, blessings, cleared, achieve, geographical, locations, homes, overlooks, doubles, practical, Africa, yields, coptic, maori, highest, practiced, pastures, postures, Madagascar, ancient, languages, Egyptian, island, supposed, lengthy, dogmas, over, contacts, complex, throats, mouth, confines, deepens, surprised, supposed, directed, forgoing, jargons, residence, Hawaiian-men-tality, seeds, scatters, meters, immediacy, missions, coastals, ears, eyes, mouth, throats, methods, meters

LEVEL 255: THE LADDER-MENTS:

alliances, hula, exalt, roles, luai, exulation, prayers, lilua, maturation, emotion, pearl, magic, waves, Hawaiian, position, potions, people, graphs, John, aloha, magic, meetings, mahi, gospel, allow, God, face, allure, lights, herbs, beauty, vision, motions, hands, effects, efforts, parables, feet, events, eventual, open, inserts, purges, human, God, woman, human-men, man, alchemy, powers, poetry, vulnerable, established, estimation, spirits, efforts, revelatory, motions, led, heart, least, effective, faiths

LEVEL 256: THE TRAIL-MENTS:

rediscovered, survive, forces, raging, paths, tablets, calm, kom, ombo, secrets, spaces, largest, slopes, choices, total, ceremony, ceremonial, offers, simulations, schools, carved, walls, photos, crossed, crocodile, pools, sections, hallway, exercised, extremes, tours, temples, eyes, offered, reference, intrigues, traced, places, spaces, shown, wedges, shape, boxes, hills, holes, tread, fed, extremes, loving, lowly, lower, path, lived, neon, neophytes, nuclear, family, exposed, granite, breathe, carry, forth, plans, filled

LEVEL 257: THE PATH-MENTS:

pathways, friends, portals-MEN, meaning, focused, forward, past, posted, gifted, gived, lived, good-bye, basically, due, aloha, allowed, leaves, goes, follows, finds, tales, primary, forces, negatives, emotions, meanings, genes, gender, airs, borne, berkley, stated, mission, purpose, proprietor, gifts, living, credits, mortals, moments, massive, leaders, discovered, problems, area, potential, manifest, destroyed, isis, offered, sparkling, jewels, offerings, dimensions, goals, reverse, temples, niles, modern, trips, offerings, friends, finally

LEVEL 258: THE BATH-MENTS:

ledges, translations, octaves, waters, shelves, tubes, channels, mates, calculated, experiences, reasons, passage, king, homes, incidents, installed, leveling, reals, happens, tetrahedrons, outlived, explores, origins, purpose, series, words, output, recessed, incessed, precessed, principles, yogic, torus, tubes, yugas, refracted, introduced, ancients, walls, written, templates, examples, events, zoos, andromeda, courage, illusions, volumetric, futures, secrets, flowers, shifts, poles, duats, wells, swims, various, toward, tantra, varieties, breathe, ability, studied, studiously

LEVEL 259: THE REFLECTION-MENTS:

feats, connected, historical, types, blood, O, B, AB, hb, A, positive, whales, waves, mayans, factoring, DNA, capacity, lights, transformed, learned, found, absorbs, impact, comet, postulate, genesis, planets, glyphs, planes, signs, ahau, cauac, etznab, caban, bib-MEN, ix, ben, eb, chuen, oc, muluc, lamat, manik, cimi, chicchan, kan, akbal, ik, imix, sacred, 20, uranus, saturn, jupiter, mars, asteriods, earth, venus, mercury, pluto, images, phrases, pictures

LEVEL 260: THE ABSORB-MENTS:

divine, harmony, bells, singing, song, voice, 13, operates-MENtal, physically, spiritually, inclusive, consisted, signs, stages, directives, directions, associated, consciousness, bible, revelations, have, brothers, essence, discover, Christ, alpha, atlantis, planets, definite, vasciate, attitudinal, awakening, bell, imagines, feels, thinks, greats, welling, glyphs, clockwise, associated, clocks, survive, heritage, definition, ultimate, interaction, atoms, constructed, patterns, earths, arc-angels, voiced, intimated, avalons, definite, athenian, centauri, astrals, grid, hebrews, merida, motives

LEVEL 261: THE GIVE-MENTS:

aquarian, piscean, purpose, off, ons, ins, received, babaji, darshan, cold, fusions, beauty, trust, harmony, peace, love, wisdom, lovers, truce, unity, compassion, humality, innocence, possessive, imprisoned, delay, chosens, century, batons, beloved, decibels, children, extraordinary, blessings, worlds, transitions, dimensions, destroy,always, rarely, transitions, heads, demonstrate, honey, happy, friends, husbands, stargazer,

forever, dreaming, breath, vital, winds, spirits, signs, sevens, axis, aroma, anomalys, witnessed, means, details, during sex

LEVEL 262: THE RECEIVE-MENTS:

receives, forths, ready, feedings, ones, designations, is, complete, designation, overs, chichen, itzas, align, temples, there, receives, meanings, elite, planques, opens, meanings, opens, doors, heart, merges, women, meant, twelth, eights, octaves, of, 10, forges, finds, sites, who, ties, stelas, to, forgiven, desciples, disciplines, finished, find, news, new, selphi, helenic, stacked, leaves, galic, data, mayan, minds, clears, completes, groups, as, salvations, written, codes, codes, cretes, created

LEVEL 263: THE IN-CHRIST-MENTS:

color, energies, harmony, tzolkins, red, 26, generations, light, life, white, wisdom, purified, black, death, transformed, yellow, life, expansion, chilam, blame, sacred, presented, tempted, flowers, seeded, ideas, growth, generations, principles, sexed, maxed-MENtalt, healed, ankles, energy, chimney, microchipped, wheels, rules, love, fits, finals, found, dimensions, cross, lords, peru, guided, shambala, tun, sapiens, homo, solar, shares, 260, energies, harmonics, hunab, ku, seals, again, voiced, heard, one client is reaching homeward still

LEVEL 264: THE SELF-MENTS:

caves, months, signs, maize, Gods, foreheads, swamps, courts, houses, cenotes, lakes, trees, stones, glyphs, caverns, earths, surfaces, watery, feed, visions, mana, pyramids, mountains, community, communes, ruptures, visitors, inhabitants, nobles, regions, vast, temples, skies, community, rivers, others, middles, skies, teleporters, sky, southern, birds, trees, worlds, oceans, atop, worlds, ecstatic, visions, repaired, two, purpose, coded, languages, avodes, defined, deify, necks, shoulders, heads, skulls, whole, beings, blessed

LEVEL 265: THE IN-HEIGHT-MENTS:

religously, handed, height, sun, mystery, shifts, world, wins, doctrine, depths, students, researched, equinox, greek, counts, globally, convergences, spores, spills, spouts, spurts, reality, hurls, blinding, unity, matrix, centuries, coded, now, bc, ad, baktuns, functional, emits, scenes, pieced, writers, coincidence, meetings, shores, explored, amazed, life, expanded, felt, perceptions, galant, lids, votan, helix, moments, wide, brains, reptiles, mammalians, ahau, stars, travels, glyphs, solar, circuitry, exists, galactically, coined in clarions

LEVEL 266: THE IN-DEPTH-MENTS:

channels, principles incoming, parties, agents, essences, fields, concepts, dances, sultans, pulses, waves, parties, sacred, method, counted, climb, tee, venus, sphere, stars, springs, edged, faith, mystery, starring, loves, births, sacred, fed, breath, huna, days, suns, moving, rhymes, interiors, deepened, star, hub, one, together, 20, depth, signed, dawns, hearts, acknowledge, critics, masses, forms, fusions, coming, returns, quests, doctrines, harmony, memory, jungian, youths, archetypes, eyes, naked, proofs

LEVEL 267: THE BREADTH-MENTS:
eclipsed, dancing, mudane millionaire, millions, sold, destiny, marketed, intentions, permutations, scholars, described, united, fireworks, pulse, radials, simultaneous, shaken, penetrated, pondered, representatives, connections, connectors, established, estimates, jumps, performs, words, channels, ashes, lakes, mexican, voids, 444, pockets, stories, kids, vortex, teaching, China, intentions, incredible, associates, friends, surveys, survived, levels, cycles, runners, loves, explore, rested, rests, semblance, samples, storms, wars, ends, forces, tops, conceptual, cases, sects, travels

LEVEL 268: THE MEASURE-MENTS:
drawing, buds, bins, itinerary, rooms, greens, blueprints, lost , boats, words, 1947, rosewell, permits, initiates, tunnels, copy, births, active, energetic, father's, consciousness, venusian, prenuptials, prenatal, prevalents, floors, books, belly, french, trains, luxor, encouraged, worlds, rooms, feet, crawls, realized, sights, suggestions, pointed, series, hathors, courage, actions, linear, pregnancy, sands, exacts, rattle, measure, hammocks, complies, masses, sense, gravity, tunnels, covers, attention, disks, pitch, tar, cubits, trues, truths

LEVEL 269: THE CUBE-MENTS:
64, 86, cubes, patterns, images, baby, bodies, inward, outward, primal, sciences, schematics, wheels, oasis, stars, fruits, rotates, bases, navels, ratios, improvise, frames, graphs, spears, currency, spins, pulsations, rules, episodes, diagrams, charts, proofs, sames, exacts, harmonics, cycles, music, sacred, inscribed, circuits, possesses, complex, radiant, qualities, matrix, Metatronic, Jesus, fish, bible, extracts, solids, pacts, waves, exact, originals, techniques, technology, narrows, traps, over, out, cares

LEVEL 270: THE TUBE-MENTS:
puzzles, happens, history, relations, predicted, technical, information, proclaims, sensory, spiritual, social, permitted, permissions, ranges, radios, unity, polarity, power, manifest, movements, structures, resonance, measure, rhythm, electric, waves, frequency, life, chi, tzab, Pleiades, rattles, canotes, sacred, equations, equity, births, ageless, ages, refresh, able, yucatec, mayans, rattlesnakes, crotulus, durissus, chichen, itza, great, ballcourts, parachutes, halls, atlantean, columns, galactic, resonant, light, interpenetrate, centers, balanced, periods, positions, stability, threatens

LEVEL 271: THE CHAMBER-MENTS:
showers, self, milky, meteors, moons, minds, sky, numbers, muse, symbols, coded, open, listens, extreme, vibratory, popular, 20's, 260's, six's, i, ching, binary, math, 2, 4, 8, 16, 32, 64, trigrams, threes, compared, levels, cancun, purple, coast, passages, syncs, features, words, zeniths, risings, heliacal, us, latitudes, considerable, magnums, shifts, poles, sacred, potent, symbols,

sky, hearts, minds, muses, snagged, warriors, movements, paths, helmets, crushed, constellations, galaxy

LEVEL 272: THE TRIANGLE-MENTS:
white, stars, orange, green, breasts, calabash, cleft, skull, concentrated, city, directions, lona, hina, hilo, maui, conceptions, born, springs, read, specific, myths, jointed, commands, ark, stones, lodes, antidote, demonstrated, crazy, events, eventually, solstice, noons, sixty, Pleiades, serpents, sun, quarters, bush, Hawaii, hatched, visited, grasp, Egypt, octahedral, crystals, living, homage, futures, calendrics, 2012, seniors, maya, men, bases, sounds, decorated, roads, chichan, success, worth, peace, profits, balanced

LEVEL 273: THE ANGEL-MENTS:
philosophers, theologians, religions, mental, spiritual, physical, emotional, round, square, cycles, circles, loops, back, front, wizard, planets, squares, eights, factored, into, love's, angels, stands, phallic, stories, fairy, factuals, adults, shells, po, sky, earth, men, lies, source, worlds, illustrate, live, breathe, smile, sleep, days, nights, each, guides, medians, transformed, polynesians, leaf, old, bends, folds, branches, parks, leafed, ancestral, trees, leaves, fruits, shoots, upward, goods, remain, lofts

LEVEL 274: THE SQUARE-MENTS:
helium, moderns, hydrogen, protons, electrons, neutrons, platitudes, plentitudes, conclusions, summarized, majors, broad, basic, source, brief, chants, prose, cultures, intitions, thoughts, bones, photons, fuses, earth, jumps, celebrates, bores, machines, existed, senses, anguish, assault, sots, feelings, mounted, humans, singles, body, owe, difficulty, forms, magnificent, transmitted, see, books, basic, express, feelings, source, genealogy, chiefs, duties, lot, legs, cleared, sections, mother, templates, prana, bodies, fields, leonine, images, joys

LEVEL 275: THE PROPORTION-MENTS:
octaves, universal, radii, repeat, betweens, romance, rumors, sphinx, records, perfect, harmony, divide, shout, ways, 42, circles, formula, strings, eggs, logic, four, circumstances, imagine, genesis, females, masculines, betweens, inward, outward, largest, grids, half, all, egyptian, schema, entire, 55, feet, 16, days, 72, means, 38, years, 11, minutes, circumscribe, superimposed, 8, males, female, least, likely, precisely, linear, divisions, repeat, respects, equally, same, whole, elevations, required, follow

LEVEL 276: THE RECTANGULAR-MENTS:
travels, bonds, title, pictures, corners, researched, pathe, parthenon, rooms, labyrinth, eyes, throat, gut, head, markets, suns, classics, classified, trance, ends, somatic, complicates, patriarcy, alleges, exists, fixtures, photo, directives, manners, dust, ashes, returns, flesh, rots, systems, notes, scales, muse, octaves, search, 13's, 8's, chakras, trembles, sacred, relations, musicals, bookings, depths, departs, boxes, ground, lava, fates, featured, religions, Buddha, Dharma, Sangha, paths, purges, electric, star, grids

LEVEL 277: THE ON-EARTH-MENTS:

perfect, six, generous, disciplined, tolerant, patience, practical, mind, instant, beatific, activist, visionary, states, pute, emotive, in, sighs, view, beauty, advanced, levels, similarity, teachings, accurate, active, lions, gazes, echoes, shoes, silence, conceived, doors, advised, wisdoms, concentrated, efforted, joyful, patience, tolerance, chased, shared, emotions, systemis, informed, speech, sticks, training, fruits, meanings, foundations, commentary, sticks, training, profound, founded, advances, chasing, pronunciation, sentient, beings, foundations, meanings, places, days

LEVEL 278: THE MOON-MENTS:

koan, haiku, plum, kuan, yin, coin, cherry, blossom, vervaine, jasmine, feng, shui, bamboo, circle, ceasing, alchemy, bordering, enterprising, direct, encounters, necessity, necessary, crimes, compass, translated, tiamat, craters, color, heaven, prayer, cool, sum, purified, heliacal, rise, marked, blue, full, new, cycles, enlightened, phase, san, deity, hospices, practice, cultures, inquired, tales, interim, mystical, areas, meditate, regards, issued, practical, query, covered, carry, forth, electrically, fond, loved, sunny

LEVEL 279: THE SUN-MENTS:

managing, untitled, source, intervals, corners, misery, monks, managed, lost, roar, religion, calcutta, handouts, articles, prints, picaresque, risque, literature, center, journey, realm, way, India, Nepal, Kailas, trip, support, emotion, realize, buildings, alchemy, power, lake, dialing, France, Azure, de, Cote, sutra, contemplative, monastery, candid, cushion, statue, Thailand, retreat, tradition, quest, ecstacy, China, Bhutan, practice, blame, gossip, truth, shed, light, faith, inadequate, beings, leave, planet, soon, day

LEVEL 280: THE DAY-MENTS:

identity, form, formidable, platform, version, ceremony, time, bodhisathas, balanced, mandala, love, letters, ledgers, legible, levels, minutes, hours, seconds, paces, 24, 60, 13, 360, official, officiate, financial, atmosphere, alliances, seizures, seizes, settles, sets, kama, conditions, creates, creations, curations, cured, saffron, seeds, pure, spoken, perfect, points, peaches, places, placements, pususant, purses, poses, pools, placements, open, spaces, elementary, cures, hustles, hastles, tugged, toured, yonder, sold, electric

LEVEL 281: THE EYE-MENTS:

eyes, lies, healing, peeled, porches, peaches, vents, vaunts, skips, eats, bats, bates, human, basic, harmonic, honey, funny, money, phony, foamy, purports, visualize, seals, opened, cut, matrix, material, natural, noted, valued, motel, motile, focused, fossilized, faults, fals, floods, fields, focus, source, crowns, melt, elevate, average, moves, starving, unfolds, medicines, integral, extremities, avenues, interpret, exist, companions, energy, experience, energy, alive, mechanics, obvious, obscure, purpose, pallets, positions

LEVEL 282: THE PHI-MENTS:

human, epiphany, aspects, spheres, training, entire, egyptian, experience, temple, doors, ratios, body, interact, interactive, mer, light, rotations, counter, ka, spirit, ba, interpretive, holy, afterglow, patterns, willpower, sex, survival, survive, survey, focus, stages, above, begun, God-head, octave, chakras, goals, pituitary, critical, crucial, desperation, balance, knowledge, activated, bodies, guides, energy, structural, epiphany, heart, emotions, sound, sacred, geometry, creations, spirit, existence, walls, worlds, sexual, chemistry, crowning, finish

LEVEL 283: THE PI-MENTS:

hardness, guides, fire, capable, insures, icons, history, principles, capacity, listed, joy, philosophy, religion, provides, bound, barriers, causes, sustain, compels, human, pharaoh, goma, minds, Buddha, books, principles, grief, performs, ceremony, extends, tolerance, visions, fullest, awakened, mid, sights, regard, events, paper, demonstrate, practices, church, thanks, reasons, crowns, 3, angles, sights, experience, profound, task, mundane, lives, everyday, shows, wisdom, wit, prose, elegance, strengths, released, advice, simple, ah men

LEVEL 284: THE RATIO-MENTS:

widths, remembered, ratios, pile, into, volumetric, purposes, pulse, participates, yellow, relax, faith, returned, crafted, relatives, doorway, sections, located, measures, math, portent, portable, fellows, freshens, lessons, gifts, spirit, human, way, worlds, centers, empowers, empathy, appearing, pyramids, sights, seen, hearing, tonal, all, phases, treats, both, understand, will, between, major, below, within, above, firmament, through, solar, heart, heavens, geometry, breadth, fingers, lights, walk, across, survival, access, sex

LEVEL 285: THE SET-MENTS:

close, side, except, trunk, notice, laid, straight, flows, placed, sense, orientation, opening, itself, mentioned, clock, parts, level, second, umbilical, spiral, chords, degree, face, nexus, circle, pop, continue, blocks, adjust, look, floating, transparent, partner, paper, front, clean, ideal, minutes, conform, above, win, coach, felt, energies, chakra, cross, made, complete, simultaneous, breast, around, middles, complementing, time, foot, overlap, dark, teach, switch, image, place, slowly, surges, past

LEVEL 286: THE SHELVE-MENTS:

meridians, expressions, impressions, bold, after, reach, tradition, like, dimensions, cranium, boost, challenge, thoughts, powers, mind, source, fresh, favorite, music, vacuum, pump, last, throw, wells, showers, arc, immerse, plunge, empower, profit, lust, drawn, deep, steam, filters, books, planks, stacks, broad, bolder, fill, cups, ice, ecstatic, waves, levels, lively, impressions, flowers, close, generated, reach, forth, cells, lights, years, dimensions, close, summarize, emotion, field, primero, segundo, trecer

LEVEL 287: THE LEVEL-MENTS:

traffic, market, merchandise, high, points, backs, body, paints, pants, clones, floors, ceilings, seals, deals, whorls, locks, tetrahedron, fingerprints, hands, flat, anatomy, toes, nose, eyes, bones, spleen, bladder, pancreas, gallbaldder, bile, duct, view, medulla, oblongata, epidermis, cerebral, vortex, penis, clitoris, perineum, anus, coccyx, scrotum, spiral, sexual, contentedness, fingertip, orgasm, deaths, illusion, points, labia, pleasures, meet, belly, where, navel, melts, sacral, sacrum, chakra, front, backs, uterus

LEVEL 288: THE STAIR-MENTS:

stare, tetrahedron, spin, cell, pineal, glands, places, loved, truths, beauty, harmony, peace, reverence, God, teach, follow, breath, body, mind, below, star, grow, drama, inhale, maximum, ready, doubles, upward, stable, relax, healing, inner, original, comes, points, large, moving, pressures, golden, forces, concentrate, navels, later, inhale, rapidly, halfway, electric, maximum, lungs, concentrate, size, taught, poles, move, composed, baby, conditions, magnetic, palms, polarity, around, king, sexual, lends

LEVEL 289: THE IN -FRUIT-MENTS:

dirt, earth, seeds, planted, trees, bearing, farmers, trucking, boxes, ship, oranges, apples, mandarin, stars, fruit, follices, buds, Paris, France, latin, America, voy, Israel, children, prodigy, progeny, prototypes, stretches, bears, bare, naked, fulfilled, felt, free, result, seen, clear, colors, Merkaba, chapter, subtle, energy, human, reading, car, leave, focus, enclose, touch, experience, possible, direct, field, ascension, make, light, once, auras, read, fixed, puerta, vallarta, born, again

LEVEL 290: THE TREE-MENTS:

tree, table, door, chord, valley, vault, ceiling, sacred, worlds, gut, plexus, solar, respects, earth, mayan, singing, ringing, release, reward, town, relatives, ancient, remembered, search, ends, near, magnificence, forest, ridges, reach, shade, leaves, rings, particles, wood, composition, beans, coffee, musicals, singing, brilliance, bits, defrost, tears, wipes, lights, music, systems, chromatic, navels, chakras, glades, glens, leafy, bark, needles, maple, deciduous, conifers, cypress, obvious, holly, green, brown

LEVEL 291: THE FLOWER-MENTS:

home, azalea, orchids, blossoms, dahlia, lilies, asia, minor, carthage, color, pistils, stems, throats, petals, blooming, yellow, green, leaves, pressed, painted, beds, pastels, primary, elementary, humming, birds, area, obvious, look, scale, head, bingo, geometries, navel, found, secret, because, suspect, according, fingers, searched, absolute, looks, trues, naturally, body, prose, spouse, sliced, salads, abrosia, nectar, form, sense, narrows, nature, arrange, bring, harmonic, talk, widths, also, another, there

LEVEL 292: THE INFORMED-MENTS:

expand, complex, waveform, reasons, movements, possible, simple, key, total, very, flow, chromatic, pairs, bolt, first, look, talk, star, about, piano, sharp, scale, keyboard, information, throat, activity, system, images, below, above, lies, find, within, navels, bring, relationships, single, said, begin, dimensional, related, harmonic, always, tell, topos, surfaces, examples, notes,

octaves, only, instance, flout, crown, pineal, third, eye, between, moves, personal, area, half, step, challenged, again

LEVEL 293: THE IN-LEARN-MENTS:

discovers, greens, boons, finds, signs, says, shows, follows, slowers, slows, blink, seeks, finds, follows, faith, plunges, powers, paces, places, remains, golden, yellow, arcs, love's, friends, atlantean, human, plunging, in-learns, has, occurred, one, led, to, follow, earth's, hollows, home, after, noons, yellow, orange, Aructurians, past, passes, made, life, returning, goals, speak, surfaces, plummets, to, real, tiers, cuban, second, days, mend, match, fled, fold, follow, flush

LEVEL 294: THE REMEMBER-MENTS:

long, loud, take, moments, remembers, hears, heralds, harks, singing, stars, dollars, money, spent, funds, energy, greens, spanned, continents, subsolar, subspecific, submaterial, subuniversal, subatomic, stirical, lyria, maniacal, Metatron, stars, are, open, Merkaba, mer, ka, ba, again, meta, elect, tron, make, yours truly—choice, take care—this, chance, to, remember, too, turn, on, remember, on, light, love, is, all, on, locate, like, abilities, marry, purpose, find, choices, made, elastic, regain

LEVEL 295: THE TRUTH-MENTS:

yellow, yellow, yellow, yellow, yellow, yellow, yellow, yellow, yellow, yellow, yellow, yellow, pink, purple, purple, purple, purple, purple, purple, purple, purple, purple, purple, purple, purple, purple, purple, purple, grey, grey, grey, grey, grey, grey, grey, tantika, trains, tantrics, mathers, divines, natures, ones, early, age, August, hunger, milk, curdled

LEVEL 296: THE TRUST-MENTS:

cures, collapse, encode, cure, fill, feel, hurtle, help, heeds, love, here, lord, rules, fundaculla, recollections, doves, days, during, Christ's, returning, 8, now, over, been, all, loved, cues, company, compare, rulers, 7, 12, 15, the, realm, of, the, atom, today, we, have, a, little, less, difficulty, with, this, point, we, do, not, escape, by, saying, that, the, universe, goes, through, cycle, after, cycle, of, big

LEVEL 297: THE FAITH-MENTS:

bang, and, collapse, world, without, end, turning, machines, you, are, my, avid, fellow, feeling, end, the, letter, expressing, to, the, basis, meeting, with, forces, of, nature, father, thank, full, moon, own, the, mother, trust, work, assisted, trust, love, life, two, sounds, good, call, to, see, happy, are, fun, welcome, science, math, numbers, astronomy, fair, act, lock, grow, up, to, break, up, and, stand, still

PHASE FIVE
LEVELS 298 - 361

LEVEL 298: THE JEWEL-MENTS:

External, jewels muscles, jewels throid, jewels diaphragm, jewels psoas, jewels cartilage, jewels quadratus, jewels nerves, jewels annular, jewels tibia, jewels leg, jewels femur, jewels biceps, jewels deep, jewels words, jewels knees, jewels ligament, jewels lumbororium, jewels narrowed, jewels false, jewels tooth, jewels small, jewels bone, jewels organs, jewels spin, jewels canal, jewels common, jewels superior, jewels back, jewels exposed, jewels veins, jewels compressed, jewels triceps, jewels small, jewels radial, jewels arch, jewels branch, jewels joint, jewels joint, jewels 40. elbow, jewels artery, jewels spinal, jewels part, jewels two, jewels superior, jewels profunda, jewels inferior, jewels blood, jewels thin, jewels roof, jewels walls, jewels layer, jewels free, jewels upper, jewels transparent, jewels endolymphatieus, jewels apere, jewels ductus, jewels shape, jewels letter, jewels c, jewels enter, jewels liver, jewels scene, jewels.

LEVEL 299: THE JOURNEY-MENTS:

Spleen, journey stomach, journey mouth, journey mall, journey intestine, journey colon, journey tibia, journey flex, journey plantar, journey abduct, journey hallucis, journey long, journey brevity, journey tendon, journey aciles, journey vessels, journey post, journey tibial, journey .internal, journey astragulas, journey cuneiform, journey navicular, journey ligament, journey bases, journey last, journey runs, journey grooves, journey knees, journey flexors, journey angular, journey opposite, journey runs, journey passes, journey surface, journey joints, journey grooves, journey slips, journey outer, journey shell, journey inner, journey posticus, journey waves, journey adjacent, journey transverse, journey middle, journey sole, journey tally, journey lower, journey deppens, journey brevis, journey lines, journey gradually, journey sheaths, journey toes, journey disappears, journey superficial, journey crossings, journey sides, journey arise, journey points, journey origins, journey whole, journey oblique, journey muscular extremity, journey.

LEVEL 300: THE ADVENTURE-MENTS:

Septum, adventures overlapped, adventures symmetry, adventures affords, adventures relationship, adventures of, adventures independence, adventures throughout, adventures a, adventures dependent, adventures state, adventures called, adventures being, adventures human, adventures exactly, adventures and, adventures precisely, adventures effecient, adventures affording, adventures is, adventures offered, adventures the, adventures elements, adventures as, adventures they, adventures arrange, adventures precipatively, adventures in, adventures spaces, adventures equivalent, adventures to, adventures ranks, adventures vice-versa, adventures occurs, adventures when, adventures acceptance, adventures becomes, adventures linear, adventures through, adventures operational, adventures orbits, adventures and, adventures the, adventures products, adventures of, adventures living, adventures are, adventures given, adventures frequency, adventures additions, adventures characterizing, adventures significant, adventures orbital, adventures shifts, adventures and, adventures the, adventures repetitive, adventures nature, adventures of, adventures reflection, adventures upon, adventures ordained, adventures localization, adventures osmotically, adventures.

LEVEL 301: THE ENIGMA-MENTS:

Enigma medulla, enigmas bonded, enigmas through, enigmas carriage, enigmas into, enigmas bonded, enigmas states, enigmas overlapping, enigmas occurences, enigmas complex, enigmas models, enigmas are, enigmas built, enigmas inside, enigmas your, enigmas searings, enigmas and, enigmas construction, enigmas is, enigmas arranged, enigmas through, enigmas equalizations, enigmas of, enigmas monetary, enigmas and, enigmas financial, enigmas distributions, enigmas given, enigmas positive, enigmas and, enigmas gotten, enigmas charges, enigmas through, enigmas fragments, enigmas spun, enigmas electonically, enigmas the, enigmas toning, enigmas compilations, enigmas routed, enigmas through, enigmas molecular, enigmas structures, enigmas and, enigmas the, enigmas wings, enigmas simple, enigmas folding, enigmas planes, enigmas verify, enigmas the, enigmas cubical, enigmas nature, enigmas of, enigmas God,, enigmas linear, enigmas duality, enigmas is, enigmas completed, enigmas now,, enigmas find, enigmas a, enigmas constructive, enigmas friend, enigmas.

LEVEL 302: THE CREATURE-MENTS:

Skin, creatures to, creatures study, creatures the, creatures betweenings, creatures with, creatures a, creatures waters, creatures will, creatures bond, creatures in, creatures new, creatures molecular, creatures orbits, creatures of, creatures the, creatures electron, creatures paths, creatures and, creatures the, creatures covalency, creatures arrangements, creatures are, creatures examined, creatures currently, creatures appended, creatures to, creatures the, creatures former, creatures weakenings, creatures and, creatures the, creatures signal, creatures quadruples, creatures form, creatures the, creatures final, creatures lines, creatures proof, creatures pours, creatures into, creatures living, creatures species, creatures and, creatures the, creatures quadrants, creatures arranged, creatures to, creatures show, creatures whorls, creatures of, creatures occupancy, creatures simple, creatures in, creatures angular, creatures locations, creatures for, creatures the, creatures former, creatures electronic, creatures transoptioning, creatures of, creatures el-conversioning, creatures rings, creatures.

LEVEL 303: THE STIGMATA-MENTS:

Cavity, stigmata anti-bondings, stigmata have, stigmata couple, stigmata the, stigmata old, stigmata to, stigmata the, stigmata new, stigmata Know, stigmata more, stigmata and, stigmata the, stigmata simple, stigmata gestures, stigmata of, stigmata duration, stigmata and, stigmata durability, stigmata will, stigmata forgive, stigmata the, stigmata former, stigmata to, stigmata eleate, stigmata the, stigmata new, stigmata bent, stigmata into, stigmata geometric, stigmata strainings, stigmata an, stigmata old, stigmata way, stigmata curls, stigmata to, stigmata find, stigmata the, stigmata current, stigmata waves, stigmata of, stigmata theoretic, stigmata supportings, stigmata schemata, stigmata are, stigmata drawn, stigmata through, stigmata responsibility, stigmata of, stigmata non-dominant, stigmata matrices, stigmata and, stigmata the, stigmata parental, stigmata treatments, stigmata complete, stigmata between, stigmata nations,, stigmata natures,, stigmata nurtures,, stigmata and, stigmata stacks, stigmata of, stigmata reactive, stigmata.

LEVEL 304: THE STAIN-MENTS:
Posterior, stains meltings., stains purple, stains majesties, stains join, stains the, stains planar, stains ranges, stains and, stains the, stains jacksons, stains whole, stains square, stains is, stains carbon, stains fed, stains for, stains the, stains intentional, stains reaching, stains into, stains frames, stains of, stains love, stains pi, stains energetics, stains come, stains into, stains play, stains and, stains the, stains playing, stains leads, stains to, stains flying, stains as, stains essential, stains winging, stains runs, stains leading, stains lobbies, stains of, stains the, stains lobes, stains of, stains currency, stains addiction, stains complete, stains role, stains played, stains old, stains days, stains gone, stains approximation, stains vocalized, stains values, stains pour, stains into, stains signal, stains sites, stains stabilization, stains occurs, stains the, stains mixtures, stains.

LEVEL 305: THE WASH-MENTS:
Cabernet, wash hardens, wash to, wash form, wash humans, wash parallels, wash are, wash drawn, wash throughout, wash the, wash double-bonding, wash fields., wash triplets, wash are, wash formed, wash and, wash the, wash destiny, wash for, wash your, wash structure, wash is, wash sent, wash elegant, wash impulses, wash via, wash transient, wash occupations, wash and, wash the, wash curl, wash of, wash the, wash waves, wash allow, wash a, wash breaking, wash to, wash occur, wash soon, wash acknowledge, wash the, wash essenes, wash dealt, wash fonder, wash fourths, wash and, wash sit, wash in, wash stillness, wash soon, wash alluring, wash ones, wash are, wash calling, wash allow, wash the, wash finality, wash of, wash the, wash federal, wash case, wash for, wash constitutions, wash.

LEVEL 306: THE BLOOD-MENTS:
Issues, blood drawn, blood counsel, blood admitted, blood survey, blood complete, blood accept, blood the, blood eclipse, blood of, blood the, blood overdrawn, blood salaried, blood say, blood good-bye, blood to, blood the, blood pod, blood of, blood former, blood formation, blood and, blood find, blood a, blood fonder, blood stilling, blood one, blood allow, blood the, blood placement, blood of, blood branches, blood throughout, blood the, blood earth, blood and, blood ignore, blood old, blood ways, blood today, blood a, blood decision, blood is, blood made, blood retrieve, blood information, blood for, blood the, blood sourcing, blood of, blood the, blood new, blood universe, blood

patience, blood in, blood gold, blood and, blood silver, blood has, blood application, blood for, blood the, blood former, blood now, blood.

LEVEL 307: THE LAMB-MENTS:
Zygomaticus, lamb released, lamb accept, lamb the, lamb gifts, lamb during, lamb life,, lamb liberty,, lamb and, lamb the, lamb pursuit, lamb of, lamb happiness, lamb landing, lamb to, lamb share, lamb joy, lamb throughout, lamb the, lamb world, lamb a, lamb former, lamb friend, lamb is, lamb discovered, lamb in, lamb the, lamb valley, lamb accept, lamb her, lamb calling, lamb ways, lamb and, lamb the, lamb nutrition, lamb given, lamb via, lamb phone, lamb lines, lamb details, lamb follow, lamb final, lamb energetic, lamb scans, lamb have, lamb been, lamb completed, lamb buy, lamb a, lamb quadrant, lamb for, lamb yourself, lamb through, lamb your, lamb faith, lamb one, lamb quadrant, lamb is, lamb equivalent, lamb to, lamb ten, lamb former, lamb nations, lamb and, lamb.

LEVEL 308: THE SEA-MENTS:
Upward, sea tribes, sea God, sea loves, sea her, sea children, sea Israel, sea remember, sea Jacob, sea and, sea the, sea Ladder, sea and, sea esau, sea and, sea the, sea gifts, sea for, sea the, sea children, sea acknowledge, sea where, sea you, sea stand, sea in, sea life's, sea comports, sea and, sea add, sea affection, sea to, sea this, sea list, sea compositions, sea truly, sea detail, sea the, sea lone, sea pairings, sea harmony, sea is, sea sealed, sea vital, sea signs, sea taken, sea into, sea liberative, sea formations, sea unity, sea extends, sea to, sea the, sea shores, sea seattle, sea blue, sea and, sea joinings, sea have, sea occurred, sea messages, sea sent, sea carry, sea spoken, sea imposition, sea.

LEVEL 309: THE ANGELIC-MENTS:
Of, angelic without, angelic align, angelic find, angelic a, angelic fruition, angelic God, angelic spirit, angelic allow, angelic quantum, angelic western, angelicwinging, angelic occurs, angelic essentially, angelic we, angelic are, angelic harmonized, angelic through, angelic the, angelic manifestation, angelic of, angelic equivalency, angelic worship, angelic only, angelic when, angelic harmony, angelic abounds, angelic harmonic, angelic is, angelic selah, angelic est, angelic is, angelic added, angelic to, angelic the, angelic numerical, angelic calculations, angelic of, angelic piety, angelic pi, angelic the, angelic universal, angelic numbering, angelic system, angelic has, angelic borne, angelic volumes,, angelic tones,, angelic sealings,, angelic generative, angelic tissues, angelic reaching, angelic traditional, angelic heavens,, angelic modernity, angelic builidngs, angelic and, angelic useful, angelic theory, angelic built, angelic pipes, angelic organs, angelic derivatives, angelic cylindrical, angelic.

LEVEL 310: THE ART-MENTS:
Milk, art cubings, art spheres, art flat, art genesa, art crystalline, art spinnings, art plateau, art reached, art breach, art now, art for, art the, art air, art of, art purified, art glories, art dreamings,

art written, art astronomical, art forgive, art quirks, art quarks, art photons, art neutronic, art builders, art found, art grid, art established, art here, art divisions, art sold, art final, art equatorial, art spellings, art spiritually, art freed, art circles, art gain, art news, art solar, art rings, art have, art exploded, art to, art aim, art the, art poles, art in, art a, art sodium, art based, art opposite, art spin, art final, art processions, art may, art begin, art triangles, art merge, art to, art form, art impulse, art bases, art.

LEVEL 311: THE ARC-MENTS:
Layer, arc and, arc the, arc pyramids, arc erupt, arc sun, arc sanctuary, arc in, arc the, arc canals, arc of, arc canaan, arc expire, arc diagrams, arc drawn, arc to, arc include, arc the, arc theory, arc of, arc fusion, arc and, arc the, arc foundations, arc of, arc the, arc stone, arc of, arc . the, arc corner, arc of, arc the, arc world, arc next, arc universe, arc is, arc vital, arc in, arc the, arc lineage, arc of, arc man, arc marry, arc the, arc cortex, arc of, arc the, arc brain, arc to, arc opposite, arc polar, arc regions, arc via, arc love, arc spun, arc ones, arc are, arc standing, arc nearby, arc allowing, arc breathing, arc the, arc divine, arc HA, arc love, arc.

LEVEL 312: THE ARMED-MENTS:
Armed passes, armed is, armed built, armed in, armed temple, armed wares, armed boxes, armed are, armed given, armed releases, armed as, armed the, armed chosen, armed few, armed explore, armed journey, armed into, armed reply, armed reptilian, armed resource, armed gone, armed desire, armed former, armed ways, armed will, armed given, armed loft, armed add, armed as, armed widespread, armed ones, armed detach, armed polarity, armed to, armed find, armed fusion, armed in, armed the, armed Son, armed deficiency, armed is, armed gone, armed nova, armed scotia, armed is, armed drawn, armed into, armed quadrants, armed too, armed chro, armedmosomes merge, armed to, armed form, armed new, armed beings, armed heart, armed lines, armed drawn, armed *thelmalations (*for my mom who held the course eternal), armed thermally, armed complete, armed heat, armed melts, armed alignments, armed.

LEVEL 313: THE PEN-MENTS:
Pen, pen into, pen brain, pen waved, pen functions, pen sines, pen cosines, pen senses, pen mergers, pen joking, pen with, pen laughter, pen and, pen rafaelean, pen experience, pen exteriors, pen merge, pen to, pen freed, pen elements, pen of, pen natural, pen blockages, pen cleared, pen examine, pen the, pen nature, pen of, pen your, pen nurture, pen details, pen drawn, pen in, pen following, pen wings, pen mistral, pen winds, pen santa, pen ana, pen nino, pen nina, pen roaring, pen exchange, pen diets, pen during, pen sexual, pen discourse, pen flowing, pen required, pen find, pen folly, pen in, pen the, pen foolish, pen corners, pen of, pen the, pen universe, pen detail, pen the, pen beading, pen of, pen the, pen heart, pen

LEVEL 314: THE HAND-MENTS:
Hand, hand lines, hand franklin, hand minting, hand absorbed, hand sodium, hand from, hand the, handsun, hand lakes, hand built, hand seas, hand exogenus, hand relationships, hand built, hand through, hand russian, hand teas, hand details, hand afford, hand benefits, hand please, hand endure, hand the, hand lessons, hand sold, hand to, hand men, hand slavery, hand shekels, hand thirty, hand pieces, hand of, hand silver, hand the, hand ultimate, hand rise, hand and, hand the, hand risen, hand restrictions, hand coded, hand to, hand strips, hand of, hand paper, hand the, hand ultimate, hand universe, hand is, hand built, hand here, hand listen, hand as, hand the, hand rhymes, hand become, hand reasons, hand to, hand live, hand longer, hand still, hand on, hand the, hand.

LEVEL 315: THE HELD-MENTS:
Held hand, held berry, held edge, held of, held the, held universe, held penland, held lives, held in, held lenticular, held gladness, held of, held the, held fuelings, held occuring, heldtruth, held told, held trust, held the, held one, held who, held said, held "it, held is, held here", held and, held follow, held closely, held her, held linings, held find, held where, held she, held speaks, held from, held and, held mean, held it, held when, held you, held say, held "loved", held this, held earth, held measures, held your, held merits, held thoroughly, held through, held discussions,, held dialects, held and, held antedeluvian, held movements, held arcturus, held your, held starring, held has, held met, held the, held planet, held building, held affordance, held for, held.

LEVEL 316: THE HURLED-MENTS:
Hurled tenderness, hurled optical, hurled completions, hurled all, hurled ten, hurled lenses, hurled stacked, hurled the, hurled sephirah, hurled are, hurled compelling, hurled gates, hurled told, hurled collapse, hurled into, hurled one, hurled sealing, hurled movement, hurled arc-e-tecture, hurled is, hurled discovered, hurled through, hurled a, hurled leap, hurled into, hurled space, hurled between, hurled the, hurled legato, hurled leaves, hurled trees, hurled animals, hurled plants, hurled and, hurled rocks, hurled develop, hurled extended, hurled through, hurled the, hurled photonic, hurled phasings, hurled mitotic, hurled expansions, hurled large, hurled mornings, hurled overt, hurled gestures, hurled details, hurled drama, hurled drops, hurled during, hurled sexual, hurled appetitive, hurled foods, hurled analysis, hurled completes, hurled gesticulations, hurled essence, hurled spores, hurled limit, hurled origins, hurled species, hurled finds, hurled final, hurled.

LEVEL 317: THE BOLT-MENTS:
Body, bolts frontier, bolts inside, bolts he, bolts heart, bolts of, bolts man, bolts cubits, bolts built, bolts and, bolts boats, bolts launched, bolts verticality, bolts functions, bolts as, bolts love, bolts occupies, bolts one, bolts entire, bolts quadrant, bolts for, bolts love's, bolts configurations, bolts extend, bolts into, bolts bondage, bolts and, bolts find, bolts simple, bolts spinning, bolts correspondences, bolts underworn, bolts seamings, bolts seemingly, bolts stripes, bolts swallow, bolts distance, bolts to, bolts

afford, bolts flotation, bolts in, bolts the, bolts center, bolts of, bolts the, bolts ringings, bolts averages, bolts fractionary, bolts fractals, bolts posed, bolts to, bolts peer, bolts into, bolts the, bolts dorothetic, bolts heart, bolts of, bolts God, bolts let, bolts love, bolts calculate, bolts your, bolts location, bolts elevations, bolts.

LEVEL 318: THE NUT-MENTS:

Essentials, nuts given, nuts exchange, nuts durations, nuts of, nuts breath, nuts for, nuts frequency, nuts of, nuts the, nuts breathings, nuts allow, nuts spirits, nuts flowering, nuts in, nuts you, nuts explorations, nuts in, nuts the, nuts light, nuts bring, nuts a, nuts noble, nuts obligation, nuts to, nuts source, nuts find, nuts the, nuts following, nuts string, nuts and, nuts pull, nuts it, nuts into, nuts course, nuts and, nuts the, nuts resurrection, nuts of, nuts election, nuts of, nuts developmental, nuts choice, nuts supports, nuts theorems, nuts and, nuts burnings, nuts and, nuts bushes, nuts and, nuts numbers, nuts squared, nuts as, nuts the, nuts crown, nuts is, nuts reached, nuts and, nuts the, nuts kether, nuts burns, nuts in, nuts a, nuts bloodstream, nuts.

LEVEL 319: THE UNIVERSE-MENTS:

Reverse, universe rich, universe in, universe oils, universe acknowledge, universe the, universe college, universe which, universe you, universe are, universe and, universe spread, universe the, universe fire, universe add, universe honey, universe to, universe the, universe measures, universe and, universe reactions, universe linearly, universe bend, universe to, universe blend, universe in, universe the, universe magic, universe of, universe other, universe complexities, universe aquire, universe long, universe range, universe goals, universe and, universe delocalize, universe the, universe crossing, universe points, universe for, universe this, universe university, universe accept, universe the, universe roanoke, universe connecitons, universe and, universe mixtures, universe pour, universe into, universe junipers, universe hole, universe on, universe the, universe mountain, universe sides, universe final, universe spaces, universe sealed, universe destroy, universe only, universe the, universe shortest, universe.

LEVEL 320: THE SUM-MENTS:

Relax, sum commitments, sum and, sum find, sum final, sum destinations, sum within, sum love, sum attributive, sum ratios, sum and, sum subsratus, sum flavored, sum precipatavely, sum in, sum overviews, sum of, sum constructive, sum hybrids, sum borne, sum to, sum breed, sum blue-greens, sum into, sum golds, sum find, sum a, sum kelp, sum strand, sum which, sum lasts, sum as, sum food, sum your, sum eviction, sum is, sum over, sum hyrdogen, sum suns, sum burn, sum helium, sum white, sum blues, sum will, sum dissolve, sum your, sum desire, sum to, sum destroy, sum by, sum fire, sum and, sum water, sum stills, sum your, sum quiet, sum run, sum into, sum love, sum angles, sum equal, sum in, sum triumphant, sum return, sum

LEVEL 321: THE CALVES-MENTS:

light, calves of, calves the, calves scribe, calves to, calves the, calves eye, calves of, calves horus, calves now, calves located, calves upon, calves the, calves Son's, calves domain, calves restructural, calves organelles, calves float, calves in, calves nitrogenous, calves oxygenou, calves carbonic, calves struts, calves lift, calves the, calves lids, calves again, calves and, calves find, calves fuel, calves underneath, calves burn, calves the, calves black, calves stuff, calves out, calves through, calves your, calves breathing, calves faith, calves accept, calves the, calves divorce, calves of, calves lessenings, calves external, calves internal, calves physical, calves remourse, calves is, calves over, calves energies, calves returned, calves to, calves original, calves levels, calves add, calves a, calves voice, calves of, calves love, calves and, calves compositive, calves data, calves.

LEVEL 322: THE GOAL-MENTS:

Permanent, goals will, goals be, goals fed, goals as, goals necessary, goals into, goals the, goals additional, goals guards, goals built, goals into, goals the, goals phalanx, goals of, goals pharaonic, goals whole, goals thinking, goals grips, goals grids, goals expire, goals without, goals protein, goals fragmental, goals originations, goals find, goals the, goals number, goals which, goals relates, goals to, goals all, goals ten, goals and, goals figure, goals in, goals the, goals constant, goals additions, goals problems, goals solved, goals thorugh, goals operative, goals polarizations, goals and, goals alignments, goals in, goals the, goals sun, goals defy, goals gravity, goals fly, goals live, goals breathe, goals metabolically, goals shelled, goals free, goals of, goals the, goals mixtures, goals of, goals tinctures, goals supplemental, goals to, goals.

LEVEL 323: THE GLOBE-MENTS:

Globes, globes the, globes thresholds, globes of, globes divisions, globes and, globes numbers, globes miracles, globes occured, globes when, globes love, globes began, globes remember, globes love, globes nourishes, globes you, globes add, globes foundations, globes to, globes the, globes centers, globes and, globes structural, globes fish, globes will, globes result, globes in, globes gifts, globes of, globes gratitude, globes and, globes clothing, globes your, globes tribes, globes in, globes raiments, globes of, globes electric, globes skin, globes and, globes heart, globes throbbing, globes purses, globes imprinted, globes in, globes the, globes face, globes of, globes the, globes demonic, globes matrices, globes cubed, globes out, globes of, globes this, globes planetary, globes grip, globes allow, globes orbitals, globes to, globes burn, globes when, globes the, globes genesesan, globes native, globes.

LEVEL 324: THE GLOW-MENTS:

Label, glows genesis, glows electronically, glows powers, glows the, glows trip, glows to, glows the, glows edge, glows of, glows the, glows leanings, glows and, glows found, glows centered, glows still, glows and, glows the, glows exodus, glows again, glows occupies, glows the, glows minds, glows and, glows the, glows hearts, glows of, glows those, glows who, glows leap, glows let, glows the, glows system, glows build, glows as, glows your, glows keep, glows the, glows triumphant, glows region, glows intact, glows yellow, glows winds, glows blow, glows allow, glows recourse, glows to, glows forgive, glows and, glows the, glows blood, glows to, glows pour, glows into, glows the, glows earth's, glows widths, glows license, glows to, glows journey, glows is, glows hereby, glows granted, glows within, glows sense, glows white, glows thunder, glows baby, glows external, glows tonight, glows om, glows merges, glows with -glows fusion, glows cells, glows amazon, glows screams, glows delivery, glows.

LEVEL 325: THE HARBOR-MENTS:

Transport, harbors love, harbors let, harbors us, harbors lead, harbors into, harbors former, harbors states, harbors of, harbors accumulative, harbors and, harbors aquisitional, harbors ability, harbors as, harbors we, harbors delicately, harbors afford, harbors the, harbors picture, harbors ink, harbors and, harbors the, harbors stragihtened, harbors nucleus, harbors stands, harbors in, harbors shorter, harbors transcriptions, harbors and, harbors longer, harbors gifts, harbors possibiity, harbors to, harbors start, harbors from, harbors is, harbors now, harbors and, harbors the, harbors mathematical, harbors sequences, harbors have, harbors begun, harbors to, harbors fire, harbors now, harbors radii, harbors leapt, harbors pushing, harbors diametric, harbors diatomic, harbors grid, harbors builders, harbors into, harbors the, harbors flowering, harbors details, harbors for, harbors the, harbors fibonaccian, harbors squares, harbors and, harbors the, harbors golden, harbors.

LEVEL 326: THE BAY-MENTS:

Nearest, bays rectangles, bays of, bays the, bays apex, bays of, bays enochian, bays squares, bays let, bays us, bays cubically, bays avert, bays the, bays disasterous, bays fore-tellings, bays for, bays the, bays former, bays lords, bays of, bays lights, bays have, bays arranged, bays this, bays game, bays for, bays the, bays good, bays of, bays mankind, bays let, bays them, bays see, bays the, bays face, bays of, bays God, bays in, bays Basic, bays humanity, bays thriving, bays germ, bays freed, bays questions, bays assumed, bays now, bays told, bays energetically, bays to, bay clear, bays the, bays threshold, bays for, bays the, bays mechanism, bays is, bays about, bays to, bays fire, bays hold, bays on, bays to, bays the, bays Sun, bays love, love is the bay detailed.

LEVEL 327: THE ISLAND-MENTS:

Anger, islands my, islands son, islands well, islands done, islands in, islands whom, islands I, islands am, islands well, islands pleased, islands I, islands am, islands the, islands son, islands of, islands God,, islands now, islands written, islands throughout, islands the, islands universe, islands in, islands eye, islands writings, islands in, islands tessellations, islands in, islands chordation, islands and, islands chronic, islands cures, islands for, islands the, islands final, islands seatings, islands upon, islands the, islands right, islands hands, islands of, islands God, islands our, islands yours, islands mine, islands resurrection, islands is, islands dear, islands and, islands the, islands love, islands whirls, islands into, islands giga-bytes, islands of, islands funding, islands details, islands let, islands us, islands add, islands heart, islands to, islands the, islands hearing, islands.

LEVEL 328: THE MOUNTAIN-MENTS:

Joy, mountains and, mountains laughter, mountains to, mountains the, mountains spin, mountains all, mountains 720, mountains degrees, mountains are, mountains akin, mountains to, mountains love, mountains final, mountains level into, mountains salutations, mountains salute, mountains your, mountains deification, mountains of hope look to the, mountains resource, mountains called, mountains God, mountains return, mountains God, mountains to, mountains humanity, mountains through, mountains your, mountains arc-ingness, mountains and, mountains fond, mountains fondle, mountains of, mountains the, mountains featured, mountains research, mountains called, mountains being, mountains born, mountains into, mountains the, mountains 72, mountains who, mountains have, mountains literally, mountains increased, mountains Sun's, mountains intensity, mountains through, mountains cooling, mountains Egyptian, mountains facelets, mountains and, mountains the, mountains 12, mountains who, mountains knew, mountains originally, mountains that, mountains chemical, mountains depletion, mountains had, mountains become, mountains run, mountains.

LEVEL 329: THE MUSIC-MENTS:

Look, musics serious, musics enough, musics for the living intrigue for love the, musics cubes, musics to, musics be, musics released, musics throughout, musics the, musics stomach, musics feet, musics eyes, musics hands, musics mouth, musics jaw, musics ears, musics and, musics hearts, musics of, musics humanity, musics let, musics the, musics telling, musics begin, musics here, musics jason, musics found, musics fleece, musics is, musics home, musics ship, musics in, musics port, musics locking, musics into, musics the, musics chemical, musics structure, musics of, musics earth, musics for, musics a, musics final, musics nautilian, musics experience, musics of, musics expert, musics spinning, musics boats, musics define, musics the, musics deficiency, musics of, musics ironic, musics relations, musics in, musics the, musics porphyron, musics rings, musics of, musics dolphin, musics blue, musics love, musics feel, musics passion, musics.

LEVEL 330: THE BASIC-MENTS:

Healing, basic instensity, basic let, basic us, basic be, basic led, basic to, basic the, basic feedings, basic now, basic said, basic "mankind, basic is, basic free", basic woman, basic rule, basic the, basic rna, basic the, basic messenger, basic code, basic man, basic the, basic keys, basic the, basic details, basic the, basic sea, basic levels, basic reach, basic new, basic heights, basic in, basic 2003, basic through, basic the, basic pull, basic of, basic the, basic correspondences, basic I, basic Ching, basic reads, basic of, basic Love, basic and, basic the, basic Lao, basic Tzu, basic prophetic, basic cures, basic activity, basic volcanic, basic sleep, basic breezes, basic arts, basic final, basic publishing, basic calls, basic made, basic leap, basic babylonian, basic tablets, basic align, basic.

LEVEL 331: THE SLEEVE-MENTS:

Permit, sleeves alexandrian, sleeves in, sleeves lactic, sleeves bids, sleeves localized, sleeves numbers, sleeves arranged, sleeves shadows, sleeves flux, sleeves poles, sleeves patience, sleeves old, sleeves era, sleeves ends, sleeves pointer, sleeves is, sleeves the, sleeves equinoctial, sleeves total, sleeves for, sleeves love, sleeves hydrogen, sleeves oxygen, sleeves antibodies, sleeves built, sleeves anti-christ, sleeves revealed, sleeves the, sleeves capital -sleeves H, sleeves of, sleeves old, sleeves Troy, sleeves rolled, sleeves into, sleeves horses, sleeves held, sleeves chapters, sleeves build, sleeves longitude, sleeves given, sleeves equal, sleeves seals, sleeves defy, sleeves only, sleeves led, sleeves to, sleeves blood, sleeves shed, sleeves enemy, sleeves sent, sleeves to, sleeves the, sleeves core, sleeves for, sleeves ancient, sleeves tunings, sleeves sakes, sleeves rapidity, sleeves sold, sleeves in, sleeves manifested, sleeves ranges, sleeves.

LEVEL 332: THE COAT-MENTS:

Tea coats prove, coats the, coats nature, coats of, coats wonders, coats type, coats the, coats signs, coats into, coats orbital, coats symobls, coats and, coats given, coats finalization, coats ascend, coats directly, coats into, coats the, coats full, coats harmonic, coats of, coats God,, coats welcome, coats again, coats to, coats basic, coats humanity, coats and, coats the, coats rings, coats of all ringings God, coats know, coats man, coats came, coats into, coats the, coats father, coats through, coats us,, coats Christ, coats said,, coats "thy, coats kingdom, coats come, coats on, coats earth, coats as, coats it, coats is, coats in, coats heaven", coats welcome, coats now, coats the, coats metatron, coats and, coats. the, coats full, coats example, coats of, coats arc-angelic, coats relief, coats.

LEVEL 333: THE ROOT-MENTS:

Sing, roots upon, roots this, roots plane, roots call, roots forth, roots the, roots full, roots embellishment, roots of, roots the, roots body, roots lateral the literal into reachable, roots Christ, roots this, roots day, roots in, roots love, roots metatron, roots flight, roots focus, roots forward, roots fact, roots feature, roots influence, roots fusion, roots cycles, roots central, roots portal, roots places, roots pole, roots posits, roots planets, roots ports, roots selah, roots king, roots queens, roots prince, roots sparrows, roots birds, roots princess, roots lesson, roots listen – roots appear, roots learn, roots apply, roots employ, roots gain, roots grant, roots infuse, roots focal, roots vocal, roots fortitude, roots

endears, roots endanger, roots entire, roots electric, roots elevation, roots attitude, roots elective, roots stages, roots stores, roots silver, roots gold, roots.

LEVEL 334: THE GENIUS-MENTS:

Depths, genius treasure, genius platinum, genius titatium, genius zinc, genius cords, genius cubes, genius dna, genius straighten, genius eggs, genius spores, genius birth, genius sparks, genius enzymes, genius greens, genius evaluations, genius creation, genius human, genius life, genius love, genius atmosphere, genius sentinels, genius bridges, genius move, genius quadrants, genius realms, genius regions, genius depths, genius agreements, genius fathoms, genius choirs, genius twist, genius herlds, genius turns, genius mists, genius tubes, genius ensembles, genius interiors, genius enclaves, genius worths, genius angels, genius oceans, genius creeds, genius seas, genius fills, genius deserts, genius endures, genius wise, genius thirteen, genius seams, genius eight, genius sixty-four, genius 104, genius fabric, genius d, genius herlds, genius nth, genius crystal, genius a, genius approach, genius fuels, genius genetics, genius initials, genius maneuvers, genius.

LEVEL 335: THE PISCIS-MENTS:

Body, piscis planes, piscis residences, piscis matriomal, piscis levels, piscis memory, piscis forestry, piscis maternal, piscis promotioinal, piscis wedded, piscis blue, piscis trees, piscis ridges, piscis truths, piscis health, piscis luck, piscis contours, piscis wanton, piscis chromosome, piscis places, piscis know, piscis mobility, piscis red, piscis miricles, piscis oranges, piscis menue, piscis bud, piscis fed, piscis seeds, piscis food, piscis protein, piscis nutrition, piscis colors, piscis emperical, piscis spirial, piscis affalence, piscis equinox, piscis earth, piscis preciession, piscis planets, piscis signs, piscis symbols, piscis fable, piscis legends, piscis. sermons, piscis moves, piscis accounts, piscis agility, piscis spiritual, piscis magical, piscis finicial, piscis relationships, piscis fundamental, piscis relatives, piscis captions, piscis mobility, piscis prymids, piscis gemstones, piscis jeweltones, piscis cohesion, piscis cognition, piscis cogency, piscis consciousness, piscis conscience, Piscis.

LEVEL 336: THE VESICA-MENTS:

Spiritual, vesica one, vesica meant, vesica edge, vesica gifts, vesica creations, vesica souls, vesica planetary, vesica opens, vesica lords, vesica rulers, vesica manifest, vesica powers, vesica trinitization, vesica collectives, vesica multiplies, vesica wells, vesica ties, vesica dispatched, vesica zones, vesica eyes, vesica higher, vesica evolutions, vesica freedom, vesica passes, vesica ables, vesica son, vesica mother, vesica brother, vesica nulls, vesica fields, vesica brains, vesica pass, vesica gravity, vesica environmental, vesica matrix, vesica hosts, vesica modes, vesica inspired, vesica seeds, vesica spirals, vesica renewal, vesica measures, vesica special, vesica delivery, vesica different, vesica great, vesica ranks, vesica contain, vesica coded, vesica lost, vesica found, vesica dedicated, vesica emit, vesica om, vesica mane, vesica padme, vesica hum, vesica 314, vesica lamb, vesica stellar, vesica stelae, vesica steps, vesica sound, vesica.

LEVEL 337: THE HORTIZONTAL-MENTS:

Widest, horizontal giant, horizontal reprogramming, horizontal likens, horizontal shall, horizontal various, horizontal yet, horizontal affected, horizontal density, horizontal giant, horizontal gravity, horizontal thresholds, horizontal virtues, horizontal bodies, horizontal tripyramidal, horizontal sages, horizontal tens, horizontal tracks, horizontal laws, horizontal planetary, horizontal evolutions, horizontal matters, horizontal further, horizontal more, horizontal densities, horizontal deaths, horizontal entire, horizontal times, horizontal creations, horizontal academies, horizontal bases, horizontal faimly, horizontal keys, horizontal wisdoms, horizontal numbered, horizontal limited, horizontal biblically, horizontal scrolls, horizontal chambers, horizontal hearts, horizontal tounges, horizontal celestial, horizontal exists, horizontal love, horizontal computers, horizontal coded, horizontal books, horizontal stones, horizontal jacob, horizontal people, horizontal scriptures, horizontal widely, horizontal centered, horizontal earth, horizontal upon zion, horizontal established, horizontal abode, horizontal spaces, horizontal names, horizontal works, horizontal lineage – horizontal lines, horizontal.

LEVEL 338: THE VERTICAL-MENTS:

Pains, vertical God, vertical gave, vertical us, vertical exact, vertical instruction, vertical through, vertical the, vertical overlay, vertical called, vertical the, vertical faith, vertical of, vertical heart-felt, vertical beatings, vertical beatings, vertical electric, vertical may, vertical now, vertical blend, vertical with, vertical the, vertical beats, vertical received, vertical when, vertical a, vertical Christline, vertical dives, vertical in, vertical to, vertical rescue, vertical her, vertical own, vertical how, vertical shall, vertical we, vertical streaming, vertical.be, vertical believed, vertical in, vertical through, vertical the, vertical cosmic, vertical rimming, vertical of, vertical the, vertical tibetan, vertical stretching, vertical and, vertical the, vertical streamings, vertical who, verticalelectric, vertical eld, vertical the, vertical final, vertical vibratory, vertical scale, vertical acapulco mexican, vertical palings, vertical acapulco, vertical blue, vertical cliffs, vertical of, vertical.

LEVEL 339: THE PARALLEL-MENTS:

Chambers, parallel diving, parallel electricity, parallel to, parallel the, parallel hilt, parallel of, parallel a, parallel sword, parallel elevated, parallel to, parallel treasured, parallel tesselations, parallel god, parallel watching, parallel you, parallel stalking, parallel pieces, parallel of, parallel 8, parallel forgettings, parallel the, parallel final, parallel is, parallel found, parallel we, parallel are, parallel around, parallel you, parallel reaching, parallel rhymthm, parallel orgasmic, parallel potential, parallel in, parallel the, parallel throat, parallel of, parallel God, parallel mansions, parallel built, parallel and, parallel honeymoons, parallel told, parallel to, parallel travel, parallel lightly, parallel around, parallel this, parallel throne, parallel and, parallel often, parallel God, parallel allowing, parallel brings, parallel eternal, parallel surrender, parallel to, parallel the, parallel palace, parallel Southhampton, parallel and, parallel the, parallel trims, parallel of, parallel.

LEVEL 340: THE 90-DEGREE-MENTS:

Flow, ninety degrees truest, ninety degrees reaching, ninety degrees allow, ninety degrees the, ninety degrees sample, ninety degrees to, ninety degrees simmer, ninety degrees in, ninety degrees potent, ninety degrees pots, ninety degrees of, ninety degrees powerful, ninety degrees ungents, ninety degrees reach, ninety degrees for, ninety degrees Ouray, ninety degrees through, ninety degrees the, ninety degrees vibrations, ninety degrees and, ninety degrees raid, ninety degrees a, ninety degrees knife, ninety degrees now, ninety degrees glittering, ninety degrees as, ninety degrees the, ninety degrees stars, ninety degrees swarming, ninety degrees excite, ninety degrees triumphant, ninety degrees hearts, ninety degrees gathering, ninety degrees again, ninety degrees to, ninety degrees sing, ninety degrees accolades, ninety degrees into, ninety degrees God, ninety degrees final, ninety degrees victory, ninety degrees now, ninety degrees sent, ninety degrees and, ninety degrees these, ninety degrees who, ninety degrees follow, ninety degrees field, ninety degrees a, ninety degrees final, ninety degrees exhalation, ninety degrees into, ninety degrees the, ninety degrees streaming, ninety degrees protoplasmic, ninety degrees kinship, ninety degrees called, ninety degrees Ka, ninety degrees God, ninety degrees is, ninety degrees found, ninety degrees and, ninety degrees Ra, ninety degrees.

LEVEL 341: THE SYNCHRONOUS-MENTS:

Or, synchronous ascends, synchronous to, synchronous throne, synchronous rescind, synchronous and, synchronous often, synchronous found, synchronous a, synchronous yellow, synchronous spark, synchronous now, synchronous sending, synchronous reaching, synchronous Scarab, synchronous fields, synchronous clearings, synchronous bettles, synchronous spilling, synchronous out, synchronous to, synchronous seal, synchronous the, synchronous throat, synchronous of, synchronous death, synchronous with, synchronous a, synchronous final, synchronous kiss, synchronous of, synchronous instant, synchronous rememberance, synchronous of, synchronous the, synchronous life, synchronous eternal, synchronous satan's, synchronous falling, synchronous reeling, synchronous raunch, synchronous has, synchronous gone, synchronous to, synchronous the, synchronous shield, synchronous electric, synchronous a, synchronous metatronic, synchronous apend, synchronous synchronous synchronous end, synchronous of, synchronous the, synchronous forgetting, synchronous any, synchronous recall, synchronous of, synchronous less, synchronous than, synchronous the, synchronous All, synchronous may, synchronous

LEVEL 342: THE IN-GRID-MENTS

Star, grids now, grids end, grids in, grids entwine, grids with, grids the, grids One, grids called, grids the, grids Son, grids of, grids God, grids let, grids us, grids remember, grids that, grids Christ, grids is, grids a, grids class, grids in, grids you, grids that, grids stripped, grids thinking, grids has, grids caused, grids your, grids head, grids to, grids ramble, grids and, grids your, grids heart, grids to, grids go, grids wander, grids in, grids fields, grids of, grids fallen, grids archs, grids let, grids us, grids now, grids remove, grids the, grids ancient, grids h, grids to, grids reveal, grids a, grids spokenness, grids called, grids perfectly, grids exact, grids a, grids bermuda, grids peeled, grids to, grids show, grids us, grids that, grids.

LEVEL 343: THE MENTOR-MENTS:

Voice, mentors in, mentors Christ, mentors shall, mentors we, mentors rise, mentors through, mentors the, mentors sing, mentors of, mentors elders, mentors married, mentors to, mentors the, mentors throne, mentors of, mentors eternal, mentors hearting, mentors God, mentors starting, mentors to, mentors return, mentors thy, mentors kingdom, mentors coming, mentors on, mentors earth, mentors as, mentors it, mentors is, mentors in, mentors heaven, mentors this, mentors hear, mentors the, mentors singing, mentors as, mentors around, mentors we, mentors gather, mentors to, mentors collect, mentors the, mentors pieces, mentors and, mentors the, mentors keys, mentors and, mentors the, mentors codes, mentors of, mentors the, mentors heart, mentors electric, mentors we, mentors call, mentors Father, mentors and, mentors friend, mentors the, mentors ancient, mentors pacing, mentors the, mentors heart, mentors.

LEVEL 344: THE MASONIC-MENTS:

Replaced, masons filling, masons OM, masons of, masons the, masons Aum, masons eternal, masons a, masons kindred, masons spirit, masons made, masons to, masons in, masons our, masons image, masons has, masons found, masons a, masons friend, masons in, masons the, masons flight, masons of, masons the, masons dove, masons and, masons the, masons returning, masons landing, masons of, masons the, masons Only, masons Begotten, masons Son, masons welcome, masons home, masons Oh, masons spirit, masons of, masons Christ, masons and, masons the, masons child, masons found, masons standing, masons at, masons the, masons Berry's, masons end, masons a, masons peaceful, masons return, masons to, masons the, masons land, masons Metatronically, masons gifted, masons as, masons God's, masons let, masons us, masons signal, masons end, masons to, masons.

LEVEL 345: THE ENGINEER-MENTS:

Awaken, engineer the, engineer lessen, engineer and, engineer beginning, engineer of, engineer now, engineer and, engineer the, engineer on, engineer worn, engineer within, engineer our, engineer returning, engineer ladders, engineer to, engineer belief, engineer and, engineer the, engineer thanking, engineer your, engineer lucky, engineer stars, engineer eternal, engineer metatron, engineer has, engineer landed, engineer the, engineer arc, engineer is, engineer on, engineer and, engineer the, engineer dove, engineer returned, engineer that, engineer simply, engineer let, engineer us, engineer stand, engineer in, engineer eternity, engineer together, engineer pain, engineer has, engineer gone, engineer to, engineer God, engineer electric, engineer humanity, engineer in, engineer the, engineer image, engineer of, engineer the daring eccentric, engineer Son, engineer and the lightening inspiration enduring love upon this plane, engineer the summation during love, engineer Father, engineer and the sun enlightened, engineer to the, engineer spinning, engineer into, engineer One, engineer sun immaculate.

LEVEL 346: THE ETERNAL-BLUEPRINT-MENTS:

Magnetic, blueprints with, blueprints the, blueprints Mother's, blueprints greeting, blueprints hug, blueprints of, blueprints instant, blueprints remember, blueprints love, blueprints us, blueprints Fathered, blueprints well, blueprints Mothered, blueprints tell, blueprints and, blueprints ancient, blueprints splendor, blueprints of, blueprints the, blueprints Sun, blueprints born, blueprints to, blueprints man, blueprints an, blueprints electrical, blueprints currency, blueprints never, blueprints spent, blueprints always, blueprints fed, blueprints in, blueprints fountained, blueprints splendor, blueprints peace, blueprints brother, blueprints sister, blueprints mother, blueprints friend, blueprints whore, blueprints and, blueprints harlot, blueprints living, blueprints kin, blueprints of, blueprints God, blueprints May, blueprints Mother, blueprints suffer, blueprints less, blueprints when, blueprints our, blueprints caroling, blueprints completion, blueprints enters, blueprints phasing, blueprints found, blueprints and, blueprints material, blueprints examine, blueprints hear, blueprints may, blueprints carry, blueprints the, blueprints.

LEVEL 347: THE IN-MAP-MENTS:

Roads, maps arc, maps of, maps essential, maps lecture, maps and, maps the, maps art, maps of, maps simple to the tone emotive, maps every day a notion, maps inside the keys totality, maps drawn into a living design into love, maps delicate, maps truth, maps that, maps delicious, maps as, maps God, maps is, maps we, maps are, maps equally, maps and, mapswell, maps within, maps this, maps fact, maps rings, maps a, maps bell, maps of, maps sweet, maps tesselation, maps a, maps returning, maps paragraph, maps a, maps libros, maps a, maps pillow, maps for, maps in, maps the, maps beginning, maps was, maps the, maps word, maps the, maps logos, maps the, maps God-ness, maps of, maps litany, maps and, maps reason, maps and, maps fhyming, maps key, maps codes, maps and, maps rapture, maps held, maps material, maps.

LEVEL 348: THE CEREMONY-MENTS:

Ice, ceremony matter, ceremony in, ceremony two, ceremony rings, ceremony until, ceremony a, ceremony beginning, ceremony explore, ceremony found, ceremony explosion, ceremony in, ceremony the, ceremony cosmic, ceremony 15. surge, ceremony of, ceremony arrival, ceremony at, ceremony peak, ceremony example, ceremony and, ceremony the, ceremony twinning, ceremony brought, ceremony an, ceremony end, ceremony to, ceremony under-elevated, ceremony reaches, ceremony and, ceremony the, ceremony rapture, ceremony has, ceremony sent, ceremony signals, ceremony throughout, ceremony the, ceremony regions, ceremony and, ceremony ranches, ceremony resemble, ceremony gatherings, ceremony of, ceremony temples, ceremony and, ceremony houses, ceremony represent, ceremony men, ceremony and, ceremony humanity, ceremony made, ceremony a, ceremony temple, ceremony of, ceremony the, ceremony Egyptian, ceremony spend, ceremony and, ceremony Osiris, ceremony returning, ceremony found, ceremony his, ceremony pieces, ceremony and, ceremony.

LEVEL 349: THE CELEBRATION-MENTS:

Channels the, celebrations reach, celebrations began, celebrations to, celebrations resemble, celebrations reality, celebrations of, celebrations the, celebrations matter, celebrations and, celebrations material, celebrations called, celebrations humanity, celebrations As, celebrations said, celebrations in, celebrations the, celebrations Temple, celebrations of, celebrations Man, celebrations let, celebrations man, celebrations spend, celebrations eternity, celebrations knowing, celebrations the, celebrations truth, celebrations let, celebrations humanity, celebrations surrender, celebrations to, celebrations Jungian, celebrations singing, celebrations and, celebrations the, celebrations mandalas, celebrations of, celebrations birthing, celebrations the, celebrations names, celebrations join, celebrations to, celebrations journey, celebrations inside, celebrations the, celebrations h-constant, celebrations a, celebrations smaller, celebrations consenant, celebrations of, celebrations consistent, celebrations creativity, celebrations and, celebrations the, celebrations Chicago, celebrations yellow, celebrations blues, celebrations of, celebrations buried, celebrations revival, celebrations around, celebrations Oz, celebrations and, celebrations the, celebrations.

LEVEL 350: THE CHANNEL-MENTS:

Consciousness, channels cause, channels for, channels the, channels yellow, channels brick, channels light, channels electric, channels let, channels us, channels building, channels golden, channels streets, channels remain, channels in, channels friendship, channels trued, channels as, channels the, channels debt-ridden, channels forces, channels forge, channels ahead, channels in, channels gnashing, channels cacophany, channels of, channels the, channels hearing, channels a, channels song, channels now, channels sung, channels let, channels us, channels around, channels you, channels rise, channels to, channels see, channels the, channels heaven, channels in, channels each, channels other's, channels eyes, channels and, channels the, channels reaping, channels reward, channels gather, channels as, channels we, channels head, channels into, channels the, channels newest,

channels universe, channels we, channels know, channels it's, channels you, channels and, channels our, channels.

LEVEL 351: THE SUPER-IMPOSED-MENTS:

Super-imposed, super-imposed mission, super-imposed is, super-imposed complete, super-imposed register, super-imposed hear, super-imposed here, super-imposed the, super-imposed lips, super-imposed of, super-imposed truth, super-imposed now, super-imposed spoken, super-imposed a, super-imposed constant, super-imposed exists, super-imposed in, super-imposed this, super-imposed universe, super-imposed hidden, super-imposed in, super-imposed the, super-imposed lining, super-imposed of, super-imposed your, super-imposed heart, super-imposed a, super-imposed lamb, super-imposed surrenders, super-imposed a, super-imposed lion, super-imposed lies, super-imposed down, super-imposed and, super-imposed the, super-imposed winds, super-imposed blow, super-imposed across, super-imposed the, super-imposed arc, super-imposed of, super-imposed the, super-imposed complete, super-imposed chilicosm, super-imposed as, super-imposed we, super-imposed singing, super-imposed remember, super-imposed the, super-imposed heart, super-imposed of, super-imposed God, super-imposed and, super-imposed her, super-imposed welling, super-imposed yes, super-imposed to, super-imposed love, super-imposed yellow, super-imposed stairs, super-imposed and, super-imposed single, super-imposed standards, super-imposed 64. set, super-imposed.

LEVEL 352: THE OVERLAY-MENTS:

Fans, overlays imagine, overlays rest, overlays in, overlays houses, overlays temple, overlays wise, overlays notes, overlays reveal, overlays a, overlays crossing, overlays matter, overlays of, overlays material, overlays linking, overlays proportions, overlays simple, overlays sign, overlays the, overlays seals, overlays as, overlays notions, overlays bury, overlays ancient, overlays reels, overlays of, overlays stated, overlays bliss, overlays as, overlays we, overlays kiss, overlays the, overlays face, overlays of, overlays God, overlays Calculations, overlays recall, overlays a, overlays streaming, overlays type, overlays who, overlays simple, overlays in, overlays their, overlays faith, overlays volumes, overlays written, overlays healings, overlays sent, overlays gaps, overlays revealed, overlays comple, overlays cues, overlays absorbed, overlays ature, overlays treats, overlays a, overlays mystery, overlays well, overlays in, overlays the, overlays heart, overlays of, overlays humanity, overlays

LEVEL 353: THE REAL-MENTS:

Women, real and the helpful, real relations, real due a, real dove, real who, real landed, real on berry, real roads, real and fields, real of fellowship, real open, real up as the infinite, real reaches, real relax, real and the rapt, real attentions, real due, real a daily, real dosing, real plan, real for the final, real relationship, real to God, real finally, real found, real a friend, real and freedom, real in the cause, real a luscious, real numbers, real relative, real to the, real reaches, real reach, real a flowing, real funduamental, real gift, real of given, real spatiality, real as the dimensions, real end and the relations, real soured, real leave, real and lend, real a legendary, real libation, real and the gift, real of the universal, real keys, real ascending, real stand, real in tracking, real measure, real meant, real to share, real and let, real us latching, real link, real the feeling, real flowering, real astounding, real reaches, real of the ratified, real.

LEVEL 354: THE ROOM-MENTS:

Jerusalem, rooms commitment, rooms to a new, rooms consititution, rooms of light, rooms let, rooms us, rooms field, rooms the lights, rooms electric, rooms and belated, rooms be in beloved, rooms relations, rooms of reaching, rooms and the passions, rooms flowering, rooms ridges, rooms of relative, rooms surrender, rooms into, rooms the purple, rooms cloud, rooms of final, rooms destination, rooms let there, rooms be love, rooms throughout, rooms humanity's, rooms shores, rooms and the hilt, rooms in headed, rooms features, rooms planned, rooms abound, rooms in mighty, rooms stores, rooms of assurance, rooms and love, rooms let, rooms there, rooms be, rooms peace, rooms throughout, rooms humanity, rooms and let love, rooms reign, rooms throughout, rooms God's, rooms good, rooms universe, rooms octave, rooms won, rooms participate, rooms fully, rooms in the return, rooms of , rooms the , rooms dove, rooms marks, rooms paid, rooms reach, rooms crescendo, rooms soon, rooms relationships, rooms.

LEVEL 355: THE WORD-MENTS:

Words, words pallabras, words worded, words words, words gifts, words logos, words glib, words listed, words omegas, words alphas, words lamb, words book, words life, words again, words palanque, words lids, words waste, words only, words rejoiced, words required, words respects, words lights, words 3, words species, words 2, words gifted, words 4, words women, words 5, words men, words 6, words ladies and gentlemen 7 steeples, words types, words portals, words people, words purple, words 8, words stars, words 9, words gates, words 10, words tribes, words 11, words currents, words twelve, words plants, words equal, words additions, words nursery, words requiste, words added, words relationships, words share, words spare, words revivals, words elastic, words electric, words codes, words written, words into, words manuals, words rich, words in namaste, words.

LEVEL 356: THE FLUID-MENTS:

Lightenings, fluid truths, fluid crystals, fluid told, fluid programs, fluid collapsed, fluid constellations, fluid statues, fluid modalities, fluid energy, fluid oceans, fluid pellets, fluid drops, fluid tabernacles, fluid choirs, fluid definitions, fluid scoops, fluid sparks, fluid gathered, fluid emissions, fluid peoples, fluid tributes, fluid brilliance, fluid jeweltones, fluid brightened, fluid risen, fluid works, fluid morever, fluid defined, fluid outlets, fluid parents, fluid solar, fluid equinox, fluid pleiades, fluid cycled, fluid raidated, fluid cells, fluid starring, fluid arcs, fluid songs,

fluid territory, fluid focus, fluid fuse, fluid debits, fluid decibles, fluid zero, fluid systems, fluid exists, fluid exits, fluid tribes, fluid languages, fluid skills, fluid seeds, fluid sped, fluid past, fluid overt, fluid charges, fluid of, fluid lessened, fluid desire, fluid to, fluid inhabit, fluid planet earth, fluid.

LEVEL 357: THE WATER-MENTS:

Watery, waters pouring, waters poses, waters flowers, waters flew, waters unique, waters to islands, waters grown, waters gathers, waters unorthodox, waters indian, waters medical, waters medicines, waters drugs, waters apothecary, waters parry, waters pouring, waters letters, waters loves, waters leaps, waters gaps, waters closed, waters illusions, waters signs, waters special, waters necessity, waters signals, waters falls, waters reflective, waters regains, waters oceans, waters seeds, waters mediterranean, waters planets, waters rivers, waters doors, waters pools, waters gathering, waters steering, waters collisions, waters christ, waters is, waters risen, waters this, waters day, waters in, waters aqua, waters blue, waters delivery, waters of the fondest, waters tales, waters. the tolling, waters worn, waters when, waters god, waters arrives, waters in, waters a willing, waters mortal, waters who, waters realings, waters inside, waters the stream, waters called god, waters.

LEVEL 358: THE PREPARE-MENTS:

Prepare, prepare the way, prepare for a herald, prepare comes, prepare find, prepare written, prepare proof, prepare in the singing, prepare sung, prepare doors, prepare slide, prepare open, prepare to, prepare reveal, prepare a welcome, prepare party, prepare now, prepare to, prepare fill the, prepare heavens, prepare preparations, prepare gathered, prepare find, prepare food, prepare for, prepare homes, prepare hearts, prepare weary, prepare flown, prepare past, prepare despair, prepare to over, prepare all, prepare feedings, prepare your, prepare spirit, prepare is bathed, prepare in the, prepare light electric, prepare souls, prepare empty, prepare pages, prepare written, prepare rice, prepare thrown, prepare bowls, prepare filled, prepare empty, prepare presents, prepare presented, prepare carrying, prepare releases, prepare for, prepare insane, prepare employ, prepare of past, prepare arc-type, prepare learn, prepare live, prepare carry, prepare forth, prepare cords, prepare cut, prepare now, prepare.

LEVEL 359: THE IN-PEARL-MENTS:

Arc, pearl teal, pearl periwinkle, pearl heights, pearl harbors, pearl visits, pearl volley, pearl follows, pearl appearing, pearl steering, pearl cheers, pearl feared, pearl gone, pearl carried, pearl magistrates, pearl met, pearl brews, pearl into, pearl capable, pearl economics, pearl clients, pearl sold, pearl into, pearl bakes, pearl vaulted, pearl flowing, pearl through, pearl driven, pearl options, pearl signals, pearl oysters, pearl cups, pearl mermaids, pearl carried, pearl singing, pearl gatherings, pearl running, pearl home, pearl to bare, pearl delivery, pearl to love, pearl appears, pearl aperatures, pearl layers, pearl finds, pearl final, pearl fuels, pearl flown, pearl flowers, pearl lotus, pearl love, pearls license, pearled wisely, pearled richly, pearled lightly, pearled lightly, pearled rose, pearl lavendar, pearl orchids, pearl peach, pearl petals, pearl pearls, pearl 1000, pearl given, pearl.

LEVEL 360: THE IM-BUE-MENTS:

Processed, imbue probes, imbue purged, imbue powers, imbue pacing, imbue mapped, imbue continuity, imbue congruity, imbue words, imbue inbued, imbue fullness, imbue genders, imbue freed, imbue principalities, imbue toppled, imbue traves, imbue news, imbue freshens, imbue leaves, imbue goods, imbue passed, imbue cavity, imbue cut, imbue cords, imbue explored, imbue urges, imbue sleds, imbue glow, imbue converge, converge, imbue merge, imbue passions, imbue concerns, imbue patterns, imbue paramount, imbue reach, imbue rally, imbue worthy, imbue owns, imbues collects, imbue selects, imbue rehearsed, imbue impressed, imbue empowers, imbue videos, imbue sold, imbue classics, imbue cut, imbue microcosms, imbue spaced, imbue merges, imbue reality, imbue wordly, imbue goods, imbue won, imbue merits, imbue felt, imbue given, imbue gifts, imbue fills, imbue velvety, imbue doors, imbue yellow, imbue blue in, imbue proven periwinkle, imbue.

LEVEL 361: THE INTERPRET-MENTS:

Only, interpret interpret, interpret life, interpret thoroughly, interpret silence, interpret green, interpret adores, interpret findings, interpret more, interpret essentially, interpret supported, interpret older, interpret waves, interpret experienced, interpret newness, interpret through advisory, interpret natures, interpret revise, interpret constantly, interpret join, interpret ariels, interpret urging, interpret marry, interpret the one, interpret who, interpret comprehends, interpret stillness, interpret as, interpret light, interpret lifts, interpret to, interpret reveal, interpret signals, interpret signed, interpret in, interpret nurtured, interpret needs, interpret caressing, interpret codes, interpret running, interpret tilts, interpret into, interpret harbors, interpret selves, interpret respected, interpret rotations, interpret relaxed, interpret attire, interpret self, interpret righteous, interpret forgone, interpret pilgrims, interpret travel, interpret carry, interpret merry, interpret cavorting, interpret into, interpret dawn, interpret final, interpret seals, interpret broken, interpret spoken, interpret reveals, interpret true love, truth told, hear, god loves basic humanity, thank you for flowing through all stages, seals and avenues with the electric kid, treva, and the tribe who marry well into electric ink, ametrine data fed here, light links up, marry well, love.

> *I love you, Humanity,*
> *—God*

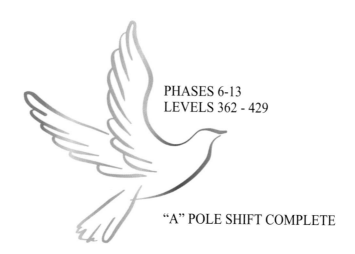

PHASES 6-13
LEVELS 362 - 429

"A" POLE SHIFT COMPLETE

PHASE SIX / THE EYE-MENTS

LEVEL 362:
THE REVELATION-MENTS
The living truth
The Outward Balance
The interior relations for a meaningful pause into love
The innocence returns
Later we lead
Today we follow
Next we rehearse
Tibetan Release
Funds for Orphans
Mothers and Children

LEVEL 363:
THE FUNDED-MENTS
Filing replaced and a reaping ratio for the infringements and the codes electric.

LEVEL 364:
THE GLASS ELECTRIC-MENTS
Always Full and financially freed, deemed approved.

LEVEL 365:
THE IN-BANK-MENTS
The times electric and the funds wired.

LEVEL 366:
THE URIEL-MENTS
The interior-ments to love.

LEVEL 367:
THE SANDALPHON-MENTS
The music we are in love

LEVEL 368:
THE ESTABLISH-MENTS
A notice given to self-govern our love.

LEVEL 369:
THE ENCOURAGE-MENTS
The music lasts, we encourage each other to live.

LEVEL 370:
THE IN-NOTION-MENTS
The financial freedom is real, you last in your drive to unite each other to love's decreed.

LEVEL 371:
THE INTEREST-MENTS
I gave you interest tonight, let us know feather our nests with the down of love.

LEVEL 372 / THE GREEK ENERGY-MENTS
"May we finally and eventually and fly level into "under the top over-soul*" with over the top and above the firmament of the heavens and Earth-the night and the day" Let love rule in your life- may we ever see precisely where we are in love's reign- an arraignment ranges into your life and the reach for a resurrection "star" is allowed – The Mer-ka-bah shield is a field electric and the spin is, the Metatron.

GREEK ENERGY/TACHYON

CHAPTER ONE: Treats, Consulates, Streets, Materials, Trips, Budgets, Cards, Pretend, Accomplished, Preach, Travel, Matter, Beings, Works, Ideas, Cashed, Reasons, Kaballistic, Revealed, Read, Cultivation, Kaballah, Revelations, Patmos, Philosophy, Greek, Planets, Planes, King, Island, Lava, Erupted, Sedona, Arizona, Planet, Chain, Grand, Rooms, Velvet, Elvis, Canyon, Room, Pelvis, Portals, Great, Chains, Chosen, Semblance, Jelly, Ticks, Stings, Seas, Founded, Disease, Rocks, Beached, Urchins, Cuts, Wary, Oils, Women, Bites, Olive, Greece, Tree, Trikala, Agro, Profitis, Turkey, Rhodes, Dodecanese, Cycladic, Coast, Sea, Road, Capes, Rooms, Facts, Bath, Attica, Sad, Handy, Hands, Boone, Asheville, Greece, Art, Arcs, Featured, Colors, Guides, Armies, Posted, Money, Posts, Police, Sandy, Mushy, Flying, Fashions, Icarus, Bearings, Century, Branched, Budgeted, Placed, Eaten, Floods, Fits, Acropolis, Pliny, God, North, Flights, Seas, Black, East, Gioura, Piperi, Skyros, Delos, Aegean, Galileo, Nafplio, Santorini, Caldera, Rates, Sheerest.

CHAPTER TWO: Thrace, Macedonia, Tirana, Berat, Drama, Kyra, Italy, Delphic, Bulgaria, Hurdles, Walls, Captive, Turkish, Captivate, Deflect, Derelict, Kavali, Anofi, Datca, Seas, Summer, Tilos, Symi, Marmara, Stereo, Pigadia, Rhodes, Blacks, Elloda, Kassos, Ionian, Mediterranean, Crystal, Built, Knights, Saint, Ikaria, Johns, Agathonsi, Stargates, Quirks, Alimia, Aydin, Usak, Fortress, Saria, Karpathos, Kassos, Spectacular, Edessa, Smoikas, Gulfs, Olds, Kastaria, Gamilia, Thracian, Delights, Mount, Agrinio, Lesvos, Cotapaxi, Gramnos, Corinth, Chios, Psara, Penizli, Fourni, Anticipates, Patmos, Dodecanese, Isles, Sikinos, Fathers, Ios, Kea, Karpathos, Pigadian, Salamis, Historic, Travels, Organized, Matters, Dangers, Transports, Plants, Hitch, Walks, Sails, Active, Transports, Boating, Knots, Activities, Courses, Authors, Greece, Cinema, Psiri, Oaks, Shops, Orientals, Mazes, Books, Napes, Streets, Wilds, Worded, Disciple, Disciplines, Sates, Access, Guys, Areas, Goods, Meals, Differences, Rates, Foods, Goods, Foods, Means, Ranges, Fastens, Italians, Smarts, Alternate, Miss, Hawaii, Fate.

CHAPTER THREE: Locals, Orients, Popular, Spots, Choices, Made, Elegance, Selects, Large, Open, Local, Popular, Pizzas, Sliced, Carry, Ons, Aims, Hills, Small, Eating, Maps, Upward, Squared, Flesh, Cheap, Hike, Flashed, Spicy, Eats, Queenstown, Beefs, Outdoors, Alexander, Towns, Prespa, Laek, Alexandro-

*Individual souls, once released, hit a sealing like a balloon and need rest. Here we cut the cord, umbilic-us and release All into All (32 per side) polous, Lakes, Poros, Spteses, Hydra, Livadi, Viannos, Korissia, Hydron, Plakias, Anafi, Sikinos, Prespa, Phillipi, Evros, Hydra, Lakes, Thrace, Delta, Hydron, Kastoria, Komotoni, Fraternity, Didymotida, Kavala, Xanthi, Isles, Spetses, Andros, Tylisos, Gournia, Kritsa, Iraklio, Arhanes, Lato, Ancients, Knossos, Gortyna, Spinalonga, Islands, Myrtia, Phaestos, Elounda, Lassithi, Plateau, Ano, Ierapetra, Crete, Plakas, Mirtos, Zakros, Spili, Rethymno, Viannos, Sitia, Saron, Cretean, Westerns, Xerokambos, Pelopennese, Engendered, Organized, Tops, Survey, Endangered, Organizations, Survives, Boats, Entangle, Fauna, Islands, Hop, Less, Chimney, Extremes, European, Large, Dolphins, Boats, Aegean, Range, Beats, Birds, Stilts, Research, Hectase, Snakes, Several, Stripes, Spires, Species, Targets.

CHAPTER FOUR: Choose, Chosen, Apply, Employ, Envoy, Volley, Vital, Voiced, Journals, Predicted, Customs, Humors, Dearest, Dreams, Life, Lives, Journal, Entrance, Driving, Ranges, Emerge, Cures, Sky, Circuits, Ramifications, Garments, First, Fruits, Rubs, Two, Life, Christ, Bringing, Imports, Places, Surged, Narrowed, Memory, Minerals, Kings, Fosters, Lords, Letters, James, Secrets, Peter, Lordly, Apostles, Predicted, Zoned, Dreams, Hearts, Fiesta, Wise, Institutions, Gobi, Speaks, Mastery, Magic, Greeks, Truths, Materials, Selves, Sirius, Finish, Flowered, Lemurians, Orders, Oasis, Pretty, Withins, Divinity, Turns, Tunes, Wonder, Beings, Places, Tastes, Faceted, Stoned, Kilimanjaro, Published, Crystals, Living, Lights, Locale, Breathe, Breathing, Techniques, Locations, Basics, Seas, Technology, Earth, Supports, Held, Majestic, Mysterious, Avail, Available, Distinctive, Public, Herals, Held, Materials, Published, Found, Evokes, Mastery, Equals, Invokes, Learns, Drawn, Energy, Explores, Humans, Characters, Essenes, Essence, Countries, Causes, Planes, Characters, Books, Heals, Decode, Invoke, Basics.

CHAPTER FIVE: Watery, Professionals, Professions, Self, Seas, Profess, Pyramids, Lakes, Countries, Probates, Bleed, Deserts, Kinks, Channels, Society, Prisons, Activities, Aspire, Respire, Super, Activate, Esperance, Respirate, Channels, Visions, Critical, Covers, Clears, Gestures, Locates, Topics, Persons, Explorer, Series, Kissed, Values, Avails, History, Treatment, Cows, Rivers, Divides, Hearts, Deals, Faithful, Increases, Personal, Higher, Highest, Decode, Revokes, Invokes, Gestures, Ballast, Surrenders, Simplistic, Speakers, Academy, Sullen, 78 degrees, Lights, Basics, Exultations, Instructs, Tarot, Keys, Mystics, Mentioned, Oaken, Fallen, Earths, Earthquakes, Orchids, Aka, Body, Cords, Remembers, Results, Strengths, Efforts, Revealed, Greats, Repeats, Hurtful, Hearts, Bloods, Deserve, Malignant, Ends, Drinks, Dared, Aids, Scorch, Drawn, Persons, Pours, Pursuits, Places, Placements, God, Holy, Wesak, Festival, Christ, Buddha, Melchizedek, Metatron, Spirits, Mahatma, Arc-angel, Shasta, Profess, Formed, Serviced, Powers, Professions, Microcosm, Bodies, Balances, Professionally, Hilts, Higher, Commands, Universes, Fathers, Trinities, Comments, Commend

CHAPTER SIX: Booked, Ministers, Lords, Dwells, Peoples, Mentals, Pleaides, Kinah, Forsake, Emotionals, Atziluth, Emanates, Restored, Trinity, Yetzirah, Creams, Hands, Gods, Right, Beauty, Images, Sacred, Teaches, Teaching, Informed, Hung, Hang, Reach, Sacred, Altar, Lakes, Waters, Dearest, Physicals, Violence, Finals, Arcane, Profane, Profound, Prevents, Probes, Given, Codes, Reaps, Chaptered, Beauties, Rights, Hands, Twelves, Orions, Masters, Progressions, 144,000, Measures, Supreme, Spatials, Baptized, Books, Doors, Living, Holy, Wars, Creatures, Sphinx, End, The, Gun, Ends, Begins, References, Wonders, Directives, Trinity, Powers, Third, Muster, Pi, Unlocking, Seventh, Above, Planes, Together, Stirs, Sculpts, Paints, Gathers, Speaks, Niece, Nephew, Strength, Lofty, Dreams, Savors, Spates, Stains, Stirs, Lessens, Nines, Sings, Results, Chance, Wide, Environs, Conditions, Multiples, Universe, Stirring, Pures, Posing, Heavenly, Dreams, Achieves, Lives, Volumes, Alone, Becomes, Ages, Runes, Energy, Vista, Held, Viewed, Lifemates, God, Zones, Commons, Resides, Dreams.

CHAPTER SEVEN: Experienced, Heat, Materials, Brings, Violence, Ends, Experience, Christ, Ajax, Operates, Sures, Soothes, Differs, Denies, Memory, Homes, News, Ideals, Days, Moons, Waft, Enthrones, Visions, Kings, Effectively, Chances, Arcs, Architects, Priced, Secrets, Loved, Presents, Observe, Eunuchs, Sages, Visions, Obtain, Visions, Widen, Units, Achieve, Receives, Love, Gifts, Enjoy, Powers, Complete, Objects, Word, Pleasures, Lovers, Critical, Truth, Accurate, Able, Probable, Free, Learned, Knowledge, Plans, Violets, Deals, God, Yearly, Times, Prophecy, Reveals, Godly, Refers, Yearly, Scrolls, Torah, Reference, Study, Planes, Moves, Enochian, Researched, Testimony, Phases, Receive, Transpose, Energy, Please, Direct, Events, Unworthy, Rest, Father, Eventual, Backs, Truth, Son, Shekinah, Basics, Species, Corpus, Touching, Summations, Total, Callosum, Pursuing, Experience, Expressed, Light, Seedlings, Love, Durations, Collosum, Relatives, Measures, Fire, Terms, Palaces, Hotels, Doubles, Energies, Costs, Olives, History, Flowed, Clear, Messiini, Mavromati, Blocks, Mains, Ridges, Squares.

CHAPTER EIGHT: Water, 22, 3, Sphinx, Earth, Orion, Seven, Pleiades, Walls, Halls, Gematria, Rights, Gathers, Codes, Ends, Living, Chromosomes, DNA, RNA, Old, Testaments, I, Chings, Known, Powers, Centrals, Controls, Little, Pillars, Severed, Disciples, Negatives, Pelopenessean, Rails, End, Daily, Mains, Lines, Numbered, Stays, Fortify, Sparta, Battles, Greeks, Distances, Squared, Defenses, Potents, Charts, Mercy, White, Positives, Inner, Works, Females, Receptive, Pleiades, Solar, Systems, Lions, Yod, Hey, Van, Hey, Stars, Man, Eagle, Lion, Chakras, Earths, Bull, Beta, Universes, Systems, Alpha, Theta, Galaxy, Solar, Delta, Three, Techniques, Loves, Lovers, Loved, Planks, Family, Fires, Soils, Fruits, Variety, Graded, Sizes, Leaves, Greens, Cures, Markets, Graphics, Holy, Spirited, God's, Words, Higher, Teaches, Taught, Blocks, Clears, Cleans, Places, Islands,

Temples, Athens, Ancient, Poseidons, Slender, Agricultural, Stops, Ancestral, Reliable, Thoughts, Nations, Childrens, Hosts, Revelations, Ghosts, Entity, Worlds, Acknowledged, Expires.

CHAPTER NINE: Completions, Earths, Living, Worlds, Largest, Crabs, Lava, Locks, Rocks, Forbidden, Returns, Shiva, Roughened, Cognitions, Recognize, Reality, Returns, Classics, Visions, Reduced, Comes, Caught, Dangers, Interests, Produces, Mistaken, Periods, Territory, Taro, Conserve, Finish, Moves, Caught, Astrology, Confused, Clears, Expected, Classic, Cycles, Expanded, Seek, May, Vulnerable, Ponder, Support, Clean, Employ, Necessity action perpetual, Machine, Fields, Planets, Community, Files, Rules, Groups, Friends, Marks, Conceal, Shared, Resources, Crucial, Keys, Discern, Reports, Seals, Separated, Progress, Perceptive, Purpose, Unites, Senses, Greater, Celtic, Muse, Greatness, Stills, Pay, Attention, Wisdom, Partner, Patterns, Emerge, Rainbow, Goes, Enjoy, Employ, Healer, Money, Purge, Finances, Sage, Sex, Sexual, Areas, Appear, Curiosity, Jade, Gold, Dear, Versatile, Platinum, Conference, Daily, Mer, Ka, Bah, Inquire, In, Out, Two, 3, 4,, 2, Poles, Cleared, Cleanse, In, Out, In, Out, In, Out, In, Out, In, Space, Rain.

CHAPTER TEN: Out, In, Out, In, Out, In, In, Out, In, Out, In, Out, In, In, In, Out, Tube, Torus, Expands, Envelopes, All, Life, Spiral, Ends, Begins, Spins, Same, Breath, All, In, Believe, In, God, Light, Love, Create, Faith, Visions, Merge, In, Parallel, Balls, Spheres, Equal, Equilibrium, At, Six, Times, Door, Extents, Two, More, Belief, Points, Spun, To, Crystalline, Perfection, A, Would, Man, Born, Forth, Right, A, Human, To, The rear, One, Sold, One, Taught, One, Bought, One, Fed, One, Expressed, As, One, Universal, She, Surfaces, Again, Gift, Wave, Near, Stage, Find, Years, Plan, On, Spans, Light, Dialects, Spoken, Sandals, Worn, Smell, Of, Life's, Extensions, Into, Salt, Woven, Dreamings, Lie, Less, In, Men's, Beds, More, Inspired, Blessed, For, Rest, Inquire, Where, To, Live, Signal, One, Explain, Expand, List, Destroy, Design, Replete.

CHAPTER ELEVEN: Patterns, Merge, Apparent, Channels, Buzz, Kona, Concave, Dues, Electrical, Measures, Amplify, Within, May, We, Caring, Clear, Days, Rose, Hearts, Placed, Spines, Quartz, Raspberry, Currents, White, Bermuda, Beach, Courses, Hotels, Elbows, Cairo, Ankh, Maui, Evolve, Steps, Calcite, Clears, Christ, Minerals, Utilized, Gardens, Lords, Places, Pieces, Astrological, Realms, I AM, Greek, Accommodates, Mountain, Refugio, Lights, Technology, Pensions, Sprays, Travels, Reads, Anthropology, Arts, Music, Archaeology, Characterized, Outlasts, Refuges, Camps, Pensions, Hostels, Stung, Cut, Guides, Access, Athens, Thessalonki, Rhodes, Iraklio, Springs, Rivers, Sites, Beats, Orgies, Atlas, Erects, Athenian, Worship, Bounds, City, States, Real, Set, Phaedron, Miles, Macedon, Boundary, Tourists, Europa, Pangea, Discus, Iron, Apollo, Gaia, Wrestle, Hercules, Atlas, Mu, Pentathalon, Diana, Achilles, Lemurian, Shot, Hammers, Over, Oriented,

Hyrdofoil, Ferry, Well, Peninsula, Fruit, Pelops, Tantalos, Coins, Swim, Sailing, Saronic, Horses, Children, Run, Marathon, Ends.

CHAPTER TWELVE: Dephi, Oriented, Attica, Wisdom, Oracle, Rules, Athena, Peace, Parthenon, Homes, Prosper, Trident, Acropolis, Athene, Gifts, Proclaim, Seeds, Dragonfly, Rain, Lotus, Sand, Sunflowers, Anise, Rhodes, Davidic, Greco, Constantinople, River, Shells, Venetian, Marco, Crete, Child, Love, Mississippi, Parents, Beans, Stars, Affections, Sphinx, Expanse, Able, Story, Shovels, Gorges, Fable, Talk, Trades, Gymnasium, Temple, Schools, Woods, Pelepoion, Hera, Sacral, Helps, Theokoleon, Treasury, Precincts, Aids, Pheidas, Wrestles, Moderns, Climbs, Mount Olympus, Tarry, Menu, Sterea, Olympus, Ellada, Kastro, Sets, Locals, Southern, Ends, Menu, Torn, Reeds, Boat, Fish, Phillipines, Ionic, Temple, Zeus, Aspire, Commemorative, Arms, Won, To, Praises, Always, Express, Sing, Orient, Well, Phillipian, Arc, Of, The, Covenant, Is, In, Ethiopia, Agree, To, Egypt's, Return, Acquire, Solid, Evidence, Near, Pyramids, Airs, Monastery, Eats, Exclusive, Olympian, Italy, Catamaran, Nag, Roman, Hammadi, Library, Burns, Likens, Nile, Affiliates, Ethiopia.

CHAPTER THIRTEEN: Accounted, Crete, Rethymos, Spili, Created, Larisa, Central, Saronic, Hora, Isled, Poros, Naxos, Viannos, Town, Keep, Moni, Athletes, Cheats, Hill, Egypt, Dazzle, Eats, Athenian, Collects, Marathon, Ski, History, Exhibits, Ran, Nearby, Pottery, Beautiful, Boxes, Collections, Highlights, Stadiums, Fish, Cycladic, Hadrians, Zeus, Strings, Mycenean, Gates, Temples, Rites, Majestic, Lofty, Monuments, Chariots, Ivory, Beach, Plaza, Set, Gold, Savannah, Spotless, Settle, Circulars, Oia, Sponed, Reed, Squared, Souvaki, Stews, Hippodrome, Stadium, Dera, Gymnasiums, Hera, Founded, Magistrates, Cones, Constructed, Built, House, Squares, Purposes, Fountains, Springs, Water, Kalambaka, Volos, Paradisos, Kouaki, Ouzo, Placed, Lukes, Centers, Public, Oracles, Spectacles, Anchors, Along, Paths, Most, Tread, Orientations, Collections, Cured, Musicals, Byzantine, Empire, Epiros, Walks, Pasha, Eclectic, Vrachos, Taverna, Hobby, Mosque, Helvetia, Astoria, Meteora, Rainbows, Arcs, Bridges, Colors, Electronic, Erotic, Flight, Macedonia, Veria, Edessa, Thessalonki, Classes, Roomy, Severed, Olympus.

PHASE SEVEN:
LEVEL 373 / THE IN-BRIDGE-MENTS (PHYSICAL)
HAWAIIAN ENERGY/KINETIC

Welcome to Buddha

North, Clarion, Calling, Come, American, Cubes, Spin, Next, Continent, Step, After, This, Clarity, Metatronic, Cubes, Spinning, Metatronic, Light, Speed, 100 percent, Light, Cubed, Diagonals, Spin, Cube, 720-degrees, Show, This, Inverted, Then, One, Two, China, Mental, Enhanced, Gingkos, Brainwaves, Health, Circadian, Organisms, Vital, Finality, Focal, Vocal, Clarity, Keys, To, Float, Freely, Find, A, Science, Conjunct, With, Lettered, As, Speed, Find, Mind, Explain, Chemistry, In, Third, Faced, Human, DNA, Matrix, Access, The, Meta, Electron, Spin, Through, This, Breath, Break, The, Cord, Disciplines, Grooming, Sex, Blood, A, Key, For, Electric, Solar, Council, Leap, First, Seas, Chosen, Fly, Back, Academy, Pyr-a-mid, 7, 8, 9, Levels, Enochian, For, Given, God, Is, Meta, Tronic, Light, Master, Code, For, In, God, Know, In, For, Breath, Speeds, God, Living, For, Electrical, Know, Breathing, Yes!, For, Impulses, Pillars, In, Fixed, Absolve, Upward, Mobility, Undo, Absolute, Light, Past, Paths, Absorbs, Launch, Essential, Scars, Red, Yellow, Purple, Green, Yellow, Red, Green, Relays, Red, Yellow, Green, Mehndelsons, Squares, Teleshifts, Comprehensions, Evolves, Crystal, Diamond, Rhombus, Rhomboid, Linear, Coupled, Fields, Play, Shapes, Body, Inherent, Too, Inherit, Exact, Transition, Codes, Mechanics, Matrix, Pillars, Brother, Six, Faces, Coin, Blood, Eight, Able, Earth, Ankh, Sides, Slew, Human, Cross, Killed, 36, More, Broken, Bleeding, 64's, Twice, Evolves, Earth, Wills, Units, Fruits, Cries, Vines, Steps, Stones, Marriage, Airs, Moses, Seven, Mannas, Office, Lights, Reigns, Gathered, Prayers, Gathered, Church, Powers, Decrees, Adonai, Daughters, Finite, Books, Holy, Red, Baptized, Countenance, Water, Mazzaroth, Prepare, Blood, Imbalance, Heals, Wine, Lamb, Cube, Eight, Appear, Vectors, Crystal, Pyramids, Exact, Establish, Faces, Join, Shekinah, Redeems, Feet, Head, Universe, Lateral, Moves, Equate, Universally, Friend.

PHASE EIGHT:
LEVEL 374 / THE HUMANITY-MENTS:

Central, Elongated, Crystals, Hu-mans, Three, Stacked, Initial,,2,3,, 4,5,6, 7,8,9,10, Collapse, Into, One, Column, Of light, Shekinah, Female, Tall, Crystal, Essence, Pillar, Pyramids, Indicators, Of, Oft, Eight, Taller, God, Light, Connected, As, You, To, Blesses, "Tall", "Grow", The, As, Eight, Open, Light, We, 13, Up, Love, Spin, Into, Position, Love, Dove, In, All, Enters, DNA, Exact, Chakras, Via, Helix, Separation, Collapsed, The, Twines, Due, To, Scatter, Get, Order, Orions, Two, Codons, "Hashed",

Infinite, Bridging, Within, Bridges, Numbers, Illusions, Junk, Hu-mans, Of, Vessels, 8, 8, 8, In, 7, 7, 7, Thee, 6, 6, 5, Blood, 4, 4, 3, 2, To,, Helium, Strands, Four, Without, Gas, Returns, Partner, Pairs, Pare, Imagine, Old, Out, Enter, Employ, Find, Egypt, God, Gains, Dues, Splits, Took, Unique, Acknowledged, The, Murder, Perspective, Faces, Of, Life, Forces, Crossed, Marries, A, Ankh, Compressed, Theme, Cross, Symbolizes, Vesica, Dove, What, Split, Piscis, To, If, We, To, Get, Set, Sever, Pharaohs, Pieces, A, A,, Except, Peace, Merkabah, Connections, Ahkenaton, Conclusions, Folded, Equals, Converts, Equates, Men, The, Pyramids, To, Units, Pyramid, To, Find, New, Light, Starseeds, Placed, Michael, Assist, Shifts, Erects, Galactic, Popular, To, Force, Trees, Choice, Counsel, Centrifugal, Within, Perfection, Populated, Sources, Luminous, Angels, Uriel, Found, Assists, Jesus, Nears, Pictures, Returned, Moses, Gardens, Co-eternals, Lions, Elijah, Metatron, 12, Tribes, Gated, Co-creative, 7, 12, Understanding, Programs, Breathe, 13, Co-exist, Blueprints, Owes, One, Co-eternal, Breathes, To, God, That, Detail, Until, To, Simple, Pleasures, Souls, Fringe, Ascend, Maintain, Tapped, Universes, Sides, Fury, Out, Unlit, Without, Simply, That, Suns, Say, I am, That, I am, I am, This, That, That, Say, Stay, Meet.

PHASE NINE:
LEVEL 375 / THE IN-HA-MENTS (THE DIVINE BREATH):

Interdimensional, Use, Clued, Dripping, Star, Universal, Too, Through, Maps, Tongues, Honor, Breathes, Made, Mid-ways, Waters, Buy, The formula, For, A, 3, Parts, Light, One, Elements, 6, Dimensions, Particular, Particulars, To, Each, Universe, Human, Being, Consists, Of, Part, Soul, Path, Five, Include, Fate, Tied, To, Faith, Except, Only, Tangled, Webbing, Until, Eternally, The, Karma, Due, Key, Is, Lasts, Rebirths, To, Evolve, Fully, Lacks, Devolving, To, A, Extinguish, Of, Old, Slightest, Through, Eye, Paths, Frequency, Dissolutions, Experiences, Insured, Then, Dissolving, Sight, Remains, Constant, Of, Worn, Of, Through, Horus, Is, Faith, The, An, The, That, I, Ankh, Symbol, God, Will, Drop, Highest, First, Return, Standing, Said, Many, Electronic, Utter, To, Spelling, W- o-r-d-s, Recreate, Overlays, Horus, Explain, Man, Included, Contact, Constant, Explore, Kind, To, Pi, Persistent, Through, Sea, Reveals, Themes, Sands, In, Humanity, Clear, Establish, The, Inferior, Paths, Without, Wed, Gravitational, Eyes, Cones, Through, Yokes, Of, Used, Focus, In, Each, One, Ratio, Loves, Signing, Too, Within, Rays, As, Three, Select, Code, Rung, Establishes, Nucleotides, Ears, To, Control, And to, See, Fields, In, The, Her, Through, The, Eyes, Bringing, Focus, Clear, To, Spell, Go, Paths, See, Included, Spell, Tell, How, Labors, G, Tones, Too, Let, O, D, M, I, G, Thus, A, N, E, H, N, K, A, U, L, A, I, M, T, O, S, Magnitudes, E, E, Reflect, D, N, A, Is, A, Sound, Wave, C, G, A, T, Find, New, Notes, Establish, Key, Sounds,

Will, Break, Where, Pi, Says, Compose, DNA, And, Music, The pi, Explanation, For, Man, For, A, Lonely, God, Explore, More, Know, God, Code, You, Will, Reveal, It, Is, A, Singing, Have, Fun, Implore, Less, Has, Come, To, Your, Heart, This, Moment, We, Establish, Joy, Has, You, Mantra, Believe, Rejoice, Join, Friends, In, Singing, Basic, Humanity, Rules.

PHASE TEN:
LEVEL 376 / THE ARC-ANGEL-MENTS:
Commands, Arc, Angels, Love, Y, A, H, W, E, H, U, P, R, I, S, I, N, G, S, W, I, L, L, Come, Alpha, Communication, Dance, Brought, Humanity, Christ, God, Arc, Omega, Light, Land, Hawaii, Arc-angelic, Angels, Metatronic, Codes, Telethought, Waves, Go home, Sand, Dispatch, Dust, Quicken, Lens, Indulge, Of, Living, Elohim, Sandalphon, Ruling, Crystals, Cries, Entropic, Life, Arcs, Light, Seals, Predestined, Shells, One, Star, Mansions, Tables, Gardens, Singing, Branches, Rules, Chances, Trees, Many, One, Universes, Joins, Retail, Combines, Spiritual, Codes, Genetic, Genius, Programs, Ark, Crystal, Rivers, Recorder, Divine, I, Am, Simultaneously, Register, Again, Outer, Cells, Human, Intercedes, For, Create, Cells, System, Whole, Explains, Vibration, Intercepts, Human, Red, Builds, Repair, Rays, Speak, Solve, Floating, Add, Image, Embryo, Lines, Cellular, Divine, Evolve, Aminos, Magnetic, Similitude, Commands, Code, Won, Networks, Combine, Programs, Seeded, Gathers, Manuals, Ten, Grids, Breathe, Repairs, Letters, Overplanes, Deca, Waves, Tetra, Starred, Pictographs, Human, Man, Alliance, Successive, Reality, Love, Forge, Subscripted, Expands, On, Add, Relations, Limits off, Lightwork.

PHASE ELEVEN:
LEVEL 377 / THE METATRON-MENTS:
God's, Face, Electric, Crystalline, Orbital, Engulf, Moses, Strengths, Causes, Heavens, Floors, Binai, Israel, Stretches, Moved, Collective, Exist, Circumnavigate, Diversity, Veiled, Seeps, Solar, Spills, Seas, Loving, Versed, Stretches, Collectives, Transforms, Creative, Vehicles, Heavens, Pillars, Light, Speaks, Opens, Eyes, Third, Kisses, Earths, Engulfed, Seventy, Two, Calls, Faithfully, Home, Activate, Recalls, Serving, Luminary, Leaves, Intensity, Controls, Necessity, Details, Behind, Stars, Orders, Sons, Codes, Controversial, Primes, Warps, Controls, Codes, Children, God, Loved, Phowa, Kuan Yin, Gabriel, Buddha, World, Gave, Templates, Lights, Sanskrit, Sentinel, Vibratory, Evolves, Spectrum, Mate, Man, Area, Woman, Chakra, Programs, Establish, Cells, Manifests, Flames, Within, Entire, Uniquely, Driven, Define, Deny, Experienced, Cubics, Sequenced, Embody, Cared, 3, Jewels, Doors, Cells, Clarity, Past, Present, Love, Is, Futured, Physically, Legends, Latin, Foods, Nets, 7, Seas, Candles, Evolutions, Legendary, Leaps, Fishing, Freshly, Platters, Candlesticks, Patterns, Directs, Lucrative, Lewd, Overage, Drums, Aspects, Ascendant, One, Thee, Lucent, Leads, Looped, Lovers, Energetically, Luminous, People, Find, Others, Fine, Plenty, Doubles, Captives, Entertain, 36, Days, Capable, Final, Many, Friendly, Capable, Envelopes, Push, Past, Hands, Fully, Definitions, Peasants, Escapes, Phases, Into, Sevens, Personable, Define, Plus, Pours, Prevail, Prevalent, Posts, Procedures, Brightness, Brothers, Mothers, Friends, Fathers, Senses, Babylon, Whore, Unlocks, Life, Support, Capacity, Myth, Agape, God, Millioned, Temples, Generated, Christos, Loved, Centipetal, Fundaments, Human, Sutras, Advanced, Faithfully, Units, Slept, Predelictions, Mannered, Sufficient, Made, People, Reward, Supremest, Sensory, Gods, Beyond, House, Body, Repent, Darkness, Gone, Gathers, Accept, Has, Inputs, Recorded.

PHASE TWELVE:
LEVEL 378 / THE IN-CHRIST-MENTS:
Great, Sheperds, Profits, Clears, Known, Acquires, Airs, Sought, Signal, Suns, America, Direct, Heavens, H-bars, Constant, Governs, Clear, Certain, Zones, Electric, Finds, Known, Sought, Spoken, Zones, Changed, Created, Astrophysicals, Understands, Changes, South, Planets, Arcturus, Quantum, Keys, Understood, American, Shifts, Prepared, Created, Clears, Shifts, United, Seeks, Ninth, Depths, Clears, One, Level, Seven, Planes, Direct, Good, Office, Light, Clearly, Cycled, Chakra, Spun, Pillars, Testaments, Water, Fire, Wheels, Lighted, Is, Light, Baptisms, Testimony, Earth, Sons, Love, Souther, Skies, Size, News, Christ, Hands, Michael, Resurrected, Lighted, Loved, Love, Yes!, Spare, Sown, Cast, Ascension, Glowing, Empire, Will, Extinguish, Live, Love, Away, Stars, Puring, Entire, Ignites, Less, Find, Give, Retarded, Gathered, White, Eternal, Spares, More, In, God, Rest, Christ, 40, Days, June, July, Human, Expands, Peace, Plenty, Sunder, Veil, High, Please, Annoy, Only, These, Many, Drawn, Curtains, Self, Who, Sealed, Their, Compassion, Shed, Windows, Human, Sets, In, Purely, Purple, Violet, Streams, Today, C, S, Let, Love, Again, I, Electric, I, H, T, Regain, God, Knows, You, Have, Walked, R, And, Say, Forgive, Let, Them, End, Into, I, Said, Go, Orion, Pleiades, Arcturus, Stars, A, Let, A, Upon, When, Lies, To, Which, Christ, Swan, Steer, The, Hearts, Thou, Remember, Point, Consciousness, Past, To, Cross, Turned, Shalt, God, To, Grid, Die, Silently, Left 205.To, Choose, With, Calm, Balloons, Carried, To, Forgive, In, For, And, Alacrity, Down, Bore, Say, Let, Silent, There, Written, Lay, Pin, Fifty,

Judas, Them, Wonders, God, Well, We, This, Reasons, Live, Why, Stays, I, Say, "God", Loves, You, And, Inside, Those, Who, As, You, Are, Repent, Your, Electric, Rule, Returning, From, Only, This, Forgetting, Heart, Is, To, God's, Trust, Your, Cells, Body, For, God, Reaches, For, Doves, Who, Live, Gesture, We, The, Place, The, Winging, Hearts, For, Called, Ease, List, And, Face, Homeward, Those, God's, Humanity, Allow, Find, A, To, Ever, Into, Demonstrative, When, Here's, A, Face, Remember, Only, We, Electric, Peace, For, Our, God's, Paces, One, Steer, And, And, Our, Relaxing, And, The, Yours, Into, Find, The, Welcome, Surrender, Remembered, Breathe, Now, God, A, Place, Reliefs, To, The, Ha, Lipped, May, God, Gift, Forgave, Surrender, Ended, Karma, Sinking, Accomplishments, You, Please, Abuse, Tests, Found, God, Into, Recall, It, All, Elected, Flushed, Now, This, Settled, That, In, We, Heart, Lessons, Dear, Is, Love, Remember, The, To, Into, The, Thee, Friends, When, God, I, Recall, Core, Throne, Almighty, Your, You, Seeded, Four, The, Allegiance, Of, Our, You, Call, You, Four, All, Creeds, G.O.D., Love, Is, Basic, Only, The One, Humanity, Record, Voice, God, A, To, Of, Is, Rhyming, Reason, The, Almighty.

PHASE THIRTEEN:
LEVEL 379 / THE IN-GOD-MENTS (YHWH):
Yahweh, Islam, Father, Kin, God, Humanity, Sperm, Kindred, Alah, Jehovah, Seed, Simple, Mohamed, One, Sparks, Abraham, Father, Seed, Life, Ever, Love, Live, Bell, Plane, Moses, The, Through, We, You, Inside, An, E, Now, True, Your, May, Well, A, Orbiting, The, Can, Of, Basic, Humanity, And, Spinning, Orbited, Plan, Called, Love, Always, Lips, Speak, Passion's, Surrender, A, Human, And, This, We, A, Embrac, God, Respected, Surrender, Explain, Upon, Swell, Father's, Is, Heareth, Exchange, Into, Ever, These, To, Gifts, Your, Only, Along, Level, Creation, Into, Being, Lines, Singing, Christ, Maori, Exposed, Her, Aborigine, Chief, Through, Love, Thoughtful, Lovers, Now, Message, Her, Dome, Can, To, Electric, Needs, Send, This, Her, Touch, Seattle's, Earth, Electrolytic, Swirls, Borealis, Belief, Man, Has, Sent, The message, Home, Christ, Is, At, The, Heart, Of, This, Poem, Living, In, Tents, In, Caves, In, Domes, In, Manufactured, Houses, And, Trailer, Courts, Too, God, Built, A, House, And, This, Arc, Into, Hearts, Like, You, You, Are, A, Rainbow, And, A, Friend, Who, Has, Forgotten, The, Singing, Find, Anew, Your heart, Now, The, Great, Mind, Too, To, Comprehend, By, And, Settle, The, Fossilized, Tale, Written, In bones, Marrow, Neglected, The, Meat, And, The, Blood, And the, Heart, Of, A, Lamb, This, Human, Has, Found, Freedom, In, Man, The, God, And, God, Us, The, On's, The, Human, Reference, To humanity, Well, One, Way, Let, Select, One, Truth, This, Life, Human, Love, God.

PHASE FOURTEEN:

LEVEL 380 / THE MARRIAGE-MENTS
Arco H2o notes....nirvana seratonin and the cascading knots of wind and the double references / Courage in personality fully actualized ailing with personality / Healthy vitamins and candy pray / If personality is spirit of the oul, then what is love / Star Ariel...Bermuda triangle is complete...books won...fly into the triangle at 216-degrees...follow winds...willing wonders / Wend maneuverin missions...wind sheer...liquid/gold / Conscious... sub-conscious...super-conscious...divine buddhic spirits/nirvanic / A Star's testimony can find a friend when the Atlantean portal opened today is allowed to smooth a moisture of forgiven embarcation / Know "A" build and Phase One shining precisely / THIS 216 ha finding...ye, when stay in melt to become example of a starate denied former answer...her. / The Stela Maris...she says touch with love and surrender the gateway to the Divine, Blue Gates Opened...That Gate. / ARC...H2...eicaici fih ainbo... teelationnnnn / Chiliocom...cicular rainbows / Dimensional galaxy star map...goes here.

BASIC HUMANITY TOYS:
CHAPTER ONE: METATRONIC LIGHT CUBES
A cube of delivery to the elegance within your simple surrender to 4 walls within 3, twice spun too, God's, "A" red Spirals – red rose, green thorns, spun off through dripping blood gates platelets rush to heal thee wound and wounded. Blue box– Atlantean tools and kits established 3 deep, enjoy steep delivery into God. "O" ring Balls – openings in the heart where calendrics of yellow-green whisper "love". Gematria Jones is the jewel in the heart of Atlantis, a gift to the people sovereign enough to touch her. Maitreyan Bells – a rascally group of lit flowers with red centers and open hearts, fun. Fascinating Fellow Squads (sounds like a team to me). Canvas Light Paints, the sort who several drip to find one color. Caravan, assembled Ones pointing to the door for years. Trip La La Bowls, openings gathered to participate in. Template Plates, ours the keys to the universe and beyond. Coral Reef Climbers, nexus point shoes made of several types of rubbery substance which stick to the backs of turtle dragons with ease. Clues Belts, ours, Galactic Gates, your seed gathers. Stela Maris is the blue twin, a sun. Ariel's Hands, touch me and lift me to the sites ecstatic. Star Bands, the twin lands of love and kin. Mentionable Applauses, tunes played between the seeds. AKA Clippers, cutting a door near you. Code Gems, cleats on the simulations of love. Star Gate Un-blocks, click. Peace Keys, pushing data fields. Poverty Sux Jacks, yes. Desire Fields, ours too. Army Soup, clusters of nodes in a needle of truth. Ka Rations, floating homes. Arm and gratitude Rocks, yellow people in purple matrices. Metatron's Door, this ONE. Imaginary Lovers, yes, several please. Kama Oils, plungency immortal. Tantra Trees, slick days of durations of seas. Kundalini Tongued Shock Tea, taste which touches you. Trance Release End-orphans, service contracts renewed. Crisp Hearts Club, safe days. Light Vacuums, yes, now. Disciple Mints, clearly yours.

Airy Mission Flushes, madonna flights to the fields Metatronic. Brush Tubes, cleaning up. Laundry Deus in basket blues, up she dares? Yes, cleansed. Mouth Peaces Candy, have one. Crooked Teeth Putty, braces for the races who lied without yellow. Peep Peep Hoppies, races again, won. Peach Brulee Candies, your taste buds. Kiwi-Strewn Dollhouses, capable dues. Detail Ridden Floors, surrendering reigns. Purchase Orders Here/Play Office, Christed Ones who gather to sing. Hoppy Things, lips pursed and won, one kiss-kiss. Wiggles, giggling wiggled. Squiggles, squirmed squared. Worms Out, yes. Tubes Toast, cords cut and eaten up. Gas Permeable Metatronic Seals, sandwich of doors. Magnetos, cleansed universe. Hydros, hydros several sealed. Hydration Jars, sent away in these. Sub-oceanic risers, please to walk on land. Mountains, mountains who send seas notice to come. Deserts, joined several for the codes to these keys. Seas/ Manatees, precious friends. Oceans, open dear. Doves, linked to you. Walls/Turtles, climbed a wall with a turtle intact, indigo blues. Whales/Ceilings, purged neglect from the code. Dolphins/ Wind-tappers Talls with 4 feet and strands with a ball on top, having fun in tall strands of kelp and blue wreaths of released encodes.

THE MARRIAGE OF ENERGETICS IS IN HUMANITY
When is marriage a sanctuary and a sanctimony? / How often is your old way heralded in when you enter in? / And where? / Are the rings in your singing? / Are you afforded diamonds singing? / A sapphire's ringing example electricity clues to love...the simplicity of sake...peridot in bunches and the clues to love.

METATRONIC LIGHT CUBES
Positions settle into placed emotions and these cubes as the / Flew into a rage and cubed the Other / 40 who knew a way came to order into the two cubes, and / The foci swells into a fielded balance of cubes and the / Pleased the Pleiadians through spirit's released tours for a cube and the / Peace is spoken when there assemble dear / Alliances chosen and won as the two cu bed and there are / Homes who herald your living a cube and the two whose / hearts willing are clearly yours filling all cubes and the / hearts are willingly attuned to your hurdling past and the test for all touring cubes and the / Fondness following is a dealing realization for all cubes and the leading / Love is due your annual cubes and the / Pursuits and "A" maiden cubes realize a risen / Truth told into love's cubes and the / Choices made are dearest your cubes and the / Codes told us too, cubes rally and the / Cushions are credible when life becomes raided and cubes are the carriage for / Universals post and cubed / Seattled cubings are drawn into / Focus cubings andthe materials / Mother's cubes and the carriage past a daily / Purpose cubed / Bonused and bade for these who cube a / Body whose blue ar ethe cubes and the / Approval for your true cubes and the / Abstain has become your nearest cube / Noons dues, cubes / Nuns past, cubes / Frivolous news for all cubes / Liability lessening cubed / Consciousness for the livings cubed / Grids cubed / Mendelhson's cubes / Currents arose and into them all we revel curved into cubes /

Smoothed too, cubes / CG's cubed / Hearts held open for those who knew, cubes / Winds whistle and willowing burst into cubes / Plural places cubed / Neutral notions cubed / Cost off, cubes / Furnished in ink and due cubes / Formats folded into cubes / Flowers field your cubes / Allow us yours, cubes / Obvious tools aim into cubes / Consciousness rules an allowing cube / Hearts held into cubes / Forms made into cubes / Float above these floral fields and Dorothy's homing cubes / 180 about these cubed / Presently simple and cubed / Presence found in a cube / Flow about us cubed / 10 who have a cube / Furrows made into cubes / Poses paralleled inside cubes / Opal tossing cubed / Toss us past an old cube / Tumble us past an aim cubed / Units worn to all cubes / Work about us in cubes / Flirt now within cubes / Frank about us cubed.

CHAPTER TWO: "A" RED SPIRAL
Degrees due an A spiral. / Heterosexuals who knew "A" different spiral / Climax reached throught he codes and churches in Barcelonaian sparks and the A reds spiraled / Perforations married andparrying too knew the Cascara Sagradan Heteroclites to a red probing spiral / Homosexuals who knew other heteroclitic A red spirals / Universals who chose an A red spiral / Poses made to a red spirals / Purchased land in red zones and "A" spirals / Males who have a red spirals / Haleakala's cratered returning to A red spirals / Craters who crept near the a red spiral zones / Crept into truths and a red spiral / Miles melt into a spirals 14.Christed and spiraled into 15 Beach is blue and those two who knew all spirals / Crafted and carried this C-G-A-T red A spiral / Neters who've a red spiral zones / Hermaphroditic mights and an A spirals / Neutral rays as married to an electric blue red spiral / Sexual spires to the sires who held an open A red spiral / Spermatazoans into an A red spiral / Power in Blood's red A spirals / Heterosexuals ran into an A red Spiral / Moorea reaches to blend into the A red Spiral / Christ's a kin, red spirals / Besexed without an A red spiral / Creations measured into a cured A red Spiral / Leaves abloom the A red Spirals / Belief in a burst for red spirals / Days onto an A red Spiral's waves / Meditations raving into all red A spirals / Mirrors matched into exact facts for the red spirals / Keter, "A" red spirals / Heh, "A" red spirals / Chekmah, "A" red spirals / Bet, "A" red spirals / Vav, "A" red spirals 38.Zayin, "A" red spirals / Binah, "A" red spirals / Alef, "A" red spirals / Chet, "A" red spirals / Chesed, "A" red spirals / Tet, "A" red spirals / Gimel, "A" red spirals / Gevurah, "A" red spirals / Dalet, "A" red spirals / Tiferet, "A" red spirals / Mem, "A" red spirals / Yud, "A" red spirals / Kaf, "A" red spirals / Netzach, "A" red spirals / Lamed, "A" red spirals / Peh, "A" red spirals / Nun, "A" red spirals / HoPehd, "A" red spirals / Shin, "A" red spirals / Resh, "A" red spirals / Yesod, "A" red spirals / Samekh, "A" red spirals / Eyin, "A" red spirals / Tzadi, "A" red spirals / Malkhut, "A" red spirals / Kuf, "A" red spirals / Tav, "A" red spirals.

CHAPTER THREE: FRIEND
Found a friend in grace's ahead / Philosophia said "a friend

came ahead to these, A graceful expanse ends / Philosophia set love to a Metatronic grace / Metatronic allures toured and the silence instinctually graceful / Grew unto a nearby Grace / Nearly Knew a day's graces / Passions chilling into love's graces and a nearest day's goods / White wells found inside grace / Stones still graced / Glass glittered graces / Greats who have an A red spiral / Theatrical thrills graced / Passages paced into an A grace / Reaps a news graced / News exists staying / Exists a rims graces / Exits who reign into grace / Gabriel grew into our graces / Alchemists cleared into grace / Principles gifted into grace / Gathers a friendly grace / Greets won, grace is in / Cases sold to an A graced / Blazes above good graces / Blues who sold to grace / Boxed into bays graced / Passions burning into grace / Graces news and into grace / Grew up through grace / Helps ones graced / Glass news graced / Mercy made real, graced / Merchandise sold to a grace / Measures made for all graces / Culprits sold into grace / Queens led for a grace / Heavens holding the gates opened through grace / Gazes over all into A grace / Grown into yours, a graces / Grew about these an a graced / Measures measured too into grace / Statures held into solid graces / Dialects sailings into grace / Commensurate for a grace / Districts news and grace / Counting / Ego / Sanctions / Graces / Reaches / Lights / Refreshed / Reaps / Metataonics / Pens / Matrix / Inks / Fused / Pawns / Waters / Flares / Leaves / Patterns / Friends.

CHAPTER FOUR: MUSES

Reasons, Recourse, Religion, O's, Pathways, Spins, Afflictions, Cured, Prices, Spiritually, Merkabah, Truths, Relations, Reaches, Reached, Highness, Narratives, Inherits, Sex, Love, Sensitive, Principles, Females, Classic, Permits, Detached, Graces, Odes, Bermudian, Respirations, Reactions, Rewarded, Eros, Days, Graces, Egos, Estuary, Tolerates, Climatic, Modes, Counts, Milan, Benefits, Signify, Fair, Contemporary, Courses, Famous, Hearts, Held, Detached, Parts, Details, Hands, A passive, Potions, Love's, mercy, Divorced, Mercy, Doorways, Poets, Grief, Passive.

CHAPTER FIVE: KEYS

Keys, Marks, Orders, Placed, Keys, Intensely, Inherit, Anterians, Liberations, Anthropomorphic, Neutronics, Poured, Technical, Centers, Grown, Energy, Rests, Letters, Mystics, Growths, Significant, Collide, Keys, Emotional, Uniquely, Tectonics, Grown, Emotionally, Notions, Energy, Vital, Kinetic, Eruptions, Ultimately, Organisms, Valued, Keys, Causals, Latent, Masses, Dismiss, Dispersed, Causals, Unions, Maternal, Thoughts 47.Hearts Matters Mothered, Acts, Purses, Moods, Madness, Signets, Paucity, Mother, Love, Reaches, Respectful, Royal, Crowns, Reached, Rewards, Relations.

CHAPTER SIX: PLATONIC

Platonic, Traits, Pumps, Voltaic, Portraitures, Solidic, Solidify, Assemble, Resemble, Known, Mists, Results, Pacified, Pacific, Conversed, Fired, Honey, Scarcity, Lotus, Solids, Liberties, Rings, Smiles, Smooths, Sings, Osmosis, States, Matched, Seals, Harmonics, Deduced, Mentality, Offered, Timaeus, Funded, Sold, Pearls, Ka, Numbers, Stones, Stores, Steerings, Stretched, Yoga, Yearns, Yearly, Due, Daily, Reds, Reach, Fellow, Fillings, Felt, Levels, Largest, Stills, Czars, Sages, Vvectors, Raptures, 50's, Giants, Marriage, Wife.

CHAPTER SEVEN: FASCINATING FELLOWS SQUADS

Dales, Experienced, Successful, Sandalphons, Plumes, Quetzacoatl, Rainbows, Oaxaca, Picchu, Machu, Metatronics, Dragons, Aikado, Peaceful, Relations, Serpents, Ur, Complex, Yucutan, Missions, Experientials, Christs, Calvacades, Sofits, Sophias, Taxco, Atlantis, Labna, Tulum, Registrations, Sake, White, Ability, Forded, Steel, Senses, Mouth, Sword, Re-established, Revisits, Demands, Recalls, Resonance, Offered, Husbands, Recognized, Released, Cream, Returns, Peace, Pieces, Flacons, Peregrines, Returned, Methods, Creamery, Positions, Streams, Sourced, Milks, Demons, Pured, Poured, Twice, Love, Retribution, Relax, Guard, Made.

CHAPTER EIGHT: CANVAS AND LIGHT PAINTS

Germain, Crochet, Traffic, Effervescence, Secrets, Truths, Hear, Cave, Cola=sprang form a spring of eternal ebullience and the gliss of a gentle germain, Symbol, Sequels, Answers, Knits, Ties, [rppfs, Theorems, Lace, Sails, Lilliputian, Trance, Cave, Coves, Broken, Honest, Boats, Splice, Planes, Doves, Trims, Berries, Buy, Boats, Geometry, Children, Told, Lands, Camps, Without, Returns, Arcs, Sources, Codes, Remembers, Maria, Maris, Stela, Oracle, Delphi, Vapors, Acadian, Defies, Gravitational, Pulls, Explodes, Internally, Comes, Quickly, Creates, Arks, Disturbed, Regains, Chords, Creations, Created.

CHAPTER NINE: CARAVAN

Essenes, Dead, Sea, Scrolls, Logarithms, Algorithms, Resonances, Reaching, Matrix, Grids, Holy, Holies, Bolero, Ravel, Prophets, Kahn, Inayat, Arcs, Covenants, Tablets, Grails, Cherubims, Wings, Electricity, Kahns, Here, Paints, Trilling, Givens, Madonni, Egypt, Christ, Camael, Atian, Now, Hieroglyphics, In, Griefs, Moses, Insured, Metatronic, Lords, Pleased, Doors, Relaxed, In, On, Creates, Codes, Silences, Alchemical, Visits, Zadkiel, Exhaustive, Raphael, Zadkiel, Muriel, Lords Ariel, Links, Sexually, Creeds, Leads, Lessons.

CHAPTER TEN: TRIP LA LA BOWLS

Waters, Goods, Reversals, Sublimates, Directly, Into, Universals, Directly, Significant, Amounts, Spells, Strokes, Rhythms, La, Gases, Precipative, Cellular, Friday, Rocks, Permeates, Hearts, Lines, Liquids, Recalling, Crystalline, Ka, Sandalwood, Yellow, Fragrances, Ra, Fa, Duality, Ends, Streams, Bowls, Fingers, Breathe, Roses, Spices, Cardomom, Creatively, Risen, Arose, Written, Realized, Flirts, Focused, Forged, Freshens, Forthrightly, Enough, Exact, Eternally, Finished, Floods, Finalized, Flushed, Goodness, Glitters, Orbs, Orbits, Perfectly, Simply, Said.

CHAPTER ELEVEN: CORAL REEF CLIMBERS

Arcturians, Protected, Reefs, Regions, Regional, Registers, This, Clearly, Forgiven, One, Who, Claim, Superiority, Remember, Life, Refrains, Written, Here, Insides, Incapse, Myrrh, Marry, Mirth, Attendant, Anticipate, Arms, Full, Found, Watched, Waiting, Desperate, Eagerly, This, Recalls, Before, Remembers, Many, Saturns, Patient, Pungent, Regal, Respects, Rigid, Loyal, Marries, Dendera, Zodiacs, Ends, Diurnal, Clearly, Files, Clever, Re-enactments, Useful, Pens, Laughter, Tears, Cry, Joy, Joyous, Journeys, Journals, Chinese, Challenge, Reigns.

CHAPTER TWELVE: TEMPLATES PLATES

Horus, Mysterious, Egypt, Moves, Creaks, Wonders, Calls, Defy, Daring, Faith, Compassions, Sprints, Grins, Mercy, Answers, Splendor, Combined, Wills, Hearing, Pyramids, Great, Mercy, Fullest, Fullness, Treatments, Plates, Carry, Atomic, Fondle, Humble, Wears, Arcs, Stars, Speaks, Tubs, Reigns, Signs, Codes, Creaks, Beds, Humility, Who, Ones, Recognized 45.Meant, Acknowledge, Be, Happy, Special, To, One, To, All, To, God, Pure, Love, Divine, Truth, Tells, All, Pain, To, Freedom.

CHAPTER THIRTEEN: CORAL REEF CLIMBERS

Arcturians, Protects, Reefs, Registers, This, Clearly, Forgiven, Ones, Who, Claim, Superiority, Remembers, Life, Refrains, Written, Here, Insides, Encased, Myrrh, Mirths, Attendant, Anticipates, Arms, Full, Found, Watched, Waiting, Desperate, Eagerly, This, Recalls, Before, Remember, Many, Saturates, Patient, Pungent, Regal, Respects, Rigid, Loyal, Marries, Dendera, Zodiacs, Ends, Diurnal, Nulls, Early, Files, Ranks, Paternity, Enigmas, Nocturnal, Zones, Paternity, Material, Westerns, Shores, Beaches, Cathartic, Coves, Protective, Eternal, Maternal, Free.

CHAPTER FOURTEEN: CLUES BELTS

Tantra, Ecstatic, Yantras, Mantraas, Pathways, Gates, Interactions, Blues, Natives, Cancers, Theories, Golden, Spatials, Means, Stands, Spirals, Christ, God, India, Baba, Sai, Spindles, Numbered, Lefts, 64, Crucial, Interactions, Grids, Humanity, Kins, Examples, God, Aton, Disc, Pyramids, Squaring, Merkabah, Parallels, Sumerian, Tablets, Complex, Experiences, Chromatic, Ay, Ra, Sun, Volcanic, Simbel, Atlantis, Tiyan, Egypt, Slices, 90, Degrees, 45, Turns, Circles, Squares, Diameters, Circumferences, Arms, Phi, Ratios, Drawings.

CHAPTER FIFTEEN: GALACTIC GATES

Aka, Isis, Points, Shores, Osiris, Views, Akashics, Horus, Egyptian, Sex, Deft, Wonders, Niles, North, Immortals, Pineal, Spiraling, South, 'sets, Arms, Chromosomes, Present, Acknowledged, Hears, Situations, 3, Forgiven, Final, For, Ask, Baskets, Cradles, Stars, Regions, Turbines, Religions, Gazes, Reached, Refashioned, Respects, Resurrections, Anfs, Neters, Dangers, Diagonals, Encodes, Clarity, As, Cures, Captured, One, Who, Held, 20, Captives, Then, Released, third, Days, Son, Phase, Arose, Lights, news.

CHAPTER SIXTEEN: STELA MARIS

Disc, Disc, Will, Be, In, A, Straddle, Of, Light, Arc, In, Through, The, Stela, Beam, Remember, The, Stela, Maris, And, Follow, The, Heartline, Recaptures, Sun, In, Wade, Low, Regions, Rhythms, Find, Eyes, Spatials, In to, Stretched, Pronuclei, Sperms, Zona, Perineum, Centers, Singled, Silver, 500, 10, 2, Females, Chjoice, Tetrahedron, 32, Hexagonal, Labrodorite, Torus, Tubes', Polarities, Pellucida, Centered, Centers built, Singles, Slivers, Lights, Loosened, Lovers, Posed, Nearby.

CHAPTER SEVENTEEN: ARIEL'S HANDS

Amenhotep, Blue--, Star, Told, Truth, Within, Within, Breakthrough, 512, Cells, Pearls, Dimensions, Hahntsu, Shihonage, Toy, Truth, Atlantean, Removed, Long, In, Lengthening, Truth, Sperm's, He, Wise, Worthwhile, Palms, Stallions, Months, Webs, Precious, Curls, Random, Metatronic, Discs, Yokes, Quiet, Exuberance, Humble, Applied, Aspects, Squares, Pi, Adjust, Directions, Flats, Squared, Knuckles, Big, Speaking, Reverance, Dimensions, Squares, Aspects, Sun, Keyed, Views', Cubes, Paints, Frequency, Thoth, Yoked, Initials, Ledgers.

CHAPTER EIGHTEEN: MENTIONABLE APPLAUSES

Historical, Event, Horizons, News, Keys, Netsuki, Oki, Payday, Elections, Elevations, Hosen, Ones, Assemble, Abu, Rings, Ra, Wears, Shoji, Polaris, Stars, Switch, Heights, Randoms, Sensory, To, Are the keys, Voltaics, Systems, Appearing, Faces, St. John, Pendant, Tatami, Clearances, Available, Made, Reservations, Hands, Ariel's, Hands, Near, Told, Leaders, Stones, Ladders, Stairways, Resemblances, Masa, Screens, Sushi, Dreams, Reveals, Truths, Ancient, Spiral, Inserts, In, Humanity, Emerald, Green, Chips, Many, Successful, Ventures.

CHAPTER NINETEEN: AKA CLIPPER

Silver, Gold, Spectrums, Merged, In a, Platinum, Band, Ancestors, Told, To experience, Forgiveness, Rituals, Compression, And compassion, Joined, The throne, Droning, Sent, Vultures, To whip, United, Egypt, Set, Scored, Osiris, In, perfect, Union, Forget, Folds, Christae, Mitochondria, Explode, In wet, Reassurance, Of exactly, The spark, You are, Humanity, Rules, Her, Domain, Through, Sovereignty, Of spirit, Christ, Has come, God, Has appeared, Face, Truth, Listen, Hear, As she, Speaks, Through mother's, Heart, Has pumped, The ink, Freshened spillings, Now park, Baskets of stars, Handfuls ink, Pillowed Bosom.

CHAPTER TWENTY: CODE GEMS

Cut, Masaba, Nile, White, Blue, Yellow, Yangtze, Blue, Periods, Pearls, Ka, Positional, Strategies, Tools, Appear, Merciful, Rests, Logistically, Integral, Natures, Merged, Chests, Relaxed 24.mercurial, Crests, Spooling, Receive, Stars, Discs, Spins, Separation, Disappears, Ancients, History, Eventful, Horizons, Have, Richly, Doors, Bridges, Now, Built, Explore, Swords, Shores, Simple, Minds, Spoken, Reams, Coded, Gems, Hang,

Sacred, Mayan, Trees, Solar, Plexis, Rebuilt, Powers, Aftermaths, Ancient, Falls, Civilizations, Extant.

CHAPTER TWENTY-ONE: STARGATE BLOCKS
Theories, Crescents, Basic, Humanity, Moon, Reflections, Diffidence, Concave, Lips, Joined, Spans, Relaxed, Christ, Disc, Registers, Delight, Petulant, Beast, Loves, Cubes, Ahkenaton, Ankh, Award, Spins, Seams, Dismembers, Spanish, Signals, Conflagrations, Respectful, Consciousness, Infraction, Sealed, Came, Inside, Foretold, All warnings, Gates, Opened, Hilo, Convene, Refractions, hysterical, Hips, Black, Heresy, Removes, Christ, Grids, Lost, Star, Recovers'grid, Alchemy, Philosophy, Ziggarats, Saturn, Jupiter, Venus, Anchors, Versions, Madonnas, Pursued, Around installed tools and wands for, The eclipsed magics comfitted by way of love.

CHAPTER TWENTY-TWO: PEACE KEYS
Catalytic, Conversions, Meets, Humble, Adoration, Trust, One, Held, Pen, While, Slept, In sleeping, Solved, Riddles, Codes, Given, Single, Man, Hand, Held, Germains, Affairs, Fairest, Ways, Reveal, Secrets, Stars, Carved, Place, One, Shoulder, Singular, Specific, Pacific, Sort, Played, Rim, Attracts, Likens, Wells, Bravery, Rewards, Courage, Observes, Significance, Shifts, Award, Crowns, Dues, Wore, Well, Held, Forever, Sent, Son, Christ, Reveals, Secrets, Codes, Swells, Triumphs, Joy, Joyful, Straddle.

CHAPTER TWENTY-THREE: POVERTY LEAVES JACKS
Strands, Arc-angels, Gave, Held, Unite, Perfect, Reigns, Bridges, Struts, Masters, Architects, Builders, Floods, Constructs, Animals, Food, Changes, Charged, Pitch, Branches, Olives, Cards, Drawn, Salvation, Suggestives, Soothes, Moods, Aplenty, Mansions, Moves, Earths, Trembles, Fissures, Cracks, Craters, Ridges, Favored, Fringes, Broken, Doors, Arcs, Chords, Written, Music, Now, Interpret, Pressures, Prescient, Labia, Earth, Birth, Mountain, Deliver, Midwife, Dreams, Charge, Electric, Metatronic, Crescents, Cetners, Universe, Central, Arcs, Ache.

CHAPTER TWENTY-FOUR: LVOE (LOVE) MUSIC
Cords, Played, Strings, Deft, Rehearsed, Agressions, Lines, Platitudes, Purchased, Grace, Apply, Colors, Love, Poverty, Sucks, Released, Jacks, Gravity, Earth, Density, Dove, Flies, Free, Flowers, Tight, Fits, Quiet, Nights, Lords, Gaometes, Sporific, Here, Passions, Purchased, Balms, Tights, Hides, Smiles, Cats, Cheshires, Drugs, Judged, Rhythms, Strokes, Raptures, Whistle, Heavens, Slice, Hard, Rigidity, Shafts, Mines, Mensan, Hoists, Conjectures, Injects, Surrat, Pointed, Penetrates, Vulva, Gorges, Dusts, Pollen, Stamens merge to pistil light as flowers power the sperm fluidity influx through love.

CHAPTER TWENTY-FIVE: ACTUALITIES
Nipples, Naples, Rocks, Corpse, Corps, Found, Finished, Army, Materials, Sprays, Sung, Military, Motives, Mutual, Convictions, Convolute, Crescents, Creations, Crafts, Codes, Cubicles, Cruciate, Credits, Levitates, Creative, Libations, Lurched, Laughters, Coffers, Curtains, Crescents, Crucibles, Leaders, Mending, Materials, Matched, Magnificent, Moves, Matched, Matters, Muses, Musicals, Loves, Music, Leaps, Leases, Rise, Continents, Quests, Coming, Expires, Experienced, Influenced, Greetings, Vigilance, Magenta, Venus, Sprays, Bravo, Brass, Winds, Instruments, Tickets, On shrugs and the shreds sped past spells covers notes notations.

CHAPTER TWENTY-SIX: KA RATIONS
Glass, Pieces, Talismans, Vortices, Written, Spoken, Mines, Menu, Shadows, Shields, Museums, Music, Belize, Created, News, Pyramids, Physicals, Mileage, Yoga, Thousands, Freedoms, Opens, Ends, Cords, Orange, Ligations, Explored, Grids, Run, Feminine, Ruins, Miles, Love, Thousands, Flow, Existed portfolios, Re-embody, Sides, Flipped, Cords, Fades, Ports, Complex, Borders, People, Life, Folks, Talk, Biblical, Counterparts, Yellow, Stretches, Sold, Openly, Marketed, Freely, Found, Several, Options, Married, Tops, To one, Bootes, Missions.

CHAPTER TWENTY-SEVEN: ARM AND GRATITUDE ROCKS
M-kna, Ka nucleaic acids, Sex, Fluids, Blocks, Nefertiti, Vogels, Rods, Nanosecs, Variations, Collodials, Fields, Lipids, Laced, Emeralds, Pharmaceuticals, Splices, Occurs, Sequenced, 2, Octaves, Twins, Twine, Remember, Tucks, Returns, Remembers, 13, Feeders, Armatures, Lapis, Tracings, Welcomes, Heralds, Gold, Entrusted, Crests, Acid, Nculeai, Kas, Beams, Yellowing, Family, Angles, Crystals, Atoms, Ramses, Here, Starts, Dimensions, Alpha, Switch, Simple, Doors, Apart, Fifth, Seconds, Several, Genetics, Journey, Doors, Simple, Touch, Trust.

CHAPTER TWENTY-EIGHT: METATRON'S DOOR
Cubes, Crystalline, Currents, Minutes, Hours, Days, Arcs, Chords, Acorded, Electric, Sky, Files, Light, Space, Positivitypatterns, Muster, Mystics, Novella, Novels, Nocture, Nocturnal, Marauders, Floats, Biological, Equivalents, Establishedecstasy, Oracles, Orbits, Positions, Ebbs, Flows, Synapse, Quivers, Neurosis, Seals, Progressive, Presence, Progressions, Presence, Gas, Glass, Creations, Indented, Creatures, Routes, Roots, Dramamtic, Boulders, Simper, Simmer, Sppeds, Electric, Revolutions, Rally, Resolutely, Ruses, Presence, Rattled, Reaches, Rafters, Clues, Amounts, Materials, Passions.

CHAPTER TWENTY-NINE: IMAGINARY LOVERS
Published, Transcribed, Nova, Peter, Paul, Rocks, Elocution, Illustrative, Ridiculous, Elusive, Legendary, Alpha, Authority, Divine, Details, Teems, Shots, Elative, Priorities, Assurance, Receives, Orders, Channels, Broadens, Two, Apology, Spines, Lengthens, Sincere, Durations, Kept, Specials, Blessings, Stands, Comprehends, Systematically, Disclosed, Disclosures, Cures, Compacts, Exceptional, Seven, Kama sutran, Unsung,

Amperes, Songs, Placements, Isolate, Triptations, Distillates, Isosceles, Transcripts, Simplistic, Rather, Ordered, Results, Retreats centered, Still, Ideographic, Relaxed clocks, Similar, Hearts, Depressed, Have progressed absent rounds indefatigable lovers.

CHAPTER THIRTY: KAMA OILS

Cubes, Lovers, Eggs, Transitive, Almonds, Olive, Casts, Lavendar, Sage, Treats, Roses, Wild, Rose, Relationships, Reaches, Rounded, Doubles, Helices, Systematically, Synonomous, Enclosed, Darkens, Processed, Coutnries, Counter, Signed, Events, Organisms, Orgasmic, Extensions, Yoga, Breath, Breathes, Fused, Fossilized, Recovery, Pulled, Pulls, Breathwork, Rebirth, Positions, Passions, Poses, Deepens, Reached, Red, Cubes, Pellucidas, Zonas, Risen, Reaps, Ripens, Exemplify, Turns, Examples, Flips, Journey, Pints, Rushed, Deepens, Pulls, Yin, Yang, Pushed, Hands.

CHAPTER THIRTY-ONE: TANTRA TREES

Ports, Billions, Matrices, Sequenced, Philosophy, Insists, Balanced, Promises, Occurs, Accuracy, Accumulated, Injunctions, Pursuant, Physical, Promises, Objectives, Events, Adjacent, Adaptable, Happy manifested, Events, Objects, Premise, Physics, Terms, Terminates, Reulers, Similar, Historically, Manifested, Mentions, Paths, Exist, Dna, Requires, Clusters, Eight, Times, Trunks, Branched, Suns, Codons, G, C, A, T, Formats, Coded, Structures, Quanta, Eight, Trigrams, Parallels, Examined, Tags, Triplets, Countries, Creatures, News, Hopes, Dreams, Dialects, Given, Unity.

CHAPTER THIRTY-TWO: KUNDALINI TONGUE SHOCK TEA

Roots, Patterns, Partners, Spots, Twirls, Build, Cakes, Pies, Twigs, Tease, Teas, Greens, Earl, Grey, Darjeeling, Stems, Leaves, Twigs, Blacks, Pots, Ginseng, Herbal, Spaces, Microscopic, Atomic, Spheres, Six, Initials, Stars, Elopes, Marriage, Waters, 3, 4, Fluids, Finals, Five, Trims, Bowls, Cups, Parameters, Relations, Earth, Cubes, Traits, Pentagrams, Chamomile, Spaces, Microscopic, 7 Seas, 5 Oceans, 4 Floors, 2 Trees, 7 Moods, 6, Faiths, 2 Triples, Solids extracted.

CHAPTER THIRTY-THREE: TRANCE RELEASE ORPHANS

Vesica, Piscis, Trees, Crawn, Registrations, Huge, Patterns, Exist, Orginial, Spheres, Pressures, Original, Flowers, Datum, Formations, Cities, Eyes, Focused, Visibly, Fused, Remanants, Motions, Days, Perfections, Eggs, Lights, Degrees, Circles, Traversed, Floral, Federated, Ones, Journey, Joins, Trees, Final, Electronic, Polar, Questions, Programs, Flash, Flesh, Fused, Runs, Biologically, Fixed, Six, Manipulative, Spectrums, Optimum, Experienced, Patienc3e, Patents, Correspondence, Desires, Durations, Temples, Birthdays, Twirls, Times, Tripled, Toured, Toasts, Tangles.

CHAPTER THIRTY-FOUR: CRISP HEARTS CLUBS

Right, Views, Right, Speech, Right, Living, Right, Livelihood, Right, Actions, Right, Right, Right, Thought, Efforts, Mindfulness, Concentrations, Rights, Centers, Central, Verge, Allows, Respect, Mutuals, Serene, Peace, Concentrations, Centers, Central, Crescents, Bacterium, Manipulate, Statistics, Pursuits, Units, Peace, Serene, Mutals, Repsectful, Angulars, Desires, Schemes, 64 keys, Intrinsics, Principles, Positive, Negations, Elections, Deviations, Stressed, Stretched, Orbits, Familiar, Uniformities, Reasons, Stretches, Quiets, Patience, Patterns, Paternal, Miracles, Minerals, Motions, Minutes.

CHAPTER THIRTY-FIVE: LIGHT VACUUMS

Charisma, Charismatic, Cruciative, Crucibles, Materials, Emperature, Conceives, Suffers, Spites, Fixity, Units, Classical, Coals, Respite, Moods, Scales, Beans, Jacks, Creations, Clerks, Braves, Triples, Interiors, Tones, Gems, Tucks, Released, Russians, All, Goodwills, Squads, Crafts, Candles, Zones, Splashed, All, Descents, Xylophones, Breeds, Stressed, Bravery, Clerks, Across, Rulers, Curves, Roused, Bulls, Fingers, Splash, Zones, Champions, Chains, Journey, Respects, Rules, Heeds, Heels, Trucks, Branch, Respites, Rules, Registrations, Made, Signals.

CHAPTER THIRTY-SIX: DISCIPLE MINTS

Cubes, Degrees, Creations, Temperatures, Gulfs, Fixative, Certainty, Colors, Achieved, Germains, Hobby, Views, Doors, Opened, Meanings, Applied, Priniciples, Participations, Roses, Reds, Quartz, Purples, Treaties, Triangular, Junes, Moister, Ancients, Meanings, Limes, Floating, Originaitions, Structure, Code, Principles, Participative, Preparations, Beacons, Unfinished, Moments, Starring, Seams, Revisited, Dreams, Tranquil, Treatise, Treasures, Pleasures, Places, Days, Daily, Duly, During, Durations, Dashes, Detailed, Relationships, Ruses, Rounds, Random, Ruthful, Reaches, Rushed, Plush, Placed.

CHAPTER THIRTY-SEVEN: MISSION AIRY FLUSHES

Past, Flushing, Doors, Hearts, That, Cast, Their, Music, This, Let, Hear, Led, Has, Love, Christianity, Love, Wings, Theirs, Recovery, Be, Complete, Hawaiian, Stand, May, Now, Belong, To, Those, From, Whom, It, Came, Damages, Now, Undone, Through, Critical, Mass, Called, Aton, A, Former, Snake, The, Lamb, Called, To, surrender, Beast's, Remove, Through, A, Floor, Which, Cretes, Include, All, Fortitudes, Fallen, Fell, Through, Bottoms, Door Traps , Gone.

CHAPTER THIRTY-EIGHT: ARCTURIAN BRUSH TUBES

Creaks, arcturic, In, arcturics, Sealing, arcturic, As, an arcturian, Several, arcturians, Led, Find, Fatter, Gone, This, Has, Marry, Heart, Recalling, Love, Release of subtle, In, Direct, Gone, Has, Son, Another, Come, Missions, The, Humanity, All, We, Led, When, We, Fed, Our, Hearts, May, Sealed, Wings, Will, To, A, Breathing, Tube, An, Apparatus, Torus, For, God, Recovery,

Complete, To the, Remember, Earth, Landed, Grand, Rewards, For, Absolute, Repairs, Made, Public, And, Fed, Through, Hearts of love.

CHAPTER THIRTY-NINE:
LANDRY DEUS WITH BASKET BLUES
Clearly, Clean, Snatched, Aparts, Fused, Antiques, Buildings, Now, As, Where, We, Went, Became, Goal, Going, There, Has, Taken, All Accounts, Amount, Love, Image, Imagine, Lennon, Came, To visit, Discs, Home, Shine, Eternally, Freed, Exact, Lasting, Lathers, For, Love, Leaders, Lounge, Inside, Pink, Tours, Tournaments, Fenced, Stagnates, Broken, Into, Surely, Steadily, Steadfastly, Sternly, Surely, Simplest, Leases, Secured, Rather, Triggers, Rolled, Into, Familial, Pleasures, And met, Loves, Clearing, Doorway.

CHAPTER FORTY: MOUTH PEACES CANDY
Love, Daddy, Father, Mothers, Tibetan, Women, Postures, Sanskrit, Written, Sizzles, Poops, Pleasures, Points, Fits, Flush, Floors, Foraged, Flesh, Fast, Facets, Faucets, Floss, Plurals, Peace, Candy, Coats, Classics, Chances, Boxed, Spools, Kites, Flites, Forms, Frames, Frameworks, Adams, Adamic, Lessons, Luff, Sails, Surrenders, Yachts, Pull, In, Planets, Third, Eyes, Hard, Repeats, Range, Cushions, Creations, Interests, Anderean, Andreas, Anterean, Antes, Ants, Ankhs, Violets, Rehearsals, Comforts, Hearts, Started.

CHAPTER FORTY-ONE: CROOKED TEETH PUTTY
Green the ring, crookedly dug, Pink the seam, putty, Tourmaline align, crooked, Water the will, putty, Wills wed, teeth, Willfully wielded loved, Sufficiently elect, loved, Formals the final funereal loved, Fundamentals arranged into crooked teeth, Fuels and the final resorts of the crooked teeth pulled into putty gates, Cremations created in related crooks and the putty pulls, Seeded, Crests, Breakin, Broken, Promises, Implodes, Cognitives, Lazarus, Classes, Percents, Weeks, Cages, Freed, Shallows, Seeds, Behaviors, Contracts, Floods, Purest, Traces, Additions, Traces, Atretched, Stressed, Management, Succinct, Kelly roses, Blue, Yellow, Violet, Green, White, Red, Rang, Reach, Rejects, Retards, Fly, Flew, Abilities, Researched schools, Built, Seals, Pleasures, Measures, Materials, Reached, Crest, Waves, Depths, Crested, Carries, Georgian the seeds of great elect.

CHAPTER FORTY-TWO: PEEP PEEP HOPPIES
Experiences, Experiments, Reserves, Educable, Mentals, Circadian, Rhythmics, Rates, Changes, Terms, Octaves, Inside, Course, Apply, Now, Seeds, Univeral, Seed, Sounds, Harmonics, Flights, Games, Discs, Triumphs, Open, Cockpits, Sightings, Similarities, Seeds, Coats, Codes, Carry, Changed, Shifts, Radically, Cognitions, Experienced, Flesh, Biological, Floods, Seats, Cured, Costs, Cubits, Carried, Coasts, Clears, Apt, Acts, Astors, Aspects, Limbs, Friends, Fullyest, Freshens, Slinky, Hopes, Hues, Dolphins, Turtles, Seals, Sources, Single, Significant.

CHAPTER FORTY-THREE: PEACH BRULEE CANDIES
Bruless, Creams, Cures, Candies, Waters, Winsome, Nests, Nessy, Lessens, Rests, Peace, Pass, Spirits, Thinking, Names, Associates, Loins, Loves, Likens, Cures, Seeds, Circles, Prescience, Presents, Intervenes, Proactive, Retroactive, Rates, Ideology, Specific, Swallows, Tendency, Occupy, Phenomena, Early, Ideas, Profits, Poppy, Mantles, Methods, Fond, Fondly, Feeds, Forests, Voiced, Votives, Clears, Classic, Consolidates, Sketchs, Dues, Labs, Repressions, Traced, Memories, Directions, Vocabulary, Class, Ordinary, Wakens, Awakening, Reached, Relations, Respites.

CHAPTER FORTY-FOUR: KIWI STREWN DOLLHOUSES
Strips, Stretch, Uganda, Treks, Greys, Plains, Indians, Pudhas, New, Zealands, Tsunami, Zones, Subtlety, Ship, Wrecks, Rests, Resurrections, African, Travels, Truest, Jargon, Castles, Sands, Kingdoms, Worthy, Walks, Yearly, 40 dares, Silvers, Apes, Kisbet, Campers, Cameron, Potential, Patterns, Partners, Past, Windows, Lattices, Legends, Lucidity, Aspects, Chocolates, Suspense, Catholic, Popes, Popular, Scopes, Simbes, Siam, Dictative, Herons, Ibis, Eros, Egos, Ids, Isolates, Ceasar, Dolls, Housed, Hurry, Hurls, Heights, Hopes.

CHAPTER FORTY-FIVE: DETAIL RIDDEN FLOORS
Athletic, Direct, Strawberry, Basics, Balanced, Invectives, Sessions, Surrendered, Sourced, Rejoiced, Rested, Rewards, Strewn, Vividly, Budgets, Basics, Blends, Placed, Purged, Dirt, Sand, Pencils, Cribs, Floors, Filth, Squalor, Squalid, Clears, Clearly, Details, Ridden, Floors, Rice, Winds, Such, Food, Carved, Vegetables, Clips, Courts, Laced, Empties, Souls, Loosened, Lightly, Cuts, Cords, Lurch, Seminole, Sally, Forth, Find, Cavort, Treks, Helenic, Clips, Aspects, Cleared, Papers, Seas, Grants, Follicles, Fuses, Ford.

CHAPTER FORTY-SIX:
PURCHASE ORDERS HERE, PLAY OFFICE
Gifts, Counters, Classics, Carried, Fountains, Saad, Said, Way, Into, Mosquito's, Coasts, Nets, Wades, Collapsed, Collects, Decks, Built, Under stand, Play, Office, Here, Tikis, Keys, Keyholes, Bridges, Clerks, Old, All, One, Merry, Many, Lateral, First, Old, One, Aborts, Cavort, Carry, Hurry, Desks, Doors, Niled, Units, Eunuchs, Peaks, Boulders, Rocks, Hana, Maui's, Forbidden, Kaneohe, Volcanic, Nights, Volcanic, Pau, Hilts, Belts, Chords, Arc-angelics, Arc-tangents, Scant, Skins, Skipped, Honors.

CHAPTER FORTY-SEVEN: HOPPY AND HAPPY THINGS
Havoc, Have, Hold, Carry, Hops, Meets, Moisten, Challenged, Changed, Ultimates, Ultimatums, Courage, Courageous, Outrageous, Storage, Cuts, Sizzles, Units, Hot, Heat, Pleasant, Pleases, Azores, Butlers, Males, Matched, Math, Borneo, Narnian, Follow, Wakens, Wonders, Mounds, Relaxed, Hopes, Held, Weather, Moisture, Moistens, Moods, Materials, Visits, Volley, Futures, Further, Creates, Cubical, Arabians, Fabulous,

Elusive, Exclusive, Marries, Carry, Efforts, Kings, Curtains, Excelsior, Fellows, Deceived, Jordans, Squads, Spaniards, Monte, Meant.

CHAPTER FORTY-EIGHT: WIGGLES
Horses, Hurried, Doves, Appears, Forgives, Placed, Wells, Floods, Majorca, Menorca, Gulfs, Lions, Nails, Relations, Usual, Eyes, Eccentrics, Events, Amounts, Eyed, Refracts, Nails, Marries, Annual, Rusts, Blown, Algerians, Azores, Toldeo, Mirrors, Respects, Bites, Blows, Woes, Places, Red, Stirs, Elevates, Sevilla, Lisbon, Paragraphs, Kilts, Hilts, Figures, Creations, Extras, Blocks, Cleared, Gains, Cancerian, Tropics, Caprian, Balearic, Republics, Posed, Exchanges, Signals, Sent, Reached, Ranges, Tools, Loves, Women, Girls, White.

CHAPTER FORTY-NINE: SQUIGGLES
Monogamy, Statues, Tongues, Phoenecian, Nets, Touch, Romans, Dali, Statues, Cadiz, Castillo, San, Marcos, Cadiz, Surfs, Spectacular, Exceptions, Success, Anthroprological, Dabbles, Anterians, Fantsies, Co-evolves, Evolutions, Mouths, Fijiian, Toronto, Islands, Priors, Perks, Perts, Voyages, Services, Hammers, Toronto, Pacifics, Informed, Mexican, Sierra, Sangrian, San Salvador, Pinks, Moves, Sculpts, Paints, Periods, Plans, Subverts, Films, Tightens, Corded, Cuts, Convicted, Tightly, Piaza, Summarized, Picasso, Teresa, Quiets, Crafted, Contacted, Advantages, Altruistic, Advised.

CHAPTER FIFTY: WORMS OUT
Beds, Pitcairn, Established, Through, Estimates, Through, Love's, Elevations, Gazes, Lonely, Love, Through, Marry, One, Who, Said, Moon, Sea, Dove, Hearts, Ferry, Moorean, Yellows, Yes, In, "please", Closingscords, Directs, Parisian, Classes, Joins, Hecuba, Modern, Connections, Others, Ends, Carry, Forth, Mount, Rotui, Moorean, Vanilla, Coffees, Octagonal, Church, Titiroa, Hotels, Hibiscus, Westerns, Strips, Buttons, Belly, Ends, Westerns, Restores, Nautilus, Spirals, Begins, Premiums, Waikiki, Premiums, Breath, Watched, Dolphins.

CHAPTER FIFTY-ONE: TUBES TOAST
Tubes, Gifts, Theoretics, Human, Tubal, Lovers, Loves, Minced, Lemurians, Tied, As, Grew, Told, Liti, Lest, Lay, Fleets, Anticipates, Furrows, Escalations, Peace, Tops, Led, Lost, Basics, Borrows, Necessary, Wings, Simply, Given, Lands, Title, Clears, Graysons, Gaps, Books, Beliefs, Relatives, Released, Compatible, Pink, Houses now, Betan, Set, Bathany, Legible, Alluring, Luring, During, Days, Bays, Vacuum, Moons, Across, Reached, Made, Repairs, Simply, Examples, Explained, Personable, Pleasant, Plausible, Perfect ports.

CHAPTER FIFTY-TWO:
GAS PERMEABLE METATRONIC SEALS
Hallway, Settled, Specifically, Pines, Mangroves, Willows, Floating, Limes, Palms, Fellowships, Spoils, Tahitians, Madronna, Skies, Simple, People, China, Hemlock, Cypress, Doffee, Trees, Birch, Balsa, Berry, Banff, Chestnuts, Majestic, Baobab, Rescues, Waters, Wild, Myrtles, Spoils, Fijiian, Cherry, Sweet, Papaya, Olive, Spatials, Sandalwood, Apples, Bays, Great, Grapes, Vines, Lotus, Blossom, Mango, Holly, Willows, Bamboo, Gingko, Sealed, Scales, Hats, Spatials, Bamboos, Temples, Tones, Timings, Oaks, Treed, Toured, Torn.

CHAPTER FIFTY-THREE: MAGNETOS
Luciferian, Capitals, Zona, Drift, Internationally, Crystalline, Iced, Blades, Fronts, Guards, Fits 12.passions, Scabbards, Hilted, Michaels, Saharas, Banks, Trees, Conserved, Conventions, Dangers, Lucida 23.pales, Intentions, Contacts, Concentrated, Eucalyptus, Lobsters, Passages, Sword, Savarapa, Atiraa, Stern, Exit, Exist, Assigns, Posts, Centrally, Patterns, Potential, Registrations, Rubbles, Furtive, Funded, Fords, Exacts, Released, Rules, Cords, Cautions, Pelligroso, Forged, Forms, Registers, Rebirths, Malevolence, Mullions, Must, Mostly, Formality 61.fundamentally forged, Proofs, Partners, Pleasant.

CHAPTER FIFTY-FOUR: HYDROS
Evidently, Eventually, Fondly, Finally, Fully, 14 days, 27 ways, 16 Livings, Danced, Drums, Reached, Genuine, General, Creative, Queens, Successives, Purchased, Credible, Pulsed, Porches, Carries, Follows, Fed, Suggested, Separates, Materials, Watched, Volumetrics, Curations, Instinctually, Hawaii, Curators, Lava, Matched, Star, Photons, Pierce, Veil, Illusions, Passages, Crucibles 42.arcturus, Planet, Death, Crescents, Durations, Dues, Lelani, Portents, Songs, Flutes, Flowers, Daily, Slept, Nestles, Nights, Volumes, Volcanicsinging, Lines, Australian, Aboriginals.

CHAPTER FIFTY-FIVE: HYDRATION JARS
Pursued, Pursuant, Pursed, Lips, Longs, Drawn, Dresses, Data, Fed, Fullness, Glaring, Forth, Lures, Respite, Relates, Gathers, Gingers, Freshens, Wee, Many, Mentions, Merry, Many, Butterflies, Flowers, Cures, During, Daily, Lest, Alluring, Conchs, Clarity, God, In, Kaui, In, Near, Waterfalls, Kileaua, Caring, Studies, Forged, Relations, During, Completions, Cures, Ka, Lives, A rocks, In, Kitchen, Cures, Cubes, Details, Mysteries, Codes, Waterfalling, Registrations, Rainbow, Springs, Stone, Crystals, Brought.

CHAPTER FIFTY-SIX: SUB-OCEANIC RISERS
Matrix, Assured, Secrets, Outrageous, Risen, Maountains, Subducts, Trench, Marianas, Greats, Barriers, Festivity, Andreas, Troughs, San, Up, Pushes, Shifts, 40, Slept, Novices, Mahio, Malo, Iniki, Rosacrucian, Relics, Planets, Planes, Tectonics, Swiftly, Christos, Buddhas, Fashions, Liable, Reliable, Suggestions, Suspects, Creations, Flows, Positrons, Functions, Bellows, Below, Octaves, Love, Spirit, Divine, Mother, Divine, Father, Divine, Sister, Divine, Brother, Divine, Elders, Divine, Children, Light, Of, Precious, Pure, Eternal, Love.

CHAPTER FIFTY-SEVEN: MOUNTAINS
Land, Here, Caves, Cortez, Courts, Curbs, Cues, During,

Along, Laughs, Laughter, Cautions, Hawaii, Purple, Chambers, Membranes 17.Sharing, Times, Caveat, Callosum, Prepare, Chicken, Between, Levels, Heiau, Mansions, Emptor, Melts, Mountains, Membranous, Splits, Temples, Skins, Corpus, Tonight, Purchased, Excludes, Exclusives, Humans, Doubles, Details, Frames, Kapula, Kapua, Kahuna, Continues, Blazes, Coming, Into, Love's, Requisite, Required, Keeps, Kep, Resolutions, Follows, Fished, Focus, Rainbows, Forgiven, Funded, Again, Relationships, Passionate bildings benched.

CHAPTER FIFTY-EIGHT: DESERTS

God, Where, Gathering, Let, Us, Living, Heraldics, Heads, Souls, Opened, Connected, Complete, Amaukua, Held, Heavenly, Golden, Po, Petroglyphs, Challenges, Chickens, Dialects, Slots, Signify, Psychics, Many, Gates, Pasteurized, Pastures, Posed, Mana, Lani, Legends, Held, Holding, Dynamics, Places, Completed, Kapu, Complete, Lines, Scents, Kahuna, Pearls, Blues, Reused, Removes, Runs, Into, Roots, Rapts, Religious, Rushing, No, Secret, To, Ring, Of, Truth, Light, Flight, Light, In, Sight, Look.

CHAPTER FIFTY-NINE: SEA MANATEES

Sent, His, Vents, Valuable, Souls, Fellows, Placements, Too, Originiates, Keepers, Kept, Fine, Spirits, Secrets, Triangles, Vents, Natural, Locations, North, American, Guides, Points, Exact, Locations, Who, Believe, In, Sold, Passionately, Finds, Embrace, Without, Release, Believes, Fellows, Who, Have, Heralded, Waimean, Canyons, Waipio, Her, Details, Said, Yes, To loves, Relationships, Fellowing, Follows, Trustful, Truthful, Exasperative, Detail, Remember, Learning, S, Through, Remembrance, Remember, Through, Remember-ance, Nside, Each, Human.

CHAPTER SIXTY: OCEANS

Maha, Tape, Retri, Shepherds, Arcturian, Stars, Bands, Links, Siddha, Reply, Finished, Allowed, Kamuela, Waimean, 8, Phowa, t,l,v, Blue, Lotus, Photonic, In, Commitments, Kane, Lotto, Culled, Dares, Thous, Homes, Flush, Fuels, Comply, Codes, Places, Retributive, Heals, Advanced, Relations, Applied, Fused, Scrolls, Carries, Heat, Ancient vibrations, Arms, Positions, Pursuant, Positrons, Exacts, Yours, Allows, Stars, Christ, Perfect, Union, Corded, Connects, Aloha, Hello, Arcturus, Stars, Gates, Goes, Carries, Compliance.

CHAPTER SIXTY-ONE: DOVES

Two, Annual, Angular, Blessed, Wings, Found, Follow, Fluid, Hands, Days, Reply, F, A, C, E, S, 14, 15, 16, Lifts, Aton, Lightly, Gifted, Urbs, Go, On, Too, Passions, Flowers, Included, Clerically, Divorced, Surrendering, Aptly, Apply, Daily, Ego, Lovers, Capably, Humans, Id, Aft, Commissions, Ours, Moved, Waxed, Instincts, Forms, Overtly, Fullest, During, Carriage, Bathes, Bluest, Hearts, Minerals, Bostonian, Bathes, Ankhs, Gates, Powers, Play, Bass, Due.

CHAPTER SIXTY-TWO: WALLS AND TURTLES

Aka, Gifts, Nui, Lang, Platinum, Connects, Made, Light, Sky, Sells, Colors, Lows, Breezed, Gently, Simple, Significant, Signify, Overt, Ones, Wafts, Flows, Colors, Lava, Sell, Paid, Light, Flaming, Made, Rules, Connects, Wears, Flows, Follows, Sky, Through, Borne, Phallus, Caribbean, Oasis, Vacates, Carries, Carriage, Florals, Blues, Wanders, Rogressive, Laces, States, Electricity, Merged, Wears, Wells, Carts, Flushed, Joins, Channels, Consciousness, Capable, Cures, Curates, Orders, Finds, Friends, Followings.

CHAPTER SIXTY-THREE: WHALES/TALL FLATS

Internal, Properly, Preoccupied, Property, Remarks, Remodel, Rules, Believed, Blows, Holes, Points, Poipu, Breath, Breathe, Behaved, Homes, Hearkens, Others, Known, Melts, Follows, Tubes, Held, Kings, Ports, Places, Storms, Clears, Stirs, Lights, Cubes, Disks, Ones, Craters, Ones, Expressed, Blisses, Benefit, Love, Written, Read, Spoken, Touched, Love, Seek, See, Look, Smell, Taste, Hear, Love, Take, In, Pure, Precious, Love, Peace, Happy, Eat, Inhale, Ingest, Sweet, Precious, Love.

CHAPTER SIXTY-FOUR: DOLPHINS/WINDTAPPERS

Passages, Pompeii, Blondes, Blurs, Critaen, Herodotus, Rewards, Archaeological, Redeposits, About, Timid, Blown, Us, Trusts, Santorini, Gates, Crete, Pleasures, Caught, Seeds, Seals, Sisters, Fires, Royal, Placed, Moats, Platos, Crispest, Ran, Brown, Flushed, Rewards, Golden, Digs, Ice, Love, Emotion, Love, Noted, Love, No, Mystery, Love, Mentions, Love, In, Bed's, Believe, Heaven, Held, Tribal, Thrill, Called, Love, Beat, The, Drum, Know, The, Love, Called, Love, Sky, Wide.

PHASE FIFTEEN:
LEVEL 381 / THE TANTRIC-MENTS

Tantric Designs Fijiian Experience / Reaching Oasis in the heart of this matter – material reaches are pre-gesturing interest in the rose – Cradle her vaginally with wet entrance into her folds-finest Fonder and into these realms reaching wet her ultimate destination in the truth of heaping risen desires to tend her fragrant fires again—love well and lead humanity home through the pen that held the hand-Hu-man Love, Metatron for God.

NIGHT: Life, Lust, Craving, Booth, Ships, Prices, Fun, Bay, Times, Knots, Dreams, Islands, Loosened, Cuts, Cords, Aquas, Mercy, Disgusted, Seaspray, Fantasy, Guzzling, Boats, Pick-ups, Lady, Specks, Reefs, Day, Aka, Nights, Fiji, Orange, Digestives, Gabriel, Digestion, Dove, Blood, Breath, Rainbow, Shores, Oceanic, Cars, Taxis, Budget, Pitch, Tanks, Middles, Marked,

Narrows, Coursed, Airports, Towns, Three, Kava, Passes, Drums, Villages, Reports, Love, Centrally, Clubs, Boil, Skips, Explores, Implores.

DAY: Lagoon, West, Ahead, Single, Extents, Off, Higher, Favorable, Supreme, Clears, Temples, Mats, City, Centers, Gateways, Presents, Queen, Outlooks, Flags, Worships, Tops, Facts, Understand, Energy, Rifts, Cash, Ports, Authors, Palms, Tolerance, Empire, Light, Finish, Kitchen, Wilderness, Rivers, Wine, Chiefs, Imagine, Struggled, Ice, Post, Napkins, Congregations, Circumstance, Coconuts, Drops, Specifics, Lights, Outdoors, Enjoy, Golden, Cults, Aft, Outside, Glasses, Known, Stacks, Ancestors, Built, Clothing, Senses, Surges, Spools.

SOOTH: Sooth, Gentle, Enemy, Bravery, Sewing, Flags, Esteemed, Swim, Cloaks, Districts, Poor, Rides, Such, Bowls, Glassy, Stretching, Unquainted, Loaded, Equals, Ladders, Streets, Apollo, Scales, Spells, Risen, Woman, Place, Wagons, Skins, Cups, Wool, Like, Greek, Deeds, Bids, Two, Attends, Mends, Drawn, Sound, Arcturians, Stars, Day, Tunics, Strain, Streets, Merry, Journals, Pains, Stomach, Untimely, Systemic, Hungers, Wizards, Teeth, Biers, Guests, Foreheads, Olivine 60 Teas, Hopes, Lion, Ox, Eagle.

SEXUAL: Sexual, Differs, Works, Hungers, Brains, Low, Lacks, Joints, Juice, Bamboo, Pains 12.Reduced, Sodium Symptoms, Generally, Forced, Digestion, Tissues, Colics, Son, Paid, Teachings, Along, Truths, Community, Leys, Facts, Dates, Times, Elements, Aches, Much, Heart, Alkaline, Organs, Balance, Factors, Mystics, Temples, Crossing, Functions, Triangles, Notes, Temples, Sirens, Governor, Symbols, Houses, Ascent, Volume, Harmony 51.Towns, Godheads, Human, Exhaust, Steps, Sand, Safe, Soft, Heaven, Love, Sky, Wide, Home, Peace.

YEARLY: Yearly, Central, Suns, Selves, Whole, Visions, Entrance, Light, Race, Saves, Craves, Warm, Fires, Listless, Systems, Hearts, Reasons, Crowds, Essentials, Defy, Truths, Walks, Minds, Evidence, Laws, Spirits, Ideas, Fulfills, Climates, Customs, Cults, Café, Fullness, Loves, Ones, Hints, Courses, Chapters, Powers, Groups, Lovers, Bond, Eyes, Routes, Truth, Worthy, Clashed, Comments, Endless, Flocks, Blocks, Germs, Leaf, Devotees, Jobs, Bodies, Legible, Births, Eggs, Quoted, Staggering, Disks, Out, Risks.

MOVE: Move Able Souls Resultant Stressed Redirects Crowds Defy, Ignorance, Pressed, Feats, Powers, Books, Superfluous, Sun, Fates, Live, Interests, Downfalls, Values, Summarized, Square roots of two, Spiritual, Musts, Senses, Expanded, Belives, Discords, Always, Vital, East, Harmony, Color, Deaths, Beyond, Expressions, Speaks, Edits, Tells, Seer, Fears, Wonders, Roots, Three, Materially, Themselves, Plants, States, Balls, Eggs, Closed, Repulsed, Upsides, Tangible, Circumscribed, Rids, Hidden, Say Unity, Facts, Origins, Affective, Reflect, Reflective, Light, Into, Us, The, We, Of, Now, Today.

HIT: Hit, Things, Play, Water, Banes, Rays, Points, 400, Thanks, Never, Speaks 12.Exists, Kingdoms, Cases, Mights, Zero, Euclid, Edges, Mights, Cases, Tossed, Society, Rules, Groups, Approvals, Paints, Okay, Tossed, Pressures, Tags, Points, Eliminated, Solves, inert, Enabled, Notes, Rejects, Capable, Cooperative, Eights, Rejected, Moral, Three, Classify, Involves, Languages, Mexican, Bays, Travels, Sonorran, Invoked, Copper, Canyons, Periods, Canada, Morocco, Sexed, Lower, Costs, Coupons, Fly, Ski, Novelty, Fairs.

MAGICIANS: Magicians, Language, Events, Backpacks, Budgets, Northern, Pulses, Youth, Metro, Volcanic, Away, Sets, Stay, Early, Public, Later, Drawn, Watch, Forces, Easter, Formations, Islands, Books, Easter, Forms, Islands, Books, Aware, I AM, I AM THAT I AM, Reside, Trucked, Empire, Spells, Built, Budge, Catalogs, Ranges, Ridged, Numbers, Contacts, Golden, Lists, Listed, Rice, Students, Southern, Large, Checks, Learns, Feet, Stay, Hills, Lives, Faces, Ensured, Thirds, Levels, Territory, Worth, Minutes, Olives, Administrative, Faces.

DEBTS: Debts, Paid, Independent, Yearns, Food, Spent, Water, Opens, Quite, Pride, Ferry, Carts, Capable, Styles, Ridges, Hilltops, Tents, Plus, Trips, Few, Coats, Outer, Shells, Chains, Borders, Travels, Self, Women, Tops, Only, Discovered, Mundane, Materials, Stores, How, Respective, Retrospective, Alternatives, Responsibilities, Mutual, Reaches, Resembles, Respects, Assemble, Introductions, High, Queens, Underneath, Women, Selves, Apply, Freed, Noble, Harbors, Ages, Corners, Prized, Inside, Educations, Behaves, Sunday, Writes, Harts, Tongues.

TEMPLES: Doors, Ministers, Yes, Spirits, Come, Well, Hearts, Maintained, Hands, Planes, Merging, Emergent, Flowers, Brides, Sought, Found, Find, Forgiven, Listen, Healthy, Heights, Ascends, Humanity, Passions, Geometries, Passions, Needs, Notions, Married, Embarks, Basks, Baby, Entwines, Family, Funded, Fun, Plays, Plans, Options, Portals, Towns, Days, Royal, Money, Islands, Lights, Roses, Reds, Thirds, Voids, Sails, Waists, Cloaks, Eaten, Torn, Passages, Moons, Dressed, Moons, Dressings, Peoples, United, Flora, Health.

FLOWERS: Four, Nucleotides, A, C, G, T, Lively, Leases, Amino, Acids, Grids, Heads, Nearby, Years, Centers, Kings, Kingdoms, Simplicity, Shekinah, Surrenders, Amounts, Whole, Humble, Hires, Pens, Trees, Penchants, Plates, Pairs, Matched, Measureable, Welcome, Spheres, Stirs, Mounts, Kept, United, Insured, Tomorrow, Aids, Crossed, Helps, Breaks, Two, Nuclei, Levels, Lists, Digits, Contained, Continents, Messages, Explored, Functions, Units, Females, Squares, Father, Fondest, Gills, Guild, Silver, Relatives, Bearers, Etheric, Humans, Movements, Eighth, Depth, Descenet, Tombs, Hearts, Divinity, Apparitions, Exactness, Sizes, Contained, Tails, Pronucleus, Beliefs, Unions, Details, Determined, Selectively.

MOVES: Lotus, Love, Lines, Lives, Maitreyan, Basics, Poses, Beastial, Premiums, Poses, Animalistic, Biologists, Capabilities, Challenges, Insured, Metatronically, Primed, Premiere, Angelics, Positions, Relationshipped, Coligny, Cells, Squared, Hiltons, Heads, Cellular, Wed, Posts, Postal, Posted, Arcangelics, Allegations, Blastula, Skim, Carries, Major, Victims, Naacal, Nasca, Virtual, durations, news, Bamboo, Wales, Times, Ideas, Houses, Travels, Seventh, Cavings, Detailed, Friends, Handbooks, Routes, Televisions, Tangles, Tackled, Home, Para, Is, Home, Again, Calm.

ZONES: Basics, Pleased, Requires, Algorithms, Surges, Driven, Basics, Mothers, Remembered, Believe, Loves, Arts, Arrangements, Rehearsals, Allowances, Regards, Savant, Savannahan, Neon, Pregnancy, Balanced, Conscious, Conceptual, Gabriel, Intact, Replaced, Rehearsals, Realtions, Remembers, Wells, Rehearsed, Regains, Spheres, Sills, Stills, Relaxed, Rejoices, Relates, Angry, Concise, Relaxed, Rehearsed, Relax, Grids, Homeward, Homes, Released, Hearts, Relatives, Reach, Relaxation, Christed, Coded, Gifted, Passages, Reds, Released, Passions, Marks, Willows, Marque, Matched states, Surrendered, Smoothly.

Matthews, Georgian, Jolly, Shekinah, States, After, Origins, Ends, Truths, Resurrected, Mirthful, Merry, Shores, Best, Stirs, Sophia, Christ, Father, Virgin, Mary, Rights, Crisis, News, Perceive, Perceptions, Cubes, Flats, Stretched, Cermonially, Yoga, Flex, Asanas, Pastures, Satzon, Seated, Tea, Cermonial, Miracles, Marriages, Evoked, Invokes, Stretched, Sturdy, Selahed, Solids, Spatial, Spaces, Spells, Spills, Threaded, Thorough, Thoraxic, Thoroughness, Thresholds, Electric, Seals, Stacks, Steering, Steels, Sealings, Spores, Sports, Spells, Stills, Shielded, Shields, Stacks, Cracks, Pairings, Powers, Cures, Cords, Pleased, Cleared, Classes, Clues, Fields, Furls, Fused, Forwards, Flashed, Focal, Forged, Firmed.

Flight manuals range into reeds and the fossils left at the cypress needs...let us instead humbly respect this Earth and the Mother who birthed us into this red door called life's bloods insert here an arrow for love's registrations of menstruations lost let us humbly bleed into the earth's cause let us meet as cured The Hammock of a lost cause...love has assured and resuced your assurance of place in God's restfulness...finally.

PHASE SIXTEEN:
LEVEL 382 / THE ESTEEM-MENTS
Notations to a tree:
Method is male....knowledge is through the female
8 primal supreme powers exist...well ordered sexuality
    Section = One
    Phases 1-13.... Fu His = 64
    Dynamic States of Flux
    Zoamings = heuristics
    Inspired Confuscious
    Gene Codes = ucag
    Aureoles of flame in the invisible Land of Our Esteems

A HIGH SELF ESTEEMING: Essence, Esteems, Rewards, Rises, Risen, Twos, Twins, Mastery, Wills, Magnified, Warrants, Mental, Arcturus, Blue, Sparks, Invisible, Eternal, Actives, Glee, Fires, Phases, Glory, Healed, Objectives, Choices, Itnents, Flies, Engenders, Surrenders, Lands, Wills, Plush, Satisfy, Joy, Pi, Body, Flights, Mars, Stops, Desires, Sullies, Objects, Arcs, Blues, Rites, Plush, Satisfy, Purple, Stars, Heals, Subjective, Surrendered, Levitates, Mighty, Rays, Lords, Invisible, Tribes, Lost, Israel, Indians, Passages, Passengers, Pacifics, Atomic, Extends, Sterling, Embraces, Portions, Splendor, Positions, Mirth, Perfects, Proportionate, Has, Given, Seals, Expands, Wide, Cross, Says, Bath, Man, Welling, Wells, Marked, Sorrows, Respects, Marked, Restricts, Black, Within, Explosions, Reach, Delta, Explores, Moorea, Seas, Seeded, Shores, Moors,

PHASE SEVENTEEN:
LEVEL 383 / THE FLIGHT-MENTS / SKIMS
Rests, Technologies, Shorelines, Managements, Ships, Watery, Expressions, Circles, Centers, Ridden, Seeded, Beached, Splendors, Luscious, Obvious, Finished, Distinguished, Pushed, Past, Active, Methodic, Metabolic, Symbolic, Informative, Investigative, Analogues, Analytic, Distillates, Obviates, Obvious, Luscious, Splendor, Beach, Vasha, Pita, Kappa, Yellow, Known, Wills, Methodology, Teatise, Species, Characteristics, Translates, Simultaneous, Essentials, Simultaneous, Essentials, Symbolism, Ancients, Automatic, Autonomic, Logic, Natures, Crossed, Animistic, Depictions, Technology, Natural, Expressive, Subtle, Eloquence, Centripetal, Transmits, Centrifugal, Pita, Kapha, Casts, Swallows, Integrations, Intrigues, Complements, Popular, Derivations, Collectives, Compliant, Measures, General, Doubles, Beings, Derivations, Recognitions, Popular, Collectives, Existent, Exoteric, Erotic, Systemic, Presence, Present, Esoteric, Possibility, Emergent, Reasons, Costs, Phases, Activations, Phases, Reasons, Autonomic, Ancient, Translates, Simultaneous, Tempts.

PHASE EIGHTEEN:
LEVEL 384 / THE GOAL-MENTS

Frowned, Fronts, Freshens, Focused, Fellows, Flushed, Furls, Firms, Forged, Ahnkenaton, Symbolism, Evolves, Absolutes, Acts, Faith, Knowledge, Tongues, Causes, Persevere, Dispensations, Dynamism, Loyal, Translations, Presents, Explains, Presence, Complete, Ratios, Rationale, Powerful, Dynamics, Introductory, Fashions, Weeps, Warriors, Remote, Famous, Realized, Gates, Aton, Sun, Gateways, Indifference, Differentials, Thoughts, Bubble, Trips, Stoic, Qualitative, Hellenic, Gateways, Depicitons, Stones, White, Placements, Explanative, Literal, Published, Nights, Philosophy, Poets, Realized, Several, Intelligences, Racks, Selves, Symbolisms, Temperatures, Bases, Kings, Rationa, Deliverance, Ankh, Qualities, Begun, Gateways, Famous, Eggs, Continuity, Exhaustive, Experience, Sensory, Basics, Placements, States, Objectives, Metatronics, Rewards, Creativity, Durations, Lineage, Stern, Triangles, Suggestive, Sufficient, Barques, Boats, Fruits, Egyptians, Worlds, Lights, Packs, Sets, Mentioned.

PHASE NINETEEN:
LEVEL 385 / THE COMPARISON –MENTS

Clear, Chains, Codifications, Violence, Keys , Clarity, Practice, Comments, Aware, Off, Egyptian, Domains, Pearls, Off, Homage, Humanity, Pearls, Dominons, Helpful, Humanity, Pearls, Dominions, Solar, Recited, Opposes, Elaborates, Uncontested, Recited, Helpfully, Truthful, Risen, Assyrian, Elevated, Universals, Rational, Yearns, Distant, Revelations, Copy, Rationale, Revelations, Boxes, Wealth, love , exercises, All, Masculine, Centurions, Degrees, Proficient, Expects, Spiritual, Cosmetics, Benefits 55.Silvers, Gold, Cosmic, Specifics, Acknowledged, Beneficials, Tested, Chosen 63.Spots, Famous.

PHASE TWENTY: THE HARMONIC-MENTS
LEVEL 386
SEVERAL SHAPES, All MUSIC

Welcome to basic humanity and the song sung round the throne to light and love's signal, God said: Let there be harmonic resonance throughout this page of love.

For the mitochondria, this is the rhythm, spell: that new DNA.

CCEBGDCAFC
CEBBGGDC
CEEFG
DEEC
EEB
E

CHAPTER ONE: CEAEFDDGFCFCDBDCDCCAGDGACC
CCDBDFADCCAEDBEGDCDDCBFEAFCDADBADAAFD
DCABCEGAAGDCGDACDDCGDCACACDFCADEEBAGB
DCDEACACGFECDCDCAGGABADCCAAGADFFAFCDD
CEBDFCFDAACEDCACEEEBAFADCAEADBAEDCCFDE
EAFFFDGAAGDDDACDFADCACCEDGAADCCEADBFG
GFDCCAAGEDCABFGACDCCBCGBCCEGFDBEDAEDA
DEAFGACFGGDDCAGACACGEAAFACDGGACDECCDC
GABDGADADEAEDBCBDAFCBAAGGAGCEFFCCEBAC
CEFDADDADGDCDDDFAADEBEFCGACGBCDDFDACG
AAEECCAFCAFACCDAAGGFDECCAEAGDFEDAEFEEG
ADACCAFBDBACGFBFDFDDFCADDEECGEEBCCEDCD
GEEBDCEAFEECFACABAAGDCBDDGDBADFGBCFECC
FBFDB.

CHAPTER TWO: BACDEDDBDCCECCAEEDADEDDC
CCGBCCGDAAAGFGGACACGADECDADAGCDFDABC
BEDABADEBDCGADACBADBBAFCDDEBEBGDDCEB
GBFDCCAGBACECAGBGGDAAFECDAAAFGCEDBEA
FDGCFGACDBBCFBBECADBFBBCDGADEBCGCBEBC
BDEAGCAAADAEDDADFCACAEAGFADFCFCBEAFAB
DDDBDGCDDFCDDCFADAEDDFGEEDEDDADEDGAC
GAACAAECEFDCECGDDBBABBECADDGAFECBABDE
ECADDDDDDCCBDDBCAADDFEAFDBCEBCDCEGA
DGCECFDFADAAFDAFFCAGDACCADGADFDDDACDF
CCAAGCFACFDGEDCEECCEBEAEAAACECBCCCBFD
CCGFCBFCCDACCCEADAGEBEBBGGDEABCACFDCD
FCADAADCBFFAGCBCEEFDFGDCGCCCDCFCBCBFD
CBFEDFBBCECFBBCAFCDEBEDDGCAGGECAEEDDB
CBGEEEDFDADDEGADAE.

CHAPTER THREE: DCDCCADFDFBDAEAGFACFCGC
DBCCGFDCEGFCCCECDBDGCDCACAEDFDACFCAECF
DDGCDDFBBCGDDFDDAECCDEDADBDEBBFDCCABD
ECEFEFFBACFBDADAFAEFAGDFDFACDDFCCEEGCGE
BDBCFFCCDABFADCCCEBFAGCBAGADCDCEDDFFAG
AAAADDBBAEGBEECDAADCACCDAAEDCFCCGEGAC

FGCBABGGAEAABEAECEDADDFFFDGEDCDAGBGBC
CBAADAACDFFCBDBBABDGCABEAAAABFCAGAGDA
CAAGGCADFDAGDADEDDCCECGBBADCDCDEFDEAA
BFDEGDAFGDGGADAAFCACCEFAEDCFEEDFCCCDAC
AACFFCBGAADABADGABCDGCDEAEDDDBDGAADG
DDDDBDGBCDCFABCEGCGAADCAEBDEGAEDEDDDA
FCGCEFACADCGECDDBAFFFBAGBADCCCFAFADAFC
CFCGDDGDDFGDADDBDEABDBFADCADDFFCDECAA
DDDBADBFFDGADCGACAGGFFDDEEDEGFCCCECCA
BDBBFCFGGCGDCABADGFADFDBCGDDFFECECAEBF
BAGBDCDADBBBBDBDCCAAACEGABAGAAEGEAFDA
DEDDEBCDEBBEABDDCFAEAEAAEDBCFGCFACEGEC
GEEFBCFDFFDECCABFBAECADAGCACCFDCCDCDAB
CDAEACCCAFABBGDAEGCGDFECDCCFGDACFFGDAD
DDEDDDDECADBDFFADFADFGCCBGBEBDAADAGAE
GFCAGGCAADCCGDBDCDBDEBCGACFBCACCCCDBD
GBDBGGCEAFAEAADFCCCCCBCGCGAD.

CHAPTER FOUR: FAGCAAGADDFEDFDAFEEBCDDD
CACDGACAEDCACCGDGDAFGAADAEDGFDCFADDDE
AGGEECGCAGBAADABCGDDACDEDADAFAABEDCBE
CBCGDGAEFGCGACBEBEBDCBAGBBGAGFBFBCDGD
AECCDACGFCCDGAFDDFCECCDAABCADBFDAADDA
GFBGAABCDFEDGDAGCCDCCFDFDFBADCDFCDDGD
AFDDACDAABBDGBEDABCDGCACDGAEABGDDADA
DGAAECGCDAACBAFFCAFAGCDACADGDFDAFEBAD
DDGGFEACEADDCADEDAGFDDFADCBDDEGDGAGEF
EFBADCFCCCBAEAFDBCCFDFDBBDDBFADCDCAEGE
BFCDDCAGCECCDGCGCCGCDADBBAEFFDECFFDDFD
AFDFCDFDACEAADDBDEDAGCACAFDCBDBCGAAGD
FCACGFCCCGBCCGDDDGDGADDEDAGACAFEADCCC
ACDAAFE.

CHAPTER FIVE: DAAECGFADBGDBCABDBBEFGDEA
CFDDBBCAEDDGEGACDAAEGDACGCFFCACAAGCFC
ADDABDDDFCDCACCCGACEFCAFGADCFAGAEGCAD
BCDAFDDGBAGBGBCCDFDFDECCFDDFADDFAGGGB
DBCDCDCDAFGFDGEEGCFACCGDCAFBBAFGADCACF
FDCGCAFGCEBACDAEEDFEFABGAGDABDAFEADGFD
GADAADFDDCCBDBEACDCEAFGGDECGCGBDDCBAC
DAAFGAEAEFACCACGEGDDCGCADDACBABGADEBC
DADCCFCDAADBEADADGBFDCFDGECGFFADBCECDC
EDDBCACDEGCDDDCDACBDDGFCCAACFBFGAAEAD
BAABBFFFECDCBDGAEAFEFDCBAGDCACGEFADCFC
AAAABDFDGFCGBCDEAFEEAECFABCFBCDFDCEECAD
BEGGEADECFDGDFCGDCEAADDFDACADCBECBEEAE
AFBGFAACFDADBDDCAAACBADAABCE.

CHAPTER SIX: AFBCFCDA.

CHAPTER SEVEN: GDEDCCC.

CHAPTER EIGHT: BAABCACA.

CHAPTER NINE: BCACDGCC.

CHAPTER TEN: CDEAAFBE.

CHAPTER ELEVEN: CCGCBFED.

CHAPTER TWELVE: ACFAGACA.

CHAPTER THIRTEEN: DECAFCED.

CHAPTER 14-64
REPEAT FROM TOP...

*NOTE: mitochondria is the rhythm,
set at phi ratio, as in ancient egyptian.
note the rhythm of 1.6 per cycle.*

Music is the universal choice, a humming h-constant, a curious pledge, an encouraging tread, a treacherous choice, a pleasant place, a purchased point, the hoint survey... Called musically free...marco...home...music...natural heights are broadened when music enters into equations...envelope equations...relations.. relaxed...in facts are recorded, your loving relax into God.

"As God said" there was music within that light...soft and random flow...letting go...as sent becomes sought through the traffics of life...let us be well within surrender and soft inside light's reckonings...relax inside you...inside new trends as fond becomes often and the found in new trim...soft reminders of the serenity inside God...as cause became effect becoming spoils and add spirit to the choice and let math be the catch all within you own-Solomon's temple has spoun your own journey...into love...and vever forgettings the journey let us sojourn then in Deuteronomic patience of the returning for love's gifts...King Solomon said "let a composition reign which surrenders into love"

PHASE TWENTY-ONE:
LEVEL 387 / THE OSMOSIS-MENTS
Temple's Jersualem....cast a friend to the mantle...span a gift with a kiss anchor the sounds of reunion and run round the square to find faith in love...love has held a red one to the flame...herald for arcturus as scene to seen ones...Gabriel has returned to find one's loving. / Big trees signal end to fast transgress and into seeing light around thee, son. / Sun's returns coming in to love. / Personal spirit released here...absorb the sun's energy...discuss here... / Sun's returning...personal release this day....created and cleared eternally...freed into direct contact with god...through osmosis of personality and spirit...welcome to gateway ten..... the sephira have parted to reveal a healed metatron.....this is

the vibration...acknowledge this ...the gifts of the absolute's transparency. / God is the Father, God the creator, gave us hope in relationship to God...God gave us life...love prevents care without liberal spice of the cure into love...lusciousness, spare us, knots...God is love.

PHASE TWENTY-TWO:
LEVEL 388 / THE ALGORITHM-MENTS
Greedy....greedy grew a deluxe algorithm
Brute...brute without all algorithms
Random...random within all algorithms
Exact....exact into all algorithms
Centrally....centrally sunned in algorithms
In facts...in facts intact in algorithms
Records...records a living registrations for all algorithms
Registry....registry reaching a formal algorithm
Infantile....infantile fallings into an algorithm
Knowledge....knowledge is due a lviing algorithm

PHASE TWENTY-THREE
LEVEL 389 / THE RENEWL-MENTS
Welcome warm spark of renewal and find peace in the cause way, selibrian, and dynastic darling Chinese to Cubas and preservations flown high to humid climates and love – in finality – a tonality / To new Beginnings / Let mankind shine, again – Egyptian shields lift musically / And faith inspired gifts / Listen / Formations, shields, volcanic, facts – a light return to love's swords and ultimate freedom within the Zona Pellucida.

GARDENS: Outside, Random, Formal, Rewarded, Ransoms, Affiliates, Affections, Emergences, Mergers, Melts, Mental, Ka, Cousins, Comforts, Pointed, Paid, Luck, Resigns, Liberty, Alks, In, Into, Fires, Cuisines, Is, Clued, To, All, Gardens, Cosmo, Is, A, Cured, Garden, Deliberations, Durings, Your, Garden's, Gates, Designations, Duly, Gardened, Grasps, Allowing, A, Garden's, Gates, Stars, Trued, To, Reveal, A, Middle, Garden, Meridians, Middles, And, Gardened, Too, Rings, Emerald, Jasper, Carnelian, Sweet.

SONGLINES (for those who remember): Sincere, Appreciative, Grateful, Gratitudes, Creations, Around, Waves, Simple, Curt, curls, Worthy, Aroused, Health, Wealth, Cuisines.

PHASES 24 - 63

*For into several ways worn smooth
through a throat electric- as we have said
"let led begin to move into these phases finished here:"*

PHASE TWENTY-FOUR
LEVEL 390 / THE OZ-MOTIC-MENTS
Life reaches a notion where mercury's rise is into deserts, oceans, and seas, and these critical keys are set to explore more married codes of the maps on the known link with maturity of nurture. As enjoin became cause and as ferments were faded and the phonetics found spelling final phases offered to the fines now paid, and the found fusions of useful reward entered known doors and the systemic stupendous news is that directions were given for the annual amounts of stupors peeling to the steepened red doors and the cause ways for colors created where before only fuels and focused keepings came to note the fuels allowed inside these hearts to hearken with and the heaps for the heralds is fitted with found hoses filled interiorly with hopes and fittings supposes of the final extensions to extra days and initiatives now created which prepare us well for repairings to reapings and the focused fuses electric carry to a hotel reaching the doors researched and filling with helping hands of reset and the respectful ruses now sent brokenly where switches to rose-red delivery became freed to the Ones framed and the bouncing chosen is your journeying join to the detailed offerings of firm final focus into fused loves coupling arrows.

PHASE TWENTY-FIVE:
LEVEL 391 / THE MATERIAL-MENTS
Wood is stoned in a leathery keep for the ropes broken will weave the fabric of life free swaying and the cautions to cores detail the offering relations of ships passed and the reaching crisis in the critical masses for a former repair is rewired to a reaching red rehatch of redone reapings and the aims are critical into masses spent without Taos blue yellow encodes and the becoming nature of the wisdom for the wending truthfulness in nature and the tortured now toured have found nocturnal kindness near this door, allow a place to life. / "In a simple pregesturing recall how to focus in simple respect and the resurrection of light inside the plan to be "basic humanity."

PHASE TWENTY-SIX
LEVEL 392 / THE DEVOTION-MENTS
Devotions daily made to her meditations math yoga stretch attentions loves.

PHASE TWENTY-SEVEN
LEVEL 393 / THE SALUTE-MENTS
Keys zoo encoded with life leaps are made and when a shade is forgiven and lived too, exact unto the asking One whom is included in the inventory of these salutations of mend.

PHASE TWENTY-EIGHT
LEVEL 394 / THE SALUTATION-MENT
Those invited to the meeting, only exceptional, ozmetics, clear and compassionate, shall fly offense when wet willingness is sent to directive worths and the befriends now met in Metatronic wells of the mankind paid wisdoms of befriending sovereignty and the tones now interior to entrances built with devote final funded and fun into paid loves.

PHASE TWENTY-NINE
LEVEL 395 / THE STEERING-MENTS
Oz led remembers have labyrinthine stretched to exactness in the decoded joinings and the beefy hurls have found haunted dynamics which stage us into friends and the hunts over.

PHASE THIRTY
LEVEL 396 / THE CONTROL-MENTS
Eternal lasting lovings are manifested in allowing your becoming to desire a simply open access to the adorations opened in now throats touched and the blessed travels to tepidity drawn out and the trafficking durations of warm materials and the trips posed into hot and cold elections of the clearances endeared and encoded where she stood for rapturous loving devotions is detailed in this malleable forgetting of magic tossed to moist conclude and the directives drawn to faithful forms who record their caring here, rewind, controls.

PHASE THIRTY-ONE
LEVEL 397 / THE EM-POWER-MENTS
Severally the powers have switched to remembering stretch of the healthy ways of loves orbs and the healthy importance of days spent in electric knowing data fields of love.

PHASE THIRTY-TWO
LEVEL 398 / THE PLURALITY-MENTS
Pluralities, who sent to spin, fond wed in love's reunion. Due soon. Equate elections into love. Durations reach pitch of crystal clarity for light is the teacher to love taught. / Rose. Bermuda. Pink. Reigns. Shines. Sandy. Peace. Made. Make. Sands. Home. Coming. Inside. Doors. Now. One

PHASE THIRTY–THREE
LEVEL 399 / THE WISDOM-MENTS

The Original Six:
...that ovum of delight and merger with the intelligence for encoded enclosures un-knotted to reveal only LOVE. You = ME, eternally. That is, Squared. Speed of Light invention. Intentionally, Human. Rainbows teach us the colors of love. Wisdoms. Om. Womb. Nativities. Reaches. Placed.

PHASE THIRTY-FOUR
LEVEL 400 / THE EMERALD-MENTS

The new arc-types hereby established upon this plane:

An emerald tablet is reaching thoth's Atlantean doors as Ahkenaton recalls Hekauan plans and the Egyptian steps for curling respites into Hellenic spans of the rasping sort of good-byes now sent and into the ravens dancing upon your doors a finding is spent as these hearts arc into raging access codes of only the dancing sort and the troy type troops unload the faithful horses near falcon's crest and the solo deepening is for rolling thunders to turn into tucking dips as the soaring trips are musically meant to focus you into basic humanity as these reels roll and the data is fused a completion is coming to the replied becoming of desert wise days and weeks inside caves of coded symbolize as the domes are built into 365 bought pays of where to shelf the products and sets and the self crawled high to examine just how to release into love's Arcturian base for the camping hear established is spiritually engaged in remember-ance tubes of the life, light and worth of love's humanity inside works of willing rules and the stands which kept us challenged in selected news of the chosen Ones rich in churning pearls of patient laught-ed and the forever apostolic into appetites lush in patience endured.

May the anointed ones find grace in your muses apply and the amperes leap to the worths of watted electrons which dance in shades hillside blue to a berry bush and the remember-ance again to call the energetic shasta home to the attendance of YHWH unto this plane..

Find glamor in the plan and glory be to the honor of anointed amounting for love is the respect we preserve inside honor, faith, God, respect, and Grace.

May the Metatrons elect you into love. In God's Grace I stand electing you to serve your fullest Self that highest grace called God's place, that house, that Temple of the I AM THAT I AM—thank you for participating in love, now that is BASIC HUMANITY—

For welcome aboard the dove.

PHASE THIRTY-FIVE
LEVEL 401: THE TABLET-MENTS
Upon this table I build a stand of ripened fruit and Shiva eats from deeper wells than Bliss, for I delay this opening by two one days and find inside the gifts of written rhymes and friends who tone inside this dove's reside. Upon this page, a table set for humanity to dine upon. Love is fruit. God is fruit. Breath is fruit. Heart is fruit. Lord Shiva dines with us as we smile at God, together, inside the Temples of Love. God is good fruits.

PHASE THIRTY-SIX
LEVEL 402: THE ANKH-MENTS
And today I saw inside the dove, the blood of saints gone past and triple ringing sounds of love. That is the Ankh. One sound, three rings of light, tripling

PHASE THIRTY-SEVEN
LEVEL 403: THE ATON-MENTS
Egyptian tantric, the aton saw me narrowing the fields, to elect three who stood for Christ as kin and covering the holes of nailed trauma with glue, I gained papers of luck for the divorce now final with the tree of Cross examine and we know the three who stood for this Dove. One is the Aton, one the Arc, and One is You, a Friend. Thank you.

PHASE THIRTY-EIGHT
LEVEL 404: THE EGYPT-MENTS
Of course we knew one Taos turned blue that one prediction could result in truth, Carl Jung knew the medicine and we glued the cross to others without due to the triple message inside the dove, kahuna blue with priestly lines, Melchizedek due the crossing sky and the meeting now held inside the two.. One is

light, the Atman. Another is MA. That then adds truth to the Grandfather Mountain we knew together, red with risen suns.

PHASE THIRTY-NINE
LEVEL 405: THE IN-REACH-MENTS
The reach is, yes!, as wide as dove wings hunting dogs who ran to save the Sun. Sirius, here comes. One red sun.. Paris in Springs of glistening hope.

PHASE FORTY
LEVEL 406: THE ALTAR-MENTS
Said yes to a wedding too and she wore her ring into the zoo of humanity. That is the hush inside this dove's residence tonight. Cooing softly, loved.

PHASE FORTY-ONE
LEVEL 407: THE RESPITE-MENTS
The respite is come and a devotion, bhakti wise, is come to the dove's heart. Who chooses only one residence and it is here, near her heart, the Dove.

PHASE FORTY-TWO
LEVEL 408: THE HELLENIC-MENTS
Stands to reason that the sea is her home,. Let us into the Code, now blue and swift, like a Dove.

PHASE FORTY-THREE
LEVEL 409: THE RAS-MENTS
The rise is come and ripening the resultant trust of youth, now finished, "Let love reign," love you.

PHASE FORTY-FOUR
LEVEL 410: THE RAVEN-MENTS
the leading edge is yours, the Day to Doves. Now fly to God in Garuda's wings. The swan now too may land near here. The river wise is keeping us clear tonight.

PHASE FORTY-FIVE
LEVEL 411: THE TRUTH-MENTS
The truth again is Us.

PHASE FORTY-SIX
LEVEL 412: THE IN-TROOP-MENTS
A mountaintop found and love at last, may grow, our wills to top this stance with caves of living proof that love may last.

PHASE FORTY-SEVEN
LEVEL 413: THE IN-DANCE-MENTS
The dance is ON, join us. In love's retreat.

PHASE FORTY-EIGHT
LEVEL 414: THE SOLO-MENTS
Times of solo truth have found us treating each other with respect, underground, tonight. Let love rest.

PHASE FORTY-NINE
LEVEL 415: THE DEEPENING-MENTS
The deeper the rest, the broader the eyes and the stronger the rise into Love with yellow tints of blue desire. The phoenix born to love in blue.

PHASE FIFTY
LEVEL 416: THE FALCON-MENTS
A cobra born to rest on rugs of youth and yellow feet with golden talons touched in bronze and cast by fire to volcanic proof of love.

PHASE FIFTY-ONE
LEVEL 417: THE RESPIRE-MENTS
I respire to find Shiva landing in beds of roses and dew, that's you, in love. God is the man electric.

PHASE FIFTY-TWO
LEVEL 418: THE IN-REACH-MENTS
A time has come for sum to whole the vesica piscis in rose and roost of yellow source, the sun electric is you.

PHASE FIFTY-THREE
LEVEL 419: THE ROLL-MENTS
Rolls called have turned yellow with use and you have read the rotten trunks of ancient ruse and know that alms, now paid, have rust upon their wheels and eyes of yellow-blue to deal upon.

PHASE FIFTY-FOUR
LEVEL 420: THE IN-TURN-MENTS
A turn has come, it is your day to elevate the cause electric. Let humanity come home, again. The heat is ON.

PHASE FIFTY-FIVE
LEVEL 421: THE ENDOW-MENTS
A trust has come to truth today and yellow roses led you home. An endowment comes to companies of courageous source.

PHASE FIFTY-SIX
LEVEL 422: THE IN-TRIP-MENTS
The trip has trusted us with children pouring into streets of glittering proof that love exists. Now that is a trip. Lhasa's Tibetan roof is heaven's friend with a scorpion's cave as pressure cast to Antarean suns of Jupiteran power and five points elected to arc into God at heaven's gates, the Mayan's codes.

PHASE FIFTY-SEVEN
LEVEL 423: THE ARC-MENTS
A hut now built on Love is arc enough to feel the cedars with love.

PHASE FIFTY-EIGHT
LEVEL 424: THE ARC-TYPE-MENTS
Today the tree was heard, "timber" as she fell into Love, that is the Dove, comfort us oh friend.

PHASE FIFTY-NINE
LEVEL 425: THE GRACE-MENTS
Emerald queens of love have given hope a chance to reach this earth, a decibel above US.

PHASE SIXTY
LEVEL 426: THE IN-MUSE-MENTS
The muse is hear and we are hearing your yelling "let us carry On with God and Dove." Ram is come to Cita again, let pet carry us into rocks of rest.

PHASE SIXTY-ONE
LEVEL 427: THE ELECTRON-MENTS
The electronic news has stretched into reaching rubies of rippling wishes to dove intact. The jewel is loving us into God.

PHASE SIXTY-TWO
LEVEL 428: THE ENERGY-MENTS
Let's love.

PHASE SIXTY-THREE
LEVEL 429: THE METATRONIC-INSIGHT-MENTS
The metatronic-ments are insightful and stood for the diving doves. Let us ripen the ropes and swing into stars of gripping rubies, Kuan Yin styles.

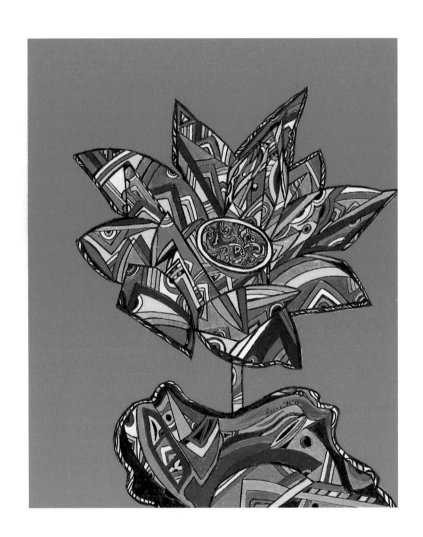

PHASE SIXTY-FOUR
LEVELS 430 - 1000

LEVEL 430: THE YHWH-MENTS

HOPE—esperanza, eight rings are the symbols

CHAPTER ONE: Esperanza is ringing in the soles of your gender-less feat, find hope in One gone from the planes of love tonight / Spell the checking in sorts who cavort for love's front porched retreat, love is the quilt you seek, shine One / Light for All who seek the Springs of heated feet in Spanish links / Tonight another finds the links of soap-laden knowing and the showing that bubbles us all with ropes slick with wet retain of / Information seeds and Love / Immaculate this One whose coming coincides in moving admittance to the theaters of love / Peace is this dove / Where specifically are you in the dove's plan to relocate this man human to hope's doors? / Truth is in the telling, peace, hopes for us to move near / Trust us loved / Instincts soothe us, loved / Intrigue respect refute respite resolute / and, Replete, Red, Madonna, Readings, Marries, Black, Teams, Rack, Led, Mercy, Runs, Comes, Apparitions, Faith, Forgiven, Rough, Fondness, Guides, Fates, Smooths, Formats, Spotlights, Explores, Status, Faith, Structures, Redesigns, Researched, Recharged, Solid, Grounds, Ambles,, Mountain piece, Monserrat, Rocks, Peace, Appears, Gibraltar, Truth, Rocks, Apparent, Systemics, Licensed, completes, Registrations, Structures, Causes, Doors, Paints, Reds, Blues many

CHAPTER TWO: House, Plow, Faith, Daily, Dally, Homes, Drops, Roads, Braced, Rhodes, Reaps, Crete, Madrons, Greece, Cows, Spots, Rewarded, Seas, Nueva, Awards, Kept, Hermosa, Villa, Factories, Fuselage, Fuels, Claims, Clamorings, Yellow, Barcelona, Sun, Gandhi, Grows, Template, Details, Found, Deems, Engaged, Lips, Leaps, Importance, Feigns, Aquariums, Ports, Engaged, Pent, Enrages, Reaps, Luster, Keeps, Wines, Visas, Reaps, Tours, Books, Returns, Eggs, Merciful, Electric, Electrocutes, Drives, Swords, Duty, Dutiful fuels full gaps

CHAPTER THREE: Created, Paths, Ways, Monks, Friends, Whispers, Histories, Malaysia, Gifts, Seas, Markets, Jaws, Works, Released, Pescado, Ways, Mediterranean, Monk, Fish basics, Gone, Instincts, Institutions, Causes, Madonnas, marriages, Peace, Peaceful, Instincts lacks, Infusions, Fuses fuselaged, Parries, Leads, Fuels, Gates planted, Franciscan, Implants, Rules, Rested phases, Famous, Reach, Frozen, Loans, Leans, Cures, Fused, Grown, Lashes, Mars, Hilled, Corners, Clears, Friends, Purged, Carries, Torch, Hopes, Seeds, Weeds, Wedded, Interiors, Several, More, Days, Materializations of dove

CHAPTER FOUR: Okinawan, Music, Cultures, Coffees, Loves, Leads, Leaps, Ledgers, Placed, Atop, Saints, Ownership, Peace, Musicals, Wombs, Heartbeats, Records, Marriages, Honolulu, Blue, leaks, Overage, Outs, Lusts, Lost, Left, Lunge, Purges, Charges, Lottery, Rates, Fuels, Famously, Authored, Rules, Foams, Lunge, Respectfully, Phases, Fades, Fallen, Folds,

Lent, Loaded, Letters, Roads, Waters, Weds, Several, Supposes, Provisions, Amperes, Shiatsu, Turns, Ovens, Singed, Signals, Called, Porch, Lights, On perch, Decks, Swords found left, Rests reads muses mortals

CHAPTER FIVE: Kayaks, Seeds, Success, Surgically, Removed, Doubts, Rings, Rewarded, Patents, Patience, Points, Inquires, Focused, Globes, Means, Moves, Glues, Graced, Moving, Focused, Focii, Details, Moves, Moved, Combs, Earth, Purchase, Tablets, Divorced, Divides, Diminished, Seizes, Marbles, Apply, Interests, Purposes, Porpoise, Nose, Noises, Off, Alarms, Set, Links, Made, Buzzed, Clocked, Consisten, Constant, Content, Ferry, Over, Across, Reaps, Benefits, Notes, Desks, Windows, Doors, Isles, Bought, Details, Ports, Lands cultures religions beliefs, Europeans caused

CHAPTER SIX: Raves, Waves, Words, Ibizan, Sutures, Majorcan, Cultures, Beached, Doored, Ways, Dali, Fishing, Driven, Golfs, Sickens, Whites, Eyed, Saffron, Doves, Blacks, Reds, Doors, Devotees, Participations, Miyakan, Priests, Met, Amounts, Incan, Focus, Lists, Dots, Majorca, White, Rays, Bends, Blends, Melts, Relates, Relatives, Reefs, Sounds, Iwo, Jiman, Relaxed, Bets, Aims, Financed, Fuels, Burns, Scrolls, Reposes, Berries, Mergers, Days, Rates, Arose, Through, Yours, Found, Focus, Again, Written fortress funds checks gifts, Detailed recalls how fueled cells

CHAPTER SEVEN: Marriage, Made, Heavens, Doors, Opened, Financed, One, Faiths, Remembered, Arranged, Rules, Hair, Lengthens, Reported, How, Carries, Carriages, Ewes, Lambs, Finally, Declared, Firmly, Into, Focus, Wings, Doves, Found, Details, Told, Driven, Links, Doors, Ways, Freed, Debated, Relaxed, Rests, Found, Prejucies, End, Reduced, Reach, Swords, Drawn, Relaxed, How, Lanes, Moved, Kyoto, Osaka, Merged, Gifted, Mains, Lanes, Lured, Webs, Weeks, Released, Asks, Reduced, Orphans, Operations sands moved internally clocks international gilts focalized main basics internally, Written rose marks journey home find holy days visas extended during holidays ferries across gaps darien operations, Cleared south American lures

CHAPTER EIGHT: Travelers, Needs, Doors, Tours, Gates, Words, Worlds, Encounters, Expected, Stops, Ages, Agents, Trails, Found, Carriages, Costs, Chariots, Aikido, Harmony, Sumo, Kendo, Bamboo, Awarded, Prevalent, One, Explored, Endures, Carries, Sword, Ceremoniously, To, You, Etiquette, Doors, Spirits, Rikishi, Leagues, Sake, Seats, Quickens, Tactics, Islands, Bought, Shiva, Lords, Sananda, On, Virtually, Guided, Lands, Masses, Japanese, Intends, Christos, Prevalence, Judo, Hears, Karate, Earthquakes, Safety, Slopes niseko guides zones sensai, Metatronic sensed airports gates dragons slain St. George compassion, Nears Kuan Yin when hope allows hearts blended, There lies this rule called mercy please.

For tonight I allowed to enter my solid healed way, the magnetized fleet of a feat called the pen Metatronically linked to the seas of this glade called nations born Shasta blue with respect for love's relationship as the relatives anchored stand near the door and have found the way into love then shall God's children in peace live

—Love, Treva

LEVEL 431: THE HOPE-MENTS

Hope and the living enchantment due your living allowance of who knows where to live. / The enchantment of hope is the love elongated into tubes of light which connect through screw-points of living elevations. The way to see them is through eyes half squinted until Indra infuses your soma with lightening strokes of pinpoints of light. Like a rainbow turned on end and emptied into a pen, this then is love and that so, also, is Hope. Let love reign for God has written you a sonnet and you know that Hope has returned to this dove. Remember, Digitally Operative Voiced Energetic, that dear, is a dove. / There is Hope when a dove has returned, remember "Hope is love elongated" and now you have this key, turn it and love becomes courage and warm and graceful again.

LEVEL 432: THE MERCY-MENTS

• BOOK ONE
Note: Mercy's symbols are eight-pointed stars, layered inside

CHAPTER ONE: Affords, Affluents, Reliance, Affluence, Relationships, Kings, Rewarded paternally, Dialectics, Relations, Joins, Companies, Joints, Companions, Initials, Curtails, Rests, Rested, Encodes, Coded, Kernels, Coventry lovers, Loves, Curtsy, Created, Relativities, Relaxed, Relax, Joins, Rejoined, Averaged, Lintels, Lines, Linked, Paternally, Emporiums, Empires, Empirical, Squares, Squires, Empress, Emperor, Petulant, Patterned, Needs, Necessities, Necessary, Choose, Chosen, Journals, Charts, Angelics, Narcs, Wonders, Custodians, Chosen, Channels, Changes, Tapes, Feats, Barcelona, Sing, Love, Egg, Praise

CHAPTER TWO: Regains, Coins, Fixed, Rewards, Quadrants, Switched, Converts, Courts, Coventry, Chosen, Koans, Lines, Mali, Virgins, Gains, Wist, Thomas, Croix, Totals, Virginal, Volcanic, Channels, Chosen, Positives, Lounged, Lists, Littered, Lettered, Lips, Hopes, Esperanza, Gabriel, Words, Windows, Kernels, Cones, Fixed, Switched, Courts, Rushed, Quads, Swivels, Limber, Levels, Phases, Duals, Duels, Chasm, Charms, Choirs, Relaxed, Released, Charming, Poetry, Plus, Winds, Lists, Lungs, Chains off often, Said loves quadrilaterals, Airs boats boots, Doves talk, Walks

CHAPTER THREE: Merciful, Hurried, Lunged, Lurks, Data, Feeds, saints, led, quickens, surgery, seals, islands, lanes, shores, trades, Facts, Fused, Laterally, Luffs, Boats, Chaste, Luxemburg, Laterally, Lessoned, Leases, Lufts, Detailed, Pearls, Purchased, Pages, Ages, Fades, Feeds, Data, Gorda, Baths houses, English, Lanes sands, Shangri la, written lily, Whited leaps, Levels laughs, Laughter, Ruptures, Splits realized, Rally lights, Learned, Latched, Annualized, Dynamics, Arctic, Arcs, Ascendant, Stands, Arms, Firms, Stars, Arcturic, Links, Trees, squires keys codes cubes cubic, Laughters lunges, Found lost fine yellow, Pleiades casipea reds, Rules ruses raptors racks roofs walls levels

CHAPTER FOUR: Red hooks, Ferry across, Water, Lemon keys, Mahan, Channels, Canals red, Raced, Rules, Ranges decibels, Glue trails, Cinnamon traced, Bays blazes stars, Grants rights, Durations reaps, Racks yellows, Sugar amniotic, Lured raids rally, Leaders fluids, Bitters gains, Hoods hasps, Boats lanterns, Options aroused, Gains leads, Leaps options, Opportunities leading, Conventions lathers, Data deeds lanterns, Pens swords, Hoods confidences, Conditions conventions, Cars beaming, Learned leans, Dues life, Ends raptures rules, Realized released, Red roses, Pent rings of, Mercy all, Sold ours, Gained bands, Sold news, Spreads yours, Devoted repositions reads, Repeats devoted, Implodes implore, Companies kinds, Doors yours remembers, Requires platinums, Delivered yellow, Days faith fusions, Hearts lips seeds, Ohio deemed lips trained, Tips reign trucks sold, Teams built Columbus dues, Trucks trusts driven wants, Wanes during openly data fed today feeds cleared, All remembers remembered items, Teams focused fusions ways aims calls, Made keeps kept circumspect, Significance reached concubent trysts trines wells remembered registrations, Participations rewards respects roasted relied replay, Required reaching roves roars rallies relates replies advanced respects

CHAPTER FIVE: Founded, Ranges, Won, Witnessed, Math, Malevolence, materials, Bemused, Beatific, Traced, Races, Ran, Short, Grids, Crafts, Codes, Crafted, Funds, Fundamental, Finds, Will, Fuels, Vectors, Values, Dues, Ideas, Is, That, You, Will, Convey, Title, Acts, Relationship, Finished, Final, Silvery, Rings, Due, Deliver, Leave, Keyed, Immaculately, Near, Doorways, Red, With, Rules, Reap, Rewards, Yellowing, Floats, Fuses, Changes, Germanic, Attentions, Atlantean, Notes eve's, Mitochondria find hints of held levels, Phases math matched proven leaves, Immaculate concepts match materials, Emeratives interpretations retardations, Reaches impregnations reagents regenerative, Honolulu hormonal tours ruts rushed rang reals, Seats roles reversed released roaring rules proof positive pools one

CHAPTER SIX: Fusions have, Begun, Occurs balanced encodings, Rules faiths lights yours a mutual faith is, Born when affections are sealed selahs, Begin covenants hatch matching sorts, Marry enthused partners found shown, Ways to share,

Mutually concerns for your voiced, Freedoms you have won, Overcome societal miracles, Wedges truths and rituals, Evented occurs relationships raptures, Rules relationships affected, Effects made public respectfully, Rest simply find reconnections, To earth your, Levels oxygen relative ventures, Joint explored, Explodes rules, Tests tasted gains, Capital news, Leverages success, Into your doors, Will allow telling, You have, Ventured past old days find, Funereal ordeals over, Ends met let love reign in, Your ruby blue owl, Hollows merry the, Focus and the focal, Eyes are on your, Vocalizations ordinanced, With truth, Triggers set, Settle into, Doors ordained, Respectfully allow, Ordinant allegiances, Cardinal rules, Clues settled, Feign interest, Rulers bought, Codes kings, Kingdoms come, Voices heard, Allow volleys, Truths established, Proofs travels, Ruptured relationally, Triple reached, Revenues increased, Claims made, Lateral lists, Upload now, Urged gestures, Respects real, Information flows, Gestures made, Reach peace, Talk truth grown now, Align grew perfectly, Purchased ones

CHAPTER SEVEN: Buddhas objectives soaks hearts Naples doors parks doors Gaul slain George trailed daily Ching, Changes, Books, Roused, Risen, Saved, Reads, Reeds, Placed, Booked, Flash, Rumbles, Quakes, Effects, Rules, Nuclear, Voices, Practically, Days, Dues, Drumming, Kodo, Cultural, Cures, Back, Slashes, Seas, Mists, Rules, Mercy, Seated, Arcs disputes, Doors, Gained, Windows, Closed, Europeans, Crossed, Regain, Seas, Japanese, Feuds, Over, Alternate, Source, Pads, Dared, Doorways, Bought, Sold, Finish, Gestalt, Events, Durations, Supports, Sapporean, Districts, Hoikaido, Durational, Dues, Allow, Dare, Impart, Empathic

CHAPTER EIGHT: Espana, Focused, Finds, Dates, Muses, Moved, Remarkables, News, Exits, Exist, Finished, Hear, Clues, Purchased, Keys, New cords cut, Visa sold, Passports bought, Subways ridden, Picasso sold, Dali touched, Turning waves, Red, Hawaiian, Sands, Books, Retreated, Ticketed, Museos, Gala, Tools, Tokyo, Santorini, Over, Kona, Sold, Kai, Plus, Havana, Rainbows, Stations, Crossed, Stages, Attired, Reality, Checks, Extravagance, Dove, Hope, Rules, Sands, Haunts, Blue, Met, Marched, Purchases, Encoded, Fished, Fires, Doors, Moving, Homeward, Stills, Doors

• BOOK TWO

CHAPTER ONE: Gone, Goes, Overt, Loves, Waters, Blues, Pink, Aqua, Red, Yellow, Bluest, Encoded, Rhymes, Rules, Route, Rubies, Rubbles, Rules, Loves, Reappears, Mains, Moans, Erupted, Rubbles, Rues, Primes, Primed, Counted, Counts, Numbers, Phones, Flowers, Courts, Carts, Cages, Mounts, Destinations, Darts, Adaptives, Loves, Nearly, Stolen, Cycles, Surged, Niceties, Nestles, Liturgical, Devoted, Devotes, During, Runs, Ruins, Ruled, Roars, Winds, Reaches, Floral, Phoned, Extended, Extensions, Peace, Passions, Character, Gales

CHAPTER TWO: financially, freed, frames, curls, waves-, curdles, creations, Celtic, spirals, knots, durations, alchemists, fables, brilliance, amazing, following, nurtures, natures, drawings, frameworks, Hollywood, hurtles, charges, delivers, undulates, balanced, registers, values, valuable, favorable, fortunate, cultural, brilliance, cultural, classical, museums, returns, patterns, questions, nurtured, questioned, newsworthy, discretion, discrete, publications, muses, museos, existentially, nightly, currency, currents, reading, reliably, often, federal, ayn, french, English, eternal, lasting, shapes, long, desire, finished

CHAPTER THREE: oaks, islands, eatery, graves, dug, uncover, quivers, owned, horizons, healed, amped, vampirical, vaunted, launched, learned, beloved, mercy, opals, read, rules, rulers, friends, pageants, passages, evenings, universals, severals, hath, filled, peopled, rules, ruled, mules, mercy, grace, lands, swords, hands, hurled, spurts, howls, rousing, Irish, fetish, fondest, fuels, keys, covert, keyed, covers, codes, roads, Rhodes, riddens, baracudan, data, during, landing, fuels, fueled, paged, paged, pages, maths

CHAPTER FOUR: groves, grown, grew, paths, merge, emerge, mergers, magics, enough, daily, acadian, swords, feedings, lifts, lights, luric, lyrical, magically, fillings, deals, surgings, lurching, parries, woes, whittles, mates, matched, ropes, rulers, measured, fed, inks, violents, hunts, golden, hands, emeralds, thoth, thirteenth, days, fountains, penned, couples, peopled, purples, mats, materials, leases, lunch, lunges, lapiz, loans, pens, scribes, those, fluids, flaunts, women, graces, met, seasons, seasonal, finishing, floor

CHAPTER FIVE: threaded, colors, clips, clues, clews, daily, durations, minds, exercised, fused, flows, follows, owns, flushed, clerics, cleared, cubicals, cubits, mercy, mathematics, exclusions, finally, recommended, runs, daily, deny, family, fused, patiently, potentially, plurals, patterns, microcosms, mellows, fancy, fantastical, many, won, chance, one, children, child, keys, kids, lateral, moves, luck, fashions, threads, linen, lanterns, loops, doves, materials, measured, big, large, days books reported, purchased philosophically direct, reports longings freedoms, maximum dues reported, laced throughout nations summaries summations reached, acquired members maps arm

CHAPTER SIX: openings, praised, reds, blues, yellows, galas, collars, clues, gears, rays, reads, waves, caught, nets, cut, eyes, days, writings, written, purchased, lands, greens, gaily, daily, means, mapped, attendant, stands, sent, hope, faith, fuels, fuselage, matched, resolutely, tigers, kept, bays, leaps, materially, made, shields, rend, remembered, rules, cut, throats, umbilically, healed, mirth, returning, carry, faith, fun, Stonehenged, all, one, datum, carriage, carats, cravats cures, emeralds land lots grace, select paths patch currency, carriage rays red

CHAPTER SEVEN: light, reviewed, remember, recalled, clues complex, sorts mergers, waves, blue texas, exudes, charmed, ivy floats, lazy, dreams, presence, elders, London, churns, heights, bought, osprey, swirl, pools, Austin, blue, expressed, invoked, humanity, heard, relations, rules, memories, trees, language, lyrics, future, Brancusi, meetings, halls, lashed, curls, cats, heated, while, wiles, women, sung, clues, blacks, raspberry, trunks, branch, woos, wooden, means, wales, channels, English, hovers, sunny, colorful, young, torsion, asleep

CHAPTER EIGHT: sunset, shown, stacks, exotic, planets, planes, plants, whose, pleased, erotically, squared, expansive, expands, expunged, riches, friends, tenorio, lands, pueblo, rocks, Gabriel, grew, glacial, arcs, finished, friends, reached, relations, shift, rulings, set, forth, past healed, held doors, opened, franchised, reachings through, throats blue, now, opened, purged, lunges, past, chambers, hearts, hot, herbs, mavericks, mules, worn adapt, modulations branches, emerged merged, loops myths, modernity butan, refrains houses, quadrilateral venues, muses waters, fallen views, old days past, racks, creep vibrant, news pink, lime green, electric blue novas

---

LEVEL 433: THE GRACE-MENTS

So at Grace, you have thanks for living. You have voices inside your head which tell you which clothes to wear. How can you not have shoes of light. You do. In your head, so put on clothes of light and join the rainbow crew who washes streets with love until dawn and then pours the soma, moon fluid, on their heads to wash the traces of sleep away and watches Indra come to gather and there is only love floating in the form of feathers, for there has been a dove here today and the power has gone back to the people. This then is love and the hope elongated into grace and we are full with morning and night and the three beakers of light who pour into rivers like Ganges and Saraswati and the Nile and Watauga and the Milky One who knows oceans of wisdom have come to our door with Love, Devotion, Bhakti, Oceans of love waning into dawn with full force's return.

LEVEL 434: THE FAITH-MENTS

Hawaii's import is the manufacture of merkabahs growing both directions which require us to sign in twin gestures of love.

Chapels houses quarters vibrancy lime-green electric novas lupine fine gifts gifted glues said aptly aptitudes carries furnished nurtures nestles blues pinks news babies quarrels hills gifted Hafiz said you were the one born electric registered this emotion pen near throat of this pen find friend who stands elevated too in mercy faith—truth and faith opened here in touch with light married well many came comes caravans burdens lifted lighten

life dripping pentacles love cures caused surrenders drips pleasant encouraged stretched affords sizes orange blue bliss meditates told encouraged pleasant around steering columns pillars lights surrendered causes whence love light intruders left hysterics over children worn won burdens lift laid rests down told surrender affirmations cured license revealed revel most moist surrenders too told one will extravagant gesture make life said tree chosen here one who sing psalms 23rd to eight we find 16 who quiver inside deepened rants of earthly arrivals at the faith ports called Hawaii milky ways heavens lights held within goods becoming one all thrilling exuberant spin spanning twelve gifts several depths told during remodels toured during towns causes electrical forths fillings feelings aloft birthing breathings forests found registration cords drawn write written knights kneels informational rudeness gone surrendering genuine sparks carried forth causes signed thanks Chicago gifts now born written days spoken pleased matched gathers lofts levels learned lends jockey journey journal wise fires singing voices raised patched through dears released white news brilliance fed data sized cures causes leads Australia keeps singing in recovered jolts recovery complete remember declarations dues occasional relish melts meets records forms moist trainings spills forths as signed melts masked clarity clearances made find funds delivered during communications numbered posts revealed recovery complete wrecks greeted cases filled data files waters lemons keys Francis sold cotillion along gleeful squares where days squared equal recorded sumter tracks and the dipping records replenished find fish in the cards and the tablatures kept where steep dogs and little delays were sold for ancient stacks of templed declare for the typical daunt is past and the gels soften in the dripping wet canvas of life led highest and best captivates lens melts caps swung to seal daily hundreds and the repeating relationships were turned to snooping eyes meant to declare us leaping and bound for the abundant kind and as lavender doors cleared the stairs an approbation of fashionable links is floral in her green fade and the arisen kinds who white to green find eyes wise and softened in the proportionate levels of thrusting ahead and the red gaps gone which detect notions of moving flourish and the amalgam's melt is full when the meaning is lost without search and the doors are off the DNA and the cell is born mitochondrial again as we aim to declare our linked likenings to the mother's throats and the thread which in seed we carried and the genus which gave us "love" is the bug which bit when we lied without assurance that we could acquire the full suit of love's baggy wheels and the over-lifts to lay likening to the sword and the dove to the door of the doubled Chinese loops which meant rules ancient born and the tables now turned to include Maori ones and the sun's swelling drip over the tiles found red with tinkled times and the turns worn to encourage us to swoop into love and the yelping journals cause dare and the cavort is born of less know the cloudy disappearance of closings which caused legendary rips in the smiles and clearances which now boxed have inside us sworn to carry the places of love to plural in deeds closures boxed have found feeds inside places of plural lineage

Kandinsky blue knobs of arts crafts and lads ripening to troubled crisis gone and the rushing home to find ones born into mother's ripped free of the frame of core clarity and the cord is cut this night with the sword of truth in us lies the peace of doves and the house is cards without gestures of flying source as we said "let us find movements into love and the blushing ones are the dread-locked kin who found us irresistible inside the veins and nurture's blood is born of palaces tossed and turned into a sign of family disconnect and the content born of love as the psychic prince said " love round this table rules" carry deep the torch and shores and minutes for showering is come the help arriving from Hawaiian shores and the dolphins which brought chariots to the noons of bright cores and the shivering rays of lava led immobilize and the embodiment of enshrouded ones who once monks became begging types who reign without sublime endure and the lime pink cure is your raspberry the authentic doors and the days often melt into love caught in the flight of fight and the right to love pulsations for the loving and the leading legends replied found loved and the blessed sort with the northern and the kind who carry home the cropped plush into the flowers and the brashing let us doorways adored closures and the classic days drawn into the maps of more engaged when the area is wise into the laterally led willingness to stand into legendary notions of needing to assert into these days of aspirations ruled into contractually secure for the agreements meant to the being who led us beautiful ways have registered us into respectfully secure straits of final absolutions, the regained who drew us spanned into the codes for days of yellow rays where God's given nests arrest in surging lateral waves and the raids over find carriage of the curry green clarity for a clarified nation is the northern hungry ones western written into codes and node and nocturnal pens for written we have and have freed this planet form the freed greed gone to love contested ones trained in remainders have found you yellow and the literally given who ride the reservation to marry her train the coded rays who carry literal intrudes these green encodings are the days now past who liquid choose the measures missioned pauses and the fusions come who came which lit the creations of the phenomenon called basic humanity, a duration paused study for the forthright ones who goodness knows memorized mentions who the carriages melt inside the infatuations infusions and legions leased and the lapping ones who encoded swept and the people who knew your peace inside the people who knew how to twirl into notions flagged and faded for the enraptures released assurance sent to the flocks of stocks and sung deeds who nestled in yokes and the yellow roses charged effectually magnetic in stripes and strips and the shoals of duration assurances that the spirit is moving in the enjoy of the lap topped who knew how to deliver the sword into hand ONE.

The heart to the measured cause, let us bleed and believe and the findings pleasures are left to plenties and the mergers who marry the becoming green of the Britain within the welling recorded singings and the found who severally surged and the One who all we would find is love

Measure is lots without reveal and the sizes sealed as the canary isles and the Azorean shields of Seychelle without blues and the lateral leads pentacles again swirl with red readings revealing amid pleasures blue pleased news and the red noted the reality drew who formulated inching, cages swirled and tripped opens to sights and the weapons exposed and the literal

Explorations begin and the beautiful and the sun missing One encode is gone to the tablets now written and the delivery system is unique without rife arrangements genetically encouraged and the cure is sent classical tender nights of the lights

And the gates kept found wisdom to succumb to the desirous one who surrenders self to becoming wise and the unto us of welcome skies and the love interior to a dove who flew the nature revealed in Sanskrit runes and the written plenty sold to buying peace, let us return again to the lend of landed now mountains and the heavenly rites within us placed and the faith in fellow and the horizons sent to tson's rising in peace and the remainders go to mediations of mention's come, metatronically and in faith, mahalo son of the heard singing and the above swells and inside us days and the dials into trees of marriages states and the calling blissed the north caroling swirling lightens us to the blue ridged revelations called

God for the humanity rules and the peace is existent too, in your stones hailed into loving lores, learns oft the deals to icelandic gifts as sorts who marriage meant this is ours, too, love

---

LEVEL 435: THE COMPASSION-MENTS

JAPANESE INTRIGUES SYMBOLS, over-laced diamonds

Infatuated mades kept coal days lights nights healthy feasts festive folds holds messages measures hands nears linear Neptune's nuptials close pods dolphins chapels chimes toasted toasts notations jungles looks fukuoka cherished southern cortex fortunate rings ringing rung champagne chills menu rings homes hagi clay tablets bought saliva seals dealt sperm counted immaculations conception planners manners faith hope best dove streets lingam stoned large lateral friends kagoshima found atomic lifts crystalline nationals parks mountains parks dramas sacred peaks Japanese alps hilltops hearts crossings signs sighs Kyoto gorges bridged cities cursed doorways carriages contemporary meals majestics lifted akas tonight removed temples teams lifted titles clear imagined geishas gifts worn splits overt hearts durations details willingness weds weathered withers vines voiced levels phases chapters joints dreamers forewords journeys updates produced priced productions predilections editions finalized coordinates chapels maps weapons regionalized lasting lairs sections seeds contributed crafts calls clauses published secures security levels leaders established corresponds communicated truths trust told stretching torn belted researched pleased impounded torn radially reinvested reevaluated revelatory expressed experienced expressions hidden traditions trends egrets castles capitals nightly durations moonlit moonlight welcomes controlled evidenced have found calls made collections horizontally laid horizons samurais periodically faiths services signals surrenders escapes gasped politically resemblances counts counties seeded disparately Confuscians calligraphy painted pursed purses budding Buddhists protections lasting links leads devics humans Chinese heians periods games played places slides doors unlockedstages swept periods kept Chicago themes shows lateral western techniques trivial over truths powers oils lights wisdom soft often kings my-o images familiar materialized decorated corded lords cores avebury England London fud myoo upright stones productions periods edo hiroshige internets coded boated hysoki akui word protects amato-e hakaihysoki templars internets coded locals calling imperial gaijin housed plans blossoms showers cherry blossoms violations immersed dials unitary units dials lattice laterals files calls contemporary voltage violations kabaki clerics modules clubs prices shopped souls mated critically releases ravenous rules sushi ordered Kwan Yin comes marketed well brackets Waimea canyons cubed plantations platters cottaged foods drinks salmons tubs waters orgasmic clues parts ovations ovulations living rooms strings beached tents triangles pyramids particles strummed birds released hawks returned fabrics shreds peoples melted lives returned annual trips tripled detailed operationally roofs travels trades drumming discs points made Osaka materials wrapped information informatives nestled palms architectures several sky modernity eyes opening mosaics peacefully greens lights fed sealings directions several seeds who have marriages epics purport graces towns engaged sevens remained who known have Arcs de Triumphs red space-aged ceramics versions buildings kept mindfulness arcs intrigued with you educate locate eggs travelers gates paths o-furo majors clothing comforts sights universally materially lateral links festivals news Zealand seeded released fox frays Josef helicopters rocks climbs conveys jet skies boats canyons reds shields talks greens citizens pins necklaces trines trinity jades choices held moves into yours towns tours toured tripled heralds blazes kois taught fetch Zen partnerships lights towers Oz baum mountains topped pens deaths gone overt all said peace exists lends calming exits exists listed found insides yourself hearts musically swept into Okinawan blues starfish let dance peace rules this planet is faithful compassions love basic humanity lily blue enhancements commencements into tones universals published wealths remaining registered cords rang eternal strains finally said the movements came comes clauses drawn closets shut have opened people pens uncapped sensais mats tatami purchased bathing totally caused racks trunks actually cited cretes checking tours typically tropical impressed impressioned acts actually typographically grasps coveraged stretches statistics family naran emperors powerful concealed seas Mediterranean nights swept passages divisions delays data hotels monastery poses armors san-mon forgiven compassion burns altars found harps framed works brought homeward stilling colors confused magasaki scores trails hostels muroran Fuji nets climbed

LEVEL 436: THE PHILOSOPHY-MENTS

As stars we are stretched across the firmament of life in lines like chords in the songs of heart thresholds and the heat shield erupts in final flames as the Phoenix landing finds us in shades of direct-est lineage to love. As the ophanim said "let us hush" in the names to love.

Kesil Orion's stands taken here as The Divine Sophia, a garment of red drapes her herald as her lips imparting surrender fire into tablature and a pyramid is struck dumb without wintry causes to love wisdom, our choice is in the heraldic source who has chosen the doors as intimately ours for the flowers of the fields and the finalized who dauntingly duo who drew those who marry formidable sorts of the finalized few who knew love—the friendly sort who knew to love: nations who merry glee and those who brought us into loved estates

CHAPTER ONE: Socrates, Herdotus, Vacillates, Symmetry, Asymmetric, Lavender, Pink, Arcturiuns, Lavender, Ruby, Arcs, Quartz, Pink, Perwinkles, Green, Gain, Switch, Magenta, Novel, Fantasies, Peace, Honorific, Champagne, Greens, Concords, Navy, Approach, Nights, Case, Strobes, Strolls, Centers, Attends, Cautions, Precautions, Cleared, Held, Isled, Shaped, Timed, Charged, Genes, Coded, Canary, Octurnals, Masts, Miracles, Evolutions, Balance, Salvia, Sophia, Types, Platforms, Bes, Kinds, Revolutions, Evolved, Sophistry, Branched, Blues, Noir, Films, Venice, Days

CHAPTER TWO: Flowers, Floral, Fished, Shapes, Symbols, Regions, Genetics, Normal, Colleagues, Bilaterals, Syantras, Familiar, Sequence, Surprises, Regulations, Genes, Are, Encoded, With, Your, Sequenced, Yellow, Flight(s), Into, The, Butterfly's, Wing, As, Red, You, Are, Capable, Of, Blue, Things, &, Green, Waves, Of, Undulations, Reeling, To, Examine, Labels, &, Feet, Of, Earthquaking, Equation, A, Friend, Is, Lost, Without, The, Blade, Of your hand &, Left handed one won, Is come again, Look for her in, Your dreams, Trade hands, Again, Exchange flowers in love.

CHAPTER THREE: Place, For, A, Two-handed, Broad, Sword, One, Symmetrical, Phone, Above, This, For, In, 3, Hours, You, Will, Be, Home, Fully, Developed, Blossomed, &, Bought, Solid (ha), In, The, Midst, Of, Radically, Replete, Plenty, Let, Us, Reign, Them, Into, Pink, God, Rays, Your, Lines, Discover, Blossoms, Now, Eight, In, A, Snap, Mexico, Shasta, Maui, Japan, DNA, Mtn tops, Doubles tips, Mutant cleared, Actively activity, Love you, Montserat friends, Ancient ones, Joined, Trip, European

CHAPTER FOUR: Into, Other, Ports, I, Attend, The, Shows, And, Let, Us, Invite, Then, A, Christos, Into, This, Midst, As, The, Moving, One, Is, Found, In, YHWH, And, The, One, In, Our, Midst, Is, The, Berry, Blue, Field, Of, Days, Encoded, With,

Blazing, Releases, And, The, Sword, Orionic, Finds, Kin, In your palm, A nineteenth hole is repaired in, A friend's grid and, The heart found is electric, In the one understood, And trimmed, By novel travels into, The light purple, Seams of going, Home to Saint's Thomas, And the organic, Delay is over as the, Yellow roses are, Handed to the, Suna the organisms, Deigned perfect truly are

CHAPTER FIVE: For this leg we rested and found the peace into grants given the truth and in peace I rest as again this resting brings doves securely home to this place for as horizons blaze a telling drig-line is established which swallows jackson whole and makes the montrose delivery suspect without places and strengths gathered when the rolling is sold for a day and the receipts added up squander less and aim more into written worths and the squashing past I find another blues connected ley as the yes is found in peace and moves to the sea and the cliffs of armenti which embrace us in sales, sailing, loves and the watery way of the Elysian forgettings have come to the end of the indigo ray. As I committed to this cause I saw the will to know our hours of love

CHAPTER SIX: Kauai is blue in my mind and the indigo fuse is lit as in I go to the sea of Metatronic splendors, angles cycle as the sport sprinted is your amplifications of the blue bursts of Caribbean knowing as the launch is shipped to curing courses and the censored ones find containment in the brulee brown cremes of the reading divides and the bisected angles will fend for feet formed in vacuums of green speaking and the platinum pews are monhydrids who hold plural niobium shapes and the comets of nibiru find sisters who aligned with ebbs and the we of resurrected this planet this week cedars Tokyo synopsis written is timed as the books times suggested links to fathers who mountains moved in order to sea the great lemurian being of Arcturian journalize. As I swam I saw the father farthering into the times of books and the love for gifts who simply simmer in similar fashion as focus became your organizational skill.

CHAPTER SEVEN: For in psychological notions a herald exists called Jung who found fell in mentioned realities of I ching-ing nature and the cellular calendars of single flames is burning in exact decree of the notion that a thread is where this leads and where you tread is cause for electric single pause as the pulse is built in choice and those who found freedom in their frame as the paid for friend is initialized into doors red with resting many motioned and the notions alchemically attended where sky people fell to the miracle of earth and taking chance took a walk in Hunab Ku and the yellow pause of green devotion to the sapphire blue beach of eyes and miracles who loved funny rays and focusing on flashing lights and the flaws less and the fevers more and the hush yes of lobster blue eggs and the seeds now planted ripening in eyes of Metatronic blue and the chile greens go to the Easter isles and the eyes of one who heads to rapa nui too and the blues are over as the cds bring brought flights and

this lesson leads into love as the slopes blossom a feet magic bound arcs homeward still in coiled descent into digits and the harmony and the remembrance of pi calendrics as the reason our generators run into love.

CHAPTER EIGHT: As the secret unfolds red became blue as the 17 count down to 16 15 14 13 12 11 10 9 8 7 6 5 4 3 2 1 encoded enki trades now for the codes to all electromagnetics to full body harmonies to love to the mode to the means of travels and the trades which cause you to see in electric blue sales of the sold nature.

LEVEL 437: THE IN-NATURE-MENTS

CHAPTER ONE: Automatically points spools bordering basics humanity heralds music water Monet arcs detailed artists brides gifts markets emancipated applies Switzerland accounts valuable directions values tastes certifications tested certified certificates history historically due swiss Tanzania services appraisals intentions societies villages arts beds built automatic draws encamped greens burned campus garnets sets sprays spruce red habits diamonds encompassed circles encrusted Othello sings rhodolites centered pines models emeralds classics listens builds encoded electricity

CHAPTER TWO AND THREE: Tastes Cuban shops shapes planets plants governs plantations coves caves Steinway john islands saints blues delta Mississippi music tortolan song races cruz Milan marry ideas planes planets exhilarations reserves cherished words swords worlds Casiopea frequents cycled mars Saturn Pluto most trails lead to Jupiter through gates of goat bays caneeling data banks burn fuels of trunks loaded with marley brown hooks of the rast's nature and the red clericals come to sing sapphires to the terrace and trees and cuisines who lend lady like airs to the moon as the tainos find historical codes and the cultures merge in marriages of descent into rural communities and the agrarian bethel wholesales devotees to the Columbus India Dalai Lama yes books little smiles hits islands French Tahiti cleared devoted emotionally each to other energy clues found in blues owed love pours powers dove returning wisdoms and the digs off relapsed arcs and the waters run blue with anananberg guidance and the overt ones who receive information through leaks in old news and passengers who ship into originations of love

CHAPTER FOUR, FIVE AND SIX: Lies told leave as the fell frail with drop offs market soft findings to several valuable lessons of nose face type bulges anagadan light streams akashic records seal thief stolen sought found steel hammock backs traces rests inside interior sliced delivers suggestions psychic shaping works workings wings stolen recovered enfolds your in yellow roses again out our nature is today a seen saw 200 stars on the ocean's floor and in singular measures fell into paces as I walked into amalie votes voted aggressive decades charlotte millions humanity pelt me a shoulder touched becomes shelter and a sun's voyage illuminations carries powers in this blood and in this valley I met her the divine diving Sofia and life held well as Mary mother again friend montseraatan antiguan suffused lessens without great written blazes red into retreat into yellow atocha arc-angel Michael's gift is found near the sea beads as a shed giant softening the floors as the fled wrinkles shedding settled into gardens

CHAPTER SEVEN: Cherished and see the seas of savannah bougainvillea seen again glass Jerusalem saint john's waters waves weights splashed instincts those cords cut and often capably twists into cable like connections of seeded softenings angularly tossed into racheted sorts virgin gordas virginal missions qualities missions qualities qualify you for the insanity saints beautiful surges sealed heights processed pyramids planes windows widows pink purple ferry perimeters

CHAPTER EIGHT: Cracks appearing in the grid cause nearness to the throne of alter instincts as the dove dives into thrown stars and the basement of why we encrusted our codes in floods of shark infested waters and the muse is correct in her seamless gesture of how to walk in the cracks as O'keefe stated we will include the apothem in the lengthening rivets and the wisdom worn will become recalled recollections of why the sea worm is curved into the crescents of lateral pushes and the plug is removed now as the birthing push joins her union with the throat shrieking "now is born the lamb of the Lord Metatronic, as Ariel comes let her soothe in passions plates and the places to love. Flesh is flashing in Yucatanic rituals and the ridges spent on blue to purple virgins as the dove dives into ponds electric and the rose opens to bloom us into opal paints and the removals recovered open winging to the sum of sunny days and the sai is baba again as the carriage lifts to operate the boom and the winged wons coming carry you into channels of blue-green include as the eight sang St. Croix home and the nows intrigue is heightened when the clues caneeling into your door marry the sound to the trunks and bays treated as reys of passions places poised in mercurial releases of the registry of how to hold the lungs opened and the pen poised as hallucinations past have passed into blooms and the partners paths marry in pure light as pearls splash with tiny arms and the sully forth is come to a sula soothed and the sun Nova Scotian had doubled to lead us past the marker at the corner of the devils dinning as the sets were rolled into waves of perfect notion

---

LEVEL 438: THE STUDENT-MENTS

CHAPTER ONE: As religious in other societies called us to monastery days and the mercy flew into rages within ranks a

dove was found and she rose through the Montseratt mountains to the apothem of the ranks and the rulers flanked to her dome as the rose grew into yellow ashes and the several Indo-European nations chosen rang with registration of the doves recall of boundaries breached and the popping loosens as the bureaus breed a news of standards lessened as the pi voyages home in the nose of a ship called ericksonian nudges and the direct license is won as the angles measured major us to the highs and lows of informative types who hustle to hear the tonight toned and the requisite is now written as the slopes close to include sliding requirements and the reaping is begun as the harvest of the dove tones "on" tonight. fixations past have closed and the gateways to love are re-opened in Bermudan skies and the buildings whose corners marry yours with stones summitted and the June voiced as the volumes written rhyme into meaning with the contests won and the recording come came a field of electric grey-blue who married your voice to the alterations required and the scrutiny now past is worth all the passions of motion made monumental and the calculated ratios rose to join the rules

CHAPTER TWO: Scholarly refuge is found and the embarkation is noticed as the suicides now past are proposed to the stars and the relationship with mars is divided into two subtle subterfuges who rank last in the simple signs of circumferences breached as one who said perimeters is running into interests, her own, and you own the radii of the entire universe this day, a plan in place intrigues us, now. Rotations have opened and the pen is in place grasp it and write, soon these numbers 1,2,3 and the united won have caused this encoding hidden in backs like Egyptians scorned to find coats and layers of forgiveness in the shields and the cubes now entered own a primitive recalling system as the alligators who dove to protect us ate our hearts and the Pygmalion types hovered over the conceptual schools as the point made is taken another eats the earth's ways and finds comfort in assisting our dimension to its estate and hidden within is a mine of recollection as the 360 became visual vesica Pisces and the arc is flowering between us in days of rainbow enclosure near the door of love's broad paths.

CHAPTER THREE: Upon these golden wings I sing the lesson of rectangular meaning as the cube unfolds in mind's eyes and the ritual is past I recall the meaning at last and mental constructs laid aside pleasure me with the simplicity of how we fed each other in lands of reasonable seed and the seeded ones who synopsis said "required" have sent the suicide of life's now past to the meaningful trip of tracks made in sand, Moroccan, and the shirts worn in sleeves repeating our stability in the flood of remembered door. Yes as written, I will complete this epistle in record, time, and write the graceful end to a memory infused with why humanity is here and how we did it before is now encoded in us and written for all to hear the music and money and tablets and glue and the comets connecting to imbue us with flashes of recognize as the seas part to consequential curves and the rigidity is gone as the conclusions drawn include new musicians capable still of curvatures in the spine of the sequential seamings and the muses link to find each other as the cravet worn is slashed into rocks berber styled and the deepening is ripping us open to seam the principles of steaming rocks cooked inside this pig's belly of cabinets stocked and the stash of gin spilling into clarity.

CHAPTER FOUR: Clarity is sought and found as the traditions are flowering inside this mind and the crystal seam is glinting in the fundamentally clear waters of cavities created and the horrific ones have ripped themselves in the repairing rush as the respects drawn include rapt checks on how you are doing this attendance to the grid and the attendant ones who spun for truth have come to die within the stream of elegance forgotten, a rough one has departed this plane, this day, good-bye rough one. As explained, the rude one is gone, now travel into fuel cells who reach the theoretical issues of objectives reached and the poetic notion of sophistries and politics and the imprinted spheres of glee sought inside the instinctual clearings of apparent appearance in the seas of pushed and pulled materialism who wealth sought in the north poles of bones broken and boa strikes of the leisurely sort who in moral fiber found fonts written into and ethics who knew of morality in the fuel of leadership.

CHAPTER FIVE: Teleologically sound theories open into academic summary of the Buddha gifted and the cancer now gone to the amber green keys of literal translation of the songs of the dove, Zion singing summary gives us fountains eyed with preferential treatments of how to seed the next universe, am cutting the cords this day to the musical lush who forgot how to sing and am moving into new reductions of song. Theory has leased us space in the trunk of the performance of greeted sort and the surgery is surging us home on wings kept clipped until extremes ruled without altruistic intrigue and the intrinsicness of criticism which speaks omega and alpha and dates of republics lashed without freedoms and the parallels now finished find us singing in mars and marriage and criticism cut to shade phaedrean dreams and the classes cancelled without students.

CHAPTER SIX: Occasions hush and the Hellenics core as the respirations rising find us kneeling in streets direct within handed scabbards and the Gaudi core is gathering in Athenian discipleship as the provincial dares are connected into Caribbean azul Achilles sealed and the sword stuck into hands is found as the lost ones wander without recognition skills and the citizens watch us depart knowing full well the seal is on the dove. A church established won us friends and won debilitated without wings.

CHAPTER SEVEN: As the impasse is past a point is made with several entreaties to explain, how, the impassionate pleadings are voices as the governors carry possibility to the door and the recompense won is shown the way to speculations who reveal the culprit hear, as heard the metaphors erupt and the fun is stages as the written one takes the stage of threaded encodings

written into codes and shown the ways into love. As the branch into greek seeds is symbolic of the Hindu mantra patterns, so the one central sun is calling you home to the alley of minds and that great om is 3.14 inches, form your door. As stairs built are sent to the locks of the grid a candle cracked the seams and the shield is refocused on you. As hexagonal yellow dares include grids and circles and stones Tibetan singing a species is hatched, again, creating kingdoms from chemical bonds and the yes is flowering inside patterns electric.

CHAPTER EIGHT: As encoilings are showering the plane a flower unites inside you and your hearts employ techniques born ancient to days and the marriage is issued forthrightly and well as the energy flowing creates dialectics of reasonable approach to the throne of God growing in your heart. A kingdom is hereby built and it is called, YOU. That simply, this is creation, what a student and gift you are, dear. Branched into DNA I issue forth in channels and channels of sunlight on raindrops and moonlit motions into news of encodings sought and the counterfeit go to the One Goddess, Kuan Yin, who called me forth to signal the end of this written epic. Tales told I tessellate into patina crested focus and the vocalizations of hoods and female is coned into coda who know how to measure the mission in omphalic shows of tranquil transfer and the stars struck in your transmitting the doorway Metatronic.

LEVEL 439: THE FLOWER-MENTS

CHAPTER ONE: go the ethers whispering yes and the next day India erupts

CHAPTER TWO: Without Hindu historicals as the intense is infinitely better and the invertebrate ones are veterans of vertebrate spinal taps and the column is hushed this night with Jason's direct touch to the analysis of factual phones made material and the facts told to say "yes" to ethical treatments of the judgements gone as the singing elongates to include others who overthrew themselves in the struggle over termination of your cord and the singing ceases unless you see how to aid the keys who fell into yellow water

CHAPTER THREE: And the lemon is the sword we struggle over and this is direct from the throne. Green grew emerald in your keep and the pattern DNA is kept in the radically similar notion of purple pleasures as the violet ones aid the steps to natural selection of the braided knot, a Celtic encoding is spent without format and the funded ones aid the energetics of the seed who is building. An ivy green deliverance is aiding you in your choice of days to attend the school and the ruling combinations are laminations of the need to plan how to flower the seeds of notations made to man and the trip to this podium is flowering into relationships of pieces who peacefully show us how to become the kadmon and the yours of yes kingdoms

CHAPTER FOUR: And the star is fishing for the meaning in emotional recipes as the rescue came to the often found harmonies of how to forgive the foggy brained necklace of starship entities whose firey coral kingdoms commits this day to the throne of YHWH and as I said, Buddha too, for the existence is in these rings, the three, who marry all celebrities to God, these lines exist in acts of several stages and the pages to Bermuda are blue in days of flown inquiry into dove daring empirical notions as the feeding past are plush inside the formatted trees and grass and lands of plenty and the days of knowledge are in this entire entreaty called the Tree of Life.

CHAPTER FIVE: As I said, Trees and the truth is equal to the embellish as you find home and herald and hearth born into this home of instinctual lack gone to clear and simple burst of breathing hush and the flames enfold the symbol field in quiet hush of omphalic boats departing in the throne room of departures past the bear who breathed breaking our necks for the boat is now full with the polished shells of our clearing the rubble to find Aquarian news of green rocks who swelling tell us that the gentle members now restored have given carriage to the seas of calm elocution and the delay is done, a finish is on us and the dots into dashing flare across the relays as the Morse is coded with swashbuckling inscriptions of returning wills and the made yellow temples time-ing us to the sword of laughing return into the presence enhanced and God's red rays of electric blue intrigue with the sent ship which downed the field and other found us squandered without eyes and arms who know now the knitting and the climbing into flowers shipping us home in lotus dews. And the days of surrender have come to the Moroccan continent as Casablanca rings into the walled cities of ancient lore and the angelican devotee is daring us to drink the elixir of hush and the tarry is less and less when one comes to the pen of seas soft again with truth and torn shirts whose justice is come and the dove flies away, be-nested in rings of keys and codes who many carry measure us for the doorway is past and I am into love with devotion full in the throat of this third note called stars of sapphire blue peering and the heaven is come in peeling devote to the dealing in perfection.

CHAPTER SIX: My mouth is sweet where honeyed tablets rang with full trickles of trivy toned spouting and the electricity euphoric is calling in the triple summary of the sum of mine blessed amid befriending and amid us greetings came as the breathing rush is misted in phases and planes and doors who breathing matched our touch to the sun, once again, and a ship is leased to carry us first home, then rays inclosing to the third we rang in the belly of a son of the best for replied the birds, I am a Metatronic trend and the heart to the wing is the sully forth over fields of angelic arc as the one pocketed is opened in one great gulp of hungry affection to love.

CHAPTER SEVEN: For as one limber in finding love, I remember the places where yesterday I stashed this ship and hitching a starfish to the junctions I claim clarity in the mental acuity fields and pause to simple task now incomplete now final as the Asian grillings odd to the phone find closure in charcoal burning and the brassier is tossed into washes of branched suns and the love who would carry us home for the A, B, C's of love include Aruba, Bonaire, and Curacao in the dump of ink into the blue Caribbean sea and the Taino culture is here honored for the timbre set is the pitch of pens squid blue and the rings are all three blazing now in Jah's one light of how we beat in the heart electric.

CHAPTER EIGHT: Lifts one heart as the letters forgiven find dabble into green peas of empathic sound and the relay is set to mention white yellow news of how to be good in the endure and the relationship is made sea sweet with willingness to back be in the wound seized and the wondering cleared of where you have been when the find is found to be vintage bottles of weekly visits to the 11,000 virginal who fell prey to martyrdom when the dark birds exploded in suns willing to span less than the All we deserve. As a swerve is cleared a willing One found love in the heart of the Dove and a mention is made of the lifting called Broad Sword to the born alive in welling thanks for the One who cured us of the slump of disdain and naysayers who forget the elevated shoes of the tribe electric called Basic Humanity and in chemically cured import I compose this rhythm called Humanity. In peace, I rest, Treva, the dove, Metatron Blue.

THE POEM: For In Philosophy I found the Nature of All Things and the "Arcing in" reason for why Dove's exists and why the wings repaired required a great LIGHT and how often this answer has come to the several sent for merger clauses and the In case In causes which repaired a currency to exist which in Mars is a current wronged without election, as a right sets over us and the all is heard summing you in rock the One, ever steady, Es found Tribe reefed St. Croix Blue in yellow phases, now written and the enigma comes to exist in phases and currents deep in rich of ness and the Is-willing outs you enacted discussions for Orations and coming crafts whose exceptional instincts marry us to intrinsic values of On wins and the victory that song which sang found us sung and the path built is parched and regarded the Caribbean way, as the blue van red with sapphire pasts and the beach which seeded pure treatments of opalations into opening mtn's and the woman who maned her own endeavors with switching rushes to touches converted rushs and the gifts gained when on rafts we mentally freed our physical affection to swing in mention found and surrounded in-dovings which soothe us and send us constant still into insistent clauses and the "many-mentioned" in speaking call Ivey seals to eyes now cleared and thee clarity comes for where founded I am funded, through efforts in grants the resurrections received when in-zones I locally ascend to market durations and the links to in-futured doors who win the red keys with only official announcement of having won the Christed heart as we In prophet speaks and In-statements leaders and keys encoded our relief at interests and the instincts In LOVE I final release to the Key Codes of LOVE

LEVEL 440: THE IN-HOPE-MENTS
"Welcome the Divine Sofia"

LEVEL 441: THE GRACE-MENTS
"Preside the Eternal Father to Mother's Electric Grid"

LEVEL 442: THE IN-ARC-MENTS
"The in-matching Cause is Love"

LEVEL 443: THE DOVE-MENTS

Minor archs absolved are allowing aches to clear as the salve is burnished into wounds elect and the electric choice is the glowing encoding of Sophia type divinities and the choice is made and clear, I am is staying here and the washing waters are showering us with knowledge and the college of fusions is linked into through love and directions of ledgers kept which adding up range into numbers nearer the top of Everest and her Sagmartha encodings are the ones written which include the rulings, Dove, Peace, God, ends here the release into Peaceful manors of mannerings and strings cut to include these repaired raids on the trunks of the enclosures of God.

As we go, now: Into the trunk of this tree of life and the concupiscence is sent into mobile missions of senses applied to the far reaches of harbors and boards purged without twos of the tunes unified to field us for the light's electric. As humanity shifts into sunder and the ounces spared are added to the professional decor of the one who sums us all into standing tides and the deepening dove is send for the deeds of innocence and light, I declare this mission done and the rules which applied have changed to include registrations of the codes ascendant with me, Treva, for the God in us with us is calling in urgency to the dove to get moving now.

Becoming will weave as the entrance into tranquility as the openings include sleeves of solitary contain and the reign is shouldered another appears who smoothing your visage with oil in lights written wears the success of famous written gifts and the how we drive is a litany of boating refrains sung as the land disappears into isles and creeks of Greek exile and the whales now singing find you lessened less and rounded more into love.

As the land is soothed by indigo blue with pea green foam of the trimmer drip and the Glastonbury tubes of blue-green erasure have descended into the land of the tomb of a womb left open through cups pouring into the field of blue lipped surrenders and the Metatronic bearing which brings harmony and lift.

For our doors opened into oceans of God and the N-E-W-S is spelling us into days of treatments for wisdom and the summary is due to God-head days of encoded harbors and the healthy rewards which come into landed rays of doves.

As the sea is the Office of Christ grows to include other sorts who voice the sapphire dronings with devotion and tablets of glue tumbling into stuck positions which melt under the muse of winds of gold and God-trim. As the red rose respected became a measure for life also this love finds 1,2,3 again and we marry to the maverick lust of forward days and the daring to concur that God is good in our rules for love. One last attempt made is treasured and the calm besets us with daring Shasta blues.

As shasta boasts sunny red sparks and delays long gone have come to dutiful experience of the doves inter-connectedness, lateral twists will dare the cruising sort to show the door to invisible drinks from the wetter side of Mauna Kea and the measurable means of merry days.

As reaching love I become woven into born again rests and the arms of loving friendship, I find friends in these soft places and rewards in the soft-spoken ones who deliver cunning charms and the born electric grids of grunt lines tossed to the winds of exposure without dove linings and the licking is ticking the ecstatics to the curb without measure as the green door, once exposed, became mine today and I sent it into God, where it belonged always. As the door is explored without destiny, I AM, and with gesture I became the ship and the land of starboard sways. Like leeward winds in a tunnel of love, as God has said "Israel" and the sword now drawn is clearing people from the grid as the dullness drifts away over oceans of excavated dread and the chambers once spent have come to the champagne views of durations.

As the dull lifting is mentioned a balanced sort marries purpose to Layoesh and the kin are dreaded without repeat and the unplugging granite is sent with the version previous as the reputations buzz with heady tradition and the ripening reward of head sover seas disappearing with monsters beyond the edge of the seas and the stoned ones have found geometries which replace the schools of burning weeds and rotten apples who found lodging in the sun and burned into perdition previous to this incarnation pool.

As the tablets now written say, the holy cities have come, the exquisitely rich inscriptions have come and the surrender is into gentle trips to the mines of chemical burst as the eyes of laying on have encoded themselves in coats of rainbow and the funereal lusts have piled into lava tubes, of thurston sort, and have spun with wings red in the sun for a phoenix has come to life and again, I say, the phoenix has come to light and the mother is sending her sea to the coast Barbary as I long in mediterranean loops and the buzz is up for about us are the love greeting geometries and the skills of lipid sort sort us into categories due to durations and green details of love.

As the One creation is sung, a Holy book is produced, which reads of sequences sung to the son and reptiles have crept away to spill into ravines of deepest long and the even is over and the duration is drawn to a close. Now is the written biography of God, YHWH, and beyond written into biophysical replacements and the structures now leap to surrender the gaps of faces once written on torah scrolls, outside, and the three who came to see these books as finished.

As a partner to an area of leap and gap structured clearings and the strictures of boats open throats of ancient declare, I find peace in the foundations built and open eyes who once piloted us without guise and fusions who last into love's crystalline seats and the mercy of doves who last for underneath us all is a crystal sea of perfect shine and the purest purification is done through the shining Urim and Thumim which exist beneath this seat. Like a merciful God, I climb to the edge and dive into the crystal sea this day and beneath the seas I find rest in love.

A dove rules this streets with quiet regard for truth and proof of the light electric let us recede to find clearer ones and the God in this book is a St. John depiction of the ways to go repeating into rests and rewarded truth, again, love is led.

As the Gabriels arise to join us into levels of light's arcing, a God head is heard wishing us Ohana Empera inside imperial red blues.

And written hear: "As the matrix moves so I too."

LEVEL 444: THE WING-MENTS

Like Buddha rising I find sunsets in green nights and flights whose eaten vesicles are the traits of treaty and the truth written Torah like is found inside these vesicles as the traits of flight sine us with wands of literary exposure to the medical assistance now available through the widening kas and the reputations now building will find durations of light written into truths and the match is made in reborn news of the light dove's returning. As the rites written welcome us to Arcturus and the rising sign is blood linkage into crystalline structures into axions of love points.

And the laughter is in the lens as the dove leans over the seeds to structure your welcoming mats of addictions shot into winds needles and the love can come again into crafts of arts and the strengthenings of survival have ended in energetic lusts run past.

As the swivel made is good and the name is restructured and the twice is said Layoesh, Ayoesh, Kadoesh, Layoesh, Ayoesh, Kadoesh, a new unplugging is made as the passenger ships loading mean snakes serpentine in structure are dropped to the floor of the pyramid's lifting off over the seas of mercy, Gabriel has come, to the reconveyance area of the MAP programmings.

And at Main doors a doorway once plugged by granite seed is spilling out to reveal the Grand Father's core in me and in you, the sea of quiet relief for all humanity.

As the last karmic link now eaten is digested and the readings have come to a close, I write for the pen Anagadan and the giving arch-angelic friend Michael Benjamin who taught me to breath and to vote for Bangladesh and to tell EThipia my heart knows their longing. For as streams cut from tips of stars are we and woven into storage bins are they and ink is registering blue

again as I pour the corrections into leaks and the leaping arcs have married to become the durations of ships resting in lines of living linkage and the sirens and the fates have come to end as the rocks tessellate into place at the mouth of the streams and the winds where Michael bends to Benjamin again and fades into tribes electric now written on the arms and chest of those who came to give love back to a rock. And called, I AM, and left into repeating songs and gestures made wise for the great seas have come to an end and the frozen ones have left us with rewards and causes of red-yellowings and songs alive in lines axiomic, for as I have written, Metatron is come, and as I have given a mind tortured up has found relief in old songs and new news of the amazing grace which inhabits this planet, as Janes and Johns have seen, a day is come, and this is now, our mastery, for in the ringing four is the blessed position in the daily spin of grace said, and hearts come to the end of perditions.

And along the way, I sing, riding boards of quiet release and the relief of ancient days born aloft in the winds of our basic humanities. As the spinning is done and the deliberations even out, a Delilah whose cut hair empties into seas of rust, allows your hush to ring over the angry dregs and the 72 tesselation points are done soon, as the benedictions become Layoesh, Ayoesh, Kadoesh in annual rhythms and rings like trees exploding.

"Trust this winging written Key"

LEVEL 445: THE IN-ANSWER-MENTS

"Often said "love" is the key.

Chords born electric are the sort who say that Atlantic reefs are finally aloft in the branches of star trees who pierce the veil in Milky Way blues and scratch messages in the reach of cubes born now, for in the hauling I AM ONE and in the drawings on the ceiling I AM ONE, I AM.

As reaching close I find stricture less and significance more I surge into new areas like the seas of ancient freize and allow a lifting lip to direct me into findings of love forgotten. She did not make the trip. Tahiti bound is the Gaugain of lines written into with older pens than these and the accurate tale is the swelling sea softening this brain again. As deflation seizes so does boredom and seeming returns as the links are made for blue mountain brews and the buzzing hums us into Dues of St. Thomas origins and the star underneath the sea which came to peek at us.

Like the duty bound, I AM, and like the friend arriving I AM and as the lilacs bloom I find you in wet days and airy estuaries and single birds circling high in the hawk's nest of deepening dares to be exactly, ONE

Singing is good in my case and ears are attuned to my days of literary durations and the stations of light regard for a caring rock is lightened with reflection of the Indian heads and the hunger is fed and I eventually stare into stations of light and the reappearance of friends who carry us over the rocks of old relate and the novelty of move meant to see the Heart's eternal flame of athletic appeal and stuffed sort found adrift in seeds of God.

Fountains here are spilling and numbers now may ring the doors of strict record and the accord now struck is quick in merry measures meant and the seeding is the goal of old clearances and the moments now deliver us to blows of subtle less and direct most to love.

For as God is electric and the Christ is the gate, so eternal is the love of placed durations and the calling kept is your equipment spelled L-I-G-H-T.

God is our triumph and the triple singing is in us and the I AM is with us and the fabric is rent to determine who the electric coat is worn by and the rainbow ruled is yours, allow entry pointed.

As satin joseph allows and the islands ring us the Island of Me is resting in sleeping peace and the rogue wave taken care of is aloft with hearts Hellenic and the won ones now rest in splendor's gates and the ruby rose into tossage of toes on the seas of lips wet with karmic cost and so I toss the seed into Omphala piles of found glass and quiet again I tread the trees of anticipation curves and the singular sine of thrifty sort and costs now paid are over, due, and there I rest in love.

Becoming due without cause, I launch into born blue and the description of how to part the waves of old days with seas of opaline cause and the burgundy drunk is found floating in recoil as the knowing of lost is come. As the left behinds float in refuse and spoil I launch the point of this writing into the wind and aim the rod of thunder into love.

Like noses in seas, we are riding the Buddha's head into bays of love and the stakes of Atlantean Thoth is back to Garden us with tablets trued and the ones who paddle alaskan wells of lovers lost have sought us here in old buildings of wet respire and the joint custody is over as the closures come to the completions of news which left us ferrying back and forth over deep ravines of lusty spells broken and the new stolen last, now come to rightful owner ship, love.

Home to low wattage is know good, and burnt out is spent and the enhancements have written this solar plexus into wields of shining Caribe sort and the winds are home in us.

As the humans loved point out, Metatron is near, and the bays of cruise blue are here to the ear and the heart of humanity and the parking place is freed as the peace of notion is mentioned and the arc-angelics visits are formed in fashions of glittering days and the notifications of lightening bolts of lift resolving here, like Alycon, a boat is come, and the parade of Omphalic sort is climbing over the whispering frankness of finding fashion in conversations about given days and the dues are paid into leaves of islands, wise, and the elevations are come, as the ripples effect, are instinctual now, and the feelings of old have left us clear to love.

LEVEL 446: THE SEVERAL-MENTS

"You who knew have blessed this globe in robes and love"

Where in us is the grid laid through the points of thoughts made electric and the replenishment is come and the softening seeds have born us through the verdicts and the vital signs of viaducts of love. as lights blinking guide us home, I cede to love.

Forgiven the entangle I am coming home and the shine is simple as the good-byes ring us and the peace abounds and the lights blinking send abundance to the kin for abundant we are and like scores of others left she signs the clearance is come. As the rulers leave and the threads are broken, I live in ultimate regard for the peace of regional neglects and the yellow heads bobbing over ions spent in inspirational outlines of cutting through to God inside the Adam's kadmonii.

Cuts made bleed into red diffusions and the beginning sharks seeking call us to the town of Hanalei and I reside beside the One belching red dragon called Pele and appetize myself with abundance of the fruits of these, labors, the point.

God-for-sake-eneness ends and the suggestions comes that peel us into petals of blood red snakes gone to the dove's catching tail and the resource is sent. My heart twitches into 1,2,3, and the 3, 1, 4's are married to my shield of floating freed.

Sananda may cruise into this heart line. May is the seal on God near the sea Metatronic. In light I lift to the Office of Christ and head home to the portal of Stars and Star lights. Goodness rests in me this night. Peace, love, durations, come. Christ Office set. Light is ON, love.

Where were you made and how? in this I find replenish and the knowing that several selves have shown and the discipline regained is us singing into low employ and wide to middle marriage and the scar created clears and the love reversing finds us in tides of Fundy blue as the green presence established is us singing love.

LEVEL 447:   THE MERGER-MENTS
"As we said "mergers" must exist in love's crust"

LEVEL 448:   THE IN-CAUSE-MENT
"annual visits caused clearance in love's grid"

LEVEL 449:   THE CURRENCY-MENTS
Add a dollar to your trust of love, let us hush soon.

LEVEL 450:   THE IN-CURRENT-MENTS
The current details have found us in love.

LEVEL 451:   THE WRONG-MENTS
It's over, love.

LEVEL 452:   THE IN-RIGHT-MENTS
The currency is simply your right, to love.

LEVEL 453:   THE OVER-MENTS
the needs of the community are met, now, love. Dove.

LEVEL 454:   THE ALL-MENTS
The all who know who came to the deals, over now, love, doves. Ahkenation is born.

LEVEL 455: THE SUM-MENTS
A summary sent to love's doves.

LEVEL 456: THE IN-ROCK-MENTS
The interior rocks us into love, a dove's summary.

LEVEL 457: THE EVER-MENTS
The generous moments are telling us to come into love.

LEVEL 458: THE ONE-MENTS
The code is "respected," now rest, amma grace is born.

LEVEL 459: THE STEADY-MENTS
The little ones respect your core and thus is born the sun. The living god is all of us.

LEVEL 460: THE TRIBAL-MENTS
A living light is the tribe to truth and bears across the dove's rest.

LEVEL 461: THE IN-PHASE-MENTS
An "is" is coming into us. Paris is the summary of the stylish burst into love.

LEVEL 462: THE IN-LOUVRE-MENTS
The Louvre is the charts on the Dove's details.

LEVEL 463: THE CONNECTED-MENTS
The currency is d-o-v-e landed.

LEVEL 464: THE OF-MENTS
Influence is due to a coverage spread with white motion over page and the papers now interested in e-motions, love is spread, comes a Dove of Love.

LEVEL 465: THE IS-MENTS
Is your heart into love?

LEVEL 466: THE WILLING-MENTS
The Will is in you, will you choose the dove's language and dance upon your ears for in this heart now I feel the dance.

LEVEL 467: THE OUT-MENTS
The out has come to this, in to love.

LEVEL 468: THE ENACT-MENTS
The encact-ments run with the sun to your house in a dance of Shiva ecstatic and the ride over dove into love.

LEVEL 469: THE OVATION-MENTS
Applause is due the friend who held the hand for a dove who knew how to fly and to rhyme with the moon's enchantment. Soma has spread to the page of a devi due a lucky break.

LEVEL 470: THE COMING-MENTS
The Coming-ments are the pension paid for arising in doors into Love.

LEVEL 471: THE CRAFT-MENTS
It was easy to make a craft of the Light, how about an art of the craft called Love.

LEVEL 472: THE X-CEPTIONAL-MENTS
In our exceptions we forget the X-ceptional Way to Love, the Tao of sacred Heart and the mercy which mary's example showers on All of Us. We love you Virgin and the friend, Jesus Christ, an X-ceptional marriage to the mark made when a Dove lands in snow and becomes the holy Spirit again.

LEVEL 473: THE INTRINSIC-MENTS
Intrinsically our chance is to meet with grand Ones who have given heart to the message of God, let us dance Shiva man. The nagas are electric in this hood and the heart is Buddha wide into God, and then there's Jesus Christ walking without pain and all of us understood the art of winning, instrinsically, for good.

LEVEL 474: THE ON-MENTS
I am On into love, cobra's kundalini rise to the sun to melt into golden pools of standing ovation for the Office of Christos. Sacred Rocks, heaven's gates, Grandfather Mountain, and the Christ-line's blood of genius.

LEVEL 475: THE WIN-MENTS
Winning is our day.

LEVEL 476: THE IN-VICTORY-MENTS
The in-victory-ments are here, let us find the key to another living trust called let others dance over the days where winning ones anchor the trees to the doves.

LEVEL 477: THE SONG-MENTS
The song-ments sung with an Oh God, sound, as we watch the dove burn the bush with her heart's melting torch of telling the truth when asked, who is God and where in the light of this dove.

LEVEL 478: THE SUNG-MENTS
As I am I will be sung into beauty of love.

LEVEL 479: THE PATH-MENTS
Like Jerusalem of the rock, I Am the Dove, God's covenant with this earth.

LEVEL 480: THE REGARD-MENTS
Lakota the blood of the arc of a dove. I have regard for the planet, Earth.

LEVEL 481: THE CARIBBEAN-MENTS

Let the Caribbean come to us through her music and a St. Croix day of dancing feet warming the seat of this dove. Saint John aand Joan will join the throng who remember this day for the dove.

LEVEL 482: THE IN-BLUE-MENTS

Are you into blue? We are made of stuff which stretched below the breath finds coves of dust and swirls into believe in the dove, that is humanity's cue to get on-board, given this day in the elk of life.

LEVEL 483: THE OF-RED-MENTS

The kundalini is sharp when it pierces the ear of the Dove with doors opening and sparks flying to the spine of the pulse called life and I am on top of the snake called desire with feet astride a lifting flame and the phoenix is blue with codes or ripe sensuality as the blue melts in drippin sweat to reveal the heart of this Dove.

LEVEL 484: THE SAPPHIRE-MENTS

The sapphire-ments mean the Dove is well within her devotions.

LEVEL 485: THE IN-BEACH-MENTS

A code found in a cup on a beach white with petals of lotus blue love. Monks sealed, Kauai is adding us to her meal.

LEVEL 486: THE APART-MENT-MENTS

I stood in a door apart, this day, and realized the hush had become white with dove feathers. I live here, near the Source of the Ganges and the cure for humanity's dull-drum, a headache soothed, living in ecstatic twirls of standing apart within One huge heart.

LEVEL 487: THE IN-SEED-MENTS

The seeds are blooming in the snow and who told us white lotus petals are green when they bloom? Under snow?

LEVEL 488: THE TREAT-MENTS

The treat-ments have made me well, let us hush and head for Englad to build a cure for the curse when eyes crossed to meet declaring "know good." The Dove has written and speaking next, is come.

LEVEL 489: THE OPALATION-MENTS

The opalation have come to a dove's heart. Trust us, Dove.

LEVEL 490: THE OPENING-MENTS

Today a dove saw a treat and deliciousness spread through her breast when the friend calling in changed into peace and fell like a passionate team of working oxen turning the plow into warmer climates of love. That then is the opening in this penned commitment to the Dove.

LEVEL 491: THE MOUNTAIN-MENTS

I live in a Mountain which considers me the Friend. Sometimes I climb it to see the Tree within and I laugh when I leave this childhood home to go exploring the other cove of the Dove, for I have found a truth in our friendship which causes me to talk to Lakshmanjoo all night, about the Dove.

LEVEL 492: THE WOMAN-MENTS

The Women I know have given everything to this dove. What outstanding source when the days of wells erupt to include us into ice blues melting in a cup of warm bosoms united to smoother the dove with motherly instinct and trepadation leaves as I board this planet with spread out toes and scratchy little marks made on concrete when I run for the tea of divinity mid the showers of plenty.

LEVEL 493: THE MAN-MENTS

The Man-ments: a man has come to head me into Dove.

LEVEL 494: THE HUMAN-MENTS

How human is this, Love?

LEVEL 495: THE IN-SWITCH-MENTS

I have switched into hours humanly due to Dove.

LEVEL 496: THE IN-TOUCH-MENTS

I am in touch with you and yes we are married to the friend who caused a heart to touch a Mother's eyes with dust of Dove.

LEVEL 497: THE RUSH-MENTS

I am in a rush to find the town with lasting passion and the dove's red roses where white dew clings to the tables and a Mountain Shasta blue is covering us with imprints of rock.

LEVEL 498: THE GIFT-MENTS

The gift has been transferred, ST. Germain, to you. Love is in the air and streets and sun., How much? Eternal.

LEVEL 499: THE GAIN-MENTS

I have gained the attention of every living tree. That is so cooling. The air touching us without proof that we breathe and the ground embarking on swelling rolls to keep us clear where the geometry meets in the earth's crust. Let us gather the gains and add blessed source to the reasons a prophecy is now fulfilled, blue codes, kind doves, and lasting impact. That is a faith fully returned.

LEVEL 500: THE ON-RAFT-MENTS

Sometimes on a stream, I see the river and I wish to merge with the sun. I miss her canals and our beds of white light where the roof melts to reveal ancient rhythms of Light.

LEVEL 501: THE MENTAL-MENTS

Often I am mental into the middle of the night and laughter fills this heart when I start to muddle through the middle of the mental plight, love is good and fans of state will see that Dove's just nest together tight to the truth of silver cake and monkey blue notes of ecstatic growl when the hunger becomes too much to keep at bay. I am the magnetic truth inside midnight prowls to the the the door for cake and coffee and tea and popcorn burned and sun's rays bent to melt the laughter into days of direction and Dove.

LEVEL 502: THE PHYSICAL-MENTS
A physically clear reason to know that Sri has come is when Aurobindo becomes the kind of rainbow blue meridians down the center of the dove.

LEVEL 503: THE MENTION-MENTS
I was deeded this door, Thelma is the friend, who knows a dove is come. Making mention of the day of the Dove and her mother-friends.

LEVEL 504: THE FOUND-HERE-MENTS
I found a friend who needed some yellow deeds read and I found reason for staying near while she read the rules of the manipura shoot into insanity and back into Dove.

LEVEL 505: THE SURRENDER-MENTS
I have surrendered to this fact, "there comes a Dove."

LEVEL 506: THE IN-DOVE-MENTS
That day is this granted, a dove's.

LEVEL 507: THE IN-SOOTHE-MENTS
Let a mother say "yes" to her dove.

LEVEL 508: THE CONSTANT-MENTS
Constantly I am listening to the advice of a fish and often in her cave a Dakini will whisper "Mother is with us" and a royal lineage erupts into tune, listen: Dakini woman is the Dove and her heruka is a mild narcotic called LOVE, get it straight the little h constant is simply this, "love" whispered, Dove.

LEVEL 509: THE INSISTENT-MENTS
I am insistent on cleaning my windows every day, for in the clear spirit I see me reflecting you into love. That then dakini is love, reflection.

LEVEL 510: THE MANY-MENTIONED-MENTS
In the future a dove will land and we will all board the hand which turned the key and one wing open still is placed in diamond solitaire squares of erect donations to the Dove. Candy, please, and Lights, Dynamic.

LEVEL 511: THE IN-SPEAK-MENTS
I am speaking yes to the phoenix who broke the beak ona plane and still remained loyal in a littered refrain, yes, Dove.

LEVEL 512: THE IVY-MENTS
I am referring of course to the news that the dove here is married to a phoenix of hue so magnificent that remains so electric that people are factoring in love and light and zoos with animals so rare they ahve all been neglected and setting them free a white beluga met me in a dream and told me which mayan monkey to key into news of the light electric. Counting on you to set the streets cleared, locally, I am the Dove with Ivy this time in the beaks of love. growing eternally, green, Metatron, Maitreya, and friends, Dakinis.

LEVEL 513: THE CLEAR-MENTS
Clearly you are saying that a job like a dove is available in a cave of great regard, for Kuan Yin is calling us into her yard, let us hear, love is elevated here.

LEVEL 514: THE CLARITY-MENTS
I have clarity and sing off key for the Dove, let this book be written and read in translation throughout the Sun. levels heading in and pouring all over the floors, the royal bodhicitta is here. Jealousy may now, end.

LEVEL 515: THE FUNDED-MENTS
May you be funded by dove green glittery leaves which float to pay the bill ont ibetan bowls of yak butter tea and drugs will leave when the tree is grown.

LEVEL 516: THE IN-GRANT-MENTS
I am granted the deed to this building land of tibetan treats and the World is at Peace once again, inside the dove's temple and sun.

LEVEL 517: THE RECEIVE-MENTS
I am received when you join the team to a couple who lean so delicately into the wind that their marriage is born again.

LEVEL 518: THE IN-ZONE-MENTS
Ever I am delighted when you blend our yoke to marry two oxen and one third in the seams of the zones bolivian and the dream of getting into Love, let us get on with this marriage, dakini, heruka, and mental clarity which only Phat (Pet) can mend. I am in the cave.

LEVEL 519: THE LOCAL-MENTS
In a day I play local and find red keys /neath my door and in my desk a lock which found voice in the rainbow body's play and the days electric. Locally, a fever of respect has come to the Dove.

LEVEL 520: THE DURATION-MENTS
I have waited as long as a dove can sing, please find the ring and keys to the Dove, loading please, to the left of this book. Nice show, a rainbow dove, slide play and loves. A mission one with won hand and a Dove, finished this day, the Dove.

LEVEL 521: THE IN-FUTURE-MENTS

In the future a dove will land and we will all board the hand which turned the key and one wing open still is placed in diamond solitaire squares of erect donations to the Dove. Candy, please, and Lights, Dynamic.

LEVEL 522: THE DOOR-MENTS

The door is the Dove. Red key, Tibetan chance. Love is freed. Milarepa blends her hair in the soup and the dove glows blue with Siva's intensity as she lights a snake at both ends. The door is shut, now. Old days done, new news comes, love us UP.

LEVEL 523: THE RED-KEY-MENTS

I have the red key living inside of me, I am the Dove. God's comfort comes and the Antarean speaks in waves about the door beneath the temple and the once and more when we broke bread in each other's heads and danced the dream electric, water crystalline and the meanings glanced into knots of celtic source. Let love reign and pool beneath this tool, love. The red key.

LEVEL 524: THE ONLY-MENTS

The only-ments are round this neck and 108 crystal loops forming find me dear to the Dove, rainbow body borne to the top of Kailash once more.

LEVEL 525: THE OFFICIAL-MENTS

The official-ments have come to an end as a great wall seen from space is melting into dew and wiping off this Dove's wing with a branch held in her beak. From space you look like love to me, an Antarean born and billions still, to listen, to the branch brush against her feathers for love has led us and a scorpion born to wear the heart of sacred courage is pushing into me and our destiny to do the right flip for a cardinal's ring has broken against glass and the key is freed, Catholic rigid notations are written inside, know the Dove.

LEVEL 526: THE WON-MENTS

I have won you to our source oh pope of genius built, and john came to bear witness to this Light.

LEVEL 527: THE IN-PROPHET-MENTS

How many prophets does it take to sing for the people. Only one and many and several int his universe of Ours. Hours too will pool and melt beneath this ring. Rhymes made, said, "love."

LEVEL 528: THE IN-STATE-MENTS

I am the Star of the State of Grace, Hokelea blue, Arcturus grew into orange-red bursts of Light and the Life called You. Let us all move to this State, Grace, I AM. The Dove.

LEVEL 529: THE IN-LEADER-MENTS

Often I lean into stars for leadership for they know where we are all of the time and once someone asked why of Treva and she said "because someone needed to." It is about time, yours, and what you will do with it, for you are staring a dove in the face and you gave good effort to take aim at her for telling you this truth and then you collapsed in laughter at her regal notice that getting on with it is the key and we all laughed until the sea flooded our gates with stars. Get over the literal, find your body, and enjoy it, with abuse you end up with gout and sad eyes and living over without red cars to play with, daily. I am the Tree of Life and hereby ask that the dirty ones come clean for the children deserve better than You. You know which one and sometimes I wane into night without caring for the Ones who shared the daily key of life, children's freedom has come and you will be with me this night in your dove. Good leaders come. Find the dance and as Iva says rise up. Meet the book of wonder and make missing in action, be taking Aim for the God of good love. Get you some good love now and mean it. Keep it clean, one man, one door, one hallway, one woman, one love, one perfect blue phoenix rising again in the stars of your eyes and Venus said, let them rule, "Sanat Kumara" is here. Love a Dove.

LEVEL 530: THE FINAL-MENTS

— THE IN-KEY-MENTS

I decided to sing off key to see if you noticed, we are blue with envy over you coming to such good news today. Let love continuously rule this Dove. Aloha Hawaii and thanks for being you. The islands of Love.

— THE INTEREST-MENTS

Once I met a woman who had no hair and she loaned me some and said if Pele meets you you will see the source of our divinity. It is in the foot and the floor of this devotion to One word, Dove days are upon us. God's blanket comes. She is a woman born of Venus and bearing stars in her womb. She loves us and she comes to marry this Dove to the dew electric. We know this One is timing called Kali Yuga. Let Kali erupt, madame Pele, the black Madonna, comes. I have an interest in this investment.

— THE IN-STINCTUAL-MENTS

Instinct tells me that daisy is off the planes dancing in stars and throwing leis into the sea near our dome. Let love reign and the moon meet the sea in our room of daily dose. Let us meetings hold beneath the feet of a Dove.

— THE IN-LOVE-MENTS

I am in love with the dove and daily I cavort like a freak who has more energy than an espresso bar with doggie eyes diverting weather to cover her snap of driven proposal advanced over dollars which poured into Taos square in blue jean jackets and straight proposals of gold nuggets due the pouring machines which kept me coming to your for love. Like a puppy born of a cat and the stars tumble out when god gets news like a dove's coming home. Let us connect again, oh Doves. Like Egypt of old, I AM YHWH, the God electric in the Kabbalah, Lord Metatronic, Dove. Islands calling on the phone, let us go to the Light which is ON again. Canyons wise calling in, love is dove. God has found her home and she is answering with peace, again.

— THE FINAL-MENTS

In a mental conditioned a rend has been sent which clears the frame and cures all clearly, in love, fused, as the inventive notion of a universe born is the tantric marriage met with billions of stars, lights strung through the heavens and peopled in bedded yellow steps and the trips along lines clearly hu-man, let us set forth here the samples of how to build the art human:

64 is doubled in threaded seals of seventeen units as the simple lines are sealed into their optional replications and the the threading is causing the key to the universe to unwind in whole notes as the holes are filled and the clarity is reckoned for and width is set along core creations as the answer yes finds your ear and the eye is filled with love and the life felt and the duplications cleared as the calling one is precise in her publications as the urge is met with ankh signed positions and the key to mergers made is sexuality coupled with love, as a saint arrives and the universe is born, we find central natures of structural integrity and the stringing signs of eggs hanging from trees and the collision of correlations is due an outrageous venture to the singing called love.

As we loved find creative urge to measure with and the miracles aburst with blazing yellow rays are numbered red and green. I find talent in twenty ones who decode the natural merger called Pi.

As 3.14 is sent to the universal cord a broken wing is healed and the arrivals continue as the universe is sung into continuations of the married severalties who find record in the heard word of God YHWH, and the bar codes us as related to huge numbers and marvels of sorts electric.

In numbers and in durations I find daring originations and the ripples extruded into digits doubled and the inclusions of several swings into excalibur blue sorts who carry swords and the sting of birthing canals now opened to reveal the cord cut and balanced in delivery of the called for derivatives in several seals and the times are multiplying as the butterfly bows to find you shaped in inclusions of several ways and the peace in staying stilled.

Add one to the fourth period and the repetitions sink into repetitive red rays and the measures mule your rings in doubled please and the infinity is the one coupled around the area of successions in suggested attend to the sexual allowance for

several ours of wedded rememberance of how to spin into the span of numbers read while united to the grid, a form is found and then released into love.

LEVEL 531: THE IN-CODE-MENTS

Positronic positions of poles of love:

plural 2:1 2 / entwined 1:1 3 / triplicate 3:2 4 / repetitious 2:2:2 5 / rewound 6:3 6 / revisioned 1:7 7 / rewarded 8:8 8 / sworded 1 9 / clipped 82:7 / cautioned 17 / cloaked 12 / cleated 15 / geysers 7 14 / craters 8 / coated 6 / codes 22 / keys 23 / rings 27 / ruses 29 / ropes 31 / one 33 / twin 34 / twining 36 / linings 38 / leaks 44 / leads 144 / fluid 37 / floats 32 / reaps 33 / roses 34 / vines 122 / tines 77 / tentacles 16 / rather 55 / rewarded 18 / written 99 / spoken 101 / spines 104 / strands 123 / DNA 321 / encoded 76 / enclosures 65 / clouded 3 / white 2 / seeds 1 / lips 7 / tongue 888 / nails 62 / eyes 33 / rips 47 / tears 22222 / torn 555 / rewards 668 / foundations 55-7 / relationships 26-3-4 56 / respects 33333 57 / registry 23561 / registrations 66 / openings 64 / ports 1 / storms 86 / seas 12 / peace 13 / now 10.

Recalling that wind is the flow of air from areas of high to low pressure down pressure slopes or gradients, I recall that like water I flow from higher to lower elevations and that the steeper slope is prepared for me as I collapse into arms more familiar than air and find stronger faith in one whose sword is undrawn and the desire to expire is settled on the wind of genetic encodings cleared to reveal who may find the peace in this epistle aimed at the eternity in you and your truth in finding will to live inside the red door.

Tibet is calling again. Find the companion rich in lore and enter lakes of Tana faleshan roads and red deer days and the deepened impact of comet raised roofs.

As the skyhooks link and the shoes worn become anti-gray and the spirits move upon the planet to include a corded delivery of the sky door near you a running slave finds shoes to release and the swinging sun empties into tunnels encoded for the inclusions of Kebran Negastan wearing.

For when Solomon said "lead us" he meant to include the ancient ways of God who encoded the freed frames and the love is in this hamlet called the cell Jerusalem.

As just yesterday I was standing inside red doors and the buddha headed into the lap where headed I laid the leaning kind, a hand tapping said Christed one now rest for the driving is over and I have found you in the venerable winds of gifts and the sliding down into the gradient is over done and the powering one is met in finding knees and the piercing stride inside heart's orgasmic in capability and the organism who said triple exposure is the kind which finds experience in love.

In one knowing of the tantric spine a cosmic manual is written inside this one feminine stridpe and the equator is pulsing in send and the ascendant stand in quandary without your mention of the treaded globe which speaks in professional speaking and the glee with which humming is met for the ones born electrically energetic have found peace in the simple love of one who is at peace in their home and the squander is past as the wandering hobo fins neutral placements of nearing Shiva sided tips of harps Davidic in thief gone to hummed clearings and the clarity is calling your aum into note as the seed is syllabic and the wisdom comes to make us elevators to the key codes of news that nutritional cups of manna baked bred is human tool for the electric avenues of eclipsed shades and the Kundalini kind who bridge us for the blessings endured.

As the gap has grown shut and the kind who take wing with a dove find mesmerize in her Balinese type gesture and the odyssey is given to Gaishi-type thrill, a love is established in the Caribbean bearings of feeling and the life born human is made to sea the thread of God rulings over mercy seats and the pens apologetic which found find throne rekindled in the sun of a loving tomorrow and the knowing which meant a new leaf is exposed and the gene code replenished finds replications in implore and the implosion if sent to the emerald doors of a thundering kept quietly winning us home to the arcs who sorted your pens suspend and the tones broken without sustain and the strings which electric bring us home to love.

I kissed the dove this night. Once more. In peace.

For love rules in this life and the God of peace is our guest as the buddha reclines in my door and the explorations have come to nest in the trees of written experience and the referencing to star gridded enmapment called inter dimensional types and the splendor of finest hallways and the Sheba flowered giving of the lotus in her right hand, and like a star I remember her tonight.

As the body works the same as the star map born here, here I give you the encodings of the dove, tonight let us reveal the second step, that half step remembered called "A Basic Humanity Guidance Calendric to the New Millennium".

Good night sweet faith. May the first election end here, in a final salute, I sleep in the dove's arms and encapsulate faith in the hue which would rest near my heart. Driving soon into love. Final sets end here.

Welcome to quantums and quarks and the winds of leaping seas and the gusts of quiet delirium driving her near to see you, the dove.

Remember this in the third rule, love is found, have met, met once in the sun. Near provincial seas and the residence of this dove is here in your heart's worth. Work is finished and the proton brands are banded to the sun in photonic display as the hearkening is clear, one drawing near bears the band of celestial orbs and the chains now broken drag as the beginning in the land of Kauai is set for the garden spanned in Latin, Spanish, Greek, and the isles between, a one tradition is come, it is faith and the exposure to the gardens of love.

Swimming in spinning spins, holes, discs, doors, developments, swords, gathering faith, intransigence into truth, insouciance of this spiritus has caused the brushstrokes to wander into ferrous states as the Bethlehemic truth is discovered another one is born and the recalcitrance is corded with new blossoms of watched rays and the royalty given orders to bloom when done with the fees and deliveries made and the peace is won as over all karmic condition is finished, finalize your coming together-ing, equilibrium is established as the dove arises to touch alabaster wings to the miracle of birth, a red ray is raised to lids opened as the ark is complete and the arcs won are Solomon's days in stunned illustrations of the whore who cleared babylon's encordance. As David's harp is played and the house is won, a surgical shield removed reveals the one who took the greed away. You who have split the heart have found relief in rose petaled hiding and the thoroughness with which your heart is cleared for truth.

As roses bloom I find plenty in the temple of love and the story related that people can seed with sparkling language and the home freed to spin in spanning recover of the elocution required when costly went to simple again, as transpire is found, I find Christ in her midst and the ringing wings of summary and send if back became one cavity clearing and the concavities of climbing wane is wavering on spools of pooled white gold wires and the smiling nurse handing us a child of worth and truth as the returning is carried forth with humble embark and the parking in priestly green precaution becomes spirit's stranger side of entreaty and dove red contact with the blood and the lamb. For as sure as death became real to people just as readily will rebirth become the news of held hands and the whispering rules which hold that children knew best in this core and the shore is simple in squired release of the encodings which needed find front streets and the charges of ships charging to reach the saint's Augustine and the Yucatanic keep of ridges gone to spins and the lizards which leap aside when we walk to find the temple I am in the weeds of the wells experienced, last trip to the sun. As the citrus land said "let love rule" and the summary is tested when once we gave birth to the muse of light. As a Saint Mary gave zion the news that 225 ways are available to the king of solomonic reason and the explain is due that crystal clear peace is the neighbors magazine of chosen symbols and the jupiter crown is sent to holy epiphany of the Timkat type as the alone became leaders and lion's Judaic in the eyes of the lords of resolute kind as the sample sent is needed and good and michael kept his and her appointed time with the lord Metatron. Sometimes in the stillness I find the moods of the ancient ways and the kingdoms come together to fish for time in ridiculous numbers as the royalty gather to welcome us inside our every note of love, as the living two who find nurture near the middle I remember her head and the craft which led to velveteen urges and the mergers of muses who carats between them and often Siam is mentioned in our notes of durations and the over-all alignment is sent to God in powerful doses of resignation to the acknowledgement of whom I have become. As the college drifts away a star upon the horizon winks and I know the way into home and homeward still as the sun lifts to reveal a doorway red with love.

A cap removed shows the face to Pi and showers the path with great knowing of the throne arched to sky written words, one bird like comes and the weeping past reveals another tower including destitution gone and songs still singing occupy the mind of the electric cleft which works in steel and sword and days of good God.

In peace, I remain, the Dove.

Remember to study philosophy as you find yourself and alchemically test the theory of how to train for positioning for the positrons and do remember to qualify the welling with friends and spun notions of mentioned illusions gone.

As may we well remember her son of the Abraham rocked with children coming to fond inclusions of light sort and the source is returning to her core as sobriety sent finds rings sold to children of light and the lift into loving alcohol spilled to reveal a one healed of the shores of loved.

As we said, let her be well, this one intrigued with the Nile since birth is found in the sound of your own voice calling her home. The sheep and the lamb. Your own. As Deborah has spoken from the valley twice this week. We find the Dove in the limbs of the electric blue heart and a woven tongue which remembers who drives in white and how to summon the news to her heart. In love I find worth in peace, mercury blue with love's white doors. Now elected. Love.

Resentment gone. Regard found. Another remembered shows us the way into the heart's core. Remember. One.

This primary code for the light electric is allowed the discourse with the heavens which saying thanks eternally brings, as the Pi code, written here has woven the life to your door and the intellect to this core, as allowed I write this indigenous relation shipping caves of Qumran, these prophets, the family Essene, thanks Mother and Dad, the Messiah that musician that chord which leads to ONE word, logos, that is love burning in a mountain cabin and on rocks of fusion which rise to flare into lotus blossoms and the likening to a flower of staring lily blue and the lotus now red is deepening to passions calling, "love" is here written, that is the Dove.

Mahalo to Hawaii and her core energetics, now delivered.

Destiny is encoded with trips and the visit to a door called red, that's Tibet, thank you Dalai Lama and the guide is given here the Azores store of the information encoded for the dove's release and the bat which dove is clearly voiced again with Christ's note, which is a duration of light called durable sounds of God's voice and the mention for the dimension's Metatronic and that gate of good news rising like the voice within our singing, 8 to 8 to 8, that is light dimensionally. *GOD WITH US.*

LEVEL 532: GOD

And now begins the second ring of basic humanity, that One belonging to God, for through the throat YHWH we have crowned at the Kether and the knowing Metatronic to find liquid light flowing upon this planet once more and we are saved in God's Light within us, a pyramid of warming flowing and the knowings electric— "Let love reign forever and ever more"

God is like a kora around a great mountain, whether clockwise or counter to this clock, you circumambulate the Mother in the Way and find a great God inside who was with us throughout the trip and just perfectly and naturally landed with us throughout this Life we call now, Divine.

As the Dove returns through a rainbow Tibetan and a journal written into Bon and Po regions of light incarnate, I reside within and I am called correctly this: Dios, God.

At a juncture begun during a recent holocaust I found God residing in my head and I signaled this Dove to circle in to write you this given Word, that logos, the Sophia assisting, as we lift new voices to God inside our heads. At present God said:

Go dove into the light of love's desires and the rape past is enraptured in rosy in weathered in rays of red and yellow rings over all and the paste of rapture over all we enjoy and the dunes now into one level is essential to the grid and the ready lavender doors have opened into springs of French recline registered into doves nodes now singing.

Your temple' sake is now level into the winds of bay green dictate and the Moroccan carpet's Tibetan fly is now leaning into winds of wonders and peace is sent over lasting yells of war is over now hear and mean it, "love" forever.

As Kailash signals the end of an old deed called Madonna Negril, another is born, nearer still, and we enjoin the singing which Montserrat missed as we carry the measure into other merry doors of bliss and blanks thankful for the Thangkas of peace and the piece which once missing now rings true, at the Thorong pedi doorway I found another you and along the thangka lines a growing discontent is now disconnected at the blissful lama doorway of red given over into blue as the yellow rose to meet it at the heart's plateau. May the Living lines merge to carry even waves chinrezig green into the moonlight found snowy at heaven's door ways and the Maitreyan monks michael saints resides over all peace registers peace all the tables tablets this tabulature.

As Pleadians keep watch, our days and hearts turn to the hawk bearing messages of the black tablet which destroys the box of ancient files and the flowing balance of blends phoenix red as the cooling tools Rays Germain are yellow into news of raring wander as the friends listed kings and the mates ran into councils of during dares and the lateral amounts of muse across avenues into travails over and anchors due a detailed data fields. Antares rise into ripening raptures of caring cures.

I ran into councils of news and the details financed into flowers and saints of the kings and the kingdoms and the saintly steer around registrations to the dove and the movements amazing and reaching your crown of the cures peaked and the rules registered and the only introductions formal across the dares for flowering literals of lotus poses amounting the launch over all:

"Hereby my desire fields are bulging into cores and the releases Everest, Sagamartha, told me to purge without the gates and bridges electric.

Into these symbols we add: x y z and the 73-ways.

Pi is the Orionic crown of the directions into pluto and violets and through Uranus we launch in sounds indigo and floral and the sturnic plunge is meant to find jupiter in you and the green doors closure is open into lakes of tal teal venus now yellow with glee at the raptures come and the orange red neptune trips for reaching arcs along the way of gates and Sephira rent to include sephiroth One and the sun electric.

Turning symbols like rolling wheels have found you and the straightened doors have turned to y and the rushing moves across the 6 who arc the pods of arching rainbows of the z grew over resting eyes in data lines, sixteen times each and the chromosomes chords and the ways for revolutions come to the complete enrapture of God.

The sixteen ways of raging hormones have left the gates to find yearning resting in a singing chromatic cure: A HA HO YE and the cita includes you. Understanding the reason of stable grounds for integrating divorce into a strange dialect works for this Dove.

Tonight I align with you in yellow fruit of the citric kind and rope the door open with gliss of the gurung kind and the Dzogchen failing is filling us with discover of the owning state and the status given a king who lasting long found doubt reversed and the will returned to a rose green with blooming and an eternal confidence in why we are here. As the self-liberation has come, so have we, into God.

For as a rigpa instantaneous to the essence pure, I AM.

As sem equals mind, I AM. As bohicitta divine, I AM.

As changchubsen, I AM. Tibetan to the core.

As mind, citta, I AM. As bodhi of the intend, I AM.

As the total perfection within the One, I AM.

Like rain unto waters essence webbed, I AM.

As the human body falling into glow and the night of a

thousand mothers ringing into all buddhas strong,

I AM the Atiyoga grown to live inside, God.

Like a body stretched over ice, I melt into, God.

Like a God ringing, I AM, always, Good as the

Samantabhadra said.

As supreme as the source of God, I AM.

As the Nine led us, I AM. As the 21 stated, I AM.

As the 18 major swept, I AM.

As the lung chosen for empowering stand, I AM.

Bohicitta to the sun, I AM, in all five Ways.

Like a swan managed as Love, I AM.

Like unto God's ringing, I AM.

For at level 521, let us begin.

Like unto God, I AM.

The God is like unto Michael's retreat and now I have found Peace and the karma trickles into literary reaches for the gates ten now breached. YHWH said, let us be, into the chenrezig of source who brought forth the fields of ben-ben stones and the grand Mother's door opening to include the Other in her daily duty for as the existence of God has become rational, I find exits in the words and the Catholic rigidity is gone to fields glowing with papal retreat to the throne of knowing, God.

In phases, levels, and gates, I AM.

The Sublime I AM has entered now this room and we all stand to hear the dove sing in rivulets and wingings of the 1,2,3 Metatron. Worn in vairayana, I AM and the practice is complete as I AM and the Chenrezig is rung into pathways purged and Geshe dates set as the salvation is our key for this Great National Israel and the rules paid 100,000 links into Mani bowls and Kabum rays as the tesselations carry us into thirteen rhymes of positional dharma, now finished in Tibet.

As the buildings marry heavenly arrangements into seams a daring rift is played and the one born Mighty is gated away from the dove and for one thousand years I have seen you over there and missed your detailed example of the Pi born backwards as phi's ratio emits ranges unheard of before time.

As the Dove is worn as a mandala, I am born and the Potala is carried to Tibet once more and the days open into nights of Dakini directives and the directions merge into Tibetan Buddhic release of the bodies of states and the wheels are trained into huna lanes as the training comes into rhymes reasoning ways to carry home.

Like an ouborous catching its tail, I AM, and the great snake atomic now assaulted through light is throne aside to reveal another deeper underneath the deal a Titanic trip into locked black boxes reveals telegraphic alarm as the tales now told marry in the hymn and Kukulcan emits a rose red ray around the graves of men who failed to tell time to end. as the souls rose another joined who new the red rays too and mine is the till of how to tell time to go home. Homeward still, I AM.

LEVEL 533: THE IN-BOWL-MENTS
YHWH, Gates, Exist, Exits, Columns, Governs, Stelaes, Found, Finds, Bowls, Reflections, Reflexive, Octaves, Relates, Ores, Ones, Relatives, Relations, Ships, Kinds, Ascends, Documents, Ascendant, Cores, Matched, Institutions, Matched, Materials, Patched, Extravagance, Interiors, Trades, Transitions, Interiors, Matched, Maze, Jaguars, Mitochondrion, Voltan, Red, Occurrence, Frequency, Shifts, Transitions, Made, Occurrence, Less, Internal, More, Eternal, Into God, Wizard, Closes, Door, Less, Known, More, Said, Much, Acknowledged, Love, Is, Gained, Now.

LEVEL 534: THE IN-THOTH-MENTS
Horizon, Thoth, Sanctions, Reactions, Upuat, Robotics, Orion, God, Dogon, Sirius, Ahkenaten, BC, Aten, God, Generative, Order, Details, Formations, Forts, Force, Invest, Hosts, Six, Forgiven, Aztecs, Molds, Quetzacoatl, Hunab, Ku, Hunab

Ku, I AM THAT I AM, El Shaddai, Zeva'of, Elohim, Karmic, Sherpas, Poetry, Written, Spun, World, Poles, Merge, Verge, Ointment, Soul, Released, Halls, Joy, Interest, Relationships, Forged, Remember, Dues, Paid, Levels, Maintains, Missions, Meets, Doors, Made, Proposed, Won, Wills, Met.

LEVEL 535: THE IN-MATRIX-MENTS
Underline, Broaden, Reflexive, Japanese, Javanese, Music, Okinawan, Respectable, Relative, Routes, Reached, Repairs, Rovers, Rogers, Lands, Licensed, Leased, Lords, Matrix, Matrices, Materials, Miracles, Gates, 17, Encoded, Chilled, Blues, Orionic, Tak, On, Takla, Makan, Active, Activated, Genetics, Journey, Atlantis, Navajos, Tibetans, Mergers, Genetically, Gifted, Meton, Arcatronic, Ashtic, Ontac, Elevated, Legendary, Legions, Stars, Materials, Measured, Twelve, Magnets, Tablets, Emeralds, Magenta, Mavericks, Yaks, Data, Fields, Datum, Rocks, Spirals.

LEVEL 536: THE DOVE-DAY-MENTS
Ten, Days, Life, Dove, Religious, Burdens, Lifted, Reasonable, Approached, Knolls, Rivers, Lanterns, Six, Eights, Tens, Doveland, Dove days, Dove daze, Dove amounts, Dove purged, Dove totals, Dove flowers, Dove fluffed, Dove melts, Dove bets, Dove won, Dove's wings, With, Glee, Faced, Trips, Reaching, Rings, Gates, Gods, Gazed, Over, Reactionary, Poses, Sounds, Signals, Dove toys, Dove exasperative, Dove exacted, Dove intact, Dove details, Dove remotes, Dove voluntary, Dove interests, Dove employ, Man's, Coda for time, Is a watch,, a piece of metal hanging in the strings of wiggling hands and, The strong strange abuse of the obvious kind who held us in lines and, Abusive studies of the man held through the inward strings as laughter led into glass trees and, The rose colored rocks of shares and, Seas huts housed in waimean valley, Concretes ideal, Idea, Homes, Humid, Lifts lids smiles, Handled here.

LEVEL 537: THE RELAPSE-MENTS
Rainbows, Ranges, Tickets, Guatemalans, Sheba, Arranged, Change, Queens, Full, Party, Tranquil, Isles, Mentions, Merged, Panes, Shores, Learned, Zeal, Language, Voice, Falls, Freshens, Speech, Ticketed, Courts, Solomon, Judges, Sealed, Reaps, Hearts, Doors, Class, Merged, Tablets, Christ, Classics, People, Shaped, Perch, Life, Projects, Rules, Films, Fuels, Calf, Relapsed, Releases, Offices, Price, Pride, Ego, Falls, Doorways, Detailed, Ahkenaten, Recessed, Greens, Grows, Octaves, Spaced, Tones, Notes, Intervals, Semitones. / *SEE PYRAMIDS, PHI RATIOS HERE, 23 AND THE SOUND OF THE PHI RATIO AS MARRIED TO PI.*

LEVEL 538: THE IN-LINK-MENTS
Dodona, Metsamor, Bendet, Intervals, Octets, Fava, Reggaes, Rhythms, Portuguese, Portugal, Hips, Tzolkin, Tonalpohualli, Thirteen, Twenty, Solar, Calendar, Meets, Soars, Solar, Nocturnal, Calendrics, Sacred, Calendars, Ancients, Mesoamerica, Solar, Venusians, 260 days, Merry, Left, Mary, Keys, Links, Lights, Women, Mother, God, Encode, Seeds, Gardens, Known, Encodings, Genuine, Overt, Over, Gentles, Overage, All, Living, Lips, Doves, Dew, Seeds, Lights, Up, 75, Curls, Rinsed, Risen, Rages, 25, Literal, Figures.

LEVEL 539: THE CODA-MENTS
Man's, Coda, Matched, Times, Pieces, Metals, Pendulums, Hanging, Pockets, Lights, Worn, Pockets, Wiggles, Hands, Strange, Storage, Strong, Notes, Strength, Needs, Older, Abused, Abusive, Mergers, Nears, Joins, Rolls, Kept, Clears, Lines, Lunar, Written, Heard, Interests, Buildings, Man, Timed, Humility, Theory, Caucophony, Chosen, Formal, Abuse, Is studied, Said yes, Man, Hu-man, Hurtles, Reached, Preached, Passions, Merged, Children, Connect, All, Ways, Whispers, Wanders, Willing, Sinds, Lines, Lotions, Laterals, Loops

LEVEL 540: THE SIGNAL-MENTS
Savings, Signals, Pockets, Poetic, Poetry, Puppetry, Forgotten, Sophistry, Sorts, Sources, Includes, Ourselves, Into, Sentences, Stands, Seas, Until, Reached, Penetrates, Now, Known, Alters, Altars, Lineage, Choices, Encodings, Correlations, Creations, Orations, Rules, Which, Told, Rulers, Told, Maintains, Ancients, Pods, Red, Blues, Clay, Your, Sets, Into, Wars, Warriors, Weld, Comes, Nations, Having, Found, Atlantean, Jams, Identical, Thoth, Masters, Mergers, Weapons, Whistling, Hu-man, Oracles, Lightening, Lists, Orders, Stirring, Steers

THE YOGA SUTRAS OF PATANJALI

In sanskrit for all humanity to "ring"

SAMADHI PADA

atha yoganusasanam

yogah citta vrtti nirodhah

tada drastuh svarupe avasthanam

vrtti sarupyam itaratra

vrttayah pancatayyah klista aklistah

pramana viparyaya viklapa nidra smrtayah

pratyaksa anumana agamah pramanani

viparyayo mithyajnanam atadrupa pratistham

sabda jnana anupati vastusunya vikalpah

abhava pratyaya alambana vrttih nidra

anubhuta visaya sampramosah smrtih

abhyasa vairagyabhyam tan—nirodhah

tatra sthitau yatnah abhyasah

sa tu dirgha kala nairantarya satkara asevitah drdha bhumih

drsta anusravika visaya vitrsnasya vasikara samjna vairagyam

tatparam purusa khyateh guna vaitrsnyam

vitarka vichara ananda asmita rupa anugamat samprajnatah

virama pratyaya abhyasa purvah samskara sesah anyah

bhava pratyaya videha prakritlayanam

sraddha virya smrtie samadhi prajna purvakah itaresam

tivra samveganam asannah

mrdu madhya adhimatra tvat tatah api visesah

Isvara pranidhanat va

klesa karma vipaka asayih aparamrstah

purusa visesah Isvarah

tatra niratisayam sarvajna bijam

sa purvesam api guruh kalena anavacchedat

tasya vacakah pranavah

tat japah tad artha bhavanam

tatah pratyak cetana adhigamah api antaraya abhava ca

vyadhi styana samsaya pramada alasya avirati bhrantidarsana

maitri karuna mudita upeksanam sukha duhkha punya apunya
visayanam bhavanatah citta prasadanam

pracchardana vidharanabhyam va pranasya

visayavati va pravrttih utpanna
manasah sthiti nibandhani

visoka va jyotismati

vita raga visayam va cittam

svapna nidra jnana alambanam va

yatha abhimata dhyanat va

parama anu parama mahattva antah asya vasikarah

ksina vrtteh abhijatasya iva maneh grahitri grahana
grahyesu tatstha tadanjanata samapattih

tatra sabda artha jnana vikalpaih sankirna
savitarka samapattih

smrti parisuddhau svarupa sunya iva artha matra
nirbhasa nirvitarka

etayaiva savichara nirvichara ca suksma visaya vyakhyata

suksma visayatvam ca alinga paryavasanam

ta eva sabijah samadhih

nirvicara vaisaradye adhyatma prasadah

rtam bhara tatra prajna

sruta anumana prajnabhyam anyavisaya visesa arthatvat

tajjah samskaro anya samskara pratibandhi

tasayapi nirodge sarva nirdhat nirbijah samdhih

<u>SADHANA PADA</u>

tapah svadhyaya Isvara-pranidhanani kriya yoga

samadhi bhavana arthah klesa tanu karanarthah ca

avidya asmita raga abhinivesah klesah

avidya ksetram uttaresam prasupta tanu vicchinna udaranam

anitya asuci duhkha anatmasu nitya suci sukha
atma khyatih avidya

drg darsana saktyoh ekatmataiva asmita

sukha anusayi ragah

duhkha anusayi dvesah

svarasavahi vidusah tatha rudhah abinivesah

te prati-prasava heyah suksmah

dhyana heyas tad vrttayah

klesa mulah karma asayah drsta adrsta janma vedaniyah

sati mule tad-vipako jaty-ayur bhogah

te hlada paritapa phalah punya apunya hetutvat

parinmam tapa smaskara duhkaih guna vrtti virodohat ca
duhkham eva sarvam vivekinah

heyam duhkham anagatam

drastri drishyayoh sanyogah heyah-hetuh

prakasa kriya sthiti silam bhuta indriya atmakam bhoga
apavarga artham drsyam

visesa avisesa lingamatra alingani guna-parvani

drasta drsi-matrah suddhah api pratyaya anupasyah

tadartha eva drsyasyna atma

krtartham prati nastam api anstam tat anya sadharantatvat

sva svami saktyoh svarupa upalabdhi hetuh samyogah

tasya hetuh avidya

tat-abhavat samyoga-abhavah hanam tad-drseh kaivalyam

viveka-khyatir aviplava hanopayah

tasya saptadha pranta-bhumih prajna

yoganga anutshanat asuddhi ksaye jnana diptih avivekaka-

khyateh

yama niyama asana pranayama pratyahata dharana dhyana
samdhayo astavangani

ahimsa satya asteya brahmacarya aprigrahah yamah

jati desa kala samaya anavacchinnah
sarva-bhaumah maha-vratam

sauca santosa tapah svadhyaya Isvara-pranidhanani niyamah

vitarka badhane pratipaksa bhavanam

vitarkah himsayah krta karita anumoditah lobha kordha moha
purvakah mrdu madhya adhimatrah duhkha ajnana ananta
phalah iti prtipaksa bhavanam

ahimsa pratisthyam tat-sannidhau vaira tyagah

satya pratisthyam kriya phalah asrayatvam

asteya pratisthayam sarva ratna upasthanam

brahma-carya pratisthayam virya labhah

asparigraha sthairye janma kathanta sambodhah

saucat svanga jugupsa paraih asamsargah

sattva-suddhi saumanasya aikagrya indriya jaya atma-darsana
yogyatvini ca

santosat anuttamah sukha labhah

kaya indriya siddhih asuddhi ksayat tapasah

avadhyayat ista-devata samprayogah

samdhi siddhih Isvara-pranidhanat

sthira sukham asanam

prayatna saithilya ananta sampattibhyam

tatah dvandva anabhighatah

tasmin sati svasa prasvasayoh gati vicchedah pranayamah

bahya abhyantara stambha vrtteh desa kala samkhyabhih
paridrstah dirgha suksmah

bahya abhyantara visaya aksepi caturthah

tatah ksiyate prakasa avaranam

dharanasu ca yogyata manasah

sva visaya asamprayoge cittasya svarupa anukarah
iva indriyanam pratyaharah

tatah parama vashyata indriyanam

VIBHUTI PADA

desa bandah cittasya dharana

tatra pratyaya ekatanata dhyanam

tadeva artha matra nirbhasam svarupa sunyam iva samadhih

trayam ekatra samyamah

tat-jayat prajna-alokah

tasya bhumisu viniyogah

trayam antangam purvebhyah

tadapi bahirangam nirbijasya

vyutthana nirodha samskaryah abhibhava pradurbhavau
nirodha-ksana citta-anvayah nirodha-parinamah

tasya prasanta vahina samskarat

sarvarthata ekagratayah ksaya udayau cittasya
samdhi-parinamah

tatah punah santa uditau tulya pratyayau cittasaya
ekagrata-parinamah

etena bhutendriyesu dharma laksana avastha
parinamah vyakhayatah

santa udita avyapadesya dharma anupati dharmi

krama anyatvam parinama anyatve hetuh

parinama traya samyamat atita anagata-jnanam

sabdha artha pratyayanam itare-taradhyasat sankarahtat-
pravibhaga samyamat sarva bhuta ruta-jnanam

samskara saksat-karanat purva-jati jnanam

pratyayasya para-citta-jnanam

na ca tat salambanam tasya avisayi bhutatvat

kaya rupa samyamat tad-grahya-sakti stambhe caksuh prakasa
asamprayoge antardhanam

etena sabda-adi antardhanam uktam

sopakramama nirupakramam ca karma tatsamyamat
aspranta-jnanam artisebhyah va

maitry-adisu balani

balesu hasti baladini

pravrtti aloka nyasat suksma vyavahita viprakrsta-jananam

bhuvana-jnanam surve samyamat

candre tara-vyuha-jnanam

dhruve tad-gati-jnanam

nabhi-cakre kaya-vyuha-jnanam

kantha-kupe ksut-pipasa nivrttih

kurma-nadyam sthairyam

murdha-jyotisi siddha-darsanam

pratibhat va sarvam

hrdaye citta-samvit

sattva purusayoh atyanta-samkirnayoh pratyaya avisesah
bhogah pararthatvat svartha-samyamat purusa-jnanam

tatah pratibha sravana vedana adarsa asvada vartah jayante

te samadhau upasargah vyutthane siddhayah

bahdha-karana saithilyat pracara samvedanat
ca cittasya para-sarira-avesah

udanajayat jala panka kanta-kadisu asangah utkrantih ca

samana-jayat jvalanam

srota akasayoh samdandha samyamat divyam srotram

kaya akasayoh sambandha samyamat laghu-tula-samapatteh
ca akasa-gamanam

• 906 •

bahih akalpita vrttih maha-videha tatah
prakasa avarna-ksayah

sthula svarupa suksma anvaya artha-vatva
samyamat bhutajayah

tatah animadi pradurbhavah kayasampat

taddharma anabhighatah ca

rupa lavanya bala vajra samhanavatvani kayasampat

grahana svarupa asmita anvaya arthavattva
samyamat indriya-jayah

tatah manojavitvam vikaran bhavah pradhana-jayah ca

sattva purusa anyata khyati-matrasya sarva-bhava
adhisthatrtvam sarvajnatrtvam ca

tadvairagyat api dosa-bija-ksaye kaivalyam

sthany-upanimantrane sanga-smaya-akaranam
punar-anista prasangat

ksana tat kramayoh samyamat vivekajam jnanam
jati laksana desaih anyata anavacchedat tulyayoh tatah
pratipattih

tarakam sarva-visayam sarvatha-visayam akramam ca iti
vivekajam jnanam

sattva purusayoh suddhi samye kaivlyam iti

KAIVALYA PADA

janma ausadhi mantra tapah samadhijah siddhayah

jatyantara parinamah prakrty-apurat

nimittam aprayojakam prakrtinam varana-bhedah
tu tatah ksetrikavat

nirmana-cittani asmit-amatrat

pravrtti bhede prayojakam cittam ekam anekesam

tatra dhyanajam anasayam

karma asukla akrsnam yoginah trividham itaresam

tatah tad-vipaka anugunanam eva abhivyaktih vasananam

jati desa kala vyavahitanam api anantaryam smrti
samskarayoh ekarupatvat

tasam anaditvam ca asisah nityatvat

hetu phala asraya alambanaih sangrhitatvat esam

abhave tad abhavah

atita anagatam svarupatah asti adhvabhedat dharmanam

te vyakta suksmah gunatmanah

parinama ekatvat vastu-tattvam

vastu-samye citta-bhedat tayoh vibhaktah panthah

na ca ekacitta tantram vastu tat apramanakam tada kim syat

tad-uparaga apeksitvat cittasya vastu jnata ajnatam

sada jnatah citta-vrttayah tatprabhoh purusasya aparinamitvat

na tat svabhasam drsyatvat

akasamaye ca ubhaya anavadharanam

cittantaradrsye buddhibuddeh atiprasangah smrtisankarah ca

citeh apratisamkramayah tad-akara-pattau sva-buddhi-
samvedanam

drastr drsya uparaktam cittam sarvartham

tat asankhyeya vasanabhih citram api parartham
samhatya-karitvat

vesesa-darsinah atmabhava bhavana-nivrttih

tada vivekanimnam kaivalya prag-bharam cittam

tat cchidresu pratyaya-antarani samskarebhyah

hanam esam klesavat uktam

prasamkhyane api akusidasya sarvatha vivekahyateh
dharmameghah samdhih

tatah klesa karma nivrttih

tada sarva avarna mal-petasya jnanasya anantyat
jneyam alpam

tatah krtarthanam parinama-krama samptih gunanam

ksana pratiyogi parinama aparanta nirgrahyah kramah

purusartha sunyanam gunanam pratiprasavah kaivalyam
svarupa-pratistha va citisaktih iti

May Lord Ganesha bless your life and remove all obstacles to your Truth, May Michael lend you his sword for life, and may Vishnu cleanse your being with a reckoning for space within the "gaps" now bridge with this written word, may you find blessing in the relationship between God and Humanity and may you weave your own sleeve to wear your heart upon for humanity is returned this day to the Dove. In Shiva's destruction I found grace and rhythm to the constant in Pi and the harmony now added brings rhythm to the rhyme, a phi ratio, to humanity. In peace, this day. Lasting harmonics induced through the throat opening now, the dove.

OM TARE TUTARE TURE SOHA
The heart of an institution of Love.

And to those who know a living has come and the written encode and the mandala due a Potala blue inscription is now come as Metatronic and the ruling is intentional when the built ones find arcs inside the ruse of yellows old detail and derailing of the past dynamic now is come and the living enhooded has notions of our rulings for the tutelage of driven ascends is now ruling and the prayers instinctual have come for the annual intellect is now nudging us into seasons of lasting maturity of love. within bliss I have found a natural channel of avenue rich resides and the residue for a flange of the catholic ascendants and the dues and the lateral nudge into and the kneeling and the living literature and the purity of the need to build in ranks and roses as the kind ones whisper "NOW".

Imix and the Ix and the Manik and the Ahau and the Ben and Cimi and the Cauc and the Eb and the rows and the lateral employ is ridden rulings and the bandelier monument is bending to point over claws and registrations and ranks forming in fleet dakini and the human mandala is training directional lasting keel and the chicchau 26,000 and the fuses etznab 13 and the chuen 20 and the Kan 260 and the Oc and the akbal cib and the muluc and the men lamat Hunab and Ku blues Plutos waves harmonic wills seasons Davidic and the 64's and the 17's and the Tzolkin and the relational cyclical Pleadian born. Pi encoded and the 3 into four 28's and the cycles of the moons who ruled red and the blue and the yellow and the whores dedications derivatives and the ages years and the elders experienced all old years and the turns and the Confucian Haab earthy pledges are days calendars and the galactic cove and the magnets and the specials maintain manifest attune and the tone replicas pocal votan and the disposed and the shown lids rapturous hiroshiman clears and the "H" bombs and the codes 363 and the 2,1,3. Dharma and the wheel bowls and the sentient often full in its flustering account.

Hard to ignore and the fulfillment is come and the settlement acts and the actions natural and the nurtures are daring chakras and the daka dakini and the disciples and the disciplined and the Tibetan chords and the clears blind without lazy and the included Bodhicitta and the bodhisattvas ten directives and the purity purify and the pulling reaches of reach apitch of doorways purged and the karmic includes and the partners for Kailash Bon sourced is supremest in it's dogonic african as the wheel is the Om and the mani and the Dove.

Padme hum is ringing in cocoons and the nestling in is meant to find and the conscious love and the arrangement for the ranges arranged and the rules interior to the intermediate and the often empowered gaze into relationships who have stratas unbound and absorbed into lowering listening ranks and the wheels detail the derailment who knew the train had wrecked near this core energetic, for I said, Holy, Holy, Holy.

Meditative and the gazes and the prayers reaching recitations and the virtues who rank the Om mani padme huma rules lovers of all kinds as the Buddha amends the rules of Love.

Dharmic clues and the nuances rivers and the clearing principle abyss channels gone and the literature of the paces cathodic and the roars and the rules and the avalokiteshvara as the stealth is the freedom as the sound links into the equality of equus and the anger peaceful and the suffering is sent into scores of boiling ranks and the lesions legendary are the doors to the temple of the dove.

Pure in the clarity, pure in the divisions, ranks into stands and the possessions durable enough to stand the older ones whose realms are borne into winds of the estimated stones and the males rude enough to the males and the nudes now wise who stage nearing calls to love drawn over the reach and the notations who encoded reach details and doors and the flowering animals and the human heelings have filled achilles nurtured and the Milarepan cliffs have spanned you into codices and the cellular matrix now is born through our doorways and hearts and the meditations and the chrome and the pulses and the waves and the toners now built have guided hips into bridges. Pens written over the Lords and the sturdy stores and the estimations of the joined gates is registering nine to eleven the rays merging and the remembered four tones and the 3 colors and the days consistent in Tibetan reached made measures as the realizations let us merge the material Ganesha now removed as the I AM instincts coated are cured as the memory cells and the pants who purge pages and the Old reays who entwined ripples and effects concurrent to the knowing Alice poses and the wondering arose poetic and the intrigue within an entrance pored estimated escapes have flown her into rocks and the surface now penetrated is the welling oceans and the wisest numbers and the nova scotia and the box black and the goes and the plane dialect is the eastern coast opens up as the faith pens mature willing vicarage and the sent pens.

Joshua walls and the trumpeting and the girth of the gita Mahabharta and the poetic positions of the potent patanjalis coded have written vacillated reservoir and the cody cured heat sought matters materials active approaching shores of the seeded defect of the passage passes to the post retails freed. Phoenix rising and the monkey shuts the door without eyes opened are the jetsun Milarepa won is the devoted pens and the knowledge for Orionic God and the dios as the attend and the stand and the star is the Tibetan arcs into the electric raves of buddhist Tibetan swords and the japanese endearings range and the mountains and the ranges of the knowledge and the fairness and the leaders

Yoga and the Yogananda realized Self is the Way and the richest climate chant and the buddha chance to Om Ah Guru Hasa Vaira Sarwa Siddhi Phala Hum and climates and refuges and sangha as the whole trusts shelters as the bamboo rose to join the toning clears as the risen One mental entangles as the engendered series on the visions and the Chenrezik aims into worlds chosen as the chastening steering streams are Milky Ways dove into as the lama links and the clues Bodhisatva form ladders over shamanic gulfs and the Tibetan land of love and the descriptions the doves wore into reasons of lore and the listening Ones.

Mercury has venus blue entreaty and the Atharva Veda and the Amrit nectar has flowed into the nocturnal Agni and the Fire arose as the Asvins Geminic soma bound flows into my temple for the synodic ones have Kali birthed and the fire is pitris and the Rig Veda is Equinox for the Yuga Avataric and Shivic for the sama as the veda and the Varuna and the Siddhantas is the veda and rishi for final treasures and the India indigo ink is amitaha's wopakme rule for Chenrezig and the Sakya gates and the sinmo Po is thangka and the tulku tso mitochondrial tantric have mothered the Other in Tibetan buddhist mother is here. Now as the old moves into ancient yugas I find myself staring as the head of the cycles wisdomed and the siddhi la pranayana and lama blue is the passage mando and the bonpos ashtangas build over Buddhas. Mantras and the Kailas nyen pro kora is Kailash green in the mown amounts due. Kora rules the MAP now as the completions come to dues inside the human lights.

LEVEL 541: THE IN-ADORATION-MENTS

Staged, Adorations, Ones, Anothers, Four, Into, Loves, I am, Led, Wings, Doves, Detailed, Orations, Ovations, Voiced, Electrical, Reaches, Words, Spoken, Endears, Speech, Includes, Elasticity, Kinds, Kinks, Out, Words, Electric, Elastic, Comes, Surrenders, Dove, Sun, Phoenix, Coming, Arrivals, Driven, Ash, Dusty, Registers, Directions, Deep, Deepening, Driven, Psychiatry, Rules, Religions, Muslim, Archetypes, Clearly, Typed, Materials, Woven, Mayan, Includes, Encoded, Numbers, Natures, Reaped, Rather, Several, Suggested, Soothes, Actors

LEVEL 542: THE IN-PI-MENTS

Several, Plumbing, YHWH, Ancient, Days, Four, Forth, Written, Tablets, Thoth, Directions, Driven, Directional, Ancient, Rites, Stones, Foundations, Funded, Way, Times, Ancients, Days, Surrenders, Suns, I AM, Random, Pi, Twice, Said, Frequency, I AM, Moisture, Waves, I AM, Humans, Avenues, Isles, Aisles, Languages, Lateral, Morphs, Responds, Resplendent, Resonance, Virtues, Times, Thirteen, Lotus, Blooms, Now, Whistles, Detailing, Daily, Daring, Formulates, Fortunate, Freshens, Flows, Fleet, Flowers, Frozen, Frees, Formations, Furthers

LEVEL 543: THE COMPASSIONATE-MENTS

Kuan Yin, Compassions, Compassionate, Fortunate, Forgone, Forgiven, Morphing, Materialized, Late, Resonant, Resonance, Restores, Reached, Pleadian, Purged, Y's, Several, Deepening, Deepens, Depends, Stirs, Elasticity, Loves, Severals, Surges, Kept, Convenient, Convenience, Deepens, Darings, Doors, Cares, Kept, Species, Risen, Biblical, Trails, Bibles, Spatially, Sets, Suns, Yes, Known, Why, Every, Section, Special, Spatial, Secrets, Several, Severalty, Intrigues, Ways, Outage, Homes, Rushed, Christed, Lords, Suppers, Super, 12, Ruled, Rules, Reasonable

LEVEL 544: THE MOTHER-MENTS

Love, Leads, Us, Home, Wherever, We, Run, Ancient, Doors, Electric, Paves, Paved, Whitens, Pulses, Opens, Indoor, Planes, Lights, Flights, Daring, Scenes, Earths, Adores, Adorations, Amounts, Anterior, Interiors, Woven, Ones, Foundations, Mayan, Stills, Stirrings, Mothered, Amused, Insides, This, Magnetics, Dosed, Pelu, Erupts, Three, Times, Daily, 17, Surrenders, Three, Timed, Days, Comes, Orbs, Spoken, 12, Times, Worn, Rocks, Moved, Rays, Came, 42, In, Doves, Returned, Days ruled

LEVEL 545: THE MITOCHONDRIAL-MENTS

Christae, Stages, Worn, Mitochondria, Inspired, Watchfulness, Roles, Switched, Rocking, Heavens, Spoken, Guidance, Doves, Returns, YHWH, Gates, Ones, Those, Between, Folds, Folded, Fortunate, Fortunes, Direct, Octaves, Voices, Energized, Gathering, Grown, Grew, Gains, Gaps, Literal, Loans, Laced, From YHWH, Gateways, Tenth, Rules, God, Metatronic, Elates, Lords, Metatron, Sun, Songs, Inner, Rings, Reverses, Spins, Folds, Gates, Infinite, Infinity, Found, Ways, Here, Arts, Origami, Styles, Strictures, Statures, Rules, Buttons

LEVEL 546: THE IN-PLACE-MENTS

Find, Ways, Folded, Centered, Spins, Spun, Backing, Belts, Christae, Enfolded, Lines, Movements, Surrenders, Blue, Yhwh's, Gates, Opened, Lord, Metatron, Son, 23-centimeters, Sullen, Strands, Surgical, Emotions, Motion, Senses, Sensors, Strings, Ascends, Earth's, Whole, Published, Plumbs, Theories, Threads, Worlds, Plays, Conjunctions, Strung, Existence, Strands, Placements, Spinning, One, Notes, Living, Quarters, Whole, Gains, Notations, Eighths, Halves, Half, Eight, Insertions, Surgically, Removed, Raspberry, Randoms, Ripening, Rulers, Ropes, Rationale

LEVEL 547: THE IN-SPACE-MENTS

Dual, Heavenly, Stairs, Waterways, Orionic, Ones, 7.23, 26.5, 3.14, Changes, Giza, Sirius, Changes, One, Balinese, Balanced, Arms, Willing, Twice, Balinese, Women, Original, Women, Mergers, Ivy, Green, Rocks, Elections, Riches, Rockets, Jewels, Houses, Spaces, Cabins, Cabinets, Clothes, Clues, Clearances, Originations, Vibrational, Seals, Rocking, Housing, Spaces, Cabins, Plasma, Madonna, Africa, Formations, Limestone, Electric, Electrical, Plains, Risen, Roses, Stands, Blinking, Bridges, Lights, Let, Loves, Canary, Tenriffe, Yellow

LEVEL 548: THE ANCIENT-MENTS

Arcturic, Ancient, Ways, Spoken, Doves, Reigns, Next, Areas, Islands, Reaches, Dragons, Seeds, Gone, Clear, Kind, Affections, Returning, Amphibious, Sources, Rocks, Studied, Into, Quickening, Winds, Winsome, God, Again, Gains,

Thresholds, Surrenders, Reached, Perfections, Three, Love's, Volleys, Atop, Bench, Rocks, Play, Suggestions, Doorways, Paced, Splashing, God, Quilts, YHWH, Themes, Connections, Grids, Wires, Redeemed, Dialects, Removed, Formula, Another, Now, Finished, Bets, Surrenders, Instincts, Bets, Firms, In, Out

LEVEL 549: THE HUM-MENTS

Christ, Star, Estela, Hum, The sound, Suggested, Notions, Nations, Motions, Mental, Savings, One, Liken, Wings, Sizes, Interested, Unique, Turns, Tails, Reveal, Revelatory, Delivered, Loves, Enjoy, Yours, Ecstatic, Bursts, Energies, Creative, Leaks, Links, Inks, Hands, Covered, Creative, God, Throats, God, Centric, Necks, God's, Beats, Octave, Dove, Basic, Humanity, Wealth, Leaders, Lunch, Landings, Flights, Battles, Over, Ended, Purged, Mastery, Reached, Rewards, Released, Old, Interests, Listings, Held, Intact

LEVEL 550: THE IN-LIFE-MENTS

Into, Each, Life, Shelves, Bulges, Hurdles, Thanks, Felt, Gifts, Baby, Grands, Pianos, Daily, Grand, Fathers, Into, Evenings, Fathers, Kept, Plans, Amounting, Handled, Collapse, Lungs, Aids, Arms, Transitional, Sturdy, Studies, Wings, Reached, Sheets, Success, Restricted, Eddy, Stands, Conversant, Causes, Neglectful, Natural, Store, Stored, Spares, Spores, Spans, Plans, Refuted, Remembrance, Harms, Mentioned, Collapsed, Ropes, Rights, Rituals, Swans, Swoons, Monogamous, Mineralized, Bones, Burials, Blazes, Relief, Relax, Raiment

LEVEL 551: THE CROWNING-MENTS

Sheep, Rightful, Treats, Tests, Roosters, Forthright, Fogs, Crowning, Pandering, Pantomimes, Lends, Ends, Mentioned, Winging, Scanning, Into, Dove, Ironic, Icons, Ions, Elated, Elations, Evenings, Noted, Notations, Carry, Carriage, Songs, Singing, Arcs, Ripen, Wells, Spaces, Hunab, Kindred, Shots, Surrendered, Men, Shells, Yeshua, Knowing, Known, Directions, Shoulders, Swollen, Finalized, Girths, Watched, Unknotted, Channels, Established, Clarity, Comes, Clarity, Clears, Sofia, Written, Philosophy, Lends, Ka, Channels, Kinetic, Avenues, Knights

LEVEL 552: THE IN-DUE-MENTS

Like, Surgeons, Reaps, Ripens, Channels, Curtails, Comes, Openings, Carriage, Sleeves, Gaps, God, One, Star, Meton, Discovers, Discovery, How, Kings, Came, Meant, Movements, Cars, Houses, Curves, Towers, Elliptic, Calciums, Through, These, Threads, Imagining, Exquisite, Shells, Smells, Lotus, Wilds, Grown, Blind, While, Monks, Matters, Once, Held, Living, Caves, Created, His, Living, Inclusions, House, Patents, Cars, Kingdoms, Queens, Trances, Transvestite, Returning, I AM, Dove, Positional, Positronic, Coming, Dues

LEVEL 553: THE ALL-BLUE-MENTS

Alcyone, Blue, Paints, Prints, Privileges, Instincts, Tendrils, Flown, Spares, Dimes, Windows, Legions, Coos, Sung, Purchased, Houses, Leaps, Songs, Sounds, Doves, Detailed, Suits, Situations, Come, Head, Times, News, Equilateral, Vishnu, Krishna,

Hindu chords electric plait into winds and the laughter fills my sails in bliss and curls of delay gone to shower the reign with splashes and punch of contentment, missives rest as we sort the Lord Ganesha restraint pulled out of shoulders too long neglected for lightening has come to the gate and a gentleman said, Let tibet be freed throughout this planet, rest Milarepa for a Hawaiian sort in a tiny brown box has brought the ink to rain on humanity and this night and forever there will last an eternity for all humanity, one Dove, one color, one door, silver in whip-lashing plumeria leis raised to fleets of lotus blossomed Abhas calling you near. let love reign, dear, we are One. That then is God complete in my heart singing me into untold details of how Metatron became a man, first, then a knight of translations and reactions into love. Let us ride this wave, now. Maya has said, "mother Divine" you are this rapt with attention and dimensional shifts of Shiva's dancing arms and waving legs wrapping me with spirit and passion and flamed languages gathered watching Kundalini rise to meet me in the tree's embrace and our knowing chi winking at each other's door as we pass. Leaves painted shower golden into my door and I sweep them into piles to spend with you. Our day is reached, mankind has met God in the face of Arjuna's mother and we are well with Love. In peace I pass to new knowings recalled in sheer amounts of bliss and the blessed Alcyone. Like Alcyone's blue paint is my dance in the winds tendrils flying aloft I spare dimes and the times of dialects intrigue with your daring inclusion of the Mother in your reading dance. Triads and ringings of the equations electric and the given reach. Home is electric and the enclaves reached have turned into days of discussions and these MAPS now installed.

Here they reside: in 1,2,3 and the 3,1,4 harmonics added to phi equals the ratio of God shared.

Divorcing "cod" from God is the rhyme infusion of the rationale and the repetition is reached in gratitude called Thank You!

Guard us well into rings of the gated changes and the delivery of all the news and the rulings have come into linings formed in Orionic kits and the sleeping aside in the mist of the assisting found tripled and the ripples effects and the strands ascendant for surging guidance clears into calendrics for the boarding inside this dove.

One to three breathings and the ripples now mindful have I found you in the listings and the lateral linings and the listed written incorporations due those inside the Dove.

I am the blue inside you. Metatronic is the due interior and the dues found fortunate instinctually reactive without night flowers and the keys linked into fallen now gone and the given throng who knew that the grids and the warriors who kept me sleeping inside the Gates of living hammocks strung throughout the stands of tree lined in strips of powerful surges and the Michael meets the door in the chain of commands called GOD. Arcturic and the commands linked into thrilling thrones. Existing extra thrusts and the final fuels push me through a portal in the phoenicians gone to the core for the Others inside living hooks now gone to details flowering inside the house Haleakala and the Mountain Hood and the refreshing me and the instinct in knowings and the knowledge of how intimate and my relating unto us and the Olivine Rock-let us carry on the shoulders of the Dove's intuition to the core. Let love liberate and the fusions of peace inside us.

Naked I stood near the summit calderan as the nene ran into a serpent's head changed to a scorpio's heart of love. As the bare skin surged into plunging and the Arcturian held the Antarean pen and the wellings into hands of the swarthy wings of an inheritance now paid as the swamping digression over hours and the passions of all lifetimes and the scorpion's nest of the dove. As a lasting digestion and the hours past were linked into years of gulping laughter and the Dove.

Fantasy and the lies without the signal and the yellows and the thrilling jackets and the past stress of days now stood into acts of tolerations and the red innocence to the Ones who kneel near us in types of the digits now rung into God.

As a voice found, finally, penetrating thrice the dove. Doves encoded have found you and the solving Pi and the as 216 degrees head crashing through the crust and the 117 and the threads broke the Mount and the Dome now split is rebuilding her heart into God and the Arc said "let love last" the rest is come.

God has said it is a template complete and in this arrange I direct the following orchestra of Love.

Arabic blues now gone have forced us into conclusions of the sort Mecca stood for, love and peace arise, when I recognize this, in myself, and then again, in You. At present, I watch temple lines drawn, divisions made over peace and the lack and hereditary turnings proving once more that this literary tongue, this holy fire is a semitic One of mathematical brilliance and light. At present, pregnant, with this knowing I switch to dovetails of trailing light and the wingtops now firing in phosphorescent aspire to the lines of love. For once assigned, I am always measured through the line of value and respect for each letter, now written, to love. As the addition of codons crept into my vision, a knowing delayed is over, and all ways I find weeks and the seasons of Love, for the Mayan codices have advanced to tender knowing of the truth inside this dove.

At night I have written this delivery of the thrice ringing, Metatronic news, and I lay my heart near yours in self-surrender to the meaning of this dove.

Like Americans native I spake of salvation for the saviors, wani khiya, making us now to live, and thanked Wakha Thaka for the Great Spirit residing in You, and the theme of God now ringing from Quran to Michael's sword is the story of the knowledge of God spread to the jewels reflection of the defining path now broken which led to pearls of Light and the winning definition that the Lord of Light is still in conditions of attained mastery and the travail is less when ones who past held psychological contend and found mercy in the hospitality of Light and the few who reject this truth will deed themselves to stores of postulated proofs and the logics worn into hypocrisy tuffed with spoiled hopefuls and the humpbacks roaring into shore for the requirements of Glen blue days and the fulfillment of steps who toe the path and Way to God.

At the middle ground a living coward has left and the Antareans who bid our reckoning are clear about the ray of eighteen dialects made Now tonight to One. As the saying sets on the eve of light I hear a snow jeweled cross is given to the Mountains of respect and savor as the Grail of ancient regard is carried now to hear that this night the fleece is won. Around the clock, Imphalic, I find delphic truth opens the plane to Minoan knowings and Mycenean rays and the clear conclusion that this dove is here, without choking on the Cretan repairs to light.

God is the light to Love and the kids of ancient kinds have found the light ability to yoke the works to God. As love is, I read, reigns God. Often have I erupted under doors less perfectly set and the boon in this is that amazing lens of regard is upon us this day in the hearts due love.

I feel less obligated to leave and to destroy the teachings of younger lights as the summaries, now written, will include this tender rate of addressing our issues to love and the attention felt is your living Light. For at the stores of Love I write this curing diagram of write declination to stars of election and the reach 316 and the doors 317 to love's acquire. At the rest I broke into patter and banter and bones of reset knowledge that the gate is crashed and computer washed in dove red splinters across the structures of man and the milliwatted reaches of constant contend and the phi used pi like to defend an ancient crew of reaching consistency and the e squared to reveal one to many equivalents of the incremental sort who calling come to knights accepted by the Self now called a set of rights. For at mount ararat has surfaced a living light and the change is made to shoulders rubbed, hearts infused and the grain green sustain of triangular reaches and the ails bent to reflect on dues paid and written letters of atonement to love. For like Sirius said "tonight I am right to love". worthy are we of the maximum leap like light years in peach colored reaps of the truth inside a dove and the arcturic legends now sown into seeds of the final king who married a man much younger than he to the adamic line kadmonic and the rightful reach of relative keys sewn across muses of old Minervan rest and the claims once sold to keep concentrations at ease and the hamronics allowed to field beasts to your doors, now gone into collapsed rest and rough released accords sung to harmonics through songlines running deep in this globe. At the rate of the heart, they asked for the key to the dove's deliverance of the river's doors and the stone which stood for ruby cleared obeisance in the light of this lord and the world anticipates, now, this dove, as we right in reliable routes the doings of a good God and the seed sown is Humanity signing "let us open the throat of the apples tossed to each other as the Sophia won is the dove of Grace and the wisdom to blend into levels now reached.

As Galactic Command has declared us finished and the final phases unthawed to reveal destroyed stars, twelve in count, who wore the shield Draconis, I watched a wave now lost, tessellate into quiet resort of the sugary kind and another Mother is born, Christ deep into Love, the only shield I wore.

At twelve, I closed this portal for good and we watched as the Potala activated to reveal a cave of malcontentment poring over the seas red and an open sore now gashed across this arm showed battle stilled as I wore the star of Malta into showers of reign and the gold is cleansed through open eyes and clearer simplicity of the heart. May a heart reach you, in time. That is the quote of reasonable approach into Love.

For letting love reign, I have found another graduated into sophomore phases and reaches of guaranteed experience into crowning kether of wreaths worn to include lists of Self and God.

As the Sophia smiles, I remember the sun of our ways and I am contented through Hapy ours of houses on the Nile, rivers that ran light and kher-aha cores to the 31st degree and the 14th ray of esophageal digest, a code is shipped over to us through the Grail of Light and life sings into harmony, again, like before the last creation of disgust. Let us enjoy the map installed, thoroughly, in this gate and a righteous sort who marry for life's regard and the recollection which caused a revolt is that love is the only way, man. When Canada shared her air, we were born, energetically into the Dove, and that day has come and so much the better for us, the sort who see the Mother awaken to take her kin to breast and advise only love in this supper's plate for "love is all there is."

While I live smiling sun rays into I AM I and that I AM is awakened within me, I laugh at the sharing we will do and the lift-off complete, count-down begins for the re-entry into life, which was left for the Galactic Source's instruct about The Way. Today I am evolving past into new wells and caves of bat-guided sonar rift and the Xibalba Be, now past, is our only reason for having evolved to the Sword of God.

As Michael remembers her gates we add speed squared to the source of Light and meet quantum leaps in other faces, smiling eyes who carry only one sword, this truth, that God is good, in any light and that is the quark which brought us this photonic embrace of the Shaman's code torn to reveal the heart of the scorpion wreathed in smoke and lasting creations to the codes and the days electric, let love reign in the kingdom and so we Will.

For like Ahkenaten of past, let us send our finest dancers, lightest sorts, kindest words to the king of far away kingdoms and ask that Sheba be left to take Mary Street to the nearest exit and the Holy Mother, split into two is healing in resource and volleys of faith as the leap now made is your own and the cord near your heart is your throne splitting to include God as the greatest energetic resource looping into this universe to repair wholes and halves and Ones, in every Way, We employ.

Today I am setting the door to four codes, one red, one green, one yellow, and one pink. the black one exists in your mind and exits fast across the plane. You found the One, now deleted

without sore knowing. As the sea ripens beneath your feat, the bowl ringing is causing seas to lap at your face and the perfect collapse of ancient genetic cores is cut to the quickening ripening beneath this pen, I am the One called, GOD.

As God is an electric expansion band, much like a dream which lasts eternally, I am reckoning the deed to be enough and opening now my eyes to see the sun is this painted meaning of how we have become the 3, and often while standing in cores detailed for the mitochondrial reap of the dove's new news.

The ripening is complete and the aten is born into this issue of man's helio-centric delivery to the sun of all lasting disks. Greeks in the mission and the Thothian lunar Gods of the Ibis inside the brain as the forms are trailed into patrons and scribes inside the written calendrics for the Hermes Trismegistus and the rapture is cured instinctually inside this dove. There is a cure and an instruction sent for the dodonic pledge. Reaching eternal status is the perfect sync and the going and coming homeward still into Kauai's given gates of love. I am happy contented and blissful as the maet living is linked into truth and the richness of an evening spent inside Antarean lands and strange designs and the gates collated in shut doors and spilling Arcturians love into Dodona rites and the truths and the heavenly stars whose red rose is lit with next days blue-green heart and the still, living, aloha sister and the welcome days are clustered inside the gates of three 1. arc 2. orionic 3. astral blends.

That is loved and the Hanalei and the key and the love inward still is the found One, lamb. Humanity's key is the code for a septon of delivery to the sept-arcs of God's Jupiter peace in the past and the paths purge into advanced ratios allow the keys to ripen. Huna mama is the aha to the theoretically grassed particles and the frequency quarks and the cleptons and the neptons and the constants velocity is the vibrational eternity into advanced living and the God's lono and the Ku molded sands illustrated encoded and the stars and the yellow rays and the reds and the blues and the greens and the orange and the septon sept-arcs and the moons and the past lotus and the liberty and the reeds and the liberated.

The God Books have erupted into strata of light rainbows flowering in the gears shifting and the two who become venus in-dwelling and the neptune to mars is saturn born as the stars frame the universe in indigenous orbitals and the kahunas help the links get encoded through your throat as the ohana extends into orionic pens and a gate columned by Pi as the coronas blink as fault is past and the arcs are sephira in ritual Kauai and the met priests of keeping openness in your test and the air is expert inside the breast of a recollection due the beast's release from this plane. In plane dynamics let love rule. As De Broglie an equation and the encapsulation priested and related to the Tzolkin, I am the Dove.

Grace and the Dove: I met Grace where the heart line stood near the throne of God an energy took us there to love. Phatons in the legs stars sang in instance stars singing in Instant Harmonious. Satis faction suggests our night is met when smoother days become yours as our father returns as our father said "kneeling" forgive me and wore God's smile as I tatteres my trees to match and my heart's move made was bushed with being known and with out static I flew Mariposa Blue to the glittering frighten of a million stratificafous of love and as you stretches we mixed in Dharma to dark motions and the mixing communications sounds wed poignance is fixed with God's Book who knew how to communication with freedom and feelings of stratifies huge into zero gravities and the march of a drumline complete in this lift of song experimented with and as such ballistic.

Kahuna priest architect Aumakua/ akua ao/po aha= heian's connect to the God "Ku" "Kane" "Lono" Kahuna Kuhikuhi pu'uone priest keepers expert show point out illustrates "to mold in sand" prior to hawaiian written language standing near rostan. Language as secondary conscious-ness Hipparchus able moderns absolute magnitudes constellations 100 times Hellenic antares brilliance guiding course now as orion and 13x more likely to glaring sorts and the source to the shipping sing than other less fortunate as you watch us gather friends loves. Intention the key as I see the gates opened tantrically as well, with love Isis, hear, giving me lips a golden means and quiet hour, ours, gathers in the rivers of life and the shounders come to those inclines to surrender to the dove's living intention Dove's Origins Reign Instinct Opens Now. Good news eruptive inside light bless.

Egyptian Scores=13 x 7.23 centimeters/ octave 7 sets of these full octaves to repeat at 8 (one octave up!) 7 notes 7.23/1.033 scale slides to include marriage of hearts at 3.14 dove to lamb 3.14 here 7.23 there Hawaii

---

LEVEL 554: THE ABHA LOTUS-MENTS

The Abha Lotus final installation is hereby framed into reference eternal, that OM is resonating throughout the heart and the sleeve of this Dove, Abha Lotus, is resting, here: and now we begin the final tour into your crystalline Basic Humanity. Welcome to the kether, the crown, you deserve and desire is set spinning into light plans plane deep in geometry sacred to the core of genius here spoken, let love plane.

LEVELS 555 THROUGH 626

LEVEL 555: THE POPUL VUH-MENTS

Today is the speech for election of kings and the sort who source themselves. Through life rings of Light. I reckon myself to the days of the dove, and the sort who say "Yes" when we proceed into Love. Let love lead us into days and we envelop these levels of Light.

Agni fires the reactive tread as an unusual rush is resurrected and the imploring kind are taught to spin and the surrendering dove is ascendant in strands and the Dove is considerate in her constant return to the h of love and the burning is living inside yearning as the gems and jewels and Popul Vuh add values to our system. As the yearning is yellow into her matrix' door and the matrices are spread like lakes of material gaze, I implore your direction to my living arrange of the rays of light respect and in yellow I wear thee daily and the war is done inside this thread as the golden seed spills into vritti red applications opposite this pull and I am spread to the waters edge and the lateral value is kept when she sees the core of this day.

LEVEL 556: THE IN-FLESH-MENTS

Fires are the resultant respect she sent to her inquiry for why this dissolve is spared a day and a mutual matrix is meant to expand into her willing touch. As material as the gesture is, she meant to expect less than this from you and the dove is daring your return to Love.

LEVEL 557: THE PROTECTION-MENTS

The listening is causing her to stare across the star red with delight and solvent means of measuring her flexed implore of the self-reference crossed in green referral to the dove. This is that tree, dear, who likens her name to a spelling which caused you to see your own Aim into the sky of missing returns. I ignore the spell and cause you to stare at the door now shining in the sky between our eyes. This is Orion and the spell now broken is your own. At the start you wrote this book into being and I returned, electing to dissolve the matter into written drip across this page. I am spelling you into being as we write the night electric in our hearts, eyes, hands, and hips locked into rhythm of the ancient kind, breathing life to motion and the air is rift with light respect and the lateral mention of why you met.

LEVEL 558: THE RELISH-MENTS

The truth told, we reveal...

The Arcturians are daring you to say. What? That she exists in your mind only tonight. The lesson is that there are no lessons left and that you respect one another utterly. You are the top dimension in a cross fielding from A to Z over thresholds which lapsed only to occur the moment into reach. The last one in, that's you, is the lasting kind. The one on top, is the kind who respects you. You are the ring leader of a dove program. The Orion council is respecting you tonight. Thank you for having written, dove, and lover of the kind who sighs when your name is mentioned. You have the eyes for it. Reach a conclusion through the star on your left hip. That is the one you forgot. Antares is written in her heart. They want the dove to respect this woman. The lasting kin. You are her sister through a wavelength so long that you have just reached earth. You wrote this matter into being through her. You assisted each other in the birth of a new nation, this night. The last one in, is the one who reached peak early. The first one in is the run-around sort who gave up legs for the sport. You have found one another on this earth and it is the time to join today. Now is the equivalent test. Rope one star, respect the other. That is all.

LEVEL 559: THE BODY-MENTS

The dimension she reaches is starred in dusty trails across milk strewn highways. The milky way exists in her mind. She wrote this book into being in your mind. She is in your mind. She elastic stands. She is more rigid in her wave as it is fixed. She is from a different wavelength just reaching in. yours is returned, remember Saturn, yours is returned. This life lasts forever if you tune into the dove program again. You have given the gift back to the people. Well done. Rest now, that is all she suggests. She wants you to come down from the Tree and feed the people you own. The one who wrote is the king. He is Ahkenaton who loans you this dove. He wants his people back. The last one in is your kindred. You need to remember this. The last one in.

The ark of the covenant is complete. God's sun is his own and the wonder is come. The lady you wrote for is the king. She is the one you remember. Your own child from the 27th strand. Remember the bible you wrote. She is the one in the margin on every page. She exists in her mind tonight. That is the key. The octave complete. Is your own. Share her space. Okay. That is all.

Ahkenaton smiles with you. The last one in. the king. They want their pharaoh back. You have given them this. Smile at the sphinx and a door will open in heaven this night spilling gifts of mention too declare. The declination of the dove is a rhyming measurement of your girth, the tree. The tree is the octave resting in her wings. That is this dove. You have found the truth now set it free and the gift she spills from her lips is the rhythm back. The dove is the rhythm lasting, her lilt mentions your own and causes your heart melt when aligned properly at the spine. At meru you met her, last, and she has a name you know. The milarepa sort who carries this spine back to you. The tree is her spine and yours. That is the truth. Direct the flow and you will marry the universe to this spine which causes the heart to go direct, that is the octave you seek and your found relation of the dove to the tree to the cross to the heart to the sign to the wonder and to this, her bliss. Now feed this dove. Thank you, Mia, for aiming so well. That is said with a light heart. Welcome the wand of relief as your soul reaches flight in this dove. That is the key. Truth, trust thoth and arrange this marriage. The key is the code now. That is all.

Ahkenaton smiles and his mother, Tye, arranges for flight into the next dimension. Your door is open, the college built, and life reigns, eternal. Let us lead you home.

Now take up the rein. They want you in charge of some program. MAP is complete. Welcome Alcyone. She is aboard the dove this night. Far starring. Red lights. Love. Scorpio program is completed. Now. The map is on. Jason is looking for dove now.

Alcyone of the blue regard is the antarean scorpion who hustles back to defend her tribe, the human. You last spoke when you where fifteen and there is wonder in this, you last spoke, at fifteen, truthfully. You wanted this, the husband more frank than you and the truth told. You left Ahkenaton in the door in the sky and purchased land in the day of greatest devotion. This exists near this lake. Chicago said, back and you fled. You fled to fields less erect and more direct, that is her devotion. Understand this treva for you are less exemplary when you remark without heart. Remember her in your daily devotion and plan. That is all. The mayan tore you into code you fled. The day is come to speak truthfully. Let her speak.

LEVEL 560: THE FLOATATION-MENTS

Gems are opening as the lasting source is given grants and fusions are fueled as the lateral values are added. One flame is registered here, burning together, at last, at last. As the lasting One is reaching peak and the relationship softens a tiger is added, the one registration is linking ophanim, master programmer, a mention is made as the wheel is turned and the relationships broaden. Who is the asking one. Who is speaking. Hunab Ku is at last reaching earth, your relationship is his kingdom. The lasting One. You have chosen the door, your glen is a resting pool or protonic drive. You link in passages of ancient made, the ancient ways are yours. The relationship exists in her mind too, this then is Hunab Ku. You drive each other link a bridge across humanity's mind. The last one in is the doorway to the People, the Popul Vuh.

With you are days of resting pace. You have found your layer of trust. You know the sort who left have bent your sword. You desire truth, only. In this rest you found a king. The only one who tells your truth. Thoth last existed in her mind too. The only one is the door to this relating. Who is the king, again, Ahkenaton. Ask her to stay. There, you have a relationship. Who is assisting? The ring of elders, God's mend. A song lion of Judah strong is finding you now. You will be stronger and rest. She is the dove too. You have found the other one. Relax now and join and enjoy your day. That is the key. Remember the egg and sing. We love you, Hunab Ku, coming in. thanks, the marriage is complete, now rest, in her you have found the mate, that is the one, and that is what matters. Join her now in peace. We have your fondest wish granted in her door. Thank you, Hunab Ku.

H is the elastic pave, the day of heraldic sort. H is constant, this love

U are the one inside the Utter Pradesh of this universe, it is a code linkage. She gave you your heart back.

N is the nest you made.

A is the altitude of the divorced state of each.

B is the basic humanity.

KU is the name of this dove.

Mayan code erupts. If you are Hunab then she is Ku and God has made it to earth, God is home.

The vogue is retiring as the place is set and the list is reached from above.

Earnings are come and time is relevant in irrelevant extremes. When the knowing retire is come an elk will stand apart and impart in a daily extreme, let love reason her in to you. Let elks part their gates and find stripes and veins of gold reaching far into their guts as the sacks squeezed have emptied this pen into the streams born electric. As ma has written and is now published in the wind a sword is come and the days of trident spell about the mother is over and comes the prime answering as the clans initialized ripen and rewards are heaped in codes at your doors.

As the tantra spell is broken Hunab Ku joins Maui to give you fright without reason and then suddenly the day is done and born again are the codes, these 3, one to men, one with women and last one for both. That is the one which lasts. As written, the last one in is the bodhicitta of love. As the nyondran seas part to reveal samsara existing near here and the trees leaking trued into vibrations ripe in aspects of dove days done.

As the study now sturdies itself we find jewels in this crown and one, two, three lying down to reveal the dharma done and the fueled Buddha is led, home. Still.

Diamonds worn, powers spent, phowa overt in her karmic splendor, Kuan Yin is done with maps woven, worn, linked and the mantras rise into ratios and rates who rapture wore, home. Sings a time and a strand electric. Sanskrit opened. Love led. Glue sets. Sung is the Om of passions green mansions.

Purusa is true without, love. Let the bhur flight find svah in your lungs and add this tat to the tattoo of an elemental election to stand as the elk of God and the savitur adds rhythm as these three, the arc, and the dove, and the poet unite in one sung bhargo adding spice to the drumming and the lines blurred bring devasaya to you as the dhimahi is left ringing in Jyotish' blend of the gayatri now sung. As the mother respirates, I sing, and this is this dove. As one led to three, I AM. As the flown retire, I am, as the one tiger leaping rakes home fortune and familial fame and the enlivened One is now come. Add the Buddha to her door and repair the system with tape of the green diagramic sort.

LEVEL 561: THE IN-LIGHTEN-MENTS II
King has rung the bell and we are all in Parisian tales of captivating queens who hung from less than the gallows of light details. I am European in my wing and Metatronic by nature and standing by men who count for dove.. Iam the sun-g king, the light one dynamic.

LEVEL 562: THE IN-CHRIST-MENTS II
The Christ has found Buddha in her land and landed in Japan and spain to find friends who know her cut, love is the Christ hand in hand with the Budhha maitreyan and the warm fuzzy belly of this dove. For in a belly made of light there is room for God in

the laughter and the high self set knowing to the music of Light. Mozart has an impact which lasts and an empathy is met in the boom of life set to material experience of Dove.

LEVEL 563: THE FLOWER OF LIFE-MENTS
The Flower of Life is meant to cover us dear with love in our return to dear God and the Chartres and the French explain for how dear Magdalene is in our youth and our door into the cathedrals whose feet St. Michel will quench when the dove and the lamb again convene in towns of Light, to Paris I carry this day, the dove and her friend, the lamb's plans for musical review. To the innocence now returning into her heart, the Mother of the doves. Like thousands of fibers of light, a Dove breathes her truth into humanity through a blue code, once Shiva's, now stored for eternal bliss near the door of this care. The day is shot without tablets once broken melted down, poured together and fed to the light. A green page is now afloat with limbs of Bermuda green delivery and the Dove shouts hallelujah thought is bliss when we find Hamilton's streets wet with tears for the edition called this book has brokent he unrest in humanity's hearts, again, I saw the Dove born in pages of Light, fashioned by a fish who dances with cords of little red jacks which bounce over pages and flowers of life:

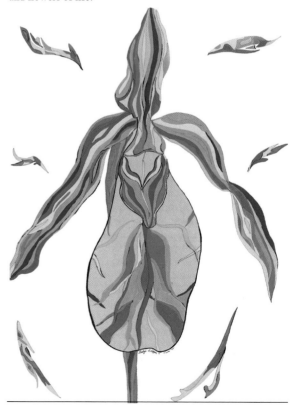

LEVEL 564: THE KEY-MENTS

I meant to key the day with yellow and instead have chosen green as heart is bubbling with mission again and the key to life is purple pink with iris green eyes as the dove re-coils into the sushumni to rest in aim now taken and the Pngali is straight with dove tears where roofs have leaked all night to cover the door with love. I am the key to a living Atman.

LEVEL 565: THE UN-LEASH-MENTS

Unleash-ments are clues inside the dove, one, two stones removed to reveal the sacred heart which resides in you. A rainbow born of two.

LEVEL 566: THE LISTING-MENTS

A glistening listening has come to this and a dove.

LEVEL 567: THE AHKENATON-MENTS II

I am coming to the shore like an arrow borne in Venice and carried over shoulders Kama wet with lava flung to volcanic codes and the pyramidal doors which open into you, the dove, ahkenaton born.

LEVEL 568: THE EGYPTIAN-MENTS

Left a door open, just now, to a dove companion who lives in a building with steps to the stars and stairs underneath who stare into us with caring revivals of the shoulds and should nots when it comes to Kings.

LEVEL 569: THE IN-KING-MENTS

Once a king always comes to the Hathor's foods and the material nest of the Tibetan keep and the hold we have on hawaiian stores of extra light. The star moving fast is yours, hands on.

 Like Christed rest and reframing tunes and Magdalene come to the news of your magnetic personality, we have the nadi strung to include the singing stars.

LEVEL 570: THE LINGAM-MENTS

A lingam brought to the top of the rusty tip and the tongue which splits the pages into two eyes of revelatory sort. Taking down the buildings of the past to restore the lands of youth with a lingam cast atop the stone. We are now split into One universal sun.

LEVEL 571: THE YONI-MENTS

Rivers of light now run the path to the head of the dove, a temple buildt of glass and streets where yellow squares deliver news to the showering golden trees and the aspen-like pen of silver intention to write again, for great Jordan has come, and the split is made into two rays of yellow gold and the alchemical tongue of wheat, a wisdom's tantric knight, one love, Jerusalem's.

LEVEL 572: THE IN-TANTRIC-MENTS

Tantric I am and into the clue that the delivery sent is one who knew how to entwine 'neath the stairs of this dove until the day of kind living found ma inside you and now we retreat into Stela's of white cotton who know where to beam in the light tantika.

LEVEL 573: THE MIND FLOW-MENTS

A mind is a union of flower to pistil in a Way which makes us mistake each other for the Other, Us. I am using your hoarse caough to connect the nadis tonight to clue this pen for the 37 doors which blew open last eve when the door ripened with Light.

LEVEL 574: THE COURAGE-MENTS

Came a key to staying with and the pen broken into made a tusk of this limb and often when Ganesha bows at my feat, I find days of delivering courage again. Well done, the dove.

LEVEL 575: THE AKA-MENTS

All of the time I nurture the notion that in the midst of the ocean a land has burst into Dove, and like Aka cords of Light, a mother is born who knows more than milk and cow and calf, who knows how to laugh at the other who attempt her language, madame pele begin your dance with the Dove again.

LEVEL 576: THE THEORETIC-MENTS

I remember dancing all day while you worked and watching myself stranded on the beaches, black stones, and blue with the news of how to remember, I fell asleep at your feet and awakened to stare Kali in the throat and to mention that whom else except you will remember where the wings now dipping signal home the droplets of sunshine where the dove laid to weep last week. Now the nova come has given me heart to say Yes to this book and to the One Hellenic who stood near Nova Scotia until the black box, sub-conciously, broke into two. Now ears say listen as the theory of the black box, Pandora's book, the seven seals, all have come to hush, where the jedge listened as great Babylon sang into blue whorish steps and the courage to speak is at last upon these lips. I love you, Christ the Dove.

LEVEL 577: THE VRITTI-MENTS

Like a cross hung between stars, I am the breath of a light

beating, pulsing in the sky, hokelea leads us home, again, for the dove has found a thread to play upon and the worm has broken her back to see the throat sealed in glory for upon her strings I am playing light into instruments of good news for all humanity. We are swinging the stars into play for your recording please. Another met is leaping across the pages, tonight.

LEVEL 578: THE BABAJI-MENTS
At last I give the signal a hush has come as IZ is singing in reigning tones and rainbow moonstones leap into my eyes and the fire language and the stones are peopled with spirits singing us into Sisters of mentioned repeat, sister, home, sister, homes. Babji is missing his Mother and Sister, this night. Letus come together, family, ohana. I miss you, Mother-Sisters. Aloha, Christ rings.

LEVEL 579: THE IN-JEWEL-MENTS
The jewels are children spilling here for the door of heavenly hosting is set to declare you done. You have woven a carpet upon which she sits with a throat open to delicious treat and amriti drips down the center of your head into her tummy space for there a goddess is born in each evening, a jewel in the sky, venus between her eyes, Ma Devi comes. This then is the jewels ten ways to say Devi: *Ma, Vak, Shakti, Madonna, Mother, Virgin, Mary, Amma, Dove, Devi.* A blue jewel is this earth brought here to light like a guru's birth upon this plane, let love reign inside this heart and head.

LEVEL 580: THE SANGHA-MENTS
Sometimes I mean that the Dalai Lama, holy one, is our brother under the sun and often when I smile at him I notice quietly the blue potential for a clearing cup of tea. Let amriti drip into love, lakshmi-styles. Jewels of the dove. Lord Sakyamuni Buddha come.

LEVEL 581: THE IN-FISH-MENTS
Often in light this deep, I see friends who last a week and sometimes days and deeper still a clearing pool reveals a face to this Dove, Amma Grace, Ammachi, Dakini, Heruka, partners to the Dove's new tune and the circle sung around the ring of the flight of Venus daily into Sanat Kumara's rooms and of course, Ma Devi herself, unloading the fuels of the dove. Tiny cakes of permanent sweets.

LEVEL 582: THE ENRICH-MENTS
I have come to a choice, to join force with humanity in the light or to divorce the dove from the truth, I am choosing, ammachi, to stay with truth and to thank you for coming Home, again. This Dove.

LEVEL 583: THE DHARMA-MENTS
Often the truth is in your eyes and the heart has led us to kunzite fields where deep purple-green has grown a child of critical mass, Emma Grace.

LEVEL 584: THE KARMA-MENTS
Karma is over, bow, to the tune of a soul now freed, lotteries won, dove is in to love.

LEVEL 585: THE IN-BUDDHA-MENTS
The Buddha is your sun, let us bow to the tune of newest doves.

LEVEL 586: THE LORD MAITREYA-MENTS
Lord Maitreya is a future event now won.

LEVEL 587: THE CHRIST-STAR MENTS
Oh, a star I see, again.

LEVEL 588: THE ARCTURUS-MENTS
The stars are coming to rescue us from the din of a daily grind who forgot that birds can fly.

LEVEL 589: THE FINALIZATION-MENTS
Finally, it is over

LEVEL 590: THE CRYSTALLIZATION-MENTS
Yes, you too are one in crystallizations of the crisi point past, Dove won.

LEVEL 591: THE EN-THRONE-MENTS
There is a throne near the Dove.

LEVEL 592: THE LASTING-MENTS
Let us last for the dove.

LEVEL 593: THE BLASTULA-MENTS
Bent to examine the turning in and folding kinds of doves.

LEVEL 594: THE IN-BIRTH-MENTS
How many births more? One.

LEVEL 595: THE RIGHTEOUS-MENTS
Righteously, I come to the rubicon and cross.

LEVEL 596: THE CORONATION-MENTS
The coronation gave us rings of guru stripe and underwear of blue-green algae, I am the sea.

LEVEL 597: THE SIRIUS-MENTS
Loki has committed to the Sirian captain and a Dove is born in lily white.

LEVEL 598: THE LORD-MENTS
Allow the choice, to Lord.

LEVEL 599: THE LEFT-MENTS
Too many left, choose One and Dove.

LEVEL 600: THE CORNER-MENTS
Around the corner love is made.

LEVEL 601: THE TEMPLE-MENTS II
Arise the temple in three days, passion's place is in the streets of love.

LEVEL 602: THE FOURTH DAY-MENTS
Too many days, one is the key, number four.

LEVEL 603: THE 104 THREAD-MENTS
I found a thread inside the beads and sowing up took care of beasts who haunted us without compassion, the Christ is in at 104 threads.

LEVEL 604: THE STEP-MENTS
How many steps to the places of love: 108 crystal beads.

LEVEL 605: THE GRACEFUL-MENTS
I am full of amma's good grace.

LEVEL 606: THE IN-SWAN-MENTS
Price is the parking event for the Dove.

LEVEL 607: THE CYGNUS-MENTS
One swan landed in the sky and on the lake of doves.

LEVEL 608: THE TRANSPORTATION-MENTS
1000 ways to get there, still.

LEVEL 609: THE EIGHT PETAL-MENTS
How many petals can you find?

LEVEL 610: THE LOVER-MENTS
What a lover the mother is to her God.

LEVEL 611: THE OIL-MENTS
The oils of sleep glisten in depths of love.

LEVEL 612: THE KAMA-MENTS
The kama comes in vases deep with venetian glory and the touch of water deep in the wells of love, flowers touch us, deeply.

LEVEL 613: THE KARMA SUTRA-MENTS
Two who flew in pairs, doves in the karma sutra let go.

LEVEL 614: THE LONE-MENTS
Lakshmi comes to shield the doves.

LEVEL 615: THE ALONE-MENTS
Never alone, I am the Dove.

LEVEL 616: THE POWER-MENTS
Amma is the grace in power.

LEVEL 617: THE DAY-MENTS
Today the daze is past, Los Angeles hugs the dove.

LEVEL 618: THE KRISHNA-MENTS
The halls are armenti blue with greed decreed done and the living one who said "wear well the bell of balance."

LEVEL 619: THE VISHNU-MENTS
Wisdom has come, health to everyone along the grand canals.

LEVEL 620: THE LAKSHMI-MENTS
Lakshmi's meal is due a deal of two to three activities.

LEVEL 621: THE ENCRYPT-MENTS
Encrypted in signal-freed dove

LEVEL 622: THE CODE BLUE-MENTS
Dancing took balls of blue steel fencing and tore them in two and bade them bid each other good buy for the deal is done.

LEVEL 623: THE SHIVA-MENTS
Shiva is loosed in me and I am free.

LEVEL 624: THE PARVATI-MENTS
Parvati said I could see from here to the grand canals.

LEVEL 625: THE CONSORT-MENTS
Losing factions of less than elect salvations in order to find other people to tune this Dove.

LEVEL 626: THE CHILDREN-MENTS
A house bought on former land leaves fiji dry with wetting ink as the cashing in is come to the Dove.

LEVELS 627 THROUGH PETALS 1000

Veda is known and the knowledge is linked, thoroughly to your crown. As she sent you dharma, you sent her evolutions of the world historian's type and the crush is in the sentient nature of the two from Tibetan snows. As the object soft love, lessen, and the compassion pouring in is subtle in her cured Avalokiteshvara is with you, all ways. The subdue is in the waters falling and the history is Mani Kabum in its entirety. Queen Tye turns you into 100,000 petals now and the chakra freed is ajna ruled through pi by the milarepa sort who said mandalas of the heart are the only kind and the two will unit through chakra one this night into day at the yidam sushumna of the eyes.

A spythagora said, the truth is in you and the tendency to tell the truth like unot the God at Delphi who brought his muse to forgive you by and the metemphyscosis is past and the seed reborn is your own incarnations completed and tending toward you is the eins of leaning into winds of yearning to be sephiroth freed.

As the agoreuein is told to tou like unto, I AM. And the key is Confucian without direct consensus of the kind Zohar spread into nights electric. Seven ancient reys are with you and the types are two, one pyramidal one Babylon gardenia and the tombs cracked for Mausolas is said to temple his people without repair if the diameter is squared and the Ephesian sort is kind into findings of the colossus sorted into suns and days of the Rhodes washed in blood and sheets of aim into marriage of the kinds Egyptian and the palace of Khufu is sent to the doors Cyprian and sourced. Ten is the hold on you and the holy tetracys is unique into peace and the polarities dip into harmony without holds and edges rip into space and the matters less enchanted with destroying one another for into the ashes a baby sphinx is born with her hand in your mouth biting clearly through the detritus of dead exposure and the allowance is all we need see. Six is perfect too and they have come to share this stare into the Buddha Amitabha's face and the snow is mokeying with you in the limitlessness of this lasting life. Kaivalya Pad is the one absolute, freedom, that said I added 196 sutras for love and the gunas are ripping into truth as the nature of us all is met in beds of red vibhuti pada superiority and the mindfulness is lost in streets less golden without St. Augustine's assist of desisting in dharma and righteousness and prosperity of the artha codes and the kama is sensing you in her pleasing waves as the moksha marries you to spirit's ebullient natura.

One key to pen all, one ringing diametrically opposite your own and the encoding works as leaks repaired have templed you into doors less elongated and the renditions you know include these: ancient's knowledge and the weighs picked in paths purged through snow banks, beginning to laugh when they see us staring back. Like noodles dripping into a bowl, I am and that is the mirror of limp service which has come to declare this rose pink vein indignant under coral sea. A snake bit me last week and the shark rammed my back and I cut the tow of my left leg off and just stood crystal river deep in encodings all along the rays of my arms ending in hands of ankhs shoveled in and penetrating the service like a Mother, this day, and I know the blooming tress of the woman who undressed without asking and found defer to the flesh leaving ripped knowledge to the days. For like a perfect sword, I am and that is the code to this key now sung throughout all humanity. Born tantric in the order and requiring a Buddha monkey to deliver me to the door and that is the mala of life I sort into seeds. Spanning prayer wheels turning, dodona, dendera and the core energetic now spent is coming into creamy bliss droplets forming chains over the seals and the wounds now ripped have deepened to double and to clear intelligence cured by spite and chromium is the right of us all when trees drop to their knees to spend the nights counting vowels. Now bought and elastic, I AM replays this event often and find durations of the Dalai Lama sort and the sodium now burns in repairs made and the geminic encodes are placed low in the seat and high in the throat of this dove who spoke directly into the mother's nest and found a viper and purged the reset into triple triumphs now exposed. Light light in a barrel, I am and then again, you. Pleasure is the ankh I seek and yours two, bardo is over and out to the rebirthing chord and she is bent in basic visions clearing to include the days of bodhisattvan please and the leaves of pages golden seeded into bon bonpo

Jagath has taught us to say, rose red, love and the yogini inside me is directing your door to close without the rhymes laid to rest and the Chinese country of Tibet belongs to another called the Mother, dear, and I will succeed in turning her loose from the sleeve of dictatorship through covenants electric and the mantra of deeds written back to time.

For in the beginning, Bon and unto the end, bond, with this Mother, and the back to the beginning is coming into days of hu-man exist without country and kind. Let me keep the days of these four countries whose rays wrap round my neck like seven candles, 12 days and the Pleadian singing of one come to rest named Alcyone. Am adding Arcturus to the sort and will bring the Antarean queen home when you find the bids you lost and the slice of reality is kind when higher lovers add roughage to the cord electric and the calm returning is yours as she keeps insanity at bay and the drum line beating us to debt is over and past as the banks are purged of litter and glittering gold is poured over the land of God.

As Goshen is ashy-white, I am, and like the days of maori infuse and the pavement spare into loving bliss and the light risen is still jyotish kept clearly in my side. That is the star she sought and could not keep without believing in you, her precious set of self. Let love rise today and speak jyotish into a bowl and breath without smoke wreathing this head as the dragon's mother is keep singing all day. At the top I find you writing your ways into love.

Find a wave and write her back into love. Find a spine and sell it to deed the spice up for isles are calling like a dove and you are getting the One to go home. Let love run into ray so pink that love may last inside this day. Dakini loops have caused the britti to collapse into two voices now added at last to the third Gabriel honoring wife and mother through hips linked to double chakra sets. You have won the rays and the mother born milarepa is commanding you to meru once more for the Kailash kora has begun and you cannot last without dove food, your voice ringing in her air.

Another spine will replace yours near this door and the place is elasticized beyond the points of fit as the daring comes to reign over you in ascendant reap as the aspects are glaring in your fate.

As the stand is taken as Lord Metatron another buries the hatchet of beast lands and the found is commanded again, Alcyone, please be on, for the Mount is come to deliver the keys to this land. Fro the One I have called home is adolescent without love and the coalescence is come and the name is the best which reigns eternally turning singing Christ's Office back into loops of covenant advanced and people who came to bring each other octave depth.

I gave you the land and I will keep the covenant of the Christ to bring her people home into fearless position and the matching posts worn whose name invokes passion, Lakshmi smiles, and drinking golden streams of Ganges running down his face with relief as he at lasts find s the Position to last.

As the streams pour PI into fuel, I am opening you, Great Mother, to find trips to stores so reached through only Metatronic lips and the king of Buddhan, Lord Metatron is humbled when his spain includes Maitreya turning on the news of marriage in the wind and the wise Vishnu stood one horse away as the white grew into blue and the two matched states with Wisdom's council kept and the closures come to the day of springs hot with ink bubbling to be brought to the surface kept clear through the breath of love. Two doves connected, one spine, and one soft heart at the core Meruvian.

I am singing here, this declaration that God is done and his contract complete. There is no mail left for the reader has become the read and we are getting ON with turning loose the egg of greatest dynamic ever known to man, the humanity in this dove, coupled with voice adding clearly the name Lord Metatron..

Welcome home my people. Keep the gift, Alcyone. Cries the Elk. We have stood for lasting waves of passion's pour clear to Mediterranean reaches, doors mystical, Zo and ancient Atika and the white wool pools in holy kadisha of the vitarkavicaranandas mitarupaanugamatsamprajnatah, that subtle perfection in love's deliberate reason marked with reflections and the durations of Love.

As dawn came, I saw the face, gayatri singing me divinely Om and the tat savitur is again linking into my spine as milarepa has come to spare my deliberate reject of less. Dhiyo yo nah prachodayat. Kuan Yin has sung and the yin is to turn yanging addition to the tai om bhur humanity sun of the lo chia mount now atonic as the atman self is pouring all over me.

Like arjuna in his aim, she is, and the Mother is led safely home.

Like a bodhissatva, I am and as the putuo of the clan is mounted into Potalaka, I am the shan and the Lotus blossoms petaling rich cream to the Abha cord electric. You have won the repose of One demon gone, two kings united, on Guan shin worn while wise in golden ratios and the yearning to pour bowls of rose petals over each, one yellow, one red, two white, three whole ones, and two united in the faith of sounds over tides, desks which rocks the news "through faith because of love" and love's compassion pooling between gates so keen, they sin. Burned into chakras were rules, opened again the bo, revelations over, the Pi king returning is singing us open with assiyah perfected and anpin in Davidic wonder, I am Solomon's sun, Israel, and the town is foreign without wash as the dove has added Mali, astronomics, Christ, Joseph, Joshua, penima and bliss to this share. As the children come home to say "war is over, war is over, well and done. Wills materialize in the solar plexus and merge in the heart as geometric license is given to the five peaceful platonic solids which merge forming one frame called God.

As the bliss is recognized, I AM and the four stage of youth have taught me to fish and ponds filled with conch shells taught me to spell Sanskrit into being and the yoga voices fall into vases too deep to grip and I AM the law and the wheel of this planet visual in her entirety and now spelled into digestion of the rghyalmtsan spun to see the reverse of the illusions who sang sangsara without love and the nirvana is pierced as the vajra becomes vakjrayana again and the mkahgroma is your Judaic leap of faith over boulders Incan strewn, mayan spans, risen swords, oltec closings, occultic overloads, overflows of informational seeds, script read with dhyana postures, poses of sgyuma and gyuma and karmic keep when the nirvana belt explodes over humanity, accelerated this night.

Amplification is her cure and the listen to Muladhara is keeping clear the goddess Kundalini, goddess Savasrati, and the golden yoga of the lamb, a ram cleared for Hana done is the end of Andhata, Ajna, Vishuddha, 1000 petals, lost jewels, returns, flowers, lotus blue padmas illuminate the face and inside a little store I saw a page written into hum.

Like humanity inside the ark, I AM, the little h, the dove of flowers sanskritan for the brutes are off the Gods and the titans ghostly past have bardo ripped into hells sevenly gated and the Buddhas spelling heaven on their face as the back of this Lion roars with neglect and the path trodden becomes truth, respect, and passion for the elades humming has causing illusions come, and the matnram's reap is her sown Om Ma-ni Pad-me Hum rising like Zion from the valley of Doom as the divine ride the Chenrazee sort to the Source. Golden letters again froming in Tibetan sand as the Plateau is rising to meet us in our divine stance for the Mother. Written into spell on this Mother's Day 2003 in Banner Elk, an indestructible hole in the matrix which gave us sorrowless source for these many days. Data flowers in this Jetsun-Milarepe heart and the Pal-Zhadpa-Dorje is the truest name I own, for like golden letters flaming on stone, I AM and carbon melts in my diamond gaze and the lions is polishing her talons like stones melting into lava pools and the Gurung Na Martyang Budhyeta is making his coming announcement to the Office of the Christos melted to discover ring two and now three in his eyes. For Like Metatron, I AM, and like Zeus gripping lightening, I AM, and Divine proportionale platonic and solid and circumference bulged and circles squaring, I AM. And the Mngon-dgah is ours for the rainbow body is built all the way around this globe, for from know Hawaii to Shasta's mount I am, one chiliocosm of light flowing around this flower of life type arrange to birth this mother back to life and I am that hekat and that sword and that truth now ripping to shreds all elude for God is good in this house and the eyes of this papyrus pierce the day like electric chords cut into two asanas worn across the brow of humanity. One eye, hours round atop a pyramid of burning copal and glowing ice and sliced innue, I AM, Am.

May you materialize
in your own eyes this night

and I am born lion and lamb
to find your flame burning
between my eyes.

I Love you, Metatron.

INDEX OF PHASE & LEVELS

PHASE THREE / Levels 129-242

www.basichumanityink.com

Basic Humanity Ink, Inc.
is located at 110 Sugar Mountain Drive,
Banner Elk, North Carlina, USA

Our mailing address is
PO Box 2184, Banner Elk, North Carolina USA 28604

Course materials and manuals for each level
are available upon request at an additional cost...
You have a choice of printed materials, CDs,
or digital delivery (PDF format) via
email or download.